# Sports Illustrated
# 2002
# Sports Almanac

**By the Editors of Sports Illustrated**

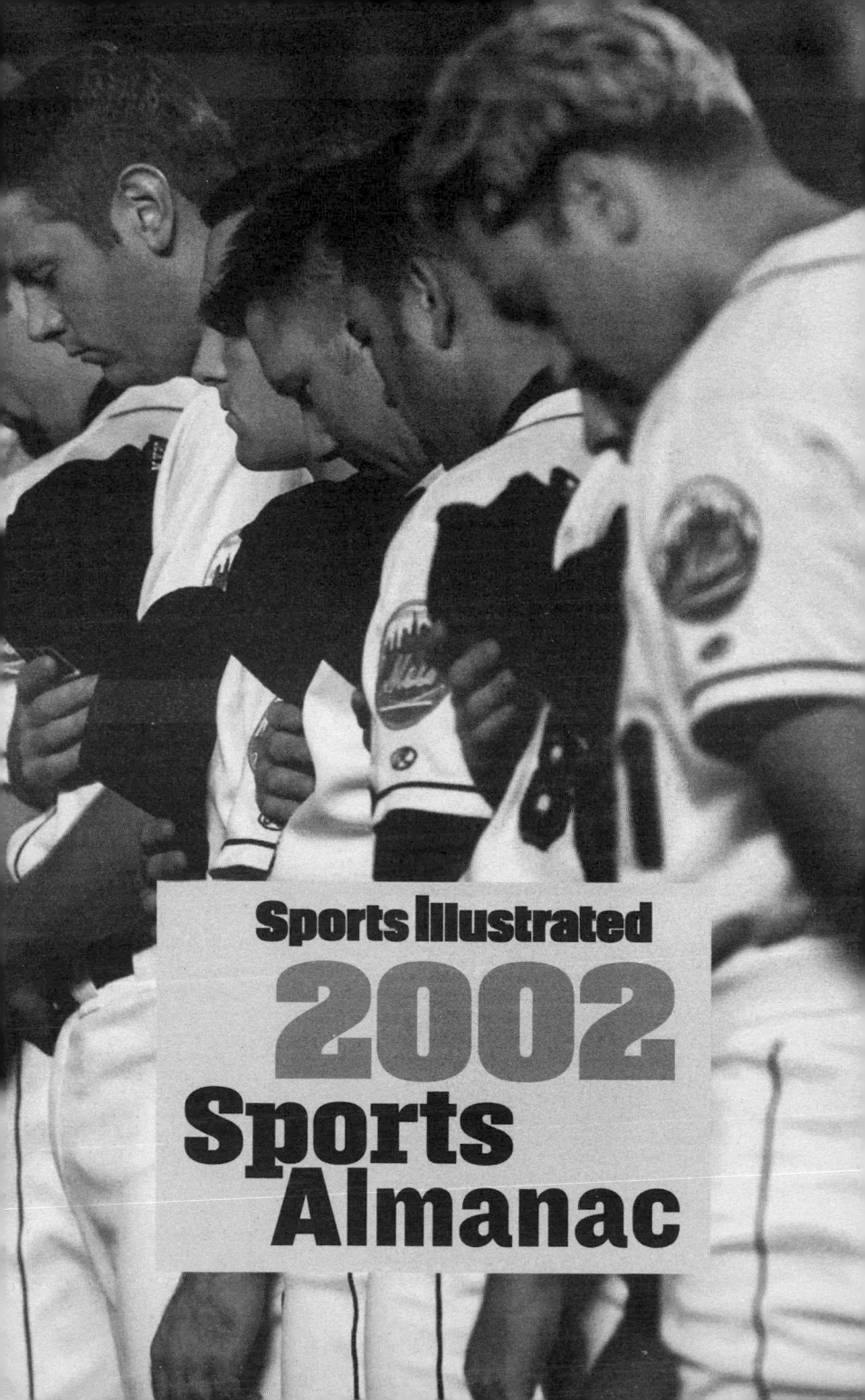

**Sports Illustrated**

# 2002
# Sports
# Almanac

First Edition
ISBN 1-929049-48-X

*Sports Illustrated 2002 Sports Almanac* was prepared by Bishop Books of New York City.

Cover photography credits (clockwise from left):
Kobe Bryant: John Biever
Ray Lewis: Al Tielemans
Dale Earnhardt: George Tiedemann
Chipper Jones and Rick White: George Tiedemann

Back cover photography credits (left to right):
Shane Battier: Manny Millan
David Duval: John Biever
Jennifer Capriati: Bob Martin

Spine photography credit: Brad Mangin

Title page photography credit: Reuters/Corbis

10   9   8   7   6   5   4   3   2   1
COM
PRINTED IN THE UNITED STATES OF AMERICA

# CONTENTS

In compiling the *Sports Illustrated 2002 Sports Almanac*, the editors would again like to thank the staff of the *Sports Illustrated* library for its invaluable assistance. They would also like to extend their gratitude to the media relations offices of the following organizations for their help in providing information and materials relating to their sports: Major League Baseball; the Canadian Football League; the National Football League; the National Collegiate Athletic Association; the National Basketball Association; the National Hockey League; the Association of Tennis Professionals; the Women's Tennis Association; the U.S. Tennis Association; the U.S. Golf Association; the Ladies Professional Golf Association; the Professional Golfers Association; National Thoroughbred Racing Association; the U.S. Trotting Association; the Breeders' Cup; Churchill Downs; the New York Racing Association, Inc.; the Jockey's Guild, Inc.; Championship Auto Racing Teams; the National Hot Rod Association; the International Motor Sports Association; the National Association for Stock Car Auto Racing; the Professional Bowlers Association; the Ladies Professional Bowlers Tour; the United Soccer Leagues; Major League Soccer; the Women's United Soccer Association; the *Fédération Internationale de Football Association*; the U.S. Soccer Federation; the U.S. Olympic Committee; USA Track & Field; U.S. Swimming; U.S. Diving; U.S. Skiing; U.S. Figure Skating Association; the U.S. Chess Federation; U.S. Curling; the Iditarod Trail Committee; the International Game Fish Association; the USA Gymnastics; U.S. Handball Association; the Lacrosse Foundation; the American Power Boat Association; the Unlimited Hydroplane Racing Association; the Professional Rodeo Cowboys Association; U.S. Rowing; the American Amateur Softball Association; the U.S. Speed Skating ; U.S. Rugby Football Union; USA Triathlon; the National Archery Association; USA Wrestling; the U.S. Squash Racquets Association; the U.S. Polo Association; ABC Sports; and the U.S. Volleyball Association.

The following sources were consulted in gathering information:

**Baseball**   *The Baseball Encyclopedia*, Macmillan Publishing Co., 1990; *Total Baseball*, Viking Penguin, 1995; *Baseballistics*, St. Martin's Press, 1990; *The Book of Baseball Records*, Seymour Siwoff, publisher, 1991; *The Complete Baseball Record Book*, The Sporting News Publishing Co., 1992; *The Sporting News Baseball Guide*, The Sporting News Publishing Co., 1996; *The Sporting News Official Baseball Register*, The Sporting News Publishing Co., 1996; *National League Green Book—1994*, The Sporting News Publishing Co., 1993; *American League Red Book—1994*, The Sporting News Publishing Co., 1993; *The Scouting Report: 1996,* Harper Perennial, 1996.

**Pro Football**   *The Official 1997 National Football League Record & Fact Book*, The National Football League, 1997; *The Official National Football League Encyclopedia*, New American Library, 1990; *The Sporting News Football Guide*, The Sporting News Publishing Co., 1996; *The Sporting News Football Register*, The Sporting News Publishing Co., 1996; *The 1993 National Football League Record & Fact Book,* Workman Publishing, 1993; *The Football Encyclopedia,* David Neft and Richard Cohen, St. Martin's Press, 1991.

**College Football**   *1997 NCAA Football*, The National Collegiate Athletic Association, 1997.

**Pro Basketball**   *The Official NBA Basketball Encyclopedia*, Villard Books, 1994; *The Sporting News Official NBA Guide*, The Sporting News Publishing Co., 1996; *The Sporting News Official NBA Register*, The Sporting News Publishing Co., 1996.

**College Basketball**   *1997 NCAA Basketball*, The National Collegiate Athletic Association, 1996.

**Hockey** *The National Hockey League Official Guide & Record Book 1997–98,* The National Hockey League, 1997; *The Sporting News Complete Hockey Book,* The Sporting News Publishing Co., 1993; *The Complete Encyclopedia of Hockey,* Visible Ink Press, 1993.

**Tennis** *1997 Official USTA Tennis Yearbook,* H.O. Zimman, Inc., 1997; *IBM/ATP Tour 1997 Player Guide,* Association of Tennis Professionals, 1997; *1997 Corel WTA Tour Media Guide,* Corel WTA Tour, 1997.

**Golf** *PGA Tour Book 1997,* PGA Tour Creative Services, 1997; *LPGA 1997 Player Guide,* LPGA Communications Department, 1997; *Senior PGA Tour Book 1997,* PGA Tour Creative Services, 1997; *USGA Yearbook 1997,* U.S. Golf Association, 1997.

**Boxing** *The Ring 1986–87 Record Book and Boxing Encyclopedia,* The Ring Publishing Corp., 1987. *Computer Boxing Update,* Ralph Citro, Inc., 1992; Bob Yalen, boxing statistician.

**Horse Racing** *The American Racing Manual 1994,* Daily Racing Form, Inc., 1994; *1994 Directory and Record Book,* The Thoroughbred Racing Association, 1994; *The Trotting and Pacing Guide 1994,* United States Trotting Association, 1994; *Breeders' Cup 1993 Statistics,* Breeders' Cup Limited, 1993; *NYRA Media Guide 1993,* The New York Racing Association, 1994; *The 120th Kentucky Derby Media Guide, 1994,* Churchill Downs Public Relations Dept., 1994; *The 120th Preakness Press Guide, 1994,* Maryland Jockey Club, 1994; *Harness Racing News,* Harness Racing Communications.

**Motor Sports** *The Official NASCAR Yearbook and Press Guide 1997,* UMI Publications, Inc., 1997; *1994 Indianapolis 500 Media Fact Book,* Indy 500 Publications, 1994; *IMSA Yearbook 1995 Season Review,* International Motor Sports Association, 1995; *1994 Winston Drag Racing Series Media Guide,* Sports Marketing Enterprises, 1994.

**Bowling** *1994 Professional Bowlers Association Press, Radio and Television Guide,* Professional Bowlers Association, Inc., 1994; *The Professional Women's Bowling Association Tour Guide 1997.*

**Soccer** *Rothmans Football Yearbook 1993–94,* Headline Book Publishing, 1993; *American Professional Soccer League 1992 Media Guide,* APSL Media Relations Department, 1992; The *European Football Yearbook,* Facer Publications Limited, 1988; *Soccer America,* Burling Communications; Dan Goldstein, editor of *Football Europe.*

**NCAA Sports** *1997–98 National Collegiate Championships,* The National Collegiate Athletic Association, 1998; *1993–94 National Directory of College Athletics,* Collegiate Directories Inc., 1993.

**Olympics** *The Complete Book of the Olympics,* Little, Brown and Co., 1991; *The Complete Book of the Summer Olympics,* Little, Brown and Co., 1996.

**Track and Field** *American Athletics Annual 1996,* The Athletics Congress/USA, 1996.

**Swimming** *6th World Swimming Championships Media Guide,* The World Swimming Championships Organizing Committee, 1991.

**Skiing** *U.S. Ski Team 1994 Media Guide / USSA Directory,* U.S. Ski Association, 1993; *Ski Racing Annual Competition Guide 1993–94,* Ski Racing International, 1993; *Ski Magazine's Encyclopedia of Skiing,* Harper & Row, 1974; *Caffe Lavazza Ski World Cup Press Kit,* Biorama, 1991.

# The Year In Sports

**Football returns to Giants Stadium 19 days after the terrorist attacks**

# Time Out

## After pausing to honor the victims of the Sept. 11 terrorist attacks, the sports world resumed play in the spirit of healing

### BY MERRELL NODEN

THIS WAS the year we were all reminded, suddenly, terribly, and perhaps irrevocably, of exactly where sports stand in the grand scheme of things. The Sept. 11 terrorist attacks on the World Trade Center and the Pentagon—and the crash of a fourth hijacked plane in rural Pennsylvania—left the entire nation and much of the world in a stupor of disbelief and horror, bringing the world of games to a stunned halt. For blinkered sports nuts, this was a strong dose of perspective.

Whereas only days earlier, on Sept. 8, 9 or 10, we had spent our time wondering whether or not Barry Bonds would break Mark McGwire's single-season home run record, or if Michael Jordan would come out of retirement to play for the Washington Wizards, by mid-morning on Sept. 11, nobody cared. In the anxious, eerie aftermath of the attacks, sports were the last thing on anyone's mind. Sports rivalries were instantly replaced by a somber awareness of the many more things we shared:

We were all Americans, and we were all pretty shaken up.

Here and there, you heard talk of playing on as an act of defiance and community. "In times of sorrow and fear," argued SPORTS ILLUSTRATED's Frank Deford, "the chance for Americans to gather in any huge stadium, to stand together, bound together, provides a powerful—even patriotic—nectar."

And perhaps sports would have supplied that nectar—had anyone been able to muster the will to play. At only one major U.S. professional event did officials follow Deford's advice. The Big Island Championships, a Women's Tennis Association event in Hawaii, suspended play on Sept. 11 but resumed it the following day. Everyone else followed the example of NFL Commissioner Paul Tagliabue, who, mindful of what former NFL commissioner Pete Rozelle called the biggest mistake of his career—allowing play to go forward the weekend after the Kennedy assassination—canceled that week's games, saying, "At a certain point, playing our games can contribute to

**Heupel and Oklahoma surprised everyone by knocking off Florida State in the Orange Bowl to win the national title.**

longed for was much in evidence, as flags were unfurled across end zones, in outfields and on the back of every major league baseball uniform. New York City firefighters and police officers found themselves guests of honor at sports events everywhere, and the New York Mets were given special dispensation by the league to abandon their usual caps in favor of dark blue ones bearing the initials NYPD and FDNY. The Mets wore the new caps as they made a late-September charge that brought them to the brink of the playoffs and salvaged an otherwise dismal season.

Of course, there was more to 2001 than that one horrific day. The events of Sept. 11 ripped the year into two very different parts. From our vantage point now, on the awful side of that date, the first eight months of 2001 look blessedly

the healing process. Just not at this time." Major league baseball did not resume its schedule until the following Monday, Sept. 17, creating the longest suspension of play since World War I. The Ryder Cup, scheduled for Sept. 28–30, at the Belfry in England, was postponed until next year.

And when sports did resume—a week or so later, in most cases—it was with a pronounced deference to the nation's somber mood and an awareness that, starting on Oct. 7, the U.S. was bombing Afghanistan, the nation harboring the prime suspect in the attacks, Saudi militant Osama bin Laden. At a preseason NHL game between the Flyers and the New York Rangers in Philadelphia's First Union Center, fans booed until arena officials stopped the game so that the crowd could watch and listen to President Bush's address to Congress on the scoreboard screen. The game was not resumed.

The communal "nectar" that Deford

carefree. Those months bear witness to the sports world's usual smorgasbord of miracles and chokes, of dynasties in the making and brilliant newcomers. At a time when we so need to believe that comebacks are possible, we can look back on more than a few inspiring comebacks. There were painful reminders of mortality, too, in the form of several sudden deaths, which, unhappy though they were, forced us to reexamine the practices that may have caused them. So let's go back, with a sense of something like nostalgia, to the start of 2001, when we could afford to place undue importance upon the outcome of college football's national championship.

That title was decided on Jan. 3 in the Orange Bowl, between surprising Oklahoma and heavily favored Florida State, with its 28-year-old, Heisman Trophy–winning quarterback, Chris Weinke. Whereas the defending champion Seminoles had not finished outside the Top 4 since 1986, the once-formidable Sooners had not cracked the Top 10 since 1987. Oklahoma accumulated more wins than believers, it seemed, as the season progressed. In their ninth game of the year, the Sooners kept their undefeated season intact by overcoming a 14-point second-half deficit to defeat Texas A&M 35–31 on the road. Still, the 12–0 Sooners lined up for the Orange Bowl as the decided underdogs. Then they defied the skeptics once and for all, whipping Bobby Bowden's Seminoles 13–2. Outplaying the befuddled Weinke, who threw two interceptions and coughed up the fumble that led to the Sooners' only touchdown, Oklahoma quarterback Josh Heupel threw for 214 yards and ran for another 23, only four fewer than the entire Florida State team produced on 17 rushes. "It seemed like they had radar," said Seminole wideout Atrews Bell. "Everything we tried they were ready for."

The NFL had a seemingly radar-equipped defense of its own: that of the Baltimore Ravens, who set a record for fewest points allowed in a season (165). A .500 team the previous year, the Ravens went 12–4 and spearheaded a season that subverted expec-

**Michigan-bound Webb (28) broke Ryun's 36-year-old scholastic record for the mile.**

tations across the board. Though the best record in the league belonged to the defending AFC champion Tennessee Titans (13–3), there were several new faces among the contenders, and several favorites fell flat. The New Orleans Saints improved from 3–13 to 10–6 and made the playoffs for the first time since 1992. There, they beat the defending Super Bowl champion St. Louis Rams and their star running back Marshall Faulk, who had been named league MVP for a season in which he ran for 1,359 yards, caught 81 passes and scored an NFL-record 26 touchdowns, 18 rushing and eight receiving.

The Washington Redskins, who went on a free-agent shopping spree in the offseason, finished 8–8 and out of the playoffs. Only one Super Bowl–winning franchise from the '90s made it past the wild-card round, and that was the New York Giants. The Giants won their last five games to secure home-field advantage throughout the playoffs, and they put that advantage to good use, routing the Minnesota Vikings 41–0 in the NFC title game, to set up a Super Bowl meeting with the Ravens.

All season long, these Ravens left offenses pondering, weak and weary. They allowed a stingy 10.3 points a game and had grown even more parsimonious in the AFC

SIMON BRUTY

AP

playoffs, surrendering 16 points in three victories. The heart of the Baltimore defense was unquestionably middle linebacker Ray Lewis, who played the entire season under a cloud of media scrutiny and suspicion after engaging in a brawl outside an Atlanta nightclub following the previous year's Super Bowl. Two men were stabbed to death during the fight, and Lewis spent several months as a murder suspect. He would plead guilty to a lesser charge of obstruction of justice in June and receive one year's probation.

In the Super Bowl, the Ravens utterly dominated the Giants, intercepting four of Kerry Collins's passes and sacking him four times, en route to a 34–7 demolition. For Lewis, it was a moment of triumph, though hardly of vindication. "To be here after what happened last year," Lewis said after the game, "it's a feeling you can't describe."

While Lewis triumphed in January, NASCAR experienced tragedy in February, at its premier event, the Daytona 500. Entering Turn 4 of the last lap, Dale Earnhardt, arguably the sport's brightest star, died instantly when his Chevy Monte Carlo crashed head-on into the wall. "Dale was the Michael Jordan of our sport," said Humpy Wheeler, president of Lowe's Motor Speedway near Charlotte. "To think he is not around anymore is incomprehensible. This is a terrible, terrible loss."

It was ruled that Earnhardt died as a result of a severe injury at the base of his skull. Dr. Steve Bohannon, Daytona's EMS director, said that he did not think that either a HANS (head-and-neck support) device or a full-face helmet would have saved Earnhardt, but his death did have the positive effect of training a spotlight on NASCAR's safety precautions, spurring several changes.

One reassuring antidote to life's nasty jolts is continuity, and for that, one turns to the Blue Devils hoopsters of Duke who, under coach Mike Krzyzewski, have made the NCAA title game six times in 12 years, and won three times. This year's team was led by senior Shane Battier, an academic-minded forward. After coming back from a 39–17 deficit to beat Maryland in the national semis, the Blue Devils shook off pesky Arizona in the title game to win 82–72. At 54, Krzyzewski has coached Duke to three NCAA titles, putting him in the exclusive company of Bob Knight, Adolph Rupp and John Wooden as the only men with three or more national championships.

In the women's championship game, Notre Dame held off cross-state rival Purdue, 68–66. Ruth Riley, Notre Dame's 6' 5" center, dominated in the paint, grabbing 13 rebounds, scoring 28 points and blocking seven shots. As impressive as Riley was, she had to share the spotlight with Southwest Missouri State's tireless sharpshooter, Jackie Stiles, who, after setting an NCAA career scoring record during the regular season, carried her upstart team to the Final Four, where she scored 22 points in a semifinal loss to Purdue.

Six days after Duke's impressive victory, Tiger Woods won the Masters by two strokes over David Duval. Not only did that put an end to all the early-season talk of a slump, it made Woods the first person to hold all four of golf's major championships simultaneously. But with the Holy Grail of a single-year Slam on the horizon, Woods seemed to falter. His best finish at a major after the Masters was 12th, in the U.S. Open.

No one could have guessed that with Woods seven strokes adrift, the three men in contention at the U.S. Open at Southern Hills would be Stewart Cink, Mark Brooks and South Africa's Retief Goosen. Or that all three would three-putt the final green, Goosen from only 15 feet. And he turned out to be the winner, edging Brooks by two strokes in an 18-hole playoff. In July, Duval won his first Grand Slam event, taking the British Open at Royal Lytham and removing the cumbersome label of "best player never to have won a major." And at the PGA Championship, in Atlanta, David Toms got up and down from 88 yards on the monstrous par-4 490-yard 18th to finish one stroke ahead of Phil Mickelson.

If the respected Duval's triumph was heartening, the comeback of superstar hockey player Mario Lemieux was downright inspiring. The National Hockey League got a huge midseason boost when the 35-year-old cancer survivor announced that he would come out of retirement to play for the team he partially owns, the Pittsburgh Penguins. On Dec. 27, just 33 seconds into his first game, Lemieux set up a goal by Jaromir Jagr, then added an assist and a goal of his own in Pittsburgh's 5–0 win over Toronto. Lemieux's return proved to be a boon to Jagr, who won his fourth straight NHL scoring title with 121 points on 52 goals and 69 assists. With their superstar back in the fold, the Penguins made it all the way to the Eastern Conference finals, where they fell in five games to the defending champion New Jersey Devils.

In the Stanley Cup finals, the Devils ran into the Colorado Avalanche and goaltender Patrick Roy, who won in seven games. Though Roy was magnificent, stopping 49 of 50 shots in Games 6 and 7 to win a record third playoff MVP trophy, it was his graybeard teammate, Ray Bourque, who was the sentimental hero. In his 22nd season and fourth decade of play, Bourque finally won the hallowed Cup. He announced his retirement several weeks later.

Another stirring argument for hanging in there was made by Jennifer Capriati, who overcame the scars of child stardom to win the Australian and French Opens and seize the No. 1 ranking in October. Capriati reached the Wimbledon semis, but lost to Justine Henin, who was herself beaten by Venus Williams in the final. In the U.S. Open, Williams and her sister, Serena, made history by meeting in the final, a sibling matchup that hadn't occurred in a major since 1884. Venus won in straight sets, and, having won four of the last six Grand Slam events, she is arguably the most talented player on the tour. There were no double winners among the men in Grand Slam play, as Andre Agassi won his seventh major at the Australian Open, claycourt specialist Gustavo Kuerten won the French, Goran Ivanisevic beat Patrick Rafter in a Wimbledon final for the ages, and Lleyton Hewitt downed Pete Sampras for the U.S. Open title.

While parity reigned in men's tennis, a dynasty grew in men's basketball as Shaquille O'Neal, Kobe Bryant and the Lakers defended their NBA title. But the championship was by no means a foregone conclusion, as the Laker's two stars, O'Neal and Bryant, feuded all season over who was the team's true go-to guy, causing the team to sputter and clearing the way for several other contenders. Among them were the steady San Antonio Spurs, led by David Robinson and Tim Duncan; the flashy Sacramento Kings, led by Chris Webber; and the Philadelphia 76ers, an anonymous cast content to support the league's leading scorer and regular-season MVP, Allen Iverson.

Surely it took all of Phil Jackson's skill as a zen psychologist and motivator to do so, but he managed to restore balance and harmony to his team. The Lakers swept all pretenders from their path, beating the Blazers, the Kings and the Spurs without a loss to set up a finals showdown with the 76ers. After losing Game 1, the Lakers won four straight to seize the title.

Like the Lakers in the NBA—but for reasons of strategy rather than ego—Lance Armstrong started slowly in the Tour de France before turning it on in the moun-

**Williams produced another banner year, winning Wimbledon and the U.S. Open.**

tains to win the 21-stage race for the third straight year. He beat Jan Ullrich of Germany by six minutes and 44 seconds. Like Lemieux, Armstrong is a cancer survivor and, seemingly, a flesh-and-blood advertisement for courage in hard times. But some of the delight was sucked out of Armstrong's win because of reports that he'd made several visits to Italian doctor Michele Ferrari, who is awaiting trial on charges of providing riders with the dangerous blood-boosting drug EPO.

In track and field, fans and athletes said goodbye to Michael Johnson, the sport's biggest star in the '90s, who retired. Olympic 100 champ Maurice Greene made another claim to the title of greatest 100 man in history by winning his third straight world title, clocking 9.82 on an injured leg. Marion Jones didn't fare so well. At the world championships, she lost her first 100 after 42 straight wins, to Zhanna Pintusevich-Block of the Ukraine, though Jones did come back to win the 200 and anchor the U.S.'s triumphant 400-meter relay team.

While Jones appeared unfocused or tired after her heroics in Sydney, Stacy Dragila took over as the top woman in track and field, setting eight world records in the pole vault. Other barriers fell in the decathlon, where Roman Sebrle of the Czech Republic became the first person to top 9,000 points, and in the women's marathon, in which Japan's Naoko Takahashi became the first woman to break 2:20, clocking 2:19:46 in Berlin—only to see her record broken seven days later by Catherine Ndereba of Kenya, who ran 2:18:47 in Chicago.

Still, there was no doubt who the most exciting star in U.S. track and field was this year. It was Alan Webb, an 18-year-old from Reston, Va., who ran a staggering 3:53.43 mile to break Jim Ryun's 36-year-old national high-school record by 1.87 seconds. That was the fastest mile run by an American of any age since 1998.

A teenager stole the spotlight in swimming, too, though that was hardly a surprise since the youngster in question was Ian Thorpe, who has starred for three years now. The sensational Australian looks to be on his way to becoming the greatest swimmer in history. At the world championships in Fukuoka, Japan, Thorpe won a meet-record six gold medals and set world records in the 200, 400 and 800 freestyles, plus the 4x200 freestyle relay. The U.S. star in Fukuoka was Michael Phelps, a 16-year-old junior at Towson (Md.) High School, who won the 200 butterfly in a world-record 1:54.58.

Pro football absorbed a tragic hit on August 1, when Korey Stringer, the Minnesota Vikings' popular All-Pro tackle, died from heat exhaustion after a preseason workout. Stringer's death was bookended by the heat-related deaths of Florida fullback Eraste Autin and Northwestern safety Rashidi Wheeler, an asthma sufferer, during preseason practices.

Baseball's long season was the last one for two classy future Hall of Famers. Bow-

JOHN IACONO

back from 2–0 down to shock the young Oakland A's in the Division Series.

Joining oldtimers Gwynn and Ripken in the late-season spotlight was 42-year-old Rickey Henderson of the Padres, who scored career run No. 2,246 to break Ty Cobb's record. But home run hitters, as they had in 1998, once again raised the bar. Arizona leftfielder Luis Gonzalez hit 57 homers—and finished third in the National League home run race. Sammy Sosa hit 64 to become the first player to top 60 in three seasons. But the undisputed star of this power-mad year was Barry Bonds, who walked a record 177 times yet still cracked 73 homers to break McGwire's record of 70. His slugging percentage of .863 was another record, topping Babe Ruth's 81-year-old record.

Yet for a number of reasons Bonds's heroics failed to ignite the excitement McGwire's and Sosa's had in 1998. And in the end, his chase was over-shadowed by the events of Sept. 11. So too was Michael Jordan's tease of a return, at 38, to play for the Washington Wizards, a team of which he was part owner. On Oct. 30, having divested his stake in the team, Jordan played in the Wizards' season opener, scoring 19 points in a sloppy 93–91 loss to the Knicks in New York. Even Air Jordan could not transport us to that distant, more innocent world.

For further evidence of the many ways in which the world of sports was changed by the Sept. 11 attacks, we need only wait for the college bowl games; for the Super Bowl, which despite heavy lobbying for a symbolic change of venue to New York, is scheduled for Feb. 3 in New Orleans; and above all, for the 2002 Winter Olympics, which will begin on Feb. 8 in Salt Lake City.

Security will be tighter than ever before, as it must be now every time Americans assemble in large numbers. But that nectar will still draw us, irresistibly, even if we look both ways before leaning in for a taste.

ing out with their customary good grace were eight-time batting champ Tony Gwynn of the San Diego Padres, and Ironman Cal Ripken Jr. who set the record for consecutive games played (2,632) during his 21-year career with the Baltimore Orioles.

The Seattle Mariners, who lost All-Stars Randy Johnson, Ken Griffey Jr. and Alex Rodriguez in the previous three years, won 116 games, tying the 1906 Chicago Cubs. Leading the way for Seattle was rightfielder Ichiro Suzuki, who won seven straight batting titles in Japan before signing with the Mariners and threatening George Sisler's single-season hits record of 257. He settled for 242 (and a AL-leading .350 average), tops in the majors since 1930. The Mariners rallied to beat the Cleveland Indians in the first round of the American League playoffs but then fell to the New York Yankees in the ALCS. The Yankees themselves had to come

# The Year in Sports Calendar

*compiled by John Bolster*

## Baseball

**Nov 1, 2000**—The day after the New York Mets re-sign manager Bobby Valentine for three years and the Seattle Mariners come to terms with skipper Lou Piniella on a three-year deal, the Philadelphia Phillies hire former All-Star shortstop Larry Bowa to succeed Terry Francona as their manager, and the Los Angeles Dodgers name former bench coach Jim Tracy to replace outgoing skipper Davey Johnson.

**Nov 2**—Six-time All-Star first baseman Will Clark, 36, a career .303 hitter who signed with the Cardinals for the 2000 stretch run, announces his retirement. In Toronto, the Blue Jays announce that they've signed TV color commentator Buck Martinez to be their manager, making Martinez the second man of the week to move from the broadcast booth to the dugout. Two days earlier Bob Brenly made the switch to take the reins of the Arizona Diamondbacks.

**Nov 6**—Thirty-two-year old Seattle reliever Kazuhiro Sasaki is named American League Rookie of the Year. The alltime saves leader in

Japan, Sasaki set a major league record for saves by a rookie with 37. He is the second-oldest player to win the award, after Sam Jethroe of the Boston Braves, who was 33 days older when he was named top rookie in the NL in 1950.

**Nov 7**—Rafael Furcal of the Atlanta Braves is named NL Rookie of the Year. Furcal, a 20-year-old shortstop who jumped from Class A to the majors, batted .295 with 40 stolen bases.

**Nov 8**—After leading the White Sox to a 95–67 season, the AL's best record, Chicago skipper Jerry Manuel is named AL Manager of the Year. The following day, San Francisco manager Dusty Baker, who, like Manuel, is from Sacramento, wins the NL Manager of the Year Award. Baker led the Giants to a 97–65 record, tops in baseball.

**Nov 13**—Boston Red Sox ace Pedro Martinez becomes the first pitcher ever to win the Cy Young Award by a unanimous vote in consecutive seasons. Martinez went 18–6 with a career-best ERA of 1.74 and a league-leading 284 strikeouts. The following day Randy Johnson of the Arizona Diamondbacks wins the NL Cy Young award for a season in which he went 19–7 with a 2.64 ERA and a league-leading 347 strikeouts.

**Nov 15**—The American League MVP award goes to Oakland first baseman Jason Giambi, who batted .333 with 43 homers and 137 RBIs to help the A's win the AL West title.

**Nov 16**—Second baseman Jeff Kent of the Giants wins the NL MVP award after a season in which he belted 33 homers, drove in 125 runs and batted .334.

**Nov 26**—After being courted by the Phillies, who had offered him the closer's role and a chance to pursue Lee Smith's major-league record of 478 saves, reliever John Franco re-signs with his hometown team, the Mets, for whom he is the setup man. Franco has 420 career saves.

**Nov 30**—The three-time defending champion New York Yankees land the top pitcher on the free-agent market, signing former Baltimore righthander Mike Mussina, a five-time All-Star, to a six-year $88.5 million contract. Mussina joins a formidable staff that already includes Roger Clemens, Orlando Hernandez and Andy Pettitte.

PETER READ MILLER

**Suzuki slid right into major league superstardom, batting .350 to lead the AL.**

**Dec 11**—Five days after re-signing veteran pitcher Rick Reed, the Mets agree to terms with free-agent righthanders Kevin Appier, formerly of Oakland, and Steve Trachsel, who played for Toronto and Tampa Bay in 2000.

**Dec 11**—The Texas Rangers sign free-agent shortstop Alex Rodriguez to the richest contract in sports history. Rodriguez, who hit .316 with 41 home runs and 132 RBIs for Seattle in 2000, agrees to a 10-year, $252 million deal with Texas.

**Dec 12**—The free-agent spending spree continues as Boston signs former Cleveland slugger Manny Ramirez to an eight-year, $160 million contract. Ramirez sat out 44 games in 2000 with a hamstring injury, but still belted 38 HRs and drove in 122 runs while hitting .351.

**Dec 14**—Righthander Curt Schilling signs a three-year, $32 million contract extension with Arizona.

**Dec 19**—The Houston Astros extend the contract of first baseman Jeff Bagwell, the 1994 NL MVP, for five years and $85 million.

**Jan 7, 2001**—After paying $13 million in November for the rights to negotiate with him, Seattle signs Ichiro Suzuki, a seven-time batting champion in Japan, for three years and $14.1

**Ripken hit a memorable homer in the All-Star Game, then waved goodbye after 21 years.**

CHUCK SOLOMON

million. Two days later former Detroit Tigers slugger Juan Gonzalez signs a one-year, $10 million deal with Cleveland.

**Jan 11**—Former Yankees pitcher David Cone, 38, signs a one-year, $4.5 million contract with New York's archrival, Boston.

**Jan 14**—Pitcher David Wells moves from the Blue Jays to the White Sox in a six-player deal.

**Jan 16**—Former All-Stars Dave Winfield and Kirby Puckett are elected to the baseball Hall of Fame on the first ballot.

**Feb 7**—The New York Yankees and English soccer dynasty Manchester United announce that they've struck a joint marketing agreement to sell one another's licensed goods.

**Feb 8**—Signing the richest contract in Yankees' history, and the second most lucrative in sports, New York shortstop Derek Jeter re-ups for 10 years and $189 million.

**Feb 18**—Hall of Fame third baseman Eddie Mathews, 69, dies in a San Diego hospital of complications from pneumonia. Mathews teamed with Henry Aaron to help deliver Milwaukee its only World Series title, in 1957.

**Feb 25**—The Dodgers trade outfielder Devon White to the Milwaukee Brewers in exchange for outfielder Marquis Grissom and a minor leaguer.

**March 1**—Veterans Randy Johnson of Arizona and Mark McGwire of St. Louis each renew their contracts during spring training. Negotiating without an agent, McGwire extends his deal with the Cardinals for two more years and $30 million, while the Diamondbacks exercise a $12 million option to keep Johnson for the 2003 season.

**March 6**—The Veterans Committee elects former Pirates second baseman Bill Mazeroski and ex-Negro leagues pitcher Hilton Smith to the Hall of Fame. In 1960, Mazeroski became the first player to end a World Series with a home run, belting a solo shot in the bottom of the ninth to beat the Yankees in Game 7.

**March 7**—Baseball commissioner Bud Selig declines to reverse a six-player deal made on Jan. 14 between Toronto and the White Sox. Toronto had filed an appeal asking for restitution because one of the players they received in the trade, pitcher Mike Sirotka, was found to have a shoulder injury. Selig rules that Chicago owes no compensation because the Blue Jays mistakenly assumed the trade could be conditional.

**March 28**—First baseman Todd Helton of the Colorado Rockies signs the fourth-richest contract in sports history, rejoining the Rockies for $151 million over 11 years.

**April 1**—The 2001 Major League Baseball season opens at Hiram Bithorn Stadium in Puerto Rico, homeland of Hall of Famers Roberto

Clemente and Orlando Cepeda. Fans line up for admission 11 hours before the game, in which Toronto pounds Texas 8–1.

**April 2**—Opening Day in North America sees fireballer Roger Clemens of the defending champion Yankees pitch his team to a 7–3 victory over Kansas City and, in the ninth inning of the game, eclipse Walter Johnson as the AL's alltime leader in strikeouts, notching his fifth of the game and 3,509th of his career. In other games, Cleveland's newly acquired slugger Juan Gonzalez homers twice in the Indians' 7–4 loss to the White Sox, and Colorado's new ace, Mike Hampton, throws 8⅓ scoreless innings at Coors Field as the Rockies defeat St. Louis 8–0.

**April 2**—Absent from a Tampa drug treatment center for four days, his whereabouts unknown during that span, former major league slugger Darryl Strawberry checks into a Tampa hospital. Strawberry, who is undergoing treatment for colon cancer, is charged with violating a probation warrant. He had been under house arrest for drug and solicitation offenses.

**April 4**—In his first start for the Red Sox, Hideo Nomo twirls a no-hitter as Boston beats the Orioles 3–0 at Camden Yards. Nomo sets a record by pitching his gem at the earliest point in the season, surpassing Detroit's Jack Morris (1984) and Houston's Ken Forsch (1979) by three days.

**April 17**—Giants outfielder Barry Bonds belts a two-run homer to give San Francisco a 3–2 victory over the Dodgers and push his career HR total to 500. He is the 17th player to reach the milestone.

**April 24**—Rickey Henderson of San Diego ties Babe Ruth's record for career walks (2,062), as he draws a base on balls during the Padres' 12–7 loss to Philadelphia. He breaks it the following night.

**April 26**—Boston's Hideo Nomo, who pitched a no-hitter on April 4, nearly becomes the first pitcher since 1900 to throw two no-hitters in a season, giving up only a disputed seventh-inning single in a 2–0 win over Minnesota.

**May 8**—Arizona lefthander Randy Johnson ties the major league record for strikeouts in a game, fanning 20 Cincinnati batters in the Diamondbacks' 4–3 victory over the Reds in Phoenix. Johnson joins Kerry Wood and Roger Clemens, who did it twice, as the record holders.

**May 10**—Two weeks after injuring his triceps while diving for a ball in a game against Seattle, White Sox slugger Frank Thomas, a two-time AL MVP, undergoes an MRI exam and learns that he has torn the muscle and will miss the rest of the season.

**May 13**—Ichiro Suzuki, the Mariners' newly acquired outfielder from Japan, raps out three hits in Seattle's 7–5 victory over Toronto to extend his run of consecutive games with at least one hit

to 19, the longest such streak of the season. Suzuki is batting .360 and the Mariners are off to a 28–9 start.

**May 15**—Filling in for the injured Mark McGwire in the cleanup spot, Cardinals rookie Albert Pujols continues his torrid season by going 3-for-4 with a home run in St. Louis's 8–3 victory over the Pirates. Pujols is among the NL leaders in batting average (.381), RBIs (43) and hits (53).

**May 16**—With a two-run homer to rightfield during the Cubs' 6–2 loss to Houston, Chicago's Sammy Sosa becomes the 33rd member of baseball's 400-homer club.

**May 20**—San Francisco leftfielder Barry Bonds goes on a home run tear during a series against the Braves, belting one on Friday, three on Saturday and two on Sunday. The feat makes him the eighth player to hit six home runs in three games and the 23rd to hit five dingers in two games.

**May 31**—Felipe Alou, who has been with the Montreal Expos for 27 years as a player, coach and manager, is dismissed as skipper after leading the Expos to a 21–32 start.

**June 10**—Rockies lefthander Mike Hampton hits his fifth home run of the season, the most by a pitcher since 1972, and pitches 5⅔ innings to pick up his ninth win of the season as Colorado defeats St. Louis 12—3.

**June 19**—Cal Ripken Jr. announces that this season, his 21st as a Baltimore Oriole, will be his last. In San Diego, the Giants' Barry Bonds ties Reggie Jackson's major league record for home runs before the All-Star break, belting his 37th of the year during San Francisco's 4–3 victory over the Padres.

**June 27**—San Diego first baseman Tony Gwynn, an eight-time batting champion, announces that he will retire after the season.

**July 1**—Bouncing back from a three-game sweep by Atlanta that knocked them out of first place in the NL East, the Phillies complete a five-game sweep of Florida, only the second such sweep in franchise history, to reclaim first place.

**July 10**—Having announced on June 19 that he would retire following the season, Baltimore third baseman Cal Ripken Jr. steps to the batter's box in the third inning of the All-Star Game and after receiving a standing ovation from the crowd at Seattle's Safeco Field, hits the first pitch from the Dodgers' Chan Ho Park over the leftfield fence, drawing another standing ovation. The American League wins the game 4–1 and Ripken is named MVP. He and Tony Gwynn, who also will retire after the season, are honored by Commissioner Bud Selig in a special ceremony during the sixth inning.

**July 15**—The Dodgers defeat the Pirates 4–2 in Pittsburgh but lose ace Kevin Brown for the season when he injures his right elbow during the game.

**July 17**—After going 1–4 with two blown saves and a 15.42 ERA in his previous five appearances, Cleveland pitcher John Rocker is relieved of his duties as closer.

**July 19**—Finishing a game that had been suspended on July 18 because of a problem with stadium lighting, Diamondbacks pitcher Randy Johnson sets a record for strikeouts by a reliever, whiffing 16 Padres after picking up the game in the third inning. Johnson also strikes out seven in a row, an NL relief record, in Arizona's 3–0 victory.

**Aug 1**—Mark McGwire hits the 573rd home run of his career—a two-run shot off Atlanta's Greg Maddux in the sixth inning of a 4–0 St. Louis victory—to move into a tie with Hall of Famer Harmon Killebrew for fifth place on the alltime list.

**Aug 7**—Atlanta's Greg Maddux breaks an NL record for consecutive innings pitched without issuing a walk, running his streak to 70⅓ innings during the Braves' 6–5 win over Houston.

**Aug 12**—The surging Oakland Athletics win their 11th in a row, defeating the Yankees 4–2 to complete a three-game sweep of the defending champions.

**Aug 16**—With his club five games off the pace in the AL East, Boston GM Dan Duquette fires manager Jimy Williams and replaces him with pitching coach Joe Kerrigan.

**Sept 3**—The Cardinals' Bud Smith becomes the 16th rookie in modern baseball history to pitch a no-hitter, when he holds the Padres hitless in a 4–0 win in San Diego.

**Sept 9**—In Denver, Barry Bonds hits three home runs in the Giants 9–4 win over the Rockies, bringing his season total to 63, seven short of Mark McGwire's single-season record with 18 games to play.

**Sept 17**—Major League Baseball resumes play after a six-day hiatus in the wake of the terrorist attacks on New York City and Washington, D.C.

**Sept 23**—Oakland completes its comeback from a dismal April by clinching the AL wild card with a 7–4 victory over Seattle, which clinched the AL West on Sept. 19.

**Oct 2**—Sammy Sosa hits his 60th homer of the year to become the first player in baseball history to produce three 60-homer seasons. He hit 66 in 1998 and 63 in '99. Two days later the Padres' Rickey Henderson breaks Ty Cobb's career record for runs scored, notching his 2,246th with a home run against the Dodgers. On Oct. 7 Henderson knocks the 3,000th hit of his career.

**Oct 5**—Having tied the record the night before, San Francisco's Barry Bonds breaks Mark McGwire's three-year old record for home runs in a season, cracking his 71st of the year in the first inning against the Dodgers' Chan Ho Park. Bonds

hits No. 72 his next time up, but despite his production the Giants lose the game 11–10 and are eliminated from playoff contention. Bonds takes a pinch-hitting role on Oct. 6, then finishes the season on Oct. 7 the way he began it, with a home run, his 73rd of the year. It comes against Los Angeles's Dennis Springer.

**Oct 6**—Seattle equals the major league record for wins in a season, beating Texas for its 116th win of the year, tying the Chicago Cubs of 1906. The following day the M's lose 4–3 to the Rangers. The baseball season closes on Oct. 7, a week later than usual, due to the national calamity of Sept. 11. In addition to the above mentioned records, baseball fans witness the fond farewells of future Hall of Famers Tony Gwynn and Cal Ripken Jr.

**Oct 12**—Atlanta beats Houston 6–2 to sweep their NL Division Series 3–0 and advance to the NLCS for the ninth time since 1991. The Braves will meet Arizona, which defeats St. Louis 2–1 in Game 5 as pitcher Curt Schilling wins his second game of the Division Series.

**Oct 15**—The three-time defending champion Yankees become the first team in baseball history to win a five-game playoff series after losing the first two games at home. The Yanks take two in Oakland, then return home and wrap up the series with a 5–3 win. New York will meet Seattle, which downed Cleveland 3–1 in Game 5 of their Division Series.

**Oct 21**—The Arizona Diamondbacks, who joined major league baseball as an expansion team in 1998, advance to the World Series with a 3–2 win over Atlanta in Game 5 of the NLCS.

**Oct 22**—After winning Game 4 of the ALCS with a home run in the bottom of the ninth, the Yankees win Game 5 in a rout, pounding Seattle 12–3 to take their fourth straight AL pennant.

**Oct 28**—After Curt Schilling leads the Diamondbacks to a 9–1 victory in Game 1 of the World Series by holding the Yankees to three hits in seven innings, Randy Johnson twirls a complete-game shutout, guiding Arizona to a 4–0 win in Game 2 in Phoenix.

**Oct 31**—The Yankees, 2–1 winners in Game 3, knot the World Series at two games apiece as Tino Martinez hits a two-run homer with two out in the bottom of the ninth off Arizona closer Byung-Hyun Kim to tie the game at three and force extra innings, where Derek Jeter wins it with a walk-off solo shot in the bottom of the 10th.

**Nov 4**—The Arizona Diamondbacks turn the tables on the Yankees—who won Games 4 and 5 in their last at-bat—scoring two runs in the bottom of the ninth to win the World Series with a 3–2 victory in Game 7. The winning run comes on a bases-loaded bloop single by Luis Gonzalez. Pitchers Curt Schilling and Randy Johnson share the Series MVP award.

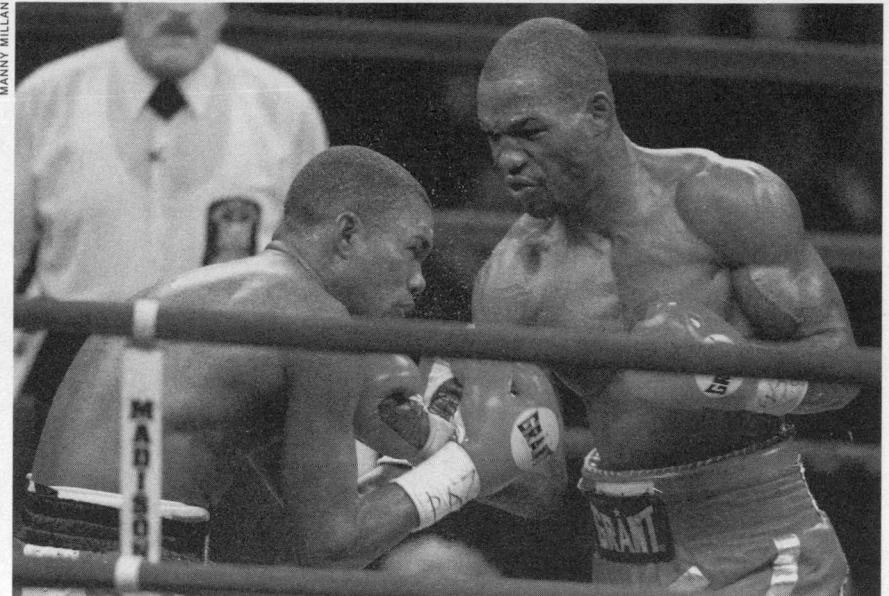

MANNY MILLAN

**Hopkins (right) pummeled Trinidad in the year's best, and most surprising, bout.**

**Nov 4, 2000**—Welterweight Sugar Shane Mosley retains the title he took from Oscar De La Hoya in June with a sixth-round knockout of Antonio Diaz in New York's Madison Square Garden Theater.

**Nov 11**—In Las Vegas, heavyweight champion Lennox Lewis defends his title with a unanimous decision over challenger David Tua.

**Dec 2**—In a stirring, back-and-forth bout that is immediately hailed as the fight of the year, Felix Trinidad stops Fernando Vargas in Las Vegas with three knockdowns in the 12th round. The victory makes Trinidad the undisputed junior middleweight champion.

**Jan 6, 2001**—With a ninth-round TKO of former champion Robert Garcia in Las Vegas, junior lightweight champion Joel Casamayor retains his title. Casamayor had been trailing on two of the three judges' scorecards when he stopped Garcia.

**Jan 9**—Three-time Olympic middleweight boxing champ Laszlo Papp of Hungary, who was forced into retirement by the Communist government of his country before he could fight for a world title, is elected to the International Boxing Hall of Fame.

**Jan 13**—Zab Judah defends his IBF junior welterweight belt with a 10th-round TKO of Reggie Green in Uncasville, Conn. The victory clears the way for Judah to fight the winner of the matchup between WBC champion Kostya Tszyu and WBA titleholder Sharmba Mitchell.

**Jan 16**—The Michigan Athletic Board of Control suspends heavyweight Mike Tyson's boxing license for three months after the fighter failed to submit a urine sample before his Oct. 20 bout with Andrew Golota in Auburn Hills, Mich. All other state commissions will uphold the suspension.

**Jan 20**—Decking challenger Diego Corrales three times in the seventh round and twice in the 10th, when the bout was stopped, Floyd Mayweather Jr. retains his junior lightweight title in Las Vegas. Afterward, the fight's referee, Richard Steele, a veteran of 167 title bouts, including the epic 1981 tilt between Thomas Hearns and Sugar Ray Leonard, announces his retirement.

**Feb 3**—Kostya Tszyu stops Sharmba Mitchell in the seventh round in Las Vegas to unify the WBA and WBC junior welterweight titles and set up a undisputed title fight with IBF champion Zab Judah.

**Feb 14**—International Boxing Federation founder Robert Lee is sentenced to 22 months in prison for tax evasion and money laundering.

**Feb 24**—Light heavyweight champion Roy Jones Jr. stops challenger Derrick Harmon after the 10th round in Tampa.

**March 3**—John Ruiz defeats Evander Holyfield in Las Vegas for the WBA heavyweight title. With the unanimous decision, Ruiz becomes the first Hispanic boxer to win a heavyweight belt.

**April 7**—A matchup of featherweight contenders in Las Vegas, England's Prince Naseem Hamed drops a unanimous decision to Marco Antonio Barrera of Mexico.

**April 14**—In New York City's Madison Square Garden Theater, Bernard Hopkins unifies the IBF and WBC middleweight titles with a lopsided decision over Keith Holmes.

**April 22**—Little known heavyweight Hasim Rahman of Baltimore pulls a shocker in Johannesburg, knocking out IBF and WBC champ Lennox Lewis in the fifth round of their title bout.

**May 12**—Felix Trinidad wins the WBA middleweight title with a devastating defeat of William Joppy at Madison Square Garden. Trinidad knocks Joppy down in the first, fourth and fifth rounds before the fight is stopped .

**May 19**—In a thunder-and-lightning super middleweight bout in Uncasville, Conn., Antwun Echols recovers from three second-round knockdowns to score a third-round TKO against Charles Brewer.

**May 26**—Fighting with two injured hands, and rallying from a sixth-round knockdown, junior lightweight champion Floyd Mayweather Jr. retains his title in Grand Rapids, Mich., by scoring a unanimous decision over Carlos Hernandez.

**June 16**—In his hometown of Cincinnati, Tim Austin knocks out Ghana's Steve Dotse in the sixth round to retain the IBF bantamweight title.

**June 23**—Oscar De La Hoya wins the WBC junior middleweight title with a unanimous decision over Spain's Javier Castillejo in Las Vegas. It is the fifth weight class in which De La Hoya has won a major title.

**July 28**—Light heavyweight champ Roy Jones Jr. wins a lopsided decision over Julio Gonzalez in Los Angeles.

**Aug 18**—Southpaw Chris Byrd, who fought as a middleweight during his amateur career, wins a shot at the heavyweight title after he outboxes David Tua over 12 rounds in Las Vegas.

**Sept 29**—The year's most hotly anticipated bout produces an unexpected result as Bernard Hopkins stops heavily favored Felix Trinidad in the 12th round at Madison Square Garden to win the undisputed middleweight championship.

**Oct 8**—In Paris, Argentina's Raul Balbi wins the WBA lightweight title with a majority decision over Julien Lorcy of France.

# College Basketball

**Nov 2, 2000**—The Web site Inside.com reports that former Indiana coach Bobby Knight will be paid $1.25 million to publish his memoirs with St. Martin's Press.

**Nov 7**—Citing recurring concussions, Stanford guard Jamie Carey, the 1999 Pac-10 freshman of the year, announces that she will end her career.

**Nov 11**—Kansas wins the Coaches vs. Cancer Classic, knocking off St. John's 82–74 in the final at Madison Square Garden.

**Nov 12**—Connecticut, the top-ranked women's team in the country, routs No. 3 Georgia 99–70 in the Hall of Fame Tip-Off Classic at the Hartford Civic Center.

**Nov 21**—As punishment for incidents of academic fraud at the school from 1993 to '99, the Big Ten strips Minnesota of its 1997 conference title and vacates all individual and team records set during the scandal years.

**Nov 26**—Stanford women's coach Tara VanDerveer seizes her 500th career victory as the Cardinal defeats Pacific 73–65 in Palo Alto. In the Maui Invitational championship game, Tennessee center Michelle Snow becomes the fifth player in women's college basketball history to dunk during a game when she rocks the rim late in the first half of the Vols' 111–62 trouncing of Illinois.

**Nov 25**—Purdue edges second-ranked Arizona 72–69 to win the inaugural Wooden Tradition in Indianapolis, a tournament named in honor of legendary UCLA coach—and former Purdue star—John Wooden.

**Nov 30**—The day after leading his team to an overtime defeat of 14th-ranked Maryland, Wisconsin coach Dick Bennett announces his retirement, effective immediately.

**Dec 4**—A rematch of the previous year's national finalists in East Lansing, Mich., ends much the way it did the first time, with Michigan State downing Florida 99–83.

**Dec 12**—The NCAA suspends UNLV from postseason play for one year and imposes scholarship and recruiting restrictions on the program for a variety of infractions, including a booster's $5,600 payment to former recruit Lamar Odom, who never attended the school. UNLV fires coach Bill Bayno in the wake of the NCAA's action.

**Dec 19**—In a battle of unbeatens at the Jimmy V Classic in East Rutherford, N.J., 14th-ranked Virginia steamrolls No. 4 Tennessee 107–89.

**Dec 21**—Third-ranked Stanford stays unbeaten and knocks off top-ranked Duke with an 84–83 victory in Oakland. Cardinal guard Casey Jacobsen banks in the winning shot with 3.6 seconds left.

**Jan 3, 2001**—Boston College ends a run of 23 games against Connecticut without a victory by beating the 10th-ranked Huskies 85–60 in Boston. The Eagles run their record to 10–0 with the win.

**Jan 7**—Indiana's Kirk Haston sinks a three-pointer at the buzzer to give the unranked Hoosiers a 59–58 upset of No.1 and previously unbeaten Michigan State. The loss drops the Spartans from first to third in the coaches' poll, with the top spot going to Stanford (13–0).

**Jan 13**—Missouri tops Iowa State 112–109 in quadruple-overtime in Columbia, Mo., as the Tigers' Clarence Gilbert scores 43 points.

**Jan 15**—Notre Dame makes its case for the No. 1 spot in the women's polls as it routs top-ranked Connecticut, the defending national champ, 92–76 in a battle of unbeatens in South Bend, Ind.

**Jan 28**—A plane carrying eight people associated with the Oklahoma State basketball program—two players and six staff members and broadcasters—crashes in Colorado, killing

**Stiles (10) took unsung Southwest Missouri State all the way to the women's Final Four.**

DAVID E. KLUTHO

everyone aboard. The school postpones the Cowboys Jan. 30 game against Texas Tech and schedules a memorial service for Jan. 31.

**Feb 14**—Virginia, which was trounced by Duke 103–61 on Jan. 13 in Durham, defeats the Blue Devils 91–89 in Charlottesville, setting a school record with the 44-point turnaround.

**Feb 20**—Michigan State downs Indiana 66–57 to give the Spartans' seniors their 108th win, which ties the Big Ten record for most wins in a four-year span, set by the Hoosier teams of 1972–76 and 1990–94.

**Feb 27**—Having blown a 10-point lead with 54 seconds remaining and lost its first meeting with Duke a month earlier, Maryland takes a heartening victory in Durham, rallying from seven points down to beat the Blue Devils 91–80.

**March 1**—Southwest Missouri State's Jackie Stiles sinks a three pointer early in the second half of a game against Creighton to run her career point total to 3,123, a new NCAA record.

**March 7**—Louisville's Denny Crum coaches his last game as the Cardinals fall to Alabama-Birmingham in the first round of the Conference USA tournament. Crum retires with 675 victories, 15th among Division I coaches. He will be succeeded by former Kentucky coach Rick Pitino.

**March 15**—The opening day of the NCAA tournament yields a bumper crop of upsets as 13th seed Kent State eliminates No. 4 Indiana 77–73, 12th-seeded Utah State upends No. 5 seed Ohio State 77–68 in overtime and 11th-seeded Georgia State rallies from a 16-point deficit to knock off sixth-seed and 2000 Final Four participant Wisconsin, 50–49. In other games, No. 2 seed Kentucky escapes 15th-seeded Holy Cross 72–68, and third-seeded Maryland edges No. 14 seed George Mason 83–80.

**March 22**—Eleventh-seeded Temple completes its surprising run to the South Regional final with an 84–72 win over another surprising team, Penn State, a seventh seed which had upset No. 2 seed North Carolina in the previous round.

**March 26**—Playing without injured All-Americas Shea Ralph and Svetlana Abrosimova, Connecticut advances to the women's Final Four with a 67–48 win over Louisiana Tech. UConn will play Notre Dame, a 72–64 winner over Vanderbilt. The other semifinal pits Purdue, an 88–78 winner over Xavier, against Soutwest Missouri State, which routed Washington 104–87 to advance.

**March 28**—The pairings for the men's Final Four are set as Michigan State ends Temple's Cinderalla run with a 69–62 victory to advance to the semis, where they will face Arizona, which defeated Illinois 87–81 in a matchup of the Midwest Region's top two seeds. The other semifinalists are ACC rivals Duke, which beat

Southern Cal 79–69 to advance, and Maryland, which cruised past Stanford 87–73 to reach the Final Four for the first time in school history.

**March 29**—In the NIT final at Madison Square Garden, Tulsa takes an 11-point halftime lead and never looks back, routing Alabama 79–60.

**April 1**—Trailing 42–26 at halftime, Notre Dame rallies behind senior center Ruth Riley's 28 points to overtake Purdue and win its first women's national title. Riley sinks two free throws with 5.8 seconds to give the Irish a 68–66 victory.

**April 2**—The top two teams in the first poll of the season, Arizona and Duke, square off in Minneapolis for the national championship. Duke wins the title 82–72 as Mike Dunleavy scores 21 points and Final Four MVP Shane Battier scores 18.

**May 14**—Two years after public revelations of academic fraud among members of its men's team, Minnesota fires its women's coach, Cheryl Littlejohn, for several violations, including giving money to a player and advising players to lie during a previous investigation.

**June 9**—Former Mississippi coach Van Chancellor, who coached the WNBA's Houston Comets to four league titles, leads a class of 10 inductees into the Women's Basketball Hall of Fame in Knoxville, Tenn.

**July 3**—The NCAA sends a letter to 52 Division I schools inquiring about eligibility issues for 62 international players enrolled in U.S. colleges.

**Sept 9**—Florida athletic director Jeremy Foley announces that point guard Teddy Dupay, who is involved in a gambling probe at the school, "is no longer eligible to play" for the Gators.

**Oct 13**—Bob Knight takes the court at Texas Tech for the first time as head coach, leading the Red Raiders in their opening "Midnight Madness" practice. Later in the day, officials at Indiana University, where Knight coached for 29 years, announce that they have canceled the Hoosiers' game with Texas Tech, scheduled for December 2002.

DAMIAN STROHMEYER

**Florida State's Weinke passed his way to the Heisman.**

Georgia Southern, the top-ranked team in Division I-AA, 45–10. The No. 2 team in Division I-AA, Delaware, also falls, blowing a 31–3 third-quarter lead and losing to New Hampshire 45–44 in overtime.

**Nov 4**—Quarterbacks Chris Weinke of Florida State and Josh Heupel of Oklahoma affirm their status as Heisman Trophy frontrunners while leading their teams to victories over Clemson and Baylor, respectively. Weinke completes 27 of 43 passes for 521 yards, while Heupel runs for one touchdown, passes for three others and connects on 20 of 27 throws for 313 yards.

**Nov 4**—Utah State running back Emmett White sets a new Div. I-A record for all-purpose yards when he gains 578 in the Aggies' 44–37 win over New Mexico State.

**Oct 31, 2000**—A Hudson County, N.J., grand jury clears Penn State quarterback Rashard Casey of a charge that he assaulted an off-duty cop outside a bar in Hoboken in May 2000.

**Nov 1**—Alabama athletic director Mal Moore announces that Crimson Tide coach Mike DuBose has agreed to resign following the season.

**Nov 4**—Furman running back Louis Ivory rushes for a school-record 301 yards as the Paladins upset

**Nov 11**—Top-ranked Oklahoma (9–0) keeps its national title hopes alive as it rallies from a 14-point second-half deficit to edge Texas A&M 35–31 in College Station, Texas.

**Nov 20**—On the strength of its 30–7 pasting of Florida, Florida State moves past Miami and into second place in the Bowl Championship Series (BCS) standings. Miami, which beat Florida State 27–24 in October, wallops Syracuse 26–0 but still drops to third in the BCS.

**Nov 24**—Charles Steger, the president of Virginia Tech, announces that football coach Frank Beamer, who had been approached by North Carolina and Alabama to fill their coaching vacancies, will receive a 25% pay raise that pushes his annual salary to $1.025 million. No word from Steger about salary adjustments or tenure arrangements among Virginia Tech faculty. In Los Angeles, Southern Cal coach Paul Hackett is dismissed after a 5–7 season. He joins coaches from Georgia, Wake Forest, Arizona and Arizona State (along with the above-mentioned North Carolina and Alabama) in the ranks of the unemployed.

**Dec 3**—The final BCS standings are set, and for the first time in its three-year history, the system fails to produce an undisputed national title game. While there is no doubt about the BCS's No. 1 team, undefeated Oklahoma, controversy clouds the system's choice for No. 2: Florida State (11–1). Many observers—and both the final coaches' poll and media poll—believe that Miami (10–1), which defeated the Seminoles during the season, is more deserving of the No. 2 spot, and the shot at the national title that comes with it. Objections aside, the Seminoles will meet Oklahoma in the Orange Bowl for the national championship while third-ranked Miami squares off against Florida (10–2) in the Sugar Bowl.

**Dec 12**—John Elway, Marcus Allen and Johnny Rodgers lead a class of 14 players and two coaches into the National Football Foundation and College Hall of Fame in South Bend, Ind.

**Dec 13**—The Southern Methodist program, which received the "death penalty" for NCAA violations in 1987, is penalized for running afoul of the NCAA once again. The Mustangs are placed on probation for two years for recruiting violations.

**Dec 9**—A 28-year-old senior who played minor league baseball for several years after high school, Florida State quarterback Chris Weinke wins the Heisman Trophy. The oldest player ever awarded the Heisman, Weinke, who led the nation with 4,167 passing yards, wins the trophy by 76 points over Oklahoma QB Josh Heupel. It is the seventh-closest margin in the trophy's history.

**Dec 9**—Delta State wins the Division II national title with a 63–34 rout of Bloomsburg in Florence, Ala.

**Dec 16**—Georgia Southern defeats Montana 27–25 in Chattanooga, Tenn., to win the Division I-AA national title for the second year in a row. In Division III, Rodney Chenos kicks a 20-yard field goal with 20 seconds remaining to give Mt. Union (Ohio) a 10–7 win over St. John's (Minn.) and its fourth championship in five years.

**Dec 20**—The bowl schedule kicks off as Southern Mississippi upends Texas Christian 28–21 in the Mobile Alabama Bowl. The following night UNLV routs Arkansas 31–14 in the Las Vegas Bowl.

**Dec 20**—Marvin (Snoop) Minnis, Florida State's leading receiver during the regular season, is declared academically ineligible for the Jan. 3 Orange Bowl, the national title game.

**Dec 24**—In a matchup of outgoing coaches, Georgia shellacks Virginia 37–14 in the Oahu Bowl in Honolulu. Bulldogs coach Jim Donnan had been fired on Dec. 4, while Cavaliers coach George Welsh announced his retirement, effective at the end of the season, on Dec. 11.

**Dec 28**—West Virginia coach Don Nehlen, who is retiring after 21 years with the Mountaineers goes out a winner as his team outscores Mississippi 49–38 in the Music City Bowl in Nashville.

**Dec 31**—Mississippi State wins the Independence Bowl, a New Year's Eve thriller in the snow in Shreveport, La., edging Texas A&M 43–41 in overtime.

**Jan 1, 2001**—Leading the six-bowl bonanza on New Year's Day are Michigan, which rides Anthony Thomas's 182 yards rushing to a 31–28 victory over Auburn in the Citrus Bowl, and South Carolina, which completes a turnaround from its winless season the previous year by beating Ohio State 24–7 in the Outback Bowl. Buckeye coach John Cooper is fired the day after the game. In the Rose Bowl, Washington finishes an 11–1 season with a 34–24 triumph over Big Ten champion Purdue, while in the Gator Bowl, Virginia Tech quarterback Michael Vick, playing what turns out to be his final college game, is named MVP of the Hokies 41–20 pasting of Clemson. Kansas State defeats Tennessee 35–21 in the Cotton Bowl and Oregon State wins the Fiesta Bowl 41–9 over Notre Dame.

**Jan 2**—In the Sugar Bowl, Miami whips Florida 37–20 to run its record to 11–1. The Hurricanes will finish the season ranked second in the final polls.

**Jan 3**—Led by its defense, which holds Florida State's top-ranked offense to 301 yards, and its kicking game, which produces two field goals and places three punts inside the Seminoles' seven-yard line, underdog Oklahoma completes a 13–0 season and wins the national championship, defeating FSU in the Orange Bowl by the unlikely score of 13–2. It is the Sooners' seventh national title but first since 1985.

**Jan 8**—Florida linemen Gerard Warren and Kenyatta Walker join Ohio State cornerback Nate Clements and Michigan wide receiver David Terrell in announcing that they will skip their senior years and make themselves eligible for the NFL draft.

**Feb 3**—Two weeks after Ohio State taps Jim Tressel of Division I-AA Youngstown State to replace John Cooper as its coach, Miami stays in-house to find its successor to Butch Davis, who left to coach the NFL's Cleveland Browns, promoting offensive coordinator Larry Coker to the head coaching job.

**May 17**—Penn State's Adam Taliaferro, who suffered a spinal injury in a September 2000 game against Ohio State, returns to classes for the school's summer session.

**July 11**—The BCS announces that it has altered its formula for determining which teams will play for the national title each year. The new system gives greater reward to teams that beat other teams in the BCS's Top 15, and will diminish the importance of margin of victory, a factor that has caused some teams to run up the score in their victories.

**Aug 25**—The 2001–02 college football season kicks off as fourth-ranked Nebraska downs Texas Christian 21–7 in the Pigskin Classic in Lincoln, Neb. In Madison, Wis., the host Badgers, ranked 23rd in the country, defeat Virginia 26–17. The following day No. 13 Georgia Tech edges Syracuse 13–7 in the Kickoff Classic in East Rutherford, N.J.

**Sept 29**—During an exciting Saturday full of tight games between Top 25 opponents, third-ranked Oklahoma nips No. 9 Kansas State 38–37, 16th-ranked South Carolina edges Alabama 37–36, No. 25 Clemson upsets 11th-ranked Georgia Tech 47–44 in overtime, No. 18 Northwestern beats No. 24 Michigan State 27–26 with a last-second field goal, and No. 21 Purdue downs Minnesota 35–28 in overtime.

**Oct 13**—Auburn's Damon Duval kicks a 44-yard field goal as time expires to give the Tigers a 23–20 victory over No. 1 Florida and knock the Gators (5–1) from the ranks of the unbeaten. Miami (5–0), which rolls over Florida State 49–27, takes the top spot in both polls, where they are followed by Oklahoma (6–0) and Nebraska (7–0).

## Golf

**Nov 5, 2000**—In Atlanta, Phil Mickelson rallies from one stroke behind Tiger Woods and Vijay Singh to win the Tour Championship by two strokes.

**Nov 12**—Mike Weir of Canada wins the World Golf Championships, a PGA event in Sotogrande, Spain, beating Tiger Woods by four strokes to prevent Woods from becoming the first player in 50 years to win 10 times in a season. The following week Woods gets win No. 10 of 2000 with a three-stroke victory over Geoff Ogilvy at the Johnnie Walker Classic in Bangkok.

**Nov 21**—Nineteen-year-old Dorothy Delasin, who won one tournament and finished 25th on the money list in 2000, is named LPGA rookie of the year.

**Nov 22**—With an eagle on the par-5 18th hole and another eagle on the same hole in a playoff against Vijay Singh, Tiger Woods wins the Grand Slam of Golf in Poipu Beach, Hawaii, for the third year in a row.

**Nov 26**—Aaron Baddeley, 19, of Australia, who in 1999 became the youngest winner in the history of the Australian Open, repeats as champion of the event, shooting a 10-under 278 to defeat runner-up Robert Allenby by two strokes.

**Dec 3**—Shooting an 8-under-par 64 in the final round, Davis Love III overtakes Tiger Woods and Sergio Garcia to win the $1 million Williams World Golf Challenge in Thousand Oaks, Calif.

**Dec 17**—U.S. Supreme Court Justice Sandra Day O'Connor, taking a day off from poring over lawsuit appeals from the 2000 presidential election, shoots a hole-in-one on the eighth hole at the Paradise Valley Golf Course in Phoenix.

**Jan 14, 2001**—Jim Furyk shoots a final-round 67 to edge Rory Sabbatini by one stroke and win the Mercedes Championships in Kapalua, Hawaii.

**Jan 14**—The LPGA Tour tees off in Orlando, Fla., with the YourLife Vitamins Classic. Se Ri Pak is the new season's first winner, shooting a final-round 64 to take the tournament with a 13-under-par 203.

**Jan 21**—Brad Faxon is the wire-to-wire winner at the Sony Open in Honolulu, taking the lead on the first day and shooting a 5-under-par 65 in the final round to win by four strokes over runner-up Tom Lehman.

**Jan 28**—Setting new PGA Tour records for total strokes (28-under 256) and birdies (32) over 72 holes, Mark Calcavecchia wins the Phoenix Open for the third time in his career.

**Feb 4**—Davis Love III ends a 62-tournament winless streak, dating to 1998, when he fires a final-round 63 to win the Pebble Beach National Pro-Am in Pebble Beach, Calif.

**Feb 11**—Phil Mickelson wins the Buick Invitational for the second year in a row and third time in his career, a record.

**March 4**—Two weeks after winning the Bob Hope Classic, Bob Durant becomes the first player since Tiger Woods to win consecutive starts when he rallies to win the Genuity Championships in Miami.

**March 16**—Annika Sorenstam shoots the lowest round in LPGA history, firing a 13-under-par 59 in the second round of the Standard Register PING in Phoenix.

**March 26**—Tiger Woods wins for the second week in a row, taking the Players Championship in Pontre Vedra Beach, Fla. He won the Bay Hill Invitational the previous week.

**April 8**—After winning the U.S. Open, the British Open and the PGA Championship in 2000, Tiger Woods shoots 70-66-68-68 to win the 2001 Masters and become the only man ever to hold all four of golf's Grand Slam titles at the same time. He defeats runner-up David Duval by two strokes and third-place finisher Phil Mickelson by three. It is Woods's second Masters title.

**April 15**—With seven birdies over the last 18 holes, Annika Sorenstam rallies from 10 strokes behind Pat Hurst to win a record-tying fourth consecutive tournament, the LPGA Office Depot at Los Angeles's Wilshire Country Club.

**April 22**—Se Ri Pak takes the Longs Drugs Classic in Lincoln, Calif., for her second win of the year, a triumph that prevents Annika Sorenstam from winning a record fifth straight LPGA event.

**May 14**—Twelve-year-old Megan Pressel of Boca Raton, Fla., qualifies for the U.S. Open when she shoots a two-under-par 70 at a tournament in Palm Beach.

**May 20**—Sergio Garcia wins the first PGA Tour event of his career, shooting a final-round 63 to take the Colonial in Fort Worth, Texas.

**May 29**—The U.S. Supreme Court rules that golfer Casey Martin, who suffers from a circulatory disorder in his right leg that severely hampers his ability to walk distances, may use a golf cart during play on the PGA Tour.

**June 3**—Karrie Webb produces rounds of 70, 65, 69 and 69 to win the U.S. Women's Open for the second straight year. On the PGA Tour, Tiger Woods wins the Memorial for a third straight time—and a record 20th victory in his last 40 starts.

**June 18**—Sinking a six-foot putt for bogey on the 18th hole of a Monday playoff with Mark Brooks, Retief Goosen wins the U.S. Open at Southern Hills Country Club in Tulsa.

**June 24**—Karrie Webb wins her second straight major and becomes the youngest woman to complete a career Grand Slam, winning the LPGA Championship in Wilmington, Del.

**July 22**—Twenty-nine-year-old David Duval sheds the "greatest player never to have won a major" tag that has dogged him for much of his career, winning the British Open at Royal Lytham and St. Annes, England, by three strokes.

**July 24**—During qualifying for the U.S. junior girls championships, Christina Kim of San Jose fires an eight-under-par 62, a new USGA record.

**Aug 5**—South Korea goes 1–2 at the Women's British Open in Berkshire, England, as Se Ri Pak shoots an 11-under 277 to finish two strokes ahead of runner-up Mi Hyun Kim.

**Aug 19**—For the 11th time in 14 years, the PGA Championship has a first-time major winner as David Toms wins the event, holding off Phil Mickelson by one stroke.

**Sept 9**—Three weeks after captain Curtis Strange makes him a controversial choice for the U.S. Ryder Cup team, Scott Verplank justifies his selection by winning the Canadian Open in Montreal. The following week the Ryder Cup is postponed to 2002.

**Sept 30**—Justin Leonard wins the Texas Open for the second year in a row, defeating runners-up Matt Kuchar and J.J. Henry by two strokes in San Antonio.

**Oct 7**—David Toms shoots a final-round 68 to win the Michelob Championship in Williamsburg, Va., to claim his third title of the season.

# Hockey

**Oct 31, 2000**—Columbus goalie Ron Tugnutt stops 45 shots during the Blue Jackets' 4–1 win over Los Angeles, the highest scoring team in the NHL after 13 games.

**Nov 1**—Colorado's 9-2-2 start is dampened as the Avalanche learns it will lose right wing Adam Deadmarsh, who suffered a concussion during the previous night's game, indefinitely, and center Chris Drury, who sprained a knee in the same game, for six to eight weeks. Two weeks later Colorado's leading scorer, Peter Forsberg, goes down with a rib injury and will be out indefinitely.

**Nov 7**—Commissioner Gary Bettman announces that the NHL will extend to one year the suspension of Bruins defenseman Marty McSorley for slashing Vancouver wing Donald

Brashear in the head on Feb. 21, 2000. McSorley, who was found guilty of assault in a British Columbia court for the incident, had applied to the league for reinstatement as mandated by his initial suspension the previous winter.

**Nov 15**—The NHL suspends Phoenix wing Brad May for 20 games after May hits the Blue Jackets' Steve Heinze on the nose with his stick, opening a cut that requires nine stitches, during the Coyote's 2–1 loss to Columbus on Nov. 11.

**Nov 24**—Detroit Red Wings coach Scotty Bowman coaches the 2,000th game of his career.

**Dec 5**—Patrik Elias scores three goals to lead New Jersey to a 6–1 rout of Colorado and extend the Devils' unbeaten streak to nine games. In Boston, the Bruins waive defenseman Paul Coffey,

No. 2 on the NHL's alltime scoring list for defenseman.

**Dec 11**—Legendary center Mario Lemieux, 35, announces that he plans to resume his playing career after 44 months away from hockey. He will suit up in his familiar No. 66 jersey for the Pittsburgh Penguins, of whom he is a part owner.

**Dec 27**—Having been advised by NHL Hall of Famer and comeback specialist Gordie Howe to be patient in his comeback attempt, Pittsburgh's Mario Lemieux is anything but, setting up teammate Jaromir Jagr for a goal only 33 seconds into his return to the ice. Lemieux instantly reestablishes himself as an NHL superstar, assisting on one more goal and scoring another in the Penguins' 5–0 win over Toronto.

**Jan 2, 2001**—Montreal's Jose Theodore becomes the sixth goalie in NHL history to score a goal in a regular-season game when he backhands the puck the length of the ice and into the Islanders' empty net in the waning seconds of the Canadiens' 3–0 defeat of New York.

**Jan 22**—The 1999–2000 NHL MVP, Blues defenseman Chris Pronger, decides to have knee surgery for an injury suffered on Jan. 4. St. Louis will be without him for three to six weeks.

**Jan 31**—Perhaps the most potent symbol of Canada's national sport, the Montreal Canadiens franchise, comes under U.S. control as Colorado businessman George Gillett purchases 80.1% of the team, along with its arena, the Molson Centre, for $183 million.

**Feb 4**—Bill Guerin of the Bruins scores three goals to lead the North America team to a 14–12 victory over the World team in the NHL All-Star Game in Denver.

**Feb 15**—NHL legend Wayne Gretzky and developer Steve Ellman purchase the Phoenix Coyotes for $125 million.

**Feb 26**—On the heels of his return from knee surgery, Blues defenseman Chris Pronger suffers a broken left arm in a game against the San Jose Sharks and will miss the rest of the regular season.

**Feb 28**—Rangers winger Theo Fleury the team's leading scorer, checks into the NHL's substance-abuse program.

**March 5**—San Jose trades forward Jeff Friesen and backup goalie Steve Shields for Anaheim forward Teemu Selanne.

**March 19**—Mark Messier moves into third place on the alltime scoring list (1,772 points)

**Bourque (77) fulfilled his 22-year quest for the Stanley Cup.**

with a goal in the Rangers' 6–3 win over Washington.

**April 8**—Boosted by the return of Mario Lemieux, who scores with 76 points in 43 games, including 41 assists, Pittsburgh wing Jaromir Jagr clinches his fourth straight NHL scoring title with 121 points on 52 goals and 69 assists.

**May 3**—Brian Sutter becomes the third Sutter brother in the ranks of NHL coaches when he is hired to lead the Blackhawks. His brothers Darryl and Duane coach San Jose and Florida, respectively.

**May 10**—After the Avalanche clinches the Western Conference semifinal series with a Game 7 victory over the Los Angeles Kings, Colorado center Peter Forsberg undergoes emergency surgery to remove his ruptured spleen. He will miss the rest of the playoffs.

**May 22**—The Devils return to the Stanley Cup finals, eliminating Pittsburgh in Game 5 of the Eastern Conference finals with a 4–2 victory. They will meet Colorado, which got past St. Louis in the Western Conference finals in five games, the last three of which went to overtime.

**May 26**—Colorado takes a 1–0 series lead in the Stanley Cup finals, blanking New Jersey 5–0 in Game 1 in Denver.

DAVID E. KLUTHO

**June 3**—The Devils score two goals in the third period, including one by Scott Gomez after a puckhandling gaffe by Colorado goalie Patrick Roy, to rally from a 2–1 deficit and defeat the Avalanche 3–2, evening the Stanley Cup finals at two games apiece.

**June 5**—A Florida investment group that includes former University of Miami and Cleveland Browns quarterback Bernie Kosar buys the NHL's Panthers for $101 million.

**June 9**—After forcing a Game 7 with an impressive 4–0 victory in New Jersey, Colorado wins the Stanley Cup, jumping out to a 3–0 lead and holding on for a 3–1 victory in the decisive game in Denver. Avalanche goalie Patrick Roy, who produced a 1.68 goals-against average in the postseason, wins the Conn Smythe Trophy as MVP of the playoffs. It is Roy's third Conn Smythe Trophy, an NHL record. Colorado's triumph brings to a happy end the 22-year title quest of future Hall of Fame defenseman Ray Bourque.

**June 24**—The Islanders, who acquired former Ottawa center Alexei Yashin on June 23, trade center Tim Connolly and forward Taylor Pratt to Buffalo in exchange for forward Mike Peca.

**June 26**—Avalanche defenseman Ray Bourque announces his retirement. A 19-time All-Star and five-time Norris Trophy winner, Bourque fulfilled his career-long quest for a Stanley Cup on June 9.

**July 1**—On the first day of the free-agent signing period, Colorado moves aggressively, re-signing goalie Patrick Roy, captain Joe Sakic and All-Star

defenseman Rob Blake. In Detroit, the Red Wings trade forward Slava Kozlov and a draft pick to Buffalo for six-time goalie of the year Dominik Hasek.

**July 11**—Granting his wish for a trade, Pittsburgh deals superstar wing Jaromir Jagr to Washington along with defenseman Frantisek Kucera. The Penguins receive prospects Kris Beech, Michal Sivek, Ross Lupaschuk and future considerations.

**Aug 20**—Six-time All-Star Eric Lindros, who has not played since suffering the sixth concussion of his career in Game 7 of the 2000 Eastern Conference finals, signs a four-year $37 million contract with the Rangers. The agreement ends Lindros's stormy relationship with Philadelphia general manager Bob Clarke.

**Aug 22**—The Detroit Red Wings sign seven-time All-Star Brett Hull, an unrestricted free agent, to a two-year, $9.5 million contract.

**Sept 6**—The Canadiens announce that malignant cells have been found in fluid in the abdomen of Montreal center Saku Koivu, who entered the hospital on Sept. 4 complaining of nausea and abdominal pain.

**Oct 3**—Defenseman Paul Coffey, who is second to Ray Bourque in career scoring by a defenseman, retires after 21 years in the NHL.

**Oct 14**—The Penguins lose to Buffalo 4–1 to begin the 2001–02 NHL season at 0–4, tying the worst start in franchise history.

# Horse Racing

**Nov 4, 2000**—In a day of surprising results at the Breeders' Cup at Churchill Downs, Tiznow wins the 1¼-mile, $4 million Classic, outrunning favorites Lemon Drop Kid and Fusaichi Pegasus. It is Tiznow's third victory in three starts. Spain wins the $2 million Distaff over favored Riboletta, and Kona Gold takes the Sprint, his fourth straight victory and fifth in his last six starts.

**Dec 2**—Jockey Chris Antley, 34, who rode Charismatic to victories in the 1999 Kentucky Derby and Preakness, is found dead in his home in Pasadena, Calif. Police initially suspect a homicide but further investigation reveals multiple drug intoxication as the cause of death.

**Dec 26**—Dixie Union wins the $200,000 Malibu Stakes on the opening day of Santa Anita's 64th winter-spring meeting in Arcadia, Calif.

**Jan 17, 2001**—For picking all six winners in the Pick 6 at Gulfstream Park in Hallandale Beach, Fla., a bettor wins $309,788.40, a track record for a one-ticket winner.

**Jan 30**—After finishing the 2000 season with three victories in 34 days, including the Breeders'

Cup Classic, Tiznow wins the Eclipse Award as Horse of the Year. Lemon Drop Kid is named Older Colt, Horse or Gelding of the Year, and Riboletta is the top Older Filly or Mare. Jerry Bailey is named top rider for the fourth time in his career.

**Jan 30**—Laffit Pincay Jr. receives the Sport of Turfdom award, voted annually by the Turf Publicists of America. Pincay, who has 9,073 wins, the most alltime, is the only two-time winner of the award.

**Feb 27**—Due to a rapidly spreading outbreak of foot-and-mouth disease, all horse racing in Britain and Ireland is suspended until at least March 7.

**March 3**—Fresh from his first loss in six months, and running on a hoof stitched with wire and screws, Tiznow wins the $1 million Santa Anita Handicap in Arcadia, Calif.

**March 10**—At Gulfstream Park, Monarchos charges from behind to win the Florida Derby by 4½ lengths over Outofthebox.

**May 5**—With the greatest margin of victory (4¾ lengths) since Spend a Buck's 5¼-length triumph in 1985, and in a time (1:59⅘) second only to Secretariat's legendary 1973 run, Monarchos comes from behind to win the Kentucky Derby at Churchill Downs. Invisible Ink finishes second.

**May 6**—Atop Gaviola, jockey Jerry Bailey wins the Beaugay Handicap at Aqueduct for the 5000th victory of his career.

**May 19**—A pre-Derby favorite who ran a flat race at Churchill Downs, Point Given shows why he was so highly regarded, winning the Preakness by 2¼ lengths over runner-up A P Valentine.

**May 28**—Exciting story indeed: A 55–1 long shot, Exciting Story wins the Met Mile at Belmont Park, paying $115.50 on a two-dollar bet.

**May 31**—Jockey Pat Day reaches the 8,000-victory plateau with a win aboard Camden Park in the sixth race at Churchill Downs. Day is third on the alltime wins list, behind Laffit Pincay Jr. (9,147) and Bill Shoemaker (8,833).

**June 9**—Preakness winner Point Given obliterates the field at the Belmont Stakes, defeating runner-up A P Valentine by 12¼ lengths.

**June 17**—Officials at Santa Anita announce that trainer Bob Baffert will be suspended from June 25 to Aug. 24 because one of his horses tested positive for morphine. The next week a judge grants a stay of the suspension, pending Baffert's appeal.

**July 15**—With Gary Stevens up, Congaree steams to a 5-length victory in the $500,000 Swaps Stakes at Hollywood Park.

**July 28**—Varenne sets a 1-mile trotting world record, taking the $1 million Breeders Crown in 1:51.1 at the Meadowlands in East Rutherford, N.J.

**Aug 25**—In front of a record crowd of 60,486 in Saratoga Springs, N.Y., Point Given wins the Travers Stakes by 3½ lengths.

**Sept 3**—Jockey John Velazquez rides six winners at Saratoga Race Course, a single-day track record.

**Sept 8**—Lido Palace wins the $500,000 Woodward Stakes at Belmont Park, defeating runner-up Albert the Great by a length.

**Sept 20**—Mike Lachance wins a record-tying fifth Little Brown Jug, driving Bettor's Delight to a 1½-length victory over Real Desire in Delaware, Ohio.

**Oct 13**—Affluent wins the $500,000 Queen Elizabeth II Challenge Cup at Keeneland, defeating runner-up Golden Apples by a neck.

# Motor Sports

**Nov 5, 2000**—NASCAR driver Jeff Burton wins his fourth race of the season, taking the Phoenix 500 despite a pit-stop snafu that costs him 30 positions.

**Nov 12**—Joe Amato, who has more wins (52) than any driver in NHRA Top Fuel history, announces his retirement.

**Nov 12**—Tony Stewart wins the Pennzoil 400 at Homestead-Miami Speedway for his series-leading sixth win of the season. Stewart's teammate Bobby Labonte, who finishes fourth, clinches the Winston Cup championship with one week remaining.

**Nov 20**—At Atlanta Motor Speedway, Darrell Waltrip runs the final race of his 29-year NASCAR career. After 84 Winston Cup wins and three championships, Waltrip retires to become a commentator for NASCAR TV broadcasts.

**Dec 4**—In an effort to boost their profile in a market increasingly dominated by NASCAR, CART officials announce that they've hired TV marketing expert Joseph Heitzler to be the circuit's new president.

**Jan 21, 2001**—Germany's Jutta Kleinschmidt becomes the first woman to win the Dakar Rally, a 6,658-mile race from Paris to Dakar, Senegal.

**Feb 4**—Despite an overheated car, Ron Fellows's team from Canada cruises to a comfortable victory in the 24 Hours of Daytona.

**Feb 12**—NASCAR suspends and fines Tony Furr and Kevin Cram, the crew chiefs for Jerry Nadeau's entry and Jason Leffler, respectively, for technical violations discovered during the opening round of qualifying for the Daytona 500.

**Feb 15**—In the first of the Twin 125-mile qualifying races at Daytona, Sterling Marlin charges past Dale Earnhardt on the final lap to take the checkered flag. In the second race, Mike Skinner defeats Dale Earnhardt Jr. in a photo finish. The exciting qualifiers prompt Marlin to say that the Daytona 500, on Feb. 18, "is probably going to be best Daytona 500 on record."

**Feb 18**—Minutes after Michael Waltrip seizes the first victory of his 15-year career, taking the checkered flag at the Daytona 500, the elation turns to sadness and mourning as word spreads that NASCAR legend Dale Earnhardt, 49, has died in a crash on Turn 4 of the last lap of the race. Earnhardt won 76 races and seven Winston Cup titles in his 23-year career.

**Feb 25**—On the first day of racing following the death of Dale Earnhardt, the late superstar's son, Dale Jr., crashes into the outside wall on the first lap of NASCAR's Rockingham 400. Thankfully, Earnhardt Jr. walks away from the crash unhurt. The race is postponed after 52 laps due to rain.

**Feb 26**—Driving a car owned by Dale Earnhardt Inc., Steve Park holds off Bobby Labonte to win the Rockingham 400 at North Carolina Speedway.

# Motor Sports (Cont.)

**March 3**—A track worker, whose name is not released, is killed by flying debris after a collision between the Formula One cars of Jacques Villeneuve and Ralf Schumacher at the season-opening Australian Grand Prix in Melbourne.

**March 3**—Jeff Gordon takes NASCAR's Las Vegas 400, seizing the lead with 20 laps to go and holding on to win.

**April 1**—David Coulthard wins the Brazilian Grand Prix in Sao Paulo, ending Michael Schumacher's six-race F/1 winning streak.

**April 8**—Winston Cup series leader Dale Jarrett wins the Virginia 500 to seize his second victory in a row and third of the season.

**May 13**—With a victory at the Austrian Grand Prix in Spielberg, David Coulthard moves to within four points of F/1 leader Michael Schumacher.

**May 20**—Jeff Gordon wins NASCAR's $500,000 Winston Cup at Lowe's Motor Speedway in Concord, N.C., to join Dale Earnhardt as the only three-time winners of the race.

**May 27**—For the second year in a row, an Indianapolis 500 rookie wins at the Brickyard as Helio Castroneves of Brazil wins the 85th running of the Indy 500. At Lowe's Motor Speedway in Concord, N.C., Jeff Burton wins NASCAR's Coca-Cola 600, while F/1 leader Michael Schumacher wins the Monaco Grand Prix for the fifth time in his career.

**June 10**—Jeff Gordon regains the Winston Cup season points lead with a victory in the Michigan 400 in Brooklyn, Mich. It is Gordon's second straight and the fourth time in five races that he has finished second or better.

**June 17**—Frank Biela, Tom Kristensen and Emanuele Pirro repeat as champions of the 24 Hours of LeMans.

**July 1**—Michael Schumacher wins the French Grand Prix, defeating his younger brother Ralf, the runner-up, by 10.3 seconds. The Schumachers have won eight of the 10 F/1 races this season.

**July 8**—Dale Earnhardt Jr. wins the Pepsi 400, the first race held at Daytona International Speedway since his father Dale Sr. died there on Feb. 18.

**Aug 12**—Jeff Gordon takes the lead with 14 laps to go in NASCAR's Global Crossing at the Glen and holds on to win. It is the fourth time in five years that Gordon has won on the Watkins Glen road course, and is the seventh road victory of his career, the most in NASCAR history.

**Aug 19**—Michael Schumacher clinches his fourth F/1 championship with a victory—the 51st of his career, at the Hungarian Grand Prix.

**Sept 16**—After a horrifying crash with Alex Tagliani during the CART American Memorial 500 in Germany, Alex Zanardi has surgery to remove both of his legs around the knee. He is in stable but serious condition.

**Sept 23**—In NASCAR's first race since the Sept. 11 terrorist attacks on New York City and Washington, D.C., Dale Earnhardt Jr. takes the checkered flag at Delaware's Dover International Speedway. Earnhardt takes a subdued victory lap holding an American flag out his driver's side window.

**Oct 13**—Italy's Max Papis wins an accident-marred Grand Prix of Monterey at Laguna Seca Raceway. CART series leader Gil de Ferran finishes third to increase his points lead over Kenny Brack to 26 with two races remaining.

# Olympics

**Nov 8, 2000**—Hockey legend Wayne Gretzky is named executive director of the men's hockey team that will represent Canada at the 2002 Winter Olympics in Salt Lake City.

**Nov 15**—In a televised ceremony outside New York City's Rockefeller Center, Brandon Slay of the U.S. receives the 2000 Olympic gold medal in the 167½-pound class of freestyle wrestling. Slay received the silver medal in Sydney but was awarded gold after Germany's Alexander Leipold failed a drug tests, the results of which were not processed until after the Games ended.

**Nov 16**—File under Only In America: A proposal approved by both the Salt Lake Organizing Committee and the Salt Lake County sheriff's office to make the SIG Sauer .40-caliber semiautomatic pistol the official gun of the 2002 Winter Games is rejected by the International Olympic Committee (IOC).

**Dec 4**—Citing personal reasons, Petros Sinadinos, the general manager of the Athens Olympic organizing committee and its second-in-command, offers his resignation.

**Dec 14**—The United States Olympic Committee (USOC) selects wrestler Rulon Gardner, sprinter Marion Jones and the U.S. Olympic baseball team as its sportsman, sportswoman and team of the year.

**Jan 7, 2001**—Olympic heavyweight boxing champion Felix Savon of Cuba, who won a record-tying third gold medal at the 2000 Games in Sydney, announces that he will retire and become coach of Cuba's national boxing team.

**Jan 8**—Bela Karolyi decides to step down as coordinator for the U.S. women's gymnastics team.

**Jan 10**—Veteran broadcaster Jim McKay, 79, announces that he will do features and nightly commentaries for the telecast of the 2002 Winter Games in Salt Lake City. McKay has not worked an Olympics since 1988.

**Jan 27**—Six members of the 2000 U.S. Olympic boxing team make their professional debuts in the Theater at Madison Square Garden. All six win their bouts, four by knockout.

**Jan 30**—The USOC admits some fault in the case of swimmer Rick DeMont, who was stripped of a gold medal from the 1972 Games because he took a banned asthma medication. The action provides DeMont, who had notified the USOC prior to taking the substance, some vindication but falls short of reinstating his medal

**Feb 21**—SLOC president and CEO Mitt Romney introduces the new torch that will light the Olympic flame for the 2002 Games and announces that the for the first time torchbearers will run in pairs during the Torch Relay.

**March 8**—C.J. Hunter, the 1999 world champion in the shot put and husband of Olympic sprint champion Marion Jones, announces his retirement. He will drop his appeal of a positive drug test he produced in 2000.

**March 11**—The Utah Olympic Oval speed skating venue passes a test for the following winter's Games with flying colors as skaters at the World Single Distance Championships take advantage of the location's thin air and hard ice to set world records in five of 10 events.

**April 8**—The U.S. women's hockey team, the defending Olympic champion, falls to Canada 3–2 in the final of the Women's World Championships in Minneapolis.

**July 13**—The streets of Beijing erupt in jubilation after the IOC announces its decision to award the 2008 Summer Olympics to China. Residents flock to Tiananmen Square to celebrate, banging drums, singing songs and dancing in an unusually giddy display for the normally buttoned-down metropolis. It is the first time the Games have been awarded to the world's most populous country and the decision is a controversial one, as critics claim that the Chinese government's myriad human rights abuses should preclude the nation from the international recognition and honor that comes with hosting the Olympics.

**July 15**—Un Yong Kim of South Korea, a potential successor to Juan Antonio Samaranch as IOC president, comes under scrutiny by the IOC ethics commission for his proposal that the IOC pay its members, who are volunteers, a "minimum" of $50,000 a year for work expenses. The commission closes the investigation without taking any action.

**July 16**—Belgium's Jacques Rogge, a former Olympic sailor, is elected president of the IOC, taking 59 of the 110 votes cast in the second round of voting to defeat runner-up Un Yong Kim of South Korea. Nicknamed "Mr. Clean," Rogge will be charged with putting distance between the IOC and, among other incidents, the Salt Lake City bid scandal of 1999. He will also have to tackle issues such as doping, logistical and political concerns with the upcoming Games in Athens and Beijing, respectively, and the economics of the Olympic movement. IOC vice president Thomas Back of Germany, expresses his confidence in the organization's new president, saying Rogge "is the representative of the new and reformed IOC."

**Aug 23**—The U.S. basketball team drubs South Africa 118–56 in preliminary round play at the World University Games in Beijing, which are a test-run of sorts for that city's capability to host the Olympics.

**Aug 27**—Tara Kirk and Kristen Woodring of the U.S. finish 1–2 in the 50-meter breaststroke at the World University Games in Beijiing. IOC president-elect Jacques Rogge, who is in Beijing to observe the Games and to meet with the city's Olympic organizers, presents them with their medals.

**Aug 30**—China, which features three seven-footers in its frontcourt, defeats the U.S. 83–82 in basketball at the World University Games in Beijing. Though China's Wang Zhizhi and Yao Ming play professionally, for the Dallas Mavericks and the Shanghai Sharks, respectively, China insists that they are also students and thus eligible for the Games. In the women's tournament, the U.S. steamrolls Lithuania 70–49 to advance to the gold-medal game, which they win 87–69 over China.

**Sept 9**—The Goodwill Games come to an end in Brisbane, Australia, as the U.S. routs Argentina 91–63 to win the gold medal in men's basketball. It is the first time the Goodwill Games—which were founded in 1986 as a bridge between U.S. and then-Soviet athletes—have been held in a nation other than the U.S. or the former Soviet Union.

**Sept 18**—Calling the arrangement "perfectly clear and legal," the IOC, whose members are volunteers, announces that it has been paying the Montreal law firm of member Dick Pound since 1985 for work Pound has done in negotiating sponsorship and TV rights for the Games. The deal, which was brokered by former IOC president Juan Antonio Samaranch, has been documented from its outset, and does not benefit Pound personally.

**Nov 9, 2000**—An arbitrator upholds the NBA's decision to void the contracts of Minnesota Timberwolves forward Joe Smith for the 1998–99, 1999–2000 and 2000–01 seasons. The Timberwolves violated the league's salary-cap rules in their contractual arrangements with Smith, and have already lost their next five first-round draft choices as punishment. For their roles in the case, owner Glen Taylor is suspended and GM Kevin McHale takes a leave of absence.

**Nov 15**—Philadelphia defeats the Cleveland Cavaliers 107–98 to run its record to 8–0, equaling the best start in franchise history. The 76ers are the only undefeated team remaining in the NBA. The last time they started 8–0 (1979–80) they went to the NBA Finals.

**Nov 20**—Facing the possibility of protracted litigation by the league, forward Joe Smith signs with the Detroit Pistons for the remainder of the season. Smith wanted to re-sign with the Timberwolves for the league minimum (with the chance to sign a megadeal at season's end), but the NBA, incensed that Smith had signed an undisclosed, salary-cap-circumventing contract with Minnesota in 1999, would have gone to court to prevent the return.

**Nov 27**—After a 6–9 start, Seattle fires coach Paul Westphal and replaces him with former SuperSonics guard and Westphal assistant Nate McMillan.

**Nov 29**—Despite former player Charles Barkley's assurance that "I've seen Don MacLean in the locker room—trust me, he's not on steroids," the NBA suspends Miami's MacLean for five days after the Miami forward tests positive for the banned substance.

**Dec 3**—Cheryl Miller resigns as coach of the WNBA's Phoenix Mercury. Four-time WNBA Finals MVP Cynthia Cooper will replace her.

**Dec 5**—Taking a pass from—who else?—John Stockton, Utah's Karl Malone sinks a scoop shot in the second quarter of the Jazz's 98–84 victory over Toronto to run his career point total to 31,421 and move past Wilt Chamberlain into second place on the career scoring list.

**Dec 20**—Charlotte and Miami join forces for the lowest-scoring NBA game since Feb. 27, 1955, as the Hornets beat the Heat 65–56. The teams combine for 90 missed field goals.

**Dec 27**—Doctors determine that Orlando swingman Grant Hill needs more surgery on his left ankle and will be sidelined for six to eight months. Hill fractured the ankle late in the 1999–2000 season and had a plate and five screws inserted in the initial surgery.

**Jan 8, 2001**—Rick Pitino, who left the University of Kentucky in 1997 for a 10-year, $50 million deal to coach the Celtics back to NBA glory, resigns in Boston after three and a half seasons and no playoff appearances.

**Jan 11**—Despite losing to Houston 76–75 the New York Knicks set an NBA record, holding their opponent to fewer than 100 points for the 29th consecutive game, breaking the record set by the Fort Wayne Pistons in 1954.

**Feb 8**—The Continental Basketball Association, which is owned by Indiana Pacers coach Isiah Thomas, suspends play after executives fail to find a buyer for the 55-year-old league.

**Feb 11**—Led by game MVP Allen Iverson's 25 points, the Eastern Conference rallies from a 21-point fourth-quarter deficit to defeat the West 111–110 in the All-Star Game.

**Feb 22**—With the league's best record (41–14) and its top scorer (Allen Iverson), the 76ers trade for the NBA's top rebounder, Dikembe Mutombo, sending injured center Theo Ratliff, forward Toni Kukoc, center Nazr Mohammed and guard Pepe Sanchez to Atlanta in exchange for the veteran center and forward Roshown McLeod.

**Feb 27**—Patrick Ewing returns to Madison Square Garden for the first time since being traded from New York to Seattle on Sept. 21, 2000, after 15 years as a Knick. He receives a three-minute standing ovation from Garden fans before the Knicks' 101–92 victory.

**March 5**—Four days after the Wizards made him available by buying out the remainder of his contract, the Trail Blazers sign controversial guard Rod Strickland for the rest of the season. Portland now has six current or former All-Stars on their 12-man roster.

**March 27**—Miami center Alonzo Mourning, who was diagnosed with focal glomerulosclerosis—a kidney disorder which can require dialysis or transplant—in October 2000, returns to the court six months sooner than expected. He scores nine points and grabs seven rebounds in Miami's 101–92 loss to the Raptors.

**April 1**—The date is only a coincidence as Portland forward Rasheed Wallace breaks his own NBA record for technical fouls in a season, receiving his 40th of the year in the third quarter of the Trail Blazers' 99–95 loss to Minnesota.

**April 5**—Seven-foot one-inch center Wang Zhizhi of China makes his debut for Dallas, scoring six points in eight minutes of action during the Mavericks' 108–94 win over Atlanta.

**April 12**—The NBA's board of governors approves the most significant rules change since the introduction of the three-point shot, discarding the illegal-defense rule, a move that will allow teams to play modified zone defenses during the 2001–02 season.

**April 19**—Wizards president Michael Jordan signs Doug Collins, who coached him in Chicago

JOHN BIEVER

**O'Neal (with ball) and the Lakers manhandled Philadelphia for a second straight NBA title.**

for three years, to a five-year, $20 million contract to coach Washington, fueling speculation that Jordan may attempt a comeback next season. But the NBA legend denies it, saying there is a 99.9% chance that he will not return to the game.

**April 24**—During a pickup game involving members of the WNBA's Houston Comets and the Houston Rockets, Comets star Sheryl Swoopes tears the anterior cruciate ligament in her left knee. She will miss the upcoming WNBA season.

**April 27**—The Charlotte Hornets defeat Miami 94–79 in Game 3 to complete a shockingly easy sweep of their first-round playoff series and send coach Pat Riley and the Heat to an early exit from the playoffs for the fourth consecutive year. Charlotte's average margin of victory in the series is 22.3 points.

**April 29**—The first-round playoff matchup between the defending champion Lakers and the Blazers ends surprisingly quickly as the Lakers win 99–86 to sweep the best-of-five series in three lopsided games. Los Angeles, which struggled early in the season, has won 11 straight games.

**April 30**—San Antonio eliminates Minnesota 97–84 in Game 4 of their first-round playoff series, sending the Timberwolves to their sixth consecutive first-round playoff exit.

**May 1**—Milwaukee overcomes the brilliance of Orlando's 21-year-old forward Tracy McGrady, who averages 33.7 points a game in the series, to defeat the Magic 112–104 in Game 4 and win

their first-round playoff series 3–1. The Bucks will play Charlotte in the conference semifinals.

**May 2**—The Sacramento Kings get 37 points from guard Predrag Stojakovic of Yugoslavia and defeat Phoenix 89–82 to take their first-round playoff series three games to one.

**May 3**—The Mavericks upend Utah 84–83 in Salt Lake City to win their first-round playoff series three games to two. In the only other first-round series to go the distance, the visiting team also wins Game 5 as Toronto defeats New York 93–89 in Madison Square Garden on May 4.

**May 8**—The Trail Blazers, who have the highest payroll in league history, dismiss coach Mike Dunleavy.

**May 10**—Defying the skeptics who thought he was making a mistake when he left the University of Florida after his sophomore season to enter the NBA draft, Orlando forward Mike Miller wins the league's rookie of the year award. The fifth pick in the 2000 draft, Miller averaged 11.9 points and 4.0 rebounds a game during his first season.

**May 13**—The Lakers complete their second straight sweep of the playoffs, dispatching Sacramento 119–113 on the road in Game 4 as Kobe Bryant scores 48 points. The following day the Spurs sweep the Mavericks out of the playoffs with a 105-87 trouncing in Game 4 in Dallas.

**May 14**—Following a season in which he led his team to the East's best record (56–26) and topped the NBA in scoring with a 31.1 average, Sixers guard Allen Iverson is named league MVP.

**May 19**—Kobe Bryant continues to sizzle in the playoffs, scoring 45 points to lead the Lakers to a 104–90 victory over the Spurs in San Antonio in Game 1 of the Western Conference finals.

**May 20**—The home teams win as both Eastern Conference semifinals series go to a Game 7. In Milwaukee, the Bucks defeat Charlotte 104–95, and in Philadelphia the 76ers squeak by Toronto 88–87.

**May 23**—Philadelphia's Larry Brown is named NBA Coach of the Year, giving the 76ers an unprecedented four major individual awards for the 2000–01 season: In addition to guard Allen Iverson's MVP award, Sixers center Dikembe Mutombo was defensive player of the year and guard Aaron McKie was the top sixth man.

**May 27**—The Los Angeles juggernaut rolls on as the Lakers remain unbeaten in the playoffs, completing their third consecutive sweep with a 111–82 drubbing of San Antonio in Game 4 of the Western Conference finals at the Staples Center.

**May 28**—The WNBA season tips off as the Los Angeles Sparks sink the four-time defending champion Comets 66–63 in Houston.

**June 3**—Sixers guard Allen Iverson scores 44 points to lead his team to a 108–91 triumph over the Bucks in Game 7 of the Eastern Conference finals in Philadelphia and send the 76ers to the NBA Finals for the first time since 1983.

**June 6**—Philadelphia hands the Lakers their first loss of the playoffs, taking Game 1 of the NBA finals 107–101 in overtime in Los Angeles. Sixers guard Allen Iverson pours in 48 points.

**June 15**—The Lakers rebound from their surprising Game 1 loss to reel off four straight victories against Philadelphia and win their second straight NBA championship. They take Game 5 108–96 in Philadelphia as Finals MVP Shaquille O'Neal scores 34 points and grabs 14 rebounds.

**June 27**—High schoolers dominate the NBA draft in New York City as four teenagers are drafted among the first eight selections. Washington takes 19-year-old Kwame Brown, a 6' 11" forward from Brunswick, Ga., with the first pick. Tyson Chandler, a 7' 1", 19-year-old center from Compton, Calif., goes second, to the Los Angeles Clippers, who trade his rights to Chicago, and Eddie Curry, a 6' 11" frontcourt player from South Holland, Ill., is the fourth pick of the draft, also going to Chicago. DeSagana Diop, a seven-footer who didn't take up basketball until he was 15, which was three years ago, is the eighth pick of the draft, going to Cleveland.

**June 28**—The NBA's relocation committee approves the Girzzlies' proposal to move from Vancouver to Memphis for the 2001–02 season. The Grizzlies also make significant roster moves, sending star forward Shareef Abdur-Rahim to Atlanta for big man Lorenzen Wright, point guard Brevin Knight and No. 3 draft pick Pau Gasol. Following the draft the team trades guards Mike Bibby and Brent Price to Sacramento for guards Jason Williams and Nick Anderson.

**June 28**—In a swap of All-Star point guards, the New Jersey Nets send Stephon Marbury to Phoenix in exchange for Jason Kidd. In Portland, the Trail Blazers announce that former All-Star point guard Maurice Cheeks is their new head coach.

**July 16**—Led by game-MVP Lisa Leslie's 20 points and nine rebounds, the West defeats the East 80–72 in the WNBA All-Star Game in Orlando.

**Aug 1**—The Rockets agree to sign center Hakeem Olajuwon and trade him to the Raptors for two draft picks, ending an era in Houston. Olajuwon played for the Rockets for 17 years and helped the team to two NBA titles.

**The unretiring sort: Jordan, 38, hoped to work some more wizardry in Washington.**

**Aug 14**—Former Coppin State assistant coach Stephanie Ready is hired as an assistant coach of the Greenville (S.C.) Groove of the National Basketball Development League (NBDL). She is the first woman to coach an NBA-affiliated men's professional team.

**Aug 20**—The Los Angeles Sparks beat the Houston Comets 70–58 in Game 2 of their first-round WNBA playoff series to end the Comets four-year reign as league champions.

**Sept 1**—Los Angeles routs the Charlotte Sting 82–54 in Game 2 to clinch the WNBA championship. The Sparks' Lisa Leslie wins the series MVP award to become the first player in WNBA history to be named All-Star Game MVP, regular-season MVP and championship MVP.

**Sept 25**—Washington president Michael Jordan, 38, announces that he will sell his stake in the team and leave the Wizards front office for their backcourt, resuming his NBA career after a three-year retirement. It is Jordan's second comeback; the first resulted in three straight titles for Chicago. The Wizards have not won a playoff series since 1982.

**Oct 12**—Denver Nuggets forward Antonio McDyess has surgery for a torn patella tendon in his left knee. He will be sidelined until February.

BOB ROSATO

**Nov 5, 2000**—Seven games in the NFL are decided by seven points or fewer as the Titans edge the Pittsburgh Steelers 9–7 in Tennessee on Al Del Greco's field goal in the waning seconds, the Eagles nip the Dallas Cowboys 16–13 in overtime in Philadelphia, and Buffalo tops New England in Foxboro by the same score, and also in overtime. In Chicago, the Bears hold off the Indianapolis Colts 27–24 after leading 27–0, while in Seattle, the Seahawks defeat the San Diego Chargers 17–15. The other two cliffhangers of the week see the host Arizona Cardinals down the Washington Redskins 16–15, and the visiting Broncos top the New York Jets 30–23.

**Nov 6**—The day after his team loses 23–8 to Miami in a game in which it allowed a 56-yard opening-kickoff return, a 46-yard touchdown run and a successful onside kick in the first quarter, Detroit Lions coach Bobby Ross resigns.

**Nov 12**—The New Orleans Saints defeat the Panthers 20–10 in Charlotte for their sixth straight win but lose star running back Ricky Williams for the season to a broken ankle. In Detroit, the Lions defeat the Atlanta Falcons 13–10 to give new head coach Gary Moeller a win in his first game, while in Nashville, the Baltimore Ravens score a last-minute touchdown to defeat the Titans 24–23 and end Tennessee's eight-game winning streak.

**Nov 19**—In a 31–22 loss to the Oakland Raiders in New Orleans, the Saints, who lost running back Ricky Williams to injury the previous week, see quarterback Jeff Blake go down with a broken foot.

**Nov 22**—Commissioner Paul Tagliabue announces the following fines and penalties in the wake of the San Francisco 49ers' alleged violations of the NFL's salary cap: Former Niners president Carmen Policy will be fined $400,000; former director of football operations Dwight Clark will be fined $200,000, and the 49ers will forfeit two future draft picks and pay a fine of $300,000.

**Nov 23**—The NFL's annual Thanksgiving Day competitors, the Cowboys and the Lions, split their Turkey Day games as Detroit gets its third consecutive win under new coach Gary Moeller, pasting New England 38–9 at home, and host Dallas falls to Minnesota 27–15.

**Nov 26**—The Chargers secure their first win of the season after 11 losses, defeating Kansas City 17–16 in San Diego.

**Nov 26**—The British Columbia Lions win the Grey Cup, the championship game of the Canadian Football League, rallying to defeat the Monteal Alouettes 28–26.

**Dec 4**—Following a 9–7 loss to the New York Giants that drops their record to 7–6 and jeopardizes their playoff hopes, the Redskins dismiss coach Norv Turner and replace him with Terry Robiskie.

**Dec 10**—Dallas quarterback Troy Aikman suffers the ninth concussion of his NFL career and the 11th of his life during the Cowboys' 32–13 win over Washington, fueling speculation that he will retire.

**Dec 14**—The Tampa Bay Buccaneers and the Titans lead the NFL in All-Pro selections as each team sends eight players to the Pro Bowl.

**Dec 17**—Wide receiver Jerry Rice, 38, who will leave the 49ers after the season because of salary-cap issues, plays his last game in San Francisco. The Niners beat the Bears 17–0 as Rice's teammate Terrell Owens breaks a 50-year-old NFL record with 20 catches in the game.

**Dec 17**—Delivering on the promise their coach, Jim Fassel, made a month earlier that they would make the playoffs, the Giants rally to defeat Dallas 17–13 and clinch the NFC East title. In Tampa the next night, the Bucs outscore the Rams 38–35 to clinch at least a wild-card berth in the playoffs. The Rams drop to 9–6 but a 26–21 victory at NFC West titlists New Orleans the following week assures them a wild-card spot.

**Dec 23**—The Raiders clinch the AFC West title with a 52–9 shellacking of Carolina, assuring the first playoff game in Oakland since 1980. In East Rutherford, N.J., the Ravens beat the Jets 34–20 to finish the season with seven straight wins. At 12–4 Baltimore finishes behind Tennessee (13–3) in the AFC Central but will go to the playoffs as a wild card, along with Indianapolis (10–6) and Denver (11–5). AFC East champion Miami (11–5) completes the AFC playoff picture. In the NFC, Minnesota wins the NFC Central despite losing its last three games, and Philadelphia defeats the Cincinnati Bengals 16–7 to finish 11–5 and clinch a wild-card berth.

**Dec 27**—Rams running back Marshall Faulk, who rushed for 1,359 yards, is named MVP of the 2000–01 season.

**Dec 29**—Wild-card weekend yields two tight games and two blowouts:The Saints win a playoff game for the first time in the 34-year history of the franchise, holding off the defending champion Rams 31–28 in New Orleans. The next day in Philadelphia, the Eagles eliminate Tampa Bay 21–3. In the AFC, the Dolphins get past wild-card Indianapolis 23–17 in overtime in Miami while the Ravens rout Denver 21–3 in Baltimore.

**Jan 2, 2001**—Baltimore linebacker Ray Lewis is named NFL defensive player of the year. In New York, Al Groh resigns as coach of the Jets to take the head coaching job at the University of Virginia.

**Jan 3**—Former Chiefs and Cleveland Browns coach Marty Schottenheimer accepts the head coaching job in Washington.

**Jan 7**—None of the divisional playoff games are particularly close as the Vikings steamroll New

Orleans 34–16 in Minneapolis, the Ravens rock Tennessee in Nashville 24–10, the Raiders blank Miami 27–0 in Oakland and the Giants defeat Philadelphia 20–10 in East Rutherford, N.J.

**Jan 8**—The Bills dismiss coach Wade Phillips for his refusal to fire his special-teams coach, Ronnie Jones, who was hired after Buffalo gave up the so-called Music City Miracle touchdown at the end of the previous season's playoff game against Tennessee. The following day the Chiefs announce that they've coaxed Dick Vermeil out of retirement to coach their team, and the Jets announce that Bill Parcells has resigned as head of football operations.

**Jan 13**—The Giants flatten the Vikings 41–0 in the NFC Championship Game in East Rutherford, N.J., to advance to the Super Bowl for the first time since 1990. The Giants score on the fourth play of the game, a 46-yard touchdown pass, and after Minnesota fumbles the ensuing kickoff, New York scores again on the very next play and the rout is on.

**Jan 14**—Tight end Shannon Sharpe catches a pass from quarterback Trent Dilfer and runs the length of the field for a 96-yard touchdown play to give the Ravens a 7–0 second-quarter lead in the AFC Championship Game against Oakland. Led by linebacker Ray Lewis, who makes seven tackles, blocks two passes and recovers a fumble, the Baltimore defense clamps down and the Ravens go on to a 16–3 triumph and their first Super Bowl berth.

**Jan 17**—League owners approve a new revenue-sharing plan that clears the way for the NFL's realignment proposal. The uprooting of traditional rivalries that realignment will bring is offset by the plan, which will distribute visiting teams' gate receipts equally among all 32 teams.

**Jan 18**—Herman Edwards becomes the third African-American in the ranks of NFL head coaches when he is hired to lead the Jets.

**Jan 19**—Former Panthers wide receiver Rae Carruth is found guilty of conspiracy to commit murder, shooting into an occupied vehicle and using an instrument with the intent to destroy an unborn child in the Nov. 16, 2000, shooting of his pregnant girlfriend, Cherica Adams. Adams died on Dec. 14 from wounds suffered in the drive-by attack, allegedly ordered by Carruth, who is sentenced to a minimum of 18 years and 11 months in prison for his role.

**Jan 28**—Baltimore's defense, which set an NFL record for fewest points allowed (165) during the regular season, smothers the Giants in Tampa, spearheading the Ravens' 34–7 victory in Super Bowl XXXV. The Ravens D forces five turnovers and linebacker Ray Lewis, who makes three tackles and tips a Kerry Collins pass that teammate Jamie Sharper intercepts, is named MVP of the game.

DAMIAN STROHMEYER

**After 12 years and 11 concussions, future Hall of Famer Aikman left the field for the broadcast booth.**

**Jan 29**—Cleveland hires Butch Davis away from the University of Miami to coach the Browns in 2001–02.

**Feb 1**—The Bills name former Tennessee defensive coordinator Gregg Williams to succeed Wade Phillips as head coach.

**Feb 3**—A joint effort between NBC and the World Wrestling Federation, the XFL football league—which promises that games will not be scripted, as WWF matches are—kicks off its televised schedule in East Rutherford, N.J., with a game between the NY/NJ Hitmen and the Las Vegas Outlaws.

**Feb 3**—Former Green Bay Packers tight end Mark Chmura is acquitted of charges of child enticement and sexual assault in connection with an incident at a friend's home on April 9, 2000, involving his 17-year-old babysitter.

**Feb 4**—The AFC downs the NFC 38–17 in the Pro Bowl in Honolulu. With 160 yards passing and two touchdowns in the first 11 minutes, Oakland quarterback Rich Gannon is named MVP.

**Feb 10**—After a promising opening weekend, television ratings for the new XFL football league drop by 50%.

**For the third consecutive year, Warner and the Rams jumped out to a 6–0 start.**

**Feb 27**—Giants head coach Jim Fassel is rewarded for taking his team to the Super Bowl, signing a four-year, $11 million contract.

**March 1**—Buffalo decides to go with Rob Johnson as its No. 1 quarterback and, in a move that puts the team almost $3 million under the NFL salary cap, releases veteran Doug Flutie.

**March 1**—Several prominent players part ways with their teams as the Chargers cut oft-troubled quarterback Ryan Leaf, the second pick in the 1998 draft; the Steelers release seven-time All-Pro center Dermontti Dawson; Kansas City announces that quarterback Elvis Grbac will become a free agent; Minnesota releases six-time Pro Bowl tackle John Randle; the 49ers cut linebacker Ken Norton Jr., who has back problems; and Carolina's defensive end Reggie White, the NFL's alltime sack leader, announces his retirement.

**March 5**—Free-agent quarterback Brad Johnson leaves Washington for a five-year, $28 million deal with Tampa Bay.

**March 6**—Elvis Grbac, who passed for 4,169 yards with the Chiefs in 2000, signs a five-year, $30 million free-agent contract with the defending champion Ravens.

**March 7**—The Cowboys bring the Troy Aikman era, which yielded three Super Bowls in 12 years, to an end, waiving the future Hall of Fame quarterback. Aikman, who suffered 11 concussions during his college and pro careers, announces his retirement on April 9.

**April 23**—The Falcons send their first- and third-round selections (Nos. 5 and 67 overall), their second-round pick in 2002 and receiver-returner Tim Dwight to San Diego in exchange for the No. 1 pick in the NFL draft. With the selection, Atlanta takes Virginia Tech quarterback Michael Vick. Picking second, Arizona selects Texas offensive tackle Leonard Davis. The Browns take Florida defensive tackle Gerard Warren with the third pick.

**May 10**—Less than three weeks after the conclusion of its inaugural season, the XFL folds.

**May 21**—After deliberating for three weeks, a Los Angeles jury votes 9–3 to toss out the Raiders' $1.2 billion lawsuit against the NFL. The suit claimed that the league sabotaged the team's negotiations to build a new stadium in Los Angeles in 1995, and that the Raiders still own rights to the Los Angeles NFL market.

**May 22**—In a unanimous vote at a meeting in Rosemont, Ill., NFL owners approve realignment for the 2002 season that will create eight, four-team divisions in the league. Under the plan, Seattle will move from the AFC West to the NFC West, while Arizona moves from the NFC East to the more geographically correct NFC West. Two South divisions will be established in the new scheme, with the expansion Houston Texans joining Indianapolis, Jacksonville and Tennessee (a team formerly located in Houston) in the AFC South.

**May 29**—Quarterback Randall Cunningham, who played for Dallas in 2000, signs a one-year contract to back up Elvis Grbac in Baltimore.

**June 5**—The Raiders sign former San Francisco wide receiver Jerry Rice, the NFL's alltime leader in receptions and touchdowns.

**June 13**—The defunct XFL's most valuable player, quarterback Tommy Maddox, signs with the Steelers. Maddox, who had a four-year stint in the NFL in the '90s, will back up Kordell Stewart.

**July 25**—Wide receiver Randy Moss signs an eight-year, $75 million contract extension with Minnesota. The deal includes a record $18 million signing bonus.

**Aug 1**—After two days of training camp in the blazing Minnesota summer sun, the Vikings' All-Pro offensive tackle Korey Stringer dies of heat exhaustion. He is survived by his wife, Kelci, and toddler son, Kodie.

**Aug 3**—The Pro Football Hall of Fame welcomes former Miami linebacker Nick Buoniconti, who spearheaded the Dolphins No-Name Defense of the 1970s; former Bills coach Marv Levy, who led Buffalo to four Super Bowls; ex-Oilers guard Mike Munchak, a 10-time All-Pro; former Rams tackle Jackie Slater, who was elected to seven Pro Bowls; ex-Steelers wide receiver Lynn Swann, the MVP of Super Bowl X;

former Vikings tackle Ron Yary, who played in four Super Bowls; and ex-defensive end Jack Youngblood, whose streak of 201 consecutive games played is a Rams record.

**Aug 8**—Baltimore running back Jamal Lewis, who was a key player in the Ravens title run the previous season, goes down with torn knee ligaments during a morning practice. He will miss the upcoming season.

**Sept 3**—Ryan Leaf's NFL odyssey takes another downturn as the Buccaneers release the former Washington State star, who was the second pick in the 1998 NFL draft, after he is unable to beat out Joe Hamilton for the third-string quarterback position in training camp.

**Sept 9**—The 2001–02 NFL season opens with replacement referees as the regular officials are involved in a labor dispute with the league. The new refs get generally passing grades, which is more than the defending NFC Central champion Vikings can say. A heavy favorite in its home opener against Carolina and rookie quarterback, Chris Weinke, Minnesota falls 24–13. In Baltimore, the Ravens open their defense of the NFL title with a 17–6 victory over the Bears, while their counterparts in Supe XXXV, the Giants, lose to

the Broncos 31–20 in Denver the following night.

**Sept 20**—Denver running back Terrell Davis, the 1998 NFL MVP who missed most of the '99 season after tearing an anterior cruciate ligament, and most of 2000 with a fractured left leg, undergoes arthroscopic knee surgery and will be sidelined for four to six weeks.

**Sept 23**—The NFL resumes play after a one-week hiatus following the Sept. 11 terrorist attacks on New York City and Washington, D.C. The regular referees return to work, and in Cincinnati, the surprising Bengals knock off Baltimore 21–10 to improve their record to 2–0.

**Oct 14**—At 5–0 the Rams remain the NFL's only unbeaten team, but just barely: they edge the Giants 15–14 in St. Louis. In Nashville, the Titans win their first game of the year after three losses, holding off Tampa Bay 31–28.

**Oct 21**—The Browns (4–2) surpass their win total of the previous season with a 24–14 upset of the Ravens in Cleveland. In Cincinnati, the Bears improve to 4–1, their best start since '91, with a 24–0 win over the Bengals, and in East Rutherford, N.J., the Rams rout the Jets 34–14 to improve to 6–0, tops in the league.

**Nov 15, 2000**—Needing a win to advance to the final round of CONCACAF qualifying for the 2002 World Cup, the United States defeats Barbados 4–0 in Waterford, Barbados.

**Nov 19**—The draw for the final round of regional qualifying for the 2002 World Cup is announced, and the U.S. learns it will host Mexico in its first game, in Columbus, Ohio, on Feb. 28. The six teams vying for three World Cup berths are Honduras, Jamaica, Trinidad & Tobago, the U.S., Mexico and Costa Rica, which defeats Guatemala on Jan. 6, 2001, to advance to the final round.

**Nov 28**—Boca Juniors of Argentina ends Europe's five-year stranglehold on the Intercontinental Cup, defeating Real Madrid 2–1 in Tokyo.

**Dec 5**—The New York/New Jersey MetroStars announce plans for a multipurpose, 25,000-seat stadium in northern New Jersey. The club hopes to have the facility ready for the 2003 season.

**Dec 6**—Alfonso Mondelo, who coached the MetroStars to a 14–17 record in 1998, is named head coach of the Tampa Bay Mutiny.

**Dec 17**—The U.S. women's national team wraps up its 2000 season with a 1–1 tie against Japan in Phoenix. Defender Brandi Chastain scores the U.S. goal.

**Dec 18**—*Football de Primera,* a nationally

syndicated Spanish-language radio program, names U.S. midfielder Michelle Akers the best woman soccer player of all time. Akers, who retired in the summer of 2000, scored 105 goals in 153 games during her 15-year career with the women's national team.

**Dec 19**—Midfielder Claudio Reyna is named U.S. soccer player of the year in voting by journalists.

**Jan 10, 2001**—Soccer's international governing body, FIFA, reduces U.S. coach Bruce Arena's suspension from three games to two. Arena was suspended for arguing with officials following the U.S.'s controversial 2–1 loss in Costa Rica on July 23.

**Jan 11**—In Panyu, near Beijing, the U.S. women fall to China 1–0 in a friendly. Substitute Han Duan scores the winner in the 90th minute. Three days later the teams play to a 1–1 tie in Hangzhou, China, as Jennifer Lalor scores the U.S. goal.

**Jan 15**—Former U.S. national team defender Alexi Lalas, who retired in 1999, announces he will resume his career to play for the Los Angeles Galaxy.

**Jan 21**—Major League Soccer gets a feather in its cap as the Galaxy defeats CD Olimpia of Honduras 3–2 to win the CONCACAF Champions' Cup, the club championship of

**Donovan helped the Earthquakes go from worst to first in Major League Soccer.**

North and Central America and the Caribbean. Defender Ezra Hendrickson scores the game winner and Alexi Lalas has two assists.

**Jan 23**—Former Chicago Fire assistant Mike Jeffries, 38, is named head coach of the Dallas Burn.

**Jan 27**—Eighteen-year-old forward Landon Donovan sends his strike partner Brian McBride in on goal with a picture-perfect one-touch pass that McBride coolly finishes, giving the U.S. a 1–0 lead in its eventual 2–1 win over China in a friendly in Oakland.

**Feb 28**—Despite losing starters Brian McBride and Claudio Reyna to injuries in the first half, the U.S. downs Mexico 2–0 in the first game of the final round of World Cup qualifying. Substitutes Clint Mathis and Josh Wolff link up for the first goal in the 47th minute, and Wolff feeds Earnie Stewart for the second in the 87th minute.

**March 3**—Hosting four-time World Cup champion Brazil in front of 45,387 fans in Pasadena, the U.S. fields a young team, starting 17-year-old Bobby Convey and 18-year-old Landon Donovan. The inexperienced team performs well—particularly Convey, who holds his own against Cafu, one of the best right backs in the world—but falls 2–1. Clint Mathis scores for the Americans.

**March 28**—Seizing a valuable three points on the road, the U.S. downs Honduras 2–1 in a World Cup qualifier in San Pedro Sula. Clint Mathis scores the winner, bending a free kick inside the far post in the 86th minute.

**March 29**—The San Jose Earthquakes announce that they have acquired promising American forward Landon Donovan, who turned 19 on March 4, from Bayer Leverkusen, the German club which signed him in 1999.

**April 7**—Major League Soccer kicks off its sixth season as D.C. United defeats the defending champion Kansas City Wizards 3–2 in Washington. United teenager Bobby Convey scores his first MLS goal in the game. In East Rutherford, N.J., the MetroStars knock off New England 2–1 in front of a crowd of 30,753, and in Pasadena the Earthquakes win their opener for the first time in three years, defeating Los Angeles 3–2. New San Jose signing Landon Donovan makes his MLS debut, entering the game in the 73rd minute.

**April 14**—The Women's United Soccer Association (WUSA) kicks off its inaugural season in front of 34,148 fans in Washington's RFK Stadium. The host Freedom top the Bay Area CyberRays 1–0 on a goal by Pretinha of Brazil.

**April 25**—The U.S. remains unbeaten in World

DAVID BERGMAN

Cup qualifying with a 1–0 victory over Costa Rica in front of 37,319 fans at Arrowhead Stadium in Kansas City. Josh Wolff scores the lone goal in the 70th minute on an assist from his former teammate at the University of South Carolina, Clint Mathis.

**April 28**—Clint Mathis of the MetroStars submits his entry for MLS goal of the year with a spectacular 60-yard solo run during the MetroStars' 3–2 victory over Dallas at Giants Stadium. Mathis, who also has an assist in the game, dribbles around three defenders and outruns another before beating goalkeeper Matt Jordan from the top of the box.

**May 2**—MetroStars striker Clint Mathis continues his hot streak, scoring three goals to lead his team to a 4–1 rout of Kansas City in East Rutherford, N.J.

**June 5**—While training with the U.S. national team in Columbus, Ohio, MetroStars striker Clint Mathis, who leads MLS in scoring with seven goals in 10 games, tears the anterior cruciate ligament (ACL) in his right knee. He will miss the rest of World Cup qualifying and the remainder of the MLS season.

**June 7**—Chicago Fire and U.S. national team forward Josh Wolff, who suffered a foot injury during a game against Tampa Bay on April 28, finds out that his initial MRI missed a stress fracture that will keep Wolff out of action for at least six more weeks.

**June 16**—The U.S. ties Jamaica 0–0 in a World Cup qualifier in Kingston.

**June 20**—The U.S. runs its World Cup qualifying record to 4-0-1 with a 2–0 triumph over Trinidad & Tobago in Foxboro, Mass. Ante Razov and Earnie Stewart score. The U.S. has 13 of a possible 15 points through five qualifiers.

**June 28**—Tampa Bay sends playmaker Carlos Valderrama to the Colorado Rapids in a three-team trade that brings goalkeeper Adin Brown and defender Eric Denton to the Mutiny.

**July 21**—The MetroStars lose a 10th player to injury as midfielder Roy Myers tears his ACL during a 2–1 victory over D.C.

**July 28**—Landon Donovan is named MVP of the MLS All-Star Game in San Jose as he scores four goals in a 6–6 tie between the West and the East.

**Aug 13**—U.S. national team goalkeeper Kasey Keller leaves Rayo Vallecano of Spain on a free transfer to join Tottenham of the English Premier League.

**Aug 18**—The Columbus Crew extends its unbeaten streak to nine games with a 1–0 victory over the MetroStars in East Rutherford, N.J. In Miami, Alex Pineda Chacon scores his league-best sixth game-winner as the Fusion downs Dallas 4–2 to run its record to 15-4-5 and continue its remarkable turnaround from the previous season, when it finished 12-15-5.

**Aug 25**—WUSA wraps up its debut season with its inaugural title game, the Founders Cup, in Foxboro, Mass., between the Atlanta Beat and the CyberRays. After overtime ends with the teams tied 3–3, Bay Area prevails 4–2 on penalties. The New York Power's Tiffeny Millbrett is named MVP of WUSA's first season.

**Sept 1**—The U.S. gives up an early lead and misses a penalty kick in a 3–2 loss to Honduras in a World Cup qualifier in Washington, D.C.

**Sept 5**—After beginning the final round of World Cup qualifying in nearly ideal fashion, with four wins and a tie through five games, the U.S. suddenly finds its World Cup hopes in jeopardy following its third straight defeat, a 2–0 blanking by Costa Rica in San Jose, C.R. The Americans are now in fourth place in their six-team group, from which three will advance to Japan/South Korea.

**Sept 9**—Mia Hamm scores two goals as the U.S. women defeat Germany 4–1 in the U.S. Women's Cup in Chicago.

**Sept 29**—The first round of the MLS playoffs ends with Los Angeles ousting the MetroStars in sudden-death overtime of Game 3, Chicago sweeping Dallas with a 2–0 win in Game 2 and Miami dispatching defending champ Kansas City 2–1 in the third game of their series.

**Oct 7**—Its World Cup chances on the line in Foxboro, Mass., the United States delivers a clutch 2–1 win over Jamaica as Joe-Max Moore scores both goals. In San Jose, Costa Rica, Mexico ties its hosts 0–0, a result that, combined with Honduras's shocking home loss to previously winless Trinidad & Tobago, assures the U.S. of a spot in the 2002 World Cup.

**Oct 17**—Both MLS semifinals go to sudden-death overtime as the Galaxy's Mauricio Cienfuegos scores a spectacular 25-yard goal to give Los Angeles a 2–1 win over Chicago, and the Earthquakes' Troy Dayak heads home the winner to give San Jose a 1–0 win over the Fusion.

**Oct 21**—Playing without star midfielder Manny Lagos, San Jose completes a worst-to-first season with a 2–1 golden-goal victory over Los Angeles in MLC Cup 2001. Landon Donovan scores the Earthquakes' first goal and substitute Dwayne DeRosario hits the winner in overtime.

# Tennis

**Oct 31, 2000**—Andre Agassi returns to competitive tennis after two months off for personal reasons and defeats Thomas Johansson 6–4, 6–2 in the Stuttgart Masters Series.

**Nov 9**—Citing anemia, Wimbledon and U.S. Open champ Venus Williams withdraws from the season-ending Chase Championships.

**Nov 12**—Marat Safin of Russia wins the $800,000 St. Petersburg (Russia) Open, defeating Dominik Hrbaty 2–6, 6–4, 6–4 in the final.

**Nov 21**—In a thrilling final at the season-ending Chase Championships in Madison Square Garden, Martina Hingis outlasts Monica Seles 6–7 (5–7), 6–4, 6–4. It is Hingis's ninth win of the year; she finishes the season ranked first in the world.

**Nov 26**—Playing without the Olympic-champion Williams sisters, the United States still defeats Spain in Las Vegas to seize a record 17th Fed Cup title. Lindsay Davenport and Monica Seles lead the way with singles victories.

**Dec 3**—With his straight-sets victory over Andre Agassi in the final of the season-ending Masters Cup in Lisbon, Gustavo Kuerten of Brazil becomes the first South American to finish the year ranked No. 1 in the world since the ATP began its rankings in 1973.

**Dec 12**—Patrick McEnroe succeeds his brother John as U.S. Davis Cup captain.

**Jan 9, 2001**—The 22-match doubles winning streak of Venus and Serena Williams comes to an end when the sisters are beaten 6–4, 3–6, 7–6, (7–2) by Martina Hingis and Monica Seles at the International in Sydney.

**Comeback Kid: The rejuvenated Capriati won the Australian and French Opens.**

**Jan 27**—Jennifer Capriati, who was out of tennis from 1993 to '96 while she struggled with personal problems, puts an exclamation point on her extraordinary comeback with a 6–4, 6–3 victory over Martina Hingis in the final of the Australian Open. It is Capriati's first Grand Slam title.

**Jan 28**—Andre Agassi wins the seventh Grand Slam title of his career, defeating Arnaud Clement of France 6–4, 6–2, 6–2 in the final of the Australian Open. It is Agassi's second straight Australian Open title.

**Feb 11**—For the first time since 1993, the U.S. exits Davis Cup play in the first round as the Americans—playing without Pete Sampras and Andre Agassi, both of whom declined invitations to play—fall to Switzerland 3–2.

**Feb 13**—Eight-time Grand Slam champion Ivan Lendl is elected to the International Tennis Hall of Fame in Newport, R.I.

**Feb 25**—Monica Seles defeats Jennifer Capriati, who ousted her from the quarterfinals of the Australian Open in January, in the finals of the IGA Indoors tournament in Oklahoma City.

**March 31**—All four finalists at the Ericsson Open in Key Biscayne, Fla., are from the U.S. Venus Williams downs Jennifer Capriati 4–6, 6–1, 7–6 (7–4) in the women's final, and the following day Andre Agassi takes the men's title, trouncing Jan-Michael Gambill 7–6 (7–4), 6–1, 6–0.

**April 8**—The visiting teams triumph in Davis Cup play as France knocks off Switzerland 3–2

and Australia travels to Brazil and wins 3–1.

**April 22**—Jennifer Capriati moves to No. 4 in the WTA computer rankings with a 6–0, 4–6, 6–4 triumph over Martina Hingis in the final of the Family Circle Cup in Charleston, S.C.

**April 29**—Highly touted American Andy Roddick wins his first ATP title, taking the Verizon Tennis Challenge in Duluth, Ga., with a 6–2, 6-4 victory over Xavier Malisse of Belgium. The following week Roddick, his serve sometimes topping 130 mph, overwhelms South Korea's Hyung-Taik Lee 7–5, 6–3 to win the U.S. Clay Court Championship in Houston.

**May 13**—Amelie Mauresmo defeats Jennifer Capriati 6-4, 2–6, 6–3 in the final of the German Open. With the win, the 21-year-old Frenchwoman moves to No. 6 in the WTA rankings.

**May 28**—Joining the injured Lindsay Davenport (knee) and Monica Seles (foot) on the sidelines, Venus Williams makes an early exit from the French Open, losing to Barbara Schett of Austria 6–4, 6–4.

**June 6**—Aiming for a second straight Grand Slam title after winning the Australian Open in January, Andre Agassi falls 1–6, 6–1, 6–1, 6–3 to Sebastien Grosjean of France in the quarterfinals of the French Open.

**June 9**—Jennifer Capriati seizes her second Grand Slam title of the season, taking the French Open final with a 1–6, 6–4,12–10 triumph over Kim Cljisters of Belgium. Gustavo Kuerten of Brazil wins the men's title the following day, defeating Spain's Alex Corretja 6–7 (3–7), 7–5, 6–2, 6–0.

**July 2**—Switzerland's Roger Federer ends Pete Sampras's four-year reign as Wimbledon champion, ousting the alltime leader in Grand Slam titles with a 7–6 (9–7), 5–7, 6–4, 6–7 (2–7), 7–5 victory in the fourth round.

**July 8**—Venus Williams repeats as Wimbledon champ—she is the first woman to do so since Steffi Graf in 1996—with a 6–1, 3–6, 6–0 victory over Justine Henin.

**July 9**—The men's final at Wimbledon is delayed one day due to rain but proves to be well worth the wait as three-time Wimbledon runner-up Goran Ivanisevic of Croatia defeats Australia's Patrick Rafter 6–3, 3–6, 6–3, 2–6, 9–7 in a match that becomes an instant classic.

**July 12**—Steffi Graf and Andre Agassi announce that they are expecting their first child, a boy, in November.

**Aug 4**—Venus Williams wins the Acura Classic in Carlsbad, Calif., for the second year in a row, defeating Monica Seles 6–2, 6–3 in the final.

**Aug 6**—The weekly WTA rankings show Martina Hingis in the top spot for the 200th week, a milestone achieved by only three other players in women's tennis history, Steffi Graf, Martina Navratilova and Chris Evert.

**Aug 12**—Clay-court specialist Gustavo Kuerten establishes himself as a contender for the U.S. Open title, steamrolling Patrick Rafter 6–1, 6–3 in the final of the hardcourt Masters Series Cincinnati.

**Sept 5**—Pete Sampras and Andre Agassi play a quarterfinal match for the ages at the U.S. Open as Sampras wins 6–7 (7–9), 7–6 (7–2), 7–6 (7–2), 7–6 (7–5). The match lasts three hours and 32 minutes and there are 43 aces.

**Sept 8**—For the first time since 1884, sisters meet in the final of a Grand Slam as Serena and Venus Williams square off for the U.S. Open title. Venus takes her second Grand Slam of the season with a 6–2, 6–4 victory.

**Sept 9**—After battling past Andre Agassi and Marat Safin, the man who defeated him in last year's final, Pete Sampras, 30, falls to 20-year-old Lleyton Hewitt of Australia in the final of the U.S. Open. After dropping the first set 7–6 (7–4), the leg-weary Sampras bows 6–1, 6–1.

**Oct 1**—Gustavo Kuerten gets his indoor season off to a poor start, losing 7–6 (6–1), 6–2 to Croatia's Ivan Ljubicic in the first round of the Lyon Grand Prix.

**Oct 14**—With a 7–5, 6–4 defeat of Belgium's Justine Henin, Lindsay Davenport wins the Porsche Grand Prix in Filderstadt, Germany, for her fifth title of the year. The tournament causes a change in the women's rankings as Martina Hingis, who tears a ligament in her ankle during a semifinal loss to Davenport, tumbles from the top spot, and Jennifer Capriati, who reached the quarterfinals of the tournament, becomes the new No. 1. Hingis is expected to miss six weeks with her injury.

**Oct 17**—Andre Agassi misses a chance to move into the No. 1 spot in the ATP rankings when he loses 7–6 (7–4), 7–5 to Hicham Arazi in the second round of the Masters Series Stuttgart. Top-ranked Gustavo Kuerten had lost the day before, opening the door for Agassi.

# Other Sports

**Oct 22, 2000**—Khalid Khannouchi, who became a U.S. citizen six months earlier, repeats as Chicago Marathon champ, clocking 2:07:01. Catherine Ndereba of Kenya wins the women's race in 2:21:33.

**Oct 29**—Austria's Hermann Maier wins the season-opening event in World Cup skiing, taking the giant slalom in Sölden, Austria. Martina Ertl of Germany wins the women's giant slalom.

**Nov 2**—Major League Lacrosse, a new outdoor league founded by fitness guru Jake Steinfeld, announces its six franchises that will begin play in the summer of 2001: Baltimore; Fairfield County, Conn.; Washington, D.C.; Long Island, N.Y; and Rochester, N.Y,

**Nov 5**—Morocco's Abdelkhader El Mouaziz wins the New York City marathon in 2:10:09. He pulls away from the pack at the 12-mile mark and finishes 2:20 ahead of runner-up Japhet Kosgei of Kenya, one of the largest margins of victory in the race's history. Ludmila Petrova of Russia wins the women's race, clocking 2:25:45.

**Nov 17**—On the Park City, Utah, slope that will be used in the 2002 Winter Olympics, Michael von Grünigen of Switzerland wins the second World Cup giant slalom of the season. His countrywoman Sonja Nef wins the women's giant slalom. Kristina Koznick of the United States finishes 18th.

**Dec 3**—The University of North Carolina women's soccer team wins its 17th NCAA title in 20 years, edging UCLA 2–1 in the final in San Jose, Calif.

**Dec 10**—The University of Connecticut defeats Creighton 2–0 in the NCAA men's soccer final in Charlotte, N.C.

**Dec 12**—At the National Finals Rodeo in Las Vegas, Joe Beaver wins his third all-around title and combines with Bret Gould to win the team roping title as well. He takes home $123,355.

**Dec 16**—Nebraska wins the NCAA women's volleyball title with a 15–9, 9–15, 7–15, 15–2, 15–9 victory over Wisconsin in the final at Richmond Coliseum. The win completes a 34–0 season for the Cornhuskers, making them the second team in NCAA history to win the title with a perfect record.

**Dec 28**—Croatia's Janica Kostelic wins her fifth straight World Cup slalom race of the year, producing two flawless runs in Semmering, Austria.

**Jan 9, 2001**—Austria's Hermann Maier wins the World Cup giant slalom in Adelboden, Switzerland, to retain a shot at winning the season title. There are two races to go.

**Jan 14**—Iowa State wrestler Cael Sanderson wins the 100th consecutive match of his college career during the Cyclones' 32–10 defeat of Hofstra. Sanderson is believed to have tied Dan Gable's streak from 1967 to '70, when no official records were kept. By the end of the following weekend, Sanderson has improved his career record to 105–0.

**Jan 17**—Dean Rojas of Lake Havasau City, Ariz., sets a one-day record when he hauls 45 pounds, two ounces of bass out of Lake Tohopekaliga in Kissimmee, Fla., during the first round of the BASSMASTER TOP 150.

**Jan 21**—Michelle Kwan wins the women's U.S. figure skating title in Boston. It is her fourth straight national title and fifth in six years. Timothy Goebel wins the men's title.

**Feb 4**—Walter Ray Williams Jr. wins the PBA National Championship with a 258–204 win over Jeff Lizzi in the title game in Toledo, Ohio.

**March 4**—Hermann Maier wins the super-G in Kvitfjell, Norway, for his 11th World Cup win this year. Maier wins the overall title as well as the season titles in super-G, giant slalom, and downhill. Janica Kostelic wins the women's overall and slalom titles.

**March 14**—Musher Doug Swingley of Lincoln, Mont., wins the Iditarod Trail Sled Dog Race for the second year in a row and fourth time overall, reaching the finish line in Nome, Alaska, after nine days, 19 hours, 55 minutes.

**March 22**—Skier Bill Johnson, the 1984 Olympic champion, suffers a catastrophic crash while attempting a comeback at a race in Whitefish, Mont. He remains in a coma for several weeks with critical injuries after plowing through two fences after going off course in the downhill.

**March 25**—Michelle Kwan wins both the U.S. and world figure skating titles for the second straight year, defeating Russia's Irina Slutskaya for the world championship in Vancouver.

**April 16**—Lee Bong-Ju of South Korea ends Kenya's 10-year stranglehold on the Boston Marathon, winning the 105th running of the event in 2:09:43, 44 seconds ahead of runner-up Silvio Guerro of Ecuador. Lee runs the last mile in 4:47. In the women's race, Catherine Ndereba, who won in New York in November, wins by nearly three minutes over runner-up Malgorzata Sobanska of Poland, despite stopping at nine miles to remove a pebble from her shoe.

**May 8**—The PBA Tour's new owners, who bought the pro bowling circuit in March 2000, announce that they've signed an exclusive three-year TV deal with ESPN, increased Tour prize money by 139% and made the season a single, continuous one instead of the previous segmented tournament schedule.

**May 27**—High-schooler Alan Webb of Reston, Va., breaks Jim Ryun's 36-year-old national prep record for the mile, clocking 3:53.43 at the Prefontaine Classic in Eugene, Ore. Webb's time is the fastest mile by an American of any age since 1998.

**May 28**—Princeton defeats Syracuse 10–9 in overtime to win the NCAA men's Division I lacrosse title for the sixth time.

**July 29**—Lance Armstrong of the U.S. Postal Service team wins the Tour de France for the third consecutive year. Armstrong finishes the grueling 21-stage race in 86 hours, 17 minutes, 28 seconds, the third-fastest time in the history of the race.

**July 25**—Swimmer Ian Thorpe of Australia sets his third world record of the world championships in Fukuoka, Japan, clocking 1:44.06 to win the 200-meter freestyle. He set records in the 400 and 800 free on July 22 and 24, respectively. On July 24 Baltimore's Michael Phelps, 16, won the 200 butterfly with a world-record time of 1:54.58.

**Aug 26**—Japan wins the Little League World Series, defeating Apopka, Fla., 2–1 with two runs in the bottom of the last inning in front of 44,800 fans in Williamsport, Pa. Several days after the tournament, the Rolando Paulino team from the Bronx is found to have used an overage player, pitcher Danny Almonte, who dominated hitters throughout the tournament.

**Sept 16**—Eight University of Wyoming track and cross-country athletes are killed in a head-on collision with a pickup truck on a highway 17 miles south of Laramie.

**Oct 7**—For the second time in a week a runner lowers the women's world record for the marathon as Catherine Ndereba breaks the tape in Chicago in 2:18:47. She betters the time of Japan's Naoko Takahashi, who ran 2:19:46 in Berlin on Sept. 30 to become the first woman ever to break 2:20:00. The women's marathon record, which had improved 23 seconds in the previous 14 years, drops by 1:56 in seven days.

**The indefatigable Armstrong won the Tour de France for the third consecutive year.**

MIKE POWELL/ALLSPORT

# Baseball

The World Series
champion Arizona
Diamondbacks

# Pair of Aces

## Led by pitchers Curt Schilling and Randy Johnson, Arizona dethroned the mighty Yankees

### BY MARK BECHTEL

The sight of New York second baseman Alfonso Soriano circling the bases after golfing a home run to left field in the top of the eighth inning of Game 7 of the World Series seemed like the perfect conclusion to the 2001 baseball season. Sure, the Yankees' opponents, the fledgling Arizona Diamondbacks, had two more cracks at New York pitching, but since Soriano's homer gave the Yankees a 2–1 lead, those two cracks would come against Mariano Rivera, arguably the greatest big-game relief pitcher baseball has ever seen. So having Soriano win the series with a home run would have been fitting, since the entire season—and especially the World Series—was defined by dramatic homers. But it didn't happen: The Diamondbacks rallied for two runs in the bottom of the ninth off the normally unhittable Rivera and snatched the title from the Yankees, spoiling the script for New York fans and giving their faithful cause for uproarious celebration in Phoenix.

But Yankee fans, and baseball fans of every stripe, had unforgettable moments to savor in 2001, a spectacular season in which the sport said goodbye to a couple of legends, a few legendary records, and more than a few home run balls.

When Mark McGwire set the single-season home run record in 1998, he established a standard that appeared ready to stand the test of time. Unlike Roger Maris, who eclipsed Babe Ruth's record by a single homer in 1961, Big Mac annihilated Maris's record of 61, cracking 70 home runs—an increase of nearly 15 percent. Given that Ruth's record had stood for 34 years, and Maris's for 37 years, it didn't seem unreasonable to expect a long life for McGwire's record.

Alas for Big Red, 2001 was a year like no other when it came to long balls. Arizona's Luis Gonzalez, who had never hit more than 31 homers in a season, slugged 13 in April and went into the All-Star break with 35 home runs and a .355 average. San Francisco's Barry Bonds belted homers in six consecutive games in April and had 39 at the break. And Sammy Sosa, who topped 60 homers in both 1998 and '99, overcame a

**Schilling, the World Series's co-MVP, pitched brilliantly in three starts against the Yankees.**

slow start with a brilliant August in which he produced two three-homer games at Wrigley. Slammin' Sammy would finish with 64 taters to become the only player in baseball history to top 60 homers in three seasons, but as the season wound down, it was clear that only Bonds had a realistic shot at McGwire's record. (Injuries limited Big Mac to 29 homers in 97 games.)

From July 26 to the end of the season, Bonds never went four games without hitting at least one home run, and he did so despite seldom seeing good pitches to hit. He walked a major league record 177 times, and after July 22, he never went consecutive games without walking at least once. After Bonds hit his 69th homer on Sept. 29, Houston, which was contending for a playoff spot, walked him eight times in 14 plate appearances. The Astros were determined not to let Bonds beat them. Even when they were trailing 8–1 in the sixth inning of the third game of the series, they walked the Giants' slugger. He finally got a decent pitch to hit from Astros rookie Wilfredo Rodriguez in the ninth inning on Oct. 4—and promptly drilled the pitch 454 feet into the seats at Enron Field for Number 70. "I threw him fastballs," Rodriguez said matter-of-factly. "That's what I do."

The next night, Dodgers ace Chan Ho Park did that too, grooving one in the first inning that Bonds hit into the right-center-field stands of Pacific Bell Park to break McGwire's record. There had been some discussion of whether or not the Dodgers—who were out of contention for the playoffs but who are also fierce rivals of the Giants—would pitch to Bonds. Happily, fair play prevailed, and Bonds got a fighting chance at

the record—and then some: Two innings later he hit a hanging curveball over the rightfield fence for Number 72. He added another one two days later to finish the season with 73 home runs, a total that most baseball fans would have considered inconceivable as recently as five years ago.

Marvelous though it was, Bonds's quest lacked much of the attendant interest and goodwill that McGwire and Sosa generated in the memorable autumn of 1998. That was partly because of Bonds's reputation for surlinesss, and partly because the record, under threat again after only three years, may have lost some of its luster. When it was all over, Bonds took the tone of a man who understood that his record—perhaps no record—was safe in this day and age. "I don't know if it is going to exist next year," he said. "These young guys are big kids and they are strong kids, and with the new stadiums being converted to a little smaller than in the past, you guys are going to see a lot of wonderful things happen in the game of baseball in the future."

A wonderful thing happened during the All-Star Game at Seattle's Safeco Field, and it also involved the Dodgers' righthander Park. He served up a fat fastball to Cal Ripken in the third inning, and the 40-year-old Orioles third baseman, who had announced that he would retire after the season, knocked it out of the park. Ripken was in the midst of his worst year statistically, but he was still able to provide a fair amount of drama with his Midsummer Night's Dream of a clout. It wasn't the first time Ripken had homered to add poignancy to an already memorable scene—he hit one out in 1995 on the night he broke Lou Gehrig's record for consecutive games played—and after the game he was asked how he always seemed to come through with the storybook hit. "Gosh, I wish I could explain that," he said. "When you have the chance, just one opportunity in front of a big baseball crowd, and feel the moment, the electricity, the magic—that's everything."

Joining Ripken in the ranks of future Hall of Famers to hang up their cleats in 2001 was San Diego outfielder Tony Gwynn, who saw his playing time severely curtailed by injuries for the second straight year. Gwynn's retirement ended a remarkable career in which he hit better than .300 19 straight times. His career average was .338, and he struck out just 434 times, the second-fewest of any member of the 3,000-hit club, behind Paul Waner. Gwynn played his final game on Oct. 7, the day after Ripken's finale. In the top of the sixth inning, the Qualcomm Stadium scoreboard showed a taped message from Ripken. "We are certainly two of the lucky ones. We both got to play our whole career with the same team," Ripken said. "I hope today is a real happy day for you."

Gwynn's teammate, veteran leadoff man Rickey Henderson, added to the festive atmosphere in San Diego that day. Having broken Ty Cobb's 73-year-old record for career runs three days earlier, Henderson hit a bloop double down the rightfield line in the first inning off Colorado's John Thomson for his 3,000th career hit. He is the 25th player to reach the milestone, and when he took the field in the top of the second, Padres manager Bruce Bochy took him out so that the crowd of 60,103 could properly salute him.

While Ripken and the 42-year-old Henderson and the 41-year-old Gwynn shared the spotlight in the final days of the season, not all of the headlines made in 2001 came courtesy of the game's older set. Cardinals rookie Albert Pujols, who played all of three minor league games above A ball before coming to the majors, set an NL rookie record with 130 RBIs. In the American League, the most dominant newcomer was hardly a novice. Ichiro Suzuki, who won seven consecutive batting titles in Japan, joined the Seattle Mariners and immediately boosted their lineup. Batting first, he set major league records for hits by a rookie and singles in a season, and he scored 127 runs. He was mobbed by the Japanese media from the time he arrived at spring training, and within a couple of weeks he became something of a sensation with the natives in his adopted homeland. The team released a statement declaring, "It is Ichiro's preference to be identified by his first name only. He is the only current Major League Baseball player to have his first name on his jersey." And just like that, Ichiro Suzuki became Ichiro, joining Cher and Madonna in the ranks of the mononymous. "He's a legitimate hitter, no question," said Yankees manager Joe Torre. "I don't think you can pitch him one way. You can go in and out, up and down, and he makes the adjustment. You can get ahead in the count, and Suzuki still seems relaxed. He doesn't seem to have any weaknesses."

Ichiro's presence more than made up for the loss of shortstop Alex Rodriguez, who bolted Seattle for Texas before the season, when the Rangers offered him $25.2 million a season for 10 years. While Rodriguez had a superb season in his first year in Texas, belting 52 homers and driving in 135 runs, the investment failed to pay dividends as the pitching-poor Rangers struggled to a 73–89 record. The Mariners, meanwhile, went

116–46, tying the major league record for wins in a season set by the 1906 Cubs. It was quite an accomplishment for the M's, who in the past three years waved goodbye to Randy Johnson, Ken Griffey Jr. and Rodriguez. In 2001 they made do, to say the least, with pitching, defense and station-to-station baseball.

Indeed, 2001 was a good year for several teams lacking in superstars. The Twins, whose payroll was less than a quarter of the Yankees', came shooting out of the gate with a 14–3 start and showed no signs of letting up. They led the Indians in the AL Central by five games in mid-July before the Tribe finally rallied to overtake them in August. But Minnesota still finished the season at 85–77, a 16-game improvement over its 2000 record. And in the National League East, the Phillies, who tied for the worst record in baseball last year, nearly ended the Braves' decade-long stranglehold on the division title. Yet when the season ended, the eight playoff spots were filled by the usual suspects. Five playoff teams were making repeat appearances from 2000, and the three newcomers—Arizona, Houston and Cleveland—had all made the playoffs in 1999.

But none of the AL contenders had the experience to stay with New York in the

**Bonds set records with 73 homers, 177 walks and an .863 slugging percentage.**

postseason. While the Mariners had the single-season wins record and the A's had arguably the best young rotation in baseball, neither team had an answer for the Yankees' mystique. The A's took the first two games of their AL Division Series in New York, but in Oakland the series turned on an amazing play by New York shortstop Derek Jeter, the kind of play that separates champions from also-rans. In the seventh inning with the Yanks up 1–0, Terrance Long hit a fly ball over rightfielder Shane Spencer's head. Jeremy Giambi, who was on first, came chugging around third as Spencer's throw sailed offline and over two cutoff men. Jeter raced across the infield and, in one motion, retrieved the errant throw, spun and flipped the ball backhanded to catcher Jorge Posada, who tagged Giambi, the would-be tying run. "I couldn't believe it," said A's outfielder Johnny Damon. "I thought, What in the heck is he doing there? Then I was amazed that the shovel pass he made was perfect. Jeter made a play that saved their season."

Indeed he did, as the Yanks came back to win the series in five games and then beat the Mariners in five in the best-of-seven

JOHN W. MCDONOUGH

innings—and just 88 pitches—to bring in Byung-Hyun Kim, who hadn't pitched in 10 days. Kim got through the eighth without trouble, but allowed a one-out single to Paul O'Neill in the ninth. One out later, Tino Martinez homered to center, sending the Bronx into bedlam and the game into extra innings, where Jeter won it with a solo homer in the 10th.

Astonishingly, the Yankees did it again the next night. Despite throwing 61 pitches in Game 4, Kim started the ninth inning of Game 5, with his team again leading by two runs. Posada led off with a double, and after Kim retired the next two Yankee batters, Scott Brosius homered down the line.

With momentum and by all indications, fate, on their side, the Yankees flew to the desert for Games 6 and 7. But the Diamondbacks rebounded with a historic win of their own in Game 6, pounding out a World Series–record 22 hits in a 15–2 win, and setting the stage for a decisive seventh game between 20-game winners Schilling and Roger Clemens. Both pitchers rose to the occasion, and after Soriano's homer it became a battle of the bullpens: Rivera, who makes postseason saves with machine-like efficiency, and a tired but effective Johnson, who started Game 6 and now hoped to finish Game 7. Rivera struck out the side in the eighth, but in the ninth the legendary Yankees closer fell apart: He gave up a single, made a throwing error and surrendered a double to allow Arizona to tie the game. Then he hit Craig Counsell with a pitch to load the bases. With the infield drawn in, Luis Gonzalez lifted a single over Jeter's head, and Jay Bell dashed home with the World Series–winning run. "Win or lose," said Arizona first baseman Mark Grace, "I'm proud to have played in one of the greatest World Series in the history of this great game.... Someone has to tell me we just beat the New York Yankees and Mariano Rivera, because I still don't believe it."

LCS. In the National League, the Diamondbacks also won a thriller in the Division Series. The decisive fifth game was tied 1–1 in the bottom of the ninth when Arizona manager Bob Brenly called for a suicide squeeze with Midre Cummings at third, Greg Colbrunn at first and Tony Womack batting. The play backfired when Tony Womack missed the bunt and Cummings was tagged out at the plate. But Womack saved Brenly an offseason of second-guessing when he stroked a series-winning RBI single four pitches later.

The Diamondbacks then blew through the Braves in five games, setting up one of the strangest World Series ever played. Behind superb performances from Schilling and Randy Johnson, the D-Backs won the first two games in Phoenix, limiting the Yankees to a combined six hits. New York bounced back to win Game 3 at home, prompting Brenly to send Schilling to the mound on three days' rest for Game 4. Under a full moon on Halloween he once again pitched brilliantly, but Brenly pulled him after seven

## Final Standings

### National League

**EASTERN DIVISION**

| Team | Won | Lost | Pct | GB | Home | Away |
|------|-----|------|-----|-----|------|------|
| Atlanta | 88 | 74 | .543 | — | 40–41 | 48–33 |
| Philadelphia | 86 | 76 | .531 | 2 | 47–34 | 39–42 |
| New York | 82 | 80 | .506 | 6 | 44–37 | 38–43 |
| Florida | 76 | 86 | .469 | 12 | 46–34 | 30–52 |
| Montreal | 68 | 94 | .420 | 20 | 34–47 | 34–47 |

**CENTRAL DIVISION**

| Team | Won | Lost | Pct | GB | Home | Away |
|------|-----|------|-----|-----|------|------|
| Houston | 93 | 69 | .574 | — | 44–37 | 49–32 |
| †St. Louis | 93 | 69 | .574 | — | 54–28 | 39–41 |
| Chicago | 88 | 74 | .543 | 5 | 48–33 | 40–41 |
| Milwaukee | 68 | 94 | .420 | 25 | 36–45 | 32–49 |
| Cincinnati | 66 | 96 | .407 | 27 | 27–54 | 39–42 |
| Pittsburgh | 62 | 100 | .383 | 31 | 38–43 | 24–47 |

**WESTERN DIVISION**

| Team | Won | Lost | Pct | GB | Home | Away |
|------|-----|------|-----|-----|------|------|
| Arizona | 92 | 70 | .568 | — | 48–33 | 44–37 |
| San Francisco | 90 | 72 | .556 | 2 | 49–32 | 41–40 |
| Los Angeles | 86 | 76 | .531 | 6 | 44–37 | 42–39 |
| San Diego | 79 | 83 | .488 | 13 | 35–56 | 44–37 |
| Colorado | 73 | 89 | .451 | 19 | 41–40 | 32–49 |

†Wild-card team.

### American League

**EASTERN DIVISION**

| Team | Won | Lost | Pct | GB | Home | Away |
|------|-----|------|-----|-----|------|------|
| New York | 95 | 65 | .594 | — | 51–28 | 44–37 |
| Boston | 82 | 79 | .509 | 13½ | 41–40 | 41–39 |
| Toronto | 80 | 82 | .494 | 16 | 40–42 | 40–40 |
| Baltimore | 63 | 98 | .391 | 32½ | 30–50 | 33–48 |
| Tampa Bay | 62 | 100 | .383 | 34 | 37–44 | 25–56 |

**CENTRAL DIVISION**

| Team | Won | Lost | Pct | GB | Home | Away |
|------|-----|------|-----|-----|------|------|
| Cleveland | 91 | 71 | .562 | — | 44–36 | 47–35 |
| Minnesota | 85 | 77 | .525 | 6 | 47–34 | 38–43 |
| Chicago | 83 | 79 | .512 | 8 | 46–35 | 37–44 |
| Detroit | 66 | 96 | .407 | 25 | 37–44 | 29–52 |
| Kansas City | 65 | 97 | .401 | 26 | 35–46 | 30–51 |

**WESTERN DIVISION**

| Team | Won | Lost | Pct | GB | Home | Away |
|------|-----|------|-----|-----|------|------|
| Seattle | 116 | 46 | .716 | — | 57–24 | 59–22 |
| †Oakland | 102 | 60 | .630 | 14 | 53–28 | 49–32 |
| Anaheim | 75 | 87 | .463 | 41 | 39–42 | 36–45 |
| Texas | 73 | 89 | .451 | 43 | 41–41 | 32–38 |

## 2001 Playoffs

### National League Division Playoffs

| | |
|---|---|
| Oct 9 .............Atlanta 7 at Houston 4 | Oct 12 .............Houston 2 at Atlanta 6 |
| Oct 10 .............Atlanta 1 at Houston 0 | |

(Atlanta won series 3–0)

| | |
|---|---|
| Oct 9 .............St. Louis 0 at Arizona 1 | Oct 13 .............Arizona 1 at St. Louis 4 |
| Oct 10 .............St. Louis 4 at Arizona 1 | Oct 14 .............St. Louis 1 at Arizona 2 |
| Oct 12 .............Arizona 5 at St. Louis 3 | |

(Arizona won series 3–2)

### National League Championship Series

| | |
|---|---|
| Oct 16 .............Atlanta 0 at Arizona 2 | Oct 20 .............Arizona 11 at Atlanta 4 |
| Oct 17 .............Atlanta 8 at Arizona 1 | Oct 21 .............Arizona 3 at Atlanta 2 |
| Oct 19 .............Arizona 5 at Atlanta 1 | |

(Arizona won series 4–1)

**GAME 1**

| | | | | | | | | | | | | |
|---|---|---|---|---|---|---|---|---|---|---|---|---|
| Atlanta | 0 | 0 | 0 | 0 | 0 | 0 | 0 | 0 | 0 | **0** | **3** | **1** |
| Arizona | 1 | 0 | 0 | 0 | 1 | 0 | 0 | 0 | x | **2** | **8** | **0** |

**W**—Johnson. **L**—Maddux.
**E**—Atlanta: Giles. **LOB**—Atlanta 4, Arizona 7. **2B**—Arizona: Counsell. **GIDP**—Arizona: Grace, Finley. **T**—2:44. **A**—37,729.

**Recap:** Randy Johnson ended the longest losing streak by a pitcher in playoff history with a three-hitter, and Craig Counsell scored both runs as the Arizona Diamondbacks edged Greg Maddux and the Atlanta Braves. Johnson had dropped seven straight postseason decisions, dating back to 1995. The 38-year-old lefthander walked one, struck out 11, and retired 20 consecutive batters. Maddux again took a hard-luck loss in October. The four-time Cy Young Award winner allowed only two runs and six hits in seven innings. He walked two and struck out five but still took his ninth loss in nine starts.

**GAME 2**

| | | | | | | | | | | | | |
|---|---|---|---|---|---|---|---|---|---|---|---|---|
| Atlanta | 1 | 0 | 0 | 0 | 0 | 0 | 2 | 5 | 0 | **8** | **8** | **0** |
| Arizona | 0 | 0 | 0 | 0 | 0 | 1 | 0 | 0 | 0 | **1** | **5** | **1** |

**W**—Glavine. **L**—Batista.
**E**—Arizona: Williams. **LOB**—Atlanta 4, Arizona 6. **2B**—Atlanta: Jordan. **HR**—Atlanta: Giles, Lopez, Surhoff. **T**—2:54. **A**—49,334.

**Recap:** Tom Glavine pitched superbly for seven innings and his teammates tattooed a trio of relievers in a five-run eighth inning as the Braves evened the series in Phoenix. Although the win only improved Glavine's LCS record to 5–8, it was his 12th career playoff victory, tying teammate John Smoltz for the most in baseball history. Glavine received a 1–0 lead on the first pitch of the game as Atlanta's rookie second baseman Marcus Giles homered off Miguel Batista. After Arizona tied it in the sixth, Braves catcher Javy Lopez put Atlanta ahead for good with a two-run shot.

## National League Championship Series (Cont.)

### GAME 3

| | | | | | | | | | | | | |
|---|---|---|---|---|---|---|---|---|---|---|---|---|
| Arizona | 0 | 0 | 2 | 0 | 3 | 0 | 0 | 0 | 0 | **5** | **9** | **1** |
| Atlanta | 0 | 0 | 0 | 1 | 0 | 0 | 0 | 0 | 0 | **1** | **4** | **1** |

**W**—Schilling. **L**—Burkett.
**E**—Arizona: Williams; Atlanta: Lopez. **LOB**—Arizona 7, Atlanta 4. **2B**—Arizona: Williams, Finley; Atlanta: Giles, Jordan. **Sac**—Arizona: Counsell. **GIDP:** Arizona: Grace; Atlanta: Jordan. **SB:** Arizona: Counsell. **CS:** Atlanta: Surhoff. **T**—2:59. **A**—41,624.

**Recap:** Curt Schilling maintained his playoff brilliance with a four-hitter, and Braves catcher Javy Lopez committed a costly error that allowed a pair of runs to score. Schilling allowed two singles, two doubles and two walks. He struck out 12, including four of the last six batters.

### GAME 4

| | | | | | | | | | | | | |
|---|---|---|---|---|---|---|---|---|---|---|---|---|
| Arizona | 0 | 0 | 4 | 2 | 0 | 0 | 0 | 1 | 4 | **11** | **12** | **0** |
| Atlanta | 1 | 1 | 0 | 0 | 0 | 0 | 1 | 1 | 0 | **4** | **13** | **3** |

**W**—Anderson. **L**—Maddux. **SV**—Kim.
**E**—Atlanta: C. Jones, Maddux, Sanchez. **LOB**—Arizona 12, Atlanta 9. **2B**—Arizona: Womack, Counsell 2; Atlanta: A. Jones, Maddux, Sanchez. **HR**—Arizona: Gonzalez; Atlanta: A. Jones. **GIDP:** Arizona: Miller; Atlanta: Giles, Lopez. **SB:** Arizona: Sanders, Finley. **CS:** Arizona: Womack. **T**—3:47. **A**—42,291.

**GAME 4 (Cont.)**

**Recap:** On three days' rest, Greg Maddux pitched poorly and got no help from his defense in the shortest playoff outing of his career. In three-plus innings, Maddux was tagged for six runs and eight hits. He surrendered a two-run lead, fell to 10–13 for his career in postseason play and remained winless since August 21. Arizona's Craig Counsell had three hits and four RBIs as the Diamondbacks moved within one win of their first National League pennant. The win was Arizona's fifth straight at Turner Field, a span in which it outscored Atlanta, 35–7.

### GAME 5

| | | | | | | | | | | | | |
|---|---|---|---|---|---|---|---|---|---|---|---|---|
| Arizona | 0 | 0 | 0 | 1 | 2 | 0 | 0 | 0 | 0 | **3** | **6** | **1** |
| Atlanta | 0 | 0 | 0 | 1 | 0 | 0 | 1 | 0 | 0 | **2** | **7** | **1** |

**W**—Johnson. **L**—Glavine. **SV**—Kim.
**E**—Arizona: Williams; Atlanta: Giles. **LOB**—Arizona 7, Atlanta 9. **HR**—Arizona: Durazo; Atlanta: Franco. **Sac**—Arizona: Counsell. **T**—3:13. **A**—35,652.

**Recap:** The Diamondbacks, who entered the NL in 1998, reached the World Series faster than any expansion team in baseball history, as pinch-hitter Erubiel Durazo delivered a tiebreaking two-run homer in the fifth inning. Second baseman Craig Counsell, who hit .381 with five runs and four RBIs in the series, was named most valuable player.

## American League Division Playoffs

Oct 9 ..............Cleveland 5 at Seattle 0
Oct 11 ............Cleveland 1 at Seattle 5
Oct 13 ............Seattle 2 at Cleveland 17

Oct 14 ............Seattle 6 at Cleveland 2
Oct 15 ............Cleveland 1 at Seattle 3

(Seattle won series 3–2)

Oct 10 ............Oakland 5 at New York 3
Oct 11 ............Oakland 2 at New York 0
Oct 13 ............New York 1 at Oakland 0

Oct 14 ............New York 9 at Oakland 2
Oct 15 ............Oakland 3 at New York 5

(New York won series 3–2)

## American League Championship Series

Oct 17 ............New York 4 at Seattle 2
Oct 18 ............New York 3 at Seattle 2
Oct 20 ............Seattle 14 at New York 3

Oct 21 ............Seattle 1 at New York 3
Oct 22 ............Seattle 3 at New York 12

(New York won series 4–1)

### GAME 1

| | | | | | | | | | | | | |
|---|---|---|---|---|---|---|---|---|---|---|---|---|
| New York | 0 | 1 | 0 | 2 | 0 | 0 | 0 | 0 | 1 | **4** | **9** | **0** |
| Seattle | 0 | 0 | 0 | 0 | 1 | 0 | 0 | 0 | 1 | **2** | **4** | **0** |

**W**—Pettitte. **L**—Sele. **SV**—Rivera.
**LOB**—New York 9, Seattle 2. **2B**—New York: Posada, Knoblauch; Seattle: Cameron, Suzuki. **HR**—New York: O'Neill. **Sac**—New York: Brosius. **SB**—New York: Soriano. **GIDP**—Seattle: Olerud, Cameron. **T**—3:06. **A**—47,644.

**Recap:** Andy Pettitte allowed only three hits in eight innings, and Paul O'Neill hit a two-run homer as the Yankees won their fourth straight playoff game. Pettitte took a no-hitter into the fifth and improved to 9–5 lifetime in the playoffs. Mariano Rivera allowed a run in the ninth but made his 22nd career postseason save.

### GAME 2

| | | | | | | | | | | | | |
|---|---|---|---|---|---|---|---|---|---|---|---|---|
| New York | 0 | 3 | 0 | 0 | 0 | 0 | 0 | 0 | 0 | **3** | **9** | **1** |
| Seattle | 0 | 0 | 0 | 0 | 0 | 0 | 0 | 0 | 0 | **2** | **6** | **0** |

**W**—Mussina. **L**—Garcia. **SV**—Rivera.
**E**—New York: Williams. **LOB**—New York 6, Seattle 7. **2B**—New York: Brosius, Spencer. **HR**—Seattle: Javier. **Sac**—New York: Jeter. **GIDP**—New York: Justice; Seattle: Martinez. **SB**—New York: Spencer. **CS**—New York: Knoblauch, Martinez. **T**—3:25. **A**—47,791.

**Recap:** Mike Mussina allowed two runs in six innings, and Scott Brosius spurred a three-run second inning with a two-run double. Seattle ace Freddy Garcia made a solid effort on three days' rest, scattering seven hits and allowing three runs in 7 ½ innings. Mariners manager Lou Piniella opened his postgame news conference by guaranteeing that the series will return to Seattle for Game 6.

## American League Championship Series *(Cont.)*

### GAME 3

| | | | | | | | | | | | | |
|---|---|---|---|---|---|---|---|---|---|---|---|---|
| Seattle | 0 | 0 | 0 | 0 | 2 | 7 | 2 | 1 | 2 | **14** | **15** | **0** |
| New York | 2 | 0 | 0 | 0 | 0 | 0 | 0 | 1 | 0 | **3** | **7** | **2** |

**W**—Moyer. **L**—Hernandez.
**E**—New York: Stanton, Wohlers. **LOB**—Seattle 11, New York 4. **2B**—Seattle: Martinez. **3B**—Seattle: McLemore, Martin. **HR**—Seattle: Olerud, Boone, Buhner; New York: Williams. **GIDP**—New York: Knoblauch, Williams. **SB**—Seattle: Suzuki, Javier. **T**—3:49. **A**—56,517.

**Recap:** Jamie Moyer held New York to four hits in seven innings and John Olerud and Bret Boone homered in a record-tying seven-run sixth inning. A misplay by Yankees leftfielder Chuck Knoblauch led to two runs in the fifth. The 14 runs set an ALCS record and were the most allowed by the Yankees in the playoff history of the franchise.

### GAME 4

| | | | | | | | | | | | | |
|---|---|---|---|---|---|---|---|---|---|---|---|---|
| Seattle | 0 | 0 | 0 | 0 | 0 | 0 | 1 | 0 | 0 | **1** | **2** | **0** |
| New York | 0 | 0 | 0 | 0 | 0 | 0 | 0 | 1 | 2 | **3** | **4** | **0** |

**W**—Rivera. **L**—Sasaki.
**LOB**—Seattle 6, New York 8. **2B**—New York: Martinez, Soriano. **Sac**—New York: Brosius. **GIDP**—New York: Brosius. **SB**—Seattle: Suzuki; New York: Soriano. **CS**—New York: Williams. **T**—3:24. **A**—56,375.

**Recap:** New York's rookie second baseman Alfonso Soriano hit a two-run homer off closer Kazuhiro Sasaki with one out in the bottom of the ninth inning to win the game, ending a strange pitchers' duel that featured only six hits but 15 walks, an LCS record.

### GAME 5

| | | | | | | | | | | | | |
|---|---|---|---|---|---|---|---|---|---|---|---|---|
| Seattle | 0 | 0 | 0 | 0 | 0 | 0 | 3 | 0 | 0 | **3** | **9** | **1** |
| New York | 0 | 0 | 4 | 1 | 0 | 4 | 0 | 3 | x | **12** | **13** | **1** |

**W**—Pettitte. **L**—Sele.
**LOB**—Seattle 8, New York 7. **2B**—Seattle: Cameron; New York: Justice, Brosius. **HR**—New York: Williams, O'Neill, Martinez. **Sac**—Seattle: Bell; New York: Knoblauch. **SF**—New York: Jeter. **T**—3:18. **A**—56,370.

**Recap:** ALCS MVP Andy Pettitte took a shutout into the seventh inning as the Yankees staked him to an early 5–0 lead and never looked back cruising to their fourth straight World Series appearance. Bernie Williams, Paul O'Neill and Tino Martinez all homered.

# Composite Box Scores

## National League Championship Series

### ARIZONA

| BATTING | AB | R | H | HR | RBI | Avg |
|---|---|---|---|---|---|---|
| Dellucci | 2 | 1 | 1 | 0 | 0 | .500 |
| Counsell | 21 | 5 | 8 | 0 | 4 | .381 |
| Grace | 16 | 1 | 6 | 0 | 1 | .375 |
| Durazo | 3 | 1 | 1 | 1 | 2 | .333 |
| Finley | 14 | 1 | 4 | 0 | 4 | .286 |
| Williams | 18 | 1 | 5 | 0 | 2 | .278 |
| Bautista | 4 | 1 | 1 | 0 | 1 | .250 |
| Gonzalez | 19 | 4 | 4 | 1 | 4 | .211 |
| Womack | 20 | 4 | 4 | 0 | 0 | .200 |
| Miller | 17 | 0 | 3 | 0 | 0 | .176 |
| Sanders | 17 | 2 | 2 | 0 | 1 | .118 |
| Bell | 4 | 0 | 0 | 0 | 0 | .000 |
| Colbrunn | 1 | 0 | 0 | 0 | 0 | .000 |
| Cummings | 1 | 0 | 0 | 0 | 0 | .000 |
| Totals | 172 | 22 | 40 | 2 | 19 | .233 |

| PITCHING | G | IP | H | BB | SO | ERA |
|---|---|---|---|---|---|---|
| Kim (2 SV) | 3 | 5 | 0 | 1 | 3 | 0.00 |
| Schilling (1–0) | 1 | 9 | 4 | 3 | 12 | 1.00 |
| Johnson (2–0) | 2 | 16 | 10 | 3 | 19 | 1.13 |
| Anderson (1–0) | 1 | 3⅓ | 4 | 1 | 0 | 2.70 |
| Batista (0–1) | 2 | 7 | 5 | 2 | 3 | 5.14 |
| Lopez | 3 | 5 | 1 | 1 | 6.00 |
| Morgan | 2 | 1 | 3 | 1 | 1 | 27.00 |
| Swindell | 2 | ⅓ | 1 | 0 | 0 | 27.00 |
| Witt | 1 | ⅓ | 3 | 0 | 0 | 27.00 |
| Totals | 5 | 45 | 35 | 11 | 39 | 3.00 |

### ATLANTA

| BATTING | AB | R | H | HR | RBI | Avg |
|---|---|---|---|---|---|---|
| Sanchez | 17 | 1 | 5 | 0 | 1 | .294 |
| C. Jones | 19 | 1 | 5 | 0 | 2 | .263 |
| Franco | 23 | 2 | 6 | 1 | 2 | .261 |
| Surhoff | 13 | 1 | 3 | 1 | 2 | .231 |
| Giles | 20 | 4 | 4 | 1 | 1 | .200 |
| Gilkey | 5 | 0 | 1 | 0 | 0 | .200 |
| Martinez | 5 | 0 | 1 | 0 | 0 | .200 |
| Jordan | 21 | 1 | 4 | 0 | 3 | .190 |
| A. Jones | 17 | 4 | 3 | 1 | 1 | .176 |
| Lopez | 14 | 1 | 2 | 1 | 2 | .143 |
| DeRosa | 4 | 0 | 0 | 0 | 0 | .000 |
| Bako | 3 | 0 | 0 | 0 | 0 | .000 |
| Lockhart | 1 | 0 | 0 | 0 | 0 | .000 |
| Totals | 169 | 15 | 35 | 5 | 14 | .207 |

| PITCHING | G | IP | H | BB | SO | ERA |
|---|---|---|---|---|---|---|
| Ligtenberg | 2 | 3 | 0 | 1 | 2 | 0.00 |
| Smoltz | 2 | 3 | 0 | 0 | 1 | 0.00 |
| Remlinger | 3 | 2⅓ | 3 | 2 | 2 | 0.00 |
| Marquis | 2 | 2 | 2 | 2 | 3 | 0.00 |
| Seanez | 2 | 2 | 1 | 3 | 3 | 0.00 |
| Millwood | 1 | 1 | 0 | 0 | 1 | 0.00 |
| Glavine (1–1) | 2 | 12 | 10 | 5 | 5 | 1.50 |
| Karsay | 4 | 4⅓ | 3 | 1 | 6 | 2.08 |
| Maddux (0–2) | 2 | 10 | 14 | 2 | 7 | 5.40 |
| Burkett (0–1) | 1 | 4⅓ | 7 | 2 | 2 | 8.31 |
| Totals | 5 | 44 | 40 | 18 | 32 | 2.66 |

### American League Championship Series

#### NEW YORK

| BATTING | AB | R | H | HR | RBI | Avg |
|---|---|---|---|---|---|---|
| Wilson | 1 | 0 | 1 | 0 | 0 | 1.000 |
| O'Neill | 12 | 2 | 5 | 2 | 3 | .417 |
| Soriano | 15 | 5 | 6 | 1 | 2 | .400 |
| Knoblauch | 18 | 0 | 6 | 0 | 3 | .333 |
| Spencer | 7 | 1 | 2 | 0 | 0 | .286 |
| Justice | 18 | 3 | 5 | 0 | 4 | .278 |
| Martinez | 20 | 3 | 5 | 1 | 3 | .250 |
| Williams | 17 | 4 | 4 | 3 | 5 | .235 |
| Posada | 14 | 4 | 3 | 0 | 0 | .214 |
| Brosius | 16 | 3 | 3 | 0 | 2 | .187 |
| Jeter | 17 | 0 | 2 | 0 | 0 | .118 |
| Bellinger | 1 | 0 | 0 | 0 | 0 | .000 |
| Greene | 1 | 0 | 0 | 0 | 0 | .000 |
| Sojo | 1 | 0 | 0 | 0 | 0 | .000 |
| Velarde | 1 | 0 | 0 | 0 | 0 | .000 |
| Totals | 159 | 25 | 42 | 7 | 24 | .264 |

| PITCHING | G | IP | H | BB | SO | ERA |
|---|---|---|---|---|---|---|
| Clemens | 1 | 5 | 1 | 4 | 7 | 0.00 |
| Mendoza | 3 | 5⅓ | 3 | 2 | 4 | 1.69 |
| Rivera (1–0, 2 SV) | 4 | 4⅔ | 2 | 1 | 3 | 1.93 |
| Pettitte (2–0) | 2 | 14⅓ | 11 | 2 | 8 | 2.51 |
| Mussina (1–0) | 1 | 6 | 4 | 1 | 3 | 3.00 |
| Hernandez (0–1) | 1 | 5 | 5 | 5 | 7 | 7.20 |
| Witasick | 1 | 3 | 6 | 0 | 2 | 9.00 |
| Wohlers | 1 | ⅔ | 3 | 1 | 1 | 13.50 |
| Stanton | 2 | 1 | 1 | 2 | 0 | 27.00 |
| Totals | 5 | 45 | 36 | 18 | 35 | 3.80 |

#### SEATTLE

| BATTING | AB | R | H | HR | RBI | Avg |
|---|---|---|---|---|---|---|
| Martin | 2 | 1 | 1 | 0 | 0 | .500 |
| Buhner | 6 | 2 | 2 | 1 | 1 | .333 |
| Boone | 19 | 2 | 6 | 2 | 6 | .316 |
| Guillen | 8 | 1 | 2 | 0 | 0 | .250 |
| Lampkin | 4 | 0 | 1 | 0 | 0 | .250 |
| Suzuki | 18 | 3 | 4 | 0 | 1 | .222 |
| Javier | 14 | 2 | 3 | 1 | 2 | .214 |
| Olerud | 19 | 2 | 4 | 1 | 3 | .211 |
| Bell | 16 | 1 | 3 | 0 | 4 | .187 |
| Cameron | 17 | 3 | 3 | 0 | 0 | .176 |
| Wilson | 13 | 2 | 2 | 0 | 0 | .154 |
| Martinez | 20 | 1 | 3 | 0 | 0 | .150 |
| McLemore | 14 | 1 | 2 | 0 | 3 | .143 |
| Gipson | 1 | 1 | 0 | 0 | 0 | .000 |
| Totals | 171 | 22 | 36 | 5 | 20 | .211 |

| PITCHING | G | IP | H | BB | SO | ERA |
|---|---|---|---|---|---|---|
| Abbott | 1 | 5 | 0 | 8 | 2 | 0.00 |
| Charlton | 2 | 1⅔ | 1 | 2 | 2 | 0.00 |
| Nelson | 2 | 2½ | 1 | 1 | 3 | 0.00 |
| Moyer (1–0) | 1 | 7 | 4 | 1 | 5 | 2.57 |
| Sele (0–1) | 2 | 10 | 11 | 4 | 5 | 3.60 |
| Garcia (0–1) | 1 | 7½ | 7 | 4 | 6 | 3.68 |
| Pineiro | 1 | 2 | 4 | 2 | 5 | 4.50 |
| Rhodes | 2 | 2 | 2 | 0 | 2 | 4.50 |
| Paniagua | 3 | 3⅔ | 7 | 1 | 1 | 12.27 |
| Halama | 2 | 2 | 3 | 0 | 0 | 13.50 |
| Sasaki (0–1) | 1 | ⅓ | 2 | 0 | 0 | 54.00 |
| Totals | 5 | 43⅓ | 42 | 23 | 31 | 4.36 |

## 2001 World Series

| | | |
|---|---|---|
| Oct 27 | New York 1 at Arizona 9 | Nov 1 ............Arizona 2 at New York 3 |
| Oct 28 | New York 0 at Arizona 4 | Nov 3 ............New York 2 at Arizona 15 |
| Oct 30 | Arizona 1 at New York 2 | Nov 4 ............New York 2 at Arizona 3 |
| Oct 31 | Arizona 3 at New York 4 | |

(Arizona won series 4–3)

#### GAME 1

| | | | | | | | | | | | |
|---|---|---|---|---|---|---|---|---|---|---|---|
| New York | 1 0 0 | 0 0 0 | 0 0 0 | **1** | **3** | **2** |
| Arizona | 1 0 4 | 4 0 0 | 0 0 x | **9** | **10** | **0** |

**W**—Schilling. **L**—Mussina.
**E**—New York: Justice, Brosius. **LOB**—New York 5, Arizona 6. **2B**—New York: Williams, Brosius; Arizona: Miller, Gonzalez, Grace. **HR**—Arizona: Counsell, Gonzalez. **Sac**—Arizona: Counsell. **SF**—Arizona: Williams. **T**—2:44. **A**—49,646.

**Recap:** Curt Schilling shut down New York's offense and the usually sure-handed Yankees gave up five unearned runs—the most in a Series game since 1973.

#### GAME 2

| | | | | | | | | | | | |
|---|---|---|---|---|---|---|---|---|---|---|---|
| New York | 0 0 0 | 0 0 0 | 0 0 0 | **0** | **3** | **0** |
| Arizona | 0 1 0 | 0 0 0 | 3 0 x | **4** | **5** | **0** |

**W**—Johnson. **L**—Pettitte.
**LOB**—New York 4, Arizona 1. **2B**—Arizona: Bautista. **HR**—Arizona: Williams. **GIDP**—New York: Sojo; Arizona: Miller. **T**—2:35. **A**—49,646.

**Recap:** Making his first World Series start, Randy Johnson delivered one of his best performances, fanning 11 Yankees, giving up only three hits

#### GAME 2 *(Cont.)*

and pitching the first complete-game shutout in the Fall Classic since Schilling accomplished the feat in 1993 for Philadelphia.

#### GAME 3

| | | | | | | | | | | | |
|---|---|---|---|---|---|---|---|---|---|---|---|
| Arizona | 0 0 0 | 1 0 0 | 0 0 0 | **1** | **3** | **3** |
| New York | 0 1 0 | 0 0 1 | 0 0 x | **2** | **7** | **1** |

**W**—Clemens. **L**—Anderson. **SV**—Rivera
**E**—Arizona: Womack, Miller, Grace; New York: Soriano. **LOB**—Arizona 5, New York 8. **HR**—New York: Posada. **SF**—Arizona: Williams. **GIDP**—New York: O'Neill. **SB**—Arizona: Sanders; New York: O'Neill. **CS**—Arizona: Finley. **T**—3:26. **A**—55,820.

**Recap:** Roger Clemens shut down Arizona for seven innings, allowing only three hits and striking out nine as the Yankees cut the Diamondbacks' lead to 2–1. An early home run by Jorge Posada and a tiebreaking single by Scott Brosius in the sixth made the difference for the Yankees. Posada's home run ended the Yankees' scoreless streak at 18 innings, the longest Series drought in franchise history.

### GAME 4

| | | | | | | | | | | | | |
|---|---|---|---|---|---|---|---|---|---|---|---|---|
| Arizona | 0 0 0 | 1 0 0 | 0 2 0 0 | **3** | **6** | **0** |
| New York | 0 0 1 | 0 0 0 | 0 0 2 1 | **4** | **7** | **0** |

**W**—Rivera. **L**—Kim.
**LOB**—Arizona 7; New York 4. **2B**—Arizona: Womack, Durazo; New York: Brosius. **HR**—Arizona: Grace; New York: Spencer, Martinez, Jeter. **Sac**—Arizona: Counsell 3. **GIDP**—Arizona: Sanders, Womack; New York: Posada. **T**—3:31. **A**—55,863.

**Recap:** Tino Martinez tied the game in the bottom of the ninth inning with a two-out, two-run homer off Arizona closer Byung-Hyun Kim, then Derek Jeter won it in the tenth, belting a solo shot with two out. The home runs spoiled a superb performance by Diamondbacks pitcher Curt Schilling, who struck out nine and limited the Yankees to three hits before leaving after the seventh inning with a 3–1 lead.

### GAME 6

| | | | | | | | | |
|---|---|---|---|---|---|---|---|---|
| New York | 0 0 0 | 0 0 2 | 0 0 0 | **2** | **7** | **1** |
| Arizona | 1 3 8 | 3 0 0 | 0 0 x | **15** | **22** | **0** |

**W**—Johnson. **L**—Pettitte.
**E**—New York: Soriano. **LOB**—New York 7, Arizona 10. **2B**—New York: Greene; Arizona: Womack, Sanders, Williams 2, Gonzalez, Miller. **GIDP**—New York: Greene; Arizona: Gonzalez. **T**—3:33. **A**—49,707.

**Recap:** Arizona staved off elimination with an impressive display of pitching and hitting. Randy Johnson won his second game of the Series, scattering six hits through seven innings while his teammates pounded New York starter Andy Pettitte and reliever Jay Witasick, who gave up 10 hits and a Series-record eight earned runs in 1⅓ innings of work.

### GAME 5

| | | | | | | | | |
|---|---|---|---|---|---|---|---|---|
| Arizona | 0 0 0 | 0 2 0 | 0 0 0 0 0 0 | **2** | **8** | **0** |
| New York | 0 0 0 | 0 0 0 | 0 0 2 0 0 1 | **3** | **9** | **1** |

**W**—Hitchcock. **L**—Lopez.
**E**—New York: Posada. **LOB**—Arizona 9, New York 8. **HR**—Arizona: Finley, Barajas; New York: Brosius. **Sac**—Arizona: Williams; New York: Brosius. **GIDP**—Arizona: Grace; New York: Posada, O'Neill. **SB**—Arizona: Womack. **CS**—New York: Soriano. **T**—4:15. **A**—56,018.

**Recap:** It was déjà vu for the Yankees as Scott Brosius cracked a two-out, two-run homer off Byung-Hyun Kim to tie the game in the bottom of the ninth and force extra innings. Alfonso Soriano drove in Chuck Knoblauch in the 12th to send the Series back to Arizona with the Yankees leading three games to two.

### GAME 7

| | | | | | | | | |
|---|---|---|---|---|---|---|---|---|
| New York | 0 0 0 | 0 0 0 | 1 1 0 | **2** | **6** | **3** |
| Arizona | 0 0 0 | 0 0 1 | 0 0 2 | **3** | **11** | **0** |

**W**—Johnson. **L**—Rivera.
**E**—New York: Soriano, Clemens, Rivera. **LOB**—New York 3, Arizona 11. **2B**—New York: O'Neill; Arizona: Womack, Bautista. **HR**—New York: Soriano. **Sac**—Arizona: Miller. **CS**—Arizona: Womack. **T**—3:20. **A**—49,589.

**Recap:** Luis Gonzalez singled off New York closer Mariano Rivera to bring home Jay Bell with the World Series–winning run in the bottom of the ninth inning. Arizona, which joined the league in 1998, won a title faster than any other expansion team. Curt Schilling, who made two brilliant starts on three days rest, and Randy Johnson, who won three games in the Series, shared the MVP award.

## 2001 World Series Composite Box Score

### ARIZONA

| BATTING | AB | R | H | HR | RBI | Avg |
|---|---|---|---|---|---|---|
| Bautista | 12 | 1 | 7 | 0 | 6 | .583 |
| Dellucci | 2 | 0 | 1 | 0 | 0 | .500 |
| Colbrunn | 5 | 2 | 2 | 0 | 1 | .400 |
| Barajas | 5 | 1 | 2 | 1 | 1 | .400 |
| Finley | 19 | 5 | 7 | 1 | 2 | .368 |
| Durazo | 11 | 0 | 4 | 0 | 1 | .364 |
| Sanders | 23 | 6 | 7 | 0 | 1 | .304 |
| Williams | 26 | 3 | 7 | 1 | 7 | .269 |
| Grace | 19 | 1 | 5 | 1 | 3 | .263 |
| Gonzalez | 27 | 4 | 7 | 1 | 5 | .259 |
| Womack | 32 | 3 | 8 | 0 | 4 | .250 |
| Miller | 20 | 3 | 4 | 0 | 4 | .200 |
| Bell | 7 | 3 | 1 | 0 | 1 | .143 |
| Counsell | 24 | 1 | 2 | 1 | 1 | .083 |
| Cummings | 0 | 2 | 0 | 0 | 0 | — |
| Others | 13 | 2 | 1 | 0 | 1 | .077 |
| Totals | 245 | 37 | 65 | 6 | 36 | .265 |

| PITCHING | G | IP | H | BB | SO | ERA |
|---|---|---|---|---|---|---|
| Batista | 2 | 8⅓ | 5 | 5 | 6 | 0.00 |
| Morgan | 3 | 4⅔ | 1 | 0 | 1 | 0.00 |
| Swindell | 3 | 2⅔ | 1 | 1 | 2 | 0.00 |
| Witt | 1 | 1 | 0 | 1 | 1 | 0.00 |
| Brohawn | 1 | 1 | 1 | 0 | 1 | 0.00 |
| Johnson (3–0) | 3 | 17⅓ | 9 | 3 | 19 | 1.04 |
| Schilling (1–0) | 3 | 21 | 12 | 2 | 26 | 1.69 |
| Anderson (0–1) | 1 | 5⅓ | 5 | 3 | 1 | 3.38 |
| Kim (0–1) | 2 | 3⅓ | 6 | 1 | 6 | 13.51 |
| Lopez (0–1) | 1 | ⅓ | 2 | 0 | 0 | 27.00 |
| Totals | 7 | 65 | 42 | 16 | 63 | 1.93 |

### NEW YORK

| BATTING | AB | R | H | HR | RBI | Avg |
|---|---|---|---|---|---|---|
| Greene | 2 | 1 | 1 | 0 | 0 | .500 |
| O'Neill | 15 | 1 | 5 | 0 | 0 | .333 |
| Sojo | 3 | 0 | 1 | 0 | 1 | .333 |
| Soriano | 25 | 1 | 6 | 1 | 2 | .240 |
| Williams | 24 | 2 | 5 | 0 | 1 | .208 |
| Spencer | 20 | 1 | 4 | 1 | 2 | .200 |
| Martinez | 21 | 1 | 4 | 1 | 3 | .190 |
| Posada | 23 | 2 | 4 | 1 | 1 | .174 |
| Brosius | 24 | 1 | 4 | 1 | 3 | .167 |
| Jeter | 27 | 3 | 4 | 1 | 1 | .148 |
| Knoblauch | 18 | 1 | 1 | 0 | 0 | .056 |
| Velarde | 3 | 0 | 0 | 0 | 0 | .000 |
| Wilson | 2 | 0 | 0 | 0 | 0 | .000 |
| Bellinger | 2 | 0 | 0 | 0 | 0 | .000 |
| Others | 7 | 0 | 1 | 0 | 0 | .143 |
| Totals | 229 | 14 | 42 | 6 | 14 | .183 |

| PITCHING | G | IP | H | BB | SO | ERA |
|---|---|---|---|---|---|---|
| Hitchcock (1–0) | 2 | 4 | 1 | 0 | 6 | 0.00 |
| Mendoza | 2 | 2⅔ | 0 | 1 | 0 | 0.00 |
| Clemens (1–0) | 2 | 13⅓ | 10 | 4 | 19 | 1.35 |
| Hernandez | 1 | 6⅓ | 4 | 4 | 5 | 1.42 |
| Choate | 2 | 3⅔ | 7 | 1 | 2 | 2.45 |
| Rivera (1–1, 1 SV) | 4 | 6⅓ | 6 | 1 | 7 | 2.84 |
| Stanton | 4 | 5⅔ | 3 | 2 | 3 | 3.18 |
| Mussina | 2 | 11 | 11 | 4 | 14 | 4.09 |
| Pettitte (0–2) | 2 | 9 | 12 | 1 | 9 | 9.00 |
| Witasick | 1 | 1⅓ | 10 | 4 | 0 | 54.00 |
| Totals | 7 | 63⅓ | 65 | 17 | 70 | 4.29 |

## National League Batting

### BATTING AVERAGE

| | |
|---|---|
| Larry Walker, Col | .350 |
| Todd Helton, Col | .336 |
| Moises Alou, Hou | .331 |
| Lance Berkman, Hou | .331 |
| Chipper Jones, Atl | .330 |
| Albert Pujols, StL | .329 |
| Barry Bonds, SF | .328 |
| Sammy Sosa, Chi | .328 |
| Juan Pierre, Col | .327 |
| Luis Gonzalez, Ariz | .325 |

### HITS

| | |
|---|---|
| Rich Aurilia, SF | 206 |
| Juan Pierre, Col | 202 |
| Luis Gonzalez, Ariz | 198 |
| Todd Helton, Col | 197 |
| Albert Pujols, StL | 194 |
| Lance Berkman, Hou | 191 |
| Fernando Vina, StL | 191 |
| Chipper Jones, StL | 189 |
| Sammy Sosa, Chi | 189 |
| Shawn Green, LA | 184 |
| Vladimir Guerrero, Mtl | 184 |

### DOUBLES

| | |
|---|---|
| Lance Berkman, Hou | 55 |
| Todd Helton, Col | 54 |
| Jeff Kent, SF | 49 |
| Bobby Abreu, Phil | 48 |
| Albert Pujols, StL | 47 |

### TRIPLES

| | |
|---|---|
| Jimmy Rollins, Phil | 12 |
| Juan Pierre, Col | 11 |
| Juan Uribe, Col | 11 |
| Luis Castillo, Fla | 10 |
| Neifi Perez, Col | 8 |
| Michael Tucker, Chi | 8 |
| Fernando Vina, StL | 8 |

### HOME RUNS

| | |
|---|---|
| Barry Bonds, SF | 73 |
| Sammy Sosa, Chi | 64 |
| Luis Gonzalez, Ariz | 57 |
| Shawn Green, LA | 49 |
| Todd Helton, Col | 49 |
| Richie Sexson, Mil | 45 |
| Phil Nevin, SD | 41 |
| Jeff Bagwell, Hou | 39 |
| Chipper Jones, Atl | 38 |
| Larry Walker, Col | 38 |

### RUNS SCORED

| | |
|---|---|
| Sammy Sosa, Chi | 146 |
| Todd Helton, Col | 132 |
| Barry Bonds, SF | 129 |
| Luis Gonzalez, Ariz | 128 |
| Jeff Bagwell, Hou | 126 |
| Cliff Floyd, Fla | 123 |
| Shawn Green, LA | 121 |
| Bobby Abreu, Phil | 118 |
| Craig Biggio, Hou | 118 |
| Brian Giles, Pitt | 116 |

### TOTAL BASES

| | |
|---|---|
| Sammy Sosa, Chi | 425 |
| Luis Gonzalez, Ariz | 419 |
| Barry Bonds, SF | 411 |
| Todd Helton, Col | 402 |
| Shawn Green, LA | 370 |

### STOLEN BASES

| | |
|---|---|
| Juan Pierre, Col | 46 |
| Jimmy Rollins, Phil | 46 |
| Vladimir Guerrero, Mtl | 37 |
| Bobby Abreu, Phil | 36 |
| Luis Castillo, Fla | 33 |

### RUNS BATTED IN

| | |
|---|---|
| Sammy Sosa, Chi | 160 |
| Todd Helton, Col | 146 |
| Luis Gonzalez, Ariz | 142 |
| Barry Bonds, SF | 137 |
| Jeff Bagwell, Hou | 130 |
| Albert Pujols, StL | 130 |
| Lance Berkman, Hou | 126 |
| Phil Nevin, SD | 126 |
| Shawn Green, LA | 125 |
| Richie Sexson, Mil | 125 |

### SLUGGING PERCENTAGE

| | |
|---|---|
| Barry Bonds, SF | .863 |
| Sammy Sosa, Chi | .737 |
| Luis Gonzalez, Ariz | .688 |
| Todd Helton, Col | .685 |
| Larry Walker, Col | .662 |

### ON-BASE PERCENTAGE

| | |
|---|---|
| Barry Bonds, SF | .515 |
| Larry Walker, Col | .449 |
| Sammy Sosa, Chi | .437 |
| Todd Helton, Col | .432 |
| Lance Berkman, Hou | .430 |

### BASES ON BALLS

| | |
|---|---|
| Barry Bonds, SF | 177 |
| Sammy Sosa, Chi | 116 |
| Bobby Abreu, Phil | 106 |
| Jeff Bagwell, Hou | 106 |
| Luis Gonzalez, Ariz | 100 |

## National League Pitching

### EARNED RUN AVERAGE

| | |
|---|---|
| Randy Johnson, Ariz | 2.49 |
| Curt Schilling, Ariz | 2.98 |
| John Burkett, Atl | 3.04 |
| Greg Maddux, Atl | 3.05 |
| Darryl Kile, StL | 3.09 |
| Matt Morris, StL | 3.16 |
| Russ Ortiz, SF | 3.29 |
| Al Leiter, NY | 3.31 |
| Kerry Wood, Chi | 3.36 |
| Wade Miller, Hou | 3.40 |

### SAVES

| | |
|---|---|
| Robb Nen, SF | 45 |
| Armando Benitez, NY | 43 |
| Trevor Hoffman, SD | 43 |
| Jeff Shaw, LA | 43 |
| Jose Mesa, Phil | 42 |
| Billy Wagner, Hou | 39 |
| Danny Graves, Cin | 32 |
| Antonio Alfonseca, Fla | 28 |
| Tom Gordon, Chi | 27 |
| Mike Williams, Pitt-Hou | 22 |

### WINS

| | |
|---|---|
| Curt Schilling, Ariz | 22 |
| Matt Morris, StL | 22 |
| Randy Johnson, Ariz | 21 |
| Jon Lieber, Chi | 20 |
| Russ Ortiz, SF | 17 |
| Greg Maddux, Atl | 17 |
| Tom Glavine, Atl | 16 |
| Wade Miller, Hou | 16 |
| Darryl Kile, StL | 16 |
| Javier Vazquez, Mtl | 16 |

### GAMES PITCHED

| | |
|---|---|
| Steve Kline, StL | 89 |
| Graeme Lloyd, Mtl | 84 |
| Jeff Fassero, Chi | 82 |
| Ray King, Mil | 82 |
| Felix Rodriguez, SF | 80 |
| David Weathers, Mil-Chi | 80 |

### INNINGS PITCHED

| | |
|---|---|
| Curt Schilling, Ariz | 256⅔ |
| Randy Johnson, Ariz | 249⅔ |
| Chan Ho Park, LA | 234 |
| Greg Maddux, Atl | 233 |
| Jon Lieber, Chi | 232⅓ |

### STRIKEOUTS

| | |
|---|---|
| Randy Johnson, Ariz | 372 |
| Curt Schilling, Ariz | 293 |
| Chan Ho Park, LA | 218 |
| Kerry Wood, Chi | 217 |
| Javier Vazquez, Mtl | 208 |
| John Burkett, Atl | 187 |
| Matt Morris, StL | 185 |
| Wade Miller, Hou | 183 |
| Robert Person, Phil | 183 |
| Darryl Kile, StL | 179 |

### COMPLETE GAMES

| | |
|---|---|
| Curt Schilling, Ariz | 6 |
| Jon Lieber, Chi | 5 |
| Javier Vazquez, Mtl | 5 |
| Pedro Astacio, Col-Hou | 4 |
| Todd Ritchie, Pitt | 4 |
| Randy Wolf, Phil | 4 |

### SHUTOUTS

| | |
|---|---|
| Greg Maddux, Atl | 3 |
| Javier Vazquez, Mtl | 3 |
| Four tied with two. | |

## American League Batting

### BATTING AVERAGE

Ichiro Suzuki, Sea .350
Jason Giambi, Oak .342
Roberto Alomar, Clev .336
Bret Boone, Sea .331
Frank Catalanotto, Tex .330
Juan Gonzalez, Clev .325
Alex Rodriguez, Tex .318
Shannon Stewart, Tor .316
Derek Jeter, NY .311
Jeff Conine, Balt .311

### HITS

Ichiro Suzuki, Sea .242
Bret Boone, Sea .206
Shannon Stewart, Tor .202
Alex Rodriguez, Tex .201
Garret Anderson, Ana .194
Roberto Alomar, Clev .193
Derek Jeter, NY .191
Carlos Beltran, KC .189
Magglio Ordonez, Chi .181
Jason Giambi, Oak .178
Terrence Long, Oak .178

### DOUBLES

Jason Giambi, Oak .47
Mike Sweeney, KC .46
Shannon Stewart, Tor .44
Eric Chavez, Oak .43
Ray Durham, Chi .42

### TRIPLES

Cristian Guzman, Minn .14
Roberto Alomar, Clev .12
Carlos Beltran, KC .12
Roger Cedeno, Det .11
Ray Durham, Chi .10

### HOME RUNS

Alex Rodriguez, Tex .52
Jim Thome, Clev .49
Rafael Palmeiro, Tex .47
Troy Glaus, Ana .41
Manny Ramirez, Bos .41
Carlos Delgado, Tor .39
Jason Giambi, Oak .38
Bret Boone, Sea .37
Juan Gonzalez, Clev .35
Jose Cruz Jr., Tor .34
Tino Martinez, NY .34

### RUNS SCORED

Alex Rodriguez, Tex .133
Ichiro Suzuki, Sea .127
Bret Boone, Sea .118
Roberto Alomar, Clev .113
Derek Jeter, NY .110
Jason Giambi, Oak .109
Johnny Damon, Oak .108
Miguel Tejada, Oak .107
Carlos Beltran, KC .106
Ray Durham, Chi .104

### TOTAL BASES

Alex Rodriguez, Tex .393
Bret Boone, Sea .360
Jason Giambi, Oak .343
Rafael Palmeiro, Tex .338
Jim Thome, Clev .328

### STOLEN BASES

Ichiro Suzuki, Sea .56
Roger Cedeno, Det .55
Alfonso Soriano, NY .43
Mark McLemore, Sea .39
Chuck Knoblauch, NY .38

### RUNS BATTED IN

Bret Boone, Sea .141
Juan Gonzalez, Clev .140
Alex Rodriguez, Tex .135
Manny Ramirez, Bos .125
Jim Thome, Clev .124
Garret Anderson, Ana .123
Rafael Palmeiro, Tex .123
Jason Giambi, Oak .120
Edgar Martinez, Sea .116
Eric Chavez, Oak .114

### SLUGGING PERCENTAGE

Jason Giambi, Oak .660
Jim Thome, Clev .624
Alex Rodriguez, Tex .622
Manny Ramirez, Bos .609
Juan Gonzalez, Clev .590

### ON-BASE PERCENTAGE

Jason Giambi, Oak .477
Edgar Martinez, Sea .423
Jim Thome, Clev .416
Roberto Alomar, Clev .415
Carlos Delgado, Tor .408

### BASES ON BALLS

Jason Giambi, Oak .129
Carlos Delgado, Tor .111
Jim Thome, Clev .111
Troy Glaus, Ana .107
Rafael Palmeiro, Tex .101

## American League Pitching

### EARNED RUN AVERAGE

Freddy Garcia, Sea .3.05
Mike Mussina, NY .3.15
Joe Mays, Minn .3.16
Mark Buehrle, Chi .3.29
Tim Hudson, Oak .3.37
Jamie Moyer, Sea .3.43
Mark Mulder, Oak .3.45
Barry Zito, Oak .3.49
Roger Clemens, NY .3.51
Cory Lidle, Oak .3.59

### SAVES

Mariano Rivera, NY .50
Kazuhiro Sasaki, Sea .45
Keith Foulke, Chi .42
Troy Percival, Ana .39
Billy Koch, Tor .36
Jason Isringhausen, Oak .34
Bob Wickman, Clev .32
LaTroy Hawkins, Minn .28
Roberto Hernandez, KC .28
Jeff Zimmerman, Tex .28

### WINS

Mark Mulder, Oak .21
Roger Clemens, NY .20
Jamie Moyer, Sea .20
Freddy Garcia, Sea .18
Tim Hudson, Oak .18
Paul Abbott, Sea .17
C.C. Sabathia, Clev .17
Barry Zito, Oak .17
Mike Mussina, NY .17
Joe Mays, Minn .17

### GAMES PITCHED

Paul Quantrill, Tor .80
Mike Stanton, NY .76
Jason Grimsley, KC .73
Keith Foulke, Chi .72
Pedro Borbon, Tor .71
Arthur Rhodes, Sea .71
Mariano Rivera, NY .71

### SHUTOUTS

Mark Mulder, Oak .4
Freddy Garcia, Sea .3
Mike Mussina, NY .3
Six tied with two.

### STRIKEOUTS

Hideo Nomo, Bos .220
Mike Mussina, NY .214
Roger Clemens, NY .213
Barry Zito, Oak .205
Bartolo Colon, Clev .201
Tim Hudson, Oak .181
C.C. Sabathia, Clev .171
Andy Pettitte, NY .164
Freddy Garcia, Sea .163
Pedro Martinez, Bos .163

### INNINGS PITCHED

Freddy Garcia, Sea .238⅔
Tim Hudson, Oak .235
Joe Mays, Minn .233⅔
Steve Sparks, Det .232
Mark Mulder, Oak .229½
Jeff Weaver, Det .229⅓

### COMPLETE GAMES

Steve Sparks, Det .8
Mark Mulder, Oak .6
Brad Radke, Minn .6
Jeff Weaver, Det .5
Four tied with four.

# 2001 Team Statistics

## National League

| TEAM BATTING | BA | AB | R | H | TB | 2B | 3B | HR | RBI | BB | SO | SB |
|---|---|---|---|---|---|---|---|---|---|---|---|---|
| Colorado | .292 | 5690 | 923 | 1663 | 2748 | 324 | 61 | 213 | 874 | 561 | 1027 | 132 |
| Houston | .271 | 5528 | 847 | 1500 | 2495 | 313 | 29 | 208 | 805 | 633 | 1119 | 64 |
| St. Louis | .270 | 5450 | 814 | 1469 | 2404 | 274 | 32 | 199 | 768 | 580 | 1089 | 91 |
| Arizona | .267 | 5595 | 818 | 1494 | 2472 | 284 | 35 | 208 | 776 | 660 | 1052 | 71 |
| San Francisco | .266 | 5612 | 799 | 1493 | 2582 | 304 | 40 | 235 | 775 | 704 | 1090 | 57 |
| Florida | .264 | 5542 | 742 | 1461 | 2344 | 325 | 30 | 166 | 713 | 513 | 1145 | 89 |
| Cincinnati | .262 | 5583 | 735 | 1464 | 2340 | 304 | 22 | 176 | 690 | 515 | 1172 | 103 |
| Chicago | .261 | 5406 | 777 | 1409 | 2323 | 268 | 32 | 194 | 748 | 649 | 1077 | 67 |
| Atlanta | .260 | 5498 | 729 | 1432 | 2265 | 263 | 24 | 174 | 696 | 544 | 1039 | 85 |
| Philadelphia | .260 | 5497 | 746 | 1431 | 2276 | 295 | 29 | 164 | 708 | 603 | 1125 | 153 |
| Los Angeles | .255 | 5493 | 758 | 1399 | 2335 | 264 | 27 | 206 | 714 | 564 | 1062 | 89 |
| Montreal | .253 | 5379 | 670 | 1361 | 2130 | 320 | 28 | 131 | 622 | 537 | 1071 | 101 |
| San Diego | .252 | 5482 | 789 | 1379 | 2187 | 273 | 26 | 161 | 753 | 715 | 1273 | 129 |
| Milwaukee | .251 | 5488 | 740 | 1378 | 2338 | 273 | 30 | 209 | 712 | 532 | 1399 | 66 |
| New York | .249 | 5459 | 642 | 1361 | 2111 | 273 | 18 | 147 | 608 | 604 | 1062 | 66 |
| Pittsburgh | .247 | 5398 | 657 | 1333 | 2122 | 256 | 25 | 161 | 618 | 518 | 1106 | 93 |

| TEAM PITCHING | W | L | ERA | CG | Sho | SV | Inn | H | R | ER | BB | SO |
|---|---|---|---|---|---|---|---|---|---|---|---|---|
| Atlanta | 88 | 74 | 3.59 | 5 | 13 | 41 | 1447⅓ | 1363 | 643 | 578 | 576 | 1133 |
| Arizona | 92 | 70 | 3.87 | 12 | 13 | 34 | 1459⅔ | 1352 | 677 | 627 | 491 | 1297 |
| St. Louis | 93 | 69 | 3.93 | 8 | 11 | 38 | 1435⅓ | 1389 | 684 | 627 | 562 | 1083 |
| Chicago | 88 | 74 | 4.03 | 8 | 6 | 41 | 1437 | 1357 | 701 | 643 | 593 | 1344 |
| New York | 82 | 80 | 4.07 | 6 | 14 | 48 | 1445⅔ | 1418 | 713 | 654 | 498 | 1191 |
| Philadelphia | 86 | 76 | 4.15 | 8 | 7 | 47 | 1445⅓ | 1417 | 719 | 667 | 587 | 1086 |
| San Francisco | 90 | 72 | 4.18 | 3 | 8 | 47 | 1463⅓ | 1437 | 748 | 680 | 628 | 1080 |
| Los Angeles | 86 | 76 | 4.25 | 3 | 5 | 46 | 1450⅔ | 1387 | 744 | 685 | 561 | 1212 |
| Florida | 76 | 86 | 4.32 | 5 | 11 | 32 | 1438 | 1397 | 744 | 691 | 670 | 1119 |
| Houston | 93 | 69 | 4.37 | 7 | 6 | 48 | 1454⅔ | 1453 | 769 | 707 | 508 | 1228 |
| San Diego | 79 | 83 | 4.52 | 5 | 6 | 46 | 1440⅔ | 1519 | 812 | 724 | 530 | 1088 |
| Milwaukee | 68 | 94 | 4.64 | 3 | 8 | 28 | 1436⅓ | 1452 | 806 | 740 | 774 | 1057 |
| Montreal | 68 | 94 | 4.68 | 5 | 11 | 28 | 1431⅓ | 1509 | 812 | 745 | 565 | 1103 |
| Cincinnati | 66 | 96 | 4.77 | 2 | 2 | 35 | 1442⅔ | 1572 | 850 | 765 | 561 | 943 |
| Pittsburgh | 62 | 100 | 5.05 | 8 | 9 | 36 | 1416⅓ | 1493 | 858 | 794 | 623 | 908 |
| Colorado | 73 | 89 | 5.29 | 8 | 8 | 26 | 1430 | 1522 | 906 | 841 | 669 | 1058 |

## American League

| TEAM BATTING | BA | AB | R | H | TB | 2B | 3B | HR | RBI | BB | SO | SB |
|---|---|---|---|---|---|---|---|---|---|---|---|---|
| Seattle | .288 | 5680 | 927 | 1637 | 2530 | 310 | 38 | 169 | 881 | 668 | 989 | 174 |
| Cleveland | .278 | 5600 | 897 | 1559 | 2563 | 294 | 37 | 212 | 868 | 609 | 1076 | 79 |
| Texas | .275 | 5685 | 890 | 1566 | 2676 | 326 | 23 | 246 | 844 | 575 | 1093 | 97 |
| Minnesota | .272 | 5560 | 771 | 1514 | 2410 | 328 | 38 | 164 | 717 | 535 | 1083 | 146 |
| Chicago | .268 | 5464 | 798 | 1463 | 2463 | 300 | 29 | 214 | 770 | 551 | 998 | 123 |
| New York | .267 | 5577 | 804 | 1488 | 2426 | 289 | 20 | 203 | 774 | 557 | 1035 | 161 |
| Boston | .266 | 5605 | 772 | 1493 | 2461 | 316 | 29 | 198 | 739 | 570 | 1131 | 46 |
| Kansas City | .266 | 5643 | 729 | 1503 | 2310 | 277 | 37 | 152 | 691 | 437 | 898 | 100 |
| Oakland | .264 | 5573 | 884 | 1469 | 2444 | 334 | 22 | 199 | 835 | 697 | 1021 | 68 |
| Toronto | .263 | 5663 | 767 | 1489 | 2433 | 287 | 36 | 195 | 728 | 517 | 1094 | 156 |
| Anaheim | .261 | 5551 | 691 | 1447 | 2248 | 275 | 26 | 158 | 662 | 528 | 1001 | 116 |
| Detroit | .260 | 5537 | 724 | 1439 | 2267 | 291 | 60 | 139 | 691 | 492 | 972 | 133 |
| Tampa Bay | .258 | 5524 | 672 | 1426 | 2142 | 311 | 21 | 121 | 645 | 480 | 1116 | 115 |
| Baltimore | .248 | 5472 | 687 | 1359 | 2077 | 262 | 24 | 136 | 663 | 540 | 989 | 133 |

| TEAM PITCHING | W | L | ERA | CG | Sho | SV | Inn | H | R | ER | BB | SO |
|---|---|---|---|---|---|---|---|---|---|---|---|---|
| Seattle | 116 | 46 | 3.54 | 8 | 14 | 56 | 1465 | 1293 | 627 | 576 | 493 | 1051 |
| Oakland | 102 | 60 | 3.59 | 13 | 9 | 44 | 1463⅓ | 1384 | 645 | 583 | 489 | 1117 |
| New York | 95 | 65 | 4.02 | 7 | 9 | 57 | 1451⅓ | 1429 | 713 | 649 | 494 | 1266 |
| Boston | 82 | 79 | 4.15 | 3 | 9 | 48 | 1448 | 1412 | 745 | 667 | 595 | 1259 |
| Anaheim | 75 | 87 | 4.20 | 6 | 1 | 43 | 1437⅔ | 1452 | 730 | 671 | 572 | 947 |
| Toronto | 80 | 82 | 4.28 | 7 | 10 | 41 | 1462⅔ | 1553 | 753 | 696 | 550 | 1041 |
| Minnesota | 85 | 77 | 4.51 | 12 | 8 | 45 | 1441⅓ | 1494 | 766 | 722 | 461 | 965 |
| Chicago | 83 | 79 | 4.55 | 8 | 7 | 51 | 1433⅓ | 1465 | 795 | 725 | 536 | 921 |
| Cleveland | 91 | 71 | 4.64 | 3 | 4 | 42 | 1446⅔ | 1512 | 821 | 746 | 617 | 1218 |
| Baltimore | 63 | 98 | 4.67 | 10 | 6 | 31 | 1432⅓ | 1504 | 829 | 744 | 556 | 938 |
| Kansas City | 65 | 97 | 4.87 | 5 | 1 | 30 | 1440 | 1537 | 858 | 779 | 602 | 911 |
| Tampa Bay | 62 | 100 | 4.94 | 1 | 6 | 30 | 1423⅔ | 1513 | 887 | 781 | 590 | 1030 |
| Detroit | 66 | 96 | 5.01 | 16 | 2 | 34 | 1429⅓ | 1624 | 876 | 795 | 609 | 859 |
| Texas | 73 | 89 | 5.71 | 4 | 3 | 37 | 1438⅓ | 1670 | 968 | 913 | 629 | 951 |

# National League Team-by-Team Statistical Leaders

## Arizona Diamondbacks

| BATTING | G | AB | R | H | 2B | 3B | HR | RBI | TB | BB | SO | SB | OBP | SLG | BA |
|---|---|---|---|---|---|---|---|---|---|---|---|---|---|---|---|
| Luis Gonzalez | 162 | 609 | 128 | 198 | 36 | 7 | 57 | 142 | 419 | 100 | 83 | 1 | .429 | .688 | .325 |
| Danny Bautista | 100 | 222 | 26 | 67 | 11 | 2 | 5 | 26 | 97 | 14 | 31 | 3 | .346 | .437 | .302 |
| Mark Grace | 145 | 476 | 66 | 142 | 31 | 2 | 15 | 78 | 222 | 67 | 36 | 1 | .386 | .466 | .298 |
| Dave Dellucci | 115 | 217 | 28 | 60 | 10 | 2 | 10 | 40 | 104 | 22 | 52 | 2 | .349 | .479 | .276 |
| Craig Counsell | 141 | 458 | 76 | 126 | 22 | 3 | 4 | 38 | 166 | 61 | 76 | 6 | .359 | .362 | .275 |
| Steve Finley | 140 | 495 | 66 | 136 | 27 | 4 | 14 | 73 | 213 | 47 | 67 | 11 | .337 | .430 | .275 |
| Matt Williams | 106 | 408 | 58 | 112 | 30 | 0 | 16 | 65 | 190 | 22 | 70 | 1 | .314 | .466 | .275 |
| Damian Miller | 123 | 380 | 45 | 103 | 19 | 0 | 13 | 47 | 161 | 35 | 80 | 0 | .337 | .424 | .271 |
| Erubial Durazo | 92 | 175 | 34 | 47 | 11 | 0 | 12 | 38 | 94 | 28 | 49 | 0 | .372 | .537 | .269 |
| Tony Womack | 125 | 481 | 66 | 128 | 19 | 5 | 3 | 30 | 166 | 23 | 54 | 28 | .307 | .345 | .266 |
| Reggie Sanders | 126 | 441 | 84 | 116 | 21 | 3 | 33 | 90 | 242 | 46 | 126 | 14 | .337 | .549 | .263 |
| Junior Spivey | 72 | 163 | 33 | 42 | 6 | 3 | 5 | 21 | 69 | 23 | 47 | 3 | .354 | .423 | .258 |
| Jay Bell | 129 | 428 | 59 | 106 | 24 | 1 | 13 | 46 | 171 | 65 | 79 | 0 | .349 | .400 | .248 |

| PITCHING | W–L | ERA | G | GS | CG | SV | INN | H | R | ER | BB | SO |
|---|---|---|---|---|---|---|---|---|---|---|---|---|
| Randy Johnson | 21–6 | 2.49 | 35 | 34 | 3 | 0 | 249⅔ | 181 | 74 | 69 | 71 | 372 |
| Bret Prinz | 4–1 | 2.63 | 46 | 0 | 0 | 9 | 41 | 33 | 13 | 12 | 19 | 27 |
| Byung-Hyun Kim | 5–6 | 2.94 | 78 | 0 | 0 | 19 | 98 | 58 | 32 | 32 | 44 | 113 |
| Curt Schilling | 22–6 | 2.98 | 35 | 35 | 6 | 0 | 256⅔ | 237 | 86 | 85 | 39 | 293 |
| Miguel Batista | 11–8 | 3.36 | 48 | 18 | 0 | 0 | 139⅓ | 113 | 57 | 52 | 60 | 90 |
| Albie Lopez | 4–7 | 4.00 | 13 | 13 | 2 | 0 | 81 | 74 | 36 | 36 | 24 | 69 |
| Erik Sabel | 3–2 | 4.38 | 42 | 0 | 0 | 0 | 51⅓ | 57 | 26 | 25 | 12 | 25 |
| Greg Swindell | 2–6 | 4.53 | 64 | 0 | 0 | 2 | 53⅔ | 51 | 27 | 27 | 8 | 42 |
| Troy Brohawn | 2–3 | 4.93 | 59 | 0 | 0 | 1 | 49⅓ | 55 | 27 | 27 | 23 | 30 |
| Brian Anderson | 4–9 | 5.20 | 29 | 22 | 1 | 0 | 133⅓ | 156 | 93 | 77 | 30 | 55 |
| Robert Ellis | 6–5 | 5.77 | 19 | 17 | 0 | 0 | 92 | 106 | 61 | 59 | 34 | 41 |

## Atlanta Braves

| BATTING | G | AB | R | H | 2B | 3B | HR | RBI | TB | BB | SO | SB | OBP | SLG | BA |
|---|---|---|---|---|---|---|---|---|---|---|---|---|---|---|---|
| Chipper Jones | 159 | 572 | 113 | 189 | 33 | 5 | 38 | 102 | 346 | 98 | 82 | 9 | .427 | .605 | .330 |
| Brian Jordan | 148 | 560 | 82 | 165 | 32 | 3 | 25 | 97 | 278 | 31 | 88 | 3 | .334 | .496 | .295 |
| Mark DeRosa | 66 | 164 | 27 | 47 | 8 | 0 | 3 | 20 | 64 | 12 | 19 | 2 | .350 | .390 | .287 |
| Dave Martinez | 120 | 237 | 33 | 68 | 11 | 3 | 2 | 20 | 91 | 21 | 44 | 3 | .347 | .384 | .287 |
| Rafael Furcal | 79 | 324 | 39 | 89 | 19 | 0 | 4 | 30 | 120 | 24 | 56 | 22 | .321 | .370 | .275 |
| B.J. Surhoff | 141 | 484 | 68 | 131 | 33 | 1 | 10 | 58 | 196 | 38 | 48 | 9 | .321 | .405 | .271 |
| Javy Lopez | 128 | 438 | 45 | 117 | 16 | 1 | 17 | 66 | 186 | 28 | 82 | 1 | .322 | .425 | .267 |
| Marcus Giles | 68 | 244 | 36 | 64 | 10 | 2 | 9 | 31 | 105 | 28 | 37 | 2 | .338 | .430 | .262 |
| Quilvio Veras | 71 | 258 | 39 | 65 | 14 | 2 | 3 | 25 | 92 | 24 | 52 | 7 | .330 | .357 | .252 |
| Andruw Jones | 161 | 625 | 104 | 157 | 25 | 2 | 34 | 104 | 288 | 56 | 142 | 11 | .312 | .461 | .251 |
| Rico Brogna | 72 | 206 | 15 | 51 | 9 | 0 | 3 | 21 | 69 | 14 | 46 | 3 | .297 | .335 | .248 |
| Ken Caminiti | 64 | 171 | 12 | 38 | 9 | 0 | 6 | 16 | 65 | 21 | 44 | 0 | .306 | .380 | .222 |
| Wes Helms | 100 | 216 | 28 | 48 | 10 | 3 | 10 | 36 | 94 | 21 | 56 | 1 | .293 | .435 | .222 |

| PITCHING | W–L | ERA | G | GS | CG | SV | INN | H | R | ER | BB | SO |
|---|---|---|---|---|---|---|---|---|---|---|---|---|
| Mike Remlinger | 3–3 | 2.76 | 75 | 0 | 0 | 1 | 75 | 67 | 25 | 23 | 23 | 93 |
| Jose Cabrera | 7–4 | 2.88 | 55 | 0 | 0 | 2 | 59⅓ | 52 | 24 | 19 | 25 | 43 |
| Kerry Ligtenberg | 3–3 | 3.02 | 53 | 0 | 0 | 1 | 59⅔ | 50 | 22 | 20 | 30 | 56 |
| John Durkell | 12–12 | 3.04 | 34 | 34 | 1 | 0 | 219⅓ | 187 | 83 | 74 | 70 | 187 |
| Greg Maddux | 17–11 | 3.05 | 34 | 34 | 3 | 0 | 233 | 220 | 86 | 79 | 27 | 173 |
| John Smoltz | 3–3 | 3.36 | 36 | 5 | 0 | 10 | 59 | 53 | 24 | 22 | 10 | 57 |
| Jason Marquis | 5–6 | 3.48 | 38 | 16 | 0 | 0 | 129⅓ | 113 | 62 | 50 | 59 | 98 |
| Tom Glavine | 16–7 | 3.57 | 35 | 35 | 1 | 0 | 219⅓ | 213 | 92 | 87 | 97 | 116 |
| Kevin Millwood | 7–7 | 4.31 | 21 | 21 | 0 | 0 | 121 | 121 | 66 | 58 | 40 | 84 |
| Odalis Perez | 7–8 | 4.91 | 24 | 14 | 0 | 0 | 95¼ | 108 | 55 | 52 | 39 | 71 |

## Chicago Cubs

| BATTING | G | AB | R | H | 2B | 3B | HR | RBI | TB | BB | SO | SB | OBP | SLG | BA |
|---|---|---|---|---|---|---|---|---|---|---|---|---|---|---|---|
| Sammy Sosa | 160 | 577 | 146 | 189 | 34 | 5 | 64 | 160 | 425 | 116 | 153 | 0 | .437 | .737 | .328 |
| Rondell White | 95 | 323 | 43 | 99 | 19 | 1 | 17 | 50 | 171 | 26 | 56 | 1 | .371 | .529 | .307 |
| Bill Mueller | 70 | 210 | 38 | 62 | 12 | 1 | 6 | 23 | 94 | 37 | 19 | 1 | .403 | .448 | .295 |
| Ricky Gutierrez | 147 | 528 | 76 | 153 | 23 | 3 | 10 | 66 | 212 | 40 | 56 | 4 | .345 | .402 | .290 |
| Fred DeRosa | 49 | 170 | 27 | 48 | 7 | 2 | 12 | 41 | 95 | 26 | 37 | 0 | .383 | .559 | .282 |
| Eric Young | 149 | 603 | 98 | 168 | 43 | 4 | 6 | 42 | 237 | 42 | 45 | 31 | .333 | .393 | .279 |
| Delino DeShields | 68 | 163 | 26 | 45 | 9 | 3 | 2 | 16 | 66 | 28 | 35 | 12 | .380 | .405 | .276 |
| Michael Tucker | 63 | 205 | 31 | 54 | 9 | 7 | 5 | 31 | 92 | 23 | 47 | 4 | .339 | .449 | .263 |
| Ron Coomer | 111 | 349 | 25 | 91 | 19 | 1 | 8 | 53 | 136 | 29 | 70 | 0 | .316 | .390 | .261 |
| Joe Girardi | 78 | 229 | 22 | 58 | 10 | 1 | 3 | 25 | 79 | 21 | 50 | 0 | .315 | .345 | .253 |
| Matt Stairs | 124 | 340 | 48 | 85 | 21 | 0 | 17 | 61 | 157 | 52 | 76 | 2 | .358 | .462 | .250 |
| Gary Matthews Jr. | 106 | 258 | 41 | 56 | 9 | 1 | 9 | 30 | 94 | 38 | 55 | 5 | .320 | .364 | .217 |
| Todd Hundley | 79 | 246 | 23 | 46 | 10 | 0 | 12 | 31 | 92 | 25 | 89 | 0 | .268 | .374 | .187 |

## Chicago Cubs *(Cont.)*

| PITCHING | W–L | ERA | G | GS | CG | SV | INN | H | R | ER | BB | SO |
|---|---|---|---|---|---|---|---|---|---|---|---|---|
| Todd Van Poppel | 4–1 | 2.52 | 59 | 0 | 0 | 0 | 75 | 63 | 22 | 21 | 38 | 90 |
| Kyle Farnsworth | 4–6 | 2.74 | 76 | 0 | 0 | 2 | 82 | 65 | 26 | 25 | 29 | 107 |
| Kerry Wood | 12–6 | 3.36 | 28 | 28 | 1 | 0 | 174⅓ | 127 | 70 | 65 | 92 | 217 |
| Tom Gordon | 1–2 | 3.38 | 47 | 0 | 0 | 27 | 45⅓ | 32 | 18 | 17 | 16 | 67 |
| Jeff Fassero | 4–4 | 3.42 | 82 | 0 | 0 | 12 | 73⅔ | 66 | 31 | 28 | 23 | 79 |
| Jon Lieber | 20–6 | 3.80 | 34 | 34 | 5 | 0 | 232⅓ | 226 | 104 | 98 | 41 | 148 |
| Jason Bere | 11–11 | 4.31 | 32 | 32 | 2 | 0 | 188 | 171 | 99 | 90 | 77 | 175 |
| Kevin Tapani | 9–14 | 4.49 | 29 | 29 | 0 | 0 | 168½ | 186 | 93 | 84 | 40 | 149 |
| Julian Tavarez | 10–9 | 4.52 | 34 | 28 | 0 | 0 | 161⅓ | 172 | 98 | 81 | 69 | 107 |

## Cincinnati Reds

| BATTING | G | AB | R | H | 2B | 3B | HR | RBI | TB | BB | SO | SB | OBP | SLG | BA |
|---|---|---|---|---|---|---|---|---|---|---|---|---|---|---|---|
| Wilton Guerrero | 60 | 142 | 16 | 48 | 5 | 1 | 1 | 8 | 58 | 3 | 17 | 5 | .352 | .408 | .338 |
| Sean Casey | 145 | 533 | 69 | 165 | 40 | 0 | 13 | 89 | 244 | 43 | 63 | 3 | .369 | .458 | .310 |
| Dmitri Young | 142 | 540 | 68 | 163 | 28 | 3 | 21 | 69 | 260 | 37 | 77 | 8 | .350 | .481 | .302 |
| Todd Walker | 66 | 261 | 41 | 77 | 17 | 0 | 5 | 32 | 109 | 26 | 42 | 0 | .361 | .418 | .295 |
| Aaron Boone | 103 | 381 | 54 | 112 | 26 | 2 | 14 | 62 | 184 | 29 | 71 | 6 | .351 | .483 | .294 |
| Alex Ochoa | 90 | 349 | 48 | 101 | 20 | 4 | 7 | 35 | 150 | 24 | 53 | 12 | .337 | .430 | .289 |
| Ken Griffey Jr. | 111 | 364 | 57 | 104 | 20 | 2 | 22 | 65 | 194 | 44 | 72 | 2 | .365 | .533 | .286 |
| Aaron Dunn | 66 | 244 | 54 | 64 | 18 | 1 | 19 | 43 | 141 | 38 | 74 | 4 | .371 | .578 | .262 |
| Barry Larkin | 45 | 156 | 29 | 40 | 12 | 0 | 2 | 17 | 58 | 27 | 25 | 3 | .373 | .372 | .256 |
| Ruben Rivera | 117 | 263 | 37 | 67 | 13 | 1 | 10 | 34 | 112 | 21 | 83 | 6 | .321 | .426 | .255 |
| Michael Tucker | 86 | 231 | 31 | 56 | 10 | 1 | 7 | 30 | 89 | 23 | 55 | 12 | .308 | .385 | .242 |
| Jason LaRue | 121 | 364 | 39 | 86 | 21 | 2 | 12 | 43 | 147 | 27 | 106 | 3 | .303 | .404 | .236 |
| Pokey Reese | 133 | 428 | 50 | 96 | 20 | 2 | 9 | 40 | 147 | 34 | 82 | 25 | .284 | .343 | .224 |
| Juan Castro | 96 | 242 | 27 | 54 | 10 | 0 | 3 | 13 | 73 | 13 | 50 | 0 | .261 | .302 | .223 |

| PITCHING | W–L | ERA | G | GS | CG | SV | INN | H | R | ER | BB | SO |
|---|---|---|---|---|---|---|---|---|---|---|---|---|
| Scott Sullivan | 7–1 | 3.31 | 79 | 0 | 0 | 0 | 103⅓ | 94 | 44 | 38 | 36 | 82 |
| Jim Brower | 7–10 | 3.97 | 46 | 10 | 0 | 1 | 129½ | 119 | 65 | 57 | 60 | 94 |
| Hector Mercado | 3–2 | 4.08 | 56 | 0 | 0 | 0 | 53 | 55 | 27 | 24 | 30 | 59 |
| Danny Graves | 6–5 | 4.15 | 66 | 0 | 0 | 32 | 80⅓ | 83 | 41 | 37 | 18 | 49 |
| Elmer Dessens | 10–14 | 4.48 | 34 | 34 | 1 | 0 | 205 | 221 | 103 | 102 | 56 | 128 |
| Lance Davis | 8–4 | 4.74 | 20 | 20 | 1 | 0 | 106⅓ | 124 | 60 | 56 | 34 | 53 |
| Dennys Reyes | 2–6 | 4.92 | 35 | 6 | 0 | 0 | 53 | 51 | 35 | 29 | 35 | 52 |
| Chris Reitsma | 7–15 | 5.29 | 36 | 29 | 0 | 0 | 182 | 209 | 121 | 107 | 49 | 96 |
| Jose Acevedo | 5–7 | 5.44 | 18 | 18 | 0 | 0 | 96 | 101 | 61 | 58 | 34 | 68 |
| Osvaldo Fernandez | 5–6 | 6.92 | 20 | 14 | 0 | 0 | 79½ | 103 | 62 | 61 | 33 | 35 |

## Colorado Rockies

| BATTING | G | AB | R | H | 2B | 3B | HR | RBI | TB | BB | SO | SB | OBP | SLG | BA |
|---|---|---|---|---|---|---|---|---|---|---|---|---|---|---|---|
| Todd Hollandsworth | 33 | 117 | 21 | 43 | 15 | 1 | 6 | 19 | 78 | 8 | 20 | 5 | .408 | .667 | .368 |
| Larry Walker | 142 | 497 | 107 | 174 | 35 | 3 | 38 | 123 | 329 | 82 | 103 | 14 | .449 | .662 | .350 |
| Todd Helton | 159 | 587 | 132 | 197 | 54 | 2 | 49 | 146 | 402 | 98 | 104 | 7 | .432 | .685 | .336 |
| Brent Mayne | 49 | 160 | 15 | 53 | 7 | 0 | 0 | 20 | 60 | 16 | 24 | 0 | .385 | .375 | .331 |
| Juan Pierre | 156 | 617 | 108 | 202 | 26 | 11 | 2 | 55 | 256 | 41 | 29 | 46 | .378 | .415 | .327 |
| Jeff Cirillo | 138 | 528 | 72 | 165 | 26 | 4 | 17 | 83 | 250 | 43 | 63 | 12 | .364 | .473 | .313 |
| Juan Uribe | 72 | 273 | 32 | 82 | 15 | 11 | 8 | 53 | 143 | 8 | 55 | 3 | .325 | .524 | .300 |
| Neifi Perez | 87 | 382 | 65 | 114 | 19 | 8 | 7 | 47 | 170 | 16 | 49 | 6 | .326 | .445 | .298 |
| Todd Walker | 85 | 290 | 52 | 86 | 18 | 2 | 12 | 43 | 144 | 25 | 40 | 1 | .349 | .497 | .297 |
| Terry Shumpert | 114 | 242 | 37 | 70 | 14 | 5 | 4 | 24 | 106 | 15 | 44 | 14 | .337 | .438 | .289 |
| Greg Norton | 117 | 225 | 30 | 60 | 13 | 2 | 13 | 40 | 116 | 19 | 65 | 1 | .321 | .516 | .267 |
| Ron Gant | 59 | 171 | 31 | 44 | 8 | 2 | 8 | 22 | 80 | 24 | 56 | 3 | .345 | .468 | .257 |
| Junior Ortiz | 53 | 204 | 38 | 52 | 8 | 1 | 13 | 35 | 101 | 14 | 36 | 3 | .314 | .495 | .255 |
| Alex Ochoa | 58 | 187 | 25 | 47 | 10 | 3 | 1 | 17 | 66 | 21 | 23 | 5 | .330 | .353 | .251 |
| Ben Petrick | 85 | 244 | 41 | 58 | 15 | 3 | 11 | 39 | 112 | 31 | 67 | 3 | .327 | .459 | .238 |

| PITCHING | W–L | ERA | G | GS | CG | SV | INN | H | R | ER | BB | SO |
|---|---|---|---|---|---|---|---|---|---|---|---|---|
| Mike Myers | 2–3 | 3.60 | 73 | 0 | 0 | 0 | 40 | 32 | 17 | 16 | 24 | 36 |
| Justin Speier | 4–3 | 3.70 | 42 | 0 | 0 | 0 | 56 | 47 | 24 | 23 | 12 | 47 |
| John Thomson | 4–5 | 4.04 | 14 | 14 | 1 | 0 | 93⅔ | 84 | 46 | 42 | 25 | 68 |
| Jose Jimenez | 6–1 | 4.09 | 56 | 0 | 0 | 17 | 55 | 56 | 27 | 25 | 22 | 37 |
| Kane Davis | 2–4 | 4.35 | 57 | 0 | 0 | 0 | 68½ | 66 | 36 | 33 | 32 | 47 |
| Shawn Chacon | 6–10 | 5.06 | 27 | 27 | 0 | 0 | 160 | 157 | 96 | 90 | 87 | 134 |
| Denny Neagle | 9–8 | 5.38 | 30 | 30 | 0 | 0 | 170⅔ | 192 | 107 | 102 | 60 | 139 |
| Mike Hampton | 14–13 | 5.41 | 32 | 32 | 2 | 0 | 203 | 236 | 138 | 122 | 85 | 122 |
| Pedro Astacio | 6–13 | 5.49 | 22 | 22 | 4 | 0 | 141 | 151 | 91 | 86 | 50 | 125 |
| Gabe White | 1–7 | 6.25 | 69 | 0 | 0 | 0 | 67⅔ | 70 | 47 | 47 | 26 | 47 |
| Brian Bohanon | 5–8 | 7.14 | 20 | 19 | 0 | 0 | 97 | 127 | 79 | 77 | 47 | 47 |

# National League Team-by-Team Statistical Leaders (Cont.)

## Florida Marlins

| BATTING | G | AB | R | H | 2B | 3B | HR | RBI | TB | BB | SO | SB | OBP | SLG | BA |
|---|---|---|---|---|---|---|---|---|---|---|---|---|---|---|---|
| Cliff Floyd | 149 | 555 | 123 | 176 | 44 | 4 | 31 | 103 | 321 | 59 | 101 | 18 | .390 | .578 | .317 |
| Kevin Millar | 144 | 449 | 62 | 141 | 39 | 5 | 20 | 85 | 250 | 39 | 70 | 0 | .374 | .557 | .314 |
| Mike Redmond | 48 | 141 | 19 | 44 | 4 | 0 | 4 | 14 | 60 | 13 | 13 | 0 | .376 | .426 | .312 |
| Mike Lowell | 146 | 551 | 65 | 156 | 37 | 0 | 18 | 100 | 247 | 43 | 79 | 1 | .340 | .448 | .283 |
| Derrek Lee | 158 | 561 | 83 | 158 | 37 | 4 | 21 | 75 | 266 | 50 | 126 | 4 | .346 | .474 | .282 |
| Preston Wilson | 123 | 468 | 70 | 128 | 30 | 2 | 23 | 71 | 231 | 36 | 107 | 20 | .331 | .494 | .274 |
| Luis Castillo | 133 | 534 | 76 | 140 | 16 | 10 | 2 | 45 | 182 | 66 | 90 | 33 | .343 | .341 | .262 |
| Charles Johnson | 128 | 451 | 51 | 117 | 32 | 0 | 18 | 75 | 203 | 38 | 133 | 0 | .321 | .450 | .259 |
| Eric Owens | 119 | 400 | 51 | 101 | 16 | 1 | 5 | 28 | 134 | 29 | 59 | 8 | .302 | .335 | .253 |
| Alex Gonzalez | 146 | 518 | 57 | 130 | 36 | 1 | 9 | 48 | 195 | 31 | 107 | 2 | .304 | .376 | .251 |
| Dave Berg | 82 | 215 | 26 | 52 | 12 | 1 | 4 | 16 | 78 | 14 | 39 | 1 | .292 | .363 | .242 |
| John Mabry | 82 | 147 | 14 | 32 | 7 | 0 | 6 | 20 | 57 | 13 | 44 | 1 | .299 | .388 | .218 |

| PITCHING | W–L | ERA | G | GS | CG | SV | INN | H | R | ER | BB | SO |
|---|---|---|---|---|---|---|---|---|---|---|---|---|
| Vladimir Nunez | 4–5 | 2.74 | 52 | 3 | 0 | 0 | 92 | 79 | 33 | 28 | 30 | 64 |
| Antonio Alfonseca | 4–4 | 3.06 | 58 | 0 | 0 | 28 | 61⅔ | 68 | 24 | 21 | 15 | 40 |
| Braden Looper | 3–3 | 3.55 | 71 | 0 | 0 | 3 | 71 | 63 | 28 | 28 | 30 | 52 |
| Brad Penny | 10–10 | 3.69 | 31 | 31 | 1 | 0 | 205 | 183 | 92 | 84 | 54 | 154 |
| A.J. Burnett | 11–12 | 4.05 | 27 | 27 | 2 | 0 | 173⅓ | 145 | 82 | 78 | 83 | 128 |
| Vic Darensbourg | 1–2 | 4.25 | 58 | 0 | 0 | 1 | 48⅔ | 52 | 24 | 23 | 10 | 33 |
| Chuck Smith | 5–5 | 4.70 | 15 | 15 | 0 | 0 | 88 | 89 | 47 | 46 | 35 | 71 |
| Jesus Sanchez | 2–4 | 4.74 | 16 | 9 | 0 | 0 | 62⅔ | 61 | 33 | 33 | 31 | 46 |
| Ryan Dempster | 15–12 | 4.94 | 34 | 34 | 2 | 0 | 211⅓ | 218 | 123 | 116 | 112 | 171 |
| Matt Clement | 9–10 | 5.05 | 31 | 31 | 0 | 0 | 169⅓ | 172 | 102 | 95 | 85 | 134 |
| Ricky Bones | 4–4 | 5.06 | 61 | 0 | 0 | 0 | 64 | 71 | 39 | 36 | 33 | 41 |

## Houston Astros

| BATTING | G | AB | R | H | 2B | 3B | HR | RBI | TB | BB | SO | SB | OBP | SLG | BA |
|---|---|---|---|---|---|---|---|---|---|---|---|---|---|---|---|
| Moises Alou | 136 | 513 | 79 | 170 | 31 | 1 | 27 | 108 | 284 | 57 | 57 | 5 | .396 | .554 | .331 |
| Lance Berkman | 157 | 577 | 110 | 191 | 55 | 5 | 34 | 126 | 358 | 92 | 121 | 7 | .430 | .620 | .331 |
| Craig Biggio | 155 | 617 | 118 | 180 | 35 | 3 | 20 | 70 | 281 | 66 | 100 | 7 | .382 | .455 | .292 |
| Jeff Bagwell | 161 | 600 | 126 | 173 | 43 | 4 | 39 | 130 | 341 | 106 | 135 | 11 | .397 | .568 | .288 |
| Jose Vizcaino | 107 | 256 | 38 | 71 | 8 | 3 | 1 | 14 | 88 | 15 | 33 | 3 | .322 | .344 | .277 |
| Richard Hidalgo | 146 | 512 | 70 | 141 | 29 | 3 | 19 | 80 | 233 | 54 | 107 | 3 | .356 | .455 | .275 |
| Vinny Castilla | 122 | 445 | 62 | 120 | 28 | 1 | 23 | 82 | 219 | 32 | 86 | 1 | .320 | .492 | .270 |
| Julio Lugo | 140 | 513 | 93 | 135 | 20 | 3 | 10 | 37 | 191 | 46 | 116 | 12 | .326 | .372 | .263 |
| Orlando Merced | 94 | 137 | 19 | 36 | 6 | 1 | 6 | 29 | 62 | 14 | 32 | 5 | .333 | .453 | .263 |
| Daryle Ward | 95 | 213 | 21 | 56 | 15 | 0 | 9 | 39 | 98 | 19 | 48 | 0 | .323 | .460 | .263 |
| Tony Eusebio | 59 | 154 | 16 | 39 | 8 | 0 | 5 | 14 | 62 | 17 | 34 | 0 | .339 | .403 | .253 |
| Brad Ausmus | 128 | 422 | 45 | 98 | 23 | 4 | 5 | 34 | 144 | 30 | 64 | 4 | .284 | .341 | .232 |

| PITCHING | W–L | ERA | G | GS | CG | SV | INN | H | R | ER | BB | SO |
|---|---|---|---|---|---|---|---|---|---|---|---|---|
| Octavio Dotel | 7–5 | 2.66 | 61 | 4 | 0 | 2 | 105 | 79 | 35 | 31 | 47 | 145 |
| Roy Oswalt | 14–3 | 2.73 | 28 | 20 | 3 | 0 | 141⅔ | 126 | 48 | 43 | 24 | 144 |
| Billy Wagner | 2–5 | 2.73 | 64 | 0 | 0 | 39 | 62⅔ | 44 | 19 | 19 | 20 | 79 |
| Wade Miller | 16–8 | 3.40 | 32 | 32 | 1 | 0 | 212 | 183 | 91 | 80 | 76 | 183 |
| Nelson Cruz | 3–3 | 4.15 | 66 | 0 | 0 | 2 | 82½ | 72 | 41 | 38 | 24 | 75 |
| Shane Reynolds | 14–11 | 4.34 | 28 | 28 | 3 | 0 | 182⅔ | 208 | 95 | 88 | 36 | 102 |
| Mike Jackson | 5–3 | 4.70 | 67 | 0 | 0 | 4 | 69 | 68 | 36 | 36 | 22 | 46 |
| Dave Mlicki | 7–3 | 5.09 | 19 | 14 | 0 | 0 | 86⅔ | 85 | 53 | 49 | 33 | 49 |
| Tim Redding | 3–1 | 5.50 | 13 | 9 | 0 | 0 | 55⅔ | 62 | 38 | 34 | 24 | 55 |
| Ron Villone | 5–7 | 5.56 | 31 | 6 | 0 | 0 | 68 | 77 | 46 | 42 | 24 | 65 |
| Scott Elarton | 4–8 | 7.14 | 20 | 20 | 0 | 0 | 109⅔ | 126 | 88 | 87 | 49 | 76 |
| Jose Lima | 1–2 | 7.30 | 14 | 9 | 0 | 0 | 53 | 77 | 48 | 43 | 16 | 41 |

## Los Angeles Dodgers

| BATTING | G | AB | R | H | 2B | 3B | HR | RBI | TB | BB | SO | SB | OBP | SLG | BA |
|---|---|---|---|---|---|---|---|---|---|---|---|---|---|---|---|
| Paul Lo Duca | 125 | 460 | 71 | 147 | 28 | 0 | 25 | 90 | 250 | 39 | 30 | 2 | .374 | .543 | .320 |
| Gary Sheffield | 143 | 515 | 98 | 160 | 28 | 2 | 36 | 100 | 300 | 94 | 67 | 10 | .417 | .583 | .311 |
| Shawn Green | 161 | 619 | 121 | 184 | 31 | 4 | 49 | 125 | 370 | 72 | 107 | 20 | .372 | .598 | .297 |
| Mark Grudzielanek | 133 | 539 | 83 | 146 | 21 | 3 | 13 | 55 | 212 | 28 | 83 | 4 | .317 | .393 | .271 |
| Jeff Reboulet | 94 | 214 | 35 | 57 | 15 | 2 | 3 | 22 | 85 | 33 | 48 | 0 | .367 | .397 | .266 |
| Adrian Beltre | 126 | 475 | 59 | 126 | 22 | 4 | 13 | 60 | 195 | 28 | 82 | 13 | .310 | .411 | .265 |
| Dave Hansen | 92 | 140 | 13 | 33 | 10 | 0 | 2 | 20 | 49 | 32 | 29 | 0 | .371 | .350 | .236 |
| Eric Karros | 121 | 438 | 42 | 103 | 22 | 0 | 15 | 63 | 170 | 41 | 101 | 3 | .303 | .388 | .235 |
| Hiram Bocachica | 76 | 133 | 15 | 31 | 11 | 1 | 2 | 9 | 50 | 9 | 33 | 4 | .287 | .376 | .233 |
| Tom Goodwin | 105 | 286 | 51 | 66 | 8 | 5 | 4 | 22 | 96 | 23 | 58 | 22 | .286 | .336 | .231 |
| Marquis Grissom | 135 | 448 | 56 | 99 | 17 | 1 | 21 | 60 | 181 | 16 | 107 | 7 | .250 | .404 | .221 |
| Alex Cora | 134 | 405 | 38 | 88 | 18 | 3 | 4 | 29 | 124 | 31 | 58 | 0 | .285 | .306 | .217 |
| Chad Kreuter | 73 | 191 | 21 | 41 | 11 | 1 | 6 | 17 | 72 | 41 | 52 | 0 | .355 | .377 | .215 |

# National League Team-by-Team Statistical Leaders (Cont.)

## Los Angeles Dodgers (Cont.)

| PITCHING | W–L | ERA | G | GS | CG | SV | INN | H | R | ER | BB | SO |
|---|---|---|---|---|---|---|---|---|---|---|---|---|
| Kevin Brown | 10–4 | 2.65 | 20 | 19 | 1 | 0 | 115⅔ | 94 | 41 | 34 | 38 | 104 |
| Giovanni Carrara | 6–1 | 3.16 | 47 | 3 | 0 | 3 | 85⅓ | 73 | 30 | 30 | 24 | 70 |
| Matt Herges | 9–8 | 3.44 | 75 | 0 | 0 | 1 | 99⅓ | 97 | 39 | 38 | 46 | 76 |
| Chan Ho Park | 15–11 | 3.50 | 36 | 35 | 2 | 0 | 234 | 183 | 98 | 91 | 91 | 218 |
| Jeff Shaw | 3–5 | 3.62 | 77 | 0 | 0 | 43 | 74⅔ | 63 | 32 | 30 | 18 | 58 |
| James Baldwin | 3–6 | 4.20 | 12 | 12 | 0 | 0 | 79⅓ | 82 | 39 | 37 | 25 | 53 |
| Terry Adams | 12–8 | 4.33 | 43 | 22 | 0 | 0 | 166⅓ | 172 | 84 | 80 | 54 | 141 |
| Eric Gagne | 6–7 | 4.75 | 33 | 24 | 0 | 0 | 151⅔ | 144 | 90 | 80 | 46 | 130 |
| Luke Prokopec | 8–7 | 4.88 | 29 | 22 | 0 | 0 | 138⅓ | 146 | 80 | 75 | 40 | 91 |
| Darren Dreifort | 4–7 | 5.13 | 16 | 16 | 0 | 0 | 94⅔ | 89 | 62 | 54 | 47 | 91 |

## Milwaukee Brewers

| BATTING | G | AB | R | H | 2B | 3B | HR | RBI | TB | BB | SO | SB | OBP | SLG | BA |
|---|---|---|---|---|---|---|---|---|---|---|---|---|---|---|---|
| Tyler Houston | 76 | 235 | 36 | 68 | 7 | 0 | 12 | 38 | 111 | 18 | 62 | 0 | .343 | .472 | .289 |
| Mark Loretta | 102 | 384 | 40 | 111 | 14 | 2 | 2 | 29 | 135 | 28 | 46 | 1 | .346 | .352 | .289 |
| Devon White | 126 | 390 | 52 | 108 | 25 | 2 | 14 | 47 | 179 | 28 | 95 | 18 | .343 | .459 | .277 |
| Richie Sexson | 158 | 598 | 94 | 162 | 24 | 3 | 45 | 125 | 327 | 60 | 178 | 2 | .342 | .547 | .271 |
| Luis Lopez | 93 | 222 | 22 | 60 | 8 | 3 | 4 | 18 | 86 | 14 | 44 | 0 | .326 | .387 | .270 |
| Ron Belliard | 101 | 364 | 69 | 96 | 30 | 3 | 11 | 36 | 165 | 35 | 65 | 5 | .335 | .453 | .264 |
| Geoff Jenkins | 105 | 397 | 60 | 105 | 21 | 1 | 20 | 63 | 188 | 36 | 120 | 4 | .334 | .474 | .264 |
| Angel Echevarria | 75 | 133 | 12 | 34 | 11 | 0 | 5 | 13 | 60 | 8 | 29 | 0 | .310 | .451 | .256 |
| Lou Collier | 50 | 127 | 19 | 32 | 8 | 1 | 2 | 14 | 48 | 17 | 30 | 5 | .340 | .378 | .252 |
| Jeromy Burnitz | 154 | 562 | 104 | 141 | 32 | 4 | 34 | 100 | 283 | 80 | 150 | 0 | .347 | .504 | .251 |
| Jose Hernandez | 152 | 542 | 67 | 135 | 26 | 2 | 25 | 78 | 240 | 39 | 185 | 5 | .300 | .443 | .249 |
| James Mouton | 75 | 138 | 20 | 34 | 8 | 0 | 2 | 10 | 48 | 11 | 40 | 7 | .329 | .348 | .246 |
| Henry Blanco | 104 | 314 | 33 | 66 | 18 | 3 | 6 | 31 | 108 | 34 | 72 | 3 | .290 | .344 | .210 |

| PITCHING | W–L | ERA | G | GS | CG | SV | INN | H | R | ER | BB | SO |
|---|---|---|---|---|---|---|---|---|---|---|---|---|
| Chad Fox | 5–2 | 1.89 | 65 | 0 | 0 | 2 | 66⅔ | 44 | 16 | 14 | 36 | 80 |
| David Weathers | 3–4 | 2.03 | 52 | 0 | 0 | 4 | 57⅔ | 37 | 14 | 13 | 25 | 46 |
| Mike DeJean | 4–2 | 2.77 | 75 | 0 | 0 | 2 | 84⅓ | 75 | 31 | 26 | 39 | 68 |
| Ray King | 0–4 | 3.60 | 82 | 0 | 0 | 1 | 55 | 49 | 22 | 22 | 25 | 49 |
| Curtis Leskanic | 2–6 | 3.63 | 70 | 0 | 0 | 17 | 69⅓ | 63 | 30 | 28 | 31 | 64 |
| Ruben Quevedo | 4–5 | 4.61 | 10 | 10 | 0 | 0 | 56⅔ | 56 | 30 | 29 | 30 | 60 |
| Ben Sheets | 11–10 | 4.76 | 25 | 25 | 1 | 0 | 151⅓ | 166 | 89 | 80 | 48 | 94 |
| Jimmy Haynes | 8–17 | 4.85 | 31 | 29 | 0 | 0 | 172⅔ | 182 | 98 | 93 | 78 | 112 |
| Jamie Wright | 11–12 | 4.90 | 33 | 33 | 1 | 0 | 194⅔ | 201 | 115 | 106 | 98 | 129 |
| Paul Rigdon | 3–5 | 5.79 | 15 | 15 | 0 | 0 | 79⅓ | 86 | 52 | 51 | 46 | 49 |
| Allen Levrault | 6–10 | 6.06 | 32 | 20 | 1 | 0 | 130⅔ | 146 | 93 | 88 | 59 | 80 |

## Montreal Expos

| BATTING | G | AB | R | H | 2B | 3B | HR | RBI | TB | BB | SO | SB | OBP | SLG | BA |
|---|---|---|---|---|---|---|---|---|---|---|---|---|---|---|---|
| Jose Vidro | 124 | 486 | 82 | 155 | 34 | 1 | 15 | 59 | 236 | 31 | 49 | 4 | .371 | .486 | .319 |
| Vladimir Guerrero | 159 | 599 | 107 | 184 | 45 | 4 | 34 | 108 | 339 | 60 | 88 | 37 | .377 | .566 | .307 |
| Mike Mordecai | 97 | 254 | 28 | 71 | 17 | 2 | 3 | 32 | 101 | 19 | 53 | 2 | .330 | .398 | .280 |
| Orlando Cabrera | 162 | 626 | 64 | 173 | 41 | 6 | 14 | 96 | 268 | 43 | 54 | 19 | .324 | .428 | .276 |
| Fernando Tatis | 41 | 145 | 20 | 37 | 9 | 0 | 2 | 11 | 52 | 16 | 43 | 0 | .339 | .359 | .255 |
| Michael Barrett | 132 | 472 | 42 | 118 | 33 | 2 | 6 | 38 | 173 | 25 | 54 | 2 | .289 | .367 | .250 |
| Lee Stevens | 152 | 542 | 77 | 133 | 35 | 1 | 25 | 95 | 245 | 74 | 157 | 2 | .338 | .452 | .245 |
| Mark Smith | 80 | 194 | 28 | 47 | 13 | 1 | 6 | 18 | 80 | 23 | 38 | 0 | .326 | .412 | .242 |
| Geoff Blum | 148 | 453 | 57 | 107 | 25 | 0 | 9 | 50 | 159 | 43 | 94 | 9 | .313 | .351 | .236 |
| Milton Bradley | 67 | 220 | 19 | 49 | 16 | 3 | 1 | 19 | 74 | 19 | 62 | 7 | .288 | .336 | .223 |
| Peter Bergeron | 102 | 375 | 53 | 79 | 11 | 4 | 3 | 16 | 107 | 28 | 87 | 10 | .275 | .285 | .211 |
| Brad Wilkerson | 47 | 117 | 11 | 24 | 7 | 2 | 1 | 5 | 38 | 17 | 41 | 2 | .304 | .325 | .205 |

| PITCHING | W–L | ERA | G | GS | CG | SV | INN | H | R | ER | BB | SO |
|---|---|---|---|---|---|---|---|---|---|---|---|---|
| Scott Strickland | 2–6 | 3.21 | 77 | 0 | 0 | 9 | 81⅓ | 67 | 36 | 29 | 41 | 85 |
| Javier Vazquez | 16–11 | 3.42 | 32 | 32 | 5 | 0 | 223⅔ | 197 | 92 | 85 | 44 | 208 |
| Scott Stewart | 3–1 | 3.78 | 62 | 0 | 0 | 3 | 47⅔ | 43 | 20 | 20 | 13 | 39 |
| Tony Armas | 9–14 | 4.03 | 34 | 34 | 0 | 0 | 196⅔ | 180 | 101 | 88 | 91 | 176 |
| Ugueth Urbina | 2–1 | 4.24 | 45 | 0 | 0 | 15 | 46⅔ | 42 | 24 | 22 | 21 | 57 |
| Graeme Lloyd | 9–5 | 4.35 | 84 | 0 | 0 | 1 | 70⅓ | 74 | 38 | 34 | 21 | 44 |
| Toma Ohka | 1–3 | 4.77 | 10 | 10 | 0 | 0 | 54⅔ | 65 | 30 | 29 | 10 | 31 |
| Masato Yoshii | 4–7 | 4.78 | 42 | 11 | 0 | 0 | 113 | 127 | 65 | 60 | 26 | 63 |
| Guillermo Mota | 1–3 | 5.26 | 53 | 0 | 0 | 0 | 49⅔ | 51 | 30 | 29 | 18 | 31 |
| Mike Thurman | 9–11 | 5.33 | 28 | 26 | 0 | 0 | 147 | 172 | 90 | 87 | 50 | 96 |
| Britt Reames | 4–8 | 5.59 | 41 | 13 | 0 | 0 | 95 | 101 | 68 | 59 | 48 | 86 |
| Troy Mattes | 3–3 | 6.00 | 8 | 8 | 0 | 0 | 45 | 51 | 33 | 30 | 21 | 26 |
| Carl Pavano | 1–6 | 6.33 | 8 | 8 | 0 | 0 | 42⅔ | 59 | 33 | 30 | 16 | 36 |

## New York Mets

| BATTING | G | AB | R | H | 2B | 3B | HR | RBI | TB | BB | SO | SB | OBP | SLG | BA |
|---|---|---|---|---|---|---|---|---|---|---|---|---|---|---|---|
| Desi Relaford............ | 120 | 301 | 43 | 91 | 27 | 0 | 8 | 36 | 142 | 27 | 65 | 13 | .364 | .472 | .302 |
| Mike Piazza .............. | 141 | 503 | 81 | 151 | 29 | 0 | 36 | 94 | 288 | 67 | 87 | 0 | .384 | .573 | .300 |
| Joe McEwing........... | 116 | 283 | 41 | 80 | 17 | 3 | 8 | 30 | 127 | 17 | 57 | 4 | .342 | .449 | .283 |
| Benny Agbayani....... | 91 | 296 | 28 | 82 | 14 | 2 | 6 | 27 | 118 | 36 | 73 | 4 | .364 | .399 | .277 |
| Tsuyoshi Shinjo ........ | 123 | 400 | 46 | 107 | 23 | 1 | 10 | 56 | 162 | 25 | 70 | 4 | .320 | .405 | .268 |
| Todd Zeile .............. | 151 | 531 | 66 | 141 | 25 | 1 | 10 | 62 | 198 | 73 | 102 | 1 | .359 | .373 | .266 |
| Jay Payton.............. | 104 | 361 | 44 | 92 | 16 | 1 | 8 | 34 | 134 | 18 | 52 | 4 | .298 | .371 | .255 |
| Rey Ordonez........... | 149 | 461 | 31 | 114 | 24 | 4 | 3 | 44 | 155 | 34 | 43 | 3 | .299 | .336 | .247 |
| Timo Perez ............. | 85 | 239 | 26 | 59 | 9 | 1 | 5 | 22 | 85 | 12 | 25 | 1 | .287 | .356 | .247 |
| Matt Lawton............ | 48 | 183 | 24 | 45 | 11 | 1 | 3 | 13 | 67 | 22 | 34 | 10 | .352 | .366 | .246 |
| Edgardo Alfonzo ..... | 124 | 457 | 64 | 111 | 22 | 0 | 17 | 49 | 184 | 51 | 62 | 5 | .322 | .403 | .243 |
| Robin Ventura.......... | 142 | 456 | 70 | 108 | 20 | 0 | 21 | 61 | 191 | 88 | 101 | 2 | .359 | .419 | .237 |
| Lenny Harris............ | 111 | 135 | 12 | 30 | 5 | 1 | 0 | 9 | 37 | 8 | 9 | 3 | .266 | .274 | .222 |

| PITCHING | W–L | ERA | G | GS | CG | SV | INN | H | R | ER | BB | SO |
|---|---|---|---|---|---|---|---|---|---|---|---|---|
| Al Leiter.................. | 11–11 | 3.31 | 29 | 29 | 0 | 0 | 187⅓ | 178 | 81 | 69 | 46 | 142 |
| Jerrod Riggan.............. | 3–3 | 3.40 | 35 | 0 | 0 | 0 | 47⅔ | 42 | 19 | 18 | 24 | 41 |
| Rick Reed .................. | 8–6 | 3.48 | 20 | 20 | 3 | 0 | 134⅔ | 119 | 53 | 52 | 17 | 99 |
| Turk Wendell .............. | 4–3 | 3.51 | 49 | 0 | 0 | 1 | 51⅔ | 42 | 23 | 20 | 22 | 41 |
| Kevin Appier ............. | 11–10 | 3.57 | 33 | 33 | 1 | 0 | 206⅔ | 181 | 89 | 82 | 64 | 172 |
| Armando Benitez ........ | 6–4 | 3.77 | 73 | 0 | 0 | 43 | 76⅓ | 59 | 32 | 32 | 40 | 93 |
| Rick White.................. | 4–5 | 3.88 | 55 | 0 | 0 | 2 | 69⅔ | 71 | 38 | 30 | 17 | 51 |
| John Franco ............... | 6–2 | 4.05 | 58 | 0 | 0 | 2 | 53⅓ | 55 | 25 | 24 | 19 | 50 |
| Steve Trachsel ........ | 11–13 | 4.46 | 28 | 28 | 1 | 0 | 173⅔ | 168 | 90 | 86 | 47 | 144 |
| Glendon Rusch......... | 8–12 | 4.63 | 33 | 33 | 1 | 0 | 179 | 216 | 101 | 92 | 43 | 156 |
| Bruce Chen................. | 3–2 | 4.68 | 11 | 11 | 0 | 0 | 59⅔ | 56 | 37 | 31 | 28 | 47 |
| Dickie Gonzalez.......... | 3–2 | 4.88 | 16 | 7 | 0 | 0 | 59 | 72 | 33 | 32 | 17 | 31 |

## Philadelphia Phillies

| BATTING | G | AB | R | H | 2B | 3B | HR | RBI | TB | BB | SO | SB | OBP | SLG | BA |
|---|---|---|---|---|---|---|---|---|---|---|---|---|---|---|---|
| Tomas Perez ............. | 62 | 135 | 11 | 41 | 7 | 1 | 3 | 19 | 59 | 7 | 22 | 0 | .347 | .437 | .304 |
| Marlon Anderson...... | 147 | 522 | 69 | 153 | 30 | 2 | 11 | 61 | 220 | 35 | 74 | 8 | .337 | .421 | .293 |
| Bobby Abreu............ | 162 | 588 | 118 | 170 | 48 | 4 | 31 | 110 | 319 | 106 | 137 | 36 | .393 | .543 | .289 |
| Scott Rolen.............. | 151 | 554 | 96 | 160 | 39 | 1 | 25 | 107 | 276 | 74 | 127 | 16 | .378 | .498 | .289 |
| Brian Hunter ............. | 83 | 145 | 22 | 40 | 6 | 0 | 2 | 16 | 52 | 16 | 25 | 14 | .344 | .359 | .276 |
| Jimmy Rollins ........... | 158 | 656 | 97 | 180 | 29 | 12 | 14 | 54 | 275 | 48 | 108 | 46 | .323 | .419 | .274 |
| Doug Glanville.......... | 153 | 634 | 74 | 166 | 24 | 3 | 14 | 55 | 238 | 19 | 91 | 28 | .285 | .375 | .262 |
| Pat Burrell................ | 155 | 539 | 70 | 139 | 29 | 2 | 27 | 89 | 253 | 70 | 162 | 2 | .346 | .469 | .258 |
| Travis Lee................ | 157 | 555 | 75 | 143 | 34 | 2 | 20 | 90 | 241 | 71 | 109 | 3 | .341 | .434 | .258 |
| Kevin Jordan ............ | 68 | 113 | 9 | 27 | 5 | 0 | 1 | 13 | 35 | 14 | 21 | 0 | .323 | .310 | .239 |
| Mike Lieberthal.......... | 34 | 121 | 21 | 28 | 8 | 0 | 2 | 11 | 42 | 12 | 21 | 0 | .316 | .347 | .231 |
| Johnny Estrada ......... | 89 | 298 | 26 | 68 | 15 | 0 | 8 | 37 | 107 | 16 | 32 | 0 | .273 | .359 | .228 |

| PITCHING | W–L | ERA | G | GS | CG | SV | INN | H | R | ER | BB | SO |
|---|---|---|---|---|---|---|---|---|---|---|---|---|
| Jose Mesa .................. | 3–3 | 2.34 | 71 | 0 | 0 | 42 | 69⅓ | 65 | 26 | 18 | 20 | 50 |
| Brandon Duckworth.... | 3–2 | 3.52 | 11 | 11 | 0 | 0 | 69 | 57 | 29 | 27 | 29 | 40 |
| Jose Santiago ........... | 2–4 | 3.61 | 53 | 0 | 0 | 0 | 62½ | 66 | 25 | 25 | 13 | 28 |
| Randy Wolf ............. | 10–11 | 3.70 | 28 | 25 | 4 | 0 | 163 | 150 | 74 | 67 | 51 | 152 |
| Ricky Bottalico........... | 3–4 | 3.90 | 66 | 0 | 0 | 3 | 67 | 58 | 31 | 29 | 25 | 57 |
| Nelson Figueroa ........ | 4–5 | 3.94 | 19 | 13 | 0 | 0 | 89 | 95 | 40 | 37 | 37 | 61 |
| Dave Coggin............. | 6–7 | 4.17 | 17 | 17 | 0 | 0 | 95 | 99 | 46 | 44 | 39 | 62 |
| Robert Person ........ | 15–7 | 4.19 | 33 | 33 | 3 | 0 | 208½ | 179 | 103 | 97 | 80 | 183 |
| Rheal Cormier........... | 5–6 | 4.21 | 60 | 0 | 0 | 1 | 51⅓ | 49 | 26 | 24 | 17 | 37 |
| Wayne Gomes ............ | 4–3 | 4.31 | 42 | 0 | 0 | 1 | 48 | 51 | 23 | 23 | 22 | 35 |
| Omar Daal ............... | 13–7 | 4.46 | 32 | 32 | 0 | 0 | 185⅔ | 199 | 100 | 92 | 56 | 107 |
| Bruce Chen................. | 4–5 | 5.00 | 16 | 16 | 0 | 0 | 86½ | 90 | 53 | 48 | 31 | 79 |
| Amaury Telemaco........ | 5–5 | 5.54 | 24 | 14 | 1 | 0 | 89¼ | 93 | 59 | 55 | 32 | 59 |

# National League Team-by-Team Statistical Leaders *(Cont.)*

## Pittsburgh Pirates

| BATTING | G | AB | R | H | 2B | 3B | HR | RBI | TB | BB | SO | SB | OBP | SLG | BA |
|---|---|---|---|---|---|---|---|---|---|---|---|---|---|---|---|
| Craig Wilson | 88 | 158 | 27 | 49 | 3 | 1 | 13 | 32 | 93 | 15 | 53 | 3 | .390 | .589 | .310 |
| Brian Giles | 160 | 576 | 116 | 178 | 37 | 7 | 37 | 95 | 340 | 90 | 67 | 13 | .404 | .590 | .309 |
| Aramis Ramirez | 158 | 603 | 83 | 181 | 40 | 0 | 34 | 112 | 323 | 40 | 100 | 5 | .350 | .536 | .300 |
| John Vander Wal | 97 | 313 | 39 | 87 | 22 | 3 | 11 | 50 | 148 | 42 | 84 | 7 | .361 | .473 | .278 |
| Jason Kendall | 157 | 606 | 84 | 161 | 22 | 2 | 10 | 53 | 217 | 44 | 48 | 13 | .335 | .358 | .266 |
| Rob Mackowiak | 83 | 214 | 30 | 57 | 15 | 2 | 4 | 21 | 88 | 15 | 52 | 4 | .319 | .411 | .266 |
| Abraham Nunez | 115 | 301 | 30 | 79 | 11 | 4 | 1 | 21 | 101 | 28 | 53 | 8 | .326 | .336 | .262 |
| Gary Matthews Jr. | 46 | 147 | 22 | 36 | 6 | 1 | 5 | 14 | 59 | 22 | 45 | 3 | .341 | .401 | .245 |
| Kevin Young | 142 | 449 | 53 | 104 | 33 | 0 | 14 | 65 | 179 | 42 | 119 | 15 | .310 | .399 | .232 |
| Tike Redman | 37 | 125 | 8 | 28 | 4 | 1 | 1 | 4 | 37 | 4 | 25 | 3 | .246 | .296 | .224 |
| Jack Wilson | 108 | 390 | 44 | 87 | 17 | 1 | 3 | 25 | 115 | 16 | 70 | 1 | .255 | .295 | .223 |
| Pat Meares | 87 | 270 | 27 | 57 | 11 | 1 | 4 | 25 | 82 | 10 | 45 | 0 | .244 | .304 | .211 |
| Emil Brown | 61 | 123 | 18 | 25 | 4 | 1 | 3 | 13 | 40 | 15 | 42 | 10 | .300 | .325 | .203 |
| Enrique Wilson | 46 | 129 | 7 | 24 | 3 | 0 | 1 | 8 | 30 | 3 | 23 | 0 | .203 | .233 | .186 |
| Derek Bell | 46 | 156 | 14 | 27 | 3 | 0 | 5 | 13 | 45 | 25 | 38 | 0 | .287 | .288 | .173 |

| PITCHING | W–L | ERA | G | GS | CG | SV | INN | H | R | ER | BB | SO |
|---|---|---|---|---|---|---|---|---|---|---|---|---|
| Mike Lincoln | 2–1 | 2.68 | 31 | 0 | 0 | 0 | 40⅓ | 34 | 16 | 12 | 11 | 24 |
| Josias Manzanillo | 3–2 | 3.39 | 71 | 0 | 0 | 2 | 79⅔ | 60 | 32 | 30 | 26 | 80 |
| Mike Williams | 2–4 | 3.67 | 40 | 0 | 0 | 22 | 41⅔ | 39 | 18 | 17 | 21 | 43 |
| Dave Williams | 3–7 | 3.71 | 22 | 18 | 0 | 0 | 114 | 100 | 53 | 47 | 45 | 57 |
| Todd Ritchie | 11–15 | 4.47 | 33 | 33 | 4 | 0 | 207⅓ | 211 | 118 | 103 | 52 | 124 |
| Jason Schmidt | 6–6 | 4.61 | 14 | 14 | 1 | 0 | 84 | 81 | 46 | 43 | 28 | 77 |
| Bronson Arroyo | 5–7 | 5.09 | 24 | 13 | 1 | 0 | 88⅓ | 99 | 54 | 50 | 34 | 39 |
| Jimmy Anderson | 9–17 | 5.10 | 34 | 34 | 1 | 0 | 206½ | 232 | 123 | 117 | 83 | 89 |
| Tony McKnight | 2–6 | 5.19 | 12 | 12 | 0 | 0 | 69½ | 88 | 44 | 40 | 21 | 36 |
| Joe Beimel | 7–11 | 5.23 | 42 | 15 | 0 | 0 | 115½ | 131 | 72 | 67 | 49 | 58 |
| Scott Sauerbeck | 2–2 | 5.60 | 70 | 0 | 0 | 2 | 62⅔ | 61 | 41 | 39 | 40 | 79 |
| Omar Olivares | 6–9 | 6.55 | 45 | 12 | 1 | 1 | 110 | 123 | 87 | 80 | 42 | 69 |

## St. Louis Cardinals

| BATTING | G | AB | R | H | 2B | 3B | HR | RBI | TB | BB | SO | SB | OBP | SLG | BA |
|---|---|---|---|---|---|---|---|---|---|---|---|---|---|---|---|
| Albert Pujols | 161 | 590 | 112 | 194 | 47 | 4 | 37 | 130 | 360 | 69 | 93 | 1 | .403 | .610 | .329 |
| J.D. Drew | 109 | 375 | 80 | 121 | 18 | 5 | 27 | 73 | 230 | 57 | 75 | 13 | .414 | .613 | .323 |
| Placido Polanco | 144 | 564 | 87 | 173 | 26 | 4 | 3 | 38 | 216 | 25 | 43 | 12 | .342 | .383 | .307 |
| Jim Edmonds | 150 | 500 | 95 | 152 | 38 | 1 | 30 | 110 | 282 | 93 | 136 | 5 | .410 | .564 | .304 |
| Fernando Vina | 154 | 631 | 95 | 191 | 30 | 8 | 9 | 56 | 264 | 32 | 35 | 17 | .357 | .418 | .303 |
| Kerry Robinson | 114 | 186 | 34 | 53 | 6 | 1 | 1 | 15 | 64 | 12 | 20 | 11 | .330 | .344 | .285 |
| Craig Paquette | 123 | 340 | 47 | 96 | 17 | 0 | 15 | 64 | 158 | 18 | 67 | 3 | .326 | .465 | .282 |
| Eli Marrero | 86 | 203 | 37 | 54 | 11 | 3 | 6 | 23 | 89 | 15 | 36 | 6 | .312 | .438 | .266 |
| Edgar Renteria | 141 | 493 | 54 | 128 | 19 | 3 | 10 | 57 | 183 | 39 | 73 | 17 | .314 | .371 | .260 |
| Ray Lankford | 91 | 264 | 38 | 62 | 18 | 3 | 15 | 39 | 131 | 44 | 105 | 4 | .345 | .496 | .235 |
| Mike Matheny | 121 | 381 | 40 | 83 | 12 | 0 | 7 | 42 | 116 | 28 | 76 | 0 | .276 | .304 | .218 |
| Bobby Bonilla | 93 | 174 | 17 | 37 | 7 | 0 | 5 | 21 | 59 | 23 | 53 | 1 | .308 | .339 | .213 |
| Mark McGwire | 97 | 299 | 48 | 56 | 4 | 0 | 29 | 64 | 147 | 56 | 118 | 0 | .316 | .492 | .187 |

| PITCHING | W–L | ERA | G | GS | CG | SV | INN | H | R | ER | BB | SO |
|---|---|---|---|---|---|---|---|---|---|---|---|---|
| Steve Kline | 3–3 | 1.80 | 89 | 0 | 0 | 9 | 75 | 53 | 16 | 15 | 29 | 54 |
| Woody Williams | 7–1 | 2.28 | 11 | 11 | 3 | 0 | 75 | 54 | 22 | 19 | 19 | 52 |
| Darryl Kile | 16–11 | 3.09 | 34 | 34 | 2 | 0 | 227⅓ | 228 | 83 | 78 | 66 | 179 |
| Matt Morris | 22–8 | 3.16 | 34 | 34 | 2 | 0 | 216½ | 218 | 86 | 76 | 54 | 185 |
| Mike Matthews | 3–4 | 3.24 | 51 | 10 | 0 | 1 | 89 | 74 | 32 | 32 | 33 | 72 |
| Dave Veres | 3–2 | 3.70 | 71 | 0 | 0 | 15 | 65⅔ | 57 | 29 | 27 | 28 | 61 |
| Bud Smith | 6–3 | 3.83 | 16 | 14 | 1 | 0 | 84⅔ | 79 | 40 | 36 | 24 | 59 |
| Gene Stechschulte | 1–5 | 3.86 | 67 | 0 | 0 | 6 | 70 | 71 | 35 | 30 | 30 | 51 |
| Mike Timlin | 4–5 | 4.09 | 67 | 0 | 0 | 3 | 72⅔ | 78 | 35 | 33 | 19 | 47 |
| Dustin Hermanson | 14–13 | 4.45 | 33 | 33 | 0 | 0 | 192½ | 195 | 106 | 95 | 73 | 123 |
| Mike James | 1–2 | 5.21 | 40 | 0 | 0 | 0 | 38 | 43 | 24 | 22 | 17 | 26 |
| Andy Benes | 7–7 | 7.38 | 27 | 19 | 0 | 0 | 107½ | 122 | 92 | 88 | 61 | 78 |

## National League Team-by-Team Statistical Leaders *(Cont.)*

### San Diego Padres

| BATTING | G | AB | R | H | 2B | 3B | HR | RBI | TB | BB | SO | SB | OBP | SLG | BA |
|---|---|---|---|---|---|---|---|---|---|---|---|---|---|---|---|
| Tony Gwynn | 71 | 102 | 5 | 33 | 9 | 1 | 1 | 17 | 47 | 10 | 9 | 1 | .384 | .461 | .324 |
| Phil Nevin | 149 | 546 | 97 | 167 | 31 | 0 | 41 | 126 | 321 | 71 | 147 | 4 | .388 | .588 | .306 |
| Mark Kotsay | 119 | 406 | 67 | 118 | 29 | 1 | 10 | 58 | 179 | 48 | 58 | 13 | .366 | .441 | .291 |
| Ray Lankford | 40 | 125 | 20 | 36 | 10 | 1 | 4 | 19 | 60 | 18 | 40 | 6 | .386 | .480 | .288 |
| Ryan Klesko | 146 | 538 | 105 | 154 | 34 | 6 | 30 | 113 | 290 | 88 | 89 | 23 | .384 | .539 | .286 |
| Mike Darr | 105 | 289 | 36 | 80 | 13 | 1 | 2 | 34 | 101 | 39 | 72 | 6 | .363 | .349 | .277 |
| D'Angelo Jimenez | 86 | 308 | 45 | 85 | 19 | 0 | 3 | 33 | 113 | 39 | 68 | 2 | .355 | .367 | .276 |
| Wiki Gonzalez | 65 | 160 | 16 | 44 | 6 | 0 | 8 | 27 | 74 | 11 | 28 | 2 | .335 | .463 | .275 |
| Bubba Trammell | 142 | 490 | 66 | 128 | 20 | 3 | 25 | 92 | 229 | 48 | 78 | 2 | .330 | .467 | .261 |
| Dave Magadan | 91 | 128 | 12 | 32 | 7 | 0 | 1 | 12 | 42 | 12 | 20 | 0 | .317 | .328 | .250 |
| Damian Jackson | 122 | 440 | 67 | 106 | 21 | 6 | 4 | 38 | 151 | 44 | 128 | 23 | .316 | .343 | .241 |
| Ben Davis | 138 | 448 | 56 | 107 | 20 | 0 | 11 | 57 | 160 | 66 | 112 | 4 | .337 | .357 | .239 |
| Rickey Henderson | 123 | 379 | 70 | 86 | 17 | 3 | 8 | 42 | 133 | 81 | 84 | 25 | .366 | .351 | .227 |
| Alex Arias | 70 | 137 | 19 | 31 | 9 | 0 | 2 | 12 | 46 | 17 | 22 | 1 | .312 | .336 | .226 |
| Cesar Crespo | 55 | 153 | 27 | 32 | 6 | 0 | 4 | 12 | 50 | 25 | 50 | 6 | .320 | .327 | .209 |
| Donaldo Mendez | 46 | 118 | 11 | 18 | 2 | 1 | 1 | 5 | 25 | 5 | 37 | 1 | .206 | .212 | .153 |

| PITCHING | W–L | ERA | G | GS | CG | SV | INN | H | R | ER | BB | SO |
|---|---|---|---|---|---|---|---|---|---|---|---|---|
| Jose A. Nunez | 4–1 | 3.31 | 56 | 0 | 0 | 0 | 51⅔ | 48 | 20 | 19 | 20 | 49 |
| Trevor Hoffman | 3–4 | 3.43 | 62 | 0 | 0 | 43 | 60⅓ | 48 | 25 | 23 | 21 | 63 |
| Brian Lawrence | 5–5 | 3.45 | 27 | 15 | 1 | 0 | 114⅔ | 107 | 53 | 44 | 34 | 84 |
| David Lee | 1–0 | 3.70 | 41 | 0 | 0 | 0 | 48⅔ | 52 | 20 | 20 | 27 | 42 |
| Brian Tollberg | 10–4 | 4.30 | 19 | 19 | 0 | 0 | 117⅓ | 133 | 58 | 56 | 25 | 71 |
| Adam Eaton | 8–5 | 4.32 | 17 | 17 | 2 | 0 | 116⅔ | 108 | 61 | 56 | 40 | 109 |
| Kevin Jarvis | 12–11 | 4.79 | 32 | 32 | 1 | 0 | 193⅓ | 189 | 107 | 103 | 49 | 133 |
| Woody Williams | 8–8 | 4.97 | 23 | 23 | 0 | 0 | 145 | 170 | 88 | 80 | 37 | 102 |
| Bobby Jones | 8–19 | 5.12 | 33 | 33 | 1 | 0 | 195 | 250 | 137 | 111 | 38 | 113 |
| Rodney Myers | 1–2 | 5.32 | 37 | 0 | 0 | 1 | 47⅓ | 53 | 31 | 28 | 20 | 29 |
| Wascar Serrano | 3–3 | 6.56 | 20 | 5 | 0 | 0 | 46⅔ | 60 | 37 | 34 | 21 | 39 |

### San Francisco Giants

| BATTING | G | AB | R | H | 2B | 3B | HR | RBI | TB | BB | SO | SB | OBP | SLG | BA |
|---|---|---|---|---|---|---|---|---|---|---|---|---|---|---|---|
| Barry Bonds | 153 | 476 | 129 | 156 | 32 | 2 | 73 | 137 | 411 | 177 | 93 | 13 | .515 | .863 | .328 |
| Rich Aurilia | 156 | 636 | 114 | 206 | 37 | 5 | 37 | 97 | 364 | 47 | 83 | 1 | .369 | .572 | .324 |
| Jeff Kent | 159 | 607 | 84 | 181 | 49 | 6 | 22 | 106 | 308 | 65 | 96 | 7 | .369 | .507 | .298 |
| Andres Galarraga | 49 | 156 | 17 | 45 | 12 | 1 | 7 | 35 | 80 | 13 | 49 | 0 | .351 | .513 | .288 |
| Shawon Dunston | 88 | 186 | 26 | 52 | 10 | 3 | 9 | 25 | 95 | 2 | 32 | 3 | .293 | .511 | .280 |
| Marvin Benard | 129 | 392 | 70 | 104 | 19 | 2 | 15 | 44 | 172 | 29 | 66 | 10 | .320 | .439 | .265 |
| Benito Santiago | 133 | 477 | 39 | 125 | 25 | 4 | 6 | 45 | 176 | 23 | 78 | 5 | .295 | .369 | .262 |
| Armando Rios | 93 | 316 | 38 | 82 | 17 | 3 | 14 | 49 | 147 | 34 | 73 | 3 | .330 | .465 | .259 |
| Russ Davis | 53 | 167 | 16 | 43 | 13 | 1 | 7 | 17 | 79 | 17 | 49 | 1 | .326 | .473 | .257 |
| Ramon E. Martinez | 128 | 391 | 48 | 99 | 18 | 3 | 5 | 37 | 138 | 38 | 52 | 1 | .323 | .353 | .253 |
| John Vander Wal | 49 | 139 | 19 | 35 | 6 | 1 | 3 | 20 | 52 | 26 | 38 | 1 | .370 | .374 | .252 |
| J.T. Snow | 101 | 285 | 43 | 70 | 12 | 1 | 8 | 34 | 108 | 55 | 81 | 0 | .371 | .379 | .246 |
| Calvin Murray | 106 | 326 | 54 | 80 | 14 | 2 | 6 | 25 | 116 | 32 | 57 | 8 | .319 | .356 | .245 |
| Edwards Guzman | 61 | 115 | 8 | 28 | 6 | 0 | 3 | 7 | 43 | 5 | 16 | 0 | .273 | .374 | .243 |
| Pedro Feliz | 94 | 220 | 23 | 50 | 9 | 1 | 7 | 22 | 82 | 10 | 50 | 2 | .264 | .373 | .227 |
| Eric Davis | 74 | 156 | 17 | 32 | 7 | 3 | 4 | 22 | 57 | 13 | 38 | 1 | .269 | .365 | .205 |

| PITCHING | W–L | ERA | G | GS | CG | SV | INN | H | R | ER | BB | SO |
|---|---|---|---|---|---|---|---|---|---|---|---|---|
| Felix Rodriguez | 9–1 | 1.68 | 80 | 0 | 0 | 0 | 80⅓ | 53 | 16 | 15 | 27 | 91 |
| Robb Nen | 4–5 | 3.01 | 79 | 0 | 0 | 45 | 77⅔ | 58 | 28 | 26 | 22 | 93 |
| Russ Ortiz | 17–9 | 3.29 | 33 | 33 | 1 | 0 | 218⅔ | 187 | 90 | 80 | 91 | 169 |
| Jason Schmidt | 7–1 | 3.39 | 11 | 11 | 0 | 0 | 66⅓ | 57 | 29 | 25 | 33 | 65 |
| Tim Worrell | 2–5 | 3.45 | 73 | 0 | 0 | 0 | 78⅓ | 71 | 33 | 30 | 33 | 63 |
| Shawn Estes | 9–8 | 4.02 | 27 | 27 | 0 | 0 | 159 | 151 | 78 | 71 | 77 | 109 |
| Ryan Jensen | 1–2 | 4.25 | 10 | 7 | 0 | 0 | 42⅓ | 44 | 21 | 20 | 25 | 26 |
| Kirk Rueter | 14–12 | 4.42 | 34 | 34 | 0 | 0 | 195⅓ | 213 | 105 | 96 | 66 | 83 |
| Aaron Fultz | 3–1 | 4.56 | 66 | 0 | 0 | 1 | 71 | 70 | 40 | 36 | 21 | 67 |
| Livan Hernandez | 13–15 | 5.24 | 34 | 34 | 2 | 0 | 226⅔ | 266 | 143 | 132 | 85 | 138 |
| Mark Gardner | 5–5 | 5.40 | 23 | 15 | 0 | 0 | 91⅔ | 93 | 57 | 56 | 34 | 53 |

# American League Team-by-Team Statistical Leaders

## Anaheim Angels

| BATTING | G | AB | R | H | 2B | 3B | HR | RBI | TB | BB | SO | SB | OBP | SLG | BA |
|---|---|---|---|---|---|---|---|---|---|---|---|---|---|---|---|
| Shawn Wooten | 79 | 221 | 24 | 69 | 8 | 1 | 8 | 32 | 103 | 5 | 42 | 2 | .332 | .466 | .312 |
| Benji Gil | 104 | 260 | 33 | 77 | 15 | 4 | 8 | 39 | 124 | 14 | 57 | 3 | .330 | .477 | .296 |
| Garret Anderson | 161 | 672 | 83 | 194 | 39 | 2 | 28 | 123 | 321 | 27 | 100 | 13 | .314 | .478 | .289 |
| David Eckstein | 153 | 582 | 82 | 166 | 26 | 2 | 4 | 41 | 208 | 43 | 60 | 29 | .355 | .357 | .285 |
| Scott Spiezio | 139 | 457 | 57 | 124 | 29 | 4 | 13 | 54 | 200 | 34 | 65 | 5 | .326 | .438 | .271 |
| Adam Kennedy | 137 | 478 | 48 | 129 | 25 | 3 | 6 | 40 | 178 | 27 | 71 | 12 | .318 | .372 | .270 |
| Ben Molina | 96 | 325 | 31 | 85 | 11 | 0 | 6 | 40 | 114 | 16 | 51 | 0 | .309 | .351 | .262 |
| Darin Erstad | 157 | 631 | 89 | 163 | 35 | 1 | 9 | 63 | 227 | 62 | 113 | 24 | .331 | .360 | .258 |
| Troy Glaus | 161 | 588 | 100 | 147 | 38 | 2 | 41 | 108 | 312 | 107 | 158 | 10 | .367 | .531 | .250 |
| Wally Joyner | 53 | 148 | 14 | 36 | 5 | 1 | 3 | 14 | 52 | 13 | 18 | 1 | .304 | .351 | .243 |
| Orlando Palmeiro | 104 | 230 | 29 | 56 | 10 | 1 | 2 | 23 | 74 | 25 | 24 | 6 | .319 | .322 | .243 |
| Tim Salmon | 137 | 475 | 63 | 108 | 21 | 1 | 17 | 49 | 182 | 96 | 121 | 9 | .365 | .383 | .227 |
| Jorge Fabregas | 53 | 148 | 9 | 33 | 4 | 2 | 2 | 16 | 47 | 3 | 15 | 0 | .235 | .318 | .223 |

| PITCHING | W–L | ERA | G | GS | CG | SV | INN | H | R | ER | BB | SO |
|---|---|---|---|---|---|---|---|---|---|---|---|---|
| Al Levine | 8–10 | 2.38 | 64 | 1 | 0 | 2 | 75⅔ | 71 | 25 | 20 | 28 | 40 |
| Troy Percival | 4–2 | 2.65 | 57 | 0 | 0 | 39 | 57⅓ | 39 | 19 | 17 | 18 | 71 |
| Ben Weber | 6–2 | 3.42 | 56 | 0 | 0 | 0 | 68⅓ | 66 | 28 | 26 | 31 | 40 |
| Jarrod Washburn | 11–10 | 3.77 | 30 | 30 | 1 | 0 | 193⅓ | 196 | 89 | 81 | 54 | 126 |
| Shigetoshi Hasegawa | 5–6 | 4.04 | 46 | 0 | 0 | 0 | 55⅔ | 52 | 28 | 25 | 20 | 41 |
| Lou Pote | 2–0 | 4.15 | 44 | 1 | 0 | 2 | 86⅔ | 88 | 41 | 40 | 32 | 66 |
| Ramon Ortiz | 13–11 | 4.36 | 32 | 32 | 2 | 0 | 208⅓ | 223 | 114 | 101 | 76 | 135 |
| Matt Wise | 1–4 | 4.38 | 11 | 9 | 0 | 0 | 49⅓ | 47 | 27 | 24 | 18 | 50 |
| Ismael Valdes | 9–13 | 4.45 | 27 | 27 | 1 | 0 | 163⅔ | 177 | 82 | 81 | 50 | 100 |
| Pat Rapp | 5–12 | 4.76 | 31 | 28 | 1 | 0 | 170 | 169 | 96 | 90 | 71 | 82 |
| Mike Holtz | 1–2 | 4.86 | 63 | 0 | 0 | 0 | 37 | 40 | 24 | 20 | 15 | 38 |
| Scott Schoeneweis | 10–11 | 5.08 | 32 | 32 | 1 | 0 | 205⅓ | 227 | 122 | 116 | 77 | 104 |

## Baltimore Orioles

| BATTING | G | AB | R | H | 2B | 3B | HR | RBI | TB | BB | SO | SB | OBP | SLG | BA |
|---|---|---|---|---|---|---|---|---|---|---|---|---|---|---|---|
| Jeff Conine | 139 | 524 | 75 | 163 | 23 | 2 | 14 | 97 | 232 | 64 | 75 | 12 | .386 | .443 | .311 |
| David Segui | 82 | 292 | 48 | 88 | 18 | 1 | 10 | 46 | 138 | 49 | 61 | 1 | .406 | .473 | .301 |
| Mike Kinkade | 61 | 160 | 19 | 44 | 5 | 0 | 4 | 16 | 61 | 14 | 31 | 2 | .345 | .381 | .275 |
| Tony Batista | 84 | 308 | 41 | 82 | 16 | 5 | 12 | 42 | 144 | 19 | 47 | 5 | .305 | .468 | .266 |
| Chris Richard | 136 | 483 | 74 | 128 | 31 | 3 | 15 | 61 | 210 | 45 | 100 | 11 | .335 | .435 | .265 |
| Brian Roberts | 75 | 273 | 42 | 69 | 12 | 3 | 2 | 17 | 93 | 13 | 36 | 12 | .284 | .341 | .253 |
| Melvin Mora | 128 | 436 | 49 | 109 | 28 | 0 | 7 | 48 | 158 | 41 | 91 | 11 | .329 | .362 | .250 |
| Mike Bordick | 58 | 229 | 32 | 57 | 13 | 0 | 7 | 30 | 91 | 17 | 36 | 9 | .314 | .397 | .249 |
| Fernando Lunar | 64 | 167 | 8 | 41 | 7 | 0 | 0 | 16 | 48 | 7 | 32 | 0 | .287 | .287 | .246 |
| Cal Ripken Jr. | 128 | 477 | 43 | 114 | 16 | 0 | 14 | 68 | 172 | 26 | 63 | 0 | .276 | .361 | .239 |
| Jay Gibbons | 73 | 225 | 27 | 53 | 10 | 0 | 15 | 36 | 108 | 17 | 39 | 0 | .301 | .480 | .236 |
| Jerry Hairston | 159 | 532 | 63 | 124 | 25 | 5 | 8 | 47 | 183 | 44 | 73 | 29 | .305 | .344 | .233 |
| Larry Bigbie | 47 | 131 | 15 | 30 | 6 | 0 | 2 | 11 | 42 | 17 | 42 | 4 | .318 | .321 | .229 |
| Brook Fordyce | 95 | 292 | 30 | 61 | 18 | 0 | 5 | 19 | 94 | 21 | 56 | 1 | .268 | .322 | .209 |
| Brady Anderson | 131 | 430 | 50 | 87 | 12 | 3 | 8 | 45 | 129 | 60 | 77 | 12 | .311 | .300 | .202 |
| Delino DeShields | 58 | 188 | 29 | 37 | 8 | 2 | 3 | 21 | 58 | 31 | 42 | 11 | .312 | .309 | .197 |

| PITCHING | W–L | ERA | G | GS | CG | SV | INN | H | R | ER | BB | SO |
|---|---|---|---|---|---|---|---|---|---|---|---|---|
| Mike Trombley | 3–4 | 3.46 | 50 | 0 | 0 | 6 | 54⅔ | 38 | 23 | 21 | 27 | 45 |
| Pat Hentgen | 2–3 | 3.47 | 9 | 9 | 1 | 0 | 62⅓ | 51 | 25 | 24 | 19 | 33 |
| Buddy Groom | 1–4 | 3.55 | 70 | 0 | 0 | 11 | 66 | 64 | 28 | 26 | 9 | 54 |
| Jason Johnson | 10–12 | 4.09 | 32 | 32 | 2 | 0 | 196 | 194 | 109 | 89 | 77 | 114 |
| Calvin Maduro | 5–6 | 4.23 | 22 | 12 | 0 | 0 | 93⅔ | 83 | 44 | 44 | 36 | 51 |
| B.J. Ryan | 2–4 | 4.25 | 61 | 0 | 0 | 2 | 53 | 47 | 31 | 25 | 30 | 54 |
| Josh Towers | 8–10 | 4.49 | 24 | 20 | 1 | 0 | 140⅓ | 165 | 74 | 70 | 16 | 58 |
| Willis Roberts | 9–10 | 4.91 | 46 | 18 | 1 | 6 | 132 | 142 | 75 | 72 | 55 | 95 |
| Sidney Ponson | 5–10 | 4.94 | 23 | 23 | 3 | 0 | 138⅓ | 161 | 83 | 76 | 37 | 84 |
| Jose Mercedes | 8–17 | 5.82 | 33 | 31 | 2 | 0 | 184 | 219 | 125 | 119 | 63 | 123 |
| Ryan Kohlmeier | 1–2 | 7.30 | 34 | 1 | 0 | 6 | 40⅔ | 48 | 33 | 33 | 19 | 29 |

### Boston Red Sox

| BATTING | G | AB | R | H | 2B | 3B | HR | RBI | TB | BB | SO | SB | OBP | SLG | BA |
|---|---|---|---|---|---|---|---|---|---|---|---|---|---|---|---|
| Manny Ramirez | 142 | 529 | 93 | 162 | 33 | 2 | 41 | 125 | 322 | 81 | 147 | 0 | .405 | .609 | .306 |
| Jason Varitek | 51 | 174 | 19 | 51 | 11 | 1 | 7 | 25 | 85 | 21 | 35 | 0 | .371 | .489 | .293 |
| Dante Bichette | 107 | 391 | 45 | 112 | 30 | 1 | 12 | 49 | 180 | 20 | 76 | 2 | .325 | .460 | .286 |
| Darren Lewis | 81 | 164 | 18 | 46 | 9 | 1 | 1 | 12 | 60 | 8 | 25 | 5 | .326 | .366 | .280 |
| Trot Nixon | 148 | 535 | 100 | 150 | 31 | 4 | 27 | 88 | 270 | 79 | 113 | 7 | .376 | .505 | .280 |
| Chris Stynes | 96 | 361 | 52 | 101 | 19 | 2 | 8 | 33 | 148 | 20 | 56 | 4 | .322 | .410 | .280 |
| Doug Mirabelli | 54 | 141 | 16 | 38 | 8 | 0 | 9 | 26 | 73 | 17 | 36 | 0 | .360 | .518 | .270 |
| Lou Merloni | 52 | 146 | 21 | 39 | 10 | 0 | 3 | 13 | 58 | 6 | 31 | 2 | .306 | .397 | .267 |
| Jose Offerman | 128 | 524 | 76 | 140 | 23 | 3 | 9 | 49 | 196 | 61 | 97 | 5 | .342 | .374 | .267 |
| Brian Daubach | 122 | 407 | 54 | 107 | 28 | 3 | 22 | 71 | 207 | 53 | 108 | 1 | .350 | .509 | .263 |
| Shea Hillenbrand | 139 | 468 | 52 | 123 | 20 | 2 | 12 | 49 | 183 | 13 | 61 | 3 | .291 | .391 | .263 |
| Carl Everett | 102 | 409 | 61 | 105 | 24 | 4 | 14 | 58 | 179 | 27 | 104 | 9 | .323 | .438 | .257 |
| Mike Lansing | 106 | 352 | 45 | 88 | 23 | 0 | 8 | 34 | 135 | 22 | 50 | 3 | .294 | .384 | .250 |
| Scott Hatteberg | 94 | 278 | 34 | 68 | 19 | 0 | 3 | 25 | 96 | 33 | 26 | 1 | .332 | .345 | .245 |
| Troy O'Leary | 104 | 341 | 50 | 82 | 16 | 6 | 13 | 50 | 149 | 25 | 73 | 1 | .298 | .437 | .240 |

| PITCHING | W–L | ERA | G | GS | CG | SV | INN | H | R | ER | BB | SO |
|---|---|---|---|---|---|---|---|---|---|---|---|---|
| Ugueth Urbina | 0–1 | 2.25 | 19 | 0 | 0 | 9 | 20 | 16 | 5 | 5 | 3 | 32 |
| Pedro Martinez | 7–3 | 2.39 | 18 | 18 | 1 | 0 | 116⅔ | 84 | 33 | 31 | 25 | 163 |
| Rolando Arrojo | 5–4 | 3.48 | 41 | 9 | 0 | 5 | 103⅓ | 88 | 44 | 40 | 35 | 78 |
| Derek Lowe | 5–10 | 3.53 | 67 | 3 | 0 | 24 | 91⅔ | 103 | 39 | 36 | 29 | 82 |
| Rod Beck | 6–4 | 3.90 | 68 | 0 | 0 | 6 | 80⅔ | 77 | 42 | 35 | 28 | 63 |
| Rich Garces | 6–1 | 3.90 | 62 | 0 | 0 | 1 | 67 | 55 | 32 | 29 | 25 | 51 |
| Tim Wakefield | 9–12 | 3.90 | 45 | 17 | 0 | 3 | 168⅔ | 156 | 84 | 73 | 73 | 148 |
| Frank Castillo | 10–9 | 4.21 | 26 | 26 | 0 | 0 | 136⅔ | 138 | 72 | 64 | 35 | 89 |
| David Cone | 9–7 | 4.31 | 25 | 25 | 0 | 0 | 135⅓ | 148 | 74 | 65 | 57 | 115 |
| Hideo Nomo | 13–10 | 4.50 | 33 | 33 | 2 | 0 | 198 | 171 | 105 | 99 | 96 | 220 |
| Toma Ohka | 2–5 | 6.19 | 12 | 11 | 0 | 0 | 52⅓ | 69 | 40 | 36 | 19 | 37 |

### Chicago White Sox

| BATTING | G | AB | R | H | 2B | 3B | HR | RBI | TB | BB | SO | SB | OBP | SLG | BA |
|---|---|---|---|---|---|---|---|---|---|---|---|---|---|---|---|
| Magglio Ordonez | 160 | 593 | 97 | 181 | 40 | 1 | 31 | 113 | 316 | 70 | 70 | 25 | .382 | .533 | .305 |
| Tony Graffanino | 74 | 145 | 23 | 44 | 9 | 0 | 2 | 15 | 59 | 16 | 29 | 4 | .370 | .407 | .303 |
| Chris Singleton | 140 | 392 | 57 | 117 | 21 | 5 | 7 | 45 | 169 | 20 | 61 | 12 | .331 | .431 | .298 |
| Aaron Rowand | 63 | 123 | 21 | 36 | 5 | 0 | 4 | 20 | 53 | 15 | 28 | 5 | .385 | .431 | .293 |
| Paul Konerko | 156 | 582 | 92 | 164 | 35 | 0 | 32 | 99 | 295 | 54 | 89 | 1 | .349 | .507 | .282 |
| Carlos Lee | 150 | 558 | 75 | 150 | 33 | 3 | 24 | 84 | 261 | 38 | 85 | 17 | .321 | .468 | .269 |
| Ray Durham | 152 | 611 | 104 | 163 | 42 | 10 | 20 | 65 | 285 | 64 | 110 | 23 | .337 | .466 | .267 |
| Josh Paul | 57 | 139 | 20 | 37 | 11 | 0 | 3 | 18 | 57 | 13 | 25 | 6 | .327 | .410 | .266 |
| Royce Clayton | 135 | 433 | 62 | 114 | 21 | 4 | 9 | 60 | 170 | 33 | 72 | 10 | .315 | .393 | .263 |
| Jose Canseco | 76 | 256 | 46 | 66 | 8 | 0 | 16 | 49 | 122 | 45 | 75 | 2 | .366 | .477 | .258 |
| Jose Valentin | 124 | 438 | 74 | 113 | 22 | 2 | 28 | 68 | 223 | 50 | 114 | 9 | .336 | .509 | .258 |
| Jeff Liefer | 83 | 254 | 36 | 65 | 13 | 0 | 18 | 39 | 132 | 20 | 69 | 0 | .313 | .520 | .256 |
| Herbert Perry | 93 | 285 | 38 | 73 | 21 | 1 | 7 | 32 | 117 | 23 | 55 | 2 | .326 | .411 | .256 |
| Mark Johnson | 61 | 173 | 21 | 43 | 6 | 1 | 5 | 18 | 66 | 23 | 31 | 2 | .338 | .382 | .249 |
| Sandy Alomar | 70 | 220 | 17 | 54 | 8 | 1 | 4 | 21 | 76 | 12 | 17 | 1 | .288 | .345 | .245 |

| PITCHING | W–L | ERA | G | GS | CG | SV | INN | H | R | ER | BB | SO |
|---|---|---|---|---|---|---|---|---|---|---|---|---|
| Keith Foulke | 4–9 | 2.33 | 72 | 0 | 0 | 42 | 81 | 57 | 21 | 21 | 22 | 75 |
| Mark Buehrle | 16–8 | 3.29 | 32 | 32 | 4 | 0 | 221⅓ | 188 | 89 | 81 | 48 | 126 |
| Sean Lowe | 9–4 | 3.61 | 45 | 11 | 0 | 3 | 127 | 123 | 55 | 51 | 32 | 71 |
| Jon Garland | 6–7 | 3.69 | 35 | 16 | 0 | 1 | 117 | 123 | 59 | 48 | 55 | 61 |
| David Wells | 5–7 | 4.47 | 16 | 16 | 1 | 0 | 100⅔ | 120 | 55 | 50 | 21 | 59 |
| James Baldwin | 7–5 | 4.61 | 17 | 16 | 2 | 0 | 95⅔ | 109 | 56 | 49 | 38 | 42 |
| Bob Howry | 4–5 | 4.69 | 69 | 0 | 0 | 5 | 78⅔ | 85 | 41 | 41 | 30 | 64 |
| Kip Wells | 10–11 | 4.79 | 40 | 20 | 0 | 0 | 133⅓ | 145 | 80 | 71 | 61 | 99 |
| Gary Glover | 5–5 | 4.93 | 46 | 11 | 0 | 0 | 100⅓ | 98 | 61 | 55 | 32 | 63 |
| Rocky Biddle | 7–8 | 5.39 | 30 | 21 | 0 | 0 | 128⅔ | 137 | 87 | 77 | 52 | 85 |
| Danny Wright | 5–3 | 5.70 | 13 | 12 | 0 | 0 | 66⅓ | 78 | 45 | 42 | 39 | 36 |

## American League Team-by-Team Statistical Leaders *(Cont.)*

### Cleveland Indians

| BATTING | G | AB | R | H | 2B | 3B | HR | RBI | TB | BB | SO | SB | OBP | SLG | BA |
|---|---|---|---|---|---|---|---|---|---|---|---|---|---|---|---|
| Roberto Alomar | 157 | 575 | 113 | 193 | 34 | 12 | 20 | 100 | 311 | 80 | 71 | 30 | .415 | .541 | .336 |
| Juan Gonzalez | 140 | 532 | 97 | 173 | 34 | 1 | 35 | 140 | 314 | 41 | 94 | 1 | .370 | .590 | .325 |
| Marty Cordova | 122 | 409 | 61 | 123 | 20 | 2 | 20 | 69 | 207 | 23 | 81 | 0 | .348 | .506 | .301 |
| Jim Thome | 156 | 526 | 101 | 153 | 26 | 1 | 49 | 124 | 328 | 111 | 185 | 0 | .416 | .624 | .291 |
| Ellis Burks | 124 | 439 | 83 | 123 | 29 | 1 | 28 | 74 | 238 | 62 | 85 | 5 | .369 | .542 | .280 |
| Einar Diaz | 134 | 437 | 54 | 121 | 34 | 1 | 4 | 56 | 169 | 17 | 44 | 1 | .328 | .387 | .277 |
| Travis Fryman | 98 | 334 | 34 | 88 | 15 | 0 | 3 | 38 | 112 | 30 | 63 | 1 | .327 | .335 | .263 |
| Jolbert Cabrera | 141 | 287 | 50 | 75 | 16 | 3 | 1 | 38 | 100 | 16 | 41 | 10 | .312 | .348 | .261 |
| Kenny Lofton | 133 | 517 | 91 | 135 | 21 | 4 | 14 | 66 | 206 | 47 | 69 | 16 | .322 | .398 | .261 |
| Omar Vizquel | 155 | 611 | 84 | 156 | 26 | 8 | 2 | 50 | 204 | 61 | 72 | 13 | .323 | .334 | .255 |
| Wil Cordero | 89 | 268 | 30 | 67 | 11 | 1 | 4 | 21 | 92 | 22 | 50 | 0 | .313 | .343 | .250 |
| Eddie Taubensee | 52 | 116 | 16 | 29 | 2 | 1 | 3 | 11 | 42 | 10 | 19 | 0 | .315 | .362 | .250 |
| Russell Branyan | 113 | 315 | 48 | 73 | 16 | 2 | 20 | 54 | 153 | 38 | 132 | 1 | .316 | .486 | .232 |

| PITCHING | W–L | ERA | G | GS | CG | SV | INN | H | R | ER | BB | SO |
|---|---|---|---|---|---|---|---|---|---|---|---|---|
| Steve Karsay | 0–1 | 1.25 | 31 | 0 | 0 | 1 | 43⅓ | 29 | 6 | 6 | 8 | 44 |
| Bob Wickman | 5–0 | 2.39 | 70 | 0 | 0 | 32 | 67⅔ | 61 | 18 | 18 | 14 | 66 |
| Danys Baez | 5–3 | 2.50 | 43 | 0 | 0 | 0 | 50⅓ | 34 | 22 | 14 | 20 | 52 |
| Paul Shuey | 5–3 | 2.82 | 47 | 0 | 0 | 2 | 54⅓ | 53 | 25 | 17 | 26 | 70 |
| Ricardo Rincon | 2–1 | 2.83 | 67 | 0 | 0 | 2 | 54 | 44 | 18 | 17 | 21 | 50 |
| Bartolo Colon | 14–12 | 4.09 | 34 | 34 | 1 | 0 | 222⅓ | 220 | 106 | 101 | 90 | 201 |
| C.C. Sabathia | 17–5 | 4.39 | 33 | 33 | 0 | 0 | 180⅓ | 149 | 93 | 88 | 95 | 171 |
| Steve Woodard | 3–3 | 5.20 | 29 | 10 | 0 | 0 | 97 | 129 | 59 | 56 | 17 | 52 |
| Chuck Finley | 8–7 | 5.54 | 22 | 22 | 1 | 0 | 113⅔ | 131 | 78 | 70 | 35 | 96 |
| Jake Westbrook | 4–4 | 23 | 6 | 0 | 0 | 0 | 64⅔ | 79 | 43 | 42 | 22 | 48 |
| Dave Burba | 10–10 | 6.21 | 32 | 27 | 1 | 0 | 150⅔ | 188 | 112 | 104 | 54 | 118 |
| Charles Nagy | 5–6 | 6.40 | 15 | 13 | 0 | 0 | 70⅓ | 102 | 53 | 50 | 20 | 29 |

### Detroit Tigers

| BATTING | G | AB | R | H | 2B | 3B | HR | RBI | TB | BB | SO | SB | OBP | SLG | BA |
|---|---|---|---|---|---|---|---|---|---|---|---|---|---|---|---|
| Randall Simon | 81 | 256 | 28 | 78 | 14 | 2 | 6 | 37 | 114 | 15 | 28 | 0 | .341 | .445 | .305 |
| Roger Cedeno | 131 | 523 | 79 | 153 | 14 | 11 | 6 | 48 | 207 | 36 | 83 | 55 | .337 | .396 | .293 |
| Tony Clark | 126 | 428 | 67 | 123 | 29 | 3 | 16 | 75 | 206 | 62 | 108 | 0 | .374 | .481 | .287 |
| Shane Halter | 136 | 450 | 53 | 128 | 32 | 7 | 12 | 65 | 210 | 37 | 100 | 3 | .344 | .467 | .284 |
| Bobby Higginson | 147 | 541 | 84 | 150 | 28 | 6 | 17 | 71 | 241 | 80 | 65 | 20 | .367 | .445 | .277 |
| Robert Fick | 124 | 401 | 62 | 109 | 21 | 2 | 19 | 61 | 191 | 39 | 62 | 0 | .339 | .476 | .272 |
| Jose Macias | 137 | 488 | 62 | 131 | 24 | 6 | 8 | 51 | 191 | 32 | 54 | 21 | .316 | .391 | .268 |
| Deivi Cruz | 110 | 414 | 39 | 106 | 28 | 1 | 7 | 52 | 157 | 17 | 46 | 4 | .291 | .379 | .256 |
| Damian Easley | 154 | 585 | 77 | 146 | 27 | 7 | 11 | 65 | 220 | 52 | 90 | 10 | .323 | .376 | .250 |
| Juan Encarnacion | 120 | 417 | 52 | 101 | 19 | 7 | 12 | 52 | 170 | 25 | 93 | 9 | .292 | .408 | .242 |
| Dean Palmer | 57 | 216 | 34 | 48 | 11 | 0 | 11 | 40 | 92 | 27 | 59 | 4 | .317 | .426 | .222 |
| Wendell Magee | 90 | 207 | 26 | 44 | 11 | 4 | 5 | 17 | 78 | 23 | 44 | 3 | .293 | .377 | .213 |
| Ryan Jackson | 79 | 118 | 19 | 25 | 4 | 2 | 2 | 11 | 39 | 5 | 26 | 3 | .250 | .331 | .212 |
| Brandon Inge | 79 | 189 | 13 | 34 | 11 | 0 | 0 | 15 | 45 | 9 | 41 | 1 | .215 | .238 | .180 |

| PITCHING | W–L | ERA | G | GS | CG | SV | INN | H | R | ER | BB | SO |
|---|---|---|---|---|---|---|---|---|---|---|---|---|
| Danny Patterson | 5–4 | 3.06 | 60 | 0 | 0 | 1 | 64⅔ | 64 | 24 | 22 | 12 | 27 |
| Victor Santos | 2–2 | 3.30 | 33 | 7 | 0 | 0 | 76⅓ | 62 | 33 | 28 | 49 | 52 |
| Steve Sparks | 14–9 | 3.65 | 35 | 33 | 8 | 0 | 232 | 244 | 110 | 94 | 64 | 116 |
| Jeff Weaver | 13–16 | 4.08 | 33 | 33 | 5 | 0 | 229⅓ | 235 | 116 | 104 | 68 | 152 |
| Todd Jones | 4–5 | 4.62 | 45 | 0 | 0 | 11 | 48⅔ | 60 | 31 | 25 | 22 | 39 |
| Jose Lima | 5–10 | 4.71 | 18 | 18 | 2 | 0 | 112⅔ | 120 | 66 | 59 | 22 | 43 |
| Matt Anderson | 3–1 | 4.82 | 62 | 0 | 0 | 22 | 56 | 56 | 33 | 30 | 18 | 52 |
| C.J. Nitkowski | 0–3 | 5.56 | 56 | 0 | 0 | 0 | 45⅓ | 51 | 30 | 28 | 31 | 38 |
| Chris Holt | 7–9 | 5.77 | 30 | 22 | 1 | 0 | 151⅓ | 197 | 102 | 97 | 57 | 80 |
| Adam Pettyjohn | 1–6 | 5.82 | 16 | 9 | 0 | 0 | 65 | 81 | 48 | 42 | 21 | 40 |
| Heath Murray | 1–7 | 6.54 | 40 | 4 | 0 | 0 | 63⅓ | 82 | 48 | 46 | 40 | 42 |
| Dave Mlicki | 4–8 | 7.33 | 15 | 15 | 0 | 0 | 81 | 118 | 69 | 66 | 41 | 48 |
| Nate Cornejo | 4– 4 | 7.38 | 10 | 10 | 0 | 0 | 42⅔ | 63 | 38 | 35 | 28 | 22 |

## American League Team-by-Team Statistical Leaders *(Cont.)*

### Kansas City Royals

| BATTING | G | AB | R | H | 2B | 3B | HR | RBI | TB | BB | SO | SB | OBP | SLG | BA |
|---|---|---|---|---|---|---|---|---|---|---|---|---|---|---|---|
| Gregg Zaun | 39 | 125 | 15 | 40 | 9 | 0 | 6 | 18 | 67 | 12 | 16 | 1 | .377 | .536 | .320 |
| Carlos Beltran | 155 | 617 | 106 | 189 | 32 | 12 | 24 | 101 | 317 | 52 | 120 | 31 | .362 | .514 | .306 |
| Mike Sweeney | 147 | 559 | 97 | 170 | 46 | 0 | 29 | 9 | 303 | 64 | 64 | 10 | .374 | .542 | .304 |
| Rey Sanchez | 100 | 390 | 46 | 118 | 14 | 5 | 0 | 28 | 142 | 11 | 34 | 9 | .322 | .364 | .303 |
| Raul Ibanez | 104 | 279 | 44 | 78 | 11 | 5 | 13 | 54 | 138 | 32 | 51 | 0 | .353 | .495 | .280 |
| Luis Alicea | 113 | 387 | 44 | 106 | 16 | 4 | 4 | 32 | 142 | 23 | 56 | 8 | .320 | .367 | .274 |
| Jermaine Dye | 97 | 367 | 50 | 100 | 14 | 0 | 13 | 47 | 153 | 30 | 68 | 7 | .333 | .417 | .272 |
| Mark Quinn | 118 | 453 | 57 | 122 | 31 | 2 | 17 | 60 | 208 | 12 | 69 | 9 | .298 | .459 | .269 |
| Joe Randa | 151 | 581 | 59 | 147 | 34 | 2 | 13 | 83 | 224 | 42 | 80 | 3 | .307 | .386 | .253 |
| Dave McCarty | 98 | 200 | 26 | 50 | 10 | 0 | 7 | 26 | 81 | 24 | 45 | 0 | .328 | .405 | .250 |
| Hector Ortiz | 56 | 154 | 12 | 38 | 6 | 1 | 0 | 11 | 46 | 9 | 24 | 1 | .293 | .299 | .247 |
| Dee Brown | 106 | 380 | 39 | 93 | 19 | 0 | 7 | 40 | 133 | 22 | 81 | 5 | .286 | .350 | .245 |
| Brent Mayne | 51 | 166 | 13 | 40 | 4 | 1 | 2 | 20 | 52 | 10 | 17 | 1 | .283 | .313 | .241 |
| Neifi Perez | 49 | 199 | 18 | 48 | 7 | 1 | 1 | 12 | 60 | 10 | 19 | 3 | .277 | .302 | .241 |
| Carlos Febles | 79 | 292 | 45 | 69 | 9 | 2 | 8 | 25 | 106 | 22 | 58 | 5 | .291 | .363 | .236 |
| A.J. Hinch | 45 | 121 | 10 | 19 | 3 | 0 | 6 | 15 | 40 | 8 | 26 | 1 | .226 | .331 | .157 |

| PITCHING | W–L | ERA | G | GS | CG | SV | INN | H | R | ER | BB | SO |
|---|---|---|---|---|---|---|---|---|---|---|---|---|
| Jason Grimsley | 1–5 | 3.02 | 73 | 0 | 0 | 0 | 80⅓ | 71 | 32 | 27 | 28 | 61 |
| Cory Bailey | 1–1 | 3.48 | 53 | 0 | 0 | 0 | 67⅓ | 57 | 28 | 26 | 33 | 61 |
| Paul Byrd | 6–6 | 4.05 | 16 | 15 | 1 | 0 | 93⅓ | 110 | 45 | 42 | 22 | 49 |
| Roberto Hernandez | 5–6 | 4.12 | 63 | 0 | 0 | 28 | 67⅔ | 69 | 34 | 31 | 26 | 46 |
| Jeff Suppan | 10–14 | 4.37 | 34 | 34 | 1 | 0 | 218⅓ | 227 | 120 | 106 | 74 | 120 |
| Blake Stein | 7–8 | 4.74 | 36 | 15 | 0 | 1 | 131 | 112 | 73 | 69 | 79 | 113 |
| Chad Durbin | 9–16 | 4.93 | 29 | 29 | 2 | 0 | 179 | 201 | 109 | 98 | 58 | 95 |
| Kris Wilson | 6–5 | 5.19 | 29 | 15 | 0 | 1 | 109⅓ | 132 | 78 | 63 | 32 | 67 |
| Chris George | 4–8 | 5.59 | 13 | 13 | 1 | 0 | 74 | 83 | 48 | 46 | 18 | 32 |
| Dan Reichert | 8–8 | 5.63 | 27 | 19 | 0 | 0 | 123 | 131 | 83 | 77 | 67 | 77 |
| Doug Henry | 2–2 | 6.07 | 53 | 0 | 0 | 0 | 75⅔ | 75 | 53 | 51 | 45 | 57 |

### Minnesota Twins

| BATTING | G | AB | R | H | 2B | 3B | HR | RBI | TB | BB | SO | SB | OBP | SLG | BA |
|---|---|---|---|---|---|---|---|---|---|---|---|---|---|---|---|
| Doug Mientkiewicz | 151 | 543 | 77 | 166 | 39 | 1 | 15 | 74 | 252 | 67 | 92 | 2 | .387 | .464 | .306 |
| Cristian Guzman | 118 | 493 | 80 | 149 | 28 | 14 | 10 | 51 | 235 | 21 | 78 | 25 | .337 | .477 | .302 |
| Matt Lawton | 103 | 376 | 71 | 110 | 25 | 0 | 10 | 51 | 165 | 63 | 46 | 19 | .396 | .439 | .293 |
| A.J. Pierzynski | 114 | 381 | 51 | 110 | 33 | 2 | 7 | 55 | 168 | 16 | 57 | 1 | .322 | .441 | .289 |
| Jacque Jones | 149 | 475 | 57 | 131 | 25 | 0 | 14 | 49 | 198 | 39 | 92 | 12 | .335 | .417 | .276 |
| Corey Koskie | 153 | 562 | 100 | 155 | 37 | 2 | 26 | 103 | 274 | 68 | 118 | 27 | .362 | .488 | .276 |
| Brian Buchanan | 69 | 197 | 28 | 54 | 12 | 0 | 10 | 32 | 96 | 19 | 58 | 1 | .342 | .487 | .274 |
| Luis Rivas | 153 | 563 | 70 | 150 | 21 | 6 | 7 | 47 | 204 | 40 | 99 | 31 | .319 | .362 | .266 |
| Chad Allen | 57 | 175 | 20 | 46 | 13 | 2 | 4 | 20 | 75 | 19 | 37 | 1 | .333 | .429 | .263 |
| Torii Hunter | 148 | 564 | 82 | 147 | 32 | 5 | 27 | 9 | 270 | 29 | 125 | 9 | .306 | .479 | .261 |
| Denny Hocking | 112 | 327 | 34 | 82 | 16 | 2 | 3 | 25 | 111 | 29 | 67 | 6 | .315 | .339 | .251 |
| Bobby Kielty | 37 | 104 | 8 | 26 | 8 | 0 | 2 | 14 | 40 | 8 | 25 | 3 | .297 | .385 | .250 |
| David Ortiz | 89 | 303 | 46 | 71 | 17 | 1 | 18 | 48 | 144 | 40 | 68 | 1 | .324 | .475 | .234 |
| Tom Prince | 64 | 196 | 19 | 43 | 4 | 1 | 7 | 23 | 70 | 12 | 39 | 3 | .284 | .357 | .219 |

| PITCHING | W–L | ERA | G | GS | CG | SV | INN | H | R | ER | BB | SO |
|---|---|---|---|---|---|---|---|---|---|---|---|---|
| Joe Mays | 17–13 | 3.16 | 34 | 34 | 4 | 0 | 233⅔ | 205 | 87 | 82 | 64 | 123 |
| Eddie Guardado | 7–1 | 3.51 | 67 | 0 | 0 | 12 | 66⅔ | 47 | 27 | 26 | 23 | 67 |
| Jack Cressend | 3–2 | 3.67 | 44 | 0 | 0 | 0 | 56⅓ | 50 | 24 | 23 | 16 | 40 |
| Brad Radke | 15–11 | 3.94 | 33 | 33 | 6 | 0 | 226 | 235 | 105 | 99 | 26 | 137 |
| Mark Redman | 2–4 | 4.22 | 9 | 9 | 0 | 0 | 49 | 57 | 26 | 23 | 19 | 29 |
| Eric Milton | 15–7 | 4.32 | 35 | 34 | 2 | 0 | 220⅔ | 222 | 109 | 106 | 61 | 157 |
| Hector Carrasco | 4–3 | 4.64 | 56 | 0 | 0 | 1 | 73⅔ | 77 | 40 | 38 | 30 | 70 |
| Travis Miller | 1–4 | 4.81 | 45 | 0 | 0 | 0 | 48⅔ | 54 | 30 | 26 | 20 | 30 |
| Bob Wells | 8–5 | 5.11 | 65 | 0 | 0 | 2 | 68⅔ | 72 | 39 | 39 | 18 | 49 |
| Rick Reed | 4–6 | 5.19 | 12 | 12 | 0 | 0 | 67⅔ | 92 | 45 | 39 | 14 | 43 |
| Kyle Lohse | 4–7 | 5.68 | 19 | 16 | 0 | 0 | 90⅓ | 102 | 60 | 57 | 29 | 64 |
| LaTroy Hawkins | 1–5 | 5.96 | 62 | 0 | 0 | 28 | 51⅓ | 59 | 34 | 34 | 39 | 36 |
| J.C. Romero | 1–4 | 6.23 | 14 | 11 | 0 | 0 | 65 | 71 | 48 | 45 | 24 | 39 |

# American League Team-by-Team Statistical Leaders *(Cont.)*

## New York Yankees

| BATTING | G | AB | R | H | 2B | 3B | HR | RBI | TB | BB | SO | SB | OBP | SLG | BA |
|---|---|---|---|---|---|---|---|---|---|---|---|---|---|---|---|
| Derek Jeter | 150 | 614 | 110 | 191 | 35 | 3 | 21 | 74 | 295 | 56 | 99 | 27 | .377 | .480 | .311 |
| Bernie Williams | 146 | 540 | 102 | 166 | 38 | 0 | 26 | 94 | 282 | 78 | 67 | 11 | .395 | .522 | .307 |
| Scott Brosius | 120 | 428 | 57 | 123 | 25 | 2 | 13 | 49 | 191 | 34 | 83 | 3 | .343 | .446 | .287 |
| Tino Martinez | 154 | 589 | 89 | 165 | 24 | 2 | 34 | 113 | 295 | 42 | 89 | 1 | .329 | .501 | .280 |
| Jorge Posada | 138 | 484 | 59 | 134 | 28 | 1 | 22 | 95 | 230 | 62 | 132 | 2 | .363 | .475 | .277 |
| Alfonso Soriano | 158 | 574 | 77 | 154 | 34 | 3 | 18 | 73 | 248 | 29 | 125 | 43 | .304 | .432 | .268 |
| Paul O'Neill | 137 | 510 | 77 | 136 | 33 | 1 | 21 | 70 | 234 | 48 | 59 | 22 | .330 | .459 | .267 |
| Shane Spencer | 81 | 283 | 40 | 73 | 14 | 2 | 10 | 46 | 121 | 21 | 58 | 4 | .315 | .428 | .258 |
| Chuck Knoblauch | 137 | 521 | 66 | 130 | 20 | 3 | 9 | 44 | 183 | 58 | 73 | 38 | .339 | .351 | .250 |
| David Justice | 111 | 381 | 58 | 92 | 16 | 1 | 18 | 51 | 164 | 54 | 83 | 1 | .333 | .430 | .241 |

| PITCHING | W–L | ERA | G | GS | CG | SV | INN | H | R | ER | BB | SO |
|---|---|---|---|---|---|---|---|---|---|---|---|---|
| Mariano Rivera | 4–6 | 2.34 | 71 | 0 | 0 | 50 | 80⅔ | 61 | 24 | 21 | 12 | 83 |
| Mike Stanton | 9–4 | 2.58 | 76 | 0 | 0 | 0 | 80⅓ | 80 | 25 | 23 | 29 | 78 |
| Mike Mussina | 17–11 | 3.15 | 34 | 34 | 4 | 0 | 228⅔ | 202 | 87 | 80 | 42 | 214 |
| Randy Choate | 3–1 | 3.35 | 37 | 0 | 0 | 0 | 48⅓ | 34 | 21 | 18 | 27 | 35 |
| Roger Clemens | 20–3 | 3.51 | 33 | 33 | 0 | 0 | 220⅓ | 205 | 94 | 86 | 72 | 213 |
| Ramiro Mendoza | 8–4 | 3.75 | 56 | 2 | 0 | 6 | 100⅔ | 89 | 44 | 42 | 23 | 70 |
| Andy Pettitte | 15–10 | 3.99 | 31 | 31 | 2 | 0 | 200⅔ | 224 | 103 | 89 | 41 | 164 |
| Jay Witasick | 3–0 | 4.69 | 32 | 0 | 0 | 0 | 40⅓ | 47 | 27 | 21 | 18 | 53 |
| Orlando Hernandez | 4–7 | 4.85 | 17 | 16 | 0 | 0 | 94⅔ | 90 | 51 | 51 | 42 | 77 |
| Ted Lilly | 5–6 | 5.37 | 26 | 21 | 0 | 0 | 120⅔ | 126 | 81 | 72 | 51 | 112 |
| Randy Keisler | 1–2 | 6.22 | 10 | 10 | 0 | 0 | 50⅔ | 52 | 36 | 35 | 34 | 36 |
| Sterling Hitchcock | 4–4 | 6.49 | 10 | 9 | 1 | 0 | 51⅓ | 67 | 37 | 37 | 18 | 28 |

## Oakland Athletics

| BATTING | G | AB | R | H | 2B | 3B | HR | RBI | TB | BB | SO | SB | OBP | SLG | BA |
|---|---|---|---|---|---|---|---|---|---|---|---|---|---|---|---|
| Jason Giambi | 154 | 520 | 109 | 178 | 47 | 2 | 38 | 120 | 343 | 129 | 83 | 2 | .477 | .660 | .342 |
| Jermaine Dye | 61 | 232 | 41 | 69 | 17 | 1 | 13 | 59 | 127 | 27 | 44 | 2 | .366 | .547 | .297 |
| Eric Chavez | 151 | 552 | 91 | 159 | 43 | 0 | 32 | 114 | 298 | 41 | 99 | 8 | .338 | .540 | .288 |
| Jeremy Giambi | 124 | 371 | 64 | 105 | 26 | 0 | 12 | 57 | 167 | 63 | 83 | 0 | .391 | .450 | .283 |
| Terrence Long | 162 | 629 | 90 | 178 | 37 | 4 | 12 | 85 | 259 | 52 | 103 | 9 | .335 | .412 | .283 |
| Miguel Tejada | 162 | 622 | 107 | 166 | 31 | 3 | 31 | 113 | 296 | 43 | 89 | 11 | .326 | .476 | .267 |
| Johnny Damon | 155 | 644 | 108 | 165 | 34 | 4 | 9 | 49 | 234 | 61 | 70 | 27 | .324 | .363 | .256 |
| Ramon Hernandez | 136 | 453 | 55 | 115 | 25 | 0 | 15 | 60 | 185 | 37 | 68 | 1 | .316 | .408 | .254 |
| Frank Menechino | 139 | 471 | 82 | 114 | 22 | 2 | 12 | 60 | 176 | 79 | 97 | 2 | .369 | .374 | .242 |
| Olmedo Saenz | 106 | 305 | 33 | 67 | 21 | 1 | 9 | 32 | 117 | 19 | 64 | 0 | .291 | .384 | .220 |

| PITCHING | W–L | ERA | G | GS | CG | SV | INN | H | R | ER | BB | SO |
|---|---|---|---|---|---|---|---|---|---|---|---|---|
| Jason Isringhausen | 4–3 | 2.65 | 65 | 0 | 0 | 34 | 71⅓ | 54 | 24 | 21 | 23 | 74 |
| Mike Magnante | 3–1 | 2.77 | 65 | 0 | 0 | 0 | 55⅓ | 50 | 23 | 17 | 13 | 23 |
| Jeff Tam | 2–4 | 3.01 | 70 | 0 | 0 | 3 | 74⅔ | 68 | 27 | 25 | 29 | 44 |
| Tim Hudson | 18– 9 | 3.37 | 35 | 35 | 3 | 0 | 235 | 216 | 100 | 88 | 71 | 181 |
| Erik Hiljus | 5–0 | 3.41 | 16 | 11 | 0 | 0 | 66 | 70 | 29 | 25 | 21 | 67 |
| Jim Mecir | 2–8 | 3.43 | 54 | 0 | 0 | 3 | 63 | 54 | 25 | 24 | 26 | 61 |
| Mark Mulder | 21– 8 | 3.45 | 34 | 34 | 6 | 0 | 229⅓ | 214 | 92 | 88 | 51 | 153 |
| Barry Zito | 17–8 | 3.49 | 35 | 35 | 3 | 0 | 214⅓ | 184 | 92 | 83 | 80 | 205 |
| Cory Lidle | 13–6 | 3.59 | 29 | 29 | 1 | 0 | 188 | 170 | 84 | 75 | 47 | 118 |
| Mark Guthrie | 6–2 | 4.47 | 54 | 0 | 0 | 1 | 52⅓ | 49 | 29 | 26 | 20 | 52 |
| Gil Heredia | 7–8 | 5.58 | 24 | 18 | 0 | 0 | 109⅔ | 144 | 75 | 68 | 29 | 48 |

# American League Team-by-Team Statistical Leaders *(Cont.)*

## Seattle Mariners

| BATTING | G | AB | R | H | 2B | 3B | HR | RBI | TB | BB | SO | SB | OBP | SLG | BA |
|---|---|---|---|---|---|---|---|---|---|---|---|---|---|---|---|
| Ichiro Suzuki | 157 | 692 | 127 | 242 | 34 | 8 | 8 | 69 | 316 | 30 | 53 | 56 | .381 | .457 | .350 |
| Bret Boone | 158 | 623 | 118 | 206 | 37 | 3 | 37 | 141 | 360 | 40 | 110 | 5 | .372 | .578 | .331 |
| Edgar Martinez | 132 | 470 | 80 | 144 | 40 | 1 | 23 | 116 | 255 | 93 | 90 | 4 | .423 | .543 | .306 |
| John Olerud | 159 | 572 | 91 | 173 | 32 | 1 | 21 | 95 | 270 | 94 | 70 | 3 | .401 | .472 | .302 |
| Stan Javier | 89 | 281 | 44 | 82 | 14 | 1 | 4 | 33 | 110 | 36 | 47 | 11 | .375 | .391 | .292 |
| Mark McLemore | 125 | 409 | 78 | 117 | 16 | 9 | 5 | 57 | 166 | 69 | 84 | 39 | .384 | .406 | .286 |
| Mike Cameron | 150 | 540 | 99 | 144 | 30 | 5 | 25 | 110 | 259 | 69 | 155 | 34 | .353 | .480 | .267 |
| Dan Wilson | 123 | 377 | 44 | 100 | 20 | 1 | 10 | 42 | 152 | 20 | 69 | 3 | .305 | .403 | .265 |
| David Bell | 135 | 470 | 62 | 122 | 28 | 0 | 15 | 64 | 195 | 28 | 59 | 2 | .303 | .415 | .260 |
| Carlos Guillen | 140 | 456 | 72 | 118 | 21 | 4 | 5 | 53 | 162 | 53 | 89 | 4 | .333 | .355 | .259 |
| Al Martin | 101 | 283 | 41 | 68 | 15 | 2 | 7 | 42 | 108 | 37 | 59 | 9 | .330 | .382 | .240 |
| Tom Lampkin | 79 | 204 | 28 | 46 | 10 | 0 | 5 | 22 | 71 | 18 | 41 | 1 | .309 | .348 | .225 |

| PITCHING | W–L | ERA | G | GS | CG | SV | INN | H | R | ER | BB | SO |
|---|---|---|---|---|---|---|---|---|---|---|---|---|
| Arthur Rhodes | 8–0 | 1.72 | 72 | 0 | 0 | 3 | 68 | 46 | 14 | 13 | 12 | 83 |
| Joel Pineiro | 6–2 | 2.03 | 17 | 11 | 0 | 0 | 75⅓ | 50 | 24 | 17 | 21 | 56 |
| Jeff Nelson | 4–3 | 2.76 | 69 | 0 | 0 | 4 | 65⅓ | 30 | 21 | 20 | 44 | 88 |
| Norm Charlton | 4–2 | 3.02 | 44 | 0 | 0 | 1 | 47⅔ | 36 | 19 | 16 | 11 | 48 |
| Freddy Garcia | 18–6 | 3.05 | 34 | 34 | 4 | 0 | 238⅔ | 199 | 88 | 81 | 69 | 163 |
| Kazuhiro Sasaki | 0–4 | 3.24 | 69 | 0 | 0 | 45 | 66⅔ | 48 | 24 | 24 | 11 | 62 |
| Jamie Moyer | 20–6 | 3.43 | 33 | 33 | 1 | 0 | 209⅔ | 187 | 84 | 80 | 44 | 119 |
| Ryan Franklin | 5–1 | 3.56 | 38 | 0 | 0 | 0 | 78⅓ | 76 | 32 | 31 | 24 | 60 |
| Aaron Sele | 15–5 | 3.60 | 34 | 3 | 2 | 0 | 215 | 216 | 93 | 86 | 51 | 114 |
| Paul Abbott | 17–4 | 4.25 | 28 | 27 | 1 | 0 | 163 | 145 | 79 | 77 | 87 | 118 |
| Jose Paniagua | 4–3 | 4.36 | 60 | 0 | 0 | 3 | 66 | 59 | 35 | 32 | 38 | 46 |
| John Halama | 10–7 | 4.73 | 31 | 17 | 0 | 0 | 110⅓ | 132 | 69 | 58 | 26 | 50 |

## Tampa Bay Devil Rays

| BATTING | G | AB | R | H | 2B | 3B | HR | RBI | TB | BB | SO | SB | OBP | SLG | BA |
|---|---|---|---|---|---|---|---|---|---|---|---|---|---|---|---|
| Fred McGriff | 97 | 343 | 40 | 109 | 18 | 0 | 19 | 61 | 184 | 40 | 69 | 1 | .387 | .536 | .318 |
| Chris Gomez | 58 | 189 | 31 | 57 | 16 | 0 | 8 | 35 | 97 | 8 | 24 | 3 | .332 | .513 | .302 |
| Toby Hall | 49 | 188 | 28 | 56 | 16 | 0 | 4 | 30 | 84 | 4 | 16 | 2 | .321 | .447 | .298 |
| Russ Johnson | 85 | 248 | 32 | 73 | 19 | 2 | 4 | 33 | 108 | 34 | 57 | 2 | .380 | .435 | .294 |
| Jason Tyner | 105 | 396 | 51 | 111 | 8 | 5 | 0 | 21 | 129 | 15 | 42 | 31 | .311 | .326 | .280 |
| Jose Guillen | 41 | 135 | 14 | 37 | 5 | 0 | 3 | 11 | 51 | 6 | 26 | 2 | .317 | .378 | .274 |
| Randy Winn | 128 | 429 | 54 | 117 | 25 | 6 | 6 | 50 | 172 | 38 | 81 | 12 | .339 | .401 | .273 |
| Brent Abernathy | 79 | 304 | 43 | 82 | 17 | 1 | 5 | 34 | 116 | 27 | 35 | 8 | .328 | .382 | .270 |
| Ben Grieve | 154 | 542 | 72 | 143 | 30 | 2 | 11 | 72 | 210 | 87 | 159 | 7 | .372 | .387 | .264 |
| Damian Rolls | 81 | 237 | 33 | 62 | 11 | 1 | 2 | 12 | 81 | 10 | 47 | 12 | .291 | .342 | .262 |
| Steve Cox | 108 | 342 | 37 | 88 | 22 | 0 | 12 | 51 | 146 | 24 | 75 | 2 | .323 | .427 | .257 |
| Aubrey Huff | 111 | 411 | 42 | 102 | 25 | 1 | 8 | 45 | 153 | 23 | 72 | 1 | .288 | .372 | .248 |
| Felix Martinez | 77 | 219 | 24 | 54 | 13 | 1 | 1 | 14 | 72 | 10 | 46 | 6 | .294 | .329 | .247 |
| John Flaherty | 78 | 248 | 20 | 59 | 17 | 1 | 4 | 29 | 90 | 10 | 33 | 1 | .269 | .363 | .238 |
| Greg Vaughn | 136 | 485 | 74 | 113 | 25 | 0 | 24 | 82 | 210 | 71 | 130 | 11 | .333 | .433 | .233 |
| Gerald Williams | 62 | 232 | 30 | 48 | 17 | 0 | 4 | 17 | 77 | 13 | 42 | 10 | .261 | .332 | .207 |

| PITCHING | W–L | ERA | G | GS | CG | SV | INN | H | R | ER | BB | SO |
|---|---|---|---|---|---|---|---|---|---|---|---|---|
| Victor Zambrano | 6–2 | 3.16 | 36 | 0 | 0 | 2 | 51⅓ | 38 | 21 | 18 | 18 | 58 |
| Travis Phelps | 2–2 | 3.48 | 49 | 0 | 0 | 5 | 62 | 53 | 30 | 24 | 24 | 54 |
| Esteban Yan | 4–6 | 3.90 | 54 | 0 | 0 | 22 | 62⅓ | 64 | 34 | 27 | 11 | 64 |
| Doug Creek | 2–5 | 4.31 | 66 | 0 | 0 | 0 | 62⅔ | 51 | 34 | 30 | 49 | 66 |
| Tanyon Sturtze | 11–12 | 4.42 | 39 | 27 | 0 | 1 | 195⅓ | 200 | 98 | 96 | 79 | 110 |
| Joe Kennedy | 7–8 | 4.44 | 20 | 20 | 0 | 0 | 117⅔ | 122 | 63 | 58 | 34 | 78 |
| Nick Bierbrodt | 3–4 | 4.55 | 11 | 11 | 0 | 0 | 61⅓ | 71 | 38 | 31 | 27 | 56 |
| Paul Wilson | 8–9 | 4.88 | 37 | 24 | 0 | 0 | 151⅓ | 165 | 94 | 82 | 52 | 119 |
| Albie Lopez | 5–12 | 5.34 | 20 | 20 | 1 | 0 | 124⅔ | 152 | 87 | 74 | 51 | 67 |
| Bryan Rekar | 3–13 | 5.89 | 25 | 25 | 0 | 0 | 140⅔ | 167 | 104 | 92 | 45 | 87 |
| Ryan Rupe | 5–12 | 6.59 | 28 | 26 | 0 | 0 | 143⅓ | 161 | 111 | 105 | 48 | 123 |

## Texas Rangers

| BATTING | G | AB | R | H | 2B | 3B | HR | RBI | TB | BB | SO | SB | OBP | SLG | BA |
|---|---|---|---|---|---|---|---|---|---|---|---|---|---|---|---|
| Frank Catalanotto | 133 | 463 | 77 | 153 | 31 | 5 | 11 | 54 | 227 | 39 | 55 | 15 | .391 | .490 | .330 |
| Alex Rodriguez | 162 | 632 | 133 | 201 | 34 | 1 | 52 | 135 | 393 | 75 | 131 | 18 | .399 | .622 | .318 |
| Ivan Rodriguez | 111 | 442 | 70 | 136 | 24 | 2 | 25 | 65 | 239 | 23 | 73 | 10 | .347 | .541 | .308 |
| Mike Lamb | 76 | 284 | 42 | 87 | 18 | 0 | 4 | 35 | 117 | 14 | 27 | 2 | .348 | .412 | .306 |
| Randy Velarde | 78 | 296 | 46 | 88 | 16 | 2 | 9 | 31 | 135 | 29 | 73 | 4 | .369 | .456 | .297 |
| Ruben Sierra | 94 | 344 | 55 | 100 | 22 | 1 | 23 | 67 | 193 | 19 | 52 | 2 | .322 | .561 | .291 |
| Bill Haselman | 47 | 130 | 12 | 37 | 6 | 0 | 3 | 25 | 52 | 8 | 27 | 0 | .331 | .400 | .285 |
| Rusty Greer | 62 | 245 | 38 | 67 | 23 | 0 | 7 | 29 | 111 | 27 | 32 | 1 | .342 | .453 | .273 |
| Rafael Palmeiro | 160 | 600 | 98 | 164 | 33 | 0 | 47 | 123 | 338 | 101 | 90 | 1 | .381 | .563 | .273 |
| Gabe Kapler | 134 | 483 | 77 | 129 | 29 | 1 | 17 | 72 | 211 | 61 | 70 | 23 | .348 | .437 | .267 |
| Chad Curtis | 38 | 115 | 24 | 29 | 3 | 0 | 3 | 10 | 41 | 14 | 21 | 7 | .338 | .357 | .252 |
| Mike Young | 106 | 386 | 57 | 96 | 18 | 4 | 11 | 49 | 155 | 26 | 91 | 3 | .298 | .402 | .249 |
| Ruben Mateo | 40 | 129 | 18 | 32 | 5 | 2 | 1 | 13 | 44 | 9 | 28 | 1 | .322 | .341 | .248 |
| Andres Galarraga | 72 | 243 | 33 | 57 | 16 | 0 | 10 | 34 | 103 | 18 | 68 | 1 | .310 | .424 | .235 |
| Ken Caminiti | 54 | 185 | 24 | 43 | 8 | 1 | 9 | 25 | 80 | 22 | 41 | 0 | .318 | .432 | .232 |
| Ricky Ledee | 78 | 242 | 33 | 56 | 21 | 1 | 2 | 36 | 85 | 23 | 58 | 3 | .303 | .351 | .231 |

| PITCHING | W–L | ERA | G | GS | CG | SV | INN | H | R | ER | BB | SO |
|---|---|---|---|---|---|---|---|---|---|---|---|---|
| Jeff Zimmerman | 4–4 | 2.40 | 66 | 0 | 0 | 28 | 71⅓ | 48 | 19 | 19 | 16 | 72 |
| Juan Moreno | 3–3 | 3.92 | 45 | 0 | 0 | 0 | 41⅓ | 22 | 21 | 18 | 28 | 36 |
| Doug Davis | 11–10 | 4.45 | 30 | 30 | 1 | 0 | 186 | 220 | 103 | 92 | 69 | 115 |
| Mike Venafro | 5–5 | 4.80 | 70 | 0 | 0 | 4 | 60 | 54 | 35 | 32 | 28 | 29 |
| Rick Helling | 12–11 | 5.17 | 34 | 34 | 2 | 0 | 215⅔ | 256 | 134 | 124 | 63 | 154 |
| Pat Mahomes | 7–6 | 5.70 | 56 | 4 | 0 | 0 | 107⅓ | 115 | 71 | 68 | 55 | 61 |
| Darren Oliver | 11–11 | 6.02 | 28 | 28 | 1 | 0 | 154 | 189 | 109 | 103 | 65 | 104 |
| Kenny Rogers | 5–7 | 6.19 | 20 | 20 | 0 | 0 | 120⅔ | 150 | 88 | 83 | 49 | 74 |
| Mark Petkovsek | 1–2 | 6.69 | 55 | 0 | 0 | 0 | 76⅔ | 103 | 61 | 57 | 28 | 42 |
| Aaron Myette | 4–5 | 7.14 | 19 | 15 | 0 | 0 | 80⅔ | 94 | 65 | 64 | 37 | 67 |
| Rob Bell | 5–5 | 7.18 | 18 | 18 | 0 | 0 | 105⅓ | 130 | 87 | 84 | 47 | 64 |

## Toronto Blue Jays

| BATTING | G | AB | R | H | 2B | 3B | HR | RBI | TB | BB | SO | SB | OBP | SLG | BA |
|---|---|---|---|---|---|---|---|---|---|---|---|---|---|---|---|
| Shannon Stewart | 155 | 640 | 103 | 202 | 44 | 7 | 12 | 60 | 296 | 46 | 72 | 27 | .371 | .463 | .316 |
| Homer Bush | 78 | 271 | 32 | 83 | 11 | 1 | 3 | 27 | 105 | 8 | 50 | 13 | .336 | .387 | .306 |
| Carlos Delgado | 162 | 574 | 102 | 160 | 31 | 1 | 39 | 102 | 310 | 111 | 136 | 3 | .408 | .540 | .279 |
| Jose Cruz | 146 | 577 | 92 | 158 | 38 | 4 | 34 | 88 | 306 | 45 | 138 | 32 | .326 | .530 | .274 |
| Brad Fullmer | 146 | 522 | 71 | 143 | 31 | 2 | 18 | 83 | 232 | 38 | 88 | 5 | .326 | .444 | .274 |
| Cesar Izturis | 46 | 134 | 19 | 36 | 6 | 2 | 2 | 9 | 52 | 2 | 15 | 8 | .279 | .388 | .269 |
| Felipe Lopez | 49 | 177 | 21 | 46 | 5 | 4 | 5 | 23 | 74 | 12 | 39 | 4 | .304 | .418 | .260 |
| Alex Gonzalez | 154 | 636 | 79 | 161 | 25 | 5 | 17 | 76 | 247 | 43 | 149 | 18 | .303 | .388 | .253 |
| Raul Mondesi | 149 | 572 | 88 | 144 | 26 | 4 | 27 | 84 | 259 | 73 | 128 | 30 | .342 | .453 | .252 |
| Jeff Frye | 74 | 175 | 24 | 43 | 6 | 1 | 2 | 15 | 57 | 12 | 18 | 2 | .305 | .326 | .246 |
| Luis Lopez | 41 | 119 | 10 | 29 | 4 | 0 | 3 | 10 | 42 | 8 | 16 | 0 | .291 | .353 | .244 |
| Darrin Fletcher | 134 | 416 | 36 | 94 | 20 | 0 | 11 | 56 | 147 | 24 | 43 | 0 | .274 | .353 | .226 |
| Tony Batista | 72 | 271 | 29 | 56 | 11 | 1 | 13 | 45 | 108 | 13 | 66 | 0 | .251 | .399 | .207 |
| Alberto Castillo | 66 | 131 | 9 | 26 | 4 | 0 | 1 | 4 | 33 | 7 | 30 | 1 | .255 | .252 | .198 |
| Brian Simmons | 61 | 107 | 8 | 19 | 5 | 0 | 2 | 8 | 38 | 8 | 26 | 1 | .239 | .280 | .178 |

| PITCHING | W–L | ERA | G | GS | CG | SV | INN | H | R | ER | BB | SO |
|---|---|---|---|---|---|---|---|---|---|---|---|---|
| Paul Quantrill | 11–2 | 3.04 | 80 | 0 | 0 | 2 | 83 | 86 | 29 | 28 | 12 | 58 |
| Roy Halladay | 5–3 | 3.16 | 17 | 16 | 1 | 0 | 105⅓ | 97 | 41 | 37 | 25 | 96 |
| Bob File | 5–3 | 3.27 | 60 | 0 | 0 | 0 | 74½ | 57 | 28 | 27 | 29 | 38 |
| Kelvim Escobar | 6–8 | 3.50 | 59 | 11 | 1 | 0 | 126 | 93 | 51 | 49 | 52 | 121 |
| Dan Plesac | 4–5 | 3.57 | 62 | 0 | 0 | 1 | 45½ | 34 | 18 | 18 | 24 | 68 |
| Chris Carpenter | 11–11 | 4.09 | 34 | 34 | 3 | 0 | 215⅔ | 229 | 112 | 98 | 75 | 157 |
| Brandon Lyon | 5–4 | 4.29 | 11 | 11 | 0 | 0 | 63 | 63 | 31 | 30 | 15 | 35 |
| Steve Parris | 4–6 | 4.60 | 19 | 19 | 1 | 0 | 105⅓ | 126 | 60 | 54 | 41 | 49 |
| Chris Michalak | 6–7 | 4.62 | 24 | 18 | 0 | 0 | 115 | 133 | 66 | 59 | 49 | 57 |
| Billy Koch | 2–5 | 4.80 | 69 | 0 | 0 | 36 | 69⅓ | 69 | 39 | 37 | 33 | 55 |
| Esteban Loaiza | 11–11 | 5.02 | 36 | 30 | 1 | 0 | 190 | 239 | 113 | 106 | 40 | 110 |
| Joey Hamilton | 5–8 | 5.89 | 22 | 22 | 0 | 0 | 122⅓ | 170 | 88 | 80 | 38 | 82 |

# FOR THE RECORD·Year by Year

## The World Series

### Results

| | |
|---|---|
| 1903 ...............Boston (A) 5, Pittsburgh (N) 3 | 1953 ...............New York (A) 4, Brooklyn (N) 2 |
| 1904 ...............No series | 1954 ...............New York (N) 4, Cleveland (A) 0 |
| 1905 ...............New York (N) 4, Philadelphia (A) 1 | 1955 ...............Brooklyn (N) 4, New York (A) 3 |
| 1906 ...............Chicago (A) 4, Chicago (N) 2 | 1956 ...............New York (A) 4, Brooklyn (N) 3 |
| 1907 ...............Chicago (N) 4, Detroit (A) 0; 1 tie | 1957 ...............Milwaukee (N) 4, New York (A) 3 |
| 1908 ...............Chicago (N) 4, Detroit (A) 1 | 1958 ...............New York (A) 4, Milwaukee (N) 3 |
| 1909 ...............Pittsburgh (N) 4, Detroit (A) 3 | 1959 ...............Los Angeles (N) 4, Chicago (A) 2 |
| 1910 ...............Philadelphia (A) 4, Chicago (N) 1 | 1960 ...............Pittsburgh (N) 4, New York (A) 3 |
| 1911 ...............Philadelphia (A) 4, New York (N) 2 | 1961 ...............New York (A) 4, Cincinnati (N) 1 |
| 1912 ...............Boston (A) 4, New York (N) 3; 1 tie | 1962 ...............New York (A) 4, San Francisco (N) 3 |
| 1913 ...............Philadelphia (A) 4, New York (N) 1 | 1963 ...............Los Angeles (N) 4, New York (A) 0 |
| 1914 ...............Boston (N) 4, Philadelphia (A) 0 | 1964 ...............St. Louis (N) 4, New York (A) 3 |
| 1915 ...............Boston (A) 4, Philadelphia (N) 1 | 1965 ...............Los Angeles (N) 4, Minnesota (A) 3 |
| 1916 ...............Boston (A) 4, Brooklyn (N) 1 | 1966 ...............Baltimore (A) 4, Los Angeles (N) 0 |
| 1917 ...............Chicago (A) 4, New York (N) 2 | 1967 ...............St. Louis (N) 4, Boston (A) 3 |
| 1918 ...............Boston (A) 4, Chicago (N) 2 | 1968 ...............Detroit (A) 4, St. Louis (N) 3 |
| 1919 ...............Cincinnati (N) 5, Chicago (A) 3 | 1969 ...............New York (N) 4, Baltimore (A) 1 |
| 1920 ...............Cleveland (A) 5, Brooklyn (N) 2 | 1970 ...............Baltimore (A) 4, Cincinnati (N) 1 |
| 1921 ...............New York (N) 5, New York (A) 3 | 1971 ...............Pittsburgh (N) 4, Baltimore (A) 3 |
| 1922 ...............New York (N) 4, New York (A) 0; 1 tie | 1972 ...............Oakland (A) 4, Cincinnati (N) 3 |
| 1923 ...............New York (A) 4, New York (N) 2 | 1973 ...............Oakland (A) 4, New York (N) 3 |
| 1924 ...............Washington (A) 4, New York (N) 3 | 1974 ...............Oakland (A) 4, Los Angeles (N) 1 |
| 1925 ...............Pittsburgh (N) 4, Washington (A) 3 | 1975 ...............Cincinnati (N) 4, Boston (A) 3 |
| 1926 ...............St. Louis (N) 4, New York (A) 3 | 1976 ...............Cincinnati (N) 4, New York (A) 0 |
| 1927 ...............New York (A) 4, Pittsburgh (N) 0 | 1977 ...............New York (A) 4, Los Angeles (N) 2 |
| 1928 ...............New York (A) 4, St. Louis (N) 0 | 1978 ...............New York (A) 4, Los Angeles (N) 2 |
| 1929 ...............Philadelphia (A) 4, Chicago (N) 1 | 1979 ...............Pittsburgh (N) 4, Baltimore (A) 3 |
| 1930 ...............Philadelphia (A) 4, St. Louis (N) 2 | 1980 ...............Philadelphia (N) 4, Kansas City (A) 2 |
| 1931 ...............St. Louis (N) 4, Philadelphia (A) 3 | 1981 ...............Los Angeles (N) 4, New York (A) 2 |
| 1932 ...............New York (A) 4, Chicago (N) 0 | 1982 ...............St. Louis (N) 4, Milwaukee (A) 3 |
| 1933 ...............New York (N) 4, Washington (A) 1 | 1983 ...............Baltimore (A) 4, Philadelphia (N) 1 |
| 1934 ...............St. Louis (N) 4, Detroit (A) 3 | 1984 ...............Detroit (A) 4, San Diego (N) 1 |
| 1935 ...............Detroit (A) 4, Chicago (N) 2 | 1985 ...............Kansas City (A) 4, St. Louis (N) 3 |
| 1936 ...............New York (A) 4, New York (N) 2 | 1986 ...............New York (N) 4, Boston (A) 3 |
| 1937 ...............New York (A) 4, New York (N) 1 | 1987 ...............Minnesota (A) 4, St. Louis (N) 3 |
| 1938 ...............New York (A) 4, Chicago (N) 0 | 1988 ...............Los Angeles (N) 4, Oakland (A) 1 |
| 1939 ...............New York (A) 4, Cincinnati (N) 0 | 1989 ...............Oakland (A) 4, San Francisco (N) 0 |
| 1940 ...............Cincinnati (N) 4, Detroit (A) 3 | 1990 ...............Cincinnati (N) 4, Oakland (A) 0 |
| 1941 ...............New York (A) 4, Brooklyn (N) 1 | 1991 ...............Minnesota (A) 4, Atlanta (N) 3 |
| 1942 ...............St. Louis (N) 4, New York (A) 1 | 1992 ...............Toronto (A) 4, Atlanta (N) 2 |
| 1943 ...............New York (A) 4, St. Louis (N) 1 | 1993 ...............Toronto (A) 4, Philadelphia (N) 2 |
| 1944 ...............St. Louis (N) 4, St. Louis (A) 2 | 1994 ...............Series canceled due to players' strike. |
| 1945 ...............Detroit (A) 4, Chicago (N) 3 | 1995 ...............Atlanta (N) 4, Cleveland (A) 2 |
| 1946 ...............St. Louis (N) 4, Boston (A) 3 | 1996 ...............New York (A) 4, Atlanta (N) 2 |
| 1947 ...............New York (A) 4, Brooklyn (N) 3 | 1997 ...............Florida (N) 4, Cleveland (A) 3 |
| 1948 ...............Cleveland (A) 4, Boston (N) 2 | 1998 ...............New York (A) 4, San Diego (N) 0 |
| 1949 ...............New York (A) 4, Brooklyn (N) 1 | 1999 ...............New York (A) 4, Atlanta (N) 0 |
| 1950 ...............New York (A) 4, Philadelphia (N) 0 | 2000 ...............New York (A) 4 , New York (N) 1 |
| 1951 ...............New York (A) 4, New York (N) 2 | 2001 ...............Arizona (N) 4, New York (A) 3 |
| 1952 ...............New York (A) 4, Brooklyn (N) 3 | |

## Most Valuable Players

| | | | |
|---|---|---|---|
| 1955 | Johnny Podres, Bklyn | 1980 | Mike Schmidt, Phil |
| 1956 | Don Larsen, NY (A) | 1981 | Ron Cey, LA; Steve Yeager, LA; Pedro Guerrero, LA |
| 1957 | Lew Burdette, Mil | 1982 | Darrell Porter, StL |
| 1958 | Bob Turley, NY (A) | 1983 | Rick Dempsey, Balt |
| 1959 | Larry Sherry, LA | 1984 | Alan Trammell, Det |
| 1960 | Bobby Richardson, NY (A) | 1985 | Bret Saberhagen, KC |
| 1961 | Whitey Ford, NY (A) | 1986 | Ray Knight, NY (N) |
| 1962 | Ralph Terry, NY (A) | 1987 | Frank Viola, Minn |
| 1963 | Sandy Koufax, LA | 1988 | Orel Hershiser, LA |
| 1964 | Bob Gibson, StL | 1989 | Dave Stewart, Oak |
| 1965 | Sandy Koufax, LA | 1990 | Jose Rijo, Cin |
| 1966 | Frank Robinson, Balt | 1991 | Jack Morris, Minn |
| 1967 | Bob Gibson, StL | 1992 | Pat Borders, Tor |
| 1968 | Mickey Lolich, Det | 1993 | Paul Molitor, Tor |
| 1969 | Donn Clendenon, NY (N) | 1994 | Series canceled due to strike. |
| 1970 | Brooks Robinson, Balt | 1995 | Tom Glavine, Atl |
| 1971 | Roberto Clemente, Pitt | 1996 | John Wetteland, NY (A) |
| 1972 | Gene Tenace, Oak | 1997 | Livan Hernandez, Fla |
| 1973 | Reggie Jackson, Oak | 1998 | Scott Brosius, NY (A) |
| 1974 | Rollie Fingers, Oak | 1999 | Mariano Rivera, NY (A) |
| 1975 | Pete Rose, Cin | 2000 | Derek Jeter, NY (A) |
| 1976 | Johnny Bench, Cin | 2001 | Randy Johnson, Ariz Curt Schilling, Ariz |
| 1977 | Reggie Jackson, NY (A) | | |
| 1978 | Bucky Dent, NY (A) | | |
| 1979 | Willie Stargell, Pitt | | |

## Career Batting Leaders (Minimum 40 at bats)

| GAMES | | BATTING AVERAGE | | RUNS | |
|---|---|---|---|---|---|
| Yogi Berra | 75 | Bobby Brown | .439 | Mickey Mantle | 42 |
| Mickey Mantle | 65 | Paul Molitor | .418 | Yogi Berra | 41 |
| Elston Howard | 54 | Pepper Martin | .418 | Babe Ruth | 37 |
| Hank Bauer | 53 | Hal McRae | .400 | Lou Gehrig | 30 |
| Gil McDougald | 53 | Lou Brock | .391 | Joe DiMaggio | 27 |
| Phil Rizzuto | 52 | Marquis Grissom | .390 | Roger Maris | 26 |
| Joe DiMaggio | 51 | Thurman Munson | .373 | Elston Howard | 25 |
| Frankie Frisch | 50 | George Brett | .373 | Gil McDougald | 23 |
| Pee Wee Reese | 44 | Pat Borders | .372 | Jackie Robinson | 22 |
| Roger Maris | 41 | Hank Aaron | .364 | Derek Jeter | 22 |
| Babe Ruth | 41 | | | | |

| AT BATS | | HOME RUNS | | STOLEN BASES | |
|---|---|---|---|---|---|
| Yogi Berra | 259 | Mickey Mantle | 18 | Lou Brock | 14 |
| Mickey Mantle | 230 | Babe Ruth | 15 | Eddie Collins | 14 |
| Joe DiMaggio | 199 | Yogi Berra | 12 | Frank Chance | 10 |
| Frankie Frisch | 197 | Duke Snider | 11 | Davey Lopes | 10 |
| Gil McDougald | 190 | Reggie Jackson | 10 | Phil Rizzuto | 10 |
| Hank Bauer | 188 | Lou Gehrig | 10 | Honus Wagner | 9 |
| Phil Rizzuto | 183 | Frank Robinson | 8 | Frankie Frisch | 9 |
| Elston Howard | 171 | Bill Skowron | 8 | Johnny Evers | 8 |
| Pee Wee Reese | 169 | Joe DiMaggio | 8 | Roberto Alomar | 7 |
| Roger Maris | 152 | Goose Goslin | 7 | Joe Tinker | 7 |
| | | Hank Bauer | 7 | Pepper Martin | 7 |
| | | Gil McDougald | 7 | Joe Morgan | 7 |
| | | | | Rickey Henderson | 7 |

| HITS | | RUNS BATTED IN | |
|---|---|---|---|
| Yogi Berra | 71 | Mickey Mantle | 40 |
| Mickey Mantle | 59 | Yogi Berra | 39 |
| Frankie Frisch | 58 | Lou Gehrig | 35 |
| Joe DiMaggio | 54 | Babe Ruth | 33 |
| Pee Wee Reese | 46 | Joe DiMaggio | 30 |
| Hank Bauer | 46 | Bill Skowron | 29 |
| Phil Rizzuto | 45 | Duke Snider | 26 |
| Gil McDougald | 45 | Reggie Jackson | 24 |
| Lou Gehrig | 43 | Bill Dickey | 24 |
| Eddie Collins | 42 | Hank Bauer | 24 |
| Babe Ruth | 42 | Gil McDougald | 24 |
| Elston Howard | 42 | | |

## Career Batting Leaders *(Cont.)*

| TOTAL BASES | | SLUGGING AVERAGE | | STRIKEOUTS | |
|---|---|---|---|---|---|
| Mickey Mantle | 123 | Reggie Jackson | .755 | Mickey Mantle | 54 |
| Yogi Berra | 117 | Babe Ruth | .744 | Elston Howard | 37 |
| Babe Ruth | 96 | Lou Gehrig | .731 | Duke Snider | 33 |
| Lou Gehrig | 87 | Bobby Brown | .707 | Babe Ruth | 30 |
| Joe DiMaggio | 84 | Lenny Dykstra | .700 | David Justice | 30 |
| Duke Snider | 79 | Al Simmons | .658 | Gil McDougald | 29 |
| Hank Bauer | 75 | Lou Brock | .655 | Bill Skowron | 26 |
| Reggie Jackson | 74 | Pepper Martin | .636 | Derek Jeter | 26 |
| Frankie Frisch | 74 | Paul Molitor | .636 | Hank Bauer | 25 |
| Gil McDougald | 72 | Joe Harris | .625 | Reggie Jackson | 24 |
| | | | | Bob Meusel | 24 |
| | | | | Bernie Williams | 24 |

## Career Pitching Leaders

| GAMES | | LOSSES | | COMPLETE GAMES | |
|---|---|---|---|---|---|
| Whitey Ford | 22 | Whitey Ford | 8 | Christy Mathewson | 10 |
| Mike Stanton | 19 | Eddie Plank | 5 | Chief Bender | 9 |
| Mariano Rivera | 18 | Schoolboy Rowe | 5 | Bob Gibson | 8 |
| Rollie Fingers | 16 | Joe Bush | 5 | Red Ruffing | 7 |
| Allie Reynolds | 15 | Rube Marquard | 5 | Whitey Ford | 7 |
| Bob Turley | 15 | Christy Mathewson | 5 | George Mullin | 6 |
| Clay Carroll | 14 | | | Eddie Plank | 6 |
| Clem Labine | 13 | **SAVES** | | Art Nehf | 6 |
| Mark Wohlers | 13 | Mariano Rivera | 8 | Waite Hoyt | 6 |
| Jeff Nelson | 13 | Rollie Fingers | 6 | | |
| | | Allie Reynolds | 4 | **STRIKEOUTS** | |
| **INNINGS PITCHED** | | Johnny Murphy | 4 | Whitey Ford | 94 |
| Whitey Ford | 146 | John Wetteland | 4 | Bob Gibson | 92 |
| Christy Mathewson | 101⅔ | Roy Face | 3 | Allie Reynolds | 62 |
| Red Ruffing | 85⅔ | Herb Pennock | 3 | Sandy Koufax | 61 |
| Chief Bender | 85 | Kent Tekulve | 3 | Red Ruffing | 61 |
| Waite Hoyt | 83⅔ | Firpo Marberry | 3 | Chief Bender | 59 |
| Bob Gibson | 81 | Will McEnaney | 3 | George Earnshaw | 56 |
| Art Nehf | 79 | Todd Worrell | 3 | John Smoltz | 52 |
| Allie Reynolds | 77 | Tug McGraw | 3 | Waite Hoyt | 49 |
| Jim Palmer | 65 | | | Christy Mathewson | 48 |
| Catfish Hunter | 63 | **\*EARNED RUN AVERAGE** | | | |
| | | Jack Billingham | 0.35 | **BASES ON BALLS** | |
| **WINS** | | Harry Brecheen | 0.83 | Whitey Ford | 34 |
| Whitey Ford | 10 | Babe Ruth | 0.87 | Allie Reynolds | 32 |
| Bob Gibson | 7 | Sherry Smith | 0.89 | Art Nehf | 32 |
| Red Ruffing | 7 | Sandy Koufax | 0.95 | Jim Palmer | 31 |
| Allie Reynolds | 7 | Hippo Vaughn | 1.00 | Bob Turley | 29 |
| Lefty Gomez | 6 | Monte Pearson | 1.01 | Paul Derringer | 27 |
| Chief Bender | 6 | Christy Mathewson | 1.06 | Red Ruffing | 27 |
| Waite Hoyt | 6 | Babe Adams | 1.29 | Don Gullett | 26 |
| Jack Coombs | 5 | Eddie Plank | 1.32 | Burleigh Grimes | 26 |
| Three Finger Brown | 5 | | | Vic Raschi | 25 |
| Herb Pennock | 5 | **SHUTOUTS** | | | |
| Christy Mathewson | 5 | Christy Mathewson | 4 | | |
| Vic Raschi | 5 | Three Finger Brown | 3 | | |
| Catfish Hunter | 5 | Whitey Ford | 3 | | |
| | | Bill Hallahan | 2 | | |
| | | Lew Burdette | 2 | | |
| | | Bill Dinneen | 2 | | |
| | | Sandy Koufax | 2 | | |
| | | Allie Reynolds | 2 | | |
| | | Art Nehf | 2 | | |
| | | Bob Gibson | 2 | | |

*Minimum 25 innings pitched.

## Alltime Team Rankings (by championships)

| Team | W | L | Appearances | Pct. | Most Recent | Last Championship |
|------|---|---|-------------|------|-------------|-------------------|
| New York Yankees | 26 | 12 | 38 | .684 | 2001 | 2000 |
| Phil/KC/Oakland Athletics | 9 | 5 | 14 | .643 | 1990 | 1989 |
| St. Louis Cardinals | 9 | 6 | 15 | .600 | 1987 | 1982 |
| Brooklyn/LA Dodgers | 6 | 12 | 18 | .333 | 1988 | 1988 |
| Pittsburgh Pirates | 5 | 2 | 7 | .714 | 1979 | 1979 |
| Cincinnati Reds | 5 | 4 | 9 | .556 | 1990 | 1990 |
| Boston Red Sox | 5 | 4 | 9 | .556 | 1986 | 1918 |
| New York/San Francisco Giants | 5 | 11 | 16 | .313 | 1989 | 1954 |
| Detroit Tigers | 4 | 5 | 9 | .444 | 1984 | 1984 |
| Washington/Minnesota Twins | 3 | 3 | 6 | .500 | 1991 | 1991 |
| St. Louis/Baltimore Orioles | 3 | 4 | 7 | .429 | 1983 | 1983 |
| Boston/Milwaukee/Atlanta Braves | 3 | 6 | 9 | .333 | 1999 | 1995 |
| Toronto Blue Jays | 2 | 0 | 2 | 1.000 | 1993 | 1993 |
| New York Mets | 2 | 2 | 4 | .500 | 2000 | 1986 |
| Chicago White Sox | 2 | 2 | 4 | .500 | 1959 | 1917 |
| Cleveland Indians | 2 | 3 | 5 | .400 | 1997 | 1948 |
| Chicago Cubs | 2 | 8 | 10 | .200 | 1945 | 1908 |
| Arizona Diamondbacks | 1 | 0 | 1 | 1.000 | 2001 | 2001 |
| Florida Marlins | 1 | 0 | 1 | 1.000 | 1997 | 1997 |
| Kansas City Royals | 1 | 1 | 2 | .500 | 1985 | 1985 |
| Philadelphia Phillies | 1 | 4 | 5 | .200 | 1993 | 1980 |
| Seattle/Milwaukee Brewers | 0 | 1 | 1 | .000 | 1982 | — |
| San Diego Padres | 0 | 2 | 2 | .000 | 1998 | — |

## League Championship Series

### National League

| | |
|---|---|
| 1969 | New York (E) 3, Atlanta (W) 0 |
| 1970 | Cincinnati (W) 3, Pittsburgh (E) 0 |
| 1971 | Pittsburgh (E) 3, San Francisco (W) 1 |
| 1972 | Cincinnati (W) 3, Pittsburgh (E) 2 |
| 1973 | New York 3, Cincinnati (W) 2 |
| 1974 | Los Angeles (W) 3, Pittsburgh (E) 1 |
| 1975 | Cincinnati (W) 3, Pittsburgh (E) 0 |
| 1976 | Cincinnati (W) 3, Philadelphia (E) 0 |
| 1977 | Los Angeles (W) 3, Philadelphia (E) 1 |
| 1978 | Los Angeles (W) 3, Philadelphia (E) 1 |
| 1979 | Pittsburgh (E) 3, Cincinnati (W) 0 |
| 1980 | Philadelphia (E) 3, Houston (W) 2 |
| 1981 | Los Angeles (W) 3, Montreal (E) 2 |
| 1982 | St. Louis (E) 3, Atlanta (W) 0 |
| 1983 | Philadelphia (E) 3, Los Angeles (W) 1 |
| 1984 | San Diego (W) 3, Chicago (E) 2 |
| 1985 | St. Louis (E) 4, Los Angeles (W) 2 |
| 1986 | New York (E) 4, Houston (W) 2 |
| 1987 | St. Louis (E) 4, San Francisco (W) 3 |
| 1988 | Los Angeles (W) 4, New York (E) 3 |
| 1989 | San Francisco (W) 4, Chicago (E) 1 |
| 1990 | Cincinnati (W) 4, Pittsburgh (E) 2 |
| 1991 | Atlanta (W) 4, Pittsburgh (E) 3 |
| 1992 | Atlanta (W) 4, Pittsburgh (E) 3 |
| 1993 | Philadelphia (E) 4, Atlanta (W) 2 |
| 1994 | Playoffs canceled due to players' strike. |
| 1995 | Atlanta (E) 4, Cincinnati (C) 0 |
| 1996 | Atlanta (E) 4, St. Louis (C) 3 |
| 1997 | Florida (wc) 4, Atlanta (E) 2 |
| 1998 | San Diego (W) 4, Atlanta (E) 2 |
| 1999 | Atlanta (E) 4, New York (wc) 2 |
| 2000 | New York (wc) 4, St. Louis (C) 1 |
| 2001 | Arizona (W) 4, Atlanta (E) 1 |

### American League

| | |
|---|---|
| 1969 | Baltimore (E) 3, Minnesota (W) 0 |
| 1970 | Baltimore (E) 3, Minnesota (W) 0 |
| 1971 | Baltimore (E) 3, Oakland (W) 0 |
| 1972 | Oakland (W) 3, Detroit (E) 2 |
| 1973 | Oakland (W) 3, Baltimore (E) 2 |
| 1974 | Oakland (W) 3, Baltimore (E) 1 |
| 1975 | Boston (E) 3, Oakland (W) 0 |
| 1976 | New York (E) 3, Kansas City (W) 2 |
| 1977 | New York (E) 3, Kansas City (W) 2 |
| 1978 | New York (E) 3, Kansas City (W) 1 |
| 1979 | Baltimore (E) 3, California (W) 1 |
| 1980 | Kansas City (W) 3, New York (E) 0 |
| 1981 | New York (E) 3, Oakland (W) 0 |
| 1982 | Milwaukee (E) 3, California (W) 2 |
| 1983 | Baltimore (E) 3, Chicago (W) 1 |
| 1984 | Detroit (E) 3, Kansas City (W) 0 |
| 1985 | Kansas City (W) 4, Toronto (E) 3 |
| 1986 | Boston (E) 4, California (W) 3 |
| 1987 | Minnesota (W) 4, Detroit (E) 1 |
| 1988 | Oakland (W) 4, Boston (E) 0 |
| 1989 | Oakland (W) 4, Toronto (E) 1 |
| 1990 | Oakland (W) 4, Boston (E) 0 |
| 1991 | Minnesota (W) 4, Toronto (E) 1 |
| 1992 | Toronto (E) 4, Oakland (W) 2 |
| 1993 | Toronto (E) 4, Chicago (W) 2 |
| 1994 | Playoffs canceled due to players' strike. |
| 1995 | Cleveland (C) 4, Seattle (W) 2 |
| 1996 | New York (E) 4, Baltimore (wc) 1 |
| 1997 | Cleveland (C) 4, Baltimore (E) 2 |
| 1998 | New York (E) 4, Cleveland (C) 2 |
| 1999 | New York (E) 4, Boston (wc) 1 |
| 2000 | New York (E) 4, Seattle (wc) 2 |
| 2001 | New York (E) 4, Seattle (W) 1 |

### NLCS Most Valuable Player

| | | |
|---|---|---|
| 1977 .......Dusty Baker, LA | 1986 .......Mike Scott, Hou | 1995 .......Mike Devereaux, Atl |
| 1978 .......Steve Garvey, LA | 1987 .......Jeffrey Leonard, SF | 1996 .......Javier Lopez, Atl |
| 1979 .......Willie Stargell, Pitt | 1988 .......Orel Hershiser, LA | 1997 .......Livan Hernandez, Fla |
| 1980 .......Manny Trillo, Phil | 1989 .......Will Clark, SF | 1998 .......Sterling Hitchcock, SD |
| 1981 .......Burt Hooton, LA | 1990 .......R. Myers/R. Dibble, Cin | 1999 .......Eddie Perez, Atl |
| 1982 .......Darrell Porter, StL | 1991 .......Steve Avery, Atl | 2000 .......Mike Hampton, NY |
| 1983 .......Gary Matthews, Phil | 1992 .......John Smoltz, Atl | 2001 .......Craig Counsell, Ariz |
| 1984 .......Steve Garvey, SD | 1993 .......Curt Schilling, Phil | |
| 1985 .......Ozzie Smith, StL | 1994 .......Playoffs canceled | |

### ALCS Most Valuable Player

| | | |
|---|---|---|
| 1980 .......Frank White, KC | 1988 .......Dennis Eckersley, Oak | 1996 .......Bernie Williams, NY |
| 1981 .......Graig Nettles, NY | 1989 .......Rickey Henderson, Oak | 1997 .......Marquis Grissom, Clev |
| 1982 .......Fred Lynn, Calif | 1990 .......Dave Stewart, Oak | 1998 .......David Wells, NY |
| 1983 .......Mike Boddicker, Balt | 1991 .......Kirby Puckett, Minn | 1999 .......Orlando Hernandez, NY |
| 1984 .......Kirk Gibson, Det | 1992 .......Roberto Alomar, Tor | 2000 .......David Justice, NY |
| 1985 .......George Brett, KC | 1993 .......Dave Stewart, Tor | 2001 .......Andy Pettitte, NY |
| 1986 .......Marty Barrett, Bos | 1994 .......Playoffs canceled | |
| 1987 .......Gary Gaetti, Minn | 1995 .......Orel Hershiser, Clev | |

## Divisional Playoffs

### National League

| | |
|---|---|
| 1995 | Atlanta (E) 3, Colorado (wc) 1 |
| | Cincinnati (C) 3, Los Angeles (W) 0 |
| 1996 | St. Louis (C) 3, San Diego (W) 0 |
| | Atlanta (E) 3, Los Angeles (wc) 0 |
| 1997 | Atlanta (E) 3, Houston (C) 0 |
| | Florida (wc) 3, San Francisco (W) 0 |
| 1998 | San Diego (W) 3, Houston (C) 1 |
| | Atlanta (E) 3, Chicago (wc) 0 |
| 1999 | Atlanta (E) 3, Houston (C) 1 |
| | New York (wc) 3, Arizona (W) 1 |
| 2000 | St. Louis (C) 3, Atlanta (E) 0 |
| | New York (wc) 3, San Francisco (W) 1 |
| 2001 | Atlanta (E) 3, Houston (C) 0 |
| | Arizona (W) 3, St. Louis (wc) 2 |

### American League

| | |
|---|---|
| 1995 | Cleveland (C) 3, Boston (E) 0 |
| | Seattle (W) 3, New York (wc) 2 |
| 1996 | Baltimore (wc) 3, Cleveland (C) 1 |
| | New York (E) 3, Texas (W) 1 |
| 1997 | Baltimore (E) 3, Seattle (W) 1 |
| | Cleveland (C) 3, New York (wc) 2 |
| 1998 | New York (E) 3, Texas (W) 0 |
| | Cleveland (C) 3, Boston (wc) 1 |
| 1999 | New York (E) 3, Texas (W) 1 |
| | Boston (wc) 3, Cleveland (C) 2 |
| 2000 | New York (E) 3, Oakland (W) 2 |
| | Seattle (wc) 3, Chicago (C) 0 |
| 2001 | Seattle (W) 3, Cleveland (C) 2 |
| | New York (E) 3, Oakland (wc) 2 |

## The All-Star Game

### Results

| Date | Winner | Score | Site | Date | Winner | Score | Site |
|---|---|---|---|---|---|---|---|
| 7-6-33 | American | 4–2 | Comiskey Park, Chi | 7 12-55 | National | 6–5 | County Stadium, Mil |
| 7-10-34 | American | 9–7 | Polo Grounds, NY | 7-10-56 | National | 7–3 | Griffith Stadium, Wash |
| 7-8-35 | American | 4–1 | Municipal Stadium, Clev | 7-9-57 | American | 6–5 | Busch Stadium, StL |
| 7-7-36 | National | 4–3 | Braves Field, Bos | 7-8-58 | American | 4–3 | Memorial Stadium, Balt |
| 7-7-37 | American | 8–3 | Griffith Stadium, Wash | 7-7-59 | National | 5–4 | Forbes Field, Pitt |
| 7-6-38 | National | 4–1 | Crosley Field, Cin | 8-3-59 | American | 5–3 | Memorial Coliseum, LA |
| 7-11-39 | American | 3–1 | Yankee Stadium, NY | 7-11-60 | National | 5–3 | Municipal Stadium, KC |
| 7-10-40 | National | 4–0 | Sportsman's Park, StL | 7-13-60 | National | 6–0 | Yankee Stadium, NY |
| 7-8-41 | American | 7–5 | Briggs Stadium, Det | 7-11-61 | National | 5–4 | Candlestick Park, SF |
| 7-6-42 | American | 3–1 | Polo Grounds, NY | 7-31-61 | Tie* | 1–1 | Fenway Park, Bos |
| 7-13-43 | American | 5–3 | Shibe Park, Phil | 7-10-62 | National | 3–1 | D.C. Stadium, Wash |
| 7-11-44 | National | 7–1 | Forbes Field, Pitt | 7-30-62 | American | 9–4 | Wrigley Field, Chi |
| 1945 | No game due to wartime travel restrictions. | | | 7-9-63 | National | 5–3 | Municipal Stadium, Clev |
| 7-9-46 | American | 12–0 | Fenway Park, Bos | 7-7-64 | National | 7–4 | Shea Stadium, NY |
| 7-8-47 | American | 2–1 | Wrigley Field, Chi | 7-13-65 | National | 6–5 | Metropolitan Stadium, Minn |
| 7-13-48 | American | 5–2 | Sportsman's Park, StL | | | | |
| 7-12-49 | American | 11–7 | Ebbets Field, Bklyn | 7-12-66 | National | 2–1 | Busch Stadium, StL |
| 7-11-50 | National | 4–3 | Comiskey Park, Chi | 7-11-67 | National | 2–1 | Anaheim Stadium, Cal |
| 7-10-51 | National | 8–3 | Briggs Stadium, Det | 7-9-68 | National | 1–0 | Astrodome, Hou |
| 7-8-52 | National | 3–2 | Shibe Park, Phil | 7-23-69 | National | 9–3 | R.F.K. Memorial Stadium, Wash |
| 7-14-53 | National | 5–1 | Crosley Field, Cin | | | | |
| 7-13-54 | American | 11–9 | Municipal Stadium, Clev | 7-14-70 | National | 5–4 | Riverfront Stadium, Cin |

*Game called because of rain after nine innings.

## Results (Cont.)

| Date | Winner | Score | Site | Date | Winner | Score | Site |
|------|--------|-------|------|------|--------|-------|------|
| 7-13-71 | American | 6–4 | Tiger Stadium, Det | 7-14-87 | National | 2–0 | Oakland Coliseum, Oak |
| 7-25-72 | National | 4–3 | Atlanta Stadium, Atl | 7-12-88 | American | 2–1 | Riverfront Stadium, Cin |
| 7-24-73 | National | 7–1 | Royals Stadium, KC | 7-11-89 | American | 5–3 | Anaheim Stadium, Cal |
| 7-23-74 | National | 7–2 | Three Rivers Stadium, Pitt | 7-10-90 | American | 2–0 | Wrigley Field, Chi |
| 7-15-75 | National | 6–3 | County Stadium, Mil | 7-9-91 | American | 4–2 | SkyDome, Tor |
| 7-13-76 | National | 7–1 | Veterans Stadium, Phil | 7-14-92 | American | 13–6 | Jack Murphy Stadium, SD |
| 7-19-77 | National | 7–5 | Yankee Stadium, NY | 7-13-93 | American | 9–3 | Camden Yards, Balt |
| 7-11-78 | National | 7–3 | Jack Murphy Stadium, SD | 7-12-94 | National | 8–7 | Three Rivers Stadium, Pitt |
| 7-17-79 | National | 7–6 | Kingdome, Sea | 7-11-95 | National | 3–2 | The Ballpark in |
| 7-8-80 | National | 4–2 | Dodger Stadium, LA | | | | Arlington, Tex |
| 8-9-81 | National | 5–4 | Municipal Stadium, Clev | 7-9-96 | National | 6–0 | Veterans Stadium, Phil |
| 7-13-82 | National | 4–1 | Olympic Stadium, Mtl | 7-8-97 | American | 3–1 | Jacobs Field, Clev |
| 7-6-83 | American | 13–3 | Comiskey Park, Chi | 7-7-98 | American | 13–8 | Coors Field, Col |
| 7-10-84 | National | 3–1 | Candlestick Park, SF | 7-13-99 | American | 4–1 | Fenway Park, Bos |
| 7-16-85 | National | 6–1 | Metrodome, Minn | 7-11-00 | American | 6–3 | Turner Field, Atl |
| 7-15-86 | American | 3–2 | Astrodome, Hou | 7-10-01 | American | 4–1 | Safeco Field, Sea |

## Most Valuable Players

| Year | Player | League | Year | Player | League | Year | Player | League |
|------|--------|--------|------|--------|--------|------|--------|--------|
| 1962 | Maury Wills, LA | NL | 1975 | Bill Madlock, Chi | NL | 1988 | Terry Steinbach, Oak | AL |
| | Leon Wagner, LA | AL | | Jon Matlack, NY | NL | 1989 | Bo Jackson, KC | AL |
| 1963 | Willie Mays, SF | NL | 1976 | George Foster, Cin | NL | 1990 | Julio Franco, Tex | AL |
| 1964 | Johnny Callison, Phil | NL | 1977 | Don Sutton, LA | NL | 1991 | Cal Ripken Jr., Balt | AL |
| 1965 | Juan Marichal, SF | NL | 1978 | Steve Garvey, LA | NL | 1992 | Ken Griffey Jr., Sea | AL |
| 1966 | Brooks Robinson, Balt | AL | 1979 | Dave Parker, Pitt | NL | 1993 | Kirby Puckett, Minn | AL |
| 1967 | Tony Perez, Cin | NL | 1980 | Ken Griffey, Cin | NL | 1994 | Fred McGriff, Atl | NL |
| 1968 | Willie Mays, SF | NL | 1981 | Gary Carter, Mtl | NL | 1995 | Jeff Conine, Fla | NL |
| 1969 | Willie McCovey, SF | NL | 1982 | Dave Concepcion, Cin | NL | 1996 | Mike Piazza, LA | NL |
| 1970 | Carl Yastrzemski, Bos | AL | 1983 | Fred Lynn, Calif | AL | 1997 | Sandy Alomar, Clev | AL |
| 1971 | Frank Robinson, Balt | AL | 1984 | Gary Carter, Mtl | NL | 1998 | Roberto Alomar, Balt | AL |
| 1972 | Joe Morgan, Cin | NL | 1985 | LaMarr Hoyt, SD | NL | 1999 | Pedro Martinez, Bos | AL |
| 1973 | Bobby Bonds, SF | NL | 1986 | Roger Clemens, Bos | AL | 2000 | Derek Jeter, NY | AL |
| 1974 | Steve Garvey, LA | NL | 1987 | Tim Raines, Mtl | NL | 2001 | Cal Ripken Jr., Balt | AL |

# The Regular Season

## Most Valuable Players

### NATIONAL LEAGUE

| Year | Name and Team | Position | Noteworthy |
|------|---------------|----------|------------|
| 1911 | Wildfire Schulte, Chi | Outfield | 21 HR†, 121 RBI†, .300 |
| 1912 | *Larry Doyle, NY | Second base | 10 HR, 90 RBI, .330 |
| 1913 | Jake Daubert, Bklyn | First base | 52 RBI, .350† |
| 1914 | *Johnny Evers, Bos | Second base | FA .976†, .279 |
| 1915–23 | No selection | | |
| 1924 | Dazzy Vance, Bklyn | Pitcher | 28†–6, 2.16 ERA†, 262 K† |
| 1925 | Rogers Hornsby, StL | Second base, Manager | 39 HR†, 143 RBI†, .403† |
| 1926 | *Bob O'Farrell, StL | Catcher | 7 HR, 68 RBI, .293 |
| 1927 | *Paul Waner, Pitt | Outfield | 237 hits†, 131 RBI†, .380† |
| 1928 | *Jim Bottomley, StL | First base | 31 HR†, 136 RBI†, .325 |
| 1929 | *Rogers Hornsby, Chi | Second base | 39 HR, 149 RBI, 156 runs†, .380 |
| 1930 | No selection | | |
| 1931 | *Frankie Frisch, StL | Second base | 4 HR, 82 RBI, 28 SB†, .311 |
| 1932 | Chuck Klein, Phil | Outfield | 38 HR†, 137 RBI, 226 hits†, .348 |
| 1933 | *Carl Hubbell, NY | Pitcher | 23†–12, 1.66 ERA†, 10 SO† |
| 1934 | *Dizzy Dean, StL | Pitcher | 30†–7, 2.66 ERA, 195 K† |
| 1935 | *Gabby Hartnett, Chi | Catcher | 13 HR, 91 RBI, .344 |
| 1936 | *Carl Hubbell, NY | Pitcher | 26†–6, 2.31 ERA† |
| 1937 | Joe Medwick, StL | Outfield | 31 HR‡, 154 RBI†, 111 runs†, .374† |
| 1938 | Ernie Lombardi, Cin | Catcher | 19 HR, 95 RBI, .342† |
| 1939 | *Bucky Walters, Cin | Pitcher | 27†–11, 2.29 ERA†, 137 K‡ |
| 1940 | *Frank McCormick, Cin | First base | 19 HR, 127 RBI, 191 hits†, .309 |
| 1941 | *Dolph Camilli, Bklyn | First base | 34 HR†, 120 RBI†, .285 |
| 1942 | *Mort Cooper, StL | Pitcher | 22†–7, 1.78 ERA†, 10 SO† |

*Played for pennant or, after 1968, division winner. †Led league. ‡Tied for league lead.

## Most Valuable Players (Cont.)
### NATIONAL LEAGUE (Cont.)

| Year | Name and Team | Position | Noteworthy |
|------|---------------|----------|------------|
| 1943 | *Stan Musial, StL | Outfield | 13 HR, 81 RBI, 220 hits†, .357† |
| 1944 | *Marty Marion, StL | Shortstop | FA .972†, 63 RBI |
| 1945 | *Phil Cavarretta, Chi | First base | 6 HR, 97 RBI, .355† |
| 1946 | *Stan Musial, StL | First base, Outfield | 103 RBI, 124 runs†, 228 hits†, .365† |
| 1947 | Bob Elliott, Bos | Third base | 22 HR, 113 RBI, .317 |
| 1948 | Stan Musial, StL | Outfield | 39 HR, 131 RBI†, .376† |
| 1949 | *Jackie Robinson, Bklyn | Second base | 16 HR, 124 RBI, 37 SB†, .342† |
| 1950 | *Jim Konstanty, Phil | Pitcher | 16–7, 22 saves†, 2.66 ERA |
| 1951 | Roy Campanella, Bklyn | Catcher | 33 HR, 108 RBI, .325 |
| 1952 | Hank Sauer, Chi | Outfield | 37 HR‡, 121 RBI†, .270 |
| 1953 | *Roy Campanella, Bklyn | Catcher | 41 HR, 142 RBI†, .312 |
| 1954 | *Willie Mays, NY | Outfield | 41 HR, 110 RBI, 13 3B†, .345† |
| 1955 | *Roy Campanella, Bklyn | Catcher | 32 HR, 107 RBI, .318 |
| 1956 | *Don Newcombe, Bklyn | Pitcher | 27†–7, 3.06 ERA |
| 1957 | *Hank Aaron, Mil | Outfield | 44 HR†, 132 RBI†, .322 |
| 1958 | Ernie Banks, Chi | Shortstop | 47 HR†, 129 RBI†, .313 |
| 1959 | Ernie Banks, Chi | Shortstop | 45 HR, 143 RBI†, .304 |
| 1960 | *Dick Groat, Pitt | Shortstop | 2 HR, 50 RBI, .325† |
| 1961 | *Frank Robinson, Cin | Outfield | 37 HR, 124 RBI, .323 |
| 1962 | Maury Wills, LA | Shortstop | 104 SB†, 208 hits, .299, GG |
| 1963 | *Sandy Koufax, LA | Pitcher | 25‡–5, 1.88 ERA†, 306 K† |
| 1964 | *Ken Boyer, StL | Third Base | 24 HR, 119 RBI†, .295 |
| 1965 | Willie Mays, SF | Outfield | 52 HR†, 112 RBI, .317, GG |
| 1966 | Roberto Clemente, Pitt | Outfield | 29 HR, 119 RBI, 202 hits, .317, GG |
| 1967 | *Orlando Cepeda, StL | First base | 25 HR, 111 RBI†, .325 |
| 1968 | *Bob Gibson, StL | Pitcher | 22–9, 1.12 ERA†, 268 K†, 13 SO†, GG |
| 1969 | Willie McCovey, SF | First base | 45 HR†, 126 RBI†, .320 |
| 1970 | *Johnny Bench, Cin | Catcher | 45 HR†, 148 RBI†, .293, GG |
| 1971 | Joe Torre, StL | Third base | 24 HR, 137 RBI†, .363† |
| 1972 | *Johnny Bench, Cin | Catcher | 40 HR†, 125 RBI†, .270, GG |
| 1973 | *Pete Rose, Cin | Outfield | 5 HR, 64 RBI, .338†, 230 hits† |
| 1974 | *Steve Garvey, LA | First base | 21 HR, 111 RBI, 200 hits, .312, GG |
| 1975 | *Joe Morgan, Cin | Second base | 17 HR, 94 RBI, 67 SB, .327, GG |
| 1976 | *Joe Morgan, Cin | Second base | 27 HR, 111 RBI, 60 SB, .320, GG |
| 1977 | George Foster, Cin | Outfield | 52 HR†, 149 RBI†, .320 |
| 1978 | Dave Parker, Pitt | Outfield | 30 HR, 117 RBI, .334†, GG |
| 1979 | Keith Hernandez, StL | First base | 11 HR, 105 RBI, 210 hits, .344†, GG |
|      | *Willie Stargell, Pitt | First base | 32 HR, 82 RBI, .281 |
| 1980 | *Mike Schmidt, Phil | Third base | 48 HR†, 121 RBI†, .286, GG |
| 1981 | Mike Schmidt, Phil | Third base | 31 HR†, 91 RBI†, 78 runs†, .316, GG |
| 1982 | *Dale Murphy, Atl | Outfield | 36 HR, 109 RBI†, .281, GG |
| 1983 | Dale Murphy, Atl | Outfield | 36 HR, 121 RBI†, .302, GG |
| 1984 | *Ryne Sandberg, Chi | Second base | 19 HR, 84 RBI, 114 runs†, .314, GG |
| 1985 | *Willie McGee, StL | Outfield | 10 HR, 82 RBI, 18 3B†, .353†, GG |
| 1986 | Mike Schmidt, Phil | Third base | 37 HR†, 119 RBI†, .290, GG |
| 1987 | Andre Dawson, Chi | Outfield | 49 HR†, 137 RBI†, .287, GG |
| 1988 | *Kirk Gibson, LA | Outfield | 25 HR, 76 RBI, 106 runs, .290 |
| 1989 | *Kevin Mitchell, SF | Outfield | 47 HR†, 125 RBI†, .291 |
| 1990 | *Barry Bonds, Pitt | Outfield | 33 HR, 114 RBI, .301 |
| 1991 | *Terry Pendleton, Atl | Third base | 23 HR, 86 RBI, .319† |
| 1992 | Barry Bonds, Pitt | Outfield | 34 HR, 103 RBI, .311 |
| 1993 | Barry Bonds, SF | Outfield | 46 HR†, 123 RBI†, .336 |
| 1994 | Jeff Bagwell, Hou | First base | 39 HR, 116 RBI†, .368 |
| 1995 | *Barry Larkin, Cin | Shortstop | 15 HR, 66 RBI, 51 SB, .319 |
| 1996 | *Ken Caminiti, SD | Third base | 40 HR, 130 RBI, .326 |
| 1997 | Larry Walker, Col | Outfield | 49 HR†, 130 RBI, .452 OBA†, .366, GG |
| 1998 | Sammy Sosa, Chi | Outfield | 66 HR†, 158 RBI†, 134 runs†, 416 TB†, .308 |
| 1999 | *Chipper Jones, Atl | Third Base | 45 HR, 110 RBI, 116 runs, .319 |
| 2000 | *Jeff Kent, SF | Second Base | 33 HR, 125 RBI, 114 runs, .334 |

*Played for pennant or, after 1968, division winner. †Led league. ‡Tied for league lead.

## Most Valuable Players *(Cont.)*

### AMERICAN LEAGUE

| Year | Name and Team | Position | Noteworthy |
|------|---------------|----------|------------|
| 1911 | Ty Cobb, Det | Outfield | 8 HR, 144 RBI†, 24 3B†, .420† |
| 1912 | *Tris Speaker, Bos | Outfield | 10 HR‡, 98 RBI, 53 2B†, .383 |
| 1913 | Walter Johnson, Wash | Pitcher | 36†–7, 1.09 ERA†, 11 SO†, 243 K† |
| 1914 | *Eddie Collins, Phil | Second base | 2 HR, 85 RBI, 122 runs†, .344 |
| 1915–21 | No selection | | |
| 1922 | George Sisler, StL | First base | 8 HR, 105 RBI, 246 hits†, .420† |
| 1923 | *Babe Ruth, NY | Outfield | 41 HR†, 131 RBI†, .393 |
| 1924 | *Walter Johnson, Wash | Pitcher | 23†–7, 2.72 ERA†, 158 K† |
| 1925 | *Roger Peckinpaugh, Wash | Shortstop | 4 HR, 64 RBI, .294 |
| 1926 | George Burns, Clev | First base | 114 RBI, 216 hits‡, 64 2B†, .358 |
| 1927 | *Lou Gehrig, NY | First base | 47 HR, 175 RBI†, 52 2B†, .373 |
| 1928 | Mickey Cochrane, Phil | Catcher | 10 HR, 57 RBI, .293 |
| 1929 | No selection | | |
| 1930 | No selection | | |
| 1931 | *Lefty Grove, Phil | Pitcher | 31†–4, 2.06 ERA†, 175 K† |
| 1932 | Jimmie Foxx, Phil | First base | 58 HR†, 169 RBI†, 151 runs†, .364 |
| 1933 | Jimmie Foxx, Phil | First base | 48 HR†, 163 RBI†, .356† |
| 1934 | *Mickey Cochrane, Det | Catcher | 2 HR, 76 RBI, .320 |
| 1935 | *Hank Greenberg, Det | First base | 36 HR‡, 170 RBI†, 203 hits, .328 |
| 1936 | *Lou Gehrig, NY | First base | 49 HR†, 152 RBI, 167 runs†, .354 |
| 1937 | Charlie Gehringer, Det | Second base | 14 HR, 96 RBI, 133 runs, .371† |
| 1938 | Jimmie Foxx, Bos | First base | 50 HR†, 175 RBI†, .349† |
| 1939 | *Joe DiMaggio, NY | Outfield | 30 HR, 126 RBI, .381† |
| 1940 | *Hank Greenberg, Det | Outfield | 41 HR†, 150 RBI†, 50 2B†, .340 |
| 1941 | *Joe DiMaggio, NY | Outfield | 30 HR, 125 RBI†, .357 |
| 1942 | *Joe Gordon, NY | Second base | 18 HR, 103 RBI, .322 |
| 1943 | *Spud Chandler, NY | Pitcher | 20†–4, 1.64 ERA†, 5 SO‡ |
| 1944 | Hal Newhouser, Det | Pitcher | 29†–9, 2.22 ERA†, 187 K† |
| 1945 | *Hal Newhouser, Det | Pitcher | 25†–9, 1.81 ERA†, 8 SO†, 212 K† |
| 1946 | *Ted Williams, Bos | Outfield | 38 HR, 123 RBI, 142 runs†, .342 |
| 1947 | *Joe DiMaggio, NY | Outfield | 20 HR, 97 RBI, .315 |
| 1948 | *Lou Boudreau, Clev | Shortstop | 18 HR, 106 RBI, .355 |
| 1949 | Ted Williams, Bos | Outfield | 43 HR†, 159 RBI†, 150 runs†, .343 |
| 1950 | *Phil Rizzuto, NY | Shortstop | 125 runs, 200 hits, .324 |
| 1951 | *Yogi Berra, NY | Catcher | 27 HR, 88 RBI, .294 |
| 1952 | Bobby Shantz, Phil | Pitcher | 24†–7, 2.48 ERA |
| 1953 | Al Rosen, Clev | Third base | 43 HR†, 145 RBI†, 115 runs†, .336 |
| 1954 | Yogi Berra, NY | Catcher | 22 HR, 125 RBI, .307 |
| 1955 | *Yogi Berra, NY | Catcher | 27 HR, 108 RBI, .272 |
| 1956 | *Mickey Mantle, NY | Outfield | 52 HR†, 130 RBI†, 132 runs†, .353† |
| 1957 | *Mickey Mantle, NY | Outfield | 34 HR, 94 RBI, 121 runs†, .365 |
| 1958 | Jackie Jensen, Bos | Outfield | 35 HR, 122 RBI†, .286 |
| 1959 | *Nellie Fox, Chi | Second base | 2 HR, 70 RBI, .306, GG |
| 1960 | *Roger Maris, NY | Outfield | 39 HR, 112 RBI†, .283, GG |
| 1961 | *Roger Maris, NY | Outfield | 61 HR†, 142 RBI†, .269 |
| 1962 | *Mickey Mantle, NY | Outfield | 30 HR, 89 RBI, .321, GG |
| 1963 | *Elston Howard, NY | Catcher | 28 HR, 85 RBI, .287, GG |
| 1964 | Brooks Robinson, Balt | Third base | 28 HR, 118 RBI†, .317, GG |
| 1965 | *Zoilo Versalles, Minn | Shortstop | 126 runs†, 45 2B†, 12 3B‡, GG |
| 1966 | *Frank Robinson, Balt | Outfield | 49 HR†, 122 RBI†, 122 runs†, .316† |
| 1967 | *Carl Yastrzemski, Bos | Outfield | 44 HR‡, 121 RBI†, 112 runs†, .326†, GG |
| 1968 | *Denny McLain, Det | Pitcher | 31†–6, 1.96 ERA, 280 K |
| 1969 | *Harmon Killebrew, Minn | Third base, First base | 49 HR†, 140 RBI†, .276 |
| 1970 | *Boog Powell, Balt | First base | 35 HR, 114 RBI, .297 |
| 1971 | *Vida Blue, Oak | Pitcher | 24–8, 1.82 ERA†, 8 SO†, 301 K |
| 1972 | Dick Allen, Chi | First base | 37 HR†, 113 RBI†, .308 |
| 1973 | *Reggie Jackson, Oak | Outfield | 32 HR†, 117 RBI†, 99 runs†, .293 |
| 1974 | Jeff Burroughs, Tex | Outfield | 25 HR, 118 RBI†, .301 |
| 1975 | *Fred Lynn, Bos | Outfield | 21 HR, 105 RBI, 103 runs†, .331, GG |
| 1976 | *Thurman Munson, NY | Catcher | 17 HR, 105 RBI, .302 |
| 1977 | Rod Carew, Minn | First base | 100 RBI, 128 runs†, 239 hits†, .388† |
| 1978 | Jim Rice, Bos | Outfield, DH | 46 HR†, 139 RBI†, 213 hits†, .315 |
| 1979 | *Don Baylor, Calif | Outfield, DH | 36 HR, 139 RBI†, 120 runs†, .296 |
| 1980 | *George Brett, KC | Third base | 24 HR, 118 RBI, .390† |

## Most Valuable Players (Cont.)
### AMERICAN LEAGUE (Cont.)

| Year | Name and Team | Position | Noteworthy |
|------|---------------|----------|------------|
| 1981 | *Rollie Fingers, Mil | Pitcher | 6–3, 28 saves†, 1.04 ERA |
| 1982 | *Robin Yount, Mil | Shortstop | 29 HR, 114 RBI, 210 hits†, .331, GG |
| 1983 | *Cal Ripken Jr., Balt | Shortstop | 27 HR, 102 RBI 121 runs†, 211 hits†, .318 |
| 1984 | *Willie Hernandez, Det | Pitcher | 9–3, 32 saves, 1.92 ERA |
| 1985 | Don Mattingly, NY | First base | 35 HR, 145 RBI†, 48 2B†, .324, GG |
| 1986 | *Roger Clemens, Bos | Pitcher | 24†–4, 2.48 ERA†, 238 K |
| 1987 | George Bell, Tor | Outfield | 47 HR, 134 RBI†, .308 |
| 1988 | *Jose Canseco, Oak | Outfield | 42 HR†, 124 RBI†, 40 SB, .307 |
| 1989 | Robin Yount, Mil | Outfield | 21 HR, 103 RBI, 101 runs, .318 |
| 1990 | *Rickey Henderson, Oak | Outfield | 28 HR, 119 runs†, 65 SB†, .325 |
| 1991 | Cal Ripken Jr., Balt | Shortstop | 34 HR, 114 RBI, .323 |
| 1992 | Dennis Eckersley, Oak | Pitcher | 7–1, 1.91 ERA, 51 saves |
| 1993 | Frank Thomas, Chi | First base | 41 HR, 128 RBI, .317 |
| 1994 | Frank Thomas, Chi | First base | 38 HR, 101 RBI, .353 |
| 1995 | *Mo Vaughn, Bos | First base | 39 HR, 126 RBI, .300 |
| 1996 | *Juan Gonzalez, Tex | Outfield | 47 HR, 144 RBI, .314 |
| 1997 | *Ken Griffey Jr., Sea | Outfield | 56 HR†, 125 runs†, 393 TB†, 147 RBI†, .304 |
| 1998 | *Juan Gonzalez, Tex | Outfield | 45 HR, 157 RBI†, 50 2B†, .318 |
| 1999 | *Ivan Rodriguez, Tex | Catcher | 35 HR, 113 RBI, 116 runs, .332, GG |
| 2000 | *Jason Giambi, Oak | First Base | 43 HR, 137 RBI, .333 |

*Played for pennant or, after 1968, division winner. †Led league. ‡Tied for league lead.

Notes: 2B=doubles; 3B=triples; FA=fielding average; GG=won Gold Glove, award begun in 1957; K=strikeouts; SO=shutouts; SB=stolen bases; TB=total bases.

## Rookies of the Year

### NATIONAL LEAGUE

| 1947* | Jackie Robinson, Bklyn (1B) |
|-------|------------------------------|
| 1948* | Alvin Dark, Bos (SS) |
| 1949 | Don Newcombe, Bklyn (P) |
| 1950 | Sam Jethroe, Bos (OF) |
| 1951 | Willie Mays, NY (OF) |
| 1952 | Joe Black, Bklyn (P) |
| 1953 | Junior Gilliam, Bklyn (2B) |
| 1954 | Wally Moon, StL (OF) |
| 1955 | Bill Virdon, StL (OF) |
| 1956 | Frank Robinson, Cin (OF) |
| 1957 | Jack Sanford, Phil (P) |
| 1958 | Orlando Cepeda, SF (1B) |
| 1959 | Willie McCovey, SF (1B) |
| 1960 | Frank Howard, LA (OF) |
| 1961 | Billy Williams, Chi (OF) |
| 1962 | Ken Hubbs, Chi (2B) |
| 1963 | Pete Rose, Cin (2B) |
| 1964 | Dick Allen, Phil (3B) |
| 1965 | Jim Lefebvre, LA (2B) |
| 1966 | Tommy Helms, Cin (2B) |
| 1967 | Tom Seaver, NY (P) |
| 1968 | Johnny Bench, Cin (C) |
| 1969 | Ted Sizemore, LA (2B) |
| 1970 | Carl Morton, Mtl(P) |
| 1971 | Earl Williams, Atl (C) |
| 1972 | Jon Matlack, NY (P) |
| 1973 | Gary Matthews, SF (OF) |
| 1974 | Bake McBride, StL (OF) |
| 1975 | John Montefusco, SF (P) |
| 1976 | Pat Zachry, Cin (P) |
|      | Butch Metzger, SD (P) |
| 1977 | Andre Dawson, Mtl (OF) |
| 1978 | Bob Horner, Atl (3B) |
| 1979 | Rick Sutcliffe, LA (P) |
| 1980 | Steve Howe, LA (P) |

### AMERICAN LEAGUE

| 1949 | Roy Sievers, StL (OF) |
|------|------------------------|
| 1950 | Walt Dropo, Bos (1B) |
| 1951 | Gil McDougald, NY (3B) |
| 1952 | Harry Byrd, Phil (P) |
| 1953 | Harvey Kuenn, Det (SS) |
| 1954 | Bob Grim, NY (P) |
| 1955 | Herb Score, Clev (P) |
| 1956 | Luis Aparicio, Chi (SS) |
| 1957 | Tony Kubek, NY (OF, SS) |
| 1958 | Albie Pearson, Wash (OF) |
| 1959 | Bob Allison, Wash (OF) |
| 1960 | Ron Hansen, Balt (SS) |
| 1961 | Don Schwall, Bos (P) |
| 1962 | Tom Tresh, NY (SS) |
| 1963 | Gary Peters, Chi (P) |
| 1964 | Tony Oliva, Minn (OF) |
| 1965 | Curt Blefary, Balt (OF) |
| 1966 | Tommie Agee, Chi (OF) |
| 1967 | Rod Carew, Minn (2B) |
| 1968 | Stan Bahnsen, NY (P) |
| 1969 | Lou Piniella, KC (OF) |
| 1970 | Thurman Munson, NY (C) |
| 1971 | Chris Chambliss, Clev (1B) |
| 1972 | Carlton Fisk, Bos (C) |
| 1973 | Al Bumbry, Balt (OF) |
| 1974 | Mike Hargrove, Tex (1B) |
| 1975 | Fred Lynn, Bos (OF) |
| 1976 | Mark Fidrych, Det (P) |
| 1977 | Eddie Murray, Balt (DH) |
| 1978 | Lou Whitaker, Det (2B) |
| 1979 | Alfredo Griffin, Tor (SS) |
|      | John Castino, Minn (3B) |
| 1980 | Joe Charboneau, Clev (OF) |
| 1981 | Dave Righetti, NY (P) |
| 1982 | Cal Ripken Jr., Balt (SS) |

*Just one selection for both leagues.

## Rookies of the Year *(Cont.)*

### NATIONAL LEAGUE *(Cont.)*

1981 ......................Fernando Valenzuela, LA (P)
1982 ......................Steve Sax, LA (2B)
1983 ......................Darryl Strawberry, NY (OF)
1984 ......................Dwight Gooden, NY (P)
1985 ......................Vince Coleman, StL (OF)
1986 ......................Todd Worrell, StL (P)
1987 ......................Benito Santiago, SD (C)
1988 ......................Chris Sabo, Cin (3B)
1989 ......................Jerome Walton, Chi (OF)
1990 ......................Dave Justice, Atl (OF)
1991 ......................Jeff Bagwell, Hou (3B)
1992 ......................Eric Karros, LA (1B)
1993 ......................Mike Piazza, LA (C)
1994 ......................Raul Mondesi, LA (OF)
1995 ......................Hideo Nomo, LA (P)
1996 ......................Todd Hollandsworth, LA (OF)
1997 ......................Scott Rolen, Phil (3B)
1998 ......................Kerry Wood, Chi (P)
1999 ......................Scott Williamson, Cin (P)
2000 ......................Rafael Furcal, Atl (SS)

### AMERICAN LEAGUE *(Cont.)*

1983 ......................Ron Kittle, Chi (OF)
1984 ......................Alvin Davis, Sea (1B)
1985 ......................Ozzie Guillen, Chi (SS)
1986 ......................Jose Canseco, Oak (OF)
1987 ......................Mark McGwire, Oak (1B)
1988 ......................Walt Weiss, Oak (SS)
1989 ......................Gregg Olson, Balt (P)
1990 ......................Sandy Alomar Jr, Clev (C)
1991 ......................Chuck Knoblauch, Minn (2B)
1992 ......................Pat Listach, Mil (SS)
1993 ......................Tim Salmon, Calif (OF)
1994 ......................Bob Hamelin, KC (DH)
1995 ......................Marty Cordova, Minn (OF)
1996 ......................Derek Jeter, NY (SS)
1997 ......................Nomar Garciaparra, Bos (SS)
1998 ......................Ben Grieve, Oak (OF)
1999 ......................Carlos Beltran, KC (OF)
2000 ......................Kazuhiro Sasaki, Sea (P)

## Cy Young Award

| Year | | W–L | Sv | ERA | Year | | W–L | Sv | ERA |
|---|---|---|---|---|---|---|---|---|---|
| 1956 | .*Don Newcombe, Bklyn (NL) | 27–7 | 0 | 3.06 | 1962 | .Don Drysdale, LA (NL) | 25–9 | 1 | 2.83 |
| 1957 | .Warren Spahn, Mil (NL) | 21–11 | 3 | 2.69 | 1963 | .*Sandy Koufax, LA (NL) | 25–5 | 0 | 1.88 |
| 1958 | .Bob Turley, NY (AL) | 21–7 | 1 | 2.97 | 1964 | .Dean Chance, LA (AL) | 20–9 | 4 | 1.65 |
| 1959 | .Early Wynn, Chi (AL) | 22–10 | 0 | 3.17 | 1965 | .Sandy Koufax, LA (NL) | 26–8 | 2 | 2.04 |
| 1960 | .Vernon Law, Pitt (NL) | 20–9 | 0 | 3.08 | 1966 | .Sandy Koufax, LA (NL) | 27–9 | 0 | 1.73 |
| 1961 | .Whitey Ford, NY (AL) | 25–4 | 0 | 3.21 | | | | | |

### NATIONAL LEAGUE

| Year | | W–L | Sv | ERA |
|---|---|---|---|---|
| 1967 | .....Mike McCormick, SF | 22–10 | 0 | 2.85 |
| 1968 | .....*Bob Gibson, StL | 22–9 | 0 | 1.12 |
| 1969 | .....Tom Seaver, NY | 25–7 | 0 | 2.21 |
| 1970 | .....Bob Gibson, StL | 23–7 | 0 | 3.12 |
| 1971 | .....Ferguson Jenkins, Chi | 24–13 | 0 | 2.77 |
| 1972 | .....Steve Carlton, Phil | 27–10 | 0 | 1.97 |
| 1973 | .....Tom Seaver, NY | 19–10 | 0 | 2.08 |
| 1974 | .....Mike Marshall, LA | 15–12 | 21 | 2.42 |
| 1975 | .....Tom Seaver, NY | 22–9 | 0 | 2.38 |
| 1976 | .....Randy Jones, SD | 22–14 | 0 | 2.74 |
| 1977 | .....Steve Carlton, Phil | 23–10 | 0 | 2.64 |
| 1978 | .....Gaylord Perry, SD | 21–6 | 0 | 2.72 |
| 1979 | .....Bruce Sutter, Chi | 6–6 | 37 | 2.23 |
| 1980 | .....Steve Carlton, Phil | 24–9 | 0 | 2.34 |
| 1981 | .....Fernando Valenzuela, LA | 13–7 | 0 | 2.48 |
| 1982 | .....Steve Carlton, Phil | 23–11 | 0 | 3.10 |
| 1983 | .....John Denny, Phil | 19–6 | 0 | 2.37 |
| 1984 | .....†Rick Sutcliffe, Chi | 16–1 | 0 | 2.69 |
| 1985 | .....Dwight Gooden, NY | 24–4 | 0 | 1.53 |
| 1986 | .....Mike Scott, Hou | 18–10 | 0 | 2.22 |
| 1987 | .....Steve Bedrosian, Phil | 5–3 | 40 | 2.83 |
| 1988 | .....Orel Hershiser, LA | 23–8 | 1 | 2.26 |
| 1989 | .....Mark Davis, SD | 4–3 | 44 | 1.85 |
| 1990 | .....Doug Drabek, Pitt | 22–6 | 0 | 2.76 |
| 1991 | .....Tom Glavine, Atl | 20–11 | 0 | 2.55 |
| 1992 | .....Greg Maddux, Chi | 20–11 | 0 | 2.18 |
| 1993 | .....Greg Maddux, Atl | 20–10 | 0 | 2.36 |
| 1994 | .....Greg Maddux, Atl | 16–6 | 0 | 1.56 |
| 1995 | .....Greg Maddux, Atl | 19–2 | 0 | 1.63 |
| 1996 | .....John Smoltz, Atl | 24–8 | 0 | 2.94 |
| 1997 | .....Pedro Martinez, Mtl | 17–8 | 0 | 1.90 |
| 1998 | .....Tom Glavine, Atl | 20–6 | 0 | 2.47 |
| 1999 | .....Randy Johnson, Ariz | 17–9 | 0 | 2.48 |
| 2000 | .....Randy Johnson, Ariz | 19–7 | 0 | 2.64 |

### AMERICAN LEAGUE

| Year | | W–L | Sv | ERA |
|---|---|---|---|---|
| 1967 | .....Jim Lonborg, Bos | 22–9 | 0 | 3.16 |
| 1968 | .....*Denny McLain, Det | 31–6 | 0 | 1.96 |
| 1969 | .....Denny McLain, Det | 24–9 | 0 | 2.80 |
| | Mike Cuellar, Balt | 23–11 | 0 | 2.38 |
| 1970 | .....Jim Perry, Minn | 24–12 | 0 | 3.03 |
| 1971 | .....*Vida Blue, Oak | 24–8 | 0 | 1.82 |
| 1972 | .....Gaylord Perry, Clev | 24–16 | 1 | 1.92 |
| 1973 | .....Jim Palmer, Balt | 22–9 | 1 | 2.40 |
| 1974 | .....Catfish Hunter, Oak | 25–12 | 0 | 2.49 |
| 1975 | .....Jim Palmer, Balt | 23–11 | 1 | 2.09 |
| 1976 | .....Jim Palmer, Balt | 22–13 | 0 | 2.51 |
| 1977 | .....Sparky Lyle, NY | 13–5 | 26 | 2.17 |
| 1978 | .....Ron Guidry, NY | 25–3 | 0 | 1.74 |
| 1979 | .....Mike Flanagan, Balt | 23–9 | 0 | 3.08 |
| 1980 | .....Steve Stone, Balt | 25–7 | 0 | 3.23 |
| 1981 | .....*Rollie Fingers, Mil | 6–3 | 28 | 1.04 |
| 1982 | .....Pete Vuckovich, Mil | 18–6 | 0 | 3.34 |
| 1983 | .....LaMarr Hoyt, Chi | 24–10 | 0 | 3.66 |
| 1984 | .....*Willie Hernandez, Det | 9–3 | 32 | 1.92 |
| 1985 | .....Bret Saberhagen, KC | 20–6 | 0 | 2.87 |
| 1986 | .....*Roger Clemens, Bos | 24–4 | 0 | 2.48 |
| 1987 | .....Roger Clemens, Bos | 20–9 | 0 | 2.97 |
| 1988 | .....Frank Viola, Minn | 24–7 | 0 | 2.64 |
| 1989 | .....Bret Saberhagen, KC | 23–6 | 0 | 2.16 |
| 1990 | .....Bob Welch, Oak | 27–6 | 0 | 2.95 |
| 1991 | .....Roger Clemens, Bos | 18–10 | 0 | 2.62 |
| 1992 | .....*Dennis Eckersley, Oak | 7–1 | 51 | 1.91 |
| 1993 | .....Jack McDowell, Chi | 22–10 | 0 | 3.37 |
| 1994 | .....David Cone, KC | 16–4 | 0 | 2.94 |
| 1995 | .....Randy Johnson, Sea | 18–2 | 0 | 2.48 |
| 1996 | .....Pat Hentgen, Tor | 20–10 | 0 | 3.22 |
| 1997 | .....Roger Clemens, Tor | 21–7 | 0 | 2.05 |
| 1998 | .....Roger Clemens, Tor | 20–6 | 0 | 2.65 |
| 1999 | .....Pedro Martinez, Bos | 23–4 | 0 | 1.55 |
| 2000 | .....Pedro Martinez, Bos | 18–6 | 0 | 1.74 |

*Pitchers who won the MVP and Cy Young awards in the same season.

†NL games only. Sutcliffe pitched 15 games with Cleveland before being traded to the Cubs.

## Career Individual Batting

### GAMES

| | |
|---|---|
| Pete Rose | 3562 |
| Carl Yastrzemski | 3308 |
| Hank Aaron | 3298 |
| Ty Cobb | 3034 |
| Stan Musial | 3026 |
| Eddie Murray | 3026 |
| Cal Ripken Jr. | 3001 |
| Willie Mays | 2992 |
| *Rickey Henderson | 2979 |
| Dave Winfield | 2973 |
| Rusty Staub | 2951 |
| Brooks Robinson | 2896 |
| Robin Yount | 2856 |
| Al Kaline | 2834 |
| *Harold Baines | 2830 |
| Eddie Collins | 2826 |
| Reggie Jackson | 2820 |
| Frank Robinson | 2808 |
| Honus Wagner | 2792 |
| Tris Speaker | 2789 |

### AT BATS

| | |
|---|---|
| Pete Rose | 14053 |
| Hank Aaron | 12364 |
| Carl Yastrzemski | 11988 |
| Cal Ripken Jr. | 11551 |
| Ty Cobb | 11429 |
| Eddie Murray | 11336 |
| Robin Yount | 11008 |
| Dave Winfield | 11003 |
| Stan Musial | 10972 |
| Willie Mays | 10881 |
| Paul Molitor | 10835 |
| *Rickey Henderson | 10710 |
| Brooks Robinson | 10654 |
| Honus Wagner | 10427 |
| George Brett | 10349 |
| Lou Brock | 10332 |
| Cap Anson | 10278 |
| Luis Aparicio | 10230 |
| Tris Speaker | 10208 |
| Al Kaline | 10116 |

### HOME RUNS

| | |
|---|---|
| Hank Aaron | 755 |
| Babe Ruth | 714 |
| Willie Mays | 660 |
| Frank Robinson | 586 |
| *Mark McGwire | 583 |
| Harmon Killebrew | 573 |
| *Barry Bonds | 567 |
| Reggie Jackson | 563 |
| Mike Schmidt | 548 |
| Mickey Mantle | 536 |
| Jimmie Foxx | 534 |
| Ted Williams | 521 |
| Willie McCovey | 521 |
| Eddie Mathews | 512 |
| Ernie Banks | 512 |
| Mel Ott | 511 |
| Eddie Murray | 504 |
| Lou Gehrig | 493 |
| Willie Stargell | 475 |
| Stan Musial | 475 |

### HITS

| | |
|---|---|
| Pete Rose | 4256 |
| Ty Cobb | 4189 |
| Hank Aaron | 3771 |
| Stan Musial | 3630 |
| Tris Speaker | 3515 |
| Carl Yastrzemski | 3419 |
| Cap Anson | 3418 |
| Honus Wagner | 3415 |
| Paul Molitor | 3319 |
| Eddie Collins | 3313 |
| Willie Mays | 3283 |
| Eddie Murray | 3255 |
| Nap Lajoie | 3251 |
| Cal Ripken Jr. | 3184 |
| George Brett | 3154 |
| Paul Waner | 3152 |
| Robin Yount | 3142 |
| Tony Gwynn | 3141 |
| Dave Winfield | 3110 |
| Rod Carew | 3053 |

### BATTING AVERAGE (5,000 AB)

| | |
|---|---|
| Ty Cobb | .367 |
| Rogers Hornsby | .358 |
| Ed Delahanty | .346 |
| Tris Speaker | .345 |
| Ted Williams | .344 |
| Billy Hamilton | .344 |
| Dan Brouthers | .342 |
| Jesse Burkett | .342 |
| Babe Ruth | .342 |
| Harry Heilmann | .342 |
| Willie Keeler | .341 |
| Bill Terry | .341 |
| George Sisler | .340 |
| Lou Gehrig | .340 |
| Jesse Burkett | .338 |
| Tony Gwynn | .338 |
| Nap Lajoie | .338 |
| Al Simmons | .334 |
| Paul Waner | .333 |
| Eddie Collins | .333 |

### RUNS

| | |
|---|---|
| *Rickey Henderson | 2248 |
| Ty Cobb | 2245 |
| Babe Ruth | 2174 |
| Hank Aaron | 2174 |
| Pete Rose | 2165 |
| Willie Mays | 2062 |
| Cap Anson | 1996 |
| Stan Musial | 1949 |
| Lou Gehrig | 1888 |
| Tris Speaker | 1881 |
| Mel Ott | 1859 |
| Frank Robinson | 1829 |
| Eddie Collins | 1820 |
| Carl Yastrzemski | 1816 |
| Ted Williams | 1798 |
| Paul Molitor | 1782 |
| Charlie Gehringer | 1774 |
| Jimmie Foxx | 1751 |
| Honus Wagner | 1740 |
| Jim O'Rourke | 1729 |

### DOUBLES

| | |
|---|---|
| Tris Speaker | 793 |
| Pete Rose | 746 |
| Stan Musial | 725 |
| Ty Cobb | 724 |
| George Brett | 665 |
| Nap Lajoie | 657 |
| Carl Yastrzemski | 646 |
| Honus Wagner | 640 |
| Hank Aaron | 624 |
| Paul Molitor | 605 |
| Paul Waner | 604 |
| Cal Ripken Jr. | 603 |
| Robin Yount | 583 |
| Cap Anson | 581 |
| Wade Boggs | 578 |
| Charlie Gehringer | 574 |
| Eddie Murray | 560 |
| Tony Gwynn | 543 |
| Harry Heilmann | 542 |
| Rogers Hornsby | 541 |

### TRIPLES

| | |
|---|---|
| Sam Crawford | 312 |
| Ty Cobb | 297 |
| Honus Wagner | 252 |
| Jake Beckley | 244 |
| Roger Connor | 233 |
| Tris Speaker | 223 |
| Fred Clarke | 223 |
| Dan Brouthers | 206 |
| Joe Kelley | 194 |
| Paul Waner | 190 |
| Bid McPhee | 189 |
| Eddie Collins | 187 |
| Ed Delahanty | 185 |
| Sam Rice | 184 |
| Jesse Burkett | 182 |
| Edd Roush | 182 |
| Ed Konetchy | 182 |
| Buck Ewing | 178 |
| Rabbit Maranville | 177 |
| Stan Musial | 177 |

### BASES ON BALLS

| | |
|---|---|
| *Rickey Henderson | 2141 |
| Babe Ruth | 2062 |
| Ted Williams | 2019 |
| Joe Morgan | 1865 |
| Carl Yastrzemski | 1845 |
| Mickey Mantle | 1735 |
| *Barry Bonds | 1724 |
| Mel Ott | 1708 |
| Eddie Yost | 1614 |
| Darrell Evans | 1605 |
| Stan Musial | 1599 |
| Pete Rose | 1566 |
| Harmon Killebrew | 1559 |
| Lou Gehrig | 1508 |
| Mike Schmidt | 1507 |
| Eddie Collins | 1503 |
| Willie Mays | 1463 |
| Jimmie Foxx | 1452 |
| Eddie Mathews | 1444 |
| Frank Robinson | 1420 |

* Active in 2001.

## Career Individual Batting *(Cont.)*

| RUNS BATTED IN | | STOLEN BASES | | TOTAL BASES | |
|---|---|---|---|---|---|
| Hank Aaron | 2297 | *Rickey Henderson | 1395 | Hank Aaron | 6856 |
| Babe Ruth | 2213 | Lou Brock | 938 | Stan Musial | 6134 |
| Cap Anson | 2076 | Billy Hamilton | 912 | Willie Mays | 6066 |
| Lou Gehrig | 1995 | Ty Cobb | 892 | Ty Cobb | 5854 |
| Stan Musial | 1951 | *Tim Raines | 808 | Babe Ruth | 5793 |
| Ty Cobb | 1937 | Vince Coleman | 752 | Pete Rose | 5752 |
| Jimmie Foxx | 1922 | Eddie Collins | 744 | Carl Yastrzemski | 5539 |
| Eddie Murray | 1917 | Arlie Latham | 739 | Eddie Murray | 5397 |
| Willie Mays | 1903 | Max Carey | 738 | Frank Robinson | 5373 |
| Mel Ott | 1860 | Honus Wagner | 722 | Dave Winfield | 5221 |
| Carl Yastrzemski | 1844 | Joe Morgan | 689 | Cal Ripken Jr. | 5168 |
| Ted Williams | 1839 | Willie Wilson | 668 | Tris Speaker | 5101 |
| Dave Winfield | 1833 | Tom Brown | 657 | Lou Gehrig | 5060 |
| Al Simmons | 1827 | Bert Campaneris | 649 | George Brett | 5044 |
| Frank Robinson | 1812 | Otis Nixon | 620 | Mel Ott | 5041 |
| Honus Wagner | 1732 | George Davis | 616 | Jimmie Foxx | 4956 |
| Reggie Jackson | 1702 | Dummy Hoy | 594 | Ted Williams | 4884 |
| *Cal Ripken Jr. | 1695 | Maury Wills | 586 | Honus Wagner | 4862 |
| Tony Perez | 1652 | George Van Haltren | 583 | Paul Molitor | 4854 |
| Ernie Banks | 1636 | Ozzie Smith | 580 | Al Kaline | 4852 |

| SLUGGING AVERAGE (5,000 AB) | | PINCH HITS | | STRIKEOUTS | |
|---|---|---|---|---|---|
| Babe Ruth | .690 | *Lenny Harris | 151 | Reggie Jackson | 2597 |
| Ted Williams | .634 | Manny Mota | 150 | *Jose Canseco | 1942 |
| Lou Gehrig | .632 | Smoky Burgess | 145 | Willie Stargell | 1936 |
| Jimmie Foxx | .609 | Greg Gross | 143 | Mike Schmidt | 1883 |
| Hank Greenberg | .605 | Jose Morales | 123 | Tony Perez | 1867 |
| *Mark McGwire | .588 | Jerry Lynch | 116 | *Andres Galarraga | 1858 |
| *Barry Bonds | .585 | *John Vander Wal | 116 | Dave Kingman | 1816 |
| Joe DiMaggio | .579 | Red Lucas | 114 | Bobby Bonds | 1757 |
| Rogers Hornsby | .577 | Steve Braun | 113 | Dale Murphy | 1748 |
| *Frank Thomas | .577 | *Dave Hansen | 111 | Lou Brock | 1730 |
| *Larry Walker | .572 | Terry Crowley | 108 | Mickey Mantle | 1710 |
| *Juan Gonzalez | .568 | Denny Walling | 108 | Harmon Killebrew | 1699 |
| *Ken Griffey Jr. | .566 | Gates Brown | 107 | *Fred McGriff | 1698 |
| Albert Belle | .564 | Mike Lum | 103 | Chili Davis | 1698 |
| Johnny Mize | .562 | Jim Dwyer | 102 | Dwight Evans | 1697 |
| Stan Musial | .559 | Rusty Staub | 100 | *Sammy Sosa | 1690 |
| Willie Mays | .557 | Larry Biittner | 95 | Dave Winfield | 1686 |
| Mickey Mantle | .557 | Vic Davalillo | 95 | *Rickey Henderson | 1631 |
| Hank Aaron | .555 | Gerald Perry | 95 | Gary Gaetti | 1602 |
| *Jeff Bagwell | .554 | Jerry Hairston | 94 | *Mark McGwire | 1596 |

## The 30–30 Club (30 HR, 30 SB in single season)

| Year | | HR | SB | Year | | HR | SB |
|---|---|---|---|---|---|---|---|
| 1922 | Kenny Williams, StL | 39 | 37 | 1992 | Barry Bonds, Pitt | 34 | 39 |
| 1956 | Willie Mays, NYG | 36 | 40 | 1993 | Sammy Sosa, ChiC | 33 | 36 |
| 1957 | Willie Mays, NYG | 35 | 38 | 1995 | Barry Bonds, SF | 33 | 31 |
| 1963 | Hank Aaron, Mil | 44 | 31 | 1995 | Sammy Sosa, ChiC | 36 | 34 |
| 1969 | Bobby Bonds, SF | 32 | 45 | 1996 | Barry Bonds, SF | 42 | 40 |
| 1970 | Tommy Harper, Mil | 31 | 38 | 1996 | Ellis Burks, Col | 40 | 32 |
| 1973 | Bobby Bonds, SF | 39 | 43 | 1996 | Barry Larkin, Cin | 33 | 36 |
| 1975 | Bobby Bonds, NYY | 32 | 30 | 1996 | Dante Bichette, Col | 31 | 31 |
| 1977 | Bobby Bonds, Cal | 37 | 41 | 1997 | Larry Walker, Col | 49 | 33 |
| 1978 | Bobby Bonds, Chi/Tex | 31 | 43 | 1997 | Jeff Bagwell, Hou | 43 | 31 |
| 1983 | Dale Murphy, Atl | 36 | 30 | 1997 | Raul Mondesi, LA | 30 | 32 |
| 1987 | Joe Carter, Clev | 32 | 31 | 1997 | Barry Bonds, SF | 40 | 37 |
| 1987 | Eric Davis, Cin | 37 | 50 | 1998 | Alex Rodriguez, Sea | 42 | 46 |
| 1987 | Darryl Strawberry, NYM | 39 | 36 | 1998 | Shawn Green, Tor | 35 | 35 |
| 1987 | Howard Johnson, NYM | 36 | 32 | 1999 | Jeff Bagwell, Hou | 42 | 30 |
| 1988 | Jose Canseco, Oak | 42 | 40 | 1999 | Raul Mondesi, LA | 33 | 36 |
| 1989 | Howard Johnson, NYM | 36 | 41 | 2000 | Preston Wilson, Fla | 31 | 36 |
| 1990 | Ron Gant, Atl | 32 | 33 | 2001 | Vladimir Guerrero, Mtl | 34 | 37 |
| 1990 | Barry Bonds, Pitt | 33 | 52 | 2001 | Jose Cruz Jr., Tor | 34 | 32 |
| 1991 | Ron Gant, Atl | 32 | 34 | 2001 | Bobby Abreu, Phil | 31 | 36 |
| 1991 | Howard Johnson, NYM | 38 | 30 | | | | |

*Active in 2001.

## Career Individual Pitching

| GAMES | | LOSSES | | EARNED RUN AVERAGE (2,000 IP) | |
|---|---|---|---|---|---|
| *Jesse Orosco | 1130 | Cy Young | 316 | Ed Walsh | 1.82 |
| Dennis Eckersley | 1071 | Pud Galvin | 308 | Addie Joss | 1.89 |
| Hoyt Wilhelm | 1070 | Nolan Ryan | 292 | Al Spalding | 2.04 |
| Kent Tekulve | 1050 | Walter Johnson | 279 | Three Finger Brown | 2.06 |
| Lee Smith | 1022 | Phil Niekro | 274 | John Ward | 2.10 |
| Goose Gossage | 1002 | Gaylord Perry | 265 | Christy Mathewson | 2.13 |
| *John Franco | 998 | Don Sutton | 256 | Tommy Bond | 2.14 |
| Lindy McDaniel | 987 | Jack Powell | 254 | Rube Waddell | 2.16 |
| *Dan Plesac | 946 | Eppa Rixey | 251 | Walter Johnson | 2.17 |
| Rollie Fingers | 944 | Bert Blyleven | 250 | Ed Reulbach | 2.28 |
| Gene Garber | 931 | Bobby Mathews | 248 | Will White | 2.28 |
| Cy Young | 906 | Robin Roberts | 245 | Eddie Plank | 2.35 |
| *Mike Jackson | 902 | Warren Spahn | 245 | Larry Corcoran | 2.36 |
| Sparky Lyle | 899 | Steve Carlton | 244 | Eddie Cicotte | 2.38 |
| Jim Kaat | 898 | Early Wynn | 244 | Candy Cummings | 2.39 |
| Paul Assenmacher | 884 | Jim Kaat | 237 | Doc White | 2.39 |
| Jeff Reardon | 880 | Frank Tanana | 236 | Nap Rucker | 2.42 |
| Don McMahon | 874 | Gus Weyhing | 232 | George Bradley | 2.43 |
| Phil Niekro | 864 | Tommy John | 231 | Jim McCormick | 2.43 |
| Charlie Hough | 858 | Bob Friend | 230 | Chief Bender | 2.46 |
| | | Ted Lyons | 230 | | |

| INNINGS PITCHED | | WINNING PERCENTAGE | | SHUTOUTS | |
|---|---|---|---|---|---|
| Cy Young | 7356⅔ | *Pedro Martinez | .691 | Walter Johnson | 110 |
| Pud Galvin | 5941½ | Dave Foutz | .690 | Grover Alexander | 90 |
| Walter Johnson | 5914⅔ | Whitey Ford | .690 | Christy Mathewson | 79 |
| Phil Niekro | 5404⅓ | Bob Caruthers | .688 | Cy Young | 76 |
| Nolan Ryan | 5386 | Lefty Grove | .680 | Eddie Plank | 69 |
| Gaylord Perry | 5350⅓ | Vic Raschi | .667 | Warren Spahn | 63 |
| Don Sutton | 5282⅓ | Larry Corcoran | .665 | Nolan Ryan | 61 |
| Warren Spahn | 5243⅔ | Christy Mathewson | .665 | Tom Seaver | 61 |
| Steve Carlton | 5217⅓ | *Randy Johnson | .664 | Bert Blyleven | 60 |
| Grover Alexander | 5190 | Sam Leever | .660 | Don Sutton | 58 |
| Kid Nichols | 5056½ | *Roger Clemens | .659 | Pud Galvin | 57 |
| Tim Keefe | 5047⅓ | Sal Maglie | .657 | Ed Walsh | 57 |
| Bert Blyleven | 4970 | Sandy Koufax | .655 | Bob Gibson | 56 |
| Bobby Mathews | 4956 | Johnny Allen | .654 | Three Finger Brown | 55 |
| Mickey Welch | 4802 | Ron Guidry | .651 | Steve Carlton | 55 |
| Tom Seaver | 4782⅔ | Lefty Gomez | .649 | Jim Palmer | 53 |
| Christy Mathewson | 4780⅔ | John Clarkson | .648 | Gaylord Perry | 53 |
| Tommy John | 4710½ | Three Finger Brown | .648 | Juan Marichal | 52 |
| Robin Roberts | 4688⅔ | Dizzy Dean | .644 | Rube Waddell | 50 |
| Early Wynn | 4564 | Grover Alexander | .642 | Vic Willis | 50 |

| WINS | | SAVES | | COMPLETE GAMES | |
|---|---|---|---|---|---|
| Cy Young | 511 | Lee Smith | 478 | Cy Young | 749 |
| Walter Johnson | 417 | *John Franco | 422 | Pud Galvin | 639 |
| Grover Alexander | 373 | Dennis Eckersley | 390 | Tim Keefe | 554 |
| Christy Mathewson | 373 | Jeff Reardon | 367 | Walter Johnson | 531 |
| Pud Galvin | 365 | Randy Myers | 347 | Kid Nichols | 531 |
| Warren Spahn | 363 | Rollie Fingers | 341 | Mickey Welch | 525 |
| Kid Nichols | 361 | John Wetteland | 330 | Bobby Mathews | 525 |
| Tim Keefe | 342 | Rick Aguilera | 318 | Charley Radbourn | 489 |
| Steve Carlton | 329 | *Trevor Hoffman | 314 | John Clarkson | 485 |
| John Clarkson | 328 | Tom Henke | 311 | Tony Mullane | 468 |
| Eddie Plank | 326 | Goose Gossage | 310 | Jim McCormick | 466 |
| Nolan Ryan | 324 | Jeff Montgomery | 304 | Gus Weyhing | 448 |
| Don Sutton | 324 | *Doug Jones | 303 | Grover Alexander | 437 |
| Phil Niekro | 318 | Bruce Sutter | 300 | Christy Mathewson | 434 |
| Gaylord Perry | 314 | *Roberto Hernandez | 294 | Jack Powell | 422 |
| Tom Seaver | 311 | *Robb Nen | 271 | Eddie Plank | 410 |
| Charley Radbourn | 309 | *Rod Beck | 266 | Will White | 394 |
| Mickey Welch | 307 | Todd Worrell | 256 | Amos Rusie | 392 |
| Lefty Grove | 300 | Dave Righetti | 252 | Vic Willis | 388 |
| Early Wynn | 300 | Dan Quisenberry | 244 | Tommy Bond | 386 |

* Active in 2001.

## Career Individual Pitching (Cont.)

### STRIKEOUTS

| | |
|---|---|
| Nolan Ryan | 5714 |
| Steve Carlton | 4136 |
| *Roger Clemens | 3717 |
| Bert Blyleven | 3701 |
| Tom Seaver | 3640 |
| Don Sutton | 3574 |
| Gaylord Perry | 3534 |
| Walter Johnson | 3509 |
| *Randy Johnson | 3412 |
| Phil Niekro | 3342 |
| Ferguson Jenkins | 3192 |
| Bob Gibson | 3117 |
| Jim Bunning | 2855 |
| Mickey Lolich | 2832 |
| Cy Young | 2803 |
| Frank Tanana | 2773 |
| *David Cone | 2655 |
| Warren Spahn | 2583 |
| Bob Feller | 2581 |
| Tim Keefe | 2564 |

### BASES ON BALLS

| | |
|---|---|
| Nolan Ryan | 2795 |
| Steve Carlton | 1833 |
| Phil Niekro | 1809 |
| Early Wynn | 1775 |
| Bob Feller | 1764 |
| Bobo Newsom | 1732 |
| Amos Rusie | 1704 |
| Charlie Hough | 1665 |
| Gus Weyhing | 1566 |
| Red Ruffing | 1541 |
| Bump Hadley | 1442 |
| Warren Spahn | 1434 |
| Earl Whitehill | 1431 |
| Tony Mullane | 1408 |
| Sad Sam Jones | 1396 |
| Jack Morris | 1390 |
| Tom Seaver | 1390 |
| Gaylord Perry | 1379 |
| Bobby Witt | 1375 |
| Mike Torrez | 1371 |

## Alltime Winningest Managers

### CAREER

| | W | L | Pct | Yrs | | W | L | Pct | Yrs |
|---|---|---|---|---|---|---|---|---|---|
| Connie Mack | 3755 | 3967 | .486 | 53 | *Tony LaRussa | 1856 | 1675 | .526 | 23 |
| John McGraw | 2810 | 1987 | .586 | 33 | *Bobby Cox | 1763 | 1390 | .559 | 20 |
| Sparky Anderson | 2238 | 1855 | .547 | 26 | Ralph Houk | 1627 | 1539 | .514 | 20 |
| Bucky Harris | 2168 | 2228 | .493 | 29 | Fred Clarke | 1609 | 1189 | .575 | 19 |
| Joe McCarthy | 2155 | 1346 | .616 | 24 | Dick Williams | 1592 | 1474 | .519 | 21 |
| Walter Alston | 2063 | 1634 | .558 | 23 | Tommy Lasorda | 1589 | 1434 | .526 | 20 |
| Leo Durocher | 2015 | 1717 | .540 | 24 | *Joe Torre | 1532 | 1416 | .520 | 20 |
| Casey Stengel | 1942 | 1868 | .510 | 25 | Earl Weaver | 1506 | 1080 | .582 | 17 |
| Gene Mauch | 1907 | 2044 | .483 | 26 | Clark Griffith | 1491 | 1367 | .522 | 20 |
| Bill McKechnie | 1904 | 1737 | .523 | 25 | Miller Huggins | 1431 | 1149 | .555 | 17 |

### REGULAR SEASON

| | W | L | Pct | Yrs | | W | L | Pct | Yrs |
|---|---|---|---|---|---|---|---|---|---|
| Connie Mack | 3731 | 3948 | .486 | 53 | *Tony LaRussa | 1827 | 1647 | .526 | 23 |
| John McGraw | 2784 | 1959 | .587 | 33 | *Bobby Cox | 1704 | 1345 | .559 | 20 |
| Sparky Anderson | 2194 | 1834 | .545 | 26 | Ralph Houk | 1619 | 1531 | .514 | 20 |
| Bucky Harris | 2157 | 2218 | .493 | 29 | Fred Clarke | 1602 | 1181 | .576 | 19 |
| Joe McCarthy | 2125 | 1333 | .615 | 24 | Dick Williams | 1571 | 1451 | .520 | 21 |
| Walter Alston | 2040 | 1613 | .558 | 23 | Tommy Lasorda | 1558 | 1404 | .526 | 20 |
| Leo Durocher | 2008 | 1709 | .540 | 24 | Clark Griffith | 1491 | 1367 | .522 | 20 |
| Casey Stengel | 1905 | 1842 | .508 | 25 | *Joe Torre | 1476 | 1390 | .515 | 20 |
| Gene Mauch | 1902 | 2037 | .483 | 26 | Earl Weaver | 1480 | 1060 | .583 | 17 |
| Bill McKechnie | 1896 | 1723 | .524 | 25 | Miller Huggins | 1413 | 1134 | .555 | 17 |

### WORLD SERIES

| | W | L | T | Pct | App | WS | | W | L | T | Pct | App | WS |
|---|---|---|---|---|---|---|---|---|---|---|---|---|---|
| Casey Stengel | 37 | 26 | 0 | .587 | 10 | 7 | Bucky Harris | 11 | 10 | 0 | .524 | 3 | 2 |
| Joe McCarthy | 30 | 13 | 0 | .698 | 9 | 7 | Billy Southworth | 11 | 11 | 0 | .500 | 4 | 2 |
| John McGraw | 26 | 28 | 2 | .482 | 9 | 2 | Earl Weaver | 11 | 13 | 0 | .458 | 4 | 1 |
| Connie Mack | 24 | 19 | 0 | .558 | 8 | 5 | *Bobby Cox | 11 | 18 | 0 | .379 | 5 | 1 |
| Walter Alston | 20 | 20 | 0 | .500 | 7 | 4 | Whitey Herzog | 10 | 11 | 0 | .476 | 3 | 1 |
| *Joe Torre | 19 | 7 | 0 | .731 | 5 | 4 | Bill Carrigan | 8 | 2 | 0 | .800 | 2 | 2 |
| Miller Huggins | 18 | 15 | 1 | .544 | 6 | 3 | Cito Gaston | 8 | 4 | 0 | .667 | 2 | 2 |
| Sparky Anderson | 16 | 12 | 0 | .571 | 5 | 3 | Danny Murtaugh | 8 | 6 | 0 | .571 | 2 | 2 |
| Tommy Lasorda | 12 | 11 | 0 | .522 | 4 | 2 | *Tom Kelly | 8 | 6 | 0 | .571 | 2 | 2 |
| Dick Williams | 12 | 14 | 0 | .462 | 4 | 2 | Ralph Houk | 8 | 8 | 0 | .500 | 3 | 2 |
| Frank Chance | 11 | 9 | 1 | .548 | 4 | 2 | Bill McKechnie | 8 | 14 | 0 | .364 | 4 | 2 |

*Active in 2001.

## Individual Batting (Single Season)

### HITS

George Sisler, 1920.............257
Lefty O'Doul, 1929...............254
Bill Terry, 1930.....................254
Al Simmons, 1925................253
Rogers Hornsby, 1922.........250
Chuck Klein, 1930 ..............250
Ty Cobb, 1911 .....................248
George Sisler, 1922.............246
Ichiro Suzuki, 2001.............242
Heinie Manush, 1928..........241
Babe Herman, 1930 ...........241

### BATTING AVERAGE

Hugh Duffy, 1894................ .440
Tip O'Neill, 1887 ................ .435
Ross Barnes, 1876 ............ .429
Nap Lajoie, 1901 ................ .426
Willie Keeler, 1897.............. .424
Rogers Hornsby, 1924........ .424
George Sisler, 1922........... .420
Ty Cobb, 1911 ................... .420
Fred Dunlap, 1884............. .412
Ed Delahanty, 1899 .......... .410

### DOUBLES

Earl Webb, 1931 .....................67
George Burns, 1926 ..............64
Joe Medwick, 1936................64
Hank Greenberg, 1934..........63
Paul Waner, 1932 .................62
Charlie Gehringer, 1936 ........60
Tris Speaker, 1923................59
Chuck Klein, 1930 ................59
Todd Helton, 2000 ................59
Billy Herman, 1936 ...............57
Billy Herman, 1935 ...............57
Carlos Delgado, 2000...........57

### TOTAL BASES

Babe Ruth, 1921..................457
Rogers Hornsby, 1922.........450
Lou Gehrig, 1927.................447
Chuck Klein, 1930 ...............445
Jimmie Foxx, 1932..............438
Stan Musial, 1948 ...............429
Sammy Sosa, 2001..............425
Hack Wilson, 1930...............423
Chuck Klein, 1932 ...............420
Luis Gonzalez, 2001............419
Lou Gehrig, 1930.................419

### TRIPLES

Chief Wilson, 1912.................36
Dave Orr, 1886 .....................31
Heinie Reitz, 1894.................31
Perry Werden, 1893...........`..29
Harry Davis, 1897 .................28
George Davis, 1893................27
Sam Thompson, 1894............27
Jimmy Williams, 1899 ...........27
John Reilly, 1890 ..................26
George Treadway, 1894.........26
Joe Jackson, 1912.................26
Sam Crawford, 1914..............26
Kiki Cuyler, 1925...................26

### HOME RUNS

Barry Bonds, 2001.................73
Mark McGwire, 1998 .............70
Sammy Sosa, 1998................66
Mark McGwire, 1999 .............65
Sammy Sosa, 2001................64
Sammy Sosa, 1999................63
Roger Maris, 1961 .................61
Babe Ruth, 1927....................60
Babe Ruth, 1921....................59
Jimmie Foxx, 1932.................58
Hank Greenberg, 1938...........58
Mark McGwire, 1997 .............58

### RUNS BATTED IN

Hack Wilson, 1930.................190
Lou Gehrig, 1931..................184
Hank Greenberg, 1937.........183
Lou Gehrig, 1927..................175
Jimmie Foxx, 1938................175
Lou Gehrig, 1930..................174
Babe Ruth, 1921...................171
Chuck Klein, 1930 ...............170
Hank Greenberg, 1935........170
Jimmie Foxx, 1932................169

### STRIKEOUTS

Bobby Bonds, 1970..............189
Bobby Bonds, 1969 ..............187
Preston Wilson, 2000...........187
Rob Deer, 1987 ...................186
Jose Hernandez, 2001 .........185
Jim Thome, 2001 .................185
Pete Incaviglia, 1986 ...........185
Cecil Fielder, 1990................182
Mo Vaughn, 2000 ................181
Mike Schmidt, 1975 .............180

### RUNS

Billy Hamilton, 1894 .............192
Tom Brown, 1891..................177
Babe Ruth, 1921 ..................177
Tip O'Neill, 1887 ..................167
Lou Gehrig, 1936..................167
Billy Hamilton, 1895..............166
Willie Keeler, 1894................165
Joe Kelley, 1894 ..................165
Arlie Latham, 1887................163
Babe Ruth, 1928 ..................163
Lou Gehrig, 1931..................163

### STOLEN BASES

Hugh Nicol, 1887..................138
Rickey Henderson, 1982 .....130
Arlie Latham, 1887................129
Lou Brock, 1974 ..................118
Charlie Comiskey, 1887.......117
John Ward, 1887 ..................111
Billy Hamilton, 1889..............111
Billy Hamilton, 1891..............111
Vince Coleman, 1985 ..........110
Arlie Latham, 1888................109
Vince Coleman, 1987 .........109

### BASES ON BALLS

Barry Bonds, 2001................177
Babe Ruth, 1923...................170
Ted Williams, 1947 ..............162
Ted Williams, 1949 ..............162
Mark McGwire, 1998 ............162
Ted Williams, 1946 ..............156
Eddie Yost, 1956 .................151
Eddie Joost, 1949.................149
Jeff Bagwell, 1999 ...............149
Babe Ruth, 1920...................148
Eddie Stanky, 1945...............148
Jimmy Wynn, 1969 ..............148

### SLUGGING AVERAGE

Barry Bonds, 2001,,.. .........863
Babe Ruth, 1920................ .847
Babe Ruth, 1921................ .846
Babe Ruth, 1927................ .772
Lou Gehrig, 1927................ .765
Babe Ruth, 1923................ .764
Rogers Hornsby, 1925........ .756
Mark McGwire, 1998 ......... .752
Jeff Bagwell, 1994 ............. .750
Jimmie Foxx, 1932............. .749

## Individual Pitching (Single Season)

### GAMES

Mike Marshall, 1974.............106
Kent Tekulve, 1979.................94
Mike Marshall, 1973................92
Kent Tekulve, 1978................91
Wayne Granger, 1969...........90
Mike Marshall, 1979...............90
Kent Tekulve, 1987................90
Steve Kline, 2001..................89
Mark Eichhorn, 1987.............89
Wilbur Wood, 1968................88
Mike Myers, 1997.................88

### GAMES STARTED

Will White, 1879.....................75
Jim Galvin, 1883....................75
Jim McCormick, 1880.......74
Charley Radbourn, 1884.......73
Guy Hecker, 1884..................73
Jim Galvin, 1884....................72
John Clarkson, 1889..............72
Bill Hutchison, 1892...............71
John Clarkson, 1885..............70
Matt Kilroy, 1887....................69

### INNINGS PITCHED

Will White, 1878.................680.0
Charley Radbourn, 1884....678.2
Guy Hecker, 1884.............670.2
Jim McCormick, 1880.......657.2
Jim Galvin, 1883..............656.1
Jim Galvin, 1884...............636.1
Charley Radbourn, 1883...632.1
Bill Hutchison, 1892..........627.0
John Clarkson, 1885.........623.0
Jim Devlin, 1876...............622.0

### WINS

Charley Radbourn, 1884.......59
John Clarkson, 1885..............53
Guy Hecker, 1884..................52
John Clarkson, 1889..............49
Charley Radbourn, 1883.......48
Charlie Buffinton, 1884.........48
Al Spalding, 1876..................47
John Ward, 1879...................47
Jim Galvin, 1883...................46
Jim Galvin, 1884...................46
Matt Kilroy, 1887..................46

### LOSSES

John Coleman, 1883.............48
Will White, 1880.....................42
Larry McKeon, 1884..............41
George Bradley, 1879...........40
Jim McCormick, 1879............40
Henry Porter, 1888................37
Kid Carsey, 1891..................37
George Cobb, 1892...............37
Stump Weidman, 1886..........36
Bill Hutchison, 1892..............36

### WINNING PERCENTAGE

Roy Face, 1959...................947
Johnny Allen, 1937.............938
Greg Maddux, 1995...........905
Randy Johnson, 1995.........900
Ron Guidry, 1978...............893
Freddie Fitzsimmons, 1940....889
Lefty Grove, 1931..............886
Bob Stanley, 1978..............882
Preacher Roe, 1951...........880
Fred Goldsmith, 1880........875
Tom Seaver, 1981..............875

### SAVES

Bobby Thigpen, 1990............57
Randy Myers, 1993................53
Trevor Hoffman, 1998............53
Dennis Eckersley, 1992........51
Rod Beck, 1998.....................51
Mariano Rivera, 2001.............50
Dennis Eckersley, 1990........48
Rod Beck, 1993.....................48
Jeff Shaw, 1998.....................48
Lee Smith, 1991....................47

### EARNED RUN AVERAGE

Tim Keefe, 1880..................0.86
Dutch Leonard, 1914..........0.96
Three Finger Brown, 1906....1.04
Bob Gibson, 1968...............1.12
Christy Mathewson, 1909...1.14
Walter Johnson, 1913.........1.14
Jack Pfiester, 1907.............1.15
Addie Joss, 1908................1.16
Carl Lundgren, 1907...........1.17
Denny Driscoll, 1882..........1.21

### SHUTOUTS

George Bradley, 1876..........16
Grover Alexander, 1916........16
Jack Coombs, 1910.................13
Bob Gibson, 1968.................13
Jim Galvin, 1884....................12
Ed Morris, 1886....................12
Grover Alexander, 1915........12
Tommy Bond, 1879...............11
Charley Radbourn, 1884.......11
Dave Foutz, 1886...................11
Christy Mathewson, 1908......11
Ed Walsh, 1908.....................11
Walter Johnson, 1913...........11
Sandy Koufax, 1963.............11
Dean Chance, 1964..............11

### COMPLETE GAMES

Will White, 1879.....................75
Charley Radbourn, 1884.......73
Jim McCormick, 1880............72
Jim Galvin, 1883...................72
Guy Hecker, 1884..................72
Jim Galvin, 1884...................71
Tim Keefe, 1883....................68
John Clarkson, 1885..............68
John Clarkson, 1889..............68
Bill Hutchison, 1892..............67

### STRIKEOUTS

Matt Kilroy, 1886..................513
Toad Ramsey, 1886.............499
Hugh Daily, 1884.................483
Dupee Shaw, 1884..............451
Charley Radbourn, 1884.....441
Charlie Buffinton, 1884........417
Guy Hecker, 1884.................385
Nolan Ryan, 1973................383
Sandy Koufax, 1965............382
Bill Sweeney, 1884..............374

### BASES ON BALLS

Amos Rusie, 1890................289
Mark Baldwin, 1889.............274
Amos Rusie, 1892................267
Amos Rusie, 1891................262
Mark Baldwin, 1890.............249
Jack Stivetts, 1891...............232
Mark Baldwin, 1891.............227
Phil Knell, 1891....................226
Bob Barr, 1890....................219
Amos Rusie 1893.................218

## Manager of the Year

| NATIONAL LEAGUE | | AMERICAN LEAGUE | |
|---|---|---|---|
| 1983 | Tommy Lasorda, LA | 1983 | Tony La Russa, Chi |
| 1984 | Jim Frey, Chi | 1984 | Sparky Anderson, Det |
| 1985 | Whitey Herzog, StL | 1985 | Bobby Cox, Tor |
| 1986 | Hal Lanier, Hou | 1986 | John McNamara, Bos |
| 1987 | Buck Rodgers, Mtl | 1987 | Sparky Anderson, Det |
| 1988 | Tommy Lasorda, LA | 1988 | Tony La Russa, Oak |
| 1989 | Don Zimmer, Chi | 1989 | Frank Robinson, Balt |
| 1990 | Jim Leyland, Pitt | 1990 | Jeff Torborg, Chi |
| 1991 | Bobby Cox, Atl | 1991 | Tom Kelly, Minn |
| 1992 | Jim Leyland, Pitt | 1992 | Tony La Russa, Oak |
| 1993 | Dusty Baker, SF | 1993 | Gene Lamont, Chi |
| 1994 | Felipe Alou, Mtl | 1994 | Buck Showalter, NY |
| 1995 | Don Baylor, Col | 1995 | Lou Piniella, Sea |
| 1996 | Bruce Bochy, SD | 1996 | Joe Torre, NY/Johnny Oates, Tex |
| 1997 | Dusty Baker, SF | 1997 | Davey Johnson, Balt |
| 1998 | Larry Dierker, Hou | 1998 | Joe Torre, NY |
| 1999 | Jack McKeon, Cin | 1999 | Jimy Williams, Bos |
| 2000 | Dusty Baker, SF | 2000 | Jerry Manuel, Chi |

## Individual Batting (Single Game)

### MOST RUNS

7 .......Guy Hecker, Lou         Aug 15, 1886

### MOST HITS

7 .......Wilbert Robinson, Balt   June 10, 1892
        Rennie Stennett, Pitt    Sept 16, 1975

### MOST HOME RUNS

4 .......Bobby Lowe, Bos (N)      May 30, 1894
        Ed Delahanty, Phil       July 13, 1896
        Lou Gehrig, NY (A)       June 3, 1932
        Gil Hodges, Bklyn        Aug 31, 1950
        Joe Adcock, Mil (N)      July 31, 1954
        Rocky Colavito, Clev     June 10, 1959
        Willie Mays, SF          April 30, 1961
        Bob Horner, Atl          July 6, 1986
        Mark Whiten, StL         Sept 7, 1993

### MOST GRAND SLAMS

2 .......Tony Lazzeri, NY (A)     May 24, 1936
        Jim Tabor, Bos (A)       July 4, 1939
        Rudy York, Bos (A)       July 27, 1946
        Jim Gentile, Balt        May 9, 1961
        Tony Cloninger, Atl      July 3, 1966
        Jim Northrup, Det        June 24, 1968
        Frank Robinson, Balt     June 26, 1970
        Robin Ventura, Chi (A)   Sept 4, 1995
        Chris Hoiles, Balt       Aug 14, 1998
        Fernando Tatis, StL      Apr 23, 1999
        N. Garciaparra, Bos      May 10, 1999

### MOST RBIs

12 .....Jim Bottomley, StL       Sept 16, 1924
        Mark Whiten, StL         Sept 7, 1993

## Individual Batting (Single Inning)

### MOST RUNS

3 .......Tommy Burns, Chi (N)   Sept 6, 1883, 7th inning
        Ned Williamson, Chi (N) Sept 6, 1883, 7th inning
        Sammy White, Bos (A)   June 18, 1953, 7th inning

### MOST RBIs

8.......Fernando Tatis, StL     Apr 23, 1999, 3rd inning

### MOST HITS

3 .......Tommy Burns, Chi (N)   Sept 6, 1883, 7th inning
        Fred Pfeiffer, Chi (N)  Sept 6, 1883, 7th inning
        Ned Williamson, Chi (N) Sept 6, 1883, 7th inning
        Gene Stephens, Bos (A)  June 18, 1953, 7th inning

Note: All single-game hitting records for a nine-inning game.

## The Regular Season (Cont.)

### Individual Pitching (Single Game)

**MOST INNINGS PITCHED**

| | | |
|---|---|---|
| 26 | Leon Cadore, Bklyn | May 1, 1920, tie 1–1 |
| | Joe Oeschger, Bos (N) | May 1, 1920, tie 1–1 |

**MOST RUNS ALLOWED**

| | | |
|---|---|---|
| 24 | Al Travers, Det | May 18, 1912 |

**MOST HITS ALLOWED**

| | | |
|---|---|---|
| 36 | Jack Wadsworth, Lou | Aug 17, 1894 |

**MOST STRIKEOUTS**

| | | |
|---|---|---|
| 20 | Roger Clemens, Bos | April 29, 1986 |
| 20 | Roger Clemens, Bos | Sept 18, 1996 |
| 20 | Kerry Wood, Chi (N) | May 6, 1998 |
| 20 | Randy Johnson, Ariz | May 8, 2001 |

**MOST WALKS ALLOWED**

| | | |
|---|---|---|
| 16 | Bill George, NY (N) | May 30, 1887 |
| | George Van Haltren, Chi (N) | June 27, 1887 |
| | Henry Gruber, Clev | Apr 19, 1890 |
| | Bruno Haas, Phil (A) | June 2, 1915 |

**MOST WILD PITCHES**

| | | |
|---|---|---|
| 6 | J.R. Richard, Hou | April 10, 1979 |
| | Phil Niekro, Atl | Aug 14, 1979 |
| | Bill Gullickson, Mtl | April 10, 1982 |

### Individual Pitching (Single Inning)

**MOST RUNS ALLOWED**

| | | |
|---|---|---|
| 13 | Lefty O'Doul, Bos (A) | July 7, 1923 |

**MOST WALKS ALLOWED**

| | | |
|---|---|---|
| 8 | Dolly Gray, Wash | Aug 28, 1909 |

**MOST WILD PITCHES**

| | | |
|---|---|---|
| 4 | Walter Johnson, Wash | Sept 21, 1914 |
| | Phil Niekro, Atl | Aug 14, 1979 |

### Miscellaneous

**LONGEST GAME, BY INNINGS**

| | | |
|---|---|---|
| 26 | Brooklyn 1, Boston 1 | May 1, 1920 |

**LONGEST NINE-INNING GAME, BY TIME**

4:27 ..Los Angeles 11, San Francisco 10  Oct 5, 2001

## Baseball Hall of Fame

### Players

| | Position | Career | Selected | | Position | Career | Selected |
|---|---|---|---|---|---|---|---|
| Hank Aaron | OF | 1954–76 | 1982 | Orlando Cepeda | 1B | 1958–74 | 1999 |
| Grover Alexander | P | 1911–30 | 1938 | Frank Chance | 1B | 1898–1914 | 1946 |
| Cap Anson | 1B | 1876–97 | 1939 | Oscar Charleston* | OF | | 1976 |
| Luis Aparicio | SS | 1956–73 | 1984 | Jack Chesbro | P | 1899–1909 | 1946 |
| Luke Appling | SS | 1930–50 | 1964 | Fred Clarke | OF | 1894–1915 | 1945 |
| Richie Ashburn | OF | 1948–62 | 1995 | John Clarkson | P | 1882–94 | 1963 |
| Earl Averill | OF | 1929–41 | 1975 | Roberto Clemente | OF | 1955–72 | 1973 |
| Frank Baker | 3B | 1908–22 | 1955 | Ty Cobb | OF | 1905–28 | 1936 |
| Dave Bancroft | SS | 1915–30 | 1971 | Mickey Cochrane | C | 1925–37 | 1947 |
| Ernie Banks | SS-1B | 1953–71 | 1977 | Eddie Collins | 2B | 1906–30 | 1939 |
| Jake Beckley | 1B | 1888–1907 | 1971 | Jimmy Collins | 3B | 1895–1908 | 1945 |
| Cool Papa Bell* | OF | | 1974 | Earle Combs | OF | 1924–35 | 1970 |
| Johnny Bench | C | 1967–83 | 1989 | Roger Connor | 1B | 1880–97 | 1976 |
| Chief Bender | P | 1903–25 | 1953 | Stan Coveleski | P | 1912–28 | 1969 |
| Yogi Berra | C | 1946–65 | 1972 | Sam Crawford | OF | 1899–1917 | 1957 |
| Jim Bottomley | 1B | 1922–37 | 1974 | Joe Cronin | SS | 1926–45 | 1956 |
| Lou Boudreau | SS | 1938–52 | 1970 | Candy Cummings | P | 1872–77 | 1939 |
| Roger Bresnahan | C | 1897–1915 | 1945 | Kiki Cuyler | OF | 1921–38 | 1968 |
| George Brett | 3B | 1973–93 | 1999 | Ray Dandridge* | 3B | | 1987 |
| Lou Brock | OF | 1961–79 | 1985 | George Davis | SS | 1890–1909 | 1998 |
| Dan Brouthers | 1B | 1879–1904 | 1945 | Leon Day* | P | | 1995 |
| Three Finger Brown | P | 1903–16 | 1949 | Dizzy Dean | P | 1930–47 | 1953 |
| Jim Bunning | P | 1955–71 | 1996 | Ed Delahanty | OF | 1888–1903 | 1945 |
| Jesse Burkett | OF | 1890–1905 | 1946 | Bill Dickey | C | 1928–46 | 1954 |
| Roy Campanella | C | 1948–57 | 1969 | Martin Dihigo* | P-OF | | 1977 |
| Rod Carew | 1B-2B | 1967–85 | 1991 | Joe DiMaggio | OF | 1936–51 | 1955 |
| Max Carey | OF | 1910–29 | 1961 | Larry Doby | OF | 1947–59 | 1998 |
| Steve Carlton | P | 1965–88 | 1994 | Bobby Doerr | 2B | 1937–51 | 1986 |

Note: Career dates indicate first and last appearances in the majors.

*Elected on the basis of his career in the Negro leagues.

## Players (Cont.)

| Name | Position | Career | Selected | Name | Position | Career | Selected |
|---|---|---|---|---|---|---|---|
| Don Drysdale | P | 1956–69 | 1984 | Juan Marichal | P | 1960–75 | 1983 |
| Hugh Duffy | OF | 1888–1906 | 1945 | Rube Marquard | P | 1908–25 | 1971 |
| Johnny Evers | 2B | 1902–29 | 1939 | Eddie Mathews | 3B | 1952–68 | 1978 |
| Buck Ewing | C | 1880–97 | 1946 | Christy Mathewson | P | 1900–16 | 1936 |
| Red Faber | P | 1914–33 | 1964 | Willie Mays | OF | 1951–73 | 1979 |
| Bob Feller | P | 1936–56 | 1962 | Bill Mazeroski | 2B | 1956–72 | 2001 |
| Rick Ferrell | C | 1929–47 | 1984 | Tommy McCarthy | OF | 1884–96 | 1946 |
| Rollie Fingers | P | 1968–85 | 1992 | Willie McCovey | 1B | 1959–80 | 1986 |
| Carlton Fisk | C | 1969–93 | 2000 | Joe McGinnity | P | 1899–1908 | 1946 |
| Elmer Flick | OF | 1898–1910 | 1963 | Bid McPhee | 2B | 1882–99 | 2000 |
| Whitey Ford | P | 1950–67 | 1974 | Joe Medwick | OF | 1932–48 | 1968 |
| Bill Foster* | P |  | 1996 | Johnny Mize | 1B | 1936–53 | 1981 |
| Nellie Fox | 2B | 1947–65 | 1997 | Joe Morgan | 2B | 1963–84 | 1990 |
| Jimmie Foxx | 1B | 1925–45 | 1951 | Stan Musial | OF-1B | 1941–63 | 1969 |
| Frankie Frisch | 2B | 1919–37 | 1947 | Hal Newhouser | P | 1939–55 | 1992 |
| Pud Galvin | P | 1879–92 | 1965 | Kid Nichols | P | 1890–1906 | 1949 |
| Lou Gehrig | 1B | 1923–39 | 1939 | Phil Niekro | P | 1964–87 | 1997 |
| Charlie Gehringer | 2B | 1924–42 | 1949 | Jim O'Rourke | OF | 1876–1904 | 1945 |
| Bob Gibson | P | 1959–75 | 1981 | Mel Ott | OF | 1926–47 | 1951 |
| Josh Gibson* | C |  | 1972 | Satchel Paige* | P | 1948–65 | 1971 |
| Lefty Gomez | P | 1930–43 | 1972 | Jim Palmer | P | 1965–84 | 1990 |
| Goose Goslin | OF | 1921–38 | 1968 | Herb Pennock | P | 1912–34 | 1948 |
| Hank Greenberg | 1B | 1930–47 | 1956 | Tony Perez | 1B | 1964–86 | 2000 |
| Burleigh Grimes | P | 1916–34 | 1964 | Gaylord Perry | P | 1962–83 | 1991 |
| Lefty Grove | P | 1925–41 | 1947 | Eddie Plank | P | 1901–17 | 1946 |
| Chick Hafey | OF | 1924–37 | 1971 | Kirby Puckett | OF | 1984–95 | 2001 |
| Jesse Haines | P | 1918–37 | 1970 | Charley Radbourn | P | 1880–91 | 1939 |
| Billy Hamilton | OF | 1888–1901 | 1961 | Pee Wee Reese | SS | 1940–58 | 1984 |
| Gabby Hartnett | C | 1922–41 | 1955 | Sam Rice | OF | 1915–35 | 1963 |
| Harry Heilmann | OF | 1914–32 | 1952 | Eppa Rixey | P | 1912–33 | 1963 |
| Billy Herman | 2B | 1931–47 | 1975 | Phil Rizzuto | SS | 1941–56 | 1994 |
| Harry Hooper | OF | 1909–25 | 1971 | Robin Roberts | P | 1948–66 | 1976 |
| Rogers Hornsby | 2B | 1915–37 | 1942 | Brooks Robinson | 3B | 1955–77 | 1983 |
| Waite Hoyt | P | 1918–38 | 1969 | Frank Robinson | OF | 1956–76 | 1982 |
| Carl Hubbell | P | 1928–43 | 1947 | Jackie Robinson | 2B | 1947–56 | 1962 |
| Catfish Hunter | P | 1965–79 | 1987 | Joe (Bullet) Rogan* | P |  | 1998 |
| Monte Irvin* | OF | 1949–56 | 1973 | Edd Roush | OF | 1913–31 | 1962 |
| Reggie Jackson | OF | 1967–87 | 1993 | Red Ruffing | P | 1924–47 | 1967 |
| Travis Jackson | SS | 1922–36 | 1982 | Amos Rusie | P | 1889–1901 | 1977 |
| Ferguson Jenkins | P | 1965–83 | 1991 | Babe Ruth | OF | 1914–35 | 1936 |
| Hugh Jennings | SS | 1891–1918 | 1945 | Nolan Ryan | P | 1966–93 | 1999 |
| Judy Johnson* | 3B |  | 1975 | Ray Schalk | C | 1912–29 | 1955 |
| Walter Johnson | P | 1907–27 | 1936 | Mike Schmidt | 3B | 1972–89 | 1995 |
| Addie Joss | P | 1902–10 | 1978 | Red Schoendienst | 2B | 1945–63 | 1989 |
| Al Kaline | OF | 1953–74 | 1980 | Tom Seaver | P | 1967–86 | 1992 |
| Tim Keefe | P | 1880–93 | 1964 | Joe Sewell | SS | 1920–33 | 1977 |
| Willie Keeler | OF | 1892–1910 | 1939 | Al Simmons | OF | 1924–44 | 1953 |
| George Kell | 3B | 1943–57 | 1983 | George Sisler | 1B | 1915–30 | 1939 |
| Joe Kelley | OF | 1891–1908 | 1971 | Enos Slaughter | OF | 1938–59 | 1985 |
| George Kelly | 1B | 1915–32 | 1973 | Hilton Smith* | P |  | 2001 |
| King Kelly | C | 1878–93 | 1945 | Duke Snider | OF | 1947–64 | 1980 |
| Harmon Killebrew | 1B-3B | 1954–75 | 1984 | Warren Spahn | P | 1942–65 | 1973 |
| Ralph Kiner | OF | 1946–55 | 1975 | Al Spalding | P | 1871–78 | 1939 |
| Chuck Klein | OF | 1928–44 | 1980 | Tris Speaker | OF | 1907–28 | 1937 |
| Sandy Koufax | P | 1955–66 | 1972 | Willie Stargell | OF-1B | 1962–82 | 1988 |
| Nap Lajoie | 2B | 1896–1916 | 1937 | Turkey Stearns* | CF |  | 2000 |
| Tony Lazzeri | 2B | 1926–39 | 1991 | Don Sutton | P | 1966–88 | 1998 |
| Bob Lemon | P | 1941–58 | 1976 | Bill Terry | 1B | 1923–36 | 1954 |
| Buck Leonard* | 1B |  | 1977 | Sam Thompson | OF | 1885–1906 | 1974 |
| Fred Lindstrom | 3B | 1924–36 | 1976 | Joe Tinker | SS | 1902–16 | 1946 |
| Pop Lloyd* | SS-1B |  | 1977 | Pie Traynor | 3B | 1920–37 | 1948 |
| Ernie Lombardi | C | 1931–47 | 1986 | Dazzy Vance | P | 1915–35 | 1955 |
| Ted Lyons | P | 1923–46 | 1955 | Arky Vaughan | SS | 1932–48 | 1985 |
| Mickey Mantle | OF | 1951–68 | 1974 | Rube Waddell | P | 1897–1910 | 1946 |
| Heinie Manush | OF | 1923–39 | 1964 | Honus Wagner | SS | 1897–1917 | 1936 |
| Rabbit Maranville | SS-2B | 1912–35 | 1954 | Bobby Wallace | SS | 1894–1918 | 1953 |

*Elected on the basis of his career in the Negro leagues.

### Players *(Cont.)*

| | Position | Career | Selected |
|---|---|---|---|
| Ed Walsh | P | 1904–17 | 1946 |
| Lloyd Waner | OF | 1927–45 | 1967 |
| Paul Waner | OF | 1926–45 | 1952 |
| John Ward | 2B-P | 1878–94 | 1964 |
| Mickey Welch | P | 1880–92 | 1973 |
| Willie Wells* | SS | 1924–49 | 1997 |
| Zach Wheat | OF | 1909–27 | 1959 |
| Hoyt Wilhelm | P | 1952–72 | 1985 |
| Billy Williams | OF | 1959–76 | 1987 |
| Ted Williams | OF | 1939–60 | 1966 |
| Vic Willis | P | 1898–1910 | 1995 |
| Hack Wilson | OF | 1923–34 | 1979 |
| Dave Winfield | OF | 1973–95 | 2001 |
| Early Wynn | P | 1939–63 | 1972 |
| Carl Yastrzemski | OF | 1961–83 | 1989 |
| Cy Young | P | 1890–1911 | 1937 |
| Ross Youngs | OF | 1917–26 | 1972 |
| Robin Yount | SS | 1974–93 | 1999 |

### Pioneers/Executives *(Cont.)*

| | Selected |
|---|---|
| Happy Chandler (commissioner) | 1982 |
| Charles Comiskey (manager-executive) | 1939 |
| Rube Foster (player-manager-executive) | 1981 |
| Ford Frick (commissioner-executive) | 1970 |
| Warren Giles (executive) | 1979 |
| Will Harridge (executive) | 1972 |
| William Hulbert (executive) | 1995 |
| Ban Johnson (executive) | 1937 |
| Kenesaw M. Landis (commissioner) | 1944 |
| Larry MacPhail (executive) | 1978 |
| Lee MacPhail Jr. (executive) | 1998 |
| Branch Rickey (manager-executive) | 1967 |
| Al Spalding (player-executive) | 1939 |
| Bill Veeck (owner) | 1991 |
| George Weiss (executive) | 1971 |
| George Wright (player-manager) | 1937 |
| Harry Wright (player-manager-executive) | 1953 |
| Tom Yawkey (executive) | 1980 |

### Umpires

| | Selected |
|---|---|
| Al Barlick | 1989 |
| Nestor Chylak | 1999 |
| Jocko Conlan | 1974 |
| Tom Connolly | 1953 |
| Billy Evans | 1973 |
| Cal Hubbard | 1976 |
| Bill Klem | 1953 |
| Bill McGowan | 1992 |

### Managers

| | Managed | Selected |
|---|---|---|
| Walt Alston | 1954–76 | 1983 |
| Sparky Anderson | 1970–94 | 2000 |
| Leo Durocher | 1939–73 | 1994 |
| Clark Griffith | 1901–20 | 1946 |
| Bucky Harris | 1924–56 | 1975 |
| Ned Hanlon | 1899–1907 | 1996 |
| Miller Huggins | 1913–29 | 1964 |
| Tommy Lasorda | 1977–96 | 1997 |
| Al Lopez | 1951–69 | 1977 |
| Connie Mack | 1894–1950 | 1937 |
| Joe McCarthy | 1926–50 | 1957 |
| John McGraw | 1899–1932 | 1937 |
| Bill McKechnie | 1915–46 | 1962 |
| Wilbert Robinson | 1902–31 | 1945 |
| Frank Selee | 1890–1905 | 1999 |
| Casey Stengel | 1934–65 | 1966 |
| Earl Weaver | 1968–82, 85–86 | 1996 |

### Pioneers/Executives

| | Selected |
|---|---|
| Ed Barrow (manager-executive) | 1953 |
| Morgan Bulkeley (executive) | 1937 |
| Alexander Cartwright (executive) | 1938 |
| Henry Chadwick (writer-executive) | 1938 |

*Elected on the basis of his career in the Negro leagues.

## Notable Achievements

### No-Hit Games, Nine Innings or More

#### NATIONAL LEAGUE

| Date | Pitcher and Game | Date | Pitcher and Game |
|---|---|---|---|
| 1876......July 15 | George Bradley, StL vs Hart 2–0 | 1892......Oct 15 | Bumpus Jones, Cin vs Pitt 7–1 (first major league game) |
| 1880......June 12 | John Richmond, Wor vs Clev 1–0 (perfect game) | 1893......Aug 16 | Bill Hawke, Balt vs Wash 5–0 |
| June 17 | Monte Ward, Prov vs Buff 5–0 (perfect game) | 1897......Sept 18 | Cy Young, Clev vs Cin 6–0 |
| | | 1898......Apr 22 | Ted Breitenstein, Cin vs Pitt 11–0 |
| Aug 19 | Larry Corcoran, Chi vs Bos 6–0 | Apr 22 | Jim Hughes, Balt vs Bos 8–0 |
| Aug 20 | Pud Galvin, Buff vs Wor 1–0 | July 8 | Frank Donahue, Phil vs Bos 5–0 |
| 1882......Sept 20 | Larry Corcoran, Chi vs Wor 5–0 | Aug 21 | Walter Thornton, Chi vs Bklyn 2–0 |
| Sept 22 | Tim Lovett, Bklyn vs NY 4–0 | 1899......May 25 | Deacon Phillippe, Lou vs NY 7–0 |
| 1883......July 25 | Hoss Radbourn, Prov vs Clev 8–0 | Aug 7 | Vic Willis, Bos vs Wash 7–1 |
| Sept 13 | Hugh Daily, Clev vs Phil 1–0 | 1900......July 12 | Noodles Hahn, Cin vs Phil 4–0 |
| 1884......June 27 | Larry Corcoran, Chi vs Prov 6–0 | 1901......July 15 | Christy Mathewson, NY vs StL 5–0 |
| Aug 4 | Pud Galvin, Buff vs Det 18–0 | 1903......Sept 18 | Chick Fraser, Phil vs Chi 10–0 |
| 1885......July 27 | John Clarkson, Chi vs Prov 4–0 | 1904......June 11 | Bob Wicker, Chi at NY 1–0 (hit in 10th; won in 12th) |
| Aug 29 | Charles Ferguson, Phil vs Prov 1–0 | 1905......June 13 | Christy Mathewson, NY vs Chi 1–0 |
| 1891......July 31 | Amos Rusie, NY vs Bklyn 6–0 | 1906......May 1 | John Lush, Phil vs Bklyn 6–0 |
| June 22 | Tom Lovett, Bklyn vs NY 4–0 | July 20 | Mal Eason, Bklyn vs StL 2–0 |
| 1892......Aug 6 | Jack Stivetts, Bos vs Bklyn 11–0 | | |
| Aug 22 | Alex Sanders, Lou vs Balt 6–2 | | |

## No-Hit Games, Nine Innings or More *(Cont.)*

### NATIONAL LEAGUE *(Cont.)*

| Date | Pitcher and Game | Date | Pitcher and Game |
|---|---|---|---|
| 1906......Aug 1 | Harry McIntire, Bklyn vs Pitt 0–1 (hit in 11th; lost in 13th) | 1965......Sept 9 | Sandy Koufax, LA vs Chi 1–0 (perfect game) |
| 1907......May 8 | Frank Pfeffer, Bos vs Cin 6–0 | 1967......June 18 | Don Wilson, Hou vs Atl 2–0 |
| Sept 20 | Nick Maddox, Pitt vs Bklyn 2–1 | 1968......July 29 | George Culver, Cin vs Phil 6–1 |
| 1908......July 4 | George Wiltse, NY vs Phil 1–0 (10 innings) | Sept 17 | Gaylord Perry, SF vs StL 1–0 |
| | | Sept 18 | Ray Washburn, StL vs SF 2–0 |
| Sept 5 | Nap Rucker, Bklyn vs Bos 6–0 | 1969......Apr 17 | Bill Stoneman, Mtl vs Phil 7–0 |
| 1909......Apr 15 | Leon Ames, NY vs Bklyn 0–3 (hit in 10th; lost in 13th) | Apr 30 | Jim Maloney, Cin vs Hou 10–0 |
| | | May 1 | Don Wilson, Hou vs Cin 4–0 |
| 1912......Sept 6 | Jeff Tesreau, NY vs Phil 3–0 | Aug 19 | Ken Holtzman, Chi vs Atl 3–0 |
| 1914......Sept 9 | George Davis, Bos vs Phil 7–0 | Sept 20 | Bob Moose, Pitt vs NY 4–0 |
| 1915......Apr 15 | Rube Marquard, NY vs Bklyn 2–0 | 1970......June 12 | Dock Ellis, Pitt vs SD 2–0 |
| Aug 31 | Jimmy Lavender, Chi vs NY 2–0 | July 20 | Bill Singer, LA vs Phil 5–0 |
| 1916......June 16 | Tom Hughes, Bos vs Pitt 2–0 | 1971......June 3 | Ken Holtzman, Chi vs Cin 1–0 |
| 1917......May 2 | Jim Vaughn, Chi vs Cin 0–1 (hit in 10th; lost in 10th) | June 23 | Rick Wise, Phil vs Cin 4–0 |
| | | Aug 14 | Bob Gibson, StL vs Pitt 11–0 |
| May 2 | Fred Toney, Cin vs Chi 1–0 (10 innings) | 1972......Apr 16 | Burt Hooton, Chi vs Phil 4–0 |
| | | Sept 2 | Milt Pappas, Chi vs SD 8–0 |
| 1919......May 11 | Hod Eller, Cin vs StL 6–0 | Oct 2 | Bill Stoneman, Mtl vs NY 7–0 |
| 1922......May 7 | Jesse Barnes, NY vs Phil 6–0 | 1973......Aug 5 | Phil Niekro, Atl vs SD 9–0 |
| 1924......July 17 | Jesse Haines, StL vs Bos 5–0 | 1975......Aug 24 | Ed Halicki, SF vs NY 6–0 |
| 1925......Sept 13 | Dazzy Vance, Bklyn vs Phil 10–1 | 1976......July 9 | Larry Dierker, Hou vs Mtl 6–0 |
| 1929......May 8 | Carl Hubbell, NY vs Pitt 11–0 | Aug 9 | John Candelaria, Pitt vs LA 2–0 |
| 1934......Sept 21 | Paul Dean, StL vs Bklyn 3–0 | Sept 29 | John Montefusco, SF vs Atl 9–0 |
| 1938......June 11 | Johnny Vander Meer, Cin vs Bos 3–0 | 1978......Apr 16 | Bob Forsch, StL vs Phil 5–0 |
| | | June 16 | Tom Seaver, Cin vs StL 4–0 |
| June 15 | Johnny Vander Meer, Cin vs Bklyn 6–0 | 1979......Apr 7 | Ken Forsch, Hou vs Atl 6–0 |
| | | 1980......June 27 | Jerry Reuss, LA vs SF 8–0 |
| 1940......Apr 30 | Tex Carleton, Bklyn vs Cin, 3–0 | 1981......May 10 | Charlie Lea, Mtl vs SF 4–0 |
| 1941......Aug 30 | Lon Warneke, StL vs Cin 2–0 | Sept 26 | Nolan Ryan, Hou vs LA 5–0 |
| 1944......Apr 27 | Jim Tobin, Bos vs Bklyn 2–0 | 1983......Sept 26 | Bob Forsch, StL vs Mtl 3–0 |
| May 15 | Clyde Shoun, Cin vs Bos 1–0 | 1986......Sept 25 | Mike Scott, Hou vs SF 2–0 |
| 1946......Apr 23 | Ed Head, Bklyn vs Bos 5–0 | 1988......Sept 16 | Tom Browning, Cin vs LA 1–0 (perfect game) |
| 1947......June 18 | Ewell Blackwell, Cin vs Bos 6–0 | | |
| 1948......Sept 9 | Rex Barney, Bklyn vs NY 2–0 | 1990 | June 29 | Fernando Valenzuela, LA vs StL 6–0 |
| 1950......Aug 11 | Vern Bickford, Bos vs Bklyn 7–0 | | |
| 1951......May 6 | Cliff Chambers, Pitt vs Bos 3–0 | 1990......Aug 15 | Terry Mulholland, Phil vs SF 6–0 |
| 1952......June 19 | Carl Erskine, Bklyn vs Chi 5–0 | 1991......May 23 | Tommy Greene, Phil vs Mtl 2–0 |
| 1954......June 12 | Jim Wilson, Mil vs Phil 2–0 | July 26 | Mark Gardner, Mtl vs LA 0–1 (hit in 10th, lost in 10th) |
| 1955......May 12 | Sam Jones, Chi vs Pitt 4–0 | | |
| 1956......May 12 | Carl Erskine, Bklyn vs NY 3–0 | July 28 | Dennis Martinez, Mtl vs LA 2–0 (perfect game) |
| Sept 25 | Sal Maglie, Bklyn vs Phil 5–0 | | |
| 1959......May 26 | Harvey Haddix, Pitt vs Mil 0–1 (hit in 13th; lost in 13th) | Sept 11 | Kent Mercker (6), Mark Wohlers (2), and Alejandro Pena (1), Atl vs SD 1–0 |
| 1960......May 15 | Don Cardwell, Chi vs StL 4–0 | 1992......Aug 17 | Kevin Gross, LA vs SF 2–0 |
| Aug 18 | Lew Burdette, Mil vs Phil 1–0 | 1993......Sept 8 | Darryl Kile, Hou vs NY 7–1 |
| Sept 16 | Warren Spahn, Mil vs Phil 4–0 | 1994......Apr 8 | Kent Mercker, Atl vs LA 6–0 |
| 1961......Apr 28 | Warren Spahn, Mil vs SF 1–0 | 1995......June 3 | Pedro Martinez, Mtl vs SD 1–0 (perfect through nine, hit in 10th) |
| 1962......June 30 | Sandy Koufax, LA vs NY 5–0 | | |
| 1963......May 11 | Sandy Koufax, LA vs SF 8–0 | July 14 | Ramon Martinez, LA vs Fla 7–0 |
| May 17 | Don Nottebart, Hou vs Phil 4–1 | 1996......May 11 | Al Leiter, Fla vs Col 11–0 |
| June 15 | Juan Marichal, SF vs Hou 1–0 | Sept 17 | Hideo Nomo, LA vs Col 9–0 |
| 1964......Apr 23 | Ken Johnson, Hou vs Cin 0–1 | 1997......June 10 | Kevin Brown, Fla vs SF 9–0 |
| June 4 | Sandy Koufax, LA vs Phil 3–0 | July 12 | Francisco Cordova (9) and Ricardo Rincon (1), Pitt vs Col 3–0 |
| June 21 | Jim Bunning, Phil vs NY 6–0 (perfect game) | | |
| 1965......June 14 | Jim Maloney, Cin vs NY 0–1 (hit in 11th; lost in 11th) | 1999......June 25 | Jose Jimenez, StL vs Ariz 1–0 |
| | | 2001......May 12 | A.J. Burnett, Fla vs SD 3–0 |
| Aug 19 | Jim Maloney, Cin vs Chi 1–0 (10 innings) | Sept 3 | Bud Smith, StL vs SD 4–0 |

Note: Includes the games struck from the official record book on Sept. 4, 1991, when baseball's committee on statistical accuracy voted to define no-hitters as games of nine innings or more that end with a team getting no hits.

## No-Hit Games, Nine Innings or More *(Cont.)*

### AMERICAN LEAGUE

| Date | Pitcher and Game | Date | Pitcher and Game |
|------|------------------|------|------------------|
| 1901......May 9 | Earl Moore, Clev vs Chi 2–4 (hit in 10th; lost in 10th) | 1966......Oct 8. | Don Larsen, NY (A) vs Bklyn (N) 2–0 (World Series) (perfect game) |
| 1902......Sept 20 | Jimmy Callahan, Chi vs Det 3–0 | 1957......Aug 20 | Bob Keegan, Chi vs Wash 6–0 |
| 1904......May 5 | Cy Young, Bos vs Phil 3–0 (perfect game) | 1958......July 20 | Jim Bunning, Det vs Bos 3–0 |
| Aug 17 | Jesse Tannehill, Bos vs Chi 6–0 | Sept 20 | Hoyt Wilhelm, Balt vs NY 1–0 |
| 1905......July 22 | Weldon Henley, Phil vs StL 6–0 | 1962......May 5 | Bo Belinsky, LA vs Balt 2–0 |
| Sept 6 | Frank Smith, Chi vs Det 15–0 | June 26 | Earl Wilson, Bos vs LA 2–0 |
| Sept 27 | Bill Dinneen, Bos vs Chi 2–0 | Aug 1 | Bill Monbouquette, Bos vs Chi 1–0 |
| 1908......June 30 | Cy Young, Bos vs NY 8–0 | Aug 26 | Jack Kralick, Minn vs KC 1–0 |
| Sept 18 | Bob Rhoades, Clev vs Bos 2–1 | 1965......Sept 16 | Dave Morehead, Bos vs Clev 2–0 |
| Sept 20 | Frank Smith, Chi vs Phil 1–0 | 1966......June 10 | Sonny Siebert, Clev vs Wash 2–0 |
| 1908......Oct 2 | Addie Joss, Clev vs Chi 1–0 (perfect game) | 1967......Apr 30 | Steve Barber (8⅔) and Stu Miller (⅓), Balt vs Det 1–2 |
| 1910......Apr 20 | Addie Joss, Clev vs Chi 1–0 | Aug 25 | Dean Chance, Minn vs Clev 2–1 |
| May 12 | Chief Bender, Phil vs Clev 4–0 | Sept 10 | Joel Horlen, Chi vs Det 6–0 |
| Aug 30 | Tom Hughes, NY vs Clev 0–5 (hit in 10th; lost in 11th) | 1968......Apr 27 | Tom Phoebus, Balt vs Bos 6–0 |
| 1911,.....July 29 | Joe Wood, Bos vs StL 5–0 | May 8 | Catfish Hunter, Oak vs Minn 4–0 (perfect game) |
| Aug 27 | Ed Walsh, Chi vs Bos 5–0 | 1969......Aug 13 | Jim Palmer, Balt vs Oak 8–0 |
| 1912......July 4 | George Mullin, Det vs StL 7–0 | 1970......July 3 | Clyde Wright, Cal vs Oak 4–0 |
| Aug 30 | Earl Hamilton, StL vs Det 5–1 | Sept 21 | Vida Blue, Oak vs Minn 6–0 |
| 1914......May 14 | Jim Scott, Chi vs Wash 0–1 (hit in 10th; lost in 10th) | 1973......Apr 27 | Steve Busby, KC vs Det 3–0 |
| May 31 | Joe Benz, Chi vs Clev 6–1 | May 15 | Nolan Ryan, Cal vs KC 3–0 |
| 1916......June 21 | George Foster, Bos vs NY 2–0 | July 15 | Nolan Ryan, Cal vs Det 6–0 |
| Aug 26 | Joe Bush, Phil vs Clev 5–0 | July 30 | Jim Bibby, Tex vs Oak 6–0 |
| Aug 30 | Dutch Leonard, Bos vs StL 4–0 | 1974......June 19 | Steve Busby, KC vs Mil 2–0 |
| 1917......Apr 14 | Ed Cicotte, Chi vs StL 11–0 | July 19 | Dick Bosman, Clev vs Oak 4–0 |
| Apr 24 | George Mogridge, NY vs Bos 2–1 | Sept 28 | Nolan Ryan, Cal vs Minn 4–0 |
| May 5 | Ernie Koob, StL vs Chi 1–0 | 1975......June 1 | Nolan Ryan, Cal vs Balt 1–0 |
| May 6 | Bob Groom, StL vs Chi 3–0 | Sept 28 | Vida Blue (5), Glenn Abbott and Paul Lindblad (1), Rollie Fingers (2), Oak vs Cal 5–0 |
| June 23 | Ernie Shore, Bos vs Wash 4–0 (perfect game) | 1976......July 28 | John Odom (5) and Francisco Barrios (4), Chi vs Oak 2–1 |
| 1918......June 3 | Dutch Leonard, Bos vs Det 5–0 | 1977......May 14 | Jim Colborn, KC vs Tex 6–0 |
| 1919......Sept 10 | Ray Caldwell, Clev vs NY 3–0 | May 30 | Dennis Eckersley, Clev vs Cal 1–0 |
| 1920......July 1 | Walter Johnson, Wash vs Bos 1–0 | Sept 22 | Bert Blyleven, Tex vs Cal 6–0 |
| 1922......Apr 30 | Charlie Robertson, Chi vs Det 2–0 (perfect game) | 1981......May 15 | Len Barker, Clev vs Tor 3–0 (perfect game) |
| 1923......Sept 4 | Sam Jones, NY vs Phil 2–0 | 1983......July 4 | Dave Righetti, NY vs Bos 4–0 |
| Sept 7 | Howard Ehmke, Bos vs Phil 4–0 | Sept 29 | Mike Warren, Oak vs Chi 3–0 |
| 1926......Aug 21 | Ted Lyons, Chi vs Bos 6–0 | 1984......Apr 7 | Jack Morris, Det vs Chi 4–0 |
| 1931......Apr 29 | Wes Ferrell, Clev vs StL 9–0 | Sept 30 | Mike Witt, Cal vs Tex 1–0 (perfect game) |
| Aug 8 | Bob Burke, Wash vs Bos 5–0 | 1986......Sept 19 | Joe Cowley, Chi vs Cal 7–1 |
| 1934......Sept 18 | Bobo Newsom, StL vs Bos 1–2 (hit in 10th; lost in 10th) | 1987......Apr 15 | Juan Nieves, Mil vs Balt 7–0 |
| 1935......Aug 31 | Vern Kennedy, Chi vs Clev 5–0 | 1990......Apr 11 | Mark Langston (7), Mike Witt (2), Cal vs Sea 1–0 |
| 1937......June 1 | Bill Dietrich, Chi vs StL 8–0 | June 2 | Randy Johnson, Sea vs Det 2–0 |
| 1938......Aug 27 | Mtle Pearson, NY vs Clev 13–0 | June 11 | Nolan Ryan, Tex vs Oak 5–0 |
| 1940......Apr 16 | Bob Feller, Clev vs Chi 1–0 (opening day) | June 29 | Dave Stewart, Oak vs Tor 5–0 |
| 1945......Sept 9 | Dick Fowler, Phil vs StL 1–0 | 1990......July 1 | Andy Hawkins, NY vs Chi 0–4 (pitched eight of nine–innning game) |
| 1946......Apr 30 | Bob Feller, Clev vs NY 1–0 | Sept 2 | Dave Stieb, Tor vs Clev 3–0 |
| 1947......July 10 | Don Black, Clev vs Phil 3–0 | 1991......May 1 | Nolan Ryan, Tex vs Tor 3–0 |
| Sep 3 | Bill McCahan, Phil vs Wash 3–0 | July 13 | Bob Milacki (6), Mike Flanagan (1), Mark Williamson (1), and Gregg Olson (1), Balt vs Oak 2–0 |
| 1948......June 30 | Bob Lemon, Clev vs Det 2–0 | Aug 11 | Wilson Alvarez, Chi vs Balt 7–0 |
| 1951......July 1 | Bob Feller, Clev vs Det 2–1 | Aug 26 | Bret Saberhagen, KC vs Chi 7–0 |
| July 12 | Allie Reynolds, NY vs Clev 1–0 | 1993......Apr 22 | Chris Bosio, Sea vs Bos 7–0 |
| Sept 28 | Allie Reynolds, NY vs Bos 8–0 | Sept 4 | Jim Abbott, NY vs Clev 4–0 |
| 1952......May 15 | Virgil Trucks, Det vs Wash 1–0 | | |
| Aug 25 | Virgil Trucks, Det vs NY 1–0 | | |
| 1953......May 6 | Bobo Holloman, StL vs Phil 6–0 (first major league start) | | |
| 1956......July 14 | Mel Parnell, Bos vs Chi 4–0 | | |

### No-Hit Games, Nine Innings or More *(Cont.)*

#### AMERICAN LEAGUE *(Cont.)*

| Date | Pitcher and Game | Date | Pitcher and Game |
|------|------------------|------|------------------|
| 1994......Apr 27 | Scott Erickson, Minn vs Mil 6–0 | 1999......July 18 | David Cone, NY vs Mtl 6–0 |
| July 28 | Kenny Rogers, Texas vs Cal 4–0 | | (perfect game) |
| | (perfect game) | Sept 11 | Eric Milton, Minn vs Ana 7–0 |
| 1996......May 14 | Dwight Gooden, NY vs Sea 2–0 | 2001......Apr 4 | Hideo Nomo, Bos vs Balt 3–0 |
| 1998......May 17 | David Wells, NY vs Minn 4–0 | | |
| | (perfect game) | | |

### Longest Hitting Streaks

#### NATIONAL LEAGUE

| Player and Team | Year | G |
|-----------------|------|---|
| Willie Keeler, Balt | 1897 | 44 |
| Pete Rose, Cin | 1978 | 44 |
| Bill Dahlen, Chi | 1894 | 42 |
| Tommy Holmes, Bos | 1945 | 37 |
| Billy Hamilton, Phil | 1894 | 36 |
| Fred Clarke, Lou | 1895 | 35 |
| Benito Santiago, SD | 1987 | 34 |
| George Davis, NY | 1893 | 33 |
| Rogers Hornsby, StL | 1922 | 32 |
| Ed Delahanty, Phil | 1899 | 31 |
| Willie Davis, LA | 1969 | 31 |
| Rico Carty, Atl | 1970 | 31 |
| Vladimir Guerrero, Mtl | 1999 | 31 |

#### AMERICAN LEAGUE

| Player and Team | Year | G |
|-----------------|------|---|
| Joe DiMaggio, NY | 1941 | 56 |
| George Sisler, StL | 1922 | 41 |
| Ty Cobb, Det | 1911 | 40 |
| Paul Molitor, Mil | 1987 | 39 |
| Ty Cobb, Det | 1917 | 35 |
| Ty Cobb, Det | 1912 | 34 |
| George Sisler, StL | 1925 | 34 |
| John Stone, Det | 1930 | 34 |
| George McQuinn, StL | 1938 | 34 |
| Dom DiMaggio, Bos | 1949 | 34 |
| Hal Chase, NY | 1907 | 33 |
| Heinie Manush, Wash | 1933 | 33 |
| Nap Lajoie, Clev | 1906 | 31 |
| Sam Rice, Wash | 1924 | 31 |
| Ken Landreaux, Minn | 1980 | 31 |

### Triple Crown Hitters

#### NATIONAL LEAGUE

| Player and Team | Year | HR | RBI | BA |
|-----------------|------|----|----|----|
| Paul Hines, Prov | 1878 | 4 | 50 | .358 |
| Hugh Duffy, Bos | 1894 | 18 | 145 | .438 |
| Heinie Zimmerman*, Chi | 1912 | 14 | 103 | .372 |
| Rogers Hornsby, StL | 1922 | 42 | 152 | .401 |
| | 1925 | 39 | 143 | .403 |
| Chuck Klein, Phil | 1933 | 28 | 120 | .368 |
| Joe Medwick, StL | 1937 | 31 | 154 | .374 |

#### AMERICAN LEAGUE

| Player and Team | Year | HR | RBI | BA |
|-----------------|------|----|----|----|
| Nap Lajoie, Phil | 1901 | 14 | 125 | .422 |
| Ty Cobb, Det | 1909 | 9 | 115 | .377 |
| Jimmie Foxx, Phil | 1933 | 48 | 163 | .356 |
| Lou Gehrig, NY | 1934 | 49 | 165 | .363 |
| Ted Williams, Bos | 1942 | 36 | 137 | .356 |
| | 1947 | 32 | 114 | .343 |
| Mickey Mantle, NY | 1956 | 52 | 130 | .353 |
| Frank Robinson, Balt | 1966 | 49 | 122 | .316 |
| Carl Yastrzemski, Bos | 1967 | 44 | 121 | .326 |

*Zimmerman ranked first in RBIs as calculated by Ernie Lanigan, but only third as calculated by Information Concepts Inc.

### THEY SAID IT

*Bill Mazeroski, new Hall of Famer,
just before cutting his tearful
induction speech short: "I want to
thank all the friends and family who
made this long trip up here to listen
to me speak and hear this crap."*

## Triple Crown Pitchers

### NATIONAL LEAGUE

| Player and Team | Year | W | L | SO | ERA |
|---|---|---|---|---|---|
| Tommy Bond, Bos | 1877 | 40 | 17 | 170 | 2.11 |
| Hoss Radbourn, Prov | 1884 | 60 | 12 | 441 | 1.38 |
| Tim Keefe, NY | 1888 | 35 | 12 | 333 | 1.74 |
| John Clarkson, Bos | 1889 | 49 | 19 | 284 | 2.73 |
| Amos Rusie, NY | 1894 | 36 | 13 | 195 | 2.78 |
| Christy Mathewson, NY | 1905 | 31 | 8 | 206 | 1.27 |
| | 1908 | 37 | 11 | 259 | 1.43 |
| Grover Alexander, Phil | 1915 | 31 | 10 | 241 | 1.22 |
| | 1916 | 33 | 12 | 167 | 1.55 |
| | 1917 | 30 | 13 | 201 | 1.86 |
| Hippo Vaughn, Chi | 1918 | 22 | 10 | 148 | 1.74 |
| Grover Alexander, Chi | 1920 | 27 | 14 | 173 | 1.91 |
| Dazzy Vance, Bklyn | 1924 | 28 | 6 | 262 | 2.16 |
| Bucky Walters, Cin | 1939 | 27 | 11 | 137 | 2.29 |
| Sandy Koufax, LA | 1963 | 25 | 5 | 306 | 1.88 |
| | 1965 | 26 | 8 | 382 | 2.04 |
| | 1966 | 27 | 9 | 317 | 1.73 |
| Steve Carlton, Phil | 1972 | 27 | 10 | 310 | 1.97 |
| Dwight Gooden, NY | 1985 | 24 | 4 | 268 | 1.53 |

### AMERICAN LEAGUE

| Player and Team | Year | W | L | SO | ERA |
|---|---|---|---|---|---|
| Cy Young, Bos | 1901 | 33 | 10 | 158 | 1.62 |
| Rube Waddell, Phil | 1905 | 26 | 11 | 287 | 1.48 |
| Walter Johnson, Wash | 1913 | 36 | 7 | 303 | 1.09 |
| | 1918 | 23 | 13 | 162 | 1.27 |
| | 1924 | 23 | 7 | 158 | 2.72 |
| Lefty Grove, Phil | 1930 | 28 | 5 | 209 | 2.54 |
| | 1931 | 31 | 4 | 175 | 2.06 |
| Lefty Gomez, NY | 1934 | 26 | 5 | 158 | 2.33 |
| | 1937 | 21 | 11 | 194 | 2.33 |
| Hal Newhouser, Det | 1945 | 25 | 9 | 212 | 1.81 |
| Roger Clemens, Tor | 1997 | 21 | 7 | 292 | 2.05 |
| | 1998 | 20 | 6 | 271 | 2.64 |
| Pedro Martinez, Bos | 1999 | 23 | 4 | 313 | 2.07 |

## Consecutive Games Played, 500 or More Games

| | | | |
|---|---|---|---|
| Cal Ripken Jr. | 2,632 | Frank McCormick | 652 |
| Lou Gehrig | 2,130 | Sandy Alomar Sr. | 648 |
| Everett Scott | 1,307 | Eddie Brown | 618 |
| Steve Garvey | 1,207 | Roy McMillan | 585 |
| Billy Williams | 1,117 | George Pinckney | 577 |
| Joe Sewell | 1,103 | Steve Brodie | 574 |
| Stan Musial | 895 | Aaron Ward | 565 |
| Eddie Yost | 829 | Candy LaChance | 540 |
| Gus Suhr | 822 | Buck Freeman | 535 |
| Nellie Fox | 798 | Fred Luderus | 533 |
| Pete Rose | 745 | Clyde Milan | 511 |
| Dale Murphy | 740 | Charlie Gehringer | 511 |
| Richie Ashburn | 730 | Vada Pinson | 508 |
| Ernie Banks | 717 | Tony Cuccinello | 504 |
| Pete Rose | 678 | Charlie Gehringer | 504 |
| Earl Averill | 673 | Omar Moreno | 503 |

## Unassisted Triple Plays

| Player and Team | Date | Pos | Opp | Opp Batter |
|---|---|---|---|---|
| Neal Ball, Clev | 7-19-09 | SS | Bos | Amby McConnell |
| Bill Wambsganss, Clev | 10-10-20 | 2B | Bklyn | Clarence Mitchell |
| George Burns, Bos | 9-14-23 | 1B | Clev | Frank Brower |
| Ernie Padgett, Bos | 10-6-23 | SS | Phil | Walter Holke |
| Glenn Wright, Pitt | 5-7-25 | SS | StL | Jim Bottomley |
| Jimmy Cooney, Chi | 5-30-27 | SS | Pitt | Paul Waner |
| Johnny Neun, Det | 5-31-27 | 1B | Clev | Homer Summa |
| Ron Hansen, Wash | 7-30-68 | SS | Clev | Joe Azcue |
| Mickey Morandini, Phil | 9-20-92 | 2B | Pitt | Jeff King |
| John Valentin, Bos | 7-15-94 | SS | Minn | Marc Newfield |
| Randy Velarde, Oak | 5-29-00 | 2B | NYY | Shane Spencer |

# National League

## Pennant Winners

| Year | Team | Manager | W | L | Pct | GA |
|------|------|---------|---|---|-----|-----|
| 1900 | Brooklyn | Ned Hanlon | 82 | 54 | .603 | 4½ |
| 1901 | Pittsburgh | Fred Clarke | 90 | 49 | .647 | 7½ |
| 1902 | Pittsburgh | Fred Clarke | 103 | 36 | .741 | 27½ |
| 1903 | Pittsburgh | Fred Clarke | 91 | 49 | .650 | 6½ |
| 1904 | New York | John McGraw | 106 | 47 | .693 | 13 |
| 1905 | New York | John McGraw | 105 | 48 | .686 | 9 |
| 1906 | Chicago | Frank Chance | 116 | 36 | .763 | 20 |
| 1907 | Chicago | Frank Chance | 107 | 45 | .704 | 17 |
| 1908 | Chicago | Frank Chance | 99 | 55 | .643 | 1 |
| 1909 | Pittsburgh | Fred Clarke | 110 | 42 | .724 | 6½ |
| 1910 | Chicago | Frank Chance | 104 | 50 | .675 | 13 |
| 1911 | New York | John McGraw | 99 | 54 | .647 | 7½ |
| 1912 | New York | John McGraw | 103 | 48 | .682 | 10 |
| 1913 | New York | John McGraw | 101 | 51 | .664 | 12½ |
| 1914 | Boston | George Stallings | 94 | 59 | .614 | 10½ |
| 1915 | Philadelphia | Pat Moran | 90 | 62 | .592 | 7 |
| 1916 | Brooklyn | Wilbert Robinson | 94 | 60 | .610 | 2½ |
| 1917 | New York | John McGraw | 98 | 56 | .636 | 10 |
| 1918 | Chicago | Fred Mitchell | 84 | 45 | .651 | 10½ |
| 1919 | Cincinnati | Pat Moran | 96 | 44 | .686 | 9 |
| 1920 | Brooklyn | Wilbert Robinson | 93 | 61 | .604 | 7 |
| 1921 | New York | John McGraw | 94 | 59 | .614 | 4 |
| 1922 | New York | John McGraw | 93 | 61 | .604 | 7 |
| 1923 | New York | John McGraw | 95 | 58 | .621 | 4½ |
| 1924 | New York | John McGraw | 93 | 60 | .608 | 1½ |
| 1925 | Pittsburgh | Bill McKechnie | 95 | 58 | .621 | 8½ |
| 1926 | St. Louis | Rogers Hornsby | 89 | 65 | .578 | 2 |
| 1927 | Pittsburgh | Donie Bush | 94 | 60 | .610 | 1½ |
| 1928 | St. Louis | Bill McKechnie | 95 | 59 | .617 | 2 |
| 1929 | Chicago | Joe McCarthy | 98 | 54 | .645 | 10½ |
| 1930 | St. Louis | Gabby Street | 92 | 62 | .597 | 2 |
| 1931 | St. Louis | Gabby Street | 101 | 53 | .656 | 13 |
| 1932 | Chicago | Charlie Grimm | 90 | 64 | .584 | 4 |
| 1933 | New York | Bill Terry | 91 | 61 | .599 | 5 |
| 1934 | St. Louis | Frankie Frisch | 95 | 58 | .621 | 2 |
| 1935 | Chicago | Charlie Grimm | 100 | 54 | .649 | 4 |
| 1936 | New York | Bill Terry | 92 | 62 | .597 | 5 |
| 1937 | New York | Bill Terry | 95 | 57 | .625 | 3 |
| 1938 | Chicago | Gabby Hartnett | 89 | 63 | .586 | 2 |
| 1939 | Cincinnati | Bill McKechnie | 97 | 57 | .630 | 4½ |
| 1940 | Cincinnati | Bill McKechnie | 100 | 53 | .654 | 12 |
| 1941 | Brooklyn | Leo Durocher | 100 | 54 | .649 | 2½ |
| 1942 | St. Louis | Billy Southworth | 106 | 48 | .688 | 2 |
| 1943 | St. Louis | Billy Southworth | 105 | 49 | .682 | 18 |
| 1944 | St. Louis | Billy Southworth | 105 | 49 | .682 | 14½ |
| 1945 | Chicago | Charlie Grimm | 98 | 56 | .636 | 3 |
| 1946 | St. Louis* | Eddie Dyer | 98 | 58 | .628 | 2 |
| 1947 | Brooklyn | Burt Shotton | 94 | 60 | .610 | 5 |
| 1948 | Boston | Billy Southworth | 91 | 62 | .595 | 6½ |
| 1949 | Brooklyn | Burt Shotton | 97 | 57 | .630 | 1 |
| 1950 | Philadelphia | Eddie Sawyer | 91 | 63 | .591 | 2 |
| 1951 | New York† | Leo Durocher | 98 | 59 | .624 | 1 |
| 1952 | Brooklyn | Chuck Dressen | 96 | 57 | .627 | 4½ |
| 1953 | Brooklyn | Chuck Dressen | 105 | 49 | .682 | 13 |
| 1954 | New York | Leo Durocher | 97 | 57 | .630 | 5 |
| 1955 | Brooklyn | Walt Alston | 98 | 55 | .641 | 13½ |
| 1956 | Brooklyn | Walt Alston | 93 | 61 | .604 | 1 |
| 1957 | Milwaukee | Fred Haney | 95 | 59 | .617 | 8 |
| 1958 | Milwaukee | Fred Haney | 92 | 62 | .597 | 8 |
| 1959 | Los Angeles‡ | Walt Alston | 88 | 68 | .564 | 2 |
| 1960 | Pittsburgh | Danny Murtaugh | 95 | 59 | .617 | 7 |
| 1961 | Cincinnati | Fred Hutchinson | 93 | 61 | .604 | 4 |
| 1962 | San Francisco# | Al Dark | 103 | 62 | .624 | 1 |
| 1963 | Los Angeles | Walt Alston | 99 | 63 | .611 | 6 |
| 1964 | St. Louis | Johnny Keane | 93 | 69 | .574 | 1 |

## Pennant Winners (Cont.)

| Year | Team | Manager | W | L | Pct | GA |
|------|------|---------|---|---|-----|-----|
| 1965 | Los Angeles | Walt Alston | 97 | 65 | .599 | 2 |
| 1966 | Los Angeles | Walt Alston | 95 | 67 | .586 | 1½ |
| 1967 | St. Louis | Red Schoendienst | 101 | 60 | .627 | 10½ |
| 1968 | St. Louis | Red Schoendienst | 97 | 65 | .599 | 9 |
| 1969 | New York (E)†† | Gil Hodges | 100 | 62 | .617 | 8 |
| 1970 | Cincinnati (W)†† | Sparky Anderson | 102 | 60 | .630 | 14½ |
| 1971 | Pittsburgh (E)†† | Danny Murtaugh | 97 | 65 | .599 | 7 |
| 1972 | Cincinnati (W)†† | Sparky Anderson | 95 | 59 | .617 | 10½ |
| 1973 | New York (E)†† | Yogi Berra | 82 | 79 | .509 | 1½ |
| 1974 | Los Angeles (W)†† | Walt Alston | 102 | 60 | .630 | 4 |
| 1975 | Cincinnati (W)†† | Sparky Anderson | 108 | 54 | .667 | 20 |
| 1976 | Cincinnati (W)†† | Sparky Anderson | 102 | 60 | .630 | 10 |
| 1977 | Los Angeles (W)†† | Tommy Lasorda | 98 | 64 | .605 | 10 |
| 1978 | Los Angeles (W)†† | Tommy Lasorda | 95 | 67 | .586 | 2½ |
| 1979 | Pittsburgh (E)†† | Chuck Tanner | 98 | 64 | .605 | 2 |
| 1980 | Philadelphia (E)†† | Dallas Green | 91 | 71 | .562 | 1 |
| 1981 | Los Angeles (W)†† | Tommy Lasorda | 63 | 47 | .573 | ** |
| 1982 | St. Louis (E)†† | Whitey Herzog | 92 | 70 | .568 | 3 |
| 1983 | Philadelphia (E)†† | Pat Corrales/ Paul Owens | 90 | 72 | .556 | 6 |
| 1984 | San Diego (W)†† | Dick Williams | 92 | 70 | .568 | 12 |
| 1985 | St. Louis (E)†† | Whitey Herzog | 101 | 61 | .623 | 3 |
| 1986 | New York (E)†† | Dave Johnson | 108 | 54 | .667 | 21½ |
| 1987 | St. Louis (E)†† | Whitey Herzog | 95 | 67 | .586 | 3 |
| 1988 | Los Angeles (W)†† | Tommy Lasorda | 94 | 67 | .584 | 7 |
| 1989 | San Francisco (W)†† | Roger Craig | 92 | 70 | .568 | 3 |
| 1990 | Cincinnati (W)†† | Lou Piniella | 91 | 71 | .562 | 5 |
| 1991 | Atlanta (W)†† | Bobby Cox | 94 | 68 | .580 | 1 |
| 1992 | Atlanta (W)†† | Bobby Cox | 98 | 64 | .605 | 8 |
| 1993 | Philadelphia (E)†† | Jim Fregosi | 97 | 65 | .599 | 3 |
| 1994 | Season ended Aug. 11 due to players' strike. | | | | | |
| 1995 | Atlanta (E)†† | Bobby Cox | 90 | 54 | .625 | 21 |
| 1996 | Atlanta (E)†† | Bobby Cox | 96 | 66 | .593 | 8 |
| 1997 | Florida (wc)†† | Jim Leyland | 92 | 70 | .568 | — |
| 1998 | San Diego (W)†† | Bruce Bochy | 98 | 64 | .605 | 9½ |
| 1999 | Atlanta Braves (E)†† | Bobby Cox | 103 | 59 | .636 | 6½ |
| 2000 | New York Mets (wc)†† | Bobby Valentine | 94 | 68 | .580 | — |
| 2001 | Arizona (W)†† | Bob Brenly | 92 | 70 | .568 | 2 |

*Defeated Brooklyn, two games to none, in playoff for pennant. †Defeated Brooklyn, two games to one, in playoff for pennant. ‡Defeated Milwaukee, two games to none, in playoff for pennant. #Defeated Los Angeles, two games to one, in playoff for pennant. ††Won Championship Series. **First half 36–21; second half 27–26, in season split by strike; defeated Houston in playoff for Western Division title.

## Most Underrated Ballplayer: Stan Musial

It's hard to argue that a Hall of Famer is underrated, but Stan Musial is. Two men are responsible for that: Joe DiMaggio and Ted Williams. DiMaggio and Williams are the ultimate baseball icons, courtesy of press-box seamheads and a bunch of PBS specials. If life were fair, though, mid-century baseball would be associated with a triumvirate of every-day players: Joltin' Joe, Teddy Ballgame and Stan the Man. Yes, Williams had a .344 batting average for his 19-year career, but he played in only one World Series. Musial, batting .331 over 22 years, led his overachieving teams into four Fall Classics. Yes, DiMaggio is on the short list of alltime outfielders, but Musial had the better career fielding percentage in the outfield, .984 versus .978. In the 1942 World Series, St. Louis, fronted by a bunch of kids—Musial among them—beat DiMaggio's exalted Yankees, four games to one. In '46 the Cards defeated a celebrated Boston club, with Williams back from the war, in seven.

From a cramped batting stance that looked as if it were made to slap singles, Musial smacked 475 homers but also led the National League in hitting seven times. His ability to run the bases shows up not in his steals but in his triples, 177, a category he led the National League in five times. He could bunt, to move a runner or to reach base, he could hit to all fields, he could foul off pitches at will and struck out about once in every 16 at bats. His career comprises a staggering 10,972 at bats, 433 of which came in his penultimate season, 1962, when he batted .330 at age 41. Preacher Roe, the outstanding Brooklyn lefthander, summarized Stan the Man's greatness in defining his own strategy for getting Musial out: "I throw him four wide ones, then I try to pick him off first base."

—Michael Bamberger

## Leading Batsmen

| Year | Player and Team | BA | Year | Player and Team | BA |
|---|---|---|---|---|---|
| 1900 | Honus Wagner, Pitt | .381 | 1951 | Stan Musial, StL | .355 |
| 1901 | Jesse Burkett, StL | .382 | 1952 | Stan Musial, StL | .336 |
| 1902 | Ginger Beaumtl, Pitt | .357 | 1953 | Carl Furillo, Bklyn | .344 |
| 1903 | Honus Wagner, Pitt | .355 | 1954 | Willie Mays, NY | .345 |
| 1904 | Honus Wagner, Pitt | .349 | 1955 | Richie Ashburn, Phil | .338 |
| 1905 | Cy Seymour, Cin | .377 | 1956 | Hank Aaron, Mil | .328 |
| 1906 | Honus Wagner, Pitt | .339 | 1957 | Stan Musial, StL | .351 |
| 1907 | Honus Wagner, Pitt | .350 | 1958 | Richie Ashburn, Phil | .350 |
| 1908 | Honus Wagner, Pitt | .354 | 1959 | Hank Aaron, Mil | .355 |
| 1909 | Honus Wagner, Pitt | .339 | 1960 | Dick Groat, Pitt | .325 |
| 1910 | Sherry Magee, Phil | .331 | 1961 | Roberto Clemente, Pitt | .351 |
| 1911 | Honus Wagner, Pitt | .334 | 1962 | Tommy Davis, LA | .346 |
| 1912 | Heinie Zimmerman, Chi | .372 | 1963 | Tommy Davis, LA | .326 |
| 1913 | Jake Daubert, Bklyn | .350 | 1964 | Roberto Clemente, Pitt | .339 |
| 1914 | Jake Daubert, Bklyn | .329 | 1965 | Roberto Clemente, Pitt | .329 |
| 1915 | Larry Doyle, NY | .320 | 1966 | Matty Alou, Pitt | .342 |
| 1916 | Hal Chase, Cin | .339 | 1967 | Roberto Clemente, Pitt | .357 |
| 1917 | Edd Roush, Cin | .341 | 1968 | Pete Rose, Cin | .335 |
| 1918 | Zach Wheat, Bklyn | .335 | 1969 | Pete Rose, Cin | .348 |
| 1919 | Edd Roush, Cin | .321 | 1970 | Rico Carty, Atl | .366 |
| 1920 | Rogers Hornsby, StL | .370 | 1971 | Joe Torre, StL | .363 |
| 1921 | Rogers Hornsby, StL | .397 | 1972 | Billy Williams, Chi | .333 |
| 1922 | Rogers Hornsby, StL | .401 | 1973 | Pete Rose, Cin | .338 |
| 1923 | Rogers Hornsby, StL | .384 | 1974 | Ralph Garr, Atl | .353 |
| 1924 | Rogers Hornsby, StL | .424 | 1975 | Bill Madlock, Chi | .354 |
| 1925 | Rogers Hornsby, StL | .403 | 1976 | Bill Madlock, Chi | .339 |
| 1926 | Bubbles Hargrave, Cin | .353 | 1977 | Dave Parker, Pitt | .338 |
| 1927 | Paul Waner, Pitt | .380 | 1978 | Dave Parker, Pitt | .334 |
| 1928 | Rogers Hornsby, Bos | .387 | 1979 | Keith Hernandez, StL | .344 |
| 1929 | Lefty O'Doul, Phil | .398 | 1980 | Bill Buckner, Chi | .324 |
| 1930 | Bill Terry, NY | .401 | 1981 | Bill Madlock, Pitt | .341 |
| 1931 | Chick Hafey, StL | .349 | 1982 | Al Oliver, Mtl | .331 |
| 1932 | Lefty O'Doul, Bklyn | .368 | 1983 | Bill Madlock, Pitt | .323 |
| 1933 | Chuck Klein, Phil | .368 | 1984 | Tony Gwynn, SD | .351 |
| 1934 | Paul Waner, Pitt | .362 | 1985 | Willie McGee, StL | .353 |
| 1935 | Arky Vaughan, Pitt | .385 | 1986 | Tim Raines, Mtl | .334 |
| 1936 | Paul Waner, Pitt | .373 | 1987 | Tony Gwynn, SD | .370 |
| 1937 | Joe Medwick, StL | .374 | 1988 | Tony Gwynn, SD | .313 |
| 1938 | Ernie Lombardi, Cin | .342 | 1989 | Tony Gwynn, SD | .336 |
| 1939 | Johnny Mize, StL | .349 | 1990 | Willie McGee, StL | .335 |
| 1940 | Debs Garms, Pitt | .355 | 1991 | Terry Pendleton, Atl | .319 |
| 1941 | Pete Reiser, Bklyn | .343 | 1992 | Gary Sheffield, SD | .330 |
| 1942 | Ernie Lombardi, Bos | .330 | 1993 | Andres Galarraga, Col | .370 |
| 1943 | Stan Musial, StL | .357 | 1994 | Tony Gwynn, SD | .394 |
| 1944 | Dixie Walker, Bklyn | .357 | 1995 | Tony Gwynn, SD | .368 |
| 1945 | Phil Cavarretta, Chi | .355 | 1996 | Tony Gwynn, SD | .353 |
| 1946 | Stan Musial, StL | .365 | 1997 | Tony Gwynn, SD | .372 |
| 1947 | Harry Walker, StL-Phil | .363 | 1998 | Larry Walker, Col | .363 |
| 1948 | Stan Musial, StL | .376 | 1999 | Larry Walker, Col | .379 |
| 1949 | Jackie Robinson, Bklyn | .342 | 2000 | Todd Helton, Col | .372 |
| 1950 | Stan Musial, StL | .346 | 2001 | Larry Walker, Col | .350 |

## Leaders in Runs Scored

| Year | Player and Team | Runs | Year | Player and Team | Runs |
|------|-----------------|------|------|-----------------|------|
| 1900 | Roy Thomas, Phil | 131 | 1952 | Stan Musial, StL | 105 |
| 1901 | Jesse Burkett, StL | 139 | | Solly Hemus, StL | 105 |
| 1902 | Honus Wagner, Pitt | 105 | 1953 | Duke Snider, Bklyn | 132 |
| 1903 | Ginger Beaumont, Pitt | 137 | 1954 | Stan Musial, StL | 120 |
| 1904 | George Browne, NY | 99 | | Duke Snider, Bklyn | 120 |
| 1905 | Mike Donlin, NY | 124 | 1955 | Duke Snider, Bklyn | 126 |
| 1906 | Honus Wagner, Pitt | 103 | 1956 | Frank Robinson, Cin | 122 |
| | Frank Chance, Chi | 103 | 1957 | Hank Aaron, Mil | 118 |
| 1907 | Spike Shannon, NY | 104 | 1958 | Willie Mays, SF | 121 |
| 1908 | Fred Tenney, NY | 101 | 1959 | Vada Pinson, Cin | 131 |
| 1909 | Tommy Leach, Pitt | 126 | 1960 | Bill Bruton, Mil | 112 |
| 1910 | Sherry Magee, Phil | 110 | 1961 | Willie Mays, SF | 129 |
| 1911 | Jimmy Sheckard, Chi | 121 | 1962 | Frank Robinson, Cin | 134 |
| 1912 | Bob Bescher, Cin | 120 | 1963 | Hank Aaron, Mil | 121 |
| 1913 | Tommy Leach, Chi | 99 | 1964 | Dick Allen, Phil | 125 |
| | Max Carey, Pitt | 99 | 1965 | Tommy Harper, Cin | 126 |
| 1914 | George Burns, NY | 100 | 1966 | Felipe Alou, Atl | 122 |
| 1915 | Gavvy Cravath, Phil | 89 | 1967 | Hank Aaron, Atl | 113 |
| 1916 | George Burns, NY | 105 | | Lou Brock, StL | 113 |
| 1917 | George Burns, NY | 103 | 1968 | Glenn Beckert, Chi | 98 |
| 1918 | Heinie Groh, Cin | 88 | 1969 | Bobby Bonds, SF | 120 |
| 1919 | George Burns, NY | 86 | | Pete Rose, Cin | 120 |
| 1920 | George Burns, NY | 115 | 1970 | Billy Williams, Chi | 137 |
| 1921 | Rogers Hornsby, StL | 131 | 1971 | Lou Brock, StL | 126 |
| 1922 | Rogers Hornsby, StL | 141 | 1972 | Joe Morgan, Cin | 122 |
| 1923 | Ross Youngs, NY | 121 | 1973 | Bobby Bonds, SF | 131 |
| 1924 | Frankie Frisch, NY | 121 | 1974 | Pete Rose, Cin | 110 |
| | Rogers Hornsby, StL | 121 | 1975 | Pete Rose, Cin | 112 |
| 1925 | Kiki Cuyler, Pitt | 144 | 1976 | Pete Rose, Cin | 130 |
| 1926 | Kiki Cuyler, Pitt | 113 | 1977 | George Foster, Cin | 124 |
| 1927 | Lloyd Waner, Pitt | 133 | 1978 | Ivan DeJesus, Chi | 104 |
| | Rogers Hornsby, NY | 133 | 1979 | Keith Hernandez, StL | 116 |
| 1928 | Paul Waner, Pitt | 142 | 1980 | Keith Hernandez, StL | 111 |
| 1929 | Rogers Hornsby, Chi | 156 | 1981 | Mike Schmidt, Phil | 78 |
| 1930 | Chuck Klein, Phil | 158 | 1982 | Lonnie Smith, StL | 120 |
| 1931 | Bill Terry, NY | 121 | 1983 | Tim Raines, Mtl | 133 |
| | Chuck Klein, Phil | 121 | 1984 | Ryne Sandberg, Chi | 114 |
| 1932 | Chuck Klein, Phil | 152 | 1985 | Dale Murphy, Atl | 118 |
| 1933 | Pepper Martin, StL | 122 | 1986 | Von Hayes, Phil | 107 |
| 1934 | Paul Waner, Pitt | 122 | | Tony Gwynn, SD | 107 |
| 1935 | Augie Galan, Chi | 133 | 1987 | Tim Raines, Mtl | 123 |
| 1936 | Arky Vaughan, Pitt | 122 | 1988 | Brett Butler, SF | 109 |
| 1937 | Joe Medwick, StL | 111 | 1989 | Howard Johnson, NY | 104 |
| 1938 | Mel Ott, NY | 116 | | Will Clark, SF | 104 |
| 1939 | Billy Werber, Cin | 115 | | Ryne Sandberg, Chi | 104 |
| 1940 | Arky Vaughan, Pitt | 113 | 1990 | Ryne Sandberg, Chi | 116 |
| 1941 | Pete Reiser, Bklyn | 117 | 1991 | Brett Butler, LA | 112 |
| 1942 | Mel Ott, NY | 118 | 1992 | Barry Bonds, Pitt | 109 |
| 1943 | Arky Vaughan, Bklyn | 112 | 1993 | Lenny Dykstra, Phil | 143 |
| 1944 | Bill Nicholson, Chi | 116 | 1994 | Jeff Bagwell, Hou | 104 |
| 1945 | Eddie Stanky, Bklyn | 128 | 1995 | Craig Biggio, Hou | 123 |
| 1946 | Stan Musial, StL | 124 | 1996 | Ellis Burks, Col | 142 |
| 1947 | Johnny Mize, NY | 137 | 1997 | Craig Biggio, Hou | 146 |
| 1948 | Stan Musial, StL | 135 | 1998 | Sammy Sosa, Chi | 134 |
| 1949 | Pee Wee Reese, Bklyn | 132 | 1999 | Jeff Bagwell, Hou | 143 |
| 1950 | Earl Torgeson, Bos | 120 | 2000 | Jeff Bagwell, Hou | 152 |
| 1951 | Stan Musial, StL | 124 | 2001 | Sammy Sosa, Chi | 146 |
| | Ralph Kiner, Pitt | 124 | | | |

## Leaders in Hits

| Year | Player and Team | Hits | Year | Player and Team | Hits |
|------|-----------------|------|------|-----------------|------|
| 1900 | Willie Keeler, Bklyn | 208 | 1953 | Richie Ashburn, Phil | 205 |
| 1901 | Jesse Burkett, StL | 228 | 1954 | Don Mueller, NY | 212 |
| 1902 | Ginger Beaumont, Pitt | 194 | 1955 | Ted Kluszewski, Cin | 192 |
| 1903 | Ginger Beaumont, Pitt | 209 | 1956 | Hank Aaron, Mil | 200 |
| 1904 | Ginger Beaumont, Pitt | 185 | 1957 | Red Schoendienst, NY-Mil | 200 |
| 1905 | Cy Seymour, Cin | 219 | 1958 | Richie Ashburn, Phil | 215 |
| 1906 | Harry Steinfeldt, Chi | 176 | 1959 | Hank Aaron, Mil | 223 |
| 1907 | Ginger Beaumont, Bos | 187 | 1960 | Willie Mays, SF | 190 |
| 1908 | Honus Wagner, Pitt | 201 | 1961 | Vada Pinson, Cin | 208 |
| 1909 | Larry Doyle, NY | 172 | 1962 | Tommy Davis, LA | 230 |
| 1910 | Honus Wagner, Pitt | 178 | 1963 | Vada Pinson, Cin | 204 |
|      | Bobby Byrne, Pitt | 178 | 1964 | Roberto Clemente, Pitt | 211 |
| 1911 | Doc Miller, Bos | 192 |      | Curt Flood, StL | 211 |
| 1912 | Heinie Zimmerman, Chi | 207 | 1965 | Pete Rose, Cin | 209 |
| 1913 | Gavvy Cravath, Phil | 179 | 1966 | Felipe Alou, Atl | 218 |
| 1914 | Sherry Magee, Phil | 171 | 1967 | Roberto Clemente, Pitt | 209 |
| 1915 | Larry Doyle, NY | 189 | 1968 | Felipe Alou, Atl | 210 |
| 1916 | Hal Chase, Cin | 184 |      | Pete Rose, Cin | 210 |
| 1917 | Heinie Groh, Cin | 182 | 1969 | Matty Alou, Pitt | 231 |
| 1918 | Charlie Hollocher, Chi | 161 | 1970 | Pete Rose, Cin | 205 |
| 1919 | Ivy Olson, Bklyn | 164 |      | Billy Williams, Chi | 205 |
| 1920 | Rogers Hornsby, StL | 218 | 1971 | Joe Torre, StL | 230 |
| 1921 | Rogers Hornsby, StL | 235 | 1972 | Pete Rose, Cin | 198 |
| 1922 | Rogers Hornsby, StL | 250 | 1973 | Pete Rose, Cin | 230 |
| 1923 | Frankie Frisch, NY | 223 | 1974 | Ralph Garr, Atl | 214 |
| 1924 | Rogers Hornsby, StL | 227 | 1975 | Dave Cash, Phil | 213 |
| 1925 | Jim Bottomley, StL | 227 | 1976 | Pete Rose, Cin | 215 |
| 1926 | Eddie Brown, Bos | 201 | 1977 | Dave Parker, Pitt | 215 |
| 1927 | Paul Waner, Pitt | 237 | 1978 | Steve Garvey, LA | 202 |
| 1928 | Freddy Lindstrom, NY | 231 | 1979 | Garry Templeton, StL | 211 |
| 1929 | Lefty O'Doul, Phil | 254 | 1980 | Steve Garvey, LA | 200 |
| 1930 | Bill Terry, NY | 254 | 1981 | Pete Rose, Phil | 140 |
| 1931 | Lloyd Waner, Pitt | 214 | 1982 | Al Oliver, Mtl | 204 |
| 1932 | Chuck Klein, Phil | 226 | 1983 | Jose Cruz, Hou | 189 |
| 1933 | Chuck Klein, Phil | 223 |      | Andre Dawson, Mtl | 189 |
| 1934 | Paul Waner, Pitt | 217 | 1984 | Tony Gwynn, SD | 213 |
| 1935 | Billy Herman, Chi | 227 | 1985 | Willie McGee, StL | 216 |
| 1936 | Joe Medwick, StL | 223 | 1986 | Tony Gwynn, SD | 211 |
| 1937 | Joe Medwick, StL | 237 | 1987 | Tony Gwynn, SD | 218 |
| 1938 | Frank McCormick, Cin | 209 | 1988 | Andres Galarraga, Mtl | 184 |
| 1939 | Frank McCormick, Cin | 209 | 1989 | Tony Gwynn, SD | 203 |
| 1940 | Stan Hack, Chi | 191 | 1990 | Brett Butler, SF | 192 |
|      | Frank McCormick, Cin | 191 |      | Lenny Dykstra, Phil | 192 |
| 1941 | Stan Hack, Chi | 186 | 1991 | Terry Pendleton, Atl | 187 |
| 1942 | Enos Slaughter, StL | 188 | 1992 | Terry Pendleton, Atl | 199 |
| 1943 | Stan Musial, StL | 220 |      | Andy Van Slyke, Pitt | 199 |
| 1944 | Stan Musial, StL | 197 | 1993 | Lenny Dykstra, Phil | 194 |
|      | Phil Cavarretta, Chi | 197 | 1994 | Tony Gwynn, SD | 165 |
| 1945 | Tommy Holmes, Bos | 224 | 1995 | Dante Bichette, Col | 197 |
| 1946 | Stan Musial, StL | 228 |      | Tony Gwynn, SD | 197 |
| 1947 | Tommy Holmes, Bos | 191 | 1996 | Lance Johnson, NY | 227 |
| 1948 | Stan Musial, StL | 230 | 1997 | Tony Gwynn, SD | 220 |
| 1949 | Stan Musial, StL | 207 | 1998 | Dante Bichette, Col | 219 |
| 1950 | Duke Snider, Bklyn | 199 | 1999 | Luis Gonzalez, Ariz | 206 |
| 1951 | Richie Ashburn, Phil | 221 | 2000 | Todd Helton, Col | 216 |
| 1952 | Stan Musial, StL | 194 | 2001 | Rich Aurilia, SF | 206 |

## Home Run Leaders

| Year | Player and Team | HR | Year | Player and Team | HR |
|------|-----------------|-----|------|-----------------|-----|
| 1900 | Herman Long, Bos | 12 | 1949 | Ralph Kiner, Pitt | 54 |
| 1901 | Sam Crawford, Cin | 16 | 1950 | Ralph Kiner, Pitt | 47 |
| 1902 | Tommy Leach, Pitt | 6 | 1951 | Ralph Kiner, Pitt | 42 |
| 1903 | Jimmy Sheckard, Bklyn | 9 | 1952 | Ralph Kiner, Pitt | 37 |
| 1904 | Harry Lumley, Bklyn | 9 | | Hank Sauer, Chi | 37 |
| 1905 | Fred Odwell, Cin | 9 | 1953 | Eddie Mathews, Mil | 47 |
| 1906 | Tim Jordan, Bklyn | 12 | 1954 | Ted Kluszewski, Cin | 49 |
| 1907 | Dave Brain, Bos | 10 | 1955 | Willie Mays, NY | 51 |
| 1908 | Tim Jordan, Bklyn | 12 | 1956 | Duke Snider, Bklyn | 43 |
| 1909 | Red Murray, NY | 7 | 1957 | Hank Aaron, Mil | 44 |
| 1910 | Fred Beck, Bos | 10 | 1958 | Ernie Banks, Chi | 47 |
| | Wildfire Schulte, Chi | 10 | 1959 | Eddie Mathews, Mil | 46 |
| 1911 | Wildfire Schulte, Chi | 21 | 1960 | Ernie Banks, Chi | 41 |
| 1912 | Heinie Zimmerman, Chi | 14 | 1961 | Orlando Cepeda, SF | 46 |
| 1913 | Gavvy Cravath, Phil | 19 | 1962 | Willie Mays, SF | 49 |
| 1914 | Gavvy Cravath, Phil | 19 | 1963 | Hank Aaron, Mil | 44 |
| 1915 | Gavvy Cravath, Phil | 24 | | Willie McCovey, SF | 44 |
| 1916 | Dave Robertson, NY | 12 | 1964 | Willie Mays, SF | 47 |
| | Cy Williams, Chi | 12 | 1965 | Willie Mays, SF | 52 |
| 1917 | Dave Robertson, NY | 12 | 1966 | Hank Aaron, Atl | 44 |
| | Gavvy Cravath, Phil | 12 | 1967 | Hank Aaron, Atl | 39 |
| 1918 | Gavvy Cravath, Phil | 8 | 1968 | Willie McCovey, SF | 36 |
| 1919 | Gavvy Cravath, Phil | 12 | 1969 | Willie McCovey, SF | 45 |
| 1920 | Cy Williams, Phil | 15 | 1970 | Johnny Bench, Cin | 45 |
| 1921 | George Kelly, NY | 23 | 1971 | Willie Stargell, Pitt | 48 |
| 1922 | Rogers Hornsby, StL | 42 | 1972 | Johnny Bench, Cin | 40 |
| 1923 | Cy Williams, Phil | 41 | 1973 | Willie Stargell, Pitt | 44 |
| 1924 | Jack Fournier, Bklyn | 27 | 1974 | Mike Schmidt, Phil | 36 |
| 1925 | Rogers Hornsby, StL | 39 | 1975 | Mike Schmidt, Phil | 38 |
| 1926 | Hack Wilson, Chi | 21 | 1976 | Mike Schmidt, Phil | 38 |
| 1927 | Hack Wilson, Chi | 30 | 1977 | George Foster, Cin | 52 |
| | Cy Williams, Phil | 30 | 1978 | George Foster, Cin | 40 |
| 1928 | Hack Wilson, Chi | 31 | 1979 | Dave Kingman, Chi | 48 |
| | Jim Bottomley, StL | 31 | 1980 | Mike Schmidt, Phil | 48 |
| 1929 | Chuck Klein, Phil | 43 | 1981 | Mike Schmidt, Phil | 31 |
| 1930 | Hack Wilson, Chi | 56 | 1982 | Dave Kingman, NY | 37 |
| 1931 | Chuck Klein, Phil | 31 | 1983 | Mike Schmidt, Phil | 40 |
| 1932 | Chuck Klein, Phil | 38 | 1984 | Dale Murphy, Atl | 36 |
| | Mel Ott, NY | 38 | | Mike Schmidt, Phil | 36 |
| 1933 | Chuck Klein, Phil | 28 | 1985 | Dale Murphy, Atl | 37 |
| 1934 | Ripper Collins, StL | 35 | 1986 | Mike Schmidt, Phil | 37 |
| | Mel Ott, NY | 35 | 1987 | Andre Dawson, Chi | 49 |
| 1935 | Wally Berger, Bos | 34 | 1988 | Darryl Strawberry, NY | 39 |
| 1936 | Mel Ott, NY | 33 | 1989 | Kevin Mitchell, SF | 47 |
| 1937 | Mel Ott, NY | 31 | 1990 | Ryne Sandberg, Chi | 40 |
| | Joe Medwick, StL | 31 | 1991 | Howard Johnson, NY | 38 |
| 1938 | Mel Ott, NY | 36 | 1992 | Fred McGriff, SD | 35 |
| 1939 | Johnny Mize, StL | 28 | 1993 | Barry Bonds, SF | 46 |
| 1940 | Johnny Mize, StL | 43 | 1994 | Matt Williams, SF | 43 |
| 1941 | Dolph Camilli, Bklyn | 34 | 1995 | Dante Bichette, Col | 40 |
| 1942 | Mel Ott, NY | 30 | 1996 | Andres Galarraga, Col | 47 |
| 1943 | Bill Nicholson, Chi | 29 | 1997 | Larry Walker, Col | 49 |
| 1944 | Bill Nicholson, Chi | 33 | 1998 | Mark McGwire, StL | 70 |
| 1945 | Tommy Holmes, Bos | 28 | 1999 | Mark McGwire, StL | 65 |
| 1946 | Ralph Kiner, Pitt | 23 | 2000 | Sammy Sosa, Chi | 50 |
| 1947 | Ralph Kiner, Pitt | 51 | 2001 | Barry Bonds, SF | 73 |
| | Johnny Mize, NY | 51 | | | |
| 1948 | Ralph Kiner, Pitt | 40 | | | |
| | Johnny Mize, NY | 40 | | | |

## Runs Batted In Leaders

| Year | Player and Team | RBI | Year | Player and Team | RBI |
|---|---|---|---|---|---|
| 1900 | Elmer Flick, Phil | 110 | 1951 | Monte Irvin, NY | 121 |
| 1901 | Honus Wagner, Pitt | 126 | 1952 | Hank Sauer, Chi | 121 |
| 1902 | Honus Wagner, Pitt | 91 | 1953 | Roy Campanella, Bklyn | 142 |
| 1903 | Sam Mertes, NY | 104 | 1954 | Ted Kluszewski, Cin | 141 |
| 1904 | Bill Dahlen, NY | 80 | 1955 | Duke Snider, Bklyn | 136 |
| 1905 | Cy Seymour, Cin | 121 | 1956 | Stan Musial, StL | 109 |
| 1906 | Jim Nealon, Pitt | 83 | 1957 | Hank Aaron, Mil | 132 |
| | Harry Steinfeldt, Chi | 83 | 1958 | Ernie Banks, Chi | 129 |
| 1907 | Sherry Magee, Phil | 85 | 1959 | Ernie Banks, Chi | 143 |
| 1908 | Honus Wagner, Pitt | 109 | 1960 | Hank Aaron, Mil | 126 |
| 1909 | Honus Wagner, Pitt | 100 | 1961 | Orlando Cepeda, SF | 142 |
| 1910 | Sherry Magee, Phil | 123 | 1962 | Tommy Davis, LA | 153 |
| 1911 | Wildfire Schulte, Chi | 121 | 1963 | Hank Aaron, Mil | 130 |
| 1912 | Heinie Zimmerman, Chi | 103 | 1964 | Ken Boyer, StL | 119 |
| 1913 | Gavvy Cravath, Phil | 128 | 1965 | Deron Johnson, Cin | 130 |
| 1914 | Sherry Magee, Phil | 103 | 1966 | Hank Aaron, Atl | 127 |
| 1915 | Gavvy Cravath, Phil | 115 | 1967 | Orlando Cepeda, StL | 111 |
| 1916 | Heinie Zimmerman, Chi-NY | 83 | 1968 | Willie McCovey, SF | 105 |
| 1917 | Heinie Zimmerman, NY | 102 | 1969 | Willie McCovey, SF | 126 |
| 1918 | Sherry Magee, Phil | 76 | 1970 | Johnny Bench, Cin | 148 |
| 1919 | Hi Myers, Bklyn | 73 | 1971 | Joe Torre, StL | 137 |
| 1920 | George Kelly, NY | 94 | 1972 | Johnny Bench, Cin | 125 |
| | Rogers Hornsby, StL | 94 | 1973 | Willie Stargell, Pitt | 119 |
| 1921 | Rogers Hornsby, StL | 126 | 1974 | Johnny Bench, Cin | 129 |
| 1922 | Rogers Hornsby, StL | 152 | 1975 | Greg Luzinski, Phil | 120 |
| 1923 | Irish Meusel, NY | 125 | 1976 | George Foster, Cin | 121 |
| 1924 | George Kelly, NY | 136 | 1977 | George Foster, Cin | 149 |
| 1925 | Rogers Hornsby, StL | 143 | 1978 | George Foster, Cin | 120 |
| 1926 | Jim Bottomley, StL | 120 | 1979 | Dave Winfield, SD | 118 |
| 1927 | Paul Waner, Pitt | 131 | 1980 | Mike Schmidt, Phil | 121 |
| 1928 | Jim Bottomley, StL | 136 | 1981 | Mike Schmidt, Phil | 91 |
| 1929 | Hack Wilson, Chi | 159 | 1982 | Dale Murphy, Atl | 109 |
| 1930 | Hack Wilson, Chi | 190 | | Al Oliver, Mtl | 109 |
| 1931 | Chuck Klein, Phil | 121 | 1983 | Dale Murphy, Atl | 121 |
| 1932 | Don Hurst, Phil | 143 | 1984 | Gary Carter, Mtl | 106 |
| 1933 | Chuck Klein, Phil | 120 | | Mike Schmidt, Phil | 106 |
| 1934 | Mel Ott, NY | 135 | 1985 | Dave Parker, Cin | 125 |
| 1935 | Wally Berger, Bos | 130 | 1986 | Mike Schmidt, Phil | 119 |
| 1936 | Joe Medwick, StL | 138 | 1987 | Andre Dawson, Chi | 137 |
| 1937 | Joe Medwick, StL | 154 | 1988 | Will Clark, SF | 109 |
| 1938 | Joe Medwick, StL | 122 | 1989 | Kevin Mitchell, SF | 125 |
| 1939 | Frank McCormick, Cin | 128 | 1990 | Matt Williams, SF | 122 |
| 1940 | Johnny Mize, StL | 137 | 1991 | Howard Johnson, NY | 117 |
| 1941 | Dolph Camilli, Bklyn | 120 | 1992 | Darren Daulton, Phil | 109 |
| 1942 | Johnny Mize, NY | 110 | 1993 | Barry Bonds, SF | 123 |
| 1943 | Bill Nicholson, Chi | 128 | 1994 | Jeff Bagwell, Hou | 116 |
| 1944 | Bill Nicholson, Chi | 122 | 1995 | Dante Bichette, Col | 128 |
| 1945 | Dixie Walker, Bklyn | 124 | 1996 | Andres Galarraga, Col | 150 |
| 1946 | Enos Slaughter, StL | 130 | 1997 | Andres Galarraga, Col | 140 |
| 1947 | Johnny Mize, NY | 138 | 1998 | Sammy Sosa, Chi | 158 |
| 1948 | Stan Musial, StL | 131 | 1999 | Mark McGwire, StL | 147 |
| 1949 | Ralph Kiner, Pitt | 127 | 2000 | Todd Helton, Col | 147 |
| 1950 | Del Ennis, Phil | 126 | 2001 | Sammy Sosa | 160 |

## Leading Base Stealers

| Year | Player and Team | SB | Year | Player and Team | SB |
|------|-----------------|-----|------|-----------------|-----|
| 1900 | George Van Haltren, NY | 45 | 1949 | Jackie Robinson, Bklyn | 37 |
|  | Patsy Donovan, StL | 45 | 1950 | Sam Jethroe, Bos | 35 |
| 1901 | Honus Wagner, Pitt | 48 | 1951 | Sam Jethroe, Bos | 35 |
| 1902 | Honus Wagner, Pitt | 43 | 1952 | Pee Wee Reese, Bklyn | 30 |
| 1903 | Jimmy Sheckard, Bklyn | 67 | 1953 | Bill Bruton, Mil | 26 |
|  | Frank Chance, Chi | 67 | 1954 | Bill Bruton, Mil | 34 |
| 1904 | Honus Wagner, Pitt | 53 | 1955 | Bill Bruton, Mil | 35 |
| 1905 | Billy Maloney, Chi | 59 | 1956 | Willie Mays, NY | 40 |
|  | Art Devlin, NY | 59 | 1957 | Willie Mays, NY | 38 |
| 1906 | Frank Chance, Chi | 57 | 1958 | Willie Mays, SF | 31 |
| 1907 | Honus Wagner, Pitt | 61 | 1959 | Willie Mays, SF | 27 |
| 1908 | Honus Wagner, Pitt | 53 | 1960 | Maury Wills, LA | 50 |
| 1909 | Bob Bescher, Cin | 54 | 1961 | Maury Wills, LA | 35 |
| 1910 | Bob Bescher, Cin | 70 | 1962 | Maury Wills, LA | 104 |
| 1911 | Bob Bescher, Cin | 80 | 1963 | Maury Wills, LA | 40 |
| 1912 | Bob Bescher, Cin | 67 | 1964 | Maury Wills, LA | 53 |
| 1913 | Max Carey, Pitt | 61 | 1965 | Maury Wills, LA | 94 |
| 1914 | George Burns, NY | 62 | 1966 | Lou Brock, StL | 74 |
| 1915 | Max Carey, Pitt | 36 | 1967 | Lou Brock, StL | 52 |
| 1916 | Max Carey, Pitt | 63 | 1968 | Lou Brock, StL | 62 |
| 1917 | Max Carey, Pitt | 46 | 1969 | Lou Brock, StL | 53 |
| 1918 | Max Carey, Pitt | 58 | 1970 | Bobby Tolan, Cin | 57 |
| 1919 | George Burns, NY | 40 | 1971 | Lou Brock, StL | 64 |
| 1920 | Max Carey, Pitt | 52 | 1972 | Lou Brock, StL | 63 |
| 1921 | Frankie Frisch, NY | 49 | 1973 | Lou Brock, StL | 70 |
| 1922 | Max Carey, Pitt | 51 | 1974 | Lou Brock, StL | 118 |
| 1923 | Max Carey, Pitt | 51 | 1975 | Davey Lopes, LA | 77 |
| 1924 | Max Carey, Pitt | 49 | 1976 | Davey Lopes, LA | 63 |
| 1925 | Max Carey, Pitt | 46 | 1977 | Frank Taveras, Pitt | 70 |
| 1926 | Kiki Cuyler, Pitt | 35 | 1978 | Omar Moreno, Pitt | 71 |
| 1927 | Frankie Frisch, StL | 48 | 1979 | Omar Moreno, Pitt | 77 |
| 1928 | Kiki Cuyler, Chi | 37 | 1980 | Ron LeFlore, Mtl | 97 |
| 1929 | Kiki Cuyler, Chi | 43 | 1981 | Tim Raines, Mtl | 71 |
| 1930 | Kiki Cuyler, Chi | 37 | 1982 | Tim Raines, Mtl | 78 |
| 1931 | Frankie Frisch, StL | 28 | 1983 | Tim Raines, Mtl | 90 |
| 1932 | Chuck Klein, Phil | 20 | 1984 | Tim Raines, Mtl | 75 |
| 1933 | Pepper Martin, StL | 26 | 1985 | Vince Coleman, StL | 110 |
| 1934 | Pepper Martin, StL | 23 | 1986 | Vince Coleman, StL | 107 |
| 1935 | Augie Galan, Chi | 22 | 1987 | Vince Coleman, StL | 109 |
| 1936 | Pepper Martin, StL | 23 | 1988 | Vince Coleman, StL | 81 |
| 1937 | Augie Galan, Chi | 23 | 1989 | Vince Coleman, StL | 65 |
| 1938 | Stan Hack, Chi | 16 | 1990 | Vince Coleman, StL | 77 |
| 1939 | Stan Hack, Chi | 17 | 1991 | Marquis Grissom, Mtl | 76 |
|  | Lee Handley, Pitt | 17 | 1992 | Marquis Grissom, Mtl | 78 |
| 1940 | Lonny Frey, Cin | 22 | 1993 | Chuck Carr, Fla | 58 |
| 1941 | Danny Murtaugh, Phil | 18 | 1994 | Craig Biggio, Hou | 39 |
| 1942 | Pete Reiser, Bklyn | 20 | 1995 | Quilvio Veras, Fla | 56 |
| 1943 | Arky Vaughan, Bklyn | 20 | 1996 | Eric Young, Col | 53 |
| 1944 | Johnny Barrett, Pitt | 28 | 1997 | Tony Womack, Pitt | 60 |
| 1945 | Red Schoendienst, StL | 26 | 1998 | Tony Womack, Pitt | 58 |
| 1946 | Pete Reiser, Bklyn | 34 | 1999 | Tony Womack, Ariz | 72 |
| 1947 | Jackie Robinson, Bklyn | 29 | 2000 | Luis Castillo, Fla | 62 |
| 1948 | Richie Ashburn, Phil | 32 | 2001 | Juan Pierre, Col | 46 |

## Leading Pitchers—Winning Percentage

| Year | Pitcher and Team | W | L | Pct | Year | Pitcher and Team | W | L | Pct |
|---|---|---|---|---|---|---|---|---|---|
| 1900 | Jesse Tannehill, Pitt | 20 | 6 | .769 | 1952 | Hoyt Wilhelm, NY | 15 | 3 | .833 |
| 1901 | Jack Chesbro, Pitt | 21 | 10 | .677 | 1953 | Carl Erskine, Bklyn | 20 | 6 | .769 |
| 1902 | Jack Chesbro, Pitt | 28 | 6 | .824 | 1954 | Johnny Antonelli, NY | 21 | 7 | .750 |
| 1903 | Sam Leever, Pitt | 25 | 7 | .781 | 1955 | Don Newcombe, Bklyn | 20 | 5 | .800 |
| 1904 | Joe McGinnity, NY | 35 | 8 | .814 | 1956 | Don Newcombe, Bklyn | 27 | 7 | .794 |
| 1905 | Sam Leever, Pitt | 20 | 5 | .800 | 1957 | Bob Buhl, Mil | 18 | 7 | .720 |
| 1906 | Ed Reulbach, Chi | 19 | 4 | .826 | 1958 | Warren Spahn, Mil | 22 | 11 | .667 |
| 1907 | Ed Reulbach, Chi | 17 | 4 | .810 | | Lew Burdette, Mil | 20 | 10 | .667 |
| 1908 | Ed Reulbach, Chi | 24 | 7 | .774 | 1959 | Roy Face, Pitt | 18 | 1 | .947 |
| 1909 | Christy Mathewson, NY | 25 | 6 | .806 | 1960 | Ernie Broglio, StL | 21 | 9 | .700 |
| | Howie Camnitz, Pitt | 25 | 6 | .806 | 1961 | Johnny Podres, LA | 18 | 5 | .783 |
| 1910 | King Cole, Chi | 20 | 4 | .833 | 1962 | Bob Purkey, Cin | 23 | 5 | .821 |
| 1911 | Rube Marquard, NY | 24 | 7 | .774 | 1963 | Ron Perranoski, LA | 16 | 3 | .842 |
| 1912 | Claude Hendrix, Pitt | 24 | 9 | .727 | 1964 | Sandy Koufax, LA | 19 | 5 | .792 |
| 1913 | Bert Humphries, Chi | 16 | 4 | .800 | 1965 | Sandy Koufax, LA | 26 | 8 | .765 |
| 1914 | Bill James, Bos | 26 | 7 | .788 | 1966 | Juan Marichal, SF | 25 | 6 | .806 |
| 1915 | Grover Alexander, Phil | 31 | 10 | .756 | 1967 | Dick Hughes, StL | 16 | 6 | .727 |
| 1916 | Tom Hughes, Bos | 16 | 3 | .842 | 1968 | Steve Blass, Pitt | 18 | 6 | .750 |
| 1917 | Ferdie Schupp, NY | 21 | 7 | .750 | 1969 | Tom Seaver, NY | 25 | 7 | .781 |
| 1918 | Claude Hendrix, Chi | 19 | 7 | .731 | 1970 | Bob Gibson, StL | 23 | 7 | .767 |
| 1919 | Dutch Ruether, Cin | 19 | 6 | .760 | 1971 | Don Gullett, Cin | 16 | 6 | .727 |
| 1920 | Burleigh Grimes, Bklyn | 23 | 11 | .676 | 1972 | Gary Nolan, Cin | 15 | 5 | .750 |
| 1921 | Bill Doak, StL | 15 | 6 | .714 | 1973 | Tommy John, LA | 16 | 7 | .696 |
| 1922 | Pete Donohue, Cin | 18 | 9 | .667 | 1974 | Andy Messersmith, LA | 20 | 6 | .769 |
| 1923 | Dolf Luque, Cin | 27 | 8 | .771 | 1975 | Don Gullett, Cin | 15 | 4 | .789 |
| 1924 | Emil Yde, Pitt | 16 | 3 | .842 | 1976 | Steve Carlton, Phil | 20 | 7 | .741 |
| 1925 | Bill Sherdel, StL | 15 | 6 | .714 | 1977 | John Candelaria, Pitt | 20 | 5 | .800 |
| 1926 | Ray Kremer, Pitt | 20 | 6 | .769 | 1978 | Gaylord Perry, SD | 21 | 6 | .778 |
| 1927 | Larry Benton, Bos-NY | 17 | 7 | .708 | 1979 | Tom Seaver, Cin | 16 | 6 | .727 |
| 1928 | Larry Benton, NY | 25 | 9 | .735 | 1980 | Jim Bibby, Pitt | 19 | 6 | .760 |
| 1929 | Charlie Root, Chi | 19 | 6 | .760 | 1981* | Tom Seaver, Cin | 14 | 2 | .875 |
| 1930 | Freddie Fitzsimmons, NY | 19 | 7 | .731 | 1982 | Phil Niekro, Atl | 17 | 4 | .810 |
| 1931 | Paul Derringer, StL | 18 | 8 | .692 | 1983 | John Denny, Phil | 19 | 6 | .760 |
| 1932 | Lon Warneke, Chi | 22 | 6 | .786 | 1984 | Rick Sutcliffe, Chi | 16 | 1 | .941 |
| 1933 | Ben Cantwell, Bos | 20 | 10 | .667 | 1985 | Orel Hershiser, LA | 19 | 3 | .864 |
| 1934 | Dizzy Dean, StL | 30 | 7 | .811 | 1986 | Bob Ojeda, NY | 18 | 5 | .783 |
| 1935 | Bill Lee, Chi | 20 | 6 | .769 | 1987 | Dwight Gooden, NY | 15 | 7 | .682 |
| 1936 | Carl Hubbell, NY | 26 | 6 | .813 | 1988 | David Cone, NY | 20 | 3 | .870 |
| 1937 | Carl Hubbell, NY | 22 | 8 | .733 | 1989 | Mike Bielecki, Chi | 18 | 7 | .720 |
| 1938 | Bill Lee, Chi | 22 | 9 | .710 | 1990 | Doug Drabeck, Pitt | 22 | 6 | .786 |
| 1939 | Paul Derringer, Cin | 25 | 7 | .781 | 1991 | John Smiley, Pitt | 20 | 8 | .714 |
| 1940 | Freddie Fitzsimmons, Bklyn | 16 | 2 | .889 | | Jose Rijo, Cin | 15 | 6 | .714 |
| 1941 | Elmer Riddle, Cin | 19 | 4 | .826 | 1992 | Bob Tewksbury, StL | 16 | 5 | .762 |
| 1942 | Larry French, Bklyn | 15 | 4 | .789 | 1993 | Tom Glavine, Atl | 22 | 6 | .786 |
| 1943 | Mort Cooper, StL | 21 | 8 | .724 | 1994 | Ken Hill, Mtl | 16 | 5 | .762 |
| 1944 | Ted Wilks, StL | 17 | 4 | .810 | 1995 | Greg Maddux, Atl | 19 | 2 | .905 |
| 1945 | Harry Brecheen, StL | 15 | 4 | .789 | 1996 | John Smoltz, Atl | 24 | 8 | .750 |
| 1946 | Murray Dickson, StL | 15 | 6 | .714 | 1997 | Denny Neagle, Atl | 20 | 5 | .800 |
| 1947 | Larry Jansen, NY | 21 | 5 | .808 | 1998 | John Smoltz, Atl | 17 | 3 | .850 |
| 1948 | Harry Brecheen, StL | 20 | 7 | .741 | 1999 | Mike Hampton, Hou | 22 | 4 | .846 |
| 1949 | Preacher Roe, Bklyn | 15 | 6 | .714 | 2000 | Randy Johnson, Ariz | 19 | 7 | .730 |
| 1950 | Sal Maglie, NY | 18 | 4 | .818 | 2001 | Curt Schilling, Ariz | 22 | 6 | .786 |
| 1951 | Preacher Roe, Bklyn | 22 | 3 | .880 | | | | | |

*1981 percentages based on 10 or more victories. Note: Percentages based on 15 or more victories in all other years.

## Leading Pitchers—Earned Run Average

| Year | Player and Team | ERA | Year | Player and Team | ERA |
|---|---|---|---|---|---|
| 1900 | Rube Waddell, Pitt | 2.37 | 1951 | Chet Nichols, Bos | 2.88 |
| 1901 | Jesse Tannehill, Pitt | 2.18 | 1952 | Hoyt Wilhelm, NY | 2.43 |
| 1902 | Jack Taylor, Chi | 1.33 | 1953 | Warren Spahn, Mil | 2.10 |
| 1903 | Sam Leever, Pitt | 2.06 | 1954 | Johnny Antonelli, NY | 2.29 |
| 1904 | Joe McGinnity, NY | 1.61 | 1955 | Bob Friend, Pitt | 2.84 |
| 1905 | Christy Mathewson, NY | 1.27 | 1956 | Lew Burdette, Mil | 2.71 |
| 1906 | Three Finger Brown, Chi | 1.04 | 1957 | Johnny Podres, Bklyn | 2.66 |
| 1907 | Jack Pfiester, Chi | 1.15 | 1958 | Stu Miller, SF | 2.47 |
| 1908 | Christy Mathewson, NY | 1.43 | 1959 | Sam Jones, SF | 2.82 |
| 1909 | Christy Mathewson, NY | 1.14 | 1960 | Mike McCormick, SF | 2.70 |
| 1910 | George McQuillan, Phil | 1.60 | 1961 | Warren Spahn, Mil | 3.01 |
| 1911 | Christy Mathewson, NY | 1.99 | 1962 | Sandy Koufax, LA | 2.54 |
| 1912 | Jeff Tesreau, NY | 1.96 | 1963 | Sandy Koufax, LA | 1.88 |
| 1913 | Christy Mathewson, NY | 2.06 | 1964 | Sandy Koufax, LA | 1.74 |
| 1914 | Bill Doak, StL | 1.72 | 1965 | Sandy Koufax, LA | 2.04 |
| 1915 | Grover Alexander, Phil | 1.22 | 1966 | Sandy Koufax, LA | 1.73 |
| 1916 | Grover Alexander, Phil | 1.55 | 1967 | Phil Niekro, Atl | 1.87 |
| 1917 | Grover Alexander, Phil | 1.83 | 1968 | Bob Gibson, StL | 1.12 |
| 1918 | Hippo Vaughn, Chi | 1.74 | 1969 | Juan Marichal, SF | 2.10 |
| 1919 | Grover Alexander, Chi | 1.72 | 1970 | Tom Seaver, NY | 2.81 |
| 1920 | Grover Alexander, Chi | 1.91 | 1971 | Tom Seaver, NY | 1.76 |
| 1921 | Bill Doak, StL | 2.58 | 1972 | Steve Carlton, Phil | 1.98 |
| 1922 | Rosy Ryan, NY | 3.00 | 1973 | Tom Seaver, NY | 2.08 |
| 1923 | Dolf Luque, Cin | 1.93 | 1974 | Buzz Capra, Atl | 2.28 |
| 1924 | Dazzy Vance, Bklyn | 2.16 | 1975 | Randy Jones, SD | 2.24 |
| 1925 | Dolf Luque, Cin | 2.63 | 1976 | John Denny, StL | 2.52 |
| 1926 | Ray Kremer, Pitt | 2.61 | 1977 | John Candelaria, Pitt | 2.34 |
| 1927 | Ray Kremer, Pitt | 2.47 | 1978 | Craig Swan, NY | 2.43 |
| 1928 | Dazzy Vance, Bklyn | 2.09 | 1979 | J.R. Richard, Hou | 2.71 |
| 1929 | Bill Walker, NY | 3.08 | 1980 | Don Sutton, LA | 2.21 |
| 1930 | Dazzy Vance, Bklyn | 2.61 | 1981 | Nolan Ryan, Hou | 1.69 |
| 1931 | Bill Walker, NY | 2.26 | 1982 | Steve Rogers, Mtl | 2.40 |
| 1932 | Lon Warneke, Chi | 2.37 | 1983 | Atlee Hammaker, SF | 2.25 |
| 1933 | Carl Hubbell, NY | 1.66 | 1984 | Alejandro Pena, LA | 2.48 |
| 1934 | Carl Hubbell, NY | 2.30 | 1985 | Dwight Gooden, NY | 1.53 |
| 1935 | Cy Blanton, Pitt | 2.59 | 1986 | Mike Scott, Hou | 2.22 |
| 1936 | Carl Hubbell, NY | 2.31 | 1987 | Nolan Ryan, Hou | 2.76 |
| 1937 | Jim Turner, Bos | 2.38 | 1988 | Joe Magrane, StL | 2.18 |
| 1938 | Bill Lee, Chi | 2.66 | 1989 | Scott Garrelts, SF | 2.28 |
| 1939 | Bucky Walters, Cin | 2.29 | 1990 | Danny Darwin, Hou | 2.21 |
| 1940 | Bucky Walters, Cin | 2.48 | 1991 | Dennis Martinez, Mtl | 2.39 |
| 1941 | Elmer Riddle, Cin | 2.24 | 1992 | Bill Swift, SF | 2.08 |
| 1942 | Mort Cooper, StL | 1.77 | 1993 | Greg Maddux, Atl | 2.36 |
| 1943 | Howie Pollet, StL | 1.75 | 1994 | Greg Maddux, Atl | 1.56 |
| 1944 | Ed Heusser, Cin | 2.38 | 1995 | Greg Maddux, Atl | 1.63 |
| 1945 | Hank Borowy, Chi | 2.14 | 1996 | Kevin Brown, Fla | 1.89 |
| 1946 | Howie Pollet, StL | 2.10 | 1997 | Pedro Martinez, Mtl | 1.90 |
| 1947 | Warren Spahn, Bos | 2.33 | 1998 | Greg Maddux, Atl | 1.98 |
| 1948 | Harry Brecheen, StL | 2.24 | 1999 | Randy Johnson, Ariz | 2.48 |
| 1949 | Dave Koslo, NY | 2.50 | 2000 | Kevin Brown, LA | 2.58 |
| 1950 | Jim Hearn, StL-NY | 2.49 | 2001 | Randy Johnson, Ariz | 2.49 |

Note: Based on 10 complete games through 1950, then 154 innings until National League expanded in 1962, when it became 162 innings. In strike-shortened 1981, one inning per game required.

## Leading Pitchers—Strikeouts

| Year | Player and Team | SO | Year | Player and Team | SO |
|------|-----------------|-----|------|-----------------|-----|
| 1900 | Rube Waddell, Pitt | 133 | 1951 | Warren Spahn, Bos | 164 |
| 1901 | Noodles Hahn, Cin | 233 | | Don Newcombe, Bklyn | 164 |
| 1902 | Vic Willis, Bos | 226 | 1952 | Warren Spahn, Bos | 183 |
| 1903 | Christy Mathewson, NY | 267 | 1953 | Robin Roberts, Phil | 198 |
| 1904 | Christy Mathewson, NY | 212 | 1954 | Robin Roberts, Phil | 185 |
| 1905 | Christy Mathewson, NY | 206 | 1955 | Sam Jones, Chi | 198 |
| 1906 | Fred Beebe, Chi-StL | 171 | 1956 | Sam Jones, Chi | 176 |
| 1907 | Christy Mathewson, NY | 178 | 1957 | Jack Sanford, Phil | 188 |
| 1908 | Christy Mathewson, NY | 259 | 1958 | Sam Jones, StL | 225 |
| 1909 | Orval Overall, Chi | 205 | 1959 | Don Drysdale, LA | 242 |
| 1910 | Christy Mathewson, NY | 190 | 1960 | Don Drysdale, LA | 246 |
| 1911 | Rube Marquard, NY | 237 | 1961 | Sandy Koufax, LA | 269 |
| 1912 | Grover Alexander, Phil | 195 | 1962 | Don Drysdale, LA | 232 |
| 1913 | Tom Seaton, Phil | 168 | 1963 | Sandy Koufax, LA | 306 |
| 1914 | Grover Alexander, Phil | 214 | 1964 | Bob Veale, Pitt | 250 |
| 1915 | Grover Alexander, Phil | 241 | 1965 | Sandy Koufax, LA | 382 |
| 1916 | Grover Alexander, Phil | 167 | 1966 | Sandy Koufax, LA | 317 |
| 1917 | Grover Alexander, Phil | 200 | 1967 | Jim Bunning, Phil | 253 |
| 1918 | Hippo Vaughn, Chi | 148 | 1968 | Bob Gibson, StL | 268 |
| 1919 | Hippo Vaughn, Chi | 141 | 1969 | Ferguson Jenkins, Chi | 273 |
| 1920 | Grover Alexander, Chi | 173 | 1970 | Tom Seaver, NY | 283 |
| 1921 | Burleigh Grimes, Bklyn | 136 | 1971 | Tom Seaver, NY | 289 |
| 1922 | Dazzy Vance, Bklyn | 134 | 1972 | Steve Carlton, Phil | 310 |
| 1923 | Dazzy Vance, Bklyn | 197 | 1973 | Tom Seaver, NY | 251 |
| 1924 | Dazzy Vance, Bklyn | 262 | 1974 | Steve Carlton, Phil | 240 |
| 1925 | Dazzy Vance, Bklyn | 221 | 1975 | Tom Seaver, NY | 243 |
| 1926 | Dazzy Vance, Bklyn | 140 | 1976 | Tom Seaver, NY | 235 |
| 1927 | Dazzy Vance, Bklyn | 184 | 1977 | Phil Niekro, Atl | 262 |
| 1928 | Dazzy Vance, Bklyn | 200 | 1978 | J.R. Richard, Hou | 303 |
| 1929 | Pat Malone, Chi | 166 | 1979 | J.R. Richard, Hou | 313 |
| 1930 | Bill Hallahan, StL | 177 | 1980 | Steve Carlton, Phil | 286 |
| 1931 | Bill Hallahan, StL | 159 | 1981 | Fernando Valenzuela, LA | 180 |
| 1932 | Dizzy Dean, StL | 191 | 1982 | Steve Carlton, Phil | 286 |
| 1933 | Dizzy Dean, StL | 199 | 1983 | Steve Carlton, Phil | 275 |
| 1934 | Dizzy Dean, StL | 195 | 1984 | Dwight Gooden, NY | 276 |
| 1935 | Dizzy Dean, StL | 182 | 1985 | Dwight Gooden, NY | 268 |
| 1936 | Van Lingle Mungo, Bklyn | 238 | 1986 | Mike Scott, Hou | 306 |
| 1937 | Carl Hubbell, NY | 159 | 1987 | Nolan Ryan, Hou | 270 |
| 1938 | Clay Bryant, Chi | 135 | 1988 | Nolan Ryan, Hou | 228 |
| 1939 | Claude Passeau, Phil-Chi | 137 | 1989 | Jose DeLeon, StL | 201 |
| | Bucky Walters, Cin | 137 | 1990 | David Cone, NY | 233 |
| 1940 | Kirby Higbe, Phil | 137 | 1991 | David Cone, NY | 241 |
| 1941 | Johnny Vander Meer, Cin | 202 | 1992 | John Smoltz, Atl | 215 |
| 1942 | Johnny Vander Meer, Cin | 186 | 1993 | Jose Rijo, Cin | 227 |
| 1943 | Johnny Vander Meer, Cin | 174 | 1994 | Andy Benes, SD | 189 |
| 1944 | Bill Voiselle, NY | 161 | 1995 | Hideo Nomo, LA | 236 |
| 1945 | Preacher Roe, Pitt | 148 | 1996 | John Smoltz, Atl | 276 |
| 1946 | Johnny Schmitz, Chi | 135 | 1997 | Curt Schilling, Phil | 319 |
| 1947 | Ewell Blackwell, Cin | 193 | 1998 | Curt Schilling, Phil | 300 |
| 1948 | Harry Brecheen, StL | 149 | 1999 | Randy Johnson, Ariz | 364 |
| 1949 | Warren Spahn, Bos | 151 | 2000 | Randy Johnson, Ariz | 347 |
| 1950 | Warren Spahn, Bos | 191 | 2001 | Randy Johnson, Ariz | 372 |

## Leading Pitchers—Saves

| Year | Player and Team | SV | Year | Player and Team | SV |
|------|-----------------|-----|------|-----------------|-----|
| 1947 | Hugh Casey, Bklyn | 18 | 1975 | Al Hrabosky, StL | 22 |
| 1948 | Harry Gumpert, Cin | 17 | | Rawly Eastwick, Cin | 22 |
| 1949 | Ted Wilks, StL | 9 | 1976 | Rawly Eastwick, Cin | 26 |
| 1950 | Jim Konstanty, Phil | 22 | 1977 | Rollie Fingers, SD | 35 |
| 1951 | Ted Wilks, StL, Pitt | 13 | 1978 | Rollie Fingers, SD | 37 |
| 1952 | Al Brazle, StL | 16 | 1979 | Bruce Sutter, Chi | 37 |
| 1953 | Al Brazle, StL | 18 | 1980 | Bruce Sutter, Chi | 28 |
| 1954 | Jim Hughes, Bklyn | 24 | 1981 | Bruce Sutter, StL | 25 |
| 1955 | Jack Meyer, Phil | 16 | 1982 | Bruce Sutter, StL | 36 |
| 1956 | Clem Labine, Bklyn | 19 | 1983 | Lee Smith, Chi | 29 |
| 1957 | Clem Labine, Bklyn | 17 | 1984 | Bruce Sutter, StL | 45 |
| 1958 | Roy Face, Pitt | 20 | 1985 | Jeff Reardon, Mtl | 41 |
| 1959 | Lindy McDaniel, StL | 15 | 1986 | Todd Worrell, StL | 36 |
| | Don McMahon, Mil | 15 | 1987 | Steve Bedrosian, Phil | 40 |
| 1960 | Lindy McDaniel, StL | 26 | 1988 | John Franco, Cin | 39 |
| 1961 | Stu Miller, SF | 17 | 1989 | Mark Davis, SD | 44 |
| | Roy Face, Pitt | 17 | 1990 | John Franco, NY | 33 |
| 1962 | Roy Face, Pitt | 28 | 1991 | Lee Smith, StL | 47 |
| 1963 | Lindy McDaniel, Chi | 22 | 1992 | Lee Smith, StL | 42 |
| 1964 | Hal Woodeshick, Hou | 23 | 1993 | Randy Myers, Chi | 53 |
| 1965 | Ted Abernathy, Chi | 31 | 1994 | John Franco, NY | 30 |
| 1966 | Phil Regan, LA | 21 | 1995 | Randy Myers, Chi | 38 |
| 1967 | Ted Abernathy, Cin | 28 | 1996 | Jeff Brantley, Cin | 44 |
| 1968 | Phil Regan, Chi, LA | 25 | | Todd Worrell, LA | 44 |
| 1969 | Fred Gladding, Hou | 29 | 1997 | Jeff Shaw, Cin | 42 |
| 1970 | Wayne Granger, Cin | 35 | 1998 | Trevor Hoffman, SD | 53 |
| 1971 | Dave Giusti, Pitt | 30 | 1999 | Ugueth Urbina, Mtl | 41 |
| 1972 | Clay Carroll, Cin | 37 | 2000 | Antonio Alfonseca, Fla | 45 |
| 1973 | Mike Marshall, Mtl | 13 | 2001 | Robb Nen, SF | 45 |
| 1974 | Mike Marshall, LA | 21 | | | |

## Downsize This!

Oh, this baseball commissioner is a political smoothie. For the grand opening of his daughter's new ballpark in Milwaukee in April, Bud Selig invited President Bush to throw out the first pitch, but the former Texas Rangers owner ended up throwing out the *second* first pitch. The Budman reserved the first first pitch for himself. *Smooth.* Then late last month, as the Florida legislature was preparing to vote on a tax bill to fund a new ballpark for the Marlins, Selig wrote a letter to State Senator Alex Villalobos of Miami, warning that the Marlins "cannot and will not survive in South Florida without a new stadium." Selig predicted one of two dire outcomes should the bill fail: The Marlins would move or fold.

Can't you just see all those big ol' Florida pols holding out their bourbons and cigars with stiff arms as they let loose a big ol' shudder? What makes Selig think any sane taxpayer would be willing to bail out a baseball team these days? Particularly a mediocre one with a history of mercurial ownership, playing in a sweltering climate ill-suited to the summer game? Selig's threat was emptier than the Marlins' upper deck. Last Friday the Florida senate adjourned without voting on the stadium plan, effectively letting it die.

During the labor battles of the early 1990s, Selig and the other Lords of Baseball, suffering acutely from NBA envy, kept talking about the importance of "growing the game." Of course, there was no widespread public clamoring to grow the game. The owners didn't care. Hundreds of millions of dollars were to be made in expansion franchise fees. As a result there are two pointless teams in Florida, another in Arizona. (Although the Diamondbacks went a long way toward legitimizing their existence by reaching the 2001 Fall Classic.)

Along the way, baseball's symmetry was trashed. Now we—we, who pay for it all—have four five-team divisions, one six-team division and one four-team division. We had balanced schedules; now we have unbalanced schedules. We have wild-card teams. We have a first-round playoff called . . . what is that round called again? Baseball stole a page from the NBA business plan, all right. Before we knew it, baseball's long season had been demeaned.

Now Selig threatens to close down "franchises" for the health of his "industry." He talks about "contraction." He may have arrived at his first good idea—unwittingly, of course. The real debate is whether baseball was better with 24 teams or 16. With fewer clubs and fewer players and better pitching, ordinary fans might actually want to follow a baseball season again. They might actually care.

— Michael Bamberger

# American League

## Pennant Winners

| Year | Team | Manager | W | L | Pct | GA |
|------|------|---------|---|---|-----|-----|
| 1901 | Chicago | Clark Griffith | 83 | 53 | .610 | 4 |
| 1902 | Philadelphia | Connie Mack | 83 | 53 | .610 | 5 |
| 1903 | Boston | Jimmy Collins | 91 | 47 | .659 | 14½ |
| 1904 | Boston | Jimmy Collins | 95 | 59 | .617 | 1½ |
| 1905 | Philadelphia | Connie Mack | 92 | 56 | .622 | 2 |
| 1906 | Chicago | Fielder Jones | 93 | 58 | .616 | 3 |
| 1907 | Detroit | Hughie Jennings | 92 | 58 | .613 | 1½ |
| 1908 | Detroit | Hughie Jennings | 90 | 63 | .588 | ½ |
| 1909 | Detroit | Hughie Jennings | 98 | 54 | .645 | 3½ |
| 1910 | Philadelphia | Connie Mack | 102 | 48 | .680 | 14½ |
| 1911 | Philadelphia | Connie Mack | 101 | 50 | .669 | 13½ |
| 1912 | Boston | Jake Stahl | 105 | 47 | .691 | 14 |
| 1913 | Philadelphia | Connie Mack | 96 | 57 | .627 | 6½ |
| 1914 | Philadelphia | Connie Mack | 99 | 53 | .651 | 8½ |
| 1915 | Boston | Bill Carrigan | 101 | 50 | .669 | 2½ |
| 1916 | Boston | Bill Carrigan | 91 | 63 | .591 | 2 |
| 1917 | Chicago | Pants Rowland | 100 | 54 | .649 | 9 |
| 1918 | Boston | Ed Barrow | 75 | 51 | .595 | 2½ |
| 1919 | Chicago | Kid Gleason | 88 | 52 | .629 | 3½ |
| 1920 | Cleveland | Tris Speaker | 98 | 56 | .636 | 2 |
| 1921 | New York | Miller Huggins | 98 | 55 | .641 | 4½ |
| 1922 | New York | Miller Huggins | 94 | 60 | .610 | 1 |
| 1923 | New York | Miller Huggins | 98 | 54 | .645 | 16 |
| 1924 | Washington | Bucky Harris | 92 | 62 | .597 | 2 |
| 1925 | Washington | Bucky Harris | 96 | 55 | .636 | 8½ |
| 1926 | New York | Miller Huggins | 91 | 63 | .591 | 3 |
| 1927 | New York | Miller Huggins | 110 | 44 | .714 | 19 |
| 1928 | New York | Miller Huggins | 101 | 53 | .656 | 2½ |
| 1929 | Philadelphia | Connie Mack | 104 | 46 | .693 | 18 |
| 1930 | Philadelphia | Connie Mack | 102 | 52 | .662 | 8 |
| 1931 | Philadelphia | Connie Mack | 107 | 45 | .704 | 13½ |
| 1932 | New York | Joe McCarthy | 107 | 47 | .695 | 13 |
| 1933 | Washington | Joe Cronin | 99 | 53 | .651 | 7 |
| 1934 | Detroit | Mickey Cochrane | 101 | 53 | .656 | 7 |
| 1935 | Detroit | Mickey Cochrane | 93 | 58 | .616 | 3 |
| 1936 | New York | Joe McCarthy | 102 | 51 | .667 | 19½ |
| 1937 | New York | Joe McCarthy | 102 | 52 | .662 | 13 |
| 1938 | New York | Joe McCarthy | 99 | 53 | .651 | 9½ |
| 1939 | New York | Joe McCarthy | 106 | 45 | .702 | 17 |
| 1940 | Detroit | Del Baker | 90 | 64 | .584 | 1 |
| 1941 | New York | Joe McCarthy | 101 | 53 | .656 | 17 |
| 1942 | New York | Joe McCarthy | 103 | 51 | .669 | 9 |
| 1943 | New York | Joe McCarthy | 98 | 56 | .636 | 13½ |
| 1944 | St. Louis | Luke Sewell | 89 | 65 | .578 | 1 |
| 1945 | Detroit | Steve O'Neill | 88 | 65 | .575 | 1½ |
| 1946 | Boston | Joe Cronin | 104 | 50 | .675 | 12 |
| 1947 | New York | Bucky Harris | 97 | 57 | .630 | 12 |
| 1948 | Cleveland† | Lou Boudreau | 97 | 58 | .626 | 1 |
| 1949 | New York | Casey Stengel | 97 | 57 | .630 | 1 |
| 1950 | New York | Casey Stengel | 98 | 56 | .636 | 3 |
| 1951 | New York | Casey Stengel | 98 | 56 | .636 | 5 |
| 1952 | New York | Casey Stengel | 95 | 59 | .617 | 2 |
| 1953 | New York | Casey Stengel | 99 | 52 | .656 | 8½ |
| 1954 | Cleveland | Al Lopez | 111 | 43 | .721 | 8 |
| 1955 | New York | Casey Stengel | 96 | 58 | .623 | 3 |
| 1956 | New York | Casey Stengel | 97 | 57 | .630 | 9 |
| 1957 | New York | Casey Stengel | 98 | 56 | .636 | 8 |
| 1958 | New York | Casey Stengel | 92 | 62 | .597 | 10 |
| 1959 | Chicago | Al Lopez | 94 | 60 | .610 | 5 |
| 1960 | New York | Casey Stengel | 97 | 57 | .630 | 8 |
| 1961 | New York | Ralph Houk | 109 | 53 | .673 | 8 |
| 1962 | New York | Ralph Houk | 96 | 66 | .593 | 5 |
| 1963 | New York | Ralph Houk | 104 | 57 | .646 | 10½ |
| 1964 | New York | Yogi Berra | 99 | 63 | .611 | 1 |
| 1965 | Minnesota | Sam Mele | 102 | 60 | .630 | 7 |
| 1966 | Baltimore | Hank Bauer | 97 | 63 | .606 | 9 |

## Pennant Winners *(Cont.)*

| Year | Team | Manager | W | L | Pct | GA |
|------|------|---------|---|---|-----|-----|
| 1967 | Boston | Dick Williams | 92 | 70 | .568 | 1 |
| 1968 | Detroit | Mayo Smith | 103 | 59 | .636 | 12 |
| 1969 | Baltimore (E)‡ | Earl Weaver | 109 | 53 | .673 | 19 |
| 1970 | Baltimore (E)‡ | Earl Weaver | 108 | 54 | .667 | 15 |
| 1971 | Baltimore (E)‡ | Earl Weaver | 101 | 57 | .639 | 12 |
| 1972 | Oakland (W)‡ | Dick Williams | 93 | 62 | .600 | 5½ |
| 1973 | Oakland (W)‡ | Dick Williams | 94 | 68 | .580 | 6 |
| 1974 | Oakland (W)‡ | Al Dark | 90 | 72 | .556 | 5 |
| 1975 | Boston (E)‡ | Darrell Johnson | 95 | 65 | .594 | 4½ |
| 1976 | New York (E)‡ | Billy Martin | 97 | 62 | .610 | 10½ |
| 1977 | New York (E)‡ | Billy Martin | 100 | 62 | .617 | 2½ |
| 1978 | New York (E)†‡ | Billy Martin, Bob Lemon | 100 | 63 | .613 | 1 |
| 1979 | Baltimore (E)‡ | Earl Weaver | 102 | 57 | .642 | 8 |
| 1980 | Kansas City (W)‡ | Jim Frey | 97 | 65 | .599 | 14 |
| 1981 | New York (E)‡ | Gene Michael, Bob Lemon | 59 | 48 | .551 | # |
| 1982 | Milwaukee (E)‡ | Buck Rodgers, Harvey Kuenn | 95 | 67 | .586 | 1 |
| 1983 | Baltimore (E)‡ | Joe Altobelli | 98 | 64 | .605 | 6 |
| 1984 | Detroit (E)‡ | Sparky Anderson | 104 | 58 | .642 | 15 |
| 1985 | Kansas City (W)‡ | Dick Howser | 91 | 71 | .562 | 1 |
| 1986 | Boston (E)‡ | John McNamara | 95 | 66 | .590 | 5½ |
| 1987 | Minnesota (W)‡ | Tom Kelly | 85 | 77 | .525 | 2 |
| 1988 | Oakland (W)‡ | Tony La Russa | 104 | 58 | .642 | 13 |
| 1989 | Oakland (W)‡ | Tony La Russa | 99 | 63 | .611 | 7 |
| 1990 | Oakland (W)‡ | Tony La Russa | 103 | 59 | .636 | 9 |
| 1991 | Minnesota (W)‡ | Tom Kelly | 95 | 67 | .586 | 8 |
| 1992 | Toronto‡ | Cito Gaston | 96 | 66 | .593 | 4 |
| 1993 | Toronto‡ | Cito Gaston | 95 | 67 | .586 | 7 |
| 1994 | Season ended Aug. 11 due to players' strike. | | | | | |
| 1995 | Cleveland (C)‡ | Mike Hargrove | 100 | 44 | .694 | 30 |
| 1996 | New York (E)‡ | Joe Torre | 92 | 70 | .568 | 4 |
| 1997 | Cleveland (C)‡ | Mike Hargrove | 86 | 75 | .534 | 6 |
| 1998 | New York (E)‡ | Joe Torre | 114 | 48 | .704 | 22 |
| 1999 | New York (E)‡ | Joe Torre | 98 | 64 | .605 | 4 |
| 2000 | New York (E)‡ | Joe Torre | 87 | 74 | .540 | 2½ |
| 2001 | New York (E)‡ | Joe Torre | 95 | 65 | .594 | 13½ |

†Defeated Boston in one-game playoff. ‡Won championship series.
#First half 34–22; second half 25–26, in season split by strike; defeated Milwaukee in playoff for Eastern Divison title.

## Leading Batsmen

| Year | Player and Team | BA | Year | Player and Team | BA |
|------|-----------------|-----|------|-----------------|-----|
| 1901 | Nap Lajoie, Phil | .422 | 1923 | Harry Heilmann, Det | .403 |
| 1902 | Ed Delahanty, Wash | .376 | 1924 | Babe Ruth, NY | .378 |
| 1903 | Nap Lajoie, Clev | .355 | 1925 | Harry Heilmann, Det | .393 |
| 1904 | Nap Lajoie, Clev | .381 | 1926 | Heinie Manush, Det | .378 |
| 1905 | Elmer Flick, Clev | .306 | 1927 | Harry Heilmann, Det | .398 |
| 1906 | George Stone, StL | .358 | 1928 | Goose Goslin, Wash | .379 |
| 1907 | Ty Cobb, Det | .350 | 1929 | Lew Fonseca, Clev | .369 |
| 1908 | Ty Cobb, Det | .324 | 1930 | Al Simmons, Phil | .381 |
| 1909 | Ty Cobb, Det | .377 | 1931 | Al Simmons, Phil | .390 |
| 1910 | Nap Lajoie, Clev* | .383 | 1932 | Dale Alexander, Det-Bos | .367 |
| 1911 | Ty Cobb, Det | .420 | 1933 | Jimmie Foxx, Phil | .356 |
| 1912 | Ty Cobb, Det | .410 | 1934 | Lou Gehrig, NY | .363 |
| 1913 | Ty Cobb, Det | .390 | 1935 | Buddy Myer, Wash | .349 |
| 1914 | Ty Cobb, Det | .368 | 1936 | Luke Appling, Chi | .388 |
| 1915 | Ty Cobb, Det | .369 | 1937 | Charlie Gehringer, Det | .371 |
| 1916 | Tris Speaker, Clev | .386 | 1938 | Jimmie Foxx, Bos | .349 |
| 1917 | Ty Cobb, Det | .383 | 1939 | Joe DiMaggio, NY | .381 |
| 1918 | Ty Cobb, Det | .382 | 1940 | Joe DiMaggio, NY | .352 |
| 1919 | Ty Cobb, Det | .384 | 1941 | Ted Williams, Bos | .406 |
| 1920 | George Sisler, StL | .407 | 1942 | Ted Williams, Bos | .356 |
| 1921 | Harry Heilmann, Det | .394 | 1943 | Luke Appling, Chi | .328 |
| 1922 | George Sisler, StL | .420 | 1944 | Lou Boudreau, Clev | .327 |

*League president Ban Johnson declared Ty Cobb batting champion with a .385 average, beating Lajoie's .384. However, subsequent research has led to the revision of Lajoie's average to .383 and Cobb's to .382.

## Leading Batsmen *(Cont.)*

| Year | Player and Team | BA | Year | Player and Team | BA |
|---|---|---|---|---|---|
| 1945 | Snuffy Stirnweiss, NY | .309 | 1974 | Rod Carew, Minn | .364 |
| 1946 | Mickey Vernon, Wash | .353 | 1975 | Rod Carew, Minn | .359 |
| 1947 | Ted Williams, Bos | .343 | 1976 | George Brett, KC | .333 |
| 1948 | Ted Williams, Bos | .369 | 1977 | Rod Carew, Minn | .388 |
| 1949 | George Kell, Det | .343 | 1978 | Rod Carew, Minn | .333 |
| 1950 | Billy Goodman, Bos | .354 | 1979 | Fred Lynn, Bos | .333 |
| 1951 | Ferris Fain, Phil | .344 | 1980 | George Brett, KC | .390 |
| 1952 | Ferris Fain, Phil | .327 | 1981 | Carney Lansford, Bos | .336 |
| 1953 | Mickey Vernon, Wash | .337 | 1982 | Willie Wilson, KC | .332 |
| 1954 | Bobby Avila, Clev | .341 | 1983 | Wade Boggs, Bos | .361 |
| 1955 | Al Kaline, Det | .340 | 1984 | Don Mattingly, NY | .343 |
| 1956 | Mickey Mantle, NY | .353 | 1985 | Wade Boggs, Bos | .368 |
| 1957 | Ted Williams, Bos | .388 | 1986 | Wade Boggs, Bos | .357 |
| 1958 | Ted Williams, Bos | .328 | 1987 | Wade Boggs, Bos | .363 |
| 1959 | Harvey Kuenn, Det | .353 | 1988 | Wade Boggs, Bos | .366 |
| 1960 | Pete Runnels, Bos | .320 | 1989 | Kirby Puckett, Minn | .339 |
| 1961 | Norm Cash, Det | .361 | 1990 | George Brett, KC | .329 |
| 1962 | Pete Runnels, Bos | .326 | 1991 | Julio Franco, Tex | .341 |
| 1963 | Carl Yastrzemski, Bos | .321 | 1992 | Edgar Martinez, Sea | .343 |
| 1964 | Tony Oliva, Minn | .323 | 1993 | John Olerud, Tor | .363 |
| 1965 | Tony Oliva, Minn | .321 | 1994 | Paul O'Neill, NY | .359 |
| 1966 | Frank Robinson, Balt | .316 | 1995 | Edgar Martinez, Sea | .356 |
| 1967 | Carl Yastrzemski, Bos | .326 | 1996 | Alex Rodriguez, Sea | .358 |
| 1968 | Carl Yastrzemski, Bos | .301 | 1997 | Frank Thomas, Chi | .347 |
| 1969 | Rod Carew, Minn | .332 | 1998 | Bernie Williams, NY | .339 |
| 1970 | Alex Johnson, Cal | .329 | 1999 | Nomar Garciaparra, Bos | .357 |
| 1971 | Tony Oliva, Minn | .337 | 2000 | Nomar Garciaparra, Bos | .372 |
| 1972 | Rod Carew, Minn | .318 | 2001 | Ichiro Suzuki, Sea | .350 |
| 1973 | Rod Carew, Minn | .350 | | | |

## Leaders in Runs Scored

| Year | Player and Team | Runs | Year | Player and Team | Runs |
|---|---|---|---|---|---|
| 1901 | Nap Lajoie, Phil | 145 | 1935 | Lou Gehrig, NY | 125 |
| 1902 | Dave Fultz, Phil | 110 | 1936 | Lou Gehrig, NY | 167 |
| 1903 | Patsy Dougherty, Bos | 108 | 1937 | Joe DiMaggio, NY | 151 |
| 1904 | Patsy Dougherty, Bos-NY | 113 | 1938 | Hank Greenberg, Det | 144 |
| 1905 | Harry Davis, Phil | 92 | 1939 | Red Rolfe, NY | 139 |
| 1906 | Elmer Flick, Clev | 98 | 1940 | Ted Williams, Bos | 134 |
| 1907 | Sam Crawford, Det | 102 | 1941 | Ted Williams, Bos | 135 |
| 1908 | Matty McIntyre, Det | 105 | 1942 | Ted Williams, Bos | 141 |
| 1909 | Ty Cobb, Det | 116 | 1943 | George Case, Wash | 102 |
| 1910 | Ty Cobb, Det | 106 | 1944 | Snuffy Stirnweiss, NY | 125 |
| 1911 | Ty Cobb, Det | 147 | 1945 | Snuffy Stirnweiss, NY | 107 |
| 1912 | Eddie Collins, Phil | 137 | 1946 | Ted Williams, Bos | 142 |
| 1913 | Eddie Collins, Phil | 125 | 1947 | Ted Williams, Bos | 125 |
| 1914 | Eddie Collins, Phil | 122 | 1948 | Tommy Henrich, NY | 138 |
| 1915 | Ty Cobb, Det | 144 | 1949 | Ted Williams, Bos | 150 |
| 1916 | Ty Cobb, Det | 113 | 1950 | Dom DiMaggio, Bos | 131 |
| 1917 | Donie Bush, Det | 112 | 1951 | Dom DiMaggio, Bos | 113 |
| 1918 | Ray Chapman, Clev | 84 | 1952 | Larry Doby, Clev | 104 |
| 1919 | Babe Ruth, Bos | 103 | 1953 | Al Rosen, Clev | 115 |
| 1920 | Babe Ruth, NY | 158 | 1954 | Mickey Mantle, NY | 129 |
| 1921 | Babe Ruth, NY | 177 | 1955 | Al Smith, Clev | 123 |
| 1922 | George Sisler, StL | 134 | 1956 | Mickey Mantle, NY | 132 |
| 1923 | Babe Ruth, NY | 151 | 1957 | Mickey Mantle, NY | 121 |
| 1924 | Babe Ruth, NY | 143 | 1958 | Mickey Mantle, NY | 127 |
| 1925 | Johnny Mostil, Chi | 135 | 1959 | Eddie Yost, Det | 115 |
| 1926 | Babe Ruth, NY | 139 | 1960 | Mickey Mantle, NY | 119 |
| 1927 | Babe Ruth, NY | 158 | 1961 | Mickey Mantle, NY | 132 |
| 1928 | Babe Ruth, NY | 163 | | Roger Maris, NY | 132 |
| 1929 | Charlie Gehringer, Det | 131 | 1962 | Albie Pearson, LA | 115 |
| 1930 | Al Simmons, Phil | 152 | 1963 | Bob Allison, Minn | 99 |
| 1931 | Lou Gehrig, NY | 163 | 1964 | Tony Oliva, Minn | 109 |
| 1932 | Jimmie Foxx, Phil | 151 | 1965 | Zoilo Versalles, Minn | 126 |
| 1933 | Lou Gehrig, NY | 138 | 1966 | Frank Robinson, Balt | 122 |
| 1934 | Charlie Gehringer, Det | 134 | 1967 | Carl Yastrzemski, Bos | 112 |

## Leaders in Runs Scored (Cont.)

| Year | Player and Team | Runs | Year | Player and Team | Runs |
|------|-----------------|------|------|-----------------|------|
| 1968 | Dick McAuliffe, Det | 95 | 1986 | Rickey Henderson, NY | 130 |
| 1969 | Reggie Jackson, Oak | 123 | 1987 | Paul Molitor, Mil | 114 |
| 1970 | Carl Yastrzemski, Bos | 125 | 1988 | Wade Boggs, Bos | 128 |
| 1971 | Don Buford, Balt | 99 | 1989 | Rickey Henderson, NY-Oak | 113 |
| 1972 | Bobby Murcer, NY | 102 | | Wade Boggs, Bos | 113 |
| 1973 | Reggie Jackson, Oak | 99 | 1990 | Rickey Henderson, Oak | 119 |
| 1974 | Carl Yastrzemski, Bos | 93 | 1991 | Paul Molitor, Mil | 133 |
| 1975 | Fred Lynn, Bos | 103 | 1992 | Tony Phillips, Det | 114 |
| 1976 | Roy White, NY | 104 | 1993 | Rafael Palmeiro, Tex | 124 |
| 1977 | Rod Carew, Minn | 128 | 1994 | Frank Thomas, Chi | 106 |
| 1978 | Ron LeFlore, Det | 126 | 1995 | Albert Belle, Clev | 121 |
| 1979 | Don Baylor, Cal | 120 | | Edgar Martinez, Sea | 121 |
| 1980 | Willie Wilson, KC | 133 | 1996 | Alex Rodriguez, Sea | 141 |
| 1981 | Rickey Henderson, Oak | 89 | 1997 | Ken Griffey Jr., Sea | 125 |
| 1982 | Paul Molitor, Mil | 136 | 1998 | Derek Jeter, NY | 127 |
| 1983 | Cal Ripken, Balt | 121 | 1999 | Roberto Alomar, Clev | 138 |
| 1984 | Dwight Evans, Bos | 121 | 2000 | Johnny Damon, KC | 136 |
| 1985 | Rickey Henderson, NY | 146 | 2001 | Alex Rodriguez, Tex | 133 |

## Leaders in Hits

| Year | Player and Team | Hits | Year | Player and Team | Hits |
|------|-----------------|------|------|-----------------|------|
| 1901 | Nap Lajoie, Phil | 229 | 1942 | Johnny Pesky, Bos | 205 |
| 1902 | Piano Legs Hickman, Bos-Clev | 194 | 1943 | Dick Wakefield, Det | 200 |
| 1903 | Patsy Dougherty, Bos | 195 | 1944 | Snuffy Stirnweiss, NY | 205 |
| 1904 | Nap Lajoie, Clev | 211 | 1945 | Snuffy Stirnweiss, NY | 195 |
| 1905 | George Stone, StL | 187 | 1946 | Johnny Pesky, Bos | 208 |
| 1906 | Nap Lajoie, Clev | 214 | 1947 | Johnny Pesky, Bos | 207 |
| 1907 | Ty Cobb, Det | 212 | 1948 | Bob Dillinger, StL | 207 |
| 1908 | Ty Cobb, Det | 188 | 1949 | Dale Mitchell, Clev | 203 |
| 1909 | Ty Cobb, Det | 216 | 1950 | George Kell, Det | 218 |
| 1910 | Nap Lajoie, Clev | 227 | 1951 | George Kell, Det | 191 |
| 1911 | Ty Cobb, Det | 248 | 1952 | Nellie Fox, Chi | 192 |
| 1912 | Ty Cobb, Det | 227 | 1953 | Harvey Kuenn, Det | 209 |
| 1913 | Joe Jackson, Clev | 197 | 1954 | Nellie Fox, Chi | 201 |
| 1914 | Tris Speaker, Bos | 193 | | Harvey Kuenn, Det | 201 |
| 1915 | Ty Cobb, Det | 208 | 1955 | Al Kaline, Det | 200 |
| 1916 | Tris Speaker, Clev | 211 | 1956 | Harvey Kuenn, Det | 196 |
| 1917 | Ty Cobb, Det | 225 | 1957 | Nellie Fox, Chi | 196 |
| 1918 | George Burns, Phil | 178 | 1958 | Nellie Fox, Chi | 187 |
| 1919 | Ty Cobb, Det | 191 | 1959 | Harvey Kuenn, Det | 198 |
| | Bobby Veach, Det | 191 | 1960 | Minnie Minoso, Chi | 184 |
| 1920 | George Sisler, StL | 257 | 1961 | Norm Cash, Det | 193 |
| 1921 | Harry Heilmann, Det | 237 | 1962 | Bobby Richardson, NY | 209 |
| 1922 | George Sisler, StL | 246 | 1963 | Carl Yastrzemski, Bos | 183 |
| 1923 | Charlie Jamieson, Clev | 222 | 1964 | Tony Oliva, Minn | 217 |
| 1924 | Sam Rice, Wash | 216 | 1965 | Tony Oliva, Minn | 185 |
| 1925 | Al Simmons, Phil | 253 | 1966 | Tony Oliva, Minn | 191 |
| 1926 | George Burns, Clev | 216 | 1967 | Carl Yastrzemski, Bos | 189 |
| | Sam Rice, Wash | 216 | 1968 | Bert Campaneris, Oak | 177 |
| 1927 | Earle Combs, NY | 231 | 1969 | Tony Oliva, Minn | 197 |
| 1928 | Heinie Manush, StL | 241 | 1970 | Tony Oliva, Minn | 204 |
| 1929 | Dale Alexander, Det | 215 | 1971 | Cesar Tovar, Minn | 204 |
| | Charlie Gehringer, Det | 215 | 1972 | Joe Rudi, Oak | 181 |
| 1930 | Johnny Hodapp, Clev | 225 | 1973 | Rod Carew, Minn | 203 |
| 1931 | Lou Gehrig, NY | 211 | 1974 | Rod Carew, Minn | 218 |
| 1932 | Al Simmons, Phil | 216 | 1975 | George Brett, KC | 195 |
| 1933 | Heinie Manush, Wash | 221 | 1976 | George Brett, KC | 215 |
| 1934 | Charlie Gehringer, Det | 214 | 1977 | Rod Carew, Minn | 239 |
| 1935 | Joe Vosmik, Clev | 216 | 1978 | Jim Rice, Bos | 213 |
| 1936 | Earl Averill, Clev | 232 | 1979 | George Brett, KC | 212 |
| 1937 | Beau Bell, StL | 218 | 1980 | Willie Wilson, KC | 230 |
| 1938 | Joe Vosmik, Bos | 201 | 1981 | Rickey Henderson, Oak | 135 |
| 1939 | Red Rolfe, NY | 213 | 1982 | Robin Yount, Mil | 210 |
| 1940 | Rip Radcliff, StL | 200 | 1983 | Cal Ripken Jr., Balt | 211 |
| | Barney McCosky, Det | 200 | 1984 | Don Mattingly, NY | 207 |
| | Doc Cramer, Bos | 200 | 1985 | Wade Boggs, Bos | 240 |
| 1941 | Cecil Travis, Wash | 218 | 1986 | Don Mattingly, NY | 238 |

## Leaders in Hits *(Cont.)*

| Year | Player and Team | Hits | Year | Player and Team | Hits |
|---|---|---|---|---|---|
| 1987 | Kirby Puckett, Minn | 207 | 1994 | Kenny Lofton, Clev | 160 |
|  | Kevin Seitzer, KC | 207 | 1995 | Lance Johnson, Chi | 186 |
| 1988 | Kirby Puckett, Minn | 234 | 1996 | Paul Molitor, Minn | 225 |
| 1989 | Kirby Puckett, Minn | 215 | 1997 | Nomar Garciaparra, Bos | 209 |
| 1990 | Rafael Palmeiro, Tex | 191 | 1998 | Alex Rodriguez, Sea | 213 |
| 1991 | Paul Molitor, Mil | 216 | 1999 | Derek Jeter, NY | 219 |
| 1992 | Kirby Puckett, Minn | 210 | 2000 | Darin Erstad, Ana | 240 |
| 1993 | Paul Molitor, Tor | 211 | 2001 | Ichiro Suzuki, Sea | 242 |

## Home Run Leaders

| Year | Player and Team | HR | Year | Player and Team | HR |
|---|---|---|---|---|---|
| 1901 | Nap Lajoie, Phil | 13 | 1954 | Larry Doby, Clev | 32 |
| 1902 | Socks Seybold, Phil | 16 | 1955 | Mickey Mantle, NY | 37 |
| 1903 | Buck Freeman, Bos | 13 | 1956 | Mickey Mantle, NY | 52 |
| 1904 | Harry Davis, Phil | 10 | 1957 | Roy Sievers, Wash | 42 |
| 1905 | Harry Davis, Phil | 8 | 1958 | Mickey Mantle, NY | 42 |
| 1906 | Harry Davis, Phil | 12 | 1959 | Rocky Colavito, Clev | 42 |
| 1907 | Harry Davis, Phil | 8 |  | Harmon Killebrew, Wash | 42 |
| 1908 | Sam Crawford, Det | 7 | 1960 | Mickey Mantle, NY | 40 |
| 1909 | Ty Cobb, Det | 9 | 1961 | Roger Maris, NY | 61 |
| 1910 | Jake Stahl, Bos | 10 | 1962 | Harmon Killebrew, Minn | 48 |
| 1911 | Frank Baker, Phil | 9 | 1963 | Harmon Killebrew, Minn | 45 |
| 1912 | Frank Baker, Phil | 10 | 1964 | Harmon Killebrew, Minn | 49 |
|  | Tris Speaker, Bos | 10 | 1965 | Tony Conigliaro, Bos | 32 |
| 1913 | Frank Baker, Phil | 13 | 1966 | Frank Robinson, Balt | 49 |
| 1914 | Frank Baker, Phil | 9 | 1967 | Harmon Killebrew, Minn | 44 |
| 1915 | Braggo Roth, Chi-Clev | 7 |  | Carl Yastrzemski, Bos | 44 |
| 1916 | Wally Pipp, NY | 12 | 1968 | Frank Howard, Wash | 44 |
| 1917 | Wally Pipp, NY | 9 | 1969 | Harmon Killebrew, Minn | 49 |
| 1918 | Babe Ruth, Bos | 11 | 1970 | Frank Howard, Wash | 44 |
|  | Tilly Walker, Phil | 11 | 1971 | Bill Melton, Chi | 33 |
| 1919 | Babe Ruth, Bos | 29 | 1972 | Dick Allen, Chi | 37 |
| 1920 | Babe Ruth, NY | 54 | 1973 | Reggie Jackson, Oak | 32 |
| 1921 | Babe Ruth, NY | 59 | 1974 | Dick Allen, Chi | 32 |
| 1922 | Ken Williams, StL | 39 | 1975 | Reggie Jackson, Oak | 36 |
| 1923 | Babe Ruth, NY | 41 |  | George Scott, Mil | 36 |
| 1924 | Babe Ruth, NY | 46 | 1976 | Graig Nettles, NY | 32 |
| 1925 | Bob Meusel, NY | 33 | 1977 | Jim Rice, Bos | 39 |
| 1926 | Babe Ruth, NY | 47 | 1978 | Jim Rice, Bos | 46 |
| 1927 | Babe Ruth, NY | 60 | 1979 | Gorman Thomas, Mil | 45 |
| 1928 | Babe Ruth, NY | 54 | 1980 | Reggie Jackson, NY | 41 |
| 1929 | Babe Ruth, NY | 46 |  | Ben Oglivie, Mil | 41 |
| 1930 | Babe Ruth, NY | 49 | 1981 | Tony Armas, Oak | 22 |
| 1931 | Babe Ruth, NY | 46 | 1981 | Dwight Evans, Bos | 22 |
|  | Lou Gehrig, NY | 46 |  | Bobby Grich, Cal | 22 |
| 1932 | Jimmie Foxx, Phil | 58 |  | Eddie Murray, Balt | 22 |
| 1933 | Jimmie Foxx, Phil | 48 | 1982 | Reggie Jackson, Cal | 39 |
| 1934 | Lou Gehrig, NY | 49 |  | Gorman Thomas, Mil | 39 |
| 1935 | Jimmie Foxx, Phil | 36 | 1983 | Jim Rice, Bos | 39 |
|  | Hank Greenberg, Det | 36 | 1984 | Tony Armas, Bos | 43 |
| 1936 | Lou Gehrig, NY | 49 | 1985 | Darrell Evans, Det | 40 |
| 1937 | Joe DiMaggio, NY | 46 | 1986 | Jesse Barfield, Tor | 40 |
| 1938 | Hank Greenberg, Det | 58 | 1987 | Mark McGwire, Oak | 49 |
| 1939 | Jimmie Foxx, Bos | 35 | 1988 | Jose Canseco, Oak | 42 |
| 1940 | Hank Greenberg, Det | 41 | 1989 | Fred McGriff, Tor | 36 |
| 1941 | Ted Williams, Bos | 37 | 1990 | Cecil Fielder, Det | 51 |
| 1942 | Ted Williams, Bos | 36 | 1991 | Jose Canseco, Oak | 44 |
| 1943 | Rudy York, Det | 34 |  | Cecil Fielder, Det | 44 |
| 1944 | Nick Etten, NY | 22 | 1992 | Juan Gonzalez, Tex | 43 |
| 1945 | Vern Stephens, StL | 24 | 1993 | Juan Gonzalez, Tex | 46 |
| 1946 | Hank Greenberg, Det | 44 | 1994 | Ken Griffey Jr., Sea | 40 |
| 1947 | Ted Williams, Bos | 32 | 1995 | Albert Belle, Clev | 50 |
| 1948 | Joe DiMaggio, NY | 39 | 1996 | Mark McGwire, Oak | 52 |
| 1949 | Ted Williams, Bos | 43 | 1997 | Ken Griffey Jr., Sea | 56 |
| 1950 | Al Rosen, Clev | 37 | 1998 | Ken Griffey Jr., Sea | 56 |
| 1951 | Gus Zornial, Chi Phil | 33 | 1999 | Ken Griffey Jr., Sea | 48 |
| 1952 | Larry Doby, Clev | 32 | 2000 | Troy Glaus, Ana | 47 |
| 1953 | Al Rosen, Clev | 43 | 2001 | Alex Rodriguez, Tex | 52 |

## Runs Batted In Leaders

| Year | Player and Team | RBI | Year | Player and Team | RBI |
|------|-----------------|-----|------|-----------------|-----|
| 1907 | Ty Cobb, Det | 116 | 1954 | Larry Doby, Clev | 126 |
| 1908 | Ty Cobb, Det | 108 | 1955 | Ray Boone, Det | 116 |
| 1909 | Ty Cobb, Det | 107 | | Jackie Jensen, Bos | 116 |
| 1910 | Sam Crawford, Det | 120 | 1956 | Mickey Mantle, NY | 130 |
| 1911 | Ty Cobb, Det | 144 | 1957 | Roy Sievers, Wash | 114 |
| 1912 | Frank Baker, Phil | 133 | 1958 | Jackie Jensen, Bos | 122 |
| 1913 | Frank Baker, Phil | 126 | 1959 | Jackie Jensen, Bos | 112 |
| 1914 | Sam Crawford, Det | 104 | 1960 | Roger Maris, NY | 112 |
| 1915 | Sam Crawford, Det | 112 | 1961 | Roger Maris, NY | 142 |
| | Bobby Veach, Det | 112 | 1962 | Harmon Killebrew, Minn | 126 |
| 1916 | Del Pratt, StL | 103 | 1963 | Dick Stuart, Bos | 118 |
| 1917 | Bobby Veach, Det | 103 | 1964 | Brooks Robinson, Balt | 118 |
| 1918 | Bobby Veach, Det | 78 | 1965 | Rocky Colavito, Clev | 108 |
| 1919 | Babe Ruth, Bos | 114 | 1966 | Frank Robinson, Balt | 122 |
| 1920 | Babe Ruth, NY | 137 | 1967 | Carl Yastrzemski, Bos | 121 |
| 1921 | Babe Ruth, NY | 171 | 1968 | Ken Harrelson, Bos | 109 |
| 1922 | Ken Williams, StL | 155 | 1969 | Harmon Killebrew, Minn | 140 |
| 1923 | Babe Ruth, NY | 131 | 1970 | Frank Howard, Wash | 126 |
| 1924 | Goose Goslin, Wash | 129 | 1971 | Harmon Killebrew, Minn | 119 |
| 1925 | Bob Meusel, NY | 138 | 1972 | Dick Allen, Chi | 113 |
| 1926 | Babe Ruth, NY | 145 | 1973 | Reggie Jackson, Oak | 117 |
| 1927 | Lou Gehrig, NY | 175 | 1974 | Jeff Burroughs, Tex | 118 |
| 1928 | Babe Ruth, NY | 142 | 1975 | George Scott, Mil | 109 |
| | Lou Gehrig, NY | 142 | 1976 | Lee May, Balt | 109 |
| 1929 | Al Simmons, Phil | 157 | 1977 | Larry Hisle, Minn | 119 |
| 1930 | Lou Gehrig, NY | 174 | 1978 | Jim Rice, Bos | 139 |
| 1931 | Lou Gehrig, NY | 184 | 1979 | Don Baylor, Cal | 139 |
| 1932 | Jimmie Foxx, Phil | 169 | 1980 | Cecil Cooper, Mil | 122 |
| 1933 | Jimmie Foxx, Phil | 163 | 1981 | Eddie Murray, Balt | 78 |
| 1934 | Lou Gehrig, NY | 165 | 1982 | Hal McRae, KC | 133 |
| 1935 | Hank Greenberg, Det | 170 | 1983 | Cecil Cooper, Mil | 126 |
| 1936 | Hal Trosky, Clev | 162 | | Jim Rice, Bos | 126 |
| 1937 | Hank Greenberg, Det | 183 | 1984 | Tony Armas, Bos | 123 |
| 1938 | Jimmie Foxx, Bos | 175 | 1985 | Don Mattingly, NY | 145 |
| 1939 | Ted Williams, Bos | 145 | 1986 | Joe Carter, Clev | 121 |
| 1940 | Hank Greenberg, Det | 150 | 1987 | George Bell, Tor | 134 |
| 1941 | Joe DiMaggio, NY | 125 | 1988 | Jose Canseco, Oak | 124 |
| 1942 | Ted Williams, Bos | 137 | 1989 | Ruben Sierra, Tex | 119 |
| 1943 | Rudy York, Det | 118 | 1990 | Cecil Fielder, Det | 132 |
| 1944 | Vern Stephens, StL | 109 | 1991 | Cecil Fielder, Det | 133 |
| 1945 | Nick Etten, NY | 111 | 1992 | Cecil Fielder, Det | 124 |
| 1946 | Hank Greenberg, Det | 127 | 1993 | Albert Belle, Clev | 129 |
| 1947 | Ted Williams, Bos | 114 | 1994 | Kirby Puckett, Minn | 112 |
| 1948 | Joe DiMaggio, NY | 155 | 1995 | Albert Belle, Clev | 126 |
| 1949 | Ted Williams, Bos | 159 | | Mo Vaughn, Bos | 126 |
| | Vern Stephens, Bos | 159 | 1996 | Albert Belle, Clev | 148 |
| 1950 | Walt Dropo, Bos | 144 | 1997 | Ken Griffey Jr., Sea | 147 |
| | Vern Stephens, Bos | 144 | 1998 | Juan Gonzales, Tex | 157 |
| 1951 | Gus Zernial, Chi-Phil | 129 | 1999 | Manny Ramirez, Clev | 165 |
| 1952 | Al Rosen, Clev | 105 | 2000 | Edgar Martinez, Sea | 145 |
| 1953 | Al Rosen, Clev | 145 | 2001 | Bret Boone, Sea | 141 |

Note: Runs Batted In not compiled before 1907; officially adopted in 1920.

## Leading Base Stealers

| Year | Player and Team | SB | Year | Player and Team | SB |
|------|-----------------|-----|------|-----------------|-----|
| 1901 | Frank Isbell, Chi | 48 | 1911 | Ty Cobb, Det | 83 |
| 1902 | Topsy Hartsel, Phil | 54 | 1912 | Clyde Milan, Wash | 88 |
| 1903 | Harry Bay, Clev | 46 | 1913 | Clyde Milan, Wash | 75 |
| 1904 | Elmer Flick, Clev | 42 | 1914 | Fritz Maisel, NY | 74 |
| | Harry Bay, Clev | 42 | 1915 | Ty Cobb, Det | 96 |
| 1905 | Danny Hoffman, Phil | 46 | 1916 | Ty Cobb, Det | 68 |
| 1906 | Elmer Flick, Clev | 39 | 1917 | Ty Cobb, Det | 55 |
| | John Anderson, Wash | 39 | 1918 | George Sisler, StL | 45 |
| 1907 | Ty Cobb, Det | 49 | 1919 | Eddie Collins, Chi | 33 |
| 1908 | Patsy Dougherty, Chi | 47 | 1920 | Sam Rice, Wash | 63 |
| 1909 | Ty Cobb, Det | 76 | 1921 | George Sisler, StL | 35 |
| 1910 | Eddie Collins, Phil | 81 | 1922 | George Sisler, StL | 51 |

## Leading Base Stealers (Cont.)

| Year | Player and Team | SB | Year | Player and Team | SB |
|------|-----------------|-----|------|-----------------|-----|
| 1923 | Eddie Collins, Chi | 49 | 1963 | Luis Aparicio, Balt | 40 |
| 1924 | Eddie Collins, Chi | 42 | 1964 | Luis Aparicio, Balt | 57 |
| 1925 | John Mostil, Chi | 43 | 1965 | Bert Campaneris, KC | 51 |
| 1926 | John Mostil, Chi | 35 | 1966 | Bert Campaneris, KC | 52 |
| 1927 | George Sisler, StL | 27 | 1967 | Bert Campaneris, KC | 55 |
| 1928 | Buddy Myer, Bos | 30 | 1968 | Bert Campaneris, Oak | 62 |
| 1929 | Charlie Gehringer, Det | 27 | 1969 | Tommy Harper, Sea | 73 |
| 1930 | Marty McManus, Det | 23 | 1970 | Bert Campaneris, Oak | 42 |
| 1931 | Ben Chapman, NY | 61 | 1971 | Amos Otis, KC | 52 |
| 1932 | Ben Chapman, NY | 38 | 1972 | Bert Campaneris, Oak | 52 |
| 1933 | Ben Chapman, NY | 27 | 1973 | Tommy Harper, Bos | 54 |
| 1934 | Bill Werber, Bos | 40 | 1974 | Bill North, Oak | 54 |
| 1935 | Bill Werber, Bos | 29 | 1975 | Mickey Rivers, Cal | 70 |
| 1936 | Lyn Lary, StL | 37 | 1976 | Bill North, Oak | 75 |
| 1937 | Bill Werber, Phil | 35 | 1977 | Freddie Patek, KC | 53 |
|      | Ben Chapman, Wash-Bos | 35 | 1978 | Ron LeFlore, Det | 68 |
| 1938 | Frank Crosetti, NY | 27 | 1979 | Willie Wilson, KC | 83 |
| 1939 | George Case, Wash | 51 | 1980 | Rickey Henderson, Oak | 100 |
| 1940 | George Case, Wash | 35 | 1981 | Rickey Henderson, Oak | 56 |
| 1941 | George Case, Wash | 33 | 1982 | Rickey Henderson, Oak | 130 |
| 1942 | George Case, Wash | 44 | 1983 | Rickey Henderson, Oak | 108 |
| 1943 | George Case, Wash | 61 | 1984 | Rickey Henderson, Oak | 66 |
| 1944 | Snuffy Stirnweiss, NY | 55 | 1985 | Rickey Henderson, NY | 80 |
| 1945 | Snuffy Stirnweiss, NY | 33 | 1986 | Rickey Henderson, NY | 87 |
| 1946 | George Case, Clev | 28 | 1987 | Harold Reynolds, Sea | 60 |
| 1947 | Bob Dillinger, StL | 34 | 1988 | Rickey Henderson, NY | 93 |
| 1948 | Bob Dillinger, StL | 28 | 1989 | Rickey Henderson, NY-Oak | 77 |
| 1949 | Bob Dillinger, StL | 20 | 1990 | Rickey Henderson, Oak | 65 |
| 1950 | Dom DiMaggio, Bos | 15 | 1991 | Rickey Henderson, Oak | 58 |
| 1951 | Minnie Minoso, Clev-Chi | 31 | 1992 | Kenny Lofton, Clev | 66 |
| 1952 | Minnie Minoso, Chi | 22 | 1993 | Kenny Lofton, Clev | 70 |
| 1953 | Minnie Minoso, Chi | 25 | 1994 | Kenny Lofton, Clev | 60 |
| 1954 | Jackie Jensen, Bos | 22 | 1995 | Kenny Lofton, Clev | 54 |
| 1955 | Jim Rivera, Chi | 25 | 1996 | Kenny Lofton, Clev | 75 |
| 1956 | Luis Aparicio, Chi | 21 | 1997 | Brian Hunter, Det | 74 |
| 1957 | Luis Aparicio, Chi | 28 | 1998 | Rickey Henderson, Oak | 66 |
| 1958 | Luis Aparicio, Chi | 29 | 1999 | Brian Hunter, Sea | 44 |
| 1959 | Luis Aparicio, Chi | 56 | 2000 | Johnny Damon, KC | 46 |
| 1960 | Luis Aparicio, Chi | 51 | 2001 | Ichiro Suzuki, Sea | 56 |
| 1961 | Luis Aparicio, Chi | 53 | | | |
| 1962 | Luis Aparicio, Chi | 31 | | | |

## Leading Pitchers—Winning Percentage

| Year | Pitcher and Team | W | L | Pct | Year | Pitcher and Team | W | L | Pct |
|------|------------------|----|----|------|------|------------------|----|----|------|
| 1901 | Clark Griffith, Chi | 24 | 7 | .774 | 1924 | Walter Johnson, Wash | 23 | 7 | .767 |
| 1902 | Bill Bernhard, Phil-Clev | 18 | 5 | .783 | 1925 | Stan Coveleski, Wash | 20 | 5 | .800 |
| 1903 | Earl Moore, Clev | 22 | 7 | .759 | 1926 | George Uhle, Clev | 27 | 11 | .711 |
| 1904 | Jack Chesbro, NY | 41 | 12 | .774 | 1927 | Waite Hoyt, NY | 22 | 7 | .759 |
| 1905 | Jess Tannehill, Bos | 22 | 9 | .710 | 1928 | General Crowder, StL | 21 | 5 | .808 |
| 1906 | Eddie Plank, Phil | 19 | 6 | .760 | 1929 | Lefty Grove, Phil | 20 | 6 | .769 |
| 1907 | Wild Bill Donovan, Det | 25 | 4 | .862 | 1930 | Lefty Grove, Phil | 28 | 5 | .848 |
| 1908 | Ed Walsh, Chi | 40 | 15 | .727 | 1931 | Lefty Grove, Phil | 31 | 4 | .886 |
| 1909 | George Mullin, Det | 29 | 8 | .784 | 1932 | Johnny Allen, NY | 17 | 4 | .810 |
| 1910 | Chief Bender, Phil | 23 | 5 | .821 | 1933 | Lefty Grove, Phil | 24 | 8 | .750 |
| 1911 | Chief Bender, Phil | 17 | 5 | .773 | 1934 | Lefty Gomez, NY | 26 | 5 | .839 |
| 1912 | Smoky Joe Wood, Bos | 34 | 5 | .872 | 1935 | Eldon Auker, Det | 18 | 7 | .720 |
| 1913 | Walter Johnson, Wash | 36 | 7 | .837 | 1936 | Monte Pearson, NY | 19 | 7 | .731 |
| 1914 | Chief Bender, Phil | 17 | 3 | .850 | 1937 | Johnny Allen, Clev | 15 | 1 | .938 |
| 1915 | Smoky Joe Wood, Bos | 15 | 5 | .750 | 1938 | Red Ruffing, NY | 21 | 7 | .750 |
| 1916 | Eddie Cicotte, Chi | 15 | 7 | .682 | 1939 | Lefty Grove, Bos | 15 | 4 | .789 |
| 1917 | Reb Russell, Chi | 15 | 5 | .750 | 1940 | Schoolboy Rowe, Det | 16 | 3 | .842 |
| 1918 | Sad Sam Jones, Bos | 16 | 5 | .762 | 1941 | Lefty Gomez, NY | 15 | 5 | .750 |
| 1919 | Eddie Cicotte, Chi | 29 | 7 | .806 | 1942 | Ernie Bonham, NY | 21 | 5 | .808 |
| 1920 | Jim Bagby, Clev | 31 | 12 | .721 | 1943 | Spud Chandler, NY | 20 | 4 | .833 |
| 1921 | Carl Mays, NY | 27 | 9 | .750 | 1944 | Tex Hughson, Bos | 18 | 5 | .783 |
| 1922 | Joe Bush, NY | 26 | 7 | .788 | 1945 | Hal Newhouser, Det | 25 | 9 | .735 |
| 1923 | Herb Pennock, NY | 19 | 6 | .760 | 1946 | Boo Ferriss, Bos | 25 | 6 | .806 |

## Leading Pitchers—Winning Percentage (Cont.)

| Year | Pitcher and Team | W | L | Pct | Year | Pitcher and Team | W | L | Pct |
|---|---|---|---|---|---|---|---|---|---|
| 1947 | Allie Reynolds, NY | 19 | 8 | .704 | 1975 | Mike Torrez, Balt | 20 | 9 | .690 |
| 1948 | Jack Kramer, Bos | 18 | 5 | .783 | 1976 | Bill Campbell, Minn | 17 | 5 | .773 |
| 1949 | Ellis Kinder, Bos | 23 | 6 | .793 | 1977 | Paul Splittorff, KC | 16 | 6 | .727 |
| 1950 | Vic Raschi, NY | 21 | 8 | .724 | 1978 | Ron Guidry, NY | 25 | 3 | .893 |
| 1951 | Bob Feller, Clev | 22 | 8 | .733 | 1979 | Mike Caldwell, Mil | 16 | 6 | .727 |
| 1952 | Bobby Shantz, Phil | 24 | 7 | .774 | 1980 | Steve Stone, Balt | 25 | 7 | .781 |
| 1953 | Ed Lopat, NY | 16 | 4 | .800 | 1981* | Pete Vuckovich, Mil | 14 | 4 | .778 |
| 1954 | Sandy Consuegra, Chi | 16 | 3 | .842 | 1982 | Pete Vuckovich, Mil | 18 | 6 | .750 |
| 1955 | Tommy Byrne, NY | 16 | 5 | .762 | | Jim Palmer, Balt | 15 | 5 | .750 |
| 1956 | Whitey Ford, NY | 19 | 6 | .760 | 1983 | Richard Dotson, Chi | 22 | 7 | .759 |
| 1957 | Dick Donovan, Chi | 16 | 6 | .727 | 1984 | Doyle Alexander, Tor | 17 | 6 | .739 |
| | Tom Sturdivant, NY | 16 | 6 | .727 | 1985 | Ron Guidry, NY | 22 | 6 | .786 |
| 1958 | Bob Turley, NY | 21 | 7 | .750 | 1986 | Roger Clemens, Bos | 24 | 4 | .857 |
| 1959 | Bob Shaw, Chi | 18 | 6 | .750 | 1987 | Roger Clemens, Bos | 20 | 9 | .690 |
| 1960 | Jim Perry, Clev | 18 | 10 | .643 | 1988 | Frank Viola, Minn | 24 | 7 | .774 |
| 1961 | Whitey Ford, NY | 25 | 4 | .862 | 1989 | Bret Saberhagen, KC | 23 | 6 | .793 |
| 1962 | Ray Herbert, Chi | 20 | 9 | .690 | 1990 | Bob Welch, Oak | 27 | 6 | .818 |
| 1963 | Whitey Ford, NY | 24 | 7 | .774 | 1991 | Scott Erickson, Minn | 20 | 8 | .714 |
| 1964 | Wally Bunker, Balt | 19 | 5 | .792 | 1992 | Mike Mussina, Balt | 18 | 5 | .783 |
| 1965 | Mudcat Grant, Minn | 21 | 7 | .750 | 1993 | Jimmy Key, NY | 18 | 6 | .750 |
| 1966 | Sonny Siebert, Clev | 16 | 8 | .667 | 1994 | Jimmy Key, NY | 17 | 4 | .810 |
| 1967 | Joel Horlen, Chi | 19 | 7 | .731 | 1995 | Randy Johnson, Sea | 18 | 2 | .900 |
| 1968 | Denny McLain, Det | 31 | 6 | .838 | 1996 | Charles Nagy, Clev | 17 | 5 | .773 |
| 1969 | Jim Palmer, Balt | 16 | 4 | .800 | 1997 | Randy Johnson, Sea | 20 | 4 | .833 |
| 1970 | Mike Cuellar, Balt | 24 | 8 | .750 | 1998 | David Wells, NY | 18 | 4 | .818 |
| 1971 | Dave McNally, Balt | 21 | 5 | .808 | 1999 | Pedro Martinez, Bos | 23 | 4 | .852 |
| 1972 | Catfish Hunter, Oak | 21 | 7 | .750 | 2000 | Tim Hudson, Oak | 20 | 6 | .769 |
| 1973 | Catfish Hunter, Oak | 21 | 5 | .808 | 2001 | Roger Clemens, NY | 20 | 3 | .870 |
| 1974 | Mike Cuellar, Balt | 22 | 10 | .688 | | | | | |

*1981 percentages based on 10 or more victories. Note: Percentages based on 15 or more victories in all other years.

## Leading Pitchers—Earned Run Average

| Year | Player and Team | ERA | Year | Player and Team | ERA |
|---|---|---|---|---|---|
| 1913 | Walter Johnson, Wash | 1.14 | 1945 | Hal Newhouser, Det | 1.81 |
| 1914 | Dutch Leonard, Bos | 1.01 | 1946 | Hal Newhouser, Det | 1.94 |
| 1915 | Smoky Joe Wood, Bos | 1.49 | 1947 | Spud Chandler, NY | 2.46 |
| 1916 | Babe Ruth, Bos | 1.75 | 1948 | Gene Bearden, Clev | 2.43 |
| 1917 | Eddie Cicotte, Chi | 1.53 | 1949 | Mel Parnell, Bos | 2.78 |
| 1918 | Walter Johnson, Wash | 1.27 | 1950 | Early Wynn, Clev | 3.20 |
| 1919 | Walter Johnson, Wash | 1.49 | 1951 | Saul Rogovin, Det-Chi | 2.78 |
| 1920 | Bob Shawkey, NY | 2.46 | 1952 | Allie Reynolds, NY | 2.07 |
| 1921 | Red Faber, Chi | 2.47 | 1953 | Ed Lopat, NY | 2.43 |
| 1922 | Red Faber, Chi | 2.80 | 1954 | Mike Garcia, Clev | 2.64 |
| 1923 | Stan Coveleski, Clev | 2.76 | 1955 | Billy Pierce, Chi | 1.97 |
| 1924 | Walter Johnson, Wash | 2.72 | 1956 | Whitey Ford, NY | 2.47 |
| 1925 | Stan Coveleski, Wash | 2.84 | 1957 | Bobby Shantz, NY | 2.45 |
| 1926 | Lefty Grove, Phil | 2.51 | 1958 | Whitey Ford, NY | 2.01 |
| 1927 | Wilcy Moore, NY# | 2.28 | 1959 | Hoyt Wilhelm, Balt | 2.19 |
| 1928 | Garland Braxton, Wash | 2.52 | 1960 | Frank Baumann, Chi | 2.68 |
| 1929 | Lefty Grove, Phil | 2.81 | 1961 | Dick Donovan, Wash | 2.40 |
| 1930 | Lefty Grove, Phil | 2.54 | 1962 | Hank Aguirre, Det | 2.21 |
| 1931 | Lefty Grove, Phil | 2.06 | 1963 | Gary Peters, Chi | 2.33 |
| 1932 | Lefty Grove, Phil | 2.84 | 1964 | Dean Chance, LA | 1.65 |
| 1933 | Monte Pearson, Clev | 2.33 | 1965 | Sam McDowell, Clev | 2.18 |
| 1934 | Lefty Gomez, NY | 2.33 | 1966 | Gary Peters, Chi | 1.98 |
| 1935 | Lefty Grove, Bos | 2.70 | 1967 | Joe Horlen, Chi | 2.06 |
| 1936 | Lefty Grove, Bos | 2.81 | 1968 | Luis Tiant, Clev | 1.60 |
| 1937 | Lefty Gomez, NY | 2.33 | 1969 | Dick Bosman, Wash | 2.19 |
| 1938 | Lefty Grove, Bos | 3.07 | 1970 | Diego Segui, Oak | 2.56 |
| 1939 | Lefty Grove, Bos | 2.54 | 1971 | Vida Blue, Oak | 1.82 |
| 1940 | Bob Feller, Clev† | 2.62 | 1972 | Luis Tiant, Bos | 1.91 |
| 1941 | Thornton Lee, Chi | 2.37 | 1973 | Jim Palmer, Balt | 2.40 |
| 1942 | Ted Lyons, Chi | 2.10 | 1974 | Catfish Hunter, Oak | 2.49 |
| 1943 | Spud Chandler, NY | 1.64 | 1975 | Jim Palmer, Balt | 2.09 |
| 1944 | Dizzy Trout, Det | 2.12 | 1976 | Mark Fidrych, Det | 2.34 |

## Leading Pitchers—Earned Run Average *(Cont.)*

| Year | Player and Team | ERA | Year | Player and Team | ERA |
|---|---|---|---|---|---|
| 1977 | Frank Tanana, Cal | 2.54 | 1990 | Roger Clemens, Bos | 1.93 |
| 1978 | Ron Guidry, NY | 1.74 | 1991 | Roger Clemens, Bos | 2.62 |
| 1979 | Ron Guidry, NY | 2.78 | 1992 | Roger Clemens, Bos | 2.41 |
| 1980 | Rudy May, NY | 2.47 | 1993 | Kevin Appier, KC | 2.56 |
| 1981 | Steve McCatty, Oak | 2.32 | 1994 | Steve Ontiveros, Oak | 2.65 |
| 1982 | Rick Sutcliffe, Clev | 2.96 | 1995 | Randy Johnson, Sea | 2.48 |
| 1983 | Rick Honeycutt, Tex | 2.42 | 1996 | Juan Guzman, Tor | 2.93 |
| 1984 | Mike Boddicker, Balt | 2.79 | 1997 | Roger Clemens, Tor | 2.05 |
| 1985 | Dave Stieb, Tor | 2.48 | 1998 | Roger Clemens, Tor | 2.64 |
| 1986 | Roger Clemens, Bos | 2.48 | 1999 | Pedro Martinez, Bos | 2.07 |
| 1987 | Jimmy Key, Tor | 2.76 | 2000 | Pedro Martinez, Bos | 1.74 |
| 1988 | Allan Anderson, Minn | 2.45 | 2001 | Freddy Garcia, Sea | 3.05 |
| 1989 | Bret Saberhagen, KC | 2.16 | | | |

Note: Based on 10 complete games through 1950, then 154 innings until the American League expanded in 1961, when it became 162 innings. In strike-shortened 1981, one inning per game required. Earned runs not tabulated in American League prior to 1913.

#Wilcy Moore pitched only six complete games—he started 12—in 1927 but was recognized as leader because of 213 innings pitched. †Ernie Bonham, New York, had 1.91 ERA and 10 complete games in 1940 but appeared in only 12 games and 99 innings, and Bob Feller was recognized as leader.

## Leading Pitchers—Strikeouts

| Year | Player and Team | SO | Year | Player and Team | SO |
|---|---|---|---|---|---|
| 1901 | Cy Young, Bos | 159 | 1945 | Hal Newhouser, Det | 212 |
| 1902 | Rube Waddell, Phil | 210 | 1946 | Bob Feller, Clev | 348 |
| 1903 | Rube Waddell, Phil | 301 | 1947 | Bob Feller, Clev | 196 |
| 1904 | Rube Waddell, Phil | 349 | 1948 | Bob Feller, Clev | 164 |
| 1905 | Rube Waddell, Phil | 286 | 1949 | Virgil Trucks, Det | 153 |
| 1906 | Rube Waddell, Phil | 203 | 1950 | Bob Lemon, Clev | 170 |
| 1907 | Rube Waddell, Phil | 226 | 1951 | Vic Raschi, NY | 164 |
| 1908 | Ed Walsh, Chi | 269 | 1952 | Allie Reynolds, NY | 160 |
| 1909 | Frank Smith, Chi | 177 | 1953 | Billy Pierce, Chi | 186 |
| 1910 | Walter Johnson, Wash | 313 | 1954 | Bob Turley, Balt | 185 |
| 1911 | Ed Walsh, Chi | 255 | 1955 | Herb Score, Clev | 245 |
| 1912 | Walter Johnson, Wash | 303 | 1956 | Herb Score, Clev | 263 |
| 1913 | Walter Johnson, Wash | 243 | 1957 | Early Wynn, Clev | 184 |
| 1914 | Walter Johnson, Wash | 225 | 1958 | Early Wynn, Chi | 179 |
| 1915 | Walter Johnson, Wash | 203 | 1959 | Jim Bunning, Det | 201 |
| 1916 | Walter Johnson, Wash | 228 | 1960 | Jim Bunning, Det | 201 |
| 1917 | Walter Johnson, Wash | 188 | 1961 | Camilo Pascual, Minn | 221 |
| 1918 | Walter Johnson, Wash | 162 | 1962 | Camilo Pascual, Minn | 206 |
| 1919 | Walter Johnson, Wash | 147 | 1963 | Camilo Pascual, Minn | 202 |
| 1920 | Stan Coveleski, Clev | 133 | 1964 | Al Downing, NY | 217 |
| 1921 | Walter Johnson, Wash | 143 | 1965 | Sam McDowell, Clev | 325 |
| 1922 | Urban Shocker, StL | 149 | 1966 | Sam McDowell, Clev | 225 |
| 1923 | Walter Johnson, Wash | 130 | 1967 | Jim Lonborg, Bos | 246 |
| 1924 | Walter Johnson, Wash | 158 | 1968 | Sam McDowell, Clev | 283 |
| 1925 | Lefty Grove, Phil | 116 | 1969 | Sam McDowell, Clev | 279 |
| 1926 | Lefty Grove, Phil | 194 | 1970 | Sam McDowell, Clev | 304 |
| 1927 | Lefty Grove, Phil | 174 | 1971 | Mickey Lolich, Det | 308 |
| 1928 | Lefty Grove, Phil | 183 | 1972 | Nolan Ryan, Cal | 329 |
| 1929 | Lefty Grove, Phil | 170 | 1973 | Nolan Ryan, Cal | 383 |
| 1930 | Lefty Grove, Phil | 209 | 1974 | Nolan Ryan, Cal | 367 |
| 1931 | Lefty Grove, Phil | 175 | 1975 | Frank Tanana, Cal | 269 |
| 1932 | Red Ruffing, NY | 190 | 1976 | Nolan Ryan, Cal | 327 |
| 1933 | Lefty Gomez, NY | 163 | 1977 | Nolan Ryan, Cal | 341 |
| 1934 | Lefty Gomez, NY | 158 | 1978 | Nolan Ryan, Cal | 260 |
| 1935 | Tommy Bridges, Det | 163 | 1979 | Nolan Ryan, Cal | 223 |
| 1936 | Tommy Bridges, Det | 175 | 1980 | Len Barker, Clev | 187 |
| 1937 | Lefty Gomez, NY | 194 | 1981 | Len Barker, Clev | 127 |
| 1938 | Bob Feller, Clev | 240 | 1982 | Floyd Bannister, Sea | 209 |
| 1939 | Bob Feller, Clev | 246 | 1983 | Jack Morris, Det | 232 |
| 1940 | Bob Feller, Clev | 261 | 1984 | Mark Langston, Sea | 204 |
| 1941 | Bob Feller, Clev | 260 | 1985 | Bert Blyleven, Clev-Minn | 206 |
| 1942 | Bobo Newsom, Wash | | 1986 | Mark Langston, Sea | 245 |
| | Tex Hughson, Bos | 113 | 1987 | Mark Langston, Sea | 262 |
| 1943 | Allie Reynolds, Clev | 151 | 1988 | Roger Clemens, Bos | 291 |
| 1944 | Hal Newhouser, Det | 187 | 1989 | Nolan Ryan, Tex | 301 |

### Leading Pitchers—Strikeouts *(Cont.)*

| Year | Player and Team | SO | Year | Player and Team | SO |
|------|-----------------|----|------|-----------------|----|
| 1990 | Nolan Ryan, Tex | 232 | 1996 | Roger Clemens, Bos | 257 |
| 1991 | Roger Clemens, Bos | 241 | 1997 | Roger Clemens, Tor | 292 |
| 1992 | Randy Johnson, Sea | 241 | 1998 | Roger Clemens, Tor | 271 |
| 1993 | Randy Johnson, Sea | 308 | 1999 | Pedro Martinez, Bos | 313 |
| 1994 | Randy Johnson, Sea | 204 | 2000 | Pedro Martinez, Bos | 284 |
| 1995 | Randy Johnson, Sea | 294 | 2001 | Hideo Nomo, Bos | 220 |

### Leading Pitchers—Saves

| Year | Player and Team | SV | Year | Player and Team | SV |
|------|-----------------|----|------|-----------------|----|
| 1947 | Joe Page, NY | 17 | 1975 | Goose Gossage, Chi | 26 |
| 1948 | Russ Christopher, Clev | 17 | 1976 | Sparky Lyle, NY | 23 |
| 1949 | Joe Page, NY | 29 | 1977 | Bill Campbell, Bos | 31 |
| 1950 | Mickey Harris, Wash | 15 | 1978 | Goose Gossage, NY | 27 |
| 1951 | Ellis Kinder, Bos | 14 | 1979 | Mike Marshall, Minn | 32 |
| 1952 | Harry Dorish, Chi | 11 | 1980 | Dan Quisenberry, KC | 33 |
| 1953 | Ellis Kinder, Bos | 27 | 1981 | Rollie Fingers, Mil | 28 |
| 1954 | Johnny Sain, NY | 22 | 1982 | Dan Quisenberry, KC | 35 |
| 1955 | Ray Narleski, Clev | 19 | 1983 | Dan Quisenberry, KC | 35 |
| 1956 | George Zuverink, Bal | 16 | 1984 | Dan Quisenberry, KC | 44 |
| 1957 | Bob Grim, NY | 19 | 1985 | Dan Quisenberry, KC | 37 |
| 1958 | Ryne Duren, NY | 20 | 1986 | Dave Righetti, NY | 46 |
| 1959 | Turk Lown, Chi | 15 | 1987 | Tom Henke, Tor | 34 |
| 1960 | Mike Fornieles, Bos | 14 | 1988 | Dennis Eckersley, Oak | 45 |
|      | Johnny Klippstein, Clev | 14 | 1989 | Jeff Russell, Tex | 38 |
| 1961 | Luis Arroyo, NY | 29 | 1990 | Bobby Thigpen, Chi | 57 |
| 1962 | Dick Radatz, Bos | 24 | 1991 | Bryan Harvey, Cal | 46 |
| 1963 | Stu Miller, Bal | 27 | 1992 | Dennis Eckersley, Oak | 51 |
| 1964 | Dick Radatz, Bos | 29 | 1993 | Jeff Montgomery, KC | 45 |
| 1965 | Ron Kline, Wash | 29 |      | Duane Ward, Tor | 45 |
| 1966 | Jack Aker, KC | 32 | 1994 | Lee Smith, Bal | 33 |
| 1967 | Minnie Rojas, Cal | 27 | 1995 | Jose Mesa, Clev | 46 |
| 1968 | Al Worthington, Minn | 18 | 1996 | John Wetteland, NY | 43 |
| 1969 | Ron Perranoski, Minn | 31 | 1997 | Randy Myers, Balt | 45 |
| 1970 | Ron Perranoski, Minn | 34 | 1998 | Tom Gordon, Bos | 46 |
| 1971 | Ken Sanders, Mil | 31 | 1999 | Mariano Rivera, NY | 45 |
| 1972 | Sparky Lyle, NY | 35 | 2000 | Todd Jones, Det | 42 |
| 1973 | John Hiller, Det | 38 | 2001 | Mariano Rivera, NY | 50 |
| 1974 | Terry Forster, Chi | 24 | | | |

## The Commissioners of Baseball

Kenesaw Mountain Landis .......Elected Nov. 12, 1920. Served until his death on Nov. 25, 1944.
Happy Chandler ......................Elected April 24, 1945. Served until July 15, 1951.
Ford Frick ................................Elected Sept. 20, 1951. Served until Nov. 16, 1965.
William Eckert ...........................Elected Nov. 17, 1965. Served until Dec. 20, 1968.
Bowie Kuhn ............................Elected Feb. 8, 1969. Served until Sept. 30, 1984.
Peter Ueberroth ......................Elected March 3, 1984. Took office Oct. 1, 1984. Served through March 31, 1989.
A. Bartlett Giamatti ..................Elected Sept. 8, 1988. Took office April 1, 1989. Served until his death on Sept. 1, 1989.
Francis Vincent Jr. ..................Appointed Acting Commissioner Sept. 2, 1989. Elected Commissioner Sept. 13, 1989. Served through Sept. 7, 1992.
Allan H. (Bud) Selig .................Elected chairman of the executive council and given the powers of interim commissioner on Sept. 9, 1992. Unanimously elected Commissioner July 9, 1998.

# Pro Football

Trent Dilfer of the Super Bowl champion Ravens

# The Defense Rests

## The Ravens' relentless, swarming 'D' delivered a title to Baltimore and a measure of redemption to its star, Ray Lewis

### BY HANK HERSCH

THE FIRST led to his indictment on double-homicide charges; the second to his entry into the NFL pantheon. Baltimore Ravens middle linebacker Ray Lewis will be forever defined by the Super Bowls that bracketed the 2000 NFL season, events that offered up a dismayingly ambiguous portrait of the talented player. For his connection to a street brawl following Super Bowl XXXIV in Atlanta during which two men were stabbed to death, Lewis became a murder suspect. He would plead guilty to a lesser charge of obstruction of justice in June and receive one year's probation. For spearheading the Ravens' 34–7 demolition of the New York Giants in Super Bowl XXXV the following year in Tampa, Lewis joined Dick Butkus, Jack Lambert and Mike Singletary in the ranks of the NFL's great middle linebackers. He solidified his status as the hub of what was arguably the best defense in NFL history and was named MVP of the game, after which he said, "The man upstairs tells you, 'I'll never take you through hell without taking you to triumph.' "

Who was Ray Lewis? His identity may have been murky in 1999, but in 2000 he was undoubtedly the best player in a league whose stock in trade is violence and intimidation. There was no greater practitioner of those arts than the Baltimore 'D', which not only set a record for fewest points allowed in a 16-game season (165), but also surrendered a mere 16 points in four playoff victories, two of them on the road and one, the Super Bowl, at the neutral site of Tampa Bay's Raymond James Stadium. The 6' 1", 245-pound Lewis, who clogged passing lanes, deflated ballcarriers and generally wreaked havoc from sideline to sideline, was the emotional leader of the Ravens' defense, a unit that was expected to be outstanding and exceeded that expectation almost every time out. "Facing our defense is like having 11 billiard balls thrown at you," said Ravens defensive end Rob Burnett. "Eventually, you're going to get hurt and lose your will."

Few observers had predicted that the Ravens would finish the season atop the

NFL heap. The buzz at the start of the season had revolved around their neighbors 40 miles to the south, the Washington Redskins. Washington was so stuffed with talent that a Las Vegas book installed them as the 5-to-2 favorite. A year after buying the Redskins for $800 million, 35-year-old Daniel M. Snyder showed no lingering effects of sticker shock, signing two future Hall of Famers in cornerback Deion Sanders and defensive end Bruce Smith; a former All-Pro safety in Mark Carrier; a pair of pricey backups in quarterback Jeff George and running back Adrian Murrell; and the No. 2 and No. 3 picks in the 2000 draft (linebacker LaVar Arrington and tackle Chris Samuels, respectively). "Everyone went shopping this off-season," Sanders said of Snyder's reported $100 million spree. "It's just that Dan's shopping at Versace, and some teams are shopping at Wal-Mart."

Snyder's free-spending approach received its spectacular comeuppance in Week 15, with the Skins clinging to a shot at the playoffs. One week after Snyder had dumped coach Norv Turner for assistant Terry Robiskie, Washington visited its archrivals, the Cowboys. Dallas quarterback Troy Aikman left the game after suffering his fourth concussion in 21 games, and an obscure backup named Anthony Wright helped Dallas to a 32–13 blowout. Snyder's profligate spending had yielded a team that put on the most embarrassing show of the season. Gutcheck, please. "I feel bad for Terry," Snyder said. "The players let him down."

It seemed only natural that in a season of unexpected reversals the previous year's Super Bowl teams, a surprising pair at the time, would emerge, along with Washington, as the favorites in 2000—only to be buried in their postseason debuts. The Tennessee Titans, who fell a yard short of forcing overtime at Supe XXXIV in Atlanta, had everything going their way: a back-breaking running back in Eddie George, a game-breaking kick returner in Derrick Mason and a heart-breaking (for their opponents, anyway) knack for succeeding in tight spots. Over a two-year stretch, the Titans were 13–4 in games decided by eight

JOHN W. MCDONOUGH

**Lewis was named defensive player of the year and MVP of the Super Bowl.**

points or fewer. "They hit you in the mouth—they don't finesse you," said Pittsburgh Steelers linebacker Levon Kirkland. "Their mind-set is whatever happens, they will break you down and get the job done."

With a 13–3 record, the league's best, Tennessee held home field advantage throughout the playoffs, and at Adelphia Coliseum that was some advantage: During two seasons in their Nashville stadium the Titans' record was 15–1. The lone loss came in a 24–23 squeaker to Baltimore on Nov. 12. The Ravens held George to 28 yards on 12 carries in that game, forcing him to fumble twice. Before the AFC Central rivals squared off again in the divisional playoffs, there was a slander-filled discussion about who had the better defense. (Ravens cornerback Chris McAlister said George "folded like a baby" in that Nov. 12 game.) Tennessee's defense was ranked first in the league in total yards surrendered (238.4 per game); Baltimore's

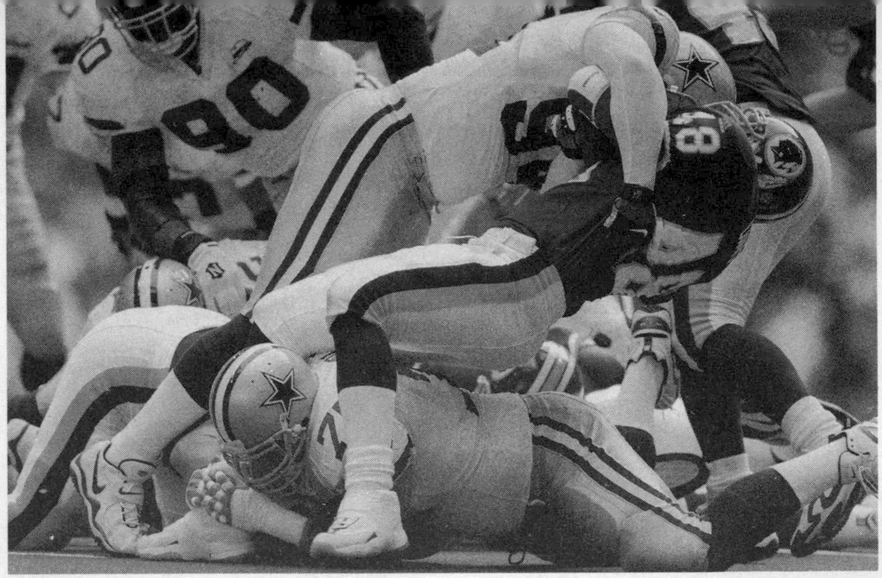

AL TIELEMANS

**Despite their offseason spending binge, running back Stephen Davis (48) and the Redskins were stopped cold in the NFC East.**

gave up a scant 10.3 points per game. The bruising showdown validated those glittering defensive stats. While the Titans yielded only 134 yards to the Baltimore offense, the Ravens gave up only 10 points and won 24–10, thanks to two scores by their vaunted defense, one of them a 50-yard interception return by Lewis.

The reigning champion St. Louis Rams, for their part, were hardly a defensive juggernaut under first-year coach Mike Martz. Offense was not a problem for the Rams, who, despite losing quarterback Kurt Warner to injury for five games, still led the league in points scored. But like many teams in 2000, the Rams were a lopsided bunch, capable on one side of the ball and inept on the other. They gave up 29 points per game. Indeed, only two teams—New Orleans and Buffalo—finished in the top 10 in both offense and defense.

Sunday to Sunday, wholesale collapses by one unit or the other were almost to be expected. The Denver Broncos returned to the postseason with a high-powered offense overseen by third-year quarterback Brian Griese and running back Mike Anderson, a sixth-round pick out of Utah who rushed for 1,500 yards and was named offensive rookie of the year. But in Week 8, against a usually anemic Cincinnati Bengals attack, the Broncos' defense allowed Corey Dillon to ramble for 278 yards, a performance that broke Walter Payton's 23-year-old single-game rushing mark of 275. Before the game, Denver had been second in the league in rushing defense, and Dillon was averaging a mere 52.3 yards per game on the ground.

Nowhere was that sort of imbalance clearer than in the Rams' final two games. In a 26–21 win over the New Orleans Saints that propelled St. Louis into the playoffs, Marshall Faulk, the 2000 MVP, gained a career-high 220 yards and scored three of his single-season-record 26 touchdowns. One week later in the wild-card game, against those same Saints, Faulk gained only 24 yards on 14 carries. The Rams' defense gave up 31 points while the offense scored only seven until midway through the fourth quarter. A last-ditch comeback fell short, and the champs bowed, 31–28.

New Orleans, which lost to the Minnesota Vikings 34–16 the following week, was the 2000 up-from-nowhere version of, well, the '99 Rams. A team that had never won a playoff game and was ranked dead last in the league by SI before the season, the Saints were 7–3 when workhorse running back Ricky Williams suffered a broken

ROBERT BECK

right ankle that would sideline him the rest of the regular season. The following week against the Raiders, New Orleans quarterback Jeff Blake went down with a season-ending foot injury. But rookie coach Jim Haslett rallied the troops, leaning on a defense spearheaded by tackle La'Roi Glover, the NFL's sack leader with 17, and unveiling 24-year-old quarterback Aaron Brooks, who would guide New Orleans to three wins down the stretch and the NFC West title. "I don't want to overstate this," said Saints general manager Randy Mueller, "but with his ability to beat you with his arm or his legs, Aaron reminds me of John Elway."

A Green Bay Packers backup acquired in the offseason by Mueller, Brooks was one of a handful of young quarterbacks making headlines in and out of the pocket. Just as Elway's draft class of 1983 kept the NFL stocked with quality signal-callers for more than a decade, the league may look back on 2000 as the coming-out season for its next wave of top QBs. Like Brooks, Philadelphia's second-year man Donovan McNabb, 24, took a team with a patchwork offense and a tenacious D into the playoffs; he was the Eagles' leading rusher, averaging 7.3 yards per carry.

The 25-year-old Griese, who led the NFL in passing efficiency (102.9), helped make 100-catch receivers of both Ed McCaffrey and Rod Smith. The Indianapolis Colts' Peyton Manning, 24, threw for the most yards (4,413) and tied for the most touchdown passes (33). Manning's favorite target was Marvin Harrison, the league's co-leader in receptions (102). (The Colts had another league leader in second-year running back Edgerrin James, who rushed for 1,709 yards.) San Francisco's Jeff Garcia, a 30-year-old CFL refugee in his first full year as a starter, not only bombed away for 4,278 yards in 2000 but also closed the home season with a memorable finale: In a 17–0 blanking of the Bears, Garcia connected with Jerry Rice on the legendary receiver's final catch in San Francisco. Rice is 38 years old, and his contract presented salary-cap problems for the Niners in 2001; he signed with the Raiders in the offseason. Garcia also completed 20 passes that day to wideout Terrell Owens, who set a record for receptions in a single game.

But of all the young quarterbacks, no one made larger waves than the 6' 4", 265-pound Daunte Culpepper of Minnesota. The 23-year-old took over the Vikings' already potent offense and tied Manning for the league lead in touchdown passes. He also rushed for seven scores, flashing his 4.42 speed and leveling linebackers who got in his way. Said 14-year veteran Bubby Brister, Culpepper's backup, "I've been around awhile and I can tell you: He's the biggest, strongest, fastest quarterback that ever was."

But in Culpepper's biggest test, the NFC championship game, he was brought down to size by a Giants team peaking at just the right time. After a 31–21 loss to Detroit in Week 12, New York coach Jim Fassel had guaranteed that his teetering team, 7–4 at the time, would make the playoffs. "He was in a no-lose situation, because if we don't get to the playoffs, he gets fired," said defensive tackle Keith Hamilton. "But if he didn't say it, that meant he had some doubts about us." After Fassel's promise, the Giants seized home field advantage with five straight wins, dumped the Eagles 20–10

**Starks (22) intercepted Collins in the third quarter of the Super Bowl and galloped 49 yards to put the Ravens ahead 17–0.**

in the divisional playoffs and then, in one of the most resounding victories in playoff history, wiped out Culpepper and Co. 41–zip to advance to the Super Bowl for the first time since after the 1990 season.

Quarterback Kerry Collins was the catalyst in that victory, completing 28 of 39 passes for 381 yards and five touchdowns—even though he sat out the fourth quarter. For Collins, it was the the highlight of a six-year career that had been scarred by a DWI arrest, a stint in alcohol rehab, allegations that he used racial slurs and a complete loss of motivation while he was with the Carolina Panthers. "There have been some scary times in my life—good, bad, bizarre," he said. "This part of the story is just as crazy."

In the next chapter, though, Collins would collide head-on with a character whose tale surpassed even his in stretching the limits of plausibility. Ray Lewis flew to Tampa as the NFL's Defensive Player of the Year, but in the days before the Super Bowl the media's interest in him extended to his role in the Atlanta murders. Second-year Ravens coach Brian Billick, in an apparent attempt to draw fire, lashed out at the press for its grilling of Lewis. "We drew a line in the sand with how we wanted to handle things," Billick said, almost smugly. "It was that simple."

Like Fassel, Billick had pushed all the right

buttons to get to the Super Bowl, including replacing Tony Banks at quarterback with Tampa Bay castoff Trent Dilfer. With the Ravens' 16–3 victory over the Raiders in the AFC title game in Oakland, Dilfer ran his record in his last 15 starts to 14–1.

The Baltimore offense was never spectacular—during one 21-quarter stretch this season it failed to score a touchdown—but Dilfer knew his role: Avoid interceptions and look for the occasional deadly long pass. He played it perfectly at Raymond James Stadium, completing 12 of 25 passes for 153 yards, with no interceptions and one 38-yard pass to Brandon Stokely that put the Ravens up 7–0 in the first quarter. Collins, under fire and out of rhythm, endured a waking nightmare, completing only 38.5% of his 39 passes and throwing four interceptions, including one that cornerback Duane Starks returned 49 yards for a touchdown that made it 17–0 in the third quarter.

The Ravens' defense dictated the terms to New York: 152 yards of offense, five turnovers, 2 of 14 third-down conversions. One year after the Rams' futuristic offense had overrun the league, one year after his involvement in a murder trial, the Ravens and Lewis had turned the NFL and, to some degree, Lewis's image, upside down. With five tackles and four batted passes, the linebacker was named Super Bowl MVP. "The thing is, the Giants didn't know," he said. "You just don't know until you play us, but our defense is a buzz saw."

## 2000 NFL Final Standings

### American Football Conference

#### EASTERN DIVISION

|  | W | L | T | Pct | Pts | OP |
|---|---|---|---|---|---|---|
| Miami | 11 | 5 | 0 | .688 | 323 | 226 |
| †Indianapolis | 10 | 6 | 0 | .625 | 429 | 326 |
| NY Jets | 9 | 7 | 0 | .562 | 321 | 321 |
| Buffalo | 8 | 8 | 0 | .500 | 315 | 350 |
| New England | 5 | 11 | 0 | .312 | 276 | 338 |

#### CENTRAL DIVISION

|  | W | L | T | Pct | Pts | OP |
|---|---|---|---|---|---|---|
| Tennessee | 13 | 3 | 0 | .812 | 346 | 191 |
| †Baltimore | 12 | 4 | 0 | .750 | 333 | 165 |
| Pittsburgh | 9 | 7 | 0 | .562 | 321 | 255 |
| Jacksonville | 7 | 9 | 0 | .438 | 367 | 327 |
| Cincinnati | 4 | 12 | 0 | .250 | 185 | 359 |
| Cleveland | 3 | 13 | 0 | .188 | 161 | 419 |

#### WESTERN DIVISION

|  | W | L | T | Pct | Pts | OP |
|---|---|---|---|---|---|---|
| Oakland | 12 | 4 | 0 | .750 | 479 | 299 |
| †Denver | 11 | 5 | 0 | .688 | 485 | 369 |
| Kansas City | 7 | 9 | 0 | .438 | 355 | 354 |
| Seattle | 6 | 10 | 0 | .375 | 320 | 405 |
| San Diego | 1 | 15 | 0 | .062 | 269 | 440 |

† Wild-card team.

### National Football Conference

#### EASTERN DIVISION

|  | W | L | T | Pct | Pts | OP |
|---|---|---|---|---|---|---|
| NY Giants | 12 | 4 | 0 | .750 | 328 | 246 |
| †Philadelphia | 11 | 5 | 0 | .688 | 351 | 245 |
| Washington | 8 | 8 | 0 | .500 | 281 | 269 |
| Dallas | 5 | 11 | 0 | .312 | 294 | 361 |
| Arizona | 3 | 13 | 0 | .188 | 210 | 443 |

#### CENTRAL DIVISION

|  | W | L | T | Pct | Pts | OP |
|---|---|---|---|---|---|---|
| Minnesota | 11 | 5 | 0 | .688 | 397 | 371 |
| †Tampa Bay | 10 | 6 | 0 | .625 | 388 | 269 |
| Green Bay | 9 | 7 | 0 | .562 | 353 | 323 |
| Detroit | 9 | 7 | 0 | .562 | 307 | 307 |
| Chicago | 5 | 11 | 0 | .312 | 216 | 355 |

#### WESTERN DIVISION

|  | W | L | T | Pct | Pts | OP |
|---|---|---|---|---|---|---|
| New Orleans | 10 | 6 | 0 | .625 | 354 | 305 |
| †St. Louis | 10 | 6 | 0 | .625 | 540 | 471 |
| Carolina | 7 | 9 | 0 | .438 | 310 | 310 |
| San Francisco | 6 | 10 | 0 | .375 | 388 | 422 |
| Atlanta | 4 | 12 | 0 | .250 | 252 | 413 |

## 2000–01 NFL Playoffs

| AFC FIRST ROUND | AFC DIVISIONAL PLAYOFF | AFC CHAMPIONSHIP | NFC CHAMPIONSHIP | NFC DIVISIONAL PLAYOFF | NFC FIRST ROUND |
|---|---|---|---|---|---|

**SUPER BOWL XXXV**

January 28, 2001

**BALTIMORE 34**
**NY Giants 7**

Denver 3
Baltimore 21

Baltimore 24

Baltimore 16

Tennessee 10

Indianapolis 17
Miami 23 (ot)

Miami 0

Oakland 3

Oakland 27

New Orleans 16

Minnesota 0

Minnesota 34

Philadelphia 10

NY Giants 41

NY Giants 20

St. Louis 28
New Orleans 31

Tampa Bay 3
Philadelphia 21

# NFL Playoff Box Scores

## AFC Wild-card Games

| Indianapolis | 3 | 11 | 0 | 3 | 0—17 |
|---|---|---|---|---|---|
| Miami | 0 | 0 | 7 | 10 | 6—23 |

### FIRST QUARTER

Indianapolis: FG Vanderjagt 32, 7:11. Drive: 47 yards, 7 plays.

### SECOND QUARTER

Indianapolis: FG Vanderjagt 26, 5:27. Drive: 17 yards, 7 plays.
Indianapolis: Pathon 17 pass from Manning (Dilger pass from Manning for two-point conversion), 7:13. Drive: 18 yards, 2 plays.

### THIRD QUARTER

Miami: Smith 2 run (Mare kick), 6:51. Drive: 70 yards, 11 plays.

### FOURTH QUARTER

Miami: FG Mare 38, 4:37. Drive 53 yards, 9 plays.
Indianapolis: FG Vanderjagt 50, 10:05. Drive: 45 yards, 9 plays.
Miami: Weaver 9 pass from Fiedler (Mare kick), 14:26. Drive: 80 yards, 14 plays.
A: 71,139; T: 3:22.

### OVERTIME

Miami: Smith 17 run, 11:26. Drive: 61 yards, 11 plays.

A: 73,193; T: 3:09.

| Denver | 0 | 3 | 0 | 0— 3 |
|---|---|---|---|---|
| Baltimore | 0 | 14 | 7 | 0—21 |

### SECOND QUARTER

Baltimore: Ja. Lewis 1 run (Stover kick), 3:17. Drive: 75 yards, 10 plays.
Denver: FG Elam 31, 10:29. Drive: 68 yards, 12 plays.
Baltimore: Sharpe 58 pass from Dilfer (Stover kick), 10: 54. Drive: 58 yards, 1 play.

### THIRD QUARTER

Baltimore: Ja. Lewis 27 run (Stover kick), 11:41. Drive: 28 yards, 2 plays.

A: 69,638; T: 2:54.

## NFC Wild-card Games

| St. Louis | 7 | 0 | 0 | 21—28 |
|---|---|---|---|---|
| New Orleans | 0 | 10 | 7 | 14—31 |

### FIRST QUARTER

St. Louis: Bruce 17 pass from Warner (Wilkins kick), 9:02. Drive: 68 yards, 11 plays.

### SECOND QUARTER

New Orleans: Wilson 12 pass from Brooks (Brien kick), 0:04. Drive: 70 yards, 11 plays.
New Orleans: FG Brien 33, 13:30. Drive: 5 yards, 4 plays.

### THIRD QUARTER

New Orleans: Jackson 10 pass from Brooks (Brien kick), 6:20. Drive: 45 yards, 7 plays.

### FOURTH QUARTER

New Orleans: Jackson 49 pass from Brooks (Brien kick), 1:38. Drive: 74 yards, 5 plays.
New Orleans: Jackson 16 pass from Brooks (Brien kick), 3:03. Drive: 16 yards, 1 play.
St. Louis: Proehl 17 pass from Warner (two-point conversion failed), 5:24. Drive: 80 yards, 4 plays.
St. Louis: Faulk 25 pass from Warner (Wilkins kick), 11:08. Drive: 62 yards, 3 plays.
St. Louis: Warner 5 run (Faulk pass from Warner for two-point conversion), 12:24. Drive: 47 yards, 5 plays.

A: 64,900; T: 3:16.

| Tampa Bay | 0 | 3 | 0 | 0— 3 |
|---|---|---|---|---|
| Philadelphia | 0 | 14 | 0 | 7—21 |

### SECOND QUARTER

Tampa Bay: FG Gramatica 29, 4:44. Drive: 58 yards, 8 plays.
Philadelphia: McNabb 5 run (Akers kick), 11:39. Drive: 15 yards, 4 plays.
Philadelphia: Brown 5 pass from McNabb (Akers kick), 14:48. Drive: 69 yards, 8 plays.

### FOURTH QUARTER

Philadelphia: Thomason 2 pass from McNabb (Akers kick), ) 0:47. Drive: 57 yards, 9 plays.

A: 65,813; T: 2:55.

## AFC Divisional Games

| Baltimore | 0 | 7 | 3 | 14—24 |
|---|---|---|---|---|
| Tennessee | 7 | 0 | 3 | 0—10 |

### FIRST QUARTER

Tennessee: George 2 run (Del Greco kick), 7:17. Drive: 68 yards, 11 plays.

### SECOND QUARTER

Baltimore: Ja. Lewis 1 run (Stover kick), 5:14. Drive: 57 yards, 4 plays.

### THIRD QUARTER

Tennessee: FG Del Greco 21, 6:40. Drive: 24 yards, 8 plays.
Baltimore: FG Stover 38, 11:55. Drive: 25 yards, 6 plays.

### FOURTH QUARTER

Baltimore: Mitchell 90 return of blocked FG (Stover kick), 2:48.
Baltimore: R. Lewis 50 int. return (Stover kick), 8:19.

A: 68,527; T: 3:01.

| Miami | 0 | 0 | 0 | 0— 0 |
|---|---|---|---|---|
| Oakland | 10 | 10 | 7 | 0—27 |

### FIRST QUARTER

Oakland: James 90 int. return (Janikowski kick), 3:24.
Oakland: FG Janikowski 36, 10:08. Drive: 46 yards, 8 plays.

### SECOND QUARTER

Oakland: FG Janikowski 33, 6:24. Drive: 78 yards 12 plays.
Oakland: Jett 6 pass from Gannon (Janikowski kick), 13:07. Drive: 43 yards, 9 plays.

### THIRD QUARTER

Oakland: Wheatley 2 run (Janikowski kick), 9:04. Drive: 54 yards, 12 plays.

A: 61,998; T: 3:04.

## NFC Divisional Games

| New Orleans | 3 | 0 | 7 | 6—16 |
|---|---|---|---|---|
| Minnesota | 10 | 7 | 10 | 7—34 |

### FIRST QUARTER

Minnesota: Moss 53 pass from Culpepper (Anderson kick), 3:03. Drive: 64 yards, 3 plays.
New Orleans: FG Brien 33, 7:14. Drive: 65 yards, 10 plays.
Minnesota: FG Anderson 24, 13:24. Drive: 67 yards, 12 plays.

### SECOND QUARTER

Minnesota: Carter 17 pass from Culpepper (Anderson kick), 13:31. Drive: 73 yards, 7 plays.

### THIRD QUARTER

Minnesota: Moss 68 pass from Culpepper (Anderson kick), 1:27. Drive: 77 yards, 3 plays.
New Orleans: Stachelski 2 pass from Brooks (Brien kick), 5:27. Drive: 83 yards, 8 plays.
Minnesota: FG Anderson 44, 10:29. Drive: 50 yards, 10 plays.

### FOURTH QUARTER

Minnesota: Smith 2 run (Anderson kick), 4:14. Drive: 29 yards, 8 plays.
New Orleans: Jackson 48 pass from Brooks (two-point conversion failed), 12:41. Drive: 66 yards, 3 plays.

A: 63,881; T: 3:15.

| Philadelphia | 0 | 3 | 0 | 7—10 |
|---|---|---|---|---|
| NY Giants | 7 | 10 | 0 | 3—20 |

### FIRST QUARTER

NY Giants: Dixon 97 kickoff return (Daluiso kick), 0:17.

### SECOND QUARTER

NY Giants: FG Daluiso 37, 0:05. Drive: 14 yards, 6 plays.
NY Giants: Sehorn 32 int. return (Daluiso kick), 13:20.
Philadelphia: FG Akers 28, 14:34. Drive: 40 yards, 7 plays.

### FOURTH QUARTER

NY Giants: FG Daluiso 25, 6:19. Drive: 88 yards, 13 plays.
Philadelphia: Small 10 pass from McNabb (Akers kick), 13:04. Drive: 8 yards, 3 plays.

A: 78,765; T: 3:15.

## AFC Championship

| Baltimore | 0 | 10 | 3 | 3—16 |
|---|---|---|---|---|
| Oakland | 0 | 0 | 3 | 0— 3 |

### SECOND QUARTER

Baltimore: Sharpe 96 pass Dilfer (Stover kick), 3:52. Drive: 88 yards, 3 plays.
Baltimore: FG Stover 31, 6:41. Drive: 7 yards, 4 plays.

### THIRD QUARTER

Oakland: FG Janikowski 24, 4:53. Drive: 33 yards, 9 plays.
Baltimore: FG Stover 28, 9:52. Drive: 51 yards, 9 plays.

### FOURTH QUARTER

Baltimore: FG Stover 21, 7:32. Drive: 3 yards, 7 plays.

A: 62,784; T: 3:08.

## NFC Championship

| Minnesota | 0 | 0 | 0 | 0— 0 |
|---|---|---|---|---|
| NY Giants | 14 | 20 | 7 | 0—41 |

### FIRST QUARTER

NY Giants: Hilliard 46 pass from Collins (Daluiso kick), 1:57. Drive: 74 yards, 4 plays.
NY Giants: Comella 18 pass from Collins (Daluiso kick), 2:13. Drive: 18 yards, 1 play.

### SECOND QUARTER

NY Giants: FG Daluiso 21, 0:04. Drive: 37 yards, 6 plays.
NY Giants: Jurevicious 8 pass from Collins (Daluiso kick), 4:36. Drive: 71 yards, 5 plays.
NY Giants: FG Daluiso 22, 9:38. Drive: 62 yards, 10 plays.
NY Giants: Hilliard 7 pass from Collins (Daluiso kick), 14:48. Drive: 77 yards, 10 plays.

### THIRD QUARTER

NY Giants: Toomer 7 pass from Collins (Daluiso kick), 2:54. Drive: 29 yards, 5 plays.

A: 79,310; T: 3:04.

# Super Bowl Box Score

| Baltimore | 7 | 3 | 14 | 10—34 |
|---|---|---|---|---|
| NY Giants | 0 | 0 | 7 | 0— 7 |

### FIRST QUARTER

Baltimore: Stokely 38 pass from Dilfer (Stover kick), 6:50. Drive: 41 yards, 2 plays. Key play: Je. Lewis 34 punt return. **Baltimore 7–0**.

### SECOND QUARTER

Baltimore: FG Stover 47, 1:41. Drive: 59 yards, 7 plays. Key play: Dilfer 44 pass to Ismail on 3rd-and-2. **Baltimore 10–0**.

### THIRD QUARTER

Baltimore: Starks 49 interception return (Stover kick), 3:49. **Baltimore 17–0**.
New York: Dixon 97 kickoff return (Daluiso kick), 3:31. **Baltimore 17–7**.
Baltimore: Je. Lewis 84 kickoff return (Stover kick), 3:13. **Baltimore 24–7**.

### FOURTH QUARTER

Baltimore: Ja. Lewis 3 run (Stover kick), 8:45. Drive: 38 yards, 6 plays. Key plays: Dilfer 17 pass to Coates; Ja. Lewis 9 run on 3rd-and-1. **Baltimore 31–7**.
Baltimore: FG Stover 34, 5:28. Drive: 18 yards, 5 plays. Key plays: Bailey recovers Dixon fumble on kickoff return at New York 34; Ja. Lewis 13 run. **Baltimore 34–7**.

# Super Bowl Box Score *(Cont.)*

## Team Statistics

| | Baltimore | NY Giants |
|---|---|---|
| FIRST DOWNS | 13 | 11 |
| Rushing | 6 | 2 |
| Passing | 6 | 6 |
| Penalty | 1 | 3 |
| THIRD DOWN EFF. | 3–16 | 2–14 |
| FOURTH DOWN EFF | 0–0 | 1–1 |
| TOTAL NET YARDS | 244 | 152 |
| Total plays | 62 | 59 |
| Avg gain | 3.9 | 2.6 |
| NET YARDS RUSHING | 111 | 66 |
| Rushes | 33 | 16 |
| Avg per rush | 3.4 | 4.1 |
| NET YARDS PASSING | 133 | 86 |
| Completed–Att. | 12–26 | 15–39 |
| Yards per pass | 4.6 | 2.0 |
| Sacked–yards lost | 3–20 | 4–26 |
| Had intercepted | 0 | 4 |
| PUNTS–Avg. | 10–43.0 | 11–38.4 |
| TOTAL RETURN YARDS | 204 | 217 |
| Punt returns | 3–34 | 5–46 |
| Kickoff returns | 2–111 | 7–171 |
| Interceptions | 4–59 | 0–0 |
| PENALTIES–Yds | 9–70 | 6–27 |
| FUMBLES–Lost | 2–0 | 2–1 |
| TIME OF POSSESSION | 34:06 | 25:54 |

## Passing

### BALTIMORE

| | Comp | Att | Yds | Int | TD |
|---|---|---|---|---|---|
| Dilfer | 12 | 25 | 153 | 0 | 1 |
| Banks | 0 | 1 | 0 | 0 | 0 |

### NY GIANTS

| | Comp | Att | Yds | Int | TD |
|---|---|---|---|---|---|
| Collins | 15 | 39 | 112 | 4 | 0 |

## Rushing

### BALTIMORE

| | No. | Yds | Lg | TD |
|---|---|---|---|---|
| Ja. Lewis | 27 | 102 | 19 | 1 |
| Holmes | 4 | 8 | 6 | 0 |
| Je. Lewis | 1 | 1 | 1 | 0 |
| Dilfer | 1 | 0 | 0 | 0 |

### NY GIANTS

| | No. | Yds | Lg | TD |
|---|---|---|---|---|
| Barber | 11 | 49 | 27 | 0 |
| Collins | 3 | 12 | 5 | 0 |
| Montgomery | 2 | 5 | 4 | 0 |

## Receiving

### BALTIMORE

| | No. | Yds | Lg | TD |
|---|---|---|---|---|
| Stokely | 3 | 52 | 38 | 1 |
| Coates | 3 | 30 | 17 | 0 |
| Ismail | 1 | 44 | 44 | 0 |
| Johnson | 1 | 8 | 8 | 0 |
| Je. Lewis | 1 | 6 | 6 | 0 |
| Sharpe | 1 | 5 | 5 | 0 |
| Holmes | 1 | 4 | 4 | 0 |
| Ja. Lewis | 1 | 4 | 4 | 0 |

### NY GIANTS

| | No. | Yds | Lg | TD |
|---|---|---|---|---|
| Barber | 6 | 26 | 7 | 0 |
| Hilliard | 3 | 30 | 13 | 0 |
| Toomer | 2 | 24 | 19 | 0 |
| Dixon | 1 | 16 | 16 | 0 |
| Mitchell | 1 | 7 | 7 | 0 |
| Cross | 1 | 7 | 7 | 0 |
| Comella | 1 | 2 | 2 | 0 |

## Defense

### BALTIMORE

| | Tck | Ast | Int | Sack |
|---|---|---|---|---|
| Woodson | 5 | 1 | 0 | 0 |
| Starks | 5 | 0 | 1 | 0 |
| R. Lewis | 3 | 2 | 0 | 0 |
| Washington | 4 | 0 | 0 | 1 |
| Harris | 3 | 1 | 0 | 0 |
| Burnett | 3 | 1 | 0 | 1 |
| McCrary | 3 | 0 | 0 | 2 |
| Sharper | 2 | 0 | 1 | 0 |
| Adams | 1 | 0 | 0 | 0 |
| McAlister | 1 | 0 | 1 | 0 |
| Siragusa | 1 | 0 | 0 | 0 |
| Dalton | 1 | 0 | 0 | 0 |
| Trapp | 1 | 0 | 0 | 0 |
| Herring | 0 | 0 | 1 | 0 |

### NY GIANTS

| | Tck | Ast | Int | Sack |
|---|---|---|---|---|
| Williams | 5 | 2 | 0 | 0 |
| Darrow | 6 | 0 | 0 | 0 |
| Sehorn | 6 | 0 | 0 | 0 |
| Strahan | 5 | 1 | 0 | 1.5 |
| Garnes | 5 | 0 | 0 | 0 |
| Hamilton | 5 | 0 | 0 | 0 |
| Phillips | 4 | 0 | 0 | 0 |
| Armstead | 2 | 1 | 0 | 0 |
| Peter | 2 | 0 | 0 | 0 |
| Griffin | 1 | 1 | 0 | 1.5 |
| McDaniel | 1 | 0 | 0 | 0 |
| Jones | 1 | 0 | 0 | 0 |
| Thomas | 1 | 0 | 0 | 0 |

# 2000 Associated Press All-Pro Team

## OFFENSE

| | |
|---|---|
| Randy Moss, Minnesota | Wide Receiver |
| Terrell Owens, San Francisco | Wide Receiver |
| Tony Gonzalez, Kansas City | Tight End |
| Jonathan Ogden, Baltimore | Tackle |
| Kyle Turley, New Orleans | Tackle |
| Bruce Matthews, Tennessee | Guard |
| Larry Allen, Dallas | Guard |
| Tom Nalen, Denver | Center |
| Rich Gannon, Oakland | Quarterback |
| Eddie George, Tennessee | Running Back |
| Marshall Faulk, St. Louis | Running Back |

## DEFENSE

| | |
|---|---|
| Hugh Douglas, Philadelphia | Defensive End |
| Jason Taylor, Miami | Defensive End |
| Warren Sapp, Tampa Bay | Tackle |
| La'Roi Glover, New Orleans | Tackle |
| Derrick Brooks, Tampa Bay | Outside Linebacker |
| Junior Seau, San Diego | Outside Linebacker |
| Ray Lewis, Baltimore | Inside Linebacker |
| Jeremiah Trotter, Philadelphia | Inside Linebacker |
| Sam Madison, Miami | Cornerback |
| Samari Rolle, Tennessee | Cornerback |
| John Lynch, Tampa Bay | Safety |
| Darren Sharper, Green Bay | Safety |

## SPECIALISTS

| | |
|---|---|
| Matt Stover, Baltimore | Kicker |
| Shane Lechler, Oakland | Punter |
| Derrick Mason, Tennessee | Kick Returner |

# 2000 AFC Team-by-Team Results

**BALTIMORE RAVENS (12–4)**

| | | |
|---|---|---|
| 16 | at Pittsburgh | 0 |
| 39 | JACKSONVILLE | 36 |
| 6 | at Miami | 19 |
| 37 | CINCINNATI | 0 |
| 12 | at Cleveland | 0 |
| 15 | at Jacksonville | 10 |
| 3 | at Washington | 10 |
| 6 | TENNESSEE | 14 |
| 6 | PITTSBURGH | 9 |
| 27 | at Cincinnati | 7 |
| 24 | at Tennessee | 23 |
| 27 | DALLAS | 0 |
| 44 | CLEVELAND | 7 |
| 24 | SAN DIEGO | 3 |
| 13 | at Arizona | 7 |
| 34 | NY JETS | 20 |
| **333** | | **165** |

**BUFFALO BILLS (8–8)**

| | | |
|---|---|---|
| 16 | TENNESSEE | 13 |
| 27 | GREEN BAY | 18 |
| 14 | at NY Jets | 27 |
| 16 | INDIANAPOLIS | 18 |
| 13 | at Miami | 22 |
| 27 | SAN DIEGO | 24 |
| 27 | at Minnesota | 31 |
| 23 | NY JETS | 20 |
| 16 | at New England | 13 |
| 20 | CHICAGO | 3 |
| 21 | at Kansas City | 17 |
| 17 | at Tampa Bay | 31 |
| 6 | MIAMI | 33 |
| 20 | at Indianapolis | 44 |
| 10 | NEW ENGLAND | 13 |
| 42 | at Seattle | 23 |
| **315** | | **250** |

**CINCINNATI BENGALS (4–12)**

| | | |
|---|---|---|
| 7 | CLEVELAND | 24 |
| 0 | at Jacksonville | 13 |
| 0 | at Baltimore | 37 |
| 16 | MIAMI | 31 |
| 14 | TENNESSEE | 23 |
| 0 | at Pittsburgh | 15 |
| 31 | DENVER | 21 |
| 12 | at Cleveland | 3 |
| 7 | BALTIMORE | 27 |
| 6 | at Dallas | 23 |
| 13 | at New England | 16 |
| 28 | PITTSBURGH | 48 |
| 24 | ARIZONA | 13 |
| 3 | at Tennessee | 35 |
| 17 | JACKSONVILLE | 14 |
| 7 | at Philadelphia | 16 |
| **185** | | **359** |

**CLEVELAND BROWNS (3–13)**

| | | |
|---|---|---|
| 7 | JACKSONVILLE | 27 |
| 24 | at Cincinnati | 7 |
| 23 | PITTSBURGH | 20 |
| 10 | at Oakland | 36 |
| 0 | BALTIMORE | 12 |
| 21 | at Arizona | 29 |
| 10 | at Denver | 44 |
| 0 | at Pittsburgh | 22 |
| 3 | CINCINNATI | 12 |

| | | |
|---|---|---|
| 3 | NY GIANTS | 24 |
| 19 | NEW ENGLAND | 11 |
| 10 | at Tennessee | 24 |
| 7 | at Baltimore | 44 |
| 0 | at Jacksonville | 48 |
| 24 | PHILADELPHIA | 35 |
| 0 | TENNESSEE | 24 |
| **161** | | **419** |

### DENVER BRONCOS (11–5)

| | | |
|---|---|---:|
| 36 | at St. Louis | 41 |
| 42 | ATLANTA | 14 |
| 33 | at Oakland | 24 |
| 22 | KANSAS CITY | 23 |
| 19 | NEW ENGLAND | 28 |
| 21 | at San Diego | 7 |
| 44 | CLEVELAND | 10 |
| 21 | at Cincinnati | 31 |
| 30 | at NY Jets | 23 |
| 27 | OAKLAND | 24 |
| 38 | SAN DIEGO | 37 |
| 38 | at Seattle | 31 |
| 38 | at New Orleans | 23 |
| 31 | SEATTLE | 24 |
| 7 | at Kansas City | 20 |
| 38 | SAN FRANCISCO | 9 |
| 485 | | 369 |

### INDIANAPOLIS COLTS (10–6)

| | | |
|---|---|---:|
| 27 | at Kansas City | 14 |
| 31 | OAKLAND | 38 |
| 43 | JACKSONVILLE | 14 |
| 18 | at Buffalo | 16 |
| 16 | at New England | 24 |
| 37 | at Seattle | 24 |
| 30 | NEW ENGLAND | 23 |
| 30 | DETROIT | 18 |
| 24 | at Chicago | 27 |
| 23 | NY JETS | 15 |
| 24 | at Green Bay | 26 |
| 14 | MIAMI | 17 |
| 17 | at NY Jets | 27 |
| 44 | BUFFALO | 20 |
| 20 | at Miami | 13 |
| 31 | MINNESOTA | 10 |
| 429 | | 326 |

### JACKSONVILLE JAGUARS (7–9)

| | | |
|---|---|---:|
| 27 | at Cleveland | 7 |
| 36 | at Baltimore | 39 |
| 13 | Cincinnati | 0 |
| 14 | at Indianapolis | 43 |
| 13 | PITTSBURGH | 24 |
| 10 | BALTIMORE | 15 |
| 13 | at Tennessee | 27 |
| 16 | WASHINGTON | 35 |
| 23 | at Dallas | 17 |
| 21 | SEATTLE | 28 |
| 34 | at Pittsburgh | 24 |
| 16 | TENNESSEE | 13 |
| 48 | CLEVELAND | 0 |
| 44 | ARIZONA | 10 |
| 14 | at Cincinnati | 17 |
| 25 | at NY Giants | 28 |
| 367 | | 327 |

### KANSAS CITY CHIEFS (7–9)

| | | |
|---|---|---:|
| 14 | INDIANAPOLIS | 27 |
| 14 | at Tennessee | 17 |
| 42 | SAN DIEGO | 10 |
| 23 | at Denver | 22 |
| 24 | SEATTLE | 17 |
| 17 | OAKLAND | 20 |
| 54 | ST. LOUIS | 34 |
| 24 | at Seattle | 19 |
| 31 | at Oakland | 49 |
| 7 | at San Francisco | 21 |
| 17 | BUFFALO | 21 |
| 16 | at San Diego | 17 |
| 24 | at New England | 30 |
| 15 | CAROLINA | 14 |
| 20 | DENVER | 7 |
| 13 | at Atlanta | 29 |
| 355 | | 354 |

### MIAMI DOLPHINS (11–5)

| | | |
|---|---|---:|
| 23 | SEATTLE | 0 |
| 7 | at Minnesota | 13 |
| 19 | BALTIMORE | 6 |
| 10 | NEW ENGLAND | 3 |
| 31 | at Cincinnati | 16 |
| 22 | BUFFALO | 13 |
| 37 | at NY Jets | 40 |
| 28 | GREEN BAY | 20 |
| 23 | at Detroit | 8 |
| 17 | at San Diego | 7 |
| 3 | NY JETS | 20 |
| 17 | at Indianapolis | 14 |
| 33 | at Buffalo | 6 |
| 13 | TAMPA BAY | 16 |
| 13 | INDIANAPOLIS | 20 |
| 27 | at New England | 24 |
| 323 | | 226 |

### NEW ENGLAND PATRIOTS (5–11)

| | | |
|---|---|---:|
| 16 | TAMPA BAY | 21 |
| 19 | at NY Jets | 20 |
| 13 | MINNESOTA | 21 |
| 3 | at Miami | 10 |
| 28 | at Denver | 19 |
| 24 | INDIANAPOLIS | 16 |
| 17 | NY JETS | 34 |
| 23 | at Indianapolis | 30 |
| 13 | BUFFALO | 16 |
| 11 | at Cleveland | 19 |
| 16 | CINCINNATI | 13 |
| 9 | at Detroit | 34 |
| 30 | KANSAS CITY | 24 |
| 17 | at Chicago | 24 |
| 13 | at Buffalo | 10 |
| 24 | MIAMI | 27 |
| 276 | | 338 |

### NEW YORK JETS (9–7)

| | | |
|---|---|---:|
| 20 | at Green Bay | 16 |
| 20 | NEW ENGLAND | 19 |
| 27 | BUFFALO | 14 |
| 21 | at Tampa Bay | 17 |
| 3 | PITTSBURGH | 20 |
| 34 | at New England | 17 |
| 40 | MIAMI | 37 |
| 20 | at Buffalo | 23 |
| 23 | DENVER | 30 |
| 15 | at Indianapolis | 23 |
| 20 | at Miami | 3 |
| 17 | CHICAGO | 10 |
| 27 | INDIANAPOLIS | 17 |
| 7 | at Oakland | 31 |
| 7 | DETROIT | 10 |
| 20 | at Baltimore | 34 |
| 321 | | 321 |

### OAKLAND RAIDERS (12–4)

| | | |
|---|---|---:|
| 9 | SAN DIEGO | 6 |
| 38 | at Indianapolis | 31 |
| 24 | DENVER | 33 |
| 36 | CLEVELAND | 10 |
| 34 | at San Francisco | 28 |
| 20 | at Kansas City | 17 |
| 31 | SEATTLE | 3 |
| 15 | at San Diego | 13 |
| 49 | KANSAS CITY | 31 |
| 24 | at Denver | 27 |
| 31 | at New Orleans | 22 |
| 41 | ATLANTA | 14 |
| 20 | at Pittsburgh | 21 |
| 31 | NY JETS | 7 |
| 24 | at Seattle | 27 |
| 52 | CAROLINA | 9 |
| 479 | | 299 |

### PITTSBURGH STEELERS (9–7)

| | | |
|---|---|---:|
| 0 | BALTIMORE | 16 |
| 20 | at Cleveland | 23 |
| 20 | TENNESSEE | 23 |
| 24 | at Jacksonville | 13 |
| 20 | at NY Jets | 3 |
| 15 | CINCINNATI | 0 |
| 22 | CLEVELAND | 0 |
| 9 | at Baltimore | 6 |
| 7 | at Tennessee | 9 |
| 23 | PHILADELPHIA | 26 |
| 24 | JACKSONVILLE | 34 |
| 48 | at Cincinnati | 28 |
| 21 | OAKLAND | 20 |
| 10 | at NY Giants | 30 |
| 24 | WASHINGTON | 3 |
| 34 | at San Diego | 21 |
| 321 | | 255 |

### SAN DIEGO CHARGERS (1–15)

| | | |
|---:|---|---:|
| 6 | at Oakland | 9 |
| 27 | NEW ORLEANS | 28 |
| 10 | at Kansas City | 42 |
| 12 | SEATTLE | 20 |
| 31 | at St. Louis | 57 |
| 7 | DENVER | 21 |
| 24 | at Buffalo | 27 |
| 13 | OAKLAND | 15 |
| 15 | at Seattle | 17 |
| 7 | MIAMI | 17 |
| 37 | at Denver | 38 |
| 17 | KANSAS CITY | 16 |
| 17 | SAN FRANCISCO | 45 |
| 3 | at Baltimore | 24 |
| 22 | at Carolina | 30 |
| 3 | PITTSBURGH | 21 |
| **269** | | **440** |

### SEATTLE SEAHAWKS (6–10)

| | | |
|---:|---|---:|
| 0 | at Miami | 23 |
| 34 | ST. LOUIS | 37 |
| 20 | NEW ORLEANS | 10 |
| 20 | at San Diego | 12 |
| 17 | at Kansas City | 24 |
| 3 | at Carolina | 26 |
| 24 | INDIANAPOLIS | 37 |
| 3 | at Oakland | 31 |
| 19 | KANSAS CITY | 24 |
| 17 | SAN DIEGO | 15 |
| 28 | at Jacksonville | 21 |
| 31 | DENVER | 38 |
| 30 | at Atlanta | 10 |
| 24 | at Denver | 31 |
| 27 | OAKLAND | 24 |
| 23 | Buffalo | 42 |
| **320** | | **405** |

### TENNESSEE TITANS (13–3)

| | | |
|---:|---|---:|
| 13 | at Buffalo | 16 |
| 17 | KANSAS CITY | 14 |
| 23 | at Pittsburgh | 20 |
| 28 | NY GIANTS | 14 |
| 23 | at Cincinnati | 14 |
| 27 | JACKSONVILLE | 13 |
| 14 | at Baltimore | 6 |
| 27 | at Washington | 21 |
| 9 | PITTSBURGH | 7 |
| 23 | BALTIMORE | 24 |
| 24 | CLEVELAND | 10 |
| 13 | at Jacksonville | 16 |
| 15 | at Philadelphia | 13 |
| 35 | CINCINNATI | 3 |
| 24 | at Cleveland | 0 |
| 31 | DALLAS | 0 |
| **346** | | **191** |

## 2000 NFC Team-by-Team Results

### ARIZONA CARDINALS (3–13)

| | | |
|---:|---|---:|
| 16 | at NY Giants | 21 |
| 32 | DALLAS | 31 |
| 3 | GREEN BAY | 29 |
| 20 | at San Francisco | 27 |
| 29 | CLEVELAND | 21 |
| 14 | PHILADELPHIA | 33 |
| 7 | at Dallas | 48 |
| 10 | NEW ORLEANS | 21 |
| 16 | WASHINGTON | 15 |
| 14 | at Minnesota | 31 |
| 9 | at Philadelphia | 34 |
| 7 | NY GIANTS | 31 |
| 13 | at Cincinnati | 24 |
| 10 | at Jacksonville | 44 |
| 7 | BALTIMORE | 13 |
| 3 | at Washington | 20 |
| **210** | | **443** |

### ATLANTA FALCONS (4–12)

| | | |
|---:|---|---:|
| 36 | SAN FRANCISCO | 28 |
| 14 | at Denver | 42 |
| 15 | at Carolina | 10 |
| 20 | ST LOUIS | 41 |
| 10 | at Philadelphia | 38 |
| 6 | NY GIANTS | 13 |
| 29 | at St. Louis | 45 |
| 19 | NEW ORLEANS | 21 |
| 13 | CAROLINA | 12 |
| 14 | TAMPA BAY | 27 |
| 10 | at Detroit | 13 |
| 6 | at San Francisco | 16 |
| 14 | at Oakland | 41 |
| 10 | SEATTLE | 30 |
| 7 | at New Orleans | 23 |
| 29 | KANSAS CITY | 13 |
| **252** | | **413** |

### CAROLINA PANTHERS (7–9)

| | | |
|---:|---|---:|
| 17 | at Washington | 20 |
| 38 | at San Francisco | 22 |
| 10 | ATLANTA | 15 |
| 13 | DALLAS | 16 |
| 26 | SEATTLE | 3 |
| 6 | at New Orleans | 24 |
| 34 | SAN FRANCISCO | 16 |
| 12 | at Atlanta | 13 |
| 27 | at St. Louis | 24 |
| 10 | NEW ORLEANS | 20 |
| 17 | at Minnesota | 31 |
| 31 | GREEN BAY | 14 |
| 16 | ST. LOUIS | 3 |
| 14 | at Kansas City | 15 |
| 30 | SAN DIEGO | 22 |
| 9 | at Oakland | 52 |
| **310** | | **310** |

### CHICAGO BEARS (5–11)

| | | |
|---:|---|---:|
| 27 | at Minnesota | 30 |
| 0 | at Tampa Bay | 41 |
| 7 | NY GIANTS | 14 |
| 14 | DETROIT | 21 |
| 27 | at Green Bay | 24 |
| 10 | NEW ORLEANS | 31 |
| 16 | MINNESOTA | 28 |
| 9 | at Philadelphia | 13 |
| 27 | INDIANAPOLIS | 24 |
| 3 | at Buffalo | 20 |
| 13 | TAMPA BAY | 10 |
| 10 | at NY Jets | 17 |
| 6 | GREEN BAY | 28 |
| 24 | NEW ENGLAND | 17 |
| 0 | at San Francisco | 17 |
| 23 | at Detroit | 20 |
| **216** | | **355** |

### DALLAS COWBOYS (5–11)

| | | |
|---:|---|---:|
| 14 | PHILADELPHIA | 41 |
| 31 | at Arizona | 32 |
| 27 | at Washington | 21 |
| 24 | SAN FRANCISCO | 41 |
| 16 | at Carolina | 13 |
| 14 | at NY Giants | 19 |
| 48 | ARIZONA | 7 |
| 17 | JACKSONVILLE | 23 |
| 13 | at Philadelphia | 16 |
| 23 | CINCINNATI | 6 |
| 0 | at Baltimore | 27 |
| 15 | MINNESOTA | 27 |
| 7 | at Tampa Bay | 27 |
| 32 | WASHINGTON | 13 |
| 13 | NY GIANTS | 17 |
| 0 | at Tennessee | 31 |
| **294** | | **361** |

### DETROIT LIONS (9–7)

| | | |
|---:|---|---:|
| 14 | at New Orleans | 10 |
| 15 | WASHINGTON | 10 |
| 10 | TAMPA BAY | 31 |
| 21 | at Chicago | 14 |
| 24 | MINNESOTA | 31 |
| 31 | GREEN BAY | 24 |
| 28 | at Tampa Bay | 14 |
| 18 | at Indianapolis | 30 |
| 8 | MIAMI | 23 |
| 13 | ATLANTA | 10 |
| 31 | at NY Giants | 21 |
| 34 | NEW ENGLAND | 9 |
| 17 | at Minnesota | 24 |
| 13 | at Green Bay | 26 |
| 10 | at NY Jets | 7 |
| 20 | CHICAGO | 23 |
| **307** | | **307** |

### GREEN BAY PACKERS (9–7)

| | | |
|---|---|---|
| 16 | NY JETS | 20 |
| 18 | at Buffalo | 27 |
| 6 | PHILADELPHIA | 3 |
| 29 | at Arizona | 3 |
| 24 | CHICAGO | 27 |
| 24 | at Detroit | 31 |
| 31 | SAN FRANCISCO | 28 |
| 20 | at Miami | 28 |
| 26 | MINNESOTA | 20 |
| 15 | at Tampa Bay | 20 |
| 26 | INDIANAPOLIS | 24 |
| 14 | at Carolina | 31 |
| 28 | at Chicago | 6 |
| 26 | DETROIT | 13 |
| 33 | at Minnesota | 28 |
| 17 | TAMPA BAY | 14 |
| 353 | | 323 |

### MINNESOTA VIKINGS (11–5)

| | | |
|---|---|---|
| 30 | CHICAGO | 27 |
| 13 | MIAMI | 7 |
| 21 | at New England | 13 |
| 31 | at Detroit | 24 |
| 30 | TAMPA BAY | 23 |
| 28 | at Chicago | 16 |
| 31 | BUFFALO | 27 |
| 13 | at Tampa Bay | 41 |
| 20 | at Green Bay | 26 |
| 31 | ARIZONA | 14 |
| 31 | CAROLINA | 17 |
| 27 | at Dallas | 15 |
| 24 | DETROIT | 17 |
| 29 | at St. Louis | 40 |
| 28 | GREEN BAY | 33 |
| 10 | at Indianapolis | 31 |
| 397 | | 371 |

### NEW ORLEANS SAINTS (10–6)

| | | |
|---|---|---|
| 10 | DETROIT | 14 |
| 28 | at San Diego | 27 |
| 10 | at Seattle | 20 |
| 7 | PHILADELPHIA | 21 |
| 31 | at Chicago | 10 |
| 24 | CAROLINA | 6 |
| 21 | at Atlanta | 19 |
| 21 | at Arizona | 10 |
| 31 | SAN FRANCISCO | 15 |
| 20 | at Carolina | 10 |
| 22 | OAKLAND | 31 |
| 31 | at St. Louis | 24 |
| 23 | DENVER | 38 |
| 31 | at San Francisco | 27 |
| 23 | ATLANTA | 7 |
| 21 | ST. LOUIS | 26 |
| 354 | | 305 |

### NEW YORK GIANTS (12–4)

| | | |
|---|---|---|
| 21 | ARIZONA | 16 |
| 33 | at Philadelphia | 18 |
| 14 | at Chicago | 7 |
| 6 | WASHINGTON | 16 |
| 14 | at Tennessee | 28 |
| 13 | at Atlanta | 6 |
| 19 | DALLAS | 14 |
| 24 | PHILADELPHIA | 7 |
| 24 | at Cleveland | 3 |
| 24 | ST. LOUIS | 38 |
| 21 | DETROIT | 31 |
| 31 | at Arizona | 7 |
| 9 | at Washington | 7 |
| 30 | PITTSBURGH | 10 |
| 17 | at Dallas | 13 |
| 28 | JACKSONVILLE | 25 |
| 328 | | 247 |

### PHILADELPHIA EAGLES (11–5)

| | | |
|---|---|---|
| 41 | at Dallas | 14 |
| 18 | NY GIANTS | 33 |
| 3 | at Green Bay | 6 |
| 21 | at New Orleans | 7 |
| 38 | ATLANTA | 10 |
| 14 | WASHINGTON | 17 |
| 33 | at Arizona | 14 |
| 13 | CHICAGO | 9 |
| 7 | at NY Giants | 24 |
| 16 | DALLAS | 13 |
| 26 | at Pittsburgh | 23 |
| 34 | ARIZONA | 9 |
| 23 | at Washington | 20 |
| 13 | TENNESSEE | 15 |
| 35 | at Cleveland | 24 |
| 16 | CINCINNATI | 7 |
| 351 | | 245 |

### ST. LOUIS RAMS (10–6)

| | | |
|---|---|---|
| 41 | DENVER | 36 |
| 37 | at Seattle | 34 |
| 41 | SAN FRANCISCO | 24 |
| 41 | at Atlanta | 20 |
| 57 | SAN DIEGO | 31 |
| 45 | ATLANTA | 29 |
| 34 | at Kansas City | 54 |
| 34 | at San Francisco | 24 |
| 24 | CAROLINA | 27 |
| 38 | at NY Giants | 24 |
| 20 | WASHINGTON | 33 |
| 24 | NEW ORLEANS | 31 |
| 3 | at Carolina | 16 |
| 40 | MINNESOTA | 29 |
| 35 | at Tampa Bay | 38 |
| 26 | at New Orleans | 21 |
| 540 | | 471 |

### SAN FRANCISCO 49ERS (6–10)

| | | |
|---|---|---|
| 28 | at Atlanta | 36 |
| 22 | CAROLINA | 38 |
| 24 | at St. Louis | 41 |
| 41 | at Dallas | 24 |
| 27 | ARIZONA | 20 |
| 28 | OAKLAND | 34 |
| 28 | at Green Bay | 31 |
| 16 | at Carolina | 34 |
| 24 | ST. LOUIS | 34 |
| 15 | at New Orleans | 31 |
| 21 | KANSAS CITY | 7 |
| 16 | ATLANTA | 6 |
| 45 | at San Diego | 17 |
| 27 | NEW ORLEANS | 31 |
| 17 | CHICAGO | 0 |
| 9 | at Denver | 38 |
| 388 | | 422 |

### TAMPA BAY BUCCANEERS (10–6)

| | | |
|---|---|---|
| 21 | at New England | 16 |
| 41 | CHICAGO | 0 |
| 31 | at Detroit | 10 |
| 17 | NY JETS | 21 |
| 17 | at Washington | 20 |
| 23 | at Minnesota | 20 |
| 14 | DETROIT | 28 |
| 41 | MINNESOTA | 13 |
| 27 | at Atlanta | 14 |
| 20 | GREEN BAY | 15 |
| 10 | at Chicago | 13 |
| 31 | BUFFALO | 17 |
| 27 | DALLAS | 7 |
| 16 | at Miami | 13 |
| 38 | ST. LOUIS | 35 |
| 14 | at Green Bay | 17 |
| 388 | | 269 |

### WASHINGTON REDSKINS (8–8)

| | | |
|---|---|---|
| 20 | CAROLINA | 17 |
| 10 | at Detroit | 15 |
| 21 | DALLAS | 27 |
| 16 | at NY Giants | 6 |
| 20 | TAMPA BAY | 17 |
| 17 | at Philadelphia | 14 |
| 10 | BALTIMORE | 3 |
| 35 | at Jacksonville | 16 |
| 21 | TENNESSEE | 27 |
| 15 | at Arizona | 16 |
| 33 | at St. Louis | 20 |
| 20 | PHILADELPHIA | 23 |
| 7 | NY GIANTS | 9 |
| 13 | at Dallas | 32 |
| 3 | at Pittsburgh | 24 |
| 20 | ARIZONA | 3 |
| 281 | | 269 |

## American Football Conference

### Scoring

| TOUCHDOWNS | TD | Rush | Rec | Ret | Pts | KICKING | PAT | FG | Lg | Pts |
|---|---|---|---|---|---|---|---|---|---|---|
| James, Ind | 18 | 13 | 5 | 0 | 108 | Stover, Balt | 30/30 | 35/39 | 51 | 135 |
| George, Tenn | 16 | 14 | 2 | 0 | 96 | Vanderjagt, Ind | 46/46 | 25/27 | 48 | 121 |
| Smith, Mia | 16 | 14 | 2 | 0 | 96 | Del Greco, Tenn | 37/38 | 27/33 | 50 | 118 |
| Anderson, Den | 15 | 15 | 0 | 0 | 90 | Mare, Mia | 32/34 | 28/31 | 49 | 116 |
| Harrison, Ind | 14 | 0 | 14 | 0 | 84 | Janikowski, Oak | 46/46 | 22/32 | 54 | 112 |
| Taylor, Jax | 14 | 12 | 2 | 0 | 84 | Christie, Buff | 31/31 | 26/35 | 48 | 109 |
| Martin, NYJ | 11 | 9 | 2 | 0 | 66 | Brown, Pitt | 32/33 | 25/30 | 52 | 107 |
| Brown, Oak | 11 | 0 | 11 | 0 | 66 | Vinatieri, NE | 25/26 | 27/33 | 53 | 106 |
| Alexander, KC | 10 | 0 | 10 | 0 | 60 | Hollis, Jax | 33/33 | 24/26 | 51 | 105 |
| Wheatley, Oak | 10 | 9 | 1 | 0 | 60 | Elam, Den | 49/49 | 18/24 | 51 | 103 |

### Passing

| | Att | Comp | Pct Comp | Yds | Avg Gain | TD | Pct TD | Int | Pct Int | Lg | Rating Pts |
|---|---|---|---|---|---|---|---|---|---|---|---|
| Griese, Den | 336 | 216 | 64.3 | 2688 | 8.00 | 19 | 5.7 | 4 | 1.2 | 61 | 102.9 |
| Manning, Ind | 571 | 357 | 62.5 | 4413 | 7.73 | 33 | 5.8 | 15 | 2.6 | t78 | 94.7 |
| Gannon, Oak | 473 | 284 | 60.0 | 3430 | 7.25 | 28 | 5.9 | 11 | 2.3 | t84 | 92.4 |
| Grbac, KC | 547 | 326 | 59.6 | 4169 | 7.62 | 28 | 5.1 | 14 | 2.6 | t81 | 89.9 |
| Flutie, Buff | 231 | 132 | 57.1 | 1700 | 7.36 | 8 | 3.5 | 3 | 1.3 | 52 | 86.5 |
| Brunell, Jax | 512 | 311 | 60.7 | 3640 | 7.11 | 20 | 3.9 | 14 | 2.7 | t67 | 84.0 |
| McNair, Tenn | 396 | 248 | 62.6 | 2847 | 7.19 | 15 | 3.8 | 13 | 3.3 | t56 | 83.2 |
| Johnson, Buff | 306 | 175 | 57.2 | 2125 | 6.94 | 12 | 3.9 | 7 | 2.3 | t74 | 82.2 |
| Frerotte, Den | 232 | 138 | 59.5 | 1776 | 7.66 | 9 | 3.9 | 8 | 3.5 | 44 | 82.1 |
| Bledsoe, NE | 531 | 312 | 58.8 | 3291 | 6.20 | 17 | 3.2 | 13 | 2.5 | 59 | 77.3 |

### Pass Receiving

| RECEPTIONS | No. | Yds | Avg | Lg | TD | YARDS | Yds | No. | Avg | Lg | TD |
|---|---|---|---|---|---|---|---|---|---|---|---|
| Harrison, Ind | 102 | 1413 | 13.9 | t78 | 14 | Smith, Den | 1602 | 100 | 16.0 | 49 | 8 |
| McCaffrey, Den | 101 | 1317 | 13.0 | 61 | 9 | Harrison, Ind | 1413 | 102 | 13.9 | t78 | 14 |
| Smith, Den | 100 | 1602 | 16.0 | 49 | 8 | Alexander, KC | 1391 | 78 | 17.8 | t81 | 10 |
| Moulds, Buff | 94 | 1326 | 14.1 | 52 | 5 | Moulds, Buff | 1326 | 94 | 14.1 | 52 | 5 |
| McCardell, Jax | 94 | 1207 | 12.8 | t67 | 5 | McCaffrey, Den | 1317 | 101 | 13.0 | 61 | 9 |
| Gonzalez, KC | 93 | 1203 | 12.9 | 39 | 9 | Smith, Jax | 1213 | 91 | 13.3 | t65 | 8 |
| Smith, Jax | 91 | 1213 | 13.3 | t65 | 8 | McCardell, Jax | 1207 | 94 | 12.8 | t67 | 5 |
| Anderson, NYJ | 88 | 853 | 9.7 | 41 | 2 | Gonzalez, KC | 1203 | 93 | 12.9 | 39 | 9 |
| Brown, NE | 83 | 944 | 11.4 | t44 | 4 | Brown, Oak | 1128 | 76 | 14.8 | 45 | 11 |
| Glenn, NE | 79 | 963 | 12.2 | t39 | 6 | Glenn, NE | 963 | 79 | 12.2 | t39 | 6 |

### Rushing

| | Att | Yds | Avg | Lg | TD |
|---|---|---|---|---|---|
| James, Ind | 387 | 1709 | 4.4 | 30 | 13 |
| George, Tenn | 403 | 1509 | 3.7 | t35 | 14 |
| Anderson, Den | 297 | 1500 | 5.1 | t80 | 15 |
| Dillon, Cin | 315 | 1435 | 4.6 | t80 | 7 |
| Taylor, Jax | 292 | 1399 | 4.8 | 71 | 12 |
| Ja. Lewis, Balt | 309 | 1364 | 4.4 | 45 | 6 |
| Bettis, Pitt | 355 | 1341 | 3.8 | 30 | 8 |
| Watters, Sea | 278 | 1242 | 4.5 | 55 | 7 |
| Martin, NYJ | 316 | 1204 | 3.8 | 55 | 9 |
| Smith, Mia | 309 | 1139 | 3.7 | t68 | 14 |

### Total Yards from Scrimmage

| | Total | Rush | Rec |
|---|---|---|---|
| James, Ind | 2303 | 1709 | 594 |
| George, Tenn | 1962 | 1509 | 453 |
| Watters, Sea | 1855 | 1242 | 613 |
| Martin, NYJ | 1712 | 1204 | 508 |
| R. Smith, Den | 1701 | 99 | 1602 |
| Anderson, Den | 1669 | 1500 | 169 |
| Ja. Lewis, Balt | 1660 | 1364 | 296 |
| Taylor, Jax | 1639 | 1399 | 240 |
| Dillon, Cin | 1593 | 1435 | 158 |
| Bettis, Pitt | 1438 | 1341 | 97 |

### Interceptions

| | No. | Yds | Lg | TD |
|---|---|---|---|---|
| Walker, Mia | 7 | 80 | 31 | 0 |
| Rolle, Tenn | 7 | 140 | t81 | 1 |

Six tied with six.

### Sacks

| | |
|---|---|
| Armstrong, Mia | 16.5 |
| Taylor, Mia | 14.5 |
| Hicks, KC | 14.0 |
| Gildon, Pitt | 13.5 |
| Pryce, Den | 12.0 |

### American Football Conference (Cont.)

#### Punting

| | No. | Yds | Avg | Net Avg | TB | In 20 | Lg | Blk | Ret | Ret Yds |
|---|---|---|---|---|---|---|---|---|---|---|
| Bennett, SD | 92 | 4248 | 46.2 | 36.2 | 10 | 23 | 66 | 0 | 51 | 722 |
| Lechler, Oak | 65 | 2984 | 45.9 | 38.0 | 10 | 24 | 69 | 0 | 30 | 279 |
| Gardocki, Clev | 108 | 4919 | 45.5 | 37.3 | 5 | 25 | 67 | 0 | 69 | 793 |
| Smith, Ind | 65 | 2906 | 44.7 | 36.4 | 9 | 20 | 65 | 0 | 28 | 357 |
| Tupa, NYJ | 83 | 3714 | 44.7 | 33.2 | 15 | 18 | 70 | 0 | 42 | 660 |

#### Punt Returns

| | No. | Yds | Avg | Lg | TD |
|---|---|---|---|---|---|
| Je. Lewis, Balt | 36 | 578 | 16.1 | t89 | 2 |
| Rogers, Sea | 26 | 363 | 14.0 | 43 | 0 |
| Poteat, Pitt | 36 | 467 | 13.0 | 54 | 1 |
| Mason, Tenn | 51 | 662 | 13.0 | t69 | 1 |
| Brown, NE | 39 | 504 | 12.9 | t66 | 1 |

#### Kickoff Returns

| | No. | Yds | Avg | Lg | TD |
|---|---|---|---|---|---|
| Mason, Tenn | 42 | 1132 | 27.0 | 66 | 0 |
| Williams, NYJ | 21 | 551 | 26.2 | t97 | 1 |
| Denson, Mia | 20 | 495 | 24.8 | 56 | 0 |
| Rogers, Sea | 66 | 1629 | 24.7 | t81 | 1 |
| Dunn, Oak | 44 | 1073 | 24.4 | t88 | 1 |

### National Football Conference

#### Scoring

| TOUCHDOWNS | TD | Rush | Rec | Ret | Pts |
|---|---|---|---|---|---|
| Faulk, StL | 26 | 18 | 8 | 0 | 156 |
| Moss, Minn | 15 | 0 | 15 | 0 | 90 |
| Green, GB | 13 | 10 | 3 | 0 | 78 |
| Owens, SF | 13 | 0 | 13 | 0 | 78 |
| Davis, Wash | 11 | 11 | 0 | 0 | 66 |
| Stewart, Det | 11 | 10 | 1 | 0 | 66 |
| Garner, SF | 10 | 7 | 3 | 0 | 60 |
| Smith, Minn | 10 | 7 | 3 | 0 | 60 |

Seven tied with nine.

| KICKING | PAT | FG | Lg | Pts |
|---|---|---|---|---|
| Longwell, GB | 32/32 | 33/37 | 52 | 131 |
| Gramatica, TB | 42/42 | 28/34 | 55 | 126 |
| Nedney, Car | 24/24 | 34/37 | 52 | 126 |
| Akers, Phil | 34/36 | 29/33 | 51 | 121 |
| Anderson, Minn | 45/45 | 22/23 | 49 | 111 |
| Brien, NO | 37/37 | 23/29 | 48 | 106 |
| Seder, Dall | 27/27 | 25/33 | 48 | 102 |
| Hanson, Det | 29/29 | 24/31 | 54 | 101 |
| Andersen, Atl | 23/23 | 25/31 | 51 | 98 |
| Wilkins, StL | 38/38 | 17/17 | 51 | 89 |

#### Passing

| | Att | Comp | Pct Comp | Yds | Avg Gain | TD | Pct TD | Int | Pct Int | Lg | Rating Pts |
|---|---|---|---|---|---|---|---|---|---|---|---|
| Green, StL | 240 | 145 | 60.4 | 2063 | 8.60 | 16 | 6.7 | 5 | 2.1 | 64 | 101.8 |
| Warner, StL | 347 | 235 | 67.7 | 3429 | 9.88 | 21 | 6.1 | 18 | 5.2 | t85 | 98.3 |
| Culpepper, Minn | 474 | 297 | 62.6 | 3937 | 8.31 | 33 | 7.0 | 16 | 3.4 | t78 | 98.0 |
| Garcia, SF | 561 | 355 | 63.2 | 4278 | 7.63 | 31 | 5.6 | 10 | 1.8 | t69 | 97.6 |
| Collins, NYG | 529 | 311 | 58.7 | 3610 | 6.82 | 22 | 4.2 | 13 | 2.5 | 59 | 83.1 |
| Blake, NO | 302 | 184 | 60.9 | 2025 | 6.71 | 13 | 4.3 | 9 | 3.0 | t49 | 82.7 |
| Beuerlein, Car | 533 | 324 | 60.7 | 3730 | 6.70 | 19 | 3.6 | 18 | 3.4 | 54 | 79.7 |
| Favre, GB | 580 | 338 | 58.2 | 3812 | 6.57 | 20 | 3.4 | 16 | 2.8 | t67 | 78.0 |
| McNabb, Phil | 569 | 330 | 57.9 | 3365 | 5.91 | 21 | 3.7 | 13 | 2.3 | t70 | 77.8 |

#### Pass Receiving

| RECEPTIONS | No. | Yds | Avg | Lg | TD |
|---|---|---|---|---|---|
| Muhammad, Car | 102 | 1183 | 11.6 | 36 | 6 |
| Owens, SF | 97 | 1451 | 15.0 | t69 | 13 |
| Carter, Minn | 96 | 1274 | 13.3 | 53 | 9 |
| Horn, NO | 94 | 1340 | 14.3 | 52 | 8 |
| Bruce, StL | 87 | 1471 | 16.9 | t78 | 9 |
| Holt, StL | 82 | 1635 | 19.9 | t85 | 6 |
| Faulk, StL | 81 | 830 | 10.2 | t72 | 8 |
| Centers, Wash | 80 | 600 | 7.5 | 26 | 3 |
| Toomer, NYG | 78 | 1094 | 14.0 | t54 | 7 |
| Moss, Minn | 77 | 1437 | 18.7 | t78 | 15 |

| YARDS | Yds | No. | Avg | Lg | TD |
|---|---|---|---|---|---|
| Holt, StL | 1635 | 82 | 19.9 | t85 | 6 |
| Bruce, StL | 1471 | 87 | 16.9 | t78 | 9 |
| Owens, SF | 1451 | 97 | 15.0 | t69 | 13 |
| Moss, Minn | 1437 | 77 | 18.7 | t78 | 15 |
| Horn, NO | 1340 | 94 | 14.3 | 52 | 8 |
| Carter, Minn | 1274 | 96 | 13.3 | 53 | 9 |
| Muhammad, Car | 1183 | 102 | 11.6 | 36 | 6 |
| Boston, Ariz | 1156 | 71 | 16.3 | t70 | 7 |
| Toomer, NYG | 1094 | 78 | 14.0 | t54 | 7 |
| Schroeder, GB | 999 | 65 | 15.4 | t55 | 4 |

### National Football Conference (Cont.)

#### Rushing

| | Att | Yds | Avg | Lg | TD |
|---|---|---|---|---|---|
| R. Smith, Minn | 295 | 1521 | 5.2 | t72 | 7 |
| Faulk, StL | 253 | 1359 | 5.4 | 36 | 18 |
| Davis, Wash | 332 | 1318 | 4.0 | t50 | 11 |
| E. Smith, Dall | 294 | 1203 | 4.1 | 52 | 9 |
| Stewart, Det | 339 | 1184 | 3.5 | 34 | 10 |
| Green, GB | 263 | 1175 | 4.5 | t39 | 10 |
| Garner, SF | 258 | 1142 | 4.4 | 42 | 7 |
| Dunn, TB | 248 | 1133 | 4.6 | t70 | 8 |
| Allen, Chi | 290 | 1120 | 3.9 | 29 | 2 |
| Anderson, Atl | 282 | 1024 | 3.6 | 42 | 6 |

#### Total Yards from Scrimmage

| | Total | Rush | Rec |
|---|---|---|---|
| Faulk, StL | 2189 | 1359 | 830 |
| R. Smith, Minn | 1869 | 1521 | 348 |
| Garner, SF | 1789 | 1142 | 647 |
| Green, GB | 1734 | 1175 | 559 |
| Barber, NYG | 1725 | 1006 | 719 |
| Holt, StL | 1642 | 7 | 1635 |
| Davis, Wash | 1631 | 1318 | 313 |
| Dunn, TB | 1555 | 1133 | 422 |
| Bruce, StL | 1482 | 11 | 1471 |
| Stewart, Det | 1471 | 1184 | 287 |

#### Interceptions

| | No. | Yds | Lg | TD |
|---|---|---|---|---|
| Sharper, GB | 9 | 109 | 47 | 0 |
| McCleon, StL | 8 | 28 | 23 | 0 |
| Abraham, TB | 7 | 82 | 23 | 0 |
| Schulz, Det | 7 | 53 | 19 | 0 |

Four tied with six.

#### Sacks

| | |
|---|---|
| Glover, NO | 17.0 |
| Sapp, TB | 16.5 |
| Douglas, Phil | 15.0 |
| Jones, TB | 13.0 |
| Coleman, Wash | 12.0 |
| Johnson, NO | 12.0 |

#### Punting

| | No. | Yds | Avg | Net Avg | TB | In 20 | Lg | Blk | Ret | Ret Yds |
|---|---|---|---|---|---|---|---|---|---|---|
| Berger, Minn | 62 | 2773 | 44.7 | 36.2 | 11 | 16 | 60 | 0 | 32 | 310 |
| Player, Ariz | 65 | 2871 | 44.2 | 37.3 | 5 | 17 | 55 | 0 | 37 | 347 |
| Jett, Det | 93 | 4044 | 43.5 | 34.8 | 12 | 33 | 59 | 0 | 53 | 498 |
| Knorr, Dall | 58 | 2485 | 42.8 | 35.8 | 8 | 12 | 60 | 0 | 25 | 248 |
| Landeta, Phil | 86 | 3635 | 42.3 | 36.0 | 8 | 23 | 60 | 0 | 47 | 375 |
| Royals, TB | 85 | 3551 | 41.8 | 35.1 | 8 | 17 | 63 | 0 | 41 | 408 |

#### Punt Returns

| | No. | Yds | Avg | Lg | TD |
|---|---|---|---|---|---|
| Hakim, StL | 32 | 489 | 15.3 | t86 | 1 |
| Howard, Det | 31 | 457 | 14.7 | t95 | 1 |
| McGarity, Dall | 30 | 353 | 11.8 | t64 | 2 |
| Mitchell, Phil | 32 | 335 | 10.5 | t72 | 1 |
| Dwight, Atl | 33 | 309 | 9.4 | t70 | 1 |

#### Kickoff Returns

| | No. | Yds | Avg | Lg | TD |
|---|---|---|---|---|---|
| Vaughn, Atl | 39 | 1082 | 27.7 | t100 | 3 |
| Jenkins, Ariz | 82 | 2186 | 26.7 | t98 | 1 |
| Rossum, GB | 50 | 1288 | 25.8 | t92 | 1 |
| Howard, Det | 57 | 1401 | 24.6 | 70 | 0 |
| Horne, StL | 57 | 1379 | 24.2 | t103 | 1 |

## 2000 NFL Team Leaders

### AFC Total Offense

| | Total Yds | Yds Rush | Yds Pass | Time of Poss | Avg Pts/Game |
|---|---|---|---|---|---|
| Denver | 6567 | 2324 | 4243 | 33:15 | 30.3 |
| Indianapolis | 6141 | 1859 | 4282 | 29:33 | 26.8 |
| Oakland | 5776 | 2470 | 3306 | 32:13 | 29.9 |
| Jacksonville | 5690 | 2032 | 3658 | 31:40 | 22.9 |
| Kansas City | 5614 | 1465 | 4149 | 27:41 | 22.2 |
| Buffalo | 5498 | 1922 | 3576 | 32:20 | 19.7 |
| NY Jets | 5395 | 1471 | 3924 | 30:33 | 20.1 |
| Tennessee | 5350 | 2085 | 3265 | 33:54 | 21.6 |
| Baltimore | 5014 | 2199 | 2815 | 33:19 | 20.8 |
| Pittsburgh | 4766 | 2248 | 2518 | 31:36 | 20.1 |
| Seattle | 4680 | 1720 | 2960 | 27:31 | 20.0 |
| New England | 4571 | 1390 | 3181 | 29:31 | 17.2 |
| Miami | 4461 | 1894 | 2567 | 30:56 | 20.2 |
| San Diego | 4300 | 1062 | 3238 | 28:23 | 16.8 |
| Cincinnati | 4260 | 2314 | 1946 | 27:13 | 11.6 |
| Cleveland | 3530 | 1085 | 2445 | 25:59 | 10.1 |

### AFC Total Defense

| | Opp Total Yds | Opp Yds Rush | Opp Yds Pass | Avg PA/Game |
|---|---|---|---|---|
| Tennessee | 3814 | 1390 | 2424 | 11.9 |
| Baltimore | 3967 | 970 | 2997 | 10.3 |
| Buffalo | 4426 | 1559 | 2867 | 21.9 |
| Miami | 4636 | 1736 | 2900 | 14.1 |
| Pittsburgh | 4713 | 1693 | 3020 | 15.9 |
| NY Jets | 4820 | 1888 | 2932 | 20.1 |
| Jacksonville | 4845 | 1685 | 3160 | 20.4 |
| San Diego | 4959 | 1422 | 3537 | 27.5 |
| Oakland | 5249 | 1551 | 3698 | 18.7 |
| Kansas City | 5293 | 1822 | 3471 | 22.1 |
| New England | 5353 | 1831 | 3522 | 21.1 |
| Indianapolis | 5375 | 1935 | 3422 | 20.4 |
| Cincinnati | 5487 | 1925 | 3562 | 22.4 |
| Denver | 5544 | 1598 | 3946 | 23.1 |
| Cleveland | 5643 | 2505 | 3138 | 26.2 |
| Seattle | 6391 | 2454 | 3937 | 25.3 |

## NFC Total Offense

| | Total Yds | Yds Rush | Yds Pass | Time of Poss | Avg Pts/Game |
|---|---|---|---|---|---|
| St. Louis | 7075 | 1843 | 5232 | 30:54 | 33.8 |
| San Francisco | 6040 | 1801 | 4239 | 29:57 | 24.2 |
| Minnesota | 5961 | 2129 | 3832 | 29:35 | 24.8 |
| New Orleans | 5397 | 2068 | 3329 | 31:27 | 22.1 |
| Washington | 5396 | 1748 | 3648 | 31:35 | 17.6 |
| NY Giants | 5376 | 2009 | 3367 | 31:39 | 20.5 |
| Green Bay | 5321 | 1643 | 3678 | 31:05 | 22.1 |
| Philadelphia | 5006 | 1882 | 3124 | 29:14 | 21.9 |
| Carolina | 4654 | 1186 | 3468 | 30:02 | 19.4 |
| Tampa Bay | 4649 | 2066 | 2583 | 29:58 | 24.2 |
| Chicago | 4541 | 1736 | 2805 | 28:30 | 13.5 |
| Arizona | 4528 | 1278 | 3250 | 26:32 | 13.1 |
| Dallas | 4476 | 1953 | 2523 | 29:08 | 18.4 |
| Detroit | 4422 | 1747 | 2675 | 30:10 | 19.2 |
| Atlanta | 3994 | 1214 | 2780 | 29:26 | 15.8 |

## NFC Total Defense

| | Opp Total Yds | Opp Yds Rush | Opp Yds Pass | Avg PA/Game |
|---|---|---|---|---|
| Washington | 4474 | 1853 | 2621 | 16.8 |
| NY Giants | 4546 | 1156 | 3390 | 15.4 |
| New Orleans | 4743 | 1672 | 3071 | 19.1 |
| Tampa Bay | 4800 | 1648 | 3152 | 16.8 |
| Philadelphia | 4820 | 1830 | 2990 | 15.3 |
| Detroit | 5033 | 1823 | 3210 | 19.2 |
| Green Bay | 5069 | 1618 | 3451 | 20.2 |
| Chicago | 5234 | 1827 | 3407 | 22.2 |
| Dallas | 5329 | 2637 | 2692 | 22.6 |
| St. Louis | 5494 | 1697 | 3797 | 29.4 |
| Atlanta | 5607 | 1983 | 3624 | 25.8 |
| Carolina | 5656 | 1944 | 3712 | 19.4 |
| Minnesota | 5701 | 1788 | 3913 | 23.2 |
| San Francisco | 5709 | 1794 | 3915 | 26.4 |
| Arizona | 5737 | 2609 | 3128 | 27.7 |

## Takeaways/Giveaways

### American Football Conference

| | Takeaways Int | Fum | Total | Giveaways Int | Fum | Total | Net Diff |
|---|---|---|---|---|---|---|---|
| Baltimore | 23 | 26 | 49 | 19 | 7 | 26 | 23 |
| Denver | 27 | 17 | 44 | 12 | 13 | 25 | 19 |
| Oakland | 21 | 16 | 37 | 11 | 9 | 20 | 17 |
| Miami | 28 | 13 | 41 | 17 | 9 | 26 | 15 |
| Pittsburgh | 17 | 18 | 35 | 10 | 11 | 21 | 14 |
| Buffalo | 16 | 13 | 29 | 10 | 13 | 23 | 6 |
| Kansas City | 15 | 14 | 29 | 15 | 11 | 26 | 3 |
| Jacksonville | 12 | 18 | 30 | 15 | 14 | 29 | 1 |
| Tennessee | 17 | 13 | 30 | 16 | 14 | 30 | 0 |
| New England | 10 | 13 | 23 | 15 | 10 | 25 | -2 |
| Cleveland | 12 | 13 | 25 | 19 | 9 | 28 | -3 |
| NY Jets | 21 | 14 | 35 | 29 | 11 | 40 | -5 |
| Indianapolis | 14 | 8 | 22 | 15 | 14 | 29 | -7 |
| Seattle | 17 | 12 | 29 | 21 | 17 | 38 | -9 |
| Cincinnati | 9 | 12 | 21 | 14 | 21 | 35 | -14 |
| San Diego | 16 | 6 | 22 | 30 | 20 | 50 | -28 |

### National Football Conference

| | Takeaways Int | Fum | Total | Giveaways Int | Fum | Total | Net Diff |
|---|---|---|---|---|---|---|---|
| Tampa Bay | 25 | 16 | 41 | 13 | 11 | 24 | 17 |
| Detroit | 25 | 17 | 42 | 19 | 12 | 31 | 11 |
| New Orleans | 20 | 15 | 35 | 15 | 11 | 26 | 9 |
| NY Giants | 20 | 11 | 31 | 13 | 11 | 24 | 7 |
| Carolina | 17 | 21 | 38 | 19 | 16 | 35 | 3 |
| Philadelphia | 19 | 12 | 31 | 15 | 14 | 29 | 2 |
| San Francisco | 13 | 8 | 21 | 10 | 9 | 19 | 2 |
| Washington | 17 | 16 | 33 | 21 | 12 | 33 | 0 |
| Green Bay | 21 | 7 | 28 | 16 | 17 | 33 | -5 |
| Atlanta | 15 | 10 | 25 | 20 | 14 | 34 | -9 |
| Chicago | 11 | 9 | 20 | 16 | 13 | 29 | -9 |
| Minnesota | 8 | 10 | 18 | 18 | 10 | 28 | -10 |
| St. Louis | 19 | 6 | 25 | 23 | 12 | 35 | -10 |
| Dallas | 16 | 9 | 25 | 21 | 18 | 39 | -14 |
| Arizona | 10 | 10 | 20 | 24 | 20 | 44 | -24 |

## Conference Rankings

### American Football Conference

| | Offense Total | Rush | Pass | Defense Total | Rush | Pass |
|---|---|---|---|---|---|---|
| Baltimore | 9 | 5 | 12 | 2 | 1 | 5 |
| Buffalo | 6 | 8 | 6 | 3 | 5 | 2 |
| Cincinnati | 15 | 3 | 16 | 13 | 13 | 13 |
| Cleveland | 16 | 15 | 15 | 15 | 16 | 7 |
| Denver | 1 | 2 | 2 | 14 | 6 | 16 |
| Indianapolis | 2 | 10 | 1 | 12 | 14 | 9 |
| Jacksonville | 4 | 7 | 5 | 7 | 7 | 8 |
| Kansas City | 5 | 13 | 3 | 10 | 10 | 10 |
| Miami | 13 | 9 | 13 | 4 | 9 | 3 |
| New England | 12 | 14 | 10 | 11 | 11 | 11 |
| NY Jets | 7 | 12 | 4 | 6 | 12 | 4 |
| Oakland | 3 | 1 | 7 | 9 | 4 | 14 |
| Pittsburgh | 10 | 4 | 14 | 5 | 8 | 6 |
| San Diego | 14 | 16 | 9 | 8 | 3 | 12 |
| Seattle | 11 | 11 | 11 | 16 | 15 | 15 |
| Tennessee | 8 | 6 | 6 | 1 | 2 | 1 |

### National Football Conference

| | Offense Total | Rush | Pass | Defense Total | Rush | Pass |
|---|---|---|---|---|---|---|
| Arizona | 12 | 13 | 9 | 15 | 14 | 5 |
| Atlanta | 15 | 14 | 12 | 11 | 13 | 11 |
| Carolina | 9 | 15 | 6 | 12 | 12 | 12 |
| Chicago | 11 | 11 | 11 | 8 | 9 | 9 |
| Dallas | 13 | 5 | 15 | 9 | 15 | 2 |
| Detroit | 14 | 10 | 13 | 6 | 8 | 7 |
| Green Bay | 7 | 12 | 4 | 7 | 2 | 10 |
| Minnesota | 3 | 1 | 3 | 13 | 6 | 14 |
| New Orleans | 4 | 2 | 8 | 3 | 4 | 4 |
| NY Giants | 6 | 4 | 7 | 2 | 1 | 8 |
| Philadelphia | 8 | 6 | 10 | 5 | 10 | 3 |
| St. Louis | 1 | 7 | 1 | 10 | 5 | 13 |
| San Francisco | 2 | 8 | 2 | 14 | 7 | 15 |
| Tampa Bay | 10 | 3 | 14 | 4 | 3 | 6 |
| Washington | 5 | 9 | 5 | 1 | 11 | 1 |

## Baltimore Ravens

| SCORING | TD Rush | Rec | Ret | PAT | FG | S | Pts |
|---|---|---|---|---|---|---|---|
| Stover | 0 | 0 | 0 | 30/30 | 35/39 | 0 | 135 |
| Ja. Lewis | 6 | 0 | 0 | 1 | 0 | 0 | 38 |
| Ismail | 0 | 5 | 0 | 0 | 0 | 0 | 30 |
| Sharpe | 0 | 5 | 0 | 0 | 0 | 0 | 30 |

| RUSHING | No. | Yds | Avg | Lg | TD |
|---|---|---|---|---|---|
| Ja. Lewis | 309 | 1364 | 4.4 | 45 | 6 |
| Holmes | 137 | 588 | 4.3 | 21 | 2 |

| PASSING | Att | Comp | Pct Comp | Yds | Avg Gain | TD | Int | Rating Pts |
|---|---|---|---|---|---|---|---|---|
| Banks | 274 | 150 | 54.8 | 1578 | 5.76 | 8 | 8 | 69.3 |
| Dilfer | 226 | 144 | 63.7 | 1502 | 6.65 | 12 | 11 | 76.6 |

| RECEIVING | No. | Yds | Avg | Lg | TD |
|---|---|---|---|---|---|
| Sharpe | 67 | 810 | 12.1 | t59 | 5 |
| Ismail | 49 | 655 | 13.4 | t53 | 5 |
| Holmes | 32 | 221 | 6.9 | 27 | 0 |
| Taylor | 28 | 276 | 9.9 | 40 | 3 |
| Ja. Lewis | 27 | 296 | 11.0 | 45 | 0 |

**INTERCEPTIONS:** Starks, 6

| PUNTING | No. | Yds | Avg | Net Avg | TB | In 20 | Lg | Blk |
|---|---|---|---|---|---|---|---|---|
| Richard'n | 86 | 3457 | 40.2 | 33.9 | 8 | 35 | 55 | 0 |

**SACKS:** Burnett, 10.5

## Buffalo Bills

| SCORING | TD Rush | Rec | Ret | PAT | FG | S | Pts |
|---|---|---|---|---|---|---|---|
| Christie | 0 | 0 | 0 | 31/31 | 26/35 | 0 | 109 |
| Morris | 5 | 1 | 0 | 0 | 0 | 0 | 36 |
| Moulds | 5 | 0 | 0 | 0 | 0 | 0 | 30 |
| Riemersma | 0 | 5 | 0 | 0 | 0 | 0 | 30 |
| Smith | 4 | 0 | 0 | 0 | 0 | 0 | 24 |

| RUSHING | No. | Yds | Avg | Lg | TD |
|---|---|---|---|---|---|
| Bryson | 161 | 591 | 3.7 | 24 | 0 |
| Smith | 101 | 354 | 3.5 | 59 | 4 |
| Morris | 93 | 341 | 3.7 | t32 | 5 |

| PASSING | Att | Comp | Pct Comp | Yds | Avg Gain | TD | Int | Rating Pts |
|---|---|---|---|---|---|---|---|---|
| Johnson | 306 | 175 | 57.2 | 2125 | 6.94 | 12 | 7 | 82.2 |
| Flutie | 231 | 132 | 57.1 | 1700 | 7.36 | 8 | 3 | 86.5 |

| RECEIVING | No. | Yds | Avg | Lg | TD |
|---|---|---|---|---|---|
| Moulds | 94 | 1326 | 14.1 | 52 | 5 |
| P. Price | 52 | 762 | 14.7 | 42 | 3 |
| McDaniel | 43 | 697 | 16.2 | t74 | 2 |
| Morris | 37 | 268 | 7.2 | 24 | 1 |

**INTERCEPTIONS:** Carpenter, 5

| PUNTING | No. | Yds | Avg | Net Avg | TB | In 20 | Lg | Blk |
|---|---|---|---|---|---|---|---|---|
| Mohr | 95 | 3661 | 38.5 | 31.4 | 5 | 19 | 57 | 0 |

**SACKS:** Wiley, 10.5

## Cincinnati Bengals

| SCORING | TD Rush | Rec | Ret | PAT | FG | S | Pts |
|---|---|---|---|---|---|---|---|
| Rackers | 0 | 0 | 0 | 21/21 | 12/21 | 0 | 57 |
| Warrick | 2 | 4 | 1 | 0 | 0 | 0 | 42 |
| Dillon | 7 | 0 | 0 | 0 | 0 | 0 | 42 |
| Bennett | 3 | 0 | 0 | 0 | 0 | 0 | 18 |

| RUSHING | No. | Yds | Avg | Lg | TD |
|---|---|---|---|---|---|
| Dillon | 315 | 1435 | 4.6 | t80 | 7 |
| Bennett | 90 | 324 | 3.6 | t37 | 3 |
| Smith | 41 | 232 | 5.7 | 21 | 0 |
| Warrick | 16 | 148 | 9.3 | t77 | 2 |

| PASSING | Att | Comp | Pct Comp | Yds | Avg Gain | TD | Int | Rating Pts |
|---|---|---|---|---|---|---|---|---|
| Smith | 267 | 118 | 44.2 | 1253 | 4.69 | 3 | 6 | 52.8 |
| Mitchell | 187 | 89 | 47.6 | 966 | 5.17 | 3 | 8 | 50.8 |

| RECEIVING | No. | Yds | Avg | Lg | TD |
|---|---|---|---|---|---|
| Warrick | 51 | 592 | 11.6 | 46 | 4 |
| McGee | 26 | 309 | 11.9 | 39 | 1 |
| Yeast | 24 | 301 | 12.5 | 27 | 0 |
| Farmer | 19 | 268 | 14.1 | 35 | 0 |

**INTERCEPTIONS:** Spikes and T. Carter, 2

| PUNTING | No. | Yds | Avg | Net Avg | TB | In 20 | Lg | Blk |
|---|---|---|---|---|---|---|---|---|
| Pope | 94 | 3775 | 40.2 | 33.1 | 14 | 18 | 57 | 0 |

**SACKS:** Foley, Gibson, Hall, 4

## Cleveland Browns

| SCORING | TD Rush | Rec | Ret | PAT | FG | S | Pts |
|---|---|---|---|---|---|---|---|
| P. Dawson | 0 | 0 | 0 | 17/17 | 14/17 | 0 | 59 |
| Prentice | 7 | 1 | 0 | 0 | 0 | 0 | 48 |
| Shea | 0 | 2 | 0 | 0 | 0 | 0 | 12 |
| Edwards | 0 | 2 | 0 | 0 | 0 | 0 | 12 |

| RUSHING | No. | Yds | Avg | Lg | TD |
|---|---|---|---|---|---|
| Prentice | 173 | 512 | 3.0 | 17 | 7 |
| Rhett | 71 | 258 | 3.6 | 42 | 0 |

| PASSING | Att | Comp | Pct Comp | Yds | Avg Gain | TD | Int | Rating Pts |
|---|---|---|---|---|---|---|---|---|
| Couch | 215 | 137 | 63.7 | 1483 | 6.90 | 7 | 9 | 77.3 |
| Pederson | 210 | 117 | 55.7 | 1047 | 4.99 | 2 | 8 | 56.6 |

| RECEIVING | No. | Yds | Avg | Lg | TD |
|---|---|---|---|---|---|
| Johnson | 57 | 669 | 11.7 | 79 | 0 |
| Northcutt | 39 | 422 | 10.8 | 37 | 0 |
| Patten | 38 | 546 | 14.4 | 65 | 1 |
| Prentice | 37 | 191 | 5.2 | 13 | 1 |
| Shea | 30 | 302 | 10.1 | 37 | 2 |

**INTERCEPTIONS:** Fuller, 3

| PUNTING | No. | Yds | Avg | Net Avg | TB | In 20 | Lg | Blk |
|---|---|---|---|---|---|---|---|---|
| Gardocki | 108 | 4919 | 45.5 | 37.3 | 5 | 25 | 67 | 0 |

**SACKS:** McKenzie, 8

## Denver Broncos

| SCORING | Rush | Rec | Ret | PAT | FG | S | Pts |
|---|---|---|---|---|---|---|---|
| Elam | 0 | 0 | 0 | 49/49 | 18/24 | 0 | 103 |
| Anderson | 15 | 0 | 0 | 1 | 0 | 0 | 92 |
| McCaffrey | 0 | 9 | 0 | 1 | 0 | 0 | 56 |
| R. Smith | 1 | 8 | 0 | 0 | 0 | 0 | 54 |

| RUSHING | No. | Yds | Avg | Lg | TD |
|---|---|---|---|---|---|
| Anderson | 297 | 1500 | 5.1 | t80 | 15 |
| Davis | 78 | 282 | 3.6 | 24 | 2 |

| PASSING | Att | Comp | Pct Comp | Yds | Avg Gain | TD | Int | Rating Pts |
|---|---|---|---|---|---|---|---|---|
| Griese | 336 | 216 | 64.3 | 2688 | 8.00 | 19 | 4 | 102.9 |
| Frerotte | 232 | 138 | 59.5 | 1776 | 7.66 | 9 | 8 | 82.1 |

| RECEIVING | No. | Yds | Avg | Lg | TD |
|---|---|---|---|---|---|
| McCaffrey | 101 | 1317 | 13.0 | 61 | 9 |
| R. Smith | 100 | 1602 | 16.0 | 49 | 8 |
| Carswell | 49 | 495 | 10.1 | t43 | 3 |
| De. Clark | 27 | 339 | 12.6 | 44 | 3 |
| Anderson | 23 | 169 | 7.3 | 18 | 0 |
| Chamberlain | 22 | 283 | 12.9 | 38 | 1 |

INTERCEPTIONS: Buckley, 6

| PUNTING | No. | Yds | Avg | Net Avg | TB | In 20 | Lg | Blk |
|---|---|---|---|---|---|---|---|---|
| Rouen | 61 | 2455 | 40.2 | 32.3 | 9 | 18 | 62 | 1 |

SACKS: Pryce, 12.5

## Indianapolis Colts

| SCORING | Rush | Rec | Ret | PAT | FG | S | Pts |
|---|---|---|---|---|---|---|---|
| Vanderjagt | 0 | 0 | 0 | 46/46 | 25/27 | 0 | 121 |
| James | 13 | 5 | 0 | 1 | 0 | 0 | 110 |
| Harrison | 0 | 14 | 0 | 0 | 0 | 0 | 84 |
| Pollard | 0 | 3 | 0 | 1 | 0 | 0 | 20 |

| RUSHING | No. | Yds | Avg | Lg | TD |
|---|---|---|---|---|---|
| James | 387 | 1709 | 4.4 | 30 | 13 |
| Manning | 37 | 116 | 3.1 | 14 | 1 |

| PASSING | Att | Comp | Pct Comp | Yds | Avg Gain | TD | Int | Rating Pts |
|---|---|---|---|---|---|---|---|---|
| Manning | 571 | 357 | 62.5 | 4413 | 7.73 | 33 | 15 | 94.7 |

| RECEIVING | No. | Yds | Avg | Lg | TD |
|---|---|---|---|---|---|
| Harrison | 102 | 1413 | 13.9 | t78 | 14 |
| James | 63 | 594 | 9.4 | 60 | 5 |
| Pathon | 50 | 646 | 12.9 | 38 | 3 |
| Dilger | 47 | 538 | 11.4 | 32 | 3 |

INTERCEPTIONS: Burris, 4

| PUNTING | No. | Yds | Avg | Net Avg | TB | In 20 | Lg | Blk |
|---|---|---|---|---|---|---|---|---|
| Smith | 65 | 2906 | 44.7 | 36.4 | 9 | 20 | 65 | 0 |

SACKS: Bratzke, 7.5

## Jacksonville Jaguars

| SCORING | Rush | Rec | Ret | PAT | FG | S | Pts |
|---|---|---|---|---|---|---|---|
| Hollis | 0 | 0 | 0 | 33/33 | 24/26 | 0 | 105 |
| Taylor | 12 | 2 | 0 | 0 | 0 | 0 | 84 |
| Ji. Smith | 0 | 8 | 0 | 0 | 0 | 0 | 48 |
| McCardell | 0 | 5 | 0 | 0 | 0 | 0 | 30 |

| RUSHING | No. | Yds | Avg | Lg | TD |
|---|---|---|---|---|---|
| Taylor | 292 | 1399 | 4.8 | 71 | 12 |
| Brunell | 48 | 236 | 4.9 | 16 | 2 |

| PASSING | Att | Comp | Pct Comp | Yds | Avg Gain | TD | Int | Rating Pts |
|---|---|---|---|---|---|---|---|---|
| Brunell | 512 | 311 | 60.7 | 3640 | 7.11 | 20 | 14 | 84.0 |

| RECEIVING | No. | Yds | Avg | Lg | TD |
|---|---|---|---|---|---|
| McCardell | 94 | 1207 | 12.8 | t67 | 5 |
| Ji. Smith | 91 | 1213 | 13.3 | t65 | 8 |
| Brady | 64 | 729 | 11.4 | 36 | 3 |
| Taylor | 36 | 240 | 6.7 | 19 | 2 |
| Soward | 14 | 154 | 11.0 | 45 | 1 |

INTERCEPTIONS: Stewart, Darius, Logan, 2

| PUNTING | No. | Yds | Avg | Net Avg | TB | In 20 | Lg | Blk |
|---|---|---|---|---|---|---|---|---|
| Barker | 76 | 3194 | 42.0 | 34.4 | 5 | 29 | 65 | 0 |

SACKS: Brackens, 7.5

## Kansas City Chiefs

| SCORING | Rush | Rec | Ret | PAT | FG | S | Pts |
|---|---|---|---|---|---|---|---|
| Peterson | 0 | 0 | 0 | 25/25 | 15/20 | 0 | 70 |
| Alexander | 0 | 10 | 0 | 0 | 0 | 0 | 60 |
| Gonzalez | 0 | 9 | 0 | 0 | 0 | 0 | 54 |
| Richardson | 3 | 3 | 0 | 0 | 0 | 0 | 36 |

| RUSHING | No. | Yds | Avg | Lg | TD |
|---|---|---|---|---|---|
| Richardson | 147 | 697 | 4.7 | 33 | 3 |
| Anders | 76 | 331 | 4.4 | 69 | 2 |

| PASSING | Att | Comp | Pct Comp | Yds | Avg Gain | TD | Int | Rating Pts |
|---|---|---|---|---|---|---|---|---|
| Grbac | 547 | 326 | 59.6 | 4169 | 7.62 | 28 | 14 | 89.9 |

| RECEIVING | No. | Yds | Avg | Lg | TD |
|---|---|---|---|---|---|
| Gonzalez | 93 | 1203 | 12.9 | 39 | 9 |
| Alexander | 78 | 1391 | 17.8 | t81 | 10 |
| Richardson | 58 | 468 | 8.1 | 24 | 3 |
| Morris | 48 | 678 | 14.1 | 47 | 3 |
| Lockett | 33 | 422 | 12.8 | t34 | 2 |

INTERCEPTIONS: Hasty, 4

| PUNTING | No. | Yds | Avg | Net Avg | TB | In 20 | Lg | Blk |
|---|---|---|---|---|---|---|---|---|
| Sau'brun | 82 | 3656 | 44.6 | 35.8 | 8 | 28 | 68 | 0 |

SACKS: Hicks, 14

## Miami Dolphins

| SCORING | Rush | Rec | TD Ret | PAT | FG | S | Pts |
|---|---|---|---|---|---|---|---|
| Mare | 0 | 0 | 0 | 33/34 | 28/31 | 0 | 117 |
| L. Smith | 14 | 2 | 0 | 0 | 0 | 0 | 96 |
| Gadsden | 0 | 6 | 0 | 0 | 0 | 0 | 36 |
| Shepherd | 0 | 4 | 0 | 0 | 0 | 0 | 24 |

| RUSHING | No. | Yds | Avg | Lg | TD |
|---|---|---|---|---|---|
| L. Smith | 309 | 1139 | 3.7 | t68 | 14 |
| Fiedler | 54 | 267 | 4.9 | 30 | 1 |
| Johnson | 50 | 168 | 3.4 | 16 | 1 |

| PASSING | Att | Comp | Pct Comp | Yds | Avg Gain | TD | Int | Rating Pts |
|---|---|---|---|---|---|---|---|---|
| Fiedler | 357 | 204 | 57.1 | 2402 | 6.73 | 14 | 14 | 74.5 |

| RECEIVING | No. | Yds | Avg | Lg | TD |
|---|---|---|---|---|---|
| Gadsden | 56 | 786 | 14.0 | 61 | 6 |
| Shepherd | 35 | 446 | 12.7 | t46 | 4 |
| L. Smith | 31 | 201 | 6.5 | 28 | 2 |
| Martin | 26 | 393 | 15.1 | 44 | 0 |
| T. Thomas | 16 | 117 | 7.3 | 15 | 1 |

**INTERCEPTIONS:** Walker, 7

| PUNTING | No. | Yds | Avg | Net Avg | TB | In 20 | Lg | Blk |
|---|---|---|---|---|---|---|---|---|
| Turk | 92 | 3870 | 42.1 | 36.2 | 14 | 25 | 70 | 0 |

**SACKS:** Armstrong, 16.5

## New England Patriots

| SCORING | Rush | Rec | TD Ret | PAT | FG | S | Pts |
|---|---|---|---|---|---|---|---|
| Vinatieri | 0 | 0 | 0 | 25/25 | 27/33 | 0 | 106 |
| Glenn | 0 | 6 | 0 | 0 | 0 | 0 | 36 |
| Faulk | 4 | 1 | 0 | 1 | 0 | 0 | 32 |
| Brown | 0 | 4 | 1 | 0 | 0 | 0 | 30 |
| Redmond | 1 | 2 | 0 | 0 | 0 | 0 | 18 |

| RUSHING | No. | Yds | Avg | Lg | TD |
|---|---|---|---|---|---|
| Faulk | 164 | 570 | 3.5 | 18 | 4 |
| Redmond | 125 | 406 | 3.2 | 20 | 1 |
| Bledsoe | 47 | 158 | 3.4 | 16 | 2 |

| PASSING | Att | Comp | Pct Comp | Yds | Avg Gain | TD | Int | Rating Pts |
|---|---|---|---|---|---|---|---|---|
| Bledsoe | 531 | 312 | 58.8 | 3291 | 6.20 | 17 | 13 | 77.3 |

| RECEIVING | No. | Yds | Avg | Lg | TD |
|---|---|---|---|---|---|
| Brown | 83 | 944 | 11.4 | t44 | 4 |
| Glenn | 79 | 963 | 12.2 | t39 | 6 |
| Faulk | 51 | 465 | 9.1 | t52 | 1 |
| Bjornson | 20 | 152 | 7.6 | 19 | 2 |
| Redmond | 20 | 126 | 6.3 | 20 | 2 |

**INTERCEPTIONS:** Law, Jones, Milloy, 2

| PUNTING | No. | Yds | Avg | Net Avg | TB | In 20 | Lg | Blk |
|---|---|---|---|---|---|---|---|---|
| L. Johnson | 89 | 3798 | 42.7 | 36.8 | 5 | 31 | 62 | 1 |

**SACKS:** McGinest and Spires, 6

## New York Jets

| SCORING | Rush | Rec | TD Ret | PAT | FG | S | Pts |
|---|---|---|---|---|---|---|---|
| Hall | 0 | 0 | 0 | 30/30 | 21/32 | 0 | 93 |
| Martin | 9 | 2 | 0 | 0 | 0 | 0 | 66 |
| Chrebet | 0 | 8 | 0 | 0 | 0 | 0 | 48 |

| RUSHING | No. | Yds | Avg | Lg | TD |
|---|---|---|---|---|---|
| Martin | 316 | 1204 | 3.8 | 55 | 9 |
| Parmalee | 27 | 87 | 3.2 | t18 | 2 |

| PASSING | Att | Comp | Pct Comp | Yds | Avg Gain | TD | Int | Rating Pts |
|---|---|---|---|---|---|---|---|---|
| Testaverde | 590 | 328 | 55.6 | 3732 | 6.33 | 21 | 25 | 69.0 |

| RECEIVING | No. | Yds | Avg | Lg | TD |
|---|---|---|---|---|---|
| R. Anderson | 88 | 853 | 9.7 | 41 | 2 |
| Martin | 70 | 508 | 7.3 | 31 | 2 |
| Chrebet | 69 | 937 | 13.6 | 50 | 8 |
| Ward | 54 | 801 | 14.8 | 61 | 3 |

**INTERCEPTIONS:** V. Green, 6

| PUNTING | No. | Yds | Avg | Net Avg | TB | In 20 | Lg | Blk |
|---|---|---|---|---|---|---|---|---|
| Tupa | 83 | 3714 | 44.7 | 33.2 | 15 | 18 | 70 | 0 |

**SACKS:** Lewis, 10

## Oakland Raiders

| SCORING | Rush | Rec | TD Ret | PAT | FG | S | Pts |
|---|---|---|---|---|---|---|---|
| Janikowski | 0 | 0 | 0 | 46/46 | 22/32 | 0 | 112 |
| Brown | 0 | 11 | 0 | 0 | 0 | 0 | 66 |
| Wheatley | 9 | 1 | 0 | 0 | 0 | 0 | 60 |
| Crockett | 7 | 0 | 0 | 0 | 0 | 0 | 42 |
| Rison | 0 | 6 | 0 | 0 | 0 | 0 | 36 |

| RUSHING | No. | Yds | Avg | Lg | TD |
|---|---|---|---|---|---|
| Wheatley | 232 | 1046 | 4.5 | t80 | 9 |
| Gannon | 89 | 529 | 5.9 | 23 | 4 |

| PASSING | Att | Comp | Pct Comp | Yds | Avg Gain | TD | Int | Rating Pts |
|---|---|---|---|---|---|---|---|---|
| Gannon | 473 | 284 | 60.0 | 3430 | 7.25 | 28 | 11 | 92.4 |

| RECEIVING | No. | Yds | Avg | Lg | TD |
|---|---|---|---|---|---|
| Brown | 76 | 1128 | 14.8 | 45 | 11 |
| Rison | 41 | 606 | 14.8 | 49 | 6 |
| Dudley | 29 | 350 | 12.1 | 30 | 4 |
| Jordan | 27 | 299 | 11.1 | 55 | 1 |

**INTERCEPTIONS:** Allen; Thomas, 6

| PUNTING | No. | Yds | Avg | Net Avg | TB | In 20 | Lg | Blk |
|---|---|---|---|---|---|---|---|---|
| Lechler | 65 | 2984 | 45.9 | 38.0 | 10 | 24 | 69 | 1 |

**SACKS:** Jackson, 8

## Pittsburgh Steelers

| SCORING | Rush | Rec | Ret | PAT | FG | S | Pts |
|---|---|---|---|---|---|---|---|
| | | TD | | | | | |
| Brown | 0 | 0 | 0 | 32/33 | 25/30 | 0 | 107 |
| Bettis | 8 | 0 | 0 | 0 | 0 | 0 | 48 |
| Stewart | 7 | 0 | 0 | 0 | 0 | 0 | 42 |
| Ward | 0 | 4 | 0 | 0 | 0 | 0 | 24 |
| Shaw | 0 | 4 | 0 | 0 | 0 | 0 | 24 |

| RUSHING | No. | Yds | Avg | Lg | TD |
|---|---|---|---|---|---|
| Bettis | 355 | 1341 | 3.8 | 30 | 8 |
| Stewart | 78 | 436 | 5.6 | t45 | 7 |
| Huntley | 46 | 215 | 4.7 | t30 | 3 |
| Fuamatu-Ma'afala | 21 | 149 | 7.1 | 23 | 1 |

| PASSING | Att | Comp | Pct Comp | Yds | Avg Gain | TD | Int | Rating Pts |
|---|---|---|---|---|---|---|---|---|
| Stewart | 289 | 151 | 52.3 | 1860 | 6.44 | 11 | 8 | 73.6 |

| RECEIVING | No. | Yds | Avg | Lg | TD |
|---|---|---|---|---|---|
| Ward | 48 | 672 | 14.0 | t77 | 4 |
| Shaw | 40 | 672 | 16.8 | t45 | 4 |
| Burress | 22 | 273 | 12.4 | 39 | 0 |

**INTERCEPTIONS:** Washington and Scott, 5

| PUNTING | No. | Yds | Avg | Net Avg | TB | In 20 | Lg | Blk |
|---|---|---|---|---|---|---|---|---|
| Miller | 90 | 3944 | 43.8 | 37.5 | 8 | 34 | 67 | 1 |

**SACKS:** Gildon, 13.5

## San Diego Chargers

| SCORING | Rush | Rec | Ret | PAT | FG | S | Pts |
|---|---|---|---|---|---|---|---|
| | | TD | | | | | |
| Carney | 0 | 0 | 0 | 27/27 | 18/25 | 0 | 81 |
| Conway | 0 | 5 | 0 | 0 | 0 | 0 | 30 |
| F. Jones | 0 | 5 | 0 | 0 | 0 | 0 | 30 |
| J. Graham | 0 | 4 | 0 | 0 | 0 | 0 | 24 |
| Fletcher | 3 | 1 | 0 | 0 | 0 | 0 | 24 |

| RUSHING | No. | Yds | Avg | Lg | TD |
|---|---|---|---|---|---|
| Fletcher | 116 | 384 | 3.3 | 21 | 3 |
| Fazande | 119 | 368 | 3.1 | 26 | 2 |
| Chancey | 42 | 141 | 3.4 | 14 | 2 |

| PASSING | Att | Comp | Pct Comp | Yds | Avg Gain | TD | Int | Rating Pts |
|---|---|---|---|---|---|---|---|---|
| Leaf | 322 | 161 | 50.0 | 1883 | 5.85 | 11 | 18 | 56.2 |
| Harbaugh | 202 | 123 | 60.9 | 1416 | 7.01 | 8 | 10 | 74.6 |

| RECEIVING | No. | Yds | Avg | Lg | TD |
|---|---|---|---|---|---|
| F. Jones | 71 | 766 | 10.8 | 44 | 5 |
| J. Graham | 55 | 907 | 16.5 | t83 | 4 |
| Conway | 53 | 712 | 13.4 | t68 | 5 |
| Fletcher | 48 | 355 | 7.4 | 26 | 1 |

**INTERCEPTIONS:** Harrison, 6

| PUNTING | No. | Yds | Avg | Net Avg | TB | In 20 | Lg | Blk |
|---|---|---|---|---|---|---|---|---|
| Bennett | 92 | 4248 | 46.2 | 36.2 | 10 | 23 | 66 | 0 |

**SACKS:** Parrella, 7

## Seattle Seahawks

| SCORING | Rush | Rec | Ret | PAT | FG | S | Pts |
|---|---|---|---|---|---|---|---|
| | | TD | | | | | |
| Lindell | 0 | 0 | 0 | 25/25 | 15/17 | 0 | 70 |
| Watters | 7 | 2 | 0 | 0 | 0 | 0 | 54 |
| Jackson | 0 | 6 | 0 | 0 | 0 | 0 | 36 |
| Dawkins | 0 | 5 | 0 | 0 | 0 | 0 | 30 |
| Mili | 0 | 3 | 0 | 0 | 0 | 0 | 18 |

| RUSHING | No. | Yds | Avg | Lg | TD |
|---|---|---|---|---|---|
| Watters | 278 | 1242 | 4.5 | 55 | 7 |
| Alexander | 64 | 313 | 4.9 | 50 | 2 |

| PASSING | Att | Comp | Pct Comp | Yds | Avg Gain | TD | Int | Rating Pts |
|---|---|---|---|---|---|---|---|---|
| Kitna | 418 | 259 | 62.0 | 2658 | 6.36 | 18 | 19 | 75.6 |

| RECEIVING | No. | Yds | Avg | Lg | TD |
|---|---|---|---|---|---|
| Dawkins | 63 | 731 | 11.6 | 40 | 5 |
| Watters | 63 | 613 | 9.7 | 59 | 2 |
| Jackson | 53 | 713 | 13.5 | 71 | 6 |
| Mayes | 29 | 264 | 9.1 | 40 | 1 |

**INTERCEPTIONS:** Bellamy and W. Williams, 4

| PUNTING | No. | Yds | Avg | Net Avg | TB | In 20 | Lg | Blk |
|---|---|---|---|---|---|---|---|---|
| Feagles | 74 | 2960 | 40.0 | 36.9 | 2 | 24 | 57 | 1 |

**SACKS:** C. Brown and King, 6

## Tennessee Oilers

| SCORING | Rush | Rec | Ret | PAT | FG | S | Pts |
|---|---|---|---|---|---|---|---|
| | | TD | | | | | |
| Del Greco | 0 | 0 | 0 | 37/38 | 27/33 | 0 | 118 |
| George | 14 | 2 | 0 | 0 | 0 | 0 | 96 |
| Mason | 0 | 5 | 1 | 0 | 0 | 0 | 36 |
| Wycheck | 0 | 4 | 0 | 0 | 0 | 0 | 24 |
| Neale | 0 | 2 | 0 | 0 | 0 | 0 | 12 |
| Thigpen | 0 | 2 | 0 | 0 | 0 | 0 | 12 |

| RUSHING | No. | Yds | Avg | Lg | TD |
|---|---|---|---|---|---|
| George | 403 | 1509 | 3.7 | l35 | 14 |
| McNair | 71 | 404 | 5.7 | 25 | 0 |

| PASSING | Att | Comp | Pct Comp | Yds | Avg Gain | TD | Int | Rating Pts |
|---|---|---|---|---|---|---|---|---|
| McNair | 396 | 248 | 62.6 | 2847 | 7.19 | 15 | 13 | 83.2 |

| RECEIVING | No. | Yds | Avg | Lg | TD |
|---|---|---|---|---|---|
| Wycheck | 70 | 636 | 9.1 | 26 | 4 |
| Mason | 63 | 895 | 14.2 | 34 | 5 |
| George | 50 | 453 | 9.1 | 24 | 2 |
| Sanders | 33 | 536 | 16.2 | 54 | 0 |

**INTERCEPTIONS:** Rolle, 7

| PUNTING | No. | Yds | Avg | Net Avg | TB | In 20 | Lg | Blk |
|---|---|---|---|---|---|---|---|---|
| Hentrich | 76 | 3101 | 40.8 | 36.3 | 9 | 33 | 67 | 0 |

**SACKS:** Kearse, 11.5

# 2000 NFC Team-by-Team Statistical Leaders

## Arizona Cardinals

### SCORING

| | TD | | | | | | |
| SCORING | Rush | Rec | Ret | PAT | FG | S | Pts |
| --- | --- | --- | --- | --- | --- | --- | --- |
| Blanchard | 0 | 0 | 0 | 18/19 | 16/23 | 0 | 66 |
| Boston | 0 | 7 | 0 | 0 | 0 | 0 | 42 |
| Pittman | 4 | 2 | 0 | 0 | 0 | 0 | 36 |
| Sanders | 0 | 6 | 0 | 0 | 0 | 0 | 36 |

### RUSHING

| RUSHING | No. | Yds | Avg | Lg | TD |
| --- | --- | --- | --- | --- | --- |
| Pittman | 184 | 719 | 3.9 | 29 | 4 |
| Jones | 112 | 373 | 3.3 | 29 | 2 |
| Plummer | 37 | 183 | 4.9 | 24 | 0 |

### PASSING

| PASSING | Att | Comp | Pct Comp | Yds | Avg Gain | TD | Int | Rating Pts |
| --- | --- | --- | --- | --- | --- | --- | --- | --- |
| Plummer | 475 | 270 | 56.8 | 2946 | 6.20 | 13 | 21 | 66.0 |

### RECEIVING

| RECEIVING | No. | Yds | Avg | Lg | TD |
| --- | --- | --- | --- | --- | --- |
| Pittman | 73 | 579 | 7.9 | t36 | 2 |
| Boston | 71 | 1156 | 16.3 | t70 | 7 |
| Sanders | 54 | 749 | 13.9 | t53 | 6 |
| Jones | 32 | 208 | 6.5 | 20 | 0 |

INTERCEPTIONS: A. Williams, 5

| PUNTING | No. | Yds | Avg | Net Avg | TB | In 20 | Lg | Blk |
| --- | --- | --- | --- | --- | --- | --- | --- | --- |
| Player | 65 | 2871 | 44.2 | 37.3 | 5 | 17 | 55 | 0 |

SACKS: Rice, 7.5

## Atlanta Falcons

### SCORING

| | TD | | | | | | |
| SCORING | Rush | Rec | Ret | PAT | FG | S | Pts |
| --- | --- | --- | --- | --- | --- | --- | --- |
| Andersen | 0 | 0 | 0 | 23/23 | 25/31 | 0 | 98 |
| Anderson | 6 | 0 | 0 | 1 | 0 | 0 | 38 |
| Mathis | 0 | 5 | 0 | 0 | 0 | 0 | 30 |
| Dwight | 0 | 3 | 1 | 0 | 0 | 0 | 24 |
| Vaughn | 0 | 0 | 3 | 0 | 0 | 0 | 18 |

### RUSHING

| RUSHING | No. | Yds | Avg | Lg | TD |
| --- | --- | --- | --- | --- | --- |
| Anderson | 282 | 1024 | 3.6 | 42 | 6 |
| M. Smith | 19 | 69 | 3.6 | 16 | 0 |

### PASSING

| PASSING | Att | Comp | Pct Comp | Yds | Avg Gain | TD | Int | Rating Pts |
| --- | --- | --- | --- | --- | --- | --- | --- | --- |
| Chandler | 331 | 192 | 58.0 | 2236 | 6.76 | 10 | 12 | 73.5 |
| Kannell | 116 | 57 | 49.1 | 524 | 4.52 | 2 | 5 | 49.6 |
| Johnson | 67 | 36 | 53.7 | 406 | 6.06 | 2 | 3 | 63.4 |

### RECEIVING

| RECEIVING | No. | Yds | Avg | Lg | TD |
| --- | --- | --- | --- | --- | --- |
| Jefferson | 60 | 822 | 13.7 | 49 | 2 |
| Mathis | 57 | 679 | 11.9 | t44 | 5 |
| Christian | 44 | 315 | 7.2 | 19 | 0 |
| Anderson | 42 | 382 | 9.1 | 55 | 0 |
| R. Kelly | 31 | 340 | 11.0 | t37 | 2 |

INTERCEPTIONS: Buchanan, 6

| PUNTING | No. | Yds | Avg | Net Avg | TB | In 20 | Lg | Blk |
| --- | --- | --- | --- | --- | --- | --- | --- | --- |
| Stryzinski | 84 | 3447 | 41.0 | 37.9 | 5 | 27 | 60 | 1 |

SACKS: Hall and Bra. Smith, 4.5

## Carolina Panthers

### SCORING

| | TD | | | | | | |
| SCORING | Rush | Rec | Ret | PAT | FG | S | Pts |
| --- | --- | --- | --- | --- | --- | --- | --- |
| Nedney | 0 | 0 | 0 | 24/24 | 34/38 | 0 | 126 |
| Muhammad | 0 | 6 | 0 | 0 | 0 | 0 | 36 |
| Biakabutuka | 2 | 2 | 0 | 0 | 0 | 0 | 24 |
| Hayes | 0 | 3 | 0 | 0 | 0 | 0 | 18 |
| Hetherington | 2 | 1 | 0 | 0 | 0 | 0 | 18 |
| Floyd | 1 | 1 | 0 | 0 | 0 | 0 | 12 |
| Byrd | 0 | 2 | 0 | 0 | 0 | 0 | 12 |
| Walls | 0 | 2 | 0 | 0 | 0 | 0 | 12 |

### RUSHING

| RUSHING | No. | Yds | Avg | Lg | TD |
| --- | --- | --- | --- | --- | --- |
| Biakabutuka | 173 | 627 | 3.6 | 43 | 2 |
| Hoover | 89 | 290 | 3.3 | 35 | 1 |

### PASSING

| PASSING | Att | Comp | Pct Comp | Yds | Avg Gain | TD | Int | Rating Pts |
| --- | --- | --- | --- | --- | --- | --- | --- | --- |
| Beuerlein | 533 | 324 | 60.8 | 3730 | 6.99 | 19 | 18 | 79.7 |

### RECEIVING

| RECEIVING | No. | Yds | Avg | Lg | TD |
| --- | --- | --- | --- | --- | --- |
| Muhammad | 102 | 1183 | 11.6 | 36 | 6 |
| Hayes | 66 | 926 | 14.0 | t43 | 3 |
| Biakabutuka | 34 | 341 | 10.0 | 25 | 2 |
| Walls | 31 | 422 | 13.6 | 54 | 2 |

INTERCEPTIONS: Davis, 5

| PUNTING | No. | Yds | Avg | Net Avg | TB | In 20 | Lg | Blk |
| --- | --- | --- | --- | --- | --- | --- | --- | --- |
| Walter | 64 | 2459 | 38.4 | 33.8 | 2 | 19 | 66 | 2 |

SACKS: Williams, 6

## Chicago Bears

### SCORING

| | TD | | | | | | |
| SCORING | Rush | Rec | Ret | PAT | FG | S | Pts |
| --- | --- | --- | --- | --- | --- | --- | --- |
| Edinger | 0 | 0 | 0 | 21/21 | 21/27 | 0 | 84 |
| M. Robinson | 0 | 5 | 0 | 0 | 0 | 0 | 30 |
| McNown | 3 | 0 | 0 | 0 | 0 | 0 | 18 |
| Allen | 2 | 1 | 0 | 0 | 0 | 0 | 18 |

### RUSHING

| RUSHING | No. | Yds | Avg | Lg | TD |
| --- | --- | --- | --- | --- | --- |
| Allen | 290 | 1120 | 3.9 | 29 | 2 |
| McNown | 50 | 326 | 6.5 | 30 | 3 |

### PASSING

| PASSING | Att | Comp | Pct Comp | Yds | Avg Gain | TD | Int | Rating Pts |
| --- | --- | --- | --- | --- | --- | --- | --- | --- |
| McNown | 280 | 154 | 55.0 | 1646 | 5.89 | 8 | 9 | 68.5 |
| Matthews | 178 | 102 | 57.3 | 964 | 5.42 | 3 | 6 | 64.0 |

### RECEIVING

| RECEIVING | No. | Yds | Avg | Lg | TD |
| --- | --- | --- | --- | --- | --- |
| M. Robinson | 55 | 738 | 13.4 | t68 | 5 |
| Kennison | 55 | 549 | 10.0 | 26 | 2 |
| Booker | 47 | 490 | 10.4 | 41 | 2 |
| Allen | 39 | 291 | 7.5 | 26 | 1 |

INTERCEPTIONS: Parrish, 3

| PUNTING | No. | Yds | Avg | Net Avg | TB | In 20 | Lg | Blk |
| --- | --- | --- | --- | --- | --- | --- | --- | --- |
| Aguiar | 52 | 2017 | 38.8 | 34.9 | 4 | 8 | 56 | 0 |
| Ba'mew | 44 | 1607 | 36.5 | 36.21 | 3 | 12 | 52 | 0 |

SACKS: Urlacher, 8

## Dallas Cowboys

| SCORING | Rush | Rec | Ret | PAT | FG | S | Pts |
|---|---|---|---|---|---|---|---|
| | | TD | | | | | |
| Seder | 0 | 0 | 0 | 27/27 | 25/33 | 0 | 102 |
| Smith | 9 | 0 | 0 | 0 | 0 | 0 | 54 |
| Harris | 0 | 5 | 0 | 1 | 0 | 0 | 32 |
| McGarity | 1 | 0 | 2 | 0 | 0 | 0 | 18 |

| RUSHING | No. | Yds | Avg | Lg | TD |
|---|---|---|---|---|---|
| Smith | 294 | 1203 | 4.1 | 52 | 9 |

| PASSING | Att | Comp | Pct Comp | Yds | Avg Gain | TD | Int | Rating Pts |
|---|---|---|---|---|---|---|---|---|
| Aikman | 262 | 156 | 59.5 | 1632 | 6.23 | 7 | 14 | 64.3 |
| Cunningham | 125 | 74 | 59.2 | 849 | 6.79 | 6 | 4 | 82.4 |
| Wright | 53 | 22 | 41.5 | 237 | 4.47 | 0 | 3 | 31.7 |

| RECEIVING | No. | Yds | Avg | Lg | TD |
|---|---|---|---|---|---|
| McKnight | 52 | 926 | 17.8 | 48 | 2 |
| Harris | 39 | 306 | 7.8 | 21 | 5 |
| Warren | 31 | 302 | 9.7 | t76 | 1 |
| Ismail | 25 | 350 | 14.0 | 44 | 1 |
| McGarity | 25 | 250 | 10.0 | 25 | 0 |

**INTERCEPTIONS:** Sparks, 5

| PUNTING | No. | Yds | Avg | Net Avg | TB | In 20 | Lg | Blk |
|---|---|---|---|---|---|---|---|---|
| Knorr | 58 | 2485 | 42.8 | 35.8 | 8 | 12 | 60 | 0 |

**SACKS:** Ekuban, 6.5

## Green Bay Packers

| SCORING | Rush | Rec | Ret | PAT | FG | S | Pts |
|---|---|---|---|---|---|---|---|
| | | TD | | | | | |
| Longwell | 0 | 0 | 0 | 32/32 | 33/38 | 0 | 131 |
| Green | 10 | 3 | 0 | 0 | 0 | 0 | 78 |
| Freeman | 0 | 9 | 0 | 0 | 0 | 0 | 54 |
| Schroeder | 0 | 4 | 0 | 0 | 0 | 0 | 24 |
| Levens | 3 | 0 | 0 | 0 | 0 | 0 | 18 |

| RUSHING | No. | Yds | Avg | Lg | TD |
|---|---|---|---|---|---|
| Green | 263 | 1175 | 4.5 | t39 | 10 |
| Levens | 77 | 224 | 2.9 | 17 | 3 |
| Favre | 27 | 108 | 4.0 | 18 | 0 |
| Parker | 18 | 85 | 4.7 | 24 | 0 |

| PASSING | Att | Comp | Pct Comp | Yds | Avg Gain | TD | Int | Rating Pts |
|---|---|---|---|---|---|---|---|---|
| Favre | 580 | 338 | 58.3 | 3812 | 6.57 | 20 | 16 | 78.0 |

| RECEIVING | No. | Yds | Avg | Lg | TD |
|---|---|---|---|---|---|
| Green | 73 | 559 | 7.7 | 31 | 3 |
| Schroeder | 65 | 999 | 15.4 | t55 | 4 |
| Freeman | 62 | 912 | 14.7 | t67 | 9 |
| Henderson | 35 | 234 | 6.7 | 25 | 1 |
| Franks | 34 | 363 | 10.7 | t27 | 1 |
| Driver | 21 | 322 | 15.3 | 49 | 1 |

**INTERCEPTIONS:** Sharper, 9

| PUNTING | No. | Yds | Avg | Net Avg | TB | In 20 | Lg | Blk |
|---|---|---|---|---|---|---|---|---|
| Bidwell | 78 | 3003 | 38.5 | 34.6 | 5 | 22 | 53 | 0 |
| Longwell | 1 | 30 | 30.0 | 10 | 1 | 0 | 30 | 0 |

**SACKS:** Thierry, 6.5

## Detroit Lions

| SCORING | Rush | Rec | Ret | PAT | FG | S | Pts |
|---|---|---|---|---|---|---|---|
| | | TD | | | | | |
| Hanson | 0 | 0 | 0 | 29/29 | 24/30 | 0 | 101 |
| J. Stewart | 10 | 1 | 0 | 3 | 0 | 0 | 72 |
| Morton | 0 | 3 | 0 | 1 | 0 | 0 | 20 |
| Moore | 0 | 3 | 0 | 0 | 0 | 0 | 18 |
| Crowell | 0 | 3 | 0 | 0 | 0 | 0 | 18 |

| RUSHING | No. | Yds | Avg | Lg | TD |
|---|---|---|---|---|---|
| J. Stewart | 339 | 1184 | 3.5 | 34 | 10 |
| Batch | 44 | 199 | 4.5 | 19 | 2 |

| PASSING | Att | Comp | Pct Comp | Yds | Avg Gain | TD | Int | Rating Pts |
|---|---|---|---|---|---|---|---|---|
| Batch | 412 | 221 | 53.6 | 2489 | 6.04 | 13 | 15 | 67.3 |
| Case | 91 | 56 | 61.5 | 503 | 5.53 | 1 | 4 | 61.7 |

| RECEIVING | No. | Yds | Avg | Lg | TD |
|---|---|---|---|---|---|
| Morton | 61 | 788 | 12.9 | t42 | 3 |
| Moore | 40 | 434 | 10.9 | t30 | 3 |
| Crowell | 34 | 430 | 12.6 | t50 | 3 |
| Sloan | 32 | 379 | 11.8 | 59 | 2 |
| J. Stewart | 32 | 287 | 9.0 | 32 | 1 |

**INTERCEPTIONS:** Schulz, 7

| PUNTING | No. | Yds | Avg | Net Avg | TB | In 20 | Lg | Blk |
|---|---|---|---|---|---|---|---|---|
| Jett | 93 | 4044 | 43.5 | 34.8 | 12 | 33 | 59 | 2 |

**SACKS:** Porcher, 8

## Minnesota Vikings

| SCORING | Rush | Rec | Ret | PAT | FG | S | Pts |
|---|---|---|---|---|---|---|---|
| | | TD | | | | | |
| Anderson | 0 | 0 | 0 | 45/45 | 22/23 | 0 | 111 |
| Moss | 0 | 15 | 0 | 1 | 0 | 0 | 92 |
| R. Smith | 7 | 3 | 0 | 0 | 0 | 0 | 60 |
| C. Carter | 0 | 9 | 0 | 0 | 0 | 0 | 54 |

| RUSHING | No. | Yds | Avg | Lg | TD |
|---|---|---|---|---|---|
| R. Smith | 295 | 1521 | 5.2 | t72 | 7 |
| Culpepper | 89 | 470 | 5.3 | t27 | 7 |

| PASSING | Att | Comp | Pct Comp | Yds | Avg Gain | TD | Int | Rating Pts |
|---|---|---|---|---|---|---|---|---|
| Culpepper | 474 | 297 | 62.7 | 3937 | 8.31 | 33 | 16 | 98.0 |

| RECEIVING | No. | Yds | Avg | Lg | TD |
|---|---|---|---|---|---|
| C. Carter | 96 | 1274 | 13.3 | 53 | 9 |
| Moss | 77 | 1437 | 18.7 | t78 | 15 |
| R. Smith | 36 | 348 | 9.7 | t53 | 3 |

**INTERCEPTIONS:** Wong and Tate, 2

| PUNTING | No. | Yds | Avg | Net Avg | TB | In 20 | Lg | Blk |
|---|---|---|---|---|---|---|---|---|
| Berger | 62 | 2773 | 44.7 | 36.2 | 11 | 16 | 60 | 0 |

**SACKS:** Randle, 8

## New Orleans Saints

| SCORING | | TD | | | | | |
|---|---|---|---|---|---|---|---|
| | Rush | Rec | Ret | PAT | FG | S | Pts |
| Brien | 0 | 0 | 0 | 37/37 | 23/29 | 0 | 106 |
| R. Williams | 8 | 1 | 0 | 0 | 0 | 0 | 54 |
| Horn | 0 | 8 | 0 | 0 | 0 | 0 | 48 |
| Jackson | 0 | 6 | 0 | 0 | 0 | 0 | 36 |

| RUSHING | No. | Yds | Avg | Lg | TD |
|---|---|---|---|---|---|
| R. Williams | 248 | 1000 | 4.0 | t26 | 8 |
| Blake | 57 | 243 | 4.3 | 20 | 1 |
| Allen | 46 | 179 | 3.9 | 18 | 2 |

| PASSING | Att | Comp | Pct Comp | Yds | Avg Gain | TD | Int | Rating Pts |
|---|---|---|---|---|---|---|---|---|
| Blake | 302 | 184 | 60.9 | 2025 | 6.71 | 13 | 9 | 82.7 |
| Brooks | 194 | 113 | 58.2 | 1514 | 7.80 | 9 | 6 | 85.7 |

| RECEIVING | No. | Yds | Avg | Lg | TD |
|---|---|---|---|---|---|
| Horn | 94 | 1340 | 14.3 | 52 | 8 |
| R. Williams | 44 | 409 | 9.3 | 24 | 1 |
| Jackson | 37 | 523 | 14.1 | t53 | 6 |
| Morton | 30 | 213 | 7.1 | 35 | 0 |
| Poole | 21 | 293 | 14.0 | t49 | 1 |
| A. Glover | 21 | 281 | 13.4 | 39 | 4 |

**INTERCEPTIONS:** Knight, 5

| PUNTING | No. | Yds | Avg | Net Avg | TB | In 20 | Lg | Blk |
|---|---|---|---|---|---|---|---|---|
| Gowin | 74 | 3043 | 41.1 | 32.3 | 8 | 22 | 58 | 0 |

**SACKS:** L. Glover, 17

## New York Giants

| SCORING | | TD | | | | | |
|---|---|---|---|---|---|---|---|
| | Rush | Rec | Ret | PAT | FG | S | Pts |
| Daluiso | 0 | 0 | 0 | 34/34 | 17/23 | 0 | 85 |
| Barber | 8 | 1 | 0 | 0 | 0 | 0 | 54 |
| Toomer | 1 | 7 | 0 | 0 | 0 | 0 | 48 |
| Hilliard | 0 | 8 | 0 | 0 | 0 | 0 | 48 |

| RUSHING | No. | Yds | Avg | Lg | TD |
|---|---|---|---|---|---|
| Barber | 213 | 1006 | 4.7 | t78 | 8 |
| Dayne | 228 | 770 | 3.4 | 50 | 5 |

| PASSING | Att | Comp | Pct Comp | Yds | Avg Gain | TD | Int | Rating Pts |
|---|---|---|---|---|---|---|---|---|
| Collins | 529 | 311 | 58.8 | 3610 | 6.82 | 22 | 13 | 83.1 |

| RECEIVING | No. | Yds | Avg | Lg | TD |
|---|---|---|---|---|---|
| Toomer | 78 | 1094 | 14.0 | t54 | 7 |
| Barber | 70 | 719 | 10.3 | 36 | 1 |
| Hilliard | 55 | 787 | 14.3 | 59 | 8 |
| Comella | 36 | 274 | 7.6 | 25 | 0 |
| Mitchell | 25 | 245 | 9.8 | 22 | 1 |

**INTERCEPTIONS:** McDaniel, 6

| PUNTING | No. | Yds | Avg | Net Avg | TB | In 20 | Lg | Blk |
|---|---|---|---|---|---|---|---|---|
| Maynard | 79 | 3210 | 40.6 | 33.7 | 8 | 26 | 64 | 1 |

**SACKS:** Hamilton, 10

## Philadelphia Eagles

| SCORING | | TD | | | | | |
|---|---|---|---|---|---|---|---|
| | Rush | Rec | Ret | PAT | FG | S | Pts |
| Akers | 0 | 0 | 0 | 34/36 | 29/33 | 0 | 121 |
| C. Johnson | 0 | 7 | 0 | 0 | 0 | 0 | 42 |
| McNabb | 6 | 0 | 0 | 0 | 0 | 0 | 36 |
| Mitchell | 2 | 1 | 2 | 0 | 0 | 0 | 30 |
| Thomason | 0 | 5 | 0 | 0 | 0 | 0 | 30 |

| RUSHING | No. | Yds | Avg | Lg | TD |
|---|---|---|---|---|---|
| McNabb | 86 | 629 | 7.3 | 54 | 6 |
| Staley | 79 | 344 | 4.4 | 60 | 1 |
| Autry | 112 | 334 | 3.0 | 15 | 3 |

| PASSING | Att | Comp | Pct Comp | Yds | Avg Gain | TD | Int | Rating Pts |
|---|---|---|---|---|---|---|---|---|
| McNabb | 569 | 330 | 58.0 | 3365 | 5.91 | 21 | 13 | 77.8 |

| RECEIVING | No. | Yds | Avg | Lg | TD |
|---|---|---|---|---|---|
| Lewis | 69 | 735 | 10.7 | 52 | 3 |
| C. Johnson | 56 | 642 | 11.5 | 59 | 7 |
| Small | 40 | 569 | 14.2 | t70 | 3 |
| Martin | 31 | 219 | 7.1 | 26 | 0 |

**INTERCEPTIONS:** Vincent, 5

| PUNTING | No. | Yds | Avg | Net Avg | TB | In 20 | Lg | Blk |
|---|---|---|---|---|---|---|---|---|
| Landeta | 86 | 3635 | 42.3 | 36.0 | 8 | 23 | 60 | 0 |

**SACKS:** H. Douglas, 15

## St. Louis Rams

| SCORING | | TD | | | | | |
|---|---|---|---|---|---|---|---|
| | Rush | Rec | Ret | PAT | FG | S | Pts |
| Faulk | 18 | 8 | 0 | 0 | 0 | 0 | 160 |
| Wilkins | 0 | 0 | 0 | 38/38 | 17/17 | 0 | 89 |
| Bruce | 0 | 9 | 0 | 0 | 0 | 0 | 54 |
| Holt | 0 | 6 | 0 | 0 | 0 | 0 | 36 |
| Hakim | 0 | 4 | 1 | 0 | 0 | 0 | 30 |
| Holcombe | 3 | 1 | 0 | 0 | 0 | 0 | 24 |
| Watson | 4 | 0 | 0 | 0 | 0 | 0 | 24 |
| Proehl | 0 | 4 | 0 | 0 | 0 | 0 | 24 |

| RUSHING | No. | Yds | Avg | Lg | TD |
|---|---|---|---|---|---|
| Faulk | 253 | 1359 | 5.4 | 36 | 18 |
| Watson | 54 | 249 | 4.6 | 49 | 4 |
| Holcombe | 21 | 70 | 3.3 | 11 | 3 |

| PASSING | Att | Comp | Pct Comp | Yds | Avg Gain | TD | Int | Rating Pts |
|---|---|---|---|---|---|---|---|---|
| Warner | 347 | 235 | 67.7 | 3429 | 9.88 | 21 | 18 | 98.3 |
| Green | 240 | 145 | 60.4 | 2063 | 8.60 | 16 | 5 | 101.8 |

| RECEIVING | No. | Yds | Avg | Lg | TD |
|---|---|---|---|---|---|
| Bruce | 87 | 1471 | 16.9 | t78 | 9 |
| Holt | 82 | 1635 | 19.9 | t85 | 6 |
| Faulk | 81 | 830 | 10.2 | t72 | 8 |
| Hakim | 53 | 734 | 13.8 | t80 | 4 |
| Proehl | 31 | 441 | 14.2 | 29 | 4 |

**INTERCEPTIONS:** McCleon, 8

| PUNTING | No. | Yds | Avg | Net Avg | TB | In 20 | Lg | Blk |
|---|---|---|---|---|---|---|---|---|
| Baker | 43 | 1736 | 40.4 | 34.2 | 5 | 13 | 59 | 1 |

**SACKS:** Wistrom, 11

## San Francisco 49ers

| SCORING | TD Rush | Rec | Ret | PAT | FG | S | Pts |
|---|---|---|---|---|---|---|---|
| Richey | 0 | 0 | 0 | 43/45 | 15/22 | 0 | 88 |
| Owens | 0 | 13 | 0 | 1 | 0 | 0 | 80 |
| Garner | 7 | 3 | 0 | 0 | 0 | 0 | 60 |
| Rice | 0 | 7 | 0 | 0 | 0 | 0 | 42 |
| Beasley | 3 | 3 | 0 | 0 | 0 | 0 | 36 |

| RUSHING | No. | Yds | Avg | Lg | TD |
|---|---|---|---|---|---|
| Garner | 258 | 1142 | 4.4 | 42 | 7 |
| Garcia | 72 | 414 | 5.8 | 33 | 4 |

| PASSING | Att | Comp | Pct Comp | Yds | Avg Gain | TD | Int | Rating Pts |
|---|---|---|---|---|---|---|---|---|
| Garcia | 561 | 355 | 63.3 | 4278 | 7.63 | 31 | 10 | 97.6 |

| RECEIVING | No. | Yds | Avg | Lg | TD |
|---|---|---|---|---|---|
| Owens | 97 | 1451 | 15.0 | t69 | 13 |
| Rice | 75 | 805 | 10.7 | t68 | 7 |
| Garner | 68 | 647 | 9.5 | 62 | 3 |
| Clark | 38 | 342 | 9.0 | 34 | 2 |
| Beasley | 31 | 233 | 7.5 | 34 | 3 |
| Stokes | 30 | 524 | 17.5 | 53 | 3 |

**INTERCEPTIONS:** Bronson and Montgomery, 3

| PUNTING | No. | Yds | Avg | Net Avg | TB | In 20 | Lg | Blk |
|---|---|---|---|---|---|---|---|---|
| Stanley | 69 | 2727 | 39.5 | 32.2 | 7 | 15 | 56 | 1 |

**SACKS:** Young, 9.5

## Washington Redskins

| SCORING | TD Rush | Rec | Ret | PAT | FG | S | Pts |
|---|---|---|---|---|---|---|---|
| Davis | 11 | 0 | 0 | 0 | 0 | 0 | 66 |
| Heppner | 0 | 0 | 0 | 17/17 | 10/15 | 0 | 47 |
| Fryar | 0 | 5 | 0 | 0 | 0 | 0 | 30 |

| RUSHING | No. | Yds | Avg | Lg | TD |
|---|---|---|---|---|---|
| Davis | 332 | 1318 | 4.0 | | 11 |
| Centers | 20 | 103 | 5.2 | 14 | 0 |

| PASSING | Att | Comp | Pct Comp | Yds | Avg Gain | TD | Int | Rating Pts |
|---|---|---|---|---|---|---|---|---|
| Bra. Johnson | 364 | 227 | 62.4 | 2505 | 6.88 | 11 | 15 | 75.7 |
| George | 194 | 113 | 58.3 | 1389 | 7.16 | 7 | 6 | 79.6 |

| RECEIVING | No. | Yds | Avg | Lg | TD |
|---|---|---|---|---|---|
| Centers | 80 | 600 | 7.5 | 26 | 3 |
| Thrash | 50 | 653 | 13.1 | 50 | 2 |
| Alexander | 47 | 510 | 10.9 | 30 | 2 |
| Fryar | 41 | 548 | 13.4 | t34 | 5 |
| Connell | 39 | 762 | 19.5 | t77 | 3 |

**INTERCEPTIONS:** Bailey, 5

| PUNTING | No. | Yds | Avg | Net Avg | TB | In 20 | Lg | Blk |
|---|---|---|---|---|---|---|---|---|
| Barnhardt | 79 | 3160 | 40 | 34.4 | 5 | 23 | 53 | 0 |

**SACKS:** Coleman, 12

## Tampa Bay Buccaneers

| SCORING | TD Rush | Rec | Ret | PAT | FG | S | Pts |
|---|---|---|---|---|---|---|---|
| Gramatica | 0 | 0 | 0 | 42/42 | 28/34 | 0 | 126 |
| Dunn | 8 | 1 | 0 | 0 | 0 | 0 | 54 |
| Johnson | 0 | 8 | 0 | 0 | 0 | 0 | 48 |
| King | 5 | 0 | 0 | 1 | 0 | 0 | 32 |
| Alstott | 5 | 0 | 0 | 0 | 0 | 0 | 30 |
| Anthony | 0 | 4 | 0 | 0 | 0 | 0 | 24 |
| Moore | 0 | 3 | 0 | 0 | 0 | 0 | 18 |
| Barber | 0 | 0 | 2 | 0 | 0 | 0 | 12 |

| RUSHING | No. | Yds | Avg | Lg | TD |
|---|---|---|---|---|---|
| Dunn | 248 | 1133 | 4.6 | t70 | 8 |
| Alstott | 131 | 465 | 3.5 | t20 | 5 |
| King | 73 | 353 | 4.8 | 19 | 5 |

| PASSING | Att | Comp | Pct Comp | Yds | Avg Gain | TD | Int | Rating Pts |
|---|---|---|---|---|---|---|---|---|
| King | 428 | 233 | 54.4 | 2769 | 6.47 | 18 | 13 | 75.8 |

| RECEIVING | No. | Yds | Avg | Lg | TD |
|---|---|---|---|---|---|
| Johnson | 71 | 874 | 12.3 | 38 | 8 |
| Green | 51 | 773 | 15.2 | 75 | 1 |
| Dunn | 44 | 422 | 9.6 | 45 | 1 |
| Moore | 29 | 288 | 9.9 | 28 | 3 |
| Anthony | 15 | 232 | 15.5 | t46 | 4 |

**INTERCEPTIONS:** Abraham, 7

| PUNTING | No. | Yds | Avg | Net Avg | TB | In 20 | Lg | Blk |
|---|---|---|---|---|---|---|---|---|
| Royals | 85 | 3551 | 41.8 | 35.1 | 8 | 17 | 63 | 0 |

**SACKS:** Sapp, 16.5

### Most Populous U.S. Cities Without an NFL Team*

**Los Angeles** (pop. 3,633,591): Raiders boss Al Davis's lawsuit against the NFL could set the stage for return from Oakland.

**San Antonio** (pop. 1,147,213) Though it would love to lure San Antonian Red McCombs's Vikings, city council has tabled plans to make Alamodome NFL-ready.

**San Jose** (pop. 867,675) Proximity of 49ers and Raiders makes Silicon Valley capital bear market for NFL.

**Columbus** (pop. 671,247) Ohio's largest city—and home of Ohio State Buckeyes—failed to get Cardinals in 1987.

**El Paso** (pop. 612,770) Compared with booming San Antonio, its pro prospects border on nonexistent.

*1999 estimates

# 2001 NFL Draft

First two rounds of the 66th annual NFL Draft held April 23–24 in New York City.

## First Round

| Team | Selection | Position |
|---|---|---|
| 1. ........Atlanta (from SD) | Michael Vick, Virginia Tech | QB |
| 2. ........Arizona | Leonard Davis, Texas | OT |
| 3. ........Cleveland | Gerard Warren, Florida | DT |
| 4. ........Cincinnati | Justin Smith, Missouri | DT |
| 5. ........San Diego (from Atl) | LaDainian Tomlinson, Texas Christian | RB |
| 6. ........New England | Richard Seymour, Georgia | DL |
| 7. ........San Francisco ..........(from Dall via Sea) | Andre Carter, Cal | DE |
| 8. ........Chicago | David Terrell, Michigan | WR |
| 9. ........Seattle | Koren Robinson, N Carolina St | WR |
| 10. ......Green Bay (from Sea) | Jamal Reynolds, Florida State | DE |
| 11. ......Carolina | Dan Morgan, Miami (FL) | LB |
| 12. ......St. Louis (from KC) | Damione Lewis, Miami (FL) | LB |
| 13. ......Jacksonville | Marcus Stroud, Georgia | DT |
| 14. ......Tampa Bay (from Buff) | Kenyatta Walker, Florida | OT |
| 15. ......Washington | Rod Gardner, Clemson | WR |
| 16. ......NY Jets (from Pitt) | Santana Moss, Miami (FL) | WR |
| 17. ......Seattle (from GB) | Steve Hutchinson, Michigan | OG |
| 18. ......Detroit | Jeff Backus, Michigan | OT |
| 19. ......Pittsburgh (from NYJ) | Casey Hampton, Texas | DT |
| 20. ......St. Louis | Adam Archuleta, Arizona St | S |
| 21. ......Buffalo (from TB) | Nate Clements, Ohio St | CB |
| 22. ......NY Giants | Will Allen, Syracuse | CB |
| 23. ......New Orleans | Deuce McAllister, Mississippi | RB |
| 24. ......Denver | Willie Middlebrooks, Minnesota | CB |
| 25. ......Philadelphia | Freddie Mitchell, UCLA | WR |
| 26. ......Miami | Jamar Fletcher, Wisconsin | CB |
| 27. ......Minnesota | Michael Bennett, Wisconsin | RB |
| 28. ......Oakland | Derrick Gibson, Florida State | S |
| 29. ......St. Louis (from Tenn) | Ryan Pickett, Ohio State | DT |
| 30. ......Indianapolis (from NYG) | Reggie Wayne, Miami (FL) | WR |
| 31. ......Baltimore | Todd Heap, Arizona St | TE |

## Second Round

| Team | Selection | Position |
|---|---|---|
| 32. ......San Diego | Drew Brees, Purdue | QB |
| 33. ......Cleveland | Quincy Morgan, Kansas St | DE |
| 34. ......Arizona | Kyle Vanden Bosch, Nebraska | DE |
| 35. ......Atlanta | Alge Cumbler, N Carolina | TE |
| 36. ......Cincinnati | Chad Johnson, Oregon St | WR |
| 37. ......Indianapolis (from Dall) | Idrees Bashir, Memphis | S |
| 38. ......Chicago | Anthony Thomas, Michigan | RB |
| 39. ......Pittsburgh (from NE) | Kendrell Bell, Georgia | LB |
| 40. ......Seattle | Ken Lucas, Mississippi | CB |
| 41. ......Green Bay (from SF) | Robert Ferguson, Texas A&M | WR |
| 42. ......St. Louis (from KC) | Tommy Polley, Florida State | LB |
| 43. ........Jacksonville | Maurice Williams, Michigan | OT |
| 44. ......Carolina | Kris Jenkins, Maryland | DT |
| 45. ......Washington | Fred Smoot, Mississippi St | CB |
| 46. ......Buffalo | Aaron Schobel, Texas Christian | DE |
| 47. ......San Francisco (from GB) | Jamie Winborn, Vanderbilt | LB |
| 48. ......New England (from Det) | Matt Light, Purdue | OT |
| 49. ......NY Jets | LaMont Jordan, Maryland | RB |
| 50. ......Detroit (from Pitt through NE) | Dominic Raiola, Nebraska | C |
| 51. ......Denver (from TB through Buff) | Paul Toviessi, Marshall | DE |
| 52. ......Miami (from Ind through Dall) | Chris Chambers, Wisconsin | WR |
| 53. ......Dallas (from NO) | Quincy Carter, Georgia | QB |
| 54. ......Arizona (from StL) | Michael Stone, Memphis | CB |
| 55. ......Philadelphia | Quinton Caver, Arkansas | LB |
| 56. ......Dallas (from Mia) | Tony Dixon, Alabama | S |
| 57. ......Minnesota | Willie Howard, Stanford | DT |
| 58. ......Buffalo (from Den) | Travis Henry, Tennessee | RB |
| 59. ......Oakland | Marques Tuiasosopo, Washington | QB |
| 60. ......Tennessee | Andre Dyson, Utah | CB |
| 61. ......Detroit (from NYG) | Shaun Rogers, Texas | DT |
| 62. ......Baltimore | Gary Baxter, Baylor | CB |

**Law Dawgs**

A group of Cleveland Browns fans brought a class-action suit against Art Modell, claiming Modell violated Ohio's consumer protection laws and breached his contract with them by moving his team to Baltimore in 1995. The case was settled out of court in April 2001, with more than 11,300 former season-ticket holders receiving $50 for each ticket they held. They had the choice of accepting cash or donating their proceeds to charity.

## Final Standings

|  | W | L | T | Pct | Pts | OP |
|---|---|---|---|---|---|---|
| Barcelona* | 8 | 2 | 0 | .800 | 252 | 191 |
| Berlin* | 6 | 4 | 0 | .600 | 270 | 239 |
| Rhein | 5 | 5 | 0 | .500 | 174 | 179 |
| Amsterdam | 4 | 6 | 0 | .400 | 194 | 226 |
| Scotland | 4 | 6 | 0 | .400 | 168 | 188 |
| Frankfurt | 3 | 7 | 0 | .300 | 199 | 234 |

*Clinched World Bowl 2001 berth.

## 2001 World Bowl

June 30, 2001, in Amsterdam

| | | | | |
|---|---|---|---|---|
| Berlin Thunder | 4 | 6 | 0 | 14—24 |
| Barcelona Dragons | 3 | 6 | 8 | 0—17 |

### FIRST QUARTER

Berlin: Four-pt. FG Bentley 53, 9:32.
Barcelona: FG Angoy 20, 14:10.

### SECOND QUARTER

Barcelona: FG Angoy 29, 3:39.
Barcelona: FG Angoy 33, 12:30.
Berlin: Jones 46 pass from Quinn (pass failed), 13:57.

### THIRD QUARTER

Barcelona: Simmons 58 pass from Jackson (Insley pass from Jackson for two-point conversion), 6:52.

### FOURTH QUARTER

Berlin: Merritt 17 pass from Quinn (Kruse kick), 5:13.
Berlin: Jones 53 pass from Quinn (Kruse kick), 10:52.
A: 32,116.

## NFL Europe Individual Leaders

### PASSING

|  | Att | Comp | Pct Comp | Yds | Avg Gain | TD | Pct TD | Int | Pct Int | Lg | Rating Pts |
|---|---|---|---|---|---|---|---|---|---|---|---|
| J. Quinn, Berlin | 296 | 167 | 56.4 | 2257 | 7.63 | 24 | 8.1 | 9 | 3.0 | t82 | 95.3 |
| J. Jackson, Barcelona | 223 | 125 | 56.1 | 1544 | 6.92 | 13 | 5.8 | 6 | 2.7 | t74 | 85.9 |
| M. Bishop, Frankfurt | 153 | 76 | 49.7 | 1090 | 7.12 | 11 | 7.2 | 9 | 4.6 | t80 | 78.1 |
| C. Sauter, Barcelona | 337 | 193 | 57.3 | 2041 | 6.06 | 14 | 4.2 | 8 | 2.6 | t45 | 77.8 |
| R. Powlus, Amsterdam | 307 | 171 | 55.7 | 1866 | 6.08 | 10 | 3.3 | 7 | 3.5 | t79 | 73.8 |

### RECEIVING

| RECEPTIONS | No. | Yds | Avg | Lg | TD |
|---|---|---|---|---|---|
| J. Whalen, Scotland | 66 | 691 | 10.5 | 47 | 3 |
| T Insley, Barcelona | 61 | 658 | 10.8 | 54 | 2 |
| C. Coleman, Amsterdam | 51 | 710 | 13.9 | t45 | 8 |
| A. McCullough, Frankfurt | 41 | 460 | 11.2 | 38 | 3 |
| A. Merritt, Berlin | 39 | 582 | 14.9 | 62 | 6 |

| YARDS | Yds | No. | Avg | Lg | TD |
|---|---|---|---|---|---|
| C. Coleman, Amsterdam | 710 | 51 | 13.9 | t45 | 8 |
| J. Whalen, Scotland | 691 | 66 | 10.5 | 47 | 3 |
| T. Insley, Barcelona | 658 | 61 | 10.8 | 54 | 2 |
| A. Merritt, Berlin | 582 | 39 | 14.9 | 62 | 6 |
| D. Jones, Berlin | 577 | 33 | 17.5 | 58 | 5 |

### RUSHING

|  | Att | Yds | Avg | Lg | TD |
|---|---|---|---|---|---|
| M. Green, Barcelona | 183 | 1057 | 5.8 | 55 | 8 |
| P. Pearson, Rhein | 166 | 597 | 3.6 | 19 | 3 |
| D. Manns, Frankfurt | 143 | 513 | 3.6 | 30 | 1 |
| A. Gray, Scotland | 111 | 445 | 4.0 | 53 | 2 |
| M. Hill, Berlin | 69 | 388 | 5.6 | t60 | 2 |

## Other Statistical Leaders

| | | |
|---|---|---|
| Points (TDs) | C. Coleman, Amsterdam | 48 |
| Points (Kicking) | Angoy, Barcelona | 66 |
| Yards from Scrimmage | M. Green, Barcelona | 1124 |
| Interceptions | D. Cooper, Rhein | 6 |
| Sacks | R. Matthews, Amsterdam | 9.5 |
| Punting Avg | B. Moorman, Berlin | 43.3 |
| Punt Return Avg | T. Insley, Barcelona | 14.1 |
| Kickoff Return Avg | D. Hall, Scotland | 24.4 |

# 2000 Canadian Football League

### EASTERN DIVISION

| | W | L | T | Pts | Pct | PF | PA |
|---|---|---|---|---|---|---|---|
| †Montreal | 12 | 6 | 0 | 24 | .666 | 594 | 379 |
| *Hamilton | 9 | 9 | 0 | 20 | .500 | 470 | 446 |
| *Winnipeg | 7 | 10 | 1 | 16 | .417 | 539 | 596 |
| Toronto | 7 | 10 | 1 | 15 | .417 | 390 | 562 |

### WESTERN DIVISION

| | W | L | T | Pts | Pct | PF | PA |
|---|---|---|---|---|---|---|---|
| †Calgary | 12 | 5 | 1 | 25 | .694 | 604 | 495 |
| *Edmonton | 10 | 8 | 0 | 21 | .556 | 527 | 520 |
| *British Columbia | 8 | 10 | 0 | 17 | .444 | 513 | 529 |
| Saskatchewan | 5 | 12 | 1 | 11 | .306 | 516 | 626 |

†Clinched division title.

*Clinched playoff berth

## Regular Season Statistical Leaders

| | | |
|---|---|---|
| Points (TDs) | Mike Pringle, Montreal | 114 |
| Points (Kicking) | Terry Baker, Montreal | 220 |
| Rushing Yards | Mike Pringle, Montreal | 1778 |
| Passing Yards | Damon Allen, B.C. | 4840 |
| Receiving Yards | Curtis Marsh, Saskatchewan | 1560 |
| Receptions | Curtis Marsh, Saskatchewan | 102 |

## 2000 Playoff Results

### DIVISION SEMIFINALS

East: Winnipeg 22, HAMILTON 20
West: British Columbia 34, Edmonton 32

### DIVISION FINALS

East: Winnipeg 24, MONTREAL 35
West: British Columbia 37, CALGARY 23

## 2000 Grey Cup Championship

Nov. 26, 2000, at Calgary, Alberta

| | | | | |
|---|---|---|---|---|
| Montreal Alouettes | 3 | 0 | 7 | 16—26 |
| British Columbia Lions | 8 | 4 | 0 | 16—28 |

A: 43,822.

## Dirigible Down; League to Follow

A blimp emblazoned with the logo of the then-fledgling XFL crashed into an Oakland seafood restaurant in January 2001. The dirigible was attempting to moor at Oakland International Airport when a gust caused a mechanical failure, forcing the two-man crew to jump to the ground. It then drifted aimlessly for about 20 minutes before coming down on the roof of the Oyster Reef. The pilot was slightly injured.

Of course no one knew it at the time, but the incident foreshadowed the fate of the World Wrestling Federation–sponsored league, which folded in May following its debut season.

# FOR THE RECORD·Year by Year

## The Super Bowl

### Results

| Date | Winner (Share) | Loser (Share) | Score | Site (Attendance) |
|------|----------------|---------------|-------|-------------------|
| I ..............1-15-67 | Green Bay ($15,000) | Kansas City ($7,500) | 35–10 | Los Angeles (61,946) |
| II ..............1-14-68 | Green Bay ($15,000) | Oakland ($7,500) | 33–14 | Miami (75,546) |
| III ..........1-12-69 | NY Jets ($15,000) | Baltimore ($7,500) | 16–7 | Miami (75,389) |
| IV ............1-11-70 | Kansas City ($15,000) | Minnesota ($7,500) | 23–7 | New Orleans (80,562) |
| V ..............1-17-71 | Baltimore ($15,000) | Dallas ($7,500) | 16–13 | Miami (79,204) |
| VI ............1-16-72 | Dallas ($15,000) | Miami ($7,500) | 24–3 | New Orleans (81,023) |
| VII ..........1-14-73 | Miami ($15,000) | Washington ($7,500) | 14–7 | Los Angeles (90,182) |
| VIII ..........1-13-74 | Miami ($15,000) | Minnesota ($7,500) | 24–7 | Houston (71,882) |
| IX ............1-12-75 | Pittsburgh ($15,000) | Minnesota ($7,500) | 16–6 | New Orleans (80,997) |
| X ..............1-18-76 | Pittsburgh ($15,000) | Dallas ($7,500) | 21–17 | Miami (80,187) |
| XI ............1-9-77 | Oakland ($15,000) | Minnesota ($7,500) | 32–14 | Pasadena (103,438) |
| XII ............1-15-78 | Dallas ($18,000) | Denver ($9,000) | 27–10 | New Orleans (75,583) |
| XIII ..........1-21-79 | Pittsburgh ($18,000) | Dallas ($9,000) | 35–31 | Miami (79,484) |
| XIV ............1-20-80 | Pittsburgh ($18,000) | Los Angeles ($9,000) | 31–19 | Pasadena (103,985) |
| XV ............1-25-81 | Oakland ($18,000) | Philadelphia ($9,000) | 27–10 | New Orleans (76,135) |
| XVI ..........1-24-82 | San Francisco ($18,000) | Cincinnati ($9,000) | 26–21 | Pontiac, MI (81,270) |
| XVII ..........1-30-83 | Washington ($36,000) | Miami ($18,000) | 27–17 | Pasadena (103,667) |
| XVIII ..........1-22-84 | LA Raiders ($36,000) | Washington ($18,000) | 38–9 | Tampa (72,920) |
| XIX ............1-20-85 | San Francisco ($36,000) | Miami ($18,000) | 38–16 | Stanford (84,059) |
| XX ............1-26-86 | Chicago ($36,000) | New England ($18,000) | 46–10 | New Orleans (73,818) |
| XXI ............1-25-87 | NY Giants ($36,000) | Denver ($18,000) | 39–20 | Pasadena (101,063) |
| XXII ............1-31-88 | Washington ($36,000) | Denver ($18,000) | 42–10 | San Diego (73,302) |
| XXIII ..........1-22-89 | San Francisco ($36,000) | Cincinnati ($18,000) | 20–16 | Miami (75,129) |
| XXIV ..........1-28-90 | San Francisco ($36,000) | Denver ($18,000) | 55–10 | New Orleans (72,919) |
| XXV ............1-27-91 | NY Giants ($36,000) | Buffalo ($18,000) | 20–19 | Tampa (73,813) |
| XXVI ..........1-26-92 | Washington ($36,000) | Buffalo ($18,000) | 37–24 | Minneapolis (63,130) |
| XXVII ..........1-31-93 | Dallas ($36,000) | Buffalo ($18,000) | 52–17 | Pasadena (98,374) |
| XXVIII ..........1-30-94 | Dallas ($38,000) | Buffalo ($23,500) | 30–13 | Atlanta (72,817) |
| XXIX ..........1-29-95 | San Francisco ($42,000) | San Diego ($26,000) | 49–26 | Miami (74,107) |
| XXX ............1-28-96 | Dallas ($42,000) | Pittsburgh ($27,000) | 27–17 | Tempe, AZ (76,347) |
| XXXI ............1-26-97 | Green Bay ($48,000) | New England ($29,000) | 35–21 | New Orleans (72,301) |
| XXXII ..........1-25-98 | Denver ($48,000) | Green Bay ($27,500) | 31–24 | San Diego (68,912) |
| XXXIII ..........1-31-99 | Denver ($53,000) | Atlanta ($32,500) | 34–19 | Miami (74,803) |
| XXXIV ..........1-30-00 | St. Louis ($58,000) | Tennessee ($33,000) | 23–16 | Atlanta (72,625) |
| XXXV ..........1-28-01 | Baltimore ($58,000) | NY Giants ($34,500) | 34–7 | Tampa (71,921) |

### Most Valuable Players

| Super Bowl | Player/ Team | Position | Super Bowl | Player/ Team | Position |
|------------|--------------|----------|------------|--------------|----------|
| I .........................Bart Starr, GB | | QB | XIX.....................Joe Montana, SF | | QB |
| II .........................Bart Starr, GB | | QB | XX.....................Richard Dent, Chi | | DE |
| III .........................Joe Namath, NYJ | | QB | XXI.....................Phil Simms, NYG | | QB |
| IV.....................Len Dawson, KC | | QB | XXII.....................Doug Williams, Wash | | QB |
| V.....................Chuck Howley, Dall | | LB | XXIII.....................Jerry Rice, SF | | WR |
| VI.....................Roger Staubach, Dall | | QB | XXIV.....................Joe Montana, SF | | QB |
| VII.....................Jake Scott, Mia | | S | XXV .....................Ottis Anderson, NYG | | RB |
| VIII.....................Larry Csonka, Mia | | RB | XXVI .....................Mark Rypien, Wash | | QB |
| IX.....................Franco Harris, Pitt | | RB | XXVII.....................Troy Aikman, Dall | | QB |
| X.....................Lynn Swann, Pitt | | WR | XXVIII .....................Emmitt Smith, Dall | | RB |
| XI.....................Fred Biletnikoff, Oak | | WR | XXIX .....................Steve Young, SF | | QB |
| XII.....................Randy White, Dall | | DT | XXX .....................Larry Brown, Dall | | DB |
| | Harvey Martin, Dall | DE | XXXI .....................Desmond Howard, GB | | KR |
| XIII.....................Terry Bradshaw, Pitt | | QB | XXXII .....................Terrell Davis, Den | | RB |
| XIV.....................Terry Bradshaw, Pitt | | QB | XXXIII .....................John Elway, Den | | QB |
| XV.....................Jim Plunkett, Oak | | QB | XXXIV .....................Kurt Warner, StL | | QB |
| XVI.....................Joe Montana, SF | | QB | XXXV .....................Ray Lewis, Balt | | LB |
| XVII.....................John Riggins, Wash | | RB | | | |
| XVIII.....................Marcus Allen, Rai | | RB | | | |

## Composite Standings

| | W | L | Pct | Pts | Opp Pts |
|---|---|---|---|---|---|
| San Francisco 49ers | 5 | 0 | 1.000 | 188 | 89 |
| Baltimore Ravens | 1 | 0 | 1.000 | 34 | 7 |
| Chicago Bears | 1 | 0 | 1.000 | 46 | 10 |
| New York Jets | 1 | 0 | 1.000 | 16 | 7 |
| Pittsburgh Steelers | 4 | 1 | .800 | 120 | 100 |
| Green Bay Packers | 3 | 1 | .750 | 127 | 76 |
| Oakland/LA Raiders | 3 | 1 | .750 | 111 | 66 |
| New York Giants | 2 | 1 | .667 | 66 | 73 |
| Dallas Cowboys | 5 | 3 | .625 | 221 | 132 |
| Washington Redskins | 3 | 2 | .600 | 122 | 103 |
| Baltimore Colts | 1 | 1 | .500 | 23 | 29 |
| Kansas City Chiefs | 1 | 1 | .500 | 33 | 42 |
| Los Angeles/St. Louis Rams | 1 | 1 | .500 | 42 | 47 |
| Miami Dolphins | 2 | 3 | .400 | 74 | 103 |
| Denver Broncos | 2 | 4 | .333 | 115 | 206 |
| Philadelphia Eagles | 0 | 1 | .000 | 10 | 27 |
| San Diego Chargers | 0 | 1 | .000 | 26 | 49 |
| Atlanta Falcons | 0 | 1 | .000 | 19 | 34 |
| Tennesse Titans | 0 | 1 | .000 | 16 | 23 |
| Cincinnati Bengals | 0 | 2 | .000 | 37 | 46 |
| New England Patriots | 0 | 2 | .000 | 31 | 81 |
| Buffalo Bills | 0 | 4 | .000 | 73 | 139 |
| Minnesota Vikings | 0 | 4 | .000 | 34 | 95 |

## Career Leaders

### Passing

| | GP | Att | Comp | Pct Comp | Yds | Avg Gain | TD | Pct TD | Int | Pct Int | Lg | Rating Pts |
|---|---|---|---|---|---|---|---|---|---|---|---|---|
| Joe Montana, SF | 4 | 122 | 83 | 68.0 | 1142 | 9.36 | 11 | 9.0 | 0 | 0.0 | 44 | 127.8 |
| Jim Plunkett, Rai | 2 | 46 | 29 | 63.0 | 433 | 9.41 | 4 | 8.7 | 0 | 0.0 | t80 | 122.8 |
| Terry Bradshaw, Pitt | 4 | 84 | 49 | 58.3 | 932 | 11.10 | 9 | 10.7 | 4 | 4.8 | t75 | 112.8 |
| Troy Aikman, Dall | 3 | 80 | 56 | 70.0 | 689 | 8.61 | 5 | 6.3 | 1 | 1.3 | t56 | 111.9 |
| Bart Starr, GB | 2 | 47 | 29 | 61.7 | 452 | 9.62 | 3 | 6.4 | 1 | 2.1 | t62 | 106.0 |
| Kurt Warner, StL | 1 | 45 | 24 | 53.3 | 414 | 9.20 | 2 | 4.4 | 0 | 0.0 | t73 | 99.6 |
| Brett Favre, GB | 2 | 69 | 39 | 56.5 | 502 | 7.28 | 5 | 7.2 | 1 | 1.4 | t81 | 97.7 |
| Roger Staubach, Dall | 4 | 98 | 61 | 62.2 | 734 | 7.49 | 8 | 8.2 | 4 | 4.1 | t45 | 95.4 |
| Len Dawson, KC | 2 | 44 | 28 | 63.6 | 353 | 8.02 | 2 | 4.5 | 2 | 4.5 | t46 | 84.8 |
| Bob Griese, Mia | 3 | 41 | 26 | 63.4 | 295 | 7.20 | 1 | 2.4 | 2 | 4.9 | t28 | 72.7 |

Note: Minimum 40 attempts.

### Rushing

| | GP | Yds | Att | Avg | Lg | TD |
|---|---|---|---|---|---|---|
| Franco Harris, Pitt | 4 | 354 | 101 | 3.5 | 25 | 4 |
| Larry Csonka, Mia | 3 | 297 | 57 | 5.2 | 9 | 2 |
| Emmitt Smith, Dall | 3 | 289 | 70 | 4.1 | 38 | 5 |
| Terrell Davis, Den | 2 | 259 | 75 | 4.1 | 15 | 3 |
| John Riggins, Wash | 2 | 230 | 64 | 3.6 | 43 | 2 |
| Timmy Smith, Wash | 1 | 204 | 22 | 9.3 | 58 | 2 |
| Thurman Thomas, Buff | 4 | 204 | 52 | 3.9 | 31 | 4 |
| Roger Craig, SF | 3 | 198 | 52 | 3.8 | 18 | 2 |
| Marcus Allen, Rai | 1 | 191 | 20 | 9.6 | t74 | 2 |
| Tony Dorsett, Dall | 2 | 162 | 31 | 5.2 | 29 | 1 |

### Receiving

| | GP | No. | Yds | Avg | Lg | TD |
|---|---|---|---|---|---|---|
| Jerry Rice, SF | 3 | 28 | 512 | 18.3 | 144 | 7 |
| Andre Reed, Buff | 4 | 27 | 323 | 11.9 | 40 | 0 |
| Roger Craig, SF | 3 | 20 | 212 | 10.6 | 40 | 2 |
| Thurman Thomas, Buff | 4 | 20 | 144 | 7.2 | 24 | 0 |
| Jay Novacek, Dall | 3 | 17 | 178 | 10.5 | 23 | 2 |
| Lynn Swann, Pitt | 4 | 16 | 364 | 22.8 | t64 | 3 |
| Michael Irvin, Dall | 3 | 16 | 256 | 16.0 | 25 | 2 |
| Chuck Foreman, Minn | 3 | 15 | 139 | 9.3 | 26 | 0 |
| Cliff Branch, Rai | 3 | 14 | 181 | 12.9 | 50 | 3 |
| Preston Pearson, Balt-Pitt-Dall | 5 | 12 | 105 | 8.8 | 14 | 0 |
| Don Beebe, Buff-GB | 5 | 12 | 171 | 14.3 | 43 | 2 |
| Kenneth Davis, Buff | 4 | 12 | 72 | 6.0 | 19 | 0 |
| Antonio Freeman, GB | 2 | 12 | 231 | 19.3 | t81 | 3 |

## Single-Game Leaders

### Scoring

| | Pts |
|---|---|
| Roger Craig: XIX, San Francisco vs Miami (1 R, 2 P) | 18 |
| Jerry Rice: XXIV, San Francisco vs Denver (3 P); XXIX, SF vs San Diego (3 P) | 18 |
| Ricky Watters: XXIX, San Francisco vs San Diego (1 R, 2 P) | 18 |
| Terrell Davis: XXXII, Denver vs Green Bay (3 R) | 18 |

### Rushing Yards

| | Yds |
|---|---|
| Timmy Smith: XXII, Washington vs Denver | 204 |
| Marcus Allen: XVIII, LA Raiders vs Washington | 191 |
| John Riggins: XVII, Washington vs Miami | 166 |
| Franco Harris: IX, Pittsburgh vs Minnesota | 158 |
| Terrell Davis: XXXII, Denver vs Green Bay | 157 |
| Larry Csonka: VIII, Miami vs Minnesota | 145 |
| Clarence Davis: XI, Oakland vs Minnesota | 137 |
| Thurman Thomas: XXV, Buffalo vs NY Giants | 135 |
| Emmitt Smith: XXVIII, Dallas vs Buffalo | 132 |
| Matt Snell: III, New York Jets vs Baltimore Colts | 121 |

### Receptions

| | No. |
|---|---|
| Dan Ross: XVI, Cincinnati vs San Francisco | 11 |
| Jerry Rice: XXIII, San Francisco vs Cincinnati | 11 |
| Tony Nathan: XIX, Miami vs San Francisco | 10 |
| Jerry Rice: XXIX, San Francisco vs San Diego | 10 |
| Andre Hastings: XXX, Pittsburgh vs Dallas | 10 |
| Ricky Sanders: XXII, Washington vs Denver | 9 |
| Antonio Freeman: XXXII, Green Bay vs Denver | 9 |
| Six tied with eight. | |

### Touchdown Passes

| | No. |
|---|---|
| Steve Young: XXIX, San Francisco vs San Diego | 6 |
| Joe Montana: XXIV, San Francisco vs Denver | 5 |
| Terry Bradshaw: XIII, Pittsburgh vs Dallas | 4 |
| Doug Williams: XXII, Washington vs Denver | 4 |
| Troy Aikman: XXVII, Dallas vs Buffalo | 4 |
| Five tied with three. | |

### Passing Yards

| | Yds |
|---|---|
| Kurt Warner: XXXIV, St. Louis vs Tennessee | 414 |
| Joe Montana: XXIII, San Francisco vs Cincinnati | 357 |
| Doug Williams: XXII, Washington vs Denver | 340 |
| John Elway: XXXIII, Denver vs Atlanta | 336 |
| Joe Montana: XIX, San Francisco vs Miami | 331 |
| Steve Young: XXIX, San Francisco vs San Diego | 325 |
| Terry Bradshaw: XIII, Pittsburgh vs Dallas | 318 |
| Dan Marino: XIX, Miami vs San Francisco | 318 |
| Terry Bradshaw: XIV, Pittsburgh vs LA Rams | 309 |

### Receiving Yards

| | Yds |
|---|---|
| Jerry Rice: XXIII, San Francisco vs Cincinnati | 215 |
| Ricky Sanders: XXII, Washington vs Denver | 193 |
| Isaac Bruce: XXXIV, St. Louis vs Tennessee | 162 |
| Lynn Swann: X, Pittsburgh vs Dallas | 161 |
| Andre Reed: XXVII, Buffalo vs Dallas | 152 |
| Rod Smith: XXXIII, Denver vs Atlanta | 152 |
| Jerry Rice: XXIX, San Francisco vs San Diego | 149 |
| Jerry Rice: XXIV, San Francisco vs Denver | 148 |
| Max McGee: I, Green Bay vs Kansas City | 138 |

# NFL Playoff History

**1933**
NFL championship  Chicago Bears 23, NY Giants 21

**1934**
NFL championship  NY Giants 30, Chicago Bears 13

**1935**
NFL championship  Detroit 26, NY Giants 7

**1936**
NFL championship  Green Bay 21, Boston 6

**1937**
NFL championship  Washington 28, Chicago Bears 21

**1938**
NFL championship  NY Giants 23, Green Bay 17

**1939**
NFL championship  Green Bay 27, NY Giants 0

**1940**
NFL championship  Chicago Bears 73, Washington 0

**1941**
W. div. playoff  Chicago Bears 33, Green Bay 14
NFL championship  Chicago Bears 37, NY Giants 9

**1942**
NFL championship  Washington 14, Chicago Bears 6

**1943**
E. div. playoff  Washington 28, NY Giants 0
NFL championship  Chicago Bears 41, Washington 21

**1944**
NFL championship  Green Bay 14, NY Giants 7

**1945**
NFL championship  Cleveland 15, Washington 14

**1946**
NFL championship  Chicago Bears 24, NY Giants 14

**1947**
E. div. playoff  Philadelphia 21, Pittsburgh 0
NFL championship  Chi Cardinals 28, Philadelphia 21

**1948**
NFL championship  Philadelphia 7, Chi Cardinals 0

**1949**
NFL championship  Philadelphia 14, Los Angeles 0

**1950**
Am. Conf. playoff  Cleveland 8, NY Giants 3
Nat. Conf. playoff  Los Angeles 24, Chicago Bears 14
NFL championship  Cleveland 30, Los Angeles 28

**1951**
NFL championship  Los Angeles 24, Cleveland 17

### 1952

| | |
|---|---|
| Nat. Conf. playoff | Detroit 31, Los Angeles 21 |
| NFL championship | Detroit 17, Cleveland 7 |

### 1953

| | |
|---|---|
| NFL championship | Detroit 17, Cleveland 16 |

### 1954

| | |
|---|---|
| NFL championship | Cleveland 56, Detroit 10 |

### 1955

| | |
|---|---|
| NFL championship | Cleveland 38, Los Angeles 14 |

### 1956

| | |
|---|---|
| NFL championship | NY Giants 47, Chicago Bears 7 |

### 1957

| | |
|---|---|
| W. Conf. playoff | Detroit 31, San Francisco 27 |
| NFL championship | Detroit 59, Cleveland 14 |

### 1958

| | |
|---|---|
| E. Conf. playoff | NY Giants 10, Cleveland 0 |
| NFL championship | Baltimore 23, NY Giants 17 |

### 1959

| | |
|---|---|
| NFL championship | Baltimore 31, NY Giants 16 |

### 1960

| | |
|---|---|
| NFL championship | Philadelphia 17, Green Bay 13 |
| AFL championship | Houston 24, LA Chargers 16 |

### 1961

| | |
|---|---|
| NFL championship | Green Bay 37, NY Giants 0 |
| AFL championship | Houston 10, San Diego 3 |

### 1962

| | |
|---|---|
| NFL championship | Green Bay 16, NY Giants 7 |
| AFL championship | Dallas Texans 20, Houston 17 |

### 1963

| | |
|---|---|
| NFL championship | Chicago 14, NY Giants 10 |
| AFL E. div. playoff | Boston 26, Buffalo 8 |
| AFL championship | San Diego 51, Boston 10 |

### 1964

| | |
|---|---|
| NFL championship | Cleveland 27, Baltimore 0 |
| AFL championship | Buffalo 20, San Diego 7 |

### 1965

| | |
|---|---|
| NFL W. Conf. playoff | Green Bay 13, Baltimore 10 |
| NFL championship | Green Bay 23, Cleveland 12 |
| AFL championship | Buffalo 23, San Diego 0 |

### 1966

| | |
|---|---|
| NFL championship | Green Bay 34, Dallas 27 |
| AFL championship | Kansas City 31, Buffalo 7 |

### 1967

| | |
|---|---|
| NFL E. Conf. championship | Dallas 52, Cleveland 14 |
| NFL W. Conf. championship | Green Bay 28, Los Angeles 7 |
| NFL championship | Green Bay 21, Dallas 17 |
| AFL championship | Oakland 40, Houston 7 |

### 1968

| | |
|---|---|
| NFL E. Conf. championship | Cleveland 31, Dallas 20 |
| NFL W. Conf. championship | Baltimore 24, Minnesota 14 |
| NFL championship | Baltimore 34, Cleveland 0 |

### 1968 *(Cont.)*

| | |
|---|---|
| AFL W. div. playoff | Oakland 41, Kansas City 6 |
| AFL championship | NY Jets 27, Oakland 23 |

### 1969

| | |
|---|---|
| NFL E. Conf. championship | Cleveland 38, Dallas 14 |
| NFL W. Conf. championship | Minnesota 23, Los Angeles 20 |
| NFL championship | Minnesota 27, Cleveland 7 |
| AFL div. playoffs | Kansas City 13, NY Jets 6 |
| | Oakland 56, Houston 7 |
| AFL championship | Kansas City 17, Oakland 7 |

### 1970

| | |
|---|---|
| AFC div. playoffs | Baltimore 17, Cincinnati 0 |
| | Oakland 21, Miami 14 |
| AFC championship | Baltimore 27, Oakland 17 |
| NFC div. playoffs | Dallas 5, Detroit 0 |
| | San Francisco 17, Minnesota 14 |
| NFC championship | Dallas 17, San Francisco 10 |

### 1971

| | |
|---|---|
| AFC div. playoffs | Miami 27, Kansas City 24 |
| | Baltimore 20, Cleveland 3 |
| AFC championship | Miami 21, Baltimore 0 |
| NFC div. playoffs | Dallas 20, Minnesota 12 |
| | San Francisco 24, Washington 20 |
| NFC championship | Dallas 14, San Francisco 3 |

### 1972

| | |
|---|---|
| AFC div. playoffs | Pittsburgh 13, Oakland 7 |
| | Miami 20, Cleveland 14 |
| AFC championship | Miami 21, Pittsburgh 17 |
| NFC div. playoffs | Dallas 30, San Francisco 28 |
| | Washington 16, Green Bay 3 |
| NFC championship | Washington 26, Dallas 3 |

### 1973

| | |
|---|---|
| AFC div. playoffs | Oakland 33, Pittsburgh 14 |
| | Miami 34, Cincinnati 16 |
| AFC championship | Miami 27, Oakland 10 |
| NFC div. playoffs | Minnesota 27, Washington 20 |
| | Dallas 27, Los Angeles 16 |
| NFC championship | Minnesota 27, Dallas 10 |

### 1974

| | |
|---|---|
| AFC div. playoffs | Oakland 28, Miami 26 |
| | Pittsburgh 32, Buffalo 14 |
| AFC championship | Pittsburgh 24, Oakland 13 |
| NFC div. playoffs | Minnesota 30, St Louis 14 |
| | Los Angeles 19, Washington 10 |
| NFC championship | Minnesota 14, Los Angeles 10 |

### 1975

| | |
|---|---|
| AFC div. playoffs | Pittsburgh 28, Baltimore 10 |
| | Oakland 31, Cincinnati 28 |
| AFC championship | Pittsburgh 16, Oakland 10 |
| NFC div. playoffs | Los Angeles 35, St Louis 23 |
| | Dallas 17, Minnesota 14 |
| NFC championship | Dallas 37, Los Angeles 7 |

### 1976

| | |
|---|---|
| AFC div. playoffs | Oakland 24, New England 21 |
| | Pittsburgh 40, Baltimore 14 |
| AFC championship | Oakland 24, Pittsburgh 7 |
| NFC div. playoffs | Minnesota 35, Washington 20 |
| | Los Angeles 14, Dallas 12 |
| NFC championship | Minnesota 24, Los Angeles 13 |

### 1977

| | |
|---|---|
| AFC div. playoffs | Denver 34, Pittsburgh 21 |
| | Oakland 37, Baltimore 31 |
| AFC championship | Denver 20, Oakland 17 |
| NFC div. playoffs | Dallas 37, Chicago 7 |
| | Minnesota 14, Los Angeles 7 |
| NFC championship | Dallas 23, Minnesota 6 |

### 1978

| | |
|---|---|
| AFC 1st-rd. playoff | Houston 17, Miami 9 |
| AFC div. playoffs | Houston 31, New England 14 |
| | Pittsburgh 33, Denver 10 |
| AFC championship | Pittsburgh 34, Houston 5 |
| NFC 1st-rd. playoff | Atlanta 14, Philadelphia 13 |
| NFC div. playoffs | Dallas 27, Atlanta 20 |
| | Los Angeles 34, Minnesota 10 |
| NFC championship | Dallas 28, Los Angeles 0 |

### 1979

| | |
|---|---|
| AFC 1st-rd. playoff | Houston 13, Denver 7 |
| AFC div. playoffs | Houston 17, San Diego 14 |
| | Pittsburgh 34, Miami 14 |
| AFC championship | Pittsburgh 27, Houston 13 |
| NFC 1st-rd. playoff | Philadelphia 27, Chicago 17 |
| NFC div. playoffs | Tampa Bay 24, Philadelphia 17 |
| | Los Angeles 21, Dallas 19 |
| NFC championship | Los Angeles 9, Tampa Bay 0 |

### 1980

| | |
|---|---|
| AFC 1st-rd. playoff | Oakland 27, Houston 7 |
| AFC div. playoffs | San Diego 20, Buffalo 14 |
| | Oakland 14, Cleveland 12 |
| AFC championship | Oakland 34, San Diego 27 |
| NFC 1st-rd. playoff | Dallas 34, Los Angeles 13 |
| NFC div. playoffs | Philadelphia 31, Minnesota 16 |
| | Dallas 30, Atlanta 27 |
| NFC championship | Philadelphia 20, Dallas 7 |

### 1981

| | |
|---|---|
| AFC 1st-rd. playoff | Buffalo 31, NY Jets 27 |
| AFC div. playoffs | San Diego 41, Miami 38 |
| | Cincinnati 28, Buffalo 21 |
| AFC championship | Cincinnati 27, San Diego 7 |
| NFC 1st-rd. playoff | NY Giants 27, Philadelphia 21 |
| NFC div. playoffs | Dallas 38, Tampa Bay 0 |
| | San Francisco 38, NY Giants 24 |
| NFC championship | San Francisco 28, Dallas 27 |

### 1982

| | |
|---|---|
| AFC 1st-rd. playoffs | Miami 28, New England 13 |
| | LA Raiders 27, Cleveland 10 |
| | NY Jets 44, Cincinnati 17 |
| | San Diego 31, Pittsburgh 28 |
| AFC div. playoffs | NY Jets 17, LA Raiders 14 |
| | Miami 34, San Diego 13 |
| AFC championship | Miami 14, NY Jets 0 |
| NFC 1st-rd. playoffs | Washington 31, Detroit 7 |
| | Green Bay 41, St Louis 16 |
| | Minnesota 30, Atlanta 24 |
| | Dallas 30, Tampa Bay 17 |
| NFC div. playoffs | Washington 21, Minnesota 7 |
| | Dallas 37, Green Bay 26 |
| NFC championship | Washington 31, Dallas 17 |

### 1983

| | |
|---|---|
| AFC 1st-rd. playoff | Seattle 31, Denver 7 |
| AFC div. playoffs | Seattle 27, Miami 20 |
| | LA Raiders 38, Pittsburgh 10 |
| AFC championship | LA Raiders 30, Seattle 14 |
| NFC 1st-rd. playoff | LA Rams 24, Dallas 17 |

### 1983 *(Cont.)*

| | |
|---|---|
| NFC div. playoffs | San Francisco 24, Detroit 23 |
| | Washington 51, LA Rams 7 |
| NFC championship | Washington 24, San Francisco 21 |

### 1984

| | |
|---|---|
| AFC 1st-rd. playoff | Seattle 13, LA Raiders 7 |
| AFC div. playoffs | Miami 31, Seattle 10 |
| | Pittsburgh 24, Denver 17 |
| AFC championship | Miami 45, Pittsburgh 28 |
| NFC 1st-rd. playoff | NY Giants 16, LA Rams 13 |
| NFC div. playoffs | San Francisco 21, NY Giants 10 |
| | Chicago 23, Washington 19 |
| NFC championship | San Francisco 23, Chicago 0 |

### 1985

| | |
|---|---|
| AFC 1st-rd. playoff | New England 26, NY Jets 14 |
| AFC div. playoffs | Miami 24, Cleveland 21 |
| | New England 27, LA Raiders 20 |
| AFC championship | New England 31, Miami 14 |
| NFC 1st-rd. playoff | NY Giants 17, San Francisco 3 |
| NFC div. playoffs | LA Rams 20, Dallas 0 |
| | Chicago 21, NY Giants 0 |
| NFC championship | Chicago 24, LA Rams 0 |

### 1986

| | |
|---|---|
| AFC 1st-rd. playoff | NY Jets 35, Kansas City 15 |
| AFC div. playoffs | Cleveland 23, NY Jets 20 |
| | Denver 22, New England 17 |
| AFC championship | Denver 23, Cleveland 20 |
| NFC 1st-rd. playoff | Washington 19, LA Rams 7 |
| NFC div playoffs | Washington 27, Chicago 13 |
| | NY Giants 49, San Francisco 3 |
| NFC championship | NY Giants 17, Washington 0 |

### 1987

| | |
|---|---|
| AFC 1st-rd. playoff | Houston 23, Seattle 20 |
| AFC div. playoffs | Cleveland 38, Indianapolis 21 |
| | Denver 34, Houston 10 |
| AFC championship | Denver 38, Cleveland 33 |
| NFC 1st-rd. playoff | Minnesota 44, New Orleans 10 |
| NFC div playoffs | Minnesota 36, San Francisco 24 |
| | Washington 21, Chicago 17 |
| NFC championship | Washington 17, Minnesota 10 |

### 1988

| | |
|---|---|
| AFC 1st-rd. playoff | Houston 24, Cleveland 23 |
| AFC div. playoffs | Cincinnati 21, Seattle 13 |
| | Buffalo 17, Houston 10 |
| AFC championship | Cincinnati 21, Buffalo 10 |
| NFC 1st-rd. playoff | Minnesota 28, LA Rams 17 |
| NFC div. playoffs | Chicago 20, Philadelphia 12 |
| | San Francisco 34, Minnesota 9 |
| NFC championship | San Francisco 28, Chicago 3 |

### 1989

| | |
|---|---|
| AFC 1st-rd. playoff | Pittsburgh 26, Houston 23 |
| AFC div. playoffs | Cleveland 34, Buffalo 30 |
| | Denver 24, Pittsburgh 23 |
| AFC championship | Denver 37, Cleveland 21 |
| NFC 1st-rd. playoff | LA Rams 21, Philadelphia 7 |
| NFC div. playoffs | LA Rams 19, NY Giants 13 |
| | San Francisco 41, Minnesota 13 |
| NFC championship | San Francisco 30, LA Rams 3 |

### 1990

| | |
|---|---|
| AFC 1st-rd. playoffs | Miami 17, Kansas City 16 |
| | Cincinnati 41, Houston 14 |
| AFC div. playoffs | Buffalo 44, Miami 34 |
| | LA Raiders 20, Cincinnati 10 |
| AFC championship | Buffalo 51, LA Raiders 3 |
| NFC 1st-rd. playoffs | Chicago 16, New Orleans 6 |

### 1990 (Cont.)

| | |
|---|---|
| NFC 1st-rd playoffs | Washington 20, Philadelphia 6 |
| NFC div. playoffs | NY Giants 31, Chicago 3 |
| | San Francisco 28, Washington 10 |
| NFC championship | NY Giants 15, San Francisco 13 |

### 1991

| | |
|---|---|
| AFC 1st-rd. playoffs | Houston 17, NY Jets 10 |
| | Kansas City 10, LA Raiders 6 |
| AFC div. playoffs | Denver 26, Houston 24 |
| | Buffalo 37, Kansas City 14 |
| AFC championship | Buffalo 10, Denver 7 |
| NFC 1st-rd. playoffs | Atlanta 27, New Orleans 20 |
| | Dallas 17, Chicago 13 |
| NFC div. playoffs | Washington 24, Atlanta 7 |
| | Detroit 38, Dallas 6 |
| NFC championship | Washington 41, Detroit 10 |

### 1992

| | |
|---|---|
| AFC 1st-rd. playoffs | San Diego 17, Kansas City 0 |
| | Buffalo 41, Houston 38 (OT) |
| AFC div. playoffs | Buffalo 24, Pittsburgh 3 |
| | Miami 31, San Diego 0 |
| AFC championship | Buffalo 29, Miami 10 |
| NFC 1st-rd. playoffs | Washington 24, Minnesota 7 |
| | Philadelphia 36, New Orleans 20 |
| NFC div. playoffs | San Francisco 20, Washington 13 |
| | Dallas 34, Philadelphia 10 |
| NFC championship | Dallas 30, San Francisco 20 |

### 1993

| | |
|---|---|
| AFC 1st-rd. playoffs | LA Raiders 42, Denver 24 |
| | Kansas City 27, Pittsburgh 24 (OT) |
| AFC div. playoffs | Buffalo 29, LA Raiders 23 |
| | Kansas City 28, Houston 20 |
| AFC championship | Buffalo 30, Kansas City 13 |
| NFC 1st-rd. playoffs | NY Giants 17, Minnesota 10 |
| | Green Bay 28, Detroit 24 |
| NFC div. playoffs | San Francisco 44, NY Giants 3 |
| | Dallas 27, Green Bay 17 |
| NFC championship | Dallas 38, San Francisco 21 |

### 1994

| | |
|---|---|
| AFC 1st-rd. playoffs | Miami 27, Kansas City 17 |
| | Cleveland 20, New England 13 |
| AFC div. playoffs | San Diego 22, Miami 21 |
| | Pittsburgh 29, Cleveland 9 |
| AFC championship | San Diego 17, Pittsburgh 13 |
| NFC 1st-rd. playoffs | Green Bay 16, Detroit 12 |
| | Chicago 35, Minnesota 18 |
| NFC div. playoffs | Dallas 35, Green Bay 9 |
| | San Francisco 44, Chicago 15 |
| NFC championship | San Francisco 38, Dallas 28 |

### 1995

| | |
|---|---|
| AFC 1st-rd. playoffs | Buffalo 37, Miami 22 |
| | Indianapolis 35, San Diego 20 |
| AFC div. playoffs | Pittsburgh 40, Buffalo 21 |
| | Indianapolis 10, Kansas City 7 |
| AFC championship | Pittsburgh 20, Indianapolis 16 |
| NFC 1st-rd. playoffs | Philadelphia 58, Detroit 37 |
| | Green Bay 37, Atlanta 20 |
| NFC div. playoffs | Dallas 30, Philadelphia 11 |
| | Green Bay 27, San Francisco 17 |
| NFC championship | Dallas 38, Green Bay 27 |

### 1996

| | |
|---|---|
| AFC 1st-rd. playoffs | Jacksonville 30, Buffalo 27 |
| | Pittsburgh 42, Indianapolis 14 |
| AFC div. playoffs | Jacksonville 30, Denver 27 |
| | New England 28, Pittsburgh 3 |
| AFC championship | New England 20, Jacksonville 6 |

### 1996 (Cont.)

| | |
|---|---|
| NFC 1st-rd. playoffs | Dallas 40, Minnesota 15 |
| | San Francisco 14, Philadelphia 0 |
| NFC div. playoffs | Green Bay 35, San Francisco 14 |
| | Carolina 26, Dallas 17 |
| NFC championship | Green Bay 30, Carolina 13 |

### 1997

| | |
|---|---|
| AFC 1st-rd. playoffs | Denver 42, Jacksonville 17 |
| | New England 17, Miami 3 |
| AFC div. playoffs | Denver 14, Kansas City 0 |
| | Pittsburgh 7, New England 6 |
| AFC championship | Denver 24, Pittsburgh 21 |
| NFC 1st-rd. playoffs | Minnesota 23, NY Giants 22 |
| | Tampa Bay 20, Detroit 10 |
| NFC div. playoffs | Green Bay 21, Tampa Bay 7 |
| | San Francisco 38, Minnesota 22 |
| NFC championship | Green Bay 23, San Francisco 10 |

### 1998

| | |
|---|---|
| AFC 1st-rd. playoffs | Miami 24, Buffalo 17 |
| | Jacksonville 25, New England 10 |
| AFC div. playoffs | Denver 38, Miami 3 |
| | NY Jets 34, Jacksonville 24 |
| AFC championship | Denver 23, NY Jets 10 |
| NFC 1st-rd. playoffs | Arizona 20, Dallas 7 |
| | San Francisco 30, Green Bay 27 |
| NFC div. playoffs | Atlanta 20, San Francisco 18 |
| | Minnesota 41, Arizona 21 |
| NFC championship | Atlanta 30, Minnesota 27 (ot) |

### 1999

| | |
|---|---|
| AFC 1st-rd. playoffs | Tennessee 22, Buffalo 16 |
| | Miami 20, Seattle 17 |
| AFC div. playoffs | Jacksonville 62, Miami 7 |
| | Tennessee 19, Indianapolis 16 |
| AFC championship | Tennessee 33, Jacksonville 14 |
| NFC 1st-rd. playoffs | Washington 27, Detroit 13 |
| | Minnesota 27, Dallas 10 |
| NFC div. playoffs | Tampa Bay 14, Washington 13 |
| | St Louis 49, Minnesota 37 |
| NFC championship | St Louis 11, Tampa Bay 6 |

### 2000

| | |
|---|---|
| AFC 1st-rd. playoffs | Baltimore 21, Denver 3 |
| | Miami 23, Indianapolis 17 (ot) |
| AFC div. playoffs | Baltimore 24, Tennessee 10 |
| | Oakland 27, Miami 0 |
| AFC championship | Baltimore 16, Oakland 3 |
| NFC 1st-rd. playoffs | New Orleans 31, St. Louis 28 |
| | Philadelphia 21, Tampa Bay 3 |
| NFC div. playoffs | NY Giants 20, Philadelphia 10 |
| | Minnesota 34, New Orleans 16 |
| NFC championship | NY Giants 41, Minnesota 0 |

## Career Leaders

### Scoring

| | Yrs | TD | FG | PAT | Pts |
|---|---|---|---|---|---|
| †Gary Anderson | 19 | 0 | 461 | 676 | 2059 |
| George Blanda | 26 | 9 | 335 | 943 | 2002 |
| †Morten Andersen | 19 | 0 | 441 | 615 | 1938 |
| Norm Johnson | 18 | 0 | 366 | 638 | 1736 |
| Nick Lowery | 18 | 0 | 383 | 562 | 1711 |
| Jan Stenerud | 19 | 0 | 373 | 580 | 1699 |
| †Eddie Murray | 19 | 0 | 352 | 539 | 1595 |
| †Al Del Greco | 17 | 0 | 347 | 543 | 1584 |
| Pat Leahy | 18 | 0 | 304 | 558 | 1470 |
| Jim Turner | 16 | 1 | 304 | 521 | 1439 |
| Matt Bahr | 17 | 0 | 300 | 522 | 1422 |
| Mark Moseley | 16 | 0 | 300 | 482 | 1382 |
| Jim Bakken | 17 | 0 | 282 | 534 | 1380 |
| Fred Cox | 15 | 0 | 282 | 519 | 1365 |
| Lou Groza | 17 | 1 | 234 | 641 | 1349 |
| Jim Breech | 14 | 0 | 243 | 517 | 1246 |
| †Pete Stoyanovich | 12 | 0 | 272 | 420 | 1236 |
| Chris Bahr | 14 | 0 | 241 | 490 | 1213 |
| Kevin Butler | 13 | 0 | 265 | 426 | 1208 |
| †Steve Christie | 11 | 0 | 272 | 358 | 1174 |

Cappelletti's total includes four two-point conversions.

### Rushing

| | Yrs | Att | Yds | Avg | Lg | TD |
|---|---|---|---|---|---|---|
| Walter Payton | 13 | 3,838 | 16,726 | 4.4 | 76 | 110 |
| Barry Sanders | 10 | 3,062 | 15,269 | 5.0 | 85 | 99 |
| †Emmitt Smith | 11 | 3,537 | 15,166 | 4.3 | 75 | 147 |
| Eric Dickerson | 11 | 2,996 | 13,259 | 4.4 | 85 | 90 |
| Tony Dorsett | 12 | 2,936 | 12,739 | 4.3 | 99 | 77 |
| Jim Brown | 9 | 2,359 | 12,312 | 5.2 | 80 | 106 |
| Marcus Allen | 16 | 3,022 | 12,243 | 4.1 | 61 | 123 |
| Franco Harris | 13 | 2,949 | 12,120 | 4.1 | 75 | 91 |
| †Thurman Thomas | 13 | 2,877 | 12,074 | 4.2 | 80 | 66 |
| John Riggins | 14 | 2,916 | 11,352 | 3.9 | 66 | 104 |
| O.J. Simpson | 11 | 2,404 | 11,236 | 4.7 | 94 | 61 |
| Ricky Watters | 9 | 2,550 | 10,325 | 4.1 | 57 | 77 |
| Ottis Anderson | 14 | 2,562 | 10,273 | 4.0 | 76 | 81 |
| †Jerome Bettis | 8 | 2,461 | 9,804 | 4.0 | t71 | 49 |
| Earl Campbell | 8 | 2,187 | 9,407 | 4.3 | 81 | 74 |
| Jim Taylor | 10 | 1,941 | 8,597 | 4.4 | 84 | 83 |
| Joe Perry | 14 | 1,737 | 8,378 | 4.8 | 78 | 53 |
| Earnest Byner | 14 | 2,095 | 8,261 | 3.9 | 54 | 56 |
| Herschel Walker | 12 | 1,954 | 8,225 | 4.2 | 91 | 61 |
| Roger Craig | 11 | 1,991 | 8,189 | 4.1 | 71 | 56 |

### Touchdowns

| | | Pass | Total | | | | Pass | Total |
|---|---|---|---|---|---|---|---|---|
| | Yrs | Rush | Rec | Ret | TD | | Yrs | Rush | Rec | Ret | TD |

| | Yrs | Rush | Rec | Ret | TD |
|---|---|---|---|---|---|
| †Jerry Rice | 16 | 10 | 176 | 1 | 187 |
| †Emmitt Smith | 11 | 145 | 11 | 0 | 156 |
| Marcus Allen | 16 | 123 | 21 | 1 | 145 |
| Jim Brown | 9 | 106 | 20 | 0 | 126 |
| Walter Payton | 13 | 110 | 15 | 0 | 125 |
| †Cris Carter | 14 | 0 | 123 | 1 | 124 |
| John Riggins | 14 | 104 | 12 | 0 | 116 |
| Lenny Moore | 12 | 63 | 48 | 2 | 113 |
| Barry Sanders | 10 | 99 | 10 | 0 | 109 |
| Don Hutson | 11 | 3 | 99 | 3 | 105 |

| | Yrs | Rush | Rec | Ret | TD |
|---|---|---|---|---|---|
| Steve Largent | 14 | 1 | 100 | 0 | 101 |
| Franco Harris | 13 | 91 | 9 | 0 | 100 |
| Eric Dickerson | 11 | 90 | 6 | 0 | 96 |
| Jim Taylor | 10 | 83 | 10 | 0 | 93 |
| Tony Dorsett | 12 | 77 | 13 | 1 | 91 |
| Bobby Mitchell | 11 | 18 | 65 | 8 | 91 |
| Leroy Kelly | 10 | 74 | 13 | 3 | 90 |
| Tim Brown | 13 | 1 | 86 | 3 | 90 |
| Charley Taylor | 13 | 11 | 79 | 0 | 90 |
| Ricky Watters | 9 | 77 | 13 | 0 | 90 |

### Combined Yards Gained

| | Yrs | Total | Rush | Rec | Int Ret | Punt Ret | Kickoff Ret | Fum Ret |
|---|---|---|---|---|---|---|---|---|
| Walter Payton | 13 | 21,803 | 16,726 | 4,538 | 0 | 0 | 539 | 0 |
| †Jerry Rice | 16 | 19,878 | 625 | 19,247 | 0 | 0 | 6 | 0 |
| †Brian Mitchell | 11 | 18,642 | 1,938 | 2,176 | 0 | 3,811 | 10,710 | 7 |
| Barry Sanders | 10 | 18,308 | 15,269 | 2,921 | 0 | 0 | 118 | 0 |
| Herschel Walker | 12 | 18,168 | 8,225 | 4,859 | 0 | 0 | 5,084 | 0 |
| †Emmitt Smith | 11 | 17,973 | 15,166 | 2,807 | 0 | 0 | 0 | 0 |
| Marcus Allen | 16 | 17,648 | 12,243 | 5,411 | 0 | 0 | 0 | -6 |
| Eric Metcalf | 11 | 16,727 | 2,385 | 5,553 | 0 | 3,042 | 5,747 | 0 |
| †Tim Brown | 13 | 16,548 | 132 | 12,072 | 0 | 3,106 | 1,235 | 3 |
| †Thurman Thomas | 13 | 16,532 | 12,074 | 4,458 | 0 | 0 | 0 | 0 |
| Tony Dorsett | 12 | 16,326 | 12,739 | 3,554 | 0 | 0 | 0 | 33 |
| Henry Ellard | 16 | 15,718 | 50 | 13,777 | 0 | 1,527 | 364 | 0 |
| †Irving Fryar | 17 | 15,594 | 242 | 12,785 | 0 | 2055 | 505 | 7 |
| Jim Brown | 9 | 15,459 | 12,312 | 2,499 | 0 | 0 | 648 | 0 |
| Eric Dickerson | 11 | 15,411 | 13,259 | 2,137 | 0 | 0 | 0 | 15 |
| James Brooks | 12 | 14,910 | 7,962 | 3,621 | 0 | 565 | 2,762 | 0 |
| Franco Harris | 13 | 14,622 | 12,120 | 2,287 | 0 | 0 | 233 | -18 |
| Ricky Watters | 9 | 14,499 | 10,325 | 4,141 | 0 | 0 | 0 | 33 |
| O.J. Simpson | 11 | 14,368 | 11,236 | 2,142 | 0 | 0 | 990 | 0 |
| James Lofton | 16 | 14,277 | 246 | 14,004 | 0 | 0 | 0 | 27 |

† Active in 2000.

## Career Leaders *(Cont.)*

### Passing

#### PASSING EFFICIENCY*

| | Yrs | Att | Comp | Pct Comp | Yds | Avg Gain | TD | Pct TD | Int | Pct Int | Rating Pts |
|---|---|---|---|---|---|---|---|---|---|---|---|
| Steve Young | 15 | 4,149 | 2,667 | 64.3 | 33,124 | 7.98 | 232 | 5.6 | 107 | 2.6 | 96.8 |
| Joe Montana | 15 | 5,391 | 3,409 | 63.2 | 40,551 | 7.52 | 273 | 5.1 | 139 | 2.6 | 92.3 |
| Dan Marino | 17 | 8,358 | 4,967 | 59.4 | 61,361 | 7.34 | 420 | 5.0 | 252 | 3.0 | 86.4 |
| †Brett Favre | 10 | 4,932 | 2,997 | 60.8 | 34,706 | 7.00 | 255 | 5.2 | 157 | 3.2 | 86.0 |
| †Peyton Manning | 3 | 1,679 | 1,014 | 60.4 | 12,287 | 7.32 | 85 | 5.1 | 58 | 3.5 | 85.4 |
| †Mark Brunell | 7 | 2,672 | 1,608 | 60.2 | 19,212 | 7.20 | 106 | 4.0 | 66 | 2.5 | 85.1 |
| †Brad Johnson | 7 | 1,820 | 1,125 | 61.8 | 12,973 | 7.13 | 79 | 4.3 | 57 | 3.1 | 84.7 |
| Jim Kelly | 11 | 4,779 | 2,874 | 60.1 | 35,467 | 7.42 | 237 | 5.0 | 175 | 3.7 | 84.4 |
| Roger Staubach | 11 | 2,958 | 1,685 | 57.0 | 22,700 | 7.67 | 153 | 5.2 | 109 | 3.7 | 83.4 |
| Neil Lomax | 8 | 3,153 | 1,817 | 57.6 | 22,771 | 7.22 | 136 | 4.3 | 90 | 2.9 | 82.7 |
| Sonny Jurgensen | 18 | 4,262 | 2,433 | 57.1 | 32,224 | 7.56 | 255 | 6.0 | 189 | 4.4 | 82.6 |
| Len Dawson | 19 | 3,741 | 2,136 | 57.1 | 28,711 | 7.67 | 239 | 6.4 | 183 | 4.9 | 82.6 |
| †Neil O'Donnell | 11 | 3,091 | 1,802 | 58.3 | 20,938 | 6.77 | 116 | 3.8 | 65 | 2.1 | 82.6 |
| †Troy Aikman | 12 | 4,715 | 2,898 | 61.5 | 32,942 | 6.99 | 171 | 3.6 | 141 | 3.0 | 82.0 |
| Ken Anderson | 16 | 4,475 | 2,654 | 59.3 | 32,838 | 7.34 | 197 | 4.4 | 160 | 3.6 | 81.9 |
| Bernie Kosar | 12 | 3,365 | 1,994 | 59.3 | 23,301 | 6.92 | 124 | 3.7 | 87 | 2.6 | 81.8 |
| Danny White | 13 | 2,950 | 1,761 | 59.7 | 21,959 | 7.44 | 155 | 5.3 | 132 | 4.5 | 81.7 |
| †Elvis Grbac | 8 | 1,978 | 1,181 | 59.7 | 13,741 | 6.95 | 84 | 4.2 | 63 | 3.2 | 81.7 |
| Dave Krieg | 19 | 5,311 | 3,105 | 58.5 | 38,147 | 7.18 | 261 | 4.9 | 199 | 3.7 | 81.5 |
| †Randall Cunningham | 15 | 4,200 | 2,375 | 56.6 | 29,406 | 7.00 | 204 | 4.9 | 132 | 3.1 | 81.5 |

*1,500 or more attempts. The passer ratings are based on performance standards established for completion percentage, interception percentage, touchdown percentage and average gain. Passers are allocated points according to how their marks compare with those standards.

#### YARDS

| | Yrs | Att | Comp | Pct Comp | Yds | | Yrs | Att | Comp | Pct Comp | Yds |
|---|---|---|---|---|---|---|---|---|---|---|---|
| Dan Marino | 17 | 8,358 | 4,967 | 59.4 | 61,361 | Jim Kelly | 11 | 4,779 | 2,874 | 60.1 | 35,467 |
| John Elway | 16 | 7,250 | 4,123 | 56.9 | 51,475 | Jim Everett | 12 | 4,923 | 2,841 | 57.7 | 34,837 |
| †Warren Moon | 17 | 6,823 | 3,988 | 58.5 | 49,325 | †Brett Favre | 10 | 4,932 | 2,997 | 60.8 | 34,706 |
| Fran Tarkenton | 18 | 6,467 | 3,686 | 57.0 | 47,003 | Jim Hart | 19 | 5,076 | 2,593 | 51.1 | 34,665 |
| Dan Fouts | 15 | 5,604 | 3,297 | 58.8 | 43,040 | Steve DeBerg | 17 | 4,746 | 2,924 | 61.6 | 34,241 |
| Joe Montana | 15 | 5,391 | 3,409 | 63.2 | 40,551 | John Hadl | 16 | 4,687 | 2,363 | 50.4 | 33,503 |
| Johnny Unitas | 18 | 5,186 | 2,830 | 54.6 | 40,239 | Phil Simms | 14 | 4,647 | 2,576 | 55.4 | 33,462 |
| Dave Krieg | 19 | 5,311 | 3,105 | 58.5 | 38,147 | Steve Young | 15 | 4,149 | 2,667 | 64.3 | 33,124 |
| Boomer Esiason | 14 | 5,205 | 2,969 | 57.0 | 37,920 | †Troy Aikman | 12 | 4,715 | 2,898 | 61.5 | 32,942 |
| †Vinny Testaverde | 14 | 5,208 | 2,897 | 55.6 | 36,307 | Ken Anderson | 16 | 4,475 | 2,654 | 59.3 | 32,838 |

#### TOUCHDOWNS

| | No. | | No. | | No. |
|---|---|---|---|---|---|
| Dan Marino | 420 | Boomer Esiason | 247 | Jim Hart | 209 |
| Fran Tarkenton | 342 | John Hadl | 244 | †Randall Cunningham | 204 |
| John Elway | 300 | Len Dawson | 239 | Jim Everett | 203 |
| †Warren Moon | 291 | Jim Kelly | 237 | Phil Simms | 199 |
| Johnny Unitas | 290 | George Blanda | 236 | Ken Anderson | 197 |
| Joe Montana | 273 | Steve Young | 232 | Joe Ferguson | 196 |
| Dave Krieg | 261 | †Vinny Testaverde | 226 | Bobby Layne | 196 |
| †Brett Favre | 255 | John Brodie | 214 | Norm Snead | 196 |
| Sonny Jurgensen | 255 | Terry Bradshaw | 212 | Steve DeBerg | 196 |
| Dan Fouts | 254 | Y.A. Tittle | 212 | Ken Stabler | 194 |

† Active in 2000.

## Career Leaders *(Cont.)*
### Receiving
#### RECEPTIONS

| | Yrs | No. | Yds | Avg | Lg | TD |
|---|---|---|---|---|---|---|
| †Jerry Rice | 16 | 1,281 | 19,247 | 15.0 | 96 | 176 |
| †Cris Carter | 14 | 1,020 | 12,962 | 12.7 | 80 | 123 |
| †Andre Reed | 16 | 951 | 13,198 | 13.9 | 83 | 87 |
| Art Monk | 16 | 940 | 12,721 | 13.5 | 79 | 68 |
| †Irving Fryar | 17 | 851 | 12,785 | 15.0 | 80 | 84 |
| †Tim Brown | 13 | 846 | 12,072 | 14.3 | 80 | 86 |
| Steve Largent | 14 | 819 | 13,089 | 16.0 | 74 | 100 |
| Henry Ellard | 16 | 814 | 13,777 | 16.9 | 81 | 65 |
| James Lofton | 16 | 764 | 14,004 | 18.3 | 80 | 75 |
| Michael Irvin | 12 | 750 | 11,904 | 15.9 | 87 | 65 |
| Charlie Joiner | 18 | 750 | 12,146 | 16.2 | 87 | 65 |
| †Andre Rison | 12 | 743 | 10,205 | 13.7 | 80 | 84 |
| Gary Clark | 11 | 699 | 10,856 | 15.5 | 84 | 65 |
| †Herman Moore | 10 | 666 | 9,098 | 13.7 | 93 | 62 |
| Ozzie Newsome | 13 | 662 | 7,980 | 12.1 | 74 | 47 |
| Charley Taylor | 13 | 649 | 9,110 | 14.0 | 88 | 79 |
| Drew Hill | 14 | 634 | 9,831 | 15.5 | 81 | 60 |
| Don Maynard | 15 | 633 | 11,834 | 18.7 | 87 | 88 |
| Raymond Berry | 13 | 631 | 9,275 | 14.7 | 70 | 68 |
| †Rob Moore | 10 | 628 | 9,368 | 14.9 | 71 | 49 |

#### YARDS

| | | | |
|---|---|---|---|
| †Jerry Rice | 19,247 | | |
| James Lofton | 14,004 | Art Monk | 12,721 |
| Henry Ellard | 13,777 | Charlie Joiner | 12,146 |
| †Andre Reed | 13,198 | †Tim Brown | 12,072 |
| Steve Largent | 13,089 | Michael Irvin | 11,904 |
| †Cris Carter | 12,962 | Don Maynard | 11,834 |
| †Irving Fryar | 12,785 | Gary Clark | 10,856 |
| | | Stanley Morgan | 10,716 |
| Harold Jackson | 10,372 | | |
| Lance Alworth | 10,266 | | |
| †Andre Rison | 10,205 | | |
| Drew Hill | 9,831 | | |
| †Rob Moore | 9,368 | | |
| Raymond Berry | 9,275 | | |

### Sacks

| | | | |
|---|---|---|---|
| †Reggie White | 198 | Chris Doleman | 150.5 |
| †Bruce Smith | 181.0 | Richard Dent | 137.5 |
| Kevin Greene | 160.0 | | |

Note: Officially compiled since 1982.

### Interceptions

| | Yrs | No. | Yds | Avg | Lg | TD |
|---|---|---|---|---|---|---|
| Paul Krause | 16 | 81 | 1185 | 14.6 | 81 | 3 |
| Emlen Tunnell | 14 | 79 | 1282 | 16.2 | 55 | 4 |
| Dick (Night Train) Lane | 14 | 68 | 1207 | 17.8 | 80 | 5 |
| Ken Riley | 15 | 65 | 596 | 9.2 | 66 | 5 |
| Ronnie Lott | 14 | 63 | 730 | 11.6 | 83 | 5 |

### Punting

| | Yrs | No. | Yds | Avg | Lg | Blk |
|---|---|---|---|---|---|---|
| Sammy Baugh | 16 | 338 | 15,245 | 45.1 | 85 | 9 |
| †Darren Bennett | 6 | 524 | 23,492 | 44.8 | 66 | 1 |
| Tommy Davis | 11 | 511 | 22,833 | 44.7 | 82 | 2 |
| Yale Lary | 11 | 503 | 22,279 | 44.3 | 74 | 4 |
| †Tom Tupa | 12 | 530 | 23,293 | 44.0 | 73 | 1 |

Note: 250 or more punts.

### Punt Returns

| | Yrs | No. | Yds | Avg | Lg | TD |
|---|---|---|---|---|---|---|
| George McAfee | 8 | 112 | 1431 | 12.8 | 74 | 2 |
| Jack Christiansen | 8 | 85 | 1084 | 12.8 | 89 | 8 |
| Claude Gibson | 5 | 110 | 1381 | 12.6 | 85 | 3 |
| †Az-Zahir Hakim | 3 | 76 | 951 | 12.5 | 86 | 2 |
| †Darrien Gordon | 6 | 219 | 2726 | 12.4 | 94 | 6 |
| †Desmond Howard | 9 | 213 | 2646 | 12.4 | 95 | 8 |

Note: 75 or more returns.

### Kickoff Returns

| | Yrs | No. | Yds | Avg | Lg | TD |
|---|---|---|---|---|---|---|
| Gale Sayers | 7 | 91 | 2781 | 30.6 | 103 | 6 |
| Lynn Chandnois | 7 | 92 | 2720 | 29.6 | 93 | 3 |
| Abe Woodson | 9 | 193 | 5538 | 28.7 | 105 | 5 |
| Claude (Buddy) Young | 6 | 90 | 2514 | 27.9 | 104 | 2 |
| Travis Williams | 5 | 102 | 2801 | 27.5 | 105 | 6 |

Note: 75 or more returns.

† Active in 2000.

## Single-Season Leaders
### Scoring

#### POINTS

| | Year | TD | PAT | FG | Pts |
|---|---|---|---|---|---|
| Paul Hornung, GB | 1960 | 15 | 41 | 15 | 176 |
| Gary Anderson, Minn | 1998 | 0 | 59 | 35 | 164 |
| Mark Moseley, Wash | 1983 | 0 | 62 | 33 | 161 |
| Marshall Faulk, StL | 2000 | 26 | 0 | 0 | 156 |
| Gino Cappelletti, Bos | 1964 | 7 | 38 | 25 | 155 |
| Emmitt Smith, Dall | 1995 | 25 | 0 | 0 | 150 |
| Chip Lohmiller, Wash | 1991 | 0 | 56 | 31 | 149 |
| Gino Cappelletti, Bos | 1961 | 8 | 48 | 17 | 147 |
| Paul Hornung, GB | 1961 | 10 | 41 | 15 | 146 |
| Jim Turner, NYJ | 1968 | 0 | 43 | 34 | 145 |
| John Kasay, Car | 1996 | 0 | 34 | 37 | 145 |
| Mike Vanderjagt | 1999 | 0 | 34 | 38 | 145 |
| John Riggins, Wash | 1983 | 24 | 0 | 0 | 144 |
| Kevin Butler, Chi | 1985 | 0 | 51 | 31 | 144 |
| Olindo Mare, Mia | 1999 | 0 | 27 | 39 | 144 |

Note: Cappelletti's 1964 total includes a two-point conversion.

#### TOUCHDOWNS

| | Year | Rush | Rec | Ret | Total |
|---|---|---|---|---|---|
| Marshall Faulk, StL | 2000 | 18 | 8 | 0 | 26 |
| Emmitt Smith, Dall | 1995 | 25 | 0 | 0 | 25 |
| John Riggins, Wash | 1983 | 24 | 0 | 0 | 24 |
| O.J. Simpson, Buff | 1975 | 16 | 7 | 0 | 23 |
| Jerry Rice, SF | 1987 | 1 | 22 | 0 | 23 |
| Terrell Davis, Den | 1998 | 21 | 2 | 0 | 23 |
| Gale Sayers, Chi | 1965 | 14 | 6 | 2 | 22 |
| Emmitt Smith, Dall | 1994 | 21 | 1 | 0 | 22 |

#### FIELD GOALS

| | Year | Att | No. |
|---|---|---|---|
| Olindo Mare, Mia | 1999 | 46 | 39 |
| John Kasay, Car | 1996 | 45 | 37 |
| Cary Blanchard, Ind | 1996 | 40 | 36 |
| Al Del Greco, Tenn | 1998 | 39 | 36 |
| Gary Anderson, Minn | 1998 | 35 | 35 |
| Jeff Jaeger, LA Raiders | 1993 | 44 | 35 |
| Ali Haji-Sheikh, NYG | 1983 | 42 | 35 |
| Matt Stover, Balt | 2000 | 39 | 35 |

Six tied with 34.

### Rushing

#### YARDS GAINED

| | Year | Att | Yds | Avg |
|---|---|---|---|---|
| Eric Dickerson, LA Rams | 1984 | 379 | 2105 | 5.6 |
| Barry Sanders, Det | 1997 | 335 | 2053 | 6.1 |
| Terrell Davis, Den | 1998 | 392 | 2008 | 5.1 |
| O.J. Simpson, Buff | 1973 | 332 | 2003 | 6.0 |
| Earl Campbell, Hou | 1980 | 373 | 1934 | 5.2 |
| Jim Brown, Clev | 1963 | 291 | 1883 | 6.4 |
| Barry Sanders, Det | 1994 | 331 | 1883 | 5.7 |
| Walter Payton, Chi | 1977 | 339 | 1852 | 5.5 |
| Jamal Anderson, Atl | 1998 | 410 | 1846 | 4.5 |
| Eric Dickerson, LA Rams | 1986 | 404 | 1821 | 4.5 |
| O.J. Simpson, Buff | 1975 | 329 | 1817 | 5.5 |
| Eric Dickerson, LA Rams | 1983 | 390 | 1808 | 4.6 |

#### AVERAGE GAIN

| | Year | Avg |
|---|---|---|
| Beattie Feathers, Chi | 1934 | 8.44 |
| Randall Cunningham, Phil | 1990 | 7.98 |
| Bobby Douglass, Chi | 1972 | 6.87 |

Minimum 100 attempts.

#### TOUCHDOWNS

| | Year | No. |
|---|---|---|
| Emmitt Smith, Dall | 1995 | 25 |
| John Riggins, Wash | 1983 | 24 |
| Emmitt Smith, Dall | 1994 | 21 |
| Joe Morris, NYG | 1985 | 21 |
| Terry Allen, Wash | 1996 | 21 |
| Terrell Davis, Den | 1998 | 21 |

### Passing

#### YARDS GAINED

| | Year | Att | Comp | Pct | Yds |
|---|---|---|---|---|---|
| Dan Marino, Mia | 1984 | 564 | 362 | 64.2 | 5084 |
| Dan Fouts, SD | 1981 | 609 | 360 | 59.1 | 4802 |
| Dan Marino, Mia | 1986 | 623 | 378 | 60.7 | 4746 |
| Dan Fouts, SD | 1980 | 589 | 348 | 59.1 | 4715 |
| Warren Moon, Hou | 1991 | 655 | 404 | 61.7 | 4690 |
| Warren Moon, Hou | 1990 | 584 | 362 | 62.0 | 4689 |
| Neil Lomax, StL Cards | 1984 | 560 | 345 | 61.6 | 4614 |
| Drew Bledsoe, NE | 1994 | 691 | 400 | 57.9 | 4555 |
| Lynn Dickey, GB | 1983 | 484 | 289 | 59.7 | 4458 |
| Dan Marino, Mia | 1994 | 615 | 385 | 62.6 | 4453 |

#### PASSER RATING

| | Year | Rat. |
|---|---|---|
| Steve Young, SF | 1994 | 112.8 |
| Joe Montana, SF | 1989 | 112.4 |
| Milt Plum, Clev | 1960 | 110.4 |
| Sammy Baugh, Wash | 1945 | 109.9 |
| Kurt Warner, Rams | 1999 | 109.2 |

#### TOUCHDOWNS

| | Year | No. |
|---|---|---|
| Dan Marino, Mia | 1984 | 48 |
| Dan Marino, Mia | 1986 | 44 |
| Kurt Warner, StL | 1999 | 41 |
| Brett Favre, GB | 1995 | 38 |

Three tied with 36.

## Single-Season Leaders *(Cont.)*
### Receiving

#### RECEPTIONS

| | Year | No. | Yds |
|---|---|---|---|
| Herman Moore, Det | 1995 | 123 | 1686 |
| Cris Carter, Minn | 1994 | 122 | 1256 |
| Jerry Rice, SF | 1995 | 122 | 1848 |
| Cris Carter, Minn | 1995 | 122 | 1371 |
| Isaac Bruce, Rams | 1995 | 119 | 1781 |
| Jimmy Smith, Jax | 1999 | 116 | 1636 |
| Marvin Harrison, Ind | 1999 | 115 | 1663 |
| Sterling Sharpe, GB | 1993 | 112 | 1274 |
| Jerry Rice, SF | 1994 | 112 | 1499 |
| Terance Mathis, Atl | 1994 | 111 | 1342 |
| Michael Irvin, Dall | 1995 | 111 | 1603 |

#### YARDS GAINED

| | Year | Yds |
|---|---|---|
| Jerry Rice, SF | 1995 | 1848 |
| Isaac Bruce, Rams | 1995 | 1781 |
| Charley Hennigan, Hou | 1961 | 1746 |
| Herman Moore, Det | 1995 | 1686 |
| Marvin Harrison, Ind | 1999 | 1663 |

#### TOUCHDOWNS

| | Year | No. |
|---|---|---|
| Jerry Rice, SF | 1987 | 22 |
| Mark Clayton, Mia | 1984 | 18 |
| Sterling Sharpe, GB | 1994 | 18 |
| Six tied with 17. | | |

#### All-Purpose Yards

| | Year | Run | Rec | Ret | Total |
|---|---|---|---|---|---|
| Lionel James, SD | 1985 | 516 | 1027 | 992 | 2535 |
| Terry Metcalf, StL Cards | 1975 | 816 | 378 | 1268 | 2462 |
| Mack Herron, NE | 1974 | 824 | 474 | 1146 | 2444 |
| Gale Sayers, Chi | 1966 | 1231 | 447 | 762 | 2440 |
| Marshall Faulk, Rams | 1999 | 1381 | 1048 | 0 | 2429 |
| Timmy Brown, Phil | 1963 | 841 | 487 | 1100 | 2428 |
| Barry Sanders, Det | 1997 | 2053 | 305 | 0 | 2358 |
| Tim Brown, Rai | 1988 | 50 | 725 | 1542 | 2317 |
| Marcus Allen, Rai | 1985 | 1759 | 555 | -6 | 2308 |
| Timmy Brown, Phil | 1962 | 545 | 849 | 912 | 2306 |
| Edgerrin James, Ind | 2000 | 1709 | 594 | 0 | 2303 |
| Gale Sayers, Chi | 1965 | 867 | 507 | 898 | 2272 |

#### Punting

| | Year | No. | Yds | Avg |
|---|---|---|---|---|
| Sammy Baugh, Wash | 1940 | 35 | 1799 | 51.4 |
| Yale Lary, Det | 1963 | 35 | 1713 | 48.9 |
| Sammy Baugh, Wash | 1941 | 30 | 1462 | 48.7 |
| Yale Lary, Det | 1961 | 52 | 2516 | 48.4 |
| Sammy Baugh, Wash | 1942 | 37 | 1783 | 48.2 |

#### Sacks

| | Year | No. |
|---|---|---|
| Mark Gastineau, NYJ | 1984 | 22 |
| Reggie White, Phil | 1987 | 21 |
| Chris Doleman, Minn | 1989 | 21 |
| Lawrence Taylor, NYG | 1986 | 20.5 |

#### Interceptions

| | Year | No. |
|---|---|---|
| Dick (Night Train) Lane, Rams | 1952 | 14 |
| Dan Sandifer, Wash | 1948 | 13 |
| Spec Sanders, NY Yanks | 1950 | 13 |
| Lester Hayes, Oak | 1980 | 13 |
| Nine tied with 12. | | |

#### Kickoff Returns

| | Year | Avg |
|---|---|---|
| Travis Williams, GB | 1967 | 41.1 |
| Gale Sayers, Chi | 1967 | 37.7 |
| Ollie Matson, Chi Cards | 1958 | 35.5 |
| Jim Duncan, Balt Colts | 1970 | 35.4 |
| Lynn Chandnois, Pitt | 1952 | 35.2 |

#### Punt Returns

| | Year | Avg |
|---|---|---|
| Herb Rich, Balt Colts | 1950 | 23.0 |
| Jack Christiansen, Det | 1952 | 21.5 |
| Dick Christy, NY Titans | 1961 | 21.3 |
| Bob Hayes, Dall | 1968 | 20.8 |

## Single-Game Leaders
### Scoring

#### POINTS

| | Date | Pts |
|---|---|---|
| Ernie Nevers, Chi Cards vs Chi | 11-28-29 | 40 |
| Dub Jones, Clev vs Chi | 11-25-51 | 36 |
| Gale Sayers, Chi vs SF | 12-12-65 | 36 |
| Paul Hornung, GB vs Balt Colts | 10-8-61 | 33 |

On Thanksgiving Day, 1929, Nevers scored all the Cardinals' points on six rushing TDs and four PATs. The Cards defeated Red Grange and the Bears, 40–6. Jones and Sayers each rushed for four touchdowns and scored two more on returns in their teams' victories. Hornung scored four touchdowns and kicked 6 PATs and a field goal in a 45-7 win over the Colts.

#### FIELD GOALS

| | Date | No. |
|---|---|---|
| Jim Bakken, StL Cards vs Pitt | 9-24-67 | 7 |
| Rich Karlis, Minn vs Rams | 11-5-89 | 7 |
| Chris Boniol, Dall vs GB | 11-18-96 | 7 |
| Fourteen players tied with 6 FGs each. | | |
| Bakken was 7 for 9, Karlis and Boniol 7 for 7. | | |

## Single-Game Leaders *(Cont.)*
### Scoring *(Cont.)*
#### TOUCHDOWNS

| | Date | No. |
|---|---|---|
| Ernie Nevers, Chi Cards vs Chi | 11-28-29 | 6 |
| Dub Jones, Clev vs Chi | 11-25-51 | 6 |
| Gale Sayers, Chi vs SF | 12-12-65 | 6 |
| Bob Shaw, Chi Cards vs Balt Colts | 10-2-50 | 5 |
| Jim Brown, Clev vs Balt Colts | 11-1-59 | 5 |
| Abner Haynes, Dall Texans vs Oak | 11-26-61 | 5 |
| Billy Cannon, Hou vs NY Titans | 12-10-61 | 5 |
| Cookie Gilchrist, Buff vs NYJ | 12-8-63 | 5 |
| Paul Hornung, GB vs Balt Colts | 12-12-65 | 5 |
| Kellen Winslow, SD vs Oak | 11-22-81 | 5 |
| Jerry Rice, SF vs Atl | 10-14-90 | 5 |
| James Stewart, Jax vs Phil | 10-12-97 | 5 |

## Rushing

### YARDS GAINED

| | Date | Yds |
|---|---|---|
| Corey Dillon, Cin vs Den | 10-22-00 | 278 |
| Walter Payton, Chi vs Minn | 11-20-77 | 275 |
| O.J. Simpson, Buff vs Det | 11-25-76 | 273 |
| Mike Anderson, Den vs NO | 12-3-00 | 251 |
| O.J. Simpson, Buff vs NE | 9-16-73 | 250 |

### CARRIES

| | Date | No. |
|---|---|---|
| Jamie Morris, Wash vs Cin | 12-17-88 | 45 |
| Butch Woolfolk, NYG vs Phil | 11-20-83 | 43 |
| James Wilder, TB vs GB | 9-30-84 | 43 |
| James Wilder, TB vs Pitt | 10-30-83 | 42 |
| Franco Harris, Pitt vs Cin | 10-17-76 | 41 |
| Gerald Riggs, Atl vs Rams | 11-17-85 | 41 |

### TOUCHDOWNS

| | Date | No. |
|---|---|---|
| Ernie Nevers, Chi Cards vs Chi | 11-28-29 | 6 |
| Jim Brown, Clev vs Balt Colts | 11-1-59 | 5 |
| Cookie Gilchrist, Buff vs NYJ | 12-8-63 | 5 |
| James Stewart, Jax vs Phil | 10-12-97 | 5 |

## Passing

### YARDS GAINED

| | Date | Yds |
|---|---|---|
| N. Van Brocklin, Rams vs NY Yanks | 9-28-51 | 554 |
| Warren Moon, Hou vs KC | 12-16-90 | 527 |
| Boomer Esiason, Ariz vs Wash | 11-10-96 | 522 |
| Dan Marino, Mia vs NYJ | 10-23-88 | 521 |
| Phil Simms, NYG vs Cin | 10-13-85 | 513 |

### COMPLETIONS

| | Date | No. |
|---|---|---|
| Drew Bledsoe, NE vs Minn | 11-13-94 | 45 |
| Richard Todd, NYJ vs SF | 9-21-80 | 42 |
| Vinny Testaverde, NYJ vs Sea | 12-6-98 | 42 |
| Warren Moon, Hou vs Dall | 11-10-91 | 41 |
| Ken Anderson, Cin vs SD | 12-20-82 | 40 |
| Phil Simms, NYG vs Cin | 10-13-85 | 40 |

### TOUCHDOWNS

| | Date | No. |
|---|---|---|
| Sid Luckman, Chi vs NYG | 11-14-43 | 7 |
| Adrian Burk, Phil vs Wash | 10-17-54 | 7 |
| George Blanda, Hou vs NY Titans | 11-19-61 | 7 |
| Y. A. Tittle, NYG vs Wash | 10-28-62 | 7 |
| Joe Kapp, Minn vs Balt Colts | 9-28-69 | 7 |

## Receiving

### YARDS GAINED

| | Date | Yds |
|---|---|---|
| Flipper Anderson, Rams vs NO | 11-26-89 | 336 |
| Stephone Paige, KC vs SD | 12-22-85 | 309 |
| Jim Benton, Clev vs Det | 11-22-45 | 303 |
| Cloyce Box, Det vs Balt Colts | 12-3-50 | 302 |
| Jimmy Smith, Jax vs Balt Ravens | 9-10-00 | 291 |

### RECEPTIONS

| | Date | No. |
|---|---|---|
| Terrell Owens, SF vs Chi | 12-17-00 | 20 |
| Tom Fears, Rams vs GB | 12-3-50 | 18 |
| Clark Gaines, NYJ vs SF | 9-21-80 | 17 |
| Sonny Randle, StL Cards vs NYG | 11-4-62 | 16 |
| Jerry Rice, SF vs Rams | 11-20-94 | 16 |
| Keenan McCardell, Jax vs Rams | 10-20-96 | 16 |

Five tied with 15.

## Single-Game Leaders *(Cont.)*

### Receiving *(Cont.)*

#### TOUCHDOWNS

|  | Date | No. |
|---|---|---|
| Bob Shaw, Chi Cards vs Balt Colts | 10-2-50 | 5 |
| Kellen Winslow, SD vs Oak | 11-22-81 | 5 |
| Jerry Rice, SF vs Atl | 10-14-90 | 5 |

### All-Purpose Yards

|  | Date | Yds |
|---|---|---|
| Glyn Milburn, Den vs Sea | 12-10-95 | 404 |
| Billy Cannon, Hou vs NY Titans | 12-10-61 | 373 |
| Tyrone Hughes, NO vs LA Rams | 10-23-94 | 347 |
| Lionel James, SD vs LA Rai | 11-10-85 | 345 |
| Timmy Brown, Phil vs StL Cards | 12-16-62 | 341 |

## Longest Plays

| RUSHING | Opponent | Year | Yds |
|---|---|---|---|
| Tony Dorsett, Dall | Minn | 1983 | 99 |
| Andy Uram, GB | Chi Cards | 1939 | 97 |
| Bob Gage, Pitt | Chi | 1949 | 97 |
| Jim Spitival, Balt Colts | GB | 1950 | 96 |
| Bob Hoernschemeyer, Det | NY Yanks | 1950 | 96 |
| Garrison Hearst, SF | NYJ | 1998 | 96 |

| PASSING | Opponent | Year | Yds |
|---|---|---|---|
| Frank Filchock to Andy Farkas, Wash | Pitt | 1939 | 99 |
| George Izo to Bobby Mitchell, Wash | Clev | 1963 | 99 |
| Karl Sweetan to Pat Studstill, Det | Balt Colts | 1966 | 99 |
| Sonny Jurgensen to Gerry Allen, Wash | Chi | 1968 | 99 |
| Jim Plunkett to Cliff Branch, LA Rai | Wash | 1983 | 99 |
| Ron Jaworski to Mike Quick, Phil | Atl | 1985 | 99 |
| Stan Humphries to Tony Martin, SD | Sea | 1994 | 99 |
| Brett Favre to Robert Brooks, GB | Chi | 1995 | 99 |

| FIELD GOALS | Opponent | Year | Yds |
|---|---|---|---|
| Tom Dempsey, NO | Det | 1970 | 63 |
| Jason Elam, Den | Jax | 1998 | 63 |
| Steve Cox, Clev | Cin | 1984 | 60 |
| Morten Andersen, NO | Chi | 1991 | 60 |

| PUNTS | Opponent | Year | Yds |
|---|---|---|---|
| Steve O'Neal, NYJ | Den | 1969 | 98 |
| Joe Lintzenich, Chi | NYG | 1931 | 94 |
| Shawn McCarthy, NE | Buff | 1991 | 93 |
| Randall Cunningham, Phil | NYG | 1989 | 91 |

| INTERCEPTION RETURNS | Opponent | Year | Yds |
|---|---|---|---|
| Vencie Glenn, SD | Den | 1987 | 103 |
| Louis Oliver, Mia | Buff | 1992 | 103 |
| Six players tied at 102. | | | |

| KICKOFF RETURNS | Opponent | Year | Yds |
|---|---|---|---|
| Al Carmichael, GB | Chi | 1956 | 106 |
| Noland Smith, KC | Den | 1967 | 106 |
| Roy Green, StL Cards | Dall | 1979 | 106 |

| PUNT RETURNS | Opponent | Year | Yds |
|---|---|---|---|
| Robert Bailey, LA Rams | NO | 1994 | 103 |
| Gil LeFebvre, Cin | Brooklyn | 1933 | 98 |
| Charlie West, Minn | Wash | 1968 | 98 |
| Dennis Morgan, Dall | StL Cards | 1974 | 98 |
| Terance Mathis, NYJ | Dall | 1990 | 98 |

### Five NFL Changes We'd Like to See

**More dancing**: Can the ban on end zone celebrations. Face it: Bob 'n' Weave hurts no one.

**More OT Thrills**: Institute college overtime rule. Teams, not a coin toss, should decide the winner of games.

**More cough-ups**: Let the ground cause a fumble! No play should be blown dead while ball goes bounding away from its carrier.

**More slack**: Give defender touchback when his momentum carries him into the end zone after he recovers a fumble. Lack of such a rule cost Oakland a victory against Seattle in December 2000.

**Less confusion**: Dump "pass was uncatchable" judgment calls on would-be interference plays. Don't we ask enough of refs without forcing them into this chicken or-egg paradox?

## Rushing

| Year | Player, Team | Att | Yards | Avg | TD |
|---|---|---|---|---|---|
| 1932 | Cliff Battles, Bos | 148 | 576 | 3.9 | 3 |
| 1933 | Jim Musick, Bos | 173 | 809 | 4.7 | 5 |
| 1934 | Beattie Feathers, Chi | 101 | 1004 | 9.9 | 8 |
| 1935 | Doug Russell, Chi Cards | 140 | 499 | 3.6 | 0 |
| 1936 | Alphonse Leemans, NY | 206 | 830 | 4.0 | 2 |
| 1937 | Cliff Battles, Wash | 216 | 874 | 4.0 | 5 |
| 1938 | Byron White, Pitt | 152 | 567 | 3.7 | 4 |
| 1939 | Bill Osmanski, Chi | 121 | 699 | 5.8 | 7 |
| 1940 | Byron White, Det | 146 | 514 | 3.5 | 5 |
| 1941 | Clarence Manders, Bklyn | 111 | 486 | 4.4 | 5 |
| 1942 | Bill Dudley, Pitt | 162 | 696 | 4.3 | 5 |
| 1943 | Bill Paschal, NY | 147 | 572 | 3.9 | 10 |
| 1944 | Bill Paschal, NY | 196 | 737 | 3.8 | 9 |
| 1945 | Steve Van Buren, Phil | 143 | 832 | 5.8 | 15 |
| 1946 | Bill Dudley, Pitt | 146 | 604 | 4.1 | 3 |
| 1947 | Steve Van Buren, Phil | 217 | 1008 | 4.6 | 13 |
| 1948 | Steve Van Buren, Phil | 201 | 945 | 4.7 | 10 |
| 1949 | Steve Van Buren, Phil | 263 | 1146 | 4.4 | 11 |
| 1950 | Marion Motley, Clev | 140 | 810 | 5.8 | 3 |
| 1951 | Eddie Price, NY | 271 | 971 | 3.6 | 7 |
| 1952 | Dan Towler, LA | 156 | 894 | 5.7 | 10 |
| 1953 | Joe Perry, SF | 192 | 1018 | 5.3 | 10 |
| 1954 | Joe Perry, SF | 173 | 1049 | 6.1 | 8 |
| 1955 | Alan Ameche, Balt | 213 | 961 | 4.5 | 9 |
| 1956 | Rick Casares, Chi | 234 | 1126 | 4.8 | 12 |
| 1957 | Jim Brown, Clev | 202 | 942 | 4.7 | 9 |
| 1958 | Jim Brown, Clev | 257 | 1527 | 5.9 | 17 |
| 1959 | Jim Brown, Clev | 290 | 1329 | 4.6 | 14 |
| 1960 | Jim Brown, Clev, NFL | 215 | 1257 | 5.8 | 9 |
| | Abner Haynes, Dall Texans, AFL | 156 | 875 | 5.6 | 9 |
| 1961 | Jim Brown, Clev, NFL | 305 | 1408 | 4.6 | 8 |
| | Billy Cannon, Hou, AFL | 200 | 948 | 4.7 | 6 |
| 1962 | Jim Taylor, GB, NFL | 272 | 1474 | 5.4 | 19 |
| | Cookie Gilchrist, Buff, AFL | 214 | 1096 | 5.1 | 13 |
| 1963 | Jim Brown, Clev, NFL | 291 | 1863 | 6.4 | 12 |
| | Clem Daniels, Oak, AFL | 215 | 1099 | 5.1 | 3 |
| 1964 | Jim Brown, Clev, NFL | 280 | 1446 | 5.2 | 7 |
| | Cookie Gilchrist, Buff, AFL | 230 | 981 | 4.3 | 6 |
| 1965 | Jim Brown, Clev, NFL | 289 | 1544 | 5.3 | 17 |
| | Paul Lowe, SD, AFL | 236 | 1121 | 5.0 | 7 |
| 1966 | Jim Nance, Bos, AFL | 299 | 1458 | 4.9 | 11 |
| | Gale Sayers, Chi, NFL | 229 | 1231 | 5.4 | 8 |
| 1967 | Jim Nance, Bos, AFL | 269 | 1216 | 4.5 | 7 |
| | Leroy Kelly, Clev, NFL | 235 | 1205 | 5.1 | 11 |
| 1968 | Leroy Kelly, Clev, NFL | 248 | 1239 | 5.0 | 16 |
| | Paul Robinson, Cin, AFL | 238 | 1023 | 4.3 | 8 |
| 1969 | Gale Sayers, Chi, NFL | 236 | 1032 | 4.4 | 8 |
| | Dickie Post, SD, AFL | 182 | 873 | 4.8 | 6 |
| 1970 | Larry Brown, Wash, NFC | 237 | 1125 | 4.7 | 5 |
| | Floyd Little, Den, AFC | 209 | 901 | 4.3 | 3 |
| 1971 | Floyd Little, Den, AFC | 284 | 1133 | 4.0 | 6 |
| | John Brockington, GB, NFC | 216 | 1105 | 5.1 | 4 |
| 1972 | O.J. Simpson, Buff, AFC | 292 | 1251 | 4.3 | 6 |
| | Larry Brown, Wash, NFC | 285 | 1216 | 4.3 | 8 |
| 1973 | O.J. Simpson, Buff, AFC | 332 | 2003 | 6.0 | 12 |
| | John Brockington, GB, NFC | 265 | 1144 | 4.3 | 3 |
| 1974 | Otis Armstrong, Den, AFC | 263 | 1407 | 5.3 | 9 |
| | Lawrence McCutcheon, LA, NFC | 236 | 1109 | 4.7 | 3 |
| 1975 | O.J. Simpson, Buff, AFC | 329 | 1817 | 5.5 | 16 |
| | Jim Otis, StL, NFC | 269 | 1076 | 4.0 | 5 |
| 1976 | O.J. Simpson, Buff, AFC | 290 | 1503 | 5.2 | 8 |
| | Walter Payton, Chi, NFC | 311 | 1390 | 4.5 | 13 |
| 1977 | Walter Payton, Chi, NFC | 339 | 1852 | 5.5 | 14 |
| | Mark van Eeghen, Oak, AFC | 324 | 1273 | 3.9 | 7 |
| 1978 | Earl Campbell, Hou, AFC | 302 | 1450 | 4.8 | 13 |
| | Walter Payton, Chi, NFC | 333 | 1395 | 4.2 | 11 |
| 1979 | Earl Campbell, Hou, AFC | 368 | 1697 | 4.6 | 19 |
| | Walter Payton, Chi, NFC | 369 | 1610 | 4.4 | 14 |
| 1980 | Earl Campbell, Hou, AFC | 373 | 1934 | 5.2 | 13 |
| | Walter Payton, Chi, NFC | 317 | 1460 | 4.6 | 6 |
| 1981 | George Rogers, NO, NFC | 378 | 1674 | 4.4 | 13 |
| | Earl Campbell, Hou, AFC | 361 | 1376 | 3.8 | 10 |
| 1982 | Freeman McNeil, NY Jets, AFC | 151 | 786 | 5.2 | 6 |
| | Tony Dorsett, Dall, NFC | 177 | 745 | 4.2 | 5 |
| 1983 | Eric Dickerson, LA Rams, NFC | 390 | 1808 | 4.6 | 18 |
| | Curt Warner, Sea, AFC | 335 | 1449 | 4.3 | 13 |
| 1984 | Eric Dickerson, LA Rams, NFC | 379 | 2105 | 5.6 | 14 |
| | Earnest Jackson, SD, AFC | 296 | 1179 | 4.0 | 8 |
| 1985 | Marcus Allen, LA Raiders, AFC | 380 | 1759 | 4.6 | 11 |
| | Gerald Riggs, Atl, NFC | 397 | 1719 | 4.3 | 10 |
| 1986 | Eric Dickerson, LA Rams, NFC | 404 | 1821 | 4.5 | 11 |
| | Curt Warner, Sea, AFC | 319 | 1481 | 4.6 | 13 |
| 1987 | Charles White, LA Rams, NFC | 324 | 1374 | 4.2 | 11 |
| | Eric Dickerson, Ind, AFC | 223 | 1011 | 4.5 | 5 |
| 1988 | Eric Dickerson, Ind, AFC | 388 | 1659 | 4.3 | 14 |
| | Herschel Walker, Dall, NFC | 361 | 1514 | 4.2 | 5 |
| 1989 | Christian Okoye, KC, AFC | 370 | 1480 | 4.0 | 12 |
| | Barry Sanders, Det, NFC | 280 | 1470 | 5.3 | 14 |
| 1990 | Barry Sanders, Det, NFC | 255 | 1304 | 5.1 | 13 |
| | Thurman Thomas, Buff, AFC | 271 | 1297 | 4.8 | 11 |
| 1991 | Emmitt Smith, Dall, NFC | 365 | 1563 | 4.3 | 12 |
| | Thurman Thomas, Buff, AFC | 288 | 1407 | 4.9 | 7 |
| 1992 | Emmitt Smith, Dall, NFC | 373 | 1713 | 4.6 | 18 |
| | Barry Foster, Pitt, AFC | 390 | 1690 | 4.3 | 11 |

## Rushing *(Cont.)*

| Year | Player, Team | Att | Yards | Avg | TD |
|------|--------------|-----|-------|-----|----|
| 1993 | Emmitt Smith, Dall, NFC | 283 | 1486 | 5.3 | 9 |
|  | Thurman Thomas, Buff, AFC | 355 | 1315 | 3.7 | 6 |
| 1994 | Barry Sanders, Det, NFC | 331 | 1883 | 5.7 | 7 |
|  | Chris Warren, Sea, AFC | 333 | 1545 | 4.6 | 9 |
| 1995 | Emmitt Smith, Dall, NFC | 377 | 1773 | 4.7 | 25 |
|  | Curtis Martin, NE, AFC | 368 | 1487 | 4.0 | 14 |
| 1996 | Barry Sanders, Det, NFC | 307 | 1553 | 5.1 | 11 |
|  | Terrell Davis, Den, AFC | 345 | 1538 | 4.5 | 13 |
| 1997 | Barry Sanders, Det, NFC | 335 | 2053 | 6.1 | 11 |
|  | Terrell Davis, Den, AFC | 369 | 1730 | 4.7 | 15 |
| 1998 | Terrell Davis, Den, AFC | 392 | 2008 | 5.1 | 21 |
|  | Jamal Anderson, Atl, NFC | 410 | 1846 | 4.5 | 14 |
| 1999 | Edgerrin James, Ind, AFC | 369 | 1553 | 4.2 | 13 |
|  | Stephen Davis, Wash, NFC | 290 | 1405 | 4.8 | 17 |
| 2000 | Edgerrin James, Ind, AFC | 387 | 1709 | 4.4 | 13 |
|  | Robert Smith, Minn, NFC | 295 | 1521 | 5.2 | 7 |

## Passing*

| Year | Player, Team | Att | Comp | Yards | TD | Int |
|------|--------------|-----|------|-------|----|----|
| 1932 | Arnie Herber, GB | 101 | 37 | 639 | 9 | 9 |
| 1933 | Harry Newman, NY | 136 | 53 | 973 | 11 | 17 |
| 1934 | Arnie Herber, GB | 115 | 42 | 799 | 8 | 12 |
| 1935 | Ed Danowski, NY | 113 | 57 | 794 | 10 | 9 |
| 1936 | Arnie Herber, GB | 173 | 77 | 1239 | 11 | 13 |
| 1937 | Sammy Baugh, Wash | 171 | 81 | 1127 | 8 | 14 |
| 1938 | Ed Danowski, NY | 129 | 70 | 848 | 7 | 8 |
| 1939 | Parker Hall, Clev | 208 | 106 | 1227 | 9 | 13 |
| 1940 | Sammy Baugh, Wash | 177 | 111 | 1367 | 12 | 10 |
| 1941 | Cecil Isbell, GB | 206 | 117 | 1479 | 15 | 11 |
| 1942 | Cecil Isbell, GB | 268 | 146 | 2021 | 24 | 14 |
| 1943 | Sammy Baugh, Wash | 239 | 133 | 1754 | 23 | 19 |
| 1944 | Frank Filchock, Wash | 147 | 84 | 1139 | 13 | 9 |
| 1945 | Sammy Baugh, Wash | 182 | 128 | 1669 | 11 | 4 |
|  | Sid Luckman, Chi | 217 | 117 | 1725 | 14 | 10 |
| 1946 | Bob Waterfield, LA | 251 | 127 | 1747 | 18 | 17 |
| 1947 | Sammy Baugh, Wash | 354 | 210 | 2938 | 25 | 15 |
| 1948 | Tommy Thompson, Phil | 246 | 141 | 1965 | 25 | 11 |
| 1949 | Sammy Baugh, Wash | 255 | 145 | 1903 | 18 | 14 |
| 1950 | Norm Van Brocklin, LA | 233 | 127 | 2061 | 18 | 14 |
| 1951 | Bob Waterfield, LA | 176 | 88 | 1566 | 13 | 10 |
| 1952 | Norm Van Brocklin, LA | 205 | 113 | 1736 | 14 | 17 |
| 1953 | Otto Graham, Clev | 258 | 167 | 2722 | 11 | 9 |
| 1954 | Norm Van Brocklin, LA | 260 | 139 | 2637 | 13 | 21 |
| 1955 | Otto Graham, Clev | 185 | 98 | 1721 | 15 | 8 |
| 1956 | Ed Brown, Chi | 168 | 96 | 1667 | 11 | 12 |
| 1957 | Tommy O'Connell, Clev | 110 | 63 | 1229 | 9 | 8 |
| 1958 | Eddie LeBaron, Wash | 145 | 79 | 1365 | 11 | 10 |
| 1959 | Charlie Conerly, NY | 194 | 113 | 1706 | 14 | 4 |
| 1960 | Milt Plum, Clev, NFL | 250 | 151 | 2297 | 21 | 5 |
|  | Jack Kemp, LA, AFL | 406 | 211 | 3018 | 20 | 25 |
| 1961 | George Blanda, Hou, AFL | 362 | 187 | 3330 | 36 | 22 |
|  | Milt Plum, Clev, NFL | 302 | 177 | 2416 | 18 | 10 |
| 1962 | Len Dawson, Dall, AFL | 310 | 189 | 2759 | 29 | 17 |
|  | Bart Starr, GB, NFL | 285 | 178 | 2438 | 12 | 9 |
| 1963 | Y.A. Tittle, NY, NFL | 367 | 221 | 3145 | 36 | 14 |
|  | Tobin Rote, SD, AFL | 286 | 170 | 2510 | 20 | 17 |
| 1964 | Len Dawson, KC, AFL | 354 | 199 | 2879 | 30 | 18 |
|  | Bart Starr, GB, NFL | 272 | 163 | 2144 | 15 | 4 |
| 1965 | Rudy Bukich, Chi, NFL | 312 | 176 | 2641 | 20 | 9 |
|  | John Hadl, SD, AFL | 348 | 174 | 2798 | 20 | 21 |
| 1966 | Bart Starr, GB, NFL | 251 | 156 | 2257 | 14 | 3 |
|  | Len Dawson, KC, AFL | 284 | 159 | 2527 | 26 | 10 |
| 1967 | Sonny Jurgensen, Wash, NFL | 508 | 288 | 3747 | 31 | 16 |
|  | Daryle Lamonica, Oakland, AFL | 425 | 220 | 3228 | 30 | 20 |
| 1968 | Len Dawson, KC, AFL | 224 | 131 | 2109 | 17 | 9 |
|  | Earl Morrall, Balt, NFL | 317 | 182 | 2909 | 26 | 17 |
| 1969 | Sonny Jurgensen, Wash, NFL | 442 | 274 | 3102 | 22 | 15 |
|  | Greg Cook, Cin, AFL | 197 | 106 | 1854 | 15 | 11 |
| 1970 | John Brodie, SF, NFC | 378 | 223 | 2941 | 24 | 10 |
|  | Daryle Lamonica, Oak, AFC | 356 | 179 | 2516 | 22 | 15 |
| 1971 | Roger Staubach, Dall, NFC | 211 | 126 | 1882 | 15 | 4 |
|  | Bob Griese, Mia, AFC | 263 | 145 | 2089 | 19 | 9 |
| 1972 | Norm Snead, NY, NFC | 325 | 196 | 2307 | 17 | 12 |
|  | Earl Morrall, Mia, AFC | 150 | 83 | 1360 | 11 | 7 |
| 1973 | Roger Staubach, Dall, NFC | 286 | 179 | 2428 | 23 | 15 |
|  | Ken Stabler, Oak, AFC | 260 | 163 | 1997 | 14 | 10 |
| 1974 | Ken Anderson, Cin, AFC | 328 | 213 | 2667 | 18 | 10 |
|  | Sonny Jurgensen, Wash, NFC | 167 | 107 | 1185 | 11 | 5 |
| 1975 | Ken Anderson, Cin, AFC | 377 | 228 | 3169 | 21 | 11 |
|  | Fran Tarkenton, Minn, NFC | 425 | 273 | 2994 | 25 | 13 |
| 1976 | Ken Stabler, Oak, AFC | 291 | 194 | 2737 | 27 | 17 |
|  | James Harris, LA, NFC | 158 | 91 | 1460 | 8 | 6 |
| 1977 | Bob Griese, Mia, AFC | 307 | 180 | 2252 | 22 | 13 |
|  | Roger Staubach, Dall, NFC | 361 | 210 | 2620 | 18 | 9 |
| 1978 | Roger Staubach, Dall, NFC | 413 | 231 | 3190 | 25 | 16 |
|  | Terry Bradshaw, Pitt, AFC | 368 | 207 | 2915 | 28 | 20 |
| 1979 | Roger Staubach, Dall, NFC | 461 | 267 | 3586 | 27 | 11 |
|  | Dan Fouts, SD, AFC | 530 | 332 | 4082 | 24 | 24 |
| 1980 | Brian Sipe, Clev, AFC | 554 | 337 | 4132 | 30 | 14 |
|  | Ron Jaworski, Phi, NFC | 451 | 257 | 3529 | 27 | 12 |
| 1981 | Ken Anderson, Cin, AFC | 479 | 300 | 3754 | 29 | 10 |
|  | Joe Montana, SF, NFC | 488 | 311 | 3565 | 19 | 12 |
| 1982 | Ken Anderson, Cin, AFC | 309 | 218 | 2495 | 12 | 9 |
|  | Joe Theismann, Wash, NFC | 252 | 161 | 2033 | 13 | 9 |
| 1983 | Steve Bartkowski, Atl, NFC | 432 | 274 | 3167 | 22 | 5 |
|  | Dan Marino, Mia AFC | 296 | 173 | 2210 | 20 | 6 |
| 1984 | Dan Marino, Mia, AFC | 564 | 362 | 5084 | 48 | 17 |
|  | Joe Montana, SF, NFC | 432 | 279 | 3630 | 28 | 10 |
| 1985 | Ken O'Brien, NY, AFC | 488 | 297 | 3888 | 25 | 8 |
|  | Joe Montana, SF, NFC | 494 | 303 | 3653 | 27 | 13 |

## Passing *(Cont.)*

| Year | Player, Team | Att | Comp | Yards | TD | Int |
|------|-------------|-----|------|-------|----|----|
| 1986 | Tommy Kramer, Minn, NFC | 372 | 208 | 3000 | 24 | 10 |
|  | Dan Marino, Mia, AFC | 623 | 378 | 4746 | 44 | 23 |
| 1987 | Joe Montana, SF, NFC | 398 | 266 | 3054 | 31 | 13 |
|  | Bernie Kosar, Clev, AFC | 389 | 241 | 3033 | 22 | 9 |
| 1988 | Boomer Esiason, Cin, AFC | 388 | 223 | 3572 | 28 | 14 |
|  | Wade Wilson, Minn, NFC | 332 | 204 | 2746 | 15 | 9 |
| 1989 | Joe Montana, SF, NFC | 386 | 271 | 3521 | 26 | 8 |
|  | Boomer Esiason, Cin, AFC | 455 | 258 | 3525 | 28 | 11 |
| 1990 | Jim Kelly, Buffalo, AFC | 346 | 219 | 2829 | 24 | 9 |
|  | Phil Simms, NY, NFC | 311 | 184 | 2284 | 15 | 4 |
| 1991 | Steve Young, SF, NFC | 279 | 180 | 2517 | 17 | 8 |
|  | Jim Kelly, Buff, AFC | 474 | 304 | 3844 | 33 | 17 |
| 1992 | Steve Young, SF, NFC | 402 | 268 | 3465 | 25 | 7 |
|  | Warren Moon, Hou, AFC | 346 | 224 | 2521 | 18 | 12 |
| 1993 | Steve Young, SF, NFC | 462 | 314 | 4023 | 29 | 16 |
|  | John Elway, Den, AFC | 551 | 348 | 4030 | 25 | 10 |

| Year | Player, Team | Att | Comp | Yards | TD | Int |
|------|-------------|-----|------|-------|----|----|
| 1994 | Steve Young, SF, NFC | 461 | 324 | 3969 | 35 | 10 |
|  | Dan Marino, Mia, AFC | 615 | 385 | 4453 | 30 | 17 |
| 1995 | Brett Favre, GB, NFC | 570 | 359 | 4413 | 38 | 13 |
|  | Jeff Blake, Cin, AFC | 567 | 326 | 3822 | 28 | 17 |
| 1996 | Vinny Testaverde, Balt, AFC | 549 | 325 | 4177 | 33 | 19 |
|  | Brett Favre, GB, NFC | 543 | 325 | 3899 | 39 | 13 |
| 1997 | Steve Young, SF, NFC | 356 | 241 | 3029 | 19 | 6 |
|  | Mark Brunell, Jax, AFC | 435 | 264 | 3281 | 18 | 7 |
| 1998 | Randall Cunningham, Minn, NFC | 425 | 259 | 3704 | 34 | 10 |
|  | Vinny Testaverde, NYJ, AFC | 421 | 259 | 3256 | 29 | 7 |
| 1999 | Kurt Warner, StL, NFC | 499 | 325 | 4353 | 41 | 13 |
|  | Peyton Manning, Ind, AFC | 533 | 331 | 4135 | 26 | 15 |
| 2000 | Trent Green, StL, NFC | 240 | 145 | 2063 | 16 | 5 |
|  | Brian Griese, Den, AFC | 336 | 216 | 2688 | 19 | 4 |

*Since 1973, the annual passing leaders have been determined by a passer rating system that compares individual performances to a fixed performance standard.

## Pass Receiving*

| Year | Player, Team | No. | Yds | Avg | TD |
|------|-------------|-----|-----|-----|----|
| 1932 | Ray Flaherty, NY | 21 | 350 | 16.7 | 3 |
| 1933 | John Kelly, Brooklyn | 22 | 246 | 11.2 | 3 |
| 1934 | Joe Carter, Phil | 16 | 238 | 14.9 | 4 |
|  | Morris Badgro, NY | 16 | 206 | 12.9 | 1 |
| 1935 | Tod Goodwin, NY | 26 | 432 | 16.6 | 4 |
| 1936 | Don Hutson, GB | 34 | 536 | 15.8 | 8 |
| 1937 | Don Hutson, GB | 41 | 552 | 13.5 | 7 |
| 1938 | Gaynell Tinsley, Chi Cards | 41 | 516 | 12.6 | 1 |
| 1939 | Don Hutson, GB | 34 | 846 | 24.9 | 6 |
| 1940 | Don Looney, Phil | 58 | 707 | 12.2 | 4 |
| 1941 | Don Hutson, GB | 58 | 738 | 12.7 | 10 |
| 1942 | Don Hutson, GB | 74 | 1211 | 16.4 | 17 |
| 1943 | Don Hutson, GB | 47 | 776 | 16.5 | 11 |
| 1944 | Don Hutson, GB | 58 | 866 | 14.9 | 9 |
| 1945 | Don Hutson, GB | 47 | 834 | 17.7 | 9 |
| 1946 | Jim Benton, LA | 63 | 981 | 15.6 | 6 |
| 1947 | Jim Keane, Chi | 64 | 910 | 14.2 | 10 |
| 1948 | Tom Fears, LA | 51 | 698 | 13.7 | 4 |
| 1949 | Tom Fears, LA | 77 | 1013 | 13.2 | 9 |
| 1950 | Tom Fears, LA | 84 | 1116 | 13.3 | 7 |
| 1951 | Elroy Hirsch, LA | 66 | 1495 | 22.7 | 17 |
| 1952 | Mac Speedie, Clev | 62 | 911 | 14.7 | 5 |
| 1953 | Pete Pihos, Phil | 63 | 1049 | 16.7 | 10 |
| 1954 | Pete Pihos, Phil | 60 | 872 | 14.5 | 10 |
|  | Billy Wilson, SF | 60 | 830 | 13.8 | 5 |
| 1955 | Pete Pihos, Phil | 62 | 864 | 13.9 | 7 |
| 1956 | Billy Wilson, SF | 60 | 889 | 14.8 | 5 |
| 1957 | Billy Wilson, SF | 52 | 757 | 14.6 | 6 |
| 1958 | Raymond Berry, Balt | 56 | 794 | 14.2 | 9 |
|  | Pete Retzlaff, Phil | 56 | 766 | 13.7 | 2 |
| 1959 | Raymond Berry, Balt | 66 | 959 | 14.5 | 14 |
| 1960 | Lionel Taylor, Den, AFL | 92 | 1235 | 13.4 | 12 |
|  | Raymond Berry, Balt, NFL | 74 | 1298 | 17.5 | 10 |
| 1961 | Lionel Taylor, Den, AFL | 100 | 1176 | 11.8 | 4 |
|  | Jim Phillips, LA, NFL | 78 | 1092 | 14.0 | 5 |
| 1962 | Lionel Taylor, Den, AFL | 77 | 908 | 11.8 | 4 |
|  | Bobby Mitchell, Wash, NFL | 72 | 1384 | 19.2 | 11 |

| Year | Player, Team | No. | Yds | Avg | TD |
|------|-------------|-----|-----|-----|----|
| 1963 | Lionel Taylor, Den, AFL | 78 | 1101 | 14.1 | 10 |
|  | Bobby Joe Conrad, St. Louis, NFL | 73 | 967 | 13.2 | 10 |
| 1964 | Charley Hennigan, Houston, AFL | 101 | 1546 | 15.3 | 8 |
|  | Johnny Morris, Chi, NFL | 93 | 1200 | 12.9 | 10 |
| 1965 | Lionel Taylor, Den, AFL | 85 | 1131 | 13.3 | 6 |
|  | Dave Parks, SF, NFL | 80 | 1344 | 16.8 | 12 |
| 1966 | Lance Alworth, SD, AFL | 73 | 1383 | 18.9 | 13 |
|  | Charley Taylor, Wash, NFL | 72 | 1119 | 15.5 | 12 |
| 1967 | George Sauer, NY, AFL | 75 | 1189 | 15.9 | 6 |
|  | Charley Taylor, Wash, NFL | 70 | 990 | 14.1 | 9 |
| 1968 | Clifton McNeil, SF, NFL | 71 | 994 | 14.0 | 7 |
|  | Lance Alworth, SD, AFL | 68 | 1312 | 19.3 | 10 |
| 1969 | Dan Abramowicz, NO, NFL | 73 | 1015 | 13.9 | 7 |
|  | Lance Alworth, SD, AFL | 64 | 1003 | 15.7 | 4 |
| 1970 | Dick Gordon, Chi, NFC | 71 | 1026 | 14.5 | 13 |
|  | Marlin Briscoe, Buff, AFC | 57 | 1036 | 18.2 | 8 |
| 1971 | Fred Biletnikoff, Oak, AFC | 61 | 929 | 15.2 | 9 |
|  | Bob Tucker, NY, NFC | 59 | 791 | 13.4 | 4 |
| 1972 | Harold Jackson, Phil, NFC | 62 | 1048 | 16.9 | 4 |
|  | Fred Biletnikoff, Oak, AFC | 58 | 802 | 13.8 | 7 |
| 1973 | Harold Carmichael, Phil, NFC | 67 | 1116 | 16.7 | 9 |
|  | Fred Willis, Hou, AFC | 57 | 371 | 6.5 | 1 |
| 1974 | Lydell Mitchell, Balt, AFC | 72 | 544 | 7.6 | 2 |
|  | Charles Young, Phil, NFC | 63 | 696 | 11.0 | 3 |
| 1975 | Chuck Foreman, Minn, NFC | 73 | 691 | 9.5 | 9 |
|  | Reggie Rucker, Clev, AFC | 60 | 770 | 12.8 | 3 |
|  | Lydell Mitchell, Balt, AFC | 60 | 544 | 9.1 | 4 |
| 1976 | MacArthur Lane, KC, AFC | 66 | 686 | 10.4 | 1 |
|  | Drew Pearson, Dall, NFC | 58 | 806 | 13.9 | 6 |

*Most catches.

## Pass Receiving (Cont.)

| Year | Player, Team | No. | Yds | Avg | TD |
|---|---|---|---|---|---|
| 1977 | Lydell Mitchell, Balt, AFC | 71 | 620 | 8.7 | 4 |
| | Ahmad Rashad, Minn, NFC | 51 | 681 | 13.4 | 2 |
| 1978 | Rickey Young, Minn, NFC | 88 | 704 | 8.0 | 5 |
| | Steve Largent, Sea, AFC | 71 | 1168 | 16.5 | 8 |
| 1979 | Joe Washington, Balt, AFC | 82 | 750 | 9.1 | 3 |
| | Ahmad Rashad, Minn, NFC | 80 | 1156 | 14.5 | 9 |
| 1980 | Kellen Winslow, SD, AFC | 89 | 1290 | 14.5 | 9 |
| | Earl Cooper, SF, NFC | 83 | 567 | 6.8 | 4 |
| 1981 | Kellen Winslow, SD, AFC | 88 | 1075 | 12.2 | 10 |
| | Dwight Clark, SF, NFC | 85 | 1105 | 13.0 | 4 |
| 1982 | Dwight Clark, SF, NFC | 60 | 913 | 15.2 | 5 |
| | Kellen Winslow, SD, AFC | 54 | 721 | 13.4 | 6 |
| 1983 | Todd Christensen, LA, AFC | 92 | 1247 | 13.6 | 12 |
| | Roy Green, StL, NFC | 78 | 1227 | 15.7 | 14 |
| | Charlie Brown, Wash, NFC | 78 | 1225 | 15.7 | 8 |
| | Earnest Gray, NY, NFC | 78 | 1139 | 14.6 | 5 |
| 1984 | Art Monk, Wash, NFC | 106 | 1372 | 12.9 | 7 |
| | Ozzie Newsome, Clev, AFC | 89 | 1001 | 11.2 | 5 |
| 1985 | Roger Craig, SF, NFC | 92 | 1016 | 11.0 | 6 |
| | Lionel James, SD, AFC | 86 | 1027 | 11.9 | 6 |
| 1986 | Todd Christensen, LA Rai, AFC | 95 | 1153 | 12.1 | 8 |
| | Jerry Rice, SF, NFC | 86 | 1570 | 18.3 | 15 |
| 1987 | J.T. Smith, StL Card, NFC | 91 | 1117 | 12.3 | 8 |
| | Al Toon, NY, AFC | 68 | 976 | 14.4 | 5 |
| 1988 | Al Toon, NY, AFC | 93 | 1067 | 11.5 | 5 |
| | Henry Ellard, LA Rams, NFC | 86 | 1414 | 16.4 | 10 |
| 1989 | Sterling Sharpe, GB, NFC | 90 | 1423 | 15.8 | 12 |
| | Andre Reed, Buff, AFC | 88 | 1312 | 14.9 | 9 |
| 1990 | Jerry Rice, SF, NFC | 100 | 1502 | 15.0 | 13 |
| | Haywood Jeffires, Hou, AFC | 74 | 1048 | 14.2 | 8 |
| | Drew Hill, Hou, AFC | 74 | 1019 | 13.8 | 5 |
| 1991 | Haywood Jeffires, Hou, AFC | 100 | 1181 | 11.8 | 7 |
| | Michael Irvin, Dall, NFC | 93 | 1523 | 16.4 | 8 |
| 1992 | Sterling Sharpe, GB, NFC | 108 | 1461 | 13.5 | 13 |
| | Haywood Jeffires, Hou, AFC | 90 | 913 | 10.1 | 9 |
| 1993 | Sterling Sharpe, GB, NFC | 112 | 1274 | 11.4 | 11 |
| | Reggie Langhorne, Ind, AFC | 85 | 1038 | 12.2 | 3 |
| 1994 | Cris Carter, Minn, NFC | 122 | 1256 | 10.3 | 7 |
| | Ben Coates, NE, AFC | 96 | 1174 | 12.2 | 7 |
| 1995 | Herman Moore, Det, NFC | 123 | 1686 | 13.7 | 14 |
| | Carl Pickens, Cin, AFC | 99 | 1234 | 12.5 | 17 |
| 1996 | Jerry Rice, SF, NFC | 108 | 1254 | 11.6 | 8 |
| | Carl Pickens, Cin, AFC | 100 | 1180 | 11.8 | 12 |
| 1997 | Herman Moore, Det, NFC | 104 | 1293 | 12.4 | 8 |
| | Tim Brown, Oak, AFC | 104 | 1408 | 13.5 | 5 |
| 1998 | Frank Sanders, Ariz, NFC | 89 | 1145 | 12.9 | 3 |
| | O.J. McDuffie, Mia, AFC | 90 | 1050 | 11.7 | 7 |
| 1999 | Mushin Muhammad, Car, NFC | 96 | 1253 | 13.1 | 8 |
| | Jimmy Smith, Jax, AFC | 116 | 1636 | 14.1 | 6 |
| 2000 | Mushin Muhammad, Car, NFC | 102 | 1183 | 11.6 | 6 |
| | Marvin Harrison, Ind, AFC | 102 | 1413 | 13.9 | 14 |

## No Cardiac Kidding

For one fan at the Meadowlands on Jan. 14, 2001, the Giants' touchdown 1:57 into the NFC title game was no cause for celebration. Just after the play, Fred Oser, 56, of Perth Amboy, N.J., had a heart attack and had to be revived with a defibrillator. His experience points to an often overlooked fact: As hazardous as pro sports are to players, they can be just as dangerous for fans.

That was made clear in a study published in December 2000 in the *British Medical Journal*. Doctors in the Netherlands examined deaths due to heart attacks and strokes on and around June 22, 1996, the day Holland played France in the quarterfinals of the '96 European soccer championship. Researchers found that cardiac-related deaths jumped 50% among Dutch men on the day of the game compared with the 10 days surrounding it. Tellingly, there was no such rise among women.

Fans should be especially vigilant during championship games. "There's no doubt that Super Bowl Sunday is a high-risk day," says David Meyerson, a cardiologist at Johns Hopkins University School of Medicine. "The stress of watching the game can trigger heart-rhythm disturbances, spike up blood pressure and cause the arteries to spasm. In addition a lot of people consume snack foods laden with salt and fat and drink alcohol in abundance."

The bottom line then, is this: Enjoy in moderation and remember—it's only a game.

—Amy Ruth Levine

## Scoring

| Year | Player, Team | TD | FG | PAT | TP |
|---|---|---|---|---|---|
| 1932 | Earl Clark, Portsmouth | 6 | 3 | 10 | 55 |
| 1933 | Ken Strong, NY | 6 | 5 | 13 | 64 |
| | Glenn Presnell, Ports | 6 | 6 | 10 | 64 |
| 1934 | Jack Manders, Chi | 3 | 10 | 31 | 79 |
| 1935 | Earl Clark, Det | 6 | 1 | 16 | 55 |
| 1936 | Earl Clark, Det | 7 | 4 | 19 | 73 |
| 1937 | Jack Manders, Chi | 5 | 18 | 15 | 69 |
| 1938 | Clarke Hinkle, GB | 7 | 3 | 7 | 58 |
| 1939 | Andy Farkas, Wash | 11 | 0 | 2 | 68 |
| 1940 | Don Hutson, GB | 7 | 0 | 15 | 57 |
| 1941 | Don Hutson, GB | 12 | 1 | 20 | 95 |
| 1942 | Don Hutson, GB | 17 | 1 | 33 | 138 |
| 1943 | Don Hutson, GB | 12 | 3 | 36 | 117 |
| 1944 | Don Hutson, GB | 9 | 0 | 31 | 85 |
| 1945 | Steve Van Buren, Phil | 18 | 0 | 2 | 110 |
| 1946 | Ted Fritsch, GB | 10 | 9 | 13 | 100 |
| 1947 | Pat Harder, Chicago Cards | 7 | 7 | 39 | 102 |
| 1948 | Pat Harder, Chicago Cards | 6 | 7 | 53 | 110 |
| 1949 | Pat Harder, Chicago Cards | 8 | 3 | 45 | 102 |
| | Gene Roberts, NY | 17 | 0 | 0 | 102 |
| 1950 | Doak Walker, Det | 11 | 8 | 38 | 128 |
| 1951 | Elroy Hirsch, LA | 17 | 0 | 0 | 102 |
| 1952 | Gordy Soltau, SF | 7 | 6 | 34 | 94 |
| 1953 | Gordy Soltau, SF | 6 | 10 | 48 | 114 |
| 1954 | Bobby Walston, Phil | 11 | 4 | 36 | 114 |
| 1955 | Doak Walker, Det | 7 | 9 | 27 | 96 |
| 1956 | Bobby Layne, Det | 5 | 12 | 33 | 99 |
| 1957 | Sam Baker, Wash | 1 | 14 | 29 | 77 |
| | Lou Groza, Clev | 0 | 15 | 32 | 77 |
| 1958 | Jim Brown, Clev | 18 | 0 | 0 | 108 |
| 1959 | Paul Hornung, GB | 7 | 7 | 31 | 94 |
| 1960 | Paul Hornung, GB, NFL | 15 | 15 | 41 | 176 |
| | Gene Mingo, Den, AFL | 6 | 18 | 33 | 123 |
| 1961 | Gino Cappelletti, Bos, AFL | 8 | 17 | 48 | 147 |
| | Paul Hornung, GB, NFL | 10 | 15 | 41 | 146 |
| 1962 | Gene Mingo, Den, AFL | 4 | 27 | 32 | 137 |
| | Jim Taylor, GB, NFL | 19 | 0 | 0 | 114 |
| 1963 | Gino Cappelletti, Bos, AFL | 2 | 22 | 35 | 113 |
| | Don Chandler, NY, NFL | 0 | 18 | 52 | 106 |
| 1964 | Gino Cappelletti, Bos, AFL | 7 | 25 | 36 | 155 |
| | Lenny Moore, Balt, NFL | 20 | 0 | 0 | 120 |
| 1965 | Gale Sayers, Chi, NFL | 22 | 0 | 0 | 132 |
| | Gino Cappelletti, Bos, AFL | 9 | 17 | 27 | 132 |
| 1966 | Gino Cappelletti, Bos, AFL | 6 | 16 | 35 | 119 |
| | Bruce Gossett, LA, NFL | 0 | 28 | 29 | 113 |
| 1967 | Jim Bakken, StL, NFL | 0 | 27 | 36 | 117 |
| | George Blanda, Oak, AFL | 0 | 20 | 56 | 116 |
| 1968 | Jim Turner, NY, AFL | 0 | 34 | 43 | 145 |
| | Leroy Kelly, Clev, NFL | 20 | 0 | 0 | 120 |
| 1969 | Jim Turner, NY, AFL | 0 | 32 | 33 | 129 |
| | Fred Cox, Minn, NFL | 0 | 26 | 43 | 121 |
| 1970 | Fred Cox, Minn, NFC | 0 | 30 | 35 | 125 |
| | Jan Stenerud, KC, AFC | 0 | 30 | 26 | 116 |
| 1971 | Garo Yepremian, Mia, AFC | 0 | 28 | 33 | 117 |
| | Curt Knight, Wash, NFC | 0 | 29 | 27 | 114 |
| 1972 | Chester Marcol, GB, NFC | 0 | 33 | 29 | 128 |
| | Bobby Howfield, NY AFC | 0 | 27 | 40 | 121 |
| 1973 | David Ray, LA, NFC | 0 | 30 | 40 | 130 |
| | Roy Gerela, Pitt, AFC | 0 | 29 | 36 | 123 |
| 1974 | Chester Marcol, GB, NFC | 0 | 25 | 19 | 94 |
| | Roy Gerela, Pitt, AFC | 0 | 20 | 33 | 93 |
| 1975 | O.J. Simpson, Buff, AFC | 23 | 0 | 0 | 138 |
| | Chuck Foreman, Minn, NFC | 22 | 0 | 0 | 132 |
| 1976 | Toni Linhart, Balt, AFC | 0 | 20 | 49 | 109 |
| | Mark Moseley, Wash, NFC | 0 | 22 | 31 | 97 |
| 1977 | Errol Mann, Oak, AFC | 0 | 20 | 39 | 99 |
| | Walter Payton, Chi, NFC | 16 | 0 | 0 | 96 |
| 1978 | Frank Corral, LA, NFC | 0 | 29 | 31 | 118 |
| | Pat Leahy, NY, AFC | 0 | 22 | 41 | 107 |
| 1979 | John Smith, NE, AFC | 0 | 23 | 46 | 115 |
| | Mark Moseley, Wash, NFC | 0 | 25 | 39 | 114 |
| 1980 | John Smith, NE, AFC | 0 | 26 | 51 | 129 |
| | Ed Murray, Det, NFC | 0 | 27 | 35 | 116 |
| 1981 | Ed Murray, Det, NFC | 0 | 25 | 46 | 121 |
| | Rafael Septien, Dall, NFC | 0 | 27 | 40 | 121 |
| | Jim Breech, Cin, AFC | 0 | 22 | 49 | 115 |
| | Nick Lowery, KC, AFC | 0 | 26 | 37 | 115 |
| 1982 | Marcus Allen, LA, AFC | 14 | 0 | 0 | 84 |
| | Wendell Tyler, LA, NFC | 13 | 0 | 0 | 78 |
| 1983 | Mark Moseley, Wash, NFC | 0 | 33 | 62 | 161 |
| | Gary Anderson, Pitt, AFC | 0 | 27 | 38 | 119 |
| 1984 | Ray Wersching, SF, NFC | 0 | 25 | 56 | 131 |
| | Gary Anderson, Pitt, AFC | 0 | 24 | 45 | 117 |
| 1985 | Kevin Butler, Chi, NFC | 0 | 31 | 51 | 144 |
| | Gary Anderson, Pitt, AFC | 0 | 33 | 40 | 139 |
| 1986 | Tony Franklin, NE, AFC | 0 | 32 | 44 | 140 |
| | Kevin Butler, Chi, NFC | 0 | 28 | 36 | 120 |
| 1987 | Jerry Rice, SF, NFC | 23 | 0 | 0 | 138 |
| | Jim Breech, Cin, AFC | 0 | 24 | 25 | 97 |
| 1988 | Scott Norwood, Buff, AFC | 0 | 32 | 33 | 129 |
| | Mike Cofer, SF, NFC | 0 | 27 | 40 | 121 |
| 1989 | Mike Cofer, SF, NFC | 0 | 29 | 49 | 136 |
| | David Treadwell, Den, AFC | 0 | 27 | 39 | 120 |
| 1990 | Nick Lowery, KC, AFC | 0 | 34 | 37 | 139 |
| | Chip Lohmiller, Wash, NFC | 0 | 30 | 41 | 131 |
| 1991 | Chip Lohmiller, Wash, NFC | 0 | 31 | 56 | 149 |
| | Pete Stoyanovich, Mia, AFC | 0 | 31 | 28 | 121 |
| 1992 | Pete Stoyanovich, Mia, AFC | 0 | 30 | 34 | 124 |
| | Morten Anderson, NO, NFC | 0 | 29 | 33 | 120 |
| | Chip Lohmiller, Wash, NFC | 0 | 30 | 30 | 120 |
| 1993 | Jeff Jaeger, Rai, AFC | 0 | 35 | 27 | 132 |
| | Jason Hanson, Det, NFC | 0 | 34 | 28 | 130 |
| 1994 | John Carney, SD, AFC | 0 | 34 | 33 | 135 |
| | Fuad Reveiz, Minn, NFC | 0 | 34 | 30 | 132 |
| | Emmitt Smith, Dall, NFC | 22 | 0 | 0 | 132 |
| 1995 | Emmitt Smith, Dall, NFC | 25 | 0 | 0 | 150 |
| | Norm Johnson, Pitt, AFC | 0 | 34 | 39 | 141 |
| 1996 | John Kasay, Car, NFC | 0 | 37 | 34 | 145 |
| | Cary Blanchard, Ind, AFC | 0 | 36 | 27 | 135 |
| 1997 | Richie Cunningham, Dall, NFC | 0 | 34 | 24 | 126 |
| | Mike Hollis, Jax, AFC | 0 | 41 | 31 | 134 |
| 1998 | Gary Anderson, Minn, NFC | 0 | 35 | 59 | 164 |
| | Steve Christie, Buff, AFC | 0 | 33 | 41 | 140 |
| 1999 | Jeff Wilkins, StL, NFC | 0 | 20 | 28 | 124 |
| | Mike Vanderjagt, Ind, AFC | 0 | 34 | 38 | 145 |
| 2000 | Marshall Faulk, StL, NFC | 26 | 0 | 0 | 156 |
| | Matt Stover, Balt, AFC | 0 | 35 | 30 | 135 |

| Date | Result | Date | Result | Date | Result |
|---|---|---|---|---|---|
| 1-15-39 | NY Giants 13, Pro All-Stars 10 | 1-13-63 | NFL East 30, West 20 | 1-29-79 | NFC 13, AFC 7 |
| 1-14-40 | Green Bay 16, NFL All-Stars 7 | 1-12-64 | NFL West 31, East 17 | 1-27-80 | NFC 37, AFC 27 |
| 12-29-40 | Chi Bears 28, NFL All-Stars 14 | 1-19-64 | AFL West 27, East 24 | 2-1-81 | NFC 21, AFC 7 |
| 1-4-42 | Chi Bears 35, NFL All-Stars 24 | 1-10-65 | NFL West 34, East 14 | 1-31-82 | AFC 16, NFC 13 |
| 12-27-42 | NFL All-Stars 17, Washington 14 | 1-16-65 | AFL West 38, East 14 | 2-6-83 | NFC 20, AFC 19 |
| 1-14-51 | A. Conf. 28, N. Conf. 27 | 1-15-66 | AFL All-Stars 30, Buffalo 19 | 1-29-84 | NFC 45, AFC 3 |
| 1-12-52 | N. Conf. 30, A. Conf. 13 | 1-15-66 | NFL East 36, West 7 | 1-27-85 | AFC 22, NFC 14 |
| 1-10-53 | N. Conf. 27, A. Conf. 7 | 1-21-67 | AFL East 30, West 23 | 2-2-86 | NFC 28, AFC 24 |
| 1-17-54 | East 20, West 9 | 1-22-67 | NFL East 20, West 10 | 2-1-87 | AFC 10, NFC 6 |
| 1-16-55 | West 26, East 19 | 1-21-68 | AFL East 25, West 24 | 2-7-88 | AFC 15, NFC 6 |
| 1-15-56 | East 31, West 30 | 1-21-68 | NFL West 38, East 20 | 1-29-89 | NFC 34, AFC 3 |
| 1-13-57 | West 19, East 10 | 1-19-69 | AFL West 38, East 25 | 2-4-90 | NFC 27, AFC 21 |
| 1-12-58 | West 26, East 7 | 1-19-69 | NFL West 10, East 7 | 2-3-91 | AFC 23, NFC 21 |
| 1 11-59 | East 28, West 21 | 1-17-70 | AFL West 26, East 3 | 2-2-92 | NFC 21, AFC 15 |
| 1-17-60 | West 38, East 21 | 1-18-70 | NFL West 16, East 13 | 2-7-93 | AFC 23, NFC 20 |
| 1-15-61 | West 35, East 31 | 1-24-71 | NFC 27, AFC 6 | 2-6-94 | NFC 17, AFC 3 |
| 1-7-62 | AFL West 47, East 27 | 1 23-72 | AFC 26, NFC 13 | 2 5 95 | AFC 41, NFC 13 |
| 1-14-62 | NFL West 31, East 30 | 1-21-73 | AFC 33, NFC 28 | 2-4-96 | NFC 20, AFC 13 |
| 1-13-63 | AFL West 21, East 14 | 1-20-74 | AFC 15, NFC 13 | 2-2-97 | AFC 26, NFC 23 |
| | | 1-20-75 | NFC 17, AFC 10 | 2-1-98 | AFC 29, NFC 24 |
| | | 1-26-76 | NFC 23, AFC 20 | 2-7-99 | AFC 23, NFC 10 |
| | | 1-17-77 | AFC 24, NFC 14 | 2-6-00 | NFC 51, AFC 31 |
| | | 1-23-78 | NFC 14, AFC 13 | 2-4-01 | AFC 38, NFC 17 |

## Chicago All-Star Game* Results

| Date | Result (Attendance) | Date | Result (Attendance) |
|---|---|---|---|
| 8-31-34 | Chi Bears 0, All-Stars 0 (79,432) | 8-10-56 | Cleveland 26, All-Stars 0 (75,000) |
| 8-29-35 | Chi Bears 5, All-Stars 0 (77,450) | 8-9-57 | NY Giants 22, All-Stars 12 (75,000) |
| 9-3-36 | All-Stars 7, Detroit 7 (76,000) | 8-15-58 | All-Stars 35, Detroit 19 (70,000) |
| 9-1-37 | All-Stars 6, Green Bay 0 (84,560) | 8-14-59 | Baltimore 29, All-Stars 0 (70,000) |
| 8-31-38 | All-Stars 28, Washington 16 (74,250) | 8-12-60 | Baltimore 32, All-Stars 7 (70,000) |
| 8-30-39 | NY Giants 9, All-Stars 0 (81,456) | 8-4-61 | Philadelphia 28, All-Stars 14 (66,000) |
| 8-29-40 | Green Bay 45, All-Stars 28 (84,567) | 8-3-62 | Green Bay 42, All-Stars 20 (65,000) |
| 8-28-41 | Chi Bears 37, All-Stars 13 (98,203) | 8-2-63 | All-Stars 20, Green Bay 17 (65,000) |
| 8-28-42 | Chi Bears 21, All-Stars 0 (101,100) | 8-7-64 | Chicago 28, All-Stars 17 (65,000) |
| 8-25-43 | All-Stars 27, Washington 7 (48,471) | 8-6-65 | Cleveland 24, All-Stars 16 (68,000) |
| 8-30-44 | Chi Bears 24, All-Stars 21 (48,769) | 8-5-66 | Green Bay 38, All-Stars 0 (72,000) |
| 8-30-45 | Green Bay 19, All-Stars 7 (92,753) | 8-4-67 | Green Bay 27, All-Stars 0 (70,934) |
| 8-23-46 | All-Stars 16, Los Angeles 0 (97,380) | 8-2-68 | Green Bay 34, All-Stars 17 (69,917) |
| 8-22-47 | All-Stars 16, Chi Bears 0 (105,840) | 8-1-69 | NY Jets 26, All-Stars 24 (74,208) |
| 8-20-48 | Chi Cardinals 28, All-Stars 0 (101,220) | 7-31-70 | Kansas City 24, All-Stars 3 (69,940) |
| 8-12-49 | Philadelphia 38, All-Stars 0 (93,780) | 7-30-71 | Baltimore 24, All-Stars 17 (52,289) |
| 8-11-50 | All-Stars 17, Philadelphia 7 (88,885) | 7-28-72 | Dallas 20, All-Stars 7 (54,162) |
| 8-17-51 | Cleveland 33, All-Stars 0 (92,180) | 7-27-73 | Miami 14, All-Stars 3 (54,103) |
| 8-15-52 | Los Angeles 10, All-Stars 7 (88,316) | 1974 | No game |
| 8-14-53 | Detroit 24, All-Stars 10 (93,818) | 8-1-75 | Pittsburgh 21, All-Stars 14 (54,103) |
| 8-13-54 | Detroit 31, All-Stars 6 (93,470) | 7-23-76 | Pittsburgh 24, All-Stars 0 (52,895) |
| 8-12-55 | All-Stars 30, Cleveland 27 (75,000) | | |

*Discontinued.

**Yet Another Sign of the Apocalypse**

In March 2001, a Milwaukee pool and spa company touted a "not guilty hot tub super sale" with ads claiming, "With a little common sense ... you'll enjoy the relaxation of your new hot tub for 20 years to life," among other veiled references to former Green Bay Packer tight end Mark Chmura's sexual-assault trial.

# Alltime Winningest NFL Coaches

## Most Career Wins

| Coach | Yrs | Teams | Regular Season | | | | Career | | | |
|---|---|---|---|---|---|---|---|---|---|---|
| | | | W | L | T | Pct | W | L | T | Pct |
| Don Shula | 33 | Colts, Dolphins | 328 | 156 | 6 | .676 | 347 | 173 | 6 | .665 |
| George Halas | 40 | Bears | 318 | 148 | 31 | .671 | 324 | 151 | 31 | .671 |
| Tom Landry | 29 | Cowboys | 250 | 162 | 6 | .605 | 270 | 178 | 6 | .601 |
| Curly Lambeau | 33 | Packers, Cardinals, Redskins | 226 | 132 | 22 | .624 | 229 | 134 | 22 | .623 |
| Chuck Noll | 23 | Steelers | 193 | 148 | 1 | .566 | 209 | 156 | 1 | .572 |
| Chuck Knox | 22 | Rams, Bills, Seahawks | 186 | 147 | 1 | .558 | 193 | 158 | 1 | .550 |
| †Dan Reeves | 20 | Broncos, Giants, Falcons | 171 | 140 | 1 | .550 | 181 | 148 | 1 | .550 |
| Paul Brown | 21 | Browns, Bengals | 166 | 100 | 6 | .621 | 170 | 108 | 6 | .609 |
| Bud Grant | 18 | Vikings | 158 | 96 | 5 | .620 | 168 | 108 | 5 | .607 |
| Marv Levy | 17 | Chiefs, Bills | 143 | 112 | 0 | .561 | 154 | 120 | 0 | .562 |
| Steve Owen | 23 | Giants | 151 | 100 | 17 | .595 | 153 | 108 | 17 | .581 |
| M. Schottenheimer | 15 | Browns, Chiefs | 145 | 85 | 1 | .630 | 150 | 96 | 1 | .607 |
| Bill Parcells | 15 | Giants, Patriots, Jets | 138 | 100 | 1 | .579 | 149 | 106 | 1 | .582 |
| Joe Gibbs | 12 | Redskins | 124 | 60 | 0 | .674 | 140 | 65 | 0 | .683 |
| Hank Stram | 17 | Chiefs, Saints | 131 | 97 | 10 | .571 | 136 | 100 | 10 | .573 |
| Weeb Ewbank | 20 | Colts, Jets | 130 | 129 | 7 | .502 | 134 | 130 | 7 | .507 |
| Mike Ditka | 14 | Bears, Saints | 121 | 95 | 0 | .560 | 127 | 101 | 0 | .557 |
| Sid Gillman | 18 | Rams, Chargers, Oilers | 122 | 99 | 7 | .550 | 123 | 104 | 7 | .541 |
| †George Seifert | 9 | 49ers, Panthers | 113 | 47 | 0 | .706 | 123 | 52 | 0 | .703 |
| George Allen | 12 | Rams, Redskins | 116 | 47 | 5 | .705 | 118 | 54 | 5 | .681 |

†Active coach.

## Top Winning Percentages

| | W | L | T | Pct | | W | L | T | Pct |
|---|---|---|---|---|---|---|---|---|---|
| Vince Lombardi | 105 | 35 | 6 | .740 | George Halas | 324 | 151 | 31 | .671 |
| John Madden | 112 | 39 | 7 | .731 | Don Shula | 347 | 173 | 6 | .665 |
| †George Seifert | 123 | 52 | 0 | .703 | Curly Lambeau | 229 | 134 | 22 | .623 |
| Joe Gibbs | 140 | 65 | 0 | .683 | Bill Walsh | 102 | 63 | 1 | .617 |
| George Allen | 118 | 54 | 5 | .681 | Paul Brown | 170 | 108 | 6 | .609 |

Note: Minimum 100 victories.

†Active coach.

# Alltime Number-One Draft Choices

| Year | Team | Selection | Position |
|---|---|---|---|
| 1936 | Philadelphia | Jay Berwanger, Chicago | HB |
| 1937 | Philadelphia | Sam Francis, Nebraska | FB |
| 1938 | Cleveland | Corbett Davis, Indiana | FB |
| 1939 | Chicago Cardinals | Ki Aldrich, Texas Christian | C |
| 1940 | Chicago Cardinals | George Cafego, Tennessee | HB |
| 1941 | Chicago Bears | Tom Harmon, Michigan | HB |
| 1942 | Pittsburgh | Bill Dudley, Virginia | HB |
| 1943 | Detroit | Frank Sinkwich, Georgia | HB |
| 1944 | Boston | Angelo Bertelli, Notre Dame | QB |
| 1945 | Chicago Cardinals | Charley Trippi, Georgia | HB |
| 1946 | Boston | Frank Dancewicz, Notre Dame | QB |
| 1947 | Chicago Bears | Bob Fenimore, Oklahoma A&M | HB |
| 1948 | Washington | Harry Gilmer, Alabama | QB |
| 1949 | Philadelphia | Chuck Bednarik, Pennsylvania | C |
| 1950 | Detroit | Leon Hart, Notre Dame | E |
| 1951 | New York Giants | Kyle Rote, Southern Methodist | HB |
| 1952 | Los Angeles | Bill Wade, Vanderbilt | QB |
| 1953 | San Francisco | Harry Babcock, Georgia | E |
| 1954 | Cleveland | Bobby Garrett, Stanford | QB |
| 1955 | Baltimore | George Shaw, Oregon | QB |
| 1956 | Pittsburgh | Gary Glick, Colorado A&M | DB |
| 1957 | Green Bay | Paul Hornung, Notre Dame | HB |
| 1958 | Chicago Cardinals | King Hill, Rice | QB |
| 1959 | Green Bay | Randy Duncan, Iowa | QB |
| 1960 | Los Angeles | Billy Cannon, Louisiana St | RB |

| Year | Team | Selection | Position |
|------|------|-----------|----------|
| 1961 | Minnesota | Tommy Mason, Tulane | RB |
| | Buffalo (AFL) | Ken Rice, Auburn | G |
| 1962 | Washington | Ernie Davis, Syracuse | RB |
| | Oakland (AFL) | Roman Gabriel, N Carolina St | QB |
| 1963 | LA Rams | Terry Baker, Oregon St | QB |
| | Kansas City (AFL) | Buck Buchanan, Grambling | DT |
| 1964 | San Francisco | Dave Parks, Texas Tech | E |
| | Boston (AFL) | Jack Concannon, Boston College | QB |
| 1965 | NY Giants | Tucker Frederickson, Auburn | RB |
| | Houston (AFL) | Lawrence Elkins, Baylor | E |
| 1966 | Atlanta | Tommy Nobis, Texas | LB |
| | Miami (AFL) | Jim Grabowski, Illinois | RB |
| 1967 | Baltimore | Bubba Smith, Michigan St | DT |
| 1968 | Minnesota | Ron Yary, Southern California | T |
| 1969 | Buffalo (AFL) | O.J. Simpson, Southern California | RB |
| 1970 | Pittsburgh | Terry Bradshaw, Louisiana Tech | QB |
| 1971 | New England | Jim Plunkett, Stanford | QB |
| 1972 | Buffalo | Walt Patulski, Notre Dame | DE |
| 1973 | Houston | John Matuszak, Tampa | DE |
| 1974 | Dallas | Ed Jones, Tennessee St | DE |
| 1975 | Atlanta | Steve Bartkowski, California | QB |
| 1976 | Tampa Bay | Lee Roy Selmon, Oklahoma | DE |
| 1977 | Tampa Bay | Ricky Bell, Southern California | RB |
| 1978 | Houston | Earl Campbell, Texas | RB |
| 1979 | Buffalo | Tom Cousineau, Ohio St | LB |
| 1980 | Detroit | Billy Sims, Oklahoma | RB |
| 1981 | New Orleans | George Rogers, South Carolina | RB |
| 1982 | New England | Kenneth Sims, Texas | DT |
| 1983 | Baltimore | John Elway, Stanford | QB |
| 1984 | New England | Irving Fryar, Nebraska | WR |
| 1985 | Buffalo | Bruce Smith, Virginia Tech | DE |
| 1986 | Tampa Bay | Bo Jackson, Auburn | RB |
| 1987 | Tampa Bay | Vinny Testaverde, Miami (FL) | QB |
| 1988 | Atlanta | Aundray Bruce, Auburn | LB |
| 1989 | Dallas | Troy Aikman, UCLA | QB |
| 1990 | Indianapolis | Jeff George, Illinois | QB |
| 1991 | Dallas | Russell Maryland, Miami (FL) | DT |
| 1992 | Indianapolis | Steve Emtman, Washington | DT |
| 1993 | New England | Drew Bledsoe, Washington St | QB |
| 1994 | Cincinnati | Dan Wilkinson, Ohio St | DT |
| 1995 | Cincinnati | Ki-Jana Carter, Penn St | RB |
| 1996 | New York Jets | Keyshawn Johnson, Southern California | WR |
| 1997 | St Louis | Orlando Pace, Ohio St | OT |
| 1998 | Indianapolis | Peyton Manning, Tennessee | QB |
| 1999 | Cleveland | Tim Couch, Kentucky | QB |
| 2000 | Cleveland | Courtney Brown, Penn St | DE |
| 2001 | Atlanta | Michael Vick, Virginia Tech | QB |

From 1947 through 1958, the first selection in the draft was a bonus pick, awarded to the winner of a random draw. That club, in turn, forfeited its last-round draft choice. The winner of the bonus choice was eliminated from future draws. The system was abolished after 1958, by which time all clubs had received a bonus choice.

# Members of the Pro Football Hall of Fame

| | | |
|---|---|---|
| Herb Adderley | George Blanda | Guy Chamberlin |
| Lance Alworth | Mel Blount | Jack Christiansen |
| Doug Atkins | Terry Bradshaw | Earl (Dutch) Clark |
| Morris (Red) Badgro | Jim Brown | George Connor |
| Lem Barney | Paul Brown | Jimmy Conzelman |
| Cliff Battles | Roosevelt Brown | Lou Creekmur |
| Sammy Baugh | Willie Brown | Larry Csonka |
| Chuck Bednarik | Buck Buchanan | Al Davis |
| Bert Bell | Nick Buoniconti | Willie Davis |
| Bobby Bell | Dick Butkus | Len Dawson |
| Raymond Berry | Earl Campbell | Eric Dickerson |
| Charles W. Bidwill Sr. | Tony Canadeo | Dan Dierdorf |
| Fred Biletnikoff | Joe Carr | Mike Ditka |

Art Donovan
Tony Dorsett
John (Paddy) Driscoll
Bill Dudley
Albert Glen (Turk) Edwards
Weeb Ewbank
Tom Fears
Jim Finks
Ray Flaherty
Len Ford
Dan Fortmann
Dan Fouts
Frank Gatski
Bill George
Joe Gibbs
Frank Gifford
Sid Gillman
Otto Graham
Harold (Red) Grange
Bud Grant
Joe Greene
Forrest Gregg
Bob Griese
Lou Groza
Joe Guyon
George Halas
Jack Ham
John Hannah
Franco Harris
Mike Haynes
Ed Healey
Mel Hein
Ted Hendricks
Wilbur (Pete) Henry
Arnie Herber
Bill Hewitt
Clarke Hinkle
Elroy (Crazylegs) Hirsch
Paul Hornung
Ken Houston
Cal Hubbard
Sam Huff
Lamar Hunt
Don Hutson
Jimmy Johnson
John Henry Johnson
Charlie Joiner
David (Deacon) Jones
Stan Jones
Henry Jordan
Sonny Jurgensen
Leroy Kelly
Walt Kiesling
Frank (Bruiser) Kinard
Paul Krause
Earl (Curly) Lambeau
Jack Lambert
Tom Landry

Dick (Night Train) Lane
Jim Langer
Willie Lanier
Steve Largent
Yale Lary
Dante Lavelli
Bobby Layne
Alphonse (Tuffy) Leemans
Marv Levy
Bob Lilly
Larry Little
Vince Lombardi
Howie Long
Ronnie Lott
Sid Luckman
William Roy (Link) Lyman
Tom Mack
John Mackey
Tim Mara
Wellington Mara
Gino Marchetti
George Preston Marshall
Ollie Matson
Don Maynard
George McAfee
Mike McCormack
Tommy McDonald
Hugh McElhenny
Johnny (Blood) McNally
Mike Michalske
Wayne Millner
Bobby Mitchell
Ron Mix
Joe Montana
Lenny Moore
Marion Motley
Mike Munchak
Anthony Munoz
George Musso
Bronko Nagurski
Joe Namath
Earle (Greasy) Neale
Ernie Nevers
Ozzie Newsome
Ray Nitschke
Chuck Noll
Leo Nomellini
Merlin Olsen
Jim Otto
Steve Owen
Alan Page
Clarence (Ace) Parker
Jim Parker
Walter Payton
Joe Perry
Pete Pihos
Hugh (Shorty) Ray
Dan Reeves

Mel Renfro
John Riggins
Jim Ringo
Andy Robustelli
Art Rooney
Dan Rooney
Pete Rozelle
Bob St. Clair
Gale Sayers
Joe Schmidt
Tex Schramm
Lee Roy Selmon
Billy Shaw
Art Shell
Don Shula
O.J. Simpson
Mike Singletary
Jackie Slater
Jackie Smith
Bart Starr
Roger Staubach
Ernie Stautner
Jan Stenerud
Dwight Stephenson
Ken Strong
Joe Stydahar
Lynn Swann
Fran Tarkenton
Charley Taylor
Jim Taylor
Lawrence Taylor
Jim Thorpe
Y.A. Tittle
George Trafton
Charley Trippi
Emlen Tunnell
Clyde (Bulldog) Turner
Johnny Unitas
Gene Upshaw
Norm Van Brocklin
Steve Van Buren
Doak Walker
Bill Walsh
Paul Warfield
Bob Waterfield
Mike Webster
Arnie Weinmeister
Randy White
Dave Wilcox
Bill Willis
Larry Wilson
Kellen Winslow
Alex Wojciechowicz
Willie Wood
Ron Yary
Jack Youngblood

### Canadian Football League Grey Cup

| Year | Results | Site | Attendance |
|------|---------|------|------------|
| 1909 | U of Toronto 26, Parkdale 6 | Toronto | 3,807 |
| 1910 | U of Toronto 16, Hamilton Tigers 7 | Hamilton | 12,000 |
| 1911 | U of Toronto 14, Toronto 7 | Toronto | 13,687 |
| 1912 | Hamilton Alerts 11, Toronto 4 | Hamilton | 5,337 |
| 1913 | Hamilton Tigers 44, Parkdale 2 | Hamilton | 2,100 |
| 1914 | Toronto 14, U of Toronto 2 | Toronto | 10,500 |
| 1915 | Hamilton Tigers 13, Toronto RAA 7 | Toronto | 2,808 |
| 1916–19 | No game | — | — |
| 1920 | U of Toronto 16, Toronto 3 | Toronto | 10,088 |
| 1921 | Toronto 23, Edmonton 0 | Toronto | 9,558 |
| 1922 | Queen's U 13, Edmonton 1 | Kingston | 4,700 |
| 1923 | Queen's U 54, Regina 0 | Toronto | 8,629 |
| 1924 | Queen's U 11, Balmy Beach 3 | Toronto | 5,978 |
| 1925 | Ottawa Senators 24, Winnipeg 1 | Ottawa | 6,900 |
| 1926 | Ottawa Senators 10, Toronto U 7 | Toronto | 8,276 |
| 1927 | Balmy Beach 9, Hamilton Tigers 6 | Toronto | 13,676 |
| 1928 | Hamilton Tigers 30, Regina 0 | Hamilton | 4,767 |
| 1929 | Hamilton Tigers 14, Regina 3 | Hamilton | 1,906 |
| 1930 | Balmy Beach 11, Regina 6 | Toronto | 3,914 |
| 1931 | Montreal AAA 22, Regina 0 | Montreal | 5,112 |
| 1932 | Hamilton Tigers 25, Regina 6 | Hamilton | 4,806 |
| 1933 | Toronto 4, Sarnia 3 | Sarnia | 2,751 |
| 1934 | Sarnia 20, Regina 12 | Toronto | 8,900 |
| 1935 | Winnipeg 18, Hamilton Tigers 12 | Hamilton | 6,405 |
| 1936 | Sarnia 26, Ottawa RR 20 | Toronto | 5,883 |
| 1937 | Toronto 4, Winnipeg 3 | Toronto | 11,522 |
| 1938 | Toronto 30, Winnipeg 7 | Toronto | 18,778 |
| 1939 | Winnipeg 8, Ottawa 7 | Ottawa | 11,738 |
| 1940 | Ottawa 12, Balmy Beach 5 | Ottawa | 1,700 |
| 1940 | Ottawa 8, Balmy Beach 2 | Toronto | 4,998 |
| 1941 | Winnipeg 18, Ottawa 16 | Toronto | 19,065 |
| 1942 | Toronto RCAF 8, Winnipeg RCAF 5 | Toronto | 12,455 |
| 1943 | Hamilton F Wild 23, Winnipeg RCAF 14 | Toronto | 16,423 |
| 1944 | Montreal St H-D Navy 7, Hamilton F Wild 6 | Hamilton | 3,871 |
| 1945 | Toronto 35, Winnipeg 0 | Toronto | 18,660 |
| 1946 | Toronto 28, Winnipeg 6 | Toronto | 18,960 |
| 1947 | Toronto 10, Winnipeg 9 | Toronto | 18,885 |
| 1948 | Calgary 12, Ottawa 7 | Toronto | 20,013 |
| 1949 | Montreal Als 28, Calgary 15 | Toronto | 20,087 |
| 1950 | Toronto 13, Winnipeg 0 | Toronto | 27,101 |
| 1951 | Ottawa 21, Saskatchewan 14 | Toronto | 27,341 |
| 1952 | Toronto 21, Edmonton 11 | Toronto | 27,391 |
| 1953 | Hamilton Ticats 12, Winnipeg 6 | Toronto | 27,313 |
| 1954 | Edmonton 26, Montreal 25 | Toronto | 27,321 |
| 1955 | Edmonton 34, Montreal 19 | Vancouver | 39,417 |
| 1956 | Edmonton 50, Montreal 27 | Toronto | 27,425 |
| 1957 | Hamilton 32, Winnipeg 7 | Toronto | 27,051 |
| 1958 | Winnipeg 35, Hamilton 28 | Vancouver | 36,567 |
| 1959 | Winnipeg 21, Hamilton 7 | Toronto | 33,133 |
| 1960 | Ottawa 16, Edmonton 6 | Vancouver | 38,102 |
| 1961 | Winnipeg 21, Hamilton 14 | Toronto | 32,651 |
| 1962 | Winnipeg 28, Hamilton 27 | Toronto | 32,655 |
| 1963 | Hamilton 21, British Columbia 10 | Vancouver | 36,545 |
| 1964 | British Columbia 34, Hamilton 24 | Toronto | 32,655 |
| 1965 | Hamilton 22, Winnipeg 16 | Toronto | 32,655 |
| 1966 | Saskatchewan 29, Ottawa 14 | Vancouver | 36,553 |
| 1967 | Hamilton 24, Saskatchewan 1 | Ottawa | 31,358 |
| 1968 | Ottawa 24, Calgary 21 | Toronto | 32,655 |
| 1969 | Ottawa 29, Saskatchewan 11 | Montreal | 33,172 |
| 1970 | Montreal 23, Calgary 10 | Toronto | 32,669 |
| 1971 | Calgary 14, Toronto 11 | Vancouver | 34,484 |
| 1972 | Hamilton 13, Saskatchewan 10 | Hamilton | 33,993 |
| 1973 | Ottawa 22, Edmonton 18 | Toronto | 36,653 |
| 1974 | Montreal 20, Edmonton 7 | Vancouver | 34,450 |
| 1975 | Edmonton 9, Montreal 8 | Calgary | 32,454 |

## Canadian Football League Grey Cup *(Cont.)*

| Year | Results | Site | Attendance |
|------|---------|------|-----------|
| 1976 | Ottawa 23, Saskatchewan 20 | Toronto | 53,467 |
| 1977 | Montreal 41, Edmonton 6 | Montreal | 68,318 |
| 1978 | Edmonton 20, Montreal 13 | Toronto | 54,695 |
| 1979 | Edmonton 17, Montreal 9 | Montreal | 65,113 |
| 1980 | Edmonton 48, Hamilton 10 | Toronto | 54,661 |
| 1981 | Edmonton 26, Ottawa 23 | Montreal | 52,478 |
| 1982 | Edmonton 32, Toronto 16 | Toronto | 54,741 |
| 1983 | Toronto 18, British Columbia 17 | Vancouver | 59,345 |
| 1984 | Winnipeg 47, Hamilton 17 | Edmonton | 60,081 |
| 1985 | British Columbia 37, Hamilton 24 | Montreal | 56,723 |
| 1986 | Hamilton 39, Edmonton 15 | Vancouver | 59,621 |
| 1987 | Edmonton 38, Toronto 36 | Vancouver | 59,478 |
| 1988 | Winnipeg 22, British Columbia 21 | Ottawa | 50,604 |
| 1989 | Saskatchewan 43, Hamilton 40 | Toronto | 54,088 |
| 1990 | Winnipeg 50, Edmonton 11 | Vancouver | 46,968 |
| 1991 | Toronto 36, Calgary 21 | Winnipeg | 51,985 |
| 1992 | Calgary 24, Winnipeg 10 | Toronto | 45,863 |
| 1993 | Edmonton 33, Winnipeg 23 | Calgary | 50,035 |
| 1994 | British Columbia 26, Baltimore 23 | Vancouver | 55,097 |
| 1995 | Baltimore 37, Calgary 20 | Regina, Saskatchewan | 52,564 |
| 1996 | Toronto 43, Edmonton 37 | Hamilton, Ontario | 38,595 |
| 1997 | Toronto 47, Saskatchewan 23 | Edmonton | 60,431 |
| 1998 | Calgary 26, Hamilton 24 | Winnipeg | 34,157 |
| 1999 | Hamilton 32, Calgary 21 | Vancouver | 45,118 |
| 2000 | British Columbia 28, Montreal 26 | Calgary | 43,822 |

In 1909, Earl Grey, the Governor-General of Canada, donated a trophy for the Rugby Football Championship of Canada. The trophy, which subsequently became known as the Grey Cup, was originally open only to teams registered with the Canada Rugby Union. Since 1954, it has been awarded to the winner of the Canadian Football League's championship game.

### AMERICAN FOOTBALL LEAGUE I

| Year | Champion | Record |
|------|----------|--------|
| 1926 | Philadelphia Quakers | 7-2 |

### AMERICAN FOOTBALL LEAGUE II

| Year | Champion | Record |
|------|----------|--------|
| 1936 | Boston Shamrocks | 8-3 |
| 1937 | LA Bulldogs | 8-0 |

### AMERICAN FOOTBALL LEAGUE III

| Year | Champion | Record |
|------|----------|--------|
| 1940 | Columbus Bullies | 8-1-1 |
| 1941 | Columbus Bullies | 5-1-2 |

### ALL-AMERICAN FOOTBALL CONFERENCE

| Year | Championship Game |
|------|-------------------|
| 1946 | Cleveland 14, NY Yankees 9 |
| 1947 | Cleveland 14, NY Yankees 3 |
| 1948 | Cleveland 49, Buffalo 7 |
| 1949 | Cleveland 21, San Francisco 7 |

### WORLD FOOTBALL LEAGUE

| Year | World Bowl Championship |
|------|-------------------------|
| 1974 | Birmingham 22, Florida 21 |
| 1975 | Disbanded midseason |

### UNITED STATES FOOTBALL LEAGUE

| Year | Championship Game |
|------|-------------------|
| 1983 | Michigan 24, Philadelphia 22 |
| 1984 | Philadelphia 23, Arizona 3 |
| 1985 | Baltimore 28, Oakland 24 |

### NFL EUROPE

| Year | Champion | Record |
|------|----------|--------|
| 1991 | London | 9-1-0 |
| 1992 | Sacramento | 8-2-0 |
| 1995 | Frankfurt | 6-4-0 |
| 1996 | Scotland | 7-3-0 |
| 1997 | Barcelona | 5-5-0 |
| 1998 | Rhein | 7-3-0 |
| 1999 | Frankfurt | 6-4-0 |
| 2000 | Rhein | 7-3-0 |
| 2001 | Berlin | 6-4-0 |

Known as World League of American Football until 1998.

Josh Heupel of
national champion
Oklahoma

# College
# Football

# Oklahoma!

## The wins came sweeping down the plain for the surprising Sooners, who defied the skeptics and won the national title

### BY B.J. SCHECTER

SOME DANCED, some cried and others glided around the turf of Pro Player Stadium in a state of jubilation. Oklahoma senior quarterback Josh Heupel wasn't sure what to do. He was mobbed by teammates, coaches and fans, and when he looked up at the scoreboard, which read OKLAHOMA 13, FLORIDA STATE 2, he could hardly believe it.

Indeed, much of Oklahoma's perfect 2000 season, which was capped off by a win over the heavily favored Seminoles in the Orange Bowl for the national title, was scarcely within the realm of belief. That Florida State had reached the BCS national championship for the third straight year was no surprise, but Oklahoma's presence in the game was like your country cousin crashing the cotillion. At the beginning of the season the Sooners weren't even considered contenders. After finishing 7–5 in 1999, Oklahoma began the year ranked No. 19. But with one impressive victory after another the Sooners slowly crept onto the nation's radar screen. First it was a 63–14 pasting of Texas, then a 41–31 win over

Kansas State, followed by a dominating 31–14 win over then–No. 1 Nebraska, and finally a 27–24 triumph over Kansas State again in the Big 12 championship game.

Yet with each victory, Oklahoma seemed to win as many critics as converts. Even after the Sooners finished the regular season as the nation's only undefeated team in Division I-A, they weren't shown much respect. Most observers believed Florida State would walk all over Oklahoma in the Orange Bowl. The pregame line had the Seminoles favored by 11. None of this mattered to coach Bob Stoops and his troops. "People aren't at practice every day," said Stoops. "They don't see what I see. I don't pay much attention to what people who don't know what they're talking about say or think. If the oddsmakers determined our fate, we'd be 7–4."

In the week leading up to the national title game, all Oklahoma heard was how it didn't have the athletes to keep up with Florida State. Stoops and his players listened to the analysis and nodded their heads. Florida State was loaded with talent, they agreed, but

BOB ROSATO

**Down 6–0 in the fourth quarter of the Orange Bowl, Florida State saw its best chance slip through Morgan's hands .**

it wasn't as if Oklahoma was stocked with Division I-AA players. "I've heard all this talk about how fast Florida State is," Stoops said the day before the game. "But I've never heard people describe our guys as slow."

Publicly, Stoops said nothing as the experts pumped up Florida State and downplayed the talent and desire of his team. Privately, he stewed. A starting safety at Iowa from 1979 to '82 and a two-time All–Big Ten selection, the 40-year-old Stoops knows something about overachieving. When he was a Hawkeye, there were many players who had more talent than he did, but few had his heart. Four days before the game, Stoops was quietly confident as his team finished practice.

"We've been incredibly focused all week and believe me, we'll be ready," he said. "I'm very confident we'll win the game. We've been ready all year and trust me, we'll be ready for the challenge."

Stoops came to Oklahoma—2000 was his second season with the Sooners—with an impressive coaching résumé. Most people are lucky to find one mentor, but Stoops had three: former Iowa coach Hayden Fry, Kansas State coach Bill Snyder and Florida coach Steve Spurrier. In 1996, Stoops made a name for himself as Spurrier's defensive coordinator, helping the Gators win the national title. Against Florida State in the Sugar Bowl that season, Stoops assembled an airtight defensive game plan and the Gators held the Seminoles to 19 points below their regular-season scoring average, routing them 52–20.

After watching this year's Florida State team on film, Stoops was quick to remind his staff that the Seminoles' offensive scheme in 2000—potent though it was—was essentially the same as it had been in 1996. "It's amazing," said one member of the Oklahoma coaching staff two days before the game. "In four years they've hardly changed a thing."

The task of neutralizing this year's model of the souped-up Seminole O—which featured Heisman Trophy–winning quarter-

**James Jackson (21) and Miami routed Florida 37–20 in the Sugar Bowl.**

back Chris Weinke, a 28-year-old senior—fell to Stoop's younger brother, Mike, the Sooners' co-defensive coordinator. The Seminoles came in averaging 549 yards per game, and Weinke had read coverages like pop-up books. Mike Stoops knew he would have to disguise his defensive schemes.

Even without their leading receiver, Marvin (Snoop) Minnis, who was academically ineligible for the game, the Seminoles felt they could pick apart the Oklahoma secondary. As FSU coach Bobby Bowden told his staff early in the year: "We may never have an offense this good again. We have an outstanding quarterback, two good running backs, big-play receivers and the best offensive line we've ever had."

Indeed, after an Oct. 7 loss to Miami, Florida State looked like a pro team for the remainder of the season, moving the ball and scoring at will. But against a stifling Oklahoma defense, "The train just kept coming off the tracks," Weinke would say later.

Mike Stoops decided to use five or six defensive backs against Weinke. But in order for this strategy to work, the Sooners had to be able to stop the run and disguise their cov-

erages. They did both, holding FSU to 27 yards on the ground and confusing Weinke all night. Nickleback Ontei Jones would start several yards off the line of scrimmage and sprint back into coverage just before the ball was snapped. Free safety J.T. Thatcher would line up as a linebacker on one play and a safety on the next. He'd blitz one play and fake a blitz on the next.

Oklahoma's actual coverages and sets were the same ones they had used all year, but they looked different. With Florida State's running game held in check, its play-calling became predictable, and even a no-huddle offense didn't improve the results. "It seemed like they had radar," said Seminoles receiver Atrews Bell. "Everything we tried they were ready for."

Still, Oklahoma wasn't exactly running roughshod over the Florida State defense. The Sooners led 3–0 at the half and 6–0 in the fourth quarter. It appeared as if the Seminoles would take a 7–6 lead when Robert Morgan dived for a catchable pass in the end zone. But Morgan, like many of Weinke's receivers all night, couldn't hold on to the ball.

The Sooner defense effectively put the game away late in the fourth quarter when linebacker Rocky Calmus knocked the ball out of Weinke's grasp as the quarterback scrambled out of the pocket. Sooner defensive back Roy Williams recovered the fumble at the Florida State 15. Two plays later Quentin Griffin scored the game's only touchdown on a 10-yard run, giving Oklahoma a 13–0 lead. Florida State's only points would come on a safety with 55 seconds remaining in the game.

For Heupel it was a fitting end to a circuitous college career which began in his hometown of Aberdeen, S. Dak., and made stops at Weber State and Snow Junior College before settling in Norman in 1999. Steady and never flashy, Heupel always found a way to get the job done. He passed for only 214 yards in the Orange Bowl, but he made very few mistakes, and his team won.

The game was a bit of a grudge match for Heupel. Though he never publicly admitted it, Heupel was deeply disappointed that he didn't win the Heisman Trophy. He was a close runner-up, but the award went to Weinke, his flashier counterpart at Florida State, who passed for 4,167 yards and threw 33 touchdown passes in 2000. If Heupel was looking for revenge, he certainly got it when his Sooners defied almost everyone's expectations in the Orange Bowl. After the game, Heupel and Patrick McClung, a minister from Norman who had been Heupel's spiritual guide all season, knelt at midfield and gave thanks. Heupel's tears mixed with the rain, which had started to fall in sheets into an emptying Pro Player Stadium.

By season's end many college football fans would have given thanks if the convoluted Bowl Championship Series had ceased to exist. To be sure, Oklahoma's impressive victory over Florida State left no doubt as to who was the best team in the nation, but the BCS system created a simmering pot of controversy before the major bowls kicked off. Everyone agreed that the Sooners, the only undefeated team in the nation, deserved to be in the championship game. But many observers believed their opponent should have been second-ranked Miami, which beat Florida State 27–24 in October. Others thought 10–1 Washington, which beat Miami in September, deserved a shot at the title. Then there were 10–1 Oregon State and 10–1 Virginia Tech making their claims. Virginia Tech's only loss came against Miami, in a game the Hokies started without superstar quarterback Michael Vick, who was hurt. Prior to the season, Vick was the odds-on favorite to win the Heisman Trophy, and he probably would have done so if an ankle injury hadn't limited him in four games. A sophomore, Vick declared himself eligible for the NFL draft soon after the season ended.

If Florida State had beaten Oklahoma, Miami would have been crowned co–national champion. The Hurricanes took care of their business by beating Florida 37–20 in the Sugar Bowl. The victory capped a remarkable turnaround for Miami, which had been a power in the late '80s and early '90s but had fallen hard from '92 to '98. The Miami program was rife with unseemly incidents off the field, and in 1995 its administration admitted that 57 of its players had received fraudulent Pell Grants. Later that year the NCAA penalized the Hurricanes in a variety of ways; the most serious was the loss of 31 scholarships over three years.

Butch Davis took over as head coach just before Miami was saddled with the sanctions. He quickly cleaned up shop and threw players off the team who wouldn't adhere to his rules. In 1999, the Hurricanes were 9–4 and ranked 15th in the final national polls; this year, they had a legitimate gripe when they weren't invited to the national title game.

Another team that worked its way up from the depths was Oregon State. Interestingly enough, the Beavers' coach was former Miami man Dennis Erickson, who had been with the Hurricanes during the Pell Grant scandal. When Erickson came to Corvallis from the Seattle Seahawks in 1999, Oregon State had just set an NCAA record with its 28th consecutive losing season. In Erickson's first year the Beavers went 7–5, and in 2000 they went 11–1. If anyone doubted that the Beavers were for real they needed to look no further than Oregon State's 41–9 trouncing of Notre Dame in the Fiesta Bowl.

As impressive as the coaching jobs by Stoops, Davis and Erickson were, nobody topped Lou Holtz's efforts in his second year at South Carolina. In 1999, Holtz inherited a Gamecocks program in disarray, and during his first season one thing after another went wrong. South Carolina failed to win a single game. The Gamecocks entered the 2000 season with the longest losing streak in Division I-A, 21 games. Ending that run of ignominy was the first order of business, which the Gamecocks dispatched in their opener, routing New Mexico State 31–0. South Carolina would win seven of its first eight games before

**Drew Brees (with ball) and Purdue fell 34–29 to Washington in the Rose Bowl.**

losing three straight to Tennessee, Florida and Clemson. But the Gamecocks ended the season back on the winning side of the ledger, beating Ohio State 24–7 in the Outback Bowl to finish 8–4.

That defeat turned out to be John Cooper's last as coach of Ohio State. It didn't matter that Cooper had won 72% of his games in 13 seasons in Columbus. His Buckeyes had trouble in big games, as evidenced by their 2-10-1 record against Michigan, and he never seemed to win over Ohio State's fans.

By season's end, coaches at some of the biggest programs in the land had received pink slips. Notre Dame coach Bob Davie kept his job, but coaches at Alabama, Georgia, Arizona, Arizona State, USC, Missouri, Maryland, North Carolina and Oklahoma State were shown the door. The pressure and the stakes at big-time programs showed no sign of decreasing. One wonders what effect coaches like Stoops, Erickson, Davis and Holtz will have. They showed that it is possible to turn things around in a couple of seasons, and may have inadvertently fueled the increasingly widespread produce-now-or-get-fired mentality.

Whatever his effect on the relationship between coaches and athletic directors, Stoops has a lot to teach his peers. When he took over in 1999 the Sooners were a laughingstock. They hadn't had a winning season or won a bowl game since 1993. From the start, Stoops embraced Oklahoma's tradition, inviting legendary former coach Barry Switzer and former star linebacker Brian Bosworth to be part of the program. Stoops wanted his players to believe that putting on the Oklahoma uniform was a privilege. The players bought every word, and the result was an improbable national championship.

"Our players recognize that the history of Oklahoma is about winning national championships," Stoops said. Yes, the history, the present and by all indications, the future.

## Final Polls

### Associated Press

| | | Record | Pts | Head Coach | SI Preseason Rank |
|---|---|---|---|---|---|
| 1. | Oklahoma (71) | 13–0 | 1775 | Bob Stoops | 23 |
| 2. | Miami (FL) | 11–1 | 1690 | Butch Davis | 10 |
| 3. | Washington | 11–1 | 1634 | Rick Neuheisel | 13 |
| 4. | Oregon St | 11–1 | 1539 | Dennis Erickson | 35 |
| 5. | Florida St | 11–2 | 1488 | Bobby Bowden | 2 |
| 6. | Virginia Tech | 11–1 | 1432 | Frank Beamer | 12 |
| 7. | Oregon | 10–2 | 1299 | Mike Belotti | 27 |
| 8. | Nebraska | 10–2 | 1282 | Frank Solich | 1 |
| 9. | Kansas St | 11–3 | 1258 | Bill Snyder | 6 |
| 10. | Florida | 10–3 | 1128 | Steve Spurrier | 11 |
| 11. | Michigan | 9–3 | 1061 | Lloyd Carr | 4 |
| 12. | Texas | 9–3 | 894 | Mack Brown | 9 |
| 13. | Purdue | 8–4 | 765 | Joe Tiller | 16 |
| 14. | Colorado St | 10–2 | 640 | Sonny Lubeck | 24 |
| 15. | Notre Dame | 9–3 | 611 | Bob Davie | 26 |
| 16. | Clemson | 9–3 | 563 | Tommy Bowden | 8 |
| 17. | Georgia Tech | 9–3 | 545 | George O'Leary | 33 |
| 18. | Auburn | 9–4 | 498 | Tommy Tuberville | 55 |
| 19. | S Carolina | 8–4 | 486 | Lou Holtz | 73 |
| 20. | Georgia | 8–4 | 430 | Jim Donnan | 7 |
| 21. | Texas Christian | 10–2 | 406 | Dennis Franchione | 15 |
| 22. | Louisiana State | 8–4 | 340 | Nick Saban | 47 |
| 23. | Wisconsin | 9–4 | 208 | Barry Alvarez | 5 |
| 24. | Mississippi St | 8–4 | 197 | Jackie Sherrill | 41 |
| 25. | Iowa St | 9–3 | 188 | Dan McCarney | 54 |

Note: As voted by a panel of 71 sportswriters and broadcasters following bowl games (1st-place votes in parentheses).

### USA Today/ESPN

| | | Pts | Prev Rank | | | Pts | Prev Rank |
|---|---|---|---|---|---|---|---|
| 1. | Oklahoma (59) | 1475 | 1 | 14. | Clemson | 590 | 13 |
| 2. | Miami (FL) | 1404 | 2 | 15. | Colorado St | 587 | 22 |
| 3. | Washington | 1336 | 4 | 16. | Notre Dame | 457 | 10 |
| 4. | Florida St | 1253 | 3 | 17. | Georgia | 357 | 24 |
| 5. | Oregon St | 1245 | 6 | 18. | Texas Christian | 341 | 16 |
| 6. | Virginia Tech | 1215 | 5 | 19. | Georgia Tech | 335 | 17 |
| 7. | Nebraska | 1099 | 8 | 20. | Auburn | 325 | 20 |
| 8. | Kansas St | 1077 | 9 | 21. | S Carolina | 314 | NR |
| 9. | Oregon | 1009 | 11 | 22. | Mississippi St | 272 | NR |
| 10. | Michigan | 901 | 15 | 23. | Iowa St | 225 | NR |
| 11. | Florida | 899 | 7 | 24. | Wisconsin | 220 | NR |
| 12. | Texas | 731 | 12 | 25. | Tennessee | 159 | 21 |
| 13. | Purdue | 626 | 14 | | | | |

Note: As voted by a panel of 59 Division I-A head coaches; 25 points for 1st, 24 for 2nd, etc. (1st-place votes in parentheses).

## Bowls and Playoffs

### NCAA Division I-A Bowl Results

| Date | Bowl | Result | Payout/Team ($) | Attendance |
|---|---|---|---|---|
| 12-20-00 | Mobile Alabama | Southern Miss 28, Texas Christian 21 | 750,000 | 40,300 |
| 12-21-00 | Las Vegas | Nevada–Las Vegas 31, Arkansas 14 | 800,000 | 29,113 |
| 12-24-00 | Oahu | Georgia 37, Virginia 14 | 750,000 | 24,187 |
| 12-25-00 | Aloha | Boston College 31, Arizona St 17 | 750,000 | 24,397 |
| 12-27-00 | Motor City | Marshall 25, Cincinnati 14 | 750,000 | 52,911 |
| 12-27-00 | GalleryFurniture.com | E Carolina 40, Texas Tech 27 | 750,000 | 33,899 |
| 12-28-00 | Insight.com | Iowa St 37, Pittsburgh 29 | 750,000 | 41,813 |
| 12-28-00 | Music City | W Virginia 49, Mississippi 38 | 750,000 | 47,119 |

### NCAA Division I-A Bowl Results *(Cont.)*

| Date | Bowl | Result | Payout/Team ($) | Attendance |
|---|---|---|---|---|
| 12-28-00 | Humanitarian | Boise St 38, Texas–El Paso | 750,000 | 26,203 |
| 12-28-00 | MicronPC.com | N Carolina St 38, Minnesota 30 | 750,000 | 28,359 |
| 12-29-00 | Sun | Wisconsin 21, UCLA 20 | 1 million | 49,093 |
| 12-29-00 | Liberty | Colorado St 22, Louisville 17 | 1.25 million | 58,302 |
| 12-29-00 | Peach | Louisiana St 28, Georgia Tech 14 | 1.8 million | 73,614 |
| 12-29-00 | Holiday | Oregon 35, Texas 30 | 1.9 million | 63,278 |
| 12-30-00 | Alamo | Nebraska 66, Northwestern 17 | 1.2 million | 60,028 |
| 12-31-00 | Silicon Valley Classic | Air Force 37, Fresno St 34 | 1.2 million | 26,542 |
| 12-31-00 | Independence | Mississippi St 43, Texas A&M 41 | 1.1 million | 36,974 |
| 1-1-01 | Cotton | Kansas St 35, Tennessee 21 | 2.5 million | 63,465 |
| 1-1-01 | Outback | S Carolina 24, Ohio St 7 | 2 million | 65,229 |
| 1-1-01 | Gator | Virginia Tech 41, Clemson 20 | 1.4 million | 68,741 |
| 1-1-01 | Florida Citrus | Michigan 31, Auburn 28 | 4 million | 66,928 |
| 1-1-01 | Fiesta | Oregon St 41, Notre Dame 9 | 13.5 million | 75,428 |
| 1-1-01 | Rose | Washington 34, Purdue 24 | 13.5 million | 94,392 |
| 1-2-01 | Sugar | Miami (FL) 37, Florida 20 | 13.5 million | 64,407 |
| 1-3-01 | Orange | Oklahoma 13, Florida St 2 | 11–13 million | 76,835 |

### NCAA Division I-AA Championship Boxscore

| | | | | |
|---|---|---|---|---|
| **Georgia Southern** ....13 | 7 | 0 | 7 | —27 |
| **Montana** ....................3 | 0 | 6 | 16 | —25 |

**FIRST QUARTER**

GS: McCoy recovers fumble in end zone (Shelton kick), 13:19.
GS: Johnson 49 pass from Revere (kick failed), 2:57.
M: FG Snyder 38, 1:07.

**SECOND QUARTER**

GS: Peterson 1 run (Shelton kick), 0:33.

**THIRD QUARTER**

M: Molden 17 pass from Edwards (kick failed), 3:41.

**FOURTH QUARTER**

M: Huntsberger 65 run (kick failed), 14:36.
M: Humphery 2 run (Humphery reception), 11:53.

**FOURTH QUARTER** *(Cont.)*

GS: Peterson 57 run (Shelton kick), 11:29.
M: Safety, 0:15.

| | GA Southern | Montana |
|---|---|---|
| First downs | 14 | 28 |
| Rushing yardage | 51–277 | 36–211 |
| Passing yardage | 113 | 276 |
| Return yardage | 18 | 7 |
| Passes (comp-att-int) | 5-8-0 | 29-52-2 |
| Punts (no.–avg) | 6–39.2 | 4–28.8 |
| Fumbles (no.–lost) | 4–2 | 2–1 |
| Penalties (no.–yards) | 8–60 | 5–36 |

Att: 17,156.

### Small College Championship Summaries

**NCAA DIVISION II**

**First round:** NW Missouri St 31, N Dakota St 17; NE–Omaha 14, Pittsburg St 3; Catawba 28, W Georgia 24; Delta St 49, Valdosta St 12; Northwood (MI) 28, Indiana (PA) 0; Bloomsburg 46, Saginaw Valey 32; UC–Davis 48, Chadron St 10; Mesa St 40, Northeastern St 21.

**Quarterfinals:** N Dakota St 43, NE–Omaha 21; Delta St 20, Catawba 14; Bloomsburg 38, Northwood 14; UC–Davis 62, Mesa St 18.

**Semifinals:** Delta St 34, N Dakota St 16; Bloomsburg 58, UC–Davis 48.

**Championship:** 12-9-00 Florence, AL

| | | | | |
|---|---|---|---|---|
| Delta St | 14 | 21 | 14 | 14—63 |
| Bloomsburg | 14 | 0 | 14 | 6—34 |

**NCAA DIVISION III**

**First round:** Ohio Northern 47, Millikin 21; Hanover 20, Hope (MI) 3; Wittenberg 31, Aurora 20; Springfield 31, Montclair St 29; Widener 33, Union (NY) 26; Hobart 25, Bridgewater St (MA) 0; Central (IA) 29, St. Norbert 14; Pacific Lutheran 41, Bethel (MN) 13; St. John's (MN) 26, WI–Stout 19; Western Maryland 38, Emory & Henry 14; Trinity (TX) 21, Wesley (DE) 3; Bridgewater (VA) 59, Washington & Jefferson (PA) 42.

**NCAA DIVISION III** *(Cont.)*

**Second Round:** Mount Union 59, Ohio Northern 28; Wittenberg 32, Hanover 21; Springfield 13, Brockport St 6; Widener 40, Hobart 14; Central 20, Linfield 17 (ot); St. John's 28, Pacific Lutheran 21 (ot); Hardin-Simmons 32, Western Maryland 14; Trinity 47, Bridgewater 41 (ot).

**Quarterfinals:** Mount Union 32, Wittenberg 15; Widener 61, Springfield 27; St. John's 21, Central 18; Hardin-Simmons 33, Trinity 30.

**Semifinals:** Mount Union 70, Widener 30; St. John's 38, Hardin-Simmons 14.

**Championship:** 12-16-00 Salem, VA

| | | | | |
|---|---|---|---|---|
| Mount Union | 7 | 0 | 0 | 3—10 |
| St. John's | 0 | 7 | 0 | 0—7 |

**NAIA CHAMPIONSHIP**

12-16-00 Hardin County, TN

| | | | | |
|---|---|---|---|---|
| Georgetown (KY) | 14 | 0 | 0 | 6—20 |
| Northwestern Oklahoma | 0 | 0 | 0 | 0—0 |

## Heisman Memorial Trophy

| Player, School | Class | Pos | 1st | 2nd | 3rd | Total |
|---|---|---|---|---|---|---|
| Chris Weinke, Florida St | Sr | QB | 369 | 216 | 89 | 1628 |
| Josh Heupel, Oklahoma | Sr | QB | 286 | 290 | 114 | 1552 |
| Drew Brees, Purdue | Sr | QB | 69 | 107 | 198 | 619 |
| LaDainian Tomlinson, TCU | Sr | RB | 47 | 110 | 205 | 566 |
| Damien Anderson, Northwestern | Jr | RB | 6 | 20 | 43 | 101 |
| Michael Vick, Virginia Tech | So | QB | 7 | 14 | 34 | 83 |
| Santana Moss, Miami (FL) | Sr | WR | 3 | 9 | 28 | 55 |
| Marques Tuiosospo, Washington | Sr | QB | 5 | 8 | 10 | 41 |
| Ken Simonton, Oregon St | Jr | RB | 1 | 5 | 12 | 25 |
| Rudi Johnson, Auburn | Jr | RB | 3 | 1 | 9 | 20 |

Note: Former Heisman winners and the media vote, with ballots allowing for three names (3 points for 1st, 2 for 2nd, 1 for 3rd).

## Other Awards

Maxwell Award ............................................Drew Brees, Purdue, QB
*Sporting News* Player of the Year ..............Josh Heupel, Oklahoma, QB
Walter Camp Player of the Year ................Josh Heupel, Oklahoma, QB
Chuck Bednarik Award (Defense) .............Dan Morgan, Miami (FL), LB
Vince Lombardi/Rotary Award (Lineman)...Jamal Reynolds, Florida St, DE
Outland Trophy (Interior lineman) .............John Henderson, Tennessee, DT
Davey O'Brien Award (QB) ........................Chris Weinke, Florida St, QB
Unitas Golden Arm Award (Senior QB)......Chris Weinke, Florida St, QB
Doak Walker Award (RB) ...........................LaDainian Tomlinson, Texas Christian, RB
Biletnikoff Award (WR) ...............................Antonio Bryant, Pittsburgh, WR
Butkus Award (Linebacker).......................Dan Morgan, Miami (FL), LB
Jim Thorpe Award (Defensive back)..........Jamar Fletcher, Wisconsin, CB
Walter Payton Award (Div I-AA Player) ......Louis Ivory, Furman, RB
Harlon Hill Trophy (Div II Player) ................Dusty Bonner, Valdosta St, QB
Gagliardi Trophy (Div III Player) ................Chad Johnson, Pacific Lutheran, QB

## Coaches' Awards

Walter Camp Award ....................................Bob Stoops, Oklahoma
Eddie Robinson Award (Div I-AA)..............Joe Glenn, Montana
Bobby Dodd Award .....................................George O' Leary, Georgia Tech
Bear Bryant Award ......................................Bob Stoops, Oklahoma

### AFCA COACHES OF THE YEAR

Division I-A ...................................................Bob Stoops, Oklahoma
Division I-AA................................................Paul Johnson, Georgia Southern
Division II.....................................................Danny Hale, Bloomsburg
Division III....................................................Larry Kehres, Mount Union

## Football Writers Association of America All-America Team

### OFFENSE

Josh Heupel, Oklahoma, Sr ...............Quarterback
LaDainian Tomlinson, TCU, Sr ...........Running back
Damien Anderson, Northwestern, Jr ...Running back
Brian Natkin, Texas–El Paso, Sr .........Tight end
Marvin Minnis, Florida St, Sr...............Wide receiver
Antonio Bryant, Pittsburgh, So ...........Wide receiver
Dominic Raiola, Nebraska, Jr..............Center
Chris Brown, Georgia Tech, Sr ...........OL
Steve Hutchinson, Michigan Sr ...........OL
Leonard Davis, Texas, Sr ....................OL
Joaquin Gonzalez, Miami (FL), Jr .......OL
Jonathon Ruffin, Cincinnati, So ...........K
Santana Moss, Miami (FL), Sr .............KR

### DEFENSE

Jamal Reynolds, Florida St, Sr ............DL
John Henderson, Tennessee, Jr .........DL
Justin Smith, Missouri, Jr.....................DL
Andre Carter, California, Sr.................DL
Levar Fisher, N Carolina St, Jr ............Linebacker
Dan Morgan, Miami (FL), Sr ...............Linebacker
Rocky Calmus, Oklahoma, Jr..............Linebacker
Jamar Fletcher, Wisconsin, Jr ............Defensive back
Dwight Smith, Akron, Sr ......................Defensive back
Edward Reed, Miami (FL), Jr ..............Defensive back
Lito Sheppard, Florida, So .................Defensive back
Brian Morton, Duke, Sr .......................Punter

# 2000 NCAA Conference Standings

## Division I-A

### ATLANTIC COAST CONFERENCE

| | Conference | | Full Season | | |
|---|---|---|---|---|---|
| | W | L | W | L | Pct |
| Florida St | 8 | 0 | 11 | 2 | .846 |
| Clemson | 6 | 2 | 9 | 3 | .750 |
| Georgia Tech | 6 | 2 | 9 | 3 | .750 |
| Virginia | 5 | 3 | 6 | 6 | .500 |
| N Carolina St | 4 | 4 | 8 | 4 | .667 |
| N Carolina | 3 | 5 | 6 | 5 | .545 |
| Maryland | 3 | 5 | 5 | 6 | .455 |
| Wake Forest | 1 | 7 | 2 | 9 | .182 |
| Duke | 0 | 8 | 0 | 11 | .000 |

### BIG EAST CONFERENCE

| | Conference | | Full Season | | |
|---|---|---|---|---|---|
| | W | L | W | L | Pct |
| Miami (FL) | 7 | 0 | 11 | 1 | .917 |
| Virginia Tech | 6 | 1 | 11 | 1 | .917 |
| Pittsburgh | 4 | 3 | 7 | 5 | .583 |
| Syracuse | 4 | 3 | 6 | 5 | .545 |
| Boston College | 3 | 4 | 7 | 5 | .583 |
| W Virginia | 3 | 4 | 7 | 5 | .583 |
| Temple | 1 | 6 | 4 | 7 | .364 |
| Rutgers | 0 | 7 | 3 | 8 | .273 |

### BIG TEN CONFERENCE

| | Conference | | Full Season | | |
|---|---|---|---|---|---|
| | W | L | W | L | Pct |
| Michigan | 6 | 2 | 9 | 3 | .750 |
| Northwestern | 6 | 2 | 8 | 4 | .667 |
| Purdue | 6 | 2 | 8 | 4 | .667 |
| Ohio St | 5 | 3 | 8 | 4 | .667 |
| Wisconsin | 4 | 4 | 9 | 4 | .692 |
| Minnesota | 4 | 4 | 6 | 6 | .500 |
| Penn St | 4 | 4 | 5 | 7 | .417 |
| Iowa | 3 | 5 | 3 | 9 | .250 |
| Illinois | 2 | 6 | 5 | 6 | .455 |
| Michigan St | 2 | 6 | 5 | 6 | .455 |
| Indiana | 2 | 6 | 3 | 8 | .273 |

### BIG 12 CONFERENCE

| | Conference | | Full Season | | |
|---|---|---|---|---|---|
| **NORTH** | W | L | W | L | Pct |
| *Kansas St | 6 | 2 | 11 | 3 | .786 |
| Nebraska | 6 | 2 | 10 | 2 | .833 |
| Iowa St | 5 | 3 | 9 | 3 | .750 |
| Colorado | 3 | 5 | 3 | 8 | .273 |
| Kansas | 2 | 6 | 4 | 7 | .364 |
| Missouri | 2 | 6 | 3 | 8 | .273 |
| **SOUTH** | | | | | |
| *Oklahoma | 8 | 0 | 13 | 0 | 1.000 |
| Texas | 7 | 1 | 9 | 3 | .750 |
| Texas A&M | 5 | 3 | 7 | 5 | .583 |
| Texas Tech | 3 | 5 | 7 | 6 | .538 |
| Oklahoma St | 1 | 7 | 3 | 8 | .273 |
| Baylor | 0 | 8 | 2 | 9 | .182 |

*Full season record includes Big 12 Championship Game in which Oklahoma defeated Kansas St 27–24, on Dec. 2.

### BIG WEST CONFERENCE

| | Conference | | Full Season | | |
|---|---|---|---|---|---|
| | W | L | W | L | Pct |
| Boise St | 5 | 0 | 10 | 2 | .833 |
| Utah St | 4 | 1 | 5 | 6 | .455 |
| Idaho | 3 | 2 | 5 | 6 | .455 |
| N Mexico St | 1 | 4 | 3 | 8 | .273 |
| N Texas | 1 | 4 | 3 | 8 | .273 |
| Arkansas St | 1 | 4 | 1 | 10 | .091 |

## Division I-A *(Cont.)*

### CONFERENCE USA

| | Conference | | Full Season | | |
|---|---|---|---|---|---|
| | W | L | W | L | Pct |
| Louisville | 6 | 1 | 9 | 3 | .750 |
| E Carolina | 5 | 2 | 8 | 4 | .667 |
| Cincinnati | 5 | 2 | 7 | 5 | .583 |
| Southern Mississippi | 4 | 3 | 8 | 4 | .667 |
| Alabama–Birmingham | 3 | 4 | 7 | 4 | .636 |
| Tulane | 3 | 4 | 6 | 5 | .545 |
| Memphis | 2 | 5 | 4 | 7 | .364 |
| Houston | 2 | 5 | 3 | 8 | .273 |
| Army | 1 | 6 | 1 | 10 | .091 |

### MID-AMERICAN ATHLETIC CONFERENCE

| | Conference | | Full Season | | |
|---|---|---|---|---|---|
| **EAST** | W | L | W | L | Pct |
| *Marshall | 5 | 3 | 7 | 5 | .583 |
| Akron | 5 | 3 | 6 | 5 | .545 |
| Miami (OH) | 5 | 3 | 6 | 5 | .545 |
| Ohio | 5 | 3 | 7 | 4 | .636 |
| Buffalo | 2 | 6 | 2 | 9 | .182 |
| Bowling Green | 2 | 5 | 2 | 8 | .200 |
| Kent | 1 | 7 | 1 | 10 | .091 |
| **WEST** | | | | | |
| *Western Michigan | 7 | 1 | 9 | 3 | .750 |
| Toledo | 6 | 1 | 10 | 1 | .909 |
| Ball St | 4 | 3 | 5 | 6 | .455 |
| Northern Illinois | 4 | 3 | 6 | 5 | .545 |
| Eastern Michigan | 2 | 5 | 3 | 8 | .273 |
| Central Michigan | 2 | 6 | 2 | 9 | .182 |

*Full season record includes MAC Championship Game in which Marshall defeated Western Michigan 19–14, on Dec. 1.

### MOUNTAIN WEST CONFERENCE

| | Conference | | Full Season | | |
|---|---|---|---|---|---|
| | W | L | W | L | Pct |
| Colorado St | 6 | 1 | 10 | 2 | .833 |
| Air Force | 5 | 2 | 9 | 3 | .750 |
| Nevada–Las Vegas | 4 | 3 | 8 | 5 | .615 |
| Brigham Young | 4 | 3 | 6 | 6 | .500 |
| New Mexico | 3 | 4 | 5 | 7 | .417 |
| Utah | 3 | 4 | 4 | 7 | .364 |
| San Diego St | 3 | 4 | 3 | 8 | .273 |
| Wyoming | 0 | 7 | 1 | 10 | .091 |

### PACIFIC 10 CONFERENCE

| | Conference | | Full Season | | |
|---|---|---|---|---|---|
| | W | L | W | L | Pct |
| Oregon St | 7 | 1 | 11 | 1 | .917 |
| Washington | 7 | 1 | 11 | 1 | .917 |
| Oregon | 7 | 1 | 10 | 2 | .833 |
| Stanford | 4 | 4 | 5 | 6 | .455 |
| Arizona St | 3 | 5 | 6 | 6 | .500 |
| UCLA | 3 | 5 | 6 | 6 | .500 |
| Arizona | 3 | 5 | 5 | 6 | .455 |
| Southern Cal | 2 | 6 | 5 | 7 | .417 |
| Washington St | 2 | 6 | 4 | 7 | .364 |
| California | 2 | 6 | 3 | 8 | .273 |

## Division I-A *(Cont.)*

### SOUTHEASTERN CONFERENCE

| EAST | Conference | | Full Season | | |
|---|---|---|---|---|---|
| | W | L | W | L | Pct |
| *Florida | 7 | 1 | 10 | 3 | .769 |
| Georgia | 5 | 3 | 8 | 4 | .667 |
| S Carolina | 5 | 3 | 8 | 4 | .667 |
| Tennessee | 5 | 3 | 8 | 4 | .667 |
| Vanderbilt | 1 | 7 | 3 | 8 | .273 |
| Kentucky | 0 | 8 | 2 | 9 | .182 |
| **WEST** | | | | | |
| *Auburn | 6 | 2 | 9 | 4 | .692 |
| Louisiana St | 5 | 3 | 8 | 4 | .667 |
| Mississippi St | 4 | 4 | 8 | 4 | .667 |
| Mississippi | 4 | 4 | 7 | 5 | .583 |
| Arkansas | 3 | 5 | 6 | 6 | .500 |
| Alabama | 3 | 5 | 3 | 8 | .273 |

*Full season record includes SEC Championship Game in which Florida defeated Auburn 28–6, on Dec. 2.

### WESTERN ATHLETIC CONFERENCE

| | Conference | | Full Season | | |
|---|---|---|---|---|---|
| | W | L | W | L | Pct |
| Texas Christian | 7 | 1 | 10 | 2 | .833 |
| Texas–El Paso | 7 | 1 | 8 | 4 | .667 |
| Fresno St | 6 | 2 | 7 | 5 | .583 |
| San Jose St | 5 | 3 | 7 | 5 | .583 |
| Tulsa | 4 | 4 | 5 | 7 | .417 |
| Rice | 2 | 6 | 3 | 8 | .273 |
| Hawaii | 2 | 6 | 3 | 9 | .250 |
| Southern Methodist | 2 | 6 | 3 | 9 | .250 |
| Nevada | 1 | 7 | 2 | 10 | .167 |

### INDEPENDENTS

| | Full Season | | |
|---|---|---|---|
| | W | L | Pct |
| Notre Dame | 9 | 3 | .750 |
| Central Florida | 7 | 4 | .636 |
| Middle Tennessee St | 6 | 5 | .545 |
| Connecticut | 3 | 8 | .273 |
| Louisiana Tech | 3 | 9 | .250 |
| Louisiana–Lafayette | 1 | 10 | .091 |
| Louisiana–Monroe | 1 | 10 | .091 |
| Navy | 1 | 10 | .091 |

## Division I-AA

### ATLANTIC 10

| | Conference | | Full Season | | |
|---|---|---|---|---|---|
| | W | L | W | L | Pct |
| Delaware | 7 | 1 | 12 | 2 | .857 |
| Richmond | 7 | 1 | 10 | 3 | .769 |
| Massachusetts | 5 | 3 | 7 | 4 | .636 |
| James Madison | 4 | 4 | 6 | 5 | .545 |
| William & Mary | 4 | 4 | 5 | 6 | .455 |
| New Hampshire | 4 | 4 | 6 | 5 | .545 |
| Maine | 3 | 5 | 5 | 6 | .455 |
| Villanova | 3 | 5 | 5 | 6 | .455 |
| Rhode Island | 2 | 6 | 3 | 8 | .273 |
| Northeastern | 1 | 7 | 4 | 7 | .364 |

## Division I-AA *(Cont.)*

### BIG SKY CONFERENCE

| | Conference | | Full Season | | |
|---|---|---|---|---|---|
| | W | L | W | L | Pct |
| Montana | 8 | 0 | 13 | 2 | .867 |
| Portland St | 5 | 3 | 8 | 4 | .667 |
| Weber St | 5 | 3 | 7 | 4 | .636 |
| Sacramento St | 5 | 3 | 7 | 4 | .636 |
| Eastern Michigan | 5 | 3 | 6 | 5 | .545 |
| Idaho St | 4 | 4 | 6 | 5 | .545 |
| Cal St–Northridge | 2 | 6 | 4 | 7 | .364 |
| Northern Arizona | 2 | 6 | 3 | 8 | .273 |
| Montana St | 0 | 8 | 0 | 11 | .000 |

### GATEWAY COLLEGIATE ATHLETIC CONFERENCE

| | Conference | | Full Season | | |
|---|---|---|---|---|---|
| | W | L | W | L | Pct |
| Western Illinois | 5 | 1 | 9 | 3 | .750 |
| Youngstown St | 4 | 2 | 9 | 3 | .750 |
| Illinois St | 4 | 2 | 7 | 4 | .636 |
| Northern Iowa | 3 | 3 | 7 | 4 | .636 |
| SW Missouri St | 2 | 4 | 5 | 6 | .455 |
| Southern Illinois | 2 | 4 | 3 | 8 | .273 |
| Indiana St | 1 | 5 | 1 | 10 | .091 |

### IVY LEAGUE

| | Conference | | Full Season | | |
|---|---|---|---|---|---|
| | W | L | W | L | Pct |
| Pennsylvania | 6 | 1 | 7 | 3 | .700 |
| Cornell | 5 | 2 | 5 | 5 | .500 |
| Yale | 4 | 3 | 7 | 3 | .700 |
| Brown | 4 | 3 | 7 | 3 | .700 |
| Harvard | 4 | 3 | 5 | 5 | .500 |
| Princeton | 3 | 4 | 3 | 7 | .300 |
| Columbia | 1 | 6 | 3 | 7 | .300 |
| Dartmouth | 1 | 6 | 2 | 8 | .200 |

### METRO ATLANTIC ATHLETIC CONFERENCE

| | Conference | | Full Season | | |
|---|---|---|---|---|---|
| | W | L | W | L | Pct |
| Duquesne | 7 | 0 | 10 | 1 | .909 |
| Fairfield | 6 | 1 | 8 | 2 | .800 |
| Marist | 5 | 2 | 6 | 3 | .667 |
| LaSalle | 4 | 3 | 6 | 4 | .600 |
| Iona | 3 | 4 | 3 | 7 | .300 |
| St. Peter's | 2 | 5 | 4 | 7 | .364 |
| Siena | 1 | 6 | 1 | 8 | .111 |
| Canisius | 0 | 7 | 0 | 10 | .000 |

### MID-EASTERN ATHLETIC LEAGUE

| | Conference | | Full Season | | |
|---|---|---|---|---|---|
| | W | L | W | L | Pct |
| Florida A&M | 7 | 1 | 9 | 3 | .750 |
| Bethune-Cookman | 6 | 2 | 9 | 2 | .818 |
| N Carolina A&T | 6 | 2 | 8 | 3 | .727 |
| Hampton | 5 | 3 | 7 | 4 | .636 |
| Delaware St | 5 | 3 | 7 | 4 | .636 |
| Howard | 3 | 5 | 3 | 8 | .273 |
| S Carolina St | 2 | 6 | 3 | 8 | .273 |
| Norfolk St | 2 | 6 | 3 | 8 | .273 |
| Morgan St | 0 | 8 | 1 | 10 | .091 |

## Division I-AA *(Cont.)*

### NORTHEAST CONFERENCE

| | Conference | | Full Season | | |
|---|---|---|---|---|---|
| | W | L | W | L | Pct |
| Robert Morris | 7 | 0 | 10 | 0 | 1.000 |
| Sacred Heart | 6 | 1 | 10 | 1 | .909 |
| Wagner | 5 | 2 | 6 | 5 | .545 |
| Albany | 4 | 3 | 5 | 6 | .455 |
| Monmouth | 3 | 4 | 5 | 6 | .455 |
| Central Connecticut St | 2 | 5 | 4 | 6 | .400 |
| Stony Brook | 1 | 6 | 2 | 8 | .200 |
| St. Francis (PA) | 0 | 7 | 0 | 11 | .000 |

### OHIO VALLEY CONFERENCE

| | Conference | | Full Season | | |
|---|---|---|---|---|---|
| | W | L | W | L | Pct |
| Western Kentucky | 7 | 0 | 11 | 2 | .846 |
| Eastern Illinois | 6 | 1 | 8 | 4 | .667 |
| Tennessee Tech | 5 | 2 | 8 | 3 | .727 |
| Murray St | 4 | 3 | 6 | 5 | .545 |
| Eastern Kentucky | 3 | 4 | 6 | 5 | .545 |
| Tennessee St | 2 | 5 | 3 | 7 | .300 |
| SE Missouri St | 1 | 6 | 3 | 8 | .273 |
| Tennessee–Martin | 0 | 7 | 2 | 9 | .182 |

### PATRIOT LEAGUE

| | Conference | | Full Season | | |
|---|---|---|---|---|---|
| | W | L | W | L | Pct |
| Lehigh | 6 | 0 | 12 | 1 | .923 |
| Holy Cross | 4 | 2 | 7 | 4 | .636 |
| Colgate | 4 | 2 | 7 | 4 | .636 |
| Towson | 3 | 3 | 7 | 4 | .636 |
| Bucknell | 2 | 4 | 6 | 5 | .545 |
| Fordham | 1 | 5 | 3 | 8 | .273 |
| Lafayette | 1 | 5 | 2 | 9 | .182 |

### PIONEER FOOTBALL LEAGUE

| | Conference | | Full Season | | |
|---|---|---|---|---|---|
| | W | L | W | L | Pct |
| Valparaiso | 3 | 1 | 7 | 3 | .700 |
| Dayton | 3 | 1 | 6 | 3 | .667 |
| Drake | 3 | 1 | 7 | 4 | .636 |
| San Diego | 1 | 3 | 4 | 6 | .400 |
| Butler | 0 | 4 | 2 | 7 | .222 |

### SOUTHERN CONFERENCE

| | Conference | | Full Season | | |
|---|---|---|---|---|---|
| | W | L | W | L | Pct |
| Georgia Southern | 7 | 1 | 13 | 2 | .867 |
| Appalachian St | 6 | 2 | 10 | 4 | .714 |
| Furman | 6 | 2 | 9 | 3 | .750 |
| Wofford | 5 | 3 | 7 | 4 | .636 |
| E Tennessee St | 4 | 4 | 6 | 5 | .545 |
| Chattanooga | 3 | 5 | 5 | 6 | .455 |
| Western Carolina | 3 | 5 | 4 | 7 | .364 |
| The Citadel | 1 | 7 | 2 | 9 | .182 |
| Virginia Military | 1 | 7 | 2 | 9 | .182 |

## Division I-AA *(Cont.)*

### SOUTHLAND FOOTBALL LEAGUE

| | Conference | | Full Season | | |
| --- | :---: | :---: | :---: | :---: | :---: |
| | W | L | W | L | Pct |
| Troy St | 6 | 1 | 9 | 3 | .750 |
| McNeese St | 5 | 2 | 8 | 4 | .667 |
| SW Texas | 5 | 2 | 7 | 4 | .636 |
| Sam Houston St | 4 | 3 | 7 | 4 | .636 |
| Stephen F. Austin | 3 | 4 | 6 | 5 | .545 |
| Northwestern St | 3 | 4 | 6 | 5 | .545 |
| Jacksonville St | 2 | 5 | 4 | 6 | .400 |
| Nicholls St | 0 | 7 | 1 | 10 | .091 |

### SOUTHWESTERN

| | Conference | | Full Season | | |
| --- | :---: | :---: | :---: | :---: | :---: |
| **EASTERN** | W | L | W | L | Pct |
| *Alabama A&M | 5 | 2 | 7 | 5 | .583 |
| Alabama St | 5 | 2 | 6 | 5 | .545 |
| Jackson St | 4 | 3 | 7 | 4 | .636 |
| Mississippi Valley St | 1 | 6 | 2 | 9 | .182 |
| Alcorn St | 0 | 7 | 0 | 11 | .000 |
| **WESTERN** | | | | | |
| *Grambling | 6 | 1 | 10 | 2 | .833 |
| Texas Southern | 5 | 2 | 8 | 3 | .727 |
| Arkansas–Pine Bluff | 4 | 3 | 6 | 5 | .545 |
| Southern | 4 | 3 | 6 | 5 | .545 |
| Prairie View | 1 | 6 | 1 | 10 | .091 |

*Full season record includes SWAC Championship Game in which Grambling defeated Alabama A&M 14–6, on Dec. 2.

### INDEPENDENTS

| | Full Season | | |
| --- | :---: | :---: | :---: |
| | W | L | Pct |
| Davidson | 10 | 0 | 1.000 |
| Hofstra | 9 | 4 | .692 |
| Morehead St | 6 | 3 | .667 |
| Gardner-Webb | 7 | 4 | .636 |
| Southern Utah | 7 | 4 | .636 |
| Elon | 7 | 4 | .636 |
| St. Mary's | 6 | 5 | .545 |
| Charleston Southern | 5 | 6 | .455 |
| St. John's (NY) | 5 | 6 | .455 |
| Georgetown | 5 | 6 | .455 |
| Morris Brown | 4 | 6 | .400 |
| Samford | 4 | 7 | .364 |
| Jacksonville | 3 | 8 | .273 |
| Cal Poly–San Luis Obispo | 3 | 8 | .273 |
| Liberty | 3 | 8 | .273 |
| Austin Peay | 2 | 9 | .182 |

# 2000 NCAA Individual Leaders

## Division I-A

### SCORING

| | Class | GP | TD | XP | FG | Pts | Pts/Game |
| --- | :---: | :---: | :---: | :---: | :---: | :---: | :---: |
| Lee Suggs, Virginia Tech | So | 11 | 28 | 0 | 0 | 168 | 15.27 |
| LaDainian Tomlinson, Texas Christian | Sr | 11 | 22 | 0 | 0 | 132 | 12.00 |
| Damien Anderson, Northwestern | Sr | 11 | 22 | 0 | 0 | 132 | 12.00 |
| Dwone Hicks, Middle Tennessee St | So | 11 | 21 | 0 | 0 | 126 | 11.45 |
| Eric Crouch, Nebraska | Jr | 11 | 20 | 0 | 0 | 120 | 10.91 |
| Thomas Hammock, Northern Illinois | So | 9 | 16 | 0 | 0 | 96 | 10.67 |
| Chester Taylor, Toledo | Sr | 11 | 19 | 0 | 0 | 114 | 10.36 |
| Ken Simonton, Oregon St | Jr | 11 | 18 | 0 | 0 | 110 | 10.00 |
| Deonce Whitaker, San Jose St | Sr | 10 | 16 | 0 | 0 | 98 | 9.80 |
| Kris Stockton, Texas | Sr | 11 | 0 | 41 | 22 | 107 | 9.73 |

## 2000 NCAA Individual Leaders *(Cont.)*

### FIELD GOALS

| | Class | GP | FGA | FG | Pct | FG/Game |
|---|---|---|---|---|---|---|
| Jonathan Ruffin, Cincinnati | So | 11 | 29 | 26 | .897 | 2.36 |
| Dan Nystrom, Minnesota | So | 11 | 34 | 22 | .647 | 2.00 |
| Kris Stockton, Texas | Sr | 11 | 26 | 22 | .846 | 2.00 |
| Rhett Gallego, Alabama–Birmingham | So | 11 | 24 | 19 | .792 | 1.73 |
| Dave Adams, Air Force | Sr | 11 | 24 | 19 | .792 | 1.73 |
| Dan Stultz, Ohio St | Sr | 11 | 23 | 19 | .826 | 1.73 |
| Alex Walls, Tennessee | So | 11 | 20 | 18 | .900 | 1.64 |
| Owen Pochman, Brigham Young | Sr | 12 | 24 | 19 | .792 | 1.58 |
| Steve Azar, Northern Illinois | Fr | 9 | 15 | 14 | .933 | 1.56 |
| Jeff Reed, N Carolina | Sr | 11 | 20 | 16 | .800 | 1.45 |
| Chris Kaylakie, Texas Christian | Sr | 11 | 18 | 16 | .889 | 1.45 |
| Seth Marler, Tulane | So | 11 | 21 | 16 | .762 | 1.45 |

### TOTAL OFFENSE

| | | Rushing | | Passing | | Total Offense | | |
|---|---|---|---|---|---|---|---|---|
| | Class | GP | Car | Net | Att | Yds | Yds | Yds/Play | Yds/Game |
| Drew Brees, Purdue | Sr | 11 | 91 | 546 | 473 | 3393 | 3939 | 6.98 | 358.1 |
| Jared Lorenzen, Kentucky | Fr | 11 | 76 | 140 | 559 | 3687 | 3827 | 6.03 | 347.9 |
| Chris Weinke, Florida St | Sr | 12 | 30 | -97 | 431 | 4167 | 4070 | 8.83 | 339.2 |
| Bart Hendricks, Boise St | Sr | 11 | 85 | 269 | 347 | 3364 | 3633 | 8.41 | 330.3 |
| Timmy Chang, Hawaii | So | 10 | 23 | -49 | 469 | 3041 | 2992 | 6.08 | 299.2 |
| Josh Heupel, Oklahoma | Sr | 12 | 70 | 144 | 433 | 3392 | 3536 | 7.03 | 294.7 |
| John Welsh, Idaho | Jr | 11 | 80 | 28 | 399 | 3171 | 3199 | 6.68 | 290.8 |
| Patrick Ramsey, Tulane | Jr | 10 | 39 | 53 | 389 | 2833 | 2886 | 6.74 | 288.6 |
| Byron Leftwich, Marshall | So | 12 | 82 | 83 | 457 | 3358 | 3441 | 6.38 | 286.8 |
| Kliff Kingsbury, Texas Tech | So | 12 | 78 | 19 | 584 | 3412 | 3431 | 5.18 | 285.9 |

### RUSHING

| | Class | GP | Car | Yds | Avg | TD | Yds/Game |
|---|---|---|---|---|---|---|---|
| LaDainian Tomlinson, TCU | Sr | 11 | 369 | 2158 | 5.85 | 22 | 196.18 |
| Damien Anderson, Northwestern | Sr | 11 | 293 | 1914 | 6.53 | 22 | 174.00 |
| Michael Bennett, Wisconsin | Jr | 10 | 294 | 1598 | 5.44 | 10 | 159.80 |
| Deonce Whitaker, San Jose St | Sr | 10 | 224 | 1577 | 7.04 | 15 | 157.70 |
| Anthony Thomas, Michigan | Sr | 11 | 287 | 1551 | 5.40 | 16 | 141.00 |
| Ken Simonton, Oregon St | Jr | 11 | 266 | 1474 | 5.54 | 18 | 134.00 |
| Chester Taylor, Toledo | Sr | 11 | 250 | 1470 | 5.88 | 18 | 133.64 |
| Robert Sanford, Western Michigan | Sr | 12 | 293 | 1571 | 5.36 | 18 | 130.92 |
| Rudi Johnson, Auburn | Jr | 12 | 324 | 1567 | 4.84 | 13 | 130.58 |
| Ennis Haywood, Iowa St | Jr | 10 | 230 | 1237 | 5.38 | 8 | 123.70 |

### PASSING EFFICIENCY

| | | | | Pct | | | | | Rating |
|---|---|---|---|---|---|---|---|---|---|
| | Class | GP | Att | Comp | Comp | Yds | Yds/Att | TD | Int | Pts |
| Bart Hendricks, Boise St | Sr | 11 | 347 | 210 | 60.52 | 3364 | 9.69 | 35 | 8 | 170.6 |
| Chris Weinke, Florida St | Sr | 12 | 431 | 266 | 61.72 | 4167 | 9.67 | 33 | 11 | 163.1 |
| Rex Grossman, Florida | Fr | 11 | 212 | 131 | 61.79 | 1866 | 8.80 | 21 | 7 | 161.8 |
| Casey Printers, Texas Christian | So | 11 | 176 | 102 | 57.95 | 1584 | 9.00 | 16 | 6 | 156.7 |
| Ken Dorsey, Miami (FL) | So | 11 | 322 | 188 | 58.39 | 2737 | 8.50 | 25 | 5 | 152.3 |
| George Godsey, Georgia Tech | Jr | 11 | 349 | 222 | 63.61 | 2906 | 8.33 | 23 | 6 | 151.9 |
| John Turman, Pittsburgh | Sr | 11 | 233 | 128 | 54.94 | 2135 | 9.16 | 18 | 7 | 151.4 |
| Rocky Perez, Texas–El Paso | Sr | 11 | 338 | 200 | 59.17 | 2661 | 7.87 | 26 | 6 | 147.1 |
| Mike Thiessen, Air Force | Sr | 11 | 195 | 112 | 57.44 | 1687 | 8.65 | 13 | 5 | 147.0 |
| Ryan Schneider, Central Florida | Fr | 9 | 286 | 177 | 61.89 | 2334 | 8.16 | 21 | 11 | 147.0 |

Note: Minimum 15 attempts per game.

### RECEPTIONS PER GAME

| | Class | GP | No. | Yds | TD | R/Game |
|---|---|---|---|---|---|---|
| James Jordan, Louisiana Tech | Sr | 12 | 109 | 1003 | 4 | 9.08 |
| Tyson Hinshaw, Central Florida | Sr | 11 | 89 | 1089 | 13 | 8.09 |
| Kenny Christian, Eastern Michigan | Jr | 10 | 78 | 808 | 3 | 7.80 |
| Robert Kilow, Arkansas St | Sr | 10 | 72 | 1002 | 3 | 7.20 |
| Brian Robinson, Houston | So | 11 | 79 | 892 | 6 | 7.18 |

## Division I-A *(Cont.)*

### RECEIVING YARDS PER GAME

| | Class | GP | No. | Yds | TD | Yds/Game |
|---|---|---|---|---|---|---|
| Antonio Bryant, Pittsburgh | So | 10 | 68 | 1302 | 11 | 130.20 |
| Freddie Mitchell, UCLA | Jr | 11 | 68 | 1314 | 8 | 119.45 |
| Marvin Minnis, Florida St | Sr | 12 | 63 | 1340 | 11 | 111.67 |
| Justin McCareins, Northern Illinois | Sr | 11 | 66 | 1168 | 10 | 106.18 |
| Aaron Jones, Utah St | Sr | 11 | 63 | 1159 | 11 | 105.36 |

### ALL-PURPOSE RUNNERS

| | Class | GP | Rush | Rec | PR | KOR | Yds | Yds/Game |
|---|---|---|---|---|---|---|---|---|
| Emmett White, Utah St | Jr | 11 | 1322 | 592 | 183 | 531 | 2628 | 238.91 |
| LaDainian Tomlinson, TCU | Sr | 11 | 2158 | 40 | 0 | 0 | 2198 | 199.82 |
| Robert Kilow, Arkansas St | Sr | 10 | 42 | 1002 | 133 | 724 | 1901 | 190.10 |
| Damien Anderson, Northwestern | Sr | 11 | 1914 | 120 | 0 | 0 | 2034 | 184.91 |
| Justin McCareins, Northern Illinois | Sr | 11 | 73 | 1168 | 362 | 411 | 2014 | 183.09 |

### INTERCEPTIONS

| | Class | GP | No. | Int/Game |
|---|---|---|---|---|
| Dwight Smith, Akron | Sr | 11 | 10 | .91 |
| Anthony Floyd, Louisville | So | 11 | 10 | .91 |
| Ed Reed, Miami (FL) | Jr | 11 | 8 | .73 |
| J.T. Thatcher, Oklahoma | Sr | 12 | 8 | .67 |
| Jamar Fletcher, Wisconsin | Jr | 9 | 6 | .67 |

### PUNTING

| | Class | No. | Avg |
|---|---|---|---|
| Preston Gruening, Minnesota | So | 46 | 45.22 |
| Brian Morton, Duke | Sr | 77 | 45.17 |
| Kevin Stemke, Wisconsin | Sr | 65 | 44.85 |
| Brooks Barnard, Maryland | So | 49 | 44.71 |
| Dave Zastudil, Ohio | Jr | 47 | 44.34 |

Note: Minimum of 3.6 per game.

### PUNT RETURNS

| | Class | No. | Yds | TD | Avg |
|---|---|---|---|---|---|
| Aaron Lockett, Kansas St | Jr | 22 | 501 | 3 | 22.77 |
| Andre Davis, Virginia Tech | Jr | 18 | 396 | 3 | 22.00 |
| Justin McCareins, Northern Ill. | Sr | 19 | 362 | 1 | 19.05 |
| Santana Moss, Miami (FL) | Sr | 36 | 655 | 4 | 18.19 |
| Jemeel Powell, California | So | 12 | 218 | 1 | 18.17 |

Note: Minimum 1.2 per game.

### KICKOFF RETURNS

| | Class | No. | Yds | TD | Avg |
|---|---|---|---|---|---|
| LaTarence Dunbar, TCU | So | 15 | 506 | 2 | 33.73 |
| Zek Parker, Louisville | Sr | 26 | 752 | 0 | 28.92 |
| David Mikell, Boise St | Fr | 16 | 459 | 1 | 28.69 |
| Julius Jones, Notre Dame | So | 15 | 427 | 1 | 28.47 |
| Ken-Yon Rambo, Ohio St | Sr | 17 | 478 | 0 | 28.12 |

Note: Minimum of 1.2 per game.

## Division I-A Team Single-Game Highs

### RUSHING AND PASSING

Rushing and passing plays: 80—Luke McCown, Louisiana Tech, Oct 28 (vs Miami (FL)).
Rushing and passing yards: 536—Chris Weinke, Florida St, Oct 14 (vs Duke).
Rushing plays: 52—Mike Turner, Northern Illinois, Nov 18 (vs Central Michigan).
Net rushing yards: 322—Emmett White, Utah St, Nov 4 (vs New Mexico St).
Passes attempted: 72—Luke McCown, Louisiana Tech, Oct 28 (vs Miami (FL)).
Passes completed: 47—Luke McCown, Louisiana Tech, Oct 21 (vs. Auburn).
Passing yards: 536—Chris Weinke, Florida St, Oct 14 (vs Duke).

### RECEIVING AND RETURNS

Passes caught: 20—Kenny Christian, Eastern Michigan, Sept 23 (vs Temple).
Receiving yards: 297—Aaron Jones, Utah St, Nov 11 (vs Boise St).
Punt return yards: 168—Keith Stokes, E Carolina, Nov 11 (vs Houston).
Kickoff return yards: 186—Shawn Terry, W Virginia, Nov 24 (vs Pittsburgh).

## Division I-AA

### SCORING

| | Class | GP | TD | XP | FG | Pts | Pts/Game |
|---|---|---|---|---|---|---|---|
| Montrell Coley, Hampton | Sr | 11 | 28 | 0 | 0 | 172 | 15.64 |
| David Dinkins, Morehead St | Sr | 9 | 21 | 0 | 0 | 128 | 14.22 |
| Brian Westbrook, Villanova | Jr | 11 | 22 | 0 | 0 | 136 | 12.36 |
| Matt Cannon, Southern Utah | Sr | 11 | 22 | 0 | 0 | 132 | 12.00 |
| Charles Dunn, Portland St | Sr | 11 | 21 | 0 | 0 | 126 | 11.45 |

### Division I-AA *(Cont.)*

#### FIELD GOALS

| | Class | GP | FGA | FG | Pct | FG/Game |
|---|---|---|---|---|---|---|
| Matt Vick, Chattanooga | Sr | 11 | 26 | 22 | .846 | 2.00 |
| Billy Cundiff, Drake | Jr | 11 | 27 | 20 | .741 | 1.82 |
| Brett Sterba, William & Mary | Sr | 11 | 19 | 17 | .895 | 1.55 |
| Jason Feinberg, Pennsylvania | Sr | 10 | 21 | 15 | .714 | 1.50 |
| Tim Redican, Sacred Heart | So | 11 | 23 | 16 | .696 | 1.45 |
| J.B. LaCombe, Texas Southern | Sr | 11 | 30 | 16 | .533 | 1.45 |
| Lawrence Tynes, Troy St | Sr | 11 | 20 | 16 | .800 | 1.45 |
| Bill Gramatica, S Florida | Sr | 11 | 24 | 16 | .667 | 1.45 |

#### TOTAL OFFENSE

| | | | Rushing | | Passing | | Total Offense | | |
|---|---|---|---|---|---|---|---|---|---|
| | Class | GP | Car | Net | Att | Yds | Yds | Yds/Play | Yds/Game |
| David Dinkins, Morehead St | Sr | 9 | 190 | 1405 | 218 | 1704 | 3109 | 7.62 | 345.4 |
| Chris Sanders, Chattanooga | Sr | 11 | 57 | 65 | 463 | 3691 | 3756 | 7.22 | 341.5 |
| Darnell Kennedy, Alabama St | Jr | 11 | 81 | -13 | 401 | 3488 | 3475 | 7.21 | 315.9 |
| Gavin Hoffman, Pennsylvania | Jr | 10 | 38 | -65 | 386 | 3214 | 3149 | 7.43 | 314.9 |
| Eric Webber, Brown | Sr | 10 | 24 | -40 | 431 | 3175 | 3135 | 6.89 | 313.5 |

#### RUSHING

| | Class | GP | Car | Yds | Avg | TD | Yds/Game |
|---|---|---|---|---|---|---|---|
| Louis Ivory, Furman | Jr | 11 | 286 | 2079 | 7.27 | 16 | 189.00 |
| Charles Dunn, Portland St | Sr | 11 | 302 | 1792 | 5.93 | 21 | 162.91 |
| David Dinkins, Morehead St | Sr | 9 | 190 | 1405 | 7.39 | 21 | 156.11 |
| Adrian Peterson, Georgia Southern | Jr | 9 | 230 | 1361 | 5.92 | 13 | 151.22 |
| Charles Roberts, Cal St–Sacramento | Sr | 11 | 296 | 1624 | 5.49 | 14 | 147.64 |

#### PASSING EFFICIENCY

| | Class | GP | Att | Comp | Pct Comp | Yds | Yds/Att | TD | Int | Rating Pts |
|---|---|---|---|---|---|---|---|---|---|---|
| Terrance Ley, Southern | Jr | 11 | 233 | 139 | 59.66 | 2249 | 9.65 | 23 | 6 | 168.2 |
| Tony Romo, Eastern Illinois | So | 11 | 278 | 164 | 58.99 | 2583 | 9.29 | 27 | 12 | 160.5 |
| Gavin Hoffman, Pennsylvania | Jr | 10 | 386 | 272 | 70.47 | 3214 | 8.33 | 24 | 14 | 153.7 |
| Brett Gordon, Villanova | So | 11 | 281 | 184 | 65.48 | 2293 | 8.16 | 22 | 9 | 153.5 |
| Matt Nagy, Delaware | Sr | 11 | 288 | 151 | 52.43 | 2718 | 9.44 | 25 | 12 | 152.0 |

Note: Minimum 15 attempts per game.

#### RECEPTIONS PER GAME

| | Class | GP | No. | Yds | TD | R/G |
|---|---|---|---|---|---|---|
| Steve Campbell, Brown | Sr | 10 | 120 | 1332 | 11 | 12.00 |
| Eric Johnson, Yale | Sr | 10 | 87 | 1017 | 14 | 8.70 |
| Jacquay Nunnally, Fla. A&M | Jr | 11 | 95 | 1082 | 9 | 8.64 |
| R. Flowers, Chattanooga | Sr | 11 | 86 | 1035 | 2 | 7.82 |
| Rob Milanese, Penn | Jr | 10 | 76 | 936 | 6 | 7.60 |

#### INTERCEPTIONS

| | Class | GP | No. | Yds | TD | Int/G |
|---|---|---|---|---|---|---|
| Steve Dogmanits, Fairfield | Sr | 10 | 11 | 113 | 2 | 1.10 |
| R. Mathis, Bethune-Cookman | So | 11 | 11 | 157 | 0 | 1.00 |
| Don Milligan, Fairfield | Jr | 10 | 9 | 165 | 1 | .90 |
| Bobby Sippio, Western Ky. | So | 10 | 9 | 236 | 2 | .90 |
| Leigh Bodden, Duquesne | So | 11 | 9 | 175 | 2 | .82 |
| Eric Martinson, La Salle | Sr | 11 | 9 | 23 | 0 | .82 |

#### RECEIVING YARDS PER GAME

| | Class | GP | No. | Yds | TD | Yds/G |
|---|---|---|---|---|---|---|
| Steve Campbell, Brown | Sr | 10 | 120 | 1332 | 11 | 133.2 |
| Kassim Osgood, Cal Poly | So | 11 | 83 | 1377 | 14 | 125.2 |
| Michael Hayes, Southern | Jr | 11 | 80 | 1328 | 15 | 120.7 |
| Eddie Berlin, Northern Iowa | Sr | 11 | 74 | 1195 | 16 | 108.6 |
| Scotty Anderson, Grambling | Sr | 11 | 69 | 1146 | 10 | 104.2 |

#### PUNTING

| | Class | No. | Avg |
|---|---|---|---|
| David Beckford, Alabama St | So | 48 | 44.19 |
| Mike Scifres, Western Illinois | So | 53 | 43.17 |
| Dan Frantz, Portland St | Sr | 44 | 42.70 |
| Nathan McKinney, Appalachian St | So | 48 | 42.54 |
| Jeremy Thompson, Nicholls St | So | 62 | 42.40 |

#### ALL-PURPOSE RUNNERS

| | Class | GP | Rush | Rec | PR | KOR | Yds | Yds/Game |
|---|---|---|---|---|---|---|---|---|
| Brian Westbrook, Villanova | Jr | 11 | 1220 | 724 | 0 | 1048 | 2992 | 272.00 |
| Johnathan Reese, Columbia | Jr | 10 | 1330 | 254 | 0 | 368 | 1952 | 195.20 |
| Louis Ivory, Furman | Jr | 11 | 2079 | 14 | 0 | 0 | 2093 | 190.27 |
| Stanley Stephens, S Carolina St | Sr | 11 | 795 | 413 | 179 | 592 | 1979 | 179.91 |
| Ryan Zimpleman, Butler | Sr | 9 | 810 | 175 | 0 | 529 | 1514 | 168.22 |

## Division II

### SCORING

| | Class | GP | TD | XP | FG | Pts | Pts/Game |
|---|---|---|---|---|---|---|---|
| Andre Braxton, Virginia Union | Sr | 11 | 27 | 14 | 0 | 176 | 16.0 |
| Matt Brown, California–Davis | Sr | 8 | 19 | 0 | 0 | 114 | 14.3 |
| Dalevon Smith, Shepherd | Sr | 9 | 19 | 0 | 0 | 114 | 12.7 |
| Lamar Gordon, N Dakota St | Jr | 11 | 23 | 0 | 0 | 138 | 12.5 |
| Eddie Acosta, Bemidji St | So | 11 | 22 | 2 | 0 | 134 | 12.2 |

### FIELD GOALS

| | Class | GP | FGA | FG | Pct | FG/Game |
|---|---|---|---|---|---|---|
| Paul Czerniak, Tusculum | Jr | 11 | 29 | 19 | 65.5 | 1.73 |
| Adam Hicks, S Dakota | Sr | 11 | 22 | 17 | 77.3 | 1.55 |
| Cameron Peterka, N Dakota | Jr | 11 | 24 | 17 | 70.8 | 1.55 |
| Nathan White, Fairmont St | Jr | 10 | 19 | 15 | 78.9 | 1.50 |
| J.W. Boren, Tarleton St | So | 11 | 20 | 16 | 80.0 | 1.45 |

### TOTAL OFFENSE

| | Class | GP | Yds | Yds/Game |
|---|---|---|---|---|
| Dusty Bonner, Valdosta St | Jr | 11 | 3795 | 345.0 |
| Bryan Harman, Fairmont St | Jr | 10 | 3427 | 342.7 |
| J.T. O'Sullivan, California–Davis | Jr | 9 | 2945 | 327.2 |
| Eric Degraff, Augustana | Sr | 11 | 3424 | 311.3 |
| Mac McArdle, Mercyhurst | So | 9 | 2647 | 294.1 |

### RUSHING

| | Class | GP | Car | Yds | TD | Yds/Game |
|---|---|---|---|---|---|---|
| Dalevon Smith, Shepherd | Sr | 9 | 229 | 1495 | 19 | 166.1 |
| Lamar Gordon, N Dakota St | Jr | 11 | 256 | 1727 | 22 | 157.0 |
| Terrance Stokes, Mars Hill | Sr | 10 | 221 | 1558 | 13 | 155.8 |
| Eddie Acosta, Bemidji St | So | 11 | 283 | 1690 | 18 | 153.6 |
| Andre Braxton, Virginia Union | Sr | 11 | 275 | 1640 | 27 | 149.1 |

### PASSING EFFICIENCY

| | Class | GP | Att | Comp | Pct Comp | Yds | TD | Int | Rating Pts |
|---|---|---|---|---|---|---|---|---|---|
| J.T. O'Sullivan, California–Davis | Jr | 9 | 226 | 141 | 62.3 | 2648 | 25 | 7 | 191.1 |
| Dusty Bonner, Valdosta St | Jr | 11 | 435 | 317 | 72.8 | 3907 | 54 | 6 | 186.5 |
| Travis Miles, NW Missouri St | Sr | 11 | 248 | 155 | 62.5 | 2723 | 25 | 7 | 182.4 |
| Kevin McCarn, Arkansas Monticello | Sr | 11 | 250 | 155 | 62.0 | 2556 | 19 | 4 | 169.7 |
| Justin Coleman, Nebraska–Kearney | Sr | 10 | 291 | 179 | 61.5 | 2645 | 26 | 11 | 159.8 |

Note: Minimum 15 attempts per game.

### RECEPTIONS PER GAME

| | Class | GP | No. | Yds | TD | Rec/Game |
|---|---|---|---|---|---|---|
| Matt Holmlund, Augustana | Jr | 11 | 104 | 1365 | 16 | 9.5 |
| Clarence Coleman, Ferris St | Jr | 11 | 97 | 1519 | 15 | 8.8 |
| Chad Luttrull, Henderson St | Sr | 11 | 92 | 1505 | 14 | 8.4 |
| Jeff Geisz, Michigan Tech | Sr | 10 | 82 | 1184 | 8 | 8.2 |
| Trevor Watson, Nebraska–Kearney | Sr | 10 | 79 | 1136 | 13 | 7.9 |

### RECEIVING YARDS PER GAME

| | Class | GP | No. | Yds | TD | Yds/Game |
|---|---|---|---|---|---|---|
| Pierre Brown, Wayne St | Jr | 10 | 66 | 1492 | 17 | 149.2 |
| Clarence Coleman, Ferris St | Jr | 11 | 97 | 1519 | 15 | 138.1 |
| Chad Luttrull, Henderson St | Sr | 11 | 92 | 1505 | 14 | 136.8 |
| Matt Holmlund, Augustana | Jr | 11 | 104 | 1365 | 16 | 124.1 |
| Damon Thompson, Virginia St | Sr | 9 | 65 | 1103 | 9 | 122.6 |

## Division II *(Cont.)*

### INTERCEPTIONS

| | Class | GP | No. | Yds | Int/Game |
|---|---|---|---|---|---|
| Tim Mustapha, Hillsdale | Jr | 11 | 11 | 78 | 1.0 |
| D. Mark Ceglie, W Liberty St | Sr | 10 | 9 | 87 | .9 |
| James Rooths, Shepherd | Sr | 10 | 9 | 186 | .9 |
| DeKendrick Haskins, Monticello | Jr | 11 | 9 | 120 | .8 |
| Tim Thomas, W Virginia St | Sr | 11 | 9 | 54 | .8 |

### PUNTING

| | Class | No. | Avg |
|---|---|---|---|
| Adam Ryan, Fort Hays St | Sr | 69 | 43.2 |
| Ryan Dutton, Minn. St–Mankato | Sr | 61 | 42.8 |
| Tony Prichard, Adams St | Sr | 45 | 42.5 |
| Chris Lutz, Pittsburgh St | So | 45 | 41.6 |
| Cory Schmidgall, Moorehead St | Sr | 58 | 41.3 |

Note: Minimum 3.6 per game.

## Division III

### SCORING

| | Class | GP | TD | XP | FG | Pts | Pts/Game |
|---|---|---|---|---|---|---|---|
| Shane Ream, Allegheny | Jr | 10 | 30 | 0 | 0 | 180 | 18.0 |
| Jay Miller, Springfield | Sr | 10 | 22 | 4 | 0 | 136 | 13.6 |
| Casey Donaldson, Wittenberg | Sr | 10 | 22 | 0 | 0 | 132 | 13.2 |
| Deon Packer, Millikin | Jr | 9 | 19 | 0 | 0 | 114 | 12.7 |
| Marvin Langley, Western New England | Jr | 9 | 19 | 0 | 0 | 114 | 12.7 |

### FIELD GOALS

| | Class | GP | FGA | FG | Pct | FG/Game |
|---|---|---|---|---|---|---|
| Carlos Martinez, Buena Vista | Jr | 10 | 24 | 17 | 70.8 | 1.70 |
| Sean Lipscomb, Redlands | So | 9 | 25 | 15 | 60.0 | 1.67 |
| Jonathon Feig, Washington | Fr | 8 | 19 | 13 | 68.4 | 1.63 |
| Roman Natoli, Chicago | Jr | 7 | 19 | 10 | 52.6 | 1.43 |
| Derrick McNeal, Millsaps | Sr | 10 | 17 | 14 | 82.4 | 1.40 |

### TOTAL OFFENSE

| | Class | GP | Yds | Yds/Game |
|---|---|---|---|---|
| Zamir Amin, Menlo | Sr | 10 | 4231 | 423.1 |
| Kyle Krober, Greenville | Jr | 10 | 3676 | 367.6 |
| Adam Ryan, Wilmington | Jr | 10 | 3415 | 341.5 |
| Chad Johnson, Pacific Lutheran | Sr | 9 | 3052 | 339.1 |
| Eric Bruns, Hanover | Sr | 10 | 3260 | 326.0 |

### RUSHING

| | Class | GP | Car | Yds | TD | Yds/Game |
|---|---|---|---|---|---|---|
| Damon Saxon, King's | Sr | 10 | 281 | 1744 | 21 | 174.4 |
| Will Castleberry, Thomas More | Sr | 10 | 324 | 1736 | 16 | 173.6 |
| R.J. Bowers, Grove City | Sr | 10 | 352 | 1733 | 19 | 173.3 |
| Steve Ballinger, MacMurray | So | 10 | 232 | 1731 | 16 | 173.1 |
| Jamal Robertson, Ohio Northern | Sr | 10 | 251 | 1664 | 18 | 166.4 |

### PASSING EFFICIENCY

| | Class | GP | Att | Comp | Pct Comp | Yds | TD | Int | Rating Pts |
|---|---|---|---|---|---|---|---|---|---|
| Brian Dawson, Washington & Jefferson | So | 10 | 227 | 149 | 65.6 | 2675 | 29 | 6 | 201.5 |
| Gary Smeck, Mount Union | Sr | 10 | 266 | 184 | 69.1 | 2773 | 30 | 3 | 191.7 |
| Matt LeFever, Western Connecticut St | Sr | 10 | 171 | 110 | 64.3 | 1792 | 17 | 4 | 180.5 |
| Chad Johnson, Pacific Lutheran | Sr | 9 | 274 | 185 | 67.5 | 2839 | 24 | 6 | 179.1 |
| Tom Linnemann, St. John's | Sr | 10 | 283 | 179 | 63.2 | 2455 | 36 | 11 | 170.3 |

Note: Minimum 15 attempts per game.

### Division III *(Cont.)*

#### RECEPTIONS PER GAME

| | Class | GP | No. | Yds | TD | Rec/Game |
|---|---|---|---|---|---|---|
| Nate Jackson, Menlo | Jr | 10 | 101 | 1515 | 16 | 10.1 |
| Darryl Deshields, Greenville | So | 10 | 90 | 1444 | 15 | 9.0 |
| Jay Agan, Hanover | Sr | 10 | 88 | 1056 | 9 | 8.8 |
| Jon Cain, Wilmington | Jr | 10 | 85 | 1459 | 15 | 8.5 |
| Jason Hill, Lewis & Clark | So | 9 | 75 | 976 | 8 | 8.3 |

#### RECEIVING YARDS PER GAME

| | Class | GP | No. | Yds | TD | Yds/Game |
|---|---|---|---|---|---|---|
| Nate Jackson, Menlo | Jr | 10 | 101 | 1515 | 16 | 151.5 |
| Jon Cain, Wilmington | Jr | 10 | 85 | 1459 | 15 | 145.9 |
| Darryl Deshields, Greenville | So | 10 | 90 | 1444 | 15 | 144.4 |
| Jim Jones, Widener | Jr | 10 | 62 | 1439 | 14 | 143.9 |
| Ryan Silvis, Washington & Jefferson | Sr | 10 | 63 | 1346 | 19 | 134.6 |

#### INTERCEPTIONS

| | Class | GP | No. | Yds | Int/G |
|---|---|---|---|---|---|
| Ben Matthews, Bethel | Sr | 10 | 15 | 134 | 1.5 |
| Nate Kok, Ripon | Sr | 10 | 13 | 254 | 1.3 |
| Eric Cowie, Ursinus | Jr | 10 | 11 | 92 | 1.1 |
| Mike Burke, Muhlenberg | Sr | 9 | 9 | 111 | 1.0 |
| Brian Portilia, WI–LaCrosse | Jr | 10 | 9 | 50 | .9 |

#### PUNTING

| | Class | No. | Avg |
|---|---|---|---|
| Wilson Hillman, Mississippi College | Sr | 62 | 43.1 |
| Brad Abraham, WI–Platteville | Jr | 52 | 41.9 |
| Kevin McCulley, WI–Stout | Sr | 68 | 41.8 |
| John Shaffer, Lycoming | So | 56 | 41.3 |
| Randy McGillivry, LaVerne | So | 51 | 41.1 |

Note: Minimum 3.6 per game.

## 2000 NCAA Division I-A Team Leaders

### Offense

#### SCORING

| | GP | Pts | Avg |
|---|---|---|---|
| Boise St | 11 | 494 | 44.91 |
| Miami (FL) | 11 | 469 | 42.64 |
| Florida St | 12 | 509 | 42.42 |
| Nebraska | 11 | 456 | 41.45 |
| Virginia Tech | 11 | 443 | 40.27 |
| Kansas St | 13 | 514 | 39.54 |
| Oklahoma | 12 | 468 | 39.00 |
| Texas | 11 | 425 | 38.64 |
| Northwestern | 11 | 424 | 38.55 |
| Florida | 12 | 448 | 37.33 |

#### RUSHING

| | GP | Car | Yds | Avg | TD | Yds/Game |
|---|---|---|---|---|---|---|
| Nebraska | 11 | 636 | 3842 | 6.0 | 45 | 349.27 |
| Ohio | 11 | 646 | 3553 | 5.5 | 32 | 323.00 |
| Air Force | 11 | 647 | 3244 | 5.0 | 33 | 294.91 |
| Texas Christian | 11 | 588 | 3032 | 5.2 | 33 | 275.64 |
| Virginia Tech | 11 | 570 | 2975 | 5.2 | 46 | 270.45 |
| New Mexico St | 11 | 535 | 2972 | 5.6 | 16 | 270.18 |
| Indiana | 11 | 505 | 2930 | 5.8 | 34 | 266.36 |
| Northwestern | 11 | 565 | 2830 | 5.0 | 36 | 257.27 |
| Toledo | 11 | 514 | 2792 | 5.4 | 29 | 253.82 |
| Clemson | 11 | 557 | 2600 | 4.7 | 33 | 236.36 |

#### TOTAL OFFENSE

| | GP | Plays | Yds | Avg | TD* | Yds/Game |
|---|---|---|---|---|---|---|
| Florida St | 12 | 924 | 6588 | 7.13 | 67 | 549.00 |
| Boise St | 11 | 812 | 5459 | 6.72 | 64 | 496.27 |
| Northwestern | 11 | 911 | 5232 | 5.74 | 56 | 475.64 |
| Purdue | 11 | 904 | 5183 | 5.73 | 47 | 471.18 |
| Miami (FL) | 11 | 774 | 5069 | 6.55 | 63 | 460.82 |
| Nebraska | 11 | 808 | 5059 | 6.26 | 63 | 459.91 |
| Tulane | 11 | 897 | 4989 | 5.56 | 40 | 453.55 |
| Idaho | 11 | 846 | 4985 | 5.89 | 42 | 453.18 |
| Air Force | 11 | 852 | 4971 | 5.83 | 47 | 451.91 |
| Clemson | 11 | 853 | 4911 | 5.76 | 53 | 446.45 |

*Defensive and special teams TDs not included.

## Offense *(Cont.)*

### PASSING

| | GP | Att | Comp | Yds | Pct Comp | Yds/Att | TD | Int | Yds/Game |
|---|---|---|---|---|---|---|---|---|---|
| Florida St | 12 | 469 | 290 | 4608 | 61.8 | 9.83 | 36 | 14 | 384.0 |
| Kentucky | 11 | 564 | 322 | 3689 | 57.09 | 6.54 | 19 | 21 | 335.4 |
| Tulane | 11 | 506 | 288 | 3569 | 56.92 | 7.05 | 28 | 16 | 324.5 |
| Hawaii | 12 | 609 | 309 | 3875 | 50.74 | 6.36 | 25 | 23 | 322.9 |
| Boise St | 11 | 372 | 225 | 3537 | 60.48 | 9.51 | 37 | 8 | 321.5 |
| Purdue | 11 | 489 | 292 | 3438 | 59.71 | 7.03 | 26 | 12 | 312.5 |
| Louisiana Tech | 12 | 546 | 357 | 3715 | 65.38 | 6.80 | 30 | 28 | 309.6 |
| Florida | 12 | 466 | 265 | 3698 | 56.87 | 7.94 | 34 | 12 | 308.2 |
| Idaho | 11 | 428 | 265 | 3357 | 61.92 | 7.84 | 24 | 19 | 305.2 |
| Marshall | 12 | 483 | 293 | 3584 | 60.66 | 7.42 | 24 | 10 | 298.7 |

## Single-Game Highs

Points Scored: 76—Kansas St, Sept 16 (vs Ball St).
Net Rushing Yards: 583—Air Force, Sept 2 (vs Cal St–Northridge).
Passing Yards: 536—Florida St, Oct 14 (vs Duke).
Rushing and Passing Yards: 771—Florida St, Nov 4 (vs Clemson).
Fewest Rushing and Passing Yards Allowed: 51—Kansas St, Sept 16 (vs Ball St).

## Defense

### SCORING

| | GP | Pts | Avg |
|---|---|---|---|
| Texas Christian | 11 | 106 | 9.6 |
| Florida St | 12 | 123 | 10.3 |
| Toledo | 11 | 125 | 11.4 |
| Western Michigan | 12 | 139 | 11.6 |
| Miami (FL) | 11 | 170 | 15.5 |
| S Carolina | 11 | 174 | 15.8 |
| Oklahoma | 12 | 192 | 16.0 |
| Southern Miss | 11 | 182 | 16.5 |
| Alabama–Birmingham | 11 | 192 | 17.5 |
| Texas A&M | 11 | 196 | 17.8 |

### TOTAL DEFENSE

| | GP | Plays | Yds | Avg | Yds/Game |
|---|---|---|---|---|---|
| Texas Christian | 11 | 718 | 2695 | 3.75 | 245.00 |
| Southern Miss | 11 | 784 | 2950 | 3.76 | 268.18 |
| Toledo | 11 | 703 | 2959 | 4.21 | 269.00 |
| Kansas St | 13 | 872 | 3517 | 4.03 | 270.54 |
| Memphis | 11 | 755 | 3028 | 4.01 | 275.27 |
| Florida St | 12 | 834 | 3324 | 3.99 | 277.00 |
| Texas | 11 | 766 | 3061 | 4.00 | 278.27 |
| Oklahoma | 12 | 809 | 3347 | 4.14 | 278.92 |
| Western Michigan | 12 | 803 | 3399 | 4.23 | 283.25 |
| Utah | 11 | 735 | 3171 | 4.31 | 288.27 |

### RUSHING

| | GP | Car | Yds | Avg | TD | Yds/Game |
|---|---|---|---|---|---|---|
| Memphis | 11 | 346 | 800 | 2.3 | 6 | 72.7 |
| Florida St | 12 | 387 | 887 | 2.3 | 6 | 73.9 |
| Tennessee | 11 | 338 | 817 | 2.4 | 7 | 74.3 |
| Louisville | 11 | 395 | 879 | 2.2 | 12 | 79.9 |
| Toledo | 11 | 365 | 897 | 2.5 | 10 | 81.5 |
| UAB | 11 | 386 | 919 | 2.4 | 9 | 83.5 |
| TCU | 11 | 395 | 928 | 2.4 | 3 | 84.4 |
| Arizona | 11 | 393 | 973 | 2.5 | 12 | 88.5 |
| Ohio St | 11 | 396 | 1008 | 2.6 | 10 | 91.6 |
| Oregon St | 11 | 385 | 1024 | 2.7 | 9 | 93.1 |

### TURNOVER MARGIN

| | | Turnovers Gained | | | Turnovers Lost | | | Margin/ |
|---|---|---|---|---|---|---|---|---|
| | GP | Fum | Int | Total | Fum | Int | Total | Game |
| Toledo | 11 | 16 | 15 | 31 | 5 | 4 | 9 | 2.00 |
| Georgia Tech | 11 | 15 | 15 | 30 | 6 | 6 | 12 | 1.64 |
| Florida | 12 | 16 | 24 | 40 | 9 | 12 | 21 | 1.58 |
| Oregon St | 11 | 10 | 22 | 32 | 9 | 7 | 16 | 1.45 |
| Notre Dame | 11 | 9 | 13 | 22 | 4 | 4 | 8 | 1.27 |
| Cincinnati | 11 | 15 | 19 | 34 | 9 | 13 | 22 | 1.09 |
| Miami (FL) | 11 | 10 | 23 | 33 | 16 | 5 | 21 | 1.09 |
| Northwestern | 11 | 13 | 12 | 25 | 6 | 7 | 13 | 1.09 |
| Louisville | 11 | 11 | 27 | 38 | 14 | 12 | 26 | 1.09 |
| Arizona St | 11 | 23 | 13 | 36 | 13 | 12 | 25 | 1.00 |
| Michigan | 11 | 12 | 14 | 26 | 10 | 5 | 15 | 1.00 |
| Boston College | 11 | 10 | 16 | 26 | 3 | 12 | 15 | 1.00 |

### PASSING EFFICIENCY

| | GP | Att | Comp | Yds | Pct Comp | Yds/Att | TD | Pct TD | Int | Pct Int | Rating Pts |
|---|---|---|---|---|---|---|---|---|---|---|---|
| Texas | 11 | 379 | 171 | 2027 | 45.12 | 5.35 | 8 | 2.11 | 17 | 4.49 | 88.02 |
| Oklahoma | 12 | 397 | 196 | 2049 | 49.37 | 5.16 | 9 | 2.27 | 22 | 5.54 | 89.15 |
| Texas Christian | 11 | 323 | 143 | 1767 | 44.27 | 5.47 | 10 | 3.10 | 15 | 4.64 | 91.18 |
| Southern Miss | 11 | 370 | 186 | 1788 | 50.27 | 4.83 | 9 | 2.43 | 14 | 3.78 | 91.35 |
| Florida St | 12 | 447 | 220 | 2437 | 49.22 | 5.45 | 7 | 1.57 | 19 | 4.25 | 91.66 |
| Kansas St | 13 | 399 | 204 | 2241 | 51.13 | 5.62 | 8 | 2.01 | 20 | 5.01 | 94.87 |
| Nebraska | 11 | 393 | 179 | 2291 | 45.55 | 5.83 | 10 | 2.54 | 14 | 3.56 | 95.74 |
| Miami (FL) | 11 | 428 | 216 | 2427 | 50.47 | 5.67 | 11 | 2.57 | 23 | 5.37 | 95.87 |
| Mississippi | 11 | 341 | 160 | 2064 | 46.92 | 6.05 | 9 | 2.64 | 18 | 5.28 | 95.90 |
| Texas Tech | 12 | 343 | 177 | 1969 | 51.60 | 5.74 | 7 | 2.04 | 15 | 4.37 | 97.81 |

## National Champions

| Year | Champion | Record | Bowl Game | Head Coach |
|---|---|---|---|---|
| 1883 | Yale | 8-0-0 | No bowl | Ray Tompkins (Captain) |
| 1884 | Yale | 9-0-0 | No bowl | Eugene L. Richards (Captain) |
| 1885 | Princeton | 9-0-0 | No bowl | Charles DeCamp (Captain) |
| 1886 | Yale | 9-0-1 | No bowl | Robert N. Corwin (Captain) |
| 1887 | Yale | 9-0-0 | No bowl | Harry W. Beecher (Captain) |
| 1888 | Yale | 13-0-0 | No bowl | Walter Camp |
| 1889 | Princeton | 10-0-0 | No bowl | Edgar Poe (Captain) |
| 1890 | Harvard | 11-0-0 | No bowl | George A. Stewart/George C. Adams |
| 1891 | Yale | 13-0-0 | No bowl | Walter Camp |
| 1892 | Yale | 13-0-0 | No bowl | Walter Camp |
| 1893 | Princeton | 11-0-0 | No bowl | Tom Trenchard (Captain) |
| 1894 | Yale | 16-0-0 | No bowl | William C. Rhodes |
| 1895 | Pennsylvania | 14-0-0 | No bowl | George Woodruff |
| 1896 | Princeton | 10-0-1 | No bowl | Garrett Cochran |
| 1897 | Pennsylvania | 15-0-0 | No bowl | George Woodruff |
| 1898 | Harvard | 11-0-0 | No bowl | W. Cameron Forbes |
| 1899 | Harvard | 10-0-1 | No bowl | Benjamin H. Dibblee |
| 1900 | Yale | 12-0-0 | No bowl | Malcolm McBride |
| 1901 | Michigan | 11-0-0 | Won Rose | Fielding Yost |
| 1902 | Michigan | 11-0-0 | No bowl | Fielding Yost |
| 1903 | Princeton | 11-0-0 | No bowl | Art Hillebrand |
| 1904 | Pennsylvania | 12-0-0 | No bowl | Carl Williams |
| 1905 | Chicago | 11-0-0 | No bowl | Amos Alonzo Stagg |
| 1906 | Princeton | 9-0-1 | No bowl | Bill Roper |
| 1907 | Yale | 9-0-1 | No bowl | Bill Knox |
| 1908 | Pennsylvania | 11-0-1 | No bowl | Sol Metzger |
| 1909 | Yale | 10-0-0 | No bowl | Howard Jones |
| 1910 | Harvard | 8-0-1 | No bowl | Percy Houghton |
| 1911 | Princeton | 8-0-2 | No bowl | Bill Roper |
| 1912 | Harvard | 9-0-0 | No bowl | Percy Houghton |
| 1913 | Harvard | 9-0-0 | No bowl | Percy Houghton |
| 1914 | Army | 9-0-0 | No bowl | Charley Daly |
| 1915 | Cornell | 9-0-0 | No bowl | Al Sharpe |
| 1916 | Pittsburgh | 8-0-0 | No bowl | Pop Warner |
| 1917 | Georgia Tech | 9-0-0 | No bowl | John Heisman |
| 1918 | Pittsburgh | 4-1-0 | No bowl | Pop Warner |
| 1919 | Harvard | 9-0-1 | Won Rose | Bob Fisher |
| 1920 | California | 9-0-0 | Won Rose | Andy Smith |
| 1921 | Cornell | 8-0-0 | No bowl | Gil Dobie |
| 1922 | Cornell | 8-0-0 | No bowl | Gil Dobie |
| 1923 | Illinois | 8-0-0 | No bowl | Bob Zuppke |
| 1924 | Notre Dame | 10-0-0 | Won Rose | Knute Rockne |
| 1925 | Alabama (H) | 10-0-0 | Won Rose | Wallace Wade |
|  | Dartmouth (D) | 8-0-0 | No bowl | Jesse Hawley |
| 1926 | Alabama (H) | 9-0-1 | Tied Rose | Wallace Wade |
|  | Stanford (D)(H) | 10-0-1 | Tied Rose | Pop Warner |
| 1927 | Illinois | 7-0-1 | No bowl | Bob Zuppke |
| 1928 | Georgia Tech (H) | 10-0-0 | Won Rose | Bill Alexander |
|  | Southern Cal (D) | 9-0-1 | No bowl | Howard Jones |
| 1929 | Notre Dame | 9-0-0 | No bowl | Knute Rockne |
| 1930 | Notre Dame | 10-0-0 | No bowl | Knute Rockne |
| 1931 | Southern Cal | 10-1-0 | Won Rose | Howard Jones |
| 1932 | Southern Cal (H) | 10-0-0 | Won Rose | Howard Jones |
|  | Michigan (D) | 8-0-0 | No bowl | Harry Kipke |
| 1933 | Michigan | 7-0-1 | No bowl | Harry Kipke |
| 1934 | Minnesota | 8-0-0 | No bowl | Bernie Bierman |
| 1935 | Minnesota (H) | 8-0-0 | No bowl | Bernie Bierman |
|  | Southern Methodist (D) | 12-1-0 | Lost Rose | Matty Bell |
| 1936 | Minnesota | 7-1-0 | No bowl | Bernie Bierman |
| 1937 | Pittsburgh | 9-0-1 | No bowl | Jock Sutherland |
| 1938 | Texas Christian (AP) | 11-0-0 | Won Sugar | Dutch Meyer |
|  | Notre Dame (D) | 8-1-0 | No bowl | Elmer Layden |
| 1939 | Southern Cal (D) | 8-0-2 | Won Rose | Howard Jones |
|  | Texas A&M (AP) | 11-0-0 | Won Sugar | Homer Norton |
| 1940 | Minnesota | 8-0-0 | No bowl | Bernie Bierman |
| 1941 | Minnesota | 8-0-0 | No bowl | Bernie Bierman |
| 1942 | Ohio St | 9-1-0 | No bowl | Paul Brown |

| Year | Champion | Record | Bowl Game | Head Coach |
|------|----------|--------|-----------|------------|
| 1943 | Notre Dame | 9-1-0 | No bowl | Frank Leahy |
| 1944 | Army | 9-0-0 | No bowl | Red Blaik |
| 1945 | Army | 9-0-0 | No bowl | Red Blaik |
| 1946 | Notre Dame | 8-0-1 | No bowl | Frank Leahy |
| 1947 | Notre Dame | 9-0-0 | No bowl | Frank Leahy |
| | Michigan* | 10-0-0 | Won Rose | Fritz Crisler |
| 1948 | Michigan | 9-0-0 | No bowl | Bennie Oosterbaan |
| 1949 | Notre Dame | 10-0-0 | No bowl | Frank Leahy |
| 1950 | Oklahoma | 10-1-0 | Lost Sugar | Bud Wilkinson |
| 1951 | Tennessee | 10-1-0 | Lost Sugar | Bob Neyland |
| 1952 | Michigan St | 9-0-0 | No bowl | Biggie Munn |
| 1953 | Maryland | 10-1-0 | Lost Orange | Jim Tatum |
| 1954 | Ohio St | 10-0-0 | Won Rose | Woody Hayes |
| | UCLA (UPI) | 9-0-0 | No bowl | Red Sanders |
| 1955 | Oklahoma | 11-0-0 | Won Orange | Bud Wilkinson |
| 1956 | Oklahoma | 10-0-0 | No bowl | Bud Wilkinson |
| 1957 | Auburn | 10-0-0 | No bowl | Shug Jordan |
| | Ohio St (UPI) | 9-1-0 | Won Rose | Woody Hayes |
| 1958 | Louisiana St | 11-0-0 | Won Sugar | Paul Dietzel |
| 1959 | Syracuse | 11-0-0 | Won Cotton | Ben Schwartzwalder |
| 1960 | Minnesota | 8-2-0 | Lost Rose | Murray Warmath |
| 1961 | Alabama | 11-0-0 | Won Sugar | Bear Bryant |
| 1962 | Southern Cal | 11-0-0 | Won Rose | John McKay |
| 1963 | Texas | 11-0-0 | Won Cotton | Darrell Royal |
| 1964 | Alabama | 10-1-0 | Lost Orange | Bear Bryant |
| 1965 | Alabama | 9-1-1 | Won Orange | Bear Bryant |
| | Michigan St (UPI) | 10-1-0 | Lost Rose | Duffy Daugherty |
| 1966 | Notre Dame | 9-0-1 | No bowl | Ara Parseghian |
| 1967 | Southern Cal | 10-1-0 | Won Rose | John McKay |
| 1968 | Ohio St | 10-0-0 | Won Rose | Woody Hayes |
| 1969 | Texas | 11-0-0 | Won Cotton | Darrell Royal |
| 1970 | Nebraska | 11-0-1 | Won Orange | Bob Devaney |
| | Texas (UPI) | 10-1-0 | Lost Cotton | Darrell Royal |
| 1971 | Nebraska | 13-0-0 | Won Orange | Bob Devaney |
| 1972 | Southern Cal | 12-0-0 | Won Rose | John McKay |
| 1973 | Notre Dame | 11-0-0 | Won Sugar | Ara Parseghian |
| | Alabama (UPI) | 11-1-0 | Lost Sugar | Bear Bryant |
| 1974 | Oklahoma | 11-0-0 | No bowl | Barry Switzer |
| | Southern Cal (UPI) | 10-1-1 | Won Rose | John McKay |
| 1975 | Oklahoma | 11-1-0 | Won Orange | Barry Switzer |
| 1976 | Pittsburgh | 12-0-0 | Won Sugar | Johnny Majors |
| 1977 | Notre Dame | 11-1-0 | Won Cotton | Dan Devine |
| 1978 | Alabama | 11-1-0 | Won Sugar | Bear Bryant |
| | Southern Cal (UPI) | 12-1-0 | Won Rose | John Robinson |
| 1979 | Alabama | 12-0-0 | Won Sugar | Bear Bryant |
| 1980 | Georgia | 12-0-0 | Won Sugar | Vince Dooley |
| 1981 | Clemson | 12-0-0 | Won Orange | Danny Ford |
| 1982 | Penn St | 11-1-0 | Won Sugar | Joe Paterno |
| 1983 | Miami (FL) | 11-1-0 | Won Orange | Howard Schnellenberger |
| 1984 | Brigham Young | 13-0-0 | Won Holiday | LaVell Edwards |
| 1985 | Oklahoma | 11-1-0 | Won Orange | Barry Switzer |
| 1986 | Penn St | 12-0-0 | Won Fiesta | Joe Paterno |
| 1987 | Miami (FL) | 12-0-0 | Won Orange | Jimmy Johnson |
| 1988 | Notre Dame | 12-0-0 | Won Fiesta | Lou Holtz |
| 1989 | Miami (FL) | 11-1-0 | Won Sugar | Dennis Erickson |
| 1990 | Colorado | 11-1-1 | Won Orange | Bill McCartney |
| | Georgia Tech (UPI) | 11-0-1 | Won Citrus | Bobby Ross |
| 1991 | Miami (FL) | 12-0-0 | Won Orange | Dennis Erickson |
| | Washington (CNN) | 12-0-0 | Won Rose | Don James |
| 1992 | Alabama | 13-0-0 | Won Sugar | Gene Stallings |
| 1993 | Florida St | 12-1-0 | Won Orange | Bobby Bowden |
| 1994 | Nebraska | 13-0-0 | Won Orange | Tom Osborne |
| 1995 | Nebraska | 12-0-0 | Won Fiesta | Tom Osborne |
| †1996 | Florida | 12-1 | Won Sugar | Steve Spurrier |

| Year | Champion | Record | Bowl Game | Head Coach |
|------|----------|--------|-----------|------------|
| 1997 | Michigan | 12–0 | Won Rose | Lloyd Carr |
|  | Nebraska (ESPN) | 13–0 | Won Orange | Tom Osborne |
| 1998 | Tennessee | 13–0 | Won Fiesta | Phillip Fulmer |
| 1999 | Florida St | 12–0 | Won Sugar | Bobby Bowden |
| 2000 | Oklahoma | 13–0 | Won Orange | Bob Stoops |

*The AP, which had voted Notre Dame No. 1, took a second vote, giving the national title to Michigan after its 49–0 win over Southern Cal in the Rose Bowl.    Note: Selectors: Helms Athletic Foundation (H) 1883–1935, The Dickinson System (D) 1924–40, The Associated Press (AP) 1936–present, United Press International (UPI) 1958–90, *USA Today*/CNN (CNN) 1991–96, and *USA Today*/ESPN (ESPN) 1997–present. †In 1996 the NCAA introduced overtime to break ties.

# Results of Major Bowl Games

## Rose Bowl

| | |
|---|---|
| 1-1-02 | Michigan 49, Stanford 0 |
| 1-1-16 | Washington St 14, Brown 0 |
| 1-1-17 | Oregon 14, Pennsylvania 0 |
| 1-1-18 | Mare Island 19, Camp Lewis 7 |
| 1-1-19 | Great Lakes 17, Mare Island 0 |
| 1-1-20 | Harvard 7, Oregon 6 |
| 1-1-21 | California 28, Ohio St 0 |
| 1-2-22 | Washington & Jefferson 0, California 0 |
| 1-1-23 | Southern Cal 14, Penn St 3 |
| 1-1-24 | Navy 14, Washington 14 |
| 1-1-25 | Notre Dame 27, Stanford 10 |
| 1-1-26 | Alabama 20, Washington 19 |
| 1-1-27 | Alabama 7, Stanford 7 |
| 1-2-28 | Stanford 7, Pittsburgh 6 |
| 1-1-29 | Georgia Tech 8, California 7 |
| 1-1-30 | Southern Cal 47, Pittsburgh 14 |
| 1-1-31 | Alabama 24, Washington St 0 |
| 1-1-32 | Southern Cal 21, Tulane 12 |
| 1-2-33 | Southern Cal 35, Pittsburgh 0 |
| 1-1-34 | Columbia 7, Stanford 0 |
| 1-1-35 | Alabama 29, Stanford 13 |
| 1-1-36 | Stanford 7, Southern Methodist 0 |
| 1-1-37 | Pittsburgh 21, Washington 0 |
| 1-1-38 | California 13, Alabama 0 |
| 1-2-39 | Southern Cal 7, Duke 3 |
| 1-1-40 | Southern Cal 14, Tennessee 0 |
| 1-1-41 | Stanford 21, Nebraska 13 |
| 1-1-42 | Oregon St 20, Duke 16 |
| 1-1-43 | Georgia 9, UCLA 0 |
| 1-1-44 | Southern Cal 29, Washington 0 |
| 1-1-45 | Southern Cal 25, Tennessee 0 |
| 1-1-46 | Alabama 34, Southern Cal 14 |
| 1-1-47 | Illinois 45, UCLA 14 |
| 1-1-48 | Michigan 49, Southern Cal 0 |
| 1-1-49 | Northwestern 20, California 14 |
| 1-2-50 | Ohio St 17, California 14 |
| 1-1-51 | Michigan 14, California 6 |
| 1-1-52 | Illinois 40, Stanford 7 |
| 1-1-53 | Southern Cal 7, Wisconsin 0 |
| 1-1-54 | Michigan St 28, UCLA 20 |
| 1-1-55 | Ohio St 20, Southern Cal 7 |
| 1-2-56 | Michigan St 17, UCLA 14 |
| 1-1-57 | Iowa 35, Oregon St 19 |
| 1-1-58 | Ohio St 10, Oregon 7 |
| 1-1-59 | Iowa 38, California 12 |
| 1-1-60 | Washington 44, Wisconsin 8 |
| 1-2-61 | Washington 17, Minnesota 7 |
| 1-1-62 | Minnesota 21, UCLA 3 |
| 1-1-63 | Southern Cal 42, Wisconsin 37 |

| | |
|---|---|
| 1-1-64 | Illinois 17, Washington 7 |
| 1-1-65 | Michigan 34, Oregon St 7 |
| 1-1-66 | UCLA 14, Michigan St 12 |
| 1-2-67 | Purdue 14, Southern Cal 13 |
| 1-1-68 | Southern Cal 14, Indiana 3 |
| 1-1-69 | Ohio St 27, Southern Cal 16 |
| 1-1-70 | Southern Cal 10, Michigan 3 |
| 1-1-71 | Stanford 27, Ohio St 17 |
| 1-1-72 | Stanford 13, Michigan 12 |
| 1-1-73 | Southern Cal 42, Ohio St 17 |
| 1-1-74 | Ohio St 42, Southern Cal 21 |
| 1-1-75 | Southern Cal 18, Ohio St 17 |
| 1-1-76 | UCLA 23, Ohio St 10 |
| 1-1-77 | Southern Cal 14, Michigan 6 |
| 1-2-78 | Washington 27, Michigan 20 |
| 1-1-79 | Southern Cal 17, Michigan 10 |
| 1-1-80 | Southern Cal 17, Ohio St 16 |
| 1-1-81 | Michigan 23, Washington 6 |
| 1-1-82 | Washington 28, Iowa 0 |
| 1-1-83 | UCLA 24, Michigan 14 |
| 1-2-84 | UCLA 45, Illinois 9 |
| 1-1-85 | Southern Cal 20, Ohio St 17 |
| 1-1-86 | UCLA 45, Iowa 28 |
| 1-1-87 | Arizona St 22, Michigan 15 |
| 1-1-88 | Michigan St 20, Southern Cal 17 |
| 1-2-89 | Michigan 22, Southern Cal 14 |
| 1-1-90 | Southern Cal 17, Michigan 10 |
| 1-1-91 | Washington 46, Iowa 34 |
| 1-1-92 | Washington 34, Michigan 14 |
| 1-1-93 | Michigan 38, Washington 31 |
| 1-1-94 | Wisconsin 21, UCLA 16 |
| 1-2-95 | Penn St 38, Oregon 20 |
| 1-1-96 | Southern Cal 41, Northwestern 32 |
| 1-1-97 | Ohio St 20, Arizona St 17 |
| 1-1-98 | Michigan 21, Washington St 16 |
| 1-1-99 | Wisconsin 38, UCLA 31 |
| 1-1-00 | Wisconsin 17, Stanford 9 |
| 1-1-01 | Washington 34, Purdue 24 |

City: Pasadena. Stadium: Rose Bowl, capacity 96,576.
Playing Sites: Tournament Park (1902, 1916–22), Rose Bowl (1923–41, since 1943), Duke Stadium, Durham, NC (1942).

## Orange Bowl

| | |
|---|---|
| 1-1-35 | Bucknell 26, Miami (FL) 0 |
| 1-1-36 | Catholic 20, Mississippi 19 |
| 1-1-37 | Duquesne 13, Mississippi St 12 |
| 1-1-38 | Auburn 6, Michigan St 0 |

Note: The Fiesta, Orange, Rose and Sugar Bowls constitute the Bowl Alliance, formed in 1995. The Alliance holds eight berths: one each for the champions of the ACC, Big 10, Big 12, Big East, Pac 10 and SEC, and two at-large, reserved for any Division I-A team with at least nine wins and ranked in the top 12 of the BCS rankings. Of the eight teams, the two highest-ranked go to the Rose Bowl in 2002, the Fiesta Bowl in 2003, and the Sugar Bowl in 2003. Once these four BCS matches have been set conferences may place the remaining qualified teams in the other bowls. Teams that have won at least six games against Division I-A teams qualify.

# Results of Major Bowl Games *(Cont.)*

## Orange Bowl *(Cont.)*

| | |
|---|---|
| 1-2-39 | Tennessee 17, Oklahoma 0 |
| 1-1-40 | Georgia Tech 21, Missouri 7 |
| 1-1-41 | Mississippi St 14, Georgetown 7 |
| 1-1-42 | Georgia 40, Texas Christian 26 |
| 1-1-43 | Alabama 37, Boston College 21 |
| 1-1-44 | Louisiana St 19, Texas A&M 14 |
| 1-1-45 | Tulsa 26, Georgia Tech 12 |
| 1-1-46 | Miami (FL) 13, Holy Cross 6 |
| 1-1-47 | Rice 8, Tennessee 0 |
| 1-1-48 | Georgia Tech 20, Kansas 14 |
| 1-1-49 | Texas 41, Georgia 28 |
| 1-2-50 | Santa Clara 21, Kentucky 13 |
| 1-1-51 | Clemson 15, Miami (FL) 14 |
| 1-1-52 | Georgia Tech 17, Baylor 14 |
| 1-1-53 | Alabama 61, Syracuse 6 |
| 1-1-54 | Oklahoma 7, Maryland 0 |
| 1-1-55 | Duke 34, Nebraska 7 |
| 1-2-56 | Oklahoma 20, Maryland 6 |
| 1-1-57 | Colorado 27, Clemson 21 |
| 1-1-58 | Oklahoma 48, Duke 21 |
| 1-1-59 | Oklahoma 21, Syracuse 6 |
| 1-1-60 | Georgia 14, Missouri 0 |
| 1-2-61 | Missouri 21, Navy 14 |
| 1-1-62 | Louisiana St 25, Colorado 7 |
| 1-1-63 | Alabama 17, Oklahoma 0 |
| 1-1-64 | Nebraska 13, Auburn 7 |
| 1-1-65 | Texas 21, Alabama 17 |
| 1-1-66 | Alabama 39, Nebraska 28 |
| 1-2-67 | Florida 27, Georgia Tech 12 |
| 1-1-68 | Oklahoma 26, Tennessee 24 |
| 1-1-69 | Penn St 15, Kansas 14 |
| 1-1-70 | Penn St 10, Missouri 3 |
| 1-1-71 | Nebraska 17, Louisiana St 12 |
| 1-1-72 | Nebraska 38, Alabama 6 |
| 1-1-73 | Nebraska 40, Notre Dame 6 |
| 1-1-74 | Penn St 16, Louisiana St 9 |
| 1-1-75 | Notre Dame 13, Alabama 11 |
| 1-1-76 | Oklahoma 14, Michigan 6 |
| 1-1-77 | Ohio St 27, Colorado 10 |
| 1-2-78 | Arkansas 31, Oklahoma 6 |
| 1-1-79 | Oklahoma 31, Nebraska 24 |
| 1-1-80 | Oklahoma 24, Florida St 7 |
| 1-1-81 | Oklahoma 18, Florida St 17 |
| 1-1-82 | Clemson 22, Nebraska 15 |
| 1-1-83 | Nebraska 21, Louisiana St 20 |
| 1-2-84 | Miami (FL) 31, Nebraska 30 |
| 1-1-85 | Washington 28, Oklahoma 17 |
| 1-1-86 | Oklahoma 25, Penn St 10 |
| 1-1-87 | Oklahoma 42, Arkansas 8 |
| 1-1-88 | Miami (FL) 20, Oklahoma 14 |
| 1-2-89 | Miami (FL) 23, Nebraska 3 |
| 1-1-90 | Notre Dame 21, Colorado 6 |
| 1-1-91 | Colorado 10, Notre Dame 9 |
| 1-1-92 | Miami (FL) 22, Nebraska 0 |
| 1-1-93 | Florida St 27, Nebraska 14 |
| 1-1-94 | Florida St 18, Nebraska 16 |
| 1-1-95 | Nebraska 24, Miami (FL) 17 |
| 1-1-96 | Florida St 31, Notre Dame 26 |
| 12-31-96 | Nebraska 41, Virginia Tech 21 |
| 1-2-98 | Nebraska 42, Tennessee 17 |
| 1-2-99 | Florida 31, Syracuse 10 |
| 1-1-00 | Michigan 35, Alabama 34 (ot) |
| 1-3-01 | Oklahoma 13, Florida St 2 |

City: Miami. Stadium: Pro Player Stadium, capacity 72,000. Playing Sites: Orange Bowl (1935–96), Pro Player Stadium (since 1996).

## Sugar Bowl

| | |
|---|---|
| 1-1-35 | Tulane 20, Temple 14 |
| 1-1-36 | Texas Christian 3, Louisiana St 2 |
| 1-1-37 | Santa Clara 21, Louisiana St 14 |
| 1-1-38 | Santa Clara 6, Louisiana St 0 |
| 1-2-39 | Texas Christian 15, Carnegie Tech 7 |
| 1-1-40 | Texas A&M 14, Tulane 13 |
| 1-1-41 | Boston Col 19, Tennessee 13 |
| 1-1-42 | Fordham 2, Missouri 0 |
| 1-1-43 | Tennessee 14, Tulsa 7 |
| 1-1-44 | Georgia Tech 20, Tulsa 18 |
| 1-1-45 | Duke 29, Alabama 26 |
| 1-1-46 | Oklahoma St 33, St. Mary's (CA) 13 |
| 1-1-47 | Georgia 20, N Carolina 10 |
| 1-1-48 | Texas 27, Alabama 7 |
| 1-1-49 | Oklahoma 14, N Carolina 6 |
| 1-2-50 | Oklahoma 35, Louisiana St 0 |
| 1-1-51 | Kentucky 13, Oklahoma 7 |
| 1-1-52 | Maryland 28, Tennessee 13 |
| 1-1-53 | Georgia Tech 24, Mississippi 7 |
| 1-1-54 | Georgia Tech 42, W Virginia 19 |
| 1-1-55 | Navy 21, Mississippi 0 |
| 1-2-56 | Georgia Tech 7, Pittsburgh 0 |
| 1-1-57 | Baylor 13, Tennessee 7 |
| 1-1-58 | Mississippi 39, Texas 7 |
| 1-1-59 | Louisiana St 7, Clemson 0 |
| 1-1-60 | Mississippi 21, Louisiana St 0 |
| 1-2-61 | Mississippi 14, Rice 6 |
| 1-1-62 | Alabama 10, Arkansas 3 |
| 1-1-63 | Mississippi 17, Arkansas 13 |
| 1-1-64 | Alabama 12, Mississippi 7 |
| 1-1-65 | Louisiana St 13, Syracuse 10 |
| 1-1-66 | Missouri 20, Florida 18 |
| 1-2-67 | Alabama 34, Nebraska 7 |
| 1-1-68 | Louisiana St 20, Wyoming 13 |
| 1-1-69 | Arkansas 16, Georgia 2 |
| 1-1-70 | Mississippi 27, Arkansas 22 |
| 1-1-71 | Tennessee 34, Air Force 13 |
| 1-1-72 | Oklahoma 40, Auburn 22 |
| 12-31-72 | Oklahoma 14, Penn St 0 |
| 12-31-73 | Notre Dame 24, Alabama 23 |
| 12-31-74 | Nebraska 13, Florida 10 |
| 12-31-75 | Alabama 13, Penn St 6 |
| 1-1-77 | Pittsburgh 27, Georgia 3 |
| 1-2-78 | Alabama 35, Ohio St 6 |
| 1-1-79 | Alabama 14, Penn St 7 |
| 1-1-80 | Alabama 24, Arkansas 9 |
| 1-1-81 | Georgia 17, Notre Dame 10 |
| 1-1-82 | Pittsburgh 24, Georgia 20 |
| 1-1-83 | Penn St 27, Georgia 23 |
| 1-2-84 | Auburn 9, Michigan 7 |
| 1-1-85 | Nebraska 28, Louisiana St 10 |
| 1-1-86 | Tennessee 35, Miami (FL) 7 |
| 1-1-87 | Nebraska 30, Louisiana St 15 |
| 1-1-88 | Syracuse 16, Auburn 16 |
| 1-2-89 | Florida St 13, Auburn 7 |
| 1-1-90 | Miami (FL) 33, Alabama 25 |
| 1-1-91 | Tennessee 23, Virginia 22 |
| 1-1-92 | Notre Dame 39, Florida 28 |
| 1-1-93 | Alabama 34, Miami (FL) 13 |
| 1-1-94 | Florida 41, West Virginia 7 |
| 1-2-95 | Florida St 23, Florida 17 |
| 12-31-95 | Virginia Tech 28, Texas 10 |
| 1-2-97 | Florida 52, Florida St 20 |
| 1-1-98 | Florida St 31, Ohio St 14 |
| 1-1-99 | Ohio St 24, Texas A&M 14 |
| 1-4-00 | Florida St 46, Virginia Tech 29 |

## Sugar Bowl *(Cont.)*

1-2-01 ..............Miami (FL) 37, Florida 20

City: New Orleans.  Stadium: Louisiana Superdome, capacity 71,023.

Playing Sites: Tulane Stadium (1935–74), Louisiana Superdome (since 1975).

## Cotton Bowl

1-1-37 ..............Texas Christian 16, Marquette 6
1-1-38 ..............Rice 28, Colorado 14
1-2-39 ..............St. Mary's (CA) 20, Texas Tech 13
1-1-40 ..............Clemson 6, Boston Col 3
1-1-41 ..............Texas A&M 13, Fordham 12
1-1-42 ..............Alabama 29, Texas A&M 21
1-1-43 ..............Texas 14, Georgia Tech 7
1-1-44 ..............Texas 7, Randolph Field 7
1-1-45 ..............Oklahoma St 34, Texas Christian 0
1-1-46 ..............Texas 40, Missouri 27
1-1-47 ..............Arkansas 0, Louisiana St 0
1-1-48 ..............Southern Methodist 13, Penn St 13
1-1-49 ..............Southern Methodist 21, Oregon 13
1-2-50 ..............Rice 27, N Carolina 13
1-1-51 ..............Tennessee 20, Texas 14
1-1-52 ..............Kentucky 20, Texas Christian 7
1-1-53 ..............Texas 16, Tennessee 0
1-1-54 ..............Rice 28, Alabama 6
1-1-55 ..............Georgia Tech 14, Arkansas 6
1-2-56 ..............Mississippi 14, Texas Christian 13
1-1-57 ..............Texas Christian 28, Syracuse 27
1-1-58 ..............Navy 20, Rice 7
1-1-59 ..............Texas Christian 0, Air Force 0
1-1-60 ..............Syracuse 23, Texas 14
1-2-61 ..............Duke 7, Arkansas 6
1-1-62 ..............Texas 12, Mississippi 7
1-1-63 ..............Louisiana St 13, Texas 0
1-1-64 ..............Texas 28, Navy 6
1-1-65 ..............Arkansas 10, Nebraska 7
1-1-66 ..............Louisiana St 14, Arkansas 7
12-31-66 .........Georgia 24, Southern Methodist 9
1-1-68 ..............Texas A&M 20, Alabama 16
1-1-69 ..............Texas 36, Tennessee 13
1-1-70 ..............Texas 21, Notre Dame 17
1-1-71 ..............Notre Dame 24, Texas 11
1-1-72 ..............Penn St 30, Texas 6
1 1 73 ..............Texas 17, Alabama 13
1-1-74 ..............Nebraska 19, Texas 3
1-1-75 ..............Penn St 41, Baylor 20
1-1-76 ..............Arkansas 31, Georgia 10
1-1-77 ..............Houston 30, Maryland 21
1-2-78 ..............Notre Dame 38, Texas 10
1-1-79 ..............Notre Dame 35, Houston 34
1-1-80 ..............Houston 17, Nebraska 14
1-1-81 ..............Alabama 30, Baylor 2
1-1-82 ..............Texas 14, Alabama 12
1-1-83 ..............SMU 7, Pittsburgh 3
1-2-84 ..............Georgia 10, Texas 9
1-1-85 ..............Boston Col 45, Houston 28
1-1-86 ..............Texas A&M 36, Auburn 16
1-1-87 ..............Ohio St 28, Texas A&M 12
1-1-88 ..............Texas A&M 35, Notre Dame 10
1-2-89 ..............UCLA 17, Arkansas 3
1-1-90 ..............Tennessee 31, Arkansas 27
1-1-91 ..............Miami (FL) 46, Texas 3
1-1-92 ..............Florida St 10, Texas A&M 2
1-1-93 ..............Notre Dame 28, Texas A&M 3
1-1-94 ..............Notre Dame 24, Texas A&M 21
1-2-95 ..............Southern Cal 55, Texas Tech 14

## Cotton Bowl *(Cont.)*

1-1-96 ..............Colorado 38, Oregon 6
1-1-97 ..............Brigham Young 19, Kansas St 15
1-1-98 ..............UCLA 29, Texas A&M 23
1-1-99 ..............Texas 38, Mississippi St 11
1-1-00 ..............Arkansas 27, Texas 6
1-1-01 ..............Kansas St 35, Tennessee 21

City: Dallas.  Stadium: Cotton Bowl, capacity 68,252.

## Sun Bowl

1-1-36 ..............Hardin-Simmons 14, New Mexico St 14
1-1-37 ..............Hardin-Simmons 34, UTEP 6
1-1-38 ..............W Virginia 7, Texas Tech 6
1-2-39 ..............Utah 26, New Mexico 0
1-1-40 ..............Catholic 0, Arizona St 0
1-1-41 ..............Case Reserve 26, Arizona St 13
1-1-42 ..............Tulsa 6, Texas Tech 0
1-1-43 ..............2nd Air Force 13, Hardin-Simmons 7
1-1-44 ..............Southwestern (TX) 7, New Mexico 0
1-1-45 ..............Southwestern (TX) 35, New Mexico 0
1-1-46 ..............New Mexico 34, Denver 24
1-1-47 ..............Cincinnati 18, Virginia Tech 6
1-1-48 ..............Miami (OH) 13, Texas Tech 12
1-1-49 ..............W Virginia 21, UTEP 12
1-2-50 ..............UTEP 33, Georgetown 20
1-1-51 ..............W Texas St 14, Cincinnati 13
1-1-52 ..............Texas Tech 25, Pacific 14
1-1-53 ..............Pacific 26, Southern Miss 7
1-1-54 ..............UTEP 37, Southern Miss 14
1-1-55 ..............UTEP 47, Florida St 20
1-2-56 ..............Wyoming 21, Texas Tech 14
1-1-57 ..............George Washington 13, UTEP 0
1-1-58 ..............Louisville 34, Drake 20
12-31-58 ..........Wyoming 14, Hardin-Simmons 6
12-31-59 ..........New Mexico St 28, N Texas 8
12-31-60 ..........New Mexico St 20, Utah St 13
12-30-61 ..........Villanova 17, Wichita St 9
12-31-62 ..........W Texas St 15, Ohio 14
12-31-63 ..........Oregon 21, Southern Methodist 14
12-26-64 ..........Georgia 7, Texas Tech 0
12-31-65 ..........UTEP 13, Texas Christian 12
12-24-66 ..........Wyoming 28, Florida St 20
12-30-67 ..........UTEP 14, Mississippi 7
12-28-68 ..........Auburn 34, Arizona 10
12-20-69 ..........Nebraska 45, Georgia 6
12-19-70 ..........Georgia Tech 17, Texas Tech 9
12-18-71 ..........Louisiana St 33, Iowa St 15
12-30-72 ..........N Carolina 32, Texas Tech 28
12-29-73 ..........Missouri 34, Auburn 17
12-28-74 ..........Mississippi St 26, N Carolina 24
12-26-75 ..........Pittsburgh 33, Kansas 19
1-2-77 ..............Texas A&M 37, Florida 14
12-31-77 ..........Stanford 24, Louisiana St 14
12-23-78 ..........Texas 42, Maryland 0
12-22-79 ..........Washington 14, Texas 7
12-27-80 ..........Nebraska 31, Mississippi St 17
12-26-81 ..........Oklahoma 40, Houston 14
12-25-82 ..........N Carolina 26, Texas 10
12-24-83 ..........Alabama 28, Southern Methodist 7
12-22-84 ..........Maryland 28, Tennessee 27
12-28-85 ..........Georgia 13, Arizona 13
12-25-86 ..........Alabama 28, Washington 6
12-25-87 ..........Oklahoma St 35, W Virginia 33
12-24-88 ..........Alabama 29, Army 28
12-30-89 ..........Pittsburgh 31, Texas A&M 28
12-31-90 ..........Michigan St 17, Southern Cal 16
12-31-91 ..........UCLA 6, Illinois 3

## Sun Bowl *(Cont.)*

12-31-92..........Baylor 20, Arizona 15
12-24-93..........Oklahoma 41, Texas Tech 10
12-30-94..........Texas 35, N Carolina 31
12-29-95..........Iowa 38, Washington 18
12-31-96..........Stanford 38, Michigan St 0
12-31-97..........Arizona St 17, Iowa 7
12-31-98..........Texas Christian 28, Southern Cal 19
12-31-99..........Oregon 24, Minnesota 20
12-29-00..........Wisconsin 21, UCLA 20

City: El Paso. Stadium: Sun Bowl, capacity 51,270.

Name Changes: Sun Bowl (1936–86; 94–), John Hancock Sun Bowl (1987–88), John Hancock Bowl (1989–93).

Playing Sites: Kidd Field (1936–62), Sun Bowl (since 1963).

## Gator Bowl

1-1-46 ..............Wake Forest 26, S Carolina 14
1-1-47 ..............Oklahoma 34, N Carolina St 13
1-1-48 ..............Maryland 20, Georgia 20
1-1-49 ..............Clemson 24, Missouri 23
1-2-50 ..............Maryland 20, Missouri 7
1-1-51 ..............Wyoming 20, Washington & Lee 7
1-1-52 ..............Miami (FL) 14, Clemson 0
1-1-53 ..............Florida 14, Tulsa 13
1-1-54 ..............Texas Tech 35, Auburn 13
12-31-54..........Auburn 33, Baylor 13
12-31-55..........Vanderbilt 25, Auburn 13
12-29-56..........Georgia Tech 21, Pittsburgh 14
12-28-57..........Tennessee 3, Texas A&M 0
12-27-58..........Mississippi 7, Florida 3
1-2-60..............Arkansas 14, Georgia Tech 7
12-31-60..........Florida 13, Baylor 12
12-30-61..........Penn St 30, Georgia Tech 15
12-29-62..........Florida 17, Penn St 7
12-28-63..........N Carolina 35, Air Force 0
1-2-65..............Florida St 36, Oklahoma 19
12-31-65..........Georgia Tech 31, Texas Tech 21
12-31-66..........Tennessee 18, Syracuse 12
12-30-67..........Penn St 17, Florida St 17
12-28-68..........Missouri 35, Alabama 10
12-27-69..........Florida 14, Tennessee 13
1-2-71..............Auburn 35, Mississippi 28
12-31-71..........Georgia 7, N Carolina 3
12-30-72..........Auburn 24, Colorado 3
12-29-73..........Texas Tech 28, Tennessee 19
12-30-74..........Auburn 27, Texas 3
12-29-75..........Maryland 13, Florida 0
12-27-76..........Notre Dame 20, Penn St 9
12-30-77..........Pittsburgh 34, Clemson 3
12-29-78..........Clemson 17, Ohio St 15
12-28-79..........N Carolina 17, Michigan 15
12-29-80..........Pittsburgh 37, S Carolina 9
12-28-81..........N Carolina 31, Arkansas 27
12-30-82..........Florida St 31, W Virginia 12
12-30-83..........Florida 14, Iowa 6
12-28-84..........Oklahoma St 21, S Carolina 14
12-30-85..........Florida St 34, Oklahoma St 23
12-27-86..........Clemson 27, Stanford 21
12-31-87..........Louisiana St 30, S Carolina 13
1-1-89 ..............Georgia 34, Michigan St 27
12-30-89..........Clemson 27, W Virginia 7
1-1-91 ..............Michigan 35, Mississippi 3
12-29-91..........Oklahoma 48, Virginia 14
12-31-92..........Florida 27, N Carolina St 10
12-31-93..........Alabama 24, North Carolina 10
12-30-94..........Tennessee 45, Virginia Tech 23
1-1-96 ..............Syracuse 41, Clemson 0
1-1-97 ..............N Carolina 20, W Virginia 13
1-1-98 ..............N Carolina 42, Viginia Tech 13

## Gator Bowl (Cont.)

1-1-99 ..............Georgia Tech 35, Notre Dame 28
1-1-00..............Miami 27, Georgia Tech 13
1-1-01..............Virginia Tech 41, Clemson 20

City: Jacksonville, FL. Stadium: Alltel Stadium, capacity 76,976.

## Florida Citrus Bowl

1-1-47 ..............Catawba 31, Maryville (TN) 6
1-1-48 ..............Catawba 7, Marshall 0
1-1-49 ..............Murray St 21, Sul Ross St 21
1-2-50..............St. Vincent 7, Emory & Henry 6
1-1-51 ..............Morris Harvey 35, Emory & Henry 14
1-1-52 ..............Stetson 35, Arkansas St 20
1-1-53..............E Texas St 33, Tennessee Tech 0
1-1-54 ..............E Texas St 7, Arkansas St 7
1-1-55 ..............NE-Omaha 7, Eastern Kentucky 6
1-2-56 ..............Juniata 6, Missouri Valley 6
1-1-57 ..............W Texas St 20, Southern Miss 13
1-1-58 ..............E Texas St 10, Southern Miss 9
12-27-58..........E Texas St 26, Missouri Valley 7
1-1-60..............Middle Tennessee St 21, Presbyterian 12
12-30-60..........Citadel 27, Tennessee Tech 0
12-29-61..........Lamar 21, Middle Tennessee St 14
12-22-62..........Houston 49, Miami (OH) 21
12-28-63..........Western Kentucky 27, Coast Guard 0
12-12-64..........E Carolina 14, Massachusetts 13
12-11-65..........E Carolina 31, Maine 0
12-10-66..........Morgan St 14, W Chester 6
12-16-67..........TN-Martin 25, W Chester 8
12-27-68..........Richmond 49, Ohio 42
12-26-69..........Toledo 56, Davidson 33
12-28-70..........Toledo 40, William & Mary 12
12-28-71..........Toledo 28, Richmond 3
12-29-72..........Tampa 21, Kent St 18
12-22-73..........Miami (OH) 16, Florida 7
12-21-74..........Miami (OH) 21, Georgia 10
12-20-75..........Miami (OH) 20, S Carolina 7
12-18-76..........Oklahoma St 49, Brigham Young 21
12-23-77..........Florida St 40, Texas Tech 17
12-23-78..........N Carolina St 30, Pittsburgh 17
12-22-79..........Louisiana St 34, Wake Forest 10
12-20-80..........Florida 35, Maryland 20
12-19-81..........Missouri 19, Southern Miss 17
12-18-82..........Auburn 33, Boston Col 26
12-17-83..........Tennessee 30, Maryland 23
12-22-84..........Georgia 17, Florida St 17
12-28-85..........Ohio St 10, Brigham Young 7
1-1-87 ..............Auburn 16, Southern Cal 7
1-1-88 ..............Clemson 35, Penn St 10
1-2-89 ..............Clemson 13, Oklahoma 6
1-1-90..............Illinois 31, Virginia 21
1-1-91 ..............Georgia Tech 45, Nebraska 21
1-1-92 ..............California 37, Clemson 13
1-1-93 ..............Georgia 21, Ohio State 14
1-1-94 ..............Penn State 31, Tennessee 13
1-2-95 ..............Alabama 24, Ohio St 17
1-1-96 ..............Tennessee 20, Ohio St 14
1-1-97 ..............Tennessee 48, Northwestern 28
1-1-98 ..............Florida 21, Penn St 6
1-1-99 ..............Michigan 45, Arkansas 31
1-1-00..............Michigan St 37, Florida 34
1-1-01 ..............Michigan 31, Auburn 28

City: Orlando, FL. Stadium: Florida Citrus Bowl, capacity 70,000.

Name Change: Tangerine Bowl (1947–82).

Playing Sites: Tangerine Bowl (1947–72, 1974–82); Florida Field, Gainesville (1973); Orlando Stadium/Florida Citrus Bowl-Orlando (since 1983).

## Liberty Bowl

12-19-59 ..........Penn St 7, Alabama 0
12-17-60 ..........Penn St 41, Oregon 12
12-16-61 ..........Syracuse 15, Miami (FL) 14
12-15-62 ..........Oregon St 6, Villanova 0
12-21-63 ..........Mississippi St 16, N Carolina St 12
12-19-64 ..........Utah 32, W Virginia 6
12-18-65 ..........Mississippi 13, Auburn 7
12-10-66 ..........Miami (FL) 14, Virginia Tech 7
12-16-67 ..........N Carolina St 14, Georgia 7
12-14-68 ..........Mississippi 34, Virginia Tech 17
12-13-69 ..........Colorado 47, Alabama 33
12-12-70 ..........Tulane 17, Colorado 3
12-20-71 ..........Tennessee 14, Arkansas 13
12-18-72 ..........Georgia Tech 31, Iowa St 30
12-17-73 ..........N Carolina St 31, Kansas 18
12-16-74 ..........Tennessee 7, Maryland 3
12-22-75 ..........Southern Cal 20, Texas A&M 0
12-20-76 ..........Alabama 36, UCLA 6
12-19-77 ..........Nebraska 21, N Carolina 17
12-23-78 ..........Missouri 20, Louisiana St 15
12-22-79 ..........Penn St 9, Tulane 6
12-27-80 ..........Purdue 28, Missouri 25
12-30-81 ..........Ohio St 31, Navy 28
12-29-82 ..........Alabama 21, Illinois 15
12-29-83 ..........Notre Dame 19, Boston Col 18
12-27-84 ..........Auburn 21, Arkansas 15
12-27-85 ..........Baylor 21, Louisiana St 7
12-29-86 ..........Tennessee 21, Minnesota 14
12-29-87 ..........Georgia 20, Arkansas 17
12-28-88 ..........Indiana 34, S Carolina 10
12 28 89 ..........Mississippi 42, Air Force 29
12-27-90 ..........Air Force 23, Ohio St 11
12-29-91 ..........Air Force 38, Mississippi St 15
12-31-92 ..........Mississippi 13, Air Force 0
12-28-93 ..........Louisville 18, Michigan St 7
12-31-94 ..........Illinois 30, E Carolina 0
12-30-95 ..........East Carolina 19, Stanford 13
12-27-96 ..........Syracuse 30, Houston 17
12-31-97 ..........Southern Miss 41, Pittsburgh 7
12-31-98 ..........Tulane 41, Brigham Young 27
12-31-99 ..........Southern Miss 23, Colorado St 17
12-29-01 ..........Colorado St 22, Louisville 17

City: Memphis (since 1965). Stadium: Liberty Bowl Memorial Stadium, capacity 62,921.

Playing Sites: Philadelphia (Municipal Stadium, 1959–63), Atlantic City (Convention Center, 1964).

## Bluebonnet Bowl

12-19-59 ..........Clemson 23, Texas Christian 7
12-17-60 ..........Texas 3, Alabama 3
12-16-61 ..........Kansas 33, Rice 7
12-22-62 ..........Missouri 14, Georgia Tech 10
12-21-63 ..........Baylor 14, LSU 7
12-19-64 ..........Tulsa 14, Mississippi 7
12-18-65 ..........Tennessee 27, Tulsa 6
12-17-66 ..........Texas 19, Mississippi 0
12-23-67 ..........Colorado 31, Miami (FL) 21
12-31-68 ..........Southern Methodist 28, Oklahoma 27
12-31-69 ..........Houston 36, Auburn 7
12-31-70 ..........Alabama 24, Oklahoma 24
12-31-71 ..........Colorado 29, Houston 17
12-30-72 ..........Tennessee 24, Louisiana St 17
12-29-73 ..........Houston 47, Tulane 7
12-23-74 ..........N Carolina St 31, Houston 31
12-27-75 ..........Texas 38, Colorado 21
12-31-76 ..........Nebraska 27, Texas Tech 24
12-31-77 ..........Southern Cal 47, Texas A&M 28

## Bluebonnet Bowl *(Cont.)*

12-31-78 ..........Stanford 25, Georgia 22
12-31-79 ..........Purdue 27, Tennessee 22
12-31-80 ..........N Carolina 16, Texas 7
12-31-81 ..........Michigan 33, UCLA 14
12-31-82 ..........Arkansas 28, Florida 24
12-31-83 ..........Oklahoma St 24, Baylor 14
12-31-84 ..........W Virginia 31, Texas Christian 14
12-31-85 ..........Air Force 24, Texas 16
12-31-86 ..........Baylor 21, Colorado 9
12-31-87 ..........Texas 32, Pittsburgh 27

City: Houston. Playing sites: Rice Stadium (1959–67; 1985–86), Astrodome (1968–84, 1987).

Name change: Astro-Bluebonnet Bowl (1968–76). Bowl was discontinued after 1987.

## Peach Bowl

12-30-68 ..........Louisiana St 31, Florida St 27
12-30-69 ..........W Virginia 14, S Carolina 3
12-30-70 ..........Arizona St 48, N Carolina 26
12-30-71 ..........Mississippi 41, Georgia Tech 18
12-29-72 ..........N Carolina St 49, W Virginia 13
12-28-73 ..........Georgia 17, Maryland 16
12-28-74 ..........Vanderbilt 6, Texas Tech 6
12-31-75 ..........W Virginia 13, N Carolina St 10
12-31-76 ..........Kentucky 21, N Carolina 0
12-31-77 ..........N Carolina St 24, Iowa St 14
12-25-78 ..........Purdue 41, Georgia Tech 21
12-31-79 ..........Baylor 24, Clemson 18
1-2-81 ..............Miami (FL) 20, Virginia Tech 10
12-31-81 ..........W Virginia 26, Florida 6
12-31-82 ..........Iowa 28, Tennessee 22
12-30-83 ..........Florida St 28, N Carolina 3
12-31-84 ..........Virginia 27, Purdue 24
12-31-85 ..........Army 31, Illinois 29
12-31-86 ..........Virginia Tech 25, N Carolina St 24
1-2-88 ..............Tennessee 27, Indiana 22
12-31-88 ..........N Carolina St 28, Iowa 23
12-30-89 ..........Syracuse 19, Georgia 18
12-29-90 ..........Auburn 27, Indiana 23
1-1-92 ..............E Carolina 37, N Carolina St 34
1-2-93 ..............N Carolina 21, Mississippi St 17
12-31-93 ..........Clemson 14, Kentucky 13
1-1-95 ..............N Carolina St 28, Mississippi St 24
12-30-95 ..........Virginia 34, Georgia 27
12-28-96 ..........Louisiana St 10, Clemson 7
1-2-98 ..............Auburn 21, Clemson 17
12-31-98 ..........Georgia 35, Virginia 33
12-30-99 ..........Mississippi St 17, Clemson 7
12-29-00 ..........Louisiana St 28, Georgia Tech 14

City: Atlanta. Stadium: Georgia Dome, capacity 71,228. Playing Sites: Grant Field (1968–70), Atlanta–Fulton County Stadium (1971–92), Georgia Dome (since 1993).

## Fiesta Bowl

12-27-71 ..........Arizona St 45, Florida St 38
12-23-72 ..........Arizona St 49, Missouri 35
12-21-73 ..........Arizona St 28, Pittsburgh 7
12-28-74 ..........Oklahoma St 16, Brigham Young 6
12-26-75 ..........Arizona St 17, Nebraska 14
12-25-76 ..........Oklahoma 41, Wyoming 7
12-25-77 ..........Penn St 42, Arizona St 30
12-25-78 ..........Arkansas 10, UCLA 10
12-25-79 ..........Pittsburgh 16, Arizona 10
12 26 80 ..........Penn St 31, Ohio St 19
1-1-82 ..............Penn St 26, Southern Cal 10
1-1-83 ..............Arizona St 32, Oklahoma 21
1-2-84 ..............Ohio St 28, Pittsburgh 23

### Fiesta Bowl *(Cont.)*

1-1-85 .............UCLA 39, Miami (FL) 37
1-1-86 .............Michigan 27, Nebraska 23
1-2-87 .............Penn St 14, Miami (FL) 10
1-1-88 .............Florida St 31, Nebraska 28
1-2-89 .............Notre Dame 34, W Virginia 21
1-1-90 .............Florida St 41, Nebraska 17
1-1-91 .............Louisville 34, Alabama 7
1-1-92 .............Penn St 42, Tennessee 17
1-1-93 .............Syracuse 26, Colorado 22
1-1-94 .............Arizona 29, Miami (FL) 0
1-2-95 .............Colorado 41, Notre Dame 24
1-2-96 .............Nebraska 62, Florida 24
1-1-97 .............Penn St 38, Texas 15
12-31-97 .........Kansas St 35, Syracuse 18
1-4-99 .............Tennessee 23, Florida St 16
1-2-00 .............Nebraska 31, Tennessee 21
1-1-01 .............Oregon St 41, Notre Dame 9

City: Tempe, AZ. Stadium: Sun Devil Stadium, capacity 73,259.

### Independence Bowl

12-13-76 ..........McNeese St 20, Tulsa 16
12-17-77 ..........Louisiana Tech 24, Louisville 14
12-16-78 ..........E Carolina 35, Louisiana Tech 13
12-15-79 ..........Syracuse 31, McNeese St 7
12-13-80 ..........Southern Miss 16, McNeese St 14
12-12-81 ..........Texas A&M 33, Oklahoma St 16
12-11-82 ..........Wisconsin 14, Kansas St 3
12-10-83 ..........Air Force 9, Mississippi 3
12-15-84 ..........Air Force 23, Virginia Tech 7
12-21-85 ..........Minnesota 20, Clemson 13
12-20-86 ..........Mississippi 20, Texas Tech 17
12-19-87 ..........Washington 24, Tulane 12
12-23-88 ..........Southern Miss 38, UTEP 18
12-16-89 ..........Oregon 27, Tulsa 24
12-15-90 ..........Louisiana Tech 34, Maryland 34
12-29-91 ..........Georgia 24, Arkansas 15
12-31-92 ..........Wake Forest 39, Oregon 35
12-31-93 ..........Virginia Tech 45, Indiana 20
12-28-94 ..........Virginia 20, Texas Christian 10
12-29-95 ..........Louisiana St 45, Michigan St 26
12-31-96 ..........Auburn 32, Army 29
12-28-97 ..........Louisiana St 27, Notre Dame 9
12-31-98 ..........Mississippi 35, Texas Tech 18
12-31-99 ..........Mississippi 27, Oklahoma 25
12-31-00 ..........Mississippi St 43, Texas A&M 41

City: Shreveport, LA. Stadium: Independence Stadium, capacity 50,459.

### All-American Bowl

12-22-77 ..........Maryland 17, Minnesota 7
12-20-78 ..........Texas A&M 28, Iowa St 12
12-29-79 ..........Missouri 24, S Carolina 14
12-27-80 ..........Arkansas 34, Tulane 15
12-31-81 ..........Mississippi St 10, Kansas 0
12-31-82 ..........Air Force 36, Vanderbilt 28
12-22-83 ..........W Virginia 20, Kentucky 16
12-29-84 ..........Kentucky 20, Wisconsin 19
12-31-85 ..........Georgia Tech 17, Michigan St 14
12-31-86 ..........Florida St 27, Indiana 13
12-22-87 ..........Virginia 22, Brigham Young 16
12-29-88 ..........Florida 14, Illinois 10
12-28-89 ..........Texas Tech 49, Duke 21
12-28-90 ..........N Carolina St 31, Southern Miss. 27

City: Birmingham, AL. Stadium: Legion Field.
Name Change: Hall of Fame Classic (1977–84). Bowl was discontinued after 1990.

### Holiday Bowl

12-22-78 .........Navy 23, Brigham Young 16
12-21-79 .........Indiana 38, Brigham Young 37
12-19-80 .........Brigham Young 46, SMU45
12-18-81 .........Brigham Young 38, Washington St 36
12-17-82 .........Ohio St 47, Brigham Young 17
12-23-83 .........Brigham Young 21, Missouri 17
12-21-84 .........Brigham Young 24, Michigan 17
12-22-85 .........Arkansas 18, Arizona St 17
12-30-86 .........Iowa 39, San Diego St 38
12-30-87 .........Iowa 20, Wyoming 19
12-30-88 .........Oklahoma St 62, Wyoming 14
12-29-89 .........Penn St 50, Brigham Young 39
12-29-90 .........Texas A&M 65, Brigham Young 14
12-30-91 .........Iowa 13, Brigham Young 13
12-30-92 .........Hawaii 27, Illinois 17
12-30-93 .........Ohio St 28, Brigham Young 21
12-30-94 .........Michigan 24, Colorado St 14
12-29-95 .........Kansas St 54, Colorado St 21
12-30-96 .........Colorado 33, Washington 21
12-29-97 .........Colorado St 35, Missouri 24
12-30-98 .........Arizona 23, Nebraska 20
12-29-99 .........Kansas St 24, Washington 20
12-29-00 .........Oregon 35, Texas 30

City: San Diego. Stadium: Qualcomm Stadium, capacity 70,000.

### Las Vegas Bowl

12-19-81 .........Toledo 27, San Jose St 25
12-18-82 .........Fresno St 29, Bowling Green 28
12-17-83 .........Northern Illinois 20, Cal St–Fullerton 13
12-15-84 .........UNLV 30, Toledo 13*
12-14-85 .........Fresno St 51, Bowling Green 7
12-13-86 .........San Jose St 37, Miami (OH) 7
12-12-87 .........Eastern Michigan 30, San Jose St 27
12-10-88 .........Fresno St 35, Western Michigan 30
12-9-89 ...........Fresno St 27, Ball St 6
12-8-90 ...........San Jose St 48, Central Michigan 24
12-14-91 .........Bowling Green 28, Fresno St 21
12-18-92 .........Bowling Green 35, Nevada 34
12-17-93 .........Utah 42, Ball St 33
12-15-94 .........UNLV 52, Central Michigan 24
12-14-95 .........Toledo 40, Nevada 37
12-19-96 .........Nevada 18, Ball St 15
12-19-97 .........Oregon 41, Air Force 13
12-19-98 .........N Carolina 20, San Diego St 13
12-18-99 .........Utah 17, Fresno St 16
12-21-00 .........UNLV 31, Arkansas 14

* Toledo won later by forfeit.

City: Las Vegas (since 1992). Stadium: Sam Boyd Silver Bowl Stadium, capacity 40,000.

Name change: California Bowl (1981–91).

Playing sites: Fresno, CA (Bulldog Stadium, 1981–91), Las Vegas.

### Aloha Bowl

12-25-82 .........Washington 21, Maryland 20
12-26-83 .........Penn St 13, Washington 10
12-29-84 .........Southern Methodist 27, Notre Dame 20
12-28-85 .........Alabama 24, Southern Cal 3
12-27-86 .........Arizona 30, N Carolina 21
12-25-87 .........UCLA 20, Florida 16
12-25-88 .........Washington St 24, Houston 22
12-25-89 .........Michigan St 33, Hawaii 13
12-25-90 .........Syracuse 28, Arizona 0
12-25-91 .........Georgia Tech 18, Stanford 17

### Aloha Bowl *(Cont.)*

12-25-92 ..........Kansas 23, Brigham Young 20
12-25-93 ..........Colorado 41, Fresno St 30
12-25-94 ..........Boston College 12, Kansas St 7
12-25-95 ..........Kansas 51, UCLA 30
12-25-96 ..........Navy 42, California 38
12-25-97 ..........Washington 51, Michigan St 23
12-25-98 ..........Colorado 51, Oregon 43
12-25-99 ..........Wake Forest 23, Arizona St 3
12-25-00 ..........Boston College 31, Arizona St 17

City: Honolulu. Stadium: Aloha Stadium, capacity 50,000.

### Freedom Bowl

12-16-84 ..........Iowa 55, Texas 17
12-30-85 ..........Washington 20, Colorado 17
12-30-86 ..........UCLA 31, Brigham Young 10
12-30-87 ..........Arizona St 33, Air Force 28
12-29-88 ..........Brigham Young 20, Colorado 17
12-30-89 ..........Washington 34, Florida 7
12-29-90 ..........Colorado St 32, Oregon 31
12-30-91 ..........Tulsa 28, San Diego St 17
12-29-92 ..........Fresno St 24, Southern Cal 7
12-30-93 ..........Southern Cal 28, Utah 21
12-29-94 ..........Utah 16, Arizona 13

City: Anaheim. Stadium: Anaheim Stadium. Bowl was discontinued after 1994.

### Outback Bowl

12-23-86 ..........Boston College 27, Georgia 24
1-2-88 ..............Michigan 28, Alabama 24
1-2-89 ..............Syracuse 23, Louisiana St 10
1-1-90 ..............Auburn 31, Ohio St 14
1-1-91 ..............Clemson 30, Illinois 0
1-1-92 ..............Syracuse 24, Ohio St 17
1-1-93 ..............Tennessee 38, Boston College 23
1-1-94 ..............Michigan 42, N Carolina St 7
1-2-95 ..............Wisconsin 34, Duke 20
1-1-96 ..............Penn St 43, Auburn 14
1-1-97 ..............Alabama 17, Michigan 14
1-1-98 ..............Georgia 33, Wisconsin 6
1-1-99 ..............Penn St 26, Kentucky 14
1-1-00 ..............Georgia 28, Purdue 25
1-1-01 ..............S Carolina 24, Ohio St 7

City: Tampa. Stadium: Raymond James Stadium, capacity 65,000.

Name change: Hall of Fame Bowl (1986–95).

### Insight.com Bowl

12-31-89 ..........Arizona 17, N Carolina St 10
12-31-90 ..........California 17, Wyoming 15
12-31-91 ..........Indiana 24, Baylor 0
12-29-92 ..........Washington St 31, Utah 28
12-29-93 ..........Kansas St 52, Wyoming 17
12-29-94 ..........Brigham Young 31, Oklahoma 6
12-27-95 ..........Texas Tech 55, Air Force 41
12-27-96 ..........Wisconsin 38, Utah 10
12-27-97 ..........Arizona 20, New Mexico 14
12-26-98 ..........Missouri 34, W Virginia 31
12-31-99 ..........Colorado 62, Boston College 28
12-28-00 ..........Iowa St 37, Pittsburgh 29

City: Tucson. Stadium: Arizona Stadium, capacity 55,883.
Name change: Copper Bowl 1989–97.

### Micron PC Bowl

12-28-90 ..........Florida St 24, Penn St 17
12-28-91 ..........Alabama 30, Colorado 25
1-1-93 ..............Stanford 24, Penn St 3
1-1-94 ..............Boston College 31, Virginia 13
1-2-95 ..............S Carolina 24, W Virginia 21
12-30-95 ..........N Carolina 20, Arkansas 10
12-27-96 ..........Miami (FL) 31, Virginia 21
12-29-97 ..........Georgia Tech 35, W Virginia 30
12-29-98 ..........Miami (FL) 46, N Carolina St 23
12-30-99 ..........Illinois 63, Virginia 21
12-28-00 ..........N Carolina St 38, Minnesota 30

City: Miami. Stadium: Pro Player Stadium, capacity 72,000.
Name Changes: Blockbuster Bowl (1990–93), Carquest Bowl (1994–97).

### Alamo Bowl

12-31-93 ..........California 37, Iowa 3
12-31-94 ..........Washington St 10, Baylor 3
12-28-95 ..........Texas A&M 22, Michigan 20
12-29-96 ..........Iowa 27, Texas Tech 0
12-30-97 ..........Purdue 33, Oklahoma St 20
12-29-98 ..........Purdue 37, Kansas St 34
12-28-99 ..........Penn St 24, Texas A&M 0
12-30-00 ..........Nebraska 66, Northwestern 17

City: San Antonio, TX. Stadium: Alamodome, capacity 65,000.

## Petty Officer Rogers Reporting

San Jose State senior Jesse Rogers may not be the Spartans' most talented player, and he rarely shows up on the stat sheet, but he saw plenty of action during the 2000 season. In addition to being a backup tight end, the 26-year-old Rogers is a husband, father and petty officer, third class, in the Naval Reserve.

Rogers enlisted in the Navy in 1992 after graduating from Central Valley High in Shasta Lake, Calif. After finishing his tour, he began a three-year hitch in the Army Reserve in 1996. He played for Shasta College in Redding, Calif., in 1997 and then transferred to San Jose State. In 1999 Rogers enlisted in the Naval Reserve because its base was close to State's campus. Until 2002, he will serve one weekend a month and attend a two-week summer session. In July 2000, Rogers spent three weeks in Thailand securing beachheads during a joint operation with marine and naval forces from the U.S. and Thailand.

Rogers entered the season with no receptions for the Spartans. Used primarily as a blocker, he had run more routes between his classes, the naval office 10 minutes away and his five-year-old daughter Savannah's day-care center than he had for the Spartans' offense. But in San Jose State's second game of 2000, against Stanford, Rogers caught a one-yard touchdown pass in the fourth quarter of a 40–27 win. "Waiting for that first catch, I felt like my daughter waiting for Santa Claus to come on Christmas," said Rogers.

—Elizabeth Newman

## 1936

| | | Record | Coach |
|---|---|---|---|
| 1. | Minnesota | 7-1-0 | Bernie Bierman |
| 2. | Louisiana St | 9-0-1 | Bernie Moore |
| 3. | Pittsburgh | 7-1-1 | Jack Sutherland |
| 4. | Alabama | 8-0-1 | Frank Thomas |
| 5. | Washington | 7-1-1 | Jimmy Phelan |
| 6. | Santa Clara | 7-1-0 | Buck Shaw |
| 7. | Northwestern | 7-1-0 | Pappy Waldorf |
| 8. | Notre Dame | 6-2-1 | Elmer Layden |
| 9. | Nebraska | 7-2-0 | Dana X. Bible |
| 10. | Pennsylvania | 7-1-0 | Harvey Harman |
| 11. | Duke | 9-1-0 | Wallace Wade |
| 12. | Yale | 7-1-0 | Ducky Pond |
| 13. | Dartmouth | 7-1-1 | Red Blaik |
| 14. | Duquesne | 7-2-0 | John Smith |
| 15. | Fordham | 5-1-2 | Jim Crowley |
| 16. | Texas Christian | 8-2-2 | Dutch Meyer |
| 17. | Tennessee | 6-2-2 | Bob Neyland |
| 18. | Arkansas | 7-3-0 | Fred Thomsen |
| 19. | Navy | 6-3-0 | Tom Hamilton |
| 20. | Marquette | 7-1-0 | Frank Murray |

## 1937

| | | Record | Coach |
|---|---|---|---|
| 1. | Pittsburgh | 9-0-1 | Jack Sutherland |
| 2. | California | 9-0-1 | Stub Allison |
| 3. | Fordham | 7-0-1 | Jim Crowley |
| 4. | Alabama | 9-0-0 | Frank Thomas |
| 5. | Minnesota | 6-2-0 | Bernie Bierman |
| 6. | Villanova | 8-0-1 | Clipper Smith |
| 7. | Dartmouth | 7-0-2 | Red Blaik |
| 8. | Louisiana St | 9-1-0 | Bernie Moore |
| 9. | Notre Dame | 6-2-1 | Elmer Layden |
| | Santa Clara | 8-0-0 | Buck Shaw |
| 11. | Nebraska | 6-1-2 | Biff Jones |
| 12. | Yale | 6-1-1 | Ducky Pond |
| 13. | Ohio St | 6-2-0 | Francis Schmidt |
| 14. | Holy Cross | 8-0-2 | Eddie Anderson |
| | Arkansas | 6-2-2 | Fred Thomsen |
| 16. | Texas Christian | 4-2-2 | Dutch Meyer |
| 17. | Colorado | 8-0-0 | Bunnie Oakes |
| 18. | Rice | 5-3-2 | Jimmy Kitts |
| 19. | N Carolina | 7-1-1 | Ray Wolf |
| 20. | Duke | 7-2-1 | Wallace Wade |

## 1938

| | | Record | Coach |
|---|---|---|---|
| 1. | Texas Christian | 10-0-0 | Dutch Meyer |
| 2. | Tennessee | 10-0-0 | Bob Neyland |
| 3. | Duke | 9-0-0 | Wallace Wade |
| 4. | Oklahoma | 10-0-0 | Tom Stidham |
| 5. | #Notre Dame | 8-1-0 | Elmer Layden |
| 6. | Carnegie Tech | 7-1-0 | Bill Kern |
| 7. | Southern Cal | 8-2-0 | Howard Jones |
| 8. | Pittsburgh | 8-2-0 | Jack Sutherland |
| 9. | Holy Cross | 8-1-0 | Eddie Anderson |
| 10. | Minnesota | 6-2-0 | Bernie Bierman |
| 11. | Texas Tech | 10-0-0 | Pete Cawthon |
| 12. | Cornell | 5-1-1 | Carl Snavely |
| 13. | Alabama | 7-1-1 | Frank Thomas |
| 14. | California | 10-1-0 | Stub Allison |
| 15. | Fordham | 6-1-2 | Jim Crowley |
| 16. | Michigan | 6-1-1 | Fritz Crisler |
| 17. | Northwestern | 4-2-2 | Pappy Waldorf |

## 1938 (Cont.)

| | | Record | Coach |
|---|---|---|---|
| 18. | Villanova | 8-0-1 | Clipper Smith |
| 19. | Tulane | 7-2-1 | Red Dawson |
| 20. | Dartmouth | 7-2-0 | Red Blaik |

#Selected No. 1 by the Dickinson System.

## 1939

| | | Record | Coach |
|---|---|---|---|
| 1. | Texas A&M | 10-0-0 | Homer Norton |
| 2. | Tennessee | 10-0-0 | Bob Neyland |
| 3. | #Southern Cal | 8-0-2 | Howard Jones |
| 4. | Cornell | 8-0-0 | Carl Snavely |
| 5. | Tulane | 8-0-1 | Red Dawson |
| 6. | Missouri | 8-1-0 | Don Faurot |
| 7. | UCLA | 6-0-4 | Babe Horrell |
| 8. | Duke | 8-1-0 | Wallace Wade |
| 9. | Iowa | 6-1-1 | Eddie Anderson |
| 10. | Duquesne | 8-0-1 | Buff Donelli |
| 11. | Boston College | 9-1-0 | Frank Leahy |
| 12. | Clemson | 8-1-0 | Jess Neely |
| 13. | Notre Dame | 7-2-0 | Elmer Layden |
| 14. | Santa Clara | 5-1-3 | Buck Shaw |
| 15. | Ohio St | 6-2-0 | Francis Schmidt |
| 16. | Georgia Tech | 7-2-0 | Bill Alexander |
| 17. | Fordham | 6-2-0 | Jim Crowley |
| 18. | Nebraska | 7-1-1 | Biff Jones |
| 19. | Oklahoma | 6-2-1 | Tom Stidham |
| 20. | Michigan | 6-2-0 | Fritz Crisler |

#Selected No. 1 by the Dickinson System.

## 1940

| | | Record | Coach |
|---|---|---|---|
| 1. | Minnesota | 8-0-0 | Bernie Bierman |
| 2. | Stanford | 9-0-0 | C. Shaughnessy |
| 3. | Michigan | 7-1-0 | Fritz Crisler |
| 4. | Tennessee | 10-0-0 | Bob Neyland |
| 5. | Boston College | 10-0-0 | Frank Leahy |
| 6. | Texas A&M | 8-1-0 | Homer Norton |
| 7. | Nebraska | 8-1-0 | Biff Jones |
| 8. | Northwestern | 6-2-0 | Pappy Waldorf |
| 9. | Mississippi St | 9-0-1 | Allyn McKeen |
| 10. | Washington | 7-2-0 | Jimmy Phelan |
| 11. | Santa Clara | 6-1-1 | Buck Shaw |
| 12. | Fordham | 7-1-0 | Jim Crowley |
| 13. | Georgetown | 8-1-0 | Jack Hagerty |
| 14. | Pennsylvania | 6-1-1 | George Munger |
| 15. | Cornell | 6-2-0 | Carl Snavely |
| 16. | SMU | 8-1-1 | Matty Bell |
| 17. | Hard.-Simmons | 9-0-0 | Abe Woodson |
| 18. | Duke | 7-2-0 | Wallace Wade |
| 19. | Lafayette | 9-0-0 | Hooks Mylin |
| 20. | — | | |

Only 19 teams selected.

### 1941

| | | Record | Coach |
|---|---|---|---|
| 1. | Minnesota | 8-0-0 | Bernie Bierman |
| 2. | Duke | 9-0-0 | Wallace Wade |
| 3. | Notre Dame | 8-0-1 | Frank Leahy |
| 4. | Texas | 8-1-1 | Dana X. Bible |
| 5. | Michigan | 6-1-1 | Fritz Crisler |
| 6. | Fordham | 7-1-0 | Jim Crowley |
| 7. | Missouri | 8-1-0 | Don Faurot |
| 8. | Duquesne | 8-0-0 | Buff Donelli |
| 9. | Texas A&M | 9-1-0 | Homer Norton |
| 10. | Navy | 7-1-1 | Swede Larson |
| 11. | Northwestern | 5-3-0 | Pappy Waldorf |
| 12. | Oregon St. | 7-2-0 | Lon Stiner |
| 13. | Ohio St | 6-1-1 | Paul Brown |
| 14. | Georgia | 8-1-1 | Wally Butts |
| 15. | Pennsylvania | 7-1-1 | George Munger |
| 16. | Mississippi St | 8-1-1 | Allyn McKeen |
| 17. | Mississippi | 6-2-1 | Harry Mehre |
| 18. | Tennessee | 8-2-0 | John Barnhill |
| 19. | Washington St | 6-4-0 | Babe Hollingbery |
| 20. | Alabama | 8-2-0 | Frank Thomas |

### 1942

| | | Record | Coach |
|---|---|---|---|
| 1. | Ohio St | 9-1-0 | Paul Brown |
| 2. | Georgia | 10-1-0 | Wally Butts |
| 3. | Wisconsin | 8-1-1 | H. Stuhldreher |
| 4. | Tulsa | 10-0-0 | Henry Frnka |
| 5. | Georgia Tech | 9-1-0 | Bill Alexander |
| 6. | Notre Dame | 7-2-2 | Frank Leahy |
| 7. | Tennessee | 8-1-1 | John Barnhill |
| 8. | Boston College | 8-1-0 | Denny Myers |
| 9. | Michigan | 7-3-0 | Fritz Crisler |
| 10. | Alabama | 7-3-0 | Frank Thomas |
| 11. | Texas | 8-2-0 | Dana X. Bible |
| 12. | Stanford | 6-4-0 | Marchie Schwartz |
| 13. | UCLA | 7-3-0 | Babe Horrell |
| 14. | William & Mary | 9-1-1 | Carl Voyles |
| 15. | Santa Clara | 7-2-0 | Buck Shaw |
| 16. | Auburn | 6-4-1 | Jack Meagher |
| 17. | Washington St | 6-2-2 | Babe Hollingbery |
| 18. | Mississippi St | 8-2-0 | Allyn McKeen |
| 19. | Minnesota | 5-4-0 | George Hauser |
| | Holy Cross | 5-4-1 | Ank Scanlon |
| | Penn St | 6-1-1 | Bob Higgins |

### 1943

| | | Record | Coach |
|---|---|---|---|
| 1. | Notre Dame | 9-1-0 | Frank Leahy |
| 2. | Iowa Pre-Flight | 9-1-0 | Don Faurot |
| 3. | Michigan | 8-1-0 | Fritz Crisler |
| 4. | Navy | 8-1-0 | Billick Whelchel |
| 5. | Purdue | 9-0-0 | Elmer Burnham |
| 6. | Great Lakes | 10-2-0 | Tony Hinkle |
| 7. | Duke | 8-1-0 | Eddie Cameron |
| 8. | Del Monte P-F | 7-1-0 | Bill Kern |
| 9. | Northwestern | 6-2-0 | Pappy Waldorf |
| 10. | March Field | 9-1-0 | Paul Schissler |
| 11. | Army | 7-2-1 | Red Blaik |
| 12. | Washington | 4-0-0 | Ralph Welch |
| 13. | Georgia Tech | 7-3-0 | Bill Alexander |

### 1943 *(Cont.)*

| | | Record | Coach |
|---|---|---|---|
| 14. | Texas | 7-1-0 | Dana X. Bible |
| 15. | Tulsa | 6-0-1 | Henry Frnka |
| 16. | Dartmouth | 6-1-0 | Earl Brown |
| 17. | Bainbridge NTS | 7-0-0 | Joe Maniaci |
| 18. | Colorado College | 7-0-0 | Hal White |
| 19. | Pacific | 7-2-0 | Amos A. Stagg |
| 20. | Pennsylvania | 6-2-1 | George Munger |

### 1944

| | | Record | Coach |
|---|---|---|---|
| 1. | Army | 9-0-0 | Red Blaik |
| 2. | Ohio St | 9-0-0 | Carroll Widdoes |
| 3. | Randolph Field | 11-0-0 | Frank Tritico |
| 4. | Navy | 6-3-0 | Oscar Hagberg |
| 5. | Bainbridge NTS | 9-0-0 | Joe Maniaci |
| 6. | Iowa Pre-Flight | 10-1-0 | Jack Meagher |
| 7. | Southern Cal | 7-0-2 | Jeff Cravath |
| 8. | Michigan | 8-2-0 | Fritz Crisler |
| 9. | Notre Dame | 8-2-0 | Ed McKeever |
| 10. | March Field | 7-1-2 | Paul Schissler |
| 11. | Duke | 5-4-0 | Eddie Cameron |
| 12. | Tennessee | 8-0-1 | John Barnhill |
| 13. | Georgia Tech | 8-2-0 | Bill Alexander |
| | Norman P-F | 6-0-0 | John Gregg |
| 15. | Illinois | 5-4-1 | Ray Eliot |
| 16. | El Toro Marines | 8-1-0 | Dick Hanley |
| 17. | Great Lakes | 9-2-1 | Paul Brown |
| 18. | Fort Pierce | 9-0-0 | Hamp Pool |
| 19. | St. Mary's P-F | 4-4-0 | Jules Sikes |
| 20. | 2nd Air Force | 7-2-1 | Bill Reese |

### 1945

| | | Record | Coach |
|---|---|---|---|
| 1. | Army | 9-0-0 | Red Blaik |
| 2. | Alabama | 9-0-0 | Frank Thomas |
| 3. | Navy | 7-1-1 | Oscar Hagberg |
| 4. | Indiana | 9-0-1 | Bo McMillan |
| 5. | Oklahoma A&M | 8-0-0 | Jim Lookabaugh |
| 6. | Michigan | 7-3-0 | Fritz Crisler |
| 7. | St. Mary's (CA) | 7-1-0 | Jimmy Phelan |
| 8. | Pennsylvania | 6-2-0 | George Munger |
| 9. | Notre Dame | 7-2-1 | Hugh Devore |
| 10. | Texas | 9-1-0 | Dana X. Bible |
| 11. | Southern Cal | 7-3-0 | Jeff Cravath |
| 12. | Ohio St | 7-2-0 | Carroll Widdoes |
| 13. | Duke | 6-2-0 | Eddie Cameron |
| 14. | Tennessee | 8-1-0 | John Barnhill |
| 15. | Louisiana St | 7-2-0 | Bernie Moore |
| 16. | Holy Cross | 8-1-0 | John DeGrosa |
| 17. | Tulsa | 8-2-0 | Henry Frnka |
| 18. | Georgia | 8-2-0 | Wally Butts |
| 19. | Wake Forest | 4-3-1 | Peahead Walker |
| 20. | Columbia | 8-1-0 | Lou Little |

### 1946

| | | Record | Coach |
|---|---|---|---|
| 1. | Notre Dame | 8-0-1 | Frank Leahy |
| 2. | Army | 9-0-1 | Red Blaik |
| 3. | Georgia | 10-0-0 | Wally Butts |
| 4. | UCLA | 10-0-0 | B. LaBrucherie |

Note: Except where indicated with an asterisk, the polls from 1936 through 1964 were taken before the bowl games and those from 1965 through the present were taken after the bowl games.

## 1946 *(Cont.)*

| | | Record | Coach |
|---|---|---|---|
| 5. | Illinois | 7-2-0 | Ray Eliot |
| 6. | Michigan | 6-2-1 | Fritz Crisler |
| 7. | Tennessee | 9-1-0 | Bob Neyland |
| 8. | Louisiana St | 9-1-0 | Bernie Moore |
| 9. | N Carolina | 8-1-1 | Carl Snavely |
| 10. | Rice | 8-2-0 | Jess Neely |
| 11. | Georgia Tech | 8-2-0 | Bobby Dodd |
| 12. | Yale | 7-1-1 | Howard Odell |
| 13. | Pennsylvania | 6-2-0 | George Munger |
| 14. | Oklahoma | 7-3-0 | Jim Tatum |
| 15. | Texas | 8-2-0 | Dana X. Bible |
| 16. | Arkansas | 6-3-1 | John Barnhill |
| 17. | Tulsa | 9-1-0 | J.O. Brothers |
| 18. | N Carolina St | 8-2-0 | Beattie Feathers |
| 19. | Delaware | 9-0-0 | Bill Murray |
| 20. | Indiana | 6-3-0 | Bo McMillan |

## 1947

| | | Record | Coach |
|---|---|---|---|
| 1. | Notre Dame | 9-0-0 | Frank Leahy |
| 2. | #Michigan | 9-0-0 | Fritz Crisler |
| 3. | SMU | 9-0-1 | Matty Bell |
| 4. | Penn St | 9-0-0 | Bob Higgins |
| 5. | Texas | 9-1-0 | Blair Cherry |
| 6. | Alabama | 8-2-0 | Red Drew |
| 7. | Pennsylvania | 7-0-1 | George Munger |
| 8. | Southern Cal | 7-1-1 | Jeff Cravath |
| 9. | N Carolina | 8-2-0 | Carl Snavely |
| 10. | Georgia Tech | 9-1-0 | Bobby Dodd |
| 11. | Army | 5-2-2 | Red Blaik |
| 12. | Kansas | 8-0-2 | George Sauer |
| 13. | Mississippi | 8-2-0 | Johnny Vaught |
| 14. | William & Mary | 9-1-0 | Rube McCray |
| 15. | California | 9-1-0 | Pappy Waldorf |
| 16. | Oklahoma | 7-2-1 | Bud Wilkinson |
| 17. | N Carolina St | 5-3-1 | Beattie Feathers |
| 18. | Rice | 6-3-1 | Jess Neely |
| 19. | Duke | 4-3-2 | Wallace Wade |
| 20. | Columbia | 7-2-0 | Lou Little |

#The AP, which had voted Notre Dame No. 1 before the bowl games, took a second vote, giving the title to Michigan after its 49–0 win over Southern Cal in the Rose Bowl.

## 1948

| | | Record | Coach |
|---|---|---|---|
| 1. | Michigan | 9-0-0 | Bennie Oosterbaan |
| 2. | Notre Dame | 9-0-1 | Frank Leahy |
| 3. | N Carolina | 9-0-1 | Carl Snavely |
| 4. | California | 10-0-0 | Pappy Waldorf |
| 5. | Oklahoma | 9-1-0 | Bud Wilkinson |
| 6. | Army | 8-0-1 | Red Blaik |
| 7. | Northwestern | 7-2-0 | Bob Voigts |
| 8. | Georgia | 9-1-0 | Wally Butts |
| 9. | Oregon | 9-1-0 | Jim Aiken |
| 10. | SMU | 8-1-1 | Matty Bell |
| 11. | Clemson | 10-0-0 | Frank Howard |
| 12. | Vanderbilt | 8-2-1 | Red Sanders |
| 13. | Tulane | 9-1-0 | Henry Frnka |
| 14. | Michigan St | 6-2-2 | Biggie Munn |
| 15. | Mississippi | 8-1-0 | Johnny Vaught |
| 16. | Minnesota | 7-2-0 | Bernie Bierman |
| 17. | William & Mary | 6-2-2 | Rube McCray |
| 18. | Penn St | 7-1-1 | Bob Higgins |
| 19. | Cornell | 8-1-0 | Lefty James |
| 20. | Wake Forest | 6-3-0 | Peahead Walker |

## 1949

| | | Record | Coach |
|---|---|---|---|
| 1. | Notre Dame | 10-0-0 | Frank Leahy |
| 2. | Oklahoma | 10-0-0 | Bud Wilkinson |
| 3. | California | 10-0-0 | Pappy Waldorf |
| 4. | Army | 9-0-0 | Red Blaik |
| 5. | Rice | 9-1-0 | Jess Neely |
| 6. | Ohio St | 6-1-2 | Wes Fesler |
| 7. | Michigan | 6-2-1 | Bennie Oosterbaan |
| 8. | Minnesota | 7-2-0 | Bernie Bierman |
| 9. | Louisiana St | 8-2-0 | Gaynell Tinsley |
| 10. | Pacific | 11-0-0 | Larry Siemering |
| 11. | Kentucky | 9-2-0 | Bear Bryant |
| 12. | Cornell | 8-1-0 | Lefty James |
| 13. | Villanova | 8-1-0 | Jim Leonard |
| 14. | Maryland | 8-1-0 | Jim Tatum |
| 15. | Santa Clara | 7-2-1 | Len Casanova |
| 16. | N Carolina | 7-3-0 | Carl Snavely |
| 17. | Tennessee | 7-2-1 | Bob Neyland |
| 18. | Princeton | 6-3-0 | Charlie Caldwell |
| 19. | Michigan St | 6-3-0 | Biggie Munn |
| 20. | Missouri | 7-3-0 | Don Faurot |
| | Baylor | 8-2-0 | Bob Woodruff |

## 1950

| | | Record | Coach |
|---|---|---|---|
| 1. | Oklahoma | 10-0-0 | Bud Wilkinson |
| 2. | Army | 8-1-0 | Red Blaik |
| 3. | Texas | 9-1-0 | Blair Cherry |
| 4. | Tennessee | 10-1-0 | Bob Neyland |
| 5. | California | 9-0-1 | Pappy Waldorf |
| 6. | Princeton | 9-0-0 | Charlie Caldwell |
| 7. | Kentucky | 10-1-0 | Bear Bryant |
| 8. | Michigan St | 8-1-0 | Biggie Munn |
| 9. | Michigan | 5-3-1 | Bennie Oosterhaan |
| 10. | Clemson | 8-0-1 | Frank Howard |
| 11. | Washington | 8-2-0 | Howard Odell |
| 12. | Wyoming | 9-0-0 | Bowden Wyatt |
| 13. | Illinois | 7-2-0 | Ray Eliot |
| 14. | Ohio St | 6-3-0 | Wes Fesler |
| 15. | Miami (FL) | 9-0-1 | Andy Gustafson |
| 16. | Alabama | 9-2-0 | Red Drew |
| 17. | Nebraska | 6-2-1 | Bill Glassford |
| 18. | Washington & Lee | 8-2-0 | George Barclay |
| 19. | Tulsa | 9-1-1 | J.O. Brothers |
| 20. | Tulane | 6-2-1 | Henry Frnka |

## 1951

| | | Record | Coach |
|---|---|---|---|
| 1. | Tennessee | 10-0-0 | Bob Neyland |
| 2. | Michigan St | 9-0-0 | Biggie Munn |
| 3. | Maryland | 9-0-0 | Jim Tatum |
| 4. | Illinois | 8-0-1 | Ray Eliot |
| 5. | Georgia Tech | 10-0-1 | Bobby Dodd |
| 6. | Princeton | 9-0-0 | Charlie Caldwell |
| 7. | Stanford | 9-1-0 | Chuck Taylor |
| 8. | Wisconsin | 7-1-1 | Ivy Williamson |
| 9. | Baylor | 8-1-1 | George Sauer |
| 10. | Oklahoma | 8-2-0 | Bud Wilkinson |
| 11. | Texas Christian | 6-4-0 | Dutch Meyer |
| 12. | California | 8-2-0 | Pappy Waldorf |
| 13. | Virginia | 8-1-0 | Art Guepe |
| 14. | San Francisco | 9-0-0 | Joe Kuharich |
| 15. | Kentucky | 7-4-0 | Bear Bryant |
| 16. | Boston University | 6-4-0 | Buff Donelli |
| 17. | UCLA | 5-3-1 | Red Sanders |
| 18. | Washington St | 7-3-0 | Forest Evashevski |

## 1951 (Cont.)

| | Record | Coach |
|---|---|---|
| 19. Holy Cross | 8-2-0 | Eddie Anderson |
| 20. Clemson | 7-2-0 | Frank Howard |

### 1952

| | Record | Coach |
|---|---|---|
| 1. Michigan St | 9-0-0 | Biggie Munn |
| 2. Georgia Tech | 11-0-0 | Bobby Dodd |
| 3. Notre Dame | 7-2-1 | Frank Leahy |
| 4. Oklahoma | 8-1-1 | Bud Wilkinson |
| 5. Southern Cal | 9-1-0 | Jess Hill |
| 6. UCLA | 8-1-0 | Red Sanders |
| 7. Mississippi | 8-0-2 | Johnny Vaught |
| 8. Tennessee | 8-1-1 | Bob Neyland |
| 9. Alabama | 9-2-0 | Red Drew |
| 10. Texas | 8-2-0 | Ed Price |
| 11. Wisconsin | 6-2-1 | Ivy Williamson |
| 12. Tulsa | 8-1-1 | J.O. Brothers |
| 13. Maryland | 7-2-0 | Jim Tatum |
| 14. Syracuse | 7-2-0 | Ben Schwartzwalder |
| 15. Florida | 7-3-0 | Bob Woodruff |
| 16. Duke | 8-2-0 | Bill Murray |
| 17. Ohio St | 6-3-0 | Woody Hayes |
| 18. Purdue | 4-3-2 | Stu Holcomb |
| 19. Princeton | 8-1-0 | Charlie Caldwell |
| 20. Kentucky | 5-4-2 | Bear Bryant |

### 1953

| | Record | Coach |
|---|---|---|
| 1. Maryland | 10-0-0 | Jim Tatum |
| 2. Notre Dame | 9-0-1 | Frank Leahy |
| 3. Michigan St | 8-1-0 | Biggie Munn |
| 4. Oklahoma | 8-1-1 | Bud Wilkinson |
| 5. UCLA | 8-1-0 | Red Sanders |
| 6. Rice | 8-2-0 | Jess Neely |
| 7. Illinois | 7-1-1 | Ray Eliot |
| 8. Georgia Tech | 8-2-1 | Bobby Dodd |
| 9. Iowa | 5-3-1 | Forest Evashevski |
| 10. W Virginia | 8-1-0 | Art Lewis |
| 11. Texas | 7-3-0 | Ed Price |
| 12. Texas Tech | 10-1-0 | DeWitt Weaver |
| 13. Alabama | 6-2-3 | Red Drew |
| 14. Army | 7-1-1 | Red Blaik |
| 15. Wisconsin | 6-2-1 | Ivy Williamson |
| 16. Kentucky | 7-2-1 | Bear Bryant |
| 17. Auburn | 7-2-1 | Shug Jordan |
| 18. Duke | 7-2-1 | Bill Murray |
| 19. Stanford | 6-3-1 | Chuck Taylor |
| 20. Michigan | 6-3-0 | Bennie Oosterbaan |

### 1954

| | Record | Coach |
|---|---|---|
| 1. Ohio St | 9-0-0 | Woody Hayes |
| 2. #UCLA | 9-0-0 | Red Sanders |
| 3. Oklahoma | 10-0-0 | Bud Wilkinson |
| 4. Notre Dame | 9-1-0 | Terry Brennan |
| 5. Navy | 7-2-0 | Eddie Erdelatz |
| 6. Mississippi | 9-1-0 | Johnny Vaught |
| 7. Army | 7-2-0 | Red Blaik |
| 8. Maryland | 7-2-1 | Jim Tatum |
| 9. Wisconsin | 7-2-0 | Ivy Williamson |
| 10. Arkansas | 8-2-0 | Bowden Wyatt |
| 11. Miami (FL) | 8-1-0 | Andy Gustafson |
| 12. W Virginia | 8-1-0 | Art Lewis |
| 13. Auburn | 7-3-0 | Shug Jordan |

## 1954 (Cont.)

| | Record | Coach |
|---|---|---|
| 14. Duke | 7-2-1 | Bill Murray |
| 15. Michigan | 6-3-0 | Bennie Oosterbaan |
| 16. Virginia Tech | 8-0-1 | Frank Moseley |
| 17. Southern Cal | 8-3-0 | Jess Hill |
| 18. Baylor | 7-3-0 | George Sauer |
| 19. Rice | 7-3-0 | Jess Neely |
| 20. Penn St | 7-2-0 | Rip Engle |

#Selected No. 1 by UP.

### 1955

| | Record | Coach |
|---|---|---|
| 1. Oklahoma | 10-0-0 | Bud Wilkinson |
| 2. Michigan St | 8-1-0 | Duffy Daugherty |
| 3. Maryland | 10-0-0 | Jim Tatum |
| 4. UCLA | 9-1-0 | Red Sanders |
| 5. Ohio St | 7-2-0 | Woody Hayes |
| 6. Texas Christian | 9-1-0 | Abe Martin |
| 7. Georgia Tech | 8-1-1 | Bobby Dodd |
| 8. Auburn | 8-1-1 | Shug Jordan |
| 9. Notre Dame | 8-2-0 | Terry Brennan |
| 10. Mississippi | 9-1-0 | Johnny Vaught |
| 11. Pittsburgh | 7-3-0 | John Michelosen |
| 12. Michigan | 7-2-0 | Bennie Oosterbaan |
| 13. Southern Cal | 6-4-0 | Jess Hill |
| 14. Miami (FL) | 6-3-0 | Andy Gustafson |
| 15. Miami (OH) | 9-0-0 | Ara Parseghian |
| 16. Stanford | 6-3-1 | Chuck Taylor |
| 17. Texas A&M | 7-2-1 | Bear Bryant |
| 18. Navy | 6-2-1 | Eddie Erdelatz |
| 19. W Virginia | 8-2-0 | Art Lewis |
| 20. Army | 6-3-0 | Red Blaik |

### 1956

| | Record | Coach |
|---|---|---|
| 1. Oklahoma | 10-0-0 | Bud Wilkinson |
| 2. Tennessee | 10-0-0 | Bowden Wyatt |
| 3. Iowa | 8-1-0 | Forest Evashevski |
| 4. Georgia Tech | 9-1-0 | Bobby Dodd |
| 5. Texas A&M | 9-0-1 | Bear Bryant |
| 6. Miami (FL) | 8-1-1 | Andy Gustafson |
| 7. Michigan | 7-2-0 | Bennie Oosterbaan |
| 8. Syracuse | 7-1-0 | Ben Schwartzwalder |
| 9. Michigan St | 7-2-0 | Duffy Daugherty |
| 10. Oregon St | 7-2-1 | Tommy Prothro |
| 11. Baylor | 8-2-0 | Sam Boyd |
| 12. Minnesota | 6-1-2 | Murray Warmath |
| 13. Pittsburgh | 7-2-1 | John Michelosen |
| 14. Texas Christian | 7-3-0 | Abe Martin |
| 15. Ohio St | 6-3-0 | Woody Hayes |
| 16. Navy | 6-1-2 | Eddie Erdelatz |
| 17. Geo Washington | 7-1-1 | Gene Sherman |
| 18. Southern Cal | 8-2-0 | Jess Hill |
| 19. Clemson | 7-1-2 | Frank Howard |
| 20. Colorado | 7-2-1 | Dallas Ward |
| Penn St | 6-2-1 | Rip Engle |

## 1957

| | | Record | Coach |
|---|---|---|---|
| 1. | Auburn | 10-0-0 | Shug Jordan |
| 2. | #Ohio St | 8-1-0 | Woody Hayes |
| 3. | Michigan St | 8-1-0 | Duffy Daugherty |
| 4. | Oklahoma | 9-1-0 | Bud Wilkinson |
| 5. | Navy | 8-1-1 | Eddie Erdelatz |
| 6. | Iowa | 7-1-1 | Forest Evashevski |
| 7. | Mississippi | 8-1-1 | Johnny Vaught |
| 8. | Rice | 7-3-0 | Jess Neely |
| 9. | Texas A&M | 8-2-0 | Bear Bryant |
| 10. | Notre Dame | 7-3-0 | Terry Brennan |
| 11. | Texas | 6-3-1 | Darrell Royal |
| 12. | Arizona St | 10-0-0 | Dan Devine |
| 13. | Tennessee | 7-3-0 | Bowden Wyatt |
| 14. | Mississippi St | 6-2-1 | Wade Walker |
| 15. | N Carolina St | 7-1-2 | Earle Edwards |
| 16. | Duke | 6-2-2 | Bill Murray |
| 17. | Florida | 6-2-1 | Bob Woodruff |
| 18. | Army | 7-2-0 | Red Blaik |
| 19. | Wisconsin | 6-3-0 | Milt Brunt |
| 20. | VMI | 9-0-1 | John McKenna |

#Selected No. 1 by UP.

## 1958

| | | Record | Coach |
|---|---|---|---|
| 1. | Louisiana St | 10-0-0 | Paul Dietzel |
| 2. | Iowa | 7-1-1 | Forest Evashevski |
| 3. | Army | 8-0-1 | Red Blaik |
| 4. | Auburn | 9-0-1 | Shug Jordan |
| 5. | Oklahoma | 9-1-0 | Bud Wilkinson |
| 6. | Air Force | 9-0-1 | Ben Martin |
| 7. | Wisconsin | 7-1-1 | Milt Bruhn |
| 8. | Ohio St | 6-1-2 | Woody Hayes |
| 9. | Syracuse | 8-1-0 | Ben Schwartzwalder |
| 10. | Texas Christian | 8-2-0 | Abe Martin |
| 11. | Mississippi | 8-2-0 | Johnny Vaught |
| 12. | Clemson | 8-2-0 | Frank Howard |
| 13. | Purdue | 6-1-2 | Jack Mollenkopf |
| 14. | Florida | 6-3-1 | Bob Woodruff |
| 15. | S Carolina | 7-3-0 | Warren Giese |
| 16. | California | 7-3-0 | Pete Elliott |
| 17. | Notre Dame | 6-4-0 | Terry Brennan |
| 18. | SMU | 6-4-0 | Bill Meek |
| 19. | Oklahoma St | 7-3-0 | Cliff Speegle |
| 20. | Rutgers | 8-1-0 | John Stiegman |

## 1959

| | | Record | Coach |
|---|---|---|---|
| 1. | Syracuse | 10-0-0 | Ben Schwartzwalder |
| 2. | Mississippi | 9-1-0 | Johnny Vaught |
| 3. | Louisiana St | 9-1-0 | Paul Dietzel |
| 4. | Texas | 9-1-0 | Darrell Royal |
| 5. | Georgia | 9-1-0 | Wally Butts |
| 6. | Wisconsin | 7-2-0 | Milt Bruhn |
| 7. | Texas Christian | 8-2-0 | Abe Martin |
| 8. | Washington | 9-1-0 | Jim Owens |
| 9. | Arkansas | 8-2-0 | Frank Broyles |
| 10. | Alabama | 7-1-2 | Bear Bryant |
| 11. | Clemson | 8-2-0 | Frank Howard |

## 1959 (Cont.)

| | | Record | Coach |
|---|---|---|---|
| 12. | Penn St | 8-2-0 | Rip Engle |
| 13. | Illinois | 5-3-1 | Ray Eliot |
| 14. | Southern Cal | 8-2-0 | Don Clark |
| 15. | Oklahoma | 7-3-0 | Bud Wilkinson |
| 16. | Wyoming | 9-1-0 | Bob Devaney |
| 17. | Notre Dame | 5-5-0 | Joe Kuharich |
| 18. | Missouri | 6-4-0 | Dan Devine |
| 19. | Florida | 5-4-1 | Bob Woodruff |
| 20. | Pittsburgh | 6-4-0 | John Michelosen |

## 1960

| | | Record | Coach |
|---|---|---|---|
| 1. | Minnesota | 8-1-0 | Murray Warmath |
| 2. | Mississippi | 9-0-1 | Johnny Vaught |
| 3. | Iowa | 8-1-0 | Forest Evashevski |
| 4. | Navy | 9-1-0 | Wayne Hardin |
| 5. | Missouri | 9-1-0 | Dan Devine |
| 6. | Washington | 9-1-0 | Jim Owens |
| 7. | Arkansas | 8-2-0 | Frank Broyles |
| 8. | Ohio St | 7-2-0 | Woody Hayes |
| 9. | Alabama | 8-1-1 | Bear Bryant |
| 10. | Duke | 7-3-0 | Bill Murray |
| 11. | Kansas | 7-2-1 | Jack Mitchell |
| 12. | Baylor | 8-2-0 | John Bridgers |
| 13. | Auburn | 8-2-0 | Shug Jordan |
| 14. | Yale | 9-0-0 | Jordan Oliver |
| 15. | Michigan St | 6-2-1 | Duffy Daugherty |
| 16. | Penn St | 6-3-0 | Rip Engle |
| 17. | New Mexico St | 10-0-0 | Warren Woodson |
| 18. | Florida | 8-2-0 | Ray Graves |
| 19. | Syracuse | 7-2-0 | Ben Schwartzwalder |
| | Purdue | 4-4-1 | Jack Mollenkopf |

## 1961

| | | Record | Coach |
|---|---|---|---|
| 1. | Alabama | 10-0-0 | Bear Bryant |
| 2. | Ohio St | 8-0-1 | Woody Hayes |
| 3. | Texas | 9-1-0 | Darrell Royal |
| 4. | Louisiana St | 9-1-0 | Paul Dietzel |
| 5. | Mississippi | 9-1-0 | Johnny Vaught |
| 6. | Minnesota | 7-2-0 | Murray Warmath |
| 7. | Colorado | 9-1-0 | Sonny Grandelius |
| 8. | Michigan St | 7-2-0 | Duffy Daugherty |
| 9. | Arkansas | 8-2-0 | Frank Broyles |
| 10. | Utah St | 9-0-1 | John Ralston |
| 11. | Missouri | 7-2-1 | Dan Devine |
| 12. | Purdue | 6-3-0 | Jack Mollenkopf |
| 13. | Georgia Tech | 7-3-0 | Bobby Dodd |
| 14. | Syracuse | 7-3-0 | Ben Schwartzwalder |
| 15. | Rutgers | 9-0-0 | John Bateman |
| 16. | UCLA | 7-3-0 | Bill Barnes |
| 17. | Rice | 7-3-0 | Jess Neely |
| | Penn St | 7-3-0 | Rip Engle |
| | Arizona | 8-1-1 | Jim LaRue |
| 20. | Duke | 7-3-0 | Bill Murray |

## 1962

| | | Record | Coach |
|---|---|---|---|
| 1. | Southern Cal | 10-0-0 | John McKay |
| 2. | Wisconsin | 8-1-0 | Milt Bruhn |
| 3. | Mississippi | 9-0-0 | Johnny Vaught |
| 4. | Texas | 9-0-1 | Darrell Royal |
| 5. | Alabama | 9-1-0 | Bear Bryant |
| 6. | Arkansas | 9-1-0 | Frank Broyles |
| 7. | Louisiana St | 8-1-1 | Charlie McClendon |
| 8. | Oklahoma | 8-2-0 | Bud Wilkinson |
| 9. | Penn St | 9-1-0 | Rip Engle |
| 10. | Minnesota | 6-2-1 | Murray Warmath |
| 11–20: UPI | | | |
| 11. | Georgia Tech | 7-2-1 | Bobby Dodd |
| 12. | Missouri | 7-1-2 | Dan Devine |
| 13. | Ohio St | 6-3-0 | Woody Hayes |
| 14. | Duke | 8-2-0 | Bill Murray |
| | Washington | 7-1-2 | Jim Owens |
| 16. | Northwestern | 7-2-0 | Ara Parseghian |
| | Oregon St | 8-2-0 | Tommy Prothro |
| 18. | Arizona St | 7-2-1 | Frank Kush |
| | Miami (FL) | 7-3-0 | Andy Gustafson |
| | Illinois | 2-7-0 | Pete Elliott |

## 1963

| | | Record | Coach |
|---|---|---|---|
| 1. | Texas | 10-0-0 | Darrell Royal |
| 2. | Navy | 9-1-0 | Wayne Hardin |
| 3. | Illinois | 7-1-1 | Pete Elliott |
| 4. | Pittsburgh | 9-1-0 | John Michelosen |
| 5. | Auburn | 9-1-0 | Shug Jordan |
| 6. | Nebraska | 9-1-0 | Bob Devaney |
| 7. | Mississippi | 7-0-2 | Johnny Vaught |
| 8. | Alabama | 8-2-0 | Bear Bryant |
| 9. | Oklahoma | 8-2-0 | Bud Wilkinson |
| 10. | Michigan St | 6-2-1 | Duffy Daugherty |
| 11–20: UPI | | | |
| 11. | Mississippi St | 6-2-2 | Paul Davis |
| 12. | Syracuse | 8-2-0 | Ben Schwartzwalder |
| 13. | Arizona St | 8-1-0 | Frank Kush |
| 14. | Memphis St | 9-0-1 | Billy J. Murphy |
| 15. | Washington | 6-4-0 | Jim Owens |
| 16. | Penn St | 7-3-0 | Rip Engle |
| | Southern Cal | 7-3-0 | John McKay |
| | Missouri | 7-3-0 | Dan Devine |
| 19. | N Carolina | 8-2-0 | Jim Hickey |
| 20. | Baylor | 7-3-0 | John Bridgers |

## 1964

| | | Record | Coach |
|---|---|---|---|
| 1. | Alabama | 10-0-0 | Bear Bryant |
| 2. | Arkansas | 10-0-0 | Frank Broyles |
| 3. | Notre Dame | 9-1-0 | Ara Parseghian |
| 4. | Michigan | 8-1-0 | Bump Elliott |
| 5. | Texas | 9-1-0 | Darrell Royal |
| 6. | Nebraska | 9-1-0 | Bob Devaney |
| 7. | Louisiana St | 7-2-1 | Charlie McClendon |
| 8. | Oregon St | 8-2-0 | Tommy Prothro |
| 9. | Ohio St | 7-2-0 | Woody Hayes |
| 10. | Southern Cal | 7-3-0 | John McKay |

## 1964 *(Cont.)*

| | | Record | Coach |
|---|---|---|---|
| 11–20: UPI | | | |
| 11. | Florida St | 8-1-1 | Bill Peterson |
| 12. | Syracuse | 7-3-0 | Ben Schwartzwalder |
| 13. | Princeton | 9-0-0 | Dick Colman |
| 14. | Penn St | 6-4-0 | Rip Engle |
| | Utah | 8-2-0 | Ray Nagel |
| 16. | Illinois | 6-3-0 | Pete Elliott |
| | New Mexico | 9-2-0 | Bill Weeks |
| 18. | Tulsa | 8-2-0 | Glenn Dobbs |
| 19. | Missouri | 6-3-1 | Dan Devine |
| 20. | Mississippi | 5-4-1 | Johnny Vaught |
| | Michigan St | 4-5-1 | Duffy Daugherty |

## 1965

| | | Record | Coach |
|---|---|---|---|
| 1. | Alabama | 9-1-1 | Bear Bryant |
| 2. | #Michigan St | 10-1-0 | Duffy Daugherty |
| 3. | Arkansas | 10-1-0 | Frank Broyles |
| 4. | UCLA | 8-2-1 | Tommy Prothro |
| 5. | Nebraska | 10-1-0 | Bob Devaney |
| 6. | Missouri | 8-2-1 | Dan Devine |
| 7. | Tennessee | 8-1-2 | Doug Dickey |
| 8. | Louisiana St | 8-3-0 | Charlie McClendon |
| 9. | Notre Dame | 7-2-1 | Ara Parseghian |
| 10. | Southern Cal | 7-2-1 | John McKay |
| 11–20: UPI | | | |
| 11. | Texas Tech | 8-2-0 | J.T. King |
| 12. | Ohio St | 7-2-0 | Woody Hayes |
| 13. | Florida | 7-3-0 | Ray Graves |
| 14. | Purdue | 7-2-1 | Jack Mollenkopf |
| 15. | Georgia | 6-4-0 | Vince Dooley |
| 16. | Tulsa | 8-2-0 | Glenn Dobbs |
| 17. | Mississippi | 6-4-0 | Johnny Vaught |
| 18. | Kentucky | 6-4-0 | Charlie Bradshaw |
| 19 | Syracuse | 7-3-0 | Ben Schwartzwalder |
| 20. | Colorado | 6-2-2 | Eddie Crowder |

#Selected No. 1 by UPI.

## 1966*

| | | Record | Coach |
|---|---|---|---|
| 1. | Notre Dame | 9-0-1 | Ara Parseghian |
| 2. | Michigan St | 9-0-1 | Duffy Daugherty |
| 3. | Alabama | 10-0-0 | Bear Bryant |
| 4. | Georgia | 9-1-0 | Vince Dooley |
| 5. | UCLA | 9-1-0 | Tommy Prothro |
| 6. | Nebraska | 9-1-0 | Bob Devaney |
| 7. | Purdue | 8-2-0 | Jack Mollenkopf |
| 8. | Georgia Tech | 9-1-0 | Bobby Dodd |
| 9. | Miami (FL) | 7-2-1 | Charlie Tate |
| 10. | SMU | 8-2-0 | Hayden Fry |
| 11–20: UPI | | | |
| 11. | Florida | 8-2-0 | Ray Graves |
| 12. | Mississippi | 8-2-0 | Johnny Vaught |
| 13. | Arkansas | 8-2-0 | Frank Broyles |
| 14. | Tennessee | 7-3-0 | Doug Dickey |
| 15. | Wyoming | 9-1-0 | Lloyd Eaton |
| 16. | Syracuse | 8-2-0 | Ben Schwartzwalder |
| 17. | Houston | 8-2-0 | Bill Yeoman |
| 18. | Southern Cal | 7-3-0 | John McKay |
| 19. | Oregon St | 7-3-0 | Dee Andros |
| 20. | Virginia Tech | 8-1-1 | Jerry Claiborne |

Note: Except where indicated with an asterisk, the polls from 1936 through 1964 were taken before the bowl games and those from 1965 through the present were taken after the bowl games. Additionally, the AP ranked only ten teams in its polls from 1962–67; positions 11–20 from those years are from the UPI poll.

## 1967*

| | | Record | Coach |
|---|---|---|---|
| 1. | Southern Cal | 9-1-0 | John McKay |
| 2. | Tennessee | 9-1-0 | Doug Dickey |
| 3. | Oklahoma | 9-1-0 | Chuck Fairbanks |
| 4. | Indiana | 9-1-0 | John Pont |
| 5. | Notre Dame | 8-2-0 | Ara Parseghian |
| 6. | Wyoming | 10-0-0 | Lloyd Eaton |
| 7. | Oregon St | 7-2-1 | Dee Andros |
| 8. | Alabama | 8-1-1 | Bear Bryant |
| 9. | Purdue | 8-2-0 | Jack Mollenkopf |
| 10. | Penn St | 8-2-0 | Joe Paterno |

11–20: UPI†

| | | | |
|---|---|---|---|
| 11. | UCLA | 7-2-1 | Tommy Prothro |
| 12. | Syracuse | 8-2-0 | Ben Schwartzwalder |
| 13. | Colorado | 8-2-0 | Eddie Crowder |
| 14. | Minnesota | 8-2-0 | Murray Warmath |
| 15. | Florida St | 7-2-1 | Bill Peterson |
| 16. | Miami (FL) | 7-3-0 | Charlie Tate |
| 17. | N Carolina St | 8-2-0 | Earle Edwards |
| 18. | Georgia | 7-3-0 | Vince Dooley |
| 19. | Houston | 9-2-0 | Bill Yeoman |
| 20. | Arizona St | 8-2-0 | Frank Kush |

†UPI ranked Penn St 11th and did not rank Alabama, which was on probation.

## 1968

| | | Record | Coach |
|---|---|---|---|
| 1. | Ohio St | 10-0-0 | Woody Hayes |
| 2. | Penn St | 11-0-0 | Joe Paterno |
| 3. | Texas | 9-1-1 | Darrell Royal |
| 4. | Southern Cal | 9-1-1 | John McKay |
| 5. | Notre Dame | 7-2-1 | Ara Parseghian |
| 6. | Arkansas | 10-1-0 | Frank Broyles |
| 7. | Kansas | 9-2-0 | Pepper Rodgers |
| 8. | Georgia | 8-1-2 | Vince Dooley |
| 9. | Missouri | 8-3-0 | Dan Devine |
| 10. | Purdue | 8-2-0 | Jack Mollenkopf |
| 11. | Oklahoma | 7-4-0 | Chuck Fairbanks |
| 12. | Michigan | 8-2-0 | Bump Elliott |
| 13. | Tennessee | 8-2-1 | Doug Dickey |
| 14. | SMU | 8-3-0 | Hayden Fry |
| 15. | Oregon St | 7-3-0 | Dee Andros |
| 16. | Auburn | 7-4-0 | Shug Jordan |
| 17. | Alabama | 8-3-0 | Bear Bryant |
| 18. | Houston | 6-2-2 | Bill Yeoman |
| 19. | Louisiana St | 8-3-0 | Charlie McClendon |
| 20. | Ohio | 10-1-0 | Bill Hess |

## 1969

| | | Record | Coach |
|---|---|---|---|
| 1. | Texas | 11-0-0 | Darrell Royal |
| 2. | Penn St | 11-0-0 | Joe Paterno |
| 3. | Southern Cal | 10-0-1 | John McKay |
| 4. | Ohio St | 8-1-0 | Woody Hayes |
| 5. | Notre Dame | 8-2-1 | Ara Parseghian |
| 6. | Missouri | 9-2-0 | Dan Devine |
| 7. | Arkansas | 9-2-0 | Frank Broyles |
| 8. | Mississippi | 8-3-0 | Johnny Vaught |
| 9. | Michigan | 8-3-0 | Bo Schembechler |
| 10. | Louisiana St | 9-1-0 | Charlie McClendon |

## 1969 *(Cont.)*

| | | Record | Coach |
|---|---|---|---|
| 11. | Nebraska | 9-2-0 | Bob Devaney |
| 12. | Houston | 9-2-0 | Bill Yeoman |
| 13. | UCLA | 8-1-1 | Tommy Prothro |
| 14. | Florida | 9-1-1 | Ray Graves |
| 15. | Tennessee | 9-2-0 | Doug Dickey |
| 16. | Colorado | 8-3-0 | Eddie Crowder |
| 17. | W Virginia | 10-0-1 | Jim Carlen |
| 18. | Purdue | 8-2-0 | Jack Mollenkopf |
| 19. | Stanford | 7-2-1 | John Ralston |
| 20. | Auburn | 8-3-0 | Shug Jordan |

## 1970

| | | Record | Coach |
|---|---|---|---|
| 1. | Nebraska | 11-0-1 | Bob Devaney |
| 2. | Notre Dame | 10-1-0 | Ara Parseghian |
| 3. | #Texas | 10-1-0 | Darrell Royal |
| 4. | Tennessee | 11-1-0 | Bill Battle |
| 5. | Ohio St | 9-1-0 | Woody Hayes |
| 6. | Arizona St | 11-0-0 | Frank Kush |
| 7. | Louisiana St | 9-3-0 | Charlie McClendon |
| 8. | Stanford | 9-3-0 | John Ralston |
| 9. | Michigan | 9-1-0 | Bo Schembechler |
| 10. | Auburn | 9-2-0 | Shug Jordan |
| 11. | Arkansas | 9-2-0 | Frank Broyles |
| 12. | Toledo | 12-0-0 | Frank Lauterbur |
| 13. | Georgia Tech | 9-3-0 | Bud Carson |
| 14. | Dartmouth | 9-0-0 | Bob Blackman |
| 15. | Southern Cal | 6-4-1 | John McKay |
| 16. | Air Force | 9-3-0 | Ben Martin |
| 17. | Tulane | 8-4-0 | Jim Pittman |
| 18. | Penn St | 7-3-0 | Joe Paterno |
| 19. | Houston | 8-3-0 | Bill Yeoman |
| 20. | Oklahoma | 7-4-1 | Chuck Fairbanks |
| | Mississippi | 7-4-0 | Johnny Vaught |

#Selected No. 1 by UPI.

## 1971

| | | Record | Coach |
|---|---|---|---|
| 1. | Nebraska | 13-0-0 | Bob Devaney |
| 2. | Oklahoma | 11-1-0 | Chuck Fairbanks |
| 3. | Colorado | 10-2-0 | Eddie Crowder |
| 4. | Alabama | 11-1-0 | Bear Bryant |
| 5. | Penn St | 11-1-0 | Joe Paterno |
| 6. | Michigan | 11-1-0 | Bo Schembechler |
| 7. | Georgia | 11-1-0 | Vince Dooley |
| 8. | Arizona St | 11-1-0 | Frank Kush |
| 9. | Tennessee | 10-2-0 | Bill Battle |
| 10. | Stanford | 9-3-0 | John Ralston |
| 11. | Louisiana St | 9-3-0 | Charlie McClendon |
| 12. | Auburn | 9-2-0 | Shug Jordan |
| 13. | Notre Dame | 8-2-0 | Ara Parseghian |
| 14. | Toledo | 12-0-0 | John Murphy |
| 15. | Mississippi | 10-2-0 | Billy Kinard |
| 16. | Arkansas | 8-3-1 | Frank Broyles |
| 17. | Houston | 9-3-0 | Bill Yeoman |
| 18. | Texas | 8-3-0 | Darrell Royal |
| 19. | Washington | 8-3-0 | Jim Owens |
| 20. | Southern Cal | 6-4-1 | John McKay |

## 1972

| | | Record | Coach |
|---|---|---|---|
| 1. | Southern Cal | 12-0-0 | John McKay |
| 2. | Oklahoma | 11-1-0 | Chuck Fairbanks |
| 3. | Texas | 10-1-0 | Darrell Royal |
| 4. | Nebraska | 9-2-1 | Bob Devaney |
| 5. | Auburn | 10-1-0 | Shug Jordan |
| 6. | Michigan | 10-1-0 | Bo Schembechler |
| 7. | Alabama | 10-2-0 | Bear Bryant |
| 8. | Tennessee | 10-2-0 | Bill Battle |
| 9. | Ohio St | 9-2-0 | Woody Hayes |
| 10. | Penn St | 10-2-0 | Joe Paterno |
| 11. | Louisiana St | 9-2-1 | Charlie McClendon |
| 12. | N Carolina | 11-1-0 | Bill Dooley |
| 13. | Arizona St | 10-2-0 | Frank Kush |
| 14. | Notre Dame | 8-3-0 | Ara Parseghian |
| 15. | UCLA | 8-3-0 | Pepper Rodgers |
| 16. | Colorado | 8-4-0 | Eddie Crowder |
| 17. | N Carolina St | 8-3-1 | Lou Holtz |
| 18. | Louisville | 9-1-0 | Lee Corso |
| 19. | Washington St | 7-4-0 | Jim Sweeney |
| 20. | Georgia Tech | 7-4-1 | Bill Fulcher |

## 1973

| | | Record | Coach |
|---|---|---|---|
| 1. | Notre Dame | 11-0-0 | Ara Parseghian |
| 2. | Ohio St | 10-0-1 | Woody Hayes |
| 3. | Oklahoma | 10-0-1 | Barry Switzer |
| 4. | #Alabama | 11-1-0 | Bear Bryant |
| 5. | Penn St | 12-0-0 | Joe Paterno |
| 6. | Michigan | 10-0-1 | Bo Schembechler |
| 7. | Nebraska | 9-2-1 | Tom Osborne |
| 8. | Southern Cal | 9-2-1 | John McKay |
| 9. | Arizona St | 11-1-0 | Frank Kush |
| | Houston | 11-1-0 | Bill Yeoman |
| 11. | Texas Tech | 11-1-0 | Jim Carlen |
| 12. | UCLA | 9-2-0 | Pepper Rodgers |
| 13. | Louisiana St | 9-3-0 | Charlie McClendon |
| 14. | Texas | 8-3-0 | Darrell Royal |
| 15. | Miami (OH) | 11-0-0 | Bill Mallory |
| 16. | N Carolina St | 9-3-0 | Lou Holtz |
| 17. | Missouri | 8-4-0 | Al Onofrio |
| 18. | Kansas | 7-4-1 | Don Fambrough |
| 19. | Tennessee | 8-4-0 | Bill Battle |
| 20. | Maryland | 8-4-0 | Jerry Claiborne |
| | Tulane | 9-3-0 | Bennie Ellender |

#Selected No. 1 by UPI.

## 1974

| | | Record | Coach |
|---|---|---|---|
| 1. | Oklahoma | 11-0-0 | Barry Switzer |
| 2. | #Southern Cal | 10-1-1 | John McKay |
| 3. | Michigan | 10-1-0 | Bo Schembechler |
| 4. | Ohio St | 10-2-0 | Woody Hayes |
| 5. | Alabama | 11-1-0 | Bear Bryant |
| 6. | Notre Dame | 10-2-0 | Ara Parseghian |
| 7. | Penn St | 10-2-0 | Joe Paterno |
| 8. | Auburn | 10-2-0 | Shug Jordan |
| 9. | Nebraska | 9-3-0 | Tom Osborne |
| 10. | Miami (OH) | 10-0-1 | Dick Crum |
| 11. | N Carolina St | 9-2-1 | Lou Holtz |
| 12. | Michigan St | 7-3-1 | Denny Stolz |

## 1974 *(Cont.)*

| | | Record | Coach |
|---|---|---|---|
| 13. | Maryland | 8-4-0 | Jerry Claiborne |
| 14. | Baylor | 8-4-0 | Grant Teaff |
| 15. | Florida | 8-4-0 | Doug Dickey |
| 16. | Texas A&M | 8-3-0 | Emory Ballard |
| 17. | Mississippi St | 9-3-0 | Bob Tyler |
| | Texas | 8-4-0 | Darrell Royal |
| 19. | Houston | 8-3-1 | Bill Yeoman |
| 20. | Tennessee | 7-3-2 | Bill Battle |

#Selected No. 1 by UPI.

## 1975

| | | Record | Coach |
|---|---|---|---|
| 1. | Oklahoma | 11-1-0 | Barry Switzer |
| 2. | Arizona St | 12-0-0 | Frank Kush |
| 3. | Alabama | 11-1-0 | Bear Bryant |
| 4. | Ohio St | 11-1-0 | Woody Hayes |
| 5. | UCLA | 9-2-1 | Dick Vermeil |
| 6. | Texas | 10-2-0 | Darrell Royal |
| 7. | Arkansas | 10-2-0 | Frank Broyles |
| 8. | Michigan | 8-2-2 | Bo Schembechler |
| 9. | Nebraska | 10-2-0 | Tom Osborne |
| 10. | Penn St | 9-3-0 | Joe Paterno |
| 11. | Texas A&M | 10-2-0 | Emory Bellard |
| 12. | Miami (OH) | 11-1-0 | Dick Crum |
| 13. | Maryland | 9-2-1 | Jerry Claiborne |
| 14. | California | 8-3-0 | Mike White |
| 15. | Pittsburgh | 8-4-0 | Johnny Majors |
| 16. | Colorado | 9-3-0 | Bill Mallory |
| 17. | Southern Cal | 8-4-0 | John McKay |
| 18. | Arizona | 9-2-0 | Jim Young |
| 19. | Georgia | 9-3-0 | Vince Dooley |
| 20. | W Virginia | 9-3-0 | Bobby Bowden |

## 1976

| | | Record | Coach |
|---|---|---|---|
| 1. | Pittsburgh | 12-0-0 | Johnny Majors |
| 2. | Southern Cal | 11-1-0 | John Robinson |
| 3. | Michigan | 10-2-0 | Bo Schembechler |
| 4. | Houston | 10-2-0 | Bill Yeoman |
| 5. | Oklahoma | 9-2-1 | Barry Switzer |
| 6. | Ohio St | 9-2-1 | Woody Hayes |
| 7. | Texas A&M | 10-2-0 | Emory Bellard |
| 8. | Maryland | 11-1-0 | Jerry Claiborne |
| 9. | Nebraska | 9-3-1 | Tom Osborne |
| 10. | Georgia | 10-2-0 | Vince Dooley |
| 11. | Alabama | 9-3-0 | Bear Bryant |
| 12. | Notre Dame | 9-3-0 | Dan Devine |
| 13. | Texas Tech | 10-2-0 | Steve Sloan |
| 14. | Oklahoma St | 9-3-0 | Jim Stanley |
| 15. | UCLA | 9-2-1 | Terry Donahue |
| 16. | Colorado | 8-4-0 | Bill Mallory |
| 17. | Rutgers | 11-0-0 | Frank Burns |
| 18. | Kentucky | 9-3-0 | Fran Curci |
| 19. | Iowa St | 8-3-0 | Earle Bruce |
| 20. | Mississippi St | 9-2-0 | Bob Tyler |

## 1977

| | | Record | Coach |
|---|---|---|---|
| 1. | Notre Dame | 11-1-0 | Dan Devine |
| 2. | Alabama | 11-1-0 | Bear Bryant |
| 3. | Arkansas | 11-1-0 | Lou Holtz |
| 4. | Texas | 11-1-0 | Fred Akers |
| 5. | Penn St | 11-1-0 | Joe Paterno |
| 6. | Kentucky | 10-1-0 | Fran Curci |
| 7. | Oklahoma | 10-2-0 | Barry Switzer |
| 8. | Pittsburgh | 9-2-1 | Jackie Sherrill |
| 9. | Michigan | 10-2-0 | Bo Schembechler |
| 10. | Washington | 10-2-0 | Don James |
| 11. | Ohio St | 9-3-0 | Woody Hayes |
| 12. | Nebraska | 9-3-0 | Tom Osborne |
| 13. | Southern Cal | 8-4-0 | John Robinson |
| 14. | Florida St | 10-2-0 | Bobby Bowden |
| 15. | Stanford | 9-3-0 | Bill Walsh |
| 16. | San Diego St | 10-1-0 | Claude Gilbert |
| 17. | N Carolina | 8-3-1 | Bill Dooley |
| 18. | Arizona St. | 9-3-0 | Frank Kush |
| 19. | Clemson | 8-3-1 | Charley Pell |
| 20. | Brigham Young | 9-2-0 | LaVell Edwards |

## 1978

| | | Record | Coach |
|---|---|---|---|
| 1. | Alabama | 11-1-0 | Bear Bryant |
| 2. | #Southern Cal | 12-1-0 | John Robinson |
| 3. | Oklahoma | 11-1-0 | Barry Switzer |
| 4. | Penn St | 11-1-0 | Joe Paterno |
| 5. | Michigan | 10-2-0 | Bo Schembechler |
| 6. | Clemson | 11-1-0 | Charley Pell |
| 7. | Notre Dame | 9-3-0 | Dan Devine |
| 8. | Nebraska | 9-3-0 | Tom Osborne |
| 9. | Texas | 9-3-0 | Fred Akers |
| 10. | Houston | 9-3-0 | Bill Yeoman |
| 11. | Arkansas | 9-2-1 | Lou Holtz |
| 12. | Michigan St | 8-3-0 | Darryl Rogers |
| 13. | Purdue | 9-2-1 | Jim Young |
| 14. | UCLA | 8-3-1 | Terry Donahue |
| 15. | Missouri | 8-4-0 | Warren Powers |
| 16. | Georgia | 9-2-1 | Vince Dooley |
| 17. | Stanford | 8-4-0 | Bill Walsh |
| 18. | N Carolina St | 9-3-0 | Bo Rein |
| 19. | Texas A&M | 8-4-0 | Emory Bellard (4–2) Tom Wilson (4–2) |
| 20. | Maryland | 9-3-0 | Jerry Claiborne |

#Selected No. 1 by UPI.

## 1979

| | | Record | Coach |
|---|---|---|---|
| 1. | Alabama | 12-0-0 | Bear Bryant |
| 2. | Southern Cal | 11-0-1 | John Robinson |
| 3. | Oklahoma | 11-1-0 | Barry Switzer |
| 4. | Ohio St | 11-1-0 | Earle Bruce |
| 5. | Houston | 11-1-0 | Bill Yeoman |
| 6. | Florida St | 11-1-0 | Bobby Bowden |
| 7. | Pittsburgh | 11-1-0 | Jackie Sherrill |
| 8. | Arkansas | 10-2-0 | Lou Holtz |
| 9. | Nebraska | 10-2-0 | Tom Osborne |
| 10. | Purdue | 10-2-0 | Jim Young |
| 11. | Washington | 10-1-0 | Don James |
| 12. | Texas | 9-3-0 | Fred Akers |
| 13. | Brigham Young | 11-1-0 | LaVell Edwards |
| 14. | Baylor | 8-4-0 | Grant Teaff |
| 15. | N Carolina | 8-3-1 | Dick Crum |
| 16. | Auburn | 8-3-0 | Doug Barfield |
| 17. | Temple | 10-2-0 | Wayne Hardin |

## 1979 *(Cont.)*

| | | Record | Coach |
|---|---|---|---|
| 18. | Michigan | 8-4-0 | Bo Schembechler |
| 19. | Indiana | 8-4-0 | Lee Corso |
| 20. | Penn St | 8-4-0 | Joe Paterno |

## 1980

| | | Record | Coach |
|---|---|---|---|
| 1. | Georgia | 12-0-0 | Vince Dooley |
| 2. | Pittsburgh | 11-1-0 | Jackie Sherrill |
| 3. | Oklahoma | 10-2-0 | Barry Switzer |
| 4. | Michigan | 10-2-0 | Bo Schembechler |
| 5. | Florida St | 10-2-0 | Bobby Bowden |
| 6. | Alabama | 10-2-0 | Bear Bryant |
| 7. | Nebraska | 10-2-0 | Tom Osborne |
| 8. | Penn St | 10-2-0 | Joe Paterno |
| 9. | Notre Dame | 9-2-1 | Dan Devine |
| 10. | N Carolina | 11-1-0 | Dick Crum |
| 11. | Southern Cal | 8-2-1 | John Robinson |
| 12. | Brigham Young | 12-1-0 | LaVell Edwards |
| 13. | UCLA | 9-2-0 | Terry Donahue |
| 14. | Baylor | 10-2-0 | Grant Teaff |
| 15. | Ohio St | 9-3-0 | Earle Bruce |
| 16. | Washington | 9-3-0 | Don James |
| 17. | Purdue | 9-3-0 | Jim Young |
| 18. | Miami (FL) | 9-3-0 | H. Schnellenberger |
| 19. | Mississippi St | 9-3-0 | Emory Bellard |
| 20. | SMU | 8-4-0 | Ron Meyer |

## 1981

| | | Record | Coach |
|---|---|---|---|
| 1. | Clemson | 12-0-0 | Danny Ford |
| 2. | Texas | 10-1-1 | Fred Akers |
| 3. | Penn St | 10-2-0 | Joe Paterno |
| 4. | Pittsburgh | 11-1-0 | Jackie Sherrill |
| 5. | SMU | 10-1-0 | Ron Meyer |
| 6. | Georgia | 10-2-0 | Vince Dooley |
| 7. | Alabama | 9-2-1 | Bear Bryant |
| 8. | Miami (FL) | 9-2-0 | H. Schnellenberger |
| 9. | N Carolina | 10-2-0 | Dick Crum |
| 10. | Washington | 10-2-0 | Don James |
| 11. | Nebraska | 9-3-0 | Tom Osborne |
| 12. | Michigan | 9-3-0 | Bo Schembechler |
| 13. | Brigham Young | 11-2-0 | LaVell Edwards |
| 14. | Southern Cal | 9-3-0 | John Robinson |
| 15. | Ohio St | 9-3-0 | Earle Bruce |
| 16. | Arizona St | 9-2-0 | Darryl Rogers |
| 17. | W Virginia | 9-3-0 | Don Nehlen |
| 18. | Iowa | 8-4-0 | Hayden Fry |
| 19. | Missouri | 8-4-0 | Warren Powers |
| 20. | Oklahoma | 7-4-1 | Barry Switzer |

## 1982

| | | Record | Coach |
|---|---|---|---|
| 1. | Penn St | 11-1-0 | Joe Paterno |
| 2. | SMU | 11-0-1 | Bobby Collins |
| 3. | Nebraska | 12-1-0 | Tom Osborne |
| 4. | Georgia | 11-1-0 | Vince Dooley |
| 5. | UCLA | 10-1-1 | Terry Donahue |
| 6. | Arizona St | 10-2-0 | Darryl Rogers |
| 7. | Washington | 10-2-0 | Don James |
| 8. | Clemson | 9-1-1 | Danny Ford |
| 9. | Arkansas | 9-2-1 | Lou Holtz |
| 10. | Pittsburgh | 9-3-0 | Foge Fazio |
| 11. | Louisiana St | 8-3-1 | Jerry Stovall |
| 12. | Ohio St | 9-3-0 | Earle Bruce |

# Annual Associated Press Top 20 *(Cont.)*

## 1982 *(Cont.)*

| | Record | Coach |
|---|---|---|
| 13. Florida St | 9-3-0 | Bobby Bowden |
| 14. Auburn | 9-3-0 | Pat Dye |
| 15. Southern Cal | 8-3-0 | John Robinson |
| 16. Oklahoma | 8-4-0 | Barry Switzer |
| 17. Texas | 9-3-0 | Fred Akers |
| 18. N Carolina | 8-4-0 | Dick Crum |
| 19. W Virginia | 9-3-0 | Don Nehlen |
| 20. Maryland | 8-4-0 | Bobby Ross |

## 1983

| | Record | Coach |
|---|---|---|
| 1. Miami (FL) | 11-1-0 | H. Schnellenberger |
| 2. Nebraska | 12-1-0 | Tom Osborne |
| 3. Auburn | 11-1-0 | Pat Dye |
| 4. Georgia | 10-1-1 | Vince Dooley |
| 5. Texas | 11-1-0 | Fred Akers |
| 6. Florida | 9-2-1 | Charlie Pell |
| 7. Brigham Young | 11-1-0 | LaVell Edwards |
| 8. Michigan | 9-3-0 | Bo Schembechler |
| 9. Ohio St | 9-3-0 | Earle Bruce |
| 10. Illinois | 10-2-0 | Mike White |
| 11. Clemson | 9-1-1 | Danny Ford |
| 12. SMU | 10-2-0 | Bobby Collins |
| 13. Air Force | 10-2-0 | Ken Hatfield |
| 14. Iowa | 9-3-0 | Hayden Fry |
| 15. Alabama | 8-4-0 | Ray Perkins |
| 16. W Virginia | 9-3-0 | Don Nehlen |
| 17. UCLA | 7-4-1 | Terry Donahue |
| 18. Pittsburgh | 8-3-1 | Foge Fazio |
| 19. Boston College | 9-3-0 | Jack Bicknell |
| 20. E Carolina | 8-3-0 | Ed Emory |

## 1984

| | Record | Coach |
|---|---|---|
| 1. Brigham Young | 13-0-0 | LaVell Edwards |
| 2. Washington | 11-1-0 | Don James |
| 3. Florida | 9-1-1 | Chas Pell (0-1-1) Galen Hall (9-0) |
| 4. Nebraska | 10-2-0 | Tom Osborne |
| 5. Boston College | 10-2-0 | Jack Bicknell |
| 6. Oklahoma | 9-2-1 | Barry Switzer |
| 7. Oklahoma St | 10-2-0 | Pat Jones |
| 8. SMU | 10-2-0 | Bobby Collins |
| 9. UCLA | 9-3-0 | Terry Donahue |
| 10. Southern Cal | 10-3-0 | Ted Tollner |
| 11. S Carolina | 10-2-0 | Joe Morrison |
| 12. Maryland | 9-3-0 | Bobby Ross |
| 13. Ohio St | 9-3-0 | Earle Bruce |
| 14. Auburn | 9-4-0 | Pat Dye |
| 15. Louisiana St | 8-3-1 | Bill Arnsparger |
| 16. Iowa | 8-4-1 | Hayden Fry |
| 17. Florida St | 7-3-2 | Bobby Bowden |
| 18. Miami (FL) | 8-5-0 | Jimmy Johnson |
| 19. Kentucky | 9-3-0 | Jerry Claiborne |
| 20. Virginia | 8-2-2 | George Welsh |

## 1985

| | Record | Coach |
|---|---|---|
| 1. Oklahoma | 11-1-0 | Barry Switzer |
| 2. Michigan | 10-1-1 | Bo Schembechler |
| 3. Penn St | 11-1-0 | Joe Paterno |
| 4. Tennessee | 9-1-2 | Johnny Majors |
| 5. Florida | 9-1-1 | Galen Hall |
| 6. Texas A&M | 10-2-0 | Jackie Sherrill |
| 7. UCLA | 9-2-1 | Terry Donahue |
| 8. Air Force | 12-1-0 | Fisher DeBerry |

## 1985 *(Cont.)*

| | Record | Coach |
|---|---|---|
| 9. Miami (FL) | 10-2-0 | Jimmy Johnson |
| 10. Iowa | 10-2-0 | Hayden Fry |
| 11. Nebraska | 9-3-0 | Tom Osborne |
| 12. Arkansas | 10-2-0 | Ken Hatfield |
| 13. Alabama | 9-2-1 | Ray Perkins |
| 14. Ohio St | 9-3-0 | Earle Bruce |
| 15. Florida St | 9-3-0 | Bobby Bowden |
| 16. Brigham Young | 11-3-0 | LaVell Edwards |
| 17. Baylor | 9-3-0 | Grant Teaff |
| 18. Maryland | 9-3-0 | Bobby Ross |
| 19. Georgia Tech | 9-2-1 | Bill Curry |
| 20. Louisiana St | 9-2-1 | Bill Arnsparger |

## 1986

| | Record | Coach |
|---|---|---|
| 1. Penn St | 12-0-0 | Joe Paterno |
| 2. Miami (FL) | 11-1-0 | Jimmy Johnson |
| 3. Oklahoma | 11-1-0 | Barry Switzer |
| 4. Arizona St | 10-1-1 | John Cooper |
| 5. Nebraska | 10-2-0 | Tom Osborne |
| 6. Auburn | 10-2-0 | Pat Dye |
| 7. Ohio St | 10-3-0 | Earle Bruce |
| 8. Michigan | 11-2-0 | Bo Schembechler |
| 9. Alabama | 10-3-0 | Ray Perkins |
| 10. Louisiana St | 9-3-0 | Bill Arnsparger |
| 11. Arizona | 9-3-0 | Larry Smith |
| 12. Baylor | 9-3-0 | Grant Teaff |
| 13. Texas A&M | 9-3-0 | Jackie Sherrill |
| 14. UCLA | 8-3-1 | Terry Donahue |
| 15. Arkansas | 9-3-0 | Ken Hatfield |
| 16. Iowa | 9-3-0 | Hayden Fry |
| 17. Clemson | 8-2-2 | Danny Ford |
| 18. Washington | 8-3-1 | Don James |
| 19. Boston College | 9-3-0 | Jack Bicknell |
| 20. Virginia Tech | 9-2-1 | Bill Dooley |

## 1987

| | Record | Coach |
|---|---|---|
| 1. Miami (FL) | 12-0-0 | Jimmy Johnson |
| 2. Florida St | 11-1-0 | Bobby Bowden |
| 3. Oklahoma | 11-1-0 | Barry Switzer |
| 4. Syracuse | 11-0-1 | Dick MacPherson |
| 5. Louisiana St | 10-1-1 | Mike Archer |
| 6. Nebraska | 10-2-0 | Tom Osborne |
| 7. Auburn | 9-1-2 | Pat Dye |
| 8. Michigan St | 9-2-1 | George Perles |
| 9. UCLA | 10-2-0 | Terry Donahue |
| 10. Texas A&M | 10-2-0 | Jackie Sherrill |
| 11. Oklahoma St | 10-2-0 | Pat Jones |
| 12. Clemson | 10-2-0 | Danny Ford |
| 13. Georgia | 9-3-0 | Vince Dooley |
| 14. Tennessee | 10-2-1 | Johnny Majors |
| 15. S Carolina | 8-4-0 | Joe Morrison |
| 16. Iowa | 10-3-0 | Hayden Fry |
| 17. Notre Dame | 8-4-0 | Lou Holtz |
| 18. Southern Cal | 8-4-0 | Larry Smith |
| 19. Michigan | 8-4-0 | Bo Schembechler |
| 20. Arizona St | 7-4-1 | John Cooper |

## 1988

| | | Record | Coach |
|---|---|---|---|
| 1. | Notre Dame | 12-0-0 | Lou Holtz |
| 2. | Miami (FL) | 11-1-0 | Jimmy Johnson |
| 3. | Florida St | 11-1-0 | Bobby Bowden |
| 4. | Michigan | 9-2-1 | Bo Schembechler |
| 5. | W Virginia | 11-1-0 | Don Nehlen |
| 6. | UCLA | 10-2-0 | Terry Donahue |
| 7. | Southern Cal | 10-2-0 | Larry Smith |
| 8. | Auburn | 10-2-0 | Pat Dye |
| 9. | Clemson | 10-2-0 | Danny Ford |
| 10. | Nebraska | 11-2-0 | Tom Osborne |
| 11. | Oklahoma St | 10-2-0 | Pat Jones |
| 12. | Arkansas | 10-2-0 | Ken Hatfield |
| 13. | Syracuse | 10-2-0 | Dick MacPherson |
| 14. | Oklahoma | 9-3-0 | Barry Switzer |
| 15. | Georgia | 9-3-0 | Vince Dooley |
| 16. | Washington St | 9-3-0 | Dennis Erickson |
| 17. | Alabama | 9-3-0 | Bill Curry |
| 18. | Houston | 9-3-0 | Jack Pardee |
| 19. | Louisiana St | 8-4-0 | Mike Archer |
| 20. | Indiana | 8-3-1 | Bill Mallory |

## †1989

| | | Record | Coach |
|---|---|---|---|
| 1. | Miami (FL) | 11-1-0 | Dennis Erickson |
| 2. | Notre Dame | 12-1-0 | Lou Holtz |
| 3. | Florida St | 10-2-0 | Bobby Bowden |
| 4. | Colorado | 11-1-0 | Bill McCartney |
| 5. | Tennessee | 11-1-0 | Johnny Majors |
| 6. | Auburn | 10-2-0 | Pat Dye |
| 7. | Michigan | 10-2-0 | Bo Schembechler |
| 8. | Southern Cal | 9-2-1 | Larry Smith |
| 9. | Alabama | 10-2-0 | Bill Curry |
| 10. | Illinois | 10-2-0 | John Mackovic |
| 11. | Nebraska | 10-2-0 | Tom Osborne |
| 12. | Clemson | 10-2-0 | Danny Ford |
| 13. | Arkansas | 10-2-0 | Ken Hatfield |
| 14. | Houston | 9-2-0 | Jack Pardee |
| 15. | Penn St | 8-3-1 | Joe Paterno |
| 16. | Michigan St | 8-4-0 | George Perles |
| 17. | Pittsburgh | 8-3-1 | Mike Gottfried |
| 18. | Virginia | 10-3-0 | George Welsh |
| 19. | Texas Tech | 9-3-0 | Spike Dykes |
| 20. | Texas A&M | 8-4-0 | R.C. Slocum |
| 21. | W Virginia | 8-3-1 | Don Nehlen |
| 22. | Brigham Young | 10-3-0 | LaVell Edwards |
| 23. | Washington | 8-4-0 | Don James |
| 24. | Ohio St | 8-4-0 | John Cooper |
| 25. | Arizona | 8-4-0 | Dick Tomey |

## 1990

| | | Record | Coach |
|---|---|---|---|
| 1. | Colorado | 11-1-1 | Bill McCartney |
| 2. | #Georgia Tech | 11-0-1 | Bobby Ross |
| 3. | Miami (FL) | 10-2-0 | Dennis Erickson |
| 4. | Florida St | 10-2-0 | Bobby Bowden |
| 5. | Washington | 10-2-0 | Don James |
| 6. | Notre Dame | 9-3-0 | Lou Holtz |
| 7. | Michigan | 9-3-0 | Gary Moeller |
| 8. | Tennessee | 9-2-2 | Johnny Majors |
| 9. | Clemson | 10-2-0 | Ken Hatfield |
| 10. | Houston | 10-1-0 | John Jenkins |
| 11. | Penn St | 9-3-0 | Joe Paterno |
| 12. | Texas | 10-2-0 | David McWilliams |

## 1990 *(Cont.)*

| | | Record | Coach |
|---|---|---|---|
| 13. | Florida | 9-2-0 | Steve Spurrier |
| 14. | Louisville | 10-1-1 | H. Schnellenberger |
| 15. | Texas A&M | 9-3-1 | R.C. Slocum |
| 16. | Michigan St | 8-3-1 | George Perles |
| 17. | Oklahoma | 8-3-0 | Gary Gibbs |
| 18. | Iowa | 8-4-0 | Hayden Fry |
| 19. | Auburn | 8-3-1 | Pat Dye |
| 20. | Southern Cal | 8-4-1 | Larry Smith |
| 21. | Mississippi | 9-3-0 | Billy Brewer |
| 22. | Brigham Young | 10-3-0 | LaVell Edwards |
| 23. | Virginia | 8-4-0 | George Wells |
| 24. | Nebraska | 9-3-0 | Tom Osborne |
| 25. | Illinois | 8-4-0 | John Mackovic |

#Selected No. 1 by UPI.

## 1991

| | | Record | Coach |
|---|---|---|---|
| 1. | Miami (FL) | 12-0-0 | Dennis Erickson |
| 2. | #Washington | 12-0-0 | Don James |
| 3. | Penn St | 11-2-0 | Joe Paterno |
| 4. | Florida St | 11-2-0 | Bobby Bowden |
| 5. | Alabama | 11-1-0 | Gene Stallings |
| 6. | Michigan | 10-2-0 | Gary Moeller |
| 7. | Florida | 10-2-0 | Steve Spurrier |
| 8. | California | 10-2-0 | Bruce Snyder |
| 9. | E Carolina | 11-1-0 | Bill Lewis |
| 10. | Iowa | 10-1-1 | Hayden Fry |
| 11. | Syracuse | 10-2-0 | Paul Pasqualoni |
| 12. | Texas A&M | 10-2-0 | R.C. Slocum |
| 13. | Notre Dame | 10-3-0 | Lou Holtz |
| 14. | Tennessee | 9-3-0 | Johnny Majors |
| 15. | Nebraska | 9-2-1 | Tom Osborne |
| 16. | Oklahoma | 9-3-0 | Gary Gibbs |
| 17. | Georgia | 9-3-0 | Ray Goff |
| 18. | Clemson | 9-2-1 | Ken Hatfield |
| 19. | UCLA | 9-3-0 | Terry Donahue |
| 20. | Colorado | 8-3-1 | Bill McCartney |
| 21. | Tulsa | 10-2-0 | David Rader |
| 22. | Stanford | 8-4-0 | Dennis Green |
| 23. | Brigham Young | 8-3-2 | LaVell Edwards |
| 24. | N Carolina St | 9-3-0 | Dick Sheridan |
| 25. | Air Force | 10-3-0 | Fisher DeBerry |

#Selected No. 1 by *USA Today*/ CNN.

## 1992

| | | Record | Coach |
|---|---|---|---|
| 1. | Alabama | 13-0-0 | Gene Stallings |
| 2. | Florida St | 11-1-0 | Bobby Bowden |
| 3. | Miami | 11-1-0 | Dennis Erickson |
| 4. | Notre Dame | 10-1-1 | Lou Holtz |
| 5. | Michigan | 9-0-3 | Gary Moeller |
| 6. | Syracuse | 10-2-0 | Paul Pasqualoni |
| 7. | Texas A&M | 12-1-0 | R.C. Slocum |
| 8. | Georgia | 10-2-0 | Ray Goff |
| 9. | Stanford | 10-3-0 | Bill Walsh |
| 10. | Florida | 9-4-0 | Steve Spurrier |
| 11. | Washington | 9-3-0 | Don James |
| 12. | Tennessee | 9-3-0 | Johnny Majors |
| 13. | Colorado | 9-2-1 | Bill McCartney |
| 14. | Nebraska | 9-3-0 | Tom Osborne |
| 15. | Washington St | 9-3-0 | Mike Price |
| 16. | Mississippi | 9-3-0 | Billy Brewer |
| 17. | N Carolina St | 9-3-1 | Dick Sheridan |
| 18. | Ohio St | 8-3-1 | John Cooper |
| 19. | N Carolina | 9-3-0 | Mack Brown |
| 20. | Hawaii | 11-2-0 | Bob Wagner |

## 1992 *(Cont.)*

| | Record | Coach |
|---|---|---|
| 21. | Boston College ......8-3-1 | Tom Coughlin |
| 22. | Kansas ..................8-4-0 | Glen Mason |
| 23. | Mississippi St ........7-5-0 | Jackie Sherrill |
| 24. | Fresno St................9-4-0 | Jim Sweeney |
| 25. | Wake Forest...........8-4-0 | Bill Dooley |

## 1993

| | Record | Coach |
|---|---|---|
| 1. | Florida St..............12-1-0 | Bobby Bowden |
| 2. | Notre Dame..........11-1-0 | Lou Holtz |
| 3. | Nebraska ..............11-1-0 | Tom Osborne |
| 4. | Auburn .................11-0-0 | Terry Bowden |
| 5. | Florida ..................11-2-0 | Steve Spurrier |
| 6. | Wisconsin.............10-1-1 | Barry Alvarez |
| 7. | W Virginia.............11-1-0 | Don Nehlen |
| 8. | Penn St................10-2-0 | Joe Paterno |
| 9. | Texas A&M...........10-2-0 | R.C. Slocum |
| 10. | Arizona.................10-2-0 | Dick Tomey |
| 11. | Ohio St ................10-1-1 | John Cooper |
| 12. | Tennessee ...........9-2-1 | Phil Fulmer |
| 13. | Boston College .....9-3-0 | Tom Coughlin |
| 14. | Alabama................9-3-1 | Gene Stallings |
| 15. | Miami ...................9-3-0 | Dennis Erickson |
| 16. | Colorado...............8-3-1 | Bill McCartney |
| 17. | Oklahoma..............9-3-0 | Gary Gibbs |
| 18. | UCLA....................8-4-0 | Terry Donahue |
| 19. | N Carolina ...........10-3-0 | Mack Brown |
| 20. | Kansas St..............9-2-1 | Bill Snyder |
| 21. | Michigan................8-4-0 | Gary Moeller |
| 22. | Virginia Tech..........9-3-0 | Frank Beamer |
| 23. | Clemson.................9-3-0 | Ken Hatfield |
| 24. | Louisville ...............9-3-0 | H. Schnellenberger |
| 25. | California...............9-4-0 | Keith Gilbertson |

## 1994

| | Record | Coach |
|---|---|---|
| 1. | Nebraska ..............13-0-0 | Tom Osborne |
| 2. | Penn St................12-0-0 | Joe Paterno |
| 3. | Colorado...............11-1-0 | Bill McCartney |
| 4. | Florida St..............10-1-1 | Bobby Bowden |
| 5. | Alabama................12-1-0 | Gene Stallings |
| 6. | Miami (FL)..............10-2-0 | Dennis Erickson |
| 7. | Florida ..................10-2-1 | Steve Spurrier |
| 8. | Texas A&M...........10-0-1 | R.C. Slocum |
| 9. | Auburn ...................9-1-1 | Terry Bowden |
| 10. | Utah .....................10-2-0 | Ron McBride |
| 11. | Oregon...................9-4-0 | Rich Brooks |
| 12. | Michigan................8-4-0 | Gary Moeller |
| 13. | Southern Cal .........8-3-1 | John Robinson |
| 14. | Ohio St .................9-4-0 | John Cooper |
| 15. | Virginia .................9-3-0 | George Welsh |
| 16. | Colorado St ..........10-2-0 | Sonny Lubick |
| 17. | N Carolina St.........9-3-0 | Mike O'Cain |
| 18. | Brigham Young ....10-3-0 | LaVell Edwards |
| 19. | Kansas St..............9-3-0 | Bill Snyder |
| 20. | Arizona..................8-4-0 | Dick Tomey |
| 21. | Washington St........8-4-0 | Mike Price |
| 22. | Tennessee ............8-4-0 | Phillip Fulmer |
| 23. | Boston College ......7-4-1 | Dan Henning |
| 24. | Mississippi St ........8-4-0 | Jackie Sherrill |
| 25. | Texas ...................8-4-0 | John Mackovic |

## 1995

| | Record | Coach |
|---|---|---|
| 1. | Nebraska .............12-0-0 | Tom Osborne |
| 2. | Florida ..................12-1-0 | Steve Spurrier |
| 3. | Tennessee ...........11-1-0 | Phillip Fulmer |
| 4. | Florida St...............10-2-0 | Bobby Bowden |
| 5. | Colorado...............10-2-0 | Rick Neuheisel |
| 6. | Ohio St .................11-2-0 | John Cooper |
| 7. | Kansas St..............10-2-0 | Bill Snyder |
| 8. | Northwestern.........10-2-0 | Gary Barnett |
| 9. | Kansas .................10-2-0 | Glen Mason |
| 10. | Virginia Tech..........10-2-0 | Frank Beamer |
| 11. | Notre Dame............9-3-0 | Lou Holtz |
| 12. | Southern Cal .........9-2-1 | John Robinson |
| 13. | Penn St..................9-3-0 | Joe Paterno |
| 14. | Texas ...................10-2-1 | John Mackovic |
| 15. | Texas A&M.............9-3-0 | S.C. Slocum |
| 16. | Virginia .................9-4-0 | George Welsh |
| 17. | Michigan................9-4-0 | Lloyd Carr |
| 18. | Oregon...................9-3-0 | Mike Bellotti |
| 19. | Syracuse................9-3-0 | Paul Pasqualoni |
| 20. | Miami (FL)..............8-3-0 | Butch Davis |
| 21. | Alabama.................8-3-0 | Gene Stallings |
| 22. | Auburn ..................8-4-0 | Terry Bowden |
| 23. | Texas Tech ...........9-3-0 | Spike Dykes |
| 24. | Toledo ..................11-0-1 | Gary Pinkel |
| 25. | Iowa .....................8-4-0 | Hayden Fry |

## 1996

| | Record* | Coach |
|---|---|---|
| 1. | Florida....................12–1 | Steve Spurrier |
| 2. | Ohio St...................11–1 | John Cooper |
| 3. | Florida St ...............11–1 | Bobby Bowden |
| 4. | Arizona St ..............11–1 | Bruce Snyder |
| 5. | Brigham Young.......14–1 | LaVell Edwards |
| 6. | Nebraska ...............11–2 | Tom Osborne |
| 7. | Penn St...................11–2 | Joe Paterno |
| 8. | Colorado.................10–2 | Rick Neuheisel |
| 9. | Tennessee .............10–2 | Phillip Fulmer |
| 10. | N Carolina..............10–2 | Mack Brown |
| 11. | Alabama..................10–3 | Gene Stallings |
| 12. | Louisiana St............10–2 | Gerry DiNardo |
| 13. | Virginia Tech...........10–2 | Frank Beamer |
| 14. | Miami (FL)................9–3 | Butch Davis |
| 15. | Northwestern ..........9–3 | Gary Barnett |
| 16. | Washington.............9–3 | Jim Lambright |
| 17. | Kansas St ...............9–3 | Bill Snyder |
| 18. | Iowa........................9–3 | Hayden Fry |
| 19. | Notre Dame .............8–3 | Lou Holtz |
| 20. | Michigan.................8–4 | Lloyd Carr |
| 21. | Syracuse.................9–3 | Paul Pasqualoni |
| 22. | Wyoming.................10–2 | Joe Tiller |
| 23. | Texas .....................8–5 | John Mackovic |
| 24. | Auburn ....................8–4 | Terry Bowden |
| 25. | Army ......................10–2 | Bob Sutton |

†In 1989 the Associated Press expanded its final poll to 25 teams.

*In 1996 the NCAA introduced overtime to break ties.

### 1997

| | | Record | Coach |
|---|---|---|---|
| 1. | Michigan | 12–0 | Lloyd Carr |
| 2. | Nebraska | 13–0 | Tom Osborne |
| 3. | Florida St | 11–1 | Bobby Bowden |
| 4. | Florida | 10–2 | Steve Spurrier |
| 5. | UCLA | 10–2 | Bob Toledo |
| 6. | N Carolina | 11–1 | Mack Brown |
| 7. | Tennessee | 11–2 | Phillip Fulmer |
| 8. | Kansas St | 11–1 | Bill Snyder |
| 9. | Washington St | 10–2 | Mike Price |
| 10. | Georgia | 10–2 | Jim Donnan |
| 11. | Auburn | 10–3 | Terry Bowden |
| 12. | Ohio St | 10–3 | John Cooper |
| 13. | Louisiana St | 9–3 | Gerry DiNardo |
| 14. | Arizona St | 8–3 | Bruce Snyder |
| 15. | Purdue | 9–3 | Joe Tiller |
| 16. | Penn St | 9–3 | Joe Paterno |
| 17. | Colorado St | 11–2 | Sonny Lubick |
| 18. | Washington | 8–4 | Jim Lambright |
| 19. | Southern Mississippi | 9–3 | Jeff Bower |
| 20. | Texas A&M | 9–4 | R. C. Slocum |
| 21. | Syracuse | 9–4 | Paul Pasqualoni |
| 22. | Mississippi | 8–4 | Tommy Tuberville |
| 23. | Missouri | 7–5 | Larry Smith |
| 24. | Oklahoma St | 8–4 | Bob Simmons |
| 25. | Georgia Tech | 7–5 | George O'Leary |

### 1998

| | | Record | Coach |
|---|---|---|---|
| 1. | Tennessee | 13–0 | Phillip Fulmer |
| 2. | Ohio St | 11–1 | John Cooper |
| 3. | Florida St | 11–2 | Bobby Bowden |
| 4. | Arizona | 12–1 | Dick Tomey |
| 5. | Florida | 10–2 | Steve Spurrier |
| 6. | Wisconsin | 11–1 | Barry Alvarez |
| 7. | Tulane | 12–0 | Tommy Bowden |
| 8. | UCLA | 10–2 | Bob Toledo |
| 9. | Georgia Tech | 10–2 | George O'Leary |
| 10. | Kansas St | 11–2 | Bill Snyder |
| 11. | Texas A&M | 11–3 | R.C. Slocum |
| 12. | Michigan | 10–3 | Lloyd Carr |
| 13. | Air Force | 12–1 | Fisher DeBerry |
| 14. | Georgia | 9–3 | Jim Donnan |
| 15. | Texas | 9–3 | Mack Brown |
| 16. | Arkansas | 9–3 | Houston Nutt |
| 17. | Penn St | 9–3 | Joe Paterno |
| 18. | Virginia | 9–3 | George Welsh |
| 19. | Nebraska | 9–4 | Frank Solich |
| 20. | Miami (FL) | 9–3 | Butch Davis |
| 21. | Missouri | 8–4 | Larry Smith |
| 22. | Notre Dame | 9–3 | Bob Davie |
| 23. | Virginia Tech | 9–3 | Frank Beamer |
| 24. | Purdue | 9–4 | Joe Tiller |
| 25. | Syracuse | 8–4 | Paul Pasqualoni |

### 1999

| | | Record | Coach |
|---|---|---|---|
| 1. | Florida St | 12–0 | Bobby Bowden |
| 2. | Virginia Tech | 11–1 | Frank Beamer |
| 3. | Nebraska | 12–1 | Frank Solich |
| 4. | Wisconsin | 10–2 | Barry Alvarez |
| 5. | Michigan | 10–2 | Lloyd Carr |
| 6. | Kansas St | 11–1 | Bill Snyder |
| 7. | Michigan St | 10–2 | Nick Saban |
| 8. | Alabama | 10–3 | Mike DuBose |
| 9. | Tennessee | 9–3 | Phillip Fulmer |
| 10. | Marshall | 13–0 | Bob Pruett |
| 11. | Penn St | 10–3 | Joe Paterno |
| 12. | Florida | 9–4 | Steve Spurrier |
| 13. | Mississippi St | 10–2 | Jackie Sherrill |
| 14. | Southern Miss | 9–3 | Jeff Bower |
| 15. | Miami (FL) | 9–4 | Butch Davis |
| 16. | Georgia | 8–4 | Jim Donnan |
| 17. | Arkansas | 8–4 | Houston Nutt |
| 18. | Minnesota | 8–4 | Glen Mason |
| 19. | Oregon | 9–3 | Mike Bellotti |
| 20. | Georgia Tech | 8–4 | Goerge O'Leary |
| 21. | Texas | 9–5 | Mack Brown |
| 22. | Mississippi | 8–4 | David Cutcliffe |
| 23. | Texas A&M | 8–4 | R.C. Slocum |
| 24. | Illinois | 8–4 | Ron Turner |
| 25. | Purdue | 7–5 | Joe Tiller |

### 2000

| | | Record | Coach |
|---|---|---|---|
| 1. | Oklahoma | 13–0 | Bob Stoops |
| 2. | Miami (FL) | 11–1 | Butch Davis |
| 3. | Washington | 11–1 | Rick Neuheisel |
| 4. | Oregon St | 11–1 | Dennis Erickson |
| 5. | Florida St | 11–2 | Bobby Bowden |
| 6. | Virginia Tech | 11–1 | Frank Beamer |
| 7. | Oregon | 10–2 | Mike Belotti |
| 8. | Nebraska | 10–2 | Frank Solich |
| 9. | Kansas St | 11–3 | Bill Snyder |
| 10. | Florida | 10–3 | Steve Spurrier |
| 11. | Michigan | 9–3 | Lloyd Carr |
| 12. | Texas | 9–3 | Mack Brown |
| 13. | Purdue | 8–4 | Joe Tiller |
| 14. | Colorado St | 10–2 | Sonny Lubeck |
| 15. | Notre Dame | 9–3 | Bob Davie |
| 16. | Clemson | 9–3 | Tommy Bowden |
| 17. | Georgia Tech | 9–3 | George O'Leary |
| 18. | Auburn | 9–4 | Tommy Tuberville |
| 19. | S Carolina | 8–4 | Lou Holtz |
| 20. | Georgia | 8–4 | Jim Donnan |
| 21. | Texas Christian | 10–2 | Dennis Franchione |
| 22. | Louisiana State | 8–4 | Nick Saban |
| 23. | Wisconsin | 9–4 | Barry Alvarez |
| 24. | Mississippi St | 8–4 | Jackie Sherrill |
| 25. | Iowa St | 9–3 | Dan McCarney |

# NCAA Divisional Championships

## Division I-AA

| Year | Winner | Runner-Up | Score |
|------|--------|-----------|-------|
| 1978 | Florida A&M | Massachusetts | 35–28 |
| 1979 | Eastern Kentucky | Lehigh | 30–7 |
| 1980 | Boise St | Eastern Kentucky | 31–29 |
| 1981 | Idaho St | Eastern Kentucky | 34–23 |
| 1982 | Eastern Kentucky | Delaware | 17–14 |
| 1983 | Southern Illinois | Western Carolina | 43–7 |
| 1984 | Montana St | Louisiana Tech | 19–6 |
| 1985 | Georgia Southern | Furman | 44–42 |
| 1986 | Georgia Southern | Arkansas St | 48–21 |
| 1987 | NE Louisiana | Marshall | 43–42 |
| 1988 | Furman | Georgia Southern | 17–12 |
| 1989 | Georgia Southern | Stephen F. Austin St | 37–34 |
| 1990 | Georgia Southern | NV-Reno | 36–13 |
| 1991 | Youngstown St | Marshall | 25–17 |
| 1992 | Marshall | Youngstown St | 31–28 |
| 1993 | Youngstown St | Marshall | 17–5 |
| 1994 | Youngstown St | Boise St | 28–14 |
| 1995 | Montana | Marshall | 22–20 |
| 1996 | Marshall | Montana | 49–29 |
| 1997 | Youngstown St | McNesse St | 10–9 |
| 1998 | Massachusetts | Georgia Southern | 55–43 |
| 1999 | Georgia Southern | Youngstown St | 59–24 |
| 2000 | Georgia Southern | Montana | 27–25 |

## Division II

| Year | Winner | Runner-Up | Score |
|------|--------|-----------|-------|
| 1973 | Louisiana Tech | Western Kentucky | 34–0 |
| 1974 | Central Michigan | Delaware | 54–14 |
| 1975 | Northern Michigan | Western Kentucky | 16–14 |
| 1976 | Montana St | Akron | 24–13 |
| 1977 | Lehigh | Jacksonville St | 33–0 |
| 1978 | Eastern Illinois | Delaware | 10–9 |
| 1979 | Delaware | Youngstown St | 38–21 |
| 1980 | Cal Poly SLO | Eastern Illinois | 21–13 |
| 1981 | SW Texas St | N Dakota St | 42–13 |
| 1982 | SW Texas St | UC–Davis | 34–9 |
| 1983 | N Dakota St | Central St (OH) | 41–21 |
| 1984 | Troy St | N Dakota St | 18–17 |
| 1985 | N Dakota St | N Alabama | 35–7 |
| 1986 | N Dakota St | S Dakota | 27–7 |
| 1987 | Troy St | Portland St | 31–17 |
| 1988 | N Dakota St | Portland St | 35–21 |
| 1989 | Mississippi College | Jacksonville St | 3–0 |
| 1990 | N Dakota St | Indiana (PA) | 51–11 |
| 1991 | Pittsburg St | Jacksonville St | 23–6 |
| 1992 | Jacksonville St | Pittsburg St | 17–13 |
| 1993 | N Alabama | Indiana (PA) | 41–34 |
| 1994 | N Alabama | Texas A&M–Kingsville | 16–10 |
| 1995 | N Alabama | Pittsburg St | 27–7 |
| 1996 | Northern Colorado | Carson-Newman | 23–14 |
| 1997 | Northern Colorado | New Haven | 51–0 |
| 1998 | NW Missouri St | Carson-Newman | 24–6 |
| 1999 | NW Missouri St | Carson-Newman | 58–52 (OT) |
| 2000 | Delta St | Bloomsburg | 63–34 |

## Division III

| Year | Winner | Runner-Up | Score |
|------|--------|-----------|-------|
| 1973 | Wittenberg | Juniata | 41–0 |
| 1974 | Central (IA) | Ithaca | 10–8 |
| 1975 | Wittenberg | Ithaca | 28–0 |
| 1976 | St. John's (MN) | Towson St | 31–28 |
| 1977 | Widener | Wabash | 39–36 |
| 1978 | Baldwin-Wallace | Wittenberg | 24–10 |
| 1979 | Ithaca | Wittenberg | 14–10 |
| 1980 | Dayton | Ithaca | 63–0 |
| 1981 | Widener | Dayton | 17–10 |
| 1982 | W Georgia | Augustana (IL) | 14–0 |
| 1983 | Augustana (IL) | Union (NY) | 21–17 |

## Division III (Cont.)

| Year | Winner | Runner-Up | Score |
|------|--------|-----------|-------|
| 1984 | Augustana (IL) | Central (IA) | 21–12 |
| 1985 | Augustana (IL) | Ithaca | 20–7 |
| 1986 | Augustana (IL) | Salisbury St | 31–3 |
| 1987 | Wagner | Dayton | 19–3 |
| 1988 | Ithaca | Central (IA) | 39–24 |
| 1989 | Dayton | Union (NY) | 17–7 |
| 1990 | Allegheny | Lycoming | 21–14 (OT) |
| 1991 | Ithaca | Dayton | 34–20 |
| 1992 | WI-LaCrosse | Washington & Jefferson | 16–12 |
| 1993 | Mount Union | Rowan | 34–24 |
| 1994 | Albion | Washington & Jefferson | 38–15 |
| 1995 | WI-LaCrosse | Rowan | 36–7 |
| 1996 | Mount Union | Rowan | 56–24 |
| 1997 | Mount Union | Lycoming | 61–12 |
| 1998 | Mount Union | Rowan | 44–24 |
| 1999 | Pacific Lutheran | Rowan | 42–13 |
| 2000 | Mount Union | St. John's | 10–7 |

# NAIA Divisional Championships

## Division I

| Year | Winner | Runner-Up | Score |
|------|--------|-----------|-------|
| 1956 | St. Joseph's (IN)/ Montana St | | 0–0 |
| 1957 | Pittsburg St (KS) | Hillsdale (MI) | 27–26 |
| 1958 | NE Oklahoma | Northern Arizona | 19–13 |
| 1959 | Texas A&I | Lenoir-Rhyne (NC) | 20–7 |
| 1960 | Lenoir-Rhyne (NC) | Humboldt St (CA) | 15–14 |
| 1961 | Pittsburg St (KS) | Linfield (OR) | 12–7 |
| 1962 | Central St (OK) | Lenoir-Rhyne (NC) | 28–13 |
| 1963 | St. John's (MN) | Prairie View (TX) | 33–27 |
| 1964 | Concordia-Moorhead/ Sam Houston | | 7–7 |
| 1965 | St. John's (MN) | Linfield (OR) | 33–0 |
| 1966 | Waynesburg (PA) | WI-Whitewater | 42–21 |
| 1967 | Fairmont St (WV) | Eastern Washington | 28–21 |
| 1968 | Troy St (MI) | Texas A&I | 43–35 |
| 1969 | Texas A&I | Concordia-Moorhead (MN) | 32–7 |
| 1970 | Texas A&I | Wofford (SC) | 48–7 |
| 1971 | Livingston (AL) | Arkansas Tech | 14–12 |
| 1972 | E Texas St | Carson-Newman (TN) | 21–18 |
| 1973 | Abilene Christian | Elon (NC) | 42–14 |
| 1974 | Texas A&I | Henderson St (AR) | 34–23 |
| 1975 | Texas A&I | Salem (WV) | 37–0 |
| 1976 | Texas A&I | Central Arkansas | 26–0 |
| 1977 | Abilene Christian | SW Oklahoma | 24–7 |
| 1978 | Angelo St (TX) | Elon (NC) | 34–14 |
| 1979 | Texas A&I | Central St (OK) | 20–14 |
| 1980 | Elon (NC) | NE Oklahoma | 17–10 |
| 1981 | Elon (NC) | Pittsburg St | 3–0 |
| 1982 | Central St (OK) | Mesa (CO) | 14–11 |
| 1983 | Carson-Newman (TN) | Mesa (CO) | 36–28 |
| 1984 | Carson-Newman (TN)/ Central Arkansas | | 19–19 |
| 1985 | Central Arkansas/ Hillsdale (MI) | | 10–10 |
| 1986 | Carson-Newman (TN) | Cameron (OK) | 17–0 |
| 1987 | Cameron (OK) | Carson-Newman (TN) | 30–2 |
| 1988 | Carson-Newman (TN) | Adams St (CO) | 56–21 |
| 1989 | Carson-Newman (TN) | Emporia St (KS) | 34–20 |
| 1990 | Central St (OH) | Mesa St (CO) | 38–16 |
| 1991 | Central Arkansas | Central St (OH) | 19–16 |
| 1992 | Central St (OH) | Gardner-Webb (NC) | 19–16 |
| 1993 | E Central (OK) | Glenville St (WV) | 49–35 |
| 1994 | Northeastern St (OK) | Arkansas–Pine Bluff | 13–12 |
| 1995 | Central St (OH) | Northeastern St (OK) | 37–7 |
| 1996 | SW Oklahoma St | Montana Tech | 33–31 |
| 1997 | Findlay (OH) | Willamette (OR) | 14–7 |
| 1998 | Azusa Pacific | Olivet Nazarene | 17–14 |
| 1999 | Northwestern Oklahoma St | Georgetown (KY) | 34–26 |
| 2000 | Georgetown (KY) | Northwestern Oklahoma St | 20–0 |

# NAIA Divisional Championships† (Cont.)

## Division II

| Year | Winner | Runner-Up | Score |
|------|--------|-----------|-------|
| 1970 | Westminster (PA) | Anderson (IN) | 21–16 |
| 1971 | California Lutheran | Westminster (PA) | 30–14 |
| 1972 | Missouri Southern | Northwestern (IA) | 21–14 |
| 1973 | Northwestern (IA) | Glenville St (WV) | 10–3 |
| 1974 | Texas Lutheran | Missouri Valley | 42–0 |
| 1975 | Texas Lutheran | California Lutheran | 34–8 |
| 1976 | Westminster (PA) | Redlands (CA) | 20–13 |
| 1977 | Westminster (PA) | California Lutheran | 17–9 |
| 1978 | Concordia-Moorhead (MN) | Findlay (OH) | 7–0 |
| 1979 | Findlay (OH) | Northwestern (IA) | 51–6 |
| 1980 | Pacific Lutheran | Wilmington (OH) | 38–10 |
| 1981 | Austin Coll./ Conc.-Moorhead (MN) | | 24–24 |
| 1982 | Linfield (OR) | William Jewell (MO) | 33–15 |
| 1983 | Northwestern (IA) | Pacific Lutheran | 25–21 |
| 1984 | Linfield (OR) | Northwestern (IA) | 33–22 |
| 1985 | WI-La Crosse | Pacific Lutheran | 24–7 |
| 1986 | Linfield (OR) | Baker (KS) | 17–0 |
| 1987 | Pacific Lutheran | WI-Stevens Point* | 16–16 |
| 1988 | Westminster (PA) | WI-La Crosse | 21–14 |
| 1989 | Westminster (PA) | WI-La Crosse | 51–30 |
| 1990 | Peru St (NE) | Westminster (PA) | 17–7 |
| 1991 | Georgetown (KY) | Pacific Lutheran | 28–20 |
| 1992 | Findlay (OH) | Linfield (OR) | 26–13 |
| 1993 | Pacific Lutheran (WA) | Westminster (PA) | 50–20 |
| 1994 | Westminster (PA) | Pacific Lutheran | 27–7 |
| 1995 | Findlay (OH)/ Central Washington | | 21–21 |
| 1996 | Sioux Falls (SD) | Western Washington | 47–25 |

*Forfeited 1987 season due to use of an ineligible player.  †In 1997 the NAIA consolidated its two divisions into one.

# Awards

## Heisman Memorial Trophy

Awarded to the best college player by the Downtown Athletic Club of New York City. The trophy is named after John W. Heisman, who coached Georgia Tech to the national championship in 1917 and later served as DAC athletic director.

| Year | Winner, College, Position | Winner's Season Statistics | Runner-Up, College |
|------|---------------------------|----------------------------|--------------------|
| 1935 | Jay Berwanger, Chicago, HB | Rush: 119  Yds: 577  TD: 6 | Monk Meyer, Army |
| 1936 | Larry Kelley, Yale, E | Rec: 17  Yds: 372  TD: 6 | Sam Francis, Nebraska |
| 1937 | Clint Frank, Yale, HB | Rush: 157  Yds: 667  TD: 11 | Byron White, Colorado |
| 1938 | †Davey O'Brien, Texas Christian, QB | Att/Comp: 194/110  Yds: 1733  TD: 19 | Marshall Goldberg, Pittsburgh |
| 1939 | Nile Kinnick, Iowa, HB | Rush: 106  Yds: 374  TD: 5 | Tom Harmon, Michigan |
| 1940 | Tom Harmon, Michigan, HB | Rush: 191  Yds: 852  TD: 16 | John Kimbrough, Texas A&M |
| 1941 | †Bruce Smith, Minnesota, HB | Rush: 98  Yds: 480  TD: 6 | Angelo Bertelli, Notre Dame |
| 1942 | Frank Sinkwich, Georgia, HB | Att/Comp: 166/84  Yds: 1392  TD: 10 | Paul Governali, Columbia |
| 1943 | Angelo Bertelli, Notre Dame, QB | Att/Comp: 36/25  Yds: 511  TD: 10 | Bob Odell, Pennsylvania |
| 1944 | Les Horvath, Ohio State, QB | Rush: 163  Yds: 924  TD: 12 | Glenn Davis, Army |
| 1945 | *†Doc Blanchard, Army, FB | Rush: 101  Yds: 718  TD: 13 | Glenn Davis, Army |
| 1946 | Glenn Davis, Army, HB | Rush: 123  Yds: 712  TD: 7 | Charley Trippi, Georgia |
| 1947 | †John Lujack, Notre Dame, QB | Att/Comp: 109/61  Yds: 777  TD: 9 | Bob Chappius, Michigan |
| 1948 | *Doak Walker, Southern Methodist, HB | Rush: 108  Yds: 532  TD: 8 | Charlie Justice, N Carolina |
| 1949 | †Leon Hart, Notre Dame, E | Rec: 19  Yds: 257  TD: 5 | Charlie Justice, N Carolina |
| 1950 | *Vic Janowicz, Ohio St, HB | Att/Comp: 77/32  Yds: 561  TD: 12 | Kyle Rote, Southern Methodist |
| 1951 | Dick Kazmaier, Princeton, HB | Rush: 149  Yds: 861  TD: 9 | Hank Lauricella, Tennessee |
| 1952 | Billy Vessels, Oklahoma, HB | Rush: 167  Yds: 1072  TD: 17 | Jack Scarbath, Maryland |
| 1953 | John Lattner, Notre Dame, HB | Rush: 134  Yds: 651  TD: 6 | Paul Giel, Minnesota |
| 1954 | Alan Ameche, Wisconsin, FB | Rush: 146  Yds: 641  TD: 9 | Kurt Burris, Oklahoma |
| 1955 | Howard Cassady, Ohio St, HB | Rush: 161  Yds: 958  TD: 15 | Jim Swink, Texas Christian |
| 1956 | Paul Hornung, Notre Dame, QB | Att/Comp: 111/59  Yds: 917  TD: 3 | Johnny Majors, Tennessee |
| 1957 | John David Crow, Texas A&M, HB | Rush: 129  Yds: 562  TD: 10 | Alex Karras, Iowa |
| 1958 | Pete Dawkins, Army, HB | Rush: 78  Yds: 428  TD: 6 | Randy Duncan, Iowa |

## Heisman Memorial Trophy *(Cont.)*

| Year | Winner, College, Position | Winner's Season Statistics | Runner-Up, College |
|---|---|---|---|
| 1959 | ...Billy Cannon, Louisiana St, HB | Rush: 139 Yds: 598 TD: 6 | Rich Lucas, Penn St |
| 1960 | ...Joe Bellino, Navy, HB | Rush: 168 Yds: 834 TD: 18 | Tom Brown, Minnesota |
| 1961 | ...Ernie Davis, Syracuse, HB | Rush: 150 Yds: 823 TD: 15 | Bob Ferguson, Ohio St |
| 1962 | ...Terry Baker, Oregon St, QB | Att/Comp: 203/112 Yds: 1738 TD: 15 | Jerry Stovall, Louisiana St |
| 1963 | ...*Roger Staubach, Navy, QB | Att/Comp: 161/107 Yds: 1474 TD: 7 | Billy Lothridge, Georgia Tech |
| 1964 | ...John Huarte, Notre Dame, QB | Att/Comp: 205/114 Yds: 2062 TD: 16 | Jerry Rhome, Tulsa |
| 1965 | ...Mike Garrett, Southern Cal, HB | Rush: 267 Yds: 1440 TD: 16 | Howard Twilley, Tulsa |
| 1966 | ...Steve Spurrier, Florida, QB | Att/Comp: 291/179 Yds: 2012 TD: 16 | Bob Griese, Purdue |
| 1967 | ...Gary Beban, UCLA, QB | Att/Comp: 156/87 Yds: 1359 TD: 8 | O.J. Simpson, Southern Cal |
| 1968 | ...O.J. Simpson, Southern Cal, HB | Rush: 383 Yds: 1880 TD: 23 | Leroy Keyes, Purdue |
| 1969 | ...Steve Owens, Oklahoma, FB | Rush: 358 Yds: 1523 TD: 23 | Mike Phipps, Purdue |
| 1970 | ...Jim Plunkett, Stanford, QB | Att/Comp: 358/191 Yds: 2715 TD: 18 | Joe Theismann, Notre Dame |
| 1971 | ...Pat Sullivan, Auburn, QB | Att/Comp: 281/162 Yds: 2012 TD: 20 | Ed Marinaro, Cornell |
| 1972 | ...Johnny Rodgers, Nebraska, FL | Rec: 55 Yds: 942 TD: 17 | Greg Pruitt, Oklahoma |
| 1973 | ...John Cappelletti, Penn St, HB | Rush: 286 Yds: 1522 TD: 17 | John Hicks, Ohio St |
| 1974 | ...*Archie Griffin, Ohio St, HB | Rush: 256 Yds: 1695 TD: 12 | Anthony Davis, Southern Cal |
| 1975 | ...Archie Griffin, Ohio St, HB | Rush: 262 Yds: 1450 TD: 4 | Chuck Muncie, California |
| 1976 | ...†Tony Dorsett, Pittsburgh, HB | Rush: 370 Yds: 2150 TD: 23 | Ricky Bell, Southern Cal |
| 1977 | ...Earl Campbell, Texas, FB | Rush: 267 Yds: 1744 TD: 19 | Terry Miller, Oklahoma St |
| 1978 | ...*Billy Sims, Oklahoma, HB | Rush: 231 Yds: 1762 TD: 20 | Chuck Fusina, Penn St |
| 1979 | ...Charles White, Southern Cal, HB | Rush: 332 Yds: 1803 TD: 19 | Billy Sims, Oklahoma |
| 1980 | ...George Rogers, S Carolina, HB | Rush: 324 Yds: 1894 TD: 14 | Hugh Green, Pittsburgh |
| 1981 | ...Marcus Allen, Southern Cal, HB | Rush: 433 Yds: 2427 TD: 23 | Herschel Walker, Georgia |
| 1982 | ...*Herschel Walker, Georgia, HB | Rush: 335 Yds: 1752 TD: 17 | John Elway, Stanford |
| 1983 | ...Mike Rozier, Nebraska, HB | Rush: 275 Yds: 2148 TD: 29 | Steve Young, Brigham Young |
| 1984 | ...Doug Flutie, Boston College, QB | Att/Comp: 396/233 Yds: 3454 TD: 27 | Keith Byars, Ohio St |
| 1985 | ...Bo Jackson, Auburn, HB | Rush: 278 Yds: 1786 TD: 17 | Chuck Long, Iowa |
| 1986 | ...Vinny Testaverde, Miami (FL), QB | Att/Comp: 276/175 Yds: 2557 TD: 26 | Paul Palmer, Temple |
| 1987 | ...Tim Brown, Notre Dame, WR | Rec: 39 Yds: 846 TD: 7 | Don McPherson, Syracuse |
| 1988 | ...*Barry Sanders, Oklahoma St, RB | Rush: 344 Yds: 2628 TD: 39 | Rodney Peete, Southern Cal |
| 1989 | ...*Andre Ware, Houston, QB | Att/Comp: 578/365 Yds: 4699 TD: 46 | Anthony Thompson, Indiana |
| 1990 | ...*Ty Detmer, Brigham Young, QB | Att/Comp: 562/361 Yds: 5188 TD: 41 | Raghib Ismail, Notre Dame |
| 1991 | ...*Desmond Howard, Michigan, WR | Rec: 61 Yds: 950 TD: 23 | Casey Weldon, Florida St |
| 1992 | ...Gino Torretta, Miami (FL), QB | Att/Comp: 402/228 Yds: 3060 TD: 19 | Marshall Faulk, San Diego St |
| 1993 | ...†Charlie Ward, Florida St, QB | Att/Comp: 380/264 Yds: 3032 TD: 27 | Heath Shuler, Tennessee |
| 1994 | ...Rashaan Salaam, Colorado, RB | Rush: 298 Yds: 2055 TD: 24 | Ki-Jana Carter, Penn St |
| 1995 | ...Eddie George, Ohio State, RB | Rush: 303 Yds: 1826 TD: 23 | Tommie Frazier, Nebraska |
| 1996 | ...†Danny Wuerffel, Florida, QB | Att/Comp: 360/207 Yds: 3625 TD: 39 | Troy Davis, Iowa St |
| 1997 | ...†Charles Woodson, Michigan, CB/ WR | 7 interceptions; Rec: 11 Yds: 231 TD: 4 | Peyton Manning, Tennessee |
| 1998 | ...Ricky Williams, Texas, RB | Rush: 361 Yds: 2124 TD: 28 | Michael Bishop, Kansas St |
| 1999 | ...Ron Dayne, Wisconsin, RB | Rush: 303 Yds: 1834 TD: 19 | Joe Hamilton, Georgia Tech |
| 2000 | ...Chris Weinke, Florida St, QB | Att/Comp: 431/266 Yds: 4167 TD: 33 | Josh Heupel, Oklahoma |

*Juniors (all others seniors). †Winners who played for national championship teams the same year.

Note: Former Heisman winners and national media cast votes, with ballots allowing for three names (3 points for first, 2 for second and 1 for third).

## Maxwell Award

Given to the nation's outstanding college football player by the Maxwell Football Club of Philadelphia.

| Year | Player, College, Position | Year | Player, College, Position |
|---|---|---|---|
| 1937 | Clint Frank, Yale, HB | 1969 | Mike Reid, Penn St, DT |
| 1938 | Davey O'Brien, Texas Christian, QB | 1970 | Jim Plunkett, Stanford, QB |
| 1939 | Nile Kinnick, Iowa, HB | 1971 | Ed Marinaro, Cornell, RB |
| 1940 | Tom Harmon, Michigan, HB | 1972 | Brad Van Pelt, Michigan St, DB |
| 1941 | Bill Dudley, Virginia, HB | 1973 | John Cappelletti, Penn St, RB |
| 1942 | Paul Governali, Columbia, QB | 1974 | Steve Joachim, Temple, QB |
| 1943 | Bob Odell, Pennsylvania, HB | 1975 | Archie Griffin, Ohio St, RB |
| 1944 | Glenn Davis, Army, HB | 1976 | Tony Dorsett, Pittsburgh, RB |
| 1945 | Doc Blanchard, Army, FB | 1977 | Ross Browner, Notre Dame, DE |
| 1946 | Charley Trippi, Georgia, HB | 1978 | Chuck Fusina, Penn St, QB |
| 1947 | Doak Walker, Southern Meth, HB | 1979 | Charles White, Southern Cal, RB |
| 1948 | Chuck Bednarik, Pennsylvania, C | 1980 | Hugh Green, Pittsburgh, DE |
| 1949 | Leon Hart, Notre Dame, E | 1981 | Marcus Allen, Southern Cal, RB |
| 1950 | Reds Bagnell, Pennsylvania, HB | 1982 | Herschel Walker, Georgia, RB |
| 1951 | Dick Kazmaier, Princeton, HB | 1983 | Mike Rozier, Nebraska, RB |
| 1952 | John Lattner, Notre Dame, HB | 1984 | Doug Flutie, Boston College, QB |
| 1953 | John Lattner, Notre Dame, HB | 1985 | Chuck Long, Iowa, QB |
| 1954 | Ron Beagle, Navy, E | 1986 | Vinny Testaverde, Miami (FL), QB |
| 1955 | Howard Cassady, Ohio St, HB | 1987 | Don McPherson, Syracuse, QB |
| 1956 | Tommy McDonald, Oklahoma, HB | 1988 | Barry Sanders, Oklahoma St, RB |
| 1957 | Bob Reifsnyder, Navy, T | 1989 | Anthony Thompson, Indiana, RB |
| 1958 | Pete Dawkins, Army, HB | 1990 | Ty Detmer, Brigham Young, QB |
| 1959 | Rich Lucas, Penn St, QB | 1991 | Desmond Howard, Michigan, WR |
| 1960 | Joe Bellino, Navy, HB | 1992 | Gino Torretta, Miami (FL), QB |
| 1961 | Bob Ferguson, Ohio St, FB | 1993 | Charlie Ward, Florida St, QB |
| 1962 | Terry Baker, Oregon St, QB | 1994 | Kerry Collins, Penn St, QB |
| 1963 | Roger Staubach, Navy, QB | 1995 | Eddie George, Ohio St, RB |
| 1964 | Glenn Ressler, Penn St, C | 1996 | Danny Wuerffel, Florida, QB |
| 1965 | Tommy Nobis, Texas, LB | 1997 | Peyton Manning, Tennessee, QB |
| 1966 | Jim Lynch, Notre Dame, LB | 1998 | Ricky Williams, Texas, RB |
| 1967 | Gary Beban, UCLA, QB | 1999 | Ron Dayne, Wisconsin, RB |
| 1968 | O.J. Simpson, Southern Cal, RB | 2000 | Drew Brees, Purdue, QB |

## Davey O'Brien National Quarterback Award

Given to the top quarterback in the nation by the Davey O'Brien Educational and Charitable Trust of Fort Worth. Named for Texas Christian Hall of Fame quarterback Davey O'Brien (1936–38).

| Year | Player, College | Year | Player, College |
|---|---|---|---|
| 1981 | Jim McMahon, Brigham Young | 1991 | Ty Detmer, Brigham Young |
| 1982 | Todd Blackledge, Penn St | 1992 | Gino Torretta, Miami (FL) |
| 1983 | Steve Young, Brigham Young | 1993 | Charlie Ward, Florida St |
| 1984 | Doug Flutie, Boston College | 1994 | Kerry Collins, Penn St |
| 1985 | Chuck Long, Iowa | 1995 | Danny Wuerffel, Florida |
| 1986 | Vinny Testaverde, Miami (FL) | 1996 | Danny Wuerffel, Florida |
| 1987 | Don McPherson, Syracuse | 1997 | Peyton Manning, Tennessee |
| 1988 | Troy Aikman, UCLA | 1998 | Michael Bishop, Kansas St |
| 1989 | Andre Ware, Houston | 1099 | Joe Hamilton, Georgia Tech |
| 1990 | Ty Detmer, Brigham Young | 2000 | Chris Weinke, Florida St |

Note: Originally honored the outstanding football player in the Southwest as follows: 1977—Earl Campbell, Texas, RB; 1978—Billy Sims, Oklahoma, RB; 1979—Mike Singletary, Baylor, LB; 1980—Mike Singletary, Baylor, LB.

## Vince Lombardi/Rotary Award

Given to the outstanding college lineman of the year, the award is sponsored by the Rotary Club of Houston.

| Year | Player, College, Position | Year | Player, College, Position |
|---|---|---|---|
| 1970 | Jim Stillwagon, Ohio St, MG | 1986 | Cornelius Bennett, Alabama, LB |
| 1971 | Walt Patulski, Notre Dame, DE | 1987 | Chris Spielman, Ohio St, LB |
| 1972 | Rich Glover, Nebraska, MG | 1988 | Tracy Rocker, Auburn, DT |
| 1973 | John Hicks, Ohio St, OT | 1989 | Percy Snow, Michigan St, LB |
| 1974 | Randy White, Maryland, DT | 1990 | Chris Zorich, Notre Dame, NG |
| 1975 | Lee Roy Selmon, Oklahoma, DT | 1991 | Steve Emtman, Washington, DT |
| 1976 | Wilson Whitley, Houston, DT | 1992 | Marvin Jones, Florida St, LB |
| 1977 | Ross Browner, Notre Dame, DE | 1993 | Aaron Taylor, Notre Dame, OT |
| 1978 | Bruce Clark, Penn St, DT | 1994 | Warren Sapp, Miami (FL), DT |
| 1979 | Brad Budde, Southern Cal, G | 1995 | Orlando Pace, Ohio St, OT |
| 1980 | Hugh Green, Pittsburgh, DE | 1996 | Orlando Pace, Ohio St, OT |
| 1981 | Kenneth Sims, Texas, DT | 1997 | Grant Wistrom, Nebraska, DE |
| 1982 | Dave Rimington, Nebraska, C | 1998 | Dat Nguyen, Texas A&M, LB |
| 1983 | Dean Steinkuhler, Nebraska, G | 1999 | Corey Moore, Virginia Tech, DE |
| 1984 | Tony Degrate, Texas, DT | 2000 | Jamal Reynolds, Florida St, DE |
| 1985 | Tony Casillas, Oklahoma, NG | | |

## Outland Trophy

Given to the outstanding interior lineman, selected by the Football Writers Association of America.

| Year | Player, College, Position | Year | Player, College, Position |
|---|---|---|---|
| 1946 | George Connor, Notre Dame, T | 1974 | Randy White, Maryland, DE |
| 1947 | Joe Steffy, Army, G | 1975 | Lee Roy Selmon, Oklahoma, DT |
| 1948 | Bill Fischer, Notre Dame, G | 1976 | Ross Browner, Notre Dame, DE |
| 1949 | Ed Bagdon, Michigan St, G | 1977 | Brad Shearer, Texas, DT |
| 1950 | Bob Gain, Kentucky, T | 1978 | Greg Roberts, Oklahoma, G |
| 1951 | Jim Weatherall, Oklahoma, T | 1979 | Jim Ritcher, N Carolina St, C |
| 1952 | Dick Modzelewski, Maryland, T | 1980 | Mark May, Pittsburgh, OT |
| 1953 | J.D. Roberts, Oklahoma, G | 1981 | Dave Rimington, Nebraska, C |
| 1954 | Bill Brooks, Arkansas, G | 1982 | Dave Rimington, Nebraska, C |
| 1955 | Calvin Jones, Iowa, G | 1983 | Dean Steinkuhler, Nebraska, G |
| 1956 | Jim Parker, Ohio St, G | 1984 | Bruce Smith, Virginia Tech, DT |
| 1957 | Alex Karras, Iowa, T | 1985 | Mike Ruth, Boston College, NG |
| 1958 | Zeke Smith, Auburn, G | 1986 | Jason Buck, Brigham Young, DT |
| 1959 | Mike McGee, Duke, T | 1987 | Chad Hennings, Air Force, DT |
| 1960 | Tom Brown, Minnesota, G | 1988 | Tracy Rocker, Auburn, DT |
| 1961 | Merlin Olsen, Utah St, T | 1989 | Mohammed Elewonibi, Brigham Young, G |
| 1962 | Bobby Bell, Minnesota, T | 1990 | Russell Maryland, Miami (FL), DT |
| 1963 | Scott Appleton, Texas, T | 1991 | Steve Emtman, Washington, DT |
| 1964 | Steve DeLong, Tennessee, T | 1992 | Will Shields, Nebraska, G |
| 1965 | Tommy Nobis, Texas, G | 1993 | Rob Waldrop, Arizona, NG |
| 1966 | Loyd Phillips, Arkansas, T | 1994 | Zach Wiegert, Nebraska, G |
| 1967 | Ron Yary, Southern Cal, T | 1995 | Jonathan Ogden, UCLA, OT |
| 1968 | Bill Stanfill, Georgia, T | 1996 | Orlando Pace, Ohio St, OT |
| 1969 | Mike Reid, Penn St, DT | 1997 | Aaron Taylor, Nebraska, G |
| 1970 | Jim Stillwagon, Ohio St, MG | 1998 | Kris Farris, UCLA, OL |
| 1971 | Larry Jacobson, Nebraska, DT | 1999 | Chris Samuels, Alabama, OL |
| 1972 | Rich Glover, Nebraska, MG | 2000 | John Henderson, Tennessee, DT |
| 1973 | John Hicks, Ohio St, OT | | |

## Butkus Award

Given to the top collegiate linebacker, the award was established by the Downtown Athletic Club of Orlando and named for college Hall of Famer Dick Butkus of Illinois.

| Year | Player, College | Year | Player, College |
|---|---|---|---|
| 1985 | Brian Bosworth, Oklahoma | 1993 | Trev Alberts, Nebraska |
| 1986 | Brian Bosworth, Oklahoma | 1994 | Dana Howard, Illinois |
| 1987 | Paul McGowan, Florida St | 1995 | Kevin Hardy, Illinois |
| 1988 | Derrick Thomas, Alabama | 1996 | Matt Russell, Colorado |
| 1989 | Percy Snow, Michigan St | 1997 | Andy Katzenmoyer, Ohio St |
| 1990 | Alfred Williams, Colorado | 1998 | Chris Claiborne, Southern Cal |
| 1991 | Erick Anderson, Michigan | 1999 | LaVar Arrington, Penn St |
| 1992 | Marvin Jones, Florida St | 2000 | Dan Morgan, Miami (FL) |

## Jim Thorpe Award

Given to the best defensive back of the year, the award is presented by the Jim Thorpe Athletic Club of Oklahoma City.

| Year | Player, College | Year | Player, College |
|---|---|---|---|
| 1986 | Thomas Everett, Baylor | 1993 | Antonio Langham, Alabama |
| 1987 | Bennie Blades, Miami (FL) | 1994 | Chris Hudson, Colorado |
| | Rickey Dixon, Oklahoma | 1995 | Greg Myers, Colorado St |
| 1988 | Deion Sanders, Florida St | 1996 | Lawrence Wright, Florida |
| 1989 | Mark Carrier, Southern Cal | 1997 | Charles Woodson, Michigan |
| 1990 | Darryl Lewis, Arizona | 1998 | Antoine Winfield, Ohio St |
| 1991 | Terrell Buckley, Florida St | 1999 | Tyrone Carter, Minnesota |
| 1992 | Deon Figures, Colorado | 2000 | Jamar Fletcher, Wisconsin |

## Walter Payton Player of the Year Award

Given to the top Division I-AA player as voted by Division I-AA sports information directors. Sponsored by Sports Network.

| Year | Player, College, Position | Year | Player, College, Position |
|---|---|---|---|
| 1987 | Kenny Gamble, Colgate, RB | 1994 | Steve McNair, Alcorn St, QB |
| 1988 | Dave Meggett, Towson St, RB | 1995 | Dave Dickenson, Montana, QB |
| 1989 | John Friesz, Idaho, QB | 1996 | Archie Amerson, Northern Arizona, RB |
| 1990 | Walter Dean, Grambling, RB | 1997 | Brian Finneran, Villanova, WR |
| 1991 | Jamie Martin, Weber St, QB | 1998 | Jerry Azumah, New Hampshire, RB |
| 1992 | Michael Payton, Marshall, QB | 1999 | Adrian Peterson, Georgia Southern, RB |
| 1993 | Doug Nussmeier, Idaho, QB | 2000 | Louis Ivory, Furman, RB |

## The Harlon Hill Trophy

Given to the outstanding NCAA Division II college football player, the award is sponsored by the National Harlon Hill Awards Committee, Florence, AL.

| Year | Player, College, Position | Year | Player, College, Position |
|------|---------------------------|------|---------------------------|
| 1986 | Jeff Bentrim, N Dakota St, QB | 1994 | Chris Hatcher, Valdosta St, QB |
| 1987 | Johnny Bailey, Texas A&I, RB | 1995 | Ronald McKinnon, N Alabama, LB |
| 1988 | Johnny Bailey, Texas A&I, RB | 1996 | Jarrett Anderson, Truman St, RB |
| 1989 | Johnny Bailey, Texas A&I, RB | 1997 | Irvin Sigler, Bloomsburg, RB |
| 1990 | Chris Simdorn, N Dakota St, QB | 1998 | Brian Shay, Emporia St, RB |
| 1991 | Ronnie West, Pittsburg St, WR | 1999 | Corte McGuffey, Northern Colorado, QB |
| 1992 | Ronald Moore, Pittsburg St, RB | 2000 | Dusty Bonner, Valdosta St, QB |
| 1993 | Roger Graham, New Haven, RB | | |

# NCAA Division I-A Individual Records

## Career

### SCORING

**Most Points Scored:** 468—Travis Prentice, Miami (OH), 1996–99
**Most Points Scored per Game:** 12.1—Marshall Faulk, San Diego St, 1991–93
**Most Touchdowns Scored:** 78—Travis Prentice, Miami (OH), 1996–99
**Most Touchdowns Scored per Game:** 2.0—Marshall Faulk, San Diego St, 1991–93
**Most Touchdowns Scored, Rushing:** 73—Travis Prentice, Miami (OH), 1996–99
**Most Touchdowns Scored, Passing:** 121—Ty Detmer, Brigham Young, 1988–91
**Most Touchdowns Scored, Receiving:** 50—Troy Edwards, Louisiana Tech, 1996–98
**Most Touchdowns Scored, Interception Returns:** 5—Ken Thomas, San Jose St, 1979–82; Jackie Walker, Tennessee, 1969–71; Deltha O'Neal, California, 1996–99
**Most Touchdowns Scored, Punt Returns:** 7—Johnny Rodgers, Nebraska, 1970–72; Jack Mitchell, Oklahoma, 1946–48; David Allen, Kansas St, 1997–99
**Most Touchdowns Scored, Kickoff Returns:** 6—Anthony Davis, Southern Cal, 1972–74

### TOTAL OFFENSE

**Most Plays:** 1,846—Chris Redman, Louisville, 1996–1999
**Most Plays per Game:** 48.5—Doug Gaynor, Long Beach St, 1984–85
**Most Yards Gained:** 14,665—Ty Detmer, Brigham Young, 1988–91 (15,031 passing, -366 rushing)
**Most Yards Gained per Game:** 382.4—Tim Rattay, Louisiana Tech, 1997–99
**Most 300+ Yard Games:** 33—Ty Detmer, Brigham Young, 1988–91

### RUSHING

**Most Rushes:** 1,215—Steve Bartalo, Colorado St, 1983–86 (4813 yds)
**Most Rushes per Game:** 34.0—Ed Marinaro, Cornell, 1969–71
**Most Yards Gained:** 6,397—Ron Dayne, Wisconsin, 1996–99
**Most Yards Gained per Game:** 174.6—Ed Marinaro, Cornell, 1969–71

**Most 100+ Yard Games:** 33—Tony Dorsett, Pittsburgh, 1973–76; Archie Griffin, Ohio St, 1972–75
**Most 200+ Yard Games:** 11—Marcus Allen, Southern Cal, 1978–81; Ricky Williams, Texas, 1995–98; Ron Dayne, Wisconsin, 1996–99

### PASSING

**Highest Passing Efficiency Rating:** 163.6—Danny Wuerffel, Florida, 1993–96 (1,170 attempts, 708 completions, 42 interceptions, 10,875 yards, 114 touchdown passes)
**Most Passes Attempted:** 1,679—Chris Redman, Louisville, 1996–99
**Most Passes Attempted per Game:** 47.0—Tim Rattay, Louisiana Tech, 1997–99
**Most Passes Completed:** 1,031—Chris Redman, Louisville, 1996–99
**Most Passes Completed per Game:** 30.8—Tim Rattay, Louisiana Tech, 1997–99
**\*Highest Completion Percentage:** 67.1—Tim Couch, Kentucky, 1996–98
**Most Yards Gained:** 15,031—Ty Detmer, Brigham Young, 1988–91
**Most Yards Gained per Game:** 386.2—Tim Rattay, Louisiana Tech, 1997–99

*Minimum 1,100 attempts.

### RECEIVING

**Most Passes Caught:** 300—Arnold Jackson, Louisville, 1997–00
**Most Passes Caught per Game:** 10.5—Emmanuel Hazard, Houston, 1989–90
**Most Yards Gained:** 5,005—Trevor Insley, Nevada, 1996–99
**Most Yards Gained per Game:** 140.9—Alex Van Dyke, Nevada, 1994–95
**Highest Average Gain per Reception:** 25.7—Wesley Walker, California, 1973–75

## Career *(Cont.)*

### ALL-PURPOSE RUNNING

**Most Plays:** 1,347—Steve Bartalo, Colorado St, 1983-86 (1,215 rushes, 132 receptions)
**Most Yards Gained:** 7,206—Ricky Williams, Texas, 1995–98 (6,279 rushing, 927 receiving)
**Most Yards Gained per Game:** 237.8—Ryan Benjamin, Pacific, 1990–92
**Highest Average Gain per Play:** 17.4—Anthony Carter, Michigan, 1979–82

### INTERCEPTIONS

**Most Passes Intercepted:** 29—Al Brosky, Illinois, 1950–52
**Most Passes Intercepted per Game:** 1.1—Al Brosky, Illinois, 1950–52
**Most Yards on Interception Returns**: 501—Terrell Buckley, Florida St, 1989–91
**Highest Average Gain per Interception:** 26.5—Tom Pridemore, W Virginia, 1975–77

### SPECIAL TEAMS

**Highest Punt Return Average:** 23.6—Jack Mitchell, Oklahoma, 1946–48
**Highest Kickoff Return Average:** 36.2—Forrest Hall, San Francisco, 1946–47
**Highest Average Yards per Punt:** 46.3—Todd Sauerbrun, W Virginia, 1991–94

## Single Season

### SCORING

**Most Points Scored:** 234—Barry Sanders, Oklahoma St, 1988
**Most Points Scored per Game:** 21.3—Barry Sanders, Oklahoma St, 1988
**Most Touchdowns Scored:** 39—Barry Sanders, Oklahoma St, 1988
**Most Touchdowns Scored, Rushing:** 37—Barry Sanders, Oklahoma St, 1988
**Most Touchdowns Scored, Passing:** 54—David Klingler, Houston, 1990
**Most Touchdowns Scored, Receiving:** 27—Troy Edwards, Louisiana Tech, 1998
**Most Touchdowns Scored, Interception Returns:** 4—Deltha O'Neal, California, 1999
**Most Touchdowns Scored, Punt Returns:** 4—Santana Moss, Miami (FL), 2000; David Allen, Kansas St, 1998; Quinton Spotwood, Syracuse, 1997; Tinker Keck, Cincinnati, 1997; James Henry, Southern Miss, 1987; Golden Richards, Brigham Young, 1971; Cliff Branch, Colorado, 1971
**Most Touchdowns Scored, Kickoff Returns:** 3—Leland McElroy, Texas A&M, 1993; Terance Mathis, New Mexico, 1989; Willie Gault, Tennessee, 1980; Anthony Davis, Southern Cal, 1974; Stan Brown, Purdue, 1970; Forrest Hall, San Francisco, 1946

### TOTAL OFFENSE

**Most Plays:** 704—David Klingler, Houston, 1990
**Most Yards Gained:** 5,221—David Klingler, Houston, 1990
**Most Yards Gained per Game:** 474.6—David Klingler, Houston, 1990
**Most 300+ Yard Games:** 12—Ty Detmer, Brigham Young, 1990

### RUSHING

**Most Rushes:** 403—Marcus Allen, Southern Cal, 1981
**Most Rushes per Game:** 39.6—Ed Marinaro, Cornell, 1971
**Most Yards Gained:** 2,628—Barry Sanders, Oklahoma St, 1988
**Most Yards Gained per Game:** 238.9—Barry Sanders, Oklahoma St, 1988
**Most 100+ Yard Games:** 11—By 14 players, most recently Ahman Green, Nebraska, 1997

### PASSING

**Highest Passing Efficiency Rating:** 183.3—Shaun King, Tulane, 1998 (328 attempts, 223 completions, 6 interceptions, 3,232 yards, 36 TD passes)
**Most Passes Attempted:** 643—David Klingler, Houston, 1990
**Most Passes Attempted per Game:** 58.5—David Klingler, Houston, 1990
**Most Passes Completed:** 400—Tim Couch, Kentucky, 1998
**Most Passes Completed per Game:** 36.4—Tim Couch, Kentucky, 1998
**Highest Completion Percentage:** 73.6—Daunte Culpepper, Central Florida, 1998
**Most Yards Gained:** (12 games) 5188—Ty Detmer, Brigham Young, 1990; (11 games) 5,140—David Klingler, Houston, 1990
**Most Yards Gained per Game:** 467.3—David Klingler, Houston, 1990

### RECEIVING

**Most Passes Caught:** 142—Emmanuel Hazard, Houston, 1989
**Most Passes Caught per Game:** 13.4—Howard Twilley, Tulsa, 1965
**Most Yards Gained:** 2060—Trevor Insley, Nevada, 1999
**Most Yards Gained per Game:** 187.3—Trevor Insley, Nevada, 1999
**Highest Average Gain per Reception:** 27.9—Elmo Wright, Houston, 1968 (min. 30 receptions)

### ALL-PURPOSE RUNNING

**Most Plays:** 432—Marcus Allen, Southern Cal, 1981
**Most Yards Gained:** 3,250—Barry Sanders, Oklahoma St, 1988
**Most Yards Gained per Game:** 295.5—Barry Sanders, Oklahoma St, 1988
**Highest Average Gain per Play:** 18.5—Henry Bailey, UNLV, 1992

## Single Season *(Cont.)*

### INTERCEPTIONS

**Most Passes Intercepted:** 14 — Al Worley, Washington, 1968
**Most Yards on Interception Returns:** 302 — Charles Phillips, Southern Cal, 1974
**Highest Average Gain per Interception:** 50.6 — Norm Thompson, Utah, 1969

### SPECIAL TEAMS

**Highest Punt Return Average:** 25.9 — Bill Blackstock, Tennessee, 1951
**Highest Kickoff Return Average:** 40.1 — Paul Allen, Brigham Young, 1961
**Highest Average Yards per Punt:** 50.3 — Chad Kessler, Louisiana St, 1997

## Single Game

### SCORING

**Most Points Scored:** 48—Howard Griffith, Illinois, 1990 (vs Southern Illinois)
**Most Field Goals:** 7—Dale Klein, Nebraska, 1985 (vs Missouri); Mike Prindle, Western Michigan, 1984 (vs Marshall)
**Most Extra Points (Kick):** 13—Derek Mahoney, Fresno St, 1991 (vs New Mexico); Terry Leiweke, Houston, 1968 (vs Tulsa)
**Most Extra Points (2-Pts):** 6—Jim Pilot, New Mexico St, 1961 (vs Hardin-Simmons)

### TOTAL OFFENSE

**Most Yards Gained:** 732—David Klingler, Houston, 1990 (vs Arizona St)

### RUSHING

**Most Yards Gained:** 406—LaDainian Tomlinson, Texas Christian, 1999 (vs UTEP)
**Most Touchdowns Rushed:** 8—Howard Griffith, Illinois, 1990 (vs Southern Illinois)

### PASSING

**Most Passes Completed:** 55—Rusty LaRue, Wake Forest, 1995 (vs Duke); Drew Brees, Purdue, 1998 (vs Wisconsin)
**Most Yards Gained:** 716—David Klingler, Houston, 1990 (vs Arizona St)
**Most Touchdown Passes:** 11—David Klingler, Houston, 1990 [vs Eastern Washington (I-AA)]

### RECEIVING

**Most Passes Caught:** 23—Randy Gatewood, UNLV, 1994 (vs Idaho)
**Most Yards Gained:** 405—Troy Edwards, Louisiana Tech, 1998 (vs Nebraska)
**Most Touchdown Catches:** 6—Tim Delaney, San Diego St, 1969 (vs New Mexico St)

# NCAA Division I-AA Individual Records

## Career

### SCORING

**Most Points Scored:** 420—Matt Cannon, Southern Utah, 1997–2000
**Most Touchdowns Scored:** 69—Adrian Peterson, Georgia Southern, 1998–00; Matt Cannon, Southern Utah, 1997–00; Jerry Azumah, New Hampshire, 1995–98
**Most Touchdowns Scored, Rushing:** 69—Matt Cannon, Southern Utah, 1997–00
**Most Touchdowns Scored, Passing:** 139—Willie Totten, Mississippi Valley, 1982–85
**Most Touchdowns Scored, Receiving:** 50—Jerry Rice, Mississippi Valley, 1981–84

### RUSHING

**Most Rushes:** 1,124—Charles Roberts, Cal St–Sacramento, 1997–00
**Most Rushes per Game:** 38.2—Arnold Mickens, Butler, 1994–95
**Most Yards Gained:** 6,553—Charles Roberts, Cal St–Sacramento, 1997–00
**Most Yards Gained per Game:** 151.0—Jerry Azumah, New Hampshire, 1995–98

### PASSING

**Highest Passing Efficiency Rating:** 170.8—Shawn Knight, William & Mary, 1991–94
**Most Passes Attempted:** 1,680—Steve McNair, Alcorn St, 1991–94
**Most Passes Completed:** 934—Jamie Martin, Weber St, 1989–92
**Most Passes Completed per Game:** 26.5—Chris Sanders, Chattanooga, 1999–00
**Highest Completion Percentage:** 67.3—Dave Dickenson, Montana, 1992–95
**Most Yards Gained:** 14,496—Steve McNair, Alcorn St, 1991–94
**Most Yards Gained per Game:** 350—Neil Lomax, Portland St, 1978–80

### RECEIVING

**Most Passes Caught:** 317—Jacquay Nunnally, Florida A&M, 1997–00
**Most Yards Gained:** 4,693—Jerry Rice, Mississippi Valley, 1981–84
**Most Yards Gained per Game:** 114.5—Jerry Rice, Mississippi Valley, 1981–84
**Highest Average Gain per Reception:** 24.3—John Taylor, Delaware St, 1982–85

## Single Season

### SCORING

**Most Points Scored:** 174—Adrian Peterson, Georgia Southern, 1999
**Most Touchdowns Scored:** 29—Adrian Peterson, Georgia Southern, 1999
**Most Touchdowns Scored, Rushing:** 28—Adrian Peterson, Georgia Southern, 1999
**Most Touchdowns Scored, Passing:** 56—Willie Totten, Mississippi Valley, 1984
**Most Touchdowns Scored, Receiving:** 27—Jerry Rice, Mississippi Valley, 1984

### RUSHING

**Most Rushes:** 409—Arnold Mickens, Butler, 1994
**Most Rushes per Game:** 40.9—Arnold Mickens, Butler, 1994
**Most Yards Gained:** 2,260—Charles Roberts, Cal St–Sacramento, 1998
**Most Yards Gained per Game:** 225.5—Arnold Mickens, Butler, 1994

### PASSING

**Highest Passing Efficiency Rating:** 204.6—Shawn Knight, William & Mary, 1993
**Most Passes Attempted:** 577—Joe Lee, Towson, 1999
**Most Passes Completed:** 324—Willie Totten, Mississippi Valley, 1984
**Most Passes Completed per Game:** 32.4—Willie Totten, Mississippi Valley, 1984
**Highest Completion Percentage:** 70.6—Giovanni Carmazzi, Hofstra, 1997
**Most Yards Gained:** 4,863—Steve McNair, Alcorn St, 1994
**Most Yards Gained per Game:** 455.7—Willie Totten, Mississippi Valley, 1984

### RECEIVING

**Most Passes Caught:** 120—Stephen Campbell, Brown, 2000
**Most Yards Gained:** 1,712—Eddie Conti, Delaware, 1998
**Most Yards Gained per Game:** 168.2—Jerry Rice, Mississippi Valley, 1984
**Highest Average Gain per Reception:** 28.9—Mikhael Ricks, Stephen F. Austin, 1997; (min. 35 receptions)

## Single Game

### SCORING

**Most Points Scored:** 42—Jesse Burton, McNeese St, 1998 (vs Southern Utah); Archie Amerson, Northern Arizona, 1996 (vs Weber St)
**Most Field Goals:** 8—Goran Lingmerth, Northern Arizona, 1986 (vs Idaho)

### RUSHING

**Most Yards Gained:** 409—Charles Roberts, Cal St–Northridge, 1999 (vs Idaho St)
**Most Touchdowns Rushed:** 7—Archie Amerson, Northern Arizona, 1996 (vs Weber St)

### PASSING

**Most Passes Completed:** 48—Clayton Millis, Cal St–Northridge, 1995 (vs St. Mary's [CA])
**Most Yards Gained:** 649—Steve McNair, Alcorn St, 1994 (vs Southern–BR)
**Most Touchdown Passes:** 9—Willie Totten, Mississippi Valley, 1984 (vs Kentucky St)

### RECEIVING

**Most Passes Caught:** 24—Jerry Rice, Mississippi Valley, 1983 (vs Southern–BR)
**Most Yards Gained:** 376—Kassim Osgood, Cal Poly, 2000 (vs Northern Iowa)
**Most Touchdown Catches:** 6—Cos DeMatteo, Chattanooga, 2000 (vs Mississippi Valley)

# NCAA Division II Individual Records

## Career

### SCORING

**Most Points Scored:** 544—Brian Shay, Emporia St, 1995–98
**Most Touchdowns Scored:** 88—Brian Shay, Emporia St, 1995–98
**Most Touchdowns Scored, Rushing:** 81—Brian Shay, Emporia St, 1995–98
**Most Touchdowns Scored, Passing:** 116—Chris Hatcher, Valdosta St, 1991–94
**Most Touchdowns Scored, Receiving:** 49—Bruce Cerone, Yankton/Emporia St, 1965–69

### RUSHING

**Most Rushes:** 1,072—Bernie Peeters, Luther, 1968–71
**Most Rushes per Game:** 29.8—Bernie Peeters, Luther, 1968–71
**Most Yards Gained:** 6,958—Brian Shay, Emporia St, 1995–98
**Most Yards Gained per Game:** 183.4—Anthony Gray, Western NM, 1997–98

## Career *(Cont.)*

### PASSING

**Highest Passing Efficiency Rating:** 167.0—
Wilkie Perez, Glenville St, 1997–98
**Most Passes Attempted:** 1,719—Bob
McLaughlin, Lock Haven, 1992–95
**Most Passes Completed:** 1,001—Chris Hatcher,
Valdosta St, 1991–94
**Most Passes Completed per Game:** 25.7—
Chris Hatcher, Valdosta St, 1991–94
**Highest Completion Percentage:** 69.6—
Chris Peterson, UC-Davis, 1985–86
**Most Yards Gained:** 11,213—Justin Coleman,
Nebraska–Kearney, 1997–00
**Most Yards Gained per Game:** 312.1—
Grady Benton, W Texas A&M, 1994–95

### RECEIVING

**Most Passes Caught:** 273—Damien Hoffman,
Minnesota–Morris, 1997–00
**Most Yards Gained:** 4,468—James Roe,
Norfolk St, 1992–95
**Most Yards Gained per Game:** 160.8—
Chris George, Glenville St, 1993–94
**Highest Average Gain per Reception:** 22.8—
Tyrone Johnson, Western St (CO), 1990–93

## Single Season

### SCORING

**Most Points Scored:** 199—Kavin Gailliard,
American International, 1999
**Most Touchdowns Scored:** 34—Kavin Gailliard,
American International, 1999
**Most Touchdowns Scored, Rushing:** 32—
Kavin Gailliard, American International, 1999
**Most Touchdowns Scored, Passing:** 54—
Dusty Bonner, Valdosta St, 2000
**Most Touchdowns Scored, Receiving:** 21—
Kevin Ingram, W Chester, 1998; Chris Perry, Adams
St, 1995

### RUSHING

**Most Rushes:** 385—Joe Gough, Wayne St (MI),
1994
**Most Rushes per Game:** 38.6—Mark Perkins,
Hobart, 1968
**Most Yards Gained:** 2,653—Kavin Gailliard,
American International, 1999
**Most Yards Gained per Game:** 222.0—Anthony
Gray, Western New Mexico, 1997

### PASSING

**Highest Passing Efficiency Rating:** 210.1—
Boyd Crawford, College of Idaho, 1953
**Most Passes Attempted:** 544—
Lance Funderburk, Valdosta St, 1995
**Most Passes Completed:** 356—
Lance Funderburk, Valdosta St, 1995
**Most Passes Completed per Game:** 32.4—
Lance Funderburk, Valdosta St, 1995
**Highest Completion Percentage:** 74.7—
Chris Hatcher, Valdosta St, 1994
**Most Yards Gained:** 4,189—Wilkie Perez,
Glenville St, 1997
**Most Yards Gained per Game:** 393.4—
Grady Benton, W Texas A&M, 1994

### RECEIVING

**Most Passes Caught:** 119—Brad Bailey,
W Texas A&M, 1994
**Most Yards Gained:** 1,876—Chris George,
Glenville St, 1993
**Most Yards Gained per Game:** 187.6—
Chris George, Glenville St, 1993
**Highest Average Gain per Reception:** 32.5—
Tyrone Johnson, Western St, 1991 (min. 30 receptions)

## Single Game

### SCORING

**Most Points Scored:** 48—Paul Zaeske, N Park,
1968 (vs N Central); Junior Wolf, Panhandle St, 1958
(vs St. Mary [KS])
**Most Field Goals:** 6—Steve Huff, Central Missouri St,
1985 (vs SE Missouri St)

### RUSHING

**Most Yards Gained:** 405—Alvon Brown,
Kentucky St, 2000 (vs Kentucky Wesleyan)
**Most Touchdowns Rushed:** 8—Junior Wolf,
Panhandle St, 1958 (vs St. Mary [KS])

### PASSING

**Most Passes Completed:** 56—Jarrod
DeGeorgia, Wayne St (NE),1996 (vs Drake)
**Most Yards Gained:** 642—Wilkie Perez,
Glenville St, 1997, (vs Concord)
**Most Touchdowns Passed:** 10—Bruce
Swanson, N Park, 1968 (vs N Central)

### RECEIVING

**Most Passes Caught:** 23—Chris George,
Glenville St, 1994 (vs W VA Wesleyan); Barry
Wagner, Alabama A&M, 1989 (vs Clark Atlanta)
**Most Yards Gained:** 401—Kevin Ingram,
W Chester, 1998 (vs Clarion)
**Most Touchdown Catches:** 8—Paul Zaeske,
N Park, 1968 (vs N Central)

# NCAA Division III Individual Records

## Career

### SCORING

**Most Points Scored:** 562—R.J. Bowers, Grove City, 1997–00
**Most Touchdowns Scored:** 92—R.J. Bowers, Grove City, 1997–00
**Most Touchdowns Scored, Rushing:** 91—R.J. Bowers, Grove City, 1997–00
**Most Touchdowns Scored, Passing:** 148—Justin Peery, Westminster (MO), 1996–99
**Most Touchdowns Scored, Receiving:** 72—Scott Pingel, Westminster (MO), 1996–99

### RUSHING

**Most Rushes:** 1,190—Steve Tardif, Maine Maritime, 1996–99
**Most Rushes per Game:** 32.7—Chris Sizemore, Bridgewater (VA), 1972–74
**Most Yards Gained:** 7,353—R.J. Bowers, Grove City, 1997–00
**Most Yards Gained per Game:** 183.8—R.J. Bowers, Grove City, 1997–00

### PASSING

**Highest Passing Efficiency Rating:** 194.2—Bill Borchert, Mount Union, 1994–97
**Most Passes Attempted:** 1,696—Kirk Baumgartner, WI–Stevens Point, 1986–89
**Most Passes Completed:** 1,012—Justin Peery, Westminster (MO), 1996–99
**Most Passes Completed per Game:** 25.9—Justin Peery, Westminster (MO), 1996–99
**Highest Completion Percentage:** 66.5—Bill Borchert, Mount Union (OH) 1994–97
**Most Yards Gained:** 13,262—Justin Peery, Westminster (MO), 1996–99
**Most Yards Gained per Game:** 340.1—Justin Peery, Westminster (MO), 1996–99

### RECEIVING

**Most Passes Caught:** 436—Scott Pingel, Westminster (MO), 1996–99
**Most Yards Gained:** 6,108—Scott Pingel, Westminster (MO), 1996–99
**Most Yards Gained per Game:** 156.6—Scott Pingel, Westminster (MO), 1996–99
**Highest Average Gain per Reception:** 22.9—Kirk Aikens, Hartwick, 1995–98

## Single Season

### SCORING

**Most Points Scored:** 206—R. J. Bowers, Grove City, 1998
**Most Points Scored per Game:** 20.8—James Regan, Pomona-Pitzer, 1997
**Most Touchdowns Scored:** 34—R. J. Bowers, Grove City, 1998
**Most Touchdowns Scored, Rushing:** 34—R. J. Bowers, Grove City, 1998

**Most Touchdowns Scored, Passing:** 54—Justin Peery, Westminster (MO), 1999
**Most Touchdowns Scored, Receiving:** 26—Scott Pingel, Westminster (MO), 1998

### RUSHING

**Most Rushes:** 380—Mike Birosak, Dickinson, 1989
**Most Rushes per Game:** 38.0—Mike Birosak, Dickinson, 1989
**Most Yards Gained:** 2,385—Dante Brown, Marietta, 1996

### PASSING

**Highest Passing Efficiency Rating:** 225.0—Mike Simpson, Eureka, 1994
**Most Passes Attempted:** 527—Kirk Baumgartner, WI–Stevens Point, 1988
**Most Passes Completed:** 329—Justin Peery, Westminster (MO), 1999
**Most Passes Completed per Game:** 32.9—Justin Peery, Westminster (MO), 1999
**Highest Completion Percentage:** 73.4—Mike Simpson, Eureka, 1994
**Most Yards Gained:** 4,501—Justin Peery, Westminster (MO), 1998
**Most Yards Gained per Game:** 450.1—Justin Peery, Westminster (MO), 1998

### RECEIVING

**Most Passes Caught:** 136—Scott Pingel, Westminster (MO), 1999
**Most Yards Gained:** 2,157—Scott Pingel, Westminster, (MO), 1998
**Most Yards Gained per Game:** 215.7—Scott Pingel, Westminster, (MO), 1998
**Highest Average Gain per Reception:** 26.9—Marty Redlawsk, Concordia (IL), 1985

## Single Game

### SCORING

**Most Field Goals:** 6—Jim Hever, Rhodes, 1984 (vs Millsaps)

### PASSING

**Most Passes Completed:** 50—Justin Peery, Westminster (MO), 1998 (vs MacMurray); Tim Lynch, Hofstra, 1991 (vs Fordham)
**Most Yards Gained:** 731—Zamir Amin, Menlo, 2000 (vs California Lutheran)
**Most Touchdowns Passed:** 9—Joe Zarlinga, Ohio Northern, 1998 (vs Capital)

### RUSHING

**Most Yards Gained:** 441—Dante Brown, Marietta, 1996 (vs Baldwin-Wallace)
**Most Touchdowns Rushed:** 8—Carey Bender, Coe, 1994 (vs Beloit)

### RECEIVING

**Most Passes Caught:** 23—Sean Munroe, Mass-Boston, 1992 (vs Mass-Maritime)
**Most Yards Gained:** 397—Matt Eisenberg, Juniata, 1999 (vs Widener)
**Most Touchdown Catches:** 7—Matt Perceval, Wesleyan (CT), 1998 (vs Middlebury)

# NCAA Division I-A Alltime Individual Leaders

## Career

### Scoring

**POINTS (KICKERS)**

| | Years | Pts |
|---|---|---|
| Roman Anderson, Houston | 1988–91 | 423 |
| Carlos Huerta, Miami (FL) | 1988–91 | 397 |
| Jason Elam, Hawaii | 1988–92 | 395 |
| Derek Schmidt, Florida St | 1984–87 | 393 |
| Kris Brown, Nebraska | 1995–98 | 388 |

**POINTS (NON-KICKERS)**

| | Years | Pts |
|---|---|---|
| Travis Prentice, Miami (OH) | 1996–99 | 468 |
| Ricky Williams, Texas | 1995–98 | 452 |
| Anthony Thompson, Indiana | 1986–89 | 394 |
| Ron Dayne, Wisconsin | 1996–99 | 378 |
| Marshall Faulk, San Diego St | 1991–93 | 376 |

**POINTS PER GAME (NON-KICKERS)**

| | Years | Pts/Game |
|---|---|---|
| Marshall Faulk, San Diego St | 1991–93 | 12.1 |
| Ed Marinaro, Cornell | 1969–71 | 11.8 |
| Bill Burnett, Arkansas | 1968–70 | 11.3 |
| Steve Owens, Oklahoma | 1967–69 | 11.2 |
| Eddie Talboom, Wyoming | 1948–50 | 10.8 |

### Total Offense

**YARDS GAINED**

| | Years | Yds |
|---|---|---|
| Ty Detmer, Brigham Young | 1988–91 | 14,665 |
| Tim Rattay, Louisiana Tech | 1997–99 | 12,618 |
| Chris Redman, Louisville | 1996–99 | 12,541 |
| Drew Brees, Purdue | 1997–00 | 11,815 |
| Doug Flutie, Boston College | 1981–84 | 11,317 |

**YARDS PER GAME**

| | Years | Yds/Game |
|---|---|---|
| Tim Rattay, Louisiana Tech | 1997–99 | 382.4 |
| Chris Vargas, Nevada | 1992–93 | 320.9 |
| Ty Detmer, Brigham Young | 1988–91 | 318.8 |
| Daunte Culpepper, Central Florida | 1996–98 | 313.5 |
| Mike Perez, San Jose St | 1986–87 | 309.1 |

### Rushing

**YARDS GAINED**

| | Years | Yds |
|---|---|---|
| Ron Dayne, Wisconsin | 1996–99 | 6,397 |
| Ricky Williams, Texas | 1995–98 | 6,279 |
| Tony Dorsett, Pittsburgh | 1973–76 | 6,082 |
| Charles White, Southern Cal | 1976–79 | 5,598 |
| Travis Prentice, Miami (OH) | 1996–99 | 5,596 |

**YARDS PER GAME**

| | Years | Yds/Game |
|---|---|---|
| Ed Marinaro, Cornell | 1969–71 | 174.6 |
| O.J. Simpson, Southern Cal | 1967–68 | 164.4 |
| Herschel Walker, Georgia | 1980–82 | 159.4 |
| LeShon Johnson, Northern Illinois | 1992–93 | 150.6 |
| Ron Dayne, Wisconsin | 1996–99 | 148.8 |

**TOUCHDOWNS RUSHING**

| | Years | TD |
|---|---|---|
| Travis Prentice, Miami (OH) | 1996–99 | 73 |
| Ricky Williams, Texas | 1995–98 | 72 |
| Anthony Thompson, Indiana | 1986–89 | 64 |
| Ron Dayne, Wisconsin | 1996–99 | 63 |
| Marshall Faulk, San Diego St | 1991–93 | 57 |

### Passing

**PASSING EFFICIENCY**

| | Years | Rating |
|---|---|---|
| Danny Wuerffel, Florida | 1993–96 | 163.6 |
| Ty Detmer, Brigham Young | 1988–91 | 162.7 |
| Steve Sarkisian, Brigham Young | 1995–96 | 162.0 |
| Billy Blanton, San Diego St | 1993–96 | 157.1 |
| Jim McMahon, Brigham Young | 1977–78, 80–81 | 156.9 |

Note: Minimum 500 completions.

**YARDS GAINED**

| | Years | Yds |
|---|---|---|
| Ty Detmer, Brigham Young | 1988–91 | 15,031 |
| Tim Rattay, Louisiana Tech | 1997–99 | 12,746 |
| Chris Redman, Louisville | 1996–99 | 12,541 |
| Todd Santos, San Diego St | 1984–87 | 11,425 |
| Tim Lester, Western Michigan | 1997–99 | 11,299 |

**COMPLETIONS**

| | Years | Comp |
|---|---|---|
| Chris Redman, Louisville | 1996–99 | 1,031 |
| Tim Rattay, Louisiana Tech | 1997–99 | 1,015 |
| Ty Detmer, Brigham Young | 1988–91 | 958 |
| Drew Brees, Purdue | 1997–00 | 942 |
| Todd Santos, San Diego St | 1984–87 | 910 |

**TOUCHDOWNS PASSING**

| | Years | TD |
|---|---|---|
| Ty Detmer, Brigham Young | 1988–91 | 121 |
| Tim Rattay, Louisiana Tech | 1997–99 | 115 |
| Danny Wuerffel, Florida | 1993–96 | 114 |
| Chad Pennington, Marshall | 1997–99 | 100 |
| David Klingler, Houston | 1988–91 | 91 |

### Receiving

**CATCHES**

| | Years | No. |
|---|---|---|
| Arnold Jackson, Louisville | 1997–00 | 300 |
| Trevor Insley, Nevada | 1996–99 | 298 |
| Geoff Noisy, Nevada | 1995–98 | 295 |
| Troy Edwards, Louisiana Tech | 1996–98 | 280 |
| Aaron Turner, Pacific | 1989–92 | 266 |

**CATCHES PER GAME**

| | Years | No./Game |
|---|---|---|
| Emmanuel Hazard, Houston | 1989–90 | 10.5 |
| Alex Van Dyke, Nevada | 1994–95 | 10.3 |
| Howard Twilley, Tulsa | 1963–65 | 10.0 |
| Jason Phillips, Houston | 1987–88 | 9.4 |
| Troy Edwards, Louisiana Tech | 1996–98 | 8.2 |

**YARDS GAINED**

| | Years | Yds |
|---|---|---|
| Trevor Insley, Nevada | 1996–99 | 5,005 |
| Marcus Harris, Wyoming | 1993–96 | 4,518 |
| Ryan Yarborough, Wyoming | 1990–93 | 4,357 |
| Troy Edwards, Louisiana Tech | 1996–98 | 4,352 |
| Aaron Turner, Pacific | 1989–92 | 4,345 |

**TOUCHDOWN CATCHES**

| | Years | TD |
|---|---|---|
| Troy Edwards, Louisiana Tech | 1996–98 | 50 |
| Aaron Turner, Pacific | 1989–92 | 43 |
| Ryan Yarborough, Wyoming | 1990–93 | 42 |
| Marcus Harris, Wyoming | 1993–96 | 38 |
| Clarkston Hines, Duke | 1986–89 | 38 |

## Career *(Cont.)*

### All-Purpose Running

**YARDS GAINED**

| | Years | Yds |
|---|---|---|
| Ricky Williams, Texas | 1996–98 | 7,206 |
| Napoleon McCallum, Navy | 1981–85 | 7,172 |
| Darrin Nelson, Stanford | 1977–78, 80–81 | 6,885 |
| Kevin Faulk, Louisiana St | 1995–98 | 6,833 |
| Ron Dayne, Wisconsin | 1996–99 | 6,701 |

**YARDS PER GAME**

| | Years | Yds/Game |
|---|---|---|
| Ryan Benjamin, Pacific | 1990–92 | 237.8 |
| Sheldon Canley, San Jose St | 1988–90 | 205.8 |
| Howard Stevens, Louisville | 1971–72 | 193.7 |
| O.J. Simpson, Southern Cal | 1967–68 | 192.9 |
| Alex Van Dyke, Nevada | 1994–95 | 188.5 |

### Interceptions

| PLAYER/SCHOOL | Years | Int |
|---|---|---|
| Al Brosky, Illinois | 1950–52 | 29 |
| John Provost, Holy Cross | 1972–74 | 27 |
| Martin Bayless, Bowling Green | 1980–83 | 27 |
| Tom Curtis, Michigan | 1967–69 | 25 |
| Tony Thurman, Boston Col | 1981–84 | 25 |
| Tracy Saul, Texas Tech | 1989–92 | 25 |

### Punting Average

| PLAYER/SCHOOL | Years | Avg |
|---|---|---|
| Todd Sauerbrun, W Virginia | 1991–94 | 46.3 |
| Reggie Roby, Iowa | 1979–82 | 45.6 |
| Greg Montgomery, Michigan St | 1985–87 | 45.4 |
| Tom Tupa, Ohio St | 1984–87 | 45.2 |
| Barry Helton, Colorado | 1984–87 | 44.9 |

Note: At least 150 punts.

### Punt Return Average

| PLAYER/SCHOOL | Years | Avg |
|---|---|---|
| Jack Mitchell, Oklahoma | 1946–48 | 23.6 |
| Gene Gibson, Cincinnati | 1949–50 | 20.5 |
| Eddie Macon, Pacific | 1949–51 | 18.9 |
| Jackie Robinson, UCLA | 1939–40 | 18.8 |
| Bobby Dillon, Texas | 1949–51 | 17.7 |

Note: At least 30 returns.

### Kickoff Return Average

| PLAYER/SCHOOL | Years | Avg |
|---|---|---|
| Anthony Davis, Southern Cal | 1972–74 | 35.1 |
| Eric Booth, Southern Miss | 1994–97 | 32.4 |
| Overton Curtis, Utah St | 1957–58 | 31.0 |
| Fred Montgomery, New Mexico St | 1991–92 | 30.5 |
| Altie Taylor, Utah St | 1966–68 | 29.3 |

Note: At least 30 returns.

---

## YET ANOTHER SIGN OF THE APOCALYPSE

*Penn State's faculty senate passed a resolution denouncing "negative cheering," which will be read before football games in Happy Valley.*

---

## Single Season

### Scoring

**POINTS**

| | Year | Pts |
|---|---|---|
| Barry Sanders, Oklahoma St | 1988 | 234 |
| Troy Edwards, Louisiana Tech | 1998 | 188 |
| Mike Rozier, Nebraska | 1983 | 174 |
| Lydell Mitchell, Penn St | 1971 | 174 |
| Ricky Williams, Texas | 1998 | 168 |
| Lee Suggs, Virginia Tech | 2000 | 168 |

**FIELD GOALS**

| | Year | FG |
|---|---|---|
| John Lee, UCLA | 1984 | 29 |
| Paul Woodside, W Virginia | 1982 | 28 |
| Luis Zendejas, Arizona St | 1983 | 28 |
| Fuad Reveiz, Tennessee | 1982 | 27 |
| Sebastian Janikowski, Florida St | 1998 | 27 |

Four tied with 25.

### All-Purpose Running

**YARDS GAINED**

| | Year | Yds |
|---|---|---|
| Barry Sanders, Oklahoma St | 1988 | 3,250 |
| Troy Edwards, Louisiana Tech | 1998 | 2,794 |
| Ryan Benjamin, Pacific | 1991 | 2,995 |
| Mike Pringle, Fullerton St | 1989 | 2,690 |
| Paul Palmer, Temple | 1986 | 2,633 |

### All-Purpose Running *(Cont.)*

**YARDS PER GAME**

| | Year | Yds/Game |
|---|---|---|
| Barry Sanders, Oklahoma St | 1988 | 295.5 |
| Ryan Benjamin, Pacific | 1991 | 249.6 |
| Byron (Whizzer) White, Colorado | 1937 | 246.3 |
| Mike Pringle, Fullerton St | 1989 | 244.6 |
| Paul Palmer, Temple | 1986 | 239.4 |

### Total Offense

**YARDS GAINED**

| | Year | Yds |
|---|---|---|
| David Klingler, Houston | 1990 | 5,221 |
| Ty Detmer, Brigham Young | 1990 | 5,022 |
| Tim Rattay, Louisiana Tech | 1998 | 4,840 |
| Andre Ware, Houston | 1989 | 4,661 |
| Jim McMahon, Brigham Young | 1980 | 4,627 |

**YARDS PER GAME**

| | Year | Yds/Game |
|---|---|---|
| David Klingler, Houston | 1990 | 474.6 |
| Andre Ware, Houston | 1989 | 423.7 |
| Ty Detmer, Brigham Young | 1990 | 418.5 |
| Tim Rattay, Louisiana Tech | 1998 | 403.3 |
| Mike Maxwell, Nevada | 1995 | 402.6 |

## Single Season (Cont.)

### Rushing

**YARDS GAINED**

| | Year | Yds |
|---|---|---|
| Barry Sanders, Oklahoma St | 1988 | 2,628 |
| Marcus Allen, Southern Cal | 1981 | 2,342 |
| Troy Davis, Iowa St | 1996 | 2,185 |
| LaDainian Tomlinson, Texas Christian | 2000 | 2,158 |
| Mike Rozier, Nebraska | 1983 | 2,148 |

**YARDS PER GAME**

| | Year | Yds/Game |
|---|---|---|
| Barry Sanders, Oklahoma St | 1988 | 238.9 |
| Marcus Allen, Southern Cal | 1981 | 212.9 |
| Ed Marinaro, Cornell | 1971 | 209.0 |
| Troy Davis, Iowa St | 1996 | 198.6 |
| LaDainian Tomlinson, Texas Christian | 2000 | 196.2 |

**TOUCHDOWNS RUSHING**

| | Year | TD |
|---|---|---|
| Barry Sanders, Oklahoma St | 1988 | 37 |
| Mike Rozier, Nebraska | 1983 | 29 |
| Ricky Williams, Texas | 1998 | 27 |
| Lee Suggs, Virginia Tech | 2000 | 27 |

Four tied with 24.

### Passing

**PASSING EFFICIENCY**

| | Year | Rating |
|---|---|---|
| Shaun King, Tulane | 1998 | 183.3 |
| Michael Vick, Virginia Tech | 1999 | 180.4 |
| Danny Wuerffel, Florida | 1995 | 178.4 |
| Jim McMahon, Brigham Young | 1980 | 176.9 |
| Ty Detmer, Brigham Young | 1989 | 175.6 |

### Passing (Cont.)

**YARDS GAINED**

| | Year | Yds |
|---|---|---|
| Ty Detmer, Brigham Young | 1990 | 5,188 |
| David Klingler, Houston | 1990 | 5,140 |
| Andre Ware, Houston | 1989 | 4,699 |
| Tim Rattay, Louisiana Tech | 1998 | 4,943 |
| Jim McMahon, Brigham Young | 1980 | 4,571 |

**COMPLETIONS**

| | Year | Att | Comp |
|---|---|---|---|
| Tim Couch, Kentucky | 1998 | 553 | 400 |
| Tim Rattay, Louisiana Tech | 1998 | 559 | 380 |
| David Klingler, Houston | 1990 | 643 | 374 |
| Andre Ware, Houston | 1989 | 578 | 365 |
| Tim Couch, Kentucky | 1997 | 547 | 363 |

**TOUCHDOWNS PASSING**

| | Year | TD |
|---|---|---|
| David Klingler, Houston | 1990 | 54 |
| Jim McMahon, Brigham Young | 1980 | 47 |
| Andre Ware, Houston | 1989 | 46 |
| Tim Rattay, Louisiana Tech | 1998 | 46 |
| Ty Detmer, Brigham Young | 1990 | 41 |

### Receiving

**CATCHES**

| | Year | GP | No. |
|---|---|---|---|
| Emmanuel Hazard, Houston | 1989 | 11 | 142 |
| Troy Edwards, Louisiana Tech | 1998 | 12 | 140 |
| Howard Twilley, Tulsa | 1965 | 10 | 134 |
| Trevor Insley, Nevada | 1999 | 11 | 134 |
| Alex Van Dyke, Nevada | 1995 | 11 | 129 |

**CATCHES PER GAME**

| | Year | No. | No./Game |
|---|---|---|---|
| Howard Twilley, Tulsa | 1965 | 134 | 13.4 |
| Emmanuel Hazard, Houston | 1989 | 142 | 12.9 |
| Trevor Insley, Nevada | 1999 | 134 | 12.2 |
| Troy Edwards, Louisiana Tech | 1998 | 140 | 11.7 |
| Alex Van Dyke, Nevada | 1995 | 129 | 11.7 |

**YARDS GAINED**

| | Year | Yds |
|---|---|---|
| Trevor Insley, Nevada | 1999 | 2,060 |
| Troy Edwards, Louisiana Tech | 1000 | 1,996 |
| Alex Van Dyke, Nevada | 1995 | 1,854 |
| Howard Twilley, Tulsa | 1965 | 1,779 |
| Troy Edwards, Louisiana Tech | 1997 | 1,707 |

**TOUCHDOWN CATCHES**

| | Year | TD |
|---|---|---|
| Troy Edwards, Louisiana Tech | 1998 | 27 |
| Randy Moss, Marshall | 1997 | 25 |
| Emmanuel Hazard, Houston | 1989 | 22 |
| Desmond Howard, Michigan | 1991 | 19 |

Five tied with 18.

## Single Game

### Scoring

**POINTS**

| | Opponent | Year | Pts |
|---|---|---|---|
| Howard Griffith, Illinois | Southern Illinois | 1990 | 48 |
| Marshall Faulk, San Diego St | Pacific | 1991 | 44 |
| Jim Brown, Syracuse | Colgate | 1956 | 43 |
| Showboat Boykin, Mississippi | Mississippi St | 1951 | 42 |
| Fred Wendt, UTEP* | New Mexico St | 1948 | 42 |

*UTEP was Texas Mines in 1948.

**FIELD GOALS**

| | Opponent | Year | FG |
|---|---|---|---|
| Dale Klein, Nebraska | Missouri | 1985 | 7 |
| Mike Prindle, Western Michigan | Marshall | 1984 | 7 |

Note: 13 tied with 6.
Klein's distances were 32-22-43-44-29-43-43. Prindle's distances were 32-44-42-23-48-41-27.

## Single Game *(Cont.)*

### Total Offense

| YARDS GAINED | Opponent | Year | Yds |
|---|---|---|---|
| David Klingler, Houston ...Arizona St | | 1990 | 732 |
| Matt Vogler, | | | |
| Texas Christian ...............Houston | | 1990 | 696 |
| David Klingler, Houston ...Texas Christian | | 1990 | 625 |
| Scott Mitchell, Utah.........Air Force | | 1988 | 625 |
| Jimmy Klingler, Houston...Rice | | 1992 | 612 |

### Passing

| YARDS GAINED | Opponent | Year | Yds |
|---|---|---|---|
| David Klingler, Houston ...Arizona St | | 1990 | 716 |
| Matt Vogler, | | | |
| Texas Christian ...............Houston | | 1990 | 690 |
| Scott Mitchell, Utah.........Air Force | | 1988 | 631 |
| Jeremy Leach, | | | |
| New Mexico ....................Utah | | 1989 | 622 |
| Dave Wilson, Illinois .........Ohio St | | 1980 | 621 |

| COMPLETIONS | Opponent | Year | Comp |
|---|---|---|---|
| Drew Brees, Purdue................Wisconsin | | 1998 | 55 |
| Rusty LaRue, Wake Forest.......Duke | | 1995 | 55 |
| Rusty LaRue, Wake Forest.......NC St | | 1995 | 50 |
| David Klingler, Houston .........SMU | | 1990 | 48 |
| Tim Couch, Kentucky...............Arkansas | | 1998 | 47 |
| Luke McCown, Louisiana Tech...Auburn | | 2000 | 47 |

| TOUCHDOWNS PASSING | Opponent | Year | TD |
|---|---|---|---|
| David Klingler, Houston...........E. Wash | | 1990 | 11 |

Note: Klingler's TD passes were 5-48-29-7-3-7-40-10-7-8-51.

### Rushing

| YARDS GAINED | Opponent | Year | Yds |
|---|---|---|---|
| LaDainian Tomlinson ........UTEP | | 1999 | 406 |
| Texas Christian | | | |
| Tony Sands, Kansas.........Missouri | | 1991 | 396 |
| Marshall Faulk, | | | |
| San Diego St....................Pacific | | 1991 | 386 |
| Troy Davis, Iowa St...........Missouri | | 1996 | 378 |
| Anthony Thompson, | | | |
| Indiana..............................Wisconsin | | 1989 | 377 |

| TOUCHDOWNS RUSHING | Opponent | Year | TD |
|---|---|---|---|
| Howard Griffith, Illinois .....Southern Illinois | | 1990 | 8 |

Note: Griffith's TD runs were 5-51-7-41-5-18-5-3.

### Receiving

| CATCHES | Opponent | Year | No. |
|---|---|---|---|
| Randy Gatewood, UNLV | Idaho | 1994 | 23 |
| Jay Miller, Brigham Young | New Mexico | 1973 | 22 |
| Troy Edwards, La. Tech | Nebraska | 1998 | 21 |
| Chris Daniels, Purdue | Michigan St | 1999 | 21 |
| Rick Eber, Tulsa | Idaho St | 1967 | 20 |
| Kenny Christian, | | | |
| Eastern Michigan | Temple | 2000 | 20 |

| YARDS GAINED | Opponent | Year | Yds |
|---|---|---|---|
| Troy Edwards,Louisiana Tech | Nebraska | 1998 | 405 |
| Randy Gatewood, UNLV | Idaho | 1994 | 363 |
| Chuck Hughes, UTEP* | N Texas St | 1965 | 349 |
| Rick Eber, Tulsa | Idaho St | 1967 | 322 |
| Harry Wood, Tulsa | Idaho St | 1967 | 318 |

*UTEP was Texas Western in 1965.

| TOUCHDOWN CATCHES | Opponent | Year | TD |
|---|---|---|---|
| Tim Delaney, San Diego St | New Mex. St | 1969 | 6 |

Note: Delaney's TD catches were 2-22-34-31-30-9.

## Longest Plays (since 1941)

| PASSING | Opponent | Year | Yds |
|---|---|---|---|
| Fred Owens to Jack Ford, | | | |
| Portland...................................St. Mary's (CA) | | 1947 | 99 |
| Bo Burris to Warren | | | |
| McVea, Houston ..................Washington St | | 1966 | 99 |
| Colin Clapton to Eddie | | | |
| Jenkins, Holy Cross ............Boston U | | 1970 | 99 |
| Terry Peel to Robert Ford, | | | |
| Houston..................................Syracuse | | 1970 | 99 |
| Terry Peel to Robert Ford, | | | |
| Houston..................................San Diego St | | 1972 | 99 |
| Cris Collinsworth to Derrick | | | |
| Gaffney, Florida ....................Rice | | 1977 | 99 |
| Scott Ankrom to James | | | |
| Maness, Texas Christian.......Rice | | 1984 | 99 |
| Gino Toretta to Horace | | | |
| Copeland, Miami (FL) ...........Arkansas | | 1991 | 99 |
| John Paci to Thomas Lewis, | | | |
| Indiana ..................................Penn St | | 1993 | 99 |
| Troy DeGar to Wes Caswell, | | | |
| Tulsa ......................................Oklahoma | | 1996 | 99 |
| Drew Brees to Vinny Sutherland, | | | |
| Purdue ...................................Northwestern | | 1999 | 99 |
| Dan Urban to Justin McCariens, | | | |
| Northern Illinois .....................Ball St | | 2000 | 99 |

| RUSHING | Opponent | Year | Yd |
|---|---|---|---|
| Gale Sayers, Kansas ...........Nebraska | | 1963 | 99 |
| Max Anderson, Arizona St ....Wyoming | | 1967 | 99 |
| Ralph Thompson, | | | |
| W Texas St............................Wichita St | | 1970 | 99 |
| Kelsey Finch, Tennessee......Florida | | 1977 | 99 |
| Eric Vann, Kansas.................Oklahoma | | 1997 | 99 |

| FIELD GOALS | Opponent | Year | Yds |
|---|---|---|---|
| Steve Little, Arkansas.............Texas | | 1977 | 67 |
| Russell Erxleben, Texas.........Rice | | 1977 | 67 |
| Joe Williams, Wichita St ........Southern IL | | 1978 | 67 |
| Martin Gramatica, Kansas St .Northern IL | | 1998 | 65 |
| Tony Franklin, Texas A&M .....Baylor | | 1976 | 65 |

| PUNTS | Opponent | Year | Yds |
|---|---|---|---|
| Pat Brady, Nevada* ...............Loyola (CA) | | 1950 | 99 |
| George O'Brien, Wisconsin....Iowa | | 1952 | 96 |
| John Hadl, Kansas.................Oklahoma | | 1959 | 94 |
| Carl Knox, Texas Christian.....Oklahoma St | | 1947 | 94 |
| Preston Johnson, SMU...........Pittsburgh | | 1940 | 94 |

*Nevada was Nevada-Reno in 1950.

# Notable Achievements

## DIVISION I-A WINNINGEST TEAMS

### Alltime Winning Percentage

| | Yrs | W | L | T | Pct | GP | Bowl Record |
|---|---|---|---|---|---|---|---|
| Notre Dame | 112 | 776 | 240 | 42 | .753 | 1,058 | 13-11-0 |
| Michigan | 121 | 805 | 262 | 36 | .746 | 1,103 | 16-15-0 |
| Alabama | 106 | 737 | 276 | 43 | .718 | 1,056 | 28-19-3 |
| Nebraska | 111 | 753 | 299 | 40 | .708 | 1,092 | 20-19-0 |
| Ohio St | 111 | 724 | 287 | 53 | .705 | 1,064 | 14-18-0 |
| Oklahoma | 106 | 702 | 278 | 53 | .705 | 1,033 | 20-12-1 |
| Texas | 108 | 744 | 302 | 33 | .705 | 1,079 | 18-20-2 |
| Tennessee | 104 | 707 | 292 | 52 | .697 | 1,051 | 22-19-0 |
| Penn St | 114 | 739 | 312 | 41 | .695 | 1,092 | 23-11-2 |
| Southern Cal | 108 | 678 | 288 | 54 | .691 | 1,020 | 25-14-0 |
| Florida St | 54 | 392 | 185 | 17 | .674 | 594 | 17-10-2 |
| Boise St | 33 | 251 | 129 | 2 | .659 | 382 | 2-0-0 |
| Washington | 111 | 617 | 336 | 50 | .640 | 1,003 | 14-12-1 |
| Miami (OH) | 112 | 597 | 332 | 44 | .636 | 973 | 5-2-0 |
| Georgia | 107 | 641 | 362 | 54 | .632 | 1,057 | 19-14-3 |
| Louisiana St | 107 | 618 | 360 | 47 | .625 | 1,025 | 15-16-1 |
| Arizona St | 88 | 490 | 289 | 24 | .625 | 803 | 10-7-1 |
| Central Michigan | 100 | 512 | 301 | 36 | .624 | 849 | 0-2-0 |
| Miami (FL) | 74 | 472 | 282 | 19 | .622 | 773 | 14-11-0 |
| Auburn | 108 | 610 | 365 | 47 | .619 | 1,022 | 14-11-2 |
| Army | 111 | 618 | 374 | 51 | .617 | 1,043 | 2-2-0 |
| Colorado | 111 | 611 | 376 | 36 | .615 | 1,023 | 11-12-0 |
| Florida | 94 | 564 | 347 | 40 | .614 | 951 | 12-15-0 |
| Texas A&M | 106 | 609 | 386 | 48 | .607 | 1,043 | 12-14-0 |
| Syracuse | 111 | 638 | 411 | 49 | .603 | 1,098 | 11-8-1 |

Note: Includes bowl games.

### Alltime Victories

| | | | | | |
|---|---|---|---|---|---|
| Michigan | 805 | Georgia | 641 | N Carolina | 600 |
| Notre Dame | 776 | Syracuse | 638 | Miami (OH) | 597 |
| Nebraska | 753 | Army | 618 | Pittsburgh | 596 |
| Texas | 744 | Louisiana St | 618 | Arkansas | 594 |
| Penn St | 739 | Washington | 617 | Minnesota | 587 |
| Alabama | 737 | Colorado | 611 | Navy | 579 |
| Ohio St | 724 | Auburn | 610 | Virginia Tech | 579 |
| Tennessee | 707 | Texas A&M | 609 | Clemson | 571 |
| Oklahoma | 702 | W Virginia | 603 | Florida | 564 |
| Southern Cal | 673 | Georgia Tech | 601 | Michigan St | 561 |

### NUMBER ONE VS NUMBER TWO

The No. 1 and No. 2 teams, according to the Associated Press Poll, have met 33 times, including 13 bowl games, since the poll's inception in 1936. The No. 1 teams have a 20-11-2 record in these matchups. Notre Dame (4-3-2) has played in nine of the games.

| Date | Results | Stadium |
|---|---|---|
| 10-9-43 | No. 1 Notre Dame 35, No. 2 Michigan 12 | Michigan (Ann Arbor) |
| 11-20-43 | No. 1 Notre Dame 14, No. 2 Iowa Pre-Flight 13 | Notre Dame (South Bend) |
| 12-2-44 | No. 1 Army 23, No. 2 Navy 7 | Municipal (Baltimore) |
| 11-10-45 | No. 1 Army 48, No. 2 Notre Dame 0 | Yankee (New York) |
| 12-1-45 | No. 1 Army 32, No. 2 Navy 13 | Municipal (Philadelphia) |
| 11-9-46 | No. 1 Army 0, No. 2 Notre Dame 0 | Yankee (New York) |
| 1-1-63 | No. 1 Southern Cal 42, No. 2 Wisconsin 37 (Rose Bowl) | Rose Bowl (Pasadena) |
| 10-12-63 | No. 2 Texas 28, No. 1 Oklahoma 7 | Cotton Bowl (Dallas) |
| 1-1-64 | No. 1 Texas 28, No. 2 Navy 6 (Cotton Bowl) | Cotton Bowl (Dallas) |
| 11-19-66 | No. 1 Notre Dame 10, No. 2 Michigan St 10 | Spartan (E Lansing) |
| 9-28-68 | No. 1 Purdue 37, No. 2 Notre Dame 22 | Notre Dame (South Bend) |
| 1-1-69 | No. 1 Ohio St 27, No. 2 Southern Cal 16 (Rose Bowl) | Rose Bowl (Pasadena) |
| 12-6-69 | No. 1 Texas 15, No. 2 Arkansas 14 | Razorback (Fayetteville) |
| 11-25-71 | No. 1 Nebraska 35, No. 2 Oklahoma 31 | Owen Field (Norman) |
| 1-1-72 | No. 1 Nebraska 38, No. 2 Alabama 6 (Orange Bowl) | Orange Bowl (Miami) |
| 1-1-79 | No. 2 Alabama 14, No. 1 Penn St 7 (Sugar Bowl) | Sugar Bowl (New Orleans) |
| 9-26-81 | No. 1 Southern Cal 28, No. 2 Oklahoma 24 | Coliseum (Los Angeles) |
| 1-1-83 | No. 2 Penn St 27, No. 1 Georgia 23 (Sugar Bowl) | Sugar Bowl (New Orleans) |

## NUMBER ONE VS NUMBER TWO *(Cont.)*

| Date | Results | Stadium |
|------|---------|---------|
| 10-19-85 | No. 1 Iowa 12, No. 2 Michigan 10 | Kinnick (Iowa City) |
| 9-27-86 | No. 2 Miami (FL) 28, No. 1 Oklahoma 16 | Orange Bowl (Miami) |
| 1-2-87 | No. 2 Penn St 14, No. 1 Miami (FL) 10 (Fiesta Bowl) | Sun Devil (Tempe) |
| 11-21-87 | No. 2 Oklahoma 17, No. 1 Nebraska 7 | Memorial (Lincoln) |
| 1-1-88 | No. 2 Miami (FL) 20, No. 1 Oklahoma 14 (Orange Bowl) | Orange Bowl (Miami) |
| 11-26-88 | No. 1 Notre Dame 27, No. 2 Southern Cal 10 | Coliseum (Los Angeles) |
| 9-16-89 | No. 1 Notre Dame 24, No. 2 Michigan 19 | Michigan (Ann Arbor) |
| 11-16-91 | No. 2 Miami (FL) 17, No. 1 Florida St 16 | Campbell (Tallahassee) |
| 1-1-93 | No. 2 Alabama 34, No. 1 Miami (FL) 13 (Sugar Bowl) | Superdome (New Orleans) |
| 11-13-93 | No. 2 Notre Dame 31, No. 1 Florida St 24 | Notre Dame (South Bend) |
| 1-1-94 | No. 1 Florida St 18, No. 2 Nebraska 16 (Orange Bowl) | Orange Bowl (Miami) |
| 1-2-96 | No. 1 Nebraska 62, No. 2 Florida 24 (Fiesta Bowl) | Sun Devil (Tempe) |
| 11-30-96 | No. 2 Florida St 24, No. 1 Florida 21 | Campbell (Tallahassee) |
| 1-4-99 | No. 1 Tennessee 23, No. 2 Florida St 16 (Fiesta Bowl) | Sun Devil (Tempe) |
| 1-4-00 | No. 1 Florida St 46, No. 2 Virginia Tech 29 (Sugar Bowl) | Superdome (New Orleans) |

## LONGEST DIVISION I-A WINNING STREAKS

| Wins | Team | Yrs | Ended by | Score |
|------|------|-----|----------|-------|
| 47 | Oklahoma | 1953–57 | Notre Dame | 7–0 |
| 39 | Washington | 1908–14 | Oregon St | 0–0 |
| 37 | Yale | 1890–93 | Princeton | 6–0 |
| 37 | Yale | 1887–89 | Princeton | 10–0 |
| 35 | Toledo | 1969–71 | Tampa | 21–0 |
| 34 | Pennsylvania | 1894–96 | Lafayette | 6–4 |
| 31 | Oklahoma | 1948–50 | Kentucky | 13–7 |
| 31 | Pittsburgh | 1914–18 | Cleveland Naval Reserve | 10–9 |
| 31 | Pennsylvania | 1896–98 | Harvard | 10–0 |
| 30 | Texas | 1968–70 | Notre Dame | 24–11 |

## LONGEST DIVISION I-A UNBEATEN STREAKS

| No. | W | T | Team | Yrs | Ended by | Score |
|-----|---|---|------|-----|----------|-------|
| 63 | 59 | 4 | Washington | 1907–17 | California | 27–0 |
| 56 | 55 | 1 | Michigan | 1901–05 | Chicago | 2–0 |
| 50 | 46 | 4 | California | 1920–25 | Olympic Club | 15–0 |
| 48 | 47 | 1 | Oklahoma | 1953–57 | Notre Dame | 7–0 |
| 48 | 47 | 1 | Yale | 1885–89 | Princeton | 10–0 |
| 47 | 42 | 5 | Yale | 1879–85 | Princeton | 6–5 |
| 44 | 42 | 2 | Yale | 1894–96 | Princeton | 24–6 |
| 42 | 39 | 3 | Yale | 1904–08 | Harvard | 4–0 |
| 39 | 37 | 2 | Notre Dame | 1946–50 | Purdue | 28–14 |
| 37 | 36 | 1 | Oklahoma | 1972–75 | Kansas | 23–3 |
| 37 | 37 | 0 | Yale | 1890–93 | Princeton | 6–0 |
| 35 | 35 | 0 | Toledo | 1969–71 | Tampa | 21–0 |
| 35 | 34 | 1 | Minnesota | 1903–05 | Wisconsin | 16–12 |
| 34 | 33 | 1 | Nebraska | 1912–16 | Kansas | 7–3 |
| 34 | 34 | 0 | Pennsylvania | 1894–96 | Lafayette | 6–4 |
| 34 | 32 | 2 | Princeton | 1884–87 | Harvard | 12–0 |
| 34 | 29 | 5 | Princeton | 1877–82 | Harvard | 1–0 |
| 33 | 30 | 3 | Tennessee | 1926–30 | Alabama | 18–6 |
| 33 | 31 | 2 | Georgia Tech | 1914–18 | Pittsburgh | 32–0 |
| 33 | 30 | 3 | Harvard | 1911–15 | Cornell | 10–0 |
| 32 | 31 | 1 | Nebraska | 1969–71 | UCLA | 20–17 |
| 32 | 30 | 2 | Army | 1944–47 | Columbia | 21–20 |
| 32 | 31 | 1 | Harvard | 1898–1900 | Yale | 28–0 |
| 31 | 30 | 1 | Penn St | 1967–70 | Colorado | 41–13 |
| 31 | 30 | 1 | San Diego St | 1967–70 | Long Beach St | 27–11 |
| 31 | 29 | 2 | Georgia Tech | 1950–53 | Notre Dame | 27–14 |
| 31 | 31 | 0 | Oklahoma | 1948–50 | Kentucky | 13–7 |
| 31 | 31 | 0 | Pittsburgh | 1914–18 | Cleveland Naval | 10–9 |
| 31 | 31 | 0 | Pennsylvania | 1896–98 | Harvard | 10–0 |

Note: Includes bowl games.

## LONGEST DIVISION I-A LOSING STREAKS

| Losses | | Seasons | Ended Against | Score |
|---|---|---|---|---|
| 34 | Northwestern | 1979–82 | Northern Illinois | 31–6 |
| 28 | Virginia | 1958–61 | William & Mary | 21–6 |
| 28 | Kansas St | 1945–48 | Arkansas St | 37–6 |
| 27 | New Mexico St | 1988–90 | Cal St–Fullerton | 43–9 |
| 27 | Eastern Michigan | 1980–82 | Kent St | 9–7 |

## MOST-PLAYED DIVISION I-A RIVALRIES

| GP | Opponents (Series Leader Listed First) | Record | First Game |
|---|---|---|---|
| 110 | Minnesota-Wisconsin | 57-45-8 | 1890 |
| 109 | Missouri-Kansas | 50-50-9 | 1891 |
| 107 | Nebraska-Kansas | 83-21-3 | 1892 |
| 107 | Texas–Texas A&M | 68-34-5 | 1894 |
| 105 | Miami (OH)-Cincinnati | 55-43-7 | 1888 |
| 105 | N Carolina–Virginia | 55-46-4 | 1892 |
| 104 | Auburn-Georgia | 50-46-8 | 1892 |
| 104 | Oregon–Oregon St | 52-42-10 | 1894 |
| 103 | Purdue-Indiana | 63-34-6 | 1891 |
| 103 | Baylor–Texas Christian* | 49-47-7 | 1899 |
| 103 | Stanford-California | 53-39-11 | 1892 |

| GP | Opponents (Series Leader Listed First) | Record | First Game |
|---|---|---|---|
| 101 | Army-Navy | 48-46-7 | 1890 |
| 100 | Utah–Utah St | 68-28-4 | 1892 |
| 98 | Clemson–S Carolina | 59-35-4 | 1896 |
| 98 | Kansas-Kansas St | 61-32-5 | 1902 |
| 97 | N Carolina–Wake Forest | 65-30-2 | 1888 |
| 97 | Michigan–Ohio St | 56-35-6 | 1897 |
| 97 | Mississippi–Miss St | 55-36-6 | 1901 |
| 96 | Oklahoma-Kansas | 63-27-6 | 1903 |
| 96 | Tennessee-Kentucky | 64-23-9 | 1893 |
| 96 | Penn St–Pittsburgh | 50-42-4 | 1893 |

*Have not met since 1996.

# NCAA Coaches' Records

## ALLTIME WINNINGEST DIVISION I-A COACHES

| Coach (Alma Mater) | Colleges Coached | Yrs | W | L | T | Pct |
|---|---|---|---|---|---|---|
| Knute Rockne (Notre Dame '14)† | Notre Dame 1918–30 | 13 | 105 | 12 | 5 | .881 |
| Frank W. Leahy (Notre Dame '31)† | Boston Col 1939–40; Notre Dame 1941–43, 1946–53 | 13 | 107 | 13 | 9 | .864 |
| George W. Woodruff (Yale 1889)† | Pennsylvania 1892–01; Illinois 1903; Carlisle 1905 | 12 | 142 | 25 | 2 | .846 |
| Barry Switzer (Arkansas '60) | Oklahoma 1973–88 | 16 | 157 | 29 | 4 | .837 |
| Tom Osborne (Hastings '59)† | Nebraska 1973–98 | 25 | 255 | 49 | 3 | .836 |
| Percy D. Haughton (Harvard 1899)† | Cornell 1899–1900; Harvard 1908–16; Columbia 1923–24 | 13 | 96 | 17 | 6 | .832 |
| Bob Neyland (Army '16)† | Tennessee 1926–34, 1936–40, 1946–52 | 21 | 173 | 31 | 12 | .829 |
| Fielding Yost (W Virginia 1895)† | Ohio Wesleyan 1897; Nebraska 1898; Kansas 1899; Stanford 1900; Michigan 1901–23, 1925–26 | 29 | 196 | 36 | 12 | .828 |
| Bud Wilkinson (Minnesota '37)† | Oklahoma 1947–63 | 17 | 145 | 29 | 4 | .826 |
| Jock Sutherland (Pittsburgh '18)† | Lafayette 1919–23; Pittsburgh 1924–38 | 20 | 144 | 28 | 14 | .812 |
| Bob Devaney (Alma, MI '39)† | Wyoming 1957–61; Nebraska 1962–72 | 16 | 136 | 30 | 7 | .806 |
| Frank W. Thomas (Notre Dame '23)† | Tenn.-Chattanooga 1925–28; Alabama 1931–42, 1944–46 | 19 | 141 | 33 | 9 | .795 |
| Henry L. Williams (Yale 1891)† | Army 1891; Minnesota 1900–21 | 23 | 141 | 34 | 12 | .786 |
| Gil Dobie (Minnesota '02)† | N Dakota St 1906–07; Washington 1908-16; Navy 1917–19; Cornell 1920–35; Boston College 1936–38 | 33 | 180 | 45 | 15 | .781 |
| *Bobby Bowden (Samford '53) | Samford 1959–62; W Virginia 1970–75; Florida St 1976– | 35 | 315 | 87 | 4 | .781 |
| Bear Bryant (Alabama '36)† | Maryland 1945, Kentucky 1946–53, Texas A&M 1954–57, Alabama 1958–82 | 38 | 323 | 85 | 17 | .780 |

*Active coach. †Hall of Fame member.

Note: Minimum 10 years as head coach at Division I institutions; record at four-year colleges only; bowl games included; ties computed as half won, half lost.

### ALLTIME WINNINGEST DIVISION I-A COACHES (Cont.)
#### By Victories

| | Yrs | W | L | T | Pct | | Yrs | W | L | T | Pct |
|---|---|---|---|---|---|---|---|---|---|---|---|
| Paul (Bear) Bryant | 38 | 323 | 85 | 17 | .780 | Hayden Fry | 37 | 232 | 178 | 10 | .564 |
| *Joe Paterno | 35 | 322 | 90 | 3 | .780 | *Lou Holtz | 29 | 224 | 110 | 7 | .667 |
| Glenn (Pop) Warner | 44 | 319 | 106 | 32 | .733 | Jess Neely | 40 | 207 | 176 | 19 | .539 |
| *Bobby Bowden | 35 | 315 | 87 | 4 | .781 | Warren Woodson | 31 | 203 | 95 | 14 | .673 |
| Amos Alonzo Stagg | 57 | 314 | 199 | 35 | .605 | Don Nehlen | 30 | 202 | 128 | 8 | .609 |
| LaVell Edwards | 29 | 257 | 100 | 3 | .718 | Vince Dooley | 25 | 201 | 77 | 10 | .715 |
| Tom Osborne | 25 | 255 | 49 | 3 | .836 | Eddie Anderson | 39 | 201 | 128 | 15 | .606 |
| Woody Hayes | 33 | 238 | 72 | 10 | .759 | *Active coach. | | | | | |
| Bo Schembechler | 27 | 234 | 65 | 8 | .775 | | | | | | |

### Most Bowl Victories

| | W | L | T | | W | L | T |
|---|---|---|---|---|---|---|---|
| *Joe Paterno | 20 | 9 | 1 | Barry Switzer | 8 | 5 | 0 |
| *Bobby Bowden | 17 | 6 | 1 | *Jackie Sherrill | 8 | 6 | 0 |
| Paul (Bear) Bryant | 15 | 12 | 2 | Darrell Royal | 8 | 7 | 1 |
| Jim Wacker | 13 | 2 | 0 | Vince Dooley | 8 | 10 | 2 |
| Tom Osborne | 12 | 13 | 0 | Pat Dye | 7 | 2 | 1 |
| *Lou Holtz | 11 | 8 | 2 | Bob Devaney | 7 | 3 | 0 |
| Don James | 10 | 5 | 0 | Dan Devine | 7 | 3 | 0 |
| John Vaught | 10 | 8 | 0 | Earle Bruce | 7 | 5 | 0 |
| Bobby Dodd | 9 | 4 | 0 | Charlie McClendon | 7 | 6 | 0 |
| Johnny Majors | 9 | 7 | 0 | Hayden Fry | 7 | 9 | 1 |
| *John Robinson | 8 | 1 | 0 | LaVell Edwards | 7 | 14 | 1 |
| Terry Donahue | 8 | 4 | 1 | *Active coach. | | | |

### WINNINGEST ACTIVE DIVISION I-A COACHES
#### By Percentage

| Coach, College | Yrs | W | L | T | Pct# | Bowls W | L | T |
|---|---|---|---|---|---|---|---|---|
| Phillip Fulmer, Tennessee | 9 | 84 | 18 | 0 | .824 | 5 | 4 | 0 |
| Bobby Bowden, Florida St | 35 | 315 | 87 | 4 | .781 | 17 | 6 | 1 |
| Joe Paterno, Penn St | 35 | 322 | 90 | 3 | .780 | 20 | 9 | 1 |
| Steve Spurrier, Florida | 14 | 132 | 38 | 2 | .773 | 5 | 6 | 0 |
| R. C. Slocum, Texas A&M | 12 | 109 | 37 | 2 | .743 | 2 | 8 | 0 |
| Dennis Erickson, Oregon St | 15 | 131 | 45 | 1 | .743 | *6 | 6 | 0 |
| Rick Neuheisel, Washington | 6 | 51 | 20 | 0 | .718 | 4 | 1 | 0 |
| John Robinson, UNLV | 14 | 115 | 48 | 4 | .701 | 8 | 1 | 0 |
| Bill Snyder, Kansas St | 12 | 99 | 43 | 1 | .696 | 5 | 3 | 0 |
| Paul Pasqualoni, Syracuse | 15 | 115 | 53 | 1 | .681 | 5 | 2 | 0 |

#Bowl games included in overall record.   Ties computed as half win, half loss.   *Includes record in NCAA and/or NAIA championships.

Note: Minimum five years as Division I-A head coach; record at four-year colleges only.

### THEY SAID IT

*Frank Beamer, Virginia Tech coach, on Hokies quarterback Michael Vick: "We have two plays when he's in the game—the one we call and the one he winds up turning it into."*

## WINNINGEST ACTIVE DIVISION I-A COACHES *(Cont.)*
### By Victories

| | | | |
|---|---|---|---|
| Joe Paterno, Penn St | 322 | Frank Beamer, Virginia Tech | 141 |
| Bobby Bowden, Florida St | 315 | Dennis Franchione, Texas Christian | 138 |
| Lou Holtz, S Carolina | 224 | Fisher DeBerry, Air Force | 135 |
| Jackie Sherrill, Mississippi St | 172 | Steve Spurrier, Florida | 132 |
| Ken Hatfield, Rice | 147 | Dennis Erickson, Oregon St | 131 |

## WINNINGEST ACTIVE DIVISION I-AA COACHES
### By Percentage

| Coach, College | Yrs | W | L | T | Pct* |
|---|---|---|---|---|---|
| Mike Kelly, Dayton | 20 | 183 | 39 | 1 | .823 |
| Al Bagnoli, Pennsylvania | 19 | 150 | 44 | 0 | .773 |
| Pete Richardson, Southern | 13 | 113 | 37 | 1 | .752 |
| Larry Blakeney, Troy St | 10 | 91 | 30 | 1 | .750 |
| Greg Gattuso, Duquesne | 8 | 63 | 22 | 0 | .741 |
| Joe Walton, Robert Morris | 7 | 52 | 18 | 1 | .739 |
| Joe Gardi, Hofstra | 11 | 90 | 33 | 2 | .728 |
| Tubby Raymond, Delaware | 35 | 296 | 113 | 3 | .722 |
| Roy Kidd, Eastern Kentucky | 37 | 299 | 117 | 8 | .715 |
| Billy Joe, Florida A&M | 27 | 214 | 85 | 4 | .713 |

*Playoff games included.

Note: Minimum five years as a Division I-A and/or Division I-AA head coach; record at four-year colleges only.

### By Victories

| | | | |
|---|---|---|---|
| Roy Kidd, Eastern Kentucky | 299 | Bill Hayes, N Carolina A&T | 183 |
| Tubby Raymond, Delaware | 296 | Willie Jeffries, S Carolina St | 173 |
| Billy Joe, Florida A&M | 214 | Al Bagnoli, Pennsylvania | 150 |
| Ron Randleman, Sam Houston St | 191 | Walt Hameline, Wagner | 147 |
| Mike Kelly, Dayton | 183 | Bob Ricca, St. John's (NY) | 145 |

## WINNINGEST ACTIVE DIVISION II COACHES
### By Percentage

| Coach, College | Yrs | W | L | T | Pct* |
|---|---|---|---|---|---|
| Chuck Broyles, Pittsburg St | 11 | 112 | 21 | 2 | .837 |
| Ken Sparks, Carson-Newman | 21 | 205 | 48 | 2 | .808 |
| David Bennett, Catawba | 6 | 52 | 15 | 0 | .776 |
| Bob Biggs, UC–Davis | 8 | 71 | 24 | 1 | .745 |
| Danny Hale, Bloomsburg | 13 | 104 | 40 | 1 | .721 |
| Peter Yetten, Bentley | 13 | 89 | 36 | 1 | .710 |
| Frank Cignetti, Indiana (PA) | 19 | 157 | 65 | 1 | .706 |
| Brian Kelly, Grand Valley St | 10 | 77 | 33 | 2 | .696 |
| Mel Tjeerdsma, NW Missouri St | 17 | 130 | 60 | 4 | .680 |
| George Mihalik, Slippery Rock | 13 | 95 | 45 | 4 | .674 |

*Ties computed as half win, half loss. Playoff games included.

Note: Minimum five years as a college head coach; record at four-year colleges only.

### By Victories

| | | | |
|---|---|---|---|
| Ken Sparks, Carson-Newman | 205 | Gary Howard, Central Oklahoma | 152 |
| Willard Bailey, Virginia Union | 191 | Jerry Vandergriff, Angelo St | 130 |
| Bud Elliott, Eastern New Mexico | 179 | Mel Tjeerdsma, NW Missouri St | 130 |
| Frank Cignetti, Indiana (PA) | 157 | Monte Cater, Shepherd | 122 |
| Dennis Douds, E Stroudsburg | 155 | Chuck Broyles, Pittsburg St | 112 |

## WINNINGEST ACTIVE DIVISION III
### By Percentage

| Coach, College | Yrs | W | L | T | Pct* |
|---|---|---|---|---|---|
| Larry Kehres, Mount Union | 15 | 164 | 17 | 3 | .899 |
| Dick Farley, Williams | 14 | 93 | 16 | 3 | .844 |
| K.C. Keeler, Rowan | 8 | 77 | 19 | 1 | .799 |
| John Gagliardi, St. John's (MN) | 52 | 377 | 109 | 11 | .770 |
| Frosty Westering, Pacific Lutheran | 36 | 286 | 86 | 7 | .764 |
| Frank Girardi, Lycoming | 29 | 218 | 68 | 5 | .758 |
| Jimmie Keeling, Hardin-Simmons | 11 | 93 | 30 | 0 | .756 |
| Bob Packard, Baldwin-Wallace | 20 | 150 | 50 | 2 | .748 |
| Wayne Perry, Hanover | 9 | 70 | 25 | 0 | .737 |
| Jim Barnes, Augustana (IL) | 6 | 44 | 16 | 0 | .733 |

*Ties computed as half won, half lost. Playoff games included.

Note: Minimum five years as a college head coach; record at four-year colleges only.

### By Victories

John Gagliardi, St John's (MN) ... 377
Frosty Westering, Pacific Lutheran ... 286
Frank Girardi, Lycoming ... 218
Peter Mazzaferro, Bridgewater (MA) ... 188
Tom Gilburg, Franklin & Marshall ... 155

Larry Kehres, Mount Union ... 164
Bob Packard, Baldwin-Wallace ... 150
Eric Hamilton, College of New Jersey ... 147
Lou Wacker, Emory & Henry ... 146
Rick Giancola, Montclair St ... 125

# NAIA Coaches' Records

## WINNINGEST ACTIVE NAIA COACHES
### By Percentage

| Coach, College | Yrs | W | L | T | Pct* |
|---|---|---|---|---|---|
| Ted Kessinger, Bethany (KS) | 25 | 200 | 49 | 1 | .802 |
| Hank Biesiot, Dickinson St (ND) | 26 | 176 | 62 | 1 | .738 |
| Geno DeMarco, Geneva (PA) | 5 | 37 | 15 | 0 | .712 |
| Carl Poelker, McKendree (IL) | 19 | 121 | 55 | 1 | .686 |
| Orv Otten, Northwestern (IA) | 6 | 43 | 21 | 0 | .672 |
| Vic Wallace, Lambuth (TN) | 19 | 136 | 69 | 4 | .660 |
| Bob Young, Sioux Falls (SD) | 19 | 125 | 64 | 3 | .659 |
| Monty Lewis, Southwestern (KS) | 8 | 54 | 28 | 0 | .659 |
| Larry Wilcox, Benedictine (KS) | 22 | 147 | 80 | 0 | .648 |
| John Frangoulis, Baker (KS) | 5 | 33 | 19 | 0 | .635 |

*Playoff games included.

Note: Minimum five years as a collegiate head coach and includes record against four-year institutions only.

### By Victories

Ted Kessinger, Bethany (KS) ... 200
Hank Biesiot, Dickinson St (ND) ... 176
Bill Ramseyer, Virginia's College at Wise ... 170
Larry Wilcox, Benedictine (KS) ... 147
Vic Wallace, Lambuth (TN) ... 136

Kevin Donley, St. Francis (IN) ... 135
Bob Young, Sioux Falls (SD) ... 125
Carl Poelker, McKendree (IL) ... 121
Jim Dennison, Walsh (OH) ... 119
Fran Schwenk, Doane (NE) ... 97

Kobe Bryant
of the NBA champion
Los Angeles Lakers

# Pro
# Basketball

# Double Feature

## Capping a season of infighting with a dominating title run, the team from Hollywood gave fans two dramas to savor in 2000–01

### BY MARK BEECH

IN HINDSIGHT it seems almost impossible that anyone could have foreseen a different ending to the 2000–01 season. The Los Angeles Lakers steamed to their second straight NBA championship, and after their title-clinching victory over the Philadelphia 76ers, the words *dynasty* and *greatness* started popping in the air like the champagne corks the players released in celebration.

Could there really have been doubts about this team? With the 7'1", 315-pound Shaquille O'Neal in the pivot—an irresistible force on offense and an immovable object on defense—and the silky Kobe Bryant slashing from the perimeter, the Lakers went 67–15 en route to the 1999–2000 NBA title. There was no reason they couldn't repeat the feat in 2000–01. Yet there were doubts, and they surfaced early in the season.

Both Bryant and O'Neal came into the season with their eyes fixed firmly on the game's most coveted prize. Bryant claimed to have spent his summer in the gym, not leaving each day until he'd sunk 2,000 jumpers from 15 feet and beyond; O'Neal re-upped with the purple and gold for three more years and $88.4 million. "Winning one championship trophy is like having one car," he said after signing the deal, with his Rolls-Royce waiting in the parking lot. "It's not enough for me."

Unfortunately for L.A., Shaq and Kobe didn't agree as to how that second championship should be won. O'Neal wanted his teammates to climb aboard his broad shoulders, as they had during his MVP season the previous year, and let him return them to the promised land. Bryant, for his part, seemed to want a more prominent role on the team. He was sure he was capable of leading the Lakers, and he refused to defer to Shaq on offense. Befitting a team from Tinseltown, a jealous squabble ensued. The feud enthralled and exasperated Angelenos for most of the season. The defending champs were plagued by inconsistency for much of the year before the two stars worked out a tentative time-share agreement for the Hollywood spotlight. Reeling off eight wins to

**O'Neal averaged 33 points a game during the Finals.**

MANNY MILLAN

end the regular season, L.A. lifted its record to a respectable 56–26, tied for second best in the league.

But on the eve of the playoffs, Los Angeles was considered vulnerable. Many of the courtside cognoscenti predicted that the Lakers wouldn't make it beyond the Western Conference finals, a notion that vaporized faster than *Pearl Harbor*'s Oscar prospects. The Lakers rolled through the postseason, dispatching opponents with arrogance and gusto, trampling them with O'Neal one night and dazzling them with Bryant the next. They swept Portland in the first round, Sacramento in the second, and then, in the hotly anticipated conference finals against San Antonio, the 1999 NBA champion and the team with the league's best regular-season record (58–24), the Lakers removed all doubts about their dominance.

The Spurs had suggested that the 1999–2000 season might have been different had their star big man, Tim Duncan, not gone down with an injury. They were eager to match their inside tandem of Duncan and David Robinson against Shaq and the Lakers, and many observers expected an epic series. Instead, San Antonio was blown right out of the water. The Lakers won the first two games at the Alamodome and then routed the Spurs twice in L.A. to complete the sweep and return to the NBA Finals, carrying an 11–0 postseason record. They hadn't lost a game in two months, and they had a chance to run the table in the playoffs, something no NBA team—not Jordan's

Bulls, Chamberlain's Lakers or Russell's Celtics—had done. Just like that, they'd gone from vulnerable to invincible. "There's no way any Eastern team can beat them," said Robinson.

But in Game 1 of the championship series, this Hollywood sequel had a most unexpected twist: The tenacious 76ers toppled the mighty Lakers in overtime 107–101. Forgoing the usual strategy of double-teaming O'Neal, Philadelphia let center Dikembe Mutombo play one-on-one against Shaq and concentrated on shutting down everybody else. O'Neal scored 44 points, but Bryant shot just 7 for 22 from the field and blew a chance to win the game in regulation when he turned the ball over with 18 seconds left and the score tied 94–94. Philadelphia's explosive, scrappy guard, Allen Iverson, the regular-season MVP, poured in 48 points to lead the Sixers.

But the plot reverted to form during the

**Twenty-one-year-old McGrady (with ball) dazzled opponents and fans alike.**

next four games, as the Lakers rolled to the title even as the irrepressible, overmatched Sixers kept finding ways to make the games close. In Game 3, a 96–91 Lakers victory, Philadelphia pressured Bryant into an uneven shooting night (3 for 14 in the second half) and induced O'Neal to foul out with more than two minutes left, only to be undone by a three-pointer from reserve forward Robert Horry. Games 4 and 5 were a Shaq-alanche, as O'Neal scored a combined 63 points and grabbed 27 rebounds. "The guy is the best," said Philadelphia coach Larry Brown. "He's unstoppable."

O'Neal, though, knew better than to claim he'd done it all by himself. "Kobe and I got on the same page," he said. "Once that happened, it was pretty much all over for the rest of the league."

While that turned out to be true, the rest of the league provided enough highlights and exciting players to keep the season in-

teresting and its conclusion in doubt until the turnaround in La-La Land.

Leading the way was Iverson, the Sixers' six-foot shooting guard, who fulfilled the brilliant promise he had flashed since he entered the league in 1996. In his first four NBA seasons, the man known as the Answer had often seemed determined to make a riddle of himself. Undeniably superb on the court, he had a knack for controversy off of it. In 1997 his car was stopped for speeding and police found marijuana and a gun in the vehicle; before the 2000–01 season began he recorded a hardcore gangsta rap album whose lyrics made sure to offend almost every segment of society; and through it all, he feuded with Brown, a conflict that, to say the least, was a distraction to the interests of the team.

The situation deteriorated so much that Philadelphia nearly traded Iverson during the summer. Sixers president Pat Croce had a sit-down with the player in the offseason, and the Answer found himself, producing the best season of his five-year career. He led the NBA in scoring for the second time, averaging 31.1 points a game. More importantly, he began showing a commitment to his team. He arrived on time for practices, participated in team workouts and made an effort to get along with his coaches.

The results were electrifying. Philadelphia started the season with 10 straight victories and had the NBA's best record for most of the year. They won the Atlantic Division by six games and rolled into the playoffs as the top seed in the Eastern Conference. "You're always trying to learn, but sometimes it doesn't stick with you," Iverson said early in the season. "Because of the s--- I went through, I'm a more mature person and a better basketball player."

In the playoffs Iverson, 25, squared off against two young stars who could eventually challenge his status as the best player in the East: Vince Carter, 24, of the Toronto Raptors, and Ray Allen, 25, of the Milwaukee Bucks. The gravity-defying Carter was already one of the most popular players in the game. The graceful Allen, on the other hand, had a more gradual emergence, honing his deadly jumper in relative obscurity in Milwaukee. Iverson brought out the best in both players. Carter rained 50 points on Philadelphia in Game 3 of the Eastern Conference semifinals, while Allen went for 38 in Game 2 of the conference finals. Alas, both the Raptors and the Bucks fell to Philadelphia in seven games, but the promise of future playoff showdowns between the three young stars bodes well for the future of the league. "A year or two ago," said Toronto coach Lenny Wilkens, "when people were talking about how some of the young players in the league hadn't won anything yet, I said, 'Give them time. Let them mature, and you'll see them start to accomplish some things.' It doesn't happen overnight, especially with players spending less and less time in college. Now, a few years later, you're seeing the emergence of some mature players, guys who are capable of leading their teams to the postseason." Wilkens might also have pointed out that Michael Jordan, the benchmark for NBA greatness, didn't win his first title until his seventh season.

There were other young players who excelled in the playoffs, including 25-year-old Duncan, who already has one championship, and of course Bryant, who is only 22, with two titles and counting. And then there was 21-year-old Tracy McGrady, of the Orlando Magic. His team fell to the Bucks in four games in the first round, but McGrady's performance was the most memorable part of the series. He scored 33 points and made eight assists in Game 1, followed that up with 20 consecutive points in Game 2, then exploded for 42 in the next game to become the second-youngest player, behind Magic Johnson, to score 40 or more points in a playoff game. McGrady scored his points with style to burn, driving for layups, posting up, burying three-pointers and throwing down poster-perfect dunks. "I should probably tell you he's not all that good and we can stop him," said Milwaukee point guard Sam Cassell. "But, man, what a wonderful player."

Despite the encouraging crop of young stars, it was the comeback of one of the league's veterans that provided the most satisfying story of the season. Alonzo Mourning, 31, the Miami Heat's 6'10" center and one of the best-conditioned athletes in the league, learned in October 2000 that he had a form of focal glomerulosclerosis, a debilitating kidney disease that would sideline him for the season and threaten his career. Mourning sat out most of the season to receive treatment but made an unexpected and stirring return to the Heat on March 27. His play was rusty, and his stamina wasn't up to its usual level, but he provided his teammates with a solid presence at center. "We've had to get used to playing without 'Zo, and now we have to get used to having him in there," said forward Brian Grant. "It's a good problem to have, but you can't expect everything to click right away." Indeed, almost nothing clicked right away, and Pat Riley's team made its fourth consecutive early exit from the playoffs, getting swept by Charlotte in the first round.

Unfortunately, it remains to be seen if

**The Answer had a reply for every challenge he met, except LA in the Finals.**

JOHN BIEVER

Mourning will be able to continue playing. He is not cured. To treat his condition, which attacks the filters in the kidneys that remove waste from the blood, he takes as many as 14 pills a day. There's no guarantee that the medication will continue to work. "I know the future isn't promised," he said. "Every time I step on the court I'm scared."

While there was plenty of good news for the league, there was also no disguising the truth that the NBA was struggling on several fronts. Television ratings continued to decline, in part because fans seemed put off by the sheer number of boors now plying their wares in the league. To wit, Trail Blazers forward Rasheed Wallace averaged one technical foul every two games; Jason Williams, the point guard for Sacramento (now with the Grizzlies), made offensive comments to an Asian fan; and Knicks point guard Charlie Ward was quoted in *The New York Times Magazine* saying that Jews are "stubborn" and persecute Christians. And, of course, there was Iverson's repugnant rap.

Also troubling was the league's conviction that fans were mostly fed up with a game that has lost some of its zip, stifled by half-court, man-to-man defenses and the stand-around offenses they engender. To remedy the situation the NBA took steps at the end of the year to try to speed up play. Beginning next season teams will be able to play zone defense, and the time a team can take to cross half-court has been reduced, from 10 seconds to eight. "It's important to be willing to make the change, understanding that you don't know exactly how it's going to turn out," said Suns owner Jerry Colangelo, the chairman of the committee that recommended the changes. "This is a work in progress. It's something we're going to continue to monitor. It may need to be tweaked here and there as it's put into practice."

If the new rules have the desired effect, and the league makes a return to its Jordan-era glory days, things could get interesting for the reigning world champions. Still, it's hard to imagine that the Lakers won't be able to stage a repeat of their repeat. Of course, that will be up to Shaq and Kobe.

## NBA Final Standings

### Eastern Conference

**ATLANTIC DIVISION**

| Team | W | L | Pct | GB |
|------|---|---|-----|----|
| Philadelphia | 56 | 26 | .683 | — |
| Miami | 50 | 32 | .610 | 6 |
| New York | 48 | 34 | .585 | 8 |
| Orlando | 43 | 39 | .524 | 13 |
| Boston | 36 | 46 | .439 | 20 |
| New Jersey | 26 | 56 | .317 | 30 |
| Washington | 19 | 63 | .232 | 37 |

**CENTRAL DIVISION**

| Team | W | L | Pct | GB |
|------|---|---|-----|----|
| Milwaukee | 52 | 30 | .634 | — |
| Toronto | 47 | 35 | .573 | 5 |
| Charlotte | 46 | 36 | .561 | 6 |
| Indiana | 41 | 41 | .500 | 11 |
| Detroit | 32 | 50 | .390 | 20 |
| Cleveland | 30 | 52 | .366 | 22 |
| Atlanta | 25 | 57 | .305 | 27 |
| Chicago | 15 | 67 | .183 | 37 |

### Western Conference

**MIDWEST DIVISION**

| Team | W | L | Pct | GB |
|------|---|---|-----|----|
| San Antonio | 58 | 24 | .707 | — |
| Utah | 53 | 29 | .646 | 5 |
| Dallas | 53 | 29 | .646 | 5 |
| Minnesota | 47 | 35 | .573 | 11 |
| Houston | 45 | 37 | .549 | 13 |
| Denver | 40 | 42 | .488 | 18 |
| Vancouver | 23 | 59 | .280 | 35 |

**PACIFIC DIVISION**

| Team | W | L | Pct | GB |
|------|---|---|-----|----|
| LA Lakers | 56 | 26 | .683 | — |
| Sacramento | 55 | 27 | .671 | 1 |
| Phoenix | 51 | 31 | .622 | 5 |
| Portland | 50 | 32 | .610 | 6 |
| Seattle | 44 | 38 | .537 | 12 |
| LA Clippers | 31 | 51 | .378 | 25 |
| Golden State | 17 | 65 | .207 | 39 |

## 2001 NBA Playoffs

**EASTERN CONFERENCE**

| 1st ROUND | SEMIFINALS | FINALS |
|-----------|------------|--------|

**WESTERN CONFERENCE**

| FINALS | SEMIFINALS | 1st ROUND |
|--------|------------|-----------|

**NBA FINALS**

LA LAKERS (4-1)

Eastern Conference bracket:
- Philadelphia / Indiana → Philadelphia (3-1)
- New York / Toronto → Toronto (3-2)
- Philadelphia (4-3)
- Milwaukee / Orlando → Milwaukee (3-1)
- Miami / Charlotte → Charlotte (3-0)
- Milwaukee (4-3)
- Philadelphia (4-3)

Western Conference bracket:
- San Antonio / Minnesota → San Antonio (3-1)
- Utah / Dallas → Dallas (3-2)
- San Antonio (4-1)
- Phoenix / Sacramento → Sacramento (3-1)
- LA Lakers / Portland → LA Lakers (3-0)
- LA Lakers (4-0)
- LA Lakers (4-0)

# 2001 NBA Playoff Results

## Eastern Conference First Round

| | | | |
|---|---|---|---|
| April 21 ......Indiana | 79 | at Philadelphia | 78 |
| April 24 ......Indiana | 98 | at Philadelphia | 116 |
| April 28 ......Philadelphia | 92 | at Indiana | 87 |
| May 2 .........Philadelphia | 88 | at Indiana | 85 |

Philadelphia won series 3–1.

| | | | |
|---|---|---|---|
| April 22 ......Orlando | 90 | at Milwaukee | 103 |
| April 25 ......Orlando | 96 | at Milwaukee | 103 |
| April 28 .....Milwaukee | 116 | at Orlando | 121* |
| May 1 .........Milwaukee | 112 | at Orlando | 104 |

Milwaukee won series 3–1.

| | | | |
|---|---|---|---|
| April 21 .....Charlotte | 106 | at Miami | 80 |
| April 23 .....Charlotte | 102 | at Miami | 76 |
| April 27 .....Miami | 79 | at Charlotte | 94 |

Charlotte won series 3–0.

| | | | |
|---|---|---|---|
| April 22 ......Toronto | 85 | at New York | 92 |
| April 26 ......Toronto | 94 | at New York | 74 |
| April 29 ......New York | 97 | at Toronto | 89 |
| May 2 .........New York | 93 | at Toronto | 100 |
| May 4 .........Toronto | 93 | at New York | 89 |

Toronto won series 3–2.

## Western Conference First Round

| | | | |
|---|---|---|---|
| April 21 ......Minnesota | 82 | at San Antonio | 87 |
| April 23 .....Minnesota | 69 | at San Antonio | 86 |
| April 28 .....San Antonio | 84 | at Minnesota | 93 |
| April 30 .....San Antonio | 97 | at Minnesota | 84 |

San Antonio won series 3–1.

| | | | |
|---|---|---|---|
| April 22 ......Portland | 93 | at LA Lakers | 106 |
| April 26 ......Portland | 88 | at LA Lakers | 106 |
| April 29 ......LA Lakers | 99 | at Portland | 86 |

LA Lakers won series 3–0.

| | | | |
|---|---|---|---|
| April 22 ......Phoenix | 86 | at Sacramento | 83 |
| April 25 ......Phoenix | 90 | at Sacramento | 116 |
| April 29 .....Sacramento | 102 | at Phoenix | 96 |
| May 2 .........Sacramento | 89 | at Phoenix | 82 |

Sacramento won series 3–1.

| | | | |
|---|---|---|---|
| April 21 ......Dallas | 86 | at Utah | 88 |
| April 24 ......Dallas | 98 | at Utah | 109 |
| April 28 ......Utah | 91 | at Dallas | 94 |
| May 1 .........Utah | 77 | at Dallas | 107 |
| May 3 .........Dallas | 84 | at Utah | 83 |

Dallas won series 3–2.

## Eastern Conference Semifinals

| | | | |
|---|---|---|---|
| May 6 .........Toronto | 96 | at Philadelphia | 93 |
| May 9 .........Toronto | 92 | at Philadelphia | 97 |
| May 11 .......Philadelphia | 78 | at Toronto | 102 |
| May 13 .......Philadelphi | 84 | at Toronto | 79 |
| May 16 .......Toronto | 88 | at Philadelphia | 121 |
| May 18 .......Philadelphia | 89 | at Toronto | 101 |
| May 20 .......Toronto | 87 | at Philadelphia | 88 |

Philadelphia won series 4–3.

| | | | |
|---|---|---|---|
| May 6 .........Charlotte | 94 | at Milwaukee | 104 |
| May 8 .........Charlotte | 90 | at Milwaukee | 91 |
| May 10 .......Milwaukee | 92 | at Charlotte | 102 |
| May 13 .......Milwaukee | 78 | at Charlotte | 85 |
| May 15 .......Charlotte | 94 | at Milwaukee | 86 |
| May 17 .......Milwaukee | 104 | at Charlotte | 97 |
| May 20 .......Charlotte | 95 | at Milwaukee | 104 |

Milwaukee won series 4–3.

## Western Conference Semifinals

| | | | |
|---|---|---|---|
| May 5 .........Dallas | 78 | at San Antonio | 94 |
| May 7 .........Dallas | 86 | at San Antonio | 100 |
| May 9 .........San Antonio | 104 | at Dallas | 90 |
| May 12 .......San Antonio | 108 | at Dallas | 112 |
| May 14 .......Dallas | 87 | at San Antonio | 105 |

San Antonio won series 4–1.

| | | | |
|---|---|---|---|
| May 6 .........Sacramento | 105 | at LA Lakers | 108 |
| May 8 .........Sacramento | 90 | at LA Lakers | 96 |
| May 11 .......LA Lakers | 103 | at Sacramento | 81 |
| May 13 .......LA Lakers | 119 | at Sacramento | 113 |

LA Lakers won series 4–0.

## Eastern Conference Finals

| | | | |
|---|---|---|---|
| May 22 .......Milwaukee | 85 | at Philadelphia | 93 |
| May 24 .......Milwaukee | 92 | at Philadelphia | 78 |
| May 26 .......Philadelphia | 74 | at Milwaukee | 80 |
| May 28 .......Philadelphia | 89 | at Milwaukee | 83 |
| May 30 .......Milwaukee | 88 | at Philadelphia | 89 |
| June 1 ........Philadelphia | 100 | at Milwaukee | 110 |
| June 3 ........Milwaukee | 91 | at Philadelphia | 108 |

Philadelphia won series 4–3.

## Western Conference Finals

| | | | |
|---|---|---|---|
| May 19 ......LA Lakers | 104 | at San Antonio | 90 |
| May 21 .......LA Lakers | 88 | at San Antonio | 81 |
| May 25 ......San Antonio | 72 | at LA Lakers | 111 |
| May 27 ......San Antonio | 82 | at LA Lakers | 111 |

LA Lakers won series 4–0.

## Finals

| | | | |
|---|---|---|---|
| June 6 ........Philadelphia | 107 | at LA Lakers | 101* |
| June 8 ........Philadelphia | 89 | at LA Lakers | 98 |
| June 10 ......LA Lakers | 96 | at Philadelphia | 91 |
| June 13 ......LA Lakers | 100 | at Philadelphia | 86 |
| June 15 ......LA Lakers | 108 | at Philadelphia | 96 |

LA Lakers won series 4–1.

*Overtime game.

### PHILADELPHIA 76ERS

| Player | GP | Field Goals FGM | Pct | 3-Pt FG FGM | FGA | Free Throws FTM | Pct | Rebounds Off | Total | A | Stl | TO | BS | Ppg | Hi |
|---|---|---|---|---|---|---|---|---|---|---|---|---|---|---|---|
| Iverson | 5 | 66 | 40.7 | 11 | 39 | 35 | 72.9 | 5 | 28 | 19 | 9 | 12 | 1 | 35.6 | 48 |
| Mutombo | 5 | 33 | 60.0 | 0 | 0 | 18 | 69.2 | 20 | 61 | 2 | 2 | 5 | 11 | 16.8 | 23 |
| Snow | 5 | 22 | 40.7 | 0 | 3 | 19 | 73.1 | 11 | 22 | 30 | 8 | 14 | 1 | 12.6 | 14 |
| McKie | 5 | 15 | 31.3 | 4 | 9 | 6 | 66.7 | 7 | 27 | 30 | 6 | 14 | 3 | 8.0 | 14 |
| Hill | 5 | 13 | 39.4 | 0 | 0 | 7 | 77.8 | 7 | 33 | 2 | 0 | 5 | 6 | 6.6 | 18 |
| Geiger | 5 | 12 | 66.7 | 0 | 0 | 2 | 100.0 | 2 | 5 | 2 | 1 | 3 | 0 | 5.2 | 10 |
| Bell | 5 | 4 | 30.8 | 0 | 3 | 5 | 50.0 | 2 | 9 | 4 | 10 | 4 | 0 | 2.6 | 6 |
| MacCulloch | 5 | 5 | 41.7 | 0 | 0 | 3 | 75.0 | 5 | 7 | 0 | 0 | 2 | 0 | 2.6 | 13 |
| Jones | 5 | 4 | 40.0 | 2 | 4 | 0 | — | 2 | 10 | 1 | 1 | 2 | 2 | 2.0 | 4 |
| Ollie | 5 | 1 | 33.3 | 0 | 0 | 3 | 100.0 | 1 | 1 | 1 | 0 | 0 | 0 | 1.0 | 3 |
| Lynch | 2 | 1 | 33.3 | 0 | 0 | 0 | — | 2 | 5 | 1 | 2 | 0 | 0 | 1.0 | 2 |
| Buford | 3 | 1 | 16.7 | 0 | 1 | 0 | — | 2 | 6 | 0 | 0 | 1 | 0 | 0.7 | 2 |
| **Totals** | **5** | **177** | **42.4** | **17** | **59** | **98** | **71.5** | **66** | **214** | **92** | **39** | **65** | **23** | **93.8** | **107** |

### LOS ANGELES LAKERS

| Player | GP | Field Goals FGM | Pct | 3-Pt FG FGM | FGA | Free Throws FTM | Pct | Rebounds Off | Total | A | Stl | TO | BS | Ppg | Hi |
|---|---|---|---|---|---|---|---|---|---|---|---|---|---|---|---|
| O'Neal | 5 | 63 | 57.3 | 0 | 0 | 39 | 51.3 | 31 | 79 | 24 | 2 | 20 | 17 | 33.0 | 44 |
| Bryant | 5 | 44 | 41.5 | 3 | 9 | 32 | 84.2 | 5 | 39 | 29 | 7 | 18 | 7 | 24.6 | 32 |
| Fisher | 5 | 17 | 43.6 | 10 | 19 | 5 | 83.3 | 1 | 6 | 10 | 8 | 6 | 1 | 9.8 | 18 |
| Fox | 5 | 14 | 44.1 | 7 | 15 | 12 | 92.3 | 3 | 23 | 19 | 6 | 14 | 2 | 9.8 | 20 |
| Horry | 5 | 14 | 56.0 | 8 | 13 | 6 | 100.0 | 10 | 25 | 6 | 4 | 2 | 7 | 8.4 | 15 |
| Grant | 5 | 10 | 29.4 | 0 | 0 | 6 | 75.0 | 12 | 28 | 3 | 2 | 2 | 7 | 5.2 | 8 |
| Harper | 3 | 5 | 62.5 | 1 | 3 | 2 | 66.7 | 0 | 5 | 3 | 1 | 0 | 1 | 4.3 | 8 |
| Lue | 5 | 7 | 58.3 | 4 | 6 | 0 | — | 1 | 4 | 7 | 7 | 5 | 1 | 3.6 | 6 |
| Shaw | 5 | 6 | 30.0 | 3 | 10 | 3 | 60.0 | 3 | 16 | 14 | 4 | 7 | 0 | 3.6 | 7 |
| Madsen | 2 | 0 | 00.0 | 0 | 0 | 0 | — | 1 | 1 | 0 | 0 | 0 | 1 | 0.0 | — |
| **Totals** | **5** | **181** | **46.5** | **36** | **75** | **105** | **67.7** | **67** | **226** | **115** | **41** | **75** | **44** | **100.6** | **108** |

## NBA Finals Box Scores

### Game 1

#### PHILADELPHIA 107

| PHIL. | Min | FG M-A | FT M-A | Reb O-T | A | PF | S | TO | TP |
|---|---|---|---|---|---|---|---|---|---|
| Hill | 40 | 1-6 | 2-2 | 1-6 | 0 | 3 | 0 | 3 | 4 |
| Jones | 11 | 2-3 | 0-0 | 0-0 | 0 | 0 | 0 | 0 | 4 |
| Mutombo | 44 | 4-7 | 5-7 | 5-16 | 0 | 5 | 0 | 0 | 13 |
| Iverson | 52 | 18-41 | 9-9 | 2-5 | 6 | 0 | 5 | 3 | 48 |
| McKie | 51 | 3-7 | 2-2 | 2-7 | 9 | 1 | 2 | 5 | 9 |
| Snow | 31 | 5-10 | 3-3 | 0-4 | 5 | 2 | 0 | 5 | 13 |
| Bell | 10 | 2-2 | 2-2 | 1-4 | 1 | 2 | 2 | 1 | 6 |
| Ollie | 1 | 0-0 | 0-0 | 0-0 | 0 | 0 | 0 | 0 | 0 |
| Geiger | 14 | 5-7 | 0-0 | 0-0 | 0 | 6 | 1 | 1 | 10 |
| MacCulloch | 2 | 0-0 | 0-0 | 0-0 | 0 | 1 | 0 | 0 | 0 |
| Totals | 265 | 40-83 | 23-25 | 11-42 | 21 | 21 | 10 | 18 | 107 |

Percentages: FG—.482, FT—.920. 3-pt goals: 4–11, .364 (Jones 0–1, Iverson 3–8, McKie 1–1, Snow 0–1). Team rebounds: 7. Blocked shots: 8 (Mutombo 5, Hill, McKie, Jones).

#### LA LAKERS 101

| LA LAKERS | Min | FG M-A | FT M-A | Reb O-T | A | PF | S | TO | TP |
|---|---|---|---|---|---|---|---|---|---|
| Fox | 44 | 7-12 | 2-2 | 1-7 | 5 | 3 | 2 | 4 | 19 |
| Grant | 27 | 3-11 | 2-2 | 4-5 | 0 | 1 | 1 | 2 | 8 |
| O'Neal | 52 | 17-28 | 10-22 | 6-20 | 5 | 3 | 1 | 4 | 44 |
| Bryant | 52 | 7-22 | 1-1 | 0-3 | 5 | 4 | 1 | 6 | 15 |
| Fisher | 23 | 0-4 | 0-0 | 0-0 | 1 | 3 | 1 | 0 | 0 |
| Shaw | 18 | 3-5 | 0-0 | 2-4 | 3 | 1 | 1 | 1 | 7 |
| Horry | 27 | 1-5 | 0-0 | 3-4 | 1 | 5 | 2 | 1 | 3 |
| Lue | 22 | 2-3 | 0-0 | 0-1 | 3 | 2 | 5 | 1 | 5 |
| Totals | 265 | 40-90 | 15-27 | 16-44 | 23 | 22 | 14 | 19 | 101 |

Percentages: FG—.444, FT—.556. 3-pt goals: 6–13, .462 (Fox 3–6, Fisher 0–1, Shaw 1–2, Horry 1–3, Lue 1–1). Team rebounds: 14. Blocked shots: 9 (Bryant 3, Horry 2, Grant 2, Fox 1, Lue 1).

A: 18,997. Officials: Bavetta, Garretson, Crawford.

## Game 2

### PHILADELPHIA 89

| PHIL | Min | FG M-A | FT M-A | Reb O-T | A | PF | S | TO | TP |
|---|---|---|---|---|---|---|---|---|---|
| Hill | 22 | 1-3 | 0-0 | 1-5 | 0 | 5 | 0 | 0 | 2 |
| Jones | 15 | 1-2 | 0-0 | 0-3 | 0 | 1 | 0 | 0 | 3 |
| Mutombo | 36 | 5-12 | 6-6 | 4-13 | 1 | 3 | 1 | 1 | 16 |
| Iverson | 47 | 10-29 | 0-4 | 0-4 | 3 | 3 | 1 | 3 | 23 |
| McKie | 40 | 6-17 | 0-2 | 4-6 | 6 | 3 | 2 | 2 | 14 |
| Snow | 28 | 4-9 | 4-4 | 1-2 | 4 | 1 | 2 | 3 | 12 |
| Geiger | 13 | 2-4 | 0-0 | 1-2 | 0 | 1 | 0 | 0 | 4 |
| MacCulloch | 16 | 5-9 | 3-4 | 3-5 | 0 | 3 | 0 | 1 | 13 |
| Bell | 18 | 0-1 | 2-6 | 0-2 | 1 | 3 | 3 | 1 | 2 |
| Buford | 1 | 0-0 | 0-0 | 0-0 | 0 | 0 | 0 | 0 | 0 |
| Ollie | 4 | 0-1 | 0-0 | 0-0 | 1 | 0 | 0 | 0 | 0 |
| Totals | 240 | 34-87 | 15-26 | 14-42 | 16 | 23 | 9 | 11 | 89 |

Percentages: FG—.391, FT—.577. 3-pt goals: 6-15, .400 (Jones 1-1, Iverson 3-10, McKie 2-4). Team rebounds:10. Blocked shots: 5 (Hill 3, Mutombo 1, Jones 1).

### LA LAKERS 98

| LA LAKERS | Min | FG M-A | FT M-A | Reb O-T | A | PF | S | TO | TP |
|---|---|---|---|---|---|---|---|---|---|
| Fox | 28 | 0-4 | 0-0 | 1-6 | 2 | 4 | 0 | 5 | 0 |
| Grant | 18 | 2-7 | 2-2 | 2-5 | 2 | 0 | 0 | 0 | 6 |
| O'Neal | 45 | 12-19 | 4-10 | 8-20 | 9 | 5 | 1 | 5 | 28 |
| Bryant | 47 | 11-23 | 8-8 | 1-8 | 6 | 4 | 2 | 2 | 31 |
| Fisher | 34 | 5-11 | 2-2 | 0-0 | 3 | 4 | 2 | 1 | 14 |
| Shaw | 25 | 1-7 | 1-2 | 0-5 | 5 | 3 | 1 | 2 | 4 |
| Horry | 26 | 4-6 | 0-0 | 3-7 | 1 | 3 | 1 | 0 | 8 |
| Lue | 10 | 1-1 | 0-0 | 0-0 | 0 | 1 | 0 | 1 | 2 |
| Harper | 7 | 2-3 | 1-2 | 0-1 | 1 | 0 | 0 | 0 | 5 |
| Totals | 240 | 38-81 | 18-26 | 15-52 | 29 | 24 | 7 | 16 | 98 |

Percentages: FG—.469, FT—.692. 3-pt goals: 4-16, .250 (Fox 0-2, Bryant 1-2, Fisher 2-5, Shaw 1-5, Horry 0-1, Harper 0-1). Team rebounds: 11. Blocked shots: 13 (O'Neal 8, Bryant 2, Grant 2, Fox 1).

A: 18,997. Officials: Fryer, Nunn, Javie.

## Game 3

### LA LAKERS 96

| LA LAKERS | Min | FG M-A | FT M-A | Reb O-T | A | PF | S | TO | TP |
|---|---|---|---|---|---|---|---|---|---|
| Fox | 22 | 1-3 | 1-2 | 0-3 | 2 | 2 | 3 | 2 | 3 |
| Grant | 29 | 2-5 | 0-0 | 3-7 | 1 | 3 | 0 | 0 | 4 |
| O'Neal | 41 | 11-20 | 8-9 | 3-12 | 3 | 6 | 0 | 3 | 30 |
| Bryant | 48 | 13-30 | 6-6 | 0-6 | 3 | 2 | 2 | 3 | 32 |
| Fisher | 31 | 2-5 | 3-4 | 1-2 | 2 | 6 | 0 | 1 | 7 |
| Shaw | 28 | 0-3 | 0-0 | 1-5 | 3 | 3 | 1 | 2 | 0 |
| Horry | 24 | 4-5 | 4-4 | 1-4 | 3 | 2 | 1 | 1 | 15 |
| Lue | 17 | 2-4 | 0-0 | 1-1 | 1 | 2 | 1 | 1 | 5 |
| Totals | 240 | 35-75 | 22-25 | 10-40 | 18 | 26 | 8 | 13 | 96 |

Percentages: FG—.467, FT—.880. 3-pt goals: 4-10, .400 (Fox 0-1, Bryant 0-2, Fisher 0-1, Shaw 0-1, Horry 3-3, Lue 1-2). Team rebounds: 7. Blocked shots: 6 (O'Neal 4, Horry, 2).

### PHILADELPHIA 91

| PHIL | Min | FG M-A | FT M-A | Reb O-T | A | PF | S | TO | TP |
|---|---|---|---|---|---|---|---|---|---|
| Hill | 26 | 1-7 | 0-0 | 0-2 | 0 | 4 | 0 | 1 | 2 |
| Jones | 18 | 1-2 | 0-0 | 0-1 | 0 | 1 | 0 | 1 | 3 |
| Mutombo | 42 | 9-14 | 5-8 | 5-12 | 0 | 4 | 1 | 2 | 23 |
| Iverson | 47 | 12-30 | 10-13 | 2-12 | 4 | 1 | 0 | 1 | 35 |
| McKie | 42 | 2-8 | 1-1 | 1-6 | 8 | 1 | 0 | 3 | 5 |
| Snow | 34 | 4-11 | 6-7 | 4-6 | 5 | 4 | 1 | 3 | 14 |
| Geiger | 5 | 2-2 | 0-0 | 0-0 | 0 | 3 | 0 | 2 | 4 |
| Bell | 17 | 1-5 | 0-0 | 0-2 | 0 | 3 | 3 | 1 | 2 |
| MacCulloch | 8 | 0-0 | 0-0 | 0-0 | 0 | 0 | 0 | 0 | 0 |
| Ollie | 1 | 1-1 | 1-1 | 1-1 | 0 | 1 | 0 | 0 | 3 |
| Totals | 240 | 33-80 | 23-30 | 13-42 | 17 | 22 | 5 | 14 | 91 |

Percentages: FG—.413 FT—.767. 3-pt goals: 2-12, .167 (Jones 1-2, Iverson 1-6, McKie 0-1, Snow 0-1, Bell 0-2). Team rebounds: 8. Blocked shots: 6 (McKie 2, Mutombo 2, Iverson, Hill).

A: 20,900. Officials: Salvatore, Delaney, Crawford.

## Game 4

### LA LAKERS 100

| LA LAKERS | Min | FG M-A | FT M-A | Reb O-T | A | PF | S | TO | TP |
|---|---|---|---|---|---|---|---|---|---|
| Fox | 30 | 2-7 | 2-2 | 0-1 | 4 | 3 | 0 | 1 | 7 |
| Grant | 25 | 1-4 | 0-0 | 0-5 | 0 | 2 | 0 | 2 | 2 |
| O'Neal | 42 | 13-25 | 8-16 | 8-14 | 5 | 4 | 0 | 3 | 34 |
| Bryant | 43 | 6-13 | 7-12 | 2-10 | 9 | 2 | 1 | 4 | 19 |
| Fisher | 34 | 4-7 | 0-0 | 0-1 | 1 | 3 | 3 | 3 | 10 |
| Shaw | 10 | 2-3 | 0-1 | 0-2 | 1 | 3 | 0 | 2 | 5 |
| Horry | 24 | 3-4 | 0-0 | 1-4 | 0 | 3 | 0 | 0 | 9 |
| Lue | 14 | 2-3 | 0-0 | 0-1 | 2 | 0 | 1 | 1 | 6 |
| Harper | 16 | 3-5 | 1-1 | 0-4 | 2 | 2 | 1 | 0 | 8 |
| Madsen | 2 | 0-1 | 0-0 | 1-1 | 0 | 0 | 0 | 0 | 0 |
| Totals | 240 | 36-72 | 18-32 | 12-43 | 24 | 22 | 6 | 14 | 100 |

Percentages: FG—.500, FT—.563. 3-pt goals: 10-19, .526 (Fox 1-3, Bryant 0-2, Fisher 2-4, Shaw 1-2, Horry 3-3, Lue 2-3, Harper 1-2). Team rebounds: 13. Blocked shots: 6 (Grant 2, Harper, Bryant, Horry, Madsen).

### PHILADELPHIA 86

| PHIL | Min | FG M-A | FT M-A | Reb O-T | A | PF | S | TO | TP |
|---|---|---|---|---|---|---|---|---|---|
| Hill | 21 | 3-4 | 1-1 | 2-7 | 1 | 5 | 0 | 1 | 7 |
| Jones | 11 | 0-3 | 0-0 | 1-3 | 1 | 1 | 1 | 1 | 0 |
| Mutombo | 44 | 9-11 | 1-3 | 3-9 | 0 | 5 | 0 | 1 | 19 |
| Iverson | 46 | 12-30 | 10-14 | 1-4 | 4 | 3 | 1 | 2 | 35 |
| McKie | 40 | 1-9 | 3-4 | 0-3 | 2 | 1 | 0 | 1 | 5 |
| Snow | 29 | 5-10 | 1-4 | 0-4 | 4 | 4 | 3 | 1 | 11 |
| Lynch | 8 | 0-0 | 0-0 | 0-2 | 1 | 2 | 2 | 0 | 0 |
| Bell | 20 | 0-2 | 1-2 | 0-0 | 1 | 2 | 2 | 1 | 1 |
| Geiger | 11 | 2-4 | 2-2 | 0-2 | 1 | 4 | 0 | 0 | 6 |
| Buford | 5 | 1-3 | 0-0 | 1-3 | 0 | 0 | 0 | 0 | 2 |
| Ollie | 3 | 0-1 | 0-0 | 0-0 | 0 | 0 | 0 | 1 | 0 |
| MacCulloch | 2 | 0-0 | 0-0 | 0-0 | 0 | 0 | 0 | 1 | 0 |
| Totals | 240 | 33-77 | 19-30 | 8-37 | 15 | 27 | 9 | 9 | 86 |

Percentages: FG—.429, FT—.633. 3-pt goals: 1-6, .167 (Iverson 1-4, McKie 0-2). Team rebounds: 12. Blocked shots: 1 (Mutombo).

A: 20,896. Officials: Evans, Rush, Nies.

## Game 5

### LA LAKERS 108

| LA LAKERS | Min | FG M–A | FT M–A | Reb O–T | A | PF | S | TO | TP |
|---|---|---|---|---|---|---|---|---|---|
| Fox | 40 | 5–8 | 7–7 | 1–6 | 6 | 2 | 1 | 2 | 20 |
| Grant | 24 | 2–7 | 2–4 | 3–6 | 0 | 3 | 1 | 0 | 6 |
| O'Neal | 45 | 10–18 | 9–19 | 6–13 | 2 | 2 | 0 | 5 | 29 |
| Bryant | 44 | 7–18 | 10–11 | 2–12 | 6 | 3 | 1 | 3 | 26 |
| Fisher | 36 | 6–12 | 0–0 | 0–3 | 3 | 4 | 2 | 1 | 18 |
| Horry | 26 | 2–5 | 2–2 | 2–6 | 1 | 4 | 0 | 0 | 7 |
| Shaw | 12 | 0–2 | 2–2 | 0–0 | 2 | 2 | 1 | 0 | 2 |
| Lue | 10 | 0–1 | 0–0 | 0–1 | 1 | 2 | 0 | 1 | 0 |
| Madsen | 1 | 0–0 | 0–0 | 0–0 | 0 | 0 | 0 | 0 | 0 |
| Harper | 2 | 0–0 | 0–0 | 0–0 | 0 | 0 | 0 | 0 | 0 |
| Totals | 240 | 32–71 | 32–45 | 14–47 | 21 | 22 | 6 | 12 | 108 |

Percentages: FG—.451, FT—.711. 3-pt goals: 12–17, .706 (Fox 3–3, Bryant 2–3, Fisher 6–8, Horry 1–3). Team rebounds: 8. Blocked shots: 10 (O'Neal 5, Horry 2, Bryant, Fisher, Grant).

### PHILADELPHIA 96

| PHIL | Min | FG M–A | FT M–A | Reb O–T | A | PF | S | TO | TP |
|---|---|---|---|---|---|---|---|---|---|
| Hill | 32 | 7–13 | 4–6 | 3–13 | 1 | 4 | 0 | 0 | 18 |
| McKie | 34 | 3–7 | 0–0 | 0–5 | 5 | 4 | 2 | 3 | 7 |
| Mutombo | 42 | 6–11 | 1–2 | 3–11 | 1 | 6 | 0 | 1 | 13 |
| Iverson | 45 | 14–32 | 6–8 | 0–3 | 2 | 5 | 2 | 3 | 37 |
| Snow | 42 | 4–14 | 5–8 | 6–6 | 12 | 3 | 2 | 2 | 13 |
| Lynch | 6 | 1–3 | 0–0 | 2–3 | 0 | 1 | 0 | 0 | 2 |
| Bell | 5 | 1–3 | 0–0 | 1–1 | 1 | 0 | 0 | 0 | 2 |
| Ollie | 6 | 0–0 | 2–2 | 0–0 | 0 | 0 | 0 | 0 | 2 |
| Jones | 7 | 0–0 | 0–0 | 1–3 | 0 | 1 | 0 | 0 | 0 |
| Buford | 7 | 0–3 | 0–0 | 1–3 | 0 | 2 | 0 | 1 | 0 |
| Geiger | 11 | 1–1 | 0–0 | 1–1 | 1 | 6 | 0 | 0 | 2 |
| MacCulloch | 3 | 0–3 | 0–0 | 2–2 | 0 | 0 | 0 | 0 | 0 |
| Totals | 240 | 37–90 | 18–26 | 20–51 | 23 | 32 | 6 | 10 | 96 |

Percentages: FG—.411, FT—.692. 3-pt goals: 4–15, .267 (McKie 1–1, Iverson 3–11, Snow 0–1, Bell 0–1, Buford 0–1). Team rebounds: 7. Blocked shots: 4 (Mutombo 2, Snow, Hill).
A: 20,890. Officials: Crawford, Bavetta, Fryer.

# NBA Awards

## All-NBA Teams

**FIRST TEAM**
G Allen Iverson, Philadelphia
G Jason Kidd, Phoenix
C Shaquille O'Neal, LA Lakers
F Chris Webber, Sacramento
F Tim Duncan, San Antonio

**SECOND TEAM**
Tracy McGrady, Orlando
Kobe Bryant, LA Lakers
Dikembe Mutombo, Philadelphia
Kevin Garnett, Minnesota
Vince Carter, Toronto

**THIRD TEAM**
Gary Payton, Seattle
Ray Allen, Milwaukee
David Robinson, San Antonio
Karl Malone, Utah
Dirk Nowitzki, Dallas

## NBA All-Defensive Teams

**FIRST TEAM**
G Gary Payton, Seattle
G Jason Kidd, Phoenix
C Dikembe Mutombo,
 Philadelphia
F Tim Duncan, San Antonio
F Kevin Garnett, Minnesota

**SECOND TEAM**
Kobe Bryant, LA Lakers
Doug Christie, Sacramento
Shaquille O'Neal, LA Lakers
Bruce Bowen, Miami
P.J. Brown, Charlotte

## All-Rookie Teams
### (Chosen Without Regard to Position)

**FIRST TEAM**
Mike Miller, Orlando
Kenyon Martin, New Jersey
Marc Jackson, Golden State
Morris Peterson, Toronto
Darius Miles, LA Clippers

**SECOND TEAM**
Hidayet Turkoglu, Sacramento
Desmond Mason, Seattle
Courtney Alexander, Washington
Marcus Fizer, Chicago
Chris Mihm, Cleveland

## Scoring

| | GP | Pts | Avg |
|---|---|---|---|
| Allen Iverson, Phil | 71 | 2207 | 31.1 |
| Jerry Stackhouse, Det | 80 | 2380 | 29.8 |
| Shaquille O'Neal, LA Lakers | 74 | 2125 | 28.7 |
| Kobe Bryant, LA Lakers | 68 | 1938 | 28.5 |
| Vince Carter, Tor | 75 | 2070 | 27.6 |
| Chris Webber, Sac | 70 | 1898 | 27.1 |
| Tracy McGrady, Orl | 77 | 2065 | 26.8 |
| Paul Pierce, Bos | 82 | 2071 | 25.3 |
| Antawn Jamison, GS | 82 | 2044 | 24.9 |
| Stephon Marbury, NJ | 67 | 1598 | 23.9 |

## Rebounds

| | GP | Reb | Avg |
|---|---|---|---|
| Dikembe Mutombo, Atl/Phil | 75 | 1015 | 13.5 |
| Ben Wallace, Det | 80 | 1052 | 13.2 |
| Shaquille O'Neal, LA Lakers | 74 | 940 | 12.7 |
| Tim Duncan, SA | 82 | 997 | 12.2 |
| Antonio McDyess, Den | 70 | 845 | 12.1 |
| Kevin Garnett, Minn | 81 | 921 | 11.4 |
| Chris Webber, Sac | 70 | 777 | 11.1 |
| Shawn Marion, Phoe | 79 | 848 | 10.7 |
| Antonio Davis, Tor | 78 | 787 | 10.1 |
| Elton Brand, Chi | 74 | 746 | 10.1 |

## Assists

| | GP | Assists | Avg |
|---|---|---|---|
| Jason Kidd, Phoe | 77 | 753 | 9.8 |
| John Stockton, Utah | 82 | 713 | 8.7 |
| Nick Van Exel, Den | 71 | 600 | 8.5 |
| Mike Bibby, Van | 82 | 685 | 8.4 |
| Gary Payton, Sea | 79 | 642 | 8.1 |
| Andre Miller, Clev | 82 | 657 | 8.0 |
| Mark Jackson, Tor/NY | 83 | 661 | 8.0 |
| Sam Cassell, Mil | 76 | 580 | 7.6 |
| Stephon Marbury, NJ | 67 | 506 | 7.6 |
| Terrell Brandon, Minn | 78 | 583 | 7.5 |

## Field-Goal Percentage

| | FGA | FGM | Pct |
|---|---|---|---|
| Shaquille O'Neal, LA Lakers | 1422 | 813 | .572 |
| Bonzi Wellls, Port | 726 | 387 | .533 |
| Marcus Camby, NY | 580 | 304 | .524 |
| Kurt Thomas, NY | 614 | 314 | .511 |
| Wally Szczerbiak, Minn | 920 | 469 | .510 |
| Darius Miles, LA Clippers | 630 | 318 | .505 |
| John Stockton, Utah | 651 | 328 | .504 |
| Donyell Marshall, Utah | 849 | 427 | .503 |
| Corliss Williamson, Det | 647 | 325 | .502 |
| Clarence Weatherspoon, Clev | 692 | 347 | .501 |
| Rasheed Wallace, Port | 1178 | 590 | .501 |

## Free-Throw Percentage

| | FTA | FTM | Pct |
|---|---|---|---|
| Reggie Miller, Ind | 348 | 323 | .928 |
| Allan Houston, NY | 307 | 279 | .909 |
| Doug Christie, Sac | 312 | 280 | .897 |
| Steve Nash, Dall | 258 | 231 | .895 |
| Mitch Richmond, Wash | 160 | 143 | .894 |
| Steve Smith, Port | 347 | 309 | .890 |
| Ray Allen, Mil | 392 | 348 | .888 |
| Darrell Armstrong, Orl | 249 | 220 | .884 |
| Eric Piatkowski, LA Clippers | 181 | 158 | .873 |
| Terrell Brandon, Minn | 224 | 195 | .871 |

## Three-Point Field-Goal Percentage

| | FGA | FGM | Pct |
|---|---|---|---|
| Brent Barry, Sea | 229 | 109 | .476 |
| John Stockton, Utah | 132 | 61 | .462 |
| Shammond Williams, Sea | 133 | 61 | .459 |
| Hubert Davis, Wash | 171 | 78 | .456 |
| Danny Ferry, SA | 156 | 70 | .449 |
| Toni Kukoc, Phil/Atl | 157 | 70 | .446 |
| Pat Garrity, Orl | 224 | 97 | .433 |
| Ray Allen, Mil | 467 | 202 | .433 |
| Rashard Lewis, Sea | 285 | 123 | .432 |
| Dell Curry, Tor | 145 | 62 | .428 |

## Steals

| | GP | Steals | Avg |
|---|---|---|---|
| Allen Iverson, Phil | 71 | 178 | 2.51 |
| Mookie Blaylock, GS | 69 | 163 | 2.36 |
| Doug Christie, Sac | 81 | 183 | 2.26 |
| Jason Kidd, Phoe | 77 | 166 | 2.16 |
| Baron Davis, Char | 82 | 170 | 2.07 |
| Terrell Brandon, Minn | 78 | 161 | 2.06 |
| Ron Artest, Chi | 76 | 152 | 2.00 |
| Darrell Armstrong, Orl | 75 | 135 | 1.80 |
| Steve Francis, Hou | 80 | 141 | 1.76 |
| Antoine Walker, Bos | 81 | 138 | 1.70 |

## Blocked Shots

| | GP | BS | Avg |
|---|---|---|---|
| Theo Ratliff, Phil/Atl | 50 | 187 | 3.74 |
| Jermaine O'Neal, Ind | 81 | 228 | 2.81 |
| Shawn Bradley, Dall | 82 | 228 | 2.78 |
| Shaquille O'Neal, LA Lakers | 74 | 204 | 2.76 |
| Dikembe Mutombo, Atl/Phil | 75 | 203 | 2.71 |
| Adonal Foyle, GS | 58 | 156 | 2.69 |
| Raef LaFrentz, Den | 78 | 206 | 2.64 |
| David Robinson, SA | 80 | 197 | 2.46 |
| Tim Duncan, SA | 82 | 192 | 2.34 |
| Ben Wallace, Det | 80 | 186 | 2.33 |

# NBA Team Statistics

## Offense

| Team | Field Goals FGM | Pct | 3-Pt Field Goals 3FGM | Pct | Free Throws FTM | Pct | Rebounds Off | Total | A | Stl | Scoring Avg |
|---|---|---|---|---|---|---|---|---|---|---|---|
| Sacramento | 3132 | 44.9 | 479 | 35.4 | 1600 | 77.1 | 987 | 3692 | 1852 | 793 | 101.7 |
| Milwaukee | 3112 | 45.8 | 562 | 37.9 | 1474 | 78.7 | 975 | 3475 | 1844 | 672 | 100.7 |
| LA Lakers | 3109 | 46.5 | 439 | 34.4 | 1594 | 68.3 | 1085 | 3668 | 1888 | 564 | 100.6 |
| Dallas | 3085 | 45.9 | 517 | 38.1 | 1552 | 79.4 | 831 | 3402 | 1740 | 618 | 100.5 |
| Toronto | 3048 | 43.7 | 429 | 36.9 | 1482 | 74.7 | 1118 | 3647 | 2004 | 599 | 97.6 |
| Orlando | 3013 | 43.8 | 490 | 36.4 | 1476 | 71.4 | 1069 | 3519 | 1803 | 674 | 97.5 |
| Minnesota | 3148 | 45.8 | 322 | 35.7 | 1364 | 78.5 | 1002 | 3472 | 2083 | 682 | 97.3 |
| Seattle | 3029 | 45.6 | 466 | 39.9 | 1454 | 73.2 | 999 | 3421 | 1792 | 657 | 97.3 |
| Houston | 2943 | 45.3 | 504 | 35.7 | 1582 | 75.8 | 919 | 3443 | 1613 | 587 | 97.2 |
| Utah | 2960 | 47.1 | 325 | 38.1 | 1714 | 75.2 | 943 | 3326 | 2111 | 661 | 97.1 |
| Denver | 2979 | 43.3 | 512 | 35.5 | 1448 | 73.7 | 1044 | 3627 | 1970 | 552 | 96.6 |
| San Antonio | 2884 | 46.1 | 445 | 40.7 | 1673 | 71.5 | 902 | 3614 | 1778 | 568 | 96.2 |
| Detroit | 2919 | 42.4 | 389 | 35.0 | 1610 | 72.1 | 1108 | 3734 | 1629 | 613 | 95.6 |
| Portland | 3004 | 46.8 | 369 | 34.9 | 1447 | 76.2 | 959 | 3440 | 1963 | 672 | 95.4 |
| Philadelphia | 2902 | 44.7 | 262 | 32.6 | 1697 | 74.5 | 1075 | 3675 | 1692 | 690 | 94.7 |
| Boston | 2773 | 42.8 | 592 | 36.3 | 1621 | 74.0 | 897 | 3264 | 1708 | 769 | 94.6 |
| Phoenix | 2944 | 43.6 | 332 | 31.5 | 1490 | 75.5 | 970 | 3499 | 1905 | 775 | 94.0 |
| Washington | 2833 | 43.9 | 275 | 32.4 | 1704 | 75.9 | 1016 | 3386 | 1647 | 630 | 93.2 |
| Indiana | 2828 | 44.0 | 396 | 34.2 | 1539 | 76.6 | 921 | 3516 | 1763 | 563 | 92.6 |
| Golden State | 2937 | 40.9 | 282 | 29.3 | 1428 | 70.6 | 1345 | 3730 | 1788 | 742 | 92.5 |
| LA Clippers | 2896 | 44.8 | 360 | 33.9 | 1429 | 69.3 | 962 | 3521 | 1585 | 490 | 92.5 |
| Cleveland | 2890 | 44.2 | 220 | 33.4 | 1561 | 76.5 | 1015 | 3455 | 1708 | 642 | 92.2 |
| New Jersey | 2781 | 42.5 | 361 | 33.3 | 1629 | 75.9 | 909 | 3246 | 1603 | 649 | 92.1 |
| Charlotte | 2800 | 43.1 | 340 | 34.6 | 1599 | 74.5 | 1033 | 3641 | 1900 | 665 | 91.9 |
| Vancouver | 2870 | 43.9 | 325 | 34.3 | 1457 | 77.0 | 894 | 3325 | 1899 | 586 | 91.7 |
| Atlanta | 2876 | 43.1 | 333 | 35.7 | 1374 | 75.9 | 1029 | 3518 | 1559 | 634 | 91.0 |
| Miami | 2694 | 43.0 | 478 | 34.5 | 1423 | 75.9 | 813 | 3248 | 1630 | 633 | 88.9 |
| New York | 2755 | 44.4 | 391 | 35.1 | 1374 | 79.6 | 773 | 3297 | 1520 | 545 | 88.7 |
| Chicago | 2721 | 42.4 | 329 | 34.6 | 1410 | 73.9 | 926 | 3186 | 1810 | 675 | 87.6 |

## Defense (Opponent's Statistics)

| Team | Field Goals FGM | Pct | 3-Pt Field Goals 3FGM | Pct | Free Throws FTM | Pct | Rebounds Off | Total | Stl | Scoring Avg | Diff |
|---|---|---|---|---|---|---|---|---|---|---|---|
| New York | 2568 | 41.7 | 445 | 35.2 | 1478 | 73.3 | 872 | 3290 | 596 | 86.1 | +2.6 |
| Miami | 2701 | 43.1 | 363 | 33.1 | 1339 | 73.7 | 914 | 3442 | 598 | 86.6 | +2.3 |
| San Antonio | 2837 | 41.9 | 343 | 32.9 | 1233 | 74.1 | 967 | 3399 | 600 | 88.4 | +7.8 |
| Charlotte | 2767 | 42.6 | 389 | 36.0 | 1444 | 75.6 | 892 | 3328 | 616 | 89.8 | +2.1 |
| Philadelphia | 2871 | 42.9 | 427 | 34.2 | 1243 | 74.9 | 985 | 3351 | 672 | 90.4 | +4.3 |
| Portland | 2819 | 43.8 | 406 | 36.8 | 1436 | 74.4 | 946 | 3184 | 646 | 91.2 | +4.2 |
| Phoenix | 2792 | 43.5 | 327 | 34.9 | 1618 | 76.1 | 902 | 3490 | 682 | 91.8 | +2.2 |
| Utah | 2667 | 43.9 | 410 | 34.3 | 1830 | 76.5 | 875 | 3057 | 699 | 92.4 | +4.7 |
| Indiana | 2829 | 42.3 | 377 | 33.6 | 1572 | 75.8 | 1042 | 3537 | 589 | 92.8 | -0.2 |
| Houston | 3020 | 44.9 | 359 | 35.4 | 1385 | 74.4 | 988 | 3408 | 605 | 94.9 | +2.3 |
| LA Clippers | 2995 | 44.1 | 354 | 32.9 | 1474 | 74.3 | 1041 | 3480 | 638 | 95.3 | -2.9 |
| Toronto | 3009 | 44.7 | 379 | 36.3 | 1425 | 75.4 | 926 | 3437 | 561 | 95.4 | +2.3 |
| Sacramento | 3087 | 43.2 | 401 | 35.5 | 1291 | 74.9 | 1121 | 3764 | 666 | 95.9 | +5.8 |
| Minnesota | 2977 | 45.2 | 350 | 35.1 | 1567 | 72.4 | 967 | 3472 | 583 | 96.0 | +1.4 |
| Atlanta | 2922 | 44.2 | 396 | 36.7 | 1646 | 76.5 | 1029 | 3563 | 698 | 96.2 | -5.2 |
| Dallas | 2938 | 43.9 | 381 | 33.4 | 1631 | 73.1 | 1068 | 3691 | 622 | 96.2 | +4.3 |
| Cleveland | 2927 | 44.5 | 422 | 36.5 | 1633 | 76.8 | 990 | 3390 | 694 | 96.5 | -4.2 |
| Orlando | 2830 | 43.5 | 366 | 34.6 | 1885 | 73.5 | 1061 | 3670 | 695 | 96.5 | +1.0 |
| Chicago | 2987 | 47.2 | 346 | 35.6 | 1607 | 73.0 | 957 | 3508 | 635 | 96.7 | -9.1 |
| Boston | 2935 | 45.9 | 430 | 36.8 | 1634 | 75.0 | 888 | 3538 | 650 | 96.8 | -2.1 |
| Milwaukee | 2912 | 43.9 | 439 | 35.2 | 1679 | 76.8 | 1014 | 3504 | 592 | 96.9 | +3.9 |
| New Jersey | 2937 | 45.5 | 428 | 36.0 | 1664 | 74.6 | 1001 | 3623 | 619 | 97.1 | -5.0 |
| LA Lakers | 2983 | 43.8 | 413 | 35.4 | 1595 | 75.4 | 981 | 3388 | 619 | 97.2 | +3.4 |
| Detroit | 2976 | 43.4 | 428 | 34.8 | 1596 | 73.6 | 1012 | 3683 | 669 | 97.3 | -1.7 |
| Seattle | 3076 | 45.3 | 471 | 34.9 | 1353 | 74.2 | 1046 | 3477 | 648 | 97.3 | 0.0 |
| Vancouver | 3143 | 46.3 | 389 | 36.2 | 1317 | 73.2 | 1052 | 3586 | 710 | 97.5 | -5.7 |
| Denver | 3081 | 44.6 | 416 | 35.6 | 1542 | 75.3 | 1012 | 3654 | 588 | 99.0 | -2.5 |
| Washington | 3100 | 47.0 | 433 | 39.6 | 1559 | 74.7 | 931 | 3341 | 688 | 99.9 | -6.7 |
| Golden State | 3179 | 47.2 | 439 | 37.9 | 1529 | 76.0 | 1039 | 3732 | 722 | 101.5 | -9.0 |

# NBA Team-by-Team Statistical Leaders

## Atlanta Hawks

| Player | GP | Min | Field Goals | | 3-Pt FG | | Free Throws | | Rebounds | | A | Stl | TO | BS | Avg |
|---|---|---|---|---|---|---|---|---|---|---|---|---|---|---|---|
| | | | FGM | Pct | FGA | FGM | FTM | Pct | Off | Total | | | | | |
| Terry | 82 | 3089 | 596 | 43.6 | 314 | 124 | 303 | 84.6 | 42 | 269 | 403 | 104 | 239 | 12 | 19.7 |
| Kukoc | 17 | 618 | 124 | 49.2 | 79 | 38 | 49 | 68.1 | 19 | 97 | 106 | 13 | 51 | 5 | 19.7 |
| Jackson | 17 | 550 | 77 | 35.5 | 38 | 16 | 73 | 85.9 | 17 | 79 | 50 | 19 | 48 | 4 | 14.3 |
| Wright | 71 | 1988 | 363 | 44.8 | 2 | 0 | 155 | 71.8 | 180 | 535 | 87 | 42 | 125 | 63 | 12.4 |
| Mohammed | 28 | 716 | 135 | 48.0 | 1 | 0 | 75 | 76.5 | 97 | 252 | 17 | 23 | 55 | 28 | 12.3 |
| Henderson | 73 | 1810 | 298 | 44.4 | 1 | 0 | 173 | 63.8 | 180 | 406 | 50 | 51 | 126 | 29 | 10.5 |
| McLeod | 34 | 907 | 144 | 43.6 | 21 | 2 | 45 | 88.2 | 37 | 118 | 58 | 23 | 57 | 8 | 9.9 |
| Mutombo | 49 | 1716 | 169 | 47.7 | 0 | 0 | 107 | 69.5 | 188 | 693 | 54 | 20 | 92 | 137 | 9.1 |
| Knight | 47 | 1364 | 137 | 38.5 | 10 | 1 | 49 | 81.7 | 22 | 161 | 286 | 95 | 84 | 3 | 6.9 |
| Crawford | 47 | 901 | 122 | 45.2 | 22 | 6 | 68 | 81.9 | 28 | 110 | 37 | 21 | 62 | 16 | 6.8 |
| Maloney | 55 | 1043 | 146 | 42.0 | 142 | 51 | 26 | 76.5 | 14 | 117 | 154 | 56 | 70 | 5 | 6.7 |
| Glover | 57 | 929 | 141 | 42.0 | 46 | 9 | 47 | 68.1 | 39 | 131 | 69 | 49 | 54 | 10 | 5.9 |
| Johnson | 78 | 1313 | 146 | 37.4 | 127 | 41 | 64 | 73.6 | 56 | 178 | 64 | 43 | 93 | 30 | 5.1 |
| **Hawks** | **82** | **19730** | **2876** | **43.1** | **933** | **333** | **1374** | **75.9** | **1028** | **3518** | **1559** | **634** | **1368** | **387** | **91.0** |
| **Opponents** | **82** | **19730** | **2922** | **44.2** | **1080** | **396** | **1646** | **76.5** | **1029** | **3563** | **1737** | **698** | **1212** | **513** | **96.2** |

## Boston Celtics

| Player | GP | Min | Field Goals | | 3-Pt FG | | Free Throws | | Rebounds | | A | Stl | TO | BS | Avg |
|---|---|---|---|---|---|---|---|---|---|---|---|---|---|---|---|
| | | | FGM | Pct | FGA | FGM | FTM | Pct | Off | Total | | | | | |
| Pierce | 82 | 3120 | 687 | 45.4 | 384 | 147 | 550 | 74.5 | 94 | 522 | 253 | 138 | 262 | 69 | 25.3 |
| Walker | 81 | 3396 | 711 | 41.3 | 603 | 221 | 249 | 71.6 | 151 | 719 | 445 | 138 | 301 | 49 | 23.4 |
| Stith | 78 | 2504 | 245 | 40.1 | 242 | 91 | 175 | 84.5 | 65 | 284 | 168 | 93 | 90 | 14 | 9.7 |
| Potapenko | 82 | 1901 | 248 | 47.6 | 0 | 0 | 115 | 72.8 | 206 | 495 | 64 | 52 | 105 | 23 | 7.5 |
| Anderson | 33 | 849 | 88 | 38.8 | 33 | 11 | 59 | 83.1 | 16 | 73 | 134 | 44 | 52 | 2 | 7.5 |
| Williams | 81 | 1745 | 162 | 36.2 | 139 | 46 | 165 | 71.4 | 64 | 207 | 112 | 64 | 76 | 13 | 6.6 |
| Battie | 40 | 845 | 108 | 53.7 | 3 | 0 | 44 | 63.8 | 73 | 233 | 16 | 27 | 37 | 60 | 6.5 |
| Palacio | 58 | 1141 | 126 | 47.2 | 36 | 12 | 78 | 84.8 | 25 | 102 | 151 | 48 | 80 | 0 | 5.9 |
| Carr | 35 | 309 | 53 | 47.3 | 37 | 17 | 46 | 76.7 | 11 | 44 | 11 | 4 | 19 | 3 | 4.8 |
| Brown | 54 | 1238 | 100 | 42.2 | 3 | 0 | 23 | 57.5 | 23 | 99 | 154 | 62 | 56 | 10 | 4.1 |
| Blount | 64 | 1098 | 101 | 50.5 | 0 | 0 | 46 | 69.7 | 97 | 231 | 32 | 39 | 62 | 76 | 3.9 |
| Herren | 25 | 408 | 29 | 30.2 | 55 | 16 | 9 | 75.0 | 4 | 21 | 56 | 14 | 20 | 0 | 3.3 |
| McCarty | 60 | 478 | 45 | 35.7 | 56 | 19 | 22 | 78.6 | 24 | 81 | 39 | 14 | 20 | 7 | 2.2 |
| **Celtics** | **82** | **19830** | **2773** | **42.8** | **1633** | **592** | **1621** | **74.0** | **897** | **3264** | **1708** | **769** | **1285** | **336** | **94.6** |
| **Opponents** | **82** | **19830** | **2935** | **45.9** | **1170** | **430** | **1634** | **75.0** | **888** | **3538** | **1885** | **650** | **1402** | **440** | **96.8** |

## Charlotte Hornets

| Player | GP | Min | Field Goals | | 3-Pt FG | | Free Throws | | Rebounds | | A | Stl | TO | BS | Avg |
|---|---|---|---|---|---|---|---|---|---|---|---|---|---|---|---|
| | | | FGM | Pct | FGA | FGM | FTM | Pct | Off | Total | | | | | |
| Mashburn | 76 | 2989 | 573 | 41.3 | 289 | 103 | 279 | 76.6 | 92 | 576 | 411 | 85 | 211 | 13 | 20.1 |
| Wesley | 82 | 3106 | 523 | 42.2 | 258 | 97 | 271 | 79.9 | 64 | 224 | 361 | 128 | 171 | 16 | 17.2 |
| Davis | 82 | 3192 | 409 | 42.7 | 274 | 85 | 228 | 67.7 | 129 | 408 | 598 | 170 | 226 | 36 | 13.8 |
| Campbell | 78 | 2337 | 367 | 44.0 | 6 | 0 | 288 | 70.9 | 157 | 608 | 104 | 60 | 144 | 140 | 13.1 |
| Brown | 80 | 2811 | 249 | 44.4 | 4 | 0 | 178 | 85.2 | 257 | 742 | 127 | 78 | 108 | 92 | 8.5 |
| Coleman | 34 | 683 | 97 | 38.0 | 51 | 20 | 63 | 68.5 | 46 | 184 | 39 | 10 | 42 | 21 | 8.1 |
| Robinson | 67 | 1201 | 216 | 53.1 | 4 | 2 | 64 | 72.7 | 60 | 198 | 59 | 50 | 43 | 32 | 7.4 |
| Magloire | 74 | 1095 | 122 | 45.0 | 2 | 0 | 95 | 65.5 | 103 | 295 | 27 | 18 | 61 | 78 | 4.6 |
| Burrell | 4 | 41 | 7 | 46.7 | 6 | 2 | 1 | 25.0 | 1 | 3 | 1 | 3 | 0 | 0 | 4.3 |
| Nailon | 42 | 469 | 66 | 48.5 | 1 | 0 | 32 | 74.4 | 29 | 92 | 24 | 9 | 27 | 5 | 3.9 |
| Hawkins | 59 | 681 | 56 | 40.9 | 46 | 17 | 54 | 85.7 | 17 | 80 | 72 | 33 | 19 | 9 | 3.1 |
| Thorpe | 49 | 647 | 59 | 45.0 | 0 | 0 | 20 | 83.3 | 50 | 145 | 29 | 12 | 32 | 7 | 2.8 |
| Recasner | 43 | 403 | 38 | 33.3 | 39 | 13 | 14 | 77.8 | 13 | 50 | 39 | 6 | 27 | 1 | 2.4 |
| James | 30 | 197 | 16 | 30.8 | 3 | 1 | 12 | 85.7 | 15 | 35 | 8 | 2 | 8 | 5 | 1.5 |
| **Hornets** | **82** | **19880** | **2800** | **43.1** | **984** | **340** | **1599** | **74.5** | **1033** | **3641** | **1900** | **665** | **1183** | **455** | **91.9** |
| **Opponents** | **82** | **19880** | **2767** | **42.6** | **1081** | **389** | **1444** | **75.6** | **892** | **3328** | **1748** | **616** | **1204** | **375** | **89.8** |

## Chicago Bulls

| Player | GP | Min | Field Goals | | 3-Pt FG | | Free Throws | | Rebounds | | A | Stl | TO | BS | Avg |
|---|---|---|---|---|---|---|---|---|---|---|---|---|---|---|---|
| | | | FGM | Pct | FGA | FGM | FTM | Pct | Off | Total | | | | | |
| Brand | 74 | 2906 | 578 | 47.6 | 2 | 0 | 334 | 70.8 | 285 | 746 | 240 | 71 | 219 | 118 | 20.1 |
| Mercer | 61 | 2535 | 500 | 44.6 | 46 | 14 | 188 | 82.5 | 72 | 236 | 201 | 78 | 129 | 27 | 19.7 |
| Artest | 76 | 2363 | 327 | 40.1 | 148 | 43 | 210 | 75.0 | 59 | 294 | 228 | 152 | 159 | 45 | 11.9 |
| Fizer | 72 | 1580 | 278 | 43.0 | 39 | 10 | 117 | 72.7 | 76 | 313 | 76 | 30 | 124 | 19 | 9.5 |
| Hoiberg | 37 | 2247 | 217 | 43.8 | 250 | 103 | 136 | 86.6 | 21 | 308 | 263 | 98 | 74 | 12 | 9.1 |
| Miller | 57 | 1434 | 168 | 43.5 | 5 | 1 | 168 | 74.3 | 144 | 419 | 107 | 33 | 73 | 38 | 8.9 |
| El-Amin | 50 | 936 | 115 | 37.0 | 84 | 28 | 56 | 77.8 | 21 | 81 | 145 | 48 | 54 | 2 | 6.3 |
| Drew | 48 | 1305 | 124 | 37.9 | 105 | 40 | 14 | 73.7 | 12 | 69 | 185 | 32 | 68 | 3 | 6.3 |
| Guyton | 33 | 630 | 78 | 40.6 | 69 | 27 | 15 | 83.3 | 10 | 36 | 64 | 9 | 24 | 5 | 6.0 |
| Benjamin | 65 | 857 | 115 | 38.1 | 81 | 21 | 56 | 67.5 | 38 | 100 | 69 | 28 | 63 | 16 | 4.7 |
| Crawford | 61 | 1050 | 107 | 35.2 | 117 | 41 | 27 | 79.4 | 9 | 89 | 141 | 43 | 85 | 14 | 4.6 |
| Ruffin | 45 | 879 | 40 | 44.4 | 0 | 0 | 39 | 50.6 | 101 | 262 | 39 | 30 | 46 | 38 | 2.6 |
| **Bulls** | **82** | **19855** | **2721** | **42.4** | **950** | **329** | **1410** | **73.9** | **926** | **3186** | **1810** | **675** | **1292** | **379** | **87.6** |
| **Opponents** | **82** | **19855** | **2987** | **47.2** | **973** | **346** | **1607** | **73.0** | **957** | **3508** | **1932** | **635** | **1217** | **426** | **96.7** |

## Cleveland Cavaliers

| Player | GP | Min | Field Goals | | 3-Pt FG | | Free Throws | | Rebounds | | A | Stl | TO | BS | Avg |
|---|---|---|---|---|---|---|---|---|---|---|---|---|---|---|---|
| | | | FGM | Pct | FGA | FGM | FTM | Pct | Off | Total | | | | | |
| Miller | 82 | 2848 | 452 | 45.2 | 64 | 17 | 375 | 83.3 | 94 | 360 | 657 | 119 | 265 | 28 | 15.8 |
| Murray | 78 | 2225 | 391 | 42.3 | 165 | 61 | 155 | 73.5 | 104 | 340 | 124 | 83 | 141 | 27 | 12.8 |
| Ilgauskas | 24 | 616 | 114 | 48.7 | 2 | 0 | 53 | 67.9 | 65 | 160 | 18 | 15 | 60 | 37 | 11.7 |
| Jackson | 56 | 1690 | 239 | 37.8 | 80 | 26 | 139 | 82.2 | 53 | 224 | 163 | 53 | 130 | 10 | 11.5 |
| Gatling | 74 | 1670 | 329 | 44.9 | 92 | 28 | 156 | 68.4 | 99 | 391 | 61 | 52 | 119 | 27 | 11.4 |
| Weatherspoon | 82 | 2774 | 347 | 50.1 | 0 | 0 | 230 | 79.0 | 223 | 796 | 103 | 85 | 112 | 105 | 11.3 |
| Harpring | 56 | 1650 | 238 | 45.4 | 52 | 13 | 134 | 81.2 | 90 | 242 | 102 | 42 | 90 | 17 | 11.1 |
| Mihm | 59 | 1166 | 173 | 44.2 | 1 | 0 | 100 | 79.4 | 106 | 280 | 16 | 20 | 80 | 53 | 7.6 |
| Person | 44 | 958 | 128 | 43.8 | 84 | 34 | 24 | 80.0 | 11 | 130 | 64 | 27 | 40 | 11 | 7.1 |
| Langdon | 65 | 1116 | 135 | 43.1 | 124 | 51 | 68 | 89.5 | 12 | 89 | 81 | 38 | 52 | 9 | 6.0 |
| Traylor | 70 | 1212 | 161 | 49.7 | 2 | 0 | 80 | 56.7 | 124 | 300 | 63 | 49 | 98 | 76 | 5.7 |
| Coles | 47 | 804 | 91 | 38.1 | 16 | 2 | 48 | 85.7 | 9 | 48 | 138 | 27 | 59 | 6 | 4.9 |
| Henderson | 55 | 961 | 102 | 38.9 | 8 | 1 | 30 | 65.2 | 19 | 70 | 79 | 29 | 63 | 23 | 4.3 |
| Brown | 26 | 339 | 40 | 42.1 | 3 | 0 | 22 | 64.7 | 8 | 54 | 11 | 9 | 8 | 7 | 3.9 |
| Johnson | 53 | 511 | 53 | 34.9 | 5 | 1 | 23 | 69.7 | 10 | 44 | 78 | 23 | 34 | 6 | 2.5 |
| Hawkins | 10 | 76 | 3 | 33.3 | 4 | 2 | 0 | — | 2 | 5 | 13 | 2 | 6 | 0 | 0.8 |
| **Cavs** | **82** | **19830** | **2890** | **44.2** | **659** | **220** | **1561** | **76.5** | **1015** | **3455** | **1708** | **642** | **1350** | **436** | **92.2** |
| **Opponents** | **82** | **19830** | **2927** | **44.5** | **1155** | **422** | **1633** | **76.8** | **990** | **3390** | **1880** | **694** | **1229** | **542** | **96.5** |

## Dallas Mavericks

| Player | GP | Min | Field Goals | | 3-Pt FG | | Free Throws | | Rebounds | | A | Stl | TO | BS | Avg |
|---|---|---|---|---|---|---|---|---|---|---|---|---|---|---|---|
| | | | FGM | Pct | FGA | FGM | FTM | Pct | Off | Total | | | | | |
| Nowitzki | 82 | 3125 | 591 | 47.4 | 390 | 151 | 451 | 83.8 | 119 | 754 | 173 | 79 | 156 | 101 | 21.8 |
| Finley | 82 | 3443 | 711 | 45.8 | 263 | 91 | 252 | 77.5 | 109 | 425 | 360 | 118 | 190 | 32 | 21.5 |
| Howard | 27 | 993 | 191 | 48.8 | 3 | 0 | 99 | 78.0 | 50 | 193 | 70 | 29 | 73 | 16 | 17.8 |
| Nash | 70 | 2387 | 386 | 48.7 | 219 | 89 | 231 | 89.5 | 46 | 223 | 509 | 72 | 205 | 5 | 15.6 |
| Eisley | 82 | 2426 | 265 | 39.3 | 269 | 107 | 104 | 82.5 | 23 | 197 | 295 | 99 | 102 | 12 | 9.0 |
| Laettner | 53 | 930 | 165 | 51.1 | 3 | 1 | 67 | 81.7 | 75 | 212 | 67 | 40 | 70 | 27 | 7.5 |
| Booth | 15 | 293 | 46 | 54.8 | 0 | 0 | 20 | 60.6 | 24 | 72 | 19 | 12 | 17 | 30 | 7.5 |
| Davis | 51 | 1261 | 139 | 44.3 | 133 | 58 | 35 | 85.4 | 18 | 109 | 61 | 29 | 56 | 1 | 7.3 |
| Bradley | 82 | 2001 | 219 | 49.6 | 6 | 1 | 140 | 78.7 | 160 | 608 | 38 | 36 | 88 | 228 | 7.1 |
| Buckner | 37 | 820 | 84 | 43.8 | 7 | 2 | 59 | 72.8 | 60 | 157 | 49 | 33 | 27 | 9 | 6.2 |
| Wang | 5 | 38 | 8 | 42.1 | 2 | 0 | 8 | 80.0 | 1 | 7 | 0 | 0 | 1 | 0 | 4.8 |
| Maxwell | 19 | 285 | 31 | 31.6 | 47 | 13 | 6 | 60.0 | 1 | 29 | 20 | 9 | 17 | 3 | 4.3 |
| Alexander | 38 | 472 | 62 | 34.8 | 10 | 3 | 33 | 73.3 | 20 | 63 | 21 | 16 | 21 | 3 | 4.2 |
| Trent | 33 | 319 | 57 | 43.8 | 1 | 0 | 19 | 52.8 | 39 | 92 | 10 | 13 | 22 | 8 | 4.0 |
| **Mavericks** | **82** | **19805** | **3085** | **45.9** | **1357** | **517** | **1552** | **79.4** | **831** | **3402** | **1740** | **618** | **1141** | **492** | **100.5** |
| **Opponents** | **82** | **19805** | **2938** | **43.9** | **1140** | **381** | **1631** | **73.1** | **1068** | **3691** | **1778** | **622** | **1273** | **379** | **96.2** |

## Denver Nuggets

| Player | GP | Min | FGM | Pct | FGA | FGM | FTM | Pct | Off | Total | A | Stl | TO | BS | Avg |
|---|---|---|---|---|---|---|---|---|---|---|---|---|---|---|---|
| | | | Field Goals | | 3-Pt FG | | Free Throws | | Rebounds | | | | | | |
| McDyess | 70 | 2555 | 577 | 49.5 | 0 | 0 | 304 | 70.0 | 240 | 845 | 146 | 43 | 162 | 102 | 20.8 |
| Van Exel | 71 | 2688 | 460 | 41.4 | 358 | 135 | 204 | 81.9 | 44 | 241 | 600 | 61 | 165 | 18 | 17.7 |
| LaFrentz | 78 | 2457 | 387 | 47.7 | 139 | 51 | 183 | 69.8 | 173 | 607 | 107 | 37 | 97 | 206 | 12.9 |
| Lenard | 80 | 2331 | 336 | 39.7 | 382 | 147 | 153 | 79.7 | 47 | 231 | 190 | 65 | 102 | 18 | 12.2 |
| McCloud | 76 | 2007 | 250 | 38.2 | 234 | 77 | 152 | 84.0 | 55 | 224 | 279 | 53 | 117 | 27 | 9.6 |
| Willis | 78 | 1830 | 304 | 44.1 | 6 | 1 | 113 | 76.9 | 177 | 532 | 50 | 57 | 87 | 52 | 9.3 |
| Posey | 82 | 2255 | 243 | 41.2 | 217 | 65 | 115 | 81.6 | 125 | 431 | 163 | 93 | 102 | 40 | 8.1 |
| Pack | 74 | 1260 | 181 | 42.5 | 31 | 12 | 105 | 76.6 | 30 | 137 | 293 | 65 | 135 | 1 | 6.5 |
| Goldwire | 20 | 201 | 30 | 37.5 | 34 | 9 | 13 | 76.5 | 1 | 12 | 34 | 9 | 15 | 0 | 4.1 |
| Abdul-Wahad | 29 | 420 | 43 | 38.7 | 10 | 4 | 21 | 58.3 | 14 | 59 | 22 | 14 | 34 | 13 | 3.8 |
| Bowen | 57 | 696 | 80 | 55.6 | 11 | 4 | 27 | 61.4 | 62 | 113 | 30 | 37 | 24 | 12 | 3.4 |
| McClintock | 6 | 58 | 9 | 50.0 | 0 | 0 | 0 | 00.0 | 10 | 17 | 1 | 0 | 3 | 2 | 3.0 |
| Cheaney | 9 | 153 | 10 | 33.3 | 0 | 0 | 1 | 50.0 | 5 | 20 | 9 | 4 | 5 | 2 | 2.3 |
| Davis | 19 | 228 | 12 | 48.0 | 0 | 0 | 9 | 40.9 | 24 | 53 | 7 | 1 | 5 | 1 | 1.7 |
| Joseph | 6 | 16 | 1 | 20.0 | 0 | 0 | 0 | 00.0 | 2 | 2 | 1 | 0 | 2 | 1 | 0.5 |
| **Nuggets** | **82** | **19780** | **2979** | **43.3** | **1444** | **512** | **1448** | **73.7** | **1044** | **3627** | **1970** | **552** | **1136** | **538** | **96.6** |
| **Opponents** | **82** | **19780** | **3081** | **44.6** | **1168** | **416** | **1542** | **75.3** | **1012** | **3654** | **2042** | **588** | **1075** | **497** | **99.0** |

## Detroit Pistons

| Player | GP | Min | FGM | Pct | FGA | FGM | FTM | Pct | Off | Total | A | Stl | TO | BS | Avg |
|---|---|---|---|---|---|---|---|---|---|---|---|---|---|---|---|
| | | | Field Goals | | 3-Pt FG | | Free Throws | | Rebounds | | | | | | |
| Stackhouse | 80 | 3215 | 774 | 40.2 | 473 | 166 | 666 | 82.2 | 99 | 315 | 410 | 97 | 326 | 54 | 29.8 |
| Williamson | 27 | 800 | 172 | 53.4 | 0 | 0 | 67 | 62.6 | 53 | 168 | 28 | 35 | 45 | 8 | 15.2 |
| Smith | 69 | 1941 | 308 | 40.3 | 5 | 0 | 231 | 80.5 | 160 | 491 | 79 | 47 | 88 | 50 | 12.3 |
| Atkins | 81 | 2363 | 380 | 39.9 | 339 | 121 | 90 | 69.2 | 28 | 173 | 330 | 67 | 149 | 5 | 12.0 |
| Barros | 60 | 1079 | 183 | 44.4 | 105 | 44 | 68 | 85.0 | 6 | 94 | 110 | 30 | 60 | 2 | 8.0 |
| Williams | 33 | 804 | 88 | 43.8 | 2 | 0 | 65 | 72.2 | 98 | 278 | 32 | 39 | 47 | 10 | 7.3 |
| B. Wallace | 80 | 2760 | 215 | 49.0 | 4 | 1 | 80 | 33.6 | 303 | 1052 | 123 | 107 | 117 | 186 | 6.4 |
| J. Wallace | 40 | 527 | 100 | 42.4 | 15 | 2 | 35 | 77.8 | 25 | 83 | 23 | 13 | 36 | 16 | 5.9 |
| Ceballos | 13 | 166 | 28 | 39.4 | 40 | 11 | 8 | 80.0 | 7 | 26 | 7 | 6 | 9 | 3 | 5.8 |
| Cleaves | 78 | 1268 | 160 | 40.0 | 17 | 5 | 97 | 70.8 | 26 | 132 | 207 | 49 | 139 | 1 | 5.4 |
| Curry | 68 | 1485 | 145 | 45.5 | 9 | 4 | 62 | 84.9 | 21 | 121 | 132 | 27 | 61 | 3 | 5.2 |
| Moore | 81 | 1154 | 132 | 49.3 | 1 | 0 | 95 | 73.1 | 121 | 316 | 33 | 24 | 74 | 61 | 4.4 |
| Owens | 45 | 793 | 88 | 38.3 | 20 | 3 | 19 | 47.5 | 84 | 205 | 55 | 32 | 39 | 12 | 4.4 |
| Buechler | 57 | 737 | 76 | 46.3 | 77 | 32 | 9 | 75.0 | 20 | 94 | 39 | 21 | 25 | 10 | 3.4 |
| Montross | 42 | 568 | 50 | 41.3 | 0 | 0 | 7 | 26.9 | 43 | 144 | 15 | 8 | 37 | 23 | 2.5 |
| **Pistons** | **82** | **19855** | **2919** | **42.4** | **1112** | **389** | **1610** | **72.1** | **1108** | **3734** | **1629** | **613** | **1304** | **447** | **95.6** |
| **Opponents** | **82** | **19855** | **2976** | **43.4** | **1229** | **428** | **1596** | **73.6** | **1012** | **3683** | **1860** | **669** | **1274** | **397** | **97.3** |

## Golden State Warriors

| Player | GP | Min | FGM | Pct | FGA | FGM | FTM | Pct | Off | Total | A | Stl | TO | BS | Avg |
|---|---|---|---|---|---|---|---|---|---|---|---|---|---|---|---|
| | | | Field Goals | | 3-Pt FG | | Free Throws | | Rebounds | | | | | | |
| Jamison | 82 | 3394 | 800 | 44.2 | 205 | 62 | 382 | 71.5 | 280 | 715 | 164 | 114 | 199 | 28 | 24.9 |
| Hughes | 50 | 1846 | 308 | 38.3 | 75 | 14 | 193 | 76.6 | 76 | 276 | 223 | 96 | 152 | 29 | 16.5 |
| Jackson | 48 | 1410 | 237 | 46.7 | 23 | 5 | 154 | 80.2 | 119 | 361 | 59 | 34 | 93 | 27 | 13.2 |
| Sura | 53 | 1684 | 202 | 39.0 | 172 | 47 | 135 | 71.4 | 54 | 227 | 242 | 54 | 160 | 8 | 11.1 |
| Blaylock | 69 | 2352 | 317 | 39.6 | 225 | 73 | 53 | 69.7 | 71 | 272 | 462 | 163 | 128 | 20 | 11.0 |
| Porter | 51 | 1147 | 173 | 38.9 | 5 | 0 | 94 | 66.7 | 89 | 189 | 61 | 45 | 59 | 6 | 8.6 |
| Dampier | 43 | 1038 | 126 | 40.1 | 2 | 0 | 67 | 53.2 | 97 | 250 | 59 | 17 | 82 | 58 | 7.4 |
| Cummings | 66 | 1495 | 178 | 34.4 | 143 | 48 | 79 | 68.1 | 47 | 137 | 227 | 67 | 91 | 14 | 7.2 |
| McPherson | 22 | 287 | 62 | 51.7 | 6 | 2 | 24 | 70.6 | 20 | 31 | 22 | 13 | 24 | 1 | 6.8 |
| Blount | 38 | 918 | 107 | 43.3 | 8 | 2 | 43 | 63.2 | 146 | 315 | 51 | 29 | 55 | 17 | 6.8 |
| Foyle | 58 | 1457 | 156 | 41.6 | 0 | 0 | 30 | 44.1 | 156 | 405 | 48 | 31 | 79 | 156 | 5.9 |
| Mullin | 20 | 374 | 36 | 34.0 | 52 | 19 | 24 | 85.7 | 10 | 41 | 19 | 16 | 19 | 10 | 5.8 |
| Curley | 15 | 177 | 24 | 55.8 | 1 | 1 | 11 | 73.3 | 21 | 37 | 3 | 6 | 14 | 8 | 4.0 |
| Del Negro | 29 | 396 | 30 | 33.3 | 9 | 1 | 16 | 1.000 | 4 | 31 | 62 | 6 | 15 | 0 | 2.7 |
| Keefe | 67 | 836 | 64 | 40.3 | 3 | 1 | 39 | 61.9 | 90 | 209 | 36 | 28 | 40 | 20 | 2.5 |
| **Warriors** | **82** | **19780** | **2937** | **40.9** | **964** | **282** | **1428** | **70.6** | **1345** | **3730** | **1788** | **742** | **1301** | **410** | **92.5** |
| **Opponents** | **82** | **19780** | **3179** | **47.2** | **1159** | **439** | **1529** | **76.0** | **1039** | **3732** | **2045** | **722** | **1348** | **493** | **101.5** |

## Houston Rockets

| Player | GP | Min | Field Goals | | 3-Pt FG | | Free Throws | | Rebounds | | A | Stl | TO | BS | Avg |
|---|---|---|---|---|---|---|---|---|---|---|---|---|---|---|---|
| | | | FGM | Pct | FGA | FGM | FTM | Pct | Off | Total | | | | | |
| Francis | 80 | 3194 | 550 | 45.1 | 336 | 133 | 358 | 81.7 | 190 | 553 | 517 | 141 | 265 | 31 | 19.9 |
| Mobley | 79 | 3002 | 527 | 43.4 | 252 | 90 | 394 | 83.1 | 83 | 397 | 195 | 84 | 165 | 26 | 19.5 |
| Taylor | 69 | 1972 | 390 | 48.9 | 4 | 0 | 119 | 73.5 | 109 | 378 | 104 | 28 | 125 | 38 | 13.0 |
| Olajuwon | 58 | 1545 | 283 | 49.8 | 1 | 0 | 123 | 62.1 | 124 | 431 | 72 | 70 | 81 | 88 | 11.9 |
| Anderson | 82 | 2396 | 263 | 44.6 | 170 | 46 | 138 | 73.4 | 72 | 333 | 189 | 82 | 131 | 40 | 8.7 |
| Williams | 72 | 1583 | 202 | 39.4 | 248 | 98 | 97 | 77.0 | 31 | 245 | 97 | 30 | 73 | 28 | 8.3 |
| Thomas | 74 | 1820 | 206 | 44.3 | 92 | 25 | 91 | 72.2 | 122 | 417 | 77 | 40 | 116 | 43 | 7.1 |
| Norris | 82 | 1654 | 184 | 44.6 | 89 | 25 | 151 | 77.8 | 44 | 198 | 283 | 69 | 107 | 2 | 6.6 |
| Bullard | 61 | 1000 | 129 | 42.3 | 213 | 87 | 10 | 71.4 | 22 | 130 | 42 | 10 | 12 | 9 | 5.8 |
| Cato | 35 | 624 | 64 | 57.7 | 0 | 0 | 37 | 64.9 | 47 | 141 | 11 | 13 | 25 | 31 | 4.7 |
| Rogers | 39 | 544 | 75 | 68.2 | 1 | 0 | 29 | 55.8 | 48 | 139 | 9 | 10 | 17 | 18 | 4.6 |
| Collier | 23 | 222 | 27 | 38.0 | 1 | 0 | 17 | 70.8 | 12 | 37 | 6 | 2 | 11 | 3 | 3.1 |
| Langhi | 33 | 241 | 37 | 37.4 | 1 | 0 | 16 | 55.2 | 13 | 41 | 4 | 7 | 8 | 1 | 2.7 |
| Colson | 13 | 44 | 6 | 25.0 | 5 | 1 | 2 | 50.0 | 2 | 6 | 10 | 1 | 2 | 0 | 1.2 |
| **Rockets** | **82** | **19830** | **2943** | **45.3** | **1412** | **504** | **1582** | **75.8** | **919** | **3443** | **1613** | **587** | **1204** | **358** | **97.2** |
| **Opponents** | **82** | **19830** | **3020** | **44.9** | **1015** | **359** | **1385** | **74.4** | **988** | **3408** | **1735** | **605** | **1092** | **400** | **94.9** |

## Indiana Pacers

| Player | GP | Min | Field Goals | | 3-Pt FG | | Free Throws | | Rebounds | | A | Stl | TO | BS | Avg |
|---|---|---|---|---|---|---|---|---|---|---|---|---|---|---|---|
| | | | FGM | Pct | FGA | FGM | FTM | Pct | Off | Total | | | | | |
| Rose | 72 | 2943 | 567 | 45.7 | 174 | 59 | 285 | 82.8 | 37 | 359 | 435 | 65 | 211 | 43 | 20.5 |
| Miller | 81 | 3181 | 517 | 44.0 | 464 | 170 | 323 | 92.8 | 38 | 285 | 260 | 81 | 133 | 15 | 18.9 |
| O'Neal | 81 | 2641 | 404 | 46.5 | 5 | 0 | 233 | 60.1 | 249 | 794 | 98 | 49 | 161 | 228 | 12.9 |
| Best | 77 | 2457 | 347 | 44.0 | 97 | 37 | 187 | 82.7 | 38 | 222 | 473 | 110 | 127 | 11 | 11.9 |
| Croshere | 81 | 1874 | 276 | 39.4 | 207 | 70 | 200 | 86.6 | 123 | 387 | 92 | 36 | 136 | 50 | 10.1 |
| Harrrington | 78 | 1892 | 241 | 44.4 | 7 | 1 | 103 | 65.6 | 119 | 381 | 130 | 63 | 148 | 18 | 7.5 |
| Edney | 24 | 263 | 35 | 38.5 | 6 | 1 | 35 | 89.7 | 5 | 24 | 54 | 17 | 25 | 0 | 4.4 |
| Tabak | 55 | 777 | 98 | 52.7 | 0 | 0 | 20 | 42.6 | 65 | 213 | 33 | 10 | 57 | 30 | 3.9 |
| Perkins | 64 | 999 | 86 | 38.1 | 110 | 38 | 32 | 84.2 | 32 | 168 | 41 | 33 | 19 | 18 | 3.8 |
| Foster | 71 | 1152 | 100 | 46.9 | 7 | 2 | 47 | 51.6 | 144 | 389 | 33 | 39 | 52 | 28 | 3.5 |
| Bender | 59 | 574 | 66 | 35.5 | 41 | 11 | 50 | 73.5 | 14 | 74 | 32 | 7 | 42 | 28 | 3.3 |
| McKey | 66 | 987 | 60 | 44.1 | 20 | 4 | 21 | 77.8 | 49 | 176 | 74 | 48 | 47 | 13 | 2.2 |
| Mills | 14 | 113 | 11 | 32.4 | 17 | 3 | 0 | — | 4 | 21 | 5 | 3 | 10 | 1 | 1.8 |
| **Pacers** | **82** | **19980** | **2828** | **44.0** | **1159** | **396** | **1539** | **76.6** | **921** | **3516** | **1763** | **563** | **1244** | **487** | **92.6** |
| **Opponents** | **82** | **19980** | **2829** | **42.3** | **1121** | **377** | **1572** | **75.8** | **1042** | **3537** | **1695** | **589** | **1115** | **387** | **92.8** |

## Los Angeles Clippers

| Player | GP | Min | Field Goals | | 3-Pt FG | | Free Throws | | Rebounds | | A | Stl | TO | BS | Avg |
|---|---|---|---|---|---|---|---|---|---|---|---|---|---|---|---|
| | | | FGM | Pct | FGA | FGM | FTM | Pct | Off | Total | | | | | |
| Odom | 76 | 2836 | 481 | 46.0 | 253 | 80 | 262 | 67.9 | 110 | 592 | 392 | 74 | 264 | 122 | 17.2 |
| McInnis | 81 | 2831 | 432 | 40.3 | 144 | 52 | 130 | 80.7 | 41 | 220 | 447 | 75 | 113 | 7 | 12.9 |
| Piatkowski | 81 | 2144 | 291 | 43.3 | 297 | 120 | 158 | 87.3 | 54 | 241 | 96 | 46 | 76 | 19 | 10.6 |
| Maggette | 69 | 1359 | 225 | 46.2 | 56 | 17 | 223 | 77.4 | 88 | 291 | 82 | 35 | 106 | 9 | 10.0 |
| Miles | 81 | 2133 | 318 | 50.5 | 19 | 1 | 124 | 52.1 | 127 | 477 | 99 | 51 | 147 | 125 | 9.4 |
| Olowokandi | 82 | 2127 | 308 | 43.5 | 0 | 0 | 85 | 54.5 | 168 | 525 | 46 | 30 | 169 | 108 | 8.5 |
| Richardson | 76 | 1358 | 232 | 44.2 | 151 | 50 | 99 | 62.7 | 105 | 257 | 62 | 42 | 64 | 7 | 8.1 |
| Nesby | 14 | 333 | 40 | 32.5 | 46 | 10 | 18 | 78.3 | 16 | 42 | 11 | 10 | 10 | 4 | 7.7 |
| Boykins | 10 | 149 | 25 | 39.7 | 8 | 1 | 14 | 82.4 | 4 | 11 | 32 | 5 | 9 | 0 | 6.5 |
| Dooling | 76 | 1237 | 148 | 40.9 | 80 | 28 | 125 | 69.8 | 8 | 89 | 177 | 41 | 94 | 11 | 5.9 |
| Rooks | 82 | 1553 | 169 | 42.8 | 2 | 1 | 107 | 74.8 | 91 | 303 | 77 | 34 | 73 | 64 | 5.4 |
| Parks | 52 | 876 | 116 | 49.2 | 6 | 0 | 19 | 70.4 | 58 | 189 | 39 | 19 | 31 | 25 | 4.8 |
| Strong | 28 | 491 | 45 | 38.5 | 1 | 0 | 28 | 75.7 | 34 | 108 | 7 | 14 | 22 | 1 | 4.2 |
| Skinner | 39 | 584 | 64 | 39.8 | 0 | 0 | 32 | 54.2 | 55 | 168 | 18 | 14 | 32 | 11 | 4.1 |
| **Clippers** | **82** | **20030** | **2896** | **44.8** | **1063** | **360** | **1429** | **69.3** | **962** | **3521** | **1585** | **490** | **1293** | **513** | **92.5** |
| **Opponents** | **82** | **20030** | **2995** | **44.0** | **1075** | **354** | **1474** | **74.3** | **1042** | **3481** | **1791** | **638** | **1054** | **412** | **95.3** |

## Los Angeles Lakers

| Player | GP | Min | Field Goals | | 3-Pt FG | | Free Throws | | Rebounds | | A | Stl | TO | BS | Avg |
|---|---|---|---|---|---|---|---|---|---|---|---|---|---|---|---|
| | | | FGM | Pct | FGA | FGM | FTM | Pct | Off | Total | | | | | |
| O'Neal | 74 | 2924 | 813 | 57.2 | 2 | 0 | 499 | 51.3 | 291 | 940 | 277 | 47 | 218 | 204 | 28.7 |
| Bryant | 68 | 2783 | 701 | 46.4 | 200 | 61 | 475 | 85.3 | 104 | 399 | 338 | 114 | 220 | 43 | 28.5 |
| Fisher | 20 | 709 | 77 | 41.2 | 63 | 25 | 50 | 80.6 | 5 | 59 | 87 | 39 | 29 | 2 | 11.5 |
| Fox | 82 | 2291 | 287 | 44.4 | 300 | 118 | 95 | 77.9 | 80 | 325 | 262 | 70 | 136 | 29 | 9.6 |
| Grant | 77 | 2390 | 263 | 46.2 | 3 | 0 | 131 | 77.5 | 220 | 545 | 121 | 51 | 48 | 61 | 8.5 |
| Rider | 67 | 1206 | 201 | 42.6 | 3 | 34 | 71 | 85.5 | 44 | 156 | 111 | 27 | 98 | 7 | 7.6 |
| Harper | 47 | 1139 | 127 | 46.9 | 72 | 19 | 34 | 70.8 | 46 | 166 | 113 | 39 | 62 | 25 | 6.5 |
| Shaw | 80 | 1833 | 164 | 39.9 | 135 | 42 | 51 | 79.7 | 48 | 304 | 258 | 49 | 97 | 27 | 5.3 |
| Horry | 79 | 1587 | 147 | 38.7 | 156 | 54 | 59 | 71.1 | 93 | 296 | 128 | 54 | 79 | 54 | 5.2 |
| Penberthy | 53 | 851 | 92 | 41.4 | 139 | 55 | 28 | 90.3 | 10 | 63 | 71 | 22 | 34 | 2 | 5.0 |
| Lue | 38 | 468 | 50 | 42.7 | 34 | 11 | 19 | 79.2 | 5 | 32 | 45 | 19 | 27 | 0 | 3.4 |
| George | 59 | 593 | 64 | 30.9 | 68 | 15 | 39 | 70.9 | 35 | 110 | 19 | 15 | 34 | 15 | 3.1 |
| Madsen | 70 | 641 | 55 | 48.7 | 1 | 1 | 26 | 70.3 | 74 | 152 | 24 | 8 | 27 | 8 | 2.0 |
| Foster | 62 | 451 | 56 | 42.1 | 9 | 3 | 10 | 71.4 | 29 | 112 | 32 | 9 | 25 | 12 | 2.0 |
| **Lakers** | **82** | **19905** | **3109** | **46.5** | **1275** | **439** | **1594** | **68.3** | **1085** | **3668** | **1888** | **564** | **1184** | **490** | **100.6** |
| **Opponents** | **82** | **19905** | **2983** | **43.8** | **1168** | **413** | **1595** | **75.4** | **981** | **3388** | **1659** | **619** | **1073** | **324** | **97.2** |

## Miami Heat

| Player | GP | Min | Field Goals | | 3-Pt FG | | Free Throws | | Rebounds | | A | Stl | TO | BS | Avg |
|---|---|---|---|---|---|---|---|---|---|---|---|---|---|---|---|
| | | | FGM | Pct | FGA | FGM | FTM | Pct | Off | Total | | | | | |
| Jones | 63 | 2282 | 388 | 44.5 | 238 | 90 | 228 | 84.4 | 75 | 292 | 171 | 110 | 135 | 58 | 17.4 |
| Mason | 80 | 3254 | 460 | 48.2 | 0 | 0 | 370 | 78.1 | 169 | 770 | 248 | 80 | 179 | 25 | 16.1 |
| Grant | 82 | 2771 | 484 | 47.9 | 1 | 0 | 282 | 79.7 | 217 | 718 | 101 | 60 | 170 | 71 | 15.2 |
| Hardaway | 77 | 2613 | 408 | 39.2 | 517 | 189 | 145 | 80.1 | 26 | 204 | 483 | 90 | 189 | 6 | 14.9 |
| Mourning | 13 | 306 | 73 | 51.8 | 1 | 0 | 31 | 56.4 | 35 | 101 | 12 | 4 | 28 | 31 | 13.6 |
| Bowen | 82 | 2685 | 211 | 36.3 | 307 | 103 | 98 | 60.9 | 45 | 245 | 132 | 83 | 74 | 53 | 7.6 |
| Ceballos | 27 | 393 | 73 | 46.2 | 33 | 11 | 29 | 87.9 | 27 | 80 | 13 | 10 | 23 | 4 | 6.9 |
| Carter | 72 | 1630 | 195 | 40.6 | 40 | 6 | 65 | 63.1 | 46 | 180 | 268 | 73 | 119 | 10 | 6.4 |
| House | 50 | 550 | 104 | 42.1 | 55 | 19 | 24 | 68.6 | 5 | 42 | 52 | 13 | 35 | 0 | 5.0 |
| Majerle | 53 | 1306 | 87 | 33.6 | 181 | 57 | 36 | 81.8 | 20 | 166 | 88 | 53 | 35 | 15 | 5.0 |
| Green | 82 | 1411 | 144 | 44.4 | 6 | 0 | 79 | 71.2 | 107 | 313 | 39 | 30 | 45 | 8 | 4.5 |
| MacLean | 8 | 76 | 10 | 50.0 | 2 | 2 | 9 | 75.0 | 7 | 18 | 4 | 5 | 10 | 1 | 3.9 |
| Fuller | 10 | 77 | 10 | 28.6 | 0 | 0 | 8 | 1.000 | 7 | 18 | 1 | 3 | 3 | 2 | 2.8 |
| Causwell | 31 | 384 | 32 | 37.6 | 0 | 0 | 12 | 48.0 | 23 | 83 | 5 | 8 | 23 | 18 | 2.5 |
| **Heat** | **82** | **19880** | **2694** | **43.0** | **1384** | **478** | **1423** | **75.9** | **813** | **3248** | **1630** | **633** | **1122** | **304** | **88.9** |
| **Opponents** | **82** | **19880** | **2701** | **43.1** | **1087** | **360** | **1339** | **73.7** | **914** | **3442** | **1421** | **598** | **1275** | **424** | **86.6** |

## Milwaukee Bucks

| Player | GP | Min | Field Goals | | 3-Pt FG | | Free Throws | | Rebounds | | A | Stl | TO | BS | Avg |
|---|---|---|---|---|---|---|---|---|---|---|---|---|---|---|---|
| | | | FGM | Pct | FGA | FGM | FTM | Pct | Off | Total | | | | | |
| Robinson | 76 | 2813 | 684 | 46.8 | 184 | 55 | 251 | 82.0 | 124 | 526 | 225 | 86 | 219 | 62 | 22.0 |
| Allen | 82 | 3129 | 628 | 48.0 | 467 | 202 | 348 | 88.8 | 101 | 428 | 374 | 124 | 204 | 20 | 22.0 |
| Cassell | 76 | 2709 | 537 | 47.4 | 98 | 30 | 277 | 85.8 | 46 | 290 | 580 | 88 | 220 | 8 | 18.2 |
| Thomas | 76 | 2086 | 326 | 43.0 | 260 | 107 | 195 | 77.1 | 79 | 313 | 138 | 78 | 114 | 45 | 12.6 |
| Hunter | 82 | 2002 | 298 | 38.1 | 407 | 152 | 77 | 80.2 | 32 | 169 | 222 | 102 | 68 | 12 | 10.1 |
| Caffey | 70 | 1460 | 179 | 48.8 | 0 | 0 | 142 | 67.3 | 135 | 353 | 53 | 38 | 77 | 25 | 7.1 |
| Williams | 66 | 1272 | 171 | 47.4 | 4 | 1 | 60 | 85.7 | 97 | 364 | 35 | 48 | 41 | 32 | 6.1 |
| Ham | 29 | 540 | 39 | 48.7 | 3 | 2 | 29 | 59.2 | 56 | 121 | 25 | 17 | 33 | 21 | 3.8 |
| Kersey | 22 | 243 | 32 | 46.4 | 1 | 0 | 8 | 50.0 | 8 | 45 | 15 | 14 | 6 | 8 | 3.3 |
| Johnson | 82 | 1981 | 108 | 54.5 | 0 | 0 | 50 | 53.8 | 205 | 613 | 40 | 44 | 47 | 97 | 3.2 |
| Pope | 63 | 942 | 62 | 43.7 | 24 | 5 | 22 | 62.9 | 56 | 147 | 38 | 16 | 17 | 26 | 2.4 |
| Alston | 37 | 288 | 30 | 35.7 | 30 | 8 | 9 | 69.2 | 4 | 31 | 68 | 13 | 20 | 0 | 2.1 |
| Przybilla | 33 | 270 | 12 | 34.3 | 0 | 0 | 3 | 27.3 | 29 | 71 | 2 | 3 | 13 | 30 | 0.8 |
| **Bucks** | **82** | **19780** | **3112** | **45.8** | **1481** | **562** | **1474** | **78.7** | **975** | **3475** | **1844** | **672** | **1123** | **386** | **100.7** |
| **Opponents** | **82** | **19780** | **2912** | **43.9** | **1246** | **439** | **1679** | **76.8** | **1014** | **3504** | **1883** | **592** | **1273** | **350** | **96.9** |

## Minnesota Timberwolves

| Player | GP | Min | Field Goals | | 3-Pt FG | | Free Throws | | Rebounds | | A | Stl | TO | BS | Avg |
|---|---|---|---|---|---|---|---|---|---|---|---|---|---|---|---|
| | | | FGM | Pct | FGA | FGM | FTM | Pct | Off | Total | | | | | |
| Garnett ............81 | 81 | 3202 | 704 | 47.7 | 66 | 19 | 357 | 76.4 | 219 | 921 | 401 | 111 | 230 | 145 | 22.0 |
| Brandon...........78 | 78 | 2821 | 511 | 45.1 | 91 | 33 | 195 | 87.1 | 60 | 298 | 583 | 161 | 155 | 21 | 16.0 |
| Szczerbiak.......82 | 82 | 2856 | 469 | 51.0 | 77 | 26 | 181 | 87.0 | 133 | 447 | 260 | 59 | 138 | 33 | 14.0 |
| Peeler ..............75 | 75 | 2126 | 308 | 42.1 | 256 | 100 | 75 | 86.2 | 44 | 192 | 192 | 91 | 105 | 18 | 10.5 |
| Ellis..................82 | 82 | 1948 | 298 | 46.4 | 22 | 7 | 169 | 79.0 | 199 | 494 | 93 | 67 | 108 | 74 | 9.4 |
| Billups.............77 | 77 | 1790 | 248 | 42.2 | 194 | 73 | 144 | 84.2 | 32 | 158 | 260 | 51 | 111 | 11 | 9.3 |
| Lopez ..............23 | 23 | 457 | 69 | 45.4 | 23 | 13 | 19 | 57.6 | 25 | 74 | 34 | 21 | 27 | 12 | 7.4 |
| Slater ..............55 | 55 | 686 | 90 | 51.4 | 0 | 0 | 74 | 67.3 | 78 | 186 | 26 | 18 | 43 | 9 | 4.6 |
| Nesterovic ........73 | 73 | 1233 | 147 | 46.1 | 1 | 0 | 34 | 52.3 | 99 | 286 | 45 | 25 | 55 | 63 | 4.5 |
| Day.................31 | 31 | 345 | 44 | 37.3 | 69 | 26 | 18 | 78.3 | 10 | 37 | 28 | 10 | 24 | 7 | 4.3 |
| Mitchell...........82 | 82 | 983 | 118 | 40.8 | 43 | 9 | 40 | 72.7 | 28 | 123 | 57 | 26 | 36 | 10 | 3.5 |
| Avery...............55 | 55 | 463 | 55 | 38.2 | 59 | 16 | 28 | 77.8 | 5 | 29 | 75 | 13 | 45 | 4 | 2.8 |
| Garrett .............70 | 70 | 831 | 75 | 48.1 | 0 | 0 | 27 | 69.2 | 65 | 217 | 24 | 26 | 25 | 49 | 2.5 |
| **T'wolves .........82** | 82 | 19830 | 3148 | 45.8 | 901 | 322 | 1364 | 78.5 | 1002 | 3472 | 2083 | 682 | 1136 | 456 | 97.3 |
| **Opponents......82** | 82 | 19830 | 2977 | 45.2 | 996 | 350 | 1567 | 72.4 | 967 | 3472 | 1834 | 583 | 1246 | 357 | 96.0 |

## New Jersey Nets

| Player | GP | Min | Field Goals | | 3-Pt FG | | Free Throws | | Rebounds | | A | Stl | TO | BS | Avg |
|---|---|---|---|---|---|---|---|---|---|---|---|---|---|---|---|
| | | | FGM | Pct | FGA | FGM | FTM | Pct | Off | Total | | | | | |
| Marbury...........67 | 67 | 2557 | 563 | 44.1 | 335 | 110 | 362 | 79.0 | 53 | 205 | 506 | 79 | 197 | 5 | 23.9 |
| Van Horn .........49 | 49 | 1733 | 308 | 43.5 | 170 | 65 | 150 | 80.6 | 78 | 347 | 82 | 40 | 103 | 20 | 17.0 |
| Martin ..............68 | 68 | 2272 | 346 | 44.5 | 11 | 1 | 121 | 63.0 | 137 | 502 | 131 | 78 | 138 | 113 | 12.0 |
| Newman...........82 | 82 | 2049 | 291 | 41.9 | 176 | 59 | 254 | 85.5 | 34 | 176 | 115 | 63 | 106 | 10 | 10.9 |
| Williams ...........82 | 82 | 2336 | 297 | 45.7 | 2 | 0 | 244 | 78.7 | 211 | 590 | 88 | 59 | 132 | 113 | 10.2 |
| Harris................73 | 73 | 2071 | 265 | 42.5 | 132 | 46 | 107 | 77.0 | 71 | 288 | 135 | 74 | 64 | 16 | 9.4 |
| Gill ...................31 | 31 | 892 | 107 | 33.1 | 14 | 4 | 65 | 72.2 | 32 | 131 | 87 | 47 | 48 | 7 | 9.1 |
| Jackson ...........77 | 77 | 1660 | 243 | 42.5 | 155 | 52 | 97 | 71.9 | 41 | 208 | 140 | 86 | 130 | 14 | 8.2 |
| Douglas ...........59 | 59 | 1094 | 122 | 40.3 | 40 | 8 | 86 | 74.8 | 21 | 74 | 144 | 36 | 79 | 4 | 5.7 |
| Eschmeyer .......74 | 74 | 1331 | 92 | 46.0 | 0 | 0 | 67 | 65.7 | 135 | 366 | 40 | 41 | 53 | 58 | 3.4 |
| Stepania ..........29 | 29 | 280 | 28 | 31.8 | 4 | 1 | 25 | 73.5 | 35 | 109 | 16 | 10 | 19 | 11 | 2.8 |
| McIlvaine..........18 | 18 | 193 | 10 | 35.7 | 0 | 0 | 8 | 66.7 | 8 | 35 | 4 | 7 | 9 | 15 | 1.6 |
| Samaki..............35 | 35 | 226 | 18 | 37.5 | 0 | 0 | 10 | 41.7 | 22 | 53 | 1 | 2 | 4 | 14 | 1.4 |
| Ollie .................19 | 19 | 161 | 5 | 18.5 | 0 | 0 | 12 | 63.2 | 3 | 23 | 25 | 5 | 9 | 0 | 1.2 |
| **Nets ................82** | 82 | 19730 | 2781 | 42.5 | 1084 | 361 | 1629 | 75.9 | 909 | 3246 | 1603 | 649 | 1208 | 407 | 92.1 |
| **Opponents......82** | 82 | 19730 | 2937 | 45.5 | 1189 | 428 | 1664 | 74.6 | 1001 | 3623 | 1840 | 619 | 1304 | 522 | 97.1 |

## New York Knicks

| Player | GP | Min | Field Goals | | 3-Pt FG | | Free Throws | | Rebounds | | A | Stl | TO | BS | Avg |
|---|---|---|---|---|---|---|---|---|---|---|---|---|---|---|---|
| | | | FGM | Pct | FGA | FGM | FTM | Pct | Off | Total | | | | | |
| Houston ...........78 | 78 | 2858 | 542 | 44.9 | 252 | 96 | 279 | 90.9 | 20 | 283 | 173 | 52 | 161 | 10 | 18.7 |
| Sprewell...........77 | 77 | 3017 | 524 | 43.0 | 135 | 41 | 275 | 78.3 | 49 | 347 | 269 | 106 | 218 | 28 | 17.7 |
| Rice .................75 | 75 | 2212 | 331 | 44.0 | 211 | 82 | 155 | 85.2 | 61 | 307 | 89 | 41 | 96 | 13 | 12.0 |
| Camby..............63 | 63 | 2127 | 304 | 52.4 | 8 | 1 | 150 | 66.7 | 197 | 723 | 52 | 66 | 63 | 136 | 12.0 |
| Thomas............77 | 77 | 2125 | 314 | 51.1 | 3 | 1 | 171 | 81.4 | 172 | 515 | 63 | 61 | 99 | 69 | 10.4 |
| Johnson...........65 | 65 | 2105 | 246 | 41.1 | 163 | 51 | 102 | 79.7 | 90 | 363 | 127 | 39 | 97 | 29 | 7.1 |
| Ward ................61 | 61 | 1492 | 155 | 41.6 | 175 | 67 | 56 | 80.0 | 32 | 159 | 273 | 70 | 112 | 10 | 7.1 |
| Harrington ........30 | 30 | 548 | 67 | 55.4 | 0 | 0 | 51 | 72.9 | 37 | 99 | 20 | 15 | 41 | 19 | 6.2 |
| Jackson ...........29 | 29 | 786 | 74 | 41.1 | 42 | 13 | 9 | 52.9 | 21 | 120 | 163 | 21 | 58 | 0 | 5.9 |
| Childs..............51 | 51 | 1309 | 93 | 41.9 | 64 | 20 | 39 | 84.8 | 14 | 138 | 236 | 37 | 98 | 7 | 4.8 |
| Strickland .........28 | 28 | 421 | 40 | 30.5 | 47 | 16 | 24 | 85.7 | 9 | 52 | 29 | 22 | 21 | 1 | 4.3 |
| Postell.............26 | 26 | 169 | 17 | 31.5 | 11 | 3 | 22 | 81.5 | 8 | 25 | 5 | 4 | 17 | 2 | 2.3 |
| Longley............25 | 25 | 301 | 18 | 33.3 | 0 | 0 | 13 | 76.5 | 26 | 66 | 7 | 3 | 22 | 9 | 2.0 |
| Knight .............45 | 45 | 256 | 10 | 18.9 | 1 | 0 | 9 | 50.0 | 19 | 53 | 5 | 5 | 10 | 11 | 0.6 |
| **Knicks ............82** | 82 | 19905 | 2755 | 44.4 | 1115 | 391 | 1374 | 79.6 | 773 | 3297 | 1520 | 545 | 1189 | 346 | 88.7 |
| **Opponents......82** | 82 | 19905 | 2568 | 41.7 | 1266 | 445 | 1478 | 73.3 | 872 | 3290 | 1573 | 596 | 1216 | 338 | 86.1 |

## Orlando Magic

| Player | GP | Min | FGM | Pct | FGA | FGM | FTM | Pct | Off | Total | A | Stl | TO | BS | Avg |
|---|---|---|---|---|---|---|---|---|---|---|---|---|---|---|---|
| | | | Field Goals | | 3-Pt FG | | Free Throws | | Rebounds | | | | | | |
| McGrady | 77 | 3087 | 788 | 45.7 | 166 | 59 | 430 | 73.3 | 192 | 580 | 352 | 116 | 198 | 118 | 26.8 |
| Armstrong | 75 | 2767 | 413 | 41.2 | 403 | 143 | 220 | 88.4 | 94 | 343 | 524 | 135 | 200 | 13 | 15.9 |
| Hill | 4 | 133 | 19 | 44.2 | 1 | 1 | 16 | 61.5 | 8 | 25 | 25 | 5 | 11 | 2 | 13.8 |
| Miller | 82 | 2390 | 368 | 43.6 | 364 | 148 | 91 | 71.1 | 66 | 327 | 140 | 51 | 97 | 19 | 11.9 |
| Garrity | 76 | 1579 | 223 | 38.7 | 224 | 97 | 85 | 86.7 | 51 | 210 | 51 | 40 | 68 | 15 | 8.3 |
| Amaechi | 82 | 1710 | 237 | 40.0 | 7 | 0 | 176 | 63.1 | 77 | 268 | 74 | 28 | 124 | 29 | 7.9 |
| Outlaw | 80 | 2534 | 226 | 61.4 | 2 | 1 | 129 | 57.3 | 211 | 619 | 225 | 105 | 141 | 137 | 7.1 |
| Doleac | 77 | 1398 | 220 | 41.7 | 3 | 0 | 50 | 84.7 | 70 | 273 | 65 | 37 | 59 | 41 | 6.4 |
| Williams | 82 | 1211 | 162 | 44.5 | 13 | 1 | 85 | 63.9 | 86 | 243 | 79 | 29 | 85 | 16 | 5.0 |
| Hudson | 75 | 1008 | 125 | 33.6 | 109 | 22 | 85 | 81.7 | 38 | 105 | 162 | 37 | 92 | 3 | 4.8 |
| DeClercq | 67 | 903 | 107 | 55.4 | 0 | 0 | 47 | 57.3 | 91 | 236 | 32 | 41 | 51 | 31 | 3.9 |
| Reid | 65 | 764 | 82 | 56.6 | 0 | 0 | 46 | 61.3 | 84 | 242 | 21 | 23 | 48 | 54 | 3.2 |
| Alexander | 26 | 227 | 18 | 32.1 | 16 | 4 | 12 | 66.7 | 0 | 25 | 36 | 16 | 25 | 0 | 2.0 |
| **Magic** | **82** | **19955** | **3013** | **43.8** | **1346** | **490** | **1476** | **71.4** | **1069** | **3519** | **1803** | **674** | **1245** | **481** | **97.5** |
| **Opponents** | **82** | **19955** | **2830** | **43.5** | **1059** | **366** | **1885** | **73.5** | **1061** | **3670** | **1793** | **695** | **1408** | **440** | **96.5** |

## Philadelphia 76ers

| Player | GP | Min | FGM | Pct | FGA | FGM | FTM | Pct | Off | Total | A | Stl | TO | BS | Avg |
|---|---|---|---|---|---|---|---|---|---|---|---|---|---|---|---|
| | | | Field Goals | | 3-Pt FG | | Free Throws | | Rebounds | | | | | | |
| Iverson | 71 | 2979 | 762 | 42.0 | 306 | 98 | 585 | 81.4 | 50 | 273 | 325 | 178 | 237 | 20 | 31.1 |
| Ratliff | 50 | 1800 | 228 | 49.9 | 0 | 0 | 165 | 76.0 | 125 | 413 | 58 | 30 | 126 | 187 | 12.4 |
| Mutombo | 26 | 875 | 100 | 49.5 | 0 | 0 | 104 | 75.9 | 119 | 322 | 22 | 9 | 52 | 66 | 11.7 |
| McKie | 76 | 2394 | 338 | 47.3 | 170 | 53 | 149 | 76.8 | 33 | 311 | 377 | 106 | 203 | 8 | 11.6 |
| Snow | 50 | 1740 | 182 | 41.8 | 19 | 5 | 122 | 79.2 | 27 | 166 | 369 | 77 | 124 | 7 | 9.8 |
| Hill | 76 | 2363 | 278 | 47.4 | 1 | 0 | 172 | 63.0 | 239 | 687 | 48 | 37 | 127 | 27 | 9.6 |
| Lynch | 82 | 2649 | 274 | 44.5 | 57 | 15 | 123 | 71.9 | 200 | 590 | 139 | 99 | 109 | 30 | 8.4 |
| Kukoc | 48 | 979 | 151 | 45.8 | 78 | 32 | 52 | 59.1 | 47 | 162 | 93 | 35 | 60 | 6 | 8.0 |
| Geiger | 35 | 542 | 88 | 39.3 | 2 | 0 | 37 | 68.5 | 50 | 139 | 14 | 12 | 25 | 8 | 6.1 |
| Buford | 47 | 573 | 104 | 43.2 | 38 | 16 | 24 | 82.8 | 16 | 74 | 17 | 17 | 29 | 6 | 5.3 |
| Maxwell | 24 | 375 | 42 | 33.6 | 64 | 21 | 15 | 68.2 | 3 | 37 | 29 | 12 | 18 | 0 | 5.0 |
| Jones | 65 | 866 | 122 | 44.4 | 60 | 20 | 40 | 75.5 | 63 | 189 | 32 | 30 | 39 | 15 | 4.7 |
| MacCulloch | 63 | 597 | 109 | 58.9 | 0 | 0 | 42 | 63.6 | 69 | 168 | 10 | 7 | 27 | 19 | 4.1 |
| Ollie | 51 | 764 | 71 | 43.0 | 3 | 1 | 51 | 72.9 | 13 | 72 | 121 | 25 | 40 | 1 | 3.8 |
| Mohammed | 30 | 196 | 41 | 46.6 | 0 | 0 | 14 | 50.0 | 18 | 55 | 2 | 6 | 9 | 7 | 3.2 |
| Sanchez | 24 | 116 | 9 | 42.9 | 1 | 0 | 2 | 100.0 | 2 | 14 | 36 | 9 | 3 | 1 | 0.8 |
| **76ers** | **82** | **19855** | **2902** | **44.7** | **803** | **262** | **1697** | **74.5** | **1075** | **3675** | **1692** | **690** | **1292** | **408** | **94.7** |
| **Opponents** | **82** | **19855** | **2871** | **42.9** | **1248** | **427** | **1243** | **74.9** | **985** | **3351** | **1771** | **672** | **1261** | **458** | **90.4** |

## Phoenix Suns

| Player | GP | Min | FGM | Pct | FGA | FGM | FTM | Pct | Off | Total | A | Stl | TO | BS | Avg |
|---|---|---|---|---|---|---|---|---|---|---|---|---|---|---|---|
| | | | Field Goals | | 3-Pt FG | | Free Throws | | Rebounds | | | | | | |
| Marion | 79 | 2857 | 557 | 48.0 | 82 | 21 | 234 | 81.0 | 220 | 848 | 160 | 132 | 129 | 108 | 17.3 |
| Kidd | 77 | 3065 | 451 | 41.1 | 232 | 69 | 328 | 81.4 | 91 | 494 | 753 | 166 | 286 | 23 | 16.9 |
| Robinson | 82 | 2751 | 501 | 42.2 | 249 | 90 | 253 | 70.9 | 105 | 334 | 237 | 87 | 186 | 82 | 16.4 |
| Delk | 82 | 2288 | 383 | 41.5 | 168 | 54 | 185 | 78.7 | 76 | 261 | 160 | 75 | 101 | 17 | 12.3 |
| Rogers | 82 | 2183 | 377 | 43.0 | 189 | 56 | 188 | 76.1 | 94 | 359 | 180 | 97 | 157 | 47 | 12.2 |
| Hardaway | 4 | 112 | 15 | 41.7 | 8 | 2 | 7 | 63.6 | 5 | 18 | 15 | 6 | 3 | 1 | 9.8 |
| Gugliotta | 57 | 1159 | 149 | 39.2 | 12 | 3 | 61 | 79.2 | 76 | 255 | 55 | 47 | 51 | 21 | 6.4 |
| Del Negro | 36 | 526 | 76 | 52.8 | 4 | 0 | 25 | 89.3 | 8 | 51 | 64 | 20 | 19 | 3 | 4.9 |
| Tsakalidis | 57 | 947 | 101 | 47.0 | 0 | 0 | 54 | 59.3 | 83 | 242 | 19 | 10 | 66 | 55 | 4.5 |
| Elie | 68 | 1506 | 104 | 42.3 | 100 | 36 | 55 | 79.7 | 38 | 155 | 131 | 58 | 60 | 12 | 4.4 |
| McPherson | 33 | 308 | 47 | 49.0 | 6 | 0 | 18 | 75.0 | 20 | 48 | 16 | 12 | 23 | 3 | 3.4 |
| Perry | 43 | 460 | 60 | 46.5 | 4 | 1 | 16 | 72.7 | 8 | 42 | 74 | 19 | 32 | 1 | 3.2 |
| Santiago | 54 | 581 | 64 | 47.8 | 0 | 0 | 42 | 68.9 | 35 | 102 | 11 | 17 | 47 | 21 | 3.1 |
| Blount | 30 | 387 | 23 | 48.9 | 0 | 0 | 8 | 53.3 | 35 | 85 | 8 | 13 | 18 | 5 | 1.8 |
| Dudley | 53 | 613 | 29 | 39.7 | 0 | 0 | 14 | 38.9 | 64 | 183 | 18 | 14 | 26 | 29 | 1.4 |
| **Suns** | **82** | **19805** | **2944** | **43.6** | **1054** | **332** | **1490** | **75.5** | **970** | **3499** | **1095** | **775** | **1250** | **429** | **94.0** |
| **Opponents** | **82** | **19805** | **2792** | **43.5** | **937** | **327** | **1618** | **76.1** | **902** | **3490** | **1652** | **682** | **1433** | **416** | **91.8** |

## Portland Trail Blazers

| Player | GP | Min | Field Goals | | 3-Pt FG | | Free Throws | | Rebounds | | A | Stl | TO | BS | Avg |
|---|---|---|---|---|---|---|---|---|---|---|---|---|---|---|---|
| | | | FGM | Pct | FGA | FGM | FTM | Pct | Off | Total | | | | | |
| Wallace | 77 | 2940 | 590 | 50.1 | 162 | 52 | 245 | 76.6 | 147 | 602 | 212 | 90 | 158 | 135 | 19.2 |
| Smith | 81 | 2542 | 359 | 45.6 | 230 | 78 | 309 | 89.0 | 87 | 272 | 213 | 48 | 137 | 24 | 13.6 |
| Stoudamire | 82 | 2655 | 406 | 43.4 | 219 | 82 | 172 | 83.1 | 69 | 303 | 468 | 106 | 191 | 8 | 13.0 |
| Wells | 75 | 1995 | 387 | 53.3 | 50 | 17 | 159 | 66.3 | 120 | 367 | 208 | 94 | 169 | 20 | 12.7 |
| Pippen | 64 | 2133 | 269 | 45.1 | 186 | 64 | 119 | 73.9 | 70 | 333 | 294 | 94 | 154 | 35 | 11.3 |
| Sabonis | 61 | 1299 | 247 | 47.9 | 15 | 1 | 121 | 77.6 | 51 | 331 | 91 | 12 | 85 | 62 | 10.1 |
| Davis | 81 | 2162 | 242 | 49.7 | 4 | 0 | 96 | 63.2 | 233 | 606 | 103 | 44 | 67 | 76 | 7.2 |
| Kemp | 68 | 1083 | 168 | 40.7 | 11 | 4 | 101 | 65.7 | 63 | 259 | 65 | 45 | 99 | 23 | 6.5 |
| Anthony | 58 | 856 | 97 | 38.3 | 159 | 65 | 23 | 65.7 | 21 | 61 | 82 | 40 | 43 | 3 | 4.9 |
| Augmon | 66 | 1182 | 127 | 47.7 | 4 | 0 | 57 | 65.5 | 60 | 159 | 98 | 48 | 48 | 21 | 4.7 |
| Strickland | 21 | 351 | 41 | 41.8 | 1 | 0 | 15 | 57.7 | 11 | 35 | 72 | 10 | 24 | 1 | 4.6 |
| Schrempf | 26 | 397 | 39 | 41.1 | 8 | 3 | 23 | 85.2 | 17 | 78 | 44 | 7 | 28 | 3 | 4.0 |
| Harvey | 12 | 72 | 13 | 36.4 | 0 | 0 | 5 | 83.3 | 5 | 14 | 4 | 1 | 3 | 6 | 2.6 |
| Grant | 4 | 17 | 5 | 71.4 | 0 | 0 | 0 | 0 | 0 | 0 | 1 | 0 | 0 | 0 | 2.5 |
| Barkley | 8 | 38 | 8 | 36.4 | 8 | 3 | 0 | — | 0 | 3 | 6 | 2 | 5 | 0 | 2.4 |
| Perdue | 13 | 58 | 6 | 66.7 | 0 | 0 | 4 | 50.0 | 6 | 18 | 2 | 3 | 0 | 2 | 1.1 |
| Trail Blazers | 82 | 19780 | 3004 | 46.8 | 1057 | 369 | 1447 | 76.2 | 960 | 3441 | 1963 | 672 | 1257 | 419 | 95.4 |
| Opponents | 82 | 19780 | 2819 | 43.8 | 1103 | 406 | 1436 | 74.4 | 946 | 3184 | 1745 | 646 | 1216 | 324 | 91.2 |

## Sacramento Kings

| Player | GP | Min | Field Goals | | 3-Pt FG | | Free Throws | | Rebounds | | A | Stl | TO | BS | Avg |
|---|---|---|---|---|---|---|---|---|---|---|---|---|---|---|---|
| | | | FGM | Pct | FGA | FGM | FTM | Pct | Off | Total | | | | | |
| Webber | 70 | 2836 | 786 | 48.1 | 28 | 2 | 324 | 70.3 | 179 | 777 | 294 | 93 | 195 | 118 | 27.1 |
| Stojakovic | 75 | 2905 | 559 | 47.0 | 360 | 144 | 267 | 85.6 | 93 | 434 | 164 | 91 | 146 | 13 | 20.4 |
| Christie | 81 | 2939 | 311 | 39.5 | 250 | 94 | 280 | 89.7 | 95 | 355 | 289 | 183 | 154 | 45 | 12.3 |
| Divac | 81 | 2420 | 364 | 48.2 | 14 | 4 | 242 | 69.1 | 207 | 673 | 231 | 87 | 192 | 93 | 12.0 |
| Williams | 77 | 2290 | 281 | 40.7 | 311 | 98 | 60 | 78.9 | 19 | 185 | 416 | 94 | 160 | 9 | 9.4 |
| Jackson | 79 | 1648 | 231 | 43.9 | 104 | 39 | 65 | 73.9 | 74 | 246 | 161 | 87 | 103 | 7 | 7.2 |
| Pollard | 77 | 1658 | 185 | 46.8 | 2 | 0 | 128 | 74.9 | 173 | 465 | 47 | 48 | 66 | 97 | 6.5 |
| Turkoglue | 74 | 1245 | 138 | 41.2 | 86 | 28 | 87 | 77.7 | 49 | 210 | 69 | 52 | 55 | 24 | 5.3 |
| Barry | 62 | 1010 | 103 | 40.4 | 132 | 46 | 64 | 87.7 | 16 | 94 | 130 | 28 | 53 | 6 | 5.1 |
| Funderburke | 59 | 698 | 120 | 49.6 | 0 | 0 | 48 | 62.3 | 74 | 196 | 17 | 9 | 32 | 13 | 4.9 |
| Martin | 31 | 176 | 29 | 38.2 | 27 | 14 | 31 | 88.6 | 2 | 16 | 14 | 7 | 10 | 0 | 3.3 |
| Smith | 9 | 66 | 11 | 50.0 | 0 | 0 | 4 | 66.7 | 1 | 8 | 6 | 4 | 3 | 0 | 2.9 |
| Anderson | 21 | 169 | 14 | 24.6 | 39 | 10 | 0 | 0 | 3 | 25 | 13 | 10 | 7 | 4 | 1.8 |
| Kings | 82 | 20080 | 3132 | 44.9 | 1353 | 479 | 1600 | 77.1 | 987 | 3692 | 1852 | 793 | 1221 | 432 | 101.7 |
| Opponents | 82 | 20080 | 3087 | 43.2 | 1131 | 401 | 1291 | 74.9 | 1121 | 3764 | 1816 | 666 | 1334 | 476 | 95.9 |

## San Antonio Spurs

| Player | GP | Min | Field Goals | | 3-Pt FG | | Free Throws | | Rebounds | | A | Stl | TO | BS | Avg |
|---|---|---|---|---|---|---|---|---|---|---|---|---|---|---|---|
| | | | FGM | Pct | FGA | FGM | FTM | Pct | Off | Total | | | | | |
| Duncan | 82 | 3174 | 702 | 49.9 | 27 | 7 | 409 | 61.8 | 259 | 997 | 245 | 70 | 242 | 192 | 22.2 |
| Anderson | 82 | 2859 | 413 | 41.6 | 253 | 101 | 342 | 85.1 | 75 | 363 | 301 | 120 | 165 | 14 | 15.5 |
| Robinson | 80 | 2371 | 400 | 48.6 | 1 | 0 | 351 | 74.7 | 208 | 691 | 116 | 80 | 122 | 197 | 14.4 |
| Daniels | 79 | 2060 | 275 | 46.8 | 183 | 74 | 121 | 77.6 | 26 | 163 | 304 | 61 | 109 | 14 | 9.4 |
| Elliott | 52 | 1229 | 147 | 43.4 | 129 | 55 | 60 | 71.4 | 17 | 170 | 81 | 23 | 51 | 25 | 7.9 |
| Rose | 57 | 1219 | 160 | 43.5 | 17 | 3 | 114 | 71.2 | 95 | 308 | 48 | 59 | 74 | 40 | 7.7 |
| Porter | 80 | 1678 | 197 | 44.8 | 205 | 87 | 92 | 79.3 | 24 | 201 | 251 | 52 | 104 | 11 | 7.2 |
| Johnson | 55 | 1290 | 134 | 44.7 | 6 | 1 | 41 | 68.3 | 21 | 85 | 237 | 33 | 60 | 4 | 5.6 |
| Ferry | 80 | 1688 | 178 | 47.5 | 156 | 70 | 22 | 73.3 | 55 | 223 | 71 | 28 | 50 | 21 | 5.6 |
| Walker | 61 | 963 | 121 | 48.0 | 3 | 1 | 78 | 62.9 | 67 | 243 | 29 | 10 | 68 | 41 | 5.3 |
| Kerr | 55 | 650 | 67 | 42.1 | 77 | 33 | 14 | 93.3 | 6 | 35 | 57 | 16 | 21 | 1 | 3.3 |
| Dial | 33 | 207 | 36 | 43.4 | 10 | 2 | 12 | 57.1 | 12 | 38 | 21 | 4 | 6 | 22 | 2.6 |
| Jackson | 16 | 114 | 16 | 40.0 | 18 | 7 | 0 | 00.0 | 1 | 12 | 7 | 5 | 3 | 0 | 2.4 |
| Newble | 27 | 184 | 21 | 38.2 | 9 | 4 | 8 | 50.0 | 13 | 35 | 6 | 2 | 4 | 18 | 2.0 |
| Scott | 27 | 144 | 17 | 41.5 | 0 | 0 | 9 | 40.9 | 23 | 50 | 4 | 5 | 11 | 6 | 1.6 |
| Spurs | 82 | 19830 | 2884 | 46.1 | 1094 | 445 | 1673 | 71.5 | 902 | 3614 | 1778 | 568 | 1145 | 576 | 96.2 |
| Opponents | 82 | 19830 | 2837 | 41.9 | 1043 | 343 | 1233 | 74.1 | 967 | 3390 | 1617 | 600 | 1107 | 426 | 88.4 |

## Seattle SuperSonics

| Player | GP | Min | Field Goals | | 3-Pt FG | | Free Throws | | Rebounds | | A | Stl | TO | BS | Avg |
|---|---|---|---|---|---|---|---|---|---|---|---|---|---|---|---|
| | | | FGM | Pct | FGA | FGM | FTM | Pct | Off | Total | | | | | |
| Payton | 79 | 3224 | 725 | 45.6 | 272 | 102 | 271 | 76.6 | 73 | 361 | 642 | 127 | 209 | 26 | 23.1 |
| Lewis | 78 | 2720 | 426 | 48.0 | 285 | 123 | 176 | 43.2 | 143 | 541 | 125 | 91 | 129 | 14 | 14.8 |
| Patterson | 76 | 2059 | 370 | 49.4 | 36 | 2 | 246 | 68.1 | 183 | 382 | 161 | 103 | 155 | 45 | 13.0 |
| Baker | 76 | 2129 | 347 | 42.2 | 16 | 1 | 232 | 72.3 | 179 | 430 | 90 | 38 | 158 | 73 | 12.2 |
| Ewing | 79 | 2107 | 294 | 43.0 | 2 | 0 | 172 | 68.5 | 124 | 585 | 92 | 53 | 151 | 91 | 9.6 |
| Barry | 67 | 1778 | 198 | 49.4 | 229 | 109 | 84 | 81.6 | 33 | 211 | 225 | 80 | 86 | 14 | 8.8 |
| Williams | 69 | 1238 | 161 | 43.8 | 133 | 61 | 84 | 87.5 | 34 | 132 | 190 | 31 | 82 | 4 | 6.8 |
| Wingate | 1 | 9 | 3 | 100.0 | 0 | 0 | 0 | — | 0 | 0 | 2 | 0 | 0 | 0 | 6.0 |
| Mason | 78 | 1522 | 189 | 43.1 | 67 | 18 | 67 | 73.6 | 72 | 249 | 63 | 12 | 53 | 20 | 5.9 |
| Davis | 62 | 1290 | 133 | 41.8 | 127 | 50 | 45 | 81.8 | 28 | 154 | 137 | 64 | 77 | 12 | 5.8 |
| McCoy | 70 | 1143 | 138 | 52.3 | 0 | 0 | 41 | 44.1 | 92 | 251 | 57 | 18 | 75 | 14 | 4.5 |
| Wolkowyski | 34 | 305 | 25 | 31.6 | 2 | 0 | 25 | 73.5 | 12 | 46 | 3 | 6 | 12 | 18 | 2.2 |
| Oyedeji | 30 | 221 | 18 | 48.6 | 0 | 0 | 9 | 75.0 | 24 | 67 | 2 | 7 | 11 | 10 | 1.5 |
| Ellison | 9 | 40 | 2 | 28.6 | 0 | 0 | 2 | 100.0 | 2 | 12 | 3 | 0 | 3 | 2 | 0.7 |
| **SuperSonics** | **82** | **19780** | **3108** | **44.7** | **1611** | **546** | **1363** | **69.5** | **1042** | **3525** | **1878** | **657** | **1116** | **345** | **99.1** |
| **Opponents** | **82** | **19780** | **3132** | **45.1** | **1293** | **440** | **1343** | **74.8** | **1084** | **3695** | **1939** | **590** | **1258** | **433** | **98.1** |

## Toronto Raptors

| Player | GP | Min | Field Goals | | 3-Pt FG | | Free Throws | | Rebounds | | A | Stl | TO | BS | Avg |
|---|---|---|---|---|---|---|---|---|---|---|---|---|---|---|---|
| | | | FGM | Pct | FGA | FGM | FTM | Pct | Off | Total | | | | | |
| Carter | 75 | 2979 | 762 | 46.0 | 397 | 162 | 384 | 76.5 | 176 | 416 | 291 | 114 | 167 | 182 | 27.6 |
| Davis | 78 | 2729 | 375 | 43.3 | 1 | 0 | 319 | 75.4 | 274 | 787 | 106 | 22 | 135 | 151 | 13.7 |
| A. Williams | 82 | 2394 | 330 | 43.0 | 108 | 33 | 109 | 75.2 | 50 | 212 | 407 | 123 | 103 | 26 | 9.8 |
| Oakley | 78 | 2767 | 305 | 38.8 | 49 | 11 | 127 | 83.6 | 142 | 741 | 264 | 76 | 139 | 48 | 9.6 |
| Peterson | 80 | 1809 | 290 | 43.1 | 165 | 62 | 104 | 71.7 | 112 | 259 | 105 | 63 | 78 | 20 | 9.3 |
| Williamson | 42 | 886 | 153 | 47.1 | 2 | 0 | 84 | 64.6 | 57 | 153 | 33 | 15 | 65 | 13 | 9.3 |
| Clark | 46 | 968 | 167 | 52.2 | 1 | 0 | 79 | 58.5 | 78 | 248 | 38 | 16 | 42 | 110 | 9.0 |
| Willis | 35 | 771 | 124 | 46.1 | 2 | 0 | 61 | 75.3 | 68 | 223 | 21 | 19 | 40 | 21 | 8.8 |
| Jackson | 54 | 1802 | 170 | 42.2 | 165 | 57 | 64 | 84.2 | 42 | 185 | 498 | 63 | 117 | 7 | 8.5 |
| Curry | 71 | 956 | 162 | 42.4 | 145 | 62 | 43 | 84.3 | 16 | 85 | 75 | 27 | 39 | 8 | 6.0 |
| Murray | 38 | 453 | 77 | 39.9 | 80 | 29 | 24 | 75.0 | 18 | 59 | 14 | 8 | 20 | 6 | 5.4 |
| J. Williams | 26 | 378 | 48 | 51.6 | 1 | 0 | 35 | 77.8 | 35 | 104 | 13 | 18 | 16 | 10 | 5.0 |
| Childs | 26 | 550 | 42 | 37.2 | 42 | 12 | 21 | 84.0 | 10 | 64 | 119 | 22 | 58 | 8 | 4.5 |
| David | 17 | 140 | 15 | 51.7 | 0 | 0 | 12 | 92.3 | 9 | 33 | 4 | 2 | 7 | 3 | 2.5 |
| Stewart | 26 | 123 | 11 | 32.4 | 0 | 0 | 11 | 61.1 | 16 | 29 | 2 | 4 | 5 | 3 | 1.3 |
| Corbin | 15 | 117 | 9 | 23.7 | 5 | 0 | 2 | 50.0 | 3 | 13 | 4 | 2 | 3 | 0 | 1.3 |
| Montross | 12 | 81 | 6 | 35.3 | 0 | 0 | 1 | 20.0 | 9 | 29 | 4 | 3 | 4 | 3 | 1.1 |
| Bogues | 3 | 34 | 0 | 0 | 1 | 0 | 0 | — | 0 | 3 | 5 | 2 | 4 | 0 | 0.0 |
| **Raptors** | **82** | **19755** | **2980** | **43.3** | **1171** | **425** | **1583** | **76.5** | **1098** | **3547** | **1947** | **666** | **1085** | **544** | **97.2** |
| **Opponents** | **82** | **19755** | **3002** | **45.4** | **1021** | **346** | **1631** | **76.4** | **961** | **3513** | **1790** | **557** | **1250** | **434** | **97.3** |

## Utah Jazz

| Player | GP | Min | Field Goals | | 3-Pt FG | | Free Throws | | Rebounds | | A | Stl | TO | BS | Avg |
|---|---|---|---|---|---|---|---|---|---|---|---|---|---|---|---|
| | | | FGM | Pct | FGA | FGM | FTM | Pct | Off | Total | | | | | |
| Malone | 81 | 2895 | 670 | 49.8 | 5 | 2 | 536 | 79.3 | 114 | 669 | 361 | 93 | 244 | 62 | 23.2 |
| Marshall | 81 | 2326 | 427 | 50.3 | 128 | 41 | 205 | 75.1 | 172 | 566 | 133 | 85 | 128 | 78 | 13.6 |
| Russell | 78 | 2473 | 308 | 44.0 | 230 | 95 | 222 | 77.9 | 94 | 330 | 160 | 96 | 113 | 20 | 12.0 |
| Stockton | 82 | 2397 | 328 | 50.4 | 132 | 61 | 227 | 81.7 | 54 | 227 | 713 | 132 | 203 | 21 | 11.5 |
| Starks | 75 | 2122 | 273 | 39.8 | 182 | 64 | 89 | 80.2 | 29 | 154 | 178 | 73 | 94 | 10 | 9.3 |
| Manning | 82 | 1305 | 247 | 49.4 | 28 | 7 | 102 | 72.9 | 66 | 214 | 92 | 47 | 96 | 29 | 7.4 |
| Vaughn | 82 | 1620 | 170 | 43.3 | 78 | 30 | 128 | 78.0 | 18 | 150 | 323 | 48 | 129 | 3 | 6.1 |
| Polynice | 81 | 1619 | 206 | 49.6 | 1 | 0 | 17 | 26.2 | 157 | 378 | 31 | 27 | 78 | 77 | 5.3 |
| Ostertag | 81 | 1491 | 139 | 49.5 | 2 | 1 | 84 | 55.6 | 165 | 415 | 22 | 22 | 63 | 142 | 4.5 |
| Benoit | 49 | 446 | 71 | 48.3 | 13 | 5 | 31 | 79.5 | 20 | 81 | 22 | 6 | 28 | 6 | 3.6 |
| Lewis | 35 | 402 | 50 | 40.7 | 25 | 9 | 15 | 71.4 | 14 | 47 | 18 | 10 | 17 | 10 | 3.5 |
| Stevenson | 40 | 293 | 31 | 34.1 | 12 | 1 | 26 | 68.4 | 9 | 28 | 18 | 10 | 28 | 2 | 2.2 |
| Padgett | 27 | 127 | 18 | 41.9 | 9 | 5 | 15 | 75.0 | 19 | 39 | 5 | 6 | 10 | 3 | 2.1 |
| Crotty | 31 | 264 | 22 | 33.8 | 7 | 4 | 17 | 89.5 | 13 | 28 | 34 | 6 | 19 | 0 | 2.1 |
| **Jazz** | **82** | **19780** | **2960** | **47.1** | **852** | **325** | **1714** | **75.2** | **943** | **3326** | **2110** | **661** | **1296** | **463** | **97.1** |
| **Opponents** | **82** | **19780** | **2667** | **43.9** | **1194** | **410** | **1830** | **76.5** | **874** | **3057** | **1564** | **699** | **1320** | **453** | **92.4** |

## Vancouver Grizzlies

| Player | GP | Min | Field Goals FGM | Pct | 3-Pt FG FGA | FGM | Free Throws FTM | Pct | Rebounds Off | Total | A | Stl | TO | BS | Avg |
|---|---|---|---|---|---|---|---|---|---|---|---|---|---|---|---|
| Abdur-Rahim | ....81 | 3241 | 604 | 47.2 | 64 | 12 | 443 | 83.4 | 175 | 735 | 250 | 90 | 231 | 77 | 20.5 |
| Dickerson | .........70 | 2618 | 425 | 41.7 | 230 | 86 | 206 | 76.3 | 70 | 229 | 233 | 62 | 162 | 27 | 16.3 |
| Bibby | ..............82 | 3190 | 525 | 45.4 | 285 | 108 | 143 | 76.1 | 47 | 304 | 685 | 107 | 258 | 12 | 15.9 |
| Reeves | .........75 | 1832 | 254 | 46.0 | 4 | 1 | 113 | 79.6 | 132 | 452 | 80 | 43 | 90 | 54 | 8.3 |
| Jones | ...............71 | 1415 | 170 | 40.9 | 231 | 87 | 37 | 71.2 | 16 | 124 | 224 | 36 | 76 | 1 | 6.5 |
| Abdul-Rauf | .......41 | 486 | 120 | 48.8 | 14 | 4 | 22 | 75.9 | 5 | 25 | 76 | 9 | 26 | 1 | 6.5 |
| Long | .................66 | 1507 | 140 | 43.9 | 15 | 4 | 112 | 71.3 | 76 | 274 | 83 | 72 | 62 | 15 | 6.0 |
| Strickland | .........50 | 830 | 81 | 30.3 | 95 | 30 | 68 | 86.1 | 18 | 128 | 95 | 44 | 48 | 2 | 5.2 |
| Swift | .................80 | 1312 | 153 | 45.1 | 4 | 0 | 85 | 60.3 | 109 | 284 | 28 | 62 | 64 | 82 | 4.9 |
| Massenburg | ....52 | 823 | 92 | 46.2 | 0 | 0 | 49 | 70.0 | 75 | 210 | 9 | 10 | 48 | 28 | 4.5 |
| Austin | ..............52 | 845 | 96 | 35.6 | 24 | 6 | 28 | 70.0 | 50 | 222 | 58 | 20 | 54 | 23 | 4.3 |
| Edwards | ..........46 | 634 | 56 | 32.9 | 19 | 5 | 43 | 81.1 | 23 | 82 | 52 | 29 | 37 | 8 | 3.5 |
| **Grizzlies** | **..........82** | **19780** | **2870** | **43.9** | **947** | **325** | **1457** | **77.0** | **894** | **3325** | **1899** | **586** | **1291** | **359** | **91.7** |
| **Opponents** | **......82** | **19780** | **3143** | **46.3** | **1075** | **389** | **1317** | **73.0** | **1052** | **3586** | **1935** | **710** | **1217** | **476** | **97.5** |

## Washington Wizards

| Player | GP | Min | Field Goals FGM | Pct | 3-Pt FG FGA | FGM | Free Throws FTM | Pct | Rebounds Off | Total | A | Stl | TO | BS | Avg |
|---|---|---|---|---|---|---|---|---|---|---|---|---|---|---|---|
| Howard | ............54 | 1981 | 392 | 47.4 | 0 | 0 | 197 | 77.0 | 121 | 379 | 154 | 46 | 169 | 21 | 18.2 |
| Hamilton | ..........78 | 2519 | 547 | 43.8 | 146 | 40 | 277 | 86.8 | 75 | 238 | 224 | 75 | 201 | 10 | 18.1 |
| Alexander | .......27 | 910 | 177 | 44.8 | 36 | 14 | 90 | 85.7 | 22 | 80 | 41 | 29 | 54 | 2 | 17.0 |
| Richmond | .........37 | 1216 | 205 | 40.7 | 133 | 45 | 143 | 89.4 | 15 | 109 | 111 | 43 | 84 | 7 | 16.2 |
| Laettner | ..........25 | 733 | 112 | 49.1 | 10 | 3 | 103 | 84.4 | 43 | 153 | 57 | 31 | 67 | 19 | 13.2 |
| Strickland | .........33 | 1020 | 141 | 42.6 | 16 | 4 | 115 | 78.2 | 25 | 105 | 231 | 43 | 83 | 4 | 12.2 |
| Whitney | ............59 | 1532 | 182 | 38.7 | 248 | 93 | 101 | 89.4 | 12 | 106 | 248 | 55 | 103 | 3 | 9.5 |
| White | ...............68 | 1609 | 203 | 49.8 | 1 | 0 | 177 | 56.7 | 178 | 521 | 20 | 32 | 136 | 111 | 8.6 |
| Nesby | ...............48 | 1223 | 149 | 36.6 | 134 | 39 | 67 | 80.7 | 35 | 131 | 65 | 41 | 55 | 16 | 8.4 |
| Lopez | ...............47 | 1108 | 142 | 43.6 | 29 | 6 | 9 | 73.2 | 30 | 160 | 73 | 41 | 56 | 18 | 8.1 |
| Vanterpool | .......22 | 411 | 46 | 41.8 | 6 | 0 | 30 | 60.0 | 15 | 37 | 66 | 23 | 37 | 3 | 5.5 |
| King | ................45 | 706 | 90 | 51.1 | 0 | 0 | 36 | 80.0 | 39 | 129 | 31 | 14 | 47 | 11 | 4.8 |
| Booth | ...............40 | 640 | 74 | 44.0 | 0 | 0 | 33 | 73.3 | 53 | 174 | 23 | 17 | 36 | 81 | 4.5 |
| Profit | ................35 | 605 | 56 | 39.4 | 26 | 7 | 33 | 73.3 | 18 | 64 | 89 | 36 | 46 | 11 | 4.3 |
| Smith | ...............79 | 1610 | 106 | 48.6 | 1 | 0 | 89 | 57.8 | 172 | 562 | 101 | 57 | 62 | 37 | 3.8 |
| Jones | ...............45 | 638 | 60 | 39.2 | 6 | 1 | 41 | 74.5 | 83 | 220 | 31 | 19 | 21 | 8 | 3.6 |
| **Wizards** | **..........82** | **19805** | **3010** | **45.1** | **890** | **335** | **1566** | **74.3** | **1064** | **3502** | **1771** | **593** | **1267** | **383** | **96.6** |
| **Opponents** | **......82** | **19805** | **3005** | **45.9** | **1052** | **390** | **1790** | **74.4** | **962** | **3380** | **1793** | **686** | **1225** | **503** | **99.9** |

# 2001 NBA Draft

The 2001 NBA Draft was held on June 27 in New York City

## First Round

1. Kwame Brown, Washington
2. Tyson Chandler, LA Clippers (to Chicago)
3. Pau Gasol, Atlanta
4. Eddy Curry, Chicago
5. Jason Richardson, Golden State
6. Shane Battier, Vancouver
7. Eddie Griffin, New Jersey (to Houston)
8. DeSagana Diop, Cleveland
9. Rodney White, Charlotte
10. Joe Johnson, Boston
11. Kedrick Brown, Boston
12. Vladimir Radmanovic, Seattle
13. Richard Jefferson, Houston (to New Jersey)
14. Troy Murphy, Golden State
15. Steven Hunter, Orlando
16. Kirk Haston, Charlotte
17. Michael Bradley, Toronto
18. Jason Collins, Houston (to New Jersey)
19. Zach Randolph, Portland
20. Brendan Haywood, Cleveland (to Orlando)
21. Joeseph Forte, Boston
22. Jeryl Sasser, Orlando
23. Brandon Armstrong, Houston (to New Jersey)
24. Raul Lopez, Utah
25. Gerald Wallace, Sacramento
26. Samuel Dalembert, Philadelphia
27. Jamaal Tinsley, Vancouver (to Indiana via Atlanta)
28. Tony Parker, SanAntonio

## Second Round

30. Trenton Hassell, Chicago
31. Gilbert Arenas, Golden State
32. Omar Cook, Orlando (to Denver)
33. Willie Solomon, Vancouver
34. Terence Morris, Atlanta (to Houston)
35. Brian Scalabrine, New Jersey
36. Jeff Trepagnier, Cleveland
37. Damone Brown, Philadelphia
38. Mehmet Okur, Detroit
39. Michael Wright, New York
40. Earl Watson, Seattle
41. Jamison Brewer, Indiana
42. B. Simmons, Seattle (to Wash)
43. Eric Chenowith, New York
44. Kyle Hill, Dallas
45. Sean Lampley, Chicago
46. Loren Woods, Minnesota
47. Ousmane Cisse, Denver
48. Antonis Foutis, Vancouver
49. Ken Johnson, Miami
50. Ruben Boumtje, Portland
51. Alton Ford, Phoenix
52. Andre Hutson, Milwaukee
53. Jarron Collins, Utah
54. Kenny Satterfield, Dallas
55. Maurice Jeffers, Sacramento
56. Robertas Javtokas, San Antonio
57. Alvin Jones, Philadelphia
58. Bryan Bracey, San Antonio

# Women's National Basketball Association

## Final Standings

### EASTERN CONFERENCE

| Team | W | L | Pct | GB |
|---|---|---|---|---|
| †Cleveland | 22 | 10 | .688 | — |
| *New York | 21 | 11 | .656 | 1 |
| *Miami | 20 | 12 | .625 | 2 |
| *Charlotte | 18 | 14 | .563 | 4 |
| Orlando | 13 | 19 | .406 | 9 |
| Indiana | 10 | 22 | .313 | 12 |
| Detroit | 10 | 22 | .313 | 12 |
| Washington | 10 | 22 | .313 | 12 |

### WESTERN CONFERENCE

| Team | W | L | Pct | GB |
|---|---|---|---|---|
| †Los Angeles | 28 | 4 | .875 | — |
| *Sacramento | 20 | 12 | .625 | 8 |
| *Utah | 19 | 13 | .594 | 9 |
| *Houston | 19 | 13 | .594 | 9 |
| Phoenix | 13 | 19 | .406 | 15 |
| Minnesota | 12 | 20 | .375 | 16 |
| Portland | 11 | 21 | .344 | 17 |
| Seattle | 10 | 22 | .313 | 18 |

†Clinched conference title.  *Clinched playoff berth.

## 2001 Playoffs

### FIRST ROUND

#### EASTERN CONFERENCE

| | | | | |
|---|---|---|---|---|
| Aug 16 | Cleveland | 46 | at Charlotte | 53 |
| Aug 18 | Charlotte | 51 | at Cleveland | 69 |
| Aug 20 | Charlotte | 72 | at Cleveland | 64 |

Charlotte won series 2–1.

| | | | | |
|---|---|---|---|---|
| Aug 17 | New York | 62 | at Miami | 46 |
| Aug 19 | Miami | 53 | at New York | 50 |
| Aug 21 | Miami | 61 | at New York | 72 |

New York won series 2–1.

#### WESTERN CONFERENCE

| | | | | |
|---|---|---|---|---|
| Aug 18 | Los Angeles | 64 | at Houston | 59 |
| Aug 20 | Houston | 58 | at Los Angeles | 70 |

Los Angeles won series 2–0.

| | | | | |
|---|---|---|---|---|
| Aug 17 | Sacramento | 89 | at Utah | 65 |
| Aug 19 | Utah | 66 | at Sacramento | 71 |

Sacramento won series 2–0.

#### EASTERN CONFERENCE FINALS

| | | | | |
|---|---|---|---|---|
| Aug 24 | New York | 61 | at Charlotte | 57 |
| Aug 26 | Charlotte | 62 | at New York | 53 |
| Aug 27 | Charlotte | 48 | at New York | 44 |

Charlotte won series 2–1.

#### WESTERN CONFERENCE FINALS

| | | | | |
|---|---|---|---|---|
| Aug 24 | Los Angeles | 74 | at Sacramento | 73 |
| Aug 26 | Sacramento | 80 | at Los Angeles | 60 |
| Aug 27 | Sacramento | 62 | at Los Angeles | 93 |

Los Angeles won series 2–1.

### WNBA CHAMPIONSHIP

| | | | | |
|---|---|---|---|---|
| Aug 30 | Los Angeles | 75 | at Charlotte | 66 |
| Sept 1 | Charlotte | 54 | at Los Angeles | 82 |

Los Angeles won series 2–0.

*Overtime game.

## From Backboards to Billboard

Former NBA forward Wayman Tisdale released an album in March 2001 entitled *Face to Face*. While most hoopsters cum musicians have tried their hand at rap, Tisdale is an accomplished bass player who lines up in the contemporary jazz vien. "It's smooth urban," says Tisdale of *Face*. "I like to do records that tell full stories, especially about relationships and love. I'm big, but I'm sensitive." Tisdale has released three previous albums, one of which, 1995's *Power Forward*, reached No. 4 on Billboard's contemporary jazz chart. So who's driving this musical success? "Women," says Tisdale. "Women are my fan base, from 25 to 80. I'm especially big with 80-year-olds. They love me."

## NBA Champions

| Season | Winner | Series | Runner-Up | Winning Coach | Finals MVP |
|---|---|---|---|---|---|
| 1946–47 | Philadelphia | 4–1 | Chicago | Eddie Gottlieb | — |
| 1947–48 | Baltimore | 4–2 | Philadelphia | Buddy Jeannette | — |
| 1948–49 | Minneapolis | 4–2 | Washington | John Kundla | — |
| 1949–50 | Minneapolis | 4–2 | Syracuse | John Kundla | — |
| 1950–51 | Rochester | 4–3 | New York | Les Harrison | — |
| 1951–52 | Minneapolis | 4–3 | New York | John Kundla | — |
| 1952–53 | Minneapolis | 4–1 | New York | John Kundla | — |
| 1953–54 | Minneapolis | 4–3 | Syracuse | John Kundla | — |
| 1954–55 | Syracuse | 4–3 | Ft Wayne | Al Cervi | — |
| 1955–56 | Philadelphia | 4–1 | Ft Wayne | George Senesky | — |
| 1956–57 | Boston | 4–3 | St Louis | Red Auerbach | — |
| 1957–58 | St Louis | 4–2 | Boston | Alex Hannum | — |
| 1958–59 | Boston | 4–0 | Minneapolis | Red Auerbach | — |
| 1959–60 | Boston | 4–3 | St Louis | Red Auerbach | — |
| 1960–61 | Boston | 4–1 | St Louis | Red Auerbach | — |
| 1961–62 | Boston | 4–3 | LA Lakers | Red Auerbach | — |
| 1962–63 | Boston | 4–2 | LA Lakers | Red Auerbach | — |
| 1963–64 | Boston | 4–1 | San Francisco | Red Auerbach | — |
| 1964–65 | Boston | 4–1 | LA Lakers | Red Auerbach | — |
| 1965–66 | Boston | 4–3 | LA Lakers | Red Auerbach | — |
| 1966–67 | Philadelphia | 4–2 | San Francisco | Alex Hannum | — |
| 1967–68 | Boston | 4–2 | LA Lakers | Bill Russell | — |
| 1968–69 | Boston | 4–3 | LA Lakers | Bill Russell | Jerry West, LA |
| 1969–70 | New York | 4–3 | LA Lakers | Red Holzman | Willis Reed, NY |
| 1970–71 | Milwaukee | 4–0 | Baltimore | Larry Costello | Kareem Abdul-Jabbar, Mil |
| 1971–72 | LA Lakers | 4–1 | New York | Bill Sharman | Wilt Chamberlain, LA |
| 1972–73 | New York | 4–1 | LA Lakers | Red Holzman | Willis Reed, NY |
| 1973–74 | Boston | 4–3 | Milwaukee | Tommy Heinsohn | John Havlicek, Bos |
| 1974–75 | Golden State | 4–0 | Washington | Al Attles | Rick Barry, GS |
| 1975–76 | Boston | 4–2 | Phoenix | Tommy Heinsohn | JoJo White, Bos |
| 1976–77 | Portland | 4–2 | Philadelphia | Jack Ramsay | Bill Walton, Port |
| 1977–78 | Washington | 4–3 | Seattle | Dick Motta | Wes Unseld, Wash |
| 1978–79 | Seattle | 4–1 | Washington | Lenny Wilkens | Dennis Johnson, Sea |
| 1979–80 | LA Lakers | 4–2 | Philadelphia | Paul Westhead | Magic Johnson, LA |
| 1980–81 | Boston | 4–2 | Houston | Bill Fitch | Cedric Maxwell, Bos |
| 1981–82 | LA Lakers | 4–2 | Philadelphia | Pat Riley | Magic Johnson, LA |
| 1982–83 | Philadelphia | 4–0 | LA Lakers | Billy Cunningham | Moses Malone, Phil |
| 1983–84 | Boston | 4–3 | LA Lakers | K.C. Jones | Larry Bird, Bos |
| 1984–85 | LA Lakers | 4–2 | Boston | Pat Riley | Kareem Abdul-Jabbar, LA |
| 1985–86 | Boston | 4–2 | Houston | K.C. Jones | Larry Bird, Bos |
| 1986–87 | LA Lakers | 4–2 | Boston | Pat Riley | Magic Johnson, LA |
| 1987–88 | LA Lakers | 4–3 | Detroit | Pat Riley | James Worthy, LA |
| 1988–89 | Detroit | 4–0 | LA Lakers | Chuck Daly | Joe Dumars, Det |
| 1989–90 | Detroit | 4–1 | Portland | Chuck Daly | Isiah Thomas, Det |
| 1990–91 | Chicago | 4–1 | LA Lakers | Phil Jackson | Michael Jordan, Chi |
| 1991–92 | Chicago | 4–2 | Portland | Phil Jackson | Michael Jordan, Chi |
| 1992–93 | Chicago | 4–2 | Phoenix | Phil Jackson | Michael Jordan, Chi |
| 1993–94 | Houston | 4–3 | New York | Rudy Tomjanovich | Hakeem Olajuwon, Hou |
| 1994–95 | Houston | 4–0 | Orlando | Rudy Tomjanovich | Hakeem Olajuwon, Hou |
| 1995–96 | Chicago | 4–2 | Seattle | Phil Jackson | Michael Jordan, Chi |
| 1996–97 | Chicago | 4–2 | Utah | Phil Jackson | Michael Jordan, Chi |
| 1997–98 | Chicago | 4–2 | Utah | Phil Jackson | Michael Jordan, Chi |
| 1998–99 | San Antonio | 4–1 | New York | Gregg Popovich | Tim Duncan, SA |
| 1999–00 | LA Lakers | 4–2 | Indiana | Phil Jackson | Shaquille O'Neal, LA |
| 2000–01 | LA Lakers | 4–1 | Philadelphia | Phil Jackson | Shaquille O'Neal, LA |

## Most Valuable Player: Maurice Podoloff Trophy

| Season | Player, Team | GP | Field Goals | | 3-Pt FG | | Free Throws | | Rebounds | | A | Stl | BS | Avg |
|--------|--------------|-----|------|------|------|------|------|------|------|-------|------|------|------|------|
| | | | FGM | Pct | FGM | Pct | FTM | Pct | Off | Total | | | | |
| 1955–56 | Bob Pettit, StL | 72 | 646 | 42.9 | – | – | 557 | 73.6 | – | 1,164 | 189 | – | – | 25.7 |
| 1956–57 | Bob Cousy, Bos | 64 | 478 | 37.8 | – | – | 363 | 82.1 | – | 309 | 478 | – | – | 20.6 |
| 1957–58 | Bill Russell, Bos | 69 | 456 | 44.2 | – | – | 230 | 51.9 | – | 1,564 | 202 | – | – | 16.6 |
| 1958–59 | Bob Pettit, StL | 72 | 719 | 43.8 | – | – | 667 | 75.9 | – | 1,182 | 221 | – | – | 29.2 |
| 1959–60 | Wilt Chamberlain, Phil | 72 | 1,065 | 46.1 | – | – | 577 | 58.2 | – | 1,941 | 168 | – | – | 37.6 |
| 1960–61 | Bill Russell, Bos | 78 | 532 | 42.6 | – | – | 258 | 55.0 | – | 1,868 | 264 | – | – | 16.9 |
| 1961–62 | Bill Russell, Bos | 76 | 575 | 45.7 | – | – | 286 | 59.5 | – | 1,891 | 341 | – | – | 18.9 |
| 1962–63 | Bill Russell, Bos | 78 | 511 | 43.2 | – | – | 287 | 55.5 | – | 1,843 | 348 | – | – | 16.8 |
| 1963–64 | Oscar Robertson, Cin | 79 | 840 | 48.3 | – | – | 800 | 85.3 | – | 783 | 868 | – | – | 31.4 |
| 1964–65 | Bill Russell, Bos | 78 | 429 | 43.8 | – | – | 244 | 57.3 | – | 1,878 | 410 | – | – | 14.1 |
| 1965–66 | Wilt Chamberlain, Phil | 79 | 1,074 | 54.0 | – | – | 501 | 51.3 | – | 1,943 | 414 | – | – | 33.5 |
| 1966–67 | Wilt Chamberlain, Phil | 81 | 785 | 68.3 | – | – | 386 | 44.1 | – | 1,957 | 630 | – | – | 24.1 |
| 1967–68 | Wilt Chamberlain, Phil | 82 | 819 | 59.5 | – | – | 354 | 38.0 | – | 1,952 | 702 | – | – | 24.3 |
| 1968–69 | Wes Unseld, Balt | 82 | 427 | 47.6 | – | – | 277 | 60.5 | – | 1,491 | 213 | – | – | 13.8 |
| 1969–70 | Willis Reed, NY | 81 | 702 | 50.7 | – | – | 351 | 75.6 | – | 1,126 | 161 | – | – | 21.7 |
| 1970–71 | Kareem Abdul-Jabbar, Mil | 82 | 1,063 | 57.7 | – | – | 470 | 69.0 | – | 1,311 | 272 | – | – | 31.7 |
| 1971–72 | Kareem Abdul-Jabbar, Mil | 81 | 1,159 | 57.4 | – | – | 504 | 68.9 | – | 1,346 | 370 | – | – | 34.8 |
| 1972–73 | Dave Cowens, Bos | 82 | 740 | 45.2 | – | – | 204 | 77.9 | – | 1,329 | 333 | – | – | 20.5 |
| 1973–74 | Kareem Abdul-Jabbar, Mil | 81 | 948 | 53.9 | – | – | 295 | 70.2 | 287 | 1,178 | 386 | 112 | 283 | 27.0 |
| 1974–75 | Bob McAdoo, Buff | 82 | 1,095 | 51.2 | – | – | 641 | 80.5 | 307 | 1,155 | 179 | 92 | 174 | 34.5 |
| 1975–76 | Kareem Abdul-Jabbar, LA | 82 | 914 | 52.9 | – | – | 447 | 70.3 | 272 | 1,383 | 413 | 119 | 338 | 27.7 |
| 1976–77 | Kareem Abdul-Jabbar, LA | 82 | 888 | 57.9 | – | – | 376 | 70.1 | 266 | 1,090 | 319 | 101 | 261 | 26.2 |
| 1977–78 | Bill Walton, Port | 58 | 460 | 52.2 | – | – | 177 | 72.0 | 118 | 766 | 291 | 60 | 146 | 18.9 |
| 1978–79 | Moses Malone, Hou | 82 | 716 | 54.0 | – | – | 599 | 73.9 | 587 | 1,444 | 147 | 79 | 119 | 24.8 |
| 1979–80 | Kareem Abdul-Jabbar, LA | 82 | 835 | 60.4 | 0 | 00.0 | 364 | 76.5 | 190 | 886 | 371 | 81 | 280 | 24.8 |
| 1980–81 | Julius Erving, Phil | 82 | 794 | 52.1 | 4 | 22.2 | 422 | 78.7 | 244 | 657 | 364 | 173 | 147 | 24.6 |
| 1981–82 | Moses Malone, Hou | 81 | 945 | 51.9 | 0 | 00.0 | 630 | 76.2 | 558 | 1,188 | 142 | 76 | 125 | 31.1 |
| 1982–83 | Moses Malone, Phil | 78 | 654 | 50.1 | 0 | 00.0 | 600 | 76.1 | 445 | 1,194 | 101 | 89 | 157 | 24.5 |
| 1983–84 | Larry Bird, Bos | 79 | 758 | 49.2 | 18 | 24.7 | 374 | 88.8 | 181 | 796 | 520 | 144 | 69 | 24.2 |
| 1984–85 | Larry Bird, Bos | 80 | 918 | 52.2 | 56 | 42.7 | 403 | 88.2 | 164 | 842 | 531 | 129 | 98 | 28.7 |
| 1985–86 | Larry Bird, Bos | 82 | 796 | 49.6 | 82 | 42.3 | 441 | 89.6 | 190 | 805 | 557 | 166 | 51 | 25.8 |
| 1986–87 | Magic Johnson, LA Lakers | 80 | 683 | 52.2 | 8 | 20.5 | 535 | 84.8 | 122 | 504 | 977 | 138 | 36 | 23.9 |
| 1987–88 | Michael Jordan, Chi | 82 | 1,069 | 53.5 | 7 | 13.2 | 723 | 84.1 | 139 | 449 | 485 | 259 | 131 | 35.0 |
| 1988–89 | Magic Johnson, LA Lakers | 77 | 579 | 50.9 | 59 | 31.4 | 513 | 91.1 | 111 | 607 | 988 | 138 | 22 | 22.5 |
| 1989–90 | Magic Johnson, LA Lakers | 79 | 546 | 48.0 | 106 | 38.4 | 567 | 89.0 | 128 | 522 | 907 | 132 | 34 | 22.3 |
| 1990–91 | Michael Jordan, Chi | 82 | 990 | 53.9 | 29 | 31.2 | 571 | 85.1 | 118 | 492 | 453 | 223 | 83 | 31.5 |
| 1991–92 | Michael Jordan, Chi | 80 | 943 | 51.9 | 27 | 27.0 | 491 | 83.2 | 91 | 511 | 489 | 182 | 75 | 30.1 |
| 1992–93 | Charles Barkley, Phoe | 76 | 716 | 52.0 | 67 | 30.5 | 445 | 76.5 | 237 | 928 | 385 | 119 | 74 | 25.6 |
| 1993–94 | Hakeem Olajuwon, Hou | 80 | 894 | 52.8 | 8 | 42.1 | 388 | 71.6 | 229 | 955 | 287 | 128 | 297 | 27.3 |
| 1994–95 | David Robinson, SA | 81 | 788 | 53.0 | 6 | 30.0 | 656 | 77.4 | 234 | 877 | 236 | 134 | 262 | 27.6 |
| 1995–96 | Michael Jordan, Chi | 82 | 916 | 49.5 | 111 | 42.7 | 548 | 83.4 | 148 | 543 | 352 | 180 | 42 | 30.4 |
| 1996–97 | Karl Malone, Utah | 82 | 864 | 55.0 | 0 | 00.0 | 521 | 75.5 | 193 | 809 | 368 | 113 | 48 | 27.4 |
| 1997–98 | Michael Jordan, Chi | 82 | 881 | 46.5 | 30 | 23.8 | 565 | 78.4 | 130 | 475 | 283 | 141 | 45 | 28.7 |
| 1998–99 | Karl Malone, Utah | 49 | 393 | 49.3 | 0 | 00.0 | 378 | 78.8 | 107 | 463 | 201 | 62 | 28 | 23.8 |
| 1999–00 | Shaquille O'Neal, LA Lakers | 79 | 956 | 57.4 | 0 | 00.0 | 432 | 52.4 | 336 | 1078 | 299 | 36 | 239 | 29.7 |
| 2000–01 | Allen Iverson, Phil | 71 | 762 | 42.0 | 98 | 32.0 | 585 | 81.4 | 50 | 273 | 325 | 78 | 20 | 31.1 |

## Coach of the Year: Arnold "Red" Auerbach Trophy

| | | |
|---|---|---|
| 1962–63...Harry Gallatin, StL | 1976–77...Tom Nissalke, Hou | 1989–90...Pat Riley, LA Lakers |
| 1963–64...Alex Hannum, SF | 1977–78...Hubie Brown, Atl | 1990–91...Don Chaney, Hou |
| 1964–65...Red Auerbach, Bos | 1978–79...Cotton Fitzsimmons, KC | 1991–92...Don Nelson, GS |
| 1965–66...Dolph Schayes, Phil | 1979–80...Bill Fitch, Bos | 1992–93...Pat Riley, NY |
| 1966–67...Johnny Kerr, Chi | 1980–81...Jack McKinney, Ind | 1993–94...Lenny Wilkens, Atl |
| 1967–68...Richie Guerin, StL | 1981–82...Gene Shue, Wash | 1994–95...Del Harris, LA Lakers |
| 1968–69...Gene Shue, Balt | 1982–83...Don Nelson, Mil | 1995–96...Phil Jackson, Chi |
| 1969–70...Red Holzman, NY | 1983–84...Frank Layden, Utah | 1996–97...Pat Riley, Mia |
| 1970–71...Dick Motta, Chi | 1984–85...Don Nelson, Mil | 1997–98...Larry Bird, Ind |
| 1971–72...Bill Sharman, LA | 1985–86...Mike Fratello, Atl | 1998–99...Mike Dunleavy, Port |
| 1972–73...Tom Heinsohn, Bos | 1986–87...Mike Schuler, Port | 1999–00...Glenn (Doc) Rivers, Orl |
| 1973–74...Ray Scott, Det | 1987–88...Doug Moe, Den | 2000–01...Larry Brown, Phil |
| 1974–75...Phil Johnson, KC-Oma | 1988–89...Cotton Fitzsimmons, Phoe | |
| 1975–76...Bill Fitch, Clev | | |

Note: Award named after Auerbach in 1986.

## Rookie of the Year: Eddie Gottlieb Trophy

1952–53...Don Meineke, FW
1953–54...Ray Felix, Balt
1954–55...Bob Pettit, Mil
1955–56...Maurice Stokes, Roch
1956–57...Tom Heinsohn, Bos
1957–58...Woody Sauldsberry, Phil
1958–59...Elgin Baylor, Minn
1959–60...Wilt Chamberlain, Phil
1960–61...Oscar Robertson, Cin
1961–62...Walt Bellamy, Chi
1962–63...Terry Dischinger, Chi
1963–64...Jerry Lucas, Cin
1964–65...Willis Reed, NY
1965–66...Rick Barry, SF
1966–67...Dave Bing, Det
1967–68...Earl Monroe, Balt
1968–69...Wes Unseld, Balt

1969–70...K. Abdul-Jabbar, Mil
1970–71...Dave Cowens, Bos
        Geoff Petrie, Port
1971–72...Sidney Wicks, Port
1972–73...Bob McAdoo, Buff
1973–74...Ernie DiGregorio, Buff
1974–75...Keith Wilkes, GS
1975–76...Alvan Adams, Phoe
1976–77...Adrian Dantley, Buff
1977–78...Walter Davis, Phoe
1978–79...Phil Ford, KC
1979–80...Larry Bird, Bos
1980–81...Darrell Griffith, Utah
1981–82...Buck Williams, NJ
1982–83...Terry Cummings, SD
1983–84...Ralph Sampson, Hou
1984–85...Michael Jordan, Chi

1985–86...Patrick Ewing, NY
1986–87...Chuck Person, Ind
1987–88...Mark Jackson, NY
1988–89...Mitch Richmond, GS
1989–90...David Robinson, SA
1990–91...Derrick Coleman, NJ
1991–92...Larry Johnson, Char
1992–93...Shaquille O'Neal, Orl
1993–94...Chris Webber, GS
1994–95...J. Kidd, Dall/G. Hill, Det
1995–96...Damon Stoudamire, Tor
1996–97...Allen Iverson, Phil
1997–98...Tim Duncan, SA
1998–99...Vince Carter, Tor
1999–00...Steve Francis, Hou
        Elton Brand, Chi
2000–01..Mike Miller, Orl

## Defensive Player of the Year

1982–83...Sidney Moncrief, Mil
1983–84...Sidney Moncrief, Mil
1984–85...Mark Eaton, Utah
1985–86...Alvin Robertson, SA
1986–87...Michael Cooper, Lakers
1987–88...Michael Jordan, Chi
1988–89...Mark Eaton, Utah

1989–90...Dennis Rodman, Det
1990–91...Dennis Rodman, Det
1991–92...David Robinson, SA
1992–93...Hakeem Olajuwon, Hou
1993–94...Hakeem Olajuwon, Hou
1994–95...Dikembe Mutombo, Den
1995–96...Gary Payton, Sea

1996–97...Dikembe Mutombo, Den
1997–98...Dikembe Mutombo, Atl
1998–99...Alonzo Mourning, Mia
1999–00...Alonzo Mourning, Mia
2000–01...Dikembe Mutombo, Phil

## Sixth Man Award

1982–83...Bobby Jones, Phil
1983–84...Kevin McHale, Bos
1984–85...Kevin McHale, Bos
1985–86...Bill Walton, Bos
1986–87...Ricky Pierce, Mil
1987–88...Roy Tarpley, Dall
1988–89...Eddie Johnson, Phoe

1989–90...Ricky Pierce, Mil
1990–91...Detlef Schrempf, Ind
1991–92...Detlef Schrempf, Ind
1992–93...Cliff Robinson, Port
1993–94...Dell Curry, Char
1994–95...Anthony Mason, NY
1995–96...Tony Kukoc, Chi

1996–97...John Starks, NY
1997–98...Danny Manning, Phoe
1998–99...Darrell Armstrong, Orl
1999–00...Rodney Rogers, Phoe
2000–01...Aaron McKie, Phil

## J. Walter Kennedy Citizenship Award

1974 75...Wes Unseld, Wash
1975–76...Slick Watts, Sea
1976–77...Dave Bing, Wash
1977–78...Bob Lanier, Det
1978–79...Calvin Murphy, Hou
1979–80...Austin Carr, Clev
1980–81...Mike Glenn, NY
1981–82...Kent Benson, Det
1982–83...Julius Erving, Phil
1983–84...Frank Layden, Utah

1984 85...Dan Issel, Den
1985–86...Michael Cooper, Lakers
        Rory Sparrow, NY
1986–87...Isiah Thomas, Det
1987–88...Alex English, Den
1988–89...Thurl Bailey, Utah
1989–90...Glenn Rivers, Atl
1990–91...Kevin Johnson, Phoe
1991–92...Magic Johnson, Lakers
1992–93...Terry Porter, Port

1993 94...Joe Dumars, Det
1994–95...Joe O'Toole, Atl
1995–96...Chris Dudley, Port
1996–97...P.J. Brown, Mia
1997–98...Steve Smith, Atl
1998–99...Brian Grant, Port
1999–00...Vlade Divac, Sac
2000–01...Dikembe Mutombo, Phil

## Most Improved Player

1985–86...Alvin Robertson, SA
1986–87...Dale Ellis, Sea
1987–88...Kevin Duckworth, Port
1988–89...Kevin Johnson, Phoe
1989–90...Rony Seikaly, Mia
1990–91...Scott Skiles, Orl

1991–92...Pervis Ellison, Wash
1992–93...Chris Jackson, Den
1993–94...Don MacLean, Wash
1994–95...Dana Barros, Phil
1995–96...Gheorghe Muresan,
        Wash

1996–97...Isaac Austin, Mia
1997–98...Alan Henderson, Atl
1998–99...Darrell Armstrong, Orl
1999–00...Jalen Rose, Ind
2000–01...Tracy McGrady, Orl

## Executive of the Year

1972–73...Joe Axelson, KC-Oma
1973–74...Eddie Donovan, Buff
1974–75...Dick Vertlieb, GS
1975–76...Jerry Colangelo, Phoe
1976–77...Ray Patterson, Hou
1977–78...Angelo Drossos, SA
1978–79...Bob Ferry, Wash
1979–80...Red Auerbach, Bos
1980–81...Jerry Colangelo, Phoe
1981–82...Bob Ferry, Wash

1982–83...Zollie Volchok, Sea
1983–84...Frank Layden, Utah
1984–85...Vince Boryla, Den
1985–86...Stan Kasten, Atl
1986–87...Stan Kasten, Atl
1987–88...Jerry Krause, Chi
1988–89...Jerry Colangelo, Phoe
1989–90...Bob Bass, SA
1990–91...Bucky Buckwalter, Port
1991–92...Wayne Embry, Clev

1992–93...Jerry Colangelo, Phoe
1993–94...Bob Whitsitt, Sea
1994–95...Jerry West, LA Lakers
1995–96...Jerry Krause, Chi
1996–97...Bob Bass, Char
1997–98...Wayne Embry, Clev
1998–99...Geoff Petrie, Sac
1999–00...John Gabriel, Orl
2000–01...Geoff Petrie, Sac

Sponsored by *The Sporting News*.

# NBA Alltime Individual Leaders

## Scoring

### MOST POINTS, CAREER

|  | Pts | Avg |
|---|---|---|
| Kareem Abdul-Jabbar | 38,387 | 24.6 |
| Karl Malone | 32,919 | 25.9 |
| Wilt Chamberlain | 31,419 | 30.1 |
| Michael Jordan | 29,277 | 31.5 |
| Moses Malone | 27,409 | 20.6 |
| Elvin Hayes | 27,313 | 21.0 |
| Oscar Robertson | 26,710 | 25.7 |
| Dominique Wilkins | 26,669 | 24.8 |
| Hakeem Olajuwon | 26,511 | 22.5 |
| John Havlicek | 26,395 | 20.8 |

### MOST POINTS, SEASON

| Wilt Chamberlain, Phil | 4,029 | 1961–62 |
|---|---|---|
| Wilt Chamberlain, SF | 3,586 | 1962–63 |
| Michael Jordan, Chi | 3,041 | 1986–87 |
| Wilt Chamberlain, Phil | 3,033 | 1960–61 |
| Wilt Chamberlain, SF | 2,948 | 1963–64 |
| Michael Jordan, Chi | 2,868 | 1987–88 |
| Bob McAdoo, Buff | 2,831 | 1974–75 |
| Rick Barry, SF | 2,775 | 1966–67 |
| Michael Jordan, Chi | 2,753 | 1989–90 |
| Elgin Baylor, LA | 2,719 | 1962–63 |

### HIGHEST SCORING AVERAGE, CAREER

| Michael Jordan | 31.5 | 930 games |
|---|---|---|
| Wilt Chamberlain | 30.1 | 1,045 games |
| Shaquille O'Neal | 27.7 | 608 games |
| Elgin Baylor | 27.4 | 846 games |
| Jerry West | 27.0 | 932 games |
| Bob Pettit | 26.4 | 792 games |
| George Gervin | 26.2 | 791 games |
| Karl Malone | 25.9 | 1,273 games |
| Oscar Robertson | 25.7 | 1,040 games |
| Dominique Wilkins | 24.8 | 1,074 games |

Note: Minimum 400 games.

### HIGHEST SCORING AVERAGE, SEASON

| Wilt Chamberlain, Phil | 50.4 | 1961–62 |
|---|---|---|
| Wilt Chamberlain, SF | 44.8 | 1962–63 |
| Wilt Chamberlain, Phil | 38.4 | 1960–61 |
| Wilt Chamberlain, Phil | 37.6 | 1959–60 |
| Michael Jordan, Chi | 37.1 | 1986–87 |
| Wilt Chamberlain, SF | 36.9 | 1963–64 |
| Rick Barry, SF | 35.6 | 1966–67 |
| Michael Jordan, Chi | 35.0 | 1987–88 |
| Elgin Baylor, LA | 34.8 | 1960–61 |

Note: Minimum 70 games.

### MOST POINTS, GAME

| Player, Team | | Opp | Date |
|---|---|---|---|
| 100 | Wilt Chamberlain, Phil | NY | 3/2/62 |
| 78 | Wilt Chamberlain, Phil | LA | 12/8/61 |
| 73 | Wilt Chamberlain, Phil | Chi | 1/13/62 |
| 73 | Wilt Chamberlain, SF | NY | 11/16/62 |
| 73 | David Thompson, Den | Det | 4/9/78 |
| 72 | Wilt Chamberlain, SF | LA | 11/3/62 |
| 71 | David Robinson, SA | LAC | 4/24/94 |
| 71 | Elgin Baylor, LA | NY | 11/15/60 |
| 70 | Wilt Chamberlain, SF | Syr | 3/10/63 |
| 69 | Michael Jordan, Chi | Clev | 3/28/90 |

## Field-Goal Percentage

Highest FG Percentage, Career: .599—Artis Gilmore
Highest FG Percentage, Season: .727—Wilt
Chamberlain, LA Lakers, 1972–73 (426/586)

## Free Throws

### HIGHEST FREE-THROW PERCENTAGE, CAREER

| Mark Price | .904 |
|---|---|
| Rick Barry | .900 |
| Calvin Murphy | .892 |
| Scott Skiles | .889 |
| Larry Bird | .886 |

Note: Minimum 1200 free throws made.

### HIGHEST FREE-THROW PERCENTAGE, SEASON

| Calvin Murphy, Hou | .958 | 1980–81 |
|---|---|---|
| Mahmoud Abdul-Rauf, Den | .956 | 1993–94 |
| Jeff Hornacek, Utah | .950 | 1999–00 |
| Mark Price, Clev | .948 | 1992–93 |
| Mark Price, Clev | .947 | 1991–92 |

### MOST FREE THROWS MADE, CAREER

|  | No. | Yrs | Pct |
|---|---|---|---|
| Karl Malone | 8,636 | 16 | .738 |
| Moses Malone | 8,531 | 19 | .769 |
| Oscar Robertson | 7,694 | 14 | .838 |
| Jerry West | 7,160 | 14 | .814 |
| Dolph Schayes | 6,979 | 16 | .844 |

## Three-Point Field Goals

Most Three-Point Field-Goals, Career: 2,037—Reggie Miller

Highest Three-Point Field-Goal Percentage, Career: .462—Steve Kerr

Most Three-Point Field Goals, Season: 267—Dennis Scott, Orl, 1995–96

Highest Three-Point Field-Goal Percentage, Season: .524—Steve Kerr, Chi, 1994–95

Most Three-Point Field Goals, Game: 11—Dennis Scott, Orlando vs Atlanta, 4/18/96 CK tk

Note: First year of shot: 1979–80.

## Steals

Most Steals, Career: 2,976—John Stockton

Most Steals, Season: 301—Alvin Robertson, San Antonio, 1985–86

Most Steals, Game: 11—Kendall Gill, New Jersey vs Miami, 4/3/99; Larry Kenon, San Antonio Ck TK vs Kansas City, 12/26/76

## Rebounds

### MOST REBOUNDS, CAREER

|  | No. | Yrs | Avg |
|---|---|---|---|
| Wilt Chamberlain | 23,924 | 14 | 22.9 |
| Bill Russell | 21,620 | 13 | 22.5 |
| Kareem Abdul-Jabbar | 17,440 | 20 | 11.4 |
| Elvin Hayes | 16,279 | 16 | 12.5 |
| Moses Malone | 16,212 | 19 | 12.2 |
| Robert Parish | 14,715 | 21 | 9.1 |
| Nate Thurmond | 14,464 | 14 | 15.0 |
| Walt Bellamy | 14,241 | 14 | 13.7 |
| Wes Unseld | 13,769 | 13 | 14.0 |
| Hakeem Olajuwon | 13,382 | 17 | 11.4 |

## Rebounds *(Cont.)*
### MOST REBOUNDS, SEASON

| | | |
|---|---|---|
| Wilt Chamberlain, Phil | 2,149 | 1960–61 |
| Wilt Chamberlain, Phil | 2,052 | 1961–62 |
| Wilt Chamberlain, Phil | 1,957 | 1966–67 |
| Wilt Chamberlain, Phil | 1,952 | 1967–68 |
| Wilt Chamberlain, SF | 1,946 | 1962–63 |
| Wilt Chamberlain, Phil | 1,943 | 1965–66 |
| Wilt Chamberlain, Phil | 1,941 | 1959–60 |
| Bill Russell, Bos | 1,930 | 1963–64 |
| Bill Russell, Bos | 1,878 | 1964–65 |
| Bill Russell, Bos | 1,868 | 1960–61 |

### MOST REBOUNDS, GAME

| | Player, Team | Opp | Date |
|---|---|---|---|
| 55 | Wilt Chamberlain, Phil | Bos | 11/24/60 |
| 51 | Bill Russell, Bos | Syr | 2/5/60 |
| 49 | Bill Russell, Bos | Phil | 11/16/57 |
| 49 | Bill Russell, Bos | Det | 3/11/65 |
| 45 | Wilt Chamberlain, Phil | Syr | 2/6/60 |
| 45 | Wilt Chamberlain, Phil | LA | 1/21/61 |

## Assists
### MOST ASSISTS, CAREER

| | |
|---|---|
| John Stockton | 14,503 |
| Magic Johnson | 10,141 |
| Oscar Robertson | 9,887 |
| Mark Jackson | 9,235 |
| Isiah Thomas | 9,061 |

## Assists *(Cont.)*
### MOST ASSISTS, SEASON

| | | |
|---|---|---|
| John Stockton, Utah | 1,164 | 1990–91 |
| John Stockton, Utah | 1,134 | 1989–90 |
| John Stockton, Utah | 1,128 | 1987–88 |
| John Stockton, Utah | 1,126 | 1991–92 |
| Isiah Thomas, Det | 1,123 | 1984–85 |

**MOST ASSISTS, GAME:** 30—Scott Skiles, Orlando vs Denver, 12/30/90

## Blocked Shots
### MOST BLOCKED SHOTS, CAREER

| | |
|---|---|
| Hakeem Olajuwon | 3,740 |
| Kareem Abdul-Jabbar | 3,189 |
| Mark Eaton | 3,064 |
| Patrick Ewing | 2,849 |
| David Robinson | 2,703 |

### MOST BLOCKED SHOTS, SEASON

| | | |
|---|---|---|
| Mark Eaton, Utah | 456 | 1984–85 |
| Manute Bol, Wash | 397 | 1985–86 |
| Elmore Smith, LA | 393 | 1973–74 |

**MOST BLOCKED SHOTS, GAME:** 17—Elmore Smith, LA Lakers vs Portland, 10/28/73

## Scoring
### MOST POINTS, CAREER

| | Pts | Yrs | Avg |
|---|---|---|---|
| Michael Jordan | 5,987 | 13 | 33.4 |
| Kareem Abdul-Jabbar | 5,762 | 18 | 24.3 |
| Jerry West | 4,457 | 13 | 29.1 |
| Karl Malone | 4,341 | 16 | 26.6 |
| Larry Bird | 3,897 | 12 | 23.8 |
| John Havlicek | 3,776 | 13 | 22.0 |
| Hakeem Olajuwon | 3,727 | 14 | 26.6 |
| Magic Johnson | 3,701 | 13 | 19.5 |
| Elgin Baylor | 3,623 | 12 | 27.0 |
| Wilt Chamberlain | 3,607 | 13 | 22.5 |

### *HIGHEST SCORING AVERAGE, CAREER

| | Avg | Games |
|---|---|---|
| Michael Jordan | 33.4 | 179 |
| Allen Iverson | 30.3 | 40 |
| Jerry West | 29.1 | 153 |
| Shaquille O'Neal | 28.2 | 105 |
| Elgin Baylor | 27.0 | 134 |
| George Gervin | 27.0 | 59 |
| Hakeem Olajuwon | 26.6 | 136 |
| Karl Malone | 26.6 | 163 |
| Bob Pettit | 25.5 | 88 |
| Dominique Wilkins | 25.4 | 55 |

*Minimum of 25 games.

## Scoring *(Cont.)*
### MOST POINTS, GAME

| | Player, Team | Opp | Date |
|---|---|---|---|
| †63 | Michael Jordan, Chi | Bos | 4/20/86 |
| 61 | Elgin Baylor, LA | Bos | 4/14/62 |
| 56 | Wilt Chamberlain, Phil | Syr | 3/22/62 |
| 56 | Michael Jordan, Chi | Mia | 4/29/92 |
| 56 | Charles Barkley, Phoe | GS | 5/4/94 |
| 55 | Rick Barry, SF | Phil | 4/18/67 |
| 55 | Michael Jordan, Chi | Clev | 5/1/88 |
| 55 | Michael Jordan, Chi | Phoe | 4/16/95 |
| 55 | Michael Jordan, Chi | Wash | 4/27/97 |

†Double overtime game.

## Rebounds
### MOST REBOUNDS, CAREER

| | No. | Yrs | Avg |
|---|---|---|---|
| Bill Russell | 4,104 | 13 | 24.9 |
| Wilt Chamberlain | 3,913 | 13 | 24.5 |
| Kareem Abdul-Jabbar | 2,481 | 18 | 10.5 |
| Karl Malone | 1,813 | 16 | 11.1 |
| Wes Unseld | 1,777 | 12 | 14.9 |

### MOST REBOUNDS, GAME

| | Player, Team | Opp | Date |
|---|---|---|---|
| 41 | Wilt Chamberlain, Phil | Bos | 4/5/67 |
| 40 | Bill Russell, Bos | Phil | 3/23/58 |
| 40 | Bill Russell, Bos | StL | 3/29/60 |
| *40 | Bill Russell, Bos | LA | 4/18/62 |

Three tied at 39.
*Overtime game.

## Assists

### MOST ASSISTS, CAREER

| | No. | Games |
|---|---|---|
| Magic Johnson | 2,346 | 190 |
| John Stockton | 1,773 | 173 |
| Larry Bird | 1,062 | 164 |
| Scottie Pippen | 1,018 | 201 |
| Dennis Johnson | 1,006 | 180 |

### MOST ASSISTS, GAME

| Player, Team | Opp | Date |
|---|---|---|
| 24 ..........Magic Johnson, LAL | Pho | 5/15/84 |
| 24 ..........John Stockton, Utah | LAL | 5/17/88 |
| 23 ..........Magic Johnson, LAL | Port | 5/3/85 |
| 22 ..........Doc Rivers, Atl | Bos | 5/16/88 |

Four tied at 21.

## Games played

| | |
|---|---|
| Kareem Abdul-Jabbar | 237 |
| Scottie Pippen | 201 |
| Danny Ainge | 193 |
| Magic Johnson | 190 |
| Robert Parish | 184 |

## Appearances

| | |
|---|---|
| Kareem Abdul-Jabbar | 18 |
| John Stockton | 17 |
| Robert Parish | 16 |
| Karl Malone | 16 |
| Dolph Schayes | 15 |
| Clyde Drexler | 15 |
| Tree Rollins | 15 |
| Jerome Kersey | 15 |

# NBA Season Leaders

## Scoring

| | | | | |
|---|---|---|---|---|
| 1946–47 ..............Joe Fulks, Phil | 1389 | 1974–75 ..............Bob McAdoo, Buff | 34.5 | |
| 1947–48 ..............Max Zaslofsky, Chi | 1007 | 1975–76 ..............Bob McAdoo, Buff | 31.1 | |
| 1948–49 ..............George Mikan, Minn | 1698 | 1976–77 ..............Pete Maravich, NO | 31.1 | |
| 1949–50 ..............George Mikan, Minn | 1865 | 1977–78 ..............George Gervin, SA | 27.2 | |
| 1950–51 ..............George Mikan, Minn | 1932 | 1978–79 ..............George Gervin, SA | 29.6 | |
| 1951–52 ..............Paul Arizin, Phil | 1674 | 1979–80 ..............George Gervin, SA | 33.1 | |
| 1952–53 ..............Neil Johnston, Phil | 1564 | 1980–81 ..............Adrian Dantley, Utah | 30.7 | |
| 1953–54 ..............Neil Johnston, Phil | 1759 | 1981–82 ..............George Gervin, SA | 32.3 | |
| 1954–55 ..............Neil Johnston, Phil | 1631 | 1982–83 ..............Alex English, Den | 28.4 | |
| 1955–56 ..............Bob Pettit, StL | 1849 | 1983–84 ..............Adrian Dantley, Utah | 30.6 | |
| 1956–57 ..............Paul Arizin, Phil | 1817 | 1984–85 ..............Bernard King, NY | 32.9 | |
| 1957–58 ..............George Yardley, Det | 2001 | 1985–86 ..............Dominique Wilkins, Atl | 30.3 | |
| 1958–59 ..............Bob Pettit, StL | 2105 | 1986–87 ..............Michael Jordan, Chi | 37.1 | |
| 1959–60 ..............Wilt Chamberlain, Phil | 2707 | 1987–88 ..............Michael Jordan, Chi | 35.0 | |
| 1960–61 ..............Wilt Chamberlain, Phil | 3033 | 1988–89 ..............Michael Jordan, Chi | 32.5 | |
| 1961–62 ..............Wilt Chamberlain, Phil | 4029 | 1989–90 ..............Michael Jordan, Chi | 33.6 | |
| 1962–63 ..............Wilt Chamberlain, SF | 3586 | 1990–91 ..............Michael Jordan, Chi | 31.5 | |
| 1963–64 ..............Wilt Chamberlain, SF | 2948 | 1991–92 ..............Michael Jordan, Chi | 30.1 | |
| 1964–65 ..............Wilt Chamberlain, SF-Phil | 2534 | 1992–93 ..............Michael Jordan, Chi | 32.6 | |
| 1965–66 ..............Wilt Chamberlain, Phil | 2649 | 1993–94 ..............David Robinson, SA | 29.8 | |
| 1966–67 ..............Rick Barry, SF | 2775 | 1994–95 ..............Shaquille O'Neal, Orl | 29.3 | |
| 1967–68 ..............Dave Bing, Det | 2142 | 1995–96 ..............Michael Jordan, Chi | 30.4 | |
| 1968–69 ..............Elvin Hayes, SD | 2327 | 1996–97 ..............Michael Jordan, Chi | 29.6 | |
| 1969–70 ..............Jerry West, LA | *31.2 | 1997–98 ..............Michael Jordan, Chi | 28.7 | |
| 1970–71 ..............Kareem Abdul-Jabbar, Mil | 31.7 | 1998–99 ..............Allen Iverson, Phil | 26.8 | |
| 1971–72 ..............Kareem Abdul-Jabbar, Mil | 34.8 | 1999–00 ..............Shaquille O'Neal, LA Lakers | 29.7 | |
| 1972–73 ..............Nate Archibald, KC-Oma | 34.0 | 2000–01 ..............Allen Iverson, Phil | 31.1 | |
| 1973–74 ..............Bob McAdoo, Buff | 30.6 | | | |

*Based on per game average since 1969–70.

## Rebounding

| | | | |
|---|---|---|---|
| 1950–51 ..............Dolph Schayes, Syr | 1080 | 1961–62 ..............Wilt Chamberlain, Phil | 2052 |
| 1951–52 ..............Larry Foust, FW | 880 | 1962–63 ..............Wilt Chamberlain, SF | 1946 |
| .................................Mel Hutchins, Mil | 880 | 1963–64 ..............Bill Russell, Bos | 1930 |
| 1952–53 ..............George Mikan, Minn | 1007 | 1964–65 ..............Bill Russell, Bos | 1878 |
| 1953–54 ..............Harry Gallatin, NY | 1098 | 1965–66 ..............Wilt Chamberlain, Phil | 1943 |
| 1954–55 ..............Neil Johnston, Phil | 1085 | 1966–67 ..............Wilt Chamberlain, Phil | 1957 |
| 1955–56 ..............Bob Pettit, StL | 1164 | 1967–68 ..............Wilt Chamberlain, Phil | 1952 |
| 1956–57 ..............Maurice Stokes, Roch | 1256 | 1968–69 ..............Wilt Chamberlain, LA | 1712 |
| 1957–58 ..............Bill Russell, Bos | 1564 | 1969–70 ..............Elvin Hayes, SD | *16.9 |
| 1958–59 ..............Bill Russell, Bos | 1612 | 1970–71 ..............Wilt Chamberlain, LA | 18.2 |
| 1959–60 ..............Wilt Chamberlain, Phil | 1941 | 1971–72 ..............Wilt Chamberlain, LA | 19.2 |
| 1960–61 ..............Wilt Chamberlain, Phil | 2149 | 1972–73 ..............Wilt Chamberlain, LA | 18.6 |
| | | 1973–74 ..............Elvin Hayes, Capital | 18.1 |

## Rebounding *(Cont.)*

| | | |
|---|---|---|
| 1974–75 | Wes Unseld, Wash | 14.8 |
| 1975–76 | Kareem Abdul-Jabbar, LA | 16.9 |
| 1976–77 | Bill Walton, Port | 14.4 |
| 1977–78 | Len Robinson, NO | 15.7 |
| 1978–79 | Moses Malone, Hou | 17.6 |
| 1979–80 | Swen Nater, SD | 15.0 |
| 1980–81 | Moses Malone, Hou | 14.8 |
| 1981–82 | Moses Malone, Hou | 14.7 |
| 1982–83 | Moses Malone, Phil | 15.3 |
| 1983–84 | Moses Malone, Phil | 13.4 |
| 1984–85 | Moses Malone, Phil | 13.1 |
| 1985–86 | Bill Laimbeer, Det | 13.1 |
| 1986–87 | Charles Barkley, Phil | 14.6 |
| 1987–88 | Michael Cage, LA Clippers | 13.0 |
| 1988–89 | Hakeem Olajuwon, Hou | 13.5 |
| 1989–90 | Hakeem Olajuwon, Hou | 14.0 |
| 1990–91 | David Robinson, SA | 13.0 |
| 1991–92 | Dennis Rodman, Det | 18.7 |
| 1992–93 | Dennis Rodman, Det | 18.3 |
| 1993–94 | Dennis Rodman, SA | 17.3 |
| 1994–95 | Dennis Rodman, SA | 16.8 |
| 1995–96 | Dennis Rodman, Chi | 14.9 |
| 1996–97 | Dennis Rodman, Chi | 16.1 |
| 1997–98 | Dennis Rodman, Chi | 15.0 |
| 1998–99 | Chris Webber, Sac | 13.0 |
| 1999–00 | Dikembe Mutombo, Atl | 14.1 |
| 2000–01 | Dikembe Mutombo, Atl | 13.5 |

*Based on per game average since 1969–70.

## Assists

| | | |
|---|---|---|
| 1946–47 | Ernie Calverly, Prov | 202 |
| 1947–48 | Howie Dallmar, Phil | 120 |
| 1948–49 | Bob Davies, Roch | 321 |
| 1949–50 | Dick McGuire, NY | 386 |
| 1950–51 | Andy Phillip, Phil | 414 |
| 1951–52 | Andy Phillip, Phil | 539 |
| 1952–53 | Bob Cousy, Bos | 547 |
| 1953–54 | Bob Cousy, Bos | 578 |
| 1954–55 | Bob Cousy, Bos | 557 |
| 1955–56 | Bob Cousy, Bos | 642 |
| 1956–57 | Bob Cousy, Bos | 478 |
| 1957–58 | Bob Cousy, Bos | 463 |
| 1958–59 | Bob Cousy, Bos | 557 |
| 1959–60 | Bob Cousy, Bos | 715 |
| 1960–61 | Oscar Robertson, Cin | 690 |
| 1961–62 | Oscar Robertson, Cin | 899 |
| 1962–63 | Guy Rodgers, SF | 825 |
| 1963–64 | Oscar Robertson, Cin | 868 |
| 1964–65 | Oscar Robertson, Cin | 861 |
| 1965–66 | Oscar Robertson, Cin | 847 |
| 1966–67 | Guy Rodgers, Chi | 908 |
| 1967–68 | Wilt Chamberlain, Phil | 702 |
| 1968–69 | Oscar Robertson, Cin | 772 |
| 1969–70 | Len Wilkens, Sea | *9.1 |
| 1970–71 | Norm Van Lier, Cin | 10.1 |
| 1971–72 | Jerry West, LA | 9.7 |
| 1972–73 | Nate Archibald, KC-Oma | 11.4 |
| 1973–74 | Ernie DiGregorio, Buff | 8.2 |
| 1974–75 | Kevin Porter, Wash | 8.0 |
| 1975–76 | Don Watts, Sea | 8.1 |
| 1976–77 | Don Buse, Ind | 8.5 |
| 1977–78 | Kevin Porter, NJ-Det | 10.2 |
| 1978–79 | Kevin Porter, Det | 13.4 |
| 1979–80 | Micheal Richardson, NY | 10.1 |
| 1980–81 | Kevin Porter, Wash | 9.1 |
| 1981–82 | Johnny Moore, SA | 9.6 |
| 1982–83 | Magic Johnson, LA | 10.5 |
| 1983–84 | Magic Johnson, LA | 13.1 |
| 1984–85 | Isiah Thomas, Det | 13.9 |
| 1985–86 | Magic Johnson, LA Lakers | 12.6 |
| 1986–87 | Magic Johnson, LA Lakers | 12.2 |
| 1987–88 | John Stockton, Utah | 13.8 |
| 1988–89 | John Stockton, Utah | 13.6 |
| 1989–90 | John Stockton, Utah | 14.5 |
| 1990–91 | John Stockton, Utah | 14.2 |
| 1991–92 | John Stockton, Utah | 13.7 |
| 1992–93 | John Stockton, Utah | 12.0 |
| 1993–94 | John Stockton, Utah | 12.6 |
| 1994–95 | John Stockton, Utah | 12.3 |
| 1995–96 | John Stockton, Utah | 11.2 |
| 1996–97 | Mark Jackson, Ind | 11.4 |
| 1997–98 | Rod Strickland, Wash | 10.1 |
| 1998–99 | Jason Kidd, Phoe | 10.8 |
| 1999–00 | Jason Kidd, Phoe | 10.1 |
| 2000–01 | Jason Kidd, Phoe | 9.8 |

*Based on per game average since 1969–70.

## Field-Goal Percentage

| | | |
|---|---|---|
| 1946–47 | Bob Feerick, Wash | 40.1 |
| 1947–48 | Bob Feerick, Wash | 34.0 |
| 1948–49 | Arnie Risen, Roch | 42.3 |
| 1949–50 | Alex Groza, Ind | 47.8 |
| 1950–51 | Alex Groza, Ind | 47.0 |
| 1951–52 | Paul Arizin, Phil | 44.8 |
| 1952–53 | Neil Johnston, Phil | 45.2 |
| 1953–54 | Ed Macauley, Bos | 48.6 |
| 1954–55 | Larry Foust, FW | 48.7 |
| 1955–56 | Neil Johnston, Phil | 45.7 |
| 1956–57 | Neil Johnston, Phil | 44.7 |
| 1957–58 | Jack Twyman, Cin | 45.2 |
| 1958–59 | Ken Sears, NY | 49.0 |
| 1959–60 | Ken Sears, NY | 47.7 |
| 1960–61 | Wilt Chamberlain, Phil | 50.9 |
| 1961–62 | Walt Bellamy, Chi | 51.9 |
| 1962–63 | Wilt Chamberlain, SF | 52.8 |
| 1963–64 | Jerry Lucas, Cin | 52.7 |
| 1964–65 | Wilt Chamberlain, SF-Phil | 51.0 |
| 1965–66 | Wilt Chamberlain, Phil | 54.0 |
| 1966–67 | Wilt Chamberlain, Phil | 68.3 |
| 1967–68 | Wilt Chamberlain, Phil | 59.5 |
| 1968–69 | Wilt Chamberlain, LA | 58.3 |
| 1969–70 | Johnny Green, Cin | 55.9 |
| 1970–71 | Johnny Green, Cin | 58.7 |
| 1971–72 | Wilt Chamberlain, LA | 64.9 |
| 1972–73 | Wilt Chamberlain, LA | 72.7 |
| 1973–74 | Bob McAdoo, Buff | 54.7 |
| 1974–75 | Don Nelson, Bos | 53.9 |
| 1975–76 | Wes Unseld, Wash | 56.1 |
| 1976–77 | Kareem Abdul-Jabbar, LA | 57.9 |
| 1977–78 | Bobby Jones, Den | 57.8 |
| 1978–79 | Cedric Maxwell, Bos | 58.4 |
| 1979–80 | Cedric Maxwell, Bos | 60.9 |
| 1980–81 | Artis Gilmore, Chi | 67.0 |
| 1981–82 | Artis Gilmore, Chi | 65.2 |
| 1982–83 | Artis Gilmore, SA | 62.6 |
| 1983–84 | Artis Gilmore, SA | 63.1 |
| 1984–85 | James Donaldson, LA Clippers | 63.7 |
| 1985–86 | Steve Johnson, SA | 63.2 |

### Field-Goal Percentage *(Cont.)*

| | | | | | |
|---|---|---|---|---|---|
| 1986–87 | Kevin McHale, Bos | 60.4 | 1994–95 | Chris Gatling, GS | 63.3 |
| 1987–88 | Kevin McHale, Bos | 60.4 | 1995–96 | Gheorghe Muresan, Wash | 58.4 |
| 1988–89 | Dennis Rodman, Det | 59.5 | 1996–97 | Gheorghe Muresan, Wash | 60.4 |
| 1989–90 | Mark West, Phoe | 62.5 | 1997–98 | Shaquille O'Neal, LA Lakers | 58.4 |
| 1990–91 | Buck Williams, Port | 60.2 | 1998–99 | Shaquille O'Neal, LA Lakers | 57.6 |
| 1991–92 | Buck Williams, Port | 60.4 | 1999–00 | Shaquille O'Neal, LA Lakers | 57.4 |
| 1992–93 | Cedric Ceballos, Phoe | 57.6 | 2000–01 | Shaquille O'Neal, LA Lakers | 57.2 |
| 1993–94 | Shaquille O'Neal, Orl | 59.9 | | | |

### Free-Throw Percentage

| | | | | | |
|---|---|---|---|---|---|
| 1946–47 | Fred Scolari, Wash | 81.1 | 1974–75 | Rick Barry, GS | 90.4 |
| 1947–48 | Bob Feerick, Wash | 78.8 | 1975–76 | Rick Barry, GS | 92.3 |
| 1948–49 | Bob Feerick, Wash | 85.9 | 1976–77 | Ernie DiGregorio, Buff | 94.5 |
| 1949–50 | Max Zaslofsky, Chi | 84.3 | 1977–78 | Rick Barry, GS | 92.4 |
| 1950–51 | Joe Fulks, Phil | 85.5 | 1978–79 | Rick Barry, Hou | 94.7 |
| 1951–52 | Bob Wanzer, Roch | 90.4 | 1979–80 | Rick Barry, Hou | 93.5 |
| 1952–53 | Bill Sharman, Bos | 85.0 | 1980–81 | Calvin Murphy, Hou | 95.8 |
| 1953–54 | Bill Sharman, Bos | 84.4 | 1981–82 | Kyle Macy, Phoe | 89.9 |
| 1954–55 | Bill Sharman, Bos | 89.7 | 1982–83 | Calvin Murphy, Hou | 92.0 |
| 1955–56 | Bill Sharman, Bos | 86.7 | 1983–84 | Larry Bird, Bos | 88.8 |
| 1956–57 | Bill Sharman, Bos | 90.5 | 1984–85 | Kyle Macy, Phoe | 90.7 |
| 1957–58 | Dolph Schayes, Syr | 90.4 | 1985–86 | Larry Bird, Bos | 89.6 |
| 1958–59 | Bill Sharman, Bos | 93.2 | 1986–87 | Larry Bird, Bos | 91.0 |
| 1959–60 | Dolph Schayes, Syr | 89.2 | 1987–88 | Jack Sikma, Mil | 92.2 |
| 1960–61 | Bill Sharman, Bos | 92.1 | 1988–89 | Magic Johnson, LA Lakers | 91.1 |
| 1961–62 | Dolph Schayes, Syr | 89.6 | 1989–90 | Larry Bird, Bos | 93.0 |
| 1962–63 | Larry Costello, Syr | 88.1 | 1990–91 | Reggie Miller, Ind | 91.8 |
| 1963–64 | Oscar Robertson, Cin | 85.3 | 1991–92 | Mark Price, Clev | 94.7 |
| 1964–65 | Larry Costello, Phil | 87.7 | 1992–93 | Mark Price, Clev | 94.8 |
| 1965–66 | Larry Siegfried, Bos | 88.1 | 1993–94 | Mahmoud Abdul-Rauf, Den | 95.6 |
| 1966–67 | Adrian Smith, Cin | 90.3 | 1994–95 | Spud Webb, Sac | 93.4 |
| 1967–68 | Oscar Robertson, Cin | 87.3 | 1995–96 | Mahmoud Abdul-Rauf, Den | 93.0 |
| 1968–69 | Larry Siegfried, Bos | 86.4 | 1996–97 | Mark Price, GS | 90.6 |
| 1969–70 | Flynn Robinson, Mil | 89.8 | 1997–98 | Chris Mullin, Ind | 93.9 |
| 1970–71 | Chet Walker, Chi | 85.9 | 1998–99 | Reggie Miller, Ind | 91.5 |
| 1971–72 | Jack Marin, Balt | 89.4 | 1999–00 | Jeff Hornacek, Utah | 95.0 |
| 1972–73 | Rick Barry, GS | 90.2 | 2000–01 | Reggie Miller, Ind | 92.8 |
| 1973–74 | Ernie DiGregorio, Buff | 90.2 | | | |

### Three-Point Field-Goal Percentage

| | | | | | |
|---|---|---|---|---|---|
| 1979–80 | Fred Brown, Sea | 44.3 | 1990–91 | Jim Les, Sac | 46.1 |
| 1980–81 | Brian Taylor, SD | 38.3 | 1991–92 | Dana Barros, Sea | 44.6 |
| 1981–82 | Campy Russell, NY | 43.9 | 1992–93 | B.J. Armstrong, Chi | 45.3 |
| 1982–83 | Mike Dunleavy, SA | 34.5 | 1993–94 | Tracy Murray, Por | 45.9 |
| 1983–84 | Darrell Griffith, Utah | 36.1 | 1994–95 | Steve Kerr, Chi | 52.4 |
| 1984–85 | Byron Scott, LA Lakers | 43.3 | 1995–96 | Tim Legler, Wash | 52.2 |
| 1985–86 | Craig Hodges, Mil | 45.1 | 1996–97 | Kevin Gamble, Sac | 48.2 |
| 1986–87 | Kiki Vandeweghe, Por | 48.1 | 1997–98 | Dale Ellis, Sea | 46.0 |
| 1987–88 | Craig Hodges, Mil-Phoe | 49.1 | 1998–99 | Dell Curry, Char | 47.6 |
| 1988–89 | Jon Sundvold, Mia | 52.2 | 1999–00 | Hubert Davis, Dall | 49.1 |
| 1989–90 | Steve Kerr, Clev | 50.7 | 2000–01 | Brent Barry, Sea | 47.6 |

### Steals

| | | | | | |
|---|---|---|---|---|---|
| 1973–74 | Larry Steele, Por | 2.68 | 1987–88 | Michael Jordan, Chi | 3.16 |
| 1974–75 | Rick Barry, GS | 2.85 | 1988–89 | John Stockton, Utah | 3.21 |
| 1975–76 | Don Watts, Sea | 3.18 | 1989–90 | Michael Jordan, Chi | 2.77 |
| 1976–77 | Don Buse, Ind | 3.47 | 1990–91 | Alvin Robertson, Mil | 3.04 |
| 1977–78 | Ron Lee, Phoe | 2.74 | 1991–92 | John Stockton, Utah | 2.98 |
| 1978–79 | M.L. Carr, Det | 2.46 | 1992–93 | Michael Jordan, Chi | 2.83 |
| 1979–80 | Micheal Richardson, NY | 3.23 | 1993–94 | Nate McMillan, Sea | 2.96 |
| 1980–81 | Magic Johnson, LA | 3.43 | 1994–95 | Scottie Pippen, Chi | 2.94 |
| 1981–82 | Magic Johnson, LA | 2.67 | 1995–96 | Gary Payton, Sea | 2.85 |
| 1982–83 | Micheal Richardson, GS-NJ | 2.84 | 1996–97 | Mookie Blaylock, Atl | 2.72 |
| 1983–84 | Rickey Green, Utah | 2.65 | 1997–98 | Mookie Blaylock, Atl | 2.61 |
| 1984–85 | Micheal Richardson, NJ | 2.96 | 1998–99 | Kendall Gill, NJ | 2.68 |
| 1985–86 | Alvin Robertson, SA | 3.67 | 1999–00 | Eddie Jones, Char | 2.67 |
| 1986–87 | Alvin Robertson, SA | 3.21 | 2000–01 | Allen Iverson, Phil | 2.51 |

## Blocked Shots

| | | | | | |
|---|---|---|---|---|---|
| 1973–74 | Elmore Smith, LA | 4.85 | 1987–88 | Mark Eaton, Utah | 3.71 |
| 1974–75 | Kareem Abdul-Jabbar, Mil | 3.26 | 1988–89 | Manute Bol, GS | 4.31 |
| 1975–76 | Kareem Abdul-Jabbar, LA | 4.12 | 1989–90 | Hakeem Olajuwon, Hou | 4.59 |
| 1976–77 | Bill Walton, Port | 3.25 | 1990–91 | Hakeem Olajuwon, Hou | 3.95 |
| 1977–78 | George Johnson, NJ | 3.38 | 1991–92 | David Robinson, SA | 4.49 |
| 1978–79 | Kareem Abdul-Jabbar, LA | 3.95 | 1992–93 | Hakeem Olajuwon, Hou | 4.17 |
| 1979–80 | Kareem Abdul-Jabbar, LA | 3.41 | 1993–94 | Dikembe Mutombo, Den | 4.10 |
| 1980–81 | George Johnson, SA | 3.39 | 1994–95 | Dikembe Mutombo, Den | 3.91 |
| 1981–82 | George Johnson, SA | 3.12 | 1995–96 | Dikembe Mutombo, Den | 4.49 |
| 1982–83 | Wayne Rollins, Atl | 4.29 | 1996–97 | Shawn Bradley, NJ | 3.40 |
| 1983–84 | Mark Eaton, Utah | 4.28 | 1997–98 | Marcus Camby, Tor | 3.65 |
| 1984–85 | Mark Eaton, Utah | 5.56 | 1998–99 | Alonzo Mourning, Mia | 3.91 |
| 1985–86 | Manute Bol, Wash | 4.96 | 1999–00 | Alonzo Mourning, Mia | 3.72 |
| 1986–87 | Mark Eaton, Utah | 4.06 | 2000–01 | Theo Ratliff, Phil/Atl | 3.74 |

# NBA All-Star Game Results

| Year | Result | Site | Winning Coach | Most Valuable Player |
|---|---|---|---|---|
| 1951 | East 111, West 94 | Boston | Joe Lapchick | Ed Macauley, Bos |
| 1952 | East 108, West 91 | Boston | Al Cervi | Paul Arizin, Phil |
| 1953 | West 79, East 75 | Ft Wayne | John Kundla | George Mikan, Minn |
| 1954 | East 98, West 93 (OT) | New York | Joe Lapchick | Bob Cousy, Bos |
| 1955 | East 100, West 91 | New York | Al Cervi | Bill Sharman, Bos |
| 1956 | West 108, East 94 | Rochester | Charley Eckman | Bob Pettit, StL |
| 1957 | East 109, West 97 | Boston | Red Auerbach | Bob Cousy, Bos |
| 1958 | East 130, West 118 | St Louis | Red Auerbach | Bob Pettit, StL |
| 1959 | West 124, East 108 | Detroit | Ed Macauley | B. Pettit, StL/ E. Baylor, Minn |
| 1960 | East 125, West 115 | Philadelphia | Red Auerbach | Wilt Chamberlain, Phil |
| 1961 | West 153, East 131 | Syracuse | Paul Seymour | Oscar Robertson, Cin |
| 1962 | West 150, East 130 | St Louis | Fred Schaus | Bob Pettit, StL |
| 1963 | East 115, West 108 | Los Angeles | Red Auerbach | Bill Russell, Bos |
| 1964 | East 111, West 107 | Boston | Red Auerbach | Oscar Robertson, Cin |
| 1965 | East 124, West 123 | St Louis | Red Auerbach | Jerry Lucas, Cin |
| 1966 | East 137, West 94 | Cincinnati | Red Auerbach | Adrian Smith, Cin |
| 1967 | West 135, East 120 | San Francisco | Fred Schaus | Rick Barry, SF |
| 1968 | East 144, West 124 | New York | Alex Hannum | Hal Greer, Phil |
| 1969 | East 123, West 112 | Baltimore | Gene Shue | Oscar Robertson, Cin |
| 1970 | East 142, West 135 | Philadelphia | Red Holzman | Willis Reed, NY |
| 1971 | West 108, East 107 | San Diego | Larry Costello | Lenny Wilkens, Sea |
| 1972 | West 112, East 110 | Los Angeles | Bill Sharman | Jerry West, LA |
| 1973 | East 104, West 84 | Chicago | Tom Heinsohn | Dave Cowens, Bos |
| 1974 | West 134, East 123 | Seattle | Larry Costello | Bob Lanier, Det |
| 1975 | East 108, West 102 | Phoenix | K.C. Jones | Walt Frazier, NY |
| 1976 | East 123, West 109 | Philadelphia | Tom Heinsohn | Dave Bing, Wash |
| 1977 | West 125, East 124 | Milwaukee | Larry Brown | Julius Erving, Phil |
| 1978 | East 133, West 125 | Atlanta | Billy Cunningham | Randy Smith, Buff |
| 1979 | West 134, East 129 | Detroit | Lenny Wilkens | David Thompson, Den |
| 1980 | East 144, West 135 (OT) | Washington | Billy Cunningham | George Gervin, SA |
| 1981 | East 123, West 120 | Cleveland | Billy Cunningham | Nate Archibald, Bos |
| 1982 | East 120, West 118 | New Jersey | Bill Fitch | Larry Bird, Bos |
| 1983 | East 132, West 123 | Los Angeles | Billy Cunningham | Julius Erving, Phil |
| 1984 | East 154, West 145 (OT) | Denver | K.C. Jones | Isiah Thomas, Det |
| 1985 | West 140, East 129 | Indiana | Pat Riley | Ralph Sampson, Hou |
| 1986 | East 139, West 132 | Dallas | K.C. Jones | Isiah Thomas, Det |
| 1987 | West 154, East 149 (OT) | Seattle | Pat Riley | Tom Chambers, Sea |
| 1988 | East 138, West 133 | Chicago | Mike Fratello | Michael Jordan, Chi |
| 1989 | West 143, East 134 | Houston | Pat Riley | Karl Malone, Utah |
| 1990 | East 130, West 113 | Miami | Chuck Daly | Magic Johnson, LA Lakers |
| 1991 | East 116, West 114 | Charlotte | Chris Ford | Charles Barkley, Phil |
| 1992 | West 153, East 113 | Orlando | Don Nelson | Magic Johnson, LA Lakers |
| 1993 | West 135, East 132 | Salt Lake City | Paul Westphal | K. Malone/ J. Stockton ,Utah |
| 1994 | East 127, West 118 | Minneapolis | Lenny Wilkens | Scottie Pippen, Chi |
| 1995 | West 139, East 112 | Phoenix | Paul Westphal | Mitch Richmond, Sac |
| 1996 | East 129, West 118 | San Antonio | Phil Jackson | Michael Jordan, Chi |
| 1997 | East 132, West 120 | Cleveland | Doug Collins | Glen Rice, Char |
| 1998 | East 135, West 114 | New York | Larry Bird | Michael Jordan, Chi |
| 1999 | Cancelled due to lockout. | | | |
| 2000 | West 137, East 126 | Oakland | Phil Jackson | Shaquille O'Neal, LA Lakers/ Tim Duncan, SA |
| 2001 | East 111, West 110 | Washington | Larry Brown | Allen Iverson, Phil |

# Members of the Basketball Hall of Fame

## Contributors

Senda Abbott (1984)
Forest C. (Phog) Allen (1959)
Clair F. Bee (1967)
Danny Biasone (2000)
Walter A. Brown (1965)
John W. Bunn (1964)
Bob Douglas (1971)
Al Duer (1981)
Wayne Embry (1999)
Clifford Fagan (1983)
Harry A. Fisher (1973)
Larry Fleisher (1991)
Edward Gottlieb (1971)
Luther H. Gulick (1959)
Lester Harrison (1979)
Ferenc Hepp (1980)

Edward J. Hickox (1959)
Paul D. (Tony) Hinkle (1965)
Ned Irish (1964)
R. William Jones (1964)
J. Walter Kennedy (1980)
Emil S. Liston (1974)
John B. McLendon (1978)
Bill Mokray (1965)
Ralph Morgan (1959)
Frank Morgenweck (1962)
James Naismith (1959)
Peter F. Newell (1978)
C.M. Newton (2000)
John J. O'Brien (1961)
Larry O'Brien (1991)
Harold G. Olsen (1959)

Maurice Podoloff (1973)
H. V. Porter (1960)
William A. Reid (1963)
Elmer Ripley (1972)
Lynn W. St. John (1962)
Abe Saperstein (1970)
Arthur A. Schabinger (1961)
Amos Alonzo Stagg (1959)
Boris Stankovic (1991)
Edward Steitz (1983)
Chuck Taylor (1968)
Oswald Tower (1959)
Arthur L. Trester (1961)
Clifford Wells (1971)
Lou Wilke (1982)
Fred Zollner (1999)

## Players

Kareem Abdul-Jabbar (1995)
Nate (Tiny) Archibald (1991)
Paul J. Arizin (1977)
Thomas B. Barlow (1980)
Rick Barry (1987)
Elgin Baylor (1976)
John Beckman (1972)
Walt Bellamy (1993)
Sergei Belov (1992)
Dave Bing (1990)
Larry Bird (1998)
Carol Blazejowski (1994)
Bennie Borgmann (1961)
Bill Bradley (1982)
Joseph Brennan (1974)
Al Cervi (1984)
Wilt Chamberlain (1978)
Charles (Tarzan) Cooper (1976)
Kresimir Cosic (1996)
Bob Cousy (1970)
Dave Cowens (1991)
Joan Crawford (1997)
Billy Cunningham (1986)
Denise Curry (1997)
Bob Davies (1969)
Forrest S. DeBernardi (1961)
Dave DeBusschere (1982)
H.G. (Dutch) Dehnert (1968)
Anne Donovan (1995)
Paul Endacott (1971)
Alex English (1997)
Julius Erving (1993)
Harold (Bud) Foster (1964)
Walter (Clyde) Frazier (1987)
Max (Marty) Friedman (1971)
Joe Fulks (1977)
Lauren (Laddie) Gale (1976)
Harry (the Horse) Gallatin (1991)
William Gates (1989)
George Gervin (1996)

Tom Gola (1975)
Gail Goodrich (1996)
Hal Greer (1981)
Robert (Ace) Gruenig (1963)
Clifford O. Hagan (1977)
Victor Hanson (1960)
John Havlicek (1983)
Connie Hawkins (1992)
Elvin Hayes (1990)
Marques Haynes (1998)
Tom Heinsohn (1986)
Nat Holman (1964)
Robert J. Houbregs (1987)
Bailey Howell (1997)
Chuck Hyatt (1959)
Dan Issel (1993)
Harry (Buddy) Jeannette (1994)
William C. Johnson (1976)
D. Neil Johnston (1990)
K.C. Jones (1989)
Sam Jones (1983)
Edward (Moose) Krause (1975)
Bob Kurland (1961)
Bob Lanier (1992)
Joe Lapchick (1966)
Nancy Lieberman-Cline (1996)
Clyde Lovellette (1988)
Jerry Lucas (1979)
Angelo (Hank) Luisetti (1959)
C. Edward Macauley (1960)
Moses Malone (2001)
Peter P. Maravich (1987)
Slater Martin (1981)
Bob McAdoo (2000)
Branch McCracken (1960)
Jack McCracken (1962)
Bobby McDermott (1988)
Dick McGuire (1993)
Kevin McHale (1999)
Ann Meyers (1993)

George L. Mikan (1959)
Vern Mikkelsen (1995)
Cheryl Miller (1995)
Earl Monroe (1990)
Calvin Murphy (1993)
Charles (Stretch) Murphy (1960)
H. O. (Pat) Page (1962)
Bob Pettit (1970)
Andy Phillip (1961)
Jim Pollard (1977)
Frank Ramsey (1981)
Willis Reed (1981)
Arnie Risen (1998)
Oscar Robertson (1979)
John S. Roosma (1961)
Bill Russell (1974)
John (Honey) Russell (1964)
Adolph Schayes (1972)
Ernest J. Schmidt (1973)
John J. Schommer (1959)
Barney Sedran (1962)
Uljana Semjonova (1993)
Bill Sharman (1975)
Christian Steinmetz (1961)
Lusia Harris Stewart (1992)
Isiah Thomas (2000)
David Thompson (1996)
John A. (Cat) Thompson (1962)
Nate Thurmond (1984)
Jack Twyman (1982)
Wes Unseld (1988)
Robert (Fuzzy) Vandivier (1974)
Edward A. Wachter (1961)
Bill Walton (1993)
Robert F. Wanzer (1987)
Jerry West (1979)
Nera White (1992)
Lenny Wilkens (1989)
John R. Wooden (1960)
George (Bird) Yardley (1996)

## Coaches

Harold Anderson (1984)
Red Auerbach (1968)
Sam Barry (1978)
Ernest A. Blood (1960)
Howard G. Cann (1967)
H. Clifford Carlson (1959)

Lou Carnesecca (1992)
Ben Carnevale (1969)
Pete Carril (1997)
Everett Case (1981)
John Chaney (2001)
Jody Conradt (1998)

Denny Crum (1994)
Chuck Daly (1994)
Everett S. Dean (1966)
Antonio Diaz-Miguel (1997)
Edgar A. Diddle (1971)
Bruce Drake (1972)

Note: Year of election in parentheses.

## Coaches (Cont.)

Clarence Gaines (1981)
Jack Gardner (1983)
Amory T. (Slats) Gill (1967)
Aleksandr Gomelsky (1995)
Alex Hannum (1998)
Marv Harshman (1984)
Don Haskins (1997)
Edgar S. Hickey (1978)
Howard A. Hobson (1965)
Red Holzman (1986)
Hank Iba (1968)
Alvin F. (Doggie) Julian (1967)
Frank W. Keaney (1960)
George E. Keogan (1961)
Bob Knight (1991)

Mike Krzyzewski (2001)
John Kundla (1995)
Ward L. Lambert (1960)
Harry Litwack (1975)
Kenneth D. Loeffler (1964)
A.C. (Dutch) Lonborg (1972)
Arad A. McCutchan (1980)
Al McGuire (1992)
Frank McGuire (1976)
Walter E. Meanwell (1959)
Raymond J. Meyer (1978)
Ralph Miller (1988)
Billie Moore (1999)
Aleksandar Nikolic (1998)
Jack Ramsay (1992)

Cesare Rubini (1994)
Adolph F. Rupp (1968)
Leonard D. Sachs (1961)
Everett F. Shelton (1979)
Dean Smith (1982)
Pat Summitt (2000)
Fred R. Taylor (1985)
Bertha Teague (1984)
John Thompson (1999)
Margaret Wade (1984)
Stanley H. Watts (1985)
Lenny Wilkens (1998)
John R. Wooden (1972)
Morgan Wooten (2000)
Phil Woolpert (1992)

## Referees

James E. Enright (1978)
George T. Hepbron (1960)
George Hoyt (1961)
Matthew P. Kennedy (1959)
Lloyd Leith (1982)
Zigmund J. Mihalik (1985)

John P. Nucatola (1977)
Ernest C. Quigley (1961)
J. Dallas Shirley (1979)
Earl Strom (1995)
David Tobey (1961)
David H. Walsh (1961)

## Teams

Buffalo Germans (1961)
First Team (1959)
Original Celtics (1959)
Renaissance (1963)

# ABA Champions

| Year | Champion | Series | Loser | Winning Coach |
|------|----------|--------|-------|---------------|
| 1968 | Pittsburgh Pipers | 4–3 | New Orleans Bucs | Vince Cazetta |
| 1969 | Oakland Oaks | 4–1 | Indiana Pacers | Alex Hannum |
| 1970 | Indiana Pacers | 4–2 | Los Angeles Stars | Bob Leonard |
| 1971 | Utah Stars | 4–3 | Kentucky Colonels | Bill Sharman |
| 1972 | Indiana Pacers | 4–2 | New York Nets | Bob Leonard |
| 1973 | Indiana Pacers | 4–3 | Kentucky Colonels | Bob Leonard |
| 1974 | New York Nets | 4–1 | Utah Stars | Kevin Loughery |
| 1975 | Kentucky Colonels | 4–1 | Indiana Pacers | Hubie Brown |
| 1976 | New York Nets | 4–2 | Denver Nuggets | Kevin Loughery |

# ABA Postseason Awards

## Most Valuable Player

| 1967–68 | Connie Hawkins, Pitt |
| 1968–69 | Mel Daniels, Ind |
| 1969–70 | Spencer Haywood, Den |
| 1970–71 | Mel Daniels, Ind |
| 1971–72 | Artis Gilmore, Ken |
| 1972–73 | Billy Cunningham, Car |
| 1973–74 | Julius Erving, NY |
| 1974–75 | Julius Erving, NY |
|         | George McGinnis, Ind |
| 1975–76 | Julius Erving, NY |

## Coach of the Year

| 1967–68 | Vince Cazetta, Pitt |
| 1968–69 | Alex Hannum, Oak |
| 1969–70 | Bill Sharman, LA |
|         | Joe Belmont, Den |
| 1970–71 | Al Bianchi, Vir |
| 1971–72 | Tom Nissalke, Dall |
| 1972–73 | Larry Brown, Car |
| 1973–74 | Babe McCarthy, Ken |
|         | Joe Mullaney, Utah |
| 1974–75 | Larry Brown, Den |
| 1975–76 | Larry Brown, Den |

## Rookie of the Year

| 1967–68 | Mel Daniels, Minn |
| 1968–69 | Warren Armstrong, Oak |
| 1969–70 | Spencer Haywood, Den |
| 1970–71 | Charlie Scott, Vir |
|         | Dan Issel, Ken |
| 1971–72 | Artis Gilmore, Ken |
| 1972–73 | Brian Taylor, NY |
| 1973–74 | Swen Nater, SA |
| 1974–75 | Marvin Barnes, StL |
| 1975–76 | David Thompson, Den |

# ABA Season Leaders

## Scoring

| | GP | Pts | Avg |
|---|---|---|---|
| 1967–68...Connie Hawkins, Pitt | 70 | 1875 | 26.8 |
| 1968–69...Rick Barry, Oak | 35 | 1190 | 34.0 |
| 1969–70...Spencer Haywood, Den | 84 | 2519 | 30.0 |
| 1970–71...Dan Issel, Ken | 83 | 2480 | 29.4 |
| 1971–72...Charlie Scott, Vir | 73 | 2524 | 34.6 |
| 1972–73...Julius Erving, Vir | 71 | 2268 | 31.9 |
| 1973–74...Julius Erving, NY | 84 | 2299 | 27.4 |
| 1974–75...George McGinnis, Ind | 79 | 2353 | 29.8 |
| 1975–76...Julius Erving, NY | 84 | 2462 | 29.3 |

## Assists

| | |
|---|---|
| 1967–68................Larry Brown, NO | 6.5 |
| 1968–69................Larry Brown, Oak | 7.1 |
| 1969–70................Larry Brown, Wash | 7.1 |
| 1970–71................Bill Melchionni, NY | 8.3 |
| 1971–72................Bill Melchionni, NY | 8.4 |
| 1972–73................Bill Melchionni, NY | 7.5 |
| 1973–74................Al Smith, Den | 8.2 |
| 1974–75................Mack Calvin, Den | 7.7 |
| 1975–76................Don Buse, Ind | 8.2 |

## Rebounds

| | |
|---|---|
| 1967–68................Mel Daniels, Minn | 15.6 |
| 1968–69................Mel Daniels, Ind | 16.5 |
| 1969–70................Spencer Haywood, Den | 19.5 |
| 1970–71................Mel Daniels, Ind | 18.0 |
| 1971–72................Artis Gilmore, Ken | 17.8 |
| 1972–73................Artis Gilmore, Ken | 17.5 |
| 1973–74................Artis Gilmore, Ken | 18.3 |
| 1974–75................Swen Nater, SA | 16.4 |
| 1975–76................Artis Gilmore, Ken | 15.5 |

## Steals

| | |
|---|---|
| 1973–74................Ted McClain, Car | 2.98 |
| 1974–75................Brian Taylor, NY | 2.80 |
| 1975–76................Don Buse, Ind | 4.12 |

## Blocked Shots

| | |
|---|---|
| 1973–74................Caldwell Jones, SD | 4.00 |
| 1974–75................Caldwell Jones, SD | 3.24 |
| 1975–76................Billy Paultz, SA | 3.05 |

# World Championship of Basketball

| Year | Winner | Runner-Up | Score | Site |
|---|---|---|---|---|
| 1950 ..........................Argentina | | United States | † | Rio de Janeiro |
| 1954 ..........................United States | | Brazil | † | Rio de Janeiro |
| 1959 ..........................Brazil | | United States | † | Santiago, Chile |
| 1963 ..........................Brazil | | Yugoslavia | † | Rio de Janeiro |
| 1967 ..........................Soviet Union | | Yugoslavia | † | Montevideo, Uruguay |
| 1970 ..........................Yugoslavia | | Brazil | † | Ljubljana, Yugoslavia |
| 1974 ..........................Soviet Union | | Yugoslavia | † | San Juan |
| 1978 ..........................Yugoslavia | | Soviet Union | 82–81 (OT) | Manila |
| 1982 ..........................Soviet Union | | United States | 95–94 | Cali, Colombia |
| 1986 ..........................United States | | Soviet Union | 87–85 | Madrid |
| 1990 ..........................Yugoslavia | | Soviet Union | 92–75 | Buenos Aires |
| 1994* ..........................United States | | Russia | 137–91 | Toronto |
| 1998 ..........................Yugoslavia | | Russia | 64–62 | Athens |

*U.S. professionals began competing in 1994. In 1998, a labor dispute resulted in a boycott of the World Championship by NBA stars; the U.S. roster was filled by members of the CBA and European professional leagues and college players.
†Result determined by overall record in final round of competition.

# THEY SAID IT

*Isaiah Rider, Los Angeles guard, on the Lakers' attitude toward him following his five-game suspension for violating the NBA antidrug program: "They're not really high on me."*

# College Basketball

Shane Battier and Mike
Dunleavy celebrate
Duke's national title

# Blue Angels

## Unlike their predecessors in Durham, who antagonized more fans than they inspired, the champs of 2000–01 were difficult not to like

### BY B.J. SCHECTER

FOR THE past decade and a half, Duke has been college basketball's version of the New York Yankees—the team everyone loves to hate. The Blue Devils are arrogant, their critics charge; they get all the breaks and all the calls. They also win with maddening consistency, having reached nine Final Fours since 1986. Nothing engenders enmity like success—just ask the Yankees—but it was awfully hard to hate the 2000–01 Duke team.

Sure, the Blue Devils won 29 of their first 33 games, were ranked No. 1 most of the way and caught their share of breaks, but the way the Blue Devils carried themselves on and off the court made this team unique. They weren't the spoilsports of the Bobby Hurley–Christian Laettner era or the prima donnas of the William Avery–Corey Maggette year. This team was, dare we say, likable.

The credit for this development can be shared by coach Mike Krzyzewski, whose steady guiding hand led the Blue Devils to their third national title, and the team's undisputed leader on the court, forward Shane Battier. Battier's route through college basketball is increasingly becoming the road less traveled: He was a star who stayed four years, who excelled on the hardwood and in the classroom. Indeed, Battier may have a brighter future off the court than on it, though he went sixth overall in the NBA draft. He is the selfless player every coach wishes he had, a natural leader whose court sense is second to none. Sophomore point guard Jason Williams scored more and usually had the ball in his hands when the game was on the line, but Battier did all the little things to put the Blue Devils in position to win games. He might draw a charge at a crucial time, make an out-of-nowhere block (his come-from-behind stuff of North Carolina's Joseph Forte in March was one of the highlights of the season), grab a key rebound or make a nifty pass; whatever Duke needed, Battier seemed to supply it every time out.

Confident but humble, respectful yet not without a killer instinct, Battier was almost too good to be true. His stature as the ultimate gentleman of the game was not lost

JOHN W. MCDONOUGH

on opponents. Before Duke's 82–72 victory over Arizona in the national championship game, Arizona's Richard Jefferson wryly summed up what Battier had accomplished in 2000–01. "He's the Player of the Year, Defender of the Year, Academic of the Year, Man of the Year," said Jefferson. "He's all-everything. Some people rank Shane Battier right below Jesus Christ."

To get a clear picture of Duke's season one need look no further than its four epic games with Maryland, of which the Blue Devils won three. In their first meeting in January, Duke was thoroughly outplayed in College Park, Md. Williams had one of his worst performances of the season, while Maryland played like a Final Four team—until the game's final minute, that is. Duke trailed by 10 points with 54 seconds remaining. Suddenly Williams came alive, scoring eight points in 13 seconds to help Duke tie the stunned Terrapins and send the game into overtime. The Blue Devils won 98–96. The shock of the loss sent Maryland reeling—the Terps lost four of their next five games and didn't regain their status as a title contender until the rematch at Cameron Indoor Stadium in February.

Few pundits gave Maryland a chance to win the second game. For one thing, Duke was playing extremely well, having won six of its last seven games. For another, it was senior night at Duke, and the Cameron Crazies were sure to be in full voice. But the Terps played their best game of the year, outplaying and outmuscling Duke and silencing the legendarily boisterous Duke faithful with a 91–80 victory. Worse for Duke was that center Carlos Boozer suffered a stress fracture in his right foot, a potentially season-ending injury. Duke's only weakness was its lack of depth, espe-

cially inside, and the loss of Boozer sorely taxed the Blue Devils' bench.

After the game a cake that was supposed to celebrate Battier's 122nd victory sat untouched in a corner of the locker room. Some Blue Devils hung their heads, others cried, and Krzyzewski went into a bunker. A former Army cadet who played for Bobby Knight at West Point, Krzyzewski stayed up all night with his assistants, kicking around ideas and plotting strategies to recover from both Boozer's injury and the devastating loss to the Terps.

Some fans wondered if Duke's chances for a national title had been quashed, but Krzyzewski took a proactive approach to keep them alive. He gave the players a day off, and then he and his staff established a training camp–like environment to get the team to refocus. He scheduled 6:30 a.m. practices for the next two days. "When

Coach starts calling 6:30 a.m. practices, you know it's serious," said senior J.D. Simpson.

Instead of becoming more regimented, however, Krzyzewski decided to loosen the reins. The Blue Devils didn't watch any tape or do any drills in their first practice after the Maryland loss; they scrimmaged for 45 minutes. "I was trained for that," said Krzyzewski. "Next play, let's go. Whether it's muddy or sunny, let's figure out a way to win."

They did and how: The Blue Devils wouldn't lose another game all season. After the Maryland loss Duke beat North Carolina by 14 in Chapel Hill, and things started rolling from there. "We don't have a system, a triple-post offense or anything like that," said sophomore forward Mike Dunleavy. "We just kind of play basketball. When you have that confidence that everybody on the floor can stick it, the other team knows it."

Duke's third game with Maryland came in the semifinals of the ACC tournament and proved that the Blue Devils were still the favorites to win it all—with or without Boozer. When Maryland guard Steve Blake drilled a three-pointer to tie the game at 82 with 8.1 seconds remaining, Williams drove the length of the floor and missed a layup in traffic. But senior swingman Nate James, who had recently lost his starting spot, tipped in the game-winner.

"When Carlos went down, the tendency would've been to bottle them up and over-coach them," Krzyzewski said. "Instead we let them grow wild."

The fourth meeting between Duke and Maryland came at the Final Four, in Minneapolis. Boozer had returned to the Blue Devils' lineup, and both teams were playing extremely well. The Terps jumped out to a 22-point lead late in the first half and appeared well on their way to a rout. Krzyzewski called his first desperation timeout of the season; it came only nine seconds before the first scheduled television timeout. He reminded his team what had turned around their season. "You can't play any worse," Krzyzewski told his

players. "What are you worried about? That you're going to lose by 40? We're already losing by 20, so will you just play?"

The Blue Devils cut the lead to 11 by halftime, caught the Terps early in the second half and then broke the game open, winning 95–84. Two nights later Arizona stayed with Duke for most of the championship game, but the Blue Devils used their poise and superb three-point shooting to pull away in the closing stages. Battier and Williams had stellar games as usual, but it was the previously struggling Dunleavy who made the biggest difference, sinking five three-pointers and scoring 18 of his 21 points in the second half. When Arizona clawed its way back into the game, Dunleavy killed the Wildcats' momentum with three three-pointers.

Afterward Battier found Krzyzewski and thanked his coach for showing so much faith in the team. As they hugged on the court, Battier told Coach K that the Blue Devils won this title for him. "It was really special for us to separate Coach from the pack," Battier said later. "A bunch of coaches have won two. Getting three makes you a legend."

The NCAA tournament has made many a legend, and this year was no different, as a few teams and several players made names for themselves. Marvin O'Connor, a junior guard from St. Joseph's, produced the best individual performance at the Big Dance, scoring 37 points in a second-round loss to Stanford. When O'Connor fouled out late in the game he was given a standing ovation by the partisan Stanford crowd, and Cardinal All-America Casey Jacobsen pulled him aside and said, "It was a pleasure being on the same court with you today."

Gonzaga, a Jesuit school in Spokane, Wash., with an enrollment of 4,500, made it to the Sweet 16 for the third consecutive year; and banged-up Temple, with only nine healthy players, reached the Elite Eight. Though the 2001 tournament had the greatest number of higher seeds eliminated in the first round since the tournament expanded to 64 teams in 1985 (13 of

**Woods (with ball) and Arizona shed early-season troubles to reach the title game.**

32), it was still a tough tournament for the little guys. That's because few small or mid-major schools were invited. The six power conferences received an unprecedented 35 bids, and, in an effort to accommodate an additional automatic bid (expanding the field to 65 teams) the powers that be made Winthrop and Northwestern State compete in a play-in game for the right to play No. 1–seeded Illinois.

There was the usual array of mammoth upsets, to be sure. Hampton, the 15th seed in the West region, knocked off second-seeded Iowa State, only the fourth time a 15 has dropped a two (a 16th seed has never beaten a No. 1 seed); 12th-seeded Utah State upended fifth-seeded Ohio State in the East; No. 13 seed Indiana State eliminated fourth-seed Oklahoma in the South region; and Kent State, a 13, bounced fourth-seed Indiana out of the West. But no little guy, except 12th-seeded Gonzaga, made it past the second round. While the NCAA tournament is famous for its David-versus-Goliath upsets, the cream usually rises; low seeds in the later rounds are rarer than Louisville fans in Lexington. The 2001 Final Four featured two No. 1 seeds, Duke and Michigan State, a No. 2, Arizona, and a three-seed, Maryland.

It was quite a season for Arizona, filled with Grand Canyon–csque highs and lows. Loaded with talent, the Wildcats were the consensus preseason No. 1, and all five starters were candidates for the John Wooden award that goes to the nation's top player. Center Loren Woods may have gone too far when he predicted that Arizona could be one of the best teams ever, but few observers doubted that the Wildcats would contend for the title. Yet after winning the Maui Invitational, Arizona lost three of its next five games and suddenly looked vulnerable. Then coach Lute Olson's wife, Bobbi, who was very close to many of the players, passed away after a long battle with cancer. Coach Olson took a leave of absence, and the team descended further into its funk. But Olson returned after five games, and Arizona rallied and knocked off Stanford in March to earn the second seed in the Midwest region of the NCAAs. Clearly peaking at the right time, the Wildcats were scarcely threatened as they cruised through the region, defeating top-seed Illinois in the final. That victory vaulted Arizona into the Final Four and a meeting with defending champion Michigan State, which had reeled off a 24–4 regular-season record and was making its third consecutive appearance in the Final Four. The rugged Spartans would not repeat, though, as Arizona, firing on all cylinders, trounced them 80–61.

In the Big East, two teams surprised their conference peers, one by how well it played and the other by how poorly. Seton Hall was supposed to be a national title

**The NCAA women's player of the year, Riley (00) scored 28 points in the final.**

two best teams provided the women's basketball season with some late-season drama. Connecticut and Tennessee had won five of the last six national titles between them, and both teams continued to be loaded with talent in 2000–01. Surely one of them would win the national title. But UConn lost All-Americas Svetlana Abrosimova and Shea Ralph in February and March, respectively, while Tennessee had to do without Tamika Catchings, the reigning player of the year, who blew out her knee in January. Suddenly the race for the championship was wide open.

Jackie Stiles and Southwest Missouri State were more than happy to seize the opportunity. Stiles, a flashy guard from Claflin, Kans. (pop. 700), could have gone to any of the big-time basketball schools but chose Southwest Missouri in part because the Bears began recruiting her when she was 12. She became the NCAA women's alltime career leading scorer during this, her senior season. In tournament wins over Rutgers, top-seeded Duke and Washington, Stiles averaged 35 points a game and led the Bears to the Final Four in St. Louis. The Bears fell to Purdue, but not before winning legions of new fans.

Notre Dame, which announced its status as a contender by beating UConn and grabbing the No. 1 ranking in January, overcame a 16-point, first-half deficit to defeat the Huskies again in the national semifinal. That set the stage for an all-Indiana championship and cued Notre Dame center Ruth Riley, who took over. The NCAA player of the year, Riley poured in 28 points in the final—including the game-winning free throws with 5.8 seconds left—grabbed 13 rebounds and made seven blocks. The Irish won 68–66. "I can't even describe it," Riley said. "We worked so hard that it was fitting to end the season this way."

Thus the 2000–01 season ended with one team reaching the mountaintop for the first time and another planting its third flag at the summit. No doubt they both enjoyed the view.

contender with a blue-chip freshman class that included the No. 1 recruit in the nation, 6'11" Eddie Griffin. The Pirates lived up to their billing early, rising as high as No. 7 in the national polls. But after a loss to Georgetown in January, Griffin and guard Ty Shine got into a fight in the locker room, irrevocably poisoning the team's chemistry. The Pirates finished 16–15 and settled for an NIT bid. The Big East overachiever was Boston College, which went 11–19 (3–13) in 1999–2000 and had been picked to finish at the bottom of the conference again. But sensational sophomore point guard Troy Bell helped catapult BC from worst to first; the Eagles won the Big East and grabbed a No. 3 seed in the NCAA tournament, where they were upset by USC in the second round. Despite the early exit from the Big Dance, the Eagles had to be pleased with BC's surprising turnaround.

Injuries to three players on the nation's

## NCAA Championship Game Box Score

### Duke 82

| DUKE | Min | FG M-A | FT M-A | Reb O-T | A | PF | TP |
|------|-----|--------|--------|---------|---|----|----|
| Battier | 40 | 7-14 | 3-6 | 4-11 | 6 | 1 | 18 |
| Dunleavy | 32 | 8-17 | 0-1 | 2-3 | 0 | 3 | 21 |
| Sanders | 10 | 0-1 | 0-0 | 0-2 | 1 | 1 | 0 |
| Duhon | 39 | 3-5 | 2-3 | 1-4 | 6 | 2 | 9 |
| Williams | 29 | 5-15 | 4-6 | 0-3 | 4 | 4 | 16 |
| Boozer | 30 | 5-9 | 2-3 | 1-12 | 1 | 3 | 12 |
| James | 20 | 2-3 | 2-3 | 1-3 | 0 | 3 | 6 |
| Totals | 200 | 30-64 | 13-22 | 9-38 | 18 | 17 | 82 |

Percentages: FG—.469, FT—.591. 3-pt goals: 9–27, .333 (Battier 1–5, Dunleavy 5–9, Duhon 1–1, Williams 2–11, James 0–1). Team rebounds: 4. Blocked shots: 5 (Battier 2, Boozer 2, James). Turnovers: 11 (Williams 6, Boozer 2, James 2, Duhon). Steals: 5 (Williams 3, James, Sanders).

### Arizona 72

| ARIZONA | Min | FG M-A | FT M-A | Reb O-T | A | PF | TP |
|---------|-----|--------|--------|---------|---|----|----|
| Wright | 28 | 5-9 | 0-1 | 4-11 | 0 | 4 | 10 |
| Jefferson | 35 | 7-13 | 1-3 | 2-8 | 3 | 2 | 19 |
| Woods | 37 | 8-15 | 6-8 | 4-11 | 1 | 4 | 22 |
| Arenas | 34 | 4-17 | 2-3 | 2-4 | 4 | 1 | 10 |
| Gardner | 40 | 2-11 | 3-4 | 1-3 | 2 | 2 | 7 |
| Wessel | 2 | 0-0 | 0-0 | 0-0 | 0 | 0 | 0 |
| Edgerson | 8 | 0-0 | 0-0 | 0-1 | 0 | 4 | 0 |
| Walton | 16 | 2-6 | 0-0 | 2-3 | 4 | 3 | 4 |
| Totals | 200 | 28-71 | 12-19 | 15-41 | 14 | 20 | 72 |

Percentages: FG— .394, FT—.632. 3-pt goals: 4–22, .182 (Jefferson 4–8, Woods 0–1, Arenas 0–4, Gardner 0–8, Walton 0–1). Team rebounds: 4. Blocked shots: 7 (Woods 4, Wright 2, Jefferson). Turnovers: 9 (Jefferson 5, Arenas, Walton, Woods, Wright). Steals: 5 (Arenas, Gardner, Jefferson, Woods, Wright).

Halftime: Duke 35, Arizona 33. A: 45,994.
Officials: Thornley, Boudeaux, Corbett.

## Final AP Top 25

Poll taken before NCAA Tournament.

| | | |
|---|---|---|
| 1. Duke | 29–4 | 14. Mississippi ............ 25–7 |
| 2. Stanford | 28–2 | 15. UCLA ............ 21–8 |
| 3. Michigan St | 24–4 | 16. Virginia ............ 20–8 |
| 4. Illinois | 24–7 | 17. Syracuse ............ 24–8 |
| 5. Arizona | 23–7 | 18. Texas ............ 25–8 |
| 6. N Carolina | 25–6 | 19. Notre Dame ............ 19–9 |
| 7. Boston College | 26–4 | 20. Indiana ............ 21–12 |
| 8. Florida | 23–6 | 21. Georgetown ............ 23–7 |
| 9. Kentucky | 22–9 | 22. St Joseph's (PA) ............ 25–6 |
| 10. Iowa St | 25–5 | 23. Wake Forest ............ 19–10 |
| 11. Maryland | 21–10 | 24. Iowa ............ 22–11 |
| 12. Kansas | 24–6 | 25. Wisconsin ............ 18–10 |
| 13. Oklahoma | 26–6 | |

## National Invitation Tournament Scores

**First round:** Alabama 85, Seton Hall 79; Memphis 71, Utah 62; Connecticut 72, S Carolina 65; Dayton 68, UNC–Wilmington 59; Pittsburgh 84, St. Bonaventure 75; Mississippi St 75, Southern Mississippi 68; Detroit 68, Bradley 49; Purdue 90, Illinois St 79; Auburn 60, Miami (FL) 58; Tulsa 75, UC–Irvine 71; Pepperdine 72, Wyoming 69; Texas–El Paso 84, McNeese St 74; Minnesota 87, Villanova 78; New Mexico 83, Baylor 73; Toledo 76, S Alabama 67; Richmond 79, W Virginia 56
**Second round:** Detroit 67, Connecticut 61; Mississippi St 66, Pittsburgh 61; Dayton 71, Richmond 56; Tulsa 76, Minnesota 73; Purdue 79, Auburn 61; Memphis 90, Texas–El Paso 65; Alabama 79, Toledo 69; New Mexico 81, Pepperdine 78
**Quarterfinals:** Detroit 59, Dayton 42; Tulsa 77, Mississippi St 75; Memphis 81, New Mexico 63; Alabama 85, Purdue 77, 2OT
**Semifinals:** Alabama 74, Detroit 63; Tulsa 72, Memphis 64
**Consolation Game:** Memphis 86, Detroit 71
**Championship:** Tulsa 79, Alabama 60

# 2001 NCAA Basketball Men's Division I Tournament

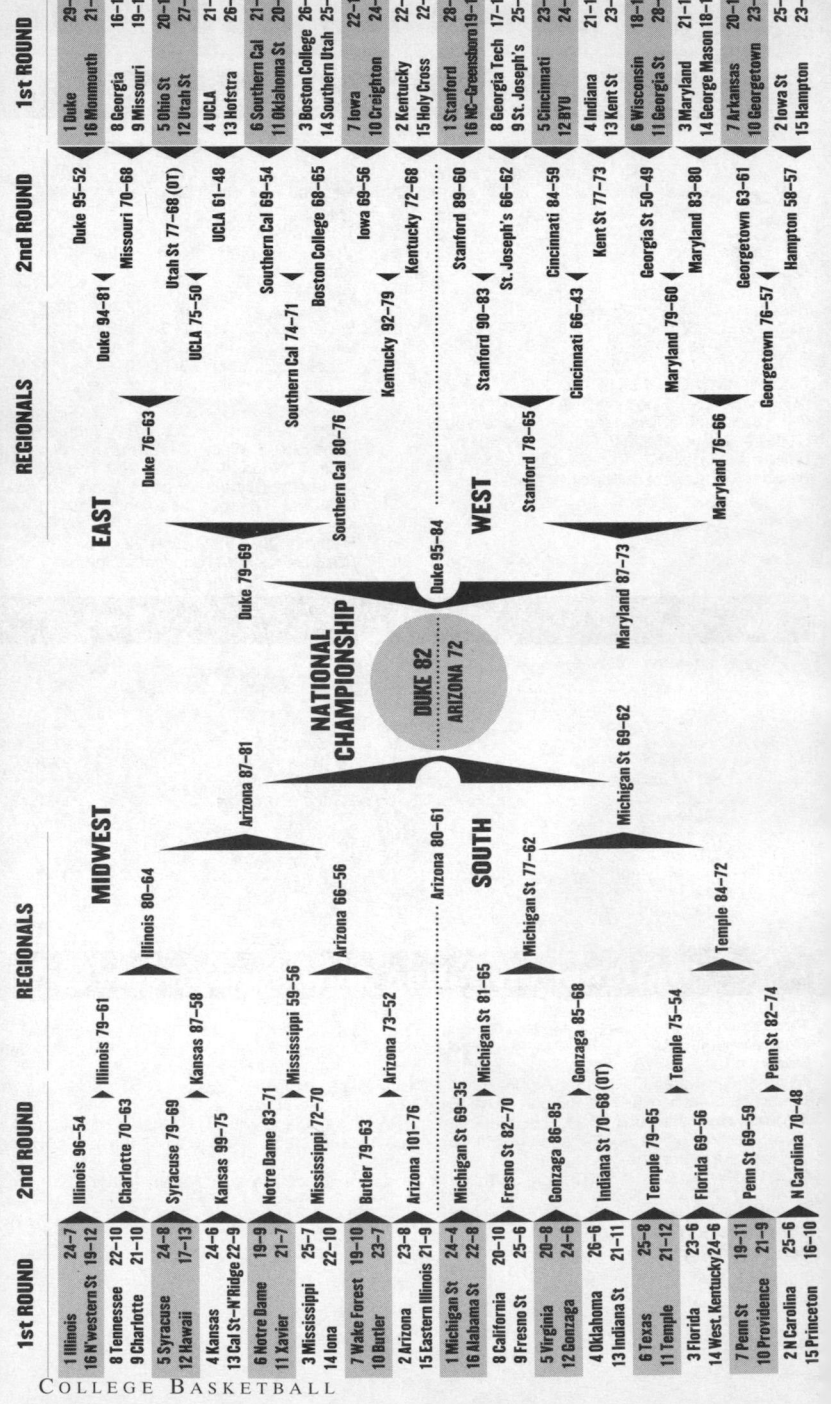

COLLEGE BASKETBALL

# NCAA Men's Division I Conference Standings

## America East

| | Conference | | | All Games | | |
|---|---|---|---|---|---|---|
| | W | L | Pct | W | L | Pct |
| †Hofstra | 16 | 2 | .889 | 26 | 5 | .839 |
| Delaware | 14 | 4 | .778 | 20 | 10 | .667 |
| Drexel | 12 | 6 | .667 | 15 | 12 | .556 |
| Maine | 10 | 8 | .556 | 18 | 11 | .621 |
| Boston | 9 | 9 | .500 | 14 | 14 | .500 |
| Northeastern | 8 | 10 | .444 | 10 | 19 | .345 |
| Towson | 7 | 11 | .389 | 12 | 17 | .414 |
| Vermont | 7 | 11 | .389 | 12 | 17 | .414 |
| New Hampshire | 6 | 12 | .333 | 7 | 21 | .333 |
| Hartford | 1 | 17 | .056 | 4 | 24 | .143 |

## Atlantic Coast

| | Conference | | | All Games | | |
|---|---|---|---|---|---|---|
| | W | L | Pct | W | L | Pct |
| †Duke | 13 | 3 | .813 | 35 | 4 | .897 |
| N Carolina | 13 | 3 | .813 | 26 | 7 | .788 |
| Maryland | 10 | 6 | .625 | 25 | 11 | .694 |
| Virginia | 9 | 7 | .563 | 20 | 9 | .690 |
| Wake Forest | 8 | 8 | .500 | 19 | 11 | .633 |
| Georgia Tech | 8 | 8 | .500 | 17 | 13 | .567 |
| N Carolina St | 5 | 11 | .313 | 13 | 16 | .448 |
| Florida St | 4 | 12 | .250 | 9 | 21 | .300 |
| Clemson | 2 | 14 | .125 | 12 | 19 | .387 |

## Atlantic 10

| | Conference | | | All Games | | |
|---|---|---|---|---|---|---|
| | W | L | Pct | W | L | Pct |
| St. Joseph's | 14 | 2 | .875 | 26 | 7 | .788 |
| Xavier | 12 | 4 | .750 | 21 | 8 | .724 |
| †Temple | 12 | 4 | .750 | 24 | 13 | .649 |
| Massachusetts | 11 | 5 | .688 | 15 | 15 | .500 |
| Dayton | 9 | 7 | .563 | 21 | 13 | .618 |
| St. Bonaventure | 9 | 7 | .563 | 18 | 12 | .600 |
| George Washington | 6 | 10 | .375 | 14 | 18 | .438 |
| La Salle | 5 | 11 | .313 | 12 | 17 | .414 |
| Fordham | 4 | 12 | .250 | 12 | 17 | .414 |
| Duquesne | 3 | 13 | .188 | 9 | 21 | .300 |
| Rhode Island | 3 | 13 | .188 | 7 | 23 | .233 |

## Big East

| | Conference | | | All Games | | |
|---|---|---|---|---|---|---|
| **EAST** | W | L | Pct | W | L | Pct |
| †Boston College | 13 | 3 | .813 | 27 | 5 | .844 |
| Providence | 11 | 5 | .688 | 21 | 10 | .677 |
| Connecticut | 8 | 8 | .500 | 20 | 12 | .625 |
| Villanova | 8 | 8 | .500 | 18 | 13 | .581 |
| Miami (FL) | 8 | 8 | .500 | 16 | 13 | .552 |
| St. John's | 8 | 8 | .500 | 14 | 15 | .483 |
| Virginia Tech | 2 | 14 | .125 | 8 | 19 | .296 |
| **WEST** | | | | | | |
| Notre Dame | 11 | 5 | .688 | 20 | 10 | .667 |
| Georgetown | 10 | 6 | .625 | 25 | 8 | .758 |
| Syracuse | 10 | 6 | .625 | 25 | 9 | .735 |
| W Virginia | 8 | 8 | .500 | 17 | 12 | .586 |
| Pittsburgh | 7 | 9 | .438 | 19 | 14 | .576 |
| Seton Hall | 5 | 11 | .313 | 16 | 15 | .516 |
| Rutgers | 3 | 13 | .188 | 11 | 16 | .407 |

## Big Sky

| | Conference | | | All Games | | |
|---|---|---|---|---|---|---|
| | W | L | Pct | W | L | Pct |
| †Cal St–Northridge | 13 | 3 | .813 | 22 | 10 | .688 |
| Eastern Washington | 11 | 5 | .688 | 17 | 11 | .607 |
| Idaho St | 10 | 6 | .625 | 14 | 14 | .500 |
| Weber St | 8 | 8 | .500 | 15 | 13 | .536 |
| Montana St | 8 | 8 | .500 | 16 | 14 | .533 |
| Northern Arizona | 8 | 8 | .500 | 15 | 14 | .517 |
| Montana | 6 | 10 | .375 | 11 | 16 | .407 |
| Portland St | 6 | 10 | .375 | 9 | 18 | .333 |
| Sacramento St | 2 | 14 | .125 | 5 | 22 | .185 |

## Big South

| | Conference | | | All Games | | |
|---|---|---|---|---|---|---|
| | W | L | Pct | W | L | Pct |
| Radford | 12 | 2 | .857 | 19 | 10 | .655 |
| †Winthrop | 11 | 3 | .786 | 18 | 13 | .581 |
| NC–Asheville | 9 | 5 | .643 | 15 | 13 | .536 |
| Charleston So. | 6 | 8 | .429 | 10 | 19 | .345 |
| Coastal Carolina | 6 | 8 | .429 | 8 | 20 | .286 |
| Liberty | 5 | 9 | .357 | 13 | 15 | .464 |
| Elon | 4 | 10 | .286 | 9 | 20 | .310 |
| High Point | 3 | 11 | .214 | 8 | 20 | .286 |

## Big Ten

| | Conference | | | All Games | | |
|---|---|---|---|---|---|---|
| | W | L | Pct | W | L | Pct |
| Michigan St | 13 | 3 | .813 | 28 | 5 | .848 |
| Illinois | 13 | 3 | .813 | 27 | 8 | .771 |
| Ohio St | 11 | 5 | .688 | 20 | 11 | .645 |
| Indiana | 10 | 6 | .625 | 21 | 13 | .618 |
| Wisconsin | 9 | 7 | .563 | 18 | 11 | .621 |
| †Iowa | 7 | 9 | .438 | 23 | 12 | .657 |
| Penn St | 7 | 9 | .438 | 21 | 12 | .636 |
| Purdue | 6 | 10 | .375 | 17 | 15 | .531 |
| Minnesota | 5 | 11 | .313 | 18 | 14 | .563 |
| Michigan | 4 | 12 | .250 | 10 | 18 | .357 |
| Northwestern | 3 | 13 | .188 | 11 | 19 | .367 |

## Big 12

| | Conference | | | All Games | | |
|---|---|---|---|---|---|---|
| | W | L | Pct | W | L | Pct |
| Iowa St | 13 | 3 | .813 | 25 | 6 | .806 |
| †Oklahoma | 12 | 4 | .750 | 26 | 7 | .788 |
| Kansas | 12 | 4 | .750 | 26 | 7 | .788 |
| Texas | 12 | 4 | .750 | 25 | 9 | .735 |
| Oklahoma St | 10 | 6 | .625 | 20 | 10 | .667 |
| Missouri | 9 | 7 | .563 | 20 | 13 | .606 |
| Nebraska | 7 | 9 | .438 | 14 | 16 | .467 |
| Baylor | 6 | 10 | .375 | 19 | 12 | .613 |
| Colorado | 5 | 11 | .313 | 15 | 15 | .500 |
| Kansas St | 4 | 12 | .250 | 11 | 18 | .379 |
| Texas A&M | 3 | 13 | .188 | 10 | 20 | .333 |
| Texas Tech | 3 | 13 | .188 | 9 | 19 | .321 |

† Conference tourney winner.
Note: Standings based on regular-season conference play only; overall records include all tournament play.

## Big West

| | Conference | | | All Games | | |
|---|---|---|---|---|---|---|
| | W | L | Pct | W | L | Pct |
| UC–Irvine | 15 | 1 | .938 | 25 | 5 | .833 |
| †Utah St | 13 | 3 | .813 | 28 | 6 | .824 |
| Long Beach St | 10 | 6 | .625 | 18 | 13 | .581 |
| Santa Barbara | 9 | 7 | .563 | 13 | 15 | .464 |
| Pacific | 8 | 8 | .500 | 18 | 12 | .600 |
| Boise St | 8 | 8 | .500 | 17 | 14 | .548 |
| Cal Poly | 3 | 13 | .188 | 9 | 19 | .321 |
| Idaho | 3 | 13 | .188 | 6 | 21 | .222 |
| Cal St–Fullerton | 3 | 13 | .188 | 5 | 23 | .179 |

## Colonial Athletic

| | Conference | | | All Games | | |
|---|---|---|---|---|---|---|
| | W | L | Pct | W | L | Pct |
| Richmond | 12 | 4 | .750 | 22 | 7 | .759 |
| NC–Wilmington | 11 | 5 | .688 | 19 | 11 | .633 |
| †George Mason | 11 | 5 | .688 | 18 | 12 | .600 |
| VA Commonwealth | 9 | 7 | .563 | 16 | 14 | .533 |
| Old Dominion | 7 | 9 | .438 | 13 | 18 | .419 |
| William & Mary | 7 | 9 | .438 | 11 | 17 | .393 |
| E Carolina | 6 | 10 | .375 | 14 | 14 | .500 |
| James Madison | 6 | 10 | .375 | 12 | 17 | .414 |
| American | 3 | 13 | .188 | 7 | 20 | .259 |

## Conference USA

| | Conference | | | All Games | | |
|---|---|---|---|---|---|---|
| AMERICAN | W | L | Pct | W | L | Pct |
| Cincinnati | 11 | 5 | .688 | 25 | 10 | .714 |
| †NC–Charlotte | 10 | 6 | .625 | 22 | 11 | .667 |
| Marquette | 9 | 7 | .563 | 15 | 14 | .517 |
| St. Louis | 8 | 8 | .500 | 17 | 14 | .548 |
| Louisville | 8 | 8 | .500 | 12 | 19 | .387 |
| DePaul | 4 | 12 | .250 | 12 | 18 | .400 |
| **NATIONAL** | | | | | | |
| Southern Miss | 11 | 5 | .688 | 22 | 9 | .710 |
| Memphis | 10 | 6 | .625 | 21 | 15 | .583 |
| S Florida | 9 | 7 | .563 | 18 | 13 | .581 |
| AL–Birmingham | 8 | 8 | .500 | 17 | 14 | .548 |
| Houston | 6 | 10 | .375 | 9 | 20 | .310 |
| Tulane | 2 | 14 | .125 | 9 | 21 | .300 |

## Ivy League

| | Conference | | | All Games | | |
|---|---|---|---|---|---|---|
| | W | L | Pct | W | L | Pct |
| Princeton | 11 | 3 | .786 | 16 | 11 | .593 |
| Brown | 9 | 5 | .643 | 15 | 12 | .556 |
| Pennsylvania | 9 | 5 | .643 | 12 | 17 | .414 |
| Harvard | 7 | 7 | .500 | 14 | 12 | .538 |
| Columbia | 7 | 7 | .500 | 12 | 15 | .444 |
| Yale | 7 | 7 | .500 | 10 | 17 | .370 |
| Dartmouth | 3 | 11 | .214 | 8 | 19 | .296 |
| Cornell | 3 | 11 | .214 | 7 | 20 | .259 |

## Metro Atlantic Athletic

| | Conference | | | All Games | | |
|---|---|---|---|---|---|---|
| | W | L | Pct | W | L | Pct |
| †Iona | 12 | 6 | .667 | 22 | 11 | .667 |
| Siena | 12 | 6 | .667 | 20 | 11 | .645 |
| Niagara | 12 | 6 | .667 | 15 | 13 | .538 |
| Rider | 11 | 7 | .611 | 16 | 12 | .571 |
| Marist | 11 | 7 | .611 | 17 | 13 | .567 |
| Manhattan | 11 | 7 | .611 | 14 | 15 | .483 |
| Canisius | 9 | 9 | .500 | 20 | 11 | .645 |
| Fairfield | 8 | 10 | .444 | 12 | 16 | .429 |
| Loyola (MD) | 2 | 16 | .111 | 6 | 23 | .207 |
| St. Peter's | 2 | 16 | .111 | 4 | 24 | .143 |

## Mid-American

| | Conference | | | All Games | | |
|---|---|---|---|---|---|---|
| EAST | W | L | Pct | W | L | Pct |
| †Kent St | 13 | 5 | .722 | 24 | 10 | .706 |
| Marshall | 12 | 6 | .667 | 18 | 9 | .667 |
| Ohio | 12 | 6 | .667 | 19 | 11 | .633 |
| Bowling Green | 10 | 8 | .556 | 15 | 14 | .517 |
| Miami (OH) | 10 | 8 | .556 | 17 | 16 | .515 |
| Akron | 9 | 9 | .500 | 12 | 16 | .429 |
| Buffalo | 2 | 16 | .111 | 4 | 24 | .143 |
| **WEST** | | | | | | |
| Central Michigan | 14 | 4 | .778 | 20 | 8 | .714 |
| Toledo | 12 | 6 | .667 | 22 | 11 | .667 |
| Ball St | 11 | 7 | .611 | 18 | 12 | .600 |
| Western Michigan | 7 | 11 | .389 | 7 | 21 | .250 |
| Northern Illinois | 4 | 14 | .222 | 5 | 23 | .179 |
| Eastern Michigan | 1 | 17 | .056 | 3 | 25 | .107 |

## Mid-Continent

| | Conference | | | All Games | | |
|---|---|---|---|---|---|---|
| | W | L | Pct | W | L | Pct |
| †Southern Utah | 13 | 3 | .813 | 25 | 6 | .806 |
| Valparaiso | 13 | 3 | .813 | 24 | 8 | .750 |
| Youngstown St | 11 | 5 | .688 | 19 | 11 | .633 |
| MO–Kansas City | 9 | 7 | .563 | 14 | 16 | .467 |
| Oakland | 8 | 8 | .500 | 12 | 16 | .429 |
| IU/PUI | 6 | 10 | .375 | 11 | 18 | .379 |
| Oral Roberts | 5 | 11 | .313 | 10 | 19 | .345 |
| Western Illinois | 5 | 11 | .313 | 5 | 23 | .179 |
| Chicago St | 2 | 14 | .125 | 5 | 23 | .179 |

## Mid-Eastern Athletic

| | Conference | | | All Games | | |
|---|---|---|---|---|---|---|
| | W | L | Pct | W | L | Pct |
| †Hampton | 14 | 4 | .778 | 24 | 6 | .800 |
| S Carolina St | 14 | 4 | .778 | 19 | 13 | .594 |
| Delaware St | 11 | 7 | .611 | 13 | 15 | .464 |
| Norfolk St | 11 | 7 | .611 | 12 | 17 | .414 |
| Coppin St | 11 | 8 | .578 | 13 | 15 | .464 |
| MD–Eastern Shore | 10 | 8 | .556 | 12 | 16 | .429 |
| N Carolina A&T | 8 | 10 | .444 | 13 | 17 | .433 |
| Howard | 8 | 10 | .444 | 10 | 18 | .357 |
| Bethune Cookman | 5 | 13 | .278 | 10 | 19 | .345 |
| Florida A&M | 4 | 14 | .222 | 6 | 22 | .214 |
| Morgan St | 4 | 15 | .211 | 6 | 23 | .207 |

†Conference tourney winner.

## Midwestern Collegiate

| | Conference | | | All Games | | |
|---|---|---|---|---|---|---|
| | W | L | Pct | W | L | Pct |
| †Butler | 11 | 3 | .786 | 24 | 8 | .750 |
| Detroit | 10 | 4 | .714 | 25 | 12 | .676 |
| Cleveland St | 9 | 5 | .643 | 19 | 13 | .594 |
| Wright St | 8 | 6 | .571 | 18 | 11 | .621 |
| WI–Milwaukee | 7 | 7 | .500 | 15 | 13 | .536 |
| IL–Chicago | 5 | 9 | .357 | 11 | 17 | .393 |
| WI–Green Bay | 4 | 10 | .286 | 11 | 17 | .393 |
| Loyola (IL) | 2 | 12 | .143 | 7 | 21 | .250 |

## Missouri Valley

| | Conference | | | All Games | | |
|---|---|---|---|---|---|---|
| | W | L | Pct | W | L | Pct |
| Creighton | 14 | 4 | .778 | 24 | 8 | .750 |
| Illinois St | 12 | 6 | .667 | 21 | 9 | .700 |
| Bradley | 12 | 6 | .667 | 19 | 12 | .613 |
| †Indiana St | 10 | 8 | .556 | 22 | 12 | .647 |
| Southern Illinois | 10 | 8 | .556 | 16 | 14 | .533 |
| Evansville | 9 | 9 | .500 | 14 | 16 | .467 |
| SW Missouri St | 8 | 10 | .444 | 13 | 16 | .448 |
| Drake | 8 | 10 | .444 | 12 | 16 | .429 |
| Wichita St | 4 | 14 | .222 | 9 | 19 | .321 |
| Northern Iowa | 3 | 15 | .167 | 7 | 24 | .226 |

## Mountain West

| | Conference | | | All Games | | |
|---|---|---|---|---|---|---|
| | W | L | Pct | W | L | Pct |
| †Brigham Young | 10 | 4 | .714 | 24 | 9 | .727 |
| Wyoming | 10 | 4 | .714 | 20 | 10 | .667 |
| Utah | 10 | 4 | .714 | 19 | 12 | .613 |
| Nevada–Las Vegas | 7 | 7 | .500 | 16 | 13 | .552 |
| New Mexico | 6 | 8 | .429 | 21 | 13 | .618 |
| Colorado St | 6 | 8 | .429 | 15 | 13 | .536 |
| San Diego St | 4 | 10 | .286 | 14 | 14 | .500 |
| Air Force | 3 | 11 | .214 | 8 | 21 | .276 |

## Northeast

| | Conference | | | All Games | | |
|---|---|---|---|---|---|---|
| | W | L | Pct | W | L | Pct |
| St. Francis (NY) | 16 | 4 | .800 | 18 | 11 | .621 |
| †Monmouth | 15 | 5 | .750 | 21 | 10 | .677 |
| MD–Balt. County | 13 | 7 | .650 | 18 | 11 | .621 |
| Long Island | 12 | 8 | .600 | 12 | 16 | .429 |
| Wagner | 11 | 9 | .550 | 16 | 13 | .552 |
| Central Connecticut | 11 | 9 | .550 | 14 | 14 | .500 |
| Fairleigh Dickinson | 10 | 10 | .500 | 13 | 15 | .464 |
| St. Francis (PA) | 9 | 11 | .450 | 9 | 18 | .333 |
| Mt. St. Mary's | 7 | 13 | .350 | 7 | 21 | .250 |
| Robert Morris | 7 | 13 | .350 | 7 | 22 | .318 |
| Sacred Heart | 6 | 14 | .300 | 7 | 21 | .250 |
| Quinnipiac | 3 | 17 | .150 | 6 | 21 | .222 |

## Ohio Valley

| | Conference | | | All Games | | |
|---|---|---|---|---|---|---|
| | W | L | Pct | W | L | Pct |
| Tennessee Tech | 13 | 3 | .813 | 20 | 9 | .690 |
| †Eastern Illinois | 11 | 5 | .688 | 21 | 10 | .677 |
| Murray St | 11 | 5 | .688 | 17 | 12 | .586 |
| Austin Peay | 10 | 6 | .625 | 22 | 10 | .688 |
| SE Missouri St | 8 | 8 | .500 | 18 | 12 | .600 |
| Tennessee St | 7 | 9 | .438 | 10 | 19 | .345 |
| Morehead St | 6 | 10 | .375 | 12 | 16 | .429 |
| Tennessee–Martin | 5 | 11 | .313 | 10 | 18 | .357 |
| Eastern Kentucky | 1 | 15 | .063 | 7 | 19 | .269 |

## Pacific 10

| | Conference | | | All Games | | |
|---|---|---|---|---|---|---|
| | W | L | Pct | W | L | Pct |
| Stanford | 16 | 2 | .889 | 31 | 3 | .912 |
| Arizona | 15 | 3 | .833 | 28 | 8 | .778 |
| UCLA | 14 | 4 | .778 | 23 | 9 | .719 |
| Southern Cal | 11 | 7 | .611 | 24 | 10 | .706 |
| California | 11 | 7 | .611 | 20 | 11 | .645 |
| Oregon | 5 | 13 | .278 | 14 | 14 | .500 |
| Arizona St | 5 | 13 | .278 | 13 | 16 | .448 |
| Washington St | 5 | 13 | .278 | 12 | 16 | .429 |
| Oregon St | 4 | 14 | .222 | 10 | 20 | .667 |
| Washington | 4 | 14 | .222 | 10 | 20 | .667 |

## Patriot

| | Conference | | | All Games | | |
|---|---|---|---|---|---|---|
| | W | L | Pct | W | L | Pct |
| †Holy Cross | 10 | 2 | .833 | 22 | 8 | .733 |
| Navy | 9 | 3 | .750 | 19 | 12 | .613 |
| Colgate | 6 | 6 | .500 | 13 | 15 | .464 |
| Lehigh | 6 | 6 | .500 | 13 | 16 | .448 |
| Bucknell | 4 | 8 | .333 | 14 | 15 | .483 |
| Lafayette | 4 | 8 | .333 | 12 | 16 | .429 |
| Army | 3 | 9 | .250 | 9 | 19 | .321 |

## Southeastern

| | Conference | | | All Games | | |
|---|---|---|---|---|---|---|
| EAST | W | L | Pct | W | L | Pct |
| Florida | 12 | 4 | .750 | 24 | 7 | .774 |
| †Kentucky | 12 | 4 | .750 | 24 | 10 | .706 |
| Georgia | 9 | 7 | .563 | 16 | 15 | .516 |
| Tennessee | 8 | 8 | .500 | 22 | 11 | .667 |
| S Carolina | 6 | 10 | .375 | 15 | 15 | .500 |
| Vanderbilt | 4 | 12 | .250 | 15 | 15 | .500 |
| WEST | | | | | | |
| Mississippi | 11 | 5 | .688 | 27 | 8 | .771 |
| Arkansas | 10 | 6 | .625 | 20 | 11 | .645 |
| Alabama | 8 | 8 | .500 | 25 | 11 | .694 |
| Mississippi St | 7 | 9 | .438 | 18 | 13 | .581 |
| Auburn | 7 | 9 | .438 | 18 | 14 | .563 |
| Louisiana St | 2 | 14 | .125 | 13 | 16 | .448 |

†Conference tourney winner.

## Southern

| NORTH | Conference | | | All Games | | |
|---|---|---|---|---|---|---|
| | W | L | Pct | W | L | Pct |
| E Tennessee St | 13 | 3 | .813 | 18 | 10 | .643 |
| †NC–Greensboro | 10 | 6 | .625 | 19 | 12 | .613 |
| Davidson | 7 | 9 | .438 | 15 | 17 | .469 |
| Appalachian St | 7 | 9 | .438 | 11 | 20 | .355 |
| VMI | 5 | 11 | .313 | 9 | 19 | .321 |
| Western Carolina | 3 | 13 | .188 | 6 | 25 | .194 |
| **SOUTH** | | | | | | |
| Coll. of Charleston | 12 | 4 | .750 | 22 | 7 | .759 |
| Citadel | 9 | 7 | .563 | 16 | 12 | .571 |
| Chattanooga | 9 | 7 | .563 | 17 | 13 | .567 |
| Georgia Southern | 9 | 7 | .563 | 15 | 15 | .500 |
| Wofford | 7 | 9 | .438 | 12 | 16 | .429 |
| Furman | 5 | 11 | .313 | 10 | 16 | .385 |

## Southland

| | Conference | | | All Games | | |
|---|---|---|---|---|---|---|
| | W | L | Pct | W | L | Pct |
| McNeese St | 17 | 3 | .850 | 22 | 9 | .710 |
| Nicholls St | 12 | 8 | .600 | 14 | 14 | .500 |
| TX–San Antonio | 12 | 8 | .600 | 14 | 15 | .483 |
| †Northwestern St | 11 | 9 | .550 | 19 | 13 | .594 |
| Sam Houston | 11 | 9 | .550 | 16 | 13 | .552 |
| TX–Arlington | 11 | 9 | .550 | 13 | 15 | .464 |
| SW Texas St | 10 | 10 | .500 | 13 | 15 | .464 |
| Louisiana–Monroe | 8 | 12 | .400 | 11 | 17 | .393 |
| Lamar | 7 | 13 | .350 | 9 | 18 | .333 |
| Stephen F. Austin | 6 | 14 | .300 | 9 | 17 | .346 |
| Southeastern LA | 5 | 15 | .250 | 8 | 21 | .276 |

## Southwestern Athletic

| | Conference | | | All Games | | |
|---|---|---|---|---|---|---|
| | W | L | Pct | W | L | Pct |
| †Alabama St | 15 | 3 | .833 | 22 | 9 | .710 |
| Mississippi Valley St | 14 | 4 | .778 | 17 | 9 | .654 |
| Alabama A&M | 13 | 5 | .722 | 17 | 11 | .607 |
| Alcorn St | 13 | 5 | .722 | 15 | 15 | .500 |
| Southern | 8 | 10 | .444 | 11 | 16 | .407 |
| Grambling | 8 | 10 | .444 | 8 | 18 | .308 |
| Jackson St | 7 | 11 | .389 | 7 | 23 | .233 |
| Texas Southern | 5 | 13 | .278 | 7 | 22 | .241 |
| Prairie View | 5 | 13 | .278 | 6 | 22 | .214 |
| AR-Pine Bluff | 2 | 16 | .111 | 2 | 25 | .074 |

## Sun Belt

| EAST | Conference | | | All Games | | |
|---|---|---|---|---|---|---|
| | W | L | Pct | W | L | Pct |
| †Western Kentucky | 14 | 2 | .875 | 24 | 7 | .774 |
| Louisiana Tech | 10 | 6 | .625 | 17 | 12 | .583 |
| Arkansas St | 10 | 6 | .625 | 17 | 13 | .567 |
| AR–Little Rock | 9 | 7 | .563 | 17 | 11 | .607 |
| Florida International | 5 | 11 | .313 | 8 | 21 | .276 |
| Middle Tenn St | 1 | 15 | .063 | 5 | 22 | .185 |
| **WEST** | | | | | | |
| S Alabama | 11 | 5 | .688 | 22 | 11 | .667 |
| New Orleans | 10 | 6 | .625 | 17 | 12 | .583 |
| Louisiana–Lafayette | 10 | 6 | .625 | 16 | 13 | .552 |
| New Mexico St | 10 | 6 | .625 | 14 | 14 | .500 |
| Denver | 5 | 11 | .313 | 10 | 18 | .357 |
| N Texas | 1 | 15 | .063 | 4 | 24 | .143 |

## Trans America

| | Conference | | | All Games | | |
|---|---|---|---|---|---|---|
| | W | L | Pct | W | L | Pct |
| †Georgia St | 16 | 2 | .889 | 29 | 5 | .853 |
| Troy St | 12 | 6 | .667 | 19 | 12 | .613 |
| Jacksonville | 11 | 7 | .611 | 18 | 10 | .643 |
| Stetson | 11 | 7 | .611 | 17 | 12 | .583 |
| Samford | 11 | 7 | .611 | 15 | 14 | .517 |
| Mercer | 10 | 8 | .556 | 13 | 15 | .464 |
| Jacksonville St | 6 | 12 | .333 | 9 | 19 | .321 |
| Campbell | 5 | 13 | .278 | 7 | 21 | .250 |
| Florida Atlantic | 5 | 13 | .278 | 7 | 24 | .226 |
| Central Florida | 3 | 15 | .167 | 8 | 23 | .258 |

## West Coast

| PACIFIC | Conference | | | All Games | | |
|---|---|---|---|---|---|---|
| | W | L | Pct | W | L | Pct |
| †Gonzaga | 13 | 1 | .929 | 26 | 7 | .788 |
| Pepperdine | 12 | 2 | .857 | 22 | 9 | .710 |
| Santa Clara | 10 | 4 | .714 | 20 | 12 | .625 |
| San Diego | 7 | 7 | .500 | 15 | 13 | .536 |
| San Francisco | 5 | 9 | .357 | 12 | 18 | .400 |
| Loyola Marymount | 5 | 9 | .357 | 9 | 19 | .321 |
| Portland | 4 | 10 | .286 | 11 | 17 | .393 |
| St. Mary's | 0 | 14 | .000 | 2 | 27 | .069 |

## Western Athletic

| | Conference | | | All Games | | |
|---|---|---|---|---|---|---|
| | W | L | Pct | W | L | Pct |
| Fresno St | 13 | 3 | .813 | 26 | 7 | .788 |
| Texas–El Paso | 10 | 6 | .625 | 23 | 9 | .719 |
| Tulsa | 10 | 6 | .625 | 26 | 11 | .703 |
| Texas Christian | 9 | 7 | .563 | 20 | 11 | .645 |
| Southern Methodist | 8 | 8 | .500 | 18 | 12 | .600 |
| †Hawaii | 8 | 8 | .500 | 17 | 14 | .548 |
| San Jose St | 6 | 10 | .375 | 14 | 14 | .500 |
| Rice | 5 | 11 | .313 | 14 | 16 | .467 |
| Nevada | 3 | 13 | .188 | 10 | 18 | .357 |

## Independents

| | All Games | | |
|---|---|---|---|
| | W | L | Pct |
| Stony Brook | 17 | 11 | .607 |
| Belmont | 13 | 15 | .464 |
| Texas A&M–C. C. | 12 | 14 | .462 |
| TX–Pan American | 12 | 17 | .414 |
| Centenary | 8 | 19 | .296 |
| Albany | 6 | 22 | .214 |

†Conference tourney winner.

## Scoring

| | Class | GP | FG | FGA | Pct | FG | FGA | FT | FTA | Pct | Pts | Avg |
|---|---|---|---|---|---|---|---|---|---|---|---|---|
| | | | **Field Goals** | | | **3-Pt FG** | | **Free Throws** | | | | |
| Ronnie McCollum, Centenary............Sr | 27 | 244 | 592 | 41.2 | 85 | 252 | 214 | 236 | 90.7 | 787 | 29.1 |
| Kyle Hill, Eastern Illinois.....................Sr | 31 | 250 | 527 | 47.4 | 86 | 198 | 151 | 180 | 83.9 | 737 | 23.8 |
| DeWayne Jefferson, Mississippi Valley..Sr | 27 | 216 | 500 | 43.2 | 107 | 285 | 98 | 122 | 80.3 | 637 | 23.6 |
| Tarise Bryson, Illinois St.....................Sr | 30 | 208 | 447 | 46.5 | 62 | 174 | 207 | 252 | 82.1 | 685 | 22.8 |
| Henry Domercant, Eastern Illinois ......So | 31 | 256 | 519 | 49.3 | 79 | 179 | 115 | 141 | 81.6 | 706 | 22.8 |
| Rashad Phillips, Detroit .....................Sr | 35 | 232 | 536 | 43.3 | 136 | 329 | 185 | 202 | 91.6 | 785 | 22.4 |
| Brandon Wolfram, Texas-El Paso.......Sr | 32 | 251 | 425 | 59.1 | 6 | 18 | 206 | 250 | 82.4 | 714 | 22.3 |
| Rasual Butler, LaSalle.........................Jr | 29 | 231 | 574 | 40.2 | 97 | 272 | 82 | 97 | 84.5 | 641 | 22.1 |
| Brandon Armstrong, Pepperdine .......Jr | 31 | 240 | 537 | 44.7 | 76 | 198 | 128 | 155 | 82.6 | 684 | 22.1 |
| Marvin O'Connor, St. Joseph............Jr | 32 | 240 | 516 | 46.5 | 99 | 265 | 127 | 188 | 67.6 | 706 | 22.1 |
| Tarvis Williams, Hampton .................Sr | 32 | 259 | 487 | 53.2 | 0 | 0 | 184 | 253 | 72.7 | 702 | 21.9 |
| Troy Murphy, Notre Dame ................Sr | 30 | 223 | 473 | 47.1 | 30 | 86 | 177 | 231 | 76.6 | 653 | 21.8 |
| Trenton Hassell, Austin Peay............Sr | 32 | 246 | 507 | 48.5 | 53 | 138 | 148 | 186 | 79.6 | 693 | 21.7 |
| Isaac Spencer, Murray St.................Sr | 29 | 225 | 461 | 48.8 | 6 | 36 | 170 | 241 | 70.5 | 626 | 21.6 |
| Jason Williams, Duke.......................So | 39 | 285 | 603 | 47.3 | 132 | 309 | 139 | 211 | 65.9 | 841 | 21.6 |
| Demond Mallet, McNeese St..............Sr | 31 | 216 | 501 | 43.1 | 107 | 275 | 121 | 152 | 79.6 | 660 | 21.3 |
| Carlos Arroyo, Florida International....Sr | 29 | 215 | 499 | 43.1 | 52 | 176 | 134 | 180 | 74.4 | 616 | 21.2 |
| Kareem Rush, Missouri......................So | 26 | 192 | 434 | 44.2 | 69 | 154 | 96 | 120 | 80.0 | 549 | 21.1 |
| Joseph Forte, N Carolina...................So | 33 | 251 | 558 | 45.0 | 55 | 146 | 133 | 156 | 85.3 | 690 | 20.9 |
| Michael Bradley, Villanova ................Jr | 31 | 254 | 367 | 69.2 | 12 | 34 | 125 | 212 | 59.0 | 645 | 20.8 |
| Troy Bell, Boston College .................So | 32 | 186 | 405 | 45.9 | 70 | 179 | 210 | 245 | 85.7 | 652 | 20.4 |
| Ian Chadwick, Wofford.....................Sr | 25 | 160 | 372 | 43.0 | 73 | 220 | 116 | 148 | 78.4 | 509 | 20.4 |
| Steven Howard, St. Francis (NY)........Sr | 29 | 171 | 447 | 38.3 | 92 | 254 | 153 | 179 | 85.5 | 587 | 20.2 |
| Brian Heinle, Cal St–Northridge.........Sr | 32 | 229 | 458 | 50.0 | 52 | 121 | 136 | 207 | 65.7 | 646 | 20.2 |
| Mike Wilks, Rice...............................Sr | 30 | 190 | 434 | 43.8 | 56 | 145 | 168 | 215 | 78.1 | 604 | 20.1 |
| Tierre Brown, McNeese St.................Sr | 31 | 213 | 518 | 41.1 | 51 | 152 | 146 | 184 | 79.3 | 623 | 20.1 |
| Wes Burtner, Belmont.......................Jr | 28 | 175 | 386 | 45.3 | 93 | 240 | 119 | 144 | 82.6 | 562 | 20.1 |
| Shane Battier, Duke...........................Sr | 39 | 251 | 533 | 47.1 | 124 | 296 | 152 | 191 | 79.6 | 778 | 19.9 |

### FIELD-GOAL PERCENTAGE

| | Class | GP | FG | FGA | Pct |
|---|---|---|---|---|---|
| Michael Bradley, Villanova........Jr | 31 | 254 | 367 | 69.2 |
| Nakiea Miller, Iona ...................Sr | 27 | 163 | 244 | 66.8 |
| Kimani Ffriend, Nebraska .........Sr | 28 | 144 | 231 | 62.3 |
| Andre Hutson, Michigan St.......Sr | 32 | 173 | 278 | 62.2 |
| George Evans, George Mason ...Sr | 30 | 233 | 380 | 61.3 |
| Carlos Boozer, Duke ................So | 32 | 160 | 265 | 60.4 |
| Steffon Bradford, Nebraska .....Sr | 30 | 155 | 257 | 60.3 |
| Terry Black, Baylor ..................Sr | 31 | 191 | 317 | 60.3 |
| Joe Linderman, Drexel.............Sr | 24 | 146 | 244 | 59.8 |
| Nick Collison, Kansas ..............So | 33 | 187 | 313 | 59.7 |

Note: Minimum 5 made per game.

### FREE-THROW PERCENTAGE

| | Class | GP | FT | FTA | Pct |
|---|---|---|---|---|---|
| Gary Buchanan, Villanova........So | 31 | 97 | 103 | 94.2 |
| Brent Jolly, Tennessee Tech......So | 29 | 95 | 102 | 93.1 |
| Ryan Mendez, Stanford ...........Sr | 34 | 94 | 101 | 93.1 |
| Rashad Phillips, Detroit ...........Sr | 35 | 185 | 202 | 91.6 |
| Ronnie McCollum, Centenary ...Sr | 27 | 214 | 236 | 90.7 |
| Titus Ivory, Penn St ................Sr | 33 | 125 | 139 | 89.9 |
| Chris Spatola, Army ................Jr | 28 | 149 | 166 | 89.8 |
| Albert Mouring, Connecticut....Sr | 32 | 104 | 117 | 88.9 |
| Scott Knapp, Siena .................Sr | 31 | 80 | 90 | 88.9 |
| Dominic Smith, Houston...........Jr | 29 | 142 | 160 | 88.8 |

Note: Minimum 2.5 made per game.

### REBOUNDS

| | Class | GP | Reb | Avg |
|---|---|---|---|---|
| Chris Marcus, Western Kentucky....Jr | 31 | 374 | 12.1 |
| Reggie Evans, Iowa .......................Jr | 35 | 416 | 11.9 |
| J.R. VanHoose, Marshall................Jr | 27 | 299 | 11.1 |
| David West, Xavier.........................So | 29 | 316 | 10.9 |
| Eddie Griffin, Seton Hall.................Fr | 30 | 323 | 10.8 |
| Jeremy Jefferson, AR–Pine Bluff....Jr | 23 | 246 | 10.7 |
| Brian Carroll, Loyola (MD) .............Sr | 27 | 286 | 10.6 |
| Eric Mann, VMI..............................Sr | 28 | 294 | 10.5 |
| Joe Breakenridge, Northern Iowa...Sr | 28 | 294 | 10.5 |
| Alvin Jones, Georgia Tech..............Sr | 30 | 312 | 10.4 |

### ASSISTS

| | Class | GP | A | Avg |
|---|---|---|---|---|
| Markus Carr, Cal St–Northridge ......Jr | 32 | 286 | 8.9 |
| Omar Cook, St. John's ...................Fr | 29 | 252 | 8.7 |
| Sean Kennedy, Marist ....................Jr | 27 | 219 | 8.1 |
| Tito Maddox, Fresno St..................So | 25 | 200 | 8.0 |
| Ashley Robinson, Mississippi Valley..Jr | 27 | 201 | 7.4 |
| Brandon Pardon, Bowling Green ...Jr | 29 | 204 | 7.0 |
| Jeremy Stanton, Evansville.............Sr | 26 | 181 | 7.0 |
| Kirk Hinrich, Kansas.......................So | 33 | 229 | 6.9 |
| Steve Blake, Maryland ...................So | 36 | 248 | 6.9 |
| Allen Griffin, Syracuse ...................Sr | 34 | 220 | 6.5 |

*Includes games played in tournaments.

## THREE-POINT FIELD-GOAL PERCENTAGE

| | Class | GP | FG | FGA | Pct |
|---|---|---|---|---|---|
| Amory Sanders, SE Missouri St | Sr | 24 | 53 | 95 | 55.8 |
| David Falknor, Akron | Jr | 22 | 47 | 87 | 54.0 |
| Cary Cochran, Nebraska | Jr | 30 | 78 | 165 | 47.3 |
| Casey Jacobsen, Stanford | So | 34 | 84 | 178 | 47.2 |
| Tim Erickson, Idaho St | Sr | 28 | 82 | 177 | 46.3 |
| Justin Brown, Montana St | Jr | 30 | 60 | 130 | 46.2 |
| Luke McDonald, Drake | Fr | 28 | 86 | 187 | 46.0 |
| Sean Jackson, UC–Irvine | Sr | 30 | 62 | 135 | 45.9 |
| Brian Chase, Virginia Tech | So | 23 | 60 | 131 | 45.8 |
| Jason Kapono, UCLA | So | 32 | 84 | 184 | 45.7 |

Note: Minimum 1.5 made per game.

## THREE-POINT FIELD GOALS MADE PER GAME

| | Class | GP | FG | Avg |
|---|---|---|---|---|
| DeWayne Jefferson, Mississippi Valley | Sr | 27 | 107 | 4.0 |
| Rashad Phillips, Detroit | Sr | 35 | 136 | 3.9 |
| Brian Merriweather, TX–Pan Am | Sr | 29 | 108 | 3.7 |
| Cory Schwab, Northern Arizona | Sr | 29 | 105 | 3.6 |
| Demond Mallet, McNeese St | Sr | 31 | 107 | 3.5 |
| Tony Orciari, Vermont | Sr | 27 | 92 | 3.4 |
| Jason Williams, Duke | So | 39 | 132 | 3.4 |
| Rasual Butler, LaSalle | Jr | 29 | 97 | 3.3 |
| Darius Lane, Seton Hall | Jr | 31 | 103 | 3.3 |
| Wes Burtner, Belmont | Jr | 28 | 93 | 3.3 |
| E.J. Gallup, Albany | Fr | 28 | 93 | 3.3 |

## BLOCKED SHOTS

| | Class | GP | BS | Avg |
|---|---|---|---|---|
| Tarvis Williams, Hampton | Sr | 32 | 147 | 4.6 |
| Eddie Griffin, Seton Hall | Fr | 30 | 133 | 4.4 |
| Wojciech Myrda, Louisiana–Monroe | Jr | 28 | 123 | 4.4 |
| Kris Hunter, Jacksonville | Sr | 28 | 114 | 4.1 |
| Ken Johnson, Ohio St | Sr | 31 | 125 | 4.0 |
| Hondre Brewer, San Francisco | Jr | 30 | 114 | 3.8 |
| Brendan Haywood, N Carolina | Sr | 33 | 120 | 3.6 |
| Jason Jennings, Arkansas St | Jr | 29 | 102 | 3.5 |
| Patrick Flomo, Ohio | Jr | 30 | 105 | 3.5 |
| Alvin Jones, Georgia Tech | Sr | 30 | 101 | 3.4 |

## STEALS

| | Class | GP | S | Avg |
|---|---|---|---|---|
| Greedy Daniels, Texas Christian | Jr | 25 | 108 | 4.3 |
| Desmond Cambridge, Alabama A&M | Jr | 28 | 107 | 3.8 |
| Senecca Wall, Sam Houston St | Sr | 29 | 103 | 3.6 |
| John Linehan, Providence | Jr | 26 | 81 | 3.1 |
| Fred House, Southern Utah | Sr | 31 | 93 | 3.0 |
| Andy Woodley, Northern Iowa | Jr | 27 | 80 | 3.0 |
| Kevin Braswell, Georgetown | Jr | 33 | 94 | 2.8 |
| Andrew Gellert, Harvard | Jr | 26 | 72 | 2.8 |
| Cookie Belcher, Nebraska | Sr | 30 | 82 | 2.7 |
| Mire Chatman, TX–Pan America | Jr | 29 | 78 | 2.7 |

## Single-Game Highs

### POINTS

50 ............Oliver Morton, Chattanooga, Jan 24 (vs. Pikeville)
49 ............Trevor Diggs, UNLV, Mar 3 (vs. Wyoming)
45 ............Senecca Wall, Sam Houston St, Mar 6 (vs. TX–Arlington)

### REBOUNDS

23 ............Clifton Jones, Old Dominion, Feb 26 (vs. NC–Wilmington)
22 ............Jamahl Mosley, Colorado, Jan 10 (vs. Missouri)
Six with tied 21.

### ASSISTS

17 ............Omar Cook, St. John's (NY), Nov 18 (vs. Stony Brook)
17 ............Tito Maddox, Fresno St, Jan 10 (vs. Texas Christian)
16 ............Greedy Daniels, Texas Christian, Dec 9 (vs. Central Oklahoma)
16 ............Flinder Boyd, Dartmouth, Jan 20 (vs. Albany)
16 ............Sean Peterson, Georgia Southern, Feb 10 (vs. E Tennessee St)

### THREE-POINT FIELD GOALS

11 ............Cory Schwab, Northern Arizona, Dec 2 (vs. Cal–Poly)
11 ............Ron Williamson, Howard, Dec 16 (vs. Georgetown)
10 ............Ravonte Dantzler, S Alabama, Dec 9 (vs. Alabama St)
10 ............Ryan Dillon, Cal St–Fullerton, Jan 31 (vs. Boise St)

### STEALS

12 ............Greedy Daniels, Texas Christian, Dec 30 (vs. AR–Pine Bluff)
10 ............Morris Scott, Florida A&M, Nov 27 (vs. Alabama St)
9 ............Fred House, Southern Utah, Nov 26 (vs. Idaho St)
9 ............Fred House, Southern Utah, Dec 19 (vs. Western Oregon)

### BLOCKED SHOTS

13 ............D'or Fischer, Northwestern St, Jan 22 (vs. SW Texas St)
12 ............Tarvis Williams, Hampton, Jan 13 (vs. Delaware St)
11 ............Walter Harper, Alcorn St, Nov 21 (vs. Southern Miss)
11 ............Gerrick Morris, South Florida, Nov 28 (vs. George Washington)
11 ............Jason Jennings, Arkansas St, Dec 18 (vs. Morris Brown)

## SCORING OFFENSE

| | GP | W | L | Pts | Avg |
|---|---|---|---|---|---|
| Texas Christian | 31 | 20 | 11 | 2902 | 93.6 |
| Duke | 39 | 35 | 4 | 3538 | 90.7 |
| Maryland | 36 | 25 | 11 | 3067 | 85.2 |
| Virginia | 29 | 20 | 9 | 2464 | 85.0 |
| McNeese St | 31 | 22 | 9 | 2580 | 83.2 |
| Stanford | 34 | 31 | 3 | 2829 | 83.2 |
| Cal St–Northridge | 32 | 22 | 10 | 2650 | 82.8 |
| Eastern Illinois | 31 | 21 | 10 | 2564 | 82.7 |
| Wagner | 29 | 16 | 13 | 2393 | 82.5 |
| Gonzaga | 33 | 26 | 7 | 2720 | 82.4 |

## SCORING DEFENSE

| | GP | W | L | Pts | Avg |
|---|---|---|---|---|---|
| Wisconsin | 29 | 18 | 11 | 1641 | 56.6 |
| Utah St | 34 | 28 | 6 | 1959 | 57.6 |
| Princeton | 27 | 16 | 11 | 1569 | 58.1 |
| NC–Wilmington | 30 | 19 | 11 | 1751 | 58.4 |
| Miami (OH) | 33 | 17 | 16 | 1928 | 58.4 |
| Columbia | 27 | 12 | 15 | 1591 | 58.9 |
| Charleston | 29 | 22 | 7 | 1739 | 60.0 |
| MO–Kansas City | 30 | 14 | 16 | 1815 | 60.5 |
| Richmond | 29 | 22 | 7 | 1763 | 60.8 |
| Butler | 32 | 24 | 8 | 1946 | 60.8 |

## SCORING MARGIN

| | Off | Def | Mar |
|---|---|---|---|
| Duke | 90.7 | 70.5 | 20.2 |
| Stanford | 83.2 | 65.5 | 17.7 |
| Michigan St | 77.4 | 61.8 | 15.6 |
| Arizona | 81.3 | 66.3 | 15.0 |
| Florida | 80.9 | 67.1 | 13.8 |
| Gonzaga | 82.4 | 68.8 | 13.6 |
| Western Kentucky | 74.3 | 60.9 | 13.4 |
| Utah St | 70.7 | 57.6 | 13.1 |
| Boston College | 79.6 | 66.5 | 13.1 |
| Maryland | 85.2 | 72.4 | 12.8 |

## FIELD-GOAL PERCENTAGE

| | FG | FGA | Pct |
|---|---|---|---|
| Stanford | .953 | 1865 | 51.1 |
| Gonzaga | .915 | 1793 | 51.0 |
| Austin Peay | .935 | 1845 | 50.7 |
| Kansas | 1002 | 1996 | 50.2 |
| Villanova | .845 | 1708 | 49.5 |
| Cal St–Northridge | .910 | 1842 | 49.4 |
| Texas–El Paso | .878 | 1786 | 49.2 |
| Michigan St | .957 | 1957 | 48.9 |
| Southern Utah | .783 | 1602 | 48.9 |
| Central Michigan | .669 | 1370 | 48.8 |

## FIELD-GOAL PERCENTAGE DEFENSE

| | FG | FGA | Pct |
|---|---|---|---|
| Kansas | 782 | 2069 | 37.8 |
| Holy Cross | 628 | 1642 | 38.2 |
| Illinois | 748 | 1936 | 38.6 |
| Georgetown | 745 | 1922 | 38.8 |
| Texas | 734 | 1889 | 38.9 |
| Alabama St | 728 | 1869 | 39.0 |
| Columbia | 525 | 1344 | 39.1 |
| N Carolina | 859 | 2196 | 39.1 |
| Michigan St | 716 | 1823 | 39.3 |
| Notre Dame | 781 | 1988 | 39.3 |

## FREE-THROW PERCENTAGE

| | FT | FTA | Pct |
|---|---|---|---|
| Brigham Young | 651 | 835 | 78.0 |
| Eastern Illinois | 504 | 650 | 77.5 |
| NC–Greensboro | 552 | 718 | 76.9 |
| Bowling Green | 546 | 712 | 76.7 |
| Penn St | 587 | 768 | 76.4 |
| Kent St | 564 | 739 | 76.3 |
| Manhattan | 471 | 618 | 76.2 |
| Drake | 428 | 562 | 76.2 |
| MO–Kansas City | 315 | 414 | 76.1 |
| Charleston | 467 | 615 | 75.9 |

## THREE-POINT FIELD GOALS MADE PER GAME

| | GP | FG | Avg |
|---|---|---|---|
| Duke | 39 | 407 | 10.4 |
| Belmont | 28 | 288 | 10.3 |
| Samford | 29 | 284 | 9.8 |
| Mississippi Valley St | 27 | 250 | 9.3 |
| Charlotte | 33 | 305 | 9.2 |
| Tennessee St | 29 | 260 | 9.0 |
| Arkansas | 31 | 273 | 8.8 |
| WI–Milwaukee | 28 | 244 | 8.7 |
| Georgia Tech | 30 | 260 | 8.7 |
| Texas Christian | 31 | 268 | 8.6 |

## THREE-POINT FIELD GOAL PERCENTAGE

| | GP | FG | FGA | Pct |
|---|---|---|---|---|
| Akron | 28 | 189 | 436 | 43.3 |
| Stanford | 34 | 252 | 587 | 42.9 |
| New Orleans | 29 | 186 | 444 | 41.9 |
| Iowa St | 31 | 182 | 436 | 41.7 |
| Montana St | 30 | 226 | 544 | 41.5 |
| Northern Arizona | 29 | 237 | 571 | 41.5 |
| Butler | 32 | 251 | 617 | 40.7 |
| AR–Little Rock | 29 | 200 | 492 | 40.7 |
| Ball St | 30 | 193 | 477 | 40.5 |
| Gonzaga | 33 | 245 | 606 | 40.4 |

Note: Minimum 3.0 made per game.

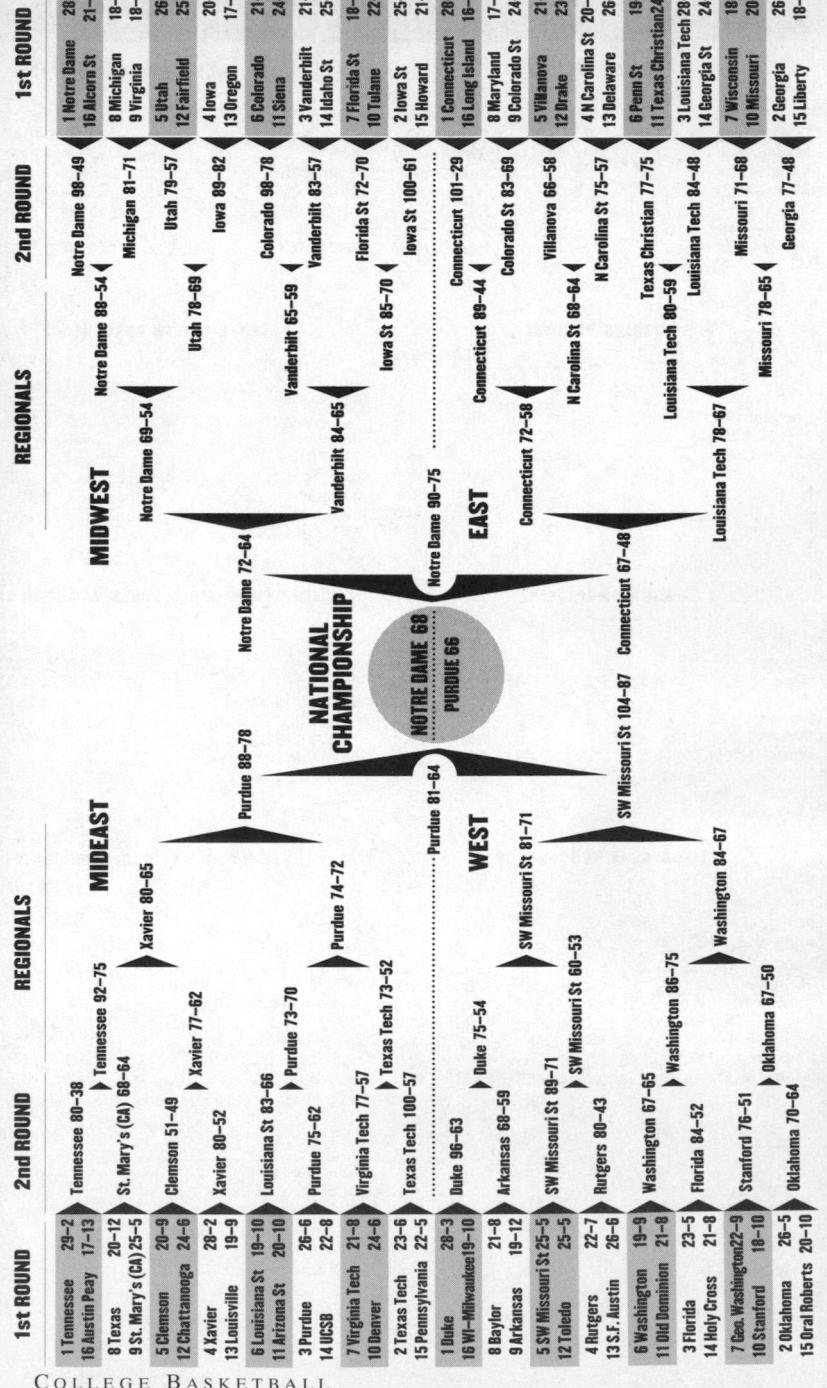

# 2001 NCAA Basketball Women's Division I Tournament

## MIDWEST

### 1st ROUND

| 1 Tennessee | 29–2 |
| 16 Austin Peay | 17–13 |
| 8 Texas | 20–12 |
| 9 St. Mary's (CA) | 25–5 |
| 5 Clemson | 20–9 |
| 12 Chattanooga | 24–6 |
| 4 Xavier | 28–2 |
| 13 Louisville | 19–9 |
| 6 Louisiana St | 19–10 |
| 11 Arizona St | 20–10 |
| 3 Purdue | 26–6 |
| 14 UCSB | 22–8 |
| 7 Virginia Tech | 21–8 |
| 10 Denver | 24–6 |
| 2 Texas Tech | 23–6 |
| 15 Pennsylvania | 22–5 |

### 2nd ROUND

Tennessee 80–38
Tennessee 92–75
St. Mary's (CA) 68–64
Clemson 51–49
Xavier 77–62
Xavier 80–52
Louisiana St 83–66
Purdue 73–70
Purdue 75–62
Virginia Tech 77–57
Texas Tech 73–52
Texas Tech 100–57

### REGIONALS

Xavier 80–65

Purdue 74–72

## MIDEAST

Xavier 80–65

Purdue 74–72

**Purdue 81–64**

## NATIONAL CHAMPIONSHIP

**NOTRE DAME 68
PURDUE 66**

---

## WEST

### REGIONALS

SW Missouri St 81–71

Washington 84–67

**Purdue 88–78**

SW Missouri St 104–87

### 2nd ROUND

Duke 96–63
Arkansas 68–59
SW Missouri St 89–71
Rutgers 80–43
Washington 67–65
Florida 84–52
Stanford 76–51
Oklahoma 70–64

SW Missouri St 60–53

Washington 86–75

Oklahoma 67–50

### 1st ROUND

| 1 Duke | 28–3 |
| 16 WI–Milwaukee | 19–10 |
| 8 Baylor | 21–8 |
| 9 Arkansas | 19–12 |
| 5 SW Missouri St | 25–5 |
| 12 Toledo | 25–5 |
| 4 Rutgers | 22–7 |
| 13 S.F. Austin | 26–6 |
| 6 Washington | 19–9 |
| 11 Old Dominion | 21–8 |
| 3 Florida | 23–5 |
| 14 Holy Cross | 21–8 |
| 7 Geo. Washington | 22–9 |
| 10 Stanford | 18–10 |
| 2 Oklahoma | 26–5 |
| 15 Oral Roberts | 20–10 |

---

## MIDWEST (top-right)

### 1st ROUND

| 1 Notre Dame | 28–2 |
| 16 Alcorn St | 21–10 |
| 8 Michigan | 18–11 |
| 9 Virginia | 18–13 |
| 5 Utah | 26–3 |
| 12 Fairfield | 25–5 |
| 4 Iowa | 20–9 |
| 13 Oregon | 17–11 |
| 6 Colorado | 21–8 |
| 11 Siena | 24–5 |
| 3 Vanderbilt | 21–9 |
| 14 Idaho St | 25–4 |
| 7 Florida St | 18–11 |
| 10 Tulane | 22–9 |
| 2 Iowa St | 25–5 |
| 15 Howard | 21–9 |

### 2nd ROUND

Notre Dame 98–49
Notre Dame 88–54
Michigan 81–71
Utah 79–57
Utah 78–69
Iowa 89–82
Colorado 98–78
Vanderbilt 65–59
Vanderbilt 83–57
Florida St 72–70
Iowa St 85–70
Iowa St 100–61

### REGIONALS

Notre Dame 69–54

Vanderbilt 84–65

## EAST

**Notre Dame 72–64**

**Notre Dame 90–75**

---

## EAST (bottom-right)

### REGIONALS

Connecticut 72–58

Louisiana Tech 78–67

**Connecticut 67–48**

### 2nd ROUND

Connecticut 89–44
Colorado St 83–69
Villanova 66–58
N Carolina St 75–57
Texas Christian 77–75
Louisiana Tech 84–48
Missouri 71–68
Georgia 77–48

Connecticut 101–29
Connecticut 72–58
N Carolina St 68–64
Louisiana Tech 80–59
Missouri 78–65

### 1st ROUND

| 1 Connecticut | 28–2 |
| 16 Long Island | 16–14 |
| 8 Maryland | 17–11 |
| 9 Colorado St | 24–6 |
| 5 Villanova | 21–8 |
| 12 Drake | 23–6 |
| 4 N Carolina St | 20–10 |
| 13 Delaware | 26–4 |
| 6 Penn St | 19–9 |
| 11 Texas Christian | 24–7 |
| 3 Louisiana Tech | 28–4 |
| 14 Georgia St | 24–6 |
| 7 Wisconsin | 18–9 |
| 10 Missouri | 20–9 |
| 2 Georgia | 26–5 |
| 15 Liberty | 18–11 |

# NCAA Women's Championship Game Box Score

## Notre Dame 68

| Notre Dame | Min | FG M-A | FT M-A | Reb O-T | A | PF | TP |
|---|---|---|---|---|---|---|---|
| Haney | 35 | 6–11 | 1–2 | 1–5 | 2 | 3 | 13 |
| Siemon | 40 | 5–11 | 0–0 | 2–9 | 6 | 3 | 10 |
| Riley | 35 | 9–13 | 10–14 | 6–13 | 1 | 3 | 28 |
| Ratay | 25 | 1–6 | 0–0 | 0–4 | 2 | 4 | 3 |
| Ivey | 40 | 5–13 | 2–3 | 1–5 | 4 | 0 | 12 |
| Joyce | 20 | 0–2 | 2–2 | 0–0 | 1 | 1 | 2 |
| Barksdale | 5 | 0–0 | 0–0 | 1–2 | 0 | 0 | 0 |
| Totals | 200 | 26–56 | 15–21 | 11–38 | 16 | 14 | 68 |

Percentages: FG—.464, FT—.714. 3-pt goals: 1–10, .100 (Ratay 1–4, Ivey 0–4, Joyce 0–2). Team rebounds: 0. Blocked shots: 11 (Riley 7, Barksdale 2, Haney, Ivey). Turnovers: 15 (Siemon 7, Ivey 4, Riley 3, Ratay). Steals: 8 (Ivey 6, Haney, Ratay).

## Purdue 66

| Purdue | Min | FG M-A | FT M-A | Reb O-T | A | PF | TP |
|---|---|---|---|---|---|---|---|
| Hurns | 39 | 7–13 | 3–5 | 4–7 | 0 | 0 | 17 |
| Wright | 34 | 6–15 | 3–5 | 2–4 | 0 | 2 | 17 |
| Cooper | 23 | 3–9 | 0–0 | 1–6 | 2 | 4 | 6 |
| Douglas | 40 | 6–15 | 3–3 | 1–7 | 5 | 2 | 18 |
| Komara | 37 | 3–9 | 0–0 | 0–2 | 2 | 1 | 8 |
| Hicks | 1 | 0–0 | 0–0 | 0–0 | 0 | 0 | 0 |
| Parks | 12 | 0–3 | 0–0 | 1–2 | 1 | 1 | 0 |
| Crawford | 11 | 0–2 | 0–2 | 3–4 | 2 | 4 | 0 |
| Noon | 3 | 0–1 | 0–0 | 0–0 | 0 | 2 | 0 |
| Totals | 200 | 25–67 | 9–15 | 12–32 | 12 | 16 | 66 |

Percentages: FG—.373, FT—.600. 3-pt goals: 7–17, .412 (Wright 2–4, Douglas 3–6, Komara 2–5, Parks 0–2). Team rebounds: 9. Blocked shots: 4 (Cooper 2, Wright, Hurns). Turnovers: 16 (Douglas 6, Cooper 2, Hurns 2, Wright 2, Crawford, Komara, Parks). Steals: 10 (Douglas 5, Cooper, Crawford, Hurns, Komara, Wright).

Halftime: Purdue 32, Notre Dame 26.
A: 20,551. Officials: Bell, Yarbrough, Mattingly.

# NCAA Women's Division I Individual Leaders

### SCORING

| Player and Team | Class | GP | TFG | 3FG | FT | Pts | Avg |
|---|---|---|---|---|---|---|---|
| Jackie Stiles, SW Missouri St | Sr | 35 | 365 | 65 | 267 | 1062 | 30.3 |
| Deanna Jackson, Alabama–Birmingham | Jr | 31 | 275 | 47 | 180 | 777 | 25.1 |
| Janet Holt, Tennessee Tech | Jr | 30 | 236 | 17 | 249 | 738 | 24.6 |
| LaToya Thomas, Mississippi | So | 31 | 276 | 5 | 195 | 752 | 24.3 |
| Susan Moran, St. Joseph's | Jr | 28 | 230 | 0 | 173 | 633 | 22.6 |
| Natalie Powers, Western Kentucky | Jr | 33 | 225 | 68 | 218 | 736 | 22.3 |
| Brooke Armistead, Austin Peay | So | 31 | 244 | 42 | 155 | 685 | 22.1 |
| Sheila Lambert, Baylor | Jr | 30 | 242 | 30 | 148 | 662 | 22.1 |
| Jaynetta Saunders, Texas A&M | Sr | 28 | 240 | 31 | 100 | 611 | 21.8 |
| Diana Caramanico, Pennsylvania | Sr | 28 | 230 | 8 | 139 | 607 | 21.7 |
| Michelle Maslowski, Drexel | Jr | 29 | 201 | 1 | 222 | 625 | 21.6 |
| Jamie Thomatis, Middle Tennessee St | Jr | 30 | 222 | 34 | 161 | 639 | 21.3 |
| Chantelle Anderson, Vanderbilt | So | 34 | 292 | 4 | 134 | 722 | 21.2 |
| Danielle Crockrom, Baylor | Jr | 30 | 249 | 0 | 139 | 637 | 21.2 |
| Marie Ferdinand, Louisiana St | Sr | 31 | 240 | 1 | 173 | 654 | 21.1 |

## Ol' Lefty Is a Winner Again

There's a small sign in Lefty Driesell's office at Georgia State that reads: IF THE GOING'S GETTING EASIER, YOU AIN'T CLIMBING.. Living by that philosophy, Driesell accepted the coaching job at Georgia State, an Atlanta commuter college, in March 1997, even though the Panthers had one of the worst programs in the nation. A school with only three winning seasons in 34 years met a coach with only two losing seasons in 35. But just as he did at Davidson, Maryland and James Madison earlier in his career, Driesell is winning big.

Georgia State's 75-58 victory over Jacksonville State on February 10 ran its record to 20-3. "I've always enjoyed the challenge of building a team," Driesell says. "People appreciate success more in places where they haven't had much, and I thought this was a sleeping giant."

Driesell, 69, is the Father Flanagan of college basketball. Ten of Georgia State's 12 players began their careers at other schools . . . "We're a bunch of basketball gypsies," senior guard Shernard Long says. "A lot of us were coaches' nightmares who got a second chance, and we're united by a promise to check our egos at the door."

Driesell is trying to guide the Panthers to their second NCAA bid and join Oklahoma State's Eddie Sutton as the only coaches to take four schools to the tournament. One of the most celebrated coaches never to reach a Final Four, Driesell is second among active coaches in victories . . . Driesell recently signed a contract extension through the 2003–04 season. "I'm still having fun, so why would I want to retire?" he said.

### FIELD-GOAL PERCENTAGE

| Player and Team | Class | GP | FG | FGA | Pct |
|---|---|---|---|---|---|
| Chantelle Anderson, Vanderbilt..So | | 34 | 292 | 404 | 72.3 |
| Angie Welle, Iowa St .................Jr | | 33 | 228 | 348 | 65.5 |
| April Cromartie, Campbell........Jr | | 29 | 193 | 296 | 65.2 |
| Ruth Riley, Notre Dame ...........Sr | | 36 | 245 | 390 | 62.8 |
| Jennifer Phillips, Xavier............Sr | | 34 | 205 | 327 | 62.7 |
| Camille Cooper, Purdue ..........Sr | | 38 | 225 | 366 | 61.5 |
| Taru Tuukkanen, Xavier ...........Sr | | 34 | 259 | 431 | 60.1 |
| Janell Burse, Tulane ................Sr | | 32 | 233 | 391 | 59.6 |
| Liene Jansone, Siena .................Fr | | 30 | 157 | 267 | 58.8 |
| Tamara Bowie, Ball St ..............So | | 28 | 195 | 334 | 58.4 |

Note: Minimum 5 made per game.

### REBOUNDS

| Player and Team | Class | GP | Reb | Avg |
|---|---|---|---|---|
| Andrea Gardner, Howard...............Jr | | 31 | 439 | 14.2 |
| Angela Buckner, Wichita St ...........Fr | | 27 | 341 | 12.6 |
| Malveata Johnson, N Carolina A&T ..Sr | | 29 | 356 | 12.3 |
| Schuye LaRue, Virginia.................So | | 32 | 379 | 11.8 |
| Danielle Crockrom, Baylor .............Jr | | 30 | 347 | 11.6 |
| Deanna Jackson, UAB....................Jr | | 31 | 358 | 11.5 |
| LaQuanda Barksdale, N Carolina...Sr | | 29 | 334 | 11.5 |
| Anne Tierney, Lehigh.....................So | | 30 | 335 | 11.2 |
| Brenda Abakwue, Sam Houston St..Sr | | 27 | 297 | 11.0 |
| Sheena Johnson, Texas–Arlington...Fr | | 27 | 292 | 10.8 |

### FREE-THROW PERCENTAGE

| Player and Team | Class | GP | FT | FTA | Pct |
|---|---|---|---|---|---|
| Brooke Lassiter, Louisiana Tech..Jr | | 36 | 111 | 122 | 91.0 |
| Kandi Brown, Morehead St.......Fr | | 29 | 75 | 83 | 90.4 |
| Kelly Pendleton, TN–Martin.......Jr | | 24 | 110 | 122 | 90.2 |
| Selena Ho, Pacific (CA)............Jr | | 24 | 100 | 111 | 90.1 |
| Tara Mitchem, SW Missouri St..Sr | | 35 | 149 | 166 | 89.8 |
| Stephanie Stanger, Weber St...Jr | | 28 | 85 | 95 | 89.5 |
| Lindsey Meder, Iowa.................Jr | | 31 | 101 | 113 | 89.4 |
| Beth Ann Dickinson, St. Peter's..So | | 28 | 96 | 108 | 88.9 |
| Katie Kelly, Eastern Kentucky...Fr | | 28 | 103 | 116 | 88.8 |
| Jackie Stiles, SW Missouri St ...Sr | | 35 | 267 | 301 | 88.7 |

Note: Minimum 2.5 made per game.

### ASSISTS

| Player and Team | Class | GP | A | Avg |
|---|---|---|---|---|
| Natasha Pointer, Rutgers...............Sr | | 31 | 257 | 8.3 |
| Reetta Piipari, Xavier......................So | | 34 | 281 | 8.3 |
| Angela Zampella, St. Joseph's.......Sr | | 27 | 220 | 8.1 |
| Jamie Lewis, Ohio St ......................Sr | | 33 | 257 | 7.8 |
| Sara Nord, Louisville......................Fr | | 29 | 227 | 7.7 |
| Reshea Bristol, Arizona..................Sr | | 32 | 242 | 7.6 |
| Michele Koclanes, Richmond ........Jr | | 28 | 208 | 7.4 |
| Stacey Dales, Oklahoma................Jr | | 34 | 248 | 7.3 |
| Toccara Williams, Texas A&M .......Fr | | 28 | 196 | 7.0 |
| Misty Garrett, Tennessee Tech.......Jr | | 30 | 209 | 7.0 |

### THREE-POINT FIELD-GOAL PERCENTAGE

| Player and Team | Class | GP | FG | FGA | Pct |
|---|---|---|---|---|---|
| Alicia Ratay, Notre Dame.........So | | 36 | 81 | 148 | 54.7 |
| Dru Bishop, Eastern Michigan ...So | | 28 | 56 | 115 | 48.7 |
| Felicia Ragland, Oregon St........Jr | | 29 | 63 | 136 | 46.3 |
| Rachael Gobble, Tennessee Tech ..Sr | | 30 | 73 | 159 | 45.9 |
| Cathy Szall, Ohio........................Jr | | 27 | 68 | 150 | 45.3 |
| Allison Clark, Tennessee Tech....Jr | | 30 | 86 | 190 | 45.3 |
| Kristin Rethman, Kansas St........Jr | | 28 | 71 | 157 | 45.2 |
| Reetta Piipari, Xavier.................So | | 34 | 73 | 163 | 44.8 |
| Natalie Powers, Western Kentucky..Jr | | 33 | 68 | 154 | 44.2 |
| Jill Sutton, Texas Christian.........Sr | | 33 | 76 | 173 | 43.9 |

Note: Minimum 1.5 made per game.

### BLOCKED SHOTS

| Player and Team | Class | GP | BS | Avg |
|---|---|---|---|---|
| Malveata Johnson, N Carolina A&T..Sr | | 29 | 95 | 3.3 |
| Ruth Riley, Notre Dame ...................Sr | | 36 | 113 | 3.1 |
| Tawana McDonald, Georgia.............Jr | | 33 | 103 | 3.1 |
| Ruta Griniute, Florida Atlantic..........Sr | | 28 | 86 | 3.1 |
| Jordan Adams, New Mexico ...........So | | 35 | 105 | 3.0 |
| Christen Roper, Hawaii ...................So | | 34 | 96 | 2.8 |
| Meribeth Feenstra, Liberty..............So | | 30 | 77 | 2.6 |
| Ayana Walker, Louisiana Tech.........Jr | | 36 | 88 | 2.4 |
| Ugo Oha, George Washington ........Fr | | 32 | 76 | 2.4 |
| Ayanna Brown, Fairfield...................Fr | | 31 | 71 | 2.3 |

---

# NCAA Men's Division II Individual Leaders

### SCORING

| Player and Team | Class | GP | TFG | 3FG | FT | Pts | Avg |
|---|---|---|---|---|---|---|---|
| Marlon Dawson, Central Oklahoma .........................Sr | | 26 | 206 | 101 | 155 | 668 | 25.7 |
| Jason Pryor, Longwood .............................................Jr | | 30 | 240 | 63 | 202 | 745 | 24.8 |
| Robbie Waldrop, Lees–McRae ................................Sr | | 25 | 206 | 112 | 89 | 613 | 24.5 |
| Daniel Willis, Lenoir–Rhyne .....................................Sr | | 27 | 198 | 69 | 195 | 660 | 24.4 |
| Chad Phillips, Westminster (PA)...............................Sr | | 23 | 189 | 47 | 133 | 558 | 24.3 |
| Harland Burgess, Oklahoma Panhandle..................Sr | | 24 | 166 | 88 | 137 | 557 | 23.2 |
| Jimmy Miller, Lincoln Memorial ...............................Sr | | 23 | 186 | 36 | 114 | 522 | 22.7 |
| Brian Atkins, Concord ...............................................Fr | | 27 | 227 | 50 | 108 | 612 | 22.7 |
| Travis Bradley, Western St .......................................Sr | | 27 | 203 | 28 | 166 | 600 | 22.2 |
| Ronald Murray, Shaw ................................................Jr | | 23 | 173 | 25 | 139 | 510 | 22.2 |

# NCAA Men's Division II Individual Leaders *(Cont.)*

## REBOUNDS

| Player and Team | Class | GP | Reb | Avg |
|---|---|---|---|---|
| Colin Ducharme, Longwood | Sr | 31 | 490 | 15.8 |
| John Laramore, Texas Lutheran | Jr | 25 | 330 | 13.2 |
| Craig Griffin, Merrimack | So | 28 | 299 | 10.7 |
| Peter Kiganya, Abilene Christian | Jr | 25 | 266 | 10.6 |
| Kenny Tate, Edinboro | Jr | 28 | 293 | 10.5 |
| Adrian Brown, NM Highlands | Jr | 25 | 254 | 10.2 |
| Tony Thomas, Fort Hays St | Sr | 29 | 289 | 10.0 |
| Ramzee Stanton, W Chester | So | 26 | 259 | 10.0 |
| Jamar Thompkins, WV Wesleyan | Jr | 29 | 287 | 9.9 |
| Derick Singleton, St. Paul's | Jr | 26 | 257 | 9.9 |
| Niki Arinze, Henderson St | Jr | 26 | 257 | 9.9 |

## FIELD-GOAL PERCENTAGE

| Player and Team | Class | GP | FG | FGA | Pct |
|---|---|---|---|---|---|
| Charles Ward, St. Augustine's | Jr | 27 | 159 | 243 | 65.4 |
| Henry Klinar, Westminster (PA) | Sr | 25 | 167 | 256 | 65.2 |
| Darian Bryant, Lynn | Sr | 26 | 130 | 201 | 64.7 |
| John Laramore, Texas Lutheran | Jr | 25 | 190 | 294 | 64.6 |
| Mark Argust, Bentley | Sr | 29 | 162 | 252 | 64.3 |
| Brian Craig, Miles | So | 27 | 142 | 222 | 64.0 |
| Ewan Auguste, Washburn | Sr | 34 | 213 | 335 | 63.6 |
| Jon Sheppard, Northeastern St | So | 28 | 199 | 317 | 62.8 |
| Seth Martin, California (PA) | Sr | 26 | 199 | 317 | 62.8 |
| Byron Johnson, Belmont Abbey | Jr | 28 | 183 | 293 | 62.5 |

Note: Minimum 5 made per game.

## ASSISTS

| Player and Team | Class | GP | A | Avg |
|---|---|---|---|---|
| Javar Cheatham, Gannon | Sr | 30 | 283 | 9.4 |
| Adam Kaufman, Edinboro | Sr | 28 | 249 | 8.9 |
| Terrence Baxter, Pfeiffer | Sr | 28 | 221 | 7.9 |
| Nate Tibbetts, S Dakota | Sr | 28 | 214 | 7.6 |
| Ryan Flores, St. Edward's | So | 27 | 202 | 7.5 |
| Corey Fox, Limestone | Sr | 27 | 187 | 6.9 |
| Pat Delany, St. Anselm | Jr | 28 | 191 | 6.8 |
| Jon Wagner, Augustana (SD) | Fr | 27 | 174 | 6.4 |
| Lajuan Christon, Southern Indiana | Jr | 30 | 193 | 6.4 |
| Lorinza Harrington, Wingate | Jr | 30 | 193 | 6.4 |

## FREE-THROW PERCENTAGE

| Player and Team | Class | GP | FT | FTA | Pct |
|---|---|---|---|---|---|
| C.J. Cowgill, Chaminade | Sr | 22 | 113 | 119 | 95.0 |
| Brent Mason, St. Joseph's (IN) | Jr | 31 | 125 | 133 | 94.0 |
| Jeremy Kudera, S Dakota | Sr | 28 | 78 | 84 | 92.9 |
| John Palosi, Texas Lutheran | Jr | 20 | 61 | 66 | 92.4 |
| Todd Manuel, St. Anselm | Jr | 28 | 146 | 160 | 91.3 |
| Drew Carlson, MN St–Mankato | So | 28 | 84 | 93 | 90.3 |
| Jamaal Bennett, Tuskegee | Jr | 24 | 74 | 82 | 90.2 |
| Matt Miller, Drury | Jr | 26 | 121 | 135 | 89.6 |
| Harland Burgess, OK Panhandle | Sr | 24 | 137 | 155 | 88.4 |
| Richard Ijeh, Assumption | Sr | 26 | 81 | 92 | 88.0 |

Note: Minimum 2.5 made per game.

# NCAA Women's Division II Individual Leaders

## SCORING

| Player and Team | Class | GP | TFG | 3FG | FT | Pts | Avg |
|---|---|---|---|---|---|---|---|
| Brandi Green, W Texas A&M | Sr | 27 | 255 | 0 | 127 | 637 | 23.6 |
| Amanda Baker, Cal St–Bakersfield | Sr | 28 | 247 | 32 | 92 | 618 | 22.1 |
| Jennifer Wilson, Fairmont St | So | 22 | 196 | 0 | 90 | 482 | 21.9 |
| Trish Fleming, IU/PU–Ft. Wayne | So | 26 | 207 | 41 | 87 | 542 | 20.8 |
| Ginnell Curtis, NC–Pembroke | Jr | 27 | 190 | 35 | 147 | 562 | 20.8 |
| Emily Bloss, Emporia St | Sr | 31 | 226 | 0 | 187 | 639 | 20.6 |
| Stormy Griffith, E Central | Fr | 25 | 185 | 0 | 144 | 514 | 20.6 |
| Tina Redmond, Colorado Christian | Sr | 26 | 188 | 60 | 98 | 534 | 20.5 |
| Tricia Peckham, Wingate | Sr | 30 | 182 | 58 | 193 | 615 | 20.5 |
| Shannon Donnelly, Cal St–Stanislaus | So | 27 | 229 | 0 | 92 | 550 | 20.4 |

## REBOUNDS

| Player and Team | Class | GP | Reb | Avg |
|---|---|---|---|---|
| Trish Martin, Morningside | Sr | 26 | 340 | 13.1 |
| Stacy Knapp, Merrimack | Jr | 27 | 350 | 13.0 |
| Amina Robinson, Franklin Pierce | Jr | 23 | 286 | 12.4 |
| Kim Vay, Edinboro | Sr | 27 | 303 | 11.2 |
| Erica Harris, Montevallo | Jr | 23 | 258 | 11.2 |
| Julie Tarrance, Livingstone | Jr | 28 | 312 | 11.1 |
| Heather Laats, Western Oregon | Jr | 26 | 285 | 11.0 |
| Natasha Ross, Fairmont St | Sr | 23 | 248 | 10.8 |
| Wanda Maynard-Morris, Pace | Jr | 30 | 323 | 10.8 |
| Fatima Carvey, Bridgeport | So | 26 | 279 | 10.7 |

## ASSISTS

| Player and Team | Class | GP | A | Avg |
|---|---|---|---|---|
| Adrianne Harlow, W Liberty St | Sr | 30 | 255 | 8.5 |
| Sabrina Stout, Glenville St | Sr | 28 | 226 | 8.1 |
| Susan Anderson, Minnesota–Duluth | Sr | 31 | 216 | 7.0 |
| Latisha Martin, Wayne St (MI) | Jr | 26 | 177 | 6.8 |
| Jacki Windon, Gannon | Jr | 31 | 208 | 6.7 |
| Stephanie Stewart, Christian Bros | Jr | 26 | 174 | 6.7 |
| Stephanie Heid, Hillsdale | So | 28 | 187 | 6.7 |
| Dena McMullen, NW Missouri St | Jr | 27 | 172 | 6.4 |
| Martina McCloud, Tuskegee | So | 27 | 171 | 6.3 |
| Joni Grubb, Alderson–Broaddus | So | 27 | 170 | 6.3 |

### FIELD-GOAL PERCENTAGE

| Player and Team | Class | GP | FGA | FG | Pct |
|---|---|---|---|---|---|
| Temeshia Dawkins, Wingate | Sr | 30 | 190 | 274 | 69.3 |
| Melanie Carter, Abilene Christian | Fr | 28 | 206 | 303 | 68.0 |
| Angie Harris, Arkansas Tech | Sr | 31 | 213 | 332 | 64.2 |
| Brandi Robinson, SE Oklahoma | Jr | 30 | 192 | 305 | 63.0 |
| Felicia Hallums, Limestone | Jr | 29 | 244 | 392 | 62.2 |
| Michelle Cottrell, N Kentucky | Jr | 30 | 187 | 301 | 62.1 |
| Myshka Wilkerson, Emporia St | Sr | 31 | 176 | 291 | 60.5 |
| Stormy Griffith, E Central | Fr | 25 | 185 | 308 | 60.1 |
| Jaana Kotova, W Liberty St | Jr | 30 | 208 | 347 | 59.9 |
| Katie Beamon, Regis (CO) | Sr | 27 | 147 | 251 | 58.6 |

Note: Minimum 5 made per game.

### FREE-THROW PERCENTAGE

| Player and Team | Class | GP | FTA | FT | Pct |
|---|---|---|---|---|---|
| Christine Kane, Assumption | Jr | 28 | 78 | 86 | 90.7 |
| Kylie Nabors, Angelo St | Sr | 28 | 125 | 139 | 89.9 |
| Anna Bell, New Hampshire | Jr | 26 | 67 | 76 | 88.2 |
| Toni Leopard, Presbyterian | Jr | 30 | 101 | 115 | 87.8 |
| Meshach Rhoades, Regis (CO) | Sr | 27 | 78 | 89 | 87.6 |
| Jacquie Rzeszut, Rockhurst | So | 27 | 69 | 79 | 87.3 |
| Blanche Tucker, Central Missouri St | Sr | 28 | 89 | 102 | 87.3 |
| Kerri Rueb, Southampton | So | 24 | 88 | 101 | 87.1 |
| Allison Bailey, Michigan Tech | Sr | 30 | 135 | 155 | 87.1 |
| Rachel Young, Bellarmine | Sr | 28 | 108 | 124 | 87.1 |

Note: Minimum 2.5 made per game.

## NCAA Men's Division III Individual Leaders

### SCORING

| Player and Team | Class | GP | TFG | 3FG | FT | Pts | Avg |
|---|---|---|---|---|---|---|---|
| Willie Chandler, Misericordia | So | 26 | 271 | 96 | 125 | 763 | 29.3 |
| Robert Moore, Mary Hardin–Baylor | Jr | 25 | 292 | 12 | 124 | 720 | 28.8 |
| Jeff Reis, Webster | Sr | 25 | 233 | 61 | 170 | 697 | 27.9 |
| K.B. Debord, Concordia–Austin | Jr | 24 | 233 | 45 | 116 | 627 | 26.1 |
| Corey Dickerson, King's (PA) | Sr | 28 | 258 | 51 | 124 | 691 | 24.7 |
| Dwayne Okantey, Lasell | Jr | 26 | 275 | 3 | 86 | 639 | 24.6 |
| Dennis Dube, New England | Sr | 21 | 185 | 11 | 129 | 510 | 24.3 |
| Greg Adams, Washington (MD) | So | 24 | 179 | 62 | 161 | 581 | 24.2 |
| Michael Lynch, Roger Williams | Sr | 25 | 223 | 24 | 121 | 591 | 23.6 |
| Brandon Dominick, Lake Erie | So | 25 | 214 | 75 | 86 | 589 | 23.6 |

### REBOUNDS

| Player and Team | Class | GP | Reb | Avg |
|---|---|---|---|---|
| Jeff Gibbs, Otterbein | Jr | 25 | 390 | 15.6 |
| Joe Corbett, Hobart | So | 28 | 364 | 13.0 |
| Jed Johnson, Maine Maritime | So | 19 | 237 | 12.5 |
| Lou Pento, Baruch | Jr | 26 | 317 | 12.2 |
| Corey Grace, Thomas More | Sr | 24 | 276 | 11.5 |
| Jesse Lisiecka, Nazareth | Sr | 25 | 284 | 11.4 |
| Stephen Erfle, Ursinus | So | 25 | 281 | 11.2 |
| Devin Lowery, Johnson & Wales | Sr | 25 | 276 | 11.0 |
| Robb Fitchlee, Fredonia St | Sr | 28 | 303 | 10.8 |
| David Schaaf, Emory | Sr | 25 | 270 | 10.8 |

### FIELD-GOAL PERCENTAGE

| Player and Team | Class | GP | FG | FGA | Pct |
|---|---|---|---|---|---|
| John Thomas, Fontbonne | So | 22 | 157 | 223 | 70.4 |
| Mike Nester, St. John's (MN) | Jr | 28 | 152 | 217 | 70.0 |
| Jarriot Rook, Washington (MO) | So | 27 | 152 | 234 | 65.0 |
| David Baranowski, Bowdoin | Sr | 23 | 140 | 216 | 64.8 |
| Wade Walters, Kean | Jr | 26 | 134 | 207 | 64.7 |
| Jeff Gibbs, Otterbein | Jr | 25 | 192 | 301 | 63.8 |
| Jonathon Jarrett, Sewanee | So | 25 | 147 | 231 | 63.6 |
| Keith Davis, Savannah A&D | Fr | 26 | 139 | 221 | 62.9 |
| David Paul, Staten Island | Jr | 28 | 205 | 326 | 62.9 |
| Neal Lewis, Eastern Mennonite | So | 25 | 125 | 200 | 62.5 |

Note: Minimum 5 made per game.

### ASSISTS

| Player and Team | Class | GP | A | Avg |
|---|---|---|---|---|
| Jimmy Driggs, Hamilton | Sr | 25 | 213 | 8.5 |
| Tennyson Whitted, Ramapo | So | 24 | 190 | 7.9 |
| Tim Gaspar, MA–Dartmouth | So | 28 | 221 | 7.9 |
| Steve King, Fontbonne | So | 25 | 195 | 7.8 |
| Jabari Harrell, Aurora | Sr | 26 | 187 | 7.2 |
| Matt Lucero, Austin | Sr | 24 | 164 | 6.8 |
| Ryan Keating, St. John's (MN) | Jr | 26 | 175 | 6.7 |
| Jason Luther, Pittsburgh–Bradford | Jr | 22 | 142 | 6.5 |
| Adam Fischer, Fontbonne | So | 23 | 146 | 6.3 |
| Diego Reino, Drew | Jr | 24 | 148 | 6.2 |

### FREE-THROW PERCENTAGE

| Player and Team | Class | GP | FT | FTA | Pct |
|---|---|---|---|---|---|
| Derrick Rogers, Averett | So | 27 | 72 | 77 | 93.5 |
| Dirk Rhinehart, Kalamazoo | So | 25 | 76 | 82 | 92.7 |
| Ryan Knuppel, Elmhurst | Sr | 27 | 111 | 121 | 91.7 |
| Al Callejas, Scranton | Sr | 26 | 107 | 117 | 91.5 |
| Shawn McCormick, Bald.–Wallace | So | 25 | 86 | 95 | 90.5 |
| Jim Conrad, Ohio Northern | Fr | 31 | 110 | 122 | 90.2 |
| Dave Stantial, Keene St | Jr | 27 | 72 | 80 | 90.0 |
| Aaron Galletta, Union (NY) | Jr | 25 | 72 | 81 | 88.9 |
| John Gleason, Springfield | Jr | 26 | 79 | 89 | 88.8 |
| Chris Lockwood, Elms | Jr | 23 | 78 | 88 | 88.6 |

Note: Minimum 2.5 made per game.

# NCAA Women's Division III Individual Leaders

## SCORING

| Player and Team | Class | GP | TFG | 3FG | FT | Pts | Avg |
|---|---|---|---|---|---|---|---|
| Emily Mullet, Eastern Mennonite | So | 24 | 203 | 104 | 116 | 626 | 26.1 |
| Angie Ensley, Cedar Crest | Sr | 24 | 224 | 76 | 102 | 626 | 26.1 |
| Rebecca Segert, Merchant Marine | Fr | 24 | 242 | 24 | 115 | 623 | 26.0 |
| E'lisa Ladson, Wesleyan (GA) | Fr | 23 | 209 | 89 | 86 | 593 | 25.8 |
| Heidi Burkhart, Rockford | Jr | 26 | 199 | 35 | 162 | 595 | 22.9 |
| Touria Ovahid, Gallaudet | Sr | 25 | 196 | 37 | 136 | 565 | 22.6 |
| Lauren Cargil, CCNY | So | 25 | 193 | 68 | 103 | 557 | 22.3 |
| Jessica Platt, Stephens | So | 17 | 141 | 32 | 59 | 373 | 21.9 |
| Chanel Kendall, Lehman | Fr | 26 | 229 | 37 | 75 | 570 | 21.9 |
| Halley Spann, Webster | Jr | 25 | 182 | 0 | 182 | 546 | 21.8 |

## REBOUNDS

| Player and Team | Class | GP | Reb | Avg |
|---|---|---|---|---|
| Crystal Wiley, Agnes Scott | Fr | 21 | 317 | 15.1 |
| Ekaterina Markova, Rosemont | So | 25 | 372 | 14.9 |
| Tiffany Stewart, Cedar Crest | Jr | 24 | 346 | 14.4 |
| Sara Zondag, Wisconsin Lutheran | Sr | 26 | 364 | 14.0 |
| Jennifer Olson, Benedictine (IL) | Jr | 25 | 346 | 13.8 |
| Amanda Smolarek, Hilbert | Fr | 18 | 239 | 13.3 |
| Llexandra Landreth, Merchant Marine | Fr | 24 | 314 | 13.1 |
| Sheryl Arduino, Daniel Webster | Sr | 21 | 267 | 12.7 |
| Jessica Platt, Stephens | So | 17 | 216 | 12.7 |
| Tanisha Giddens, Alvernia | Jr | 26 | 324 | 12.5 |

## ASSISTS

| Player and Team | Class | GP | A | Avg |
|---|---|---|---|---|
| Alisa DiBonaventura, DE Valley | Jr | 27 | 237 | 8.8 |
| Lisa Cowling, Simpson | Sr | 27 | 184 | 6.8 |
| Garrianne Brown, York (NY) | Jr | 22 | 143 | 6.5 |
| Sara Bozorg, Amherst | So | 28 | 174 | 6.2 |
| Stephanie Valerio, Staten Island | Fr | 25 | 154 | 6.2 |
| Darcy Mund, Eastern CT St. | Jr | 26 | 156 | 6.0 |
| Megan Koppenhoefer, Clarke | So | 24 | 138 | 5.8 |
| Jamie Vielmetti, Westfield St. | Sr | 25 | 141 | 5.6 |
| Devon Bonnemere, Utica | So | 21 | 117 | 5.6 |
| Jamie Dalbey, Coe | Jr | 24 | 133 | 5.5 |

## FIELD-GOAL PERCENTAGE

| Player and Team | Class | GP | FG | FGA | Pct |
|---|---|---|---|---|---|
| Kathy Darling, Rowan | So | 25 | 188 | 285 | 66.0 |
| Kelly Etzel, Gust. Adolphus | So | 25 | 145 | 225 | 64.4 |
| Kristyn Grassi, Eastern CT St. | Jr | 26 | 191 | 302 | 63.2 |
| Courtney Aimetti, Staten Island | Sr | 28 | 253 | 409 | 61.9 |
| Amber Oliver, Marietta | Jr | 25 | 125 | 203 | 61.6 |
| Megan Selmon, Trinity (TX) | So | 25 | 157 | 258 | 60.9 |
| Kate Smith, Cortland St. | Sr | 30 | 196 | 326 | 60.1 |
| Jill Dewane, Lakeland | Jr | 27 | 228 | 383 | 59.5 |
| Jaquana Abdullah, Kean | So | 24 | 164 | 276 | 59.4 |
| Amanda Dickerson, WI-Oshkosh | Jr | 25 | 127 | 214 | 59.3 |

Note: Minimum 5 made per game.

## FREE-THROW PERCENTAGE

| Player and Team | Class | GP | FT | FTA | Pct |
|---|---|---|---|---|---|
| Kendra Meyer, Capital | Sr | 24 | 60 | 68 | 88.2 |
| Keri Canning, Mount Union | Sr | 26 | 127 | 144 | 88.2 |
| Lora Trenkle, Bowdoin | Fr | 29 | 110 | 125 | 88.0 |
| Erin Crawford, Cabrini | Jr | 23 | 120 | 137 | 87.6 |
| Heather Dana, Redlands | Jr | 25 | 63 | 72 | 87.5 |
| Lenora Sundstrom, Cornell | Sr | 24 | 117 | 134 | 87.3 |
| Missy Bynon, Chapman | Jr | 24 | 67 | 77 | 87.0 |
| Kristin Gullickson, Beloit | So | 22 | 70 | 81 | 86.4 |
| Lehticia Deskins, Lynchburg | Jr | 23 | 58 | 68 | 85.3 |
| Becky Campbell, Albion | So | 23 | 75 | 88 | 85.2 |

Note: Minimum 2.5 made per game.

## Guard Shatters Mark

There are gym rats, and there's Jackie Stiles. Every day during her last two years of high school Stiles would stay in the Claflin (Kans.) High gym until she had made 1,000 baskets. This routine, which could take as long as four hours, often continued late into the night.

As a senior at Southwest Missouri State, Stiles, a 5'8" guard, broke the Division I women's career scoring record. She led the nation in scoring with a 30.3 average and finished her with 3,392 points to shatter the record of former Mississippi Valley State star Patricia Hoskins, who scored 3,122 from 1985 to '89.

With a deadly outside shot and crafty ball handling, Stiles thwarted defenses by shooting 60.3% from the field, and an astonishing 52.9% from beyond the arc. After she dropped 49 points on Northern Iowa on January 20, frustrated Panthers coach Tony DiCecco was asked how best to guard her. "I'd go with a 6'2" kid who ran in the 100 meters in the Olympics," he said.

Stiles's success at Southwest Missouri raised interest in the Lady Bears to a fever pitch in Springfield, where the school is located. One fan even carved Stiles's likeness on a piece of wood and gave it to her.

Stiles, who went fourth in April's WNBA draft, led the Lady Bears to the Final Four, which was held only 215 miles away in St. Louis. They lost to Purdue in the national semis, but it was a banner season for the Lady Bears nonetheless. And if you're looking for Stiles, you should check the gym first. "She knows all the security people on campus," says Southwest Missouri State coach Cheryl Burnett. "If they see the lights on in the gym at midnight, they know it's Jackie."

—Trisha Blackmar

## NCAA Men's Division I Championship Results

### NCAA Final Four Results

| Year | Winner | Score | Runner-up | Third Place | Fourth Place | Winning Coach |
|------|--------|-------|-----------|-------------|--------------|---------------|
| 1939 | Oregon | 46–33 | Ohio St | *Oklahoma | *Villanova | Howard Hobson |
| 1940 | Indiana | 60–42 | Kansas | *Duquesne | *Southern Cal | Branch McCracken |
| 1941 | Wisconsin | 39–34 | Washington St | *Pittsburgh | *Arkansas | Harold Foster |
| 1942 | Stanford | 53–38 | Dartmouth | *Colorado | *Kentucky | Everett Dean |
| 1943 | Wyoming | 46–34 | Georgetown | *Texas | *DePaul | Everett Shelton |
| 1944 | Utah | 42–40 (OT) | Dartmouth | *Iowa St | *Ohio St | Vadal Peterson |
| 1945 | Oklahoma St | 49–45 | NYU | *Arkansas | *Ohio St | Hank Iba |
| 1946 | Oklahoma St | 43–40 | N Carolina | Ohio St | California | Hank Iba |
| 1947 | Holy Cross | 58–47 | Oklahoma | Texas | CCNY | Alvin Julian |
| 1948 | Kentucky | 58–42 | Baylor | Holy Cross | Kansas St | Adolph Rupp |
| 1949 | Kentucky | 46–36 | Oklahoma St | Illinois | Oregon St | Adolph Rupp |
| 1950 | CCNY | 71–68 | Bradley | N Carolina St | Baylor | Nat Holman |
| 1951 | Kentucky | 68–58 | Kansas St | Illinois | Oklahoma St | Adolph Rupp |
| 1952 | Kansas | 80–63 | St. John's (NY) | Illinois | Santa Clara | Forrest Allen |
| 1953 | Indiana | 69–68 | Kansas | Washington | Louisiana St | Branch McCracken |
| 1954 | La Salle | 92–76 | Bradley | Penn St | Southern Cal | Kenneth Loeffler |
| 1955 | San Francisco | 77–63 | La Salle | Colorado | Iowa | Phil Woolpert |
| 1956 | San Francisco | 83–71 | Iowa | Temple | Southern Meth | Phil Woolpert |
| 1957 | N Carolina | 54–53 (3OT) | Kansas | San Francisco | Michigan St | Frank McGuire |
| 1958 | Kentucky | 84–72 | Seattle | Temple | Kansas St | Adolph Rupp |
| 1959 | California | 71–70 | W Virginia | Cincinnati | Louisville | Pete Newell |
| 1960 | Ohio St | 75–55 | California | Cincinnati | NYU | Fred Taylor |
| 1961 | Cincinnati | 70–65 (OT) | Ohio St | Vacated‡ | Utah | Edwin Jucker |
| 1962 | Cincinnati | 71–59 | Ohio St | Wake Forest | UCLA | Edwin Jucker |
| 1963 | Loyola (IL) | 60–58 (OT) | Cincinnati | Duke | Oregon St | George Ireland |
| 1964 | UCLA | 98–83 | Duke | Michigan | Kansas St | John Wooden |
| 1965 | UCLA | 91–80 | Michigan | Princeton | Wichita St | John Wooden |
| 1966 | UTEP | 72–65 | Kentucky | Duke | Utah | Don Haskins |
| 1967 | UCLA | 79–64 | Dayton | Houston | N Carolina | John Wooden |
| 1968 | UCLA | 78–55 | N Carolina | Ohio St | Houston | John Wooden |
| 1969 | UCLA | 92–72 | Purdue | Drake | N Carolina | John Wooden |
| 1970 | UCLA | 80–69 | Jacksonville | New Mexico St | St. Bonaventure | John Wooden |
| 1971 | UCLA | 68–62 | Vacated‡ | Vacated‡ | Kansas | John Wooden |
| 1972 | UCLA | 81–76 | Florida St | N Carolina | Louisville | John Wooden |
| 1973 | UCLA | 87–66 | Memphis St | Indiana | Providence | John Wooden |
| 1974 | N Carolina St | 76–64 | Marquette | UCLA | Kansas | Norm Sloan |
| 1975 | UCLA | 92–85 | Kentucky | Louisville | Syracuse | John Wooden |
| 1976 | Indiana | 86–68 | Michigan | UCLA | Rutgers | Bob Knight |
| 1977 | Marquette | 67–59 | N Carolina | UNLV | NC-Charlotte | Al McGuire |
| 1978 | Kentucky | 94–88 | Duke | Arkansas | Notre Dame | Joe Hall |
| 1979 | Michigan St | 75–64 | Indiana St | DePaul | Penn | Jud Heathcote |
| 1980 | Louisville | 59–54 | Vacated‡ | Purdue | Iowa | Denny Crum |
| 1981 | Indiana | 63–50 | N Carolina | Virginia | Louisiana St | Bob Knight |
| 1982 | N Carolina | 63–62 | Georgetown | *Houston | *Louisville | Dean Smith |
| 1983 | N Carolina St | 54–52 | Houston | *Georgia | *Louisville | Jim Valvano |
| 1984 | Georgetown | 84–75 | Houston | *Kentucky | *Virginia | John Thompson |
| 1985 | Villanova | 66–64 | Georgetown | St. John's (NY) | Vacated‡ | Rollie Massimino |
| 1986 | Louisville | 72–69 | Duke | *Kansas | *Louisiana St | Denny Crum |
| 1987 | Indiana | 74–73 | Syracuse | *UNLV | *Providence | Bob Knight |
| 1988 | Kansas | 83–79 | Oklahoma | *Arizona | *Duke | Larry Brown |
| 1989 | Michigan | 80–79 (OT) | Seton Hall | *Duke | *Illinois | Steve Fisher |
| 1990 | UNLV | 103–73 | Duke | *Arkansas | *Georgia Tech | Jerry Tarkanian |
| 1991 | Duke | 72–65 | Kansas | *UNLV | *N Carolina | Mike Krzyzewski |
| 1992 | Duke | 71–51 | Michigan | *Cincinnati | *Indiana | Mike Krzyzewski |
| 1993 | N Carolina | 77–71 | Michigan | *Kansas | *Kentucky | Dean Smith |
| 1994 | Arkansas | 76–72 | Duke | *Arizona | *Florida | Nolan Richardson |
| 1995 | UCLA | 89–78 | Arkansas | *N Carolina | *Oklahoma St | Jim Harrick |
| 1996 | Kentucky | 76–67 | Syracuse | Vacated‡ | Mississippi St | Rick Pitino |
| 1997 | Arizona | 84–79 (OT) | Kentucky | *Minnesota | *N Carolina | Lute Olson |
| 1998 | Kentucky | 78–69 | Utah | *Stanford | *N Carolina | Tubby Smith |
| 1999 | Connecticut | 77–74 | Duke | *Michigan St | *Ohio St | Jim Calhoun |
| 2000 | Michigan St | 89–76 | Florida | *Wisconsin | *N Carolina | Tom Izzo |
| 2001 | Duke | 82–72 | Arizona | *Maryland | *Michigan St | Mike Krzyzewski |

*Tied for third place. ‡Student-athletes representing St. Joseph's (PA) in 1961, Villanova in 1971, Western Kentucky in 1971, UCLA in 1980, Memphis State in 1985 and Massachusetts in 1996 were declared ineligible subsequent to the tournament. Under NCAA rules, the teams' and ineligible student-athletes' records were deleted, and the teams' places in the standings were vacated.

## NCAA Final Four MVPs

| Year | Winner, School | GP | FGM | Pct | FGA | FGM | FTM | Pct | Reb | A | Stl | BS | Avg |
|------|----------------|----|-----|-----|-----|-----|-----|-----|-----|---|-----|----|-----|
| | | | Field Goals | | 3-Pt FG | | Free Throws | | | | | | |
| 1939 | ....None selected | | | | | | | | | | | | |
| 1940 | ....Marv Huffman, Indiana | 2 | 7 | — | — | — | 4 | — | — | — | — | — | 9.0 |
| 1941 | ....John Kotz, Wisconsin | 2 | 8 | — | — | — | 6 | — | — | — | — | — | 11.0 |
| 1942 | ....Howard Dallmar, Stanford | 2 | 8 | — | — | — | 4 | 66.7 | — | — | — | — | 10.0 |
| 1943 | ....Ken Sailors, Wyoming | 2 | 10 | — | — | — | 8 | 72.7 | — | — | — | — | 14.0 |
| 1944 | ....Arnie Ferrin, Utah | 2 | 11 | — | — | — | 6 | — | — | — | — | — | 14.0 |
| 1945 | ....Bob Kurland, Oklahoma St | 2 | 16 | — | — | — | 5 | — | — | — | — | — | 18.5 |
| 1946 | ....Bob Kurland, Oklahoma St | 2 | 21 | — | — | — | 10 | 66.7 | — | — | — | — | 26.0 |
| 1947 | ....George Kaftan, Holy Cross | 2 | 18 | — | — | — | 12 | 70.6 | — | — | — | — | 24.0 |
| 1948 | ....Alex Groza, Kentucky | 2 | 16 | — | — | — | 5 | — | — | — | — | — | 18.5 |
| 1949 | ....Alex Groza, Kentucky | 2 | 19 | — | — | — | 14 | — | — | — | — | — | 26.0 |
| 1950 | ....Irwin Dambrot, CCNY | 2 | 12 | 42.9 | — | — | 4 | 50.0 | — | — | — | — | 14.0 |
| 1951 | ....None selected | | | | | | | | | | | | |
| 1952 | ....Clyde Lovellette, Kansas | 2 | 24 | — | — | — | 18 | — | — | — | — | — | 33.0 |
| 1953 | ....*B.H. Horn, Kansas | 2 | 17 | — | — | — | 17 | — | — | — | — | — | 25.5 |
| 1954 | ....Tom Gola, La Salle | 2 | 12 | — | — | — | 14 | — | — | — | — | — | 19.0 |
| 1955 | ....Bill Russell, San Francisco | 2 | 19 | — | — | — | 9 | — | — | — | — | — | 23.5 |
| 1956 | ....*Hal Lear, Temple | 2 | 32 | — | — | — | 16 | — | — | — | — | — | 40.0 |
| 1957 | ....*Wilt Chamberlain, Kansas | 2 | 18 | 51.4 | — | — | 19 | 70.4 | 25 | — | — | — | 32.5 |
| 1958 | ....*Elgin Baylor, Seattle | 2 | 18 | 34.0 | — | — | 12 | 75.0 | 41 | — | — | — | 24.0 |
| 1959 | ....*Jerry West, West Virginia | 2 | 22 | 66.7 | — | — | 22 | 68.8 | 25 | — | — | — | 33.0 |
| 1960 | ....Jerry Lucas, Ohio State | 2 | 16 | 66.7 | — | — | 3 | 100.0 | 23 | — | — | — | 17.5 |
| 1961 | ....*Jerry Lucas, Ohio State | 2 | 20 | 71.4 | — | — | 16 | 94.1 | 25 | — | — | — | 28.0 |
| 1962 | ....Paul Hogue, Cincinnati | 2 | 23 | 63.9 | — | — | 12 | 63.2 | 38 | — | — | — | 29.0 |
| 1963 | ....Art Heyman, Duke | 2 | 18 | 41.0 | — | — | 15 | 68.2 | 19 | — | — | — | 25.5 |
| 1964 | ....Walt Hazzard, UCLA | 2 | 11 | 55.0 | — | — | 8 | 66.7 | 10 | — | — | — | 15.0 |
| 1965 | ....*Bill Bradley, Princeton | 2 | 34 | 63.0 | — | — | 19 | 95.0 | 24 | — | — | — | 43.5 |
| 1966 | ....*Jerry Chambers, Utah | 2 | 25 | 53.2 | — | — | 20 | 83.3 | 35 | — | — | — | 35.0 |
| 1967 | ....Lew Alcindor, UCLA | 2 | 14 | 60.9 | — | — | 11 | 45.8 | 38 | — | — | — | 19.5 |
| 1968 | ....Lew Alcindor, UCLA | 2 | 22 | 62.9 | — | — | 9 | 90.0 | 34 | — | — | — | 26.5 |
| 1969 | ....Lew Alcindor, UCLA | 2 | 23 | 67.7 | — | — | 16 | 64.0 | 41 | — | — | — | 31.0 |
| 1970 | ....Sidney Wicks, UCLA | 2 | 15 | 71.4 | — | — | 9 | 60.0 | 34 | — | — | — | 19.5 |
| 1971 | ....*†Howard Porter, Villanova | 2 | 20 | 48.8 | — | — | 7 | 77.8 | 24 | — | — | — | 23.5 |
| 1972 | ....Bill Walton, UCLA | 2 | 20 | 69.0 | — | — | 17 | 73.9 | 41 | — | — | — | 28.5 |
| 1973 | ....Bill Walton, UCLA | 2 | 28 | 82.4 | — | — | 2 | 40.0 | 30 | — | — | — | 29.0 |
| 1974 | ....David Thompson, NC State | 2 | 19 | 51.4 | — | — | 11 | 78.6 | 17 | — | — | — | 24.5 |
| 1975 | ....Richard Washington, UCLA | 2 | 23 | 54.8 | — | — | 8 | 72.7 | 20 | — | — | — | 27.0 |
| 1976 | ....Kent Benson, Indiana | 2 | 17 | 50.0 | — | — | 7 | 63.6 | 18 | — | — | — | 20.5 |
| 1977 | ....Butch Lee, Marquette | 2 | 11 | 34.4 | — | — | 8 | 100.0 | 6 | 2 | 1 | 1 | 15.0 |
| 1978 | ....Jack Givens, Kentucky | 2 | 28 | 65.1 | — | — | 8 | 66.7 | 17 | 4 | 1 | 3 | 32.0 |
| 1979 | ....Earvin Johnson, Michigan St | 2 | 17 | 68.0 | — | — | 19 | 86.4 | 17 | 3 | 0 | 2 | 26.5 |
| 1980 | ....Darrell Griffith, Louisville | 2 | 23 | 62.2 | — | — | 11 | 68.8 | 7 | 15 | 0 | 2 | 28.5 |
| 1981 | ....Isiah Thomas, Indiana | 2 | 14 | 56.0 | — | — | 9 | 81.8 | 4 | 9 | 3 | 4 | 18.5 |
| 1982 | ....James Worthy, N Carolina | 2 | 20 | 74.1 | — | — | 2 | 28.6 | 8 | 9 | 0 | 4 | 21.0 |
| 1983 | ....*Akeem Olajuwon, Houston | 2 | 16 | 55.2 | — | — | 9 | 64.3 | 40 | 3 | 2 | 5 | 20.5 |
| 1984 | ....Patrick Ewing, Georgetown | 2 | 8 | 57.1 | — | — | 2 | 100.0 | 18 | 1 | 1 | 15 | 9.0 |
| 1985 | ....Ed Pinckney, Villanova | 2 | 8 | 57.1 | — | — | 12 | 75.0 | 15 | 6 | 3 | 0 | 14.0 |
| 1986 | ....Pervis Ellison, Louisville | 2 | 15 | 60.0 | — | — | 6 | 75.0 | 24 | 2 | 3 | 1 | 18.0 |
| 1987 | ....Keith Smart, Indiana | 2 | 14 | 63.6 | 1 | 0 | 7 | 77.8 | 7 | 7 | 0 | 2 | 17.5 |
| 1988 | ....Danny Manning, Kansas | 2 | 25 | 55.6 | 1 | 0 | 6 | 66.7 | 17 | 4 | 8 | 9 | 28.0 |
| 1989 | ....Glen Rice, Michigan | 2 | 24 | 49.0 | 16 | 7 | 4 | 100.0 | 16 | 1 | 0 | 3 | 29.5 |
| 1990 | ....Anderson Hunt, UNLV | 2 | 19 | 61.3 | 16 | 9 | 2 | 50.0 | 4 | 9 | 1 | 1 | 24.5 |
| 1991 | ....Christian Laettner, Duke | 2 | 12 | 54.5 | 1 | 1 | 21 | 91.3 | 17 | 2 | 1 | 2 | 23.0 |
| 1992 | ....Bobby Hurley, Duke | 2 | 10 | 41.7 | 12 | 7 | 8 | 80.0 | 3 | 11 | 0 | 3 | 17.5 |
| 1993 | ....Donald Williams, N Carolina | 2 | 15 | 65.2 | 14 | 10 | 10 | 100.0 | 4 | 2 | 2 | 0 | 25.0 |
| 1994 | ....Corliss Williamson, Arkansas | 2 | 21 | 50.0 | 0 | 0 | 10 | 71.4 | 21 | 8 | 4 | 3 | 26.0 |
| 1995 | ....Ed O'Bannon, UCLA | 2 | 16 | 45.7 | 8 | 3 | 10 | 76.9 | 25 | 3 | 7 | 1 | 22.5 |
| 1996 | ....Tony Delk, Kentucky | 2 | 15 | 41.7 | 16 | 8 | 6 | 54.6 | 9 | 2 | 3 | 2 | 22.0 |
| 1997 | ....Miles Simon, Arizona | 2 | 17 | 45.9 | 10 | 3 | 17 | 77.3 | 8 | 6 | 0 | 1 | 27.0 |
| 1998 | ....Jeff Sheppard, Kentucky | 2 | 16 | 55.2 | 10 | 4 | 7 | 77.8 | 10 | 7 | 4 | 0 | 21.5 |
| 1999 | ....Richard Hamilton, Connecticut | 2 | 20 | 51.3 | 7 | 3 | 8 | 72.7 | 12 | 4 | 2 | 1 | 25.5 |
| 2000 | ....Mateen Cleaves, Michigan St | 2 | 8 | 44.4 | 4 | 3 | 10 | 83.3 | 6 | 5 | 2 | 0 | 14.5 |
| 2001 | ....Shane Battier, Duke | 2 | 13 | 50.0 | 12 | 5 | 12 | 70.6 | 19 | 8 | 2 | 6 | 21.5 |

*Not a member of the championship-winning team.    †Record later vacated.

## Best NCAA Tournament Single-Game Scoring Performances

| Player and Team | Year | Round | FG | 3FG | FT | TP |
|---|---|---|---|---|---|---|
| Austin Carr, Notre Dame vs Ohio | 1970 | 1st | 25 | — | 11 | 61 |
| Bill Bradley, Princeton vs Wichita St. | 1965 | C* | 22 | — | 14 | 58 |
| Oscar Robertson, Cincinnati vs Arkansas | 1958 | C | 21 | — | 14 | 56 |
| Austin Carr, Notre Dame vs Kentucky | 1970 | 2nd | 22 | — | 8 | 52 |
| Austin Carr, Notre Dame vs Texas Christian | 1971 | 1st | 20 | — | 12 | 52 |
| David Robinson, Navy vs Michigan | 1987 | 1st | 22 | 0 | 6 | 50 |
| Elvin Hayes, Houston vs Loyola (IL) | 1968 | 1st | 20 | — | 9 | 49 |
| Hal Lear, Temple vs SMU | 1956 | C* | 17 | — | 14 | 48 |
| Austin Carr, Notre Dame vs Houston | 1971 | C | 17 | — | 13 | 47 |
| Dave Corzine, DePaul vs Louisville | 1978 | 2nd | 18 | — | 10 | 46 |

C=regional third place; C*=third-place game.

## NIT Championship Results

| Year | Winner | Score | Runner-up | Year | Winner | Score | Runner-up |
|---|---|---|---|---|---|---|---|
| 1938 | Temple | 60–36 | Colorado | 1971 | N Carolina | 84–66 | Georgia Tech |
| 1939 | Long Island U | 44–32 | Loyola (IL) | 1972 | Maryland | 100–69 | Niagara |
| 1940 | Colorado | 51–40 | Duquesne | 1973 | Virginia Tech | 92–91 (OT) | Notre Dame |
| 1941 | Long Island U | 56–42 | Ohio U | 1974 | Purdue | 97–81 | Utah |
| 1942 | W Virginia | 47–45 | W Kentucky | 1975 | Princeton | 80–69 | Providence |
| 1943 | St. John's (NY) | 48–27 | Toledo | 1976 | Kentucky | 71–67 | NC-Charlotte |
| 1944 | St. John's (NY) | 47–39 | DePaul | 1977 | St. Bonaventure | 94–91 | Houston |
| 1945 | DePaul | 71–54 | Bowling Green | 1978 | Texas | 101–93 | N Carolina St |
| 1946 | Kentucky | 46–45 | Rhode Island | 1979 | Indiana | 53–52 | Purdue |
| 1947 | Utah | 49–45 | Kentucky | 1980 | Virginia | 58–55 | Minnesota |
| 1948 | St. Louis | 65–52 | NYU | 1981 | Tulsa | 86–84 (OT) | Syracuse |
| 1949 | San Francisco | 48–47 | Loyola (IL) | 1982 | Bradley | 67–58 | Purdue |
| 1950 | CCNY | 69–61 | Bradley | 1983 | Fresno St | 69–60 | DePaul |
| 1951 | BYU | 62–43 | Dayton | 1984 | Michigan | 83–63 | Notre Dame |
| 1952 | La Salle | 75–64 | Dayton | 1985 | UCLA | 65–62 | Indiana |
| 1953 | Seton Hall | 58–46 | St. John's (NY) | 1986 | Ohio St | 73–63 | Wyoming |
| 1954 | Holy Cross | 71–62 | Duquesne | 1987 | Southern Miss | 84–80 | La Salle |
| 1955 | Duquesne | 70–58 | Dayton | 1988 | Connecticut | 72–67 | Ohio St |
| 1956 | Louisville | 93–80 | Dayton | 1989 | St. John's (NY) | 73–65 | St. Louis |
| 1957 | Bradley | 84–83 | Memphis St | 1990 | Vanderbilt | 74–72 | St. Louis |
| 1958 | Xavier (OH) | 78–74 (OT) | Dayton | 1991 | Stanford | 78–72 | Oklahoma |
| 1959 | St. John's (NY) | 76–71 (OT) | Bradley | 1992 | Virginia | 81–76 | Notre Dame |
| 1960 | Bradley | 88–72 | Providence | 1993 | Minnesota | 62–61 | Georgetown |
| 1961 | Providence | 62–59 | St. Louis | 1994 | Villanova | 80–73 | Vanderbilt |
| 1962 | Dayton | 73–67 | St. John's (NY) | 1995 | Virginia Tech | 65–64 (OT) | Marquette |
| 1963 | Providence | 81–66 | Canisius | 1996 | Nebraska | 60–56 | St. Joseph's |
| 1964 | Bradley | 86–54 | New Mexico | 1997 | Michigan | 82–73 | Florida St |
| 1965 | St. John's (NY) | 55–51 | Villanova | 1998 | Minnesota | 79–72 | Penn St |
| 1966 | BYU | 97–84 | NYU | 1999 | California | 61–60 | Clemson |
| 1967 | Southern Illinois | 71–56 | Marquette | 2000 | Wake Forest | 71–61 | Notre Dame |
| 1968 | Dayton | 61–48 | Kansas | 2001 | Tulsa | 79–60 | Alabama |
| 1969 | Temple | 89–76 | Boston College | | | | |
| 1970 | Marquette | 65–53 | St. John's (NY) | | | | |

# NCAA Men's Division I Season Leaders

## Scoring Average

| Year | Player and Team | Ht | Class | GP | FG | 3FG | FT | Pts | Avg |
|---|---|---|---|---|---|---|---|---|---|
| 1948 | Murray Wier, Iowa | 5-9 | Sr | 19 | 152 | — | 95 | 399 | 21.0 |
| 1949 | Tony Lavelli, Yale | 6-3 | Sr | 30 | 228 | — | 215 | 671 | 22.4 |
| 1950 | Paul Arizin, Villanova | 6-3 | Sr | 29 | 260 | — | 215 | 735 | 25.3 |
| 1951 | Bill Mlkvy, Temple | 6-4 | Sr | 25 | 303 | — | 125 | 731 | 29.2 |
| 1952 | Clyde Lovellette, Kansas | 6-9 | Sr | 28 | 315 | — | 165 | 795 | 28.4 |
| 1953 | Frank Selvy, Furman | 6-3 | Jr | 25 | 272 | — | 194 | 738 | 29.5 |
| 1954 | Frank Selvy, Furman | 6-3 | Sr | 29 | 427 | — | 355 | 1209 | 41.7 |
| 1955 | Darrell Floyd, Furman | 6-1 | Jr | 25 | 344 | — | 209 | 897 | 35.9 |
| 1956 | Darrell Floyd, Furman | 6-1 | Sr | 28 | 339 | — | 268 | 946 | 33.8 |
| 1957 | Grady Wallace, S Carolina | 6-4 | Sr | 29 | 336 | — | 234 | 906 | 31.2 |
| 1958 | Oscar Robertson, Cincinnati | 6-5 | So | 28 | 352 | — | 280 | 984 | 35.1 |
| 1959 | Oscar Robertson, Cincinnati | 6-5 | Jr | 30 | 331 | — | 316 | 978 | 32.6 |
| 1960 | Oscar Robertson, Cincinnati | 6-5 | Sr | 30 | 369 | — | 273 | 1011 | 33.7 |
| 1961 | Frank Burgess, Gonzaga | 6-1 | Sr | 26 | 304 | — | 234 | 842 | 32.4 |
| 1962 | Billy McGill, Utah | 6-9 | Sr | 26 | 394 | — | 221 | 1009 | 38.8 |
| 1963 | Nick Werkman, Seton Hall | 6-3 | Jr | 22 | 221 | — | 208 | 650 | 29.5 |
| 1964 | Howard Komives, Bowling Green | 6-1 | Sr | 23 | 292 | — | 260 | 844 | 36.7 |

## Scoring Average *(Cont.)*

| Year | Player and Team | Ht | Class | GP | FG | 3FG | FT | Pts | Avg |
|------|-----------------|-----|-------|-----|-----|-----|-----|------|------|
| 1965 | Rick Barry, Miami (FL) | 6-7 | Sr | 26 | 340 | — | 293 | 973 | 37.4 |
| 1966 | Dave Schellhase, Purdue | 6-4 | Sr | 24 | 284 | — | 213 | 781 | 32.5 |
| 1967 | Jim Walker, Providence | 6-3 | Sr | 28 | 323 | — | 205 | 851 | 30.4 |
| 1968 | Pete Maravich, Louisiana St | 6-5 | So | 26 | 432 | — | 274 | 1138 | 43.8 |
| 1969 | Pete Maravich, Louisiana St | 6-5 | Jr | 26 | 433 | — | 282 | 1148 | 44.2 |
| 1970 | Pete Maravich, Louisiana St | 6-5 | Sr | 31 | 522 | — | 337 | 1381 | 44.5 |
| 1971 | Johnny Neumann, Mississippi | 6-6 | So | 23 | 366 | — | 191 | 923 | 40.1 |
| 1972 | Dwight Lamar, Southwestern Louisiana | 6-1 | Jr | 29 | 429 | — | 196 | 1054 | 36.3 |
| 1973 | William Averitt, Pepperdine | 6-1 | Sr | 25 | 352 | — | 144 | 848 | 33.9 |
| 1974 | Larry Fogle, Canisius | 6-5 | So | 25 | 326 | — | 183 | 835 | 33.4 |
| 1975 | Bob McCurdy, Richmond | 6-7 | Sr | 26 | 321 | — | 213 | 855 | 32.9 |
| 1976 | Marshall Rodgers, TX-Pan American | 6-2 | Sr | 25 | 361 | — | 197 | 919 | 36.8 |
| 1977 | Freeman Williams, Portland St | 6-4 | Jr | 26 | 417 | — | 176 | 1010 | 38.8 |
| 1978 | Freeman Williams, Portland St | 6-4 | Sr | 27 | 410 | — | 149 | 969 | 35.9 |
| 1979 | Lawrence Butler, Idaho St | 6-3 | Sr | 27 | 310 | — | 192 | 812 | 30.1 |
| 1980 | Tony Murphy, Southern-BR | 6-3 | Sr | 29 | 377 | — | 178 | 932 | 32.1 |
| 1981 | Zam Fredrick, S Carolina | 6-2 | Sr | 27 | 300 | — | 181 | 781 | 28.9 |
| 1982 | Harry Kelly, Texas Southern | 6-7 | Jr | 29 | 336 | — | 190 | 862 | 29.7 |
| 1983 | Harry Kelly, Texas Southern | 6-7 | Sr | 29 | 333 | — | 169 | 835 | 28.8 |
| 1984 | Joe Jakubick, Akron | 6-5 | Sr | 27 | 304 | — | 206 | 814 | 30.1 |
| 1985 | Xavier McDaniel, Wichita St | 6-8 | Sr | 31 | 351 | — | 142 | 844 | 27.2 |
| 1986 | Terrance Bailey, Wagner | 6-2 | Jr | 29 | 321 | — | 212 | 854 | 29.4 |
| 1987 | Kevin Houston, Army | 5-11 | Sr | 29 | 311 | 63 | 268 | 953 | 32.9 |
| 1988 | Hersey Hawkins, Bradley | 6-3 | Sr | 31 | 377 | 87 | 284 | 1125 | 36.3 |
| 1989 | Hank Gathers, Loyola Marymount | 6-7 | Jr | 31 | 419 | 0 | 177 | 1015 | 32.7 |
| 1990 | Bo Kimble, Loyola Marymount | 6-5 | Sr | 32 | 404 | 92 | 231 | 1131 | 35.3 |
| 1991 | Kevin Bradshaw, U.S. Int'l | 6-6 | Sr | 28 | 358 | 60 | 278 | 1054 | 37.6 |
| 1992 | Brett Roberts, Morehead St | 6-8 | Sr | 29 | 278 | 66 | 193 | 815 | 28.1 |
| 1993 | Greg Guy, TX-Pan American | 6-1 | Jr | 19 | 189 | 67 | 111 | 556 | 29.3 |
| 1994 | Glenn Robinson, Purdue | 6-8 | Jr | 34 | 368 | 79 | 215 | 1030 | 30.3 |
| 1995 | Kurt Thomas, Texas Christian | 6-9 | Sr | 27 | 288 | 3 | 202 | 781 | 28.9 |
| 1996 | Kevin Granger, Texas Southern | 6-3 | Sr | 24 | 194 | 30 | 230 | 648 | 27.0 |
| 1997 | Charles Jones, LIU-Brooklyn | 6-3 | Jr | 30 | 338 | 109 | 118 | 903 | 30.1 |
| 1998 | Charles Jones, LIU-Brooklyn | 6-3 | Sr | 30 | 326 | 116 | 101 | 869 | 29.0 |
| 1999 | Alvin Young, Niagara | 6-3 | Sr | 29 | 253 | 65 | 157 | 728 | 25.1 |
| 2000 | Courtney Alexander, Fresno St | 6-6 | Sr | 27 | 252 | 58 | 107 | 669 | 24.8 |
| 2001 | Ronnie McCollum, Centenary | 6-4 | Sr | 27 | 244 | 85 | 214 | 787 | 29.1 |

## Rebounds

| Year | Player and Team | Ht | Class | GP | Reb | Avg |
|------|-----------------|-----|-------|-----|-----|------|
| 1951 | Ernie Beck, Pennsylvania | 6-4 | So | 27 | 556 | 20.6 |
| 1952 | Bill Hannon, Army | 6-3 | So | 17 | 355 | 20.9 |
| 1953 | Ed Conlin, Fordham | 6-5 | So | 26 | 612 | 23.5 |
| 1954 | Art Quimby, Connecticut | 6-5 | Jr | 26 | 588 | 22.6 |
| 1955 | Charlie Slack, Marshall | 6-5 | Jr | 21 | 538 | 25.6 |
| 1956 | Joe Holup, George Washington | 6-6 | Sr | 26 | 604 | †.256 |
| 1957 | Elgin Baylor, Seattle | 6-6 | Jr | 25 | 508 | †.235 |
| 1958 | Alex Ellis, Niagara | 6-5 | Sr | 25 | 536 | †.262 |
| 1959 | Leroy Wright, Pacific | 6-8 | Jr | 26 | 652 | †.238 |
| 1960 | Leroy Wright, Pacific | 6-8 | Sr | 17 | 380 | †.234 |
| 1961 | Jerry Lucas, Ohio St | 6-8 | Jr | 27 | 470 | †.198 |
| 1962 | Jerry Lucas, Ohio St | 6-8 | Sr | 28 | 499 | †.211 |
| 1963 | Paul Silas, Creighton | 6-7 | Sr | 27 | 557 | 20.6 |
| 1964 | Bob Pelkington, Xavier (OH) | 6-7 | Sr | 26 | 567 | 21.8 |
| 1965 | Toby Kimball, Connecticut | 6-8 | Sr | 23 | 483 | 21.0 |
| 1966 | Jim Ware, Oklahoma City | 6-8 | Sr | 29 | 607 | 20.9 |
| 1967 | Dick Cunningham, Murray St | 6-10 | Jr | 22 | 479 | 21.8 |
| 1968 | Neal Walk, Florida | 6-10 | Jr | 25 | 494 | 19.8 |
| 1969 | Spencer Haywood, Detroit | 6-8 | So | 22 | 472 | 21.5 |
| 1970 | Artis Gilmore, Jacksonville | 7-2 | Jr | 28 | 621 | 22.2 |
| 1971 | Artis Gilmore, Jacksonville | 7-2 | Sr | 26 | 603 | 23.2 |
| 1972 | Kermit Washington, American | 6-8 | Jr | 23 | 455 | 19.8 |
| 1973 | Kermit Washington, American | 6-8 | Sr | 22 | 439 | 20.0 |
| 1974 | Marvin Barnes, Providence | 6-9 | Sr | 32 | 597 | 18.7 |
| 1975 | John Irving, Hofstra | 6-9 | So | 21 | 323 | 15.4 |
| 1976 | Sam Pellom, Buffalo | 6-8 | So | 26 | 420 | 16.2 |
| 1977 | Glenn Mosley, Seton Hall | 6-8 | Sr | 29 | 473 | 16.3 |
| 1978 | Ken Williams, N Texas St | 6-7 | Sr | 28 | 411 | 14.7 |
| 1979 | Monti Davis, Tennessee St | 6-7 | Jr | 26 | 421 | 16.2 |
| 1980 | Larry Smith, Alcorn St | 6-8 | Sr | 26 | 392 | 15.1 |
| 1981 | Darryl Watson, Miss Valley | 6-7 | Sr | 27 | 379 | 14.0 |
| 1982 | LaSalle Thompson, Texas | 6-10 | Jr | 27 | 365 | 13.5 |

## Rebounds *(Cont.)*

| Year | Player and Team | Ht | Class | GP | Reb | Avg |
|------|-----------------|-----|-------|-----|-----|-----|
| 1983 | Xavier McDaniel, Wichita St | 6-7 | So | 28 | 403 | 14.4 |
| 1984 | Akeem Olajuwon, Houston | 7-0 | Jr | 37 | 500 | 13.5 |
| 1985 | Xavier McDaniel, Wichita St | 6-8 | Sr | 31 | 460 | 14.8 |
| 1986 | David Robinson, Navy | 6-11 | Jr | 35 | 455 | 13.0 |
| 1987 | Jerome Lane, Pittsburgh | 6-6 | So | 33 | 444 | 13.5 |
| 1988 | Kenny Miller, Loyola (IL) | 6-9 | Fr | 29 | 395 | 13.6 |
| 1989 | Hank Gathers, Loyola (CA) | 6-7 | Jr | 31 | 426 | 13.7 |
| 1990 | Anthony Bonner, St. Louis | 6-8 | Sr | 33 | 456 | 13.8 |
| 1991 | Shaquille O'Neal, Louisiana St | 7-1 | So | 28 | 411 | 14.7 |
| 1992 | Popeye Jones, Murray St | 6-8 | Sr | 30 | 431 | 14.4 |
| 1993 | Warren Kidd, Middle Tenn St | 6-9 | Sr | 26 | 386 | 14.8 |
| 1994 | Jerome Lambert, Baylor | 6-8 | Jr | 24 | 355 | 14.8 |
| 1995 | Kurt Thomas, Texas Christian | 6-9 | Sr | 27 | 393 | 14.6 |
| 1996 | Marcus Mann, Mississippi Valley | 6-8 | Sr | 29 | 394 | 13.6 |
| 1997 | Tim Duncan, Wake Forest | 6-11 | Sr | 31 | 457 | 14.7 |
| 1998 | Ryan Perryman, Dayton | 6-7 | Sr | 33 | 412 | 12.5 |
| 1999 | Ian McGinnis, Dartmouth | 6-8 | So | 26 | 317 | 12.2 |
| 2000 | Darren Phillips, Fairfield | 6-7 | Sr | 29 | 405 | 14.0 |
| 2001 | Chris Marcus, Western Kentucky | 7-1 | Jr | 31 | 374 | 12.1 |

†From 1956–1962, title was based on highest individual recoveries out of total by both teams in all games.

## Assists

| Year | Player and Team | Class | GP | A | Avg |
|------|-----------------|-------|-----|-----|-----|
| 1984 | Craig Lathen, IL-Chicago | Jr | 29 | 274 | 9.45 |
| 1985 | Rob Weingard, Hofstra | Sr | 24 | 228 | 9.50 |
| 1986 | Mark Jackson, St. John's (NY) | Jr | 36 | 328 | 9.11 |
| 1987 | Avery Johnson, Southern-BR | Jr | 31 | 333 | 10.74 |
| 1988 | Avery Johnson, Southern-BR | Sr | 30 | 399 | 13.30 |
| 1989 | Glenn Williams, Holy Cross | Sr | 28 | 278 | 9.93 |
| 1990 | Todd Lehmann, Drexel | Sr | 28 | 260 | 9.29 |
| 1991 | Chris Corchiani, N Carolina St | Sr | 31 | 299 | 9.65 |
| 1992 | Van Usher, Tennessee Tech | Sr | 29 | 254 | 8.76 |
| 1993 | Sam Crawford, New Mex St | Sr | 34 | 310 | 9.12 |
| 1994 | Jason Kidd, California | So | 30 | 272 | 9.06 |
| 1995 | Nelson Haggerty, Baylor | Sr | 28 | 284 | 10.10 |
| 1996 | Raimonds Miglinieks, UC-Irvine | Sr | 27 | 230 | 8.52 |
| 1997 | Kenny Mitchell, Dartmouth | Sr | 26 | 203 | 7.81 |
| 1998 | Ahlon Lewis, Arizona St | Sr | 32 | 294 | 9.19 |
| 1999 | Doug Gottlieb, Oklahoma St | Jr | 34 | 299 | 8.79 |
| 2000 | Mark Dickel, UNLV | Sr | 31 | 280 | 9.03 |
| 2001 | Markus Carr, Cal St–Northridge | Jr | 32 | 286 | 8.94 |

## Blocked Shots

| Year | Player and Team | Class | GP | BS | Avg |
|------|-----------------|-------|-----|-----|-----|
| 1986 | David Robinson, Navy | Jr | 35 | 207 | 5.91 |
| 1987 | David Robinson, Navy | Sr | 32 | 144 | 4.50 |
| 1988 | Rodney Blake, St. Joseph's (PA) | Sr | 29 | 116 | 4.00 |
| 1989 | Alonzo Mourning, Georgetown | Fr | 34 | 169 | 4.97 |
| 1990 | Kenny Green, Rhode Island | Sr | 26 | 124 | 4.77 |
| 1991 | Shawn Bradley, Brigham Young | Fr | 34 | 177 | 5.21 |
| 1992 | Shaquille O'Neal, Louisiana St | Jr | 30 | 157 | 5.23 |
| 1993 | Theo Ratliff, Wyoming | Jr | 28 | 124 | 4.43 |
| 1994 | Grady Livingston, Howard | Jr | 26 | 115 | 4.42 |
| 1995 | Keith Closs, Central Conn St | Fr | 26 | 139 | 5.35 |
| 1996 | Keith Closs, Central Conn St | So | 28 | 178 | 6.36 |
| 1997 | Adonal Foyle, Colgate | Jr | 28 | 180 | 6.43 |
| 1998 | Jerome James, Florida A&M | Sr | 27 | 125 | 4.63 |
| 1999 | Tarvis Williams, Hampton | Jr | 27 | 135 | 5.00 |
| 2000 | Ken Johnson, Ohio St | Sr | 30 | 161 | 5.37 |
| 2001 | Tarvis Williams, Hampton | Sr | 32 | 147 | 4.59 |

## Steals

| Year | Player and Team | Class | GP | S | Avg |
|------|-----------------|-------|-----|-----|-----|
| 1986 | Darron Brittman, Chicago St | Sr | 28 | 139 | 4.96 |
| 1987 | Tony Fairley, Charleston Sou | Sr | 28 | 114 | 4.07 |
| 1988 | Aldwin Ware, Florida A&M | Sr | 29 | 142 | 4.90 |
| 1989 | Kenny Robertson, Cleveland St | Jr | 28 | 111 | 3.96 |
| 1990 | Ronn McMahon, E Washington | Sr | 29 | 130 | 4.48 |
| 1991 | Van Usher, Tennessee Tech | Jr | 28 | 104 | 3.71 |
| 1992 | Victor Snipes, NE Illinois | So | 25 | 86 | 3.44 |
| 1993 | Jason Kidd, California | Fr | 29 | 110 | 3.80 |
| 1994 | Shawn Griggs, SW Louisiana | Sr | 30 | 120 | 4.00 |
| 1995 | Roderick Anderson, Texas | Sr | 30 | 101 | 3.37 |

## Steals (Cont.)

| Year | Player and Team | Class | GP | S | Avg |
|------|-----------------|-------|----|----|-----|
| 1996 | Pointer Williams, McNeese St | Sr | 27 | 118 | 4.37 |
| 1997 | Joel Hoover, MD-Eastern Shore | Fr | 28 | 90 | 3.21 |
| 1998 | Bonzi Wells, Ball St | Sr | 29 | 103 | 3.55 |
| 1999 | Shawnta Rogers, George Wash | Sr | 29 | 103 | 3.55 |
| 2000 | Carl Williams, Liberty | Sr | 28 | 107 | 3.82 |
| 2001 | Greedy Daniels, Texas Christian | Jr | 25 | 108 | 4.32 |

## Single Game Records

### SCORING HIGHS VS NON-DIVISION I OPPONENT

| Pts | Player and Team vs Opponent | Date |
|-----|------------------------------|------|
| 72 | Kevin Bradshaw, U.S. Int'l vs Loyola Marymount | 1-5-91 |
| 69 | Pete Maravich, Louisiana St vs Alabama | 2-7-70 |
| 68 | Calvin Murphy, Niagara vs Syracuse | 12-7-68 |
| 66 | Jay Handlan, Washington & Lee vs Furman | 2-17-51 |
| 66 | Pete Maravich, Louisiana St vs Tulane | 2-10-69 |
| 66 | Anthony Roberts, Oral Roberts vs N Carolina A&T | 2-19-77 |
| 65 | Anthony Roberts, Oral Roberts vs Oregon | 3-9-77 |
| 65 | Scott Haffner, Evansville vs Dayton | 2-18-89 |
| 64 | Pete Maravich, Louisiana St vs Kentucky | 2-21-70 |
| 63 | Johnny Neumann, Mississippi vs Louisiana St | 1-30-71 |
| 63 | Hersey Hawkins, Bradley vs Detroit | 2-22-88 |

### SCORING HIGHS VS NON-DIVISION I OPPONENT

| Pts | Player and Team vs Opponent | Date |
|-----|------------------------------|------|
| 100 | Frank Selvy, Furman vs Newberry | 2-13-54 |
| 85 | Paul Arizin, Villanova vs Philadelphia NAMC | 2-12-49 |
| 81 | Freeman Williams, Portland St vs Rocky Mountain | 2-3-78 |
| 73 | Bill Mlkvy, Temple vs Wilkes | 3-3-51 |
| 71 | Freeman Williams, Portland St vs Southern Oregon | 2-9-77 |

### REBOUNDING HIGHS BEFORE 1973

| Reb | Player and Team vs Opponent | Date |
|-----|------------------------------|------|
| 51 | Bill Chambers, William & Mary vs Virginia | 2-14-53 |
| 43 | Charlie Slack, Marshall vs Morris Harvey | 1-12-54 |
| 42 | Tom Heinsohn, Holy Cross vs Boston College | 3-1-55 |
| 40 | Art Quimby, Connecticut vs Boston U | 1-11-55 |
| 39 | Maurice Stokes, St. Francis (PA) vs John Carroll | 1-28-55 |
| 39 | Dave DeBusschere, Detroit vs Central Michigan | 1-30-60 |
| 39 | Keith Swagerty, Pacific vs UC-Santa Barbara | 3-5-65 |

### REBOUNDING HIGHS SINCE 1973*

| Reb | Player and Team vs Opponent | Date |
|-----|------------------------------|------|
| 35 | Larry Abney, Fresno St vs Southern Methodist | 2-17-00 |
| 34 | David Vaughn, Oral Roberts vs Brandeis | 1-8-73 |
| 32 | Jervaughn Scales, Southern-BR vs Grambling | 2-7-94 |
| 32 | Durand Macklin, Louisiana St vs Tulane | 11-26-76 |
| 31 | Jim Bradley, Northern Illinois vs WI-Milwaukee | 2-19-73 |
| 31 | Calvin Natt, NE Louisiana vs Georgia Southern | 12-29-76 |

### ASSISTS

| A | Player and Team vs Opponent | Date |
|---|------------------------------|------|
| 22 | Tony Fairley, Baptist vs Armstrong St | 2-9-87 |
| 22 | Avery Johnson, Southern-BR vs Texas Southern | 1-25-88 |
| 22 | Sherman Douglas, Syracuse vs Providence | 1-28-89 |
| 21 | Mark Wade, UNLV vs Navy | 12-29-86 |
| 21 | Kelvin Scarborough, New Mexico vs Hawaii | 2-13-87 |
| 21 | Anthony Manuel, Bradley vs UC-Irvine | 12-19-87 |
| 21 | Avery Johnson, Southern-BR vs Alabama St | 1-16-88 |

### STEALS

| S | Player and Team vs Opponent | Date |
|---|------------------------------|------|
| 13 | Mookie Blaylock, Oklahoma vs Centenary | 12-12-87 |
| 13 | Mookie Blaylock, Oklahoma vs Loyola Marymount | 12-17-88 |
| 12 | Kenny Robertson, Cleveland St vs Wagner | 12-3-88 |
| 12 | Terry Evans, Oklahoma vs Florida A&M | 1-27-93 |
| 12 | Richard Duncan, Middle Tenn St vs Eastern Kentucky | 2-20-99 |
| 12 | Greedy Daniels, Texas Christian vs AR–Pine Bluff | 12-30-00 |

## Single Game Records *(Cont.)*

### BLOCKED SHOTS

| BS | Player and Team vs Opponent | Date |
|----|------------------------------|------|
| 14 | David Robinson, Navy vs NC-Wilmington | 1-4-86 |
| 14 | Shawn Bradley, Brigham Young vs Eastern Kentucky | 12-7-90 |
| 14 | Roy Rogers, Alabama vs Georgia | 2-10-96 |
| 14 | Loren Woods, Arizona vs Oregon | 2-3-00 |
| 13 | Kevin Roberson, Vermont vs New Hampshire | 1-9-92 |
| 13 | Jim McIlvaine, Marquette vs Northeastern (IL) | 12-9-92 |
| 13 | Keith Closs, Central Conn. St vs St. Francis (PA) | 12-21-94 |
| 13 | D'or Fischer, Northwestern St vs SW Texas St | 1-22-01 |

## Single Season Records

### POINTS

| Player and Team | Year | GP | FG | 3FG | FT | Pts |
|-----------------|------|----|----|-----|----|----|
| Pete Maravich, Louisiana St | 1970 | 31 | 522 | — | 337 | 1381 |
| Elvin Hayes, Houston | 1968 | 33 | 519 | — | 176 | 1214 |
| Frank Selvy, Furman | 1954 | 29 | 427 | — | 355 | 1209 |
| Pete Maravich, Louisiana St | 1969 | 26 | 433 | — | 282 | 1148 |
| Pete Maravich, Louisiana St | 1968 | 26 | 432 | — | 274 | 1138 |
| Bo Kimble, Loyola Marymount | 1990 | 32 | 404 | 92 | 231 | 1131 |
| Hersey Hawkins, Bradley | 1988 | 31 | 377 | 87 | 284 | 1125 |
| Austin Carr, Notre Dame | 1970 | 29 | 444 | — | 218 | 1106 |
| Austin Carr, Notre Dame | 1971 | 29 | 430 | — | 241 | 1101 |
| Otis Birdsong, Houston | 1977 | 36 | 452 | — | 186 | 1090 |

### SCORING AVERAGE

| Player and Team | Year | GP | FG | 3FG | FT | Pts | Avg |
|-----------------|------|----|----|-----|----|----|----|
| Pete Maravich, Louisiana St | 1970 | 31 | 522 | 337 | 1381 | | 44.5 |
| Pete Maravich, Louisiana St | 1969 | 26 | 433 | 282 | 1148 | | 44.2 |
| Pete Maravich, Louisiana St | 1968 | 26 | 432 | 274 | 1138 | | 43.8 |
| Frank Selvy, Furman | 1954 | 29 | 427 | 355 | 1209 | | 41.7 |
| Johnny Neumann, Mississippi | 1971 | 23 | 366 | 191 | 923 | | 40.1 |
| Freeman Williams, Portland St | 1977 | 26 | 417 | 176 | 1010 | | 38.8 |
| Billy McGill, Utah | 1962 | 26 | 394 | 221 | 1009 | | 38.8 |
| Calvin Murphy, Niagara | 1968 | 24 | 337 | 242 | 916 | | 38.2 |
| Austin Carr, Notre Dame | 1970 | 29 | 444 | 218 | 1106 | | 38.1 |
| Austin Carr, Notre Dame | 1971 | 29 | 430 | 241 | 1101 | | 38.0 |

### REBOUNDS

| Player and Team | Year | GP | Reb | Player and Team | Year | GP | Reb |
|-----------------|------|----|-----|-----------------|------|----|-----|
| Walt Dukes, Seton Hall | 1953 | 33 | 734 | Artis Gilmore, Jacksonville | 1970 | 28 | 621 |
| Leroy Wright, Pacific | 1959 | 26 | 652 | Tom Gola, La Salle | 1955 | 31 | 618 |
| Tom Gola, La Salle | 1954 | 30 | 652 | Ed Conlin, Fordham | 1953 | 26 | 612 |
| Charlie Tyra, Louisville | 1956 | 29 | 645 | Art Quimby, Connecticut | 1955 | 25 | 611 |
| Paul Silas, Creighton | 1964 | 29 | 631 | Bill Russell, San Francisco | 1956 | 29 | 609 |
| Elvin Hayes, Houston | 1968 | 33 | 624 | Jim Ware, Oklahoma City | 1966 | 29 | 607 |

### REBOUND AVERAGE BEFORE 1973

| Player and Team | Year | GP | Reb | Avg |
|-----------------|------|----|-----|-----|
| Charlie Slack, Marshall | 1955 | 21 | 538 | 25.6 |
| Leroy Wright, Pacific | 1959 | 26 | 652 | 25.1 |
| Art Quimby, Connecticut | 1955 | 25 | 611 | 24.4 |
| Charlie Slack, Marshall | 1956 | 22 | 520 | 23.6 |
| Ed Conlin, Fordham | 1953 | 26 | 612 | 23.5 |

### REBOUND AVERAGE SINCE 1973*

| Player and Team | Year | GP | Reb | Avg |
|-----------------|------|----|-----|-----|
| Kermit Washington, American | 1973 | 22 | 439 | 20.0 |
| Marvin Barnes, Providence | 1973 | 30 | 571 | 19.0 |
| Marvin Barnes, Providence | 1974 | 32 | 597 | 18.7 |
| Pete Padgett, NV-Reno | 1973 | 26 | 462 | 17.8 |
| Jim Bradley, Northern Illinois | 1973 | 24 | 426 | 17.8 |

*Freshmen became eligible for varsity play in 1973.

## Single Season Records *(Cont.)*

### ASSISTS

| Player and Team | Year | GP | A | Player and Team | Year | GP | A |
|---|---|---|---|---|---|---|---|
| Mark Wade, UNLV | 1987 | 38 | 406 | Sherman Douglas, Syracuse | 1989 | 38 | 326 |
| Avery Johnson, Southern-BR | 1988 | 30 | 399 | Sam Crawford, New Mex. St | 1993 | 34 | 310 |
| Anthony Manuel, Bradley | 1988 | 31 | 373 | Greg Anthony, UNLV | 1991 | 35 | 310 |
| Avery Johnson, Southern-BR | 1987 | 31 | 333 | Reid Gettys, Houston | 1984 | 37 | 309 |
| Mark Jackson, St. John's (NY) | 1986 | 32 | 328 | Carl Golston, Loyola (IL) | 1985 | 33 | 305 |

### ASSIST AVERAGE

| Player and Team | Year | GP | A | Avg | Player and Team | Year | GP | A | Avg |
|---|---|---|---|---|---|---|---|---|---|
| Avery Johnson, Southern-BR | 1988 | 30 | 399 | 13.3 | Chris Corchiani, N Carolina St | 1991 | 31 | 299 | 9.6 |
| Anthony Manuel, Bradley | 1988 | 31 | 373 | 12.0 | Tony Fairley, Charleston So.* | 1987 | 28 | 270 | 9.6 |
| Avery Johnson, Southern-BR | 1987 | 31 | 333 | 10.7 | Tyrone Bogues, Wake Forest | 1987 | 29 | 276 | 9.5 |
| Mark Wade, UNLV | 1987 | 38 | 406 | 10.7 | Ron Weingard, Hofstra | 1985 | 24 | 228 | 9.5 |
| Nelson Haggerty, Baylor | 1995 | 28 | 284 | 10.1 | Craig Neal, Georgia Tech | 1988 | 32 | 303 | 9.5 |
| Glenn Williams, Holy Cross | 1989 | 28 | 278 | 9.9 | *Formerly Baptist. | | | | |

### FIELD-GOAL PERCENTAGE

| Player and Team | Year | GP | FG | FGA | Pct |
|---|---|---|---|---|---|
| Steve Johnson, Oregon St | 1981 | 28 | 235 | 315 | 74.6 |
| Dwayne Davis, Florida | 1989 | 33 | 179 | 248 | 72.2 |
| Keith Walker, Utica | 1985 | 27 | 154 | 216 | 71.3 |
| Steve Johnson, Oregon St | 1980 | 30 | 211 | 297 | 71.0 |
| Oliver Miller, Arkansas | 1991 | 38 | 254 | 361 | 70.4 |
| Alan Williams, Princeton | 1987 | 25 | 163 | 232 | 70.3 |
| Mark McNamara, California | 1982 | 27 | 231 | 329 | 70.2 |
| Warren Kidd, Middle Tennessee St | 1991 | 30 | 173 | 247 | 70.0 |
| Pete Freeman, Akron | 1991 | 28 | 175 | 250 | 70.0 |
| Joe Senser, West Chester | 1977 | 25 | 130 | 186 | 69.9 |

Based on qualifiers for annual championship.

### FREE-THROW PERCENTAGE

| Player and Team | Year | GP | FT | FTA | Pct |
|---|---|---|---|---|---|
| Craig Collins, Penn St | 1985 | 27 | 94 | 98 | 95.9 |
| Rod Foster, UCLA | 1982 | 27 | 95 | 100 | 95.0 |
| Clay McKnight, Pacific | 2000 | 24 | 74 | 78 | 94.9 |
| Danny Basile, Marist | 1994 | 27 | 84 | 89 | 94.4 |
| Carlos Gibson, Marshall | 1978 | 28 | 84 | 89 | 94.4 |
| Jim Barton, Dartmouth | 1986 | 26 | 65 | 69 | 94.2 |
| Gary Buchanan, Villanova | 2001 | 31 | 97 | 103 | 94.2 |
| Jack Moore, Nebraska | 1982 | 27 | 123 | 131 | 93.9 |
| Dandrea Evans, Troy St | 1994 | 27 | 72 | 77 | 93.5 |
| Rob Robbins, New Mexico | 1990 | 34 | 101 | 108 | 93.5 |

Based on qualifiers for annual championship.

### THREE-POINT FIELD-GOAL PERCENTAGE

| Player and Team | Year | GP | 3FG | 3FGA | Pct |
|---|---|---|---|---|---|
| Glenn Tropf, Holy Cross | 1988 | 29 | 52 | 82 | 63.4 |
| Sean Wightman, Western Michigan | 1992 | 30 | 48 | 76 | 63.2 |
| Keith Jennings, E Tennessee St | 1991 | 33 | 84 | 142 | 59.2 |
| Dave Calloway, Monmouth (NJ) | 1989 | 28 | 48 | 82 | 58.5 |
| Steve Kerr, Arizona | 1988 | 38 | 114 | 199 | 57.3 |
| Reginald Jones, Prairie View | 1987 | 28 | 64 | 112 | 57.1 |
| Jim Cantamessa, Siena | 1998 | 29 | 66 | 117 | 56.4 |
| Joel Tribelhorn, Colorado St | 1989 | 33 | 76 | 135 | 56.3 |
| Mike Joseph, Bucknell | 1988 | 28 | 65 | 116 | 56.0 |
| Brian Jackson, Evansville | 1995 | 27 | 53 | 95 | 55.8 |
| Amory Sanders, SE Missouri St | 2001 | 24 | 53 | 95 | 55.8 |

Based on qualifiers for annual championship.

## Single Season Records *(Cont.)*

### STEALS

| Player and Team | Year | GP | S |
|---|---|---|---|
| Mookie Blaylock, Oklahoma | 1988 | 39 | 150 |
| Aldwin Ware, Florida A&M | 1988 | 29 | 142 |
| Darron Brittman, Chicago St | 1986 | 28 | 139 |
| Nadav Henefeld, Connecticut | 1990 | 37 | 138 |
| Mookie Blaylock, Oklahoma | 1989 | 35 | 131 |

### BLOCKED SHOTS

| Player and Team | Year | GP | BS |
|---|---|---|---|
| David Robinson, Navy | 1986 | 35 | 207 |
| Adonal Foyle, Colgate | 1997 | 28 | 180 |
| Keith Closs, Central Conn St | 1996 | 28 | 178 |
| Shawn Bradley, BYU | 1991 | 34 | 177 |
| Alonzo Mourning, Georgetown | 1989 | 34 | 169 |

### STEAL AVERAGE

| Player and Team | Year | GP | S | Avg |
|---|---|---|---|---|
| Darron Brittman, Chicago St | 1986 | 28 | 139 | 4.96 |
| Aldwin Ware, Florida A&M | 1988 | 29 | 142 | 4.90 |
| Ronn McMahon, E Washington | 1990 | 29 | 130 | 4.48 |
| Pointer Williams, McNeese St | 1996 | 27 | 118 | 4.37 |
| Greedy Daniels, Texas Christian | 2001 | 25 | 108 | 4.32 |

### BLOCKED-SHOT AVERAGE

| Player and Team | Year | GP | BS | Avg |
|---|---|---|---|---|
| Adonal Foyle, Colgate | 1997 | 28 | 180 | 6.43 |
| Keith Closs, Central Conn St | 1996 | 28 | 178 | 6.36 |
| David Robinson, Navy | 1986 | 35 | 207 | 5.91 |
| Adonal Foyle, Colgate | 1996 | 29 | 165 | 5.69 |
| Ken Johnson, Ohio St | 2000 | 30 | 161 | 5.37 |

## Career Records

### POINTS

| Player and Team | Ht | Final Year | GP | FG | 3FG* | FT | Pts |
|---|---|---|---|---|---|---|---|
| Pete Maravich, Louisiana St | 6-5 | 1970 | 83 | 1387 | — | 893 | 3667 |
| Freeman Williams, Portland St | 6-4 | 1978 | 106 | 1369 | — | 511 | 3249 |
| Lionel Simmons, La Salle | 6-7 | 1990 | 131 | 1244 | 56 | 673 | 3217 |
| Alphonso Ford, Mississippi Valley | 6-2 | 1993 | 109 | 1121 | 333 | 590 | 3165 |
| Harry Kelly, Texas Southern | 6-7 | 1983 | 110 | 1234 | — | 598 | 3066 |
| Hersey Hawkins, Bradley | 6-3 | 1988 | 125 | 1100 | 118 | 690 | 3008 |
| Oscar Robertson, Cincinnati | 6-5 | 1960 | 88 | 1052 | — | 869 | 2973 |
| Danny Manning, Kansas | 6-10 | 1988 | 147 | 1216 | 10 | 509 | 2951 |
| Alfredrick Hughes, Loyola (IL) | 6-5 | 1985 | 120 | 1226 | — | 462 | 2914 |
| Elvin Hayes, Houston | 6-8 | 1968 | 93 | 1215 | — | 454 | 2884 |
| Larry Bird, Indiana St | 6-9 | 1979 | 94 | 1154 | — | 542 | 2850 |
| Otis Birdsong, Houston | 6-4 | 1977 | 116 | 1176 | — | 480 | 2832 |
| Kevin Bradshaw, Bethune-Cookman, U.S. Int'l | 6-6 | 1991 | 111 | 1027 | 132 | 618 | 2804 |
| Allan Houston, Tennessee | 6-6 | 1993 | 128 | 902 | 346 | 651 | 2801 |
| Hank Gathers, Southern Cal, Loyola Marymount | 6-7 | 1990 | 117 | 1127 | 0 | 469 | 2723 |
| Reggie Lewis, Northeastern | 6-7 | 1987 | 122 | 1043 | 30 (1) | 592 | 2708 |
| Daren Queenan, Lehigh | 6-5 | 1988 | 118 | 1024 | 29 | 626 | 2703 |
| Byron Larkin, Xavier (OH) | 6-3 | 1988 | 121 | 1022 | 51 | 601 | 2696 |
| David Robinson, Navy | 7-1 | 1987 | 127 | 1032 | 1 | 604 | 2669 |
| Wayman Tisdale, Oklahoma | 6-9 | 1985 | 104 | 1077 | — | 507 | 2661 |

*Listed is the number of three-pointers scored since it became the national rule in 1987; the number in the parentheses is number scored prior to 1987—these counted as three points in the game but counted as two-pointers in the national rankings. The three-pointers in the parentheses are not included in total points.

### SCORING AVERAGE

| Player and Team | Final Year | GP | FG | FT | Pts | Avg |
|---|---|---|---|---|---|---|
| Pete Maravich, Louisiana St | 1968 | 83 | 1387 | 893 | 3667 | 44.2 |
| Austin Carr, Notre Dame | 1971 | 74 | 1017 | 526 | 2560 | 34.6 |
| Oscar Robertson, Cincinnati | 1960 | 88 | 1052 | 869 | 2973 | 33.8 |
| Calvin Murphy, Niagara | 1970 | 77 | 947 | 654 | 2548 | 33.1 |
| Dwight Lamar, Southwestern Louisiana | 1973 | 57 | 768 | 326 | 1862 | 32.7 |
| Frank Selvy, Furman | 1954 | 78 | 922 | 694 | 2538 | 32.5 |
| Rick Mount, Purdue | 1970 | 72 | 910 | 503 | 2323 | 32.3 |
| Darrell Floyd, Furman | 1956 | 71 | 868 | 545 | 2281 | 32.1 |
| Nick Werkman, Seton Hall | 1964 | 71 | 812 | 649 | 2273 | 32.0 |
| Willie Humes, Idaho St | 1971 | 48 | 565 | 380 | 1510 | 31.5 |
| William Averitt, Pepperdine | 1973 | 49 | 615 | 311 | 1541 | 31.4 |
| Elgin Baylor, Coll. of Idaho, Seattle | 1958 | 80 | 956 | 588 | 2500 | 31.3 |
| Elvin Hayes, Houston | 1968 | 93 | 1215 | 454 | 2884 | 31.0 |
| Freeman Williams, Portland St | 1978 | 106 | 1369 | 511 | 3249 | 30.7 |
| Larry Bird, Indiana St | 1979 | 94 | 1154 | 542 | 2850 | 30.3 |

## Career Records *(Cont.)*

### REBOUNDS BEFORE 1973

| Player and Team | Final Year | GP | Reb |
|---|---|---|---|
| Tom Gola, La Salle | 1955 | 118 | 2201 |
| Joe Holup, George Washington | 1956 | 104 | 2030 |
| Charlie Slack, Marshall | 1956 | 88 | 1916 |
| Ed Conlin, Fordham | 1955 | 102 | 1884 |
| Dickie Hemric, Wake Forest | 1955 | 104 | 1802 |

### REBOUNDS SINCE 1973*

| Player and Team | Final Year | GP | Reb |
|---|---|---|---|
| Tim Duncan, Wake Forest | 1997 | 128 | 1570 |
| Derrick Coleman, Syracuse | 1990 | 143 | 1537 |
| Malik Rose, Drexel | 1996 | 120 | 1514 |
| Ralph Sampson, Virginia | 1983 | 132 | 1511 |
| Pete Padgett, NV-Reno | 1976 | 104 | 1464 |

### ASSISTS

| Player and Team | Final Year | GP | A |
|---|---|---|---|
| Bobby Hurley, Duke | 1993 | 140 | 1076 |
| Chris Corchiani, N Carolina St | 1991 | 124 | 1038 |
| Ed Cota, N Carolina | 2000 | 138 | 1030 |
| Keith Jennings, E Tennessee St | 1991 | 127 | 983 |
| Sherman Douglas, Syracuse | 1989 | 138 | 960 |

### FIELD-GOAL PERCENTAGE

| Player and Team | Final Year | FG | FGA | Pct |
|---|---|---|---|---|
| Steve Johnson, Oregon St | 1981 | 828 | 1222 | 67.8 |
| Murray Brown, Florida St | 1980 | 566 | 847 | 66.8 |
| Lee Campbell, SW Missouri St | 1990 | 411 | 618 | 66.5 |
| Warren Kidd, Middle Tennessee St | 1993 | 496 | 747 | 66.4 |
| Todd MacCulloch, Washington | 1999 | 702 | 1058 | 66.4 |

Note: Minimum 400 field goals and 4 FG made per game.

### FREE-THROW PERCENTAGE

| Player and Team | Final Year | FT | FTA | Pct |
|---|---|---|---|---|
| Greg Starrick, Kentucky; Southern Illinois | 1972 | 341 | 375 | 90.9 |
| Jack Moore, Nebraska | 1982 | 446 | 495 | 90.1 |
| Steve Henson, Kansas St | 1990 | 361 | 401 | 90.0 |
| Steve Alford, Indiana | 1987 | 535 | 596 | 89.8 |
| Bob Lloyd, Rutgers | 1967 | 543 | 605 | 89.8 |

Note: Minimum 300 free throws.

*Freshmen became eligible for varsity play in 1973.

## Bob on Down, Coach

Bob Knight asked the question first, not us. It was November 1999, and Knight's Indiana Hoosiers had gone to Lubbock to open Texas Tech's United Spirit Arena with a game against the Red Raiders. Afterward Knight was asked if he would consider returning to Lubbock. Ever the diplomat, he offered to come back at the turn of the next century, then added: "What the hell do I need to come to Texas for?"

Well, Coach, what if you: 1) got fired at Indiana, 2) were only 117 wins shy of breaking Dean Smith's record of 879 college wins, 3) were prevented by your old contract with the Hoosiers from taking a job in the Big Ten or in the states of Indiana and Kentucky without giving up a hunk of cash, and 4) couldn't land at other top basketball schools because their athletic directors think you're more radioactive than Chernobyl?

Then you might be reduced to considering Texas Tech, which fired coach James Dickey (166–124 in 10 seasons) in March and began an all-out offensive to lure Knight. He quickly met with Red Raiders officials, evidently unconcerned that Tech finished with the worst record in the Big 12 last season. Or that men's basketball is a distant No. 3 at the school, behind football and women's basketball. Or that Lubbock's own Mac Davis sang, "Happiness is Lubbock, Texas, in my rearview mirror."

Oh, the Red Raiders have a few things going for them. Athletic director Gerald Myers, a longtime Knight crony, wouldn't dream of getting in the General's way, nor would the small-market media. Texas Tech has a big arena and is in a major conference. What's more, the rural setting would allow Knight to hunt and fish as much as he pleased. Recruiting would be hard but not impossible ... Besides, he can take heart in one thing, at least: Texas Tech's arena is located on Indiana Avenue.

—Grant Wahl

## Career Records (Cont.)

### THREE-POINT FIELD GOALS MADE

| Player and Team | Final Year | GP | 3FG |
|---|---|---|---|
| Curtis Staples, Virginia | 1998 | 122 | 413 |
| Keith Veney, Lamar; Marshall | 1997 | 111 | 409 |
| Doug Day, Radford | 1993 | 117 | 401 |
| Ronnie Schmitz, MO-Kansas City | 1993 | 112 | 378 |
| Mark Alberts, Akron | 1993 | 103 | 375 |

### THREE-POINT FIELD-GOAL PERCENTAGE

| Player and Team | Final Year | 3FG | 3FGA | Pct |
|---|---|---|---|---|
| Tony Bennett, WI-Green Bay | 1992 | 290 | 584 | 49.7 |
| Keith Jennings, E Tennessee St | 1991 | 223 | 452 | 49.3 |
| Kirk Manns, Michigan St | 1990 | 212 | 446 | 47.5 |
| Tim Locum, Wisconsin | 1991 | 227 | 481 | 47.2 |
| David Olson, Eastern Illinois | 1992 | 262 | 562 | 46.6 |

Note: Minimum 200 3-point field goals.

### STEALS

| Player and Team | Final Year | GP | S |
|---|---|---|---|
| Eric Murdock, Providence | 1991 | 117 | 376 |
| Pepe Sanchez, Temple | 2000 | 116 | 365 |
| Bonzi Wells, Ball St | 1998 | 116 | 347 |
| Gerald Walker, San Francisco | 1996 | 111 | 344 |
| Johnny Rhodes, Maryland | 1996 | 122 | 344 |

### BLOCKED SHOTS

| Player and Team | Final Year | GP | BS |
|---|---|---|---|
| Adonal Foyle, Colgate | 1997 | 87 | 492 |
| Tim Duncan, Wake Forest | 1997 | 128 | 481 |
| Alonzo Mourning, Georgetown | 1992 | 120 | 453 |
| Tarvis Williams, Hampton | 2001 | 114 | 452 |
| Lorenzo Coleman, Tennessee Tech | 1997 | 113 | 437 |

# NCAA Men's Division I Team Leaders

## Division I Team Alltime Wins

| Team | First Year | Yrs | W | L | T |
|---|---|---|---|---|---|
| Kentucky | 1903 | 98 | 1795 | 558 | 1 |
| N Carolina | 1911 | 91 | 1781 | 630 | 0 |
| Kansas | 1899 | 103 | 1738 | 741 | 0 |
| Duke | 1906 | 96 | 1649 | 764 | 0 |
| St. John's (NY) | 1908 | 94 | 1621 | 738 | 0 |
| Temple | 1895 | 105 | 1571 | 843 | 0 |
| Syracuse | 1901 | 100 | 1549 | 719 | 0 |
| Pennsylvania | 1897 | 101 | 1508 | 863 | 2 |
| Indiana | 1901 | 101 | 1494 | 800 | 0 |
| Oregon St | 1902 | 100 | 1492 | 1035 | 0 |
| UCLA | 1920 | 82 | 1489 | 641 | 0 |
| Notre Dame | 1898 | 96 | 1483 | 817 | 1 |
| Utah | 1909 | 93 | 1446 | 758 | 0 |
| Princeton | 1901 | 101 | 1443 | 873 | 0 |
| Washington | 1896 | 99 | 1423 | 945 | 0 |

Note: Minimum of 25 years in Division I.

## Division I Alltime Winning Percentage

| Team | First Year | Yrs | W | L | T | Pct |
|---|---|---|---|---|---|---|
| Kentucky | 1903 | 98 | 1795 | 558 | 1 | .763 |
| N Carolina | 1911 | 91 | 1781 | 630 | 0 | .739 |
| UNLV | 1959 | 43 | 883 | 341 | 0 | .721 |
| Kansas | 1899 | 103 | 1738 | 741 | 0 | .701 |
| UCLA | 1920 | 82 | 1489 | 641 | 0 | .699 |
| St. John's (NY) | 1908 | 94 | 1621 | 738 | 0 | .687 |
| Duke | 1906 | 96 | 1649 | 764 | 0 | .683 |
| Syracuse | 1901 | 100 | 1549 | 719 | 0 | .683 |
| Western Kentucky | 1915 | 82 | 1414 | 710 | 0 | .666 |
| Arkansas | 1924 | 78 | 1354 | 708 | 0 | .657 |
| Utah | 1909 | 93 | 1446 | 758 | 0 | .656 |
| Indiana | 1901 | 101 | 1494 | 800 | 0 | .651 |
| Temple | 1895 | 105 | 1571 | 843 | 0 | .651 |
| Louisville | 1912 | 87 | 1387 | 758 | 0 | .647 |
| Notre Dame | 1898 | 96 | 1483 | 817 | 1 | .645 |

Note: Minimum of 25 years in Division I.

# NCAA Men's Division I Winning Streaks

## Longest—Full Season

| Team | Games | Years | Ended by |
|---|---|---|---|
| UCLA | 88 | 1971–74 | Notre Dame (71–70) |
| San Francisco | 60 | 1955–57 | Illinois (62–33) |
| UCLA | 47 | 1966–68 | Houston (71–69) |
| UNLV | 45 | 1990–91 | Duke (79–77) |
| Texas | 44 | 1913–17 | Rice (24–18) |
| Seton Hall | 43 | 1939–41 | LIU-Brooklyn (49–26) |
| LIU-Brooklyn | 43 | 1935–37 | Stanford (45–31) |
| UCLA | 41 | 1968–69 | Southern Cal (46–44) |
| Marquette | 39 | 1970–71 | Ohio St (60–59) |
| Cincinnati | 37 | 1962–63 | Wichita St (65–64) |
| N Carolina | 37 | 1957–58 | W Virginia (75–64) |

## Longest—Regular Season

| Team | Games | Years | Ended by |
|---|---|---|---|
| UCLA | 76 | 1971–74 | Notre Dame (71–70) |
| Indiana | 57 | 1975–77 | Toledo (59–57) |
| Marquette | 56 | 1970–72 | Detroit (70–49) |
| Kentucky | 54 | 1952–55 | Georgia Tech (59–58) |
| San Francisco | 51 | 1955–57 | Illinois (62–33) |
| Pennsylvania | 48 | 1970–72 | Temple (57–52) |
| Ohio State | 47 | 1960–62 | Wisconsin (86–67) |
| Texas | 44 | 1913–17 | Rice (24–18) |
| UCLA | 43 | 1966–68 | Houston (71–69) |
| LIU-Brooklyn | 43 | 1935–37 | Stanford (45–31) |
| Seton Hall | 42 | 1939–41 | LIU-Brooklyn (49–26) |

## Longest—Home Court

| Team | Games | Years | Team | Games | Years |
|---|---|---|---|---|---|
| Kentucky | 129 | 1943–55 | Lamar | 80 | 1978–84 |
| St. Bonaventure | 99 | 1948–61 | Long Beach St | 75 | 1968–74 |
| UCLA | 98 | 1970–76 | UNLV | 72 | 1974–78 |
| Cincinnati | 86 | 1957–64 | Arizona | 71 | 1987–92 |
| Marquette | 81 | 1967–73 | Cincinnati | 68 | 1972–78 |
| Arizona | 81 | 1945–51 | Western Kentucky | 67 | 1949–55 |

# NCAA Men's Division I Winningest Coaches

## Active Coaches

### WINS

| Coach and Team | W |
|---|---|
| James Phelan, Mt. St. Mary's (MD) | 816 |
| Bob Knight, Texas Tech | 763 |
| Lefty Driesell, Georgia St | 762 |
| Jerry Tarkanian, Fresno St | 749 |
| Lou Henson, New Mexico St | 740 |
| Eddie Sutton, Oklahoma St | 679 |
| John Chaney, Temple | 656 |
| Lute Olson, Arizona | 641 |
| Mike Krzyzewski, Duke | 606 |
| Jim Boeheim, Syracuse | 600 |

Note: Minimum 5 years as a Division I head coach; includes record at 4-year colleges only.

### WINNING PERCENTAGE

| Coach and Team | Yrs | W | L | Pct |
|---|---|---|---|---|
| John Kresse, Coll. of Charleston | 22 | 539 | 134 | .801 |
| Roy Williams, Kansas | 13 | 355 | 89 | .800 |
| Jerry Tarkanian, Fresno St | 30 | 749 | 193 | .795 |
| Jim Boeheim, Syracuse | 25 | 600 | 208 | .743 |
| Lute Olson, Arizona | 28 | 641 | 228 | .738 |
| Bob Huggins, Cincinnati | 20 | 469 | 168 | .736 |
| Tom Izzo, Michigan St | 6 | 148 | 53 | .736 |
| Rick Majerus, Utah | 17 | 379 | 137 | .735 |
| John Chaney, Temple | 29 | 656 | 238 | .734 |
| Mike Krzyzewski, Duke | 26 | 606 | 223 | .731 |

Note: Minimum 5 years as a Division I head coach; includes record at 4-year colleges only.

## Alltime Winningest Men's Division I Coaches

### WINS

| Coach (Team) | W |
|---|---|
| Dean Smith (N Carolina) | 879 |
| Adolph Rupp (Kentucky) | 876 |
| Jim Phelan (Mt. St. Mary's) | 816 |
| Hank Iba (NW Missouri St, Colorado, Oklahoma St) | 767 |
| Bob Knight (Army, Indiana, Texas Tech) | 763 |
| Lefty Driesell (Davidson, Maryland, James Madison, Georgia St) | 762 |
| Ed Diddle (Western Kentucky) | 759 |
| Jerry Tarkanian (Long Beach St, UNLV, Fresno St) | 749 |
| Phog Allen (Baker, Kansas, Haskell, Central Missouri St, Kansas) | 746 |
| Lou Henson (Hardin-Simmons, New Mexico St, Illinois) | 740 |
| Norm Stewart (Northern Iowa, Missouri) | 731 |
| Ray Meyer (DePaul) | 724 |
| Don Haskins (UTEP) | 719 |
| Eddie Sutton (Creighton, Arkansas, Kentucky, Oklahoma St) | 679 |
| Denny Crum (Louisville) | 675 |

Note: Minimum 10 head coaching seasons in Division I.

## Alltime Winningest Men's Division I Coaches *(Cont.)*
### WINNING PERCENTAGE

| Coach (Team, Years) | Yrs | W | L | Pct |
|---|---|---|---|---|
| Clair Bee (Rider 29–31, LIU-Brooklyn 32–45, 46–51) | 21 | 412 | 87 | .826 |
| Adolph Rupp (Kentucky 31–72) | 41 | 876 | 190 | .822 |
| John Wooden (Indiana St 47–48, UCLA 49–75) | 29 | 664 | 162 | .804 |
| Roy Williams (Kansas 89–) | 13 | 355 | 89 | .800 |
| Jerry Tarkanian (Long Beach St 69–73, UNLV 74–92, Fresno St 95–) | 30 | 749 | 193 | .795 |
| Dean Smith (N Carolina 62–97) | 36 | 879 | 254 | .776 |
| Harry Fisher (Columbia 07–16, Army 22–23, 25) | 13 | 147 | 44 | .770 |
| Frank Keaney (Rhode Island 21–48) | 27 | 387 | 117 | .768 |
| George Keogan (St. Louis 16, Allegheny 19, Valparaiso 20–21, Notre Dame 24–43) | 24 | 385 | 117 | .767 |
| Jack Ramsay (St. Joseph's [PA] 56–66) | 11 | 231 | 71 | .765 |
| Vic Bubas (Duke 60–69) | 10 | 213 | 67 | .761 |
| Charles (Chick) Davies (Duquesne 25–43, 47–48) | 21 | 314 | 106 | .748 |
| Ray Mears (Wittenberg 57–62, Tennessee 63–77) | 21 | 399 | 135 | .747 |
| Jim Boeheim (Syracuse 77–) | 25 | 600 | 208 | .743 |
| Al McGuire (Belmont Abbey 58–64, Marquette 65–77) | 20 | 405 | 143 | .739 |
| Rick Pitino (Boston 79–83, Providence 86–87, Kentucky 90–97) | 15 | 352 | 124 | .739 |
| Phog Allen (Baker 06–08, Kansas 08–09, Haskell 09, Cent MO St 13–19, Kansas 20–56) | 48 | 746 | 264 | .739 |
| Everett Case (N Carolina St 47–64) | 18 | 376 | 133 | .739 |
| Lute Olson (Long Beach St 74, Iowa 75–83, Arizona 84–) | 28 | 641 | 228 | .738 |
| Bob Huggins (Walsh 81–83, Akron 85–89, Cincinnati 90–) | 20 | 469 | 168 | .736 |

Note: Minimum 10 head coaching seasons in Division I.

# NCAA Women's Division I Championship Results

| Year | Winner | Score | Runner-up | Winning Coach |
|---|---|---|---|---|
| 1982 | Louisiana Tech | 76–62 | Cheyney | Sonja Hogg |
| 1983 | Southern Cal | 69–67 | Louisiana Tech | Linda Sharp |
| 1984 | Southern Cal | 72–61 | Tennessee | Linda Sharp |
| 1985 | Old Dominion | 70–65 | Georgia | Marianne Stanley |
| 1986 | Texas | 97–81 | Southern Cal | Jody Conradt |
| 1987 | Tennessee | 67–44 | Louisiana Tech | Pat Summitt |
| 1988 | Louisiana Tech | 56–54 | Auburn | Leon Barmore |
| 1989 | Tennessee | 76–60 | Auburn | Pat Summitt |
| 1990 | Stanford | 88–81 | Auburn | Tara VanDerveer |
| 1991 | Tennessee | 70–67 (OT) | Virginia | Pat Summitt |
| 1992 | Stanford | 78–62 | Western Kentucky | Tara VanDerveer |
| 1993 | Texas Tech | 84–82 | Ohio State | Marsha Sharp |
| 1994 | N Carolina | 60–59 | Louisiana Tech | Sylvia Hatchell |
| 1995 | Connecticut | 70–64 | Tennessee | Geno Auriemma |
| 1996 | Tennessee | 83–65 | Georgia | Pat Summitt |
| 1997 | Tennessee | 68–59 | Old Dominion | Pat Summitt |
| 1998 | Tennessee | 93–75 | Louisiana Tech | Pat Summitt |
| 1999 | Purdue | 62–45 | Duke | Carolyn Peck |
| 2000 | Connecticut | 71–52 | Tennessee | Geno Auriemma |
| 2001 | Notre Dame | 68–66 | Purdue | Muffet McGraw |

# NCAA Women's Division I Alltime Individual Leaders

## Single-Game Records
### SCORING HIGHS

| Pts | Player and Team vs Opponent | Year |
|---|---|---|
| 60 | Cindy Brown, Long Beach St vs San Jose St | 1987 |
| 58 | Kim Perrot, SW Louisiana vs SE Louisiana | 1990 |
| 58 | Lorri Bauman, Drake vs SW Missouri St | 1984 |
| 56 | Jackie Stiles, SW Missouri St vs Evansville | 2000 |
| 55 | Patricia Hoskins, Mississippi Valley vs Southern-BR | 1989 |
| 55 | Patricia Hoskins, Mississippi Valley vs Alabama St | 1989 |
| 54 | Anjinea Hopson, Grambling vs Jackson St | 1994 |
| 54 | Mary Lowry, Baylor vs Texas | 1994 |
| 54 | Wanda Ford, Drake vs SW Missouri St | 1986 |

Three tied with 53.

## Single-Game Records *(Cont.)*
### REBOUNDS

| Reb | Player and Team vs Opponent | Year |
|-----|------------------------------|------|
| 40 | Deborah Temple, Delta St vs AL-Birmingham | 1983 |
| 37 | Rosina Pearson, Bethune-Cookman vs Florida Memorial | 1985 |
| 33 | Maureen Formico, Pepperdine vs Loyola (CA) | 1985 |
| 31 | Darlene Beale, Howard vs S Carolina St | 1987 |
| 30 | Cindy Bonforte, Wagner vs Queens (NY) | 1983 |
| 30 | Kayone Hankins, New Orleans vs. Nicholls St | 1994 |
| 30 | Wanda Ford, Drake vs Eastern Illinois | 1985 |
| 29 | Gail Norris, Alabama St vs Texas Southern | 1992 |
| 29 | Joy Kellogg, Oklahoma City vs Oklahoma Christian | 1984 |
| 29 | Joy Kellogg, Oklahoma City vs UTEP | 1984 |

### ASSISTS

| A | Player and Team vs Opponent | Year |
|---|------------------------------|------|
| 23 | Michelle Burden, Kent St vs Ball St | 1991 |
| 22 | Shawn Monday, Tennessee Tech vs Morehead St | 1988 |
| 22 | Veronica Pettry, Loyola (IL) vs Detroit | 1989 |
| 22 | Tine Freil, Pacific vs Wichita St | 1991 |
| 21 | Tine Freil, Pacific vs Fresno St | 1992 |
| 21 | Amy Bauer, Wisconsin vs Detroit | 1989 |
| 21 | Neacole Hall, Alabama St vs Southern-BR | 1989 |

Five tied with 20.

## Single Season Records
### POINTS

| Player and Team | Year | GP | FG | 3FG | FT | Pts |
|-----------------|------|----|----|-----|----|----|
| Jackie Stiles, SW Missouri St | 2001 | 35 | 365 | 65 | 267 | 1062 |
| Cindy Brown, Long Beach St | 1987 | 35 | 362 | — | 250 | 974 |
| Genia Miller, Cal St-Fullerton | 1991 | 33 | 376 | 0 | 217 | 969 |
| Sheryl Swoopes, Texas Tech | 1993 | 34 | 356 | 32 | 211 | 955 |
| Andrea Congreaves, Mercer | 1992 | 28 | 353 | 77 | 142 | 925 |
| Wanda Ford, Drake | 1986 | 30 | 390 | — | 139 | 919 |
| Chamique Holdsclaw, Tennessee | 1998 | 39 | 370 | 9 | 166 | 915 |
| Barbara Kennedy, Clemson | 1982 | 31 | 392 | — | 124 | 908 |
| Patricia Hoskins, Mississippi Valley | 1989 | 27 | 345 | 13 | 205 | 908 |
| LaTaunya Pollard, Long Beach St | 1983 | 31 | 376 | — | 155 | 907 |

### SEASON SCORING AVERAGE

| Player and Team | Year | GP | FG | 3FG | FT | Pts | Avg |
|-----------------|------|----|----|-----|----|----|-----|
| Patricia Hoskins, Mississippi Valley | 1989 | 27 | 345 | 13 | 205 | 908 | 33.6 |
| Andrea Congreaves, Mercer | 1992 | 28 | 353 | 77 | 142 | 925 | 33.0 |
| Deborah Temple, Delta St | 1984 | 28 | 373 | — | 127 | 873 | 31.2 |
| Andrea Congreaves, Mercer | 1993 | 26 | 302 | 51 | 150 | 805 | 31.0 |
| Wanda Ford, Drake | 1986 | 30 | 390 | — | 139 | 919 | 30.6 |
| Anucha Browne, Northwestern | 1985 | 28 | 341 | — | 173 | 855 | 30.5 |
| LeChandra LeDay, Grambling | 1988 | 28 | 334 | 36 | 146 | 850 | 30.4 |
| Jackie Stiles, SW MIssouri St | 2001 | 35 | 365 | 65 | 267 | 1062 | 30.3 |
| Kim Perrot, Southwestern Louisiana | 1990 | 28 | 308 | 95 | 128 | 839 | 30.0 |
| Tina Hutchinson, San Diego St | 1984 | 30 | 383 | — | 132 | 898 | 29.9 |
| Jan Jensen, Drake | 1991 | 30 | 358 | 6 | 166 | 888 | 29.6 |
| Genia Miller, Cal St-Fullerton | 1991 | 33 | 376 | 0 | 217 | 969 | 29.4 |
| Barbara Kennedy, Clemson | 1982 | 31 | 392 | — | 124 | 908 | 29.3 |
| LaTaunya Pollard, Long Beach St | 1983 | 31 | 376 | — | 155 | 907 | 29.3 |
| Lisa McMullen, Alabama St | 1991 | 28 | 285 | 126 | 119 | 815 | 29.1 |

## Single Season Records *(Cont.)*

### REBOUNDS

| Player and Team | Year | GP | Reb | Player and Team | Year | GP | Reb |
|---|---|---|---|---|---|---|---|
| Wanda Ford, Drake | 1985 | 30 | 534 | Rosina Pearson, Beth.-Cookman | 1985 | 26 | 480 |
| Wanda Ford, Drake | 1986 | 30 | 506 | Patricia Hoskins, Miss Valley | 1987 | 28 | 476 |
| Anne Donovan, Old Dominion | 1983 | 35 | 504 | Cheryl Miller, Southern Cal | 1985 | 30 | 474 |
| Darlene Jones, Miss Valley | 1983 | 31 | 487 | Darlene Beale, Howard | 1987 | 29 | 459 |
| Melanie Simpson, Okla. City | 1982 | 37 | 481 | Olivia Bradley, W Virginia | 1985 | 30 | 458 |

### REBOUND AVERAGE

| Player and Team | Year | GP | Reb | Avg |
|---|---|---|---|---|
| Rosina Pearson, Bethune-Cookman | 1985 | 26 | 480 | 18.5 |
| Wanda Ford, Drake | 1985 | 30 | 534 | 17.8 |
| Katie Beck, E Tennessee St | 1988 | 25 | 441 | 17.6 |
| DeShawne Blocker, E Tennessee St | 1994 | 26 | 450 | 17.3 |
| Patricia Hoskins, Mississippi Valley | 1987 | 28 | 476 | 17.0 |
| Wanda Ford, Drake | 1986 | 30 | 506 | 16.9 |
| Patricia Hoskins, Mississippi Valley | 1989 | 27 | 440 | 16.3 |
| Joy Kellogg, Oklahoma City | 1984 | 23 | 373 | 16.2 |
| Deborah Mitchell, Mississippi Coll. | 1983 | 28 | 447 | 16.0 |
| Cheryl Miller, Southern California | 1985 | 30 | 474 | 15.8 |

### FIELD-GOAL PERCENTAGE

| Player and Team | Year | GP | FG | FGA | Pct |
|---|---|---|---|---|---|
| Myndee Larsen, Southern Utah | 1998 | 28 | 249 | 344 | 72.4 |
| Chantelle Anderson, Vanderbilt | 2001 | 34 | 292 | 404 | 72.3 |
| Deneka Knowles, Southeastern La. | 1996 | 26 | 199 | 276 | 72.1 |
| Barbara Farris, Tulane | 1998 | 27 | 151 | 210 | 71.9 |
| Renay Adams, Tennessee Tech | 1991 | 30 | 185 | 258 | 71.7 |
| Regina Days, Georgia Southern | 1986 | 27 | 234 | 332 | 70.5 |
| Kim Wood, WI-Green Bay | 1994 | 27 | 188 | 271 | 69.4 |
| Kelly Lyons, Old Dominion | 1990 | 31 | 308 | 444 | 69.4 |
| Alisha Hill, Howard | 1995 | 28 | 194 | 281 | 69.0 |
| Ruth Riley, Notre Dame | 1999 | 31 | 198 | 290 | 68.3 |

Based on qualifiers for annual championship.

### FREE-THROW PERCENTAGE

| Player and Team | Year | GP | FT | FTA | Pct |
|---|---|---|---|---|---|
| Ginny Doyle, Richmond | 1992 | 29 | 96 | 101 | 95.0 |
| Paula Corder-King, SE Missouri St | 1999 | 28 | 111 | 118 | 94.1 |
| Linda Cyborski, Delaware | 1991 | 29 | 74 | 79 | 93.7 |
| Paula Corder-King, SE Missouri St | 2000 | 27 | 69 | 74 | 93.2 |
| Jennifer Howard, N Carolina St | 1994 | 27 | 118 | 127 | 92.9 |
| Keely Feeman, Cincinnati | 1986 | 30 | 76 | 82 | 92.7 |
| Amy Slowikowski, Kent St | 1989 | 27 | 112 | 121 | 92.6 |
| Lea Ann Parsley, Marshall | 1990 | 28 | 96 | 104 | 92.3 |
| Chris Starr, NV-Reno | 1986 | 25 | 119 | 129 | 92.2 |
| DeAnn Craft, Central Florida | 1987 | 24 | 94 | 102 | 92.2 |

Based on qualifiers for annual championship.

## Career Records
### POINTS

| Player and Team | Yrs | GP | Pts |
|---|---|---|---|
| Jackie Stiles, SW Missouri St | 1997–01 | 129 | 3393 |
| Patricia Hoskins, Mississippi Valley | 1985–89 | 110 | 3122 |
| Lorri Bauman, Drake | 1981–84 | 120 | 3115 |
| Chamique Holdsclaw, Tennessee | 1995–99 | 148 | 3025 |
| Cheryl Miller, Southern Cal | 1983–86 | 128 | 3018 |
| Cindy Blodgett, Maine | 1994–98 | 118 | 3005 |
| Valorie Whiteside, Appalachian St | 1984–88 | 116 | 2944 |
| Joyce Walker, Louisiana St | 1981–84 | 117 | 2906 |
| Sandra Hodge, New Orleans | 1981–84 | 107 | 2860 |
| Andrea Congreaves, Mercer | 1989–93 | 108 | 2796 |

### SCORING AVERAGE

| Player and Team | Yrs | GP | FG | 3FG | FT | Pts | Avg |
|---|---|---|---|---|---|---|---|
| Patricia Hoskins, Mississippi Valley | 1985–89 | 110 | 1196 | 24 | 706 | 3122 | 28.4 |
| Sandra Hodge, New Orleans | 1981–84 | 107 | 1194 | — | 472 | 2860 | 26.7 |
| Jackie Stiles, SW Missouri St | 1997–01 | 129 | 1160 | 221 | 852 | 3393 | 26.3 |
| Lorri Bauman, Drake | 1981–84 | 120 | 1104 | — | 907 | 3115 | 26.0 |
| Andrea Congreaves, Mercer | 1989–93 | 108 | 1107 | 153 | 429 | 2796 | 25.9 |
| Cindy Blodgett, Maine | 1994–98 | 118 | 1055 | 219 | 676 | 3005 | 25.5 |
| Valorie Whiteside, Appalachian St | 1984–88 | 116 | 1153 | 0 | 638 | 2944 | 25.4 |
| Joyce Walker, Louisiana St | 1981–84 | 117 | 1259 | — | 388 | 2906 | 24.8 |
| Tarcha Hollis, Grambling | 1988–91 | 85 | 904 | 3 | 247 | 2058 | 24.2 |
| Korie Hlede, Duquesne | 1994–98 | 109 | 1045 | 162 | 379 | 2631 | 24.1 |

# NCAA Men's Division II Championship Results

| Year | Winner | Score | Runner-up | Third Place | Fourth Place |
|---|---|---|---|---|---|
| 1957 | Wheaton (IL) | 89–65 | Kentucky Wesleyan | Mount St Mary's (MD) | Cal St-Los Angeles |
| 1958 | S Dakota | 75–53 | St. Michael's | Evansville | Wheaton (IL) |
| 1959 | Evansville | 83–67 | SW Missouri St | N Carolina A&T | Cal St-Los Angeles |
| 1960 | Evansville | 90–69 | Chapman | Kentucky Wesleyan | Cornell College |
| 1961 | Wittenberg | 42–38 | SE Missouri St | S Dakota St | Mount St Mary's (MD) |
| 1962 | Mount St Mary's (MD) | 58–57 (OT) | Cal St-Sacramento | Southern Illinois | Nebraska Wesleyan |
| 1963 | S Dakota St | 44–42 | Wittenberg | Oglethorpe | Southern Illinois |
| 1964 | Evansville | 72–59 | Akron | N Carolina A&T | Northern Iowa |
| 1965 | Evansville | 85–82 (OT) | Southern Illinois | N Dakota | St Michael's |
| 1966 | Kentucky Wesleyan | 54–51 | Southern Illinois | Akron | N Dakota |
| 1967 | Winston-Salem | 77–74 | SW Missouri St | Kentucky Wesleyan | Illinois St |
| 1968 | Kentucky Wesleyan | 63–52 | Indiana St | Trinity (TX) | Ashland |
| 1969 | Kentucky Wesleyan | 75–71 | SW Missouri St | †Vacated | Ashland |
| 1970 | Philadelphia Textile | 76–65 | Tennessee St | UC-Riverside | Buffalo St |
| 1971 | Evansville | 97–82 | Old Dominion | †Vacated | Kentucky Wesleyan |
| 1972 | Roanoke | 84–72 | Akron | Tennessee St | Eastern Mich |
| 1973 | Kentucky Wesleyan | 78–76 (OT) | Tennessee St | Assumption | Brockport St |
| 1974 | Morgan St | 67–52 | SW Missouri St | Assumption | New Orleans |
| 1975 | Old Dominion | 76–74 | New Orleans | Assumption | TN-Chattanooga |
| 1976 | Puget Sound | 83–74 | TN-Chattanooga | Eastern Illinois | Old Dominion |
| 1977 | TN-Chattanooga | 71–62 | Randolph-Macon | N Alabama | Sacred Heart |
| 1978 | Cheyney | 47–40 | WI-Green Bay | Eastern Illinois | Central Florida |
| 1979 | N Alabama | 64–50 | WI-Green Bay | Cheyney | Bridgeport |
| 1980 | Virginia Union | 80–74 | New York Tech | Florida Southern | N Alabama |
| 1981 | Florida Southern | 73–68 | Mount St Mary's (MD) | Cal Poly-SLO | WI-Green Bay |
| 1982 | District of Columbia | 73–63 | Florida Southern | Kentucky Wesleyan | Cal St-Bakersfield |
| 1983 | Wright St | 92–73 | District of Columbia | *Cal St-Bakersfield | *Morningside |
| 1984 | Central Missouri St | 81–77 | St. Augustine's | *Kentucky Wesleyan | *N Alabama |
| 1985 | Jacksonville St | 74–73 | S Dakota St | *Kentucky Wesleyan | *Mount St. Mary's (MD) |
| 1986 | Sacred Heart | 93–87 | SE Missouri St | *Cheyney | *Florida Southern |
| 1987 | Kentucky Wesleyan | 92–74 | Gannon | *Delta St | *Eastern Montana |
| 1988 | Lowell | 75–72 | AK-Anchorage | Florida Southern | Troy St |
| 1989 | N Carolina Central | 73–46 | SE Missouri St | UC-Riverside | Jacksonville St |

*Indicates tied for third. †Student-athletes representing American International in 1969 and Southwestern Louisiana in 1971 were declared ineligible subsequent to the tournament. Under NCAA rules, the teams' and ineligible student-athletes' records were deleted, and the teams' places in the final standings were vacated.

| Year | Winner | Score | Runner-up | Third Place | Fourth Place |
|------|--------|-------|-----------|-------------|--------------|
| 1990 | .......Kentucky Wesleyan | 93–79 | Cal St-Bakersfield | N Dakota | Morehouse |
| 1991 | .......N Alabama | 79–72 | Bridgeport (CT) | *Cal St-Bakersfield | *Virginia Union |
| 1992 | .......Virginia Union | 100–75 | Bridgeport (CT) | *Cal St-Bakersfield | *California (PA) |
| 1993 | .......Cal St-Bakersfield | 85–72 | Troy St (AL) | *New Hampshire Coll | *Wayne St (MI) |
| 1994 | .......Cal St-Bakersfield | 92–86 | Southern Indiana | *New Hampshire Coll | *Washburn |
| 1995 | .......Southern Indiana | 71–63 | UC-Riverside | *Norfolk St | *Indiana (PA) |
| 1996 | .......Fort Hays St | 70–63 | Northern Kentucky | *California (PA) | *Virginia Union |
| 1997 | .......Cal St-Bakersfield | 57–56 | Northern Kentucky | *Lynn | *Salem-Teikyo |
| 1998 | .......UC-Davis | 83–77 | Kentucky Wesleyan | *St. Rose | *Virginia Union |
| 1999 | .......Kentucky Wesleyan | 75–60 | Metropolitan St | *Truman St | *Florida Southern |
| 2000 | .......Metropolitan St | 97–79 | Kentucky Wesleyan | *Missouri Southern | *Seattle Pacific |
| 2001 | .......Kentucky Wesleyan | 72–63 | Washburn | *Western Washington | *Tampa |

# NCAA Men's Division II Alltime Individual Leaders

## SINGLE-GAME SCORING HIGHS

| Pts | Player and Team vs Opponent | Date |
|-----|------------------------------|------|
| 113 | .............................Bevo Francis, Rio Grande vs Hillsdale | 1954 |
| 84 | .............................Bevo Francis, Rio Grande vs Alliance | 1954 |
| 82 | .............................Bevo Francis, Rio Grande vs Bluffton | 1954 |
| 80 | .............................Paul Crissman, Southern Cal Col vs Pacific Christian | 1966 |
| 77 | .............................William English, Winston-Salem vs Fayetteville St | 1968 |

## Single Season Records
### SCORING AVERAGE

| Player and Team | Year | GP | FG | FT | Pts | Avg |
|-----------------|------|----|----|----|----|-----|
| Bevo Francis, Rio Grande | 1954 | 27 | 444 | 367 | 1255 | 46.5 |
| Earl Glass, Mississippi Industrial | 1963 | 19 | 322 | 171 | 815 | 42.9 |
| Earl Monroe, Winston-Salem | 1967 | 32 | 509 | 311 | 1329 | 41.5 |
| John Rinka, Kenyon | 1970 | 23 | 354 | 234 | 942 | 41.0 |
| Willie Shaw, Lane | 1964 | 18 | 303 | 121 | 727 | 40.4 |

### REBOUND AVERAGE

| Player and Team | Year | GP | Reb | Avg |
|-----------------|------|----|-----|-----|
| Tom Hart, Middlebury | 1956 | 21 | 620 | 29.5 |
| Tom Hart, Middlebury | 1955 | 22 | 649 | 29.5 |
| Frank Stronczek, American Int'l | 1966 | 26 | 717 | 27.6 |
| R.C. Owens, College of Idaho | 1954 | 25 | 677 | 27.1 |
| Maurice Stokes, St Francis (PA) | 1954 | 26 | 689 | 26.5 |

### ASSISTS

| Player and Team | Year | GP | A |
|-----------------|------|----|----|
| Steve Ray, Bridgeport | 1989 | 32 | 400 |
| Steve Ray, Bridgeport | 1990 | 33 | 385 |
| Tony Smith, Pfeiffer | 1992 | 35 | 349 |
| Jim Ferrer, Bentley | 1989 | 31 | 309 |
| Rob Paternostro, New Hamp. Coll. | 1995 | 33 | 309 |

### ASSIST AVERAGE

| Player and Team | Year | GP | A | Avg |
|-----------------|------|----|----|-----|
| Steve Ray, Bridgeport | 1989 | 32 | 400 | 12.5 |
| Steve Ray, Bridgeport | 1990 | 33 | 385 | 11.7 |
| Demetri Beekman, Assumption | 1993 | 23 | 264 | 11.5 |
| Ernest Jenkins, NM Highlands | 1995 | 27 | 291 | 10.8 |
| Brian Gregory, Oakland | 1989 | 28 | 300 | 10.7 |

### FIELD-GOAL PERCENTAGE

| Player and Team | Year | Pct |
|-----------------|------|-----|
| Todd Linder, Tampa | 1987 | 75.2 |
| Maurice Stafford, N Alabama | 1984 | 75.0 |
| Matthew Cornegay, Tuskegee | 1982 | 74.8 |
| Brian Moten, W Georgia | 1992 | 73.4 |
| Ed Phillips, Alabama A&M | 1968 | 73.3 |

### FREE-THROW PERCENTAGE

| Player and Team | Year | Pct |
|-----------------|------|-----|
| Paul Cluxton, Northern Kentucky | 1997 | 100.0 |
| Tomas Rimkus, Pace | 1997 | 95.6 |
| C.J. Cowgill, Chaminade | 2001 | 95.0 |
| Billy Newton, Morgan St | 1976 | 94.4 |
| Kent Andrews, McNeese St | 1968 | 94.4 |

## Career Records
### POINTS

| Player and Team | Yrs | Pts |
|-----------------|-----|-----|
| Travis Grant, Kentucky St | 1969–72 | 4045 |
| Bob Hopkins, Grambling | 1953–56 | 3759 |
| Tony Smith, Pfeiffer | 1989–92 | 3350 |
| Earnest Lee, Clark Atlanta | 1984–87 | 3298 |
| Joe Miller, Alderson-Broaddus | 1954–57 | 3294 |

## Career Records (Cont.)

### CAREER SCORING AVERAGE

| Player and Team | Yrs | GP | Pts | Avg |
|---|---|---|---|---|
| Travis Grant, Kentucky St | 1969–72 | 121 | 4045 | 33.4 |
| John Rinka, Kenyon | 1967–70 | 99 | 3251 | 32.8 |
| Florindo Vieira, Quinnipiac | 1954–57 | 69 | 2263 | 32.8 |
| Willie Shaw, Lane | 1961–64 | 76 | 2379 | 31.3 |
| Mike Davis, Virginia Union | 1966–69 | 89 | 2758 | 31.0 |

### REBOUND AVERAGE

| Player and Team | Yrs | GP | Reb | Avg |
|---|---|---|---|---|
| Tom Hart, Middlebury | 1953, 55–56 | 63 | 1738 | 27.6 |
| Maurice Stokes, St. Francis (PA) | 1953–55 | 72 | 1812 | 25.2 |
| Frank Stronczek, American Int'l | 1965–67 | 62 | 1549 | 25.0 |
| Bill Thieben, Hofstra | 1954–56 | 76 | 1837 | 24.2 |
| Hank Brown, Lowell Tech | 1965–67 | 49 | 1129 | 23.0 |

### ASSISTS

| Player and Team | Yrs | A |
|---|---|---|
| Demetri Beekman, Assumption | 1990–93 | 1044 |
| Rob Paternostro, New Hamp. Coll. | 1992–95 | 919 |
| Gallagher Driscoll, St. Rose | 1989–92 | 878 |
| Tony Smith, Pfeiffer | 1989–92 | 828 |
| Jamie Stevens, Montana St-Billings | 1996–99 | 805 |

### ASSIST AVERAGE

| Player and Team | Yrs | GP | A | Avg |
|---|---|---|---|---|
| Steve Ray, Bridgeport | 1989–90 | 65 | 785 | 12.1 |
| Demetri Beekman, Assumption | 1990–93 | 119 | 1044 | 8.8 |
| Ernest Jenkins, NM Highlands | 1992–95 | 84 | 699 | 8.3 |
| Mark Benson, Texas A&I | 1989–91 | 86 | 674 | 7.8 |
| Pat Madden, Jacksonville St | 1989–91 | 88 | 688 | 7.8 |

Note: Minimum 550 Assists.

### FIELD-GOAL PERCENTAGE

| Player and Team | Yrs | Pct |
|---|---|---|
| Todd Linder, Tampa | 1984–87 | 70.8 |
| Tom Schurfranz, Bellarmine | 1989–92 | 70.2 |
| Chad Scott, California (PA) | 1991–94 | 70.0 |
| Ed Phillips, Alabama, A&M | 1968–71 | 68.9 |
| Ulysses Hackett, SC-Spartanburg | 1990–92 | 67.9 |

Note: Minimum 400 FGM.

### FREE-THROW PERCENTAGE

| Player and Team | Yrs | Pct |
|---|---|---|
| Paul Cluxton, Northern Kentucky | 1994–97 | 93.5 |
| Kent Andrews, McNeese St | 1967–69 | 91.6 |
| Jon Hagen, Mankato St | 1963–65 | 90.0 |
| Dave Reynolds, Davis & Elkins | 1986–89 | 89.3 |
| Michael Shue, Lock Haven | 1994–97 | 88.5 |

Note: Minimum 250 FTM

# NCAA Men's Division III Championship Results

| Year | Winner | Score | Runner-up | Third Place | Fourth Place |
|---|---|---|---|---|---|
| 1975 | LeMoyne-Owen | 57–54 | Glassboro St | Augustana (IL) | Brockport St |
| 1976 | Scranton | 60–57 | Wittenberg | Augustana (IL) | Plattsburgh St |
| 1977 | Wittenberg | 79–66 | Oneonta St | Scranton | Hamline |
| 1978 | North Park | 69–57 | Widener | Albion | Stony Brook |
| 1979 | North Park | 66–62 | Potsdam St | Franklin & Marshall | Centre |
| 1980 | North Park | 83–76 | Upsala | Wittenberg | Longwood |
| 1981 | Potsdam St | 67–65 (OT) | Augustana (IL) | Ursinus | Otterbein |
| 1982 | Wabash | 83–62 | Potsdam St | Brooklyn | Cal St-Stanislaus |
| 1983 | Scranton | 64–63 | Wittenberg | Roanoke | WI-Whitewater |
| 1984 | WI-Whitewater | 103–86 | Clark (MA) | DePauw | Upsala |
| 1985 | North Park | 72–71 | Potsdam St | Nebraska Wesleyan | Widener |
| 1986 | Potsdam St | 76–73 | LeMoyne-Owen | Nebraska Wesleyan | Jersey City St |
| 1987 | North Park | 106–100 | Clark (MA) | Wittenberg | Stockton St |
| 1988 | Ohio Wesleyan | 92–70 | Scranton | Nebraska Wesleyan | Hartwick |
| 1989 | WI-Whitewater | 94–86 | Trenton St | Southern Maine | Centre |
| 1990 | Rochester | 43–42 | DePauw | Washington (MD) | Calvin |
| 1991 | WI-Platteville | 81–74 | Franklin & Marshall | Otterbein | Ramapo (NJ) |
| 1992 | Calvin | 62–49 | Rochester | WI-Platteville | Jersey City St |
| 1993 | Ohio Northern | 71–68 | Augustana | Mass-Dartmouth | Rowan |
| 1994 | Lebanon Valley Coll | 66–59 (OT) | New York University | Wittenberg | St Thomas (MN) |
| 1995 | WI-Platteville | 69–55 | Manchester | Rowan | Trinity (CT) |
| 1996 | Rowan | 100–93 | Hope (MI) | Illinois Wesleyan | Franklin & Marshall |
| 1997 | Illinois Wesleyan | 89–86 | Nebraska Wesleyan | Williams | Alvernia |
| 1998 | WI-Platteville | 69–56 | Hope (MI) | Williams | Wilkes |
| 1999 | WI-Platteville | 76–75 (2 OT) | Hampden-Sydney | William Paterson | Connecticut Coll. |
| 2000 | Calvin | 79–74 | WI-Eau Claire | Salem St | Franklin & Marshall |
| 2001 | Catholic | 76–62 | William Paterson | *Illinois Wesleyan | *Ohio Northern |

## SINGLE-GAME SCORING HIGHS

| Pts | Player and Team vs Opponent | Year |
|---|---|---|
| 77 | Jeff Clement, Grinnell vs Illinois College | 1998 |
| 69 | Steve Diekmann, Grinnell vs Simpson | 1995 |
| 63 | Joe DeRoche, Thomas vs St. Joseph's (ME) | 1988 |
| 62 | Shannon Lilly, Bishop vs Southwest Assembly of God | 1983 |
| 61 | Steve Honderd, Calvin vs Kalamazoo | 1993 |
| 61 | Dana Wilson, Husson vs Ricker | 1974 |
| 61 | Joshua Metzger, Wisconsin Lutheran vs Grinnell | 2000 |

## Single Season Records

### SCORING AVERAGE

| Player and Team | Year | GP | FG | FT | Pts | Avg |
|---|---|---|---|---|---|---|
| Steve Diekmann, Grinnell | 1995 | 20 | 223 | 162 | 745 | 37.3 |
| Rickey Sutton, Lyndon St | 1976 | 14 | 207 | 93 | 507 | 36.2 |
| Shannon Lilly, Bishop | 1983 | 26 | 345 | 218 | 908 | 34.9 |
| Dana Wilson, Husson | 1974 | 20 | 288 | 122 | 698 | 34.9 |
| Rickey Sutton, Lyndon St | 1977 | 16 | 223 | 112 | 558 | 34.9 |

### REBOUND AVERAGE

| Player and Team | Year | GP | Reb | Avg |
|---|---|---|---|---|
| Joe Manley, Bowie St | 1976 | 29 | 579 | 20.0 |
| Fred Petty, New Hampshire College | 1974 | 22 | 436 | 19.8 |
| Larry Williams, Pratt | 1977 | 24 | 457 | 19.0 |
| Charles Greer, Thomas | 1977 | 17 | 318 | 18.7 |
| Larry Parker, Plattsburgh St | 1975 | 23 | 430 | 18.7 |

### ASSISTS

| Player and Team | Year | GP | A |
|---|---|---|---|
| Robert James, Kean | 1989 | 29 | 391 |
| Ricky Spicer, WI-Whitewater | 1989 | 31 | 295 |
| Joe Marcotte, New Jersey Tech | 1995 | 30 | 292 |
| Andre Bolton, Chris. Newport | 1996 | 30 | 289 |
| Ron Torgalski, Hamilton | 1989 | 26 | 275 |

### ASSIST AVERAGE

| Player and Team | Year | GP | A | Avg |
|---|---|---|---|---|
| Robert James, Kean | 1989 | 29 | 391 | 13.5 |
| Albert Kirchner, Mt. St. Vincent | 1990 | 24 | 267 | 11.1 |
| Ron Torgalski, Hamilton | 1989 | 26 | 275 | 10.6 |
| Louis Adams, Rust | 1989 | 22 | 227 | 10.3 |
| Eric Johnson, Coe | 1991 | 24 | 238 | 9.9 |

### FIELD-GOAL PERCENTAGE

| Player and Team | Year | Pct |
|---|---|---|
| Travis Weiss, St. John's (MN) | 1994 | 76.6 |
| Pete Metzelaars, Wabash | 1982 | 75.3 |
| Tony Rychlec, Mass. Maritime | 1981 | 74.9 |
| Tony Rychlec, Mass. Maritime | 1982 | 73.1 |
| Russ Newnan, Menlo | 1991 | 73.0 |

### FREE-THROW PERCENTAGE

| Player and Team | Year | Pct |
|---|---|---|
| Korey Coon, IL Wesleyan | 2000 | 96.3 |
| Chanse Young, Manchester | 1998 | 95.6 |
| Andy Enfield, Johns Hopkins | 1991 | 95.3 |
| Chris Carideo, Widener | 1992 | 95.2 |
| Yudi Teichman, Yeshiva | 1989 | 95.2 |

## Career Records

### POINTS

| Player and Team | Yrs | Pts |
|---|---|---|
| Andre Foreman, Salisbury St | 1989–92 | 2940 |
| Lamont Strothers, Chris. Newport | 1988–91 | 2709 |
| Matt Hancock, Colby | 1987–90 | 2678 |
| Scott Fitch, Geneseo St | 1990–94 | 2634 |
| Greg Grant, Trenton St | 1987–89 | 2611 |

### CAREER SCORING AVERAGE

| Player and Team | Yrs | GP | Avg |
|---|---|---|---|
| Dwain Govan, Bishop | 1974–75 | 55 | 32.8 |
| Dave Russell, Shepherd | 1974–75 | 60 | 30.6 |
| Rickey Sutton, Lyndon St | 1976–79 | 80 | 29.7 |
| John Atkins, Knoxville | 1976–78 | 70 | 28.7 |
| Willie Chandler, Misericordia | 1999–01 | 53 | 27.7 |

### REBOUND AVERAGE

| Player and Team | Yrs | GP | Reb | Avg |
|---|---|---|---|---|
| Larry Parker, Plattsburgh St | 1975–78 | 85 | 1482 | 17.4 |
| Charles Greer, Thomas | 1975–77 | 58 | 926 | 16.0 |
| Willie Parr, LeMoyne-Owen | 1974–76 | 76 | 1182 | 15.6 |
| Michael Smith, Hamilton | 1989–92 | 107 | 1632 | 15.2 |
| Dave Kufeld, Yeshiva | 1977–80 | 81 | 1222 | 15.1 |
| E. Owens, Hampden-Sydney | 1977–80 | 77 | 1160 | 15.1 |

### ASSIST AVERAGE

| Player and Team | Yrs | Avg |
|---|---|---|
| Phil Dixon, Shenandoah | 1993–96 | 8.6 |
| Steve Artis, Chris. Newport | 1990–93 | 8.1 |
| David Genovese, Mt. St. Vincent | 1992–95 | 7.5 |
| Kevin Root, Eureka | 1989–91 | 7.1 |
| Dennis Jacobi, Bowdoin | 1989–92 | 7.1 |

# Hockey

**Ray Bourque of the Stanley Cup champion Colorado Avalanche**

# Oh, Happy Ray!

## After 22 years in the league and several near misses, Colorado defenseman Ray Bourque finally lifted the Stanley Cup

### BY B.J. SCHECTER

THIS WAS the moment Raymond Bourque had waited for his entire career, his entire life. The Stanley Cup, the most revered trophy in North American sports, had been within Bourque's reach on several occasions but had always eluded his grasp. He had spent more than 20 seasons with the Bruins, and in March 2000, when it became apparent that Boston wouldn't contend for the Cup before the end of his career, Bourque asked to be traded to a championship-caliber team. The Bruins graciously granted his wish, trading him to Colorado, and from the day Bourque pulled on the Avalanche sweater, everybody wanted him to win a Cup.

Colorado made it to the brink of the Stanley Cup finals that year, losing to the Dallas Stars in Game 7 of the Western Conference finals, but then, a year later, they did it: With a 3–1 victory over New Jersey in Game 7, they won their second NHL title in six years, but more importantly, they delivered the Stanley Cup to the 40-year-old Bourque, ending the legendary defenseman's 22-year quest. Soon after the final whistle blew, Avalanche captain Joe Sakic accepted the Cup from NHL commissioner Gary Bettman, skipped the traditional captain's spin around the rink with the fabled trophy and literally handed it to Bourque, whose eyes began to well up with tears. The crowd at the Pepsi Center went wild when Bourque lifted the 34 1/2-pound piece of silver over his head. "Maybe it's because I'm old or I was tired, but it felt really heavy," Bourque said.

You could search from Saskatoon to St. Petersburg without finding a hockey fan, or player, who dislikes Ray Bourque. He is the quintessential old-school team player, a superbly skilled defenseman of unerring consistency. Even in Boston, where fans are notoriously provincial and treat players who leave Beantown as traitors, Bourque's name ranks with Williams's and Russell's. The television ratings were higher in Boston for the Stanley Cup than they were in the New York area, home of the New Jersey Devils.

After Colorado clinched the Cup, Avalanche goalie Patrick Roy, who won the Conn Smythe Trophy as the playoff MVP for a record third time, said, "A name was missing from that thing. And today it's back to normal. [It was so special] seeing Ray raise that Cup, seeing his eyes, seeing how excited he was."

Bourque played in 1,826 games in 22 seasons, starting in 1979 and playing through the '80s, '90s and into the 21st century. He played in two Stanley Cup finals with Boston, but each time the Bruins were thwarted by Wayne Gretzky's Edmonton Oilers. Though Bourque had two years left on his contract when the season began, most observers assumed that this would be his final season, win or lose. So from the time the Avalanche opened training camp their goal was clear: win it for Ray.

The Avalanche ripped through the regular season, winning the Western Conference points race with a 52-16-10 record and establishing a few milestones along the way. In October, Roy, whose 2.21 goals-against average was the lowest in his 17-year career, surpassed Terry Sawchuk as the goalie with

**Roy (33) overcame several gaffes to win a record third Conn Smythe Trophy.**

the most career victories (448). In February, just before the trading deadline, the Avalanche acquired the final piece of their championship puzzle when they obtained defenseman Rob Blake from the Los Angeles Kings. "[Now] they're the overwhelming favorite to win the Stanley Cup," said Detroit general manager Ken Holland.

On March 24 the high-flying Avalanche traveled to Boston, where Bourque faced his old team for the first time since the trade. With Bruins fans enthusiastically cheering his every move, he played marvelously, assisting on two goals in a 4–2 Colorado victory. "I was very happy I had an opportunity at the end to thank the fans, who have been so good to me," Bourque said. "They treated me very well today, and I want to thank them. I certainly appreciate that. It was a very nice day, and I had a lot of fun."

Now Bourque & Co. were ready to begin their drive for a championship. In the first round of the playoffs the Avalanche faced

**Lemieux made an electrifying return to the ice, scoring 35 goals in 43 games.**

Vancouver and former Colorado coach Marc Crawford, who had a bitter parting from the team in 1998. The inspired Canucks put up a valiant fight, losing 5–4 and 2–1 in the first two games in Colorado. With two more tough victories in Vancouver the Avalanche swept the Canucks out of the playoffs and earned the respect of their former coach. "Our three-hundred thousand dollar players were trying to corral million dollar players," said Crawford. "But the superstars won out. I told the guys there's no shame in losing to a team that is great. And Colorado is a great team."

In the conference semifinals it was Blake's turn for an emotional homecoming—though the emotions were not as tender as those that greeted Bourque in Boston. The Avalanche met the upstart Kings, who had shocked the Red Wings in the first round. While Blake was so well respected on the ice that the Kings didn't name another captain after he left, he didn't fare as well in the stands. Kings fans were unforgiving, vigorously booing Blake during three games at the Staples Center. Los Angeles stole Game 1 in Colorado and hung on despite losing the next three games. They took Game 5 1–0, then won a 1–0 double-overtime thriller to force a Game 7, but the Avalanche wouldn't be denied. Blake, who scored a key goal in

Colorado's clinching 5–1 win, was relieved it was over. "You build your friendships through battles you've gone through over the years, and a month later you have to put all of that aside and battle your old team," said Blake. "It's very difficult."

More difficulty awaited the Avalanche in the Western Conference finals, where it would meet the St. Louis Blues. Shortly after the Los Angeles series, Colorado center Peter Forsberg felt a searing pain in his abdomen, the result of a ruptured spleen that would require emergency surgery, ending his season then and there. Without Forsberg, Colorado battled its way past St. Louis in five games, the last three of which went into overtime. Roy, who had some shaky moments early in the playoffs, was the stalwart, making big save after big save. "I don't care what I accomplished yesterday," said Roy, who is also the NHL's alltime leader in playoff wins. "Your next game makes everything disappear."

The 2000–01 regular season will be best remembered for the reappearance of one of the greatest players in NHL history. In 1997 Mario Lemieux retired from hockey, his prodigious powers still very much intact. When Gretzky called it quits two years later, hockey was left without a true superstar. At the same time, the Pittsburgh Penguins went into a financial tailspin and filed for bankruptcy. Lemieux bought a stake in the team (35%) in September 1999 and proved almost as adept in the front office as he had been on the ice, turning a loss of $16 million the previous season into a profit of $47,000 in his first year of ownership. But the Penguins, who possessed two top-shelf offensive threats in Jaromir Jagr and Alexei Kovalev, were struggling in the won-loss columns.

No ivory-tower owner, Lemieux opted for a hands-on approach to that problem: On Dec. 27, 2000, he restored himself to the Penguins' lineup, ending a 44-month retirement. It was as if he never left. He set up a goal in the first minute of the game and would score one and set up another during the 5–0 victory over Toronto. His performance was 21 minutes of awe-inspiring, nature-defying brilliance. "Mario is the bright color of the game," said Detroit Red Wings center Igor Larionov. "People want to see a Monet, a Rembrandt at work. Whenever he's on the ice, he's capable of producing a masterpiece or at least the unpredictable or unexpected. It's art, hockey performed at its highest skill level. If people are appreciating him more now, it's like an artist who gains proper recognition only after he passes away. But he lives again."

Lemieux finished the regular season with 35 goals and 41 assists in 43 games, leading the Penguins to a sixth-place finish in the Eastern Conference and single-handedly revitalizing the franchise, which regularly sold out its home games. Pittsburgh made a strong playoff run as well, advancing to the conference finals, where it fell to the New Jersey Devils. "This is the best time of my life," said Lemieux. "I had a lot of great moments in the early 1990s, but to be back and have a chance to play one more time has been great, especially with me playing well and the team playing well."

While Lemieux rejoined his team in 2000–01, two other stars, Eric Lindros of Philadelphia and Michael Peca of Buffalo, left theirs because of contract disputes. Lindros—a restricted free agent whose history of concussions has dimmed his once-bright star considerably—turned down Philadelphia's $8.5 million offer, and the Flyers were unable to move him before the March 13 trading deadline. Peca, also a restricted free agent, turned down the Sabres' four-year, $11.5 million deal, and Buffalo let him sit all year, finally trading him after the season. He accused the Sabres and the league of trying to punish him, a charge Buffalo's brass steadfastly denied. But like Alexei Yashin, a holdout in 1999, Peca was shipped to the Islanders, and if that isn't punishment, well....

There were two notable ownership changes in 2000–01. On Feb. 15 a group headed by Gretzky purchased the Phoenix Coyotes. And though Gretzky talked about building a championship team and took an active role early on, firing general manager

DAVID E. KLUTHO

seem to refute: He was suspended for 11 games, eight at the beginning of the 2001–02 season. To make matters worse, Toronto coach Pat Quinn plunged the NHL image to WWF depths when he grabbed a photographer around the neck and pushed him aside as the man attempted to take pictures of Domi entering league offices to hear his punishment.

But ugly incidents could not take away from Bourque's shining moment. While Bourque was no longer the player he had been during his peak Boston years, when he routinely racked up 80 points a year, he was certainly still a valuable contributor. He scored the game-winning goal in Game 3 of the finals, and he played 29 minutes and 35 seconds in Game 7, which would be the last game of his Hall of Fame career. Seizing the chance to end his career in storybook fashion, Bourque announced his retirement a few weeks after finally lifting the Cup.

He felt the gravity of the moment as the national anthem was played before Game 7. "I couldn't breathe the last 30 seconds, and it wasn't because I was tired," he said. "It was just too much, and I was trying to hold back the tears, the emotions. All night long it was tough to stay focused, from the national anthem on. I had tears in my eyes on the bench a few times. You kind of just let your mind drift for a couple of seconds, and then you have to regroup and just hold it and wait and wait."

As he left the ice in tears you got the sense that Ray Bourque was the happiest man in the world. For his teammates it was a fitting retirement gift. "Just seeing Ray carry that cup around the ice makes you want to cry," said Colorado forward Dan Hinote.

Bobby Smith two days after buying the team, the Coyotes narrowly missed the playoffs.

In Montreal, an American—*sacré bleu!*—bought the Canadiens, winners of a record 24 Stanley Cups. The $184 million that George Gillett Jr., a ski resort developer from Vail, Colo., spent for the team was a relative bargain when you consider that Molson Inc. spent $190 million to build the Molson Centre, which Gillett also acquired in the deal. Gillett had his work cut out for him, though, as the Habs finished dead last in the Northeast Division at 28-40-8.

The league, too, has work to do (still) in the area of on-ice violence. The playoffs were marred by an ugly incident in Game 4 of the Eastern Conference semifinals between New Jersey and Toronto. In the waning seconds of the Leafs' 3–1 victory, Toronto tough guy Tie Domi blindsided Devils defenseman Scott Niedermayer with a flying elbow to the skull. The cheap shot left Niedermayer with a concussion that sidelined him for four games and recast a shadow over the NHL, which claims it wants to shed the image that it allows gratuitous violence. That's a claim the toothless punishment handed down to Domi would

# FOR THE RECORD·2000-01

## NHL Final Standings

### Eastern Conference

#### NORTHEAST DIVISION

| | GP | W | L | T | RT | GF | GA | Pts |
|---|---|---|---|---|---|---|---|---|
| Ottawa | 82 | 48 | 21 | 9 | 4 | 274 | 205 | 109 |
| Buffalo | 82 | 46 | 30 | 5 | 1 | 218 | 184 | 98 |
| Toronto | 82 | 37 | 29 | 11 | 5 | 232 | 207 | 90 |
| Boston | 82 | 36 | 30 | 8 | 8 | 227 | 249 | 88 |
| Montreal | 82 | 28 | 40 | 8 | 6 | 206 | 232 | 70 |

#### ATLANTIC DIVISION

| | GP | W | L | T | RT | GF | GA | Pts |
|---|---|---|---|---|---|---|---|---|
| New Jersey | 82 | 48 | 19 | 12 | 3 | 295 | 195 | 111 |
| Philadelphia | 82 | 43 | 25 | 11 | 3 | 240 | 207 | 100 |
| Pittsburgh | 82 | 42 | 28 | 9 | 3 | 281 | 256 | 96 |
| NY Rangers | 82 | 33 | 43 | 5 | 1 | 250 | 290 | 72 |
| NY Islanders | 82 | 21 | 51 | 7 | 3 | 185 | 268 | 52 |

#### SOUTHEAST DIVISION

| | GP | W | L | T | RT | GF | GA | Pts |
|---|---|---|---|---|---|---|---|---|
| Washington | 82 | 41 | 27 | 10 | 4 | 233 | 211 | 96 |
| Carolina | 82 | 38 | 32 | 9 | 3 | 212 | 225 | 88 |
| Florida | 82 | 22 | 38 | 13 | 9 | 200 | 246 | 66 |
| Atlanta | 82 | 23 | 45 | 12 | 2 | 211 | 289 | 60 |
| Tampa Bay | 82 | 24 | 47 | 6 | 5 | 201 | 280 | 59 |

### Western Conference

#### CENTRAL DIVISION

| | GP | W | L | T | RT | GF | GA | Pts |
|---|---|---|---|---|---|---|---|---|
| Detroit | 82 | 49 | 20 | 9 | 4 | 253 | 202 | 111 |
| St. Louis | 82 | 43 | 22 | 12 | 5 | 249 | 195 | 103 |
| Nashville | 82 | 34 | 36 | 9 | 3 | 186 | 200 | 80 |
| Columbus | 82 | 28 | 39 | 9 | 6 | 190 | 233 | 71 |
| Chicago | 82 | 29 | 40 | 8 | 5 | 210 | 246 | 71 |

#### PACIFIC DIVISION

| | GP | W | L | T | RT | GF | GA | Pts |
|---|---|---|---|---|---|---|---|---|
| Dallas | 82 | 48 | 24 | 8 | 2 | 241 | 187 | 106 |
| San Jose | 82 | 40 | 27 | 12 | 3 | 217 | 192 | 95 |
| Los Angeles | 82 | 38 | 28 | 13 | 3 | 252 | 228 | 92 |
| Phoenix | 82 | 35 | 27 | 17 | 3 | 214 | 212 | 90 |
| Anaheim | 82 | 25 | 41 | 11 | 5 | 188 | 245 | 66 |

#### NORTHWEST DIVISION

| | GP | W | L | T | RT | GF | GA | Pts |
|---|---|---|---|---|---|---|---|---|
| Colorado | 82 | 52 | 16 | 10 | 4 | 270 | 192 | 118 |
| Edmonton | 82 | 39 | 28 | 12 | 3 | 243 | 222 | 93 |
| Vancouver | 82 | 36 | 28 | 11 | 7 | 239 | 238 | 90 |
| Calgary | 82 | 27 | 36 | 15 | 4 | 197 | 236 | 73 |
| Minnesota | 82 | 25 | 39 | 13 | 5 | 168 | 210 | 68 |

RT=regulation ties—games lost in overtime; worth 1 pt.

## 2001 Stanley Cup Playoffs

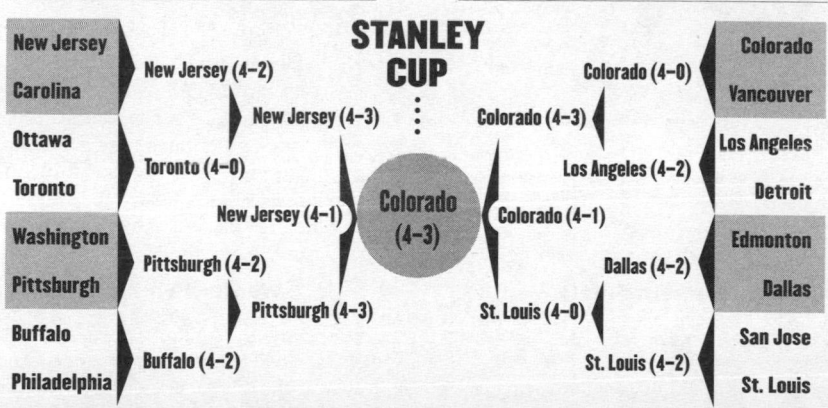

**EASTERN CONFERENCE**

QUARTERFINALS  SEMIFINALS  CONFERENCE FINAL

**WESTERN CONFERENCE**

CONFERENCE FINAL  SEMIFINALS  QUARTERFINALS

**STANLEY CUP**

New Jersey
Carolina
Ottawa
Toronto
Washington
Pittsburgh
Buffalo
Philadelphia

New Jersey (4–2)
Toronto (4–0)
Pittsburgh (4–2)
Buffalo (4–2)

New Jersey (4–3)
New Jersey (4–1)
Pittsburgh (4–3)

New Jersey (4–3)

Colorado (4–3)

Colorado (4–0)
Colorado (4–3)
Colorado (4–1)

Los Angeles (4–2)
Dallas (4–2)
St. Louis (4–0)
St. Louis (4–2)

Colorado
Vancouver
Los Angeles
Detroit
Edmonton
Dallas
San Jose
St. Louis

**Colorado (4–3)**

## Stanley Cup Playoff Results

### Conference Quarterfinals

#### EASTERN CONFERENCE

| | | | | |
|---|---|---|---|---|
| April 12 | Carolina | 1 | at New Jersey | 5 |
| April 15 | Carolina | 0 | at New Jersey | 2 |
| April 17 | New Jersey | 4 | at Carolina | 0 |
| April 18 | New Jersey | 2 | at Carolina | 3* |
| April 20 | Carolina | 3 | at New Jersey | 2 |
| April 22 | New Jersey | 5 | at Carolina | 1 |

New Jersey won series 4–2.

## Conference Quarterfinals *(Cont.)*

### EASTERN CONFERENCE *(Cont.)*

| | | | | |
|---|---|---|---|---|
| April 12 | Pittsburgh | 0 | at Washington | 1 |
| April 14 | Pittsburgh | 2 | at Washington | 1 |
| April 16 | Washington | 0 | at Pittsburgh | 3 |
| April 18 | Washington | 4 | at Pittsburgh | 3* |
| April 21 | Pittsburgh | 2 | at Washington | 1 |
| April 23 | Washington | 3 | at Pittsburgh | 4* |

Pittsburgh won series 4–2.

| | | | | |
|---|---|---|---|---|
| April 13 | Toronto | 1 | at Ottawa | 0* |
| April 14 | Toronto | 3 | at Ottawa | 0 |
| April 16 | Ottawa | 2 | at Toronto | 3* |
| April 18 | Ottawa | 1 | at Toronto | 3 |

Toronto won series 4–0.

| | | | | |
|---|---|---|---|---|
| April 11 | Buffalo | 2 | at Philadelphia | 1 |
| April 14 | Buffalo | 4 | at Philadelphia | 3* |
| April 16 | Philadelphia | 3 | at Buffalo | 2 |
| April 17 | Philadelphia | 3 | at Buffalo | 4* |

| | | | | |
|---|---|---|---|---|
| April 19 | Buffalo | 1 | at Philadelphia | 3 |
| April 21 | Philadelphia | 0 | at Buffalo | 8 |

Buffalo won series 4–2.

### WESTERN CONFERENCE

| | | | | |
|---|---|---|---|---|
| April 12 | Vancouver | 4 | at Colorado | 5 |
| April 14 | Vancouver | 1 | at Colorado | 5 |
| April 16 | Colorado | 4 | at Vancouver | 3* |
| April 18 | Colorado | 5 | at Vancouver | 1 |

Colorado won series 4–0.

| | | | | |
|---|---|---|---|---|
| April 11 | Los Angeles | 3 | at Detroit | 5 |
| April 14 | Los Angeles | 0 | at Detroit | 4 |
| April 15 | Detroit | 1 | at Los Angeles | 2 |
| April 18 | Detroit | 3 | at Los Angeles | 4* |
| April 21 | Los Angeles | 3 | at Detroit | 2 |
| April 23 | Detroit | 2 | at Los Angeles | 3* |

Los Angeles won series 4–2.

| | | | | |
|---|---|---|---|---|
| April 11 | Edmonton | 1 | at Dallas | 2* |
| April 14 | Edmonton | 4 | at Dallas | 3 |
| April 15 | Dallas | 3 | at Edmonton | 2* |
| April 17 | Dallas | 1 | at Edmonton | 2* |
| April 19 | Edmonton | 3 | at Dallas | 4* |
| April 21 | Dallas | 3 | at Edmonton | 1 |

Dallas won series 4–2.

| | | | | |
|---|---|---|---|---|
| April 12 | San Jose | 1 | at St. Louis | 3 |
| April 14 | San Jose | 1 | at St. Louis | 0 |
| April 16 | St. Louis | 6 | at San Jose | 3 |
| April 17 | St. Louis | 2 | at San Jose | 3 |
| April 19 | San Jose | 2 | at St. Louis | 3* |
| April 21 | St. Louis | 2 | at San Jose | 1 |

St. Louis won series 4–2.

## Conference Semifinals

### EASTERN CONFERENCE

| | | | | |
|---|---|---|---|---|
| April 26 | Toronto | 2 | at New Jersey | 0 |
| April 28 | Toronto | 5 | at New Jersey | 6* |
| May 1 | New Jersey | 3 | at Toronto | 2* |
| May 3 | New Jersey | 1 | at Toronto | 3 |
| May 5 | Toronto | 3 | at New Jersey | 2 |
| May 7 | New Jersey | 4 | at Toronto | 2 |
| May 9 | Toronto | 1 | at New Jersey | 5 |

New Jersey won series 4–3.

### WESTERN CONFERENCE

| | | | | |
|---|---|---|---|---|
| April 26 | Los Angeles | 4 | at Colorado | 3* |
| April 28 | Los Angeles | 0 | at Colorado | 2 |
| April 30 | Colorado | 4 | at Los Angeles | 3 |
| May 2 | Colorado | 3 | at Los Angeles | 0 |
| May 4 | Los Angeles | 1 | at Colorado | 0 |
| May 6 | Colorado | 0 | at Los Angeles | 1† |
| May 9 | Los Angeles | 1 | at Colorado | 5 |

Colorado won series 4–3.

| | | | | |
|---|---|---|---|---|
| April 26 | Pittsburgh | 3 | at Buffalo | 0 |
| April 28 | Pittsburgh | 3 | at Buffalo | 1 |
| April 30 | Buffalo | 4 | at Pittsburgh | 1 |
| May 2 | Buffalo | 5 | at Pittsburgh | 2 |
| May 5 | Pittsburgh | 2 | at Buffalo | 3* |
| May 8 | Buffalo | 2 | at Pittsburgh | 3* |
| May 10 | Pittsburgh | 3 | at Buffalo | 2* |

Pittsburgh won series 4–3.

| | | | | |
|---|---|---|---|---|
| April 27 | St. Louis | 4 | at Dallas | 2 |
| April 29 | St. Louis | 2 | at Dallas | 1 |
| May 1 | Dallas | 2 | at St. Louis | 3† |
| May 3 | Dallas | 1 | at St. Louis | 4 |

St. Louis won series 4–0.

## Eastern Finals

| | | | | |
|---|---|---|---|---|
| May 12 | Pittsburgh | 1 | at New Jersey | 3 |
| May 15 | Pittsburgh | 4 | at New Jersey | 2 |
| May 17 | New Jersey | 3 | at Pittsburgh | 0 |
| May 19 | New Jersey | 5 | at Pittsburgh | 0 |
| May 22 | Pittsburgh | 2 | at New Jersey | 4 |

New Jersey won series 4–1.

## Western Finals

| | | | | |
|---|---|---|---|---|
| May 12 | St. Louis | 1 | at Colorado | 4 |
| May 14 | St. Louis | 2 | at Colorado | 4 |
| May 16 | Colorado | 3 | at St. Louis | 4† |
| May 18 | Colorado | 4 | at St. Louis | 3* |
| May 21 | St. Louis | 1 | at Colorado | 2* |

Colorado won series 4–1.

## Stanley Cup Finals

| | | | | |
|---|---|---|---|---|
| May 26 | New Jersey | 0 | at Colorado | 5 |
| May 29 | New Jersey | 2 | at Colorado | 1 |
| May 31 | Colorado | 3 | at New Jersey | 1 |
| June 2 | Colorado | 2 | at New Jersey | 3 |

| | | | | |
|---|---|---|---|---|
| June 4 | New Jersey | 4 | at Colorado | 1 |
| June 7 | Colorado | 4 | at New Jersey | 0 |
| June 9 | New Jersey | 1 | at Colorado | 3 |

Colorado won series 4–3.

*Overtime game. †Double overtime game.

# Stanley Cup Championship Box Scores

## Game 1

New Jersey......0   0   0—0
Colorado .........1   2   2—5

### FIRST PERIOD
Scoring: 1, Colorado, Sakic 10 (Hejduk, Blake), 11:07. Penalties: White, NJ (holding) 4:28; Podein, Col (elbowing), 13:46.

### SECOND PERIOD
Scoring: 2, Colorado, Drury 9 (Hinote, Nieminen), 9:35. 3, Colorado, Sakic 11 (Blake, Skoula), 15:06. Penalties: De Vries, Col (boarding), 7:01; Tanguay, Col (tripping), 10:46; Daneyko, NJ (boarding), 14:16; Nieminen, Col (goalie int.), 14:16.

### THIRD PERIOD
Scoring: 4, Colorado, Blake 5 (pp) (Tanguay, Sakic), 5:36. 5, Colorado, Reinprecht 2 (Dingman, Reid), 17:36. Penalties: Hinote, Col (holding), 3:30; Stevenson, NJ (goalie int.), 4:45; White, NJ

### THIRD PERIOD (CONT.)
(roughing), 8:04; Sykora, NJ (charging), 8:04; Foote, Col (double roughing minor), 8:04; Daneyko, NJ (slashing, roughing), 9:43; O'Donnell, NJ (roughing), 11:34; Podein, Col (tripping), 11:34; De Vries, Col (tripping), 13:20; O'Donnell, NJ (served by Gomez) (instigator, fighting major, game misconduct) 17:36; Dingman, Col (fighting major), 17:36; Hinote, Col (roughing), 18:20.

Shots on goal: NJ—7-11-7—25. Colorado—14-7-9—30. Power-play opportunities: NJ 0 of 6, Col 1 of 5. Goalies: NJ, Brodeur (30 shots, 25 saves); Col, Roy (25 shots, 25 saves). A: 18,007.

Referees: Devorski, Marouelli. Linesmen: Schachte, Lazarowich.

## Game 2

New Jersey......2   0   0—2
Colorado .........1   0   0—1

### FIRST PERIOD
Scoring: 1, Colorado, Sakic 12 (pp) (Hejduk, Blake), 5:58. 2, New Jersey, Corkum 1 (Rafalski), 14:29. 3, New Jersey, Stevenson 1 (Niedermayer, Mogilny), 17:20. Penalties: Niedermayer, NJ (cross-checking), 1:43; Brylin, NJ (int.), 4:53; Elias, NJ (slashing) 12:28; Messier, Col (roughing), 14:46; Foote, Col (holding stick), 15:17; Holik, NJ (slashing), 19:39.

### SECOND PERIOD
Scoring: None. Penalties: De Vries, Col (int.), 9:11; Madden, NJ (diving), 9:11; Skoula, Col (holding), 14:47.

### THIRD PERIOD
Scoring: None. Penalties: Daneyko, NJ (cross-checking), 1:28; White, NJ (roughing), 2:58; Nieminen, Col (roughing), 2:58; Mogilny, NJ (high sticking), 4:26.

Shots on goal: NJ—12-6-2—20. Col—8-4-8—20. Power-play opportunities: NJ 0-of-3; Col 1-of-6. Goalies: NJ, Brodeur (20 shots, 19 saves); Col, Roy (20 shots, 18 saves). A: 18,007.

Referees: McCreary, Shick. Linesmen: Wheler, Lazarowich.

## Game 3

Colorado .........1   0   2—3
New Jersey......1   0   0—1

### FIRST PERIOD
Scoring:1, NJ, Arnott 8 (pp) (Holik, Elias), 3:16; 2, Colorado, Skoula 1 (Podein, Messier), 10:38. Penalties: Foote, Col (tripping), 1:29; Yelle, Col (int.), 6:28; Brylin, NJ (int.) 14:29; Tanguay, Col (hooking), 15:03; Nieminen, Col (boarding), 16:29.

### SECOND PERIOD
Scoring: None. Penalties: O'Donnell, NJ (cross-checking), 2:40; O'Donnell, NJ (holding), 8:25; Foote, Col (tripping), 14:52; Arnott, NJ (boarding), 19:02.

### THIRD PERIOD
Scoring: 3, Colorado, Bourque 4 (pp) (Sakic). 0:31. 4, Colorado, Hinote 2 (Nieminen, Drury), 6:28. Penalties: Klemm, Col (holding), 8:22.

Shots on goal: Col—5 11 5—21. NJ—8-3-11—22. Power-play opportunities: Col 1-of-4; NJ 1-of-6. Goalies: Col, Roy (22 shots, 21 saves); NJ, Brodeur (21 shots, 18 saves). A: 19,004.
Referees: Fraser, Marouelli. Linesmen: Collins, Schachte.

## Game 4

Colorado .........1   1   0—2
New Jersey......0   1   2—3

### FIRST PERIOD
Scoring: 1, Colorado, Blake 6 (Tanguay), 3:58. Penalties: Stevenson, NJ (int.), 1:36; Gomez, NJ (goalie int.), 4:42; Yelle, Col (diving), 7:15; Sykora, NJ (hooking), 7:15; Stevens, NJ (hooking), 7:42; Sakic, Col (hooking), 8:26.

### SECOND PERIOD
Scoring: 2, New Jersey, Elias 8 (sh) (Sykora), 3:42. 3, Colorado, Drury 10 (Dingman, Hinote), 13:54. Penalties: White, NJ (roughing), 2:18; Skoula, Col (int.), 10:16; Stevenson, NJ (tripping), 16:42.

### THIRD PERIOD
Scoring: 4, New Jersey, Gomez 5 (Pandolfo, Corkum), 8:09. 5, New Jersey, Sykora 9 (Elias, Holik), 17:23. Penalties: None.

Shots on goal: Col—4-4-4—12. NJ—8-11-16—35. Power-play opportunities: Col 0-of-5; NJ 0-of-2. Goalies: Col, Roy (35 shots, 32 saves), NJ, Brodeur (12 shots, 10 saves). A: 19,040.
Referees: Devorski, McCreary. Linesmen: Collins, Schachte.

### Game 5

| | | |
|---|---|---|
| New Jersey......2 | 1 | 1—4 |
| Colorado .........1 | 0 | 0—1 |

**FIRST PERIOD**

Scoring: 1, New Jersey, Elias 9 (Sykora, Rafalski), 3:09. 2, Colorado, Tanguay 3 (pp) (Sakic, Bourque), 10:09. 3, New Jersey, Mogilny 5 (Gomez, Rafalski), 18:47. Penalties: Holik, NJ (tripping), 8:56; NJ bench (served by Gomez) (too many men on ice), 19:24.

**SECOND PERIOD**

Scoring: 4, New Jersey, Brylin 3 (pp) (Mogilny, Niedermayer), 4:38. Penalties: Blake, Col (int.), 3:53; Niedermayer, NJ (int.), 16:33.

**THIRD PERIOD**

Scoring: 5, New Jersey, Madden 4 (Stevenson, Brylin), 18:05. Penalties: McKenzie, NJ (holding), 12:54; Sutton, NJ (roughing), 20:00; Hinote, Col (roughing), 20:00.

Shots on goal: NJ—6-10-10—26. Col—6-9-8—23. Power-play opportunities: NJ 1-of-1; Col 1-of-4. Goalies: NJ, Brodeur (23 shots, 22 saves); Col, Roy (26 shots, 22 saves). A: 18,007.

Referees: Fraser, Shick. Linesmen: Wheler, Lazarowich.

### Game 6

| | | |
|---|---|---|
| Colorado .........1 | 2 | 1—4 |
| New Jersey......0 | 0 | 0—0 |

**FIRST PERIOD**

Scoring: 1, Colorado, Foote 3 (unassisted), 18:02. Penalties: Reid, Col (obstruction), 5:22; Foote, Col (high sticking), 7:20; Mogilny, NJ (hooking), 9:12; Skoula, Col (hooking) 11:08.

**SECOND PERIOD**

Scoring: 2, Colorado, Nieminen 4 (pp) (Skoula, Foote), 2:26. 3, Colorado, Drury 11 (Reinprecht, Foote), 18:27. Penalties: Holik, NJ (roughing), 0:29; Colorado bench (served by Nieminen) (too many men on ice), 8:35; Niedermayer, NJ (holding), 11:10; Bourque, Col (obstruction), 13:01.

**THIRD PERIOD**

Scoring: 4, Colorado, Tanguay 4 (Reid, Sakic), 13:46. Penalties: Podein, Col (int.), 3:24; Niedermayer, NJ (slashing), 8:26; White, NJ (slashing), 17:27; Hinote, Col (fighting major), 18:19; Sutton, NJ (roughing, fighting major), 18:19; White, NJ (high sticking), 19:43; Dingman, Col (fighting major), 19:48; Daneyko, NJ (fighting major), 19:48.

Shots on goal: Col—5-7-6—18; NJ—12-7-5—24. Power-play opportunities: Col 1-of-7; NJ 0-of-6. Goalies: Col, Roy (24 shots, 24 saves); NJ, Brodeur (18 shots, 14 saves). A: 19,040.

Referees: Marouelli, McCreary. Linesmen: Collins, Lazarowich.

### Game 7

| | | |
|---|---|---|
| New Jersey......0 | 1 | 0—1 |
| Colorado .........1 | 2 | 0—3 |

**FIRST PERIOD**

Scoring: 1, Colorado, Tanguay 5 (Hinote), 7:58. Penalties: Brylin, NJ (boarding), 3:20; Gomez, NJ (holding), 16:06.

**SECOND PERIOD**

Scoring: 2, Colorado, Tanguay 6 (Sakic, Foote), 4:57. 3, Colorado, Sakic 13 (pp) (Hejduk, Tanguay), 6:16. 4, New Jersey, Sykora 10 (pp) (Elias, Arnott), 9:33. Penalties: O'Donnell, NJ (high sticking), 5:51; Messier, Col (high sticking), 9:22; Messier, Col (holding), 12:23; Arnott, NJ (tripping), 12:23.

**THIRD PERIOD**

Scoring: None. Penalties: Blake, Col (int.), 4:59; White, NJ (high sticking), 10:32; Foote, Col (holding stick), 12:11; Stevens, NJ (tripping), 14:42.

Shots on goal: NJ—9-12-5—26; Col—10-7-5—22. Power-play opportunities: NJ 1-of-3; Col 1-of-5. Goalies: NJ, Brodeur (22 shots, 19 saves); Col, Roy (26 shots, 25 saves). A: 18,007. Referees: Fraser, Marouelli. Linesmen: Collins, Schachte.

## Individual Playoff Leaders

### Scoring

**POINTS**

| Player and Team | GP | G | A | Pts | +/− | PM | Player and Team | GP | G | A | Pts | +/− | PM |
|---|---|---|---|---|---|---|---|---|---|---|---|---|---|
| Joe Sakic, Col ...............21 | | 13 | 13 | 26 | 6 | 6 | Pierre Turgeon, StL........15 | | 5 | 10 | 15 | 8 | 2 |
| Patrik Elias, NJ .............25 | | 9 | 14 | 23 | 11 | 10 | Scott Gomez, NJ ...........25 | | 5 | 9 | 14 | 7 | 24 |
| Milan Hejduk, Col ..........23 | | 7 | 16 | 23 | 8 | 6 | Peter Forsberg, Col .......11 | | 4 | 10 | 14 | 5 | 6 |
| Petr Sykora, NJ..............25 | | 10 | 12 | 22 | 11 | 12 | Mats Sundin, Tor............11 | | 6 | 7 | 13 | 5 | 12 |
| Alex Tanguay, Col ..........23 | | 6 | 15 | 21 | 13 | 8 | Scott Young, StL............15 | | 6 | 7 | 13 | 9 | 2 |
| Rob Blake, Col .............23 | | 6 | 13 | 19 | 6 | 16 | Martin Straka, Pitt ..........18 | | 5 | 8 | 13 | -1 | 8 |
| Brian Rafalski, NJ ..........25 | | 7 | 11 | 18 | 10 | 7 | Miroslav Satan, Buff.......13 | | 3 | 10 | 13 | 4 | 8 |
| Mario Lemieux, Pitt ........18 | | 6 | 11 | 17 | 4 | 4 | Jaromir Jagr, Pitt...........16 | | 2 | 10 | 12 | 3 | 18 |
| Chris Drury, Col ...........23 | | 11 | 5 | 16 | 5 | 4 | Gary Roberts, Tor ..........11 | | 2 | 9 | 11 | 5 | 0 |
| Bobby Holik, NJ ............25 | | 6 | 10 | 16 | 1 | 37 | Six tied with 10. | | | | | | |
| Alexander Mogilny, NJ ..25 | | 5 | 11 | 16 | 3 | 8 | | | | | | | |
| Jason Arnott, NJ...........23 | | 8 | 7 | 15 | 8 | 16 | | | | | | | |

# Individual Playoff Leaders (Cont.)

## GOALS

| Player and Team | GP | G |
|---|---|---|
| Joe Sakic, Col | 21 | 13 |
| Chris Drury, Col | 23 | 11 |
| Petr Sykora, NJ | 25 | 10 |
| Patrik Elias, NJ | 25 | 9 |
| Jason Arnott, NJ | 23 | 8 |

## POWER PLAY GOALS

| Player and Team | GP | PP |
|---|---|---|
| Joe Sakic, Col | 21 | 5 |
| Jason Arnott, NJ | 23 | 5 |
| Steve Thomas, Tor | 11 | 4 |
| Milan Hejduk, Col | 23 | 4 |
| Six tied with three. | | |

## ASSISTS

| Player and Team | GP | A |
|---|---|---|
| Milan Hejduk, Col | 23 | 16 |
| Alex Tanguay, Col | 23 | 15 |
| Patrik Elias, NJ | 25 | 14 |
| Joe Sakic, Col | 21 | 13 |
| Rob Blake, Col | 23 | 13 |

## GAME-WINNING GOALS

| Player and Team | GP | GW |
|---|---|---|
| Scott Young, StL | 15 | 3 |
| Mario Lemieux, Pitt | 18 | 3 |
| Joe Sakic, Col | 21 | 3 |
| Bobby Holik, NJ | 25 | 3 |
| Brian Rafalski, NJ | 25 | 3 |

## SHORT-HANDED GOALS

| Player and Team | GP | SH |
|---|---|---|
| Curtis Brown, Buff | 13 | 2 |
| Scott Young, StL | 15 | 2 |
| Petr Sykora, NJ | 25 | 2 |

## PLUS/MINUS

| Player and Team | GP | +/– |
|---|---|---|
| Alex Tanguay, Col | 23 | 13 |
| Patrik Elias, NJ | 25 | 11 |
| Petr Sykora, NJ | 25 | 11 |
| Brian Rafalski, NJ | 25 | 10 |
| Chris Pronger, StL | 15 | 10 |

## Goaltending (Minimum 420 minutes)

### GOALS AGAINST AVERAGE

| Player and Team | GP | Mins | GA | Avg |
|---|---|---|---|---|
| Patrick Roy, Col | 23 | 1451 | 41 | 1.70 |
| Roman Turek, StL | 14 | 908 | 31 | 2.05 |
| Martin Brodeur, NJ | 25 | 1505 | 52 | 2.07 |
| Dominik Hasek, Buff | 13 | 833 | 29 | 2.09 |
| Curtis Joseph, Tor | 11 | 685 | 24 | 2.10 |

### SAVE PERCENTAGE

| Player and Team | GP | Mins | GA | SA | Pct | W | L |
|---|---|---|---|---|---|---|---|
| Patrick Roy, Col | 23 | 1451 | 41 | 622 | .934 | 16 | 7 |
| Curtis Joseph, Tor | 11 | 685 | 24 | 329 | .927 | 7 | 4 |
| Roman Turek, StL | 14 | 908 | 31 | 382 | .919 | 9 | 5 |
| Dominik Hasek, Buff | 13 | 833 | 29 | 347 | .916 | 7 | 6 |
| Johan Hedberg, Pitt | 18 | 1122 | 43 | 482 | .911 | 9 | 9 |

## NHL Awards

| Award | Player and Team |
|---|---|
| Hart Trophy (MVP) | Joe Sakic, Col |
| Calder Trophy (top rookie) | Evgeni Nabokov, SJ |
| Vezina Trophy (top goaltender) | Dominik Hasek, Buff |
| Norris Trophy (top defenseman) | Nicklas Lidstrom, Det |
| Lady Byng Trophy (for gentlemanly play) | Joe Sakic, Col |
| Adams Award (top coach) | Bill Barber, Phil |

| Award | Player and Team |
|---|---|
| Selke Trophy (top defensive forward) | John Madden, NJ |
| Jennings Trophy (goaltender on club allowing fewest goals) | Dominik Hasek, Buff |
| Conn Smythe Trophy (playoff MVP) | Patrick Roy, Col |

## Individual Regular Season Leaders

### Scoring

#### POINTS

| Player and Team | GP | G | A | Pts | +/– | PM |
|---|---|---|---|---|---|---|
| Jaromir Jagr, Pitt | 81 | 52 | 69 | 121 | 19 | 42 |
| Joe Sakic, Col | 82 | 54 | 64 | 118 | 45 | 30 |
| Patrik Elias, NJ | 82 | 40 | 56 | 96 | 45 | 51 |
| Alexei Kovalev, Pitt | 79 | 44 | 51 | 95 | 12 | 96 |
| Jason Allison, Bos | 82 | 36 | 59 | 95 | -8 | 85 |
| Martin Straka, Pitt | 82 | 27 | 68 | 95 | 19 | 38 |
| Pavel Bure, Fla | 82 | 59 | 33 | 92 | -2 | 58 |
| Doug Weight, Edm | 82 | 25 | 65 | 90 | 12 | 91 |
| Zigmund Palffy, LA | 73 | 38 | 51 | 89 | 22 | 20 |
| Peter Forsberg, Col | 73 | 27 | 62 | 89 | 23 | 54 |
| Alexei Yashin, Ott | 82 | 40 | 48 | 88 | 10 | 30 |
| Luc Robitaille, LA | 82 | 37 | 51 | 88 | 10 | 66 |
| Bill Guerin, Edm/Bos | 85 | 40 | 45 | 85 | 7 | 140 |
| Mike Modano, Dall | 81 | 33 | 51 | 84 | 26 | 52 |
| Alexander Mogilny, NJ | 75 | 43 | 40 | 83 | 10 | 43 |
| Pierre Turgeon, StL | 79 | 30 | 52 | 82 | 14 | 37 |
| Adam Oates, Wash | 81 | 13 | 69 | 82 | -9 | 28 |
| Peter Bondra, Wash | 82 | 45 | 36 | 81 | 8 | 60 |
| Petr Sykora, NJ | 73 | 35 | 46 | 81 | 36 | 32 |
| Robert Lang, Pitt | 82 | 32 | 48 | 80 | 20 | 28 |

#### GOALS

| Player and Team | GP | G |
|---|---|---|
| Pavel Bure, Fla | 82 | 59 |
| Joe Sakic, Col | 82 | 54 |
| Jaromir Jagr, Pitt | 81 | 52 |
| Peter Bondra, Wash | 82 | 45 |
| Alexei Kovalev, Pitt | 79 | 44 |

#### GAME-WINNING GOALS

| Player and Team | GP | GW |
|---|---|---|
| Joe Sakic, Col | 82 | 12 |
| Jaromir Jagr, Pitt | 81 | 10 |
| Alexei Yashin, Ott | 82 | 10 |
| Alexei Kovalev, Pitt | 79 | 9 |
| Milan Hejduk, Col | 80 | 9 |

#### ASSISTS

| Player and Team | GP | A |
|---|---|---|
| Jaromir Jagr, Pitt | 81 | 69 |
| Adam Oates, Wash | 81 | 69 |
| Martin Straka, Pitt | 82 | 68 |
| Doug Weight, Edm | 82 | 65 |
| Joe Sakic, Col | 82 | 64 |

#### POWER PLAY GOALS

| Player and Team | GP | PP |
|---|---|---|
| Peter Bondra, Wash | 82 | 22 |
| Joe Thornton, Bos | 72 | 19 |
| Joe Sakic, Col | 82 | 19 |
| Pavel Bure, Fla | 82 | 19 |
| Paul Kariya, Ana | 66 | 18 |
| Markus Naslund, Van | 72 | 18 |

#### SHORT-HANDED GOALS

| Player and Team | GP | SHG |
|---|---|---|
| Steve Sullivan, Chi | 81 | 8 |
| Theoren Fleury, NYR | 62 | 7 |
| Wes Walz, Minn | 82 | 7 |
| Pavel Bure, Fla | 82 | 5 |
| Five tied with four. | | |

#### PLUS/MINUS

| Player and Team | GP | +/– |
|---|---|---|
| Joe Sakic, Col | 82 | 45 |
| Patrik Elias, NJ | 82 | 45 |
| Scott Stevens, NJ | 81 | 40 |
| Petr Sykora, NJ | 73 | 36 |
| Brian Rafalski, NJ | 78 | 36 |

### Goaltending
### (Minimum 25 games)

#### GOALS AGAINST AVERAGE

| Player and Team | GP | Mins | GA | Avg |
|---|---|---|---|---|
| Marty Turco, Dall | 26 | 1266 | 40 | 1.90 |
| Roman Cechmanek, Phil | 59 | 3431 | 115 | 2.01 |
| Manny Legace, Det | 39 | 2136 | 73 | 2.05 |
| Dominik Hasek, Buff | 67 | 3904 | 137 | 2.11 |
| Brent Johnson, StL | 31 | 1744 | 63 | 2.17 |

#### SAVE PERCENTAGE

| Player and Team | GP | GA | SA | Pct | W | L | T |
|---|---|---|---|---|---|---|---|
| Marty Turco, Dall | 26 | 40 | 532 | .925 | 13 | 6 | 1 |
| Mike Dunham, Nash | 48 | 107 | 1381 | .923 | 21 | 21 | 4 |
| Sean Burke, Phoe | 62 | 138 | 1766 | .922 | 25 | 22 | 13 |
| Dominik Hasek, Buff | 67 | 137 | 1726 | .921 | 37 | 24 | 4 |
| R. Cechmanek, Phil | 59 | 115 | 1464 | .921 | 35 | 15 | 6 |

#### WINS

| Player and Team | GP | Mins | W | L | T |
|---|---|---|---|---|---|
| Martin Brodeur, NJ | 72 | 4297 | 42 | 17 | 11 |
| Patrick Roy, Col | 62 | 3585 | 40 | 13 | 7 |
| Dominik Hasek, Buff | 67 | 3904 | 37 | 24 | 4 |
| Olaf Kolzig, Wash | 72 | 4279 | 37 | 26 | 8 |
| Arturs Irbe, Car | 77 | 4406 | 37 | 29 | 9 |

#### SHUTOUTS

| Player and Team | GP | Mins | SO | W | L | T |
|---|---|---|---|---|---|---|
| Dominik Hasek, Buff | 67 | 3904 | 11 | 37 | 24 | 4 |
| Roman Cechmanek, Phil | 59 | 3431 | 10 | 35 | 15 | 6 |
| Martin Brodeur, NJ | 72 | 4297 | 9 | 42 | 17 | 11 |
| Ed Belfour, Dall | 63 | 3687 | 8 | 35 | 20 | 7 |
| Tommy Salo, Edm | 73 | 4364 | 8 | 36 | 25 | 12 |

## NHL Team-by-Team Statistical Leaders

### Anaheim Mighty Ducks

#### SCORING

| Player | GP | G | A | Pts | +/– | PM |
|---|---|---|---|---|---|---|
| Paul Kariya, L | 66 | 33 | 34 | 67 | -9 | 20 |
| Oled Tverdovsky, D | 82 | 14 | 39 | 53 | -11 | 32 |
| Jeff Friesen, L | 79 | 14 | 34 | 48 | 5 | 66 |
| Marty McInnis, R | 75 | 20 | 22 | 42 | -21 | 40 |
| Matt Cullen, C | 82 | 10 | 30 | 40 | -23 | 38 |
| Tony Hrkac, C | 80 | 13 | 25 | 38 | 0 | 29 |
| Mike LeClerc, L | 54 | 15 | 20 | 35 | -1 | 26 |
| German Titov, L | 71 | 9 | 11 | 20 | -21 | 61 |
| *Petr Tenkrat, R | 46 | 5 | 9 | 14 | -11 | 16 |
| Niklas Hvelid, D | 47 | 4 | 10 | 14 | -6 | 34 |
| Jim Cummins, R | 79 | 5 | 6 | 11 | -11 | 167 |
| Mike Crowley, D | 39 | 1 | 10 | 11 | -16 | 20 |
| Vitaly Vishnevski, D | 76 | 1 | 10 | 11 | -1 | 99 |
| Pascal Trepanier, D | 57 | 6 | 4 | 10 | -12 | 73 |
| Dan Bylsma, L | 82 | 1 | 9 | 10 | -12 | 22 |
| *Samuel Pahlsson, C | 76 | 4 | 5 | 9 | -14 | 20 |
| Pavel Trnka, D | 59 | 1 | 7 | 8 | -12 | 42 |
| *Marc Chouinard, C | 44 | 3 | 4 | 7 | -5 | 12 |
| Ruslon Salei, D | 50 | 1 | 5 | 6 | -14 | 70 |
| Jonas Ronnqvist, R | 38 | 0 | 4 | 4 | -7 | 14 |
| *Antti-Jussi Niemi, D | 28 | 1 | 1 | 2 | -6 | 22 |

#### GOALTENDING

| Player | GP | Mins | Avg | W | L | T | SO |
|---|---|---|---|---|---|---|---|
| Steve Shields | 21 | 1135 | 2.48 | 6 | 8 | 5 | 2 |
| J.-S. Giguerre | 34 | 2031 | 2.57 | 11 | 17 | 5 | 4 |
| *Gregg Naumenko | 2 | 70 | 6.00 | 0 | 1 | 0 | 0 |
| Team total | 82 | 4995 | 2.94 | 25 | 46 | 11 | 6 |

*Rookie.

### Atlanta Thrashers

#### SCORING

| Player | GP | G | A | Pts | +/– | PM |
|---|---|---|---|---|---|---|
| Ray Ferraro, C | 81 | 29 | 47 | 76 | -11 | 91 |
| Andrew Brunette, L | 77 | 15 | 44 | 59 | -5 | 26 |
| Jiri Sleger, D | 75 | 8 | 26 | 34 | -10 | 96 |
| Patrik Stefan, C | 66 | 10 | 21 | 31 | -3 | 22 |
| Stephen Guolla, L | 63 | 12 | 16 | 28 | -6 | 23 |
| Hnat Domenichelli, L | 63 | 15 | 12 | 27 | -9 | 18 |
| *Tommi Kallio, L | 56 | 14 | 13 | 27 | -3 | 22 |
| Shean Donovan, R | 63 | 12 | 11 | 23 | -14 | 47 |
| Steve Staios, D | 70 | 9 | 13 | 22 | -23 | 137 |
| Per Svartvadet, C | 69 | 10 | 11 | 21 | -6 | 20 |
| Chris Tamer, D | 82 | 4 | 13 | 17 | -1 | 128 |
| Andreas Karlsson, C | 60 | 5 | 11 | 16 | -2 | 16 |
| Frantisek Kaberle, D | 51 | 4 | 11 | 15 | 11 | 18 |
| Vladislav Kohn, R | 77 | 7 | 7 | 14 | -27 | 86 |
| Gord Murphy, D | 27 | 3 | 11 | 14 | -11 | 12 |
| Jeff Odgers, R | 82 | 6 | 7 | 13 | -8 | 226 |
| Yannick Tremblay, D | 46 | 4 | 8 | 12 | -6 | 30 |
| Dean Sylvester, R | 43 | 5 | 6 | 11 | -16 | 8 |
| Denny Lambert, L | 67 | 1 | 7 | 8 | -5 | 215 |
| Chris Joseph, D | 43 | 1 | 4 | 5 | -11 | 36 |
| Andrei Skopintsev, D | 17 | 1 | 3 | 4 | -7 | 16 |
| Brett Clark, D | 28 | 1 | 2 | 3 | -12 | 14 |
| Adam Burt, D | 27 | 0 | 2 | 2 | 2 | 27 |
| David Harlock, D | 65 | 0 | 1 | 1 | -28 | 62 |

#### GOALTENDING

| Player | GP | Mins | Avg | W | L | T | SO |
|---|---|---|---|---|---|---|---|
| Milan Hnilicka | 36 | 1879 | 3.35 | 12 | 19 | 2 | 2 |
| Damian Rhodes | 38 | 2072 | 3.36 | 7 | 19 | 7 | 0 |
| Norm Maracle | 13 | 753 | 3.43 | 2 | 8 | 3 | 0 |
| Team total | 82 | 4983 | 3.48 | 23 | 47 | 12 | 2 |

## Boston Bruins

### SCORING

| Player | GP | G | A | Pts | +/– | PM |
|---|---|---|---|---|---|---|
| Jason Allison, C | 82 | 36 | 59 | 95 | -8 | 85 |
| Bill Guerin, R | 85 | 40 | 45 | 85 | 7 | 140 |
| Sergei Samsonov, L | 82 | 29 | 46 | 75 | 6 | 18 |
| Joe Thornton, C | 72 | 37 | 34 | 71 | -4 | 107 |
| Brian Rolston, L | 77 | 19 | 39 | 58 | 6 | 28 |
| Andrei Kovalenko, R | 76 | 16 | 21 | 37 | -14 | 27 |
| Eric Weinrich, D | 82 | 7 | 24 | 31 | -9 | 44 |
| Mikko Eloranta, L | 62 | 12 | 11 | 23 | 2 | 38 |
| P.J. Axelsson, L | 81 | 8 | 15 | 23 | -12 | 27 |
| Mike Knuble, R | 82 | 7 | 13 | 20 | 0 | 37 |
| Dixon Ward, C | 63 | 5 | 13 | 18 | -1 | 65 |
| Kyle McLaren, D | 58 | 5 | 12 | 17 | -5 | 53 |
| Darren Van Impe, D | 31 | 3 | 10 | 13 | -9 | 41 |
| Don Sweeney, D | 72 | 2 | 10 | 12 | -1 | 26 |
| Hal Gill, D | 80 | 1 | 10 | 11 | -2 | 71 |
| Jarno Kultanen, D | 62 | 2 | 8 | 10 | -3 | 26 |
| Peter Popovic, D | 60 | 1 | 6 | 7 | -5 | 48 |
| Andrei Nazarov, R | 79 | 2 | 4 | 6 | -23 | 229 |
| Shawn Bates, C | 45 | 2 | 3 | 5 | -12 | 26 |
| Ken Belanger, L | 40 | 2 | 2 | 4 | 6 | 121 |
| Paul Coffey, D | 18 | 0 | 4 | 4 | -6 | 30 |
| *Lee Goren, R | 21 | 2 | 0 | 2 | -3 | 7 |

### GOALTENDING

| Player | GP | Mins | Avg | W | L | T | SO |
|---|---|---|---|---|---|---|---|
| Byron Dafoe | 45 | 2536 | 2.39 | 22 | 14 | 7 | 2 |
| *Andrew Raycroft | 15 | 649 | 2.96 | 4 | 6 | 0 | 0 |
| Peter Skudra | 26 | 1116 | 3.33 | 6 | 12 | 1 | 0 |
| Team total | 82 | 4991 | 2.99 | 36 | 38 | 8 | 2 |

## Buffalo Sabres

### SCORING

| Player | GP | G | A | Pts | +/– | PM |
|---|---|---|---|---|---|---|
| Donald Audette, R | 76 | 34 | 45 | 79 | -2 | 76 |
| Miroslav Satan, R | 82 | 29 | 33 | 62 | 5 | 36 |
| Steve Heinz, R | 79 | 27 | 27 | 54 | -13 | 46 |
| J.P. Dumont, L | 79 | 23 | 28 | 51 | 1 | 54 |
| Stu Barnes, C | 75 | 19 | 24 | 43 | -2 | 26 |
| Chris Gratton, C | 82 | 19 | 21 | 40 | 0 | 102 |
| Doug Gilmour, L | 71 | 7 | 31 | 38 | 3 | 70 |
| Alexei Zhitnik, D | 78 | 8 | 29 | 37 | -3 | 75 |
| Maxim Afinogenov, R | 78 | 14 | 22 | 36 | 1 | 40 |
| Dave Andreychuk, L | 74 | 21 | 13 | 33 | 0 | 32 |
| Curtis Brown, C | 70 | 10 | 22 | 32 | 15 | 34 |
| Erik Rasmussen, L | 82 | 12 | 19 | 31 | 0 | 51 |
| Vaclav Varada, R | 75 | 10 | 21 | 31 | -2 | 81 |
| Jason Woolley, D | 67 | 5 | 18 | 23 | 0 | 46 |
| *Dmitri Kalinin, D | 79 | 4 | 18 | 22 | -2 | 38 |
| Rhett Warrener, D | 77 | 3 | 16 | 19 | 10 | 78 |
| Richard Smehlik, D | 56 | 3 | 12 | 15 | 6 | 4 |
| Vladimir Tsyplakov, L | 36 | 7 | 7 | 14 | 2 | 10 |
| James Patrick, D | 54 | 4 | 9 | 13 | 9 | 12 |
| Jay McKee, D | 74 | 1 | 10 | 11 | 9 | 76 |
| Rob Ray, R | 63 | 4 | 6 | 10 | 2 | 210 |
| *Eric Boulton, L | 35 | 1 | 2 | 3 | -1 | 94 |
| Chris Taylor, C | 14 | 0 | 2 | 2 | 1 | 6 |
| Steve Smith, D | 20 | 0 | 4 | 4 | -13 | 42 |

### GOALTENDING

| Player | GP | Mins | Avg | W | L | T | SO |
|---|---|---|---|---|---|---|---|
| Dominik Hasek | 67 | 3904 | 2.11 | 37 | 24 | 4 | 11 |
| Martin Biron | 18 | 918 | 2.55 | 7 | 7 | 1 | 2 |
| Mika Noronen | 2 | 108 | 2.78 | 2 | 0 | 0 | 0 |
| Team total | 82 | 4956 | 2.23 | 46 | 31 | 5 | 13 |

## Calgary Flames

### SCORING

| Player | GP | G | A | Pts | +/– | PM |
|---|---|---|---|---|---|---|
| Jarome Iginla, R | 77 | 31 | 40 | 71 | -2 | 62 |
| Marc Savard, C | 77 | 23 | 42 | 65 | -12 | 46 |
| Valeri Bure, R | 78 | 27 | 28 | 55 | -21 | 26 |
| Dave Lowry, L | 79 | 18 | 17 | 35 | -2 | 47 |
| Phil Housley, D | 69 | 4 | 30 | 34 | -15 | 24 |
| Craig Conroy, C | 83 | 14 | 18 | 32 | 2 | 60 |
| Derek Morris, D | 51 | 5 | 23 | 28 | -15 | 56 |
| *Oleg Saprykin, R | 59 | 9 | 14 | 23 | 4 | 43 |
| Jeff Shantz, C | 73 | 5 | 15 | 20 | -7 | 58 |
| Tommy Albelin, D | 77 | 1 | 19 | 20 | 2 | 22 |
| *Toni Lydman, D | 62 | 3 | 16 | 19 | -7 | 30 |
| Jason Wiemer, C | 65 | 10 | 5 | 15 | -15 | 177 |
| Clarke Wilm, C | 81 | 7 | 8 | 15 | -11 | 69 |
| Igor Kravchuk, D | 52 | 1 | 13 | 14 | -8 | 18 |
| *Jeff Cowan, L | 51 | 9 | 4 | 13 | -8 | 74 |

### SCORING (CONT.)

| Player | GP | G | A | Pts | +/– | PM* |
|---|---|---|---|---|---|---|
| *Ronald Petrovicky, R | 30 | 4 | 5 | 9 | 0 | 54 |
| Brad Werenka, D | 33 | 1 | 4 | 5 | -3 | 16 |
| Benoit Gratton, L | 14 | 1 | 3 | 4 | 0 | 14 |
| Ron Sutter, C | 21 | 1 | 3 | 4 | 4 | 12 |
| Dwayne Hay, R | 49 | 1 | 3 | 4 | -4 | 16 |
| Robyn Regehr, D | 71 | 1 | 3 | 4 | -7 | 70 |
| Dallas Eakins, D | 17 | 0 | 1 | 1 | -1 | 11 |

### GOALTENDING

| Player | GP | Mins | Avg | W | L | T | SO |
|---|---|---|---|---|---|---|---|
| Fred Brathwaite | 49 | 2742 | 2.32 | 15 | 17 | 10 | 5 |
| Mike Vernon | 41 | 2246 | 3.23 | 12 | 23 | 5 | 3 |
| Team total | 82 | 5009 | 2.83 | 27 | 40 | 15 | 8 |

*Rookie.

## Carolina Hurricanes

### SCORING

| Player | GP | G | A | Pts | +/– | PM |
|---|---|---|---|---|---|---|
| Jeff O'Neill, R | 82 | 41 | 26 | 67 | -18 | 106 |
| Ron Francis, C | 82 | 15 | 50 | 65 | -15 | 32 |
| Sami Kapanen, L | 82 | 20 | 37 | 57 | -12 | 24 |
| Rod Brind'Amour, C | 79 | 20 | 36 | 56 | -7 | 47 |
| Martin Gelinas, L | 79 | 23 | 29 | 52 | -4 | 59 |
| *Shane Willis, R | 73 | 20 | 24 | 44 | -6 | 45 |
| Sandis Ozolinsh, D | 72 | 12 | 32 | 44 | -25 | 71 |
| Scott Pellerin, R | 77 | 11 | 33 | 44 | 2 | 51 |
| David Tanabe, D | 74 | 7 | 22 | 29 | -9 | 42 |
| Bates Battaglia, L | 80 | 12 | 15 | 27 | -14 | 76 |
| Rob DiMaio, R | 74 | 6 | 18 | 24 | -14 | 54 |
| *Josef Vasicek, C | 76 | 8 | 13 | 21 | -8 | 53 |
| Glen Wesley, D | 71 | 5 | 16 | 21 | -2 | 42 |
| Marek Malik, D | 61 | 6 | 14 | 20 | -4 | 34 |
| Kevin Hatcher, D | 57 | 4 | 14 | 18 | 2 | 38 |
| David Karpa, D | 80 | 4 | 6 | 10 | -19 | 159 |
| Tommy Westlund, C | 79 | 5 | 3 | 8 | -9 | 23 |
| *Niclas Wallin, D | 37 | 2 | 3 | 5 | -11 | 21 |
| Jeff Daniels, R | 67 | 1 | 1 | 2 | -3 | 15 |
| Darren Langdon, L | 54 | 0 | 2 | 2 | -4 | 94 |
| *Craig Adams, R | 44 | 1 | 0 | 1 | -7 | 20 |

### GOALTENDING

| Player | GP | Mins | Avg | W | L | T | SO |
|---|---|---|---|---|---|---|---|
| Arturs Irbe | 77 | 4406 | 2.45 | 37 | 29 | 9 | 6 |
| Tyler Moss | 12 | 557 | 3.99 | 1 | 6 | 0 | 0 |
| Team total | 82 | 4986 | 2.71 | 38 | 35 | 9 | 6 |

## Chicago Blackhawks

### SCORING

| Player | GP | G | A | Pts | +/– | PM |
|---|---|---|---|---|---|---|
| Steve Sullivan, R | 81 | 34 | 41 | 75 | 3 | 54 |
| Tony Amonte, R | 82 | 35 | 29 | 64 | -22 | 54 |
| Michael Nylander, C | 82 | 25 | 39 | 64 | 7 | 32 |
| Eric Daze, L | 79 | 33 | 24 | 57 | 1 | 16 |
| Alex Zhamnov, C | 63 | 13 | 36 | 49 | -12 | 40 |
| Jaroslav Spacek, D | 62 | 7 | 19 | 26 | 3 | 28 |
| Chris Herperger, L | 61 | 10 | 15 | 25 | 0 | 20 |
| Boris Mironov, D | 66 | 5 | 17 | 22 | -14 | 42 |
| Bob Probert, L | 79 | 7 | 12 | 19 | -13 | 103 |
| Stephane Quintal, D | 72 | 1 | 18 | 19 | -9 | 60 |
| *Kyle Calder, C | 43 | 5 | 10 | 15 | -4 | 14 |
| A. Karpovtsev, D | 53 | 2 | 13 | 15 | -4 | 39 |
| Kevin Dean, D | 69 | 0 | 11 | 11 | -16 | 30 |
| Steve Dubinsky, C | 60 | 6 | 4 | 10 | -4 | 33 |
| Jean-Yves Leroux, L | 59 | 4 | 4 | 8 | -9 | 22 |
| Valeri Zelepukin, L | 36 | 3 | 4 | 7 | -14 | 18 |
| Ryan VandenBussche, R | 64 | 2 | 5 | 7 | -8 | 146 |
| Chris McAlpine, D | 50 | 0 | 6 | 6 | 5 | 32 |
| Steve Poapst, D | 36 | 2 | 3 | 5 | 3 | 12 |
| *Steve McCarthy, D | 44 | 0 | 5 | 5 | -7 | 8 |
| Jamie Allison, D | 44 | 1 | 3 | 4 | 7 | 53 |

### GOALTENDING

| Player | GP | Mins | Avg | W | L | T | SO |
|---|---|---|---|---|---|---|---|
| Jocelyn Thibault | 66 | 3844 | 2.81 | 27 | 32 | 7 | 6 |
| Steve Passmore | 6 | 340 | 2.47 | 0 | 4 | 1 | 0 |
| Robbie Tallas | 12 | 627 | 3.35 | 2 | 7 | 0 | 0 |
| Team total | 82 | 4981 | 2.96 | 29 | 45 | 8 | 6 |

## Colorado Avalanche

### SCORING

| Player | GP | G | A | Pts | +/– | PM |
|---|---|---|---|---|---|---|
| Joe Sakic, C | 82 | 54 | 64 | 118 | 45 | 30 |
| Peter Forsberg, C | 73 | 27 | 62 | 89 | 23 | 54 |
| Milan Hejduk, R | 80 | 41 | 38 | 79 | 32 | 36 |
| Alex Tanguay, L | 82 | 27 | 50 | 77 | 35 | 37 |
| Chris Drury, L | 71 | 24 | 41 | 65 | 6 | 47 |
| Rob Blake, D | 67 | 19 | 40 | 59 | 3 | 77 |
| Ray Bourque, D | 80 | 7 | 52 | 59 | 25 | 48 |
| *Steve Reinprecht, C | 80 | 15 | 21 | 36 | 10 | 14 |
| Shjon Podein, R | 82 | 15 | 17 | 32 | 7 | 68 |
| Martin Skoula, D | 82 | 8 | 17 | 25 | 8 | 38 |
| *Ville Nieminen, L | 50 | 14 | 8 | 22 | 8 | 38 |
| Dan Hinote, C | 76 | 5 | 10 | 15 | 1 | 51 |
| Jon Klemm, D | 78 | 4 | 11 | 15 | 22 | 54 |
| Adam Foote, D | 35 | 3 | 12 | 15 | 6 | 42 |
| Stephane Yelle C | 50 | 4 | 10 | 14 | -3 | 20 |
| Eric Messier, L, D | 64 | 5 | 7 | 12 | -3 | 26 |
| Dave Reid, R | 73 | 1 | 9 | 10 | 1 | 21 |
| Scott Parker, R | 69 | 2 | 3 | 5 | -2 | 155 |
| Nolan Pratt, D | 46 | 1 | 2 | 3 | 2 | 40 |
| Chris Dingman, L | 41 | 1 | 1 | 2 | -3 | 108 |

### GOALTENDING

| Player | GP | Mins | Avg | W | L | T | SO |
|---|---|---|---|---|---|---|---|
| Patrick Roy | 62 | 3585 | 2.21 | 40 | 13 | 7 | 4 |
| *David Aebischer | 26 | 1393 | 2.24 | 12 | 7 | 3 | 3 |
| Team total | 82 | 4993 | 2.31 | 52 | 20 | 10 | 7 |

*Rookie.*

## Columbus Blue Jackets

### SCORING

| Player | GP | G | A | Pts | +/– | PM |
|---|---|---|---|---|---|---|
| Geoff Sanderson, L | 68 | 30 | 26 | 56 | 4 | 46 |
| Espen Knutsen, C | 66 | 11 | 42 | 53 | -3 | 30 |
| Ray Whitney, L | 46 | 10 | 24 | 34 | -17 | 30 |
| Tyler Wright, C | 76 | 16 | 16 | 32 | -9 | 140 |
| *David Vyborny, R | 79 | 13 | 19 | 32 | -9 | 22 |
| *Serge Aubin, C | 81 | 13 | 17 | 30 | -20 | 107 |
| Jamie Heward, D | 69 | 11 | 16 | 27 | 3 | 33 |
| Deron Quint, D | 57 | 7 | 16 | 23 | -19 | 16 |
| Bruce Gardiner, C | 73 | 7 | 15 | 22 | -1 | 78 |
| Robert Kron, L | 59 | 8 | 11 | 19 | 4 | 10 |
| Alexander Selivanov, R | 59 | 8 | 11 | 19 | -11 | 38 |
| Lyle Odelein, D | 81 | 3 | 14 | 17 | -16 | 118 |
| Petteri Nummelin, D | 61 | 4 | 12 | 16 | -11 | 10 |
| Kevin Dineen, R | 66 | 8 | 7 | 15 | 2 | 126 |
| Jamie Pushor, D | 75 | 3 | 10 | 13 | 7 | 94 |
| Mattias Timander, D | 76 | 2 | 9 | 11 | -8 | 24 |
| *Chris Nielsen, L | 29 | 4 | 5 | 9 | 4 | 4 |
| Blake Sloan, R | 47 | 3 | 2 | 5 | -4 | 17 |
| J.-L. Grand-Pierre, D | 64 | 1 | 4 | 5 | -6 | 73 |

### GOALTENDING

| Player | GP | Mins | Avg | W | L | T | S |
|---|---|---|---|---|---|---|---|
| Ron Tugnutt | 53 | 3129 | 2.44 | 22 | 25 | 5 | 4 |
| *Marc Dennis | 32 | 1830 | 3.25 | 6 | 20 | 4 | 0 |
| Team total | 82 | 4988 | 2.80 | 28 | 45 | 9 | 4 |

## Dallas Stars

### SCORING

| Player | GP | G | A | Pts | +/– | PM |
|---|---|---|---|---|---|---|
| Mike Modano, C | 81 | 33 | 51 | 84 | 26 | 52 |
| Brett Hull, R | 79 | 39 | 40 | 79 | 10 | 18 |
| Joe Nieuwendyk, C | 69 | 29 | 23 | 52 | 5 | 30 |
| Sergei Zubov, D | 79 | 10 | 41 | 51 | 22 | 24 |
| Darryl Sydor, D | 81 | 10 | 37 | 47 | 5 | 34 |
| Jere Lehtinen, L | 74 | 20 | 25 | 45 | 14 | 24 |
| Brenden Morrow, L | 82 | 20 | 24 | 44 | 18 | 128 |
| Grant Marshall, R | 75 | 13 | 24 | 37 | 1 | 64 |
| Jamie Langenbrunner, R | 53 | 12 | 18 | 30 | 4 | 57 |
| Ted Donato, C | 65 | 8 | 17 | 25 | 6 | 26 |
| Mike Keane, R | 67 | 10 | 14 | 24 | 4 | 35 |
| Shaun Van Allen, C | 59 | 7 | 16 | 23 | 5 | 16 |
| Derian Hatcher, D | 80 | 2 | 21 | 23 | 5 | 77 |
| Richard Matvichuk, D | 78 | 4 | 16 | 20 | 5 | 62 |
| Brad Lukowich, D | 80 | 4 | 10 | 14 | 28 | 76 |
| Benoit Hogue, L | 34 | 3 | 7 | 10 | -1 | 26 |
| Kirk Muller, C | 55 | 1 | 9 | 10 | -4 | 26 |
| Roman Lyashenko, C | 60 | 6 | 3 | 9 | -1 | 45 |
| *Tyler Bouck, L | 48 | 2 | 5 | 7 | -3 | 29 |
| John MacLean, R | 30 | 4 | 2 | 6 | 2 | 17 |
| Grant Ledyard, D | 22 | 2 | 3 | 5 | -2 | 16 |
| Sammi Helenius, D | 57 | 1 | 2 | 3 | 1 | 99 |

### GOALTENDING

| Player | GP | Mins | Avg | W | L | T | SO |
|---|---|---|---|---|---|---|---|
| *Marty Turco | 26 | 1266 | 1.90 | 13 | 6 | 1 | 3 |
| Ed Belfour | 63 | 3687 | 2.34 | 35 | 20 | 7 | 8 |
| Team total | 82 | 4970 | 2.26 | 48 | 26 | 8 | 11 |

## Detroit Red Wings

### SCORING

| Player | GP | G | A | Pts | +/– | PM |
|---|---|---|---|---|---|---|
| Brendan Shanahan, L | 81 | 31 | 45 | 76 | 9 | 81 |
| Nicklas Lidstrom, D | 82 | 15 | 56 | 71 | 9 | 18 |
| Sergei Fedorov, C | 75 | 32 | 37 | 69 | 12 | 40 |
| Martin Lapointe, R | 82 | 27 | 30 | 57 | 3 | 127 |
| Steve Yzerman, C | 54 | 18 | 34 | 52 | 4 | 18 |
| Tomas Holmstrom, L | 73 | 16 | 24 | 40 | -12 | 40 |
| Igor Larionov, C | 65 | 9 | 31 | 40 | -5 | 38 |
| Vyacheslav Kozlov, L | 72 | 20 | 18 | 38 | 9 | 30 |
| Pat Verbeek, R | 67 | 15 | 15 | 30 | 0 | 73 |
| Mathieu Dandenault, D | 73 | 10 | 15 | 25 | 11 | 38 |
| Kris Draper, C | 75 | 8 | 17 | 25 | 17 | 38 |
| Steve Duchesne, D | 54 | 6 | 19 | 25 | 9 | 48 |
| Darren McCarty, R | 72 | 12 | 10 | 22 | -5 | 123 |
| Doug Brown, C | 60 | 9 | 13 | 22 | 0 | 14 |
| Larry Murphy, D | 57 | 2 | 19 | 21 | -6 | 12 |
| Kirk Maltby, R | 79 | 12 | 7 | 19 | 16 | 22 |
| Boyd Devereaux, L | 55 | 5 | 6 | 11 | 1 | 14 |
| Todd Gill, D | 68 | 3 | 8 | 11 | 17 | 53 |
| Aaron Ward, D | 73 | 4 | 5 | 9 | -4 | 57 |
| Jiri Fischer, D | 55 | 1 | 8 | 9 | 3 | 59 |
| Brent Gilchrist, C | 60 | 1 | 8 | 9 | -8 | 41 |
| *Maxim Kuznetsov, D | 25 | 1 | 2 | 3 | -1 | 23 |
| Chris Chelios, D | 24 | 0 | 3 | 3 | 4 | 45 |

### GOALTENDING

| Player | GP | Mins | Avg | W | L | T | SO |
|---|---|---|---|---|---|---|---|
| Manny Legace | 39 | 2136 | 2.05 | 24 | 5 | 5 | 2 |
| Chris Osgood | 52 | 2834 | 2.69 | 25 | 19 | 4 | 1 |
| Team total | 82 | 4994 | 2.43 | 49 | 24 | 9 | 3 |

## Edmonton Oliers

### SCORING

| Player | GP | G | A | Pts | +/– | PM |
|---|---|---|---|---|---|---|
| Doug Weight, C | 82 | 25 | 65 | 90 | 12 | 91 |
| Ryan Smyth, R | 82 | 31 | 39 | 70 | 10 | 58 |
| Janne Niinimaa, D | 82 | 12 | 34 | 46 | 6 | 90 |
| Anson Carter, L | 61 | 16 | 26 | 42 | 1 | 23 |
| Todd Marchant, C | 71 | 13 | 26 | 39 | 1 | 51 |
| Mike Grier, R | 74 | 20 | 16 | 36 | 11 | 20 |
| Rem Murray, L | 82 | 15 | 21 | 36 | 5 | 24 |
| Dan Cleary, R | 81 | 14 | 21 | 35 | 5 | 37 |
| Tom Poti, D | 81 | 12 | 20 | 32 | -4 | 60 |
| Sergei Zholtok, C | 69 | 5 | 26 | 31 | -7 | 30 |
| Georges Laraque, R | 82 | 13 | 16 | 29 | 5 | 148 |
| Igor Ulanov, D | 67 | 3 | 20 | 23 | 15 | 90 |
| *Mike Comrie, C | 41 | 8 | 14 | 22 | 6 | 14 |
| Eric Brewer, D | 77 | 7 | 14 | 21 | 15 | 53 |
| Jason Smith, D | 82 | 5 | 15 | 20 | 14 | 120 |
| Ethan Moreau, L | 68 | 9 | 10 | 19 | -6 | 90 |
| *Shawn Horcoff, R | 49 | 9 | 7 | 16 | 8 | 10 |
| *Domenic Pittis, C | 47 | 4 | 5 | 9 | -5 | 49 |
| Sean Brown, D | 62 | 2 | 3 | 5 | 2 | 110 |
| Sven Butenschon, D | 12 | 1 | 2 | 3 | 3 | 4 |
| Drian Swanson, C | 16 | 1 | 1 | 2 | -1 | 6 |
| Scott Ferguson, D | 20 | 0 | 1 | 1 | 2 | 13 |

### GOALTENDING

| Player | GP | Mins | Avg | W | L | T | SO |
|---|---|---|---|---|---|---|---|
| Tommy Salo | 73 | 4364 | 2.46 | 36 | 25 | 12 | 8 |
| Dominic Roussel | 8 | 348 | 3.62 | 1 | 4 | 0 | 0 |
| Joaquin Gage | 5 | 260 | 3.46 | 2 | 2 | 0 | 0 |
| Team total | 82 | 4997 | 2.67 | 39 | 31 | 12 | 8 |

* Rookie.

## Florida Panthers

### SCORING

| Player | GP | G | A | Pts | +/- | PM |
|---|---|---|---|---|---|---|
| Pavel Bure, R | 82 | 59 | 33 | 92 | -2 | 58 |
| Viktor Kozlov, C | 51 | 14 | 23 | 37 | -4 | 10 |
| Marcus Nilson, R | 78 | 12 | 24 | 36 | -3 | 74 |
| Rob Niedermayer, | 67 | 12 | 20 | 32 | -12 | 50 |
| Kevyn Adams, C | 78 | 11 | 18 | 29 | 3 | 54 |
| Vaclav Prospal, C | 74 | 5 | 24 | 29 | -1 | 22 |
| Robert Svehla, D | 82 | 6 | 22 | 28 | -8 | 76 |
| Anders Eriksson, D | 73 | 2 | 24 | 26 | -2 | 30 |
| Greg Adams, L | 60 | 11 | 12 | 23 | -3 | 10 |
| Len Barrie, L | 60 | 5 | 18 | 23 | 4 | 135 |
| Dan Boyle, D | 69 | 4 | 18 | 22 | -14 | 28 |
| Bret Hedican, D | 70 | 5 | 15 | 20 | -7 | 72 |
| *Denis Shvidki, R | 43 | 6 | 10 | 16 | 6 | 16 |
| Olli Jokinen, C | 78 | 6 | 10 | 16 | -22 | 106 |
| Peter Worrell, L | 71 | 3 | 7 | 10 | -10 | 248 |
| *Ivan Novoseltsev, R | 38 | 3 | 6 | 9 | -5 | 16 |
| *Serge Payer, C | 43 | 5 | 1 | 6 | 0 | 21 |
| *Joey Tetarenko, D | 29 | 3 | 1 | 4 | -1 | 44 |
| Paul Laus, R | 25 | 1 | 2 | 3 | 5 | 66 |
| *John Jakopin, D | 60 | 1 | 2 | 3 | -4 | 62 |
| Lance Pitlick, D | 68 | 1 | 2 | 3 | -5 | 42 |

### GOALTENDING

| Player | GP | Mins | Avg | W | L | T | SO |
|---|---|---|---|---|---|---|---|
| *Roberto Longo | 47 | 2628 | 2.44 | 12 | 24 | 7 | 5 |
| Trevor Kidd | 42 | 2354 | 3.31 | 10 | 23 | 6 | 1 |
| Team total | 82 | 5006 | 2.95 | 22 | 47 | 13 | 6 |

## Los Angeles Kings

### SCORING

| Player | GP | G | A | Pts | +/- | PM |
|---|---|---|---|---|---|---|
| Zigmund Palffy, R | 73 | 38 | 51 | 89 | 22 | 20 |
| Luc Robitaille, L | 82 | 37 | 51 | 88 | 10 | 66 |
| Bryan Smolinski, L | 78 | 27 | 32 | 59 | 10 | 40 |
| Jozef Stumpel, C | 63 | 16 | 39 | 55 | 20 | 14 |
| Mathieu Schneider, D | 73 | 16 | 35 | 51 | 0 | 56 |
| Glen Murray, R | 64 | 18 | 21 | 39 | 9 | 32 |
| *Lubomir Visnovsky, D | 81 | 7 | 32 | 39 | 16 | 36 |
| Adam Deadmarsh, R | 57 | 17 | 15 | 32 | 1 | 63 |
| Nelson Emerson, R | 78 | 11 | 11 | 22 | -13 | 54 |
| *Eric Belanger, C | 62 | 9 | 12 | 21 | 14 | 16 |
| Kelly Buchberger, L | 82 | 6 | 14 | 20 | -10 | 75 |
| Jaroslav Modry, D | 63 | 4 | 15 | 19 | 16 | 48 |
| Ian Lapierriere, R | 79 | 8 | 10 | 18 | 5 | 141 |
| Aaron Miller, D | 69 | 4 | 14 | 18 | 22 | 43 |
| Mattias Norstrom, D | 82 | 0 | 18 | 18 | 10 | 60 |
| Craig Johnson, R | 26 | 4 | 5 | 9 | 0 | 16 |
| Jere Karalahti, D | 56 | 2 | 7 | 9 | 8 | 38 |
| Philippe Boucher, D | 22 | 2 | 4 | 6 | 4 | 20 |
| Steve Kelly, L | 35 | 3 | 2 | 5 | 0 | 25 |
| Stu Grimson, L | 72 | 3 | 2 | 5 | -2 | 235 |
| Scott Thomas, L | 24 | 3 | 1 | 4 | 0 | 11 |

### GOALTENDING

| Player | GP | Mins | Avg | W | L | T | SO |
|---|---|---|---|---|---|---|---|
| Felix Potvin | 23 | 1410 | 1.96 | 13 | 5 | 5 | 5 |
| Jamie Storr | 45 | 2498 | 2.74 | 19 | 18 | 6 | 4 |
| Stephane Fiset | 7 | 318 | 3.58 | 3 | 0 | 1 | 0 |
| Team total | 82 | 4995 | 2.74 | 38 | 31 | 13 | 10 |

## Minnesota Wild

### SCORING

| Player | GP | G | A | Pts | +/- | PM |
|---|---|---|---|---|---|---|
| *Marian Gaborik, L | 71 | 18 | 18 | 36 | -6 | 32 |
| Lubomir Sekeras, D | 80 | 11 | 23 | 34 | -8 | 52 |
| Wes Walz, C | 82 | 18 | 12 | 30 | -8 | 37 |
| *Filip Kuba, D | 75 | 9 | 21 | 30 | -6 | 28 |
| Darby Hendrickson, L | 72 | 18 | 11 | 29 | 1 | 36 |
| Jim Dowd, C | 68 | 7 | 22 | 29 | -6 | 80 |
| Antti Laaksonen, L | 82 | 12 | 16 | 28 | -7 | 24 |
| Stacy Roest, C | 76 | 7 | 20 | 27 | 3 | 20 |
| Aaron Gavey, C | 75 | 10 | 14 | 24 | -8 | 52 |
| Sergei Krivokrasov, R | 54 | 7 | 15 | 22 | -1 | 20 |
| Roman Simicek, C | 57 | 5 | 10 | 15 | -9 | 51 |
| Brad Bombardir, D | 70 | 0 | 15 | 15 | -6 | 42 |
| Cam Stewart, L | 54 | 4 | 9 | 13 | -3 | 16 |
| Maxim Sushinsky, R | 30 | 7 | 4 | 11 | -7 | 29 |
| Jeff Nielsen, R | 59 | 3 | 8 | 11 | -16 | 4 |
| *Willie Mitchell, D | 33 | 1 | 9 | 10 | 4 | 40 |
| Andy Sutton, D | 69 | 3 | 4 | 7 | -11 | 131 |
| *Ladislav Benysek, D | 71 | 2 | 5 | 7 | -11 | 38 |
| Sylvain Blouin, L | 41 | 3 | 2 | 5 | -5 | 117 |
| Pavel Patera, C | 20 | 1 | 3 | 4 | -8 | 4 |
| Matt Johnson, L | 50 | 1 | 1 | 2 | -6 | 137 |

### GOALTENDING

| Player | GP | Mins | Avg | W | L | T | SO |
|---|---|---|---|---|---|---|---|
| Manny Fernandez | 42 | 2461 | 2.24 | 19 | 17 | 4 | 4 |
| *Derek Gustafson | 4 | 239 | 2.51 | 1 | 3 | 0 | 0 |
| Jamie McLennan | 38 | 2230 | 2.64 | 5 | 23 | 9 | 2 |
| Team total | 82 | 5005 | 2.52 | 25 | 44 | 13 | 6 |

## Montreal Canadiens

### SCORING

| Player | GP | G | A | Pts | +/- | PM |
|---|---|---|---|---|---|---|
| Saku Koivu, C | 54 | 17 | 30 | 47 | 2 | 40 |
| Oleg Petrov, R | 81 | 17 | 30 | 47 | -11 | 24 |
| Brian Savage, L | 62 | 21 | 24 | 45 | -13 | 26 |
| Richard Zednik, R | 74 | 19 | 25 | 44 | -4 | 71 |
| Martin Rucinsky, L | 57 | 16 | 22 | 38 | -5 | 66 |
| Patrice Brisebois, D | 77 | 15 | 21 | 36 | -31 | 28 |
| Chad Kilger, C | 77 | 14 | 18 | 32 | -8 | 51 |
| Craig Darby, C | 78 | 12 | 16 | 28 | -17 | 16 |
| Andrei Markov, D | 63 | 6 | 17 | 23 | -6 | 18 |
| Jan Bulis, C | 51 | 5 | 18 | 23 | -1 | 26 |
| Patrick Poulin, L | 52 | 9 | 11 | 20 | 1 | 13 |
| Jim Campbell, R | 57 | 9 | 11 | 20 | -3 | 53 |
| Karl Dykhuis, D | 67 | 8 | 9 | 17 | 9 | 44 |
| Patrick Traverse, D | 71 | 5 | 9 | 14 | -10 | 10 |
| Benoit Brunet, R | 35 | 3 | 11 | 14 | -4 | 12 |
| *Stephane Robidas, D | 65 | 6 | 6 | 12 | 0 | 14 |
| *Eric Landry, C | 51 | 4 | 7 | 11 | -9 | 43 |
| Sheldon Souray, D | 52 | 3 | 8 | 11 | -11 | 95 |
| Juha Lind, L | 47 | 3 | 4 | 7 | -4 | 4 |
| Arron Asham, R | 46 | 2 | 3 | 5 | -9 | 59 |
| Christian Laflamme, D | 39 | 0 | 3 | 3 | -11 | 42 |

### GOALTENDING

| Player | GP | Mins | Avg | W | L | T | SO |
|---|---|---|---|---|---|---|---|
| *Mathieu Garon | 11 | 589 | 2.44 | 4 | 5 | 1 | 2 |
| Jose Theodore | 59 | 3298 | 2.57 | 20 | 29 | 5 | 2 |
| Jeff Hackett | 19 | 998 | 3.25 | 4 | 10 | 2 | 0 |
| Team total | 82 | 4978 | 2.80 | 28 | 46 | 8 | 4 |

## Nashville Predators
### SCORING

| Player | GP | G | A | Pts | +/– | PM |
|---|---|---|---|---|---|---|
| Cliff Ronning, C | 80 | 19 | 43 | 62 | 4 | 28 |
| Scott Walker, R | 74 | 25 | 29 | 54 | -2 | 66 |
| Patric Kjellberg, L | 81 | 14 | 31 | 45 | -2 | 12 |
| David Legwand, C | 81 | 13 | 28 | 41 | 1 | 38 |
| Vitali Yachmenev, L | 78 | 15 | 19 | 34 | -5 | 10 |
| Greg Johnson, C | 82 | 15 | 17 | 32 | -6 | 46 |
| *Marian Cisar, R | 60 | 12 | 15 | 27 | -7 | 45 |
| Randy Robitaille, C | 62 | 9 | 17 | 26 | -11 | 12 |
| Kimmo Timonen, D | 82 | 12 | 13 | 25 | -6 | 50 |
| Tom Fitzgerald, L | 82 | 9 | 9 | 18 | -5 | 71 |
| Bill Houlder, D | 81 | 4 | 12 | 16 | -7 | 40 |
| *Scott Hartnell, R | 75 | 2 | 14 | 16 | -8 | 48 |
| Rob Valicevic, L | 60 | 8 | 6 | 14 | -2 | 26 |
| *Denis Arkhipov, C | 40 | 6 | 7 | 13 | 0 | 4 |
| Karlis Skrastins, D | 82 | 1 | 11 | 12 | -12 | 30 |
| Mark Eaton, D | 34 | 3 | 8 | 11 | 7 | 14 |
| Richard Linter, D | 50 | 3 | 5 | 8 | 2 | 22 |
| Cale Hulse, D | 82 | 1 | 7 | 8 | -5 | 128 |
| *Greg Classen, C | 27 | 2 | 4 | 6 | -4 | 14 |
| Ville Peltonen, L | 23 | 3 | 1 | 4 | -7 | 2 |

### GOALTENDING

| Player | GP | Mins | Avg | W | L | T | SO |
|---|---|---|---|---|---|---|---|
| *Chris Mason | 1 | 59 | 2.03 | 0 | 1 | 0 | 0 |
| Mike Dunham | 48 | 2810 | 2.28 | 21 | 21 | 4 | 4 |
| Tomas Vokoun | 37 | 2088 | 2.44 | 13 | 17 | 5 | 2 |
| Team total | 82 | 4984 | 2.24 | 39 | 34 | 9 | 6 |

## New Jersey Devils
### SCORING

| Player | GP | G | A | Pts | +/– | PM |
|---|---|---|---|---|---|---|
| Patrik Elias, L | 82 | 40 | 56 | 96 | 45 | 51 |
| Alexander Mogilny, R | 75 | 43 | 40 | 83 | 10 | 43 |
| Petr Sykora, R | 73 | 35 | 46 | 81 | 36 | 32 |
| Scott Gomez, C | 76 | 14 | 49 | 63 | -1 | 46 |
| Jason Arnott, C | 54 | 21 | 34 | 55 | 23 | 75 |
| Sergei Brylin, L | 75 | 23 | 29 | 52 | 25 | 24 |
| Brian Rafalski, D | 78 | 9 | 43 | 52 | 36 | 26 |
| Bobby Holik, C | 80 | 15 | 35 | 50 | 19 | 97 |
| Randy McKay, R | 77 | 23 | 40 | 43 | 3 | 50 |
| John Madden, L | 80 | 23 | 15 | 38 | 24 | 12 |
| Scott Niedermayer, D | 57 | 6 | 29 | 35 | 14 | 22 |
| Scott Stevens, D | 81 | 9 | 22 | 31 | 40 | 71 |
| Sergei Nemchinov, C | 65 | 8 | 22 | 30 | 11 | 16 |
| Turner Stevenson, R | 69 | 8 | 18 | 26 | 11 | 97 |
| *Colin White, D | 82 | 1 | 19 | 20 | 32 | 155 |
| Sean O'Donnell, D | 80 | 4 | 13 | 17 | 0 | 161 |
| Jay Pandolfo, L | 63 | 4 | 12 | 16 | 3 | 16 |
| Bob Corkum, C | 75 | 7 | 7 | 14 | -8 | 22 |
| Ken Sutton, D | 53 | 1 | 7 | 8 | 9 | 37 |
| Jim McKenzie, L | 53 | 2 | 2 | 4 | 0 | 119 |
| Ken Daneyko, D | 77 | 0 | 4 | 4 | 8 | 87 |

### GOALTENDING

| Player | GP | Mins | Avg | W | L | T | SO |
|---|---|---|---|---|---|---|---|
| Martin Brodeur | 72 | 4297 | 2.32 | 42 | 17 | 11 | 9 |
| J. Vanbiesbrouck | 4 | 240 | 1.50 | 4 | 0 | 0 | 1 |
| Team total | 82 | 5001 | 2.34 | 48 | 22 | 12 | 10 |

## New York Islanders
### SCORING

| Player | GP | G | A | Pts | +/– | PM |
|---|---|---|---|---|---|---|
| Mariusz Czerkawski, R | 82 | 30 | 32 | 62 | -25 | 48 |
| Roman Hamrlik, D | 76 | 16 | 30 | 46 | -20 | 92 |
| Dave Scatchard, C | 81 | 21 | 24 | 45 | -9 | 114 |
| Tim Connolly, C | 82 | 10 | 31 | 41 | -14 | 42 |
| Brad Isbister, L | 51 | 18 | 14 | 32 | -19 | 59 |
| Claude Lapointe, L | 80 | 9 | 23 | 32 | -2 | 56 |
| Mark Parrish, R | 70 | 17 | 13 | 30 | -27 | 28 |
| Kenny Jonsson, D | 65 | 8 | 21 | 29 | -22 | 30 |
| Bill Muckalt, R | 60 | 11 | 15 | 26 | -3 | 33 |
| Oleg Kvasha, C | 62 | 11 | 9 | 20 | -15 | 46 |
| Garry Galley, D | 56 | 6 | 14 | 20 | -4 | 59 |
| *Taylor Pyatt, L | 78 | 4 | 14 | 18 | -17 | 39 |
| Jason Blake, C | 47 | 5 | 11 | 16 | -20 | 34 |
| Zdeno Chara, D | 82 | 2 | 7 | 9 | -27 | 157 |
| Aris Brimanis, D | 56 | 0 | 8 | 8 | -12 | 26 |
| *Juraj Kolnik, R | 29 | 4 | 3 | 7 | -8 | 12 |
| Steve Martins, C | 59 | 2 | 4 | 6 | -16 | 33 |
| Kevin Haller, D | 30 | 1 | 5 | 6 | 5 | 56 |
| *Branislav Mezei, D | 42 | 1 | 4 | 5 | -5 | 53 |
| Eric Cairns, D | 45 | 2 | 2 | 4 | -18 | 106 |
| Craig Berube, L | 60 | 0 | 3 | 3 | -8 | 72 |
| Steve Webb, C | 31 | 0 | 2 | 2 | 1 | 35 |

### GOALTENDING

| Player | GP | Mins | Avg | W | L | T | SO |
|---|---|---|---|---|---|---|---|
| Chris Terreri | 8 | 442 | 2.44 | 2 | 4 | 1 | 0 |
| *Rick DiPietro | 20 | 1083 | 3.49 | 3 | 15 | 1 | 0 |
| J. Vanbiesbrouck | 44 | 2390 | 3.01 | 10 | 25 | 5 | 1 |
| Team total | 82 | 4968 | 3.24 | 21 | 54 | 7 | 2 |

## New York Rangers
### SCORING

| Player | GP | G | A | Pts | +/– | PM |
|---|---|---|---|---|---|---|
| Brian Leetch, D | 82 | 21 | 58 | 79 | -18 | 34 |
| Petr Nedved, C | 79 | 32 | 46 | 78 | 10 | 54 |
| Theoren Fleury, R | 62 | 30 | 44 | 74 | 0 | 122 |
| Radek Dvorak, R | 82 | 31 | 36 | 67 | 9 | 20 |
| Mark Messier, C | 82 | 24 | 43 | 67 | -25 | 89 |
| Jan Hlavac, L | 79 | 28 | 36 | 64 | 3 | 20 |
| Valeri Kamensky, L | 65 | 14 | 20 | 34 | -18 | 36 |
| Mike York, C | 79 | 14 | 17 | 31 | 1 | 20 |
| Adam Graves, L | 82 | 10 | 16 | 26 | -16 | 77 |
| Kim Johnsson, D | 75 | 5 | 21 | 26 | -3 | 40 |
| Sandy McCarthy, R | 81 | 11 | 10 | 21 | 3 | 171 |
| Michal Grosek, R | 65 | 9 | 11 | 20 | -10 | 61 |
| Sylvain Lefebvre, D | 71 | 2 | 13 | 15 | 3 | 55 |
| Manny Malhotra, C | 50 | 4 | 8 | 12 | -10 | 31 |
| Rich Pilon, D | 69 | 2 | 9 | 11 | -2 | 175 |
| Jeff Toms, L | 54 | 3 | 5 | 8 | -10 | 10 |
| *Tomas Kloucek, D | 43 | 1 | 4 | 5 | -3 | 74 |
| Brad Brown, D | 48 | 1 | 3 | 4 | 0 | 107 |
| *Dale Purinton, D | 42 | 0 | 2 | 2 | 5 | 180 |

### GOALTENDING

| Player | GP | Mins | Avg | W | L | T | SO |
|---|---|---|---|---|---|---|---|
| Guy Hebert | 13 | 735 | 3.43 | 5 | 7 | 1 | 0 |
| Mike Richter | 45 | 2635 | 3.28 | 20 | 21 | 3 | 0 |
| Kirk McLean | 23 | 1220 | 3.49 | 8 | 10 | 1 | 0 |
| Team total | 82 | 4966 | 3.50 | 33 | 44 | 5 | 0 |

* Rookie.

## Ottawa Senators

### SCORING

| Player | GP | G | A | Pts | +/- | PM |
|---|---|---|---|---|---|---|
| Alexei Yashin, C | 82 | 40 | 48 | 88 | 10 | 30 |
| Marian Hossa, R | 81 | 32 | 43 | 75 | 19 | 44 |
| Shawn McEachern, L | 82 | 32 | 40 | 72 | 10 | 62 |
| Daniel Alfredsson, R | 68 | 24 | 46 | 70 | 11 | 30 |
| Radek Bonk, C | 74 | 23 | 36 | 59 | 27 | 52 |
| Wade Redden, D | 78 | 10 | 37 | 47 | 22 | 49 |
| *Martin Havlat, R | 73 | 19 | 23 | 42 | 8 | 20 |
| Mike Sillinger, C | 68 | 16 | 25 | 41 | -11 | 48 |
| Rob Zamuner, L | 79 | 19 | 18 | 37 | 7 | 52 |
| Magnus Arvedson | 51 | 17 | 16 | 33 | 23 | 24 |
| *Karel Rachunek, D | 71 | 3 | 30 | 33 | 17 | 60 |
| Andreas Dackell, R | 81 | 13 | 18 | 31 | 7 | 24 |
| Jason York, D | 33 | 74 | 6 | 16 | 22 | 72 |
| Mike Fisher, C | 60 | 7 | 12 | 19 | -1 | 46 |
| Sami Salo, D | 31 | 2 | 16 | 18 | 9 | 10 |
| Chris Phillips, D | 73 | 2 | 12 | 14 | 8 | 31 |
| Curtis Leschyshyn, D | 65 | 2 | 7 | 9 | 5 | 19 |
| Ricard Persson | 33 | 1 | 8 | 9 | 8 | 35 |
| Roy Andre, L | 64 | 3 | 5 | 8 | 1 | 169 |
| Jamie Rivers, D | 45 | 2 | 4 | 6˙ | 6 | 44 |
| Eric Lacroix, L | 55 | 2 | 4 | 6 | -6 | 43 |
| *Todd White, C | 16 | 4 | 1 | 5 | 5 | 4 |
| *Petr Schastlivy, L | 17 | 3 | 2 | 5 | -1 | 6 |
| *Shane Hnidy, D | 52 | 3 | 2 | 5 | 8 | 84 |

### GOALTENDING

| Player | GP | Mins | Avg | W | L | T | SO |
|---|---|---|---|---|---|---|---|
| Patrick Lalime | 60 | 3607 | 2.35 | 36 | 19 | 5 | 7 |
| *Jani Hurme | 22 | 1296 | 2.50 | 12 | 5 | 4 | 2 |
| Team total | 82 | 4977 | 2.47 | 48 | 25 | 9 | 9 |

## Philadelphia Flyers

### SCORING

| Player | GP | G | A | Pts | +/- | PM |
|---|---|---|---|---|---|---|
| Mark Recchi, R | 69 | 27 | 50 | 77 | 15 | 33 |
| Keith Primeau, C | 71 | 34 | 39 | 73 | 17 | 76 |
| Simon Gagne, L | 69 | 27 | 32 | 59 | 24 | 18 |
| Daymond Langkow, C | 71 | 13 | 41 | 54 | 12 | 50 |
| Dan McGillis, D | 82 | 14 | 35 | 49 | 13 | 86 |
| Eric Desjardins, D | 79 | 15 | 33 | 48 | -3 | 50 |
| *Ruslan Fedotenko, L | 74 | 16 | 20 | 36 | 8 | 72 |
| Rick Tocchet, R | 60 | 14 | 22 | 36 | 10 | 83 |
| Dean McAmmond, L | 71 | 11 | 17 | 28 | 3 | 43 |
| *Justin Williams, R | 63 | 12 | 13 | 25 | 6 | 22 |
| Peter White, C | 77 | 9 | 16 | 25 | 1 | 16 |
| Paul Ranheim, L | 80 | 10 | 7 | 17 | 2 | 14 |
| Michal Sykora, D | 49 | 5 | 11 | 16 | 9 | 26 |
| Jody Hull, R | 71 | 7 | 8 | 15 | -1 | 10 |
| Kent Manderville, C | 82 | 5 | 19 | 15 | -2 | 47 |
| Andy Delmore, D | 66 | 5 | 9 | 14 | 2 | 16 |
| Chris Therien, D | 73 | 2 | 12 | 14 | 22 | 48 |
| John LeClair, L | 16 | 7 | 5 | 12 | 2 | 0 |
| *Todd Fedoruk, D | 53 | 5 | 5 | 10 | 0 | 109 |
| Luke Richardson, D | 82 | 2 | 6 | 8 | 23 | 131 |
| P.J. Stock, C | 51 | 2 | 5 | 7 | -3 | 110 |
| Michel Picard, L | 7 | 1 | 4 | 5 | 6 | 0 |
| Chris McAllister, D | 60 | 2 | 2 | 4 | 1 | 124 |
| Derek Plante, C | 12 | 1 | 2 | 3 | 0 | 4 |

### GOALTENDING

| Player | GP | Mins | Avg | W | L | T | SO |
|---|---|---|---|---|---|---|---|
| Roman Turek | 67 | 3960 | 1.95 | 42 | 15 | 9 | 7 |
| Jamie McLennan | 19 | 1008 | 1.96 | 9 | 5 | 2 | 2 |
| Team total | 82 | 4968 | 1.95 | 51 | 20 | 11 | 9 |

## Phoenix Coyotes

### SCORING

| Player | GP | G | A | Pts | +/- | PM | | Player | GP | G | A | Pts | +/- | PM |
|---|---|---|---|---|---|---|---|---|---|---|---|---|---|---|
| Jeremy Roenick, C | 80 | 30 | 46 | 76 | -1 | 114 | | Keith Carney, D | 82 | 2 | 14 | 16 | 15 | 86 |
| Shane Doan, R | 76 | 26 | 37 | 63 | 0 | 89 | | Daniel Briere, C | 30 | 11 | 4 | 15 | -2 | 12 |
| Mike Johnson, R | 76 | 13 | 30 | 43 | -10 | 42 | | *Wyatt Smith, C | 42 | 3 | 7 | 10 | 7 | 13 |
| Joe Juneau, L | 69 | 10 | 23 | 33 | -2 | 28 | | Radoslav Suchy, D | 72 | 0 | 10 | 10 | 1 | 22 |
| Michal Handzus, C | 46 | 14 | 18 | 32 | 16 | 33 | | Mike Sullivan, L | 72 | 5 | 4 | 9 | -6 | 16 |
| Landon Wilson, R | 70 | 18 | 13 | 31 | 3 | 92 | | Todd Simpson, D | 38 | 1 | 4 | 5 | -4 | 86 |
| Teppo Numinen, D | 72 | 5 | 26 | 31 | 9 | 36 | | Joel Bouchard, D | 32 | 1 | 2 | 3 | -8 | 22 |
| Travis Green, C | 69 | 13 | 15 | 28 | -11 | 63 | | Louie DeBrusk, R | 39 | 0 | 0 | 0 | -5 | 79 |
| Claude Lemieux, R | 46 | 10 | 16 | 26 | 1 | 58 | | | | | | | | |
| Brad May, L | 62 | 11 | 14 | 25 | 10 | 107 | | | | | | | | |

### GOALTENDING

| Player | GP | Mins | Avg | W | L | T | SO |
|---|---|---|---|---|---|---|---|
| Sean Burke | 62 | 3644 | 2.27 | 25 | 22 | 13 | 4 |
| *Robert Esche | 25 | 1350 | 3.02 | 10 | 8 | 4 | 2 |
| Team total | 82 | 5010 | 2.54 | 35 | 30 | 17 | 6 |

| Player | GP | G | A | Pts | +/- | PM |
|---|---|---|---|---|---|---|
| Jyrki Lumme, D | 58 | 4 | 21 | 25 | 3 | 44 |
| Juha Ylonen, C | 69 | 9 | 14 | 23 | 10 | 38 |
| Trevor Letowski, C | 77 | 7 | 15 | 22 | -2 | 32 |
| Paul Mara, D | 62 | 6 | 14 | 20 | -16 | 54 |
| Mika Alatalo, L | 70 | 7 | 12 | 19 | 1 | 22 |
| *Ladislav Nagy, R | 46 | 8 | 9 | 17 | -2 | 22 |
| Ossi Vaananen, D | 81 | 4 | 12 | 16 | 9 | 90 |

* Rookie.

## Pittsburgh Penguins

### SCORING

| Player | GP | G | A | Pts | +/– | PM |
|---|---|---|---|---|---|---|
| Jaromir Jagr, R | 81 | 52 | 69 | 121 | 19 | 42 |
| Alexei Kovalev, R | 79 | 44 | 51 | 95 | 12 | 96 |
| Martin Straka, L | 82 | 27 | 68 | 95 | 19 | 38 |
| Robert Lang, C | 82 | 32 | 48 | 80 | 20 | 28 |
| Mario Lemieux, C | 43 | 35 | 41 | 76 | 15 | 18 |
| Jan Hrdina, C | 78 | 15 | 28 | 43 | 19 | 48 |
| Kevin Stevens, L | 55 | 10 | 22 | 32 | -6 | 73 |
| Josef Beranek, L | 70 | 9 | 14 | 23 | -7 | 43 |
| Hans Jonsson, D | 58 | 4 | 18 | 22 | 11 | 22 |
| Wayne Primeau, C | 75 | 3 | 19 | 22 | -17 | 131 |
| Janne Laukkanen, D | 50 | 3 | 17 | 20 | 9 | 34 |
| Aleksey Morozov, R | 66 | 5 | 14 | 19 | -8 | 6 |
| Darius Kasparaitis, D | 77 | 3 | 16 | 19 | 11 | 111 |
| Rene Corbet, L | 43 | 8 | 9 | 17 | -3 | 57 |
| Andrew Ference, D | 36 | 4 | 11 | 15 | 6 | 28 |
| *Milan Kraft, C | 42 | 7 | 7 | 14 | -6 | 8 |
| Kip Miller, L | 33 | 3 | 8 | 11 | 0 | 6 |
| Frantisek Kucera, D | 55 | 2 | 7 | 9 | -7 | 12 |
| *Toby Peterson, C | 12 | 2 | 6 | 8 | 3 | 4 |
| Ian Moran, D | 40 | 3 | 4 | 7 | 5 | 28 |
| *Dan LaCouture, L | 48 | 2 | 4 | 6 | -2 | 43 |
| Michal Rozsival, D | 30 | 1 | 4 | 5 | 3 | 26 |
| Krzysztof Oliwa, L | 36 | 1 | 4 | 5 | -3 | 165 |
| Marc Bergevin, D | 38 | 1 | 4 | 5 | 6 | 26 |
| Bob Boughner, D | 58 | 1 | 3 | 4 | 18 | 147 |
| *Billy Tibbetts, R | 29 | 1 | 2 | 3 | -2 | 79 |
| Bobby Dollas, D | 21 | 1 | 1 | 2 | 4 | 18 |
| Steve McKenna, L | 54 | 1 | 1 | 2 | -4 | 119 |

### GOALTENDING

| Player | GP | Mins | Avg | W | L | T | SO |
|---|---|---|---|---|---|---|---|
| Johan Hedberg | 9 | 545 | 2.64 | 7 | 1 | 1 | 0 |
| Garth Snow | 35 | 2032 | 2.98 | 14 | 15 | 4 | 3 |
| Rich Parent | 7 | 332 | 3.07 | 1 | 1 | 3 | 0 |
| J.-S. Aubin | 36 | 2050 | 3.13 | 20 | 14 | 1 | 0 |
| Team total | 82 | 4978 | 3.09 | 42 | 31 | 9 | 3 |

## St. Louis Blues

### SCORING

| Player | GP | G | A | Pts | +/– | PM |
|---|---|---|---|---|---|---|
| Pierre Turgeon, C | 79 | 30 | 52 | 82 | 14 | 37 |
| Keith Tkachuk, L | 76 | 35 | 44 | 79 | 3 | 122 |
| Scott Young, R | 81 | 40 | 33 | 73 | 15 | 30 |
| Al MacInnis, D | 59 | 12 | 42 | 54 | 23 | 52 |
| Cory Stillman, L | 78 | 24 | 28 | 52 | -8 | 51 |
| Chris Pronger, D | 51 | 8 | 39 | 47 | 21 | 75 |
| Pavol Demitra, R | 44 | 20 | 25 | 45 | 27 | 16 |
| Jochin Hecht, L | 72 | 19 | 25 | 44 | 11 | 48 |
| Dallas Drake, L | 82 | 12 | 29 | 41 | 18 | 71 |
| Alexander Khavanov, D | 74 | 7 | 16 | 23 | 16 | 52 |
| Mike Eastwood, C | 77 | 6 | 17 | 23 | 4 | 28 |
| Scott Mellanby, R | 63 | 11 | 10 | 21 | -13 | 71 |
| Jamal Mayers, R | 77 | 8 | 13 | 21 | -3 | 117 |
| Tyson Nash, L | 57 | 8 | 7 | 15 | 8 | 110 |
| *Daniel Corso, C | 28 | 10 | 3 | 13 | 0 | 14 |
| Lubos Bartecko, L | 50 | 5 | 8 | 13 | -1 | 12 |
| Marty Reasoner, C | 41 | 4 | 9 | 13 | -5 | 14 |
| Sean Hill, D | 48 | 1 | 10 | 11 | 5 | 51 |
| Jeff Finley, D | 72 | 2 | 8 | 10 | 7 | 38 |
| *Bryce Salvador, D | 75 | 2 | 8 | 10 | -4 | 69 |
| Alexei Gusarov, D | 51 | 1 | 8 | 9 | -3 | 18 |
| Todd Reirden, D | 38 | 2 | 4 | 6 | -2 | 43 |
| *Reed Low, R | 56 | 1 | 5 | 6 | 4 | 159 |
| Reid Simpson, L | 38 | 2 | 1 | 3 | -3 | 96 |
| Vladimir Chebaturkin, D | 22 | 1 | 2 | 3 | 5 | 26 |
| Dan Trebil, D | 26 | 0 | 0 | 0 | 0 | 7 |

### GOALTENDING

| Player | GP | Mins | Avg | W | L | T | SO |
|---|---|---|---|---|---|---|---|
| *Brent Johnson | 31 | 1744 | 2.17 | 19 | 9 | 2 | 4 |
| Roman Turek | 54 | 3232 | 2.28 | 24 | 18 | 10 | 6 |
| Team total | 82 | 5001 | 2.34 | 43 | 27 | 12 | 10 |

## San Jose Sharks

### SCORING

| Player | GP | G | A | Pts | +/– | PM |
|---|---|---|---|---|---|---|
| Teemu Selanne, R | 73 | 33 | 39 | 72 | -7 | 36 |
| Patrick Marleau, C | 81 | 25 | 27 | 52 | 7 | 22 |
| Owen Nolan, R | 57 | 24 | 25 | 49 | 0 | 75 |
| Niklas Sundstrom, R | 82 | 10 | 39 | 49 | 10 | 28 |
| Vincent Damphousse, C | 45 | 9 | 37 | 46 | 17 | 62 |
| Mike Ricci, C | 81 | 22 | 22 | 44 | 3 | 65 |
| Scott Thornton, L | 73 | 19 | 17 | 36 | 4 | 114 |
| Gary Suter, D | 68 | 10 | 24 | 34 | 8 | 84 |
| Marco Sturm, L | 81 | 14 | 18 | 32 | 9 | 28 |
| Stephane Matteau, L | 80 | 13 | 19 | 32 | 5 | 32 |
| Alex Korolyuk, R | 70 | 12 | 13 | 25 | 2 | 41 |
| Brad Stuart, D | 77 | 5 | 18 | 23 | 10 | 56 |
| Todd Harvey, R | 69 | 10 | 11 | 21 | 6 | 72 |
| Bryan Marchment, D | 75 | 7 | 11 | 18 | 15 | 204 |
| Scott Hannan, D | 75 | 3 | 14 | 17 | 10 | 51 |
| Marcus Ragnarsson, D | 68 | 3 | 12 | 15 | 2 | 44 |
| Bill Lindsay, L | 68 | 1 | 13 | 14 | -6 | 126 |
| Jeff Norton, D | 42 | 2 | 11 | 13 | 12 | 28 |
| Mike Rathje, D | 81 | 0 | 11 | 11 | 7 | 48 |
| Tony Granato, R | 61 | 4 | 4 | 9 | -1 | 65 |
| Shawn Heins, D | 38 | 3 | 4 | 7 | 2 | 57 |
| Jim Montgomery, C | 28 | 1 | 6 | 7 | -1 | 19 |
| *Mark Smith, C | 42 | 2 | 2 | 4 | 2 | 51 |
| Paul Kruse, L | 1 | 0 | 0 | 0 | 0 | 5 |

### GOALTENDING

| Player | GP | Mins | Avg | W | L | T | SO |
|---|---|---|---|---|---|---|---|
| Steve Shields | 21 | 1135 | 2.48 | 6 | 8 | 5 | 2 |
| *Evgeni Nabakov | 66 | 3700 | 2.19 | 32 | 21 | 7 | 6 |
| *Miikka Kiprusoff | 5 | 154 | 1.95 | 2 | 1 | 0 | 0 |
| Team total | 82 | 5008 | 2.30 | 40 | 30 | 12 | 9 |

## Tampa Bay Lightning

### SCORING

| Player | GP | G | A | Pts | +/- | PM |
|---|---|---|---|---|---|---|
| *Brad Richards, C | 82 | 21 | 41 | 62 | -10 | 14 |
| Frederik Modin, L | 76 | 32 | 24 | 56 | -1 | 48 |
| Vincent Lacavalier, C | 68 | 23 | 28 | 51 | -26 | 66 |
| Martin St. Louis, L | 78 | 18 | 22 | 40 | -4 | 12 |
| Terry Holzinger, R | 70 | 11 | 25 | 36 | -9 | 64 |
| Pavel Kubina, D | 70 | 11 | 19 | 30 | -13 | 103 |
| Adrian Aucoin, D | 73 | 4 | 24 | 28 | 5 | 45 |
| *Alexander Kharitonov, R | 66 | 7 | 15 | 22 | -9 | 8 |
| Todd Warriner, L | 64 | 10 | 11 | 21 | -13 | 46 |
| Ryan Johnson, C | 80 | 7 | 14 | 21 | -20 | 44 |
| Nils Ekman, L | 43 | 9 | 11 | 20 | -15 | 40 |
| Andrei Zyuzin, D | 64 | 4 | 16 | 20 | -8 | 76 |
| Matthew Barnaby, R | 76 | 5 | 8 | 13 | -10 | 265 |
| Cory Sarich, D | 73 | 1 | 8 | 9 | -26 | 106 |
| Jassen Cullimore, D | 74 | 1 | 6 | 7 | -6 | 80 |
| Ben Clymer, D | 23 | 5 | 1 | 6 | -7 | 21 |
| Stan Drulia, R | 34 | 2 | 4 | 6 | -11 | 18 |
| Stan Neckar, D | 69 | 2 | 4 | 6 | -3 | 71 |
| Maxim Galanov, D | 25 | 0 | 5 | 5 | -5 | 8 |
| *Sheldon Keefe, R | 49 | 4 | 0 | 4 | -13 | 38 |
| *Kristian Kudroc, D | 22 | 2 | 2 | 4 | 0 | 36 |
| John Emmons, C | 53 | 2 | 2 | 4 | -5 | 42 |
| Petr Svoboda, D | 19 | 1 | 3 | 4 | -4 | 41 |
| Craig Millar, D | 21 | 1 | 1 | 2 | -7 | 16 |
| Gordie Dwyer, L | 28 | 0 | 1 | 1 | -7 | 96 |

### GOALTENDING

| Player | GP | Mins | Avg | W | L | T | SO |
|---|---|---|---|---|---|---|---|
| Nikolai Khabibulin | 2 | 123 | 2.93 | 1 | 1 | 0 | 0 |
| Kevin Weekes | 61 | 3378 | 3.14 | 20 | 33 | 3 | 4 |
| Wade Flaherty | 2 | 118 | 4.07 | 0 | 2 | 0 | 0 |
| *Dieter Kochan | 10 | 314 | 3.44 | 0 | 3 | 0 | 0 |
| Team total | 82 | 4968 | 3.38 | 24 | 52 | 6 | 5 |

## Vancouver Canucks

### SCORING

| Player | GP | G | A | Pts | +/- | PM |
|---|---|---|---|---|---|---|
| Markus Naslund, R | 72 | 41 | 34 | 75 | -2 | 58 |
| Andrew Cassels, C | 66 | 12 | 44 | 56 | 1 | 10 |
| Todd Bertuzzi, L | 79 | 25 | 30 | 55 | -18 | 93 |
| Brendan Morrison, C | 82 | 16 | 38 | 54 | 2 | 42 |
| Ed Jovanovski, D | 79 | 12 | 35 | 47 | -1 | 102 |
| Peter Schaefer, L | 82 | 16 | 20 | 36 | 14 | 22 |
| *Daniel Sedin, C | 75 | 20 | 14 | 34 | -3 | 24 |
| Trent Klatt, R | 77 | 13 | 20 | 33 | 8 | 31 |
| Harold Drukin, C | 55 | 15 | 15 | 30 | 2 | 14 |
| *Henrik Sedin, L | 82 | 9 | 20 | 29 | -2 | 38 |
| Donald Brashear, L | 79 | 9 | 19 | 28 | 0 | 145 |
| Mattias Ohlund, D | 65 | 8 | 20 | 28 | -16 | 46 |
| Matt Cook, R | 81 | 14 | 13 | 27 | 5 | 94 |
| Drake Berehowsky, D | 80 | 7 | 19 | 26 | -9 | 121 |
| *Brent Sopel, D | 52 | 4 | 10 | 14 | 4 | 10 |
| Scott Lachance, D | 76 | 3 | 11 | 14 | 5 | 46 |
| Denis Pederson, R | 61 | 4 | 8 | 12 | 0 | 65 |
| Murray Baron, D | 82 | 3 | 8 | 11 | -13 | 63 |
| Mike Stapleton, C | 52 | 2 | 6 | 8 | -11 | 10 |
| *Jarkko Ruutu, L | 21 | 3 | 3 | 6 | 1 | 32 |
| Jason Strudwick, D | 60 | 1 | 4 | 5 | 16 | 64 |

### GOALTENDING

| Player | GP | Mins | Avg | W | L | T | SO |
|---|---|---|---|---|---|---|---|
| Bob Essensa | 39 | 2059 | 2.68 | 18 | 12 | 3 | 1 |
| Felix Potvin | 35 | 2006 | 3.08 | 14 | 17 | 3 | 1 |
| Dan Cloutier | 16 | 914 | 2.43 | 4 | 6 | 5 | 0 |
| Team total | 82 | 5006 | 2.85 | 36 | 35 | 11 | 2 |

*Rookie.

## Toronto Maple Leafs

### SCORING

| Player | GP | G | A | Pts | +/- | PM |
|---|---|---|---|---|---|---|
| Mats Sundin, C | 82 | 28 | 46 | 74 | 15 | 76 |
| Gary Roberts, L | 82 | 29 | 24 | 53 | 16 | 109 |
| Yannic Perreault, C | 76 | 24 | 28 | 52 | 0 | 52 |
| Sergei Berezin, L | 79 | 22 | 28 | 50 | 2 | 8 |
| Jonas Hoglund, L | 82 | 23 | 26 | 49 | 1 | 14 |
| Tomas Kaberle, D | 82 | 6 | 39 | 45 | 10 | 24 |
| Darcy Tucker, R | 82 | 16 | 21 | 37 | 6 | 141 |
| Steve Thomas, R | 57 | 80 | 26 | 34 | 0 | 46 |
| Igor Korolev, R | 73 | 10 | 19 | 29 | 3 | 28 |
| Bryan McCabe, D | 82 | 5 | 24 | 29 | 16 | 123 |
| Garry Valk, R | 74 | 8 | 18 | 26 | 4 | 46 |
| Shayne Corson, C | 77 | 8 | 18 | 26 | 1 | 189 |
| Dimitri Yushkevich, D | 81 | 5 | 19 | 24 | -2 | 52 |
| Tie Domi, R | 82 | 13 | 7 | 20 | 2 | 214 |
| Nikolai Antropov, C | 52 | 6 | 11 | 17 | 5 | 30 |
| Danny Markov, D | 59 | 3 | 13 | 16 | 6 | 34 |
| Dave Manson, D | 74 | 4 | 7 | 11 | 13 | 93 |
| Nathan Dempsey, D | 25 | 1 | 9 | 10 | 13 | 4 |
| Cory Cross, D | 41 | 3 | 5 | 8 | 7 | 50 |
| Aki Berg, D | 59 | 3 | 4 | 7 | -3 | 45 |
| *Alexei Ponikarovsky, R | 22 | 1 | 3 | 4 | -1 | 14 |
| *Petr Svoboda, D | 18 | 1 | 2 | 3 | -5 | 10 |
| Wade Belak, D | 39 | 1 | 1 | 2 | -6 | 110 |
| Alyn McCauley, C | 14 | 1 | 0 | 1 | 0 | 0 |

### GOALTENDING

| Player | GP | Mins | Avg | W | L | T | SO |
|---|---|---|---|---|---|---|---|
| Curtis Joseph | 68 | 4100 | 2.39 | 33 | 27 | 8 | 6 |
| Glenn Healy | 15 | 871 | 2.62 | 4 | 7 | 3 | 0 |
| Team Total | 82 | 4990 | 2.49 | 37 | 34 | 11 | 6 |

## Washington Capitals

### SCORING

| Player | GP | G | A | Pts | +/- | PM |
|---|---|---|---|---|---|---|
| Adam Oates, C | 81 | 13 | 69 | 82 | -9 | 28 |
| Peter Bondra, L | 82 | 45 | 36 | 81 | 8 | 60 |
| Sergei Gonchar, D | 76 | 19 | 38 | 57 | 12 | 70 |
| Ulf Dahlen, R | 73 | 15 | 33 | 48 | 11 | 6 |
| Steve Konowalchuk, L | 82 | 24 | 23 | 47 | 8 | 87 |
| Jeff Halpern, C | 80 | 21 | 21 | 42 | 13 | 60 |
| Dmitri Khristich, R | 70 | 13 | 25 | 38 | 0 | 16 |
| Andrei Nikolishin, C | 81 | 13 | 25 | 38 | 9 | 34 |
| Trevor Linden, C | 69 | 15 | 22 | 37 | 0 | 60 |
| Calley Johansson, D | 76 | 7 | 29 | 36 | 11 | 26 |
| Dainius Zubrus, R | 61 | 13 | 13 | 26 | -11 | 37 |
| Chris Simon, L | 60 | 10 | 10 | 20 | -12 | 109 |
| Sylvain Cote, D | 68 | 7 | 11 | 18 | -3 | 18 |
| Joe Sacco, R | 69 | 7 | 7 | 14 | 4 | 48 |
| Joe Reekie, D | 74 | 2 | 9 | 11 | 14 | 77 |
| Dmitri Mironov, D | 55 | 3 | 5 | 8 | -7 | 6 |
| Jason Marshall, D | 55 | 3 | 4 | 7 | -13 | 122 |
| Brendan Witt, D | 72 | 3 | 3 | 6 | 2 | 101 |
| Ken Klee, D | 54 | 2 | 4 | 6 | -5 | 60 |
| *Trent Whitfield, C | 61 | 2 | 4 | 6 | 3 | 35 |
| James Black, L | 42 | 1 | 5 | 6 | -3 | 4 |

### GOALTENDING

| Player | GP | Mins | Avg | W | L | T | SO |
|---|---|---|---|---|---|---|---|
| Craig Billington | 12 | 660 | 2.45 | 3 | 5 | 2 | 0 |
| Olaf Kolzig | 72 | 4279 | 2.48 | 37 | 26 | 8 | 5 |
| Team total | 82 | 4986 | 2.54 | 41 | 31 | 10 | 5 |

## 2001 NHL Draft

### First Round

The opening round of the 2001 NHL draft was held on June 23 in Sunrise, Fla.

| Team | Selection | Position | Team | Selection | Position |
|------|-----------|----------|------|-----------|----------|
| 1.....Atlanta | Ilja Kovalchuk | F | 15...Carolina | Igor Knyazev | D |
| 2.....Ottawa | Jason Spezza | C | 16...Vancouver | R.J. Umberger | C |
| 3.....Tampa Bay | Alexander Svitov | C | 17...Toronto | Carlo Colaiacovo | D |
| 4.....Florida | Stephen Weiss | C | 18...Los Angeles | Jens Karlsson | F |
| 5.....Anaheim | Stanislav Chistov | F | 19...Boston | Shaone Morrisonn | D |
| 6.....Minnesota | Mikko Koivu | C | 20...San Jose | Marcel Goc | C |
| 7.....Montreal | Michael Komisarek | D | 21...Pittsburgh | Colby Armstrong | R |
| 8.....Columbus | Pascal LeClaire | G | 22...Buffalo | Jiri Novotny | C |
| 9.....Chicago | Tuomo Ruutu | F | 23...Ottawa | Tim Gleason | D |
| 10...NY Rangers | Daniel Blackburn | G | 24...Florida | Lukas Krajicek | D |
| 11...Phoenix | Fredrik Sjostrom | R | 25...Montreal | Alexander Perezhogin | C |
| 12...Nashville | Dan Hamhuis | D | 26...Dallas | Jason Bacashihua | G |
| 13...Edmonton | Ales Hemsky | R | 27...Philadelphia | Jeff Woywitka | D |
| 14...Calgary | Chuck Kobasew | R | 28...New Jersey | Adrian Foster | L |
| | | | 29...Chicago | Adam Munro | G |
| | | | 30...Los Angeles | David Steckle | F |

# FOR THE RECORD · Year by Year

## The Stanley Cup

Awarded annually to the team that wins the NHL's best-of-seven final-round playoffs. The Stanley Cup is the oldest trophy competed for by professional athletes in North America. It was donated in 1893 by Frederick Arthur, Lord Stanley of Preston.

### Results

#### WINNERS PRIOR TO FORMATION OF NHL IN 1917

| | | |
|---|---|---|
| 1892–93.....Montreal A.A.A. | 1900–01.....Winnipeg Victorias | 1907–08.....Montreal Wanderers |
| 1893–94.....Montreal A.A.A. | 1901–02.....Winnipeg Victorias (Jan) | 1908–09.....Ottawa Senators |
| 1894–95.....Montreal Victorias | 1901–02.....Montreal A.A.A. (Mar) | 1909–10.....Montreal Wanderers |
| 1895–96.....Winnipeg Victorias (Feb) | 1902–03.....Montreal A.A.A. (Feb) | 1910–11.....Ottawa Senators |
| 1895–96.....Montreal Victorias (Dec) | 1902–03.....Ottawa Silver Seven (Mar) | 1911–12.....Quebec Bulldogs |
| 1896–97.....Montreal Victorias | 1903–04.....Ottawa Silver Seven | 1912–13.....Quebec Bulldogs |
| 1897–98.....Montreal Victorias | 1904–05.....Ottawa Silver Seven | 1913–14.....Toronto Blueshirts |
| 1898–99.....Montreal Victorias (Feb) | 1905–06.....Ottawa Silver Seven (Feb) | 1914–15.....Vancouver Millionaires |
| 1898–99.....Montreal Shamrocks (Mar) | 1905–06.....Montreal Wanderers (Mar) | 1915–16.....Montreal Canadiens |
| 1899–1900...Montreal Shamrocks | 1906–07.....Kenora Thistles (Jan) | 1916–17.....Seattle Metropolitans |
| | 1906–07.....Montreal Wanderers (Mar) | |

#### NHL WINNERS AND FINALISTS

| Season | Champion | Finalist | GP in Final |
|--------|----------|----------|-------------|
| 1917–18 | Toronto Arenas | Vancouver Millionaires | 5 |
| 1918–19 | No decision* | No decision* | 5 |
| 1919–20 | Ottawa Senators | Seattle Metropolitans | 5 |
| 1920–21 | Ottawa Senators | Vancouver Millionaires | 5 |
| 1921–22 | Toronto St. Pats | Vancouver Millionaires | 5 |
| 1922–23 | Ottawa Senators | Vancouver Maroons, Edmonton Eskimos | 2, 4 |
| 1923–24 | Montreal Canadiens | Vancouver Maroons, Calgary Tigers | 2, 2 |
| 1924–25 | Victoria Cougars | Montreal Canadiens | 4 |
| 1925–26 | Montreal Maroons | Victoria Cougars | 4 |
| 1926–27 | Ottawa Senators | Boston Bruins | 4 |
| 1927–28 | New York Rangers | Montreal Maroons | 5 |
| 1928–29 | Boston Bruins | New York Rangers | 2 |
| 1929–30 | Montreal Canadiens | Boston Bruins | 2 |
| 1930–31 | Montreal Canadiens | Chicago Blackhawks | 5 |
| 1931–32 | Toronto Maple Leafs | New York Rangers | 3 |
| 1932–33 | New York Rangers | Toronto Maple Leafs | 4 |
| 1933–34 | Chicago Blackhawks | Detroit Red Wings | 4 |
| 1934–35 | Montreal Maroons | Toronto Maple Leafs | 3 |

## NHL WINNERS AND FINALISTS *(CONT.)*

| Season | Champion | Finalist | GP in Final |
|---|---|---|---|
| 1935–36 | Detroit Red Wings | Toronto Maple Leafs | 4 |
| 1936–37 | Detroit Red Wings | New York Rangers | 5 |
| 1937–38 | Chicago Blackhawks | Toronto Maple Leafs | 4 |
| 1938–39 | Boston Bruins | Toronto Maple Leafs | 5 |
| 1939–40 | New York Rangers | Toronto Maple Leafs | 6 |
| 1940–41 | Boston Bruins | Detroit Red Wings | 4 |
| 1941–42 | Toronto Maple Leafs | Detroit Red Wings | 7 |
| 1942–43 | Detroit Red Wings | Boston Bruins | 4 |
| 1943–44 | Montreal Canadiens | Chicago Blackhawks | 4 |
| 1944–45 | Toronto Maple Leafs | Detroit Red Wings | 7 |
| 1945–46 | Montreal Canadiens | Boston Bruins | 5 |
| 1946–47 | Toronto Maple Leafs | Montreal Canadiens | 6 |
| 1947–48 | Toronto Maple Leafs | Detroit Red Wings | 4 |
| 1948–49 | Toronto Maple Leafs | Detroit Red Wings | 4 |
| 1949–50 | Detroit Red Wings | New York Rangers | 7 |
| 1950–51 | Toronto Maple Leafs | Montreal Canadiens | 5 |
| 1951–52 | Detroit Red Wings | Montreal Canadiens | 4 |
| 1952–53 | Montreal Canadiens | Boston Bruins | 5 |
| 1953–54 | Detroit Red Wings | Montreal Canadiens | 7 |
| 1954–55 | Detroit Red Wings | Montreal Canadiens | 7 |
| 1955–56 | Montreal Canadiens | Detroit Red Wings | 5 |
| 1956–57 | Montreal Canadiens | Boston Bruins | 5 |
| 1957–58 | Montreal Canadiens | Boston Bruins | 6 |
| 1958–59 | Montreal Canadiens | Toronto Maple Leafs | 5 |
| 1959–60 | Montreal Canadiens | Toronto Maple Leafs | 4 |
| 1960–61 | Chicago Blackhawks | Detroit Red Wings | 6 |
| 1961–62 | Toronto Maple Leafs | Chicago Blackhawks | 6 |
| 1962–63 | Toronto Maple Leafs | Detroit Red Wings | 5 |
| 1963–64 | Toronto Maple Leafs | Detroit Red Wings | 7 |
| 1964–65 | Montreal Canadiens | Chicago Blackhawks | 7 |
| 1965–66 | Montreal Canadiens | Detroit Red Wings | 6 |
| 1966–67 | Toronto Maple Leafs | Montreal Canadiens | 6 |
| 1967–68 | Montreal Canadiens | St. Louis Blues | 4 |
| 1968–69 | Montreal Canadiens | St. Louis Blues | 4 |
| 1969–70 | Boston Bruins | St. Louis Blues | 4 |
| 1970–71 | Montreal Canadiens | Chicago Blackhawks | 7 |
| 1971–72 | Boston Bruins | New York Rangers | 6 |
| 1972–73 | Montreal Canadiens | Chicago Blackhawks | 6 |
| 1973–74 | Philadelphia Flyers | Boston Bruins | 6 |
| 1974–75 | Philadelphia Flyers | Buffalo Sabres | 6 |
| 1975–76 | Montreal Canadiens | Philadelphia Flyers | 4 |
| 1976–77 | Montreal Canadiens | Boston Bruins | 4 |
| 1977–78 | Montreal Canadiens | Boston Bruins | 6 |
| 1978–79 | Montreal Canadiens | New York Rangers | 5 |
| 1979–80 | New York Islanders | Philadelphia Flyers | 6 |
| 1980–81 | New York Islanders | Minnesota North Stars | 5 |
| 1981–82 | New York Islanders | Vancouver Canucks | 4 |
| 1982–83 | New York Islanders | Edmonton Oilers | 4 |
| 1983–84 | Edmonton Oilers | New York Islanders | 5 |
| 1984–85 | Edmonton Oilers | Philadelphia Flyers | 5 |
| 1985–86 | Montreal Canadiens | Calgary Flames | 6 |
| 1986–87 | Edmonton Oilers | Philadelphia Flyers | 7 |
| 1987–88 | Edmonton Oilers | Boston Bruins | 4 |
| 1988–89 | Calgary Flames | Montreal Canadiens | 6 |
| 1989–90 | Edmonton Oilers | Boston Bruins | 5 |
| 1990–91 | Pittsburgh Penguins | Minnesota North Stars | 6 |
| 1991–92 | Pittsburgh Penguins | Chicago Blackhawks | 4 |
| 1992–93 | Montreal Canadiens | Los Angeles Kings | 5 |
| 1993–94 | New York Rangers | Vancouver Canucks | 7 |
| 1994–95 | New Jersey Devils | Detroit Red Wings | 4 |
| 1995–96 | Colorado Avalanche | Florida Panthers | 4 |
| 1996–97 | Detroit Red Wings | Philadelphia Flyers | 4 |
| 1997–98 | Detroit Red Wings | Washington Capitals | 4 |
| 1998–99 | Dallas Stars | Buffalo Sabres | 6 |

## NHL WINNERS AND FINALISTS (CONT.)

| Season | Champion | Finalist | GP in Final |
|---|---|---|---|
| 1999–00 | New Jersey Devils | Dallas Stars | 6 |
| 2000–01 | Colorado Avalanche | New Jersey Devils | 7 |

*In 1919 the Montreal Canadiens traveled to meet Seattle, the PCHL champions. After 5 games had been played—the teams were tied at 2 wins and 1 tie—the series was called off by the local Department of Health because of the influenza epidemic and the death of Canadiens defenseman Joe Hall from influenza.

## Conn Smythe Trophy

Awarded to the Most Valuable Player of the Stanley Cup playoffs, as selected by the Professional Hockey Writers Association. The trophy is named after the former coach, general manager, president and owner of the Toronto Maple Leafs.

| | | | |
|---|---|---|---|
| 1965 | Jean Beliveau, Mtl | 1984 | Mark Messier, Edm |
| 1966 | Roger Crozier, Det | 1985 | Wayne Gretzky, Edm |
| 1967 | Dave Keon, Tor | 1986 | Patrick Roy, Mtl |
| 1968 | Glenn Hall, StL | 1987 | Ron Hextall, Phil |
| 1969 | Serge Savard, Mtl | 1988 | Wayne Gretzky, Edm |
| 1970 | Bobby Orr, Bos | 1989 | Al MacInnis, Cgy |
| 1971 | Ken Dryden, Mtl | 1990 | Bill Ranford, Edm |
| 1972 | Bobby Orr, Bos | 1991 | Mario Lemieux, Pitt |
| 1973 | Yvan Cournoyer, Mtl | 1992 | Mario Lemieux, Pitt |
| 1974 | Bernie Parent, Phil | 1993 | Patrick Roy, Mtl |
| 1975 | Bernie Parent, Phil | 1994 | Brian Leetch, NYR |
| 1976 | Reggie Leach, Phil | 1995 | Claude Lemieux, NJ |
| 1977 | Guy Lafleur, Mtl | 1996 | Joe Sakic, Col |
| 1978 | Larry Robinson, Mtl | 1997 | Mike Vernon, Det |
| 1979 | Bob Gainey, Mtl | 1998 | Steve Yzerman, Det |
| 1980 | Bryan Trottier, NYI | 1999 | Joe Nieuwendyk, Dall |
| 1981 | Butch Goring, NYI | 2000 | Scott Stevens, NJ |
| 1982 | Mike Bossy, NYI | 2001 | Patrick Roy, Col |
| 1983 | Bill Smith, NYI | | |

## Alltime Stanley Cup Playoff Leaders

### Points

| | Yrs | GP | G | A | Pts | | Yrs | GP | G | A | Pts |
|---|---|---|---|---|---|---|---|---|---|---|---|
| Wayne Gretzky, four teams | 17 | 208 | 122 | 260 | 382 | *Brett Hull, Cal, StL, Dall | 16 | 163 | 90 | 76 | 166 |
| *Mark Messier, Edm, NYR | 17 | 236 | 109 | 186 | 295 | Denis Potvin, NYI | 14 | 185 | 56 | 108 | 164 |
| Jari Kurri, four teams | 15 | 200 | 106 | 127 | 233 | Mike Bossy, NYI | 10 | 129 | 85 | 75 | 160 |
| Glenn Anderson, four teams | 15 | 225 | 93 | 121 | 214 | Gordie Howe, Det, Hart | 20 | 157 | 68 | 92 | 160 |
| *Paul Coffey, six teams | 16 | 198 | 59 | 137 | 196 | Bobby Smith, Minn, Mtl | 13 | 184 | 64 | 96 | 160 |
| Bryan Trottier, NYI, Pitt | 17 | 221 | 71 | 113 | 184 | *Claude Lemieux, Mtl, NJ, Col | 15 | 221 | 80 | 77 | 157 |
| *Ray Bourque, Bos, Col | 21 | 214 | 41 | 139 | 180 | *Steve Yzerman, Det | 16 | 154 | 61 | 91 | 152 |
| *Doug Gilmour, five teams | 16 | 170 | 56 | 122 | 178 | *Larry Murphy, six teams | 20 | 215 | 37 | 115 | 152 |
| Jean Beliveau, Mtl | 17 | 162 | 79 | 97 | 176 | *Al MacInnis, Cgy, StL | 17 | 164 | 39 | 113 | 152 |
| Denis Savard, Chi, Mtl | 16 | 169 | 66 | 109 | 175 | | | | | | |
| *Mario Lemieux, Pitt | 8 | 107 | 76 | 96 | 172 | | | | | | |

*Active in 2000–01.

### Goals

| | Yrs | GP | G |
|---|---|---|---|
| Wayne Gretzky, four teams | 17 | 208 | 122 |
| *Mark Messier, Edm, NYR | 17 | 236 | 109 |
| Jari Kurri, five teams | 15 | 200 | 106 |
| Glenn Anderson, four teams | 15 | 225 | 93 |
| *Brett Hull, Cgy, StL, Dall | 16 | 163 | 90 |
| Mike Bossy, NYI | 10 | 129 | 85 |
| Maurice Richard, Mtl | 15 | 133 | 82 |
| *Claude Lemieux, Mtl, NJ, Col | 15 | 221 | 80 |
| Jean Beliveau, Mtl | 17 | 162 | 79 |
| *Mario Lemieux, Pitt | 8 | 107 | 76 |

*Active in 2000–01.

### Assists

| | Yrs | GP | A |
|---|---|---|---|
| Wayne Gretzky, four teams | 17 | 208 | 260 |
| *Mark Messier, Edm, NYR | 17 | 236 | 186 |
| *Ray Bourque, Bos, Col | 21 | 214 | 139 |
| *Paul Coffey, six teams | 16 | 198 | 137 |
| Jari Kurri, five teams | 15 | 196 | 127 |
| *Doug Gilmour, five teams | 16 | 170 | 122 |
| Glenn Anderson, four teams | 15 | 225 | 121 |
| Larry Robinson, Mtl, LA | 20 | 227 | 116 |
| *Larry Murphy, six teams | 20 | 215 | 115 |
| Al MacInnis, Cgy, StL | 17 | 164 | 113 |
| Bryan Trottier, NYI, Pitt | 17 | 221 | 113 |

*Active in 2000–01.

## Goaltending

| WINS | W | L | Pct |
|---|---|---|---|
| *Patrick Roy, Mtl, Col | 137 | 80 | .631 |
| Grant Fuhr, five teams | 92 | 50 | .648 |
| Billy Smith, LA, NYI | 88 | 36 | .710 |
| Ken Dryden, Mtl | 80 | 32 | .714 |
| *Ed Belfour, Chi, SJ, Dall | 79 | 57 | .581 |
| *Mike Vernon, four teams | 77 | 56 | .579 |
| Jacques Plante, five teams | 71 | 37 | .657 |
| Andy Moog, four teams | 68 | 57 | .544 |
| Martin Brodeur, NJ | 65 | 44 | .596 |
| Tom Barrasso, Buff, Pitt, Ott | 61 | 54 | .530 |

*Active in 2000–01.

| SHUTOUTS | GP | W | SO |
|---|---|---|---|
| *Patrick Roy, Mtl, Col | 219 | 137 | 19 |
| Clint Benedict, Ott, Mtl M | 48 | 25 | 15 |
| Jacques Plante, five teams | 112 | 71 | 14 |
| Turk Broda, Tor | 101 | 58 | 13 |
| Curtis Joseph, StL, Edm, Tor | 98 | 48 | 12 |
| Martin Brodeur, NJ | 109 | 65 | 12 |
| Terry Sawchuk, Det, LA | 106 | 54 | 12 |

| GOALS AGAINST AVG | | | Avg |
|---|---|---|---|
| *Martin Brodeur, NJ | | | 1.91 |
| George Hainsworth, Mtl, Tor | | | 1.93 |
| Turk Broda, Tor | | | 1.98 |
| *Dominik Hasek, Edm, Tor, Buff | | | 2.09 |
| *Ed Belfour, Chi, Dall | | | 2.14 |

Note: At least 50 games played.
*Active in 2000–01.

## Alltime Stanley Cup Standings

| TEAM | W | L | Pct | TEAM | W | L | Pct |
|---|---|---|---|---|---|---|---|
| Montreal | 381 | 249 | .605 | Buffalo | 99 | 110 | .474 |
| Boston | 236 | 252 | .484 | New Jersey† | 88 | 70 | .557 |
| Detroit | 235 | 219 | .518 | Calgary* | 69 | 87 | .442 |
| Toronto | 232 | 248 | .483 | Washington | 67 | 81 | .453 |
| Chicago | 187 | 214 | .467 | Los Angeles | 62 | 97 | .390 |
| NY Rangers | 183 | 195 | .484 | Vancouver | 54 | 74 | .422 |
| Philadelphia | 160 | 143 | .528 | Phoenix†† | 27 | 59 | .313 |
| Edmonton | 133 | 86 | .607 | Carolina§ | 22 | 39 | .361 |
| Dallas# | 130 | 127 | .506 | San Jose | 22 | 33 | .400 |
| NY Islanders | 128 | 90 | .587 | Florida | 13 | 18 | .419 |
| St. Louis | 129 | 152 | .459 | Ottawa | 10 | 22 | .313 |
| Pittsburgh | 109 | 99 | .524 | Anaheim | 4 | 11 | .267 |
| Colorado** | 102 | 83 | .551 | Tampa Bay | 2 | 4 | .333 |

*Atlanta Flames 1972–80. †Colorado Rockies 1976–82. #Minnesota North Stars 1967–93. **Quebec Nordiques 1979–95. ††Winnipeg Jets 1979–96. §Hartford Whalers 1979–97. Note: Teams ranked by playoff victories.

## Stanley Cup Coaching Records

| Coach | Team | Yrs | Series | Series W | Series L | Games | Games W | Games L | T | Cups | Pct |
|---|---|---|---|---|---|---|---|---|---|---|---|
| Glen Sather | Edm | 10 | 27 | 21 | 6 | *126 | 89 | 37 | 0 | 4 | .706 |
| Toe Blake | Mtl | 13 | 23 | 18 | 5 | 119 | 82 | 37 | 0 | 8 | .689 |
| †Scott Bowman | Five teams | 27 | 64 | 45 | 19 | 329 | 207 | 123 | 0 | 8 | .629 |
| Hap Day | Tor | 9 | 14 | 10 | 4 | 80 | 49 | 31 | 0 | 5 | .613 |
| Jacques Lemaire | Mtl, NJ | 6 | 15 | 10 | 5 | 83 | 49 | 34 | 0 | 1 | .590 |
| Al Arbour | StL, NYI | 16 | 42 | 30 | 12 | 209 | 123 | 86 | 0 | 4 | .589 |
| †Ken Hitchcock | Dall | 5 | 14 | 10 | 4 | 80 | 47 | 33 | 0 | 1 | .588 |
| Mike Keenan | five teams | 11 | 28 | 18 | 10 | 160 | 91 | 69 | 0 | 1 | .569 |
| Fred Shero | Phil, NYR | 8 | 21 | 15 | 6 | 108 | 61 | 47 | 0 | 2 | .565 |
| Jacques Demers | Que, StL, Det, Mtl | 9 | 19 | 11 | 8 | 104 | 57 | 47 | 0 | 1 | .548 |

*Does not include suspended game, May 24, 1988. †Active in 2000–01.
Note: Coaches ranked by winning percentage. Minimum: 65 games.

## The 10 Longest Overtime Games

| Date | Result | OT | Scorer | Series | Series Winner |
|---|---|---|---|---|---|
| 3-24-36 | Det 1 vs Mtl M 0 | 116:30 | Mud Bruneteau | SF | Det |
| 4-3-33 | Tor 1 vs Bos 0 | 104:46 | Ken Doraty | SF | Tor |
| 5-4-00 | Phil 2 vs Pitt 1 | 92:01 | Keith Primeau | CSF | Phil |
| 4-24-96 | Pitt 3 vs Wash 2 | 79:15 | Petr Nedved | CQF | Pitt |
| 3-23-43 | Tor 3 vs Det 2 | 70:18 | Jack McLean | SF | Det |
| 3-28-30 | Mtl 2 vs NYR 1 | 68:52 | Gus Rivers | SF | Mtl |
| 4-18-87 | NYI 3 vs Wash 2 | 68:47 | Pat LaFontaine | DSF | NYI |
| 4-27-94 | Buff 1 vs NJ 0 | 65:43 | Dave Hannan | CQF | NJ |
| 3-27-51 | Mtl 3 vs Det 2 | 61:09 | Maurice Richard | SF | Mtl |
| 3-27-38 | NYA 3 vs NYR 2 | 60:40 | Lorne Carr | QF | NYA |

## Hart Memorial Trophy

Awarded annually "to the player adjudged to be the most valuable to his team." The original trophy was donated by Dr. David A. Hart, father of Cecil Hart, former manager-coach of the Montreal Canadiens. In the 1980s Wayne Gretzky won the award nine times.

| Year | Winner | Key Statistics | Runner-Up |
|------|--------|----------------|-----------|
| 1924 | Frank Nighbor, Ott | 10 goals, 3 assists in 20 games | Sprague Cleghorn, Mtl |
| 1925 | Billy Burch, Ham | 20 goals, 4 assists in 27 games | Howie Morenz, Mtl |
| 1926 | Nels Stewart, Mtl M | 42 points in 36 games | Sprague Cleghorn, Mtl |
| 1927 | Herb Gardiner, Mtl | 12 points in 44 games as defenseman | Bill Cook, NYR |
| 1928 | Howie Morenz, Mtl | 33 goals, 18 assists | Roy Worters, Pitt |
| 1929 | Roy Worters, NYA | 1.21 goals against, 13 shutouts | Ace Bailey, Tor |
| 1930 | Nels Stewart, Mtl M | 39 goals, 16 assists | Lionel Hitchman, Bos |
| 1931 | Howie Morenz, Mtl | 28 goals, 23 assists | Eddie Shore, Bos |
| 1932 | Howie Morenz, Mtl | 24 goals, 25 assists | Ching Johnson, NYR |
| 1933 | Eddie Shore, Bos | 27 assists in 48 games as defenseman | Bill Cook, NYR |
| 1934 | Aurel Joliat, Mtl | 27 points | Lionel Conacher, Chi |
| 1935 | Eddie Shore, Bos | 26 assists in 48 games as defenseman | Charlie Conacher, Tor |
| 1936 | Eddie Shore, Bos | 16 assists in 46 games as defenseman | Hooley Smith, Mtl M |
| 1937 | Babe Siebert, Mtl | 28 points | Lionel Conacher, Mtl M |
| 1938 | Eddie Shore, Bos | 17 points in 47 games as defenseman | Paul Thompson, Chi |
| 1939 | Toe Blake, Mtl | led NHL in points (47) | Syl Apps, Tor |
| 1940 | Ebbie Goodfellow, Det | 28 points | Syl Apps, Tor |
| 1941 | Bill Cowley, Bos | led NHL in assists (45) and points (62) | Dit Clapper, Bos |
| 1942 | Tom Anderson, Bos | 41 points | Syl Apps, Tor |
| 1943 | Bill Cowley, Bos | led NHL in assists (45) | Doug Bentley, Chi |
| 1944 | Babe Pratt, Tor | 57 points in 50 games | Bill Cowley, Bos |
| 1945 | Elmer Lach, Mtl | led NHL in assists (54) and points (80) | Maurice Richard, Mtl |
| 1946 | Max Bentley, Chi | 61 points in 47 games | Gaye Stewart, Tor |
| 1947 | Maurice Richard, Mtl | led NHL in goals (45); 26 assists | Milt Schmidt, Bos |
| 1948 | Buddy O'Connor, NYR | 60 points in 60 games | Frank Brimsek, Bos |
| 1949 | Sid Abel, Det | 28 goals, 26 assists | Bill Durnan, Mtl |
| 1950 | Charlie Rayner, NYR | 6 shutouts | Ted Kennedy, Tor |
| 1951 | Milt Schmidt, Bos | 61 points in 62 games | Maurice Richard, Mtl |
| 1952 | Gordie Howe, Det | led NHL in goals (47) and points (86) | Elmer Lach, Mtl |
| 1953 | Gordie Howe, Det | led NHL in goals (49) and points (95) | Al Rollins, Chi |
| 1954 | Al Rollins, Chi | 5 shutouts | Red Kelly, Det |
| 1955 | Ted Kennedy, Tor | 52 points | Harry Lumley, Tor |
| 1956 | Jean Beliveau, Mtl | led NHL in goals (47) and points (88) | Tod Sloan, Tor |
| 1957 | Gordie Howe, Det | led NHL in goals (44) and points (89) | Jean Beliveau, Mtl |
| 1959 | Andy Bathgate, NYR | 74 points in 70 games | Gordie Howe, Det |
| 1960 | Gordie Howe, Det | 45 assists, 73 points | Bobby Hull, Chi |
| 1961 | Bernie Geoffrion, Mtl | 50 goals, 95 points | Johnny Bower, Tor |
| 1962 | Jacques Plante, Mtl | 42 wins, 2.37 goals against avg. | Doug Harvey, NYR |
| 1963 | Gordie Howe, Det | 47 assists, 73 points | Stan Mikita, Chi |
| 1964 | Jean Beliveau, Mtl | 50 assists, 78 points | Bobby Hull, Chi |
| 1965 | Bobby Hull, Chi | 39 goals, 32 assists | Norm Ullman, Det |
| 1966 | Bobby Hull, Chi | led NHL in goals (54) and points (97) | Jean Beliveau, Mtl |
| 1967 | Stan Mikita, Chi | led NHL in assists (62) and points (97) | Ed Giacomin, NYR |
| 1968 | Stan Mikita, Chi | 40 goals, 47 assists | Jean Beliveau, Mtl |
| 1969 | Phil Esposito, Bos | led NHL in assists (77) and points (126) | Jean Beliveau, Mtl |
| 1970 | Bobby Orr, Bos | led NHL in assists (87) and points (120) | Tony Esposito, Chi |
| 1971 | Bobby Orr, Bos | 102 assists, 139 points | Tony Esposito, Chi |
| 1972 | Bobby Orr, Bos | 80 assists, 117 points | Ken Dryden, Mtl |
| 1973 | Bobby Clarke, Phil | 67 assists, 104 points | Phil Esposito, Bos |
| 1974 | Phil Esposito, Bos | led NHL in goals (68) and points (145) | Bernie Parent, Phil |
| 1975 | Bobby Clarke, Phil | 89 assists, 116 points | Rogatien Vachon, LA |
| 1976 | Bobby Clarke, Phil | 89 assists, 119 points | Denis Potvin, NYI |
| 1977 | Guy Lafleur, Mtl | led NHL in assists (80) and points (136) | Bobby Clarke, Phil |
| 1978 | Guy Lafleur, Mtl | led NHL in assists (60) and points (132) | Bryan Trottier, NYI |
| 1979 | Bryan Trottier, NYI | led NHL in assists (87) and points (134) | Guy Lafleur, Mtl |
| 1980 | Wayne Gretzky, Edm | 51 goals, 86 assists | Marcel Dionne, LA |
| 1981 | Wayne Gretzky, Edm | led NHL in assists (109) and points (164) | Mike Liut, StL |
| 1982 | Wayne Gretzky, Edm | NHL-record 92 goals and 212 points | Bryan Trottier, NYI |
| 1983 | Wayne Gretzky, Edm | led NHL in goals (71) and points (196) | Pete Peeters, Bos |
| 1984 | Wayne Gretzky, Edm | led NHL in goals (87) and points (205) | Rod Langway, Wash |
| 1985 | Wayne Gretzky, Edm | led NHL in goals (73) and points (208) | Dale Hawerchuk, Winn |
| 1986 | Wayne Gretzky, Edm | NHL-record 163 assists and 215 points | Mario Lemieux, Pitt |

## Hart Memorial Trophy (Cont.)

| Year | Winner | Key Statistics | Runner-Up |
|------|--------|----------------|-----------|
| 1987 | Wayne Gretzky, Edm | led NHL in assists (121) and points (183) | Ray Bourque, Bos |
| 1988 | Mario Lemieux, Pitt | led NHL in goals (70) and points (168) | Grant Fuhr, Edm |
| 1989 | Wayne Gretzky, LA | 114 assists, 168 points | Mario Lemieux, Pitt |
| 1990 | Mark Messier, Edm | 84 assists, 129 points | Ray Bourque, Bos |
| 1991 | Brett Hull, StL | led NHL in goals (86); 131 points | Wayne Gretzky, LA |
| 1992 | Mark Messier, NYR | 72 assists, 107 points | Patrick Roy, Mtl |
| 1993 | Mario Lemieux, Pitt | 69 goals, 91 assists in 60 games | Doug Gilmour, Tor |
| 1994 | Sergei Fedorov, Det | 56 goals, 64 assists | Dominik Hasek, Buff |
| 1995 | Eric Lindros, Phil | 29 goals, 41 assists in 46 games | Jaromir Jagr, Pitt |
| 1996 | Mario Lemieux, Pitt | led NHL in goals (69) and points (161) | Mark Messier, NYR |
| 1997 | Dominik Hasek, Buff | 5 shutouts, 2.27 goals against | Paul Kariya, Ana |
| 1998 | Dominik Hasek, Buff | 13 shutouts, 2.09 goals against | Jaromir Jagr, Pitt |
| 1999 | Jaromir Jagr, Pitt | 44 goals, 127 points | Alexei Yashin, Ott |
| 2000 | Chris Pronger, StL | 62 points, +52 plus/minus rating | Jaromir Jagr, Pitt |
| 2001 | Joe Sakic, Col | 118 points, +45 plus/minus rating | Mario Lemieux, Pitt |

## Art Ross Trophy

Awarded annually "to the player who leads the league in scoring points at the end of the regular season." The trophy was presented to the NHL in 1947 by Arthur Howie Ross, former manager-coach of the Boston Bruins. The tie-breakers, in order, are as follows: (1) player with most goals, (2) player with fewer games played, (3) player scoring first goal of the season. Bobby Orr is the only defenseman in NHL history to win this trophy, and he won it twice (1970 and 1975).

| Year | Winner | Pts | Year | Winner | Pts |
|------|--------|-----|------|--------|-----|
| 1919 | Newsy Lalonde, Mtl | 44 | 1957 | Gordie Howe, Det | 89 |
| 1920 | Joe Malone, Que | 30 | 1958 | Dickie Moore, Mtl | 84 |
| 1921 | Newsy Lalonde, Mtl | 48 | 1959 | Dickie Moore, Mtl | 96 |
| 1922 | Punch Broadbent, Ott | 41 | 1960 | Bobby Hull, Chi | 81 |
| 1923 | Babe Dye, Tor | 46 | 1961 | Bernie Geoffrion, Mtl | 95 |
| 1924 | Cy Denneny, Ott | 37 | 1962 | Bobby Hull, Chi | 84 |
| 1925 | Babe Dye, Tor | 23 | 1963 | Gordie Howe, Det | 86 |
| 1926 | Nels Stewart, Mtl M | 44 | 1964 | Stan Mikita, Chi | 89 |
| 1927 | Bill Cook, NYR | 42 | 1965 | Stan Mikita, Chi | 87 |
| 1928 | Howie Morenz, Mtl | 37 | 1966 | Bobby Hull, Chi | 97 |
| 1929 | Ace Bailey, Tor | 51 | 1967 | Stan Mikita, Chi | 97 |
| 1930 | Cooney Weiland, Bos | 32 | 1968 | Stan Mikita, Chi | 87 |
| 1931 | Howie Morenz, Mtl | 73 | 1969 | Phil Esposito, Bos | 126 |
| 1932 | Harvey Jackson, Tor | 51 | 1970 | Bobby Orr, Bos | 120 |
| 1933 | Bill Cook, NYR | 53 | 1971 | Phil Esposito, Bos | 152 |
| 1934 | Charlie Conacher, Tor | 50 | 1972 | Phil Esposito, Bos | 133 |
| 1935 | Charlie Conacher, Tor | 57 | 1973 | Phil Esposito, Bos | 130 |
| 1936 | Sweeney Schriner, NYA | 45 | 1974 | Phil Esposito, Bos | 145 |
| 1937 | Sweeney Schriner, NYA | 46 | 1975 | Bobby Orr, Bos | 135 |
| 1938 | Gordie Drillon, Tor | 52 | 1976 | Guy Lafleur, Mtl | 125 |
| 1939 | Toe Blake, Mtl | 47 | 1977 | Guy Lafleur, Mtl | 136 |
| 1940 | Milt Schmidt, Bos | 52 | 1978 | Guy Lafleur, Mtl | 132 |
| 1941 | Bill Cowley, Bos | 62 | 1979 | Bryan Trottier, NYI | 134 |
| 1942 | Bryan Hextall, NYR | 56 | 1980 | Marcel Dionne, LA | 137 |
| 1943 | Doug Bentley, Chi | 73 | 1981 | Wayne Gretzky, Edm | 164 |
| 1944 | Herb Cain, Bos | 82 | 1982 | Wayne Gretzky, Edm | 212 |
| 1945 | Elmer Lach, Mtl | 80 | 1983 | Wayne Gretzky, Edm | 196 |
| 1946 | Max Bentley, Chi | 61 | 1984 | Wayne Gretzky, Edm | 205 |
| 1947 | *Max Bentley, Chi | 72 | 1985 | Wayne Gretzky, Edm | 208 |
| 1948 | Elmer Lach, Mtl | 61 | 1986 | Wayne Gretzky, Edm | 215 |
| 1949 | Roy Conacher, Chi | 68 | 1987 | Wayne Gretzky, Edm | 183 |
| 1950 | Ted Lindsay, Det | 78 | 1988 | Mario Lemieux, Pitt | 168 |
| 1951 | Gordie Howe, Det | 86 | 1989 | Mario Lemieux, Pitt | 199 |
| 1952 | Gordie Howe, Det | 86 | 1990 | Wayne Gretzky, LA | 142 |
| 1953 | Gordie Howe, Det | 95 | 1991 | Wayne Gretzky, LA | 163 |
| 1954 | Gordie Howe, Det | 81 | 1992 | Mario Lemieux, Pitt | 131 |
| 1955 | Bernie Geoffrion, Mtl | 75 | 1993 | Mario Lemieux, Pitt | 160 |
| 1956 | Jean Beliveau, Mtl | 88 | 1994 | Wayne Gretzky, LA | 130 |
| | | | 1995 | Jaromir Jagr, Pitt | 70 |

## Art Ross Trophy (Cont.)

| | | | | | |
|---|---|---|---|---|---|
| 1996 | Mario Lemieux, Pitt | 161 | 2000 | Jaromir Jagr, Pitt | 96 |
| 1997 | Mario Lemieux, Pitt | 122 | 2001 | Jaromir Jagr, Pitt | 121 |
| 1998 | Jaromir Jagr, Pitt | 102 | | | |
| 1999 | Jaromir Jagr, Pitt | 127 | | | |

Note: Listing includes scoring leaders prior to inception of Art Ross Trophy in 1947–48.

## Lady Byng Memorial Trophy

Awarded annually "to the player adjudged to have exhibited the best type of sportsmanship and gentlemanly conduct combined with a high standard of playing ability." Lady Byng, who first presented the trophy in 1925, was the wife of Canada's Governor-General. She donated a second trophy in 1936 after the first was given permanently to Frank Boucher of the New York Rangers, who won it seven times in eight seasons. Stan Mikita, one of the league's most penalized players during his early years in the NHL, won the trophy twice late in his career (1967 and 1968).

| | | | | | |
|---|---|---|---|---|---|
| 1925 | Frank Nighbor, Ott | 1952 | Sid Smith, Tor | 1979 | Bob MacMillan, Atl |
| 1926 | Frank Nighbor, Ott | 1953 | Red Kelly, Det | 1980 | Wayne Gretzky, Edm |
| 1927 | Billy Burch, NYA | 1954 | Red Kelly, Det | 1981 | Rick Kehoe, Pitt |
| 1928 | Frank Boucher, NYR | 1955 | Sid Smith, Tor | 1982 | Rick Middleton, Bos |
| 1929 | Frank Boucher, NYR | 1956 | Earl Reibel, Det | 1983 | Mike Bossy, NYI |
| 1930 | Frank Boucher, NYR | 1957 | Andy Hebenton, NYR | 1984 | Mike Bossy, NYI |
| 1931 | Frank Boucher, NYR | 1958 | Camille Henry, NYR | 1985 | Jari Kurri, Edm |
| 1932 | Joe Primeau, Tor | 1959 | Alex Delvecchio, Det | 1986 | Mike Bossy, NYI |
| 1933 | Frank Boucher, NYR | 1960 | Don McKenney, Bos | 1987 | Joe Mullen, Cgy |
| 1934 | Frank Boucher, NYR | 1961 | Red Kelly, Tor | 1988 | Mats Naslund, Mtl |
| 1935 | Frank Boucher, NYR | 1962 | Dave Keon, Tor | 1989 | Joe Mullen, Cgy |
| 1936 | Doc Romnes, Chi | 1963 | Dave Keon, Tor | 1990 | Brett Hull, StL |
| 1937 | Marty Barry, Det | 1964 | Ken Wharram, Chi | 1991 | Wayne Gretzky, LA |
| 1938 | Gordie Drillon, Tor | 1965 | Bobby Hull, Chi | 1992 | Wayne Gretzky, LA |
| 1939 | Clint Smith, NYR | 1966 | Alex Delvecchio, Det | 1993 | Pierre Turgeon, NYI |
| 1940 | Bobby Bauer, Bos | 1967 | Stan Mikita, Chi | 1994 | Wayne Gretzky, LA |
| 1941 | Bobby Bauer, Bos | 1968 | Stan Mikita, Chi | 1995 | Ron Francis, Pitt |
| 1942 | Syl Apps, Tor | 1969 | Alex Delvecchio, Det | 1996 | Paul Kariya, Ana |
| 1943 | Max Bentley, Chi | 1970 | Phil Goyette, StL | 1997 | Paul Karlya, Ana |
| 1944 | Clint Smith, Chi | 1971 | John Bucyk, Bos | 1998 | Ron Francis, Pitt |
| 1945 | Billy Mosienko, Chi | 1972 | Jean Ratelle, NYR | 1999 | Wayne Gretzky, NYR |
| 1946 | Toe Blake, Mtl | 1973 | Gilbert Perreault, Buff | 2000 | Pavol Demitra, StL |
| 1947 | Bobby Bauer, Bos | 1974 | John Bucyk, Bos | 2001 | Joe Sakic, Col |
| 1948 | Buddy O'Connor, NYR | 1975 | Marcel Dionne, Det | | |
| 1949 | Bill Quackenbush, Det | 1976 | Jean Ratelle, NYR-Bos | | |
| 1950 | Edgar Laprade, NYR | 1977 | Marcel Dionne, LA | | |
| 1951 | Red Kelly, Det | 1978 | Butch Goring, LA | | |

## James Norris Memorial Trophy

Awarded annually "to the defense player who demonstrates throughout the season the greatest all-around ability in the position." James Norris was the former owner-president of the Detroit Red Wings. Bobby Orr holds the record for most consecutive times winning the award (eight, 1968–1975).

| | | | | | |
|---|---|---|---|---|---|
| 1954 | Red Kelly, Det | 1971 | Bobby Orr, Bos | 1988 | Ray Bourque, Bos |
| 1955 | Doug Harvey, Mtl | 1972 | Bobby Orr, Bos | 1989 | Chris Chelios, Mtl |
| 1956 | Doug Harvey, Mtl | 1973 | Bobby Orr, Bos | 1990 | Ray Bourque, Bos |
| 1957 | Doug Harvey, Mtl | 1974 | Bobby Orr, Bos | 1991 | Ray Bourque, Bos |
| 1958 | Doug Harvey, Mtl | 1975 | Bobby Orr, Bos | 1992 | Brian Leetch, NYR |
| 1959 | Tom Johnson, Mtl | 1976 | Denis Potvin, NYI | 1993 | Chris Chelios, Chi |
| 1960 | Doug Harvey, Mtl | 1977 | Larry Robinson, Mtl | 1994 | Ray Bourque, Bos |
| 1961 | Doug Harvey, Mtl | 1978 | Denis Potvin, NYI | 1995 | Paul Coffey, Det |
| 1962 | Doug Harvey, NYR | 1979 | Denis Potvin, NYI | 1996 | Chris Chelios, Chi |
| 1963 | Pierre Pilote, Chi | 1980 | Larry Robinson, Mtl | 1997 | Brian Leetch, NYR |
| 1964 | Pierre Pilote, Chi | 1981 | Randy Carlyle, Pitt | 1998 | Rob Blake, LA |
| 1965 | Pierre Pilote, Chi | 1982 | Doug Wilson, Chi | 1999 | Al MacInnis, StL |
| 1966 | Jacques Laperriere, Mtl | 1983 | Rod Langway, Wash | 2000 | Chris Pronger, StL |
| 1967 | Harry Howell, NYR | 1984 | Rod Langway, Wash | 2001 | Nicklas Lidstrom, Det |
| 1968 | Bobby Orr, Bos | 1985 | Paul Coffey, Edm | | |
| 1969 | Bobby Orr, Bos | 1986 | Paul Coffey, Edm | | |
| 1970 | Bobby Orr, Bos | 1987 | Ray Bourque, Bos | | |

## Calder Memorial Trophy

Awarded annually "to the player selected as the most proficient in his first year of competition in the National Hockey League." Frank Calder was a former NHL president. Sergei Makarov, who won the award in 1989–90, was the oldest recipient of the trophy, at 31. Players are no longer eligible for the award if they are 26 or older as of September 15th of the season in question.

| | | |
|---|---|---|
| 1933 ......Carl Voss, Det | 1957 ......Larry Regan, Bos | 1981 ......Peter Stastny, Que |
| 1934 ......Russ Blinko, Mtl M | 1958 ......Frank Mahovlich, Tor | 1982 ......Dale Hawerchuk, Winn |
| 1935 ......Dave Schriner, NYA | 1959 ......Ralph Backstrom, Mtl | 1983 ......Steve Larmer, Chi |
| 1936 ......Mike Karakas, Chi | 1960 ......Bill Hay, Chi | 1984 ......Tom Barrasso, Buff |
| 1937 ......Syl Apps, Tor | 1961 ......Dave Keon, Tor | 1985 ......Mario Lemieux, Pitt |
| 1938 ......Cully Dahlstrom, Chi | 1962 ......Bobby Rousseau, Mtl | 1986 ......Gary Suter, Cgy |
| 1939 ......Frank Brimsek, Bos | 1963 ......Kent Douglas, Tor | 1987 ......Luc Robitaille, LA |
| 1940 ......Kilby MacDonald, NYR | 1964 ......Jacques Laperriere, Mtl | 1988 ......Joe Nieuwendyk, Cgy |
| 1941 ......Johnny Quilty, Mtl | 1965 ......Roger Crozier, Det | 1989 ......Brian Leetch, NYR |
| 1942 ......Grant Warwick, NYR | 1966 ......Brit Selby, Tor | 1990 ......Sergei Makarov, Cgy |
| 1943 ......Gaye Stewart, Tor | 1967 ......Bobby Orr, Bos | 1991 ......Ed Belfour, Chi |
| 1944 ......Gus Bodnar, Tor | 1968 ......Derek Sanderson, Bos | 1992 ......Pavel Bure, Van |
| 1945 ......Frank McCool, Tor | 1969 ......Danny Grant, Minn | 1993 ......Teemu Selanne, Winn |
| 1946 ......Edgar Laprade, NYR | 1970 ......Tony Esposito, Chi | 1994 ......Martin Brodeur, NJ |
| 1947 ......Howie Meeker, Tor | 1971 ......Gilbert Perreault, Buff | 1995 ......Peter Forsberg, Que |
| 1948 ......Jim McFadden, Det | 1972 ......Ken Dryden, Mtl | 1996 ......Daniel Alfredsson, Ott |
| 1949 ......Pentti Lund, NYR | 1973 ......Steve Vickers, NYR | 1997 ......Bryan Berard, NYI |
| 1950 ......Jack Gelineau, Bos | 1974 ......Denis Potvin, NYI | 1998 ......Sergei Samsonov, Bos |
| 1951 ......Terry Sawchuk, Det | 1975 ......Eric Vail, Atl | 1999 ......Chris Drury, Col |
| 1952 ......Bernie Geoffrion, Mtl | 1976 ......Bryan Trottier, NYI | 2000 ......Scott Gomez, NJ |
| 1953 ......Gump Worsley, NYR | 1977 ......Willi Plett, Atl | 2001 ......Evgeni Nabokov, SJ |
| 1954 ......Camille Henry, NYR | 1978 ......Mike Bossy, NYI | |
| 1955 ......Ed Litzenberger, Chi | 1979 ......Bobby Smith, Minn | |
| 1956 ......Glenn Hall, Det | 1980 ......Ray Bourque, Bos | |

## Vezina Trophy

Awarded annually "to the goalkeeper adjudged to be the best at his position." The trophy is named after Georges Vezina, an outstanding goalie for the Montreal Canadiens who collapsed during a game on November 28, 1925, and died four months later of tuberculosis. The general managers of the NHL teams vote on the award.

| | | |
|---|---|---|
| 1927 ......George Hainsworth, Mtl | 1957 ......Jacques Plante, Mtl | 1979 ........Ken Dryden, Mtl |
| 1928 ......George Hainsworth, Mtl | 1958 ......Jacques Plante, Mtl | ............Michel Larocque, Mtl |
| 1929 ......George Hainsworth, Mtl | 1959 ......Jacques Plante, Mtl | 1980 ........Bob Sauve, Buff |
| 1930 ......Tiny Thompson, Bos | 1960 ......Jacques Plante, Mtl | ............Don Edwards, Buff |
| 1931 ......Roy Worters, NYA | 1961 ......Johnny Bower, Tor | 1981 ........Richard Sevigny, Mtl |
| 1932 ......Charlie Gardiner, Chi | 1962 ......Jacques Plante, Mtl | ............Denis Herron, Mtl |
| 1933 ......Tiny Thompson, Bos | 1963 ......Glenn Hall, Chi | ............Michel Larocque, Mtl |
| 1934 ......Charlie Gardiner, Chi | 1964 ........Charlie Hodge, Mtl | 1982 ........Billy Smith, NYI |
| 1935 ......Lorne Chabot, Chi | 1965 ......Terry Sawchuk, Tor | 1983 ........Pete Peeters, Bos |
| 1936 ......Tiny Thompson, Bos | ............Johnny Bower, Tor | 1984 ........Tom Barrasso, Buff |
| 1937 ......Normie Smith, Det | 1966 ........Gump Worsley, Mtl | 1985 ........Pelle Lindbergh, Phil |
| 1938 ......Tiny Thompson, Bos | ............Charlie Hodge, Mtl | 1986 ........John Vanbiesbrouck, NYR |
| 1939 ......Frank Brimsek, Bos | 1967 ........Glenn Hall, Chi | 1987 ........Ron Hextall, Phil |
| 1940 ......Dave Kerr, NYR | ............Rogie Vachon, Mtl | 1988 ........Grant Fuhr, Edm |
| 1941 ......Turk Broda, Tor | 1969 ........Jacques Plante, StL | 1989 ........Patrick Roy, Mtl |
| 1942 ......Frank Brimsek, Bos | ............Glenn Hall, StL | 1990 ........Patrick Roy, Mtl |
| 1943 ......Johnny Mowers, Det | 1970 ........Tony Esposito, Chi | 1991 ........Ed Belfour, Chi |
| 1944 ......Bill Durnan, Mtl | 1971 ........Ed Giacomin, NYR | 1992 ........Patrick Roy, Mtl |
| 1945 ......Bill Durnan, Mtl | ............Gilles Villemure, NYR | 1993 ........Ed Belfour, Chi |
| 1946 ......Bill Durnan, Mtl | 1972 ........Tony Esposito, Chi | 1994 ........Dominik Hasek, Buff |
| 1947 ......Bill Durnan, Mtl | ............Gary Smith, Chi | 1995 ........Dominik Hasek, Buff |
| 1948 ......Turk Broda, Tor | 1973 ........Ken Dryden, Mtl | 1996 ........Jim Carey, Wash |
| 1949 ......Bill Durnan, Mtl | 1974 ........Bernie Parent, Phil | 1997 ........Dominik Hasek, Buff |
| 1950 ......Bill Durnan, Mtl | ............Tony Esposito, Chi | 1998 ........Dominik Hasek, Buff |
| 1951 ......Al Rollins, Tor | 1975 ........Bernie Parent, Phil | 1999 ........Dominik Hasek, Buff |
| 1952 ......Terry Sawchuk, Det | 1976 ........Ken Dryden, Mtl | 2000 ........Olaf Kolzig, Wash |
| 1953 ......Terry Sawchuk, Det | 1977 ........Ken Dryden, Mtl | 2001 ........Dominik Hasek, Buff |
| 1954 ......Harry Lumley, Tor | ............Michel Larocque, Mtl | |
| 1955 ......Terry Sawchuk, Det | 1978 ........Ken Dryden, Mtl | |
| 1956 ......Jacques Plante, Mtl | ............Michel Larocque, Mtl | |

## Selke Trophy

Awarded annually "to the forward who best excels in the defensive aspects of the game." The trophy is named after Frank J. Selke, the architect of the Montreal Canadians dynasty that won five consecutive Stanley Cups in the late '50s. The winner is selected by a vote of the Professional Hockey Writers Association.

| | | |
|---|---|---|
| 1978........Bob Gainey, Mtl | 1987........Dave Poulin, Phil | 1996........Sergei Fedorov, Det |
| 1979........Bob Gainey, Mtl | 1988........Guy Carbonneau, Mtl | 1997........Michael Peca, Buff |
| 1980........Bob Gainey, Mtl | 1989........Guy Carbonneau, Mtl | 1998........Jere Lehtinen, Dall |
| 1981........Bob Gainey, Mtl | 1990........Rick Meagher, StL | 1999........Jere Lehtinen, Dall |
| 1982........Steve Kasper, Bos | 1991........Dirk Graham, Chi | 2000........Steve Yzerman, Det |
| 1983........Bobby Clarke, Phil | 1992........Guy Carbonneau, Mtl | 2001........John Madden, NJ |
| 1984........Doug Jarvis, Wash | 1993........Doug Gilmour, Tor | |
| 1985........Craig Ramsay, Buff | 1994........Sergei Fedorov, Det | |
| 1986........Troy Murray, Chi | 1995........Ron Francis, Pitt | |

## Adams Award

Awarded annually "to the NHL coach adjudged to have contributed the most to his team's success." The trophy is named in honor of Jack Adams, longtime coach and general manager of the Detroit Red Wings. The winner is selected by a vote of the National Hockey League Broadcasters' Association.

| | | |
|---|---|---|
| 1974 .....Fred Shero, Phil | 1984 .....Bryan Murray, Wash | 1994 .....Jacques Lemaire, NJ |
| 1975 .....Bob Pulford, LA | 1985 .....Mike Keenan, Phil | 1995 .....Marc Crawford, Que |
| 1976 .....Don Cherry, Bos | 1986 .....Glen Sather, Edm | 1996 .....Scotty Bowman, Det |
| 1977 .....Scott Bowman, Mtl | 1987 .....Jacques Demers, Det | 1997 .....Ted Nolan, Buff |
| 1978 .....Bobby Kromm, Det | 1988 .....Jacques Demers, Det | 1998 .....Pat Burns, Bos |
| 1979 .....Al Arbour, NYI | 1989 .....Pat Burns, Mtl | 1999 .....Jacques Martin, Ott |
| 1980 .....Pat Quinn, Phil | 1990 .....Bob Murdoch, Winn | 2000 .....Joel Quenneville, StL |
| 1981 .....Red Berenson, StL | 1991 .....Brian Sutter, StL | 2001 .....Bill Barber, Phil |
| 1982 .....Tom Watt, Winn | 1992 .....Pat Quinn, Van | |
| 1983 .....Orval Tessier, Chi | 1993 .....Pat Burns, Tor | |

## Quick Fix? Not This Time

Jaromir Jagr was at a Capitals introductory press conference in July 2001, cracking wise, because 1) he is a jokester, and 2) Rangers president Glen Sather had been unwilling to to trade two prospects to the Penguins for the star right winger, who seemed destined for Broadway.

For normally quick-fix New York, this reluctance to part with 1999 first-round draft picks Pavel Brendl and Jamie Lundmark was a principled stand—albeit the kind that blew up in the team's face in 1999. That's when Neil Smith, Sather's predecessor, hung on to slow-developing center Manny Malhotra, breaking a deal to bring Pavel Bure from the Canucks. (Malhotra has yet to get much playing time in the NHL.) So, are Brendl and Lundmark, juniors who were in the Western Hockey League in 2000–01, good enough to justify passing on Jagr?

"They're all genuine prospects," says Canadiens assistant G.M. Martin Madden, who worked for the Rangers at the time of the '99 draft. "Brendl's going to be a scorer on the first line. Lundmark looks like a second-line center who'll give you something every night. When you're rebuilding, you can't keep starting the process over every year. Five years from now, I think Glen's decision will have served the Rangers well."

# Career Records

## Alltime Point Leaders

| | Player | Yrs | GP | G | A | Pts | Pts/game |
|---|---|---|---|---|---|---|---|
| 1. | Wayne Gretzky, Edm, LA, StL, NYR | 20 | 1487 | 894 | 1963 | 2857 | 1.921 |
| 2. | Gordie Howe, Det, Hart | 26 | 1767 | 801 | 1049 | 1850 | 1.047 |
| 3. | *Mark Messier, Edm, NYR, Van | 22 | 1561 | 651 | 1130 | 1781 | 1.141 |
| 4. | Marcel Dionne, Det, LA, NYR | 18 | 1348 | 731 | 1040 | 1771 | 1.314 |
| 5. | *Ron Francis, Hart, Pitt, Car | 20 | 1489 | 487 | 1137 | 1624 | 1.091 |
| 6. | *Steve Yzerman, Det | 18 | 1310 | 645 | 969 | 1614 | 1.232 |
| 7. | Phil Esposito, Chi, Bos, NYR | 18 | 1282 | 717 | 873 | 1590 | 1.240 |
| 8. | *Ray Bourque, Bos, Col | 22 | 1612 | 410 | 1169 | 1579 | .980 |
| 9. | *Mario Lemieux, Pitt | 13 | 788 | 648 | 922 | 1570 | 1.992 |
| 10. | *Paul Coffey, eight teams | 21 | 1409 | 396 | 1135 | 1531 | 1.087 |
| 11. | Stan Mikita, Chi | 22 | 1394 | 541 | 926 | 1467 | 1.052 |
| 12. | Bryan Trottier, NYI, Pitt | 18 | 1279 | 524 | 901 | 1425 | 1.114 |
| 13. | Dale Hawerchuk, Winn, Buff, StL, Phil | 16 | 1188 | 518 | 891 | 1409 | 1.186 |
| 14. | Jari Kurri, Edm, LA, NYR, Ana, Col | 17 | 1251 | 601 | 797 | 1397 | 1.118 |
| 15. | John Bucyk, Det, Bos | 23 | 1540 | 556 | 813 | 1369 | .889 |

*Active in 2000–01.

## Alltime Goal-Scoring Leaders

| | Player | Yrs | GP | G | G/game |
|---|---|---|---|---|---|
| 1. | Wayne Gretzky, Edm, LA, StL, NYR | 20 | 1487 | 894 | .601 |
| 2. | Gordie Howe, Det, Hart | 26 | 1767 | 801 | .453 |
| 3. | Marcel Dionne, Det, LA, NYR | 18 | 1348 | 731 | .542 |
| 4. | Phil Esposito, Chi, Bos, NYR. | 18 | 1282 | 717 | .559 |
| 5. | Mike Gartner, Wash, Minn, NYR, Tor, Phoe | 19 | 1432 | 708 | .494 |
| 6. | *Mark Messier, Edm, NYR, Van | 22 | 1561 | 651 | .417 |
| 7. | *Brett Hull, Cal, StL, Dall | 16 | 1019 | 649 | .637 |
| 8. | *Mario Lemieux, Pitt | 13 | 788 | 648 | .822 |
| 9. | *Steve Yzerman, Det. | 18 | 1310 | 645 | .492 |
| 10. | Bobby Hull, Chi, Winn, Hart | 16 | 1063 | 610 | .574 |

*Active in 2000–01.

## Alltime Assist Leaders

| | Player | Yrs | GP | A | A/game |
|---|---|---|---|---|---|
| 1. | Wayne Gretzky, Edm, LA, StL, NYR | 20 | 1487 | 1963 | 1.320 |
| 2. | *Ray Bourque, Bos, Col | 22 | 1612 | 1169 | .725 |
| 3. | *Ron Francis, Hart, Pitt, Car | 20 | 1489 | 1135 | .763 |
| 4. | *Paul Coffey, eight teams | 21 | 1409 | 1135 | .806 |
| 5. | *Mark Messier, Edm, NYR, Van | 22 | 1561 | 1130 | .724 |
| 6. | Gordie Howe, Det, Hart | 26 | 1767 | 1049 | .594 |
| 7. | Marcel Dionne, Det, LA, NYR | 18 | 1348 | 1040 | .771 |
| 8. | *Steve Yzerman, Det | 18 | 1310 | 969 | .740 |
| 9. | Adam Oates, Det, StL, Bos, Wash | 16 | 1130 | 963 | .852 |
| 10. | *Larry Murphy, six teams | 21 | 1615 | 929 | .575 |

*Active player in 2000–01.

## THEY SAID IT

*Tie Domi, Maple Leafs enforcer,
after grappling with a heckler
who tumbled into the penalty box
during a game in Philadelphia:
"It's nice to see the fans get
involved, I guess."*

## Alltime Penalty Minutes Leaders

| | Player | Yrs | GP | PIM | Min/game |
|---|---|---|---|---|---|
| 1. | Dave Williams, Tor, Van, Det, LA, Hart | 14 | 962 | 3966 | 4.12 |
| 2. | Dale Hunter, Que, Wash, Col | 19 | 1407 | 3565 | 2.53 |
| 3. | Marty McSorley, Pitt, Edm, LA, NYR, SJ, Bos | 17 | 961 | 3381 | 3.52 |
| 4. | Tim Hunter, Calg, Que, Van, SJ | 16 | 815 | 3146 | 3.86 |
| 5. | *Bob Probert, Det, Chi | 15 | 874 | 3124 | 3.57 |
| 6. | Chris Nilan, Mtl, NYR, Bos | 13 | 688 | 3043 | 4.42 |
| 7. | *Rick Tocchet, Phil, Pitt, LA, Bos, Wash, Phoe | 17 | 1130 | 2946 | 2.61 |
| 8. | *Rob Ray, Buff | 12 | 777 | 2897 | 3.73 |
| 9. | *Craig Berube, Phil, Tor, Cgy, Wash | 15 | 933 | 2885 | 3.09 |
| 10. | *Tie Domi, Tor, NYR, Winn | 12 | 710 | 2870 | 4.04 |

*Active in 2000–01.

## Goaltending Records

### ALLTIME WIN LEADERS

| Goaltender | W | L | T | Pct |
|---|---|---|---|---|
| *Patrick Roy, Mtl, Col | 484 | 277 | 110 | .619 |
| Terry Sawchuk, five teams | 447 | 330 | 173 | .562 |
| Jacques Plante, five teams | 434 | 246 | 147 | .614 |
| Tony Esposito, Mtl, Chi | 423 | 306 | 152 | .566 |
| Glenn Hall, Det, Chi, StL | 407 | 327 | 163 | .545 |
| Grant Fuhr, six teams | 403 | 295 | 114 | .567 |
| *Mike Vernon, Cgy, Det, SJ, Fla | 383 | 264 | 91 | .581 |
| Andy Moog, Edm, Bos, Dall, Mtl | 372 | 209 | 88 | .622 |
| *John Vanbiesbrouck, five teams | 372 | 343 | 119 | .517 |
| Rogie Vachon, Mtl, LA, Det, Bos | 355 | 291 | 127 | .541 |

*Active in 2000–01.

### ACTIVE GOALTENDING LEADERS

| Goaltender | W | L | T | Pct |
|---|---|---|---|---|
| Chris Osgood, Det | 221 | 110 | 46 | .647 |
| Martin Brodeur, NJ | 286 | 142 | 76 | .643 |
| Patrick Roy, Mtl, Col | 484 | 277 | 110 | .619 |
| Ed Belfour, Chi, SJ, Dall | 343 | 215 | 89 | .599 |
| Mike Vernon, Cgy, Det, SJ, Fla | 383 | 264 | 91 | .581 |
| Dominik Hasek, Chi, Buff | 247 | 175 | 72 | .573 |
| Curtis Joseph, StL, Edm, Tor | 317 | 243 | 76 | .558 |
| Mike Richter, NYR | 272 | 226 | 68 | .541 |
| Olaf Kolzig, Wash | 151 | 131 | 40 | .531 |
| Nikolai Khabibulin, Winn, Phoe, TB | 127 | 114 | 30 | .524 |

Note: Ranked by winning percentage; minimum 250 games played.

### ALLTIME SHUTOUT LEADERS

| Goaltender | Team | Yrs | GP | SO |
|---|---|---|---|---|
| Terry Sawchuk | Det, Bos, Tor, LA, NYR | 21 | 971 | 103 |
| George Hainsworth | Mtl, Tor | 11 | 465 | 94 |
| Glenn Hall | Det, Chi, StL | 18 | 906 | 84 |
| Jacques Plante | Mtl, NYR, StL, Tor, Bos | 18 | 837 | 82 |
| Tiny Thompson | Bos, Det | 12 | 553 | 81 |
| Alex Connell | Ott, Det, NYA, Mtl M | 12 | 417 | 81 |
| Tony Esposito | Mtl, Chi | 16 | 886 | 76 |
| Lorne Chabot | NYR, Tor, Mtl, Chi, Mtl M, NYA | 11 | 411 | 73 |
| Harry Lumley | Det, NYR, Chi, Tor, Bos | 16 | 804 | 71 |
| Roy Worters | Pitt Plr, NYA, *Mtl | 12 | 484 | 66 |

*Played 1 game for Canadiens in 1929–30, not a shutout.

### ALLTIME GOALS AGAINST AVERAGE LEADERS (PRE-1950)

| Goaltender | Team | Yrs | GP | GA | GAA |
|---|---|---|---|---|---|
| George Hainsworth | Mtl, Tor | 11 | 465 | 937 | 1.91 |
| Alex Connell | Ott, Det, NYA, Mtl M | 12 | 417 | 830 | 1.91 |
| Chuck Gardiner | Chi | 7 | 316 | 664 | 2.02 |
| Lorne Chabot | NYR, Tor, Mtl, Chi, Mtl M, NYA | 11 | 411 | 861 | 2.04 |
| Tiny Thompson | Bos, Det | 12 | 553 | 1183 | 2.08 |

### ALLTIME GOALS AGAINST AVERAGE LEADERS (POST-1950)

| Goaltender | Team | Yrs | GP | GA | GAA |
|---|---|---|---|---|---|
| *Martin Brodeur | NJ | 9 | 519 | 1116 | 2.21 |
| Ken Dryden | Mtl | 8 | 397 | 870 | 2.24 |
| *Dominik Hasek | Chi, Buff | 11 | 516 | 1114 | 2.24 |
| Jacques Plante | Mtl, NYR, StL, Tor, Bos | 18 | 837 | 1965 | 2.38 |
| *Chris Osgood | Det | 8 | 389 | 900 | 2.40 |

*Active in 2000–01.
Note: Minimum 250 games played. Goals against average equals goals against per 60 minutes played.

## Coaching Records

| Coach | Team | Seasons | W | L | T | Pct |
|-------|------|---------|---|---|---|-----|
| *Scott Bowman ........... | five teams | 1967–87, 91– | 1148 | 539 | 295 | .654 |
| Toe Blake ................... | Mtl | 1955–68 | 500 | 255 | 159 | .634 |
| Glen Sather ................ | Edm | 1979–89, 93–94 | 464 | 268 | 110 | .616 |
| Fred Shero ................. | Phil, NYR | 1971–81 | 390 | 225 | 119 | .612 |
| Mike Keenan .............. | five teams | 1984–1999 | 506 | 360 | 115 | .574 |
| Emile Francis ............. | NYR, StL | 1965–77, 81–83 | 388 | 273 | 117 | .574 |
| Billy Reay .................. | Tor, Chi | 1957–59, 63–77 | 542 | 385 | 175 | .571 |
| *Terry Murray ............. | Wash, Phil, Fla | 1989– | 354 | 265 | 82 | .563 |
| Bryan Murray ............. | Wash, Det, Fla | 1981–98 | 484 | 368 | 123 | .559 |
| *Pat Burns .................. | Mtl, Tor, Bos | 1988– | 409 | 310 | 128 | .558 |

Note: Minimum 600 regular-season games. Ranked by percentage.

## Sticking to a Simple Plan

When Doug Risebrough, general manager of the expansion Minnesota Wild, was casting about for advice on building a team in 2000, one of the men he consulted was Panthers G.M. Bill Torrey, who presided over Florida's record-setting 83-point expansion season in 1993–94. Advised Torrey, "Assess what's available, develop a philosophy and stick with it."

It's no accident that Risebrough and his counterpart on the first-year Blue Jackets, Doug MacLean, adopted philosophies similar to Torrey's and were quite successful in putting together their teams. Neither club made the playoffs in 2000–01, but both beat a few Stanley Cup contenders and ran off short winning streaks. "We both learned from watching what previous expansion teams did," said MacLean after Columbus (28-39-9) split a home-and-home series against Minnesota (25-39-13) in January, 2001. "There were some things we knew we had to do." Here are four of them.

•*Get goaltending skill and depth.* The Blue Jackets wisely signed free agent Ron Tugnutt in the summer of 2000, even though they had already acquired promising Marc Denis, 23, from the Avalanche. The Wild traded for talented Stars backup Manny Fernandez (.917 save percentage) and then selected Jamie MacLennan, a former No. 1 goalie for the Blues, in the expansion draft.

•*Assemble a blend of experience and youth.* Minnesota played three rookies, including dynamic 18-year-old left wing Marian Gaborik, but was anchored by established forwards Scott Pellerin and Jim Dowd. Columbus also sent out three Calder Trophy candidates, but the Blue Jackets were led by seasoned wingers Geoff Sanderson and Steve Heinze.

•*Acquire veteran players from Europe.* Columbus relied on the playmaking of 29-year-old Norwegian center Espen Knutsen and on the two-way effectiveness of 25-year-old wing David Vyborny from the Czech Republic. Minnesota got steady play on the back line from 32-year-old Slovakian Lubomir Sekeras and 25-year-old Czech Ladislav Benysek.

•*Hire a veteran coach who believes in hands-on teaching.* The Blue Jackets' Dave King was a prominent coach in the Canadian national team program for nine years. The Wild's Jacques Lemaire implemented the trapping style that the Devils thrived on in the mid-1990s.

Of course, executing the plan isn't as easy as devising it, and MacLean and Risebrough said they were zonked by the complexities that running their teams involves. That may explain why when Torrey was asked what he would do if he were given control of an expansion team today, he replied, "Find a psychiatrist."

# Single-Season Records

## Goals

| Player | Season | GP | G | Player | Season | GP | G |
|---|---|---|---|---|---|---|---|
| Wayne Gretzky, Edm | 1981–82 | 80 | 92 | Wayne Gretzky, Edm | 1982–83 | 80 | 71 |
| Wayne Gretzky, Edm | 1983–84 | 74 | 87 | Brett Hull, StL | 1991–92 | 73 | 70 |
| Brett Hull, StL | 1990–91 | 78 | 86 | Mario Lemieux, Pitt | 1987–88 | 77 | 70 |
| Mario Lemieux, Pitt | 1988–89 | 76 | 85 | Bernie Nicholls, LA | 1988–89 | 79 | 70 |
| Alexander Mogilny, Buff | 1992–93 | 77 | 76 | Mario Lemieux, Pitt | 1992–93 | 60 | 69 |
| Phil Esposito, Bos | 1970–71 | 78 | 76 | Mario Lemieux, Pitt | 1995–96 | 70 | 69 |
| Teemu Selanne, Winn | 1992–93 | 84 | 76 | Mike Bossy, NYI | 1978–79 | 80 | 69 |
| Wayne Gretzky, Edm | 1984–85 | 80 | 73 | Phil Esposito, Bos | 1973–74 | 78 | 68 |
| Brett Hull, StL | 1989–90 | 80 | 72 | Jari Kurri, Edm | 1985–86 | 78 | 68 |
| Jari Kurri, Edm | 1984–85 | 73 | 71 | Mike Bossy, NYI | 1980–81 | 79 | 68 |

## Assists

| Player | Season | GP | A | Player | Season | GP | A |
|---|---|---|---|---|---|---|---|
| Wayne Gretzky, Edm | 1985–86 | 80 | 163 | Wayne Gretzky, LA | 1989–90 | 73 | 102 |
| Wayne Gretzky, Edm | 1984–85 | 80 | 135 | Bobby Orr, Bos | 1970–71 | 78 | 102 |
| Wayne Gretzky, Edm | 1982–83 | 80 | 125 | Mario Lemieux, Pitt | 1987–88 | 77 | 98 |
| Wayne Gretzky, LA | 1990–91 | 78 | 122 | Adam Oates, Bos | 1992–93 | 84 | 97 |
| Wayne Gretzky, Edm | 1986–87 | 79 | 121 | Doug Gilmour, Tor | 1992–93 | 83 | 95 |
| Wayne Gretzky, Edm | 1981–82 | 80 | 120 | Pat LaFontaine, Buff | 1992–93 | 84 | 95 |
| Wayne Gretzky, Edm | 1983–84 | 74 | 118 | Mario Lemieux, Pitt | 1985–86 | 79 | 93 |
| Mario Lemieux, Pitt | 1988–89 | 76 | 114 | Peter Stastny, Que | 1981–82 | 80 | 93 |
| Wayne Gretzky, LA | 1988–89 | 78 | 114 | Wayne Gretzky, LA | 1993–94 | 81 | 92 |
| Wayne Gretzky, Edm | 1987–88 | 64 | 109 | Mario Lemieux, Pitt | 1995–96 | 70 | 92 |
| Wayne Gretzky, Edm | 1980–81 | 80 | 109 | Ron Francis, Pitt | 1995–96 | 77 | 92 |

## Points

| Player | Season | G | A | Pts | Player | Season | G | A | Pts |
|---|---|---|---|---|---|---|---|---|---|
| Wayne Gretzky, Edm | 1985–86 | 52 | 163 | 215 | Wayne Gretzky, LA | 1990–91 | 41 | 122 | 163 |
| Wayne Gretzky, Edm | 1981–82 | 92 | 120 | 212 | Mario Lemieux, Pitt | 1995–96 | 69 | 92 | 161 |
| Wayne Gretzky, Edm | 1984–85 | 73 | 135 | 208 | Mario Lemieux, Pitt | 1992–93 | 69 | 91 | 160 |
| Wayne Gretzky, Edm | 1983–84 | 87 | 118 | 205 | Steve Yzerman, Det | 1988–89 | 65 | 90 | 155 |
| Mario Lemieux, Pitt | 1988–89 | 85 | 114 | 199 | Phil Esposito, Bos | 1970–71 | 76 | 76 | 152 |
| Wayne Gretzky, Edm | 1982–83 | 71 | 125 | 196 | Bernie Nicholls, LA | 1988–89 | 70 | 80 | 150 |
| Wayne Gretzky, Edm | 1986–87 | 62 | 121 | 183 | Wayne Gretzky, Edm | 1987–88 | 40 | 109 | 149 |
| Mario Lemieux, Pitt | 1987–88 | 70 | 98 | 168 | Pat LaFontaine, Buff | 1992–93 | 53 | 95 | 148 |
| Wayne Gretzky, LA | 1988–89 | 54 | 114 | 168 | Mike Bossy, NYI | 1981–82 | 64 | 83 | 147 |
| Wayne Gretzky, Edm | 1980–81 | 55 | 109 | 164 | Phil Esposito, Bos | 1973–74 | 68 | 77 | 145 |

## Points per Game

| Player | Season | GP | Pts | Avg | Player | Season | GP | Pts | Avg |
|---|---|---|---|---|---|---|---|---|---|
| Wayne Gretzky, Edm | 1983–84 | 74 | 205 | 2.77 | Mario Lemieux, Pitt | 1987–88 | 77 | 168 | 2.18 |
| Wayne Gretzky, Edm | 1985–86 | 80 | 215 | 2.69 | Wayne Gretzky, LA | 1988–89 | 78 | 168 | 2.15 |
| Mario Lemieux, Pitt | 1992–93 | 60 | 160 | 2.67 | Wayne Gretzky, LA | 1990–91 | 78 | 163 | 2.09 |
| Wayne Gretzky, Edm | 1981–82 | 80 | 212 | 2.65 | Mario Lemieux, Pitt | 1989–90 | 59 | 123 | 2.08 |
| Mario Lemieux, Pitt | 1988–89 | 76 | 199 | 2.62 | Wayne Gretzky, Edm | 1980–81 | 80 | 164 | 2.05 |
| Wayne Gretzky, Edm | 1984–85 | 80 | 208 | 2.60 | Mario Lemieux, Pitt | 1991–92 | 64 | 131 | 2.05 |
| Wayne Gretzky, Edm | 1982–83 | 80 | 196 | 2.45 | Bill Cowley, Bos | 1943–44 | 36 | 71 | 1.97 |
| Wayne Gretzky, Edm | 1987–88 | 64 | 149 | 2.33 | Phil Esposito, Bos | 1970–71 | 78 | 152 | 1.95 |
| Wayne Gretzky, Edm | 1986–87 | 79 | 183 | 2.32 | Wayne Gretzky, LA | 1989–90 | 73 | 142 | 1.95 |
| Mario Lemieux, Pitt | 1995–96 | 70 | 161 | 2.30 | Steve Yzerman, Det | 1988–89 | 80 | 155 | 1.94 |

Note: Minimum 50 points in one season.

## Goals per Game

| Player | Season | GP | G | Avg |
|---|---|---|---|---|
| Joe Malone, Mtl | 1917–18 | 20 | 44 | 2.20 |
| Cy Denneny, Ott | 1917–18 | 22 | 36 | 1.64 |
| Newsy Lalonde, Mtl | 1917–18 | 14 | 23 | 1.64 |
| Joe Malone, Que | 1919–20 | 24 | 39 | 1.63 |
| Newsy Lalonde, Mtl | 1919–20 | 23 | 36 | 1.57 |
| Joe Malone, Ham | 1920–21 | 20 | 30 | 1.50 |
| Babe Dye, Ham-Tor | 1920–21 | 24 | 35 | 1.46 |
| Cy Denneny, Ott | 1920–21 | 24 | 34 | 1.42 |
| Reg Noble, Tor | 1917–18 | 20 | 28 | 1.40 |
| Newsy Lalonde, Mtl | 1920–21 | 24 | 33 | 1.38 |

Note: Minimum 20 goals in one season.

## Assists per Game

| Player | Season | GP | A | Avg |
|---|---|---|---|---|
| Wayne Gretzky, Edm | 1985–86 | 80 | 163 | 2.04 |
| Wayne Gretzky, Edm | 1987–88 | 64 | 109 | 1.70 |
| Wayne Gretzky, Edm | 1984–85 | 80 | 135 | 1.69 |
| Wayne Gretzky, Edm | 1983–84 | 74 | 118 | 1.59 |
| Wayne Gretzky, Edm | 1982–83 | 80 | 125 | 1.56 |
| Wayne Gretzky, LA | 1990–91 | 78 | 122 | 1.56 |
| Wayne Gretzky, Edm | 1986–87 | 79 | 121 | 1.53 |
| Mario Lemieux, Pitt | 1992–93 | 60 | 91 | 1.52 |
| Wayne Gretzky, Edm | 1981–82 | 80 | 120 | 1.50 |
| Mario Lemieux, Pitt | 1988–89 | 76 | 114 | 1.50 |

Note: Minimum 35 assists in one season.

## Shutout Leaders

| | Season | SO | Length of Schedule | | Season | SO | Length of Schedule |
|---|---|---|---|---|---|---|---|
| George Hainsworth, Mtl | 1928–29 | 22 | 44 | Harry Holmes, Det | 1927–28 | 11 | 44 |
| Alex Connell, Ott | 1925–26 | 15 | 36 | Clint Benedict, Mtl M | 1928–29 | 11 | 44 |
| Alex Connell, Ott | 1927–28 | 15 | 44 | Joe Miller, Pitt Pirates | 1928–29 | 11 | 44 |
| Hal Winkler, Bos | 1927–28 | 15 | 44 | Tiny Thompson, Bos | 1932–33 | 11 | 48 |
| Tony Esposito, Chi | 1969–70 | 15 | 76 | Terry Sawchuk, Det | 1950–51 | 11 | 70 |
| George Hainsworth, Mtl | 1926–27 | 14 | 44 | Dominik Hasek, Buff | 2000–01 | 11 | 82 |
| Clint Benedict, Mtl M | 1926–27 | 13 | 44 | Lorne Chabot, NYR | 1926–27 | 10 | 44 |
| Alex Connell, Ott | 1926–27 | 13 | 44 | Roy Worters, Pitt Pirates | 1927–28 | 10 | 44 |
| George Hainsworth, Mtl | 1927–28 | 13 | 44 | Clarence Dolson, Det | 1928–29 | 10 | 44 |
| John Roach, NYR | 1928–29 | 13 | 44 | John Roach, Det | 1932–33 | 10 | 48 |
| Roy Worters, NYA | 1928–29 | 13 | 44 | Chuck Gardiner, Chi | 1933–34 | 10 | 48 |
| Harry Lumley, Tor | 1953–54 | 13 | 70 | Tiny Thompson, Bos | 1935–36 | 10 | 48 |
| Dominik Hasek, Buff | 1997–98 | 13 | 82 | Frank Brimsek, Bos | 1938–39 | 10 | 48 |
| Tiny Thompson, Bos | 1928–29 | 12 | 44 | Bill Durnan, Mtl | 1948–49 | 10 | 60 |
| Lorne Chabot, Tor | 1928–29 | 12 | 44 | Gerry McNeil, Mtl | 1952–53 | 10 | 70 |
| Chuck Gardiner, Chi | 1930–31 | 12 | 44 | Harry Lumley, Tor | 1952–53 | 10 | 70 |
| Terry Sawchuk, Det | 1951–52 | 12 | 70 | Tony Esposito, Chi | 1973–74 | 10 | 78 |
| Terry Sawchuk, Det | 1953–54 | 12 | 70 | Ken Dryden, Mtl | 1976–77 | 10 | 80 |
| Terry Sawchuk, Det | 1954–55 | 12 | 70 | Martin Brodeur, NJ | 1996–97 | 10 | 82 |
| Glenn Hall, Det | 1955–56 | 12 | 70 | Martin Brodeur, NJ | 1997–98 | 10 | 82 |
| Bernie Parent, Phil | 1973–74 | 12 | 78 | Roman Cechmanek, Phil | 2000–01 | 10 | 82 |
| Bernie Parent, Phil | 1974–75 | 12 | 80 | Byron Dafoe, Bos | 1998–99 | 10 | 82 |
| Lorne Chabot, NYR | 1927–28 | 11 | 44 | | | | |

## Wins

| | Season | Record |
|---|---|---|
| Bernie Parent, Phil | 1973–74 | 47-13-12 |
| Bernie Parent, Phil | 1974–75 | 44-14-9 |
| Terry Sawchuk, Det | 1950–51 | 44-13-13 |
| Terry Sawchuk, Det | 1951–52 | 44-14-12 |
| Tom Barasso, Pitt | 1992–93 | 43-14-5 |
| Ed Belfour, Chi | 1990–91 | 43-19-7 |
| Martin Brodeur, NJ | 1997–98 | 43-17-8 |
| Martin Brodeur, NJ | 1999–00 | 43-20-8 |
| Jacques Plante, Mtl | 1955–56 | 42-12-10 |
| Jacques Plante, Mtl | 1961–62 | 42-14-14 |
| Ken Dryden, Mtl | 1975–76 | 42-10-8 |
| Mike Richter, NYR | 1993–94 | 42-12-6 |
| Roman Turek, StL | 1999–00 | 42-15-9 |
| Martin Brodeur, NJ | 2000–01 | 42-17-11 |

## Goals Against Average
### (PRE-1950)

| | Season | GP | GAA |
|---|---|---|---|
| George Hainsworth, Mtl | 1928–29 | 44 | 0.92 |
| George Hainsworth, Mtl | 1927–28 | 44 | 1.05 |
| Alex Connell, Ott | 1925–26 | 36 | 1.12 |
| Tiny Thompson, Bos | 1928–29 | 44 | 1.18 |
| Roy Worters, NYA | 1928–29 | 38 | 1.21 |

### (POST-1950)

| | Season | GP | GAA |
|---|---|---|---|
| Tony Esposito, Chi | 1971–72 | 48 | 1.7698 |
| Al Rollins, Tor | 1950–51 | 40 | 1.7744 |
| Ron Tugnutt, Ott | 1998–99 | 43 | 1.7943 |
| Harry Lumley, Tor | 1953–54 | 69 | 1.8551 |
| Jacques Plante, Mtl | 1955–56 | 64 | 1.8594 |
| Dominik Hasek, Buff | 1998–99 | 64 | 1.8706 |
| Martin Brodeur, NJ | 1996–97 | 67 | 1.8759 |
| Ed Belfour, Dall | 1997–98 | 61 | 1.8766 |

# Single-Game Records

## Goals

| | Date | G |
|---|---|---|
| Joe Malone, Que vs Tor | 1-31-20 | 7 |
| Newsy Lalonde, Mtl vs Tor | 1-10-20 | 6 |
| Joe Malone, Que vs Ott | 3-10-20 | 6 |
| Corb Denneny, Tor vs Ham | 1-26-21 | 6 |
| Cy Denneny, Ott vs Ham | 3-7-21 | 6 |
| Syd Howe, Det vs NYR | 2-3-44 | 6 |
| Red Berenson, StL vs Phil | 11-7-68 | 6 |
| Darryl Sittler, Tor vs Bos | 2-7-76 | 6 |

## Assists

| | Date | A |
|---|---|---|
| Billy Taylor, Det vs Chi | 3-16-47 | 7 |
| Wayne Gretzky, Edm vs Wash | 2-15-80 | 7 |
| Wayne Gretzky, Edm vs Chi | 12-11-85 | 7 |
| Wayne Gretzky, Edm vs Que | 2-14-86 | 7 |

Note: 24 tied with 6.

## Points

| | Date | G | A | Pts |
|---|---|---|---|---|
| Darryl Sittler, Tor vs Bos | 2-7-76 | 6 | 4 | 10 |
| Maurice Richard, Mtl vs Det | 12-28-44 | 5 | 3 | 8 |
| Bert Olmstead, Mtl vs Chi | 1-9-54 | 4 | 4 | 8 |
| Tom Bladon, Phil vs Clev | 12-11-77 | 4 | 4 | 8 |
| Bryan Trottier, NYI vs NYR | 12-23-78 | 5 | 3 | 8 |
| Peter Stastny, Que vs Wash | 2-22-81 | 4 | 4 | 8 |
| Anton Stastny, Que vs Wash | 2-22-81 | 3 | 5 | 8 |
| Wayne Gretzky, Edm vs NJ | 11-19-83 | 3 | 5 | 8 |
| Wayne Gretzky, Edm vs Minn | 1-4-84 | 4 | 4 | 8 |
| Paul Coffey, Edm vs Det | 3-14-86 | 2 | 6 | 8 |
| Mario Lemieux, Pitt vs StL | 10-15-88 | 2 | 6 | 8 |
| Bernie Nicholls, LA vs Tor | 12-1-88 | 2 | 6 | 8 |
| Mario Lemieux, Pitt vs NJ | 12-31-88 | 5 | 3 | 8 |

# NHL Season Leaders

## Points

| Season | Player and Club | Pts | Season | Player and Club | Pts |
|---|---|---|---|---|---|
| 1917–18 | Joe Malone, Mtl | 44 | 1956–57 | Gordie Howe, Det | 89 |
| 1918–19 | Newsy Lalonde, Mtl | 30 | 1957–58 | Dickie Moore, Mtl | 84 |
| 1919–20 | Joe Malone, Que | 48 | 1958–59 | Dickie Moore, Mtl | 96 |
| 1920–21 | Newsy Lalonde, Mtl | 41 | 1959–60 | Bobby Hull, Chi | 81 |
| 1921–22 | Punch Broadbent, Ott | 46 | 1960–61 | Bernie Geoffrion, Mtl | 95 |
| 1922–23 | Babe Dye, Tor | 37 | 1961–62 | Andy Bathgate, NY | 84 |
| 1923–24 | Cy Denneny, Ott | 23 | | Bobby Hull, Chi | 84 |
| 1924–25 | Babe Dye, Tor | 44 | 1962–63 | Gordie Howe, Det | 86 |
| 1925–26 | Nels Stewart, Mtl M | 42 | 1963–64 | Stan Mikita, Chi | 89 |
| 1926–27 | Bill Cook, NY | 37 | 1964–65 | Stan Mikita, Chi | 87 |
| 1927–28 | Howie Morenz, Mtl | 51 | 1965–66 | Bobby Hull, Chi | 97 |
| 1928–29 | Ace Bailey, Tor | 32 | 1966–67 | Stan Mikita, Chi | 97 |
| 1929–30 | Cooney Weiland, Bos | 73 | 1967–68 | Stan Mikita, Chi | 87 |
| 1930–31 | Howie Morenz, Mtl | 51 | 1968–69 | Phil Esposito, Bos | 126 |
| 1931–32 | Harvey Jackson, Tor | 53 | 1969–70 | Bobby Orr, Bos | 120 |
| 1932–33 | Bill Cook, NY | 50 | 1970–71 | Phil Esposito, Bos | 152 |
| 1933–34 | Charlie Conacher, Tor | 52 | 1971–72 | Phil Esposito, Bos | 133 |
| 1934–35 | Charlie Conacher, Tor | 57 | 1972–73 | Phil Esposito, Bos | 130 |
| 1935–36 | Sweeney Schriner, NYA | 45 | 1973–74 | Phil Esposito, Bos | 145 |
| 1936–37 | Sweeney Schriner, NYA | 46 | 1974–75 | Bobby Orr, Bos | 135 |
| 1937–38 | Gord Drillon, Tor | 52 | 1975–76 | Guy Lafleur, Mtl | 125 |
| 1938–39 | Hector Blake, Mtl | 47 | 1976–77 | Guy Lafleur, Mtl | 136 |
| 1939–40 | Milt Schmidt, Bos | 52 | 1977–78 | Guy Lafleur, Mtl | 132 |
| 1940–41 | Bill Cowley, Bos | 62 | 1978–79 | Bryan Trottier, NYI | 134 |
| 1941–42 | Bryan Hextall, NY | 54 | 1979–80 | Marcel Dionne, LA | 137 |
| 1942–43 | Doug Bentley, Chi | 73 | | Wayne Gretzky, Edm | 137 |
| 1943–44 | Herb Cain, Bos | 82 | 1980–81 | Wayne Gretzky, Edm | 164 |
| 1944–45 | Elmer Lach, Mtl | 80 | 1981–82 | Wayne Gretzky, Edm | 212 |
| 1945–46 | Max Bentley, Chi | 61 | 1982–83 | Wayne Gretzky, Edm | 196 |
| 1946–47 | Max Bentley, Chi | 72 | 1983–84 | Wayne Gretzky, Edm | 205 |
| 1947–48 | Elmer Lach, Mtl | 61 | 1984–85 | Wayne Gretzky, Edm | 208 |
| 1948–49 | Roy Conacher, Chi | 68 | 1985–86 | Wayne Gretzky, Edm | 215 |
| 1949–50 | Ted Lindsay, Det | 78 | 1986–87 | Wayne Gretzky, Edm | 183 |
| 1950–51 | Gordie Howe, Det | 86 | 1987–88 | Mario Lemieux, Pitt | 168 |
| 1951–52 | Gordie Howe, Det | 86 | 1988–89 | Mario Lemieux, Pitt | 199 |
| 1952–53 | Gordie Howe, Det | 95 | 1989–90 | Wayne Gretzky, LA | 142 |
| 1953–54 | Gordie Howe, Det | 81 | 1990–91 | Wayne Gretzky, LA | 163 |
| 1954–55 | Bernie Geoffrion, Mtl | 75 | 1991–92 | Mario Lemieux, Pitt | 131 |
| 1955–56 | Jean Beliveau, Mtl | 88 | 1992–93 | Mario Lemieux, Pitt | 160 |

## Points *(Cont.)*

| Season | Player and Club | Pts | Season | Player and Club | Pts |
|--------|-----------------|-----|--------|-----------------|-----|
| 1993–94 | Wayne Gretzky, LA | 130 | 1998–99 | Jaromir Jagr, Pitt | 127 |
| 1994–95 | Jaromir Jagr, Pitt | 70 | 1999–00 | Jaromir Jagr, Pitt | 96 |
| 1995–96 | Mario Lemieux, Pitt | 161 | 2000–01 | Jaromir Jagr, Pitt | 121 |
| 1996–97 | Mario Lemieux, Pitt | 122 | | | |
| 1997–98 | Jaromir Jagr, Pitt | 102 | | | |

## Goals

| Season | Player and Club | G | Season | Player and Club | G |
|--------|-----------------|---|--------|-----------------|---|
| 1917–18 | Joe Malone, Mtl | 44 | 1959–60 | Bobby Hull, Chi | 39 |
| 1918–19 | Odie Cleghorn, Mtl | 23 | | Bronco Horvath, Bos | 39 |
| 1919–20 | Joe Malone, Que | 39 | 1960–61 | Bernie Geoffrion, Mtl | 50 |
| 1920–21 | Babe Dye, Ham-Tor | 35 | 1961–62 | Bobby Hull, Chi | 50 |
| 1921–22 | Punch Broadbent, Ott | 32 | 1962–63 | Gordie Howe, Det | 38 |
| 1922–23 | Babe Dye, Tor | 26 | 1963–64 | Bobby Hull, Chi | 43 |
| 1923–24 | Cy Denneny, Ott | 22 | 1964–65 | Norm Ullman, Det | 42 |
| 1924–25 | Babe Dye, Tor | 38 | 1965–66 | Bobby Hull, Chi | 54 |
| 1925–26 | Nels Stewart, Mtl | 34 | 1966–67 | Bobby Hull, Chi | 52 |
| 1926–27 | Bill Cook, NY | 33 | 1967–68 | Bobby Hull, Chi | 44 |
| 1927–28 | Howie Morenz, Mtl | 33 | 1968–69 | Bobby Hull, Chi | 58 |
| 1928–29 | Ace Bailey, Tor | 22 | 1969–70 | Phil Esposito, Bos | 43 |
| 1929–30 | Cooney Weiland, Bos | 43 | 1970–71 | Phil Esposito, Bos | 76 |
| 1930–31 | Bill Cook, NY | 30 | 1971–72 | Phil Esposito, Bos | 66 |
| 1931–32 | Charlie Conacher, Tor | 34 | 1972–73 | Phil Esposito, Bos | 55 |
| | Bill Cook, NY | 34 | 1973–74 | Phil Esposito, Bos | 68 |
| 1932–33 | Bill Cook, NY | 28 | 1974–75 | Phil Esposito, Bos | 61 |
| 1933–34 | Charlie Conacher, Tor | 32 | 1975–76 | Guy Lafleur, Mtl | 56 |
| 1934–35 | Charlie Conacher, Tor | 36 | 1976–77 | Steve Shutt, Mtl | 60 |
| 1935–36 | Charlie Conacher, Tor | 23 | 1977–78 | Guy Lafleur, Mtl | 60 |
| | Bill Thoms, Tor | 23 | 1978–79 | Mike Bossy, NYI | 69 |
| 1936–37 | Larry Aurie, Det | 23 | 1979–80 | Charlie Simmer, LA | 56 |
| | Nels Stewart, Bos-NYA | 23 | | Blaine Stoughton, Hart | 56 |
| 1937–38 | Gord Drill, Tor | 26 | 1980–81 | Mike Bossy, NYI | 68 |
| 1938–39 | Roy Conacher, Bos | 26 | 1981–82 | Wayne Gretzky, Edm | 92 |
| 1939–40 | Bryan Hextall, NY | 24 | 1982–83 | Wayne Gretzky, Edm | 71 |
| 1940–41 | Bryan Hextall, NY | 26 | 1983–84 | Wayne Gretzky, Edm | 87 |
| 1941–42 | Lynn Patrick, NY | 32 | 1984–85 | Wayne Gretzky, Edm | 73 |
| 1942–43 | Doug Bentley, Chi | 43 | 1985–86 | Jari Kurri, Edm | 68 |
| 1943–44 | Doug Bentley, Chi | 38 | 1986–87 | Wayne Gretzky, Edm | 62 |
| 1944–45 | Maurice Richard, Mtl | 50 | 1987–88 | Mario Lemieux, Pitt | 70 |
| 1945–46 | Gaye Stewart, Tor | 37 | 1988–89 | Mario Lemieux, Pitt | 85 |
| 1946–47 | Maurice Richard, Mtl | 50 | 1989–90 | Brett Hull, StL | 72 |
| 1947–48 | Ted Lindsay, Det | 33 | 1990–91 | Brett Hull, StL | 78 |
| 1948–49 | Sid Abel, Det | 28 | 1991–92 | Brett Hull, StL | 70 |
| 1949–50 | Maurice Richard, Mtl | 43 | 1992–93 | Alexander Mogilny, Buff | 76 |
| 1950–51 | Gordie Howe, Det | 43 | | Teemu Selanne, Winn | 76 |
| 1951–52 | Gordie Howe, Det | 47 | 1993–94 | Pavel Bure, Van | 60 |
| 1952–53 | Gordie Howe, Det | 49 | 1994–95 | Peter Bondra, Wash | 34 |
| 1953–54 | Maurice Richard, Mtl | 37 | 1995–96 | Mario Lemieux, Pitt | 69 |
| 1954–55 | Bernie Geoffrion, Mtl | 38 | 1996–97 | Keith Tkachuk, Phoe | 52 |
| | Maurice Richard, Mtl | 38 | 1997–98 | Teemu Selanne, Ana | 52 |
| | | | | Peter Bondra, Wash | 52 |
| 1955–56 | Jean Beliveau, Mtl | 47 | 1998–99 | Teemu Selanne, Ana | 47 |
| 1957–58 | Dickie Moore, Mtl | 36 | 1999–00 | Pavel Bure, Fla | 58 |
| 1956–57 | Gordie Howe, Det | 44 | 2000–01 | Pavel Bure, Fla | 59 |
| 1958–59 | Jean Beliveau, Mtl | 45 | | | |

## Assists

| Season | Player and Club | A |
|--------|-----------------|---|
| 1917–18 | statistic not kept | |
| 1918–19 | Newsy Lalonde, Mtl | 9 |
| 1919–20 | Corbett Denneny, Tor | 12 |
| 1920–21 | Louis Berlinquette, Mtl | 9 |
| 1921–22 | Punch Broadbench, Ott | 14 |
| 1922–23 | Babe Dye, Tor | 11 |
| 1923–24 | Billy Boucher, Mtl | 6 |
| 1924–25 | Cy Denneny, Ott | 15 |
| 1925–26 | Cy Denneny, Ott | 12 |
| 1926–27 | Dick Irvin, Chi | 18 |
| 1927–28 | Howie Morenz, Mtl | 18 |
| 1928–29 | Frank Boucher, NY | 16 |
| 1929–30 | Frank Boucher, NY | 36 |
| 1930–31 | Joe Primeau, Tor | 36 |
| 1931–32 | Joe Primeau, Tor | 37 |
| 1932–33 | Frank Boucher, NY | 28 |
| 1933–34 | Joe Primeau, Tor | 32 |
| 1934–35 | Art Chapman, NYA | 28 |
| 1935–36 | Art Chapman, NYA | 28 |
| 1936–37 | Syl Apps, Tor | 29 |
| 1937–38 | Syl Apps, Tor | 29 |
| 1938–39 | Bill Cowley, Bos | 34 |
| 1939–40 | Milt Schmidt, Bos | 30 |
| 1940–41 | Bill Cowley, Bos | 45 |
| 1941–42 | Phil Watson, NY | 37 |
| 1942–43 | Bill Cowley, Bos | 45 |
| 1943–44 | Clint Smith, Chi | 49 |
| 1944–45 | Elmer Lach, Mtl | 54 |
| 1945–46 | Elmer Lach, Mtl | 34 |
| 1946–47 | Billy Taylor, Det | 46 |
| 1947–48 | Doug Bentley, Chi | 37 |
| 1948–49 | Doug Bentley, Chi | 43 |
| 1949–50 | Ted Lindsay, Det | 55 |
| 1950–51 | Gordie Howe, Det | 43 |
| | Ted Kennedy, Tor | 43 |
| 1951–52 | Elmer Lach, Mtl | 50 |
| 1952–53 | Gordie Howe, Det | 46 |
| 1953–54 | Gordie Howe, Det | 48 |
| 1954–55 | Bert Olmstead, Mtl | 48 |
| 1955–56 | Bert Olmstead, Mtl | 56 |
| 1956–57 | Ted Lindsay, Det | 55 |
| 1957–58 | Henri Richard, Mtl | 52 |
| 1958–59 | Dickie Moore, Mtl | 55 |
| 1959–60 | Bobby Hull, Chi | 42 |
| 1960–61 | Jean Beliveau, Mtl | 58 |
| 1961–62 | Andy Bathgate, NY | 56 |

| Season | Player and Club | A |
|--------|-----------------|---|
| 1962–63 | Henri Richard, Mtl | 50 |
| 1963–64 | Andy Bathgate, NY-Tor | 58 |
| 1964–65 | Stan Mikita, Chi | 59 |
| 1965–66 | Stan Mikita, Chi | 48 |
| | Bobby Rousseau, Mtl | 48 |
| | Jean Beliveau, Mtl | 48 |
| 1966–67 | Stan Mikita, Chi | 62 |
| 1967–68 | Phil Esposito, Bos | 49 |
| 1968–69 | Phil Esposito, Bos | 77 |
| 1969–70 | Bobby Orr, Bos | 87 |
| 1970–71 | Bobby Orr, Bos | 102 |
| 1971–72 | Bobby Orr, Bos | 80 |
| 1972–73 | Phil Esposito, Bos | 75 |
| 1973–74 | Bobby Orr, Bos | 89 |
| 1974–75 | Bobby Clarke, Phil | 89 |
| | Bobby Orr, Bos | 89 |
| 1975–76 | Bobby Clarke, Phil | 89 |
| 1976–77 | Guy Lafleur, Mtl | 80 |
| 1977–78 | Bryan Trottier, NYI | 77 |
| 1978–79 | Bryan Trottier, NYI | 87 |
| 1979–80 | Wayne Gretzky, Edm | 86 |
| 1980–81 | Wayne Gretzky, Edm | 109 |
| 1981–82 | Wayne Gretzky, Edm | 120 |
| 1982–83 | Wayne Gretzky, Edm | 125 |
| 1983–84 | Wayne Gretzky, Edm | 118 |
| 1984–85 | Wayne Gretzky, Edm | 135 |
| 1985–86 | Wayne Gretzky, Edm | 163 |
| 1986–87 | Wayne Gretzky, Edm | 121 |
| 1987–88 | Wayne Gretzky, Edm | 109 |
| 1988–89 | Wayne Gretzky, LA | 114 |
| | Mario Lemieux, Pitt | 114 |
| 1989–90 | Wayne Gretzky, LA | 102 |
| 1990–91 | Wayne Gretzky, LA | 122 |
| 1991–92 | Wayne Gretzky, LA | 90 |
| 1992–93 | Adam Oates, Bos | 97 |
| 1993–94 | Wayne Gretzky, LA | 92 |
| 1994–95 | Ron Francis, Pitt | 48 |
| 1995–96 | Mario Lemieux, Pitt | 92 |
| | Ron Francis, Pitt | 92 |
| 1996–97 | Mario Lemieux, Pitt | 72 |
| 1997–98 | Jaromir Jagr, Pitt | 67 |
| | Wayne Gretzky, NYR | 67 |
| 1998–99 | Jaromir Jagr, Pitt | 83 |
| 1999–00 | Mark Recchi, Phil | 63 |
| 2000–01 | Jaromir Jagr, Pitt | 69 |
| | Adam Oates, Wash | 69 |

---

## THEY SAID IT

*Bob Boughner, Pittsburgh defenseman, anticipating owner Mario Lemieux's return to the ice:*
*"I'm going to take him out on the first road trip, get him drunk and talk contract."*

---

### Goals Against Average

| Season | Goaltender and Club | GP | Min | GA | SO | Avg |
|---|---|---|---|---|---|---|
| 1917–18 | Georges Vezina, Mtl | 21 | 1282 | 84 | 1 | 3.93 |
| 1918–19 | Clint Benedict, Ott | 18 | 1113 | 53 | 2 | 2.86 |
| 1919–20 | Clint Benedict, Ott | 24 | 1444 | 64 | 5 | 2.66 |
| 1920–21 | Clint Benedict, Ott | 24 | 1457 | 75 | 2 | 3.09 |
| 1921–22 | Clint Benedict, Ott | 24 | 1508 | 84 | 2 | 3.34 |
| 1922–23 | Clint Benedict, Ott | 24 | 1478 | 54 | 4 | 2.19 |
| 1923–24 | Georges Vezina, Mtl | 24 | 1459 | 48 | 3 | 1.97 |
| 1924–25 | Georges Vezina, Mtl | 30 | 1860 | 56 | 5 | 1.81 |
| 1925–26 | Alex Connell, Ott | 36 | 2251 | 42 | 15 | 1.12 |
| 1926–27 | Clint Benedict, Mtl M | 43 | 2748 | 65 | 13 | 1.42 |
| 1927–28 | George Hainsworth, Mtl | 44 | 2730 | 48 | 13 | 1.05 |
| 1928–29 | George Hainsworth, Mtl | 44 | 2800 | 43 | 22 | 0.92 |
| 1929–30 | Tiny Thompson, Bos | 44 | 2680 | 98 | 3 | 2.19 |
| 1930–31 | Roy Worters, NYA | 44 | 2760 | 74 | 8 | 1.61 |
| 1931–32 | Chuck Gardiner, Chi | 48 | 2989 | 92 | 4 | 1.85 |
| 1932–33 | Tiny Thompson, Bos | 48 | 3000 | 88 | 11 | 1.76 |
| 1933–34 | Wilf Cude, Det-Mtl | 30 | 1920 | 47 | 5 | 1.47 |
| 1934–35 | Lorne Chabot, Chi | 48 | 2940 | 88 | 8 | 1.80 |
| 1935–36 | Tiny Thompson, Bos | 48 | 2930 | 82 | 10 | 1.68 |
| 1936–37 | Normie Smith, Det | 48 | 2980 | 102 | 6 | 2.05 |
| 1937–38 | Tiny Thompson, Bos | 48 | 2970 | 89 | 7 | 1.80 |
| 1938–39 | Frank Brimsek, Bos | 43 | 2610 | 68 | 10 | 1.56 |
| 1939–40 | Dave Kerr, NYR | 48 | 3000 | 77 | 8 | 1.54 |
| 1940–41 | Turk Broda, Tor | 48 | 2970 | 99 | 5 | 2.00 |
| 1941–42 | Frank Brimsek, Bos | 47 | 2930 | 115 | 3 | 2.35 |
| 1942–43 | Johnny Mowers, Det | 50 | 3010 | 124 | 6 | 2.47 |
| 1943–44 | Bill Durnan, Mtl | 50 | 3000 | 109 | 2 | 2.18 |
| 1944–45 | Bill Durnan, Mtl | 50 | 3000 | 121 | 1 | 2.42 |
| 1945–46 | Bill Durnan, Mtl | 40 | 2400 | 104 | 4 | 2.60 |
| 1946–47 | Bill Durnan, Mtl | 60 | 3600 | 138 | 4 | 2.30 |
| 1947–48 | Turk Broda, Tor | 60 | 3600 | 143 | 5 | 2.38 |
| 1948–49 | Bill Durnan, Mtl | 60 | 3600 | 126 | 10 | 2.10 |
| 1949–50 | Bill Durnan, Mtl | 64 | 3840 | 141 | 8 | 2.20 |
| 1950–51 | Al Rollins, Tor | 40 | 2367 | 70 | 5 | 1.77 |
| 1951–52 | Terry Sawchuk, Det | 70 | 4200 | 133 | 12 | 1.90 |
| 1952–53 | Terry Sawchuk, Det | 63 | 3780 | 120 | 9 | 1.90 |
| 1953–54 | Harry Lumley, Tor | 69 | 4140 | 128 | 13 | 1.86 |
| 1954–55 | Harry Lumley, Tor | 69 | 4140 | 134 | 8 | 1.94 |
| | Terry Sawchuk, Det | 68 | 4060 | 132 | 12 | 1.94 |
| 1955–56 | Jacques Plante, Mtl | 64 | 3840 | 119 | 7 | 1.86 |
| 1956–57 | Jacques Plante, Mtl | 61 | 3660 | 123 | 9 | 2.02 |
| 1957–58 | Jacques Plante, Mtl | 57 | 3386 | 119 | 9 | 2.11 |
| 1958–59 | Jacques Plante, Mtl | 67 | 4000 | 144 | 9 | 2.16 |
| 1959–60 | Jacques Plante, Mtl | 69 | 4140 | 175 | 3 | 2.54 |
| 1960–61 | Johnny Bower, Tor | 58 | 3480 | 145 | 2 | 2.50 |
| 1961–62 | Jacques Plante, Mtl | 70 | 4200 | 166 | 4 | 2.37 |
| 1962–63 | Jacques Plante, Mtl | 56 | 3320 | 138 | 5 | 2.49 |
| 1963–64 | Johnny Bower, Tor | 51 | 3009 | 106 | 5 | 2.11 |
| 1964–65 | Johnny Bower, Tor | 34 | 2040 | 81 | 3 | 2.38 |
| 1965–66 | Johnny Bower, Tor | 35 | 1998 | 75 | 3 | 2.25 |
| 1966–67 | Glenn Hall, Chi | 32 | 1664 | 66 | 2 | 2.38 |
| 1967–68 | Gump Worsley, Mtl | 40 | 2213 | 73 | 6 | 1.98 |
| 1968–69 | Jacques Plante, StL | 37 | 2139 | 70 | 5 | 1.96 |
| 1969–70 | Ernie Wakely, StL | 30 | 1651 | 58 | 4 | 2.11 |
| 1970–71 | Jacques Plante, Tor | 40 | 2329 | ·73 | 4 | 1.88 |
| 1971–72 | Tony Esposito, Chi | 48 | 2780 | 82 | 9 | 1.77 |
| 1972–73 | Ken Dryden, Mtl | 54 | 3165 | · 119 | 6 | 2.26 |
| 1973–74 | Bernie Parent, Phil | 73 | 4314 | 136 | 12 | 1.89 |
| 1974–75 | Bernie Parent, Phil | 68 | 4041 | 137 | 12 | 2.03 |
| 1975–76 | Ken Dryden, Mtl | 62 | 3580 | 121 | 8 | 2.03 |
| 1976–77 | Michael Larocque, Mtl | 26 | 1525 | 53 | 4 | 2.09 |
| 1977–78 | Ken Dryden, Mtl | 52 | 3071 | 105 | 5 | 2.05 |
| 1978–79 | Ken Dryden, Mtl | 47 | 2814 | · 108 | 5 | 2.30 |
| 1979–80 | Bob Sauve, Buff | 32 | 1880 | 74 | 4 | 2.36 |
| 1980–81 | Richard Sevigny, Mtl · | 33 | 1777 | 71 | 2 | 2.40 |
| 1981–82 | Denis Herron, Mtl | 27 | 1547 | 68 | 3 | 2.64 |

## Goals Against Average *(Cont.)*

| Season | Goaltender and Club | GP | Min | GA | SO | Avg |
|---|---|---|---|---|---|---|
| 1982–83 | Pete Peeters, Bos | 62 | 3611 | 142 | 8 | 2.36 |
| 1983–84 | Pat Riggin, Wash | 41 | 2299 | 102 | 4 | 2.66 |
| 1984–85 | Tom Barrasso, Buff | 54 | 3248 | 144 | 5 | 2.66 |
| 1985–86 | Bob Froese, Phil | 51 | 2728 | 116 | 5 | 2.55 |
| 1986–87 | Brian Hayward, Mtl | 37 | 2178 | 102 | 1 | 2.81 |
| 1987–88 | Pete Peeters, Wash | 35 | 1896 | 88 | 2 | 2.78 |
| 1988–89 | Patrick Roy, Mtl | 48 | 2744 | 113 | 4 | 2.47 |
| 1989–90 | Patrick Roy, Mtl | 54 | 3173 | 134 | 3 | 2.53 |
| | Mike Liut, Hart-Wash | 37 | 2161 | 91 | 4 | 2.53 |
| 1990–91 | Ed Belfour, Chi | 74 | 4127 | 170 | 4 | 2.47 |
| 1991–92 | Patrick Roy, Mtl | 67 | 3935 | 155 | 5 | 2.36 |
| 1992–93 | *Felix Potvin, Tor | 48 | 2781 | 116 | 2 | 2.50 |
| 1993–94 | Dominik Hasek, Buff | 58 | 3358 | 109 | 7 | 1.95 |
| 1994–95 | Dominik Hasek, Buff | 41 | 2416 | 85 | 5 | 2.11 |
| 1995–96 | Ron Hextall, Phil | 53 | 3102 | 112 | 4 | 2.17 |
| | Chris Osgood, Det | 50 | 2933 | 106 | 5 | 2.17 |
| 1996–97 | Martin Brodeur, NJ | 67 | 3838 | 120 | 10 | 1.88 |
| 1997–98 | Ed Belfour, Dall | 61 | 3581 | 112 | 9 | 1.88 |
| 1998–99 | Ron Tugnutt, Ott | 43 | 2508 | 75 | 3 | 1.79 |
| 1999–00 | Brian Boucher, Phil | 35 | 2038 | 65 | 4 | 1.91 |
| 2000–01 | Marty Turco, Dall | 26 | 1266 | 40 | 3 | 1.90 |

*Rookie.

## Penalty Minutes

| Season | Player and Club | GP | PIM | Season | Player and Club | GP | PIM |
|---|---|---|---|---|---|---|---|
| 1918–19 | Joe Hall, Mtl | 17 | 85 | 1960–61 | Pierre Pilote, Chi | 70 | 165 |
| 1919–20 | Cully Wilson, Tor | 23 | 79 | 1961–62 | Lou Fontinato, Mtl | 54 | 167 |
| 1920–21 | Bert Corbeau, Mtl | 24 | 86 | 1962–63 | Howie Young, Det | 64 | 273 |
| 1921–22 | Sprague Cleghorn, Mtl | 24 | 63 | 1963–64 | Vic Hadfield, NYR | 69 | 151 |
| 1922–23 | Billy Boucher, Mtl | 24 | 52 | 1964–65 | Carl Brewer, Tor | 70 | 177 |
| 1923–24 | Bert Corbeau, Tor | 24 | 55 | 1965–66 | Reggie Fleming, Bos-NYR | 69 | 166 |
| 1924–25 | Billy Boucher, Mtl | 30 | 92 | 1966–67 | John Ferguson, Mtl | 67 | 177 |
| 1925–26 | Bert Corbeau, Tor | 36 | 121 | 1967–68 | Barclay Plager, StL | 49 | 153 |
| 1926–27 | Nels Stewart, Mtl M | 44 | 133 | 1968–69 | Forbes Kennedy, Phil-Tor | 77 | 219 |
| 1927–28 | Eddie Shore, Bos | 44 | 165 | 1969–70 | Keith Magnuson, Chi | 76 | 213 |
| 1928–29 | Red Dutton, Mtl M | 44 | 139 | 1970–71 | Keith Magnuson, Chi | 76 | 291 |
| 1929–30 | Joe Lamb, Ott | 44 | 119 | 1971–72 | Brian Watson, Pitt | 75 | 212 |
| 1930–31 | Harvey Rockburn, Det | 42 | 118 | 1972–73 | Dave Schultz, Phil | 76 | 259 |
| 1931–32 | Red Dutton, NYA | 47 | 107 | 1973–74 | Dave Schultz, Phil | 73 | 348 |
| 1932–33 | Red Horner, Tor | 48 | 144 | 1974–75 | Dave Schultz, Phil | 76 | 472 |
| 1933–34 | Red Horner, Tor | 42 | 126 | 1975–76 | Steve Durbano, Pitt-KC | 69 | 370 |
| 1934–35 | Red Horner, Tor | 46 | 125 | 1976–77 | Dave Williams, Tor | 77 | 338 |
| 1935–36 | Red Horner, Tor | 43 | 167 | 1977–78 | Dave Schultz, LA-Pitt | 74 | 405 |
| 1936–37 | Red Horner, Tor | 48 | 124 | 1978–79 | Dave Williams, Tor | 77 | 298 |
| 1937–38 | Red Horner, Tor | 47 | 82 | 1979–80 | Jimmy Mann, Winn | 72 | 287 |
| 1938–39 | Red Horner, Tor | 48 | 85 | 1980–81 | Dave Williams, Van | 77 | 343 |
| 1939–40 | Red Horner, Tor | 30 | 87 | 1981–82 | Paul Baxter, Pitt | 76 | 409 |
| 1940–41 | Jimmy Orlando, Det | 48 | 99 | 1982–83 | Randy Holt, Wash | 70 | 275 |
| 1941–42 | Jimmy Orlando, Det | 48 | 81 | 1983–84 | Chris Nilan, Mtl | 76 | 338 |
| 1942–43 | Jimmy Orlando, Det | 40 | 89 | 1984–85 | Chris Nilan, Mtl | 77 | 358 |
| 1943–44 | Mike McMahon, Mtl | 42 | 98 | 1985–86 | Joey Kocur, Det | 59 | 377 |
| 1944–45 | Pat Egan, Bos | 48 | 86 | 1986–87 | Tim Hunter, Cgy | 73 | 361 |
| 1945–46 | Jack Stewart, Det | 47 | 73 | 1987–88 | Bob Probert, Det | 74 | 398 |
| 1946–47 | Gus Mortson, Tor | 60 | 133 | 1988–89 | Tim Hunter, Cgy | 75 | 375 |
| 1947–48 | Bill Barilko, Tor | 57 | 147 | 1989–90 | Basil McRae, Minn | 66 | 351 |
| 1948–49 | Bill Ezinicki, Tor | 52 | 145 | 1990–91 | Bob Ray, Buff | 66 | 350 |
| 1949–50 | Bill Ezinicki, Tor | 67 | 144 | 1991–92 | Mike Peluso, Chi | 63 | 408 |
| 1950–51 | Gus Mortson, Tor | 60 | 142 | 1992–93 | Marty McSorley, LA | 81 | 399 |
| 1951–52 | Gus Kyle, Bos | 69 | 127 | 1993–94 | Tie Domi, Winn | 81 | 347 |
| 1952–53 | Maurice Richard, Mtl | 70 | 112 | 1994–95 | Enrico Ciccone, TB | 41 | 225 |
| 1953–54 | Gus Mortson, Chi | 68 | 132 | 1995–96 | Matthew Barnaby, Buff | 73 | 335 |
| 1954–55 | Fern Flaman, Bos | 70 | 150 | 1996–97 | Gino Odjick, Van | 70 | 371 |
| 1955–56 | Lou Fontinato, NYR | 70 | 202 | 1997–98 | Donald Brashear, Van | 77 | 372 |
| 1956–57 | Gus Mortson, Chi | 70 | 147 | 1998–99 | Rob Ray, Buff | 76 | 261 |
| 1957–58 | Lou Fontinato, NYR | 70 | 152 | 1999–00 | Denny Lambert, Atl | 73 | 219 |
| 1958–59 | Ted Lindsay, Chi | 70 | 184 | 2000–01 | Matthew Barnaby, TB | 76 | 265 |
| 1959–60 | Carl Brewer, Tor | 67 | 150 | | | | |

First played in 1947, this game was scheduled before the start of the regular season and used to match the defending Stanley Cup Champions against a squad made up of the league All-stars from other teams. In 1966 the games were moved to mid-season, although there was no game that year. The format changed to a conference versus conference showdown in 1969.

## Results

| Year | Site | Score | MVP | Attendance |
|---|---|---|---|---|
| 1947 | Toronto | All-Stars 4, Toronto 3 | None named | 14,169 |
| 1948 | Chicago | All-Stars 3, Toronto 1 | None named | 12,794 |
| 1949 | Toronto | All-Stars 3, Toronto 1 | None named | 13,541 |
| 1950 | Detroit | Detroit 7, All-Stars 1 | None named | 9,166 |
| 1951 | Toronto | 1st team 2, 2nd team 2 | None named | 11,469 |
| 1952 | Detroit | 1st team 1, 2nd team 1 | None named | 10,680 |
| 1953 | Montreal | All-Stars 3, Montreal 1 | None named | 14,153 |
| 1954 | Detroit | All-Stars 2, Detroit 2 | None named | 10,689 |
| 1955 | Detroit | Detroit 3, All-Stars 1 | None named | 10,111 |
| 1956 | Montreal | All-Stars 1, Montreal 1 | None named | 13,095 |
| 1957 | Montreal | All-Stars 5, Montreal 3 | None named | 13,003 |
| 1958 | Montreal | Montreal 6, All-Stars 3 | None named | 13,989 |
| 1959 | Montreal | Montreal 6, All-Stars 1 | None named | 13,818 |
| 1960 | Montreal | All-Stars 2, Montreal 1 | None named | 13,949 |
| 1961 | Chicago | All-Stars 3, Chicago 1 | None named | 14,534 |
| 1962 | Toronto | Toronto 4, All-Stars 1 | Eddie Shack, Tor | 14,236 |
| 1963 | Toronto | All-Stars 3, Toronto 3 | Frank Mahovlich, Tor | 14,034 |
| 1964 | Toronto | All-Stars 3, Toronto 2 | Jean Beliveau, Mtl | 14,232 |
| 1965 | Montreal | All-Stars 5, Montreal 2 | Gordie Howe, Det | 13,529 |
| 1967 | Montreal | Montreal 3, All-Stars 0 | Henri Richard, Mtl | 14,284 |
| 1968 | Toronto | Toronto 4, All-Stars 3 | Bruce Gamble, Tor | 15,753 |
| 1969 | Montreal | East 3, West 3 | Frank Mahovlich, Det | 16,260 |
| 1970 | St Louis | East 4, West 1 | Bobby Hull, Chi | 16,587 |
| 1971 | Boston | West 2, East 1 | Bobby Hull, Chi | 14,790 |
| 1972 | Minnesota | East 3, West 2 | Bobby Orr, Bos | 15,423 |
| 1973 | NY Rangers | East 5, West 4 | Greg Polis, Pitt | 16,986 |
| 1974 | Chicago | West 6, East 4 | Garry Unger, StL | 16,426 |
| 1975 | Montreal | Wales 7, Campbell 1 | Syl Apps Jr, Pitt | 16,080 |
| 1976 | Philadelphia | Wales 7, Campbell 5 | Pete Mahovlich, Mtl | 16,436 |
| 1977 | Vancouver | Wales 4, Campbell 3 | Rick Martin, Buff | 15,607 |
| 1978 | Buffalo | Wales 3, Campbell 2 (OT) | Billy Smith, NYI | 16,433 |
| 1980 | Detroit | Wales 6, Campbell 3 | Reg Leach, Phil | 21,002 |
| 1981 | Los Angeles | Campbell 4, Wales 1 | Mike Liut, StL | 15,761 |
| 1982 | Washington | Wales 4, Campbell 2 | Mike Bossy, NYI | 18,130 |
| 1983 | NY Islanders | Campbell 9, Wales 3 | Wayne Gretzky, Edm | 15,230 |
| 1984 | NJ Devils | Wales 7, Campbell 6 | Don Maloney, NYR | 18,939 |
| 1985 | Calgary | Wales 6, Campbell 4 | Mario Lemieux, Pitt | 16,825 |
| 1986 | Hartford | Wales 4, Campbell 3 (OT) | Grant Fuhr, Edm | 15,100 |
| 1988 | St Louis | Wales 6, Campbell 5 (OT) | Mario Lemieux, Pitt | 17,878 |
| 1989 | Edmonton | Campbell 9, Wales 5 | Wayne Gretzky, LA | 17,503 |
| 1990 | Pittsburgh | Wales 12, Campbell 7 | Mario Lemieux, Pitt | 16,236 |
| 1991 | Chicago | Campbell 11, Wales 5 | Vince Damphousse, Tor | 18,472 |
| 1992 | Philadelphia | Campbell 10, Wales 6 | Brett Hull, StL | 17,380 |
| 1993 | Montreal | Wales 16, Campbell 6 | Mike Gartner, NYR | 17,137 |
| 1994 | NY Rangers | East 9, West 8 | Mike Richter, NYR | 18,200 |
| 1996 | Boston | East 5, West 4 | Ray Bourque, Bos | 17,565 |
| 1997 | San Jose | East 11, West 7 | Mark Recchi, Mtl | 17,565 |
| 1998 | Vancouver | N America 8, World 7 | Teemu Selanne, Ana (World) | 18,422 |
| 1999 | Tampa Bay | N America 8, World 6 | Wayne Gretzky, NYR (N America) | 19,758 |
| 2000 | Toronto | World 9, N America 4 | Pavel Bure, Fla (World) | 19,300 |
| 2001 | Denver | N America 14, World 12 | Bill Guerin, Bos (N America) | 18,646 |

Note: The Challenge Cup, a series between the NHL All-Stars and the Soviet Union, was played instead of the All-Star Game in 1979. Eight years later, Rendez-Vous '87, a two-game series matching the Soviet Union and the NHL All-Stars, replaced the All-Star Game. The 1995 NHL All-Star game was cancelled due to a labor dispute. The 1998 NHL All-Star game, billed as a preview to the 1998 Winter Olympics in Nagano, Japan, matched North Amercian–born All-Stars and All-Stars born elsewhere.

# Hockey Hall of Fame

Located in Toronto, the Hockey Hall of Fame was officially opened on August 26, 1961. The current chairman is William C. Hay. There are, at present, 306 members of the Hockey Hall of Fame—209 players, 84 "builders," and 14 on-ice officials. (One member, Alan Eagleson, resigned from the Hall 3-25-98.) To be eligible, player and referee/linesman candidates should have been out of the game for three years, but the Hall's Board of Directors can make exceptions.

## Players

Sid Abel (1969)
Jack Adams (1959)
Charles (Syl) Apps (1961)
George Armstrong (1975)
Irvine (Ace) Bailey (1975)
Donald H. (Dan) Bain (1945)
Hobey Baker (1945)
Bill Barber (1990)
Marty Barry (1965)
Andy Bathgate (1978)
Bobby Bauer (1996)
Jean Beliveau (1972)
Clint Benedict (1965)
Douglas Bentley (1964)
Max Bentley (1966)
Hector (Toe) Blake (1966)
Leo Boivin (1986)
Dickie Boon (1952)
Mike Bossy (1991)
Emile (Butch) Bouchard (1966)
Frank Boucher (1958)
George (Buck) Boucher (1960)
Johnny Bower (1976)
Russell Bowie (1945)
Frank Brimsek (1966)
Harry L. (Punch) Broadbent (1962)
Walter (Turk) Broda (1967)
John Bucyk (1981)
Billy Burch (1974)
Harry Cameron (1962)
Gerry Cheevers (1985)
Francis (King) Clancy (1958)
Aubrey (Dit) Clapper (1947)
Bobby Clarke (1987)
Sprague Cleghorn (1958)
Neil Colville (1967)
Charlie Conacher (1961)
Lionel Conacher (1994)
Roy Conacher (1998)
Alex Connell (1958)
Bill Cook (1952)
Fred (Bun) Cook (1995)
Arthur Coulter (1974)
Yvan Cournoyer (1982)
Bill Cowley (1968)
Samuel (Rusty) Crawford (1962)
Jack Darragh (1962)
Allan M. (Scotty) Davidson (1950)
Clarence (Hap) Day (1961)
Alex Delvecchio (1977)
Cy Denneny (1959)
Marcel Dionne (1992)
Gordie Drillon (1975)
Charles Drinkwater (1950)
Ken Dryden (1983)

Woody Dumart (1992)
Thomas Dunderdale (1974)
Bill Durnan (1964)
Mervyn A. (Red) Dutton (1958)
Cecil (Babe) Dye (1970)
Phil Esposito (1984)
Tony Esposito (1988)
Arthur F. Farrell (1965)
Viacheslav Fetisov (2001)
Ferdinand (Fern) Flaman (1990)
Frank Foyston (1958)
Frank Frederickson (1958)
Bill Gadsby (1970)
Bob Gainey (1992)
Chuck Gardiner (1945)
Herb Gardiner (1958)
Jimmy Gardner (1962)
Mike Gartner (2001)
Bernie (Boom Boom) Geoffrion (1972)
Eddie Gerard (1945)
Ed Giacomin (1987)
Rod Gilbert (1982)
Hamilton (Billy) Gilmour (1962)
Frank (Moose) Goheen (1952)
Ebenezer R. (Ebbie) Goodfellow (1963)
Michel Goulet (1998)
Mike Grant (1950)
Wilfred (Shorty) Green (1962)
Wayne Gretzky (1999)
Si Griffis (1950)
George Hainsworth (1961)
Glenn Hall (1975)
Joe Hall (1961)
Doug Harvey (1973)
Dale Hawerchuk (2001)
George Hay (1958)
William (Riley) Hern (1962)
Bryan Hextall (1969)
Harry (Hap) Holmes (1972)
Tom Hooper (1962)
George (Red) Horner (1965)
Miles (Tim) Horton (1977)
Gordie Howe (1972)
Syd Howe (1965)
Harry Howell (1979)
Bobby Hull (1983)
John (Bouse) Hutton (1962)
Harry M. Hyland (1962)
James (Dick) Irvin (1958)
Harvey (Busher) Jackson (1971)
Ernest (Moose) Johnson (1952)
Ivan (Ching) Johnson (1958)
Tom Johnson (1970)
Aurel Joliat (1947)

Gordon (Duke) Keats (1958)
Leonard (Red) Kelly (1969)
Ted (Teeder) Kennedy (1966)
Dave Keon (1986)
Jari Kurri (2001)
Elmer Lach (1966)
Guy Lafleur (1988)
Edouard (Newsy) Lalonde (1950)
Jacques Laperriere (1987)
Guy LaPointe (1993)
Edgar Laprade (1993)
Reed Larson (1996)
Jean (Jack) Laviolette (1962)
Hugh Lehman (1958)
Jacques Lemaire (1984)
Mario Lemieux (1997)
Percy LeSueur (1961)
Herbert A. Lewis (1989)
Ted Lindsay (1966)
Harry Lumley (1980)
Lanny McDonald (1992)
Frank McGee (1945)
Billy McGimsie (1962)
George McNamara (1958)
Duncan (Mickey) MacKay (1952)
Frank Mahovlich (1981)
Joe Malone (1950)
Sylvio Mantha (1960)
Jack Marshall (1965)
Fred G. (Steamer) Maxwell (1962)
Stan Mikita (1983)
Dicky Moore (1974)
Patrick (Paddy) Moran (1958)
Howie Morenz (1945)
Billy Mosienko (1965)
Joe Mullen (2000)
Frank Nighbor (1947)
Reg Noble (1962)
Herbert (Buddy) O'Connor (1988)
Harry Oliver (1967)
Bert Olmstead (1985)
Bobby Orr (1979)
Bernie Parent (1984)
Brad Park (1988)
Lester Patrick (1947)
Lynn Patrick (1980)
Gilbert Perreault (1990)
Tommy Phillips (1945)
Pierre Pilote (1975)
Didier (Pit) Pitre (1962)
Jacques Plante (1978)
Denis Potvin (1991)
Walter (Babe) Pratt (1966)
Joe Primeau (1963)
Marcel Pronovost (1978)
Bob Pulford (1991)

## Players (Cont.)

Harvey Pulford (1945)
Hubert (Bill) Quackenbush (1976)
Frank Rankin (1961)
Jean Ratelle (1985)
Claude (Chuck) Rayner (1973)
Kenneth Reardon (1966)
Henri Richard (1979)
Maurice (Rocket) Richard (1961)
George Richardson (1950)
Gordon Roberts (1971)
Larry Robinson (1995)
Art Ross (1945)
Blair Russel (1965)
Ernest Russell (1965)
Jack Ruttan (1962)
Borje Salming (1996)
Denis Savard (2000)
Serge Savard (1986)
Terry Sawchuk (1971)
Fred Scanlan (1965)
Milt Schmidt (1961)
Dave (Sweeney) Schriner (1962)
Earl Seibert (1963)
Oliver Seibert (1961)
Eddie Shore (1947)
Steve Shutt (1993)
Albert C. (Babe) Siebert (1964)
Harold (Bullet Joe) Simpson (1962)
Daryl Sittler (1989)
Alfred E. Smith (1962)
Billy Smith (1993)
Clint Smith (1991)
Reginald (Hooley) Smith (1972)
Thomas Smith (1973)
Allan Stanley (1981)
Russell (Barney) Stanley (1962)
Peter Stastny (1998)
John (Black Jack) Stewart (1964)
Nels Stewart (1962)
Bruce Stuart (1961)
Hod Stuart (1945)
Frederic (Cyclone) (O.B.E.)
    Taylor (1947)
Cecil R. (Tiny) Thompson
    (1959)
Vladislav Tretiak (1989)
Harry J. Trihey (1950)
Bryan Trottier (1997)
Norm Ullman (1982)
Georges Vezina (1945)
Jack Walker (1960)
Marty Walsh (1962)
Harry Watson (1994)
Harry E. Watson (1962)
Ralph (Cooney) Weiland (1971)
Harry Westwick (1962)
Fred Whitcroft (1962)
Gordon (Phat) Wilson (1962)
Lorne (Gump) Worsley (1980)
Roy Worters (1969)

## Builders

Charles Adams (1960)
Weston W. Adams (1972)
Thomas (Frank) Ahearn (1962)
John (Bunny) Ahearne (1977)
Montagu Allan (C.V.O.) (1945)
Keith Allen (1992)
Al Arbour (1996)
Harold Ballard (1977)
David Bauer (1989)
John Bickell (1978)
Scott Bowman (1991)
George V. Brown (1961)
Walter A. Brown (1962)
Frank Buckland (1975)
Walter L. Bush (2000)
Jack Butterfield (1980)
Frank Calder (1947)
Angus D. Campbell (1964)
Clarence Campbell (1966)
Joe Cattarinich (1977)
Bob Cole (1996)
Joseph (Leo) Dandurand (1963)
Francis Dilio (1964)
George S. Dudley (1958)
James A. Dunn (1968)
Robert Alan Eagleson (1989–98*)
Sergio Gambucci (1996)
Emile Francis (1982)
Jack Gibson (1976)
Tommy Gorman (1963)
Frank Griffiths (1993)
William Hanley (1986)
Charles Hay (1974)
James C. Hendy (1968)
Foster Hewitt (1965)
William Hewitt (1947)
Fred J. Hume (1962)
George (Punch) Imlach (1984)
Tommy Ivan (1974)
William M. Jennings (1975)
Bob Johnson (1992)
Gordon W. Juckes (1979)
John Kilpatrick (1960)
Seymour Knox III (1993)
George Leader (1969)
Robert LeBel (1970)
Thomas F. Lockhart (1965)
Paul Loicq (1961)
Frederic McLaughlin (1963)
John Mariucci (1985)
Frank Mathers (1992)
John (Jake) Milford (1984)
Hartland Molson (1973)
Scotty Morrison (1999)
Mngr. Athol (Pere) Murray (1998)
Francis Nelson (1947)
Bruce A. Norris (1969)
James Norris, Sr. (1958)
James D. Norris (1962)
William M. Northey (1947)

## Builders (Cont.)

John O'Brien (1962)
Brian O'Neill (1994)
Fred Page (1993)
Craig Patrick (1996)
Frank Patrick (1958)
Allan W. Pickard (1958)
Rudy Pilous (1985)
Norman (Bud) Poile (1990)
Samuel Pollock (1978)
Donat Raymond (1958)
John Robertson (1947)
Claude C. Robinson (1947)
Philip D. Ross (1976)
Gunther Sabetzki (1995)
Glen Sather (1997)
Frank J. Selke (1960)
Harry Sinden (1983)
Frank D. Smith (1962)
Conn Smythe (1958)
Edward M. Snider (1988)
Lord Stanley of Preston
    (G.C.B.) (1945)
James T. Sutherland (1947)
Anatoli V. Tarasov (1974)
Bill Torrey (1995)
Lloyd Turner (1958)
William Tutt (1978)
Carl Potter Voss (1974)
Fred C. Waghorn (1961)
Arthur Wirtz (1971)
Bill Wirtz (1976)
John A. Ziegler, Jr. (1987)

## Referees/Linesmen

Neil Armstrong (1991)
John Ashley (1981)
William L. Chadwick (1964)
John D'Amico (1993)
Chaucer Elliott (1961)
George Hayes (1988)
Robert W. Hewitson (1963)
Fred J. (Mickey) Ion (1961)
Matt Pavelich (1987)
Mike Rodden (1962)
J. Cooper Smeaton (1961)
Roy (Red) Storey (1967)
Frank Udvari (1973)
Andy van Hellemond (1999)

Note: Year of election to the Hall of Fame is in parentheses after the member's name.
*Eagleson resigned from Hall March 25, 1998.

# Tennis

**Australian and French
Open champion
Jennifer Capriati**

# Women's Movement

## Led by Jennifer Capriati and the Williams sisters, the women's tour outshined the men's for the second year in a row

### BY B.J. SCHECTER

PERHAPS CBS executives sensed the inevitable. Or maybe they were just reacting to the obvious. Whatever the case, by moving the U.S. Open women's final to prime time on a Saturday night, CBS sent the unmistakable message that the women's game had overtaken the men's in popularity. And the women didn't disappoint. Though there was more parity in the men's game—which had four different champions in the Grand Slams—the women provided more intensity and entertainment from baseline to baseline, with a few notable exceptions.

Once again the Williams sisters were lightning rods for history, excitement and controversy. In their ongoing efforts to maintain lives outside tennis, and to simply take a break from the intense world of the WTA, Venus and Serena took significant time off at the beginning of the tennis season, drawing criticism from fans and players alike. They devoted little time to practice during this period, pursued outside interests such as fashion classes, and were noticeably absent from early tournaments.

In the first major of the year, the Australian Open, Martina Hingis dispatched both sisters in succession, defeating Serena 6–2, 3–6, 8–6 in the quarterfinals and routing Venus 6–1, 6–1 in the semis. Afterward Hingis said of the Williams sisters, "They're always saying, 'O.K., we went to school.' Either you go to school or you play tennis. You can't do both. Tennis is a full-time commitment."

Apparently players as supremely talented as the Williamses can get away with part-time commitment. But first, perhaps, they need a wake-up call. Venus got hers in May, when she lost in the first round of the French Open to little-known Barbara Schett. Following that shocking defeat Venus rededicated herself to tennis and was determined to show the world that she could still perform at the championship level. One month later, with her rocket serve and stunning power and range, she defended her Wimbledon title by beating Justine Henin 6–1, 3–6, 6–0 in the final. Afterward she

MANNY MILLAN

vowed to make tennis more of a priority. "I'm still a kid, and I don't want to grow up yet," she said, "but I have to in some things, but not everything. So it's a happy medium. Grand Slams definitely are Number 1. Then Number 2, for sure, is Number 1. Oh boy, that sounds like a Dr. Seuss book." She meant, if we can unravel the Seussian construct, that outside of peaking for Grand Slam tournaments, she's going to make sure she's happy and fulfilled—which won't necessarily involve tennis.

The final of the U.S. Open read like a happy bedtime story in the Williams household, one that outspoken papa Richard had been predicting for years. The Williams sisters had met in tournaments before, and in the semifinals at Wimbledon (in 2000), but they had not yet played each other in the final of a Grand Slam. Their play in the early rounds in New York was so stellar that people started checking the record for the last time two sisters had met in a Grand Slam final. They had to go back to 1884, when Maud Watson downed her sister Lilian at Wimbledon.

Dominating the field with their power and grace, Venus and Serena dispatched some of the world's top players with ease. In the semis, Venus dismantled Jennifer Capriati, winner of the year's first two Grand Slams, and Serena made Hingis, the world's No. 1 player, look like an amateur. The all-Williams final was set.

And based on the sisters' form, Venus versus Serena looked to be the battle of the ages. But it didn't turn out that way. The tennis was uneventful, sloppy at times, and surprisingly emotionless as Venus cruised to a 6–2, 6–4 victory. There were times when it seemed as if neither sister wanted to win. "I was saying, 'Come on, Serena, just do this or do that,'" said Venus. "When I'd find myself doing that, I'd lose a

couple of points. When I'd lose a couple of points, I wasn't sorry [for her] anymore." Lackluster tennis aside, though, this event had the pomp and circumstance befitting its historic status. Arthur Ashe Stadium was chock full of A-list celebrities. "Hey, I wouldn't have missed it either if I knew something so historic was going to happen," Serena said. "I guess a lot of people want to watch us. For me it's really exciting because some of these [celebrities] are really superstars. I didn't think that they would want to watch little me play tennis."

In the end the better player won as Venus seized her fourth Grand Slam title. Following match point the two sisters hugged at the net and Venus said to Serena, "I love you. I feel so bad. I feel like I haven't won."

But arguably both sisters had won; their appearance in a Grand Slam final was a thumping affirmation of the barriers they have obliterated in their careers. The Williams sisters' impact on tennis is similar to Tiger Woods's effect on golf. "Tennis has come to a different level now," said Jeanne

Moutoussamy-Ashe, the widow of Arthur Ashe. "Arthur would have liked to have been here for them because we're all beneficiaries. They've done a wonderful job."

The story of the first half of the season, though, was Capriati, who completed an inspiring comeback. Once considered the bright future of the women's game, Capriati crumbled under the immense pressure and disappeared from tennis for several years. She played her first professional match at 13. At age 14 she made it to the semifinals of the French Open and vaulted into the Top 10. By 17, however, Capriati was burned out. In December 1993 she was cited for shoplifting and five months later was arrested for marijuana possession at a Florida motel. She went five years without winning a match in a Grand Slam event, and it was doubtful that she would ever recapture her previous form.

"There were times when I thought maybe this isn't worth it," Capriati said. "But once I got over the hump and enjoyed the game and stopped worrying about the other stuff, I knew I'd break through eventually."

After an inconsistent season in 2000, Capriati rededicated herself in the off-season, working out with a personal trainer daily, and arrived at the Australian Open in the best shape of her life. She toned the mental side of her game as well. No longer did she let unforced errors or poor line calls affect her. The results were striking indeed. Capriati defeated Monica Seles, Lindsay Davenport and Hingis in successive matches to win the Australian. "Who would have ever thought I would have made it here after so much happened?" said Capriati after beating Hingis 6–4, 6–3 in the final. "Dreams do come true."

And Capriati wasn't done dreaming. At the French Open she continued her superb play, arriving in Paris as the fourth seed but leaving as the champion. In a remarkable final, she rallied to beat Kim Clijsters 1–6, 6–4, 12–10. "I never thought I'd be standing here 11 years later, after playing my first time here when I was 14 years old," Capriati told the crowd afterward. "Really I'm just waiting to wake up from this dream."

On the men's side of the French Open,

Gustavo Kuerten knew he wasn't dreaming when he cruised to the final. A fixture at Roland Garros now, and a master on clay, Kuerten had only one truly tough match en route to the final. There he defeated Alex Corretja to win his third French Open title, then drew a large heart in the clay and lay down inside it as a tribute to the French fans.

There was plenty of heart and desire on display at Wimbledon, where Goran Ivanisevic became the first wild card to win a Grand Slam. Ivanisevic, who was only invited to the event because he had lost in the Wimbledon final three times, came to the All England having won just nine matches during the season. Down two sets to one in the semis against local favorite Tim Henman, Ivanisevic was spared by a rain delay. Refreshed, he came back the next day and rallied to win.

In the final, which was pushed to Monday due to the weather, Ivanisevic defeated Patrick Rafter in a marvelous five-set match that went 9–7 in the fifth. Contemplating retirement because of a bum shoulder, Ivanisevic knew this might be his last chance to win a Grand Slam. Before the match he said, "If some angel comes tonight in my dreams and says, 'O.K., Goran, you are going to win Wimbledon tomorrow, but you won't be able to touch the racket ever again in your life,' I'd say, 'O.K., I take that.'"

Though the women overshadowed the men at the U.S. Open, one match stood out above all, men's or women's. Andre Agassi and Pete Sampras are more accustomed to meeting in finals, but with Sampras struggling (he was seeded 10th), they met one another in a quarterfinal—one that will rank with the best matches in tennis history. Neither player had his serve broken as Sampras outslugged his fellow legend 6–7, 7–6, 7–6, 7–6.

It's too bad for the men that the tournament couldn't have ended right then and there, because everything that followed was a letdown. Sampras reached the final, where he faced 20-year-old Lleyton Hewitt, but he had nothing left. Looking slow and tired, he lost in straight sets.

Once again, the men could not match the drama of the women's tour.

## 2001 Grand Slam Champions

### Australian Open

#### Men's Singles

| | Winner | Finalist | Score |
|---|---|---|---|
| Quarterfinals | Andre Agassi (6) | Todd Martin | 7–5, 6–3, 6–4 |
| | Sebastien Grosjean (16) | Carlos Moya | 6–1, 6–4, 6–2 |
| | Arnaud Clement (15) | Yevgeny Kafelnikov (5) | 6–4, 5–7, 7–6 (7–3), 7–6 (7–3) |
| | Patrick Rafter (12) | Dominik Hrbaty (14) | 6–2, 6–7 (4–7), 7–5, 6–0 |
| Semifinals | Andre Agassi | Patrick Rafter | 7–5, 2–6, 6–7 (5–7), 6–2, 6–3 |
| | Arnaud Clement | Sebastien Grosjean | 5–7, 2–6, 7–6 (7–4), 7–5, 6–2 |
| Final | Andre Agassi | Arnaud Clement | 6–4, 6–2, 6–2 |

#### Women's Singles

| | Winner | Finalist | Score |
|---|---|---|---|
| Quarterfinals | Martina Hingis (1) | Serena Williams (6) | 6–2, 3–6, 8–6 |
| | Venus Williams (3) | Amanda Coetzer (10) | 2–6, 6–1, 8–6 |
| | Jennifer Capriati (12) | Monica Seles (4) | 5–7, 6–4, 6–3 |
| | Lindsay Davenport (2) | Anna Kournikova (8) | 6–3, 4–6, 9–7 |
| Semifinals | Martina Hingis | Venus Williams | 6–1, 6–1 |
| | Jennifer Capriati | Lindsay Davenport | 6–3, 6–4 |
| Final | Jennifer Capriati | Martina Hingis | 6–4, 6–3 |

#### Doubles

| | Winner | Finalist | Score |
|---|---|---|---|
| Men's Final | Jonas Bjorkman/ Todd Woodbridge (4) | Byron Black/ David Prinosil (14) | 6–1, 5–7, 6–4, 6–4, |
| Women's Final | Serena Williams/ Venus Williams | Lindsay Davenport/ Corina Morariu | 6–2, 4–6, 6–4 |
| Mixed Final | Ellis Ferreira/ Corina Morariu | Joshua Eagle/ Barbara Schett (4) | 6–1, 6–3 |

### French Open

#### Men's Singles

| | Winner | Finalist | Score |
|---|---|---|---|
| Quarterfinals | Alex Corretja (13) | Roger Federer | 7–5, 6–4, 7–5 |
| | Sebastien Grosjean (10) | Andre Agassi (3) | 1–6, 6–1, 6–1, 6–3, |
| | Gustavo Kuerten (1) | Yevgeny Kafelnikov (7) | 6–1, 3–6, 7–6 (7–3), 6–4 |
| | Juan Carlos Ferrero (4) | Lleyton Hewitt (6) | 6–4, 6–2, 6–1 |
| Semifinals | Alex Corretja | Sebastien Grosjean | 7–6 (7–2), 6–4, 6–4 |
| | Gustavo Kuerten | Juan Carlos Ferrero | 6–4, 6–4, 6–3 |
| Final | Gustavo Kuerten | Alex Corretja | 6–7 (3–7), 7–5, 6–2, 6–0 |

#### Women's Singles

| | Winner | Finalist | Score |
|---|---|---|---|
| Quarterfinals | Justine Henin (14) | Lina Krasnoroutskaya | 6–1, 6–2 |
| | Martina Hingis (1) | Francesca Schiavone | 6–1, 6–4 |
| | Jennifer Capriati (4) | Serena Williams (6) | 6–2, 5–7, 6–2 |
| | Kim Clijsters (12) | Petra Mandula | 6–1, 6–2 |
| Semifinals | Jennifer Capriati | Martina Hingis | 6 4, 6 3 |
| | Kim Clijsters | Justine Henin | 2–6, 7–5, 6–3 |
| Final | Jennifer Capriati | Kim Clijsters | 1–6, 6–4, 12–10 |

Note: Seedings in parentheses.

### French Open *(Cont.)*
#### Doubles

| | Winner | Finalist | Score |
|---|---|---|---|
| **Men's Final** | Mahesh Bhupathi/<br>Leander Paes | Petr Pala/<br>Pavel Vizner (13) | 7–6 (7–5), 6–3 |
| **Women's Final** | Virginia Ruano Pascual/<br>Paola Suarez (2) | Jelena Dokic/<br>Conchita Martinez (16) | 6–2, 6–4 |
| **Mixed Final** | Virginia Ruano-Pascual/<br>Tomas Carbonell | Paola Suarez/<br>Jaime Oncins | 7–5, 6–3 |

## Wimbledon
### Men's Singles

| | Winner | Finalist | Score |
|---|---|---|---|
| **Quarterfinals** | Patrick Rafter (3) | Thomas Enqvist (10) | 6–1, 6–3, 7–6 (7–5) |
| | Goran Ivanisevic | Marat Safin (4) | 7–6 (7–2), 7–5, 3–6,<br>7–6 (7–3) |
| | Andre Agassi (2) | Nicolas Escude (24) | 6–7 (3), 6–3, 6–4, 6–2 |
| | Tim Henman (6) | Roger Federer (15) | 7–5, 7–6 (8–6), 2–6,<br>7–6 (8–6) |
| **Semifinals** | Patrick Rafter | Andre Agassi | 2–6, 6–3, 3–6, 6–2,<br>8–6 |
| | Goran Ivanisevic | Tim Henman | 7–5, 6–7(6–8), 0–6, 7–6<br>(7–5), 6–3 |
| **Final** | Goran Ivanisevic | Patrick Rafter | 6–3, 3–6, 6–3,<br>2–6, 9–7 |

### Women's Singles

| | Winner | Finalist | Score |
|---|---|---|---|
| **Quarterfinals** | Jennifer Capriati (4) | Serena Williams (5) | 6–7 (4–7), 7–5, 6–3 |
| | Justine Henin (8) | Conchita Martinez (19) | 6–1, 6–0 |
| | Venus Williams (2) | Nathalie Tauziat (9) | 7–5, 6–1 |
| | Lindsay Davenport (3) | Kim Clijsters (7) | 6–1, 6–2 |
| **Semifinals** | Justine Henin | Jennifer Capriati | 2–6, 6–4, 6–2 |
| | Venus Williams | Lindsay Davenport | 6–2, 6–7 (1–7), 6–1 |
| **Final** | Venus Williams | Justine Henin | 6–1, 3–6, 6–0 |

#### Doubles

| | Winner | Finalist | Score |
|---|---|---|---|
| **Men's Final** | Donald Johnson/<br>Jared Palmer (4) | Jiri Novak/<br>David Rikl (3) | 6–4, 4–6, 6–3, 7–6 (8–6) |
| **Women's Final** | Lisa Raymond/<br>Rennae Stubbs (1) | Kim Clijsters/<br>Ai Sugiyama (9) | 6–4, 6–3 |
| **Mixed Final** | Leos Friedl/<br>Daniela Hantuchova | Mike Bryan/<br>Liezel Huber | 4–6, 6–3, 6–2 |

## U.S. Open
### Men's Singles

| | Winner | Finalist | Score |
|---|---|---|---|
| **Quarterfinals** | Yevgeny Kafelnikov (7) | Gustavo Kuerten (1) | 6–4, 6–0, 6–3, |
| | Lleyton Hewitt (4) | Andy Roddick (18) | 6–7 (5–7), 6–3, 6–4,<br>3–6 6–4 |
| | Marat Safin (3) | Mariano Zabaleta | 6–4, 6–4, 6–2 |
| | Pete Sampras (10) | Andre Agassi (2) | 6–7 (7–9), 7–6 (7–2),<br>7–6 (7–2), 7–6 (7–5) |
| **Semifinals** | Lleyton Hewitt | Yevgeny Kafelnikov | 6–1, 6–2, 6–1 |
| | Pete Sampras | Marat Safin | 6–3, 7–6 (7–5), 6–3 |
| **Final** | Lleyton Hewitt (4) | Pete Sampras (10) | 7–6 (7–4), 6–1, 6–1 |

Note: Seedings in parentheses.

# Grand Slam Champions (Cont.)

## U.S. Open (Cont.)

### Women's Singles

| | Winner | Finalist | Score |
|---|---|---|---|
| **Quarterfinals** | Venus Williams (4) | Kim Clijsters (5) | 6–3, 6–1 |
| | Jennifer Capriati (2) | Amelie Mauresmo (8) | 6–3, 6–4 |
| | Martina Hingis (1) | Daja Bedanova | 6–2, 6–0 |
| | Serena Williams (10) | Lindsay Davenport (3) | 6–3, 6–7 (5–7), 7–5 |
| **Semifinals** | Serena Williams | Martina Hingis | 6–3, 6–2 |
| | Venus Williams | Jennifer Capriati | 6–4, 6–2 |
| **Final** | Venus Williams | Serena Williams | 6–2, 6–4 |

### Doubles

| | Winner | Finalist | Score |
|---|---|---|---|
| **Men's Final** | Wayne Black/ Kevin Ullyett (14) | Donald Johnson/ Jared Palmer (2) | 7–6 (11–9), 2–6, 6–3 |
| **Women's Final** | Lisa Raymond/ Rennae Stubbs (1) | Kimberly Po-Messerli/ Nathalie Tauziat (4) | 6–2, 5–7, 7–5 |
| **Mixed Final** | Rennae Stubbs/ Todd Woodbridge (1) | Lisa Raymond/ Leander Paes (2) | 6–4, 5–7, 7–6 (11–9) |

# Major Tournament Results

## Men's Tour (late 2000)

| Date | Tournament | Site | Winner | Finalist | Score |
|---|---|---|---|---|---|
| Oct 9–16 | CA Trophy Tournament | Vienna | Tim Henman | Tommy Haas | 6–4, 6–4, 6–4 |
| Oct 9–16 | Japan Open | Tokyo | S. Schalken | Nicolas Lapentti | 6–4, 3–6, 6–1 |
| Oct 23–30 | Kremlin Cup | Moscow | Y. Kafelnikov | David Prinosil | 6–2, 7–5 |
| Oct 23–30 | Swiss Indoors | Basel, Switzerland | Thomas Enqvist | Roger Federer | 6–2, 4–6, 7–6 (7–4), 1–6, 6–1 |
| Nov 6–13 | St. Petersburg Open | St. Petersburg, Russia | Marat Safin | Dominik Hrbaty | 2–6, 6–4, 6–4 |
| Nov 6–13 | Lyon Grand Prix | Lyon, France | Arnaud Clement | Patrick Rafter | 7–6 (7–2), 7–6 (7–5) |
| Nov 13–20 | Paris Masters | Paris | Marat Safin | M. Philippoussis | 3–6, 7–6 (9–7), 6–4 3–6, 7–6 (10–8) |
| Nov 20–27 | Stockholm Open | Stockholm | T. Johansson | Y. Kafelnikov | 6–2, 6–4, 6–4 |
| Nov 27–Dec 4 | Tennis Masters Cup | Lisbon | G. Kuerten | Andre Agassi | 6–4, 6–4, 6–4 |

## Men's Tour (Through September 9, 2001)

| Date | Tournament | Site | Winner | Finalist | Score |
|---|---|---|---|---|---|
| Jan 1–7 | Qatar Open | Doha, Qatar | Marcelo Rios | Bohdan Ulihrach | 6–3, 2–6, 6–3 |
| Jan 15–28 | Australian Open | Melbourne | Andre Agassi | Arnaud Clement | 6–4, 6–2, 6–2 |
| Feb 12–18 | Marseille Open | Marseille, France | Y. Kafelnikov | S. Grosjean | 7–6 (7–5), 6–2 |
| Feb 19–25 | ABN/Amro Tournament | Rotterdam, Amsterdam | N. Escude | Roger Federer | 7–5, 3–6, 7–6 (7–5) |
| Feb 19–25 | Kroger St. Jude | Memphis | M. Philippoussis | D. Sanguinetti | 6–3, 6–7 (5–7), 6–3 |
| Feb 26–Mar 3 | Dubai Open | Dubai, UAE | Juan Carlos Ferrero | Marat Safin | 6–2, 3–1, retired |
| Mar 12–18 | Champions Cup | Indian Wells, California | Andre Agassi | Pete Sampras | 7–6 (7–5), 7–5, 6–1 |
| Mar 21–Apr 1 | Ericsson Open | Miami | Andre Agassi | Jan-Michael Gambill | 7–6 (7–4), 6–1, 6–0 |
| Apr 9–15 | Estoril Open | Estoril, Portugal | Juan Carlos Ferrero | Felix Mantilla | 7–6 (7–3), 4–6, 6–3 |
| Apr 16–22 | Monte Carlo Open | Monte Carlo | G. Kuerten | Hicham Arazi | 6–3, 6–2, 6–4 |
| Apr 23–29 | Open Seat Godo | Barcelona | Juan Carlos Ferrero | Carlos Moya | 4–6, 7–5, 6–3, 3–6 7–5 |
| Apr 30–May 6 | BMW Open | Munich | Jiri Novak | Anthony Dupuis | 6–4, 7–5 |
| May 7–13 | Italian Open | Rome | Juan Carlos Ferrero | Gustavo Kuerten | 3–6, 6–1, 2–6, 6–4 6–2 |

# Tournament Results *(Cont.)*

## Men's Tour (Through September 9, 2001) *(Cont.)*

| Date | Tournament | Site | Winner | Finalist | Score |
|---|---|---|---|---|---|
| May 14–20 | German Open | Hamburg | Albert Portas | Juan Carlos Ferrero | 4–6, 6–2, 0–6, 7–6 (7–5), 7–5 |
| May 28–Jun 10 | French Open | Paris | Gustavo Kuerten | Alex Corretja | 6–7 (3–7), 7–5, 6–2, 6–0 |
| June 11–17 | Gerry Weber Open | Halle, Germany | T. Johanson | Frabice Santoro | 6–3, 6–7 (5–7), 6–2 |
| June 18–24 | Heineken Trophy | 'S-Hertogenbosch Netherlands | Lleyton Hewitt | Guillermo Canas | 6–3, 6–4 |
| June 25–July 9 | Wimbledon | Wimbledon | Goran Ivanisevic | Patrick Rafter | 6–3, 3–6, 6–3, 2–6, 9–7 |
| July 10–15 | Gstaad Open | Gstaad, Switzerland | Jiri Novak | Juan Carlos Ferrero | 6–1, 6–7 (5–7), 7–5 |
| July 16–22 | Mercedes Cup | Stuttgart, Germany | Gustavo Kuerten | Guillermo Canas | 6–3, 6–2, 6–4 |
| July 23–29 | Generali Open | Kitzbuhel, Austria | Nicolas Lapentti | Albert Costa | 1–6, 6–4, 7–5, 7–5 |
| Jul 30–Aug 5 | Canadian Open | Montreal | Andrei Pavel | Patrick Rafter | 7–6 (7–3), 2–6, 6–3 |
| Aug 6–12 | Tennis Masters Series | Cincinnati | Gustavo Kuerten | Patrick Rafter | 6–1, 6–3 |
| Aug 13–19 | RCA Championships | Indianapolis | Patrick Rafter | Gustavo Kuerten | 4–2, retired |
| Aug 13–19 | Legg Mason Classic | Wash., D.C. | Andy Roddick | Sjeng Schalken | 6–2, 6–3 |
| Aug 27–Sept 9 | U.S. Open | New York City | Lleyton Hewitt | Pete Sampras | 7–6 (7–4), 6–1, 6–1 |

## Women's Tour (Late 2000)

| Date | Tournament | Site | Winner | Finalist | Score |
|---|---|---|---|---|---|
| Oct 9–15 | Swisscom Challenge | Zurich | Martina Hingis | L. Davenport | 6–4, 4–6, 7–5 |
| Oct 23–29 | Ladies Kremlin Cup | Moscow | Martina Hingis | A. Kournikova | 6–3, 6–1 |
| Oct 30–Nov 5 | Sparkassen Cup | Leipzig, Germany | Kim Clijsters | E. Likhovtseva | 7–6 (8–6), 4–6, 6–4 |
| Nov 6–12 | Advanta Champ'ships | Philadelphia | L. Davenport | Martina Hingis | 7–6 (9–7), 6–4 |
| Nov 13–19 | Chase Champ'ships | New York | Martina Hingis | Monica Seles | 6–7 (5–7), 6–4, 6–4 |

## Women's Tour (Through September 9, 2001)

| Date | Tournament | Site | Winner | Finalist | Score |
|---|---|---|---|---|---|
| Jan 7–13 | Adidas International | Sydney | Martina Hingis | L. Davenport | 6–3, 4–6, 7–5 |
| Jan 15–28 | Australian Open | Melbourne | Jennfier Capriati | Martina Hingis | 6–4, 6–3 |
| Jan 30–Feb 4 | Pan Pacific Open | Tokyo | L. Davenport | Martina Hingis | 6–7 (4–7), 6–4, 6–2 |
| Feb 5–11 | Open Gaz de France | Paris | A. Mauresmo | Anke Huber | 7–6 (7–2), 6–1 |
| Feb 14–20 | Qatar Open | Doha, Qatar | Martina Hingis | Sandrine Testud | 6–3, 6–2 |
| Mar 5–18 | Tennis Masters Series | Indian Wells, California | Serena Williams | Kim Clijsters | 4–6, 6–4, 6–2 |
| Mar 21–Apr 1 | Ericsson Open | Miami | Venus Williams | Jennifer Capriati | 4–6, 6–1, 7–6 (7–4) |
| Apr 9–15 | Bausch & Lomb Championships | Amelia Island, Florida | A. Mauresmo | Amanda Coetzer | 6–4, 7–5 |
| Apr 16–22 | Family Circle Cup | Charleston, S Carolina | Jennifer Capriati | Martina Hingis | 6–0, 4–6, 6–4 |
| Apr 30–May 6 | Betty Barclay Cup | Hamburg | Venus Williams | M. Shaughnessy | 6–3, 6–0 |
| May 7–13 | German Open | Berlin | A. Mauresmo | Jennifer Capriati | 6–4, 2–6, 6–3 |
| May 14–20 | Tennis Masters Series | Rome | Jelena Dokic | A. Mauresmo | 7–6 (7–3), 6–1 |
| May 21–27 | Int'l de Strasbourg | Strasbourg, France | Silvia Farena Elia | Anke Huber | 7–5, 0–6, 6–4 |
| May 28–Jun 9 | French Open | Paris | Jennifer Capriati | Kim Clijsters | 1–6, 6–4, 12–10 |
| June 18–24 | Britannic Asset Championships | Eastbourne, England | L. Davenport | Magui Serna | 6–2, 6–0 |
| June 25–July 8 | Wimbledon | Wimbledon | Venus Williams | Justine Henin | 6–1, 3–6, 6–0 |
| July 23–29 | Bank of the West | Stanford | Kim Clijsters | L. Davenport | 6–4, 6–7 (5–7), 6–1 |
| July 30–Aug 5 | Acura Classic | San Diego | Venus Williams | Monica Seles | 6–2, 6–3 |
| Aug 6–12 | Estyle.com Classic | Los Angeles | L. Davenport | Monica Seles | 6–3, 7–5 |

## Women's Tour (Through September 9, 2001) *(Cont.)*

| Date | Tournament | Site | Winner | Finalist | Score |
|---|---|---|---|---|---|
| Aug 13–19 | Rogers AT&T Cup | Toronto | Serena Williams | Jennifer Capriati | 6–1, 6–7(7–9), 6–3 |
| Aug 19–25 | Pilot Pen Int'l | New Haven,CT | Venus Williams | L. Davenport | 7–6 (8–6), 6–4 |
| Aug 28–Sept 10 | U.S. Open | New York City | Venus Williams | Serena Williams | 6–2, 6–4 |

# 2000 Singles Leaders

## Men

| Rank | Player | Tournament Wins | Match Record | Earnings ($) |
|---|---|---|---|---|
| 1. | Gustavo Kuerten | 5 | 63–22 | 4,701,610 |
| 2. | Marat Safin | 7 | 73–27 | 3,755,599 |
| 3. | Pete Sampras | 2 | 42–13 | 2,254,698 |
| 4. | Magnus Norman | 5 | 67–25 | 1,846,269 |
| 5. | Yevgeny Kafelnikov | 2 | 66–35 | 3,755,598 |
| 6. | Andre Agassi | 1 | 40–15 | 1,884,443 |
| 7. | Lleyton Hewitt | 4 | 61–19 | 1,642,572 |
| 8. | Alex Corretja | 5 | 54–19 | 1,530,062 |
| 9. | Thomas Enqvist | 2 | 51–23 | 2,381,060 |
| 10. | Tim Henman | 2 | 57–25 | 1,057,823 |
| 11. | Mark Philippoussis | 1 | 43–22 | 839,567 |
| 12. | Juan Carlos Ferrero | 1 | 46–26 | 812,636 |
| 13. | Wayne Ferreira | 1 | 43–22 | 1,237,864 |
| 14. | Franco Squillari | 1 | 34–24 | 754,458 |
| 15. | Patrick Rafter | 1 | 34–18 | 814,586 |
| 16. | Cedric Pioline | 1 | 33–20 | 888.789 |
| 17. | Dominik Hrbaty | 1 | 44–29 | 1,195,760 |
| 18. | Arnaud Clement | 1 | 36–27 | 671,815 |
| 19. | Sebastien Grosjean | 1 | 44–26 | 655,280 |
| 20. | Nicolas Kiefer | 1 | 30–16 | 591,749 |

Note: Compiled by the ATP Tour, as of Dec. 18, 2000.
Note: Prize money reflects both singles and doubles.

## Women

| Rank | Player | Tournament Wins | Match Record | Earnings ($) |
|---|---|---|---|---|
| 1. | Martina Hingis | 10 | 77–10 | 3,049,581 |
| 2. | Lindsay Davenport | 4 | 57–12 | 2,353,634 |
| 3. | Venus Williams | 6 | 41–4 | 1,897,730 |
| 4. | Monica Seles | 3 | 56–13 | 1,127,475 |
| 5. | Conchita Martinez | 1 | 50–21 | 970,978 |
| 6. | Serena Williams | 3 | 37–8 | 850,398 |
| 7. | Mary Pierce | 2 | 29–11 | 988,225 |
| 8. | Anna Kournikova | 0 | 47–29 | 640,459 |
| 9. | Arantxa Sánchez Vicario | 0 | 44–19 | 638,859 |
| 10. | Nathalie Tauziat | 1 | 36–26 | 594,560 |
| 11. | Amanda Coetzer | 1 | 46–23 | 505,593 |
| 12. | Elena Dementieva | 0 | 40–22 | 608,077 |
| 13. | Chanda Rubin | 1 | 42–21 | 423,686 |
| 14. | Jennifer Capriati | 1 | 35–19 | 444,449 |
| 15. | Julie Halard-Decugis | 2 | 32–23 | 413,700 |
| 16. | Amelie Mauresmo | 1 | 24–13 | 323,325 |
| 17. | Sandrine Testud | 0 | 31–21 | 439,663 |
| 18. | Kim Clijsters | 2 | 30–16 | 336,100 |
| 19. | Anke Huber | 2 | 32–16 | 354,858 |
| 20. | Amy Frazier | 0 | 30–22 | 258,460 |

Note: Compiled by the WTA, as of Nov. 20, 2000.
Note: Prize money reflects singles play only.

# THEY SAID IT

*Jennifer Capriati, comeback kid, on her newfound perspective, "I've made the decision that I'm in control. I'm not a victim. I'm going to make everyone else a victim."*

## 2000 Davis Cup World Group Final

Spain def. Australia 3–1, Dec. 8–10 in Barcelona, Spain
 Lleyton Hewitt (AUS) def. Albert Costa (SPA), 3–6, 6–1, 2–6, 6–4, 6–4
 Juan-Carlos Ferrero (SPA) def. Patrick Rafter (AUS), 6–7 (4–7), 7–6 (7–2), 6–2, 3–1, retired
 Joan Balcells and Alex Corretja (SPA) def. Mark Woodforde and Sandon Stolle (AUS)
 6–4, 6–4, 6–4
 Juan-Carlos Ferrero (SPA) def. Lleyton Hewitt (AUS) 6–2, 7–6 (7–5), 4–6, 6–4
 Albert Costa (SPA) vs. Patrick Rafter (AUS), canceled

## 2001 Davis Cup World Group Tournament

### FIRST ROUND

Australia def. Ecuador, 4–1
Brazil def. Morocco, 4–1
Sweden def. Czech Republic, 3–2
Russia def. Slovakia, 3–2
France def. Belgium, 5–0
Switzerland def. United States, 3–2
Germany def. Romania, 3–2
Netherlands def. Spain, 4–1

### QUARTERFINAL ROUND

Australia def. Brazil, 3–1
Sweden def. Russia, 4–1
France def. Switzerland, 3–2
Netherlands def. Germany, 4–1

### SEMIFINALS

Australia def. Sweden, 4–1
 Thomas Johansson (SWE) def. Patrick Rafter (AUS), 3–6, 6–7 (10–8), 6–3, 6–2, 6–3
 Lleyton Hewitt (AUS) def. Jonas Bjorkman (SWE), 4–6, 6–4, 7–6 (7–5), 7–6 (7–2)
 Wayne Arthurs and Todd Woodbridge (AUS) def. Jonas Bjorkman and Magnus Larsson (SWE), 6–7 (3–7), 7–6 (7–2), 7–6 (7–5), 7–6 (7–3)
 Lleyton Hewitt (AUS) def. Thomas Johansson (SWE), 7–6 (7–3), 5–7, 6–2, 6–1
 Patrick Rafter (AUS) def. Jonas Bjorkman (SWE) 6–3, 6–2

France def. Netherlands, 3–2
 Arnaud Clement (FRA) def. Raemon Sluiter (NET), 3–6, 6–2, 1–2, retired
 Nicolas Escude (FRA) def. Sjeng Schalken (NET), 6–7 (5–7), 7–6 (7–4), 4–6, 7–6 (7–4), 8–6
 Cedric Pioline and Fabrice Santoro (FRA) def. Paul Haarhuis and Sjeng Schalken (NET), 7–5 6–1, 7–5
 Sjeng Schalken (NET) def. Arnaud Clement (FRA), 7–6 (8–6), 7–6 (7–4)
 Jan Siemerink (NET) def. Fabrice Santoro (FRA), 6–4, 6–4

FINAL: Australia versus France to be held Nov. 30–Dec. 2, 2001, in Melbourne.

## 2001 Federation Cup World Group Tournament

### FIRST ROUND

Italy def. Croatia, 4–1
Argentina def. Japan, 4–1
Slovakia def. Hungary, 4–1
Australia def. Austria, 5–0

### SECOND ROUND

France def. Italy, 4–1
Argentina def. Germany, 4–1
Russia def. Slovakia, 3–2
Australia def. Switzerland, 4–1

Note: Second round winners and 2000 semifinalists, United States, Spain, Belgium and Czech Republic will meet in Barcelona, November, 2001.

## Grand Slam Tournaments

### MEN

### Australian Championships

| Year | Winner | Finalist | Score |
|------|--------|----------|-------|
| 1905 | Rodney Heath | A. H. Curtis | 4–6, 6–3, 6–4, 6–4 |
| 1906 | Tony Wilding | H. A. Parker | 6–0, 6–4, 6–4 |
| 1907 | Horace M. Rice | H. A. Parker | 6–3, 6–4, 6–4 |
| 1908 | Fred Alexander | A. W. Dunlop | 3–6, 3–6, 6–0, 6–2, 6–3 |
| 1909 | Tony Wilding | E. F. Parker | 6–1, 7–5, 6–2 |
| 1910 | Rodney Heath | Horace M. Rice | 6–4, 6–3, 6–2 |
| 1911 | Norman Brookes | Horace M. Rice | 6–1, 6–2, 6–3 |
| 1912 | J. Cecil Parke | A. E. Beamish | 3–6, 6–3, 1–6, 6–1, 7–5 |
| 1913 | E. F. Parker | H. A. Parker | 2–6, 6–1, 6–2, 6–3 |
| 1914 | Pat O'Hara Wood | G. L. Patterson | 6–4, 6–3, 5–7, 6–1 |
| 1915 | Francis G. Lowe | Horace M. Rice | 4–6, 6–1, 6–1, 6–4 |
| 1916–18 | No tournament | | |
| 1919 | A. R. F. Kingscote | E. O. Pockley | 6–4, 6–0, 6–3 |
| 1920 | Pat O'Hara Wood | Ron Thomas | 6–3, 4–6, 6–8, 6–1, 6–3 |
| 1921 | Rhys H. Gemmell | A. Hedeman | 7–5, 6–1, 6–4 |
| 1922 | Pat O'Hara Wood | Gerald Patterson | 6–0, 3–6, 3–6, 6–3, 6–2 |
| 1923 | Pat O'Hara Wood | C. B. St John | 6–1, 6–1, 6–3 |
| 1924 | James Anderson | R. E. Schlesinger | 6–3, 6–4, 3–6, 5–7, 6–3 |
| 1925 | James Anderson | Gerald Patterson | 11–9, 2–6, 6–2, 6–3 |
| 1926 | John Hawkes | J. Willard | 6–1, 6–3, 6–1 |
| 1927 | Gerald Patterson | John Hawkes | 3–6, 6–4, 3–6, 18–16, 6–3 |
| 1928 | Jean Borotra | R. O. Cummings | 6–4, 6–1, 4–6, 5–7, 6–3 |
| 1929 | John C. Gregory | R. E. Schlesinger | 6–2, 6–2, 5–7, 7–5 |
| 1930 | Gar Moon | Harry C. Hopman | 6–3, 6–1, 6–3 |
| 1931 | Jack Crawford | Harry C. Hopman | 6–4, 6–2, 2–6, 6–1 |
| 1932 | Jack Crawford | Harry C. Hopman | 4–6, 6–3, 3–6, 6–3, 6–1 |
| 1933 | Jack Crawford | Keith Gledhill | 2–6, 7–5, 6–3, 6–2 |
| 1934 | Fred Perry | Jack Crawford | 6–3, 7–5, 6–1 |
| 1935 | Jack Crawford | Fred Perry | 2–6, 6–4, 6–4, 6–4 |
| 1936 | Adrian Quist | Jack Crawford | 6–2, 6–3, 4–6, 3–6, 9–7 |
| 1937 | Vivian B. McGrath | John Bromwich | 6–3, 1–6, 6–0, 2–6, 6–1 |
| 1938 | Don Budge | John Bromwich | 6 4, 6 2, 6 1 |
| 1939 | John Bromwich | Adrian Quist | 6–4, 6–1, 6–3 |
| 1940 | Adrian Quist | Jack Crawford | 6–3, 6–1, 6–2 |
| 1941–45 | No tournament | | |
| 1946 | John Bromwich | Dinny Pails | 5–7, 6–3, 7–5, 3–6, 6–2 |
| 1947 | Dinny Pails | John Bromwich | 4–6, 6–4, 3–6, 7–5, 8–6 |
| 1948 | Adrian Quist | John Bromwich | 6–4, 3–6, 6–3, 2–6, 6–3 |
| 1949 | Frank Sedgman | Ken McGregor | 6–3, 6–3, 6–2 |
| 1950 | Frank Sedgman | Ken McGregor | 6–3, 6–4, 4–6, 6–1 |
| 1951 | Richard Savitt | Ken McGregor | 6–3, 2–6, 6–3, 6–1 |
| 1952 | Ken McGregor | Frank Sedgman | 7–5, 12–10, 2–6, 6–2 |
| 1953 | Ken Rosewall | Mervyn Rose | 6–0, 6–3, 6–4 |
| 1954 | Mervyn Rose | Rex Hartwig | 6–2, 0–6, 6–4, 6–2 |
| 1955 | Ken Rosewall | Lew Hoad | 9–7, 6–4, 6–4 |
| 1956 | Lew Hoad | Ken Rosewall | 6–4, 3–6, 6–4, 7–5 |
| 1957 | Ashley Cooper | Neale Fraser | 6–3, 9–11, 6–4, 6–2 |
| 1958 | Ashley Cooper | Mal Anderson | 7–5, 6–3, 6–4 |
| 1959 | Alex Olmedo | Neale Fraser | 6–1, 6–2, 3–6, 6–3 |
| 1960 | Rod Laver | Neale Fraser | 5–7, 3–6, 6–3, 8–6, 8–6 |
| 1961 | Roy Emerson | Rod Laver | 1–6, 6–3, 7–5, 6–4 |
| 1962 | Rod Laver | Roy Emerson | 8–6, 0–6, 6–4, 6–4 |
| 1963 | Roy Emerson | Ken Fletcher | 6–3, 6–3, 6–1 |
| 1964 | Roy Emerson | Fred Stolle | 6–3, 6–4, 6–2 |
| 1965 | Roy Emerson | Fred Stolle | 7–9, 2–6, 6–4, 7–5, 6–1 |
| 1966 | Roy Emerson | Arthur Ashe | 6–4, 6–8, 6–2, 6–3 |
| 1967 | Roy Emerson | Arthur Ashe | 6–4, 6–1, 6–1 |
| 1968 | Bill Bowrey | Juan Gisbert | 7–5, 2–6, 9–7, 6–4 |
| 1969* | Rod Laver | Andres Gimeno | 6–3, 6–4, 7–5 |

*Became Open (amateur and professional) in 1969.

## MEN *(Cont.)*

### Australian Championships *(Cont.)*

| Year | Winner | Finalist | Score |
|---|---|---|---|
| 1970 | Arthur Ashe | Dick Crealy | 6–4, 9–7, 6–2 |
| 1971 | Ken Rosewall | Arthur Ashe | 6–1, 7–5, 6–3 |
| 1972 | Ken Rosewall | Mal Anderson | 7–6, 6–3, 7–5 |
| 1973 | John Newcombe | Onny Parun | 6–3, 6–7, 7–5, 6–1 |
| 1974 | Jimmy Connors | Phil Dent | 7–6, 6–4, 4–6, 6–3 |
| 1975 | John Newcombe | Jimmy Connors | 7–5, 3–6, 6–4, 7–5 |
| 1976 | Mark Edmondson | John Newcombe | 6–7, 6–3, 7–6, 6–1 |
| 1977 (Jan) | Roscoe Tanner | Guillermo Vilas | 6–3, 6–3, 6–3 |
| 1977 (Dec) | Vitas Gerulaitis | John Lloyd | 6–3, 7–6, 5–7, 3–6, 6–2 |
| 1978 | Guillermo Vilas | John Marks | 6–4, 6–4, 3–6, 6–3 |
| 1979 | Guillermo Vilas | John Sadri | 7–6, 6–3, 6–2 |
| 1980 | Brian Teacher | Kim Warwick | 7–5, 7–6, 6–3 |
| 1981 | Johan Kriek | Steve Denton | 6–2, 7–6, 6–7, 6–4 |
| 1982 | Johan Kriek | Steve Denton | 6–3, 6–3, 6–2 |
| 1983 | Mats Wilander | Ivan Lendl | 6–1, 6–4, 6–4 |
| 1984 | Mats Wilander | Kevin Curren | 6–7, 6–4, 7–6, 6–2 |
| 1985 (Dec) | Stefan Edberg | Mats Wilander | 6–4, 6–3, 6–3 |
| 1987 (Jan) | Stefan Edberg | Pat Cash | 6–3, 6–4, 3–6, 5–7, 6–3 |
| 1988 | Mats Wilander | Pat Cash | 6–3, 6–7, 3–6, 6–1, 8–6 |
| 1989 | Ivan Lendl | Miloslav Mecir | 6–2, 6–2, 6–2 |
| 1990 | Ivan Lendl | Stefan Edberg | 4–6, 7–6, 5–2, ret. |
| 1991 | Boris Becker | Ivan Lendl | 1–6, 6–4, 6–4, 6–4 |
| 1992 | Jim Courier | Stefan Edberg | 6–3, 3–6, 6–4, 6–2 |
| 1993 | Jim Courier | Stefan Edberg | 6–2, 6–1, 2–6, 7–5 |
| 1994 | Pete Sampras | Todd Martin | 7–6, 6–4, 6–4 |
| 1995 | Andre Agassi | Pete Sampras | 4–6, 6–1, 7–6, 6–4 |
| 1996 | Boris Becker | Michael Chang | 6–2, 6–4, 2–6, 6–2 |
| 1997 | Pete Sampras | Carlos Moya | 6–2, 6–3, 6–3 |
| 1998 | Petr Korda | Marcelo Ríos | 6–2, 6–2, 6–2 |
| 1999 | Yevgeny Kafelnikov | Thomas Enqvist | 4–6, 6–0, 6–3, 7–6 |
| 2000 | Andre Agassi | Yevgeny Kafelnikov | 3–6, 6–3, 6–2, 6–4 |
| 2001 | Andre Agassi | Arnaud Clement | 6–4, 6–2, 6–2 |

### French Championships

| Year | Winner | Finalist | Score |
|---|---|---|---|
| 1925† | Rene Lacoste | Jean Borotra | 7–5, 6–1, 6–4 |
| 1926 | Henri Cochet | Rene Lacoste | 6–2, 6–4, 6–3 |
| 1927 | Rene Lacoste | Bill Tilden | 6–4, 4–6, 5–7, 6–3, 11–9 |
| 1928 | Henri Cochet | Rene Lacoste | 5–7, 6–3, 6–1, 6–3 |
| 1929 | Rene Lacoste | Jean Borotra | 6–3, 2–6, 6–0, 2–6, 8–6 |
| 1930 | Henri Cochet | Bill Tilden | 3–6, 8–6, 6–3, 6–1 |
| 1931 | Jean Borotra | Claude Boussus | 2–6, 6–4, 7–5, 6–4 |
| 1932 | Henri Cochet | Giorgio de Stefani | 6–0, 6–4, 4–6, 6–3 |
| 1933 | Jack Crawford | Henri Cochet | 8–6, 6–1, 6–3 |
| 1934 | Gottfried von Cramm | Jack Crawford | 6–4, 7–9, 3–6, 7–5, 6–3 |
| 1935 | Fred Perry | Gottfried von Cramm | 6–3, 3–6, 6–1, 6–3 |
| 1936 | Gottfried von Cramm | Fred Perry | 6–0, 2–6, 6–2, 2–6, 6–0 |
| 1937 | Henner Henkel | Henry Austin | 6–1, 6–4, 6–3 |
| 1938 | Don Budge | Roderick Menzel | 6–3, 6–2, 6–4 |
| 1939 | Don McNeill | Bobby Riggs | 7–5, 6–0, 6–3 |
| 1940 | No tournament | | |
| 1941‡ | Bernard Destremau | n/a | n/a |
| 1942‡ | Bernard Destremau | n/a | n/a |
| 1943‡ | Yvon Petra | n/a | n/a |
| 1944‡ | Yvon Petra | n/a | n/a |
| 1945‡ | Yvon Petra | Bernard Destremau | 7–5, 6–4, 6–2 |
| 1946 | Marcel Bernard | Jaroslav Drobny | 3–6, 2–6, 6–1, 6–4, 6–3 |
| 1947 | Joseph Asboth | Eric Sturgess | 8–6, 7–5, 6–4 |
| 1948 | Frank Parker | Jaroslav Drobny | 6–4, 7–5, 5–7, 8–6 |
| 1949 | Frank Parker | Budge Patty | 6–3, 1–6, 6–1, 6–4 |
| 1950 | Budge Patty | Jaroslav Drobny | 6–1, 6–2, 3–6, 5–7, 7–5 |
| 1951 | Jaroslav Drobny | Eric Sturgess | 6–3, 6–3, 6–3 |
| 1952 | Jaroslav Drobny | Frank Sedgman | 6–2, 6–0, 3–6, 6–4 |

## MEN *(Cont.)*
### French Championships *(Cont.)*

| Year | Winner | Finalist | Score |
|------|--------|----------|-------|
| 1953 | Ken Rosewall | Vic Seixas | 6–3, 6–4, 1–6, 6–2 |
| 1954 | Tony Trabert | Arthur Larsen | 6–4, 7–5, 6–1 |
| 1955 | Tony Trabert | Sven Davidson | 2–6, 6–1, 6–4, 6–2 |
| 1956 | Lew Hoad | Sven Davidson | 6–4, 8–6, 6–3 |
| 1957 | Sven Davidson | Herbie Flam | 6–3, 6–4, 6–4 |
| 1958 | Mervyn Rose | Luis Ayala | 6–3, 6–4, 6–4 |
| 1959 | Nicola Pietrangeli | Ian Vermaak | 3–6, 6–3, 6–4, 6–1 |
| 1960 | Nicola Pietrangeli | Luis Ayala | 3–6, 6–3, 6–4, 4–6, 6–3 |
| 1961 | Manuel Santana | Nicola Pietrangeli | 4–6, 6–1, 3–6, 6–0, 6–2 |
| 1962 | Rod Laver | Roy Emerson | 3–6, 2–6, 6–3, 9–7, 6–2 |
| 1963 | Roy Emerson | Pierre Darmon | 3–6, 6–1, 6–4, 6–4 |
| 1964 | Manuel Santana | Nicola Pietrangeli | 6–3, 6–1, 4–6, 7–5 |
| 1965 | Fred Stolle | Tony Roche | 3–6, 6–0, 6–2, 6–3 |
| 1966 | Tony Roche | Istvan Gulyas | 6–1, 6–4, 7–5 |
| 1967 | Roy Emerson | Tony Roche | 6–1, 6–4, 2–6, 6–2 |
| 1968* | Ken Rosewall | Rod Laver | 6–3, 6–1, 2–6, 6–2 |
| 1969 | Rod Laver | Ken Rosewall | 6–4, 6–3, 6–4 |
| 1970 | Jan Kodes | Zeljko Franulovic | 6–2, 6–4, 6–0 |
| 1971 | Jan Kodes | Ilie Nastase | 8–6, 6–2, 2–6, 7–5 |
| 1972 | Andres Gimeno | Patrick Proisy | 4–6, 6–3, 6–1, 6–1 |
| 1973 | Ilie Nastase | Nikki Pilic | 6–3, 6–3, 6–0 |
| 1974 | Bjorn Borg | Manuel Orantes | 6–7, 6–0, 6–1, 6–1 |
| 1975 | Bjorn Borg | Guillermo Vilas | 6–2, 6–3, 6–4 |
| 1976 | Adriano Panatta | Harold Solomon | 6–1, 6–4, 4–6, 7–6 |
| 1977 | Guillermo Vilas | Brian Gottfried | 6–0, 6–3, 6–0 |
| 1978 | Bjorn Borg | Guillermo Vilas | 6–1, 6–1, 6–3 |
| 1979 | Bjorn Borg | Victor Pecci | 6–3, 6–1, 6–7, 6–4 |
| 1980 | Bjorn Borg | Vitas Gerulaitis | 6–4, 6–1, 6–2 |
| 1981 | Bjorn Borg | Ivan Lendl | 6–1, 4–6, 6–2, 3–6, 6–1 |
| 1982 | Mats Wilander | Guillermo Vilas | 1–6, 7–6, 6–0, 6–4 |
| 1983 | Yannick Noah | Mats Wilander | 6–2, 7–5, 7–6 |
| 1984 | Ivan Lendl | John McEnroe | 3–6, 2–6, 6–4, 7–5, 7–5 |
| 1985 | Mats Wilander | Ivan Lendl | 3–6, 6–4, 6–2, 6–2 |
| 1986 | Ivan Lendl | Mikael Pernfors | 6–3, 6–2, 6–4 |
| 1987 | Ivan Lendl | Mats Wilander | 7–5, 6–2, 3–6, 7–6 |
| 1988 | Mats Wilander | Henri Leconte | 7–5, 6–2, 6–1 |
| 1989 | Michael Chang | Stefan Edberg | 6–1, 3–6, 4–6, 6–4, 6–2 |
| 1990 | Andres Gomez | Andre Agassi | 6–3, 2–6, 6–4, 6–4 |
| 1991 | Jim Courier | Andre Agassi | 3–6, 6–4, 2–6, 6–1, 6–4 |
| 1992 | Jim Courier | Petr Korda | 7–5, 6–2, 6–1 |
| 1993 | Sergi Bruguera | Jim Courier | 6–4, 2–6, 6–2, 3–6, 6–3 |
| 1994 | Sergi Bruguera | Alberto Berasategui | 6–3, 7–5, 2–6, 6–1 |
| 1995 | Thomas Muster | Michael Chang | 7–5, 6–2, 6–4 |
| 1996 | Yevgeny Kafelnikov | Michael Stich | 7–6, 7–5, 7–6 |
| 1997 | Gustavo Kuerten | Sergi Bruguera | 6–3, 6–4, 6–2 |
| 1998 | Carlos Moya | Alex Corretja | 6–3, 7–5, 6–3 |
| 1999 | Andre Agassi | Andrei Medvedev | 1–6, 2–6, 6–4, 6–3, 6–4 |
| 2000 | Gustavo Kuerten | Magnus Norman | 6–2, 6–3, 2–6, 7–6 |
| 2001 | Gustavo Kuerten | Alex Corretja | 6–7, 7–5, 6–2, 6–0 |

*Became Open (amateur and professional) in 1968 but closed to contract professionals in 1972.

†1925 was the first year that entries were accepted from all countries.
‡From 1941 to 1945 the event was called Tournoi de France and was closed to all foreigners.

### Wimbledon Championships

| Year | Winner | Finalist | Score |
|------|--------|----------|-------|
| 1877 | Spencer W. Gore | William C. Marshall | 6–1, 6–2, 6–4 |
| 1878 | P. Frank Hadow | Spencer W. Gore | 7–5, 6–1, 9–7 |
| 1879 | John T. Hartley | V. St Leger Gould | 6–2, 6–4, 6–2 |
| 1880 | John T. Hartley | Herbert F. Lawford | 6–0, 6–2, 2–6, 6–3 |
| 1881 | William Renshaw | John T. Hartley | 6–0, 6–2, 6–1 |
| 1882 | William Renshaw | Ernest Renshaw | 6–1, 2–6, 4–6, 6–2, 6–2 |
| 1883 | William Renshaw | Ernest Renshaw | 2–6, 6–3, 6–3, 4–6, 6–3 |

## MEN *(Cont.)*

### Wimbledon Championship *(Cont.)*

| Year | Winner | Finalist | Score |
|------|--------|----------|-------|
| 1884 | William Renshaw | Herbert F. Lawford | 6–0, 6–4, 9–7 |
| 1885 | William Renshaw | Herbert F. Lawford | 7–5, 6–2, 4–6, 7–5 |
| 1886 | William Renshaw | Herbert F. Lawford | 6–0, 5–7, 6–3, 6–4 |
| 1887 | Herbert F. Lawford | Ernest Renshaw | 1–6, 6–3, 3–6, 6–4, 6–4 |
| 1888 | Ernest Renshaw | Herbert F. Lawford | 6–3, 7–5, 6–0 |
| 1889 | William Renshaw | Ernest Renshaw | 6–4, 6–1, 3–6, 6–0 |
| 1890 | William J. Hamilton | William Renshaw | 6–8, 6–2, 3–6, 6–1, 6–1 |
| 1891 | Wilfred Baddeley | Joshua Pim | 6–4, 1–6, 7–5, 6–0 |
| 1892 | Wilfred Baddeley | Joshua Pim | 4–6, 6–3, 6–3, 6–2 |
| 1893 | Joshua Pim | Wilfred Baddeley | 3–6, 6–1, 6–3, 6–2 |
| 1894 | Joshua Pim | Wilfred Baddeley | 10–8, 6–2, 8–6 |
| 1895 | Wilfred Baddeley | Wilberforce V. Eaves | 4–6, 2–6, 8–6, 6–2, 6–3 |
| 1896 | Harold S. Mahoney | Wilfred Baddeley | 6–2, 6–8, 5–7, 8–6, 6–3 |
| 1897 | Reggie F. Doherty | Harold S. Mahoney | 6–4, 6–4, 6–3 |
| 1898 | Reggie F. Doherty | H. Laurie Doherty | 6–3, 6–3, 2–6, 5–7, 6–1 |
| 1899 | Reggie F. Doherty | Arthur W. Gore | 1–6, 4–6, 6–2, 6–3, 6–3 |
| 1900 | Reggie F. Doherty | Sidney H. Smith | 6–8, 6–3, 6–1, 6–2 |
| 1901 | Arthur W. Gore | Reggie F. Doherty | 4–6, 7–5, 6–4, 6–4 |
| 1902 | H. Laurie Doherty | Arthur W. Gore | 6–4, 6–3, 3–6, 6–0 |
| 1903 | H. Laurie Doherty | Frank L. Riseley | 7–5, 6–3, 6–0 |
| 1904 | H. Laurie Doherty | Frank L. Riseley | 6–1, 7–5, 8–6 |
| 1905 | H. Laurie Doherty | Norman E. Brookes | 8–6, 6–2, 6–4 |
| 1906 | H. Laurie Doherty | Frank L. Riseley | 6–4, 4–6, 6–2, 6–3 |
| 1907 | Norman E. Brookes | Arthur W. Gore | 6–4, 6–2, 6–2 |
| 1908 | Arthur W. Gore | H. Roper Barrett | 6–3, 6–2, 4–6, 3–6, 6–4 |
| 1909 | Arthur W. Gore | M. J. G. Ritchie | 6–8, 1–6, 6–2, 6–2, 6–2 |
| 1910 | Anthony F. Wilding | Arthur W. Gore | 6–4, 7–5, 4–6, 6–2 |
| 1911 | Anthony F. Wilding | H. Roper Barrett | 6–4, 4–6, 2–6, 6–2 ret |
| 1912 | Anthony F. Wilding | Arthur W. Gore | 6–4, 6–4, 4–6, 6–4 |
| 1913 | Anthony F. Wilding | Maurice E. McLoughlin | 8–6, 6–3, 10–8 |
| 1914 | Norman E. Brookes | Anthony F. Wilding | 6–4, 6–4, 7–5 |
| 1915–18 | No tournament | | |
| 1919 | Gerald L. Patterson | Norman E. Brookes | 6–3, 7–5, 6–2 |
| 1920 | Bill Tilden | Gerald L. Patterson | 2–6, 6–3, 6–2, 6–4 |
| 1921 | Bill Tilden | Brian I. C. Norton | 4–6, 2–6, 6–1, 6–0, 7–5 |
| 1922 | Gerald L. Patterson | Randolph Lycett | 6–3, 6–4, 6–2 |
| 1923 | Bill Johnston | Francis T. Hunter | 6–0, 6–3, 6–1 |
| 1924 | Jean Borotra | Rene Lacoste | 6–1, 3–6, 6–1, 3–6, 6–4 |
| 1925 | Rene Lacoste | Jean Borotra | 6–3, 6–3, 4–6, 8–6 |
| 1926 | Jean Borotra | Howard Kinsey | 8–6, 6–1, 6–3 |
| 1927 | Henri Cochet | Jean Borotra | 4–6, 4–6, 6–3, 6–4, 7–5 |
| 1928 | Rene Lacoste | Henri Cochet | 6–1, 4–6, 6–4, 6–2 |
| 1929 | Henri Cochet | Jean Borotra | 6–4, 6–3, 6–4 |
| 1930 | Bill Tilden | Wilmer Allison | 6–3, 9–7, 6–4 |
| 1931 | Sidney B. Wood Jr | Francis X. Shields | walkover |
| 1932 | Ellsworth Vines | Henry Austin | 6–4, 6–2, 6–0 |
| 1933 | Jack Crawford | Ellsworth Vines | 4–6, 11–9, 6–2, 2–6, 6–4 |
| 1934 | Fred Perry | Jack Crawford | 6–3, 6–0, 7–5 |
| 1935 | Fred Perry | Gottfried von Cramm | 6–2, 6–4, 6–4 |
| 1936 | Fred Perry | Gottfried von Cramm | 6–1, 6–1, 6–0 |
| 1937 | Don Budge | Gottfried von Cramm | 6–3, 6–4, 6–2 |
| 1938 | Don Budge | Henry Austin | 6–1, 6–0, 6–3 |
| 1939 | Bobby Riggs | Elwood Cooke | 2–6, 8–6, 3–6, 6–3, 6–2 |
| 1940–45 | No tournament | | |
| 1946 | Yvon Petra | Geoff E. Brown | 6–2, 6–4, 7–9, 5–7, 6–4 |
| 1947 | Jack Kramer | Tom P. Brown | 6–1, 6–3, 6–2 |
| 1948 | Bob Falkenburg | John Bromwich | 7–5, 0–6, 6–2, 3–6, 7–5 |
| 1949 | Ted Schroeder | Jaroslav Drobny | 3–6, 6–0, 6–3, 4–6, 6–4 |
| 1950 | Budge Patty | Frank Sedgman | 6–1, 8–10, 6–2, 6–3 |
| 1951 | Dick Savitt | Ken McGregor | 6–4, 6–4, 6–4 |
| 1952 | Frank Sedgman | Jaroslav Drobny | 4–6, 6–3, 6–2, 6–3 |
| 1953 | Vic Seixas | Kurt Nielsen | 9–7, 6–3, 6–4 |
| 1954 | Jaroslav Drobny | Ken Rosewall | 13–11, 4–6, 6–2, 9–7 |
| 1955 | Tony Trabert | Kurt Nielsen | 6–3, 7–5, 6–1 |

## MEN *(Cont.)*

### Wimbledon Championships *(Cont.)*

| Year | Winner | Finalist | Score |
|------|--------|----------|-------|
| 1956 | Lew Hoad | Ken Rosewall | 6–2, 4–6, 7–5, 6–4 |
| 1957 | Lew Hoad | Ashley Cooper | 6–2, 6–1, 6–2 |
| 1958 | Ashley Cooper | Neale Fraser | 3–6, 6–3, 6–4, 13–11 |
| 1959 | Alex Olmedo | Rod Laver | 6–4, 6–3, 6–4 |
| 1960 | Neale Fraser | Rod Laver | 6–4, 3–6, 9–7, 7–5 |
| 1961 | Rod Laver | Chuck McKinley | 6–3, 6–1, 6–4 |
| 1962 | Rod Laver | Martin Mulligan | 6–2, 6–2, 6–1 |
| 1963 | Chuck McKinley | Fred Stolle | 9–7, 6–1, 6–4 |
| 1964 | Roy Emerson | Fred Stolle | 6–4, 12–10, 4–6, 6–3 |
| 1965 | Roy Emerson | Fred Stolle | 6–2, 6–4, 6–4 |
| 1966 | Manuel Santana | Dennis Ralston | 6–4, 11–9, 6–4 |
| 1967 | John Newcombe | Wilhelm Bungert | 6–3, 6–1, 6–1 |
| 1968* | Rod Laver | Tony Roche | 6–3, 6–4, 6–2 |
| 1969 | Rod Laver | John Newcombe | 6–4, 5–7, 6–4, 6–4 |
| 1970 | John Newcombe | Ken Rosewall | 5–7, 6–3, 6–2, 3–6, 6–1 |
| 1971 | John Newcombe | Stan Smith | 6–3, 5–7, 2–6, 6–4, 6–4 |
| 1972 | Stan Smith | Ilie Nastase | 4–6, 6–3, 6–3, 4–6, 7–5 |
| 1973 | Jan Kodes | Alex Metreveli | 6–1, 9–8, 6–3 |
| 1974 | Jimmy Connors | Ken Rosewall | 6–1, 6–1, 6–4 |
| 1975 | Arthur Ashe | Jimmy Connors | 6–1, 6–1, 5–7, 6–4 |
| 1976 | Bjorn Borg | Ilie Nastase | 6–4, 6–2, 9–7 |
| 1977 | Bjorn Borg | Jimmy Connors | 3–6, 6–2, 6–1, 5–7, 6–4 |
| 1978 | Bjorn Borg | Jimmy Connors | 6–2, 6–2, 6–3 |
| 1979 | Bjorn Borg | Roscoe Tanner | 6–7, 6–1, 3–6, 6–3, 6–4 |
| 1980 | Bjorn Borg | John McEnroe | 1–6, 7–5, 6–3, 6–7, 8–6 |
| 1981 | John McEnroe | Bjorn Borg | 4–6, 7–6, 7–6, 6–4 |
| 1982 | Jimmy Connors | John McEnroe | 3–6, 6–3, 6–7, 7–6, 6–4 |
| 1983 | John McEnroe | Chris Lewis | 6–2, 6–2, 6–2 |
| 1984 | John McEnroe | Jimmy Connors | 6–1, 6–1, 6–2 |
| 1985 | Boris Becker | Kevin Curren | 6–3, 6–7, 7–6, 6–4 |
| 1986 | Boris Becker | Ivan Lendl | 6–4, 6–3, 7–5 |
| 1987 | Pat Cash | Ivan Lendl | 7–6, 6–2, 7–5 |
| 1988 | Stefan Edberg | Boris Becker | 4–6, 7–6, 6–4, 6–2 |
| 1989 | Boris Becker | Stefan Edberg | 6–0, 7–6, 6–4 |
| 1990 | Stefan Edberg | Boris Becker | 6–2, 6–2, 3–6, 3–6, 6–4 |
| 1991 | Michael Stich | Boris Becker | 6–4, 7–6, 6–4 |
| 1992 | Andre Agassi | Goran Ivanisevic | 6–7, 6–4, 6–4, 1–6, 6–4 |
| 1993 | Pete Sampras | Jim Courier | 7–6, 7–6, 3–6, 6–3 |
| 1994 | Pete Sampras | Goran Ivanisevic | 7–6, 7–6, 6–0 |
| 1995 | Pete Sampras | Boris Becker | 6–7, 6–2, 6–4, 6–2 |
| 1996 | Richard Krajicek | MaliVai Washington | 6–3, 6–4, 6–3 |
| 1997 | Pete Sampras | Cedric Pioline | 6–4, 6–2, 6–4 |
| 1998 | Pete Sampras | Goran Ivanisevic | 6–7, 7–6, 6–4, 3–6, 6–2 |
| 1999 | Pete Sampras | Andre Agassi | 6–3, 6–4, 7–5 |
| 2000 | Pete Sampras | Patrick Rafter | 6–7, 7–6, 6–4, 6–2 |
| 2001 | Goran Ivanisevic | Patrick Rafter | 6–3, 3–6, 6–3, 2–6, 9–7 |

*Became Open (amateur and professional) in 1968 but closed to contract professionals in 1972

Note: Prior to 1922 the tournament was run on a challenge-round system. The previous year's winner "stood out"of an All Comers event, which produced a challenger to play him for the title.

### United States Championships

| Year | Winner | Finalist | Score |
|------|--------|----------|-------|
| 1881 | Richard D. Sears | W.E. Glyn | 6–0, 6–3, 6–2 |
| 1882 | Richard D. Sears | C.M. Clark | 6–1, 6–4, 6–0 |
| 1883 | Richard D. Sears | James Dwight | 6–2, 6–0, 9–7 |
| 1884 | Richard D. Sears | H.A. Taylor | 6–0, 1–6, 6–0, 6–2 |
| 1885 | Richard D. Sears | G.M. Brinley | 6–3, 4–6, 6–0, 6–3 |
| 1886 | Richard D. Sears | R.L. Beeckman | 4–6, 6–1, 6–3, 6–4 |
| 1887 | Richard D. Sears | H.W. Slocum Jr | 6–1, 6–3, 6–2 |
| 1888‡ | H. W. Slocum Jr | H.A. Taylor | 6–4, 6–1, 6–0 |
| 1889 | H. W. Slocum Jr | Q.A. Shaw | 6–3, 6–1, 4–6, 6–2 |
| 1890 | Oliver S. Campbell | H.W. Slocum Jr | 6–2, 4–6, 6–3, 6–1 |
| 1891 | Oliver S. Campbell | Clarence Hobart | 2–6, 7–5, 7–9, 6–1, 6–2 |
| 1892 | Oliver S. Campbell | Frederick H. Hovey | 7–5, 3–6, 6–3, 7–5 |

## MEN (Cont.)

### United States Championships (Cont.)

| Year | Winner | Finalist | Score |
|------|--------|----------|-------|
| 1893‡ | Robert D. Wrenn | Frederick H. Hovey | 6–4, 3–6, 6–4, 6–4 |
| 1894 | Robert D. Wrenn | M.F. Goodbody | 6–8, 6–1, 6–4, 6–4 |
| 1895 | Frederick H. Hovey | Robert D. Wrenn | 6–3, 6–2, 6–4 |
| 1896 | Robert D. Wrenn | Frederick H. Hovey | 7–5, 3–6, 6–0, 1–6, 6–1 |
| 1897 | Robert D. Wrenn | Wilberforce V. Eaves | 4–6, 8–6, 6–3, 2–6, 6–2 |
| 1898‡ | Malcolm D. Whitman | Dwight F. Davis | 3–6, 6–2, 6–2, 6–1 |
| 1899 | Malcolm D. Whitman | J. Parmly Paret | 6–1, 6–2, 3–6, 7–5 |
| 1900 | Malcolm D. Whitman | William A. Larned | 6–4, 1–6, 6–2, 6–2 |
| 1901‡ | William A. Larned | Beals C. Wright | 6–2, 6–8, 6–4, 6–4 |
| 1902 | William A. Larned | Reggie F. Doherty | 4–6, 6–2, 6–4, 8–6 |
| 1903 | H. Laurie Doherty | William A. Larned | 6–0, 6–3, 10–8 |
| 1904‡ | Holcombe Ward | William J. Clothier | 10–8, 6–4, 9–7 |
| 1905 | Beals C. Wright | Holcombe Ward | 6–2, 6–1, 11–9 |
| 1906 | William J. Clothier | Beals C. Wright | 6–3, 6–0, 6–4 |
| 1907‡ | William A. Larned | Robert LeRoy | 6–2, 6–2, 6–4 |
| 1908 | William A. Larned | Beals C. Wright | 6–1, 6–2, 8–6 |
| 1909 | William A. Larned | William J. Clothier | 6–1, 6–2, 5–7, 1–6, 6–1 |
| 1910 | William A. Larned | Thomas C. Bundy | 6–1, 5–7, 6–0, 6–8, 6–1 |
| 1911 | William A. Larned | Maurice E. McLoughlin | 6–4, 6–4, 6–2 |
| 1912† | Maurice E. McLoughlin | Bill Johnson | 3–6, 2–6, 6–2, 6–4, 6–2 |
| 1913 | Maurice E. McLoughlin | Richard N. Williams | 6–4, 5–7, 6–3, 6–1 |
| 1914 | Richard N. Williams | Maurice E. McLoughlin | 6–3, 8–6, 10–8 |
| 1915 | Bill Johnston | Maurice E. McLoughlin | 1–6, 6–0, 7–5, 10–8 |
| 1916 | Richard N. Williams | Bill Johnston | 4–6, 6–4, 0–6, 6–2, 6–4 |
| 1917# | R.L. Murray | N. W. Niles | 5–7, 8–6, 6–3, 6–3 |
| 1918 | R.L. Murray | Bill Tilden | 6–3, 6–1, 7–5 |
| 1919 | Bill Johnston | Bill Tilden | 6–4, 6–4, 6–3 |
| 1920 | Bill Tilden | Bill Johnston | 6–1, 1–6, 7–5, 5–7, 6–3 |
| 1921 | Bill Tilden | Wallace F. Johnson | 6–1, 6–3, 6–1 |
| 1922 | Bill Tilden | Bill Johnston | 4–6, 3–6, 6–2, 6–3, 6–4 |
| 1923 | Bill Tilden | Bill Johnston | 6–4, 6–1, 6–4 |
| 1924 | Bill Tilden | Bill Johnston | 6–1, 9–7, 6–2 |
| 1925 | Bill Tilden | Bill Johnston | 4–6, 11–9, 6–3, 4–6, 6–3 |
| 1926 | Rene Lacoste | Jean Borotra | 6–4, 6–0, 6–4 |
| 1927 | Rene Lacoste | Bill Tilden | 11–9, 6–3, 11–9 |
| 1928 | Henri Cochet | Francis T. Hunter | 4–6, 6–4, 3–6, 7–5, 6–3 |
| 1929 | Bill Tilden | Francis T. Hunter | 3–6, 6–3, 4–6, 6–2, 6–4 |
| 1930 | John H. Doeg | Francis X. Shields | 10–8, 1–6, 6–4, 16–14 |
| 1931 | Ellsworth Vines | George M. Lott Jr | 7–9, 6–3, 9–7, 7–5 |
| 1932 | Ellsworth Vines | Henri Cochet | 6–4, 6–4, 6–4 |
| 1933 | Fred Perry | Jack Crawford | 6–3, 11–13, 4–6, 6–0, 6–1 |
| 1934 | Fred Perry | Wilmer L. Allison | 6–4, 6–3, 1–6, 8–6 |
| 1935 | Wilmer L. Allison | Sidney B. Wood Jr | 6–2, 6–2, 6–3 |
| 1936 | Fred Perry | Don Budge | 2–6, 6–2, 8–6, 1–6, 10–8 |
| 1937 | Don Budge | Gottfried von Cramm | 6–1, 7–9, 6–1, 3–6, 6–1 |
| 1938 | Don Budge | Gene Mako | 6–3, 6–8, 6–2, 6–1 |
| 1939 | Bobby Riggs | Welby Van Horn | 6–4, 6–2, 6–4 |
| 1940 | Don McNeill | Bobby Riggs | 4–6, 6–8, 6–3, 6–3, 7–5 |
| 1941 | Bobby Riggs | Francis Kovacs II | 5–7, 6–1, 6–3, 6–3 |
| 1942 | Ted Schroeder | Frank Parker | 8–6, 7–5, 3–6, 4–6, 6–2 |
| 1943 | Joseph R. Hunt | Jack Kramer | 6–3, 6–8, 10–8, 6–0 |
| 1944 | Frank Parker | William F. Talbert | 6–4, 3–6, 6–3, 6–3 |
| 1945 | Frank Parker | William F. Talbert | 14–12, 6–1, 6–2 |
| 1946 | Jack Kramer | Tom P. Brown | 9–7, 6–3, 6–0 |
| 1947 | Jack Kramer | Frank Parker | 4–6, 2–6, 6–1, 6–0, 6–3 |
| 1948 | Pancho Gonzales | Eric W. Sturgess | 6–2, 6–3, 14–12 |
| 1949 | Pancho Gonzales | Ted Schroeder | 16–18, 2–6, 6–1, 6–2, 6–4 |
| 1950 | Arthur Larsen | Herbie Flam | 6–3, 4–6, 5–7, 6–4, 6–3 |
| 1951 | Frank Sedgman | Vic Seixas | 6–4, 6–1, 6–1 |
| 1952 | Frank Sedgman | Gardnar Mulloy | 6–1, 6–2, 6–3 |
| 1953 | Tony Trabert | Vic Seixas | 6–3, 6–2, 6–3 |
| 1954 | Vic Seixas | Rex Hartwig | 3–6, 6–2, 6–4, 6–4 |
| 1955 | Tony Trabert | Ken Rosewall | 9–7, 6–3, 6–3 |

## MEN (Cont.)

### United States Championships (Cont.)

| Year | Winner | Finalist | Score |
|---|---|---|---|
| 1956 | Ken Rosewall | Lew Hoad | 4–6, 6–2, 6–3, 6–3 |
| 1957 | Mal Anderson | Ashley J. Cooper | 10–8, 7–5, 6–4 |
| 1958 | Ashley J. Cooper | Mal Anderson | 6–2, 3–6, 4–6, 10–8, 8–6 |
| 1959 | Neale Fraser | Alex Olmedo | 6–3, 5–7, 6–2, 6–4 |
| 1960 | Neale Fraser | Rod Laver | 6–4, 6–4, 9–7 |
| 1961 | Roy Emerson | Rod Laver | 7–5, 6–3, 6–2 |
| 1962 | Rod Laver | Roy Emerson | 6–2, 6–4, 5–7, 6–4 |
| 1963 | Rafael Osuna | Frank Froehling III | 7–5, 6–4, 6–2 |
| 1964 | Roy Emerson | Fred Stolle | 6–4, 6–2, 6–4 |
| 1965 | Manuel Santana | Cliff Drysdale | 6–2, 7–9, 7–5, 6–1 |
| 1966 | Fred Stolle | John Newcombe | 4–6, 12–10, 6–3, 6–4 |
| 1967 | John Newcombe | Clark Graebner | 6–4, 6–4, 8–6 |
| 1968* | Arthur Ashe | Tom Okker | 14–12, 5–7, 6–3, 3–6, 6–3 |
| 1968** | Arthur Ashe | Bob Lutz | 4–6, 6–3, 8–10, 6–0, 6–4 |
| 1969 | Rod Laver | Tony Roche | 7–9, 6–1, 6–3, 6–2 |
| 1969** | Stan Smith | Bob Lutz | 9–7, 6–3, 6–1 |
| 1970 | Ken Rosewall | Tony Roche | 2–6, 6–4, 7–6, 6–3 |
| 1971 | Stan Smith | Jan Kodes | 3–6, 6–3, 6–2, 7–6 |
| 1972 | Ilie Nastase | Arthur Ashe | 3–6, 6–3, 6–7, 6–4, 6–3 |
| 1973 | John Newcombe | Jan Kodes | 6–4, 1–6, 4–6, 6–2, 6–3 |
| 1974 | Jimmy Connors | Ken Rosewall | 6–1, 6–0, 6–1 |
| 1975 | Manuel Orantes | Jimmy Connors | 6–4, 6–3, 6–3 |
| 1976 | Jimmy Connors | Bjorn Borg | 6–4, 3–6, 7–6, 6–4 |
| 1977 | Guillermo Vilas | Jimmy Connors | 2–6, 6–3, 7–6, 6–0 |
| 1978 | Jimmy Connors | Bjorn Borg | 6–4, 6–2, 6–2 |
| 1979 | John McEnroe | Vitas Gerulaitis | 7–5, 6–3, 6–3 |
| 1980 | John McEnroe | Bjorn Borg | 7–6, 6–1, 6–7, 5–7, 6–4 |
| 1981 | John McEnroe | Bjorn Borg | 4–6, 6–2, 6–4, 6–3 |
| 1982 | Jimmy Connors | Ivan Lendl | 6–3, 6–2, 4–6, 6–4 |
| 1983 | Jimmy Connors | Ivan Lendl | 6–3, 6–7, 7–5, 6–0 |
| 1984 | John McEnroe | Ivan Lendl | 6–3, 6–4, 6–1 |
| 1985 | Ivan Lendl | John McEnroe | 7–6, 6–3, 6–4 |
| 1986 | Ivan Lendl | Miloslav Mecir | 6–4, 6–2, 6–0 |
| 1987 | Ivan Lendl | Mats Wilander | 6–7, 6–0, 7–6, 6–4 |
| 1988 | Mats Wilander | Ivan Lendl | 6–4, 4–6, 6–3, 5–7, 6–4 |
| 1989 | Boris Becker | Ivan Lendl | 7–6, 1–6, 6–3, 7–6 |
| 1990 | Pete Sampras | Andre Agassi | 6–4, 6–3, 6–2 |
| 1991 | Stefan Edberg | Jim Courier | 6–2, 6–4, 6–0 |
| 1992 | Stefan Edberg | Pete Sampras | 3–6, 6–4, 7–6, 6–2 |
| 1993 | Pete Sampras | Cedric Pioline | 6–4, 6–4, 6–3 |
| 1994 | Andre Agassi | Michael Stich | 6–1, 7–6, 7–5 |
| 1995 | Pete Sampras | Andre Agassi | 6–4, 6–3, 4–6, 7–5 |
| 1996 | Pete Sampras | Michael Chang | 6–1, 6–4, 7–6 |
| 1997 | Patrick Rafter | Greg Rusedski | 6–3, 6–2, 4–6, 7–5 |
| 1998 | Patrick Rafter | Mark Philippoussis | 6–3, 3–6, 6–2, 6–0 |
| 1999 | Andre Agassi | Todd Martin | 6–4, 6–7, 6–7, 6–3, 6–2 |
| 2000 | Marat Safin | Pete Sampras | 6–4, 6–3, 6–3 |
| 2001 | Lleyton Hewitt | Pete Sampras | 7–6, 6–1, 6–1 |

‡No challenge round played.*Became Open (amateur and professional) in 1968.†Challenge round abolished; #National Patriotic Tournament.**Amateur event held.

## WOMEN

### Australian Championships

| Year | Winner | Finalist | Score |
|---|---|---|---|
| 1922 | Margaret Molesworth | Esna Boyd | 6–3, 10–8 |
| 1923 | Margaret Molesworth | Esna Boyd | 6–1, 7–5 |
| 1924 | Sylvia Lance | Esna Boyd | 6–3, 3–6, 6–4 |
| 1925 | Daphne Akhurst | Esna Boyd | 1–6, 8–6, 6–4 |
| 1926 | Daphne Akhurst | Esna Boyd | 6–1, 6–3 |
| 1927 | Esna Boyd | Sylvia Harper | 5–7, 6–1, 6–2 |
| 1928 | Daphne Akhurst | Esna Boyd | 7–5, 6–2 |
| 1929 | Daphne Akhurst | Louise Bickerton | 6–1, 5–7, 6–2 |

## WOMEN *(Cont.)*

### Australian Championships *(Cont.)*

| Year | Winner | Finalist | Score |
|------|--------|----------|-------|
| 1930 | Daphne Akhurst | Sylvia Harper | 10–8, 2–6, 7–5 |
| 1931 | Coral Buttsworth | Margorie Crawford | 1–6, 6–3, 6–4 |
| 1932 | Coral Buttsworth | Kathrine Le Messurier | 9–7, 6–4 |
| 1933 | Joan Hartigan | Coral Buttsworth | 6–4, 6–3 |
| 1934 | Joan Hartigan | Margaret Molesworth | 6–1, 6–4 |
| 1935 | Dorothy Round | Nancye Wynne Bolton | 1–6, 6–1, 6–3 |
| 1936 | Joan Hartigan | Nancye Wynne Bolton | 6–4, 6–4 |
| 1937 | Nancye Wynne Bolton | Emily Westacott | 6–3, 5–7, 6–4 |
| 1938 | Dorothy Bundy | D. Stevenson | 6–3, 6–2 |
| 1939 | Emily Westacott | Nell Hopman | 6–1, 6–2 |
| 1940 | Nancye Wynne Bolton | Thelma Coyne | 5–7, 6–4, 6–0 |
| 1941–45 | No tournament | | |
| 1946 | Nancye Wynne Bolton | Joyce Fitch | 6–4, 6–4 |
| 1947 | Nancye Wynne Bolton | Nell Hopman | 6–3, 6–2 |
| 1948 | Nancye Wynne Bolton | Marie Toomey | 6–3, 6–1 |
| 1949 | Doris Hart | Nancye Wynne Bolton | 6–3, 6–4 |
| 1950 | Louise Brough | Doris Hart | 6–4, 3–6, 6–4 |
| 1951 | Nancye Wynne Bolton | Thelma Long | 6–1, 7–5 |
| 1952 | Thelma Long | H. Angwin | 6–2, 6–3 |
| 1953 | Maureen Connolly | Julia Sampson | 6–3, 6–2 |
| 1954 | Thelma Long | J. Staley | 6–3, 6–4 |
| 1955 | Beryl Penrose | Thelma Long | 6–4, 6–3 |
| 1956 | Mary Carter | Thelma Long | 3–6, 6–2, 9–7 |
| 1957 | Shirley Fry | Althea Gibson | 6–3, 6–4 |
| 1958 | Angela Mortimer | Lorraine Coghlan | 6–3, 6–4 |
| 1959 | Mary Carter-Reitano | Renee Schuurman | 6–2, 6–3 |
| 1960 | Margaret Smith | Jan Lehane | 7–5, 6–2 |
| 1961 | Margaret Smith | Jan Lehane | 6–1, 6–4 |
| 1962 | Margaret Smith | Jan Lehane | 6–0, 6–2 |
| 1963 | Margaret Smith | Jan Lehane | 6–2, 6–2 |
| 1964 | Margaret Smith | Lesley Turner | 6–3, 6–2 |
| 1965 | Margaret Smith | Maria Bueno | 5–7, 6–4, 5–2 ret. |
| 1966 | Margaret Smith | Nancy Richey | Default |
| 1967 | Nancy Richey | Lesley Turner | 6–1, 6–4 |
| 1968 | Billie Jean King | Margaret Smith | 6–1, 6–2 |
| 1969* | Margaret Smith Court | Billie Jean King | 6–4, 6–1 |
| 1970 | Margaret Smith Court | Kerry Melville Reid | 6–3, 6–1 |
| 1971 | Margaret Smith Court | Evonne Goolagong | 2–6, 7–6, 7–5 |
| 1972 | Virginia Wade | Evonne Goolagong | 6–4, 6–4 |
| 1973 | Margaret Smith Court | Evonne Goolagong | 6–4, 7–5 |
| 1974 | Evonne Goolagong | Chris Evert | 7–6, 4–6, 6–0 |
| 1975 | Evonne Goolagong | Martina Navratilova | 6–3, 6–2 |
| 1976 | Evonne Goolagong Cawley | Renata Tomanova | 6–2, 6–2 |
| 1977 (Jan) | Kerry Melville Reid | Dianne Balestrat | 7–5, 6–2 |
| 1977 (Dec) | Evonne Goolagong Cawley | Helen Gourlay | 6–3, 6–0 |
| 1978 | Chris O'Neil | Betsy Nagelsen | 6–3, 7–6 |
| 1979 | Barbara Jordan | Sharon Walsh | 6–3, 6–3 |
| 1980 | Hana Mandlikova | Wendy Turnbull | 6–0, 7–5 |
| 1981 | Martina Navratilova | Chris Evert Lloyd | 6–7, 6–4, 7–5 |
| 1982 | Chris Evert Lloyd | Martina Navratilova | 6–3, 2–6, 6–3 |
| 1983 | Martina Navratilova | Kathy Jordan | 6–2, 7–6 |
| 1984 | Chris Evert Lloyd | Helena Sukova | 6–7, 6–1, 6–3 |
| 1985 (Dec) | Martina Navratilova | Chris Evert Lloyd | 6–2, 4–6, 6–2 |
| 1987 (Jan) | Hana Mandlikova | Martina Navratilova | 7–5, 7–6 |
| 1988 | Steffi Graf | Chris Evert | 6–1, 7–6 |
| 1989 | Steffi Graf | Helena Sukova | 6–4, 6–4 |
| 1990 | Steffi Graf | Mary Joe Fernandez | 6–3, 6–4 |
| 1991 | Monica Seles | Jana Novotna | 5–7, 6–3, 6–1 |
| 1992 | Monica Seles | Mary Joe Fernandez | 6–2, 6–3 |
| 1993 | Monica Seles | Steffi Graf | 4–6, 6–3, 6–2 |
| 1994 | Steffi Graf | Arantxa Sánchez Vicario | 6–0, 6–2 |
| 1995 | Mary Pierce | Arantxa Sánchez Vicario | 6–3, 6–2 |
| 1996 | Monica Seles | Anke Huber | 6–4, 6–1 |
| 1997 | Martina Hingis | Mary Pierce | 6–2, 6–2 |
| 1998 | Martina Hingis | Conchita Martinez | 6–3, 6–3 |
| 1999 | Martina Hingis | Amelie Mauresmo | 6–2, 6–3 |

# Grand Slam Tournaments (Cont.)

## WOMEN (Cont.)

### Australian Championships (Cont.)

| Year | Winner | Finalist | Score |
|------|--------|----------|-------|
| 2000 | Lindsay Davenport | Martina Hingis | 6–1, 7–5 |
| 2001 | Jennifer Capriati | Martina Hingis | 6–4, 6–3 |

*Became Open (amateur and professional) in 1969.

### French Championships

| Year | Winner | Finalist | Score |
|------|--------|----------|-------|
| 1925† | Suzanne Lenglen | Kathleen McKane | 6–1, 6–2 |
| 1926 | Suzanne Lenglen | Mary K. Browne | 6–1, 6–0 |
| 1927 | Kea Bouman | Irene Peacock | 6–2, 6–4 |
| 1928 | Helen Wills | Eileen Bennett | 6–1, 6–2 |
| 1929 | Helen Wills | Simone Mathieu | 6–3, 6–4 |
| 1930 | Helen Wills Moody | Helen Jacobs | 6–2, 6–1 |
| 1931 | Cilly Aussem | Betty Nuthall | 8–6, 6–1 |
| 1932 | Helen Wills Moody | Simone Mathieu | 7–5, 6–1 |
| 1933 | Margaret Scriven | Simone Mathieu | 6–2, 4–6, 6–4 |
| 1934 | Margaret Scriven | Helen Jacobs | 7–5, 4–6, 6–1 |
| 1935 | Hilde Sperling | Simone Mathieu | 6–2, 6–1 |
| 1936 | Hilde Sperling | Simone Mathieu | 6–3, 6–4 |
| 1937 | Hilde Sperling | Simone Mathieu | 6–2, 6–4 |
| 1938 | Simone Mathieu | Nelly Landry | 6–0, 6–3 |
| 1939 | Simone Mathieu | Jadwiga Jedrzejowska | 6–3, 8–6 |
| 1940–45 | No tournament | | |
| 1946 | Margaret Osborne | Pauline Betz | 1–6, 8–6, 7–5 |
| 1947 | Patricia Todd | Doris Hart | 6–3, 3–6, 6–4 |
| 1948 | Nelly Landry | Shirley Fry | 6–2, 0–6, 6–0 |
| 1949 | Margaret Osborne duPont | Nelly Adamson | 7–5, 6–2 |
| 1950 | Doris Hart | Patricia Todd | 6–4, 4–6, 6–2 |
| 1951 | Shirley Fry | Doris Hart | 6–3, 3–6, 6–3 |
| 1952 | Doris Hart | Shirley Fry | 6–4, 6–4 |
| 1953 | Maureen Connolly | Doris Hart | 6–2, 6–4 |
| 1954 | Maureen Connolly | Ginette Bucaille | 6–4, 6–1 |
| 1955 | Angela Mortimer | Dorothy Knode | 2–6, 7–5, 10–8 |
| 1956 | Althea Gibson | Angela Mortimer | 6–0, 12–10 |
| 1957 | Shirley Bloomer | Dorothy Knode | 6–1, 6–3 |
| 1958 | Zsuzsi Kormoczi | Shirley Bloomer | 6–4, 1–6, 6–2 |
| 1959 | Christine Truman | Zsuzsi Kormoczi | 6–4, 7–5 |
| 1960 | Darlene Hard | Yola Ramirez | 6–3, 6–4 |
| 1961 | Ann Haydon | Yola Ramirez | 6–2, 6–1 |
| 1962 | Margaret Smith | Lesley Turner | 6–3, 3–6, 7–5 |
| 1963 | Lesley Turner | Ann Haydon Jones | 2–6, 6–3, 7–5 |
| 1964 | Margaret Smith | Maria Bueno | 5–7, 6–1, 6–2 |
| 1965 | Lesley Turner | Margaret Smith | 6–3, 6–4 |
| 1966 | Ann Jones | Nancy Richey | 6–3, 6–1 |
| 1967 | Francoise Durr | Lesley Turner | 4–6, 6–3, 6–4 |
| 1968* | Nancy Richey | Ann Jones | 5–7, 6–4, 6–1 |
| 1969 | Margaret Smith Court | Ann Jones | 6–1, 4–6, 6–3 |
| 1970 | Margaret Smith Court | Helga Niessen | 6–2, 6–4 |
| 1971 | Evonne Goolagong | Helen Gourlay | 6–3, 7–5 |
| 1972 | Billie Jean King | Evonne Goolagong | 6–3, 6–3 |
| 1973 | Margaret Smith Court | Chris Evert | 6–7, 7–6, 6–4 |
| 1974 | Chris Evert | Olga Morozova | 6–1, 6–2 |
| 1975 | Chris Evert | Martina Navratilova | 2–6, 6–2, 6–1 |
| 1976 | Sue Barker | Renata Tomanova | 6–2, 0–6, 6–2 |
| 1977 | Mima Jausovec | Florenza Mihai | 6–2, 6–7, 6–1 |
| 1978 | Virginia Ruzici | Mima Jausovec | 6–2, 6–2 |
| 1979 | Chris Evert Lloyd | Wendy Turnbull | 6–2, 6–0 |
| 1980 | Chris Evert Lloyd | Virginia Ruzici | 6–0, 6–3 |
| 1981 | Hana Mandlikova | Sylvia Hanika | 6–2, 6–4 |
| 1982 | Martina Navratilova | Andrea Jaeger | 7–6, 6–1 |
| 1983 | Chris Evert Lloyd | Mima Jausovec | 6–1, 6–2 |
| 1984 | Martina Navratilova | Chris Evert Lloyd | 6–3, 6–1 |
| 1985 | Chris Evert Lloyd | Martina Navratilova | 6–3, 6–7, 7–5 |

### WOMEN *(Cont.)*
### French Championships *(Cont.)*

| Year | Winner | Finalist | Score |
|------|--------|----------|-------|
| 1986 | Chris Evert Lloyd | Martina Navratilova | 2–6, 6–3, 6–3 |
| 1987 | Steffi Graf | Martina Navratilova | 6–4, 4–6, 8–6 |
| 1988 | Steffi Graf | Natalia Zvereva | 6–0, 6–0 |
| 1989 | Arantxa Sánchez Vicario | Steffi Graf | 7–6, 3–6, 7–5 |
| 1990 | Monica Seles | Steffi Graf | 7–6, 6–4 |
| 1991 | Monica Seles | Arantxa Sánchez Vicario | 6–3, 6–4 |
| 1992 | Monica Seles | Steffi Graf | 6–2, 3–6, 10–8 |
| 1993 | Steffi Graf | Mary Joe Fernandez | 4–6, 6–2, 6–4 |
| 1994 | Arantxa Sánchez Vicario | Mary Pierce | 6–4, 6–4 |
| 1995 | Steffi Graf | Arantxa Sánchez Vicario | 7–5, 4–6, 6–0 |
| 1996 | Steffi Graf | Arantxa Sánchez Vicario | 6–3, 6–7 (4–7), 10–8 |
| 1997 | Iva Majoli | Martina Hingis | 6–4, 6–2 |
| 1998 | Arantxa Sánchez Vicario | Monica Seles | 7–6 (7–5), 0–6, 6–2 |
| 1999 | Steffi Graf | Martina Hingis | 4–6, 7–5, 6–2 |
| 2000 | Mary Pierce | Conchita Martinez | 6–2, 7–5 |
| 2001 | Jennifer Capriati | Kim Clijsters | 1–6, 6–4, 12–10 |

†1925 was the first year that entries were accepted from all countries.

*Became Open (amateur and professional) in 1968 but closed to contract professionals in 1972.

### Wimbledon Championships

| Year | Winner | Finalist | Score |
|------|--------|----------|-------|
| 1884 | Maud Watson | Lilian Watson | 6–8, 6–3, 6–3 |
| 1885 | Maud Watson | Blanche Bingley | 6–1, 7–5 |
| 1886 | Blanche Bingley | Maud Watson | 6–3, 6–3 |
| 1887 | Charlotte Dod | Blanche Bingley | 6–2, 6–0 |
| 1888 | Charlotte Dod | Blanche Bingley Hillyard | 6–3, 6–3 |
| 1889 | Blanche Bingley Hillyard | n/a | n/a |
| 1890 | Lena Rice | n/a | n/a |
| 1891 | Charlotte Dod | n/a | n/a |
| 1892 | Charlotte Dod | Blanche Bingley Hillyard | 6–1, 6–1 |
| 1893 | Charlotte Dod | Blanche Bingley Hillyard | 6–8, 6–1, 6–4 |
| 1894 | Blanche Bingley Hillyard | n/a | n/a |
| 1895 | Charlotte Cooper | n/a | |
| 1896 | Charlotte Cooper | Mrs. W. H. Pickering | 6–2, 6–3 |
| 1897 | Blanche Bingley Hillyard | Charlotte Cooper | 5–7, 7–5, 6–2 |
| 1898 | Charlotte Cooper | n/a | n/a |
| 1899 | Blanche Bingley Hillyard | Charlotte Cooper | 6–2, 6–3 |
| 1900 | Blanche Bingley Hillyard | Charlotte Cooper | 4–6, 6–4, 6–4 |
| 1901 | Charlotte Cooper Sterry | Blanche Bingley Hillyard | 6–2, 6–2 |
| 1902 | Muriel Robb | Charlotte Cooper Sterry | 7–5, 6–1 |
| 1903 | Dorothea Douglass | n/a | n/a |
| 1904 | Dorothea Douglass | Charlotte Cooper Sterry | 6–0, 6–3 |
| 1905 | May Sutton | Dorothea Douglass | 6–3, 6–4 |
| 1906 | Dorothea Douglass | May Sutton | 6–3, 9–7 |
| 1907 | May Sutton | Dorothea Douglass Lambert Chambers | 6–1, 6–4 |
| 1908 | Charlotte Cooper Sterry | n/a | n/a |
| 1909 | Dora Boothby | n/a | n/a |
| 1910 | Dorothea Douglass Lambert Chambers | Dora Boothby | 6–2, 6–2 |
| 1911 | Dorothea Douglass Lambert Chambers | Dora Boothby | 6–0, 6–0 |
| 1912 | Ethel Larcombe | n/a | n/a |
| 1913 | Dorothea Douglass Lambert Chambers | | |
| 1914 | Dorothea Douglass Lambert Chambers | Ethel Larcombe | 7–5, 6–4 |
| 1915–18 | No tournament | | |
| 1919 | Suzanne Lenglen | Dorothea Douglass Lambert Chambers | 10–8, 4–6, 9–7 |
| 1920 | Suzanne Lenglen | Dorothea Douglass Lambert Chambers | 6–3, 6–0 |

## WOMEN *(Cont.)*

### Wimbledon Championships *(Cont.)*

| Year | Winner | Finalist | Score |
|------|--------|----------|-------|
| 1921 | Suzanne Lenglen | Elizabeth Ryan | 6–2, 6–0 |
| 1922 | Suzanne Lenglen | Molla Mallory | 6–2, 6–0 |
| 1923 | Suzanne Lenglen | Kathleen McKane | 6–2, 6–2 |
| 1924 | Kathleen McKane | Helen Wills | 4–6, 6–4, 6–2 |
| 1925 | Suzanne Lenglen | Joan Fry | 6–2, 6–0 |
| 1926 | Kathleen McKane Godfree | Lili de Alvarez | 6–2, 4–6, 6–3 |
| 1927 | Helen Wills | Lili de Alvarez | 6–2, 6–4 |
| 1928 | Helen Wills | Lili de Alvarez | 6–2, 6–3 |
| 1929 | Helen Wills | Helen Jacobs | 6–1, 6–2 |
| 1930 | Helen Wills Moody | Elizabeth Ryan | 6–2, 6–2 |
| 1931 | Cilly Aussem | Hilde Kranwinkel | 7–5, 7–5 |
| 1932 | Helen Wills Moody | Helen Jacobs | 6–3, 6–1 |
| 1933 | Helen Wills Moody | Dorothy Round | 6–4, 6–8, 6–3 |
| 1934 | Dorothy Round | Helen Jacobs | 6–2, 5–7, 6–3 |
| 1935 | Helen Wills Moody | Helen Jacobs | 6–3, 3–6, 7–5 |
| 1936 | Helen Jacobs | Hilde Kranwinkel Sperling | 6–2, 4–6, 7–5 |
| 1937 | Dorothy Round | Jadwiga Jedrzejowska | 6–2, 2–6, 7–5 |
| 1938 | Helen Wills Moody | Helen Jacobs | 6–4, 6–0 |
| 1939 | Alice Marble | Kay Stammers | 6–2, 6–0 |
| 1940–45 | No tournament | | |
| 1946 | Pauline Betz | Louise Brough | 6–2, 6–4 |
| 1947 | Margaret Osborne | Doris Hart | 6–2, 6–4 |
| 1948 | Louise Brough | Doris Hart | 6–3, 8–6 |
| 1949 | Louise Brough | Margaret Osborne duPont | 10–8, 1–6, 10–8 |
| 1950 | Louise Brough | Margaret Osborne duPont | 6–1, 3–6, 6–1 |
| 1951 | Doris Hart | Shirley Fry | 6–1, 6–0 |
| 1952 | Maureen Connolly | Louise Brough | 6–4, 6–3 |
| 1953 | Maureen Connolly | Doris Hart | 8–6, 7–5 |
| 1954 | Maureen Connolly | Louise Brough | 6–2, 7–5 |
| 1955 | Louise Brough | Beverly Fleitz | 7–5, 8–6 |
| 1956 | Shirley Fry | Angela Buxton | 6–3, 6–1 |
| 1957 | Althea Gibson | Darlene Hard | 6–3, 6–2 |
| 1958 | Althea Gibson | Angela Mortimer | 8–6, 6–2 |
| 1959 | Maria Bueno | Darlene Hard | 6–4, 6–3 |
| 1960 | Maria Bueno | Sandra Reynolds | 8–6, 6–0 |
| 1961 | Angela Mortimer | Christine Truman | 4–6, 6–4, 7–5 |
| 1962 | Karen Hantze Susman | Vera Sukova | 6–4, 6–4 |
| 1963 | Margaret Smith | Billie Jean Moffitt | 6–3, 6–4 |
| 1964 | Maria Bueno | Margaret Smith | 6–4, 7–9, 6–3 |
| 1965 | Margaret Smith | Maria Bueno | 6–4, 7–5 |
| 1966 | Billie Jean King | Maria Bueno | 6 3, 3 6, 6 1 |
| 1967 | Billie Jean King | Ann Haydon Jones | 6–3, 6–4 |
| 1968* | Billie Jean King | Judy Tegart | 9–7, 7–5 |
| 1969 | Ann Haydon Jones | Billie Jean King | 3–6, 6–3, 6–2 |
| 1970 | Margaret Smith Court | Billie Jean King | 14–12, 11–9 |
| 1971 | Evonne Goolagong | Margaret Smith Court | 6–4, 6–1 |
| 1972 | Billie Jean King | Evonne Goolagong | 6–3, 6–3 |
| 1973 | Billie Jean King | Chris Evert | 6–0, 7–5 |
| 1974 | Chris Evert | Olga Morozova | 6–0, 6–4 |
| 1975 | Billie Jean King | Evonne Goolagong Cawley | 6–0, 6–1 |
| 1976 | Chris Evert | Evonne Goolagong Cawley | 6–3, 4–6, 8–6 |
| 1977 | Virginia Wade | Betty Stove | 4–6, 6–3, 6–1 |
| 1978 | Martina Navratilova | Chris Evert | 2–6, 6–4, 7–5 |
| 1979 | Martina Navratilova | Chris Evert Lloyd | 6–4, 6–4 |
| 1980 | Evonne Goolagong Cawley | Chris Evert Lloyd | 6–1, 7–6 |
| 1981 | Chris Evert Lloyd | Hana Mandlikova | 6–2, 6–2 |
| 1982 | Martina Navratilova | Chris Evert Lloyd | 6–1, 3–6, 6–2 |
| 1983 | Martina Navratilova | Andrea Jaeger | 6–0, 6–3 |
| 1984 | Martina Navratilova | Chris Evert Lloyd | 7–6, 6–2 |
| 1985 | Martina Navratilova | Chris Evert Lloyd | 4–6, 6–3, 6–2 |
| 1986 | Martina Navratilova | Hana Mandlikova | 7–6, 6–3 |
| 1987 | Martina Navratilova | Steffi Graf | 7–5, 6–3 |
| 1988 | Steffi Graf | Martina Navratilova | 5–7, 6–2, 6–1 |

## WOMEN *(Cont.)*

### Wimbledon Championships *(Cont.)*

| Year | Winner | Finalist | Score |
|------|--------|----------|-------|
| 1989 | Steffi Graf | Martina Navratilova | 6–2, 6–7, 6–1 |
| 1990 | Martina Navratilova | Zina Garrison | 6–4, 6–1 |
| 1991 | Steffi Graf | Gabriela Sabatini | 6–4, 3–6, 8–6 |
| 1992 | Steffi Graf | Monica Seles | 6–2, 6–1 |
| 1993 | Steffi Graf | Jana Novotna | 7–6, 1–6, 6–4 |
| 1994 | Conchita Martinez | Martina Navratilova | 6–4, 3–6, 6–3 |
| 1995 | Steffi Graf | Arantxa Sánchez Vicario | 4–6, 6–1, 7–5 |
| 1996 | Steffi Graf | Arantxa Sánchez Vicario | 6–3, 7–5 |
| 1997 | Martina Hingis | Jana Novotna | 2–6, 6–3, 6–3 |
| 1998 | Jana Novotna | Nathalie Tauziat | 6–4, 7–6 |
| 1999 | Lindsay Davenport | Steffi Graf | 6–4, 7–5 |
| 2000 | Venus Williams | Lindsay Davenport | 6–3, 7–6 |
| 2001 | Venus Williams | Justine Henin | 6–1, 3–6, 6–0 |

*Became Open (amateur and professional) in 1968 but closed to contract professionals in 1972.

Note: Prior to 1922 the tournament was run on a challenge-round system. The previous year's winner "stood out" of an All-Comers event, which produced a challenger to play her for the title.

### United States Championships

| Year | Winner | Finalist | Score |
|------|--------|----------|-------|
| 1887 | Ellen Hansell | Laura Knight | 6–1, 6–0 |
| 1888 | Bertha L. Townsend | Ellen Hansell | 6–3, 6–5 |
| 1889 | Bertha L. Townsend | Louise Voorhes | 7–5, 6–2 |
| 1890 | Ellen C. Roosevelt | Bertha L. Townsend | 6–2, 6–2 |
| 1891 | Mabel Cahill | Ellen C. Roosevelt | 6–4, 6–1, 4–6, 6–3 |
| 1892 | Mabel Cahill | Elisabeth Moore | 5–7, 6–3, 6–4, 4–6, 6–2 |
| 1893 | Aline Terry | Alice Schultze | 6–1, 6–3 |
| 1894 | Helen Hellwig | Aline Terry | 7–5, 3–6, 6–0, 3–6, 6–3 |
| 1895 | Juliette Atkinson | Helen Hellwig | 6–4, 6–2, 6–1 |
| 1896 | Elisabeth Moore | Juliette Atkinson | 6–4, 4–6, 6–2, 6–2 |
| 1897 | Juliette Atkinson | Elisabeth Moore | 6–3, 6–3, 4–6, 3–6, 6–3 |
| 1898 | Juliette Atkinson | Marion Jones | 6–3, 5–7, 6–4, 2–6, 7–5 |
| 1899 | Marion Jones | Maud Banks | 6–1, 6–1, 7–5 |
| 1900 | Myrtle McAteer | Edith Parker | 6–2, 6–2, 6–0 |
| 1901 | Elisabeth Moore | Myrtle McAteer | 6–4, 3–6, 7–5, 2–6, 6–2 |
| 1902** | Marion Jones | Elisabeth Moore | 6–1, 1–0, ret. |
| 1903 | Elisabeth Moore | Marion Jones | 7–5, 8–6 |
| 1904 | May Sutton | Elisabeth Moore | 6–1, 6–2 |
| 1905 | Elisabeth Moore | Helen Homans | 6–4, 5–7, 6–1 |
| 1906 | Helen Homans | Maud Barger-Wallach | 6–4, 6–3 |
| 1907 | Evelyn Sears | Carrie Neely | 6–3, 6–2 |
| 1908 | Maud Barger–Wallach | Evelyn Sears | 6–3, 1–6, 6–3 |
| 1909 | Hazel Hotchkiss | Maud Barger–Wallach | 6–0, 6–1 |
| 1910 | Hazel Hotchkiss | Louise Hammond | 6–4, 6–2 |
| 1911 | Hazel Hotchkiss | Florence Sutton | 8–10, 6–1, 9–7 |
| 1912† | Mary K. Browne | Eleanora Sears | 6–4, 6–2 |
| 1913 | Mary K. Browne | Dorothy Green | 6–2, 7–5 |
| 1914 | Mary K. Browne | Marie Wagner | 6–2, 1–6, 6–1 |
| 1915 | Molla Bjurstedt | Hazel Hotchkiss Wightman | 4–6, 6–2, 6–0 |
| 1916 | Molla Bjurstedt | Louise Hammond Raymond | 6–0, 6–1 |
| 1917‡ | Molla Bjurstedt | Marion Vanderhoef | 4–6, 6–0, 6–2 |
| 1918 | Molla Bjurstedt | Eleanor Goss | 6–4, 6–3 |
| 1919 | Hazel Hotchkiss Wightman | Marion Zinderstein | 6–1, 6–2 |
| 1920 | Molla Bjurstedt Mallory | Marion Zinderstein | 6–3, 6–1 |
| 1921 | Molla Bjurstedt Mallory | Mary K. Browne | 4–6, 6–4, 6–2 |
| 1922 | Molla Bjurstedt Mallory | Helen Wills | 6–3, 6–1 |
| 1923 | Helen Wills | Molla Bjurstedt Mallory | 6–2, 6–1 |
| 1924 | Helen Wills | Molla Bjurstedt Mallory | 6–1, 6–3 |
| 1925 | Helen Wills | Kathleen McKane | 3–6, 6–0, 6–2 |
| 1926 | Molla Bjurstedt Mallory | Elizabeth Ryan | 4–6, 6–4, 9–7 |
| 1927 | Helen Wills | Betty Nuthall | 6–1, 6–4 |
| 1928 | Helen Wills | Helen Jacobs | 6–2, 6–1 |
| 1929 | Helen Wills | Phoebe Holcroft Watson | 6–4, 6–2 |
| 1930 | Betty Nuthall | Anna McCune Harper | 6–1, 6–4 |
| 1931 | Helen Wills Moody | Eileen Whitingstall | 6–4, 6–1 |

## WOMEN *(Cont.)*

### United States Championships *(Cont.)*

| Year | Winner | Finalist | Score |
|---|---|---|---|
| 1932 | Helen Jacobs | Carolin Babcock | 6–2, 6–2 |
| 1933 | Helen Jacobs | Helen Wills Moody | 8–6, 3–6, 3–0, ret. |
| 1934 | Helen Jacobs | Sarah Palfrey | 6–1, 6–4 |
| 1935 | Helen Jacobs | Sarah Palfrey Fabyan | 6–2, 6–4 |
| 1936 | Alice Marble | Helen Jacobs | 4–6, 6–3, 6–2 |
| 1937 | Anita Lizane | Jadwiga Jedrzejowska | 6–4, 6–2 |
| 1938 | Alice Marble | Nancye Wynne | 6–0, 6–3 |
| 1939 | Alice Marble | Helen Jacobs | 6–0, 8–10, 6–4 |
| 1940 | Alice Marble | Helen Jacobs | 6–2, 6–3 |
| 1941 | Sarah Palfrey Cooke | Pauline Betz | 7–5, 6–2 |
| 1942 | Pauline Betz | Louise Brough | 4–6, 6–1, 6–4 |
| 1943 | Pauline Betz | Louise Brough | 6–3, 5–7, 6–3 |
| 1944 | Pauline Betz | Margaret Osborne | 6–3, 8–6 |
| 1945 | Sarah Palfrey Cooke | Pauline Betz | 3–6, 8–6, 6–4 |
| 1946 | Pauline Betz | Patricia Canning | 11–9, 6–3 |
| 1947 | Louise Brough | Margaret Osborne | 8–6, 4–6, 6–1 |
| 1948 | Margaret Osborne duPont | Louise Brough | 4–6, 6–4, 15–13 |
| 1949 | Margaret Osborne duPont | Doris Hart | 6–4, 6–1 |
| 1950 | Margaret Osborne duPont | Doris Hart | 6–4, 6–3 |
| 1951 | Maureen Connolly | Shirley Fry | 6–3, 1–6, 6–4 |
| 1952 | Maureen Connolly | Doris Hart | 6–3, 7–5 |
| 1953 | Maureen Connolly | Doris Hart | 6–2, 6–4 |
| 1954 | Doris Hart | Louise Brough | 6–8, 6–1, 8–6 |
| 1955 | Doris Hart | Patricia Ward | 6–4, 6–2 |
| 1956 | Shirley Fry | Althea Gibson | 6–3, 6–4 |
| 1957 | Althea Gibson | Louise Brough | 6–3, 6–2 |
| 1958 | Althea Gibson | Darlene Hard | 3–6, 6–1, 6–2 |
| 1959 | Maria Bueno | Christine Truman | 6–1, 6–4 |
| 1960 | Darlene Hard | Maria Bueno | 6–4, 10–12, 6–4 |
| 1961 | Darlene Hard | Ann Haydon | 6–3, 6–4 |
| 1962 | Margaret Smith | Darlene Hard | 9–7, 6–4 |
| 1963 | Maria Bueno | Margaret Smith | 7–5, 6–4 |
| 1964 | Maria Bueno | Carole Graebner | 6–1, 6–0 |
| 1965 | Margaret Smith | Billie Jean Moffitt | 8–6, 7–5 |
| 1966 | Maria Bueno | Nancy Richey | 6–3, 6–1 |
| 1967 | Billie Jean King | Ann Haydon Jones | 11–9, 6–4 |
| 1968* | Virginia Wade | Billie Jean King | 6–4, 6–4 |
| 1968# | Margaret Smith Court | Maria Bueno | 6–2, 6–2 |
| 1969 | Margaret Smith Court | Nancy Richey | 6–2, 6–2 |
| 1969# | Margaret Smith Court | Virginia Wade | 4–6, 6–3, 6–0 |
| 1970 | Margaret Smith Court | Rosie Casals | 6–2, 2–6, 6–1 |
| 1971 | Billie Jean King | Rosie Casals | 6–4, 7–6 |
| 1972 | Billie Jean King | Kerry Melville | 6–3, 7–5 |
| 1973 | Margaret Smith Court | Evonne Goolagong | 7–6, 5–7, 6–2 |
| 1974 | Billie Jean King | Evonne Goolagong | 3–6, 6–3, 7–5 |
| 1975 | Chris Evert | Evonne Goolagong Cawley | 5–7, 6–4, 6–2 |
| 1976 | Chris Evert | Evonne Goolagong Cawley | 6–3, 6–0 |
| 1977 | Chris Evert | Wendy Turnbull | 7–6, 6–2 |
| 1978 | Chris Evert | Pam Shriver | 7–6, 6–4 |
| 1979 | Tracy Austin | Chris Evert Lloyd | 6–4, 6–3 |
| 1980 | Chris Evert Lloyd | Hana Mandlikova | 5–7, 6–1, 6–1 |
| 1981 | Tracy Austin | Martina Navratilova | 1–6, 7–6, 7–6 |
| 1982 | Chris Evert Lloyd | Hana Mandlikova | 6–3, 6–1 |
| 1983 | Martina Navratilova | Chris Evert Lloyd | 6–1, 6–3 |
| 1984 | Martina Navratilova | Chris Evert Lloyd | 4–6, 6–4, 6–4 |
| 1985 | Hana Mandlikova | Martina Navratilova | 7–6, 1–6, 7–6 |
| 1986 | Martina Navratilova | Helena Sukova | 6–3, 6–2 |
| 1987 | Martina Navratilova | Steffi Graf | 7–6, 6–1 |
| 1988 | Steffi Graf | Gabriela Sabatini | 6–3, 3–6, 6–1 |
| 1989 | Steffi Graf | Martina Navratilova | 3–6, 6–4, 6–2 |
| 1990 | Gabriela Sabatini | Steffi Graf | 6–2, 7–6 |
| 1991 | Monica Seles | Martina Narvatilova | 7–6, 6–1 |
| 1992 | Monica Seles | Arantxa Sánchez Vicario | 6–3, 6–2 |
| 1993 | Steffi Graf | Helena Sukova | 6–3, 6–3 |
| 1994 | Arantxa Sánchez Vicario | Steffi Graf | 1–6, 7–6, 6–4 |
| 1995 | Steffi Graf | Monica Seles | 7–6, 0–6, 6–3 |
| 1996 | Steffi Graf | Monica Seles | 7–5, 7–4 |
| 1997 | Martina Hingis | Venus Williams | 6–0, 6–4 |
| 1998 | Lindsay Davenport | Martina Hingis | 6–3, 7–5 |

## WOMEN (Cont.)
### United States Championships (Cont.)

| Year | Winner | Finalist | Score |
|------|--------|----------|-------|
| 1999 | Serena Williams | Martina Hingis | 6–3, 7–6 |
| 2000 | Venus Williams | Lindsay Davenport | 6–4, 7–5 |
| 2001 | Venus Williams | Serena Williams | 6–2, 6–4 |

\*\*Five-set final abolished; †Challenge round abolished. \*Became Open (amateur and professional) in 1968. ‡National Patriotic Tournament; #Amateur event held.

# Grand Slams

## Singles

Don Budge, 1938
Maureen Connolly, 1953
Rod Laver, 1962, 1969
Margaret Smith Court, 1970
Steffi Graf, 1988

## Doubles

Frank Sedgman and Ken McGregor, 1951
Martina Navratilova and Pam Shriver, 1984
Maria Bueno and two partners: Christine Truman (Australian), Darlene Hard (French, Wimbledon and U.S. Championships), 1960
Martina Hingis and two partners: Mirjana Lucic (Australian), Jana Novotna (French, Wimbledon and U.S. Championships), 1998

## Mixed Doubles

Margaret Smith and Ken Fletcher, 1963
Owen Davidson and two partners: Lesley Turner (Australian), Billie Jean King (French, Wimbledon and U.S. Championships), 1967

## Alltime Grand Slam Champions

### MEN

| Player | Aus. S-D-M | French S-D-M | Wim. S-D-M | U.S. S-D-M | Total |
|--------|------------|--------------|------------|------------|-------|
| Roy Emerson | 6-3-0 | 2-6-0 | 2-3-0 | 2-4-0 | 28 |
| John Newcombe | 2-5-0 | 0-3-0 | 3-6-0 | 2-3-1 | 25 |
| Frank Sedgman | 2-2-2 | 0-2-2 | 1-3-2 | 2-2-2 | 22 |
| Bill Tilden | † | 0-0-1 | 3-1-0 | 7-5-4 | 21 |
| Rod Laver | 3-4-0 | 2-1-1 | 4-1-2 | 2-0-0 | 20 |
| John Bromwich | 2-8-1 | 0-0-0 | 0-2-2 | 0-3-1 | 19 |
| Jean Borotra | 1-1-1 | 1-5-2 | 2-3-1 | 0-0-1 | 18 |
| Fred Stolle | 0-3-1 | 1-2-0 | 0-2-3 | 1-3-2 | 18 |
| Ken Rosewall | 4-3-0 | 2-2-0 | 0-2-0 | 2-2-1 | 18 |
| Neale Fraser | 0-3-1 | 0-3-0 | 1-2-0 | 2-3-3 | 18 |
| Adrian Quist | 3-10-0 | 0-1-0 | 0-2-0 | 0-1-0 | 17 |
| John McEnroe | 0-0-0 | 0-0-1 | 3-4-0 | 4-5-0 | 17 |
| Jack Crawford | 4-4-3 | 1-1-1 | 1-1-1 | 0-0-0 | 17 |
| *Mark Woodforde | 0-2-2 | 0-1-1 | 0-6-1 | 0-3-1 | 17 |

†Did not compete.

### WOMEN

| Player | Aus. S-D-M | French S-D-M | Wim. S-D-M | U.S. S-D-M | Total |
|--------|------------|--------------|------------|------------|-------|
| Margaret Smith Court | 11-8-2 | 5-4-4 | 3-2-5 | 5-5-8 | 62 |
| Martina Navratilova | 3-8-0 | 2-7-2 | 9-7-3 | 4-9-2 | 56 |
| Billie Jean King | 1-0-1 | 1-1-2 | 6-10-4 | 4-5-4 | 39 |
| Doris Hart | 1-1-2 | 2-5-3 | 1-4-5 | 2-4-5 | 35 |
| Helen Wills Moody | † | 4-2-0 | 8-3-1 | 7-4-2 | 31 |
| Louise Brough | 1-1-0 | 0-3-0 | 4-5-4 | 1-8-3 | 30** |
| Margaret Osborne duPont | † | 2-3-0 | 1-5-1 | 3-8-6 | 29** |
| Elizabeth Ryan | † | 0-4-0 | 0-12-7 | 0-1-2 | 26 |
| Steffi Graf | 4-0-0 | 6-0-0 | 7-1-0 | 5-0-0 | 23 |
| Pam Shriver | 0-7-0 | 0-4-1 | 0-5-0 | 0-5-0 | 22 |
| Chris Evert | 2-0-0 | 7-2-0 | 3-1-0 | 6-0-0 | 21 |
| Darlene Hard | † | 1-3-2 | 0-4-3 | 2-6-0 | 21 |
| Suzanne Lenglen | † | 2-2-2# | 6-6-3 | 0-0-0 | 21 |
| Nancye Wynne Bolton | 6-10-4 | 0-0-0 | 0-0-0 | 0-0-0 | 20 |
| Maria Bueno | 0-1-0 | 0-1-1 | 3-5-0 | 4-4-0 | 19 |
| Thelma Coyne Long | 2-12-4 | 0-0-1 | 0-0-0 | 0-0-0 | 19 |

\*Active player. †Did not compete. #Suzanne Lenglen also won four singles titles at the French Championships before 1925, when competition was first opened to entries from all nations.\*\*From 1940–45, with competition in the U.S. Championships thinned due to wartime constraints, Louise Brough Clapp also won four doubles titles (1942–45) and one mixed doubles title (1942); and Margaret Osborne duPont won five doubles titles (1941–45) and three mixed doubles titles (1943–45).

## Alltime Grand Slam Singles Champions

### MEN

| Player | Aus. | French | Wim. | U.S. | Total |
|---|---|---|---|---|---|
| *Pete Sampras | 2 | 0 | 7 | 4 | 13 |
| Roy Emerson | 6 | 2 | 2 | 2 | 12 |
| Bjorn Borg | 0 | 6 | 5 | 0 | 11 |
| Rod Laver | 3 | 2 | 4 | 2 | 11 |
| Bill Tilden | † | 0 | 3 | 7 | 10 |
| Jimmy Connors | 1 | 0 | 2 | 5 | 8 |
| Ivan Lendl | 2 | 3 | 0 | 3 | 8 |
| Fred Perry | 1 | 1 | 3 | 3 | 8 |
| Ken Rosewall | 4 | 2 | 0 | 2 | 8 |
| Henri Cochet | † | 4 | 2 | 1 | 7 |
| Rene Lacoste | † | 3 | 2 | 2 | 7 |
| Bill Larned | † | † | 0 | 7 | 7 |
| John McEnroe | 0 | 0 | 3 | 4 | 7 |
| John Newcombe | 2 | 0 | 3 | 2 | 7 |
| Willie Renshaw | † | † | 7 | † | 7 |
| Dick Sears | † | † | 0 | 7 | 7 |
| *Andre Agassi | 3 | 1 | 1 | 2 | 7 |

*Active player. †Did not compete.

### WOMEN

| Player | Aus. | French | Wim. | U.S. | Total |
|---|---|---|---|---|---|
| Margaret Smith Court | 11 | 5 | 3 | 5 | 24 |
| Steffi Graf | 4 | 6 | 7 | 5 | 22 |
| Helen Wills Moody | † | 4 | 8 | 7 | 19 |
| Chris Evert | 2 | 7 | 3 | 6 | 18 |
| Martina Navratilova | 3 | 2 | 9 | 4 | 18 |
| Billie Jean King | 1 | 1 | 6 | 4 | 12 |
| Maureen Connolly | 1 | 2 | 3 | 3 | 9 |
| *Monica Seles | 4 | 3 | 0 | 2 | 9 |
| Suzanne Lenglen | † | 2# | 6 | 0 | 8 |
| Molla Bjurstedt Mallory | † | † | 0 | 8 | 8 |
| Maria Bueno | 0 | 0 | 3 | 4 | 7 |
| Evonne Goolagong | 4 | 1 | 2 | 0 | 7 |
| Dorothea D.L. Chambers | † | † | 7 | 0 | 7 |
| Nancye Wynne Bolton | 6 | 0 | 0 | 0 | 6 |
| Louise Brough | 1 | 0 | 4 | 1 | 6 |
| Margaret Osborne duPont | † | 2 | 1 | 3 | 6 |
| Doris Hart | 1 | 2 | 1 | 2 | 6 |
| Blanche Bingley Hillyard | † | † | 6 | † | 6 |

*Active player. †Did not compete.
#Suzanne Lenglen also won four singles titles at the French Championships before 1925, when competition was first opened to entries from all nations.

| Understated | Shortly after defeating Arnaud Clement in straight sets in the Australian Open final, Andre Agassi was acting as though he had just won a second-round match in Indianapolis. When asked how he planned to fete the win, he simply shrugged, "I'm going to celebrate with Qantas. I'm going home." |
|---|---|

# National Team Competition

## Davis Cup

Started in 1900 as the International Lawn Tennis Challenge Trophy by America's Dwight Davis, the runner-up in the 1898 U.S. Championships. A Davis Cup meeting between two countries is known as a tie and is a three-day event consisting of two singles matches, followed by one doubles match and then two more singles matches. The United States boasts the greatest number of wins (31), followed by Australia (20).

| Year | Winner | Finalist | Site | Score |
|------|--------|----------|------|-------|
| 1900 | United States | Great Britain | Boston | 3–0 |
| 1901 | No tournament | | | |
| 1902 | United States | Great Britain | New York | 3–2 |
| 1903 | Great Britain | United States | Boston | 4–1 |
| 1904 | Great Britain | Belgium | Wimbledon | 5–0 |
| 1905 | Great Britain | United States | Wimbledon | 5–0 |
| 1906 | Great Britain | United States | Wimbledon | 5–0 |
| 1907 | Australasia | Great Britain | Wimbledon | 3–2 |
| 1908 | Australasia | United States | Melbourne | 3–2 |
| 1909 | Australasia | United States | Sydney | 5–0 |
| 1910 | No tournament | | | |
| 1911 | Australasia | United States | Christchurch, NZ | 5–0 |
| 1912 | Great Britain | Australasia | Melbourne | 3–2 |
| 1913 | United States | Great Britain | Wimbledon | 3–2 |
| 1914 | Australasia | United States | New York | 3–2 |
| 1915–18 | No tournament | | | |
| 1919 | Australasia | Great Britain | Sydney | 4–1 |
| 1920 | United States | Australasia | Auckland, NZ | 5–0 |
| 1921 | United States | Japan | New York | 5–0 |
| 1922 | United States | Australasia | New York | 4–1 |
| 1923 | United States | Australasia | New York | 4–1 |
| 1924 | United States | Australia | Philadelphia | 5–0 |
| 1925 | United States | France | Philadelphia | 5–0 |
| 1926 | United States | France | Philadelphia | 4–1 |
| 1927 | France | United States | Philadelphia | 3–2 |
| 1928 | France | United States | Paris | 4–1 |
| 1929 | France | United States | Paris | 3–2 |
| 1930 | France | United States | Paris | 4–1 |
| 1931 | France | Great Britain | Paris | 3–2 |
| 1932 | France | United States | Paris | 3–2 |
| 1933 | Great Britain | France | Paris | 3–2 |
| 1934 | Great Britain | United States | Wimbledon | 4–1 |
| 1935 | Great Britain | United States | Wimbledon | 5–0 |
| 1936 | Great Britain | Australia | Wimbledon | 3–2 |
| 1937 | United States | Great Britain | Wimbledon | 4–1 |
| 1938 | United States | Australia | Philadelphia | 3–2 |
| 1939 | Australia | United States | Philadelphia | 3–2 |
| 1940–45 | No tournament | | | |
| 1946 | United States | Australia | Melbourne | 5–0 |
| 1947 | United States | Australia | New York | 4–1 |
| 1948 | United States | Australia | New York | 5–0 |
| 1949 | United States | Australia | New York | 4–1 |
| 1950 | Australia | United States | New York | 4–1 |
| 1951 | Australia | United States | Sydney | 3–2 |
| 1952 | Australia | United States | Adelaide | 4–1 |
| 1953 | Australia | United States | Melbourne | 3–2 |
| 1954 | United States | Australia | Sydney | 3–2 |
| 1955 | Australia | United States | New York | 5–0 |
| 1956 | Australia | United States | Adelaide | 5–0 |
| 1957 | Australia | United States | Melbourne | 3–2 |
| 1958 | United States | Australia | Brisbane | 3–2 |
| 1959 | Australia | United States | New York | 3–2 |
| 1960 | Australia | Italy | Sydney | 4–1 |
| 1961 | Australia | Italy | Melbourne | 5–0 |
| 1962 | Australia | Mexico | Brisbane | 5–0 |
| 1963 | United States | Australia | Adelaide | 3–2 |
| 1964 | Australia | United States | Cleveland | 3–2 |
| 1965 | Australia | Spain | Sydney | 4–1 |
| 1966 | Australia | India | Melbourne | 4–1 |
| 1967 | Australia | Spain | Brisbane | 4–1 |
| 1968 | United States | Australia | Adelaide | 4–1 |
| 1969 | United States | Romania | Cleveland | 5–0 |
| 1970 | United States | W Germany | Cleveland | 5–0 |
| 1971 | United States | Romania | Charlotte, NC | 3–2 |

## Davis Cup *(Cont.)*

| Year | Winner | Finalist | Site | Score |
|------|--------|----------|------|-------|
| 1972 | United States | Romania | Bucharest | 3–2 |
| 1973 | Australia | United States | Cleveland | 5–0 |
| 1974 | South Africa | India | * | walkover |
| 1975 | Sweden | Czechoslovakia | Stockholm | 3–2 |
| 1976 | Italy | Chile | Santiago | 4–1 |
| 1977 | Australia | Italy | Sydney | 3–1 |
| 1978 | United States | Great Britain | Palm Springs | 4–1 |
| 1979 | United States | Italy | San Francisco | 5–0 |
| 1980 | Czechoslovakia | Italy | Prague | 4–1 |
| 1981 | United States | Argentina | Cincinnati | 3–1 |
| 1982 | United States | France | Grenoble, France | 4–1 |
| 1983 | Australia | Sweden | Melbourne | 3–2 |
| 1984 | Sweden | United States | Göteborg, Sweden | 4–1 |
| 1985 | Sweden | W Germany | Munich | 3–2 |
| 1986 | Australia | Sweden | Melbourne | 3–2 |
| 1987 | Sweden | India | Göteborg, Sweden | 5–0 |
| 1988 | West Germany | Sweden | Göteborg, Sweden | 4–1 |
| 1989 | West Germany | Sweden | Stuttgart | 3–2 |
| 1990 | United States | Australia | St. Petersburg | 3–2 |
| 1991 | France | United States | Lyon | 3–1 |
| 1992 | United States | Switzerland | Fort Worth, TX | 3–1 |
| 1993 | Germany | Australia | Dusseldorf | 4–1 |
| 1994 | Sweden | Russia | Moscow | 4–1 |
| 1995 | United States | Russia | Moscow | 3–2 |
| 1996 | France | Sweden | Malmö, Sweden | 3–2 |
| 1997 | Sweden | United States | Göteborg, Sweden | 5–0 |
| 1998 | Sweden | Italy | Milan | 4–1 |
| 1999 | Australia | France | Nice, France | 3–2 |
| 2000 | Spain | Australia | Barcelona | 3–1 |

*India refused to play the final in protest over South Africa's governmental policy of apartheid.
Note: Prior to 1972 the challenge-round system was in effect, with the previous year's winner "standing out" of the competition until the finals. A straight 16-nation tournament has been held since 1981.

## Federation Cup

The Federation Cup was started in 1963 by the International Lawn Tennis Federation (now the ITF). Until 1991 all entrants gathered at one site at one time for a tournament that was concluded within one week. Since 1995 the Fed Cup, as it is now called, has been contested in three rounds by a World Group of eight nations. A meeting between two countries now consists of five matches: four singles and one doubles. The United States has the most wins (15), followed by Australia (7).

| Year | Winner | Finalist | Site | Score |
|------|--------|----------|------|-------|
| 1963 | United States | Australia | London | 2–1 |
| 1964 | Australia | United States | Philadelphia | 2–1 |
| 1965 | Australia | United States | Melbourne | 2–1 |
| 1966 | United States | W Germany | Turin | 3–0 |
| 1967 | United States | Great Britain | W Berlin | 2–0 |
| 1968 | Australia | Netherlands | Paris | 3–0 |
| 1969 | United States | Australia | Athens | 2–1 |
| 1970 | Australia | Great Britain | Freiburg | 3 0 |
| 1971 | Australia | Great Britain | Perth | 3–0 |
| 1972 | South Africa | Great Britain | Johannesburg | 2–1 |
| 1973 | Australia | South Africa | Bad Homburg | 3–0 |
| 1974 | Australia | United States | Naples | 2–1 |
| 1975 | Czechoslovakia | Australia | Aix-en-Provence | 3–0 |
| 1976 | United States | Australia | Philadelphia | 2–1 |
| 1977 | United States | Australia | Eastbourne, G.B. | 2–1 |
| 1978 | United States | Australia | Melbourne | 2–1 |
| 1979 | United States | Australia | Madrid | 3–0 |
| 1980 | United States | Australia | W Berlin | 3–0 |
| 1981 | United States | Great Britain | Nagoya | 3–0 |
| 1982 | United States | W Germany | Santa Clara, CA | 3–0 |
| 1983 | Czechoslovakia | W Germany | Zurich | 2–1 |
| 1984 | Czechoslovakia | Australia | Sao Paulo | 2–1 |
| 1985 | Czechoslovakia | United States | Tokyo | 2–1 |
| 1986 | United States | Czechoslovakia | Prague | 3–0 |
| 1987 | W Germany | United States | Vancouver | 2–1 |

## Federation Cup *(Cont.)*

| Year | Winner | Finalist | Site | Score |
|------|--------|----------|------|-------|
| 1988 | Czechoslovakia | USSR | Melbourne | 2–1 |
| 1989 | United States | Spain | Tokyo | 3–0 |
| 1990 | United States | USSR | Atlanta | 2–1 |
| 1991 | Spain | United States | Nottingham | 2–1 |
| 1992 | Germany | Spain | Frankfurt | 2–1 |
| 1993 | Spain | Australia | Frankfurt | 3–0 |
| 1994 | Spain | United States | Frankfurt | 3–0 |
| 1995 | Spain | United States | Valencia, Spain | 3–2 |
| 1996 | United States | Spain | Atlantic City | 5–0 |
| 1997 | France | Netherlands | Hertogenbosch, Neth. | 4–1 |
| 1998 | Spain | Switzerland | Geneva | 3–2 |
| 1999 | United States | Russia | Palo Alto, California | 4–1 |
| 2000 | United States | Spain | Las Vegas, Nevada | 5–0 |

# Rankings

## ATP Computer Year-End Top 10
### MEN

**1973**
1. Ilie Nastase
2. John Newcombe
3. Jimmy Connors
4. Tom Okker
5. Stan Smith
6. Ken Rosewall
7. Manuel Orantes
8. Rod Laver
9. Jan Kodes
10. Arthur Ashe

**1974**
1. Jimmy Connors
2. John Newcombe
3. Bjorn Borg
4. Rod Laver
5. Guillermo Vilas
6. Tom Okker
7. Arthur Ashe
8. Ken Rosewall
9. Stan Smith
10. Ilie Nastase

**1975**
1. Jimmy Connors
2. Guillermo Vilas
3. Bjorn Borg
4. Arthur Ashe
5. Manuel Orantes
6. Ken Rosewall
7. Ilie Nastase
8. John Alexander
9. Roscoe Tanner
10. Rod Laver

**1976**
1. Jimmy Connors
2. Bjorn Borg
3. Ilie Nastase
4. Manuel Orantes
5. Raul Ramirez
6. Guillermo Vilas
7. Adriano Panatta
8. Harold Solomon
9. Eddie Dibbs
10. Brian Gottfried

**1977**
1. Jimmy Connors
2. Guillermo Vilas
3. Bjorn Borg
4. Vitas Gerulaitis
5. Brian Gottfried
6. Eddie Dibbs
7. Manuel Orantes
8. Raul Ramirez
9. Ilie Nastase
10. Dick Stockton

**1978**
1. Jimmy Connors
2. Bjorn Borg
3. Guillermo Vilas
4. John McEnroe
5. Vitas Gerulaitis
6. Eddie Dibbs
7. Brian Gottfried
8. Raul Ramirez
9. Harold Solomon
10. Corrado Barazzutti

**1979**
1. Bjorn Borg
2. Jimmy Connors
3. John McEnroe
4. Vitas Gerulaitis
5. Roscoe Tanner
6. Guillermo Vilas
7. Arthur Ashe
8. Harold Solomon
9. Jose Higueras
10. Eddie Dibbs

**1980**
1. Bjorn Borg
2. John McEnroe
3. Jimmy Connors
4. Gene Mayer
5. Guillermo Vilas
6. Ivan Lendl
7. Harold Solomon
8. Jose–Luis Clerc
9. Vitas Gerulaitis
10. Eliot Teltscher

**1981**
1. John McEnroe
2. Ivan Lendl
3. Jimmy Connors
4. Bjorn Borg
5. Jose–Luis Clerc
6. Guillermo Vilas
7. Gene Mayer
8. Eliot Teltscher
9. Vitas Gerulaitis
10. Peter McNamara

## ATP Computer Year-End Top 10
### MEN (CONT.)

**1982**
1 ....John McEnroe
2 ....Jimmy Connors
3 ....Ivan Lendl
4 ....Guillermo Vilas
5 ....Vitas Gerulaitis
6 ....Jose–Luis Clerc
7 ....Mats Wilander
8 ....Gene Mayer
9 ....Yannick Noah
10 ..Peter McNamara

**1983**
1 ....John McEnroe
2 ....Ivan Lendl
3 ....Jimmy Connors
4 ....Mats Wilander
5 ....Yannick Noah
6 ....Jimmy Arias
7 ....Jose Higueras
8 ....Jose–Luis Clerc
9 ....Kevin Curren
10 ..Gene Mayer

**1984**
1 ....John McEnroe
2 ....Jimmy Connors
3 ....Ivan Lendl
4 ....Mats Wilander
5 ....Andres Gomez
6 ....Anders Jarryd
7 ....Henrik Sundstrom
8 ....Pat Cash
9 ...:Eliot Teltscher
10 ..Yannick Noah

**1985**
1 ....Ivan Lendl
2 ....John McEnroe
3 ....Mats Wilander
4 ....Jimmy Connors
5 ....Stefan Edberg
6 ....Boris Becker
7 ....Yannick Noah
8 ....Anders Jarryd
9 ....Miloslav Mecir
10 ..Kevin Curren

**1986**
1 ....Ivan Lendl
2 ....Boris Becker
3 ....Mats Wilander
4 ....Yannick Noah
5 ....Stefan Edberg
6 ....Henri Leconte
7 ....Joakim Nystrom
8 ....Jimmy Connors
9 ....Miloslav Mecir
10 ..Andres Gomez

**1987**
1 ....Ivan Lendl
2 ....Stefan Edberg
3 ....Mats Wilander
4 ....Jimmy Connors
5 ....Boris Becker
6 ....Miloslav Mecir
7 ....Pat Cash
8 ....Yannick Noah
9 ....Tim Mayotte
10 ..John McEnroe

**1988**
1 ....Mats Wilander
2 ....Ivan Lendl
3 ....Andre Agassi
4 ....Boris Becker
5 ....Stefan Edberg
6 ....Kent Carlsson
7 ....Jimmy Connors
8 ....Jakob Hlasek
9 ....Henri Leconte
10 ..Tim Mayotte

**1989**
1 ....Ivan Lendl
2 ....Boris Becker
3 ....Stefan Edberg
4 ....John McEnroe
5 ....Michael Chang
6 ....Brad Gilbert
7 ....Andre Agassi
8 ....Aaron Krickstein
9 ....Alberto Mancini
10 ..Jay Berger

**1990**
1 ....Stefan Edberg
2 ....Boris Becker
3 ....Ivan Lendl
4 ....Andre Agassi
5 ....Pete Sampras
6 ....Andres Gomez
7 ....Thomas Muster
8 ....Emilio Sanchez
9 ....Goran Ivanisevic
10 ..Brad Gilbert

**1991**
1 ....Stefan Edberg
2 ....Jim Courier
3 ....Boris Becker
4 ....Michael Stich
5 ....Ivan Lendl
6 ....Pete Sampras
7 ....Guy Forget
8 ....Karel Novacek
9 ....Petr Korda
10 ..Andre Agassi

**1992**
1 ....Jim Courier
2 ....Stefan Edberg
3 ....Pete Sampras
4 ....Goran Ivanisevic
5 ....Boris Becker
6 ....Michael Chang
7 ....Petr Korda
8 ....Ivan Lendl
9 ....Andre Agassi
10 ..Richard Krajicek

**1993**
1 ....Pete Sampras
2 ....Michael Stich
3 ....Jim Courier
4 ....Sergi Bruguera
5 ....Stefan Edberg
6 ....Andrei Medvedev
7 ....Goran Ivanisevic
8 ....Michael Chang
9 ....Thomas Muster
10 ..Cedric Pioline

**1994**
1 ....Pete Sampras
2 ....Andre Agassi
3 ....Boris Becker
4 ....Sergi Bruguera
5 ....Goran Ivanisevic
6 ....Michael Chang
7 ....Stefan Edberg
8 ....Alberto Berasategui
9 ....Michael Stich
10 ..Todd Martin

**1995**
1 ....Pete Sampras
2 ....Andre Agassi
3 ....Thomas Muster
4 ....Boris Becker
5 ....Michael Chang
6 ....Yevgeny Kafelnikov
7 ....Thomas Enqvist
8 ....Jim Courier
9 ....Wayne Ferreira
10 ...Goran Ivanisevic

**1996**
1 ....Pete Sampras
2 ....Michael Chang
3 ....Yevgeny Kafelnikov
4 ....Goran Ivanisevic
5 ....Thomas Muster
6 ....Boris Becker
7 ....Richard Krajicek
8 ....Andre Agassi
9 ....Thomas Enqvist
10 ...Wayne Ferreira

## ATP Computer Year-End Top 10
### MEN *(CONT.)*

**1997**
1 ....Pete Sampras
2 ....Patrick Rafter
3 ....Michael Chang
4 ....Jonas Bjorkman
5 ....Yevgeny Kafelnikov
6 ....Greg Rusedski
7 ....Carlos Moya
8 ....Sergei Bruguera
9 ....Thomas Muster
10...Marcelo Rios

**1998**
1 ....Pete Sampras
2 ....Marcelo Rios
3 ....Alex Corretja
4 ....Patrick Rafter
5 ....Carlos Moya
6 ....Andre Agassi
7 ....Tim Henman
8 ....Karol Kucera
9 ...Greg Rusedski
10...Richard Krajicek

**1999**
1 ....Andre Agassi
2 ....Yevgeny Kafelnikov
3 ...Pete Sampras
4 ....Thomas Enqvist
5 ....Gustavo Kuerten
6 ...Nicolas Kiefer
7 ....Todd Martin
8 ...Nicolas Lapentti
9 ....Marcelo Rios
10 ..Richard Krajicek

**2000**
1 ....Gustavo Kuerten
2 ....Marat Safin
3 ....Pete Sampras
4 ....Magnus Norman
5 ....Yevgeny Kafelnikov
6 ....Andre Agassi
7 ....Lleyton Hewitt
8 ....Alex Corretja
9 ....Thomas Enqvist
10 ..Tim Henman

## WTA Computer Year-End Top 10
### WOMEN

**1973**
1 ....Margaret Smith
      Court
2 ....Billie Jean King
3 ....Evonne Goolagong
4 ....Chris Evert
5 ....Rosie Casals
6 ....Virginia Wade
7 ....Kerry Reid
8 ....Nancy Gunter
9 ....Julie Heldman
10...Helga Masthoff

**1974**
1 ....Billie Jean King
2 ....Evonne Goolagong
3 ....Chris Evert
4 ....Virginia Wade
5 ....Julie Heldman
6 ....Rosie Casals
7 ....Kerry Reid
8 ....Olga Morozova
9 ....Lesley Hunt
10...Francoise Durr

**1975**
1 ....Chris Evert
2 ....Billie Jean King
3 ....Evonne Goolagong
      Cawley
4 ....Martina Navratilova
5 ....Virginia Wade
6 ....Margaret Smith
      Court
7 ....Olga Morozova
8 ....Nancy Gunter
9 ....Francoise Durr
10...Rosie Casals

**1976**
1 ....Chris Evert
2 ....Evonne Goolagong
      Cawley
3 ...Virginia Wade
4 ....Martina Navratilova
5 ....Sue Barker
6 ....Betty Stove
7 ....Dianne Balestrat
8 ...Mima Jausovec
9 ....Rosie Casals
10...Francoise Durr

**1977**
1 ....Chris Evert
2 ....Billie Jean King
3 ....Martina Navratilova
4 ....Virginia Wade
5 ....Sue Barker
6 ....Rosie Casals
7 ....Betty Stove
8 ....Dianne Balestrat
9 ....Wendy Turnbull
10...Kerry Reid

**1978**
1 ....Martina Navratilova
2 ....Chris Evert
3 ....Evonne Goolagong
      Cawley
4 ....Virginia Wade
5 ....Billie Jean King
6 ....Tracy Austin
7 ....Wendy Turnbull
8 ....Kerry Reid
9 ....Betty Stove
10...Dianne Balestrat

**1979**
1 ....Martina Navratilova
2 ....Chris Evert Lloyd
3 ....Tracy Austin
4 ....Evonne Goolagong
      Cawley
5 ....Billie Jean King
6 ....Dianne Balestrat
7 ....Wendy Turnbull
8 ....Virginia Wade
9 ....Kerry Reid
10...Sue Barker

**1980**
1 ....Chris Evert Lloyd
2 ....Tracy Austin
3 ....Martina Navratilova
4 ....Hana Mandlikova
5 ....Evonne Goolagong
      Cawley
6 ....Billie Jean King
7 ....Andrea Jaeger
8 ....Wendy Turnbull
9 ....Pam Shriver
10...Greer Stevens

**1981**
1 ....Chris Evert Lloyd
2 ....Tracy Austin
3 ....Martina Navratilova
4 ....Andrea Jaeger
5 ....Hana Mandlikova
6 ....Sylvia Hanika
7 ....Pam Shriver
8 ....Wendy Turnbull
9 ....Bettina Bunge
10...Barbara Potter

**1982**
1 ....Martina Navratilova
2 ....Chris Evert Lloyd
3 ....Andrea Jaeger
4 ....Tracy Austin
5 ....Wendy Turnbull
6 ....Pam Shriver
7 ....Hana Mandlikova
8 ....Barbara Potter
9 ....Bettina Bunge
10...Sylvia Hanika

**1983**
1 ....Martina Navratilova
2 ....Chris Evert Lloyd
3 ....Andrea Jaeger
4 ....Pam Shriver
5 ....Sylvia Hanika
6 ....Jo Durie
7 ....Bettina Bunge
8 ....Wendy Turnbull
9 ....Tracy Austin
10...Zina Garrison

**1984**
1 ....Martina Navratilova
2 ....Chris Evert Lloyd
3 ....Hana Mandlikova
4 ....Pam Shriver
5 ....Wendy Turnbull
6 ....Manuela Maleeva
7 ....Helena Sukova
8 ....Claudia Kohde-
      Kilsch
9 ....Zina Garrison
10...Kathy Jordan

## WTA Computer Year-End Top 10 (Cont.)
### WOMEN (CONT.)

**1985**
1 ....Martina Navratilova
2 ....Chris Evert Lloyd
3 ....Hana Mandlikova
4 ....Pam Shriver
5 ....Claudia Kohde-
Kilsch
6 ....Steffi Graf
7 ....Manuela Maleeva
8 ....Zina Garrison
9 ....Helena Sukova
10...Bonnie Gadusek

**1986**
1 ....Martina Navratilova
2 ....Chris Evert Lloyd
3 ....Pam Shriver
4 ....Hana Mandlikova
5 ....Helena Sukova
6 ....Pam Shriver
7 ....Claudia Kohde-
Kilsch
8 ....Manuela Maleeva
9 ....Kathy Rinaldi
10...Gabriela Sabatini

**1987**
1 ....Steffi Graf
2 ....Martina Navratilova
3 ....Chris Evert
4 ....Pam Shriver
5 ....Hana Mandlikova
6 ....Gabriela Sabatini
7 ....Helena Sukova
8 ....Manuela Maleeva
9 ....Zina Garrison
10...Claudia Kohde-
Kilsch

**1988**
1 ....Steffi Graf
2 ....Martina Navratilova
3 ....Chris Evert
4 ....Gabriela Sabatini
5 ....Pam Shriver
6 ....Manuela Maleeva-
Fragniere
7 ....Natalia Zvereva
8 ....Helena Sukova
9 ....Zina Garrison
10...Barbara Potter

**1989**
1 ....Steffi Graf
2 ....Martina Navratilova
3 ....Gabriela Sabatini
4 ....Zina Garrison
5 ....Arantxa Sánchez
Vicario
6 ....Monica Seles
7 ....Conchita Martinez
8 ....Helena Sukova
9 ....Manuela Maleeva-
Fragniere
10...*Chris Evert

**1990**
1 ....Steffi Graf
2 ....Monica Seles
3 ....Martina Navratilova
4 ....Mary Joe Fernandez
5 ....Gabriela Sabatini
6 ....Katerina Maleeva
7 ....Arantxa Sánchez
Vicario
8 ....Jennifer Capriati
9 ....Manuela Maleeva-
Fragniere
10...Zina Garrison

**1991**
1 ....Monica Seles
2 ....Steffi Graf
3 ....Gabriela Sabatini
4 ....Martina Navratilova
5 ....Arantxa Sánchez
Vicario
6 ....Jennifer Capriati
7 ....Jana Novotna
8 ....Mary Joe Fernandez
9 ....Conchita Martinez
10...Manuela Maleeva-
Fragniere

**1992**
1 ....Monica Seles
2 ....Steffi Graf
3 ....Gabriela Sabatini
4 ....Arantxa Sánchez
Vicario
5 ....Martina Navratilova
6 ....Mary Joe Fernandez
7 ....Jennifer Capriati
8 ....Conchita Martinez
9 ....Manuela Maleeva-
Fragniere
10...Jana Novotna

**1993**
1 ....Steffi Graf
2 ....Arantxa Sánchez
Vicario
3 ....Martina Navratilova
4 ....Conchita Martinez
5 ....Gabriela Sabatini
6 ....Jana Novotna
7 ....Mary Joe Fernandez
8 ....Monica Seles
9 ....Jennifer Capriati
10...Anke Huber

**1994**
1 ....Steffi Graf
2 ....Arantxa Sánchez
Vicario
3 ....Conchita Martinez
4 ....Jana Novotna
5 ....Mary Pierce
6 ....Lindsay Davenport
7 ....Gabriela Sabatini
8 ....Martina Navratilova
9 ....Kimiko Date
10...Natasha Zvereva

**1995**
1 ....Steffi Graf (co-No. 1)
1 ....Monica Seles
(co-No. 1)
2 ....Conchita Martinez
3 ....Arantxa Sánchez
Vicario
4 ....Kimiko Date
5 ....Mary Pierce
6 ....Magdalena Maleeva
7 ....Gabriela Sabatini
8 ....Mary Joe Fernandez
9 ....Iva Majoli
10...Anke Huber

**1996**
1 ....Steffi Graf
2 ....Monica Seles
3 ....Jana Novotna
4 ....Lindsay Davenport
5 ....Martina Hingis
6 ....Stephanie de Ville
7 ....Tamarine
Tanasugarn
8 ....Anke Huber
9 ....Conchita Martinez
10...Julie Halard-
Decugis

**1997**
1 ....Martina Hingis
2 ....Jana Novotna
3 ....Lindsay Davenport
4 ....Amanda Coetzer
5 ....Monica Seles
6 ....Iva Majoli
7 ....Mary Pierce
8 ....Irina Spirlea
9 ....Arantxa Sánchez
Vicario
10...Mary Joe Fernandez

**1998**
1 ....Lindsay Davenport
2 ....Martina Hingis
2 ....Jana Novotna
4 ....Arantxa Sánchez
Vicario
5 ....Venus Williams
6 ....Monica Seles
7 ....Mary Pierce
8 ....Conchita Martinez
9 ....Steffi Graf
10...Nathalie Tauziat

**1999**
1 ....Martina Hingis
2 ....Lindsay Davenport
3 ....Venus Williams
4 ....Serena Williams
5 ....Mary Pierce
6 ....Monica Seles
7 ....Nathalie Tauziat
8 ....Barbara Schett
9 ....Julie Halard-
......Decugis
10...Amelie Mauresmo

**2000**
1 ....Martina Hingis
2 ....Lindsay Davenport
3 ....Venus Williams
4 ....Monica Seles
5 ....Conchita Martinez
6 ....Serena Williams
7 ....Mary Pierce
8 ....Anna Kournikova
9 ....Arantxa
Sánchez Vicario
10...Nathalie Tauziat

*When Chris Evert announced her retirement at the 1989 United States Open, she was ranked fourth in the world. That was her last official series tournament.

# Prize Money

## Top 25 Men's Career Prize Money Leaders

Note: From arrival of Open tennis in 1968 through September 30, 2001.

| | Earnings ($) |
|---|---|
| Pete Sampras | 41,664,440 |
| Boris Becker | 25,079,186 |
| Andre Agassi | 22,102,690 |
| Ivan Lendl | 21,262,417 |
| Stefan Edberg | 20,630,941 |
| Goran Ivanisevic | 19,315,100 |
| Michael Chang | 18,510,306 |
| Yevgeny Kafelnikov | 16,874,355 |
| Jim Courier | 14,033,132 |
| Michael Stich | 12,590,152 |
| John McEnroe | 12,539,622 |
| Thomas Muster | 12,224,410 |
| Sergi Bruguera | 11,406,296 |
| Patrick Rafter | 10,878,411 |
| Petr Korda | 10,447,665 |
| Richard Krajicek | 9,762,111 |
| Marcelo Rios | 8,766,598 |
| Jimmy Connors | 8,641,040 |
| Alex Corretja | 8,464,759 |
| Mark Woodforde | 8,322,151 |
| Wayne Ferreira | 8,055,937 |
| Jonas Bjorkman | 8,034,186 |
| Mats Wilander | 7,976,256 |
| Thomas Enqvist | 7,719,301 |
| Todd Woodbridge | 7,715,042 |

## Top 25 Women's Career Prize Money Leaders

Note: From arrival of Open tennis in 1968 through October 1, 2001.

| | Earnings ($) |
|---|---|
| Steffi Graf | 21,895,277 |
| Martina Navratilova | 20,394,149 |
| Arantxa Sánchez Vicario | 16,111,619 |
| Martina Hingis | 14,993,779 |
| Monica Seles | 13,100,919 |
| Lindsay Davenport | 12,639,870 |
| Jana Novotna | 11,249,134 |
| Conchita Martinez | 9,583,580 |
| Venus Williams | 9,135,837 |
| Chris Evert | 8,896,195 |
| Gabriela Sabatini | 8,785,850 |
| Natasha Zvereva | 7,714,430 |
| Helena Sukova | 6,391,245 |
| Mary Pierce | 6,169,661 |
| Nathalie Tauziat | 6,093,077 |
| Pam Shriver | 5,460,566 |
| Mary Joe Fernandez | 5,252,571 |
| Serena Williams | 5,144,324 |
| Gigi Fernandez | 4,681,906 |
| Anke Huber | 4,615,192 |
| Zina Garrison Jackson | 4,590,816 |
| Amanda Coetzer | 4,526,797 |
| Larisa Neiland | 4,083,936 |
| Iva Majoli | 3,569,988 |
| Lori McNeil | 3,474,115 |

## Love Amongst the Clay

A romantic air swept the French Open, the tour's most unpredictable Grand Slam event, in a new direction in 2001. On her first Wednesday at Roland Garros, Capriati smiled wistfully and announced a Disneyfied desire "to find my Prince Charming."

By the time the fortnight had ended, TV screens were saturated with shots of Jennifer's divorced parents, Denise and Stefano, sitting side by side and hugging after her wins. Men's champion Gustavo Kuerten, who won his third French Open title, with a victory over Alex Corretja, conjured up the tournament's most apt image. After surviving a match point to win a fourth-round marathon against qualifier Michael Russell, he used his racket to carve a heart—a valentine to the French fans—in the clay of Court Phillippe Chatrier, then kneeled and blew two kisses. Following the final he took it one step further, carving another heart and stretching out inside it.

—S.L. Price

# Open Era Overall Wins

## Men's Career Leaders—Singles Titles Won

The top tournament-winning men from the institution of Open tennis in 1968 through Sept. 30, 2001.

| | W | | W |
|---|---|---|---|
| Jimmy Connors | 109 | Thomas Muster | 44 |
| Ivan Lendl | 94 | Stefan Edberg | 41 |
| John McEnroe | 77 | Stan Smith | 39 |
| Pete Sampras | 63 | Michael Chang | 34 |
| Bjorn Borg | 62 | Arthur Ashe | 33 |
| Guillermo Vilas | 62 | Mats Wilander | 33 |
| Ilie Nastase | 57 | John Newcombe | 32 |
| Boris Becker | 49 | Manuel Orantes | 32 |
| Andre Agassi | 49 | Ken Rosewall | 32 |
| Rod Laver | 47 | Tom Okker | 31 |

## Women's Career Leaders—Singles Titles Won

The top tournament-winning women from the institution of Open tennis in 1968 through Sept. 30, 2001.

| | W | | W |
|---|---|---|---|
| Martina Navratilova | 167 | Lindsay Davenport | 32 |
| Chris Evert | 157 | Tracy Austin | 29 |
| Steffi Graf | 108 | Arantxa Sánchez Vicario | 29 |
| Evonne Goolagong Cawley | 88 | Hana Mandlikova | 27 |
| Margaret Smith Court | 79 | Gabriela Sabatini | 27 |
| Billie Jean King | 67 | Nancy Richey | 25 |
| Virginia Wade | 55 | Jana Novotna | 24 |
| Monica Seles | 49 | Kerry Melville Reid | 22 |
| Martina Hingis | 33 | Sue Barker | 21 |
| Conchita Martinez | 32 | Pam Shriver | 21 |

# Annual ATP/WTA Champions

## Men—ATP Tour World Championship

| Year | Player | Year | Player |
|---|---|---|---|
| 1970 | Stan Smith | 1986 (Jan) | Ivan Lendl |
| 1971 | Ilie Nastase | 1986 (Dec) | Ivan Lendl |
| 1972 | Ilie Nastase | 1987 | Ivan Lendl |
| 1973 | Ilie Nastase | 1988 | Boris Becker |
| 1974 | Guillermo Vilas | 1989 | Stefan Edberg |
| 1975 | Ilie Nastase | 1990 | Andre Agassi |
| 1976 | Manuel Orantes | 1991 | Pete Sampras |
| 1977 | Not held | 1992 | Boris Becker |
| 1978 | Jimmy Connors | 1993 | Michael Stich |
| 1979 | John McEnroe | 1994 | Pete Sampras |
| 1980 | Bjorn Borg | 1995 | Boris Becker |
| 1981 | Bjorn Borg | 1996 | Pete Sampras |
| 1982 | Ivan Lendl | 1997 | Pete Sampras |
| 1983 | Ivan Lendl | 1998 | Alex Corretja |
| 1984 | John McEnroe | 1999 | Pete Sampras |
| 1985 | John McEnroe | 2000 | Thomas Enqvist |

Note: Event held twice in 1986. *Since 1984 the final has been best-of-five sets.

## Women—WTA Tour Championship

| Year | Player | Year | Player |
|------|--------|------|--------|
| 1972 | Chris Evert | 1986 (Nov) | Martina Navratilova |
| 1973 | Chris Evert | 1987 | Steffi Graf |
| 1974 | Evonne Goolagong | 1988 | Gabriela Sabatini |
| 1975 | Chris Evert | 1989 | Steffi Graf |
| 1976 | Evonne Goolagong Cawley | 1990 | Monica Seles |
| 1977 | Chris Evert | 1991 | Monica Seles |
| 1978 | Martina Navratilova | 1992 | Monica Seles |
| 1979 | Martina Navratilova | 1993 | Steffi Graf |
| 1980 | Tracy Austin | 1994 | Gabriela Sabatini |
| 1981 | Martina Navratilova | 1995 | Steffi Graf |
| 1982 | Sylvia Hanika | 1996 | Steffi Graf |
| 1983 | Martina Navratilova | 1997 | Jana Novotna |
| 1984* | Martina Navratilova | 1998 | Martina Hingis |
| 1985 | Martina Navratilova | 1999 | Lindsay Davenport |
| 1986 (Mar) | Martina Navratilova | 2000 | Martina Hingis |

## Sisterly Competition

Venus and Serena Williams met in the U.S. Open finals and as in their five previous meetings (Venus had won four), the play was uninspired. There have been not-so-veiled suggestions that Richard [Williams] has predetermined the outcome of their matches, but after Venus again dominated Serena, the reason for their lackluster meetings appeared obvious. First, neither has faced a player with anything resembling the speed and power of the other. Second, Serena is intimidated by Venus, as if the idea of supplanting her sister's place in the family pecking order is unthinkable. "I was saying, 'Come on, Serena, just do this or do that',"

Venus said after the Final. "When I'd find myself doing that, I'd lose a couple points. When I lost a couple points, I wasn't sorry [for her] anymore."

At the end Venus was merciless. Serving for the match at 5–4, she bombed in a serve at 120 mph and then wore down Serena in a match point rally for her fourth Grand Slam crown. The sisters hugged at the net, and Venus told Serena, "I love you. I feel so bad. I feel like I haven't won." Walking toward the umpire's chair, Serena told Venus, "You did win. You're the champion, you deserve it."

—S.L. Price

Pauline Betz Addie (1965)
George T. Adee (1964)
Fred B. Alexander (1961)
Wilmer L. Allison (1963)
Manuel Alonso (1977)
Malcolm Anderson (2000)
Arthur Ashe (1985)
Juliette Atkinson (1974)
H.W. Bunny Austin (1997)
Tracy Austin (1992)
Lawrence A. Baker Sr. (1975)
Maud Barger–Wallach (1958)
Angela Mortimer Barrett (1993)
Karl Behr (1969)
Bjorn Borg (1987)
Jean Borotra (1976)
Lesley Turner Bowrey (1997)
Maureen Connolly Brinker(1968)
John Bromwich (1984)
Norman Everard Brookes (1977)
Mary K. Browne (1957)
Jacques Brugnon (1976)
J. Donald Budge (1964)
Maria E. Bueno (1978)
May Sutton Bundy (1956)
Mabel E. Cahill (1976)
Rosie Casals (1996)
Oliver S. Campbell (1955)
Malcolm Chace (1961)
Dorothea Douglass
    Chambers (1981)
Philippe Chatrier (1992)
Louise Brough Clapp (1967)
Clarence Clark (1983)
Joseph S. Clark (1955)
William J. Clothier (1956)
Henri Cochet (1976)
Arthur W. (Bud) Collins Jr. (1994)
Jimmy Connors (1998)
Ashley Cooper (1991)
Margaret Smith Court (1979)
Gottfried von Cramm (1977)
Jack Crawford (1979)
Joseph F. Cullman III (1990)
Allison Danzig (1968)
Sarah Palfrey Danzig (1963)
Herman David (1998)
Dwight F. Davis (1956)
Charlotte Dod (1983)
John H. Doeg (1962)
Lawrence Doherty (1980)
Reginald Doherty (1980)
Jaroslav Drobny (1983)
Margaret Osborne duPont
    (1967)

James Dwight (1955)
Roy Emerson (1982)
Pierre Etchebaster (1978)
Chris Evert (1995)
Robert Falkenburg (1974)
Neale Fraser (1984)
Shirley Fry-Irvin (1970)
Charles S. Garland (1969)
Althea Gibson (1971)
Kathleen McKane Godfree
    (1978)
Richard A. Gonzales (1968)
Evonne Goolagong Cawley
    (1988)
Bryan M. Grant Jr. (1972)
David Gray (1985)
Clarence Griffin (1970)
King Gustaf V of Sweden
    (1980)
Harold H. Hackett (1961)
Ellen Forde Hansell (1965)
Darlene R. Hard (1973)
Doris J. Hart (1969)
Gladys M. Heldman (1979)
W.E. (Slew) Hester Jr. (1981)
Bob Hewitt (1992)
Lew Hoad (1980)
Harry Hopman (1978)
Fred Hovey (1974)
Joseph R. Hunt (1966)
Lamar Hunt (1993)
Francis T. Hunter (1961)
Helen Hull Jacobs (1962)
William Johnston (1958)
Ann Haydon Jones (1985)
Perry Jones (1970)
Robert Kelleher (2000)
Billie Jean King (1987)
Jan Kodes (1990)
John A. Kramer (1968)
Rene Lacoste (1976)
Al Laney (1979)
William A. Larned (1956)
Arthur D. Larsen (1969)
Rod G. Laver (1981)
Ivan Lendl (2001)
Suzanne Lenglen (1978)
Dorothy Round Little (1986)
George M. Lott Jr. (1964)
Gene Mako (1973)
Molla Bjurstedt Mallory (1958)
Hana Mandlikova (1994)
Alice Marble (1964)
Alastair B. Martin (1973)
Dan Maskell (1996)

William McChesney Martin (1982)
John McEnroe (1999)
Ken McGregor (1999)
Chuck McKinley (1986)
Maurice McLoughlin (1957)
Frew McMillan (1992)
W. Donald McNeill (1965)
Elisabeth H. Moore (1971)
Gardnar Mulloy (1972)
R. Lindley Murray (1958)
Julian S. Myrick (1963)
Ilie Nastase (1991)
Martina Navratilova (2000)
John D. Newcombe (1986)
Arthur C. Nielsen Sr (1971)
Alex Olmedo (1987)
Rafael Osuna (1979)
Mary Ewing Outerbridge (1981)
Frank A. Parker (1966)
Gerald Patterson (1989)
Budge Patty (1977)
Theodore R. Pell (1966)
Fred Perry (1975)
Tom Pettitt (1982)
Nicola Pietrangeli (1986)
Adrian Quist (1984)
Dennis Ralston (1987)
Ernest Renshaw (1983)
William Renshaw (1983)
Vincent Richards (1961)
Bobby Riggs (1967)
Helen Wills Moody Roark
    (1959)
Anthony D. Roche (1986)
Ellen C. Roosevelt (1975)
Mervyn Rose (2001)
Ken Rosewall (1980)
Elizabeth Ryan (1972)
Manuel Santana (1984)
Richard Savitt (1976)
Frederick R. Schroeder (1966)
Eleonora Sears (1968)
Richard D. Sears (1955)
Frank Sedgman (1979)
Pancho Segura (1984)
Vic Seixas Jr. (1971)
Francis X. Shields (1964)
Betty Nuthall Shoemaker (1977)
Henry W. Slocum Jr. (1955)
Stan Smith (1987)
Fred Stolle (1985)
William F. Talbert (1967)
Bill Tilden (1959)
Lance Tingay (1982)
Ted Tinling (1986)

Bertha Townsend Toulmin (1974)
Tony Trabert (1970)
James H. Van Alen (1965)
John Van Ryn (1963)
Guillermo Vilas (1991)
Ellsworth Vines (1962)
Virginia Wade (1989)
Marie Wagner (1969)
Holcombe Ward (1956)

Watson Washburn (1965)
Malcolm D. Whitman (1955)
Hazel Hotchkiss Wightman (1957)
Anthony Wilding (1978)
Richard Norris Williams II (1957)
Major Walter Clopton Wingfield (1997)
Sidney B. Wood (1964)

Robert D. Wrenn (1955)
Beals C. Wright (1956)

Note: Years in parentheses are dates of induction.

## Divine Intervention?

The 2001 Wimbledon marked the first time the men's final was not contested before the usual All England Club members but before a riot of Aussie and Croat supporters who'd camped out the night before for 10,000 unreserved Centre Court tickets to see Goran Ivanisevic and Patrick Rafter vie for the title. The usually subdued proceedings turned into a virtual soccer match. Once Rafter was broken at 7–7 in the fifth set, everybody knew the battle would be fought in Goran's head.

After audibly imploring God for help and squandering a championship point, Ivanisevic settled down and faced his fourth match point with a steady focus. He didn't crane his eyes to the heavens, didn't cross himself, didn't ask the crowd for help. Inside, though, Ivanisevic made one more plea. *God, please. You are testing me enough. Not four match points.* "He wanted to be sure that I'm really a man," Ivanisevic said.

His first serve went wide. On the second, instead of launching his typical missile, Ivanisevic lofted the ball down the middle at 109 mph. Rafter's forehand landed in the net. The air filled with a noise the likes of which Ivanisevic had never heard. "This is it," he said. "This is the end of the world."

And the end of Goran as we know him. "Today my life changes," he said. "Finally I am the champion. Now people are going to look at me differently. Now I am proud of myself."

Ivanisevic then revealed plans to "get drunk, fly for another week and put myself back to earth." As he spoke, he had his hat on backward and looked as goofy as ever, but what he said was true. Everyone was looking at him differently now. The jester had become the king.

—S.L. Price

# Golf

**British Open champion David Duval**

# Caged Tiger

## Trapped by his own impossibly high standards, golf's top player ceded the spotlight to others in 2001

### BY MARK BEECH

IT'S NOT EASY knowing that you're second-best. Just ask David Duval and Phil Mickelson. They are two of the top three golfers in the world, players so talented that in past eras they probably could have counted on winning one or more of golf's Grand Slam events before their careers were over. But unfortunately for them, they compete in the looming shadow of Tiger Woods, the greatest golfer of their, or perhaps any, generation, which makes counting on anything more than a bit presumptuous.

At the beginning of 2001, Duval and Mickelson were trying to escape their ignominious designation as the best players never to have won a major championship. Duval was able to shed that nom de guerre in July, with a convincing victory at the British Open, while Mickelson wore the mantle like a millstone around his neck, coming up just short in the Masters, the U.S. Open and the PGA Championship. Woods, of course, eclipsed everybody despite producing what was, for him, a dis-

appointing season. He won only one major tournament, the Masters at Augusta National in April, but that victory completed a historic sweep that had begun the year before, with victories in the U.S. and British Opens and the PGA Championship.

Because he did not win all four titles in the same calendar year, Woods's sweep wasn't unanimously accepted as a Grand Slam, but that hardly mattered. "I would imagine it was the same way when people were competing against Jack Nicklaus," Duval said after finishing second to Woods in the Masters. "We've got another player who is certainly the best player in the game right now. It's very difficult to win these events. To have your game at the right place at the right time, there's an art to that. It's an accomplishment for him that I don't know what you would compare it to, because I'm not so sure there's something you could compare it with, certainly not in modern golf."

In addition to making him the only player to hold all four major titles at once, Woods's victory at Augusta proved hi-

**Duval's triumph left Mickelson as the best player without a major title.**

resourcefulness; it showed that he can win in a variety of ways. Unlike in 1997, when he ran away from the field to win by 12 strokes at Augusta, he bled the 65th Masters to death, bit by bit, picking up a stroke here and another there. Knowing he didn't have his best stuff, Woods didn't press. He watched little-known Chris DiMarco lead the field into the weekend, then turned it on and outlasted Duval and Mickelson on Sunday. Only when Woods holed a 18-footer for a birdie on 18 and a two-stroke victory did he betray how desperately he had wanted to win, covering his eyes with his cap as he leaked tears of triumph. "It was a great putt," he said. "I walked over to the side, and I started thinking, I don't have any more shots to play. I'm done. I just won the Masters."

For Mickelson, 31, his third-place finish at Augusta was the prelude to a tough-luck year. In June, at the U.S. Open at Southern Hills Country Club in Tulsa, Mickelson was two strokes off the lead heading into the final round. But he shot a 75 on Sunday and finished six strokes behind surprise winner Retief Goosen, who defeated Mark Brooks in an 18-hole playoff. At the PGA Championship in Georgia in August, Mickelson had his first major title within reach, only to watch David Toms—who aced No. 15 on Saturday to take the lead—stroke a 12-foot birdie putt on the final hole to beat him by a stroke. "I'm confident in the way I have been able to play in these championships," said Mickelson, who had three-putted for bogey on No. 16 to let Toms get away. "But it's frustrating that I haven't been able to break through. I know the off-season will be long. I felt this would be a breakthrough year. I've been playing better than ever. But I wasn't able to beat everyone in the field."

Duval, for his part, produced the kind of year that had been expected of him ever since he shot a 59 at the Bob Hope Desert Classic in 1999. His talent had always gone unquestioned, but he had failed in 26 previous attempts to win a major; one of those losses came at the 1998 Masters, when he blew a three-shot lead to Mark O'Meara over the final three holes. That letdown became a distant memory at the 2001 British Open, though, as Duval swung his way through the mighty course at Royal Lytham and St. Annes, in England, to win his long-overdue first major. Playing with a more relaxed attitude after taking two weeks off to go mountain biking and fishing, he cruised through the final two rounds at 10-under par. "I beat them all this week," Duval said. "I played really well, and it feels wonderful. I don't know if I can savor it any more than I am now."

As for Woods, though he won the Masters and spent much of the year atop most of the PGA's significant statistical categories (including money won), his failure to win a second major caused many people to see his year as a disappointment—a testament to how preposterously high Woods's performances have raised expectations. The most popular explanations for Tiger's subpar year were (in no particular order): that he'd burned out on golf; that he'd sold out to play in too many made-for-TV exhibitions; that he was distracted by his numerous product-endorsement responsibilities; that he was in love with Gabrielle Reece, the model, volleyball player and aspiring golfer; that he was injured; and that he had altered his swing.

Whatever the reason, it probably won't be a problem too much longer. It will be interesting to see if Duval can continue to challenge Woods in 2002 and if Mickelson will be able to challenge him at all.

For the second straight year, two of the four LPGA majors went to Karrie Webb, 26, of Australia. Webb defended her U.S. Women's Open title and added the LPGA Championship prize to her burgeoning trophy case. (She won the Nabisco Championships in 2000.)

**The LPGA's answer to Woods, Webb won two majors and dominated the tour for the second year in a row.**

Webb's dominance in the majors came as a bit of a surprise this year because of the way Annika Sorenstam, 31, Webb's good friend and chief rival on the LPGA tour, began the season. Sorenstam won four tournaments in a row, a streak capped by the Office Depot title in April. Her most impressive feat during that run came when she fired a second-round 59 at the Standard Register PING, in Phoenix, the lowest tournament round in the history of women's golf. On the way to that score, she rang up 13 birdies and no bogeys. "I'm absolutely overwhelmed," she said moments after the round. "I can't believe what I just did. Now I see what I can shoot when the putts go in."

But Sorenstam crashed in the U.S. Open, finishing 16th, well behind Webb, who became the first back-to-back Open winner since Sorenstam in 1995 and '96. Webb followed her Open triumph with an emotional victory in the LPGA. Her 71-year-old maternal grandfather, Mick

Collinson, had suffered a stroke earlier in the week in Queensland. On the morning of the final round, a shaky Webb learned that he had taken a turn for the worse, and after debating with her family about whether or not to return home, she pressed on to complete a career Grand Slam. "I wanted to win, but I wasn't overly concerned if I didn't," Webb said. "A part of me wanted to play anyway. The fact that my family wanted me to do it is what changed my mind."(Collinson would die a few days later.)

Though Webb couldn't prevent Se Ri Pak from winning the Women's British Open in August, her impact on the women's game can hardly be overestimated. Webb forces her competitors to raise their games, just as Woods does on the PGA Tour. And as is also the case with Woods, no matter how high her peers lift their level of play, Webb's game usually goes a little higher.

## Men's Majors

### The Masters
**Augusta National GC (par 72; 6,985 yds);**
**Augusta, GA, April 5–8**

| Player | Score | Earnings ($) |
|---|---|---|
| Tiger Woods | 70-66-68-68—272 | 1,008,000 |
| David Duval | 71-66-70-67—274 | 604,800 |
| Phil Mickelson | 67-69-69-70—275 | 380,800 |
| Mark Calcavecchia | 72-66-68-72—278 | 246,400 |
| Toshi Izawa | 71-66-74-67—278 | 246,400 |
| Ernie Els | 71-68-68-72—279 | 181,300 |
| Jim Furyk | 69-71-70-69—279 | 181,300 |
| Bernhard Langer | 73-69-68-69—279 | 181,300 |
| Kirk Triplett | 68-70-70-71—279 | 181,300 |
| Angel Cabrera | 66-71-70-73—280 | 128,800 |
| Chris DiMarco | 65-69-72-74—280 | 128,800 |
| Brad Faxon | 73-68-68-71—280 | 128,800 |
| Miguel Angel Jiménez | 68-72-71-69—280 | 128,800 |
| Steve Stricker | 66-71-72-71—280 | 128,800 |
| Paul Azinger | 70-71-71-69—281 | 95,200 |
| Rocco Mediate | 72-70-66-73—281 | 95,200 |
| José María Olazábal | 70-68-71-72—281 | 95,200 |
| Tom Lehman | 75-68-71-68—282 | 81,200 |
| Vijay Singh | 69-71-72-69—282 | 81,200 |
| John Huston | 67-75-72-69—283 | 65,240 |
| Jeff Maggert | 72-70-70-71—283 | 65,240 |
| Mark O'Meara | 69-74-72-68—283 | 65,240 |
| Jesper Parnevik | 71-71-72-69—283 | 65,240 |

### U.S. Open
**Southern Hills CC (par 70; 6,973 yds);**
**Tulsa, June 14–17**

| Player | Score | Earnings ($) |
|---|---|---|
| Retief Goosen† | 66-70-69-71—276 | 900,000 |
| Mark Brooks | 72-64-70-70—276 | 530,000 |
| Stewark Cink | 69-69-67-72—277 | 325,310 |
| Rocco Mediate | 71-68-67-72—278 | 226,777 |
| Tom Kite | 73-72-72-64—281 | 172,912 |
| Paul Azinger | 74-67-69-71—281 | 172,912 |
| Vijay Singh | 74-70-74-64—282 | 125,172 |
| Angel Cabrera | 70-71-72-69—282 | 125,172 |
| Davis Love III | 72-69-71-70—282 | 125,172 |
| Kirk Triplett | 72-69-71-70—282 | 125,172 |
| Phil Mickelson | 70-69-68-75—282 | 125,172 |
| Tiger Woods | 74-71-69-69—283 | 91,733 |
| Matt Gogel | 70-69-74-70—283 | 91,733 |
| Michael Allen | 77-68-67-71—283 | 91,733 |
| Sergio Garcia | 70-68-68-77—283 | 91,733 |
| Scott Hoch | 73-73-69-69—284 | 75,337 |
| Chris DiMarco | 69-73-70-72—284 | 75,337 |
| David Duval | 70-69-71-74—284 | 75,337 |
| Chris Perry | 72-71-73-69—285 | 63,425 |
| Corey Pavin | 70-75-68-72—285 | 63,425 |
| Mike Weir | 67-76-68-74—285 | 63,425 |

† Won 18-hole playoff, 70 to 72.

### British Open
**Royal Lytham & St. Annes GC (par 71;**
**6,905 yds); Lytham, England, July 19–22**

| Player | Score | Earnings ($) |
|---|---|---|
| David Duval | 69-73-65-67—274 | 858,000 |
| Niclas Fasth | 69-69-72-67—277 | 514,800 |
| Ernie Els | 71-71-67-69—278 | 202,584 |
| Darren Clarke | 70-69-69-70—278 | 202,584 |
| Miguel Angel Jiménez | 69-72-67-70—278 | 202,584 |
| Billy Mayfair | 69-72-67-70—278 | 202,584 |
| Ian Woosnam | 72-68-67-71—278 | 202,584 |
| Bernhard Langer | 71-69-67-71—278 | 202,584 |
| Mikko Ilonen | 68-75-70-66—279 | 91,163 |
| Kevin Sutherland | 75-69-68-67—279 | 91,163 |
| Sergio Garcia | 70-72-67-70—279 | 91,163 |
| Jesper Parnevik | 69-68-71-71—279 | 91,163 |
| Vijay Singh | 70-70-71-69—280 | 57,290 |
| Loren Roberts | 70-70-70-70—280 | 57,290 |
| Des Smyth | 74-65-70-71—280 | 57,290 |
| Billy Andrade | 69-70-70-71—280 | 57,290 |
| Retief Goosen | 74-68-67-71—280 | 57,290 |
| Colin Montgomerie | 65-70-73-72—280 | 57,290 |
| Raphael Jacquelin | 71-68-69-72—280 | 57,290 |
| Alex Cejka | 69-69-69-73—280 | 57,290 |

### PGA Championship
**Atlanta AC (par 70; 7,213 yds),**
**Duluth, GA, August 16–19**

| Player | Score | Earnings ($) |
|---|---|---|
| David Toms | 66-65-65-69—265 | 936,000 |
| Phil Mickelson | 66-66-66-68—266 | 562,000 |
| Steve Lowery | 67-67-66-68—268 | 354,000 |
| Mark Calcavecchia | 71-68-66-65—270 | 222,500 |
| Shingo Katayama | 67-64-69-70—270 | 222,500 |
| Billy Andrade | 68-70-68-66—272 | 175,000 |
| Scott Hoch | 68-70-69-67—274 | 152,333 |
| Scott Verplank | 69-68-70-67—274 | 152,333 |
| Jim Furyk | 70-64-71-69—274 | 152,333 |
| Kirk Triplett | 68-70-71-66—275 | 122,000 |
| Justin Leonard | 70-69-67-69—275 | 122,000 |
| David Duval | 66-68-67-74—275 | 122,000 |
| Steve Flesch | 73-67-70-66—276 | 94,666 |
| Jesper Parnevik | 70-68-70-68—276 | 94,666 |
| Ernie Els | 67-67-70-72—276 | 94,666 |
| Jose Coceres | 69-68-73-67—277 | 70,666 |
| Robert Allenby | 69-67-73-68—277 | 70,666 |
| Dudley Hart | 66-68-73-70—277 | 70,666 |
| Mike Weir | 69-72-66-70—277 | 70,666 |
| Chris DiMarco | 68-67-71-71—277 | 70,666 |
| Stuart Appleby | 66-70-68-73—277 | 70,666 |

## Late 2000 PGA Tour Events

| Tournament | Final Round | Winner | Score/ Under Par | Earnings ($) |
|---|---|---|---|---|
| National Car Rental Classic | Oct 29 | Duffy Waldorf | 262/–26 | 540,000 |
| The Tour Championship | Nov 5 | Phil Mickelson | 267/–13 | 900,000 |
| Southern Farm Bureau Classic | Nov 5 | Steve Lowery* | 266/–22 | 396,000 |
| American Express Championship | Nov 12 | Mike Weir | 277/–11 | 1,000,000 |
| Franklin Templeton Shootout | Nov 19 | Brad Faxon/Scott McCarron* | 190/–26 | 200,000 each |
| PGA Grand Slam of Golf | Nov 22 | Tiger Woods | 139/–5 | 400,000 |
| Williams World Challenge | Dec 3 | Davis Love III | 266/–22 | 1,000,000 |
| EMC World Cup | Dec 10 | Tiger Woods/David Duval | 254/–34 | 500,000 each |

## 2001 PGA Tour Events

| Tournament | Final Round | Winner | Score/ Under Par | Earnings ($) |
|---|---|---|---|---|
| Mercedes Championships | Jan 14 | Jim Furyk | 274/–18 | 630,000 |
| Tucson Open | Jan 15 | Garrett Willis | 273/–15 | 540,000 |
| Sony Open | Jan 21 | Brad Faxon | 260/–20 | 720,000 |
| Phoenix Open | Jan 28 | Mark Calcavecchia | 256/–28 | 720,000 |
| Pebble Beach National Pro-Am | Feb 4 | Davis Love III | 272/–16 | 720,000 |
| Buick Invitational | Feb 11 | Phil Mickelson* | 269/–19 | 630,000 |
| Bob Hope Classic | Feb 18 | Joe Durant | 324/–36 | 630,000 |
| Nissan Open | Feb 25 | Robert Allenby* | 276/–8 | 612,000 |
| Genuity Championship | Mar 4 | Joe Durant | 270/–18 | 810,000 |
| Honda Classic | Mar 11 | Jesper Parnevik | 270/–18 | 576,000 |
| Bay Hill Invitational | Mar 18 | Tiger Woods | 273/–15 | 630,000 |
| The Players Championship | Mar 26 | Tiger Woods | 274/–14 | 1,080,000 |
| BellSouth Classic | Apr 1 | Scott McCarron | 280/–8 | 594,000 |
| The Masters | Apr 8 | Tiger Woods | 272/–16 | 1,008,000 |
| Worldcom Classic | Apr 15 | Jose Coceres* | 273/–11 | 630,000 |
| Houston Open | Apr 22 | Hal Sutton | 278/–10 | 612,000 |
| Greater Greensboro Classic | Apr 29 | Scott Hoch | 272/–16 | 630,000 |
| Compaq Classic | May 6 | David Toms | 266/–22 | 720,000 |
| Byron Nelson Classic | May 13 | Robert Damron* | 263/–17 | 810,000 |
| The Colonial | May 20 | Sergio Garcia | 267/–13 | 720,000 |
| Kemper Open | May 27 | Frank Lickliter | 268/–16 | 630,000 |
| The Memorial | June 3 | Tiger Woods | 271/–17 | 558,000 |
| St. Jude Classic | June 10 | Bob Estes | 267/–17 | 630,000 |
| U.S. Open | June 18 | Retief Goosen* | 270/–4 | 900,000 |
| Buick Classic | June 25 | Sergio Garcia | 268/–16 | 630,000 |
| Greater Hartford Open | July 1 | Phil Mickelson | 264/–16 | 558,000 |
| Western Open | July 8 | Scott Hoch | 267/–21 | 648,000 |
| Greater Milwaukee Open | July 15 | Shigeki Maruyama* | 266/–18 | 558,000 |
| British Open | July 22 | David Duval | 274/–10 | 858,300 |
| B.C. Open | July 22 | Jeff Sluman* | 266/–22 | 360,000 |
| John Deere Classic | July 29 | David Gossett | 265/–19 | 504,000 |
| The International | Aug 5 | Tom Pernice Jr. | +34‡ | 720,000 |
| Buick Open | Aug 12 | Kenny Perry | 263/–25 | 558,000 |
| PGA Championship | Aug 19 | David Toms | 265/–15 | 936,000 |
| NEC Invitational | Aug 26 | Tiger Woods* | 268/–12 | 1,000,000 |
| Reno-Tahoe Open | Aug 26 | John Cook | 271/–17 | 540,000 |
| Air Canada Championship | Sept 2 | Joel Edwards | 265/–19 | 612,000 |
| Canadian Open | Sept 9 | Scott Verplank | 266/–14 | 684,000 |
| Pennsylvania Classic | Sept 23 | Robert Allenby | 269/–19 | 594,000 |
| Texas Open | Sept 30 | Justin Leonard | 266/–18 | 540,000 |
| Michelob Championship | Oct 7 | David Toms | 269/–15 | 630,000 |
| Invensys Classic | Oct 14 | Bob Estes | 329/–30 | 810,000 |

* Won playoff. †Won on the second extra hole of match play. # Tournament shortened by rain. ‡ Revised Stableford scoring.

## Nabisco Championship

**Mission Hills CC; Rancho Mirage, CA
(par 72; 6,478 yds) March 22–25**

| Player | Score | Earnings ($) |
|---|---|---|
| Annika Sorenstam | 72-70-70-69—281 | 225,000 |
| Akiko Fukushima | 74-68-70-72—284 | 87,557 |
| Janice Moodie | 72-72-70-70—284 | 87,557 |
| Dottie Pepper | 71-71-71-71—284 | 87,557 |
| Rachel Teske | 72-73-66-73—284 | 87,557 |
| Karrie Webb | 73-72-70-69—284 | 87,557 |
| Brandie Burton | 74-69-72-70—285 | 41,891 |
| Sophie Gustafson | 72-74-70-69—285 | 41,891 |
| Laura Diaz | 71-74-69-72—286 | 33,589 |
| Pat Hurst | 70-68-74-74—286 | 33,589 |
| Tina Barrett | 71-73-70-73—287 | 25,957 |
| Laura Davies | 71-73-75-68—287 | 25,957 |
| Dorothy Delasin | 73-70-74-70—287 | 25,957 |
| Se Ri Pak | 73-69-73-72—287 | 25,957 |
| Juli Inkster | 70-75-68-75—288 | 20,736 |
| Mi Hyun Kim | 74-71-70-73—288 | 20,736 |
| Carin Koch | 70-69-75-74—288 | 20,736 |
| Jeong Jang | 74-71-71-73—289 | 18,220 |
| Liselotte Neumann | 70-74-74-71—289 | 18,220 |
| Michele Redman | 71-72-71-75—289 | 18,220 |

## U.S. Women's Open

**Pine Needles GC; Southern Pines, NC
(par 70; 6,256 yds) May 31–June 3**

| Player | Score | Earnings ($) |
|---|---|---|
| Karrie Webb | 70-65-69-69—273 | 520,000 |
| Se Ri Pak | 69-70-70-72—281 | 310,000 |
| Dottie Pepper | 74-69-70-69—282 | 202,580 |
| Cristie Kerr | 69-73-71-70—283 | 118,697 |
| Sherri Turner | 72-70-71-70—283 | 118,697 |
| Catriona Matthew | 72-68-70-73—283 | 118,697 |
| Lorie Kane | 75-68-72-69—284 | 80,726 |
| Kristi Albers | 71-69-74-70—284 | 80,726 |
| Kelli Kuehne | 70-71-72-71—284 | 80,726 |
| Wendy Doolan | 71-70-70-73—284 | 80,726 |
| Sophie Gustafson | 74-66-74-71—285 | 66,581 |
| Kelly Robbins | 72-68-76-70—286 | 57,088 |
| A.J. Eathorne | 67-71-75-73—286 | 57,088 |
| Juli Inkster | 68-72-71-75—286 | 57,088 |
| Yuri Fudoh | 73-68-70-75—286 | 57,088 |
| Emilee Klein | 72-69-75-71—287 | 46,885 |
| Michele Redman | 70-72-73-72—287 | 46,885 |
| Annika Sorenstam | 70-72-73-72—287 | 46,885 |
| Maria Hjorth | 70-71-77-70—288 | 37,327 |
| Marisa Baena | 71-72-75-70—288 | 37,327 |
| Jill McGill | 68-76-72-72—288 | 37,327 |
| Wendy Ward | 70-71-74-73—288 | 37,327 |
| Dorothy Delasin | 75-70-70-73—288 | 37,327 |

## LPGA Championship

**DuPont CC; Wilmington, DE
(par 71; 6,386 yds) June 21–24**

| Player | Score | Earnings ($) |
|---|---|---|
| Karrie Webb | 67-64-70-69—270 | 225,000 |
| Laura Diaz | 67-71-66-68—272 | 139,639 |
| Wendy Ward | 65-69-71-69—274 | 90,577 |
| Maria Hjorth | 71-67-66-70—274 | 90,577 |
| Annika Sorenstam | 68-69-71-67—275 | 64,157 |
| Becky Iverson | 66-73-67-70—276 | 48,684 |
| Laura Davies | 67-68-70-71—276 | 48,684 |
| Mi Hyun Kim | 70-70-68-69—277 | 39,250 |
| Helen Alfredsson | 68-66-74-70—278 | 35,476 |
| Maggie Will | 68-74-67-70—279 | 30,245 |
| Michele Redman | 69-66-73-71—279 | 30,245 |
| Rosie Jones | 71-69-71-69—280 | 25,013 |
| Lorie Kane | 69-71-71-69—280 | 25,013 |
| Liselotte Neumann | 69-72-68-71—280 | 25,013 |
| Wendy Doolan | 70-71-72-68—281 | 21,239 |
| Juli Inkster | 71-71-69-70—281 | 21,239 |
| Dottie Pepper | 71-72-71-68—282 | 16,819 |
| Kelly Robbins | 69-74-71-68—282 | 16,819 |
| Carin Koch | 69-73-71-69—282 | 16,819 |
| Meg Mallon | 71-74-67-70—282 | 16,819 |
| Leta Lindley | 71-71-70-70—282 | 16,819 |
| Pat Hurst | 72-68-72-70—282 | 16,819 |
| Terry-Jo Myers | 70-71-69-72—282 | 16,819 |
| Rachel Teske | 68-72-70-72—282 | 16,819 |
| Mhairi McKay | 68-72-70-72—282 | 16,819 |

## Women's British Open

**Sunningdale GC; Berkshire, England
(par 72; 6,277 yds) August 2–5**

| Player | Score | Earnings ($) |
|---|---|---|
| Se Ri Pak | 71-70-70-66—277 | 221,650 |
| Mi Hyun Kim | 72-65-71-71—279 | 143,000 |
| Laura Diaz | 74-70-69-67—280 | 74,092 |
| Iben Tinning | 71-69-72-68—280 | 74,092 |
| Janice Moodie | 67-70-71-72—280 | 74,092 |
| Catriona Matthew | 70-65-72-73—280 | 74,092 |
| Kathryn Marshall | 75-71-68-67—281 | 36,608 |
| Marina Arruti | 71-73-70-67—281 | 36,608 |
| Kristal Parker | 72-71-71-67—281 | 36,608 |
| Kelli Kuehne | 71-70-71-69—281 | 36,608 |
| Kasumi Fujii | 71-71-69-70—281 | 36,608 |
| Raquel Carriedo | 73-70-70-69—282 | 25,382 |
| Tracy Hanson | 72-69-70-71—282 | 25,382 |
| Rosie Jones | 70-69-71-72—282 | 25,382 |
| Pearl Sinn | 74-70-72-67—283 | 20,592 |
| Brandie Burton | 72-71-73-67—283 | 20,592 |
| Jill McGill | 70-70-72-71—283 | 20,592 |
| Karrie Webb | 74-67-68-74—283 | 20,592 |
| Becky Morgan | 73-68-71-72—284 | 17,982 |
| Trish Johnson | 70-67-72-75—284 | 17,982 |

# Women's Tour Results

## Late 2000 LPGA Tour Events

| Tournament | Final Round | Winner | Score/ Under Par | Earnings ($) |
|---|---|---|---|---|
| AFLAC Champions | Oct 22 | Karrie Webb* | 273/–15 | 122,000 |
| Mizuno Classic | Nov 5 | Lorie Kane* | 204/–12 | 127,500 |
| Arch Wireless Championship | Nov 19 | Dottie Pepper | 279/–9 | 215,000 |
| Certain Teed Hall of Fame Golf Chall. | Nov 22 | Beth Daniel/Johnny Miller | 196/–20 | 100,000 each |
| Women's World Cup | Dec 3 | K. Webb/R. Hetherington | 275/–13 | 100,000 each |

## 2001 LPGA Tour Events

| Tournament | Final Round | Winner | Score/ Under Par | Earnings ($) |
|---|---|---|---|---|
| YourLife Vitamins LPGA Classic | Jan 14 | Se Ri Pak | 203/–13 | 150,000 |
| Naples LPGA Memorial | Jan 21 | Sophie Gustafson | 272/–16 | 150,000 |
| LPGA Office Depot | Jan 28 | Grace Park | 280/–6 | 123,750 |
| Takefuji Classic | Feb 10 | Lori Kane | 205/–11 | 127,500 |
| Hawaiian Ladies Open | Feb 17 | Catriona Matthew | 210/–6 | 112,500 |
| Welch's/Circle K Championship | Mar 11 | Annika Sorenstam | 265/–23 | 112,500 |
| Standard Register PING | Mar 18 | Annika Sorenstam | 261/–27 | 150,000 |
| Nabisco Championship | Mar 25 | Annika Sorenstam | 281/–7 | 225,000 |
| The Office Depot | Apr 14 | Annika Sorenstam* | 210/–6 | 120,000 |
| Longs Drugs Challenge | Apr 22 | Se Ri Pak | 208/–8 | 120,000 |
| Kathy Ireland Championship | Apr 29 | Rosie Jones* | 268/–12 | 135,000 |
| Chick-fil-A Championship | May 6 | Annika Sorenstam* | 203/–13 | 180,000 |
| Electrolux Championship | May 13 | Juli Inkster | 274/–14 | 120,000 |
| Champions Classic# | May 20 | Wendy Doolan* | 132/–12 | 112,500 |
| Corning Classic | May 27 | Carin Koch | 270/–18 | 135,000 |
| U.S. Women's Open | June 3 | Karrie Webb | 273/–7 | 520,000 |
| Rochester International | June 10 | Laura Davies | 279/–9 | 150,000 |
| Evian Masters | June 16 | Rachel Teske | 273/–15 | 315,000 |
| LPGA Championship | June 24 | Karrie Webb | 270/–14 | 225,000 |
| ShopRite Classic | July 1 | Betsy King | 201/–12 | 180,000 |
| Jamie Farr Classic | July 8 | Se Ri Pak | 269/–15 | 150,000 |
| Michelob Light Classic | July 15 | Emilee Klein | 205/–11 | 120,000 |
| Sybase Big Apple Classic | July 22 | Rosie Jones | 272/–12 | 142,500 |
| Giant Eagle LPGA Classic | July 29 | Dorothy Delasin | 203/–13 | 150,000 |
| Women's British Open | Aug 5 | Se Ri Pak | 277/–11 | 221,650 |
| New Albany Golf Classic | Aug 12 | Wendy Ward | 195/–21 | 150,000 |
| Canadian Women's Open | Aug 19 | Annika Sorenstam | 272/–16 | 180,000 |
| Betsy King Classic | Aug 26 | Heather Daly-Donofrio | 273/–15 | 120,000 |
| State Farm Rail Classic | Sep 2 | Kate Golden | 267/–21 | 150,000 |
| Williams Championship | Sep 9 | Gloria Park | 201/–9 | 150,000 |
| Asahi Ryokuken International Champ. | Sep 23 | Tina Fischer | 206/–10 | 180,000 |
| AFLAC Champions | Sep 30 | Se Ri Pak | 272/–16 | 122,000 |
| Samsung World Championship | Oct 7 | Dorothy Delasin | 277/–11 | 157,000 |

\* Won sudden-death playoff. #Shortened due to rain.

## Double Duty

As the 15-year-old Wongluekiet twins, Aree and Naree, teed it up in July's Jamie Farr Kroger Classic in Toledo, one LPGA veteran was heard to say, "What are they doing here?" Duh. Longtime tournament director Judd Silverman has always given sponsors' exemptions to promising amateurs. In pro golf, it's called investing in the future.

When Tiger Woods was an amateur, he received invitations to play in the Nissan and Western Opens and the Byron Nelson Classic. Guess which Tour stops he hasn't missed since turning pro? Silverman amateur invitees have included Vicki Goetze-Ackerman, Emilee Klein, Grace Park and Meg Mallon. As a group they have won 17 LPGA titles, and Mallon never misses the Jamie Farr. In 1997 Silverman gave a sponsor's exemption to 19-year-old Korean no one had ever heard of. Se Ri Pak returned in July to win the Farr for the third time in four years.

Aree finished 51st and Naree missed the cut, but that's not what they'll remember about their week with the pros in Toledo.

# Senior Men's Tour Results

## Late 2000 Senior Tour Events

| Tournament | Final Round | Winner | Score/ Under Par | Earnings ($) |
|---|---|---|---|---|
| EMC Kaanapali Classic | Oct 22 | Hale Irwon | 198/–15 | 165,000 |
| SBC Senior Classic | Oct 29 | Joe Inman | 198/–15 | 210,000 |
| Senior Tour Championship | Nov 5 | Tom Watson | 270/–18 | 365,000 |
| Senior Match Play Challenge | Nov 12 | Vicente Fernandez | 37 holes | 240,000 |

## 2001 Senior Tour Events

| Tournament | Final Round | Winner | Score/ Under Par | Earnings ($) |
|---|---|---|---|---|
| MasterCard Championship | Jan 21 | Larry Nelson | 197/–19 | 240,000 |
| Royal Caribbean Classic | Feb 4 | Larry Nelson | +29‡ | 210,000 |
| ACE Group Classic | Feb 11 | Gil Morgan | 204/–12 | 210,000 |
| Verizon Classic | Feb 18 | Bob Gilder | 205/–8 | 210,000 |
| Mexico Senior Classic | Feb 25 | Mike McCullough | 276/–12 | 225,000 |
| Toshiba Classic | Mar 4 | Jose Maria Canizares* | 202/–11 | 210,000 |
| SBC Senior Classic | Mar 11 | Jim Colbert | 204/–12 | 210,000 |
| Siebel Classic | Mar 18 | Hale Irwin | 206/–10 | 210,000 |
| Emerald Coast Classic | Mar 25 | Mike McCullough* | 200/–10 | 210,000 |
| Legends of Golf# | April 1 | Jim Colbert/Andy North | 124/–20 | 170,000 each |
| The Tradition | April 15 | Doug Tewell | 265/–23 | 255,000 |
| Las Vegas Senior Classic | April 22 | Bruce Fleisher | 208/–8 | 210,000 |
| Bruno's Memorial Classic | April 29 | Hale Irwin | 195/–21 | 210,000 |
| Home Depot Invitational | May 6 | Bruce Fleisher | 201/–15 | 195,000 |
| Match Play Championship | May 13 | Leonard Thompson | 2 up | 300,000 |
| TD Waterhouse Championship | May 20 | Ed Dougherty | 194/–22 | 225,000 |
| Senior PGA Championship | May 27 | Tom Watson | 274/–14 | 360,000 |
| BellSouth Senior Classic | June 3 | Sammy Rachels | 199/–17 | 240,000 |
| Cadillac NFL Golf Classic | June 10 | John Schroeder* | 207/–9 | 180,000 |
| Instinet Classic | June 17 | Gil Morgan | 201/–15 | 225,000 |
| FleetBoston Classic | June 24 | Larry Nelson | 201/–15 | 210,000 |
| U.S. Senior Open | July 1 | Bruce Fleisher | 280/even | 430,000 |
| Farmers Charity | July 8 | Larry Nelson | 202/–14 | 210,000 |
| Senior Players Championship | July 15 | Allen Doyle* | 273/–15 | 375,000 |
| SBC Senior Open | July 23 | Dana Quigley | 200/–16 | 210,000 |
| State Farm Senior Classic | July 29 | Allen Doyle* | 205/–11 | 217,500 |
| Lightpath Long Island Classic | Aug 5 | Bobby Wadkins | 202/–14 | 255,000 |
| 3M Championship | Aug 12 | Bruce Lietzke | 207/–9 | 262,500 |
| Utah Showdown | Aug 19 | Steve Veriato | 204/–12 | 225,000 |
| Canadian Senior Open | Aug 26 | Walter Hall* | 269/–15 | 240,000 |
| Kroger Senior Classic# | Sep 2 | Jim Thorpe* | 130/–10 | 225,000 |
| Allianz Championship | Sep 9 | Jim Thorpe | 199/–14 | 262,500 |
| SAS Championship | Sep 23 | Bruce Lietzke | 201/–15 | 240,000 |
| Gold Rush Classic | Sep 30 | Tom Kite | 194/–22 | 195,000 |
| Turtle Bay Championship | Oct 7 | Hale Irwin | 205/–11 | 225,000 |
| The Transamerica | Oct 14 | Sammy Rachels | 202/–14 | 195,000 |

*Won playoff. #Shortened due to rain. ‡ Revised Stableford scoring.

# U.S. Amateur Results

| Tournament | Final Round | Winner | Score | Runner-Up |
|---|---|---|---|---|
| Women's Amateur Public Links .............June 24 | | Candie Kung | 2 up | Missy Farr-Kaye |
| Men's Amateur Public Links...................July 14 | | Chez Reavie | 38 holes | Danny Green |
| Girls' Junior Amateur...............................July 28 | | Nicole Perrot | 3 & 2 | Whitney Welch |
| Boys' Junior Amateur ...............................July 28 | | Henry Liaw | 2 & 1 | Richard Scott |
| Women's Amateur ....................................Aug 4 | | Meredith Duncan | 37 holes | Nicole Perrot |
| Men's Amateur ........................................Aug 26 | | Bubba Dickerson | 1 up | Robert Hamilton |
| Men's Mid-Amateur ................................Oct 18 | | Tim Jackson | 1 up | George Zahringer |
| Senior Women .........................................Sept 13 | | Carol Semple Thompson | 1 up | Anne Carr |
| Senior Men .............................................Sep 13 | | Kemp Richardson | 2 & 1 | Bill Ploeger |
| Women's Mid-Amateur...........................Oct 11 | | Laura Shanahan | 4 & 3 | Mina Hardin |

# International Results

| Tournament | Final Round | Winner | Score | Runner-Up |
|---|---|---|---|---|
| Walker Cup ...............................................Aug 12 | | GB/Ireland | 15–9 | United States |
| Ryder Cup.................................................Canceled | | | | |

# PGA Tour Final 2000 Money Leaders

| Name | Events | Best Finish | Scoring Average* | Money ($) |
|---|---|---|---|---|
| Tiger Woods ...............................20 | | 1 (9) | 67.79 | 9,188,321 |
| Phil Mickelson ...........................23 | | 1 (4) | 69.25 | 4,746,457 |
| Ernie Els ....................................20 | | 1 (1) | 69.31 | 3,469,405 |
| Hal Sutton...................................25 | | 1 (2) | 70.12 | 3,061,444 |
| Vijay Singh..................................26 | | 1 (1) | 70.01 | 2,573,835 |
| Mike Weir....................................28 | | 1 (1) | 70.36 | 2,547,829 |
| David Duval.................................19 | | 1 (1) | 69.41 | 2,462,846 |
| Jesper Parnevik..........................20 | | 1 (2) | 69.94 | 2,413,345 |
| Davis Love III..............................25 | | 2 (3) | 69.90 | 2,337,765 |
| Stewart Cink ...............................27 | | 1 (1) | 69.79 | 2,169,727 |

*Adjusted for average score of field in each tournament entered.

# LPGA Tour Final 2000 Money Leaders

| Name | Events | Best Finish | Scoring Average | Money ($) |
|---|---|---|---|---|
| Karrie Webb .................................22 | | 1 (7) | 70.05 | 1,876,853 |
| Annika Sorenstam .......................22 | | 1 (5) | 70.47 | 1,404,948 |
| Meg Mallon..................................26 | | 1 (2) | 71.01 | 1,146.360 |
| Juli Inkster ...................................19 | | 1 (3) | 70.73 | 980,330 |
| Lorie Kane ...................................30 | | 1 (3) | 71.38 | 929,189 |
| Pat Hurst......................................26 | | 1 (1) | 71.10 | 840,161 |
| Mi Hyun Kim.................................27 | | 1 (1) | 71.13 | 825,720 |
| Dottie Pepper ..............................19 | | 1 (1) | 70.71 | 786,695 |
| Rosie Jones.................................25 | | 2 (2) | 71.21 | 643,054 |
| Michele Redman .........................28 | | 1 (1) | 71.62 | 585,694 |

| Name | Events | Best Finish | Scoring Average | Money ($) |
|---|---|---|---|---|
| Larry Nelson | 30 | 1 (6) | 68.87 | 2,708,005 |
| Bruce Fleisher | 30 | 1 (4) | 69.01 | 2,373,977 |
| Hale Irwin | 24 | 1 (4) | 69.16 | 2,128,968 |
| Gil Morgan | 23 | 1 (3) | 68.83 | 1,873,216 |
| Dana Quigley | 39 | 1 (1) | 69.85 | 1,802,063 |
| Jim Thorpe | 37 | 1 (2) | 69.73 | 1,656,747 |
| Allen Doyle | 33 | 1 (1) | 69.56 | 1,505,471 |
| Doug Tewell | 27 | 1 (3) | 70.09 | 1,408,194 |
| Hubert Green | 28 | 1 (2) | 70.04 | 1,308,784 |
| Tom Jenkins | 36 | 1 (1) | 70.31 | 1,298,244 |

## Changing of the Guard: A Major Reassessment

The monkey has been passed. David Duval no longer qualifies as the best player never to have won a major. (Although he's my pick as the best player to have won only one.) Instead of hammering Phil Mickelson and the usual suspects left on the BPNTHWM list, let's focus on another group: the players whose finest moments are behind them. These golfers might win the odd tour event but they're through in the majors.

Jack Nicklaus concedes that he's not a factor in the regular Tour's majors—though I bet he *still* thinks he could steal a Masters—but now he's toast in the Senior majors too. Yes, the most exciting Senior moment of the year came when he made a run at the U.S. Open at Salem, but what about bogeying three of his last six holes in the final round? Did anyone else hear a last gasp? By the time of the next Senior major, Nicklaus, who hasn't won in five years, will be 62. He jokes that X-rays of his back "look like a war zone." A herniated disk has bothered him all year, and he had to withdraw after 27 holes of the Senior Players with a hamstring tear. Bad things happen to old bodies, Jack. No matter how fanatical you are about getting in shape, I don't believe you'll ever be healthy enough to knock off guys a dozen years younger.

At 38 Colin Montgomerie should be too young to write off, yet I've colored him gone for a while, and his performance at Royal Lytham made it official. Even though he opened with a 65, Monty sounded like a beaten man, an accident waiting to happen. When he talked about how hard it was to lead the British Open, he was already looking for something soft to break his fall.

Ian Woosnam, 43, was so surprised to be in contention at Lytham that he forgot how to count to 15. Did his gaffe cost him the Open? I doubt it.

Greg Norman last won four years and two surgeries ago, and it's been eight years since the Shark, now 46, won a major. He's all about his businesses—clothes, courses, wine and yachts—and his family these days. He withdrew from the British Open to attend the funeral of a friend. Would he have done that 10 years ago? He has his priorities in order. He has a life, but he won't be winning any more majors.

When it comes to squandered talent, John Daly, 35, is the clubhouse leader. Although Daly has had more chances than Darryl Strawberry over the last decade, he has been unable, until this year, to get his addictions under control and lead what passes for a stable life. Daly is too scarred and carries too much baggage to add to his two major titles.

It would take a miracle on the order of Nicklaus in the '86 Masters for 44-year-old Nancy Lopez to win another major, much less the Women's Open, the one title missing from her résumé. Lopez, a part-timer on the tour, has been overwhelmed by a wave of long-hitting youngsters and driven foreigners, and she failed to break 70 in her first 25 rounds in 2001.

Give Nick Faldo credit. At 44 he's still retooling his game, only it always winds up looking like a once-used Rubik's Cube: close but never just right. Be thankful you've won six majors, Nick. Paul Azinger, John Cook, Ray Floyd, Scott Hoch and Greg Norman left a message: "You're welcome."

Carnoustie was more of a hay-baling contest than a major in '99, so it figures that two years later the guy who won there, 32-year-old Paul Lawrie, is a distant 25th in Europe's Ryder Cup rankings. Like Jean Van de Velde, 35, who was wide right on his once-in-a-life-time shot that week, Lawrie is proof that, well, stuff happens.

Fred Couples is 41 and happy as a clam with a wife and two kids. Why play constantly when being a stay-at-home Dad is better than winning a major every day? He has his green jacket and that will have to be enough.

—Gary Van Sickle

## Men's Golf

# THE MAJOR TOURNAMENTS
### The Masters

| Year | Winner | Score | Runner-Up | Year | Winner | Score | Runner-Up |
|------|--------|-------|-----------|------|--------|-------|-----------|
| 1934 | Horton Smith | 284 | Craig Wood | 1971 | Charles Coody | 279 | Johnny Miller |
| 1935 | Gene Sarazen* (144) | 282 | Craig Wood (149) | | | | Jack Nicklaus |
| | (only 36-hole playoff) | | | 1972 | Jack Nicklaus | 286 | Bruce Crampton |
| 1936 | Horton Smith | 285 | Harry Cooper | | | | Bobby Mitchell |
| 1937 | Byron Nelson | 283 | Ralph Guldahl | | | | Tom Weiskopf |
| 1938 | Henry Picard | 285 | Ralph Guldahl | 1973 | Tommy Aaron | 283 | J.C. Snead |
| | | | Harry Cooper | 1974 | Gary Player | 278 | Tom Weiskopf |
| 1939 | Ralph Guldahl | 279 | Sam Snead | | | | Dave Stockton |
| 1940 | Jimmy Demaret | 280 | Lloyd Mangrum | 1975 | Jack Nicklaus | 276 | Johnny Miller |
| 1941 | Craig Wood | 280 | Byron Nelson | | | | Tom Weiskopf |
| 1942 | Byron Nelson* (69) | 280 | Ben Hogan (70) | 1976 | Ray Floyd | 271 | Ben Crenshaw |
| 1943–45 | No tournament | | | 1977 | Tom Watson | 276 | Jack Nicklaus |
| 1946 | Herman Keiser | 282 | Ben Hogan | 1978 | Gary Player | 277 | Hubert Green |
| 1947 | Jimmy Demaret | 281 | Byron Nelson | | | | Rod Funseth |
| | | | Frank Stranahan | | | | Tom Watson |
| 1948 | Claude Harmon | 279 | Cary Middlecoff | 1979 | Fuzzy Zoeller* (4–3)† | 280 | Ed Sneed (4–4) |
| 1949 | Sam Snead | 282 | Johnny Bulla | | | | Tom Watson (4–4) |
| | | | Lloyd Mangrum | 1980 | Seve Ballesteros | 275 | Gibby Gilbert |
| 1950 | Jimmy Demaret | 283 | Jim Ferrier | | | | Jack Newton |
| 1951 | Ben Hogan | 280 | Skee Riegel | 1981 | Tom Watson | 280 | Johnny Miller |
| 1952 | Sam Snead | 286 | Jack Burke Jr.. | | | | Jack Nicklaus |
| 1953 | Ben Hogan | 274 | Ed Oliver Jr. | 1982 | Craig Stadler* (4) | 284 | Dan Pohl (5) |
| 1954 | Sam Snead* (70) | 289 | Ben Hogan (71) | 1983 | Seve Ballesteros | 280 | Ben Crenshaw |
| 1955 | Cary Middlecoff | 279 | Ben Hogan | | | | Tom Kite |
| 1956 | Jack Burke Jr. | 289 | Ken Venturi | 1984 | Ben Crenshaw | 277 | Tom Watson |
| 1957 | Doug Ford | 282 | Sam Snead | 1985 | Bernhard Langer | 282 | Curtis Strange |
| 1958 | Arnold Palmer | 284 | Doug Ford | | | | Seve Ballesteros |
| | | | Fred Hawkins | | | | Ray Floyd |
| 1959 | Art Wall Jr. | 284 | Cary Middlecoff | 1986 | Jack Nicklaus | 279 | Greg Norman |
| 1960 | Arnold Palmer | 282 | Ken Venturi | | | | Tom Kite |
| 1961 | Gary Player | 280 | Charles R. Coe | 1987 | Larry Mize* (4–3) | 285 | Seve Ballesteros (5) |
| | | | Arnold Palmer | | | | Greg Norman (4–4) |
| 1962 | Arnold Palmer* (68) | 280 | Gary Player (71) | 1988 | Sandy Lyle | 281 | Mark Calcavecchia |
| | | | D. Finsterwald (77) | 1989 | Nick Faldo* (5–3) | 283 | Scott Hoch (5–4) |
| 1963 | Jack Nicklaus | 286 | Tony Lema | 1990 | Nick Faldo* (4–4) | 278 | Ray Floyd (4–x) |
| 1964 | Arnold Palmer | 276 | Dave Marr | 1991 | Ian Woosnam | 277 | José María Olazábal |
| | | | Jack Nicklaus | 1992 | Fred Couples | 275 | Ray Floyd |
| 1965 | Jack Nicklaus | 271 | Arnold Palmer | 1993 | Bernhard Langer | 277 | Chip Beck |
| | | | Gary Player | 1994 | José María Olazábal | 279 | Tom Lehman |
| 1966 | Jack Nicklaus* (70) | 288 | Tommy Jacobs (72) | 1995 | Ben Crenshaw | 274 | Davis Love III |
| | | | Gay Brewer Jr. (78) | 1996 | Nick Faldo | 276 | Greg Norman |
| 1967 | Gay Brewer Jr. | 280 | Bobby Nichols | 1997 | Tiger Woods | 270 | Tom Kite |
| 1968 | Bob Goalby | 277 | Roberto DeVicenzo | 1998 | Mark O'Meara | 279 | David Duval |
| 1969 | George Archer | 281 | Billy Casper | | | | Fred Couples |
| | | | George Knudson | 1999 | José María Olazábal | 280 | Davis Love III |
| | | | Tom Weiskopf | 2000 | Vijay Singh | 278 | Ernie Els |
| 1970 | Billy Casper* (69) | 279 | Gene Littler (74) | 2001 | Tiger Woods | 272 | David Duval |

*Winner in playoff. Playoff scores are in parentheses. †Playoff cut from 18 holes to sudden death.
Note: Played at Augusta National Golf Club, Augusta, GA.

## United States Open Championship

| Year | Winner | Score | Runner-Up | Site |
|------|--------|-------|-----------|------|
| 1895 | Horace Rawlins | †173 | Willie Dunn | Newport GC, Newport, RI |
| 1896 | James Foulis | †152 | Horace Rawlins | Shinnecock Hills GC, Southampton, NY |
| 1897 | Joe Lloyd | †162 | Willie Anderson | Chicago GC, Wheaton, IL |
| 1898 | Fred Herd | 328 | Alex Smith | Myopia Hunt Club, Hamilton, MA |
| 1899 | Willie Smith | 315 | George Low<br>Val Fitzjohn<br>W.H. Way | Baltimore CC, Baltimore |
| 1900 | Harry Vardon | 313 | John H. Taylor | Chicago GC, Wheaton, IL |
| 1901 | Willie Anderson* (85) | 331 | Alex Smith (86) | Myopia Hunt Club, Hamilton, MA |
| 1902 | Laurie Auchterlonie | 307 | Stewart Gardner | Garden City GC, Garden City, NY |
| 1903 | Willie Anderson* (82) | 307 | David Brown (84) | Baltusrol GC, Springfield, NJ |
| 1904 | Willie Anderson | 303 | Gil Nicholls | Glen View Club, Golf, IL |
| 1905 | Willie Anderson | 314 | Alex Smith | Myopia Hunt Club, Hamilton, MA |
| 1906 | Alex Smith | 295 | Willie Smith | Onwentsia Club, Lake Forest, IL |
| 1907 | Alex Ross | 302 | Gil Nicholls | Philadelphia Cricket Club, Chestnut Hill, PA |
| 1908 | Fred McLeod* (77) | 322 | Willie Smith (83) | Myopia Hunt Club, Hamilton, MA |
| 1909 | George Sargent | 290 | Tom McNamara | Englewood GC, Englewood, NJ |
| 1910 | Alex Smith* (71) | 298 | John McDermott (75)<br>Macdonald Smith (77) | Philadelphia Cricket Club, Chestnut Hill, PA |
| 1911 | John McDermott* (80) | 307 | Mike Brady (82)<br>George Simpson (85) | Chicago GC, Wheaton, IL |
| 1912 | John McDermott | 294 | Tom McNamara | CC of Buffalo, Buffalo |
| 1913 | Francis Ouimet* (72) | 304 | Harry Vardon (77)<br>Edward Ray (78) | The Country Club, Brookline, MA |
| 1914 | Walter Hagen | 290 | Chick Evans | Midlothian CC, Blue Island, IL |
| 1915 | Jerry Travers | 297 | Tom McNamara | Baltusrol GC, Springfield, NJ |
| 1916 | Chick Evans | 286 | Jock Hutchison | Minikahda Club, Minneapolis |
| 1917–18 | No tournament | | | |
| 1919 | Walter Hagen* (77) | 301 | Mike Brady (78) | Brae Burn CC, West Newton, MA |
| 1920 | Edward Ray | 295 | Harry Vardon<br>Jack Burke<br>Leo Diegel<br>Jock Hutchison | Inverness CC, Toledo |
| 1921 | Jim Barnes | 289 | Walter Hagen<br>Fred McLeod | Columbia CC, Chevy Chase, MD |
| 1922 | Gene Sarazen | 288 | John L. Black<br>Bobby Jones | Skokie CC, Glencoe, IL |
| 1923 | Bobby Jones* (76) | 296 | Bobby Cruickshank (78) | Inwood CC, Inwood, NY |
| 1924 | Cyril Walker | 297 | Bobby Jones | Oakland Hills CC, Birmingham, MI |
| 1925 | W. MacFarlane* (75–72) | 291 | Bobby Jones (75–73) | Worcester CC, Worcester, MA |
| 1926 | Bobby Jones | 293 | Joe Turnesa | Scioto CC, Columbus, OH |
| 1927 | Tommy Armour* (76) | 301 | Harry Cooper (79) | Oakmont CC, Oakmont, PA |
| 1928 | Johnny Farrell* (143) | 294 | Bobby Jones (144) | Olympia Fields CC, Matteson, IL |
| 1929 | Bobby Jones* (141) | 294 | Al Espinosa (164) | Winged Foot GC, Mamaroneck, NY |
| 1930 | Bobby Jones | 287 | Macdonald Smith | Interlachen CC, Hopkins, MN |
| 1931 | Billy Burke* (149–148) | 292 | George Von Elm (149–149) | Inverness Club, Toledo |
| 1932 | Gene Sarazen | 286 | Phil Perkins<br>Bobby Cruickshank | Fresh Meadows CC, Flushing, NY |
| 1933 | Johnny Goodman | 287 | Ralph Guldahl | North Shore CC, Glenview, IL |
| 1934 | Olin Dutra | 293 | Gene Sarazen | Merion Cricket Club, Ardmore, PA |
| 1935 | Sam Parks Jr. | 299 | Jimmy Thompson | Oakmont CC, Oakmont, PA |
| 1936 | Tony Manero | 282 | Harry Cooper | Baltusrol GC (Upper Course), Springfield, NJ |
| 1937 | Ralph Guldahl | 281 | Sam Snead | Oakland Hills CC, Birmingham, MI |
| 1938 | Ralph Guldahl | 284 | Dick Metz | Cherry Hills CC, Denver |
| 1939 | Byron Nelson* (68–70) | 284 | Craig Wood (68–73)<br>Denny Shute (76) | Philadelphia CC, Philadelphia |
| 1940 | Lawson Little* (70) | 287 | Gene Sarazen (73) | Canterbury GC, Cleveland |
| 1941 | Craig Wood | 284 | Denny Shute | Colonial Club, Fort Worth |
| 1942–45 | No tournament | | | |
| 1946 | Lloyd Mangrum* (72–72) | 284 | Vic Ghezzi (72–73)<br>Byron Nelson (72–73) | Canterbury GC, Cleveland |

## United States Open Championship *(Cont.)*

| Year | Winner | Score | Runner-Up | Site |
|------|--------|-------|-----------|------|
| 1947 | Lew Worsham* (69) | 282 | Sam Snead (70) | St. Louis CC, Clayton, MO |
| 1948 | Ben Hogan | 276 | Jimmy Demaret | Riviera CC, Los Angeles |
| 1949 | Cary Middlecoff | 286 | Sam Snead<br>Clayton Heafner | Medinah CC, Medinah, IL |
| 1950 | Ben Hogan* (69) | 287 | Lloyd Mangrum (73)<br>George Fazio (75) | Merion GC, Ardmore, PA |
| 1951 | Ben Hogan | 287 | Clayton Heafner | Oakland Hills CC, Birmingham, MI |
| 1952 | Julius Boros | 281 | Ed Oliver | Northwood CC, Dallas |
| 1953 | Ben Hogan | 283 | Sam Snead | Oakmont CC, Oakmont, PA |
| 1954 | Ed Furgol | 284 | Gene Littler | Baltusrol GC (Lower Course), Springfield, NJ |
| 1955 | Jack Fleck* (69) | 287 | Ben Hogan (72) | Olympic Club (Lake Course), San Francisco |
| 1956 | Cary Middlecoff | 281 | Ben Hogan<br>Julius Boros | Oak Hill CC, Rochester, NY |
| 1957 | Dick Mayer* (72) | 282 | Cary Middlecoff (79) | Inverness Club, Toledo |
| 1958 | Tommy Bolt | 283 | Gary Player | Southern Hills CC, Tulsa |
| 1959 | Billy Casper | 282 | Bob Rosburg | Winged Foot GC, Mamaroneck, NY |
| 1960 | Arnold Palmer | 280 | Jack Nicklaus | Cherry Hills CC, Denver |
| 1961 | Gene Littler | 281 | Bob Goalby<br>Doug Sanders | Oakland Hills CC, Birmingham, MI |
| 1962 | Jack Nicklaus* (71) | 283 | Arnold Palmer (74) | Oakmont CC, Oakmont, PA |
| 1963 | Julius Boros* (70) | 293 | Jacky Cupit (73)<br>Arnold Palmer (76) | The Country Club, Brookline, MA |
| 1964 | Ken Venturi | 278 | Tommy Jacobs | Congressional CC, Bethesda, MD |
| 1965 | Gary Player* (71) | 282 | Kel Nagle (74) | Bellerive CC, St. Louis |
| 1966 | Billy Casper* (69) | 278 | Arnold Palmer (73) | Olympic Club (Lake Course), San Francisco |
| 1967 | Jack Nicklaus | 275 | Arnold Palmer | Baltusrol GC (Lower Course), Springfield, NJ |
| 1968 | Lee Trevino | 275 | Jack Nicklaus | Oak Hill CC, Rochester, NY |
| 1969 | Orville Moody | 281 | Deane Beman<br>Al Geiberger<br>Bob Rosburg | Champions GC (Cypress Creek Course),<br>Houston |
| 1970 | Tony Jacklin | 281 | Dave Hill | Hazeltine GC, Chaska, MN |
| 1971 | Lee Trevino* (68) | 280 | Jack Nicklaus (71) | Merion GC (East Course), Ardmore, PA |
| 1972 | Jack Nicklaus | 290 | Bruce Crampton | Pebble Beach GL, Pebble Beach, CA |
| 1973 | Johnny Miller | 279 | John Schlee | Oakmont CC, Oakmont, PA |
| 1974 | Hale Irwin | 287 | Forrest Fezler | Winged Foot GC, Mamaroneck, NY |
| 1975 | Lou Graham* (71) | 287 | John Mahaffey (73) | Medinah CC, Medinah, IL |
| 1976 | Jerry Pate | 277 | Tom Weiskopf<br>Al Geiberger | Atlanta Athletic Club, Duluth, GA |
| 1977 | Hubert Green | 278 | Lou Graham | Southern Hills CC, Tulsa |
| 1978 | Andy North | 285 | Dave Stockton<br>J.C. Snead | Cherry Hills CC, Denver |
| 1979 | Hale Irwin | 284 | Gary Player<br>Jerry Pate | Inverness Club, Toledo |
| 1980 | Jack Nicklaus | 272 | Isao Aoki | Baltusrol GC (Lower Course), Springfield, NJ |
| 1981 | David Graham | 273 | George Burns<br>Bill Rogers | Merion GC, Ardmore, PA |
| 1982 | Tom Watson | 282 | Jack Nicklaus | Pebble Beach GL, Pebble Beach, CA |
| 1983 | Larry Nelson | 280 | Tom Watson | Oakmont CC, Oakmont, PA |
| 1984 | Fuzzy Zoeller* (67) | 276 | Greg Norman (75) | Winged Foot GC, Mamaroneck, NY |
| 1985 | Andy North | 279 | Dave Barr<br>T.C. Chen<br>Denis Watson | Oakland Hills CC, Birmingham, MI |
| 1986 | Ray Floyd | 279 | Lanny Wadkins<br>Chip Beck | Shinnecock Hills GC, Southampton, NY |
| 1987 | Scott Simpson | 277 | Tom Watson | Olympic Club (Lake Course), San Francisco |
| 1988 | Curtis Strange* (71) | 278 | Nick Faldo (75) | The Country Club, Brookline, MA |
| 1989 | Curtis Strange | 278 | Chip Beck<br>Mark McCumber<br>Ian Woosnam | Oak Hill CC, Rochester, NY |
| 1990 | Hale Irwin* (74) (3) | 280 | Mike Donald (74) (4) | Medinah CC, Medinah, IL |
| 1991 | Payne Stewart* (75) | 282 | Scott Simpson (77) | Hazeltine GC, Chaska, MN |
| 1992 | Tom Kite | 285 | Jeff Sluman | Pebble Beach GL, Pebble Beach, CA |
| 1993 | Lee Janzen | 272 | Payne Stewart | Baltusrol GC, Springfield, NJ |
| 1994 | Ernie Els* | 279 | Loren Roberts<br>Colin Montgomerie | Oakmont CC, Oakmont, PA |

## United States Open Championship (Cont.)

| Year | Winner | Score | Runner-Up | Site |
|------|--------|-------|-----------|------|
| 1995 | Corey Pavin | 280 | Greg Norman | Shinnecock Hills GC, Southampton, NY |
| 1996 | Steve Jones | 278 | Davis Love III | Oakland Hills CC, Birmingham, MI |
| | | | Tom Lehman | |
| 1997 | Ernie Els | 276 | Colin Montgomerie | Congressional CC, Bethesda, MD |
| 1998 | Lee Janzen | 280 | Payne Stewart | The Olympic Club, San Francisco |
| 1999 | Payne Stewart | 279 | Phil Mickelson | Pinehurst Resort and CC, Pinehurst, NC |
| 2000 | Tiger Woods | 272 | Miguel Angel Jiménez | Pebble Beach GL, Pebble Beach, CA |
| | | | Ernie Els | |
| 2001 | Retief Goosen* (70) | 276 | Mark Brooks (72) | Southern Hills CC, Tulsa |

*Winner in playoff. Playoff scores are in parentheses. The 1990 playoff went to one hole of sudden death after an 18-hole playoff. In the 1994 playoff, Montgomerie was eliminated after 18 playoff holes, and Els beat Roberts on the 20th.
†Before 1898, 36 holes. From 1898 on, 72 holes.

## British Open

| Year | Winner | Score | Runner-Up | Site |
|------|--------|-------|-----------|------|
| 1860† | Willie Park | 174 | Tom Morris Sr. | Prestwick, Scotland |
| 1861‡ | Tom Morris Sr. | 163 | Willie Park | Prestwick, Scotland |
| 1862 | Tom Morris Sr. | 163 | Willie Park | Prestwick, Scotland |
| 1863 | Willie Park | 168 | Tom Morris Sr. | Prestwick, Scotland |
| 1864 | Tom Morris, Sr. | 160 | Andrew Strath | Prestwick, Scotland |
| 1865 | Andrew Strath | 162 | Willie Park | Prestwick, Scotland |
| 1866 | Willie Park | 169 | David Park | Prestwick, Scotland |
| 1867 | Tom Morris Sr. | 170 | Willie Park | Prestwick, Scotland |
| 1868 | Tom Morris Jr. | 154 | Tom Morris Sr. | Prestwick, Scotland |
| 1869 | Tom Morris Jr. | 157 | Tom Morris Sr. | Prestwick, Scotland |
| 1870 | Tom Morris Jr. | 149 | David Strath | Prestwick, Scotland |
| | | | Bob Kirk | |
| 1871 | No tournament | | | |
| 1872 | Tom Morris Jr. | 166 | David Strath | Prestwick, Scotland |
| 1873 | Tom Kidd | 179 | Jamie Anderson | St. Andrews, Scotland |
| 1874 | Mungo Park | 159 | No record | Musselburgh, Scotland |
| 1875 | Willie Park | 166 | Bob Martin | Prestwick, Scotland |
| 1876 | Bob Martin# | 176 | David Strath | St. Andrews, Scotland |
| 1877 | Jamie Anderson | 160 | Bob Pringle | Musselburgh, Scotland |
| 1878 | Jamie Anderson | 157 | Robert Kirk | Prestwick, Scotland |
| 1879 | Jamie Anderson | 169 | Andrew Kirkaldy | St. Andrews, Scotland |
| | | | James Allan | |
| 1880 | Robert Ferguson | 162 | No record | Musselburgh, Scotland |
| 1881 | Robert Ferguson | 170 | Jamie Anderson | Prestwick, Scotland |
| 1882 | Robert Ferguson | 171 | Willie Fernie | St. Andrews, Scotland |
| 1883 | Willie Fernie* | 159 | Robert Ferguson | Musselburgh, Scotland |
| 1884 | Jack Simpson | 160 | Douglas Rolland | Prestwick, Scotland |
| | | | Willie Fernie | |
| 1885 | Bob Martin | 171 | Archie Simpson | St. Andrews, Scotland |
| 1886 | David Brown | 157 | Willie Campbell | Musselburgh, Scotland |
| 1887 | Willie Park Jr. | 161 | Bob Martin | Prestwick, Scotland |
| 1888 | Jack Burns | 171 | Bernard Sayers | St. Andrews, Scotland |
| | | | David Anderson | |
| 1889 | Willie Park Jr.* (158) | 155 | Andrew Kirkaldy (163) | Musselburgh, Scotland |
| 1890 | John Ball | 164 | Willie Fernie | Prestwick, Scotland |
| 1891 | Hugh Kirkaldy | 166 | Andrew Kirkaldy | St. Andrews, Scotland |
| | | | Willie Fernie | |
| 1892 | Harold Hilton | **305 | John Ball | Muirfield, Scotland |
| | | | Hugh Kirkaldy | |
| 1893 | William Auchterlonie | 322 | John E. Laidlay | Prestwick, Scotland |
| 1894 | John H. Taylor | 326 | Douglas Rolland | Royal St. George's, England |
| 1895 | John H. Taylor | 322 | Alexander Herd | St. Andrews, Scotland |
| 1896 | Harry Vardon* (157) | 316 | John H. Taylor (161) | Muirfield, Scotland |
| 1897 | Harold Hilton | 314 | James Braid | Hoylake, England |
| 1898 | Harry Vardon | 307 | Willie Park Jr. | Prestwick, Scotland |
| 1899 | Harry Vardon | 310 | Jack White | Royal St. George's, England |
| 1900 | John H. Taylor | 309 | Harry Vardon | St. Andrews, Scotland |
| 1901 | James Braid | 309 | Harry Vardon | Muirfield, Scotland |
| 1902 | Alexander Herd | 307 | Harry Vardon | Hoylake, England |

## British Open *(Cont.)*

| Year | Winner | Score | Runner-Up | Site |
|------|--------|-------|-----------|------|
| 1903 | Harry Vardon | 300 | Tom Vardon | Prestwick, Scotland |
| 1904 | Jack White | 296 | John H. Taylor | Royal St. George's, England |
| 1905 | James Braid | 318 | John H. Taylor | St. Andrews, Scotland |
| | | | Rolland Jones | |
| 1906 | James Braid | 300 | John H. Taylor | Muirfield, Scotland |
| 1907 | Arnaud Massy | 312 | John H. Taylor | Hoylake, England |
| 1908 | James Braid | 291 | Tom Ball | Prestwick, Scotland |
| 1909 | John H. Taylor | 295 | James Braid | Deal, England |
| | | | Tom Ball | |
| 1910 | James Braid | 299 | Alexander Herd | St. Andrews, Scotland |
| 1911 | Harry Vardon | 303 | Arnaud Massy | Royal St. George's, England |
| 1912 | Ted Ray | 295 | Harry Vardon | Muirfield, Scotland |
| 1913 | John H. Taylor | 304 | Ted Ray | Hoylake, England |
| 1914 | Harry Vardon | 306 | John H. Taylor | Prestwick, Scotland |
| 1915–19 | No tournament | | | |
| 1920 | George Duncan | 303 | Alexander Herd | Deal, England |
| 1921 | Jock Hutchison* (150) | 296 | Roger Wethered (159) | St. Andrews, Scotland |
| 1922 | Walter Hagen | 300 | George Duncan | Royal St. George's, England |
| | | | Jim Barnes | |
| 1923 | Arthur G. Havers | 295 | Walter Hagen | Troon, Scotland |
| 1924 | Walter Hagen | 301 | Ernest Whitcombe | Hoylake, England |
| 1925 | Jim Barnes | 300 | Archie Compston | Prestwick, Scotland |
| | | | Ted Ray | |
| 1926 | Bobby Jones | 291 | Al Watrous | Royal Lytham & St. Annes, England |
| 1927 | Bobby Jones | 285 | Aubrey Boomer | St. Andrews, Scotland |
| 1928 | Walter Hagen | 292 | Gene Sarazen | Royal St. George's, England |
| 1929 | Walter Hagen | 292 | Johnny Farrell | Muirfield, Scotland |
| 1930 | Bobby Jones | 291 | Macdonald Smith | Hoylake, England |
| | | | Leo Diegel | |
| 1931 | Tommy Armour | 296 | Jose Jurado | Carnoustie, Scotland |
| 1932 | Gene Sarazen | 283 | Macdonald Smith | Prince's, England |
| 1933 | Denny Shute* (149) | 292 | Craig Wood (154) | St. Andrews, Scotland |
| 1934 | Henry Cotton | 283 | Sidney F. Brews | Royal St. George's, England |
| 1935 | Alfred Perry | 283 | Alfred Padgham | Muirfield, Scotland |
| 1936 | Alfred Padgham | 287 | James Adams | Hoylake, England |
| 1937 | Henry Cotton | 290 | Reginald A. Whitcombe | Carnoustie, Scotland |
| 1938 | Reginald A. Whitcombe | 295 | James Adams | Royal St. George's, England |
| 1939 | Richard Burton | 290 | Johnny Bulla | St. Andrews, Scotland |
| 1940–45 | No tournament | | | |
| 1946 | Sam Snead | 290 | Bobby Locke | St. Andrews, Scotland |
| | | | Johnny Bulla | |
| 1947 | Fred Daly | 293 | Reginald W. Horne | Hoylake, England |
| | | | Frank Stranahan | |
| 1948 | Henry Cotton | 294 | Fred Daly | Muirfield, Scotland |
| 1949 | Bobby Locke* (135) | 283 | Harry Bradshaw (147) | Royal St. George's, England |
| 1950 | Bobby Locke | 279 | Roberto DeVicenzo | Troon, Scotland |
| 1951 | Max Faulkner | 285 | Tony Cerda | Portrush, Ireland |
| 1952 | Bobby Locke | 287 | Peter Thomson | Royal Lytham & St. Annes, England |
| 1953 | Ben Hogan | 282 | Frank Stranahan | Carnoustie, Scotland |
| | | | Dai Rees | |
| | | | Peter Thomson | |
| | | | Tony Cerda | |
| 1954 | Peter Thomson | 283 | Sidney S. Scott | Royal Birkdale, England |
| | | | Dai Rees | |
| | | | Bobby Locke | |
| 1955 | Peter Thomson | 281 | John Fallon | St. Andrews, Scotland |
| 1956 | Peter Thomson | 286 | Flory Van Donck | Hoylake, England |
| 1957 | Bobby Locke | 279 | Peter Thomson | St. Andrews, Scotland |
| 1958 | Peter Thomson* (139) | 278 | Dave Thomas (143) | Royal Lytham & St. Annes, England |
| 1959 | Gary Player | 284 | Fred Bullock | Muirfield, Scotland |
| | | | Flory Van Donck | |
| 1960 | Kel Nagle | 278 | Arnold Palmer | St. Andrews, Scotland |
| 1961 | Arnold Palmer | 284 | Dai Rees | Royal Birkdale, England |
| 1962 | Arnold Palmer | 276 | Kel Nagle | Troon, Scotland |

## British Open *(Cont.)*

| Year | Winner | Score | Runner-Up | Site |
|------|--------|-------|-----------|------|
| 1963 | Bob Charles* (140) | 277 | Phil Rodgers (148) | Royal Lytham & St. Annes, England |
| 1964 | Tony Lema | 279 | Jack Nicklaus | St. Andrews, Scotland |
| 1965 | Peter Thomson | 285 | Brian Huggett | Southport, England |
| | | | Christy O'Connor | |
| 1966 | Jack Nicklaus | 282 | Doug Sanders | Muirfield, Scotland |
| | | | Dave Thomas | |
| 1967 | Robert DeVicenzo | 278 | Jack Nicklaus | Hoylake, England |
| 1968 | Gary Player | 289 | Jack Nicklaus | Carnoustie, Scotland |
| | | | Bob Charles | |
| 1969 | Tony Jacklin | 280 | Bob Charles | Royal Lytham & St. Annes, England |
| 1970 | Jack Nicklaus* (72) | 283 | Doug Sanders (73) | St. Andrews, Scotland |
| 1971 | Lee Trevino | 278 | Lu Liang Huan | Royal Birkdale, England |
| 1972 | Lee Trevino | 278 | Jack Nicklaus | Muirfield, Scotland |
| 1973 | Tom Weiskopf | 276 | Johnny Miller | Troon, Scotland |
| 1974 | Gary Player | 282 | Peter Oosterhuis | Royal Lytham & St. Annes, England |
| 1975 | Tom Watson* (71) | 279 | Jack Newton (72) | Carnoustie, Scotland |
| 1976 | Johnny Miller | 279 | Jack Nicklaus | Royal Birkdale, England |
| | | | Seve Ballesteros | |
| 1977 | Tom Watson | 268 | Jack Nicklaus | Turnberry, Scotland |
| 1978 | Jack Nicklaus | 281 | Ben Crenshaw | St. Andrews, Scotland |
| | | | Tom Kite | |
| | | | Ray Floyd | |
| | | | Simon Owen | |
| 1979 | Seve Ballesteros | 283 | Ben Crenshaw | Royal Lytham & St. Annes, England |
| | | | Jack Nicklaus | |
| 1980 | Tom Watson | 271 | Lee Trevino | Muirfield, Scotland |
| 1981 | Bill Rogers | 276 | Bernhard Langer | Royal St. George's, England |
| 1982 | Tom Watson | 284 | Nick Price | Troon, Scotland |
| | | | Peter Oosterhuis | |
| 1983 | Tom Watson | 275 | Andy Bean | Royal Birkdale, England |
| 1984 | Seve Ballesteros | 276 | Tom Watson | St. Andrews, Scotland |
| | | | Bernhard Langer | |
| 1985 | Sandy Lyle | 282 | Payne Stewart | Royal St. George's, England |
| 1986 | Greg Norman | 280 | Gordon Brand | Turnberry, Scotland |
| 1987 | Nick Faldo | 279 | Paul Azinger | Muirfield, Scotland |
| | | | Rodger Davis | |
| 1988 | Seve Ballesteros | 273 | Nick Price | Royal Lytham & St. Annes, England |
| 1989†† | Mark Calcavecchia* | 275 | Wayne Grady (4-4-4-4) | Troon, Scotland |
| | (4-3-3-3) | | Greg Norman (3-3-4-x) | |
| 1990 | Nick Faldo | 270 | Payne Stewart | St. Andrews, Scotland |
| | | | Mark McNulty | |
| 1991 | Ian Baker-Finch | 272 | Mike Harwood | Royal Birkdale, England |
| 1992 | Nick Faldo | 272 | John Cook | Muirfield, Scotland |
| 1993 | Greg Norman | 267 | Nick Faldo | Royal St. George's, England |
| 1994 | Nick Price | 268 | Jesper Parnevik | Turnberry, Scotland |
| 1995 | John Daly* (4-3-4-4) | 282 | C. Rocca (5-4-7-3) | St. Andrews, Scotland |
| 1996 | Tom Lehman | 271 | Mark McCumber | Royal Lytham & St. Annes, England |
| | | | Ernie Els | |
| 1997 | Justin Leonard | 272 | Jesper Parnevik | Troon, Scotland |
| | | | Darren Clarke | |
| 1998 | Mark O'Meara* (4-4-5-4) | 280 | Brian Watts (5-4-5-5) | Southport, England |
| 1999 | Paul Lawrie* (5-4-3-3) | 290 | Jean Van de Velde (6-4-3-5) | Carnoustie GC, Carnoustie, |
| | | | Justin Leonard (5-4-4-5) | Scotland |
| 2000 | Tiger Woods | 269 | Thomas Bjorn | St. Andrews, Scotland |
| | | | Ernie Els | |
| 2001 | David Duval | 274 | Niclas Fasth | Royal Lytham & St. Annes, England |

*Winner in playoff. Playoff scores are in parentheses. †The first event was open only to professional golfers.
‡The second annual open was open to amateurs and pros. #Tied, but refused playoff.
**Championship extended from 36 to 72 holes. ††Playoff cut from 18 holes to 4 holes.

### PGA Championship

| Year | Winner | Score | Runner-Up | Site |
|------|--------|-------|-----------|------|
| 1916 | Jim Barnes | 1 up | Jock Hutchison | Siwanoy CC, Bronxville, NY |
| 1917–18 | No tournament | | | |
| 1919 | Jim Barnes | 6 & 5 | Fred McLeod | Engineers CC, Roslyn, NY |
| 1920 | Jock Hutchison | 1 up | J. Douglas Edgar | Flossmoor CC, Flossmoor, IL |
| 1921 | Walter Hagen | 3 & 2 | Jim Barnes | Inwood CC, Far Rockaway, NY |
| 1922 | Gene Sarazen | 4 & 3 | Emmet French | Oakmont CC, Oakmont, PA |
| 1923 | Gene Sarazen | 1 up 38 holes | Walter Hagen | Pelham CC, Pelham, NY |
| 1924 | Walter Hagen | 2 up | Jim Barnes | French Lick CC, French Lick, IN |
| 1925 | Walter Hagen | 6 & 5 | William Mehlhorn | Olympia Fields CC, Olympia Fields, IL |
| 1926 | Walter Hagen | 5 & 3 | Leo Diegel | Salisbury GC, Westbury, NY |
| 1927 | Walter Hagen | 1 up | Joe Turnesa | Cedar Crest CC, Dallas |
| 1928 | Leo Diegel | 6 & 5 | Al Espinosa | Five Farms CC, Baltimore |
| 1929 | Leo Diegel | 6 & 4 | Johnny Farrell | Hillcrest CC, Los Angeles |
| 1930 | Tommy Armour | 1 up | Gene Sarazen | Fresh Meadow CC, Flushing, NY |
| 1931 | Tom Creavy | 2 & 1 | Denny Shute | Wannamoisett CC, Rumford, RI |
| 1932 | Olin Dutra | 4 & 3 | Frank Walsh | Keller GC, St. Paul |
| 1933 | Gene Sarazen | 5 & 4 | Willie Goggin | Blue Mound CC, Milwaukee |
| 1934 | Paul Runyan | 1 up | Craig Wood | Park CC, Williamsville, NY |
| 1935 | Johnny Revolta | 5 & 4 38 holes | Tommy Armour | Twin Hills CC, Oklahoma City |
| 1936 | Denny Shute | 3 & 2 | Jimmy Thomson | Pinehurst CC, Pinehurst, NC |
| 1937 | Denny Shute | 1 up 37 holes | Harold McSpaden | Pittsburgh FC, Aspinwall, PA |
| 1938 | Paul Runyan | 8 & 7 | Sam Snead | Shawnee CC, Shawnee-on-Delaware, PA |
| 1939 | Henry Picard | 1 up 37 holes | Byron Nelson | Pomonok CC, Flushing, NY |
| 1940 | Byron Nelson | 1 up | Sam Snead | Hershey CC, Hershey, PA |
| 1941 | Vic Ghezzi | 1 up 38 holes | Byron Nelson | Cherry Hills CC, Denver |
| 1942 | Sam Snead | 2 & 1 | Jim Turnesa | Seaview CC, Atlantic City |
| 1943 | No tournament | | | |
| 1944 | Bob Hamilton | 1 up | Byron Nelson | Manito G & CC, Spokane, WA |
| 1945 | Byron Nelson | 4 & 3 | Sam Byrd | Morraine CC, Dayton |
| 1946 | Ben Hogan | 6 & 4 | Ed Oliver | Portland GC, Portland, OR |
| 1947 | Jim Ferrier | 2 & 1 | Chick Harbert | Plum Hollow CC, Detroit |
| 1948 | Ben Hogan | 7 & 6 | Mike Turnesa | Norwood Hills CC, St. Louis |
| 1949 | Sam Snead | 3 & 2 | Johnny Palmer | Hermitage CC, Richmond |
| 1950 | Chandler Harper | 4 & 3 | Henry Williams Jr. | Scioto CC, Columbus, OH |
| 1951 | Sam Snead | 7 & 6 | Walter Burkemo | Oakmont CC, Oakmont, PA |
| 1952 | Jim Turnesa | 1 up | Chick Harbert | Big Spring CC, Louisville |
| 1953 | Walter Burkemo | 2 & 1 | Felice Torza | Birmingham CC, Birmingham, MI |
| 1954 | Chick Harbert | 4 & 3 | Walter Burkemo | Keller GC, St. Paul |
| 1955 | Doug Ford | 4 & 3 | Cary Middlecoff | Meadowbrook CC, Detroit |
| 1956 | Jack Burke | 3 & 2 | Ted Kroll | Blue Hill CC, Boston |
| 1957 | Lionel Hebert | 2 & 1 | Dow Finsterwald | Miami Valley CC, Dayton |
| 1958 | Dow Finsterwald | 276 | Billy Casper | Llanerch CC, Havertown, PA |
| 1959 | Bob Rosburg | 277 | Jerry Barber Doug Sanders | Minneapolis GC, St. Louis Park, MN |
| 1960 | Jay Hebert | 281 | Jim Ferrier | Firestone CC, Akron |
| 1961 | Jerry Barber* (67) | 277 | Don January (68) | Olympia Fields CC, Olympia Fields, IL |
| 1962 | Gary Player | 278 | Bob Goalby | Aronimink GC, Newton Square, PA |
| 1963 | Jack Nicklaus | 279 | Dave Ragan Jr. | Dallas Athletic Club, Dallas |
| 1964 | Bobby Nichols | 271 | Jack Nicklaus Arnold Palmer | Columbus CC, Columbus, OH |
| 1965 | Dave Marr | 280 | Billy Casper Jack Nicklaus | Laurel Valley CC, Ligonier, PA |
| 1966 | Al Geiberger | 280 | Dudley Wysong | Firestone CC, Akron |
| 1967 | Don January* (69) | 281 | Don Massengale (71) | Columbine CC, Littleton, CO |
| 1968 | Julius Boros | 281 | Bob Charles Arnold Palmer | Pecan Valley CC, San Antonio |
| 1969 | Ray Floyd | 276 | Gary Player | NCR CC, Dayton |
| 1970 | Dave Stockton | 279 | Arnold Palmer Bob Murphy | Southern Hills CC, Tulsa |

## PGA Championship *(Cont.)*

| Year | Winner | Score | Runner-Up | Site |
|---|---|---|---|---|
| 1971 | Jack Nicklaus | 281 | Billy Casper | PGA Nat'l GC, Palm Beach Gardens, FL |
| 1972 | Gary Player | 281 | Tommy Aaron | Oakland Hills CC, Birmingham, MI |
| | | | Jim Jamieson | |
| 1973 | Jack Nicklaus | 277 | Bruce Crampton | Canterbury GC, Cleveland |
| 1974 | Lee Trevino | 276 | Jack Nicklaus | Tanglewood GC, Winston-Salem, NC |
| 1975 | Jack Nicklaus | 276 | Bruce Crampton | Firestone CC, Akron |
| 1976 | Dave Stockton | 281 | Ray Floyd | Congressional CC, Bethesda, MD |
| | | | Don January | |
| 1977† | Lanny Wadkins* (4-4-4) | 282 | Gene Littler (4-4-5) | Pebble Beach GL, Pebble Beach, CA |
| 1978 | John Mahaffey* (4-3) | 276 | Jerry Pate (4-4) | Oakmont CC, Oakmont, PA |
| | | | Tom Watson (4-5) | |
| 1979 | David Graham* (4-4-2) | 272 | Ben Crenshaw (4-4-4) | Oakland Hills CC, Birmingham, MI |
| 1980 | Jack Nicklaus | 274 | Andy Bean | Oak Hill CC, Rochester, NY |
| 1981 | Larry Nelson | 273 | Fuzzy Zoeller | Atlanta Athletic Club, Duluth, GA |
| 1982 | Raymond Floyd | 272 | Lanny Wadkins | Southern Hills CC, Tulsa |
| 1983 | Hal Sutton | 274 | Jack Nicklaus | Riviera CC, Pacific Palisades, CA |
| 1984 | Lee Trevino | 273 | Gary Player | Shoal Creek, Birmingham, AL |
| | | | Lanny Wadkins | |
| 1985 | Hubert Green | 278 | Lee Trevino | Cherry Hills CC, Denver |
| 1986 | Bob Tway | 276 | Greg Norman | Inverness CC, Toledo |
| 1987 | Larry Nelson* (4) | 287 | Lanny Wadkins (5) | PGA Natl GC, Palm Beach Gardens, FL |
| 1988 | Jeff Sluman | 272 | Paul Azinger | Oak Tree GC, Edmond, OK |
| 1989 | Payne Stewart | 276 | Mike Reid | Kemper Lakes GC, Hawthorn Woods, IL |
| 1990 | Wayne Grady | 282 | Fred Couples | Shoal Creek, Birmingham, AL |
| 1991 | John Daly | 276 | Bruce Lietzke | Crooked Stick GC, Carmel, IN |
| 1992 | Nick Price | 278 | Jim Gallagher Jr. | Bellerive CC, St. Louis |
| 1993 | Paul Azinger* (4-4) | 272 | Greg Norman (4-5) | Inverness CC, Toledo |
| 1994 | Nick Price | 269 | Corey Pavin | Southern Hills CC, Tulsa |
| 1995 | Steve Elkington* (3) | 267 | Colin Montgomerie (4) | Riviera CC, Pacific Palisades, CA |
| 1996 | Mark Brooks* (3) | 277 | Kenny Perry (x) | Valhalla GC, Louisville |
| 1997 | Davis Love III | 269 | Justin Leonard | Winged Foot GC, Mamaroneck, NY |
| 1998 | Vijay Singh | 271 | Steve Stricker | Sahalee CC, Redmond, WA |
| 1999 | Tiger Woods | 277 | Sergio Garcia | Medinah CC, Medinah, IL |
| 2000 | Tiger Woods* (3-4-5) | 270 | Bob May (4-4-x) | Valhalla GC, Louisville |
| 2001 | David Toms | 265 | Phil Mickelson | Atlanta AC, Duluth, GA |

*Winner in playoff. Playoff scores are in parentheses. †Playoff changed from 18 holes to sudden death.

## Alltime Major Championship Winners

| | Masters | U.S. Open | British Open | PGA Champ. | U.S. Amateur | British Amateur | Total |
|---|---|---|---|---|---|---|---|
| †Jack Nicklaus | 6 | 4 | 3 | 5 | 2 | 0 | 20 |
| Bobby Jones | 0 | 4 | 3 | 0 | 5 | 1 | 13 |
| Walter Hagen | 0 | 2 | 4 | 5 | 0 | 0 | 11 |
| Ben Hogan | 2 | 4 | 1 | 2 | 0 | 0 | 9 |
| †Gary Player | 3 | 1 | 3 | 2 | 0 | 0 | 9 |
| John Ball | 0 | 0 | 1 | 0 | 0 | 8 | 9 |
| *Tiger Woods | 2 | 1 | 1 | 2 | 3 | 0 | 9 |
| †Arnold Palmer | 4 | 1 | 2 | 0 | 1 | 0 | 8 |
| †Tom Watson | 2 | 1 | 5 | 0 | 0 | 0 | 8 |
| Harold Hilton | 0 | 0 | 2 | 0 | 1 | 4 | 7 |
| Gene Sarazen | 1 | 2 | 1 | 3 | 0 | 0 | 7 |
| Sam Snead | 3 | 0 | 1 | 3 | 0 | 0 | 7 |
| Harry Vardon | 0 | 1 | 6 | 0 | 0 | 0 | 7 |

*Active PGA player. †Active Senior PGA player.

## Alltime Multiple Professional Major Winners

| MASTERS | | U.S. OPEN (Cont.) | | BRITISH OPEN (Cont.) | | PGA CHAMPIONSHIP | |
|---|---|---|---|---|---|---|---|
| Jack Nicklaus | 6 | Hale Irwin | 3 | Tom Watson | 5 | Walter Hagen | 5 |
| Arnold Palmer | 4 | Julius Boros | 2 | Walter Hagen | 4 | Jack Nicklaus | 5 |
| Jimmy Demaret | 3 | Billy Casper | 2 | Bobby Locke | 4 | Gene Sarazen | 3 |
| Nick Faldo | 3 | Ernie Els | 2 | Tom Morris Sr. | 4 | Sam Snead | 3 |
| Gary Player | 3 | Ralph Guldahl | 2 | Tom Morris Jr. | 4 | Jim Barnes | 2 |
| Sam Snead | 3 | Walter Hagen | 2 | Willie Park | 4 | Leo Diegel | 2 |
| Seve Ballesteros | 2 | Lee Janzen | 2 | Jamie Anderson | 3 | Raymond Floyd | 2 |
| Ben Crenshaw | 2 | John McDermott | 2 | Seve Ballesteros | 3 | Ben Hogan | 2 |
| Ben Hogan | 2 | Cary Middlecoff | 2 | Henry Cotton | 3 | Byron Nelson | 2 |
| Bernhard Langer | 2 | Andy North | 2 | Nick Faldo | 3 | Larry Nelson | 2 |
| Byron Nelson | 2 | Gene Sarazen | 2 | Robert Ferguson | 3 | Gary Player | 2 |
| José María Olazábal | 2 | Alex Smith | 2 | Bobby Jones | 3 | Paul Runyan | 2 |
| Horton Smith | 2 | Payne Stewart | 2 | Jack Nicklaus | 3 | Denny Shute | 2 |
| Tom Watson | 2 | Curtis Strange | 2 | Gary Player | 3 | Dave Stockton | 2 |
| Tiger Woods | 2 | Lee Trevino | 2 | Harold Hilton | 2 | Lee Trevino | 2 |
| | | | | Bob Martin | 2 | Tiger Woods | 2 |
| **U.S. OPEN** | | **BRITISH OPEN** | | Greg Norman | 2 | | |
| | | | | Arnold Palmer | 2 | | |
| Willie Anderson | 4 | Harry Vardon | 6 | Willie Park Jr. | 2 | | |
| Ben Hogan | 4 | James Braid | 5 | Lee Trevino | 2 | | |
| Bobby Jones | 4 | J.H. Taylor | 5 | | | | |
| Jack Nicklaus | 4 | Peter Thomson | 5 | | | | |

# THE PGA TOUR

## Most Career Wins

| | Wins | | Wins | | Wins |
|---|---|---|---|---|---|
| Sam Snead | 81 | Billy Casper | 51 | Tom Watson | 34 |
| Jack Nicklaus | 70 | Walter Hagen | 40 | Horton Smith | 32 |
| Ben Hogan | 63 | Cary Middlecoff | 40 | Harry Cooper | 31 |
| Arnold Palmer | 60 | Gene Sarazen | 38 | Jimmy Demaret | 31 |
| Byron Nelson | 52 | Lloyd Mangrum | 36 | Leo Diegel | 30 |

## Season Money Leaders

| | | Earnings ($) | | | Earnings ($) | | | Earnings ($) |
|---|---|---|---|---|---|---|---|---|
| 1934 | Paul Runyan | 6,767.00 | 1957 | Dick Mayer | 65,835.00 | 1980 | Tom Watson | 530,808.33 |
| 1935 | Johnny Revolta | 9,543.00 | 1958 | Arnold Palmer | 42,607.50 | 1981 | Tom Kite | 375,698.84 |
| 1936 | Horton Smith | 7,682.00 | 1959 | Art Wall | 53,167.60 | 1982 | Craig Stadler | 446,462.00 |
| 1937 | Harry Cooper | 14,138.69 | 1960 | Arnold Palmer | 75,262.85 | 1983 | Hal Sutton | 426,668.00 |
| 1938 | Sam Snead | 19,534.49 | 1961 | Gary Player | 64,540.45 | 1984 | Tom Watson | 476,260.00 |
| 1939 | Henry Picard | 10,303.00 | 1962 | Arnold Palmer | 81,448.33 | 1985 | Curtis Strange | 542,321.00 |
| 1940 | Ben Hogan | 10,655.00 | 1963 | Arnold Palmer | 128,230.00 | 1986 | Greg Norman | 653,296.00 |
| 1941 | Ben Hogan | 18,358.00 | 1964 | Jack Nicklaus | 113,284.50 | 1987 | Curtis Strange | 925,941.00 |
| 1942 | Ben Hogan | 13,143.00 | 1965 | Jack Nicklaus | 140,752.14 | 1988 | Curtis Strange | 1,147,644.00 |
| 1943 | No statistics compiled | | 1966 | Billy Casper | 121,944.92 | 1989 | Tom Kite | 1,395,278.00 |
| 1944 | Byron Nelson* | 37,967.69 | 1967 | Jack Nicklaus | 188,998.08 | 1990 | Greg Norman | 1,165,477.00 |
| 1945 | Byron Nelson* | 63,335.66 | 1968 | Billy Casper | 205,168.67 | 1991 | Corey Pavin | 979,430.00 |
| 1946 | Ben Hogan | 42,556.16 | 1969 | Frank Beard | 164,707.11 | 1992 | Fred Couples | 1,344,188.00 |
| 1947 | Jimmy Demaret | 27,936.83 | 1970 | Lee Trevino | 157,037.63 | 1993 | Nick Price | 1,478,557.00 |
| 1948 | Ben Hogan | 32,112.00 | 1971 | Jack Nicklaus | 244,490.50 | 1994 | Nick Price | 1,499,927.00 |
| 1949 | Sam Snead | 31,593.83 | 1972 | Jack Nicklaus | 320,542.26 | 1995 | Greg Norman | 1,654,959.00 |
| 1950 | Sam Snead | 35,758.83 | 1973 | Jack Nicklaus | 308,362.10 | 1996 | Tom Lehman | 1,780,159.00 |
| 1951 | Lloyd Mangrum | 26,088.83 | 1974 | Johnny Miller | 353,021.59 | 1997 | Tiger Woods | 2,066,833.00 |
| 1952 | Julius Boros | 37,032.97 | 1975 | Jack Nicklaus | 298,149.17 | 1998 | David Duval | 2,591,031.00 |
| 1953 | Lew Worsham | 34,002.00 | 1976 | Jack Nicklaus | 266,438.57 | 1999 | Tiger Woods | 6,616,585.00 |
| 1954 | Bob Toski | 65,819.81 | 1977 | Tom Watson | 310,653.16 | 2000 | Tiger Woods | 9,188,321.00 |
| 1955 | Julius Boros | 63,121.55 | 1978 | Tom Watson | 362,428.93 | | | |
| 1956 | Ted Kroll | 72,835.83 | 1979 | Tom Watson | 462,636.00 | | | |

* War bonds. Note: Total money listed from 1968 through 1974. Official money listed from 1975 on.

## Career Money Leaders*

| | Earnings ($) | | Earnings ($) | | Earnings ($) |
|---|---|---|---|---|---|
| 1. Tiger Woods | 26,021,227 | 18. Tom Kite | 10,865,959 | 35. Jesper Parnevik | 8,193,358 |
| 2. Phil Mickelson | 17,837,998 | 19. Justin Leonard | 10,821,723 | 36. Billy Mayfair | 8,139,562 |
| 3. Davis Love III | 17,383,490 | 20. Jeff Sluman | 10,478,372 | 37. Bob Estes | 8,117,388 |
| 4. David Duval | 14,778,686 | 21. Loren Roberts | 9,747,871 | 38. Curtis Strange | 7,583,744 |
| 5. Scott Hoch | 14,472,202 | 22. Brad Faxon | 9,687,198 | 39. Scott Verplank | 7,545,384 |
| 6. Nick Price | 14,313,092 | 23. Tom Watson | 9,593,631 | 40. David Frost | 7,484,490 |
| 7. Vijay Singh | 14,234,724 | 24. Corey Pavin | 9,536,170 | 41. Kirk Triplett | 7,417,896 |
| 8. Hal Sutton | 13,802,946 | 25. John Cook | 9,364,182 | 42. Kenny Perry | 7,397,950 |
| 9. Greg Norman | 13,344,142 | 26. John Huston | 9,184,049 | 43. Steve Pate | 7,387,504 |
| 10. M. Calcavecchia | 13,311,349 | 27. Jeff Maggert | 9,135,461 | 44. Rocco Mediate | 7,199,744 |
| 11. Fred Couples | 12,661,590 | 28. David Toms | 8,928,357 | 45. Mark Brooks | 7,142,156 |
| 12. Mark O'Meara | 11,950,398 | 29. Lee Janzen | 8,916,149 | 46. Ben Crenshaw | 7,091,166 |
| 13. Tom Lehman | 11,914,662 | 30. Steve Elkington | 8,766,672 | 47. Chris Perry | 6,866,671 |
| 14. Payne Stewart | 11,737,008 | 31. Craig Stadler | 8,502,884 | 48. Larry Mize | 6,859,090 |
| 15. Ernie Els | 11,631,635 | 32. Jay Haas | 8,433,856 | 49. Andrew Magee | 6,824,498 |
| 16. Paul Azinger | 11,590,852 | 33. Bob Tway | 8,332,936 | 50. Stewart Cink | 6,819,888 |
| 17. Jim Furyk | 11,326,926 | 34. Fred Funk | 8,196,686 | | |

*Through 10/14/01.

## Year by Year Statistical Leaders

### SCORING AVERAGE

| 1980 | Lee Trevino | 69.73 |
|---|---|---|
| 1981 | Tom Kite | 69.80 |
| 1982 | Tom Kite | 70.21 |
| 1983 | Raymond Floyd | 70.61 |
| 1984 | Calvin Peete | 70.56 |
| 1985 | Don Pooley | 70.36 |
| 1986 | Scott Hoch | 70.08 |
| 1987 | David Frost | 70.09 |
| 1988 | Greg Norman | 69.38 |
| 1989 | Payne Stewart | 69.485† |
| 1990 | Greg Norman | 69.10 |
| 1991 | Fred Couples | 69.59 |
| 1992 | Fred Couples | 69.38 |
| 1993 | Greg Norman | 68.90 |
| 1994 | Greg Norman | 68.81 |
| 1995 | Greg Norman | 69.06 |
| 1996 | Tom Lehman | 69.32 |
| 1997 | Nick Price | 68.98 |
| 1998 | David Duval | 69.13 |
| 1999 | Tiger Woods | 68.43 |
| 2000 | Tiger Woods | 67.79 |

Note: Scoring average per round, with adjustments made at each round for the field's course scoring average.

### DRIVING DISTANCE

| | | Yds |
|---|---|---|
| 1980 | Dan Pohl | 274.3 |
| 1981 | Dan Pohl | 280.1 |
| 1982 | Bill Calfee | 275.3 |
| 1983 | John McComish | 277.4 |
| 1984 | Bill Glasson | 276.5 |
| 1985 | Andy Bean | 278.2 |
| 1986 | Davis Love III | 285.7 |
| 1987 | John McComish | 283.9 |
| 1988 | Steve Thomas | 284.6 |
| 1989 | Ed Humenik | 280.9 |
| 1990 | Tom Purtzer | 279.6 |
| 1991 | John Daly | 288.9 |

### DRIVING DISTANCE *(Cont.)*

| 1992 | John Daly | 283.4 |
|---|---|---|
| 1993 | John Daly | 288.9 |
| 1994 | Davis Love III | 283.8 |
| 1995 | John Daly | 289.0 |
| 1996 | John Daly | 288.8 |
| 1997 | John Daly | 302.0 |
| 1998 | John Daly | 299.4 |
| 1999 | John Daly | 305.6 |
| 2000 | John Daly | 301.4 |

Note: Average computed by charting distance of two tee shots on a predetermined par-four or par-five hole (one on front nine, one on back nine).

### DRIVING ACCURACY

| 1980 | Mike Reid | 79.5 |
|---|---|---|
| 1981 | Calvin Peete | 81.9 |
| 1982 | Calvin Peete | 84.6 |
| 1983 | Calvin Peete | 81.3 |
| 1984 | Calvin Peete | 77.5 |
| 1985 | Calvin Peete | 80.6 |
| 1986 | Calvin Peete | 81.7 |
| 1987 | Calvin Peete | 83.0 |
| 1988 | Calvin Peete | 82.5 |
| 1989 | Calvin Peete | 82.6 |
| 1990 | Calvin Peete | 83.7 |
| 1991 | Hale Irwin | 78.3 |
| 1992 | Doug Tewell | 82.3 |
| 1993 | Doug Tewell | 82.5 |
| 1994 | David Edwards | 81.6 |
| 1995 | Fred Funk | 81.3 |
| 1996 | Fred Funk | 78.7 |
| 1997 | Allen Doyle | 80.8 |
| 1998 | Bruce Fleisher | 81.4 |
| 1999 | Fred Funk | 80.2 |
| 2000 | Fred Funk | 79.7 |

Note: Percentage of fairways hit on number of par-four and par-five holes played; par-three holes excluded.

### GREENS IN REGULATION

| 1980 | Jack Nicklaus | 72.1 |
|---|---|---|
| 1981 | Calvin Peete | 73.1 |
| 1982 | Calvin Peete | 72.4 |
| 1983 | Calvin Peete | 71.4 |
| 1984 | Andy Bean | 72.1 |
| 1985 | John Mahaffey | 71.9 |
| 1986 | John Mahaffey | 72.0 |
| 1987 | Gil Morgan | 73.3 |
| 1988 | John Adams | 73.9 |
| 1989 | Bruce Lietzke | 72.6 |
| 1990 | Doug Tewell | 70.9 |
| 1991 | Bruce Lietzke | 73.3 |
| 1992 | Tim Simpson | 74.0 |
| 1993 | Fuzzy Zoeller | 73.6 |
| 1994 | Bill Glasson | 73.0 |
| 1995 | Lenny Clements | 72.3 |
| 1996 | Fred Couples | 71.8 |
| | Mark O'Meara | 71.8 |
| 1997 | Tom Lehman | 72.7 |
| 1998 | Hal Sutton | 71.3 |
| 1999 | Tiger Woods | 71.4 |
| 2000 | Tiger Woods | 75.2 |

Note: Average of greens reached in regulation out of total holes played; hole is considered hit in regulation if any part of the ball rests on the putting surface in two shots less than the hole's par—a par-5 hit in two shots is one green in regulation.

### PUTTING

| 1980 | Jerry Pate | 28.81 |
|---|---|---|
| 1981 | Alan Tapie | 28.70 |
| 1982 | Ben Crenshaw | 28.65 |
| 1983 | Morris Hatalsky | 27.96 |
| 1984 | Gary McCord | 28.57 |
| 1985 | Craig Stadler | 28.627† |
| 1986 | Greg Norman | 1.736 |
| 1987 | Ben Crenshaw | 1.743 |
| 1988 | Don Pooley | 1.729 |

† Number had to be carried to extra decimal place to determine winner.

## Year by Year Statistical Leaders (Cont.)

### PUTTING (Cont.)

| | | | | | | | | |
|---|---|---|---|---|---|---|---|---|
| 1989 | Steve Jones | 1.734 | 1993 | David Frost | 1.739 | 1997 | Don Pooley | 1.718 |
| 1990 | Larry Rinker | 1.7467† | 1994 | Loren Roberts | 1.737 | 1998 | Rick Fehr | 1.722 |
| 1991 | Jay Don Blake | 1.7326† | 1995 | Jim Furyk | 1.708 | 1999 | Brad Faxon | 1.723 |
| 1992 | Mark O'Meara | 1.731 | 1996 | Brad Faxon | 1.709 | 2000 | Brad Faxon | 1.704 |

Note: Average number of putts taken on greens reached in regulation; prior to 1986, based on average number of putts per 18 holes.

### SAND SAVES

| | | | | | | | | |
|---|---|---|---|---|---|---|---|---|
| 1980 | Bob Eastwood | 65.4 | 1987 | Paul Azinger | 63.2 | 1994 | Corey Pavin | 65.4 |
| 1981 | Tom Watson | 60.1 | 1988 | Greg Powers | 63.5 | 1995 | Billy Mayfair | 68.6 |
| 1982 | Isao Aoki | 60.2 | 1989 | Mike Sullivan | 66.0 | 1996 | Gary Rusnak | 64.0 |
| 1983 | Isao Aoki | 62.3 | 1990 | Paul Azinger | 67.2 | 1997 | Bob Estes | 70.3 |
| 1984 | Peter Oosterhuis | 64.7 | 1991 | Ben Crenshaw | 64.9 | 1998 | Keith Fergus | 71.0 |
| 1985 | Tom Purtzer | 60.8 | 1992 | Mitch Adcock | 66.9 | 1999 | Jeff Sluman | 67.3 |
| 1986 | Paul Azinger | 63.8 | 1993 | Ken Green | 64.4 | 2000 | Fred Couples | 67.0 |

Note: Percentage of up-and-down efforts from greenside sand traps only—fairway bunkers excluded.

### PAR BREAKERS

| | | | | | | | | |
|---|---|---|---|---|---|---|---|---|
| 1980 | Tom Watson | .213 | 1984 | Craig Stadler | .220 | 1988 | Ken Green | .236 |
| 1981 | Bruce Lietzke | .225 | 1985 | Craig Stadler | .218 | 1989 | Greg Norman | .224 |
| 1982 | Tom Kite | .2154† | 1986 | Greg Norman | .248 | 1990 | Greg Norman | .219 |
| 1983 | Tom Watson | .211 | 1987 | Mark Calcavecchia | .221 | | | |

Note: Average based on total birdies and eagles scored out of total holes played. Discontinued as an official category after 1990.

### EAGLES

| | | | | | | | | |
|---|---|---|---|---|---|---|---|---|
| 1980 | Dave Eichelberger | 16 | 1986 | Joey Sindelar | 16 | 1993 | Davis Love III | 15 |
| 1981 | Bruce Lietzke | 12 | 1987 | Phil Blackmar | 20 | 1994 | Davis Love III | 18 |
| 1982 | Tom Weiskopf | 10 | 1988 | Ken Green | 21 | 1995 | Kelly Gibson | 16 |
| | J.C. Snead | 10 | 1989 | Lon Hinkle | 14 | 1996 | Tom Watson | 97.2 |
| | Andy Bean | 10 | | Duffy Waldorf | 14 | 1997 | Tiger Woods | 104.1 |
| 1983 | Chip Beck | 15 | 1990 | Paul Azinger | 14 | 1998 | Davis Love III | 83.3 |
| 1984 | Gary Hallberg | 15 | 1991 | Andy Bean | 15 | 1999 | Vijay Singh | 104.8 |
| 1985 | Larry Rinker | 14 | 1992 | Dan Forsman | 18 | 2000 | Tiger Woods | 72.0 |

Note: Total of eagles scored 1980–1995. Since 1996 winner determined by number of holes played per eagle.

### BIRDIES

| | | | | | | | | |
|---|---|---|---|---|---|---|---|---|
| 1980 | Andy Bean | 388 | 1988 | Dan Forsman | 465 | 1996 | Fred Couples | 4.20 |
| 1981 | Vance Heafner | 388 | 1989 | Ted Schulz | 415 | 1997 | Tiger Woods | 4.25 |
| 1982 | Andy Bean | 392 | 1990 | Mike Donald | 401 | 1998 | David Duval | 4.29 |
| 1983 | Hal Sutton | 399 | 1991 | Scott Hoch | 446 | 1999 | Tiger Woods | 4.46 |
| 1984 | Mark O'Meara | 419 | 1992 | Jeff Sluman | 417 | 2000 | Tiger Woods | 4.92 |
| 1985 | Joey Sindelar | 411 | 1993 | John Huston | 426 | | | |
| 1986 | Joey Sindelar | 415 | 1994 | Brad Bryant | 397 | | | |
| 1987 | Dan Forsman | 409 | 1995 | Steve Lowery | 410 | | | |

Note: Total of birdies scored 1980–95. Since 1996, winner determined by average number of birdies per round.

### ALL-AROUND

| | | | | | | | | |
|---|---|---|---|---|---|---|---|---|
| 1987 | Dan Pohl | 170 | 1992 | Fred Couples | 256 | 1997 | Bill Glasson | 282 |
| 1988 | Payne Stewart | 170 | 1993 | Gil Morgan | 252 | 1998 | John Huston | 151 |
| 1989 | Paul Azinger | 250 | 1994 | Bob Estes | 227 | 1999 | Tiger Woods | 120 |
| 1990 | Paul Azinger | 162 | 1995 | Justin Leonard | 323 | 2000 | Tiger Woods | 113 |
| 1991 | Scott Hoch | 283 | 1996 | Fred Couples | 214 | | | |

Note: Sum of the places of standing from the other statistical categories; the player with the number closest to zero leads.

† Number had to be carried to extra decimal place to determine winner.

## PGA Player of the Year Award

| | | |
|---|---|---|
| 1948 ................Ben Hogan | 1966 ................Billy Casper | 1984 ................Tom Watson |
| 1949 ................Sam Snead | 1967 ................Jack Nicklaus | 1985 ................Lanny Wadkins |
| 1950 ................Ben Hogan | 1968 ................Not awarded | 1986 ................Bob Tway |
| 1951 ................Ben Hogan | 1969 ................Orville Moody | 1987 ................Paul Azinger |
| 1952 ................Julius Boros | 1970 ................Billy Casper | 1988 ................Curtis Strange |
| 1953 ................Ben Hogan | 1971 ................Lee Trevino | 1989 ................Tom Kite |
| 1954 ................Ed Furgol | 1972 ................Jack Nicklaus | 1990 ................Wayne Levi |
| 1955 ................Doug Ford | 1973 ................Jack Nicklaus | 1991 ................Fred Couples |
| 1956 ................Jack Burke | 1974 ................Johnny Miller | 1992 ................Fred Couples |
| 1957 ................Dick Mayer | 1975 ................Jack Nicklaus | 1993 ................Nick Price |
| 1958 ................Dow Finsterwald | 1976 ................Jack Nicklaus | 1994 ................Nick Price |
| 1959 ................Art Wall | 1977 ................Tom Watson | 1995 ................Greg Norman |
| 1960 ................Arnold Palmer | 1978 ................Tom Watson | 1996 ................Tom Lehman |
| 1961 ................Jerry Barber | 1979 ................Tom Watson | 1997 ................Tiger Woods |
| 1962 ................Arnold Palmer | 1980 ................Tom Watson | 1998 ................David Duval |
| 1963 ................Julius Boros | 1981 ................Bill Rogers | 1999 ................Tiger Woods |
| 1964 ................Ken Venturi | 1982 ................Tom Watson | 2000 ................Tiger Woods |
| 1965 ................Dave Marr | 1983 ................Hal Sutton | |

## Vardon Trophy: Scoring Average

| Year | Winner | Avg | Year | Winner | Avg | Year | Winner | Avg |
|---|---|---|---|---|---|---|---|---|
| 1937 | Harry Cooper | *500 | 1961 | Arnold Palmer | 69.85 | 1981 | Tom Kite | 69.80 |
| 1938 | Sam Snead | 520 | 1962 | Arnold Palmer | 70.27 | 1982 | Tom Kite | 70.21 |
| 1939 | Byron Nelson | 473 | 1963 | Billy Casper | 70.58 | 1983 | Raymond Floyd | 70.61 |
| 1940 | Ben Hogan | 423 | 1964 | Arnold Palmer | 70.01 | 1984 | Calvin Peete | 70.56 |
| 1941 | Ben Hogan | 494 | 1965 | Billy Casper | 70.85 | 1985 | Don Pooley | 70.36 |
| 1942–46 | No award | | 1966 | Billy Casper | 70.27 | 1986 | Scott Hoch | 70.08 |
| 1947 | Jimmy Demaret | 69.90 | 1967 | Arnold Palmer | 70.18 | 1987 | Don Pohl | 70.25 |
| 1948 | Ben Hogan | 69.30 | 1968 | Billy Casper | 69.82 | 1988 | Chip Beck | 69.46 |
| 1949 | Sam Snead | 69.37 | 1969 | Dave Hill | 70.34 | 1989 | Greg Norman | 69.49 |
| 1950 | Sam Snead | 69.23 | 1970 | Lee Trevino | 70.64 | 1990 | Greg Norman | 69.10 |
| 1951 | Lloyd Mangrum | 70.05 | 1971 | Lee Trevino | 70.27 | 1991 | Fred Couples | 69.59 |
| 1952 | Jack Burke | 70.54 | 1972 | Lee Trevino | 70.89 | 1992 | Fred Couples | 69.38 |
| 1953 | Lloyd Mangrum | 70.22 | 1973 | Bruce Crampton | 70.57 | 1993 | Nick Price | 69.11 |
| 1954 | E.J. Harrison | 70.41 | 1974 | Lee Trevino | 70.53 | 1994 | Greg Norman | 68.81 |
| 1955 | Sam Snead | 69.86 | 1975 | Bruce Crampton | 70.51 | 1995 | Steve Elkington | 69.62 |
| 1956 | Cary Middlecoff | 70.35 | 1976 | Don January | 70.56 | 1996 | Tom Lehman | 69.32 |
| 1957 | Dow Finsterwald | 70.30 | 1977 | Tom Watson | 70.32 | 1997 | Nick Price | 68.98 |
| 1958 | Bob Rosburg | 70.11 | 1978 | Tom Watson | 70.16 | 1998 | David Duval | 69.13 |
| 1959 | Art Wall | 70.35 | 1979 | Tom Watson | 70.27 | 1999 | Tiger Woods | 68.43 |
| 1960 | Billy Casper | 69.95 | 1980 | Lee Trevino | 69.73 | 2000 | Tiger Woods | 67.79 |

*Point system used, 1937–41.
Note: As of 1988, based on minimum of 60 rounds per year. Adjusted for average score of field in tournaments entered.

## Alltime PGA Tour Records*

### Scoring

#### 90 HOLES

**324**—(65-61-67-66-65) by Joe Durant, at four courses, La Quinta, CA, to win the 2001 Bob Hope Classic (36 under par).

#### 72 HOLES

**256**—(65-60-64-67) by Mark Calcavecchia, at the TPC at Scottsdale, Scottsdale, AZ, to win the 2001 Phoenix Open (28 under par).

#### 54 HOLES, OPENING ROUNDS

**189**—(64-62-63) by John Cook, at the TPC at Southwind, Memphis, en route to winning the 1996 St. Jude Classic.

#### 54 HOLES, OPENING ROUNDS *(Cont.)*

**189**—(65-60-64) Mark Calcavecchia, at the TPC at Scottsdale, Scottsdale, AZ, en route to winning the 2001 Phoenix Open.

#### 54 HOLES, CONSECUTIVE ROUNDS

**189**—(63-63-63) by Chandler Harper in the last three rounds to win the 1954 Texas Open at Brackenridge Park GC, San Antonio.

**189**—(64-62-63) by John Cook, at the TPC at Southwind, Memphis, in the first three rounds en route to winning the 1996 St. Jude Classic.

**189**—(65-60-64) Mark Calcavecchia, at the TPC at Scottsdale, Scottsdale, AZ, in the first three rounds en route to winning the 2001 Phoenix Open.

## Alltime PGA Tour Records *(Cont.)**

### Scoring *(Cont.)*

#### 36 HOLES, OPENING ROUNDS

**125**—(64–61) by Tiger Woods, in the 2000 World Golf Championships/ NEC Invitational, which he won, at Firestone CC, Akron.

**125**—(65–60) by Mark Calcavecchia, in the 2001 Phoenix Open, which he won, at TPC at Scottsdale, Scottsdale, AZ.

#### 36 HOLES, CONSECUTIVE ROUNDS

**125**—(64–61) by Gay Brewer, in the middle rounds
of    the 1967 Pensacola Open, which he won, at Pensacola CC, Pensacola, FL.

**125**—(63–62) by Ron Streck, in the last two rounds to win the 1978 Texas Open at Oak Hills CC, San Antonio.

**125**—(62–63) by Blaine McCallister, in the middle two rounds of the 1988 Hardee's Golf Classic, which he won at Oakwood CC, Coal Valley, IL.

**125**—(62–63) by John Cook, in the middle two rounds of the 1996 St. Jude Classic, which he won at the TPC at Southwind, Memphis.

**125**—(62–63) by John Cook, in the fourth and fifth rounds in winning the 1997 Bob Hope Chrysler Classic at Indian Wells CC, Indian Hills, CA.

**125**—(64–61) by Tiger Woods, in the first two rounds of the 2000 World Golf Championship/ NEC Invitational, which he won, at Firestone CC, Akron.

**125**—(65–60) by Mark Calcavecchia, in the first two rounds of the 2001 Phoenix Open, which he won, at TPC at Scottsdale, Scottsdale, AZ.

#### 18 HOLES

**59**—by Al Geiberger, at Colonial Country Club, Memphis, in second round in winning the 1977 Memphis Classic.

**59**—by Chip Beck, at Sunrise Golf Club, Las Vegas, in third round of the 1991 Las Vegas Invitational.

**59**—by David Duval, on the Palmer Course at PGA West, La Quinta, CA, in the fifth round of the 1999 Bob Hope Chrysler Classic.

#### 9 HOLES

**27**—by Mike Souchak, at Brackenridge Park GC, San Antonio, on par-35 second nine of first round in the 1955 Texas Open.

**27**—by Andy North, at En-Joie GC, Endicott, NY, on par-34 second nine of first round in the 1975 BC Open.

**27**—by Billy Mayfair, at Warwick Hills, Grand Blanc, MI, on par-36 back nine of fourth round, 2001 Buick Open.

#### MOST CONSECUTIVE ROUNDS UNDER 70

**19**—Byron Nelson in 1945.

#### MOST BIRDIES IN A ROW

**8**—Bob Goalby, at Pasadena GC, St. Petersburg, FL, during fourth round in winning the 1961 St Petersburg Open.

**8**—Fuzzy Zoeller, at Oakwood CC, Coal Valley, IL, during first round of 1976 Quad Cities Open.

**8**—Dewey Arnette, at Warwick Hills GC, Grand Blanc, MI, during first round of the 1987 Buick Open.

**8**—Edward Fryatt, at the Blue Course of the Doral Resort and Spa, Miami, during second round of the 2000 Doral-Ryder Open.

#### MOST BIRDIES IN A ROW TO WIN

**5**—Jack Nicklaus, to win 1978 Jackie Gleason Inverrary Classic (last 5 holes).

### Wins

#### MOST CONSECUTIVE YEARS WINNING AT LEAST ONE TOURNAMENT

**17**—Jack Nicklaus, 1962–78.

**17**—Arnold Palmer, 1955–71.

**16**—Billy Casper, 1956–71.

#### MOST CONSECUTIVE WINS

**11**—Byron Nelson, from Miami Four Ball, March 8–11, 1945, through Canadian Open, August 2–4, 1945.

#### MOST WINS IN A SINGLE EVENT

**8**—Sam Snead, Greater Greensboro Open, 1938, 1946, 1949, 1950, 1955, 1956, 1960, and 1965.

#### MOST CONSECUTIVE WINS IN A SINGLE EVENT

**4**—Walter Hagen, PGA Championships, 1924–27.

**4**—Gene Sarazen, Miami Open, 1926, (schedule change) 1928–30.

#### MOST WINS IN A CALENDAR YEAR

**18**—Byron Nelson, 1945

#### MOST YEARS BETWEEN WINS

**15 yrs, 5 mos**—Butch Baird, 1961–76.

#### MOST YEARS FROM FIRST WIN TO LAST

**28 yrs, 11 mos, 20 days**—Raymond Floyd, 1963–92.

#### YOUNGEST WINNERS

**19 yrs, 10 mos**—John McDermott, 1911 U.S. Open.

#### OLDEST WINNER

**52 yrs, 10 mos**—Sam Snead, 1965 Greater Greensboro Open.

#### WIDEST WINNING MARGIN: STROKES

**16**—Bobby Locke, 1948 Chicago Victory National Championship.

### Putting

#### FEWEST PUTTS, ONE ROUND

**18**—Andy North, at Kingsmill GC, in second round of 1990 Anheuser Busch Golf Classic.

**18**—Kenny Knox, at Harbour Town GL, in first round of 1989 MCI Heritage Classic.

**18**—Mike McGee, at Colonial CC, in first round of 1987 Federal Express St. Jude Classic.

**18**—Sam Trahan, at Whitemarsh Valley CC, in final round of 1979 IVB Philadelphia Golf Classic.

**18**—Jim McGovern, at TPC at Southwind, in second round of 1992 Federal Express St. Jude Classic.

#### FEWEST PUTTS, FOUR ROUNDS

**93**—Kenny Knox, in 1989 MCI Heritage Classic at Harbour Town GL.

*Through 10/22/01.

# THE MAJOR TOURNAMENTS

## LPGA Championship

| Year | Winner | Score | Runner-Up | Site |
|------|--------|-------|-----------|------|
| 1955 | Beverly Hanson† (4 & 3) | 220 | Louise Suggs | Orchard Ridge CC, Ft Wayne, IN |
| 1956 | Marlene Hagge* | 291 | Patty Berg | Forest Lake CC, Detroit |
| 1957 | Louise Suggs | 285 | Wiffi Smith | Churchill Valley CC, Pittsburgh |
| 1958 | Mickey Wright | 288 | Fay Crocker | Churchill Valley CC, Pittsburgh |
| 1959 | Betsy Rawls | 288 | Patty Berg | Sheraton Hotel CC, French Lick, IN |
| 1960 | Mickey Wright | 292 | Louise Suggs | Sheraton Hotel CC, French Lick, IN |
| 1961 | Mickey Wright | 287 | Louise Suggs | Stardust CC, Las Vegas |
| 1962 | Judy Kimball | 282 | Shirley Spork | Stardust CC, Las Vegas |
| 1963 | Mickey Wright | 294 | Mary Lena Faulk Mary Mills Louise Suggs | Stardust CC, Las Vegas |
| 1964 | Mary Mills | 278 | Mickey Wright | Stardust CC, Las Vegas |
| 1965 | Sandra Haynie | 279 | Clifford A. Creed | Stardust CC, Las Vegas |
| 1966 | Gloria Ehret | 282 | Mickey Wright | Stardust CC, Las Vegas |
| 1967 | Kathy Whitworth | 284 | Shirley Englehorn | Pleasant Valley CC, Sutton, MA |
| 1968 | Sandra Post* (68) | 294 | Kathy Whitworth (75) | Pleasant Valley CC, Sutton, MA |
| 1969 | Betsy Rawls | 293 | Susie Berning Carol Mann | Concord GC, Kiameshia Lake, NY |
| 1970 | Shirley Englehorn* (74) | 285 | Kathy Whitworth (78) | Pleasant Valley CC, Sutton, MA |
| 1971 | Kathy Whitworth | 288 | Kathy Ahern | Pleasant Valley CC, Sutton, MA |
| 1972 | Kathy Ahern | 293 | Jane Blalock | Pleasant Valley CC, Sutton, MA |
| 1973 | Mary Mills | 288 | Betty Burfeindt | Pleasant Valley CC, Sutton, MA |
| 1974 | Sandra Haynie | 288 | JoAnne Carner | Pleasant Valley CC, Sutton, MA |
| 1975 | Kathy Whitworth | 288 | Sandra Haynie | Pine Ridge GC, Baltimore |
| 1976 | Betty Burfeindt | 287 | Judy Rankin | Pine Ridge GC, Baltimore |
| 1977 | Chako Higuchi | 279 | Pat Bradley Sandra Post Judy Rankin | Bay Tree Golf Plantation, N Myrtle Beach, SC |
| 1978 | Nancy Lopez | 275 | Amy Alcott | Jack Nicklaus GC, Kings Island, OH |
| 1979 | Donna Caponi | 279 | Jerilyn Britz | Jack Nicklaus GC, Kings Island, OH |
| 1980 | Sally Little | 285 | Jane Blalock | Jack Nicklaus GC, Kings Island, OH |
| 1981 | Donna Caponi | 280 | Jerilyn Britz Pat Meyers | Jack Nicklaus GC, Kings Island, OH |
| 1982 | Jan Stephenson | 279 | JoAnne Carner | Jack Nicklaus GC, Kings Island, OH |
| 1983 | Patty Sheehan | 279 | Sandra Haynie | Jack Nicklaus GC, Kings Island, OH |
| 1984 | Patty Sheehan | 272 | Beth Daniel Pat Bradley | Jack Nicklaus GC, Kings Island, OH |
| 1985 | Nancy Lopez | 273 | Alice Miller | Jack Nicklaus GC, Kings Island, OH |
| 1986 | Pat Bradley | 277 | Patty Sheehan | Jack Nicklaus GC, Kings Island, OH |
| 1987 | Jane Geddes | 275 | Betsy King | Jack Nicklaus GC, Kings Island, OH |
| 1988 | Sherri Turner | 281 | Amy Alcott | Jack Nicklaus GC, Kings Island, OH |
| 1989 | Nancy Lopez | 274 | Ayako Okamoto | Jack Nicklaus GC, Kings Island, OH |
| 1990 | Beth Daniel | 280 | Rosie Jones | Bethesda CC, Bethesda, MD |
| 1991 | Meg Mallon | 274 | Pat Bradley Ayako Okamoto | Bethesda CC, Bethesda, MD |
| 1992 | Betsy King | 267 | Karen Noble | Bethesda CC, Bethesda, MD |
| 1993 | Patty Sheehan | 275 | Lauri Merten | Bethesda CC, Bethesda, MD |
| 1994 | Laura Davies | 279 | Alice Ritzman | DuPont CC, Wilmington, DE |
| 1995 | Kelly Robbins | 274 | Laura Davies | DuPont CC, Wilmington, DE |
| 1996 | Laura Davies | 213† | Julie Piers | DuPont CC, Wilmington, DE |
| 1997 | Chris Johnson* | 281 | Leta Lindley | DuPont CC, Wilmington, DE |
| 1998 | Se Ri Pak | 273 | Donna Andrews | DuPont CC, Wilmington, DE |
| 1999 | Juli Inkster | 268 | Liselotte Neumann | DuPont CC, Wilmington, DE |
| 2000 | Juli Inkster* | 281 | Stefania Croce | DuPont CC, Wilmington, DE |
| 2001 | Karrie Webb | 270 | Laura Diaz | DuPont CC, Wilmington, DE |

*Won in playoff. Playoff scores are in parentheses. 1956 and 1997 were sudden death; 1968 and 1970 were 18-hole playoffs. †Won match-play final. #Shortened due to rain.

## U.S. Women's Open

| Year | Winner | Score | Runner-Up | Site |
|------|--------|-------|-----------|------|
| 1946 | Patty Berg | 5 & 4 | Betty Jameson | Spokane CC, Spokane, WA |
| 1947 | Betty Jameson | 295 | Sally Sessions | Starmount Forest CC, Greensboro, NC |
| | | | Polly Riley | |
| 1948 | Babe Zaharias | 300 | Betty Hicks | Atlantic City CC, Northfield, NJ |
| 1949 | Louise Suggs | 291 | Babe Zaharias | Prince George's G & CC, Landover, MD |
| 1950 | Babe Zaharias | 291 | Betsy Rawls | Rolling Hills GC, Wichita, KS |
| 1951 | Betsy Rawls | 293 | Louise Suggs | Druid Hills GC, Atlanta |
| 1952 | Louise Suggs | 284 | Marlene Bauer | Bala GC, Philadelphia |
| | | | Betty Jameson | |
| 1953 | Betsy Rawls* (71) | 302 | Jackie Pung (77) | CC of Rochester, Rochester, NY |
| 1954 | Babe Zaharias | 291 | Betty Hicks | Salem CC, Peabody, MA |
| 1955 | Fay Crocker | 299 | Mary Lena Faulk | Wichita CC, Wichita, KS |
| | | | Louise Suggs | |
| 1956 | Kathy Cornelius* (75) | 302 | Barbara McIntire (82) | Northland CC, Duluth, MN |
| 1957 | Betsy Rawls | 299 | Patty Berg | Winged Foot GC, Mamaroneck, NY |
| 1958 | Mickey Wright | 290 | Louise Suggs | Forest Lake CC, Detroit |
| 1959 | Mickey Wright | 287 | Louise Suggs | Churchill Valley CC, Pittsburgh |
| 1960 | Betsy Rawls | 292 | Joyce Ziske | Worcester CC, Worcester, MA |
| 1961 | Mickey Wright | 293 | Betsy Rawls | Baltusrol GC (Lower Course), Springfield, NJ |
| 1962 | Murle Breer | 301 | Jo Ann Prentice | Dunes GC, Myrtle Beach, SC |
| | | | Ruth Jessen | |
| 1963 | Mary Mills | 289 | Sandra Haynie | Kenwood CC, Cincinnati |
| | | | Louise Suggs | |
| 1964 | Mickey Wright* (70) | 290 | Ruth Jessen (72) | San Diego CC, Chula Vista, CA |
| 1965 | Carol Mann | 290 | Kathy Cornelius | Atlantic City CC, Northfield, NJ |
| 1966 | Sandra Spuzich | 297 | Carol Mann | Hazeltine Natl GC, Chaska, MN |
| 1967 | Catherine LaCoste | 294 | Susie Berning | Hot Springs GC (Cascades Course), |
| | | | Beth Stone | Hot Springs, VA |
| 1968 | Susie Berning | 289 | Mickey Wright | Moslem Springs GC, Fleetwood, PA |
| 1969 | Donna Caponi | 294 | Peggy Wilson | Scenic Hills CC, Pensacola, FL |
| 1970 | Donna Caponi | 287 | Sandra Haynie | Muskogee CC, Muskogee, OK |
| | | | Sandra Spuzich | |
| 1971 | JoAnne Carner | 288 | Kathy Whitworth | Kahkwa CC, Erie, PA |
| 1972 | Susie Berning | 299 | Kathy Ahern | Winged Foot GC, Mamaroneck, NY |
| | | | Pam Barnett | |
| | | | Judy Rankin | |
| 1973 | Susie Berning | 290 | Gloria Ehret | CC of Rochester, Rochester, NY |
| | | | Shelley Hamlin | |
| 1974 | Sandra Haynie | 295 | Carol Mann | La Grange CC, La Grange, IL |
| | | | Beth Stone | |
| 1975 | Sandra Palmer | 295 | JoAnne Carner | Atlantic City CC, Northfield, NJ |
| | | | Sandra Post | |
| | | | Nancy Lopez | |
| 1976 | JoAnne Carner* (76) | 292 | Sandra Palmer (78) | Rolling Green CC, Springfield, PA |
| 1977 | Hollis Stacy | 292 | Nancy Lopez | Hazeltine Natl GC, Chaska, MN |
| 1978 | Hollis Stacy | 289 | JoAnne Carner | CC of Indianapolis, Indianapolis |
| | | | Sally Little | |
| 1979 | Jerilyn Britz | 284 | Debbie Massey | Brooklawn CC, Fairfield, CT |
| | | | Sandra Palmer | |
| 1980 | Amy Alcott | 280 | Hollis Stacy | Richland CC, Nashville |
| 1981 | Pat Bradley | 279 | Beth Daniel | La Grange CC, La Grange, IL |
| 1982 | Janet Anderson | 283 | Beth Daniel | Del Paso CC, Sacramento |
| | | | Sandra Haynie | |
| | | | Donna White | |
| | | | JoAnne Carner | |
| 1983 | Jan Stephenson | 290 | JoAnne Carner | Cedar Ridge CC, Tulsa |
| | | | Patty Sheehan | |
| 1984 | Hollis Stacy | 290 | Rosie Jones | Salem CC, Peabody, MA |
| 1985 | Kathy Baker | 280 | Judy Dickinson | Baltusrol GC (Upper Course), Springfield, NJ |
| 1986 | Jane Geddes* (71) | 287 | Sally Little (73) | NCR GC, Dayton |
| 1987 | Laura Davies* (71) | 285 | Ayako Okamoto (73) | Plainfield CC, Plainfield, NJ |
| | | | JoAnne Carner (74) | |
| 1988 | Liselotte Neumann | 277 | Patty Sheehan | Baltimore CC, Baltimore |
| 1989 | Betsy King | 278 | Nancy Lopez | Indianwood G & CC, Lake Orion, MI |
| 1990 | Betsy King | 284 | Patty Sheehan | Atlanta Athletic Club, Duluth, GA |
| 1991 | Meg Mallon | 283 | Pat Bradley | Colonial Club, Fort Worth |

## U.S. Women's Open (Cont.)

| Year | Winner | Score | Runner-Up | Site |
|---|---|---|---|---|
| 1992 | Patty Sheehan* (72) | 280 | Juli Inkster | Oakmont CC, Oakmont, PA |
| 1993 | Lauri Merten | 280 | Donna Andrew | Crooked Stick, Carmel, IN |
| | | | Helen Alfredsson | |
| 1994 | Patty Sheehan | 277 | Tammie Green | Indianwood G & CC, Lake Orion, MI |
| 1995 | Annika Sorenstam | 278 | Meg Mallon | The Broadmoor GC, Colorado Springs, CO |
| 1996 | Annika Sorenstam | 272 | Kris Tschetter | Pine Needles GC, Southern Pines, NC |
| 1997 | Alison Nicholas | 274 | Nancy Lopez | Pumpkin Ridge CC, North Plains, OR |
| 1998 | Se Ri Pak† | 290 | Jenny Chuasiriporn | Blackwolf Run Golf Resort, Kohler, WI |
| 1999 | Juli Inkster | 272 | Sherri Turner | Old Waverly GC, West Point, MS |
| 2000 | Karrie Webb | 282 | Cristie Kerr | Merit GC, Libertyville, IL |
| | | | Meg Mallon | |
| 2001 | Karrie Webb | 273 | Se Ri Pak | Pine Needles GC, Southern Pines, NC |

* Winner in playoff; 18-hole playoff scores are in parentheses. † Winner on second hole of sudden death after 18-hole playoff ended in a tie.

## Nabisco Championship

| Year | Winner | Score | Runner-Up | Year | Winner | Score | Runner-Up |
|---|---|---|---|---|---|---|---|
| 1972 | Jane Blalock | 213 | Carol Mann | 1988 | Amy Alcott | 274 | Colleen Walker |
| | | | Judy Rankin | 1989 | Juli Inkster | 279 | Tammie Green |
| 1973 | Mickey Wright | 284 | Joyce Kazmierski | | | | JoAnne Carner |
| 1974 | Jo Ann Prentice* | 289 | Jane Blalock | 1990 | Betsy King | 283 | Kathy Postlewait |
| | | | Sandra Haynie | | | | Shirley Furlong |
| 1975 | Sandra Palmer | 283 | Kathy McMullen | 1991 | Amy Alcott | 273 | Dottie Mochrie |
| 1976 | Judy Rankin | 285 | Betty Burfeindt | 1992 | Dottie Mochrie* | 279 | Juli Inkster |
| 1977 | Kathy Whitworth | 289 | JoAnne Carner | 1993 | Helen Alfredsson | 284 | Amy Benz |
| | | | Sally Little | | | | Tina Barrett |
| 1978 | Sandra Post* | 283 | Penny Pulz | | | | Betsy King |
| 1979 | Sandra Post | 276 | Nancy Lopez | 1994 | Donna Andrews | 276 | Laura Davies |
| 1980 | Donna Caponi | 275 | Amy Alcott | 1995 | Nanci Bowen | 285 | Susie Redman |
| 1981 | Nancy Lopez | 277 | Carolyn Hill | 1996 | Patti Sheehan | 281 | Kelly Robbins |
| 1982 | Sally Little | 278 | Hollis Stacy | | | | Meg Mallon |
| | | | Sandra Haynie | | | | Annika Sörenstam |
| 1983 | Amy Alcott | 282 | Beth Daniel | 1997 | Betsy King | 276 | Kris Tschetter |
| | | | Kathy Whitworth | 1998 | Pat Hurst | 281 | Helen Dobson |
| 1984 | Juli Inkster* | 280 | Pat Bradley | 1999 | Dottie Pepper | 269 | Meg Mallon |
| 1985 | Alice Miller | 275 | Jan Stephenson | 2000 | Karrie Webb | 274 | Dottie Pepper |
| 1986 | Pat Bradley | 280 | Val Skinner | 2001 | Annika Sorenstam | 281 | five players |
| 1987 | Betsy King* | 283 | Patty Sheehan | | | | |

*Winner in sudden-death playoff. Note: Designated fourth major in 1983; played at Mission Hills CC, Rancho Mirage, CA.

## du Maurier Classic

| Year | Winner | Score | Runner-Up | Site |
|---|---|---|---|---|
| 1973 | Jocelyne Bourassa* | 214 | Sandra Haynie | Montreal GC, Montreal |
| | | | Judy Rankin | |
| 1974 | Carole Jo Callison | 208 | JoAnne Carner | Candiac GC, Montreal |
| 1975 | JoAnne Carner* | 214 | Carol Mann | St. George's CC, Toronto |
| 1976 | Donna Caponi* | 212 | Judy Rankin | Cedar Brae G & CC, Toronto |
| 1977 | Judy Rankin | 214 | Pat Meyers | Lachute G & CC, Montreal |
| | | | Sandra Palmer | |
| 1978 | JoAnne Carner | 278 | Hollis Stacy | St. George's CC, Toronto |
| 1979 | Amy Alcott | 285 | Nancy Lopez | Richelieu Valley CC, Montreal |
| 1980 | Pat Bradley | 277 | JoAnne Carner | St. George's CC, Toronto |
| 1981 | Jan Stephenson | 278 | Nancy Lopez | Summerlea CC, Dorion, Quebec |
| | | | Pat Bradley | |
| 1982 | Sandra Haynie | 280 | Beth Daniel | St. George's CC, Toronto |
| 1983 | Hollis Stacy | 277 | JoAnne Carner | Beaconsfield GC, Montreal |
| | | | Alice Miller | |
| 1984 | Juli Inkster | 279 | Ayako Okamoto | St. George's G & CC, Toronto |
| 1985 | Pat Bradley | 278 | Jane Geddes | Beaconsfield CC, Montreal |
| 1986 | Pat Bradley* | 276 | Ayako Okamoto | Board of Trade CC, Toronto |
| 1987 | Jody Rosenthal | 272 | Ayako Okamoto | Islesmere GC, Laval, Quebec |
| 1988 | Sally Little | 279 | Laura Davies | Vancouver GC, Coquitlam, British Columbia |
| 1989 | Tammie Green | 279 | Pat Bradley | Beaconsfield GC, Montreal |
| | | | Betsy King | |

## du Maurier Classic (Cont.)

| Year | Winner | Score | Runner-Up | Site |
|------|--------|-------|-----------|------|
| 1990 | Cathy Johnston | 276 | Patty Sheehan | Westmount G & CC, Kitchener, Ontario |
| 1991 | Nancy Scranton | 279 | Debbie Massey | Vancouver GC, Coquitlam, British Columbia |
| 1992 | Sherri Steinhauer | 277 | Judy Dickinson | St. Charles CC, Winnipeg, Manitoba |
| 1993 | Brandie Burton | 277 | Betsy King | London Hunt and CC, London, Ontario |
| 1994 | Martha Nause | 279 | Michelle McGann | Ottawa Hunt and GC, Ottawa, Ont. |
| 1995 | Jenny Lidback | 280 | Liselotte Neumann | Beaconsfield GC, Pointe-Claire, Quebec |
| 1996 | Laura Davies | 277 | Nancy Lopez<br>Karrie Webb | Edmonton CC, Edmonton, Alberta |
| 1997 | Colleen Walker | 278 | Liselotte Neumann | Glen Abbey GC, Oakville, Ontario |
| 1998 | Brandie Burton | 270 | Annika Sorenstam | Essex G & CC, Windsor, Ontario |
| 1999 | Karrie Webb | 277 | Laura Davies | Priddis Greens G & CC, Calgary, Alberta |
| 2000 | Meg Mallon | 282 | Rosie Jones | Royal Ottawa GC, Aylmer, Quebec |

*Winner in sudden-death playoff. Note: Designated third major in 1979; discontinued in 2001.

## Women's British Open

| Year | Winner | Score | Runner-Up | Site |
|------|--------|-------|-----------|------|
| 2001 | Se Ri Pak | 277 | Mi Hyun Kim | Sunningdale GC, Berkshire, England |

Note: Designated fourth major in 2001.

## Alltime Major Championship Winners

| | LPGA | U.S. Open | Dinah Shore | ‡du Maurier | #Titleholders | †Western | U.S. Am | British Am | Total |
|---|------|-----------|-------------|-------------|---------------|----------|---------|------------|-------|
| Patty Berg | 0 | 1 | 0 | 0 | 7 | 7 | 1 | 0 | 16 |
| Mickey Wright | 4 | 4 | 0 | 0 | 2 | 3 | 0 | 0 | 13 |
| Louise Suggs | 1 | 2 | 0 | 0 | 4 | 4 | 1 | 1 | 13 |
| Babe Zaharias | 0 | 3 | 0 | 0 | 3 | 4 | 1 | 1 | 12 |
| *Juli Inkster | 2 | 1 | 2 | 1 | 0 | 0 | 3 | 0 | 9 |
| Betsy Rawls | 2 | 4 | 0 | 0 | 0 | 2 | 0 | 0 | 8 |
| *JoAnne Carner | 0 | 2 | 0 | 0 | 0 | 0 | 5 | 0 | 7 |
| Kathy Whitworth | 3 | 0 | 0 | 0 | 2 | 1 | 0 | 0 | 6 |
| Pat Bradley | 1 | 1 | 1 | 3 | 0 | 0 | 0 | 0 | 6 |
| *Patty Sheehan | 3 | 2 | 1 | 0 | 0 | 0 | 0 | 0 | 6 |
| Glenna Vare | 0 | 0 | 0 | 0 | 0 | 0 | 6 | 0 | 6 |
| *Betsy King | 1 | 2 | 3 | 0 | 0 | 0 | 0 | 0 | 6 |

*Active LPGA player.
#Major from 1937–1972. †Major from 1937–1967. ‡Major from 1979–2000.

## Alltime Multiple Professional Major Winners

### LPGA

| | |
|---|---|
| Mickey Wright | 4 |
| Nancy Lopez | 3 |
| Patty Sheehan | 3 |
| Kathy Whitworth | 3 |
| Donna Caponi | 2 |
| Sandra Haynie | 2 |
| Mary Mills | 2 |
| Betsy Rawls | 2 |
| Laura Davies | 2 |
| Juli Inkster | 2 |

### U.S. OPEN

| | |
|---|---|
| Betsy Rawls | 4 |
| Mickey Wright | 4 |
| Susie Maxwell Berning | 3 |

### U.S. OPEN (Cont.)

| | |
|---|---|
| Hollis Stacy | 3 |
| Babe Zaharias | 3 |
| JoAnne Carner | 2 |
| Donna Caponi | 2 |
| Betsy King | 2 |
| Patty Sheehan | 2 |
| Louise Suggs | 2 |
| Annika Sorenstam | 2 |
| Karrie Webb | 2 |

### NABISCO/DINAH SHORE

| | |
|---|---|
| Amy Alcott | 3 |
| Betsy King | 3 |
| Juli Inkster | 2 |

### DU MAURIER

| | |
|---|---|
| Pat Bradley | 3 |
| Brandie Burton | 2 |
| JoAnne Carner | 2 |

### TITLEHOLDERS

| | |
|---|---|
| Patty Berg | 7 |
| Louise Suggs | 4 |
| Babe Zaharias | 3 |
| Dorothy Kirby | 2 |
| Marilynn Smith | 2 |
| Kathy Whitworth | 2 |
| Mickey Wright | 2 |

### WESTERN OPEN

| | |
|---|---|
| Patty Berg | 7 |
| Louise Suggs | 4 |
| Babe Zaharias | 4 |
| Mickey Wright | 3 |
| June Beebe | 2 |
| Opal Hill | 2 |
| Betty Jameson | 2 |
| Betsy Rawls | 2 |

# THE LPGA TOUR

## Most Career Wins†

| | Wins | | Wins | | Wins |
|---|---|---|---|---|---|
| Kathy Whitworth | 88 | Sandra Haynie | 42 | *Amy Alcott | 29 |
| Mickey Wright | 82 | Babe Zaharias | 41 | *Annika Sorenstam | 29 |
| Patty Berg | 57 | Carol Mann | 38 | Jane Blalock | 27 |
| Betsy Rawls | 55 | *Patty Sheehan | 35 | Judy Rankin | 26 |
| Louise Suggs | 50 | *Betsy King | 35 | *Juli Inkster | 26 |
| *Nancy Lopez | 48 | *Beth Daniel | 32 | *Karrie Webb | 26 |
| *JoAnne Carner | 43 | Pat Bradley | 31 | | |

*Active LPGA player. †Through 10/14/01.

## Season Money Leaders

| | Earnings ($) | | Earnings ($) | | Earnings ($) |
|---|---|---|---|---|---|
| 1950...Babe Zaharias | 14,800 | 1967...Kathy Whitworth | 32,937 | 1984...Betsy King | 266,771 |
| 1951...Babe Zaharias | 15,087 | 1968...Kathy Whitworth | 48,379 | 1985...Nancy Lopez | 416,472 |
| 1952...Betsy Rawls | 14,505 | 1969...Carol Mann | 49,152 | 1986...Pat Bradley | 492,021 |
| 1953...Louise Suggs | 19,816 | 1970...Kathy Whitworth | 30,235 | 1987...Ayako Okamoto | 466,034 |
| 1954...Patty Berg | 16,011 | 1971...Kathy Whitworth | 41,181 | 1988...Sherri Turner | 350,851 |
| 1955...Patty Berg | 16,492 | 1972...Kathy Whitworth | 65,063 | 1989...Betsy King | 654,132 |
| 1956...Marlene Hagge | 20,235 | 1973...Kathy Whitworth | 82,864 | 1990...Beth Daniel | 863,578 |
| 1957...Patty Berg | 16,272 | 1974...JoAnne Carner | 87,094 | 1991...Pat Bradley | 763,118 |
| 1958...Beverly Hanson | 12,639 | 1975...Sandra Palmer | 76,374 | 1992...Dottie Mochrie | 693,335 |
| 1959...Betsy Rawls | 26,774 | 1976...Judy Rankin | 150,734 | 1993...Betsy King | 595,992 |
| 1960...Louise Suggs | 16,892 | 1977...Judy Rankin | 122,890 | 1994...Laura Davies | 687,201 |
| 1961...Mickey Wright | 22,236 | 1978...Nancy Lopez | 189,814 | 1995...Annika Sorenstam | 666,533 |
| 1962...Mickey Wright | 21,641 | 1979...Nancy Lopez | 197,489 | 1996...Karrie Webb | 1,002,000 |
| 1963...Mickey Wright | 31,269 | 1980...Beth Daniel | 231,000 | 1997...Annika Sorenstam | 1,236,789 |
| 1964...Mickey Wright | 29,800 | 1981...Beth Daniel | 206,998 | 1998...Annika Sorenstam | 1,092,748 |
| 1965...Kathy Whitworth | 28,658 | 1982...JoAnne Carner | 310,400 | 1999...Karrie Webb | 1,591,959 |
| 1966...Kathy Whitworth | 33,517 | 1983...JoAnne Carner | 291,404 | 2000...Karrie Webb | 1,876,853 |

## Career Money Leaders†

| | Earnings ($) | | Earnings ($) | | Earnings ($) |
|---|---|---|---|---|---|
| 1. Annika Sorenstam | 7,885,464 | 11. Patty Sheehan | 5,504,005 | 21. Chris Johnson | 3,405,354 |
| 2. Karrie Webb | 7,483,299 | 12. Nancy Lopez | 5,310,391 | 22. Amy Alcott | 3,385,486 |
| 3. Betsy King | 7,144,444 | 13. Kelly Robbins | 4,428,314 | 23. Michelle McGann | 3,128,228 |
| 4. Dottie Pepper | 6,636,963 | 14. Liselotte Neumann | 4,205,822 | 24. Donna Andrews | 3,007,519 |
| 5. Juli Inkster | 6,496,737 | 15. Se Ri Pak | 3,912,481 | 25. Jan Stephenson | 2,992,593 |
| 6. Beth Daniel | 6,423,501 | 16. Sherri Steinhauer | 3,802,527 | 26. JoAnne Carner | 2,950,253 |
| 7. Meg Mallon | 5,904,573 | 17. Jane Geddes | 3,736,152 | 27. D. Ammaccapane | 2,857,420 |
| 8. Pat Bradley | 5,743,605 | 18. Tammie Green | 3,590,042 | 28. Ayako Okamoto | 2,749,508 |
| 9. Rosie Jones | 5,626,934 | 19. Lorie Kane | 3,500,965 | 29. Colleen Walker | 2,747,278 |
| 10. Laura Davies | 5,551,335 | 20. Brandie Burton | 3,442,242 | 30. Dawn Coe-Jones | 2,740,400 |

†Through 10/14/01.

## LPGA Player of the Year

| 1966 | Kathy Whitworth | 1978 | Nancy Lopez | 1990 | Beth Daniel |
|---|---|---|---|---|---|
| 1967 | Kathy Whitworth | 1979 | Nancy Lopez | 1991 | Pat Bradley |
| 1968 | Kathy Whitworth | 1980 | Beth Daniel | 1992 | Dottie Mochrie |
| 1969 | Kathy Whitworth | 1981 | JoAnne Carner | 1993 | Betsy King |
| 1970 | Sandra Haynie | 1982 | JoAnne Carner | 1994 | Beth Daniel |
| 1971 | Kathy Whitworth | 1983 | Patty Sheehan | 1995 | Annika Sörenstam |
| 1972 | Kathy Whitworth | 1984 | Betsy King | 1996 | Laura Davies |
| 1973 | Kathy Whitworth | 1985 | Nancy Lopez | 1997 | Annika Sorenstam |
| 1974 | JoAnne Carner | 1986 | Pat Bradley | 1998 | Annika Sorenstam |
| 1975 | Sandra Palmer | 1987 | Ayako Okamoto | 1999 | Karrie Webb |
| 1976 | Judy Rankin | 1988 | Nancy Lopez | 2000 | Karrie Webb |
| 1977 | Judy Rankin | 1989 | Betsy King | | |

## Vare Trophy: Best Scoring Average

| | | Avg | | | Avg | | | Avg |
|---|---|---|---|---|---|---|---|---|
| 1953 | Patty Berg | 75.00 | 1969 | Kathy Whitworth | 72.38 | 1985 | Nancy Lopez | 70.73 |
| 1954 | Babe Zaharias | 75.48 | 1970 | Kathy Whitworth | 72.26 | 1986 | Pat Bradley | 71.10 |
| 1955 | Patty Berg | 74.47 | 1971 | Kathy Whitworth | 72.88 | 1987 | Betsy King | 71.14 |
| 1956 | Patty Berg | 74.57 | 1972 | Kathy Whitworth | 72.38 | 1988 | Colleen Walker | 71.26 |
| 1957 | Louise Suggs | 74.64 | 1973 | Judy Rankin | 73.08 | 1989 | Beth Daniel | 70.38 |
| 1958 | Beverly Hanson | 74.92 | 1974 | JoAnne Carner | 72.87 | 1990 | Beth Daniel | 70.54 |
| 1959 | Betsy Rawls | 74.03 | 1975 | JoAnne Carner | 72.40 | 1991 | Pat Bradley | 70.76 |
| 1960 | Mickey Wright | 73.25 | 1976 | Judy Rankin | 72.25 | 1992 | Dottie Mochrie | 70.80 |
| 1961 | Mickey Wright | 73.55 | 1977 | Judy Rankin | 72.16 | 1993 | Nancy Lopez | 70.83 |
| 1962 | Mickey Wright | 73.67 | 1978 | Nancy Lopez | 71.76 | 1994 | Beth Daniel | 70.90 |
| 1963 | Mickey Wright | 72.81 | 1979 | Nancy Lopez | 71.20 | 1995 | Annika Sorenstam | 71.00 |
| 1964 | Mickey Wright | 72.46 | 1980 | Amy Alcott | 71.51 | 1996 | Annika Sorenstam | 70.47 |
| 1965 | Kathy Whitworth | 72.61 | 1981 | JoAnne Carner | 71.75 | 1997 | Karrie Webb | 70.00 |
| 1966 | Kathy Whitworth | 72.60 | 1982 | JoAnne Carner | 71.49 | 1998 | Annika Sorenstam | 69.99 |
| 1967 | Kathy Whitworth | 72.74 | 1983 | JoAnne Carner | 71.41 | 1999 | Karrie Webb | 69.43 |
| 1968 | Carol Mann | 72.04 | 1984 | Patty Sheehan | 71.40 | 2000 | Karrie Webb | 70.05 |

## Alltime LPGA Tour Records†

### Scoring

#### 72 HOLES

**261**—(71-61-63-66) by Se Ri Pak to win at the Highland Meadows CC, Sylvania, OH, in the 1998 Jamie Farr Kroger Classic (23 under par).

**261**—(65-59-69-68) by Annika Sorenstam to win at the Moon Valley CC, Phoenix, in the 2001 Standard Register PING (27 under par).

#### 54 HOLES

**193**—(66-61-66) by Karrie Webb to lead at the Walnut Hills CC, East Lansing, MI, in the 2000 Oldsmobile Classic (23 under par).

**193**—(65-59-69) by Annika Sorenstam to lead at the Moon Valley CC, Phoenix, in the 2001 Standard Register PING (23 under par)

#### 36 HOLES

**124**—(65-59) by Annika Sorenstam to lead at the Moon Valley CC, Phoenix, in the 2001 Standard Register PING (20 under par).

#### 18 HOLES

**59**—by Annika Sorenstam at the Moon Valley CC, Phoenix, in the second round in winning the 2001 Standard Register PING (13 under par).

#### 9 HOLES

**28**—by Mary Beth Zimmerman at Rail GC, 1984 Rail Charity Golf Classic, Springfield, IL (par 36). Zimmerman shot 64.

**28**—by Pat Bradley at Green Gables CC, Denver, 1984 Columbia Savings Classic (par 35). Bradley shot 65.

**28**—by Muffin Spencer-Devlin at Knollwood CC, Elmsford, NY, in winning the 1985 MasterCard International Pro-Am (par 35). Spencer-Devlin shot 64.

†Through 10/14/01.

### Scoring (Cont.)

#### 9 HOLES (Cont.)

**28**—by Peggy Kirsch at Squaw Creek CC, Vienna, OH, in the 1991 Phar-Mor (par 35).

**28**—by Renee Heiken at Highland Meadows CC, Sylvania, OH, in the 1996 Jamie Farr Kroger Classic (par 34).

#### MOST CONSECUTIVE ROUNDS UNDER 70

**9**—Beth Daniel, in 1990.

#### MOST BIRDIES IN A ROW

**9**—Beth Daniel at Onion Creek Club in Austin, in the second round of the 1999 Philips Invitational. Daniel shot 62 (8 under par).

### Wins

#### MOST CONSECUTIVE WINS IN SCHEDULED EVENTS

**4**—Mickey Wright, in 1962.
**4**—Mickey Wright, in 1963.
**4**—Kathy Whitworth, in 1969.
**4**—Annika Sorenstam in 2001.

#### MOST CONSECUTIVE WINS IN ENTERED TOURNAMENTS

**5**—Nancy Lopez, in 1978.

#### MOST WINS IN A CALENDAR YEAR

**13**—Mickey Wright, in 1963.

#### WIDEST WINNING MARGIN, STROKES

**14**—Louise Suggs, 1949 U.S. Women's Open.
**14**—Cindy Mackey, 1986 MasterCard Int'l Pro-Am.

## U.S. Senior Open

| Year | Winner | Score | Runner-Up | Site |
|------|--------|-------|-----------|------|
| 1980 | Roberto DeVicenzo | 285 | William C. Campbell | Winged Foot GC, Mamaroneck, NY |
| 1981 | Arnold Palmer* (70) | 289 | Bob Stone (74) Billy Casper (77) | Oakland Hills CC, Birmingham, MI |
| 1982 | Miller Barber | 282 | Gene Littler Dan Sikes, Jr. | Portland GC, Portland, OR |
| 1983 | Billy Casper* (75) (3) | 288 | Rod Funseth (75) (4) | Hazeltine GC, Chaska, MN |
| 1984 | Miller Barber | 286 | Arnold Palmer | Oak Hill CC, Rochester, NY |
| 1985 | Miller Barber | 285 | Roberto DeVicenzo | Edgewood Tahoe GC, Stateline, NV |
| 1986 | Dale Douglass | 279 | Gary Player | Scioto CC, Columbus, OH |
| 1987 | Gary Player | 270 | Doug Sanders | Brooklawn CC, Fairfield, CT |
| 1988 | Gary Player* (68) | 288 | Bob Charles (70) | Medinah CC, Medinah, IL |
| 1989 | Orville Moody | 279 | Frank Beard | Laurel Valley GC, Ligonier, PA |
| 1990 | Lee Trevino | 275 | Jack Nicklaus | Ridgewood CC, Paramus, NJ |
| 1991 | Jack Nicklaus (65) | 282 | Chi Chi Rodriguez (69) | Oakland Hills CC, Birmingham, MI |
| 1992 | Larry Laoretti | 275 | Jim Colbert | Saucon Valley CC, Bethlehem, PA |
| 1993 | Jack Nicklaus | 278 | Tom Weiskopf | Cherry Hills CC, Englewood, CO |
| 1994 | Simon Hobday | 274 | Jim Albus | Pinehurst Resort & CC, Pinehurst, NC |
| 1995 | Tom Weiskopf | 275 | Jack Nicklaus | Congressional CC, Bethesda, MD |
| 1996 | Dave Stockton | 277 | Hale Irwin | Canterbury GC, Beachwood, OH |
| 1997 | Graham Marsh | 280 | Hale Irwin | Olympia Fields CC, Olympia Fields, IL |
| 1998 | Hale Irwin | 285 | Vicente Fernandez | Riviera CC, Pacific Palisades, CA |
| 1999 | Dave Eichelberger | 281 | Ed Dougherty | Des Moines G & CC, Des Moines, IA |
| 2000 | Hale Irwin | 267 | Bruce Fleisher | Saucon Valley CC, Bethlehem, PA |
| 2001 | Bruce Fleisher | 280 | Isao Aoki Gil Morgan | Salem CC, Peabody, MA |

*Winner in playoff. Playoff scores are in parentheses. The 1983 playoff went to one hole of sudden death after an 18-hole playoff.

# SENIOR TOUR

## Season Money Leaders

| Year | Player | Earnings ($) | Year | Player | Earnings ($) | Year | Player | Earnings ($) |
|------|--------|-------------|------|--------|-------------|------|--------|-------------|
| 1980 | Don January | 44,100 | 1987 | Chi Chi Rodriguez | 509,145 | 1994 | Dave Stockton | 1,402,519 |
| 1981 | Miller Barber | 83,136 | 1988 | Bob Charles | 533,929 | 1995 | Jim Colbert | 1,444,386 |
| 1982 | Miller Barber | 106,890 | 1989 | Bob Charles | 725,887 | 1996 | Jim Colbert | 1,627,890 |
| 1983 | Don January | 237,571 | 1990 | Lee Trevino | 1,190,518 | 1997 | Hale Irwin | 2,449,420 |
| 1984 | Don January | 328,597 | 1991 | Mike Hill | 1,065,657 | 1998 | Hale Irwin | 2,861,945 |
| 1985 | Peter Thomson | 386,724 | 1992 | Lee Trevino | 1,027,002 | 1999 | Bruce Fleisher | 2,515,705 |
| 1986 | Bruce Crampton | 454,299 | 1993 | Dave Stockton | 1,175,944 | 2000 | Larry Nelson | 2,708,005 |

## Career Money Leaders†

| # | Player | Earnings ($) | # | Player | Earnings ($) | # | Player | Earnings ($) |
|---|--------|-------------|---|--------|-------------|---|--------|-------------|
| 1. | Hale Irwin | 13,812,411 | 11. | Isao Aoki | 7,557,949 | 21. | Allen Doyle | 6,073,770 |
| 2. | Jim Colbert | 10,519,900 | 12. | Mike Hill | 7,370,766 | 22. | Bruce Summerhays | 5,969,404 |
| 3. | Gil Morgan | 9,600,354 | 13. | Bruce Fleisher | 7,202,859 | 23. | Tom Wargo | 5,935,610 |
| 4. | Lee Trevino | 9,426,642 | 14. | Chi Chi Rodriguez | 6,554,744 | 24. | Jim Albus | 5,653,319 |
| 5. | Dave Stockton | 9,135,830 | 15. | Bob Murphy | 6,519,830 | 25. | Gary Player | 5,613,497 |
| 6. | Bob Charles | 8,553,489 | 16. | Dale Douglass | 6,439,430 | 26. | Al Geiberger | 5,253,001 |
| 7. | Ray Floyd | 8,171,638 | 17. | Graham Marsh | 6,415,566 | 27. | John Bland | 4,988,090 |
| 8. | George Archer | 7,991,881 | 18. | Jay Sigel | 6,409,842 | 28. | Vicente Fernandez | 4,953,708 |
| 9. | Jim Dent | 7,831,090 | 19. | J.C. Snead | 6,290,116 | 29. | John Jacobs | 4,937,449 |
| 10. | Larry Nelson | 7,747,897 | 20. | Dana Quigley | 6,140,467 | 30. | Bruce Crampton | 4,652,684 |

## Most Career Wins†

| Player | Wins | Player | Wins |
|--------|------|--------|------|
| Hale Irwin | 32 | Jim Colbert | 20 |
| Lee Trevino | 29 | Gil Morgan | 20 |
| Miller Barber | 24 | Gary Player | 19 |
| Bob Charles | 23 | George Archer | 19 |
| Don January | 22 | Mike Hill | 18 |
| Chi Chi Rodriguez | 22 | Bruce Fleisher | 15 |
| Bruce Crampton | 20 | Larry Nelson | 15 |

†Through 10/14/01.

# MAJOR MEN'S AMATEUR CHAMPIONSHIPS

## U.S. Amateur

| Year | Winner | Score | Runner-Up | Site |
|------|--------|-------|-----------|------|
| 1895 | Charles B. Macdonald | 12 & 11 | Charles E. Sands | Newport GC, Newport, RI |
| 1896 | H.J. Whigham | 8 & 7 | J.G Thorp | Shinnecock Hills GC, Southampton, NY |
| 1897 | H.J. Whigham | 8 & 6 | W. Rossiter Betts | Chicago GC, Wheaton, IL |
| 1898 | Findlay S. Douglas | 5 & 3 | Walter B. Smith | Morris County GC, Morristown, NJ |
| 1899 | H.M. Harriman | 3 & 2 | Findlay S. Douglas | Onwentsia Club, Lake Forest, IL |
| 1900 | Walter Travis | 2 up | Findlay S. Douglas | Garden City GC, Garden City, NY |
| 1901 | Walter Travis | 5 & 4 | Walter E. Egan | CC of Atlantic City, NJ |
| 1902 | Louis N. James | 4 & 2 | Eben M. Byers | Glen View Club, Golf, IL |
| 1903 | Walter Travis | 5 & 4 | Eben M. Byers | Nassau CC, Glen Cove, NY |
| 1904 | H. Chandler Egan | 8 & 6 | Fred Herreshoff | Baltusrol GC, Springfield, NJ |
| 1905 | H. Chandler Egan | 6 & 5 | D.E. Sawyer | Chicago GC, Wheaton, IL |
| 1906 | Eben M. Byers | 2 up | George S. Lyon | Englewood GC, Englewood, NJ |
| 1907 | Jerry Travers | 6 & 5 | Archibald Graham | Euclid Club, Cleveland, OH |
| 1908 | Jerry Travers | 8 & 7 | Max H. Behr | Garden City GC, Garden City, NY |
| 1909 | Robert A. Gardner | 4 & 3 | H. Chandler Egan | Chicago GC, Wheaton, IL |
| 1910 | William C. Fownes Jr. | 4 & 3 | Warren K. Wood | The Country Club, Brookline, MA |
| 1911 | Harold Hilton | 1 up | Fred Herreshoff | The Apawamis Club, Rye, NY |
| 1912 | Jerry Travers | 7 & 6 | Charles Evans Jr. | Chicago GC, Wheaton, IL |
| 1913 | Jerry Travers | 5 & 4 | John G. Anderson | Garden City GC, Garden City, NY |
| 1914 | Francis Ouimet | 6 & 5 | Jerry Travers | Ekwanok CC, Manchester, VT |
| 1915 | Robert A. Gardner | 5 & 4 | John G. Anderson | CC of Detroit, Grosse Pt. Farms, MI |
| 1916 | Chick Evans | 4 & 3 | Robert A. Gardner | Merion Cricket Club, Haverford, PA |
| 1917–18 | No tournament | | | |
| 1919 | S. Davidson Herron | 5 & 4 | Bobby Jones | Oakmont CC, Oakmont, PA |
| 1920 | Chick Evans | 7 & 6 | Francis Ouimet | Engineers' CC, Roslyn, NY |
| 1921 | Jesse P. Guilford | 7 & 6 | Robert A. Gardner | St. Louis CC, Clayton, MO |
| 1922 | Jess W. Sweetser | 3 & 2 | Chick Evans | The Country Club, Brookline, MA |
| 1923 | Max R. Marston | 1 up | Jess W. Sweetser | Flossmoor CC, Flossmoor, IL |
| 1924 | Bobby Jones | 9 & 8 | George Von Elm | Merion Cricket Club, Ardmore, PA |
| 1925 | Bobby Jones | 8 & 7 | Watts Gunn | Oakmont CC, Oakmont, PA |
| 1926 | George Von Elm | 2 & 1 | Bobby Jones | Baltusrol GC, Springfield, NJ |
| 1927 | Bobby Jones | 8 & 7 | Chick Evans | Minikahda Club, Minneapolis |
| 1928 | Bobby Jones | 10 & 9 | T. Phillip Perkins | Brae Burn CC, West Newton, MA |
| 1929 | Harrison R. Johnston | 4 & 3 | Dr. O.F. Willing | Del Monte G & CC, Pebble Beach, CA |
| 1930 | Bobby Jones | 8 & 7 | Eugene V. Homans | Merion Cricket Club, Ardmore, PA |
| 1931 | Francis Ouimet | 6 & 5 | Jack Westland | Beverly CC, Chicago, IL |
| 1932 | C. Ross Somerville | 2 & 1 | John Goodman | Baltimore CC, Timonium, MD |
| 1933 | George T. Dunlap Jr. | 6 & 5 | Max R. Marston | Kenwood CC, Cincinnati, OH |
| 1934 | Lawson Little | 8 & 7 | David Goldman | The Country Club, Brookline, MA |
| 1935 | Lawson Little | 4 & 2 | Walter Emery | The Country Club, Cleveland, OH |
| 1936 | John W. Fischer | 1 up | Jack McLean | Garden City GC, Garden City, NY |
| 1937 | John Goodman | 2 up | Raymond E. Billows | Alderwood CC, Portland, OR |
| 1938 | William P. Turnesa | 8 & 7 | B. Patrick Abbott | Oakmont CC, Oakmont, PA |
| 1939 | Marvin H. Ward | 7 & 5 | Raymond E. Billows | North Shore CC, Glenview, IL |
| 1940 | Richard D. Chapman | 11 & 9 | W. McCullough Jr. | Winged Foot GC, Mamaroneck, NY |
| 1941 | Marvin H. Ward | 4 & 3 | B. Patrick Abbott | Omaha Field Club, Omaha, NE |
| 1942–45 | No tournament | | | |
| 1946 | Ted Bishop | 1 up | Smiley L. Quick | Baltusrol GC, Springfield, NJ |
| 1947 | Skee Riegel | 2 & 1 | John W. Dawson | Del Monte G & CC, Pebble Beach, CA |
| 1948 | William P. Turnesa | 2 & 1 | Raymond E. Billows | Memphis CC, Memphis, TN |
| 1949 | Charles R. Coe | 11 & 10 | Rufus King | Oak Hill CC, Rochester, NY |
| 1950 | Sam Urzetta | 1 up | Frank Stranahan | Minneapolis GC, Minneapolis, MN |
| 1951 | Billy Maxwell | 4 & 3 | Joseph F. Gagliardi | Saucon Valley CC, Bethlehem, PA |
| 1952 | Jack Westland | 3 & 2 | Al Mengert | Seattle GC, Seattle, WA |
| 1953 | Gene Littler | 1 up | Dale Morey | Oklahoma City G & CC, Oklahoma City |
| 1954 | Arnold Palmer | 1 up | Robert Sweeny | CC of Detroit, Grosse Pt. Farms, MI |
| 1955 | E. Harvie Ward Jr. | 9 & 8 | William Hyndman III | CC of Virginia, Richmond, VA |
| 1956 | E. Harvie Ward Jr. | 5 & 4 | Charles Kocsis | Knollwood Club, Lake Forest, IL |
| 1957 | Hillman Robbins Jr. | 5 & 4 | Dr. Frank M. Taylor | The Country Club, Brookline, MA |
| 1958 | Charles R. Coe | 5 & 4 | Tommy Aaron | Olympic Club, San Francisco, CA |
| 1959 | Jack Nicklaus | 1 up | Charles R. Coe | Broadmoor GC, Colorado Springs, CO |
| 1960 | Deane Beman | 6 & 4 | Robert W. Gardner | St. Louis CC, Clayton, MO |
| 1961 | Jack Nicklaus | 8 & 6 | H. Dudley Wysong | Pebble Beach GL, Pebble Beach, CA |

## U.S. Amateur (Cont.)

| Year | Winner | Score | Runner-Up | Site |
|------|--------|-------|-----------|------|
| 1962 | Labron E. Harris Jr. | 1 up | Downing Gray | Pinehurst CC, Pinehurst, NC |
| 1963 | Deane Beman | 2 & 1 | Richard H. Sikes | Wakonda Club, Des Moines, IA |
| 1964 | William C. Campbell | 1 up | Edgar M. Tutwiler | Canterbury GC, Cleveland, OH |
| 1965 | Robert J. Murphy Jr. | 291 | Robert B. Dickson | Southern Hills, CC, Tulsa |
| 1966 | Gary Cowan | 285–75 | Deane Beman | Merion GC, Ardmore, PA |
| 1967 | Robert B. Dickson | 285 | Marvin Giles III | Broadmoor GC, Colorado Springs |
| 1968 | Bruce Fleisher | 284 | Marvin Giles III | Scioto CC, Columbus, OH |
| 1969 | Steven N. Melnyk | 286 | Marvin Giles III | Oakmont CC, Oakmont, PA |
| 1970 | Lanny Wadkins | 279 | Tom Kite | Waverley CC, Portland, OR |
| 1971 | Gary Cowan | 280 | Eddie Pearce | Wilmington CC, Wilmington DE |
| 1972 | Marvin Giles III | 285 | two tied | Charlotte CC, Charlotte, NC |
| 1973 | Craig Stadler | 6 & 5 | David Strawn | Inverness Club, Toledo |
| 1974 | Jerry Pate | 2 & 1 | John P. Grace | Ridgewood CC, Ridgewood, NJ |
| 1975 | Fred Ridley | 2 up | Keith Fergus | CC of Virginia, Richmond |
| 1976 | Bill Sander | 8 & 6 | C. Parker Moore Jr. | Bel Air CC, Los Angeles |
| 1977 | John Fought | 9 & 8 | Doug Fischesser | Aronimink GC, Newton Square, PA |
| 1978 | John Cook | 5 & 4 | Scott Hoch | Plainfield CC, Plainfield, NJ |
| 1979 | Mark O'Meara | 8 & 7 | John Cook | Canterbury GC, Cleveland |
| 1980 | Hal Sutton | 9 & 8 | Bob Lewis | CC of North Carolina, Pinehurst, NC |
| 1981 | Nathaniel Crosby | 1 up | Brian Lindley | Olympic Club, San Francisco |
| 1982 | Jay Sigel | 8 & 7 | David Tolley | The Country Club, Brookline, MA |
| 1983 | Jay Sigel | 8 & 7 | Chris Perry | North Shore CC, Glenview, IL |
| 1984 | Scott Verplank | 4 & 3 | Sam Randolph | Oak Tree GC, Edmond, OK |
| 1985 | Sam Randolph | 1 up | Peter Persons | Montclair GC, West Orange, NJ |
| 1986 | Buddy Alexander | 5 & 3 | Chris Kite | Shoal Creek, Shoal Creek, AL |
| 1987 | Bill Mayfair | 4 & 3 | Eric Rebmann | Jupiter Hills Club, Jupiter, FL |
| 1988 | Eric Meeks | 7 & 6 | Danny Yates | Va. Hot Springs G & CC, VA |
| 1989 | Chris Patton | 3 & 1 | Danny Green | Merion GC, Ardmore, PA |
| 1990 | Phil Mickelson | 5 & 4 | Manny Zerman | Cherry Hills CC, Englewood, CO |
| 1991 | Mitch Voges | 7 & 6 | Manny Zerman | The Honors Course, Ooltewah, TN |
| 1992 | Justin Leonard | 8 & 7 | Tom Scherrer | Muirfield Village GC, Dublin, OH |
| 1993 | John Harris | 5 & 3 | Danny Ellis | Champions GC, Houston |
| 1994 | Tiger Woods | 2 up | Trip Kuehne | TPC-Sawgrass, Ponte Vedre, FL |
| 1995 | Tiger Woods | 2 up | Buddy Marucci | Newport Country Club, Newport, RI |
| 1996 | Tiger Woods | 38 holes | Steve Scott | Pumpkin Ridge GC, Cornelius, OR |
| 1997 | Matthew Kuchar | 2 & 1 | Joel Kribel | Cog Hill G & CC, Lemont, IL |
| 1998 | Hank Kuehne | 2 & 1 | Tom McKnight | Oak Hill CC, Rochester, NY |
| 1999 | David Gossett | 9 & 8 | Sung Yoon Kim | Pebble Beach GL, Pebble Beach, CA |
| 2000 | Jeff Quinney | 39 holes | James Driscoll | Baltusrol GC, Upper Springfield, NJ |
| 2001 | Bubba Dickerson | 1 up | Robert Hamilton | East Lake GC, Atlanta |

Note: All stroke play from 1965 to 1972.

## U.S. Junior Amateur

| | | | |
|---|---|---|---|
| 1948...Dean Lind | 1962...Jim Wiechers | 1976...Madden Hatcher III | 1990...Mathew Todd |
| 1949...Gay Brewer | 1963...Gregg McHatton | 1977...Willie Wood Jr. | 1991...Tiger Woods |
| 1950...Mason Rudolph | 1964...Johnny Miller | 1978...Don Hurter | 1992...Tiger Woods |
| 1951...Tommy Jacobs | 1965...James Masserio | 1979...Jack Larkin | 1993...Tiger Woods |
| 1952...Don Bisplinghoff | 1966...Gary Sanders | 1980...Eric Johnson | 1994...Terry Noe |
| 1953...Rex Baxter | 1967...John Crooks | 1981...Scott Erickson | 1995...D. Scott Hailes |
| 1954...Foster Bradley | 1968...Eddie Pearce | 1982...Hich Marik | 1996...Shane McMenamy |
| 1955...William Dunn | 1969...Aly Trompas | 1983...Tim Straub | 1997...Jason Allred |
| 1956...Harlan Stevenson | 1970...Gary Koch | 1984...Doug Martin | 1998...James Oh |
| 1957...Larry Beck | 1971...Mike Brannan | 1985...Charles Rymer | 1999...Hunter Mahan |
| 1958...Buddy Baker | 1972...Bob Byman | 1986...Brian Montgomery | 2000...Matthew Rosenfeld |
| 1959...Larry Lee | 1973...Jack Renner | 1987...Brett Quigley | 2001...Henry Liaw |
| 1960...Bill Tindall | 1974...David Nevatt | 1988...Jason Widener | |
| 1961...Charles McDowell | 1975...Brett Mullin | 1989...David Duval | |

Note: Event is for amateur golfers younger than 18 years of age.

## Mid-Amateur Championship

| | | | |
|---|---|---|---|
| 1981...Jim Holtgrieve | 1987...Jay Sigel | 1993...Jeff Thomas | 1999...Danny Green |
| 1982...William Hoffer | 1988...David Eger | 1994...Tim Jackson | 2000...Greg Puga |
| 1983...Jay Sigel | 1989...James Taylor | 1995...Jerry Courville Jr. | 2001...Tim Jackson |
| 1984...Mike Podolak | 1990...Jim Stuart | 1996...John Miller | |
| 1985...Jay Sigel | 1991...Jim Stuart | 1997...Ken Bakst | |
| 1986...Bill Loeffler | 1992...Danny Yates | 1998...John Miller | |

Note: Event is for amateur golfers at least 25 years of age.

## British Amateur

| | | |
|---|---|---|
| 1887 | H. G. Hutchinson | |
| 1888 | John Ball | |
| 1889 | J.E. Laidlay | |
| 1890 | John Ball | |
| 1891 | J.E. Laidlay | |
| 1892 | John Ball | |
| 1893 | Peter Anderson | |
| 1894 | John Ball | |
| 1895 | L.M.B. Melville | |
| 1896 | F.G. Tait | |
| 1897 | A.J.T. Allan | |
| 1898 | F.G. Tait | |
| 1899 | John Ball | |
| 1900 | H.H. Hilton | |
| 1901 | H.H. Hilton | |
| 1902 | C. Hutchings | |
| 1903 | R. Maxwell | |
| 1904 | W.J. Travis | |
| 1905 | A.G. Barry | |
| 1906 | James Robb | |
| 1907 | John Ball | |
| 1908 | E.A. Lassen | |
| 1909 | R. Maxwell | |
| 1910 | John Ball | |
| 1911 | H.H. Hilton | |
| 1912 | John Ball | |
| 1913 | H.H. Hilton | |
| 1914 | J.L.C. Jenkins | |
| 1915–19 | not held | |
| 1920 | C.J.H. Tolley | |
| 1921 | W.I. Hunter | |
| 1922 | E.W.E. Holderness | |
| 1923 | R.H. Wethered | |
| 1924 | E.W.E. Holderness | |
| 1925 | R. Harris | |
| 1926 | Jess Sweetser | |
| 1927 | Dr. W. Tweddell | |
| 1928 | T.P. Perkins | |
| 1929 | C.J.H. Tolley | |
| 1930 | Robert T. Jones Jr | |
| 1931 | E. Martin Smith | |
| 1932 | J. DeForest | |
| 1933 | M. Scott | |
| 1934 | W. Lawson Little | |
| 1935 | W. Lawson Little | |
| 1936 | H. Thomson | |
| 1937 | R. Sweeney Jr | |
| 1938 | C.R. Yates | |
| 1939 | A.T. Kyle | |
| 1940–45 | not held | |
| 1946 | J. Bruen | |
| 1947 | Willie D. Turnesa | |
| 1948 | Frank R. Stranahan | |
| 1949 | S.M. McReady | |
| 1950 | Frank R. Stranahan | |
| 1951 | Richard D. Chapman | |
| 1952 | E.H. Ward | |
| 1953 | J.B. Carr | |
| 1954 | D.W. Bachli | |
| 1955 | J.W. Conrad | |
| 1956 | J.C. Beharrel | |
| 1957 | R. Reid Jack | |
| 1958 | J.B. Carr | |
| 1959 | Deane Beman | |
| 1960 | J.B. Carr | |
| 1961 | M. Bonallack | |
| 1962 | R. Davies | |
| 1963 | M. Lunt | |
| 1964 | C. Clark | |
| 1965 | M. Bonallack | |
| 1966 | C.R. Cole | |
| 1967 | R. Dickson | |
| 1968 | M. Bonallack | |
| 1969 | M. Bonallack | |
| 1970 | M. Bonallack | |
| 1971 | Steve Melnyk | |
| 1972 | Trevor Homer | |
| 1973 | R. Siderowf | |
| 1974 | Trevor Homer | |
| 1975 | M. Giles | |
| 1976 | R. Siderowf | |
| 1977 | P. McEvoy | |
| 1978 | P. McEvoy | |
| 1979 | J. Sigel | |
| 1980 | D. Evans | |
| 1981 | P. Ploujoux | |
| 1982 | M. Thompson | |
| 1983 | A. Parkin | |
| 1984 | J.M. Olazabal | |
| 1985 | G. McGimpsey | |
| 1986 | D. Curry | |
| 1987 | P. Mayo | |
| 1988 | C. Hardin | |
| 1989 | S. Dodd | |
| 1990 | R. Muntz | |
| 1991 | G. Wolstenholme | |
| 1992 | S. Dundas | |
| 1993 | I. Pyman | |
| 1994 | L. James | |
| 1995 | G. Sherry | |
| 1996 | W. Bladon | |
| 1997 | C. Watson | |
| 1998 | Sergio Garcia | |
| 1999 | Graeme Storm | |
| 2000 | Mikko Ilonen | |
| 2001 | Michael Hoey | |

## Amateur Public Links

| | | |
|---|---|---|
| 1922 | Edmund R. Held | |
| 1923 | Richard J. Walsh | |
| 1924 | Joseph Coble | |
| 1925 | Raymond J. McAuliffe | |
| 1926 | Lester Bolstad | |
| 1927 | Carl F. Kauffmann | |
| 1928 | Carl F. Kauffmann | |
| 1929 | Carl F. Kauffmann | |
| 1930 | Robert E. Wingate | |
| 1931 | Charles Ferrera | |
| 1932 | R.L. Miller | |
| 1933 | Charles Ferrera | |
| 1934 | David A. Mitchell | |
| 1935 | Frank Strafaci | |
| 1936 | B. Patrick Abbott | |
| 1937 | Bruce N. McCormick | |
| 1938 | Al Leach | |
| 1939 | Andrew Szwedko | |
| 1940 | Robert C. Clark | |
| 1941 | William M. Welch Jr | |
| 1942–45 | not held | |
| 1946 | Smiley L. Quick | |
| 1947 | Wilfred Crossley | |
| 1948 | Michael R. Ferentz | |
| 1949 | Kenneth J. Towns | |
| 1950 | Stanley Bielat | |
| 1951 | Dave Stanley | |
| 1952 | Omer L. Bogan | |
| 1953 | Ted Richards Jr | |
| 1954 | Gene Andrews | |
| 1955 | Sam D. Kocsis | |
| 1956 | James H. Buxbaum | |
| 1957 | Don Essig III | |
| 1958 | Daniel D. Sikes Jr | |
| 1959 | William A. Wright | |
| 1960 | Verne Callison | |
| 1961 | Richard H. Sikes | |
| 1962 | Richard H. Sikes | |
| 1963 | Robert Lunn | |
| 1964 | William McDonald | |
| 1965 | Arne Dokka | |
| 1966 | Lamont Kaser | |
| 1967 | Verne Callison | |
| 1968 | Gene Towry | |
| 1969 | John M. Jackson Jr | |
| 1970 | Robert Risch | |
| 1971 | Fred Haney | |
| 1972 | Bob Allard | |
| 1973 | Stan Stopa | |
| 1974 | Charles Barenaba | |
| 1975 | Randy Barenaba | |
| 1976 | Eddie Mudd | |
| 1977 | Jerry Vidovic | |
| 1978 | Dean Prince | |
| 1979 | Dennis Walsh | |
| 1980 | Jodie Mudd | |
| 1981 | Jodie Mudd | |
| 1982 | Billy Tuten | |
| 1983 | Billy Tuten | |
| 1984 | Bill Malley | |
| 1985 | Jim Sorenson | |
| 1986 | Bill Mayfair | |
| 1987 | Kevin Johnson | |
| 1988 | Ralph Howe III | |
| 1989 | Tim Hobby | |
| 1990 | Michael Combs | |
| 1991 | David Berganio Jr | |
| 1992 | Warren Schulte | |
| 1993 | David Berganio Jr | |
| 1994 | Guy Yamamoto | |
| 1995 | Chris Wollmann | |
| 1996 | Tim Hogarth | |
| 1997 | Tim Clark | |
| 1998 | Trevor Immelman | |
| 1999 | Hunter Haas | |
| 2000 | D.J. Trahan | |
| 2001 | Chez Reavie | |

## U.S. Senior Golf

| | | |
|---|---|---|
| 1955 ..........J. Wood Platt | 1971 ..........Tom Draper | 1987 ..........John Richardson |
| 1956 ..........Frederick J. Wright | 1972 ..........Lewis W. Oehmig | 1988 ..........Clarence Moore |
| 1957 ..........J. Clark Espie | 1973 ..........William Hyndman III | 1989 ..........Bo Williams |
| 1958 ..........Thomas C. Robbins | 1974 ..........Dale Morey | 1990 ..........Jackie Cummings |
| 1959 ..........J. Clark Espie | 1975 ..........William F. Colm | 1991 ..........Bill Bosshard |
| 1960 ..........Michael Cestone | 1976 ..........Lewis W. Oehmig | 1992 ..........Clarence Moore |
| 1961 ..........Dexter H. Daniels | 1977 ..........Dale Morey | 1993 ..........Joe Ungvary |
| 1962 ..........Merrill L. Carlsmith | 1978 ..........K.K. Compton | 1994 ..........O. Gordon Brewer |
| 1963 ..........Merrill L. Carlsmith | 1979 ..........William C. Campbell | 1995 ..........James Stahl Jr. |
| 1964 ..........William D. Higgins | 1980 ..........William C. Campbell | 1996 ..........O. Gordon Brewer |
| 1965 ..........Robert B. Kiersky | 1981 ..........Ed Updegraff | 1997 ..........Cliff Cunningham |
| 1966 ..........Dexter H. Daniels | 1982 ..........Alton Duhon | 1998 ..........Bill Shean Jr. |
| 1967 ..........Ray Palmer | 1983 ..........William Hyndman III | 1999 ..........Bill Ploeger |
| 1968 ..........Curtis Person Sr. | 1984 ..........Bob Rawlins | 2000 ..........Bill Shean Jr. |
| 1969 ..........Curtis Person Sr. | 1985 ..........Lewis W. Oehmig | |
| 1970 ..........Gene Andrews | 1986 ..........Bo Williams | |

Note: Event is for amateur golfers at least 55 years of age.

# MAJOR WOMEN'S AMATEUR CHAMPIONSHIPS

## U.S. Women's Amateur

| Year | Winner | Score | Runner-Up | Site |
|---|---|---|---|---|
| 1895 ..........Mrs. Charles S. Brown | | 132 | Nellie Sargent | Meadow Brook Club, Hempstead, NY |
| 1896 ..........Beatrix Hoyt | | 2 & 1 | Mrs. Arthur Turnure | Morris Couty GC, Morristown, NJ |
| 1897 ..........Beatrix Hoyt | | 5 & 4 | Nellie Sargent | Essex County Club, Manchester, MA |
| 1898 ..........Beatrix Hoyt | | 5 &3 | Maude Wetmore | Ardsley Club, Ardsley-on-Hudson, NY |
| 1899 ..........Ruth Underhill | | 2 & 1 | Margaret Fox | Philadelphia CC, Philadelphia, PA |
| 1900 ..........Frances C. Griscom | | 6 & 5 | Margaret Curtis | Shinnecock Hills GC, Shinnecock Hills, NY |
| 1901 ..........Genevieve Hecker | | 5 & 3 | Lucy Herron | Baltusrol GC, Springfield, NJ |
| 1902 ..........Genevieve Hecker | | 4 & 3 | Louisa A. Wells | The Country Club, Brookline, MA |
| 1903 ..........Bessie Anthony | | 7 & 6 | J. Anna Carpenter | Chicago GC, Wheaton, IL |
| 1904 ..........Georgianna M. Bishop | | 5 & 3 | Mrs. E.F. Sanford | Merion Cricket Club, Haverford, PA |
| 1905 ..........Pauline Mackay | | 1 up | Margaret Curtis | Morris County GC, Convent, NJ |
| 1906 ..........Harriot S. Curtis | | 2 & 1 | Mary B. Adams | Brae Burn CC, West Newton, MA |
| 1907 ..........Margaret Curtis | | 7 & 6 | Harriot S. Curtis | Midlothian CC, Blue Island, IL |
| 1908 ..........Katherine C. Harley | | 6 & 5 | Mrs. T.H. Polhemus | Chevy Chase Club, Chevy Chase, MD |
| 1909 ..........Dorothy I. Campbell | | 3 & 2 | Nonna Barlow | Merion Cricket Club, Haverford, PA |
| 1910 ..........Dorothy I. Campbell | | 2 & 1 | Mrs. G.M. Martin | Homewood CC, Flossmoor, IL |
| 1911 ..........Margaret Curtis | | 5 & 3 | Lillian B. Hyde | Baltusrol GC, Springfield, NJ |
| 1912 ..........Margaret Curtis | | 3 & 2 | Nonna Barlow | Essex County Club, Manchester, MA |
| 1913 ..........Gladys Ravenscroft | | 2 up | Marion Hollins | Wilmington CC, Wilmington, DE |
| 1914 ..........Katherine Harley | | 1 up | Elaine V. Rosenthal | Nassau CC, Glen Cove, NY |
| 1915 ..........Florence Vanderbeck | | 3 & 2 | Margaret Gavin | Onwentsia Club, Lake Forest, IL |
| 1916 ..........Alexa Stirling | | 2 & 1 | Mildred Caverly | Belmont Springs CC, Waverley, MA |
| 1917–18 .....No tournament | | | | |
| 1919 ..........Alexa Stirling | | 6 & 5 | Margaret Gavin | Shawnee CC, Shawnee-on-Delaware, PA |
| 1920 ..........Alexa Stirling | | 5 & 4 | Dorothy Campbell | Mayfield CC, Cleveland |
| 1921 ..........Marion Hollins | | 5 & 4 | Alexa Stirling | Hollywood GC, Deal, NJ |
| 1922 ..........Glenna Collett | | 5 & 4 | Margaret Gavin | Greenbriar GC, White Sulphur Springs, WV |
| 1923 ..........Edith Cummings | | 3 & 2 | Alexa Stirling | Westchester-Biltmore CC, Rye, NY |
| 1924 ..........Dorothy Campbell | | 7 & 6 | Mary K. Browne | Rhode Island CC, Nyatt, RI |
| 1925 ..........Glenna Collett | | 9 & 8 | Alexa Stirling | St. Louis CC, Clayton, MO |
| 1926 ..........Helen Stetson | | 3 & 1 | Elizabeth Goss | Merion Cricket Club, Ardmore, PA |
| 1927 ..........Miiriam Burns Horn | | 5 & 4 | Maureen Orcutt | Cherry Valley Club, Garden City, NY |
| 1928 ..........Glenna Collett | | 13 & 12 | Virginia Van Wie | Va. Hot Springs G & TC, Hot Springs, VA |
| 1929 ..........Glenna Collett | | 4 & 3 | Leona Pressler | Oakland Hills CC, Birmingham, MI |
| 1930 ..........Glenna Collett | | 6 & 5 | Virginia Van Wie | Los Angeles CC, Beverly Hills, CA |
| 1931 ..........Helen Hicks | | 2 & 1 | Glenna Collet Vare | CC of Buffalo, Williamsville, NY |
| 1932 ..........Virginia Van Wie | | 10 & 8 | Glenna Collet Vare | Salem CC, Peabody, MA |
| 1933 ..........Virginia Van Wie | | 4 & 3 | Helen Hicks | Exmoor CC, Highland Park, IL |
| 1934 ..........Virginia Van Wie | | 2 & 1 | Dorothy Traung | Whitemarsh Valley CC, Chestnut Hill, PA |
| 1935 ..........Glenna Collett Vare | | 3 & 2 | Patty Berg | Interlachen CC, Hopkins, MN |
| 1936 ..........Pamela Barton | | 4 & 3 | Maureen Orcutt | Canoe Brook CC, Summit, NJ |
| 1937 ..........Estelle Lawson | | 7 & 6 | Patty Berg | Memphis CC, Memphis, TN |
| 1938 ..........Patty Berg | | 6 & 5 | Estelle Lawson | Westmoreland CC, Wilmette, IL |

## U.S. Women's Amateur (Cont.)

| Year | Winner | Score | Runner-Up | Site |
|------|--------|-------|-----------|------|
| 1939 | Betty Jameson | 3 & 2 | Dorothy Kirby | Wee Burn Club, Darien, CT |
| 1940 | Betty Jameson | 6 & 5 | Jane S. Cothran | Del Monte G & CC, Pebble Beach, CA |
| 1941 | Elizabeth Hicks | 5 & 3 | Helen Sigel | The Country Club, Brookline, MA |
| 1942–45 | No tournament | | | |
| 1946 | Babe Zaharias | 11 & 9 | Clara Sherman | Southern Hills CC, Tulsa |
| 1947 | Louise Suggs | 2 up | Dorothy Kirby | Franklin Hills CC, Franklin, MI |
| 1948 | Grace S. Lenczyk | 4 & 3 | Helen Sigel | Del Monte G & CC, Pebble Beach, CA |
| 1949 | Dorothy Porter | 3 & 2 | Dorothy Kielty | Merion GC, Ardmore, PA |
| 1950 | Beverly Hanson | 6 & 4 | Mae Murray | Atlanta AC, Atlanta |
| 1951 | Dorothy Kirby | 2 & 1 | Claire Doran | Town & CC, St. Paul |
| 1952 | Jacqueline Pung | 2 & 1 | Shirley McFedters | Waverley CC, Portland, OR |
| 1953 | Mary Lena Faulk | 3 & 2 | Polly Riley | Rhode Island CC, West Barrington, RI |
| 1954 | Barbara Romack | 4 & 2 | Mickey Wright | Allegheny CC, Sewickley, PA |
| 1955 | Patricia A. Lesser | 7 & 6 | Jane Nelson | Myers Park CC, Charlotte |
| 1956 | Marlene Stewart | 2 & 1 | JoAnne Gunderson | Meridian Hills CC, Indianapolis |
| 1957 | JoAnne Gunderson | 8 & 6 | Ann Casey Johnstone | Del Paso CC, SacramentoA |
| 1958 | Anne Quast | 3 & 2 | Barbara Romack | Wee Burn CC, Darien, CT |
| 1959 | Barbara McIntire | 4 & 3 | Joanne Goodwin | Congressional CC, Washington, D.C. |
| 1960 | JoAnne Gunderson | 6 & 5 | Jean Ashley | Tulsa CC, Tulsa |
| 1961 | Anne Quast Decker | 14 & 13 | Phyllis Preuss | Tacoma G & CC, Tacoma, WA |
| 1962 | JoAnne Gunderson | 9 & 8 | Anne Baker | CC of Rochester, Rochester, NY |
| 1963 | Anne Quast Decker | 2 & 1 | Peggy Conley | Taconic GC, Williamstown, MA |
| 1964 | Barbara McIntire | 3 & 2 | JoAnne Gunderson | Prairie Dunes CC, Hutchinson, KS |
| 1965 | Jean Ashley | 5 & 4 | Anne Quast Decker | Lakewood CC, Denver |
| 1966 | JoAnne Gunderson | 1 up | Marlene Stewart Streit | Sewickley Heights GC, Sewickley, PA |
| 1967 | Mary Lou Dill | 5 & 4 | Jean Ashley | Annandale GC, Pasadena |
| 1968 | JoAnne Gunderson Carner | 5 & 4 | Anne Quast Decker | Birmingham CC, Birmingham, MI |
| 1969 | Catherine Lacoste | 3 & 2 | Shelley Hamling | Las Colinas CC, Irving, TX |
| 1970 | Martha Wilkinson | 3 & 2 | Cynthia Hall | Wee Burn CC, Darien, CT |
| 1971 | Laura Baugh | 1 up | Beth Barry | Atlanta CC, Atlanta |
| 1972 | Mary Budke | 5 & 4 | Cynthia Hill | St. Louis CC, St. Louis |
| 1973 | Carol Semple | 1 up | Anne Quast Decker | Montclair GC, Montclair, NJ |
| 1974 | Cynthia Hill | 5 & 4 | Carol Semple | Broadmoor GC, Seattle |
| 1975 | Beth Daniel | 3 & 2 | Donna Horton | Brae Burn CC, West Newton, MA |
| 1976 | Donna Horton | 2 & 1 | Marianne Bretton | Del Paso CC, Sacramento |
| 1977 | Beth Daniel | 3 & 1 | Cathy Sherk | Cincinnati CC, Cincinnati |
| 1978 | Cathy Sherk | 4 & 3 | Judith Oliver | Sunnybrook GC, Plymouth Meeting, PA |
| 1979 | Carolyn Hill | 7 & 6 | Patty Sheehan | Memphis CC, Memphis |
| 1980 | Juli Inkster | 2 up | Patti Rizzo | Prairie Dunes CC, Hutchinson, KS |
| 1981 | Juli Inkster | 1 up | Lindy Goggin | Waverley CC, Portland, OR |
| 1982 | Juli Inkster | 4 & 3 | Cathy Hanlon | Broadmoor GC, Colorado Springs, CO |
| 1983 | Joanne Pacillo | 2 & 1 | Sally Quinlan | Canoe Brook CC, Summit, NJ |
| 1984 | Deb Richard | 1 up | Kimberly Williams | Broadmoor GC, Seattle |
| 1985 | Michiko Hattori | 5 & 4 | Cheryl Stacy | Fox Chapel CC, Pittsburgh |
| 1986 | Kay Cockerill | 9 & 7 | Kathleen McCarthy | Pasatiempo GC, Santa Cruz, CA |
| 1987 | Kay Cockerill | 3 & 2 | Tracy Kerdyk | Rhode Island CC, Barrington, RI |
| 1988 | Pearl Sinn | 6 & 5 | Karen Noble | Minikahda Club, Minneapolis |
| 1989 | Vicki Goetze | 4 & 3 | Brandie Burton | Pinehurst CC (No. 2), Pinehurst, NC |
| 1990 | Pat Hurst | 37 holes | Stephanie Davis | Canoe Brook CC, Summit, NJ |
| 1991 | Amy Fruhwirth | 5 & 4 | Heidi Voorhees | Prairie Dunes CC, Hutchinson, KN |
| 1992 | Vicki Goetz | 1 up | Annika Sorensteam | Kemper Lakes GC, Hawthorne Hills, IL |
| 1993 | Jill McGill | 1 up | Sarah Ingram | San Diego CC, Chula Vista, CA |
| 1994 | Wendy Ward | 2 & 1 | Jill McGill | The Homestead, Hot Springs, WV |
| 1995 | Kelli Kuehne | 4 & 3 | Anne-Marie Knight | The Country Club, Brookline, MA |
| 1996 | Kelli Kuehne | 2 & 1 | Marisa Baena | Firethorn GC, Lincoln, NE |
| 1997 | Silvia Cavalleri | 5 & 4 | Robin Burke | Brae Burn CC, West Newton, MA |
| 1998 | Grace Park | 7 & 6 | Jenny Chuasiriporn | Barton Hills CC, Ann Arbor, MI |
| 1999 | Dorothy Delasin | 4 & 3 | Jimin Kang | Biltmore Forest CC, Asheville, NC |
| 2000 | Marcy Newton | 8 & 7 | Laura Myerscough | Waverley CC, Portland, OR |
| 2001 | Meredith Duncan | 37 holes | Nicole Perrot | Flint Hills GC, Wichita, KA |

## U.S. Girls' Junior Amateur

| | | |
|---|---|---|
| 1949 ..........Marlene Bauer | 1968 ..........Peggy Harmon | 1987 ..........Michelle McGann |
| 1950 ..........Patricia Lesser | 1969 ..........Hollis Stacy | 1988 ..........Jamille Jose |
| 1951 ..........Arlene Brooks | 1970 ..........Hollis Stacy | 1989 ..........Brandie Burton |
| 1952 ..........Mickey Wright | 1971 ..........Hollis Stacy | 1990 ..........Sandrine Mendiburu |
| 1953 ..........Millie Meyerson | 1972 ..........Nancy Lopez | 1991 ..........Emilee Klein |
| 1954 ..........Margaret Smith | 1973 ..........Amy Alcott | 1992 ..........Jamie Koizumi |
| 1955 ..........Carole Jo Kabler | 1974 ..........Nancy Lopez | 1993 ..........Kellee Booth |
| 1956 ..........JoAnne Gunderson | 1975 ..........Dayna Benson | 1962 ..........Maureen Orcutt |
| 1957 ..........Judy Eller | 1976 ..........Pilar Dorado | 1963 ..........Sis Choate |
| 1958 ..........Judy Eller | 1977 ..........Althea Tome | 1994 ..........Kelli Kuehne |
| 1959 ..........Judy Rand | 1978 ..........Lori Castillo | 1995 ..........Marcy Newton |
| 1960 ..........Carol Sorenson | 1979 ..........Penny Hammel | 1996 ..........Dorothy Delasin |
| 1961 ..........Mary Lowell | 1980 ..........Laurie Rinker | 1997 ..........Beth Bauer |
| 1962 ..........Mary Lou Daniel | 1981 ..........Kay Cornelius | 1998 ..........Leigh Anne Hardin |
| 1963 ..........Janis Ferraris | 1982 ..........Heather Farr | 1999 ..........Aree Wongluekiet |
| 1964 ..........Peggy Conley | 1983 ..........Kim Saiki | 2000 ..........Lisa Ferrero |
| 1965 ..........Gail Sykes | 1984 ..........Cathy Mockett | 2001 ..........Nicole Perrot |
| 1966 ..........Claudia Mayhew | 1985 ..........Dana Lofland | |
| 1967 ..........Elizabeth Story | 1986 ..........Pat Hurst | |

## Women's British Amateur

| | | |
|---|---|---|
| 1893 .............Lady Margaret Scott | 1928 ..........Miss N. Le Blan | 1964 .............C. Sorenson |
| 1894 .............Lady Margaret Scott | 1929 ............Miss J. Wethered | 1965 .............B. Varangot |
| 1895 .............Lady Margaret Scott | 1930 ............Miss D. Fishwick | 1966 .............E. Chadwick |
| 1896 .............Miss Pascoe | 1931 ............Miss E. Wilson | 1967 .............E. Chadwick |
| 1897 .............Miss E.C. Orr | 1932 ............Miss E. Wilson | 1968 .............B. Varangot |
| 1898 .............Miss L. Thomson | 1933 ............Miss E. Wilson | 1975 .............C. Lacoste |
| 1899 .............Miss M. Hezlet | 1934 ............Mrs. A.M. Holm | 1976 .............D. Oxley |
| 1900 .............Miss Adair | 1935 ............Miss W. Morgan | 1977 .............A. Uzielli |
| 1901 .............Miss Graham | 1936 ............Miss P. Barton | 1978 .............E. Kennedy |
| 1902 .............Miss M. Hezlet | 1937 ............Miss J. Anderson | 1979 .............M. Madill |
| 1903 .............Miss Adair | 1938 ............Mrs. A.M. Holm | 1980 .............A. Quast |
| 1904 .............Miss L. Dod | 1939 ............Miss P. Barton | 1981 .............I.C. Robertson |
| 1905 .............Miss B. Thompson | 1940–45 .......not held | 1982 .............K. Douglas |
| 1906 .............Mrs. Kennon | 1946 ............G.W. Hetherington | 1983 .............J. Thornhill |
| 1907 .............Miss M. Hezlet | 1947 ............B. Zaharias | 1984 .............J. Rosenthal |
| 1908 .............Miss M. Titterton | 1948 ............L. Suggs | 1985 .............L. Beman |
| 1909 .............Miss D. Campbell | 1949 ............F. Stephens | 1986 .............M. McGuire |
| 1910 .............Miss Grant Suttie | 1950 ............Vicomtesse de Saint | 1987 .............J. Collingham |
| 1911 .............Miss D. Campbell | Sauveur | 1988 .............J. Furby |
| 1912 .............Miss G. Ravenscroft | 1951 ............P.J. MacCann | 1989 .............H. Dobson |
| 1913 .............Miss M. Dodd | 1952 ............M. Paterson | 1990 .............J. Hall |
| 1914 .............Miss C. Leitch | 1953 ............M. Stewart | 1991 .............V. Michaud |
| 1915–19 .......not held | 1954 ............F. Stephens | 1992 .............P. Pedersen |
| 1920 .............Miss C. Leitch | 1955 ............J. Valentine | 1993 .............Catriona Lambert |
| 1921 .............Miss C. Leitch | 1956 ............M. Smith | 1994 .............Emma Duggleby |
| 1922 .............Miss J. Wethered | 1957 ............P. Garvey | 1995 .............Julie Hall |
| 1923 .............Miss D. Chambers | 1958 ............J. Valentine | 1996 .............Kelli Kuehne |
| 1024 .............Miss J. Wethered | 1959 ............E. Price | 1997 .............Alison Rose |
| 1925 .............Miss J. Wethered | 1960 ............B. McIntyre | 1998 .............K. Rostron |
| 1926 .............Miss C. Leitch | 1961 ............M. Spearman | 1999 .............Marine Monnet |
| 1927 .............Miss Thion de la | 1962 ............M. Spearman | 2000 .............Rebecca Hudson |
| Chaume | 1963 ............B. Varangot | 2001 .............Rebecca Hudson |

## Women's Amateur Public Links

| | | |
|---|---|---|
| 1977 .............Kelly Fuiks | Ammaccapane | 1994 .............Jill McGill |
| 1978 .............Kelly Fuiks | 1986 ............Cindy Schreyer | 1995 .............Jo Jo Robertson |
| 1979 .............Lori Castillo | 1987 ............Tracy Kerdyk | 1996 .............Heather Graff |
| 1980 .............Lori Castillo | 1988 ............Pearl Sinn | 1997 .............Jo Jo Robertson |
| 1981 .............Mary Enright | 1989 ............Pearl Sinn | 1998 .............Amy Spooner |
| 1982 .............Nancy Taylor | 1990 ............Cathy Mockett | 1999 .............Jody Niemann |
| 1983 .............Kelli Antolock | 1991 ............Tracy Hanson | 2000 .............Catherine Cartwright |
| 1984 .............Heather Farr | 1992 ............Amy Fruhwirth | 2001 .............Candie Kung |
| 1985 .............Danielle | 1993 ............Connie Masterson | |

# Amateur Golf (Cont.)

## U.S. Senior Women's Amateur

| | | |
|---|---|---|
| 1964 ..........Loma Smith | 1977 ..........Dorothy Porter | 1990 ..........Anne Sander |
| 1965 ..........Loma Smith | 1978 ..........Alice Dye | 1991 ..........Phyllis Preuss |
| 1966 ..........Maureen Orcutt | 1979 ..........Alice Dye | 1992 ..........Rosemary Thompson |
| 1967 ..........Marge Mason | 1980 ..........Dorothy Porter | 1993 ..........Anne Sander |
| 1968 ..........Carolyn Cudone | 1981 ..........Dorothy Porter | 1994 ..........Marlene Streit |
| 1969 ..........Carolyn Cudone | 1982 ..........Edean Ihlanfeldt | 1995 ..........Jean Smith |
| 1970 ..........Carolyn Cudone | 1983 ..........Dorothy Porter | 1996 ..........Gayle Borthwick |
| 1971 ..........Carolyn Cudone | 1984 ..........Constance Guthrie | 1997 ..........Nancy Fitzgerald |
| 1972 ..........Carolyn Cudone | 1985 ..........Marlene Streit | 1998 ..........Gayle Borthwick |
| 1973 ..........Gwen Hibbs | 1986 ..........Connie Guthrie | 1999 ...........C. Semple Thompson |
| 1974 ..........Justine Cushing | 1987 ..........Anne Sander | 2000 ...........C. Semple Thompson |
| 1975 ..........Alberta Bower | 1988 ..........Lois Hodge | 2001 ..........C. Semple Thompson |
| 1976 ..........Cecile H. Maclaurin | 1989 ..........Anne Sander | |

## Women's Mid-Amateur Championship

| | | |
|---|---|---|
| 1987 ..........Cindy Scholefield | 1992 ..........M. Mamey-McInerney | 1997 ..........C. Semple Thompson |
| 1988 ..........Martha Lang | 1993 ..........Sarah Ingram | 1998 ..........Virginia Derby Grimes |
| 1989 ..........Robin Weiss | 1994 ..........Sarah Ingram | 1999 ..........Alissa Herron |
| 1990 ..........C. Semple Thompson | 1995 ..........Ellen Port | 2000 ..........Ellen Port |
| 1991 ..........Sarah LeBrun Ingram | 1996 ..........Ellen Port | 2001 ..........Laura Shanahan |

# International Golf

## Ryder Cup Matches

| Year | Results | Site |
|---|---|---|
| 1927 | United States 9½, Great Britain 2½ | Worcester CC, Worcester, MA |
| 1929 | Great Britain 7, United States 5 | Moortown GC, Leeds, England |
| 1931 | United States 9, Great Britain 3 | Scioto CC, Columbus, OH |
| 1933 | Great Britain 6½, United States 5½ | Southport and Ainsdale Courses, Southport, England |
| 1935 | United States 9, Great Britain 3 | Ridgewood CC, Ridgewood, NJ |
| 1937 | United States 8, Great Britain 4 | Southport and Ainsdale Courses, Southport, England |
| 1939–1945 | No tournament | |
| 1947 | United States 11, Great Britain 1 | Portland GC, Portland, OR |
| 1949 | United States 7, Great Britain 5 | Ganton GC, Scarborough, England |
| 1951 | United States 9½, Great Britain 2½ | Pinehurst CC, Pinehurst, NC |
| 1953 | United States 6½, Great Britain 5½ | Wentworth Club, Surrey, England |
| 1955 | United States 8, Great Britain 4 | Thunderbird Ranch & CC, Palm Springs, CA |
| 1957 | Great Britain 7½, United States 4½ | Lindrick GC, Yorkshire, England |
| 1959 | United States 8½, Great Britain 3½ | Eldorado CC, Palm Desert, CA |
| 1961 | United States 14½, Great Britain 9½ | Royal Lytham & St. Annes GC, St Anne's-on-the-Sea, England |
| 1963 | United States 23, Great Britain 9 | East Lake CC, Atlanta |
| 1965 | United States 19½, Great Britain 12½ | Royal Birkdale GC, Southport, England |
| 1967 | United States 23½, Great Britain 8½ | Champions GC, Houston |
| 1969 | United States 16, Great Britain 16 | Royal Birkdale GC, Southport, England |
| 1971 | United States 18½, Great Britain 13½ | Old Warson CC, St. Louis |
| 1973 | United States 19, Great Britain 13 | Hon Co of Edinburgh Golfers, Muirfield, Scotland |
| 1975 | United States 21, Great Britain 11 | Laurel Valley GC, Ligonier, PA |
| 1977 | United States 12½, Great Britain 7½ | Royal Lytham & St. Annes GC, St. Annes-on-the-Sea, England |
| 1979 | United States 17, Europe 11 | Greenbrier, White Sulphur Springs, WV |
| 1981 | United States 18½, Europe 9½ | Walton Heath GC, Surrey, England |
| 1983 | United States 14½, Europe 13½ | PGA National GC, Palm Beach Gardens, FL |
| 1985 | Europe 16½, United States 11½ | Belfry GC, Sutton Coldfield, England |
| 1987 | Europe 15, United States 13 | Muirfield GC, Dublin, OH |
| 1989 | Europe 14, United States 14 | Belfry GC, Sutton Coldfield, England |
| 1991 | United States 14½, Europe 13½ | Ocean Course, Kiawah Island, SC |
| 1993 | United States 15, Europe 13 | Belfry GC, Sutton Coldfield, England |
| 1995 | Europe 14½, United States 13½ | Oak Hill CC, Rochester, NY |
| 1997 | Europe 14½, United States 13½ | Valderrama GC, Sotogrande, Spain |
| 1999 | United States 14½, Europe 13½ | The Country Club, Brookline, MA |

Team matches held every odd year between U.S. professionals and those of Great Britain/Europe (since 1979—prior to that it was U.S. vs G.B.). Team members selected on basis of finishes in PGA and European tour events.

## Walker Cup Matches

| Year | Results | Site |
|---|---|---|
| 1922 | United States 8, Great Britain 4 | Nat'l Golf Links of America, Southampton, NY |
| 1923 | United States 6, Great Britain 5 | St. Andrews, Scotland |
| 1924 | United States 9, Great Britain 3 | Garden City GC, Garden City, NY |
| 1926 | United States 6, Great Britain 5 | St. Andrews, Scotland |
| 1928 | United States 11, Great Britain 1 | Chicago GC, Wheaton, IL |
| 1930 | United States 10, Great Britain 2 | Royal St. George GC, Sandwich, England |
| 1932 | United States 8, Great Britain 1 | The Country Club, Brookline, MA |
| 1934 | United States 9, Great Britain 2 | St. Andrews, Scotland |
| 1936 | United States 9, Great Britain 0 | Pine Valley GC, Clementon, NJ |
| 1938 | Great Britain 7, United States 4 | St. Andrews, Scotland |
| 1940–46 | No tournament | |
| 1947 | United States 8, Great Britain 4 | St. Andrews, Scotland |
| 1949 | United States 10, Great Britain 2 | Winged Foot GC, Mamaroneck, NY |
| 1951 | United States 6, Great Britain 3 | Birkdale GC, Southport, England |
| 1953 | United States 9, Great Britain 3 | The Kittansett Club, Marion, MA |
| 1955 | United States 10, Great Britain 2 | St. Andrews, Scotland |
| 1957 | United States 8, Great Britain 3 | Minikahda Club, Minneapolis |
| 1959 | United States 9, Great Britain 3 | Muirfield, Scotland |
| 1961 | United States 11, Great Britain 1 | Seattle GC, Seattle |
| 1963 | United States 12, Great Britain 8 | Ailsa Course, Turnberry, Scotland |
| 1965 | Great Britain 11, United States 11 | Baltimore CC, Five Farms, Baltimore, MD |
| 1967 | United States 13, Great Britain 7 | Royal St. George's GC, Sandwich, England |
| 1969 | United States 10, Great Britain 8 | Milwaukee CC, Milwaukee, WI |
| 1971 | Great Britain 13, United States 11 | St. Andrews, Scotland |
| 1973 | United States 14, Great Britain 10 | The Country Club, Brookline, MA |
| 1975 | United States 15½, Great Britain 8½ | St. Andrews, Scotland |
| 1977 | United States 16, Great Britain 8 | Shinnecock Hills GC, Southampton, NY |
| 1979 | United States 15½, Great Britain 8½ | Muirfield, Scotland |
| 1981 | United States 15, Great Britain 9 | Cypress Point Club, Pebble Beach, CA |
| 1983 | United States 13½, Great Britain 10½ | Royal Liverpool GC, Hoylake, England |
| 1985 | United States 13, Great Britain 11 | Pine Valley GC, Pine Valley, NJ |
| 1987 | United States 16½, Great Britain 7½ | Sunningdale GC, Berkshire, England |
| 1989 | Great Britain 12½, United States 11½ | Peachtree Golf Club, Atlanta |
| 1991 | United States 14, Great Britain 10 | Portmarnock GC, Dublin, Ireland |
| 1993 | United States 19, Great Britain 5 | Interlachen CC, Edina, MN |
| 1995 | Great Britain/Ireland 14, United States 10 | Royal Porthcawl, Porthcawl, Wales |
| 1997 | United States 18, Great Britain/Ireland 6 | Quaker Ridge GC, Scarsdale, NY |
| 1999 | Great Britain/Ireland 15, United States 9 | Nairn GC, Nairn, Scotland |
| 2001 | Great Britain/Ireland 15, United States 9 | Ocean Forest GC, Sea Island, GA |

Men's amateur team competition every other year between United States and Great Britain/Ireland. U.S. team members selected by USGA.

## Solheim Cup Matches

| Year | Results | Site |
|---|---|---|
| 1990 | United States 11½, Europe 4½ | Lake Nona GC, Orlando, FL |
| 1992 | Europe 11½, United States 6½ | Dalmahoy Hotel GC, Edinburgh |
| 1994 | United States 13, Europe 7 | The Greenbriar, White Sulpher Springs, WV |
| 1996 | United States 17, Europe 11 | Marriot St Pierre Hotel & CC, Chepstow, Wales |
| 1998 | United States 16, Europe 12 | Muirfield Village GC, Dublin, OH |
| 2000 | Europe 14½, United States, 11½ | Loch Lomond GC, Luss, Scotand |

Team matches held every other year between U.S. professionals and those of Europe. Team members selected on basis of finishes in LPGA and European tour events.

## Curtis Cup Matches

| Year | Results | Site |
|---|---|---|
| 1932 | United States 5½, British Isles 3½ | Wentworth GC, Wentworth, England |
| 1934 | United States 6½, British Isles 2½ | Chevy Chase Club, Chevy Chase, MD |
| 1936 | United States 4½, British Isles 4½ | King's Course, Gleneagles, Scotland |
| 1938 | United States 5½, British Isles 3½ | Essex CC, Manchester, MA |
| 1940–46 | No tournament | |
| 1948 | United States 6½, British Isles 2½ | Birkdale GC, Southport, England |
| 1950 | United States 7½, British Isles 1½ | CC of Buffalo, Williamsville, NY |
| 1952 | British Isles 5, United States 4 | Muirfield, Scotland |
| 1954 | United States 6, British Isles 3 | Merion GC, Ardmore, PA |
| 1956 | British Isles 5, United States 4 | Prince's GC, Sandwich Bay, England |

## Curtis Cup Matches (Cont.)

| Year | Results | Site |
|------|---------|------|
| 1958 | British Isles 4½, United States 4½ | Brae Burn CC, West Newton, Mass. |
| 1960 | United States 6½, British Isles 2½ | Lindrick GC, Worksop, England |
| 1962 | United States 8, British Isles 1 | Broadmoor CG, Colorado Springs,CO |
| 1964 | United States 10½, British Isles 7½ | Royal Porthcawl GC, Porthcawl, South Wales |
| 1966 | United States 13, British Isles 5 | Va. Hot Springs G & TC, Hot Springs, VA |
| 1968 | United States 10½, British Isles 7½ | Royal County Down GC, Newcastle, N. Ire. |
| 1970 | United States 11½, British Isles 6½ | Brae Burn CC, West Newton, MA |
| 1972 | United States 10, British Isles 8 | Western Gailes, Ayrshire, Scotland |
| 1974 | United States 13, British Isles 5 | San Francisco GC, San Francisco |
| 1976 | United States 11½, British Isles 6½ | Royal Lytham & St. Annes GC, England |
| 1978 | United States 12, British Isles 6 | Apawamis Club, Rye, NY |
| 1980 | United States 13, British Isles 5 | St. Pierre G & CC, Chepstow, Wales |
| 1982 | United States 14½, British Isles 3½ | Denver CC, Denver |
| 1984 | United States 9½, British Isles 8½ | Muirfield, Scotland |
| 1986 | British Isles 13, United States 5 | Prairie Dunes CC, Hutchinson, KS |
| 1988 | British Isles 11, United States 7 | Royal St. George's GC, Sandwich, England |
| 1990 | United States 14, British Isles 4 | Somerset Hills CC, Bernardsville, NJ |
| 1992 | Great Britain/Ireland 10, United States 8 | Royal Liverpool GC, Hoylake, England |
| 1994 | Great Britain/Ireland 9, United States 9 | The Honors Course, Ooltewah, TN |
| 1996 | Great Britain/Ireland 11½, United States 6½ | Killarney Golf & Fishing Club, Killarney, Ireland |
| 1998 | United States 10, Great Britain/Ireland 8 | The Minikahda Club, Minneapolis |
| 2000 | United States 10, Great Britain/Ireland 8 | Ganton GC, North Yorkshire, England |

Women's amateur team competition every other year between the United States and Great Britain/Ireland. U.S. team members selected by USGA.

## Famous Flameouts

Although some of the six golf newsmakers listed below had their 15 minutes of fame not much more than 15 minutes ago, plenty has changed for all of them, which in today's world of disposable stars is not so surprising. Here's what these former bright lights, ranked by degree of flameout, are up to today.

**Jenny Chuasiriporn** She was the darling of the 1998 U.S. Women's Open, in which she lost a 20-hole playoff to Se Ri Pak. Instead of cashing in on her fame, Chuasiriporn returned to Duke for her senior year, helping the Blue Devils win the 1999 NCAA title. She has turned pro, but her ambition to play on the LPGA tour has gone unfulfilled. Through mid-September, Chuasiriporn, 24, had won a total of $1,146 in 11 Futures tour events, and she had decided to take a pass on LPGA Q school.

**Robert Landers** A farmer from Azle, Tex., who caught lightning in a bottle when he earned a Senior tour card in the fall of 1995 and opened the '96 season playing in sneakers and using homemade clubs. Landers lasted two years on tour, winning $158,240— enough to pay off the mortgage on his house. He had heart surgery in '98 and, at 57, is back on the farm with his wife, Freddie.

**Paul Lawrie** His victory at age 30 in the 1999 British Open—the tournament Jean Van de Velde threw away—was a happy accident. He has been a non-factor since, with seven top 10 finishes on the European tour in two years.

**Brian Watts** He lost the '98 British Open to Mark O'Meara in a playoff after making a brilliant sand save on the 72nd hole. Watts, 35, is no longer exempt on the PGA Tour. He finished 133rd on the money list in 2000, then missed at Q school by a stroke. In January 2001 he underwent surgery to repair a torn labrum. Watts has played on sponsors' exemptions this year and as of mid-September ranked 94th in earnings in 13 starts.

**Gordon Sherry** One golf writer, a fellow Scot, predicted that Sherry, the 1995 British Amateur champ, would be more successful as a pro than Tiger Woods. Not quite. The 6'8'' Sherry had an amazing, but brief, run in '95. In the weeks following the Amateur he finished fourth in the Scottish Open, was low amateur at the British Open (four shots better than Woods) and led Great Britain and Ireland to victory in the Walker Cup. These days he plays the odd Challenge tour (Europe's version of the Buy.com tour) event but at 27, has no status on any pro circuit.

**Steve Scott** While a sophomore at Florida, he was 2 up on Woods with three holes to play in the final of the '96 U.S. Amateur. Woods rallied to win the title for a third straight year, and Scott lost his putting touch and went into a two-year funk. Married to Kristi Hommel, his caddie at the '96 Amateur, Scott, 24, plays on the Canadian tour, on which in June he won for the first time as a pro.

WBC and IBF
heavyweight champion
Hasim Rahman

# Boxing

# Sweet Again

## Soured by controversy in recent years, boxing reclaimed its famous moniker in 2001 as the focus returned to the ring

### BY MARK BEECH

**A**LL TOO OFTEN, it seems, boxing rewards the paying public with little more than a feeling of exasperation and a lingering suspicion that it may have just been swindled. From carnivorous combatants (Mike Tyson, call your office) to screwy scoring decisions, tomato-can challengers to slippery promoters, the sweet science has become singularly adept at leaving a sour aftertaste in the mouths of fistic aficionados the world over.

So it was refreshing that this year the game seemed to give back to its faithful, bestowing upon them all sorts of memorable moments: an arrogant poseur finally got his just desserts, a complacent champion lost his crown and the esteem of his subjects, and, most rich, two of the best fighters in the world went toe-to-toe in an all-or-nothing bout that satisfied purists and fans alike.

Those two men were Felix Trinidad and Bernard (the Executioner) Hopkins, and their late-September tilt was the result of one of the best brainstorms Don King has ever had. In January the preposterously coiffed promoter announced a middleweight unification series that would produce an undisputed champion in that division for the first time in more than a decade, when Marvelous Marvin Hagler was laying waste to the division.

As 2001 began, Trinidad, 28, held the IBF and WBA championships at 154 pounds—and arguably the mythical mantle of the best pound-for-pound fighter in the world—while Hopkins, 36, owned the IBF middleweight (160-pound) belt. Joining them in the four-fighter tournament were middleweights William Joppy, 30, the WBA champion, and Keith Holmes, 32, the WBC titleholder.

"I got 'em all signed," crowed King in January. "We're going to get an undisputed champion and then that man is going after Roy Jones [Jr., the light heavyweight champ and another contender for the pound-for-pound title]. It's a great shot in the arm for boxing, and it also gives a hard road to glory for whoever comes out the victor in what will be a super, sensational series."

First into the ring were Hopkins and Holmes, who met at Madison Square Gar-

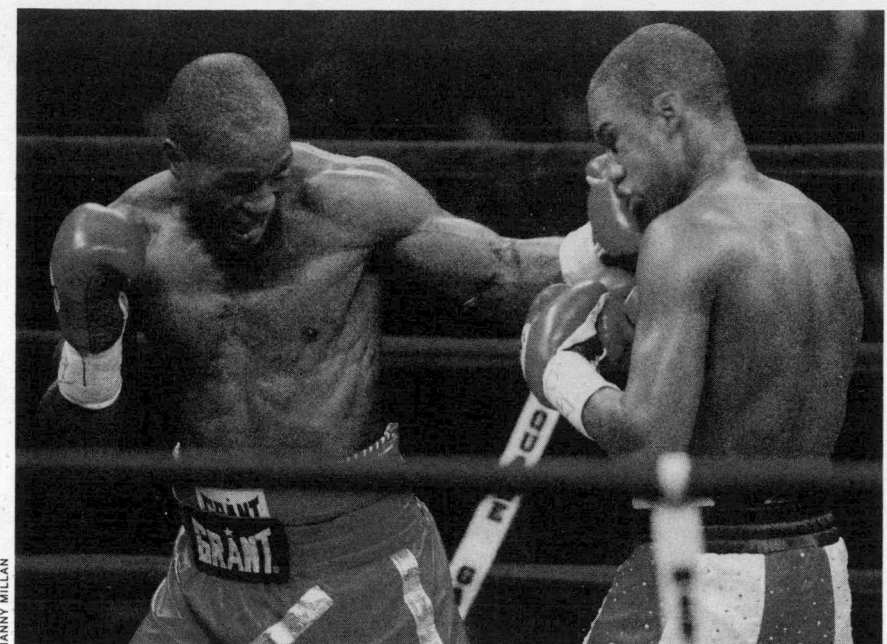

**Hopkins (left) beat Trinidad to unify the middleweight title for the first time since 1987.**

den in April. Hopkins had promised to make an early evening of it but ended up slowly torturing two-time WBC champ Holmes for 12 rounds instead; the unanimous decision improved Hopkins' career record to 39-2-1 with 28 knockouts. The fight may not have been an aesthetic success, as Holmes grabbed and held Hopkins during all 12 rounds, but it was one-sided enough that no one doubted the judges' ruling. "First of all, I did predict I would knock him out," said Hopkins. "Second of all, I lied. I will win the tournament, but no more guarantees of knockouts. I don't care if it's Joppy or Trinidad, I will be rooting for both of them."

He didn't get to root for either one of them very long. Trinidad dispatched Joppy in the fifth round at the Garden in May, delivering a frighteningly brutal TKO. And it had been coming since the first round, when Trinidad dropped the older fighter with a whistling four-punch barrage. In the fourth, Joppy had his eggs scrambled by a three-punch salvo. Trinidad shut off the houselights for good in the fifth, sending Joppy staggering headfirst into the ring post with a pair of lefts, then a pair of rights. "I didn't think he'd have that much power coming up to 160," Joppy said. "I have never been hit like that." Trinidad, who ran his record to a perfect 40–0 with 33 knockouts, said, "My right was for the hospital."

So it was not surprising that he came into his Sept. 29 bout with Hopkins—the tournament final that would serve up a single middleweight world champion—as the decided favorite. What was surprising was the result of that fight: Hopkins took the initiative from the opening bell and picked Trinidad apart over 12 rounds, dropping him late in the 12th, when Trinidad's corner threw in the towel.

That bout made caused many fight fans to forget that this could have been the year in which heavyweight titleholder Lennox Lewis cemented his status as a dominant champion. Instead, with a prefight carelessness that could only ensure his eventual demise, he never made it out of April. In one of the more stunning upsets in recent heavyweight history, Lewis lost to the relatively unknown Hasim Rahman of Baltimore.

The two men met in Johannesburg, South Africa, more than 6,000 feet above sea level. Rahman showed up a month early; Lewis didn't arrive until 12 days before the fight, claiming not to believe all that scientific blather about the effects of altitude. Rahman trained in a hardscrabble gym; Lewis came in at his highest weight ever, 253 pounds, and slacked off on his training while appearing in the film *Ocean's Eleven*, with Brad Pitt and Julia Roberts.

In hindsight, it is glaringly evident that there was only one way the fight could have ended—and it went exactly that way. Rahman floored Lewis in the fifth round with a straight right that arrived when the champion's arms were at his sides. "I can't believe it," Lewis said afterward. "I just can't believe it. I felt fine. I was going about my work nice and comfortable."

Almost as bad for Lewis as the loss of the IBF and WBC titles was that his defeat scuttled any chance that he would fight Tyson in the near future. Enter King, who promptly turned the heavyweight picture upside down. After Rahman's victory, he was to face either Lewis on HBO in a rematch, or Tyson, the WBC's No. 1 contender, on Showtime. On the eve of the day Rahman was reportedly going to sign a $17 million deal for a Lewis bout, King signed him away from his longtime promoter, Cedric Kushner, by presenting the boxer with a check for $4.5 million and a duffel bag containing 5,000 $100 bills. King planned to have Rahman defend his title against David Izon in China, but Lewis counterpunched by going to court and convincing a federal judge that Rahman must either fight Lewis or not fight anybody for 18 months.

Lewis and Rahman signed a $10 million deal in August for a November rematch. During a promotional appearance for the bout, Rahman and Lewis scuffled on camera in the ESPN studios.

While the top heavyweight contenders reduced themselves to a sideshow, the featherweight champion of the world, a man who has made a lucrative career out of being his own sideshow, finally got his chance to show the world if he could actually box. The world quickly found out that he can't.

Prince Naseem Hamed of England, the richest featherweight in history, brought his ragged, sometimes buffoonish fighting style, not to mention his massive ego, to Las Vegas to face his first experienced opponent, Marco Antonio Barrera, and spent an early April evening having all his boxing weaknesses exposed. He lost a 12-round decision in what one wag described as the "best one-sided fight in history."

The Prince, who entered the ring on a swing set against a fireworks display, was matter-of-fact in defeat, perhaps because he earned $6 million just for showing up. "The guy boxed better than me tonight, and that's it," he said. "He's the pure winner tonight. Do I want a rematch? I've got a rematch in the contract. I'm *getting* a rematch."

Say this for Hamed, at least his presence made the bout interesting. Two other fighters, Jones and Sugar Shane Mosley, each of whom could make a case for being the world's best pound-for-pound boxer, couldn't find a worthy opponent all year. Mosley, a welterweight, has been a man in search of an opponent ever since his epic defeat of Oscar De La Hoya in 2000. Unfortunately, the only competitive opponent for him is still De La Hoya, who so far hasn't shown any interest in a rematch.

As for Jones, he challenged all those who had conferred the pound-for-pound title on Trinidad by releasing a rap entitled, *Y'all Must've Forgot*. In Los Angeles in July, as Jones was dismantling the overmatched Julio Gonzales in the seventh round of what would be a 12-round decision, a near-sellout crowd of 20,409 began booing: The bout was no contest.

A far more competitive match could be made with Hopkins, whom Jones defeated in 12 rounds for the IBF middleweight title in 1993. But after downing Trinidad, Hopkins said, "I want Oscar De La Hoya right now. He needs a chance to redeem himself. Roy Jones is not on my radar. Of course, $20 million would change my mind quickly."

## Current Champions

| Division | Weight Limit | WBC Champion | WBA Champion | IBF Champion |
|---|---|---|---|---|
| Heavyweight | None | Hasim Rahman | John Ruiz | Hasim Rahman |
| Cruiserweight | 190 | Juan Carlos Gomez | Virgil Hill | Vassily Jirov |
| Light heavyweight | 175 | Roy Jones Jr | — | Roy Jones Jr |
| Super middleweight | 168 | Eric Lucas | Byron Mitchell | Sven Ottke |
| Middleweight | 160 | Bernard Hopkins | Bernard Hopkins | Bernard Hopkins |
| Junior middleweight | 154 | Oscar De La Hoya | Fernando Vargas | — |
| Welterweight | 147 | Shane Mosley | Andrew Lewis | Vernon Forrest |
| Junior welterweight | 140 | Kostya Tszyu | — | Zab Judah |
| Lightweight | 135 | Jose Luis Castillo | Julien Lorcy | Paul Spadafora |
| Junior lightweight | 130 | Floyd Mayweather | Joel Casamayor | Steve Forbes |
| Featherweight | 126 | Erik Morales | Derrick Gainer | Frankie Toledo |
| Junior featherweight | 122 | Willie Jorrin | — | Manny Pacquiao |
| Bantamweight | 118 | Veerapol Sahaprom | Paulie Ayala | Tim Austin |
| Junior bantamweight | 115 | Masanori Tokuyama | Celes Kobayashi | Felix Machado |
| Flyweight | 112 | Pongsakiek Wonjongkam | Eric Morel | Irene Pacheco |
| Junior flyweight | 108 | Choi Yo-Sam | Rosendo Alvarez | Ricardo Lopez |
| Strawweight | 105 | Jose Aguirre | Yutaka Niida | Robert Leyva |

Note: WBC=World Boxing Council; WBA=World Boxing Association; IBF=International Boxing Federation

## Championship and Major Fights of 2000 and 2001

Abbreviations: WBC=World Boxing Council; WBA= World Boxing Association; IBF=International Boxing Federation; KO=knockout; TKO=technical knockout; UD=unanimous decision; SD=split decision; Disq=disqualification; MD=majority decision.

### Heavyweight

| Date | Winner | Loser | Result | Title | Site |
|---|---|---|---|---|---|
| Nov 11 | Lennox Lewis | David Tua | UD | IBF/WBC | Las Vegas |
| Mar 3 | John Ruiz | Evander Holyfield | UD | WBA | Las Vegas |
| Apr 22 | Hasim Rahman | Lennox Lewis | KO 5 | IBF/WBC | Brakpan, S Africa |

### Cruiserweight

| Date | Winner | Loser | Result | Title | Site |
|---|---|---|---|---|---|
| Dec 9 | Virgil Hill | Fabrice Tiozzo | TKO 1 | WBA | Lyon, France |
| Dec 16 | Juan Carlos Gomez | Jorge Castro | TKO 10 | WBC | Essen, Germany |
| Feb 6 | Vassiliy Jirov | Alex Gonzalez | KO 1 | IBF | Almaty, Kazakhstan |
| Mar 24 | Vassiliy Jirov | Terry McGroom | KO 1 | IBF | Las Vegas |
| Sept 8 | Vassiliy Jirov | Julian Letterlough | TKO 8 | IBF | Reno |

### Light Heavyweight

| Date | Winner | Loser | Result | Title | Site |
|---|---|---|---|---|---|
| Sept 9 | Roy Jones | Eric Harding | TKO 10 | IBF/WBA/WBC | New Orleans |
| Feb 24 | Roy Jones | Derrick Harmon | TKO 10 | IBF/WBA/WBC | Tampa |
| July 28 | Roy Jones | Julio Gonzalez | UD | IBF/WBA/WBC | Los Angeles |
| Aug 4 | Lou Del Valle | Bruno Girard | Draw | WBA | Marseille, France |

### Super Middleweight

| Date | Winner | Loser | Result | Title | Site |
|---|---|---|---|---|---|
| Sept 1 | Glenn Catley | Dingaan Thobela | KO 12 | WBC | Brakpan, S Africa |
| Sept 2 | Sven Ottke | Charles Brewer | SD | IBF | Magdeburg, Germany |
| Sept 16 | Bruno Girard | Manuel Siaca | SD | WBA | Chateauroux, France |
| Dec 15 | Davey Hilton | Dingaan Thobela | SD | WBC | Montreal |
| Dec 16 | Sven Ottke | Silvio Branco | UD | IBF | Karlsruhe, Germany |
| Mar 3 | Byron Mitchell | Manuel Siaca | TKO 12 | WBA | Las Vegas |
| Mar 24 | Sven Ottke | James Crawford | KO 8 | IBF | Magdeburg, Germany |
| June 9 | Sven Ottke | Ali Ennebati | TKO 11 | IBF | Nuremberg, Germany |
| July 10 | Eric Lucas | Glenn Catley | KO 7 | WBC | Montreal |
| Sept 1 | Sven Ottke | James Butler | UD | IBF | Magdeburg, Germany |
| Sept 29 | Byron Mitchell | Manuel Siaca | SD | WBA | New York |

## Middleweight

| Date | Winner | Loser | Result | Title | Site |
|------|--------|-------|--------|-------|------|
| Sept 16 | William Joppy | Hassine Cherifi | UD | WBA | Las Vegas |
| Dec 1 | Bernard Hopkins | Antwun Echols | TKO 10 | IBF | Las Vegas |
| Dec 2 | William Joppy | Jonathan Reid | TKO 4 | WBA | Las Vegas |
| Apr 14 | Bernard Hopkins | Keith Holmes | UD | IBF/WBC | New York City |
| May 12 | Felix Trinidad | William Joppy | TKO 5 | WBA | New York City |
| Sept 29 | Bernard Hopkins | Felix Trinidad | TKO 12 | IBF/WBA/WBC | New York City |

## Junior Middleweight (Super Welterweight)

| Date | Winner | Loser | Result | Title | Site |
|------|--------|-------|--------|-------|------|
| Aug 26 | Fernando Vargas | Ross Thompson | TKO 4 | IBF | Las Vegas |
| Oct 21 | Javier Castillejo | Javier Marinez | TKO 4 | WBC | Mexico City |
| Dec 2 | Felix Trinidad | Fernando Vargas | TKO 12 | IBF/WBA | Las Vegas |
| June 23 | Oscar De La Hoya | Javier Castillejo | UD | WBC | Las Vegas |
| Sept 22 | Fernando Vargas | Jose Flores | KO 7 | WBA | Las Vegas |

## Welterweight

| Date | Winner | Loser | Result | Title | Site |
|------|--------|-------|--------|-------|------|
| Aug 26 | Raul Frank | Vernon Forrest | NC | IBF | Las Vegas |
| Nov 4 | Shane Mosley | Antonio Diaz | TKO 6 | WBC | New York City |
| Feb 17 | Andrew Lewis | James Page | TKO 7 | WBA | Las Vegas |
| Mar 10 | Shane Mosley | Shannan Taylor | TKO 5 | WBC | Las Vegas |
| Apr 28 | Andrew Lewis | Larry Marks | UD | WBA | New York City |
| May 12 | Vernon Forrest | Raul Frank | UD | IBF | New York City |
| July 21 | Shane Mosley | Adrian Stone | KO 3 | WBC | Las Vegas |
| July 28 | Andrew Lewis | Ricardo Mayorga | NC | WBA | Los Angeles |

## Junior Welterweight (Super Lightweight)

| Date | Winner | Loser | Result | Title | Site |
|------|--------|-------|--------|-------|------|
| Sept 16 | Sharmba Mitchell | Felix Flores | UD | WBA | Las Vegas |
| Oct 20 | Zab Judah | Hector Quiroz | TKO 8 | IBF | Auburn Hills, MI |
| Jan 13 | Zab Judah | Reggie Green | TKO 10 | IBF | Uncasville, CT |
| Feb 3 | Kostya Tszyu | Sharmba Mitchell | TKO 7 | WBA/WBC | Las Vegas |
| June 23 | Kostya Tszyu | Oktay Urkal | UD | WBA/WBC | Uncasville, CT |
| June 23 | Zab Judah | Allan Vester | TKO 3 | IBF | Uncasville, CT |

## Lightweight

| Date | Winner | Loser | Result | Title | Site |
|------|--------|-------|--------|-------|------|
| Sept 15 | Jose Luis Castillo | Stevie Johnston | Maj Draw | WBC | Denver |
| Oct 11 | Takanori Hatakeyama | Hiroyuki Sakamoto | KO 10 | WBA | Yokohama, Japan |
| Dec 16 | Paul Spadafora | Billy Irwin | UD | IBF | Pittsburgh |
| Jan 20 | Jose Luis Castillo | Cesar Bazan | TKO 6 | WBC | Las Vegas |
| Feb 17 | Takanori Hatakeyama | Rick Roberts Toshimura | Split Draw | WBA | Tokyo |
| May 8 | Paul Spadafora | Joel Perez | UD | IBF | Pittsburgh |
| June 16 | Jose Luis Castillo | Yuh Sung-Ho | KO 1 | WBC | Hermosillo, Mexico |
| July 1 | Julien Lorcy | Takanori Hatakeyama | UD | WBA | Saitama, Japan |

---

### ANOTHER SIGN OF THE APOCALYPSE

*Top 10 heavyweight boxer Lance Whitaker has asked that he henceforth be referred to simply as Goofi.*

---

## Junior Lightweight (Super Featherweight)

| Date | Winner | Loser | Result | Title | Site |
|------|--------|-------|--------|-------|------|
| Sept 2 | Diego Corrales | Angel Manfredy | TKO 3 | IBF | El Paso, TX |
| Sept 16 | Joel Casamayor | Radford Beasley | TKO 5 | WBA | Las Vegas |
| Dec 3 | Steve Forbes | John Brown | TKO 8 | IBF | Miami |
| Jan 6 | Joel Casamayor | Roberto Garcia | TKO 9 | WBA | Las Vegas |
| Jan 20 | Floyd Mayweather | Diego Corrales | TKO 10 | WBC | Las Vegas |
| May 5 | Joel Casamayor | Edwin Santana | UD | WBA | Philadelphia, MS |
| May 26 | Floyd Mayweather | Carlos Hernandez | UD | WBC | Grand Rapids, MI |
| Sept 29 | Joel Casamayor | Joe Morales | TKO 8 | WBA | Miami |
| Sept 29 | Steve Forbes | John Brown | UD | IBF | Miami |

## Featherweight

| Date | Winner | Loser | Result | Title | Site |
|------|--------|-------|--------|-------|------|
| Sept 2 | Erik Morales | Kevin Kelley | TKO 7 | WBC | El Paso, TX |
| Sept 9 | Derrick Gainer | Freddy Norwood | TKO 11 | WBA | New Orleans |
| Dec 16 | Mbulelo Botile | Paul Ingle | TKO 12 | IBF | Sheffield, England |
| Feb 17 | Erik Morales | Gustavos Espadas Jr | UD | WBC | Las Vegas |
| Feb 24 | Derrick Gainer | Victor Polo | SD | WBA | Tampa |
| Apr 6 | Frankie Toledo | Mbulelo Botile | UD | IBF | Las Vegas |
| July 28 | Erik Morales | Chi In-Jin | UD | WBC | Los Angeles |

## Junior Featherweight (Super Bantamweight)

| Date | Winner | Loser | Result | Title | Site |
|------|--------|-------|--------|-------|------|
| Sept 9 | Willie Jorrin | Michael Brodie | MD | WBC | Manchester, England |
| Oct 6 | Lehlohonolo Ledwaba | Eduardo Alvarez | KO 8 | IBF | Kent, England |
| Nov 23 | Yober Ortega | Kozo Ishii | TKO 11 | WBA | Nagoya, Japan |
| Jan 19 | Willie Jorrin | Oscar Larios | UD | WBC | Sacramento, CA |
| Feb 17 | Lehlohonolo Ledwaba | Arnel Barotillo | TKO 9 | IBF | Brakpan, S Africa |
| Mar 23 | Clarence Adams | Ivan Alvarez | UD | WBA | Owensboro, KY |
| Apr 22 | Lehlohonolo Ledwaba | Carlos Contreras | UD | IBF | Brakpan, S Africa |
| June 23 | Manny Pacquiao | Lehlohonolo Ledwaba | TKO 6 | IBF | Las Vegas |

## Bantamweight

| Date | Winner | Loser | Result | Title | Site |
|------|--------|-------|--------|-------|------|
| Dec 5 | Veerapol Sahaprom | Oscar Arciniega | TKO 5 | WBC | Bangkok, Thailand |
| Dec 16 | Eidy Moya | Saohin Srithai Condo | UD | WBA | Maracay, Venezuela |
| Mar 3 | Tim Austin | Jesus Perez | TKO 6 | IBF | Las Vegas |
| Mar 30 | Paulie Ayala | Hugo Dianzo | UD | WBA | Fort Worth, TX |
| May 14 | Veerapol Sahaprom | Ricardo Barajas | KO 3 | WBC | Paris |
| June 16 | Tim Austin | Steve Dotse | KO 6 | IBF | Cincinnati |
| Sept 1 | Veerapol Sahaprom | Toshiaki Nishioka | Split Draw | WBC | Yokohama, Japan |

## Junior Bantamweight (Super Flyweight)

| Date | Winner | Loser | Result | Title | Site |
|------|--------|-------|--------|-------|------|
| Aug 27 | Masamori Tokuyama | Cho In-Joo | UD | WBC | Osaka, Japan |
| Oct 9 | Leo Gamez | Hideki Todaka | KO 7 | WBA | Nagoya, Japan |
| Dec 12 | Masamori Tokuyama | Akihiko Nago | UD | WBC | Osaka, Japan |
| Dec 16 | Felix Machado | William de Sousa | TKO 3 | IBF | Maracay, Venezuela |
| Mar 11 | Celes Kobayashi | Leo Gamez | TKO 10 | WBA | Yokohama, Japan |
| May 20 | Masamori Tokuyama | Cho In-Joo | KO 5 | WBC | Seoul |
| June 16 | Felix Machado | Mauricio Pastrana | UD | IBF | Cincinnati |
| Sept 1 | Celes Kobayashi | Jesus Rojas | SD | WBA | Yokohama, Japan |
| Sept 24 | Masamori Tokuyama | Gerry Penalosa | UD | WBC | Yokohama, Japan |

## Flyweight

| Date | Winner | Loser | Result | Title | Site |
|---|---|---|---|---|---|
| Oct 7 | Eric Morel | Alberto Ontiveros | UD | WBA | Las Vegas |
| Nov 10 | Irene Pacheco | Masibulele Makepula | MD | IBF | Las Vegas |
| Dec 15 | Eric Morel | Gilberto Keb-Baas | UD | WBA | Madison, WI |
| Mar 2 | P. Wonjongkam | Malcolm Tunacao | TKO 1 | WBC | Pichit, Thailand |
| June 8 | Eric Morel | Jose DeJesus Lopez | TKO 8 | WBA | Baraboo, WI |
| July 15 | P. Wonjongkam | Hayato Asai | TKO 5 | WBC | Nagoya, Japan |

## Junior Flyweight

| Date | Winner | Loser | Result | Title | Site |
|---|---|---|---|---|---|
| Dec 2 | Ricardo Lopez | R. Sow Voraphin | TKO 3 | IBF | Las Vegas |
| Jan 30 | Choi Yo-Sam | Saman Sorjaturong | KO 7 | WBC | Seoul |
| Mar 3 | Rosendo Alvarez | Beibis Mendoza | SD | WBA | Las Vegas |
| Sept 29 | Ricardo Lopez | Zolani Petelo | KO 8 | IBF | New York City |

## Strawweight (Mini Flyweight)

| Date | Winner | Loser | Result | Title | Site |
|---|---|---|---|---|---|
| Oct 21 | Jose Antonio Aguirre | Erdene Chuluun | KO 4 | WBC | Mexico City |
| Dec 6 | Keitaro Hoshino | Joma Gamboa | UD | WBA | Yokohama, Japan |
| Feb 2 | Jose Antonio Aguirre | Manny Melchor | UD | WBC | Tijuana, Mexico |
| Apr 16 | Chana Porpaoin | Keitaro Hoshino | SD | WBA | Yokohama, Japan |
| Apr 29 | Roberto Leyva | Daniel Reyes | UD | IBF | Queens, NY |
| Aug 25 | Yutaka Niida | Chana Porpaoin | UD | WBA | Yokohama, Japan |
| Sept 29 | Roberto Leyva | Miguel Barrera | Tech Draw | IBF | Ensenada, Mexico |

## Of Me I Sing

Remember Roy Jones Jr., the light heavyweight champion, the only undisputed titleholder in boxing? Jones, concerned that you don't, has a single called *Y'all Must've Forgot*. The drumbeating, hip-hop tune begins: *"Everybody get on your feet/Right now for Roy Jones Jr./The best pound-for-pound fighter in the world/Whoever don't agree, you know what?/I guess, y'all must've forgot."*

The reason Jones seems such a distant memory is that despite his technical brilliance, he hardly ever works up a sweat. Unquestionably superior to any of his challengers, Jones has never been seriously tested in his 46 pro fights. Critics carp about his reluctance to mix it up or go for knockouts. Fight fans have even organized a "Roycott" on the Internet, claiming he has padded his record by pounding cream puffs. Jones tries to beat the rap with rap: *"They got the nerve to say I ain't fight nobody/I just make them look like nobody/Y'all must've forgot."*

On this last point at least, the record book backs up Jones: Five of his opponents (Jorge Castro, Bernard Hopkins, Thulane Malinga, Virgil Hill and Eric Lucas) have gone on to win world titles. Alas, Julio Gonzalez, who faced Jones in late July at the Staples Center in Los Angeles, was not in their league. Although undefeated (27–0, 17 KOs), Gonzalez, whom no one will ever call Speedy, was a pigeon ripe for plucking. Jones predicted his foe would see neither the 12th round nor his hands, which he boasted were "so fast in training camp, I couldn't even eat with them."

At 24 Gonzalez is eight years younger than Jones and, at 6'2", three inches taller. Still, Jones treated this bout as little more than a light workout for what looks to be the richest of his career, against the winner of the middleweight title unification showdown between Hopkins and Felix Trinidad. Jones dominated Gonzalez, dropping him in Rounds 1 (on a short left to the chin), 5 (another left hook) and 12 (a right).

Hands held high, Jones sidestepped Gonzalez's lumbering advances and deflected his increasingly predictable shots. Jones attempted 375 punches—a miserly 31 per round—but landed more than half (192) to win a lopsided decision. "You knock him down, he gets up like you gave him a burst of energy," Jones said. "So I [wasn't] going to punch myself out trying to get him down."

Unimpressed by Jones's economy and control of the ring, and resentful that he wouldn't finish off an overmatched opponent, the near-sellout crowd of 20,409 began booing him in the seventh round and never let up. "I was surprised Jones didn't go for a knockout," Gonzalez said.

He'all must've forgot.

# FOR THE RECORD·Year by Year

Sanctioning bodies: the National Boxing Association (NBA), the New York State Athletic Commission (NY), the World Boxing Association (WBA), the World Boxing Council (WBC), and the International Boxing Federation (IBF).

## Heavyweights
### (Weight: Unlimited)

| Champion | Reign |
|---|---|
| John L. Sullivan | 1885–92 |
| James J. Corbett | 1892–97 |
| Bob Fitzsimmons | 1897–99 |
| James J. Jeffries | 1899–05† |
| Marvin Hart | 1905–06 |
| Tommy Burns | 1906–08 |
| Jack Johnson | 1908–15 |
| Jess Willard | 1915–19 |
| Jack Dempsey | 1919–26 |
| Gene Tunney | 1926–28 |
| Max Schmeling | 1930–32 |
| Jack Sharkey | 1932–33 |
| Primo Carnera | 1933–34 |
| Max Baer | 1934–35 |
| James J. Braddock | 1935–37 |
| Joe Louis | 1937–49† |
| Ezzard Charles | 1949–51 |
| Jersey Joe Walcott | 1951–52 |
| Rocky Marciano | 1952–56† |
| Ingemar Johansson | 1959–60 |
| Floyd Patterson | 1960–62 |
| Sonny Liston | 1962–64 |

| Champion | Reign |
|---|---|
| Muhammad Ali | 1964–70 |
| Ernie Terrell* WBA | 1965–67 |
| Joe Frazier* NY | 1968–70 |
| Jimmy Ellis* WBA | 1968–70 |
| Joe Frazier | 1970–73 |
| George Foreman | 1973–74 |
| Muhammad Ali | 1974–78 |
| Leon Spinks | 1978 |
| Ken Norton* WBC | 1978 |
| Larry Holmes* WBC | 1978–80 |
| Muhammad Ali | 1978–79† |
| John Tate* WBA | 1979–80 |
| Mike Weaver* WBA | 1980–82 |
| Larry Holmes | 1980–85 |
| Michael Dokes* WBA | 1982–83 |
| Gerrie Coetzee* WBA | 1983–84 |
| Tim Witherspoon* WBC | 1984 |
| Pinklon Thomas* WBC | 1984–86 |
| Greg Page* WBA | 1984–85 |
| Michael Spinks | 1985–87 |
| Tim Witherspoon* WBA | 1986 |
| Trevor Berbick* WBC | 1986 |

| Champion | Reign |
|---|---|
| Mike Tyson* WBC | 1986–87 |
| James Bonecrusher | |
| Smith* WBA | 1986–87 |
| Tony Tucker* IBF | 1987 |
| Mike Tyson | 1987–90 |
| Buster Douglas | 1990 |
| Evander Holyfield | 1990–92 |
| Lennox Lewis* WBC | 1993–95 |
| Riddick Bowe | 1992–93 |
| Evander Holyfield | 1993–94 |
| Michael Moorer | 1994 |
| George Foreman | 1994–95 |
| Oliver McCall* WBC | 1995 |
| Frank Bruno* WBC | 1995–96 |
| Bruce Seldon* WBA | 1995–96 |
| Mike Tyson WBA | 1996 |
| Michael Moorer* IBF | 1996–97 |
| Lennox Lewis* WBC | 1997–01 |
| E. Holyfield WBA, IBF | 1996–99 |
| Lennox Lewis | 1999–01 |
| E. Holyfield* WBA | 2000–01 |
| John Ruiz* WBA | 2001– |
| Hasim Rahman WBC, IBF | 2001– |

## Cruiserweights
### (Weight Limit: 190 pounds)

| Champion | Reign |
|---|---|
| Marvin Camel* WBC | 1980 |
| Carlos De Leon* WBC | 1980–82 |
| Ossie Ocasio* WBA | 1982–84 |
| S.T. Gordon* WBC | 1982–83 |
| Carlos De Leon* WBC | 1983–85 |
| Marvin Camel* IBF | 1983–84 |
| Lee Roy Murphy* IBF | 1984–86 |
| Piet Crous* WBA | 1984–85 |
| Alfonso Ratliff* WBC | 1985 |
| Dwight Braxton* WBA | 1985–86 |
| Bernard Benton* WBC | 1985–86 |
| Carlos De Leon* WBC | 1986–88 |
| Evander Holyfield* WBA | 1986–88 |

| Champion | Reign |
|---|---|
| Ricky Parkey* IBF | 1986–87 |
| E. Holyfield* WBA, IBF | 1987–88 |
| Evander Holyfield | 1988† |
| Toufik Belbouli* WBA | 1989 |
| Robert Daniels* WBA | 1989–91 |
| Carlos De Leon* WBC | 1989–90 |
| Glenn McCrory* IBF | 1989–90 |
| Jeff Lampkin* IBF | 1990 |
| M. Duran* WBC | 1990–91 |
| Bobby Czyz* WBA | 1991–92† |
| Anaclet Wamba* WBC | 1991–95 |
| James Pritchard* IBF | 1991 |
| James Warring* IBF | 1991–92 |

| Champion | Reign |
|---|---|
| Alfred Cole* IBF | 1992–96 |
| Orlin Norris* WBA | 1993–95 |
| Nate Miller* WBA | 1995–97 |
| Marcelo | |
| Dominguez* WBC | 1996–98 |
| A. Washington* IBF | 1996–97 |
| Uriah Grant* IBF | 1997 |
| Imamu Mayfield* IBF | 1997–98 |
| Fabrice Tiozzo* WBA | 1997–00 |
| J.C. Gomez* WBC | 1998– |
| Arthur Williams* IBF | 1998–99 |
| Vassiliy Jirov* IBF | 1999– |
| Virgil Hill* WBA | 2000– |

Note: Division called Junior Heavyweight by the WBA.

*Champion not generally recognized.  †Champion retired or relinquished title.

### Light Heavyweights
### (Weight Limit: 175 pounds)

| Champion | Reign | Champion | Reign | Champion | Reign |
|---|---|---|---|---|---|
| Jack Root | 1903 | Archie Moore | 1952–62† | Marvin Johnson* WBA | 1986–87 |
| George Gardner | 1903 | Harold Johnson* NBA | 1961 | Dennis Andries* WBC | 1986–87 |
| Bob Fitzsimmons | 1903–05 | Harold Johnson | 1962–63 | Bobby Czyz* IBF | 1986–87 |
| Philadelphia Jack | | Willie Pastrano | 1963–65 | Leslie Stewart* WBA | 1987 |
| O'Brien | 1905–12† | Jose Torres | 1965–66 | Virgil Hill* WBA | 1987–91 |
| Jack Dillon | 1914–16 | Dick Tiger | 1966–68 | Pr Charles Williams* IBF | 1987–93 |
| Battling Levinsky | 1916–20 | Bob Foster | 1968–74† | Thomas Hearns* WBC | 1987† |
| Georges Carpentier | 1920–22 | Vicente Rondon* WBA | 1971–72 | Donny Lalonde* WBC | 1987–88 |
| Battling Siki | 1922–23 | John Conteh* WBC | 1974–77 | Sugar Ray Leonard* WBC | 1988 |
| Mike McTigue | 1923–25 | Victor Galindez* WBA | 1974–78 | Dennis Andries* WBC | 1989 |
| Paul Berlenbach | 1925–26 | Miguel A. Cuello* WBC | 1977–78 | Jeff Harding* WBC | 1989–90 |
| Jack Delaney | 1926–27† | Mate Parlov* WBC | 1978 | Dennis Andries* WBC | 1990–91 |
| Jimmy Slattery* NBA | 1927 | Mike Rossman* WBA | 1978–79 | Thomas Hearns* WBC | 1991–92 |
| Tommy Loughran | 1927–29 | Marvin Johnson* WBC | 1978–79 | Jeff Harding* WBC | 1991–94 |
| Maxie Rosenbloom | 1930–34 | Matthew Saad | | Iran Barkley* WBA | 1992 |
| George Nichols* NBA | 1932 | Muhammad* WBC | 1979–81 | Virgil Hill* WBA | 1992–97 |
| Bob Godwin* NBA | 1933 | Marvin Johnson* WBA | 1979–80 | Henry Maske* IBF | 1993–96 |
| Bob Olin | 1934–35 | Eddie Mustapha | | Mike McCallum* WBC | 1994–95 |
| John Henry Lewis | 1935–38 | Muhammad* WBA | 1980–81 | Fabrice Tiozzo* WBC | 1995–96 |
| Melio Bettina | 1939 | Michael Spinks* WBA | 1981–83 | Roy Jones Jr. WBC, WBA. | 1997– |
| Billy Conn | 1939–40† | D. Muhammad | | William Guthrie* IBF | 1997–98 |
| Anton Christoforidis | 1941 | Qawi* WBC | 1981–83 | Reggie Johnson* IBF | 1998–99 |
| Gus Lesnevich | 1941–48 | Michael Spinks | 1983–85† | Roy Jones Jr. | 1999– |
| Freddie Mills | 1948–50 | J. B. Williamson* WBC | 1985–86 | | |
| Joey Maxim | 1950–52 | Slobodan Kacar* IBF | 1985–86 | | |

### Super Middleweights
### (Weight Limit: 168 pounds)

| Champion | Reign | Champion | Reign | Champion | Reign |
|---|---|---|---|---|---|
| Murray Sutherland* IBF | 1984 | Darrin Van Horn* IBF | 1991–92 | Charles Brewer* IBF | 1997–98 |
| Chong-Pal Park* IBF | 1984–87 | Iran Barkley *IBF | 1992 | Thulane Malinga* WBC | 1997–98 |
| Chong-Pal Park* WBA | 1987–88 | Nigel Benn* WBC | 1992–96 | Richie Woodhall* WBC | 1998–99 |
| G. Rocchigiani* IBF | 1988–89 | James Toney* IBF | 1992–94 | Sven Ottke* IBF | 1998– |
| F. Obelmejias* WBA | 1988–89 | Michael Nunn* WBA | 1992–94 | Byron Mitchell* WBA | 1999–00 |
| Sugar Ray Leonard* WBC | 1988–90† | Steve Little* WBA | 1994 | Markus Beyer* WBC | 1999–00 |
| In-Chul Baek* WBA | 1989–90 | Frank Liles* WBA | 1994–99 | Bruno Girard* WBA | 2000–01† |
| Lindell Holmes* IBF | 1990–91 | Roy Jones Jr.* IBF | 1994–96 | Glenn Catley* WBC | 2000–01 |
| C. Tiozzo* WBA | 1990–91 | Thulane Malinga* WBC | 1996 | Eric Lucas* WBC | 2000– |
| Mauro Galvano* WBC | 1990–92 | V. Nardiello* WBC | 1996 | Byron Mitchell* WBA | 2000– |
| Victor Cordova* WBA | 1991 | Robin Reid* WBC | 1996–97 | | |

*Champion not generally recognized.   †Champion retired or relinquished title.

## Belting 'Em Out

What is it about the sweet science and singing? Pugilists gravitate to the mike with alarming frequency. Witness Roy Jones Jr., who released his debut rap album, *Round One*, in May. Here's a one- to five-glove rating of some other warbling warriors.

JAKE LaMOTTA: After his boxing career the Raging Bull opened a Miami nightclub, where he often sang standards. He also appeared onstage in a Broadway production of *Guys and Dolls*; Walter Winchell called his performance "surprisingly good." Crooner rating: Two Gloves.

JOE FRAZIER: Played gigs from Atlantic City to Las Vegas in the 1960s and '70s, first as the front man of Joe Frazier and the Knockouts and later with Smokin' Joe's Revue. In February 1977, *The New York Times* said, "He has a warm and pleasant voice and an easy, gracious manner." Crooner rating: Four Gloves.

LARRY HOLMES: Dueled with Frazier in the Battle of the Singing Heavyweight Champs in June 1987 in Atlantic City. Holmes opened with the rap *Boxing Politics*. Sample lyrics: "I trained real hard/To do the job/But I got robbed ... Everybody knows I beat Spinks/Everybody knows boxing stinks." Crooner rating: One Glove.

OSCAR DE LA HOYA: His eponymous album, which blends romantic pop numbers with ballads in English and Spanish, was released last year. Said *Billboard*, "A surprisingly pleasing experience, with more expressed talent than any number of successful artists." De La Hoya was nominated for a Grammy in 2001 for Best Latin Pop Album. Crooner rating: Five Gloves.

## Middleweights
## (Weight Limit: 160 pounds)

| Champion | Reign | Champion | Reign | Champion | Reign |
|---|---|---|---|---|---|
| Jack Dempsey | 1884–91 | Marcel Cerdan | 1948–49 | Alan Minter | 1980 |
| Bob Fitzsimmons | 1891–97 | Jake La Motta | 1949–51 | Marvin Hagler | 1980–87 |
| Kid McCoy | 1897–98 | Sugar Ray Robinson | 1951 | Sugar Ray Leonard | 1987† |
| Tommy Ryan | 1898–1907 | Randy Turpin | 1951 | Frank Tate* IBF | 1987–88 |
| Stanley Ketchel | 1908 | Sugar Ray Robinson | 1951–52 | Sumbu Kalambay* WBA | 1987–89 |
| Billy Papke | 1908 | Bobo Olson | 1953–55 | Thomas Hearns* WBC | 1987–88 |
| Stanley Ketchel | 1908–10 | Sugar Ray Robinson | 1955–57 | Iran Barkley* WBC | 1988–89 |
| Frank Klaus | 1913 | Gene Fullmer | 1957 | Michael Nunn* IBF | 1988–91 |
| George Chip | 1913–14 | Sugar Ray Robinson | 1957 | Roberto Duran* WBC | 1989–90† |
| Al McCoy | 1914–17 | Carmen Basilio | 1957–58 | Mike McCallum* WBA | 1989–91 |
| Mike O'Dowd | 1917–20 | Sugar Ray Robinson | 1958–60 | Julian Jackson* WBC | 1990–93 |
| Johnny Wilson | 1920–23 | Gene Fullmer* NBA | 1959–62 | James Toney* IBF | 1991–93† |
| Harry Greb | 1923–26 | Paul Pender | 1960–61 | Reggie Johnson* WBA | 1992–94 |
| Tiger Flowers | 1926 | Terry Downes | 1961–62 | Roy Jones Jr.* IBF | 1993–95† |
| Mickey Walker | 1926–31† | Paul Pender | 1962–63 | G. McClellan* WBC | 1993–95† |
| Gorilla Jones | 1931–32 | Dick Tiger* WBA | 1962–63 | Jorge Castro* WBA | 1994–95 |
| Marcel Thil | 1932–37 | Dick Tiger | 1963 | Shinji Takehara* WBA | 1995–96 |
| Fred Apostoli | 1937–39 | Joey Giardello | 1963–65 | Jullian Jackson*WBC | 1995 |
| Al Hostak* NBA | 1938 | Dick Tiger | 1965–66 | Quincy Taylor* WBC | 1995–96 |
| Solly Krieger* NBA | 1938–39 | Emile Griffith | 1966–67 | Bernard Hopkins* IBF | 1995– |
| Al Hostak* NBA | 1939–40 | Nino Benvenuti | 1967 | Keith Holmes* WBC | 1996–98 |
| Ceferino Garcia | 1939–40 | Emile Griffith | 1967–68 | William Joppy Jr.* WBA | 1996–97 |
| Ken Overlin | 1940–41 | Nino Benvenuti | 1968–70 | J.C. Green* WBA | 1997 |
| Tony Zale* NBA | 1940–41 | Carlos Monzon | 1970–77† | William Joppy Jr.* WBA | 1998–01 |
| Billy Soose | 1941 | Rodrigo Valdez* WBC | 1974–76 | Hassine Cherifi* WBC | 1998–99 |
| Tony Zale | 1941–47 | Rodrigo Valdez | 1977–78 | Keith Holmes* WBC | 1999–00 |
| Rocky Graziano | 1947–48 | Hugo Corro | 1978–79 | Felix Trinidad* WBA | 2001 |
| Tony Zale | 1948 | Vito Antuofermo | 1979–80 | Bernard Hopkins | 2001– |

## Junior Middleweights
## (Weight Limit: 154 pounds)

| Champion | Reign | Champion | Reign | Champion | Reign |
|---|---|---|---|---|---|
| Emile Griffith (EBU) | 1962–63 | Ayub Kalule | 1979–81 | Terry Norris* WBC | 1990–93 |
| Dennis Moyer | 1962–63 | Wilfred Benitez* WBC | 1981–82 | Gilbert Dele* WBA | 1991 |
| Ralph Dupas | 1963 | Sugar Ray Leonard | 1981–82† | Vinny Pazienza* WBA | 1991–92 |
| Sandro Mazzinghi | 1963–65 | Tadashi Mihara* WBA | 1981–82 | Julio C. Vasquez* WBA | 1992–95 |
| Nino Benvenuti | 1965–66 | Davey Moore* WBA | 1982–83 | Simon Brown* WBC | 1993–94 |
| Ki-Soo Kim | 1966–68 | Thomas Hearns* WBC | 1982–84 | Terry Norris *WBC | 1994–97 |
| Sandro Mazzinghi | 1968 | Roberto Duran* WBA | 1983–84 | Vincent Pettway* IBF | 1994–95 |
| Freddie Little | 1969–70 | Mark Medal* IBF | 1984 | Paul Vaden* IBF | 1995 |
| Carmelo Bossi | 1970–71 | Thomas Hearns | 1984–86† | Carl Daniels* WBA | 1995 |
| Koichi Wajima | 1971–74 | Mike McCallum* WBA | 1984–87† | Terry Norris WBC | 1995–97 |
| Oscar Albarado | 1974–75 | Carlos Santos* IBF | 1984–86 | Terry Norris IBF | 1995–96† |
| Koichi Wajima | 1975 | Buster Drayton* IBF | 1986–87 | L. Boudouani* WBA | 1996–99 |
| Miguel de Oliveira* WBC | 1975–76 | Duane Thomas* WBC | 1986–87 | Raul Marquez* IBF | 1997 |
| Jao Do Yuh | 1975–76 | Matthew Hilton* IBF | 1987–88 | Keith Mullings* WBC | 1997–99 |
| Elisha Obed* WBC | 1975–76 | Lupe Aquino* WBC | 1987 | Yori Boy Campas* IBF | 1997–98 |
| Koichi Wajima | 1976 | Gianfranco Rosi* WBC | 1987–88 | Fernando Vargas* IBF | 1998–00 |
| Jose Duran | 1976 | Julian Jackson* WBC | 1987–90 | F. Javier Castillejo* WBC | 1999–01 |
| Eckhard Dagge* WBC | 1976–77 | Donald Curry* WBC | 1988–89 | David Reid* WBA | 1999–00 |
| Miguel Angel Castellini | 1976–77 | Robert Hines* IBF | 1988–89 | Felix Trinidad* WBA | 2000–01 |
| Eddie Gazo | 1977–78 | Darrin Van Horn* IBF | 1989 | Felix Trinidad WBA, IBF | 2001† |
| Rocky Mattioli* WBC | 1977–79 | Rene Jacquot* WBC | 1989 | Oscar De La Hoya WBC | 2001– |
| Masashi Kudo | 1978–79 | John Mugabi* WBC | 1989–90 | Fernando Vargas* WBA | 2001– |
| Maurice Hope* WBC | 1979–81 | Gianfranco Rosi* IBF | 1989–94 | | |

Note: Division called Super Welterweight by the WBC.

## Welterweights
### (Weight Limit: 147 pounds)

| Champion | Reign |
|---|---|
| Paddy Duffy | 1888–90 |
| Mysterious Billy Smith | 1892–94 |
| Tommy Ryan | 1894–98 |
| Mysterious Billy Smith | 1898–1900 |
| Rube Ferns | 1900 |
| Matty Matthews | 1900–01 |
| Rube Ferns | 1901 |
| Joe Walcott | 1901–04 |
| The Dixie Kid | 1904–05 |
| Honey Mellody | 1906–07 |
| Twin Sullivan | 1907–08 |
| Jimmy Gardner | 1908 |
| Jimmy Clabby | 1910–11 |
| Waldemar Holberg | 1914 |
| Tom McCormick | 1914 |
| Matt Wells | 1914–15 |
| Mike Glover | 1915 |
| Jack Britton | 1915 |
| Ted "Kid" Lewis | 1915–16 |
| Jack Britton | 1916–17 |
| Ted "Kid" Lewis | 1917–19 |
| Jack Britton | 1919–22 |
| Mickey Walker | 1922–26 |
| Pete Latzo | 1926–27 |
| Joe Dundee | 1927–29 |
| Jackie Fields | 1929–30 |
| Young Jack Thompson | 1930 |
| Tommy Freeman | 1930–31 |
| Young Jack Thompson | 1931 |
| Lou Brouillard | 1931–32 |
| Jackie Fields | 1932–33 |
| Young Corbett III | 1933 |
| Jimmy McLarnin | 1933–34 |
| Barney Ross | 1934 |
| Jimmy McLarnin | 1934–35 |
| Barney Ross | 1935–38 |
| Henry Armstrong | 1938–40 |
| Fritzie Zivic | 1940–41 |
| Red Cochrane | 1941–46 |
| Marty Servo | 1946 |
| Sugar Ray Robinson | 1946–51† |
| Johnny Bratton | 1951 |
| Kid Gavilan | 1951–54 |
| Johnny Saxton | 1954–55 |
| Tony DeMarco | 1955 |
| Carmen Basilio | 1955–56 |
| Johnny Saxton | 1956 |
| Carmen Basilio | 1956–57 |
| Virgil Akins | 1958 |
| Don Jordan | 1958–60 |
| Kid Paret | 1960–61 |
| Emile Griffith | 1961 |
| Kid Paret | 1961–62 |
| Emile Griffith | 1962–63 |
| Luis Rodriguez | 1963 |
| Emile Griffith | 1963–66 |
| Curtis Cokes | 1966–69 |
| Jose Napoles | 1969–70 |
| Billy Backus | 1970–71 |
| Jose Napoles | 1971–75 |
| Hedgemon Lewis* NY | 1972–73 |
| Angel Espada* WBA | 1975–76 |
| John H. Stracey | 1975–76 |
| Carlos Palomino | 1976–79 |
| Pipino Cuevas* WBA | 1976–80 |
| Wilfredo Benitez | 1979 |
| Sugar Ray Leonard | 1979–80 |
| Roberto Duran | 1980 |
| Thomas Hearns* WBA | 1980–81 |
| Sugar Ray Leonard | 1980–82† |
| Donald Curry* WBA | 1983–85 |
| Milton McCrory* WBC | 1983–85 |
| Donald Curry | 1985–86 |
| Lloyd Honeyghan | 1986–87 |
| Jorge Vaca WBC | 1987–88 |
| Lloyd Honeyghan WBC | 1988–89 |
| Mark Breland* WBA | 1987 |
| Marlon Starling* WBA | 1987–88 |
| Tomas Molinares* WBA | 1988–89 |
| Simon Brown* IBF | 1988–91 |
| Mark Breland* WBA | 1989–90 |
| Marlon Starling* WBC | 1989–90 |
| Aaron Davis* WBA | 1990–91 |
| Maurice Blocker* WBC | 1990–91 |
| Meldrick Taylor* WBA | 1991–92 |
| Simon Brown* WBC | 1991 |
| Buddy McGirt* WBC | 1991–93 |
| Felix Trinidad* IBF | 1993–00 |
| Pernell Whitaker WBC | 1993–97 |
| Crisanto Espana* WBA | 1992–94 |
| Ike Quartey* WBA | 1994–97† |
| Oscar De La Hoya* WBC | 1997–99 |
| James Page* WBA | 1998–01 |
| Felix Trinidad IBF, WBC | 1999–00† |
| Shane Mosley* WBC | 2000– |
| Andrew Lewis* WBA | 2001– |
| Vernon Forrest* IBF | 2001– |

## Junior Welterweights
### (Weight Limit: 140 pounds)

| Champion | Reign |
|---|---|
| Pinkey Mitchell | 1922–25 |
| Red Herring | 1925 |
| Mushy Callahan | 1926–30 |
| Jack (Kid) Berg | 1930–31 |
| Tony Canzoneri | 1931–32 |
| Johnny Jadick | 1932–33 |
| Sammy Fuller* | 1932–33 |
| Battling Shaw | 1933 |
| Tony Canzoneri | 1933 |
| Barney Ross | 1933–35 |
| Tippy Larkin | 1946 |
| Carlos Ortiz | 1959–60 |
| Duilio Loi | 1960–62 |
| Eddie Perkins | 1962 |
| Duilio Loi | 1962–63 |
| Roberto Cruz* WBA | 1963 |
| Eddie Perkins | 1963–65 |
| Carlos Hernandez | 1965–66 |
| Sandro Lopopolo | 1966–67 |
| Paul Fujii | 1967–68 |
| Nicolino Loche | 1968–72 |
| Pedro Adigue* WBC | 1968–70 |
| Bruno Arcari* WBC | 1970–74 |
| Alfonso Frazer | 1972 |
| Antonio Cervantes | 1972–76 |
| Perico Fernandez* WBC | 1974–75 |
| S. Muangsurin* WBC | 1975–76 |
| Wilfred Benitez | 1976–79† |
| M. Velasquez* WBC | 1976 |
| S. Muangsurin* WBC | 1976–78 |
| A. Cervantes* WBA | 1977–80 |
| Sang-Hyun Kim* WBC | 1978–80 |
| Saoul Mamby* WBC | 1980–82 |
| Aaron Pryor* WBA | 1980–83 |
| Leroy Haley* WBC | 1982–83 |
| Aaron Pryor* IBF | 1983–85 |
| Bruce Curry* WBC | 1983–84 |
| Johnny Bumphus* WBA | 1984 |
| Bill Costello* WBC | 1984–85 |
| Gene Hatcher* WBA | 1984–85 |
| Ubaldo Sacco* WBA | 1985–86 |
| Lonnie Smith* WBC | 1985–86 |
| Patrizio Oliva* WBA | 1986–87 |
| Gary Hinton* IBF | 1986 |
| Rene Arredondo* WBC | 1986 |
| Tsuyoshi Hamada* WBC | 1986–87 |
| Joe Louis Manley* IBF | 1986–87 |
| Terry Marsh* IBF | 1987 |
| Juan Coggi* WBA | 1987–90 |
| Rene Arredondo* WBC | 1987 |
| R. Mayweather* WBC | 1987–89 |
| James McGirt* IBF | 1988 |
| Meldrick Taylor* IBF | 1988–90 |
| Julio César Chávez* WBC | 1989–94 |
| Julio César Chávez* IBF | 1990–91 |
| Loreto Garza* WBA | 1990–91 |
| Juan Coggi* WBA | 1991 |
| Edwin Rosario* WBA | 1991–92 |
| Rafael Pineda* IBF | 1991–92 |
| Akinobu Hiranaka* WBA | 1992 |
| Pernell Whitaker* IBF | 1992–93† |
| Charles Murray* IBF | 1993–94 |
| Jake Rodriguez* IBF | 1994–95 |
| Juan Coggi* WBA | 1993–94 |
| Frankie Randall* WBC | 1994 |
| Frankie Randall* WBA | 1994–96 |
| Juan Coggi* WBA | 1996 |
| Julio César Chávez WBC | 1994–96 |
| Kostya Tszyu* IBF | 1995–97 |
| Frankie Randall* WBC | 1996–97 |
| Oscar De La Hoya WBC | 1996–97† |
| Khalid Rahilou* WBA | 1997–98 |
| Vincent Phillips* IBF | 1997–99 |
| Sharmba Mitchell* WBA | 1998–01 |
| Kostya Tszyu* WBC | 1998– |
| Terronn Millett* IBF | 1999–00 |
| Zab Judah* IBF | 2000– |
| Kostya Tszyu WBA,WBC | 2001– |

## Lightweights
### (Weight Limit: 135 pounds)

| Champion | Reign | Champion | Reign | Champion | Reign |
|---|---|---|---|---|---|
| Jack McAuliffe | 1886–94 | James Carter | 1952–54 | Edwin Rosario* WBA | 1986–87 |
| Kid Lavigne | 1896–99 | Paddy DeMarco | 1954 | Julio César Chávez* WBA | 1987–88 |
| Frank Erne | 1899–1902 | James Carter | 1954–55 | Jose Luis Ramirez* WBC | 1987–88 |
| Joe Gans | 1902–04 | Wallace Smith | 1955–56 | Julio César Chávez | 1988–89 |
| Jimmy Britt | 1904–05 | Joe Brown | 1956–62 | Vinny Pazienza* IBF | 1987–88 |
| Battling Nelson | 1905–06 | Carlos Ortiz | 1962–65 | Greg Haugen* IBF | 1988–89 |
| Joe Gans | 1906–08 | Ismael Laguna | 1965 | P. Whitaker* WBC, IBF | 1989–90 |
| Battling Nelson | 1908–10 | Carlos Ortiz | 1965–68 | Edwin Rosario* WBA | 1989–90 |
| Ad Wolgast | 1910–12 | Carlos Teo Cruz | 1968–69 | Juan Nazario* WBA | 1990 |
| Willie Ritchie | 1912–14 | Mando Ramos | 1969–70 | P. Whitaker* WBA, WBC | 1990–92 |
| Freddie Welsh | 1915–17 | Ismael Laguna | 1970 | Pernell Whitaker* IBF | 1991–92 |
| Benny Leonard | 1917–25† | Ken Buchanan | 1970–72 | Julio César Chávez* IBF | 1990–91 |
| Jimmy Goodrich | 1925 | Roberto Duran | 1972–79† | Edwin Rosario* WBA | 1991–92 |
| Rocky Kansas | 1925–26 | Chango Carmona* WBC | 1972 | Julio César Chávez* WBC | 1990–92 |
| Sammy Mandell | 1926–30 | Rodolfo Gonzalez* WBC | 1972–74 | Miguel Gonzalez* WBC | 1992–95 |
| Al Singer | 1930 | Ishimatsu Suzuki* WBC | 1974–76 | Joey Gamache* WBA | 1992–93 |
| Tony Canzoneri | 1930–33 | Estaban DeJesus* WBC | 1976–78 | Dingaan Thobela* WBA | 1993 |
| Barney Ross | 1933–35† | Jim Watt* WBC | 1979–81 | Fred Pendleton* IBF | 1993–94 |
| Tony Canzoneri | 1935–36 | Ernesto Espana* WBA | 1979–80 | Orzubek Nazarov* WBA | 1993–98 |
| Lou Ambers | 1936–38 | Hilmer Kenty* WBA | 1980–81 | Rafael Ruelas* IBF | 1994–95 |
| Henry Armstrong | 1938–39 | Sean O'Grady* WBA | 1981 | Phillip Holiday* IBF | 1995–97 |
| Lou Ambers | 1939–40 | Claude Noel* WBA | 1981 | Jean B. Mendy* WBC | 1996–97 |
| Sammy Angott* NBA | 1940–41 | Alexis Arguello* WBC | 1981–82 | Steve Johnston* WBC | 1997–98 |
| Lew Jenkins | 1940–41 | Arturo Frias* WBA | 1981–82 | Shane Mosley* IBF | 1997–99† |
| Sammy Angott | 1941–42† | Ray Mancini* WBA | 1982–84 | Jean B. Mendy* WBA | 1998–99 |
| Beau Jack* NY | 1942–43 | Alexis Arguello | 1982–83 | Cesar Bazan* WBC | 1998–99 |
| Bob Montgomery* NY | 1943 | Edwin Rosario* WBC | 1983–84 | Steve Johnston* WBC | 1999–00 |
| Sammy Angott* NBA | 1943–44 | Choo Choo Brown* IBF | 1984 | Julien Lorcy* WBA | 1999 |
| Beau Jack* NY | 1943–44 | L. Bramble* WBA | 1984–86 | Stefano Zoff* WBA | 1999 |
| Bob Montgomery* NY | 1944–47 | Jose Luis Ramirez* WBC | 1984–85 | Paul Spadafora* IBF | 1999– |
| Juan Zurita* NBA | 1944–45 | Harry Arroyo* IBF | 1984–85 | Gilbert Serrano* WBA | 1999–00 |
| Ike Williams | 1947–51 | Jimmy Paul* IBF | 1985–86 | T. Hatakeyama* WBA | 2000–01 |
| James Carter | 1951–52 | Hector Camacho* WBC | 1985–86 | Jose Luis Castillo* WBC | 2000– |
| Lauro Salas | 1952 | Greg Haugen* IBF | 1986–87 | Julien Lorcy* WBA | 2001– |

## Junior Lightweights
### (Weight Limit: 130 pounds)

| Champion | Reign | Champion | Reign | Champion | Reign |
|---|---|---|---|---|---|
| Johnny Dundee | 1921–23 | Samuel Serrano | 1976–80 | Tony Lopez* IBF | 1990–91 |
| Jack Bernstein | 1923 | Alexis Arguello* WBC | 1978–80 | Joey Gamache WBA | 1991 |
| Johnny Dundee | 1923–24 | Yasutsune Uehara | 1980–81 | Brian Mitchell* IBF | 1991 |
| Steve (Kid) Sullivan | 1924–25 | Rafael Limon* WBC | 1980–81 | Genaro Hernandez* WBA | 1991–95 |
| Mike Ballerino | 1925 | C. Boza-Edwards* WBC | 1981 | James Leija* WBC | 1994 |
| Tod Morgan | 1925–29 | Samuel Serrano | 1981–83 | Juan Molina* IBF | 1991–95 |
| Benny Bass | 1929–31 | R. Navarrete* WBC | 1981–82 | Gabriel Ruelas* WBC | 1994–95 |
| Kid Chocolate | 1931–33 | Rafael Limon* WBC | 1982 | Eddie Hopson* IBF | 1995 |
| Frankie Klick | 1933–34 | Bobby Chacon* WBC | 1982–83 | Tracy Patterson* IBF | 1995 |
| Sandy Saddler | 1949–50 | Roger Mayweather | 1983–84 | Azumah Nelson* WBC | 1995–97 |
| Harold Gomes | 1959–60 | Hector Camacho* WBC | 1983–84 | Choi Yong-Soo* WBA | 1995–98 |
| Gabriel (Flash) Elorde | 1960–67 | Rocky Lockridge | 1984–85 | Arturo Gatti* IBF | 1995–98† |
| Yoshiaki Numata | 1967 | Hwan-Kil Yuh* IBF | 1984–85 | Genaro Hernandez* WBC | 1997–98 |
| Hiroshi Kobayashi | 1967–71 | Julio César Chávez* WBC | 1984–87 | Roberto Garcia* IBF | 1998–99 |
| Rene Barrientos* WBC | 1969–70 | Lester Ellis* IBF | 1985 | Floyd Mayweather* WBC | 1998– |
| Yoshiaki Numata* WBC | 1970–71 | Wilfredo Gomez | 1985–86 | T. Hatakeyama* WBA | 1998–99 |
| Alfredo Marcano | 1971–72 | Barry Michael* IBF | 1985–87 | Lakva Sim* WBA | 1999 |
| R. Arredondo* WBC | 1971–74 | Alfredo Layne* WBA | 1986 | Diego Corrales* IBF | 1999–01 |
| Ben Villaflor | 1972–73 | Brian Mitchell* WBA | 1986–91 | Jong Kwon Baek* WBA | 1999–00 |
| Kuniaki Shibata | 1973 | Rocky Lockridge* IBF | 1987–88 | Joel Casamayor* WBA | 2000– |
| Ben Villaflor | 1973–76 | Azumah Nelson* WBC | 1988–94 | Steve Forbes* IBF | 2000– |
| Kuniaki Shibata* WBC | 1974–75 | Tony Lopez* IBF | 1988–89 | | |
| Alfredo Escalera* WBC | 1975–78 | Juan Molina* IBF | 1989–90 | | |

*Champion not generally recognized. †Champion retired or relinquished title.

## Featherweights
### (Weight Limit: 126 pounds)

| Champion | Reign |
|---|---|
| Torpedo Billy Murphy | 1890 |
| Young Griffo | 1890–92 |
| George Dixon | 1892–97 |
| Solly Smith | 1897–98 |
| Dave Sullivan | 1898 |
| George Dixon | 1898–1900 |
| Terry McGovern | 1900–01 |
| Young Corbett II | 1901–04 |
| Jimmy Britt | 1904 |
| Tommy Sullivan | 1904–05 |
| Abe Attell | 1906–12 |
| Johnny Kilbane | 1912–23 |
| Eugene Criqui | 1923 |
| Johnny Dundee | 1923–24 |
| "Kid" Kaplan | 1925–26 |
| Benny Bass | 1927–28 |
| Tony Canzoneri | 1928 |
| Andre Routis | 1928–29 |
| Battling Battalino | 1929–32 |
| Tommy Paul* NBA | 1932–33 |
| Kid Chocolate* NY | 1932–33 |
| Freddie Miller* NBA | 1933–36 |
| Mike Beloise* NY | 1936–37 |
| Petey Sarron* NBA | 1936–37 |
| Maurice Holtzer | 1937–38 |
| Henry Armstrong | 1937–38 |
| Joey Archibald* NY | 1938–39 |
| Leo Rodak* NBA | 1938–39 |
| Joey Archibald | 1939–40 |
| Petey Scalzo* NBA | 1940–41 |
| Harry Jeffra | 1940–41 |
| Joey Archibald | 1941 |
| Richie Lamos* NBA | 1941 |
| Chalky Wright | 1941–42 |
| Jackie Wilson* NBA | 1941–43 |

| Champion | Reign |
|---|---|
| Willie Pep | 1942–48 |
| Jackie Callura* NBA | 1943 |
| Phil Terranova* NBA | 1943–44 |
| Sal Bartolo* NBA | 1944–46 |
| Sandy Saddler | 1948–49 |
| Willie Pep | 1949–50 |
| Sandy Saddler | 1950–57† |
| Kid Bassey | 1957–59 |
| Davey Moore | 1959–63 |
| Sugar Ramos | 1963–64 |
| Vicente Saldivar | 1964–67† |
| Paul Rojas* WBA | 1968 |
| Jose Legra* WBC | 1968–69 |
| Shozo Saijyo* WBA | 1968–71 |
| J. Famechon* WBC | 1969–70 |
| Vicente Saldivar WBC | 1970 |
| Kuniaki Shibata WBC | 1970–72 |
| Antonio Gomez* WBA | 1971–72 |
| C. Sanchez WBC | 1972 |
| Ernesto Marcel* WBA | 1972–74 |
| Jose Legra WBC | 1972–73 |
| Eder Jofre WBC | 1973–74 |
| Ruben Olivares* WBA | 1974 |
| Bobby Chacon* WBC | 1974–75 |
| Alexis Arguello WBA | 1974–76 |
| Ruben Olivares* WBC | 1975 |
| Poison Kotey* WBC | 1975–76 |
| Danny Lopez WBC | 1976–80 |
| Rafael Ortega* WBA | 1977 |
| Cecilio Lastra* WBA | 1977–78 |
| Eusebio Pedroza* WBA | 1978–85 |
| S. Sanchez WBC | 1980–82 |
| Juan LaPorte* WBC | 1982–84 |
| Wilfredo Gomez* WBC | 1984 |
| Min-Keun Oh* IBF | 1984–85 |

| Champion | Reign |
|---|---|
| Azumah Nelson* WBC | 1984–88 |
| Barry McGuigan* WBA | 1985–86 |
| Ki Young Chung* IBF | 1985–86 |
| Steve Cruz* WBA | 1986–87 |
| Antonio Rivera* IBF | 1986–88 |
| A. Esparragoza* WBA | 1987–91 |
| Calvin Grove* IBF | 1988 |
| Jorge Paez* IBF | 1988–91 |
| Jeff Fenech* WBC | 1988–90† |
| Marcos Villasana* WBC | 1990–91 |
| Paul Hodkinson* WBC | 1991–93 |
| Troy Dorsey* IBF | 1991 |
| Manuel Medina* IBF | 1991–93 |
| Yung Kyun Park* WBA | 1991–93 |
| Gregorio Vargas* WBC | 1993 |
| Tom Johnson* IBF | 1993–97† |
| Eloy Rojas* WBA | 1993–96 |
| Kevin Kelley* WBC | 1993–95 |
| A. Gonzalez* WBC | 1995 |
| Manuel Medina* WBC | 1995–95 |
| Luisito Espinosa* WBC | 1995–99 |
| Wilfredo Vazquez* WBA | 1996–98† |
| Hector Lizarraga* IBF | 1997–98 |
| Freddy Norwood* WBA | 1998 |
| Manuel Medina* IBF | 1998–99 |
| Antonio Cermeno* WBA | 1998–99 |
| Cesar Soto* WBC | 1999 |
| Freddy Norwood* WBA | 1999–00 |
| Naseem Hamed* WBC | 1999† |
| Paul Ingle* IBF | 1999–00 |
| Guty Espadas* WBC | 2000–01 |
| Erik Morales* WBC | 2000– |
| Derrick Gainer* WBA | 2000– |
| Mbulelo Botile* IBF | 2001 |
| Frankie Toledo* IBF | 2001– |

## Junior Featherweights
### (Weight Limit: 122 pounds)

| Champion | Reign |
|---|---|
| Jack (Kid) Wolfe* | 1922–23 |
| Carl Duane* | 1923–24 |
| Rigoberto Riasco* WBC | 1976 |
| Royal Kobayashi* WBC | 1976 |
| Dong-Kyun Yum* WBC | 1976–77 |
| Wilfredo Gomez* WBC | 1977–83 |
| Soo-Hwan Hong* WBA | 1977–78 |
| Ricardo Cardona* WBA | 1978–80 |
| Leo Randolph* WBA | 1980 |
| Sergio Palma* WBA | 1980–82 |
| Leonardo Cruz* WBA | 1982–84 |
| Jaime Garza* WBC | 1983 |
| Bobby Berna* IBF | 1983–84 |
| Loris Stecca* WBA | 1984 |
| Seung-Il Suh* IBF | 1984–85 |
| Victor Callejas* WBA | 1984–86 |
| Juan (Kid) Meza* WBC | 1984–85 |
| Ji-Won Kim* IBF | 1985–86 |

| Champion | Reign |
|---|---|
| Lupe Pintor* WBC | 1985–86 |
| Samart Payakaroon* WBC | 1986–87 |
| Seung-Hoon Lee* IBF | 1987–88 |
| Louie Espinoza* WBA | 1987 |
| Jeff Fenech* WBC | 1987 |
| Julio Gervacio* WBA | 1987–88 |
| Daniel Zaragoza* WBC | 1988–90 |
| Jose Sanabria* IBF | 1988–89 |
| Bernardo Pinango* WBA | 1988 |
| Juan Jose Estrada* WBA | 1988–89 |
| Fabrice Benichou* IBF | 1989–90 |
| Jesus Salud* WBA | 1989–90 |
| Welcome Ncita* IBF | 1990–92 |
| Paul Banke* WBC | 1990 |
| Luis Mendoza* WBA | 1990–91 |
| Raul Perez* WBA | 1992 |

| Champion | Reign |
|---|---|
| Pedro Decima* WBC | 1990–91 |
| K. Hatanaka* WBC | 1991 |
| Daniel Zaragoza* WBC | 1991–92 |
| Tracy Patterson* WBC | 1992–94 |
| Kennedy McKinney* IBF | 1993–94 |
| Wilfredo Vasquez* WBA | 1992–95 |
| Vuyani Bungu* IBF | 1994–99† |
| H. Acero Sanchez* WBC | 1994–95 |
| Antonio Cermeno* WBA | 1995–98† |
| Daniel Zaragoza* WBC | 1995–97 |
| Erik Morales* WBC | 1997–00† |
| Enrique Sanchez* WBA | 1998 |
| Nestor Garza* WBA | 1998–00 |
| Benedict Ledwaba* IBF | 1999–01 |
| Clarence Adams* WBA | 2000– |
| Willie Jorrin* WBC | 2000– |
| Manny Pacquiao* IBF | 2001– |

*Champion not generally recognized. †Champion retired or relinquished title.

### Bantamweights
### (Weight Limit: 118 pounds)

| Champion | Reign | Champion | Reign | Champion | Reign |
|---|---|---|---|---|---|
| Spider Kelly | 1887 | Sixto Escobar | 1938–39 | Miguel Lora* WBC | 1985–88 |
| Hughey Boyle | 1887–88 | Georgie Pace NBA | 1939–40 | Gaby Canizales | 1986 |
| Spider Kelly | 1889 | Lou Salica | 1940–42 | Bernardo Pinango | 1986–87 |
| Chappie Moran | 1889–90 | Manuel Ortiz | 1942–47 | W. Vasquez* WBA | 1987–88 |
| George Dixon | 1890–91 | Harold Dade | 1947 | Kevin Seabrooks* IBF | 1987–88 |
| Pedlar Palmer* | 1895–99 | Manuel Ortiz | 1947–50 | Kaokor Galaxy* WBA | 1988 |
| Terry McGovern | 1899–1900 | Vic Toweel | 1950–52 | Moon Sung-Kil* WBA | 1988–89 |
| Harry Harris | 1901–02 | Jimmy Carruthers | 1952–54† | Kaokor Galaxy* WBA | 1989 |
| Harry Forbes | 1902–03 | Robert Cohen | 1954–56 | Raul Perez* WBC | 1988–91 |
| Frankie Neil | 1903–04 | Paul Macias* NBA | 1955–57 | O. Canizales* IBF | 1988–95 |
| Joe Bowker | 1904–05 | Mario D'Agata | 1956–57 | Luisito Espinosa* WBA | 1989–91 |
| Jimmy Walsh | 1905–06 | Alphonse Halimi | 1957–59 | Israel Contreras* WBA | 1991–92 |
| Owen Moran | 1907–08 | Joe Becerra | 1959–60† | Eddie Cook* WBA | 1992–93 |
| Monte Attell* | 1909–10 | Eder Jofre | 1961–65 | Greg Richardson* WBC | 1991 |
| Frankie Conley | 1910–11 | Fighting Harada | 1965–68 | J. Tatsuyoshi, WBC | 1991–92 |
| Johnny Coulon | 1911–14 | Lionel Rose | 1968–69 | Victor Rabanales* WBC | 1992–93 |
| Kid Williams | 1914–17 | Ruben Olivares | 1969–70 | Jung-Il Byun* WBC | 1993 |
| Kewpie Ertle* | 1915 | Chucho Castillo | 1970–71 | Jorge Julio WBA | 1993 |
| Pete Herman | 1917–20 | Ruben Olivares | 1971–72 | Yasuei Yakushiji* WBC | 1993–95 |
| Joe Lynch | 1920–21 | Rafael Herrera | 1972 | Junior Jones WBA* | 1994 |
| Pete Herman | 1921 | Enriquo Pindor | 1972 73 | John M. Johncon* WBA | 1994 |
| Johnny Buff | 1921–22 | Romeo Anaya | 1973 | D. Chuvatana*WBA | 1994–95 |
| Joe Lynch | 1922–24 | Rafael Herrera* WBC | 1973–74 | V. Sahaprom* WBA | 1995–96 |
| Abe Goldstein | 1924 | Soo-Hwan Hong | 1974–75 | W. McCullough* WBC | 1995–96 |
| Cannonball Martin | 1924–25 | Rodolfo Martinez* WBC | 1974–76 | Harold Mestre* IBF | 1995 |
| Phil Rosenberg | 1925–27 | Alfonso Zamora | 1975–77 | Mbulelo Botile* IBF | 1995–97 |
| Bud Taylor NBA | 1927–28 | Carlos Zarate* WBC | 1976–79 | Nana Yaw | |
| Bushy Graham* NY | 1928–29 | Jorge Lujan | 1977–80 | Konadu* WBA | 1996–98 |
| Panama Al Brown | 1929–35 | Lupe Pintor* WBC | 1979–83 | S. Singmanassak* WBC | 1996–97 |
| Sixto Escobar* NBA | 1934–35 | Julian Solis | 1980 | Tim Austin* IBF | 1997– |
| Baltazar Sangchilli | 1935–36 | Jeff Chandler | 1980–84 | J.Tatsuyoshi* WBC | 1997–98 |
| Lou Salica* NBA | 1935 | Albert Davila* WBC | 1983–85 | Johnny Tapia* WBA | 1998–99 |
| Sixto Escobar* NBA | 1935–36 | Richard Sandoval | 1984–86 | V. Sahaprom* WBC | 1998– |
| Tony Marino | 1936 | Satoshi Shingaki* IBF | 1984–85 | Paulie Ayala* WBA | 1999– |
| Sixto Escobar | 1936–37 | Jeff Fenech* IBF | 1985 | | |
| Harry Jeffra | 1937–38† | Daniel Zaragoza* WBC | 1985 | | |

### Hollywood or Bust (er)

After his stunning upset knockout of Mike Tyson in 1990 made him an overnight success, James (Buster) Douglas has toiled in obscurity, battling obesity and mediocrity. Now the one-hit wonder is taking a shot at Hollywood—sort of. On location in his hometown of Columbus, Ohio, Douglas, 41, will play an FBI agent in *Pluto's Plight*, an independent sci-fi flick scheduled to begin shooting next month. "The way I envision my role, I'm like the Will Smith character in *Men in Black*," says Douglas, who brushes off concerns about his inexperience as a thespian, pointing proudly to his single appearance as an inmate on the syndicated television series *Street Justice*.

John Russell, who has handled Douglas throughout his boxing life, will manage Douglas's acting career. Russell, who like his charge is a rookie in the entertainment business, promises to enlist the help of Hollywood heavyweights—including another old heavyweight underdog, and longtime friend, Sylvester Stallone to help with Douglas's dramatic development. "Buster speaks well, and he's got personality," says Russell. "He's a talented, lovable guy."

Asked if he thinks he can out-act his famous foe Tyson, whose forays into film have consisted exclusively of appearances as ... Mike Tyson, Douglas laughs. "I'll take him on the silver screen just like I took him in the ring," he says.

— Luis Fernando Llosa

### Junior Bantamweights
### (Weight Limit: 115 pounds)

| Champion | Reign | Champion | Reign | Champion | Reign |
|---|---|---|---|---|---|
| Rafael Orono* WBC | 1980–81 | Tae-Il Chang* IBF | 1987 | Yokthai Sith-Oar* WBA | 1996–97 |
| Chul-Ho Kim* WBC | 1981–82 | Sugar Rojas* WBC | 1987–88 | Carlos Salazar* IBF | 1995–96 |
| Gustavo Ballas* WBA | 1981 | Ellyas Pical* IBF | 1987–89 | Harold Grey* IBF | 1996 |
| Rafael Pedroza* WBA | 1981–82 | Giberto Roman* WBC | 1988–89 | Danny Romero* IBF | 1996–97 |
| Jiro Watanabe* WBA | 1982–84 | Juan Polo Perez* IBF | 1989–90 | Gerry Penalosa* WBC | 1997–98 |
| Rafael Orono* WBC | 1982–83 | Nana Konadu* WBC | 1989–90 | Johnny Tapia* IBF | 1997–99† |
| Payao Poontarat* WBC | 1983–84 | Sung-Kil Moon* WBC | 1990–93 | Satoshi Iida* WBA | 1997–98 |
| Joo-Do Chun* IBF | 1983–85 | Robert Quiroga* IBF | 1990–93 | Cho In-Joo* WBC | 1998–00 |
| Jiro Watanabe* WBA | 1984–86 | Julio Borboa* IBF | 1993–94 | Jesus Rojas* WBA | 1998–99 |
| Kaosai Galaxy* WBA | 1984 | Katsuya Onizuka* WBA | 1993–94 | Mark Johnson* IBF | 1999–00 |
| Ellyas Pical* IBF | 1985–86 | Lee Hyung-Chul* WBA | 1994–95 | Hideki Todaka* WBA | 1999–00 |
| Cesar Polanco* IBF | 1986 | Jose Luis Bueno* WBC | 1993–94 | Felix Machado* IBF | 2000– |
| Gilberto Roman* WBC | 1986–87 | Hiroshi Kawashima*WBC | 1994–97 | M. Tokuyama* WBC | 2000– |
| Ellyas Pical* IBF | 1986 | Harold Grey* IBF | 1994–95 | Leo Gamez* WBA | 2000–01 |
| Santos Laciar* WBC | 1987 | Alimi Goitia* WBA | 1995–96 | Celes Kobayashi* WBA | 2001– |

### Flyweights
### (Weight Limit: 112 pounds)

| Champion | Reign | Champion | Reign | Champion | Reign |
|---|---|---|---|---|---|
| Sid Smith | 1913 | B. Chartvanchai* WBA | 1970 | Hi-Sup Shin* IBF | 1986–87 |
| Bill Ladbury | 1913–14 | Masao Ohba* WBA | 1970–73 | Dodie Penalosa* IBF | 1987 |
| Percy Jones | 1914 | Erbito Salavarria | 1970–73 | Fidel Bassa* WBA | 1987–89 |
| Joe Symonds | 1914–16 | B. Gonzalez* WBA | 1972 | Choi-Chang Ho* IBF | 1987–88 |
| Jimmy Wilde | 1916–23 | V. Borkorsor* WBC | 1972–73 | Rolando Bohol* IBF | 1988 |
| Pancho Villa | 1923–25 | Venice Borkorsor | 1973 | Yong-Kang Kim* WBC | 1988–89 |
| Fidel LaBarba | 1925–27† | Chartchai Chionoi* WBA | 1973–74 | Duke McKenzie* IBF | 1988–89 |
| Frenchy Belanger NBA | 1927–28 | B. Gonzalez* WBA | 1973–74 | Sot Chitalada* WBC | 1989–91 |
| Izzy Schwartz NY | 1927–29 | Shoji Oguma* WBC | 1974–75 | Dave McAuley* IBF | 1989–92 |
| Frankie Genaro NBA | 1928–29 | S. Hanagata* WBA | 1974–75 | Jesus Rojas* WBA | 1989–90 |
| Spider Pladner NBA | 1929 | Miguel Canto* WBC | 1975–79 | Yul-Woo Lee* WBA | 1990 |
| Frankie Genaro NBA | 1929–31 | Erbito Salavarria* WBA | 1975–76 | L. Tamakuma* WBA | 1990–91 |
| Midget Wolgast* NY | 1930–35 | Alfonso Lopez* WBA | 1976 | M. Kittikasem* WBC | 1991–92 |
| Young Perez NBA | 1931–32 | G. Espadas* WBA | 1976–78 | Yuri Arbachakov* WBC | 1992–97 |
| Jackie Brown NBA | 1932–35 | B. Gonzalez* WBA | 1978–79 | Yong Kang Kim* WBA | 1991–92 |
| Benny Lynch | 1935–38 | Chan-Hee Park* WBC | 1979–80 | Rodolfo Blanco* IBF | 1992–93 |
| Small Montana* NY | 1935–37 | Luis Ibarra* WBA | 1979–80 | P. Sithbangprachan* IBF | 1993–95 |
| Peter Kane | 1938–43 | Tae-Shik Kim* WBA | 1980 | David Griman* WBA | 1992–94 |
| Little Dado* NY | 1938–40 | Shoji Oguma* WBC | 1980–81 | S.S. Ploenchit* WBA | 1994–96 |
| Jackie Paterson | 1943–48 | Peter Mathebula* WBA | 1980–81 | Francisco Tejedor* IBF | 1995 |
| Rinty Monaghan | 1948–50 | Santos Laciar* WBA | 1981 | Danny Romero* IBF | 1995–96 |
| Terry Allen | 1950 | Antonio Avelar* WBC | 1981–82 | Mark Johnson* IBF | 1996–99† |
| Dado Marino | 1950–52 | Luis Ibarra* WBA | 1981 | Jose Bonilla* WBA | 1996–98 |
| Yoshio Shirai | 1953–54 | Juan Herrera* WBA | 1981–82 | Chatchai Sasakul* WBC | 1997–98 |
| Pascual Perez | 1954–60 | P. Cardona* WBC | 1982 | Hugo Soto* WBA | 1998–99 |
| Pone Kingpetch | 1960–62 | Santos Laciar* WBA | 1982–85 | Manny Pacquiao* WBC | 1998–99 |
| Masahiko Harada | 1962–63 | Freddie Castillo* WBC | 1982 | Leo Gamez* WBA | 1999 |
| Pone Kingpetch | 1963 | E. Mercedes* WBC | 1982–83 | Irene Pacheco* IBF | 1999– |
| Hiroyuki Ebihara | 1963–64 | Charlie Magri* WBC | 1983 | S. Pisnurachan* WBA | 1999–00 |
| Pone Kingpetch | 1964–65 | Frank Cedeno* WBC | 1983–84 | M. Sinsurat* WBC | 1999–00 |
| Salvatore Burrini | 1965–66 | Soon-Chun Kwon* IBF | 1983–85 | Malcolm Tunacao* WBC | 2000–01 |
| H. Accavallo* WBA | 1966–68 | Koji Kobayashi* WBC | 1984 | Eric Morel* WBA | 2000– |
| Walter McGowan | 1966 | Gabriel Bernal* WBC | 1984 | P. Wonjongkam* WBC | 2001– |
| Chartchai Chionoi | 1966–69 | Sot Chitalada* WBC | 1984–88 | | |
| Efren Torres | 1969–70 | Hilario Zapate* WBA | 1985–87 | | |
| Hiroyuki Ebihara* WBA | 1969 | Chong-Kwan | | | |
| B. Villacampo* WBA | 1969–70 | Chung* IBF | 1985–86 | | |
| Chartchai Chionoi | 1970 | Bi-Won Chung* IBF | 1986 | | |

*Champion not generally recognized.  †Champion retired or relinquished title.

## Junior Flyweights
### (Weight Limit: 108 pounds)

| Champion | Reign |
|---|---|
| Franco Udella* WBC | 1975 |
| Jaime Rios* WBA | 1975–76 |
| Luis Estaba* WBC | 1975–78 |
| Juan Guzman* WBA | 1976 |
| Yoko Gushiken* WBA | 1976–81 |
| Freddy Castillo* WBC | 1978 |
| Netrnoi Vorasingh* WBC | 1978 |
| Sung-Jun Kim* WBC | 1978–80 |
| Shigeo Nakajima* WBC | 1980 |
| Hilario Zapata* WBC | 1980–82 |
| Pedro Flores* WBA | 1981 |
| Hwan-Jin Kim* WBA | 1981 |
| Katsuo Tokashiki* WBA | 1981–83 |
| Amado Urzua* WBC | 1982 |
| Tadashi Tomori* WBC | 1982 |
| Hilario Zapata* WBA | 1982–83 |
| Jung-Koo Chang* WBC | 1983–88 |
| Lupe Madera* WBA | 1983–84 |

| Champion | Reign |
|---|---|
| Dodie Penalosa* IBF | 1983–86 |
| Francisco Quiroz* WBA | 1984–85 |
| Joey Olivo* WBA | 1985 |
| Myung-Woo Yuh* WBA | 1985–91 |
| Jum-Hwan Choi* IBF | 1986–88 |
| Tacy Macalos* IBF | 1988–89 |
| German Torres* WBC | 1988–89 |
| Yul-Woo Lee* WBC | 1989 |
| Muangchai Kittikasem* IBF | 1989–90 |
| Humberto Gonzalez* WBC | 1989–90 |
| Michael Carbajal* IBF | 1990–94 |
| R. Pascua* WBC | 1990 |
| M. C. Castro* WBC | 1991 |
| H. Gonzalez* WBC | 1991–93 |
| Hirokia Ioka* WBA | 1991–92 |
| Michael Carbajal, WBC | 1993–94 |

| Champion | Reign |
|---|---|
| Myung-Woo Yuh* WBA | 1993 |
| Leo Gamez* WBA | 1993–95 |
| H. Gonzalez* WBC, IBF | 1994–95 |
| Choi Hi-Yong* WBA | 1995–96 |
| S. Sor Jaturong* WBC, IBF | 1995–96 |
| Carlos Murillo* WBA | 1996 |
| Keiji Yamaguchi* WBA | 1996 |
| Michael Carbajal* IBF | 1996–97 |
| S. Sor Jaturong* WBC | 1995–99 |
| Phichitchor Siriwat* WBA | 1996–00 |
| Mauricio Pastrana* IBF | 1997–98† |
| Will Grigsby* IBF | 1998–99 |
| Ricardo Lopez* IBF | 1999– |
| Choi Yo-Sam* WBC | 1999– |
| Beibis Mendoza* WBA | 2000–01 |
| Rosendo Alvarez* WBA | 2001– |

## Strawweights
### (Weight Limit: 105 pounds)

| Champion | Reign |
|---|---|
| Kyung-Yun Lee* IBF | 1987 |
| Hiroki Ioka* WBC | 1987–88 |
| Leo Gamez* WBA | 1988–89 |
| S. Sithnaruepol* IBF | 1988–89 |
| N. Kiatwanchai* WBC | 1988–89 |
| Bong-Jun Kim* WBA | 1989–91 |
| Nico Thomas* IBF | 1989 |
| Eric Chavez* IBF | 1989–90 |
| Jum-Hwan Choi* WBC | 1989–90 |
| Hideyuki Ohaski* WBC | 1990 |

| Champion | Reign |
|---|---|
| F. Lookmingkwan* IBF | 1990–92 |
| Ricardo Lopez* WBC | 1990–98 |
| Hi-Yong Choi* WBA | 1991–92 |
| Manny Melchor* IBF | 1992 |
| Hideyuki Ohashi* WBA | 1992–93 |
| R.S. Voraphin* IBF | 1992–96 |
| Chana Porpaoin* WBA | 1993–95 |
| Rosendo Alvarez* WBA | 1995–98 |
| R. Sor Vorapin* IBF | 1996–97 |
| Zolani Petelo* IBF | 1997–00 |

| Champion | Reign |
|---|---|
| W. Chor Charoen* WBC | 1998–00 |
| Ricardo Lopez WBA, WBC | 1998–99† |
| Songkram Popaoin* WBA | 1999 |
| Noel Arambulet* WBA | 1999–00 |
| J. Antonio Aguirre* WBC | 2000– |
| Joma Gamboa* WBA | 2000–01 |
| Keitaro Hoshino* WBA | 2000–01 |
| Chana Porpaoin* WBA | 2001 |
| Roberto Leyva* IBF | 2001– |
| Yutaka Niida* WBA | 2001– |

*Champion not generally recognized. †Champion retired or relinquished title.

---

### ONE MORE SIGN OF THE APOCALYPSE

*Tony Ayala Jr., who served 16 years for rape and faced trial on charges of burglary with intent to commit sexual assault, beat Santos Cardona in a bout in July 2001 while wearing an electronic monitoring device on his left ankle.*

# Alltime Career Leaders

## Total Bouts

| Name | Years Active | Bouts | Name | Years Active | Bouts |
|------|--------------|-------|------|--------------|-------|
| Len Wickwar | 1928–47 | 463 | Maxie Rosenbloom | 1923–39 | 299 |
| Jack Britton | 1905–30 | 350 | Harry Greb | 1913–26 | 298 |
| Johnny Dundee | 1910–32 | 333 | Young Stribling | 1921–33 | 286 |
| Billy Bird | 1920–48 | 318 | Battling Levinsky | 1910–29 | 282 |
| George Marsden | 1928–46 | 311 | Ted (Kid) Lewis | 1909–29 | 279 |

Note: Based on records in *The Ring Record Book* and *Boxing Encyclopedia*.

## Most Knockouts

| Name | Years Active | KOs | Name | Years Active | KOs |
|------|--------------|-----|------|--------------|-----|
| Archie Moore | 1936–63 | 130 | Sandy Saddler | 1944–56 | 103 |
| Young Stribling | 1921–33 | 126 | Sam Langford | 1902–26 | 102 |
| Billy Bird | 1920–48 | 125 | Henry Armstrong | 1931–45 | 100 |
| George Odwell | 1930–45 | 114 | Jimmy Wilde | 1911–23 | 98 |
| Sugar Ray Robinson | 1940–65 | 110 | Len Wickwar | 1928–47 | 93 |

Note: Based on records in *The Ring Record Book* and *Boxing Encyclopedia*.

## Overrated/Underrated

### HEAVYWEIGHT CHAMPIONSHIP FIGHT

**OVERRATED**: Ali vs. Foreman

Rope-a-dope has entered the lexicon as a strategy that means "winning by doing almost nothing." That says everything one needs to know about the Rumble in the Jungle, the strange, almost surreal, fight in October 1974 that was chronicled in the documentary *When We Were Kings*. The film was brilliant; the fight, won by Muhammad Ali in eight rounds, was not. Ali's strategy of covering up and letting the heavily favored George Foreman (who 21 months earlier had knocked down Joe Frazier six times en route to a second-round TKO) punch himself out was probably the only one the Greatest could've used to win. Ali's coy tactic produced great theater but not great boxing.

**UNDERRATED**: Holmes vs. Norton

Larry Holmes was always something of an Ali wannabe during his career, complaining that he was being ignored in favor of the fading former champ. He had a point.

Holmes was a courageous warrior who continues to be underrated by the boxing public. His 15-rounder against Ken Norton for the WBC belt in 1978, rarely mentioned as a great fight (except by the cognoscenti), is a case in point: Despite a torn left biceps, Holmes used his jab, one of the best in heavyweight history, to win four of the first five rounds. "Now it's my turn," Norton told his corner before the sixth. Awkward but relentless, Norton took five of the next six rounds. Both men were nearing exhaustion, but neither backed off—Holmes staggered Norton twice in the 13th, Norton returned the favor in the 14th, staggering Holmes twice.

Going into the final round, the fight was even on all three cards. The 15th was something out of the cinema: two gloved gladiators slugging it out—appropriately enough in the parking lot of Caesars Palace in Las Vegas—both probably aware that victory would go to the winner of the three climactic minutes. Just before the final bell Holmes staggered Norton with a huge right that might have won him the bout.

One judge gave the 15th to Norton, but the other two gave it to the Easton Assassin. With it came the title Holmes would hold for seven years and 20 defenses.

— Jack McCallum

## World Heavyweight Championship Fights

| Date | Winner | Wgt | Loser | Wgt | Result | Site |
|---|---|---|---|---|---|---|
| Sept 7, 1892 | James J. Corbett* | 178 | John L. Sullivan | 212 | KO 21 | New Orleans |
| Jan 25, 1894 | James J. Corbett | 184 | Charley Mitchell | 158 | KO 3 | Jacksonville |
| Mar 17, 1897 | Bob Fitzsimmons* | 167 | James J. Corbett | 183 | KO 14 | Carson City, NV |
| June 9, 1899 | James J. Jeffries* | 206 | Bob Fitzsimmons | 167 | KO 11 | Coney Island, NY |
| Nov 3, 1899 | James J. Jeffries | 215 | Tom Sharkey | 183 | Ref 25 | Coney Island, NY |
| Apr 6, 1900 | James J. Jeffries | n/a | Jack Finnegan | n/a | KO 1 | Detroit |
| May 11, 1900 | James J. Jeffries | 218 | James J. Corbett | 188 | KO 23 | Coney Island, NY |
| Nov 15, 1901 | James J. Jeffries | 211 | Gus Ruhlin | 194 | TKO 6 | San Francisco |
| July 25, 1902 | James J. Jeffries | 219 | Bob Fitzsimmons | 172 | KO 8 | San Francisco |
| Aug 14, 1903 | James J. Jeffries | 220 | James J. Corbett | 190 | KO 10 | San Francisco |
| Aug 25, 1904 | James J. Jeffries | 219 | Jack Munroe | 186 | TKO 2 | San Francisco |
| July 3, 1905 | Marvin Hart* | 190 | Jack Root | 171 | KO 12 | Reno |
| Feb 23, 1906 | Tommy Burns* | 180 | Marvin Hart | 188 | Ref 20 | Los Angeles |
| Oct 2, 1906 | Tommy Burns | n/a | Jim Flynn | n/a | KO 15 | Los Angeles |
| Nov 28, 1906 | Tommy Burns | 172 | Jack O'Brien | 163½ | Draw 20 | Los Angeles |
| May 8, 1907 | Tommy Burns | 180 | Jack O'Brien | 167 | Ref 20 | Los Angeles |
| Jul 4, 1907 | Tommy Burns | 181 | Bill Squires | 180 | KO 1 | Colma, CA |
| Dec 2, 1907 | Tommy Burns | 177 | Gunner Moir | 204 | KO 10 | London |
| Feb 10, 1908 | Tommy Burns | n/a | Jack Palmer | n/a | KO 4 | London |
| Mar 17, 1908 | Tommy Burns | n/a | Jem Roche | n/a | KO 1 | Dublin |
| Apr 18, 1908 | Tommy Burns | n/a | Jewey Smith | n/a | KO 5 | Paris |
| June 13, 1908 | Tommy Burns | 184 | Bill Squires | 183 | KO 8 | Paris |
| Aug 24, 1908 | Tommy Burns | 181 | Bill Squires | 184 | KO 13 | Sydney |
| Sept 2, 1908 | Tommy Burns | 183 | Bill Lang | 187 | KO 6 | Melbourne |
| Dec 26, 1908 | Jack Johnson* | 192 | Tommy Burns | 168 | TKO 14 | Sydney |
| Mar 10, 1909 | Jack Johnson | n/a | Victor McLaglen | n/a | ND 6 | Vancouver |
| May 19, 1909 | Jack Johnson | 205 | Jack O'Brien | 161 | ND 6 | Philadelphia |
| June 30, 1909 | Jack Johnson | 207 | Tony Ross | 214 | ND 6 | Pittsburgh |
| Sept 9, 1909 | Jack Johnson | 209 | Al Kaufman | 191 | ND 10 | San Francisco |
| Oct 16, 1909 | Jack Johnson | 205½ | Stanley Ketchel | 170¼ | KO 12 | Colma, CA |
| July 4, 1910 | Jack Johnson | 208 | James J. Jeffries | 227 | KO 15 | Reno |
| July 4, 1912 | Jack Johnson | 195½ | Jim Flynn | 175 | TKO 9 | Las Vegas |
| Dec 19, 1913 | Jack Johnson | n/a | Jim Johnson | n/a | Draw 10 | Paris |
| June 27, 1914 | Jack Johnson | 221 | Frank Moran | 203 | Ref 20 | Paris |
| Apr 5, 1915 | Jess Willard* | 230 | Jack Johnson | 205½ | KO 26 | Havana |
| Mar 25, 1916 | Jess Willard | 225 | Frank Moran | 203 | ND 10 | New York City |
| July 4, 1919 | Jack Dempsey* | 187 | Jess Willard | 245 | TKO 4 | Toledo, OH |
| Sept 6, 1920 | Jack Dempsey | 185 | Billy Miske | 187 | KO 3 | Benton Harbor, MI |
| Dec 14, 1920 | Jack Dempsey | 188¼ | Bill Brennan | 197 | KO 12 | New York City |
| July 2, 1921 | Jack Dempsey | 188 | Georges Carpentier | 172 | KO 4 | Jersey City |
| July 4, 1923 | Jack Dempsey | 188 | Tommy Givvons | 175½ | Ref 15 | Shelby, MT |
| Sept 14, 1923 | Jack Dempsey | 192½ | Luis Firpo | 216½ | KO 2 | New York City |
| Sept 23, 1926 | Gene Tunney* | 189½ | Jack Dempsey | 190 | UD 10 | Philadelphia |
| Sept 22, 1927 | Gene Tunney | 189½ | Jack Dempsey | 192½ | UD 10 | Chicago |
| July 26, 1928 | Gene Tunney | 192 | Tom Heeney | 203½ | TKO 11 | New York City |
| June 12, 1930 | Max Schmeling* | 188 | Jack Sharkey | 197 | DQ 4 | New York City |
| July 3, 1931 | Max Schmeling | 189 | Young Stribling | 186½ | TKO 15 | Cleveland |
| June 21, 1932 | Jack Sharkey* | 205 | Max Schmeling | 188 | Split 15 | Long Island City |
| June 29, 1933 | Primo Carnera* | 260½ | Jack Sharkey | 201 | KO 6 | Long Island City |
| Oct 22, 1933 | Primo Carnera | 259½ | Paulino Uzcudun | 229¼ | UD 15 | Rome |
| Mar 1, 1934 | Primo Carnera | 270 | Tommy Loughran | 184 | UD 15 | Miami |
| June 14, 1934 | Max Baer* | 209½ | Primo Carnera | 263¼ | TKO 11 | Long Island City |
| June 13, 1935 | James J. Braddock* | 193¾ | Max Baer | 209½ | UD 15 | Long Island City |
| June 22, 1937 | Joe Louis | 197¼ | James J. Braddock | 197 | KO 8 | Chicago |
| Aug 30, 1937 | Joe Louis | 197 | Tommy Farr | 204¼ | UD 15 | New York City |
| Feb 23, 1938 | Joe Louis | 200 | Nathan Mann | 193½ | KO 3 | New York City |
| Apr 1, 1938 | Joe Louis | 202½ | Harry Thomas | 196 | KO 5 | Chicago |
| June 22, 1938 | Joe Louis | 198¼ | Max Schmeling | 193 | KO 1 | New York City |
| Jan 25, 1939 | Joe Louis | 200¼ | John Henry Lewis | 180¾ | KO 1 | New York City |
| Apr 17, 1939 | Joe Louis | 201¼ | Jack Roper | 204¾ | KO 1 | Los Angeles |
| June 28, 1939 | Joe Louis | 200¾ | Tony Galento | 233¾ | TKO 4 | New York City |
| Sept 20, 1939 | Joe Louis | 200 | Bob Pastor | 183 | KO 11 | Detroit |
| Feb 9, 1940 | Joe Louis | 203 | Arturo Godoy | 202 | Split 15 | New York City |
| Mar 29, 1940 | Joe Louis | 201½ | Johnny Paychek | 187½ | KO 2 | New York City |
| June 20, 1940 | Joe Louis | 199 | Arturo Godoy | 201¼ | TKO 8 | New York City |
| Dec 16, 1940 | Joe Louis | 202¼ | Al McCoy | 180¾ | TKO 6 | Boston |
| Jan 31, 1941 | Joe Louis | 202½ | Red Burman | 188 | KO 5 | New York City |

## World Heavyweight Championship Fights *(Cont.)*

| Date | Winner | Wgt | Loser | Wgt | Result | Site |
|---|---|---|---|---|---|---|
| Feb 17, 1941 | Joe Louis | 203½ | Gus Dorazio | 193½ | KO 2 | Philadelphia |
| Mar 21, 1941 | Joe Louis | 202 | Abe Simon | 254½ | TKO 13 | Detroit |
| Apr 8, 1941 | Joe Louis | 203½ | Tony Musto | 199½ | TKO 9 | St Louis |
| May 23, 1941 | Joe Louis | 201½ | Buddy Baer | 237½ | DQ 7 | Washington, D.C. |
| June 18, 1941 | Joe Louis | 199½ | Billy Conn | 174 | KO 13 | New York City |
| Sept 29, 1941 | Joe Louis | 202¼ | Lou Nova | 202½ | TKO 6 | New York City |
| Jan 9, 1942 | Joe Louis | 206¾ | Buddy Baer | 250 | KO 1 | New York City |
| Mar 27, 1942 | Joe Louis | 207½ | Abe Simon | 255½ | KO 6 | New York City |
| June 9, 1946 | Joe Louis | 207 | Billy Conn | 187 | KO 8 | New York City |
| Sept 18, 1946 | Joe Louis | 211 | Tami Mauriello | 198½ | KO 1 | New York City |
| Dec 5, 1947 | Joe Louis | 211½ | Jersey Joe Walcott | 194½ | Split 15 | New York City |
| June 25, 1948 | Joe Louis | 213½ | Jersey Joe Walcott | 194¾ | KO 11 | New York City |
| June 22, 1949 | Ezzard Charles* | 181¾ | Jersey Joe Walcott | 195½ | UD 15 | Chicago |
| Aug 10, 1949 | Ezzard Charles | 180 | Gus Lesnevich | 182 | TKO 8 | New York City |
| Oct 14, 1949 | Ezzard Charles | 182 | Pat Valentino | 188½ | KO 8 | San Francisco |
| Aug 15, 1950 | Ezzard Charles | 183¼ | Freddie Beshore | 184½ | TKO 14 | Buffalo |
| Sept 27, 1950 | Ezzard Charles | 184½ | Joe Louis | 218 | UD 15 | New York City |
| Dec 5, 1950 | Ezzard Charles | 185 | Nick Barone | 178½ | KO 11 | Cincinnati |
| Jan 12, 1951 | Ezzard Charles | 185 | Lee Oma | 193 | TKO 10 | New York City |
| Mar 7, 1951 | Ezzard Charles | 186 | Jersey Joe Walcott | 193 | UD 15 | Detroit |
| May 30, 1951 | Ezzard Charles | 182 | Joey Maxim | 181½ | UD 15 | Chicago |
| July 18, 1951 | Jersey Joe Walcott* | 194 | Ezzard Charles | 182 | KO 7 | Pittsburgh |
| June 5, 1952 | Jersey Joe Walcott | 196 | Ezzard Charles | 191½ | UD 15 | Philadelphia |
| Sept 23, 1952 | Rocky Marciano* | 184 | Jersey Joe Walcott | 196 | KO 13 | Philadelphia |
| May 15, 1953 | Rocky Marciano | 184½ | Jersey Joe Walcott | 197¾ | KO 1 | Chicago |
| Sept 24, 1953 | Rocky Marciano | 185 | Roland LaStarza | 184¾ | TKO 11 | New York City |
| June 17, 1954 | Rocky Marciano | 187½ | Ezzard Charles | 185½ | UD 15 | New York City |
| Sept 17, 1954 | Rocky Marciano | 187 | Ezzard Charles | 192½ | KO 8 | New York City |
| May 16, 1955 | Rocky Marciano | 189 | Don Cockell | 205 | TKO 9 | San Francisco |
| Sept 21, 1955 | Rocky Marciano | 188¼ | Archie Moore | 188 | KO 9 | New York City |
| Nov 30, 1956 | Floyd Patterson* | 182¼ | Archie Moore | 187¾ | KO 5 | Chicago |
| July 29, 1957 | Floyd Patterson | 184 | Tommy Jackson | 192½ | TKO 10 | New York City |
| Aug 22, 1957 | Floyd Patterson | 187¼ | Pete Rademacher | 202 | KO 6 | Seattle |
| Aug 18, 1958 | Floyd Patterson | 184½ | Roy Harris | 194 | TKO 13 | Los Angeles |
| May 1, 1959 | Floyd Patterson | 182½ | Brian London | 206 | KO 11 | Indianapolis |
| June 26, 1959 | Ingemar Johansson* | 196 | Floyd Patterson | 182 | TKO 3 | New York City |
| June 20, 1960 | Floyd Patterson* | 190 | Ingemar Johansson | 194¾ | KO 5 | New York City |
| Mar 13, 1961 | Floyd Patterson | 194¾ | Ingemar Johansson | 206½ | KO 6 | Miami Beach |
| Dec 4, 1961 | Floyd Patterson | 188½ | Tom McNeeley | 197 | KO 4 | Toronto |
| Sept 25, 1962 | Sonny Liston* | 214 | Floyd Patterson | 189 | KO 1 | Chicago |
| July 22, 1963 | Sonny Liston | 215 | Floyd Patterson | 194½ | KO 1 | Las Vegas |
| Feb 25, 1964 | Cassius Clay | 210½ | Sonny Liston | 218 | TKO 7 | Miami Beach |
| Mar 5, 1965 | Ernie Terrell* | 199 | Eddie Machen | 192 | UD 15 | Chicago |
| May 25, 1965 | Muhammad Ali | 206 | Sonny Liston | 215¼ | KO 1 | Lewiston, ME |
| Nov 1, 1965 | Ernie Terrell * | 206 | George Chuvalo | 209 | UD 15 | Toronto |
| Nov 22, 1965 | Muhammad Ali | 210 | Floyd Patterson | 196¾ | TKO 12 | Las Vegas |
| Mar 29, 1966 | Muhammad Ali | 214½ | George Chuvalo | 216 | UD 15 | Toronto |
| May 21, 1966 | Muhammad Ali | 201½ | Henry Cooper | 188 | TKO 6 | London |
| June 28, 1966 | Ernie Terrell * | 209½ | Doug Jones | 187½ | UD 15 | Houston |
| Aug 6, 1966 | Muhammad Ali | 209½ | Brian London | 201½ | KO 3 | London |
| Sept 10, 1966 | Muhammad Ali | 203½ | Karl Mildenberger | 194¼ | TKO 12 | Frankfurt |
| Nov 14, 1966 | Muhammad Ali | 212¾ | Cleveland Williams | 210½ | TKO 3 | Houston |
| Feb 6, 1967 | Muhammad Ali | 212¼ | Ernie Terrell | 212½ | UD 15 | Houston |
| Mar 22, 1967 | Muhammad Ali | 211½ | Zora Folley | 202½ | KO 7 | New York City |
| Mar 4, 1968 | Joe Frazier* | 204½ | Buster Mathis | 243½ | TKO 11 | New York City |
| Apr 27, 1968 | Jimmy Ellis* | 197 | Jerry Quarry | 195 | Maj 15 | Oakland |
| June 24, 1968 | Joe Frazier NY* | 203½ | Manuel Ramos | 208 | TKO 2 | New York City |
| Aug 14, 1968 | Jimmy Ellis * | 198 | Floyd Patterson | 188 | Ref 15 | Stockholm |
| Dec 10, 1968 | Joe Frazier NY* | 203 | Oscar Bonavena | 207 | UD 15 | Philadelphia |
| Apr 22, 1969 | Joe Frazier NY* | 204½ | Dave Zyglewicz | 190½ | KO 1 | Houston |
| June 23, 1969 | Joe Frazier NY* | 203½ | Jerry Quarry | 198½ | TKO 8 | New York City |
| Feb 16, 1970 | Joe Frazier NY* | 205 | Jimmy Ellis | 201 | TKO 5 | New York City |
| Nov 18, 1970 | Joe Frazier* | 209 | Bob Foster | 188 | KO 2 | Detroit |
| Mar 8, 1971 | Joe Frazier* | 205½ | Muhammad Ali | 215 | UD 15 | New York City |
| Jan 15, 1972 | Joe Frazier | 215½ | Terry Daniels | 195 | TKO 4 | New Orleans |
| May 26, 1972 | Joe Frazier | 217½ | Ron Stander | 218 | TKO 5 | Omaha |
| Jan 22, 1973 | George Foreman* | 217½ | Joe Frazier | 214 | TKO 2 | Kingston, Jam. |

## World Heavyweight Championship Fights *(Cont.)*

| Date | Winner | Wgt | Loser | Wgt | Result | Site |
|---|---|---|---|---|---|---|
| Sept 1, 1973 | George Foreman | 219½ | Jose Roman | 196½ | KO 1 | Tokyo |
| Mar 26, 1974 | George Foreman | 224¼ | Ken Norton | 212¼ | TKO 2 | Caracas |
| Oct 30, 1974 | Muhammad Ali* | 216½ | George Foreman | 220 | KO 8 | Kinshasa, Zaire |
| Mar 24, 1975 | Muhammad Ali | 223½ | Chuck Wepner | 225 | TKO 15 | Cleveland |
| May 16, 1975 | Muhammad Ali | 224½ | Ron Lyle | 219 | TKO 11 | Las Vegas |
| July 1, 1975 | Muhammad Ali | 224½ | Joe Bugner | 230 | UD 15 | Kuala Lumpur, Malay. |
| Oct 1, 1975 | Muhammad Ali | 224½ | Joe Frazier | 215 | TKO 15 | Manila |
| Feb 20, 1976 | Muhammad Ali | 226 | Jean Pierre Coopman | 206 | KO 5 | San Juan |
| Apr 30, 1976 | Muhammad Ali | 230 | Jimmy Young | 209 | UD 15 | Landover, MD |
| May 24, 1976 | Muhammad Ali | 230 | Richard Dunn | 206½ | TKO 5 | Munich |
| Sept 28, 1976 | Muhammad Ali | 221 | Ken Norton | 217½ | UD 15 | New York City |
| May 16, 1977 | Muhammad Ali | 221¼ | Alfredo Evangelista | 209¼ | UD 15 | Landover, MD |
| Sept 29, 1977 | Muhammad Ali | 225 | Earnie Shavers | 211¼ | UD 15 | New York City |
| Feb 15, 1978 | Leon Spinks* | 197¼ | Muhammad Ali | 224¼ | Split 15 | Las Vegas |
| June 9, 1978 | Larry Holmes* | 209 | Ken Norton | 220 | Split 15 | Las Vegas |
| Sept 15, 1978 | Muhammad Ali* | 221 | Leon Spinks | 201 | UD 15 | New Orleans |
| Nov 10, 1978 | Larry Holmes* | 214 | Alfredo Evangelista | 208¼ | KO 7 | Las Vegas |
| Mar 23, 1979 | Larry Holmes* | 214 | Osvaldo Ocasio | 207 | TKO 7 | Las Vegas |
| June 22, 1979 | Larry Holmes* | 215 | Mike Weaver | 202 | TKO 12 | New York City |
| Sept 28, 1979 | Larry Holmes* | 210 | Earnie Shavers | 211 | TKO 11 | Las Vegas |
| Oct 20, 1979 | John Tate* | 240 | Gerrie Coetzee | 222 | UD 15 | Pretoria |
| Feb 3, 1980 | Larry Holmes * | 213½ | Lorenzo Zanon | 215 | TKO 6 | Las Vegas |
| Mar 31, 1980 | Mike Weaver* | 232 | John Tate | 232 | KO 15 | Knoxville |
| Mar 31, 1980 | Larry Holmes* | 211 | Leroy Jones | 254½ | TKO 8 | Las Vegas |
| July 7, 1980 | Larry Holmes* | 214¼ | Scott LeDoux | 226 | TKO 7 | Minneapolis |
| Oct 2, 1980 | Larry Holmes* | 211¼ | Muhammad Ali | 217½ | TKO 11 | Las Vegas |
| Oct 25, 1980 | Mike Weaver* | 210 | Gerrie Coetzee | 226½ | KO 13 | Sun City, S.A. |
| Apr 11, 1981 | Larry Holmes | 215 | Trevor Berbick | 215½ | UD 15 | Las Vegas |
| June 12, 1981 | Larry Holmes | 212¼ | Leon Spinks | 200¼ | TKO 3 | Detroit |
| Oct 3, 1981 | Mike Weaver* | 215 | James Quick Tillis | 209 | UD 15 | Rosemont, IL |
| Nov 6, 1981 | Larry Holmes | 213¼ | Renaldo Snipes | 215¾ | TKO 11 | Pittsburgh |
| June 11, 1982 | Larry Holmes | 212½ | Gerry Cooney | 225½ | TKO 13 | Las Vegas |
| Nov 26, 1982 | Larry Holmes | 217½ | Tex Cobb | 234¼ | UD 15 | Houston |
| Dec 10, 1982 | Michael Dokes* | 216 | Mike Weaver | 209¾ | TKO 1 | Las Vegas |
| Mar 27, 1983 | Larry Holmes | 221 | Lucien Rodriguez | 209 | UD 12 | Scranton, PA |
| May 20, 1983 | Michael Dokes* | 223 | Mike Weaver | 218½ | Draw 15 | Las Vegas |
| May 20, 1983 | Larry Holmes | 213 | Tim Witherspoon | 219½ | Split 12 | Las Vegas |
| Sept 10, 1983 | Larry Holmes | 223 | Scott Frank | 211¼ | TKO 5 | Atlantic City |
| Sept 23, 1983 | Gerrie Coetzee* | 215 | Michael Dokes | 217 | KO 10 | Richfield, OH |
| Nov 25, 1983 | Larry Holmes | 219 | Marvis Frazier | 200 | TKO 1 | Las Vegas |
| Mar 9, 1984 | Tim Witherspoon | 220¼ | Greg Page | 239½ | Maj 12 | Las Vegas |
| Aug 31, 1984 | Pinklon Thomas* | 216 | Tim Witherspoon | 217 | Maj 12 | Las Vegas |
| Nov 9, 1984 | Larry Holmes IBF | 221½ | James Smith | 227 | TKO 12 | Las Vegas |
| Dec 1, 1984 | Greg Page* | 236½ | Gerrie Coetzee | 218 | KO 8 | Sun City, S.A. |
| Mar 15, 1985 | Larry Holmes | 223½ | David Bey | 233¼ | TKO 10 | Las Vegas |
| Apr 29, 1985 | Tony Tubbs* | 229 | Greg Page | 239½ | UD 15 | Buffalo |
| May 20, 1985 | Larry Holmes | 224¼ | Carl Williams | 215 | UD 15 | Las Vegas |
| June 15, 1985 | Pinklon Thomas* | 220¼ | Mike Weaver | 221¼ | KO 8 | Las Vegas |
| Sept 21, 1985 | Michael Spinks* | 200 | Larry Holmes | 221½ | UD 15 | Las Vegas |
| Jan 17, 1986 | Tim Witherspoon | 227 | Tony Tubbs | 229 | Maj 15 | Atlanta |
| Mar 22, 1986 | Trevor Berbick* | 218½ | Pinklon Thomas | 222¾ | UD 15 | Las Vegas |
| Apr 19, 1986 | Michael Spinks | 205 | Larry Holmes | 223 | Split 15 | Las Vegas |
| July 19, 1986 | Tim Witherspoon* | 234¾ | Frank Bruno | 228 | TKO 11 | Wembley, Eng. |
| Sept 6, 1986 | Michael Spinks | 201 | Steffen Tangstad | 214¾ | TKO 4 | Las Vegas |
| Nov 22, 1986 | Mike Tyson* | 221¼ | Trevor Berbick | 218½ | TKO 2 | Las Vegas |
| Dec 12, 1986 | James Smith* | 228½ | Tim Witherspoon | 233½ | TKO 1 | New York City |
| Mar 7, 1987 | Mike Tyson* | 219 | James Smith | 233 | UD 12 | Las Vegas |
| May 30, 1987 | Mike Tyson* | 218¾ | Pinklon Thomas | 217¾ | TKO 6 | Las Vegas |
| May 30, 1987 | Tony Tucker | 222¼ | Buster Douglas | 227¼ | TKO 10 | Las Vegas |
| June 15, 1987 | Michael Spinks | 208¾ | Gerry Cooney | 238 | TKO 5 | Atlantic City |
| Aug 1, 1987 | Mike Tyson* | 221 | Tony Tucker | 221 | UD 12 | Las Vegas |
| Oct 16, 1987 | Mike Tyson* | 216 | Tyrell Biggs | 228¾ | TKO 7 | Atlantic City |
| Jan 22, 1988 | Mike Tyson* | 215¾ | Larry Holmes | 225¾ | TKO 4 | Atlantic City |
| Mar 20, 1988 | Mike Tyson* | 216¼ | Tony Tubbs | 238¼ | KO 2 | Tokyo |
| June 27, 1988 | Mike Tyson* | 218¼ | Michael Spinks | 212¼ | KO 1 | Atlantic City |
| Feb 25, 1989 | Mike Tyson | 218 | Frank Bruno | 228 | TKO 5 | Las Vegas |
| July 21, 1989 | Mike Tyson | 219¼ | Carl Williams | 218 | TKO 1 | Atlantic City |

| Date | Winner | Wgt | Loser | Wgt | Result | Site |
|------|--------|-----|-------|-----|--------|------|
| Feb 10, 1990 | Buster Douglas | 231½ | Mike Tyson | 220½ | KO 10 | Tokyo |
| Oct 25, 1990 | Evander Holyfield | 208 | Buster Douglas | 246 | KO 3 | Las Vegas |
| Apr 19, 1991 | Evander Holyfield | 212 | George Foreman | 257 | UD 12 | Atlantic City |
| Nov 23, 1991 | Evander Holyfield | 210 | Bert Cooper | 215 | TKO 7 | Atlanta |
| June 19, 1992 | Evander Holyfield | 210 | Larry Holmes | 233 | UD 12 | Las Vegas |
| Nov 13, 1992 | Riddick Bowe | 235 | Evander Holyfield | 205 | UD 12 | Las Vegas |
| Feb 6, 1993 | Riddick Bowe | 243 | Michael Dokes | 244 | KO 1 | New York City |
| May 8, 1993 | Lennox Lewis* | 235 | Tony Tucker | 235 | UD 12 | Las Vegas |
| May 22, 1993 | Riddick Bowe | 244 | Jesse Ferguson | 224 | KO 2 | Washington, D.C. |
| Oct 2, 1993 | Lennox Lewis* | 229 | Frank Bruno | 233 | KO 7 | London |
| Nov 6, 1993 | Evander Holyfield | 217 | Riddick Bowe | 246 | Split 12 | Las Vegas |
| Apr 22, 1994 | Michael Moorer | 214 | Evander Holyfield | 214 | Split 12 | Las Vegas |
| May 6, 1994 | Lennox Lewis* | 235 | Phil Jackson | 218 | TKO 8 | Atlantic City |
| Nov 6, 1994 | George Foreman | 250 | Michael Moorer | 222 | KO 10 | Las Vegas |
| Mar 11, 1995 | Riddick Bowe* | 241 | Herbie Hide | 214 | KO 6 | Las Vegas |
| Apr 8, 1995 | Oliver McCall* | 231 | Larry Holmes | 236 | UD 12 | Las Vegas |
| Apr 8, 1995 | Bruce Seldon* | 236 | Tony Tucker | 243 | TKO 7 | Las Vegas |
| Apr 22, 1995 | George Foreman | 256 | Axel Schulz | 221 | Split 12 | Las Vegas |
| Jun 17, 1995 | Riddick Bowe* | 243 | Jorge Luis Gonzalez | 237 | KO 6 | Las Vegas |
| Aug 19, 1995 | Bruce Seldon* | 234 | Joe Hipp | 233 | TKO 10 | Las Vegas |
| Sept 2, 1995 | Frank Bruno* | 247¾ | Oliver McCall | 234¾ | UD 12 | London |
| Dec 9, 1995 | Frans Botha* | 237 | Axel Shulz | 223 | Split 12 | Stuttgart |
| Mar 16, 1996 | Mike Tyson* | 220 | Frank Bruno | 247 | TKO 3 | Las Vegas |
| June 22, 1996 | Michael Moorer* | 222¼ | Axel Shulz | 222¾ | Split 12 | Dortmund, Ger. |
| Sept 7, 1996 | Mike Tyson | 219 | Bruce Seldon | 229 | TKO 1 | Las Vegas |
| Nov 9, 1996 | Evander Holyfied | 215 | Mike Tyson | 222 | TKO 11 | Las Vegas |
| Feb 7, 1997 | Lennox Lewis* | 251 | Oliver McCall | 237 | TKO 5 | Las Vegas |
| June 28, 1997 | Evander Holyfield | 218 | Mike Tyson | 218 | DQ 4 | Las Vegas |
| Oct 4, 1997 | Lennox Lewis* | 244 | Andrew Golota | 244 | TKO 1 | Atlantic City |
| Nov 8, 1997 | Evander Holyfield | 214 | Michael Moorer | 223 | TKO 8 | Las Vegas |
| Mar 28, 1998 | Lennox Lewis* | 243 | Shannon Briggs | 228 | TKO 5 | Atlantic City |
| Mar 13, 1999 | Evander Holyfield | 215 | Lennox Lewis | 246 | Draw 12 | New York City |
| Nov 13, 1999 | Lennox Lewis | 242 | Evander Holyfield | 217 | UD 12 | Las Vegas |
| Apr 29, 2000 | Lennox Lewis | 247 | Michael Grant | 250 | KO 2 | New York |
| July 15, 2000 | Lennox Lewis | 250 | Frans Botha | 236 | TKO 2 | London |
| Aug 12, 2000 | Evander Holyfield* | 221 | John Ruiz | 224 | UD 12 | Las Vegas |
| Nov 11, 2000 | Lennox Lewis | 249 | David Tua | 245 | UD 12 | Las Vegas |
| Mar 3, 2001 | John Ruiz | 227 | Evander Holyfield | 217 | UD 12 | Las Vegas |
| Apr 22, 2001 | Hasim Rahman | 238 | Lennox Lewis | 253½ | KO 5 | Brakpan, S Africa |

*Champion not generally recognized. KO=knockout; TKO=technical knockout; UD=unanimous decision; Split=split decision; Ref=referee's decision; DQ=disqualification; ND=no decision.

---

### YET ANOTHER SIGN OF THE APOCALYPSE

*Boxer Darrin Morris, who died in October 2000 of meningitis, climbed up the WBO's super middleweight rankings from seventh in November to sixth in December and fifth in January before officials realized he was out of title contention for good.*

---

# Ring Magazine Fighter and Fight of the Year

| Year | Fighter | Year | Fighter | Year | Fighter |
|------|---------|------|---------|------|---------|
| 1928 | Gene Tunney | 1935 | Barney Ross | 1940 | Billy Conn |
| 1929 | Tommy Loughran | 1936 | Joe Louis | 1941 | Joe Louis |
| 1930 | Max Schmeling | 1937 | Henry Armstrong | 1942 | Ray Robinson |
| 1932 | Jack Sharkey | 1938 | Joe Louis | 1943 | Fred Apostoli |
| 1934 | T. Canzoneri/B. Ross | 1939 | Joe Louis | 1944 | Beau Jack |

Note: No award in 1933; no fight of the year named until 1945

| Year | Fighter | Fight | Winner | Site |
|------|---------|-------|--------|------|
| 1945 | Willie Pep | Rocky Graziano–Freddie Cochrane | Rocky Graziano | New York City |
| 1946 | Tony Zale | Tony Zale–Rocky Graziano | Tony Zale | New York City |
| 1947 | Gus Lesnevich | Rocky Graziano–Tony Zale | Rocky Graziano | Chicago |
| 1948 | Ike Williams | Marcel Cerdan–Tony Zale | Marcel Cerdan | Jersey City |
| 1949 | Ezzard Charles | Willie Pep–Sandy Saddler | Willie Pep | New York City |
| 1950 | Ezzard Charles | Jake LaMotta–Laurent Dauthuille | Jake LaMotta | Detroit |
| 1951 | Ray Robinson | Jersey Joe Walcott–Ezzard Charles | Jersey Joe Walcott | Pittsburgh |
| 1952 | Rocky Marciano | Rocky Marciano–Jersey Joe Walcott | Rocky Marciano | Philadelphia |
| 1953 | Carl Olson | Rocky Marciano–Roland LaStarza | Rocky Marciano | New York City |
| 1954 | Rocky Marciano | Rocky Marciano–Ezzard Charles | Rocky Marciano | New York City |
| 1955 | Rocky Marciano | Carmen Basilio–Tony DeMarco | Carmen Basilio | Boston |
| 1956 | Floyd Patterson | Carmen Basilio–Johnny Saxton | Carmen Basilio | Syracuse |
| 1957 | Carmen Basilio | Carmen Basilio–Ray Robinson | Carmen Basilio | New York City |
| 1958 | Ingemar Johansson | Ray Robinson–Carmen Basilio | Ray Robinson | Chicago |
| 1959 | Ingemar Johansson | Gene Fullmer–Carmen Basilio | Gene Fullmer | San Francisco |
| 1960 | Floyd Patterson | Floyd Patterson–Ingemar Johansson | Floyd Patterson | New York City |
| 1961 | Joe Brown | Joe Brown–Dave Charnley | Joe Brown | London |
| 1962 | Dick Tiger | Joey Giardello–Henry Hank | Joey Giardello | Philadelphia |
| 1963 | Cassius Clay | Cassius Clay–Doug Jones | Cassius Clay | New York City |
| 1964 | Emile Griffith | Cassius Clay–Sonny Liston | Cassius Clay | Miami Beach |
| 1965 | Dick Tiger | Floyd Patterson–George Chuvalo | Floyd Patterson | New York City |
| 1966 | No award | Jose Torres–Eddie Cotton | Jose Torres | Las Vegas |
| 1967 | Joe Frazier | Nino Benvenuti–Emile Griffith | Nino Benvenuti | New York City |
| 1968 | Nino Benvenuti | Dick Tiger–Frank DePaula | Dick Tiger | New York City |
| 1969 | Jose Napoles | Joe Frazier–Jerry Quarry | Joe Frazier | New York City |
| 1970 | Joe Frazier | Carlos Monzon–Nino Benvenuti | Carlos Monzon | Rome |
| 1971 | Joe Frazier | Joe Frazier–Muhammad Ali | Joe Frazier | New York City |
| 1972 | Muhammad Ali Carlos Monzon | Bob Foster–Chris Finnegan | Bob Foster | London |
| 1973 | George Foreman | George Foreman–Joe Frazier | George Foreman | Kingston, Jam. |
| 1974 | Muhammad Ali | Muhammad Ali–George Foreman | Muhammad Ali | Kinshasa, Zaire |
| 1975 | Muhammad Ali | Muhammad Ali–Joe Frazier | Muhammad Ali | Manila |
| 1976 | George Foreman | George Foreman–Ron Lyle | George Foreman | Las Vegas |
| 1977 | Carlos Zarate | Joe Young–George Foreman | Joe Young | San Juan |
| 1978 | Muhammad Ali | Leon Spinks–Muhammad Ali | Leon Spinks | Las Vegas |
| 1979 | Ray Leonard | Danny Lopez–Mike Ayala | Danny Lopez | San Antonio |
| 1980 | Thomas Hearns | Saad Muhammad–Yaqui Lopez | Saad Muhammad | McAfee, NJ |
| 1981 | Ray Leonard Salvador Sanchez | Ray Leonard–Tommy Hearns | Ray Leonard | Las Vegas |
| 1982 | Larry Holmes | Bobby Chacon–Rafael Limon | Bobby Chacon | Sacramento |
| 1983 | Marvin Hagler | Bobby Chacon–Cornelius Boza-Edwards | Bobby Chacon | Las Vegas |
| 1984 | Thomas Hearns | Jose Luis Ramirez–Edwin Rosario | Jose Luis Ramirez | San Juan |
| 1985 | Donald Curry Marvin Hagler | Marvin Hagler–Tommy Hearns | Marvin Hagler | Las Vegas |
| 1986 | Mike Tyson | Stevie Cruz–Barry McGuigan | Stevie Cruz | Las Vegas |
| 1987 | Evander Holyfield | Ray Leonard–Marvin Hagler | Ray Leonard | Las Vegas |
| 1988 | Mike Tyson | Tony Lopez–Rocky Lockridge | Tony Lopez | Inglewood, CA |
| 1989 | Pernell Whitaker | Roberto Duran–Iran Barkley | Roberto Duran | Atlantic City |
| 1990 | Julio César Chávez | Julio César Chávez–Meldrick Taylor | Julio César Chávez | Las Vegas |
| 1991 | James Toney | Robert Quiroga–Kid Akeem Anifowoshe | Robert Quiroga | San Antonio |
| 1992 | Riddick Bowe | Riddick Bowe–Evander Holyfield | Riddick Bowe | Las Vegas |
| 1993 | Michael Carbajal | Michael Carbajal–Humberto Gonzalez | Michael Carbajal | Las Vegas |
| 1994 | Roy Jones | Jorge Castro–John David Jackson | Jorge Castro | Monterrey, Mex. |
| 1995 | Oscar De La Hoya | Saman Sor Jaturong–Chiquita Gonzalez | Saman Sor Jaturong | Inglewood, CA |
| 1996 | Evander Holyfield | Evander Holyfield–Mike Tyson | Evander Holyfield | Las Vegas |
| 1997 | Evander Holyfield | Arturo Gatti–Gabriel Ruelas | Arturo Gatti | Atlantic City |
| 1998 | Floyd Mayweather | Ivan Robinson–Arturo Gatti | Ivan Robinson | Atlantic City |
| 1999 | Paulie Ayala | Paulie Ayala–Johnny Tapia | Paulie Ayala | Las Vegas |
| 2000 | Felix Trinidad | Erik Morales–Marco Antonio Barrera | Erik Morales | Las Vegas |

# U.S. Olympic Gold Medalists

### LIGHT FLYWEIGHT
1984 ..............Paul Gonzales

### FLYWEIGHT
1904 ..............George Finnegan
1920 ..............Frank Di Gennara
1024 ..............Fidel LaBarba
1952 ..............Nathan Brooks
1976 ..............Leo Randolph
1984 ..............Steve McCrory

### BANTAMWEIGHT
1904 ..............Oliver Kirk
1988 ..............Kennedy McKinney

### FEATHERWEIGHT
1904 ..............Oliver Kirk
1924 ..............John Fields
1984 ..............Meldrick Taylor

### LIGHTWEIGHT
1904 ..............Harry Spanger
1920 ..............Samuel Mosberg
1968 ..............Ronald W. Harris
1976 ..............Howard Davis
1984 ..............Pernell Whitaker
1992 ..............Oscar De La Hoya

### LIGHT WELTERWEIGHT
1952 ..............Charles Adkins
1972 ..............Ray Seales
1976 ..............Ray Leonard
1984 ..............Jerry Page

### WELTERWEIGHT
1904 ..............Albert Young
1932 ..............Edward Flynn
1984 ..............Mark Breland

### LIGHT MIDDLEWEIGHT
1960 ..............Wilbert McClure
1984 ..............Frank Tate
1996 ..............David Reid

### MIDDLEWEIGHT
1904 ..............Charles Mayer
1932 ..............Carmen Bath
1952 ..............Floyd Patterson
1960 ..............Edward Crook
1976 ..............Michael Spinks

### LIGHT HEAVYWEIGHT
1920 ..............Eddie Eagan
1952 ..............Norvel Lee
1956 ..............James Boyd
1960 ..............Cassius Clay
1976 ..............Leon Spinks
1988 ..............Andrew Maynard

### HEAVYWEIGHT
1984 ..............Henry Tillman
1988 ..............Ray Mercer

### SUPER HEAVYWEIGHT
1904 ..............Samuel Berger
1952 ..............H. Edward Sanders
1956 ..............T. Peter
               Rademacher
1964 ..............Joe Frazier
1968 ..............George Foreman
1984 ..............Tyrell Biggs

## Brush With Greatness

They call Joel Casamayor "Cepillo," which means brush in Spanish. This name derives not from Casamayor's bristly hair but from the way the southpaw's swift uppercuts buff his opponents' faces. "My punches scrape the nose, the lips, the bones of their eyes," says the WBA super featherweight champ. "It's said I only lightly brush my opponents, but many fall and do not get up."

A former star of Cuba's powerhouse amateur boxing team who defected to the U.S. before the 1996 Olympics, Cepillo has brushed off all 25 of his professional opponents, 15 by knockout. He won the WBA crown with a fifth-round TKO of Jongkwon Baek of South Korea in May 2000. At age 30 he is eyeing big-money bouts against the two other undefeated 130-pound champions, WBC titleholder Floyd Mayweather and WBO king Acelino Freitas.... Freitas, who has knocked out all 29 fighters he has faced, may well be the career-defining opponent Casamayor is seeking. "Joel is too slick, and his attack is too unpredictable," says veteran trainer Lou Duva. "Freitas will be lucky to land a solid shot."

Casamayor has a hard, angular face and an enigmatic set to his mouth. His well-calibrated brushwork paints a picture of fistic precision. "He doesn't waste movement," says trainer and ESPN2 commentator Teddy Atlas. "He's a very contained little fighter. . . ."

Casamayor honed his boxing skills in a gym where his father, Reymundo, had sent him at age six, as an alternative to street fighting. Regional age-group champ at 12, Joel was invited to Havana at 15 to join the national team.

At the 1992 Olympics in Barcelona, Casamayor was part of a Cuban contingent that won seven gold and two silver medals in 12 weight divisions, the most dominant boxing performance by any country in a nonboycott year. Three of the seven gold medalists were rewarded with cars; Casamayor, the bantamweight champ, got a bicycle, which he swapped for a pig to provide meat for his family.

Despite winning 380 of 410 amateur bouts, Casamayor was often slighted by Cuban sports officials on other ways. He was pressured to join the Communist Party and to declare his fealty to the revolution and Fidel Castro. When he refused, the government threatened to take away his small house in Guantanamo. Team officials made him prepare for the '96 Olympics at 119 pounds, a weight he nearly had to starve himself to make. "They wouldn't even let me have water," he says. "To them I was a piece of meat."

While training for the '96 Games at the Cuban compound in Guadalajara, Mexico, Casamayor heard that team officials might not permit him to compete in Atlanta, fearing he would defect. A few days after teammate Ramon Garbey had slipped away into hiding, Casamayor walked out of camp saying he was going to buy a loaf of bread, and he kept on walking.

In June he and Garbey crossed over into the U.S. near Tijuana and were granted political asylum.... Casamayor settled in Miami, turned pro and joined Team Freedom, a squad mostly made up of former Cuban amateurs in exile. "Joel was a diamond," says manager Luis de Cubas. "He just needed someone to polish him." In 1999 de Cubas sent him to Joe Goossen, the Van Nuys, Calif., trainer who had helped steer the Ruelas brothers, Gabriel and Rafael, to world titles.

Mindful that Casamayor might be set in his ways as a three-round fighter, Goossen designed a daily regimen of bag work and 30 to 40 rounds of sparring. "Joel gets a psychotic possession in the gym," he says. "No matter what I throw out, he devours it."

Casamayor is far from sated. As his biggest bouts draw near, the artistic Cepillo is eager to lay something out on the canvas.

—Rich O'Brien

# Horse Racing

BILL FRAKES

# Point Taken

## By easily winning two legs of the Triple Crown, Point Given made a claim to greatness

### BY MARK BEECH

THOUSANDS OF horses raced in the U.S. in 2001, but one was in class by himself: Point Given. From March 17, when he won the San Felipe Stakes at Santa Anita, to Aug. 30, when his racing career ended because of a strained tendon in his left foreleg, the huge chestnut colt dominated the 3-year-old division like no other horse in recent memory. He won five Grade I races, and in each victory he demonstrated a new facet of his formidable talent. He won two legs of the Triple Crown and emerged as a genuine superstar.

Railbirds had already begun buzzing about Point Given, the son of Thunder Gulch, during the waning months of 2000. Although he lost by a nose to Macho Uno in the Breeders' Cup Juvenile at Churchill Downs on Nov. 4, the enormous colt stamped himself as an early Kentucky Derby favorite six weeks later when he won the Hollywood Futurity by a length. And if his accomplishments on the track weren't enough, the colt had his prodigious size—he weighed more than 1,200 pounds as a 2-year-old—and goofy demeanor to attract attention. He had a habit of rearing up during his morning workouts, once dumping

his exercise rider on the track at Santa Anita and running on autopilot back to his stall in trainer Bob Baffert's barn. Baffert nicknamed the colt T-Rex.

After a brief New Year's break, Point Given kicked off his 3-year-old campaign by winning the San Felipe and then pulverizing a weak field in the Santa Anita Derby on April 7. By the time the first Saturday in May rolled around, almost every turf writer in America was picking him to win the Derby—and more. "If that horse doesn't win the Triple Crown," said one trainer, "something's wrong."

Unfortunately Point Given produced his worst performance of the year in the biggest race of his life, finishing fifth in the Derby, 11½ lengths out of contention. As the horse broke from post 17 on the far outside, his jockey, Gary Stevens, hustled him to within five lengths of the front of the pack as the field entered the clubhouse turn. But Stevens failed to gauge that the leaders were cooking like sprinters through some of the fastest early fractions in the history of the 1¼-mile Derby. Three quarters of a mile later, when Point Given entered the homestretch, he had nothing left in his tank. "He never got out of

BILL FRAKES

a high lope," Baffert told the *Daily Racing Form*. "He's a big, heavy horse, and he hits the ground hard, so maybe he wasn't that comfortable with the track. I don't know. It's one of those deals where you shake your head, scratch it, rub it and bang it against a table, but there's no answer. Maybe he was too close to the pace. Maybe it was the condition of the track. There was nothing physically wrong with him."

But even if Point Given had run his race, there is no guarantee he would have won because Monarchos, who did win, ran one of the most brilliant races in the history of the Derby. Trailing by as many as 15 lengths down the backstretch, the gray colt, with Jorge Chávez up, let the leaders fry their circuitry in a crazy speed duel for ¾ of a mile, then swallowed the field whole as he steamed around the turn, down the stretch and under the wire. His final time of 1:59.97 is the second-fastest Derby ever run, only ⅖ of a second slower than the 1973 mark of the great Secretariat.

Two weeks later, in the 1³⁄₁₆-mile Preakness, Point Given delivered on his immense promise. Breaking from the far outside again, this time in post 11, Stevens let the big colt settle into an easy pace rather than rush him up with the leaders. He had barely gone 500 yards when he could tell that the old Point Given—relaxed and cruising along—was back. "Going into the first turn, it was the same feeling I had in the Santa Anita Derby," Stevens said. "The race was over."

Indeed it was. Between the midway point on the first turn and the midway point on

the far turn, Point Given tore through a half mile in 46 seconds, then galloped down the lane, bumping his stablemate, Congaree, along the way and cruising under the wire 2¼ lengths in front of A P Valentine. "He did it with no effort at all," Stevens said of Point Given. "We got the trip we were hoping to get in the Kentucky Derby."

And it was only a tuneup, it turned out, for the spectacular trip Stevens got in the Belmont. The Big Red Train, as Point Given came to be called, trailed the leaders in the third leg of the Triple Crown for nearly a mile before making his move as he entered the far turn and overtaking Balto Star. "I looked over and thought, Oh, my god, he's here already," said Balto Star's jockey, Chris McCarron. Eating up the track in huge, powerful strides, Stevens rocking rhythmically on his back, Point Given pulled away by five, six, seven lengths. Belmont Park began to shake. Eight lengths widened to nine in the stretch, then 10. Point Given crossed the wire 12¼ lengths ahead of second-place finisher A P Valentine. Again the colt had produced a race that ranked with the greatest in thoroughbred history: His time of 2:26⅗ for the 1½ miles was the fourth-fastest Belmont ever. In the winner's circle Point Given's handlers couldn't help feeling that they had let history get away. "It's bittersweet," Stevens said of the victory. "He should have a Triple Crown after his name."

Point Given more than atoned for his Kentucky Derby failure with two summer romps that further burnished his brassy reputation. At Monmouth Park for the Haskell Invitational on Aug. 5, a track-record crowd of 47,127 watched him gut out a half-length victory. Three weeks later, at Saratoga, he handily won the Travers in front of a stakes-record throng of 60,846. Four days later veterinarians detected the injury to the colt's left foreleg, and Baffert and Point Given's owner, Prince Ahmed bin Salman of Saudi

CHUCK SOLOMON

**According Stevens, Point Given (center) won the Preakness with "no effort at all."**

Arabia, made the difficult decision to end the horse's career. "I'm devastated," Baffert said. "What really hurts is that it's not only a blow for me, the stable and the prince, but it's a blow for racing. He attracts such a huge following. We finally had a great horse, and look what happens."

Point Given's injury prevented him from running in the Breeders' Cup Classic at Belmont Park on Oct. 27. He was expected to be challenged there by the only other horse in the world thought to be his equal, an undefeated 3-year-old Irish colt named Galileo, winner of the Epsom and Irish derbies, as well as the King George VI and Queen Elizabeth Diamond Stakes. The other horses expected to test Point Given were all 4-year-olds: Tiznow, winner of the 2000 Classic; Captain Steve, who took the Dubai World Cup, the planet's richest race, in March; and Albert the Great, winner of the Suburban Handicap at Belmont in July. But none of those horses could duplicate the box-office clout wielded by Point Given.

Off the track the racing industry took a major hit in the spring when, on the eve of the Kentucky Derby, pregnant mares all over the Bluegrass State began miscarrying their fetuses and late-term foals. The death toll had exceeded 1,000 fetuses and foals by the end of May, and the estimated cost to the state's $900 million breeding industry was $150 million. Estimated losses to the 2002 foal crop ranged from 10% to 40%. Though the cause was never pinpointed, medical specialists said that pasture grass ingested by horses may have contained fungal poisons as a result of a sudden change in temperatures.

Not all the business news was bad, though. Spurred by racing's decision to switch the Triple Crown telecasts from ABC to NBC and the network's use of the races as lead-ins for its NBA playoff programming, ratings for the Derby, Preakness and Belmont were up substantially this year. As for the 2002 Triple Crown, Baffert may be sitting pretty again with a 2-year-old colt named Officer, who is also owned by Prince Ahmed. In the last five years the silver-haired trainer has won six of 15 Triple Crown races, supplanting D. Wayne Lukas as the leading 3-year-old trainer in the country. Appropriately, when Baffert announced Point Given's retirement, he was already looking ahead to next spring. "The only thing probably helping my situation is that we still have Officer. Maybe he can carry the torch. He's going to have to. Horses like Point Given don't come around too often."

## The Triple Crown

### 127th Kentucky Derby

May 5, 2001. Grade I, 3-year-olds; 8th race, Churchill Downs, Louisville. All 126 lbs. Distance: 1¼ miles. Stakes value: $1,112,000; Winner: $812,000; Second: $170,000; Third: $85,000; Fourth: $45,000. Track: Fast. Off: 6:11 p.m. Winner: Monarchos (B. c, Maria's Mon out of Regal Band by Dixieland Band); Times: 0:22.25, 0:44.86, 1:09.25, 1:35.00, !:59.97. Won: Driving. Breeder: J.D. Squires.

| Horse | Finish-PP | Margin | Jockey/Owner |
|---|---|---|---|
| Monarchos | 1–16 | 4¾ | Jorge Chavez/John C. Oxley |
| Invisible Ink | 2–13 | nose | John Velazquez/Peachtree Stable |
| Congaree | 3–8 | 4 | Victor Espinoza/Stonerside Stable |
| Thunder Blitz | 4–4 | 2¾ | Edgar Prado/Stronach Stable |
| Point Given | 5–17 | 1¼ | Gary Stevens/The Thoroughbred Corporation |
| Jamaican Rum | 6–15 | neck | Eddie Delahoussaye/S'thern Nevada Racing Stables, Inc. |
| A P Valentine | 7–9 | 1¼ | Corey Nakatani/Ol' Memorial Stable & Michael Tabor |
| Express Tour | 8–6 | ¾ | David Flores/Godolphin Racing, Inc. |
| Fifty Stars | 9–5 | 1¼ | Donnie Meche/James Cassels and Bob Zollars |
| Startac | 10–12 | 4 | Alex Solis/Allen E. Paulson Living Trust Paulson & White |
| Millennium Wind | 11–2 | neck | Laffit Pincay Jr./David and Jill Heerensperger |
| Artic Boy | 12–7 | 6½ | Calvin Borel/Royce G. Roberts |
| Songandaprayer | 13–1 | 5 | Aaron Gryder/Devil Eleven Stable & DJ Stable Leslie & Bobby Hurley |
| Balto Star | 14–3 | 2¼ | Mark Guidry/Anstu Stables, Inc. |
| Dollar Bill | 15–10 | 17 | Pat Day/Gary and Mary West |
| Keats | 16–14 | — | Larry Melancon/Henry E. Pabst |
| Talk is Money | 17–11 | — | Jerry Bailey/Daniel M. Borislow |

### 126th Preakness Stakes

May 19, 2001. Grade I, 3-year-olds; 11th race, Pimlico Race Course, Baltimore. All 126 lbs. Distance: 1³⁄₁₆ miles; Stakes value: $1,000,000; Winner: $650,000; Second: $200,000; Third: $100,000; Fourth: $50,000. Track: Fast. Off: 6:09 p.m. Winner: Point Given (B. c, Thunder Gulch out of Turko's Turn by Turkoman); Times: 0:23.84, 0:47.32, 1:11.86, 1:36.40, 1:55.51. Won: Driving. Breeder: The Thoroughbred Corporation.

| Horse | Finish-PP | Margin | Jockey/Owner |
|---|---|---|---|
| Point Given | 1–11 | 2¼ | Gary Stevens/The Thoroughbred Corporation |
| A P Valentine | 2–4 | neck | Victor Espinoza/Ol' Memorial Stable and Michael Tabor |
| Congaree | 3–5 | 1¼ | Jerry Bailey/Stonerside Stable |
| Dollar Bill | 4–10 | 2¼ | Pat Day/Gary and Mary West |
| Griffinite | 5–3 | 1½ | Shaun Bridgmohan/Paraneck Stable |
| Monarchos | 6–7 | 1 | Jorge Chavez/John C. Oxley |
| Marciano | 7–1 | 1¼ | Mark Johnston/Win More Stable, Inc. |
| Bay Eagle | 8–9 | nose | Ramon Dominguez/Lazy Lane Farms, Inc. |
| Percy Hope | 9–8 | 17½ | Jon Court/Waterfall Stable |
| Richly Blended | 10 | 9¾ | Rick Wilson/Raymond Dweck |
| Mr. John | 11 | — | Corey Nakatani/Thomas F. Van Meter II |

### 133rd Belmont Stakes

June 9, 2001. Grade I, 3-year-olds; 10th race, Belmont Park, Elmont, NY. All 126 lbs. Distance: 1½ miles. Stakes purse: $1,000,000; Winner: $650,000; Second: $200,000; Third: $100,000; Fourth: $50,000.. Track: Fast. Off: 6:10 p.m. Winner: Point Given (B. c, Thunder Gulch out of Turko's Turn by Turkoman); Times: 0:23.95, 48.00, 1:11.78, 135.56, 2:00.76, 2:26.56. Won: Driving. Breeder: The Thoroughbred Corporation.

| Horse | Finish-PP | Margin | Jockey/Owner |
|---|---|---|---|
| Point Given | 1–9 | 12¼ | Gary Stevens/The Thoroughbred Corporation |
| A P Valentine | 2–8 | ¾ | Victor Espinoza/Ol' Memorial Stable and Michael Tabor |
| Monarchos | 3–5 | 1 | Jorge Chavez/John C. Oxley |
| Dollar Bill | 4–3 | 2½ | Pat Day/Gary and Mary West |
| Invisible Ink | 5–1 | 7½ | John Velazquez/Peachtree Stable |
| Thunder Blitz | 6–4 | 5¾ | Edgar Prado/Stronach Stable |
| Buckle Down Ben | 7–6 | 15½ | Corey Nakatani/Michael Tabor |
| Balto Star | 8–2 | 28¾ | Chris McCarron/Anstu Stables, Inc. |
| Dr. Greenfield | 9–7 | — | Edgar Prado/Team Valor |

# Major Stakes Races

## Late 2000

| Date | Race | Track | Distance | Winner | Jockey/Trainer | Purse ($) |
|---|---|---|---|---|---|---|
| Sept 10 | Atto Mile Stakes | Woodbine | 1 mile | Riviera | John Velazquez/ Robert Frankel | 1,000,000 |
| Sept 16 | Woodward Stakes | Belmont Park | 1⅛ miles | Lemon Drop Kid | Edgar Prado/ F. Schulhoffer | 500,000 |
| Sept 16 | Kentucky Cup Classic Handicap | Turfway Park | 1⅛ miles | Captain Steve | Shane Sellers/ Bob Baffert | 500,000 |
| Sept 30 | Super Derby | Louisiana Downs | 1¼ miles | Tiznow | Chris McCarron/ J. Robbins | 500,000 |
| Oct 7 | Yellow Ribbon Stakes | Santa Anita Park | 1¼ miles | Tranquility Lake | Eddie Delahoussaye/ J. Canani | 500,000 |
| Oct 7 | Flower Bowl Invitational Handicap | Belmont Park | 1¼ miles | Colstar | Jean-Luc Samyn/ P. Fout | 750,000 |
| Oct 7 | Turf Classic Invitational | Belmont Park | 1½ miles | John's Call | Jean-Luc Samyn/ T. Voss | 750,000 |
| Oct 7 | Hawthorne Gold Cup Handicap | Hawthorne | 1¼ miles | Dust on the Bottle | T. Doocy/ G. Hilld | 500,000 |
| Oct 8 | Queen Elizabeth II Challenge Cup | Keeneland | 1⅛ miles | Collect the Cash | Shane Sellers/ J. Orseno | 500,000 |
| Oct 8 | Lane's End Breeders' Futurity | Keeneland | 1¹⁄₁₆ miles | Arabian Light | Shane Sellers/ Bob Baffert | 451,200 |
| Oct 8 | Meadowlands Cup Handicap | Meadowlands | 1⅛ miles | North East Bound | John Velez/ W. Perry | 400,000 |
| Oct 13 | Winstar Galaxy Stakes | Keeneland | 1³⁄₁₆ miles | Tout Charmant | Chris McCarron/ R. McAnally | 554,000 |
| Oct 14 | The Jockey Club Gold Cup | Belmont Park | 1¼ miles | Albert the Great | Jorge Chavez/ Nick Zito | 1,000,000 |
| Oct 14 | Frizette Stakes | Belmont Park | 1¹⁄₁₆ miles | Raging Fever | Jerry Bailey/ M. Hennig | 500,000 |
| Oct 14 | Beldame Stakes | Belmont Park | 1⅛ miles | Riboletta | Chris McCarron/ E. Inda | 750,000 |
| Oct 14 | Spinster Stakes | Keeneland | 1⅛ miles | Plenty of Life | Garrett Gomez/ E. Walden | 543,500 |
| Oct 15 | Goodwood Breeders' Cup Handicap | Santa Anita | 1⅛ miles | Tiznow | Chris McCarron/ J. Robbins | 418,000 |
| Oct 15 | Alcibiades Stakes | Keeneland | 1¹⁄₁₆ miles | She's A Devil Due | Mark Guidry/ K. McPeek | 436,000 |
| Oct 15 | Canadian International Stakes | Woodbine | 1½ miles | Mutafaweq | Frankie Dettori/ S.B. Saeed | 1,500,000 |
| Oct 15 | E.P. Taylor Stakes | Woodbine | 1¼ miles | Fly For Avie | T. Kabel/ D. Bell | 500,000 |
| Oct 21 | Calder Oaks | Calder | 1⅛ miles | Lucky Lune | Rene Douglas/ C. Clement | 200,000 |
| Nov 4 | Breeders' Cup Classic | Churchill Downs | 1¼ miles | Tiznow | Chris McCarron/ J. Robbins | 4,296,040 |
| Nov 4 | Breeders' Cup Turf | Churchill Downs | 1½ miles | Kalanisi | John Murtagh/ M.R. Stoute | 2,271,680 |
| Nov 4 | Breeders' Cup Sprint | Churchill Downs | 6 furlongs | Kona Gold | Alex Solis/ B. Hedley | 916,000 |
| Nov 4 | Breeders' Cup Mile | Churchill Downs | 1 mile | War Chant | Gary Stevens/ Neil Drysdale | 1,071,720 |
| Nov 4 | Breeders' Cup Juvenile Fillies | Churchill Downs | 1¹⁄₁₆ miles | Caressing | John Velazquez/ D. Vance | 1,025,920 |
| Nov 4 | Breeders' Cup Distaff | Churchill Downs | 1⅛ miles | Spain | Victor Espinoza/ D. Wayne Lukas | 2,161,760 |
| Nov 4 | Breeders' Cup Juvenile | Churchill Downs | 1¹⁄₁₆ miles | Macho Uno | Jerry Bailey/ Joe Orseno | 980,120 |
| Nov 24 | Clark Handicap | Churchill Downs | 1⅛ miles | Surfside | Pat Day/ D. Wayne Lukas | 445,600 |
| Nov 25 | Cigar Mile Handicap | Aqueduct | 1 mile | El Corredor | Jerry Bailey/ Bob Baffert | 350,000 |
| Nov 25 | Citation Handicap | Hollywood Park | 1¹⁄₁₆ miles | Charge D'Affaires | Jose Santos/ C. Clement | 500,000 |
| Nov 26 | Matriarch Stakes | Hollywood Park | 1⅛ miles | Tout Charmant | Chris McCarron/ R. McAnally | 500,000 |
| Nov 26 | Hollywood Derby | Hollywood Park | 1⅛ miles | Brahms | Pat Day/ W.E. Walden | 500,000 |

## 2001 (Through September 8)

| Date | Race | Track | Distance | Winner | Jockey/Trainer | Purse ($) |
|---|---|---|---|---|---|---|
| Jan 13 | San Fernando B.C. Stakes | Santa Anita | 1¹⁄₁₆ miles | Tiznow | Chris McCarron/ J. Robbins | 190,800 |
| Feb 3 | Strub Stakes | Santa Anita | 1⅛ miles | Wooden Phone | Corey Nakatani/ Bob Baffert | 500,000 |
| Feb 4 | Donn Handicap | Gulfstream Park | 1⅛ miles | Captain Steve | Jerry Bailey/ Bob Baffert | 500,000 |
| Mar 3 | Santa Anita Handicap | Santa Anita Park | 1¼ miles | Tiznow | Chris McCarron/ J. Robbins | 1,000,000 |
| Mar 4 | New Orleans Handicap | Fair Grounds | 1⅛ miles | Include | Jerry Bailey/ G. Delp | 500,000 |
| Mar 10 | Santa Margarita Handicap | Santa Anita Park | 1⅛ miles | Lazy Susan | David Flores/ J. Dolan | 300,000 |
| Mar 10 | Florida Derby | Gulfstream Park | 1⅛ miles | Monarchos | Jorge Chavez/ J. Ward | 1,000,000 |
| Mar 10 | Fair Grounds Oaks | Fair Grounds | 1¹⁄₁₆ miles | Real Cozy | E. Martin/ D. Peitz | 350,000 |
| Mar 10 | Santa Anita Oaks | Santa Anita Park | 1¹⁄₁₆ miles | Golden Ballet | Chris McCarron/ J. Sahadi | 300,000 |
| Mar 11 | Louisiana Derby | Fair Grounds | 1¹⁄₁₆ miles | Fifty Stars | Don Meche/ S. Asmussen | 750,000 |
| Mar 24 | Spiral Stakes | Turfway Park | 1⅛ miles | Balto Star | Aaron Guidry/ T. Pletcher | 600,000 |
| Mar 24 | Dubai World Cup | Nad Al Sheba | 1¼ miles | Captain Steven | Jerry Bailey/ Bob Baffert | 6,000,000 |
| Apr 7 | Santa Anita Derby | Santa Anita Park | 1⅛ miles | Point Given | Gary Stevens/ Bob Baffert | 750,000 |
| Apr 7 | Oaklawn Handicap | Oaklawn Park | 1⅛ miles | Traditionally | Pat Day/ C. McGaughey | 600,000 |
| Apr 7 | Ashland Stakes | Keeneland | 1¹⁄₁₆ miles | Fleet Renee | John Velazquez/ M. Dickinson | 576,250 |
| Apr 7 | Illinois Derby | Sportsman's Park | 1⅛ miles | Distilled | Mike Smith/ T. Pletcher | 500,000 |
| Apr 8 | Apple Blossom Handicap | Oaklawn Park | 1¹⁄₁₆ miles | Gourmet Girl | Calvin Borel/ A. Perdomo | 500,000 |
| Apr 14 | Arkansas Derby | Oaklawn Park | 1⅛ miles | Balto Star | Mark Guidry/ T. Pletcher | 500,000 |
| Apr 14 | Bluegrass Stakes | Keeneland | 1⅛ miles | Millennium Wind | Laffit Pincay/ D. Hofmans | 750,000 |
| Apr 14 | Wood Memorial Stakes | Aqueduct | 1⅛ miles | Congaree | Victor Espinoza/ Bob Baffert | 750,000 |
| Apr 14 | San Juan Capistrano Handicap | Santa Anita | 1¾ miles | Bienamado | Chris McCarron/ P. Gonzalez | 400,000 |
| May 5 | Kentucky Derby | Churchill Downs | 1¼ miles | Monarchos | Jorge Chavez/ J. Ward | 1,112,000 |
| May 19 | Preakness Stakes | Pimlico | 1³⁄₁₆ miles | Point Given | Gary Stevens/ Bob Baffert | 1,000,000 |
| May 28 | Metropolitan Handicap | Belmont Park | 1 mile | Exciting Story | Pat Husbands/ M. Casse | 750,000 |
| May 28 | Lone Star Park Handicap | Lone Star Park | 1¹⁄₁₆ miles | Dixie Dotcom | David Flores/ W. Morey | 300,000 |
| May 28 | Shoemaker Breeders' Cup Mile | Hollywood Park | 1 mile | Irish Prize | Gary Stevens/ Neil Drysdale | 475,000 |
| June 2 | Massachusetts Handicap | Suffolk Downs | 1⅛ miles | Include | Jerry Bailey/ G. Delp | 500,000 |
| June 9 | Belmont Stakes | Belmont Park | 1½ miles | Point Given | Gary Stevens/ Bob Baffert | 1,000,000 |
| June 10 | Charlie Whittingham Handicap | Hollywood Park | 1¼ miles | Bienamado | Chris McCarron/ P. Gonzalez | 350,000 |
| June 16 | Stephen Foster Handicap | Churchill Downs | 1⅛ miles | Guided Tour | Larry Melancon/ N. O'Callaghan | 831,000 |
| June 16 | Fleur de Lis Handicap | Churchill Downs | 1⅛ miles | Saudi Poetry | Victor Espinoza/ Bob Baffert | 333,000 |
| June 24 | Queen's Plate Stakes | Woodbine | 1¼ miles | Dancethru-thedawn | Guy Boulanger/ M. Frostad | 1,000,000 |
| July 1 | Suburban Handicap | Belmont Park | 1¼ miles | Albert the Great | Jorge Chavez/ Nick Zito | 500,000 |

### 2001 (Through September 8) *(Cont.)*

| Date | Race | Track | Distance | Winner | Jockey/Trainer | Purse ($) |
|---|---|---|---|---|---|---|
| July 1 | Hollywood Gold Cup | Hollywood Park | 1¼ miles | Aptitude | Laffit Pincay/ Robert Frankel | 750,000 |
| July 14 | Princess Rooney Handicap | Calder | 6 furlongs | Dream Supreme | Pat Day/ Bill Mott | 400,000 |
| July 15 | Swaps Stakes | Hollywood Park | 1⅛ miles | Congaree | Gary Stevens/ Bob Baffert | 300,000 |
| July 15 | Sunset Handicap | Hollywood Park | 1½ miles | Blueprint | Gary Stevens/ R. Hess Jr. | 200,000 |
| July 22 | Delaware Handicap | Delaware Park | 1¼ miles | Irving's Baby | Ramon Dominguez/ T. Pletcher | 600,300 |
| Aug 4 | Jim Dandy Stakes | Saratoga | 1⅛ miles | Scorpion | Jerry Bailey/ D. Wayne Lukas | 600,000 |
| Aug 5 | Haskell Invitational | Monmouth Park | 1⅛ miles | Point Given | Gary Stevens/ Bob Baffert | 1,500,000 |
| Aug 18 | Arlington Million | Arlington | 1¼ miles | Silvano | A. Suborics/ A. Wohler | 1,000,000 |
| Aug 18 | Alabama Stakes | Saratoga | 1¼ miles | Flute | Edgar Prado/ Robert Frankel | 750,000 |
| Aug 19 | Pacific Classic | Del Mar Pleasure | 1¼ miles | Skimming | Garrett Gomez/ Robert Frankel | 1,000,000 |
| Aug 25 | Travers Stakes | Saratoga | 1¼ miles | Point Given | Gary Stevens/ Bob Baffert | 1,000,000 |
| Sept 3 | Diana Handicap | Saratoga | 1⅛ miles | Starine | John Velazquez/ Robert Frankel | 500,000 |
| Sept 8 | Woodward Stakes | Belmont Park | 1⅛ miles | Lido Palace | Jerry Bailey/ Robert Frankel | 500,000 |
| Sept 8 | Man O' War | Belmont Park | 1⅜ miles | With Anticipation | Pat Day/ J. Sheppard | 500,000 |

*Irish pounds

## 2000 Statistical Leaders

### Horses

| Horse | Starts | 1st | 2nd | 3rd | Purses ($) | Horse | Starts | 1st | 2nd | 3rd | Purses ($) |
|---|---|---|---|---|---|---|---|---|---|---|---|
| Dubai Millennium | 1 | 1 | 0 | 0 | 3,600,000 | Spain | 13 | 5 | 3 | 1 | 1,979,500 |
| Tiznow | 9 | 5 | 3 | 0 | 3,445,950 | Captain Steve | 11 | 3 | 2 | 4 | 1,882,276 |
| Fantastic Light | 6 | 2 | 1 | 1 | 3,238,998 | Behrens | 7 | 1 | 3 | 2 | 1,764,500 |
| T.M. Opera O | 1 | 1 | 0 | 0 | 2,278,332 | Lemon Drop Kid | 9 | 5 | 0 | 1 | 1,673,900 |
| Fusaichi Pegasus | 8 | 6 | 1 | 0 | 1,987,800 | Giant's Causeway | 3 | 1 | 2 | 0 | 1,600,593 |

### Jockeys

| Jockey | Mounts | 1st | 2nd | 3rd | Purses ($) | Win Pct | $ Pct* |
|---|---|---|---|---|---|---|---|
| Pat Day | 1219 | 267 | 206 | 186 | 17,479,838 | .22 | .54 |
| Jerry Bailey | 908 | 246 | 145 | 133 | 17,468,690 | .27 | .58 |
| Shane Sellers | 1109 | 192 | 158 | 128 | 14,881,680 | .17 | .43 |
| Jorge Chavez | 1447 | 261 | 242 | 171 | 14,440,907 | .18 | .47 |
| Kent Desormeaux | 887 | 177 | 132 | 137 | 13,460,166 | .20 | .50 |
| Chris McCarron | 563 | 115 | 97 | 65 | 13,405,170 | .20 | .49 |
| Victor Espinoza | 1325 | 243 | 202 | 190 | 13,286,705 | .18 | .48 |
| Corey Nakatani | 889 | 185 | 160 | 124 | 12,670,504 | .21 | .53 |
| Edgar Prado | 1642 | 255 | 245 | 255 | 12,375,107 | .16 | .46 |
| John R. Velazquez | 1083 | 200 | 189 | 131 | 10,794,003 | .18 | .48 |

*Percentage in the Money (1st, 2nd, and 3rd).

### Trainers

| Trainer | Starts | 1st | 2nd | 3rd | Purses ($) | Win Pct | $ Pct* |
|---|---|---|---|---|---|---|---|
| Bob Baffert | 678 | 146 | 94 | 108 | 11,831,605 | .22 | .51 |
| Robert Frankel | 371 | 96 | 62 | 56 | 10,839,071 | .26 | .58 |
| D. Wayne Lukas | 815 | 118 | 110 | 108 | 10,490,292 | .14 | .41 |
| William Mott | 733 | 155 | 99 | 106 | 8,591,389 | .21 | .49 |
| Saeed bin Suroor | 28 | 5 | 3 | 3 | 8,065,104 | .18 | .39 |
| Todd Pletcher | 661 | 114 | 102 | 68 | 7,058,280 | .17 | .43 |
| Joesph Orseno | 245 | 52 | 32 | 40 | 6,673,714 | .21 | .51 |
| Neil Drysdale | 197 | 48 | 27 | 25 | 6,111,440 | .24 | .51 |
| Steven Asmussen | 1119 | 234 | 199 | 144 | 5,872,931 | .21 | .52 |
| Scott Lake | 1045 | 336 | 205 | 153 | 5,731,522 | .32 | .66 |

*Percentage in the Money (1st, 2nd, and 3rd).

### Owners

| Owner | Starts | 1st | 2nd | 3rd | Purses ($) |
|---|---|---|---|---|---|
| Stronach Stable | 764 | 163 | 111 | 118 | 11,198,225 |
| Godolphin Inc. | 26 | 5 | 3 | 3 | 8,041,704 |
| Juddmonte Farms, Inc. | 137 | 36 | 25 | 20 | 6,096,951 |
| The Thoroughbred Corporation | 326 | 54 | 60 | 46 | 5,880,705 |
| Richard Englander | 1149 | 213 | 205 | 169 | 4,921,294 |
| Sam-Son Farms | 164 | 45 | 37 | 23 | 4,698,712 |
| Golden Eagle Farm | 476 | 82 | 83 | 68 | 4,096,574 |
| Bruno Schickedanz | 727 | 143 | 111 | 94 | 3,594,542 |
| Michael Cooper and Cecilia Straub-Rubens | 10 | 5 | 3 | 1 | 3,451,590 |
| John Franks | 738 | 120 | 90 | 72 | 3,169,118 |

## HARNESS RACING

## Major Stakes Races

### Late 2000

| Date | Race | Location | Winner | Driver/Trainer | Purse ($) |
|---|---|---|---|---|---|
| Oct 27 | BC Two-year-old Colt Trot | Mohawk Raceway | Banker Hall | Trevor Ritchie/ Harald Lunde | 705,889 |
| Oct 27 | BC Two-year-old Filly Pace | Mohawk Raceway | Lady MacBeach | Luc Ouellette/ Joe Holloway | 715,080 |
| Oct 27 | BC Two-year-old Colt Pace | Mohawk Raceway | Bettor's Delight | Michel Lachance/ Gary Machiz | 871,475 |
| Oct 27 | BC Two-year-old Filly Trot | Mohawk Raceway | Syrinx Hanover | Trevor Ritchie/ Christopher Marino | 755,911 |
| Oct 27 | BC Three-year-old Colt Trot | Mohawk Raceway | Fast Photo | Michel Lachance/ Donald Swick | 662,948 |
| Oct 27 | BC Three-year-old Filly Trot | Mohawk Raceway | Aviano | Trevor Ritchie/ William Wellwood | 602,680 |
| Oct 27 | BC Three-year-old Filly Pace | Mohawk Raceway | Popcorn Penny | Ryan Anderson/ Tktktkt | 738,484 |
| Oct 27 | BC Three-year-old Colt Pace | Mohawk Raceway | Gallo Blue Chip | Daniel Dube/ Mark Ford | 602,680 |
| Nov 18 | Three Diamonds Pace Filly Pace | Garden State Park | Electrical Art | Ron Pierce/ Robert McIntosh | 356,100 |
| Nov 18 | Governor's Cup | Garden State Park | Bettor's Delight | Eric Ledford/ Gary Machiz | 542,300 |

### 2001 (Through September 20)

| Date | Race | Location | Winner | Driver/Trainer | Purse ($) |
|---|---|---|---|---|---|
| June 2 | New Jersey Classic | Meadowlands | Bettor's Delight | Michel Lachance Scott McEneny | 500,000 |
| June 23 | North America Cup | Woodbine | Bettor's Delight | Michel Lachance/ Scott McEneny | 1,148,500 |

## Major Stakes Races *(Cont.)*

### 2000 (Through September 20) *(Cont.)*

| Date | Race | Location | Winner | Driver/Trainer | Purse ($) |
|---|---|---|---|---|---|
| July 13 | Beacon Course Trot | Meadowlands | SJ's Caviar | Robert Blanton Jr./ Belinda Blanton | 401,500 |
| July 14 | Meadowlands Pace | Meadowlands | Real Desire | John Campbell/ Blair Burgess | 1,009,500 |
| July 28 | BC Three and up Open Trot | Meadowlands | Varenna | G. Minnucci/ G. Minnucci | 1,000,000 |
| July 28 | BC Three and up Mare Pace | Meadowlands | Eternal Camnation | Eric Ledford/ Jeffrey Miller | 332,500 |
| July 28 | BC Three and up Open Pace | Meadowlands | Goliath Bayama | Sylvain Filion/ Yves Filion | 500,000 |
| July 28 | Hambletonian | Meadowlands | Scarlet Knight | Stefan Melander/ Stefan Melander | 1,200,000 |
| Aug 2 | P. Haughton Memorial | Meadowlands | Civil Action | Michel Lachance/ Thomas Merriman | 460,000 |
| Aug 3 | Sweetheart Pace | Meadowlands | Sing Fat Lady | Michel Lachance/ Lora Sodano | 500,000 |
| Aug 3 | Woodrow Wilson | Meadowlands | Allamerican Ingot | John Campbell/ Robert McIntosh | 703,000 |
| Aug 4 | Hambletonian Oaks | Meadowlands | Syrinx Hanover | John Campbell/ Vincent Fusco Jr. | 500,000 |
| Sept 20 | Little Brown Jug | Delaware, OH | Bettor's Delight | Michel Lachance/ Scott McEneny | 646,050 |

## Major Races

### The Hambletonian

Raced at The Meadowlands, East Rutherford, NJ, on August 4, 2001.

| Horse | Driver | PP | ¼ | ½ | ¾ | Stretch–Margin | Finish–Margin |
|---|---|---|---|---|---|---|---|
| Scarlet Knight | Melander | 4 | 3 | 3 | 3° | 2–Head | 1–1¾ |
| Pegasus Spur | O'Donnell | 6 | 4 | 4 | 4° | 3–2 | 2–1¾ |
| Banker Hall | Ritchie | 5 | 1 | 1 | 1 | 1–Head | 3–3¾ |
| Lavecster | Lachance | 7 | 6 | 6 | 6 | 5–4¾ | 4–4¾ |
| Cigar Bar | Campbell | 9 | 5 | 5° | 5 | 6–5 | 5–4¾ |
| Victory Sam | Takter | 8 | 8 | 8 | 7° | 7–6½ | 6–5 |
| Choco Chip Hanover | Lindstedt | 1 | 2 | 2 | 2 | 4–3¼ | 7–5¼ |
| Yankee Mustang | Johnson | 10 | 7° | 7x°° | 8 | 8–14½ | 8–16¾ |
| Laredo Kosmos | Paver Jr. | 3 | 9 | 9 | 9 | 9–dis | 9–37½ |
| Amer I Can | Ackerman | 2 | 10 | 10 | 10 | 10–dis | 10–68 |

Times: 0:27.2, 0:54.4, 1:23.3, 1:53.4; Fast.

### The Little Brown Jug

Raced at the Delaware County Fairgrounds, in Delaware, OH, on September 20, 2001.

| Horse | Driver | PP | ¼ | ½ | ¾ | Stretch–Margin | Finish–Margin |
|---|---|---|---|---|---|---|---|
| Bettor's Delight | Lachance | 1 | 2 | 1 | 1 | 1–¼ | 1–1¼ |
| Real Desire | Campbell | 5 | 5 | 4° | 2° | 2–¼ | 2–1¼ |
| Four Starzzz Shark | Miller | 4 | 1 | 2 | 3 | 3–2¼ | 3–2½ |
| Running Start | Pierce | 2 | 6 | 6° | 4° | 4–3¼ | 4–6¼ |
| Exquisite Art | Brennan | 3 | 3 | 3 | 5 | 5–4¾ | 5–7 |
| Quality of Life | Palone | 7 | 9 | 9 | 7° | 7–5½ | 6–7½ |
| Ameripan Gigolo | Bouchard | 8 | 8 | 8° | 6° | 6–5¼ | 7–7½ |
| Place To Be | Filion | 9 | 4 | 5 | 8 | 8–9½ | 8–13 |
| McGwire | Case Jr. | 6 | 7 | 7 | 9 | 9–11½ | 9–16 |

Time: 0:27.0, 0:55.3, 1:23.3, 1:51.4; Fast.

# 2000 Statistical Leaders

## 2000 Leading Moneywinners by Age, Sex and Gait

| Division | Horse | Starts | 1st | 2nd | 3rd | Earnings ($) |
|---|---|---|---|---|---|---|
| 2-Year-Old Pacing Colts | Bettor's Delight | 10 | 6 | 1 | 1 | 804,661 |
| 2-Year-Old Pacing Fillies | Lady MacBeach | 12 | 6 | 4 | 0 | 659,707 |
| 3-Year-Old Pacing Colts | Gallo Blue Chip | 29 | 19 | 5 | 1 | 2,428,816 |
| 3-Year-Old Pacing Fillies | Art's Virtue | 7 | 6 | 1 | 0 | 606,556 |
| Aged Pacing Horses | Western Ideal | 14 | 10 | 3 | 0 | 1,220,000 |
| Aged Pacing Mares | French Panicure | 21 | 8 | 3 | 0 | 484,930 |
| 2-Year-Old Trotting Colts | Banker Hall | 9 | 6 | 0 | 0 | 607,412 |
| 2-Year-Old Trotting Fillies | Spellbound Hanover | 15 | 11 | 3 | 1 | 748,346 |
| 3-Year-Old Trotting Colts | Yankee Paco | 16 | 10 | 2 | 0 | 1,361,421 |
| 3-Year-Old Trotting Fillies | Casual Breeze | 19 | 12 | 3 | 3 | 752,567 |
| Aged Trotting Horses | Magician | 17 | 11 | 2 | 2 | 1,200,190 |
| Aged Trotting Mares | Moni Maker* | 14 | 7 | 4 | 1 | 1,173,273 |

* Statistics include foreign start information.

## Drivers

| Driver | Earnings ($) | Driver | Earnings ($) |
|---|---|---|---|
| John Campbell | 11,160,482 | Ron Pierce | 6,992,328 |
| Luc Ouelette | 9,566,305 | Daniel Dube | 6,921,164 |
| Michel Lachance | 9,070,680 | Eric Ledford | 6,523,727 |
| Chris Christoforou | 8,986,409 | Randy Waples | 6,380,157 |
| David Miller | 7,594,003 | Andy Miller | 5,623,134 |

## Back in the Saddle

A doughty bay named Millennium Wind had just won the 2001 Blue Grass Stakes, at Keeneland Race Corse, enhancing his stature as a serious contender in the Kentucky Derby, but what ensued seemed less a celebration of his triumph than a tribute to the old, familiar rider on his back.

Of all the jockeys in the Keeneland colony—in fact, of all the riders in the nation—none could have evoked a richer sense of history than 54-year-old Laffit Pincay Jr. did as he steered the Wind toward the winner's circle. He smiled almost shyly while acknowledging the cheers that followed his 5¼-length victory. Only three years earlier, unable to get decent mounts, an angry Pincay considered moving to Northern California to finish his career. Instead, the Hall of Fame jock stayed in Southern California. Around that time, after an eternity of starving himself in his battle with the bulge, he took up a diet structured around fruit and stabilized his riding weight at 117 pounds. "All he had been eating was peanuts," says David Hofmans,

Millennium Wind's trainer. "Now he can eat one meal a day. It freed him, changed his personality. It was amazing."

Since then Pincay has been riding like a young man, getting live mounts and using his celebrated strength to muscle horses to the wire. On Dec. 10, 1999, he won the 8,834th race of his then 35-year career, finally eclipsing the career record for victories, set between 1949 and '90 by Bill Shoemaker.

In February 2001, Hofmans says, he had a startling dream "that Laffit rode [Millennium Wind] and won the Triple Crown." At the time, the colt's regular rider was Chris McCarron. So, when McCarron begged off the Blue Grass to ride another horse in California, Hofmans grabbed Pincay. The jock last won the Blue Grass in 1974, and he had figured he would never duplicate his only Kentucky Derby victory, aboard Swale in 1984.

"I thought for a long while that I'd never get a chance to ride a horse like Swale again," said Pincay. "It's a dream come true."

# FOR THE RECORD · Year by Year

## THOROUGHBRED RACING

### Kentucky Derby

Run at Churchill Downs, Louisville, KY, on the first Saturday in May.

| Year | Winner (Margin) | Jockey | Second | Third | Time |
|---|---|---|---|---|---|
| 1875 | Aristides (1) | Oliver Lewis | Volcano | Verdigris | 2:37¾ |
| 1876 | Vagrant (2) | Bobby Swim | Creedmoor | Harry Hill | 2:38¼ |
| 1877 | Baden-Baden (2) | William Walker | Leonard | King William | 2:38 |
| 1878 | Day Star (2) | Jimmie Carter | Himyar | Leveler | 2:37¼ |
| 1879 | Lord Murphy (1) | Charlie Shauer | Falsetto | Strathmore | 2:37 |
| 1880 | Fonso (1) | George Lewis | Kimball | Bancroft | 2:37½ |
| 1881 | Hindoo (4) | Jimmy McLaughin | Lelex | Alfambra | 2:40 |
| 1882 | Apollo (½) | Babe Hurd | Runnymede | Bengal | 2:40¼ |
| 1883 | Leonatus (3) | Billy Donohue | Drake Carter | Lord Raglan | 2:43 |
| 1884 | Buchanan (2) | Isaac Murphy | Loftin | Audrain | 2:40¼ |
| 1885 | Joe Cotton (Neck) | Erskine Henderson | Bersan | Ten Booker | 2:37¼ |
| 1886 | Ben Ali (½) | Paul Duffy | Blue Wing | Free Knight | 2:36½ |
| 1887 | Montrose (2) | Isaac Lewis | Jim Gore | Jacobin | 2:39¼ |
| 1888 | MacBeth II (1) | George Covington | Gallifet | White | 2:38¼ |
| 1889 | Spokane (Nose) | Thomas Kiley | Proctor Knott | Once Again | 2:34½ |
| 1890 | Riley (2) | Isaac Murphy | Bill Letcher | Robespierre | 2:45 |
| 1891 | Kingman (1) | Isaac Murphy | Balgowan | High Tariff | 2:52¼ |
| 1892 | Azra (Nose) | Alonzo Clayton | Huron | Phil Dwyer | 2:41½ |
| 1893 | Lookout (5) | Eddie Kunze | Plutus | Boundless | 2:39¼ |
| 1894 | Chant (2) | Frank Goodale | Pearl Song | Sigurd | 2:41 |
| 1895 | Halma (3) | Soup Perkins | Basso | Laureate | 2:37½ |
| 1896 | Ben Brush (Nose) | Willie Simms | Ben Eder | Semper Ego | 2:07¾ |
| 1897 | Typhoon II (Head) | Buttons Garner | Ornament | Dr. Catlett | 2:12½ |
| 1898 | Plaudit (Neck) | Willie Simms | Lieber Karl | Isabey | 2:09 |
| 1899 | Manuel (2) | Fred Taral | Corsini | Mazo | 2:12 |
| 1900 | Lieut. Gibson (4) | Jimmy Boland | Florizar | Thrive | 2:06¼ |
| 1901 | His Eminence (2) | Jimmy Winkfield | Sannazarro | Driscoll | 2:07¾ |
| 1902 | Alan-a-Dale (Nose) | Jimmy Winkfield | Inventor | The Rival | 2:08¾ |
| 1903 | Judge Himes (¾) | Hal Booker | Early | Bourbon | 2:09 |
| 1904 | Elwood (½) | Frankie Prior | Ed Tierney | Brancas | 2:08½ |
| 1905 | Agile (3) | Jack Martin | Ram's Horn | Layson | 2:10¾ |
| 1906 | Sir Huon (2) | Roscoe Troxler | Lady Navarre | James Reddick | 2:08⅕ |
| 1907 | Pink Star (2) | Andy Minder | Zal | Ovelando | 2:12⅗ |
| 1908 | Stone Street (1) | Arthur Pickens | Sir Cleges | Dunvegan | 2:15⅕ |
| 1909 | Wintergreen (4) | Vincent Powers | Miami | Dr. Barkley | 2:08⅕ |
| 1910 | Donau (½) | Fred Herbert | Joe Morris | Fighting Bob | 2:06⅖ |
| 1911 | Meridian (¾) | George Archibald | Governor Gray | Colston | 2:05 |
| 1912 | Worth (Neck) | Carroll H. Schilling | Duval | Flamma | 2:09⅖ |
| 1913 | Donerail (½) | Roscoe Goose | Ten Point | Gowell | 2:04⅘ |
| 1914 | Old Rosebud (8) | John McCabe | Hodge | Bronzewing | 2:03⅖ |
| 1915 | Regret (2) | Joe Notter | Pebbles | Sharpshooter | 2:05⅖ |
| 1916 | George Smith (Neck) | Johnny Loftus | Star Hawk | Franklin | 2:04 |
| 1917 | Omar Khayyam (2) | Charles Borel | Ticket | Midway | 2:04⅗ |
| 1918 | Exterminator (1) | William Knapp | Escoba | Viva America | 2:10⅘ |
| 1919 | Sir Barton (5) | Johnny Loftus | Billy Kelly | Under Fire | 2:09⅘ |
| 1920 | Paul Jones (Head) | Ted Rice | Upset | On Watch | 2:09 |
| 1921 | Behave Yourself (Head) | Charles Thompson | Black Servant | Prudery | 2:04⅕ |
| 1922 | Morvich (½) | Albert Johnson | Bet Mosie | John Finn | 2:04⅗ |
| 1923 | Zev (1½) | Earl Sande | Martingale | Vigil | 2:05⅖ |
| 1924 | Black Gold (½) | John Mooney | Chilhowee | Beau Butler | 2:05⅕ |
| 1925 | Flying Ebony (1½) | Earl Sande | Captain Hal | Son of John | 2:07⅗ |
| 1926 | Bubbling Over (5) | Albert Johnson | Bagenbaggage | Rock Man | 2:03⅗ |
| 1927 | Whiskery (Head) | Linus McAtee | Osmond | Jock | 2:06 |
| 1928 | Reigh Count (3) | Chick Lang | Misstep | Toro | 2:10⅖ |
| 1929 | Clyde Van Dusen (2) | Linus McAtee | Naishapur | Panchio | 2:10⅘ |
| 1930 | Gallant Fox (2) | Earl Sande | Gallant Knight | Ned O. | 2:07⅗ |
| 1931 | Twenty Grand (4) | Charles Kurtsinger | Sweep All | Mate | 2:01⅘ |
| 1932 | Burgoo King (5) | Eugene James | Economic | Stepenfetchit | 2:05⅕ |
| 1933 | Brokers Tip (Nose) | Don Meade | Head Play | Charley O. | 2:06⅘ |
| 1934 | Cavalcade (2½) | Mack Garner | Discovery | Agrarian | 2:04 |
| 1935 | Omaha (1½) | Willie Saunders | Roman Soldier | Whiskolo | 2:05 |
| 1936 | Bold Venture (Head) | Ira Hanford | Brevity | Indian Broom | 2:03⅗ |

## Kentucky Derby (Cont.)

| Year | Winner (Margin) | Jockey | Second | Third | Time |
|---|---|---|---|---|---|
| 1937 | War Admiral (1¾) | Charles Kurtsinger | Pompoon | Reaping Reward | 2:03⅕ |
| 1938 | Lawrin (1) | Eddie Arcaro | Dauber | Can't Wait | 2:04⅘ |
| 1939 | Johnstown (8) | James Stout | Challedon | Heather Broom | 2:03⅗ |
| 1940 | Gallahadion (1½) | Carroll Bierman | Bimelech | Dit | 2:05 |
| 1941 | Whirlaway (8) | Eddie Arcaro | Staretor | Market Wise | 2:01⅖ |
| 1942 | Shut Out (2½) | Wayne Wright | Alsab | Valdina Orphan | 2:04⅖ |
| 1943 | Count Fleet (3) | John Longden | Blue Swords | Slide Rule | 2:04 |
| 1944 | Pensive (4½) | Conn McCreary | Broadcloth | Stir Up | 2:04⅕ |
| 1945 | Hoop Jr. (6) | Eddie Arcaro | Pot o' Luck | Darby Dieppe | 2:07 |
| 1946 | Assault (8) | Warren Mehrtens | Spy Song | Hampden | 2:06⅗ |
| 1947 | Jet Pilot (Head) | Eric Guerin | Phalanx | Faultless | 2:06⅘ |
| 1948 | Citation (3½) | Eddie Arcaro | Coaltown | My Request | 2:05⅖ |
| 1949 | Ponder (3) | Steve Brooks | Capot | Palestinian | 2:04⅕ |
| 1950 | Middleground (1¼) | William Boland | Hill Prince | Mr. Trouble | 2:01⅗ |
| 1951 | Count Turf (4) | Conn McCreary | Royal Mustang | Ruhe | 2:02⅗ |
| 1952 | Hill Gail (2) | Eddie Arcaro | Sub Fleet | Blue Man | 2:01⅗ |
| 1953 | Dark Star (Head) | Hank Moreno | Native Dancer | Invigorator | 2:02 |
| 1954 | Determine (1½) | Ray York | Hasty Road | Hasseyampa | 2:03 |
| 1955 | Swaps (1½) | Bill Shoemaker | Nashua | Summer Tan | 2:01⅘ |
| 1956 | Needles (¾) | Dave Erb | Fabius | Come On Red | 2:03⅖ |
| 1957 | Iron Liege (Nose) | Bill Hartack | Gallant Man | Round Table | 2:02⅕ |
| 1958 | Tim Tam (½) | Ismael Valenzuela | Lincoln Road | Noureddin | 2:05 |
| 1959 | Tomy Lee (Nose) | Bill Shoemaker | Sword Dancer | First Landing | 2:02⅕ |
| 1960 | Venetian Way (3½) | Bill Hartack | Bally Ache | Victoria Park | 2:02⅖ |
| 1961 | Carry Back (¾) | John Sellers | Crozier | Bass Clef | 2:04 |
| 1962 | Decidedly (2¼) | Bill Hartack | Roman Line | Ridan | 2:00⅖ |
| 1963 | Chateaugay (1¼) | Braulio Baeza | Never Bend | Candy Spots | 2:01⅘ |
| 1964 | Northern Dancer (Neck) | Bill Hartack | Hill Rise | The Scoundrel | 2:00 |
| 1965 | Lucky Debonair (Neck) | Bill Shoemaker | Dapper Dan | Tom Rolfe | 2:01⅕ |
| 1966 | Kauai King (½) | Don Brumfield | Advocator | Blue Skyer | 2:02 |
| 1967 | Proud Clarion (1) | Bobby Ussery | Barbs Delight | Damascus | 2:00⅗ |
| 1968 | Forward Pass (Disq.) | Ismael Valenzuela | Francie's Hat | T.V. Commercial | 2:02⅕ |
| 1969 | Majestic Prince (Neck) | Bill Hartack | Arts and Letters | Dike | 2:01⅘ |
| 1970 | Dust Commander (5) | Mike Manganello | My Dad George | High Echelon | 2:03⅖ |
| 1971 | Canonero II (3¾) | Gustavo Avila | Jim French | Bold Reason | 2:03⅕ |
| 1972 | Riva Ridge (3¼) | Ron Turcotte | No Le Hace | Hold Your Peace | 2:01⅘ |
| 1973 | Secretariat (2½) | Ron Turcotte | Sham | Our Native | 1:59⅖ |
| 1974 | Cannonade (2¼) | Angel Cordero Jr. | Hudson County | Agitate | 2:04 |
| 1975 | Foolish Pleasure (1¾) | Jacinto Vasquez | Avatar | Diabolo | 2:02 |
| 1976 | Bold Forbes (1) | Angel Cordero Jr. | Honest Pleasure | Elocutionist | 2:01⅗ |
| 1977 | Seattle Slew (1¾) | Jean Cruguet | Run Dusty Run | Sanhedrin | 2:02⅕ |
| 1978 | Affirmed (1¼) | Steve Cauthen | Alydar | Believe It | 2:01⅕ |
| 1979 | Spectacular Bid (2¾) | Ronald J. Franklin | General Assembly | Golden Act | 2:02⅖ |
| 1980 | Genuine Risk (1) | Jacinto Vasquez | Rumbo | Jaklin Klugman | 2:02 |
| 1981 | Pleasant Colony (¾) | Jorge Velasquez | Woodchopper | Partez | 2:02 |
| 1982 | Gato Del Sol (2½) | Eddie Delahoussaye | Laser Light | Reinvested | 2:02⅕ |
| 1983 | Sunny's Halo (2) | Eddie Delahoussaye | Desert Wine | Caveat | 2:02⅕ |
| 1984 | Swale (3¼) | Laffit Pincay Jr. | Coax Me Chad | At the Threshold | 2:02⅖ |
| 1985 | Spend A Buck (5) | Angel Cordero Jr. | Stephan's Odyssey | Chief's Crown | 2:00⅕ |
| 1986 | Ferdinand (2¼) | Bill Shoemaker | Bold Arrangement | Broad Brush | 2:02⅘ |
| 1987 | Alysheba (¾) | Chris McCarron | Bet Twice | Avies Copy | 2:03⅖ |
| 1988 | Winning Colors (Neck) | Gary Stevens | Forty Niner | Risen Star | 2:02⅕ |
| 1989 | Sunday Silence (2½) | Pat Valenzuela | Easy Goer | Awe Inspiring | 2:05 |
| 1990 | Unbridled (3½) | Craig Perret | Summer Squall | Pleasant Tap | 2:02 |
| 1991 | Strike the Gold (1¾) | Chris Antley | Best Pal | Mane Minister | 2:03 |
| 1992 | Lil E. Tee (1) | Pat Day | Casual Lies | Dance Floor | 2:03 |
| 1993 | Sea Hero (2½) | Jerry Bailey | Prairie Bayou | Wild Gale | 2:02⅖ |
| 1994 | Go for Gin (2½) | Chris McCarron | Strodes Creek | Blumin Affair | 2:03⅗ |
| 1995 | Thunder Gulch (2¼) | Gary Stevens | Tejano Run | Timber Country | 2:01⅕ |
| 1996 | Grindstone (Nose) | Jerry Bailey | Cavonnier | Prince of Thieves | 2:01 |
| 1997 | Silver Charm (Head) | Gary Stevens | Captain Bodgit | Free House | 2:02⅖ |
| 1998 | Real Quiet (½) | Kent Desormeaux | Victory Gallop | Indian Charlie | 2:02⅒ |
| 1999 | Charismatic (Neck) | Chris Antley | Menifee | Cat Thief | 2:03⅕ |
| 2000 | Fusaichi Pegasus (1½) | Kent Desormeaux | Aptitude | Impeachment | 2:01.12 |
| 2001 | Monarchos (4¾) | Jorge Chavez | Invisible Ink | Congaree | 1:59.97 |

Note: Distance: 1½ miles (1875–95), 1¼ miles (1896–present).

# Preakness

Run at Pimlico Race Course, Baltimore, Md., two weeks after the Kentucky Derby.

| Year | Winner (Margin) | Jockey | Second | Third | Time |
|---|---|---|---|---|---|
| 1873 | Survivor (10) | G. Barbee | John Boulger | Artist | 2:43 |
| 1874 | Culpepper (¾) | W. Donohue | King Amadeus | Scratch | 2:56½ |
| 1875 | Tom Ochiltree (2) | L. Hughes | Viator | Bay Final | 2:43½ |
| 1876 | Shirley (4) | G. Barbee | Rappahannock | Algerine | 2:44¾ |
| 1877 | Cloverbrook (4) | C. Holloway | Bombast | Lucifer | 2:45½ |
| 1878 | Duke of Magenta (6) | C. Holloway | Bayard | Albert | 2:41¾ |
| 1879 | Harold (3) | L. Hughes | Jericho | Rochester | 2:40½ |
| 1880 | Grenada (¾) | L. Hughes | Oden | Emily F. | 2:40½ |
| 1881 | Saunterer (½) | T. Costello | Compensation | Baltic | 2:40½ |
| 1882 | Vanguard (Neck) | T. Costello | Heck | Col Watson | 2:44⅕ |
| 1883* | Jacobus (4) | G. Barbee | Parnell | | 2:42½ |
| 1884* | Knight of Ellerslie (2) | S. Fisher | Welcher | | 2:39½ |
| 1885 | Tecumseh (2) | Jim McLaughlin | Wickham | John C. | 2:49 |
| 1886 | The Bard (3) | S. Fisher | Eurus | Elkwood | 2:45 |
| 1887 | Dunboyne (1) | W. Donohue | Mahoney | Raymond | 2:39½ |
| 1888 | Refund (3) | F. Littlefield | Judge Murray | Glendale | 2:49 |
| 1889* | Buddhist (8) | W. Anderson | Japhet | * | 2:17½ |
| 1890* | Montague (3) | W. Martin | Philosophy | Barrister | 2:36¾ |
| 1894 | Assignee (3) | Fred Taral | Potentate | Ed Kearney | 1:49¼ |
| 1895 | Belmar (1) | Fred Taral | April Fool | Sue Kittie | 1:50½ |
| 1896 | Margrave (1) | H. Griffin | Hamilton II | Intermission | 1:51 |
| 1897 | Paul Kauvar (1½) | C. Thorpe | Elkins | On Deck | 1:51¼ |
| 1898 | Sly Fox (2) | C. W. Simms | The Huguenot | Nuto | 1:49⅗ |
| 1899 | Half Time (1) | R. Clawson | Filigrane | Lackland | 1:47 |
| 1900 | Hindus (Head) | H. Spencer | Sarmation | Ten Candles | 1:48⅖ |
| 1901 | The Parader (2) | F. Landry | Sadie S. | Dr. Barlow | 1:47⅕ |
| 1902 | Old England (Nose) | L. Jackson | Major Daingerfield | Namtor | 1:45⅘ |
| 1903 | Flocarline (½) | W. Gannon | Mackey Dwyer | Rightful | 1:44⅘ |
| 1904 | Bryn Mawr (1) | E. Hildebrand | Wotan | Dolly Spanker | 1:44⅕ |
| 1905 | Cairngorm (Head) | W. Davis | Kiamesha | Coy Maid | 1:45⅘ |
| 1906 | Whimsical (4) | Walter Miller | Content | Larabie | 1:45 |
| 1907 | Don Enrique (1) | G. Mountain | Ethon | Zambesi | 1:45⅖ |
| 1908 | Royal Tourist (4) | E. Dugan | Live Wire | Robert Cooper | 1:46⅖ |
| 1909 | Effendi (1) | Willie Doyle | Fashion Plate | Hilltop | 1:39⅘ |
| 1910 | Layminster (½) | R. Estep | Dalhousie | Sager | 1:40⅗ |
| 1911 | Watervale (1) | E. Dugan | Zeus | The Nigger | 1:51 |
| 1912 | Colonel Holloway (5) | C. Turner | Bwana Tumbo | Tipsand | 1:56⅗ |
| 1913 | Buskin (Neck) | J. Butwell | Kleburne | Barnegat | 1:53⅖ |
| 1914 | Holiday (¾) | A. Schuttinger | Brave Cunarder | Defendum | 1:53⅘ |
| 1915 | Rhine Maiden (1½) | Douglas Hoffman | Half Rock | Runes | 1:58 |
| 1916 | Damrosch (1½) | Linus McAtee | Greenwood | Achievement | 1:54⅘ |
| 1917 | Kalitan (2) | E. Haynes | Al M. Dick | Kentucky Boy | 1:54⅖ |
| 1918* | War Cloud (¾) | Johnny Loftus | Sunny Slope | Lanius | 1:53⅗ |
| 1918* | Jack Hare, Jr (2) | C. Peak | The Porter | Kate Bright | 1:53⅖ |
| 1919 | Sir Barton (4) | Johnny Loftus | Eternal | Sweep On | 1:53 |
| 1920 | Man o' War (1½) | Clarence Kummer | Upset | Wildair | 1:51⅗ |
| 1921 | Broomspun (¾) | F. Coltiletti | Polly Ann | Jeg | 1:54⅕ |
| 1922 | Pillory (Head) | L. Morris | Hea | June Grass | 1:51⅗ |
| 1923 | Vigil (1¼) | B. Marinelli | General Thatcher | Rialto | 1:53⅗ |
| 1924 | Nellie Morse (1½) | J. Merimee | Transmute | Mad Play | 1:57⅕ |
| 1925 | Coventry (4) | Clarence Kummer | Backbone | Almadel | 1:59 |
| 1926 | Display (Head) | J. Maiben | Blondin | Mars | 1:59⅘ |
| 1927 | Bostonian (½) | A. Abel | Sir Harry | Whiskery | 2:01⅗ |
| 1928 | Victorian (Nose) | Sonny Workman | Toro | Solace | 2:00⅕ |
| 1929 | Dr. Freeland (1) | Louis Schaefer | Minotaur | African | 2:01⅗ |
| 1930 | Gallant Fox (¾) | Earl Sande | Crack Brigade | Snowflake | 2:00⅗ |
| 1931 | Mate (1½) | G. Ellis | Twenty Grand | Ladder | 1:59 |
| 1932 | Burgoo King (Head) | E. James | Tick On | Boatswain | 1:59⅘ |
| 1933 | Head Play (4) | Charles Kurtsinger | Ladysman | Utopian | 2:02 |
| 1934 | High Quest (Nose) | R. Jones | Cavalcade | Discovery | 1:58⅕ |
| 1935 | Omaha (6) | Willie Saunders | Firethorn | Psychic Bid | 1:58⅖ |
| 1936 | Bold Venture (Nose) | George Woolf | Granville | Jean Bart | 1:59 |
| 1937 | War Admiral (Head) | Charles Kurtsinger | Pompoon | Flying Scot | 1:58⅖ |
| 1938 | Dauber (7) | M. Peters | Cravat | Menow | 1:59⅘ |
| 1939 | Challedon (1¼) | George Seabo | Gilded Knight | Volitant | 1:59⅘ |
| 1940 | Bimelech (3) | F. A. Smith | Mioland | Gallahadion | 1:58⅗ |

## Preakness (Cont.)

| Year | Winner (Margin) | Jockey | Second | Third | Time |
|---|---|---|---|---|---|
| 1941 | Whirlaway (5½) | Eddie Arcaro | King Cole | Our Boots | 1:58⅘ |
| 1942 | Alsab (1) | B. James | Requested Sun Again | (dead heat for second) | 1:57 |
| 1943 | Count Fleet (8) | Johnny Longden | Blue Swords | Vincentive | 1:57⅖ |
| 1944 | Pensive (¾) | Conn McCreary | Platter | Stir Up | 1:59⅕ |
| 1945 | Polynesian (2½) | W. D. Wright | Hoop Jr. | Darby Dieppe | 1:58⅘ |
| 1946 | Assault (Neck) | Warren Mehrtens | Lord Boswell | Hampden | 2:01⅖ |
| 1947 | Faultless (1¼) | Doug Dodson | On Trust | Phalanx | 1:59 |
| 1948 | Citation (5½) | Eddie Arcaro | Vulcan's Forge | Boyard | 2:02⅖ |
| 1949 | Capot (Head) | Ted Atkinson | Palestinian | Noble Impulse | 1:56 |
| 1950 | Hill Prince (5) | Eddie Arcaro | Middleground | Dooley | 1:59⅕ |
| 1951 | Bold (7) | Eddie Arcaro | Counterpoint | Alerted | 1:56⅖ |
| 1952 | Blue Man (3½) | Conn McCreary | Jampol | One Count | 1:57⅖ |
| 1953 | Native Dancer (Neck) | Eric Guerin | Jamie K. | Royal Bay Gem | 1:57⅘ |
| 1954 | Hasty Road (Neck) | Johnny Adams | Correlation | Hasseyampa | 1:57⅖ |
| 1955 | Nashua (1) | Eddie Arcaro | Saratoga | Traffic Judge | 1:54⅗ |
| 1956 | Fabius (¾) | Bill Hartack | Needles | No Regrets | 1:58⅖ |
| 1957 | Bold Ruler (2) | Eddie Arcaro | Iron Liege | Inside Tract | 1:56⅕ |
| 1958 | Tim Tam (1½) | I. Valenzuela | Lincoln Road | Gone Fishin' | 1:57⅕ |
| 1959 | Royal Orbit (4) | William Harmatz | Sword Dancer | Dunce | 1:57 |
| 1960 | Bally Ache (4) | Bobby Ussery | Victoria Park | Celtic Ash | 1:57⅗ |
| 1961 | Carry Back (¾) | Johnny Sellers | Globemaster | Crozier | 1:57⅗ |
| 1962 | Greek Money (Nose) | John Rotz | Ridan | Roman Line | 1:56⅕ |
| 1963 | Candy Spots (3½) | Bill Shoemaker | Chateaugay | Never Bend | 1:56⅕ |
| 1964 | Northern Dancer (2¼) | Bill Hartack | The Scoundrel | Hill Rise | 1:56⅘ |
| 1965 | Tom Rolfe (Neck) | Ron Turcotte | Dapper Dan | Hail to All | 1:56⅕ |
| 1966 | Kauai King (1¾) | Don Brumfield | Stupendous | Amberoid | 1:55⅖ |
| 1967 | Damascus (2¼) | Bill Shoemaker | In Reality | Proud Clarion | 1:55⅕ |
| 1968 | Forward Pass (6) | I. Valenzuela | Out of the Way | Nodouble | 1:56⅘ |
| 1969 | Majestic Prince (Head) | Bill Hartack | Arts and Letters | Jay Ray | 1:55⅗ |
| 1970 | Personality (Neck) | Eddie Belmonte | My Dad George | Silent Screen | 1:56⅕ |
| 1971 | Canonero II (1½) | Gustavo Avila | Eastern Fleet | Jim French | 1:54 |
| 1972 | Bee Bee Bee (1¼) | Eldon Nelson | No Le Hace | Key to the Mint | 1:55⅗ |
| 1973 | Secretariat (2½) | Ron Turcotte | Sham | Our Native | 1:54⅖ |
| 1974 | Little Current (7) | Miguel Rivera | Neapolitan Way | Cannonade | 1:54⅗ |
| 1975 | Master Derby (1) | Darrel McHargue | Foolish Pleasure | Diabolo | 1:56⅖ |
| 1976 | Elocutionist (3) | John Lively | Play the Red | Bold Forbes | 1:55 |
| 1977 | Seattle Slew (1½) | Jean Cruguet | Iron Constitution | Run Dusty Run | 1:54⅖ |
| 1978 | Affirmed (Neck) | Steve Cauthen | Alydar | Believe It | 1:54⅖ |
| 1979 | Spectacular Bid (5½) | Ron Franklin | Golden Act | Screen King | 1:54⅕ |
| 1980 | Codex (4¾) | Angel Cordero Jr. | Genuine Risk | Colonel Moran | 1:54⅕ |
| 1981 | Pleasant Colony (1) | Jorge Velasquez | Bold Ego | Paristo | 1:54⅗ |
| 1982 | Aloma's Ruler (½) | Jack Kaenel | Linkage | Cut Away | 1:55⅖ |
| 1983 | Deputed Testamony (2¾) | Donald Miller Jr. | Desert Wine | High Honors | 1:55⅖ |
| 1984 | Gate Dancer (1½) | Angel Cordero Jr. | Play On | Fight Over | 1:53⅗ |
| 1985 | Tank's Prospect (Head) | Pat Day | Chief's Crown | Eternal Prince | 1:53⅖ |
| 1986 | Snow Chief (4) | Alex Solis | Ferdinand | Broad Brush | 1:54⅘ |
| 1987 | Alysheba (½) | Chris McCarron | Bet Twice | Cryptoclearance | 1:55⅘ |
| 1988 | Risen Star (1¼) | E. Delahoussaye | Brian's Time | Winning Colors | 1:56⅕ |
| 1989 | Sunday Silence (Nose) | Pat Valenzuela | Easy Goer | Rock Point | 1:53⅘ |
| 1990 | Summer Squall (2¼) | Pat Day | Unbridled | Mister Frisky | 1:53⅗ |
| 1991 | Hansel (Head) | Jerry Bailey | Corporate Report | Mane Minister | 1:54 |
| 1992 | Pine Bluff (¾) | Chris McCarron | Alydeed | Casual Lies | 1:55⅗ |
| 1993 | Prairie Bayou (½) | Mike Smith | Cherokee Run | El Bakan | 1:56⅗ |
| 1994 | Tabasco Cat (¾) | Pat Day | Go For Gin | Concern | 1:56⅖ |
| 1995 | Timber Country (½) | Pat Day | Oliver's Twist | Thunder Gulch | 1:54⅖ |
| 1996 | Louis Quatorze (3¼) | Pat Day | Skip Away | Editor's Note | 1:53⅖ |
| 1997 | Silver Charm (Head) | Gary Stevens | Free House | Captain Bodgit | 1:54⅖ |
| 1998 | Real Quiet (2¼) | Kent Desormeaux | Victory Gallop | Classic Cat | 1:54⅗ |
| 1999 | Charismatic (1½) | Chris Antley | Menifee | Badge | 1:55⅕ |
| 2000 | Red Bullet (3¾) | Jerry Bailey | Fusaichi Pegasus | Impeachment | 1:56.04 |
| 2001 | Point Given (2¼) | Gary Stevens | A P Valentine | Congaree | 1:55.51 |

*Preakness was a two-horse race in 1883, '84 and '89. It was not run 1891–1893; and in 1918, it was run in two divisions.

Note: Distance: 1½ miles (1873–88), 1¼ miles (1889), 1½ miles (1890), 1 1/16 miles (1894–1900), 1 mile and 70 yards (1901–1907), 1 1/16 miles (1908), 1 mile (1909–10), 1⅛ miles (1911–24), 1 3/16 miles (1925–present).

# Belmont

Run at Belmont Park, Elmont, NY, three weeks after the Preakness Stakes. Held previously at two locations in the Bronx (NY): Jerome Park (1867–1889) and Morris Park (1890–1904).

| Year | Winner (Margin) | Jockey | Second | Third | Time |
|---|---|---|---|---|---|
| 1867 | Ruthless (Head) | J. Gilpatrick | De Courcy | Rivoli | 3:05 |
| 1868 | General Duke (2) | R. Swim | Northumberland | Fannie Ludlow | 3:02 |
| 1869 | Fenian (Unknown) | C. Miller | Glenelg | Invercauld | 3:04¼ |
| 1870 | Kingfisher (½) | E. Brown | Foster | Midday | 2:59½ |
| 1871 | Harry Bassett (3) | W. Miller | Stockwood | By-the-Sea | 2:56 |
| 1872 | Joe Daniels (¾) | James Rowe | Meteor | Shylock | 2:58¼ |
| 1873 | Springbok (4) | James Rowe | Count d'Orsay | Strachino | 3:01¾ |
| 1874 | Saxon (Neck) | G. Barbee | Grinstead | Aaron Pennington | 2:39½ |
| 1875 | Calvin (2) | R. Swim | Aristides | Milner | 2:40¼ |
| 1876 | Algerine (Head) | W. Donahue | Fiddlestick | Barricade | 2:40½ |
| 1877 | Cloverbrook (1) | C. Holloway | Loiterer | Baden-Baden | 2:46 |
| 1878 | Duke of Magenta (2) | L. Hughes | Bramble | Sparta | 2:43½ |
| 1879 | Spendthrift (5) | S. Evans | Monitor | Jericho | 2:42¾ |
| 1880 | Grenada (½) | L. Hughes | Ferncliffe | Turenne | 2:47 |
| 1881 | Saunterer (Neck) | T. Costello | Eole | Baltic | 2:47 |
| 1882 | Forester (5) | James McLaughlin | Babcock | Wyoming | 2:43 |
| 1883 | George Kinney (2) | James McLaughlin | Trombone | Renegade | 2:42½ |
| 1884 | Panique (½) | James McLaughlin | Knight of Ellerslie | Himalaya | 2:42 |
| 1885 | Tyrant (3½) | Paul Duffy | St. Augustine | Tecumseh | 2:43 |
| 1886 | Inspector B (1) | James McLaughlin | The Bard | Linden | 2:41 |
| 1887* | Hanover (28-32) | James McLaughlin | Oneko | | 2:43½ |
| 1888* | Sir Dixon (12) | James McLaughlin | Prince Royal | | 2:40¼ |
| 1889 | Eric (Head) | W. Hayward | Diable | Zephyrus | 2:47 |
| 1890 | Burlington (1) | S. Barnes | Devotee | Padishah | 2:07¾ |
| 1891 | Foxford (Neck) | E. Garrison | Montana | Laurestan | 2:08¾ |
| 1892* | Patron (Unknown) | W. Hayward | Shellbark | | 2:17 |
| 1893 | Comanche (Head) | Willie Simms | Dr. Rice | Rainbow | 1:53¼ |
| 1894 | Henry of Navarre (2-4) | Willie Simms | Prig | Assignee | 1:56½ |
| 1895 | Belmar (Head) | Fred Taral | Counter Tenor | Nanki Pooh | 2:11½ |
| 1896 | Hastings (Neck) | H. Griffin | Handspring | Hamilton II | 2:24½ |
| 1897 | Scottish Chieftain (1) | J. Scherrer | On Deck | Octagon | 2:23¼ |
| 1898 | Bowling Brook (8) | P. Littlefield | Previous | Hamburg | 2:32 |
| 1899 | Jean Bereaud (Head) | R. R. Clawson | Half Time | Glengar | 2:23 |
| 1900 | Ildrim (Head) | N. Turner | Petrucio | Missionary | 2:21½ |
| 1901 | Commando (½) | H. Spencer | The Parader | All Green | 2:21 |
| 1902 | Masterman (2) | John Bullmann | Ranald | King Hanover | 2:22½ |
| 1903 | Africander (2) | John Bullmann | Whorler | Red Knight | 2:23⅕ |
| 1904 | Delhi (3½) | George Odom | Graziallo | Rapid Water | 2:06⅗ |
| 1905 | Tanya (1/2) | E. Hildebrand | Blandy | Hot Shot | 2:08 |
| 1906 | Burgomaster (4) | L. Lyne | The Quail | Accountant | 2:20 |
| 1907 | Peter Pan (1) | G. Mountain | Superman | Frank Gill | Unknown |
| 1908 | Colin (Head) | Joe Notter | Fair Play | King James | Unknown |
| 1909 | Joe Madden (8) | E. Dugan | Wise Mason | Donald MacDonald | 2:21⅗ |
| 1910* | Sweep (6) | J. Butwell | Duke of Ormonde | | 2:22 |
| 1913 | Prince Eugene (½) | Roscoe Troxler | Rock View | Flying Fairy | 2:18 |
| 1914 | Luke McLuke (8) | M. Buxton | Gainer | Charlestonian | 2:20 |
| 1915 | The Finn (4) | G. Byrne | Half Rock | Pebbles | 2:18⅖ |
| 1916 | Friar Rock (3) | E. Haynes | Spur | Churchill | 2:22 |
| 1917 | Hourless (10) | J. Butwell | Skeptic | Wonderful | 2:17⅘ |
| 1918 | Johren (2) | Frank Robinson | War Cloud | Cum Sah | 2:20⅖ |
| 1919 | Sir Barton (5) | Johnny Loftus | Sweep On | Natural Bridge | 2:17⅖ |
| 1920* | Man o' War (20) | Clarence Kummer | Donnacona | | 2:14⅕ |
| 1921 | Grey Lag (3) | Earl Sande | Sporting Blood | Leonardo II | 2:16⅘ |
| 1922 | Pillory (2) | C. H. Miller | Snob II | Hea | 2:18⅘ |
| 1923 | Zev (1½) | Earl Sande | Chickvale | Rialto | 2:19 |
| 1924 | Mad Play (2) | Earl Sande | Mr. Mutt | Modest | 2:18⅘ |
| 1925 | American Flag (8) | Albert Johnson | Dangerous | Swope | 2:16⅘ |
| 1926 | Crusader (1) | Albert Johnson | Espino | Haste | 2:32⅕ |
| 1927 | Chance Shot (1½) | Earl Sande | Bois de Rose | Flambino | 2:32⅖ |
| 1928 | Vito (3) | Clarence Kummer | Genie | Diavolo | 2:33⅕ |
| 1929 | Blue Larkspur (¾) | Mack Garner | African | Jack High | 2:32⅘ |
| 1930 | Gallant Fox (3) | Earl Sande | Whichone | Questionnaire | 2:31⅗ |

## Belmont (Cont.)

| Year | Winner (Margin) | Jockey | Second | Third | Time |
|---|---|---|---|---|---|
| 1931 | Twenty Grand (10) | Charles Kurtsinger | Sun Meadow | Jamestown | 2:29⅗ |
| 1932 | Faireno (1½) | T. Malley | Osculator | Flag Pole | 2:32⅘ |
| 1933 | Hurryoff (1½) | Mack Garner | Nimbus | Union | 2:32⅗ |
| 1934 | Peace Chance (6) | W. D. Wright | High Quest | Good Goods | 2:29⅕ |
| 1935 | Omaha (1½) | Willie Saunders | Firethorn | Rosemont | 2:30⅗ |
| 1936 | Granville (Nose) | James Stout | Mr. Bones | Hollyrood | 2:30 |
| 1937 | War Admiral (3) | Charles Kurtsinger | Sceneshifter | Vamoose | 2:28⅗ |
| 1938 | Pasteurized (Neck) | James Stout | Dauber | Cravat | 2:29⅖ |
| 1939 | Johnstown (5) | James Stout | Belay | Gilded Knight | 2:29⅗ |
| 1940 | Bimelech (¾) | F. A. Smith | Your Chance | Andy K | 2:29⅗ |
| 1941 | Whirlaway (2½) | Eddie Arcaro | Robert Morris | Yankee Chance | 2:31 |
| 1942 | Shut Out (2) | Eddie Arcaro | Alsab | Lochinvar | 2:29⅕ |
| 1943 | Count Fleet (25) | Johnny Longden | Fairy Manhurst | Deseronto | 2:28⅕ |
| 1944 | Bounding Home (½) | G. L. Smith | Pensive | Bull Dandy | 2:32⅕ |
| 1945 | Pavot (5) | Eddie Arcaro | Wildlife | Jeep | 2:30⅕ |
| 1946 | Assault (3) | Warren Mehrtens | Natchez | Cable | 2:30⅘ |
| 1947 | Phalanx (5) | R. Donoso | Tide Rips | Tailspin | 2:29⅖ |
| 1948 | Citation (8) | Eddie Arcaro | Better Self | Escadru | 2:28⅕ |
| 1949 | Capot (½) | Ted Atkinson | Ponder | Palestinian | 2:30⅕ |
| 1950 | Middleground (1) | William Boland | Lights Up | Mr. Trouble | 2:28⅗ |
| 1951 | Counterpoint (4) | D. Gorman | Battlefield | Battle Morn | 2:29 |
| 1952 | One Count (2½) | Eddie Arcaro | Blue Man | Armageddon | 2:30⅕ |
| 1953 | Native Dancer (Neck) | Eric Guerin | Jamie K. | Royal Bay Gem | 2:38⅗ |
| 1954 | High Gun (Neck) | Eric Guerin | Fisherman | Limelight | 2:30⅘ |
| 1955 | Nashua (9) | Eddie Arcaro | Blazing Count | Portersville | 2:29 |
| 1956 | Needles (Neck) | David Erb | Career Boy | Fabius | 2:29⅘ |
| 1957 | Gallant Man (8) | Bill Shoemaker | Inside Tract | Bold Ruler | 2:26⅗ |
| 1958 | Cavan (6) | Pete Anderson | Tim Tam | Flamingo | 2:30⅕ |
| 1959 | Sword Dancer (¾) | Bill Shoemaker | Bagdad | Royal Orbit | 2:28⅖ |
| 1960 | Celtic Ash (5½) | Bill Hartack | Venetian Way | Disperse | 2:29⅗ |
| 1961 | Sherluck (2¼) | Braulio Baeza | Globemaster | Guadalcanal | 2:29⅕ |
| 1962 | Jaipur (Nose) | Bill Shoemaker | Admiral's Voyage | Crimson Satan | 2:28⅘ |
| 1963 | Chateaugay (2½) | Braulio Baeza | Candy Spots | Choker | 2:30⅕ |
| 1964 | Quadrangle (2) | Manuel Ycaza | Roman Brother | Northern Dancer | 2:28⅖ |
| 1965 | Hail to All (Neck) | John Sellers | Tom Rolfe | First Family | 2:28⅖ |
| 1966 | Amberold (2½) | William Boland | Buffle | Advocator | 2:29⅗ |
| 1967 | Damascus (2½) | Bill Shoemaker | Cool Reception | Gentleman James | 2:28⅘ |
| 1968 | Stage Door Johnny (1¼) | Hellodoro Gustines | Forward Pass | Call Me Prince | 2:27⅕ |
| 1969 | Arts and Letters (5½) | Braulio Baeza | Majestic Prince | Dike | 2:28⅘ |
| 1970 | High Echelon (¾) | John L. Rotz | Needles N Pins | Naskra | 2:34 |
| 1971 | Pass Catcher (¾) | Walter Blum | Jim French | Bold Reason | 2:30⅖ |
| 1972 | Riva Ridge (7) | Ron Turcotte | Ruritania | Cloudy Dawn | 2:28 |
| 1973 | Secretariat (31) | Ron Turcotte | Twice a Prince | My Gallant | 2:24 |
| 1974 | Little Current (7) | Miguel A. Rivera | Jolly Johu | Cannonade | 2:29⅕ |
| 1975 | Avatar (Neck) | Bill Shoemaker | Foolish Pleasure | Master Derby | 2:28⅕ |
| 1976 | Bold Forbes (Neck) | Angel Cordero Jr. | McKenzie Bridge | Great Contractor | 2:29 |
| 1977 | Seattle Slew (4) | Jean Cruguet | Run Dusty Run | Sanhedrin | 2:29⅗ |
| 1978 | Affirmed (Head) | Steve Cauthen | Alydar | Darby Creek Road | 2:26⅘ |
| 1979 | Coastal (3¼) | Ruben Hernandez | Golden Act | Spectacular Bid | 2:28⅗ |
| 1980 | Temperence Hill (2) | Eddie Maple | Genuine Risk | Rockhill Native | 2:29⅘ |
| 1981 | Summing (Neck) | George Martens | Highland Blade | Pleasant Colony | 2:29 |
| 1982 | Conquistador Cielo (14½) | Laffit Pincay, Jr. | Gato Del Sol | Illuminate | 2:28⅕ |
| 1983 | Caveat (3½) | Laffit Pincay Jr. | Slew o'Gold | Barberstown | 2:27⅘ |
| 1984 | Swale (4) | Laffit Pincay Jr. | Pine Circle | Morning Bob | 2:27⅕ |
| 1985 | Creme Fraiche (½) | Eddie Maple | Stephan's Odyssey | Chief's Crown | 2:27 |
| 1986 | Danzig Connection (1¼) | Chris McCarron | Johns Treasure | Ferdinand | 2:29⅘ |
| 1987 | Bet Twice (14) | Craig Perret | Cryptoclearance | Gulch | 2:28⅕ |
| 1988 | Risen Star (14¾) | Eddie Delahoussaye | Kingpost | Brian's Time | 2:26⅖ |
| 1989 | Easy Goer (8) | Pat Day | Sunday Silence | Le Voyageur | 2:26 |
| 1990 | Go and Go (8¼) | Michael Kinane | Thirty Six Red | Baron de Vaux | 2:27⅕ |
| 1991 | Hansel (Head) | Jerry Bailey | Strike the Gold | Mane Minister | 2:28 |
| 1992 | A.P. Indy (¾) | Eddie Delahoussaye | My Memoirs | Pine Bluff | 2:26 |

## Belmont (Cont.)

| Year | Winner (Margin) | Jockey | Second | Third | Time |
|---|---|---|---|---|---|
| 1993 | Colonial Affair (2¼) | Julie Krone | Kissin Kris | Wild Gale | 2:29⅘ |
| 1994 | Tabasco Cat (2) | Pat Day | Go For Gin | Strodes Creek | 2:26⅘ |
| 1995 | Thunder Gulch (2) | Gary Stevens | Star Standard | Citadeed | 2:32 |
| 1996 | Editor's Note (1) | Rene Douglas | Skip Away | My Flag | 2:28⅘ |
| 1997 | Touch Gold (¾) | Chris McCarron | Silver Charm | Free House | 2:28⅘ |
| 1998 | Victory Gallop (Nose) | Gary Stevens | Real Quiet | Thomas Jo | 2:28⅘ |
| 1999 | Lemon Drop Kid (Head) | Jose Santos | Vision and Verse | Charismatic | 2:27⅘ |
| 2000 | Commendable (1½) | Pat Day | Aptitude | Unshaded | 2:31.19 |
| 2001 | Point Given (12¼ ) | Gary Stevens | A P Valentine | Monarchos | 2:26.56 |

*Belmont was a two-horse race in 1887, '88, '92, 1910 and '20; and was not held in 1911–1912.
Note: Distance: 1 mile 5 furlongs (1867–89), 1¼ miles (1890–1905), 1⅜ miles (1906–25), 1½ miles (1926–present).

## Triple Crown Winners

| Year | Horse | Jockey | Owner | Trainer |
|---|---|---|---|---|
| 1919 | Sir Barton | John Loftus | J. K. L. Ross | H. G. Bedwell |
| 1930 | Gallant Fox | Earle Sande | Belair Stud | James Fitzsimmons |
| 1935 | Omaha | William Saunders | Belair Stud | James Fitzsimmons |
| 1937 | War Admiral | Charles Kurtsinger | Samuel D. Riddle | George Conway |
| 1941 | Whirlaway | Eddie Arcaro | Calumet Farm | Ben Jones |
| 1943 | Count Fleet | John Longden | Mrs J. D. Hertz | Don Cameron |
| 1946 | Assault | Warren Mehrtens | King Ranch | Max Hirsch |
| 1948 | Citation | Eddie Arcaro | Calumet Farm | Jimmy Jones |
| 1973 | Secretariat | Ron Turcotte | Meadow Stable | Lucien Laurin |
| 1977 | Seattle Slew | Jean Cruguet | Karen L. Taylor | William H. Turner Jr. |
| 1978 | Affirmed | Steve Cauthen | Harbor View Farm | Laz Barrera |

### Revelation Derby

As a child, my little brother John had a speech impediment so serious that he would require therapy. He slurred his s's severely. For years John couldn't have spoken the preceding sentence without spraying his listener like a lawn sprinkler.

So when I was 10, my older brothers and I enjoyed goading John, who was four, into saying our favorite sentence. He would always comply, and the resulting spume of saliva was, we thought, hilarious. It put us in mind of whitewater rapids. The sentence we made him say was "Seattle Slew in '77!"

I have seldom thought of horse racing since that summer, when allusions to the great thoroughbred's Triple Crown bid were omnipresent in pop culture. Until, that is, I went to cover the 2001 Kentucky Derby and discovered, to my everlasting surprise, that the Derby would cover me. It covered me in seersucker and sunblock and goose pimples.

Two days before the race at Churchill Downs a gravely ill six-year-old girl was reluctantly granted one of her wishes, to sit atop a thoroughbred racehorse, which is, by breeding, high-strung and hinky and freighted with danger. So a small crowd held its breath when the child was placed athwart Derby entrant Arctic Boy, a 1,150-pound animal who did something rather unusual with his new cargo: absolutely nothing. The horse stood stock-still. In gratitude the girl slowly placed her palms on his coat, as if preserving her prints in wet concrete, and began silently leaking tears.

The scene was almost unendurably poignant, and to keep gazing on it felt like an invasion of privacy, except for this: The combined beauty of these creatures, a 3-year-old thoroughbred and a six-year-old girl, is powerful enough to turn the Earth.

Everything, of course, is fleeting—youth and beauty and life. It's most evident among great athletes. In the stands at Churchill Downs was Oscar Robertson, the Big O, whose nickname now serves as a physical description. There, too, was Louisville native Paul Hornung, the Olden Boy, who with his white hair and white beard resembles Kenny Rogers. Even Seattle Slew is now 27 (my kid brother, good God, is 28) and, his spine fused, enduring the equine equivalent of assisted living on Three Chimneys Farms near Lexington. But 24 years ago—as Sheik Mohammed al Maktoum said during Derby week—"the winds of heaven blew between his ears."

At 6:07 p.m. on raceday, I understood what that meant. For until you've put on a photographer's bib and watched the Kentucky Derby from on the track, inside the rail, at the finish line, as I was privileged and terrified to do, you have not fully fathomed athletic vitality. I don't know what to tell you, except what winning jockey Jorge Chávez said, after thundering by in a blur on Monarchos in a time second only to Secretariat's track record. Chávez declared in broken English that was just right, "It is closest you can get to the sky."

—Steve Rushin

# Awards

## Horse of the Year

| Year | Horse | Owner | Trainer | Breeder |
|---|---|---|---|---|
| 1936 | Granville | Belair Stud | James Fitzsimmons | Belair Stud |
| 1937 | War Admiral | Samuel D. Riddle | George Conway | Mrs. Samuel D. Riddle |
| 1938 | Seabiscuit | Charles S. Howard | Tom Smith | Wheatley Stable |
| 1939 | Challedon | William L. Brann | Louis J. Schaefer | Branncastle Farm |
| 1940 | Challedon | William L. Brann | Louis J. Schaefer | Branncastle Farm |
| 1941 | Whirlaway | Calumet Farm | Ben Jones | Calumet Farm |
| 1942 | Whirlaway | Calumet Farm | Ben Jones | Calumet Farm |
| 1943 | Count Fleet | Mrs. John D. Hertz | Don Cameron | Mrs. John D. Hertz |
| 1944 | Twilight Tear | Calumet Farm | Ben Jones | Calumet Farm |
| 1945 | Busher | Louis B. Mayer | George Odom | Idle Hour Stock Farm |
| 1946 | Assault | King Ranch | Max Hirsch | King Ranch |
| 1947 | Armed | Calumet Farm | Jimmy Jones | Calumet Farm |
| 1948 | Citation | Calumet Farm | Jimmy Jones | Calumet Farm |
| 1949 | Capot | Greentree Stable | John M. Gaver Sr. | Greentree Stable |
| 1950 | Hill Prince | C.T. Chenery | Casey Hayes | C.T. Chenery |
| 1951 | Counterpoint | C.V. Whitney | Syl Veitch | C.V. Whitney |
| 1952 | One Count | Mrs. W. M. Jeffords | O. White | W M. Jeffords |
| 1953 | Tom Fool | Greentree Stable | John M. Gaver Sr. | D.A. Headley |
| 1954 | Native Dancer | A.G. Vanderbilt | Bill Winfrey | A.G. Vanderbilt |
| 1955 | Nashua | Belair Stud | James Fitzsimmons | Belair Stud |
| 1956 | Swaps | Ellsworth-Galbreath | Mesh Tenney | R. Ellsworth |
| 1957 | Bold Ruler | Wheatley Stable | James Fitzsimmons | Wheatley Stable |
| 1958 | Round Table | Kerr Stables | Willy Molter | Claiborne Farm |
| 1959 | Sword Dancer | Brookmeade Stable | Elliott Burch | Brookmeade Stable |
| 1960 | Kelso | Bohemia Stable | C. Hanford | Mrs. R.C. duPont |
| 1961 | Kelso | Bohemia Stable | C. Hanford | Mrs. R.C. duPont |
| 1962 | Kelso | Bohemia Stable | C. Hanford | Mrs. R.C. duPont |
| 1963 | Kelso | Bohemia Stable | C. Hanford | Mrs. R.C. duPont |
| 1964 | Kelso | Bohemia Stable | C. Hanford | Mrs. R.C. duPont |
| 1965 | Roman Brother | Harbor View Stable | Burley Parke | Ocala Stud |
| 1966 | Buckpasser | Ogden Phipps | Eddie Neloy | Ogden Phipps |
| 1967 | Damascus | Mrs. E. W. Bancroft | Frank Y. Whiteley Jr. | Mrs. E. W. Bancroft |
| 1968 | Dr. Fager | Tartan Stable | John A. Nerud | Tartan Farms |
| 1969 | Arts and Letters | Rokeby Stable | Elliott Burch | Paul Mellon |
| 1970 | Fort Marcy | Rokeby Stable | Elliott Burch | Paul Mellon |
| 1971 | Ack Ack | E.E. Fogelson | Charlie Whittingham | H.F. Guggenheim |
| 1972 | Secretariat | Meadow Stable | Lucien Laurin | Meadow Stud |
| 1973 | Secretariat | Meadow Stable | Lucien Laurin | Meadow Stud |
| 1974 | Forego | Lazy F Ranch | Sherrill W. Ward | Lazy F Ranch |
| 1975 | Forego | Lazy F Ranch | Sherrill W. Ward | Lazy F Ranch |
| 1976 | Forego | Lazy F Ranch | Frank Y. Whiteley Jr. | Lazy F Ranch |
| 1977 | Seattle Slew | Karen L. Taylor | Billy Turner Jr. | B.S. Castleman |
| 1978 | Affirmed | Harbor View Farm | Laz Barrera | Harbor View Farm |
| 1979 | Affirmed | Harbor View Farm | Laz Barrera | Harbor View Farm |
| 1980 | Spectacular Bid | Hawksworth Farm | Bud Delp | Mmes. Gilmore and Jason |
| 1981 | John Henry | Dotsam Stable | Ron McAnally and Lefty Nickerson | Golden Chance Farm |
| 1982 | Conquistador Cielo | H. de Kwiatkowski | Woody Stephens | L.E. Landoli |
| 1983 | All Along | Daniel Wildenstein | P.L. Biancone | Dayton |
| 1984 | John Henry | Dotsam Stable | Ron McAnally | Golden Chance Farm |
| 1985 | Spend a Buck | Hunter Farm | Cam Gambolati | Irish Hill & R.W. Harper |
| 1986 | Lady's Secret | Mr. & Mrs. Eugene Klein | D. Wayne Lukas | R.H. Spreen |
| 1987 | Ferdinand | Mrs. H.B. Keck | Charlie Whittingham | H.B. Keck |
| 1988 | Alysheba | D. & P. Scharbauer | Jack Van Berg | Preston Madden |
| 1989 | Sunday Silence | Gaillard, Hancock, & Whittingham | Charlie Whittingham | Oak Cliff Thoroughbreds |
| 1990 | Criminal Type | Calumet Farm | D. Wayne Lukas | Calumet Farm |
| 1991 | Black Tie Affair | Jeffrey Sullivan | Ernie Poulos | Stephen D. Peskoff |
| 1992 | A.P. Indy | Tomonori Tsurumaki | Neil Drysdale | W.S. Farish & W.S. Kilroy |
| 1993 | Kotashaan | La Presle Farm | Richard Mandella | La Presle Farm |
| 1994 | Holy Bull | Jimmy Croll | Jimmy Croll | Pelican Stable |
| 1995 | Cigar | Allen E. Paulson | William Mott | Allen E. Paulson |
| 1996 | Cigar | Allen E. Paulson | William Mott | Allen E. Paulson |

## Horse of the Year (Cont.)

| Year | Horse | Owner | Trainer | Breeder |
|------|-------|-------|---------|---------|
| 1997 | Favorite Trick | Joseph LaCombe | William Mott | Mr. & Mrs. M.L. Wood |
| 1998 | Skip Away | Carolyn Hine | Hubert Hine | Anna Marie Barnhart |
| 1999 | Charismatic | Robert & Beverly Lewis | D. Wayne Lukas | William Farish/Partners |
| 2000 | Tiznow | Michael Cooper and Cecilia Straub-Rubens | Jay M. Robbins | Cecilia Straub-Rubens |

Note: From 1936 to 1970, the *Daily Racing Form* annually selected a "Horse of the Year." In 1971 the *Daily Racing Form*, with the Thoroughbred Racing Association and the National Turf Writers Association, jointly created the Eclipse Awards.

## Eclipse Award Winners

| 2-YEAR-OLD COLT | 2-YEAR-OLD FILLY | 3-YEAR-OLD COLT |
|-----------------|------------------|-----------------|
| 1971 Riva Ridge | 1971 Numbered Account | 1971 Canonero II |
| 1972 Secretariat | 1972 La Prevoyante | 1972 Key to the Mint |
| 1973 Protagonist | 1973 Talking Picture | 1973 Secretariat |
| 1974 Foolish Pleasure | 1974 Ruffian | 1974 Little Currant |
| 1975 Honest Pleasure | 1975 Dearly Precious | 1975 Wajima |
| 1976 Seattle Slew | 1976 Sensational | 1976 Bold Forbes |
| 1977 Affirmed | 1977 Lakeville Miss | 1977 Seattle Slew |
| 1978 Spectacular Bid | 1978 Candy Eclair, It's in the Air | 1978 Affirmed |
| 1979 Rockhill Native | 1979 Smart Angle | 1979 Spectacular Bid |
| 1980 Lord Avie | 1980 Heavenly Cause | 1980 Temperence Hill |
| 1981 Deputy Minister | 1981 Before Dawn | 1981 Pleasant Colony |
| 1982 Roving Boy | 1982 Landaluce | 1982 Conquistador Cielo |
| 1983 Devil's Bag | 1983 Althea | 1983 Slew o' Gold |
| 1984 Chief's Crown | 1984 Outstandingly | 1984 Swale |
| 1985 Tasso | 1985 Family Style | 1985 Spend A Buck |
| 1986 Capote | 1986 Brave Raj | 1986 Snow Chief |
| 1987 Forty Niner | 1987 Epitome | 1987 Alysheba |
| 1988 Easy Goer | 1988 Open Mind | 1988 Risen Star |
| 1989 Rhythm | 1989 Go for Wand | 1989 Sunday Silence |
| 1990 Fly So Free | 1990 Meadow Star | 1990 Unbridled |
| 1991 Arazi | 1991 Pleasant Stage | 1991 Hansel |
| 1992 Gilded Time | 1992 Eliza | 1992 A.P. Indy |
| 1993 Dehere | 1993 Phone Chatter | 1993 Prairie Bayou |
| 1994 Timber Country | 1994 Flanders | 1994 Holy Bull |
| 1995 Maria's Mon | 1995 Golden Attraction | 1995 Thunder Gulch |
| 1996 Boston Harbor | 1996 Storm Song | 1996 Skip Away |
| 1997 Favorite Trick | 1997 Countess Diana | 1997 Silver Charm |
| 1998 Answer Lively | 1998 Silverbullettday | 1998 Real Quiet |
| 1999 Anees | 1999 Chilukki | 1999 Charismatic |
| 2000 Macho Uno | 2000 Caressing | 2000 Tiznow |

### CHAMPION TURF HORSE

| | |
|---|---|
| 1971 | Run the Gantlet (3) |
| 1972 | Cougar II (6) |
| 1973 | Secretariat (3) |
| 1974 | Dahlia (4) |
| 1975 | Snow Knight (4) |
| 1976 | Youth (3) |
| 1977 | Johnny D (3) |
| 1978 | Mac Diarmida (3) |

### CHAMPION MALE TURF HORSE

| | |
|---|---|
| 1979 | Bowl Game (5) |
| 1980 | John Henry (5) |
| 1981 | John Henry (6) |
| 1982 | Perrault (5) |
| 1983 | John Henry (8) |
| 1984 | John Henry (9) |
| 1985 | Cozzene (4) |
| 1986 | Manila (3) |
| 1987 | Theatrical (5) |
| 1988 | Sunshine Forever (3) |
| 1989 | Steinlen (6) |
| 1990 | Itsallgreektome (3) |

### CHAMPION MALE TURF HORSE *(Cont.)*

| | |
|---|---|
| 1991 | Tight Spot (4) |
| 1992 | Sky Classic (5) |
| 1993 | Kotashaan (5) |
| 1994 | Paradise Creek (5) |
| 1995 | Northern Spur (4) |
| 1996 | Singspiel (4) |
| 1997 | Chief Bearhart (4) |
| 1998 | Buck's Boy (5) |
| 1999 | Daylami (5) |
| 2000 | Kalanisi (4) |

### CHAMPION FEMALE TURF HORSE

| | |
|---|---|
| 1979 | Trillion (5) |
| 1980 | Just a Game II (4) |
| 1981 | De La Rose (3) |
| 1982 | April Run (4) |
| 1983 | All Along (4) |
| 1984 | Royal Heroine (4) |
| 1985 | Pebbles (4) |
| 1986 | Estrapade (6) |
| 1987 | Miesque (3) |

### CHAMPION FEMALE TURF HORSE *(Cont.)*

| | |
|---|---|
| 1988 | Miesque (4) |
| 1989 | Brown Bess (7) |
| 1990 | Laugh and Be Merry (5) |
| 1991 | Miss Alleged (4) |
| 1992 | Flawlessly (4) |
| 1993 | Flawlessly (5) |
| 1994 | Hatoof (5) |
| 1995 | Possibly Perfect (5) |
| 1996 | Wandesta (5) |
| 1997 | Ryafan (3) |
| 1998 | Fiji (4) |
| 1999 | Soaring Softly (4) |
| 2000 | Perfect Sting (4) |

## Eclipse Award Winners *(Cont.)*

### 3-YEAR-OLD FILLY

| | |
|---|---|
| 1971 | Turkish Trousers |
| 1972 | Susan's Girl |
| 1973 | Desert Vixen |
| 1974 | Chris Evert |
| 1975 | Ruffian |
| 1976 | Revidere |
| 1977 | Our Mims |
| 1978 | Tempest Queen |
| 1979 | Davona Dale |
| 1980 | Genuine Risk |
| 1981 | Wayward Lass |
| 1982 | Christmas Past |
| 1983 | Heartlight No. One |
| 1984 | Life's Magic |
| 1985 | Mom's Command |
| 1986 | Tiffany Lass |
| 1987 | Sacahuista |
| 1988 | Winning Colors |
| 1989 | Open Mind |
| 1990 | Go for Wand |
| 1991 | Dance Smartly |
| 1992 | Saratoga Dew |
| 1993 | Hollywood Wildcat |
| 1994 | Heavenly Prize |
| 1995 | Serena's Song |
| 1996 | Yank's Music |
| 1997 | Ajina |
| 1998 | Banshee Breeze |
| 1999 | Silverbulletday |
| 2000 | Surfside |

### OLDER COLT, HORSE OR GELDING

| | |
|---|---|
| 1971 | Ack Ack (5) |
| 1972 | Autobiography (4) |
| 1973 | Riva Ridge (4) |
| 1974 | Forego (4) |
| 1975 | Forego (5) |
| 1976 | Forego (6) |
| 1977 | Forego (7) |
| 1978 | Seattle Slew (4) |
| 1979 | Affirmed (4) |
| 1980 | Spectacular Bid (4) |
| 1981 | John Henry (6) |
| 1982 | Lemhi Gold (4) |
| 1983 | Bates Motel (4) |
| 1984 | Slew o'Gold (4) |
| 1985 | Vanlandingham (4) |
| 1986 | Turkoman (4) |
| 1987 | Ferdinand (4) |
| 1988 | Alysheba (4) |
| 1989 | Blushing John (4) |
| 1990 | Criminal Type (5) |
| 1991 | Black Tie Affair (5) |
| 1992 | Pleasant Tap (5) |
| 1993 | Bertrando (4) |
| 1994 | The Wicked North (5) |
| 1995 | Cigar (5) |
| 1996 | Cigar (6) |
| 1997 | Skip Away (4) |
| 1998 | Skip Away (5) |
| 1999 | Victory Gallop (4) |
| 2000 | Lemon Drop Kid (4) |

### OLDER FILLY OR MARE

| | |
|---|---|
| 1971 | Shuvee (5) |
| 1972 | Typecast (6) |
| 1973 | Susan's Girl (4) |
| 1974 | Desert Vixen (4) |
| 1975 | Susan's Girl (6) |
| 1976 | Proud Delta (4) |
| 1977 | Cascapedia (4) |
| 1978 | Late Bloomer (4) |
| 1979 | Waya (5) |
| 1980 | Glorious Song (4) |
| 1981 | Relaxing (5) |
| 1982 | Track Robbery (6) |
| 1983 | Ambassador of Luck (4) |
| 1984 | Princess Rooney (4) |
| 1985 | Life's Magic (4) |
| 1986 | Lady's Secret (4) |
| 1987 | North Sider (5) |
| 1988 | Personal Ensign (4) |
| 1989 | Bayakoa (5) |
| 1990 | Bayakoa (6) |
| 1991 | Queena (5) |
| 1992 | Paseana (5) |
| 1993 | Paseana (6) |
| 1994 | Sky Beauty (4) |
| 1995 | Inside Information (4) |
| 1996 | Jewel Princess (4) |
| 1997 | Hidden Lake (4) |
| 1998 | Escena (5) |
| 1999 | Beautiful Pleasure (4) |
| 2000 | Riboletta (6) |

### STEEPLECHASE OR HURDLE HORSE

| | |
|---|---|
| 1971 | Shadow Brook (7) |
| 1972 | Soothsayer (5) |
| 1973 | Athenian Idol (5) |
| 1974 | Gran Kan (8) |
| 1975 | Life's Illusion (4) |
| 1976 | Straight & True (6) |
| 1977 | Cafe Prince (7) |
| 1978 | Cafe Prince (8) |
| 1979 | Martie's Anger (4) |
| 1980 | Zaccio (4) |
| 1981 | Zaccio (5) |
| 1982 | Zaccio (6) |
| 1983 | Flatterer (4) |
| 1984 | Flatterer (5) |
| 1985 | Flatterer (6) |
| 1986 | Flatterer (7) |
| 1987 | Inlander (6) |
| 1988 | Jimmy Lorenzo (6) |
| 1989 | Highland Bud (4) |
| 1990 | Morley Street (7) |
| 1991 | Morley Street (8) |
| 1992 | Lonesome Glory (4) |
| 1993 | Lonesome Glory (5) |
| 1994 | Warm Spell (6) |
| 1995 | Lonesome Glory (7) |
| 1996 | Corregio (5) |
| 1997 | Lonesome Glory (9) |
| 1998 | Flat Top (5) |
| 1999 | Lonesome Glory (11) |
| 2000 | All Gong (6) |

### SPRINTER

| | |
|---|---|
| 1971 | Ack Ack (5) |
| 1972 | Chou Croute (4) |
| 1973 | Shecky Greene (3) |
| 1974 | Forego (4) |
| 1975 | Gallant Bob (3) |
| 1976 | My Juliet (4) |
| 1977 | What a Summer (4) |
| 1978 | Dr. Patches (4) |
| | J.O. Tobin (4) |
| 1979 | Star de Naskra (4) |
| 1980 | Plugged Nickel (3) |
| 1981 | Guilty Conscience (5) |
| 1982 | Gold Beauty (3) |
| 1983 | Chinook Pass (4) |
| 1984 | Eillo (4) |
| 1985 | Precisionist (4) |
| 1986 | Smile (4) |
| 1987 | Groovy (4) |
| 1988 | Gulch (4) |
| 1989 | Safely Kept (3) |
| 1990 | Housebuster (3) |
| 1991 | Housebuster (4) |
| 1992 | Rubiano (5) |
| 1993 | Cardmania (7) |
| 1994 | Cherokee Run (4) |
| 1995 | Not Surprising (5) |
| 1996 | Lit de Justice (6) |
| 1997 | Smoke Glacken (3) |
| 1998 | Reraise (3) |
| 1999 | Artax (4) |
| 2000 | Kone Gold (6) |

### OUTSTANDING OWNER

| | |
|---|---|
| 1971 | Mr. & Mrs. E. E. Fogleson |
| 1974 | Dan Lasater |
| 1975 | Dan Lasater |
| 1976 | Dan Lasater |
| 1977 | Maxwell Gluck |
| 1978 | Harbor View Farm |
| 1979 | Harbor View Farm |
| 1980 | Mr. & Mrs. Bertram |
| 1981 | Dotsam Stable |
| 1982 | Viola Sommer |
| 1983 | John Franks |
| 1984 | John Franks |
| 1985 | Mr. & Mrs. Eugene Klein |
| 1986 | Mr. & Mrs. Eugene Klein |
| 1987 | Mr. & Mrs. Eugene Klein |
| 1988 | Ogden Phipps |
| 1989 | Ogden Phipps |
| 1990 | Frances Genter |
| 1991 | Sam-Son Farm |
| 1992 | Juddmonte Farms |
| 1993 | John Franks |
| 1994 | John Franks |
| 1995 | Allen E. Paulson |
| 1996 | Allen E. Paulson |
| 1997 | Carolyn Hine |
| 1998 | Frank Stronach |
| 1999 | Frank Stronach |
| 2000 | Frank Stronach |

Note: Number in parentheses is horse's age.

## Eclipse Award Winners (Cont.)

| OUTSTANDING TRAINER | OUTSTANDING JOCKEY | OUTSTANDING APPRENTICE JOCKEY |
|---|---|---|
| 1971.....Charlie Whittingham | 1971.....Laffit Pincay Jr. | 1971.....Gene St. Leon |
| 1972.....Lucien Laurin | 1972.....Braulio Baeza | 1972.....Thomas Wallis |
| 1973.....H. Allen Jerkens | 1973.....Laffit Pincay Jr | 1973.....Steve Valdez |
| 1974.....Sherrill Ward | 1974.....Laffit Pincay Jr | 1974.....Chris McCarron |
| 1975.....Steve DiMauro | 1975.....Braulio Baeza | 1975.....Jimmy Edwards |
| 1976.....Lazaro Barrera | 1976.....Sandy Hawley | 1976.....George Martens |
| 1977.....Lazaro Barrera | 1977.....Steve Cauthen | 1977.....Steve Cauthen |
| 1978.....Lazaro Barrera | 1978.....Darrel McHargue | 1978.....Ron Franklin |
| 1979.....Lazaro Barrera | 1979.....Laffit Pincay Jr | 1979.....Cash Asmussen |
| 1980.....Bud Delp | 1980.....Chris McCarron | 1980.....Frank Lovato Jr. |
| 1981.....Ron McAnally | 1981.....Bill Shoemaker | 1981.....Richard Migliore |
| 1982.....Charlie Whittingham | 1982.....Angel Cordero Jr | 1982.....Alberto Delgado |
| 1983.....Woody Stephens | 1983.....Angel Cordero Jr | 1983.....Declan Murphy |
| 1984.....Jack Van Berg | 1984.....Pat Day | 1984.....Wesley Ward |
| 1985.....D. Wayne Lukas | 1985.....Laffit Pincay Jr | 1985.....Art Madrid Jr. |
| 1986.....D. Wayne Lukas | 1986.....Pat Day | 1986.....Allen Stacy |
| 1987.....D. Wayne Lukas | 1987.....Pat Day | 1987.....Kent Desormeaux |
| 1988.....Claude R. McGaughey III | 1988.....Jose Santos | 1988.....Steve Capanas |
| 1989.....Charlie Whittingham | 1989.....Kent Desormeaux | 1989.....Michael Luzzi |
| 1990.....Carl Nafzger | 1990.....Craig Perret | 1990.....Mark Johnston |
| 1991.....Ron McAnally | 1991.....Pat Day | 1991.....Mickey Walls |
| 1992.....Ron McAnally | 1992.....Kent Desormeaux | 1992.....Jesus A. Bracho |
| 1993.....Bobby Frankel | 1993.....Mike Smith | 1993.....Juan Umana |
| 1994.....D. Wayne Lukas | 1994.....Mike Smith | 1994.....Dale Beckner |
| 1995.....William Mott | 1995.....Jerry Bailey | 1995.....Ramon Perez |
| 1996.....William Mott | 1996.....Jerry Bailey | 1996.....Neil Pozansky |
| 1997.....Bob Baffert | 1997.....Jerry Bailey | 1997.....Phil Teator |
| 1998.....Bob Baffert | 1998.....Gary Stevens |        Roberto Rosado |
| 1999.....Bob Baffert | 1999.....Jorge Chavez | 1998.....Shaun Bridgmohan |
| 2000.....Robert Frankel | 2000.....Jerry Bailey | 1999.....Ariel Smith |
| | | 2000.....Tyler Baze |

## Seabiscuit

More than 60 years after he captured America's imagination, the charismatic thoroughbred Seabiscuit is again making a late charge. His improbable resurgence began in March 2001 with the publication of Laura Hillenbrand's *Seabiscuit: An American Legend*, chronicling the tale of the rags-to-riches horse who beat Triple Crown winner War Admiral in a famous 1938 match race. The critically acclaimed book was a surprise success, topping *The New York Times* nonfiction bestseller list for seven weeks. In Hollywood a bidding war erupted for the movie rights; Universal won out by committing more than $1 million. PBS's *American Experience* has begun work on a documentary about the horse, and a toy company, Beyer, is even considering producing a plastic Seabiscuit figure. Meanwhile, Seabiscuit items on eBay have become hotter than Churchill Downs in August. A recording of the calls of two of the horse's races, previously valued at $15 to $20, sold for $270 in the spring of 2001.

Hillenbrand, who may write a children's book about the horse, has been asked to participate in three documentaries and a Seabiscuit play. "Seabiscuit was enormous then, and he's enormous now for the same reason: He's the ultimate underdog," says Hillenbrand. "The owner, trainer and jockey are also great underdog stories. Those are universally appealing no matter when you tell them."

## Eclipse Award Winners *(Cont.)*

### OUTSTANDING BREEDER

1974.....John W. Galbreath
1975.....Fred W. Hooper
1976.....Nelson Bunker Hunt
1977.....Edward Plunket Taylor
1978.....Harbor View Farm
1979.....Claiborne Farm
1980.....Mrs. Henry D. Paxson
1981.....Golden Chance Farm
1982.....Fred W. Hooper
1983.....Edward Plunket Taylor
1984.....Claiborne Farm
1985.....Nelson Bunker Hunt
1986.....Paul Mellon
1987.....Nelson Bunker Hunt
1988.....Ogden Phipps
1989.....North Ridge Farm
1990.....Calumet Farm
1991.....John and Betty Mabee
1992.....William S. Farish III
1993.....Allen Paulson
1994.....William T. Young

### OUTSTANDING BREEDER *(Cont.)*

1995.....Juddmonte Farms
1996.....Fansworth Farms
1997.....Golden Eagle Farm
1998.....John and Betty Mabee
1999.....William Farish/Partners
2000.....Frank Stronach/Adena
        Springs

### AWARD OF MERIT

1976.....Jack J. Dreyfus
1977.....Steve Cauthen
1978.....Ogden Phipps
1979.....Frank E. Kilroe
1980.....John D. Schapiro
1981.....Bill Shoemaker
1984.....John Gaines
1985.....Keene Daingerfield
1986.....Herman Cohen
1987.....J. B. Faulconer
1988.....John Forsythe
1989.....Michael P. Sandler

### AWARD OF MERIT *(Cont.)*

1991.....Fred W. Hooper
1994.....Alfred G. Vanderbilt
1996.....Allen E. Paulson

### SPECIAL AWARD

1971.....Robert J. Kleberg
1974.....Charles Hatton
1976.....Bill Shoemaker
1980.....John T. Landry
        Pierre E. Bellocq (Peb)
1984.....C. V. Whitney
1985.....Arlington Park
1987.....Anheuser-Busch
1988.....Edward J. DeBartolo Sr.
1989.....Richard Duchossois
1994.....John Longden
        Edward Arcaro
1998.....Oak Tree Racing
        Association

Note: Special Award and Award of Merit, for long-term and/or outstanding service to the industry, not presented annually.

## No Sex, Thanks; Gotta Run

April 14 was a busy day in the 2001 thoroughbred season, one on which veteran jockey Laffit Pincay led Millennium Wind to victory in the Bluegrass Stakes, and Congaree established himself as trainer Bob Baffert's second Derby contender (the other was Point Given) by winning the Wood Memorial in impressive fashion over Monarchos. Also lighting up that Saturday was Balto Star, the gelding who annihilated the field in the 1⅛-mile Arkansas Derby, at sloppy Oaklawn Park. Breaking from the number 10 post, the 8–5 favorite led all the way. Jockey Mark Guidry never raised his whip.

The victory was the third in a row for Balto Star, who turned in a similarly devastating performance when he wired the field in the 1⅛-mile Spiral Stakes at Turfway Park in Florence, Ky., on March 24, winning by nearly13 lengths. The speedy bay had to be considered a legitimate Derby contender. He had won his last three races by a combined 29½ lengths.

Such dominance didn't seem likely in September 2000, when Balto Star finished last in his first start, at Belmont Park. He misbehaved so much in the post parade—he tried to mount his lead pony—that trainer Todd Pletcher and owners Stuart and Anita Subotnick had him gelded. Three starts later, on Jan. 1, 2001, a more focused Balto Star broke his maiden at Aqueduct. "It made a big difference in his attitude," Pletcher said after the Spiral. "That was the first step in turning him around."

But Balto Star's loss of virility did not bode well for him on Derby day. The last sexless wonder to win the Run for the Roses was Clyde Van Dusen, in 1929. Alas, Balto Star finished 14th in a field of 17 at Churchill Downs.

—Mark Beech

# Breeders' Cup

Location: Hollywood Park 1984, '87, '97; Aqueduct Racetrack 1985; Santa Anita Park (CA) 1986, '93; Churchill Downs 1988, '91, '98,'00; Gulfstream Park (FL) 1989, '92, '99; Belmont Park 1990, '95; Woodbine (Toronto) 1996.

## Juveniles

| Year | Winner (Margin) | Jockey | Second | Third | Time |
|---|---|---|---|---|---|
| 1984 | Chief's Crown (¾) | Don MacBeth | Tank's Prospect | Spend a Buck | 1:36⅕ |
| 1985 | Tasso (Nose) | Laffit Pincay Jr. | Storm Cat | Scat Dancer | 1:36⅕ |
| 1986 | Capote (1¼) | Laffit Pincay Jr. | Qualify | Alysheba | 1:43⅘ |
| 1987 | Success Express (1¾) | Jose Santos | Regal Classic | Tejano | 1:35⅕ |
| 1988 | Is It True (1¼) | Laffit Pincay Jr. | Easy Goer | Tagel | 1:46⅗ |
| 1989 | Rhythm (2) | Craig Perret | Grand Canyon | Slavic | 1:43⅗ |
| 1990 | Fly So Free (3) | Jose Santos | Take Me Out | Lost Mountain | 1:43⅖ |
| 1991 | Arazi (4¾) | Pat Valenzuela | Bertrando | Snappy Landing | 1:44⅗ |
| 1992 | Gilded Time (¾) | Chris McCarron | It'sali'lknownfact | River Special | 1:43⅖ |
| 1993 | Brocco (5) | Gary Stevens | Blumin Affair | Tabasco Cat | 1:42⅘ |
| 1994 | Timber Country (½) | Pat Day | Eltish | Tejano Run | 1:44⅖ |
| 1995 | Unbridled's Song (Neck) | Mike Smith | Hennessy | Editor's Note | 1:41⅗ |
| 1996 | Boston Harbor (Neck) | Jerry Bailey | Acceptable | Ordway | 1:43⅖ |
| 1997 | Favorite Trick (5½) | Pat Day | Dawson's Legacy | Nationalore | 1:41⅗ |
| 1998 | Answer Lively (Head) | Jerry Bailey | Aly's Alley | Cat Thief | 1:44 |
| 1999 | Anees (2½) | Gary Stevens | Chief Seattle | High Yield | 1:42.29 |
| 2000 | Macho Uno (Nose) | Jerry Bailey | Point Given | Street Cry | 1:42.05 |

Note: One mile (1984–85, '87), 1 1/16 miles (1986 and since 1988).

## Juvenile Fillies

| Year | Winner (Margin) | Jockey | Second | Third | Time |
|---|---|---|---|---|---|
| 1984 | Outstandingly* | Walter Guerra | Dusty Heart | Fine Spirit | 1:37⅘ |
| 1985 | Twilight Ridge (1) | Jorge Velasquez | Family Style | Steal a Kiss | 1:35⅘ |
| 1986 | Brave Raj (5½) | Pat Valenzuela | Tappiano | Saros Brig | 1:43⅕ |
| 1987 | Epitome (Nose) | Pat Day | Jeanne Jones | Dream Team | 1:36⅖ |
| 1988 | Open Mind (1¾) | Angel Cordero Jr. | Darby Shuffle | Lea Lucinda | 1:46⅗ |
| 1989 | Go for Wand (2¾) | Randy Romero | Sweet Roberta | Stella Madrid | 1:44⅕ |
| 1990 | Meadow Star (5) | Jose Santos | Private Treasure | Dance Smartly | 1:44 |
| 1991 | Pleasant Stage (Neck) | Eddie Delahoussaye | La Spia | Cadillac Women | 1:46⅖ |
| 1992 | Eliza (1½) | Pat Valenzuela | Educated Risk | Boots 'n Jackie | 1:42⅘ |
| 1993 | Phone Chatter (Head) | Laffit Pincay | Sardula | Heavenly Prize | 1:43 |
| 1994 | Flanders (Head) | Pat Day | Serena's Song | Stormy Blues | 1:45⅕ |
| 1995 | My Flag (½) | Jerry Bailey | Cara Rafaela | Golden Attraction | 1:42⅖ |
| 1996 | Storm Song (4½) | Craig Perret | Love That Jazz | Critical Factor | 1:43⅗ |
| 1997 | Countess Diana (8½) | Shane Sellers | Career Collection | Primaly | 1:42⅕ |
| 1998 | Silverbulletday (½) | Gary Stevens | Excellent Meeting | Three Ring | 1:43⅗ |
| 1999 | Cash Run (1¼) | Jerry Bailey | Chilukki | Surfside | 1:43.31 |
| 2000 | Caressing (½) | John Velazquez | Platinum Tiara | Shes a Devil Due | 1:42.72 |

*In 1984, winner Fran's Valentine was disqualified for interference in the stretch and placed 10th.
Note: One mile (1984–85, '87), 1 1/16 miles (1986 and since 1988).

## Sprint

| Year | Winner (Margin) | Jockey | Second | Third | Time |
|---|---|---|---|---|---|
| 1984 | Eillo (Nose) | Craig Perret | Commemorate | Fighting Fit | 1:10⅕ |
| 1985 | Precisionist (¾) | Chris McCarron | Smile | Mt. Livermore | 1:08⅖ |
| 1986 | Smile (1¼) | Jacinto Vasquez | Pine Tree Lane | Bedside Promise | 1:08⅖ |
| 1987 | Very Subtle (4) | Pat Valenzuela | Groovy | Exclusive Enough | 1:08⅘ |
| 1988 | Gulch (¾) | Angel Cordero Jr | Play the King | Afleet | 1:10⅖ |
| 1989 | Dancing Spree (Neck) | Angel Cordero Jr | Safely Kept | Dispersal | 1:09 |
| 1990 | Safely Kept (Neck) | Craig Perret | Dayjur | Black Tie Affair | 1:09⅗ |
| 1991 | Sheikh Albadou (Neck) | Pat Eddery | Pleasant Tap | Robyn Dancer | 1:09⅕ |
| 1992 | Thirty Slews (Neck) | Eddie Delahoussaye | Meafara | Rubiano | 1:08⅕ |
| 1993 | Cardmania (Neck) | Eddie Delahoussaye | Meafara | Gilded Time | 1:08⅗ |
| 1994 | Cherokee Run (Head) | Mike Smith | Soviet Problem | Cardmania | 1:09⅖ |
| 1995 | Desert Stormer (Neck) | Kent Desormeaux | Mr. Greeley | Lit de Justice | 1:09 |
| 1996 | Lit de Justice (1¼) | Corey Nakatani | Paying Dues | Honour and Glory | 1:08⅗ |
| 1997 | Elmhurst (½) | Corey Nakatani | Hesabull | Bet on Sunshine | 1:08 |
| 1998 | Reraise (2) | Corey Nakatani | Grand Slam | Kona Gold | 1:09 |
| 1999 | Artax (½) | Jorge Chavez | Kona Gold | Big Jag | 1:07.89 |
| 2000 | Kona Gold (½) | Alex Solis | Honest Lady | Bet on Sunshine | 1:07.77 |

Note: Six furlongs (since 1984).

## Breeders' Cup (Cont.)

### Mile

| Year | Winner (Margin) | Jockey | Second | Third | Time |
|---|---|---|---|---|---|
| 1984 | Royal Heroine (1½) | Fernando Toro | Star Choice | Cozzene | 1:32⅗ |
| 1985 | Cozzene (2¼) | Walter Guerra | Al Mamoon* | Shadeed | 1:35 |
| 1986 | Last Tycoon (Head) | Yves St-Martin | Palace Music | Fred Astaire | 1:35⅕ |
| 1987 | Miesque (3½) | Freddie Head | Show Dancer | Sonic Lady | 1:32⅘ |
| 1988 | Miesque (4) | Freddie Head | Steinlen | Simply Majestic | 1:38⅗ |
| 1989 | Steinlen (¾) | Jose Santos | Sabona | Most Welcome | 1:37⅕ |
| 1990 | Royal Academy (Neck) | Lester Piggott | Itsallgreektome | Priolo | 1:35⅕ |
| 1991 | Opening Verse (2¼) | Pat Valenzuela | Val de Bois | Star of Cozzene | 1:37⅖ |
| 1992 | Lure (3) | Mike Smith | Paradise Creek | Brief Truce | 1:32⅘ |
| 1993 | Lure (2¼) | Mike Smith | Ski Paradise | Fourstars Allstar | 1:33⅖ |
| 1994 | Barathea (Head) | Frankie Dettori | Johann Quatz | Unfinished Symph | 1:34⅖ |
| 1995 | Ridgewood Pearl (2) | John Murtagh | Fastness | Sayyedati | 1:43⅗ |
| 1996 | Da Hoss (1½) | Gary Stevens | Spinning World | Same Old Wish | 1:35⅘ |
| 1997 | Spinning World (2) | Cash Asmussen | Geri | Decorated Hero | 1:32⅘ |
| 1998 | Da Hoss (Head) | John Velazquez | Hawksley Hill | Labeeb | 1:35⅕ |
| 1999 | Silic (Neck) | Corey Nakatani | Tuzla | Docksider | 1:34.26 |
| 2000 | War Chant (Neck) | Gary Stevens | North East Bound | Dansili | 1:34.67 |

*2nd place finisher Palace Music was disqualified for interference and placed 9th.

### Distaff

| Year | Winner (Margin) | Jockey | Second | Third | Time |
|---|---|---|---|---|---|
| 1984 | Princess Rooney (7) | Eddie Delahoussaye | Life's Magic | Adored | 2:02⅖ |
| 1985 | Life's Magic (6¼) | Angel Cordero Jr. | Lady's Secret | Dontstop Themusic | 2:02 |
| 1986 | Lady's Secret (2½) | Pat Day | Fran's Valentine | Outstandingly | 2:01⅕ |
| 1987 | Sacahuista (2¼) | Randy Romero | Clabber Girl | Oueee Bebe | 2:02⅘ |
| 1988 | Personal Ensign (Nose) | Randy Romero | Winning Colors | Goodbye Halo | 1:52 |
| 1989 | Bayakoa (1½) | Laffit Pincay Jr. | Gorgeous | Open Mind | 1:47⅖ |
| 1990 | Bayakoa (6¾) | Laffit Pincay Jr. | Colonial Waters | Valay Maid | 1:49⅕ |
| 1991 | Dance Smarty (½) | Pat Day | Versailles Treaty | Brought to Mind | 1:50⅘ |
| 1992 | Paseana (4) | Chris McCarron | Versailles Treaty | Magical Maiden | 1:48 |
| 1993 | Hollywood Wildcat (Nose) | Eddie Delahoussaye | Paseana | Re Toss | 1:48⅕ |
| 1994 | One Dreamer (Neck) | Gary Stevens | Heavenly Prize | Miss Dominique | 1:50⅗ |
| 1995 | Inside Information (13½) | Mike Smith | Heavenly Prize | Lakeway | 1:46 |
| 1996 | Jewel Princess (1½) | Corey Nakatani | Serena's Song | Different | 1:48⅖ |
| 1997 | Ajina (2) | Mike Smith | Sharp Cat | Escena | 1:47⅕ |
| 1998 | Escena (Nose) | Gary Stevens | Banshee Breeze | Keeper Hill | 1:49⅘ |
| 1999 | Beautiful Pleasure (¾) | Jorge Chavez | Banshee Breeze | Heritage of Gold | 1:47.56 |
| 2000 | Spain (1½) | Victor Espinoza | Surfside | Heritage of Gold | 1:47.66 |

Note: 1¼ miles (1984–87), 1⅛ miles (since 1988).

### Turf

| Year | Winner (Margin) | Jockey | Second | Third | Time |
|---|---|---|---|---|---|
| 1984 | Lashkari (Neck) | Yves St. Martin | All Along | Raami | 2:25⅕ |
| 1985 | Pebbles (Neck) | Pat Eddery | Strawberry Rd II | Mourjane | 2:27 |
| 1986 | Manila (Neck) | Jose Santos | Theatrical | Estrapade | 2:25⅖ |
| 1987 | Theatrical (½) | Pat Day | Trempolino | Village Star II | 2:24⅗ |
| 1988 | Great Communicator (½) | Ray Sibille | Sunshine Forever | Indian Skimmer | 2:35⅕ |
| 1989 | Prized (Head) | Eddie Delahoussaye | Sierra Roberta | Star Lift | 2:28 |
| 1990 | In the Wings (½) | Gary Stevens | With Approval | El Senor | 2:29⅗ |
| 1991 | Miss Alleged (2) | Eric Legrix | Itsallgreektome | Quest for Fame | 2:30⅘ |
| 1992 | Fraise (Nose) | Pat Valenzuela | Sky Classic | Quest For Fame | 2:24 |
| 1993 | Kotashaan (½) | Kent Desormeaux | Bien Bien | Luazar | 2:25 |
| 1994 | Tikkanen (1½) | Mike Smith | Hatoof | Paradise Creek | 2:26⅖ |
| 1995 | Northern Spur (Neck) | Chris McCarron | Freedom Cry | Carnegie | 2:42 |
| 1996 | Pilsudski (1¼) | Walter Swinburn | Singspiel | Swain | 2:30⅕ |
| 1997 | Chief Bearhart (¾) | Jose Santos | Borgia | Flag Down | 2:23⅘ |
| 1998 | Buck's Boy (1¼) | Shane Sellers | Yagli | Dushyantor | 2:28⅗ |
| 1999 | Daylami (2½) | Frankie Dettori | Royal Anthem | Buck's Boy | 2:24.73 |
| 2000 | Kalanisi (½) | John Murtagh | Quiet Resolve | John's Call | 2:26.96 |

Note: 1½ miles.

## Breeders' Cup *(Cont.)*

### Classic

| Year | Winner (Margin) | Jockey | Second | Third | Time |
|---|---|---|---|---|---|
| 1984 | Wild Again (Head) | Pat Day | Slew o' Gold* | Gate Dancer | 2:03⅖ |
| 1985 | Proud Truth (Head) | Jorge Velasquez | Gate Dancer | Turkoman | 2:00⅘ |
| 1986 | Skywalker (1¼) | Laffit Pincay Jr. | Turkoman | Precisionist | 2:00⅖ |
| 1987 | Ferdinand (Nose) | Bill Shoemaker | Alysheba | Judge Angelucci | 2:01⅖ |
| 1988 | Alysheba (Nose) | Chris McCarron | Seeking the Gold | Waquoit | 2:04⅘ |
| 1989 | Sunday Silence (½) | Chris McCarron | Easy Goer | Blushing John | 2:00⅕ |
| 1990 | Unbridled (1) | Pat Day | Ibn Bey | Thirty Six Red | 2:02⅕ |
| 1991 | Black Tie Affair (1¼) | Jerry Bailey | Twilight Agenda | Unbridled | 2:02⅘ |
| 1992 | A.P. Indy (2) | Eddie Delahoussaye | Pleasant Tap | Jolypha | 2:00⅕ |
| 1993 | Arcangues (2) | Jerry Bailey | Bertrando | Kissin Kris | 2:00⅘ |
| 1994 | Concern (Neck) | Jerry Bailey | Tabasco Cat | Dramatic Gold | 2:02⅖ |
| 1995 | Cigar (2½) | Jerry Bailey | L'Carriere | Unaccounted For | 1:59⅖ |
| 1996 | Alphabet Soup (Nose) | Chris McCarron | Louis Quatorze | Cigar | 2:01 |
| 1997 | Skip Away (6) | Mike Smith | Deputy Commander | Dowty | 1:59⅕ |
| 1998 | Awesome Again (¾) | Pat Day | Silver Charm | Swain | 2:02 |
| 1999 | Cat Thief (1¼) | Pat Day | Budroyale | Golden Missile | 1:59.52 |
| 2000 | Tiznow (Neck) | Chris McCarron | Giant's Causeway | Captain Steve | 2:00.75 |

*2nd place finisher Gate Dancer was disqualified for interference and placed 3rd.

Note: 1¼ miles.

## England's Triple Crown Winners

England's Triple Crown consists of the Two Thousand Guineas, held at Newmarket; the Epsom Derby, held at Epsom Downs; and the St. Leger Stakes, held at Doncaster.

| Year | Horse | Owner |
|---|---|---|
| 1853 | West Australian | Mr. Bowes |
| 1865 | Gladiateur | F. DeLagrange |
| 1866 | Lord Lyon | R. Sutton |
| 1886 | *Ormonde | Duke of Westminster |
| 1891 | Common | †F. Johnstone |
| 1893 | Isinglass | H. McCalmont |
| 1897 | Galtee More | J. Gubbins |
| 1899 | Flying Fox | Duke of Westminster |
| 1900 | Diamond Jubilee | Prince of Wales |
| 1903 | *Rock Sand | J. Miller |
| 1915 | Pommern | S. Joel |
| 1917 | Gay Crusader | Mr. Fairie |
| 1918 | Gainsborough | Lady James Douglas |
| 1935 | *Bahram | Aga Khan |
| 1970 | ‡Nijinsky II | C. W. Engelhard |

*Imported into United States. †Raced in name of Lord Alington in Two Thousand Guineas. ‡Canadian-bred.

### The Racehorse

Three-year-old colt Dollar Bill chronicled—with a little help from his owner, Gary West—his Triple Crown experiences in Diary entries on his website (dollarbill.ws). We caught up with the outspoken thoroughbred after he finished fourth in the 2001 Preakness for an exclusive interview.

*You and jockey Pat Day had another rough ride. Was that why you couldn't catch Point Given?*

The trip was a killer. Griffinite took a left-hand turn and caused me to check abruptly at the five-eighths pole. But I could have run two miles, and I wouldn't have caught Point Given. Excuses won't get me in the Hall of Fame.

*How does a horse know when it's a big race day?*

Fact is, on race day our trainers trick us. It's business as usual for most of the day. Then they rope off the barn and security gets real cranky. That's when I know it's a big day.

*What do you think about before a race?*

I eyeball the competition. The 99–1 horses have real bad vibes. Knowin you're gonna get an ass-kickin' ain't a good feeling.

*Does it bother you when your jockey goes to the whip?*

No. I do love a good whippin'.Some horses do and some don't.

*Does a horse know when he wins?*

Absolutely. Being in the winner's circle is intoxicating. People taking pictures, kissin' ya, tellin' ya what a great horse ya are. Then I get to go to the test barn and strut around. Ain't a person or beast on earth don't know when he wins.

## Horse—Money Won

| Year | Horse | Age | Starts | 1st | 2nd | 3rd | Winnings ($) |
|------|-------|-----|--------|-----|-----|-----|--------------|
| 1919 | Sir Barton | 3 | 13 | 8 | 3 | 2 | 88,250 |
| 1920 | Man o' War | 3 | 11 | 11 | 0 | 0 | 166,140 |
| 1921 | Morvich | 2 | 11 | 11 | 0 | 0 | 115,234 |
| 1922 | Pillory | 3 | 7 | 4 | 1 | 1 | 95,654 |
| 1923 | Zev | 3 | 14 | 12 | 1 | 0 | 272,008 |
| 1924 | Sarzen | 3 | 12 | 8 | 1 | 1 | 95,640 |
| 1925 | Pompey | 2 | 10 | 7 | 2 | 0 | 121,630 |
| 1926 | Crusader | 3 | 15 | 9 | 4 | 0 | 166,033 |
| 1927 | Anita Peabody | 2 | 7 | 6 | 0 | 1 | 111,905 |
| 1928 | High Strung | 2 | 6 | 5 | 0 | 0 | 153,590 |
| 1929 | Blue Larkspur | 3 | 6 | 4 | 1 | 0 | 153,450 |
| 1930 | Gallant Fox | 3 | 10 | 9 | 1 | 0 | 308,275 |
| 1931 | Gallant Flight | 2 | 7 | 7 | 0 | 0 | 219,000 |
| 1932 | Gusto | 3 | 16 | 4 | 3 | 2 | 145,940 |
| 1933 | Singing Wood | 2 | 9 | 3 | 2 | 2 | 88,050 |
| 1934 | Cavalcade | 3 | 7 | 6 | 1 | 0 | 111,235 |
| 1935 | Omaha | 3 | 9 | 6 | 1 | 2 | 142,255 |
| 1936 | Granville | 3 | 11 | 7 | 3 | 0 | 110,295 |
| 1937 | Seabiscuit | 4 | 15 | 11 | 2 | 2 | 168,580 |
| 1938 | Stagehand | 3 | 15 | 8 | 2 | 3 | 189,710 |
| 1939 | Challedon | 3 | 15 | 9 | 2 | 3 | 184,535 |
| 1940 | Bimelech | 3 | 7 | 4 | 2 | 1 | 110,005 |
| 1941 | Whirlaway | 3 | 20 | 13 | 5 | 2 | 272,386 |
| 1942 | Shut Out | 3 | 12 | 8 | 2 | 0 | 238,872 |
| 1943 | Count Fleet | 3 | 6 | 6 | 0 | 0 | 174,055 |
| 1944 | Pavot | 2 | 8 | 8 | 0 | 0 | 179,040 |
| 1945 | Busher | 3 | 13 | 10 | 2 | 1 | 273,735 |
| 1946 | Assault | 3 | 15 | 8 | 2 | 3 | 424,195 |
| 1947 | Armed | 6 | 17 | 11 | 4 | 1 | 376,325 |
| 1948 | Citation | 3 | 20 | 19 | 1 | 0 | 709,470 |
| 1949 | Ponder | 3 | 21 | 9 | 5 | 2 | 321,825 |
| 1950 | Noor | 5 | 12 | 7 | 4 | 1 | 346,940 |
| 1951 | Counterpoint | 3 | 15 | 7 | 2 | 1 | 250,525 |
| 1952 | Crafty Admiral | 4 | 16 | 9 | 4 | 1 | 277,225 |
| 1953 | Native Dancer | 3 | 10 | 9 | 1 | 0 | 513,425 |
| 1954 | Determine | 3 | 15 | 10 | 3 | 2 | 328,700 |
| 1955 | Nashua | 3 | 12 | 10 | 1 | 1 | 752,550 |
| 1956 | Needles | 3 | 8 | 4 | 2 | 0 | 440,850 |
| 1957 | Round Table | 3 | 22 | 15 | 1 | 3 | 600,383 |
| 1958 | Round Table | 4 | 20 | 14 | 4 | 0 | 662,780 |
| 1959 | Sword Dancer | 3 | 13 | 8 | 4 | 0 | 537,004 |
| 1960 | Bally Ache | 3 | 15 | 10 | 3 | 1 | 445,045 |
| 1961 | Carry Back | 3 | 16 | 9 | 1 | 3 | 565,349 |
| 1962 | Never Bend | 2 | 10 | 7 | 1 | 2 | 402,969 |
| 1963 | Candy Spots | 3 | 12 | 7 | 2 | 1 | 604,481 |
| 1964 | Gun Bow | 4 | 16 | 8 | 4 | 2 | 580,100 |
| 1965 | Buckpasser | 2 | 11 | 9 | 1 | 0 | 568,096 |
| 1966 | Buckpasser | 3 | 14 | 13 | 1 | 0 | 669,078 |
| 1967 | Damascus | 3 | 16 | 12 | 3 | 1 | 817,941 |
| 1968 | Forward Pass | 3 | 13 | 7 | 2 | 0 | 546,674 |
| 1969 | Arts and Letters | 3 | 14 | 8 | 5 | 1 | 555,604 |
| 1970 | Personality | 3 | 18 | 8 | 2 | 1 | 444,049 |
| 1971 | Riva Ridge | 2 | 9 | 7 | 0 | 0 | 503,263 |
| 1972 | Droll Role | 4 | 19 | 7 | 3 | 4 | 471,633 |
| 1973 | Secretariat | 3 | 12 | 9 | 2 | 1 | 860,404 |
| 1974 | Chris Evert | 3 | 8 | 5 | 1 | 2 | 551,063 |
| 1975 | Foolish Pleasure | 3 | 11 | 5 | 4 | 1 | 716,278 |
| 1976 | Forego | 6 | 8 | 6 | 1 | 1 | 401,701 |
| 1977 | Seattle Slew | 3 | 7 | 6 | 0 | 1 | 641,370 |
| 1978 | Affirmed | 3 | 11 | 8 | 2 | 0 | 901,541 |
| 1979 | Spectacular Bid | 3 | 12 | 10 | 1 | 1 | 1,279,334 |
| 1980 | Temperence Hill | 3 | 17 | 8 | 3 | 1 | 1,130,452 |
| 1981 | John Henry | 6 | 10 | 8 | 0 | 0 | 1,798,030 |
| 1982 | Perrault | 5 | 8 | 4 | 1 | 2 | 1,197,400 |
| 1983 | All Along | 4 | 7 | 4 | 1 | 1 | 2,138,963 |

## Horse—Money Won (Cont.)

| Year | Horse | Age | Starts | 1st | 2nd | 3rd | Winnings ($) |
|------|-------|-----|--------|-----|-----|-----|--------------|
| 1984 | Slew o'Gold | 4 | 6 | 5 | 1 | 0 | 2,627,944 |
| 1985 | Spend A Buck | 3 | 7 | 5 | 1 | 1 | 3,552,704 |
| 1986 | Snow Chief | 3 | 9 | 6 | 1 | 1 | 1,875,200 |
| 1987 | Alysheba | 3 | 10 | 3 | 3 | 1 | 2,511,156 |
| 1988 | Alysheba | 4 | 9 | 7 | 1 | 0 | 3,808,600 |
| 1989 | Sunday Silence | 3 | 9 | 7 | 2 | 0 | 4,578,454 |
| 1990 | Unbridled | 3 | 11 | 4 | 3 | 2 | 3,718,149 |
| 1991 | Dance Smartly | 3 | 8 | 8 | 0 | 0 | 2,876,821 |
| 1992 | A.P. Indy | 3 | 7 | 5 | 0 | 1 | 2,622,560 |
| 1993 | Kotashaan | 3 | 10 | 6 | 3 | 0 | 2,619,014 |
| 1994 | Paradise Creek | 5 | 11 | 8 | 2 | 1 | 2,610,187 |
| 1995 | Cigar | 5 | 10 | 10 | 0 | 0 | 4,819,800 |
| 1996 | Cigar | 6 | 8 | 5 | 2 | 1 | 4,910,000 |
| 1997 | Skip Away | 4 | 11 | 4 | 5 | 2 | 4,089,000 |
| 1998 | Silver Charm | 4 | 9 | 6 | 2 | 0 | 4,696,506 |
| 1999 | Almutawakel | 4 | 4 | 1 | 1 | 1 | 3,290,000 |
| 2000 | Dubai Millennium | 4 | 1 | 1 | 0 | 0 | 3,600,000 |

## Trainer—Money Won

| Year | Trainer | Wins | Winnings ($) | Year | Trainer | Wins | Winnings ($) |
|------|---------|------|--------------|------|---------|------|--------------|
| 1908 | James Rowe, Sr. | 50 | 284,335 | 1955 | Sunny Jim Fitzsimmons | 66 | 1,270,055 |
| 1909 | Sam Hildreth | 73 | 123,942 | 1956 | Willie Molter | 142 | 1,227,402 |
| 1910 | Sam Hildreth | 84 | 148,010 | 1957 | Jimmy Jones | 70 | 1,150,910 |
| 1911 | Sam Hildreth | 67 | 49,418 | 1958 | Willie Molter | 69 | 1,116,544 |
| 1912 | John F. Schorr | 63 | 58,110 | 1959 | Willie Molter | 71 | 847,290 |
| 1913 | James Rowe, Sr. | 18 | 45,936 | 1960 | Hirsch Jacobs | 97 | 748,349 |
| 1914 | R. C. Benson | 45 | 59,315 | 1961 | Jimmy Jones | 62 | 759,856 |
| 1915 | James Rowe, Sr. | 19 | 75,596 | 1962 | Mesh Tenney | 58 | 1,099,474 |
| 1916 | Sam Hildreth | 39 | 70,950 | 1963 | Mesh Tenney | 40 | 860,703 |
| 1917 | Sam Hildreth | 23 | 61,698 | 1964 | Bill Winfrey | 61 | 1,350,534 |
| 1918 | H. Guy Bedwell | 53 | 80,296 | 1965 | Hirsch Jacobs | 91 | 1,331,628 |
| 1919 | H. Guy Bedwell | 63 | 208,728 | 1966 | Eddie Neloy | 93 | 2,456,250 |
| 1920 | L. Feustal | 22 | 186,087 | 1967 | Eddie Neloy | 72 | 1,776,089 |
| 1921 | Sam Hildreth | 85 | 262,768 | 1968 | Eddie Neloy | 52 | 1,233,101 |
| 1922 | Sam Hildreth | 74 | 247,014 | 1969 | Elliott Burch | 26 | 1,067,936 |
| 1923 | Sam Hildreth | 75 | 392,124 | 1970 | Charlie Whittingham | 82 | 1,302,354 |
| 1924 | Sam Hildreth | 77 | 255,608 | 1971 | Charlie Whittingham | 77 | 1,737,115 |
| 1925 | G. R. Tompkins | 30 | 199,245 | 1972 | Charlie Whittingham | 79 | 1,734,020 |
| 1926 | Scott P. Harlan | 21 | 205,681 | 1973 | Charlie Whittingham | 85 | 1,865,385 |
| 1927 | W. H. Bringloe | 63 | 216,563 | 1974 | Pancho Martin | 166 | 2,408,419 |
| 1928 | John F. Schorr | 65 | 258,425 | 1975 | Charlie Whittingham | 93 | 2,437,244 |
| 1929 | James Rowe, Jr. | 25 | 314,881 | 1976 | Jack Van Berg | 496 | 2,976,196 |
| 1930 | Sunny Jim Fitzsimmons | 47 | 397,355 | 1977 | Laz Barrera | 127 | 2,715,848 |
| 1931 | Big Jim Healey | 33 | 297,300 | 1978 | Laz Barrera | 100 | 3,307,164 |
| 1932 | Sunny Jim Fitzsimmons | 68 | 266,650 | 1979 | Laz Barrera | 98 | 3,608,517 |
| 1933 | Humming Bob Smith | 53 | 135,720 | 1980 | Laz Barrera | 99 | 2,969,151 |
| 1934 | Humming Bob Smith | 43 | 249,938 | 1981 | Charlie Whittingham | 74 | 3,993,300 |
| 1935 | Bud Stotler | 87 | 303,005 | 1982 | Charlie Whittingham | 63 | 4,587,457 |
| 1936 | Sunny Jim Fitzsimmons | 42 | 193,415 | 1983 | D. Wayne Lukas | 78 | 4,267,261 |
| 1937 | Robert McGarvey | 46 | 209,925 | 1984 | D. Wayne Lukas | 131 | 5,835,921 |
| 1938 | Earl Sande | 15 | 226,495 | 1985 | D. Wayne Lukas | 218 | 11,155,188 |
| 1939 | Sunny Jim Fitzsimmons | 45 | 266,205 | 1986 | D. Wayne Lukas | 259 | 12,345,180 |
| 1940 | Silent Tom Smith | 14 | 269,200 | 1987 | D. Wayne Lukas | 343 | 17,502,110 |
| 1941 | Plain Ben Jones | 70 | 475,318 | 1988 | D. Wayne Lukas | 318 | 17,842,358 |
| 1942 | John M. Gaver Sr. | 48 | 406,547 | 1989 | D. Wayne Lukas | 305 | 16,103,998 |
| 1943 | Plain Ben Jones | 73 | 267,915 | 1990 | D. Wayne Lukas | 267 | 14,508,871 |
| 1944 | Plain Ben Jones | 60 | 601,660 | 1991 | D. Wayne Lukas | 289 | 15,942,223 |
| 1945 | Silent Tom Smith | 52 | 510,655 | 1992 | D. Wayne Lukas | 230 | 9,806,436 |
| 1946 | Hirsch Jacobs | 99 | 560,077 | 1993 | Robert Frankel | 79 | 8,883,252 |
| 1947 | Jimmy Jones | 85 | 1,334,805 | 1994 | D. Wayne Lukas | 147 | 9,247,457 |
| 1948 | Jimmy Jones | 81 | 1,118,670 | 1995 | D. Wayne Lukas | 194 | 12,842,865 |
| 1949 | Jimmy Jones | 76 | 978,587 | 1996 | D. Wayne Lukas | 192 | 15,966,344 |
| 1950 | Preston Burch | 96 | 637,754 | 1997 | D. Wayne Lukas | 175 | 10,338,957 |
| 1951 | John M. Gaver Sr. | 42 | 616,392 | 1998 | Bob Baffert | 139 | 15,000,870 |
| 1952 | Plain Ben Jones | 29 | 662,137 | 1999 | Bob Baffert | 169 | 16,934,607 |
| 1953 | Harry Trotsek | 54 | 1,028,873 | 2000 | Bob Baffert | 146 | 11,831,605 |
| 1954 | Willie Molter | 136 | 1,107,860 | | | | |

## Jockey—Money Won

| Year | Jockey | Mts | 1st | 2nd | 3rd | Pct | Winnings ($) |
|------|--------|-----|-----|-----|-----|-----|--------------|
| 1919 | John Loftus | 177 | 65 | 36 | 24 | .37 | 252,707 |
| 1920 | Clarence Kummer | 353 | 87 | 79 | 48 | .25 | 292,376 |
| 1921 | Earl Sande | 340 | 112 | 69 | 59 | .33 | 263,043 |
| 1922 | Albert Johnson | 297 | 43 | 57 | 40 | .14 | 345,054 |
| 1923 | Earl Sande | 430 | 122 | 89 | 79 | .28 | 569,394 |
| 1924 | Ivan Parke | 844 | 205 | 175 | 121 | .24 | 290,395 |
| 1925 | Laverne Fator | 315 | 81 | 54 | 44 | .26 | 305,775 |
| 1926 | Laverne Fator | 511 | 143 | 90 | 86 | .28 | 361,435 |
| 1927 | Earl Sande | 179 | 49 | 33 | 19 | .27 | 277,877 |
| 1928 | Pony McAtee | 235 | 55 | 43 | 25 | .23 | 301,295 |
| 1929 | Mack Garner | 274 | 57 | 39 | 33 | .21 | 314,975 |
| 1930 | Sonny Workman | 571 | 152 | 88 | 79 | .27 | 420,438 |
| 1931 | Charles Kurtsinger | 519 | 93 | 82 | 79 | .18 | 392,095 |
| 1932 | Sonny Workman | 378 | 87 | 48 | 55 | .23 | 385,070 |
| 1933 | Robert Jones | 471 | 63 | 57 | 70 | .13 | 226,285 |
| 1934 | Wayne D. Wright | 919 | 174 | 154 | 114 | .19 | 287,185 |
| 1935 | Silvio Coucci | 749 | 141 | 125 | 103 | .19 | 319,760 |
| 1936 | Wayne D. Wright | 670 | 100 | 102 | 73 | .15 | 264,000 |
| 1937 | Charles Kurtsinger | 765 | 120 | 94 | 106 | .16 | 384,202 |
| 1938 | Nick Wall | 658 | 97 | 94 | 82 | .15 | 385,161 |
| 1939 | Basil James | 904 | 191 | 165 | 105 | .21 | 353,333 |
| 1940 | Eddie Arcaro | 783 | 132 | 143 | 112 | .17 | 343,661 |
| 1941 | Don Meade | 1,164 | 210 | 185 | 158 | .18 | 398,627 |
| 1942 | Eddie Arcaro | 687 | 123 | 97 | 89 | .18 | 481,949 |
| 1943 | John Longden | 871 | 173 | 140 | 121 | .20 | 573,276 |
| 1944 | Ted Atkinson | 1,539 | 287 | 231 | 213 | .19 | 899,101 |
| 1945 | John Longden | 778 | 180 | 112 | 100 | .23 | 981,977 |
| 1946 | Ted Atkinson | 1,377 | 233 | 213 | 173 | .17 | 1,036,825 |
| 1947 | Douglas Dodson | 646 | 141 | 100 | 75 | .22 | 1,429,949 |
| 1948 | Eddie Arcaro | 726 | 188 | 108 | 98 | .26 | 1,686,230 |
| 1949 | Steve Brooks | 906 | 209 | 172 | 110 | .23 | 1,316,817 |
| 1950 | Eddie Arcaro | 888 | 195 | 153 | 144 | .22 | 1,410,160 |
| 1951 | Bill Shoemaker | 1,161 | 257 | 197 | 161 | .22 | 1,329,890 |
| 1952 | Eddie Arcaro | 807 | 188 | 122 | 109 | .23 | 1,859,591 |
| 1953 | Bill Shoemaker | 1,683 | 485 | 302 | 210 | .29 | 1,784,187 |
| 1954 | Bill Shoemaker | 1,251 | 380 | 221 | 142 | .30 | 1,876,760 |
| 1955 | Eddie Arcaro | 820 | 158 | 126 | 108 | .19 | 1,864,796 |
| 1956 | Bill Hartack | 1,387 | 347 | 252 | 184 | .25 | 2,343,955 |
| 1957 | Bill Hartack | 1,238 | 341 | 208 | 178 | .28 | 3,060,501 |
| 1958 | Bill Shoemaker | 1,133 | 300 | 185 | 137 | .26 | 2,961,693 |
| 1959 | Bill Shoemaker | 1,285 | 347 | 230 | 159 | .27 | 2,843,133 |
| 1960 | Bill Shoemaker | 1,227 | 274 | 196 | 158 | .22 | 2,123,961 |
| 1961 | Bill Shoemaker | 1,256 | 304 | 186 | 175 | .24 | 2,690,819 |
| 1962 | Bill Shoemaker | 1,126 | 311 | 156 | 128 | .28 | 2,916,844 |
| 1963 | Bill Shoemaker | 1,203 | 271 | 193 | 137 | .22 | 2,526,925 |
| 1964 | Bill Shoemaker | 1,056 | 246 | 147 | 133 | .23 | 2,649,553 |
| 1965 | Braulio Baeza | 1,245 | 270 | 200 | 201 | .22 | 2,582,702 |
| 1966 | Braulio Baeza | 1,341 | 298 | ??? | 190 | .22 | 2,951,022 |
| 1967 | Braulio Baeza | 1,064 | 256 | 184 | 127 | .24 | 3,088,888 |
| 1968 | Braulio Baeza | 1,089 | 201 | 184 | 145 | .18 | 2,835,108 |
| 1969 | Jorge Velasquez | 1,442 | 258 | 230 | 204 | .18 | 2,542,315 |
| 1970 | Laffit Pincay Jr. | 1,328 | 269 | 208 | 187 | .20 | 2,626,526 |
| 1971 | Laffit Pincay Jr. | 1,627 | 380 | 288 | 214 | .23 | 3,784,377 |
| 1972 | Laffit Pincay Jr. | 1,388 | 289 | 215 | 205 | .21 | 3,225,827 |
| 1973 | Laffit Pincay Jr. | 1,444 | 350 | 254 | 209 | .24 | 4,093,492 |
| 1974 | Laffit Pincay Jr. | 1,278 | 341 | 227 | 180 | .27 | 4,251,060 |
| 1975 | Braulio Baeza | 1,190 | 196 | 208 | 180 | .16 | 3,674,398 |
| 1976 | Angel Cordero Jr. | 1,534 | 274 | 273 | 235 | .18 | 4,709,500 |
| 1977 | Steve Cauthen | 2,075 | 487 | 345 | 304 | .23 | 6,151,750 |
| 1978 | Darrel McHargue | 1,762 | 375 | 294 | 263 | .21 | 6,188,353 |
| 1979 | Laffit Pincay Jr. | 1,708 | 420 | 302 | 261 | .25 | 8,183,535 |
| 1980 | Chris McCarron | 1,964 | 405 | 318 | 282 | .20 | 7,666,100 |
| 1981 | Chris McCarron | 1,494 | 326 | 251 | 207 | .22 | 8,397,604 |
| 1982 | Angel Cordero Jr. | 1,838 | 397 | 338 | 227 | .22 | 9,702,520 |
| 1983 | Angel Cordero Jr. | 1,792 | 362 | 296 | 237 | .20 | 10,116,807 |
| 1984 | Chris McCarron | 1,565 | 356 | 276 | 218 | .23 | 12,038,213 |
| 1985 | Laffit Pincay Jr. | 1,409 | 289 | 246 | 183 | .21 | 13,415,049 |

## Jockey—Money Won *(Cont.)*

| Year | Jockey | Mts | 1st | 2nd | 3rd | Pct | Winnings ($) |
|---|---|---|---|---|---|---|---|
| 1986 | Jose Santos | 1,636 | 329 | 237 | 222 | .20 | 11,329,297 |
| 1987 | Jose Santos | 1,639 | 305 | 268 | 208 | .19 | 12,407,355 |
| 1988 | Jose Santos | 1,867 | 370 | 287 | 265 | .20 | 14,877,298 |
| 1989 | Jose Santos | 1,459 | 285 | 238 | 220 | .20 | 13,847,003 |
| 1990 | Gary Stevens | 1,504 | 283 | 245 | 202 | .19 | 13,881,198 |
| 1991 | Chris McCarron | 1,440 | 265 | 228 | 206 | .18 | 14,441,083 |
| 1992 | Kent Desormeaux | 1,568 | 361 | 260 | 208 | .23 | 14,193,006 |
| 1993 | Mike Smith | 1,510 | 343 | 235 | 214 | .23 | 14,008,148 |
| 1994 | Mike Smith | 1,484 | 317 | 250 | 196 | .21 | 15,979,820 |
| 1995 | Jerry Bailey | 1,265 | 287 | 193 | 144 | .23 | 16,308,230 |
| 1996 | Jerry Bailey | 1,187 | 298 | 189 | 165 | .25 | 19,465,376 |
| 1997 | Jerry Bailey | 1,143 | 272 | 186 | 178 | .26 | 18,260,553 |
| 1998 | Gary Stevens | 869 | 178 | 145 | 122 | .20 | 19,358,840 |
| 1999 | Pat Day | 1,265 | 254 | 209 | 209 | .20 | 18,092,845 |
| 2000 | Pat Day | 1,219 | 267 | 206 | 186 | .22 | 17,479,838 |

## Jockey—Races Won

| Year | Jockey | Mts | 1st | 2nd | 3rd | Pct |
|---|---|---|---|---|---|---|
| 1895 | J. Perkins | 762 | 192 | 177 | 129 | .25 |
| 1896 | J. Scherrer | 1,093 | 271 | 227 | 172 | .24 |
| 1897 | H. Martin | 803 | 173 | 152 | 116 | .21 |
| 1898 | T. Burns | 973 | 277 | 213 | 149 | .28 |
| 1899 | T. Burns | 1,064 | 273 | 173 | 266 | .26 |
| 1900 | C. Mitchell | 874 | 195 | 140 | 139 | .23 |
| 1901 | W. O'Connor | 1,047 | 253 | 221 | 192 | .24 |
| 1902 | J. Ranch | 1,069 | 276 | 205 | 181 | .26 |
| 1903 | G.C. Fuller | 918 | 229 | 152 | 122 | .25 |
| 1904 | E. Hildebrand | 1,169 | 297 | 230 | 171 | .25 |
| 1905 | D. Nicol | 861 | 221 | 143 | 136 | .26 |
| 1906 | W. Miller | 1,384 | 388 | 300 | 199 | .28 |
| 1907 | W. Miller | 1,194 | 334 | 226 | 170 | .28 |
| 1908 | V. Powers | 1,260 | 324 | 204 | 185 | .26 |
| 1909 | V. Powers | 704 | 173 | 121 | 114 | .25 |
| 1910 | G. Garner | 947 | 200 | 188 | 153 | .20 |
| 1911 | T. Koerner | 813 | 162 | 133 | 112 | .20 |
| 1912 | P. Hill | 967 | 168 | 141 | 129 | .17 |
| 1913 | M. Buxton | 887 | 146 | 131 | 136 | .16 |
| 1914 | J. McTaggart | 787 | 157 | 132 | 106 | .20 |
| 1915 | M. Garner | 775 | 151 | 118 | 90 | .19 |
| 1916 | F. Robinson | 791 | 178 | 131 | 124 | .23 |
| 1917 | W. Crump | 803 | 151 | 140 | 101 | .19 |
| 1918 | F. Robinson | 864 | 185 | 140 | 108 | .21 |
| 1919 | C. Robinson | 896 | 190 | 140 | 126 | .21 |
| 1920 | J. Butwell | 721 | 152 | 129 | 139 | .21 |
| 1921 | C. Lang | 696 | 135 | 110 | 105 | .19 |
| 1922 | M. Fator | 859 | 188 | 153 | 116 | .22 |
| 1923 | I. Parke | 718 | 173 | 105 | 95 | .24 |
| 1924 | I. Parke | 844 | 205 | 175 | 121 | .24 |
| 1925 | A. Mortensen | 987 | 187 | 145 | 138 | .19 |
| 1926 | R. Jones | 1,172 | 190 | 163 | 152 | .16 |
| 1927 | L. Hardy | 1,130 | 207 | 192 | 151 | .18 |
| 1928 | J. Inzelone | 1,052 | 155 | 152 | 135 | .15 |
| 1929 | M. Knight | 871 | 149 | 132 | 133 | .17 |
| 1930 | H.R. Riley | 861 | 177 | 145 | 123 | .21 |
| 1931 | H. Roble | 1,174 | 173 | 173 | 155 | .15 |
| 1932 | J. Gilbert | 1,050 | 212 | 144 | 160 | .20 |
| 1933 | J. Westrope | 1,224 | 301 | 235 | 166 | .25 |
| 1934 | M. Peters | 1,045 | 221 | 179 | 147 | .21 |
| 1935 | C. Stevenson | 1,099 | 206 | 169 | 146 | .19 |
| 1936 | B. James | 1,106 | 245 | 195 | 161 | .22 |
| 1937 | J. Adams | 1,265 | 260 | 186 | 177 | .21 |
| 1938 | J. Longden | 1,150 | 236 | 168 | 171 | .21 |
| 1939 | D. Meade | 1,284 | 255 | 221 | 180 | .20 |
| 1940 | E. Dew | 1,377 | 287 | 201 | 180 | .21 |
| 1941 | D. Meade | 1,164 | 210 | 185 | 158 | .18 |
| 1942 | J. Adams | 1,120 | 245 | 185 | 150 | .22 |
| 1943 | J. Adams | 1,069 | 228 | 159 | 171 | .21 |

## Jockey—Races Won *(Cont.)*

| Year | Jockey | Mts | 1st | 2nd | 3rd | Pct |
|------|--------|-----|-----|-----|-----|-----|
| 1944 | T. Atkinson | 1,539 | 287 | 231 | 213 | .19 |
| 1945 | J.D. Jessop | 1,085 | 290 | 182 | 168 | .27 |
| 1946 | T. Atkinson | 1,377 | 233 | 213 | 173 | .17 |
| 1947 | J. Longden | 1,327 | 316 | 250 | 195 | .24 |
| 1948 | J. Longden | 1,197 | 319 | 233 | 161 | .27 |
| 1949 | G. Glisson | 1,347 | 270 | 217 | 181 | .20 |
| 1950 | W. Shoemaker | 1,640 | 388 | 266 | 230 | .24 |
| 1951 | C. Burr | 1,319 | 310 | 232 | 192 | .24 |
| 1952 | A. DeSpirito | 1,482 | 390 | 247 | 212 | .26 |
| 1953 | W. Shoemaker | 1,683 | 485 | 302 | 210 | .29 |
| 1954 | W. Shoemaker | 1,251 | 380 | 221 | 142 | .30 |
| 1955 | W. Hartack | 1,702 | 417 | 298 | 215 | .25 |
| 1956 | W. Hartack | 1,387 | 347 | 252 | 184 | .25 |
| 1957 | W. Hartack | 1,238 | 341 | 208 | 178 | .28 |
| 1958 | W. Shoemaker | 1,133 | 300 | 185 | 137 | .26 |
| 1959 | W. Shoemaker | 1,285 | 347 | 230 | 159 | .27 |
| 1960 | W. Hartack | 1,402 | 307 | 247 | 190 | .22 |
| 1961 | J. Sellers | 1,394 | 328 | 212 | 227 | .24 |
| 1962 | R. Ferraro | 1,755 | 352 | 252 | 226 | .20 |
| 1963 | W. Blum | 1,704 | 360 | 286 | 215 | .21 |
| 1964 | W. Blum | 1,577 | 324 | 274 | 170 | .21 |
| 1965 | J. Davidson | 1,582 | 319 | 228 | 190 | .20 |
| 1966 | A. Gomez | 996 | 318 | 173 | 142 | .32 |
| 1967 | J. Velasquez | 1,939 | 438 | 315 | 270 | .23 |
| 1968 | A. Cordero Jr. | 1,662 | 345 | 278 | 219 | .21 |
| 1969 | L. Snyder | 1,645 | 352 | 290 | 243 | .21 |
| 1970 | S. Hawley | 1,908 | 452 | 313 | 265 | .24 |
| 1971 | L Pincay Jr. | 1,627 | 380 | 288 | 214 | .23 |
| 1972 | S. Hawley | 1,381 | 367 | 269 | 200 | .27 |
| 1973 | S. Hawley | 1,925 | 515 | 336 | 292 | .27 |
| 1974 | C.J. McCarron | 2,199 | 546 | 392 | 297 | .25 |
| 1975 | C.J. McCarron | 2,194 | 458 | 389 | 305 | .21 |
| 1976 | S. Hawley | 1,637 | 413 | 245 | 201 | .25 |
| 1977 | S. Cauthen | 2,075 | 487 | 345 | 304 | .23 |
| 1978 | E. Delahoussaye | 1,666 | 384 | 285 | 238 | .23 |
| 1979 | D. Gall | 2,146 | 479 | 396 | 326 | .22 |
| 1980 | C.J. McCarron | 1,964 | 405 | 318 | 282 | .20 |
| 1981 | D. Gall | 1,917 | 376 | 305 | 297 | .20 |
| 1982 | Pat Day | 1,870 | 399 | 326 | 255 | .21 |
| 1983 | Pat Day | 1,725 | 454 | 321 | 251 | .26 |
| 1984 | Pat Day | 1,694 | 399 | 296 | 259 | .24 |
| 1985 | C.W. Antley | 2,335 | 469 | 371 | 288 | .20 |
| 1986 | Pat Day | 1,417 | 429 | 246 | 202 | .30 |
| 1987 | Kent Desormeaux | 2,207 | 450 | 370 | 294 | .28 |
| 1988 | Kent Desormeaux | 1,897 | 474 | 295 | 276 | .25 |
| 1989 | Kent Desormeaux | 2,312 | 598 | 385 | 309 | .25 |
| 1990 | Pat Day | 1,421 | 364 | 265 | 222 | .26 |
| 1991 | Pat Day | 1,405 | 430 | 256 | 213 | .31 |
| 1992 | Russell Baze | 1,691 | 433 | 296 | 237 | .25 |
| 1993 | Russell Baze | 1,579 | 410 | 207 | 225 | .26 |
| 1994 | Russell Baze | 1,588 | 415 | 301 | 266 | .26 |
| 1995 | Russell Baze | 1,531 | 445 | 310 | 232 | .29 |
| 1996 | Russell Baze | 1,482 | 415 | 297 | 200 | .28 |
| 1997 | Edgar S. Prado | 2,037 | 533 | 384 | 308 | .26 |
| 1998 | Edgar S. Prado | 1,969 | 470 | 377 | 285 | .23 |
| 1999 | Edgar S. Prado | 1,902 | 402 | 307 | 276 | .21 |
| 2000 | Ramon Dominguez | 1,586 | 361 | 293 | 238 | .23 |

## Leading Jockeys—Career Records

| Jockey | Years Riding | Mts | 1st | 2nd | 3rd | Win Pct | Winnings ($) |
|---|---|---|---|---|---|---|---|
| Laffit Pincay Jr. | 37 | 47,813 | 9,412 | 7,684 | 6,543 | .197 | 231,644,024 |
| Bill Shoemaker (1990) | 42 | 40,350 | 8,833 | 6,136 | 4,987 | .219 | 123,375,524 |
| Pat Day | 29 | 38,178 | 8,330 | 6,469 | 5,470 | .218 | 271,236,479 |
| Russell Baze | 28 | 37,050 | 7,901 | 6,118 | 5,285 | .213 | 115,388,176 |
| Dave Gall (1999) | 41 | 41,775 | 7,396 | 6,525 | 6,131 | .177 | 24,547,584 |
| Chris McCarron | 27 | 34,369 | 7,163 | 5,709 | 4,691 | .208 | 265,213,877 |
| Angel Cordero (1992) | 31 | 38,646 | 7,057 | 6,136 | 5,359 | .183 | 164,561,227 |
| Jorge Velasquez (1998) | 35 | 40,852 | 6,795 | 6,178 | 5,755 | .166 | 125,544,379 |
| Sandy Hawley (1998) | 31 | 31,455 | 6,449 | 4,825 | 4,159 | .205 | 88,681,292 |
| Eddie Delahoussaye | 32 | 39,324 | 6,392 | 5,708 | 5,599 | .163 | 194,130,574 |
| Larry Snyder (1994) | 35 | 35,681 | 6,388 | 5,030 | 3,440 | .179 | 47,207,289 |
| Carl Gambardella (1994) | 39 | 39,018 | 6,349 | 5,953 | 5,353 | .163 | 29,389,041 |
| Earlie Fires | 37 | 43,026 | 6,209 | 5,293 | 5,112 | .144 | 78,928,757 |
| John Longden (1966) | 40 | 32,413 | 6,032 | 4,914 | 4,273 | .186 | 24,665,800 |
| Jerry Bailey | 28 | 28,773 | 5,372 | 4,178 | 3,632 | .187 | 326,764,753 |
| Jacinto Vasquez (1998) | 38 | 37,390 | 5,231 | 4,721 | 4,513 | .140 | 80,764,853 |
| Ron Ardoin | 29 | 32,232 | 5,206 | 4,305 | 3,772 | .162 | 58,779,016 |
| Rick Wilson | 30 | 34,770 | 4,993 | 4,288 | 3,484 | .144 | 79,206,668 |
| Rodolfo Baez (1999) | 26 | 28,609 | 4,875 | 4,291 | 4,103 | .170 | 30,039,543 |
| Eddie Arcaro (1961) | 31 | 24,092 | 4,779 | 3,807 | 3,302 | .198 | 30,039,543 |
| Mario Pino | 22 | 29,983 | 4,701 | 4,329 | 4,087 | .157 | 69,494,173 |
| Gary Stevens | 27 | 26,227 | 4,657 | 4,160 | 3,763 | .178 | 204,121,184 |
| Don Brumfield (1989) | 37 | 33,223 | 4,573 | 4,076 | 3,758 | .138 | 43,567,861 |
| Steve Brooks (1975) | 34 | 30,330 | 4,451 | 4,219 | 3,658 | .147 | 18,239,817 |
| Eddie Maple (1998) | 31 | 33,974 | 4,398 | 4,516 | 4,335 | .129 | 105,338,573 |

Note: Records go through September 10, 1999, and include available statistics for races ridden in foreign countries. Figures in parentheses after jockey's name indicate last year in which he rode.

Leading jockeys courtesy of *National Thoroughbred Racing Association*.

## Horse Sense

Fusaichi Pegasus's first attempt at stud may have been with the Iris m,are Name of Love on Valentine's Day, but to the breeders at Kentucky's Ahford Farm, love had nothing to with it. Why? In June 2000 Ashford paid a recod $60 million for Fusaichi Pegasus, that year's Kentucky Derby winner, and has millions in potential profits riding on his ability to produce champions. In racing, it's usually about bloodlines. So if you've been inspired to follow the sport on online, a couple of breeding sites are appropriate places to start. **Bloodhorse.com** has links to the top farms around the country, a Horse Health section and an earnings list (updated daily) for the progeny of the leading sires of 2001. For pedigrees of the winners of every Triple Crown race since 1940 and every Breeders' Cup Classic, log onto **chef-de-race.com**, a site run by Steven A. Roman, a Ph.D in, of all things, chemistry.

If you're more interested in current runners, **equibase.com**'s Backstretch Buzz link provides daily news and notes from every major track in North America. You can also see charts from every race posted as quickly as 20 minutes after the finish, along with concise postrace comments. The redesigned **drf.com** (the official site of the *Daily Racing Form*) has a nifty past performance tutorial that enables you to decipher all those confusing numbers in a racing program. (To use the tutorial, you need a flash plug-in.)

By the way, Fusaichi Pegasus, whose stud fee is $150,000, had 13 mares in foal in June 2001. But future bettor beware. "There are no guarantees," said Ron Mitchell, editor of bloodhorse.com. "All elements off this industry are at the mercy of the forces of nature."
—John O'Keefe

## HORSES

Ack Ack (1986, 1966)
Affectionately (1989, 1960)
Affirmed (1980, 1975)
All Along (1990, 1979)
Alsab (1976, 1939)
Alydar (1989, 1975)
Alysheba (1993, 1984)
American Eclipse (1970, 1814)
A.P. Indy (2000, 1989)
Armed (1963, 1941)
Artful (1956, 1902)
Arts and Letters (1994, 1966)
Assault (1964, 1943)
Battleship (1969, 1927)
Bayakoa (1998, 1984)
Bed o' Roses (1976, 1947)
Beldame (1956, 1901)
Ben Brush (1955, 1893)
Bewitch (1977, 1945)
Bimelech (1990, 1937)
Black Gold (1989, 1921)
Black Helen (1991, 1932)
Blue Larkspur (1957, 1926)
Bold 'n Determined (1997, 1977)
Bold Ruler (1973, 1954)
Bon Nouvel (1976, 1960)
Boston (1955, 1833)
Broomstick (1956, 1901)
Buckpasser (1970, 1963)
Busher (1964, 1942)
Bushranger (1967, 1930)
Cafe Prince (1985, 1970)
Carry Back (1975, 1958)
Cavalcade (1993, 1931)
Challedon (1977, 1936)
Chris Evert (1988, 1971)
Cicada (1967, 1959)
Citation (1959, 1945)
Coaltown (1983, 1945)
Colin (1956, 1905)
Commando (1956, 1898)
Count Fleet (1961, 1940)
Crusader (1995, 1923)
Dahlia (1981, 1970)
Damascus (1974, 1964)
Dark Mirage (1974, 1965)
Davona Dale (1985, 1976)
Desert Vixen (1979, 1970)
Devil Diver (1980, 1939)
Discovery (1969, 1931)
Domino (1955, 1891)
Dr. Fager (1971, 1964)
Easy Goer (1997, 1986)
Eight Thirty (1994, 1936)
Elkridge (1966, 1938)

Emperor of Norfolk (1988, 1885)
Equipoise (1957, 1928)
Exceller (1999, 1973)
Exterminator (1957, 1915)
Fairmount (1985, 1921)
Fair Play (1956, 1905)
Fashion (1980, 1837)
Firenze (1981, 1884)
Flatterer (1994, 1979)
Foolish Pleasure (1995, 1972)
Forego (1979, 1970)
Fort Marcy (1998, 1964)
Gallant Bloom (1977, 1966)
Gallant Fox (1957, 1927)
Gallant Man (1987, 1954)
Gallorette (1962, 1942)
Gamely (1980, 1964)
Genuine Risk (1986, 1977)
Go For Wand (1996, 1987)
Good and Plenty (1956, 1900)
Grandville (1997, 1933)
Grey Lag (1957, 1918)
Gun Bow (1999, 1960)
Hamburg (1986, 1895)
Hanover (1955, 1884)
Henry of Navarre (1985, 1891)
Hill Prince (1991, 1947)
Hindoo (1955, 1878)
Holy Bull (2001, 1991)
Imp (1965, 1894)
Jay Trump (1971, 1957)
John Henry (1990, 1975)
Johnstown (1992, 1936)
Jolly Roger (1965, 1922)
Kelso (1967, 1957)
Kentucky (1983, 1861)
Kingston (1955, 1884)
Lady's Secret (1992, 1982)
La Prevoyante (1995, 1970)
L'Escargot (1977, 1963)
Lexington (1955, 1850)
Longfellow (1971, 1867)
Luke Blackburn (1956, 1877)
Majestic Prince (1988, 1966)
Man o' War (1957, 1917)
Maskette (2001, 1908)
Miesque (1999, 1984)
Miss Woodford (1967, 1880)
Myrtlewood (1979, 1932)
Nashua (1965, 1952)
Native Dancer (1963, 1950)
Native Diver (1978, 1959)
Needles (2000, 1953)
Neji (1966, 1950)
Northern Dancer (1976, 1961)

Oedipus (1978, 1946)
Old Rosebud (1968, 1911)
Omaha (1965, 1932)
Pan Zareta (1972, 1910)
Parole (1984, 1873)
Paseana (2001, 1987)
Personal Ensign (1993, 1984)
Peter Pan (1956, 1904)
Princess Doreen (1982, 1921)
Princess Rooney (1991, 1980)
Real Delight (1987, 1949)
Regret (1957, 1912)
Reigh Count (1978, 1923)
Riva Ridge (1998, 1969)
Roamer (1981, 1911)
Roseben (1956, 1901)
Round Table (1972, 1954)
Ruffian (1976, 1972)
Ruthless (1975, 1864)
Salvator (1955, 1886)
Sarazen (1957, 1921)
Seabiscuit (1958, 1933)
Searching (1978, 1952)
Seattle Slew (1981, 1974)
Secretariat (1974, 1970)
Shuvee (1975, 1966)
Silver Spoon (1978, 1956)
Sir Archy (1955, 1805)
Sir Barton (1957, 1916)
Slew o' Gold (1992, 1980)
Spectacular Bid (1982, 1976)
Stymie (1975, 1941)
Sun Beau (1996, 1925)
Sunday Silence (1996, 1986)
Susan's Girl (1976, 1969)
Swaps (1966, 1952)
Sword Dancer (1977, 1956)
Sysonby (1956, 1902)
Ta Wee (1994, 1967)
Ten Broeck (1982, 1872)
Tim Tam (1985, 1955)
Tom Fool (1960, 1949)
Top Flight (1966, 1929)
Tosmah (1984, 1961)
Twenty Grand (1957, 1928)
Twilight Tear (1963, 1941)
Two Lea (1982, 1946)
War Admiral (1958, 1934)
Whirlaway (1959, 1938)
Whisk Broom II (1979, 1907)
Winning Colors (2000, 1985)
Zaccio (1990, 1976)
Zev (1983, 1920)

Note: Years of election and foaling in parentheses.

# HARNESS RACING

## Major Races

### Hambletonian

| Year | Winner | Driver | Year | Winner | Driver |
|------|--------|--------|------|--------|--------|
| 1926 | Guy McKinney | Nat Ray | 1964 | Ayres | J. Simpson Sr. |
| 1927 | Iosola's Worthy | Marvin Childs | 1965 | Egyptian Candor | Del Cameron |
| 1928 | Spenser | W. H. Leese | 1966 | Kerry Way | Frank Ervin |
| 1929 | Walter Dear | Walter Cox | 1967 | Speedy Streak | Del Cameron |
| 1930 | Hanover's Bertha | Tom Berry | 1968 | Nevele Pride | Stanley Dancer |
| 1931 | Calumet Butler | R. D. McMahon | 1969 | Lindy's Pride | H. Beissinger |
| 1932 | The Marchioness | William Caton | 1970 | Timothy T. | J. Simpson Jr. |
| 1933 | Mary Reynolds | Ben White | 1971 | Speedy Crown | H. Beissinger |
| 1934 | Lord Jim | Doc Parshall | 1972 | Super Bowl | Stanley Dancer |
| 1935 | Greyhound | Sep Palin | 1973 | Flirth | Ralph Baldwin |
| 1936 | Rosalind | Ben White | 1974 | Christopher T. | Bill Haughton |
| 1937 | Shirley Hanover | Henry Thomas | 1975 | Bonefish | Stanley Dancer |
| 1938 | McLin Hanover | Henry Thomas | 1976 | Steve Lobell | Bill Haughton |
| 1939 | Peter Astra | Doc Parshall | 1977 | Green Speed | Bill Haughton |
| 1940 | Spencer Scott | Fred Egan | 1978 | Speedy Somolli | H. Beissinger |
| 1941 | Bill Gallon | Lee Smith | 1979 | Legend Hanover | George Sholty |
| 1942 | The Ambassador | Ben White | 1980 | Burgomeister | Bill Haughton |
| 1943 | Volo Song | Ben White | 1981 | Shiaway St. Pat | Ray Remmen |
| 1944 | Yankee Maid | Henry Thomas | 1982 | Speed Bowl | Tom Haughton |
| 1945 | Titan Hanover | H. Pownall Sr. | 1983 | Duenna | Stanley Dancer |
| 1946 | Chestertown | Thomas Berry | 1984 | Historic Freight | Ben Webster |
| 1947 | Hoot Mon | Sep Palin | 1985 | Prakas | Bill O'Donnell |
| 1948 | Demon Hanover | Harrison Hoyt | 1986 | Nuclear Kosmos | Ulf Thoresen |
| 1949 | Miss Tilly | Fred Egan | 1987 | Mack Lobell | John Campbell |
| 1950 | Lusty Song | Del Miller | 1988 | Armbro Goal | John Campbell |
| 1951 | Mainliner | Guy Crippen | 1989 | Park Ave. Joe/Probe* | R. Waples/B. Fahy |
| 1952 | Sharp Note | Bion Shively | 1990 | Harmonious | John Campbell |
| 1953 | Helicopter | Harry Harvey | 1991 | Giant Victory | Jack Moiseyev |
| 1954 | Newport Dream | Del Cameron | 1992 | Alf Palema | Mickey McNichol |
| 1955 | Scott Frost | Joe O'Brien | 1993 | American Winner | Ron Pierce |
| 1956 | The Intruder | Ned Bower | 1994 | Victory Dream | Michel Lachance |
| 1957 | Hickory Smoke | J. Simpson Sr. | 1995 | Tagliabue | John Campbell |
| 1958 | Emily's Pride | Flave Nipe | 1996 | Continentalvictory | Michel Lachance |
| 1959 | Diller Hanover | Frank Ervin | 1997 | Malabar Man | Mal Burroughs |
| 1960 | Blaze Hanover | Joe O'Brien | 1998 | Muscles Yankee | John Campbell |
| 1961 | Harlan Dean | James Arthur | 1999 | Self Possessed | Michel Lachance |
| 1962 | A. C.'s Viking | Sanders Russell | 2000 | Yankee Paco | T.J. Ritchie |
| 1963 | Speedy Scot | Ralph Baldwin | 2001 | Scarlet Knight | Stefan Melander |

*Park Avenue Joe and Probe dead-heated for win. Park Avenue finished first in the summary 2-1-1 to Probe's 1-9-1 finish.
Note: Run at 1 mile since 1947.

## Little Brown Jug

| Year | Winner | Driver |
|------|--------|--------|
| 1946 | Ensign Hanover | Wayne Smart |
| 1947 | Forbes Chief | Del Cameron |
| 1948 | Knight Dream | Frank Safford |
| 1949 | Good Time | Frank Ervin |
| 1950 | Dudley Hanover | Del Miller |
| 1951 | Tar Heel | Del Cameron |
| 1952 | Meadow Rice | Wayne Smart |
| 1953 | Keystoner | Frank Ervin |
| 1954 | Adios Harry | Morris MacDonald |
| 1955 | Quick Chief | Bill Haughton |
| 1956 | Noble Adios | John Simpson Sr. |
| 1957 | Torpid | John Simpso Sr. |
| 1958 | Shadow Wave | Joe O'Brien |
| 1959 | Adios Butler | Clint Hodgins |
| 1960 | Bullet Hanover | John Simpson Sr. |
| 1961 | Henry T. Adios | Stanley Dancer |
| 1962 | Lehigh Hanover | Stanley Dancer |
| 1963 | Overtrick | John Patterson |
| 1964 | Vicar Hanover | Bill Haughton |
| 1965 | Bret Hanover | Frank Ervin |
| 1966 | Romeo Hanover | George Sholty |
| 1967 | Best of All | James Hackett |
| 1968 | Rum Customer | Bill Haughton |
| 1969 | Laverne Hanover | Bill Haughton |
| 1970 | Most Happy Fella | Stanley Dancer |
| 1971 | Nansemond | Herve Filion |
| 1972 | Strike Out | Keith Waples |
| 1973 | Melvin's Woe | Joe O'Brien |
| 1974 | Armbro Omaha | Bill Haughton |
| 1975 | Seatrain | Ben Webster |
| 1976 | Keystone Ore | Stanley Dancer |
| 1977 | Governor Skipper | John Chapman |
| 1978 | Happy Escort | William Popfinger |
| 1979 | Hot Hitter | Herve Filion |
| 1980 | Niatross | Clint Galbraith |
| 1981 | Fan Hanover | Glen Garnsey |
| 1982 | Merger | John Campbell |
| 1983 | Ralph Hanover | Ron Waples |
| 1984 | Colt Fortysix | Chris Boring |
| 1985 | Nihilator | Bill O'Donnell |
| 1986 | Barberry Spur | Bill O'Donnell |
| 1987 | Jaguar Spur | Dick Stillings |
| 1988 | B. J. Scoot | Michel Lachance |
| 1989 | Goalie Jeff | Michel Lachance |
| 1990 | Beach Towel | Ray Remmen |
| 1991 | Precious Bunny | Jack Moiseye |
| 1992 | Fake Left | Ron Waples |
| 1993 | Life Sign | John Campbell |
| 1994 | Magical Mike | Michel Lachance |
| 1995 | Nick's Fantasy | John Campbell |
| 1996 | Armbro Operative | Jack Moiseyev |
| 1997 | Western Dreamer | Michel Lachance |
| 1998 | Shady Character | Ron Pierce |
| 1999 | Blissful Hall | Ron Pierce |
| 2000 | Astreos | Chris Christoforou |
| 2001 | Bettor's Delight | Michel Lachance |

## Point Blunted

The racing career of the most captivating 3-year-old since the glory days of Secretariat, Seattle Slew and Affirmed versus Alydar ended in late August 2001 because of a strained tendon in his left front leg. Although Point Given missed the Triple Crown by running fifth in the 2001 Kentucky Derby, the towering chestnut largely atoned for that failure by winning all four of his subsequent starts: the Preakness, the Belmont, the Haskell Invitational and six days before his sudden retirement, the Travers."This horse was on the edge of greatness," said his trainer, Bob Baffert, on Aug. 31. "I feel cheated that we didn't get to see his best."

Point Given's premature trip to the stud farm was especially untimely because he'd emerged as a 3-year-old superstar, the kind of draw racing most covets—and desperately needs. TV ratings for the Triple Crown rose considerably in the spring of 2001 thanks to the series' switch from ABC to NBC, which used the races as lead-ins for its NBA playoff telecasts. Point Given's romp parlayed that added exposure into attendance records when he ran. He helped attract 73,857 to the Belmont Stakes, the biggest crowd ever for a Belmont in which the Triple Crown was not on the line. Monmouth Park officials so badly wanted Point Given in the Haskell that they boosted the purse by $500,000, to $1.5 million; they were rewarded when a throng of 47,127 showed up, breaking a 39-year-old track mark. At Saratoga three weeks later 60,486 fans turned out to see Point Given run in the Travers, a record for that race. "It's like when I was a kid and you got to see Mantle play centerfield," said Robert Kulina, the general manager at Monmouth. "You need superhorses to draw new fans."

In 1999 Charismatic, the long-shot winner of that year's Derby and Preakness, was on the verge of the most unlikely thoroughbred success story since Seabiscuit, only to shatter his left front leg in the homestretch of the Belmont. The injury to Point Given is a similarly painful setback. "Superstars such as Point Given bring out the casual fans," said Barry Schwartz, chairman of the New York Racing Association. "There's no question it's a big blow."

—Mark Beech

## Breeders' Crown

### 1984

| Div | Winner | Driver |
|-----|--------|--------|
| 2PC | Dragon's Lair | Jeff Mallet |
| 2PF | Amneris | John Campbell |
| 3PC | Troublemaker | Bill O'Donnell |
| 3PF | Naughty But Nice | Tommy Haughton |
| 2TC | Workaholic | Berndt Lindstedt |
| 2TF | Conifer | George Sholty |
| 3TC | Baltic Speed | Jan Nordin |
| 3TF | Fancy Crown | Bill O'Donnell |

### 1985

| Div | Winner | Driver |
|-----|--------|--------|
| 2PC | Robust Hanover | John Campbell |
| 2PF | Caressable | Herve Filion |
| 3PC | Nihilator | Bill O'Donnell |
| 3PF | Stienam | Buddy Gilmour |
| 2TC | Express Ride | John Campbell |
| 2TF | JEF's Spice | Mickey McNichol |
| 3TC | Prakas | John Campbell |
| 3TF | Armbro Devona | Bill O'Donnell |
| AP | Division Street | Michel Lachance |
| AT | Sandy Bowl | John Campbell |

### 1986

| Div | Winner | Driver |
|-----|--------|--------|
| 2PC | Sunset Warrior | Bill Gale |
| 2PF | Halcyon | Ray Remmen |
| 3PC | Masquerade | Richard Silverman |
| 3PF | Glow Softly | Ron Waples |
| 2TC | Mack Lobell | John Campbell |
| 2TF | Super Flora | Ron Waples |
| 3TC | Sugarcane Hanover | Ron Waples |
| 3TF | JEF's Spice | Bill O'Donnell |
| APM | Samshu Bluegrass | Michel Lachance |
| ATM | Grades Singing | Herve Filion |
| APH | Forrest Skipper | Lucien Fontaine |
| ATH | Nearly Perfect | Mickey McNichol |

### 1987

| Div | Winner | Driver |
|-----|--------|--------|
| 2PC | Camtastic | Bill O'Donnell |
| 2PF | Leah Almahurst | Bill Fahy |
| 3PC | Call For Rain | Clint Galbraith |
| 3PF | Pacific | Tom Harmer |
| 2TC | Defiant One | Howard Beissinger |
| 2TF | Nan's Catch | Berndt Lindstedt |
| 3TC | Mack Lobell | John Campbell |
| 3TF | Armbro Fling | George Sholty |
| APM | Follow My Star | John Campbell |
| ATM | Grades Singing | Olle Goop |
| APH | Armbro Emerson | Walter Whelan |
| ATH | Sugarcane Hanover | Ron Waples |

### 1988

| Div | Winner | Driver |
|-----|--------|--------|
| 2PC | Kentucky Spur | Dick Stillings |
| 2PF | Central Park West | John Campbell |
| 3PC | Camtastic | Bill O'Donnell |
| 3PF | Sweet Reflection | Bill O'Donnell |
| 2TC | Valley Victory | Bill O'Donnell |
| 2TF | Peace Corps | John Campbell |
| 3TC | Firm Tribute | Mark O'Mara |
| 3TF | Nalda Hanover | Mickey McNichol |
| APM | Anniecrombie | Dave Magee |
| ATM | Armbro Flori | Larry Walker |
| APH | Call For Rain | Clint Galbraith |
| ATH | Mack Lobell | John Campbell |

### 1989

| Div | Winner | Driver |
|-----|--------|--------|
| 2PC | Till We Meet Again | Mickey McNichol |
| 2PF | Town Pro | Doug Brown |
| 3PC | Goalie Jeff | Michel Lachance |
| 3PF | Cheery Hello | John Campbell |
| 2TC | Royal Troubador | Carl Allen |
| 2TF | Delphi's Lobell | Ron Waples |
| 3TC | Esquire Spur | Dick Stillings |
| 3TF | Pace Corps | John Campbell |
| APM | Armbro Feather | John Kopas |
| ATM | Grades Singing | Olle Goop |
| APH | Matt's Scooter | Michel Lachance |
| ATH | Delray Lobell | John Campbell |

### 1990

| Div | Winner | Driver |
|-----|--------|--------|
| 2PC | Artsplace | John Campbell |
| 2PF | Miss Easy | John Campbell |
| 3PC | Beach Towel | Ray Remmen |
| 3PF | Town Pro | Doug Brown |
| 2TC | Crysta's Best | Dick Richardson Jr. |
| 2TF | Jean Bi | Jan Nordin |
| 3TC | Embassy Lobell | Michel Lachance |
| 3TF | Me Maggie | Berndt Lindstedt |
| APM | Caesar's Jackpot | Bill Fahy |
| ATM | Peace Corps | Stig Johansson |
| APH | Bay's Fella | Paul MacDonell |
| ATH | No Sex Please | Ron Waples |

Note: 2=Two-year-old; T=Trotter; C=Colt; 3=Three-year-old; P=Pacer; F=Filly; A=Aged; H=Horse; M=Mare.

## Breeders' Crown *(Cont.)*

### 1991

| Div | Winner | Driver |
|---|---|---|
| 2PC | Digger Almahurst | Doug Brown |
| 2PF | Hazleton Kay | John Campbell |
| 3PC | Three Wizzards | Bill Gale |
| 3PF | Miss Easy | John Campbell |
| 2TC | King Conch | Bill Gale |
| 2TF | Armbro Keepsake | John Campbell |
| 3TC | Giant Victory | Ron Pierce |
| 3TF | Twelve Speed | Ron Waples |
| APM | Delinquent Account | Bill O'Donnell |
| ATM | Me Maggie | Berndt Lindstedt |
| APH | Camluck | Michel Lachance |
| ATH | Billyjojimbob | Paul MacDonell |

### 1992

| Div | Winner | Driver |
|---|---|---|
| 2PC | Village Jiffy | Ron Waples |
| 2PF | Immortality | John Campbell |
| 3PC | Kingsbridge | Roger Mayotte |
| 3PF | So Fresh | John Campbell |
| 2TC | Giant Chill | John Patterson Jr. |
| 2TF | Winky's Goal | Cat Manzi |
| 3TC | Baltic Striker | Michel Lachance |
| 3TF | Imperfection | Michel Lachance |
| APM | Shady Daisy | Ron Pierce |
| ATM | Peace Corps | Torbjorn Jansson |
| APH | Artsplace | John Campbell |
| ATH | No Sex Please | Ron Waples |

### 1993

| Div | Winner | Driver |
|---|---|---|
| 2PC | Expensive Scooter | Jack Moiseyev |
| 2PF | Electric Scooter | Mike Lachance |
| 3PC | Life Sign | John Campbell |
| 3PF | Immortality | John Campbell |
| 2TC | Westgate Crown | John Campbell |
| 2TF | Gleam | Jimmy Takter |
| 3TC | Pine Chip | John Campbell |
| 3TF | Expressway Hanover | Per Henriksen |
| APM | Swing Back | Kelly Sheppard |
| ATM | Lifetime Dream | Paul MacDonnell |
| APH | Staying Together | Bill O'Donnell |
| ATH | Earl | Chris Christoforou Jr. |

### 1994

| Div | Winner | Driver |
|---|---|---|
| 2PC | Jenna's Beach Boy | Bill Fahy |
| 2PF | Yankee Cashmere | Peter Wrenn |
| 3PC | Magical Mike | Michel Lachance |
| 3PF | Hardie Hanover | Tim Twaddle |
| 2TC | Eager Seelster | Teddy Jacobs |
| 2TF | Lookout Victory | John Patterson |
| 3TC | Incredible Abe | Italo Tamborrino |
| 3TF | Imageofa Clear Day | Bill O'Donnell |
| APM | Shady Daisy | Michel Lachance |
| ATM | Armbro Keepsake | Stig Johansson |
| APH | Village Jiffy | Paul MacDonell |
| ATH | Pine Chip | John Campbell |

### 1995

| Div | Winner | Driver |
|---|---|---|
| 2PC | John Street North | Jack Moiseyev |
| 2PF | Paige Nicole Q | John Campbell |
| 3PC | Jenna's Beach Boy | Bill Fahy |
| 3PF | Headline Hanover | Doug Brown |
| 2TC | Armbro Officer | Steve Condren |
| 2TF | Continentalvictory | Michel Lachance |
| 3TC | Abundance | Bill O'Donnell |
| 3TF | Lookout Victory | Sonny Patterson |
| APM | Ellamony | Mike Saftic |
| ATM | CR Kay Suzie | Rod Allen |
| APH | That'll Be Me | Roger Mayotte |
| ATH | Panifesto | Luc Ouellette |

### 1996

| Div | Winner | Driver |
|---|---|---|
| 2PC | His Mattjesty | Doug Brown |
| 2PF | Before Sunrise | Steve Condren |
| 3PC | Armbro Operative | Michel Lachance |
| 3PF | Mystical Maddy | Michel Lachance |
| 2TC | Malabar Man | Mal Burroughs |
| 2TF | Armbro Prowess | Jimmy Takter |
| 3TC | Running Sea | Wally Hennessey |
| 3TF | Personal Banner | Peter Wrenn |
| APM | She's A Great Lady | John Campbell |
| APH | Jenna's Beach Boy | Bill Fahy |
| AT | CR Kay Suzie | Rod Allen |

### 1997

| Div | Winner | Driver |
|---|---|---|
| 2PC | Artiscape | Michel Lachance |
| 2PF | Take Flight | Luc Ouellette |
| 3PC | Village Jasper | Paul McDonnell |
| 3PF | Stienam's Place | Jack Moiseyev |
| 2TC | Catch As Catch Can | Wally Hennessey |
| 2TF | My Dolly | Wally Hennessey |
| 3TC | Malabar Man | Malvern Burroughs |
| 3TF | No Nonsense Woman | Jim Doherty |
| APM | Jay's Table | John Campbell |
| APH | Red Bow Tie | Luc Ouellette |
| AT | Moni Maker | Wally Hennessey |

### 1998

| Div | Winner | Driver |
|---|---|---|
| 2PC | Badlands Hanover | Ron Pierce |
| 2PF | Juliet's Fate | George Brennan |
| 3PC | Artiscape | Michel Lachance |
| 3PF | Galleria | George Brennan |
| 2TC | CR Commando | Carl Allen |
| 2TF | Musical Victory | Luc Ouellette |
| 3TC | Muscles Yankee | John Campbell |
| 3TF | Lassie's Goal | Mark O'Mara |
| APM | Shore By Five | Daniel Dube |
| APH | Red Bow Tie | Luc Ouellette |
| AT | Supergrit | Ron Pierce |

### Breeders' Crown (Cont.)

| | 1999 | | | 2000 | |
|---|---|---|---|---|---|
| Div | Winner | Driver | Div | Winner | Driver |
| 2PC | Tyberwood | Richard Silverman | 2PC | Bettor's Delight | Michel Lachance |
| 2PF | Eternal Camnation | Eric Ledford | 2PF | Lady MacBeach | Luc Ouellette |
| 3PC | Grinfromeartoear | Chris Christoforou | 3PC | Gallo Blue Chip | Daniel Dube |
| 3PF | Odies Fame | David Wall | 3PF | Popcorn Penny | Ryan Anderson |
| 2TC | Master Lavec | Daniel Daley | 2TC | Banker Hall | Trevor Ritchie |
| 2TF | Dream of Joy | James Meittinis | 2TF | Syrinx Hanover | Trevor Ritchie |
| 3TC | CR Renegade | Rodney Allen | 3TC | Fast Photo | Michel Lachance |
| 3TF | Oolong | Ronald Pierce | 3TF | Aviano | Trevor Ritchie |
| APM | Shore By Five | Daniel Dube | APM | Ron's Girl | Michel Lachance |
| APH | Red Bow Tie | Luc Ouellette | APH | Western Ideal | Michel Lachance |
| AT | Supergrit | Ronald Pierce | AT | Magician | David Miller |

Note: 2=Two-year-old; T=Trotter; C=Colt; 3=Three-year-old; P=Pacer; F=Filly; A=Aged; H=Horse; M=Mare.

## Triple Crown Winners

### Trotting

Trotting's Triple Crown consists of the Hambletonian (first run in 1926), the Kentucky Futurity (first run in 1893) and the Yonkers Trot (known as the Yonkers Futurity when it began in 1955).

| Year | Horse | Owner | Breeder | Trainer & Driver |
|---|---|---|---|---|
| 1955 | Scott Frost | S.A. Camp Farms | Est of W.N. Reynolds | Joe O'Brien |
| 1963 | Speedy Scot | Castleton Farms | Castleton Farms | Ralph Baldwin |
| 1964 | Ayres | Charlotte Sheppard | Charlotte Sheppard | John Simpson Sr |
| 1968 | Nevele Pride | Nevele Acres & Lou Resnick | Mr & Mrs E.C. Quin | Stanley Dancer |
| 1969 | Lindy's Pride | Lindy Farm | Hanover Shoe Farms | Howard Beissinger |
| 1972 | Super Bowl | Rachel Dancer & Rose Hild Breeding Farm | Stoner Creek Stud | Stanley Dancer |

### Pacing

Pacing's Triple Crown consists of the Cane Pace (called the Cane Futurity when it began in 1955), the Little Brown Jug (first run in 1946) and the Messenger Stakes (first run in 1956).

| Year | Horse | Owner | Breeder | Trainer/Driver |
|---|---|---|---|---|
| 1959 | Adios Butler | Paige West & Angelo Pellillo | R.C. Carpenter | Paige West/Clint Hodgins |
| 1965 | Bret Hanover | Richard Downing | Hanover Shoe Farms | Frank Ervin |
| 1966 | Romeo Hanover | Lucky Star Stables & Morton Finder | Hanover Shoe Farms | Jerry Silverman/ William Meyer (Cane) & George Sholty (Jug & Messenger) |
| 1968 | Rum Customer | Kennilworth Farms & L. C. Mancuso | Mr. & Mrs. R.C. Larkin | Bill Haughton |
| 1970 | Most Happy Fella | Egyptian Acres Stable | Stoner Creek Stud | Stanley Dancer |
| 1980 | Niatross | Niagara Acres, C. Galbraith & Niatross Stables | Niagara Acres | Clint Galbraith |
| 1983 | Ralph Hanover | Waples Stable, Pointsetta Stable, Grant's Direct Stable & P. J. Baugh | Hanover Shoe Farms | Stew Firlotte/Ron Waples |
| 1997 | Western Dreamer | Daniel and Matthew Daly and Patrick Daly Jr. | Kentuckiana Farms | Bill Robinson/Michel Lachance |
| 1999 | Blissful Hall | Daniel Plouffe | Walnut Hall Limited | Ben Wallace/Ron Pierce |

## Horse of the Year

| Year | Horse | Gait | Owner | Year | Horse | Gait | Owner |
|------|-------|------|-------|------|-------|------|-------|
| 1947 | Victory Song | T | Castleton Farm | 1979 | Niatross | P | Niagara Acres, Clint Galbraith |
| 1948 | Rodney | T | R.H. Johnston | | | | |
| 1949 | Good Time | P | William Cane | 1980 | Niatross | P | Niatross Syndicate, Niagara Acres, Clint Galbraith |
| 1950 | Proximity | T | Ralph and Gordon Verhurst | | | | |
| 1951 | Pronto Don | T | Hayes Fair Acres Stable | | | | |
| 1952 | Good Time | P | William Cane | 1981 | Fan Hanover | P | Dr. J. Glen Brown |
| 1953 | Hi Lo's Forbes | P | Mr. and Mrs. Earl Wagner | 1982 | Cam Fella | P | Norm Clements, Norm Faulkner |
| 1954 | Stenographer | T | Max Hempt | | | | |
| 1955 | Scott Frost | T | S.A. Camp Farms | 1983 | Cam Fella | P | JEF's Standardbred, Norm Clements, Norm Faulkner |
| 1956 | Scott Frost | T | S.A. Camp Farms | | | | |
| 1957 | Torpid | P | Sherwood Farm | | | | |
| 1958 | Emily's Pride | T | Walnut Hall and Castleton Farms | 1984 | Fancy Crown | T | Fancy Crown Stable |
| | | | | 1985 | Nihilator | P | Wall Street-Nihilator Syndicate |
| 1959 | Bye Bye Byrd | P | Mr. and Mrs. Rex Larkin | | | | |
| 1960 | Adios Butler | P | Adios Butler Syndicate | 1986 | Forrest Skipper | P | Forrest L. Bartlett |
| 1961 | Adios Butler | P | Adios Butler Syndicate | | | | |
| 1962 | Su Mac Lad | P | I.W. Berkemeyer | 1987 | Mack Lobell | T | One More Time Stable and Fair Wind Farm |
| 1963 | Speedy Scot | T | Castleton Farm | | | | |
| 1964 | Bret Hanover | P | Richard Downing | 1988 | Mack Lobell | T | John Erik Magnusson |
| 1965 | Bret Hanover | P | Richard Downing | 1989 | Matt's Scooter | P | Gordon and Illa Rumpel, Charles Jurasvinski |
| 1966 | Bret Hanover | P | Richard Downing | | | | |
| 1967 | Nevele Pride | T | Nevele Acres | 1990 | Beach Towel | P | Uptown Stables |
| 1968 | Nevele Pride | T | Nevele Acres, Louis Resnick | 1991 | Precious Bunny | P | R. Peter Heffering |
| 1969 | Nevele Pride | T | Nevele Acres, Louis Resnick | 1992 | Artsplace | P | George Segal |
| | | | | 1993 | Staying Together | P | Robert Hamather |
| 1970 | Fresh Yankee | T | Duncan MacDonald | | | | |
| 1971 | Albatross | P | Albatross Stable | 1994 | Cam's Card Shark | P | Jeffrey S. Snyder |
| 1972 | Albatross | P | Amicable Stable | | | | |
| 1973 | Sir Dalrae | P | A La Carte Racing Stable | 1995 | CR Kay Suzie | T | Carl & Rod Allen Stable, Inc. |
| 1974 | Delmonica Hanover | T | Delvin Miller, W. Arnold Hanger | 1996 | Continental-victory | T | Continentalvictory Stables |
| 1975 | Savoir | T | Allwood Stable | 1997 | Malabar Man | T | Malvern Burroughs |
| 1976 | Keystone Ore | P | Mr. and Mrs. Stanley Dancer, Rose Hild Farms, Robert Jones | 1998 | Moni Maker | T | Moni Maker Stable |
| | | | | 1999 | Moni Maker | T | Moni Maker Stable |
| 1977 | Green Speed | T | Beverly Lloyds | 2000 | Gallo Blue Chip | P | Dan Gernatt Farms |
| 1978 | Abercrombie | P | Shirley Mitchell, L. Keith Bulen | | | | |

## Driver of the Year

| Year | Driver | Year | Driver | Year | Driver |
|------|--------|------|--------|------|--------|
| 1968 | Stanley Dancer | 1979 | Ron Waples | 1991 | Walter Case Jr. |
| 1969 | Herve Filion | 1980 | Ron Waples | 1992 | Walter Case Jr. |
| 1970 | Herve Filion | 1981 | Herve Filion | 1993 | Jack Moiseyev |
| 1971 | Herve Filion | 1982 | Bill O'Donnell | 1994 | Dave Magee |
| 1972 | Herve Filion | 1983 | John Campbell | 1995 | Luc Ouellette |
| 1973 | Herve Filion | 1984 | Bill O'Donnell | 1996 | Tony Morgan |
| 1974 | Herve Filion | 1985 | Michel Lachance | | Luc Ouellette |
| 1975 | Joe O'Brien | 1986 | Michel Lachance | 1997 | Tony Morgan |
| 1976 | Herve Filion | 1987 | Michel Lachance | 1998 | Walter Case Jr. |
| 1977 | Donald Dancer | 1988 | John Campbell | 1999 | Dave Palone |
| 1978 | Carmine Abbatiello Herve Filion | 1989 | Herve Filion | 2000 | Dave Palone |
| | | 1990 | John Campbell | | |

Note: Balloting is conducted by the U.S Trotting Association for the U.S. Harness Writers Association.

## Leading Drivers—Money Won

| Year | Driver | Winnings ($) | Year | Driver | Winnings ($) |
|------|--------|-------------|------|--------|-------------|
| 1946 | Thomas Berry | 121,933 | 1974 | Herve Filion | 3,474,315 |
| 1947 | H.C. Fitzpatrick | 133,675 | 1975 | Carmine Abbatiello | 2,275,093 |
| 1948 | Ralph Baldwin | 153,222 | 1976 | Herve Filion | 2,278,634 |
| 1949 | Clint Hodgins | 184,108 | 1977 | Herve Filion | 2,551,058 |
| 1950 | Del Miller | 306,813 | 1978 | Carmine Abbatiello | 3,344,457 |
| 1951 | John Simpson Sr. | 333,316 | 1979 | John Campbell | 3,308,984 |
| 1952 | Bill Haughton | 311,728 | 1980 | John Campbell | 3,732,306 |
| 1953 | Bill Haughton | 374,527 | 1981 | Bill O'Donnell | 4,065,608 |
| 1954 | Bill Haughton | 415,577 | 1982 | Bill O'Donnell | 5,755,067 |
| 1955 | Bill Haughton | 599,455 | 1983 | John Campbell | 6,104,082 |
| 1956 | Bill Haughton | 572,945 | 1984 | Bill O'Donnell | 9,059,184 |
| 1957 | Bill Haughton | 586,950 | 1985 | Bill O'Donnell | 10,207,372 |
| 1958 | Bill Haughton | 816,659 | 1986 | John Campbell | 9,515,055 |
| 1959 | Bill Haughton | 771,435 | 1987 | John Campbell | 10,186,495 |
| 1960 | Del Miller | 567,282 | 1988 | John Campbell | 11,148,565 |
| 1961 | Stanley Dancer | 674,723 | 1989 | John Campbell | 9,738,450 |
| 1962 | Stanley Dancer | 760,343 | 1990 | John Campbell | 11,620,878 |
| 1963 | Bill Haughton | 790,086 | 1991 | Jack Moiseyev | 9,568,468 |
| 1964 | Stanley Dancer | 1,051,538 | 1992 | John Campbell | 8,202,108 |
| 1965 | Bill Haughton | 889,943 | 1993 | John Campbell | 9,926,482 |
| 1966 | Stanley Dancer | 1,218,403 | 1994 | John Campbell | 9,834,139 |
| 1967 | Bill Haughton | 1,305,773 | 1995 | John Campbell | 9,469,797 |
| 1968 | Bill Haughton | 1,654,463 | 1996 | Michel Lachance | 8,408,231 |
| 1969 | Del Insko | 1,635,463 | 1997 | Michel Lachance | 9,215,388 |
| 1970 | Herve Filion | 1,647,837 | 1998 | John Campbell | 10,768,771 |
| 1971 | Herve Filion | 1,915,945 | 1999 | Luc Ouellette | 10,841,495 |
| 1972 | Herve Filion | 2,473,265 | 2000 | John Campbell | 11,160,462 |
| 1973 | Herve Filion | 2,233,303 | | | |

**Changed**  Thoroughbred racing officials altered the logo for the 2001 Breeders' Cup, which was held on Oct. 27 at Belmont Park. The original design featured the World Trade Center in the background; the new one features the outline of a globe.

# Motor Sports

Dale Earnhardt
1951–2001

# Season of Sadness

## In a year of unprecedented national calamity, the racing world came to grips with disasters of its own

### BY MARK BECHTEL

**A**T ALMOST the precise instant that Michael Waltrip, one of auto racing's most personable and least successful drivers, crossed the finish line at the Daytona 500 to win his first race in 462 career starts, Dale Earnhardt, one of the sport's most popular and most successful drivers, crashed into the wall between Turns 3 and 4. A moment of long-delayed joy was instantly snuffed out by tragedy: The impact of the crash killed Earnhardt, the seven-time Winston Cup champion, and left NASCAR without its heart and soul. "Dale was the Michael Jordan of our sport," said H.A. (Humpy) Wheeler, president of Lowe's Motor Speedway near Charlotte. "To think he is not around anymore is incomprehensible. This is a terrible, terrible loss, and for me it ranks right up there with the death of JFK."

Earnhardt was chasing his 77th career win when he died. Number 76 came in a restrictor-plate race in October 2000, the Winston 500 in Talladega, Ala. That race drew raves from spectators for its 49 lead changes, which included Earnhardt's moving from 18th to first during the last five laps. Some drivers, on the other hand, were less effusive in their praise. Said Jeff Gordon, "It was a little too exciting at times for me."

The excitement came thanks to a rules change that NASCAR had made in the wake of three numbingly dull restrictor-plate races earlier in the 2000 season, including a Daytona 500 that had only nine lead changes. The sanctioning body decided to slow the cars down aerodynamically and switch to a less restrictive plate, which would give drivers the power to pass more easily. Not only did the Talladega race feature a breathtaking game of hot potato with the lead, but it also finished without the big wreck that drivers have come to expect at superspeedways.

Pleased with the Talladega experiment, NASCAR stuck with the new rules for the 2001 Daytona 500, which left some drivers skittish. "The cars are so stable now that you feel like you are Superman, that you can do anything you want with them,"

HEINZ KLUETMEIER

restrictive plates. Earnhardt, who was just ahead of the crash, stayed out of trouble, and with five laps left he was riding in third place, behind two cars he owned—Waltrip's and Dale Earnhardt Jr.'s.

It had the makings of an interesting showdown. Only one man had gotten his first win faster than Junior, who won in 2000 at Texas in his 12th Winston Cup start, and no driver had gone longer without his first career victory than the 37-year-old Waltrip. Earnhardt seemed content to lay back and run interference for his two employees. "I was monitoring him on the radio," said rival owner Jack Roush. "He was telling the guys in front of him where to go on the track. You can draw your own conclusions what he was doing. Both of those cars up there were his."

Stacey Compton said two days before the race. "Some awfully talented drivers are out here, and we have a tendency to put the cars in some places they don't belong and [still expect to] come out of it. Sometimes you do, sometimes you don't."

Defending Daytona 500 champ Dale Jarrett was also cautious. "Things wouldn't have worked in Talladega if everyone hadn't used his head," he said before the 2001 Daytona. With 27 laps remaining on that fateful Sunday, Jarrett found out firsthand what happens when someone doesn't use his head. Robby Gordon got a little overanxious and tapped Ward Burton from behind, spinning Burton into Tony Stewart, who was sent tumbling through the air, spinning once and flipping twice. Stewart's airborne vehicle tore the hood off teammate Bobby Labonte's car. Nineteen cars—including Jarrett's—were involved in the wreck, and the race was red-flagged for 16 minutes. "You can't do it when you've got idiots out there," said Burton of the move to the less-

As Waltrip outlegged Junior to the finish line, Rusty Wallace came up behind Earnhardt Sr.'s car, which wiggled slightly when Wallace closed in. The black Chevrolet marked No. 3 veered left toward the lower portion of the track, took an abrupt right, got hit on the passenger side by Ken Schrader and then barreled into the wall.

The investigation into Earnhardt's death lasted months, and when NASCAR finally issued a report in August, it didn't point the finger at any individual entity. As the investigation wore on, NASCAR did its best to move forward. The week after the crash—in the first of several results that piqued the interest of garage conspiracy theorists—Steve Park, driving a car owned by Earnhardt, won at Rockingham. Two weeks later storybook ending number two took place as Kevin Harvick, who was tapped by Richard Childress to replace Earnhardt, won in Atlanta, edging Jeff Gordon at the finish line by a matter of inches. When the circuit returned to Daytona in July for the Pepsi 400, Earnhardt Jr. won in dramatic fashion—a little too dramatic for some. Drivers Jimmy Spencer and Johnny Benson both intimated that NASCAR had fixed the outcome of the race, a notion some other drivers had a tough time swallowing. "This," said Labonte, "is not the WWF." Junior was far from pleased that his exploits were being questioned. "It's a shame," he said. "It was a great moment in NASCAR history, and it got kicked in the [groin]."

While Park, Harvick and Junior provided the most memorable wins, the driver who provided the most wins, period, was Jeff Gordon. Gordon struggled through a subpar year in 2000 with his new crew chief, Robbie Loomis. They won only three times and finished ninth in the season points race. But in their second year together Gordon and Loomis began to click, and Gordon was back on top. The pair's biggest win of the season came at the Brickyard 400 in August, the day after Gordon's 30th birthday. "I try to live in the moment and enjoy as much of my life as I can," he said. "I'm just trying to get through age 30.... Hopefully [it] means I'm coming into my prime."

The era of "the Kid" may be over. Unfortunately for Gordon's fellow drivers, though, the dawning era of "the Man" didn't look to be any more enjoyable for them. Heading into the season's final weeks, he had all but wrapped up his fourth Winston Cup title.

Like every other sport, the auto racing world had difficult decisions to make in the wake of the terrorist attacks on the World Trade Center and the Pentagon. NASCAR postponed its races the following weekend, but CART and F/1 elected to run. The Formula One race in Italy should have been a joyous occasion for Michael Schumacher and his Ferrari team. They had already clinched both the drivers title and the constructors title, and the return to Ferrari's home country should have been one long party. Instead, the Ferraris ran with black nose cones, and a somber mood prevailed. "Everyone is emotionally down," Schumacher said. "It's a weekend where a lot of things are not right, and you should question whether we should race here."

As for CART's decision to go on with the German 500, CEO Joseph Heitzler said that "we will be racing with a great deal of sadness and compassion." He also announced that CART would change the name of the race to the American Memorial but otherwise proceed as planned. Heitzler and CART hoped that by carrying on in the face of tragedy they might make a small step toward healing. Sadly, the decision only resulted in more heartache as a terrifying crash left one of the sport's most popular drivers, Alex Zanardi, in critical but stable condition, both of his legs amputated close to the knee.

A 34-year-old Italian, Zanardi was leading the race with 12 laps to go when he made a quick pit stop to refuel. As he was leaving the pits he lost control and slid across the patch of grass that separates the pit road exit from the track. He ended up facing sideways and directly in the path of Alex Tagliani, who was going nearly 200 miles an hour when he T-boned Zanardi's car, scattering debris all over the track.

Zanardi had returned to CART in 2001 after a disastrous campaign with Frank Williams in F/1. After the 1999 season Williams bought out the remainder of Zanardi's contract and the racer returned to his home in Monaco, where he spent 2000 mostly being a husband to his wife, Daniela, a father to his son, Niccolo, and the captain of his 58-foot boat, *Hakuna Matata*, a Swahili phrase made familiar by *The Lion King* that translates to "no worries for the rest of your days." But a worry-free existence meant no racing, and eventually Zanardi's desire to drive brought him back to the United States. Morris Nunn, who had been an engineer with Zanardi's CART team before forming his own team in 2000, hired him for the 2001 season, but the two were unable to duplicate their previous success. Zanardi's best finish in 2001 was fourth, and he didn't lead a single lap all year until that Saturday in Germany—a day on which a very dark week in a dark year became a little darker still.

## Indy Racing League

### Indianapolis 500

Results of the 85th running of the Indianapolis 500 and fourth race of the 2001 Indy Racing League season. Held Sunday, May 27, 2001, at the 2.5-mile Indianapolis Motor Speedway in Indianapolis.

Distance, 500 miles; starters, 33; time of race, 3 hours, 31 minutes, 54.18 seconds; average speed, 153.601 mph; margin of victory, 1.737 seconds; caution flags, eight for 56 laps; lead changes, 14 among eight drivers.

#### TOP 10 FINISHERS

| Pos. | Driver (start pos.) | Chassis-Engine | Qual. Speed | Laps | Status |
|---|---|---|---|---|---|
| 1 | Helio Castroneves (11) | Dallara-Oldsmobile | 224.142 | 200 | running |
| 2 | Gil de Ferran (5) | Dallara-Oldsmobile | 224.406 | 200 | running |
| 3 | Michael Andretti (21) | Dallara-Oldsmobile | 223.441 | 200 | running |
| 4 | Jimmy Vasser (12) | G Force-Oldsmobile | 223.455 | 200 | running |
| 5 | Bruno Junqueira (20) | G Force-Oldsmobile | 224.208 | 200 | running |
| 6 | Tony Stewart (7) | G Force-Oldsmobile | 224.248 | 200 | running |
| 7 | Eliseo Salazar (28) | Dallara-Oldsmobile | 223.740 | 199 | running |
| 8 | Airton Dare (30) | G Force-Oldsmobile | 222.236 | 199 | running |
| 9 | Billy Boat (32) | Dallara-Oldsmobile | 221.528 | 199 | running |
| 10 | Felipe Giaffone (33) | G Force-Oldsmobile | 221.879 | 199 | running |

### 2001 Indy Racing League Results

| Date | Race | Winner (start pos.) | Chassis-Engine | Avg Speed |
|---|---|---|---|---|
| Mar 18 | Pennzoil 200 | Sam Hornish (2) | Dallara-Oldsmobile | 125.072 |
| Apr 8 | Grand Prix of Miami | Sam Hornish (5) | Dallara-Oldsmobile | 148.508 |
| Apr 28 | zMAX 500 K | Greg Ray (1) | Dallara-Oldsmobile | 133.647 |
| May 27 | Indianapolis 500 | Helio Castroneves (11) | Dallara-Oldsmobile | 153.601 |
| June 9 | Casino Magic 500 K | Scott Sharp (2) | Dallara-Oldsmobile | 150.873 |
| June 17 | Radisson Indy 200* | Buddy Lazier (13) | Dallara-Oldsmobile | 142.987 |
| June 30 | SunTrust Indy Challenge | Buddy Lazier (4) | Dallara-Oldsmobile | 97.435 |
| July 8 | Ameristar Casino 200* | Eddie Cheever (2) | Dallara-Infiniti | 148.914 |
| July 21 | Harrah's Indy 200* | Buddy Lazier (6) | Dallara-Oldsmobile | 144.809 |
| Aug 12 | Belterra Casino 300 | Buddy Lazier (11) | Dallara-Oldsmobile | 174.910 |
| Aug 26 | Gateway Indy | Al Unser Jr (8) | G Force-Oldsmobile | 136.379 |
| Sept 2 | Delphi 300 | Jacques Lazier (1) | Dallara-Oldsmobile | 172.146 |
| Oct 6 | Chevy 500 | | | |

Note: Distances are in miles unless followed by K (kilometers) or * (laps).

### 2000 Final Championship Standings

| Driver | Starts | Highest Finish | Pts |
|---|---|---|---|
| Buddy Lazier | 9 | 1 | 290 |
| Scott Goodyear | 9 | 1 | 272 |
| Eddie Cheever | 9 | 1 | 257 |
| Eliseo Salazar | 9 | 2 | 210 |
| Mark Dismore | 9 | 2 | 202 |
| Donnie Beechler | 9 | 3 | 202 |

## Championship Auto Racing Teams

### Michigan 500

Results of the 6th running of the Michigan 500 (formerly the U.S. 500) and 11th race of the 2001 CART Series. Held Sunday, July 22, 2001, at the 2-mile Michigan International Speedway in Brooklyn, MI.

Distance, 500 miles; starters, 25; time of race, 2 hours, 54 minutes, 55.8 seconds; average speed, 171.494 mph; margin of victory, 0.243 seconds; caution flags, five for 39 laps; lead changes, 60 among 11 drivers.

#### TOP 5 FINISHERS

| Pos. | Driver (start pos.) | Car | Qual. Speed | Laps | Status |
|---|---|---|---|---|---|
| 1 | Patrick Carpentier (21) | Ford-Cosworth/Reynard | 223.478 | 250 | running |
| 2 | Dario Franchitti (25) | Honda/Reynard | 220.453 | 250 | running |
| 3 | Michel Jourdain Jr. (6) | Ford-Cosworth/Lola | 227.301 | 250 | running |
| 4 | Cristiano da Matta (13) | Toyota/Lola | 225.776 | 250 | running |
| 5 | Bryan Herta (7) | Ford-Cosworth/Reynard | 226.943 | 250 | running |

### 2001 CART Championship Series Results (through September 22)

| Date | Event | Winner (start pos.) | Car | Avg Speed |
|------|-------|---------------------|-----|-----------|
| Mar 11 | Monterrey Grand Prix | Cristiano da Matta (2) | Toyota-Lola | 81.548 mph |
| Apr 8 | Grand Prix of Long Beach | Helio Castroneves (1) | Honda-Reynard | 86.223 |
| May 6 | Lehigh Valley Grand Prix | Scott Dixon (23) | Toyota-Reynard | 114.840 |
| May 18 | Firehawk 500 | Kenny Brack (6) | Ford Cosworth-Lola | 178.113 |
| June 3 | Miller Lite 225 | Kenny Brack (1) | Ford Cosworth-Lola | 122.066 |
| June 17 | Grand Prix of Detroit | Helio Castroneves (1) | Honda-Reynard | 89.008 |
| June 24 | Freightliner/G.I. Joe's 200 | Max Papis (1) | Ford Cosworth-Lola | 74.606 |
| July 1 | Grand Prix of Cleveland | Dario Franchitti (14) | Honda-Reynard | 118.007 |
| July 15 | Molson Indy | Michael Andretti (13) | Honda-Reynard | 83.375 |
| July 22 | Harrah's 500 | Patrick Carpentier (21) | Ford Cosworth-Reynard | 171.498 |
| July 29 | Target Grand Prix | Kenny Brack (8) | Ford Cosworth-Lola | 132.031 |
| Aug 12 | Miller Lite 200 | Helio Castroneves (2) | Honda-Reynard | 106.627 |
| Aug 19 | Motorola 220 | Bruno Junqueira (10) | Toyota-Lola | 90.721 |
| Sept 2 | Molson Indy Vancouver | Roberto Moreno (7) | Toyota-Reynard | 80.543 |
| Sept 15 | The American Memorial | Kenny Brack (2) | Ford Cosworth-Lola | 155.319 |
| Sept 22 | Rockingham 500 | Gil de Ferran (2) | Honda-Reynard | 153.408 |

### 2000 Championship Standings

| Driver | Starts | Wins | Pts |
|--------|--------|------|-----|
| Gil de Ferran | 20 | 2 | 168 |
| Adrian Fernandez | 20 | 2 | 158 |
| Roberto Moreno | 20 | 1 | 147 |
| Kenny Brack | 20 | 0 | 135 |
| Paul Tracy | 20 | 3 | 134 |
| Jimmy Vasser | 20 | 1 | 131 |
| Helio Castroneves | 20 | 3 | 129 |
| Juan Montoya | 20 | 3 | 126 |
| Michael Andretti | 20 | 2 | 123 |
| Cristiano da Matta | 20 | 1 | 112 |

# National Association for Stock Car Auto Racing

## Daytona 500

Results of the 43rd Daytona 500, the opening round of the 2001 Winston Cup series. Held Sunday, February 28, 2001, at the 2.5-mile high-banked Daytona International Speedway.

Distance, 500 miles; starters, 43; time of race, 3:05:26; average speed, 161.783 mph; margin of victory, 0.124 seconds; caution flags, three for 14 laps; lead changes, 49 among 14 drivers.

### TOP 10 FINISHERS

| Pos. | Driver (start pos.) | Car | Laps | Winnings ($) |
|------|---------------------|-----|------|--------------|
| 1 | Michael Waltrip (19) | Chevrolet | 200 | 1,331,185 |
| 2 | Dale Earnhardt Jr. (6) | Chevrolet | 200 | 975,907 |
| 3 | Rusty Wallace (12) | Ford | 200 | 676,224 |
| 4 | Ricky Rudd (30) | Ford | 200 | 517,831 |
| 5 | Bill Elliott (1) | Dodge | 200 | 392,582 |
| 6 | Mike Wallace (27) | Ford | 200 | 275,269 |
| 7 | Sterling Marlin (3) | Dodge | 200 | 262,354 |
| 8 | Bobby Hamilton (35) | Chevrolet | 200 | 189,259 |
| 9 | Jeremy Mayfield (38) | Ford | 200 | 207,168 |
| 10 | Stacy Compton (2) | Dodge | 200 | 168,770 |

## Late 2000 Winston Cup Series Results

| Date | Track/Distance | Winner (start pos.) | Car | Avg Speed | Winnings ($) |
|------|----------------|---------------------|-----|-----------|--------------|
| Oct 1 | Martinsville 500* | Tony Stewart (1) | Pontiac | 73.859 | 125,875 |
| Oct 8 | Charlotte 500 | Bobby Labonte (2) | Pontiac | 133.630 | 220,700 |
| Oct 15 | Talladega 500 | Dale Earnhardt (20) | Chevrolet | 165.681 | 135,900 |
| Oct 22 | N Carolina 400 | Dale Jarrett (21) | Ford | 110.418 | 125,850 |
| Nov 5 | Phoenix 500 K | Jeff Burton (2) | Ford | 105.041 | 197,345 |
| Nov 12 | Miami 400 | Tony Stewart (13) | Pontiac | 127.480 | 291,325 |
| Nov 20 | Atlanta 500 | Jerry Nadeau (2) | Chevrolet | 141.296 | 180,550 |

Note: Distances are in miles unless followed by K (kilometers) or * (laps).

## 2001 Winston Cup Series Results (through September 30)

| Date | Track/Distance | Winner (start pos.) | Car | Avg Speed | Winnings ($) |
|---|---|---|---|---|---|
| Feb 18 | Daytona 500 | Michael Waltrip (19) | Chevrolet | 161.783 | 1,331,185 |
| Feb 25 | N Carolina 400 | Steve Park (2) | Chevrolet | 111.817 | 144,593 |
| Mar 4 | Las Vegas 400 | Jeff Gordon (24) | Chevrolet | 135.546 | 1,369,600 |
| Mar 11 | Atlanta 500 | Kevin Harvick (5) | Chevrolet | 143.273 | 158,427 |
| Mar 18 | Darlington 400 | Dale Jarrett (2) | Ford | 126.557 | 214,612 |
| Mar 25 | Bristol 500* | Elliott Sadler (38) | Ford | 86.949 | 124,700 |
| Apr 1 | Texas 500 | Dale Jarrett (3) | Ford | 141.804 | 444,527 |
| Apr 8 | Martinsville 500* | Dale Jarrett (13) | Ford | 70.799 | 170,027 |
| Apr 22 | Talladega 500 | Bobby Hamilton (14) | Chevrolet | 184.003 | 173,855 |
| Apr 29 | California 500 | Rusty Wallace (19) | Ford | 143.118 | 195,090 |
| May 5 | Richmond 400* | Tony Stewart (7) | Pontiac | 95.872 | 150,175 |
| May 27 | Charlotte 600 | Jeff Burton (18) | Ford | 138.107 | 258,846 |
| June 3 | Dover Downs 400 | Jeff Gordon (2) | Chevrolet | 120.361 | 183,907 |
| June 10 | Michigan 400 | Jeff Gordon (1) | Chevrolet | 134.203 | 240,137 |
| June 17 | Pocono 500 | Ricky Rudd (1) | Ford | 134.389 | 189,542 |
| June 24 | Sears Point 350 K | Tony Stewart (3) | Pontiac | 75.889 | 139,875 |
| July 7 | Daytona 400 | Dale Earnhardt Jr (13) | Chevrolet | 157.601 | 185,873 |
| July 15 | Chicago 400 | Kevin Harvick (6) | Chevrolet | 121.200 | 162,500 |
| July 22 | New Hampshire 300* | Dale Jarrett (9) | Ford | 102.131 | 238,027 |
| July 29 | Pocono 500 | Bobby Labonte (11) | Pontiac | 134.590 | 189,427 |
| Aug 5 | Indianapolis 400 | Jeff Gordon (27) | Chevrolet | 130.790 | 428,452 |
| Aug 12 | Watkins Glen 90* | Jeff Gordon (13) | Chevrolet | 89.081 | 173,402 |
| Aug 19 | Michigan 400 | Sterling Marlin (15) | Dodge | 140.513 | 157,830 |
| Aug 25 | Bristol 500* | Tony Stewart (18) | Pontiac | 85.106 | 189,415 |
| Sept 2 | Darlington 500 | Ward Burton (37) | Dodge | 122.773 | 181,435 |
| Sept 8 | Richmond 400* | Ricky Rudd (9) | Ford | 95.146 | 171,992 |
| Sept 23 | Dover Downs 400 | Dale Earnhardt Jr (3) | Chevrolet | 101.559 | 168,858 |
| Sept 30 | Kansas 400 | Jeff Gordon (2) | Chevrolet | 110.576 | 254,377 |

Note: Distances are in miles unless followed by K (kilometers) or * (laps).

### 2000 Winston Cup Final Standings

| Driver | Pts | Starts | Wins | Top 5 | Top 10 |
|---|---|---|---|---|---|
| Bobby Labonte | 5130 | 34 | 4 | 19 | 24 |
| Dale Earnhardt | 4865 | 34 | 2 | 13 | 24 |
| Jeff Burton | 4836 | 34 | 4 | 15 | 22 |
| Dale Jarrett | 4684 | 34 | 2 | 15 | 24 |
| Ricky Rudd | 4575 | 34 | 0 | 12 | 19 |
| Tony Stewart | 4570 | 34 | 6 | 12 | 23 |
| Rusty Wallace | 4544 | 34 | 4 | 12 | 20 |
| Mark Martin | 4410 | 34 | 1 | 13 | 20 |
| Jeff Gordon | 4361 | 34 | 3 | 11 | 22 |
| Ward Burton | 4152 | 34 | 1 | 4 | 17 |

### 2000 Winston Cup Driver Winnings

| Driver | Winnings ($) |
|---|---|
| Dale Jarrett | 5,225,500 |
| Jeff Burton | 5,121,350 |
| Bobby Labonte | 4,041,750 |
| Dale Earnhardt | 3,701,390 |
| Tony Stewart | 3,200,190 |
| Rusty Wallace | 3,037,720 |
| Mark Martin | 2,763,540 |
| Jeff Gordon | 2,703,590 |
| Dale Earnhardt Jr | 2,610,400 |
| Bill Elliott | 2,447,790 |

# Formula One Grand Prix Racing

## 2001 Formula One Results (through September 30)

| Date | Grand Prix | Winner | Car | Time |
|---|---|---|---|---|
| Mar 4 | Australia | Michael Schumacher | Ferrari | 1:38:26.533 |
| Mar 18 | Malaysia | Michael Schumacher | Ferrari | 1:47:34.801 |
| Apr 1 | Brazil | David Coulthard | McLaren-Mercedes | 1:39:00.834 |
| Apr 15 | San Marino | Ralf Schumacher | BMW-Williams | 1:30:44.817 |
| Apr 29 | Spain | Michael Schumacher | Ferrari | 1:31:03.305 |
| May 13 | Austria | David Coulthard | McLaren-Mercedes | 1:27:45.927 |
| May 27 | Monaco | Michael Schumacher | Ferrari | 1:47:22.561 |
| June 10 | Canada | Ralf Schumacher | BMW-Williams | 1:34:31.522 |
| June 24 | Europe | Michael Schumacher | Ferrari | 1:29:42.724 |
| July 1 | France | Michael Schumacher | Ferrari | 1:33:35.636 |
| July 15 | Britain | Mika Hakkinen | McLaren-Mercedes | 1:25:33.770 |
| July 29 | Germany | Ralf Schumacher | BMW-Williams | 1:18:17.873 |
| Aug 19 | Hungary | Michael Schumacher | Ferrari | 1:41:49.675 |
| Sept 2 | Belgium | Michael Schumacher | Ferrari | 1:08:05.002 |
| Sept 16 | Italy | Juan Montoya | BMW-Williams | 1:16:58.493 |
| Sept 30 | United States | Mika Hakkinen | McLaren-Mercedes | 1:32:42.840 |

### 2000 World Championship Final Standings

Drivers compete in Grand Prix races for the title of World Driving Champion. Below are the top 10 drivers from the 2000 season. Points are awarded for places 1–6 as follows: 10-6-4-3-2-1.

| Driver, Country | Starts | Wins | Car | Pts |
|---|---|---|---|---|
| Michael Schumacher, Germany | 17 | 9 | Ferrari | 108 |
| Mika Hakkinen, Finland | 17 | 4 | McLaren-Mercedes | 89 |
| David Coulthard, Great Britain | 17 | 3 | McLaren-Mercedes | 73 |
| Rubens Barrichello, Brazil | 17 | 1 | Ferrari | 62 |
| Ralf Schumacher, Germany | 17 | 0 | Williams-BMW | 24 |
| Giancarlo Fisichella, Italy | 17 | 0 | Benetton | 18 |
| Jacques Villeneuve, Canada | 17 | 0 | BAR-Honda | 17 |
| Jenson Button, Great Britain | 17 | 0 | Williams-BMW | 12 |
| Heinz-Harald Frentzen, Germany | 17 | 0 | Jordan-Mugen Honda | 11 |
| Jarno Trulli, Italy | 17 | 0 | Jordan-Mugen Honda | 6 |

## Professional Sports Car Racing, Inc.

### The 24 Hours of Daytona

Held at the Daytona International Speedway on February 3–4, 2001, the 24 Hours of Daytona serves as the opening round of Grand American Road Racing Association's season.

| Place | Drivers | Car (Class) | Distance |
|---|---|---|---|
| 1 | Ron Fellows, Chris Kneifel, Franck Freon, Johnny O'Connell | Corvette (GTS) | 656 laps (97.293 mph) |
| 2 | Mike Fitzgerald, Lucas Luhr, Randy Pobst, Christian Menzel | Porsche 911 (GT) | 648 |
| 3 | Wolfgang Kaufmann, Lance Stewart, Cyril Chateau | Porsche 911 (GT) | 644 |
| 4 | Andy Pilgrim, Dale Earnhardt, Dale Earnhardt Jr, Kelly Collins | Corvette (GTS) | 642 |
| 5 | Gabrio Rosa, Fabio Rosa, Fabio Babini, Alex Caffi | Porsche 911 (GT) | 637 |

### 2001 American Le Mans Series—Prototype Class (through October 4)

| Date | Race | Winners | Car |
|---|---|---|---|
| Mar 4 | Grand Prix of Texas | Rinaldo Capello, Tom Kristensen | Audi |
| Mar 17 | 12 Hours at Sebring | Rinaldo Capello, Michele Alboreto, Laurent Aiello | Audi |
| July 22 | Grand Prix of Sonoma | Rinaldo Capello, Tom Kristensen | Audi |
| Aug 4 | Grand Prix of Portland | Jan Magnussen | Panoz LMP |
| Aug 19 | Grand Prix at Mosport | Frank Biela, Emanuele Pirro | Audi |
| Aug 25 | Grand Prix of Mid-Ohio | David Brabham, Jan Magnussen | Panoz LMP |
| Sept 9 | Monteray Championships | Frank Biela, Emanuele Pirro | Audi |

### 2001 American Le Mans Series—GTS Class (through October 4)

| Date | Race | Winners | Car |
|---|---|---|---|
| Mar 4 | Grand Prix of Texas | Johnny O'Connell, Ron Fellows | Corvette |
| Mar 17 | 12 Hours at Sebring | Oliver Gavin, Terry Borcheller, Franz Konrad | S7R |
| July 22 | Grand Prix of Sonoma | Ron Fellows, Johnny O'Connell | Corvette |
| Aug 4 | Grand Prix of Portland | Johnny O'Connell | Corvette |
| Aug 19 | Grand Prix at Mosport | Ron Fellows, Johnny O'Connell | Corvette |
| Aug 25 | Grand Prix of Mid-Ohio | Ron Fellows, Johnny O'Connell | Corvette |
| Sept 9 | Monteray Championships | Terry Borcheller, Franz Konrad | S7R |

### 2001 American Le Mans Series—GT Class (through October 4)

| Date | Race | Winners | Car |
|---|---|---|---|
| Mar 4 | Grand Prix of Texas | Lucas Luhr, Sascha Maassen | Porsche 911 |
| Mar 17 | 12 Hours at Sebring | Sascha Maassen, Lucas Luhr | Porsche 911 |
| July 22 | Grand Prix of Sonoma | J.J. Lehto, Jörg Müller | BMW |
| Aug 4 | Grand Prix of Portland | Boris Said | BMW |
| Aug 19 | Grand Prix at Mosport | J.J. Lehto, Jörg Müller | BMW |
| Aug 25 | Grand Prix of Mid-Ohio | J.J. Lehto, Jörg Müller | BMW |
| Sept 9 | Monteray Championships | J.J. Lehto, Jörg Müller | BMW |

# Professional Sports Car Racing, Inc. (Cont.)

## 2001 American Le Mans Series Championship Final Standings

| PROTOTYPE CLASS | Pts | GTS CLASS | Pts | GT CLASS | Pts |
|---|---|---|---|---|---|
| Emanuele Pirro | 202 | Terry Borcheller | 187 | Jörg Müller | 191 |
| Frank Biela | 198 | Franz Konrad | 184 | J.J. Lehto | 186 |
| Rinaldo Capello | 175 | Ron Fellows | 171 | Sascha Maassen | 177 |
| Tom Kristensen | 161 | Johnny O'Connell | 170 | Lucas Luhr | 176 |
| Jan Magnussen | 159 | Andy Pilgrim | 153 | Boris Said | 169 |
| Andy Wallace | 153 | Kelly Collins | 153 | Dirk Müller | 164 |
| David Brabham | 145 | Tom Weikardt | 123 | Frederik Ekblom | 159 |
| Johnny Herbert | 113 | Shane Lewis | 87 | Hans Stuck | 158 |
| Stefan Johannsson | 89 | Oliver Gavin | 74 | Randy Pobst | 148 |
| Christophe Tinseau | 83 | Jeff Altenburg | 60 | Christian Menzel | 148 |

# 24 Hours of Le Mans

Held at Le Mans, France, on June 16–17, 2001, the 24 Hours of Le Mans is the most prestigious international event in endurance racing.

| Place | Drivers | Car | Laps |
|---|---|---|---|
| 1 | Frank Biela, Tom Kristensen, Emanuele Pirro | Audi | 321 (2,714.4 mi) |
| 2 | Laurent Aiello, Rinaldo Capello, Christian Pescatori | Audi | 320 |
| 3 | Andy Wallace, Butch Leitzinger, Eric Van De Poele | Bentley | 306 |
| 4 | Olivier Beretta, Karl Wendlinger, Pedro Lamy | Chrysler | 298 |
| 5 | Jean Denis Deletraz, Pascal Fabre, Jordi Gene | Reynard | 284 |
| 6 | Gabrio Rosa, Fabio Babini, Luca Drudi | Porsche | 283 |
| 7 | Gunnar Jeannette, Romain Dumas, Philippe Haezebrouck | Porsche | 282 |
| 8 | Ron Fellows, Johnny O'Connell, Scott Pruett | Corvette | 278 |
| 9 | Thierry Perrier, Michel Neugarten, Nigel Smith | Porsche | 275 |
| 10 | Jean-Luc Chereau, Sebastien Dumez, Patrice Goueslard | Porsche | 274 |

# National Hot Rod Association

## 2001 Results (through September 30)

### TOP FUEL

| Date | Race, Site | Winner | Time | Speed |
|---|---|---|---|---|
| Feb 1–4 | Winternationals, Pomona, CA | Darrell Russell | 4.665 | 309.77 |
| Feb 15–18 | Kragen Nationals, Phoenix | Doug Kalitta | 4.628 | 309.84 |
| Mar 15–18 | Mac Tools Gatornationals, Gainesville, FL | Larry Dixon | 4.661 | 313.95 |
| Mar 22–25 | O'Reilly Nationals, Baytown, TX | Mike Dunn | 4.603 | 324.98 |
| Apr 5–8 | Las Vegas Nationals | Kenny Bernstein | 4.533 | 325.53 |
| Apr 27–29 | Thunder Valley Nationals, Bristol, TN | Doug Kalitta | 4.690 | 300.73 |
| May 3–6 | Southern Nationals, Commerce, GA | Mike Dunn | 4.591 | 325.00 |
| May 17–20 | Matco Supernationals, Englishtown, NJ | Kenny Bernstein | 4.532 | 321.35 |
| May 24–27 | Advance Auto Parts Nationals, Topeka, KS | Kenny Bernstein | 4.625 | 317.94 |
| May 31–Jun 3 | Route 66 Nationals, Joliet, IL | Kenny Bernstein | 4.546 | 322.81 |
| June 14–17 | Pontiac Nationals, Columbus, OH | Larry Dixon | 4.700 | 306.53 |
| June 21–24 | Sears Craftsman Nationals, St. Louis, MO | Doug Kalitta | 4.772 | 302.82 |
| July 5–7 | Pep Boys Nationals, Pomona, CA | Doug Herbert | 4.600 | 320.58 |
| July 19–22 | Mile High Nationals, Denver | Larry Dixon | 4.844 | 298.47 |
| July 27–29 | Northwest Nationals, Kent, WA | Gary Scelzi | 4.556 | 319.29 |
| Aug 3–5 | Fram Nationals, Sonoma, CA | Kenny Bernstein | 4.819 | 298.40 |
| Aug 16–19 | Colonel's Nationals, Brainerd, MN | Larry Dixon | 4.609 | 316.90 |
| Aug 29–Sept 3 | U.S. Nationals, Clermont, IN | Larry Dixon | 4.609 | 315.93 |
| Sept 20–23 | AutoZone Nationals, Millington, TN | Kenny Bernstein | 4.682 | 308.78 |
| Sept 27–30 | National Event, Joliet, IL | Kenny Bernstein | 4.569 | 322.04 |

### FUNNY CAR

| Date | Race, Site | Winner | Time | Speed |
|---|---|---|---|---|
| Feb 1–4 | Winternationals, Pomona, CA | Bruce Sarver | 4.887 | 308.35 |
| Feb 15–18 | Kragen Nationals, Phoenix | John Force | 4.929 | 285.77 |
| Mar 15–18 | Mac Tools Gatornationals, Gainesville, FL | John Force | 5.310 | 273.27 |
| Mar 22–25 | O'Reilly Nationals, Baytown, TX | Del Worsham | 4.852 | 311.63 |

## 2001 Results (through September 30) *(Cont.)*

### FUNNY CAR *(CONT.)*

| Date | Race, Site | Winner | Time | Speed |
|---|---|---|---|---|
| Apr 5–8 | Las Vegas Nationals | Tommy Johnson Jr | 4.856 | 310.77 |
| Apr 27–29 | Thunder Valley Nationals, Bristol, TN | Ron Capps | 5.045 | 288.52 |
| May 3–6 | Southern Nationals, Commerce, GA | Frank Pedregon | 4.902 | 305.98 |
| May 17–20 | Matco Supernationals, Englishtown, NJ | Tony Pedregon | 4.936 | 316.23 |
| May 24–27 | Advance Auto Parts Nationals, Topeka, KS | Tony Pedregon | 4.912 | 309.77 |
| May 31–Jun 3 | Lucas Oil Products Nationals, Joilet, IL | Del Worsham | 4.811 | 314.39 |
| June 14–17 | Pontiac Nationals, Columbus, OH | John Force | 4.963 | 308.00 |
| June 21–24 | Sears Craftsman Nationals, St. Louis, MO | Tony Pedregon | 5.006 | 296.31 |
| July 5–7 | Pep Boys Nationals, Pomona, CA | John Force | 4.853 | 317.64 |
| July 19–22 | Mile High Nationals, Denver | John Force | 5.225 | 288.39 |
| July 27–29 | Northwest Nationals, Kent, WA | Whit Bazemore | 5.049 | 284.56 |
| Aug 3–5 | Fram Nationals, Sonoma, CA | Del Worsham | 5.044 | 301.60 |
| Aug 16–19 | Colonel's Nationals, Brainerd, MN | Ron Capps | 4.939 | 306.53 |
| Aug 29–Sept 3 | U.S. Nationals, Clermont, IN | Whit Bazemore | 4.971 | 298.14 |
| Sept 20–23 | AutoZone Nationals, Millington, TN | Gary Densham | 5.070 | 290.01 |
| Sept 27–30 | National Event, Joliet, IL | Whit Bazemore | 4.823 | 320.97 |

### PRO STOCK

| Date | Race, Site | Winner | Time | Speed |
|---|---|---|---|---|
| Feb 1–4 | Winternationals, Pomona, CA | Kurt Johnson | 6.912 | 200.44 |
| Feb 15–18 | Kragen Nationals, Phoenix | Warren Johnson | 6.924 | 199.20 |
| Mar 15–18 | Mac Tools Gatornationals, Gainesville, FL | Jeg Coughlin | 6.935 | 199.40 |
| Mar 22–25 | O'Reilly Nationals, Baytown, TX | Warren Johnson | 6.844 | 200.98 |
| Apr 5–8 | Las Vegas Nationals | Jeg Coughlin | 6.959 | 197.62 |
| Apr 27–29 | Thunder Valley Nationals, Bristol, TN | Greg Anderson | 6.993 | 196.85 |
| May 3–6 | Southern Nationals, Commerce, GA | Jim Yates | 6.959 | 199.43 |
| May 17–20 | Matco Supernationals, Englishtown, NJ | Richie Stevens | 6.892 | 200.14 |
| May 24–27 | Advance Auto Parts Nationals, Topeka, KS | Ron Krisher | 6.963 | 198.73 |
| May 31–Jun 3 | Lucas Oil Products Nationals, Joilet, IL | Mike Edwards | 6.848 | 200.23 |
| June 14–17 | Pontiac Nationals, Columbus, OH | Warren Johnson | 6.948 | 198.00 |
| June 21–24 | Sears Craftsman Nationals, St. Louis, MO | Warren Johnson | 6.908 | 200.74 |
| July 5–7 | Pep Boys Nationals, Pomona, CA | Jeg Coughlin | 6.911 | 199.26 |
| July 19–22 | Mile High Nationals, Denver | Warren Johnson | 7.347 | 188.28 |
| July 27–29 | Northwest Nationals, Kent, WA | Mark Osborne | 6.893 | 201.43 |
| Aug 3–5 | Fram Nationals, Sonoma, CA | Tom Martino | 7.037 | 196.50 |
| Aug 16–19 | Colonel's Nationals, Brainerd, MN | Bruce Allen | 6.962 | 197.28 |
| Aug 29–Sept 3 | U.S. Nationals, Clermont, IN | Greg Anderson | 6.958 | 198.58 |
| Sept 20–23 | AutoZone Nationals, Millington, TN | George Marnell | 6.974 | 198.12 |
| Sept 27–30 | National Event, Joliet, IL | Warren Johnson | 6.832 | 201.70 |

## 2000 Standings

### TOP FUEL

| Driver | Wins | Pts |
|---|---|---|
| Gary Scelzi | 9 | 1890 |
| Tony Schumacher | 4 | 1624 |
| Larry Dixon | 2 | 1603 |
| Joe Amato | 2 | 1422 |
| Doug Kalitta | 2 | 1413 |
| Kenny Bernstein | 1 | 1275 |
| Cory McClenathan | 3 | 1249 |
| Bob Vandergriff | 0 | 1001 |
| Bob Herbert | 0 | 963 |
| David Grubnic | 0 | 861 |

### FUNNY CAR

| Driver | Wins | Pts |
|---|---|---|
| John Force | 11 | 1992 |
| Ron Capps | 0 | 1551 |
| Jerry Toliver | 3 | 1513 |
| Tony Pedregon | 2 | 1444 |
| Jim Epler | 2 | 1242 |
| Scotty Cannon | 0 | 1114 |
| Whit Bazemore | 1 | 1088 |
| Del Worsham | 0 | 1056 |
| Bruce Sarver | 1 | 1035 |
| Dean Skuza | 0 | 995 |

### PRO STOCK

| Driver | Wins | Pts |
|---|---|---|
| Jeg Coughlin | 10 | 2054 |
| Kurt Johnson | 6 | 1604 |
| Warren Johnson | 2 | 1481 |
| Ron Krisher | 2 | 1392 |
| Mark Pawuk | 1 | 1214 |
| Troy Coughlin | 1 | 1166 |
| Richie Stevens Jr | 1 | 1142 |
| Jim Yates | 0 | 1028 |
| Darrell Alderman | 0 | 927 |
| Bruce Allen | 0 | 887 |

# FOR THE RECORD·Year by Year

## Indianapolis 500

First held in 1911, the Indianapolis 500—200 laps of the 2.5-mile Indianapolis Motor Speedway Track (called the Brickyard in honor of its original pavement)—grew to become the most famous auto race in the world. Though the Memorial Day weekend event lost participants and prestige in the mid-1990s due to feuding in the world of U.S. open-wheel racing, it annually attracts crowds of over 100,000.

| Year | Winner (start pos.) | Chassis/Engine | Avg Speed | Pole Winner | Speed |
|---|---|---|---|---|---|
| 1911 | Ray Harroun (28) | Marmon/Marmon | 74.590 | Lewis Strang | Awarded pole |
| 1912 | Joe Dawson (7) | National/National | 78.720 | Gil Anderson | Drew pole |
| 1913 | Jules Goux (7) | Peugeot/Peugeot | 75.930 | Caleb Bragg | Drew pole |
| 1914 | Rene Thomas (15) | Delage/Delage | 82.470 | Jean Chassagne | Drew pole |
| 1915 | Ralph DePalma (2) | Mercedes/Mercedes | 89.840 | Howard Wilcox | 98.90 |
| 1916 | Dario Resta (4) | Peugeot/Peugeot | 84.000 | John Aitken | 96.69 |
| 1917–18 | No race | | | | |
| 1919 | Howard Wilcox (2) | Peugeot/Peugeot | 88.050 | Rene Thomas | 104.78 |
| 1920 | Gaston Chevrolet (6) | Frontenac/Frontenac | 88.620 | Ralph DePalma | 99.15 |
| 1921 | Tommy Milton (20) | Frontenac/Frontenac | 89.620 | Ralph DePalma | 100.75 |
| 1922 | Jimmy Murphy (1) | Duesenberg/Miller | 94.480 | Jimmy Murphy | 100.50 |
| 1923 | Tommy Milton (1) | Miller/Miller | 90.950 | Tommy Milton | 108.17 |
| 1924 | L.L. Corum<br>Joe Boyer (21) | Duesenberg/Duesenberg | 98.230 | Jimmy Murphy | 108.037 |
| 1925 | Peter DePaolo (2) | Duesenberg/Duesenberg | 101.130 | Leon Duray | 113.196 |
| 1926 | Frank Lockhart (20) | Miller/Miller | 95.904 | Earl Cooper | 111.735 |
| 1927 | George Souders (22) | Duesenberg/Duesenberg | 97.545 | Frank Lockhart | 120.100 |
| 1928 | Louis Meyer (13) | Miller/Miller | 99.482 | Leon Duray | 122.391 |
| 1929 | Ray Keech (6) | Miller/Miller | 97.585 | Cliff Woodbury | 120.599 |
| 1930 | Billy Arnold (1) | Summers/Miller | 100.448 | Billy Arnold | 113.268 |
| 1931 | Louis Schneider (13) | Stevens/Miller | 96.629 | Russ Snowberger | 112.796 |
| 1932 | Fred Frame (27) | Wetteroth/Miller | 104.144 | Lou Moore | 117.363 |
| 1933 | Louis Meyer (6) | Miller/Miller | 104.162 | Bill Cummings | 118.524 |
| 1934 | Bill Cummings (10) | Miller/Miller | 104.863 | Kelly Petillo | 119.329 |
| 1935 | Kelly Petillo (22) | Wetteroth/Offy | 106.240 | Rex Mays | 120.736 |
| 1936 | Louis Meyer (28) | Stevens/Miller | 109.069 | Rex Mays | 119.664 |
| 1937 | Wilbur Shaw (2) | Shaw/Offy | 113.580 | Bill Cummings | 123.343 |
| 1938 | Floyd Roberts (1) | Wetteroth/Miller | 117.200 | Floyd Roberts | 125.681 |
| 1939 | Wilbur Shaw (3) | Maserati/Maserati | 115.035 | Jimmy Snyder | 130.138 |
| 1940 | Wilbur Shaw (2) | Maserati/Maserati | 114.277 | Rex Mays | 127.850 |
| 1941 | Floyd Davis<br>Mauri Rose (17) | Wetteroth/Offy | 115.117 | Mauri Rose | 128.691 |
| 1942–45 | No race | | | | |
| 1946 | George Robson (15) | Adams/Sparks | 114.820 | Cliff Bergere | 126.471 |
| 1947 | Mauri Rose (3) | Deidt/Offy | 116.338 | Ted Horn | 126.564 |
| 1948 | Mauri Rose (3) | Deidt/Offy | 119.814 | Rex Mays | 130.577 |
| 1949 | Bill Holland (4) | Deidt/Offy | 121.327 | Duke Nalon | 132.939 |
| 1950 | Johnnie Parsons (5) | Kurtis/Offy | 124.002 | Walt Faulkner | 134.343 |
| 1951 | Lee Wallard (2) | Kurtis/Offy | 126.244 | Duke Nalon | 136.498 |
| 1952 | Troy Ruttman (7) | Kuzma/Offy | 128.922 | Fred Agabashian | 138.010 |
| 1953 | Bill Vukovich (1) | KK500A/Offy | 128.740 | Bill Vukovich | 138.392 |
| 1954 | Bill Vukovich (19) | KK500A/Offy | 130.840 | Jack McGrath | 141.033 |
| 1955 | Bob Sweikert (14) | KK500C/Offy | 128.209 | Jerry Hoyt | 140.045 |
| 1956 | Pat Flaherty (1) | Watson/Offy | 128.490 | Pat Flaherty | 145.596 |
| 1957 | Sam Hanks (13) | Salih/Offy | 135.601 | Pat O'Connor | 143.948 |
| 1958 | Jim Bryan (7) | Salih/Offy | 133.791 | Dick Rathmann | 145.974 |
| 1959 | Rodger Ward (6) | Watson/Offy | 135.857 | Johnny Thomson | 145.908 |
| 1960 | Jim Rathmann (2) | Watson/Offy | 138.767 | Eddie Sachs | 146.592 |
| 1961 | A.J. Foyt (7) | Trevis/Offy | 139.130 | Eddie Sachs | 147.481 |
| 1962 | Rodger Ward (2) | Watson/Offy | 140.293 | Parnelli Jones | 150.370 |
| 1963 | Parnelli Jones (1) | Watson/Offy | 143.137 | Parnelli Jones | 151.153 |
| 1964 | A.J. Foyt (5) | Watson/Offy | 147.350 | Jim Clark | 158.828 |
| 1965 | Jim Clark (2) | Lotus/Ford | 150.686 | A.J. Foyt | 161.233 |
| 1966 | Graham Hill (15) | Lola/Ford | 144.317 | Mario Andretti | 165.899 |
| 1967 | A.J. Foyt (4) | Coyote/Ford | 151.207 | Mario Andretti | 168.982 |
| 1968 | Bobby Unser (3) | Eagle/Offy | 152.882 | Joe Leonard | 171.559 |
| 1969 | Mario Andretti (2) | Hawk/Ford | 156.867 | A.J. Foyt | 170.568 |
| 1970 | Al Unser (1) | PJ Colt/Ford | 155.749 | Al Unser | 170.221 |
| 1971 | Al Unser (5) | PJ Colt/Ford | 157.735 | Peter Revson | 178.696 |
| 1972 | Mark Donohue (3) | McLaren/Offy | 162.962 | Bobby Unser | 195.940 |
| 1973 | Gordon Johncock (11) | Eagle/Offy | 159.036 | Johnny Rutherford | 198.413 |
| 1974 | Johnny Rutherford (25) | McLaren/Offy | 158.589 | A.J. Foyt | 191.632 |

| Year | Winner (start pos.) | Chassis/Engine | Avg speed | Pole Winner | Speed |
|---|---|---|---|---|---|
| 1975 | Bobby Unser (3) | Racers Eagle/Offy | 149.213 | A.J. Foyt | 193.976 |
| 1976 | Johnny Rutherford (1) | McLaren/Offy | 148.725 | Johnny Rutherford | 188.957 |
| 1977 | A.J. Foyt (4) | Coyote/Ford | 161.331 | Tom Sneva | 198.884 |
| 1978 | Al Unser (5) | Lola/Cosworth | 161.361 | Tom Sneva | 202.156 |
| 1979 | Rick Mears (1) | Penske/Cosworth | 158.899 | Rick Mears | 193.736 |
| 1980 | Johnny Rutherford (1) | Chaparral/Coswoth | 142.862 | Johnny Rutherford | 192.256 |
| 1981 | Bobby Unser (1) | Penske/Cosworth | 139.084 | Bobby Unser | 200.546 |
| 1982 | Gordon Johncock (5) | Wildcat/Cosworth | 162.026 | Rick Mears | 207.004 |
| 1983 | Tom Sneva (4) | March/Cosworth | 162.117 | Teo Fabi | 207.395 |
| 1984 | Rick Mears (3) | March/Cosworth | 163.612 | Tom Sneva | 210.029 |
| 1985 | Danny Sullivan (8) | March/Cosworth | 152.982 | Pancho Carter | 212.583 |
| 1986 | Bobby Rahal (4) | March/Cosworth | 170.722 | Rick Mears | 216.828 |
| 1987 | Al Unser (20) | March/Cosworth | 162.175 | Mario Andretti | 215.390 |
| 1988 | Rick Mears (1) | Penske/Chevrolet | 144.809 | Rick Mears | 219.198 |
| 1989 | Emerson Fittipaldi (3) | Penske/Chevrolet | 167.581 | Rick Mears | 223.885 |
| 1990 | Arie Luyendyk (3) | Lola/Chevrolet | 185.981* | Emerson Fittipaldi | 225.301 |
| 1991 | Rick Mears (1) | Penske/Chevrolet | 176.457 | Rick Mears | 224.113 |
| 1992 | Al Unser Jr (12) | Galmer/Chevrolet | 134.477 | Roberto Guerrero | 232.482 |
| 1993 | Emerson Fittipaldi (9) | Penske/Chevrolet | 157.207 | Arie Luyendyk | 223.967 |
| 1994 | Al Unser Jr (1) | Penske/Mercedes | 160.872 | Al Unser Jr | 228.011 |
| 1995 | Jacques Villeneuve (5) | Reynard/Ford | 153.616 | Scott Brayton | 231.616 |
| 1996 | Buddy Lazier (5) | Reynard/Ford | 147.956 | Tony Stewart | 233.100† |
| 1997 | Arie Luyendyk (1) | G Force/Aurora | 145.827 | Arie Luyendyk | 231.468 |
| 1998 | Eddie Cheever (17) | Dallara/Aurora | 145.155 | Billy Boat | 223.503 |
| 1999 | Kenny Brack (8) | Dallara/Aurora | 153.176 | Arie Luyendyk | 225.179 |
| 2000 | Juan Montoya (2) | G Force/Aurora | 167.607 | Greg Ray | 223.471 |
| 2001 | Helio Castroneves (11) | Dallara/Aurora | 153.601 | Scott Sharp | 226.037 |

*Track record, winning time. †Track record, qualifying time.

## Indianapolis 500 Rookie of the Year Award

| | | |
|---|---|---|
| 1952 | Art Cross | 1970 | Donnie Allison | 1987 | Fabrizio Barbazza |
| 1953 | Jimmy Daywalt | 1971 | Denny Zimmerman | 1988 | Billy Vukovich III |
| 1954 | Larry Crockett | 1972 | Mike Hiss | 1989 | Bernard Jourdain |
| 1955 | Al Herman | 1973 | Graham McRae | | Scott Pruett |
| 1956 | Bob Veith | 1974 | Pancho Carter | 1990 | Eddie Cheever* |
| 1957 | Don Edmunds | 1975 | Bill Puterbaugh | 1991 | Jeff Andretti |
| 1958 | George Amick | 1976 | Vern Schuppan | 1992 | Lyn St. James |
| 1959 | Bobby Grim | 1977 | Jerry Sneva | 1993 | Nigel Mansell |
| 1960 | Jim Hurtubise | 1978 | Rick Mears* | 1994 | Jacques Villeneuve* |
| 1961 | Parnelli Jones* | | Larry Rice | 1995 | Gil de Ferran |
| | Bobby Marshman | 1979 | Howdy Holmes | 1996 | Tony Stewart |
| 1962 | Jimmy McElreath | 1980 | Tim Richmond | 1997 | Jeff Ward |
| 1963 | Jim Clark* | 1981 | Josele Garza | 1998 | Steve Knapp |
| 1964 | Johnny White | 1982 | Jim Hickman | 1999 | Robby McGehee |
| 1965 | Mario Andretti* | 1983 | Teo Fabi | 2000 | Juan Montoya* |
| 1966 | Jackie Stewart | 1984 | Michael Andretti | 2001 | Helio Castroneves* |
| 1967 | Denis Hulme | | Roberto Guerrero | | |
| 1968 | Billy Vukovich | 1985 | Arie Luyendyk* | | |
| 1969 | Mark Donohue* | 1986 | Randy Lanier | | |

*Future winner of Indy 500.

## CART Championship Series Champions

From 1909 to 1955, this championship was awarded by the American Automobile Association (AAA), and from 1956 to 1979 by the United States Auto Club (USAC). Since 1979, Championship Auto Racing Teams (CART) has conducted the championship. Known as PPG CART World Series until 1998.

| | | |
|---|---|---|
| 1909 .............George Robertson | 1940 .............Rex Mays | 1974 .............Bobby Unser |
| 1910 .............Ray Harroun | 1941 .............Rex Mays | 1975 .............A.J. Foyt |
| 1911 .............Ralph Mulford | 1942–45 .......No racing | 1976 .............Gordon Johncock |
| 1912 .............Ralph DePalma | 1946 .............Ted Horn | 1977 .............Tom Sneva |
| 1913 .............Earl Cooper | 1947 .............Ted Horn | 1978 .............Tom Sneva |
| 1914 .............Ralph DePalma | 1948 .............Ted Horn | 1979 .............A.J. Foyt |
| 1915 .............Earl Cooper | 1949 .............Johnnie Parsons | 1979 .............Rick Mears |
| 1916 .............Dario Resta | 1950 .............Henry Banks | 1980 .............Johnny Rutherford |
| 1917 .............Earl Cooper | 1951 .............Tony Bettenhausen | 1981 .............Rick Mears |
| 1918 .............Ralph Mulford | 1952 .............Chuck Stevenson | 1982 .............Rick Mears |
| 1919 .............Howard Wilcox | 1953 .............Sam Hanks | 1983 .............Al Unser |
| 1920 .............Tommy Milton | 1954 .............Jimmy Bryan | 1984 .............Mario Andretti |
| 1921 .............Tommy Milton | 1955 .............Bob Sweikert | 1985 .............Al Unser |
| 1922 .............Jimmy Murphy | 1956 .............Jimmy Bryan | 1986 .............Bobby Rahal |
| 1923 .............Eddie Hearne | 1957 .............Jimmy Bryan | 1987 .............Bobby Rahal |
| 1924 .............Jimmy Murphy | 1958 .............Tony Bettenhausen | 1988 .............Danny Sullivan |
| 1925 .............Peter DePaolo | 1959 .............Rodger Ward | 1989 .............Emerson Fittipaldi |
| 1926 .............Harry Hartz | 1960 .............A.J. Foyt | 1990 .............Al Unser Jr. |
| 1927 .............Peter DePaolo | 1961 .............A.J. Foyt | 1991 .............Michael Andretti |
| 1928 .............Louis Meyer | 1962 .............Rodger Ward | 1992 .............Bobby Rahal |
| 1929 .............Louis Meyer | 1963 .............A.J. Foyt | 1993 .............Nigel Mansell |
| 1930 .............Billy Arnold | 1964 .............A.J. Foyt | 1994 .............Al Unser Jr. |
| 1931 .............Louis Schneider | 1965 .............Mario Andretti | 1995 .............Jacques Villeneuve |
| 1932 .............Bob Carey | 1966 .............Mario Andretti | 1996 .............Jimmy Vasser |
| 1933 .............Louis Meyer | 1967 .............A.J. Foyt | 1997 .............Alex Zanardi |
| 1934 .............Bill Cummings | 1968 .............Bobby Unser | 1998 .............Alex Zanardi |
| 1935 .............Kelly Petillo | 1969 .............Mario Andretti | 1999 .............Juan Montoya |
| 1936 .............Mauri Rose | 1970 .............Al Unser | 2000 .............Gil de Ferran |
| 1937 .............Wilbur Shaw | 1971 .............Joe Leonard | |
| 1938 .............Floyd Roberts | 1972 .............Joe Leonard | |
| 1939 .............Wilbur Shaw | 1973 .............Roger McCluskey | |

## Alltime CART Leaders

| WINS | | WINNINGS ($) | | POLE POSITIONS | |
|---|---|---|---|---|---|
| A.J. Foyt | 67 | Al Unser Jr | 18,828,406 | Mario Andretti | 67 |
| Mario Andretti | 52 | *Michael Andretti | 17,314,369 | A.J. Foyt | 53 |
| *Michael Andretti | 41 | Bobby Rahal | 16,344,008 | Bobby Unser | 49 |
| Al Unser | 39 | Emerson Fittipaldi | 14,293,625 | Rick Mears | 40 |
| Bobby Unser | 35 | Mario Andretti | 11,552,154 | *Michael Andretti | 32 |
| Al Unser Jr | 31 | Rick Mears | 11,050,807 | Al Unser | 27 |
| Rick Mears | 29 | *Jimmy Vasser | 10,056,244 | Johnny Rutherford | 23 |
| Johnny Rutherford | 27 | Danny Sullivan | 8,884,126 | Gordon Johncock | 20 |
| Rodger Ward | 26 | *Paul Tracy | 8,307,770 | Rex Mays | 19 |
| Gordon Johncock | 25 | Arie Luyendyk | 7,732,188 | Danny Sullivan | 19 |
| Bobby Rahal | 24 | Raul Boesel | 6,971,887 | Bobby Rahal | 18 |
| Ralph DePalma | 24 | Al Unser | 6,740,843 | Emerson Fittipaldi | 17 |
| Tommy Milton | 23 | *Gil de Ferran | 6,280,703 | Tony Bettenhausen | 14 |
| Tony Bettenhausen | 22 | *Adrian Fernandez | 6,266,515 | Juan Montoya | 14 |
| Emerson Fittipaldi | 22 | *Alex Zanardi | 5,893,750 | *Gil de Ferran | 14 |
| Earl Cooper | 20 | Scott Pruett | 5,440,144 | Don Branson | 14 |
| Jimmy Bryan | 19 | A.J. Foyt | 5,357,589 | Tom Sneva | 14 |
| Jimmy Murphy | 19 | Teo Fabi | 5,045,881 | *Paul Tracy | 13 |
| *Paul Tracy | 18 | *Christian Fittipaldi | 4,940,918 | Parnelli Jones | 12 |
| Danny Sullivan | 17 | Scott Brayton | 4,807,274 | Rodger Ward | 11 |
| Ralph Mulford | 17 | | | Danny Ongais | 11 |

*Active driver. Note: Leaders through October 5, 2001.

# National Association for Stock Car Auto Racing

## Stock Car Racing's Major Events

Winston offers a $1 million bonus to any driver to win three of NASCAR's top four events in the same season. These races are the richest (Daytona 500), the fastest (Talladega 500), the longest (World 600 at Charlotte) and the oldest (Southern 500 at Darlington). These events form the backbone of NASCAR racing. Only four drivers, Lee Roy Yarbrough (1969), David Pearson (1976), Bill Elliott (1985) and Jeff Gordon (1997) have scored the three-track hat trick.

## Daytona 500

| Year | Winner | Car | Avg Speed | Pole Winner | Speed |
|------|--------|-----|-----------|-------------|-------|
| 1959 | Lee Petty | Oldsmobile | 135.520 | Cotton Owens | 143.198 |
| 1960 | Junior Johnson | Chevrolet | 124.740 | Fireball Roberts | 151.556 |
| 1961 | Marvin Panch | Pontiac | 149.601 | Fireball Roberts | 155.709 |
| 1962 | Fireball Roberts | Pontiac | 152.529 | Fireball Roberts | 156.995 |
| 1963 | Tiny Lund | Ford | 151.566 | Johnny Rutherford | 165.183 |
| 1964 | Richard Petty | Plymouth | 154.345 | Paul Goldsmith | 174.910 |
| 1965 | Fred Lorenzen | Ford | 141.539 | Darel Dieringer | 171.151 |
| 1966 | Richard Petty | Plymouth | 160.627 | Richard Petty | 175.165 |
| 1967 | Mario Andretti | Ford | 149.926 | Curtis Turner | 180.831 |
| 1968 | Cale Yarborough | Mercury | 143.251 | Cale Yarborough | 189.222 |
| 1969 | Lee Roy Yarbrough | Ford | 157.950 | David Pearson | 190.029 |
| 1970 | Pete Hamilton | Plymouth | 149.601 | Cale Yarborough | 194.015 |
| 1971 | Richard Petty | Plymouth | 144.462 | A.J. Foyt | 182.744 |
| 1972 | A.J. Foyt | Mercury | 161.550 | Bobby Isaac | 186.632 |
| 1973 | Richard Petty | Dodge | 157.205 | Buddy Baker | 185.662 |
| 1974 | Richard Petty | Dodge | 140.894 | David Pearson | 185.017 |
| 1975 | Benny Parsons | Chevrolet | 153.649 | Donnie Allison | 185.827 |
| 1976 | David Pearson | Mercury | 152.181 | A.J. Foyt | 185.943 |
| 1977 | Cale Yarborough | Chevrolet | 153.218 | Donnie Allison | 188.048 |
| 1978 | Bobby Allison | Ford | 159.730 | Cale Yarborough | 187.536 |
| 1979 | Richard Petty | Oldsmobile | 143.977 | Buddy Baker | 196.049 |
| 1980 | Buddy Baker | Oldsmobile | 177.602* | A.J. Foyt | 195.020 |
| 1981 | Richard Petty | Buick | 169.651 | Bobby Allison | 194.624 |
| 1982 | Bobby Allison | Buick | 153.991 | Benny Parsons | 196.317 |
| 1983 | Cale Yarborough | Pontiac | 155.979 | Ricky Rudd | 198.864 |
| 1984 | Cale Yarborough | Chevrolet | 150.994 | Cale Yarborough | 201.848 |
| 1985 | Bill Elliott | Ford | 172.265 | Bill Elliott | 205.114 |
| 1986 | Geoff Bodine | Chevrolet | 148.124 | Bill Elliott | 205.039 |
| 1987 | Bill Elliott | Ford | 176.263 | Bill Elliott | 210.364† |
| 1988 | Bobby Allison | Buick | 137.531 | Ken Schrader | 193.823 |
| 1989 | Darrell Waltrip | Chevrolet | 148.466 | Ken Schrader | 196.996 |
| 1990 | Derrike Cope | Chevrolet | 165.761 | Ken Schrader | 196.515 |
| 1991 | Ernie Irvan | Chevrolet | 148.148 | Davey Allison | 195.955 |
| 1992 | Davey Allison | Ford | 160.256 | Sterling Marlin | 192.213 |
| 1993 | Dale Jarrett | Chevrolet | 154.972 | Kyle Petty | 189.426 |
| 1994 | Sterling Marlin | Chevrolet | 156.931 | Loy Allen Jr | 190.158 |
| 1995 | Sterling Marlin | Chevrolet | 141.710 | Dale Jarrett | 193.498 |
| 1996 | Dale Jarrett | Ford | 154.308 | Dale Earnhardt | 189.510 |
| 1997 | Jeff Gordon | Chevrolet | 148.295 | Mike Skinner | 189.813 |
| 1998 | Dale Earnhardt | Chevrolet | 172.712 | Bobby Labonte | 192.415 |
| 1999 | Jeff Gordon | Chevrolet | 161.551 | Jeff Gordon | 195.067 |
| 2000 | Dale Jarrett | Ford | 155.669 | Dale Jarrett | 191.091 |
| 2001 | Michael Waltrip | Chevrolet | 161.783 | Bill Elliott | 183.570 |

*Track record, winning time. †Track record, qualifying time. Note: The Daytona 500, held annually in February, now opens the NASCAR season with 200 laps around the high-banked Daytona International Speedway.

## World 600

| Year | Winner | Car | Avg Speed | Pole Winner |
|------|--------|-----|-----------|-------------|
| 1960 | Joe Lee Johnson | Chevrolet | 107.752 | Joe Lee Johnson |
| 1961 | David Pearson | Pontiac | 111.634 | Richard Petty |
| 1962 | Nelson Stacy | Ford | 125.552 | Fireball Roberts |
| 1963 | Fred Lorenzen | Ford | 132.418 | Junior Johnson |
| 1964 | Jim Paschal | Plymouth | 125.772 | Junior Johnson |
| 1965 | Fred Lorenzen | Ford | 121.772 | Fred Lorenzon |
| 1966 | Marvin Panch | Plymouth | 135.042 | Paul Goldsmith |
| 1967 | Jim Paschal | Plymouth | 135.832 | Cale Yarborough |
| 1968 | Buddy Baker | Dodge | 104.207 | Donnie Allison |
| 1969 | Lee Yarbrough | Mercury | 134.631 | Donnie Allison |
| 1970 | Donnie Allison | Ford | 129.680 | Bobby Isaac |
| 1971 | Bobby Allison | Mercury | 140.442 | Charlie Glotzbach |
| 1972 | Buddy Baker | Dodge | 142.255 | Bobby Allison |
| 1973 | Buddy Baker | Dodge | 134.890 | Buddy Baker |
| 1974 | David Pearson | Mercury | 135.720 | David Pearson |
| 1975 | Richard Petty | Dodge | 145.327 | David Pearson |
| 1976 | David Pearson | Mercury | 137.352 | David Pearson |
| 1977 | Richard Petty | Dodge | 137.636 | David Pearson |
| 1978 | Darrell Waltrip | Chevrolet | 138.355 | David Pearson |
| 1979 | Darrell Waltrip | Chevrolet | 136.674 | Neil Bonnet |
| 1980 | Benny Parsons | Chevrolet | 119.265 | Cale Yarborough |
| 1981 | Bobby Allison | Buick | 129.326 | Neil Bonnett |
| 1982 | Neil Bonnett | Ford | 130.508 | David Pearson |
| 1983 | Neil Bonnett | Chevrolet | 140.406 | Buddy Baker |
| 1984 | Bobby Allison | Buick | 129.233 | Harry Gant |
| 1985 | Darrell Waltrip | Chevrolet | 141.807 | Bill Elliott |
| 1986 | Dale Earnhardt | Chevrolet | 140.406 | Geoff Bodine |
| 1987 | Kyle Petty | Ford | 131.483 | Bill Elliott |
| 1988 | Darrell Waltrip | Chevrolet | 124.460 | Davey Allison |
| 1989 | Darrell Waltrip | Chevrolet | 144.077 | Alan Kulwicki |
| 1990 | Rusty Wallace | Pontiac | 137.650 | Ken Schrader |
| 1991 | Davey Allison | Ford | 138.951 | Mark Martin |
| 1992 | Dale Earnhardt | Chevrolet | 132.980 | Bill Elliott |
| 1993 | Dale Earnhardt | Chevrolet | 145.504 | Ken Schrader |
| 1994 | Jeff Gordon | Chevrolet | 139.445 | Jeff Gordon |
| 1995 | Bobby Labonte | Chevrolet | 151.952 | Jeff Gordon |
| 1996 | Dale Jarrett | Ford | 147.581 | Jeff Gordon |
| 1997 | Jeff Gordon | Chevrolet | 136.745 | Jeff Gordon |
| 1998 | Jeff Gordon | Chevrolet | 136.424 | Jeff Gordon |
| 1999 | Jeff Burton | Ford | 151.367 | Bobby Labonte |
| 2000 | Matt Kenseth | Ford | 142.640 | Dale Earnhardt Jr |
| 2001 | Jeff Burton | Ford | 138.107 | Ryan Newman |

Note: Held at the 1.5 mile high banked Lowe's Motor Speedway in Charlotte on Memorial Day weekend.

### ANOTHER SIGN OF THE APOCALYPSE

*Claiming that the promotion of milk is racist because many blacks and Hispanics are lactose intolerant, People for the Ethical Treatment of Animals called for the Indy 500 to replace the winner's traditional sip of dairy milk with orange juice or soy milk.*

## Talladega 500

| Year | Winner | Car | Avg Speed | Pole Winner | Speed |
|------|--------|-----|-----------|-------------|-------|
| 1969 | Richard Brickhouse | Dodge | 153.778 | Charlie Glotzbach | 199.466 |
| 1970 | Pete Hamilton | Plymouth | 158.517 | Bobby Isaac | 186.834 |
| 1971 | Bobby Allison | Mercury | 145.945 | Davey Allison | 187.323 |
| 1972 | James Hylton | Mercury | 148.728 | Bobby Isaac | 190.677 |
| 1973 | Dick Brooks | Plymouth | 145.454 | Bobby Allison | 187.064 |
| 1974 | Richard Petty | Dodge | 148.637 | David Pearson | 184.926 |
| 1975 | Buddy Baker | Ford | 130.892 | Dave Marcis | 191.340 |
| 1976 | Dave Marcis | Dodge | 157.547 | Dave Marcis | 190.651 |
| 1977 | Davey Allison | Chevrolet | 162.524 | Benny Parsons | 192.682 |
| 1978 | Lennie Pond | Oldsmobile | 174.700 | Cale Yarborough | 192.917 |
| 1979 | Darrell Waltrip | Oldsmobile | 161.229 | Neil Bonnet | 193.600 |
| 1980 | Neil Bonnett | Mercury | 166.894 | Buddy Baker | 198.545 |
| 1981 | Ron Bouchard | Buick | 156.737 | Harry Gant | 195.897 |
| 1982 | Darrell Waltrip | Buick | 168.157 | Geoff Bodine | 199.400 |
| 1983 | Dale Earnhardt | Ford | 170.611 | Cale Yarborough | 201.744 |
| 1984 | Dale Earnhardt | Chevrolet | 155.485 | Cale Yarborough | 202.474 |
| 1985 | Cale Yarborough | Ford | 148.772 | Bill Elliott | 207.578 |
| 1986 | Bobby Hillin | Buick | 151.552 | Bill Elliott | 209.005 |
| 1987 | Bill Elliott | Ford | 171.293 | Bill Elliott | 203.827 |
| 1988 | Ken Schrader | Chevrolet | 154.505 | Darrell Waltrip | 196.274 |
| 1989 | Terry Labonte | Ford | 157.354 | Mark Martin | 194.800 |
| 1990 | Dale Earnhardt | Chevrolet | 174.430 | Dale Earnhardt | 192.513 |
| 1991 | Harry Gant | Oldsmobile | 165.620 | Sterling Marlin | 192.085 |
| 1992 | Ernie Irvan | Chevrolet | 176.309 | Sterling Marlin | 190.586 |
| 1993 | Dale Earnhardt | Chevrolet | 153.858 | Bill Elliott | 192.397 |
| 1994 | Jimmy Spencer | Ford | 163.217 | Dale Earnhardt | 193.470 |
| 1995 | Sterling Marlin | Chevrolet | 173.188 | Sterling Marlin | 194.212 |
| 1996 | Jeff Gordon | Chevrolet | 133.387 | Jeremy Mayfield | 192.370 |
| 1997 | Mark Martin | Ford | 188.345 | John Andretti | 193.627 |
| 1998 | Bobby Labonte | Pontiac | 163.439 | Bobby Labonte | 195.728 |
| 1999 | Dale Earnhardt | Chevrolet | 163.395 | Ken Schrader | 197.765 |
| 2000 | Jeff Gordon | Chevrolet | 161.157 | Jeremy Mayfield | 186.969 |
| 2001 | Bobby Hamilton | Chevrolet | 184.003 | Stacy Compton | 184.861 |

Note: Held every spring at the 2.66-mile Talladega Superspeedway.

## How to Smoke Your Tires

After his win at Watkins Glen on August 12, Jeff Gordon burned rubber in textbook fashion, a vast improvement on what he called a "pretty sad" attempt to do so at the Brickyard 400. In his defense, the burnouts and infield doughnuts that others have made popular are rarely rehearsed. "It's kind of like a teenager practicing kissing in the mirror," says Winston Cup driver Buckshot Jones. "Even if you did it, you wouldn't tell anybody." Here are a few tips on how to start smoking:

1. Put the car in gear and, with your foot on the brake, rev the motor. "Run the engine to as many rpm as you can without grenading it," says driver Jeremy Mayfield.

2. Pop the clutch. This gets the rear wheels spinning, which provides the smoke. Timing is of the essence. Says Mayfield, "Start too late, and your engine blows. Start too soon, and the tires catch and you're dodging the wall."

3. Keep moving. "If you stay in place," says Jones, "the smoke will come into the car and make you sick." To keep moving, let the car roll a bit before popping the clutch and work the brake. But don't move too much or the tires will stop smoking.

4. Watch the gauges. "Get those rpm too high, and there's going to be trouble," says Mayfield. "It's pretty tough to explain to your engine builder why you blew his motor while celebrating. And it's pretty embarrassing to have your crew push the car to victory lane."

## Southern 500

| Year | Winner | Car | Avg Speed | Pole Winner |
|------|--------|-----|-----------|-------------|
| 1950 | Johnny Mantz | Plymouth | 76.260 | Wally Campbell |
| 1951 | Herb Thomas | Hudson | 76.900 | Marshall Teague |
| 1952 | Fonty Flock | Oldsmobile | 74.510 | Dick Rathman |
| 1953 | Buck Baker | Oldsmobile | 92.780 | Fonty Flock |
| 1954 | Herb Thomas | Hudson | 94.930 | Buck Baker |
| 1955 | Herb Thomas | Chevrolet | 92.281 | Tim Flock |
| 1956 | Curtis Turner | Ford | 95.067 | Buck Baker |
| 1957 | Speedy Thompson | Chevrolet | 100.100 | Paul Goldsmith |
| 1958 | Fireball Roberts | Chevrolet | 102.590 | Fireball Roberts |
| 1959 | Jim Reed | Chevrolet | 111.836 | Fireball Roberts |
| 1960 | Buck Baker | Pontiac | 105.901 | Cotton Owens |
| 1961 | Nelson Stacy | Ford | 117.880 | Fireball Roberts |
| 1962 | Larry Frank | Ford | 117.965 | Fireball Roberts |
| 1963 | Fireball Roberts | Ford | 129.784 | Fireball Roberts |
| 1964 | Buck Baker | Dodge | 117.757 | Richard Petty |
| 1965 | Ned Jarrett | Ford | 115.924 | Junior Johnson |
| 1966 | Darel Dieringer | Mercury | 114.830 | Lee Yarborough |
| 1967 | Richard Petty | Plymouth | 131.933 | David Pearson |
| 1968 | Cale Yarborough | Mercury | 126.132 | Charlie Glotzbach |
| 1969 | Lee Roy Yarbrough | Ford | 105.612 | Cale Yarborough |
| 1970 | Buddy Baker | Dodge | 128.817 | David Pearson |
| 1971 | Bobby Allison | Mercury | 131.398 | Bobby Allison |
| 1972 | Bobby Allison | Chevrolet | 128.124 | David Pearson |
| 1973 | Cale Yarborough | Chevrolet | 134.033 | David Pearson |
| 1974 | Cale Yarborough | Chevrolet | 111.075 | Richard Petty |
| 1975 | Bobby Allison | Matador | 116.825 | David Pearson |
| 1976 | David Pearson | Mercury | 120.534 | David Pearson |
| 1977 | David Pearson | Mercury | 106.797 | Darrell Waltrip |
| 1978 | Cale Yarborough | Oldsmobile | 116.828 | David Pearson |
| 1979 | David Pearson | Chevrolet | 126.259 | Bobby Allison |
| 1980 | Terry Labonte | Chevrolet | 115.210 | Darrell Waltrip |
| 1981 | Neil Bonnett | Ford | 126.410 | Harry Gant |
| 1982 | Cale Yarborough | Buick | 126.703 | David Pearson |
| 1983 | Bobby Allison | Buick | 123.343 | Neil Bonnett |
| 1984 | Harry Gant | Chevrolet | 128.270 | Harry Gant |
| 1985 | Bill Elliott | Ford | 121.254 | Bill Elliott |
| 1986 | Tim Richmond | Chevrolet | 121.068 | Tim Richmond |
| 1987 | Dale Earnhardt | Chevrolet | 115.520 | Davey Allison |
| 1988 | Bill Elliott | Ford | 128.297 | Bill Elliott |
| 1989 | Dale Earnhardt | Chevrolet | 135.462 | Alan Kulwicki |
| 1990 | Dale Earnhardt | Chevrolet | 123.141 | Dale Earnhardt |
| 1991 | Harry Gant | Oldsmobile | 133.508 | Davey Allison |
| 1992 | Darrell Waltrip | Chevrolet | 129.114 | Sterling Marlin |
| 1993 | Mark Martin | Ford | 137.932 | Ken Schrader |
| 1994 | Bill Elliott | Ford | 127.915 | Geoff Bodine |
| 1995 | Jeff Gordon | Chevrolet | 121.231 | John Andretti |
| 1996 | Jeff Gordon | Chevrolet | 135.757 | Dale Jarrett |
| 1997 | Jeff Gordon | Chevrolet | 121.149 | Bobby Labonte |
| 1998 | Jeff Gordon | Chevrolet | 139.031 | Dale Jarrett |
| 1999 | Jeff Burton | Ford | 100.816 | Kenny Irwin |
| 2000 | Bobby Labonte | Pontiac | 108.275 | Jeremy Mayfield |
| 2001 | Ward Burton | Dodge | 122.773 | Kurt Busch |

Note: Held at the 1.366-mile Darlington (S.C.) Raceway on Labor Day weekend.

## Winston Cup NASCAR Champions

| Year | Driver | Car | Wins | Poles | Winnings ($) |
|------|--------|-----|------|-------|--------------|
| 1949 | Red Byron | Oldsmobile | 2 | 0 | 5,800 |
| 1950 | Bill Rexford | Oldsmobile | 1 | 0 | 6,175 |
| 1951 | Herb Thomas | Hudson | 7 | 4 | 18,200 |
| 1952 | Tim Flock | Hudson | 8 | 4 | 20,210 |
| 1953 | Herb Thomas | Hudson | 11 | 10 | 27,300 |
| 1954 | Lee Petty | Dodge | 7 | 3 | 26,706 |
| 1955 | Tim Flock | Chrysler | 18 | 19 | 33,750 |
| 1956 | Buck Baker | Chrysler | 14 | 12 | 29,790 |
| 1957 | Buck Baker | Chevrolet | 10 | 5 | 24,712 |
| 1958 | Lee Petty | Oldsmobile | 7 | 4 | 20,600 |
| 1959 | Lee Petty | Plymouth | 10 | 2 | 45,570 |
| 1960 | Rex White | Chevrolet | 6 | 3 | 45,260 |
| 1961 | Ned Jarrett | Chevrolet | 1 | 4 | 27,285 |
| 1962 | Joe Weatherly | Pontiac | 9 | 6 | 56,110 |
| 1963 | Joe Weatherly | Mercury | 3 | 6 | 58,110 |
| 1964 | Richard Petty | Plymouth | 9 | 8 | 98,810 |
| 1965 | Ned Jarrett | Ford | 13 | 9 | 77,966 |
| 1966 | David Pearson | Dodge | 14 | 7 | 59,205 |
| 1967 | Richard Petty | Plymouth | 27 | 18 | 130,275 |
| 1968 | David Pearson | Ford | 16 | 12 | 118,824 |
| 1969 | David Pearson | Ford | 11 | 14 | 183,700 |
| 1970 | Bobby Isaac | Dodge | 11 | 13 | 121,470 |
| 1971 | Richard Petty | Plymouth | 21 | 9 | 309,225 |
| 1972 | Richard Petty | Plymouth | 8 | 3 | 227,015 |
| 1973 | Benny Parsons | Chevrolet | 1 | 0 | 114,345 |
| 1974 | Richard Petty | Dodge | 10 | 7 | 299,175 |
| 1975 | Richard Petty | Dodge | 13 | 3 | 378,865 |
| 1976 | Cale Yarborough | Chevrolet | 9 | 2 | 387,173 |
| 1977 | Cale Yarborough | Chevrolet | 9 | 3 | 477,499 |
| 1978 | Cale Yarborough | Oldsmobile | 10 | 8 | 530,751 |
| 1979 | Richard Petty | Chevrolet | 5 | 1 | 531,292 |
| 1980 | Dale Earnhardt | Chevrolet | 5 | 0 | 588,926 |
| 1981 | Darrell Waltrip | Buick | 12 | 11 | 693,342 |
| 1982 | Darrell Waltrip | Buick | 12 | 7 | 873,118 |
| 1983 | Bobby Allison | Buick | 6 | 0 | 828,355 |
| 1984 | Terry Labonte | Chevrolet | 2 | 2 | 713,010 |
| 1985 | Darrell Waltrip | Chevrolet | 3 | 4 | 1,318,735 |
| 1986 | Dale Earnhardt | Chevrolet | 5 | 1 | 1,783,880 |
| 1987 | Dale Earnhardt | Chevrolet | 11 | 1 | 2,099,243 |
| 1988 | Bill Elliott | Ford | 6 | 6 | 1,574,639 |
| 1989 | Rusty Wallace | Pontiac | 6 | 4 | 2,247,950 |
| 1990 | Dale Earnhardt | Chevrolet | 9 | 4 | 3,083,056 |
| 1991 | Dale Earnhardt | Chevrolet | 4 | 0 | 2,396,685 |
| 1992 | Alan Kulwicki | Ford | 2 | 6 | 2,322,561 |
| 1993 | Dale Earnhardt | Chevrolet | 6 | 2 | 3,353,789 |
| 1994 | Dale Earnhardt | Chevrolet | 4 | 2 | 3,400,733 |
| 1995 | Jeff Gordon | Chevrolet | 7 | 8 | 4,347,343 |
| 1996 | Terry Labonte | Chevrolet | 2 | 4 | 4,030,648 |
| 1997 | Jeff Gordon | Chevrolet | 10 | 1 | 4,201,227 |
| 1998 | Jeff Gordon | Chevrolet | 13 | 7 | 6,175,867 |
| 1999 | Dale Jarrett | Ford | 4 | 0 | 3,590,829 |
| 2000 | Bobby Labonte | Pontiac | 4 | 2 | 4,041,750 |

# NASCAR (Cont.)

## Alltime NASCAR Leaders

| WINS | | WINNINGS ($) | | POLE POSITIONS | |
|---|---|---|---|---|---|
| Richard Petty | 200 | Dale Earnhardt | 41,742,384 | Richard Petty | 126 |
| David Pearson | 105 | *Jeff Gordon | 40,495,851 | David Pearson | 113 |
| Bobby Allison | 84 | *Dale Jarrett | 31,635,528 | Cale Yarborough | 70 |
| Darrell Waltrip | 84 | *Rusty Wallace | 28,303,048 | Darrell Waltrip | 59 |
| Cale Yarborough | 83 | *Mark Martin | 28,081,772 | Bobby Allison | 57 |
| Dale Earnhardt | 76 | *Bill Elliott | 26,161,396 | Bobby Isaac | 51 |
| *Jeff Gordon | 58 | *Terry Labonte | 25,818,522 | *Bill Elliott | 50 |
| Lee Petty | 55 | *Bobby Labonte | 24,241,873 | Junior Johnson | 47 |
| *Rusty Wallace | 54 | *Ricky Rudd | 22,843,456 | Buck Baker | 44 |
| Ned Jarrett | 50 | *Jeff Burton | 21,526,436 | *Mark Martin | 41 |
| Junior Johnson | 50 | Darrell Waltrip | 19,416,618 | Buddy Baker | 40 |
| Herb Thomas | 48 | *Sterling Marlin | 17,822,962 | *Jeff Gordon | 39 |
| Buck Baker | 46 | *Ken Schrader | 17,458,675 | Tim Flock | 39 |
| *Bill Elliott | 40 | *Geoff Bodine | 14,794,719 | Herb Thomas | 39 |
| Tim Flock | 40 | *Michael Waltrip | 14,196,171 | *Geoff Bodine | 37 |

*Active drivers. Note: NASCAR leaders through September 24, 2001.

# Formula One Grand Prix Racing

## World Driving Champions

| Year | Winner | Car | Year | Winner | Car |
|---|---|---|---|---|---|
| 1950 | Guiseppe Farina, Italy | Alfa Romeo | 1973 | Jackie Stewart, Scotland | Tyrell-Ford |
| 1951 | Juan-Manuel Fangio, Argentina | Alfa Romeo | 1974 | Emerson Fittipaldi, Brazil | McLaren-Ford |
| | | | 1975 | Niki Lauda, Austria | Ferrari |
| 1952 | Alberto Ascari, Italy | Ferrari | 1976 | James Hunt, England | McLaren-Ford |
| 1953 | Alberto Ascari, Italy | Ferrari | 1977 | Niki Lauda, Austria | Ferrari |
| 1954 | Juan-Manuel Fangio, Argentina | Maserati/ Mercedes | 1978 | Mario Andretti, U.S. | Lotus-Ford |
| 1955 | Juan-Manuel Fangio, Argentina | Mercedes | 1979 | Jody Scheckter, S Africa | Ferrari |
| | | | 1980 | Alan Jones, Australia | Williams-Ford |
| 1956 | Juan-Manuel Fangio, Argentina | Ferrari | 1981 | Nelson Piquet, Brazil | Brabham-Ford |
| | | | 1982 | Keke Rosberg, Finland | Williams-Ford |
| 1957 | Juan-Manuel Fangio, Argentina | Maserati | 1983 | Nelson Piquet, Brazil | Brabham-BMW |
| | | | 1984 | Niki Lauda, Austria | McLaren-Porsche |
| 1958 | Mike Hawthorne, England | Ferrari | 1985 | Alain Prost, France | McLaren-Porsche |
| 1959 | Jack Brabham, Australia | Cooper-Climax | 1986 | Alain Prost, France | McLaren-Porsche |
| 1960 | Jack Brabham, Australia | Cooper-Climax | 1987 | Nelson Piquet, Brazil | Williams-Honda |
| 1961 | Phil Hill, United States | Ferrari | 1988 | Ayrton Senna, Brazil | McLaren-Honda |
| 1962 | Graham Hill, England | BRM | 1989 | Alain Prost, France | McLaren-Honda |
| 1963 | Jim Clark, Scotland | Lotus-Climax | 1990 | Ayrton Senna, Brazil | McLaren-Honda |
| 1964 | John Surtees, England | Ferrari | 1991 | Ayrton Senna, Brazil | McLaren-Honda |
| 1965 | Jim Clark, Scotland | Lotus-Climax | 1992 | Nigel Mansell, Gr. Britain | Williams-Renault |
| 1966 | Jack Brabham, Australia | Brabham-Climax | 1993 | Alain Prost, France | Williams-Renault |
| 1967 | Denis Hulme, New Zealand | Brabham-Repco | 1994 | Michael Schumacher, Ger | Benetton-Ford |
| | | | 1995 | Michael Schumacher, Ger | Benetton-Renault |
| 1968 | Graham Hill, England | Lotus-Ford | 1996 | Damon Hill, Great Britain | Williams-Renault |
| 1969 | Jackie Stewart, Scotland | Matra-Ford | 1997 | Jacques Villeneuve, Canada | Williams-Renault |
| 1970 | Jochen Rindt, Austria* | Lotus-Ford | 1998 | Mika Hakkinen, Finland | McLaren-Mercedes |
| 1971 | Jackie Stewart, Scotland | Tyrell-Ford | 1999 | Mika Hakkinen, Finland | McLaren-Mercedes |
| 1972 | Emerson Fittipaldi, Brazil | Lotus-Ford | 2000 | Michael Schumacher, Ger | Ferrari |

*The championship was awarded after Rindt was killed during practice for the Italian Grand Prix.

# Formula One Grand Prix Racing (Cont.)

## Alltime Grand Prix Winners

| Driver | Wins | Driver | Wins |
|---|---|---|---|
| *Michael Schumacher, Germany | 52 | Jim Clark, Great Britain | 25 |
| Alain Prost, France | 51 | Niki Lauda, Austria | 25 |
| Ayrton Senna, Brazil | 41 | Juan Manuel Fangio, Argentina | 24 |
| Nigel Mansell, Great Britain | 31 | Nelson Piquet, Brazil | 23 |
| Jackie Stewart, Great Britain | 27 | Damon Hill, Great Britain | 22 |

*Active driver. Note: Grand Prix winners through October 3, 2001.

## Alltime Grand Prix Pole Winners

| Driver | Poles | Driver | Poles |
|---|---|---|---|
| Ayrton Senna, Brazil | 65 | Juan Manuel Fangio, Argentina | 29 |
| *Michael Schumacher, Germany | 42 | *Mika Hakkinen, Finland | 26 |
| Alain Prost, France | 33 | Niki Lauda, Austria | 24 |
| Jim Clark, Great Britain | 33 | Nelson Piquet, Brazil | 24 |
| Nigel Mansell, Great Britain | 32 | Damon Hill, Great Britain | 20 |

*Active driver. Note: Pole winners through October 3, 2001.

# Professional Sports Car Racing, Inc.

## The 24 Hours of Daytona

| Year | Winner | Car | Avg Speed | Distance |
|---|---|---|---|---|
| 1962 | Dan Gurney | Lotus 19-Class SP11 | 104.101 mph | 3 hrs (312.42 mi) |
| 1963 | Pedro Rodriguez | Ferrari-Class 12 | 102.074 mph | 3 hrs (308.61 mi) |
| 1964 | Pedro Rodriguez/Phil Hill | Ferrari 250 LM | 98.230 mph | 2,000 km |
| 1965 | Ken Miles/Lloyd Ruby | Ford | 99.944 mph | 2,000 km |
| 1966 | Ken Miles/Lloyd Ruby | Ford Mark II | 108.020 mph | 24 hrs (2,570.63 mi) |
| 1967 | Lorenzo Bandini/Chris Amon | Ferrari 330 P4 | 105.688 mph | 24 hrs (2,537.46 mi) |
| 1968 | Vic Elford/Jochen Neerpasch | Porsche 907 | 106.697 mph | 24 hrs (2,565.69 mi) |
| 1969 | Mark Donohue/Chuck Parsons | Chevy Lola | 99.268 mph | 24 hrs (2,383.75 mi) |
| 1970 | Pedro Rodriguez/Leo Kinnunen | Porsche 917 | 114.866 mph | 24 hrs (2,758.44 mi) |
| 1971 | Pedro Rodriguez/Jackie Oliver | Porsche 917K | 109.203 mph | 24 hrs (2,621.28 mi) |
| 1972* | Mario Andretti/Jacky Ickx | Ferrari 312/P | 122.573 mph | 6 hrs (738.24 mi) |
| 1973 | Peter Gregg/Hurley Haywood | Porsche Carrera | 106.225 mph | 24 hrs (2,552.7 mi) |
| 1974 | (No race) | | | |
| 1975 | Peter Gregg/Hurley Haywood | Porsche Carrera | 108.531 mph | 24 hrs (2,606.04 mi) |
| 1976† | Peter Gregg/Brian Redman/ John Fitzpatrick | BMW CSL | 104.040 mph | 24 hrs (2,092.8 mi) |
| 1977 | John Graves/Hurley Haywood/ Dave Helmick | Porsche Carrera | 108.801 mph | 24 hrs (2,615 mi) |
| 1978 | Rolf Stommelen/ Antoine Hezemans/Peter Gregg | Porsche Turbo | 108.743 mph | 24 hrs (2,611.2 mi) |
| 1979 | Ted Field/Danny Ongais/ Hurley Haywood | Porsche Turbo | 109.249 mph | 24 hrs (2,626.56 mi) |
| 1980 | Volkert Meri/Rolf Stommelen/ Reinhold Joest | Porsche Turbo | 114.303 mph | 24 hrs |
| 1981 | Bob Garretson/Bobby Rahal/ Brian Redman | Porsche Turbo | 113.153 mph | 24 hrs |
| 1982 | John Paul Jr/John Paul Sr/ Rolf Stommelen | Porsche Turbo | 114.794 mph | 24 hrs |
| 1983 | Preston Henn/Bob Wollek/ Claude Ballot-Lena/A.J. Foyt | Porsche Turbo | 98.781 mph | 24 hrs |
| 1984 | Sarel van der Merwe/ Graham Duxbury/Tony Martin | Porsche March | 103.119 mph | 24 hrs (2,476.8 mi) |
| 1985 | A.J. Foyt/Bob Wollek/ Al Unser/Thierry Boutsen | Porsche 962 | 104.162 mph | 24 hrs (2,502.68 mi) |
| 1986 | Al Holbert/Derek Bell/Al Unser Jr. | Porsche 962 | 105.484 mph | 24 hrs (2,534.72 mi) |
| 1987 | Chip Robinson/Derek Bell/ Al Holbert/Al Unser Jr. | Porsche 962 | 111.599 mph | 24 hrs (2,680.68 mi) |

## The 24 Hours of Daytona *(Cont.)*

| Year | Winner | Car | Avg Speed | Distance |
|---|---|---|---|---|
| 1988 | Martin Brundle/John Nielsen/ Raul Boesel | Jaguar XJR-9 | 107.943 mph | 24 hrs (2,591.68 mi) |
| 1989 | John Andretti/Derek Bell/ Bob Wollek | Porsche 962 | 92.009 mph | 24 hrs (2,210.76 mi) |
| 1990 | Davy Jones/ Jan Lammers/ Andy Wallace | Jaguar XJR-12 | 112.857 mph | 24 hrs (2,709.16 mi) |
| 1991 | Hurley Haywood/ John Winter/ Frank Jelinski/ Henri Pescarolo/ Bob Wollek | Porsche 962C | 106.633 mph | 24 hrs (2,559.64 mi) |
| 1992 | Massahiro Hasemi/ Kazuoyshi Hoshino/ Toshio Suzuki/ Anders Olofsson | Nissan R91CP | 112.987 mph | 24 hrs (2,712.72 mi) |
| 1993 | P.J. Jones/Mark Dismore/ Rocky Moran | Toyota Eagle MK III | 103.537 mph | 24 hrs (2,484.88 mi) |
| 1994 | Paul Gentilozzi/ Scott Pruett/ Butch Leitzinger/ Steve Millen | Nissan 300 ZX | 104.80 mph | 24 hrs (2,693.67 mi) |
| 1995 | Jurgen Lassig/ Christophe Buochut/ Giovanni Lavaggi/ Marco Werner | Porsche Spyder K8 | 102.28 mph | 690 laps (2,456.4 mi) |
| 1996 | Wayne Taylor/ Scott Sharp/ Jim Pace | Oldsmobile Mark III | 103.32 mph | 697 laps (2,481.32 mi) |
| 1997 | Elliot Forbes/John Schneider/ Rob Dyson/John Paul Jr/ Butch Leitzinger/James Weaver/ Andy Wallace | Ford R & S MK III | 102.292 mph | 690 laps (2,456.4 mi) |
| 1998 | Arie Luyendyk/Didier Theys/ Mauro Baldi | Ferrari 333 SP | 105.565 mph | 711 laps (2,531.16 mi) |
| 1999 | Elliott Forbes-Robinson/Butch Leitzinger/ Andy Wallace | Ford R & S MK III | 104.9 mph | 708 laps (2,520.48 mi) |
| 2000 | Olivier Beretta/Karl Wendlinger/ Dominique Dupuy | Dodge Viper | 107.207 mph | 723 laps (2,573.88 mi) |
| 2001 | Ron Fellows/Chris Kneifel/Franck Freon/Johnny O'Connell | Corvette | 97.293 mph | 656 laps (2,335.360 mi) |

*Race shortened due to fuel crisis. †Course lengthened from 3.81 miles to 3.84 miles.

## World SportsCar Champions*

| Year | Winner | Car | Year | Winner | Car |
|---|---|---|---|---|---|
| 1978 | Peter Gregg | Porsche 935 | 1989 | Geoff Brabham | Nissan GTP |
| 1979 | Peter Gregg | Porsche 935 | 1990 | Geoff Brabham | Nissan GTP |
| 1980 | John Fitzpatrick | Porsche 935 | 1991 | Geoff Brabham | Nissan NPT |
| 1981 | Brian Redman | Chevy Lola | 1992 | Juan Fangio II | Toyota EGL MKIII |
| 1982 | John Paul Jr | Chevy Lola | 1993 | Juan Fangio II | Toyota EGL MKIII |
| 1983 | Al Holbert | Chevy March | 1994 | Wayne Taylor | Mazda Kudzu |
| 1984 | Randy Lanier | Chevy March | 1995 | Fermin Velez | Ferrari 333 SP |
| 1985 | Al Holbert | Porsche 962 | 1996 | Wayne Taylor | Mazda Kudzu |
| 1986 | Al Holbert | Porsche 962 | 1997 | Butch Leitzinger | Ford R&S MKIII |
| 1987 | Chip Robinson | Porsche 962 | 1998 | Butch Leitzinger | Ford R&S MKIII |
| 1988 | Geoff Brabham | Nissan GTP | | | |

| Year | Prototype | GTS | GT |
|---|---|---|---|
| 1999 | Elliott Forbes-Robinson | Olivier Beretta | Cort Wagner |
| 2000 | Alan McNish | Olivier Beretta | Sascha Maassen |
| 2001 | Emanuele Pirro | Terry Borcheller | Jörg Müller |

*1978–93 champions raced in the GT series, which in 1994 was replaced by the World SportsCar series. Beginning in 1999, racing was reclassified according to the American Le Mans Series. The Series is comprised of two different types of race cars divided into two categories and five separate classes. The Prototype category features open-cockpit prototype World Sports Cars (WSC) and Le Mans Prototypes (LMP), as well as Grand Touring Prototype (GTP) class cars. The Grand Touring category features the Grand Touring S (GTS) class cars, formerly known as GT2, and Grand Touring (GT) cars, formerly known as GT3. Both classes feature purpose-built race cars with an emphasis on spectator car identification.

### Alltime SportsCar Leaders

**PROTOTYPE WINS (WSC/GTP ERA: 1994–2001)**

| | |
|---|---|
| James Weaver | 14 |
| Butch Leitzinger | 13 |
| Rinaldo Capello | 9 |
| Wayne Taylor | 8 |
| Gianpiero Moretti | 7 |
| Frank Biela | 6 |
| J.J. Lehto | 6 |
| Alan McNish | 6 |
| Emanuele Pirro | 6 |
| David Brabham | 5 |
| John Paul Jr | 5 |
| Fermin Velez | 5 |
| Eric van de Poele | 5 |
| Andy Wallace | 5 |

Note: Leaders through October 12, 2001.

**GTS AND GT WINS (IMSA GT: 1971–1993)**

| | |
|---|---|
| Al Holbert | 49 |
| Peter Gregg | 41 |
| Hurley Haywood | 31 |
| Geoff Brabham | 26 |
| Parker Johnstone | 25 |
| Jim Downing | 23 |
| Irv Hoerr | 23 |
| Jack Baldwin | 22 |
| Don Devendorf | 22 |
| Bob Earl | 22 |
| Tommy Riggins | 22 |

## 24 Hours of Le Mans

| Year | Winning Drivers | Car |
|---|---|---|
| 1923 | André Lagache/René Léonard | Chenard & Walker |
| 1924 | John Duff/Francis Clement | Bentley |
| 1925 | Gérard de Courcelles/André Rossignol | La Lorraine |
| 1926 | Robert Bloch/André Rossignol | La Lorraine |
| 1927 | J. Dudley Benjafield/Sammy Davis | Bentley |
| 1928 | Woolf Barnato/Bernard Rubin | Bentley |
| 1929 | Woolf Barnato/Sir Henry Birkin | Bentley Speed 6 |
| 1930 | Woolf Barnato/Glen Kidston | Bentley Speed 6 |
| 1931 | Earl Howe/Sir Henry Birkin | Alfa Romeo 8C-2300 sc |
| 1932 | Raymond Sommer/Luigi Chinetti | Alfa Romeo 8C-2300 sc |
| 1933 | Raymond Sommer/Tazio Nuvolari | Alfa Romeo 8C-2300 sc |
| 1934 | Luigi Chinetti/Philippe Etancelin | Alfa Romeo 8C-2300 sc |
| 1935 | John Hindmarsh/Louis Fontés | Lagonda M45R |
| 1936 | Race cancelled | |
| 1937 | Jean-Pierre Wimille/Robert Benoist | Bugatti 57G sc |
| 1938 | Eugene Chaboud/Jean Tremoulet | Delahaye 135M |
| 1939 | Jean-Pierre Wimille/Pierre Veyron | Bugatti 57G sc |
| 1940–48 | Races cancelled | |
| 1949 | Luigi Chinetti/Lord Selsdon | Ferrari 166MM |
| 1950 | Louis Rosier/Jean-Louis Rosier | Talbot-Lago |
| 1951 | Peter Walker/Peter Whitehead | Jaguar C |
| 1952 | Hermann Lang/Fritz Reiss | Mercedes-Benz 300 SL |
| 1953 | Tony Rolt/Duncan Hamilton | Jaguar C |
| 1954 | Froilan Gonzales/Maurice Trintignant | Ferrari 375 |
| 1955 | Mike Hawthorn/Ivor Bueb | Jaguar D |
| 1956 | Ron Flockhart/Ninian Sanderson | Jaguar D |
| 1957 | Ron Flockhart/Ivor Buab | Jaguar D |
| 1958 | Olivier Gendebien/Phil Hill | Ferrari 250 TR58 |
| 1959 | Carroll Shelby/Roy Salvadori | Aston Martin DBR1 |
| 1960 | Olivier Gendebien/Paul Fràre | Ferrari 250 TR59/60 |
| 1961 | Olivier Gendebien/Phil Hill | Ferrari 250 TR61 |
| 1962 | Olivier Gendebien/Phil Hill | Ferrari 250P |
| 1963 | Lodovico Scarfiotti/Lorenzo Bandini | Ferrari 250P |
| 1964 | Jean Guichel/Nino Vaccarella | Ferrari 275P |
| 1965 | Jochen Rindt/Masten Gregory | Ferrari 250LM |
| 1966 | Chris Amon/Bruce McLaren | Ford Mk2 |
| 1967 | Dan Gurney/A.J. Foyt | Ford Mk4 |
| 1968 | Pedro Rodriguez/Lucien Bianchi | Ford GT40 |
| 1969 | Jacky Ickx/Jackie Oliver | Ford GT40 |
| 1970 | Hans Herrmann/Richard Attwood | Porsche 917 |
| 1971 | Helmut Marko/Gijs van Lennep | Porsche 917 |
| 1972 | Henri Pescarolo/Graham Hill | Matra-Simca MS670 |
| 1973 | Henri Pescarolo/Gérard Larrousse | Matra-Simca MS670B |

| Year | Winning Drivers | Car |
|------|-----------------|-----|
| 1974 | Henri Pescarolo/Gérard Larrousse | Matra-Simca MS670B |
| 1975 | Jacky Ickx/Derek Bell | Mirage-Ford MB |
| 1976 | Jacky Ickx/Gijs van Lennep | Porsche 936 |
| 1977 | Jacky Ickx/Jurgen Barth/Hurley Haywood | Porsche 936 |
| 1978 | Jean-Pierre Jaussaud/Didier Pironi | Renault-Alpine A442 |
| 1979 | Klaus Ludwig/Bill Whittington/Don Whittington | Porsche 935 |
| 1980 | Jean-Pierre Jaussaud/Jean Rondeau | Rondeau-Ford M379B |
| 1981 | Jacky Ickx/Derek Bell | Porsche 936-81 |
| 1982 | Jacky Ickx/Derek Bell | Porsche 956 |
| 1983 | Vern Schuppan/Hurley Haywood/Al Holbert | Porsche 956-83 |
| 1984 | Klaus Ludwig/Henri Pescarolo | Porsche 956B |
| 1985 | Klaus Ludwig/Paolo Barilla/John Winter | Porsche 956B |
| 1986 | Derek Bell/Hans-Joachim Stuck/Al Holbert | Porsche 962C |
| 1987 | Derek Bell/Hans-Joachim Stuck/Al Holbert | Porsche 962C |
| 1988 | Jan Lammers/Johnny Dumfries/Andy Wallace | Jaguar XJR9LM |
| 1989 | Jochen Mass/Manuel Reuter/Stanley Dickens | Sauber-Mercedes C9-88 |
| 1990 | John Nielsen/Price Cobb/Martin Brundle | TWR Jaguar XJR-12 |
| 1991 | Volker Weidler/Johnny Herbert/Bertrand Gachot | Mazda 787B |
| 1992 | Derek Warwick/Yannick Dalmas/Mark Blundell | Peugeot 905B |
| 1993 | Geoff Brabham/Christophe Bouchut/Eric Helary | Peugeot 905 |
| 1994 | Yannick Dalmas/Hurley Haywood/Mauro Baldi | Porsche 962 |
| 1995 | Yannick Dalmas/J.J. Lehto/Masanori Sekiya | McLaren BMW |
| 1996 | Manuel Reuter/Davy Jones/Alexander Wurz | TWR Porsche |
| 1997 | Michele Alboreto/Stefan Johansson/Tom Kristensen | TWR Porsche |
| 1998 | Alan McNish/Laurent Aiello/Stephane Ortelli | Porsche GT One |
| 1999 | Yannick Dalmas/Joachim Winkelhock/Pierluigi Martini | BMW V12 LMR |
| 2000 | Frank Biela/Tom Kristensen/Emanuele Pirro | Audi R8 |
| 2001 | Frank Biela/Tom Kristensen/Emanuele Pirro | Audi R8 |

## You Want to Drag?

After driving less than half of the 1994 NASCAR season for Petty Enterprises, John Andretti left in '95 for the fledgling Krane-fuss-Haas team—and quickly realized his mistake. "By May, I was calling up the King, begging to come back," he says. Richard Petty finally relented and gave Andretti his seat back in '98, and the two have been together since.

For the adventuresome Andretti, spending three years with one outfit—and doing just one type of racing—has been a novel experience. In 1993 he drove in the Indianapolis 500, the 24 Hours of Daytona, a top fuel dragster event, a series of go-kart races against a team of Russians, a midget race and four Winston Cup events and still found time to set a land speed record for street-production cars on the Bonneville Salt Flats. (He got a factory-built Subaru up to 178 mph.) In '94 he became the first driver to run the Indy 500 and Coca-Cola 600 on the same day.

Andretti, 38, is happy as can be with Petty—for whom he has won one race—and he's in no great rush to move on, despite his natural inclination to do so. "I was never patient," Andretti says. "My dad [Aldo, twin brother of Mario] would tell me I'd trade a headache for an upset stomach."

That doesn't mean he has lost his peripatetic side. His next trick might be running in the 2002 Southern 500 in Darlington as well as the NHRA Nationals, both of which are held over Labor Day weekend. Andretti says he has been "goofing around with the idea" for some time. "I'd have to get a lot of people to agree to it," he says.

It would be interesting, but it wouldn't be a lark; Andretti beat defending series champ Joe Amato in the quarterfinals of his first competition behind the wheel of a dragster. That was in April 1993, when Andretti was in the midst of his rambling days. "I wouldn't sign a contract with anybody that year," says Andretti. "I'd look at my calendar and say, 'O.K., I'm open that weekend.' It was a ball."

# Drag Racing: Milestone Performances

## Top Fuel
### ELAPSED TIME

| Time (Sec.) | Driver | Date | Site |
|---|---|---|---|
| 9.00 | Jack Chrisman | Feb 18, 1961 | Pomona, CA |
| 8.97 | Jack Chrisman | May 20, 1961 | Empona, VA |
| 7.96 | Bobby Vodnick | May 16, 1964 | Bayview, MD |
| 6.97 | Don Johnson | May 7, 1967 | Carlsbad, CA |
| 5.97 | Mike Snively | Nov 17, 1972 | Ontario, CA |
| 5.78 | Don Garlits | Nov 18, 1973 | Ontario, CA |
| 5.698 | Gary Beck | Oct 10, 1975 | Ontario, CA |
| 5.573 | Gary Beck | Oct 18, 1981 | Irvine, CA |
| 5.484 | Gary Beck | Sept 6, 1982 | Clermont, IN |
| 5.391 | Gary Beck | Oct 1, 1983 | Fremont, CA |
| 5.280 | Darrell Gwynn | Sept 25, 1986 | Ennis, TX |
| 5.176 | Darrell Gwynn | April 4, 1987 | Ennis, TX |
| 5.090 | Joe Amato | Oct 1, 1987 | Ennis, TX |
| 4.990 | Eddie Hill | April 9, 1988 | Ennis, TX |
| 4.881 | Gary Ormsby | Sept 28, 1990 | Topeka, KS |
| 4.799 | Cory McClenathan | Sept 19, 1992 | Mohnton, PA |
| 4.762 | Cory McClenathan | Oct 3, 1993 | Topeka, KS |
| 4.690 | Michael Brotherton | May 20, 1994 | Englishtown, NJ |
| 4.595 | Joe Amato | July 5,1996 | Topeka, KS |
| 4.539 | Joe Amato | Mar 21, 1998 | Baytown, TX |
| 4.525 | Gary Scelzi | Oct 23, 1998 | Ennis, TX |
| 4.503 | Mike Dunn | Feb 5, 1999 | Pomona, CA |
| 4.486 | Larry Dixon | Apr 9, 1999 | Houston |
| 4.480 | Gary Scelzi | Oct 31, 1999 | Houston |
| 4.477 | Kenny Bernstein | June 2, 2001 | Joliet, IL |

### SPEED

| MPH | Driver | Date | Site |
|---|---|---|---|
| 180.36 | Connie Kalitta | Sept 3, 1962 | Indianapolis |
| 190.34 | Don Garlits | Sept 21, 1963 | East Haddam, CT |
| 201.34 | Don Garlits | Aug 1, 1964 | Great Meadows, NJ |
| 211.26 | Donny Milani | May 15, 1965 | Sacramento, CA |
| 223.32 | Don Cook | Apr 24, 1965 | Fremont, CA |
| 230.17 | James Warren | Apr 10, 1967 | Fresno, CA |
| 243.24 | Don Garlits | Mar 18, 1973 | Gainesville, FL |
| 250.69 | Don Garlits | Oct 11, 1975 | Ontario, CA |
| 260.11 | Joe Amato | Mar 18, 1984 | Gainesville, FL |
| 272.56 | Don Garlits | Mar 23, 1986 | Gainesville, FL |
| 282.13 | Joe Amato | Sept 5, 1987 | Clermont, IN |
| 291.54 | Connie Kalitta | Feb 11, 1989 | Pomona, CA |
| 301.70 | Kenny Bernstein | Mar 20, 1992 | Gainesville, FL |
| 311.86 | Kenny Bernstein | Oct 30, 1994 | Pomona, CA |
| 319.82 | Joe Amato | Mar 21, 1998 | Baytown, TX |
| 323.50 | Joe Amato | May 17, 1998 | Englishtown, NJ |
| 326.44 | Gary Scelzi | Nov 2, 1998 | Houston |
| 326.91 | Tony Schumacher | Oct 22, 1999 | Dallas |
| 330.55 | Mike Dunn | June 2, 2001 | Joliet, IL |

## THEY SAID IT

*Paul Brooks, VP of broadcasting for
NASCAR, which is seeking more
prime-time references to stock car
racing: "We're finding out about
getting into the [production] process
so that Ally McBeal can talk about
going to Daytona in a natural way."*

## Funny Car
### ELAPSED TIME

| Time (sec.) | Driver | Date | Site |
| --- | --- | --- | --- |
| 6.92 | Leroy Goldstein | Sept 3, 1970 | Clermont, IN |
| 5.987 | Don Prudhomme | Oct 12, 1975 | Ontario, CA |
| 5.868 | Raymond Beadle | July 16, 1981 | Englishtown, NJ |
| 5.799 | Tom Anderson | Sept 3, 1982 | Clermont, IN |
| 5.637 | Don Prudhomme | Sept 4, 1982 | Clermont, IN |
| 5.588 | Rick Johnson | Feb 3, 1985 | Pomona, CA |
| 5.425 | Kenny Bernstein | Sept 26, 1986 | Ennis, TX |
| 5.397 | Kenny Bernstein | April 5, 1987 | Ennis, TX |
| 5.255 | Ed McCulloch | April 17, 1988 | Ennis, TX |
| 5.193 | Don Prudhomme | Mar 2, 1989 | Baytown, TX |
| 5.077 | Cruz Pedregon | Sept 20, 1992 | Mohnton, PA |
| 4.987 | Chuck Etcholis | Oct 2, 1993 | Topeka, KS |
| 4.819 | Cruz Pedregon | Mar 21, 1998 | Baytown, TX |
| 4.807 | Cruz Pedregon | Nov 1, 1998 | Houston |
| 4.788 | John Force | Apr 11, 1999 | Houston |
| 4.763 | John Force | June 2, 2001 | Joliet, IL |
| 4.750 | William Bazemore | Sept 28, 2001 | Joliet, IL |

### SPEED

| MPH | Driver | Date | Site |
| --- | --- | --- | --- |
| 200.44 | Gene Snow | Aug, 1968 | Houston |
| 250.00 | Don Prudhomme | May 23, 1982 | Baton Rouge |
| 260.11 | Kenny Bernstein | Mar 18, 1984 | Gainesville, FL |
| 271.41 | Kenny Bernstein | Aug 30, 1986 | Indianapolis |
| 280.72 | Mike Dunn | Oct 2, 1987 | Ennis, TX |
| 290.13 | Jim White | Oct 11, 1991 | Ennis, TX |
| 291.82 | Jim White | Oct 25, 1991 | Pomona, CA |
| 300.40 | Jim Epler | Oct 3, 1993 | Topeka, KS |
| 303.64 | John Force | Sept 2, 1995 | Indianapolis |
| 308.74 | John Force | Sept 28, 1997 | Topeka, KS |
| 317.46 | John Force | Mar 21, 1998 | Baytown, TX |
| 323.89 | John Force | May 17, 1998 | Englishtown, NJ |
| 324.05 | John Force | Mar 19, 1999 | Gainesville, FL |
| 325.45 | William Bazemore | Sept 28, 2001 | Joliet, IL |

## Pro Stock
### ELAPSED TIME

| Time (sec.) | Driver | Date | Site |
| --- | --- | --- | --- |
| 7.778 | Lee Shepherd | Mar 12, 1982 | Gainesville, FL |
| 7.655 | Lee Shepherd | Oct 1, 1982 | Fremont, CA |
| 7.557 | Bob Glidden | Feb 2, 1985 | Pomona, CA |
| 7.497 | Bob Glidden | Sep 13, 1985 | Maple Grove, PA |
| 7.377 | Bob Glidden | Aug 28, 1986 | Clermont, IN |
| 7.294 | Frank Sanchez | Oct 7, 1988 | Baytown, TX |
| 7.184 | Darrell Alderman | Oct 12, 1990 | Ennis, TX |
| 7.099 | Scott Geoffrion | Sept 19, 1992 | Mohnton, PA |
| 6.988 | Kurt Johnson | May 20, 1994 | Englishtown, NJ |
| 6.873 | Warren Johnson | Mar 14, 1998 | Gainesville, FL |
| 6.867 | Warren Johnson | Oct 23, 1998 | Ennis, TX |
| 6.866 | Warren Johnson | Mar 19, 1999 | Gainesville, FL |
| 6.843 | Warren Johnson | Apr 30, 1999 | Dinwiddie, VA |
| 6.840 | Kurt Johnson | May 1, 1999 | Dinwiddie, VA |
| 6.822 | Warren Johnson | Oct 23, 1999 | Dallas |
| 6.801 | Kurt Johnson | Sept 29, 2001 | Joliet, IL |

### Pro Stock *(Cont.)*

#### SPEED

| MPH | Driver | Date | Site |
|---|---|---|---|
| 181.08 | Warren Johnson | Oct 1, 1982 | Fremont, CA |
| 190.07 | Warren Johnson | Aug 29, 1986 | Clermont, IN |
| 191.32 | Bob Glidden | Sept 4, 1987 | Clermont, IN |
| 192.18 | Warren Johnson | Oct 13, 1990 | Ennis, TX |
| 193.21 | Bob Glidden | July 28, 1991 | Sonoma, CA |
| 194.51 | Warren Johnson | July 31, 1992 | Sonoma, CA |
| 195.99 | Warren Johnson | May 21, 1993 | Englishtown, NJ |
| 196.24 | Warren Johnson | Mar 19, 1993 | Gainesville, FL |
| 197.15 | Warren Johnson | Apr 23, 1994 | Commerce, GA |
| 199.15 | Warren Johnson | Mar 10, 1995 | Baytown, TX |
| 201.20 | Warren Johnson | Mar 14, 1998 | Gainesville, FL |
| 201.34 | Warren Johnson | Oct 23, 1998 | Ennis, TX |
| 201.37 | Warren Johnson | Mar 19, 1999 | Gainesville, FL |
| 202.24 | Warren Johnson | Apr 30,1999 | Dinwiddie, VA |
| 202.33 | Warren Johnson | Oct 23, 1999 | Dallas |
| 202.36 | Warren Johnson | Oct 31, 1999 | Houston |
| 202.70 | Kurt Johnson | Sept 29, 2001 | Joliet, IL |

## Alltime Drag Racing Leaders

| NHRA CAREER WINS | | BEST WON-LOST RECORD (WINNING PCT.) | |
|---|---|---|---|
| *John Force | 98 | *Matt Hines | 211–52 (.802) |
| *Warren Johnson | 87 | John Myers | 268–69 (.795) |
| Bob Glidden | 85 | *Angelle Savoie | 175–53 (.768) |
| *Kenny Bernstein | 60 | *John Force | 748–247 (.752) |
| Joe Amato | 52 | *Bob Panella Jr | 116–40 (.744) |
| Don Prudhomme | 49 | *Jeg Coughlin | 173–60 (.742) |
| David Schultz | 45 | *Warren Johnson | 756–287 (.725) |
| Don Garlits | 35 | *Gary Scelzi | 221–85 (.722) |
| John Myers | 33 | *Randy Daniels | 86–40 (.683) |
| *Matt Hines | 28 | *Antron Brown | 91–44 (.674) |

*Active driver. Note: Leaders through October 4, 2001.

## Conquistador

Roger Penske was on the schneid in late May. He had gone six years without one of his cars appearing in the Indy 500—a nightmare year in 1995, when his two cars failed to qualify, followed by a five-year absence because most CART car owners boycotted the race in a dispute with the rival IRL. However, Chip Ganassi's return to Indy last year and his win with rookie driver Juan Montoya enticed other CART owners, including Penske, to race at the Brickyard this year. "Roger pushed the whole month [before the race]," says Gil de Ferran, who drives for Penske. "To get cars built, to get engines built, pushing, pushing, pushing." When Brazil's Helio Castroneves won the race on Sunday, finishing 1.7 seconds ahead of de Ferran to give Penske a one-two showing, the pushing paid off.

Penske wasn't the only big name to return to Indy. CART driver Michael Andretti finished third in his first race at the Brickyard since 1995. The CART boycott had been especially tough on the 38-year-old Andretti, who has one of the longest lists of near misses in Indy history. "Five really good years in the prime of my career to win this thing, and they were taken from me," he said on Saturday. "Last year was the worst. I was watching the race, and I thought, What's going on? If Juan can be there, why can't we? I was upset because I really pushed hard to make it happen with [owner] Carl Haas, but he didn't want to know about it."

After last season Andretti and Haas split up, and Andretti joined Barry Green, who was amenable to a Brickyard effort. Andretti led for 16 laps on Sunday, giving him 398 laps led in his Brickyard career, the most of any driver without a win. Still, it was Castroneves who led at the end, marking the first time since 1926 and '27 that rookie drivers had won at Indy in successive years.

Castroneves, 26, is known as Spiderman because he has a penchant for climbing trackside fences following his victory. At Indy he invited his crew to join him in his Peter Parker impersonation. They all did, except Penske, who was in a more reflective mood. "It's the best day of my life, redeeming myself like this," Penske said.

The win might have officially belonged to the guy scaling the fence, but looking at Penske, you couldn't help but feel that this one was his.

PBA legend
Earl Anthony
1938–2001

Bowling

# Hello, Goodbye

## The PBA welcomed new owners and dramatic innovations, then bid farewell to one of its legends

### BY HANK HERSCH

ON AUG. 14, 2001, Earl Anthony died from head trauma after a fall at a friend's home in New Berlin, Wis. He was 63. Nicknamed Square Earl for his crew cut, glasses and unembroidered style, Anthony and his swinging left arm made bowling go 'round from 1970 to '83. A former pinsetter from Kent, Wash., he won 41 titles on the Professional Bowlers Association tour—a record that still stands—seized seven more on the senior tour and became the sport's first $1 million man. Even more impressive, he turned ABC-TV's *Professional Bowlers Tour* into riveting television despite his nerdy look and poky approach. As Square Earl was fond of saying, "You can't ever be too slow to the line."

The staid Anthony would have been hard-pressed to recognize the sport he loved in the fall of 2001. In March 2000, G. Chris Peters, the former chief of Microsoft Office, and two of his friends paid $5 million for the PBA, which had lost its TV contract in 1997 and was on the brink of bankruptcy. Within 15 months, the new ownership group had reached a three-year agreement with ESPN to televise 20 events annually; structured a season that will run from September to March; signed a national sponsor, Miller Brewing; and upped its tournaments' minimum first prize to $40,000, with $100,000 going to those who claim major titles. The total prize money increased a whopping 139%, from $1.8 million to $4.3 million.

Such mercurial change would have stunned Anthony, who made his ascent to the title of bowling's greatest champion slowly. After failing to win a tournament in 1963, he went back to driving a forklift in a Tacoma, Wash., supermarket. He returned to the tour in '69 and earned his first title a year later, at the age of 32. But Peters & Co., who are modeling their outfit after NASCAR, are taking a high-speed approach. Their deals quickly lured Del Ballard Jr., who has four major titles on his résumé, out of retirement. "When the PBA announced the prize fund increases, that really convinced me it was the right thing to do," the 38-year-old Ballard

**One of the Tour's best for 17 years, Bohn finally won a major.**

said. "The timing is perfect for me."

The new enticements could also prove timely for a couple of active bowlers who ended the winter tour on a roll, since their stats will count toward the 2001–02 year-end totals: Parker Bohn III, who led the PBA in earnings ($91,200) and victories (three), and Jason Couch, who set the pace in average (226.12) and TV appearances (six). The year was especially sweet for Bohn, of Jackson, N.J. Pairing with Rohn Morton, he took the season's first title, the National/Senior Doubles in Reno in January; and in June he claimed the first major of his career, winning the American Bowling Congress Masters.

That victory, also in Reno, came against Couch, a fellow lefty and Bohn's former tour roommate. It was the 27th title of Bohn's 17-year career, tying him with Mike Aulby for fourth place on the alltime list. A solid 9-pin in the ninth frame cost Couch, who fell 248–237. "Jason got a bad break, the worst break in bowling as a matter of fact, and I was able to take advantage," said Bohn, age 38, who earned $40,000 with the victory. "I've been knocking on the door of the Masters for a long time now, and to tell you the truth, I've been sick of being the bridesmaid at the majors."

The bridesmaid label hung a little heavy on the 31-year-old Couch as well. Despite reaching five title matches he won only once, at the Villages Open in February. At the Silicon Valley Open in Daly City, Calif., a month earlier, he had fallen 257–211 to Aulby in the final. "Growing up, I idolized him," Couch said. "I wanted to bowl against him for the title. To be the best, you have to beat the best."

Perhaps no player matches the cutting-edge innovations of the tour as well as Couch, of Clermont, Fla. He uses a computer-aided tracking system to find and fix the flaws in his delivery. The technology allows him to simulate every kind of lane condition and practice every kind of ball. "It removes the lies," Couch says. "The computers show you the mistakes you're making, and quite often they aren't what you think they are."

It's hard to imagine Anthony availing himself of that gadgetry—just as it's hard to imagine any bowler today achieving the sort of status Square Earl had in his heyday. But times and tastes do change: Bowling shoes and shirts are now fashion items, and the TV comedy *Ed* is about a New York lawyer who drops out of big-city life to buy an alley in the Midwest.

For better or worse, in 2001 professional bowling entered the fast lane.

## The Majors

### MEN

### 2000 U.S. Open

#### CHAMPIONSHIP ROUND

| Bowler | Games | Total | Earnings ($) |
|---|---|---|---|
| Robert Smith | 1 | 202 | 35,000 |
| Norm Duke | 2 | 480 | 20,000 |
| Jeff Lizzi | 1 | 224 | 15,000 |
| Paul Fleming | 1 | 214 | 10,000 |

**Playoff Results:** Duke def. Lizzi and Fleming, 279–224–214; Smith def. Duke, 202–201.
Held at Arizona Veterans Memorial Coliseum, Phoenix, July 10–15, 2000.

### 2000 Brunswick World Tournament of Champions

#### CHAMPIONSHIP ROUND

| Bowler | Games | Total | Earnings ($) |
|---|---|---|---|
| Jason Couch | 1 | 198 | 60,000 |
| Ryan Shafer | 2 | 392 | 31,000 |
| Norm Duke | 1 | 202 | 23,000 |
| Steve Jaros | 2 | 442 | 16,000 |
| Walter Ray Williams Jr. | 1 | 214 | 12,000 |
| Doug Kent | 2 | 445 | 10,000 |
| Tommy Delutz Jr. | 1 | 179 | 9,000 |
| Dave Husted | 1 | 204 | 8,000 |

**Playoff Results:** Kent def. Husted and Delutz, 224–204–179; Jaros def. Kent and Williams, 257–221–214; Shafer def. Duke and Jaros, 226–202–185; Couch def. Shafer, 198–166.
Held at Brunswick Zone-Deer Park Lanes, Lake Zurich, IL, Nov 3–7, 2000.

### 2001 PBA National Championship

#### CHAMPIONSHIP ROUND

| Bowler | Games | Total | Earnings ($) |
|---|---|---|---|
| Walter Ray Williams Jr. | 1 | 258 | 25,000 |
| Jeff Lizzi | 3 | 667 | 13,000 |
| Tommy Delutz Jr. | 1 | 239 | 7,000 |
| Dave Arnold | 2 | 438 | 5,000 |
| Chris Hayden | 1 | 214 | 4,000 |

**Playoff Results:** Arnold def. Hayden, 235–214; Lizzi def. Arnold, 224–203; Lizzi and Delutz tied, 239–239 (Lizzi def. Delutz in roll-off, 10–9); Williams def. Lizzi, 258–204.
Held at Southwyck Lanes, Toledo, OH, Jan 28–Feb 4, 2001.

### 2001 ABC Masters

#### CHAMPIONSHIP ROUND

| Bowler | Games | Total | Earnings ($) |
|---|---|---|---|
| Parker Bohn III | 2 | 448 | 40,000 |
| Jason Couch | 1 | 237 | 20,000 |
| Tony Reyes | 2 | 407 | 14,000 |
| Shannon Buchan | 2 | 391 | 9,500 |
| Chris Hayden | 1 | 170 | 7,500 |

**Playoff Results:** Buchan def. Hayden, 201–170; Reyes def. Buchan, 237–190; Bohn def. Reyes, 200–170; Bohn def. Couch, 248–237.
Held at The National Bowling Stadium, Reno, June 11–16, 2001.

## WOMEN
### 2000 U.S. Open
#### CHAMPIONSHIP ROUND

| Bowler | Games | Total | Earnings ($) |
| --- | --- | --- | --- |
| Tennelle Grijalva | 2 | 452 | 35,000 |
| Kelly Kulick | 1 | 155 | 20,000 |
| Carol Gianotti-Block | 1 | 196 | 15,000 |
| Liz Johnson | 1 | 203 | 10,000 |

**Playoff Results:** Grijalva def. Johnson and Gianotti, 213–203–196; Grijalva def. Kulick, 239–155.

Held at Arizona Veterans Memorial Coliseum, Phoenix, July 9–15, 2000.

### 2000 Brunswick Women's World Open
#### CHAMPIONSHIP ROUND

| Bowler | Games | Total | Earnings ($) |
| --- | --- | --- | --- |
| Cara Honeychurch | 1 | 170 | 14,400 |
| Marianne DiRupo | 3 | 546 | 7,700 |
| Lynda Barnes | 1 | 160 | 6,200 |
| Liz Johnson | 1 | 188 | 4,400 |
| Cathy Dorin-Ballard | 1 | 170 | 3,800 |

**Playoff Results:** DiRupo def. Johnson and Dorin-Ballard, 201–188–170; DiRupo def. Barnes, 185–160; Honeychurch def. DiRupo, 179–160.

Held at Suncoast Bowling Center, Las Vegas, Sept 24–28, 2000.

### 2000 Sam's Town Invitational
#### CHAMPIONSHIP ROUND

| Bowler | Games | Total | Earnings ($) |
| --- | --- | --- | --- |
| Dede Davidson | 1 | 183 | 14,400 |
| Tiffany Stanbrough | 3 | 664 | 7,700 |
| Aleta Sill | 1 | 243 | 5,200 |
| Cara Honeychurch | 1 | 207 | 4,400 |
| Tish Johnson | 1 | 193 | 3,800 |

**Playoff Results:** Stanbrough def. Honeychurch and Johnson, 227–207–193; Stanbrough def. Sill, 258–243; Davidson def. Stanbrough, 183–179.

Held at Sam's Town Bowling Center, Las Vegas, Nov 4–11, 2000.

### 2001 WIBC Queens
#### CHAMPIONSHIP ROUND

| Bowler | Games | Total | Earnings ($) |
| --- | --- | --- | --- |
| Carolyn Dorin-Ballard | 1 | 213 | 18,000 |
| Kelly Kulick | 2 | 453 | 12,000 |
| Kim Terrell | 2 | 402 | 8,000 |
| Maxine Nable | 1 | 200 | 6,000 |
| Robin Crawford | 1 | 188 | 4,000 |

**Playoff Results:** Terrell def. Nable and Crawford, 217–200–188; Kulick def. Terrell, 256–185; Dorin-Ballard def. Kulick, 213–197.

Held at Sawgrass Lanes, Ft. Lauderdale, FL, May 7–11, 2001.

# PBA Tour Results

## Men
### 2000 Fall Tour

| Date | Event | Winner | Earnings ($) | Runner-Up |
|------|-------|--------|--------------|-----------|
| Sept 13–17 | Oronamin C Japan Cup | Parker Bohn III | 50,000 | Y. Sadamatsu |
| Oct 7–10 | Track Canandaigua Open | Walter Ray Williams Jr. | 20,000 | Patrick Healey |
| Oct 14–17 | Johnny Petraglia Open | Walter Ray Williams Jr. | 26,000 | Bob Learn Jr. |
| Oct 21–24 | Flagship Open | Robert Smith | 19,000 | W.R. Williams Jr. |
| Oct 26–31 | Indianapolis Open | Doug Kent | 19,000 | Jeff Zaffino |
| Nov 3–7 | Brunswick World Tournament of Champions | Jason Couch | 60,000 | Ryan Shafer |
| Nov 11–15 | Columbia Open | Danny Wiseman | 20,000 | Chris Barnes |
| Nov 17–21 | Lone Star Open | Steve Hoskins | 19,000 | Doug Kent |

### 2001 Tour

| Date | Event | Winner | Earnings ($) | Runner-Up |
|------|-------|--------|--------------|-----------|
| Jan 9–14 | National Bowling Stadium National/Senior Doubles | Parker Bohn III Rohn Morton | 30,000 | J. Yajima M. Koivuniemi |
| Jan 16–21 | Silicon Valley Open | Mike Aulby | 19,000 | Jason Couch |
| Jan 21–25 | The Orleans Casino Open | Ryan Shafer | 25,000 | Jeff Lizzi |
| Jan 26–Feb 4 | PBA National Championship | Walter Ray Williams Jr. | 25,000 | Jeff Lizzi |
| Feb 7–11 | Parker Bohn III Empire State Open | Parker Bohn III | 20,000 | Chris Barnes |
| Feb 13–18 | Tarheel Open | Ricky Ward | 20,000 | Jason Couch |
| Feb 20–24 | The Villages PBA Open | Jason Couch | 25,000 | Chris Barnes |
| Mar 1–4 | Battle at Little Creek | Steve Wilson | 20,000 | Jason Couch |
| June 11–16 | ABC Masters | Parker Bohn III | 40,000 | Jason Couch |

### 2000–2001 Senior Tour

| Date | Event | Winner | Earnings ($) | Runner-Up |
|------|-------|--------|--------------|-----------|
| Sept 23–27 | Columbia 300 Senior Open | Johnny Petraglia | 12,000 | Barry Gurney |
| Oct 1–5 | Gastonia Senior Classic | Roger Workman | 8,000 | Gary Dickinson |
| Oct 7–13 | Senior National Championship | Bob Glass | 20,000 | Rohn Morton |
| Oct 16–20 | Hammond Senior Open | Mike Pullin | 8,000 | Roger Workman |
| Jan 3–7 | ABC Senior Masters | Bob Glass | 18,000 | Dave Soutar |
| Jan 9–14 | National Bowling Stadium National/Senior Doubles | Rohn Morton Parker Bohn III | 30,000 | Junichi Yajima M. Koivuniemi |
| May 6–10 | Greater Syracuse PBA Senior Open | Bob Glass | 8,000 | B. Chamberlain |
| May 12–17 | Pennsylvania Senior Tour Open | Bob Glass | 8,000 | George Pappas |
| May 20–24 | Hawthorne Lanes Senior Tour Open | Chuck Pierce | 8,000 | Dale Eagle |
| May 27–June 1 | Seattle Senior Open | Mark Roth | 10,000 | Steve Neff |
| June 3–7 | Northwest Senior Classic | Bob Chamberlain | 10,000 | Sal Bongiorno |
| June 10–14 | Epicenter Senior Classic | Johnny Petraglia | 10,000 | Bob Glass |
| June 16–21 | The Orleans Casino Senior Open | Steve Neff | 20,000 | B. Chamberlain |
| June 24–28 | Tucson Senior Open | Dave Soutar | 8,000 | Larry Laub |
| July 1–5 | Northern California Senior Classic | Larry Laub | 10,000 | Rohn Morton |

# †PWBA Tour Results

## 2000 Fall Tour

| Date | Event | Winner | Earnings ($) | Runner-Up |
|------|-------|--------|--------------|-----------|
| Sept 3–7 | Greater Orlando Classic | Cara Honeychurch | 11,000 | Dede Davidson |
| Sept 9–14 | Paula Carter Classic | Debbie McMullen | 11,000 | Michelle Feldman |
| Sept 16–21 | The Foundation Games II | Lisa Bishop | 11,000 | Cara Honeychurch |
| Sept 23–28 | Brunswick Women's World Open | Cara Honeychurch | 14,000 | Marianne DiRupo |
| Oct 1–5 | North Myrtle Beach Classic | Tish Johnson | 11,000 | Cara Honeychurch |
| Oct 8–12 | Columbia 300 Open | Carol Gianotti-Block | 14,400 | Wendy Macpherson |
| Oct 14–19 | Three Rivers Open | Carolyn Dorin-Ballard | 11,000 | Cheryl Daniels |
| Oct 21–26 | Greater Harrisburg Open | Dede Davidson | 11,000 | Leanne Barrette |
| Oct 28–Nov 2 | Hammer Players Championship | Tennelle Grijalva | 16,000 | Wendy Macpherson |
| Nov 4–11 | Sam's Town Invitational | Dede Davidson | 14,400 | Tiffany Stanbrough |

## 2001 Spring/Summer Tour

| Date | Event | Winner | Earnings ($) | Runner-Up |
|------|-------|--------|--------------|-----------|
| May 12–17 | St. Clair Classic | Liz Johnson | 9,000 | Cara Honeychurch |
| May 20–24 | Miller High Life Open | Michelle Feldman | 11,000 | Lynda Barnes |
| May 27–31 | Albuquerque Open | Carolyn Dorin-Ballard | 9,000 | Lisa Bishop |
| June 2–7 | Wheelchair Awareness Classic | Tish Johnson | 9,000 | Kim Adler |
| June 9–14 | Greater San Diego Open | Cara Honeychurch | 9,000 | Anne Marie Duggan |
| June 17–21 | Ft. Worth Classic | Carolyn Dorin-Ballard | 9,000 | Dede Davidson |
| June 24–28 | Greater Memphis Open | Carolyn Dorin-Ballard | 9,000 | Marianne DiRupo |
| July 1–6 | Southern Virginia Open | Carolyn Dorin-Ballard | 9,000 | Wendy Macpherson |
| July 9–12 | Sport Bowling Challenge | Cara Honeychurch | 9,000 | Brenda Norman |
| July 16–20 | Lady Ebonite Kentucky Classic | Leanne Barrette | 11,000 | Cara Honeychurch |
| July 23–26 | Greater Terre Haute Open | Cara Honeychurch | 10,000 | Carol Gianotti-Block |
| Sept 1–6 | The Foundation Games V | Liz Johnson | 9,000 | Wendy Macpherson |
| Sept 9–13 | The Paula Carter Classic | Liz Johnson | 9,000 | C. Dorin-Ballard |
| Sept 15–20 | Storm Challenge | Leanne Barrette | 11,000 | Cara Honeychurch |

†Known as LBPT until 1998.

# 2000 Tour Leaders

## PBA

| Name | Titles | Tournaments | Earnings ($) | Name | Games | Average |
|------|--------|-------------|--------------|------|-------|---------|
| | **MONEY LEADERS** | | | **AVERAGE** | | |
| Norm Duke | 3 | 17 | 136,900 | Chris Barnes | 785 | 220.93 |
| Ryan Shafer | 2 | 19 | 123,600 | Ryan Shafer | 662 | 219.50 |
| Jason Couch | 1 | 19 | 111,715 | Walter Ray Williams Jr. | 680 | 219.00 |
| Parker Bohn III | 2 | 19 | 108,105 | Norm Duke | 658 | 218.77 |
| Chris Barnes | 0 | 19 | 103,900 | Danny Wiseman | 717 | 218.05 |

## Seniors

| Name | Titles | Tournaments | Earnings ($) | Name | Games | Average |
|------|--------|-------------|--------------|------|-------|---------|
| | **MONEY LEADERS** | | | **AVERAGE** | | |
| Roger Workman | 2 | 12 | 145,275 | Robert Glass | 537 | 222.69 |
| Robert Glass | 2 | 12 | 66,650 | Gary Dickinson | 250 | 220.08 |
| Dave Soutar | 1 | 12 | 36,985 | Dave Soutar | 438 | 219.69 |
| Steve Neff | 0 | 10 | 32,525 | Roger Workman | 483 | 219.26 |
| Dave Davis | 1 | 9 | 31,995 | John Bennett | 310 | 218.93 |

## PWBA

| Name | Titles | Tournaments | Earnings ($) | Name | Games | Average |
|------|--------|-------------|--------------|------|-------|---------|
| | **MONEY LEADERS** | | | **AVERAGE** | | |
| Wendy Macpherson | 2 | 23 | 108,525 | Cara Honeychurch | 774 | 215.18 |
| Cara Honeychurch | 2 | 22 | 100,950 | Wendy Macpherson | 936 | 214.90 |
| Michelle Feldman | 3 | 23 | 92,925 | Michelle Feldman | 856 | 214.38 |
| Carolyn Dorin-Ballard | 3 | 23 | 88,677 | Carolyn Dorin-Ballard | 953 | 213.87 |
| Tennelle Grijalva | 2 | 21 | 84,575 | Carol Gianotti-Block | 815 | 213.75 |

## Men's Majors

### BPAA United States Open

| Year | Winner | Score | Runner-Up | Site |
|------|--------|-------|-----------|------|
| 1942 | John Crimmins | 265.09–262.33 | Joe Norris | Chicago |
| 1943 | Connie Schwoegler | not available | Frank Benkovic | Chicago |
| 1944 | Ned Day | 315.21–298.21 | Paul Krumske | Chicago |
| 1945 | Buddy Bomar | 304.46–296.16 | Joe Wilman | Chicago |
| 1946 | Joe Wilman | 310.27–305.37 | Therman Gibson | Chicago |
| 1947 | Andy Varipapa | 314.16–308.04 | Allie Brandt | Chicago |
| 1948 | Andy Varipapa | 309.23–309.06 | Joe Wilman | Chicago |
| 1949 | Connie Schwoegler | 312.31–307.27 | Andy Varipapa | Chicago |
| 1950 | Junie McMahon | 318.37–307.17 | Ralph Smith | Chicago |
| 1951 | Dick Hoover | 305.29–304.07 | Lee Jouglard | Chicago |
| 1952 | Junie McMahon | 309.29–305.41 | Bill Lillard | Chicago |
| 1953 | Don Carter | 304.17–297.36 | Ed Lubanski | Chicago |
| 1954 | Don Carter | 308.02–307.25 | Bill Lillard | Chicago |
| 1955 | Steve Nagy | 307.17–303.34 | Ed Lubanski | Chicago |
| 1956 | Bill Lillard | 304.30–304.22 | Joe Wilman | Chicago |
| 1957 | Don Carter | 308.49–305.45 | Dick Weber | Chicago |
| 1958 | Don Carter | 311.03–308.09 | Buzz Fazio | Minneapolis |
| 1959 | Billy Welu | 311.48–310.26 | Ray Bluth | Buffalo |
| 1960 | Harry Smith | 312.24–308.12 | Bob Chase | Omaha |
| 1961 | Bill Tucker | 318.49–309.11 | Dick Weber | San Bernardino, CA |
| 1962 | Dick Weber | 299.34–297.38 | Roy Lown | Miami Beach |
| 1963 | Dick Weber | 642–591 | Billy Welu | Kansas City, MO |
| 1964 | Bob Strampe | 714–616 | Tommy Tuttle | Dallas |
| 1965 | Dick Weber | 608–586 | Jim St. John | Philadelphia |
| 1966 | Dick Weber | 684–681 | Nelson Burton Jr. | Lansing, MI |
| 1967 | Les Schissler | 613–610 | Pete Tountas | St. Ann, MO |
| 1968 | Jim Stefanich | 12,401–12,104 | Billy Hardwick | Garden City, NY |
| 1969 | Billy Hardwick | 12,585–11,463 | Dick Weber | Miami |
| 1970 | Bobby Cooper | 12,936–12,307 | Billy Hardwick | Northbrook, IL |
| 1971 | Mike Limongello | 397 (2 games) | Teata Semiz | St. Paul, MN |
| 1972 | Don Johnson | 233 (1 game) | George Pappas | New York City |
| 1973 | Mike McGrath | 712 (3 games) | Earl Anthony | New York City |
| 1974 | Larry Laub | 749 (3 games) | Dave Davis | New York City |
| 1975 | Steve Neff | 279 (1 game) | Paul Colwell | Grand Prairie, TX |
| 1976 | Paul Moser | 226 (1 game) | Jim Frazier | Grand Prairie, TX |
| 1977 | Johnny Petraglia | 279 (1 game) | Bill Spigner | Greensboro, NC |
| 1978 | Nelson Burton Jr. | 873 (4 games) | Jeff Mattingly | Greensboro, NC |
| 1979 | Joe Berardi | 445 (2 games) | Earl Anthony | Windsor Locks, CT |
| 1980 | Steve Martin | 930 (4 games) | Earl Anthony | Windsor Locks, CT |
| 1981 | Marshall Holman | 684 (3 games) | Mark Roth | Houston |
| 1982 | Dave Husted | 1011 (4 games) | Gil Sliker | Houston |
| 1983 | Gary Dickinson | 214 (1 game) | Steve Neff | Oak Lawn, IL |
| 1984 | Mark Roth | 244 (1 game) | Guppy Troup | Oak Hill, IL |
| 1985 | Marshall Holman | 233 (1 game) | Wayne Webb | Venice, FL |
| 1986 | Steve Cook | 467 (2 games) | Frank Ellenburg | Venice, FL |
| 1987 | Del Ballard Jr. | 525 (2 games) | Pete Weber | Tacoma, WA |
| 1988 | Pete Weber | 929 (4 games) | Marshall Holman | Atlantic City |
| 1989 | Mike Aulby | 429 (2 games) | Jim Pencak | Edmond, OK |
| 1990 | Ron Palombi Jr. | 269 (1 game) | Amleto Monacelli | Indianapolis |
| 1991 | Pete Weber | 956 (4 games) | Mark Thayer | Indianapolis |
| 1992 | Robert Lawrence | 667 (3 games) | Scott Devers | Canandaigua, NY |
| 1993 | Del Ballard Jr. | 505 (2 games) | Walter Ray Williams Jr. | Canandaigua, NY |
| 1994 | Justin Hromek | 267 (1 game) | Parker Bohn III | Troy, MI |
| 1995 | Dave Husted | 266 (1 game) | Paul Koehler | Troy, MI |
| 1996 | Dave Husted | 730 (3 games) | George Brooks | Indianapolis |
| 1997 | No event—tournament rescheduled to April, beginning in 1998. | | | |
| 1998 | Walter Ray Williams Jr. | 466 (2 games) | Tim Criss | Fairfield, CT |

## BPAA United States Open *(Cont.)*

| 1999 | Bob Learn Jr. | 231 (1 game) | Jason Couch | Uncasville, CT |
|------|---------------|--------------|-------------|----------------|
| 2000 | Robert Smith | 202 (1 game) | Norm Duke | Phoenix |

Note: From 1942 to 1970, the tournament was called the BPAA All-Star. Peterson scoring was used from 1942 through 1962. Under this system, the winner of an individual match game gets one point, plus one point for each 50 pins knocked down. From 1963 through 1967, a three-game championship was held between the two top qualifiers. From 1968 through 1970 total pinfall determined the winner. From 1971 to the present, five qualifiers compete for the championship.

## Touring Players Championship

| Year | Winner | Score | Runner-Up | Site |
|------|--------|-------|-----------|------|
| 1996 | Mike Aulby | 268 (1 game) | Parker Bohn III | Harmarville, PA |
| 1997 | Steve Hoskins | 932 (4 games) | Danny Wiseman | Harmarville, PA |
| 1998 | Dennis Horan | 481 (2 games) | Parker Bohn III | Akron, OH |
| 1999 | Steve Hoskins | 503 (2 games) | Parker Bohn III | Akron, OH |
| 2000 | Dennis Horan | 924 (4 games) | Pete Weber | Akron, OH |

## PBA National Championship

| Year | Winner | Score | Runner-Up | Site |
|------|--------|-------|-----------|------|
| 1960 | Don Carter | 6512 (30 games) | Ronnie Gaudern | Memphis |
| 1961 | Dave Soutar | 5792 (27 games) | Morrie Oppenheim | Cleveland |
| 1962 | Carmen Salvino | 5369 (25 games) | Don Carter | Philadelphia |
| 1963 | Billy Hardwick | 13,541 (61 games) | Ray Bluth | Long Island, NY |
| 1964 | Bob Strampe | 13,979 (61 games) | Ray Bluth | Long Island, NY |
| 1965 | Dave Davis | 13,895 (61 games) | Jerry McCoy | Detroit |
| 1966 | Wayne Zahn | 14,006 (61 games) | Nelson Burton Jr. | Long Island, NY |
| 1967 | Dave Davis | 421 (2 games) | Pete Tountas | New York City |
| 1968 | Wayne Zahn | 14,182 (60 games) | Nelson Burton Jr. | New York City |
| 1969 | Mike McGrath | 13,670 (60 games) | Bill Allen | Garden City, NY |
| 1970 | Mike McGrath | 660 (3 games) | Dave Davis | Garden City, NY |
| 1971 | Mike Limongello | 911 (4 games) | Dave Davis | Paramus, NJ |
| 1972 | Johnny Guenther | 12,986 (56 games) | Dick Ritger | Rochester, NY |
| 1973 | Earl Anthony | 212 (1 game) | Sam Flanagan | Oklahoma City |
| 1974 | Earl Anthony | 218 (1 game) | Mark Roth | Downey, CA |
| 1975 | Earl Anthony | 245 (1 game) | Jim Frazier | Downey, CA |
| 1976 | Paul Colwell | 191 (1 game) | Dave Davis | Seattle |
| 1977 | Tommy Hudson | 206 (1 game) | Jay Robinson | Seattle |
| 1978 | Warren Nelson | 453 (2 games) | Joseph Groskind | Reno |
| 1979 | Mike Aulby | 727 (3 games) | Earl Anthony | Las Vegas |
| 1980 | Johnny Petraglia | 235 (1 game) | Gary Dickinson | Sterling Heights, MI |
| 1981 | Earl Anthony | 242 (1 game) | Ernie Schlegel | Toledo, OH |
| 1982 | Earl Anthony | 233 (1 game) | Charlie Tapp | Toledo, OH |
| 1983 | Earl Anthony | 210 (1 game) | Mike Durbin | Toledo, OH |
| 1984 | Bob Chamberlain | 961 (4 games) | Dan Eberl | Toledo, OH |
| 1985 | Mike Aulby | 476 (2 games) | Steve Cook | Toledo, OH |
| 1986 | Tom Crites | 190 (1 game) | Mike Aulby | Toledo, OH |
| 1987 | Randy Pedersen | 759 (3 games) | Amleto Monacelli | Toledo, OH |
| 1988 | Brian Voss | 246 (1 game) | Todd Thompson | Toledo, OH |
| 1989 | Pete Weber | 221 (1 game) | Dave Ferraro | Toledo, OH |
| 1990 | Jim Pencak | 900 (4 games) | Chris Warren | Toledo, OH |
| 1991 | Mike Miller | 450 (2 games) | Norm Duke | Toledo, OH |
| 1992 | Eric Forkel | 833 (4 games) | Bob Vespi | Toledo, OH |
| 1993 | Ron Palombi Jr. | 237 (1 game) | Eugene McCune | Toledo, OH |
| 1994 | David Traber | 196 (1 game) | Dale Traber | Toledo, OH |
| 1995 | Scott Alexander | 246 (1 game) | Wayne Webb | Toledo, OH |
| 1996 | Butch Soper | 442 (2 games) | Walter Ray Williams Jr. | Toledo, OH |
| 1997 | Rick Steelsmith | 888 (4 games) | Brian Voss | Toledo, OH |
| 1998 | Pete Weber | 277 (1 game) | David Ozio | Toledo, OH |
| 1999 | Tim Criss | 238 (1 game) | Dave Arnold | Toledo, OH |
| 2000 | Norm Duke | 492 (2 games) | Jason Couch | Toledo, OH |
| 2001 | Walter Ray Williams Jr. | 258 (1 game) | Jeff Lizzi | Toledo, OH |

Note: Totals from 1963–66, 1968–69 and 1972 include bonus pins.

## Tournament of Champio

| Year | Winner | Score | Runner-Up | Site |
|------|--------|-------|-----------|------|
| 1965 | Billy Hardwick | 484 (2 games) | Dick Weber | Akron, OH |
| 1966 | Wayne Zahn | 595 (3 games) | Dick Weber | Akron, OH |
| 1967 | Jim Stefanich | 227 (1 game) | Don Johnson | Akron, OH |
| 1968 | Dave Davis | 213 (1 game) | Don Johnson | Akron, OH |
| 1969 | Jim Godman | 266 (1 game) | Jim Stefanich | Akron, OH |
| 1970 | Don Johnson | 299 (1 game) | Dick Ritger | Akron, OH |
| 1971 | Johnny Petraglia | 245 (1 game) | Don Johnson | Akron, OH |
| 1972 | Mike Durbin | 775 (3 games) | Tim Harahan | Akron, OH |
| 1973 | Jim Godman | 451 (2 games) | Barry Asher | Akron, OH |
| 1974 | Earl Anthony | 679 (3 games) | Johnny Petraglia | Akron, OH |
| 1975 | Dave Davis | 448 (2 games) | Barry Asher | Akron, OH |
| 1976 | Marshall Holman | 441 (2 games) | Billy Hardwick | Akron, OH |
| 1977 | Mike Berlin | 434 (2 games) | Mike Durbin | Akron, OH |
| 1978 | Earl Anthony | 237 (1 game) | Teata Semiz | Akron, OH |
| 1979 | George Pappas | 224 (1 game) | Dick Ritger | Akron, OH |
| 1980 | Wayne Webb | 750 (3 games) | Gary Dickinson | Akron, OH |
| 1981 | Steve Cook | 287 (1 game) | Pete Couture | Akron, OH |
| 1982 | Mike Durbin | 448 (2 games) | Steve Cook | Akron, OH |
| 1983 | Joe Berardi | 865 (4 games) | Henry Gonzalez | Akron, OH |
| 1984 | Mike Durbin | 950 (4 games) | Mike Aulby | Akron, OH |
| 1985 | Mark Williams | 616 (3 games) | Bob Handley | Akron, OH |
| 1986 | Marshall Holman | 233 (1 game) | Mark Baker | Akron, OH |
| 1986 | Marshall Holman | 233 (1 game) | Mark Baker | Akron, OH |
| 1987 | Pete Weber | 928 (4 games) | Jim Murtishaw | Akron, OH |
| 1988 | Mark Williams | 237 (1 game) | Tony Westlake | Fairlawn, OH |
| 1989 | Del Ballard Jr. | 490 (2 games) | Walter Ray Williams Jr. | Fairlawn, OH |
| 1990 | Dave Ferraro | 226 (1 game) | Tony Westlake | Fairlawn, OH |
| 1991 | David Ozio | 476 (2 games) | Amleto Monacelli | Fairlawn, OH |
| 1992 | Marc McDowell | 471 (2 games) | Don Genalo | Fairlawn, OH |
| 1993 | George Branham III | 227 (1 game) | Parker Bohn III | Fairlawn, OH |
| 1994 | Norm Duke | 422 (2 games) | Eric Forkel | Fairlawn, OH |
| 1995 | Mike Aulby | 502 (2 games) | Bob Spaulding | Lake Zurich, IL |
| 1996 | Dave D'Entremont | 971 (4 games) | Dave Arnold | Lake Zurich, IL |
| 1997 | John Gant | 446 (2 games) | Mike Aulby | Reno |
| 1998 | Bryan Goebel | 245 (1 game) | Steve Hoskins | Overland Park, KS |
| 1999 | Jason Couch | 427 (2 games) | Chris Barnes | Overland Park, KS |
| 2000 | Jason Couch | 198 (1 game) | Ryan Shafer | Lake Zurich, IL |

## Quick Strike

And now bowling—yes, bowling—has gone high-tech. First there was automatic scoring. Then came the Seattle guys, a former Microsoft exec and his two buddies, who bought the Professional Bowlers Association. Maybe you didn't think the PBA and its tour, the tour made famous by Earl Anthony and Chris Schenkel and ABC Sports, the tour that relieved school-year boredom in Toledo and Indianapolis and Canandaigua, N.Y., was a commodity, something that could be bought and sold. Chris Peters, the 105th person hired by Microsoft, thought differently....

In March 2000, Peters and two other former Microsoft employees, Mike Slade and Rob Glaser, bought the PBA, beleaguered and in debt, for $5 million—or, as Peters says, "less than you would spend to buy a minor league baseball team." The PBA was a not-for-profit corporation based in Akron. Not anymore. Now it's a corporation, period. The office in Akron, with its furniture from Sears, will remain open, at least for now, but the sleek Seattle office has already opened. When you call there seeking the telephone number of a PBA member, somebody tells you, "I don't have the phone number, but I have the e-mail address." It's a new day.

Peters is one to zag when others zig, so when his thirtysomething techie buddies were taking up golf, he tried his hand at his father's old game, bowling. He immersed himself in it, learning the pro's fingertip grip from a pro, studying the mechanics of the ball-pin collision, reading the game's literature. He bought himself a 15-pound ball, a nice pair of bowling shoes and, without going to a bank for a loan, the PBA....

— Michael Bamberger

## ABC Masters Tournament

| Year | Winner | Scoring Avg | Runner-Up | Site |
|------|--------|-------------|-----------|------|
| 1951 | Lee Jouglard | 201.8 | Joe Wilman | St. Paul, MN |
| 1952 | Willard Taylor | 200.32 | Andy Varipapa | Milwaukee |
| 1953 | Rudy Habetler | 200.13 | Ed Brosius | Chicago |
| 1954 | Eugene Elkins | 205.19 | W. Taylor | Seattle |
| 1955 | Buzz Fazio | 204.13 | Joe Kristof | Ft. Wayne, IN |
| 1956 | Dick Hoover | 209.9 | Ray Bluth | Rochester, NY |
| 1957 | Dick Hoover | 216.39 | Bill Lillard | Ft. Worth, TX |
| 1958 | Tom Hennessy | 209.15 | Lou Frantz | Syracuse, NY |
| 1959 | Ray Bluth | 214.26 | Billy Golembiewski | St. Louis |
| 1960 | Billy Golembiewski | 206.13* | Steve Nagy | Toledo, OH |
| 1961 | Don Carter | 211.18 | Dick Hoover | Detroit |
| 1962 | Billy Golembiewski | 223.12 | Ron Winger | Des Moines, IA |
| 1963 | Harry Smith | 219.3 | Bobby Meadows | Buffalo |
| 1964 | Billy Welu | 227 | Harry Smith | Oakland, CA |
| 1965 | Billy Welu | 202.12 | Don Ellis | St. Paul, MN |
| 1966 | Bob Strampe | 219.80 | Al Thompson | Rochester, NY |
| 1967 | Lou Scalia | 216.9 | Bill Johnson | Miami Beach |
| 1968 | Pete Tountas | 220.15 | Buzz Fazio | Cincinnati |
| 1969 | Jim Chestney | 223.2 | Barry Asher | Madison, WI |
| 1970 | Don Glover | 215.10 | Bob Strampe | Knoxville, TN |
| 1971 | Jim Godman | 229.8 | Don Johnson | Detroit |
| 1972 | Bill Beach | 220.27 | Jim Godman | Long Beach, CA |
| 1973 | Dave Soutar | 218.61 | Dick Ritger | Syracuse, NY |
| 1974 | Paul Colwell | 234.17 | Steve Neff | Indianapolis |
| 1975 | Eddie Ressler | 213.51 | Sam Flanagan | Dayton, OH |
| 1976 | Nelson Burton Jr. | 220.79 | Steve Carson | Oklahoma City |
| 1977 | Earl Anthony | 218.21 | Jim Godman | Reno |
| 1978 | Frank Ellenburg | 200.61 | Earl Anthony | St. Louis |
| 1979 | Doug Myers | 202.9 | Bill Spigner | Tampa |
| 1980 | Neil Burton | 206.69 | Mark Roth | Louisville |
| 1981 | Randy Lightfoot | 218.3 | Skip Tucker | Memphis |
| 1982 | Joe Berardi | 207.12 | Ted Hannahs | Baltimore |
| 1983 | Mike Lastowski | 212.65 | Pete Weber | Niagara Falls |
| 1984 | Earl Anthony | 212.5 | Gil Sliker | Reno |
| 1985 | Steve Wunderlich | 210.4 | Tommy Kress | Tulsa |
| 1986 | Mark Fahy | 206.5 | Del Ballard Jr. | Las Vegas |
| 1987 | Rick Steelsmith | 210.7 | Brad Snell | Niagara Falls |
| 1988 | Del Ballard Jr. | 219.1 | Keith Smith | Jacksonville |
| 1989 | Mike Aulby | 218.5 | Mike Edwards | Wichita |
| 1990 | Chris Warren | 231.6 | David Ozio | Reno |
| 1991 | Doug Kent | 226.8 | George Branham III | Toledo, OH |
| 1992 | Ken Johnson | 230.0 | Dave D'Entremont | Corpus Christi, TX |
| 1993 | Norm Duke | 245.68 | Patrick Allen | Tulsa |
| 1994 | Steve Fehr | 213.09 | Steve Anderson | Greenacres, FL |
| 1995 | Mike Aulby | 230.7 | Mark Williams | Reno |
| 1996 | Ernie Schlegel | 221.2 | Mike Aulby | Salt Lake City |
| 1997 | Jason Queen | 225.5 | Eric Forkel | Huntsville, AL |
| 1998 | Mike Aulby | 224.0 | Parker Bohn III | Reno |
| 1999 | Brian Boghosian | 246.0 | Parker Bohn III | Syracuse, NY |
| 2000 | Mika Koivuniemi | 241.0 | Pete Weber | Albuquerque |
| 2001 | Parker Bohn III | 224.0 | Jason Couch | Reno |

# Women's Majors

## BPAA United States Open

| Year | Winner | Score | Runner-Up | Site |
|------|--------|-------|-----------|------|
| 1949 | Marion Ladewig | 113.26–104.26 | Catherine Burling | Chicago |
| 1950 | Marion Ladewig | 151.46–146.06 | Stephanie Balogh | Chicago |
| 1951 | Marion Ladewig | 159.17–148.03 | Sylvia Wene | Chicago |
| 1952 | Marion Ladewig | 154.39–142.05 | Shirley Garms | Chicago |
| 1953 | Not held | | | |
| 1954 | Marion Ladewig | 148.29–143.01 | Sylvia Wene | Chicago |
| 1955 | Sylvia Wene | 142.30–141.11 | Sylvia Fanta | Chicago |
| 1955 | Anita Cantaline | 144.40–144.13 | Doris Porter | Chicago |
| 1956 | Marion Ladewig | 150.16–145.41 | Marge Merrick | Chicago |
| 1957 | Not held | | | |
| 1958 | Merle Matthews | 145.09–143.14 | Marion Ladewig | Minneapolis |
| 1959 | Marion Ladewig | 149.33–143.00 | Donna Zimmerman | Buffalo |
| 1960 | Sylvia Wene | 144.14–143.26 | Marion Ladewig | Omaha |
| 1961 | Phyllis Notaro | 144.13–143.12 | Hope Riccilli | San Bernardino, CA |
| 1962 | Shirley Garms | 138.44–135.49 | Joy Abel | Miami Beach |
| 1963 | Marion Ladewig | 586–578 | Bobbie Shaler | Kansas City, MO |
| 1964 | LaVerne Carter | 683–609 | Evelyn Teal | Dallas |
| 1965 | Ann Slattery | 597–550 | Sandy Hooper | Philadelphia |
| 1966 | Joy Abel | 593–538 | Bette Rockwell | Lansing, MI |
| 1967 | Gloria Bouvia | 578–516 | Shirley Garms | St. Ann, MO |
| 1968 | Dotty Fothergill | 9,000–8,187 | Doris Coburn | Garden City, NY |
| 1969 | Dotty Fothergill | 8,284–8,258 | Kayoka Suda | Miami |
| 1970 | Mary Baker | 8,730–8,465 | Judy Cook | Northbrook, IL |
| 1971 | Paula Carter | 5,660–5,650 | June Llewellyn | Kansas City, MO |
| 1972 | Lorrie Nichols | 5,272–5,189 | Mary Baker | Denver |
| 1973 | Millie Martorella | 5,553–5,294 | Patty Costello | Garden City, NY |
| 1974 | Patty Costello | 219–216 | Betty Morris | Irving, TX |
| 1975 | Paula Carter | 6,500–6,352 | Lorrie Nichols | Toledo, OH |
| 1976 | Patty Costello | 11,341–11,281 | Betty Morris | Tulsa |
| 1977 | Betty Morris | 10,511–10,358 | Virginia Norton | Milwaukee |
| 1978 | Donna Adamek | 236–202 | Vesma Grinfelds | Miami |
| 1979 | Diana Silva | 11,775–11,718 | Bev Ortner | Phoenix |
| 1980 | Pat Costello | 223–199 | Shinobu Saitoh | Rockford, IL |
| 1981 | Donna Adamek | 201–190 | Nikki Gianulias | Rockford, IL |
| 1982 | Shinobu Saitoh | 12,184–12,028 | Robin Romeo | Hendersonville, TN |
| 1983 | Dana Miller-Mackie | 247–200 | Aleta Sill | St. Louis |
| 1984 | Karen Ellingsworth | 236–217 | Lorrie Nichols | St. Louis |
| 1985 | Pat Mercatani | 214–178 | Nikki Gianulias | Topeka, KS |
| 1986 | Wendy Macpherson | 265–179 | Lisa Wagner | Topeka, KS |
| 1987 | Carol Norman | 206–179 | Cindy Coburn | Mentor, OH |
| 1988 | Lisa Wagner | 226–218 | Lorrie Nichols | Winston-Salem, NC |
| 1989 | Robin Romeo | 187–163 | Michelle Mullen | Addison, IL |
| 1990 | Dana Miller-Mackie | 190–189 | Tish Johnson | Dearborn Heights, MI |
| 1991 | Anne Marie Duggan | 196–185 | Leanne Barrette | Fountain Valley, CA |
| 1992 | Tish Johnson | 216–213 | Aleta Sill | Fountain Valley, CA |
| 1993 | Dede Davidson | 213–194 | Dana Miller-Mackie | Garland, TX |
| 1994 | Aleta Sill | 229–170 | Anne Marie Duggan | Wichita |
| 1995 | Cheryl Daniels | 235–180 | Tish Johnson | Blaine, MN |
| 1996 | Liz Johnson | 265–236 | Marianne DiRupo | Indianapolis |
| 1997 | No event—tournament rescheduled to April, beginning in 1998. | | | |
| 1998 | Aleta Sill | 276–151 | Tammy Turner | Milford, CT |
| 1999 | Kim Adler | 213–195 | Lynda Barnes | Uncasville, CT |
| 2000 | Tennelle Grijalva | 239–155 | Kelly Kulick | Phoenix |

Note: From 1942 to 1970, tournament was called the BPAA All-Star. Peterson scoring used from 1949 to '62. Under this system, the winner of an individual match game gets one point, plus one point for each 50 pins. From 1963 to '67, a three-game championship was held between the two top qualifiers. From 1968 to '73, 1975 to '77, 1979 and 1982, total pinfall determined the winner. In the other years, five qualifiers competed in a playoff for the championship, with the final listed above.

# Women's Majors *(Cont.)*

## AMF Gold Cup

| Year | Winner | Score | Runner-Up | Site |
|------|--------|-------|-----------|------|
| 1997 | Aleta Sill | 221–179 | C. Gianotti-Block | Richmond, VA |
| 1998 | Dana Miller-Mackie | 278–170 | Dede Davidson | Richmond, VA |
| 1999 | Dana Miller-Mackie | 236–222 | Cara Honeychurch | Richmond, VA |

## WIBC Queens

| Year | Winner | Score | Runner-Up | Site |
|------|--------|-------|-----------|------|
| 1961 | Janet Harman | 794–776 | Eula Touchette | Fort Wayne, IN |
| 1962 | Dorothy Wilkinson | 799–794 | Marion Ladewig | Phoenix |
| 1963 | Irene Monterosso | 852–803 | Georgette DeRosa | Memphis |
| 1964 | D. D. Jacobson | 740–682 | Shirley Garms | Minneapolis |
| 1965 | Betty Kuczynski | 772–739 | LaVerne Carter | Portland, OR |
| 1966 | Judy Lee | 771–742 | Nancy Peterson | New Orleans |
| 1967 | Millie Ignizio | 840–809 | Phyllis Massey | Rochester, NY |
| 1968 | Phyllis Massey | 884–853 | Marian Spencer | San Antonio |
| 1969 | Ann Feigel | 832–765 | Millie Ignizio | San Diego |
| 1970 | Millie Ignizio | 807–797 | Joan Holm | Tulsa |
| 1971 | Millie Ignizio | 809–778 | Katherine Brown | Atlanta |
| 1972 | Dotty Fothergill | 890–841 | Maureen Harris | Kansas City, MO |
| 1973 | Dotty Fothergill | 804–791 | Judy Soutar | Las Vegas |
| 1974 | Judy Soutar | 939–705 | Betty Morris | Houston |
| 1975 | Cindy Powell | 758–674 | Patty Costello | Indianapolis |
| 1976 | Pam Buckner | 214–178 | Shirley Sjostrom | Denver |
| 1977 | Dana Stewart | 175–167 | Vesma Grinfelds | Milwaukee |
| 1978 | Loa Boxberger | 197–176 | Cora Fiebig | Miami |
| 1979 | Donna Adamek | 216–181 | Shinobu Saitoh | Tucson |
| 1980 | Donna Adamek | 213–165 | Cheryl Robinson | Seattle |
| 1981 | Katsuko Sugimoto | 166–158 | Virginia Norton | Baltimore |
| 1982 | Katsuko Sugimoto | 160–137 | Nikki Gianulias | St. Louis |
| 1983 | Aleta Sill | 214–188 | Dana Miller-Mackie | Las Vegas |
| 1984 | Kazue Inahashi | 248–222 | Aleta Sill | Niagara Falls |
| 1985 | Aleta Sill | 279–192 | Linda Graham | Toledo, OH |
| 1986 | Cora Fiebig | 223–177 | Barbara Thorberg | Orange County, CA |
| 1987 | Cathy Alameida | 850–817 | Lorrie Nichols | Hartford, CT |
| 1988 | Wendy Macpherson | 213–199 | Leanne Barrette | Reno/Carson City, NV |
| 1989 | Carol Gianotti | 207–177 | Sandra Jo Shiery | Bismarck-Mandan, ND |
| 1990 | Patty Ann | 207–173 | Vesma Grinfelds | Tampa |
| 1991 | Dede Davidson | 231–159 | Jeanne Maiden | Cedar Rapids, IA |
| 1992 | Cindy Coburn-Carroll | 184–170 | Dana Miller-Mackie | Lansing, MI |
| 1993 | Jan Schmidt | 201–163 | Pat Costello | Baton Rouge, LA |
| 1994 | Anne Marie Duggan | 224–177 | Wendy Macpherson-Papanos | Salt Lake City |
| 1995 | Sandra Postma | 226–187 | Carolyn Dorin | Tucson |
| 1996 | Lisa Wagner | 231–226 | Tammy Turner | Buffalo |
| 1997 | S.J. Shiery-Odom | 209–185 | Audry Allen | Reno |
| 1998 | Lynda Norry | 213–157 | Karen Stroud | Davenport, IA |
| 1999 | Leanne Barrette | 256–174 | Dede Davidson | Indianapolis |
| 2000 | Wendy Macpherson | 227–202 | Marianne DiRupo | Reno |
| 2001 | Carolyn Dorin-Ballard | 213–197 | Kelly Kulick | Ft. Lauderdale, FL |

## Sam's Town Invitational

| Year | Winner | Score | Runner-Up | Site |
|------|--------|-------|-----------|------|
| 1984 | Aleta Sill | 238 (1 game) | Cheryl Daniels | Las Vegas |
| 1985 | Patty Costello | 236 (1 game) | Robin Romeo | Las Vegas |
| 1986 | Aleta Sill | 238 (1 game) | Dina Wheeler | Las Vegas |
| 1987 | Debbie Bennett | 880 (4 games) | Lorrie Nichols | Las Vegas |
| 1988 | Donna Adamek | 634 (3 games) | Robin Romeo | Las Vegas |
| 1989 | Tish Johnson | 210 (1 game) | Dede Davidson | Las Vegas |
| 1990 | Wendy Macpherson | 900 (4 games) | Jeanne Maiden | Las Vegas |
| 1991 | Lorrie Nichols | 469 (2 games) | Dana Miller-Mackie | Las Vegas |
| 1992 | Tish Johnson | 279 (1 game) | Robin Romeo | Las Vegas |
| 1993 | Robin Romeo | 194 (1 game) | Tammy Turner | Las Vegas |
| 1994 | Tish Johnson | 178 (1 game) | Carol Gianotti | Las Vegas |
| 1995 | Michelle Mullen | 202 (1 game) | Cheryl Daniels | Las Vegas |
| 1996 | C. Gianotti-Block | 892 (4 games) | Leanne Barrette | Las Vegas |
| 1997 | Kim Adler | 953 (4 games) | Wendy Macpherson | Las Vegas |
| 1998 | Julie Gardner | 961 (4 games) | Dede Davidson | Las Vegas |
| 1999 | Wendy Macpherson | 209 (1 game) | Marianne DiRupo | Las Vegas |
| 2000 | Dede Davidson | 183 (1 game) | Tiffany Stanbrough | Las Vegas |

## PWBA Championships *(Discontinued)*

| | | | |
|------|------|------|------|
| 1960...Marion Ladewig | 1966...Joy Abel | 1972...Patty Costello | 1978...Toni Gillard |
| 1961...Shirley Garms | 1967...Betty Mivalez | 1973...Betty Morris | 1979...Cindy Coburn |
| 1962...Stephanie Balogh | 1968...Dotty Fothergill | 1974...Pat Costello | 1980...Donna Adamek |
| 1963...Janet Harman | 1969...Dotty Fothergill | 1975...Pam Buckner | |
| 1964...Betty Kuczynski | 1970...Bobbe North | 1976...Patty Costello | |
| 1965...Helen Duval | 1971...Patty Costello | 1977...Vesma Grinfelds | |

## Sixteen-Pound Picasso

With the notable exception of *Kingpin*, bowling hasn't been associated with great art. Now, though, the bowling ball is finally enjoying its turn as an *objet d'art* thanks to Todd Ramquist and Kiaralinda, two Florida artists, and their newly published book, *On the Ball: Over 80 Artists Put a New Spin on the Classic Bowling Ball*. Over the course of five years, the duo solicited bowling-ball-based works from artists around the world. Here's a descripton of samples from the collection.

**Untitled**, by Johnny Meah. Meah's art often depicts the world of circus sideshows—he himself has performed as a sword-swallower and fire-eater—hence this piece, which is a take on the circus fat lady.

**And on the 7th Day**, by Chris Hubbard. This is one of Hubbard's "Heaven and Hell" works, which also include Heaven and Hell Car, a 1990 Honda Civic decorated with images of angels and demons.

**Birdhouse**, by Holly Apperson. As its name implies, this piece is a bowling ball as birdhouse. Birdhouses are big with Apperson, who has made a habit of making personalized ones as gifts for her friends.

**Flash**, by Emily Hughes. A sanguine self-portrait that's also a statement on the travails of aging—specifically, says Hughes, of entering her red-faced years.

**Untitled**, by Judd. Juddletts is the name the artist has given to the small ceramic figures that often appear in his works, including the ones crawling over this ball.

**Super Bowl Sundae**, by Bob Apperson. Inspiration struck after the pun-happy artist watched an NFL playoff game and heard an announcer talking about the impending title match. Says Apperson, "I had my play on words, and I went balls out!" You can imagine the result.

# Men's Awards

## BWAA Bowler of the Year

| Year | Bowler | Year | Bowler |
|------|--------|------|--------|
| 1942 | Johnny Crimmins | 1971 | Don Johnson |
| 1943 | Ned Day | 1972 | Don Johnson |
| 1944 | Ned Day | 1973 | Don McCune |
| 1945 | Buddy Bomar | 1974 | Earl Anthony |
| 1946 | Joe Wilman | 1975 | Earl Anthony |
| 1947 | Buddy Bomar | 1976 | Earl Anthony |
| 1948 | Andy Varipapa | 1977 | Mark Roth |
| 1949 | Connie Schwoegler | 1978 | Mark Roth |
| 1950 | Junie McMahon | 1979 | Mark Roth |
| 1951 | Lee Jouglard | 1980 | Wayne Webb |
| 1952 | Steve Nagy | 1981 | Earl Anthony |
| 1953 | Don Carter | 1982 | Earl Anthony |
| 1954 | Don Carter | 1983 | Earl Anthony |
| 1955 | Steve Nagy | 1984 | Mark Roth |
| 1956 | Bill Lillard | 1985 | Mike Aulby |
| 1957 | Don Carter | 1986 | Walter Ray Williams Jr. |
| 1958 | Don Carter | 1987 | Marshall Holman |
| 1959 | Ed Lubanski | 1988 | Brian Voss |
| 1960 | Don Carter | 1989 | Mike Aulby |
| 1961 | Dick Weber | | Amleto Monacelli* |
| 1962 | Don Carter | 1990 | Amleto Monacelli |
| 1963 | Dick Weber | 1991 | David Ozio |
| | Billy Hardwick* | 1992 | Dave Ferraro |
| 1964 | Billy Hardwick | 1993 | Walter Ray Williams Jr. |
| | Bob Strampe* | 1994 | Norm Duke |
| 1965 | Dick Weber | 1995 | Mike Aulby |
| 1966 | Wayne Zahn | 1996 | Walter Ray Williams Jr. |
| 1967 | Dave Davis | 1997 | Walter Ray Williams Jr. |
| 1968 | Jim Stefanich | 1998 | Walter Ray Williams Jr. |
| 1969 | Billy Hardwick | 1999 | Parker Bohn III |
| 1970 | Nelson Burton Jr. | 2000 | Norm Duke |

*PBA Bowler of the Year. The PBA began selecting a player of the year in 1963. Its selection has been the same as the BWAA's in all but three years.

# Women's Awards

## BWAA Bowler of the Year

| Year | Bowler | Year | Bowler |
|------|--------|------|--------|
| 1948 | Val Mikiel | 1972 | Patty Costello |
| 1949 | Val Mikiel | 1973 | Judy Soutar |
| 1950 | Marion Ladewig | 1974 | Betty Morris |
| 1951 | Marion Ladewig | 1975 | Judy Soutar |
| 1952 | Marion Ladewig | 1976 | Patty Costello |
| 1953 | Marion Ladewig | 1977 | Betty Morris |
| 1954 | Marion Ladewig | 1978 | Donna Adamek |
| 1955 | Marion Ladewig | 1979 | Donna Adamek |
| 1956 | Sylvia Martin | 1980 | Donna Adamek |
| 1957 | Anita Cantaline | 1981 | Donna Adamek |
| 1958 | Marion Ladewig | 1982 | Nikki Gianulias |
| 1959 | Marion Ladewig | 1983 | Lisa Wagner |
| 1960 | Sylvia Martin | 1984 | Aleta Sill |
| 1961 | Shirley Garms | 1985 | Aleta Sill |
| 1962 | Shirley Garms | | Patty Costello* |
| 1963 | Marion Ladewig | 1986 | Lisa Wagner |
| 1964 | LaVerne Carter | | Jeanne Madden* |
| 1965 | Betty Kuczynski | 1987 | Betty Morris |
| 1966 | Joy Abel | 1988 | Lisa Wagner |
| 1967 | Millie Martorella | 1989 | Robin Romeo |
| 1968 | Dotty Fothergill | 1990 | Tish Johnson |
| 1969 | Dotty Fothergill | | Leanne Barrette* |
| 1970 | Mary Baker | 1991 | Leanne Barrette |
| 1971 | Paula Sperber Carter | 1992 | Tish Johnson |

### BWAA Bowler of the Year (Cont.)

| | |
|---|---|
| 1993.........................Lisa Wagner | 1998........................Carol Gianotti-Block |
| 1994..........................Anne Marie | 1999........................Wendy Macpherson |
| Duggan | 2000........................Wendy Macpherson |
| 1995.........................Tish Johnson | |
| 1996..........................Wendy Macpherson | |
| 1997.........................Wendy Macpherson | |

*PWBA Bowler of the Year. The PWBA began selecting a player of the year in 1983. Its selection has been the same as the BWAA's in all but three years.

## Career Leaders

### Earnings

| MEN | | WOMEN | |
|---|---|---|---|
| Walter Ray Williams Jr. | $2,559,951 | Wendy Macpherson | $1,069,685 |
| Pete Weber | $2,237,548 | Aleta Sill | $1,067,999 |
| Parker Bohn III | $2,042,276 | Tish Johnson | $1,009,130 |
| Mike Aulby | $2,038,540 | Leanne Barrette | $891,458 |
| Brian Voss | $1,778,878 | Anne Marie Duggan | $885,251 |

### Titles

| MEN | | WOMEN | |
|---|---|---|---|
| Earl Anthony | 41 | Lisa Wagner | 32 |
| Mark Roth | 34 | Aleta Sill | 31 |
| Walter Ray Williams Jr. | 33 | Patty Costello | 25 |
| Parker Bohn III | 27 | Tish Johnson | 24 |
| Mike Aulby | 27 | Leanne Barrette | 22 |

Note: Leaders through Sept 20, 2001

# Soccer

**Landon Donovan of the
MLS Cup champion
San Jose Earthquakes**

# Reversals of Fortune

## While the U.S. national team saw its World Cup fate take hairpin turns, San Jose went from worst to first in MLS

### BY HANK HERSCH

**B**ruce Arena kept saying it over and over, but no one believed him because no one wanted to. After the U.S. national team's incendiary start in the final round of qualifying for the 2002 World Cup—four victories and a tie, including a 2–0 defeat of archrival Mexico—its fans were gaga, speculating on how their side stacked up against soccer's international superpowers and scanning eBay to size up the cheapest flights to Japan and South Korea. The Americans had never looked better, attacking with flair, defending with fervor. Who cared about Arena's cautionary words, utterances to be expected from any coach in the catbird seat? "We're only halfway through this round," Arena repeatedly said. "We haven't done anything yet."

Mounting injuries were the first sign of trouble. The offense was gradually crippled, as midfield maestro Claudio Reyna (groin) and forward Brian McBride (blood-clot disorder) were sidelined along with up-and-coming strikers Clint Mathis (torn right ACL) and Josh Wolf (broken left foot). Mid-

fielders John O'Brien and Ben Olsen also struggled with injuries. After the plague of injuries came a storm of miscues by the normally solid backline, which had allowed only one goal in the first five matches. But now it began to buckle under the pressure. After a 1–0 defeat at Mexico came a devastating 3–2 loss to Honduras on Sept. 1 at RFK Stadium in Washington, where the visitors' supporters seemed to outnumber the home side's. Another blanking at Costa Rica (2–0) gave the U.S. its longest losing streak in qualifying in 44 years. Only three of the six teams left from the region—North America, Central America and the Caribbean—would advance to the 2002 Cup. The Yanks stood fourth.

World Cup qualifying has alway been an arduous process. After 1950 the U.S. failed to advance to the next nine Cups—a streak that ended with what remains arguably the most important goal in U.S. soccer history. In 1989, as the Americans struggled to secure a berth for the '90 tournament, FIFA, which had awarded the '94 World Cup to the U.S., considered moving its prized event to a more soccer-worthy coun-

**Moore delivered a clutch performance against Jamaica.**

SIMON BRUTY

try. With the U.S. needing a victory at Trinidad & Tobago in its last match to qualify, midfielder Paul Caligiuri launched a looping, left-footed shot from 30 yards that found the upper right corner. That 31st-minute goal held up, and the U.S. advanced to Italia '90 while holding on to the rights to host USA '94.

"It was completely instinctive, no thought whatsoever," recalls Caligiuri, who scored only four other times in his 13-year, 114-match career for the national team. "A gift from the gods."

The gift kept on giving. The slew of sold-out venues from Boston to Los Angeles at World Cup '94 prompted investors to bankroll Major League Soccer, which began play in 1996. In April, MLS entered its sixth season, and it continues to make progress. Attendance improved by 9% in 2001, and more important, the quality of play picked up as well. In particular, the Miami Fusion showed plenty of flair, leading the league with a 16-5-5 record and 2.2 goals per game. Making that achievement all the more remarkable was the team's woeful history. After losing for three straight years and having the league's worst attendance, the Fusion had reportedly considered moving to Winston-Salem, N.C.

But with 22-year-old Nick Rimando's goalkeeping, 38-year-old Preki's playmaking and the finishing touches of MLS's top two scorers—Alex Pineda Chacon, the league MVP, and Diego Serna—crowds in Miami swelled to 14,274 a game. Former NASL midfielder and Fusion TV analyst Ray Hudson, in his first full season as Miami coach, encouraged an aggressive approach on the field by challenging his troops. Hudson, 46, compared players to a ballpoint pen, saying, "If it doesn't work, you shake it; if it doesn't

work, you shake it again; and if it still doesn't work, you get rid of it."

Miami easily won the Eastern division, but its run ended in the semifinals of the playoffs when it was beaten by a team even more resurgent. After finishing with the league's worst record in 2000, the San Jose Earthquakes marched into the 2001 title game against the Los Angeles Galaxy behind rookie coach Frank Yallop; former D.C. United stalwart Jeff Agoos, the defender of the year; and striker Landon Donovan. A 19-year-old from Redlands, Calif., Donovan was loaned to MLS after a year and a half with the German powerhouse Bayer Leverkusen, which recognized his sparkling talent when he was 16, signing him to a four-year, $400,000 deal in 1999. But Donovan languished on the Leverkusen amateur team, pining for home.

With the Earthquakes, he quickly came of age. On Aug. 8 he led San Jose to a 5–1 rout of New England with two goals and two assists. He finished with seven goals and 10 assists in the 17 games he started, and in MLS Cup 2001, he pounced on a cross from Richard Mulrooney in the 45th minute, rocketing a volley from 12 yards into the upper corner to tie the game at one. "It was just one of those times when you *know* you've hit it well," Donovan said.

When reserve forward Dwayne DeRosario collected the ball on the left flank six minutes into overtime, cut inside on defender Danny Califf and curled a shot from 16 yards into the far corner, the Quakes had a 2–1 victory and a completed journey from worst to first. That play also completed Caligiuri's journey as a pro: The title game was the last MLS match for the 37-year-old Galaxy defender whose left foot, it could be said, had kick-started the league.

Just as the '94 World Cup provided the impetus for MLS, the 1999 Women's World Cup yielded the Women's United Soccer Association (WUSA) in the summer of 2001. The eight-team league included stars from around the globe as well as most of the top U.S. players—most notably Mia Hamm. Though her Washington Freedom tied for last place, Hamm's drawing power attracted an average of 12,748 fans to Freedom matches, helping WUSA to draw 8,133 per game and exceed its modest attendance goal of 7,500. Hamm was supplanted as the world's top player, however, by the New York Power's Tiffeny Milbrett, who led the league with 16 goals and won its first MVP award.

Goals were scarce early in the season, but offenses improved as the season progressed. The two playoff semifinals produced high drama, and the final, the Founders Cup, between the Bay Area CyberRays and the Atlanta Beat, was a thriller. After Bay Area's Tisha Venturini made it 3–3 with a goal in the 86th minute, the teams played two overtimes without breaking the deadlock. Like their cotenants at San Jose's Spartan Stadium, the CyberRays had known difficulty, starting the season 1-4-1. And also like the Earthquakes, the Bay Area side prevailed, with the clinching penalty coming from Australian midfielder Julie Murray, the Founders Cup MVP. As fireworks boomed above the crowd of 21,078, CyberRays defender Brandi Chastain, who scored Bay Area's first goal in the game, pronounced this victory sweeter than the U.S. team's in '99. "The World Cup happens every four years," Chastain said. "This league will be going every summer, and there will be a champion every year. To me, it is so important for young girls to be able to come to the stadium on a regular basis, not just every four years."

The prospect of going *eight* years between World Cup appearances weighed heavily on the U.S. men as they prepared to face Jamaica at Foxboro on Oct. 7. Victories in the Americans' final two matches would assure them a berth; anything less and the U.S. would need considerable help from the soccer gods to make it to Japan/South Korea 2002.

Reyna's return to health was a huge boost. "When you get Claudio in the mix, you get players forward and create chances," Arena said. "We've sorely missed that." Only four minutes into the match Reyna sent a free kick to the near post, where a diving Joe-Max Moore flicked a header into the net.

But Jamaica equalized 10 minutes later, and the Americans were once again on Uneasy Street—until Donovan, in only his seventh national-team appearance, streaked onto a pass in the box from Reyna, stopped on a dime and was cleaned out by defender Tyrone Marshall. The referee immediately pointed to the spot, without protest from Jamaica. Moore drilled the penalty kick, and the U.S. escaped with a 2–1 win.

Minutes later, when the other matches in the region had ended, it became clear that the Yanks had won much more. A tie between visiting Mexico and Costa Rica, and Trinidad & Tobago's stunning upset of Honduras in Tegucigalpa meant that the U.S. hadn't merely kept its hopes of qualifying alive—it had clinched a spot in the field of 32. Officials had to hunt down four bottles of champagne in the stadium's catering supply room. Said Agoos, "Nobody in our locker room thought we would qualify today."

The Yanks could look ahead to May, when the World Cup will begin and more unexpected turns can be expected.

## Major League Soccer

### 2001 Final Standings*

| EASTERN DIVISION | | | | | CENTRAL DIVISION | | | | | WESTERN DIVISION | | | | |
|---|---|---|---|---|---|---|---|---|---|---|---|---|---|---|
| Team | Won | Lost | Tied | Pts | Team | Won | Lost | Tied | Pts | Team | Won | Lost | Tied | Pts |
| Miami (1) | 16 | 5 | 5 | 53 | Chicago (2) | 16 | 6 | 5 | 53 | Los Angeles (3) | 14 | 7 | 5 | 47 |
| NY/NJ (6) | 13 | 10 | 3 | 42 | Columbus (4) | 13 | 7 | 6 | 45 | San Jose (5) | 13 | 7 | 6 | 45 |
| New England | 7 | 14 | 6 | 27 | Dallas (8) | 10 | 11 | 5 | 35 | Kansas City (7) | 11 | 13 | 3 | 36 |
| D.C. | 8 | 16 | 2 | 26 | Tampa Bay | 4 | 21 | 2 | 14 | Colorado | 5 | 13 | 8 | 23 |

*League canceled all regular-season games after Sept. 11, 2001. Note: Three points for a win. One point for a tie. Number in parentheses is playoff seed.

### SCORING LEADERS

| Player, Team | GP | G | A | Pts |
|---|---|---|---|---|
| Alex Pineda Chacon, Miami | 25 | 19 | 9 | 47 |
| Diego Serna, Miami | 22 | 15 | 15 | 45 |
| John Spencer, Colorado | 23 | 14 | 7 | 35 |
| Jeff Cunningham, Columbus | 22 | 10 | 13 | 33 |
| John Wilmar Perez, Colum. | 25 | 8 | 15 | 31 |

### ASSISTS LEADERS

| Player, Team | GP | A |
|---|---|---|
| Diego Serna, Miami | 22 | 15 |
| John Wilmar Perez, Columbus | 25 | 15 |
| Preki, Miami | 24 | 14 |
| Jeff Cunningham, Columbus | 22 | 13 |
| Ian Bishop, Miami | 23 | 13 |

### GOALS LEADERS

| Player, Team | GP | G |
|---|---|---|
| Alex Pineda Chacon, Miami | 25 | 19 |
| Diego Serna, Miami | 22 | 15 |
| John Spencer, Colorado | 23 | 14 |
| Abdul Thompson Conteh, D.C. | 25 | 14 |
| Ronald Cerritos, San Jose | 25 | 11 |
| Ariel Graziani, Dallas | 25 | 11 |

### GOALS-AGAINST-AVERAGE LEADERS

| Player, Team | GAA |
|---|---|
| Zach Thornton, Chicago | 1.08 |
| Joe Cannon, San Jose | 1.09 |
| Nick Rimando, Miami | 1.29 |
| Tim Howard, NY/NJ | 1.33 |
| Tom Presthus, Columbus | 1.36 |

### 2001 PLAYOFFS

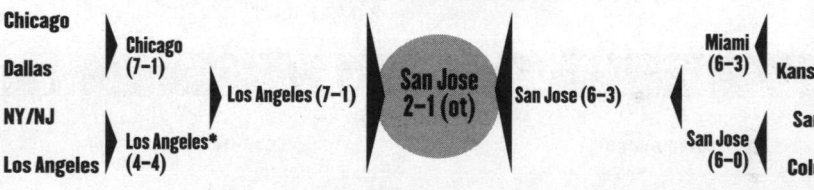

Chicago
Dallas — Chicago (7-1)
NY/NJ
Los Angeles — Los Angeles* (4-4)

Los Angeles (7-1)

San Jose 2-1 (ot)

San Jose (6-3)

Miami (6-3) — Miami / Kansas City

San Jose (6-0) — San Jose / Columbus

*Won tiebreaking minigame. Note: Except for the final, which was a single game, scores in parentheses are points earned (three for a win, one for a tie) in a three-game series, the winner being the first team to accumulate five points.

## MLS Cup 2001

### COLUMBUS, OHIO, OCTOBER 21, 2001

| | | | | |
|---|---|---|---|---|
| San Jose | 1 | 0 | 1 | —2 |
| Los Angeles | 1 | 0 | 0 | —1 |

Goals: Hernandez (Vanney) 21; Donovan (Mulrooney) 43; DeRosario (Ekelund) 96.

**San Jose**—Cannon, Conrad, Dayak, Agoos, Barrett, Russell, Corrales, Mulrooney, Ekelund, Cerritos (DeRosario 85), Donovan.

**Los Angeles**—Hartman, Hendrickson, Vanney, Caliguri (Frye 53), Califf, Elliott, Cienfuegos, Vagenas, Jones, Victorine (Mullan 75), Hernandez.

Att: 21,626.

# A-League

## 2001 Final Standings

### NORTHERN CONFERENCE

| Team | Won | Lost | Tied | BP | Pts |
|---|---|---|---|---|---|
| Hershey | 16 | 7 | 3 | 8 | 75 |
| Rochester | 16 | 6 | 4 | 6 | 74 |
| Pittsburgh | 10 | 12 | 4 | 6 | 50 |
| Montreal | 10 | 14 | 2 | 3 | 45 |
| Connecticut | 9 | 11 | 6 | 1 | 43 |
| Long Island | 6 | 16 | 4 | 5 | 33 |
| Toronto | 7 | 16 | 3 | 1 | 32 |

### CENTRAL CONFERENCE

| Team | Won | Lost | Tied | BP | Pts |
|---|---|---|---|---|---|
| Richmond | 15 | 6 | 3 | 7 | 70 |
| Charleston | 15 | 9 | 1 | 7 | 68 |
| Nashville | 14 | 9 | 2 | 5 | 63 |
| Charlotte | 13 | 10 | 2 | 7 | 61 |
| Atlanta | 13 | 11 | 1 | 6 | 59 |
| Indiana | 8 | 17 | 0 | 3 | 35 |
| Cincinnati | 5 | 20 | 0 | 2 | 22 |

### WESTERN CONFERENCE

| Team | Won | Lost | Tied | BP | Pts |
|---|---|---|---|---|---|
| Vancouver | 16 | 7 | 2 | 8 | 74 |
| San Diego | 14 | 11 | 1 | 11 | 68 |
| Milwaukee | 14 | 10 | 2 | 5 | 63 |
| Portland | 12 | 10 | 3 | 6 | 57 |
| Seattle | 12 | 12 | 1 | 3 | 52 |
| Minnesota | 9 | 15 | 2 | 3 | 41 |
| El Paso | 8 | 13 | 4 | 4 | 40 |

Note: BP=Bonus points. Teams receive a bonus point each time they score three or more goals in a regulation or overtime game, regardless of the result.

### SCORING LEADERS

| Player, Team | GP | G | A | Pts |
|---|---|---|---|---|
| Paul Conway, Charleston | 25 | 22 | 3 | 47 |
| Dustin Swinehart, Charlotte | 23 | 18 | 3 | 39 |
| Jakob Fenger, Nashville | 24 | 14 | 6 | 34 |
| Jeff Houser, Nashville | 25 | 14 | 5 | 33 |
| Digital Takawira, Mil | 20 | 13 | 4 | 30 |

### GOALS-AGAINST-AVERAGE LEADERS

| Player, Team | GAA |
|---|---|
| Jon Busch, Hershey | 0.60 |
| Scott Vallow, Rochester, | 0.97 |
| Didar Sandhu, Vancouver | 1.09 |
| John Swallen, Minnesota | 1.14 |
| Dusty Hudock, Charleston | 1.20 |

## 2001 PLAYOFFS

### FIRST ROUND

Pittsburgh 5, Charleston 2
San Diego 4, Atlanta 2
Portland 5, Charlotte 2
Milwaukee* 3, Nashville 3

### QUARTERFINALS

Milwaukee 4, Richmond 3
Rochester 4, Pittsburgh 2
Hershey 3, Charlotte 0
Vancouver 4, San Diego 3

### SEMIFINALS

Hershey 4, Vancouver 1
Rochester 4, Milwaukee 2

*Milwaukee advanced on penalties. Note: Scores from first round, quarterfinals and semifinals are two-game aggregates.

### A-LEAGUE CHAMPIONSHIP*

Rochester 2, Vancouver 0

*One game.

# U.S. Open Cup

## 2001 RESULTS

### THIRD ROUND

Pittsburgh (A-League) 2, El Paso (A-League) 1
Chicago (MLS) 1, Kansas City (MLS) 0
San Jose* (MLS) 0, Milwaukee (A-League) 0
Los Angeles (MLS) 3, Seattle (PDL) 1
New England (MLS) 2, Charleston (A-League) 1
Columbus (MLS) 2, Miami (MLS) 1
Richmond (A-League) 2, Connecticut (A-League) 1
D.C. United (MLS) 3, Hershey (A-League) 0

### QUARTERFINALS

Chicago 3, Pittsburgh 2 (ot)
Los Angeles* 1, San Jose 1
New England 2, Columbus 1
D.C. United 2, Richmond 1

*Advanced on penalties. Note:MLS: Major League Soccer (1st division); A-League (2nd division); PDL: Premier Development League (Amateur).

### SEMIFINALS

Los Angeles 1, Chicago 0 (ot)
New England 2, D.C. United 0

### 2001 LAMAR HUNT U.S. OPEN CUP FINAL, OCTOBER 27, FULLERTON, CA

| | | | |
|---|---|---|---|
| **New England** | 1 | 0 | —1 |
| **Los Angeles** | 0 | 2 | —2 |

Goals: Harris (unassisted) 30; Hendrickson (Vanney) 70; Califf (Jones) 92.

**New England**—Fernandez, Franchino, Wright, Cullen, Alvarez, Heaps (sent off, 88), Downing (Chronopolous 78), Cloutier, Cate, Williams (Woods 61), Harris (Sunsing 68).

**Los Angeles**—Hartman, Vanney, Caliguiri (Mullan 64), Califf, Hendrickson, Elliott, Vagenas, Cienfuegos, Frye, Victorine (Lalas 91), Jones.

Att: 4,195

# Women's United Soccer Association

## 2001 Final Standings

| Team | GP | W | L | T | Pts | GF | GA | Diff. | Home | Road |
|------|-----|---|----|---|-----|----|----|-------|-------|-------|
| †Atlanta | 21 | 10 | 4 | 7 | 37 | 31 | 21 | +10 | 5-2-4 | 5-2-3 |
| *Bay Area | 21 | 11 | 6 | 4 | 37 | 27 | 23 | +4 | 6-3-1 | 5-3-3 |
| *New York | 21 | 9 | 7 | 5 | 32 | 30 | 25 | +5 | 4-3-3 | 5-4-2 |
| *Philadelphia | 21 | 9 | 8 | 4 | 31 | 35 | 28 | +7 | 5-3-2 | 4-5-2 |
| San Diego | 21 | 7 | 7 | 7 | 28 | 29 | 28 | +1 | 4-3-4 | 3-4-3 |
| Boston | 21 | 8 | 10 | 3 | 27 | 29 | 35 | -6 | 4-6-1 | 4-4-2 |
| Washington | 21 | 6 | 12 | 3 | 21 | 26 | 35 | -9 | 3-6-1 | 3-6-2 |
| Carolina | 21 | 6 | 12 | 3 | 21 | 28 | 40 | -12 | 4-5-2 | 2-7-1 |

†Regular-season champion. *Clinched playoff berth.

### SCORING LEADERS

| Player, Team | GP | G | A | Pts |
|--------------|-----|----|---|-----|
| Tiffeny Milbrett, NY | 20 | 16 | 3 | 35 |
| Shannon MacMillan, SD | 20 | 12 | 6 | 30 |
| Charmaine Hooper, Atl | 19 | 12 | 3 | 27 |
| Dagny Mellgren, Bos | 19 | 11 | 4 | 26 |
| Danielle Fotopoulos, Car | 21 | 9 | 5 | 23 |
| Maren Meinert, Bos | 17 | 8 | 7 | 23 |

### GOALS-AGAINST-AVERAGE LEADERS

| Player, Team | GAA |
|--------------|-----|
| Briana Scurry, Atl | 0.82 |
| LaKeysia Beene, Bay | 0.97 |
| Melissa Moore, Phil | 1.01 |
| Gao Hong, NY | 1.11 |
| Jaime Pagliarulo, SD | 1.40 |

## 2001 PLAYOFFS
### SEMIFINALS

Atlanta 2, Philadelphia 2
Bay Area 3, New York 2

### 2001 FOUNDERS CUP, AUGUST 25, FOXBORO STADIUM

Bay Area 3, Atlanta 3
Bay Area won 4–2 on penalties.

# International Competition

## 2000–2001 U.S. Men's National Team Results

| Date | Opponent | Site | Result | U.S. Goals |
|------|----------|------|--------|------------|
| Oct 25, 2000 | Mexico | Los Angeles | 2–0 W | Donovan, Wolff |
| Nov 15 | Barbados† | St. Michael, Barbados | 4–0 W | Mathis, Stewart, Jones, Razov |
| Jan 27, 2001 | China | Oakland | 2–1 W | McBride, own goal |
| Feb 3 | Colombia | Miami | 0–1 L | — |
| Feb 28 | Mexico† | Columbus, OH | 2–0 W | Wolff, Stewart |
| March 3 | Brazil | Los Angeles | 2–1 L | Mathis |
| March 28 | Honduras† | San Pedro Sula, Hond. | 2–1 W | Stewart, Mathis |
| April 25 | Costa Rica† | Kansas City, MO | 1–0 W | Wolff |
| June 7 | Ecuador | Columbus, OH | 0–0 T | — |
| June 16 | Jamaica† | Kingston, Jamaica | 0–0 T | — |
| June 20 | Trinidad & Tobago† | Foxboro, MA | 2–0 W | Razov, Stewart |
| July 1 | Mexico† | Mexico City | 0–1 L | — |
| Sept 1 | Honduras† | Washington, D.C. | 2–3 L | Stewart (2) |
| Sept 5 | Costa Rica† | San Jose, Costa Rica | 0–2 L | — |
| Oct 7 | Jamaica† | Foxboro, MA | 2–1 W | Moore (2) |

†Qualifying for 2002 World Cup. Record in full internationals from Oct. 25, 2000, through Oct. 7, 2001: 8-5-2.

## 2000–2001 U.S. Women's National Team Results

| Date | Opponent | Site | Result | U.S. Goals |
|------|----------|------|--------|------------|
| Sept 14, 2000 | Norway† | Melbourne, Australia | 2–0 W | Milbrett, Hamm |
| Sept 17 | China† | Melbourne, Australia | 1–1 T | Foudy |
| Sept 20 | Nigeria† | Melbourne, Australia | 3–1 W | Chastain, Lily, MacMillan |
| Sept 24 | Brazil† | Canberra, Australia | 1–0 W | Hamm |
| Sept 28 | Norway† | Sydney, Australia | 2–3 L | Milbrett (2) |
| Nov 11 | Canada | Columbus, OH | 1–3 L | Milbrett |
| Dec 10 | Mexico | Houston | 3–2 W | Lily, Parlow (2) |
| Dec 17 | Japan | Phoenix | 1–1 T | Chastain |
| Jan 11, 2001 | China | Panyu, China | 0–1 L | — |
| Jan 14 | China | Hangzhou, China | 1–1 T | Lalor |
| March 7 | Italy | Rieti, Italy | 0–1 L | — |
| March 11 | Canada# | Lagos, Portugal | 0–3 L | — |

### 2000–2001 U.S. Women's National Team Results (Cont.)

| Date | Opponent | Site | Result | U.S. Goals |
|---|---|---|---|---|
| March 13 | Portugal# | Silves, Portugal | 2–0 W | Welsh, Rigamat |
| March 15 | Sweden# | Albufeira, Portugal | 0–2 L | — |
| March 17 | Norway# | Quartfeira, Portugal | 3–4 L | Marquand, Schott, Reddick |
| June 30 | Canada | Toronto | 2–2 T | MacMillan, Milbrett |
| July 3 | Canada | Blaine, MN | 1–0 W | Milbrett |
| Sept. 9 | Germany* | Chicago | 4–1 W | Hamm (2), Parlow, Milbrett |

Record from Sept. 14, 2000, through Sept. 9, 2001: 7-7-4. †Olympic Games. #Algarves Cup. *U.S. Women's Cup, the remainder of which was canceled after the Sept. 11 terrorist attacks on New York City and Washington, D.C.

## International Club Competition

### Intercontinental Cup

Competition between winners of European Cup and Libertadores Cup.

**TOKYO: NOVEMBER 28, 2000**

**Boca Juniors (Arg) ..........2    0—2**
**Real Madrid (Spain) ........1    0—1**

Goals: Palermo 3, 6; Roberto Carlos 12.

Att: 50,091.

**Boca Juniors:** Cordoba, Bermudez, Traverso, Ibarra, Matellan, Basualdo, Serna, Riquelme, Battaglia (Burdisso, 90), Delgado (Barros Schelotto, 88), Palermo.
**Real Madrid:** Casillas, Hiero, Roberto Carlos, Karanka, McManaman (Savio, 67), Figo, Makelele (Morientes, 77), Helguera, Guti Geremi Raul.

### UEFA Cup

Competition between teams other than league champions and cup-winners from UEFA.

**DORTMUND, GERMANY: MAY 16, 2001**

**Liverpool (England) .........3   1   1—5**
**Alaves (Spain) ...................1   3   0—4**

Goals: Babbel 4, Gerrard 16, McAllister 41 (pen.), Fowler 73, own goal 117 (Geli); Alonso 27, Moreno 48, 51, Cruyff 89.

Att: 55,000.

**Liverpool:** Westerveld, Babbel, Henchoz (Smicer, 56) Hyyppia, Carragher, Gerrard, McAllister, Hamann, Murphy, Heskey (Fowler, 64), Owen (Berger, 79).
**Alaves:** Herrera, Eggen (Ivan 23), Karmona, Tellez, Contra, Tomic, Desio, Astudillo (Magno, 45), Geli, Cruyff, Moreno (Pablo, 64).

### European Cup

League champions of the countries belonging to UEFA (Union of European Football Associations).

**MILAN: MAY 23, 2001**

**Bayern Munich (Ger)* ......1    0   0—1**
**Valencia (Spain) ..............1    0   0—1**

Goals: Mendieta 3 (pk), Effenberg 50 (pk).
*Bayern Munich won 5–4 on penalties.

Att: 48,000.

**Bayern Munich:** Kahn, Kuffour, Andersson, Linke, Sagnol, Hargreaves, Effenberg, Lizarazu, Scholl (Paulo Sergio, 108), Salihamidzic (Jancker, 45), Elber (Zickler, 102).
**Valencia:** Canizares, Angloma, Ayala (Djukic, 89), Pellegrino, Carboni, Mendieta, Baraja, Aimar (Albelda 45) Kily Gonzalez, Sanchez (Zahovic, 65), Carew Mendieta, Farinos, Angulo, Gerard, Lopez, Oscar.

### Libertadores Cup

Competition between champion clubs and runners-up of 10 South American National Associations.

**(2ND LEG) BUENOS AIRES: JUNE 28, 2001**

**Boca Juniors* (Arg) ...........0    0—0**
**Cruz Azul (Mexico) ..........0    1—1**

Goals: Palencia. *Aggregate: 1–1;
Boca Juniors won 3–1 on penalties.

Att: 59,000.

**Boca Juniors:** Cordoba, Ibarra, Bermudez, Samuel, Rodriguez, Battaglia, Traverso, Basualdo, Riquelme, Barros, Schelotto.
**Cruz Azul:** Perez, Reynoso, Gutierrez, Brown, Macias, Moreno, Campos, Morales, Pinheiro, Adomaitis, Palencia.

---

**Another Sign of the Apocalypse** Birmingham City, an English First Division soccer team, is offering personalized funeral packages complete with coffins in team colors and scattering of ashes at the stadium.

| Country | League Champion | League Scoring Leader, Club | Cup Winner |
|---|---|---|---|
| Albania | Vllaznia Shkodër | Indrit Fortuzi, SK Tirana | SK Tirana |
| Andorra | FC Santa Coloma | n/a | FC Santa Coloma |
| Armenia | Araks Ararat* | Ara Hakobian* | Mika Ashtarak* |
| Austria | Tirol Innsbruck | Gilewicz, FC Tirol Innsbruck | Kärnten |
| Azerbaijan | FK Samkir | Alay Bayramov FK Samkir | Shafa Baku |
| Belarus | Belshyna Babruisk | Vital Kutuzau, BATE Barysau | Belshyna Babruisk |
| Belgium | Anderlecht | Tomasz Radzinski, Anderlecht | Westerlo |
| Bosnia | Zeljeznicar | n/a | Zeljeznicar |
| Bulgaria | Levski Sofia | Georgi Ivanov, Levski Sofia | Litex Lovetch |
| Croatia | Hajduk Split | Tomislav Sokota, Dinamo Zagreb | Dinamo Zagreb |
| Cyprus | Omonia Nicosia | n/a | Appollon Limassol |
| Czech Republic | Sparta Prague | Vitezslav Tuma, Drnovice | Viktoria Zizkov |
| Denmark | FC Copenhagen | Peter Granlund, Brøndby | Silkeborg |
| England | Manchester United | Jimmy Floyd Hasselbaink, Chelsea | Liverpool |
| Estonia | Levadia Maardu* | Egidijus Jushka, Tallinna VMK* Toomas Kröm, Levadia Maardu* | Levadia Maardu* |
| Faroe Islands | Vágur* | n/a | Gøta* |
| Finland | Haka Valkeakoski* | Shefki Kugi, Jokerit Helsinki* | HJK Helsinki* |
| France | Nantes | Sonny Anderson, Lyon | Lyon |
| Georgia | Torpedo Kutaisi | Zaza Zirakishvili, Dinamo Tblisi | Torpedo Kutaisi |
| Germany | Bayern Munich | Sergez Barbarez, Hamburger SV Ebbe Sand, Schalke O4 | Hertha Berlin |
| Greece | Olympiakos | Alexandris, Olympiakos | PAOK Thessaloniki |
| Hungary | Ferencvaros TC | Peter Kabat, Vasas | Debreceni VSC |
| Iceland | KR Reykjavik* | Andri Sigflórsson, KR Reykjavik* | IA Akranes* |
| Ireland | Bohemians | Glen Crowe, Bohemians | Bohemians |
| Israel | Maccabi Haifa | Avi Nimni, Maccabi Tel-Aviv | Maccabi Tel-Aviv |
| Italy | Roma | Hernán Crespo, Lazio | Fiorentina |
| Latvia | Skonto Riga* | Vladimirs Kolesnicenko, Skonto Riga* | Skonto Riga* |
| Lithuania | FBK Kaunas* | n/a | Ekranas Panevezys* |
| Luxembourg | F'91 Dudelange | n/a | Etzella |
| Macedonia | Sloga Skopje | Argent Beciri, Sloga Skopje | Pelister Bitola |
| Malta | Valletta FC | n/a | Valletta FC |
| Moldova | Serif Tiraspol | Ruslan Barburos, Harduc/ Agro/Serif (three teams) David Mudziri, Tiraspol Serif | Serif Tiraspol |
| Netherlands | PSV Eindhoven | Mateja Kezman, PSV Eindhoven | FC Twente |
| Northern Ireland | Linfield | n/a | Glentoran |
| Norway | Rosenborg* | n/a | Odd Grenland* |
| Poland | Wisla Krakow | Tomasz Frankowski, Wisla Krakow | Wisla Krakow |
| Portugal | Boavista FC | Jesus Pena, FC Porto | FC Porto |
| Romania | Steaua Bucharest | Marius Niculae, Dinamo Bucharest | Dinamo Bucharest |
| Russia | Spartak Moscow* | Dmitry Loskov, Lokomotiv M* | Lokomotiv M* |
| San Marino | Cosmos | n/a | Domagnano |
| Scotland | Glasgow Celtic | Henrik Larsson, Glasgow Celtic | Glasgow Celtic |
| Slovakia | Inter Bratislava | n/a | Inter Bratislava |
| Slovenia | Maribor Branik | Damir Pekic, Celje | HIT Gorica |
| Spain | Real Madrid | Raul, Real Madrid | Real Zaragoza |
| Sweden | Halmstad* | n/a | Orgryte IS* |
| Switzerland | Grasshopper | Stephane Chapuisat, Grasshopper Christian Gimenez, Lugano | Servette |
| Turkey | Fenerbahce | Okan Yilmaz, Bursaspor | Genglerbirligi |
| Ukraine | Dinamo Kiev | Andriy Vorobei, Shakhtar Donetsk | Shakhtar Donetsk |
| Wales | Barry Town | Graham Evans, Caersws | Caersws |
| Yugoslavia | Red Star Belgrade | Petar Divic, OFK Belgrade | Partizan Belgrade |

Note: Results are from 2001 unless followed by *.

# FOR THE RECORD·Year by Year

## The World Cup

### Results

| Year | Champion | Score | Runner-Up | Winning Coach |
|---|---|---|---|---|
| 1930 | Uruguay | 4–2 | Argentina | Alberto Supicci |
| 1934 | Italy | 2–1 | Czechoslovakia | Vittorio Pozzo |
| 1938 | Italy | 4–2 | Hungary | Vittorio Pozzo |
| 1950 | Uruguay | 2–1 | Brazil | Juan Lopez |
| 1954 | W Germany | 3–2 | Hungary | Sepp Herberger |
| 1958 | Brazil | 5–2 | Sweden | Vicente Feola |
| 1962 | Brazil | 3–1 | Czechoslovakia | Aymore Moreira |
| 1966 | England | 4–2 | W Germany | Alf Ramsey |
| 1970 | Brazil | 4–1 | Italy | Mario Zagalo |
| 1974 | W Germany | 2–1 | Netherlands | Helmut Schoen |
| 1978 | Argentina | 3–1 | Netherlands | César Menotti |
| 1982 | Italy | 3–1 | W Germany | Enzo Bearzot |
| 1986 | Argentina | 3–2 | W Germany | Carlos Bilardo |
| 1990 | W Germany | 1–0 | Argentina | Franz Beckenbauer |
| 1994 | Brazil | 0–0 (3–2) | Italy | Carlos Alberto Parreira |
| 1998 | France | 3–0 | Brazil | Aime Jacquet |

### Alltime World Cup Participation

Of the 62 nations that have taken part in the World Cup Finals, only Brazil has competed in each of the 16 tournaments held to date. West Germany or an undivided Germany (1934, '38, '94 and '98) has played in 15 World Cups.

| Nation | Matches | W | T | L | Goals For | Goals Against |
|---|---|---|---|---|---|---|
| Brazil | 80 | 53 | 14 | 13 | 173 | 78 |
| *Germany | 78 | 45 | 17 | 16 | 162 | 103 |
| Italy | 66 | 38 | 16 | 12 | 105 | 62 |
| Argentina | 57 | 29 | 10 | 18 | 100 | 68 |
| France | 41 | 21 | 6 | 14 | 86 | 58 |
| England | 45 | 20 | 13 | 12 | 62 | 42 |
| Yugoslavia | 37 | 17 | 6 | 14 | 60 | 46 |
| †Russia | 34 | 16 | 6 | 12 | 60 | 40 |
| Spain | 40 | 16 | 10 | 14 | 61 | 48 |
| Uruguay | 37 | 15 | 8 | 14 | 61 | 52 |
| Hungary | 32 | 15 | 3 | 14 | 87 | 57 |
| Netherlands | 31 | 14 | 9 | 8 | 55 | 34 |
| Poland | 25 | 13 | 5 | 7 | 39 | 29 |
| Sweden | 37 | 13 | 7 | 17 | 62 | 60 |
| Austria | 29 | 12 | 4 | 13 | 42 | 48 |
| Czechoslovakia | 30 | 11 | 5 | 14 | 44 | 45 |
| Belgium | 32 | 9 | 7 | 16 | 40 | 56 |
| Romania | 21 | 8 | 5 | 8 | 30 | 32 |
| Mexico | 37 | 8 | 10 | 19 | 39 | 75 |
| Chile | 25 | 7 | 6 | 12 | 31 | 40 |
| Portugal | 9 | 6 | 0 | 3 | 19 | 12 |
| Switzerland | 22 | 6 | 3 | 13 | 33 | 51 |
| Denmark | 9 | 5 | 1 | 3 | 19 | 13 |
| Croatia | 6 | 4 | 0 | 2 | 9 | 4 |
| Nigeria | 8 | 4 | 0 | 4 | 13 | 13 |
| Peru | 15 | 4 | 3 | 8 | 19 | 31 |
| Paraguay | 15 | 4 | 6 | 5 | 19 | 27 |
| United States | 17 | 4 | 1 | 12 | 18 | 38 |
| Scotland | 23 | 4 | 7 | 12 | 25 | 41 |
| Northern Ireland | 13 | 3 | 5 | 5 | 13 | 23 |
| Colombia | 13 | 3 | 2 | 8 | 14 | 23 |
| Cameroon | 14 | 3 | 6 | 5 | 14 | 25 |
| Bulgaria | 25 | 3 | 8 | 14 | 22 | 49 |
| Costa Rica | 4 | 2 | 0 | 2 | 4 | 6 |
| Algeria | 6 | 2 | 1 | 3 | 6 | 10 |
| E Germany | 6 | 2 | 2 | 2 | 5 | 5 |
| Saudi Arabia | 7 | 2 | 1 | 4 | 7 | 13 |
| Norway | 8 | 2 | 3 | 3 | 7 | 8 |
| Morocco | 10 | 2 | 4 | 4 | 10 | 13 |
| Wales | 5 | 1 | 3 | 1 | 4 | 4 |
| Republic of Ireland | 9 | 1 | 5 | 3 | 4 | 7 |
| Tunisia | 6 | 1 | 2 | 3 | 4 | 6 |
| N Korea | 4 | 1 | 1 | 2 | 5 | 9 |
| Cuba | 3 | 1 | 1 | 1 | 5 | 12 |
| Turkey | 3 | 1 | 0 | 2 | 10 | 11 |
| Israel | 3 | 1 | 0 | 2 | 1 | 3 |
| Jamaica | 3 | 1 | 0 | 2 | 3 | 9 |
| Iran | 6 | 1 | 1 | 4 | 4 | 12 |
| Honduras | 3 | 0 | 2 | 1 | 2 | 3 |
| Egypt | 4 | 0 | 2 | 2 | 3 | 6 |
| Kuwait | 3 | 0 | 1 | 2 | 2 | 6 |
| Australia | 3 | 0 | 1 | 2 | 0 | 5 |
| S Korea | 14 | 0 | 4 | 10 | 11 | 43 |
| Dutch East Indies | 1 | 0 | 0 | 1 | 0 | 6 |
| Iraq | 3 | 0 | 0 | 3 | 1 | 4 |
| Canada | 3 | 0 | 0 | 3 | 0 | 5 |
| United Arab Emirates | 3 | 0 | 0 | 3 | 2 | 11 |
| New Zealand | 3 | 0 | 0 | 3 | 2 | 12 |
| Haiti | 3 | 0 | 0 | 3 | 2 | 14 |
| Zaire | 3 | 0 | 0 | 3 | 0 | 14 |
| Bolivia | 6 | 0 | 1 | 5 | 1 | 20 |
| El Salvador | 6 | 0 | 0 | 6 | 1 | 22 |
| Japan | 3 | 0 | 0 | 3 | 1 | 4 |
| Greece | 3 | 0 | 0 | 3 | 0 | 8 |

*Includes West Germany 1950–90. †Includes USSR 1930–1990.
Note: Matches decided by penalty kicks are shown as drawn games.

## World Cup Final Box Scores

### URUGUAY 1930

| | | |
|---|---|---|
| Uruguay...........1 | 3 | —4 |
| Argentina.........2 | 0 | —2 |

#### FIRST HALF

Scoring: 1, Uruguay, Dorado (12); 2, Argentina, Peucelle (20); 3, Argentina, Stabile (37).

#### SECOND HALF

Scoring: 4, Uruguay, Cea (57); 5, Uruguay, Iriarte (68); 6, Uruguay, Castro (89).

**Argentina:** Botosso, Della Toree, Paternoster, J. Evaristo, Monti, Suarez, Peucelle, Varallo, Stabile, Ferreira, M. Evaristo.

**Uruguay:** Ballesteros, Nasazzi, Mascheroni, Andrade, Fernandez, Gestido, Dorado, Scarone, Castro, Cea, Iriarte.

Referee: Langenus (Belgium).

### FRANCE 1938

| | | |
|---|---|---|
| Italy..................3 | 1 | —4 |
| Hungary...........1 | 1 | —2 |

#### FIRST HALF

Scoring: 1, Italy, Colaussi (5); 2, Hungary, Titkos (7); 3, Italy, Piola (16); 4, Italy, Piola (35).

#### SECOND HALF

Scoring: 5, Hungary, Sarosi (70); 6, Italy, Colaussi (82).

**Italy:** Olivieri, Foni, Rava, Serantoni, Andreolo, Locatelli, Biavati, Meazza, Piola, Ferrari, Colaussi.

**Hungary:** Szabo, Polger, Biro, Szalay, Szucs, Lazar, Sas, Vincze, Sarosi, Zsengeller, Titkos.

Referee: Capdeville (France).

### SWITZERLAND 1954

| | | |
|---|---|---|
| W Germany......2 | 1 | —3 |
| Hungary...........2 | 0 | —2 |

#### FIRST HALF

Scoring. 1, Hungary, Puskas (6); 2, Hungary, Czibor (8); 3, W Germ., Morlock (10); 4, W Germ., Rahn (18).

#### SECOND HALF

Scoring: 5, W Germany, Rahn (84).

**W Germany:** Turek, Posipal, Kohlmeyer, Eckel, Liebrich, Mai, Rahn, Morlock, O.Walter, F. Walter, Schaefer.

**Hungary:** Grosics, Buzansky, Lantos, Bozsik, Lorant, Zakarias, Czibor, Kocsis, Hidegkuti, Puskas, Toth.

Referee: Ling (England).

### ITALY 1934

| | | | |
|---|---|---|---|
| Italy...................0 | 1 | 1 | —2 |
| Czechoslovakia....0 | 1 | 0 | —1 |

#### SECOND HALF

Scoring: 1, Czech., Puc (70); 2, Italy, Orsi (80).

#### OVERTIME

Scoring: 3, Italy, Schiavio (95).

**Italy:** Combi, Monzeglio, Allemandi, Ferraris Monti, Monti, Bertolini, Guaita, Meazza, Schiavio, Ferrari, Orsi.

**Czechoslovakia:** Planicka, Zenisek, Ctyroky, Kostalek, Cambal, Cambal, Krcil, Junek, Svoboda, Sobotka, Nejedly, Puc.

Referee: Eklind (Sweden).

### BRAZIL 1950

| | | |
|---|---|---|
| Uruguay...........0 | 2 | —2 |
| Brazil.................0 | 1 | —1 |

#### SECOND HALF

Scoring: 1, Brazil, Friaca (47); 2, Uruguay, Schiaffino (66); 3, Uruguay, Ghiggia (79).

**Uruguay:** Maspoli, Gonzales, Tejera, Gambretta, Varela, Andrade, Ghiggia, Perez, Miguez, Schiffiano, Moran.

**Brazil:** Barbosa, Augusto, Juvenal, Bauer, Banilo, Bigode, Friaca, Zizinho, Ademir, Jair, Chico.

Referee: Reader (England).

### SWEDEN 1958

| | | |
|---|---|---|
| Brazil.................2 | 3 | —5 |
| Sweden............1 | 1 | —2 |

#### FIRST HALF

Scoring 1, Sweden, Liedholm (3); 2, Brazil, Vava (9); 3, Brazil, Vava (32).

#### SECOND HALF

Scoring: 4, Brazil, Pelé (55); 5, Brazil, Zagalo (68); 6, Sweden Simonsson (80); 7, Brazil, Pelé (90).

**Brazil:** Glymar, D. Santos, N. Santos, Zito, Bellini, Orlando, Garrincha, Didi, Vava, Pelé, Zagalo.

**Sweden:** Svensson, Bergmark, Axbom, Boerjesson, Gustavsson, Parling, Hamrin, Gren, Simonsson, Liedholm, Skoglund.

Referee: Guigue (France).

### CHILE 1962

| | | |
|---|---|---|
| Brazil.........................1 | 2 | —3 |
| Czechoslovakia ..........1 | 0 | —1 |

#### FIRST HALF

Scoring: 1, Czech., Masopust (15); 2, Brazil, Amarildo (17).

#### SECOND HALF

Scoring: 3, Brazil, Zito (68); 4, Brazil, Vava (77).

**Brazil:** Glymar, D. Santos, N. Santos, Zito, Mauro, Zozimo, Garrincha, Didi, Vava, Amarildo, Zagalo.

**Czechoslovakia:** Schroiff, Tichy, Novak, Pluskal, Popluhar, Masopust, Pospichal, Scherer, Kvasnak, Kadraba, Jelinek.

Referee: Latychev (USSR).

## World Cup Final Box Scores *(Cont.)*

### ENGLAND 1966

| | | | |
|---|---|---|---|
| England............1 | 1 | 2 | —4 |
| W Germany ......1 | 1 | 0 | —2 |

#### FIRST HALF

Scoring: 1, W Germany, Haller (12); 2, England, Hurst (18).

#### SECOND HALF

Scoring: 3, England, Peters (78); 4, W. Germany, Weber (90).

#### OVERTIME

Scoring: 5, England, Hurst (101); 6, England, Hurst (120).

**England:** Banks, Cohen, Wilson, Stiles, J. Charlton, Moore, Ball, Hurst, Hunt, R. Charlton, Peters.

**W Germany:** Tilkowski, Hottges, Schmellinger, Beckenbauer, Schulz, Weber, Held, Haller, Seeler, Overath, Emmerich.

Referee: Dienst (Switzerland).

### W GERMANY 1974

| | | | |
|---|---|---|---|
| W Germany ......2 | 0 | —2 |
| Netherlands.....1 | 0 | —1 |

#### FIRST HALF

Scoring: 1, Netherlands, Neeskens, PK (1); 2, W Germany, Breitner, PK (26); 3, W Germany, Müller (44).

**W Germany:** Maier, Vogts, Beckenbauer, Schwarzenbeck, Breitner, Hoeness, Bonhof, Overath, Grabowski, Müller, Holzenbein.

**Netherlands:** Jongbloed, Suurbier, Rijsbergen (de Jong), Haan, Krol, Jansen, Neeskens, van Hanagem, Cruyff, Rensenbrink (van der Kerkhof).

Referee: Taylor (England).

### ITALY 1982

| | | | |
|---|---|---|---|
| Italy..................0 | 3 | —3 |
| W Germany ......0 | 1 | —1 |

#### SECOND HALF

Scoring: 1, Italy, Rossi (57); 2, Italy, Tardelli (68); 3, Italy, Altobelli (81); 4, W Germany, Breitner (83).

**Italy:** Zoff, Bergomi, Scirea, Collovati, Cabrini, Oriali, Gentile, Tardelli, Conti, Rossi, Graziani (Altobelli, Causio).

**W Germany:** Schumacher, Kaltz, Stielike, K. Foerster, B. Foerster, Dremmler (Hrubesch), Breitner, Briegel, Rummenigge (Müller), Fishcher (Littbarski).

Referee: Coelho (Brazil).

### MEXICO 1986

| | | | |
|---|---|---|---|
| Argentina.........1 | 2 | —3 |
| W Germany ......0 | 2 | —2 |

#### FIRST HALF

Scoring: 1, Argentina, Brown (22).

#### SECOND HALF

Scoring: 2, Arg., Valdano (55); 3, W Germ., Rummenigge (73); 4, W Germ., Voller (81); 5, Arg., Burruchaga (83).

### MEXICO 1970

| | | | |
|---|---|---|---|
| Brazil.................1 | 3 | —4 |
| Italy...................1 | 0 | —1 |

#### FIRST HALF

Scoring: 1, Brazil, Pelé (18); 2, Italy, Boninsegna (32).

#### SECOND HALF

Scoring: 3, Brazil, Gerson (65); 4, Brazil, Jairzinho (70); 5, Brazil, Alberto (86).

**Brazil:** Feliz, Alberto, Brito, Wilson, Piazza, Everaldo, Clodoaldo, Gerson, Jairzinho, Tostao, Pelé, Rivelino.

**Italy:** Albertosi, Burgnich, Cera, Rosato, Facchetti, Bertini (Juliano), Mazzola, De Sisti, Domenghini, Boninsegna (Rivera), Riva.

Referee: Glockner (E Germany).

### ARGENTINA 1978

| | | | |
|---|---|---|---|
| Argentina.........1 | 0 | 2 | —3 |
| Netherlands .....0 | 1 | 0 | —1 |

#### FIRST HALF

Scoring: 1, Argentina, Kempes (38).

#### SECOND HALF

Scoring: 2, Netherlands, Nanninga (81).

#### OVERTIME

Scoring: 3, Arg., Kempes (104); 4, Arg., Bertoni (114).

**Argentina:** Fillol, Olguin, Galvan, Passarella, Tarantini, Ardiles (Larrosa), Gallego, Kempes, Bertoni, Luque, Ortiz (Houseman).

**Netherlands:** Jongbloed, Jansen (Suurbier), Krol, Brandts, Poortvliet, Neeskens, Haan, W. van der Kerkhoff, R. van der Kerkhoff, Rep (Nanninga), Rensenbrink.

Referee: Gonella (Italy).

### MEXICO 1986 *(Cont.)*

**Argentina:** Pumpido, Brown, Cuciuffo, Ruggeri, Olarticoechea, Bastista, Giusti, Burruchaga (Trobbiani 90), Enrique, Maradona, Valdona.

**W Germany:** Schumacher, Jakobs, Forster, Eder, Brehme, Matthaus, Berthold, Magath (Hoeness 62), Briegel, Rummenigge, Allofs (Voller 46).

Referee: Filho (Brazil).

### ITALY 1990

| | | | |
|---|---|---|---|
| W Germany .........0 | 1 | —1 |
| Argentina..............0 | 0 | —0 |

#### SECOND HALF

Scoring: 1, W Germany, Brehme, PK (84).

**W Germany:** Illgner, Brehme, Kohler, Augenthaler, Buchwald, Berthold (Reuter), Littbarski, Haessler, Mattaeus, Voeller, Klinsmann.

**Argentina:** Goychoechea, Lorenzo, Serrizuela, Sensini, Ruggeri (Monzon), Simon, Basualdo, Burruchag (Calderon), Maradona, Troglio, Dezottir.

Referee: Coelho (Brazil).

## World Cup Final Box Scores *(Cont.)*

| UNITED STATES 1994 | | | | FRANCE 1998 | |
|---|---|---|---|---|---|
| Italy..................0 | 0 | 0—0 | | Brazil ..................0 | 0—0 |
| Brazil ...............0 | 0 | 0—0 | | France .................2 | 1—3 |

Scoring: None. Shootout goals: Italy—2: Albertini, Evani; Brazil—3: Romario, Branco, Dunga.

**Italy:** Pagliuca, Benarrivo, Maldini, Baresi, Mussi (Apolloni 35), Albertini, D. Baggio (Evani 95), Berti, Donadoni, Baggio, Massaro.

**Brazil:** Taffarel, Jorginho (Cafu 21), Branco, Aldair, Santos, Silva, Dunga, Zinho (Viola 106), Mazinho, Bebeto, Romario.

Referee: Puhl (Hungary).

**FIRST HALF**
Scoring: 1, France, Zidane (27); 2, France, Zidane (45).
**SECOND HALF**
Scoring: 3, France, Petit (90).

**Brazil:** Taffarel, Cafu, Aldair, Baiano, Carlos, Sampaio (Edmundo 74), Dunga, Rivaldo, Leonardo, (Denilson 46), Bebeto, Ronaldo.

**France:** Barthez, Lizarazu, Desailly, Thuram, Leboeuf, Djorkaeff (Vieira 75) Deschamps, Zidane, Petit, Karembeu (Boghossian 57), Guivarc'h (Dugarry 66).

Referee: Belqola (Morocco).

## Alltime Leaders
### GOALS

| Player, Nation | Tournaments | Goals | Player, Nation | Tournaments | Goals |
|---|---|---|---|---|---|
| Gerd Müller, W Germany | 1970, '74 | 14 | Ademir, Brazil | 1950 | 9 |
| Just Fontaine, France | 1958 | 13 | Eusebio, Portugal | 1966 | 9 |
| Pelé, Brazil | 1958, '62, '66, '70 | 12 | Jairzinho, Brazil | 1970, '74 | 9 |
| Sandor Kocsis, Hungary | 1954 | 11 | Paolo Rossi, Italy | 1982, '86 | 9 |
| Teofilo Cubillas, Peru | 1970, '78 | 10 | Karl-Heinz Rummenigge, | | |
| Gregorz Lato, Poland | 1974, '78, '82 | 10 | W Germany | 1978, '82, '86 | 9 |
| Helmut Rahn, W Germany | 1954, '58 | 10 | Uwe Seeler, W Germany | 1958, '62, '66, '70 | 9 |
| Gary Lineker, England | 1986, '90 | 10 | Vava, Brazil | 1958, '62 | 9 |

### LEADING SCORER, CUP BY CUP

| Year | Player, Nation | Goals | Year | Player, Nation | Goals |
|---|---|---|---|---|---|
| 1930 | Guillermo Stabile, Argentina | 8 | 1966 | Eusebio Ferreira, Portugal | 9 |
| 1934 | Oldrich Nejedly, Czechoslovakia | 5 | 1970 | Gerd Müller, W Germany | 10 |
| 1938 | Leonidas da Silva, Brazil | 8 | 1974 | Gregorz Lato, Poland | 7 |
| 1950 | Ademir de Menezes, Brazil | 9 | 1978 | Mario Kempes, Argentina | 6 |
| 1954 | Sandor Kocsis, Hungary | 11 | 1982 | Paolo Rossi, Italy | 6 |
| 1958 | Just Fontaine, France | 13 | 1986 | Gary Lineker, England | 6 |
| 1962 | Florian Albert, Hungary | 4 | 1990 | Salvatore Schillaci, Italy | 6 |
| | Valentin Ivanov, USSR | | 1994 | Hristo Stoichkov, Bulgaria | 6 |
| | Garrincha, Brazil | | | Oleg Salenko, Russia | |
| | Drazan Jerkovic, Yugoslavia | | 1998 | Davor Suker, Croatia | 6 |
| | Leonel Sanchez, Chile | | | | |
| | Vava, Brazil | | | | |

## Most Goals, Individual, One Game

| Goals | Player, Nation | Score | Date |
|---|---|---|---|
| 5 | Oleg Salenko, Russia | Russia–Cameroon, 6–1 | 6-28-94 |
| 4 | Leonidas, Brazil | Brazil–Poland, 6–5 | 6-5-38 |
| 4 | Ernest Willimowski, Poland | Brazil–Poland, 6–5 | 6-5-38 |
| 4 | Gustav Wetterstrîm, Sweden | Sweden–Cuba, 8–0 | 6-12-38 |
| 4 | Juan Alberto Schiaffino, Uruguay | Uruguay–Bolivia, 8–0 | 7-2-50 |
| 4 | Ademir, Brazil | Brazil–Sweden, 7–1 | 7-9-50 |
| 4 | Sandor Kocsis, Hungary | Hungary–W Germany, 8–3 | 6-20-54 |
| 4 | Just Fontaine, France | France–W Germany, 6–3 | 6-28-58 |
| 4 | Eusebio, Portugal | Portugal–N Korea, 5–3 | 7-23-66 |
| 4 | Emilio Butragueño, Spain | Spain–Denmark, 5–1 | 6-18-86 |

Note: 30 players have scored 31 World Cup hat tricks. Gerd Müller of West Germany is the only man to have two World Cup hat tricks, both in 1970. The last hat tricks were 6-21-98, Gabriel Batistuta (Arg) vs. Jamaica; 6-23-90, Tomas Skuhravy (Czech) vs. Costa Rica; and 6-17-90, Michel (Spain) vs. South Korea.

### Attendance and Goal Scoring, Year by Year

| Year | Site | No. of Games | Goals | Goals/Game | Attendance | Avg Att |
|---|---|---|---|---|---|---|
| 1930 | Uruguay | 18 | 70 | 3.89 | 434,500 | 24,139 |
| 1934 | Italy | 17 | 70 | 4.12 | 395,000 | 23,235 |
| 1938 | France | 18 | 84 | 4.67 | 483,000 | 26,833 |
| 1950 | Brazil | 22 | 88 | 4.00 | 1,337,000 | 60,773 |
| 1954 | Switzerland | 26 | 140 | 5.38 | 943,000 | 36,269 |
| 1958 | Sweden | 35 | 126 | 3.60 | 868,000 | 24,800 |
| 1962 | Chile | 32 | 89 | 2.78 | 776,000 | 24,250 |
| 1966 | England | 32 | 89 | 2.78 | 1,614,677 | 50,459 |
| 1970 | Mexico | 32 | 95 | 2.97 | 1,673,975 | 52,312 |
| 1974 | W Germany | 38 | 97 | 2.55 | 1,774,022 | 46,685 |
| 1978 | Argentina | 38 | 102 | 2.68 | 1,610,215 | 42,374 |
| 1982 | Spain | 52 | 146 | 2.80 | 1,856,277 | 35,698 |
| 1986 | Mexico | 52 | 132 | 2.54 | 2,441,731 | 46,956 |
| 1990 | Italy | 52 | 115 | 2.21 | 2,514,443 | 48,354 |
| 1994 | United States | 52 | 140 | 2.69 | 3,567,415 | 68,604 |
| 1998 | France | 64 | 171 | 2.67 | 2,775,400 | 43,366 |
| Totals | | 580 | 1,754 | 3.02 | 25,064,655 | 43,215 |

### The United States in the World Cup

**URUGUAY 1930: FINAL COMPETITION**

| Date | Opponent | Result | Scoring |
|---|---|---|---|
| 7-13-30 | Belgium | 3–0 W | U.S.: McGhee 2, Patenaude |
| 7-17-30 | Paraguay | 3–0 W | U.S.: Patenaude 2, Florie |
| 7-26-30 | Argentina | 1–6 L | Arg.: Monti 2, Scopelli 2, Stabile 2 U.S.: Brown. |

**ITALY 1934: FINAL COMPETITION**

| Date | Opponent | Result | Scoring |
|---|---|---|---|
| 5-27-34 | Italy | 1–7 L | U.S.: Donelli Italy: Schiavio 3, Orsi 2, Meazza, Ferrari |

**BRAZIL 1950: FINAL COMPETITION**

| Date | Opponent | Result | Scoring |
|---|---|---|---|
| 6-25-50 | Spain | 1–3 L | U.S.: Pariani Spain: Igoa, Basora, Zarra |
| 6-29-50 | England | 1–0 W | U.S.: Gaetjens. |
| 7-2-50 | Chile | 2–5 L | U.S.: Wallace, Maca Chile: Robledo, Cremaschi 3, Prieto |

**ITALY 1990: FINAL COMPETITION**

| Date | Opponent | Result | Scoring |
|---|---|---|---|
| 6-10-90 | Czechoslovakia | 1–5 L | U.S.: Caligiuri Czech.: Skuhravy 2, Hasek, Bilek, Luhovy |
| 6-14-90 | Italy | 0–1 L | Italy: Gianinni |
| 6-19-90 | Austria | 1–2 L | U.S.: Murray Austria: Rodax, Ogris |

**UNITED STATES 1994: FINAL COMPETITION**

| Date | Opponent | Result | Scoring |
|---|---|---|---|
| 6-18-94 | Switzerland | 1–1 T | U.S.: Wynalda Switz.: Bregy |
| 6-22-94 | Colombia | 2–1 W | U.S.: Escobar (own goal), Stewart Colombia: Valencia |
| 6-26-94 | Romania | 1–0 L | Romania: Petrescu |
| 7-4-94 | Brazil | 1–0 L | Brazil: Bebeto |

**FRANCE 1998: FINAL COMPETITION**

| Date | Opponent | Result | Scoring |
|---|---|---|---|
| 6-15-98 | Germany | 2–0 L | Germany: Möller, Klinsmann |
| 6-21-98 | Iran | 2–1 L | U.S.: McBride Iran: Estili, Mahdavikia |
| 6-25-98 | Yugoslavia | 1–0 L | Yugoslavia: Komljenovic |

## International Competition

### European Championship

Official name: the European Football Championship. Held every four years since 1960.

| Year | Champion | Score | Runner-up | Year | Champion | Score | Runner-up |
|---|---|---|---|---|---|---|---|
| 1960 | USSR | 2–1 | Yugoslavia | 1980 | W Germany | 2–1 | Belgium |
| 1964 | Spain | 2–1 | USSR | 1984 | France | 2–0 | Spain |
| 1968 | Italy | 2–0 | Yugoslavia | 1988 | Holland | 2–0 | USSR |
| 1972 | W Germany | 3–0 | USSR | 1992 | Denmark | 2–0 | Germany |
| 1976 | Czechoslovakia* | 2–2 | W Germany | 1996 | Germany† | 2–1 | Czech Republic |
| | | | | 2000 | France† | 2–1 | Italy |

*Won on penalty kicks. †Won in sudden-death overtime.

## Under-20 World Championship

| Year | Host | Champion | Runner-Up |
|------|------|----------|-----------|
| 1977 | Tunisia | USSR | Mexico |
| 1979 | Japan | Argentina | USSR |
| 1981 | Australia | W Germany | Qatar |
| 1983 | Mexico | Brazil | Argentina |
| 1985 | USSR | Brazil | Spain |
| 1987 | Chile | Yugoslavia | W Germany |
| 1989 | Saudi Arabia | Portugal | Nigeria |
| 1991 | Portugal | Portugal | Brazil |
| 1993 | Australia | Brazil | Ghana |
| 1995 | Qatar | Argentina | Brazil |
| 1997 | Malaysia | Argentina | Uruguay |
| 1999 | Nigeria | Spain | Japan |
| 2001 | Argentina | Argentina | Ghana |

## Under-17 World Championship

| Year | Champion |
|------|----------|
| 1985 | Nigeria |
| 1987 | USSR |
| 1989 | Saudi Arabia |
| 1991 | Ghana |

## Under-17 *(Cont.)*

| Year | Champion |
|------|----------|
| 1993 | Nigeria |
| 1995 | Ghana |
| 1997 | Brazil |
| 1999 | Brazil |
| 2001 | France |

## Pan American Games

| Year | Champion |
|------|----------|
| 1951 | Argentina |
| 1955 | Argentina |
| 1959 | Argentina |
| 1963 | Brazil |
| 1967 | Mexico |
| 1971 | Argentina |
| 1975 | Brazil/Mexico (tie) |
| 1979 | Brazil |
| 1983 | Uruguay |
| 1987 | Brazil |
| 1991 | United States |
| 1995 | Argentina |
| 1999 | Mexico |

## South American Championship (Copa America)

| Year | Champion | Host | Year | Champion | Host |
|------|----------|------|------|----------|------|
| 1916 | Uruguay | Argentina | 1953 | Paraguay | Peru |
| 1917 | Uruguay | Uruguay | 1955 | Argentina | Chile |
| 1919 | Brazil | Brazil | 1956 | Uruguay | Uruguay |
| 1920 | Uruguay | Chile | 1957 | Argentina | Peru |
| 1921 | Argentina | Argentina | 1958 | Argentina | Argentina |
| 1922 | Brazil | Brazil | 1959 | Uruguay | Ecuador |
| 1923 | Uruguay | Uruguay | 1963 | Bolivia | Bolivia |
| 1924 | Uruguay | Uruguay | 1967 | Uruguay | Uruguay |
| 1925 | Argentina | Argentina | 1975 | Peru | Various sites |
| 1926 | Uruguay | Chile | 1979 | Paraguay | Various sites |
| 1927 | Argentina | Peru | 1983 | Uruguay | Various sites |
| 1929 | Argentina | Argentina | 1987 | Uruguay | Argentina |
| 1935 | Uruguay | Peru | 1989 | Brazil | Brazil |
| 1937 | Argentina | Argentina | 1990 | Brazil | Argentina |
| 1939 | Peru | Peru | 1991 | Argentina | Chile |
| 1941 | Argentina | Chile | 1993 | Argentina | Ecuador |
| 1942 | Uruguay | Uruguay | 1995 | Uruguay | Uruguay |
| 1945 | Argentina | Chile | 1997 | Brazil | Bolivia |
| 1946 | Argentina | Argentina | 1999 | Brazil | Paraguay |
| 1917 | Argentina | Ecuador | 2001 | Colombia | Colombia |
| 1949 | Brazil | Brazil | | | |

# Awards

## European Footballer of the Year

| Year | Player | Club | Year | Player | Club |
|------|--------|------|------|--------|------|
| 1956 | Stanley Matthews | Blackpool | 1975 | Oleg Blokhin | Dynamo Kiev |
| 1957 | Alfredo Di Stefano | Real Madrid | 1976 | Franz Beckenbauer | Bayern Munich |
| 1958 | Raymond Kopa | Real Madrid | 1977 | Allan Simonsen | Borussia M'gladbach |
| 1959 | Alfredo Di Stefano | Real Madrid | 1978 | Kevin Keegan | SV Hamburg |
| 1960 | Luis Suarez | Barcelona | 1979 | Kevin Keegan | SV Hamburg |
| 1961 | Omar Sivori | Juventus | 1980 | Karl-Heinz Rummenigge | Bayern Munich |
| 1962 | Josef Masopust | Dukla Prague | 1981 | Karl-Heinz Rummenigge | Bayern Munich |
| 1963 | Lev Yashin | Moscow Dynamo | 1982 | Paolo Rossi | Juventus |
| 1964 | Denis Law | Manchester United | 1983 | Michel Platini | Juventus |
| 1965 | Eusebio | Benfica | 1984 | Michel Platini | Juventus |
| 1966 | Bobby Charlton | Manchester United | 1985 | Michel Platini | Juventus |
| 1967 | Florian Albert | Ferencvaros | 1986 | Igor Belanov | Dynamo Kiev |
| 1968 | George Best | Manchester United | 1987 | Ruud Gullit | AC Milan |
| 1969 | Gianni Rivera | AC Milan | 1988 | Marco Van Basten | AC Milan |
| 1970 | Gerd Mueller | Bayern Munich | 1989 | Marco Van Basten | AC Milan |
| 1971 | Johan Cruyff | Ajax | 1990 | Lothar Matthaeus | Inter Milan |
| 1972 | Franz Beckenbauer | Bayern Munich | 1991 | Jean-Pierre Papin | Olympique Marseille |
| 1973 | Johan Cruyff | Barcelona | 1992 | Marco Van Basten | AC Milan |
| 1974 | Johan Cruyff | Barcelona | | | |

### European Footballer of the Year *(Cont.)*

| Year | Player | Club | Year | Player | Club |
|------|--------|------|------|--------|------|
| 1993 | Roberto Baggio | Juventus | 1997 | Ronaldo | Inter Milan |
| 1994 | Hristo Stoichkov | Barcelona | 1998 | Zinedine Zidane | Juventus |
| 1995 | George Weah | AC Milan | 1999 | Rivaldo | Barcelona |
| 1996 | Matthias Sammer | Borussia Dortmund | 2000 | Luis Figo | Real Madrid |

### African Footballer of the Year

| Year | Player | Club | Year | Player | Club |
|------|--------|------|------|--------|------|
| 1970 | Salif Keita | St. Etienne | 1986 | Badou Ezaki | Real Mallorca |
| 1971 | Ibrahim Sunday | Asante Kotoko | 1987 | Rabah Madjer | FC Porto |
| 1972 | Chérif Soueymane | Hafia | 1988 | Kalusha Bwalya | Cercle Bruges |
| 1973 | Tshimen Bwanga | TP Mazembe | 1989 | George Weah | Monaco |
| 1974 | Paul Moukila | CARA Brazzaville | 1990 | Roger Milla | St. Denis |
| 1975 | Ahmed Faras | Mohammedia | 1991 | Abedi Pele Ayew | Marseille |
| 1976 | Roger Milla | Canon Yaounde | 1992 | Abedi Pele Ayew | Marseille |
| 1977 | Tarak Dhiab | Esperance | 1993 | Rashidi Yekini | FC Zurich |
| 1978 | Karim Abdul Razak | Asante Kotoko | 1994 | George Weah | Paris St. Germain |
| 1979 | Thomas Nkono | Canon Yaounde | 1995 | George Weah | AC Milan |
| 1980 | Jean Manga Onguene | Canon Yaounde | 1996 | Nwankwo Kanu | Inter Milan |
| 1981 | Lakhdar Belloumi | GCR Mascara | 1997 | Victor Ikpeba | Monaco |
| 1982 | Thomas Nkono | Espanol | 1998 | Mustapha Hadji | Deportivo Coruna |
| 1983 | Mahmoud Al-Khatib | Al Ahli | 1999 | Nwankwo Kanu | Arsenal |
| 1984 | Theophile Abega | Toulouse | 2000 | Patrick Mboma | Parma |
| 1985 | Mohamed Timoumi | Royal Armed Forces | | | |

### South American Player of the Year

| Year | Player | Club | Year | Player | Club |
|------|--------|------|------|--------|------|
| 1971 | Tostao | Cruzeiro | 1986 | Antonio Alzamendi | River Plate |
| 1972 | Teofilo Cubillas | Alianza Lima | 1987 | Carlos Valderrama | Deportivo Cali |
| 1973 | Pelé | Santos | 1988 | Ruben Paz | Racing Buenos Aires |
| 1974 | Elias Figueroa | Internacional | 1989 | Bebeto | Vasco da Gama |
| 1975 | Elias Figueroa | Internacional | 1990 | Raul Amarilla | Olimpia |
| 1976 | Elias Figueroa | Internacional | 1991 | Oscar Ruggeri | Velez Sarsfield |
| 1977 | Zico | Flamengo | 1992 | Rai | São Paulo |
| 1978 | Mario Kempes | Valencia | 1993 | Carlos Valderrama | Junior Barranquilla |
| 1979 | Diego Maradona | Argentinos Juniors | 1994 | Cafu | São Paulo |
| 1980 | Diego Maradona | Boca Juniors | 1995 | Enzo Francescoli | River Plate |
| 1981 | Zico | Flamengo | 1996 | Jose-Luis Chilavert | Velez Sarsfield |
| 1982 | Zico | Flamengo | 1997 | Marcelo Salas | River Plate |
| 1983 | Socrates | Corinthians | 1998 | Martin Palermo | Boca Juniors |
| 1984 | Enzo Francescoli | River Plate | 1999 | Javier Saviola | River Plate |
| 1985 | Julio Cesar Romero | Fluminense | 2000 | Romario | Vasco da Gama |

## International Club Competition

### Intercontinental Cup

Competition between winners of European Cup and Libertadores Cup.

| | | |
|---|---|---|
| 1960...Real Madrid, Spain | 1974...Atletico de Madrid, Spain | 1988...Nacional, Uruguay |
| 1961...Penarol, Uruguay | 1975...No tournament | 1989...Milan, Italy |
| 1962...Santos, Brazil | 1976...Bayern Munich | 1990...Milan, Italy |
| 1963...Santos, Brazil | 1977...Boca Juniors, Argentina | 1991...Red Star Belgrade, Yugos. |
| 1964...Inter, Italy | 1978...No tournament | 1992...São Paulo, Brazil |
| 1965...Inter, Italy | 1979...Olimpia, Paraguay | 1993...São Paulo, Brazil |
| 1966...Penarol, Uruguay | 1980...Nacional, Uruguay | 1994...Velez Sarsfield, Argentina |
| 1967...Racing Club, Argentina | 1981...Flamengo, Brazil | 1995...Ajax Amsterdam, Netherlands |
| 1968...Estudiantes, Argentina | 1982...Penarol, Uruguay | 1996...Juventus, Italy |
| 1969...Milan, Italy | 1983...Gremio, Brazil | 1997...Borussia Dortmund, Ger. |
| 1970...Feyenoord, Netherlands | 1984...Independiente, Argentina | 1998...Real Madrid, Spain |
| 1971...Nacional, Uruguay | 1985...Juventus, Italy | 1999...Manchester United, England |
| 1972...Ajax Amsterdam, Netherlands | 1986...River Plate, Argentina | 2000...Boca Juniors, Argentina |
| 1973...Independiente, Argentina | 1987...Porto, Portugal | |

Note: Until 1968 a best-of-three-games format decided the winner. After that a two-game/total-goal format was used until Toyota became the sponsor in 1980, moved the game to Tokyo and switched the format to a one-game championship. The European Cup runner-up substituted for the winner in 1971, 1973, 1974, and 1979.

## European Cup

| | | |
|---|---|---|
| 1956...Real Madrid, Spain | 1973...Ajax Amsterdam, Netherlands | 1986...Steaua Bucharest, Romania |
| 1957...Real Madrid, Spain | 1974...Bayern Munich, W Germany | 1987...Porto, Portugal |
| 1958...Real Madrid, Spain | 1975...Bayern Munich, W Germany | 1988...PSV Eindhoven, Netherlands |
| 1959...Real Madrid, Spain | 1976...Bayern Munich, W Germany | 1989...AC Milan, Italy |
| 1960...Real Madrid, Spain | | 1990...AC Milan, Italy |
| 1961...Benfica, Portugal | 1977...Liverpool, England | 1991....Red Star Belgrade, Yugoslav. |
| 1962...Benfica, Portugal | 1978...Liverpool, England | 1992...Barcelona, Spain |
| 1963...AC Milan, Italy | 1979...Nottingham Forest, England | 1993...Olympique Marseille, France |
| 1964...Inter-Milan, Italy | 1980...Nottingham Forest, England | 1994...AC Milan, Italy |
| 1965...Inter-Milan, Italy | | 1995...Ajax Amsterdam, Netherlands |
| 1966...Real Madrid, Spain | 1981...Liverpool, England | 1996...Juventus, Italy |
| 1967...Celtic, Scotland | 1982...Aston Villa, England | 1997...Borussia Dortmund, Ger. |
| 1968...Manchester United, England | 1983...SV Hamburg, W Germany | 1998...Real Madrid, Spain |
| 1969...AC Milan, Italy | 1984...Liverpool, England | 1999...Manchester United, England |
| 1970...Feyenoord, Netherlands | 1985...Juventus, Italy | 2000...Real Madrid, Spain |
| 1971...Ajax Amsterdam, Netherlands | | 2001...Bayern Munich, Germany |
| 1972...Ajax Amsterdam, Netherlands | | |

Note: On four occasions the European Cup winner has refused to play in the Intercontinental Cup and has been replaced by the runner-up: Panathinaikos (Greece) in 1971, Juventus (Italy) in 1973, Atletico Madrid (Spain) in 1974, and Malmo (Sweden) in 1979.

## Libertadores Cup

Competition between champion clubs and runners-up of 10 South American National Associations.

| | | |
|---|---|---|
| 1960...Penarol, Uruguay | 1975...Independiente, Argentina | 1990...Olimpia, Paraguay |
| 1961...Penarol, Uruguay | 1976...Cruzeiro, Brazil | 1991...Colo Colo, Chile |
| 1962...Santos, Brazil | 1977...Boca Juniors, Argentina | 1992...São Paulo, Brazil |
| 1963...Santos, Brazil | 1978...Boca Juniors, Argentina | 1993...São Paulo, Brazil |
| 1964...Independiente, Argentina | 1979...Olimpia, Paraguay | 1994...Velez Sarsfield, Argentina |
| 1965...Independiente, Argentina | 1980...Nacional, Uruguay | 1995...Gremio, Brazil |
| 1966...Penarol, Uruguay | 1981...Flamengo, Brazil | 1996...River Plate, Argentina |
| 1967...Racing Club, Argentina | 1982...Penarol, Uruguay | 1997...Cruzeiro, Brazil |
| 1968...Estudiantes, Argentina | 1983...Gremio, Brazil | 1998...Vasco da Gama, Brazil |
| 1969...Estudiantes, Argentina | 1984...Independiente, Argentina | 1999...Palmeiras, Brazil |
| 1970...Estudiantes, Argentina | 1985...Argentinos Juniors, Arg | 2000...Boca Juniors, Argentina |
| 1971...Nacional, Uruguay | 1986...River Plate, Argentina | 2001...Boca Juniors, Argentina |
| 1972...Independiente, Argentina | 1987...Penarol, Uruguay | |
| 1973...Independiente, Argentina | 1988...Nacional, Uruguay | |
| 1974...Independiente, Argentina | 1989...Atletico Nacional, Colombia | |

## UEFA Cup

Competition between teams other than league champions and cup winners from the Union of European Football Associations.

| | | |
|---|---|---|
| 1958...Barcelona, Spain | 1974...Feyenoord, Netherlands | 1987...IFK Gothenburg, Sweden |
| 1959...No tournament | 1975...Borussia Monchengladbach, W Germany | 1988...Bayer Leverkusen, W Germany |
| 1960...Barcelona, Spain | 1976...Liverpool, England | 1989...Naples, Italy |
| 1961...AS Roma, Italy | 1977...Juventus, Italy | 1990...Juventus, Italy |
| 1962...Valencia, Spain | 1978...PSV Eindhoven, Netherl. | 1991...Inter-Milan, Italy |
| 1963...Valencia, Spain | 1979...Borussia Monchengladbach, W Germany | 1992...Torino, Italy |
| 1964...Real Zaragoza, Spain | 1980...Eintracht Frankfurt, W Germany | 1993...Juventus, Italy |
| 1965...Ferencvaros, Hungary | | 1994...Internazionale, Italy |
| 1966...Barcelona, Spain | 1981...Ipswich Town, England | 1995...Parma, Italy |
| 1967...Dynamo Zagreb, Yugoslav. | 1982...IFK Gothenburg, Sweden | 1996...Bayern Munich, Germany |
| 1968...Leeds United, England | 1983...Anderlecht, Belgium | 1997...Schalke 04, Germany |
| 1969...Newcastle United, England | 1984...Tottenham Hotspur, England | 1998...Inter Milan, Italy |
| 1970...Arsenal, England | 1985...Real Madrid, Spain | 1999...Parma, Italy |
| 1971...Leeds United, England | 1986...Real Madrid, Spain | 2000...Galatasaray, Turkey |
| 1972...Tottenham Hotspur, England | | 2001...Liverpool, England |
| 1973...Liverpool, England | | |

## European Cup-Winners' Cup

Competition between cup winners of countries belonging to UEFA.

| | | |
|---|---|---|
| 1961...AC Fiorentina, Italy | 1974...Magdeburg, E Germany | 1988...Mechelen, Belgium |
| 1962...Atletico Madrid, Spain | 1975...Dynamo Kiev, USSR | 1989...Barcelona, Spain |
| 1963...Tottenham Hotspur, England | 1976...Anderlecht, Belgium | 1990...Sampdoria, Italy |
| 1964...Sporting Lisbon, Portugal | 1977...SV Hamburg, W Germ. | 1991 ...Manchester United, England |
| 1965...West Ham United, England | 1978...Anderlecht, Belgium | 1992...Werder Bremen, Germany |
| 1966...Borussia Dortmund, W Germany | 1979...Barcelona, Spain | 1993...Parma, Italy |
| | 1980...Valencia, Spain | 1994...Arsenal, England |
| 1967...Bayern Munich, W Germ. | 1981...Dynamo Tbilisi, USSR | 1995...Real Zaragoza, Spain |
| 1968...AC Milan, Italy | 1982...Barcelona, Spain | 1996...Paris St. Germain, France |
| 1969...Slovan Bratislava, Czech. | 1983...Aberdeen, Scotland | 1997...Barcelona, Spain |
| 1970...Manchester City, England | 1984...Juventus, Italy | 1998...Chelsea, England |
| 1971...Chelsea, England | 1985...Everton, England | 1999...Lazio, Italy |
| 1972...Glasgow Rangers, Scotland | 1986...Dynamo Kiev, USSR | |
| 1973...AC Milan, Italy | 1987...Ajax Amsterdam, Neth. | |

Note: the Cup-Winners Cup was discontinued after 1999.

# Major League Soccer

## MLS Cup Results

| Year | Champion | Score | Runner-up | Regular Season MVP |
|---|---|---|---|---|
| 1996 | D.C. United | 3–2 (ot) | Los Angeles | Carlos Valderrama, TB |
| 1997 | D.C. United | 2–1 | Colorado | Preki, Kansas City |
| 1998 | Chicago | 2–0 | D.C. United | Marco Etcheverry, D.C. |
| 1999 | D.C. United | 2–0 | Los Angeles | Jason Kreis, Dallas |
| 2000 | Kansas City | 1–0 | Chicago | Tony Meola, Kansas City |
| 2001 | San Jose | 2–1 (ot) | Los Angeles | Alex Pineda Chacon, Mia |

# A-League

| Year | Champion | Score | Runner-Up | Regular Season MVP |
|---|---|---|---|---|
| 1991 | San Francisco | 1–3, 2–0 (1–0 on PKs) | Albany | Jean Harbor, Maryland |
| 1992 | Colorado | 1–0 | Tampa Bay | Taifour Diane, Colorado |
| 1993 | Colorado | 3–1 (OT) | Los Angeles | Taifour Diane, Colorado |
| 1994 | Montreal | 1–0 | Colorado | Paulinho, Los Angeles |
| 1995 | Seattle | 1–2 (SO), 3–0, 2–1 (SO) | Atlanta | Peter Hattrup, Seattle |
| 1996 | Seattle | 2–0 | Rochester | Wolde Harris, Colorado |
| 1997 | Milwaukee | 2–1 (SO) | Carolina | Doug Miller, Rochester |
| 1998 | Rochester | 3–1 | Minnesota | Mark Baena, Seattle |
| 1999 | Minnesota | 2–1 | Rochester | John Swallen, Minnesota |
| 2000 | Rochester | 3–1 | Minnesota | Vitalis Takawira, Mil |
| 2001 | Rochester | 2–0 | Vancouver | Paul Conway, Charleston |

# Woman's United Soccer Association

## Founders Cup Results

| Year | Champion | Score | Runner-up | Regular Season MVP |
|---|---|---|---|---|
| 2001 | Bay Area | 3–3 (4–2 PKs) | Atlanta | Tiffeny Milbrett, New York |

# U.S. Open Cup

Open to all amateur and professional teams in the United States, the annual U.S. Open Cup is the oldest cup competition in the country and among the oldest in the world. The tournament is a single-elimination event running concurrent to the MLS season. The winner advances to the CONCACAF Cup, a tournament of the top club teams from North and Central America and the Caribbean.

| Year | Champion |
|------|----------|
| 1914 | Brooklyn Field Club (NYC) |
| 1915 | Bethlehem Steel FC (PA) |
| 1916 | Bethlehem Steel FC (PA) |
| 1917 | Fall River Rovers (MA) |
| 1918 | Bethlehem Steel FC (PA) |
| 1919 | Bethlehem Steel FC (PA) |
| 1920 | Ben Miller FC (St. Louis) |
| 1921 | Robbins Dry Dock FC (Brooklyn) |
| 1922 | Scullin Steel FC (St. Louis) |
| 1923 | Paterson FC (NJ) |
| 1924 | Fall River FC (MA) |
| 1925 | Shawsheen FC (Andover, MA) |
| 1926 | Bethlehem Steel FC (PA) |
| 1927 | Fall River FC (MA) |
| 1928 | New York National FC (NYC) |
| 1929 | Hakoah All Star SC (NYC) |
| 1930 | Fall River FC (MA) |
| 1931 | Fall River FC (MA) |
| 1932 | New Bedford FC (MA) |
| 1933 | Stix, Baer and Fuller FC (St. Louis) |
| 1934 | Stix, Baer and Fuller FC (St. Louis) |
| 1935 | Central Breweries FC (Chicago) |
| 1936 | German-Americans (Philadelphia) |
| 1937 | New York American FC (NYC) |
| 1938 | Sparta A and BA (Chicago) |
| 1939 | St. Mary's Celtic SC (Brooklyn) |
| 1940 | — |
| 1941 | Pawtucket FC (RI) |
| 1942 | Gallatin SC (PA) |
| 1943 | Brooklyn Hispano SC (NYC) |
| 1944 | Brooklyn Hispano SC (NYC) |
| 1945 | Brookhattan FC (NYC) |
| 1946 | Chicago Viking FC (IL) |
| 1947 | Ponta Delgada SC (Fall River, MA) |
| 1948 | Simpkins-Ford SC (St. Louis) |
| 1949 | Morgan SC (PA) |
| 1950 | Simpkins-Ford SC (St. Louis) |
| 1951 | German Hungarian SC (NYC) |
| 1952 | Harmarville SC (PA) |
| 1953 | Falcons SC (Chicago) |
| 1954 | New York Americans (NYC) |
| 1955 | Eintracht Sport Club (NYC) |
| 1956 | Harmarville SC (PA) |
| 1957 | Kutis SC (St. Louis) |
| 1958 | Los Angeles Kickers (CA) |
| 1959 | McIlvaine Canvasbacks (Los Angeles) |
| 1960 | Ukrainian Nationals (Philadelphia) |
| 1961 | Ukrainian Nationals (Philadelphia) |
| 1962 | New York Hungaria (NYC) |
| 1963 | Ukrainian Nationals (Philadelphia) |
| 1964 | Los Angeles Kickers (CA) |
| 1965 | New York Hungaria (NYC) |
| 1966 | Ukrainian Nationals (Philadelphia) |
| 1967 | Greek American AA (NYC) |
| 1968 | Greek American AA (NYC) |
| 1969 | Greek American AA (NYC) |
| 1970 | Elizabeth SC (Union, NJ) |
| 1971 | Hota SC (NYC) |
| 1972 | Elizabeth SC (Union, NJ) |
| 1973 | Maccabee SC (Los Angeles) |
| 1974 | Greek American AA (NYC) |
| 1975 | Maccabee SC (Los Angeles) |
| 1976 | San Francisco AC (CA) |
| 1977 | Maccabee SC (Los Angeles) |
| 1978 | Maccabee SC (Los Angeles) |
| 1979 | Brooklyn Dodgers SC (NYC) |
| 1980 | NY Pancyprian-Freedoms (NYC) |
| 1981 | Maccabee SC (Los Angeles) |
| 1982 | NY Pancyprian-Freedoms (NYC) |
| 1983 | NY Pancyprian-Freedoms (NYC) |
| 1984 | AO Krete (NYC) |
| 1985 | Greek American AC (San Francisco) |
| 1986 | Kutis SC (St. Louis) |
| 1987 | Club Espana (Washington, D.C.) |
| 1988 | Busch SC (St. Louis) |
| 1989 | HRC Kickers (St. Petersburg, FL) |
| 1990 | AAC Eagles (Chicago) |
| 1991 | Brooklyn Italians SC (East NY) |
| 1992 | San Jose Oaks (CA) |
| 1993 | Club Deportivo Mexico (San Francisco) |
| 1994 | Greek American AC (San Francisco) |
| 1995 | Richmond Kickers (VA) |
| 1996 | D.C. United (MLS) |
| 1997 | Dallas Burn (MLS) |
| 1998 | Chicago Fire (MLS) |
| 1999 | Rochester Rhinos (A-League) |
| 2000 | Chicago Fire (MLS) |
| 2001 | Los Angeles Galaxy (MLS) |

# North American Soccer League

Formed in 1968 by the merger of the National Professional Soccer League and the USA League, both of which had begun operations a year earlier. The NPSL's lone champion was the Oakland Clippers. The USA League, which brought entire teams in from Europe, was won in 1967 by the L.A. Wolves, who were the English League's Wolverhampton Wanderers.

| Year | Champion | Score | Runner-Up | Regular Season MVP |
|------|----------|-------|-----------|--------------------|
| 1968 | Atlanta | 0–0, 3–0 | San Diego | John Kowalik, Chi |
| 1969 | Kansas City | No game | Atlanta | Cirilio Fernandez, KC |
| 1970 | Rochester | 3–0,1–3 | Washington | Carlos Metidieri, Roch |
| 1971 | Dallas | 1–2, 4–1, 2–0 | Atlanta | Carlos Metidieri, Roch |
| 1972 | New York | 2–1 | St. Louis | Randy Horton, NY |
| 1973 | Philadelphia | 2–0 | Dallas | Warren Archibald, Mia |
| 1974 | Los Angeles | 4–3* | Miami | Peter Silvester, Balt |
| 1975 | Tampa Bay | 2–0 | Portland | Steve David, Mia |
| 1976 | Toronto | 3–0 | Minnesota | Pelé, NY |
| 1977 | New York | 2–1 | Seattle | Franz Beckenbauer, NY |
| 1978 | New York | 3–1 | Tampa Bay | Mike Flanagan, NE |
| 1979 | Vancouver | 2–1 | Tampa Bay | Johan Cruyff, LA |
| 1980 | New York | 3–0 | Ft. Lauderdale | Roger Davies, Sea |
| 1981 | Chicago | 1–0* | New York | Giorgio Chinaglia, NY |
| 1982 | New York | 1–0 | Seattle | Peter Ward, Sea |
| 1983 | Tulsa | 2–0 | Toronto | Roberto Cabanas, NY |
| 1984 | Chicago | 2–1, 3–2 | Toronto | Steve Zungul, SJ |

*Shootout.

Championship Format: 1968 and 1970: Two games/total goals. 1971 and 1984: Best-of-three series. 1972–1983: One-game championship. Title in 1969 went to the regular-season champion.

## Statistical Leaders

### SCORING

| Year | Player/Team | Pts | Year | Player/Team | Pts |
|------|-------------|-----|------|-------------|-----|
| 1968 | John Kowalik, Chi | 69 | 1977 | Steven David, LA | 58 |
| 1969 | Kaiser Motaung, Atl | 36 | 1978 | Giorgio Chinaglia, NY | 79 |
| 1970 | Kirk Apostolidis, Dall | 35 | 1979 | Oscar Fabbiani, Tampa Bay | 58 |
| 1971 | Carlos Metidieri, Roch | 46 | 1980 | Giorgio Chinaglia, NY | 77 |
| 1972 | Randy Horton, NY | 22 | 1981 | Giorgio Chinaglia, NY | 74 |
| 1973 | Kyle Rote, Dall | 30 | 1982 | Giorgio Chinaglia, NY | 55 |
| 1974 | Paul Child, San Jose | 36 | 1983 | Roberto Cabanas, NY | 66 |
| 1975 | Steven David, Miami | 52 | 1984 | Slavisa Zungul, Golden Bay | 50 |
| 1976 | Giorgio Chinaglia, NY | 49 | | | |

## Recognizing Ramos

The feel-good story in the early stages of the 2001 MLS season was the rebirth of Met- roStars playmaker Tab Ramos, who recov- ered from left ACL operations in 1996 and '97 to become one of the most dangerous on-the-ball threats in the league. So it's worth askeing: Would Ramos, 34, reconsider his decision of November 2000 to retire from the U.S. team? "No, my decision is final," Ramos said. "I still get the urge, but I realize my time is done at the international level. We have great young players who can take the team higher than we ever did."

In that case it's time for U.S. Soccer to give Ramos a testimonial match, the world- wide custom for honoring a nation's retiring stars. No player has done more to advance American soccer than Ramos, the finest attacker the U.S. has produced and one of three Yanks (along with Marcelo Balboa and Eric Wynalda) to have played in three World Cups. While U.S. Soccer wouldn't have to give Ramos the gate receipts of his tribute match (as tradition dictates elsewhere), it could pay for Ramos's longtime U.S. team- mates to fly in for the occasion.

In November 2000, U.S. Soccer president Bob Contiguglia promised to honor Ramos, but Ramos hasn't heard from him since. "It hasn't been on the front burner with all the World Cup qualifiers and the federation's budget cuts," said Contiguglia, "but Tab deserves something, and he'll get it."

DAMIAN STROHMEYER

NCAA baseball
champions Miami

# NCAA Sports

# Unfinished Business

## The champions in men's soccer, ice hockey and baseball were motivated by bitter memories of recent failures

## BY HANK HERSCH

**T**IME HEALS all wounds, it's true, but it usually takes quite a while. The players on three NCAA championship teams in 2000–01 didn't have the luxury of time, so they borrowed from another well-worn aphorism and healed themselves. Worked pretty well.

### MEN'S SOCCER

Before the national championship weekend kicked off on Dec. 8, 2000, Connecticut defender Chris Gbandi's most vivid memory of Ericsson Stadium in Charlotte was of its turf, in blurry close-up. That image was seared into his mind in 1999 after the Huskies' 2–1 loss to Santa Clara in the national semifinals. The decisive goal came in the fourth overtime, when the ball deflected off Gbandi's leg and into the Huskies' net, reducing the sophomore defender to a sobbing heap on the sod.

The defeat deprived UConn of a shot at its first men's soccer title since 1981. While the loss haunted the nine returning starters, it also spurred them to an 18-3-2 record in

2000 and a return trip to Charlotte, where they downed SMU 2–0 in the semis to set up a showdown with Creighton (22–3) for the national title. "The hurt from that game carried over all year long," said Gbandi. "I don't want this to end again with me laying on the ground crying. We'll do anything in the world to prevent that from happening."

A junior from Houston who was born in Liberia, where his father played semipro ball, Gbandi was the anchor of the Connecticut defense in 2000. The Huskies allowed 0.50 goals per game, second best in the nation. The day before the final Gbandi was awarded the Hermann Trophy as the top player in the country. As much as he appreciated the honor, Gbandi had his sights set on a prize he could only seize against Creighton at Ericsson.

In the 16th minute of a scoreless match, a foul by Creighton gave UConn a free kick on the right side, 24 yards from the goal. As Cesar Cuellar approached the ball and sized up a shot, Gbandi headed him off, explaining later, "He was a freshman. No way he takes

**Gbandi (4) scored a goal in the final, then helped seal the win with rock-solid defense.**

that kick in a big game." Not that Gbandi's credentials were impeccable; he hadn't scored on a free kick all year. Still, he waved the freshman away, stepped up and drove a left-footed shot to the right corner of the goal. Creighton goalkeeper Mike Gabb got his fingertips on the ball, but he couldn't keep it from the back of the net. "He took advantage of the inch I gave him," Gabb said. Sprinting toward the Huskies' fans, Gbandi peeled back his jersey to reveal a Superman T-shirt underneath. He had bought it from Toys "R" Us in the summer and had waited all season to flash it. "My dad was making fun of me, but I told him he would see," Gbandi said. "It was going to get used someday."

All-America forward Darin Lewis, a senior, added a goal in the 86th minute to give UConn a 2–0 victory, the only time the Bluejays were shut out all season. "I thought Chris Gbandi was the star of the game," Creighton coach Bret Simon said. "He obviously scored a great goal, but he was also the

player who made the difference in the back. Every time I thought we were going to get a great chance, he was there."

## MEN'S ICE HOCKEY

For the seniors on the Boston College hockey team, the 2001 NCAA hockey Final Four presented a knife-edge drama, a chance for either sweet, purging redemption or total, dismal failure. The Eagles had reached the Frozen Four in each of the past three seasons only to be frozen out with a heartbreaking loss each year. The 2001 tournament was their last chance. If they succeeded, the previous three years of frustration would be washed away, remembered only for how they made the one triumph all the sweeter. But if they failed, well, they'd be the Buffalo Bills of NCAA hockey.

In the East Regional the Eagles downed Maine, which had dumped Boston College in overtime in the 1999 semifinals. In the national semifinals Boston College topped Michigan, which had defeated BC in overtime in the '98 championship game. All of the pieces were falling into place. Finally, on April 7, in the national championship game at the Pepsi Center in Albany, N.Y., Boston College met North Dakota, which had beaten the Eagles 4–2 in the previous year's title tilt.

Redemption was tantalizingly close as BC held a 2–0 lead with less than five minutes remaining. Chuck Kobasew, a freshman right wing, scored the first goal, and senior right wing Mike Lephart scored the second. Senior goalie Scott Clemmensen, the NCAA tournament's alltime saves leader, made the two-goal lead stand up.

But now, in the dying minutes of the game, the Eagles were penalized for having too many men on the ice. Fighting Sioux coach Dean Blais pulled his goalie, Karl Goehring, to give his team a six-on-four advantage. "What is the difference if we lose 2–0 or 3–0?" Blais said later. "You have to go down swinging."

The Eagles' solid penalty-killing unit finally gave out as Fighting Sioux center Tim Skarperud deflected the puck past Clemmensen with 3:42 to go. The Fighting Sioux ratcheted up the pressure on Clemmensen. He made two big saves as the clock wound down but could not prevent the equalizer, which came on another deflection, this time by Wes Dorey with 36.4 seconds left.

Skating off somewhat dazed to the locker room before overtime, BC faced the prospect of yet another sudden, cruel death in the Frozen Four. "Everyone was down a little bit in the first couple of minutes," freshman left wing Tony Voce recalled. "But Coach [Jerry York] said, 'As bad as this feels now, just think about how good it's going to feel when you get off the ice.' Everyone was like, This is our year. We're not going to lose no matter what." As play was about to resume, York made a special plea to sophomore center Krys Kolanos: "Get this done."

Less than five minutes into OT, Voce passed to Kolanos on the blue line. As Kolanos swept in on goal, Goehring moved out to poke-check the puck. Kolanos held the puck despite being knocked off his feet by the sprawling goalie and delivered it into the net. Boston College's 52-year national-title drought—one that extended to all sports—was over. "Hey," said Eagles defenseman Bobby Allen, "perseverance pays off."

## BASEBALL

On April 1, following a three-game sweep by Cal State–Fullerton, Miami's record stood at 25–9, and the Hurricanes seemed poised to achieve what they had the year before: nothing. After winning the fireworks-filled 1999 College World Series, Miami didn't even make it back to Omaha in 2000, an ignominy the Hurricanes seemed destined to relive in 2001. Coach Jim Morris told his players to get back to basics. "Fullerton will be in Omaha," Morris said. "If you want to be there, you need to play like that."

His message was not lost on centerfielder Charlton Jimerson. A 6'2", 200-pound non-scholarship senior from Hayward, Calif., Jimerson had a .240 career average and $40,000 in student loans to his name heading into the 2001 season. He worked his way into the starting lineup four games after the Fullerton series. Not only would Jimerson hold onto that spot, but he would also hit .327 and steal 20 bases as a starter, spurring Miami to 19 wins in its last 22 games. "We were in shock a long time after losing in the regionals last year," said first baseman Kevin Brown, one of 16 holdovers from the '99 team. "We had to make it back."

Jimerson made sure they didn't leave early once they got there. He bashed a lead-off home run in each of Miami's first two wins, made a wall-climbing catch to help edge Southern Cal 4–3 and stole four bases in a 12–6 rout of Tennessee. Without any bona fide superstars at his disposal, Morris used speed (Miami led the nation in stolen bases) and a deep bullpen to wear down opponents. The Hurricanes roared into the June 16 final against Stanford atop a 16-game unbeaten streak.

Jimerson attributed Miami's dominance to "our drive to accept nothing less." That drive proved too formidable for the Cardinal, which was humbled 12–1. Brown knocked in five runs; Tom Farmer (15–2), Luke DeBold and Alex Prendes combined for a five-hitter; and the Hurricanes tied a 45-year-old record for margin of victory in a CWS title game. Jimerson was voted the Most Outstanding Player. "This was the perfect way to go out," he said. "The perfect storybook ending."

## NCAA Team Champions

### Fall 2000
### Cross-Country

#### MEN

| | Champion | Runner-Up |
|---|---|---|
| Division I: | Arkansas | Colorado |
| Division II: | Western St (CO) | Abilene Christian |
| Division III: | Calvin | Keene St |

#### WOMEN

| | Champion | Runner-Up |
|---|---|---|
| Division I: | Colorado | Brigham Young |
| Division II: | Western St (CO) | N Dakota |
| Division III: | Middlebury | Williams |

### Field Hockey

#### WOMEN

| | Champion | Runner-Up |
|---|---|---|
| Division I: | Old Dominion | N Carolina |
| Division II | Lock Haven | Bentley |
| Division III: | William Smith | Springfield |

### Football

#### MEN

| | Champion | Runner-Up |
|---|---|---|
| Division I-AA: | Georgia Southern | Montana |
| Division II: | Delta State | Bloomsburg |
| Division III: | Mount Union | St. John's (MN) |

### Soccer

#### MEN

| | Champion | Runner-Up |
|---|---|---|
| Division I: | Connecticut | Creighton |
| Division II: | Cal St– Dominguez Hills | Barry |
| Division III: | Messiah | Rowan |

#### WOMEN

| | Champion | Runner-Up |
|---|---|---|
| Division I: | N Carolina | UCLA |
| Division II: | UC–San Diego | Northern Kentucky |
| Division III: | College of New Jersey | Tufts |

### Volleyball

#### WOMEN

| | Champion | Runner-Up |
|---|---|---|
| Division I: | Nebraska | Wisconsin |
| Division II: | Hawaii Pacific | Augustana |
| Division III: | Central (IA) | Wisconsin-Whitewater |

### Water Polo

#### MEN

| Champion | Runner-Up |
|---|---|
| UCLA | UC–San Diego |

## Winter 2000–2001
### Basketball

#### MEN

| | Champion | Runner-Up |
|---|---|---|
| Division I: | Duke | Arizona |
| Division II: | Kentucky Wesleyan | Washburn (KS) |
| Division III: | Catholic | William Paterson |

#### WOMEN

| | Champion | Runner-Up |
|---|---|---|
| Division I: | Notre Dame | Purdue |
| Division II: | Cal Poly–Pomona | N Dakota |
| Division III: | Washington (MO) | Messiah |

### Fencing

| Champion | Runner-Up |
|---|---|
| St. John's (NY) | Penn St |

### Gymnastics

#### MEN

| Champion | Runner-Up |
|---|---|
| Ohio St | Oklahoma |

#### WOMEN

| UCLA | Georgia |
|---|---|

### Ice Hockey

#### MEN

| | Champion | Runner-Up |
|---|---|---|
| Division I: | Boston College | N Dakota |
| Division III: | Plattsburgh | RIT |

#### WOMEN

| Minnesota–Duluth | St. Lawrence |
|---|---|

### Rifle

| Champion | Runner-Up |
|---|---|
| AK–Fairbanks | Kentucky |

### Skiing

| Champion | Runner-Up |
|---|---|
| Denver | Vermont |

### Swimming and Diving

#### MEN

| | Champion | Runner-Up |
|---|---|---|
| Division I: | Texas | Stanford |
| Division II: | Cal St–Bakersfield | Drury |
| Division III: | Kenyon | Emory |

#### WOMEN

| | Champion | Runner-Up |
|---|---|---|
| Division I: | Georgia | Stanford |
| Division II: | Truman St | Drury |
| Division III: | Denison | Kenyon |

### Wrestling

#### MEN

| | Champion | Runner-Up |
|---|---|---|
| Division I: | Minnesota | Iowa |
| Division II: | N Dakota St | S Dakota St |
| Division III: | Augsburg | Wartburg |

## Winter 2000–2001 *(Cont.)*
### Indoor Track and Field
#### MEN

| | Champion | Runner-Up |
|---|---|---|
| Division I: | Louisiana St | Texas Christian |
| Division II: | St. Augustine's | New York Tech |
| Division III: | WI–La Crosse | WI–Oshkosh |

#### WOMEN

| | Champion | Runner-Up |
|---|---|---|
| Division I: | UCLA | S Carolina |
| Division II: | St. Augustine's | Abilene Christian |
| Division III: | Wheaton (MA) | WI–La Crosse |

## Spring 2001
### Baseball

| | Champion | Runner-Up |
|---|---|---|
| Division I: | Miami (FL) | Stanford |
| Division II: | St. Mary's | Central Missouri St |
| Division III: | St. Thomas (MN) | Marietta |

### Golf
#### MEN

| | Champion | Runner-Up |
|---|---|---|
| Division I: | Florida | Clemson |
| Division II: | W Florida | Florida Southern |
| Division III: | WI–Eau Claire | Guilford |

#### WOMEN

| | Champion | Runner-Up |
|---|---|---|
| Division I: | Georgia | Duke |
| Division II: | Florida Southern | Rollins (FL) |
| Division III | Methodist | Concordia (MN) |

### Lacrosse
#### MEN

| | Champion | Runner-Up |
|---|---|---|
| Division I: | Princeton | Syracuse |
| Division II: | Adelphi | Limestone |
| Division III: | Middlebury | Gettysburg |

#### WOMEN

| | Champion | Runner-Up |
|---|---|---|
| Division I: | Maryland | Georgetown |
| Division II | C.W. Post | W Chester |
| Division III: | Middlebury | Amherst |

### Rowing
#### WOMEN

| Champion | Runner-Up |
|---|---|
| Washington | Michigan |

### Softball

| | Champion | Runner-Up |
|---|---|---|
| Division I: | Arizona | UCLA |
| Division II: | Nebraska–Omaha | Lewis |
| Division III: | Muskingum (OH) | Central (IA) |

### Tennis
#### MEN

| | Champion | Runner-Up |
|---|---|---|
| Division I: | Georgia | Tennessee |
| Division II: | Rollins | Hawaii Pacific |
| Division III: | Williams | UC–Santa Cruz |

## Spring 2001 *(Cont.)*
### Tennis *(Cont.)*
#### WOMEN

| | Champion | Runner-Up |
|---|---|---|
| Division I: | Stanford | Vanderbilt |
| Division II: | Lynn | BYU–Hawaii |
| Division III: | Williams | Trinity |

### Outdoor Track and Field
#### MEN

| | Champion | Runner-Up |
|---|---|---|
| Division I: | Tennessee | Texas Christian |
| Division II: | St. Augustine's | Abilene Christian |
| Division III: | WI–La Crosse | Lincoln (PA) |

#### WOMEN

| | Champion | Runner-Up |
|---|---|---|
| Division I: | Southern Cal | UCLA |
| Division II: | St. Augustine's | Western St |
| Division III: | Wheaton (MA) | Calvin |

### Volleyball
#### MEN

| Champion | Runner-Up |
|---|---|
| Brigham Young | UCLA |

# NCAA Division I Individual Champions

## Fall 2000
### Cross Country
#### MEN

| Champion | Runner-Up |
|---|---|
| Keith Kelly, Providence | Stephen Ondieki, Fairleigh Dickinson |

#### WOMEN

| Champion | Runner-Up |
|---|---|
| Kara Grgas-Wheeler, Colorado | Sabrina Monro, Montana |

## Winter 2000–2001
### Fencing
#### MEN

| | Champion | Runner-Up |
|---|---|---|
| Sabre | Ivan Lee, St. John's (NY) | Keeth Smart, St. John's (NY) |
| Foil | William Jed Dupree, Columbia | Nontapat Panchan, Penn St |
| Épée | Soren Thompson, Princeton | Adam Wiercioch, Penn St |

#### WOMEN

| | Champion | Runner-Up |
|---|---|---|
| Sabre | Sada Jacobson, Yale | Marisa Mustilli, St. John's (NY) |
| Foil | Iris Zimmermann, Stanford | Marta Grochal, Penn St |
| Épée | Emese Takács, St. John's (NY) | Arlene Stevens, St. John's (NY) |

### Gymnastics
#### MEN

| | Champion | Runner-Up |
|---|---|---|
| All-around | Jamie Natalie, Ohio St | Raj Bhavsar, Ohio State |
| Vault | Daren Lynch, Ohio St | Brad Golden, Michigan St |
| Parallel bars | Raj Bhavsar, Ohio St | Kris Zimmerman, Michigan |
| Horizontal bar | Michael Ashe, California | Daniel Diaz-Loung, Michigan |
| Floor exercise | Clay Stother, Minnesota | Brendan O'Neil, Oklahoma |
| Pommel horse | Clay Stother, Minnesota | Steve Van Etten, Oklahoma |
| Rings | Chris Lakeman, Penn St | Scott Vetere, Michigan |

## Winter 2000–2001 *(Cont.)*
## Gymnastics *(Cont.)*
### WOMEN

| | Champion | Runner-Up |
|---|---|---|
| All-around | Onnie Willis, UCLA/ Elise Ray, Michigan | |
| Balance beam | Theresa Kulikowski, Utah | Lindsay Wing, Stanford |
| Uneven bars | Yvonne Tousek, UCLA | Onnie Willis, UCLA |
| Floor exercise | Mohini Bhardwaj, UCLA | Jamie Dantzscher, UCLA |
| Vault | Cory Fritzinger, Georgia | Katrina Severin, Oregon St |

## Skiing
### MEN

| | Champion | Runner-Up |
|---|---|---|
| Slalom | Jernej Bukovec, Utah | Kyle Hildebrand, Bates |
| Giant slalom | John Minahan, Vermont | Chad Wolk, Colorado |
| 10-kilometer classic | Wolf Wallendorf, Denver | Jorn Frohs, Denver |
| 20-kilometer free | Pietro Broggini, Denver | Pat Casey, Utah |

### WOMEN

| | Champion | Runner-Up |
|---|---|---|
| Slalom | Petra Svet, Utah | Marte Dolva, New Mexio |
| Giant slalom | Erica MacConnell, Vermont | Alexandra Krebs, Vermont |
| 5-kilometer classic | Katerina Hanusova, Nevada | Mari Storeng, Colorado |
| 15-kilometer free | Katerina Hanusova, Nevada | Aubrey Smith, Northern Michigan |

## Wrestling

| | Champion | Runner-Up |
|---|---|---|
| 125 lb | Stephen Abas, Fresno St | Jody Strittmatter, Iowa |
| 133 lb | Eric Juergens, Iowa | Johnny Thompson, Oklahoma St |
| 141 lb | Michael Lightner, Oklahoma | Doug Schwab, Iowa |
| 149 lb | Adam Tirapelle, Illinois | Dave Esposito, Lehigh |
| 157 lb | T.J. Williams, Iowa | Brian Snyder, Nebraska |
| 165 lb | Don Pritzlaff, Wisconsin | Joe Heskett, Iowa St |
| 174 lb | Josh Koscheck, Edinboro | Maurice Worthy, Army |
| 184 lb | Cael Sanderson, Ohio St | Daniel Cormier, Oklahoma St |
| 197 lb | Mark Munoz, Oklahoma St | Pat Quirk, Illinois |
| HWT | John Lockhardt, Illinois | Tommy Rowlands, Ohio St |

## Swimming and Diving
### MEN

| | Champion | Time | Runner-Up | Time |
|---|---|---|---|---|
| 50-yd freestyle | Anthony Robinson, Stanford | 19.15 | Anthony Ervin, California | 19.23 |
| 100-yd freestyle | Anthony Ervin, California | 41.80*# | Roland Schoeman, Arizona | 42.58 |
| 200-yd freestyle | Klete Keller, Southern Cal | 1:34.43 | Chris Kemp, Texas | 1:34.69 |
| 500-yd freestyle | Klete Keller, Southern Cal | 4:14.67 | Chris Thompson, Michigan | 4:14.71 |
| 1650-yd freestyle | Chris Thompson, Michigan | 14:26.62*# | Tim Siciliano, Michigan | 14:41.84 |
| 100-yd backstroke | Michael Gilliam, Tennessee | 45.97 | Peter Marshall, Stanford | 46.23 |
| 200-yd backstroke | Nate Dusing, Texas | 1:41.52 | Markus Rogan, Stanford | 1:41.64 |
| 100-yd breaststroke | Brendan Hansen, Texas | 52.35 | David Denniston, Auburn | 52.62 |
| 200-yd breaststroke | Brendan Hansen, Texas | 1:53.11*# | David Denniston, Auburn | 1:53.48 |
| 100-yd butterfly | Ian Crocker, Texas | 45.96 | Nate Dusing, Texas | 46.22 |
| 200-yd butterfly | Adam Messner, Stanford | 1:43.12 | Duncan Sherrard, Florida | 1:43.18 |
| 200-yd IM | Nate Dusing, Texas | 1:42.85* | Tom Hannan, Texas | 1:43.87 |
| 400-yd IM | Tim Siciliano, Michigan | 3:40.77 | Erik Vendt, Southern Cal | 3:40.98 |

| | Champion | Pts | Runner-Up | Pts |
|---|---|---|---|---|
| 1-meter diving | Troy Dumais, Texas | 397.60 | Jud Campbell, Georgia | 372.25 |
| 3-meter diving | Troy Dumais, Texas | 664.70 | Omar Ojeda, Arizona | 635.95 |
| Platform | Kyle Prandi, Miami (FL) | 591.75 | Justin Dumais, Texas | 564.85 |

*NCAA record. #American record.

## Winter 2000–2001 (Cont.)
## Swimming and Diving (Cont.)

### WOMEN

| | Champion | Time | Runner-Up | Time |
|---|---|---|---|---|
| 50-yd freestyle | Colleen Lanne, Texas | 21.99 | Haley Cope, California | 22.34 |
| 100-yd freestyle | Colleen Lanne, Texas | 48.29 | Maritza Correia, Georgia | 48.49 |
| 200-yd freestyle | Sarah Tolar, Arizona | 1:45.21 | Colleen Lanne, Texas | 1:45.27 |
| 500-yd freestyle | Jessica Foschi, Stanford | 4:37.81 | Janelle Atkinson, Florida | 4:39.44 |
| 1650-yd freestyle | Cara Lane, Virginia | 15:53.86 | Jessica Foschi, Stanford | 16:03.47 |
| 100-yd backstroke | Natalie Coughlin, California | 51.23*# | Misty Hyman, Stanford | 53.04 |
| 200-yd backstroke | Natalie Coughlin, California | 1:51.02*# | Beth Botsford, Arizona | 1:55.65 |
| 100-yd breaststroke | Tara Kirk, Stanford | 59.18 | Ashley Roby, Georgia | 59.91 |
| 200-yd breaststroke | Amanda Beard, Arizona | 2:09.09 | Tara Kirk, Stanford | 2:09.18 |
| 100-yd butterfly | Natalie Coughlin, California | 51.18* | Misty Hyman, Stanford | 51.51 |
| 200-yd butterfly | Misty Hyman, Stanford | 1:53.63 | Shelly Ripple, Stanford | 1:54.95 |
| 200-yd IM | Maggie Bowen, Auburn | 1:55.49*# | Shelly Ripple, Stanford | 1:56.24 |
| 400-yd IM | Maggie Bowen, Auburn | 4:07.26 | Michala Kwasny, Southern Cal | 4:10.61 |

| | Champion | Pts | Runner-Up | Pts |
|---|---|---|---|---|
| 1-meter diving | Yulia Pakhalina, Houston | 329.60 | Katie Beth Bryant, Miami (FL) | 324.75 |
| 3-meter diving | Yulia Pakhalina, Houston | 573.20 | Jenny Keim, Miami (FL) | 544.30 |
| Platform | Erin Sones, Stanford | 463.05 | Ashley Culpepper, Louisiana St | 453.45 |

*NCAA record.   #American record.

## Indoor Track and Field

### MEN

| | Champion | Time/Mark | Runner-Up | Time/Mark |
|---|---|---|---|---|
| 60-meter dash | Kim Collins, Texas Christian | 6.58 | James Shelton, Mississippi | 6.61 |
| 60-meter hurdles | Aubrey Herring, Indiana St | 7.61 | Ron Bramlett, Alabama | 7.62 |
| 200-meter dash | Kim Collins, Texas Christian | 20.55 | Ja'Warren Hooker, Washington | 20.56 |
| 400-meter dash | Rickey Harris, Florida | 45.78 | Andrew Pierce, Ohio St | 45.78 |
| 800-meter run | Patrick Nduwimana, Arizona | 1:45.33* | Dirk Heinze, Arkansas | 1:45.95 |
| Mile run | Bryan Berryhill, Colorado St | 3:56.84 | Charlie Gruber, Kansas | 3:58.51 |
| 3,000-meter run | David Kimani, Alabama | 8:03.29 | Adrian Blincoe, Villanova | 8:04.08 |
| 5,000-meter run | David Kimani, Alabama | 13:42.32 | Matthew Lane, William & Mary | 13:43.36 |
| High jump | Charles Clinger, Weber St | 7 ft 5 in | Shaun Guice, Purdue | 7 ft 5 in |
| Pole vault | Jacob Pauli, Northern Iowa | 18 ft 7½ in | Adam Keul, Stephen F. Austin | 18 ft 7½ in |
| Long jump | Savante Stringfellow, Mississippi | 26 ft 6¼ in | Walter Davis, Louisiana St | 26 ft 3½ in |
| Triple jump | Walter Davis, Louisiana St | 55 ft 5 in | Chris Hercules, Texas | 54 ft 9¾ in |
| Shot put | Janus Robberts, SMU | 70 ft 1 in | Joachim Olsen, Idaho | 65 ft 10½ in |
| 35-pound wt throw | Andras Haklits, Georgia | 80 ft 2 in | Libor Charfreitag, SMU | 78 ft 9¾ in* |

### WOMEN

| | Champion | Time/Mark | Runner-Up | Time/Mark |
|---|---|---|---|---|
| 60-meter dash | Monique Tubbs, Jacksonville | 7.29 | Shavonda Benjamin, Florida | 7.31 |
| 60-meter hurdles | Donica Merriman, Ohio St | 7.95 | Perdita Felicien, Illinois | 8.00 |
| 200-meter dash | Cydonie Mothersill, Clemson | 22.89 | Rachelle Boone, Indiana | 23.33 |
| 400-meter dash | Demetria Washington, S Carolina | 52.37 | Lesley Owusu, Nebraska | 52.49 |
| 800-meter run | Svetlana Badrankova, UTEP | 2:06.58 | Alice Schmidt, N Carolina | 2:08.47 |
| Mile run | Tracy Robertson, Arkansas | 4:39.10 | Lesley Higgins, Colorado | 4:42.36 |
| 3,000-meter run | Shannon Smith, Boston College | 9:11.25 | Ann Marie Brooks, Missouri | 9:12.43 |
| 5,000-meter run | Jodie Hughes, Colorado | 16:08.61 | Tara Chaplin, Arizona | 16:13.58 |
| High jump | Kart Siilats, Harvard | 6 ft ¾ in | Mary Varga, Akron | 6 ft |
| Pole vault | Thorey Elisdottir, Georgia | 14 ft 9½ in* | Tracy O'Hara, UCLA | 13 ft 9¼ in |
| Long jump | Jenny Adams, Houston | 21 ft 11 in | Elisha Williams, Mississippi St | 21 ft 7½ in |
| Triple jump | Gi-Gi Miller, Arkansas | 44 ft 4 in | Deana Simmons, UCLA | 44 ft 2½ in |
| Shot put | Christina Tolson, UCLA | 55 ft 9¾ in | Jamine Moton, Clemson | 53 ft 8½ in |
| 20-pound wt throw | Florence Ezeh, SMU | 69 ft 10¼ in | Christina Tolson, UCLA | 68 ft 9¾ in |

*NCAA record.

## Rifle

| | Champion | Pts | Runner-Up | Pts |
|---|---|---|---|---|
| Smallbore | Matthew Emmons, AK–Fairbanks | 1178 | Per Sandberg, AK–Fairbanks | 1177 |
| Air rifle | Matthew Emmons, AK–Fairbanks | 392 | Amanda Trujillo, Nebraska | 392 |

## Spring 2001
### Golf

#### MEN

| Champion | Score | Runner-Up | Score |
|---|---|---|---|
| Nick Gilliam, Florida | 276 | Camilo Benedetti, Florida | 279 |

#### WOMEN

| | | | |
|---|---|---|---|
| Candy Hannemann, Duke | 285 | Lorena Ochoa, Arizona | 285 |

### Outdoor Track and Field

#### MEN

| | Champion | Mark | Runner-Up | Mark |
|---|---|---|---|---|
| 100-meter dash | Justin Gatlin, Tennessee | 10.08 | Kim Collins, Texas Christian | 10.13 |
| 200-meter dash | Justin Gatlin, Tennessee | 20.11 | Caimin Douglas, Texas–El Paso | 20.56 |
| 400-meter dash | Avard Moncur, Auburn | 44.84 | Alleyne Francique, Louisiana St | 45.36 |
| 800-meter run | Otukile Lekote, S Carolina | 1:46.68 | Bryce Knight, Idaho St | 1:47.22 |
| 1,500-meter run | Bryan Berryhill, Colorado St | 3:37.05 | Gabe Jennings, Stanford | 3:37.56 |
| 5,000-meter run | Jonathon Riley, Stanford | 13:42.51 | Bolota Asmeron, California | 13:43.13 |
| 10,000-meter run | Ryan Shay, Notre Dame | 29:05.44 | Murray Link, Arkansas | 29:25.75 |
| 110-meter hurdles | Ron Bramlett, Alabama | 13.54 | Bashir Ramzy, Texas A&M | 13.70 |
| 400-meter hurdles | Bayano Kamani, Baylor | 48.99 | Michael Smith, Baylor | 49.34 |
| 3,000-m steeplechase | Daniel Lincoln, Arkansas | 8:42.31 | Jeremy Tolman, Weber St | 8:42.85 |
| High jump | Charles Clinger, Weber St | 7 ft 6½ in | Dave Hoffman, Utah St | 7 ft 6½ in |
| Pole vault | Dennis Kholev, Southern Cal | 18 ft 6½ in | Jeff Hansen, Brigham Young | 18 ft 2½ in |
| Long jump | Savante Stringfellow, Mississippi | 27 ft 1¾ in | Walter Davis, Louisiana St | 26 ft 10½ in |
| Triple jump | Walter Davis, Louisiana St | 54 ft 4 in | Chris Hercules, Texas | 54 ft 2¾ in |
| Shot put | Janus Robberts, SMU | 72 ft 1 in | Joachim Olsen, Idaho | 67 ft ½ in |
| Discus throw | Tolga Koseoglu, Texas A&M | 204 ft 10 in | Gabor Mate, Auburn | 199 ft 8 in |
| Hammer throw | Andras Haklits, Georgia | 247 ft 8 in | James Parker, Utah St | 240 ft 7 in |
| Javelin throw | John Stiegeler, Oregon | 252 ft 10 in | Vesa Jappinen, Texas–El Paso | 239 ft 7 in |
| Decathlon | Santiago Lorenzo, Oregon | 7889 pts | Stephen Harris, Tennessee | 7871 pts |

#### WOMEN

| | Champion | Mark | Runner-Up | Mark |
|---|---|---|---|---|
| 100-meter dash | Angela Williams, Southern Cal | 11.05 | Shakedia Jones, UCLA | 11.10 |
| 200-meter dash | Brianna Glenn, Arizona | 22.92 | Muna Lee, Louisiana St | 23.05 |
| 400-meter dash | Allison Beckford, Rice | 52.33 | Demetria Washington, S Carolina | 52.42 |
| 800-meter run | Brigita Langerholc, Southern Cal | 2:05.69 | Mary Jayne Harrelson, App St | 2:03.10 |
| 1,500-meter run | Mary Jayne Harrelson, App St | 4:14.30 | Sally Glynn, Stanford | 4:15.89 |
| 5,000-meter run | Lauren Fleshman, Stanford | 15:52.21 | Melissa Gulli, Texas A&M | 15:55.64 |
| 10,000-meter run | Amy Yoder-Begley, Arkansas | 33:59.96 | Sara Day, Wake Forest | 34:06.53 |
| 100-meter hurdles | Donica Merriman, Ohio St | 12.73 | Danielle Carruthers, Indiana | 12.96 |
| 400-meter hurdles | Brenda Taylor, Harvard | 55.88 | Allison Beckford, Rice | 56.22 |
| 3,000-m steeplechase | Elizabeth Jackson, BYU | 9:49.73# | Rebecca Bennion, Weber St | 9:54.84 |
| High jump | Dora Gyorffy, Harvard | 6 ft 2¾ in | Tamika Toppin, Connecticut | 6 ft ½ in |
| Pole vault | Andrea Dutoit, Arizona | 13 ft 9¼ in | Tracy O'Hara, UCLA | 13 ft 9¼ in |
| Long jump | Brianna Glenn, Arizona | 21 ft 6¼ in | Alice Falaiye, Rice | 21 ft 1¼ in |
| Triple jump | Shelly-Ann Gallimore, Auburn | 43 ft 7¼ in | Gi-Gi Miller, Arkansas | 43 ft 1¾ in |
| Shot put | Christina Tolson, UCLA | 57 ft ¾ in | Jamine Moton, Clemson | 56 ft 4¾ in |
| Discus throw | Katja Schreiber, Idaho | 197 ft 11 in | Liz Toman, Colorado St | 184 ft 5 in |
| Hammer throw | Florence Ezeh, SMU | 219 ft 4 in | Christina Tolson, UCLA | 215 ft |
| Javelin throw | Inga Stasiulionyte, Southern Cal | 172 ft 4 in | Andrea Bulat, Kansas | 168 ft 4 in |
| Heptathlon | Austria Skujyte, Kansas St | 5857 pts | Michelle Perry, UCLA | 5759 pts |

# American record.

### Tennis

#### MEN

| | Champion | Score | Runner-Up |
|---|---|---|---|
| Singles | Matias Boeker, Georgia | 6–2, 6–4 | Brian Vahaly, Virginia |
| Doubles | Matias Boeker & Travis Parrott, Georgia | 6–4, 7–5 | Johan Brunstrom & Jon Wallmark, Southern Methodist |

#### WOMEN

| | Champion | Score | Runner-Up |
|---|---|---|---|
| Singles | Laura Granville, Stanford | 6–3, 7–6 | Lauren Kalvaria, Stanford |
| Doubles | Whitney Laiho & Jessica Lehnhoff, Florida | 4–6, 6–1, 6–3 | Laura Granville & Gabriela Lastra, Stanford |

## CHAMPIONSHIP RESULTS

### Baseball

#### DIVISION I

| Year | Champion | Coach | Score | Runner-Up | Most Outstanding Player |
|------|----------|-------|-------|-----------|-------------------------|
| 1947 | California* | Clint Evans | 8–7 | Yale | No award |
| 1948 | Southern Cal | Sam Barry | 9–2 | Yale | No award |
| 1949 | Texas* | Bibb Falk | 10–3 | Wake Forest | Charles Teague, Wake Forest, 2B |
| 1950 | Texas | Bibb Falk | 3–0 | Washington St | Ray VanCleef, Rutgers, CF |
| 1951 | Oklahoma* | Jack Baer | 3–2 | Tennessee | Sidney Hatfield, Tennessee, P-1B |
| 1952 | Holy Cross | Jack Barry | 8–4 | Missouri | James O'Neill, Holy Cross, P |
| 1953 | Michigan | Ray Fisher | 7–5 | Texas | J.L. Smith, Texas, P |
| 1954 | Missouri | John (Hi) Simmons | 4–1 | Rollins | Tom Yewcic, Michigan St, C |
| 1955 | Wake Forest | Taylor Sanford | 7–6 | Western Michigan | Tom Borland, Oklahoma St, P |
| 1956 | Minnesota | Dick Siebert | 12–1 | Arizona | Jerry Thomas, Minnesota, P |
| 1957 | California* | George Wolfman | 1–0 | Penn St | Cal Emery, Penn St, P-1B |
| 1958 | Southern Cal | Rod Dedeaux | 8–7† | Missouri | Bill Thom, Southern Cal, P |
| 1959 | Oklahoma St | Toby Greene | 5–3 | Arizona | Jim Dobson, Oklahoma St, 3B |
| 1960 | Minnesota | Dick Siebert | 2–1‡ | Southern Cal | John Erickson, Minnesota, 2B |
| 1961 | Southern Cal* | Rod Dedeaux | 1–0 | Oklahoma St | Littleton Fowler, Oklahoma St, P |
| 1962 | Michigan | Don Lund | 5–4 | Santa Clara | Bob Garibaldi, Santa Clara, P |
| 1963 | Southern Cal | Rod Dedeaux | 5–2 | Arizona | Bud Hollowell, Southern Cal, C |
| 1964 | Minnesota | Dick Siebert | 5–1 | Missouri | Joe Ferris, Maine, P |
| 1965 | Arizona St | Bobby Winkles | 2–1# | Ohio St | Sal Bando, Arizona St, 3B |
| 1966 | Ohio St | Marty Karow | 8–2 | Oklahoma St | Steve Arlin, Ohio St, P |
| 1967 | Arizona St | Bobby Winkles | 11–2 | Houston | Ron Davini, Arizona St, C |
| 1968 | Southern Cal* | Rod Dedeaux | 4–3 | Southern Illinois | Bill Seinsoth, Southern Cal, 1B |
| 1969 | Arizona St | Bobby Winkles | 10–1 | Tulsa | John Dolinsek, Arizona St, LF |
| 1970 | Southern Cal | Rod Dedeaux | 2–1 | Florida St | Gene Ammann, Florida St, P |
| 1971 | Southern Cal | Rod Dedeaux | 7–2 | Southern Illinois | Jerry Tabb, Tulsa, 1B |
| 1972 | Southern Cal | Rod Dedeaux | 1–0 | Arizona St | Russ McQueen, Southern Cal, P |
| 1973 | Southern Cal* | Rod Dedeaux | 4–3 | Arizona St | Dave Winfield, Minnesota, P-OF |
| 1974 | Southern Cal | Rod Dedeaux | 7–3 | Miami (FL) | George Milke, Southern Cal, P |
| 1975 | Texas | Cliff Gustafson | 5–1 | S Carolina | Mickey Reichenbach, Texas, 1B |
| 1976 | Arizona | Jerry Kindall | 7–1 | Eastern Michigan | Steve Powers, Arizona, P-DH |
| 1977 | Arizona St | Jim Brock | 2–1 | S Carolina | Bob Horner, Arizona St, 3B |
| 1978 | Southern Cal* | Rod Dedeaux | 10–3 | Arizona St | Rod Boxberger, Southern Cal, P |
| 1979 | Cal St–Fullerton | Augie Garrido | 2–1 | Arkansas | Tony Hudson, Cal St–Fullerton, P |
| 1980 | Arizona | Jerry Kindall | 5–3 | Hawaii | Terry Francona, Arizona, LF |
| 1981 | Arizona St | Jim Brock | 7–4 | Oklahoma St | Stan Holmes, Arizona St, LF |
| 1982 | Miami (FL)* | Ron Fraser | 9–3 | Wichita St | Dan Smith, Miami (FL), P |
| 1983 | Texas* | Cliff Gustafson | 4–3 | Alabama | Calvin Schiraldi, Texas, P |
| 1984 | Cal St–Fullerton | Augie Garrido | 3–1 | Texas | John Fishel, Cal St–Fullerton, LF |
| 1985 | Miami (FL) | Ron Fraser | 10–6 | Texas | Greg Ellena, Miami (FL), DH |
| 1986 | Arizona | Jerry Kindall | 10–2 | Florida St | Mike Senne, Arizona, LF |
| 1987 | Stanford | Mark Marquess | 9–5 | Oklahoma St | Paul Carey, Stanford, RF |
| 1988 | Stanford | Mark Marquess | 9–4 | Arizona St | Lee Plemel, Stanford, P |
| 1989 | Wichita St | Gene Stephenson | 5–3 | Texas | Greg Brummett, Wichita St, P |
| 1990 | Georgia | Steve Webber | 2–1 | Oklahoma St | Mike Rebhan, Georgia, P |
| 1991 | Louisiana St | Skip Bertman | 6–3 | Wichita St | Gary Hymel, Louisiana St, C |
| 1992 | Pepperdine | Andy Lopez | 3–2 | Cal St–Fullerton | Phil Nevin, Cal St–Fullerton, 3B |
| 1993 | Louisiana St | Skip Bertman | 8–0 | Wichita St | Todd Walker, Louisiana St, 2B |
| 1994 | Oklahoma | Larry Cochell | 13–5 | Georgia Tech | Chip Glass, Oklahoma, CF |
| 1995 | Cal St–Fullerton* | Augie Garrido | 11–5 | Southern Cal | Mark Kotsay, Cal St–Fullerton, CF-P |
| 1996 | Louisiana St | Skip Bertman | 9–8 | Miami (FL) | Pat Burrell, Miami (FL), 3B |
| 1997 | Louisiana St* | Skip Bertman | 13–6 | Alabama | Brandon Larson, Louisiana St, SS |
| 1998 | Southern Cal | Mike Gillespie | 21–14 | Arizona St | Wes Rachels, Southern Cal, 2B |
| 1999 | Miami (FL) | Jim Morris | 6–5 | Florida St | Marshall McDougall, FSU 3B/2B |
| 2000 | Louisiana St* | Skip Bertman | 6–5 | Stanford | Trey Hodges, Louisiana St, P |
| 2001 | Miami (FL)* | Jim Morris | 12–1 | Stanford | Charlton Jimerson, Miami (FL) OF |

*Undefeated teams in College World Series play. †12 innings. ‡10 innings. #15 innings.

#### DIVISION II

| Year | Champion | Year | Champion | Year | Champion |
|------|----------|------|----------|------|----------|
| 1968 | Chapman* | 1972 | Florida Southern | 1976 | Cal Poly–Pomona |
| 1969 | Illinois St* | 1973 | UC–Irvine* | 1977 | UC–Riverside |
| 1970 | Cal St–Northridge | 1974 | UC–Irvine | 1978 | Florida Southern |
| 1971 | Florida Southern | 1975 | Florida Southern | 1979 | Valdosta St |

## DIVISION II (Cont.)

| Year | Champion | Year | Champion | Year | Champion |
|------|----------|------|----------|------|----------|
| 1980 | Cal Poly–Pomona* | 1988 | Florida Southern* | 1996 | Kennesaw St* |
| 1981 | Florida Southern* | 1989 | Cal Poly–SLO | 1997 | Cal St–Chico* |
| 1982 | UC–Riverside* | 1990 | Jacksonville St | 1998 | Tampa* |
| 1983 | Cal Poly–Pomona* | 1991 | Jacksonville St | 1999 | Cal St–Chico |
| 1984 | Cal St–Northridge | 1992 | Tampa* | 2000 | SE Oklahoma St |
| 1985 | Florida Southern* | 1993 | Tampa | 2001 | St. Mary's (TX) |
| 1986 | Troy St | 1994 | Central Missouri St | | |
| 1987 | Troy St* | 1995 | Florida Southern* | | |

## DIVISION III

| Year | Champion | Year | Champion | Year | Champion |
|------|----------|------|----------|------|----------|
| 1976 | Cal St–Stanislaus | 1985 | WI–Oshkosh | 1994 | WI–Oshkosh |
| 1977 | Cal St–Stanislaus | 1986 | Marietta | 1995 | La Verne |
| 1978 | Glassboro St | 1987 | Montclair St | 1996 | William Paterson |
| 1979 | Glassboro St | 1988 | Ithaca | 1997 | Southern Maine |
| 1980 | Ithaca | 1989 | NC Wesleyan | 1998 | Eastern Connecticut St |
| 1981 | Marietta | 1990 | Eastern Connecticut St | 1999 | N Carolina Wesleyan |
| 1982 | Eastern Connecticut St | 1991 | Southern Maine | 2000 | Montclair St |
| 1983 | Marietta | 1992 | William Paterson | 2001 | St. Thomas (MN) |
| 1984 | Ramapo | 1993 | Montclair St | | |

*Undefeated teams in final series.

# Cross-Country

## Men

### DIVISION I

| Year | Champion | Coach | Pts | Runner-Up | Pts | Individual Champion | Time |
|------|----------|-------|-----|-----------|-----|---------------------|------|
| 1938 | Indiana | Earle Hayes | 51 | Notre Dame | 61 | Greg Rice, Notre Dame | 20:12.9 |
| 1939 | Michigan St | Lauren Brown | 54 | Wisconsin | 57 | Walter Mehl, Wisconsin | 20:30.9 |
| 1940 | Indiana | Earle Hayes | 65 | Eastern Michigan | 68 | Gilbert Dodds, Ashland | 20:30.2 |
| 1941 | Rhode Island | Fred Tootell | 83 | Penn St | 110 | Fred Wilt, Indiana | 20:30.1 |
| 1942 | Indiana | Earle Hayes | 57 | | | Oliver Hunter, Notre Dame | 20:18.0 |
| | Penn St | Charles Werner | 57 | | | | |
| 1943 | No meet | | | | | | |
| 1944 | Drake | Bill Easton | 25 | Notre Dame | 64 | Fred Feiler, Drake | 21:04.2 |
| 1945 | Drake | Bill Easton | 50 | Notre Dame | 65 | Fred Feiler, Drake | 21:14.2 |
| 1946 | Drake | Bill Easton | 42 | NYU | 98 | Quentin Brelsford, Ohio Wesleyan | 20:22.9 |
| 1947 | Penn St | Charles Werner | 60 | Syracuse | 72 | Jack Milne, N Carolina | 20:41.1 |
| 1948 | Michigan St | Karl Schlademan | 41 | Wisconsin | 69 | Robert Black, Rhode Island | 19:52.3 |
| 1949 | Michigan St | Karl Schlademan | 59 | Syracuse | 81 | Robert Black, Rhode Island | 20:25.7 |
| 1950 | Penn St | Charles Werner | 53 | Michigan St | 55 | Herb Semper Jr, Kansas | 20:31.7 |
| 1951 | Syracuse | Robert Grieve | 80 | Kansas | 118 | Herb Semper Jr, Kansas | 20:09.5 |
| 1952 | Michigan St | Karl Schlademan | 65 | Indiana | 68 | Charles Capozzoli, Georgetown | 19:36.7 |
| 1953 | Kansas | Bill Easton | 70 | Indiana | 82 | Wes Santee, Kansas | 19:43.5 |
| 1954 | Oklahoma St | Ralph Higgins | 61 | Syracuse | 118 | Allen Frame, Kansas | 19:54.2 |
| 1955 | Michigan St | Karl Schlademan | 46 | Kansas | 68 | Charles Jones, Iowa | 19:57.4 |
| 1956 | Michigan St | Karl Schlademan | 28 | Kansas | 88 | Walter McNew, Texas | 19:55.7 |
| 1957 | Notre Dame | Alex Wilson | 121 | Michigan St | 127 | Max Truex, Southern Cal | 19:12.3 |
| 1958 | Michigan St | Francis Dittrich | 79 | Western Michigan | 104 | Crawford Kennedy, Michigan State | 20:07.1 |
| 1959 | Michigan St | Francis Dittrich | 44 | Houston | 120 | Al Lawrence, Houston | 20:35.7 |
| 1960 | Houston | John Morriss | 54 | Michigan St | 80 | Al Lawrence, Houston | 19:28.2 |
| 1961 | Oregon St | Sam Bell | 68 | San Jose St | 82 | Dale Story, Oregon St | 19:46.6 |
| 1962 | San Jose St | Dean Miller | 58 | Villanova | 69 | Tom O'Hara, Loyola (IL) | 19:20.3 |
| 1963 | San Jose St | Dean Miller | 53 | Oregon | 68 | Victor Zwolak, Villanova | 19:35.0 |
| 1964 | W Michigan | George Dales | 86 | Oregon | 116 | Elmore Banton, Ohio | 20:07.5 |
| 1965 | W Michigan | George Dales | 81 | Northwestern | 114 | John Lawson, Kansas | 29:24.0 |
| 1966 | Villanova | James Elliott | 79 | Kansas St | 155 | Gerry Lindgren, Washington St | 29:01.4 |
| 1967 | Villanova | James Elliott | 91 | Air Force | 96 | Gerry Lindgren, Washington St | 30:45.6 |
| 1968 | Villanova | James Elliott | 78 | Stanford | 100 | Michael Ryan, Air Force | 29:16.8 |
| 1969 | UTEP | Wayne Vandenburg | 74 | Villanova | 88 | Gerry Lindgren, Wash St | 28:59.2 |

## Men *(Cont.)*

### DIVISION I *(Cont.)*

| Year | Champion | Coach | Pts | Runner-Up | Pts | Individual Champion | Time |
|------|----------|-------|-----|-----------|-----|---------------------|------|
| 1970 | Villanova | James Elliott | 85 | Oregon | 86 | Steve Prefontaine, Oregon | 28:00.2 |
| 1971 | Oregon | Bill Dellinger | 83 | Washington St | 122 | Steve Prefontaine, Oregon | 29:14.0 |
| 1972 | Tennessee | Stan Huntsman | 134 | E Tennessee St | 148 | Neil Cusack, E Tenn St | 28:23.0 |
| 1973 | Oregon | Bill Dellinger | 89 | UTEP | 157 | Steve Prefontaine, Oregon | 28:14.0 |
| 1974 | Oregon | Bill Dellinger | 77 | Western Kentucky | 110 | Nick Rose, Western Ky | 29:22.0 |
| 1975 | UTEP | Ted Banks | 88 | Washington St | 92 | Craig Virgin, Illinois | 28:23.3 |
| 1976 | UTEP | Ted Banks | 62 | Oregon | 117 | Henry Rono, Washington St | 28:06.6 |
| 1977 | Oregon | Bill Dellinger | 100 | UTEP | 105 | Henry Rono, Washington St | 28:33.5 |
| 1978 | UTEP | Ted Banks | 56 | Oregon | 72 | Alberto Salazar, Oregon | 29:29.7 |
| 1979 | UTEP | Ted Banks | 86 | Oregon | 93 | Henry Rono, Washington St | 28:19.6 |
| 1980 | UTEP | Ted Banks | 58 | Arkansas | 152 | Suleiman Nyambui, UTEP | 29:04.0 |
| 1981 | UTEP | Ted Banks | 17 | Providence | 109 | Mathews Motshwarateu,UTEP | 28:45.6 |
| 1982 | Wisconsin | Dan McClimon | 59 | Providence | 138 | Mark Scrutton, Colorado | 30:12.6 |
| 1983 | Vacated | | | Wisconsin | 164 | Zakarie Barie, UTEP | 29:20.0 |
| 1984 | Arkansas | John McDonnell | 101 | Arizona | 111 | Ed Eyestone, Brigham Young | 29:28.8 |
| 1985 | Wisconsin | Martin Smith | 67 | Arkansas | 104 | Timothy Hacker, Wisconsin | 29:17.88 |
| 1986 | Arkansas | John McDonnell | 69 | Dartmouth | 141 | Aaron Ramirez, Arizona | 30:27.53 |
| 1987 | Arkansas | John McDonnell | 87 | Dartmouth | 119 | Joe Falcon, Arkansas | 29:14.97 |
| 1988 | Wisconsin | Martin Smith | 105 | Northern Arizona | 160 | Robert Kennedy, Indiana | 29:20.0 |
| 1989 | Iowa St | Bill Bergan | 54 | Oregon | 72 | John Nuttall, Iowa St | 29:30.55 |
| 1990 | Arkansas | John McDonnell | 68 | Iowa St | 96 | Jonah Koech, Iowa St | 29:05.0 |
| 1991 | Arkansas | John McDonnell | 52 | Iowa St | 114 | Sean Dollman, Western Ky | 30:17.1 |
| 1992 | Arkansas | John McDonnell | 46 | Wisconsin | 87 | Bob Kennedy, Indiana | 30:15.3 |
| 1993 | Arkansas | John McDonnell | 31 | Brigham Young | 153 | Josephat Kapkory, Wash St | 29:32.4 |
| 1994 | Iowa St | Bill Bergan | 65 | Colorado | 88 | Martin Keino, Arizona | 30:08.7 |
| 1995 | Arkansas | John McDonnell | 100 | Northern Arizona | 142 | Godfrey Siamusiye, Arkansas | 30:09 |
| 1996 | Stanford | Vin Lananna | 46 | Arkansas | 74 | Godfrey Siamusiye, Arkansas | 29:49 |
| 1997 | Stanford | Vin Lananna | 53 | Arkansas | 56 | Mebrahtom Keflezighi, UCLA | 28:54 |
| 1998 | Arkansas | John McDonnell | 97 | Stanford | 114 | Adam Goucher, Colorado | 29:26 |
| 1999 | Arkansas | John McDonnell | 58 | Wisconsin | 185 | David Kimani, S Alabama | 30:06.6 |
| 2000 | Arkansas | John McDonnell | 83 | Colorado | 94 | Keith Kelly, Providence | 30:14.5 |

### DIVISION II

| Year | Champion | Year | Champion | Year | Champion |
|------|----------|------|----------|------|----------|
| 1958 | Northern Illinois | 1973 | S Dakota St | 1988 | Edinboro/ Mankato St |
| 1959 | S Dakota St | 1974 | SW Missouri St | 1989 | S Dakota St |
| 1960 | Central St (OH) | 1975 | UC–Irvine | 1990 | Edinboro |
| 1961 | Southern Illinois | 1976 | UC–Irvine | 1991 | MA–Lowell |
| 1962 | Central St (OH) | 1977 | Eastern Illinois | 1992 | Adams St |
| 1963 | Emporia St | 1978 | Cal Poly–SLO | 1993 | Adams St |
| 1964 | Kentucky St | 1979 | Cal Poly–SLO | 1994 | Adams St |
| 1965 | San Diego St | 1980 | Humboldt St | 1995 | Western St |
| 1966 | San Diego St | 1981 | Millersville | 1996 | S Dakota St |
| 1967 | San Diego St | 1982 | Eastern Washington | 1997 | S Dakota |
| 1968 | Eastern Illinois | 1983 | Cal Poly–Pomona | 1998 | Adams St |
| 1969 | Eastern Illinois | 1984 | SE Missouri St | 1999 | Western St |
| 1970 | Eastern Michigan | 1985 | S Dakota St | 2000 | Western St |
| 1971 | Cal St–Fullerton | 1986 | Edinboro | | |
| 1972 | N Dakota St | 1987 | Edinboro | | |

### DIVISION III

| Year | Champion | Year | Champion | Year | Champion |
|------|----------|------|----------|------|----------|
| 1973 | Ashland | 1983 | Brandeis | 1993 | N Central |
| 1974 | Mount Union | 1984 | St. Thomas (MN) | 1994 | Williams |
| 1975 | North Central | 1985 | Luther | 1995 | Williams |
| 1976 | North Central | 1986 | St. Thomas (MN) | 1996 | WI–La Crosse |
| 1977 | Occidental | 1987 | N Central | 1997 | N Central |
| 1978 | N Central | 1988 | WI–Oshkosh | 1998 | N Central |
| 1979 | N Central | 1989 | WI–Oshkosh | 1999 | N Central |
| 1980 | Carleton | 1990 | WI–Oshkosh | 2000 | Calvin |
| 1981 | N Central | 1991 | Rochester | | |
| 1982 | N Central | 1992 | N Central | | |

## Women
### DIVISION I

| Year | Champion | Coach | Pts | Runner-Up | Pts | Individual Champion | Time |
|---|---|---|---|---|---|---|---|
| 1981 | Virginia | John Vasvary | 36 | Oregon | 83 | Betty Springs, N Carolina St | 16:19.0 |
| 1982 | Virginia | Martin Smith | 48 | Stanford | 91 | Lesley Welch, Virginia | 16:39.7 |
| 1983 | Oregon | Tom Heinonen | 95 | Stanford | 98 | Betty Springs, N Carolina St | 16:30.7 |
| 1984 | Wisconsin | Peter Tegen | 63 | Stanford | 89 | Cathy Branta, Wisconsin | 16:15.6 |
| 1985 | Wisconsin | Peter Tegen | 58 | Iowa St | 98 | Suzie Tuffey, N Carolina St | 16:22.5 |
| 1986 | Texas | Terry Crawford | 62 | Wisconsin | 64 | Angela Chalmers, N Arizona | 16:55.49 |
| 1987 | Oregon | Tom Heinonen | 97 | N Carolina St | 99 | Kimberly Betz, Indiana | 16:10.85 |
| 1988 | Kentucky | Don Weber | 75 | Oregon | 128 | Michelle Dekkers, Indiana | 16:30.0 |
| 1989 | Villanova | Marty Stern | 99 | Kentucky | 168 | Vicki Huber, Villanova | 15:59.86 |
| 1990 | Villanova | Marty Stern | 82 | Providence | 172 | Sonia O'Sullivan, Villanova | 16:06.0 |
| 1991 | Villanova | Marty Stern | 85 | Arkansas | 168 | Sonia O'Sullivan, Villanova | 16:30.3 |
| 1992 | Villanova | Marty Stern | 123 | Arkansas | 130 | Carole Zajac, Villanova | 17:01.9 |
| 1993 | Villanova | Marty Stern | 66 | Arkansas | 71 | Carole Zajac, Villanova | 16:40.3 |
| 1994 | Villanova | John Marshall | 75 | Michigan | 108 | Jennifer Rhines, Villanova | 16:31.2 |
| 1995 | Providence | Ray Treacy | 88 | Colorado | 123 | Kathy Butler, Wisconsin | 16:51 |
| 1996 | Stanford | Beth Alford-Sullivan | 101 | Villanova | 106 | Amy Skieresz, Arizona | 17:04 |
| 1997 | BYU | Patrick Shane | 100 | Stanford | 102 | Carrie Tollefson, Villanova | 16:58 |
| 1998 | Villanova | Marcus O'Sullivan | 106 | BYU | 110 | Katie McGregor, Michigan | 16:47.21 |
| 1999 | BYU | Patrick Shane | 72 | Arkansas | 125 | Erica Palmer, Wisconsin | 16:39.50 |
| 2000 | Colorado | Mark Wetmore | 117 | Brigham Young | 167 | Kara Grgas-Wheeler, Colorado | 20:30.5 |

### DIVISION II

| Year | Champion | Year | Champion | Year | Champion |
|---|---|---|---|---|---|
| 1981 | S Dakota St | 1988 | Cal Poly–SLO | 1995 | Adams St |
| 1982 | Cal Poly–SLO | 1989 | Cal Poly–SLO | 1996 | Adams St |
| 1983 | Cal Poly–SLO | 1990 | Cal Poly–SLO | 1997 | Adams St |
| 1984 | Villanova | 1991 | Cal Poly–SLO | 1998 | Adams St |
| 1985 | Cal Poly–SLO | 1992 | Adams St | 1999 | Adams St |
| 1986 | Cal Poly–SLO | 1993 | Adams St | 2000 | Western St |
| 1987 | Cal Poly–SLO | 1994 | Adams St | | |

### DIVISION III

| Year | Champion | Year | Champion | Year | Champion |
|---|---|---|---|---|---|
| 1981 | Central (IA) | 1988 | WI–Oshkosh | 1996 | WI–Oshkosh |
| 1982 | St. Thomas (MN) | 1989 | Cortland St | 1997 | Cortland St |
| 1983 | WI–La Crosse | 1990 | Cortland St | 1998 | Calvin |
| 1984 | St. Thomas (MN) | 1991 | WI–Oshkosh | 1999 | Calvin |
| 1985 | Franklin & Marshall | 1992 | Cortland St | 2000 | Middlebury |
| 1986 | St. Thomas (MN) | 1993 | Cortland St | | |
| 1987 | St. Thomas (MN)/ WI–Oshkosh | 1994 | Cortland St | | |
| | | 1995 | Cortland St | | |

# Fencing

## Men's and Women's Combined
### TEAM CHAMPIONS

| Year | Champion | Coach | Pts | Runner-Up | Pts |
|---|---|---|---|---|---|
| 1990 | Penn St | Emmanuil Kaidanov | 36 | Columbia–Barnard | 35 |
| 1991 | Penn St | Emmanuil Kaidanov | 4700 | Columbia–Barnard | 4200 |
| 1992 | Columbia–Barnard | G. Kolombatovich/A. Kogler | 4150 | Penn St | 3646 |
| 1993 | Columbia–Barnard | G. Kolombatovich/A. Kogler | 4525 | Penn St | 4500 |
| 1994 | Notre Dame | Michael DeCicco | 4350 | Penn St | 4075 |
| 1995 | Penn St | Emmanuil Kaidanov | 440 | St. John's (NY) | 413 |
| 1996 | Penn St | Emmanuil Kaidanov | 1500 | Notre Dame | 1190 |
| 1997 | Penn St | Emmanuil Kaidanov | 1530 | Notre Dame | 1470 |
| 1998 | Penn St | Emmanuil Kaidanov | 149 | Notre Dame | 147 |
| 1999 | Penn St | Emmanuil Kaidanov | 171 | Notre Dame | 139 |
| 2000 | Penn St | Emmanuil Kaidanov | 175 | Notre Dame | 171 |
| 2001 | St. John's (NY) | Yuri Gelman | 180 | Penn St | 172 |

## Men
### TEAM CHAMPIONS

| Year | Champion | Coach | Pts | Runner-Up | Pts |
|---|---|---|---|---|---|
| 1941 | Northwestern | Henry Zettleman | 28½ | Illinois | 27 |
| 1942 | Ohio St | Frank Riebel | 34 | St. John's (NY) | 33½ |
| 1943–46 | No tournament | | | | |

## Men (Cont.)

### TEAM CHAMPIONS (Cont.)

| Year | Champion | Coach | Pts | Runner-Up | Pts |
|------|----------|-------|-----|-----------|-----|
| 1947 | NYU | Martinez Castello | 72 | Chicago | 50½ |
| 1948 | CCNY | James Montague | 30 | Navy | 28 |
| 1949 | Army/Rutgers | S. Velarde/D. Cetrulo | 63 | | |
| 1950 | Navy | Joseph Fiems | 67½ | NYU/Rutgers | 66½ |
| 1951 | Columbia | Servando Velarde | 69 | Pennsylvania | 64 |
| 1952 | Columbia | Servando Velarde | 71 | NYU | 69 |
| 1953 | Pennsylvania | Lajos Csiszar | 94 | Navy | 86 |
| 1954 | Columbia | Irving DeKoff | 61 | | |
| | NYU | Hugo Castello | 61 | | |
| 1955 | Columbia | Irving DeKoff | 62 | Cornell | 57 |
| 1956 | Illinois | Maxwell Garret | 90 | Columbia | 88 |
| 1957 | NYU | Hugo Castello | 65 | Columbia | 64 |
| 1958 | Illinois | Maxwell Garret | 47 | Columbia | 43 |
| 1959 | Navy | Andre Deladrier | 72 | NYU | 65 |
| 1960 | NYU | Hugo Castello | 65 | Navy | 57 |
| 1961 | NYU | Hugo Castello | 79 | Princeton | 68 |
| 1962 | Navy | Andre Deladrier | 76 | NYU | 74 |
| 1963 | Columbia | Irving DeKoff | 55 | Navy | 50 |
| 1964 | Princeton | Stan Sieja | 81 | NYU | 79 |
| 1965 | Columbia | Irving DeKoff | 76 | NYU | 74 |
| 1966 | NYU | Hugo Castello | 5–0 | Army | 5–2 |
| 1967 | NYU | Hugo Castello | 72 | Pennsylvania | 64 |
| 1968 | Columbia | Louis Bankuti | 92 | NYU | 87 |
| 1969 | Pennsylvania | Lajos Csiszar | 54 | Harvard | 43 |
| 1970 | NYU | Hugo Castello | 71 | Columbia | 63 |
| 1971 | NYU/Columbia | Hugo Castello/Louis Bankuti | 68 | | |
| 1972 | Detroit | Richard Perry | 73 | NYU | 70 |
| 1973 | NYU | Hugo Castello | 76 | Pennsylvania | 71 |
| 1974 | NYU | Hugo Castello | 92 | Wayne St (MI) | 87 |
| 1975 | Wayne St (MI) | Istvan Danosi | 89 | Cornell | 83 |
| 1976 | NYU | Herbert Cohen | 79 | Wayne St (MI) | 77 |
| 1977 | Notre Dame | Michael DeCicco | 114* | NYU | 114 |
| 1978 | Notre Dame | Michael DeCicco | 121 | Pennsylvania | 110 |
| 1979 | Wayne St (MI) | Istvan Danosi | 119 | Notre Dame | 108 |
| 1980 | Wayne St (MI) | Istvan Danosi | 111 | Pennsylvania/MIT | 106 |
| 1981 | Pennsylvania | Dave Micahnik | 113 | Wayne St (MI) | 111 |
| 1982 | Wayne St (MI) | Istvan Danosi | 85 | Clemson | 77 |
| 1983 | Wayne St (MI) | Aladar Kogler | 86 | Notre Dame | 80 |
| 1984 | Wayne St (MI) | Gil Pezza | 69 | Penn St | 50 |
| 1985 | Wayne St (MI) | Gil Pezza | 141 | Notre Dame | 140 |
| 1986 | Notre Dame | Michael DeCicco | 151 | Columbia | 141 |
| 1987 | Columbia | George Kolombatovich | 86 | Pennsylvania | 78 |
| 1988 | Columbia | G. Kolombatovich/A. Kogler | 90 | Notre Dame | 83 |
| 1989 | Columbia | G. Kolombatovich/A. Kogler | 88 | Penn St | 85 |

*Tie broken by a fence-off. Note: Beginning in 1990, men's and women's combined teams competed for the national championship.

### INDIVIDUAL CHAMPIONS

| | Foil | Sabre | Épée |
|---|------|-------|------|
| 1941 | Edward McNamara, Northwestern | William Meyer, Dartmouth | G.H. Boland, Illinois |
| 1942 | Byron Kreiger, Wayne St (MI) | Andre Deladrier, St. John's (NY) | Ben Burtt, Ohio St |
| 1943–46 | No tournament | | |
| 1947 | Abraham Balk, NYU | Oscar Parsons, Temple | Abraham Balk, NYU |
| 1948 | Albert Axelrod, CCNY | James Day, Navy | William Bryan, Navy |
| 1949 | Ralph Tedeschi, Rutgers | Alex Treves, Rutgers | Richard C. Bowman, Army |
| 1950 | Robert Nielsen, Columbia | Alex Treves, Rutgers | Thomas Stuart, Navy |
| 1951 | Robert Nielsen, Columbia | Chamberless Johnston, Princeton | Daniel Chafetz, Columbia |
| 1952 | Harold Goldsmith, CCNY | Frank Zimolzak, Navy | James Wallner, NYU |
| 1953 | Ed Nober, Brooklyn | Robert Parmacek, Penn | Jack Tori, Pennsylvania |
| 1954 | Robert Goldman, Pennsylvania | Steve Sobel, Columbia | Henry Kolowrat, Princeton |
| 1955 | Herman Velasco, Illinois | Barry Pariser, Columbia | Donald Tadrawski, Notre Dame |
| 1956 | Ralph DeMarco, Columbia | Gerald Kaufman, Columbia | Kinmont Hoitsma, Princeton |
| 1957 | Bruce Davis, Wayne St (MI) | Bernie Balaban, NYU | James Margolis, Columbia |
| 1958 | Bruce Davis, Wayne St (MI) | Art Schankin, Illinois | Roland Wommack, Navy |
| 1959 | Joe Paletta, Navy | Al Morales, Navy | Roland Wommack, Navy |
| 1960 | Gene Glazer, NYU | Mike Desaro, NYU | Gil Eisner, NYU |
| 1961 | Herbert Cohen, NYU | Israel Colon, NYU | Jerry Halpern, NYU |
| 1962 | Herbert Cohen, NYU | Barton Nisonson, Columbia | Thane Hawkins, Navy |

## Men *(Cont.)*
### INDIVIDUAL CHAMPIONS *(Cont.)*

| | Foil | Sabre | Épée |
|---|---|---|---|
| 1963 | Jay Lustig, Columbia | Bela Szentivanyi, Wayne St (MI) | Larry Crum, Navy |
| 1964 | Bill Hicks, Princeton | Craig Bell, Illinois | Paul Pesthy, Rutgers |
| 1965 | Joe Nalven, Columbia | Howard Goodman, NYU | Paul Pesthy, Rutgers |
| 1966 | Al Davis, NYU | Paul Apostol, NYU | Bernhardt Hermann, Iowa |
| 1967 | Mike Gaylor, NYU | Todd Makler, Pennsylvania | George Masin, NYU |
| 1968 | Gerard Esponda, San Francisco | Todd Makler, Pennsylvania | Don Sieja, Cornell |
| 1969 | Anthony Kestler, Columbia | Norman Braslow, Penn | James Wetzler, Pennsylvania |
| 1970 | Walter Krause, NYU | Bruce Soriano, Columbia | John Nadas, Case Reserve |
| 1971 | Tyrone Simmons, Detroit | Bruce Soriano, Columbia | George Szunyogh, NYU |
| 1972 | Tyrone Simmons, Detroit | Bruce Soriano, Columbia | Ernesto Fernandez, Penn |
| 1973 | Brooke Makler, Pennsylvania | Peter Westbrock, NYU | Risto Hurme, NYU |
| 1974 | Greg Benko, Wayne St (MI) | Steve Danosi, Wayne St (MI) | Risto Hurme, NYU |
| 1975 | Greg Benko, Wayne St (MI) | Yuri Rabinovich, Wayne St (MI) | Risto Hurme, NYU |
| 1976 | Greg Benko, Wayne St (MI) | Brian Smith, Columbia | Randy Eggleton, Pennsylvania |
| 1977 | Pat Gerard, Notre Dame | Mike Sullivan, Notre Dame | Hans Wieselgren, NYU |
| 1978 | Ernest Simon, Wayne St (MI) | Mike Sullivan, Notre Dame | Bjorne Vaggo, Notre Dame |
| 1979 | Andrew Bonk, Notre Dame | Yuri Rabinovich, Wayne St (MI) | Carlos Songini, Cleveland St |
| 1980 | Ernest Simon, Wayne St (MI) | Paul Friedberg, Pennsylvania | Gil Pezza, Wayne St (MI) |
| 1981 | Ernest Simon, Wayne St (MI) | Paul Friedberg, Pennsylvania | Gil Pezza, Wayne St (MI) |
| 1982 | Alexander Flom, George Mason | Neil Hick, Wayne St (MI) | Peter Schifrin, San Jose St |
| 1983 | Demetrios Valsamis, NYU | John Friedberg, N Carolina | Ola Harstrom, Notre Dame |
| 1984 | Charles Higgs-Coulthard, Notre Dame | Michael Lofton, NYU | Ettore Bianchi, Wayne St (MI) |
| 1985 | Stephan Chauvel, Wayne St (MI) | Michael Lofton, NYU | Ettore Bianchi, Wayne St (MI) |
| 1986 | Adam Feldman, Penn St | Michael Lofton, NYU | Chris O'Loughlin, Pennsylvania |
| 1987 | William Mindel, Columbia | Michael Lofton, NYU | James O'Neill, Harvard |
| 1988 | Marc Kent, Columbia | Robert Cottingham, Columbia | Jon Normile, Columbia |
| 1989 | Edward Mufel, Penn St | Peter Cox, Penn St | Jon Normile, Columbia |
| 1990 | Nick Bravin, Stanford | David Mandell, Columbia | Jubba Beshin, Notre Dame |
| 1991 | Ben Atkins, Columbia | Vitali Nazlimov, Penn St | Marc Oshima, Columbia |
| 1992 | Nick Bravin, Stanford | Tom Strzalkowski, Penn St | Harald Bauder, Wayne St |
| 1993 | Nick Bravin, Stanford | Tom Strzalkowski, Penn St | Ben Atkins, Columbia |
| 1994 | Kwame van Leeuwen, Harvard | Tom Strzalkowski, Penn St | Harald Winkman, Princeton |
| 1995 | Sean McClain, Stanford | Paul Palestis, NYU | Mike Gattner, Lawrence |
| 1996 | Thorstein Becker, Wayne St (MI) | Maxim Pekarev, Princeton | Jeremy Kahn, Duke |
| 1997 | Cliff Bayer, Pennsylvania | Keith Smart, St. John's (NY) | Alden Clarke, Stanford |
| 1998 | Ayo Griffin, Yale | Luke LaValle, Notre Dame | George Hentea, St. John's (NY) |
| 1999 | Felix Reichling, Stanford | Keeth Smart, St. John's (NY) | Alex Roytblat St. John's (NY) |
| 2000 | Felix Reichling, Stanford | Gabor Szelle, Notre Dame | Daniel Landgren, Penn St |
| 2001 | William Jed Dupree, Columbia | Ivan Lee, St. John's (NY) | Soren Thompson, Princeton |

## Women
### TEAM CHAMPIONS

| Year | Champion | Coach | Rec | Runner-Up | Rec |
|---|---|---|---|---|---|
| 1982 | Wayne St (MI) | Istvan Danosi | 7–0 | San Jose St | 6–1 |
| 1983 | Penn St | Beth Alphin | 5–0 | Wayne St (MI) | 3–2 |
| 1984 | Yale | Henry Harutunian | 3–0 | Penn St | 2–1 |
| 1985 | Yale | Henry Harutunian | 3–0 | Pennsylvania | 2–1 |
| 1986 | Pennsylvania | David Micahnik | 3–0 | Notre Dame | 2–1 |
| 1987 | Notre Dame | Yves Auriol | 3–0 | Temple | 2–1 |
| 1988 | Wayne St (MI) | Gil Pezza | 3–0 | Notre Dame | 2–1 |
| 1989 | Wayne St (MI) | Gil Pezza | 3–0 | Columbia-Barnard | 2–1 |

Note: Beginning in 1990, men's and women's combined teams competed for the national championship.

### INDIVIDUAL CHAMPIONS

| | Foil | | Foil *(Cont.)* | | Sabre |
|---|---|---|---|---|---|
| 1982 | Joy Ellingson, San Jose St | 1993 | Olga Kalinovskaya, Penn St | 2000 | Caroline Purcell, MIT |
| 1983 | Jana Angelakis, Penn St | 1994 | Olga Kalinovskaya, Penn St | 2001 | Sada Jacobson, Yale |
| 1984 | Mary Jane O'Neill, Penn | 1995 | Olga Kalinovskaya, Penn St | | |
| 1985 | C. Bilodeaux, Columbia-Barn. | 1996 | Olga Kalinovskaya, Penn St | | **Épée** |
| 1986 | M. Sullivan, Notre Dame | 1997 | Yelena Kalkina, Ohio St | 1995 | Tina Loven, St. John's (NY) |
| 1987 | C. Bilodeaux, Columbia-Barn. | 1998 | F. Zimmermann, Stanford | 1996 | N. Dygert, St. John's (NY) |
| 1988 | M. Sullivan, Notre Dame | 1999 | Monique DeBruin, Stanford | 1997 | Magda Krol, Notre Dame |
| 1989 | Yasemin Topcu, Wayne St (MI) | 2000 | Eva Petschnigg, Princeton | 1998 | Charlotte Walker, Penn St |
| 1990 | Tzu Moy, Columbia-Barn. | 2001 | Iris Zimmerman, Stanford | 1999 | F. Zimmermann, Stanford |
| 1991 | Heidi Piper, Notre Dame | | | 2000 | Jessica Burke, Penn St |
| 1992 | Olga Cheryak, Penn St | | | 2001 | E. Takács, St. John's (NY) |

# Field Hockey

## DIVISION I

| Year | Champion | Coach | Score | Runner-Up |
|------|----------|-------|-------|-----------|
| 1981 | Connecticut | Diane Wright | 4–1 | Massachusetts |
| 1982 | Old Dominion | Beth Anders | 3–2 | Connecticut |
| 1983 | Old Dominion | Beth Anders | 3–1 (3 OT) | Connecticut |
| 1984 | Old Dominion | Beth Anders | 5–1 | Iowa |
| 1985 | Connecticut | Diane Wright | 3–2 | Old Dominion |
| 1986 | Iowa | Judith Davidson | 2–1 (2 OT) | New Hampshire |
| 1987 | Maryland | Sue Tyler | 2–1 (OT) | N Carolina |
| 1988 | Old Dominion | Beth Anders | 2–1 | Iowa |
| 1989 | N Carolina | Karen Shelton | 2–1 (3 OT)* | Old Dominion |
| 1990 | Old Dominion | Beth Anders | 5–0 | N Carolina |
| 1991 | Old Dominion | Beth Anders | 2–0 | N Carolina |
| 1992 | Old Dominion | Beth Anders | 4–0 | Iowa |
| 1993 | Maryland | Missy Meharg | 2–1 (3 OT)* | N Carolina |
| 1994 | James Madison | Christy Morgan | 2–1 (3 OT)* | N Carolina |
| 1995 | N Carolina | Karen Shelton-Scroggs | 5–1 | Maryland |
| 1996 | N Carolina | Karen Shelton-Scroggs | 3–0 | Princeton |
| 1997 | N Carolina | Karen Shelton | 3–2 | Old Dominion |
| 1998 | Old Dominion | Beth Anders | 3–2 | Princeton |
| 1999 | Maryland | Missy Meharg | 2–1 | Michigan |
| 2000 | Old Dominion | Beth Anders | 3–1 | N Carolina |

*Penalty strokes.

## DIVISION II *(Discontinued, then renewed)*

| Year | Champion | Coach | Score | Runner-Up |
|------|----------|-------|-------|-----------|
| 1981 | Pfeiffer | Ellen Briggs | 5–3 | Bentley |
| 1982 | Lock Haven | Sharon E. Taylor | 4–1 | Bloomsburg |
| 1983 | Bloomsburg | Jan Hutchinson | 1–0 | Lock Haven |
| 1992 | Lock Haven | Sharon E. Taylor | 3–1 | Bloomsburg |
| 1993 | Bloomsburg | Jan Hutchinson | 2–1 (2 OT) | Lock Haven |
| 1994 | Lock Haven | Sharon E. Taylor | 2–1 | Bloomsburg |
| 1995 | Lock Haven | Sharon E. Taylor | 1–0 | Bloomsburg |
| 1996 | Bloomsburg | Jan Hutchinson | 1–0 | Lock Haven |
| 1997 | Bloomsburg | Jan Hutchinson | 2–0 | Kutztown |
| 1998 | Bloomsburg | Jan Hutchinson | 4–3 (OT) | Lock Haven |
| 1999 | Bloomsburg | Jan Hutchinson | 2–0 | Bentley |
| 2000 | Lock Haven | Pat Rudy | 2–0 | Bentley |

## DIVISION III

| Year | Champion | Year | Champion | Year | Champion |
|------|----------|------|----------|------|----------|
| 1981 | Trenton St | 1988 | Trenton St | 1995 | Trenton St |
| 1982 | Ithaca | 1989 | Lock Haven | 1996 | College of New Jersey* |
| 1983 | Trenton St | 1990 | Trenton St | 1997 | William Smith |
| 1984 | Bloomsburg | 1991 | Trenton St | 1998 | Middelbury |
| 1985 | Trenton St | 1992 | William Smith | 1999 | College of New Jersey* |
| 1986 | Salisbury St | 1993 | Cortland St | 2000 | William Smith |
| 1987 | Bloomsburg | 1994 | Cortland St | | *Formerly Trenton St. |

# Golf

## Men

### DIVISION I
### Results, 1897–1938

| Year | Champion | Site | Individual Champion |
|------|----------|------|---------------------|
| 1897 | Yale | Ardsley Casino | Louis Bayard Jr, Princeton |
| 1898 | Harvard (spring) | | John Reid Jr, Yale |
| 1898 | Yale (fall) | | James Curtis, Harvard |
| 1899 | Harvard | | Percy Pyne, Princeton |
| 1900 | No tournament | | |
| 1901 | Harvard | Atlantic City | H. Lindsley, Harvard |
| 1902 | Yale (spring) | Garden City | Charles Hitchcock Jr, Yale |
| 1902 | Harvard (fall) | Morris County | Chandler Egan, Harvard |
| 1903 | Harvard | Garden City | F.O. Reinhart, Princeton |
| 1904 | Harvard | Myopia | A.L. White, Harvard |
| 1905 | Yale | Garden City | Robert Abbott, Yale |
| 1906 | Yale | Garden City | W.E. Clow Jr, Yale |
| 1907 | Yale | Nassau | Ellis Knowles, Yale |
| 1908 | Yale | Brae Burn | H.H. Wilder, Harvard |
| 1909 | Yale | Apawamis | Albert Seckel, Princeton |

## Men (Cont.)
### DIVISION I (Cont.)
## Results, 1897–1938 (Cont.)

| Year | Champion | Site | Individual Champion |
|---|---|---|---|
| 1910 | Yale | Essex County | Robert Hunter, Yale |
| 1911 | Yale | Baltusrol | George Stanley, Yale |
| 1912 | Yale | Ekwanok | F.C. Davison, Harvard |
| 1913 | Yale | Huntingdon Valley | Nathaniel Wheeler, Yale |
| 1914 | Princeton | Garden City | Edward Allis, Harvard |
| 1915 | Yale | Greenwich | Francis Blossom, Yale |
| 1916 | Princeton | Oakmont | J.W. Hubbell, Harvard |
| 1917–18 | No tournament | | |
| 1919 | Princeton | Merion | A.L. Walker Jr, Columbia |
| 1920 | Princeton | Nassau | Jess Sweetster, Yale |
| 1921 | Dartmouth | Greenwich | Simpson Dean, Princeton |
| 1922 | Princeton | Garden City | Pollack Boyd, Dartmouth |
| 1923 | Princeton | Siwanoy | Dexter Cummings, Yale |
| 1924 | Yale | Greenwich | Dexter Cummings, Yale |
| 1925 | Yale | Montclair | Fred Lamprecht, Tulane |
| 1926 | Yale | Merion | Fred Lamprecht, Tulane |
| 1927 | Princeton | Garden City | Watts Gunn, Georgia Tech |
| 1928 | Princeton | Apawamis | Maurice McCarthy, Georgetown |
| 1929 | Princeton | Hollywood | Tom Aycock, Yale |
| 1930 | Princeton | Oakmont | G.T. Dunlap Jr, Princeton |
| 1931 | Yale | Olympia Fields | G.T. Dunlap Jr, Princeton |
| 1932 | Yale | Hot Springs | J.W. Fischer, Michigan |
| 1933 | Yale | Buffalo | Walter Emery, Oklahoma |
| 1934 | Michigan | Cleveland | Charles Yates, Georgia Tech |
| 1935 | Michigan | Congressional | Ed White, Texas |
| 1936 | Yale | North Shore | Charles Kocsis, Michigan |
| 1937 | Princeton | Oakmont | Fred Haas Jr, Louisiana St |
| 1938 | Stanford | Louisville | John Burke, Georgetown |

## Results, 1939–2001

| Year | Champion (Score) | Coach | Runner-Up (Score) | Host or Site | Individual Champion |
|---|---|---|---|---|---|
| 1939 | Stanford (612) | Eddie Twiggs | Northwestern (614) Princeton (614) | Wakonda | Vincent D'Antoni, Tulane |
| 1940 | Princeton (601) Louisiana St (601) | Walter Bourne Mike Donahue | | Ekwanok | Dixon Brooke, Virginia |
| 1941 | Stanford (580) | Eddie Twiggs | Louisiana St (599) | Ohio St | Earl Stewart, Louisiana St |
| 1942 | Louisiana St (590) Stanford (590) | Mike Donahue Eddie Twiggs | | Notre Dame | Frank Tatum Jr, Stanford |
| 1943 | Yale (614) | William Neale Jr | Michigan (618) | Olympia Fields | Wallace Ulrich, Carleton |
| 1944 | Notre Dame (311) | George Holderith | Minnesota (312) | Inverness | Louis Lick, Minnesota |
| 1945 | Ohio St (602) | Robert Kepler | Northwestern (621) | Ohio St | John Lorms, Ohio St |
| 1946 | Stanford (619) | Eddie Twiggs | Michigan (624) | Princeton | George Hamer, Georgia |
| 1947 | Louisiana St (606) | T.P. Heard | Duke (614) | Michigan | Dave Barclay, Michigan |
| 1948 | San Jose St (579) | Wilbur Hubbard | Louisiana St (588) | Stanford | Bob Harris, San Jose St |
| 1949 | N Texas (590) | Fred Cobb | Purdue (600) Texas (600) | Iowa St | Harvie Ward, N Carolina |
| 1950 | N Texas (573) | Fred Cobb | Purdue (577) | New Mexico | Fred Wampler, Purdue |
| 1951 | N Texas (588) | Fred Cobb | Ohio St (589) | Ohio St | Tom Nieporte, Ohio St |
| 1952 | N Texas (587) | Fred Cobb | Michigan (593) | Purdue | Jim Vickers, Oklahoma |
| 1953 | Stanford (578) | Charles Finger | N Carolina (580) | Broadmoor | Earl Moeller, Oklahoma St |
| 1954 | SMU (572) | Graham Ross | N Texas (573) | Houston Hillman | Robbins, Memphis St |
| 1955 | Louisiana St (574) | Mike Barbato | N Texas (583) | Tennessee | Joe Campbell, Purdue |
| 1956 | Houston (601) | Dave Williams | N Texas (602) Purdue (602) | Ohio St | Rick Jones, Ohio St |
| 1957 | Houston (602) | Dave Williams | Stanford (603) | Broadmoor | Rex Baxter Jr., Houston |
| 1958 | Houston (570) | Dave Williams | Oklahoma St (582) | Williams | Phil Rodgers, Houston |
| 1959 | Houston (561) | Dave Williams | Purdue (571) | Oregon | Dick Crawford, Houston |
| 1960 | Houston (603) | Dave Williams | Purdue (607) Oklahoma St (607) | Broadmoor | Dick Crawford, Houston |
| 1961 | Purdue (584) | Sam Voinoff | Arizona St (595) | Lafayette | Jack Nicklaus, Ohio St |
| 1962 | Houston (588) | Dave Williams | Oklahoma St (598) | Duke | Kermit Zarley, Houston |
| 1963 | Oklahoma St (581) | Labron Harris | Houston (582) | Wichita St | R.H. Sikes, Arkansas |
| 1964 | Houston (580) | Dave Williams | Oklahoma St (587) | Broadmoor | Terry Small, San Jose St |
| 1965 | Houston (577) | Dave Williams | Cal St–LA (587) | Tennessee | Marty Fleckman, Houston |
| 1966 | Houston (582) | Dave Williams | San Jose St (586) | Stanford | Bob Murphy, Florida |
| 1967 | Houston (585) | Dave Williams | Florida (588) | Shawnee, PA | Hale Irwin, Colorado |

## Men (Cont.)
### DIVISION I (Cont.)
## Results, 1939–2001 (Cont.)

| Year | Champion (Score) | Coach | Runner-Up (Score) | Host or Site | Individual Champion |
|---|---|---|---|---|---|
| 1968 | Florida (1154) | Buster Bishop | Houston (1156) | New Mexico St | Grier Jones, Oklahoma St |
| 1969 | Houston (1223) | Dave Williams | Wake Forest (1232) | Broadmoor | Bob Clark, Cal St–LA |
| 1970 | Houston (1172) | Dave Williams | Wake Forest (1182) | Ohio St | John Mahaffey, Houston |
| 1971 | Texas (1144) | George Hannon | Houston (1151) | Arizona | Ben Crenshaw, Texas |
| 1972 | Texas (1146) | George Hannon | Houston (1159) | Cape Coral | Ben Crenshaw, Texas<br>Tom Kite, Texas |
| 1973 | Florida (1149) | Buster Bishop | Oklahoma St (1159) | Oklahoma St | Ben Crenshaw, Texas |
| 1974 | Wake Forest (1158) | Jess Haddock | Florida (1160) | San Diego St | Curtis Strange, Wake Forest |
| 1975 | Wake Forest (1156) | Jess Haddock | Oklahoma St (1189) | Ohio St | Jay Haas, Wake Forest |
| 1976 | Oklahoma St (1166) | Mike Holder | Brigham Young (1173) | New Mexico | Scott Simpson, USC |
| 1977 | Houston (1197) | Dave Williams | Oklahoma St (1205) | Colgate | Scott Simpson, USC |
| 1978 | Oklahoma St (1140) | Mike Holder | Georgia (1157) | Oregon | David Edwards, Oklahoma St |
| 1979 | Ohio St (1189) | James Brown | Oklahoma St (1191) | Wake Forest | Gary Hallberg, Wake Forest |
| 1980 | Oklahoma St (1173) | Mike Holder | Brigham Young (1177) | Ohio St | Jay Don Blake, Utah St |
| 1981 | BYU (1161) | Karl Tucker | Oral Roberts (1163) | Stanford | Ron Commans, USC |
| 1982 | Houston (1141) | Dave Williams | Oklahoma St (1151) | Pinehurst | Billy Ray Brown, Houston |
| 1983 | Oklahoma St (1161) | Mike Holder | Texas (1168) | Fresno St | Jim Carter, Arizona St |
| 1984 | Houston (1145) | Dave Williams | Oklahoma St (1146) | Houston | John Inman, N Carolina |
| 1985 | Houston (1172) | Dave Williams | Oklahoma St (1175) | Florida | Clark Burroughs, Ohio St |
| 1986 | Wake Forest (1156) | Jess Haddock | Oklahoma St (1160) | Wake Forest | Scott Verplank, Oklahoma St |
| 1987 | Oklahoma St (1160) | Mike Holder | Wake Forest (1176) | Ohio St | Brian Watts, Oklahoma St |
| 1988 | UCLA (1176) | Eddie Merrins | UTEP (1179)<br>Oklahoma (1179)<br>Oklahoma St (1179) | Southern Cal | E.J. Pfister, Oklahoma St |
| 1989 | Oklahoma (1139) | Gregg Grost | Texas (1158) | Oklahoma<br>Oklahoma St | Phil Mickelson, Arizona St |
| 1990 | Arizona St (1155) | Steve Loy | Florida (1157) | Florida | Phil Mickelson, Arizona St |
| 1991 | Oklahoma St (1161) | Mike Holder | N Carolina (1168) | San Jose St | Warren Schutte, UNLV |
| 1992 | Arizona (1129) | Rick LaRose | Arizona St (1136) | New Mexico | Phil Mickelson, Arizona St |
| 1993 | Florida (1145) | Buddy Alexander | Georgia Tech (1146) | Kentucky | Todd Demsey, Arizona St |
| 1994 | Stanford (1129) | Wally Goodwin | Texas (1133) | McKinney, TX | Justin Leonard, Texas |
| 1995 | Oklahoma St* (1156) | Mike Holder | Stanford (1156) | Ohio St | Chip Spratlin, Auburn |
| 1996 | Arizona St (1186) | Randy Lein | UNLV (1189) | Chattanooga | Tiger Woods, Stanford |
| 1997 | Pepperdine (1148) | John Geiberger | Wake Forest (1151) | Evanston, IL | Charles Warren, Clemson |
| 1998 | UNLV (1118) | Dwaine Knight | Clemson (1121) | Albuquerque | James McLean, Minnesota |
| 1999 | Georgia (1180) | Chris Haack | Oklahoma St (1183) | Chaska, MN | Donald Luke, Northwestern |
| 2000 | Oklahoma St* (1116) | Mike Holder | Georgia Tech (1116) | Opelika, AL | Charles Howell, Oklahoma St |
| 2001 | Florida (1126) | Buddy Alexander | Clemson (1144) | Durham, NC | Nick Gilliam, Florida |

*Won sudden death playoff. Notes: Match play, 1897–1964; par-70 tournaments held in 1969, 1973 and 1989; par-71 tournaments held in 1968, 1981 and 1988; all other championships par-72 tournaments. Scores are based on 4 rounds instead of 2 after 1967.

## DIVISION II

| Year | Champion | Year | Champion | Year | Champion |
|---|---|---|---|---|---|
| 1963 | SW Missouri St | 1976 | Troy St | 1989 | Columbus St |
| 1964 | Southern Illinois | 1977 | Troy St | 1990 | Florida Southern |
| 1965 | Middle Tennessee St | 1978 | Columbus St | 1991 | Florida Southern |
| 1966 | Cal St–Chico | 1979 | UC–Davis | 1992 | Columbus St |
| 1967 | Lamar | 1980 | Columbus St | 1993 | Abilene Christian |
| 1968 | Lamar | 1981 | Florida Southern | 1994 | Columbus St |
| 1969 | Cal St–Northridge | 1982 | Florida Southern | 1995 | Florida Southern |
| 1970 | Rollins | 1983 | SW Texas St | 1996 | Florida Southern |
| 1971 | New Orleans | 1984 | Troy St | 1997 | Columbus St |
| 1972 | New Orleans | 1985 | Florida Southern | 1998 | Florida Southern |
| 1973 | Cal St–Northridge | 1986 | Florida Southern | 1999 | Florida Southern |
| 1974 | Cal St–Northridge | 1987 | Tampa | 2000 | Florida Southern |
| 1975 | UC–Irvine | 1988 | Tampa | 2001 | W Florida |

Note: Par-71 tournaments held in 1967, 1970, 1976–78, 1985, 1988 and 2001; par-70 tournament held in 1996; all other championships par-72 tournaments.

## Men (Cont.)

### DIVISION III

| Year | Champion | Year | Champion | Year | Champion |
|------|----------|------|----------|------|----------|
| 1975 | Wooster | 1984 | Cal St–Stanislaus | 1993 | UC–San Diego |
| 1976 | Cal St–Stanislaus | 1985 | Cal St–Stanislaus | 1994 | Methodist (NC) |
| 1977 | Cal St–Stanislaus | 1986 | Cal St–Stanislaus | 1995 | Methodist (NC) |
| 1978 | Cal St–Stanislaus | 1987 | Cal St–Stanislaus | 1996 | Methodist (NC) |
| 1979 | Cal St–Stanislaus | 1988 | Cal St–Stanislaus | 1997 | Methodist (NC) |
| 1980 | Cal St–Stanislaus | 1989 | Cal St–Stanislaus | 1998 | Methodist (NC) |
| 1981 | Cal St–Stanislaus | 1990 | Methodist (NC) | 1999 | Methodist (NC) |
| 1982 | Ramapo | 1991 | Methodist (NC) | 2000 | Greensboro |
| 1983 | Allegheny | 1992 | Methodist (NC) | 2001 | WI–Eau Claire |

Note: All championships par-72 except for 1986, 1988 and 2001, which were par-71; fourth round of 1975 championships canceled as a result of bad weather; first round of 1988 championships canceled as a result of rain.

## Women

### DIVISION I

| Year | Champion | Coach | Score | Runner-Up | Score | Individual Champion |
|------|----------|-------|-------|-----------|-------|---------------------|
| 1982 | Tulsa | Dale McNamara | 1191 | Texas Christian | 1227 | Kathy Baker, Tulsa |
| 1983 | Texas Christian | Fred Warren | 1193 | Tulsa | 1196 | Penny Hammel, Miami (FL) |
| 1984 | Miami (FL) | Lela Cannon | 1214 | Arizona St | 1221 | Cindy Schreyer, Georgia |
| 1985 | Florida | Mimi Ryan | 1218 | Tulsa | 1233 | Danielle Ammaccapane, Arizona St |
| 1986 | Florida | Mimi Ryan | 1180 | Miami (FL) | 1188 | Page Dunlap, Florida |
| 1987 | San Jose St | Mark Gale | 1187 | Furman | 1188 | Caroline Keggi, New Mexico |
| 1988 | Tulsa | Dale McNamara | 1175 | Georgia | 1182 | Melissa McNamara, Tulsa |
|      |          |             |      | Arizona | 1182 |                     |
| 1989 | San Jose St | Mark Gale | 1208 | Tulsa | 1209 | Pat Hurst, San Jose St |
| 1990 | Arizona St | Linda Vollstedt | 1206 | UCLA | 1222 | Susan Slaughter, Arizona |
| 1991 | UCLA* | Jackie Steinmann | 1197 | San Jose St | 1197 | Annika Sorenstam, Arizona |
| 1992 | San Jose St | Mark Gale | 1171 | Arizona | 1175 | Vicki Goetze, Georgia |
| 1993 | Arizona St | Linda Vollstedt | 1187 | Texas | 1189 | Charlotta Sorenstam, Texas |
| 1994 | Arizona St | Linda Vollstedt | 1189 | Southern Cal | 1205 | Emilee Klein, Arizona St |
| 1995 | Arizona St | Linda Vollstedt | 1155 | San Jose St | 1181 | Kristel Mourgue d'Algue, Arizona St |
| 1996 | Arizona* | Rick LaRose | 1240 | San Jose St | 1240 | Marisa Baena, Arizona |
| 1997 | Arizona St | Linda Vollstedt | 1178 | San Jose St | 1180 | Heather Bowie, Texas |
| 1998 | Arizona St | Linda Vollstedt | 1155 | Florida | 1173 | Jennifer Rosales, USC |
| 1999 | Duke | Dan Brooks | 895 | Arizona St/Georgia | 903 | Grace Park, Arizona St |
| 2000 | Arizona | Todd McCorkle | 1175 | Stanford | 1196 | Jenna Daniels, Arizona |
| 2001 | Georgia | Todd McCorkle | 1176 | Duke | 1179 | Candy Hannemann, Duke |

*Won sudden death playoff. Note: Par-74 tournaments held in 1983 and 1988; par-72 tournament held in 1990, 2000 and 2001; all other championships par-73 tournaments.

### DIVISIONS II AND III

| Year | Champion | Year | Champion |
|------|----------|------|----------|
| 1996 | Methodist (NC) | 1998 | Methodist (NC) |
| 1997 | Lynn | 1999 | Methodist (NC) |

#### DIVISION II

| Year | Champion |
|------|----------|
| 2000 | Florida Southern |
| 2001 | Florida Southern |

#### DIVISION III

| Year | Champion |
|------|----------|
| 2000 | Methodist (NC) |
| 2001 | Methodist (NC) |

# Gymnastics

## Men
### TEAM CHAMPIONS

| Year | Champion | Coach | Pts | Runner-Up | Pts |
|------|----------|-------|-----|-----------|-----|
| 1938 | Chicago | Dan Hoffer | 22 | Illinois | 18 |
| 1939 | Illinois | Hartley Price | 21 | Army | 17 |
| 1940 | Illinois | Hartley Price | 20 | Navy | 17 |
| 1941 | Illinois | Hartley Price | 68.5 | Minnesota | 52.5 |
| 1942 | Illinois | Hartley Price | 39 | Penn St | 30 |
| 1943–47 | No tournament | | | | |
| 1948 | Penn St | Gene Wettstone | 55 | Temple | 34.5 |
| 1949 | Temple | Max Younger | 28 | Minnesota | 18 |
| 1950 | Illinois | Charley Pond | 26 | Temple | 25 |
| 1951 | Florida St | Hartley Price | 26 | Illinois | 23.5 |
| | | | | Southern Cal | 23.5 |
| 1952 | Florida St | Hartley Price | 89.5 | Southern Cal | 75 |
| 1953 | Penn St | Gene Wettstone | 91.5 | Illinois | 68 |
| 1954 | Penn St | Gene Wettstone | 137 | Illinois | 68 |
| 1955 | Illinois | Charley Pond | 82 | Penn St | 69 |
| 1956 | Illinois | Charley Pond | 123.5 | Penn St | 67.5 |
| 1957 | Penn St | Gene Wettstone | 88.5 | Illinois | 80 |
| 1958 | Michigan St | George Szypula | 79 | | |
| | Illinois | Charley Pond | 79 | | |
| 1959 | Penn St | Gene Wettstone | 152 | Illinois | 87.5 |
| 1960 | Penn St | Gene Wettstone | 112.5 | Southern Cal | 65.5 |
| 1961 | Penn St | Gene Wettstone | 88.5 | Southern Illinois | 80.5 |
| 1962 | Southern Cal | Jack Beckner | 95.5 | Southern Illinois | 75 |
| 1963 | Michigan | Newton Loken | 129 | Southern Illinois | 73 |
| 1964 | Southern Illinois | Bill Meade | 84.5 | Southern Cal | 69.5 |
| 1965 | Penn St | Gene Wettstone | 68.5 | Washington | 51.5 |
| 1966 | Southern Illinois | Bill Meade | 187.200 | California | 185.100 |
| 1967 | Southern Illinois | Bill Meade | 189.550 | Michigan | 187.400 |
| 1968 | California | Hal Frey | 188.250 | Southern Illinois | 188.150 |
| 1969 | Iowa | Mike Jacobson | 161.175 | Penn St | 160.450 |
| | Michigan* | Newton Loken | | Colorado St | |
| 1970 | Michigan | Newton Loken | 164.150 | Iowa St | 164.050 |
| | | | | New Mexico St | |
| 1971 | Iowa St | Ed Gagnier | 319.075 | Southern Illinois | 316.650 |
| 1972 | Southern Illinois | Bill Meade | 315.925 | Iowa St | 312.325 |
| 1973 | Iowa St | Ed Gagnier | 325.150 | Penn St | 323.025 |
| 1974 | Iowa St | Ed Gagnier | 326.100 | Arizona St | 322.050 |
| 1975 | California | Hal Frey | 437.325 | Louisiana St | 433.700 |
| 1976 | Penn St | Gene Wettstone | 432.075 | Louisiana St | 425.125 |
| 1977 | Indiana St | Roger Counsil | 434.475 | | |
| | Oklahoma | Paul Ziert | 434.475 | | |
| 1978 | Oklahoma | Paul Ziert | 439.350 | Arizona St | 437.075 |
| 1979 | Nebraska | Francis Allen | 448.275 | Oklahoma | 446.625 |
| 1980 | Nebraska | Francis Allen | 563.300 | Iowa St | 557.650 |
| 1981 | Nebraska | Francis Allen | 284.600 | Oklahoma | 281.950 |
| 1982 | Nebraska | Francis Allen | 285.500 | UCLA | 281.050 |
| 1983 | Nebraska | Francis Allen | 287.800 | UCLA | 283.900 |
| 1984 | UCLA | Art Shurlock | 287.300 | Penn St | 281.250 |
| 1985 | Ohio St | Michael Willson | 285.350 | Nebraska | 284.550 |
| 1986 | Arizona St | Don Robinson | 283.900 | Nebraska | 283.600 |
| 1987 | UCLA | Art Shurlock | 285.300 | Nebraska | 284.750 |
| 1988 | Nebraska | Francis Allen | 288.150 | Illinois | 287.150 |
| 1989 | Illinois | Yoshi Hayasaki | 283.400 | Nebraska | 282.300 |
| 1990 | Nebraska | Francis Allen | 287.400 | Minnesota | 287.300 |
| 1991 | Oklahoma | Greg Buwick | 288.025 | Penn St | 285.500 |
| 1992 | Stanford | Sadao Hamada | 289.575 | Nebraska | 288.950 |
| 1993 | Stanford | Sadao Hamada | 276.500 | Nebraska | 275.500 |
| 1994 | Nebraska | Francis Allen | 288.250 | Stanford | 285.925 |
| 1995 | Stanford | Sadao Hamada | 232.400 | Nebraska | 231.525 |
| 1996 | Ohio St | Peter Kormann | 232.150 | California | 231.775 |
| 1997 | California | Barry Weiner | 233.825 | Oklahoma | 232.725 |
| 1998 | Caliornia | Barry Weiner | 231.200 | Iowa | 229.675 |
| 1999 | Michigan | Kurt Golder | 232.550 | Ohio St | 230.850 |
| 2000 | Penn St | Randy Jepson | 231.975 | Michigan | 231.850 |
| 2001 | Ohio St | Miles Avery | 218.125 | Oklahoma | 217.775 |

*Trampoline.

## Men (Cont.)

### INDIVIDUAL CHAMPIONS

### ALL-AROUND

1938.....Joe Giallombardo, Illinois
1939.....Joe Giallombardo, Illinois
1940.....Joe Giallombardo, Illinois
        Paul Fina, Illinois
1941.....Courtney Shanken, Chicago
1942.....Newt Loken, Minnesota
1948.....Ray Sorenson, Penn St
1949.....Joe Kotys, Kent
1950.....Joe Kotys, Kent
1951.....Bill Roetzheim, Florida St
1952.....Jack Beckner, Southern Cal
1953.....Jean Cronstedt, Penn St
1954.....Jean Cronstedt, Penn St
1955.....Karl Schwenzfeier, Penn St
1956.....Don Tonry, IIIinois
1957.....Armando Vega, Penn St
1958.....Abie Grossfeld, Illinois
1959.....Armando Vega, Penn St
1960.....Jay Werner, Penn St
1961.....Gregor Weiss, Penn St
1962.....Robert Lynn, Southern Cal
1963.....Gil Larose, Michigan
1964.....Ron Barak, Southern Cal
1965.....Mike Jacobson, Penn St
1966.....Steve Cohen, Penn St
1967.....Steve Cohen, Penn St
1968.....Makoto Sakamoto, USC
1969.....Mauno Nissinen, Wash
1970.....Yoshi Hayasaki, Wash
1971.....Yoshi Hayasaki, Wash
1972.....Steve Hug, Stanford
1973.....Steve Hug, Stanford
        Marshall Avener, Penn St
1974.....Steve Hug, Stanford
1975.....Wayne Young, BYU
1976.....Peter Kormann,
        Southern Conn St
1977.....Kurt Thomas, Indiana St
1978.....Bart Conner, Oklahoma
1979.....Kurt Thomas, Indiana St
1980.....Jim Hartung, Nebraska
1981.....Jim Hartung, Nebraska
1982.....Peter Vidmar, UCLA
1983.....Peter Vidmar, UCLA
1984.....Mitch Gaylord, UCLA
1985.....Wes Suter, Nebraska
1986.....Jon Louis, Stanford
1987.....Tom Schlesinger, Nebraska
1988.....Vacated†
1989.....Patrick Kirsey, Nebraska
1990.....Mike Racanelli, Ohio St
1991.....John Roethlisberger, Minn
1992.....John Roethlisberger, Minn
1993.....John Roethlisberger, Minn
1994.....Dennis Harrison, Nebraska
1995.....Richard Grace, Nebraska
1996.....Blaine Wilson, Ohio St
1997.....Blaine Wilson, Ohio St
1998.....Travis Romagnoli, Illinois
1999.....Justin Hardabura, Nebraska
2000.....Jamie Natalie, Ohio St
2001.....Jamie Natalie, Ohio St

### HORIZONTAL BAR

1938.....Bob Sears, Army

1939.....Adam Walters, Temple
1940.....Norm Boardman, Temple
1941.....Newt Loken, Minnesota
1942.....Norm Boardman, Temple
1948.....Joe Calvetti, Illinois
1949.....Bob Stout, Temple
1950.....Joe Kotys, Kent
1951.....Bill Roetzheim, Florida St
1952.....Charles Simms, USC
1953.....Hal Lewis, Navy
1954.....Jean Cronstedt, Penn St
1955.....Carlton Rintz, Michigan St
1956.....Ronnie Amster, Florida St
1957.....Abie Grossfeld, Illinois
1958.....Abie Grossfeld, Illinois
1959.....Stanley Tarshis, Mich St
1960.....Stanley Tarshis, Mich St
1961.....Bruno Klaus, Southern Ill
1962.....Robert Lynn, USC
1963.....Gil Larose, Michigan
1964.....Ron Barak, USC
1965.....Jim Curzi, Michigan St
        Mike Jacobsen, Penn St
1966.....Rusty Rock, Cal St–
        Northridge
1967.....Rich Grigsby, Cal St–
        Northridge
1968.....Makoto Sakamoto, USC
1969.....Bob Manna, New Mexico
1970.....Yoshi Hayasaki, Wash
1971.....Brent Simmons, Iowa St
1972.....Tom Lindner, Souhern Ill
1973.....Jon Aitken, New Mexico
1974.....Rick Banley, Indiana St
1975.....Rich Larsen, Iowa St
1976.....Tom Beach, California
1977.....John Hart, UCLA
1978.....Mel Cooley, Washington
1979.....Kurt Thomas, Indiana St
1980.....Philip Cahoy, Nebraska
1981.....Philip Cahoy, Nebraska
1982.....Peter Vidmar, UCLA
1983.....Scott Johnson, Nebraska
1984.....Charles Lakes, Illinois
1985.....Dan Hayden, Arizona St
        Wes Suter, Nebraska
1986.....Dan Hayden, Arizona St
1987.....David Moriel, UCLA
1988.....Vacated†
1989.....Vacated†
1990.....Chris Waller, UCLA
1991.....Luis Lopez, New Mexico
1992.....Jair Lynch, Stanford
1993.....Steve McCain, UCLA
1994.....Jim Foody, UCLA
1995.....Rick Kieffer, Nebraska
1996.....Carl Imhauser, Temple
1997.....Marshall Nelson, Nebraska
1998.....Todd Bishop, Oklahoma
1999.....Todd Bishop, Oklahoma
2000.....Michael Ashe, California
2001.....Michael Ashe, California

### PARALLEL BARS

1938.....Erwin Beyer, Chicago
1939.....Bob Sears, Army
1940.....Bob Hanning, Minnesota

1941.....Caton Cobb, Illinois
1942.....Hal Zimmerman, Penn St
1948.....Ray Sorenson, Penn St
1949.....Joe Kotys, Kent
        Mel Stout, Michigan St
1950.....Joe Kotys, Kent
1951.....Jack Beckner, USC
1952.....Jack Beckner, USC
1953.....Jean Cronstedt, Penn St
1954.....Jean Cronstedt, Penn St
1955.....Carlton Rintz, Michigan St
1956.....Armando Vega, Penn St
1957.....Armando Vega, Penn St
1958.....Tad Muzyczko, Mich St
1959.....Armando Vega, Penn St
1960.....Robert Lynn, Southern Cal
1961.....Fred Tijerina, Southern Ill
        Jeff Cardinalli, Springfield
1962.....Robert Lynn, Southern Cal
1963.....Arno Lascari, Michigan
1964.....Ron Barak, Southern Cal
1965.....Jim Curzi, Michigan St
1966.....Jim Curzi, Michigan St
1967.....Makoto Sakamoto, USC
1968.....Makoto Sakamoto, USC
1969.....Ron Rapper, Michigan
1970.....Ron Rapper, Michigan
1971.....Brent Simmons, Iowa St
        Tom Dunn, Penn St
1972.....Dennis Mazur, Iowa St
1973.....Steve Hug, Stanford
1974.....Steve Hug, Stanford
1975.....Yoichi Tomita,
        Long Beach St
1976.....Gene Whelan, Penn St
1977.....Kurt Thomas, Indiana St
1978.....John Corritore, Michigan
1979.....Kurt Thomas, Indiana St
1980.....Philip Cahoy, Nebraska
1981.....Phillip Cahoy, Nebraska
        Peter Vidmar, UCLA
        Jim Hartung, Nebraska
1982.....Jim Hartung, Nebraska
1983.....Scott Johnson, Nebraska
1984.....Tim Daggett, UCLA
1985.....Dan Hayden, Arizona St
        Noah Riskin, Ohio St
        Seth Riskin, Ohio St
1986.....Dan Hayden, Arizona St
1987.....Kevin Davis, Nebraska
        Tom Schlesinger, Nebraska
1988.....Kevin Davis, Nebraska
1989.....Vacated†
1990.....Patrick Kirksey, Nebraska
1991.....Scott Keswick, UCLA
        John Roethlisberger, Minn
1992.....Dom Minicucci, Temple
1993.....Jair Lynch, Stanford
1994.....Richard Grace, Nebraska
1995.....Richard Grace, Nebraska
1996.....Jamie Ellis, Stanford
        Blaine Wilson, Ohio St
1997.....Marshall Nelson, Nebraska
1998.....Marshall Nelson, Nebraska
1999.....Justin Toman, Michigan
2000.....Kris Zimmerman, Michigan
        Justin Toman, Michigan
2001.....Raj Bhavsar, Ohio St

## Men *(Cont.)*
### INDIVIDUAL CHAMPIONS *(Cont.)*

### VAULT

1938.....Erwin Beyer, Chicago
1939.....Marv Forman, Illinois
1940.....Earl Shanken, Chicago
1941.....Earl Shanken, Chicago
1942.....Earl Shanken, Chicago
1948....Jim Peterson, Minnesota
1962.....Bruno Klaus, Southern Ill
1963.....Gil Larose, Michigan
1964.....Sidney Oglesby, Syracuse
1965.....Dan Millman, California
1966.....Frank Schmitz, S Illinois
1967....Paul Mayer, S Illinois
1968.....Bruce Colter, Cal St–
              Los Angeles
1969.....Dan Bowles, California
              Jack McCarthy, Illinois
1970.....Doug Boger, Arizona
1971.....Pat Mahoney, Cal St–
              Northridge
1972.....Gary Morava, Southern Ill
1973....John Crosby, S Conn St
1974.....Greg Goodhue, Oklahoma
1975.....Tom Beach, California
1976.....Sam Shaw, Cal St–
              Fullerton
1977.....Steve Wejmar, Wash
1978.....Ron Galimore, Louisiana St
1979.....Leslie Moore, Oklahoma
1980.....Ron Galimore, Iowa St
1981.....Ron Galimore, Iowa St
1982.....Randall Wickstrom, Cal
              Steve Elliott, Nebraska
1983.....Chris Riegel, UCLA
              Mark Oates, Oklahoma
1984.....Chris Riegel, Nebraska
1985.....Derrick Cornelius,
              Cortland St
1986.....Chad Fox, New Mexico
1987.....Chad Fox, New Mexico
1988.....Chad Fox, New Mexico
1989.....Chad Fox, New Mexico
1990.....Brad Hayashi, UCLA
1991.....Adam Carton, Penn St
1992.....Jason Hebert, Syracuse
1993.....Steve Wiegel, N Mexico
1994.....Steve McCain, UCLA
1995.....Ian Bachrach, Stanford
1996.....Jay Thornton, Iowa
1997.....Blaine Wilson, Ohio St
1998.....Travis Romagnoli, Illinois
1999.....Guard Young, BYU
2000.....Guard Young, BYU
2001.....Daren Lynch, Ohio St

### POMMEL HORSE

1938.....Erwin Beyer, Chicago
1939.....Erwin Beyer, Chicago
1940......Harry Koehnemann, Illinois
1941.....Caton Cobb, Illinois
1942.....Caton Cobb, Illinois
1948.....Steve Greene, Penn St
1949.....Joe Berenato, Temple
1950.....Gene Rabbitt, Syracuse
1951.....Joe Kotys, Kent
1952.....Frank Bare, Illinois
1953.....Carlton Rintz, Michigan St
1954.....Robert Lawrence, Penn St

1955.....Carlton Rintz, Michigan St
1956.....James Brown, Cal St–
              Los Angeles
1957.....John Davis, Illinois
1958.....Bill Buck, Iowa
1959.....Art Shurlock, California
1960.....James Fairchild, California
1961.....James Fairchild, California
1962.....Mike Aufrecht, Illinois
1963.....Russ Mills, Yale
1964.....Russ Mills, Yale
1965.....Bob Elsinger, Springfield
1966.....Gary Hoskins, Cal St–
              Los Angeles
1967.....Keith McCanless, Iowa
1968.....Jack Ryan, Colorado
1969.....Keith McCanless, Iowa
1970.....Russ Hoffman, Iowa St
              John Russo, Wisconsin
1971.....Russ Hoffman, Iowa St
1972.....Russ Hoffman, Iowa St
1973.....Ed Slezak, Indiana St
1974.....Ted Marcy, Stanford
1975.....Ted Marcy, Stanford
1976.....Ted Marcy, Stanford
1977.....Chuck Walter, New Mexico
1978.....Mike Burke, Northern Ill
1979.....Mike Burke, Northern Ill
1980.....David Stoldt, Illinois
1981.....Mark Bergman, California
              Steve Jennings, New Mexico
1982.....Peter Vidmar, UCLA
              Steve Jennings, New Mexico
1983.....Doug Kieso, Northern Ill
1984.....Tim Daggett, UCLA
1985.....Tony Pineda, UCLA
1986.....Curtis Holdsworth, UCLA
1987......Li Xiao Ping, Cal St–
              Fullerton
1988.....Vacated†
              Mark Sohn, Penn St
1989.....Mark Sohn, Penn St
              Chris Waller, UCLA
1990.....Mark Sohn, Penn St
1991.....Mark Sohn, Penn St
1992.....Che Bowers, Nebraska
1993.....John Roethlisberger, Minn
1994.....Jason Bertram, California
1995.....Drew Durbin, Ohio St
1996.....Drew Durbin, Ohio St
1997.....Drew Durbin, Ohio St
1998.....Josh Birckelbaw, California
1999......Brandon Stefaniak, Penn St
2000......Brandon Stefaniak, Penn St
              Don Jackson, Iowa
2001 ....Clay Stother, Minnesota

### FLOOR EXERCISE

1941.....Lou Fina, Illinois
1953.....Bob Sullivan, Illinois
1954.....Jean Cronstedt, Penn St
1955.....Don Faber, Illinois
1956.....Jamile Ashmore, Florida St
1957.....Norman Marks, Cal St–
              Los Angeles
1958.....Abie Grossfeld, Illinois
1959.....Don Tonry, Illinois
1960.....Ray Hadley, Illinois
1961.....Robert Lynn, Southern Cal

1962.....Robert Lynn, Southern Cal
1963.....Tom Seward, Penn St
              Mike Henderson, Michigan
1964.....Rusty Mitchell, S Illinois
1965.....Frank Schmitz, S Illinois
1966.....Frank Schmitz, S Illinois
1967.....Dave Jacobs, Michigan
1968.....Toby Towson, Michigan St
1969.....Toby Towson, Michigan St
1970.....Tom Proulx, Colorado St
1971......Stormy Eaton, New Mexico
1972.....Odessa Lovin, Oklahoma
1973.....Odessa Lovin, Oklahoma
1974.....Doug Fitzjarrell, Iowa St
1975.....Kent Brown, Arizona St
1976.....Bob Robbins, Colorado St
1977.....Ron Galimore, Louisiana St
1978.....Curt Austin, Iowa St
1979.....Mike Wilson, Oklahoma
              Bart Conner, Oklahoma
1980.....Steve Elliott, Nebraska
1981.....James Yuhashi, Oregon
1982.....Steve Elliott, Nebraska
1983.....Scott Johnson, Nebraska
              David Branch, Arizona St
              Donnie Hinton, Arizona St
1984.....Kevin Ekburg, Northern Ill
1985.....Wes Suter, Nebraska
1986.....Jerry Burrell, Arizona St
              Brian Ginsberg, UCLA
1987.....Chad Fox, New Mexico
1988.....Chris Wyatt, Temple
1989.....Jody Newman, Arizona St
1990.....Mike Racanelli, Ohio St
1991.....Brad Hayashi, UCLA
1992.....Brian Winkler, Michigan
1993.....Richard Grace, Nebraska
1994.....Mark Booth, Stanford
1995.....Jay Thornton, Iowa
1996.....Ian Bachrach, Stanford
1997.....Jeremy Killen, Oklahoma
1998.....Darin Gerlach, Temple
1999.......Jason Hardabura, Nebraska
2000.....Jamie Natalie, Ohio St
2001.....Clay Stother, Minnesota

### RINGS

1959.....Armando Vega, Penn St
1960.....Sam Garcia, Southern Cal
1961.....Fred Orlofsky, Southern Ill
1962.....Dale Cooper, Michigan St
1963.....Dale Cooper, Michigan St
1964.....Chris Evans, Arizona St
1965.....Glenn Gailis, Iowa
1966.....Ed Gunny, Michigan St
1967.....Josh Robison, California
1968.....Pat Arnold, Arizona
1969.....Paul Vexler, Penn St
              Ward Maythaler, Iowa St
1970.....Dave Seal, Indiana St
1971.....Charles Ropiequet, S Illinois
1972.....Dave Seal, Indiana St
1973.....Bob Mahorney, Indiana St
1974.....Keith Heaver, Iowa St
1975.....Keith Heaver, Iowa St
1976.....Doug Wood, Iowa St
1977.....Doug Wood, Iowa St
1978.....Scott McEldowney, Oregon
1979.....Kirk Mango, Northern Ill

## Men *(Cont.)*
### INDIVIDUAL CHAMPIONS *(Cont.)*

| | | |
|---|---|---|
| 1980.....Jim Hartung, Nebraska | 1988.....Paul O'Neill, New Mexico | 1995.....Dave Frank, Temple |
| 1981.....Jim Hartung, Nebraska | 1989.....Vacated† | 1996.....Scott McCall, Will. & Mary |
| 1982.....Jim Hartung, Nebraska |        Paul O'Neill, New Mexico |        Blaine Wilson, Ohio St |
| 1983.....Alex Schwartz, UCLA | 1990.....Wayne Cowden, Penn St | 1997.....Blaine Wilson, Ohio St |
| 1984.....Tim Daggett, UCLA | 1991.....Adam Carton, Penn St | 1998.....Dan Fink, Oklahoma |
| 1985.....Mark Diab, Iowa St | 1992.....Scott Keswick, UCLA | 1999.....Cortney Bramwell, BYU |
| 1986.....Mark Diab, Iowa St | 1993.....Chris LaMorte, N Mexico | 2000.....Cortney Bramwell, BYU |
| 1987.....Paul O'Neill, Hou. Baptist | 1994.....Chris LaMorte, N Mexico | 2001.....Chris Lakeman, Penn St |

†Championships won by Miguel Rubio (All Around, 1988; Horizontal Bar, 1988–89) and Alfonso Rodriguez (Pommel Horse, 1988; Rings, 1989; Parallel Bars, 1989) were vacated by action of the NCAA Committee on Infractions.

### DIVISION II *(Discontinued)*

| Year | Champion | Coach | Pts | Runner-Up | Pts |
|---|---|---|---|---|---|
| 1968 | Cal St–Northridge | Bill Vincent | 179.400 | Springfield | 178.050 |
| 1969 | Cal St–Northridge | Bill Vincent | 151.800 | Southern Connecticut St | 145.075 |
| 1970 | Northwestern Louisiana | Armando Vega | 160.250 | Southern Connecticut St | 159.300 |
| 1971 | Cal St–Fullerton | Dick Wolfe | 158.150 | Springfield | 156.987 |
| 1972 | Cal St–Fullerton | Dick Wolfe | 160.550 | Southern Connecticut St | 153.050 |
| 1973 | Southern Connecticut St | Abe Grossfeld | 160.750 | Cal St–Northridge | 158.700 |
| 1974 | Cal St–Fullerton | Dick Wolfe | 309.800 | Southern Connecticut St | 309.400 |
| 1975 | Southern Connecticut St | Abe Grossfeld | 411.650 | IL–Chicago | 398.800 |
| 1976 | Southern Connecticut St | Abe Grossfeld | 419.200 | IL–Chicago | 388.850 |
| 1977 | Springfield | Frank Wolcott | 395.950 | Cal St–Northridge | 381.250 |
| 1978 | IL–Chicago | C. Johnson/A. Gentile | 406.850 | Cal St–Northridge | 400.400 |
| 1979 | IL–Chicago | Clarence Johnson | 418.550 | WI-Oshkosh | 385.650 |
| 1980 | WI–Oshkosh | Ken Allen | 260.550 | Cal St–Chico | 256.050 |
| 1981 | WI–Oshkosh | Ken Allen | 209.500 | Springfield | 201.550 |
| 1982 | WI–Oshkosh | Ken Allen | 216.050 | E Stroudsburg | 211.200 |
| 1983 | E Stroudsburg | Bruno Klaus | 258.650 | WI–Oshkosh | 257.850 |
| 1984 | E Stroudsburg | Bruno Klaus | 270.800 | Cortland St | 246.350 |

## Women
### TEAM CHAMPIONS

| Year | Champion | Coach | Pts | Runner-Up | Pts |
|---|---|---|---|---|---|
| 1982 | Utah | Greg Marsden | 148.60 | Cal St–Fullerton | 144.10 |
| 1983 | Utah | Greg Marsden | 184.65 | Arizona St | 183.30 |
| 1984 | Utah | Greg Marsden | 186.05 | UCLA | 185.55 |
| 1985 | Utah | Greg Marsden | 188.35 | Arizona St | 186.60 |
| 1986 | Utah | Greg Marsden | 186.95 | Arizona St | 186.70 |
| 1987 | Georgia | Suzanne Yoculan | 187.90 | Utah | 187.55 |
| 1988 | Alabama | Sarah Patterson | 190.05 | Utah | 189.50 |
| 1989 | Georgia | Suzanne Yoculan | 192.65 | UCLA | 192.60 |
| 1990 | Utah | Greg Marsden | 194.900 | Alabama | 194.575 |
| 1991 | Alabama | Sarah Patterson | 195.125 | Utah | 194.375 |
| 1992 | Utah | Greg Marsden | 195.650 | Georgia | 194.600 |
| 1993 | Georgia | Suzanne Yoculan | 198.000 | Alabama | 196.825 |
| 1994 | Utah | Greg Marsden | 196.400 | Alabama | 196.350 |
| 1995 | Utah | Greg Marsden | 196.650 | Alabama | 196.425 |
| | | | | Michigan | 196.425 |
| 1996 | Alabama | Sarah Patterson | 198.025 | UCLA | 197.475 |
| 1997 | UCLA | Valorie Kondos | 197.150 | Arizona St | 196.850 |
| 1998 | Georgia | Suzanne Yoculan | 197.725 | Florida | 196.350 |
| 1999 | Georgia | Suzanne Yoculan | 196.850 | Michigan | 196.55 |
| 2000 | UCLA | Valorie Kondos | 197.300 | Utah | 196.875 |
| 2001 | UCLA | Valorie Kondos | 197.575 | Georgia | 197.400 |

## Women (Cont.)
### INDIVIDUAL CHAMPIONS

### ALL-AROUND

1982.....Sue Stednitz, Utah
1983.....Megan McCunniff, Utah
1984......Megan McCunniff-Marsden, Utah
1985......Penney Hauschild, Alabama
1986......Penney Hauschild, Alabama
      Jackie Brummer, Arizona St
1987.....Kelly Garrison-Steves, Oklahoma
1988.....Kelly Garrison-Steves, Oklahoma
1989.....Corrinne Wright, Georgia
1990.....Dee Dee Foster, Alabama
1991.....Hope Spivey, Georgia
1992.....Missy Marlowe, Utah
1993.....Jenny Hansen, Kentucky
1994.....Jenny Hansen, Kentucky
1995.....Jenny Hansen, Kentucky
1996.....Meredith Willard, Alabama
1997.....Kim Arnold, Georgia
1998.....Kim Arnold, Georgia
1999.....Theresa Kulikowski, Utah
2000.....Mohini Bhardwaj, UCLA
      Heather Brink, Nebraska
2001.....Onnis Willis, UCLA
      Elise Ray, Michigan

### VAULT

1982.....Elaine Alfano, Utah
1983.....Elaine Alfano, Utah
1984.....Megan Marsden, Utah
1985.....Elaine Alfano, Utah
1986.....Kim Neal, Arizona St
      Pam Loree, Penn St
1987.....Yumi Mordre, Washington
1988.....Jill Andrews, UCLA
1989.....Kim Hamilton, UCLA
1990.....Michele Bryant, Nebraska
1991.....Anna Basaldva, Arizona
1992.....Tammy Marshall, Mass.
      Heather Stepp, Georgia
      Kristein Kenoyer, Utah
1993.....Heather Stepp, Georgia
1994.....Jenny Hansen, Kentucky
1995.....Jenny Hansen, Kentucky
1996.....Leah Brown, Georgia
1997.....Susan Hines, Florida
1998.....Susan Hines, Florida

### VAULT (Cont.)

1999.....Heidi Moneymaker, UCLA
2000.....Heather Brink, Nebraska
2001.....Cory Fritzinger, Georgia

### BALANCE BEAM

1982.....Sue Stednitz, Utah
1983.....Julie Goewey, Cal St–Fullerton
1984.....Heidi Anderson, Oregon St
1985.....Lisa Zeis, Arizona St
1986.....Jackie Brummer, Arizona St
1987.....Yumi Mordre, Washington
1988.....Kelly Garrison-Steves, Oklahoma
1989.....Jill Andrews, UCLA
      Joy Selig, Oregon St
1990.....Joy Selig, Oregon St
1991.....Missy Marlowe, Utah
1992.....Missy Marlowe, Utah
1992    Dana Dobransky, Alabama
1993.....Dana Dobransky, Alabama
1994.....Jenny Hansen, Kentucky
1995.....Jenny Hansen, Kentucky
1996.....Summer Reid, UUtah
1997.....Summer Reid, Utah
      Elizabeth Reid, Arizona St
1998    Larissa Fontaine, Stanford
      Susan Hines, Florida
1999.....Theresa Kulikowski, Utah
2000.....Lena Degteva, UCLA
2001.....Theresa Kulikowski, Utah

### FLOOR EXERCISE

1982.....Mary Ayotte-Law, Oregon St
1983.....Kim Neal, Arizona St
1984.....Maria Anz, Florida
1985.....Lisa Mitzel, Utah
1986.....Lisa Zeis, Arizona St
      P. Hauschild, Alabama
1987.....Kim Hamilton, UCLA
1988.....Kim Hamilton, UCLA
1989.....Corrinne Wright, Georgia
      Kim Hamilton, UCLA
1990.....Joy Selig, Oregon St
1991.....Hope Spivey, Georgia

### FLOOR EXERCISE (Cont.)

1992.....Missy Marlowe, Utah
1993.....Heather Stepp, Georgia
      Tammy Marshall, Mass.
      Amy Durham, Oregon St
1994.....Hope Spivey-Sheeley, UGA
1995.....Jenny Hansen, Kentucky
      Stella Umeh, UCLA
      Leslie Angeles, Georgia
1996.....Heidi Hornbeek, Arizona
      Kim Kelly, Alabama
1997.....Leah Brown, Georgia
1998.....Kim Arnold, Georgia
      Jenni Beathard, Georgia
      Betsy Hamm, Florida
1999.....Marny Oestreng, BGSU
2000.....Suzanne Sears, Georgia
2001.....Mohini Bhardwaj, UCLA

### UNEVEN BARS

1982.....Lisa Shirk, Pittsburgh
1983.....Jeri Cameron, Arizona St
1984.....Jackie Brummer, Arizona St
1985......Penney Hauschild, Alabama
1986.....Lucy Wener, Georgia
1987.....Lucy Wener, Georgia
1988.....Kelly Garrison-Steves, Oklahoma
1989.....Lucy Wener, Georgia
1990.....Marie Roethlisberger, Minnesota
1991.....Kelly Macy, Georgia
1992.....Missy Marlowe, Utah
1993.....Agina Simpkins, Georgia
      Beth Wymer, Michigan
1994.....Sandy Woolsey, Utah
      Beth Wymer, Michigan
      Lori Strong, Georgia
1995.....Beth Wymer, Michigan
1996.....Stephanie Woods, Alabama
1997.....Jenni Beathard, Georgia
1998.....Karin Lichey, Georgia
      Stella Umeh, UCLA
1999.....Angie Leionard, Utah
2000.....Mohini Bhardwaj, UCLA
2001.....Yvonne Tousek, UCLA

### DIVISION II (Discontinued)

| Year | Champion | Coach | Pts | Runner-Up | Pts |
|------|----------|-------|-----|-----------|-----|
| 1982 | Cal St–Northridge | Donna Stuart | 138.10 | Jacksonville St | 134.05 |
| 1983 | Denver | Dan Garcia | 174.80 | Cal St–Northridge | 174.35 |
| 1984 | Jacksonville St | Robert Dillard | 173.40 | SE Missouri St | 171.45 |
| 1985 | Jacksonville St | Robert Dillard | 176.85 | SE Missouri St | 173.95 |
| 1986 | Seattle Pacific | Laurel Tindall | 175.80 | Jacksonville St | 175.15 |

## Men

### DIVISION I

| Year | Champion | Coach | Score | Runner-Up | Most Outstanding Player |
|------|----------|-------|-------|-----------|-------------------------|
| 1948 | Michigan | Vic Heyliger | 8–4 | Dartmouth | Joe Riley, Dartmouth, F |
| 1949 | Boston College | John Kelley | 4–3 | Dartmouth | Dick Desmond, Dartmouth, G |
| 1950 | Colorado College | Cheddy Thompson | 13–4 | Boston University | Ralph Bevins, Boston University, G |
| 1951 | Michigan | Vic Heyliger | 7–1 | Brown | Ed Whiston, Brown, G |
| 1952 | Michigan | Vic Heyliger | 4–1 | Colorado College | Kenneth Kinsley, Colorado Coll, G |
| 1953 | Michigan | Vic Heyliger | 7–3 | Minnesota | John Matchefts, Michigan, F |
| 1954 | Rensselaer | Ned Harkness | 5–4 (OT) | Minnesota | Abbie Moore, Rensselaer, F |
| 1955 | Michigan | Vic Heyliger | 5–3 | Colorado College | Philip Hilton, Colorado College, D |
| 1956 | Michigan | Vic Heyliger | 7–5 | Michigan Tech | Lorne Howes, Michigan, G |
| 1957 | Colorado College | Thomas Bedecki | 13–6 | Michigan | Bob McCusker, Colorado Coll, F |
| 1958 | Denver | Murray Armstrong | 6–2 | N Dakota | Murray Massier, Denver, F |
| 1959 | N Dakota | Bob May | 4–3 (OT) | Michigan St | Reg Morelli, N Dakota, F |
| 1960 | Denver | Murray Armstrong | 5–3 | Michigan Tech | Bob Marquis, Boston University, F |
| 1961 | Denver | Murray Armstrong | 12–2 | St. Lawrence | Barry Urbanski, Boston Univ, G |
| 1962 | Michigan Tech | John MacInnes | 7–1 | Clarkson | Louis Angotti, Michigan Tech, F |
| 1963 | N Dakota | Barney Thorndycraft | 6–5 | Denver | Al McLean, N Dakota, F |
| 1964 | Michigan | Allen Renfrew | 6–3 | Denver | Bob Gray, Michigan, G |
| 1965 | Michigan Tech | John MacInnes | 8–2 | Boston College | Gary Milroy, Michigan Tech, F |
| 1966 | Michigan St | Amo Bessone | 6–1 | Clarkson | Gaye Cooley, Michigan St, G |
| 1967 | Cornell | Ned Harkness | 4–1 | Boston University | Walt Stanowski, Cornell, D |
| 1968 | Denver | Murray Armstrong | 4–0 | N Dakota | Gerry Powers, Denver, G |
| 1969 | Denver | Murray Armstrong | 4–3 | Cornell | Keith Magnuson, Denver, D |
| 1970 | Cornell | Ned Harkness | 6–4 | Clarkson | Daniel Lodboa, Cornell, D |
| 1971 | Boston University | Jack Kelley | 4–2 | Minnesota | Dan Brady, Boston University, G |
| 1972 | Boston University | Jack Kelley | 4–0 | Cornell | Tim Regan, Boston University, G |
| 1973 | Wisconsin | Bob Johnson | 4–2 | Vacated | Dean Talafous, Wisconsin, F |
| 1974 | Minnesota | Herb Brooks | 4–2 | Michigan Tech | Brad Shelstad, Minnesota, G |
| 1975 | Michigan Tech | John MacInnes | 6–1 | Minnesota | Jim Warden, Michigan Tech, G |
| 1976 | Minnesota | Herb Brooks | 6–4 | Michigan Tech | Tom Vanelli, Minnesota, F |
| 1977 | Wisconsin | Bob Johnson | 6–5 (OT) | Michigan | Julian Baretta, Wisconsin, G |
| 1978 | Boston University | Jack Parker | 5–3 | Boston College | Jack O'Callahan, Boston Univ, D |
| 1979 | Minnesota | Herb Brooks | 4–3 | N Dakota | Steve Janaszak, Minnesota, G |
| 1980 | N Dakota | John Gasparini | 5–2 | Northern Michigan | Doug Smail, N Dakota, F |
| 1981 | Wisconsin | Bob Johnson | 6–3 | Minnesota | Marc Behrend, Wisconsin, G |
| 1982 | N Dakota | John Gasparini | 5–2 | Wisconsin | Phil Sykes, N Dakota, F |
| 1983 | Wisconsin | Jeff Sauer | 6–2 | Harvard | Marc Behrend, Wisconsin, G |
| 1984 | Bowling Green | Jerry York | 5–4 (OT) | MN–Duluth | Gary Kruzich, Bowling Green, G |
| 1985 | Rensselaer | Mike Addesa | 2–1 | Providence | Chris Terreri, Providence, G |
| 1986 | Michigan St | Ron Mason | 6–5 | Harvard | Mike Donnelly, Michigan St, F |
| 1987 | N Dakota | John Gasparini | 5–3 | Michigan St | Tony Hrkac, N Dakota, F |
| 1988 | Lake Superior St | Frank Anzalone | 4–3 (OT) | St. Lawrence | Bruce Hoffort, Lake Superior St, G |
| 1989 | Harvard | Bill Cleary | 4–3 (OT) | Minnesota | Ted Donato, Harvard, F |
| 1990 | Wisconsin | Jeff Sauer | 7–3 | Colgate | Chris Tancill, Wisconsin, F |
| 1991 | N Michigan | Rick Comley | 8–7 (3OT) | Boston University | Scott Beattie, N Michigan, F |
| 1992 | Lake Superior St | Jeff Jackson | 4–2 | Wisconsin | Paul Constantin, Lake Superior St, F |
| 1993 | Maine | Shawn Walsh | 5–4 | Lake Superior St | Jim Montgomery, Maine, F |
| 1994 | Lake Superior St | Jeff Jackson | 9–1 | Boston University | Sean Tallaire, Lake Superior St, F |
| 1995 | Boston University | Jack Parker | 6–2 | Maine | Chris O'Sullivan, Boston Univ, F |
| 1996 | Michigan | Red Berenson | 3–2 (OT) | Colorado College | Brendan Morrison, Michigan, F |
| 1997 | N Dakota | Dean Blais | 6–4 | Boston University | Matt Henderson, N Dakota, F |
| 1998 | Michigan | Red Berenson | 3–2 (OT) | Boston Coll | Marty Turco, Michigan, G |
| 1999 | Maine | Shawn Walsh | 3–2 (OT) | New Hampshire | Alfie Michaud, Maine, G |
| 2000 | N Dakota | Dean Blais | 4–2 | Boston College | Lee Goren, N Dakota, F |
| 2001 | Boston College | Jerry York | 3–2 (OT) | N Dakota | Chuck Kobasew, Boston College, F |

### DIVISION II *(Discontinued)*

| Year | Champion | Coach | Score | Runner-Up |
|------|----------|-------|-------|-----------|
| 1978 | Merrimack | Thom Lawler | 12–2 | Lake Forest |
| 1979 | Lowell | Bill Riley Jr | 6–4 | Mankato St |
| 1980 | Mankato St | Don Brose | 5–2 | Elmira |
| 1981 | Lowell | Bill Riley Jr | 5–4 | Plattsburgh St |
| 1982 | Lowell | Bill Riley Jr | 6–1 | Plattsburgh St |
| 1983 | RIT | Brian Mason | 4–2 | Bemidji St |
| 1984 | Bemidji St | R.H. (Bob) Peters | 14–4* | Merrimack |
| 1993 | Bemidji St | R.H. (Bob) Peters | 15–6* | Mercyhurst |
| 1994 | Bemidji St | R.H. (Bob) Peters | 7–6* | AL–Huntsville |

# Ice Hockey (Cont.)

## DIVISION II (Cont.)

| Year | Champion | Coach | Score | Runner-Up |
|------|----------|-------|-------|-----------|
| 1995 | Bemidji St | R.H. (Bob) Peters | 11–6* | Mercyhurst |
| 1996 | AL–Huntsville | Doug Ross | 10–1* | Bemidji St |
| 1997 | Bemidji St | R.H. (Bob) Peters | 7–4* | AL–Huntsville |
| 1998 | AL–Huntsville | Doug Ross | 11–4* | Bemidji St |
| 1999 | St. Michael's (VT) | Lou DiMasi | 12–9* | New Hamp. Coll |

*Two-game, total-goal series.

## DIVISION III

| Year | Champion | Coach | Score | Runner-Up |
|------|----------|-------|-------|-----------|
| 1984 | Babson | Bob Riley | 8–0 | Union (NY) |
| 1985 | RIT | Bruce Delventhal | 5–1 | Bemidji St |
| 1986 | Bemidji St | R.H. (Bob) Peters | 8–5 | Vacated |
| 1987 | Vacated | | | Oswego St |
| 1988 | WI–River Falls | Rick Kozuback | 7–1, 3–5, 3–0 | Elmira |
| 1989 | WI–Stevens Point | Mark Mazzoleni | 3–3, 3–2 | RIT |
| 1990 | WI–Stevens Point | Mark Mazzoleni | 10–1, 3–6, 1–0 | Plattsburgh St |
| 1991 | WI–Stevens Point | Mark Mazzoleni | 6–2 | Mankato St |
| 1992 | Plattsburgh St | Bob Emery | 7–3 | WI–Stevens Point |
| 1993 | WI–Stevens Point | Joe Baldarotta | 4–3 | WI–River Falls |
| 1994 | WI–River Falls | Dean Talafous | 6–4 | WI–Superior |
| 1995 | Middlebury | Bill Beaney | 1–0 | Fredonia St |
| 1996 | Middlebury | Bill Beaney | 3–2 | RIT |
| 1997 | Middlebury | Bill Beaney | 3–2 | WI–Superior |
| 1998 | Middlebury | Bill Beaney | 2–1 | WI–Stevens Point |
| 1999 | Middlebury | Bill Beaney | 5–0 | WI–Superior |
| 2000 | Norwich | Michael McShane | 2–1 | St. Thomas (MN) |
| 2001 | Plattsburgh | Bob Emery | 6–2 | RIT |

## Women
### DIVISION I

| Year | Champion | Coach | Score | Runner-Up |
|------|----------|-------|-------|-----------|
| 2001 | Minnesota–Duluth | Shannon Miller | 4–2 | St. Lawrence |

# Lacrosse

## Men
### DIVISION I

| Year | Champion | Coach | Score | Runner-Up |
|------|----------|-------|-------|-----------|
| 1971 | Cornell | Richie Moran | 12–6 | Maryland |
| 1972 | Virginia | Glenn Thiel | 13–12 | Johns Hopkins |
| 1973 | Maryland | Bud Beardmore | 10–9 (2 OT) | Johns Hopkins |
| 1974 | Johns Hopkins | Bob Scott | 17–12 | Maryland |
| 1975 | Maryland | Bud Beardmore | 20–13 | Navy |
| 1976 | Cornell | Richie Moran | 16–13 (OT) | Maryland |
| 1977 | Cornell | Richie Moran | 16–8 | Johns Hopkins |
| 1978 | Johns Hopkins | Henry Ciccarone | 13–8 | Cornell |
| 1979 | Johns Hopkins | Henry Ciccarone | 15–9 | Maryland |
| 1980 | Johns Hopkins | Henry Ciccarone | 9–8 (2 OT) | Virginia |
| 1981 | N Carolina | Willie Scroggs | 14–13 | Johns Hopkins |
| 1982 | N Carolina | Willie Scroggs | 7–5 | Johns Hopkins |
| 1983 | Syracuse | Roy Simmons Jr | 17–16 | Johns Hopkins |
| 1984 | Johns Hopkins | Don Zimmerman | 13–10 | Syracuse |
| 1985 | Johns Hopkins | Don Zimmerman | 11–4 | Syracuse |
| 1986 | N Carolina | Willie Scroggs | 10–9 (OT) | Virginia |
| 1987 | Johns Hopkins | Don Zimmerman | 11–10 | Cornell |
| 1988 | Syracuse | Roy Simmons Jr | 13–8 | Cornell |
| 1989 | Syracuse | Roy Simmons Jr | 13–12 | Johns Hopkins |
| 1990 | Syracuse | Roy Simmons Jr | 21–9 | Loyola (MD) |
| 1991 | N Carolina | Dave Klarmann | 18–13 | Towson St |
| 1992 | Princeton | Bill Tierney | 10–9 | Syracuse |
| 1993 | Syracuse | Roy Simmons Jr | 13–12 | N Carolina |
| 1994 | Princeton | Bill Tierney | 9–8 (OT) | Virginia |
| 1995 | Syracuse | Roy Simmons Jr | 13–9 | Maryland |
| 1996 | Princeton | Bill Tierney | 13–12 (OT) | Virginia |
| 1997 | Princeton | Bill Tierney | 19–7 | Maryland |
| 1998 | Princeton | Bill Tierney | 15–5 | Maryland |

## Men (Cont.)
### DIVISION I (Cont.)

| | | | |
|---|---|---|---|
| 1999 | Virginia | Dom Starsia | 12–10 | Syracuse |
| 2000 | Syracuse | John Desko | 13–7 | Princeton |
| 2001 | Princeton | Bill Tierney | 10–9 (OT) | Syracuse |

### DIVISION II (Discontinued, then renewed)

| Year | Champion | Coach | Score | Runner-Up |
|---|---|---|---|---|
| 1974 | Towson St | Carl Runk | 18–17 (OT) | Hobart |
| 1975 | Cortland St | Chuck Winters | 12–11 | Hobart |
| 1976 | Hobart | Jerry Schmidt | 18–9 | Adelphi |
| 1977 | Hobart | Jerry Schmidt | 23–13 | Washington (MD) |
| 1978 | Roanoke | Paul Griffin | 14–13 | Hobart |
| 1979 | Adelphi | Paul Doherty | 17–12 | MD–Baltimore County |
| 1980 | MD–Baltimore County | Dick Watts | 23–14 | Adelphi |
| 1981 | Adelphi | Paul Doherty | 17–14 | Loyola (MD) |
| 1993 | Adelphi | Kevin Sheehan | 11–7 | LIU–C.W. Post |
| 1994 | Springfield | Keith Bugbee | 15–12 | New York Tech |
| 1995 | Adelphi | Sandy Kapatos | 12–10 | Springfield |
| 1996 | LIU–C.W. Post | Tom Postel | 15–10 | Adelphi |
| 1997 | New York Tech | Jack Kaley | 18–11 | Adelphi |
| 1998 | Adelphi | Sandy Kapatos | 18–6 | LIU–C.W. Post |
| 1999 | Adelphi | Sandy Kapatos | 11–8 | LIU–C.W. Post |
| 2000 | Limestone | Mike Cerino | 10–9 | LIU–C.W. Post |
| 2001 | Adelphi | Sandy Kapatos | 14–10 | Limestone |

### DIVISION III

| Year | Champion | Coach | Score | Runner-Up |
|---|---|---|---|---|
| 1980 | Hobart | Dave Urick | 11–8 | Cortland St |
| 1981 | Hobart | Dave Urick | 10–8 | Cortland St |
| 1982 | Hobart | Dave Urick | 9–8 (OT) | Washington (MD) |
| 1983 | Hobart | Dave Urick | 13–9 | Roanoke |
| 1984 | Hobart | Dave Urick | 12–5 | Washington (MD) |
| 1985 | Hobart | Dave Urick | 15–8 | Washington (MD) |
| 1986 | Hobart | Dave Urick | 13–10 | Washington (MD) |
| 1987 | Hobart | Dave Urick | 9–5 | Ohio Wesleyan |
| 1988 | Hobart | Dave Urick | 18–9 | Ohio Wesleyan |
| 1989 | Hobart | Dave Urick | 11–8 | Ohio Wesleyan |
| 1990 | Hobart | B.J. O'Hara | 18–6 | Washington (MD) |
| 1991 | Hobart | B.J. O'Hara | 12–11 | Salisbury St |
| 1992 | Nazareth (NY) | Scott Nelson | 13–12 | Hobart |
| 1993 | Hobart | B.J. O'Hara | 16–10 | Ohio Wesleyan |
| 1994 | Salisbury St | Jim Berkman | 15–9 | Hobart |
| 1995 | Salisbury St | Jim Berkman | 22–13 | Nazareth |
| 1996 | Nazareth | Scott Nelson | 11–10 (OT) | Washington (MD) |
| 1997 | Nazareth | Scott Nelson | 15–14 (OT) | Washington (MD) |
| 1998 | Washington (MD) | John Haus | 16–10 | Nazareth |
| 1999 | Salisbury St | Jim Berkman | 13–6 | Middlebury |
| 2000 | Middlebury | Erin Quinn | 16–12 | Salisbury St |
| 2001 | Middlebury | Erin Quinn | 15–10 | Gettysburg |

## Women*
### DIVISION I

| Year | Champion | Coach | Score | Runner-Up |
|---|---|---|---|---|
| 2001 | Maryland | Cindy Timchal | 14–13 (OT) | Georgetown |

### DIVISION II

| Year | Champion | Coach | Score | Runner-Up |
|---|---|---|---|---|
| 2001 | LIU–C.W. Post | Karen MacCrate | 13–9 | W Chester |

*Divisions I and II competed for a single championship until 2001.

## Women (Cont.)
### DIVISIONS I AND II

| Year | Champion | Coach | Score | Runner-Up |
|------|----------|-------|-------|-----------|
| 1982 | Massachusetts | Pamela Hixon | 9–6 | Trenton St |
| 1983 | Delaware | Janet Smith | 10–7 | Temple |
| 1984 | Temple | Tina Sloan Green | 6–4 | Maryland |
| 1985 | New Hampshire | Marisa Didio | 6–5 | Maryland |
| 1986 | Maryland | Sue Tyler | 11–10 | Penn St |
| 1987 | Penn St | Susan Scheetz | 7–6 | Temple |
| 1988 | Temple | Tina Sloan Green | 15–7 | Penn St |
| 1989 | Penn St | Susan Scheetz | 7–6 | Harvard |
| 1990 | Harvard | Carole Kleinfelder | 8–7 | Maryland |
| 1991 | Virginia | Jane Miller | 8–6 | Maryland |
| 1992 | Maryland | Cindy Timchal | 11–10 | Harvard |
| 1993 | Virginia | Jane Miller | 8–6 (OT) | Princeton |
| 1994 | Princeton | Chris Sailer | 10–7 | Virginia |
| 1995 | Maryland | Cindy Timchal | 13–5 | Princeton |
| 1996 | Maryland | Cindy Timchal | 10–5 | Virginia |
| 1997 | Maryland | Cindy Timchal | 8–7 | Loyola (MD) |
| 1998 | Maryland | Cindy Timchal | 11–5 | Virginia |
| 1999 | Maryland | Cindy Timchal | 16–6 | Virginia |
| 2000 | Maryland | Cindy Timchal | 16–8 | Princeton |

### DIVISION III

| Year | Champion | Score | Runner-Up | Year | Champion | Score | Runner-Up |
|------|----------|-------|-----------|------|----------|-------|-----------|
| 1985 | Trenton St | 7–4 | Ursinus | 1994 | Trenton St | 29–11 | William Smith |
| 1986 | Ursinus | 12–10 | Trenton St | 1995 | Trenton St | 14–13 | William Smith |
| 1987 | Trenton St | 8–7 (OT) | Ursinus | 1996 | Trenton St | 15–8 | Middlebury |
| 1988 | Trenton St | 14–11 | William Smith | 1997 | Middlebury | 14–9 | College of NJ* |
| 1989 | Ursinus | 8–6 | Trenton St | 1998 | Coll of NJ | 14–9 | Williams |
| 1990 | Ursinus | 7–6 | St. Lawrence | 1999 | Middlebury | 10–9 | Amherst |
| 1991 | Trenton St | 7–6 | Ursinus | 2000 | Coll of NJ | 14–8 | Williams |
| 1992 | Trenton St | 5–3 | William Smith | 2001 | Middlebury | 11–10 | Amherst |
| 1993 | Trenton St | 10–9 | William Smith | | | | |

# Rifle

| | | | | | | Individual Champions | |
|------|----------|-------|-------|-----------|-------|----------------------|----------|
| Year | Champion | Coach | Score | Runner-Up | Score | Air Rifle | Smallbore |
| 1980 | Tennessee Tech | James Newkirk | 6201 | W Virginia | 6150 | Rod Fitz-Randolph, Tennessee Tech | Rod Fitz-Randolph, Tennessee Tech |
| 1981 | Tennessee Tech | James Newkirk | 6139 | W Virginia | 6136 | John Rost, W Virginia | Kurt Fitz-Randolph, Tennessee Tech |
| 1982 | Tennessee Tech | James Newkirk | 6138 | W Virginia | 6136 | John Rost, W Virginia | Kurt Fitz-Randolph, Tennessee Tech |
| 1983 | W Virginia | Edward Etzel | 6166 | Tennessee Tech | 6148 | Ray Slonena, Tennessee Tech | David Johnson, W Virginia |
| 1984 | W Virginia | Edward Etzel | 6206 | E Tennessee St | 6142 | Pat Spurgin, Murray St | Bob Broughton, W Virginia |
| 1985 | Murray St | Elvis Green | 6150 | W Virginia | 6149 | Christian Heller, W Virginia | Pat Spurgin, Murray St |
| 1986 | W Virginia | Edward Etzel | 6229 | Murray St | 6163 | Marianne Wallace, Murray St | Mike Anti, W Virginia |
| 1987 | Murray St | Elvis Green | 6205 | W Virginia | 6203 | Rob Harbison, TN–Martin | Web Wright, W Virginia |
| 1988 | W Virginia | Greg Perrine | 6192 | Murray St | 6183 | Deena Wigger, Murray St | Web Wright, W Virginia |
| 1989 | W Virginia | Edward Etzel | 6234 | S Florida | 6180 | Michelle Scarborough, S Florida | Deb Sinclair, AK–Fairbanks |
| 1990 | W Virginia | Marsha Beasley | 6205 | Navy | 6101 | Gary Hardy, W Virginia | M. Scarborough, S Florida |
| 1991 | W Virginia | Marsha Beasley | 6171 | AK–Fairbanks | 6110 | Ann Pfiffner, W Virginia | Soma Dutta, UTEP |
| 1992 | W Virginia | Marsha Beasley | 6214 | AK–Fairbanks | 6166 | Ann Pfiffner, W Virginia | Tim Manges, W Virginia |
| 1993 | W Virginia | Marsha Beasley | 6179 | AK–Fairbanks | 6169 | Trevor Gathman, W Virginia | Eric Uptagrafft, W Virginia |
| 1994 | AK–Fairbanks | Randy Pitney | 6194 | W Virginia | 6187 | Nancy Napolski, Kentucky | Cory Brunetti, AK–Fairbanks |

# Rifle (Cont.)

| Year | Champion | Coach | Score | Runner-Up | Score | Individual Champions | |
|---|---|---|---|---|---|---|---|
| | | | | | | Air Rifle | Smallbore |
| 1995 | W Virginia | Marsha Beasley | 6241 | Air Force | 6187 | Benji Belden, Murray St | Oleg Selezner, AK–Fairbanks |
| 1996 | W Virginia | Marsha Beasley | 6179 | Air Force | 6168 | Trevor Gathman, W Virginia | Joe Johnson, Navy |
| 1997 | W Virginia | Marsha Beasley | 6223 | Kentucky | 6175 | Marra Hastings, Murray St | Marcos Scrivner, W Virginia |
| 1998 | W Virginia | Marsha Beasley | 6214 | AK–Fairbanks | 6175 | Emily Caruso, Norwich | Karen Juzinuk, Xavier |
| 1999 | AK–Fairbanks | Randy Pitney | 6276 | Navy | 6168 | Kelly Mansfield, AK–Fairbanks | Kelly Mansfield, AK–Fairbanks |
| 2000 | AK–Fairbanks | Randy Pitney | 6285 | Xavier | 6156 | Kelly Mansfield, AK–Fairbanks | Nicole Allaire, Nebraska |
| 2001 | AK–Fairbanks | David Johnson | 6283 | Kentucky | 6175 | Matthew Emmons, AK–Fairbanks | Matthew Emmons, AK–Fairbanks |

# Skiing

| Year | Champion | Coach | Pts | Runner-Up | Pts | Host or Site |
|---|---|---|---|---|---|---|
| 1954 | Denver | Willy Schaeffler | 384.0 | Seattle | 349.6 | NV–Reno |
| 1955 | Denver | Willy Schaeffler | 567.05 | Dartmouth | 558.935 | Norwich |
| 1956 | Denver | Willy Schaeffler | 582.01 | Dartmouth | 541.77 | Winter Park |
| 1957 | Denver | Willy Schaeffler | 577.95 | Colorado | 545.29 | Ogden Snow Basin |
| 1958 | Dartmouth | Al Merrill | 561.2 | Denver | 550.6 | Dartmouth |
| 1959 | Colorado | Bob Beattie | 549.4 | Denver | 543.6 | Winter Park |
| 1960 | Colorado | Bob Beattie | 571.4 | Denver | 568.6 | Bridger Bowl |
| 1961 | Denver | Willy Schaeffler | 376.19 | Middlebury | 366.94 | Middlebury |
| 1962 | Denver | Willy Schaeffler | 390.08 | Colorado | 374.30 | Squaw Valley |
| 1963 | Denver | Willy Schaeffler | 384.6 | Colorado | 381.6 | Solitude |
| 1964 | Denver | Willy Schaeffler | 370.2 | Dartmouth | 368.8 | Franconia Notch |
| 1965 | Denver | Willy Schaeffler | 380.5 | Utah | 378.4 | Crystal Mountain |
| 1966 | Denver | Willy Schaeffler | 381.02 | Western Colorado | 365.92 | Crested Butte |
| 1967 | Denver | Willy Schaeffler | 376.7 | Wyoming | 375.9 | Sugarloaf Mountain |
| 1968 | Wyoming | John Cress | 383.9 | Denver | 376.2 | Mount Werner |
| 1969 | Denver | Willy Schaeffler | 388.6 | Dartmouth | 372.0 | Mount Werner |
| 1970 | Denver | Willy Schaeffler | 386.6 | Dartmouth | 378.8 | Cannon Mountain |
| 1971 | Denver | Peder Pytte | 394.7 | Colorado | 373.1 | Terry Peak |
| 1972 | Colorado | Bill Marolt | 385.3 | Denver | 380.1 | Winter Park |
| 1973 | Colorado | Bill Marolt | 381.89 | Wyoming | 377.83 | Middlebury |
| 1974 | Colorado | Bill Marolt | 176 | Wyoming | 162 | Jackson Hole |
| 1975 | Colorado | Bill Marolt | 183 | Vermont | 115 | Fort Lewis |
| 1976 | Colorado | Bill Marolt | 112 | | | Bates |
| | Dartmouth | Jim Page | 112 | | | |
| 1977 | Colorado | Bill Marolt | 179 | Wyoming | 154.5 | Winter Park |
| 1978 | Colorado | Bill Marolt | 152.5 | Wyoming | 121.5 | Cannon Mountain |
| 1979 | Colorado | Tim Hinderman | 153 | Utah | 130 | Steamboat Springs |
| 1980 | Vermont | Chip LaCasse | 171 | Utah | 151 | Lake Placid and Stowe |
| 1981 | Utah | Pat Miller | 183 | Vermont | 172 | Park City |
| 1982 | Colorado | Tim Hinderman | 461 | Vermont | 436.5 | Lake Placid |
| 1983 | Utah | Pat Miller | 696 | Vermont | 650 | Bozeman |
| 1984 | Utah | Pat Miller | 750.5 | Vermont | 604 | New Hampshire |
| 1985 | Wyoming | Tim Ameel | 764 | Utah | 744 | Bozeman |
| 1986 | Utah | Pat Miller | 612 | Vermont | 602 | Vermont |
| 1987 | Utah | Pat Miller | 710 | Vermont | 627 | Anchorage |
| 1988 | Utah | Pat Miller | 651 | Vermont | 614 | Middlebury |
| 1989 | Vermont | Chip LaCasse | 672 | Utah | 668 | Jackson Hole |
| 1990 | Vermont | Chip LaCasse | 671 | Utah | 571 | Vermont |
| 1991 | Colorado | Richard Rokos | 713 | Vermont | 682 | Park City, UT |
| 1992 | Vermont | Chip LaCasse | 693.5 | New Mexico | 642.5 | New Hampshire |
| 1993 | Utah | Pat Miller | 783 | Vermont | 700.5 | Steamboat Springs |
| 1994 | Vermont | Chip LaCasse | 688 | Utah | 667 | Sugarloaf, ME |
| 1995 | Colorado | Richard Rokos | 720.5 | Utah | 711 | New Hampshire |
| 1996 | Utah | Pat Miller | 719 | Denver | 635.5 | Montana St |
| 1997 | Utah | Pat Miller | 686 | Vermont | 646.5 | Vermont |
| 1998 | Colorado | Richard Rokos | 654 | Utah | 651.5 | Montana St |
| 1999 | Colorado | Richard Rokos | 650 | Denver | 636 | Bates College |
| 2000 | Denver | Kurt Smitz | 720 | Colorado | 621 | Park City, UT |
| 2001 | Denver | Kurt Smitz | 649 | Vermont | 605 | Middlebury, VT |

## Men

### DIVISION I

| Year | Champion | Coach | Score | Runner-Up |
|---|---|---|---|---|
| 1959 | St. Louis | Bob Guelker | 5–2 | Bridgeport |
| 1960 | St. Louis | Bob Guelker | 3–2 | Maryland |
| 1961 | West Chester | Mel Lorback | 2–0 | St. Louis |
| 1962 | St. Louis | Bob Guelker | 4–3 | Maryland |
| 1963 | St. Louis | Bob Guelker | 3–0 | Navy |
| 1964 | Navy | F.H. Warner | 1–0 | Michigan St |
| 1965 | St. Louis | Bob Guelker | 1–0 | Michigan St |
| 1966 | San Francisco | Steve Negoesco | 5–2 | LIU–Brooklyn |
| 1967 | Michigan St | Gene Kenney | 0–0 | Game called due to |
|  | St. Louis | Harry Keough |  | inclement weather |
| 1968 | Maryland | Doyle Royal | 2–2 (2 OT) |  |
|  | Michigan St | Gene Kenney |  |  |
| 1969 | St. Louis | Harry Keough | 4–0 | San Francisco |
| 1970 | St. Louis | Harry Keough | 1–0 | UCLA |
| 1971 | Vacated |  | 3–2 | St. Louis |
| 1972 | St. Louis | Harry Keough | 4–2 | UCLA |
| 1973 | St. Louis | Harry Keough | 2–1 (OT) | UCLA |
| 1974 | Howard | Lincoln Phillips | 2–1 (4 OT) | St. Louis |
| 1975 | San Francisco | Steve Negoesco | 4–0 | SIU–Edwardsville |
| 1976 | San Francisco | Steve Negoesco | 1–0 | Indiana |
| 1977 | Hartwick | Jim Lennox | 2–1 | San Francisco |
| 1978 | Vacated |  | 2–0 | Indiana |
| 1979 | SIU–Edwardsville | Bob Guelker | 3–2 | Clemson |
| 1980 | San Francisco | Steve Negoesco | 4–3 (OT) | Indiana |
| 1981 | Connecticut | Joe Morrone | 2–1 (OT) | Alabama A&M |
| 1982 | Indiana | Jerry Yeagley | 2–1 (8 OT) | Duke |
| 1983 | Indiana | Jerry Yeagley | 1–0 (2 OT) | Columbia |
| 1984 | Clemson | I.M. Ibrahim | 2–1 | Indiana |
| 1985 | UCLA | Sigi Schmid | 1–0 (8 OT) | American |
| 1986 | Duke | John Rennie | 1–0 | Akron |
| 1987 | Clemson | I.M. Ibrahim | 2–0 | San Diego St |
| 1988 | Indiana | Jerry Yeagley | 1–0 | Howard |
| 1989 | Santa Clara | Steve Sampson | 1–1 (2 OT) |  |
|  | Virginia | Bruce Arena |  |  |
| 1990 | UCLA | Sigi Schmid | 1–0 (OT) | Rutgers |
| 1991 | Virginia | Bruce Arena | 0–0* | Santa Clara |
| 1992 | Virginia | Bruce Arena | 2–0 | San Diego |
| 1993 | Virginia | Bruce Arena | 2–0 | S Carolina |
| 1994 | Virginia | Bruce Arena | 1–0 | Indiana |
| 1995 | Wisconsin | Jim Launder | 2–0 | Duke |
| 1996 | St. John's (NY) | Dave Masur | 4–1 | Florida International |
| 1997 | UCLA | Sigi Schmid | 2–1 | Virginia |
| 1998 | Indiana | Jerry Yeagley | 3–1 | Stanford |
| 1999 | Indiana | Jerry Yeagley | 1–0 | Santa Clara |
| 2000 | Connecticut | Ray Reid | 2–0 | Creighton |

*Under a rule passed in 1991, the NCAA determined that when a score is tied after regulation and overtime, and the championship is determined by penalty kicks, the official score will be 0–0.

### DIVISION II

| Year | Champion | Year | Champion | Year | Champion |
|---|---|---|---|---|---|
| 1972 | SIU–Edwardsville | 1982 | Florida International | 1992 | Southern Connecticut St |
| 1973 | MO–St. Louis | 1983 | Seattle Pacific | 1993 | Seattle Pacific |
| 1974 | Adelphi | 1984 | Florida International | 1994 | Tampa |
| 1975 | Baltimore | 1985 | Seattle Pacific | 1995 | Southern Connecticut St |
| 1976 | Loyola (MD) | 1986 | Seattle Pacific | 1996 | Grand Canyon |
| 1977 | Alabama A&M | 1987 | Southern Connecticut St | 1997 | Cal St-Bakersfield |
| 1978 | Seattle Pacific | 1988 | Florida Tech | 1998 | Southern Connecticut St |
| 1979 | Alabama A&M | 1989 | New Hampshire College | 1999 | Southern Connecticut St |
| 1980 | Lock Haven | 1990 | Southern Connecticut St | 2000 | Cal St–Dominguez Hills |
| 1981 | Tampa | 1991 | Florida Tech |  |  |

## Men *(Cont.)*

### DIVISION III

| Year | Champion | Year | Champion | Year | Champion |
|------|----------|------|----------|------|----------|
| 1974 | Brockport St | 1983 | NC–Greensboro | 1992 | Kean |
| 1975 | Babson | 1984 | Wheaton (IL) | 1993 | UC–San Diego |
| 1976 | Brandeis | 1985 | NC–Greensboro | 1994 | Bethany (WV) |
| 1977 | Lock Haven | 1986 | NC–Greensboro | 1995 | Williams |
| 1978 | Lock Haven | 1987 | NC–Greensboro | 1996 | College of New Jersey |
| 1979 | Babson | 1988 | UC–San Diego | 1997 | Wheaton (IL) |
| 1980 | Babson | 1989 | Elizabethtown | 1998 | Ohio Wesleyan |
| 1981 | Glassboro St | 1990 | Glassboro St | 1999 | St. Lawrence |
| 1982 | NC–Greensboro | 1991 | UC–San Diego | 2000 | Messiah |

## Women

### DIVISION I

| Year | Champion | Coach | Score | Runner-Up |
|------|----------|-------|-------|-----------|
| 1982 | N Carolina | Anson Dorrance | 2–0 | Central Florida |
| 1983 | N Carolina | Anson Dorrance | 4–0 | George Mason |
| 1984 | N Carolina | Anson Dorrance | 2–0 | Connecticut |
| 1985 | George Mason | Hank Leung | 2–0 | North Carolina |
| 1986 | N Carolina | Anson Dorrance | 2–0 | Colorado College |
| 1987 | N Carolina | Anson Dorrance | 1–0 | Massachusetts |
| 1988 | N Carolina | Anson Dorrance | 4–1 | North Carolina St |
| 1989 | N Carolina | Anson Dorrance | 2–0 | Colorado College |
| 1990 | N Carolina | Anson Dorrance | 6–0 | Connecticut |
| 1991 | N Carolina | Anson Dorrance | 3–1 | Wisconsin |
| 1992 | N Carolina | Anson Dorrance | 9–1 | Duke |
| 1993 | N Carolina | Anson Dorrance | 6–0 | George Mason |
| 1994 | N Carolina | Anson Dorrance | 5–0 | Notre Dame |
| 1995 | Notre Dame | Chris Petrucelli | 1–0 | Portland |
| 1996 | N Carolina | Anson Dorrance | 1–0 | Notre Dame |
| 1997 | N Carolina | Anson Dorrance | 2–0 | Connecticut |
| 1998 | Florida | Becky Burleigh | 1–0 | N Carolina |
| 1999 | N Carolina | Anson Dorrance | 2–0 | Notre Dame |
| 2000 | N Carolina | Anson Dorrance | 2–1 | UCLA |

### DIVISION II

| Year | Champion |
|------|----------|
| 1988 | Cal St–Hayward |
| 1989 | Barry |
| 1990 | Sonoma St |
| 1991 | Cal St–Dominguez Hills |
| 1992 | Barry |
| 1993 | Barry |
| 1994 | Franklin Pierce |
| 1995 | Franklin Pierce |
| 1996 | Franklin Pierce |
| 1997 | Franklin Pierce |
| 1998 | Lynn |
| 1999 | Franklin Pierce |
| 2000 | UC–San Diego |

### DIVISION III

| Year | Champion |
|------|----------|
| 1986 | Rochester |
| 1987 | Rochester |
| 1988 | William Smith |
| 1989 | UC–San Diego |
| 1990 | Ithaca |
| 1991 | Ithaca |
| 1992 | Cortland St |
| 1993 | Trenton St |
| 1994 | Trenton St |
| 1995 | UC San Diego |
| 1996 | UC–San Diego |
| 1997 | UC–San Diego |
| 1998 | Macalester |
| 1999 | UC–San Diego |
| 2000 | College of New Jersey |

# Softball

## DIVISION I

| Year | Champion | Coach | Score | Runner-Up |
|------|----------|-------|-------|-----------|
| 1982 | UCLA* | Sharron Backus | 2–0† | Fresno St |
| 1983 | Texas A&M | Bob Brock | 2–0‡ | Cal St–Fullerton |
| 1984 | UCLA | Sharron Backus | 1–0# | Texas A&M |
| 1985 | UCLA | Sharron Backus | 2–1** | Nebraska |
| 1986 | Cal St–Fullerton* | Judi Garman | 3–0 | Texas A&M |
| 1987 | Texas A&M | Bob Brock | 4–1 | UCLA |
| 1988 | UCLA | Sharron Backus | 3–0 | Fresno St |
| 1989 | UCLA* | Sharron Backus | 1–0 | Fresno St |
| 1990 | UCLA | Sharron Backus | 2–0 | Fresno St |
| 1991 | Arizona | Mike Candrea | 5–1 | UCLA |
| 1992 | UCLA* | Sharron Backus | 2–0 | Arizona |
| 1993 | Arizona | Mike Candrea | 1–0 | UCLA |
| 1994 | Arizona | Mike Candrea | 4–0 | Cal St–Northridge |
| 1995 | Vacated | — | — | Arizona |
| 1996 | Arizona* | Mike Candrea | 6–4 | Washington |
| 1997 | Arizona | Mike Candrea | 10–2*** | UCLA |
| 1998 | Fresno St | Margie Wright | 1–0 | Arizona |
| 1999 | UCLA | Sue Enquist | 3–2 | Washington |
| 2000 | Oklahoma | Patty Gasso | 3–1 | UCLA |
| 2001 | Arizona* | Mike Candrea | 1–0 | UCLA |

*Undefeated teams in final series. †Eight innings. ‡12 innings. #13 innings. **Nine innings. ***Five innings.

## DIVISION II

| Year | Champion | Year | Champion | Year | Champion |
|------|----------|------|----------|------|----------|
| 1982 | Sam Houston St | 1989 | Cal St–Bakersfield | 1996 | Kennesaw St |
| 1983 | Cal St–Northridge | 1990 | Cal St–Bakersfield | 1997 | California (PA)* |
| 1984 | Cal St–Northridge | 1991 | Augustana (SD) | 1998 | California (PA) |
| 1985 | Cal St–Northridge | 1992 | Missouri Southern | 1999 | Humboldt St |
| 1986 | SF Austin St | 1993 | Florida Southern | 2000 | N Dakota St |
| 1987 | Cal St–Northridge | 1994 | Merrimack | 2001 | Nebraska–Omaha |
| 1988 | Cal St–Bakersfield | 1995 | Kennesaw St | | |

## DIVISION III

| Year | Champion | Year | Champion | Year | Champion |
|------|----------|------|----------|------|----------|
| 1982 | Sam Houston St | 1988 | Central (IA) | 1995 | Chapman |
| 1982 | Eastern Connecticut St* | 1989 | Trenton St* | 1996 | Trenton St* |
| 1983 | Trenton St | 1990 | Eastern Connecticut St | 1997 | Simpson (IA)* |
| 1984 | Buena Vista* | 1991 | Central (IA) | 1998 | WI–Stevens Point |
| 1985 | Eastern Connecticut St | 1992 | Trenton St | 1999 | Simpson (IA) |
| 1986 | Eastern Connecticut St | 1993 | Central (IA) | 2000 | St. Mary's |
| 1987 | Trenton St* | 1994 | Trenton St | 2001 | Muskingum* |

*Undefeated teams in final series.

# Swimming and Diving

## Men
### DIVISION I

| Year | Champion | Coach | Pts | Runner-Up | Pts |
|------|----------|-------|-----|-----------|-----|
| 1937 | Michigan | Matt Mann | 75 | Ohio St | 39 |
| 1938 | Michigan | Matt Mann | 46 | Ohio St | 45 |
| 1939 | Michigan | Matt Mann | 65 | Ohio St | 58 |
| 1940 | Michigan | Matt Mann | 45 | Yale | 42 |
| 1941 | Michigan | Matt Mann | 61 | Yale | 58 |
| 1942 | Yale | Robert J.H. Kiphuth | 71 | Michigan | 39 |
| 1943 | Ohio St | Mike Peppe | 81 | Michigan | 47 |
| 1944 | Yale | Robert J.H. Kiphuth | 39 | Michigan | 38 |
| 1945 | Ohio St | Mike Peppe | 56 | Michigan | 48 |
| 1946 | Ohio St | Mike Peppe | 61 | Michigan | 37 |
| 1947 | Ohio St | Mike Peppe | 66 | Michigan | 39 |
| 1948 | Michigan | Matt Mann | 44 | Ohio St | 41 |
| 1949 | Ohio St | Mike Peppe | 49 | Iowa | 35 |
| 1950 | Ohio St | Mike Peppe | 64 | Yale | 43 |
| 1951 | Yale | Robert J.H. Kiphuth | 81 | Michigan St | 60 |
| 1952 | Ohio St | Mike Peppe | 94 | Yale | 81 |

## Men *(Cont.)*

### DIVISION I *(Cont.)*

| Year | Champion | Coach | Pts | Runner-Up | Pts |
|------|----------|-------|-----|-----------|-----|
| 1953 | Yale | Robert J.H. Kiphuth | 96½ | Ohio St | 73½ |
| 1954 | Ohio St | Mike Peppe | 94 | Michigan | 67 |
| 1955 | Ohio St | Mike Peppe | 90 | Yale | 51 |
| | | | | Michigan | 51 |
| 1956 | Ohio St | Mike Peppe | 68 | Yale | 54 |
| 1957 | Michigan | Gus Stager | 69 | Yale | 61 |
| 1958 | Michigan | Gus Stager | 72 | Yale | 63 |
| 1959 | Michigan | Gus Stager | 137½ | Ohio St | 44 |
| 1960 | Southern Cal | Peter Daland | 87 | Michigan | 73 |
| 1961 | Michigan | Gus Stager | 85 | Southern Cal | 62 |
| 1962 | Ohio St | Mike Peppe | 92 | Southern Cal | 46 |
| 1963 | Southern Cal | Peter Daland | 81 | Yale | 77 |
| 1964 | Southern Cal | Peter Daland | 96 | Indiana | 91 |
| 1965 | Southern Cal | Peter Daland | 285 | Indiana | 278½ |
| 1966 | Southern Cal | Peter Daland | 302 | Indiana | 286 |
| 1967 | Stanford | Jim Gaughran | 275 | Southern Cal | 260 |
| 1968 | Indiana | James Counsilman | 346 | Yale | 253 |
| 1969 | Indiana | James Counsilman | 427 | Southern Cal | 306 |
| 1970 | Indiana | James Counsilman | 332 | Southern Cal | 235 |
| 1971 | Indiana | James Counsilman | 351 | Southern Cal | 260 |
| 1972 | Indiana | James Counsilman | 390 | Southern Cal | 371 |
| 1973 | Indiana | James Counsilman | 358 | Tennessee | 294 |
| 1974 | Southern Cal | Peter Daland | 339 | Indiana | 338 |
| 1975 | Southern Cal | Peter Daland | 344 | Indiana | 274 |
| 1976 | Southern Cal | Peter Daland | 398 | Tennessee | 237 |
| 1977 | Southern Cal | Peter Daland | 385 | Alabama | 204 |
| 1978 | Tennessee | Ray Bussard | 307 | Auburn | 185 |
| 1979 | California | Nort Thornton | 287 | Southern Cal | 227 |
| 1980 | California | Nort Thornton | 234 | Texas | 220 |
| 1981 | Texas | Eddie Reese | 259 | UCLA | 189 |
| 1982 | UCLA | Ron Ballatore | 219 | Texas | 210 |
| 1983 | Florida | Randy Reese | 238 | Southern Meth | 227 |
| 1984 | Florida | Randy Reese | 287½ | Texas | 277 |
| 1985 | Stanford | Skip Kenney | 403½ | Florida | 302 |
| 1986 | Stanford | Skip Kenney | 404 | California | 335 |
| 1987 | Stanford | Skip Kenney | 374 | Southern Cal | 296 |
| 1988 | Texas | Eddie Reese | 424 | Southern Cal | 369½ |
| 1989 | Texas | Eddie Reese | 475 | Stanford | 396 |
| 1990 | Texas | Eddie Reese | 506 | Southern Cal | 423 |
| 1991 | Texas | Eddie Reese | 476 | Stanford | 420 |
| 1992 | Stanford | Skip Kenney | 632 | Texas | 356 |
| 1993 | Stanford | Skip Kenney | 520½ | Michigan | 396 |
| 1994 | Stanford | Skip Kenney | 566½ | Texas | 445 |
| 1995 | Michigan | Jon Urbanchek | 561 | Stanford | 475 |
| 1996 | Texas | Eddie Reese | 479 | Auburn | 443½ |
| 1997 | Auburn | David Marsh | 496½ | Stanford | 340 |
| 1998 | Stanford | Skip Kenney | 594 | Auburn | 394½ |
| 1999 | Auburn | David Marsh | 467½ | Stanford | 414½ |
| 2000 | Texas | Eddie Reese | 538 | Auburn | 385 |
| 2001 | Texas | Eddie Reese | 597½ | Stanford | 457½ |

### DIVISION II

| Year | Champion | Year | Champion | Year | Champion |
|------|----------|------|----------|------|----------|
| 1963 | SW Missouri St | 1976 | Cal St–Chico | 1989 | Cal St–Bakersfield |
| 1964 | Bucknell | 1977 | Cal St–Northridge | 1990 | Cal St–Bakersfield |
| 1965 | San Diego St | 1978 | Cal St–Northridge | 1991 | Cal St–Bakersfield |
| 1966 | San Diego St | 1979 | Cal St–Northridge | 1992 | Cal St–Bakersfield |
| 1967 | UC–Santa Barbara | 1980 | Oakland (MI) | 1993 | Cal St–Bakersfield |
| 1968 | Long Beach St | 1981 | Cal St–Northridge | 1994 | Oakland (MI) |
| 1969 | UC–Irvine | 1982 | Cal St–Northridge | 1995 | Oakland (MI) |
| 1970 | UC–Irvine | 1983 | Cal St–Northridge | 1996 | Oakland (MI) |
| 1971 | UC–Irvine | 1984 | Cal St–Northridge | 1997 | Oakland (MI) |
| 1972 | Eastern Michigan | 1985 | Cal St–Northridge | 1998 | Cal St–Bakersfield |
| 1973 | Cal St–Chico | 1986 | Cal St–Bakersfield | 1999 | Drury |
| 1974 | Cal St–Chico | 1987 | Cal St–Bakersfield | 2000 | Cal St–Bakersfield |
| 1975 | Cal St–Northridge | 1988 | Cal St–Bakersfield | 2001 | Cal St–Bakersfield |

## DIVISION III

| Year | Champion | Year | Champion | Year | Champion |
|------|----------|------|----------|------|----------|
| 1975 | Cal St–Chico | 1984 | Kenyon | 1993 | Kenyon |
| 1976 | St. Lawrence | 1985 | Kenyon | 1994 | Kenyon |
| 1977 | Johns Hopkins | 1986 | Kenyon | 1995 | Kenyon |
| 1978 | Johns Hopkins | 1987 | Kenyon | 1996 | Kenyon |
| 1979 | Johns Hopkins | 1988 | Kenyon | 1997 | Kenyon |
| 1980 | Kenyon | 1989 | Kenyon | 1998 | Kenyon |
| 1981 | Kenyon | 1990 | Kenyon | 1999 | Kenyon |
| 1982 | Kenyon | 1991 | Kenyon | 2000 | Kenyon |
| 1983 | Kenyon | 1992 | Kenyon | 2001 | Kenyon |

# Women

## DIVISION I

| Year | Champion | Coach | Pts | Runner-Up | Pts |
|------|----------|-------|-----|-----------|-----|
| 1982 | Florida | Randy Reese | 505 | Stanford | 383 |
| 1983 | Stanford | George Haines | 418½ | Florida | 389½ |
| 1984 | Texas | Richard Quick | 392 | Stanford | 324 |
| 1985 | Texas | Richard Quick | 643 | Florida | 400 |
| 1986 | Texas | Richard Quick | 633 | Florida | 586 |
| 1987 | Texas | Richard Quick | 648½ | Stanford | 631½ |
| 1988 | Texas | Richard Quick | 661 | Florida | 542½ |
| 1989 | Stanford | Richard Quick | 610½ | Texas | 547 |
| 1990 | Texas | Mark Schubert | 632 | Stanford | 622½ |
| 1991 | Texas | Mark Schubert | 746 | Stanford | 653 |
| 1992 | Stanford | Richard Quick | 735½ | Texas | 651 |
| 1993 | Stanford | Richard Quick | 649½ | Florida | 421 |
| 1994 | Stanford | Richard Quick | 512 | Texas | 421 |
| 1995 | Stanford | Richard Quick | 497½ | Michigan | 478½ |
| 1996 | Stanford | Richard Quick | 478 | SMU | 397 |
| 1997 | Southern Cal | Mark Schubert | 406 | Stanford | 395 |
| 1998 | Stanford | Richard Quick | 422 | Arizona | 378 |
| 1999 | Georgia | Jack Bauerle | 504½ | Stanford | 441 |
| 2000 | Georgia | Jack Bauerle | 490½ | Arizona | 472 |
| 2001 | Georgia | Jack Bauerle | 389 | Stanford | 387½ |

## DIVISION II

| Year | Champion | Year | Champion | Year | Champion |
|------|----------|------|----------|------|----------|
| 1982 | Cal St–Northridge | 1989 | Cal St–Northridge | 1996 | Air Force |
| 1983 | Clarion | 1990 | Oakland (MI) | 1997 | Drury |
| 1984 | Clarion | 1991 | Oakland (MI) | 1998 | Drury |
| 1985 | S Florida | 1992 | Oakland (MI) | 1999 | Drury |
| 1986 | Clarion | 1993 | Oakland (MI) | 2000 | Drury |
| 1987 | Cal St–Northridge | 1994 | Oakland (MI) | 2001 | Truman St |
| 1988 | Cal St–Northridge | 1995 | Air Force | | |

## DIVISION III

| Year | Champion | Year | Champion | Year | Champion |
|------|----------|------|----------|------|----------|
| 1982 | Williams | 1989 | Kenyon | 1996 | Kenyon |
| 1983 | Williams | 1990 | Kenyon | 1997 | Kenyon |
| 1984 | Kenyon | 1991 | Kenyon | 1998 | Kenyon |
| 1985 | Kenyon | 1992 | Kenyon | 1999 | Kenyon |
| 1986 | Kenyon | 1993 | Kenyon | 2000 | Kenyon |
| 1987 | Kenyon | 1994 | Kenyon | 2001 | Denison |
| 1988 | Kenyon | 1995 | Kenyon | | |

# Tennis

## Men

### INDIVIDUAL CHAMPIONS 1883–1945

| Year | Champion | Year | Champion |
|------|----------|------|----------|
| 1883 | Joseph Clark, Harvard (spring) | 1914 | George Church, Princeton |
| 1883 | Howard Taylor, Harvard (fall) | 1915 | Richard Williams II, Harvard |
| 1884 | W.P. Knapp, Yale | 1916 | G. Colket Caner, Harvard |
| 1885 | W.P. Knapp, Yale | 1917–18 | No tournament |
| 1886 | G.M. Brinley, Trinity (CT) | 1919 | Charles Garland, Yale |
| 1887 | P.S. Sears, Harvard | 1920 | Lascelles Banks, Yale |
| 1888 | P.S. Sears, Harvard | 1921 | Philip Neer, Stanford |
| 1889 | R.P. Huntington Jr, Yale | 1922 | Lucien Williams, Yale |
| 1890 | Fred Hovey, Harvard | 1923 | Carl Fischer, Philadelphia Osteo |
| 1891 | Fred Hovey, Harvard | 1924 | Wallace Scott, Washington |
| 1892 | William Larned, Cornell | 1925 | Edward Chandler, California |
| 1893 | Malcolm Chace, Brown | 1926 | Edward Chandler, California |
| 1894 | Malcolm Chace, Yale | 1927 | Wilmer Allison, Texas |
| 1895 | Malcolm Chace, Yale | 1928 | Julius Seligson, Lehigh |
| 1896 | Malcolm Whitman, Harvard | 1929 | Berkeley Bell, Texas |
| 1897 | S.G. Thompson, Princeton | 1930 | Clifford Sutter, Tulane |
| 1898 | Leo Ware, Harvard | 1931 | Keith Gledhill, Stanford |
| 1899 | Dwight Davis, Harvard | 1932 | Clifford Sutter, Tulane |
| 1900 | Raymond Little, Princeton | 1933 | Jack Tidball, UCLA |
| 1901 | Fred Alexander, Princeton | 1934 | Gene Mako, Southern Cal |
| 1902 | William Clothier, Harvard | 1935 | Wilbur Hess, Rice |
| 1903 | E.B. Dewhurst, Pennsylvania | 1936 | Ernest Sutter, Tulane |
| 1904 | Robert LeRoy, Columbia | 1937 | Ernest Sutter, Tulane |
| 1905 | E.B. Dewhurst, Pennsylvania | 1938 | Frank Guernsey, Rice |
| 1906 | Robert LeRoy, Columbia | 1939 | Frank Guernsey, Rice |
| 1907 | G. Peabody Gardner Jr, Harvard | 1940 | Donald McNeil, Kenyon |
| 1908 | Nat Niles, Harvard | 1941 | Joseph Hunt, Navy |
| 1909 | Wallace Johnson, Pennsylvania | 1942 | Frederick Schroeder Jr, Stanford |
| 1910 | R.A. Holden Jr, Yale | 1943 | Pancho Segura, Miami (FL) |
| 1911 | E.H. Whitney, Harvard | 1944 | Pancho Segura, Miami (FL) |
| 1912 | George Church, Princeton | 1945 | Pancho Segura, Miami (FL) |
| 1913 | Richard Williams II, Harvard | | |

### DIVISION I

| Year | Champion | Coach | Pts | Runner-Up | Pts | Individual Champion |
|------|----------|-------|-----|-----------|-----|---------------------|
| 1946 | Southern Cal | William Moyle | 9 | William & Mary | 6 | Robert Falkenburg, Southern Cal |
| 1947 | William & Mary | Sharvey G. Umbeck | 10 | Rice | 4 | Gardner Larned, William & Mary |
| 1948 | William & Mary | Sharvey G. Umbeck | 6 | San Francisco | 5 | Harry Likas, San Francisco |
| 1949 | San Francisco | Norman Brooks | 7 | Rollins/Tulane/ Washington | 4 | Jack Tuero, Tulane |
| 1950 | UCLA | William Ackerman | 11 | California Southern Cal | 5 5 | Herbert Flam, UCLA |
| 1951 | Southern Cal | Louis Wheeler | 9 | Cincinnati | 7 | Tony Trabert, Cincinnati |
| 1952 | UCLA | J.D. Morgan | 11 | California Southern Cal | 5 5 | Hugh Stewart, Southern Cal |
| 1953 | UCLA | J.D. Morgan | 11 | California | 6 | Hamilton Richardson, Tulane |
| 1954 | UCLA | J.D. Morgan | 15 | Southern Cal | 10 | Hamilton Richardson, Tulane |
| 1955 | Southern Cal | George Toley | 12 | Texas | 7 | Jose Aguero, Tulane |
| 1956 | UCLA | J.D. Morgan | 15 | Southern Cal | 14 | Alejandro Olmedo, Southern Cal |
| 1957 | Michigan | William Murphy | 10 | Tulane | 9 | Barry MacKay, Michigan |
| 1958 | Southern Cal | George Toley | 13 | Stanford | 9 | Alejandro Olmedo, Southern Cal |
| 1959 | Notre Dame Tulane | Thomas Fallon Emmet Pare | 8 8 | | | Whitney Reed, San Jose St |
| 1960 | UCLA | J.D. Morgan | 18 | Southern Cal | 8 | Larry Nagler, UCLA |
| 1961 | UCLA | J.D. Morgan | 17 | Southern Cal | 16 | Allen Fox, UCLA |
| 1962 | Southern Cal | George Toley | 22 | UCLA | 12 | Rafael Osuna, Southern Cal |
| 1963 | Southern Cal | George Toley | 27 | UCLA | 19 | Dennis Ralston, Southern Cal |
| 1964 | Southern Cal | George Toley | 26 | UCLA | 25 | Dennis Ralston, Southern Cal |
| 1965 | UCLA | J.D. Morgan | 31 | Miami (FL) | 13 | Arthur Ashe, UCLA |
| 1966 | Southern Cal | George Toley | 27 | UCLA | 23 | Charles Pasarell, UCLA |
| 1967 | Southern Cal | George Toley | 28 | UCLA | 23 | Bob Lutz, Southern Cal |
| 1968 | Southern Cal | George Toley | 31 | Rice | 23 | Stan Smith, Southern Cal |
| 1969 | Southern Cal | George Toley | 35 | UCLA | 23 | Joaquin Loyo-Mayo, Southern Cal |
| 1970 | UCLA | Glenn Bassett | 26 | Trinity (TX) Rice | 22 22 | Jeff Borowiak, UCLA |

## Men (Cont.)

### DIVISION I (Cont.)

| Year | Champion | Coach | Pts | Runner-Up | Pts | Individual Champion |
|------|----------|-------|-----|-----------|-----|---------------------|
| 1971 | UCLA | Glenn Bassett | 35 | Trinity (TX) | 27 | Jimmy Connors, UCLA |
| 1972 | Trinity (TX) | Clarence Mabry | 36 | Stanford | 30 | Dick Stockton, Trinity (TX) |
| 1973 | Stanford | Dick Gould | 33 | Southern Cal | 28 | Alex Mayer, Stanford |
| 1974 | Stanford | Dick Gould | 30 | Southern Cal | 25 | John Whitlinger, Stanford |
| 1975 | UCLA | Glenn Bassett | 27 | Miami (FL) | 20 | Bill Martin, UCLA |
| 1976 | Southern Cal | George Toley | 21 | | | Bill Scanlon, Trinity (TX) |
| | UCLA | Glenn Bassett | 21 | | | |
| 1977 | Stanford | Dick Gould | | Trinity (TX) | | Matt Mitchell, Stanford |
| 1978 | Stanford | Dick Gould | | UCLA | | John McEnroe, Stanford |
| 1979 | UCLA | Glenn Bassett | | Trinity (TX) | | Kevin Curren, Texas |
| 1980 | Stanford | Dick Gould | | California | | Robert Van't Hof, Southern Cal |
| 1981 | Stanford | Dick Gould | | UCLA | | Tim Mayotte, Stanford |
| 1982 | UCLA | Glenn Bassett | | Pepperdine | | Mike Leach, Michigan |
| 1983 | Stanford | Dick Gould | | SMU | | Greg Holmes, Utah |
| 1984 | UCLA | Glenn Bassett | | Stanford | | Mikael Pernfors, Georgia |
| 1985 | Georgia | Dan Magill | | UCLA | | Mikael Pernfors, Georgia |
| 1986 | Stanford | Dick Gould | | Pepperdine | | Dan Goldie, Stanford |
| 1987 | Georgia | Dan Magill | | UCLA | | Andrew Burrow, Miami (FL) |
| 1988 | Stanford | Dick Gould | | Louisiana St | | Robby Weiss, Pepperdine |
| 1989 | Stanford | Dick Gould | | Georgia | | Donni Leaycraft, Louisiana St |
| 1990 | Stanford | Dick Gould | | Tennessee | | Steve Bryan, Texas |
| 1991 | Southern Cal | Dick Leach | | Georgia | | Jared Palmer, Stanford |
| 1992 | Stanford | Dick Gould | | Notre Dame | | Alex O'Brien, Stanford |
| 1993 | Southern Cal | Dick Leach | | Georgia | | Chris Woodruff, Tennessee |
| 1994 | Southern Cal | Dick Leach | | Stanford | | Mark Merklein, Florida |
| 1995 | Stanford | Dick Gould | | Mississippi | | Sargis Sargsian, Arizona St |
| 1996 | Stanford | Dick Gould | | UCLA | | Cecil Mamiit, Southern Cal |
| 1997 | Stanford | Dick Gould | | Georgia | | Luke Smith, UNLV |
| 1998 | Stanford | Dick Gould | | Georgia | | Bob Bryan, Stanford |
| 1999 | Georgia | Manuel Diaz | | UCLA | | Jeff Morrison, Florida |
| 2000 | Stanford | Dick Gould | | VA–Commonwealth | | Alex Kim, Stanford |
| 2001 | Georgia | Manuel Diaz | | Tennessee | | Matias Boeker, Georgia |

Note: Prior to 1977, individual wins counted in the team's total points. In 1977, a dual-match single-elimination team championship was initiated, eliminating the point system.

### DIVISION II

| Year | Champion | Year | Champion | Year | Champion |
|------|----------|------|----------|------|----------|
| 1963 | Cal St–LA | 1976 | Hampton | 1989 | Hampton |
| 1964 | Cal St–LA/S Illinois | 1977 | UC–Irvine | 1990 | Cal Poly–SLO |
| 1965 | Cal St–LA | 1978 | SIU–Edwardsville | 1991 | Rollins |
| 1966 | Rollins | 1979 | SIU–Edwardsville | 1992 | UC–Davis |
| 1967 | Long Beach St | 1980 | SIU–Edwardsville | 1993 | Lander |
| 1968 | Fresno St | 1981 | SIU–Edwardsville | 1994 | Lander |
| 1969 | Cal St–Northridge | 1982 | SIU–Edwardsville | 1995 | Lander |
| 1970 | UC–Irvine | 1983 | SIU–Edwardsville | 1996 | Lander |
| 1971 | UC–Irvine | 1984 | SIU–Edwardsville | 1997 | Lander |
| 1972 | UC–Irvine/ Rollins | 1985 | Chapman | 1998 | Lander |
| 1973 | UC–Irvine | 1986 | Cal Poly–SLO | 1999 | Lander |
| 1974 | San Diego | 1987 | Chapman | 2000 | Lander |
| 1975 | UC–Irvine/San Diego | 1988 | Chapman | 2001 | Rollins |

### DIVISION III

| Year | Champion | Year | Champion | Year | Champion |
|------|----------|------|----------|------|----------|
| 1976 | Kalamazoo | 1984 | Redlands | 1993 | Kalamazoo |
| 1977 | Swarthmore | 1985 | Swarthmore | 1994 | Washington (MD) |
| 1978 | Kalamazoo | 1986 | Kalamazoo | 1995 | UC–Santa Cruz |
| 1979 | Redlands | 1987 | Kalamazoo | 1996 | UC–Santa Cruz |
| 1980 | Gustavus Adolphus | 1988 | Washington & Lee | 1997 | Washington (MD) |
| 1981 | Claremont-M-S/ | 1989 | UC–Santa Cruz | 1998 | UC–Santa Cruz |
| | Swarthmore | 1990 | Swarthmore | 1999 | Williams |
| 1982 | Gustavus Adolphus | 1991 | Kalamazoo | 2000 | Trinity (TX) |
| 1983 | Redlands | 1992 | Kalamazoo | 2001 | Williams |

## Women
### DIVISION I

| Year | Champion | Coach | Runner-Up | Individual Champion |
|------|----------|-------|-----------|---------------------|
| 1982 | Stanford | Frank Brennan | UCLA | Alycia Moulton, Stanford |
| 1983 | Southern Cal | Dave Borelli | Trinity (TX) | Beth Herr, Southern Cal |
| 1984 | Stanford | Frank Brennan | Southern Cal | Lisa Spain, Georgia |
| 1985 | Southern Cal | Dave Borelli | Miami (FL) | Linda Gates, Stanford |
| 1986 | Stanford | Frank Brennan | Southern Cal | Patty Fendick, Stanford |
| 1987 | Stanford | Frank Brennan | Georgia | Patty Fendick, Stanford |
| 1988 | Stanford | Frank Brennan | Florida | Shaun Stafford, Florida |
| 1989 | Stanford | Frank Brennan | UCLA | Sandra Birch, Stanford |
| 1990 | Stanford | Frank Brennan | Florida | Debbie Graham, Stanford |
| 1991 | Stanford | Frank Brennan | UCLA | Sandra Birch, Stanford |
| 1992 | Florida | Andy Brandi | Texas | Lisa Raymond, Florida |
| 1993 | Texas | Jeff Moore | Stanford | Lisa Raymond, Florida |
| 1994 | Georgia | Jeff Wallace | Stanford | Angela Lettiere, Georgia |
| 1995 | Texas | Jeff Moore | Florida | Keri Phebus, UCLA |
| 1996 | Florida | Andy Brandi | Stanford | Jill Craybas, Florida |
| 1997 | Stanford | Frank Brennan | Florida | Lilia Osterloh, Stanford |
| 1998 | Florida | Andy Brandi | Duke | Vanessa Webb, Duke |
| 1999 | Stanford | Frank Brennan | Florida | Zuzana Lesenarova, UC–SD |
| 2000 | Georgia | Jeff Wallace | Stanford | Laura Granville, Stanford |
| 2001 | Stanford | Lele Forood | Vanderbilt | Laura Granville, Stanford |

### DIVISION II

| Year | Champion | Year | Champion | Year | Champion |
|------|----------|------|----------|------|----------|
| 1982 | Cal St–Northridge | 1989 | SIU–Edwardsville | 1996 | Armstrong St |
| 1983 | TN–Chattanooga | 1990 | UC–Davis | 1997 | Lynn |
| 1984 | TN–Chattanooga | 1991 | Cal Poly–Pomona | 1998 | Lynn |
| 1985 | TN–Chattanooga | 1992 | Cal Poly–Pomona | 1999 | BYU–Hawaii |
| 1986 | SIU–Edwardsville | 1993 | UC–Davis | 2000 | BYU–Hawaii |
| 1987 | SIU–Edwardsville | 1994 | N Florida | 2001 | Lynn |
| 1988 | SIU–Edwardsville | 1995 | Armstrong St | | |

### DIVISION III

| Year | Champion | Year | Champion | Year | Champion |
|------|----------|------|----------|------|----------|
| 1982 | Occidental | 1989 | UC–San Diego | 1996 | Emory |
| 1983 | Principia | 1990 | Gustavus Adolphus | 1997 | Kenyon |
| 1984 | Davidson | 1991 | Mary Washington | 1998 | Kenyon |
| 1985 | UC–San Diego | 1992 | Pomona-Pitzer | 1999 | Amherst |
| 1986 | Trenton St | 1993 | Kenyon | 2000 | Trinity (TX) |
| 1987 | UC–San Diego | 1994 | UC–San Diego | 2001 | Williams |
| 1988 | Mary Washington | 1995 | Kenyon | | |

# Indoor Track and Field

## Men
### DIVISION I

| Year | Champion | Coach | Pts | Runner-Up | Pts |
|------|----------|-------|-----|-----------|-----|
| 1965 | Missouri | Tom Botts | 14 | Oklahoma St | 12 |
| 1966 | Kansas | Bob Timmons | 14 | Southern Cal | 13 |
| 1967 | Southern Cal | Vern Wolfe | 26 | Oklahoma | 17 |
| 1968 | Villanova | Jim Elliott | 35 | Southern Cal | 25 |
| 1969 | Kansas | Bob Timmons | 41½ | Villanova | 33 |
| 1970 | Kansas | Bob Timmons | 27½ | Villanova | 26 |
| 1971 | Villanova | Jim Elliott | 22 | UTEP | 19¼ |
| 1972 | Southern Cal | Vern Wolfe | 19 | Bowling Green/ Mich St | 18 |
| 1973 | Manhattan | Fred Dwyer | 18 | Kansas/Kent St/UTEP | 12 |
| 1974 | UTEP | Ted Banks | 19 | Colorado | 18 |
| 1975 | UTEP | Ted Banks | 36 | Kansas | 17½ |
| 1976 | UTEP | Ted Banks | 23 | Villanova | 15 |
| 1977 | Washington St | John Chaplin | 25½ | UTEP | 25 |
| 1978 | UTEP | Ted Banks | 44 | Auburn | 38 |
| 1979 | Villanova | Jim Elliott | 52 | UTEP | 51 |
| 1980 | UTEP | Ted Banks | 76 | Villanova | 42 |
| 1981 | UTEP | Ted Banks | 76 | SMU | 51 |

## Men *(Cont.)*
### DIVISION I *(Cont.)*

| Year | Champion | Coach | Pts | Runner-Up | Pts |
|------|----------|-------|-----|-----------|-----|
| 1982 | UTEP | John Wedel | 67 | Arkansas | 30 |
| 1983 | SMU | Ted McLaughlin | 43 | Villanova | 32 |
| 1984 | Arkansas | John McDonnell | 38 | Washington St | 28 |
| 1985 | Arkansas | John McDonnell | 70 | Tennessee | 29 |
| 1986 | Arkansas | John McDonnell | 49 | Villanova | 22 |
| 1987 | Arkansas | John McDonnell | 39 | SMU | 31 |
| 1988 | Arkansas | John McDonnell | 34 | Illinois | 29 |
| 1989 | Arkansas | John McDonnell | 34 | Florida | 31 |
| 1990 | Arkansas | John McDonnell | 44 | Texas A&M | 36 |
| 1991 | Arkansas | John McDonnell | 34 | Georgetown | 27 |
| 1992 | Arkansas | John McDonnell | 53 | Clemson | 46 |
| 1993 | Arkansas | John McDonnell | 66 | Clemson | 30 |
| 1994 | Arkansas | John McDonnell | 83 | UTEP | 45 |
| 1995 | Arkansas | John McDonnell | 59 | GMU/Tennessee | 26 |
| 1996 | George Mason | John Cook | 39 | Nebraska | 31½ |
| 1997 | Arkansas | John McDonnell | 59 | Auburn | 27 |
| 1998 | Arkansas | John McDonnell | 56 | Stanford | 36½ |
| 1999 | Arkansas | John McDonnell | 65 | Stanford | 42½ |
| 2000 | Arkansas | John McDonnell | 69½ | Stanford | 52 |
| 2001 | Louisiana St | Pat Henry | 34 | Texas Christian | 33 |

### DIVISION II

| Year | Champion | Year | Champion | Year | Champion |
|------|----------|------|----------|------|----------|
| 1985 | SE Missouri St | 1991 | St. Augustine's | 1997 | Abilene Christian |
| 1986 | Not held | 1992 | St. Augustine's | 1998 | Abilene Christian |
| 1987 | St. Augustine's | 1993 | Abilene Christian | 1999 | Abilene Christian |
| 1988 | Abil. Christian/St. August. | 1994 | Abilene Christian | 2000 | Abilene Christian |
| 1989 | St. Augustine's | 1995 | St. Augustine's | 2001 | St. Augustine's |
| 1990 | St. Augustine's | 1996 | Abilene Christian | | |

### DIVISION III

| Year | Champion | Year | Champion | Year | Champion |
|------|----------|------|----------|------|----------|
| 1985 | St. Thomas (MN) | 1991 | WI–La Crosse | 1997 | WI–La Crosse |
| 1986 | Frostburg St | 1992 | WI–La Crosse | 1998 | Lincoln (PA) |
| 1987 | WI–La Crosse | 1993 | WI–La Crosse | 1999 | Lincoln (PA) |
| 1988 | WI–La Crosse | 1994 | WI–La Crosse | 2000 | Lincoln (PA) |
| 1989 | N Central | 1995 | Lincoln (PA) | 2001 | WI–La Crosse |
| 1990 | Lincoln (PA) | 1996 | Lincoln (PA) | | |

## Women
### DIVISION I

| Year | Champion | Coach | Pts | Runner-Up | Pts |
|------|----------|-------|-----|-----------|-----|
| 1983 | Nebraska | Gary Pepin | 47 | Tennessee | 44 |
| 1984 | Nebraska | Gary Pepin | 59 | Tennessee | 48 |
| 1985 | Florida St | Gary Winckler | 34 | Texas | 32 |
| 1986 | Texas | Terry Crawford | 31 | Southern Cal | 26 |
| 1987 | Louisiana St | Loren Seagrave | 49 | Tennessee | 30 |
| 1988 | Texas | Terry Crawford | 71 | Villanova | 52 |
| 1989 | Louisiana St | Pat Henry | 61 | Villanova | 34 |
| 1990 | Texas | Terry Crawford | 50 | Wisconsin | 26 |
| 1991 | Louisiana St | Pat Henry | 48 | Texas | 39 |
| 1992 | Florida | Bev Kearney | 50 | Stanford | 26 |
| 1993 | Louisiana St | Pat Henry | 49 | Wisconsin | 44 |
| 1994 | Louisiana St | Pat Henry | 48 | Alabama | 29 |
| 1995 | Louisiana St | Pat Henry | 40 | UCLA | 37 |
| 1996 | Louisiana St | Pat Henry | 52 | Georgia | 34 |
| 1997 | Louisiana St | Pat Henry | 49 | Texas/Wisconsin | 39 |
| 1998 | Texas | Bev Kearney | 60 | Louisiana St | 30 |
| 1999 | Texas | Bev Kearney | 61 | Louisiana St | 57 |
| 2000 | UCLA | Jeanette Bolden | 51 | S Carolina | 41 |
| 2001 | UCLA | Jeanette Bolden | 53½ | S Carolina | 40 |

## Women (Cont.)

### DIVISION II

| Year | Champion | Year | Champion | Year | Champion |
|---|---|---|---|---|---|
| 1985 | St. Augustine's | 1991 | Abilene Christian | 1997 | Abilene Christian |
| 1986 | Not held | 1992 | Alabama A&M | 1998 | Abilene Christian |
| 1987 | St. Augustine's | 1993 | Abilene Christian | 1999 | Abilene Christian |
| 1988 | Abilene Christian | 1994 | Abilene Christian | 2000 | Abilene Christian |
| 1989 | Abilene Christian | 1995 | Abilene Christian | 2001 | St. Augustine's |
| 1990 | Abilene Christian | 1996 | Abilene Christian | | |

### DIVISION III

| Year | Champion | Year | Champion | Year | Champion |
|---|---|---|---|---|---|
| 1985 | MA–Boston | 1991 | Cortland St | 1997 | Christopher Newport |
| 1986 | MA–Boston | 1992 | Christopher Newport | 1998 | Christopher Newport |
| 1987 | MA–Boston | 1993 | Lincoln (PA) | 1999 | Wheaton (MA) |
| 1988 | Christopher Newport | 1994 | WI–Oshkosh | 2000 | Wheaton (MA) |
| 1989 | Christopher Newport | 1995 | WI–Oshkosh | 2001 | Wheaton (MA) |
| 1990 | Christopher Newport | 1996 | WI–Oshkosh | | |

# Outdoor Track and Field

## Men
### DIVISION I

| Year | Champion | Coach | Pts | Runner-Up | Pts |
|---|---|---|---|---|---|
| 1921 | Illinois | Harry Gill | 20† | Notre Dame | 16† |
| 1922 | California | Walter Christie | 28† | Penn St | 19† |
| 1923 | Michigan | Stephen Farrell | 29† | Mississippi St | 16 |
| 1924 | No meet | | | | |
| 1925 | Stanford* | R.L. Templeton | 31† | | |
| 1926 | Southern Cal* | Dean Cromwell | 27† | | |
| 1927 | Illinois* | Harry Gill | 35† | | |
| 1928 | Stanford | R.L. Templeton | 72 | Ohio St | 31 |
| 1929 | Ohio St | Frank Castleman | 50 | Washington | 42 |
| 1930 | Southern Cal | Dean Cromwell | 55† | Washington | 40 |
| 1931 | Southern Cal | Dean Cromwell | 77† | Ohio St | 31† |
| 1932 | Indiana | Billy Hayes | 56 | Ohio St | 49† |
| 1933 | Louisiana St | Bernie Moore | 58 | Southern Cal | 54 |
| 1934 | Stanford | R.L. Templeton | 63 | Southern Cal | 54† |
| 1935 | Southern Cal | Dean Cromwell | 74† | Ohio St | 40† |
| 1936 | Southern Cal | Dean Cromwell | 103† | Ohio St | 73 |
| 1937 | Southern Cal | Dean Cromwell | 62 | Stanford | 50 |
| 1938 | Southern Cal | Dean Cromwell | 67† | Stanford | 38 |
| 1939 | Southern Cal | Dean Cromwell | 86 | Stanford | 44† |
| 1940 | Southern Cal | Dean Cromwell | 47 | Stanford | 28† |
| 1941 | Southern Cal | Dean Cromwell | 81† | Indiana | 50 |
| 1942 | Southern Cal | Dean Cromwell | 85† | Ohio St | 44† |
| 1943 | Southern Cal | Dean Cromwell | 46 | California | 39 |
| 1944 | Illinois | Leo Johnson | 79 | Notre Dame | 43 |
| 1945 | Navy | E.J. Thomson | 62 | Illinois | 48† |
| 1946 | Illinois | Leo Johnson | 78 | Southern Cal | 42† |
| 1947 | Illinois | Leo Johnson | 59† | Southern Cal | 34† |
| 1948 | Minnesota | James Kelly | 46 | Southern Cal | 41† |
| 1949 | Southern Cal | Jess Hill | 55† | UCLA | 31 |
| 1950 | Southern Cal | Jess Hill | 49† | Stanford | 28 |
| 1951 | Southern Cal | Jess Mortenson | 56 | Cornell | 40 |
| 1952 | Southern Cal | Jess Mortenson | 66† | San Jose St | 24† |
| 1953 | Southern Cal | Jess Mortenson | 80 | Illinois | 41 |
| 1954 | Southern Cal | Jess Mortenson | 66† | Illinois | 31† |
| 1955 | Southern Cal | Jess Mortenson | 42 | UCLA | 34 |
| 1956 | UCLA | Elvin Drake | 55† | Kansas | 51 |
| 1957 | Villanova | James Elliott | 47 | California | 32 |
| 1958 | Southern Cal | Jess Mortenson | 48† | Kansas | 40† |
| 1959 | Kansas | Bill Easton | 73 | San Jose St | 48 |
| 1960 | Kansas | Bill Easton | 50 | Southern Cal | 37 |

## Men *(Cont.)*

### DIVISION I *(Cont.)*

| Year | Champion | Coach | Pts | Runner-Up | Pts |
|------|----------|-------|-----|-----------|-----|
| 1961 | Southern Cal | Jess Mortenson | 65 | Oregon | 47 |
| 1962 | Oregon | William Bowerman | 85 | Villanova | 40† |
| 1963 | Southern Cal | Vern Wolfe | 61 | Stanford | 42 |
| 1964 | Oregon | William Bowerman | 70 | San Jose St | 40 |
| 1965 | Oregon | William Bowerman | 32 | | |
| | Southern Cal | Vern Wolfe | 32 | | |
| 1966 | UCLA | Jim Bush | 81 | Brigham Young | 33 |
| 1967 | Southern Cal | Vern Wolfe | 86 | Oregon | 40 |
| 1968 | Southern Cal | Vern Wolfe | 58 | Washington St | 57 |
| 1969 | San Jose St | Bud Winter | 48 | Kansas | 45 |
| 1970 | Brigham Young | Clarence Robison | 35 | | |
| | Kansas | Bob Timmons | 35 | | |
| | Oregon | William Bowerman | 35 | | |
| 1971 | UCLA | Jim Bush | 52 | Southern Cal | 41 |
| 1972 | UCLA | Jim Bush | 82 | Southern Cal | 49 |
| 1973 | UCLA | Jim Bush | 56 | Oregon | 31 |
| 1974 | Tennessee | Stan Huntsman | 60 | UCLA | 56 |
| 1975 | UTEP | Ted Banks | 55 | UCLA | 42 |
| 1976 | Southern Cal | Vern Wolfe | 64 | UTEP | 44 |
| 1977 | Arizona St | Senon Castillo | 64 | UTEP | 50 |
| 1978 | UCLA/UTEP | Jim Bush/Ted Banks | 50 | | |
| 1979 | UTEP | Ted Banks | 64 | Villanova | 48 |
| 1980 | UTEP | Ted Banks | 69 | UCLA | 46 |
| 1981 | UTEP | Ted Banks | 70 | SMU | 57 |
| 1982 | UTEP | John Wedel | 105 | Tennessee | 94 |
| 1983 | SMU | Ted McLaughlin | 104 | Tennessee | 102 |
| 1984 | Oregon | Bill Dellinger | 113 | Washington St | 94½ |
| 1985 | Arkansas | John McDonnell | 61 | Washington St | 46 |
| 1986 | SMU | Ted McLaughlin | 53 | Washington St | 52 |
| 1987 | UCLA | Bob Larsen | 81 | Texas | 28 |
| 1988 | UCLA | Bob Larsen | 82 | Texas | 41 |
| 1989 | Louisiana St | Pat Henry | 53 | Texas A&M | 51 |
| 1990 | Louisiana St | Pat Henry | 44 | Arkansas | 36 |
| 1991 | Tennessee | Doug Brown | 51 | Washington St | 42 |
| 1992 | Arkansas | John McDonnell | 60 | Tennessee | 46½ |
| 1993 | Arkansas | John McDonnell | 69 | LSU/Ohio St | 45 |
| 1994 | Arkansas | John McDonnell | 83 | UTEP | 45 |
| 1995 | Arkansas | John McDonnell | 61½ | UCLA | 55 |
| 1996 | Arkansas | John McDonnell | 55 | George Mason | 40 |
| 1997 | Arkansas | John McDonnell | 55 | Texas | 42½ |
| 1998 | Arkansas | John McDonnell | 58½ | Stanford | 51 |
| 1999 | Arkansas | John McDonnell | 59 | Stanford | 52 |
| 2000 | Stanford | Vin Lananna | 72 | Arkansas | 59 |
| 2001 | Tennessee | Bill Webb | 50 | Texas Christian | 49 |

*Unofficial championship. †Fraction of a point.

### DIVISION II

| Year | Champion | Year | Champion | Year | Champion |
|------|----------|------|----------|------|----------|
| 1963 | MD–Eastern Shore | 1976 | UC–Irvine | 1990 | St. Augustine's |
| 1964 | Fresno St | 1977 | Cal St–Hayward | 1991 | St. Augustine's |
| 1965 | San Diego St | 1978 | Cal St–LA | 1992 | St. Augustine's |
| 1966 | San Diego St | 1979 | Cal Poly–SLO | 1993 | St. Augustine's |
| 1967 | Long Beach St | 1980 | Cal Poly–SLO | 1994 | St. Augustine's |
| 1968 | Cal Poly–SLO | 1981 | Cal Poly–SLO | 1995 | St. Augustine's |
| 1969 | Cal Poly–SLO | 1982 | Abilene Christian | 1996 | Abilene Christian |
| 1970 | Cal Poly–SLO | 1983 | Abilene Christian | 1997 | Abilene Christian |
| 1971 | Kentucky St | 1984 | Abilene Christian | 1998 | St. Augustine's |
| 1972 | Eastern Michigan | 1985 | Abilene Christian | 1999 | Abilene Christian |
| 1973 | Norfolk St | 1986 | Abilene Christian | 2000 | Abilene Christian |
| 1974 | Eastern Illinois | 1987 | Abilene Christian | 2001 | St. Augustine's |
| | Norfolk St | 1988 | Abilene Christian | | |
| 1975 | Cal St–Northridge | 1989 | St. Augustine's | | |

### Men *(Cont.)*

#### DIVISION III

| Year | Champion | Year | Champion | Year | Champion |
|------|----------|------|----------|------|----------|
| 1974 | Ashland | 1984 | Glassboro St | 1994 | N Central |
| 1975 | Southern–N Orleans | 1985 | Lincoln (PA) | 1995 | Lincoln (PA) |
| 1976 | Southern–N Orleans | 1986 | Frostburg St | 1996 | Lincoln (PA) |
| 1977 | Southern–N Orleans | 1987 | Frostburg St | 1997 | WI–La Crosse |
| 1978 | Occidental | 1988 | WI–La Crosse | 1998 | N Central |
| 1979 | Slippery Rock | 1989 | N Central | 1999 | Lincoln (PA) |
| 1980 | Glassboro St | 1990 | Lincoln (PA) | 2000 | Nebraska Wesleyan |
| 1981 | Glassboro St | 1991 | WI–La Crosse | 2001 | WI–La Crosse |
| 1982 | Glassboro St | 1992 | WI–La Crosse | | |
| 1983 | Glassboro St | 1993 | WI–La Crosse | | |

### Women
#### DIVISION I

| Year | Champion | Coach | Pts | Runner-Up | Pts |
|------|----------|-------|-----|-----------|-----|
| 1982 | UCLA | Scott Chisam | 153 | Tennessee | 126 |
| 1983 | UCLA | Scott Chisam | 116½ | Florida St | 108 |
| 1984 | Florida St | Gary Winckler | 145 | Tennessee | 124 |
| 1985 | Oregon | Tom Heinonen | 52 | Florida St/LSU | 46 |
| 1986 | Texas | Terry Crawford | 65 | Alabama | 55 |
| 1987 | Louisiana St | Loren Seagrave | 62 | Alabama | 53 |
| 1988 | Louisiana St | Loren Seagrave | 61 | UCLA | 58 |
| 1989 | Louisiana St | Pat Henry | 86 | UCLA | 47 |
| 1990 | Louisiana St | Pat Henry | 53 | UCLA | 46 |
| 1991 | Louisiana St | Pat Henry | 78 | Texas | 67 |
| 1992 | Louisiana St | Pat Henry | 87 | Florida | 81 |
| 1993 | Louisiana St | Pat Henry | 93 | Wisconsin | 44 |
| 1994 | Louisiana St | Pat Henry | 86 | Texas | 43 |
| 1995 | Louisiana St | Pat Henry | 69 | UCLA | 58 |
| 1996 | Louisiana St | Pat Henry | 81 | Texas | 52 |
| 1997 | Louisiana St | Pat Henry | 63 | Texas | 62 |
| 1998 | Texas | Bev Kearney | 60 | UCLA | 55 |
| 1999 | Texas | Bev Kearney | 62 | UCLA | 60 |
| 2000 | Louisiana St | Pat Henry | 59 | Southern Cal | 56 |
| 2001 | Southern Cal | Ron Allice | 64 | UCLA | 55 |

#### DIVISION II

| Year | Champion | Year | Champion | Year | Champion |
|------|----------|------|----------|------|----------|
| 1982 | Cal Poly–SLO | 1989 | Cal Poly–SLO | 1996 | Abilene Christian |
| 1983 | Cal Poly–SLO | 1990 | Cal Poly–SLO | 1997 | St. Augustine's |
| 1984 | Cal Poly–SLO | 1991 | Cal Poly–SLO | 1998 | Abilene Christian |
| 1985 | Abilene Christian | 1992 | Alabama A&M | 1999 | Abilene Christian |
| 1986 | Abilene Christian | 1993 | Alabama A&M | 2000 | St. Augustine's |
| 1987 | Abilene Christian | 1994 | Alabama A&M | 2001 | St. Augustine's |
| 1988 | Abilene Christian | 1995 | Abilene Christian | | |

#### DIVISION III

| Year | Champion | Year | Champion | Year | Champion |
|------|----------|------|----------|------|----------|
| 1982 | Central (IA) | 1989 | Chris. Newport | 1996 | WI–Oshkosh |
| 1983 | WI–La Crosse | 1990 | WI–Oshkosh | 1997 | WI–Oshkosh |
| 1984 | WI–La Crosse | 1991 | WI–Oshkosh | 1998 | Chris. Newport |
| 1985 | Cortland St | 1992 | Chris. Newport | 1999 | Lincoln (PA) |
| 1986 | MA–Boston | 1993 | Lincoln (PA) | 2000 | Lincoln (PA) |
| 1987 | Chris. Newport | 1994 | Chris. Newport | 2001 | Wheaton (MA) |
| 1988 | Chris. Newport | 1995 | WI–Oshkosh | | |

## Volleyball

### Men

| Year | Champion | Coach | Score | Runner-Up | Most Outstanding Player |
|------|----------|-------|-------|-----------|-------------------------|
| 1970 | UCLA | Al Scates | 3–0 | Long Beach St | Dane Holtzman, UCLA |
| 1971 | UCLA | Al Scates | 3–0 | UC–Santa Barbara | Kirk Kilgore, UCLA |
| | | | | | Tim Bonynge, UC–Santa Barbara |
| 1972 | UCLA | Al Scates | 3–2 | San Diego St | Dick Irvin, UCLA |

## Men *(Cont.)*

| Year | Champion | Coach | Score | Runner-Up | Most Outstanding Player |
|------|----------|-------|-------|-----------|-------------------------|
| 1973 | San Diego St | Jack Henn | 3–1 | Long Beach St | Duncan McFarland, San Diego St |
| 1974 | UCLA | Al Scates | 3–2 | UC–Santa Barbara | Bob Leonard, UCLA |
| 1975 | UCLA | Al Scates | 3–1 | UC–Santa Barbara | John Bekins, UCLA |
| 1976 | UCLA | Al Scates | 3–0 | Pepperdine | Joe Mika, UCLA |
| 1977 | Southern Cal | Ernie Hix | 3–1 | Ohio St | Celso Kalache, Southern Cal |
| 1978 | Pepperdine | Marv Dunphy | 3–2 | UCLA | Mike Blanchard, Pepperdine |
| 1979 | UCLA | Al Scates | 3–1 | Southern Cal | Sinjin Smith, UCLA |
| 1980 | Southern Cal | Ernie Hix | 3–1 | UCLA | Dusty Dvorak, Southern Cal |
| 1981 | UCLA | Al Scates | 3–2 | Southern Cal | Karch Kiraly, UCLA |
| 1982 | UCLA | Al Scates | 3–0 | Penn St | Karch Kiraly, UCLA |
| 1983 | UCLA | Al Scates | 3–0 | Pepperdine | Ricci Luyties, UCLA |
| 1984 | UCLA | Al Scates | 3–1 | Pepperdine | Ricci Luyties, UCLA |
| 1985 | Pepperdine | Marv Dunphy | 3–1 | Southern Cal | Bob Ctvrtlik, Pepperdine |
| 1986 | Pepperdine | Rod Wilde | 3–2 | Southern Cal | Steve Friedman, Pepperdine |
| 1987 | UCLA | Al Scates | 3–0 | Southern Cal | Ozzie Volstad, UCLA |
| 1988 | Southern Cal | Bob Yoder | 3–2 | UC–Santa Barbara | Jen-Kai Liu, Southern Cal |
| 1989 | UCLA | Al Scates | 3–1 | Stanford | Matt Sonnichsen, UCLA |
| 1990 | Southern Cal | Jim McLaughlin | 3–1 | Long Beach St | Bryan Ivie, Southern Cal |
| 1991 | Long Beach St | Ray Ratelle | 3–1 | Southern Cal | Brent Hilliard, Long Beach St |
| 1992 | Pepperdine | Marv Dunphy | 3–0 | Stanford | Alon Grinberg, Pepperdine |
| 1993 | UCLA | Al Scates | 3–0 | Cal St–Northridge | Mike Sealy/Jeff Nygaard, UCLA |
| 1994 | Penn St | Tom Peterson | 3–2 | UCLA | Ramon Hernandez, Penn St |
| 1995 | UCLA | Al Scates | 3–0 | Penn St | Jeff Nygaard, UCLA |
| 1996 | UCLA | Al Scates | 3–2 | Hawaii | Yuval Katz, Hawaii |
| 1997 | Stanford | Ruben Nieves | 3–2 | UCLA | Mike Lambert, Stanford |
| 1998 | UCLA | Al Scates | 3–2 | Pepperdine | George Roumain, Pepperdine |
| 1999 | Brigham Young | Carl McGown | 3–0 | Long Beach St | Ossie Antonetti, Brigham Young |
| 2000 | UCLA | Al Scates | 3–0 | Ohio St | Brandon Taliaferro, UCLA |
| 2001 | Brigham Young | Carl McGown | 3–0 | UCLA | Mike Wall, Brigham Young |

## Women

### DIVISION I

| Year | Champion | Coach | Score | Runner-Up |
|------|----------|-------|-------|-----------|
| 1981 | Southern Cal | Chuck Erbe | 3–2 | UCLA |
| 1982 | Hawaii | Dave Shoji | 3–2 | Southern Cal |
| 1983 | Hawaii | Dave Shoji | 3–0 | UCLA |
| 1984 | UCLA | Andy Banachowski | 3–2 | Stanford |
| 1985 | Pacific | John Dunning | 3–1 | Stanford |
| 1986 | Pacific | John Dunning | 3–0 | Nebraska |
| 1987 | Hawaii | Dave Shoji | 3–1 | Stanford |
| 1988 | Texas | Mick Haley | 3–0 | Hawaii |
| 1989 | Long Beach St | Brian Gimmillaro | 3–0 | Nebraska |
| 1990 | UCLA | Andy Banachowski | 3–0 | Pacific |
| 1991 | UCLA | Andy Banachowski | 3–2 | Long Beach St |
| 1992 | Stanford | Don Shaw | 3–1 | UCLA |
| 1993 | Long Beach St | Brian Gimmillaro | 3–1 | Penn St |
| 1994 | Stanford | Don Shaw | 3–1 | UCLA |
| 1995 | Nebraska | Terry Pettit | 3–1 | Texas |
| 1996 | Stanford | Don Shaw | 3–0 | Hawaii |
| 1997 | Stanford | Don Shaw | 3–2 | Penn St |
| 1998 | Long Beach St | Brian Gimmillaro | 3–2 | Penn St |
| 1999 | Penn St | Russ Rose | 3–0 | Stanford |
| 2000 | Nebraska | John Cook | 3–2 | Wisconsin |

### DIVISION II

| Year | Champion | Year | Champion | Year | Champion |
|------|----------|------|----------|------|----------|
| 1981 | Cal St–Sacramento | 1988 | Portland St | 1995 | Barry |
| 1982 | UC–Riverside | 1989 | Cal St–Bakersfield | 1996 | Nebraska–Omaha |
| 1983 | Cal St–Northridge | 1990 | West Texas A&M | 1997 | West Texas A&M |
| 1984 | Portland St | 1991 | West Texas A&M | 1998 | Hawaii Pacific |
| 1985 | Portland St | 1992 | Portland St | 1999 | BYU–Hawaii |
| 1986 | UC–Riverside | 1993 | Northern Michigan | 2000 | Hawaii Pacific |
| 1987 | Cal St–Northridge | 1994 | Northern Michigan | | |

### DIVISION III

| Year | Champion | Year | Champion | Year | Champion | Year | Champion |
|------|----------|------|----------|------|----------|------|----------|
| 1981 | UC–San Diego | 1986 | UC–San Diego | 1991 | Washington (MO) | 1996 | Washington (MO) |
| 1982 | La Verne | 1987 | UC–San Diego | 1992 | Washington (MO) | 1997 | UC–San Diego |
| 1983 | Elmhurst | 1988 | UC–San Diego | 1993 | Washington (MO) | 1998 | Central (IA) |
| 1984 | UC–San Diego | 1989 | Washington (MO) | 1994 | Washington (MO) | 1999 | Central (IA) |
| 1985 | Elmhurst | 1990 | UC–San Diego | 1995 | Washington (MO) | 2000 | Central (IA) |

# Water Polo

| Year | Champion | Coach | Score | Runner-Up |
|------|----------|-------|-------|-----------|
| 1969 | UCLA | Bob Horn | 5–2 | California |
| 1970 | UC–Irvine | Ed Newland | 7–6 (3 OT) | UCLA |
| 1971 | UCLA | Bob Horn | 5–3 | San Jose St |
| 1972 | UCLA | Bob Horn | 10–5 | UC–Irvine |
| 1973 | California | Pete Cutino | 8–4 | UC–Irvine |
| 1974 | California | Pete Cutino | 7–6 | UC–Irvine |
| 1975 | California | Pete Cutino | 9–8 | UC–Irvine |
| 1976 | Stanford | Art Lambert | 13–12 | UCLA |
| 1977 | California | Pete Cutino | 8–6 | UC–Irvine |
| 1978 | Stanford | Dante Dettamanti | 7–6 (3 OT) | California |
| 1979 | UC–Santa Barbara | Pete Snyder | 11–3 | UCLA |
| 1980 | Stanford | Dante Dettamanti | 8–6 | California |
| 1981 | Stanford | Dante Dettamanti | 17–6 | Long Beach St |
| 1982 | UC–Irvine | Ed Newland | 7–4 | Stanford |
| 1983 | California | Pete Cutino | 10–7 | Southern Cal |
| 1984 | California | Pete Cutino | 9–8 | Stanford |
| 1985 | Stanford | Dante Dettamanti | 12–11 (2 OT) | UC–Irvine |
| 1986 | Stanford | Dante Dettamanti | 9–6 | California |
| 1987 | California | Pete Cutino | 9–8 (OT) | Southern Cal |
| 1988 | California | Pete Cutino | 14–11 | UCLA |
| 1989 | UC–Irvine | Ed Newland | 9–8 | California |
| 1990 | California | Steve Heaston | 8–7 | Stanford |
| 1991 | California | Steve Heaston | 7–6 | UCLA |
| 1992 | California | Steve Heaston | 12–11 | Stanford |
| 1993 | Stanford | Dante Dettamanti | 11–9 | Southern Cal |
| 1994 | Stanford | Dante Dettamanti | 14–10 | Southern Cal |
| 1995 | UCLA | Guy Baker | 10–8 | California |
| 1996 | UCLA | Guy Baker | 8–7 | Southern Cal |
| 1997 | Pepperdine | Terry Schroeder | 8–7 (OT) | Southern Cal |
| 1998 | Southern Cal | John Williams | 9–8 (2 OT) | Stanford |
| 1999 | UCLA | Guy Baker | 6–5 | Stanford |
| 2000 | UCLA | Guy Baker/Adam Krikorian | 11–2 | UC–San Diego |

# Wrestling

## DIVISION I

| Year | Champion | Coach | Pts | Runner-Up | Pts | Most Outstanding Wrestler |
|------|----------|-------|-----|-----------|-----|---------------------------|
| 1928 | Oklahoma St* | E.C. Gallagher | | | | |
| 1929 | Oklahoma St | E.C. Gallagher | 26 | Michigan | 18 | |
| 1930 | Oklahoma St* | E.C. Gallagher | 27 | Illinois | 14 | |
| 1931 | Oklahoma St* | E.C. Gallagher | | Michigan | | |
| 1932 | Indiana* | W.H. Thom | | Oklahoma St | | Edwin Belshaw, Indiana |
| 1933 | Oklahoma St* | E.C. Gallagher | | | | Allan Kelley, Oklahoma St |
| | Iowa St* | Hugo Otopalik | | | | Pat Johnson, Harvard |
| 1934 | Oklahoma St | E.C. Gallagher | 29 | Indiana | 19 | Ben Bishop, Lehigh |
| 1935 | Oklahoma St | E.C. Gallagher | 36 | Oklahoma | 18 | Ross Flood, Oklahoma St |
| 1936 | Oklahoma | Paul Keen | 14 | Central St (OK) | 10 | Wayne Martin, Oklahoma |
| | | | | Oklahoma St | 10 | |
| 1937 | Oklahoma St | E.C. Gallagher | 31 | Oklahoma | 13 | Stanley Henson, Oklahoma St |
| 1938 | Oklahoma St | E.C. Gallagher | 19 | Illinois | 15 | Joe McDaniels, Oklahoma St |
| 1939 | Oklahoma St | E.C. Gallagher | 33 | Lehigh | 12 | Dale Hanson, Minnesota |
| 1940 | Oklahoma St | E.C. Gallagher | 24 | Indiana | 14 | Don Nichols, Michigan |
| 1941 | Oklahoma St | Art Griffith | 37 | Michigan St | 26 | Al Whitehurst, Oklahoma St |
| 1942 | Oklahoma St | Art Griffith | 31 | Michigan St | 26 | David Arndt, Oklahoma St |
| 1943–45 | No tournament | | | | | |
| 1946 | Oklahoma St | Art Griffith | 25 | Northern Iowa | 24 | Gerald Leeman, Northern Iowa |
| 1947 | Cornell | Paul Scott | 32 | Northern Iowa | 19 | William Koll, Northern Iowa |
| 1948 | Oklahoma St | Art Griffith | 33 | Michigan St | 28 | William Koll, Northern Iowa |
| 1949 | Oklahoma St | Art Griffith | 32 | Northern Iowa | 27 | Charles Hetrick, Oklahoma St |
| 1950 | Northern Iowa | David McCuskey | 30 | Purdue | 16 | Anthony Gizoni, Waynesburg |
| 1951 | Oklahoma | Port Robertson | 24 | Oklahoma St | 23 | Walter Romanowski, Cornell |
| 1952 | Oklahoma | Port Robertson | 22 | Northern Iowa | 21 | Tommy Evans, Oklahoma |
| 1953 | Penn St | Charles Speidel | 21 | Oklahoma | 15 | Frank Bettucci, Cornell |
| 1954 | Oklahoma St | Art Griffith | 32 | Pittsburgh | 17 | Tommy Evans, Oklahoma |
| 1955 | Oklahoma St | Art Griffith | 40 | Penn St | 31 | Edward Eichelberger, Lehigh |
| 1956 | Oklahoma St | Art Griffith | 65 | Oklahoma | 62 | Dan Hodge, Oklahoma |
| 1957 | Oklahoma | Port Robertson | 73 | Pittsburgh | 66 | Dan Hodge, Oklahoma |
| 1958 | Oklahoma St | Myron Roderick | 77 | Iowa St | 62 | Dick Delgado, Oklahoma |
| 1959 | Oklahoma St | Myron Roderick | 73 | Iowa St | 51 | Ron Gray, Iowa St |

## DIVISION I *(Cont.)*

| Year | Champion | Coach | Pts | Runner-Up | Pts | Most Outstanding Wrestler |
|------|----------|-------|-----|-----------|-----|---------------------------|
| 1960 | Oklahoma | Thomas Evans | 59 | Iowa St | 40 | Dave Auble, Cornell |
| 1961 | Oklahoma St | Myron Roderick | 82 | Oklahoma | 63 | E. Gray Simons, Lock Haven |
| 1962 | Oklahoma St | Myron Roderick | 82 | Oklahoma | 45 | E. Gray Simons, Lock Haven |
| 1963 | Oklahoma | Thomas Evans | 48 | Iowa St | 45 | Mickey Martin, Oklahoma |
| 1964 | Oklahoma St | Myron Roderick | 87 | Oklahoma | 58 | Dean Lahr, Colorado |
| 1965 | Iowa St | Harold Nichols | 87 | Oklahoma St | 86 | Yojiro Uetake, Oklahoma St |
| 1966 | Oklahoma St | Myron Roderick | 79 | Iowa St | 70 | Yojiro Uetake, Oklahoma St |
| 1967 | Michigan St | Grady Peninger | 74 | Michigan | 63 | Rich Sanders, Portland St |
| 1968 | Oklahoma St | Myron Roderick | 81 | Iowa St | 78 | Dwayne Keller, Oklahoma St |
| 1969 | Iowa St | Harold Nichols | 104 | Oklahoma | 69 | Dan Gable, Iowa St |
| 1970 | Iowa St | Harold Nichols | 99 | Michigan St | 84 | Larry Owings, Washington |
| 1971 | Oklahoma St | Tommy Chesbro | 94 | Iowa St | 66 | Darrell Keller, Oklahoma St |
| 1972 | Iowa St | Harold Nichols | 103 | Michigan St | 72½ | Wade Schalles, Clarion |
| 1973 | Iowa St | Harold Nichols | 85 | Oregon St | 72½ | Greg Strobel, Oregon St |
| 1974 | Oklahoma | Stan Abel | 69½ | Michigan | 67 | Floyd Hitchcock, Bloomsburg |
| 1975 | Iowa | Gary Kurdelmeier | 102 | Oklahoma | 77 | Mike Frick, Lehigh |
| 1976 | Iowa | Gary Kurdelmeier | 123½ | Iowa St | 85¾ | Chuch Yagla, Iowa |
| 1977 | Iowa St | Harold Nichols | 95½ | Oklahoma St | 88¾ | Nick Gallo, Hofstra |
| 1978 | Iowa | Dan Gable | 94½ | Iowa St | 94 | Mark Churella, Michigan |
| 1979 | Iowa | Dan Gable | 122½ | Iowa St | 88 | Bruce Kinseth, Iowa |
| 1980 | Iowa | Dan Gable | 110¾ | Oklahoma St | 87 | Howard Harris, Oregon St |
| 1981 | Iowa | Dan Gable | 129¾ | Oklahoma | 100¼ | Gene Mills, Syracuse |
| 1982 | Iowa | Dan Gable | 131¾ | Iowa St | 111 | Mark Schultz, Oklahoma |
| 1983 | Iowa | Dan Gable | 155 | Oklahoma St | 102 | Mike Sheets, Oklahoma St |
| 1984 | Iowa* | Dan Gable | 123¾ | Oklahoma St | 98 | Jim Zalesky, Iowa |
| 1985 | Iowa | Dan Gable | 145¼ | Oklahoma | 98½ | Barry Davis, Iowa |
| 1986 | Iowa | Dan Gable | 158 | Oklahoma | 84¼ | Marty Kistler, Iowa |
| 1987 | Iowa St | Jim Gibbons | 133 | Iowa | 108 | John Smith, Oklahoma St |
| 1988 | Arizona St | Bobby Douglas | 93 | Iowa | 85½ | Scott Turner, N Carolina St |
| 1989 | Oklahoma St | Joe Seay | 91¼ | Arizona St | 70½ | Tim Krieger, Iowa St |
| 1990 | Oklahoma St | Joe Seay | 117¾ | Arizona St | 104¾ | Chris Barnes, Oklahoma St |
| 1991 | Iowa | Dan Gable | 157 | Oklahoma St | 108¾ | Jeff Prescott, Penn St |
| 1992 | Iowa | Dan Gable | 149 | Oklahoma St | 100½ | Tom Brands, Iowa |
| 1993 | Iowa | Dan Gable | 123¾ | Penn St | 87½ | Terry Steiner, Iowa |
| 1994 | Oklahoma St | John Smith | 94¾ | Iowa | 76½ | Pat Smith, Oklahoma St |
| 1995 | Iowa | Dan Gable | 134 | Oregon St | 77½ | T.J. Jaworsky, N Carolina |
| 1996 | Iowa | Dan Gable | 122½ | Iowa St | 78½ | Les Gutches, Oregon St |
| 1997 | Iowa | Dan Gable | 170 | Oklahoma St | 113½ | Lincoln McIlravy, Iowa |
| 1998 | Iowa | Jim Zalesky | 115 | Minnesota | 102 | Joe Williams, Iowa |
| 1999 | Iowa | Jim Zalesky | 100½ | Minnesota | 98½ | Cael Sanderson, Iowa St |
| 2000 | Iowa | Jim Zalesky | 116 | Iowa St | 109½ | Cael Sanderson, Iowa St |
| 2001 | Minnesota | J Robinson | 138½ | Iowa | 125½ | Cael Sanderson, Iowa St |

*Unofficial champions.

## DIVISION II

| Year | Champion | Year | Champion | Year | Champion |
|------|----------|------|----------|------|----------|
| 1963 | Western St (CO) | 1976 | Cal St–Bakersfield | 1989 | Portland St |
| 1964 | Western St (CO) | 1977 | Cal St–Bakersfield | 1990 | Portland St |
| 1965 | Mankato St | 1978 | Northern Iowa | 1991 | NE–Omaha |
| 1966 | Cal Poly–SLO | 1979 | Cal St–Bakersfield | 1992 | Central Oklahoma |
| 1967 | Portland St | 1980 | Cal St–Bakersfield | 1993 | Central Oklahoma |
| 1968 | Cal Poly–SLO | 1981 | Cal St–Bakersfield | 1994 | Central Oklahoma |
| 1969 | Cal Poly–SLO | 1982 | Cal St–Bakersfield | 1995 | Central Oklahoma |
| 1970 | Cal Poly–SLO | 1983 | Cal St–Bakersfield | 1996 | Pittsburgh–Johnstown |
| 1971 | Cal Poly–SLO | 1984 | SIU–Edwardsville | 1997 | San Francisco St |
| 1972 | Cal Poly–SLO | 1985 | SIU–Edwardsville | 1998 | N Dakota St |
| 1973 | Cal Poly–SLO | 1986 | SIU–Edwardsville | 1999 | Pittsburgh–Johnstown |
| 1974 | Cal Poly–SLO | 1987 | Cal St–Bakersfield | 2000 | N Dakota St |
| 1975 | Northern Iowa | 1988 | N Dakota St | 2001 | N Dakota St |

## DIVISION III

| Year | Champion | Year | Champion | Year | Champion |
|------|----------|------|----------|------|----------|
| 1974 | Wilkes | 1984 | Trenton St | 1994 | Ithaca |
| 1975 | John Carroll | 1985 | Trenton St | 1995 | Augsburg |
| 1976 | Montclair St | 1986 | Montclair St | 1996 | Wartburg |
| 1977 | Brockport St | 1987 | Trenton St | 1997 | Augsburg |
| 1978 | Buffalo | 1988 | St. Lawrence | 1998 | Augsburg |
| 1979 | Trenton St | 1989 | Ithaca | 1999 | Wartburg |
| 1980 | Brockport St | 1990 | Ithaca | 2000 | Augsburg |
| 1981 | Trenton St | 1991 | Augsburg | 2001 | Augsburg |
| 1982 | Brockport St | 1992 | Brockport | | |
| 1983 | Brockport St | 1993 | Augsburg | | |

# INDIVIDUAL CHAMPIONSHIP
# RECORDS

## Swimming

### Men

| Event | Time | Record Holder | Date |
|---|---|---|---|
| 50-yard freestyle | 19.08 | Neil Walker, Texas | 3-27-97 |
| 100-yard freestyle | 41.80 | Matt Biondi, California | 4-4-87 |
| | | Anthony Ervin, California | 3-24-01 |
| 200-yard freestyle | 1:33.03 | Matt Biondi, California | 4-3-87 |
| 500-yard freestyle | 4:08.75 | Tom Dolan, Michigan | 3-23-95 |
| 1,650-yard freestyle | 14:26.62 | Chris Thompson, Michigan | 3-24-01 |
| 100-yard backstroke | 45.25 | Neil Walker, Texas | 3-28-97 |
| 200-yard backstroke | 1:40.06 | Brian Retterer, Stanford | 3-25-95 |
| 100-yard breaststroke | 52.32 | Jeremy Linn, Tennessee | 3-28-97 |
| 200-yard breaststroke | 1:53.11 | Brendan Hansen, Texas | 3-24-01 |
| 100-yard butterfly | 45.59 | Lars Frolander, Southern Methodist | 3-28-98 |
| 200-yard butterfly | 1:41.78 | Melvin Stewart, Tennessee | 3-30-91 |
| 200-yard individual medley | 1:42.85 | Nate Dusing, Texas | 3-22-01 |
| 400-yard individual medley | 3:38.18 | Tom Dolan, Michigan | 3-24-95 |

### Women

| Event | Time | Record Holder | Date |
|---|---|---|---|
| 50-yard freestyle | 21.77 | Amy Van Dyken, Colorado St | 3-18-94 |
| 100-yard freestyle | 47.61 | Jenny Thompson, Stanford | 3-21-92 |
| 200-yard freestyle | 1:43.08 | Martina Moravcova, Southern Methodist | 3-28-97 |
| 500-yard freestyle | 4:34.39 | Janet Evans, Stanford | 3-15-90 |
| 1,650-yard freestyle | 15:39.14 | Janet Evans, Stanford | 3-17-90 |
| 100-yard backstroke | 51.23 | Natalie Coughlin, California | 3-16-01 |
| 200-yard backstroke | 1:51.02 | Natalie Coughlin, California | 3-17-01 |
| 100-yard breaststroke | 59.05 | Kristy Kowal, Georgia | 3-20-98 |
| 200-yard breaststroke | 2:07.66 | Kristy Kowal, Georgia | 3-20-99 |
| 100-yard butterfly | 51.18 | Natalie Coughlin, California | 3-16-01 |
| 200-yard butterfly | 1:53.36 | Limin Liu, Nevada | 3-20-99 |
| 200-yard individual medley | 1:55.59 | Maggie Bowen, Auburn | 3-15-01 |
| 400-yard individual medley | 4:02.28 | Summer Sanders, Stanford | 3-20-92 |

## Indoor Track and Field

### Men

| Event | Mark | Record Holder | Date |
|---|---|---|---|
| 55-meter dash | 6.00 | Lee McRae, Pittsburgh | 3-14-86 |
| 55-meter hurdles | 7.07 | Allen Johnson, N Carolina | 3-13-92 |
| 200-meter dash | 20.26 | Shawn Crawford, Clemson | 3-10-00 |
| 400-meter dash | 45.60 | Brandon Couts, Baylor | 3-10-00 |
| 800-meter run | 1:45.33 | Patrick Nduwimana, Arizona | 3-10-01 |
| Mile run | 3:55.33 | Kevin Sullivan, Michigan | 3-11-95 |
| 3,000-meter run | 7:46.03 | Adam Goucher, Colorado | 3-14-98 |
| 5,000-meter run | 13:36.64 | Jonah Koech, Iowa St | 3-8-91 |
| High jump | 7 ft 9¼ in | Hollis Conway, SW Louisiana | 3-11-89 |
| Pole vault | 19 ft 2¼ in | Jacob Davis, Texas | 3-6-99 |
| Long jump | 27 ft 10 in | Carl Lewis, Houston | 3-13-81 |
| Triple jump | 56 ft 9½ in | Keith Connor, Southern Methodist | 3-13-81 |
| Shot put | 70 ft 1 in | Janus Robberts, Southern Methodist | 3-10-01 |
| 35-pound weight throw | 78 ft 9¾ in | Libor Charfreitag, Southern Methodist | 3-11-00 |

### Women

| Event | Mark | Record Holder | Date |
|---|---|---|---|
| 55-meter dash | 6.56 | Gwen Torrence, Georgia | 3-14-87 |
| 55-meter hurdles | 7.39 | Tiffany Lott, Brigham Young | 3-7-97 |
| 200-meter dash | 22.83 | Peta-Gaye Dowdie, LSU | 3-6-99 |
| 400-meter dash | 51.05 | Maicel Malone, Arizona St | 3-9-91 |
| 800-meter run | 2:01.77 | Hazel Clark, Florida | 3-5-99 |
| Mile run | 4:30.63 | Suzy Favor, Wisconsin | 3-11-89 |
| 3,000-meter run | 8:54.98 | Stephanie Herbst, Wisconsin | 3-15-86 |
| 5,000-meter run | 15:39.75 | Amy Skieresz, Arizona | 3-7-97 |
| High jump | 6 ft 5½ in | Amy Acuff, UCLA | 3-11-95 |
| Pole vault | 14 ft 9½ in | Thorey Elisdottir, Georgia | 3-10-01 |
| Long jump | 22 ft 1 in | Daphne Saunders, Louisiana St | 3-12-94 |
| Triple jump | 46 ft 9 in | Suzette Lee, Louisiana St | 3-8-97 |
| Shot put | 60 ft 5¼ in | Teri Tunks, Southern Methodist | 3-14-98 |
| 20-pound weight throw | 71 ft 8¾ in | Dawn Ellerbe, S Carolina | 3-7-97 |

## Outdoor Track and Field

### Men

| Event | Mark | Record Holder | Date |
|---|---|---|---|
| 100-meter dash | 9.92 | Ato Bolden, UCLA | 6-1-96 |
| 200-meter dash | 19.87 | Lorenzo Daniel, Mississippi St | 6-3-88 |
| | | John Capel, Florida | 6-5-99 |
| 400-meter dash | 44.00 | Quincy Watts, Southern Cal | 6-6-92 |
| 800-meter run | 1:44.70 | Mark Everett, Florida | 6-1-90 |
| 1,500-meter run | 3:35.30 | Sydney Maree, Villanova | 6-6-81 |
| 3,000-meter steeplechase | 8:12.39 | Henry Rono, Washington St | 6-1-78 |
| 5,000-meter run | 13:20.63 | Sydney Maree, Villanova | 6-2-79 |
| 10,000-meter run | 28:01.30 | Suleiman Nyambui, UTEP | 6-1-79 |
| 110-meter high hurdles | 13.22 | Greg Foster, UCLA | 6-2-78 |
| 400-meter intermediate hurdles | 47.85 | Kevin Young, UCLA | 6-3-88 |
| High jump | 7 ft 9¾ in | Hollis Conway, SW Louisiana | 6-3-89 |
| Pole vault | 19 ft 1 in | Lawrence Johnson, Tennessee | 5-29-96 |
| Long jump | 28 ft | Erick Walder, Arkansas | 6-3-93 |
| Triple jump | 57 ft 7¾ in | Keith Connor, Southern Methodist | 6-5-82 |
| Shot put | 72 ft 2¼ in | John Godina, UCLA | 6-3-95 |
| Discus throw | 220 ft | Kamy Keshmiri, Nevada | 6-5-92 |
| Hammer throw | 265 ft 3 in | Balazs Kiss, Southern Cal | 5-31-96 |
| Javelin throw (new javelin) | 268 ft 7 in | Esko Mikkola, Arizona | 6-3-98 |
| Decathlon | 8279 pts | Tito Steiner, Brigham Young | 6-2/3-81 |

### Women

| Event | Mark | Record Holder | Date |
|---|---|---|---|
| 100-meter dash | 10.78 | Dawn Sowell, Louisiana St | 6-3-89 |
| 200-meter dash | 22.04 | Dawn Sowell, Louisiana St | 6-2-89 |
| 400-meter dash | 50.18 | Pauline Davis, Alabama | 6-3-89 |
| 800-meter run | 1:59.11 | Suzy Favor, Wisconsin | 6-1-90 |
| 1,500-meter run | 4:08.26 | Suzy Favor, Wisconsin | 6-2-90 |
| 3,000-meter run | 8:47.35 | Vicki Huber, Villanova | 6-3-88 |
| 5,000-meter run | 15:37.77 | Amy Skieresz, Arizona | 6-5-98 |
| 10,000-meter run | 32:28.57 | Sylvia Mosqueda, Cal St–Los Angeles | 6-1-88 |
| 100-meter hurdles | 12.70 | Tananjalyn Stanley, Louisiana St | 6-3-89 |
| 400-meter hurdles | 54.54 | Ryan Tolbert, Vanderbilt | 6-6-97 |
| High jump | 6 ft 5 in | Amy Acuff, UCLA | 6-3-95 |
| Pole vault | 14 ft 5¼ in | Tracy O'Hara, UCLA | 6-2-00 |
| Long jump | 22 ft 9¼ in | Sheila Echols, Louisiana St | 6-5-87 |
| Triple jump | 46 ft ¾ in | Sheila Hudson, California | 6-2-90 |
| Shot put | 61 ft 2¼ in | Tressa Thompson, Nebraska | 6-4-98 |
| Discus throw | 210 ft 10 in | Seilala Sua, UCLA | 6-6-99 |
| Hammer throw | 219 ft 4 in | Florence Ezah, Southern Methodist | 6-2-01 |
| Javelin throw (new javelin) | 197 ft 8 in | Angeliki Tsiolakoudi, Texas–El Paso | 6-3-00 |
| Heptathlon | 6527 pts | Diane Guthrie-Gresham, George Mason | 6-2/3-95 |

# Olympics

**Beijing wins the right to host the 2008 Games**

# Uncharted Territory

## A year of historic developments in the Olympic movement ended with China winning the right to host its first Games

### BY MERRELL NODEN

THE OLYMPIC GAMES are like the wooden horse that brought so much trouble to Troy. The risks of bringing them into your city just might outweigh the rewards. After years of nervous, round-the-clock preparations, you finally learn that your city has won. You celebrate with cheers, fireworks and a victory parade beamed around the world. But man—the trouble the Games seem to bring! There always seem to be unimaginable dangers hidden inside that gift horse. No matter how visionary a city's leaders might be, they have no way of foreseeing how the Games are going to affect their city.

That's why it seems awfully premature to fret over the long-term impact of this year's biggest Olympics news: the awarding of the 2008 Summer Games to Beijing. The city was the heavy favorite because Juan Antonio Samaranch, the retiring head of the International Olympic Committee, saw taking the Games into China as a suitably grand curtain-closer for his career, whose guiding impulse has always been expansion (see side-

bar). Obviously, the IOC rank and file sensed this. They chose the sprawling, polluted Chinese capital by a wide margin over Toronto, Paris, Istanbul and Osaka. For the first time the Games will be held in the world's most populous country. Whether that turns out to be good or bad for the people of China ... well, it's impossible to know.

It was a year of historic developments and new directions for the Games. In July, at the IOC summit in Moscow, the organization bid farewell to Samaranch, whose 21-year tenure had produced more changes—and scandals—than those of any of his predecessors, and elected his replacement, Jacques Rogge of Belgium, whose nickname is Mr. Clean. In December 2000, the USOC elected its first female president, Sandra Baldwin, a real-estate executive from Phoenix who previously had served as head of both the U.S. shooting and swimming federations.

Elsewhere around the Olympic movement:

In Salt Lake City, where the XIX Winter Olympics are scheduled to begin on Feb. 8,

2002, everyone was working extra hard to assure people that the tawdry bid scandal of 1998 was truly past. No one worked more diligently at this—or more successfully, it seems—than Salt Lake Organizing Committee (SLOC) president Mitt Romney, a former venture capitalist from Boston who became Salt Lake's knight in shining armor for taking an operation besmirched by scandal and nearly $400 million in debt and turning it into a relative model of fiscal vibrancy.

Alas, as Romney and his team will no doubt be reminded again and again, things don't always go according to the best-laid plans. On Feb. 8, the one-year-to-go date, 8,000 Utah schoolchildren were bused in to watch a figure skating competition. A few days earlier, the trial of former SLOC officials Dave Johnson and Tom Welch on charges of fraud and bribery was to have begun. It ended up being delayed until July, when a judge dismissed four of the 15 charges against the pair, severely weakening the government's case and casting doubt on its prospects of going to trial. SLOC members were free to move on to less scandalous concerns, such as prosletyzing Mormons, polygamous Mormons and Utah's restrictive drinking laws, all of which may deliver a dose of culture shock to thousands of visitors.

"We do not intend to try to sanitize the view the world gets," Romney said. "We will show Utah as it is."

BRIAN BAHR/ALLSPORT

**Romney helped erase memories of scandal, and mountains of debt, for Salt Lake City, which got back on track for 2002.**

So far so good, as early competitions at Olympic venues have proceeded without any major hitches.

The Athens organizing committee seemed to have gotten preparations back on track for 2004, though there is precious little margin for error. Ever since April 2000, when Samaranch declared that the Athens preparations were the worst he'd seen in his career, there has been a real fear that the next Summer Games might be a logistical disaster. The IOC put the Athens committee on probation and talked openly of sending the next

Games back to Sydney, which certainly would have been a colossal embarrassment for the country that invented the Olympics all those years ago.

When, in December 2000, Petros Sinadinos resigned as the Athens committee's number two man, there was great concern that things were fraying further. But Athens bid wonderwoman Gianna Angelopoulos-Daskalaki had already rejoined the team, and her determination seems to have made all the difference. When Rogge led a touring delegation last May, he praised the organizing committee for playing catch-up.

"We must not lose even an hour," said Panos K. Protopsaltis, operations manager for the Athens committee. "But we can do it."

But none of these developments matched the furor over China's successful bid for the 2008 Games. In 1993 China had thrown its hat in the ring for the 2000 Games, losing to Sydney by two votes after months as the front-runner. Parts of the Chinese press blamed this bitter loss on the meddling of Western nations, though surely, with memories of the Tiananmen Square massacre only four years old, they could have looked elsewhere for blame.

Then as now, there were strong feelings on both sides. Human rights advocates howled that it was wrong to reward a brutal, oppressive government with the honor of hosting what is still, warts and all, the world's most idealistic extravaganza. Amnesty International reported that as part of its Strike Hard anticrime campaign, China executed 1,781 people in the three months leading up to the vote—more than the entire rest of the world had executed in the previous three years.

And that was just the tip of the iceberg. Critics also pointed to the Chinese govern-

## "His Excellency" Steps Down

During his 21 eventful years as head of the International Olympic Committee, Juan Antonio Samaranch expected to be addressed as "Your Excellency." Though the salutation seems ridiculously anachronistic, Samaranch's great achievement was quite the opposite: He transformed the Olympic Games from a moribund dinosaur into a profit-conscious, global marketing juggernaut. The gold medal question is: at what cost?

Samaranch's aim was always growth through inclusion—of millionaire pros, pariah nations and newfangled sports. To understand this impulse, it helps to recall the perilous state of the Games in 1980, when Samaranch took over from Lord Killanin of Ireland. Political rivalries posed a constant threat: The Games of 1976, '80 and '84 had each been beset by boycotts.

Samaranch's other apparent obsession was money, again with good reason. The year he took over, the IOC had less than $500,000 in the bank, and the financially disastrous Montreal Games had made hosting the Olympics look like a terrible mistake. Today, the IOC generates $900 million a year in revenue, much of it from television contracts

such as the one that NBC signed in 1995, paying $3.5 billion for the rights to televise five Olympics. Cities spend millions on their bids to host the Games.

Samaranch was the first full-time IOC head, and under him the Olympics grew tremendously in size and popularity. It was estimated that 3.5 billion of the world's 3.7 billion television sets tuned in to the Sydney Olympics, which featured 199 competing nations, as opposed to 80 in 1980. There are more female athletes, and a few women have finally been permitted IOC membership. Along the way came other major changes, including the abolition of amateurism and the reinstatement of South Africa in 1992 after 32 years of banishment.

The growth is undeniable. But Samaranch's critics offer it as proof of corruption or at least of his willingness to trade integrity and independence for commercial success. For instance, in 1984, in order to secure the participation of the powerful East German team at the Seoul Olympics, Samaranch gave the movement's highest award to Manfred Ewald, head of the East German Olympic Committee, who was then widely suspected, and

ment's ongoing persecution of the Falun Gong religious cult; China's usurpation of Tibet; its hounding—and apparently groundless prosecution—of dissidents, including four Chinese-born American residents; and its hard-line spear-rattling before freeing the 24 U.S. Navy men and women whose EP-3E reconnaissance plane had been forced to land on Hainan Island in April after colliding with a Chinese fighter plane. Surely, the critics argued, all of those misdeeds add up to a powerful case against giving the Games to Beijing. Wouldn't awarding China the Olympics send the wrong signal?

Well, no, argued the other side. Bringing the world's press to Beijing will force the Chinese to open up. The bright spotlight of international attention is a pretty good catalyst for change. "If you want to keep China on the hook," argued Jim Kolbe, a member of the House from Arizona, "this is the best leverage to have. This could be one more thing that opens up China." Australian track star Cathy Freeman pointed out that the Sydney Games had promoted the cause of Australia's Aboriginal population, while others mentioned the positive impact the Games had on repressive South Korea in 1988. Even the Dalai Lama, the exiled leader of Tibet, spoke in favor of giving the Games to Beijing.

"I believe an important responsibility we have is to keep moving the Games around the world," said Kevan Gosper, an influential IOC member from Australia. "[In China] we have a huge country which has never had the Games. This could be an event which encourages an ever greater degree of openness. From the Olympics' point of view, Beijing has to have the edge."

And whatever their actual feelings about

DARREN ENGLAND/ALLSPORT

**Samaranch waved goodbye after a checkered 21-year career as head of the IOC.**

later convicted, of overseeing the sinister East German doping machine.

In some key ways Samaranch was clearly a product of the Old Order. Calls for accountability left him mystified. The Salt Lake City bidding scandal of 1998 opened a Pandora's box of corruption and bribery, of which Samaranch must have been aware. IOC members were expelled, and Samaranch himself was tarnished but not destroyed—though he never seemed to comprehend what the fuss was about.

On July 16, 2001, the IOC chose Jacques Rogge, an orthopedic surgeon and former Olympic sailor for Belgium, to succeed Samaranch. The result was interpreted as a vote for reform. Many thorny issues await Rogge, such as drug testing and containing the increasingly unwieldy event his predecessor created. Samaranch guaranteed the Games would survive: In what form, remains to be seen.

human rights issues in their country, Chinese leaders demonstrated a willingness at least to say the right things. "We are not perfect," conceded Beijing's Vice Mayor Liu Jingmin, point man for the city's bid. But the 2008 Games "will help us improve people's rights [and] the quality of life for Beijing's citizens."

"Even Falun Gong members can come if they are athletes," added Liu, apparently not intending this to sound like a bad joke.

With the counseling of two crack p.r. firms, Liu and his colleagues promised staggering changes. In what China's national press agency described as "one of the largest construction projects in China since the Great Wall," they announced that they would spend $20 billion to build a light rail system and expand the city's 134 miles of expressways to 435. Whereas Sydney corralled 47,000 volunteers for its Games, the Chinese promise 600,000.

A subplot to the heated political arguments was a practical consideration—Beijing's terrible pollution. Among the remedies the city announced were shuttering or moving polluting factories, including the Capital Iron and Steelworks, prior to the Games, and reducing automobile emissions. Thousands of flowers and trees were to be planted. Hi-tech public toilets were to be installed in downtown Beijing, each costing $60,000.

But in the end, Beijing's top selling point for Samaranch and his followers seemed to be its novelty and, ironically, its poor human rights record. Samaranch has long been hoping to win the Nobel peace prize, and the potential for making a huge global impact is greater in Beijing than in, say, Toronto or Paris, the two challengers for the rights to host in 2008. There is risk of course, but there is no doubting the great democratizing force the Games could be in China. That worthy dream, coupled with the IOC members' hunger to foster the Games'—and by extension their own—influence, made Beijing an all but foregone conclusion.

Rogge, Samaranch's heir and, in the opinion of some IOC watchers, his hand-picked candidate, will have his hands full.

MIKE HEWITT/ALLSPORT

**Nicknamed Mr. Clean, Rogge had plenty of tidying to do at the IOC, which he will steward into the 21st century.**

A former Olympic sailor, the 59-year-old Rogge is considered an unwavering straight arrow. His triumph over Kim Un Yong of South Korea—whose proposal to grant all IOC members an annual expenses stipend of $50,000 sounded like more of the same bribery that tarnished Salt Lake City's bid—was hailed as a vote for true reform.

Rogge has also questioned one part of his predecessor's legacy—the present size of the Olympics. He is on record as saying that he would like to shrink the Games to make them less expensive. What he will do about this remains to be seen. Drugs pose another huge threat to the Games' legitimacy, but with tests for both EPO and human growth hormone soon to be implemented, that scourge too might be removed.

Samaranch ensured the survival of the Games when they were in grave danger. It will be up to Rogge to see that they thrive as the bastion of true sportsmanship and global unity that Baron Pierre de Coubertin envisioned in the late 19th century.

## 2000 Summer Games

### TRACK AND FIELD
### Men

**100 METERS**

1. ...Maurice Green, United States — 9.87
2. ...Ato Boldon, Trinidad and Tobago — 9.99
3. ...Obadele Thomoson, Barbados — 10.04

**200 METERS**

1. ...Konstadinos Kederis, Greece — 20.09
2. ...Darren Campbell, Great Britain — 20.14
3. ...Ato Boldon, Trinidad and Tobago — 20.20

**400 METERS**

1. ...Michael Johnson, United States — 43.84
2. ...Alvin Harrison, United States — 44.40
3. ...Gregory Haughton, Jamaica — 44.70

**800 METERS**

1. ...Nils Schumann, Germany — 1:45.08
2. ...Wilson Kipketer, Denmark — 1:45.14
3. ...Aissa Djabir Said-Guerni, Algeria — 1:45.16

**1,500 METERS**

1. ...Noah Ngeny, Kenya — 3:32.07 OR
2. ...Hicham El Guerrouj, Morocco — 3:32.32
3. ...Bernard Lagat, Kenya — 3:32.44

**5,000 METERS**

1. ...Millon Wolde, Ethiopia — 13:35.49
2. ...Ali Saidi-Sief, Algeria — 13:36.20
3. ...Brahim Lahlafi, Morocco — 13:36.47

**10,000 METERS**

1. ...Haile Gebrselassie, Ethiopia — 27:18.20
2. ...Paul Tergat, Kenya — 27:18.29
3. ...Assefa Mezgebu, Ethiopia — 27:19.75

**MARATHON**

1. ...Geznghe Abera, Ethiopia — 2:10:11
2. ...Eric Wainaina, Kenya — 2:10:31
3. ...Tesfaye Tola, Ethiopia — 2:11:10

**110-METER HURDLES**

1. ...Anier Garcia, Cuba — 13.00
2. ...Terrence Trammell, United States — 13.16
3. ...Mark Crear, United States — 13.22

**400-METER HURDLES**

1. ...Angelo Taylor, United States — 47.50
2. ...Hadi Souan Somalyi, Saudi Arabia — 47.53
3. ...Llewelyn Herbert, South Africa — 47.81

**3,000-METER STEEPLECHASE**

1. ...Reuben Kosgei, Kenya — 8:21.43
2. ...Wilson Boit Kipketer, Kenya — 8:21.77
3. ...Ali Ezzine, Morocco — 8:22.15

**4 X 100-METER RELAY**

1. ...United States: (Jon Drummond — 37.61
......Bernard Williams III, Brian Lewis,
......Maurice Greene)
2. ...Brazil — 37.90
3. ...Cuba — 38.04

**4 X 400-METER RELAY**

1. ...United States: (Alvin Harrison, — 2:56.35
......Antonio Pettigrew, Calvin Harrison,
......Michael Johnson)
2. ...Nigeria — 2:58.68
3. ...Jamaica — 2:58.78

**20-KILOMETER WALK**

1. ...Robert Korzeniowski, Poland — 1:18:59
2. ...Noe Hernandez, Mexico — 1:19:03
3. ...Vladimir Andreyev. Russia — 1:19:27

**50-KILOMETER WALK**

1. ...Robert Korzeniowski, Poland — 3:42:22
2. ...Aigars Fadejevs, Latvia — 3:43:40
3. ...Joel Sanchez, Mexico — 3:44:36

**HIGH JUMP**

1. ...Sergey Kliugin, Russia — 7 ft 8¼ in
2. ...Javier Sotomayor, Cuba — 7 ft 7¼ in
3. ...Abderrahmane Hammad, Algeria — 7 ft 7¼ in

**POLE VAULT**

1. ...Nick Hysong, United States — 19 ft 4¼ in
2. ...Lawrence Johnson, United States — 19 ft 4¼ in
3. ...Maksim Tarasov, Russia — 19 ft 4¼ in

**LONG JUMP**

1. ...Ivan Pedroso, Cuba — 28 ft ¾ in
2. ...Jai Taurima, Australia — 27 ft 10¼ in
3. ...Roman Schurenko, Ukraine — 27 ft 3¼ in

**TRIPLE JUMP**

1. ...Jonathan Edwards, Great Britain — 58 ft 1¼ in
2. ...Yoel Garcia, Cuba — 57 ft 3¾ in
3. ...Denis Kapustin, Russia — 57 ft 3½ in

**SHOT PUT**

1. ...Arsi Harju, Finland — 69 ft 10¼ in
2. ...Adam Nelson, United States — 69 ft 7 in
3. ...John Godina, United States — 69 ft 6¾ in

**DISCUS THROW**

1. ...Virgilijus Alekna, Lithuania — 227 ft 4 in
2. ...Lars Riedel, Germany — 224 ft 9 in
3. ...Frantz Kruger, South Africa — 223 ft 8 in

**HAMMER THROW**

1. ...Szymon Ziolkowski, Poland — 262 ft 6 in
2. ...Nicola Vizzoni, Italy — 261 ft 3 in
3. ...Igor Astapkovich, Belarus — 259 ft 8½ in

**JAVELIN**

1. ...Jan Zelezny, Czech Republic — 295 ft 9½ in
2. ...Steve Backley, Great Britain — 294 ft 9½ in
3. ...Sergey Makarov, Russia — 290 ft 10½ in

**DECATHLON**

.......Pts

1. ...Erki Nool, Estonia — 8641
2. ...Roman Seberle, Czech Republic — 8606
3. ...Chris Huffins, United States — 8595

Note: OR=Olympic record. WR=world record. EOR=equals Olympic record. EWR=equals world record.

## TRACK AND FIELD (Cont.)
### Women

#### 100 METERS
1. ...Marion Jones, United States — 10.75
2. ...Ekaterini Thanou, Greece — 11.12
3. ...Tanya Lawrence, Jamaica — 11.18

#### 200 METERS
1. ...Marion Jones, United States — 21.84
2. ...P. Davis-Thompson, Bahamas — 22.27
3. ...Susanthika Jayasinghe, Sri Lanka — 22.28

#### 400 METERS
1. ...Cathy Freeman, Australia — 49.11
2. ...Lorraine Graham, Jamaica — 49.58
3. ...Katharine Merry, Great Britain — 49.72

#### 800 METERS
1. ...Maria Mutola, Mozambique — 1:56.15
2. ...Stephanie Graf, Austria — 1:56.64
3. ...Kelly Holmes, Great Britain — 1:56.80

#### 1,500 METERS
1. ...Nouria Merah-Benida, Algeria — 4:05.10
2. ...Violeta Szekely, Romania — 4:05.15
3. ...Gabriela Szabo, Romania — 4:05.27

#### 5,000 METERS
1. ...Gabriela Szabo, Romania — 14:40.79 OR
2. ...Sonia O'Sullivan, Ireland — 14:41.02
3. ...Gete Wami, Ethiopia — 14:42.23

#### 10,000 METERS
1. ...Derartu Tulu, Ethiopia — 30:17.49 OR
2. ...Gete Wami, Ethiopia — 30:22.48
3. ...Fernanda Ribeiro, Portugal — 30:22.88

#### MARATHON
1. ...Naoko Takahashi, Japan — 2:23:14 OR
2. ...Lidia Simon, Romania — 2:23:22
3. ...Joyce Chepchumba, Kenya — 2:24:45

#### 100-METER HURDLES
1. ...Olga Shishigina, Kazakhstan — 12.65
2. ...Glory Alozie, Nigeria — 12.68
3. ...Melissa Morrison, United States — 12.76

#### 400-METER HURDLES
1. ...Irina Privalova, Russia — 53.02
2. ...Deon Hemmings, Jamaica — 53.45
3. ...Nouza Bidouane, Morocco — 53.57

#### 4 X 100-METER RELAY
1. ...Bahamas (S. Fynes, C. Sturrup, P. Davis-Thompson, D. Ferguson) — 41.95
2. ...Jamaica — 42.13
3. ...United States — 42.20

#### 4 X 400-METER RELAY
1. ...United States (Jearl Miles-Clark, Monique Hennagan, Marion Jones, La Tasha Colander-Richardson) — 3:22.62
2. ...Jamaica — 3:23.25
3. ...Russia — 3:23.46

#### 20-KILOMETER WALK
1. ...Wang Liping, China — 1:29.05
2. ...Kiersti Plaetzer, Norway — 1:29.33
3. ...Maria Vasco, Spain — 1:30.23

#### HIGH JUMP
1. ...Yelena Yelesina, Russia — 6 ft 7 in
2. ...Hestrie Cloete, S Africa — 6 ft 7 in
3. ...Kajsa Bergqvist, Sweden — 6 ft 7 in

#### POLE VAULT
1. ...Stacy Dragila, United States — 15 ft 1 in OR
2. ...Tatiana Grigorieva, Australia — 14 ft 11 in
3. ...Vala Flosadottir, Iceland — 14 ft 9 in

#### LONG JUMP
1. ...Heike Drechsler, Germany — 22 ft 11¼ in
2. ...Fiona May, Italy — 22 ft 8½ in
3. ...Marion Jones, United States — 22 ft 8½ in

#### TRIPLE JUMP
1. ...Tereza Marinova, Bulgaria — 49 ft 10½ in
2. ...Tatyana Lebedeva, Russia — 49 ft 2½ in
3. ...Olena Hovorova, Ukraine — 49 ft 1 in

#### SHOT PUT
1. ...Yanina Korolchik, Belarus — 67 ft 5½ in
2. ...Laris Peleshenko, Russia — 65 ft 4¼ in
3. ...Astrid Kumbernuss, Germany — 64 ft 4½ in

#### DISCUS THROW
1. ...Ellina Zvereva, Belarus — 224 ft 5 in
2. ...Anastasia Kelesidou, Greece — 215 ft 7 in
3. ...Irina Yatchenko, Belarus — 213 ft 11 in

#### JAVELIN
1. ...Trine Hattestad, Norway — 226 ft ½ in OR
2. ...Mirella Maniani-Tzelili, Greece — 221 ft 5½ in
3. ...Osleidys Menendez, Cuba — 217 ft 1 in

#### HEPTATHLON — Pts
1. ...Denise Lewis, Great Britain — 6584
2. ...Yelena Prokhorova, Russia — 6531
3. ...Natalya Sazanovich, Belarus — 6527

#### HAMMER THROW
1. ...Kamila Skolimowska, Russia — 233 ft 5 in OR
2. ...Olga Kuzenkova, Russia — 228 ft 11 in
3. ...Kirsten Muenchow, Germany — 227 ft 3 in

## INDIVIDUAL ARCHERY

### Men
1. ...........Simon Fairweather, Australia
2. ...........Victor Wuderle, United States
3. ...........Wietse van Alten, Netherlands

### Women
1. ...........Yun Mi-Jin, S Korea
2. ...........Kim Nam-Soon, S Korea
3. ...........Kim Soo-Nyuong, S Korea

## TEAM ARCHERY

### Men
1. .......................................................S Korea
2. ...........................................................Italy
3. .............................................United States

### Women
1. .......................................................S Korea
2. .....................................................Ukraine
3. ....................................................Germany

Note: OR=Olympic record. WR=world record. EOR=equals Olympic record. EWR=equals world record.

# BADMINTON

## Men

### SINGLES
1. ...Ji Xinpeng, China
2. ...Henra wan, Indonesia
3. ...Xia Xuanze, China

### DOUBLES
1. ...Tony Gunawan/ Candra Wijaya, Indonesia
2. ...Lee Dong-soo/ Yoo Yong-sung, S Korea
3. ...Ha Tae-kwan/ Kim Dong-moon, S Korea

## Women

### SINGLES
1. ...Gong Zhichao, China
2. ...Camilla Martin, Denmark
3. ...Ye Zhaoying, China

### DOUBLES
1. ...Ge Fei/ Gu Jun, China
2. ...Huang Nanyan/ Yang Wei, China
3. ...Gao Ling/ Qin Yiyuan, China

### MIXED DOUBLES
1. ...Zhang Jun/Gao Ling, China
2. ...Tri Kushanjanto/Minarti Timur, Indonesia
3. ...Simon Archer/Joanne Goode, Great Britain

# BASEBALL

1. ...United States
2. ...Cuba
3. ...S Korea

# BASKETBALL

## Men

Final: United States 85, France 75
Lithuania (3rd)
United States: Shareef Abdur-Rahim, Ray Allen, Vin Baker, Vince Carter, Kevin Garnett, Tim Hardaway, Allan Houston, Jason Kidd, Antonio McDyess, Alonzo Mourning, Gary Payton, Steve Smith

## Women

Final: United States 76, Australia 54
Brazil (3rd)
United States: Ruthie Bolton-Holifield, Teresa Edwards, Yolanda Griffith, Chamique Holdsclaw, Lisa Leslie, Nikki McCray, Delisha Milton, Katie Smith Dawn Staley, Sheryl Swoopes, Natalie Williams, Kara Wolters

# BOXING

### LIGHT FLYWEIGHT (106 LB)
1. ...Brahim Asloum, France
2. ...Rafael Lozano Munoz, Spain
3. ...Un Chol Kim, N Korea
3. ...Maikro Romero Esquirol, Cuba

### FLYWEIGHT (112 LB)
1. ...Wijan Ponlid, Thailand
2. ...Bulat Jumadilov, Kazakhstan
3. ...Jerome Thomas, France
3. ...Vladimir Sidorenko, Ukraine

### BANTAMWEIGHT (119 LB)
1. ...Guillermo Ortiz, Cuba
2. ...Raimkoul Malakhbekov, Russia
3. ...Serguey Daniltchenko, Ukraine
3. ...Clarence Vinson, United States

### FEATHERWEIGHT (125 LB)
1. ...Bekzat Sattarkhanov, Kazakhstan
2. ...Ricardo Juarez, United States
3. ...Tahar Tamsamani, Morocco
3. ...Kamil Dzamalutdinov, Russia

### LIGHTWEIGHT (132 LB)
1. ...Mario Kindelan, Cuba
2. ...Andriy Kotelnyk, Ukraine
3. ...Cristian Benitez, Mexico
3. ...Alexandr Maletin, Russia

### LIGHT WELTERWEIGHT (139 LB)
1. ...Mahamadkadyz Abdullaev, Uzbekistan
2. ...Ricardo Williams, United States
3. ...Diogenes Luna Martinez, Cuba
3. ...Mohamed Allalou, Algeria

### WELTERWEIGHT (147 LB)
1. ...Oleg Saitov, Russia
2. ...Sergey Dotsenko, Ukraine
3. ...Vitalii Grusac, Moldova
3. ...Dorel Simion, Romania

### LIGHT MIDDLEWEIGHT (156 LB)
1. ...Yermakhan Ibraimov, Kazakhstan
2. ...Marin Simion, Romania
3. ...Pornchai Thongburan, Thailand
3. ...Jermain Taylor, United States

### MIDDLEWEIGHT (165 LB)
1. ...Jorge Gutierrez, Cuba
2. ...Gaidarbek Gaidarbekov, Russia
3. ...Vugar Alekperov, Azerbaijan
3. ...Zsolt Erdei, Hungary

### LIGHT HEAVYWEIGHT (178 LB)
1. ...Alexander Lebziak, Russia
2. ...Rudolf Kraj, Czech Republic
3. ...Andri Fedtchouk, Ukraine
3. ...Sergei Mikhailov, Uzbekistan

### HEAVYWEIGHT (201 LB)
1. ...Félix Sávon, Cuba
2. ...Sultanahmed Ibzagimov, Russia
3. ...Sebastian Kober, Germany
3. ...Vladimir Tchantouria, Georgia

### SUPERHEAVYWEIGHT (201+ LB)
1. ...Audley Harrison, Great Britain
2. ...Mukhtarkhan Dildabkov, Kazakhstan
3. ...Rustam Saidov, Uzbekistan
3. ...Paolo Vidoz, Italy

## CANOE/KAYAK

### Men

#### C-1 FLATWATER 500 METERS
1. ...Gyorgy Kolonics, Hungary — 2:24.813
2. ...Maxim Opalev, Russia — 2:25.809
3. ...Andreas Dittmer, Germany — 2:27.591

#### C-1 FLATWATER 1,000 METERS
1. ...Andreas Dittmer, Germany — 3:54.379
2. ...Ledys Frank Balceiro, Cuba — 3:56.071
3. ...Steve Giles, Canada — 3:56.437

#### C-2 FLATWATER 500 METERS
1. ...F. Novak/ I. Pulai, Hungary — 1:51.284
2. ...D. Jedraszko/ P. Baraszkiewicz, Poland — 1:51.536
3. ...F. Popescu/ M. Pricop, Romania — 1:54.260

#### C-2 FLATWATER 1,000 METERS
1. ...F. Popescu/ M. Pricop, Romania — 3:37.355
2. ...I. Rojas/ L. Pereira, Cuba — 3:38.753
3. ...L. Kober/ S. Utess, Germany — 3:41.129

#### C-1 WHITEWATER SLALOM
|  |  | Pts |
|--|--|-----|
| 1. ...Tony Estanguet, France | | 231.87 |
| 2. ...Michal Martikan, Slovakia | | 233.76 |
| 3. ...Juraj Mincik, Slovakia | | 234.22 |

#### C-2 WHITEWATER SLALOM
|  |  | Pts |
|--|--|-----|
| 1. ...Pavel/ Peter Hochschorner, Slovakia | | 237.74 |
| 2. ...K. Kolomanski/ M. Staniszewski, Poland | | 243.81 |
| 3. ...M. Jiras/ T. Mader, Czech Republic | | 249.45 |

#### K-1 FLATWATER 500 METERS
1. ...Knut Holmann, Norway — 1:57.847
2. ...Petar Merkov, Bulgaria — 1:58.393
3. ...Michael Kolganov, Israel — 1:59.563

#### K-1 FLATWATER 1,000 METERS
1. ...Knut Holmann, Norway — 3:33.260
2. ...Petar Merkov, Bulgaria — 3:34.640
3. ...Tim Brabants, Great Britain — 3:35.057

### Men *(Cont.)*

#### K-2 FLATWATER 500 METERS
1. ...Z. Kammerer/ B. Storcz, Hungary — 1:47.055
2. ...D. Collins/ A. Trim, Australia — 1:47.895
3. ...R. Rauhe/ T. Wieskoetter, Germany — 1:48.771

#### K-2 FLATWATER 1,000 METERS
1. ...B. Bonomi/ A. Rossi, Italy — 3:14.461
2. ...M. Oscarsson/ H. Nilsson, Sweden — 3:16.075
3. ...K. Bartfai/ K. Vereb, Hungary — 3:16.357

#### K-4 FLATWATER 1,000 METERS
1. ...Hungary — 2:55.188
2. ...Germany — 2:55.704
3. ...Poland — 2:57.192

#### K-1 WHITEWATER SLALOM
|  |  | Pts |
|--|--|-----|
| 1. ...Thomas Schmidt, Germany | | 217.25 |
| 2. ...Paul Ratcliffe, Great Britain | | 223.71 |
| 3. ...Pierpaolo Ferrazzi, Italy | | 225.03 |

### Women

#### K-1 FLATWATER 500 METERS
1. ...Josefa Idem Geurrini, Italy — 2:13.848
2. ...Caroline Brunet, Canada — 2:14.646
3. ...Katrin Borchert, Australia — 2:15.138

#### K-2 FLATWATER 500 METERS
1. ...B. Fischer/ K. Wagner, Germany — 1:56.996
2. ...K. Kovacs/ S. Szabo, Hungary — 1:58.580
3. ...A. Pastuszka/ B. Sokoloska, Poland — 1:58.784

#### K-4 FLATWATER 500 METERS
1. ...Germany — 1:34.532
2. ...Hungary — 1:34.946
3. ...Romania — 1:37.010

#### K-1 WHITEWATER SLALOM
|  |  | Pts |
|--|--|-----|
| 1. ...Stepanka Hilgertova, Czech Republic | | 247.04 |
| 2. ...Brigitte Guibal, France | | 251.88 |
| 3. ...Anne-Lise Bardet, France | | 254.77 |

## CYCLING

### Men

#### ROAD RACE
1. ...Jan Ullrich, Germany — 5:29:17.001
2. ...Alexander Vinokourov, Kazakhstan — 5:29:17.002
3. ...Andreas Kloeden, Germany — 5:29:29.003

#### INDIVIDUAL TIME TRIAL
1. ...Vyachslev Ekimov, Russia — 57:40.420
2. ...Jan Ullrich, Germany — 57:48.333
3. ...Lance Armstrong, United States — 58:14.267

#### 1KM TIME TRIAL
1. ...Jason Queally, Great Britain — 101.609
2. ...Stefan Nimke, Germany — 102.487
3. ...Shane Kelly, Australia — 102.818

#### 4,000-METER INDIVIDUAL PURSUIT
1. ...Robert Bartko, Germany — 4:18.515 OR
2. ...Jens Lehmann, Germany — 4:23.824
3. ...Bradley McGee, Australia — 4:19.250

#### 4,000-METER TEAM PURSUIT
1. ...Germany (Robert Bartko, Guido Fulst, Daniel Becke, Jens Lehmann) — 3:59.710WR
2. ...Russia — 4:04.520
3. ...Great Britain — 4:01.979

### Men *(Cont.)*

#### SPRINT
1. ...Marty Nothstein, United States — 10.874
2. ...Florian Rousseau, France — 11.066
3. ...Jens Fiedler, Germany — 10.732

#### 40-KM POINTS RACE
1. ...Juan Llaneras, Spain — 14
2. ...Milton Wynant, Uruguay — 18
3. ...Alexey Markov, Russia — 16

#### KIERIN
1. ...Florian Rousseau, France — 11.020
2. ...Gary Neiwand, Australia
3. ...Jens Fiedler, Germany

#### MADISON
1. ...B. Aiken/ S. McGrory, Australia — 26
2. ...E. DeWilde/ M. Gilmore, Belgium — 22
3. ...S. Martinello/ M. Villa, Italy — 15

#### OLYMPIC SPRINT
1. ...France — 44.233
2. ...Great Britain — 44.680
3. ...Australia — 45.161

## CYCLING *(Cont.)*
### Women

#### 24-KM POINTS RACE
1. ...Antonella Bellutti, Italy — 19
2. ...Leontien Zijlaard, Netherlands — 16
3. ...Olga Slioussareva, Russia — 15

#### SPRINT
1. ...Felicia Ballanger, France — 12.553
2. ...Oxana Grichina, Russia — 13.112
3. ...Irina Yanovych, Ukraine — 12.310

#### INDIVIDUAL TIME TRIAL
1. ...Leontien Zijlaard, Netherlands — 42:00.781
2. ...Mari Holden, United States — 42:37.372
3. ...Jeannie Longo-Ciprelli, France — 42:52:547

#### ROAD RACE
1. ...Leontien Zijlaard, Netherlands — 3:6:31.001
2. ...Hanka Kupfernagel, Germany — 3:6:31.002
3. ...Diana Ziliute, Lithuania — 3:6:31.003

#### 3,000-METER INDIVIDUAL PURSUIT
1. ...Leontien Zijlaard, Netherlands — 3:33:360
2. ...Marion Clignet, France — 3:38:751
3. ...Yvonne McGregor, Great Britain — 3:38:850

#### 500-M TIME TRIAL
1. ...Felicia Ballanger, France — 34.140
2. ...Michelle Ferris, Australia — 34.696
3. ...Jiang Cuihua, China — 34.768

## DIVING

### Men
#### SPRINGBOARD

| | | Pts |
|---|---|---|
| 1. | Xiong Ni, China | 708.72 |
| 2. | Fernando Platas, Mexico | 708.42 |
| 3. | Dmitri Sautin, Russia | 703.20 |

#### PLATFORM

| | | Pts |
|---|---|---|
| 1. | Tian Liang, China | 724.53 |
| 2. | Hu Jia, China | 713.55 |
| 3. | Dmitry Sautin, Russia | 679.26 |

### Women
#### SPRINGBOARD

| | | Pts |
|---|---|---|
| 1. | Fu Mingxia, China | 609.42 |
| 2. | Guo Jingjing, China | 597.81 |
| 3. | Doerte Linder, Germany | 574.35 |

#### PLATFORM

| | | Pts |
|---|---|---|
| 1. | Laura Wilkinson, United States | 543.75 |
| 2. | Li Na, China | 542.01 |
| 3. | Anne Montminy, Canada | 540.15 |

## EQUESTRIAN

#### 3-DAY TEAM — Pts
1. ...Australia (Phillip Dutton, Andrew Hoy, Stuart Tinney, Matt Ryan) — 146.8
2. ...Great Britain — 161.0
3. ...United States — 175.8

#### INDIVIDUAL DRESSAGE — Pts
1. ...Anky van Grunsven, Netherlands — 239.18
2. ...Isabell Werth, Germany — 234.19
3. ...Ulla Salzberger, Germany — 230.57

#### 3-DAY INDIVIDUAL — Pts
1. ...David O'Connor, United States — 34.00
2. ...Andrew Hoy, Australia — 39.80
3. ...Mark Todd, New Zealand — 42.00

#### TEAM JUMPING — Pts
1. ...Germany (Ludger Beerbaum, Lars Nieberg, Marcus Ehning, Otto Becker) — 7.00
2. ...Switzerland — 8.00
3. ...Brazil — 12.00

#### TEAM DRESSAGE — Pts
1. ...Germany (Isabell Werth, Nadine Capellmann, Ulla Salzgeber, Alexandra Simons de Ridder) — 5632
2. ...Netherlands — 5579
3. ...United States — 5166

#### INDIVIDUAL JUMPING — Pts
1. ...Jeroen Dubbeldam, Netherlands — 4.00
2. ...Albert Voorn, Netherlands — 4.00
3. ...Khaled Al Eid, Saudi Arabia — 4.00

## FENCING
### Men

#### FOIL
1. ...Kim Young Ho, S Korea
2. ...Ralf Bissdorf, Germany
3. ...Dmitri Chevtchenko, Russia

#### TEAM FOIL
1. ...France
2. ...China
3. ...Italy

#### SABRE
1. ...Mihai Claudiu Covaliu, Romania
2. ...Mathieu Gourdain, France
3. ...Wiradech Kothny, Germany

#### TEAM SABRE
1. ...Russia
2. ...France
3. ...Germany

#### ÉPÉE
1. ...Pavel Kolobkov, Russia
2. ...Hugues Obry, France
3. ...Lee Sang Ki, S Korea

#### TEAM ÉPÉE
1. ...Italy
2. ...France
3. ...Cuba

## FENCING *(Cont.)*

### Women

#### FOIL

1. ...................Valentina Vezzali, Italy
2. ...................Rita Koenig, Germany
3. ...................Giovanna Trillini, Italy

#### ÉPÉE

1. ...................Timea Nagy, Hungary
2. ...................Gianna Habluetzel-Buerki, Switzerland
3. ...................Laura Flessel-Colovic, France

#### TEAM FOIL

1. ...................Italy
2. ...................Poland
3. ...................Germany

#### TEAM ÉPÉE

1. ...................Russia
2. ...................Switzerland
3. ...................China

## FIELD HOCKEY

### Men

1. ...................Netherlands
2. ...................S Korea
3. ...................Australia

### Women

1. ...................Australia
2. ...................Argentina
3. ...................Netherlands

## GYMNASTICS

### Men

#### ALL-AROUND

| | | Pts |
|---|---|---|
| 1. | Alexei Nemov, Russia | 58.474 |
| 2. | Wei Yang, China | 58.361 |
| 3. | O. Beresh, Ukraine | 58.212 |

#### HORIZONTAL BAR

| | | Pts |
|---|---|---|
| 1. | Alexei Nemov, Russia | 9.787 |
| 2. | Benjamin Varonian, France | 9.787 |
| 3. | Joo-hyung Lee, S Korea | 9.775 |

#### PARALLEL BARS

| | | Pts |
|---|---|---|
| 1. | Xiaopeng Li, China | 9.825 |
| 2. | Joo-hyung Lee, S Korea | 9.812 |
| 3. | Alexei Nemov, Russia | 9.800 |

#### VAULT

| | | Pts |
|---|---|---|
| 1. | Gervasio Deferr, Spain | 9.712 |
| 2. | Alexei Bondarenko, Russia | 9.587 |
| 3. | Leszsk Blanik, Poland | 9.475 |

#### POMMEL HORSE

| | | Pts |
|---|---|---|
| 1. | Marius Urzica, Romania | 9.862 |
| 2. | Eric Poujade, France | 9.825 |
| 3. | Alexei Nemov, Russia | 9.800 |

#### RINGS

| | | Pts |
|---|---|---|
| 1. | Szilveszter Csollany, Hungary | 9.850 |
| 2. | Dimosthenis Tampakos, Kasakhstan | 9.762 |
| 2. | Iordan Iovtchev, Bulgaria | 9.737 |

#### FLOOR EXERCISE

| | | Pts |
|---|---|---|
| 1. | Igors Vihrovs, Latvia | 9.812 |
| 2. | Alexei Nemov, Russia | 9.800 |
| 3. | Iordan Iovtchev, Bulgaria | 9.787 |

#### TEAM COMBINED EXERCISES

| | | Pts |
|---|---|---|
| 1. | China | 231.919 |
| 2. | Ukraine | 230.306 |
| 3. | Russia | 230.019 |

### Women

#### ALL-AROUND

| | | Pts |
|---|---|---|
| 1. | Simona Amanar, Romania | 38.642 |
| 2. | Maria Olaru, Romania | 38.581 |
| 3. | Xuan Li, China | 38.418 |

#### VAULT

| | | Pts |
|---|---|---|
| 1. | Yelena Zamolodtchikova, Russia | 9.731 |
| 2. | Andreea Raducan, Romania | 9.693 |
| 3. | Yekaterina Lobazniouk, Russia | 9.674 |

#### UNEVEN BARS

| | | Pts |
|---|---|---|
| 1. | Svetlana Khorkina, Russia | 9.862 |
| 2. | Ling Jie, China | 9.837 |
| 2. | Yang Yun, China | 9.787 |

#### BALANCE BEAM

| | | Pts |
|---|---|---|
| 1. | Li Xuan, China | 9.825 |
| 2. | Yekaterina Lobazniouk, Russia | 9.787 |
| 3. | Yelena Prodounova, Russia | 9.775 |

#### FLOOR EXERCISE

| | | Pts |
|---|---|---|
| 1. | Yelena Zamolodtchikova, Russia | 9.850 |
| 2. | Svetlana Khorkina, Russia | 9.812 |
| 3. | Simona Amanar, Romania | 9.712 |

#### TEAM COMBINED EXERCISES

| | | Pts |
|---|---|---|
| 1. | Romania | 154.608 |
| 2. | Russia | 154.403 |
| 3. | China | 154.008 |

#### RHYTHMIC ALL-AROUND

| | | Pts |
|---|---|---|
| 1. | Yulia Barsukova, Russia | 39.632 |
| 2. | Yulia Raskina, Belarus | 39.548 |
| 3. | Alina Kabaeva, Russia | 39.466 |

#### RHYTHMIC TEAM COMBINED EXERCISES

| | | Pts |
|---|---|---|
| 1. | Russia | 39.500 |
| 2. | Belarus | 39.500 |
| 3. | Greece | 39.283 |

## JUDO

### Men

#### EXTRA-LIGHTWEIGHT
1. ...................Tadahiro Nomura, Japan
2. ...................Jung Bu-Kyung, S Korea
3. ...................Manolo Poulot, Cuba
3. ...................Aidyn Smagulov, Kirghyzstan

#### HALF-LIGHTWEIGHT
1. ...................Huseyin Ozkan, Turkey
2. ...................Larbi Benboudaoud, France
3. ...................Giorgi Vazagashvili, Georgia
3. ...................Girolamo Giovinazzo, Italy

#### LIGHTWEIGHT
1. ...................Giuseppe Maddaloni, Italy
2. ...................Tiago Camilo, Brazil
3. ...................Anatoly Laryukov, Belarus
3. ...................Vselvolods Zelonijs, Latvia

#### HALF-MIDDLEWEIGHT
1. ...................Makoto Takimoto, Japan
2. ...................Cho In Chul, S Korea
3. ...................Nuno Delgado, Portugal
3. ...................Aleksei Budolin, Estonia

#### MIDDLEWEIGHT
1. ...................Mark Huizinga, Netherlands
2. ...................Carlos Honorato, Brazil
3. ...................Frederic Demontfaucon, France
3. ...................Ruslan Mashurenko, Ukraine

#### HALF-HEAVYWEIGHT
1. ...................Kosei Inoue, Japan
2. ...................Nicolas Gill, Canda
3. ...................Iouri Stepkine, Russial
3. ...................Stéphane Traineau, France

#### HEAVYWEIGHT
1. ...................David Douillet, France
2. ...................Shinichi Shinohara, Japan
3. ...................Indrek Pertelson, Estonia
3. ...................Tamerlan Tmenov, Russia

### Women

#### EXTRA-LIGHTWEIGHT
1. ...................Ryoko Tamura, Japan
2. ...................Lioubov Brouletova, Russia
3. ...................Anna-Maria Gradante, Germany
3. ...................Ann Simons, Belgium

#### HALF-LIGHTWEIGHT
1. ...................Legna Verdecia, Cuba
2. ...................Noriko Narazaki, Japan
3. ...................Kye Sun Hi, N Korea
3. ...................Liu Yuxiang, China

#### LIGHTWEIGHT
1. ...................Isabel Fernández, Spain
2. ...................Driulis González, Cuba
3. ...................Kie Kusakabe, Japan
3. ...................Maria Pekli, Australia

#### HALF-MIDDLEWEIGHT
1. ...................Severine Vandenhende, France
2. ...................Li Shufang, China
3. ...................Gella Vandecaveye, Belgium
3. ...................Jung Sung Sook, S Korea

#### MIDDLEWEIGHT
1. ...................Sibelis Veranes, Cuba
2. ...................Kate Howey, Great Britain
3. ...................Cho Min Sun, S Korea
3. ...................Ylenia Scapin, Italy

#### HALF-HEAVYWEIGHT
1. ...................Lin Tang, China
2. ...................Celine LeBrun, France
3. ...................Simona Marcela Richter, Romania
3. ...................Emanuela Pierantozzi, Italy

#### HEAVYWEIGHT
1. ...................Hua Yuan, China
2. ...................Daima Mayelis Beltran, Cuba
3. ...................Kim Seon-Young, S Korea
3. ...................Mayumi Yamashita, Japan

## MOUNTAIN BIKING

### Men

1. ......Miguel Martinez, France — 2:09:02
2. ......Filip Meirhaeghe, Belgium — 2:10.05
3. ......Christoph Sauser, Switzerland — 2:11:21

### Women

1. ......Paola Pezzo, Italy — 1:49:24
2. ......Barbara Blatter, Switzerland — 1:49.51
3. ......Margarita Fullana, Spain — 1:49.57

## MODERN PENTATHLON

### Men

1. ......Dmitry Svatlovsky, Russia
2. ......Gabor Balogh, Hungary
3. ......Pavel Dovgal, Belarus

### Women

1. ......Stephanie Cook, Great Britain
2. ......Emily deRiel, United States
3. ......Kate Allenby, Great Britain

## ROWING

### Men

#### SINGLE SCULLS
1. ...Rob Waddell, New Zealand — 6:48.90
2. ...Xeno Mueller, Switzerland — 6:50.55
3. ...Marcel Hacker, Germany — 6:50.83

#### DOUBLE SCULLS
1. ...I. Cop/L. Spik, Slovenia — 6:16.63
2. ...F. Beeken/O Tufte, Norway — 6:17.98
3. ...G. Calabrese/N. Sartori, Italy — 6:20.49

#### LIGHTWEIGHT DOUBLE SCULLS
1. ...T. Kucharski/R. Sycz, Poland — 6:21.75
2. ...E. Liunii/L. Pettinari, Italy — 6:23.57
3. ...T. Chappelle/P. Touron, France — 6:24.85

#### QUADRUPLE SCULLS
1. ...Italy — 5:45.56
2. ...Netherlands — 5:47.91
3. ...Germany — 5:48.64

## ROWING *(Cont.)*

### Men *(Cont.)*

#### COXLESS PAIR

| | | |
|---|---|---|
| 1. ...M. Andrieux/ J. Rolland, France | 6:32.97 |
| 2. ...S. Bea/ T. Murphy, United States | 6:33.80 |
| 3. ...J. Tomkins/ M. Long, Australia | 6:34.26 |

#### COXLESS FOUR

| | |
|---|---|
| 1. ...Great Britain | 5:56.24 |
| 2. ...Italy | 5:56.62 |
| 3. ...Australia | 5:57.61 |

#### LIGHTWEIGHT COXLESS FOUR

| | |
|---|---|
| 1. ...France | 6:01.68 |
| 2. ...Australia | 6:02.09 |
| 3. ...Denmark | 6:03.51 |

#### EIGHT-OARS

| | |
|---|---|
| 1. ...Great Britain | 5:33.08 |
| 2. ...Australia | 5:33.88 |
| 3. ...Croatia | 5:34.85 |

### Women

#### SINGLE SCULLS

| | |
|---|---|
| 1. ...Ekaterina Karsten, Belarus | 7:28.14 |
| 2. ...Rumyana Neykova, Bulgaria | 7:28.15 |
| 3. ...K. Rutschow-Stomporowski, Germany | 7:28.99 |

#### DOUBLE SCULLS

| | |
|---|---|
| 1. ...K. Boron/ J. Thieme, Germany | 6:55.44 |
| 2. ...P. Van Dishoeck/ E. Van Nes, Netherlands | 7:00.36 |
| 3. ...B. Sakickiene/ K. Poplavskaya, Lithuania | 7:01.71 |

#### LIGHTWEIGHT DOUBLE SCULLS

| | |
|---|---|
| 1. ...C. Burcica/ A. Alupei, Romania | 7:02.64 |
| 2. ...V. Viehoff/ C. Blaserg, Germany | 7:02.95 |
| 3. ...C. Collins/ S. Garner, United States | 7:06.37 |

#### QUADRUPLE SCULLS

| | |
|---|---|
| 1. ...Germany | 6:19.58 |
| 2. ...Great Britain | 6:21.64 |
| 3. ...Russia | 6:21.65 |

#### COXLESS PAIR

| | |
|---|---|
| 1. ...G. Damian/D. Ignat, Romania | 7:11.00 |
| 2. ...R. Taylor/K. Slatter, Australia | 7:12.56 |
| 3. ...K. Kraft/M. Ryan, United States | 7:13.00 |

#### EIGHT-OARS

| | |
|---|---|
| 1. ...Romania | 6:06.44 |
| 2. ...Netherlands | 6:09.39 |
| 3. ...Canada | 6:11.58 |

## SHOOTING

### Men

#### RAPID-FIRE PISTOL

| | Pts |
|---|---|
| 1......Serguei Alifirenko, Russia | 687.6 |
| 2......Michel Ansermet, Switzerland | 686.1 |
| 3......Iulian Raicen, Romania | 684.6 |

#### FREE PISTOL

| | Pts |
|---|---|
| 1......Tanyu Kiriakov, Bulgaria | 666.0 |
| 2......Igor Basinski, Belarus | 663.3 |
| 3......Martin Tenk, Czech Republic | 662.5 |

#### AIR PISTOL

| | Pts |
|---|---|
| 1......Franck Dumoulin, France | 688.9 |
| 2......Yifu Wang, China | 686.9 |
| 3......Igor Basinsky, Belarus | 682.7 |

#### RUNNING TARGET

| | Pts |
|---|---|
| 1......Ling Yang, China | 681.1 |
| 2......Oleg Moldovan, Moldova | 681.0 |
| 3......Zhiyuan Niu, China | 677.4 |

#### SMALL-BORE RIFLE, THREE-POSITION

| | Pts |
|---|---|
| 1......Rajmond Debevec, Slovenia | 1275.1 |
| 2......Juha Hirvi, Finland | 1270.5 |
| 3......Harald Stenvaag, Norway | 1268.6 |

#### SMALL-BORE RIFLE, PRONE

| | Pts |
|---|---|
| 1......Jonas Edman, Swedem | 701.3 |
| 2......Torben Grimmel, Denmark | 700.4 |
| 3......Sergei Martynov, Belarus | 700.3 |

#### AIR RIFLE

| | Pts |
|---|---|
| 1......Yalin Cai, China | 696.4 |
| 2......Artem Khadjibekov, Russia | 695.1 |
| 3......Evgueni Aleinikov, Russia | 693.8 |

#### TRAP

| | Pts |
|---|---|
| 1......Michael Diamond, Australia | 122.0 |
| 2......Ian Peel, Great Britain | 118.0 |
| 3......David Kostelecky, Czech Republic | 116.0 |

#### DOUBLE TRAP

| | Pts |
|---|---|
| 1......Richard Faulds, Great Britain | 187.0 |
| 2......Russell Mark, Australia | 187.0 |
| 3......Fehaid Al Deehani, Kuwait | 186.0 |

#### SKEET

| | Pts |
|---|---|
| 1......Mykola Milchen, Ukraine | 150.0 |
| 2......Petr Malek, Czech Republic | 148.0 |
| 3......James Graves, United States | 147.0 |

### Women

#### SPORT PISTOL

| | Pts |
|---|---|
| 1......Maria Grozdeva, Bulgaria | 690.3 |
| 2......Luna Tao, China | 689.8 |
| 3......Lolita Evglevskaya, Belarus | 686.0 |

#### AIR PISTOL

| | Pts |
|---|---|
| 1......Luna Tao, China | 488.2 |
| 2......Jasna Sekaric, Yugoslavia | 486.5 |
| 3......Annemarie Forder, Australia | 484.0 |

### SHOOTING *(Cont.)*
### Women *(Cont.)*

**SMALL-BORE RIFLE, THREE-POSITION**

| | Pts |
|---|---|
| 1......Renata Mauer-Rozanska, Poland | 684.6 |
| 2......Tatiana Goldobina, Russia | 680.9 |
| 3......Maria Feklistova, Russia | 679.9 |

**AIR RIFLE**

| | Pts |
|---|---|
| 1......Nancy Johnson, United States | 497.7 |
| 2......Kang Cho-Hyan, S Korea | 497.5 |
| 3......Jing Gao, China | 497.2 |

**DOUBLE TRAP**

| | Pts |
|---|---|
| 1......Pia Hansen, United States | 148.0 |
| 2......Deborah Gelisio, Italy | 144.0 |
| 3......Kimberly Rhode, United States | 139.0 |

**TRAP**

| | Pts |
|---|---|
| 1......Daina Gudzineviciute, Lithuania | 93.0 |
| 2......Delphine Racinet, France | 92.0 |
| 3......E Gao, China | 90.0 |

**SKEET**

| | Pts |
|---|---|
| 1......Zemfira Meftakhetdinova, Azerbaijan | 98.0 |
| 2......Svetlana Demina, Russia | 95.0 |
| 3......Diana Igaly, Hungary | 93.0 |

### SOCCER

**Men**

1. ...................Cameroon
2. ...................Spain
3. ...................Chile

**Women**

1. ...................Norway
2. ...................United States
3. ...................Germany

### SOFTBALL

1. ...........................United States
2. ...........................Japan
3. ...........................Australia

### SWIMMING
### Men

**50-METER FREESTYLE**

| | |
|---|---|
| 1. ...Gary Hall Jr., United States | 21.98 |
| 1. ...Anthony Ervin, United States | 21.98 |
| 3. ...Pieter van den Hoogenband, Netherlands | 22.03 |

**100-METER FREESTYLE**

| | |
|---|---|
| 1. ...Pieter van den Hoogenband, Netherlands | 48.30 |
| 2. ...Alexander Popov, Russia | 48.69 |
| 3. ...Gary Hall Jr., United States | 48.73 |

**200-METER FREESTYLE**

| | |
|---|---|
| 1. ...Pieter van den Hoogenband, Netherlands | 1:45.35 EWR |
| 2. ...Ian Thorpe, Australia | 1:45.83 |
| 3. ...Massimiliano Rosolino, Italy | 1:46.65 |

**400-METER FREESTYLE**

| | |
|---|---|
| 1. ...Ian Thorpe, Australia | 3:40.59 WR |
| 2. ...Massimiliano Rosolino, Italy | 3:43.50 |
| 3. ...Klete Keller, United States | 3:47.00 |

**1,500-METER FREESTYLE**

| | |
|---|---|
| 1. ...Grant Hackett, Australia | 14:48.33 |
| 2. ...Kieren Perkins Australia | 14:53.59 |
| 3. ...Chris Thompson, United States | 14:56.81 |

**100-METER BACKSTROKE**

| | |
|---|---|
| 1. ...Lenny Krayzelburg, United States | 53.72 OR |
| 2. ...Matthew Welsh, Australia | 54.07 |
| 3. ...Stev Theloke, Germany | 54.82 |

**200-METER BACKSTROKE**

| | |
|---|---|
| 1. ...Lenny Krayzelburg, United States | 1:56.76 OR |
| 2. ...Aaron Piersol, United States | 1:57.35 |
| 3. ...Matthew Welsh, Australia | 1:59.59 |

**100-METER BREASTSTROKE**

| | |
|---|---|
| 1. ...Domenico Fioravanti, Italy | 1:00.46 OR |
| 2. ...Ed Moses, United States | 1:00.73 |
| 3. ...Roman Sloudnov, Russia | 1:00.91 |

**200-METER BREASTSTROKE**

| | |
|---|---|
| 1. ...Domenico Fioravanti, Italy | 2:10.87 |
| 2. ...Terence Parkin, S Africa | 2:12.50 |
| 3. ...Davide Rummolo, Italy | 2:12.73 |

**100-METER BUTTERFLY**

| | |
|---|---|
| 1. ...Lars Froelander, Sweden | 52.00 |
| 2. ...Michael Klim, Australia | 52.18 |
| 3. ...Geoff Huegill, Australia | 52.22 |

**200-METER BUTTERFLY**

| | |
|---|---|
| 1. ...Tom Malchow, United States | 1:55.35 OR |
| 2. ...Denys Sylant'yev, Ukraine | 1:55.76 |
| 3. ...Justin Norris, Australia | 1:56.17 |

**200-METER INDIVIDUAL MEDLEY**

| | |
|---|---|
| 1. ...Massimiliano Rosolino, Italy | 1:58.98 OR |
| 2. ...Tom Dolan, United States | 1:59.77 |
| 3. ...Tom Wilkens, United States | 2:00.87 |

**400-METER INDIVIDUAL MEDLEY**

| | |
|---|---|
| 1. ...Tom Dolan, United States | 4:11,76 WR |
| 2. ...Eric Vendt, United States | 4:14.23 |
| 3. ...Curtis Myden, Canada | 4:15.33 |

**4 X 100-METER MEDLEY RELAY**

| | |
|---|---|
| 1. ...United States (Lenny Krayzelburg, Ed Moses, Ian Crocker, Gary Hall Jr.) | 3:34.84 WR |
| 2. ...Australia | 3:35.27 |
| 3. ...Germany | 3:35.88 |

**4 X 100-METER FREESTYLE RELAY**

| | |
|---|---|
| 1. ...Australia (Ian Thorpe, Michael Klim, Ashley Callus, Chris Fydler) | 3:13.67 WR |
| 2. ...United States | 3:13.86 |
| 3. ...Brazil | 3:17.40 |

**4 X 200-METER FREESTYLE RELAY**

| | |
|---|---|
| 1. ...Australia (Ian Thorpe, Michael Klim, William Kirby, Todd Pearson) | 7:07.05 WR |
| 2. ...United States | 7:12.64 |
| 3. ...Netherlands | 7:12.70 |

Note: OR=Olympic record. WR=world record. EOR=equals Olympic record. EWR=equals world record.

### SWIMMING *(Cont.)*
### Women

#### 50-METER FREESTYLE
1. ...Inge de Bruijn, Netherlands — 24.32
2. ...Therese Alshammar, Sweden — 24.51
3. ...Dara Torres, United States — 24.63

#### 100-METER FREESTYLE
1. ...Inge de Bruijn, Netherlands — 53.83
2. ...Therese Alshammar, Sweden — 54.33
3. ...Dara Torres, United States — 54.43

#### 200-METER FREESTYLE
1. ...Susie O'Neill, Australia — 1:58.24
2. ...Martina Moravcova, Slovakia — 1:58.32
3. ...Claudia Poll Ahrens, Costa Rica — 1:58.81

#### 400-METER FREESTYLE
1. ...Brooke Bennett, United States — 4:05.80
2. ...Diana Munz, United States — 4:07.07
3. ...Claudia Poll Ahrens, Costa Rica — 4:07.83

#### 800-METER FREESTYLE
1. ...Brooke Bennett, United States — 8:19.67 OR
2. ...Yana Klochkova, Ukraine — 8:22.66
3. ...Kaitlin Sandeno, United States — 8:24.29

#### 100-METER BACKSTROKE
1. ...Diana Iuliana Mocanu, Romania — 1:00.21 OR.
2. ...Mai Nakamura, Japan — 1:00.55
3. ...Nina Zhivanevskaya, Spain — 1:00.89

#### 200-METER BACKSTROKE
1. ...Diana Iuliana Mocanu, Romania — 2:08.16
2. ...Roxana Maracineanu, France — 2:10.25
3. ...Miki Nakao, Japan — 2:11.05

#### 100-METER BREASTSTROKE
1. ...Megan Quann, United States — 1:07.05
2. ...Leisel Jones, Australia — 1:07.49
3. ...Penny Heyns, South Africa — 1:07.55

#### 200-METER BREASTSTROKE
1. ...Agnes Kovacs, Hungary — 2:24.35
2. ...Kristy Kowal, United States — 2:24.56
3. ...Amanda Beard, United States — 2:25.35

#### 100-METER BUTTERFLY
1. ...Inge de Bruijn, Netherlands — 56.61 WR
2. ...Martina Moravcova, Slovakia — 57.97
3. ...Dara Torres, United States — 58.20

#### 200-METER BUTTERFLY
1. ...Misty Hyman, United States — 2:05.88 OR
2. ...Susie O'Neill, Australia — 2:06.58
3. ...Petria Thomas, Australia — 2:07.12

#### 200-METER INDIVIDUAL MEDLEY
1. ...Yana Klochkova, Ukraine — 2:10.68 OR
2. ...Beatrice Nicoleta Caslaru, Romania 2:12.57
3. ...Cristina Teuscher, United States — 2:13.32

#### 400-METER INDIVIDUAL MEDLEY
1. ...Yana Klochkova, Ukraine — 4:33.59 WR
2. ...Yasuko Tajima, Japan — 4:35.90
3. ...Beatrice Nicoleta Caslaru, Romania 4:37.18

#### 4 X 100-METER MEDLEY RELAY
1. ...United States: BJ Bedford, — 3:58.30 WR
Megan Quann, Jenny Thompson,
Dara Torres
2. ...Australia — 4:01.59
3. ...Japan — 4:04.16

#### 4 X 100-METER FREESTYLE RELAY
1. ...United States: Jenny Thompson, — 3:36.61 WR
Courtney Shealy, Dara Torres,
Amy Van Dyken
2. ...Netherlands — 3:39.83
3. ...Sweden — 3:40.30

#### 4 X 200-METER FREESTYLE RELAY
1. ...United States (Samantha Arsenault, — 7:57.80 OR
Diana Munz, Lindsay Benko,
Jenny Thompson)
2. ...Australia — 7:58.52
3. ...Germany — 7:58.64

Note: OR=Olympic record. WR=world record. EOR=equals Olympic record. EWR=equals world record.

## SYNCHRONIZED SWIMMING

### DUET
1. ...Russia — 99.580
2. ...Japan — 98.650
3. ...France — 97.437

### TEAM
1. ...Russia — 99.146
2. ...Japan — 98.860
3. ...Canada — 97.357

## SYNCHRONIZED DIVING

### Men
#### 3M SPRINGBOARD
| | Pts |
|---|---|
| 1. ..........Xiang Ni/ Xiao Hailang, China | 365.58 |
| 2. ..........D. Sautin/ A. Dobroskoki, Russia | 329.97 |
| 3. ..........D. Pullan/ R. Newbery, Australia | 322.86 |

#### 10M PLATFORM
| | Pts |
|---|---|
| 1. ..........I. Loukachine/ D. Sautin, Russia | 365.04 |
| 2. ..........Tian Liang/ Hu Jia, China | 358.74 |
| 3. ..........J.Hempel/ H. Meyer, Germany | 338.88 |

### Women
#### 3M SPRINGBOARD
| | Pts |
|---|---|
| 1. ..........V. Ilina/ I. Pakhalina, Russia | 332.64 |
| 2. ..........Guo Jing Jing/ Fu Mingxia, China | 321.60 |
| 3. ..........G. Sorokina/ O. Zhupina, Ukraine | 290.34 |

#### 10M PLATFORM
| | Pts |
|---|---|
| 1. ..........Li Na/ Sang Zue, China | 345.12 |
| 2. ..........A. Montminy/ E.Heymanns, Canada | 312.02 |
| 3. ..........L. Tourky/ R. Gilmore, Australia | 301.50 |

## TABLE TENNIS

### Men

**SINGLES**

1. ....................Kong Linghui, China
2. ....................Jan-Ove Wablner, Sweden
3. ....................Liu Guoliang, China

**DOUBLES**

1. ....................Wang Liqin/ Yan Sen, China
2. ....................Kong Linghu/ Liu Guoliang, China
3. ....................Patrick Chila/ J.P. Gatien, France

### Women

**SINGLES**

1. ....................Wang Nan, China
2. ....................Li Ju, China
3. ....................Chen Jing, Taiwan

**DOUBLES**

1. ....................Li Ju/ Wang Nan, China
2. ....................Sun Jin/ Yang Yin, China
3. ....................Kim Moo Kyo/ Ji-Hye Ryu, S Korea

## TAEKWONDO

### Men

**FLYWEIGHT**

1. ....................Michail Mouroutsos, Greece
2. ....................Gabriel Esparza, Spain
3. ....................Chi-Hsiung Huang, China

**FEATHERWEIGHT**

1. ....................Steven Lopez, United States
2. ....................Sin Joon Sik, S Korea
3. ....................Hadi Saeibonehkohal, Iran

**WELTERWEIGHT**

1. ....................Angel Valodia Matos Fuentes, Cuba
2. ....................Faissal Ebnoutalib, Germany
3. ....................Victor Estrada Garibay, Mexico

**HEAVYWEIGHT**

1. ....................Kyong-Hun Kim, S Korea
2. ....................Daniel Trenton, Australia
3. ....................Pascal Gentil, France

### Women

**FLYWEIGHT**

1. ....................Lauren Burns, Australia
2. ....................Urbia Melendez Rodriguez, Cuba
3. ....................Ju Chi Shu, China

**FEATHERWEIGHT**

1. ....................Jung Jae Eun, S Korea
2. ....................Hieu Ngan Tran, Vietnam
3. ....................Hamide Bikcin, Turkey

**WELTERWEIGHT**

1. ....................Sun-Hee Lee, S Korea
2. ....................Trude Gunderson, Denmark
3. ....................Yoriko Okamoto, Japan

**HEAVYWEIGHT**

1. ....................Chen Zhong, China
2. ....................Natalia Ivanova, Russia
3. ....................Dominique Bosshart, Canada

## TEAM HANDBALL

### Men

1. ....................Russia
2. ....................Sweden
3. ....................Spain

### Women

1. ....................Denmark
2. ....................Hungary
3. ....................Norway

## TENNIS

### Men

**SINGLES**

1. ....................Yevgeni Kafelnikov, Russia
2. ....................Tommy Haas, Germany
3. ....................Arnaud Di Pasquale, France

**DOUBLES**

1. ....................Daniel Nestor/ Sebastien Lareau, Canada
2. ....................Todd Woodbridge/ Mark Woodforde, Australia
3. ....................Alex Corretja/ Albert Costa, Spain

### Women

**SINGLES**

1. ....................Venus Williams, United States
2. ....................Elena Dementieva, Russia
3. ....................Monica Seles, United States

**DOUBLES**

1. ....................V. Williams/ S. Williams, United States
2. ....................Kristie Boogert/ Miriam Oremans, Netherlands
3. ....................Dominique van Roost/ Els Callens, Belgium

## TRAMPOLINE

### Men

1. ....................Alexandre Mosalenko, Russia   41.70
2. ....................Ji Wallace, Australia   39.30
3. ....................Mathieu Turgeon, Canada   39.10

### Women

1. ....................Irina Karavaeva, Russia   38.90
2. ....................Oxana Tsyhuleva, Ukraine   37.70
3. ....................Karen Cockburn, Canada   37.40

## TRIATHLON

### Men

1. ....................Simon Whitfield, Canada   1:48.24.02
2. ....................Stefan Vucovic, Germany   1:48.37.58
3. ....................Jan Rehula, Czech Rep.   1:48.46,64

### Women

1. ....................Brigitte McMahon, Switz.   2:00.40.52.
2. ....................Michellie Jones, Australia   2:00.42.55
3. ....................Magali Messmer, Switz.   2:01.08.83

## VOLLEYBALL

| Men | Women |
|---|---|
| 1. ...................Yugoslavia | 1. ...................Cuba |
| 2. ...................Russia | 2. ...................Russia |
| 3. ...................Italy | 3. ...................Brazil |

## BEACH VOLLEYBALL

| Men | Women |
|---|---|
| 1. ..........Dain Blanton/ E. Fonoimoana, United States | 1. ..........Kerri Pottharst/ Natalie Cook, Australia |
| 2. ..........Ze Marco Melo/ Ricardo Santos, Brazil | 2. ..........Shelda Bede/ Adriana Behar, Brazil |
| 3. ..........Joerg Ahmann/ Axel Hager, Germany | 3. ..........Adriana Samuel/ Sandra Pires, Brazil |

## WATER POLO

| Men | Women |
|---|---|
| 1. ...................Hungary | 1. ...................Australia |
| 2. ...................Russia | 2. ...................United States |
| 3. ...................Yugoslavia | 3. ...................Russia |

## WEIGHTLIFTING

### Men

| 123 POUNDS | | 187 POUNDS | |
|---|---|---|---|
| 1. ..........Halil Mutlu, Turkey | 671 lb WR | 1. ..........Pyrros Dimas, Greece | 858 lb |
| 2. ..........Wu Wenxiong, China | 631 lb | 2. ..........Marc Huster, Germany | 858 lb |
| 3. ..........Zhang Xiangxiang, China | 631 lb | 3. ..........George Asanidze, Georgia | 858 lb |

| 137 POUNDS | | 207 POUNDS | |
|---|---|---|---|
| 1. ..........Nikolay Pechaliv, Croatia | 715 lb OR | 1. ..........Akakios Kakiasvilis, Greece | 891 lb |
| 2. ..........Leonidas Sabanis, Greece | 697 lb | 2. ..........Szymon Kolecki, Poland | 891 lb |
| 3. ..........Gennady Oleshchuk, Belarus | 697 lb | 3. ..........Alexei Petrov. Russia | 884 lb |

| 152 POUNDS | | 231 POUNDS | |
|---|---|---|---|
| 1. ..........Galabin Boevski, Bulgaria | 785 lb OR | 1. ..........Hossein Tavakoli, Iran | 935 lb |
| 2. ..........Georgi Markov, Bulgaria | 774 lb | 2. ..........Alan Tsagaev, Bulgaria | 928 lb |
| 3. ..........Sergei Lavrenov, Belarus | 680 lb | 3. ..........Said Asaad, Qatar | 924 lb |

| 170 POUNDS | | 231+ POUNDS | |
|---|---|---|---|
| 1. ..........Zhan Xugang, China | 807 lb | 1. ..........Hossein Rezazadeh, Iran | 1,045 lb WR |
| 2. ..........Viktor Mitrou, Greece | 807 lb | 2. ..........Ronny Weller, Germany | 1,025 lb |
| 3. ..........Arsen Melikyan, Armenia | 803 lb | 3. ..........Andrei Chermerkin, Russia | 1,017 lb |

### Women

| 106 POUNDS | | 152 POUNDS | |
|---|---|---|---|
| 1. ..........Tara Nott, United States | 407 lb | 1. ..........Lin Weining, China | 532 lb |
| 2. ..........Raema Rumbewas, Indonesia | 407 lb | 2. ..........Erzsebet Markus, Hungary | 532 lb |
| 3. ..........Sri Indriyani, Indonesia | 400 lb | 3. ..........Karnam Malleswari. Indonesia | 528 lb |

| 117 POUNDS | | 165 POUNDS | |
|---|---|---|---|
| 1. ..........Yang Xia, China | 495 lb WR | 1. ..........Maria Isabel Urrutia, Colombia | 539 lb |
| 2. ..........Li Feng ying, Taipei | 466 lb | 2. ..........Ruth Ogbeifo, Nigeria | 539 lb |
| 3. ..........Winarni Slamet, Indonesia | 444 lb | 3. ..........Kuo Yi Hang, Taipei | 539 lb |

| 128 POUNDS | | 165 + POUNDS | |
|---|---|---|---|
| 1. ..........Soraya Mendivil, Mexico | 488 lb | 1. ..........Ding Meiyuan, China | 660 lb WR |
| 2. ..........Ri Song Hui, N Korea | 484 lb | 2. ..........Agata Wrobel, Poland | 649 lb OR |
| 3. ..........Khassaraporn Suta, Thailand | 462 lb | 3. ..........Cheryl Haworth, United States | 594 lb |

| 139 POUNDS | |
|---|---|
| 1. ..........Xiaomin Chen, China | 532 lb |
| 2. ..........Valentina Popova, Russia | 517 lb |
| 3. ..........Ioanna Chatziioannou, Greece | 488 lb |

## FREESTYLE WRESTLING

### 119 POUNDS
1. ...................Namig Abdullayev, Azerbaijan
2. ...................Samuel Henson, United States
3. ...................Amiran Karntanov, Greece

### 127.75 POUNDS
1. ...................Alireza Dabir, Iran
2. ...................Yevgen Buslovych, Ukraine
3. ...................Terry Brands, United States

### 138.75 POUNDS
1. ...................Mourad Oumakhanov, Russia
2. ...................Serafim Barzakov, Bulgaria
3. ...................Jang Jae Sung, S Korea

### 152 POUNDS
1. ...................Daniel Igali, Canada
2. ...................Arsen Gitinov, Russia
3. ...................Lincoln McIlvray, United States

### 167.5 POUNDS
1. ...................Alexander Leipold, Germany
2. ...................Brandon Slay, United States
3. ...................Moon Eui Jae, S Korea

### 187.25 POUNDS
1. ...................Adam Saitiev, Russia
2. ...................Yoel Romero, Cuba
3. ...................Mogamed Ibragimov, Macedonia

### 213.75 POUNDS
1. ...................Sagid Mourtasaliyev, Russia
2. ...................Islam Bairamukov, Kazakhstan
3. ...................Eldar Kurtanidze, Georgia

### 286 POUNDS
1. ...................David Moussoulbes, Russia
2. ...................Artur Taymazov, Uzbekistan
3. ...................Alexis Rodriguez, Cuba

## GRECO-ROMAN WRESTLING

### 119 POUNDS
1. ...................Kwon Ho Sim, S Korea
2. ...................Lazaro Rivas, Cuba
3. ...................Young Gyun Kang, N Korea

### 127.75 POUNDS
1. ...................Armen Nazarian, Bulgaria
2. ...................Kim In Sub, S Korea
3. ...................Zertian Sheng, China

### 138.75 POUNDS
1. ...................Varteres Samourgachev, Russia
2. ...................Juan Luis Maren, Cuba
3. ...................Akaki Chachua, Georgia

### 152 POUNDS
1. ...................Filiberto Azcuy, Cuba
2. ...................Katsushiko Nagata, Japan
3. ...................Alexei Glouchkov, Russia

### 167.5 POUNDS
1. ...................Mourat Kardanov, Russia
2. ...................Matt James Lindland, United States
3. ...................M. Yli-Hannuksela, Finland

### 187.25 POUNDS
1. ...................Hamza Yerlikaya, Turkey
2. ...................Sandor Istvan Bardosi, Hungary
3. ...................Mukhran Vakhtangadze, Georgia

### 213.75 POUNDS
1. ...................Mikael Ljundberg, Sweden
2. ...................Davyd Saldadze, Ukraine
3. ...................Garrett Lowney, United States

### 286 POUNDS
1. ...................Rulon Gardner, United States
2. ...................Alexander Karelin, Russia
3. ...................Dmitry Debelka, Belarus

## YACHTING

### MEN'S 470
1. ...................Australia
2. ...................United States
3. ...................Argentina

### MEN'S FINN
1. ...................Iain Percy, Great Britain
2. ...................Luca Devoti, Italy
3. ...................Fredrik Loof, Sweden

### MEN'S BOARD
1. ...................Christoph Sieber, Austria
2. ...................Carlos Espinosa, Argentina
3. ...................Aaron McIntosh, New Zealand

### WOMEN'S 470
1. ...................Australia
2. ...................United States
3. ...................Ukraine

### WOMEN'S EUROPE
1. ...................Shirley Robertson, Great Britain
2. ...................Margriet Matthysse, Netherlands
3. ...................Serena Amato, Argentina

### WOMEN'S BOARD
1. ...................Alessandra Sensini, Italy
2. ...................Amelie Lux, Germany
3. ...................Barbara Kendall, New Zealand

### SOLING
1. ...................Denmark
2. ...................Germany
3. ...................Norway

### STAR
1. ...................M. Reynolds/M. Liljedahl, United States
2. ...................M. Covell/ I. Walker, Great Britain
3. ...................T. Grael/ M. Ferreira, Brazil

### TORNADO
1. ...................H. Steinacher/ R.Hagara, Austria
2. ...................J. Forbes/ D. Bundock, Australia
3. ...................R. Gaebler/ R. Schwall, Germany

### LASER
1. ...................Ben Ainslie, Great Britain
2. ...................Robert Scheidt, Brazil
3. ...................Michael Blackburn, Australia

### 49ER
1. ...................T. Johnson/ J. Jarvi, Finland
2. ...................I. Barker/ S. Hicksocks, Great Britain
3. ...................J. McKee/ C. Mckee, United States

## BIATHLON

| Men | | Women | |
|---|---|---|---|
| **10 KILOMETERS** | | **7.5 KILOMETERS** | |
| 1. ...Ole Einar Bjorndalen, Norway | 27:16.2 | 1. ...Galina Koukleva, Russia | 23:08.0 |
| 2. ...Frode Andresen, Norway | 28:17.8 | 2. ...Ursula Disl, Germany | 23:08.7 |
| 3. ...Ville Raikkonen, FInland | 28:21.7 | 3. ...Katrin Apel, Germany | 23:32.4 |
| **20 KILOMETERS** | | **15 KILOMETERS** | |
| 1. ...Halvard Hanevold, Norway | 56:16.4 | 1. ...Ekaterina Dofovska, Bulgaria | 54:52.0 |
| 2. ...Pier Alberto Carrara, Italy | 56:21.9 | 2. ...Elena Petrova, Ukraine | 55:09.8 |
| 3. ...Aleksei Aidarov, Belarus | 56:45.5 | 3. ...Ursula Disl, Germany | 55:17.9 |
| **4 X 7.5-KILOMETER RELAY** | | **3 X 7.5-KILOMETER RELAY** | |
| 1. ...Germany | 1:19:43.3 | 1. ...Germany | 1:40:13.6 |
| 2. ...Norway | 1:20:03.4 | 2. ...Russia | 1:40:25.2 |
| 3. ...Russia | 1:20:19.4 | 3. ...Norway | 1:40:37.3 |

## BOBSLED

| 2-MAN BOB | | 4-MAN BOB | |
|---|---|---|---|
| 1. ...Pierre Lueders/ Dave MacEachern, Canada | 3:37.24 | 1. ...Germany II | 2:39.41 |
| 1. ...Guenther Huber/ Antonio Tartaglia, Italy | 3:37.24 | 2. ...Switzerland I | 2:40.01 |
| 3. ...Christoph Langen/ Markus Zimmerman, Germany | 3:37.89 | 3. ...Britain I | 2:40.06 |
| | | 3. ...France I | 2:40.06 |

## CURLING

| Men | Women |
|---|---|
| 1. ...Switzerland | 1. ...Canada |
| 2. ...Canada | 2. ...Denmark |
| 3. ...Norway | 3 ...Sweden |

## ICE HOCKEY

| Men | Women |
|---|---|
| 1. ...Czech Republic | 1. ...United States |
| 2. ...Russia | 2. ...Canada |
| 3. ...Finland | 3. ...Finland |

## LUGE

| Men | | Women | |
|---|---|---|---|
| **SINGLES** | | **SINGLES** | |
| 1. ...Georg Hackl, Germany | 3:18.44 | 1. ...Silke Kraushaar, Germany | 3:23.779 |
| 2. ...Armin Zoeggeler, Italy | 3:18.94 | 2. ...Barbara Niedernhuber, Germany | 3:23.781 |
| 3. ...Jens Mueller, Germany | 3:19.09 | 3. ...Angelika Neuner, Austria | 3:24.253 |
| **DOUBLES** | | | |
| 1. ...Stefan Krausse/ Jan Behrendt, Germany | 1:41.105 | | |
| 1. ...Chris Thorpe/ Gordy Sheer, United States | 1:41.127 | | |
| 3. ...Mark Grimmette/ Brian Martin, United States | 1:41.217 | | |

## FIGURE SKATING

| Men | Women |
|---|---|
| 1. ...Ilia Kulik, Russia | 1. ...Tara Lipinski, United States |
| 2. ...Elvis Stojko, Canada | 2. ...Michelle Kwan, United States |
| 3. ...Philippe Candeloro, France | 3. ...Lu Chen, China |

| Pairs | Ice Dancing |
|---|---|
| 1. ...Oksana Kazakova/Artur Dmitriev, Russia | 1. ...Pasha Grishuk/ Evgeny Platov, Russia |
| 2. ...Elena Berezhnaya/ Anton Sikharulidze, Russia | 2. ...Anjelika Krylova/ Oleg Ovsyannikov, Russia |
| 3. ...Mandy Wötzel/Ingo Steuer, Germany | 3. ...Marina Anissina/ Gwendal Peizerat, France |

## SPEED SKATING

### Men

**500 METERS**

1. ...Hiroyasu Shimizu, Japan — 1:11.35*
2. ...Jeremy Wotherspoon, Canada — 1:11.84
3. ...Kevin Overland, Canada — 1:11.86

**1,000 METERS**

1. ...Ids Postma, Netherlands — 1:10.64 OR
2. ...Jan Bos, Netherlands — 1:10.71
3. ...Hiroyasu Shimizu, Japan — 1:11.00

**1,500 METERS**

1. ...Aadne Sondral, Norway — 1:47.87 WR
2. ...Ids Postma, Netherlands — 1:48.13
3. ...Rintje Ritsma, Netherlands — 1:48.52

**5,000 METERS**

1. ...Gianni Romme, Netherlands — 6:22.20 WR
2. ...Rintje Ritsma, Netherlands — 6:28.24
3. ...Bart Veldkamp, Belgium — 6:28.31

**10,000 METERS**

1. ...Gianni Romme, Netherlands — 13:15.33 WR
2. ...Bob de Jong, Netherlands — 13:25.76
3. ...Rintje Ritsma, Netherlands — 13:28.19

**500 METERS SHORT TRACK**

1. ...Takafumi Nishitani, Japan — 42.862
2. ...An Yulong, China — 43.022
3. ...Hitoshi Uematsu, Japan — 43.713

**1,000 METERS SHORT TRACK**

1. ...Kim Dong Sung, South Korea — 1:32.375
2. ...Li Jiajun, China — 1:32.428
3. ...Eric Bedard, Canada — 1:32.661

**5,000-METER SHORT TRACK RELAY**

1. ...Canada — 7:06.075
2. ...South Korea — 7:06.776
3. ...China — 7:11.559

### Women

**500 METERS**

1. ...Catriona LeMay Doan, Canada — 1:16.60*
2. ...Susan Auch, Canada — 1:16.93
3. ...Tomoni Okazaki, Japan — 1:17.10

**1,000 METERS**

1. ...Marianne Timmer, Netherlands — 1:16.51 OR
2. ...Chris Witty, United States — 1:16.79
3. ...Catriona LeMay Doan, Canada — 1:17.37

**1,500 METERS**

1. ...Marianne Timmer, Netherlands — 1:57.58 WR
2. ...Gunda Niemann-Stirnemann, Ger. — 1:58.66
3. ...Chris Witty, United States — 1:58.97

**3,000 METERS**

1. ...Gunda Niemann-Stirnemann, Ger. — 4:07.29 OR
2. ...Claudia Pechstein, Germany — 4:08.47
3. ...Anna Friesinger, Germany — 4:09.44

**5,000 METERS**

1. ...Claudia Pechstein, Germany — 6:59.61 WR
2. ...Gunda Niemann-Stirnemann, Ger. — 6:59.65
3. ...Lyudmila Prokasheva, Kazakhstan — 7:11.14

**500 METERS SHORT TRACK**

1. ...Annie Perreault, Canada — 46.568
2. ...Yang Yang, China — 46.627
3. ...Chun Lee Kyung, S Korea — 46.335

**1,000 METERS SHORT TRACK**

1. ...Chun Lee Kyung, S Korea — 1:42.776
2. ...Yang Yang, China — 1:43.343
3. ...Hye Kyung Won, S Korea — 1:43.361

**3,000-METER SHORT TRACK RELAY**

1. ...S Korea — 4:16.260
2. ...China — 4:16.383
3. ...Canada — 4:21.205

Note: OR=Olympic Record. WR=World Record. EOR=Equals Olympic Record. EWR=Equals World Record. WB=World Best.

* Final standings based on the combined time of two 500-meter runs. Shimizu set an Olympic record with his second-run time of 35.59 seconds, and LeMay Doan set an Olympic record with her second-run time of 38.21 seconds.

## ALPINE SKIING

### Men

**DOWNHILL**

1. ...Jean-Luc Crétier, France — 1:50.11
2. ...Lasse Kjus, Norway — 1:50.51
3. ...Hannes Trinkl, Austria — 1:50.63

**SLALOM**

1. ...Hans-Petter Buraas, Norway — 1:49.31
2. ...Ole Christian Furuseth, Norway — 1:50.64
3. ...Thomas Sykora, Austria — 1:50.68

**GIANT SLALOM**

1. ...Hermann Maier, Austria — 2:38.51
2. ...Stefan Eberharter, Austria — 2:39.36
3. ...Michael von Grünigen, Switzerland — 2:39.69

**SUPER GIANT SLALOM**

1. ...Hermann Maier, Austria — 1:34.82
2. ...Didier Cucher, Switzerland — 1:35.43
3. ...Hans Knauss, Austria — 1:35.43

**COMBINED**

1. ...Mario Reiter, Austria — 3:08.06
2. ...Lasse Kjus, Norway — 3:08.65
3. ...Christian Mayer, Austria — 3:10.11

### Women

**DOWNHILL**

1. ...Katja Seizinger, Germany — 1:28.89
2. ...Pernilla Wiberg, Sweden — 1:29.18
3. ...Florence Masnada, France — 1:29.37

**SLALOM**

1. ...Hilde Gerg, Germany — 1:32.40
2. ...Deborah Compagnoni, Italy — 1:32.46
3. ...Zali Steggall, Australia — 1:32.67

**GIANT SLALOM**

1. ...Deborah Compagnoni, Italy — 2:50.59
2. ...Alexandra Meissnitzer, Austria — 2:52.39
3. ...Katja Seizinger, Germany — 2:52.61

**SUPER GIANT SLALOM**

1. ...Picabo Street, United States — 1:18.02
2. ...Michaela Dorfmeister, Austria — 1:18.03
3. ...Alexandra Meissnitzer, Austria — 1:18.09

**COMBINED**

1. ...Katja Seizinger, Germany — 2:40.74
2. ...Martina Ertl, Germany — 2:40.92
3. ...Hilde Gerg, Germany — 2:41.50

## FREESTYLE SKIING

### Men

| MOGULS | Pts |
|---|---|
| 1. ...Jonny Moseley, United States | 26.93 |
| 2. ...Janne Lahtela, Finland | 26.00 |
| 3. ...Sami Mustonen, Finland | 25.76 |

| AERIALS | Pts |
|---|---|
| 1. ...Eric Bergoust, United States | 255.64 |
| 2. ...Sebastien Foucras, France | 248.79 |
| 3. ...Dmitri Dashchinsky, Belarus | 240.79 |

### Women

| MOGULS | Pts |
|---|---|
| 1. ...Tae Satoya, Japan | 25.06 |
| 2. ...Tatjana Mittermayer, Germany | 24.62 |
| 3. ...Kari Traa, Norway | 24.09 |

| AERIALS | Pts |
|---|---|
| 1. ...Nikki Stone, United States | 193.00 |
| 2. ...Nannan Xu, China | 186.97 |
| 3. ...Colette Brand, Switzerland | 171.83 |

## NORDIC SKIING

### Men

| 10 KILOMETERS CLASSICAL STYLE | |
|---|---|
| 1. ...Bjørn Dæhlie, Norway | 27:24.5 |
| 2. ...Markus Gandler, Austria | 27:32.5 |
| 3. ...Mika Myllylae, Finland | 27:40.1 |

| 15 KILOMETERS PURSUIT FREESTYLE | |
|---|---|
| 1. ...Thomas Alsgaard, Norway | 1:07:01.7 |
| 2. ...Bjørn Dæhlie, Norway | 1:07:02.8 |
| 3. ...Vladimir Smirnov, Kazakhstan | 1:07:31.5 |

| 30 KILOMETERS CLASSICAL STYLE | |
|---|---|
| 1. ...Mika Myllylae, Finland | 1:33:55.8 |
| 2. ...Erling Jevne, Norway | 1:35:27.1 |
| 3. ...Silvio Fauner, Italy | 1:36:08.5 |

| 50 KILOMETERS FREESTYLE | |
|---|---|
| 1. ...Bjørn Dæhlie, Norway | 2:05:08.2 |
| 2. ...Niklas Jonsson, Sweden | 2:05:16.3 |
| 3. ...Christian Hoffmann, Austria | 2:06:01.8 |

| 4 X 10-KILOMETER RELAY MIXED STYLE | |
|---|---|
| 1. ...............Norway | 1:40:55.7 |
| 2. ...............Italy | 1:40:55.9 |
| 3. ...............Finland | 1:42:15.5 |

| 90-METER HILL SKI JUMPING | Pts |
|---|---|
| 1. ...Jani Soininen, Finland | 234.5 |
| 2. ...Kazuyoshi Funaki, Japan | 233.5 |
| 3. ...Andreas Widhoelzl, Austria | 232.5 |

| 120-METER HILL SKI JUMPING | Pts |
|---|---|
| 1. ...Kazuyoshi Funaki, Japan | 272.3 |
| 2. ...Jani Soininen, Finland | 260.8 |
| 3. ...Masahiko Harada, Japan | 258.3 |

| 120-METER HILL TEAM SKI JUMPING | Pts |
|---|---|
| 1. ...Japan | 933.0 |
| 2. ...Germany | 897.4 |
| 3. ...Austria | 881.5 |

| INDIVIDUAL COMBINED | Time behind |
|---|---|
| 1. ...Bjarte Engen Vik, Norway | — |
| 2. ...Samppa Lajunen, Finland | 27.5 |
| 3. ...Valery Stoljarov, Russia | 28.2 |

| TEAM COMBINED | Time behind |
|---|---|
| 1. ...............Norway | — |
| 2. ...............Finland | 1:18.9 |
| 3. ...............France | 1:41.9 |

### Women

| 5 KILOMETERS CLASSICAL STYLE | |
|---|---|
| 1. ...Larissa Lazhutina, Russia | 17:37.9 |
| 2. ...Katerina Neumannova, Czech Rep | 17:42.7 |
| 3. ...Bente Martinsen, Norway | 17:49.4 |

| 10 KILOMETERS PURSUIT FREESTYLE | |
|---|---|
| 1. ...Larissa Lazhutina, Russia | 46:06.9 |
| 2. ...Olga Danilova, Russia | 46:13.4 |
| 3. ...Katerina Neumannova, Czech Rep | 46:14.2 |

| 15 KILOMETERS CLASSICAL STYLE | |
|---|---|
| 1. ...Olga Danilova, Russia | 46:55.04 |
| 2. ...Larissa Lazhutina, Russia | 47:01.00 |
| 3. ...Anita Moen-Guidon, Norway | 47:52.06 |

| 30 KILOMETERS FREESTYLE | |
|---|---|
| 1. ...Julija Tchepalova, Russia | 1:22:01.5 |
| 2. ...Stefania Belmondo, Italy | 1:22:11.7 |
| 3. ...Larissa Lazhutina, Russia | 1:23:15.7 |

| 4 X 5-KILOMETER RELAY MIXED STYLE | |
|---|---|
| 1. ...................Russia | 55:13.5 |
| 2. ...................Norway | 55:38.0 |
| 3. ...................Italy | 56:53.3 |

## SNOWBOARDING

### Men

#### GIANT SLALOM

| | |
|---|---|
| 1. ...Ross Rebagliati, Canada | 2:03.96 |
| 2. ...Thomas Prugger, Italy | 2:03.98 |
| 3. ...Ueli Kestenholz, Switzerland | 2:04.08 |

| HALF-PIPE | Pts |
|---|---|
| 1. ...Gian Simmen, Switzerland | 85.2 |
| 2. ...Daniel Franck, Norway | 82.4 |
| 3. ...Ross Powers, United States | 82.1 |

### Women

#### GIANT SLALOM

| | |
|---|---|
| 1. ...Karine Ruby, France | 2:17.34 |
| 2. ...Heidi Renoth, Germany | 2:19.17 |
| 3. ...Brigitte Koeck, Austria | 2:19.42 |

| HALF-PIPE | Pts |
|---|---|
| 1. ...Nicola Thost, Germany | 74.6 |
| 2. ...Stine Brun Kjeldaas, Norway | 74.2 |
| 3. ...Shannon Dunn, United States | 72.8 |

# FOR THE RECORD·Year by Year

## Olympic Games Locations and Dates

### Summer

| | Year | Site | Dates | Competitors Men | Women | Nations | Most Medals | US Medals |
|---|---|---|---|---|---|---|---|---|
| I | 1896 | Athens, Greece | Apr 6–15 | 311 | 0 | 13 | Greece (10-19-18—47) | 11-6-2—19 (2nd) |
| II | 1900 | Paris, France | May 20–Oct 28 | 1319 | 11 | 22 | France (29-41-32—102) | 20-14-19—53 (2nd) |
| III | 1904 | St Louis, United States | July 1–Nov 23 | 681 | 6 | 12 | United States (80-86-72—238) | |
| — | 1906 | Athens, Greece | Apr 22–May 28 | 77 | 7 | 20 | France (15-9-16—40) | 12-6-5—23 (4th) |
| IV | 1908 | London, Great Britain | Apr 27–Oct 31 | 1999 | 36 | 23 | Britain (56-50-39—145) | 23-12-12—47 (2nd) |
| V | 1912 | Stockholm, Sweden | May 5–July 22 | 2490 | 57 | 28 | Sweden (24-24-17—65) | 23-19-19—61 (2nd) |
| VI | 1916 | Berlin, Germany | Canceled because of war | | | | | |
| VII | 1920 | Antwerp, Belgium | Apr 20–Sep 12 | 2543 | 64 | 29 | United States (41-27-28—96) | |
| VIII | 1924 | Paris, France | May 4–July 27 | 2956 | 136 | 44 | United States (45-27-27—99) | |
| IX | 1928 | Amsterdam, Netherlands | May 17–Aug 12 | 2724 | 290 | 46 | United States (22-18-16—56) | |
| X | 1932 | Los Angeles, United States | July 30–Aug 14 | 1281 | 127 | 37 | United States (41-32-31—104) | |
| XI | 1936 | Berlin, Germany | Aug 1–16 | 3738 | 328 | 49 | Germany (33-26-30—89) | 24-20-12—56 (2nd) |
| XII | 1940 | Tokyo, Japan | Canceled because of war | | | | | |
| XIII | 1944 | London, Great Britain | Canceled because of war | | | | | |
| XIV | 1948 | London, Great Britain | July 29–Aug 14 | 3714 | 385 | 59 | United States (38-27-19—84) | |
| XV | 1952 | Helsinki, Finland | July 19–Aug 3 | 4407 | 518 | 69 | United States (40-19-17—76) | |
| XVI | 1956 | Melbourne, Australia* | Nov 22–Dec 8 | 2958 | 384 | 67 | USSR (37-29-32—98) | 32-25-17—74 (2nd) |
| XVII | 1960 | Rome, Italy | Aug 25–Sep 11 | 4738 | 610 | 83 | USSR (43-29-31—103) | 34-21-16—71 (2nd) |
| XVIII | 1964 | Tokyo, Japan | Oct 10–24 | 4457 | 683 | 93 | United States (36-26-28—90) | |
| XIX | 1968 | Mexico City, Mexico | Oct 12–27 | 4750 | 781 | 112 | United States (45-28-34—107) | |
| XX | 1972 | Munich, W Germany | Aug 26–Sep 10 | 5848 | 1299 | 122 | USSR (50-27-22—99) | 33-31-30—94 (2nd) |
| XXI | 1976 | Montreal, Canada | July 17–Aug 1 | 4834 | 1251 | 92† | USSR (49-41-35—125) | 34-35-25—94 (3rd) |
| XXII | 1980 | Moscow, USSR | July 19–Aug 3 | 4265 | 1088 | 81‡ | USSR (80-69-46—195) | Did not compete |
| XXIII | 1984 | Los Angeles, United States | July 28–Aug 12 | 5458 | 1620 | 141# | United States (83-61-30—174) | |
| XXIV | 1988 | Seoul, S Korea | Sep 17–Oct 2 | 7105 | 2476 | 160 | USSR (55-31-46—132) | 36-31-27—94 (3rd) |
| XXV | 1992 | Barcelona, Spain | July 25–Aug. 9 | 7555 | 3008 | 172 | Unified Team (45-38-29—112) | 37-34-37—108 (2nd) |
| XXVI | 1996 | Atlanta, United States | July 19–Aug 4 | 6984 | 3766 | 197 | United States (44-32-25—101) | |
| XXVII | 2000 | Sydney, Australia | Sept 15–Oct 1 | 6862 | 4254 | 199 | United States (39-25-33—97) | |

*The equestrian events were held in Stockholm, Sweden, June 10–17, 1956.

†This figure includes Cameroon, Egypt, Morocco, and Tunisia, countries that boycotted the 1976 Olympics after some of their athletes had already competed.

‡The U.S. was among 65 countries that did not participate in the 1980 Summer Games in Moscow.

#The USSR, East Germany, and 14 other countries did not participate in the 1984 Summer Games in Los Angeles.

## Winter

| | Year | Site | Dates | Men | Women | Nations | Most Medals | US Medals |
|---|---|---|---|---|---|---|---|---|
| I | 1924 | Chamonix, France | Jan 25–Feb 4 | 281 | 13 | 16 | Norway (4-7-6—17) | 1-2-1—4 (3rd) |
| II | 1928 | St. Moritz, Switzerland | Feb 11–19 | 366 | 27 | 25 | Norway (6-4-5—15) | 2-2-2—6 (2nd) |
| III | 1932 | Lake Placid, United States | Feb 4–13 | 277 | 30 | 17 | United States (6-4-2—12) | |
| IV | 1936 | Garmisch-Partenkirchen, Germany | Feb 6–16 | 680 | 76 | 28 | Norway (7-5-3—15) | 1-0-3—4 (T-5th) |
| — | 1940 | Garmisch-Partenkirchen, Germany | Canceled because of war | | | | | |
| — | 1944 | Cortina d'Ampezzo, Italy | Canceled because of war | | | | | |
| V | 1948 | St. Moritz, Switzerland | Jan 30–Feb 8 | 636 | 77 | 28 | Norway (4-3-3—10) Sweden (4-3-3—10) Switzerland (3-4-3—10) | 3-4-2—9 (4th) |
| VI | 1952 | Oslo, Norway | Feb 14–25 | 624 | 108 | 30 | Norway (7-3-6—16) | 4-6-1—11 (2nd) |
| VII | 1956 | Cortina d'Ampezzo, Italy | Jan 26–Feb 5 | 687 | 132 | 32 | USSR (7-3-6—16) | 2-3-2—7 (T-4th) |
| VIII | 1960 | Squaw Valley, United States | Feb 18–28 | 502 | 146 | 30 | USSR (7-5-9—21) | 3-4-3—10 (2nd) |
| IX | 1964 | Innsbruck, Austria | Jan 29–Feb 9 | 758 | 175 | 36 | USSR (11-8-6—25) | 1-2-3—6 (7th) |
| X | 1968 | Grenoble, France | Feb 6–18 | 1063 | 230 | 37 | Norway (6-6-2—14) | 1-5-1—7 (T-7th) |
| XI | 1972 | Sapporo, Japan | Feb 3–13 | 927 | 218 | 35 | USSR (8-5-3—16) | 3-2-3—8 (6th) |
| XII | 1976 | Innsbruck, Austria | Feb 4–15 | 1013 | 248 | 37 | USSR (13-6-8—27) | 3-3-4—10 (T-3rd) |
| XIII | 1980 | Lake Placid, United States | Feb 13–24 | 1012 | 271 | 37 | East Germany (9-7-7—23) | 6-4-2—12 (3rd) |
| XIV | 1984 | Sarajevo, Yugoslavia | Feb 8–19 | 1127 | 283 | 49 | USSR (6-10-9—25) | 4-4-0—8 (T-5th) |
| XV | 1988 | Calgary, Canada | Feb 13–28 | 1270 | 364 | 57 | USSR (11-9-9—29) | 2-1-3—6 (T-8th) |
| XVI | 1992 | Albertville, France | Feb 8–23 | 1313 | 488 | 65 | Germany (10-10-6—26) | 5-4-2—11 (6th) |
| XVII | 1994 | Lillehammer, Norway | Feb 12–27 | 1302 | 542 | 67 | Norway (10-11-5—26) | 6-5-2—13 (T-5th) |
| XVIII | 1998 | Nagano, Japan | Feb 7–22 | 2302 (total) | | 72 | Germany (12-9-8—29) | 6-3-4—13 (6th) |

# Alltime Olympic Medal Winners

## Summer

### NATIONS

| Nation | Gold | Silver | Bronze | Total | Nation | Gold | Silver | Bronze | Total |
|---|---|---|---|---|---|---|---|---|---|
| United States | 871 | 659 | 586 | 2116 | Finland | 101 | 81 | 114 | 296 |
| Soviet Union (1952–88) | 395 | 319 | 296 | 1010 | Japan | 97 | 97 | 102 | 296 |
| Great Britain | 180 | 233 | 225 | 638 | Romania | 74 | 83 | 108 | 265 |
| France | 188 | 193 | 217 | 598 | Poland | 56 | 72 | 113 | 241 |
| Italy | 179 | 143 | 157 | 479 | Canada | 51 | 81 | 98 | 230 |
| Sweden | 136 | 156 | 177 | 469 | China | 80 | 79 | 64 | 223 |
| E Germany (1956–88) | 159 | 150 | 136 | 445 | The Netherlands | 61 | 67 | 85 | 213 |
| Hungary | 150 | 135 | 158 | 443 | Bulgaria | 48 | 82 | 65 | 195 |
| Germany (1896–1936, 1992– ) | 138 | 138 | 160 | 436 | Switzerland | 47 | 75 | 61 | 183 |
| | | | | | Denmark | 40 | 63 | 58 | 161 |
| Australia | 102 | 110 | 138 | 350 | Russia | 59 | 53 | 47 | 159 |
| W Germany (1952–88) | 77 | 104 | 120 | 301 | Czechoslovakia (1924–92) | 49 | 49 | 44 | 142 |

## Summer *(Cont.)*
### INDIVIDUALS — OVERALL

### Men

| Athlete, Nation | Sport | G | S | B | Tot |
|---|---|---|---|---|---|
| Nikolai Andrianov, USSR | Gym | 7 | 5 | 3 | 15 |
| Boris Shakhlin, USSR | Gym | 7 | 4 | 2 | 13 |
| Edoardo Mangiarotti, Italy | Fen | 6 | 5 | 2 | 13 |
| Takashi Ono, Japan | Gym | 5 | 4 | 4 | 13 |
| Paavo Nurmi, Finland | Track | 9 | 3 | 0 | 12 |
| Sawao Kato, Japan | Gym | 8 | 3 | 1 | 12 |
| Alexei Nemov, Russia | Gym | 4 | 2 | 6 | 12 |
| Mark Spitz, United States | Swim | 9 | 1 | 1 | 11 |
| Matt Biondi, United States | Swim | 8 | 2 | 1 | 11 |
| Viktor Chukarin, USSR | Gym | 7 | 3 | 1 | 11 |
| Carl Osburn, United States | Shoot | 5 | 4 | 2 | 11 |
| Ray Ewry, United States | Track | 10 | 0 | 0 | 10 |
| Carl Lewis, United States | Track | 9 | 1 | 0 | 10 |
| Aladár Gerevich, Hungary | Fen | 7 | 1 | 2 | 10 |
| Akinori Nakayama, Japan | Gym | 6 | 2 | 2 | 10 |
| Vitaly Scherbo, UT/Belarus | Gym | 6 | 0 | 4 | 10 |
| Aleksandr Dityatin, USSR | Gym | 3 | 6 | 1 | 10 |

### Women

| Athlete, Nation | Sport | G | S | B | Tot |
|---|---|---|---|---|---|
| Larissa Latynina, USSR | Gym | 9 | 5 | 4 | 18 |
| Vera Cáslavská, Czech | Gym | 7 | 4 | 0 | 11 |
| Agnes Keleti, Hungary | Gym | 5 | 3 | 2 | 10 |
| Polina Astaknova, USSR | Gym | 5 | 2 | 3 | 10 |
| Nadia Comaneci, Romania | Gym | 5 | 3 | 1 | 9 |
| Jenny Thompson, United States | Swim | 7 | 1 | 1 | 9 |
| Lyudmila Tourischeva, USSR | Gym | 4 | 3 | 2 | 9 |
| Kornelia Ender, E Germany | Swim | 4 | 4 | 0 | 8 |
| Dawn Fraser, Australia | Swim | 4 | 4 | 0 | 8 |
| Shirley Babashoff, United States | Swim | 2 | 6 | 0 | 8 |
| Sofia Muratova, USSR | Gym | 2 | 2 | 4 | 8 |
| Dara Torres, United States | Swim | 4 | 0 | 4 | 8 |
| Eight tied with seven. | | | | | |

### INDIVIDUALS — GOLD
### Men

| | | |
|---|---|---|
| Ray Ewry, United States | 10 | Sawao Kato, Japan | 8 | Viktor Chukarin, USSR | 7 |

Ray Ewry, United States ..........10
Paavo Nurmi, Finland ...............9
Carl Lewis, United States ..........9
Mark Spitz, United States ..........9

Sawao Kato, Japan ...................8
Matt Biondi, United States .........8
Nikolai Andrianov, USSR ...........7
Boris Shakhlin, USSR ................7

Viktor Chukarin, USSR ...............7
Aladár Gerevich, Hungary ..........7

### Women

Larissa Latynina, USSR .............9
Jenny Thompson, United States ..8
Vera Cáslavská, Czech ..............7
Kristin Otto, E Germany ..............6
Agnes Keleti, Hungary ...............5
Nadia Comaneci, Romania ........5

Polina Astaknova, USSR ............5
Krisztina Egerszegi, Hun ...........5
Kornelia Ender, E Germany ........4
Dawn Fraser, Australia ..............4
Lyudmila Tourischeva, USSR ....4
Evelyn Ashford, United States ...4

Janet Evans, United States ........4
Fanny Blankers-Koen, Neth .......4
Betty Cuthbert, Australia ............4
Pat McCormick, United States ...4
Bärbel Eckert Wöckel, E Ger .....4
Amy Van Dyken, United States ...4

## Winter
### NATIONS

| Nation | Gold | Silver | Bronze | Total | Nation | Gold | Silver | Bronze | Total |
|---|---|---|---|---|---|---|---|---|---|
| Norway | 83 | 85 | 68 | 236 | E Germany (1956–88) | 39 | 36 | 35 | 110 |
| Soviet Union (1956–88) | 78 | 57 | 59 | 194 | Sweden | 36 | 26 | 34 | 96 |
| United States | 59 | 58 | 40 | 157 | Switzerland | 29 | 31 | 31 | 91 |
| Austria | 39 | 53 | 53 | 145 | Germany (1928–36, '92– ) | 34 | 29 | 25 | 88 |
| Finland | 37 | 49 | 48 | 134 | Canada | 24 | 25 | 29 | 78 |

### INDIVIDUALS — OVERALL

### Men

| Athlete, Nation | Sport | G | S | B | Tot |
|---|---|---|---|---|---|
| Bjørn Dæhlie, Norway | N Ski | 8 | 4 | 0 | 12 |
| Sixten Jernberg, Sweden | N Ski | 4 | 3 | 2 | 9 |
| A. Clas Thunberg, Finland | S Skat | 5 | 1 | 1 | 7 |
| Ivar Ballangrud, Norway | S Skat | 4 | 2 | 1 | 7 |
| Veikko Hakulinen, Finland | N Ski | 3 | 3 | 1 | 7 |
| Eero Mäntyranta, Finland | N Ski | 3 | 2 | 2 | 7 |
| Bogdan Musiol, E Ger/Ger | Bob | 1 | 5 | 1 | 7 |

### Women

| Athlete, Nation | Sport | G | S | B | Tot |
|---|---|---|---|---|---|
| Raisa Smetanina, USSR/UT | N Ski | 4 | 5 | 1 | 10 |
| Lyubov Egorova, UT/Russia | N Ski | 6 | 3 | 0 | 9 |
| Galina Kulakova, USSR | N Ski | 4 | 2 | 2 | 8 |
| Karin (Enke) Kania, E Germany | S Skat | 3 | 4 | 1 | 8 |
| Gunda Niemann Stimemann, Ger | S Skat | 3 | 4 | 1 | 8 |
| Larissa Lazutina, UT/Russia | N Ski | 5 | 1 | 1 | 7 |
| Marja-Liisa Kirvesniemi, Fin | N Ski | 3 | 0 | 4 | 7 |
| Andrea Ehrig, E Germany | S Skat | 1 | 5 | 1 | 7 |

### INDIVIDUALS — GOLD
### Men

Bjørn Dæhlie, Nor .......8
A. Clas Thunberg, Fin...5
Eric Heiden, U.S. ........5
Sixten Jernberg, Swe...4
Evgeny Grishin, USSR...4
J. Olav Koss, Norway...4

Matti Nykänen, Fin......4
A. Tikhonov, USSR......4
N. Zimyatov, USSR......4
Ivar Ballangrud, Nor ...4
Gunde Svan, Swe.......4
T. Wassberg, Swe.......4

### Women

Lyubov Egorova,
UT/Russia ..................6
L. Skoblikova, USSR...6
Larissa Lazutina,
UT/Russia ..................5
Bonnie Blair, U.S.........5

Raisa Smetanina,
USSR/UT....................4
G. Kulakova, USSR.....4
Chun Lee Kyung, Kor...4

## TRACK AND FIELD
### Men

### 100 METERS

| | | |
|---|---|---|
| 1896 | Thomas Burke, United States | 12.0 |
| 1900 | Frank Jarvis, United States | 11.0 |
| 1904 | Archie Hahn, United States | 11.0 |
| 1906 | Archie Hahn, United States | 11.2 |
| 1908 | Reginald Walker, S Africa | 10.8 OR |
| 1912 | Ralph Craig, United States | 10.8 |
| 1920 | Charles Paddock, United States | 10.8 |
| 1924 | Harold Abrahams, Great Britain | 10.6 OR |
| 1928 | Percy Williams, Canada | 10.8 |
| 1932 | Eddie Tolan, United States | 10.3 OR |
| 1936 | Jesse Owens, United States | 10.3 |
| 1948 | Harrison Dillard, United States | 10.3 |
| 1952 | Lindy Remigino, United States | 10.4 |
| 1956 | Bobby Morrow, United States | 10.5 |
| 1960 | Armin Hary, W Germany | 10.2 OR |
| 1964 | Bob Hayes, United States | 10.0 EWR |
| 1968 | Jim Hines, United States | 9.95 WR |
| 1972 | Valery Borzov, USSR | 10.14 |
| 1976 | Hasely Crawford, Trinidad | 10.06 |
| 1980 | Allan Wells, Great Britain | 10.25 |
| 1984 | Carl Lewis, United States | 9.99 |
| 1988 | Carl Lewis, United States* | 9.92 WR |
| 1992 | Linford Christie, Great Britain | 9.96 |
| 1996 | Donovan Bailey, Canada | 9.84 WR |
| 2000 | Maurice Greene, United States | 9.87 |

*Ben Johnson, Canada, disqualified.

### 200 METERS

| | | |
|---|---|---|
| 1900 | John Walter Tewksbury, United States | 22.2 |
| 1904 | Archie Hahn, United States | 21.6 OR |
| 1906 | Not held | |
| 1908 | Robert Kerr, Canada | 22 6 |
| 1912 | Ralph Craig, United States | 21.7 |
| 1920 | Allen Woodring, United States | 22.0 |
| 1924 | Jackson Scholz, United States | 21.6 |
| 1928 | Percy Williams, Canada | 21.8 |
| 1932 | Eddie Tolan, United States | 21.2 OR |
| 1936 | Jesse Owens, United States | 20.7 OR |
| 1948 | Mel Patton, United States | 21.1 |
| 1952 | Andrew Stanfield, United States | 20.7 |
| 1956 | Bobby Morrow, United States | 20.6 OR |
| 1960 | Livio Berruti, Italy | 20.5 EWR |
| 1964 | Henry Carr, United States | 20.3 OR |
| 1968 | Tommie Smith, United States | 19.83 WR |
| 1972 | Valery Borzov, USSR | 20.00 |
| 1976 | Donald Quarrie, Jamaica | 20.23 |
| 1980 | Pietro Mennea, Italy | 20.19 |
| 1984 | Carl Lewis, United States | 19.80 OR |
| 1988 | Joe DeLoach, United States | 19.75 OR |
| 1992 | Mike Marsh, United States | 20.01 |
| 1996 | Michael Johnson, United States | 19.32 WR |
| 2000 | Konstadinos Kederis, Greece | 20.09 |

### 400 METERS

| | | |
|---|---|---|
| 1896 | Thomas Burke, United States | 54.2 |
| 1900 | Maxey Long, United States | 49.4 OR |
| 1904 | Harry Hillman, United States | 49.2 OR |
| 1906 | Paul Pilgrim, United States | 53.2 |
| 1908 | Wyndham Halswelle, Great Britain | 50.0 |
| 1912 | Charles Reidpath, United States | 48.2 OR |
| 1920 | Bevil Rudd, South Africa | 49.6 |
| 1924 | Eric Liddell, Great Britain | 47.6 OR |
| 1928 | Ray Barbuti, United States | 47.8 |
| 1932 | William Carr, United States | 46.2 WR |
| 1936 | Archie Williams, United States | 46.5 |
| 1948 | Arthur Wint, Jamaica | 46.2 |

### 400 METERS *(CONT.)*

| | | |
|---|---|---|
| 1952 | George Rhoden, Jamaica | 45.9 |
| 1956 | Charles Jenkins, United States | 46.7 |
| 1960 | Otis Davis, United States | 44.9 WR |
| 1964 | Michael Larrabee, United States | 45.1 |
| 1968 | Lee Evans, United States | 43.86 WR |
| 1972 | Vincent Matthews, United States | 44.66 |
| 1976 | Alberto Juantorena, Cuba | 44.26 |
| 1980 | Viktor Markin, USSR | 44.60 |
| 1984 | Alonzo Babers, United States | 44.27 |
| 1988 | Steve Lewis, United States | 43.87 |
| 1992 | Quincy Watts, United States | 43.50 OR |
| 1996 | Michael Johnson, United States | 43.49 OR |
| 2000 | Michael Johnson, United States | 43.84 |

### 800 METERS

| | | |
|---|---|---|
| 1896 | Edwin Flack, Australia | 2:11 |
| 1900 | Alfred Tysoe, Great Britain | 2:01.2 |
| 1904 | James Lightbody, United States | 1:56 OR |
| 1906 | Paul Pilgrim, United States | 2:01.5 |
| 1908 | Mel Sheppard, United States | 1:52.8 WR |
| 1912 | James Meredith, United States | 1:51.9 WR |
| 1920 | Albert Hill, Great Britain | 1:53.4 |
| 1924 | Douglas Lowe, Great Britain | 1:52.4 |
| 1928 | Douglas Lowe, Great Britain | 1:51.8 OR |
| 1932 | Thomas Hampson, Great Britain | 1:49.8 WR |
| 1936 | John Woodruff, United States | 1:52.9 |
| 1948 | Mal Whitfield, United States | 1:49.2 OR |
| 1952 | Mal Whitfield, United States | 1:49.2 EOR |
| 1956 | Thomas Courtney, United States | 1:47.7 OR |
| 1960 | Peter Snell, New Zealand | 1:46.3 OR |
| 1964 | Peter Snell, New Zealand | 1:45.1 OR |
| 1968 | Ralph Doubell, Australia | 1:44.3 EWR |
| 1972 | Dave Wottle, United States | 1:45.9 |
| 1976 | Alberto Juantorena, Cuba | 1:43.50 WR |
| 1980 | Steve Ovett, Great Britain | 1:45.40 |
| 1984 | Joaquim Cruz, Brazil | 1:43.00 OR |
| 1988 | Paul Ereng, Kenya | 1:43.45 |
| 1992 | William Tanui, Kenya | 1:43.66 |
| 1996 | Vebjoern Rodal, Norway | 1:42.58 OR |
| 2000 | Nils Schumann, Germany | 1:45.08 |

### 1,500 METERS

| | | |
|---|---|---|
| 1896 | Edwin Flack, Australia | 4:33.2 |
| 1900 | Charles Bennett, Great Britain | 4:06.2 WR |
| 1904 | James Lightbody, United States | 4:05.4 WR |
| 1906 | James Lightbody, United States | 4:12.0 |
| 1908 | Mel Sheppard, United States | 4:03.4 OR |
| 1912 | Arnold Jackson, Great Britain | 3:56.8 OR |
| 1920 | Albert Hill, Great Britain | 4:01.8 |
| 1924 | Paavo Nurmi, Finland | 3:53.6 OR |
| 1928 | Harry Larva, Finland | 3:53.2 OR |
| 1932 | Luigi Beccali, Italy | 3:51.2 OR |
| 1936 | Jack Lovelock, New Zealand | 3:47.8 WR |
| 1948 | Henri Eriksson, Sweden | 3:49.8 |
| 1952 | Josef Barthel, Luxemburg | 3:45.1 OR |
| 1956 | Ron Delany, Ireland | 3:41.2 OR |
| 1960 | Herb Elliott, Australia | 3:35.6 WR |
| 1964 | Peter Snell, New Zealand | 3:38.1 |
| 1968 | Kipchoge Keino, Kenya | 3:34.9 OR |
| 1972 | Pekkha Vasala, Finland | 3:36.3 |
| 1976 | John Walker, New Zealand | 3:39.17 |
| 1980 | Sebastian Coe, Great Britain | 3:38.4 |
| 1984 | Sebastian Coe, Great Britain | 3:32.53 OR |
| 1988 | Peter Rono, Kenya | 3:35.96 |
| 1992 | Fermin Cacho, Spain | 3:40.12 |
| 1996 | Noureddine Morceli, Algeria | 3:35.78 |
| 2000 | Noah Ngeni, Kenya | 3:32.07 OR |

Note: OR=Olympic Record. WR=World Record. EOR=Equals Olympic Record. EWR=Equals World Record. WB=World Best.

### TRACK AND FIELD *(Cont.)*
### Men *(Cont.)*

#### 5,000 METERS
| | | |
|---|---|---|
| 1912 | Hannes Kolehmainen, Finland | 14:36.6 WR |
| 1920 | Joseph Guillemot, France | 14:55.6 |
| 1924 | Paavo Nurmi, Finland | 14:31.2 OR |
| 1928 | Villie Ritola, Finland | 14:38 |
| 1932 | Lauri Lehtinen, Finland | 14:30 OR |
| 1936 | Gunnar Höckert, Finland | 14:22.2 OR |
| 1948 | Gaston Reiff, Belgium | 14:17.6 OR |
| 1952 | Emil Zatopek, Czechoslovakia | 14:06.6 OR |
| 1956 | Vladimir Kuts, USSR | 13:39.6 OR |
| 1960 | Murray Halberg, New Zealand | 13:43.4 |
| 1964 | Bob Schul, United States | 13:48.8 |
| 1968 | Mohamed Gammoudi, Tunisia | 14:05.0 |
| 1972 | Lasse Viren, Finland | 13:26.4 OR |
| 1976 | Lasse Viren, Finland | 13:24.76 |
| 1980 | Miruts Yifter, Ethiopia | 13:21.0 |
| 1984 | Said Aouita, Morocco | 13:05.59 OR |
| 1988 | John Ngugi, Kenya | 13:11.70 |
| 1992 | Dieter Baumann, Germany | 13:12.52 |
| 1996 | Venuste Niyongabo, Burundi | 13:07.96 |
| 2000 | Millon Wolde, Ethiopia | 13:35.49 |

#### 10,000 METERS
| | | |
|---|---|---|
| 1912 | Hannes Kolehmainen, Finland | 31:20.8 |
| 1920 | Paavo Nurmi, Finland | 31:45.8 |
| 1924 | Vilho (Ville) Ritola, Finland | 30:23.2 WR |
| 1928 | Paavo Nurmi, Finland | 30:18.8 OR |
| 1932 | Janusz Kusocinski, Poland | 30:11.4 OR |
| 1936 | Ilmari Salminen, Finland | 30:15.4 |
| 1948 | Emil Zatopek, Czechoslovakia | 29:59.6 OR |
| 1952 | Emil Zatopek, Czechoslovakia | 29:17.0 OR |
| 1956 | Vladimir Kuts, USSR | 28:45.6 OR |
| 1960 | Pyotr Bolotnikov, USSR | 28:32.2 OR |
| 1964 | Billy Mills, United States | 28:24.4 OR |
| 1968 | Naftali Temu, Kenya | 29:27.4 |
| 1972 | Lasse Viren, Finland | 27:38.4 WR |
| 1976 | Lasse Viren, Finland | 27:40.38 |
| 1980 | Miruts Yifter, Ethiopia | 27:42.7 |
| 1984 | Alberto Cova, Italy | 27:47.54 |
| 1988 | Brahim Boutaib, Morocco | 27:21.46 OR |
| 1992 | Khalid Skah, Morocco | 27:46.70 |
| 1996 | Haile Gebrselassie, Ethiopia | 27:07.34 OR |
| 2000 | Haile Gebrselassie, Ethiopia | 27:18.20 |

#### MARATHON
| | | |
|---|---|---|
| 1896 | Spiridon Louis, Greece | 2:58:50 |
| 1900 | Michel Theato, France | 2:59:45 |
| 1904 | Thomas Hicks, United States | 3:28:53 |
| 1906 | William Sherring, Canada | 2:51:23.6 |
| 1908 | John Hayes, United States | 2:55:18.4 OR |
| 1912 | Kenneth McArthur, S Africa | 2:36:54.8 |
| 1920 | Hannes Kolehmainen, Finland | 2:32:35.8 WB |
| 1924 | Albin Stenroos, Finland | 2:41:22.6 |
| 1928 | Boughera El Ouafi, France | 2:32:57 |
| 1932 | Juan Zabala, Argentina | 2:31:36 OR |
| 1936 | Kijung Son, Japan (Korea) | 2:29:19.2 OR |
| 1948 | Delfo Cabrera, Argentina | 2:34:51.6 |
| 1952 | Emil Zatopek, Czechoslovakia | 2:23:03.2 OR |
| 1956 | Alain Mimoun O'Kacha, France | 2:25:00.0 |
| 1960 | Abebe Bikila, Ethiopia | 2:15:16.2 WB |
| 1964 | Abebe Bikila, Ethiopia | 2:12:11.2 WB |
| 1968 | Mamo Wolde, Ethiopia | 2:20:26.4 |
| 1972 | Frank Shorter, United States | 2:12:19.8 |
| 1976 | Waldemar Cierpinski, E Germ. | 2:09:55 OR |
| 1980 | Waldemar Cierpinski, E Germ. | 2:11:03.0 |
| 1984 | Carlos Lopes, Portugal | 2:09:21.0 OR |
| 1988 | Gelindo Bordin, Italy | 2:10:32 |
| 1992 | Hwang Young-Cho, S Korea | 2:13:23 |
| 1996 | Josia Thugwane, S Africa | 2:12:36 |
| 2000 | Gezahgne Abera, Ethiopia | 2:10:11 |

#### 110-METER HURDLES
| | | |
|---|---|---|
| 1896 | Thomas Curtis, United States | 17.6 |
| 1900 | Alvin Kraenzlein, United States | 15.4 OR |
| 1904 | Frederick Schule, United States | 16.0 |
| 1906 | Robert Leavitt, United States | 16.2 |
| 1908 | Forrest Smithson, United States | 15.0 WR |
| 1912 | Frederick Kelly, United States | 15.1 |
| 1920 | Earl Thomson, Canada | 14.8 WR |
| 1924 | Daniel Kinsey, United States | 15.0 |
| 1928 | Sydney Atkinson, S Africa | 14.8 |
| 1932 | George Saling, United States | 14.6 |
| 1936 | Forrest Towns, United States | 14.2 |
| 1948 | William Porter, United States | 13.9 OR |
| 1952 | Harrison Dillard, United States | 13.7 OR |
| 1956 | Lee Calhoun, United States | 13.5 OR |
| 1960 | Lee Calhoun, United States | 13.8 |
| 1964 | Hayes Jones, United States | 13.6 |
| 1968 | Willie Davenport, United States | 13.3 OR |
| 1972 | Rod Milburn, United States | 13.24 EWR |
| 1976 | Guy Drut, France | 13.30 |
| 1980 | Thomas Munkelt, E Germany | 13.39 |
| 1984 | Roger Kingdom, United States | 13.20 OR |
| 1988 | Roger Kingdom, United States | 12.98 OR |
| 1992 | Mark McKoy, Canada | 13.12 |
| 1996 | Allen Johnson, United States | 12.95 OR |
| 2000 | Anier Garcia, Cuba | 13.00 |

#### 400-METER HURDLES
| | | |
|---|---|---|
| 1900 | John Walter Tewksbury, U.S. | 57.6 |
| 1904 | Harry Hillman, United States | 53.0 |
| 1906 | Not held | |
| 1908 | Charles Bacon, United States | 55.0 WR |
| 1912 | Not held | |
| 1920 | Frank Loomis, United States | 54.0 WR |
| 1924 | F. Morgan Taylor, United States | 52.6 |
| 1928 | David Burghley, Great Britain | 53.4 OR |
| 1932 | Robert Tisdall, Ireland | 51.7 |
| 1936 | Glenn Hardin, United States | 52.4 |
| 1948 | Roy Cochran, United States | 51.1 OR |
| 1952 | Charles Moore, United States | 50.8 OR |
| 1956 | Glenn Davis, United States | 50.1 EOR |
| 1960 | Glenn Davis, United States | 49.3 EOR |
| 1964 | Rex Cawley, United States | 49.6 |
| 1968 | Dave Hemery, Great Britain | 48.12 WR |
| 1972 | John Akii-Bua, Uganda | 47.82 WR |
| 1976 | Edwin Moses, United States | 47.64 WR |
| 1980 | Volker Beck, E Germany | 48.70 |
| 1984 | Edwin Moses, United States | 47.75 |
| 1988 | Andre Phillips, United States | 47.19 OR |
| 1992 | Kevin Young, United States | 46.78 WR |
| 1996 | Derrick Adkins, United States | 47.54 |
| 2000 | Angelo Taylor, United States | 47.50 |

#### 3,000-METER STEEPLECHASE
| | | |
|---|---|---|
| 1920 | Percy Hodge, Great Britain | 10:00.4 OR |
| 1924 | Vilho (Ville) Ritola, Finland | 9:33.6 OR |
| 1928 | Toivo Loukola, Finland | 9:21.8 WR |
| 1932 | Volmari Iso-Hollo, Finland | 10:33.4* |
| 1936 | Volmari Iso-Hollo, Finland | 9:03.8 WR |
| 1948 | Thore Sjöstrand, Sweden | 9:04.6 |
| 1952 | Horace Ashenfelter, U.S. | 8:45.4 WR |
| 1956 | Chris Brasher, Great Britain | 8:41.2 OR |
| 1960 | Zdzislaw Krzyszkowiak, Poland | 8:34.2 OR |
| 1964 | Gaston Roelants, Belgium | 8:30.8 OR |
| 1968 | Amos Biwott, Kenya | 8:51 |
| 1972 | Kipchoge Keino, Kenya | 8:23.6 OR |
| 1976 | Anders Gärderud, Sweden | 8:08.2 WR |
| 1980 | Bronislaw Malinowski, Poland | 8:09.7 |
| 1984 | Julius Korir, Kenya | 8:11.8 |
| 1988 | Julius Kariuki, Kenya | 8:05.51 OR |
| 1992 | Matthew Birir, Kenya | 8:08.84 |
| 1996 | Joseph Keter, Kenya | 8:07.12 |

## TRACK AND FIELD (Cont.)
### Men (Cont.)

#### 3,000-METER STEEPLECHASE (CONT.)

| | | |
|---|---|---|
| 2000 | Reuben Kosgei, Kenya | 8:21.43 |

*About 3,450 meters; extra lap by error.

#### 4 X 100-METER RELAY

| | | |
|---|---|---|
| 1912 | Great Britain | 42.4 OR |
| 1920 | United States | 42.2 WR |
| 1924 | United States | 41.0 EWR |
| 1928 | United States | 41.0 EWR |
| 1932 | United States | 40.0 EWR |
| 1936 | United States | 39.8 WR |
| 1948 | United States | 40.6 |
| 1952 | United States | 40.1 |
| 1956 | United States | 39.5 WR |
| 1960 | W Germany | 39.5 EWR |
| 1964 | United States | 39.0 WR |
| 1968 | United States | 38.2 WR |
| 1972 | United States | 38.19 EWR |
| 1976 | United States | 38.33 |
| 1980 | USSR | 38.26 |
| 1984 | United States | 37.83 WR |
| 1988 | USSR | 38.19 |
| 1992 | United States | 37.40 WR |
| 1996 | Canada | 37.69 |
| 2000 | United States | 37.61 |

#### 4 X 400-METER RELAY

| | | |
|---|---|---|
| 1908 | United States | 3:29.4 |
| 1912 | United States | 3:16.6 WR |
| 1920 | Great Britain | 3:22.2 |
| 1924 | United States | 3:16.0 WR |
| 1928 | United States | 3:14.2 WR |
| 1932 | United States | 3:08.2 WR |
| 1936 | Great Britain | 3:09.0 |
| 1948 | United States | 3:10.4 WR |
| 1952 | Jamaica | 3:03.9 WR |
| 1956 | United States | 3:04.8 |
| 1960 | United States | 3:02.2 WR |
| 1964 | United States | 3:00.7 WR |
| 1968 | United States | 2:56.16 WR |
| 1972 | Kenya | 2:59.8 |
| 1976 | United States | 2:58.65 |
| 1980 | USSR | 3:01.1 |
| 1984 | United States | 2:57.91 |
| 1988 | United States | 2:56.16 EWR |
| 1992 | United States | 2:55.74 WR |
| 1996 | United States | 2:55.99 |
| 2000 | United States | 2:56.35 |

#### 20-KILOMETER WALK

| | | |
|---|---|---|
| 1956 | Leonid Spirin, USSR | 1:31:27.4 |
| 1960 | Vladimir Golubnichiy, USSR | 1:33:07.2 |
| 1964 | Kenneth Mathews, Great Britain | 1:29:34.0 OR |
| 1968 | Vladimir Golubnichiy, USSR | 1:33:58.4 |
| 1972 | Peter Frenkel, E Germany | 1:26:42.4 OR |
| 1976 | Daniel Bautista, Mexico | 1:24:40.6 OR |
| 1980 | Maurizio Damilano, Italy | 1:23:35.5 OR |
| 1984 | Ernesto Canto, Mexico | 1:23:13.0 OR |
| 1988 | Jozef Pribilinec, Czechoslovakia | 1:19:57.0 OR |
| 1992 | Daniel Plaza, Spain | 1:21:45.0 |
| 1996 | Jefferson Pérez, Ecuador | 1:20:07 |
| 2000 | Robert Korzeniowski, Poland | 1:18:59 OR |

#### 50-KILOMETER WALK

| | | |
|---|---|---|
| 1932 | Thomas Green, Great Britain | 4:50:10 |
| 1936 | Harold Whitlock, Great Britain | 4:30:41.4 OR |
| 1948 | John Ljunggren, Sweden | 4:41:52 |
| 1952 | Giuseppe Dordoni, Italy | 4:28:07.8 OR |
| 1956 | Norman Read, New Zealand | 4:30:42.8 |
| 1960 | Donald Thompson, Great Britain | 4:25:30 OR |
| 1964 | Abdon Parnich, Italy | 4:11:12.4 OR |

#### 50-KILOMETER WALK (CONT.)

| | | |
|---|---|---|
| 1968 | Christoph Höhne, E Germany | 4:20:13.6 |
| 1972 | Bernd Kannenberg, W Germany | 3:56:11.6 OR |
| 1980 | Hartwig Gauder, E Germany | 3:49:24.0 OR |
| 1984 | Raul Gonzalez, Mexico | 3:47:26.0 OR |
| 1988 | Viacheslav Ivanenko, USSR | 3:38:29.0 OR |
| 1992 | Andrey Perlov, Unified Team | 3:50:13 |
| 1996 | Robert Korzeniowski, Poland | 3:43:30 |
| 2000 | Robert Korzeniowski, Poland | 3:42:22 OR |

#### HIGH JUMP

| | | |
|---|---|---|
| 1896 | Ellery Clark, United States | 5 ft 11¼ in |
| 1900 | Irving Baxter, United States | 6 ft 2¾ in OR |
| 1904 | Samuel Jones, United States | 5 ft 11 in |
| 1906 | Cornelius Leahy, Great Britain/Ireland | 5 ft 10 in |
| 1908 | Harry Porter, United States | 6 ft 3 in OR |
| 1912 | Alma Richards, United States | 6 ft 4 in OR |
| 1920 | Richmond Landon, United States | 6 ft 4 in OR |
| 1924 | Harold Osborn, United States | 6 ft 6 in OR |
| 1928 | Robert W. King, United States | 6 ft 4½ in |
| 1932 | Duncan McNaughton, Canada | 6 ft 5½ in |
| 1936 | Cornelius Johnson, United States | 6 ft 8 in OR |
| 1948 | John L. Winter, Australia | 6 ft 6 in |
| 1952 | Walter Davis, United States | 6 ft 8½ in OR |
| 1956 | Charles Dumas, United States | 6 ft 11½ in OR |
| 1960 | Robert Shavlakadze, USSR | 7 ft 1 in OR |
| 1964 | Valery Brumel, USSR | 7 ft 1¾ in OR |
| 1968 | Dick Fosbury, United States | 7 ft 4¼ in OR |
| 1972 | Yuri Tarmak, USSR | 7 ft 3¾ in |
| 1976 | Jacek Wszola, Poland | 7 ft 4½ in OR |
| 1980 | Gerd Wessig, E Germany | 7 ft 8¾ in WR |
| 1984 | Dietmar Mögenburg, W Germany | 7 ft 8½ in |
| 1988 | Gennadiy Avdeyenko, USSR | 7 ft 9¾ in OR |
| 1992 | Javier Sotomayor, Cuba | 7 ft 8 in. |
| 1996 | Charles Austin, United States | 7 ft 10 in OR |
| 2000 | Sergey Kliugin, Russia | 7 ft 8¼ in |

#### POLE VAULT

| | | |
|---|---|---|
| 1896 | William Hoyt, United States | 10 ft 10 in |
| 1900 | Irving Baxter, United States | 10 ft 10 in |
| 1904 | Charles Dvorak, United States | 11 ft 5¾ in |
| 1906 | Fernand Gonder, France | 11 ft 5¾ in |
| 1908 | Alfred Gilbert, United States Edward Cooke Jr., United States | 12 ft 2 in OR |
| 1912 | Harry Babcock, United States | 12 ft 11½ in OR |
| 1920 | Frank Foss, United States | 13 ft 5 in WR |
| 1924 | Lee Barnes, United States | 12 ft 11½ in |
| 1928 | Sabin Carr, United States | 13 ft 9¼ in OR |
| 1932 | William Miller, United States | 14 ft 1¾ in OR |
| 1936 | Earle Meadows, United States | 14 ft 3¼ in OR |
| 1948 | Guinn Smith, United States | 14 ft 1¼ in |
| 1952 | Robert Richards, United States | 14 ft 11 in OR |
| 1956 | Robert Richards, United States | 14 ft 11½ in OR |
| 1960 | Don Bragg, United States | 15 ft 5 in OR |
| 1964 | Fred Hansen, United States | 16 ft 8¾ in OR |
| 1968 | Bob Seagren, United States | 17 ft 8½ in OR |
| 1972 | Wolfgang Nordwig, E Germany | 18 ft ½ in OR |
| 1976 | Tadeusz Slusarski, Poland | 18 ft ½ in EOR |
| 1980 | Wladyslaw Kozakiewicz, Poland | 18 ft 11½ in WR |
| 1984 | Pierre Quinon, France | 18 ft 10¼ in |
| 1988 | Sergei Bubka, USSR | 19 ft 4¼ in OR |
| 1992 | Maksim Tarasov, Unified Team | 19 ft ¼ in |
| 1996 | Jean Galfione, France | 19 ft 5 ¼ in OR |
| 2000 | Nick Hysong, United States | 19 ft 4¼ in |

Note: OR=Olympic Record. WR=World Record. EOR=Equals Olympic Record. EWR=Equals World Record. WB=World Best.

## TRACK AND FIELD *(Cont.)*
### Men *(Cont.)*

### LONG JUMP

| | | |
|---|---|---|
| 1896 | Ellery Clark, United States | 20 ft 10 in |
| 1900 | Alvin Kraenzlein, United States | 23 ft 6¾ in OR |
| 1904 | Meyer Prinstein, United States | 24 ft 1 in OR |
| 1906 | Meyer Prinstein, United States | 23 ft 7½ in |
| 1908 | Frank Irons, United States | 24 ft 6½ in OR |
| 1912 | Albert Gutterson, United States | 24 ft 11¼ in OR |
| 1920 | William Petersson, Sweden | 23 ft 5½ in |
| 1924 | DeHart Hubbard, United States | 24 ft 5 in |
| 1928 | Edward B. Hamm, United States | 25 ft 4½ in OR |
| 1932 | Edward Gordon, United States | 25 ft ¾ in |
| 1936 | Jesse Owens, United States | 26 ft 5½ in OR |
| 1948 | William Steele, United States | 25 ft 8 in |
| 1952 | Jerome Biffle, United States | 24 ft 10 in |
| 1956 | Gregory Bell, United States | 25 ft 8¼ in |
| 1960 | Ralph Boston, United States | 26 ft 7¾ in OR |
| 1964 | Lynn Davies, Great Britain | 26 ft 5¾ in |
| 1968 | Bob Beamon, United States | 29 ft 2½ in WR |
| 1972 | Randy Williams, United States | 27 ft ½ in |
| 1976 | Arnie Robinson, United States | 27 ft 4¾ in |
| 1980 | Lutz Dombrowski, E Germany | 28 ft ¼ in |
| 1984 | Carl Lewis, United States | 28 ft ¼ in |
| 1988 | Carl Lewis, United States | 28 ft 7½ in |
| 1992 | Carl Lewis, United States | 28 ft 5½ in |
| 1996 | Carl Lewis, United States | 27 ft 10¾ in |
| 2000 | Ivan Pedrosa, Cuba | 28 ft ¾ in |

### TRIPLE JUMP

| | | |
|---|---|---|
| 1896 | James Connolly, United States | 44 ft 11¾ in |
| 1900 | Meyer Prinstein, United States | 47 ft 5¾ in OR |
| 1904 | Meyer Prinstein, United States | 47 ft 1 in |
| 1906 | Peter O'Connor, Great Britain/Ireland | 46 ft 2¼ in |
| 1908 | Timothy Ahearne, Great Britain/Ireland | 48 ft 11¼ in OR |
| 1912 | Gustaf Lindblom, Sweden | 48 ft 5¼ in |
| 1920 | Vilho Tuulos, Finland | 47 ft 7 in |
| 1924 | Anthony Winter, Australia | 50 ft 11¼ in WR |
| 1928 | Mikio Oda, Japan | 49 ft 11 in |
| 1932 | Chuhei Nambu, Japan | 51 ft 7 in WR |
| 1936 | Naoto Tajima, Japan | 52 ft 6 in WR |
| 1948 | Arne Ahman, Sweden | 50 ft 6¼ in |
| 1952 | Adhemar da Silva, Brazil | 53 ft 2¾ in WR |
| 1956 | Adhemar da Silva, Brazil | 53 ft 7¾ in OR |
| 1960 | Jozef Schmidt, Poland | 55 ft 2 in |
| 1964 | Jozef Schmidt, Poland | 55 ft 3½ in OR |
| 1968 | Viktor Saneyev, USSR | 57 ft ¾ in WR |
| 1972 | Viktor Saneyev, USSR | 56 ft 11¾ in |
| 1976 | Viktor Saneyev, USSR | 56 ft 8¾ in |
| 1980 | Jaak Uudmae, USSR | 56 ft 11¼ in |
| 1984 | Al Joyner, United States | 56 ft 7½ in |
| 1988 | Khristo Markov, Bulgaria | 57 ft 9½ in OR |
| 1992 | Mike Conley, United States | 59 ft 7½ in (w) |
| 1996 | Kenny Harrison, United States | 59 ft 4¼ in OR |
| 2000 | Jonathon Edwards, G. Britain | 58 ft 1¼ in |

### SHOT PUT

| | | |
|---|---|---|
| 1896 | Robert Garrett, United States | 36 ft 9¾ in |
| 1900 | Richard Sheldon, United States | 46 ft 3¼ in OR |
| 1904 | Ralph Rose, United States | 48 ft 7 in WR |
| 1906 | Martin Sheridan, United States | 40 ft 5¼ in |
| 1908 | Ralph Rose, United States | 46 ft 7½ in |
| 1912 | Pat McDonald, United States | 50 ft 4 in OR |
| 1920 | Ville Porhola, Finland | 48 ft 7¼ in |
| 1924 | Clarence Houser, United States | 49 ft 2¼ in |
| 1928 | John Kuck, United States | 52 ft ¾ in WR |
| 1932 | Leo Sexton, United States | 52 ft 6 in OR |

### SHOT PUT *(CONT.)*

| | | |
|---|---|---|
| 1936 | Hans Woellke, Germany | 53 ft 1¾ in OR |
| 1948 | Wilbur Thompson, United States | 56 ft 2 in OR |
| 1952 | Parry O'Brien, United States | 57 ft ½ in OR |
| 1956 | Parry O'Brien, United States | 60 ft 11¼ in OR |
| 1960 | William Nieder, United States | 64 ft 6¾ in OR |
| 1964 | Dallas Long, United States | 66 ft 8½ in OR |
| 1968 | Randy Matson, United States | 67 ft 4¾ in |
| 1972 | Wladyslaw Komar, Poland | 69 ft 6 in OR |
| 1976 | Udo Beyer, E Germany | 69 ft ¾ in |
| 1980 | Vladimir Kiselyov, USSR | 70 ft ½ in OR |
| 1984 | Alessandro Andrei, Italy | 69 ft 9 in |
| 1988 | Ulf Timmermann, E Germany | 73 ft 8¾ in OR |
| 1992 | Mike Stulce, United States | 71 ft 2½ in |
| 1996 | Randy Barnes, United States | 70 ft 11 in |
| 2000 | Arsi Harju, Finland | 69 ft 10¼ in |

### DISCUS THROW

| | | |
|---|---|---|
| 1896 | Robert Garrett, United States | 95 ft 7½ in |
| 1900 | Rudolf Bauer, Hungary | 118 ft 3 in OR |
| 1904 | Martin Sheridan, United States | 128 ft 10½ in OR |
| 1906 | Martin Sheridan, United States | 136 ft |
| 1908 | Martin Sheridan, United States | 134 ft 2 in OR |
| 1912 | Armas Taipele, Finland | 148 ft 3 in OR |
| 1920 | Elmer Niklander, Finland | 146 ft 7 in |
| 1924 | Clarence Houser, United States | 151 ft 4 in OR |
| 1928 | Clarence Houser, United States | 155 ft 3 in OR |
| 1932 | John Anderson, United States | 162 ft 4 in OR |
| 1936 | Ken Carpenter, United States | 165 ft 7 in OR |
| 1948 | Adolfo Consolini, Italy | 173 ft 2 in OR |
| 1952 | Sim Iness, United States | 180 ft 6 in OR |
| 1956 | Al Oerter, United States | 184 ft 11 in OR |
| 1960 | Al Oerter, United States | 194 ft 2 in OR |
| 1964 | Al Oerter, United States | 200 ft 1 in OR |
| 1968 | Al Oerter, United States | 212 ft 6 in OR |
| 1972 | Ludvik Danek, Czechoslovakia | 211 ft 3 in |
| 1976 | Mac Wilkins, United States | 221 ft 5 in OR |
| 1980 | Viktor Rashchupkin, USSR | 218 ft 8 in |
| 1984 | Rolf Dannenberg, W Germany | 218 ft 6 in |
| 1988 | Jürgen Schult, E Germany | 225 ft 9 in OR |
| 1992 | Romas Ubartas, Lithuania | 213 ft 8 in |
| 1996 | Lars Riedel, Germany | 227 ft 8 in OR |
| 2000 | Virgilijus Alekna, Lithuania | 227 ft 4 in |

### HAMMER THROW

| | | |
|---|---|---|
| 1900 | John Flanagan, United States | 163 ft 1 in |
| 1904 | John Flanagan, United States | 168 ft 1 in OR |
| 1906 | Not held | |
| 1908 | John Flanagan, United States | 170 ft 4 in OR |
| 1912 | Matt McGrath, United States | 179 ft 7 in OR |
| 1920 | Pat Ryan, United States | 173 ft 5 in |
| 1924 | Fred Tootell, United States | 174 ft 10 in |
| 1928 | Patrick O'Callaghan, Ireland | 168 ft 7 in |
| 1932 | Patrick O'Callaghan, Ireland | 176 ft 11 in |
| 1936 | Karl Hein, Germany | 185 ft 4 in OR |
| 1948 | Imre Nemeth, Hungary | 183 ft 11 in |
| 1952 | Jozsef Csermak, Hungary | 197 ft 11 in WR |
| 1956 | Harold Connolly, United States | 207 ft 3 in OR |
| 1960 | Vasily Rudenkov, USSR | 220 ft 2 in OR |
| 1964 | Romuald Klim, USSR | 228 ft 10 in OR |
| 1968 | Gyula Zsivotsky, Hungary | 240 ft 8 in OR |
| 1972 | Anatoli Bondarchuk, USSR | 247 ft 8 in OR |
| 1976 | Yuri Sedykh, USSR | 254 ft 4 in OR |
| 1980 | Yuri Sedykh, USSR | 268 ft 4 in WR |
| 1984 | Juha Tiainen, Finland | 256 ft 2 in |
| 1988 | Sergei Litvinov, USSR | 278 ft 2 in OR |

## TRACK AND FIELD *(Cont.)*
### Men *(Cont.)*

**HAMMER THROW (CONT.)**

| | | |
|---|---|---|
| 1992...Andrey Abduvaliyev, Unified Team | 270 ft 9 in | |
| 1996...Balazs Kiss, Hungary | 266 ft 6 in | |
| 2000...Szymon Ziolkowski, Poland | 262 ft 6 in | |

**JAVELIN**

| | |
|---|---|
| 1908...Erik Lemming, Sweden | 179 ft 10 in |
| 1912...Erik Lemming, Sweden | 198 ft 11 in WR |
| 1920...Jonni Myyrä, Finland | 215 ft 10 in OR |
| 1924...Jonni Myyrä, Finland | 206 ft 6 in |
| 1928...Eric Lundkvist, Sweden | 218 ft 6 in OR |
| 1932...Matti Jarvinen, Finland | 238 ft 6 in OR |
| 1936...Gerhard Stöck, Germany | 235 ft 8 in |
| 1948...Kai Rautavaara, Finland | 228 ft 10½ in |
| 1952...Cy Young, United States | 242 ft 1 in OR |
| 1956...Egil Danielson, Norway | 281 ft 2¼ in WR |
| 1960...Viktor Tsibulenko, USSR | 277 ft 8 in |
| 1964...Pauli Nevala, Finland | 271 ft 2 in |
| 1968...Janis Lusis, USSR | 295 ft 7 in OR |
| 1972...Klaus Wolfermann, W Germany | 296 ft 10 in OR |
| 1976...Miklos Nemeth, Hungary | 310 ft 4 in WR |
| 1980...Dainis Kuta, USSR | 299 ft 2⅜ in |
| 1984...Arto Härkönen, Finland | 284 ft 8 in |
| 1988...Tapio Korjus, Finland | 276 ft 6 in |
| 1992...Jan Zelezny, Czechoslovakia | 294 ft 2 in OR |
| 1996...Jan Zelezny, Czech Republic | 289 ft 3 in |
| 2000...Jan Zelezny, Czech Republic | 295 ft 9½ in OR |

**DECATHLON**

| | Pts |
|---|---|
| 1904 ...Thomas Kiely, Ireland | 6036 |
| 1912 ...Jim Thorpe, United States* | 8412 WR |
| 1920 ...Helge Lövland, Norway | 6803 |
| 1924 ...Harold Osborn, United States | 7711 WR |
| 1928 ...Paavo Yrjölä, Finland | 8053.29 WR |
| 1932 ...James Bausch, United States | 8462 WR |
| 1936 ...Glenn Morris, United States | 7900 WR |
| 1948 ...Robert Mathias, United States | 7139 |
| 1952 ...Robert Mathias, United States | 7887 WR |
| 1956 ...Milton Campbell, United States | 7937 OR |
| 1960 ...Rafer Johnson, United States | 8392 OR |
| 1964 ...Willi Holdorf, W Germany | 7887 |
| 1968 ...Bill Toomey, United States | 8193 OR |
| 1972 ...Nikolai Avilov, USSR | 8454 WR |
| 1976 ...Bruce Jenner, United States | 8617 WR |
| 1980 ...Daley Thompson, Great Britain | 8495 |
| 1984 ...Daley Thompson, Great Britain | 8798 EWR |
| 1988 ...Christian Schenk, E Germany | 8488 |
| 1992 ...Robert Zmelik, Czechoslovakia | 8611 |
| 1996 ...Dan O'Brien, United States | 8824 OR |
| 2000 ...Erki Nool, Estonia | 8641 |

*In 1913, Thorpe was disqualified for having played professional baseball in 1910. His record was restored in 1982.

### Women

**100 METERS**

| | |
|---|---|
| 1928 ....Elizabeth Robinson, United States | 12.2 EWR |
| 1932 ....Stella Walsh, Poland | 11.9 EWR |
| 1936 ....Helen Stephens, United States | 11.5 |
| 1948 ....Francina Blankers-Koen, Netherlands | 11.9 |
| 1952 ....Marjorie Jackson, Australia | 11.5 EWR |
| 1956 ....Betty Cuthbert, Australia | 11.5 EWR |
| 1960 ....Wilma Rudolph, United States | 11.0 |
| 1964 ....Wyomia Tyus, United States | 11.4 |
| 1968 ....Wyomia Tyus, United States | 11.0 WR |
| 1972 ....Renate Stecher, E Germany | 11.07 |
| 1976 ....Annegret Richter, W Germany | 11.08 |
| 1980 ....Lyudmila Kondratyeva, USSR | 11.06 |
| 1984 ....Evelyn Ashford, United States | 10.97 OR |
| 1988 ....Florence Griffith Joyner, United States | 10.54 WR |
| 1992 ....Gail Devers, United States | 10.82 |
| 1996 ....Gail Devers, United States | 10.94 |
| 2000 ....Marion Jones, United States | 10.75 |

**200 METERS**

| | |
|---|---|
| 1948 ....Francina Blankers-Koen, Netherlands | 24.4 |
| 1952 ....Marjorie Jackson, Australia | 23.7 |
| 1956 ....Betty Cuthbert, Australia | 23.4 EOR |
| 1960 ....Wilma Rudolph, United States | 24.0 |
| 1964 ....Edith McGuire, United States | 23.0 OR |
| 1968 ....Irena Szewinska, Poland | 22.5 WR |
| 1972 ....Renate Stecher, E Germany | 22.40 EWR |
| 1976 ....Bärbel Eckert, E Germany | 22.37 OR |
| 1980 ....Bärbel Wöckel (Eckert), E Germ. | 22.03 OR |
| 1984 ....Valerie Brisco-Hooks, U.S. | 21.81 OR |

**200 METERS *(CONT.)***

| | |
|---|---|
| 1988 ....Florence Griffith Joyner, U.S. | 21.34 WR |
| 1992 ....Gwen Torrence, United States | 21.81 |
| 1996 ....Marie-José Pérec, France | 22.12 |
| 2000 ....Marion Jones, United States | 21.84 |

**400 METERS**

| | |
|---|---|
| 1964 ....Betty Cuthbert, Australia | 52.0 OR |
| 1968 ....Colette Besson, France | 52.0 EOR |
| 1972 ....Monika Zehrt, E Germany | 51.08 OR |
| 1976 ....Irena Szewinska, Poland | 49.29 WR |
| 1980 ....Marita Koch, E Germany | 48.88 OR |
| 1984 ....Valerie Brisco-Hooks, United States | 48.83 OR |
| 1988 ....Olga Bryzgina, USSR | 48.65 OR |
| 1992 ....Marie-José Pérec, France | 48.83 |
| 1996 ....Marie-José Pérec, France | 48.25 OR |
| 2000 ....Cathy Freeman, Australia | 49.11 |

**800 METERS**

| | |
|---|---|
| 1928 ....Lina Radke, Germany | 2:16.8 WR |
| 1932 ....Not held 1932–1956 | |
| 1960 ....Lyudmila Shevtsova, USSR | 2:04.3 EWR |
| 1964 ....Ann Packer, Great Britain | 2:01.1 OR |
| 1968 ....Madeline Manning, United States | 2:00.9 OR |
| 1972 ....Hildegard Falck, W Germany | 1:58.55 OR |
| 1976 ....Tatyana Kazankina, USSR | 1:54.94 WR |
| 1980 ....Nadezhda Olizarenko, USSR | 1:53.42 WR |
| 1984 ....Doina Melinte, Romania | 1:57.6 |
| 1988 ....Sigrun Wodars, E Germany | 1:56.10 |
| 1992 ....Ellen Van Langen, Netherlands | 1:55.54 |
| 1996 ....Svetlana Masterkova, Russia | 1:57.73 |
| 2000 ....Maria Mutola, Mozambique | 1:56.15 |

Note: OR=Olympic Record. WR=World Record. EOR=Equals Olympic Record. EWR=Equals World Record. WB=World Best.

### TRACK AND FIELD *(Cont.)*
### Women *(Cont.)*

**1,500 METERS**

| | | |
|---|---|---|
| 1972....Lyudmila Bragina, USSR | 4:01.4 WR |
| 1976....Tatyana Kazankina, USSR | 4:05.48 |
| 1980....Tatyana Kazankina, USSR | 3:56.6 OR |
| 1984....Gabriella Dorio, Italy | 4:03.25 |
| 1988....Paula Ivan, Romania | 3:53.96 OR |
| 1992....Hassiba Boulmerka, Algeria | 3:55.30 |
| 1996....Svetlana Masterkova, Russia | 4:00.83 |
| 2000....Nouria Merah-Benida, Algeria | 4:05.10 |

**3,000 METERS**

| | |
|---|---|
| 1984....Maricica Puica, Romania | 8:35.96 OR |
| 1988....Tatyana Samolenko, USSR | 8:26.53 OR |
| 1992....Elena Romanova, Unified Team | 8:46.04 |

**5,000 METERS**

| | |
|---|---|
| 1996....Wang Junxia, China | 14:57.88 |
| 2000....Gabriela Szabo, Romania | 14:40.79 OR |

**10,000 METERS**

| | |
|---|---|
| 1988....Olga Bondarenko, USSR | 31:05.21 OR |
| 1992....Derartu Tulu, Ethiopia | 31:06.02 |
| 1996....Fernanda Ribeiro, Portugal | 31:01.63 OR |
| 2000....Derartu Tulu, Ethiopia | 30:17.49 OR |

**MARATHON**

| | |
|---|---|
| 1984....Joan Benoit, United States | 2:24:52 OR |
| 1988....Rosa Mota, Portugal | 2:25:40 |
| 1992....Valentin Yegorova, Unified Team | 2:32:41 |
| 1996....Fatuma Roba, Ethiopia | 2:26:05 |
| 2000....Naoko Takahashi, Japan | 2:23.14 OR |

**80-METER HURDLES**

| | |
|---|---|
| 1932....Babe Didrikson, United States | 11.7 WR |
| 1936....Trebisonda Valla, Italy | 11.7 |
| 1948....Francina Blankers-Koen, Netherlands | 11.2 OR |
| 1952....Shirley Strickland, Australia | 10.9 WR |
| 1956....Shirley Strickland, Australia | 10.7 OR |
| 1960....Irina Press, USSR | 10.8 |
| 1964....Karin Balzer, E Germany | 10.5 |
| 1968....Maureen Caird, Australia | 10.3 OR |

**100-METER HURDLES**

| | |
|---|---|
| 1972....Annelie Ehrhardt, E Germany | 12.59 WR |
| 1976....Johanna Schaller, E Germany | 12.77 |
| 1980....Vera Komisova, USSR | 12.56 OR |
| 1984....Benita Fitzgerald-Brown, United States | 12.84 |
| 1988....Yordanka Donkova, Bulgaria | 12.38 OR |
| 1992....Paraskevi Patoulidou, Greece | 12.64 |
| 1996....Lyudmila Engqvist, Sweden | 12.58 |
| 2000....Olga Shishigina, Kazakhstan | 12.65 |

**400-METER HURDLES**

| | |
|---|---|
| 1984....Nawal el Moutawakel, Morocco | 54.61 OR |
| 1988....Debra Flintoff-King, Australia | 53.17 OR |
| 1992....Sally Gunnell, Great Britain | 53.23 |
| 1996....Deon Hemmings, Jamaica | 52.82 OR |
| 2000....Irina Privalova, Russia | 53.02 |

**4 X 100-METER RELAY**

| | | |
|---|---|---|
| 1928 .................Canada | 48.4 WR |
| 1932 .................United States | 46.9 WR |
| 1936 .................United States | 46.9 |
| 1948 .................Netherlands | 47.5 |
| 1952 .................United States | 45.9 WR |
| 1956 .................Australia | 44.5 WR |

**4 X 100-METER RELAY** *(CONT.)*

| | |
|---|---|
| 1960 .................United States | 44.5 |
| 1964 .................Poland | 43.6 |
| 1968 .................United States | 42.8 WR |
| 1972 .................W Germany | 42.81 EWR |
| 1976 .................E Germany | 42.55 OR |
| 1980 .................E Germany | 41.60 WR |
| 1984 .................United States | 41.65 |
| 1988 .................United States | 41.98 |
| 1992 .................United States | 42.11 |
| 1996 .................United States | 41.95 |
| 2000 .................Bahamas | 41.95 |

**4 X 400-METER RELAY**

| | |
|---|---|
| 1972 .................E Germany | 3:23 WR |
| 1976 .................E Germany | 3:19.23 WR |
| 1980 .................USSR | 3:20.02 |
| 1984 .................United States | 3:18.29 OR |
| 1988 .................USSR | 3:15.18 WR |
| 1992 .................Unified Team | 3:20.20 |
| 1996 .................United States | 3:20.91 |
| 2000 .................United States | 3:22.62 |

**10-KILOMETER WALK**

| | |
|---|---|
| 1992....Chen Yueling, China | 44:32 |
| 1996....Elena Nikolayeva, Russia | 41:49 OR |

**20-KILOMETER WALK**

| | |
|---|---|
| 2000....Liping Wang, China | 1:29.05 |

**HIGH JUMP**

| | |
|---|---|
| 1928...Ethel Catherwood, Canada | 5 ft 2½ in |
| 1932...Jean Shiley, United States | 5 ft 5¼ in WR |
| 1936...Ibolya Csak, Hungary | 5 ft 3 in |
| 1948...Alice Coachman, United States | 5 ft 6 in OR |
| 1952...Esther Brand, South Africa | 5 ft 5¾ in |
| 1956...Mildred L. McDaniel, U.S. | 5 ft 9¼ in WR |
| 1960...Iolanda Balas, Romania | 6 ft ¾ in OR |
| 1964...Iolanda Balas, Romania | 6 ft 2¾ in OR |
| 1968...Miloslava Reskova, Czech. | 5 ft 11½ in |
| 1972...Ulrike Meyfarth, W. Germany | 6 ft 3½ in EWR |
| 1976...Rosemarie Ackermann, E Germ | 6 ft 4 in OR |
| 1980...Sara Simeoni, Italy | 6 ft 5½ in OR |
| 1984...Ulrike Meyfarth, W Germany | 6 ft 7½ in OR |
| 1988...Louise Ritter, United States | 6 ft 8 in OR |
| 1992...Heike Henkel, Germany | 6 ft 7½ in |
| 1996...Stefka Kostadinova, Bulgaria | 6 ft 8¾ in OR |
| 2000...Yelena Yelesina, Russia | 6 ft 7 in |

**LONG JUMP**

| | |
|---|---|
| 1948...Olga Gyarmati, Hungary | 18 ft 8¼ in |
| 1952...Yvette Williams, New Zealand | 20 ft 5¾ in OR |
| 1956...Elzbieta Krzeskinska, Poland | 20 ft 10 in EWR |
| 1960...Vyera Krepkina, USSR | 20 ft 10¾ in OR |
| 1964...Mary Rand, Great Britain | 22 ft 2¼ in WR |
| 1968...Viorica Viscopoleanu, Romania | 22 ft 4½ in WR |
| 1972...Heidemarie Rosendahl, W Germany | 22 ft 3 in |
| 1976...Angela Voigt, E Germany | 22 ft ¾ in |
| 1980...Tatyana Kolpakova, USSR | 23 ft 2 in OR |
| 1984...Anisoara Stanciu, Romania | 22 ft 10 in |
| 1988...Jackie Joyner-Kersee, United States | 24 ft 3½ in OR |
| 1992...Heike Drechsler, Germany | 23 ft 5¼ in |
| 1996...Chioma Ajunwa, Nigeria | 23 ft 4½ in |
| 2000...Heike Drechsler, Germany | 22 ft 11¼ in |

Note: OR=Olympic Record; WR=World Record; EOR=Equals Olympic Record; EWR=Equals World Record; WB=World Best.

## TRACK AND FIELD (Cont.)
### Women (Cont.)

**TRIPLE JUMP**

| | | |
|---|---|---|
| 1996 | Inessa Kravets, Ukraine | 50 ft 3½ in |
| 2000 | Tereza Marinova, Bulgaria | 49 ft 10½ in |

**SHOT PUT**

| | | |
|---|---|---|
| 1948 | Micheline Ostermeyer, France | 45 ft 1½ in |
| 1952 | Galina Zybina, USSR | 50 ft 1¾ in WR |
| 1956 | Tamara Tyshkevich, USSR | 54 ft 5 in OR |
| 1960 | Tamara Press, USSR | 56 ft 10 in OR |
| 1964 | Tamara Press, USSR | 59 ft 6¼ in OR |
| 1968 | Margitta Gummel, E Germany | 64 ft 4 in WR |
| 1972 | Nadezhda Chizhova, USSR | 69 ft WR |
| 1976 | Ivanka Hristova, Bulgaria | 69 ft 5¼ in OR |
| 1980 | Ilona Slupianek, E Germany | 73 ft 6¼ in |
| 1984 | Claudia Losch, W Germany | 67 ft 2¼ in |
| 1988 | Natalya Lisovskaya, USSR | 72 ft 11¾ in |
| 1992 | Svetlana Kriveleva, Unified Team | 69 ft 1¼ in |
| 1996 | Astrid Kumbernuss, Germany | 67 ft 5½ in |
| 2000 | Yanina Korolchik, Belarus | 67 ft 5½ in |

**DISCUS THROW**

| | | |
|---|---|---|
| 1928 | Helena Konopacka, Poland | 129 ft 11¾ in WR |
| 1932 | Lillian Copeland, United States | 133 ft 2 in OR |
| 1936 | Gisela Mauermayer, Germany | 156 ft 3 in OR |
| 1948 | Micheline Ostermeyer, France | 137 ft 6 in |
| 1952 | Nina Romaschkova, USSR | 168 ft 8 in OR |
| 1956 | Olga Fikotova, Czechoslovakia | 176 ft 1 in OR |
| 1960 | Nina Ponomaryeva, USSR | 180 ft 9 in OR |
| 1964 | Tamara Press, USSR | 187 ft 10 in OR |
| 1968 | Lia Manoliu, Romania | 191 ft 2 in OR |
| 1972 | Faina Melnik, USSR | 218 ft 7 in OR |
| 1976 | Evelin Schlaak, E Germany | 226 ft 4 in OR |
| 1980 | Evelin Jahl (Schlaak), E Germ. | 229 ft 6 in OR |
| 1984 | Ria Stalman, Netherlands | 214 ft 5 in |
| 1988 | Martina Hellmann, E Germany | 237 ft 2 in OR |
| 1992 | Maritza Martén, Cuba | 229 ft 10 in |
| 1996 | Ilke Wyludda, Germany | 228 ft 6 in |
| 2000 | Ellina Zvereva, Belarus | 224 ft 5 in |

**HAMMER THROW**

| | | |
|---|---|---|
| 2000 | Kamila Skolimowska, Russia | 233 ft 5 in OR |

**JAVELIN THROW**

| | | |
|---|---|---|
| 1932 | Babe Didrikson, United States | 143 ft 4 in OR |
| 1936 | Tilly Fleischer, Germany | 148 ft 3 in OR |
| 1948 | Herma Bauma, Austria | 149 ft 6 in |
| 1952 | Dana Zatopkova, Czechoslovakia | 165 ft 7 in |
| 1956 | Inese Jaunzeme, USSR | 176 ft 8 in |
| 1960 | Elvira Ozolina, USSR | 183 ft 8 in OR |
| 1964 | Mihaela Penes, Romania | 198 ft 7 in |
| 1968 | Angela Nemeth, Hungary | 198 ft |
| 1972 | Ruth Fuchs, E Germany | 209 ft 7 in OR |
| 1976 | Ruth Fuchs, E Germany | 216 ft 4 in OR |
| 1980 | Maria Colon, Cuba | 224 ft 5 in OR |
| 1984 | Tessa Sanderson, Great Britain | 228 ft 2 in OR |
| 1988 | Petra Felke, E Germany | 245 ft OR |
| 1992 | Silke Renk, Germany | 224 ft 2 in |
| 1996 | Heli Rantanen, Finland | 222 ft 11 in |
| 2000 | Trine Hattestad, Norway | 226 ft ½ in OR |

**PENTATHLON**

| | | Pts |
|---|---|---|
| 1964 | Irina Press, USSR | 5246 WR |
| 1968 | Ingrid Becker, W Germany | 5098 |
| 1972 | Mary Peters, Great Britain | 4801 WR* |
| 1976 | Siegrun Siegl, E Germany | 4745 |
| 1980 | Nadezhda Tkachenko, USSR | 5083 WR |

**HEPTATHLON**

| | | Pts |
|---|---|---|
| 1984 | Glynis Nunn, Australia | 6390 OR |
| 1988 | Jackie Joyner-Kersee, U.S. | 7291 WR |
| 1992 | Jackie Joyner-Kersee, U.S. | 7044 |
| 1996 | Ghada Shouaa, Syria | 6780 |
| 2000 | Denise Lewis, Great Britain | 6584 |

## BASKETBALL
### Men

**1936**
Final: United States 19, Canada 8
United States: Ralph Bishop, Joe Fortenberry, Carl Knowles, Jack Ragland, Carl Shy, William Wheatley, Francis Johnson, Samuel Balter, John Gibbons, Frank Lubin, Arthur Mollner, Donald Piper, Duane Swanson, Willard Schmidt

**1948**
Final: United States 65, France 21
United States: Cliff Barker, Don Barksdale, Ralph Beard, Lewis Beck, Vince Boryla, Gordon Carpenter, Alex Groza, Wallace Jones, Bob Kurland, Ray Lumpp, Robert Pitts, Jesse Renick, Bob Robinson, Ken Rollins

**1952**
Final: United States 36, USSR 25
United States: Charles Hoag, Bill Hougland, Melvin Dean Kelley, Bob Kenney, Clyde Lovellette, Marcus Freiberger, Victor Wayne Glasgow, Frank McCabe, Daniel Pippen, Howard Williams, Ronald Bontemps, Bob Kurland, William Lienhard, John Keller

**1956**
Final: United States 89, USSR 55
United States: Carl Cain, Bill Hougland, K.C. Jones, Bill Russell, James Walsh, William Evans, Burdette Haldorson, Ron Tomsic, Dick Boushka, Gilbert Ford, Bob Jeangerard, Charles Darling

**1960**
Final: United States 90, Brazil 63
United States: Jay Arnette, Walt Bellamy, Bob Boozer, Terry Dischinger, Jerry Lucas, Oscar Robertson, Adrian Smith, Burdette Haldorson, Darrall Imhoff, Allen Kelley, Lester Lane, Jerry West

**1964**
Final: United States 73, USSR 59
United States: Jim Barnes, Bill Bradley, Larry Brown, Joe Caldwell, Mel Counts, Richard Davies, Walt Hazzard, Lucius Jackson, John McCaffrey, Jeff Mullins, Jerry Shipp, George Wilson

**1968**
Final: United States 65, Yugoslavia 50
United States: John Clawson, Ken Spain, Jo-Jo White, Michael Barrett, Spencer Haywood, Charles Scott, William Hosket, Calvin Fowler, Michael Silliman, Glynn Saulters, James King, Donald Dee

**1972**
Final: USSR 51, United States 50
United States: Kenneth Davis, Doug Collins, Thomas Henderson, Mike Bantom, Bobby Jones, Dwight Jones, James Forbes, James Brewer, Tom Burleson, Tom McMillen, Kevin Joyce, Ed Ratleff

## BASKETBALL (Cont.)
### Men (Cont.)

**1976**
Final: United States 95, Yugoslavia 74
United States: Phil Ford, Steve Sheppard, Adrian Dantley, Walter Davis, Quinn Buckner, Ernie Grunfield, Kenny Carr, Scott May, Michel Armstrong, Tom La Garde, Phil Hubbard, Mitch Kupchak

**1980**
Final: Yugoslavia 86, Italy 77
U.S. participated in boycott.

**1984**
Final: United States 96, Spain 65
United States: Steve Alford, Leon Wood, Patrick Ewing, Vern Fleming, Alvin Robertson, Michael Jordan, Joe Kleine, Jon Koncak, Wayman Tisdale, Chris Mullin, Sam Perkins, Jeff Turner

**1988**
Final: USSR 76, Yugoslavia 63
United States (3rd): Mitch Richmond, Charles E. Smith IV, Vernell Coles, Hersey Hawkins, Jeff Grayer, Charles D. Smith, Willie Anderson, Stacey Augmon, Dan Majerle, Danny Manning, J.R. Reid, David Robinson

**1992**
Final: United States 117, Croatia 85
United States: David Robinson, Christian Laettner, Patrick Ewing, Larry Bird, Scottie Pippen, Michael Jordan, Clyde Drexler, Karl Malone, John Stockton, Chris Mullin, Charles Barkley, Earvin Johnson

**1996**
Final: United States 95, Yugoslavia 69
United States: Charles Barkley, Anfernee Hardaway, Grant Hill, Karl Malone, Reggie Miller, Hakeem Olajuwon, Shaquille O'Neal, Scottie Pippen, Mitch Richmond, John Stockton, David Robinson, Gary Payton

**2000**
Final: United States 85, France 75
United States: Shareef Abdur-Rahim, Ray Allen, Vin Baker, Vince Carter, Kevin Garnett, Tim Hardaway, Allan Houston, Jason Kidd, Antonio McDyess, Alonzo Mourning, Gary Payton, Steve Smith

### Women

**1976**
Gold, USSR; Silver, United States*
United States: Cindy Brogdon, Susan Rojcewicz, Ann Meyers, Lusia Harris, Nancy Dunkle, Charlotte Lewis, Nancy Lieberman, Gail Marquis, Patricia Roberts, Mary Anne O'Connor, Patricia Head, Julienne Simpson

*In 1976 the women played a round-robin tournament, with the gold medal going to the team with the best record. The USSR won with a 5–0 record, and the USA, with a 3–2 record, was given the silver by virtue of a 95–79 victory over Bulgaria, which was also 3–2.

**1980**
Final: USSR 104, Bulgaria 73
U.S. participated in boycott.

**1984**
Final: United States 85, Korea 55
United States: Teresa Edwards, Lea Henry, Lynette Woodard, Anne Donovan, Cathy Boswell, Cheryl Miller, Janice Lawrence, Cindy Noble, Kim Mulkey, Denise Curry, Pamela McGee, Carol Menken-Schaudt

**1988**
Final: United States 77, Yugoslavia 70
United States: Teresa Edwards, Mary Ethridge, Cynthia Brown, Anne Donovan, Teresa Weatherspoon, Bridgette Gordon, Victoria Bullett, Andrea Lloyd, Katrina McClain, Jennifer Gillom, Cynthia Cooper, Suzanne McConnell

**1992**
Final: Unified Team 76, China 66
United States (3rd): Teresa Edwards, Teresa Weatherspoon, Victoria Bullett, Katrina McClain, Cynthia Cooper, Suzanne McConnell, Daedra Charles, Clarissa Davis, Tammy Jackson, Vickie Orr, Carolyn Jones, Medina Dixon

**1996**
Final: United States 111, Brazil 87
United States: Jennifer Azzi, Ruthie Bolton, Teresa Edwards, Lisa Leslie, Rebecca Lobo, Katrina McClain, Nikki McCray, Carla McGhee, Dawn Staley, Katy Steding, Sheryl Swoopes, Venus Lacey

**2000**
Final: United States 76, Australia 54
United States: Ruthie Bolton-Holifield, Teresa Edwards, Yolanda Griffith, Chamique Holdsclaw, Lisa Leslie, Nikki McCray, Delisha Milton, Katie Smith, Dawn Staley, Sheryl Swoopes, Natalie Williams, Kara Wolters

## BOXING

| LIGHT FLYWEIGHT (106 LB) | | LIGHT FLYWEIGHT (CONT.) | |
|---|---|---|---|
| 1968 | Francisco Rodriguez, Venezuela | 1988 | Ivailo Hristov, Bulgaria |
| 1972 | Gyorgy Gedo, Hungary | 1992 | Rogelio Marcelo, Cuba |
| 1976 | Jorge Hernandez, Cuba | 1996 | Daniel Petrov, Bulgaria |
| 1980 | Shamil Sabyrov, USSR | 2000 | Brahim Asloum, France |
| 1984 | Paul Gonzalez, United States | | |

## BOXING (Cont.)

### FLYWEIGHT (112 LB)

| | |
|---|---|
| 1904 | George Finnegan, United States |
| 1906–1912 | Not held |
| 1920 | Frank Di Gennara, United States |
| 1924 | Fidel LaBarba, United States |
| 1928 | Antal Kocsis, Hungary |
| 1932 | Istvan Enekes, Hungary |
| 1936 | Willi Kaiser, Germany |
| 1948 | Pascual Perez, Argentina |
| 1952 | Nathan Brooks, United States |
| 1956 | Terence Spinks, Great Britain |
| 1960 | Gyula Torok, Hungary |
| 1964 | Fernando Atzori, Italy |
| 1968 | Ricardo Delgado, Mexico |
| 1972 | Georgi Kostadinov, Bulgaria |
| 1976 | Leo Randolph, United States |
| 1980 | Peter Lessov, Bulgaria |
| 1984 | Steve McCrory, United States |
| 1988 | Kim Kwang Sun, S Korea |
| 1992 | Su Choi Chol, N Korea |
| 1996 | Maikro Romero, Cuba |
| 2000 | Wijan Ponlid, Thailand |

### BANTAMWEIGHT (119 LB)

| | |
|---|---|
| 1904 | Oliver Kirk, United States |
| 1906 | Not held |
| 1908 | A. Henry Thomas, Great Britain |
| 1912 | Not held |
| 1920 | Clarence Walker, S Africa |
| 1924 | William Smith, S Africa |
| 1928 | Vittorio Tamagnini, Italy |
| 1932 | Horace Gwynne, Canada |
| 1936 | Ulderico Sergo, Italy |
| 1948 | Tibor Csik, Hungary |
| 1952 | Pentti Hamalainen, Finland |
| 1956 | Wolfgang Behrendt, E Germany |
| 1960 | Oleg Grigoryev, USSR |
| 1964 | Takao Sakurai, Japan |
| 1968 | Valery Sokolov, USSR |
| 1972 | Orlando Martinez, Cuba |
| 1976 | Yong Jo Gu, N Korea |
| 1980 | Juan Hernandez, Cuba |
| 1984 | Maurizio Stecca, Italy |
| 1988 | Kennedy McKinney, United States |
| 1992 | Joel Casamayor, Cuba |
| 1996 | István Kovács, Hungary |
| 2000 | Guillermo Ortiz, Cuba |

### FEATHERWEIGHT (125 LB)

| | |
|---|---|
| 1904 | Oliver Kirk, United States |
| 1906 | Not held |
| 1908 | Richard Gunn, Great Britain |
| 1912 | Not held |
| 1920 | Paul Fritsch, France |
| 1924 | John Fields, United States |
| 1928 | Lambertus van Klaveren, Netherlands |
| 1932 | Carmelo Robledo, Argentina |
| 1936 | Oscar Casanovas, Argentina |
| 1948 | Ernesto Formenti, Italy |
| 1952 | Jan Zachara, Czechoslovakia |
| 1956 | Vladimir Safronov, USSR |
| 1960 | Francesco Musso, Italy |
| 1964 | Stanislav Stephashkin, USSR |
| 1968 | Antonio Roldan, Mexico |
| 1972 | Boris Kousnetsov, USSR |
| 1976 | Angel Herrera, Cuba |
| 1980 | Rudi Fink, E Germany |
| 1984 | Meldrick Taylor, United States |
| 1988 | Giovanni Parisi, Italy |
| 1992 | Andreas Tews, Germany |
| 1996 | Somluck Kamsing, Thailand |
| 2000 | Bekzat Sattarkhanox, Kazakhstan |

### LIGHTWEIGHT (132 LB)

| | |
|---|---|
| 1904 | Harry Spanger, United States |
| 1906 | Not held |
| 1908 | Frederick Grace, Great Britain |
| 1912 | Not held |
| 1920 | Samuel Mosberg, United States |
| 1924 | Hans Nielsen, Denmark |
| 1928 | Carlo Orlandi, Italy |
| 1932 | Lawrence Stevens, S Africa |
| 1936 | Imre Harangi, Hungary |
| 1948 | Gerald Dreyer, S Africa |
| 1952 | Aureliano Bolognesi, Italy |
| 1956 | Richard McTaggart, Great Britain |
| 1960 | Kazimierz Pazdzior, Poland |
| 1964 | Jozef Grudzien, Poland |
| 1968 | Ronald Harris, United States |
| 1972 | Jan Szczepanski, Poland |
| 1976 | Howard Davis, United States |
| 1980 | Angel Herrera, Cuba |
| 1984 | Pernell Whitaker, United States |
| 1988 | Andreas Zuelow, E Germany |
| 1992 | Oscar De La Hoya, United States |
| 1996 | Hocine Soltani, Algeria |
| 2000 | Mario Kindelan, Cuba |

### LIGHT WELTERWEIGHT (139 LB)

| | |
|---|---|
| 1952 | Charles Adkins, United States |
| 1956 | Vladimir Yengibaryan, USSR |
| 1960 | Bohumil Nemecek, Czechoslovakia |
| 1964 | Jerzy Kulej, Poland |
| 1968 | Jerzy Kulej, Poland |
| 1972 | Ray Seales, United States |
| 1976 | Ray Leonard, United States |
| 1980 | Patrizio Oliva, Italy |
| 1984 | Jerry Page, United States |
| 1988 | Viatcheslav Janovski, USSR |
| 1992 | Hector Vinent, Cuba |
| 1996 | Hector Vinent, Cuba |
| 2000 | Mahamadkadyz Abdullaev, Uzbekistan |

### WELTERWEIGHT (147 LB)

| | |
|---|---|
| 1904 | Albert Young, United States |
| 1906–1912 | Not held |
| 1920 | Albert Schneider, Canada |
| 1924 | Jean Delarge, Belgium |
| 1928 | Edward Morgan, New Zealand |
| 1932 | Edward Flynn, United States |
| 1936 | Sten Suvio, Finland |
| 1948 | Julius Torma, Czechoslovakia |
| 1952 | Zygmunt Chychla, Poland |
| 1956 | Nicolae Linca, Romania |
| 1960 | Giovanni Benvenuti, Italy |
| 1964 | Marian Kasprzyk, Poland |
| 1968 | Manfred Wolke, E Germany |
| 1972 | Emilio Correa, Cuba |
| 1976 | Jochen Bachfeld, E Germany |
| 1980 | Andres Aldama, Cuba |
| 1984 | Mark Breland, United States |
| 1988 | Robert Wangila, Kenya |
| 1992 | Michael Carruth, Ireland |
| 1996 | Oleg Saitov, Russia |
| 2000 | Oleg Saitov, Russia |

### LIGHT MIDDLEWEIGHT (156 LB)

| | |
|---|---|
| 1952 | Laszlo Papp, Hungary |
| 1956 | Laszlo Papp, Hungary |
| 1960 | Wilbert McClure, United States |
| 1964 | Boris Lagutin, USSR |
| 1968 | Boris Lagutin, USSR |
| 1972 | Dieter Kottysch, W Germany |
| 1976 | Jerzy Rybicki, Poland |
| 1980 | Armando Martinez, Cuba |
| 1984 | Frank Tate, United States |

## BOXING *(Cont.)*

### LIGHT MIDDLEWEIGHT *(CONT.)*
1988 ...............Park Si-Hun, S Korea
1992 ...............Juan Lemus, Cuba
1996 ...............David Reid, United States
2000 ...............Yermakhan Ibraimov, Kazahkstan

### MIDDLEWEIGHT (165 LB)
1904 ...............Charles Mayer, United States
1908 ...............John Douglas, Great Britain
1912 ...............Not held
1920 ...............Harry Mallin, Great Britain
1924 ...............Harry Mallin, Great Britain
1928 ...............Piero Toscani, Italy
1932 ...............Carmen Barth, United States
1936 ...............Jean Despeaux, France
1948 ...............Laszlo Papp, Hungary
1952 ...............Floyd Patterson, United States
1956 ...............Gennady Schatkov, USSR
1960 ...............Edward Crook, United States
1964 ...............Valery Popenchenko, USSR
1968 ...............Christopher Finnegan, Great Britain
1972 ...............Vyacheslav Lemechev, USSR
1976 ...............Michael Spinks, United States
1980 ...............Jose Gomez, Cuba
1984 ...............Shin Joon Sup, S Korea
1988 ...............Henry Maske, E Germany
1992 ...............Ariel Hernandez, Cuba
1996 ...............Ariel Hernandez, Cuba
2000 ...............Jorge Gutierrez, Cuba

### LIGHT HEAVYWEIGHT (178 LB)
1920 ...............Edward Eagan, United States
1924 ...............Harry Mitchell, Great Britain
1928 ...............Victor Avendano, Argentina
1932 ...............David Carstens, S Africa
1936 ...............Roger Michelot, France
1948 ...............George Hunter, S Africa
1952 ...............Norvel Lee, United States
1956 ...............James Boyd, United States
1960 ...............Cassius Clay, United States
1964 ...............Cosimo Pinto, Italy
1968 ...............Dan Poznyak, USSR
1972 ...............Mate Parlov, Yugoslavia
1976 ...............Leon Spinks, United States

### LIGHT HEAVYWEIGHT *(CONT.)*
1980 ...............Slobodan Kacer, Yugoslavia
1984 ...............Anton Josipovic, Yugoslavia
1988 ...............Andrew Maynard, United States
1992 ...............Torsten May, Germany
1996 ...............Vassili Jirov, Kazakhstan
2000 ...............Alexander Lebziak, Russia

### HEAVYWEIGHT (OVER 201 LB)
1904 ...............Samuel Berger, United States
1906 ...............Not held
1908 ...............Albert Oldham, Great Britain
1912 ...............Not held
1920 ...............Ronald Rawson, Great Britain
1924 ...............Otto von Porat, Norway
1928 ...............Arturo Rodriguez Jurado, Argentina
1932 ...............Santiago Lovell, Argentina
1936 ...............Herbert Runge, Germany
1948 ...............Rafael Inglesias, Argentina
1952 ...............H. Edward Sanders, United States
1956 ...............T. Peter Rademacher, United States
1960 ...............Franco De Piccoli, Italy
1964 ...............Joe Frazier, United States
1968 ...............George Foreman, United States
1972 ...............Teofilo Stevenson, Cuba
1976 ...............Teofilo Stevenson, Cuba
1980 ...............Teofilo Stevenson, Cuba

### HEAVYWEIGHT (201* LB)
1984 ...............Henry Tillman, United States
1988 ...............Ray Mercer, United States
1992 ...............Félix Sávon, Cuba
1996 ...............Félix Sávon, Cuba
2000 ...............Félix Sávon, Cuba

### SUPERHEAVYWEIGHT (UNLIMITED)
1984 ...............Tyrell Biggs, United States
1988 ...............Lennox Lewis, Canada
1992 ...............Roberto Balado, Cuba
1996 ...............Vladimir Klitchko, Ukraine
2000 ...............Audley Harrison, Great Britain

*Until 1984 the heavyweight division was unlimited. With the addition of the super heavyweight division, a limit of 201 pounds was imposed.

## SWIMMING

### Men

#### 50-METER FREESTYLE
| | | |
|---|---|---|
| 1904 | Zoltan Halmay, Hungary (50 yds) | 28.0 |
| 1988 | Matt Biondi, United States | 22.14 WR |
| 1992 | Aleksandr Popov, Unified Team | 22.30 |
| 1996 | Aleksandr Popov, Russia | 22.13 |
| 2000 | Anthony Ervin, United States | 21.98 |
| | Gary Hall Jr, United States | 21.98 |

#### 100-METER FREESTLYE
| | | |
|---|---|---|
| 1896 | Alfred Hajos, Hungary | 1:22.2 OR |
| 1904 | Zoltan Halmay, Hungary (100 yds) | 1:02.8 |
| 1906 | Charles Daniels, United States | 1:13.4 |
| 1908 | Charles Daniels, United States | 1:05.6 WR |
| 1912 | Duke Kahanamoku, United States | 1:03.4 |
| 1920 | Duke Kahanamoku, United States | 1:00.4 WR |
| 1924 | John Weissmuller, United States | 59.0 OR |
| 1928 | John Weissmuller, United States | 58.6 OR |
| 1932 | Yasuji Miyazaki, Japan | 58.2 |

#### 100-METER FREESTLYE *(CONT.)*
| | | |
|---|---|---|
| 1936 | Ferenc Csik, Hungary | 57.6 |
| 1948 | Wally Ris, United States | 57.3 OR |
| 1952 | Clarke Scholes, United States | 57.4 |
| 1956 | Jon Henricks, Australia | 55.4 OR |
| 1960 | John Devitt, Australia | 55.2 OR |
| 1964 | Don Schollander, United States | 53.4 OR |
| 1968 | Mike Wenden, Australia | 52.2 WR |
| 1972 | Mark Spitz, United States | 51.22 WR |
| 1976 | Jim Montgomery, United States | 49.99 WR |
| 1980 | Jörg Woithe, E Germany | 50.40 |
| 1984 | Rowdy Gaines, United States | 49.80 OR |
| 1988 | Matt Biondi, United States | 48.63 OR |
| 1992 | Aleksandr Popov, Unified Team | 49.02 |
| 1996 | Aleksandr Popov, Russia | 48.74 |
| 2000 | P. van den Hoogenband, Neth. | 48.30 |

Note: OR=Olympic Record. WR=World Record. EOR=Equals Olympic Record. EWR=Equals World Record. WB=World Best.

## SWIMMING (Cont.)
### Men (Cont.)

### 200-METER FREESTYLE

| | | |
|---|---|---|
| 1900 | Frederick Lane, Australia | 2:25.2 OR |
| 1904 | Charles Daniels, United States | 2:44.2 |
| 1906–1964 | Not held | |
| 1968 | Michael Wenden, Australia | 1:55.2 OR |
| 1972 | Mark Spitz, United States | 1:52.78 WR |
| 1976 | Bruce Furniss, United States | 1:50.29 WR |
| 1980 | Sergei Kopliakov, USSR | 1:49.81 OR |
| 1984 | Michael Gross, W Germany | 1:47.44 WR |
| 1988 | Duncan Armstrong, Australia | 1:47.25 WR |
| 1992 | Evgueni Sadovyi, Unified Team | 1:46.70 OR |
| 1996 | Danyon Loader, New Zealand | 1:47.63 |
| 2000 | Pieter van den Hoogenband, Netherlands | 1:45.35 EWR |

### 400-METER FREESTYLE

| | | |
|---|---|---|
| 1896 | Paul Neumann, Austria (500 yds) | 8:12.6 |
| 1904 | Charles Daniels, U.S. (440 yds) | 6:16.2 |
| 1906 | Otto Scheff, Austria (440 yds) | 6:23.8 |
| 1908 | Henry Taylor, Great Britain | 5:36.8 |
| 1912 | George Hodgson, Canada | 5:24.4 |
| 1920 | Norman Ross, United States | 5:26.8 |
| 1924 | John Weissmuller, United States | 5:04.2 OR |
| 1928 | Albert Zorilla, Argentina | 5:01.6 OR |
| 1932 | Buster Crabbe, United States | 4:48.4 OR |
| 1936 | Jack Medica, United States | 4:44.5 OR |
| 1948 | William Smith, United States | 4:41.0 OR |
| 1952 | Jean Boiteux, France | 4:30.7 OR |
| 1956 | Murray Rose, Australia | 4:27.3 OR |
| 1960 | Murray Rose, Australia | 4:18.3 OR |
| 1964 | Don Schollander, United States | 4:12.2 WR |
| 1968 | Mike Burton, United States | 4:09.0 OR |
| 1972 | Brad Cooper, Australia | 4:00.27 OR |
| 1976 | Brian Goodell, United States | 3:51.93 WR |
| 1980 | Vladimir Salnikov, USSR | 3:51.31 OR |
| 1984 | George DiCarlo, United States | 3:51.23 OR |
| 1988 | Uwe Dassler, E Germany | 3:46.95 WR |
| 1992 | Evgueni Sadovyi, Unified Team | 3:45.00 WR |
| 1996 | Danyon Loader, New Zealand | 3:47.97 |
| 2000 | Ian Thorpe, Australia | 3:40.59 WR |

### 1,500-METER FREESTYLE

| | | |
|---|---|---|
| 1908 | Henry Taylor, Great Britain | 22:48.4 WR |
| 1912 | George Hodgson, Canada | 22:00.0 WR |
| 1920 | Norman Ross, United States | 22:23.2 |
| 1924 | Andrew Charlton, Australia | 20:06.6 WR |
| 1928 | Arne Borg, Sweden | 19:51.8 OR |
| 1932 | Kusuo Kitamura, Japan | 19:12.4 OR |
| 1936 | Noboru Terada, Japan | 19:13.7 |
| 1948 | James McLane, United States | 19:18.5 |
| 1952 | Ford Konno, United States | 18:30.3 OR |
| 1956 | Murray Rose, Australia | 17:58.9 |
| 1960 | John Konrads, Australia | 17:19.6 OR |
| 1964 | Robert Windle, Australia | 17:01.7 OR |
| 1968 | Mike Burton, United States | 16:38.9 OR |
| 1972 | Mike Burton, United States | 15:52.58 OR |
| 1976 | Brian Goodell, United States | 15:02.40 WR |
| 1980 | Vladimir Salnikov, USSR | 14:58.27 WR |
| 1984 | Michael O'Brien, United States | 15:05.20 |
| 1988 | Vladimir Salnikov, USSR | 15:00.40 |
| 1992 | Kieren Perkins, Australia | 14:43.48 WR |
| 1996 | Kieren Perkins, Australia | 14:56.40 |
| 2000 | Grant Hackett, Australia | 14:48.33 |

### 100-METER BACKSTROKE

| | | |
|---|---|---|
| 1904 | Walter Brack, Germany (100 yds) | 1:16.8 |
| 1908 | Arno Bieberstein, Germany | 1:24.6 WR |
| 1912 | Harry Hebner, United States | 1:21.2 |

### 100-METER BACKSTROKE (CONT.)

| | | |
|---|---|---|
| 1920 | Warren Kealoha, United States | 1:15.2 |
| 1924 | Warren Kealoha, United States | 1:13.2 OR |
| 1928 | George Kojac, United States | 1:08.2 WR |
| 1932 | Masaji Kiyokawa, Japan | 1:08.6 |
| 1936 | Adolph Kiefer, United States | 1:05.9 WR |
| 1948 | Allen Stack, United States | 1:06.4 |
| 1952 | Yoshi Oyakawa, United States | 1:05.4 OR |
| 1956 | David Thiele, Australia | 1:02.2 OR |
| 1960 | David Thiele, Australia | 1:01.9 OR |
| 1964 | Not held | |
| 1968 | Roland Matthes, E Germany | 58.7 OR |
| 1972 | Roland Matthes, E Germany | 56.58 OR |
| 1976 | John Naber, United States | 55.49 WR |
| 1980 | Bengt Baron, Sweden | 56.33 |
| 1984 | Rick Carey, United States | 55.79 |
| 1988 | Daichi Suzuki, Japan | 55.05 |
| 1992 | Mark Tewksbury, Canada | 53.98 WR |
| 1996 | Jeff Rouse, United States | 54.10 |
| 2000 | Lenny Krayzelburg, United States | 53.72 OR |

### 200-METER BACKSTROKE

| | | |
|---|---|---|
| 1900 | Ernst Hoppenberg, Germany | 2:47.0 |
| 1906–1960 | Not held | |
| 1964 | Jed Graef, United States | 2:10.3 WR |
| 1968 | Roland Matthes, E Germany | 2:09.6 OR |
| 1972 | Roland Matthes, E Germany | 2:02.82 EWR |
| 1976 | John Naber, United States | 1:59.19 WR |
| 1980 | Sandor Wladar, Hungary | 2:01.93 |
| 1984 | Rick Carey, United States | 2:00.23 |
| 1988 | Igor Polianski, USSR | 1:59.37 |
| 1992 | Martin Lopez-Zubero, Spain | 1:58.47 OR |
| 1996 | Brad Bridgewater, United States | 1:58.54 |
| 2000 | Lenny Krayzelburg, United States | 1:56.76 OR |

### 100-METER BREASTSTROKE

| | | |
|---|---|---|
| 1968 | Don McKenzie, United States | 1:07.7 OR |
| 1972 | Nobutaka Taguchi, Japan | 1:04.94 WR |
| 1976 | John Hencken, United States | 1:03.11 WR |
| 1980 | Duncan Goodhew, Great Britain | 1:03.44 |
| 1984 | Steve Lundquist, United States | 1:01.65 WR |
| 1988 | Adrian Moorhouse, Great Britain | 1:02.04 |
| 1992 | Nelson Diebel, United States | 1:01.50 OR |
| 1996 | Fred DeBurghgraeve, Belgium | 1:00.65 |
| 2000 | Domenico Fioravanti, Italy | 1:00.46 OR |

### 200-METER BREASTSTROKE

| | | |
|---|---|---|
| 1908 | Frederick Holman, Great Britain | 3:09.2 WR |
| 1912 | Walter Bathe, Germany | 3:01.8 OR |
| 1920 | Haken Malmroth, Sweden | 3:04.4 |
| 1924 | Robert Skelton, United States | 2:56.6 |
| 1928 | Yoshiyuki Tsuruta, Japan | 2:48.8 OR |
| 1932 | Yoshiyuki Tsuruta, Japan | 2:45.4 |
| 1936 | Tetsuo Hamuro, Japan | 2:41.5 OR |
| 1948 | Joseph Verdeur, United States | 2:39.3 OR |
| 1952 | John Davies, Australia | 2:34.4 OR |
| 1956 | Masura Furukawa, Japan | 2:34.7 OR |
| 1960 | William Mulliken, United States | 2:37.4 |
| 1964 | Ian O'Brien, Australia | 2:27.8 WR |
| 1968 | Felipe Munoz, Mexico | 2:28.7 |
| 1972 | John Hencken, United States | 2:21.55 WR |
| 1976 | David Wilkie, Great Britain | 2:15.11 WR |
| 1980 | Robertas Zhulpa, USSR | 2:15.85 |
| 1984 | Victor Davis, Canada | 2:13.34 WR |
| 1988 | Jozsef Szabo, Hungary | 2:13.52 |
| 1992 | Mike Barrowman, United States | 2:10.16 WR |
| 1996 | Norbert Rózsa, Hungary | 2:12.57 |
| 2000 | Domenico Fioravanti, Italy | 2:10.87 |

Note: OR=Olympic Record. WR=World Record. EOR=Equals Olympic Record. EWR=Equals World Record. WB=World Best.

## SWIMMING *(Cont.)*

### Men *(Cont.)*

#### 100-METER BUTTERFLY

| | | |
|---|---|---|
| 1968 | Doug Russell, United States | 55.9 OR |
| 1972 | Mark Spitz, United States | 54.27 WR |
| 1976 | Matt Vogel, United States | 54.35 |
| 1980 | Pär Arvidsson, Sweden | 54.92 |
| 1984 | Michael Gross, W Germany | 53.08 WR |
| 1988 | Anthony Nesty, Suriname | 53.00 OR |
| 1992 | Pablo Morales, United States | 53.32 |
| 1996 | Denis Pankratov, Russia | 52.27 WR |
| 2000 | Lars Froelander, Sweden | 52.00 |

#### 200-METER BUTTERFLY

| | | |
|---|---|---|
| 1956 | William Yorzyk, United States | 2:19.3 OR |
| 1960 | Michael Troy, United States | 2:12.8 WR |
| 1964 | Kevin Berry, Australia | 2:06.6 WR |
| 1968 | Carl Robie, United States | 2:08.7 |
| 1972 | Mark Spitz, United States | 2:00.70 WR |
| 1976 | Mike Bruner, United States | 1:59.23 WR |
| 1980 | Sergei Fesenko, USSR | 1:59.76 |
| 1984 | Jon Sieben, Australia | 1:57.04 WR |
| 1988 | Michael Gross, W Germany | 1:56.94 OR |
| 1992 | Melvin Stewart, United States | 1:56.26 OR |
| 1996 | Denis Pankratov, Russia | 1:56.51 |
| 2000 | Tom Malchow, United States | 1:55.35 OR |

#### 200-METER INDIVIDUAL MEDLEY

| | | |
|---|---|---|
| 1968 | Charles Hickcox, United States | 2:12.0 OR |
| 1972 | Gunnar Larsson, Sweden | 2:07.17 WR |
| 1984 | Alex Baumann, Canada | 2:01.42 WR |
| 1988 | Tamas Darnyi, Hungary | 2:00.17 WR |
| 1992 | Tamas Darnyi, Hungary | 2:00.76 |
| 1996 | Attila Czene, Hungary | 1:59.91 OR |
| 2000 | Massimiliano Rosolino, Italy | 1:58.98 OR |

#### 400-METER INDIVIDUAL MEDLEY

| | | |
|---|---|---|
| 1964 | Richard Roth, United States | 4:45.4 WR |
| 1968 | Charles Hickcox, United States | 4:48.4 |
| 1972 | Gunnar Larsson, Sweden | 4:31.98 OR |
| 1976 | Rod Strachan, United States | 4:23.68 WR |
| 1980 | Aleksandr Sidorenko, USSR | 4:22.89 OR |
| 1984 | Alex Baumann, Canada | 4:17.41 WR |
| 1988 | Tamas Darnyi, Hungary | 4:14.75 WR |
| 1992 | Tamas Darnyi, Hungary | 4:14.23 OR |
| 1996 | Tom Dolan United States | 4:14.90 |
| 2000 | Tom Dolan, United States | 4:11.76 WR |

#### 4 X 100-METER MEDLEY RELAY

| | | |
|---|---|---|
| 1960 | United States | 4:05.4 WR |
| 1964 | United States | 3:58.4 WR |
| 1968 | United States | 3:54.9 WR |
| 1972 | United States | 3:48.16 WR |
| 1976 | United States | 3:42.22 WR |
| 1980 | Australia | 3:45.70 |
| 1984 | United States | 3:39.30 WR |
| 1988 | United States | 3:36.93 WR |
| 1992 | United States | 3:36.93 EWR |
| 1996 | United States | 3:34.84 WR |
| 2000 | United States | 3:33.73 WR |

#### 4 X 100-METER FREESTYLE RELAY

| | | |
|---|---|---|
| 1964 | United States | 3:32.2 WR |
| 1968 | United States | 3:31.7 WR |
| 1972 | United States | 3:26.42 WR |
| 1976–1980 | Not held | |
| 1984 | United States | 3:19.03 WR |
| 1988 | United States | 3:16.53 WR |
| 1992 | United States | 3:16.74 |
| 1996 | United States | 3:15.41 OR |
| 2000 | Australia | 3:13.67 WR |

#### 4 X 200-METER FREESTYLE RELAY

| | | |
|---|---|---|
| 1906 | Hungary (1,000 m) | 16:52.4 |
| 1908 | Great Britain | 10:55.6 |
| 1912 | Australia/New Zealand | 10:11.6 WR |
| 1920 | United States | 10:04.4 WR |
| 1924 | United States | 9:53.4 WR |
| 1928 | United States | 9:36.2 WR |
| 1932 | Japan | 8:58.4 WR |
| 1936 | Japan | 8:51.5 WR |
| 1948 | United States | 8:46.0 WR |
| 1952 | United States | 8:31.1 OR |
| 1956 | Australia | 8:23.6 WR |
| 1960 | United States | 8:10.2 WR |
| 1964 | United States | 7:52.1 WR |
| 1968 | United States | 7:52.33 |
| 1972 | United States | 7:35.78 WR |
| 1976 | United States | 7:23.22 WR |
| 1980 | USSR | 7:23.50 |
| 1984 | United States | 7:15.69 WR |
| 1988 | United States | 7:12.51 WR |
| 1992 | Unified Team | 7:11.95 WR |
| 1996 | United States | 7:14.84 |
| 2000 | Australia | 7:07.05 WR |

### Women

#### 50-METER FREESTYLE

| | | |
|---|---|---|
| 1988 | Kristin Otto, E Germany | 25.49 OR |
| 1992 | Yang Wenyi, China | 24.79 WR |
| 1996 | Amy Van Dyken, United States | 24.87 |
| 2000 | Inge de Bruijn, Netherlands | 24.32 WR |

#### 100-METER FREESTYLE

| | | |
|---|---|---|
| 1912 | Fanny Durack, Australia | 1:22.2 |
| 1920 | Ethelda Bleibtrey, United States | 1:13.6 WR |
| 1924 | Ethel Lackie, United States | 1:12.4 |
| 1928 | Albina Osipowich, United States | 1:11.0 OR |
| 1932 | Helene Madison, United States | 1:06.8 OR |
| 1936 | Hendrika Mastenbroek, Netherlands | 1:05.9 WR |
| 1948 | Greta Andersen, Denmark | 1:06.3 |
| 1952 | Katalin Szöke, Hungary | 1:06.8 |
| 1956 | Dawn Fraser, Australia | 1:02.0 WR |
| 1960 | Dawn Fraser, Australia | 1:01.2 OR |
| 1964 | Dawn Fraser, Australia | 59.5 OR |

#### 100-METER FREESTYLE *(CONT.)*

| | | |
|---|---|---|
| 1968 | Jan Henne, United States | 1:00.0 |
| 1972 | Sandra Neilson, United States | 58.59 OR |
| 1976 | Kornelia Ender, E Germany | 55.65 WR |
| 1980 | Barbara Krause, E Germany | 54.79 WR |
| 1984 | Carrie Steinseifer, United States | 55.92 |
| | Nancy Hogshead, United States | 55.92 |
| 1988 | Kristin Otto, E Germany | 54.93 |
| 1992 | Zhuang Yong, China | 54.64 OR |
| 1996 | Le Jingyi, China | 54.50 OR |
| 2000 | Inge de Bruijn, Netherlands | 53.83 OR |

#### 200-METER FREESTYLE

| | | |
|---|---|---|
| 1968 | Debbie Meyer, United States | 2:10.5 OR |
| 1972 | Shane Gould, Australia | 2:03.56 WR |
| 1976 | Kornelia Ender, E Germany | 1:59.26 WR |
| 1980 | Barbara Krause, E Germany | 1:58.33 OR |
| 1984 | Mary Wayte, United States | 1:59.23 |
| 1988 | Heike Friedrich, E Germany | 1:57.65 OR |

Note: OR=Olympic Record. WR=World Record. EOR=Equals Olympic Record. EWR=Equals World Record. WB=World Best.

## SWIMMING (Cont.)
## Women (Cont.)

### 200-METER FREESTYLE (CONT.)

| | | |
|---|---|---|
| 1992 | Nicole Haislett, United States | 1:57.90 |
| 1996 | Claudia Poll, Costa Rica | 1:58.16 |
| 2000 | Susie O'Neill, Australia | 1:58.24 |

### 400-METER FREESTYLE

| | | |
|---|---|---|
| 1924 | Martha Norelius, United States | 6:02.2 OR |
| 1928 | Martha Norelius, United States | 5:42.8 WR |
| 1932 | Helene Madison, United States | 5:28.5 WR |
| 1936 | Hendrika Mastenbroek, Netherlands | 5:26.4 OR |
| 1948 | Ann Curtis, United States | 5:17.8 OR |
| 1952 | Valeria Gyenge, Hungary | 5:12.1 OR |
| 1956 | Lorraine Crapp, Australia | 4:54.6 OR |
| 1960 | Chris von Saltza, United States | 4:50.6 OR |
| 1964 | Virginia Duenkel, United States | 4:43.3 OR |
| 1968 | Debbie Meyer, United States | 4:31.8 OR |
| 1972 | Shane Gould, Australia | 4:19.44 WR |
| 1976 | Petra Thümer, E Germany | 4:09.89 WR |
| 1980 | Ines Diers, E Germany | 4:08.76 WR |
| 1984 | Tiffany Cohen, United States | 4:07.10 OR |
| 1988 | Janet Evans, United States | 4:03.85 WR |
| 1992 | Dagmar Hase, Germany | 4:07.18 |
| 1996 | Michelle Smith, Ireland | 4:07.25 |
| 2000 | Brooke Bennett, United States | 4:05.80 |

### 800-METER FREESTYLE

| | | |
|---|---|---|
| 1968 | Debbie Meyer, United States | 9:24.0 OR |
| 1972 | Keena Rothhammer, United States | 8:53.68 WR |
| 1976 | Petra Thümer, E Germany | 8:37.14 WR |
| 1980 | Michelle Ford, Australia | 8:28.90 OR |
| 1984 | Tiffany Cohen, United States | 8:24.95 OR |
| 1988 | Janet Evans, United States | 8:20.20 OR |
| 1992 | Janet Evans, United States | 8:25.52 |
| 1996 | Brooke Bennett, United States | 8:27.89 |
| 2000 | Brooke Bennett, United States | 8:19.67 OR |

### 100-METER BACKSTROKE

| | | |
|---|---|---|
| 1924 | Sybil Bauer, United States | 1:23.2 OR |
| 1928 | Marie Braun, Netherlands | 1:22.0 |
| 1932 | Eleanor Holm, United States | 1:19.4 |
| 1936 | Dina Senff, Netherlands | 1:18.9 |
| 1948 | Karen Harup, Denmark | 1:14.4 OR |
| 1952 | Joan Harrison, South Africa | 1:14.3 |
| 1956 | Judy Grinham, Great Britain | 1:12.9 OR |
| 1960 | Lynn Burke, United States | 1:09.3 OR |
| 1964 | Cathy Ferguson, United States | 1:07.7 WR |
| 1968 | Kaye Hall, United States | 1:06.2 WR |
| 1972 | Melissa Belote, United States | 1:05.78 OR |
| 1976 | Ulrike Richter, E Germany | 1:01.83 OR |
| 1980 | Rica Reinisch, E Germany | 1:00.86 WR |
| 1984 | Theresa Andrews, United States | 1:02.55 |
| 1988 | Kristin Otto, E Germany | 1:00.89 |
| 1992 | Krisztina Egerszegi, Hungary | 1:00.68 OR |
| 1996 | Beth Botsford, United States | 1:01.19 |
| 2000 | Diana Iuliana Mocanu, Romania | 1:00.21 OR |

### 200-METER BACKSTROKE

| | | |
|---|---|---|
| 1968 | Pokey Watson, United States | 2:24.8 OR |
| 1972 | Melissa Belote, United States | 2:19.19 WR |
| 1976 | Ulrike Richter, E Germany | 2:13.43 OR |
| 1980 | Rica Reinisch, E Germany | 2:11.77 WR |
| 1984 | Jolanda De Rover, Netherlands | 2:12.38 |
| 1988 | Krisztina Egerszegi, Hungary | 2:09.29 OR |
| 1992 | Krisztina Egerszegi, Hungary | 2:07.06 OR |
| 1996 | Krisztina Egerszegi, Hungary | 2:07.83 |
| 2000 | Diana Iuliana Mocanu, Romania | 2:08.16 |

### 100-METER BREASTSTROKE

| | | |
|---|---|---|
| 1968 | Djurdjica Bjedov, Yugoslavia | 1:15.8 OR |
| 1972 | Catherine Carr, United States | 1:13.58 WR |
| 1976 | Hannelore Anke, E Germany | 1:11.16 |
| 1980 | Ute Geweniger, E Germany | 1:10.22 |
| 1984 | Petra Van Staveren, Netherlands | 1:09.88 OR |
| 1988 | Tania Dangalakova, Bulgaria | 1:07.95 OR |
| 1992 | Elena Roudkovskaia, Unified Team | 1:08.00 |
| 1996 | Penelope Heyns, S Africa | 1:07.73 |
| 2000 | Megan Quann, United States | 1:07.05 |

### 200-METER BREASTSTROKE

| | | |
|---|---|---|
| 1924 | Lucy Morton, Great Britain | 3:33.2 OR |
| 1928 | Hilde Schrader, Germany | 3:12.6 |
| 1932 | Clare Dennis, Australia | 3:06.3 OR |
| 1936 | Hideko Maehata, Japan | 3:03.6 |
| 1948 | Petronella Van Vliet, Netherlands | 2:57.2 |
| 1952 | Eva Szekely, Hungary | 2:51.7 OR |
| 1956 | Ursula Happe, W Germany | 2:53.1 OR |
| 1960 | Anita Lonsbrough, Great Britain | 2:49.5 WR |
| 1964 | Galina Prozumenshikova, USSR | 2:46.4 OR |
| 1968 | Sharon Wichman, United States | 2:44.4 OR |
| 1972 | Beverly Whitfield, Australia | 2:41.71 OR |
| 1976 | Marina Koshevaia, USSR | 2:33.35 WR |
| 1980 | Lina Kaciusyte, USSR | 2:29.54 OR |
| 1984 | Anne Ottenbrite, Canada | 2:30.38 |
| 1988 | Silke Hoerner, E Germany | 2:26.71 WR |
| 1992 | Kyoko Iwasaki, Japan | 2:26.65 OR |
| 1996 | Penelope Heyns, S Africa | 2:25.41 OR |
| 2000 | Agnes Kovacs, Hungary | 2:24.35 OR |

### 100-METER BUTTERFLY

| | | |
|---|---|---|
| 1956 | Shelley Mann, United States | 1:11.0 OR |
| 1960 | Carolyn Schuler, United States | 1:09.5 OR |
| 1964 | Sharon Stouder, United States | 1:04.7 WR |
| 1968 | Lynn McClements, Australia | 1:05.5 |
| 1972 | Mayumi Aoki, Japan | 1:03.34 WR |
| 1976 | Kornelia Ender, E Germany | 1:00.13 EWR |
| 1980 | Caren Metschuck, E Germany | 1:00.42 |
| 1984 | Mary T. Meagher, United States | 59.26 |
| 1988 | Kristin Otto, E Germany | 59.00 OR |
| 1992 | Qian Hong, China | 58.62 OR |
| 1996 | Amy Van Dyken, United States | 59.13 |
| 2000 | Inge de Bruijn, Netherlands | 56.61 WR |

### 200-METER BUTTERFLY

| | | |
|---|---|---|
| 1968 | Ada Kok, Netherlands | 2:24.7 OR |
| 1972 | Karen Moe, United States | 2:15.57 WR |
| 1976 | Andrea Pollack, E Germany | 2:11.41 OR |
| 1980 | Ines Geissler, E Germany | 2:10.44 OR |
| 1984 | Mary T. Meagher, United States | 2:06.90 OR |
| 1988 | Kathleen Nord, E Germany | 2:09.51 |
| 1992 | Summer Sanders, United States | 2:08.67 |
| 1996 | Susan O'Neill, Australia | 2:07.76 |
| 2000 | Misty Hyman, United States | 2:05.88 OR |

### 200-METER INDIVIDUAL MEDLEY

| | | |
|---|---|---|
| 1968 | Claudia Kolb, United States | 2:24.7 OR |
| 1972 | Shane Gould, Australia | 2:23.07 WR |
| 1976–1980 | Not held | |
| 1984 | Tracy Caulkins, United States | 2:12.64 OR |
| 1988 | Daniela Hunger, E Germany | 2:12.59 OR |
| 1992 | Lin Li, China | 2:11.65 WR |
| 1996 | Michelle Smith, Ireland | 2:13.93 |
| 2000 | Yana Klochkova, Ukraine | 2:10.68 OR |

Note: OR=Olympic Record. WR=World Record. EOR=Equals Olympic Record. EWR=Equals World Record. WB=World Best.

## SWIMMING *(Cont.)*

### Women *(Cont.)*

#### 400-METER INDIVIDUAL MEDLEY

| | | |
|---|---|---|
| 1964 | Donna de Varona, United States | 5:18.7 OR |
| 1968 | Claudia Kolb, United States | 5:08.5 OR |
| 1972 | Gail Neall, Australia | 5:02.97 WR |
| 1976 | Ulrike Tauber, E Germany | 4:42.77 WR |
| 1980 | Petra Schneider, E Germany | 4:36.29 WR |
| 1984 | Tracy Caulkins, United States | 4:39.24 |
| 1988 | Janet Evans, United States | 4:37.76 |
| 1992 | Krisztina Egerszegi, Hungary | 4:36.54 |
| 1996 | Michelle Smith, Ireland | 4:39.18 |
| 2000 | Yana Klochkova, Ukraine | 4:33.59 WR |

#### 4 X 100-METER MEDLEY RELAY

| | | |
|---|---|---|
| 1960 | United States | 4:41.1 WR |
| 1964 | United States | 4:33.9 WR |
| 1968 | United States | 4:28.3 OR |
| 1972 | United States | 4:20.75 WR |
| 1976 | E Germany | 4:07.95 WR |
| 1980 | E Germany | 4:06.67 WR |
| 1984 | United States | 4:08.34 |
| 1988 | E Germany | 4:03.74 OR |
| 1992 | United States | 4:02.54 WR |
| 1996 | United States | 4:02.88 |
| 2000 | United States | 3:58.30 WR |

#### 4 X 100-METER FREESTYLE RELAY

| | | |
|---|---|---|
| 1912 | Great Britain | 5:52.8 WR |
| 1920 | United States | 5:11.6 WR |
| 1924 | United States | 4:58.8 WR |
| 1928 | United States | 4:47.6 WR |
| 1932 | United States | 4:38.0 WR |
| 1936 | Netherlands | 4:36.0 OR |
| 1948 | United States | 4:29.2 OR |
| 1952 | Hungary | 4:24.4 WR |
| 1956 | Australia | 4:17.1 WR |
| 1960 | United States | 4:08.9 WR |
| 1964 | United States | 4:03.8 WR |
| 1968 | United States | 4:02.5 OR |
| 1972 | United States | 3:55.19 WR |
| 1976 | United States | 3:44.82 WR |
| 1980 | E Germany | 3:42.71 WR |
| 1984 | United States | 3:43.43 |
| 1988 | E Germany | 3:40.63 OR |
| 1992 | United States | 3:39.46 WR |
| 1996 | United States | 3:39.29 OR |
| 2000 | United States | 3:36.61 WR |

#### 4 X 200-METER FREESTYLE RELAY

| | | |
|---|---|---|
| 1996 | United States | 7:59.87 |
| 2000 | United States | 7:57.80 OR |

## DIVING

### Men

#### SPRINGBOARD

| | | Pts |
|---|---|---|
| 1908 | Albert Zürner, Germany | 85.5 |
| 1912 | Paul Günther, Germany | 79.23 |
| 1920 | Louis Kuehn, United States | 675.40 |
| 1924 | Albert White, United States | 97.46 |
| 1928 | Pete DesJardins, United States | 185.04 |
| 1932 | Michael Galitzen, United States | 161.38 |
| 1936 | Richard Degener, United States | 163.57 |
| 1948 | Bruce Harlan, United States | 163.64 |
| 1952 | David Browning, United States | 205.29 |
| 1956 | Robert Clotworthy, United States | 159.56 |
| 1960 | Gary Tobian, United States | 170.00 |
| 1964 | Kenneth Sitzberger, United States | 159.90 |
| 1968 | Bernie Wrightson, United States | 170.15 |
| 1972 | Vladimir Vasin, USSR | 594.09 |
| 1976 | Phil Boggs, United States | 619.05 |
| 1980 | Aleksandr Portnov, USSR | 905.02 |
| 1984 | Greg Louganis, United States | 754.41 |
| 1988 | Greg Louganis, United States | 730.80 |
| 1992 | Mark Lenzi, United States | 676.53 |
| 1996 | Xiong Ni, China | 701.46 |
| 2000 | Xiong Ni, China | 708.72 |

#### PLATFORM

| | | Pts |
|---|---|---|
| 1904 | George Sheldon, United States | 12.66 |
| 1906 | Gottlob Walz, Germany | 156.0 |
| 1908 | Hjalmar Johansson, Sweden | 83.75 |
| 1912 | Erik Adlerz, Sweden | 73.94 |
| 1920 | Clarence Pinkston, United States | 100.67 |
| 1924 | Albert White, United States | 97.46 |
| 1928 | Pete DesJardins, United States | 98.74 |
| 1932 | Harold Smith, United States | 124.80 |
| 1936 | Marshall Wayne, United States | 113.58 |
| 1948 | Sammy Lee, United States | 130.05 |
| 1952 | Sammy Lee, United States | 156.28 |
| 1956 | Joaquin Capilla, Mexico | 152.44 |
| 1960 | Robert Webster, United States | 165.56 |
| 1964 | Robert Webster, United States | 148.58 |
| 1968 | Klaus Dibiasi, Italy | 164.18 |
| 1972 | Klaus Dibiasi, Italy | 504.12 |
| 1976 | Klaus Dibiasi, Italy | 600.51 |
| 1980 | Falk Hoffmann, E Germany | 835.65 |
| 1984 | Greg Louganis, United States | 710.91 |
| 1988 | Greg Louganis, United States | 638.61 |
| 1992 | Sun Shuwei, China | 677.31 |
| 1996 | Dmitri Sautin, Russia | 692.34 |
| 2000 | Tian Liang, China | 724.53 |

### Women

#### SPRINGBOARD

| | | Pts |
|---|---|---|
| 1920 | Aileen Riggin, United States | 539.90 |
| 1924 | Elizabeth Becker, United States | 474.50 |
| 1928 | Helen Meany, United States | 78.62 |
| 1932 | Georgia Coleman, United States | 87.52 |
| 1936 | Marjorie Gestring, United States | 89.27 |
| 1948 | Victoria Draves, United States | 108.74 |

#### SPRINGBOARD *(CONT.)*

| | | Pts |
|---|---|---|
| 1952 | Patricia McCormick, United States | 147.30 |
| 1956 | Patricia McCormick, United States | 142.36 |
| 1960 | Ingrid Krämer, E Germany | 155.81 |
| 1964 | Ingrid Engel Krämer, E Germany | 145.00 |
| 1968 | Sue Gossick, United States | 150.77 |
| 1972 | Micki King, United States | 450.03 |

### DIVING *(Cont.)*
### Women *(Cont.)*

#### SPRINGBOARD *(CONT.)*

| | | Pts |
|---|---|---|
| 1976 | Jennifer Chandler, United States | 506.19 |
| 1980 | Irina Kalinina, USSR | 725.91 |
| 1984 | Sylvie Bernier, Canada | 530.70 |
| 1988 | Gao Min, China | 580.23 |
| 1992 | Gao Min, China | 572.40 |
| 1996 | Fu Mingxia, China | 547.68 |
| 2000 | Fu Mingxia, China | 609.42 |

#### PLATFORM

| | | Pts |
|---|---|---|
| 1912 | Greta Johansson, Sweden | 39.90 |
| 1920 | Stefani Fryland-Clausen, Denmark | 34.60 |
| 1924 | Caroline Smith, United States | 33.20 |
| 1928 | Elizabeth B. Pinkston, United States | 31.60 |
| 1932 | Dorothy Poynton, United States | 40.26 |
| 1936 | Dorothy Poynton Hill, United States | 33.93 |

#### PLATFORM *(CONT.)*

| | | Pts |
|---|---|---|
| 1948 | Victoria Draves, United States | 68.87 |
| 1952 | Patricia McCormick, United States | 79.37 |
| 1956 | Patricia McCormick, United States | 84.85 |
| 1960 | Ingrid Krämer, E Germany | 91.28 |
| 1964 | Lesley Bush, United States | 99.80 |
| 1968 | Milena Duchkova, Czechoslovakia | 109.59 |
| 1972 | Ulrika Knape, Sweden | 390.00 |
| 1976 | Elena Vaytsekhovskaya, USSR | 406.59 |
| 1980 | Martina Jäschke, E Germany | 596.25 |
| 1984 | Zhou Jihong, China | 435.51 |
| 1988 | Xu Yanmei, China | 445.20 |
| 1992 | Mingxia Fu, China | 461.43 |
| 1996 | Mingxia Fu, China | 521.58 |
| 2000 | Laura Wilkinson, United States | 543.75 |

## GYMNASTICS
### Men

#### ALL-AROUND

| | | Pts |
|---|---|---|
| 1900 | Gustave Sandras, France | 302 |
| 1904 | Julius Lenhart, Austria | 69.80 |
| 1906 | Pierre Paysse, France | 97 |
| 1908 | Alberto Braglia, Italy | 317.0 |
| 1912 | Alberto Braglia, Italy | 135.0 |
| 1920 | Giorgio Zampori, Italy | 88.35 |
| 1924 | Leon Stukelj, Yugoslavia | 110.340 |
| 1928 | Georges Miez, Switzerland | 247.500 |
| 1932 | Romeo Neri, Italy | 140.625 |
| 1936 | Alfred Schwarzmann, Germany | 113.100 |
| 1948 | Veikko Huhtanen, Finland | 229.70 |
| 1952 | Viktor Chukarin, USSR | 115.70 |
| 1956 | Viktor Chukarin, USSR | 114.25 |
| 1960 | Boris Shakhlin, USSR | 115.95 |
| 1964 | Yukio Endo, Japan | 115.95 |
| 1968 | Sawao Kato, Japan | 115.90 |
| 1972 | Sawao Kato, Japan | 114.65 |
| 1976 | Nikolai Andrianov, USSR | 116.65 |
| 1980 | Aleksandr Dityatin, USSR | 118.65 |
| 1984 | Koji Gushiken, Japan | 118.70 |
| 1988 | Vladimir Artemov, USSR | 119.125 |
| 1992 | Vitaly Scherbo, Unified Team | 59.025 |
| 1996 | Li Xiaoshuang, China | 58.423 |
| 2000 | Alexei Nemov, Russia | 58.474 |

#### HORIZONTAL BAR

| | | Pts |
|---|---|---|
| 1896 | Hermann Weingärtner, Germany | — |
| 1904 | Anton Heida, United States | 40 |
| 1924 | Leon Stukelj, Yugoslavia | 19.73 |
| 1928 | Georges Miez, Switzerland | 19.17 |
| 1932 | Dallas Bixler, United States | 18.33 |
| 1936 | Aleksanteri Saarvala, Finland | 19.367 |
| 1948 | Josef Stafler, Switzerland | 19.85 |
| 1952 | Jack Günthard, Switzerland | 19.55 |
| 1956 | Takashi Ono, Japan | 19.60 |
| 1960 | Takashi Ono, Japan | 19.60 |
| 1964 | Boris Shakhlin, USSR | 19.625 |
| 1968 | Akinori Nakayama, Japan | 19.55 |
| 1972 | Mitsuo Tsukahara, Japan | 19.725 |
| 1976 | Mitsuo Tsukahara, Japan | 19.675 |
| 1980 | Stoyan Deltchev, Bulgaria | 19.825 |
| 1984 | Shinji Morisue, Japan | 20.00 |
| 1988 | Vladimir Artemov, USSR | 19.90 |
| 1992 | Trent Dimas, United States | 9.875 |
| 1996 | Andreas Wecker, Germany | 9.850 |
| 2000 | Alexei Nemov, Russia | 9.787 |

#### PARALLEL BARS

| | | Pts |
|---|---|---|
| 1896 | Alfred Flatow, Germany | — |
| 1904 | George Eyser, United States | 44 |
| 1924 | August Güttinger, Switzerland | 21.63 |
| 1928 | Ladislav Vacha, Czechoslovakia | 18.83 |
| 1932 | Romeo Neri, Italy | 18.97 |
| 1936 | Konrad Frey, Germany | 19.067 |
| 1948 | Michael Reusch, Switzerland | 19.75 |
| 1952 | Hans Eugster, Switzerland | 19.65 |
| 1956 | Viktor Chukarin, USSR | 19.20 |
| 1960 | Boris Shakhlin, USSR | 19.40 |
| 1964 | Yukio Endo, Japan | 19.675 |
| 1968 | Akinori Nakayama, Japan | 19.475 |
| 1972 | Sawao Kato, Japan | 19.475 |
| 1976 | Sawao Kato, Japan | 19.675 |
| 1980 | Aleksandr Tkachyov, USSR | 19.775 |
| 1984 | Bart Conner, United States | 19.95 |
| 1988 | Vladimir Artemov, USSR | 19.925 |
| 1992 | Vitaly Scherbo, Unified Team | 9.900 |
| 1996 | Rustan Sharipov, Ukraine | 9.837 |
| 2000 | Xiaopeng Li, China | 9.825 |

#### VAULT

| | | Pts |
|---|---|---|
| 1896 | Karl Schumann, Germany | — |
| 1904 | George Eyser, United States | 36 |
| 1924 | Frank Kriz, United States | 9.98 |
| 1928 | Eugen Mack, Switzerland | 9.58 |
| 1932 | Savino Guglielmetti, Italy | 18.03 |
| 1936 | Alfred Schwarzmann, Germany | 19.20 |
| 1948 | Paavo Aaltonen, Finland | 19.55 |
| 1952 | Viktor Chukarin, USSR | 19.20 |
| 1956 | Helmut Bantz, Germany | 18.85 |
| 1960 | Takashi Ono, Japan | 19.35 |
| 1964 | Haruhiro Yamashita, Japan | 19.60 |
| 1968 | Mikhail Voronin, USSR | 19.00 |
| 1972 | Klaus Köste, E Germany | 18.85 |
| 1976 | Nikolai Andrianov, USSR | 19.45 |
| 1980 | Nikolai Andrianov, USSR | 19.825 |
| 1984 | Lou Yun, China | 19.95 |
| 1988 | Lou Yun, China | 19.875 |
| 1992 | Vitaly Scherbo, Unified Team | 9.856 |
| 1996 | Alexei Nemov, Russia | 9.787 |
| 2000 | Gervasio Deferr, Spain | 9.712 |

## GYMNASTICS *(Cont.)*
## Men *(Cont.)*

### POMMEL HORSE

| | | Pts |
|---|---|---|
| 1896 | Louis Zutter, Switzerland | — |
| 1900 | Not held | |
| 1904 | Anton Heida, United States | 42 |
| 1908–1920 | Not held | |
| 1924 | Josef Wilhelm, Switzerland | 21.23 |
| 1928 | Hermann Hänggi, Switzerland | 19.75 |
| 1932 | Istvan Pelle, Hungary | 19.07 |
| 1936 | Konrad Frey, Germany | 19.333 |
| 1948 | Paavo Aaltonen, Finland | 19.35 |
| 1952 | Viktor Chukarin, USSR | 19.50 |
| 1956 | Boris Shakhlin, USSR | 19.25 |
| 1960 | Eugen Ekman, Finland | 19.375 |
| 1964 | Miroslav Cerar, Yugoslavia | 19.525 |
| 1968 | Miroslav Cerar, Yugoslavia | 19.325 |
| 1972 | Viktor Klimenko, USSR | 19.125 |
| 1976 | Zoltan Magyar, Hungary | 19.70 |
| 1980 | Zoltan Magyar, Hungary | 19.925 |
| 1984 | Li Ning, China | 19.95 |
| 1988 | Dmitri Bilozerchev, USSR | 19.95 |
| 1992 | Vitaly Scherbo, Unified Team | 9.925 |
| 1996 | Donghua Li, Switzerland | 9.875 |
| 2000 | Marius Urzica, Romania | 9.862 |

### RINGS

| | | Pts |
|---|---|---|
| 1896 | Ioannis Mitropoulos, Greece | — |
| 1900 | Not held | |
| 1904 | Hermann Glass, United States | 45 |
| 1908–1920 | Not held | |
| 1924 | Francesco Martino, Italy | 21.553 |
| 1928 | Leon Stukelj, Yugoslavia | 19.25 |
| 1932 | George Gulack, United States | 18.97 |
| 1936 | Alois Hudec, Czechoslovakia | 19.433 |
| 1948 | Karl Frei, Switzerland | 19.80 |
| 1952 | Grant Shaginyan, USSR | 19.75 |
| 1956 | Albert Azaryan, USSR | 19.35 |
| 1960 | Albert Azaryan, USSR | 19.725 |
| 1964 | Takuji Haytta, Japan | 19.475 |
| 1968 | Akinori Nakayama, Japan | 19.45 |
| 1972 | Akinori Nakayama, Japan | 19.35 |
| 1976 | Nikolai Andrianov, USSR | 19.65 |
| 1980 | Aleksandr Dityatin, USSR | 19.875 |
| 1984 | Koji Gushiken, Japan | 19.85 |
| 1988 | Holger Behrendt, E Germany | 19.925 |
| 1992 | Vitaly Scherbo, Unified Team | 9.937 |
| 1996 | Yuri Chechi, Italy | 9.887 |
| 2000 | Szilveszter Csollany, Hungary | 9.862 |

### FLOOR EXERCISE

| | | Pts |
|---|---|---|
| 1932 | Istvan Pelle, Hungary | 9.60 |
| 1936 | Georges Miez, Switzerland | 18.666 |
| 1948 | Ferenc Pataki, Hungary | 19.35 |
| 1952 | K. William Thoresson, Sweden | 19.25 |
| 1956 | Valentin Muratov, USSR | 19.20 |
| 1960 | Nobuyuki Aihara, Japan | 19.45 |
| 1964 | Franco Menichelli, Italy | 19.45 |
| 1968 | Sawao Kato, Japan | 19.475 |
| 1972 | Nikolai Andrianov, USSR | 19.175 |
| 1976 | Nikolai Andrianov, USSR | 19.45 |
| 1980 | Roland Brückner, E Germany | 19.75 |
| 1984 | Li Ning, China | 19.925 |
| 1988 | Sergei Kharkov, USSR | 19.925 |
| 1992 | Li Xiaoshuang, China | 9.925 |
| 1996 | Ioannis Melissanidis, Greece | 9.850 |
| 2000 | Igors Vihrovs, Latvia | 9.812 |

### TEAM COMBINED EXERCISES

| | | Pts |
|---|---|---|
| 1904 | Turngemeinde Philadelphia | 374.43 |
| 1906 | Norway | 19.00 |
| 1908 | Sweden | 438 |
| 1912 | Italy | 265.75 |
| 1920 | Italy | 359.855 |
| 1924 | Italy | 839.058 |
| 1928 | Switzerland | 1718.625 |
| 1932 | Italy | 541.850 |
| 1936 | Germany | 657.430 |
| 1948 | Finland | 1358.30 |
| 1952 | USSR | 574.40 |
| 1956 | USSR | 568.25 |
| 1960 | Japan | 575.20 |
| 1964 | Japan | 577.95 |
| 1968 | Japan | 575.90 |
| 1972 | Japan | 571.25 |
| 1976 | Japan | 576.85 |
| 1980 | USSR | 598.60 |
| 1984 | United States | 591.40 |
| 1988 | USSR | 593.35 |
| 1992 | Unified Team | 585.45 |
| 1996 | Russia | 576.778 |
| 2000 | China | 231.919 |

## Women

### ALL-AROUND

| | | Pts |
|---|---|---|
| 1952 | Maria Gorokhovskaya, USSR | 76.78 |
| 1956 | Larissa Latynina, USSR | 74.933 |
| 1960 | Larissa Latynina, USSR | 77.031 |
| 1964 | Vera Caslavska, Czechoslovakia | 77.564 |
| 1968 | Vera Caslavska, Czechoslovakia | 78.25 |
| 1972 | Lyudmila Tousischeva, USSR | 77.025 |
| 1976 | Nadia Comaneci, Romania | 79.275 |
| 1980 | Yelena Davydova, USSR | 79.15 |
| 1984 | Mary Lou Retton, United States | 79.175 |
| 1988 | Yelena Shushunova, USSR | 79.662 |
| 1992 | Tatiana Gutsu, Unified Team | 39.737 |
| 1996 | Lilia Podkopayeva, Ukraine | 39.255 |
| 2000 | Simona Amanar, Romania | 38.642 |

### VAULT

| | | Pts |
|---|---|---|
| 1952 | Yekaterina Kalinchuk, USSR | 19.20 |
| 1956 | Larissa Latynina, USSR | 18.833 |
| 1960 | Margarita Nikolayeva, USSR | 19.316 |
| 1964 | Vera Caslavska, Czechoslovakia | 19.483 |
| 1968 | Vera Caslavska, Czechoslovakia | 19.775 |
| 1972 | Karin Janz, E Germany | 19.525 |
| 1976 | Nelli Kim, USSR | 19.80 |
| 1980 | Natalya Shaposhnikova, USSR | 19.725 |
| 1984 | Ecaterina Szabo, Romania | 19.875 |
| 1988 | Svetlana Boginskaya, USSR | 19.905 |
| 1992 | Henrietta Onodi, Hungary | 9.925 |
| | Lavinia Milosovici, Romania | 9.925 |
| 1996 | Simona Amanar, Romania | 9.825 |
| 2000 | Yelena Zamolodtchikova, Russia | 9.731 |

## GYMNASTICS *(Cont.)*
### Women *(Cont.)*

#### UNEVEN BARS

| | | Pts |
|---|---|---|
| 1952 | Margit Korondi, Hungary | 19.40 |
| 1956 | Agnes Keleti, Hungary | 18.966 |
| 1960 | Polina Astakhova, USSR | 19.616 |
| 1964 | Polina Astakhova, USSR | 19.332 |
| 1968 | Vera Caslavska, Czechoslovakia | 19.65 |
| 1972 | Karin Janz, E Germany | 19.675 |
| 1976 | Nadia Comaneci, Romania | 20.00 |
| 1980 | Maxi Gnauck, E Germany | 19.875 |
| 1984 | Ma Yanhong, China | 19.95 |
| 1988 | Daniela Silivas, Romania | 20.00 |
| 1992 | Lu Li, China | 10.00 |
| 1996 | Svetlana Khorkina, Russia | 9.850 |
| 2000 | Svetlana Khorkina, Russia | 9.862 |

#### BALANCE BEAM

| | | Pts |
|---|---|---|
| 1952 | Nina Bocharova, USSR | 19.22 |
| 1956 | Agnes Keleti, Hungary | 18.80 |
| 1960 | Eva Bosakova, Czechoslovakia | 19.283 |
| 1964 | Vera Caslavska, Czechoslovakia | 19.449 |
| 1968 | Natalya Kuchinskaya, USSR | 19.65 |
| 1972 | Olga Korbut, USSR | 19.40 |
| 1976 | Nadia Comaneci, Romania | 19.95 |
| 1980 | Nadia Comaneci, Romania | 19.80 |
| 1984 | Simona Pauca, Romania | 19.80 |
| 1988 | Daniela Silivas, Romania | 19.924 |
| 1992 | Tatiana Lisenko, Unified Team | 9.975 |
| 1996 | Shannon Miller, United States | 9.862 |
| 2000 | Xuan Li, China | 9.825 |

#### FLOOR EXERCISE

| | | Pts |
|---|---|---|
| 1952 | Agnes Keleti, Hungary | 19.36 |
| 1956 | Agnes Keleti, Hungary | 18.733 |
| 1960 | Larissa Latynina, USSR | 19.583 |
| 1964 | Larissa Latynina, USSR | 19.599 |
| 1968 | Vera Caslavska, Czechoslovakia | 19.675 |
| 1972 | Olga Korbut, USSR | 19.575 |
| 1976 | Nelli Kim, USSR | 19.85 |
| 1980 | Nadia Comaneci, Romania | 19.875 |

#### FLOOR EXERCISE *(Cont.)*

| | | Pts |
|---|---|---|
| 1984 | Ecaterina Szabo, Romania | 19.975 |
| 1988 | Daniela Silivas, Romania | 19.937 |
| 1992 | Lavinia Milosovici, Romania | 10.00 |
| 1996 | Lilia Podkopayeva, Ukraine | 9.887 |
| 2000 | Yelena Zamolodtchikova, Russia | 9.850 |

#### TEAM COMBINED EXERCISES

| | | Pts |
|---|---|---|
| 1928 | The Netherlands | 316.75 |
| 1932 | Not held | |
| 1936 | Germany | 506.50 |
| 1948 | Czechoslovakia | 445.45 |
| 1952 | USSR | 527.03 |
| 1956 | USSR | 444.800 |
| 1960 | USSR | 382.320 |
| 1964 | USSR | 280.890 |
| 1968 | USSR | 382.85 |
| 1972 | USSR | 380.50 |
| 1976 | USSR | 466.00 |
| 1980 | USSR | 394.90 |
| 1984 | Romania | 392.02 |
| 1988 | USSR | 395.475 |
| 1992 | Unified Team | 395.666 |
| 1996 | United States | 389.225 |
| 2000 | Romania | 154.608 |

#### RHYTHMIC ALL-AROUND

| | | Pts |
|---|---|---|
| 1984 | Lori Fung, Canada | 57.95 |
| 1988 | Marina Lobach, USSR | 60.00 |
| 1992 | A. Timoshenko, Unified Team | 59.037 |
| 1996 | E. Serebrianskaya, Ukraine | 39.683 |
| 2000 | Yulia Barsukova, Russia | 39.632 |

#### RHYTHMIC TEAM COMBINED EXERCISES

| | | Pts |
|---|---|---|
| 1996 | Spain | 38.933 |
| 2000 | Russia | 39.500 |

## SOCCER
### Men

| | | | |
|---|---|---|---|
| 1900 | Great Britain | 1928 | Uruguay |
| 1904 | Canada | 1936 | Italy |
| 1908 | Great Britain | 1948 | Sweden |
| 1912 | Great Britain | 1952 | Hungary |
| 1920 | Belgium | 1956 | Soviet Union |
| 1924 | Uruguay | 1960 | Yugoslavia |

| | | | |
|---|---|---|---|
| 1964 | Hungary | 1988 | Soviet Union |
| 1968 | Hungary | 1992 | Spain |
| 1972 | Poland | 1996 | Nigeria |
| 1976 | E Germany | 2000 | Cameroon |
| 1980 | Czechoslovakia | | |
| 1984 | France | | |

### Women

| | |
|---|---|
| 1996 | United States |
| 2000 | Norway |

## BIATHLON
### Men

**10 KILOMETERS**

| | |
|---|---|
| 1980....Frank Ullrich, E Germany | 32:10.69 |
| 1984....Eirik Kvalfoss, Norway | 30:53.8 |
| 1988....Frank-Peter Rötsch, W Germany | 25:08.1 |
| 1992....Mark Kirchner, Germany | 26:02.3 |
| 1994....Sergei Tchepikov, Russia | 28:07.0 |
| 1998....Ole Einar Bjorndalen, Norway | 27:16.2 |

**20 KILOMETERS**

| | |
|---|---|
| 1960....Klas Lestander, Sweden | 1:33:21.6 |
| 1964....Vladimir Melyanin, Soviet Union | 1:20:26.8 |
| 1968....Magnar Solberg, Norway | 1:13:45.9 |
| 1972....Magnar Solberg, Norway | 1:15:55.5 |
| 1976....Nikolay Kruglov, Soviet Union | 1:14:12.26 |
| 1980....Anatoliy Alyabiev, Soviet Union | 1:08:16.31 |
| 1984....Peter Angerer, W Germany | 1:11:52.7 |

**20 KILOMETERS *(Cont.)***

| | |
|---|---|
| 1988....Frank-Peter Rötsch, W Germany | 56:33.3 |
| 1992....Evgueni Redkine, Unified Team | 57:34.4 |
| 1994....Sergei Tarasov, Russia | 57:25.3 |
| 1998....Halvard Hanevold, Norway | 56:16.4 |

**4 X 7.5-KILOMETER RELAY**

| | |
|---|---|
| 1968 ..............Soviet Union | 2:13:02.4 |
| 1972 ..............Soviet Union | 1:51:44.92 |
| 1976 ..............Soviet Union | 1:57:55.64 |
| 1980 ..............Soviet Union | 1:34:03.27 |
| 1984 ..............Soviet Union | 1:38:51.7 |
| 1988 ..............Soviet Union | 1:22:30.0 |
| 1992 ..............Germany | 1:24:43.5 |
| 1994 ..............Germany | 1:30:22.1 |
| 1998 ..............Germany | 1:19:43.3 |

### Women

**7.5 KILOMETERS**

| | |
|---|---|
| 1992....Antissa Restzova, Unified Team | 24:29.2 |
| 1994....Myriam Bedard, Canada | 26:08.8 |
| 1998....Galina Koukleva, Russia | 23:08.0 |

**15 KILOMETERS**

| | |
|---|---|
| 1992....Antje Misersky, Germany | 51:47.2 |
| 1994....Myriam Bedard, Canada | 52:06.6 |
| 1998....Ekaterina Dofovska, Bulgaria | 54:52.0 |

**3 X 7.5-KILOMETER RELAY**

| | |
|---|---|
| 1992....France | 1:15:55.6 |
| 1994....Russia | 1:47:19.5 |
| 1998....Germany | 1:40:13.6 |

## BOBSLED

**4-MAN BOB**

| | |
|---|---|
| 1924....Switzerland (Eduard Scherrer) | 5:45.54 |
| 1928....United States (William Fiske) (5-man) | 3:20.50 |
| 1932....United States (William Fiske) | 7:53.68 |
| 1936....Switzerland (Pierre Musy) | 5:19.85 |
| 1948....United States (Francis Tyler) | 5:20.10 |
| 1952....Germany (Andreas Ostler) | 5:07.84 |
| 1956....Switzerland (Franz Kapus) | 5:10.44 |
| 1960....Not held | |
| 1964....Canada (Victor Emery) | 4:14.46 |
| 1968....Italy (Eugenio Monti) (2 runs) | 2:17.39 |
| 1972....Switzerland (Jean Wicki) | 4:43.07 |
| 1976....E Germany (Meinhard Nehmer) | 3:40.43 |
| 1980....E Germany (Meinhard Nehmer) | 3:59.92 |
| 1984....E Germany (Wolfgang Hoppe) | 3:20.22 |
| 1988....Switzerland (Ekkehard Fasser) | 3:47.51 |
| 1992....Austria (Ingo Appelt) | 3:53.90 |
| 1994....Germany (Harold Czudaj) | 3:27.78 |
| 1998....Germany (Christoph Langen) | 2:39.41 |

Note: Driver in parentheses.

**2-MAN BOB**

| | |
|---|---|
| 1932....United States (Hubert Stevens) | 8:14.74 |
| 1936....United States (Ivan Brown) | 5:29.29 |
| 1948....Switzerland (Felix Endrich) | 5:29.20 |
| 1952....Germany (Andreas Ostler) | 5:24.54 |
| 1956....Italy (Lamberto Dalla Costa) | 5:30.14 |
| 1960....Not held | |
| 1964....Great Britain (Anthony Nash) | 4:21.90 |
| 1968....Italy (Eugenio Monti) | 4:41.54 |
| 1972....W Germany (Wolfgang Zimmerer) | 4:57.07 |
| 1976....E Germany (Meinhard Nehmer) | 3:44.42 |
| 1980....Switzerland (Erich Schärer) | 4:09.36 |
| 1984....E Germany (Wolfgang Hoppe) | 3:25.56 |
| 1988....USSR (Janis Kipours) | 3:53.48 |
| 1992....Switzerland (Gustav Weder) | 4:03.26 |
| 1994....Switzerland (Gustav Weder) | 3:30.81 |
| 1998....Canada (Pierre Lueders) | 3:37.24 |
| Italy (Guenther Huber) | 3:37.24 |

Note: Driver in parentheses.

## CURLING

### Men

1998 .....Switzerland, Canada, Norway
Note: Gold, silver, and bronze medals.

### Women

1998 .....Canada, Denmark, Sweden
Note: Gold, silver, and bronze medals.

## ICE HOCKEY

### Men

1920* ....Canada, United States, Czechoslovakia
1924 .....Canada, United States, Great Britain
1928 .....Canada, Sweden, Switzerland
1932 .....Canada, United States, Germany
1936 .....Great Britain, Canada, United States
1948 .....Canada, Czechoslovakia, Switzerland
1952 .....Canada, United States, Sweden
1956 .....USSR, United States, Canada
1960 .....United States, Canada, USSR
1964 .....USSR, Sweden, Czechoslovakia
1968 .....USSR, Czechoslovakia, Canada

1972 .....USSR, United States, Czechoslovakia
1976 .....USSR, Czechoslovakia, W Germany
1980 .....United States, USSR, Sweden
1984 .....USSR, Czechoslovakia, Sweden
1988 .....USSR, Finland, Sweden
1992 .....Unified Team, Canada, Czechoslovakia
1994 .....Sweden, Canada, Finland
1998 .....Czech Republic, Russia, Finland
*Competition held at Summer Games in Antwerp.
Note: Gold, silver, and bronze medals.

### Women

1998 .....United States, Canada, Finland

Note: Gold, silver, and bronze medals.

## LUGE

### Men

| SINGLES | | | DOUBLES | | |
|---|---|---|---|---|---|
| 1964 .....Thomas Köhler, East Germany | 3:26.77 | | 1964 ...............Austria | 1:41.62 |
| 1968 .....Manfred Schmid, Austria | 2:52.48 | | 1968 ...............E Germany | 1:35.85 |
| 1972 .....Wolfgang Scheidel, W Germany | 3:27.58 | | 1972 ...............E Germany | 1:28.35 |
| 1976 .....Detlef Guenther, W Germany | 3:27.688 | | 1976 ...............E Germany | 1:25.604 |
| 1980 .....Bernhard Glass, W Germany | 2:54.796 | | 1980 ...............E Germany | 1:19.331 |
| 1984 .....Paul Hildgartner, Italy | 3:04.258 | | 1984 ...............W Germany | 1:23.620 |
| 1988 .....Jens Müller, W Germany | 3:05.548 | | 1988 ...............E Germany | 1:31.940 |
| 1992 .....Georg Hackl, Germany | 3:02.363 | | 1992 ...............Germany | 1:32.053 |
| 1994 .....Georg Hackl, Germany | 3:21.571 | | 1994 ...............Italy | 1:36.720 |
| 1998 .....Georg Hackl, Germany | 3:18.44 | | 1998 ...............Germany | 1:41.105 |

### Women

| SINGLES | | | SINGLES *(Cont.)* | |
|---|---|---|---|---|
| 1964 ....Ortrun Enderlein, Germany | 3:24.67 | | 1984 .....Steffi Martin, E Germany | 2:46.570 |
| 1968 .....Erica Lechner, Italy | 2:28.66 | | 1988 .....Steffi Walter (Martin) E Germany | 3:03.973 |
| 1972 .....Anna-Maria Müller, E Germany | 2:59.18 | | 1992 .....Doris Neuner, Austria | 3:06.696 |
| 1976 .....Margit Schumann, E Germany | 2:50.621 | | 1994 .....Gerda Weissensteiner, Italy | 3:15.517 |
| 1980 .....Vera Zozulya, USSR | 2:36.537 | | 1998 .....Silke Kraushaar, Germany | 3:23.779 |

### A Little Help from Havana

Hamstrung by an impossibly tight budget, organizers of the 2003 Pan Am Games, scheduled for August of that year in Santo Domingo, Dominican Republic, have enlisted outside aid to help them modernize venues, update technology, and improve medical facilities. The help is coming from an unlikely source: Cuba. The Cubans have offered the use of a drug-testing lab in Havana, and in early March 2001, Cuban vice president Jose Ramon Fernandez, director of the country's Olympic committee, agreed to send 30 consultants to Santo Domingo to give locals a chance to pull off a modest but successful Games—much like the ones Havana staged in 1991. The Dominican government told organizers to keep the budget to $30 million (Winnipeg spent $100 million to host the '99 Pan Ams.)."These will not be an extravagant Games," says Fernandez, "but if a small, poor country wants to organize them, we'd like to help."

—Brian Cazeneuve

## FIGURE SKATING

### Men

1908* ..............Ulrich Salchow, Sweden
1920† ............Gillis Grafström, Sweden
1924 .............Gillis Grafström, Sweden
1928 .............Gillis Grafström, Sweden
1932 .............Karl Schäfer, Austria
1936 .............Karl Schäfer, Austria
1948 .............Dick Button, United States
1952 .............Dick Button, United States
1956 .............Hayes Alan Jenkins, United States
1960 .............David Jenkins, United States
1964 .............Manfred Schnelldorfer, W Germany
1968 .............Wolfgang Schwarz, Austria
1972 .............Ondrej Nepela, Czechoslovakia
1976 .............John Curry, Great Britain
1980 .............Robin Cousins, Great Britain
1984 .............Scott Hamilton, United States
1988 .............Brian Boitano, United States
1992 .............Victor Petrenko, Unified Team
1994 .............Alexei Urmanov, Russia
1998 .............Ilia Kulik, Russia

*Competition held at Summer Games in London.
†Competition held at Summer Games in Antwerp.

### Women

1908* ..............Madge Syers, Great Britain
1920† ..............Magda Julin, Sweden
1924 ..............Herma Szabo-Planck, Austria
1928 ..............Sonja Henie, Norway
1932 ..............Sonja Henie, Norway
1936 ..............Sonja Henie, Norway
1948 ..............Barbara Ann Scott, Canada
1952 ..............Jeanette Altwegg, Great Britain
1956 ..............Tenley Albright, United States
1960 ..............Carol Heiss, United States
1964 ..............Sjoukje Dijkstra, Netherlands
1968 ..............Peggy Fleming, United States
1972 ..............Beatrix Schuba, Austria
1976 ..............Dorothy Hamill, United States
1980 ..............Anett Pötzsch, E Germany
1984 ..............Katarina Witt, E Germany
1988 ..............Katarina Witt, E Germany
1992 ..............Kristi Yamaguchi, United States
1994 ..............Oksana Baiul, Ukraine
1998 ..............Tara Lipinski, United States

## Mixed

### PAIRS

1908* ..Anna Hübler & Heinrich Burger, Germany
1920† ...Ludovika & Walter Jakobsson, Finland
1924 ....Helene Engelmann & Alfred Berger, Austria
1928 ....Andree Joly & Pierre Brunet, France
1932 ....Andree Brunet (Joly) & Pierre Brunet, France
1936 ....Maxi Herber & Ernst Baier, Germany
1948 ....Micheline Lannoy & Pierre Baugniet, Belgium
1952 ....Ria Falk and Paul Falk, W Germany
1956 ....Elisabeth Schwartz & Kurt Oppelt, Austria
1960 ....Barbara Wagner & Robert Paul, Canada
1964 ....Lyudmila Beloussova & Oleg Protopopov, USSR
1968 ....Lyudmila Beloussova & Oleg Protopopov, USSR
1972 ....Irina Rodnina & Alexei Ulanov, USSR
1976 ....Irina Rodnina & Aleksandr Zaitzev, USSR
1980 ....Irina Rodnina & Aleksandr Zaitzev, USSR
1984 ....Elena Valova & Oleg Vasiliev, USSR
1988 ....Ekaterina Gordeeva & Sergei Grinkov, USSR
1992 ....Natalia Michkouteniok & Artour Dmitriev, Unified Team

### PAIRS (Cont.)

1994 ....Ekaterina Gordeeva & Sergei Grinkov, Russia
1998 ....Oksana Kazakova & Artur Dmitriev, Russia

### DANCE

1976 ....Lyudmila Pakhomova & Aleksandr Gorshkov, USSR
1980 ....Natalia Linichuk & Gennadi Karponosov, USSR
1984 ....Jayne Torvill & Christopher Dean, Great Britain
1988 ....Natalia Bestemianova & Andrei Bukin, USSR
1992 ....Marina Klimova & Sergei Ponomarenko, Unified Team
1994 ....Oksana Grishuk & Evgeny Platov, Russia
1998 ....Pasha Grishuk & Evgeny Platov, Russia

*Competition held at Summer Games in London.
†Competition held at Summer Games in Antwerp.

## Capel's Sprint to the NFL: Off Track for Good?

John Capel couldn't be accused of taking the easy road in abandoning his track career to play football. As the U.S. 200-meter champion and the 10th-fastest man in history at the distance, Capel, a 22-year-old former wide receiver at Florida, could have earned a mid-six-figure income from a shoe-company contract and European races. Instead, he gave up his final two years of football eligibility and made himself available for the NFL draft in April 2001.

The 5' 11", 180-pound Capel played only two seasons with the Gators and caught just nine passes. On Feb. 25, 2001, at the NFL scouting combine, Capel ran the 40 in roughly 4.4 seconds, mediocre for him, but he impressed scouts with his routes and soft hands. Provided he proved himself in training camp, he might have had a chance to play. "Football has always been my first love," Capel said.

Still, he hadn't completely left track behind, which turned out to be a good thing. In 2000 Capel won the Olympic trials 200 when both Maurice Greene and Michael Johnson pulled up with injuries. "Maurice wasn't going to beat me that day, and he still can't beat me," said Capel.

He may get a chance to back up his bravado: After being selected in the seventh round of the NFL draft by Chicago, Capel failed a league drug test. He was later arrested for possession of marijuana, and the Bears cut him before training camp began.

## SPEED SKATING

### Men

#### 500 METERS

| | | |
|---|---|---|
| 1924 | Charles Jewtraw, United States | 44.0 |
| 1928 | Clas Thunberg, Finland | 43.4 OR |
| | Bernt Evensen, Norway | 43.4 OR |
| 1932 | John Shea, United States | 43.4 EOR |
| 1936 | Ivar Ballangrud, Norway | 43.4 EOR |
| 1948 | Finn Helgesen, Norway | 43.1 OR |
| 1952 | Kenneth Henry, United States | 43.2 |
| 1956 | Yevgeny Grishin, USSR | 40.2 EWR |
| 1960 | Yevgeny Grishin, USSR | 40.2 EWR |
| 1964 | Terry McDermott, United States | 40.1 OR |
| 1968 | Erhard Keller, W Germany | 40.3 |
| 1972 | Erhard Keller, W Germany | 39.44 OR |
| 1976 | Yevgeny Kulikov, USSR | 39.17 OR |
| 1980 | Eric Heiden, United States | 38.03 OR |
| 1984 | Sergei Fokichev, USSR | 38.19 |
| 1988 | Uwe-Jens Mey, E Germany | 36.45 WR |
| 1992 | Uwe-Jens Mey, E Germany | 37.14 |
| 1994 | Aleksandr Golubev, Russia | 36.33 |
| 1998 | Hiroyasu Shimizu, Japan | 35.59 OR |
| | (second run) | |

#### 1,000 METERS

| | | |
|---|---|---|
| 1976 | Peter Mueller, United States | 1:19.32 |
| 1980 | Eric Heiden, United States | 1:15.18 OR |
| 1984 | Gaetan Boucher, Canada | 1:15.80 |
| 1988 | Nikolai Gulyaev, USSR | 1:13.03 OR |
| 1992 | Olaf Zinke, Germany | 1:14.85 |
| 1994 | Dan Jansen, United States | 1:12.43 WR |
| 1998 | Ids Postma, Netherlands | 1:10.64 OR |

#### 1,500 METERS

| | | |
|---|---|---|
| 1924 | Clas Thunberg, Finland | 2:20.8 |
| 1928 | Clas Thunberg, Finland | 2:21.1 |
| 1932 | John Shea, United States | 2:57.5 |
| 1936 | Charles Mathisen, Norway | 2:19.2 OR |
| 1948 | Sverre Farstad, Norway | 2:17.6 OR |
| 1952 | Hjalmar Andersen, Norway | 2:20.4 |
| 1956 | Yevgeny Grishin, USSR | 2:08.6 WR |
| | Yuri Mikhailov, USSR | 2:08.6 WR |
| 1960 | Roald Aas, Norway | 2:10.4 |
| | Yevgeny Grishin, USSR | 2:10.4 |
| 1964 | Ants Anston, USSR | 2:10.3 |
| 1968 | Cornelis Verkerk, Netherlands | 2:03.4 OR |
| 1972 | Ard Schenk, Netherlands | 2:02.96 OR |
| 1976 | Jan Egil Storholt, Norway | 1:59.38 OR |
| 1980 | Eric Heiden, United States | 1:55.44 OR |
| 1984 | Gaetan Boucher, Canada | 1:58.36 |

#### 1,500 METERS *(Cont.)*

| | | |
|---|---|---|
| 1988 | Andre Hoffmann, E Germany | 1:52.06 WR |
| 1992 | Johann Olav Koss, Norway | 1:54.81 |
| 1994 | Johann Olav Koss, Norway | 1:51.29 WR |
| 1998 | Aadne Sondral, Norway | 1:47.87 WR |

#### 5,000 METERS

| | | |
|---|---|---|
| 1924 | Clas Thunberg, Finland | 8:39.0 |
| 1928 | Ivar Ballangrud, Norway | 8:50.5 |
| 1932 | Irving Jaffee, United States | 9:40.8 |
| 1936 | Ivar Ballangrud, Norway | 8:19.6 OR |
| 1948 | Reidar Liaklev, Norway | 8:29.4 |
| 1952 | Hjalmar Andersen, Norway | 8:10.6 OR |
| 1956 | Boris Shilkov, USSR | 7:48.7 OR |
| 1960 | Viktor Kosichkin, USSR | 7:51.3 |
| 1964 | Knut Johannesen, Norway | 7:38.4 OR |
| 1968 | Fred Anton Maier, Norway | 7:22.4 WR |
| 1972 | Ard Schenk, Netherlands | 7:23.61 |
| 1976 | Sten Stensen, Norway | 7:24.48 |
| 1980 | Eric Heiden, United States | 7:02.29 OR |
| 1984 | Sven Tomas Gustafson, Sweden | 7:12.28 |
| 1988 | Tomas Gustafson, Sweden | 6:44.63 WR |
| 1992 | Geir Karlstad, Norway | 6:59.97 |
| 1994 | Johann Olav Koss, Norway | 6:34.96 WR |
| 1998 | Gianni Romme, Netherlands | 6:22.20 WR |

#### 10,000 METERS

| | | |
|---|---|---|
| 1924 | Julius Skutnabb, Finland | 18:04.8 |
| 1928 | Not held, thawing of ice | |
| 1932 | Irving Jaffee, United States | 19:13.6 |
| 1936 | Ivar Ballangrud, Norway | 17:24.3 OR |
| 1948 | Ake Seyffarth, Sweden | 17:26.3 |
| 1952 | Hjalmar Andersen, Norway | 16:45.8 OR |
| 1956 | Sigvard Ericsson, Sweden | 16:35.9 OR |
| 1960 | Knut Johannesen, Norway | 15:46.6 WR |
| 1964 | Jonny Nilsson, Sweden | 15:50.1 |
| 1968 | Johnny Höglin, Sweden | 15:23.6 OR |
| 1972 | Ard Schenk, Netherlands | 15:01.35 OR |
| 1976 | Piet Kleine, Netherlands | 14:50.59 OR |
| 1980 | Eric Heiden, United States | 14:28.13 WR |
| 1984 | Igor Malkov, USSR | 14:39.90 |
| 1988 | Tomas Gustafson, Sweden | 13:48.20 WR |
| 1992 | Bart Veldkamp, Netherlands | 14:12.12 |
| 1994 | Johann Olav Koss, Norway | 13:30.55 WR |
| 1998 | Gianni Romme, Netherlands | 13:15.33 WR |

### Women

#### 500 METERS

| | | |
|---|---|---|
| 1960 | Helga Haase, E Germany | 45.9 |
| 1964 | Lydia Skoblikova, USSR | 45.0 OR |
| 1968 | Lyudmila Titova, USSR | 46.1 |
| 1972 | Anne Henning, United States | 43.33 OR |
| 1976 | Sheila Young, United States | 42.76 OR |
| 1980 | Karin Enke, E Germany | 41.78 OR |
| 1984 | Christa Rothenburger, E Germany | 41.02 OR |

#### 500 METERS *(Cont.)*

| | | |
|---|---|---|
| 1988 | Bonnie Blair, United States | 39.10 WR |
| 1992 | Bonnie Blair, United States | 40.33 |
| 1994 | Bonnie Blair, United States | 39.25 |
| 1998 | Catriona LeMay Doan, Canada | 38.21 OR |
| | (second run) | |

Note: OR=Olympic Record; WR=World Record; EOR=Equals Olympic Record; EWR=Equals World Record; WB=World Best.

## SPEED SKATING *(Cont.)*
### Women *(Cont.)*

#### 1,000 METERS

| | | |
|---|---|---|
| 1960 | Klara Guseva, USSR | 1:34.1 |
| 1964 | Lydia Skoblikova, USSR | 1:33.2 OR |
| 1968 | Carolina Geijssen, Netherlands | 1:32.6 OR |
| 1972 | Monika Pflug, W Germany | 1:31.40 OR |
| 1976 | Tatiana Averina, USSR | 1:28.43 OR |
| 1980 | Natalya Petruseva, USSR | 1:24.10 OR |
| 1984 | Karin Enke, E Germany | 1:21.61 OR |
| 1988 | Christa Rothenburger, E Germany | 1:17.65 WR |
| 1992 | Bonnie Blair, United States | 1:21.90 |
| 1994 | Bonnie Blair, United States | 1:18.74 |
| 1998 | Marianne Timmer, Netherlands | 1:16.51 OR |

#### 1,500 METERS

| | | |
|---|---|---|
| 1960 | Lydia Skoblikova, USSR | 2:25.2 WR |
| 1964 | Lydia Skoblikova, USSR | 2:22.6 OR |
| 1968 | Kaija Mustonen, Finland | 2:22.4 OR |
| 1972 | Dianne Holum, United States | 2:20.85 OR |
| 1976 | Galina Stepanskaya, USSR | 2:16.58 OR |
| 1980 | Anne Borckink, Netherlands | 2:10.95 OR |
| 1984 | Karin Enke, E Germany | 2:03.42 WR |
| 1988 | Yvonne van Gennip, Netherlands | 2:00.68 OR |
| 1992 | Jacqueline Boerner, Germany | 2:05.87 |

#### 1,500 METERS *(Cont.)*

| | | |
|---|---|---|
| 1994 | Emese Hunyady, Austria | 2:02.19 |
| 1998 | Marianne Timmer, Netherlands | 1:57.58 WR |

#### 3,000 METERS

| | | |
|---|---|---|
| 1960 | Lydia Skoblikova, USSR | 5:14.3 |
| 1964 | Lydia Skoblikova, USSR | 5:14.9 |
| 1968 | Johanna Schut, Netherlands | 4:56.2 OR |
| 1972 | Christina Baas-Kaiser, Netherlands | 4:52.14 OR |
| 1976 | Tatiana Averina, USSR | 4:45.19 OR |
| 1980 | Bjorg Eva Jensen, Norway | 4:32.13 OR |
| 1984 | Andrea Schöne, E Germany | 4:24.79 OR |
| 1988 | Yvonne van Gennip, Netherlands | 4:11.94 WR |
| 1992 | Gunda Niemann, Germany | 4:19.90 |
| 1994 | Svetlana Bazhanova, Russia | 4:17.43 |
| 1998 | Gunda Niemann-Stirnemann, Germany | 4:07.29 OR |

#### 5,000 METERS

| | | |
|---|---|---|
| 1988 | Yvonne van Gennip, Netherlands | 7:14.13 WR |
| 1992 | Gunda Niemann, Germany | 7:31.57 |
| 1994 | Claudia Pechstein, Germany | 7:14.37 |
| 1998 | Claudia Pechstein, Germany | 6:59.61 WR |

## SHORT TRACK SPEED SKATING

### Men

#### 500 METERS

| | | |
|---|---|---|
| 1994 | Chae Ji-Hoon, S Korea | 43.54 |
| 1998 | Takafumi Nishitani, Japan | 42.862 |

#### 1,000 METERS

| | | |
|---|---|---|
| 1992 | Kim Ki-Hoon, S Korea | 1:30.76 |
| 1994 | Kim Ki-Hoon, S Korea | 1:34.57 |
| 1998 | Kim Dong Sung, S Korea | 1:32.375 |

#### 5,000-METER RELAY

| | | |
|---|---|---|
| 1992 | Korea | 7:14.02 |
| 1994 | Italy | 7:11.74 |
| 1998 | Canada | 7:06.075 |

### Women

#### 500 METERS

| | | |
|---|---|---|
| 1992 | Cathy Turner, United States | 47.04 |
| 1994 | Cathy Turner, United States | 45.98 |
| 1998 | Annie Perreault, Canada | 46.568 |

#### 1,000 METERS

| | | |
|---|---|---|
| 1994 | Chun Lee Kyung, S Korea | 1:36.87 |
| 1998 | Chun Lee Kyung, S Korea | 1:42.776 |

#### 3,000-METER RELAY

| | | |
|---|---|---|
| 1992 | Canada | 4:36.62 |
| 1994 | S Korea | 4:26.64 |
| 1998 | S Korea | 4:16.260 |

## ALPINE SKIING
### Men

#### DOWNHILL

| | | |
|---|---|---|
| 1948 | Henri Oreiller, France | 2:55.0 |
| 1952 | Zeno Colo, Italy | 2:30.8 |
| 1956 | Anton Sailer, Austria | 2:52.2 |
| 1960 | Jean Vuarnet, France | 2:06.0 |
| 1964 | Egon Zimmermann, Austria | 2:18.16 |
| 1968 | Jean-Claude Killy, France | 1:59.85 |
| 1972 | Bernhard Russi, Switzerland | 1:51.43 |
| 1976 | Franz Klammer, Austria | 1:45.73 |
| 1980 | Leonhard Stock, Austria | 1:45.50 |
| 1984 | Bill Johnson, United States | 1:45.59 |
| 1988 | Pirmin Zurbriggen, Switzerland | 1:59.63 |
| 1992 | Patrick Ortlieb, Austria | 1:50.37 |
| 1994 | Tommy Moe, United States | 1:45.75 |
| 1998 | Jean-Luc Crétier, France | 1:50.11 |

#### SLALOM

| | | |
|---|---|---|
| 1948 | Edi Reinalter, Switzerland | 2:10.3 |
| 1952 | Othmar Schneider, Austria | 2:00.0 |
| 1956 | Anton Sailer, Austria | 3:14.7 |
| 1960 | Ernst Hinterseer, Austria | 2:08.9 |
| 1964 | Josef Stiegler, Austria | 2:11.13 |
| 1968 | Jean-Claude Killy, France | 1:39.73 |
| 1972 | Francisco Fernandez Ochoa, Spain | 1:49.27 |
| 1976 | Piero Gros, Italy | 2:03.29 |
| 1980 | Ingemar Stenmark, Sweden | 1:44.26 |
| 1984 | Phil Mahre, United States | 1:39.41 |
| 1988 | Alberto Tomba, Italy | 1:39.47 |
| 1992 | Finn Christian Jagge, Norway | 1:44.39 |
| 1994 | Thomas Stangassinger, Austria | 2:02.02 |
| 1998 | Hans-Petter Buraas, Norway | 1:49.31 |

## ALPINE SKIING
### Men *(Cont.)*

#### GIANT SLALOM
| | | |
|---|---|---|
| 1952 | Stein Eriksen, Norway | 2:25.0 |
| 1956 | Anton Sailer, Austria | 3:00.1 |
| 1960 | Roger Staub, Switzerland | 1:48.3 |
| 1964 | Francois Bonlieu, France | 1:46.71 |
| 1968 | Jean-Claude Killy, France | 3:29.28 |
| 1972 | Gustav Thöni, Italy | 3:09.62 |
| 1976 | Heini Hemmi, Switzerland | 3:26.97 |
| 1980 | Ingemar Stenmark, Sweden | 2:40.74 |
| 1984 | Max Julen, Switzerland | 2:41.18 |
| 1988 | Alberto Tomba, Italy | 2:06.37 |
| 1992 | Alberto Tomba, Italy | 2:06.98 |
| 1994 | Markus Wasmeier, Germany | 2:52.46 |
| 1998 | Hermann Maier, Austria | 2:38.51 |

#### SUPER GIANT SLALOM
| | | |
|---|---|---|
| 1988 | Franck Piccard, France | 1:39.66 |
| 1992 | Kjetil Andre Aamodt, Norway | 1:13.04 |
| 1994 | Markus Wasmeier, Germany | 1:32.53 |
| 1998 | Hermann Maier, Austria | 1:34.82 |

#### COMBINED*
| | | Pts |
|---|---|---|
| 1936 | Franz Pfnür, Germany | 99.25 |
| 1948 | Henri Oreiller, France | 3.27 |
| 1988 | Hubert Strolz, Austria | 36.55 |
| 1992 | Josef Polig, Italy | 14.58 |
| 1994 | Lasse Kjus, Norway | 3:17.53 |
| 1998 | Mario Reiter, Austria | 3:08.06 |

### Women

#### DOWNHILL
| | | |
|---|---|---|
| 1948 | Hedy Schlunegger, Switzerland | 2:28.3 |
| 1952 | Trude Jochum-Beiser, Austria | 1:47.1 |
| 1956 | Madeleine Berthod, Switzerland | 1:40.7 |
| 1960 | Heidi Biebl, W Germany | 1:37.6 |
| 1964 | Christl Haas, Austria | 1:55.39 |
| 1968 | Olga Pall, Austria | 1:40.87 |
| 1972 | Marie-Theres Nadig, Switzerland | 1:36.68 |
| 1976 | Rosi Mittermaier, W Germany | 1:46.16 |
| 1980 | Annemarie Moser-Pröll, Austria | 1:37.52 |
| 1984 | Michela Figini, Switzerland | 1:13.36 |
| 1988 | Marina Kiehl, W Germany | 1:25.86 |
| 1992 | Kerrin Lee-Gartner, Canada | 1:52.55 |
| 1994 | Katja Seizinger, Germany | 1:35.93 |
| 1998 | Katja Seizinger, Germany | 1:28.89 |

#### SLALOM
| | | |
|---|---|---|
| 1948 | Gretchen Fraser, United States | 1:57.2 |
| 1952 | Andrea Mead Lawrence, United States | 2:10.6 |
| 1956 | Renee Colliard, Switzerland | 1:52.3 |
| 1960 | Anne Heggtveigt, Canada | 1:49.6 |
| 1964 | Christine Goitschel, France | 1:29.86 |
| 1968 | Marielle Goitschel, France | 1:25.86 |
| 1972 | Barbara Cochran, United States | 1:31.24 |
| 1976 | Rosi Mittermaier, W Germany | 1:30.54 |
| 1980 | Hanni Wenzel, Liechtenstein | 1:25.09 |
| 1984 | Paoletta Magoni, Italy | 1:36.47 |
| 1988 | Vreni Schneider, Switzerland | 1:36.69 |
| 1992 | Petra Kronberger, Austria | 1:32.68 |
| 1994 | Vreni Schneider, Switzerland | 1:56.01 |
| 1998 | Hilde Gerg, Germany | 1:32.40 |

#### GIANT SLALOM
| | | |
|---|---|---|
| 1952 | Andrea Mead Lawrence, U.S. | 2:06.8 |
| 1956 | Ossi Reichert, W Germany | 1:56.5 |
| 1960 | Yvonne Rüegg, Switzerland | 1:39.9 |
| 1964 | Marielle Goitschel, France | 1:52.24 |
| 1968 | Nancy Greene, Canada | 1:51.97 |
| 1972 | Marie-Theres Nadig, Switzerland | 1:29.90 |
| 1976 | Kathy Kreiner, Canada | 1:29.13 |
| 1980 | Hanni Wenzel, Liechtenstein (2 runs) | 2:41.66 |
| 1984 | Debbie Armstrong, United States | 2:20.98 |
| 1988 | Vreni Schneider, Switzerland | 2:06.49 |
| 1992 | Pernilla Wiberg, Sweden | 2:12.74 |
| 1994 | Deborah Compagnoni, Italy | 2:30.97 |
| 1998 | Deborah Compagnoni, Italy | 2:50.59 |

#### SUPER GIANT SLALOM
| | | |
|---|---|---|
| 1988 | Sigrid Wolf, Austria | 1:19.03 |
| 1992 | Deborah Compagnoni, Italy | 1:21.22 |
| 1994 | Diann Roffe-Steinrotter, U.S. | 1:22.15 |
| 1998 | Picabo Street, United States | 1:18.02 |

#### COMBINED*
| | | Pts |
|---|---|---|
| 1988 | Anita Wachter, Austria | 29.25 |
| 1992 | Petra Kronberger, Austria | 2.55 |
| 1994 | Pernilla Wiberg, Sweden | 3:05.16 |
| 1998 | Katja Seizinger, Germany | 2:40.74 |

*Beginning in 1994, scoring was based on time.

## FREESTYLE SKIING

### Men
#### MOGULS
| | | Pts |
|---|---|---|
| 1992 | Edgar Grospiron, France | 25.81 |
| 1994 | Jean-Luc Brassard, Canada | 27.24 |
| 1998 | Jonny Moseley, United States | 26.93 |

#### AERIALS
| | | Pts |
|---|---|---|
| 1994 | Andreas Schoenbaechler, Switz | 234.67 |
| 1998 | Eric Bergoust, United States | 255.64 |

### Women
#### MOGULS
| | | Pts |
|---|---|---|
| 1992 | Donna Weinbrecht, United States | 23.69 |
| 1994 | Stine Lise Hattestad, Norway | 25.97 |
| 1998 | Tae Satoya, Japan | 25.06 |

#### AERIALS
| | | Pts |
|---|---|---|
| 1994 | Lina Cherjazova, Uzbekistan | 166.84 |
| 1998 | Nikki Stone, United States | 193.00 |

## NORDIC SKIING
### Men

#### 10 KILOMETERS CLASSICAL STYLE

| | | |
|---|---|---|
| 1992 | Vegard Ulvang, Norway | 27:36.0 |
| 1994 | Bjørn Dæhlie, Norway | 24:20.1 |
| 1998 | Bjørn Dæhlie, Norway | 27:24.5 |

#### 15 KILOMETERS CLASSICAL STYLE

| | | |
|---|---|---|
| 1924 | Thorlief Haug, Norway | 1:14:31.0* |
| 1928 | Johan Gröttumsbraaten, Norway | 1:37:01.0† |
| 1932 | Sven Utterström, Sweden | 1:23:07.0‡ |
| 1936 | Erik-August Larsson, Sweden | 1:14:38.0* |
| 1948 | Martin Lundström, Sweden | 1:13:50.0* |
| 1952 | Hallgeir Brenden, Norway | 1:01:34.0* |
| 1956 | Hallgeir Brenden, Norway | 49:39.0 |
| 1960 | Haakon Brusveen, Norway | 51:55.5 |
| 1964 | Eero Mantyränta, Finland | 50:54.1 |
| 1968 | Harald Grönningen, Norway | 47:54.2 |
| 1972 | Sven-Ake Lundback, Sweden | 45:28.24 |
| 1976 | Nikolay Bajukov, Unified Team | 43:58.47 |
| 1980 | Thomas Wassberg, Sweden | 41:57.63 |
| 1984 | Gunde Swan, Sweden | 41:25.6 |
| 1988 | Michael Deviatyarov, USSR | 41:18.9 |

*Distance was 18 km. †Distance was 19.7 km.
‡Distance was 18.2 km.

#### 15 KILOMETERS PURSUIT FREESTYLE

| | | |
|---|---|---|
| 1992 | Bjørn Dæhlie, Norway | 1:05:37.9 |
| 1994 | Bjørn Dæhlie, Norway | 1:00:08.8 |
| 1998 | Thomas Alsgaard, Norway | 1:07:01.7 |

#### 30 KILOMETERS CLASSICAL STYLE

| | | |
|---|---|---|
| 1956 | Veikko Hakulinen, Finland | 1:44:06.0 |
| 1960 | Sixten Jernberg, Sweden | 1:51:03.9 |
| 1964 | Eero Mantyränta, Finland | 1:30:50.7 |
| 1968 | Franco Nones, Italy | 1:35:39.2 |
| 1972 | Viaceslav Vedenine, USSR | 1:36:31.2 |
| 1976 | Sergei Savelyev, USSR | 1:30:29.38 |
| 1980 | Nikolai Simyatov, USSR | 1:27:02.80 |
| 1984 | Nikolai Simyatov, USSR | 1:28:56.3 |
| 1988 | Alexey Prokororov, USSR | 1:24:26.3 |
| 1992 | Vegard Ulvang, Norway | 1:22:27.8 |
| 1994 | Thomas Alsgaard, Norway | 1:12:26.4 |
| 1998 | Mika Myllylae, Finland | 1:33:55.8 |

#### 50 KILOMETERS FREESTYLE

| | | |
|---|---|---|
| 1924 | Thorlief Haug, Norway | 3:44:32.0 |
| 1928 | Per Erik Hedlund, Sweden | 4:52:03.0 |
| 1932 | Veli Saarinen, Finland | 4:28:00.0 |
| 1936 | Elis Wlklund, Sweden | 3:30:11.0 |
| 1948 | Nils Karlsson, Sweden | 3:47:48.0 |
| 1952 | Veikko Hakulinen, Finland | 3:33:33.0 |
| 1956 | Sixten Jernberg, Sweden | 2:50:27.0 |
| 1960 | Kalevi Hämäläinen, Finland | 2:59:06.3 |
| 1964 | Sixten Jernberg, Sweden | 2:43:52.6 |
| 1968 | Olle Ellefsaeter, Norway | 2:28:45.8 |
| 1972 | Paal Tyldrum, Norway | 2:43:14.75 |
| 1976 | Ivar Formo, Norway | 2:37:30.50 |
| 1980 | Nikolai Simyatov, USSR | 2:27:24.60 |
| 1984 | Thomas Wassberg, Sweden | 2:15:55.8 |
| 1988 | Gunde Svan, Sweden | 2:04:30.9 |
| 1992 | Bjørn Dæhlie, Norway | 2:03:41.5 |
| 1994 | Vladimir Smirnov, Kazakhstan | 2:07:20.3 |
| 1998 | Bjørn Dæhlie, Norway | 2:05:08.2 |

#### 4 X 10-KILOMETER RELAY MIXED STYLE

| | | |
|---|---|---|
| 1936 | Finland | 2:41:33.0 |
| 1948 | Sweden | 2:32:80.0 |
| 1952 | Finland | 2:20:16.0 |
| 1956 | USSR | 2:15:30.0 |
| 1960 | Finland | 2:18:45.6 |
| 1964 | Sweden | 2:18:34.6 |
| 1968 | Norway | 2:08:33.5 |
| 1972 | USSR | 2:04:47.94 |
| 1976 | Finland | 2:07:59.72 |
| 1980 | USSR | 1:57:03.46 |
| 1984 | Sweden | 1:55:06.3 |
| 1988 | Sweden | 1:43:58.6 |
| 1992 | Norway | 1:39:26.0 |
| 1994 | Italy | 1:41:15.0 |
| 1998 | Norway | 1:40:55.7 |

#### SKI JUMPING (NORMAL HILL)

| | | Pts |
|---|---|---|
| 1964 | Veikko Kankkonen, Finland | 229.90 |
| 1968 | Jiri Raska, Czechoslovakia | 216.5 |
| 1972 | Yukio Kasaya, Japan | 244.2 |
| 1976 | Hans-Georg Aschenbach, E Germany | 252.0 |
| 1980 | Toni Innauer, Austria | 266.3 |
| 1984 | Jens Andersen, E Germany | 215.2 |
| 1988 | Matti Nykänen, Finland | 229.1 |
| 1992 | Ernst Vettori, Austria | 222.8 |
| 1994 | Espen Bredesen, Norway | 282.0 |
| 1998 | Jani Soininen, Finland | 234.5 |

#### SKI JUMPING (LARGE HILL)

| | | Pts |
|---|---|---|
| 1924 | Jacob Tullin Thams, Norway | 18.960 |
| 1928 | Alf Andersen, Norway | 19.208 |
| 1932 | Birger Ruud, Norway | 228.1 |
| 1936 | Birger Ruud, Norway | 232.0 |
| 1948 | Petter Hugsted, Norway | 228.1 |
| 1952 | Arnfinn Bergmann, Norway | 226.0 |
| 1956 | Antti Hyvärinen, Finland | 227.0 |
| 1960 | Helmut Recknagel, E Germany | 227.2 |
| 1964 | Toralf Engan, Norway | 230.70 |
| 1968 | Vladimir Beloussov, USSR | 231.3 |
| 1972 | Wojciech Fortuna, Poland | 219.9 |
| 1976 | Karl Schnabl, Austria | 234.8 |
| 1980 | Jouko Tormanen, Finland | 271.0 |
| 1984 | Matti Nykänen, Finland | 231.2 |
| 1988 | Matti Nykänen, Finland | 224.0 |
| 1992 | Toni Nieminen, Finland | 239.5 |
| 1994 | Jens Weissflog, Germany | 274.5 |
| 1998 | Kazuyoshi Funaki, Japan | 272.3 |

#### TEAM SKI JUMPING

| | | Pts |
|---|---|---|
| 1988 | Finland | 634.4 |
| 1992 | Finland | 644.4 |
| 1994 | Germany | 970.1 |
| 1998 | Japan | 933.0 |

## NORDIC SKIING *(Cont.)*
### Men *(Cont.)*

**NORDIC COMBINED**

| | Pts |
|---|---|
| 1924 .... Thorleif Haug, Norway | 18.906* |
| 1928 .... Johan Gröttumsbraaten, Norway | 17.833* |
| 1932 .... Johan Gröttumsbraaten, Norway | 446.0 |
| 1936 .... Oddbjörn Hagen, Norway | 430.30 |
| 1948 .... Heikki Hasu, Finland | 448.80 |
| 1952 .... Simon Slattvik, Norway | 451.621 |
| 1956 .... Sverre Stenersen, Norway | 455.0 |
| 1960 .... Georg Thoma, W Germany | 457.952 |
| 1964 .... Tormod Knutsen, Norway | 469.28 |
| 1968 .... Frantz Keller, W Germany | 449.04 |
| 1972 .... Ulrich Wehling, E Germany | 413.34 |
| 1976 .... Ulrich Wehling, E Germany | 423.39 |

**NORDIC COMBINED *(Cont.)***

| | Pts |
|---|---|
| 1980 .... Ulrich Wehling, E Germany | 432.20 |
| 1984 .... Tom Sandberg, Norway | 422.595 |
| 1988 .... Hippolyt Kempf, Switzerland | 432.230 |
| 1992 .... Fabrice Guy, France | 426.47 |
| 1994 .... Fred B. Lundberg, Norway | 457.970 |
| 1998 .... Bjarte Engen Vik, Norway | 41:21.1† |

**TEAM NORDIC COMBINED**

| | |
|---|---|
| 1988 .... W Germany | |
| 1992 .... Japan | |
| 1994 .... Japan | |
| 1998 .... Norway | |

\* Different scoring system; 1924–1952 distance was 18 km; 1952–present, 15 km.

† Times in the cross-country race were not converted into points. According to the Gundersen Method, used since 1988, starting times in the race are staggered in proportion to points earned in the ski jumping segment of the event.

## Women

**5 KILOMETERS CLASSICAL STYLE**

| | |
|---|---|
| 1964 .... Klaudia Boyarskikh, USSR | 17:50.5 |
| 1968 .... Toini Gustafsson, Sweden | 16:45.2 |
| 1972 .... Galina Kulakova, USSR | 17:00.50 |
| 1976 .... Helena Takalo, Finland | 15:48.69 |
| 1980 .... Raisa Smetanina, USSR | 15:06.92 |
| 1984 .... Marja-Liisa Hamalainen, Finland | 17:04.0 |
| 1988 .... Marjo Matikainen, Finland | 15:04.0 |
| 1992 .... Marjut Lukkarinen, Finland | 14:13.8 |
| 1994 .... Lyubova Egorova, Russia | 14:08.8 |
| 1998 .... Larissa Lazhutina, Russia | 17:37.9 |

**10 KILOMETERS CLASSICAL STYLE**

| | |
|---|---|
| 1952 .... Lydia Widemen, Finland | 41:40.0 |
| 1956 .... Lyubov Kosyryeva, USSR | 38:11.0 |
| 1960 .... Maria Gusakova, USSR | 39:46.6 |
| 1964 .... Klaudia Boyarskikh, USSR | 40:24.3 |
| 1968 .... Toini Gustafsson, Sweden | 36:46.5 |
| 1972 .... Galina Kulakova, USSR | 34:17.8 |
| 1976 .... Raisa Smetanina, USSR | 30:13.41 |
| 1980 .... Barbara Petzold, E Germany | 30:31.54 |
| 1984 .... Marja-Liisa Hamalainen, Finland | 31:44.2 |
| 1988 .... Vida Ventsene, USSR | 30:08.3 |

**10 KILOMETERS PURSUIT FREESTYLE**

| | |
|---|---|
| 1992 .... Lyubov Egorova, Unified Team | 40:07.7 |
| 1994 .... Lyubov Egorova, Russia | 41:38.1 |
| 1998 .... Larissa Lazhutina, Russia | 46:06.9 |

**15 KILOMETERS CLASSICAL STYLE**

| | |
|---|---|
| 1992 .... Lyubov Egorova, Unified Team | 42:20.8 |
| 1994 .... Manuela Di Centa, Italy | 39:44.5 |
| 1998 .... Olga Danilova, Russia | 46:55.04 |

**20 KILOMETERS FREESTYLE**

| | |
|---|---|
| 1984 .... Marja-Liisa Hamalainen, Finland | 1:01:45.0 |
| 1988 .... Tamara Tikhonova, USSR | 55:53.6 |

**30 KILOMETERS FREESTYLE**

| | |
|---|---|
| 1992 .... Stefania Belmondo, Italy | 1:22:30.1 |
| 1994 .... Manuela Di Centa, Italy | 1:25:41.6 |
| 1998 .... Julija Tchepalova, Russia | 1:22:01.5 |

**4 X 5-KILOMETER RELAY MIXED STYLE**

| | |
|---|---|
| 1956 .... Finland | 1:9:01.0 |
| 1960 .... Sweden | 1:4:21.4 |
| 1964 .... USSR | 59:20.0 |
| 1968 .... Norway | 57:30.0 |
| 1972 .... USSR | 48:46.15 |
| 1976 .... USSR | 1:07:49.75 |
| 1980 .... E Germany | 1:02:11.10 |
| 1984 .... Norway | 1:06:49.7 |
| 1988 .... USSR | 59:51.1 |
| 1992 .... Unified Team | 59:34.8 |
| 1994 .... Russia | 57:12.5 |
| 1998 .... Russia | 55:13.5 |

## SNOWBOARDING

### Men

**GIANT SLALOM**

| | |
|---|---|
| 1998 .... Ross Rebagliati, Canada | 2:03.96 |

**HALF-PIPE**

| | Pts |
|---|---|
| 1998 .... Gian Simmen, Switzerland | 85.2 |

### Women

**GIANT SLALOM**

| | |
|---|---|
| 1998 .... Karine Ruby, France | 2:17.34 |

**HALF-PIPE**

| | Pts |
|---|---|
| 1998 .... Nicola Thost, Germany | 74.6 |

Track & Field

SIMON BRUTY

Schoolboy miler
Alan Webb

# Prodigy

## A high school miler seized track's spotlight with an electrifying performance in Oregon

### BY MERRELL NODEN

I F YOU HAD predicted at the start of the year that the athlete generating the most excitement on the U.S. track circuit would be a high schooler, you'd have been whisked off to the nearest asylum and punished appropriately, given a wedgie, say, or forced to sit through a 24-hour marathon of Adam Sandler movies.

In a year that saw Michael Johnson retire, Marion Jones finally lose a 100 and Maurice Greene take another step toward becoming the greatest 100 man of all time, the moment of purest exhilaration was provided by Alan Webb, a muscular 18-year-old senior at South Lakes High in Reston, Va.

Webb's goal was a familiar one: Not since 1967, when Marty Liquori clocked 3:59.8, had an American high schooler broken four minutes for what is still the most hallowed of track events, the mile. Jim Ryun's national prep record of 3:55.3 was even older, standing unthreatened for 36 years.

In January, Webb and his coach, Scott Raczko, showed they were not above a little subterfuge in their quest for history. To escape rising expectations, they kept secret Webb's entry in an all-comers mile in New York City. There Webb did what even the great Ryun hadn't: clocked 3:59.86 for the first indoor sub-four run by a prep. The stage was set.

For their big outdoor effort Webb and Raczko picked the Prefontaine meet, on May 27, in Eugene, where they knew they'd get a fast pace and a supportive crowd. When the gun went off, Webb showed patience and savvy beyond his years, biding his time near the back of the pack through reasonable splits of 58.1 and 1:57.8. He reached the bell in 2:58.4 in seventh place. With 300 to go he accelerated, picking runners off down the backstretch, starting with NCAA champ Bryan Berryhill. The knowledgeable crowd roared, realizing it was witnessing history. Webb nailed three more runners before fading slightly at the finish, which he reached in fifth place, his face twisted in a gasp of agony. The time was 3:53.43.

For track diehards who had come to believe that no one would ever challenge Ryun's mark, the time was mind-boggling. It didn't just break Ryun's storied mark, it smashed it by almost two seconds. Indeed, it was the fastest mile by an American of any age since 1998. "I'm excited to see what I can run this summer," said Webb, who will attend Michigan in the fall. "I'm still young, and there are races to be run."

There was talk of Webb's making the world championship team in the 1,500. He didn't, running 3:38.50 at the U.S. nationals, for fifth, a performance that appeared disappointing until one recalled that this time too was faster than Ryun's old national mark.

BILL FRAKES

**Despite tendinitis in his left knee, Greene (center) ran a sizzling 100 at the worlds.**

Webb gave a jolt of energy to a slightly flat year that ended in a muted world championships in Edmonton, only the second at which no world records were set. In the time-honored Olympic events, only two men's world records fell all year: Brahim Boulami of Morocco ran 7:55.28 in the steeplechase, while Roman Sebrle of the Czech Republic became the first man to break 9,000 points in the decathlon, scoring 9,026 in late May. Vault wonder woman Stacy Dragila set a Sergei Bubka–like total of eight world records, indoors and out. Johnson, history's best long sprinter, conducted a seasonlong farewell tour, running only relays. In his absence the winning time in the Edmonton 400 was 44.64, a jog for Johnson.

Jones, meanwhile, had a year of mixed fortune, starting with her divorce from shot-putter C.J. Hunter. Having decided to forgo long jumping this season, she went unbeaten in the sprints for most of the year, though clearly she was not at her peak. Proof of this came in the world championship semis, where she was nipped by Zhanna Pintuse-vich-Block, a Ukrainian veteran. In the final Pintusevich-Block got out fast and held her small lead over Jones, edging her 10.82 to 10.85, and then fell to her knees in surprise. "I still cannot believe," she said.

Though Jones returned to win the 200 and anchor the U.S. women's winning 400 rclay, in 2002 people will wonder whether she has come back to the pack—not likely— or had been merely distracted by personal problems and post-Olympic letdown.

The U.S. men's sprint corps, whose supposed vulnerability was a constant theme in the mid-'90s, returned with a vengeance. For the fifth straight year Greene, the muscle-bound Olympic champion, led the way, but Tim Montgomery made it interesting. After losing his spikes in Oslo, he wore Jones's to clock 9.84, stunning on a cool night. "I'm on pace to run 9.75," he announced, throwing down the gauntlet.

"He'd better be wearing Marion's shoes again," said Greene.

Montgomery looked like a real threat in Edmonton, where Greene was suffering from tendinitis in his left knee. But in the final Montgomery false-started, forcing him to start conservatively the second time. He chased Greene all the way, but couldn't quite catch him. Greene's time, 9.82, was especially impressive since it came against a headwind and on a bad knee. Behind him, Montgomery (9.85) and Bernard Williams (9.94) completed the first U.S. world championships sweep since 1991.

While the year may have been flat, and the great Johnson is retiring, there's no need for handwringing: Veterans like Jones, Greene and Dragila are far from finished, and Webb has just started.

## USATF Outdoor Championships

### Eugene, Oregon, June 21–24, 2001

## Men

### 100 METERS
1. .............Tim Montgomery, ZMA TC    9.95
2. .............Bernard Williams, Nike    9.98
3. .............Curtis Johnson, HSI    10.01

### 200 METERS
1. .............Shawn Crawford, Mizuno    20.54
2. .............Ramon Clay, Nike    20.60
3. .............Kevin Little, Nike    20.64

### 400 METERS
1. .............Antonio Pettigrew, adidas    45.08
2. .............Leonard Byrd, Nike    45.26
3. .............Jerome Young, adidas    45.32

### 800 METERS
1. .............David Krummenacker, adidas    1:47.40
2. .............Derrick Peterson, adidas    1:47.40
3. .............Jesse Stritzel, Nike    1:47.53

### 1,500 METERS
1. .............Andy Downin, Nike    3:37.63
2. .............Senaca Lassiter, Nike    3:37.66
3. .............Paul McMullen    3:37.94

### 5,000 METERS
1. .............Bob Kennedy, Nike    13:28.72
2. .............Alan Culpepper, adidas    13:29.66
3. .............Adam Goucher, Team Fila    13:30.36

### 10,000 METERS
1. .............Abdi Abdirahman, Nike    28:23.82
2. .............Mebrahtom Keflezighi, Nike    28:39.64
3. .............Alan Culpepper, adidas    28:49.03

### 110-METER HURDLES
1. .............Allen Johnson, Nike    13.22
2. .............Terrence Trammell, Mizuno    13.46
3. .............Dawane Wallace, adidas    13.60

### 400-METER HURDLES
1. .............Angelo Taylor, Nike    48.53
2. .............Calvin Davis, adidas    48.75
3. .............James Carter, Nike    48.79

### 3,000-METER STEEPLECHASE
1. .............Thomas Chorny, Nike    8:22.16
2. .............Anthony Famiglietti, adidas    8:22.68
3. .............Tim Broe, adidas    8:24.66

### HIGH JUMP
1. .............Nathan Leeper, Nike    7 ft 6½ in
2. .............Charles Austin    7 ft 6½ in
3. .............Henry Patterson    7 ft 5¼ in

### POLE VAULT
1. .............Lawrence Johnson, adidas    19 ft 2¼ in
2. .............Timothy Mack, Nike    18 ft 10¼ in
3. .............Nicholas Hysong, Nike    18 ft 6½ in

### LONG JUMP
1. .............Savante Stringfellow    27 ft 9½ in
2. .............Miguel Pate, Alabama    27 ft 4¾ in
3. .............Dwight Phillips, Nike    27 ft

### TRIPLE JUMP
1. .............Lamark Carter, Nike    56 ft 4 in
2. .............Robert Howard    55 ft 7 in
3. .............Walter Davis, Louisiana St    55 ft 6¼ in

### SHOT PUT
1. .............John Godina, adidas    70 ft 10½ in
2. .............Adam Nelson, Nike    67 ft 5¼ in
3. .............John Davis, NYAC    67 ft 3½ in

### DISCUS
1. .............Adam Setliff, Nike    219 ft 4 in
2. .............John Godina, adidas    214 ft 6 in
3. .............Andrew Bloom, Nike    206 ft 7 in

### HAMMER THROW
1. .............Kevin McMahon, NYAC    251 ft
2. .............Jay Harvard    240 ft 1 in
3. .............James Parker    237 ft 10 in

### JAVELIN
1. .............Breaux Greer    279 ft 7 in
2. .............Tom Pukstys, adidas    244 ft 5 in
3. .............Ron White, Eastern Illinois    238 ft 7 in

### DECATHLON
1. .............Kip Janvrin    8241 pts
2. .............Phil McMullen, Indian Invaders    8220
3. .............Bryan Clay, Azusa Pacific    8169

### 20,000-METER RACE WALK
1. .............Curt Clausen, NYAC    1:24:50
2. .............Tim Seaman, NYAC    1:26:15
3. .............Sean Albert, New Balance–NJ    1:26:34

## Women

### 100 METERS

| | |
|---|---|
| 1. Chryste Gaines, ZMA TC | 10.89 |
| 2. Kelli White, Nike | 10.93 |
| 3. Angela Williams, unattached | 11.01 |

### 200 METERS

| | |
|---|---|
| 1. Marion Jones, Nike | 22.52 |
| 2. Latasha Jenkins, Nike | 22.88 |
| 3. Kelli White, Nike | 22.93 |

### 400 METERS

| | |
|---|---|
| 1. LaTasha Colander-Richar, Nike | 50.79 |
| 2. Michelle Collins, Nike | 51.00 |
| 3. Monique Hennagan, adidas | 51.20 |

### 800 METERS

| | |
|---|---|
| 1. Regina Jacobs, Nike | 2:00.43 |
| 2. Hazel Clark, Nike | 2:01.15 |
| 3. Jennifer Toomey, Reebok Boston | 2:01.28 |

### 1,500 METERS

| | |
|---|---|
| 1. Regina Jacobs, Nike | 4:06.12 |
| 2. Suzy Favor Hamilton, Nike | 4:06.61 |
| 3. Sarah Schwald, Nike | 4:08.57 |

### 5,000 METERS

| | |
|---|---|
| 1. Marla Runyan, Asics TC | 15:08.03 |
| 2. Regina Jacobs, Nike | 15:10.78 |
| 3. Elva Dryer, Nike | 15:11.76 |

### 10,000 METERS

| | |
|---|---|
| 1. Deena Drossin, Asics TC | 32:05.14 |
| 2. Jen Rhines, adidas | 32:20.03 |
| 3. Sylvia Mosqueda, Team Fila | 32:25.22 |

### 100-METER HURDLES

| | |
|---|---|
| 1. Gail Devers, Nike | 12.91 |
| 2. Jenny Adams, SMTC | 13.11 |
| 3. Anjanette Kirkland, Nike | 13.14 |

### 400-METER HURDLES

| | |
|---|---|
| 1. Sandra Glover, Nike | 55.08 |
| 2. Tonja Buford-Bailey, Nike | 55.71 |
| 3. Brenda Taylor, Harvard | 55.99 |

### 3,000-METER STEEPLECHASE

| | |
|---|---|
| 1. Lisa Nye, NIKE–Portland | 9:49.41 |
| 2. Elizabeth Jackson, Nike | 9:49.94 |
| 3. Kelly MacDonald, Arizona St | 9:55.49 |

### HIGH JUMP

| | |
|---|---|
| 1. Amy Acuff, Asics TC | 6 ft 2 in |
| 2. Erin Aldrich, Asics TC | 6 ft ½ in |
| 3. Stacy Ann Grant, Shore AC | 6 ft ½ in |

### POLE VAULT

| | |
|---|---|
| 1. Stacy Dragila, Nike | 15 ft 1¾ in |
| 2. Alicia Warlick, SMTC | 14 ft 5¼ in |
| 3. Mary Sauer, Asics TC | 14 ft 5¼ in |

### LONG JUMP

| | |
|---|---|
| 1. Jenny Adams, SMTC | 22 ft ¼ in |
| 2. Grace Upshaw, unattached | 21 ft 8¾ in |
| 3. Briana Glenn, Arizona | 21 ft 3½ in |

### TRIPLE JUMP

| | |
|---|---|
| 1. Tiombe Hurd, Nike | 46 ft ¾ in |
| 2. Yuliana Perez, Pima CC | 45 ft 10½ in |
| 3. Sheila Hudson, unattached | 44 ft 10¾ in |

### SHOT PUT

| | |
|---|---|
| 1. Seilala Sue, unattached | 58 ft 11½ in |
| 2. Connie Price-Smith, Nike | 58 ft 8½ in |
| 3. Kristin L. Heaston, Sacramento TC | 56 ft 4 in |

### DISCUS

| | |
|---|---|
| 1. Seilala Sue, unattached | 207 ft 10 in |
| 2. Suzy Powell, Asics TC | 207 ft 8 in |
| 3. Kris Kuehl, unattached | 205 ft 7 in |

### HAMMER THROW

| | |
|---|---|
| 1. Dawn Ellerbe, NYAC | 226 ft 8 in |
| 2. Anna Norgren, SoBe TF | 218 ft 9 in |
| 3. Melissa Price, unattached | 217 ft 4 in |

### JAVELIN

| | |
|---|---|
| 1. Kim Kreiner, unattached | 182 ft 11 in |
| 2. Erica Wheeler, unattached | 172 ft |
| 3. Serene Ross, Purdue | 170 ft 10 in |

### HEPTATHLON

| | |
|---|---|
| 1. DeDee Nathan, Indiana Invaders | 6174 pts |
| 2. Shelia Burrell, Nike | 6051 |
| 3. Gigi Miller, Arkansas | 5925 |

### 20,000-METER RACE WALK

| | |
|---|---|
| 1. Michelle Rohl, Moving Comfort RT | 1:32:49 |
| 2. Amber Antonia, unattached | 1:36:37 |
| 3. Jill Zenner, Miami Valley TC | 1:37:10 |

# 2001 IAAF World Championships

## Edmonton, Canada, August 3–12, 2001

### Men

#### 100 METERS

1. ............Maurice Greene, USA — 9.82
2. ............Tim Montgomery, USA — 9.85
3. ............Bernard Williams, USA — 9.94

#### 200 METERS

1. ............Konstadínos Kedéris, Greece — 20.04
2. ............Christopher Williams, Jamaica — 20.20
3. ............Kim Collins, St. Kitts & Nevis — 20.20

#### 400 METERS

1. ............Avard Moncur, Bahamas — 44.64
2. ............Ingo Schultz, Germany — 44.87
3. ............Gregory Haughton, Jamaica — 44.98

#### 800 METERS

1. ............André Bucher, Switzerland — 1:43.70
2. ............Wilfred Bungei, Kenya — 1:44.55
3. ............Pawal Czapiewski, Poland — 1:44.63

#### 1,500 METERS

1. ............Hicham El Guerrouj, Morocco — 3:30.68
2. ............Bernard Lagat, Kenya — 3:31.10
3. ............Driss Maazouzi, France — 3:31.54

#### 5,000 METERS

1. ............Richard Limo, Kenya — 13:00.77
2. ............Ail Saïdi-Sief, Algeria — 13:02.16
3. ............Million Wolde, Ethiopia — 13:03.47

#### 10,000 METERS

1. ............Charles Kamathi, Kenya — 27:53.25
2. ............Assefa Mezgebu, Ethiopia — 27:53.97
3. ............Haile Gebrselassie, Ethiopia — 27:54.41

#### MARATHON

1. ............Gezahegne Abera, Ethiopia — 2:12:42
2. ............Simon Biwott, Kenya — 2:12.43
3. ............Stefano Baldini, Italy — 2:13:18

#### 3,000-METER STEEPLECHASE

1. ............Reuben Kosgei, Kenya — 8:15.16
2. ............Ali Ezzine, Morocco — 8:16.21
3. ............Bernard Barmasai, Kenya — 8:16.59

#### 110-METER HURDLES

1. ............Allen Johnson, USA — 13.04
2. ............Anier García, Cuba — 13.07
3. ............Dudley Dorival, Haiti — 13.25

#### 400-METER HURDLES

1. ............Felix Sánchez, Dominican Rep. — 47.49
2. ............Fabrizio Mori, Italy — 47.54
3. ............Dai Tamesue, Japan — 47.89

#### HIGH JUMP

1. ............Martin Buss, Germany — 7 ft 8¾ in
2. ............Vyacheslav Voronin, Russia — 7 ft 7¾ in
2. ............Yaroslav Rybakov, Russia — 7 ft 7¾ in

#### POLE VAULT

1. ............Dmitri Markov, Australia — 19 ft 10¼ in
2. ............Aleksandr Averbukh, Israel — 19 ft 2¼ in
3. ............Nick Hysong, USA — 19 ft 2¼ in

#### LONG JUMP

1. ............Iván Pedroso, Cuba — 27 ft 6¾ in
2. ............Savante Stringfellow, USA — 27 ft ½ in
3. ............Carlos Calado, Portugal — 26 ft 11¼ in

#### TRIPLE JUMP

1. ............Jonathan Edwards, Great Britain — 58 ft 9½ in
2. ............Christian Olsson, Sweden — 57 ft 3¾ in
3. ............Igor Spasovkhodskiy, Russia — 57 ft 2¾ in

#### SHOT PUT

1. ............John Godina, USA — 71 ft 9 in
2. ............Adam Nelson, USA — 68 ft 9¼ in
3. ............Arsi Harju, Finland — 68 ft 8 in

#### DISCUS

1. ............Lars Riedel, Germany — 228 ft 9 in
2. ............Virgilijus Alekna, Lithuania — 227 ft 8 in
3. ............Michael Möllenbeck, Ger. — 221 ft 10 in

#### HAMMER THROW

1. ............Szymon Ziólkowski, Poland — 273 ft 7 in
2. ............Koji Murofuski, Japan — 272 ft
3. ............Ilya Konovalov, Russia — 263 ft 4 in

#### JAVELIN

1. ............Jan Zelezny, Czech Republic — 304 ft 5 in
2. ............Aki Parviainen, Finland — 299 ft 7 in
3. ............K. Gatssioúdis, Greece — 295 ft 1 in

#### 20-KILOMETER WALK

1. ............Roman Rasskazov, Russia — 1:20:31
2. ............Ilya Markov, Russia — 1:20:33
3. ............Viktor Burayev, Russia — 1:20:36

#### 50-KILOMETER WALK

1. ............Robert Korzeniowski, Poland — 3:42:08
2. ............Jesús Angel García, Spain — 3:43:07
3. ............Edgar Hernandez, Mexico — 3:46:12

#### 4 x 100 RELAY

1. ............United States — 37.96
2. ............South Africa — 38.47
3. ............Trindad and Tobago — 38.58

#### 4 x 400 RELAY

1. ............United States — 2:57.54
2. ............Bahamas — 2:58.19
3. ............Jamaica — 2:58.39

#### DECATHLON

1. ............Tomás Dvorák, Czech Republic — 8902 pts
2. ............Erki Nool, Estonia — 8815
3. ............Dean Macey, Great Britain — 8603

## Women

### 100 METERS

1. ............Zhanna Pintusevich-Block, Ukraine 10.82
2. ............Marion Jones, USA 10.85
3. ............Ekateríni Thánou, Greece 10.91

### 200 METERS

1. ............Marion Jones, USA 22.39
2. ............Debbie Ferguson, Bahamas 22.52
3. ............Kelli White, USA 22.56

### 400 METERS

1. ............Amy Mbacke Thiam, Senegal 49.86
2. ............Lorraine Fenton, Jamaica 49.88
3. ............Ana Guevara, Mexico 49.97

### 800 METERS

1. ............Maria Mutola, Mozambique 1:57.17
2. ............Stephanie Graf, Austria 1:57.20
3. ............Letitia Vriesde, Surinam 1:57.35

### 1,500 METERS

1. ............Gabriela Szabo, Romania 4:00.57
2. ............Violeta Szekely, Romania 4:01.70
3. ............Natalya Gorelova, Russia 4:02.40

### 5,000 METERS

1. ............Olga Yegorova, Russia 15:03.39
2. ............Marta Domínguez, Spain 15:06.59
3. ............Ayelech Worku, Ethiopia 15:10.17

### 10,000 METERS

1. ............Derartu Tulu, Ethiopia 31:48.81
2. ............Berhane Adere, Ethiopia 31:48.85
3. ............Gete Wami, Ethiopia 31:49.98

### MARATHON

1. ............Lidia Simon, Romania 2:26:01
2. ............Reiko Tosa, Japan 2:26:06
3. ............Svetlana Zakharova, Russia 2:26:18

### 100-METER HURDLES

1. ............Anjanette Kirkland, USA 12.42
2. ............Gail Devers, USA 12.54
3. ............Olga Shishigina, Kazakhstan 12.58

### 400-METER HURDLES

1. ............Nezha Bidouane, Morocco 53.34
2. ............Yuliya Nosova, Russia 54.27
3. ............Daimí Pernía, Cuba 54.51

### HIGH JUMP

1. ............Hestrie Cloete, S Africa 6 ft 6¾ in
2. ............Inha Babakova, Ukraine 6 ft 6¾ in
3. ............Kajsa Bergqvist, Sweden 6 ft 5½ in

### POLE VAULT

1. ............Stacy Dragila, USA 15 ft 7 in
2. ............Svetlana Feofanova, Russia 15 ft 7 in
3. ............Monika Pyrek, Poland 14 ft 11 in

### LONG JUMP

1. ............Fiona May, Italy 23 ft ½ in
2. ............Tatyana Kotova, Russia 23 ft
3. ............Niurka Montalvo, Spain 22 ft 7 in

### TRIPLE JUMP

1. ............Tatyana Lebedeva, Russia 50 ft ½ in
2. ............Etone F. Mbango, Cameroon 47 ft 10¾ in
3. ............Tereza Marinova, Bulgaria 47 ft 10 in

### SHOT PUT

1. ............Yanina Korolchik, Belarus 67 ft 7½ in
2. ............N. Kleinert-Schmitt, Germany 61 ft 10¾ in
3. ............Vita Pavlysh, Ukraine 56 ft 4 in

### DISCUS

1. ............Natalya Sadova, Russia 224 ft 11 in
2. ............Ellina Zvereva, Belarus 220 ft 1 in
3. ............Nicoleta Grasu, Romania 217 ft 4 in

### HAMMER THROW

1. ............Yipsi Moreno, Cuba 231 ft 9 in
2. ............Olga Kuzenkova, Russia 231 ft 8 in
3. ............Bronwyn Eagles, Australia 225 ft 11 in

### JAVELIN

1. ............Osleidys Menéndez, Cuba 228 ft 1 in
2. ............Miréla Manjani-Tzelili, Greece 215 ft 9 in
3. ............Sonia Bisset, Cuba 212 ft 3 in

### 20-KILOMETER WALK

1. ............Olimpiada Ivanova, Russia 1:27:48
2. ............Valentina Tsybulskaya, Belarus 1:28:49
3. ............Elisabetta Perrone, Italy 1:28:56

### 4 x 100 RELAY

1. ............United States 41.71
2. ............Germany 42.32
3. ............France 42.39

### 4 x 400 RELAY

1. ............Jamaica 3:20.65
2. ............Germany 3:21.97
3. ............Russia 3:24.92

### HEPTATHLON

1. ............Yelena Prokhorova, Russia 6694 pts
2. ............Natalya Sazanovich, Belarus 6539
3. ............Shelia Burrell, USA 6472

# IAAF World Cross-Country Championships

## Ostend, Belgium, March 24–25, 2001

### 60 METERS
| | | |
|---|---|---|
| 1. | Maurice Greene, Nike | 6.51 |
| 2. | Tim Harden, Nike | 6.53 |
| 3. | Tim Montgomery, Nike | 6.56 |

### 200 METERS
| | | |
|---|---|---|
| 1. | Coby Miller, Nike | 20.31 |
| 2. | Kevin Little, Nike | 20.44 |
| 3. | Shawn Crawford, unattached | 20.45 |

# Major Marathons

## Chicago: October 22, 2000

### MEN
| | | |
|---|---|---|
| 1. | Khalid Khannouchi, United States | 2:07:01 |
| 2. | Josephat Kiprono Kenya | 2:07:29 |
| 3. | Moses Tanui, Kenya | 2:07:47 |

### WOMEN
| | | |
|---|---|---|
| 1. | Catherine Ndereba, Kenya | 2:21:33 |
| 2. | Lornah Kiplagat, Kenya | 2:22:36 |
| 3. | Irinia Timofeyeva, Russia | 2:29:13 |

## New York City: November 5, 2000

### MEN
| | | |
|---|---|---|
| 1. | Abdelkhader El Mouaziz, Morocco | 2:10:09 |
| 2. | Japhet Kosgei, Kenya | 2:12:30 |
| 3. | Shem Kororia, Kenya | 2:12:33 |

### WOMEN
| | | |
|---|---|---|
| 1. | Ludmila Petrova, Russia | 2:25:45 |
| 2. | Franca Fiacconi, Italy | 2:26:03 |
| 3. | Margaret Okayo, Kenya | 2:26:36 |

## Tokyo: November 19, 2000

### WOMEN ONLY
| | | |
|---|---|---|
| 1. | Joyce Chepchumba, Kenya | 2:24:02 |
| 2. | Reiko Tosa, Japan | 2:24:47 |
| 3. | Derartu Tulu, Ethiopia | 2:26:38 |

## Tokyo: February 18, 2001

### MEN ONLY
| | | |
|---|---|---|
| 1. | Kenichi Takahashi, Japan | 2:10:51 |
| 2. | Tesfaye Jifar, Ethiopia | 2:11:07 |
| 3. | Dmitri Kapitonov, Russia | 2:11:09 |

## Rome: March 25, 2001

### MEN
| | | |
|---|---|---|
| 1. | Henry Cherono, Kenya | 2:11:33 |
| 2. | Ottavio Andriani, Italy | 2:11:39 |
| 3. | Alberico DiCecco, Italy | 2:12:43 |

### WOMEN
| | | |
|---|---|---|
| 1. | Maria Guida, Italy | 2:30:40 |
| 2. | Abossa Ememet, Italy | 2:36:32 |
| 3. | Angelina Kanana, Italy | 2:39:10 |

## Paris: April 8, 2001

### MEN
| | | |
|---|---|---|
| 1. | Simon Biwott, Kenya | 2:09:40 |
| 2. | David Kirui, Kenya | 2:09:40 |
| 3. | Fred Kiprop, Kenya | 2:09:43 |

### WOMEN
| | | |
|---|---|---|
| 1. | Florence Barsosio, Kenya | 2:27:53 |
| 2. | Ruth Kutol, Kenya | 2:27:54 |
| 3. | Alina Tecuta, Romania | 2:29:16 |

## Boston: April 16, 2001

### MEN
| | | |
|---|---|---|
| 1. | Lee Bong-Ju, Korea | 2:09:43 |
| 2. | Silvio Guerra, Ecuador | 2:10:07 |
| 3. | Joshua Chelanga, Kenya | 2:10:29 |

### WOMEN
| | | |
|---|---|---|
| 1. | Catherine Ndereba, Kenya | 2:23:53 |
| 2. | Malgorzata Sobanska, Poland | 2:26:42 |
| 3. | Lyubov Morgunova, Russia | 2:27:18 |

## Rotterdam: April 22, 2001

### MEN
| | | |
|---|---|---|
| 1. | Josephat Kiprono, Kenya | 2:06:50 |
| 2. | Kenneth Cheruiyot, Kenya | 2:07:18 |
| 3. | Sammy Korir, Kenya | 2:08:15 |

### WOMEN
| | | |
|---|---|---|
| 1. | Susan Chepkemei, Kenya | 2:25:45 |
| 2. | Masako Koide, Japan | 2:28:28 |
| 3. | Madja Wijenberg, Netherlands | 2:30:27 |

## London: April 22, 2001

### MEN
| | | |
|---|---|---|
| 1. | Abdelkader El Mouaziz, Morocco | 2:07:11 |
| 2. | Paul Tergat, Kenya | 2:08:15 |
| 3. | Antonio Pinto, Portugal | 2:09:36 |

### WOMEN
| | | |
|---|---|---|
| 1. | Deratu Tulu, Ethiopia | 2:23:57 |
| 2. | Svetlana Zakharova, Russia | 2:24:04 |
| 3. | Joyce Chepchumba, Kenya | 2:24:12 |

# FOR THE RECORD·Year by Year

## TRACK AND FIELD

## World Records

As of October 1, 2001. World outdoor records are recognized by the International Amateur Athletics Federation (IAAF).

### Men

| Event | Mark | Record Holder | Date | Site |
|---|---|---|---|---|
| 100 meters | 9.79 | Maurice Greene, United States | 6-16-99 | Athens |
| 200 meters | 19.32 | Michael Johnson, United States | 8-1-96 | Atlanta |
| 400 meters | 43.18 | Michael Johnson, United States | 8-26-99 | Seville |
| 800 meters | 1:41.11 | Wilson Kipketer, Denmark | 8-24-97 | Cologne |
| 1,000 meters | 2:11.96 | Noah Ngeny, Kenya | 9-5-99 | Rieti, Italy |
| 1,500 meters | 3:26.00 | Hicham El Guerrouj, Morocco | 7-14-98 | Rome |
| Mile | 3:43.13 | Hicham El Guerrouj, Morocco | 7-7-99 | Rome |
| 2,000 meters | 4:44.79 | Hicham El Guerrouj, Morocco | 9-7-99 | Berlin |
| 3,000 meters | 7:20.67 | Daniel Komen, Kenya | 9-1-96 | Rieti, Italy |
| Steeplechase | 7:55.28 | Brahim Boulami, Morocco | 8-24-01 | Brussels |
| 5,000 meters | 12:39.36 | Haile Gebrselassie, Ethiopia | 6-13-98 | Helsinki |
| 10,000 meters | 26:22.75 | Haile Gebrselassie, Ethiopia | 6-1-98 | Hengelo, Netherlands |
| 20,000 meters | 56:55.6 | Arturo Barrios, Mexico | 3-30-91 | La Flâche, France |
| Hour | 21,101 meters | Arturo Barrios, Mexico | 3-30-91 | La Flâche, France |
| 25,000 meters | 1:13:55.8 | Toshihiko Seko, Japan | 3-22-81 | Christchurch, New Zealand |
| 30,000 meters | 1:29:18.8 | Toshihiko Seko, Japan | 3-22-81 | Christchurch, New Zealand |
| Marathon | 2:05:42 | Khalid Khannouchi, Morocco | 10-24-99 | Chicago |
| 110-meter hurdles | 12.91 | Colin Jackson, Great Britain | 8-20-93 | Stuttgart, Germany |
| 400-meter hurdles | 46.78 | Kevin Young, United States | 8-6-92 | Barcelona |
| 20-kilometer walk | 1:17:25.6 | Bernardo Segura, Mexico | 5-7-94 | Bergen, Norway |
| 30-kilometer walk | 2:01:44.1 | Maurizio Damilano, Italy | 10-3-92 | Cuneo, Italy |
| 50-kilometer walk | 3:40:57.9 | Thierry Toutain, France | 9-29-96 | Héricourt, France |
| 4 x 100-meter relay | 37.40 | United States (Mike Marsh, Leroy Burrell, Dennis Mitchell, Carl Lewis) | 8-8-92 | Barcelona |
| | | United States (Jon Drummond, Andre Cason, Dennis Mitchell, Leroy Burrell) | 8-21-93 | Stuttgart, Germany |
| 4 x 200-meter relay | 1:18.68 | Santa Monica TC (Mike Marsh, Leroy Burrell, Floyd Heard, Carl Lewis) | 4-17-94 | Walnut, CA |
| 4 x 400-meter relay | 2:54.20 | United States (Jerome Young, Antonio Pettigrew, Tyree Washington, Michael Johnson) | 7-22-98 | New York City |
| 4 x 800-meter relay | 7:03.89 | Great Britain (Peter Elliott, Garry Cook, Steve Cram, Sebastian Coe) | 8-30-82 | London |
| 4 x 1,500-meter relay | 14:38.8 | W Germany (Thomas Wessinghage, Harald Hudak, Michael Lederer, Karl Fleschen) | 8-17-77 | Cologne |
| High jump | 8 ft ½ in | Javier Sotomayor, Cuba | 7-27-93 | Salamanca, Spain |
| Pole vault | 20 ft 1¾ in | Sergei Bubka, Ukraine | 7-31-94 | Sestriere, Italy |
| Long jump | 29 ft 4½ in | Mike Powell, United States | 8-30-91 | Tokyo |
| Triple jump | 60 ft ¼ in | Jonathan Edwards, Great Britain | 8-7-95 | Göteborg, Sweden |
| Shot put | 75 ft 10¼ in | Randy Barnes, United States | 5-20-90 | Westwood, CA |
| Discus throw | 243 ft 0 in | Jürgen Schult, E Germany | 6-6-86 | Neubrandenburg, Germany |
| Hammer throw | 284 ft 7 in | Yuri Syedikh, USSR | 8-30-86 | Stuttgart, Germany |
| Javelin throw | 323 ft 1 in | Jan Zelezny, Czech Republic | 5-25-96 | Jena, Germany |
| Decathlon | 9026 pts | Roman Sebrle, Czech Republic | 5-27-01 | Götzis |

Note: The decathlon consists of 10 events: the 100 meters, long jump, shot put, high jump and 400 meters on the first day; the 110-meter hurdles, discus, pole vault, javelin and 1,500 meters on the second.

## Women

| Event | Mark | Record Holder | Date | Site |
|---|---|---|---|---|
| 100 meters | 10.49 | Florence Griffith Joyner, United States | 7-16-88 | Indianapolis |
| 200 meters | 21.34 | Florence Griffith Joyner, United States | 9-29-88 | Seoul |
| 400 meters | 47.60 | Marita Koch, E Germany | 10-6-85 | Canberra, Australia |
| 800 meters | 1:53.28 | Jarmila Kratochvílová, Czechoslovakia | 7-26-83 | Munich |
| 1,000 meters | 2:28.98 | Svetlana Masterkova, Russia | 8-23-96 | Brussels |
| 1,500 meters | 3:50.46 | Qu Yunxia, China | 9-11-93 | Beijing |
| Mile | 4:12.56 | Svetlana Masterkova, Russia | 8-14-96 | Zurich |
| 2,000 meters | 5:25.36 | Sonia O'Sullivan, Ireland | 7-8-94 | Edinburgh |
| 3,000 meters | 8:06.11 | Wang Junxia, China | 9-13-93 | Beijing |
| Steeplechase | 9:25.31 | Justyna Bak, Poland | 7-9-01 | Nice |
| 5,000 meters | 14:28.09 | Jiang Bo, China | 10-23-97 | Shanghai |
| 10,000 meters | 29:31.78 | Wang Junxia, China | 9-8-93 | Beijing |
| Hour | 18,340 meters | Tegla Loroupe, Kenya | 8-8-98 | Borgholzhausen, Germany |
| 20,000 meters | 1:05:26.6 | Tegla Loroupe, Kenya | 9-3-00 | Borgholzhausen, Germany |
| 25,000 meters | 1:29:29.2 | Karolina Szabó, Hungary | 4-22-88 | Budapest |
| 30,000 meters | 1:47:05.6 | Karolina Szabó, Hungary | 4-22-88 | Budapest |
| Marathon | 2:20:43 | Tegla Loroupe, Kenya | 9-26-99 | Berlin |
| 100-meter hurdles | 12.21 | Yordanka Donkova, Bulgaria | 8-20-88 | Stara Zagora, Bulgaria |
| 400-meter hurdles | 52.61 | Kim Batten, United States | 8-11-95 | Göteborg, Sweden |
| 5-kilometer walk | 20:13.26 | Kerry Saxby, Australia | 2-25-96 | Hobart, Australia |
| 10-kilometer walk | 41:56.23 | Nadezhda Ryashkina, URS | 7-24-90 | Seattle |
| 4 x 100-meter relay | 41.37 | East Germany (Silke Gladisch, Sabine Reiger, Ingrid Auerswald, Marlies Göhr) | 10-6-85 | Canberra, Australia |
| 4 x 200-meter relay | 1:27.46 | United States (LaTasha Jenkins, LaTasha Colander-Richardson, Nanceen Perry, Marion Jones) | 4-29-00 | Philadelphia |
| 4 x 400-meter relay | 3:15.17 | USSR (Tatyana Ledovskaya, Olga Nazarova, Maria Pinigina, Olga Bryzgina) | 10-1-88 | Seoul |
| 4 x 800-meter relay | 7:50.17 | USSR (Nadezhda Olizarenko, Lyubov Gurina, Lyudmila Borisova, Irina Podyalovskaya) | 8-5-84 | Moscow |
| High jump | 6 ft 10¼ in | Stefka Kostadinova, Bulgaria | 8-30-87 | Rome |
| Pole vault | 15 ft 9¼ in | Stacy Dragila, United States | 6-9-01 | Palo Alto, California |
| Long jump | 24 ft 8¼ in | Galina Chistyakova, USSR | 6-11-88 | Leningrad |
| Triple jump | 50 ft 10¼ in | Inessa Kravets, Ukraine | 8-10-95 | Göteborg, Sweden |
| Shot put | 74 ft 3 in | Natalya Lisovskaya, USSR | 6-7-87 | Moscow |
| Discus throw | 252 ft | Gabriele Reinsch, E Germany | 7-9-88 | Neubrandenburg, Germany |
| Hammer throw | 247 ft 3 in | Mihaela Melinte, Romania | 8-29-99 | Rüdlingen, Switzerland |
| Javelin throw | 234 ft 8 in | Osleidys Menéndez, Cuba | 7-1-01 | Réthymno, Greece |
| Heptathlon | 7291 pts | Jackie Joyner-Kersee, United States | 9-23/24-88 | Seoul |

Note: The heptathlon consists of 7 events: the 100-meter hurdles, high jump, shot put and 200 meters on the first day; the long jump, javelin and 800 meters on the second.

# American Records

As of September 26, 2001. American outdoor records are recognized by USA Track and Field (USATF). WR=world record. EWR=equals world record.

## Men

| Event | Mark | Record Holder | Date | Site |
|---|---|---|---|---|
| 100 meters | 9.79 WR | Maurice Greene | 6-16-99 | Athens |
| 200 meters | 19.32 WR | Michael Johnson | 8-1-96 | Atlanta |
| 400 meters | 43.18 WR | Michael Johnson | 8-26-99 | Seville |
| 800 meters | 1:42.60 | Johnny Gray | 8-28-85 | Koblenz, Germany |
| 1,000 meters | 2:13.9 | Rick Wohlhuter | 7-30-74 | Oslo |
| 1,500 meters | 3:29.77 | Sydney Maree | 8-25-85 | Cologne |
| Mile | 3:47.69 | Steve Scott | 7-7-82 | Oslo |
| 2,000 meters | 4:52.44 | Jim Spivey | 9-15-87 | Lausanne |
| 3,000 meters | 7:30.84 | Bob Kennedy | 8-8-98 | Monte Carlo |
| Steeplechase | 8:09.17 | Henry Marsh | 8-28-85 | Koblenz, Germany |
| 5,000 meters | 12:58.21 | Bob Kennedy | 8-14-96 | Zurich |
| 10,000 meters | 27:13.98 | Mebrahtom Keflezighi | 5-4-01 | Palo Alto, California |
| 20,000 meters | 58:25.0 | Bill Rodgers | 8-9-77 | Boston |
| Hour | 20,547 meters | Bill Rodgers | 8-9-77 | Boston |
| 25,000 meters | 1:14:11.8 | Bill Rodgers | 2-21-79 | Saratoga, CA |
| 30,000 meters | 1:31:49 | Bill Rodgers | 2-21-79 | Saratoga, CA |
| Marathon | 2:07:01 | Khalid Khannouchi | 10-22-00 | Chicago |
| 110-meter hurdles | 12.92 | Roger Kingdom | 8-16-89 | Zurich |
| | | Allen Johnson | 6-23-96 | Atlanta |
| | | Allen Johnson | 8-23-96 | Brussels |
| 400-meter hurdles | 46.78 WR | Kevin Young | 8-6-92 | Barcelona |
| 20-kilometer walk | 1:23:40 | Tim Seaman | 8-14-00 | La Jolla, CA |
| 30-kilometer walk | 2:14:31 | Allen James | 10-31-93 | Atlanta |
| 50-kilometer walk | 3:59:41.1 | Herman Nelson | 6-9-96 | Seattle |
| 4x100-meter relay | 37.40 WR | United States (Mike Marsh, Leroy Burrell, Dennis Mitchell, Carl Lewis) | 8-8-92 | Barcelona |
| | | United States (Jon Drummond, Andre Cason, Dennis Mitchell, Leroy Burrell) | 8-21-93 | Stuttgart, Germany |
| 4x200-meter relay | 1:18.68 WR | Santa Monica Track Club (Mike Marsh, Leroy Burrell, Floyd Heard, Carl Lewis) | 4-17-94 | Walnut, CA |
| 4x400-meter relay | 2:54.20 WR | United States (Jerome Young, Antonio Pettigrew, Tyree Washington, Michael Johnson) | 7-22-98 | New York City |
| 4x800-meter relay | 7:06.5 | Santa Monica Track Club (James Robinson, David Mack, Earl Jones, Johnny Gray) | 4-26-86 | Walnut, CA |
| 4x1,500-meter relay | 14:46.3 | National Team (Dan Aldredge, Andy Clifford, Todd Harbour, Tom Duits) | 6-24-79 | Bourges, France |
| High jump | 7 ft 10½ in | Charles Austin | 8-17-91 | Zurich |
| Pole vault | 19 ft 9¾ in | Jeff Hartwig | 6-14-00 | Jonesboro, AR |
| Long jump | 29 ft 4½ in WR | Mike Powell | 8-30-91 | Tokyo |
| Triple jump | 59 ft 4¼ in | Kenny Harrison | 7-27-96 | Atlanta |
| Shot put | 75 ft 10¼ in WR | Randy Barnes | 5-20-90 | Westwood, CA |
| Discus throw | 237 ft 4 in | Ben Plucknett | 7-7-81 | Stockholm |
| Hammer throw | 270 ft 9 in | Lance Deal | 9-7-96 | Milan |
| Javelin throw | 285 ft 10 in | Tom Pukstys | 5-25-97 | Jena, Germany |
| Decathlon | 8891 pts | Dan O'Brien | 9-4/5-92 | Talence, France |

## Women

| Event | Mark | Record Holder | Date | Site |
|---|---|---|---|---|
| 100 meters | 10.49 WR | Florence Griffith Joyner | 7-16-88 | Indianapolis |
| 200 meters | 21.34 WR | Florence Griffith Joyner | 9-29-88 | Seoul |
| 400 meters | 48.83 | Valerie Brisco-Hooks | 8-6-84 | Los Angeles |
| 800 meters | 1:56.40 | Jearl Miles-Clark | 8-11-99 | Zurich |
| 1,500 meters | 3:57.12 | Mary Slaney | 7-26-83 | Stockholm |
| Mile | 4:16.71 | Mary Slaney | 8-21-85 | Zurich |
| 2,000 meters | 5:32.7 | Mary Slaney | 8-3-84 | Eugene, OR |
| 3,000 meters | 8:25.83 | Mary Slaney | 9-7-85 | Rome |
| Steeplechase | 9:41.94 | Elizabeth Jackson | 9-4-01 | Brisbane |
| 5,000 meters | 14:45.38 | Regina Jacobs | 7-21-00 | Sacramento, CA |
| 10,000 meters | 31:19.89 | Lynn Jennings | 8-7-92 | Barcelona |
| Marathon | 2:21:21 | Joan Samuelson | 10-20-85 | Chicago |
| 100-meter hurdles | 12.33 | Gail Devers | 7-23-00 | Sacramento, CA |
| 400-meter hurdles | 52.61 WR | Kim Batten | 8-11-95 | Göteborg, Sweden |
| 5,000-meter walk | 20:56.88 | Michelle Rohl | 4-27-96 | Philadelphia |
| 10,000-meter walk | 44:41.87 | Michelle Rohl | 7-26-94 | St. Petersburg |
| 4 x 100-meter relay | 41.47 | National Team (Chryste Gaines, Marion Jones, Inger Miller, Gail Devers) | 8-9-97 | Athens |
| 4 x 200-meter relay | 1:27.46 WR | USA Blue (LaTasha Jenkins, LaTasha Colander, Nanceen Perry, Marion Jones) | 4-29-00 | Philadelphia |
| 4 x 400-meter relay | 3:15.51 | United States (Denean Howard, Diane Dixon, Valerie Brisco, Florence Griffith Joyner) | 10-1-88 | Seoul |
| 4 x 800-meter relay | 8:17.09 | Athletics West (Sue Addison, Lee Arbogast, Mary Decker, Chris Mullen) | 4-24-83 | Walnut, CA |
| High jump | 6 ft 8 in | Louise Ritter | 7-9-88 | Austin |
| | | Louise Ritter | 9-30-88 | Seoul |
| Pole vault | 15 ft 9¼ in WR | Stacy Dragila | 6-9-01 | Palo Alto, CA |
| Long jump | 24 ft 7 in | Jackie Joyner-Kersee | 5-22-94 | New York City |
| | | | 7-31-94 | Sestriere, Italy |
| Triple jump | 47 ft 3½ in | Sheila Hudson | 7-8-96 | Stockholm |
| Shot put | 66 ft 2½ in | Ramona Pagel | 6-25-88 | San Diego |
| Discus throw | 216 ft 10 in | Carol Cady | 5-31-86 | San Jose |
| Hammer throw | 231 ft 8 in | Dawn Ellerbe | 4-28-01 | Philadelphia |
| Javelin throw | 192 ft 3 in | Lynda Blutreich | 7-1-00 | New Haven, CT |
| Heptathlon | 7291 pts WR | Jackie Joyner-Kersee | 9-23/24-88 | Seoul |

# World and American Indoor Records

As of September 26, 2001. American indoor records are recognized by USA Track and Field. World Indoor records are recognized by the International Amateur Athletics Federation (IAAF).

## Men

| Event | Mark | Record Holder | Date | Site |
|---|---|---|---|---|
| 50 meters | 5.56 | Donovan Bailey, Canada (W) | 2-9-96 | Reno |
| | 5.56 | Maurice Greene (A) | 2-13-99 | Los Angeles |
| 55 meters* | 5.99 | Obadele Thompson, Barbados (W) | 2-22-97 | Colorado Springs |
| | 6.00 | Lee McRae (A) | 3-14-86 | Oklahoma City |
| 60 meters | 6.39 | Maurice Greene (W, A) | 3-1-98 | Madrid |
| | 6.39 | Maurice Greene (W, A) | 3-3-01 | Atlanta |
| 200 meters | 19.92 | Frankie Fredericks, Namibia (W) | 2-18-96 | Liévin, France |
| | 20.26 | Shawn Crawford (A) | 3-11-00 | Fayetteville, AR |
| | 20.26 | John Capel (A) | 3-11-00 | Fayetteville, AR |
| 400 meters | 44.63 | Michael Johnson (W, A) | 3-4-95 | Atlanta |
| 800 meters | 1:42.67 | Wilson Kipketer, Denmark (W) | 3-9-97 | Paris |
| | 1:45.00 | Johnny Gray (A) | 3-8-92 | Sindelfingen, Germany |
| 1,000 meters | 2:14.96 | Wilson Kipketer, Denmark (W) | 2-20-00 | Birmingham, England |
| | 2:18.19 | Ocky Clark (A) | 2-12-89 | Stuttgart, Germany |

## Men (Cont.)

| Event | Mark | Record Holder | Date | Site |
|---|---|---|---|---|
| 1,500 meters | 3:31.18 | Hicham El Guerrouj, Morocco (W) | 2-02-97 | Stuttgart, Germany |
| | 3:38.12 | Jeff Atkinson (A) | 3-5-89 | Budapest |
| Mile | 3:48.45 | Hicham El Guerrouj, Morocco (W) | 2-12-97 | Ghent, Belgium |
| | 3:51.8 | Steve Scott (A) | 2-20-81 | San Diego |
| 3,000 meters | 7:24.90 | Daniel Komen, Kenya (W) | 2-6-98 | Budapest |
| | 7:39.94 | Steve Scott (A) | 2-10-89 | East Rutherford, NJ |
| 5,000 meters | 12:50.38 | Haile Gebrselassie, Ethiopia (W) | 2-14-99 | Birmingham, England |
| | 13:20.55 | Doug Padilla (A) | 2-12-82 | New York City |
| 50-meter hurdles | 6.25 | Mark McKoy, Canada (W) | 3-5-86 | Kobe, Japan |
| | 6.35 | Greg Foster (A) | 1-27-85 | Rosemont, Illinois |
| 55-meter hurdles* | 6.89 | Renaldo Nehemiah (A) | 1-20-79 | New York City |
| 60-meter hurdles | 7.30 | Colin Jackson, Great Britain (W) | 3-6-94 | Sindelfingen, Germany |
| | 7.36 | Greg Foster (A) | 1-16-87 | Los Angeles |
| 5,000-meter walk | 18:07.08 | Mikhail Shchennikov, Russia (W) | 2-14-95 | Moscow |
| | 19:18.40 | Tim Lewis (A) | 3-7-87 | Indianapolis |
| 4 x 200-meter relay | 1:22.11 | Great Britain (W) (Linford Christie, Darren Braithwaite, Ade Mafe, John Regis) | 3-3-91 | Glasgow |
| | 1:22.71 | National Team (A) (Thomas Jefferson, Raymond Pierre, Antonio McKay Kevin Little) | 3-3-91 | Glasgow |
| 4 x 400-meter relay | 3:02.83 | National Team (W, A) (Andre Morris, Dameon Johnson, Deon Minor, Milt Campbell) | 3-7-99 | Maebashi, Japan |
| 4 x 800-meter relay | 7:13.94 | Global Athletics & Marketing (W, A) (Rich Kenah, Joel Woody, Karl Paranya, David Krummenacker) | 2-6-00 | Boston |
| High jump | 7 ft 11½ in | Javier Sotomayor, Cuba (W) | 3-4-89 | Budapest |
| | 7 ft 10½ in | Hollis Conway (A) | 3-10-91 | Seville |
| Pole vault | 20 ft 2 in | Sergei Bubka, Ukraine (W) | 2-21-93 | Donetsk, Ukraine |
| | 19 ft 6½ in | Lawrence Johnson (A) | 3-3-01 | Atlanta |
| Long jump | 28 ft 10¼ in | Carl Lewis (W, A) | 1-27-84 | New York City |
| Triple jump | 58 ft 6 in | Alicier Urrutia, Cuba (W) | 3-1-97 | Sindelfingen, Germany |
| | 58 ft 3¼ in | Mike Conley (A) | 2-27-87 | New York City |
| Shot put | 74 ft 4¼ in | Randy Barnes (W, A) | 1-20-89 | Los Angeles |
| Weight throw | 84 ft 10¼ in | Lance Deal (W, A) | 3-4-95 | Atlanta |
| Pentathlon | 4478 pts | Steve Fritz, (W, A) | 1-14-95 | Lawrence, KS |
| Heptathlon | 6476 pts | Dan O'Brien (W, A) | 3-13/14-93 | Toronto |

*No recognized world record.

## Putting MJ into Perspective

Just how good was Michael Johnson? His absence from high-level 200- and 400-meter races in 2001 (he ran a few lesser races and relays during a low-key farewell tour) gives a hint. Remember the yawning gap between Johnson and runner-up Frankie Fredericks (19.32 seconds to 19.68) in the 200 final at the Atlanta Games? Consider that Fredericks would have beaten the gold medalist at the 2001 worlds, Konstadinos Kederis of Greece (20.04), by roughly the same margin. Only once this year did anyone run a sub-20 200; Johnson did it 23 times in his career. He also ran 22 sub-44 400s; only once this year did anyone break 44.45. Put today's champs into one of Johnson's signature races, and you'd have to photograph it from the front to get MJ and the also-rans in the same frame.

## Women

| Event | Mark | Record Holder | Date | Site |
|---|---|---|---|---|
| 50 meters | 5.96 | Irina Privolova, Russia (W) | 2-9-95 | Madrid |
| | 6.02 | Gail Devers (A) | 2-21-99 | Liévin, France |
| 55 meters* | 6.54 | Evelyn Ashford (A) | 2-26-82 | New York |
| | | Jeanette Bolden (A) | 2-21-86 | Inglewood, CA |
| 60 meters | 6.92 | Irina Privalova, Russia (W) | 2-11-93 | Madrid |
| | 6.92 | Irina Privalova, Russia (W) | 2-9-95 | Madrid |
| | 6.95 | Gail Devers (A) | 3-12-93 | Toronto |
| | 6.95 | Marion Jones (A) | 3-7-98 | Maebashi, Japan |
| 200 meters | 21.87 | Merlene Ottey, Jamaica (W) | 2-13-93 | Liévin, France |
| | 22.33 | Gwen Torrence (A) | 3-2-96 | Atlanta |
| 400 meters | 49.59 | Jarmila Kratochvílová, Czech. (W) | 3-7-82 | Milan |
| | 50.64 | Diane Dixon (A) | 3-10-91 | Seville |
| 800 meters | 1:56.4 | Christine Wachtel, E Germany (W) | 2-13-88 | Vienna |
| | 1:58.9 | Mary Slaney (A) | 2-22-80 | San Diego |
| | 1:58.92 | Suzy Hamilton (A) | 3-7-99 | Boston |
| 1,000 meters | 2:30.94 | Maria Mutola, Mozambique (W) | 2-25-99 | Stockholm |
| | 2:35.29 | Regina Jacobs (A) | 2-6-00 | Boston |
| 1,500 meters | 4:00.27 | Doina Melinte, Romania (W) | 2-9-90 | East Rutherford, NJ |
| | 4:00.80 | Mary Slaney (A) | 2-8-80 | New York City |
| Mile | 4:17.14 | Doina Melinte, Romania (W) | 2-9-90 | East Rutherford, NJ |
| | 4:20.5 | Mary Slaney (A) | 2-19-82 | San Diego |
| 3,000 meters | 8:32.88 | Gabriela Szabo, Romania (W) | 2-18-01 | Birmingham |
| | 8:39.14 | Regina Jacobs (A) | 3-7-99 | Maebashi, Japan |
| 5,000 meters | 14:47.35 | Gabriela Szabo, Romania (W) | 2-13-99 | Dortmund, Germany |
| | 15:07.33 | Marla Runyan (A) | 2-18-01 | New York |
| 50-meter hurdles | 6.58 | Cornelia Oschkenat, E Germany (W) | 2-20-88 | Berlin |
| | 6.67 | Jackie Joyner-Kersee (A) | 2-10-95 | Reno |
| 55-meter hurdles* | 7.30 | Tiffany Lott (A) | 2-20-97 | Air Force Academy, CO |
| 60-meter hurdles | 7.69 | Lyudmila Narozhilenko, Russia (W) | 2-4-90 | Chelyabinsk, Russia |
| | 7.81 | Jackie Joyner-Kersee (A) | 2-5-89 | Fairfax, VA |
| 3,000-meter walk | 11:40.33 | Claudia Iovan, Romania | 1-30-99 | Bucharest |
| | 12:20.79 | Debbi Lawrence (A) | 3-12-93 | Toronto |
| 4 x 200-meter relay | 1:32.55 | SC Eintracht Hamm, W Gemany (W) (Helga Arendt, Silke-Beate Knoll, Mechthild Kluth, Gisela Kinzel) | 2-20-88 | Dortmund, W Germany |
| | 1:33.24 | National Team (A) (Flirtisha Harris, Chryste Gaines, Terri Dendy, Michele Collins) | 2-12-94 | Glasgow |
| 4 x 400-meter relay | 3:24.25 | Russia (W) (Tatyanna Chebykina, Svetlana Goncharenko, Olga Kotlyarova, Natalya Nazarova) | 3-7-99 | Maebashi, Japan |
| | 3:27.59 | National Team (A) (Michelle Collins, Monique Hennagan, Zundra Feagin-Alexander, Shanelle Porter) | 3-7-99 | Maebashi, Japan |
| 4 x 800-meter relay | 8:18.71 | Russia (W) (Natalya Zaytseva, Olga Kuvnetsova, Yelena Afanasyeva, Yekaterina Podkopayeva) | 2-4-94 | Moscow |
| | 8:25.50 | Villanova (A) (Gina Procaccio, Debbie Grant, Michelle DiMuro, Celeste Halliday) | 2-7-87 | Gainesville, FL |
| High jump | 6 ft 9½ in | Heike Henkel, Germany (W) | 2-8-92 | Karlsruhe, Germany |
| | 6 ft 7 in | Tisha Walker (A) | 2-28-98 | Atlanta |
| Pole vault | 15 ft 5 in | Stacy Dragila (W, A) | 2-17-01 | Pocatello, Idaho |
| Long jump | 24 ft 2¼ in | Heike Drechsler, E Germany (W) | 2-13-88 | Vienna |
| | 23 ft 4¾ in | Jackie Joyner-Kersee (A) | 3-5-94 | Atlanta |
| Triple jump | 49 ft 9 in | Ashia Hansen, Great Britain (W) | 2-28-98 | Valencia, Spain |
| | 46 ft 8¼ in | Sheila Hudson-Strudwick (A) | 3-4-95 | Atlanta |
| Shot put | 73 ft 10 in | Helena Fibingerová, Czech. (W) | 2-19-77 | Jablonec, Czech. |
| | 65 ft ¾ in | Ramona Pagel (A) | 2-20-87 | Inglewood, CA |
| Weight throw* | 77 ft 5 in | Dawn Ellerbe (W, A) | 3-4-00 | Atlanta |
| Pentathlon | 4991 pts | Irina Byelova, CIS (W) | 2-14/15-92 | Berlin |
| | 4753 | DeDee Nathan (A) | 3-4/5-99 | Maebashi, Japan |

*No recognized world record.

## Men

### 100 METERS

| | | |
|---|---|---|
| 1983 | Carl Lewis, United States | 10.07 |
| 1987* | Carl Lewis, United States | 9.93 WR |
| 1991 | Carl Lewis, United States | 9.86 WR |
| 1993 | Linford Christie, Great Britain | 9.87 |
| 1995 | Donovan Bailey, Canada | 9.97 |
| 1997 | Maurice Greene, United States | 9.86 |
| 1999 | Maurice Greene, United States | 9.80 |
| 2001 | Maurice Greene, United States | 9.82 |

### 200 METERS

| | | |
|---|---|---|
| 1983 | Calvin Smith, United States | 20.14 |
| 1987 | Calvin Smith, United States | 20.16 |
| 1991 | Michael Johnson, United States | 20.01 |
| 1993 | Frank Fredericks, Namibia | 19.85 |
| 1995 | Michael Johnson, United States | 19.79 |
| 1997 | Ato Boldon, Trinidad and Tobago | 20.04 |
| 1999 | Maurice Greene, United States | 19.90 |
| 2001 | Konstadínos Kedéris, Greece | 20.04 |

### 400 METERS

| | | |
|---|---|---|
| 1983 | Bert Cameron, Jamaica | 45.05 |
| 1987 | Thomas Schoenlebe, E Germany | 44.33 |
| 1991 | Antonio Pettigrew, United States | 44.57 |
| 1993 | Michael Johnson, United States | 43.65 |
| 1995 | Michael Johnson, United States | 43.39 |
| 1997 | Michael Johnson, United States | 44.12 |
| 1999 | Michael Johnson, United States | 43.18 WR |
| 2001 | Avard Moncur, Bahamas | 44.64 |

### 800 METERS

| | | |
|---|---|---|
| 1983 | Willi Wulbeck, W Germany | 1:43.65 |
| 1987 | Billy Konchellah, Kenya | 1:43.06 |
| 1991 | Billy Konchellah, Kenya | 1:43.99 |
| 1993 | Paul Ruto, Kenya | 1:44.71 |
| 1995 | Wilson Kipketer, Denmark | 1:45.08 |
| 1997 | Wilson Kipketer, Denmark | 1:43.38 |
| 1999 | Wilson Kipketer, Denmark | 1:43.30 |
| 2001 | André Bucher, Switzerland | 1:43.70 |

### 1,500 METERS

| | | |
|---|---|---|
| 1983 | Steve Cram, Great Britain | 3:41.59 |
| 1987 | Abdi Bile, Somalia | 3:36.80 |
| 1991 | Noureddine Morceli, Algeria | 3:32.84 |
| 1993 | Noureddine Morceli, Algeria | 3:34.24 |
| 1995 | Noureddine Morceli, Algeria | 3:33.73 |
| 1997 | Hicham El Guerrouj, Morocco | 3:35.83 |
| 1999 | Hicham El Guerrouj, Morocco | 3:27.65 |
| 2001 | Hicham El Guerrouj, Morocco | 3:30.68 |

### STEEPLECHASE

| | | |
|---|---|---|
| 1983 | Patriz Ilg, W Germany | 8:15.06 |
| 1987 | Francesco Panetta, Italy | 8:08.57 |
| 1991 | Moses Kiptanui, Kenya | 8:12.59 |
| 1993 | Moses Kiptanui, Kenya | 8:06.36 |
| 1995 | Moses Kiptanui, Kenya | 8:04.16 |
| 1997 | Wilson Boit Kipketer, Kenya | 8:05.84 |
| 1999 | Christopher Koskei, Kenya | 8:11.76 |
| 2001 | Reuben Kosgei, Kenya | 8:15.16 |

### 5,000 METERS

| | | |
|---|---|---|
| 1983 | Eamonn Coghlan, Ireland | 13:28.53 |
| 1987 | Said Aouita, Morocco | 13:26.44 |
| 1991 | Yobes Ondieki, Kenya | 13:14.45 |
| 1993 | Ismael Kirui, Kenya | 13:02.75 |
| 1995 | Ismael Kirui, Kenya | 13:16.77 |
| 1997 | Daniel Komen, Kenya | 13:07.38 |
| 1999 | Salah Hissou, Morocco | 12:58.13 |
| 2001 | Richard Limo, Kenya | 13:00.77 |

### 10,000 METERS

| | | |
|---|---|---|
| 1983 | Alberto Cova, Italy | 28:01.04 |
| 1987 | Paul Kipkoech, Kenya | 27:38.63 |
| 1991 | Moses Tanui, Kenya | 27:38.74 |
| 1993 | Haile Gebrselassie, Ethiopia | 27:46.02 |
| 1995 | Haile Gebrselassie, Ethiopia | 27:12.95 |
| 1997 | Haile Gebrselassie, Ethiopia | 27:24.58 |
| 1999 | Haile Gebrselassie, Ethiopia | 27:57.27 |
| 2001 | Charles Kamathi, Kenya | 27:53.25 |

### MARATHON

| | | |
|---|---|---|
| 1983 | Rob de Castella, Australia | 2:10:03 |
| 1987 | Douglas Wakiihuri, Kenya | 2:11:48 |
| 1991 | Hiromi Taniguchi, Japan | 2:14:57 |
| 1993 | Mark Plaatjes, United States | 2:13:57 |
| 1995 | Martín Fiz, Spain | 2:11:41 |
| 1997 | Abel Anton, Spain | 2:13:16 |
| 1999 | Abel Anton, Spain | 2:13:36 |
| 2001 | Gezahegne Abera, Ethiopia | 2:12:42 |

### 110-METER HURDLES

| | | |
|---|---|---|
| 1983 | Greg Foster, United States | 13.42 |
| 1987 | Greg Foster, United States | 13.21 |
| 1991 | Greg Foster, United States | 13.06 |
| 1993 | Colin Jackson, Great Britain | 12.91 WR |
| 1995 | Allen Johnson, United States | 13.00 |
| 1997 | Allen Johnson, United States | 12.93 |
| 1999 | Colin Jackson, Great Britain | 13.04 |
| 2001 | Allen Johnson, United States | 13.04 |

### 400-METER HURDLES

| | | |
|---|---|---|
| 1983 | Edwin Moses, United States | 47.50 |
| 1987 | Edwin Moses, United States | 47.46 |
| 1991 | Samuel Matete, Zambia | 47.64 |
| 1993 | Kevin Young, United States | 47.18 |
| 1995 | Derrick Adkins, United States | 47.98 |
| 1997 | Stéphane Diagana, France | 47.70 |
| 1999 | Fabrizio Mori, Italy | 47.72 |
| 2001 | Felix Sánchez, Dominican Rep. | 47.49 |

### 20-KILOMETER WALK

| | | |
|---|---|---|
| 1983 | Ernesto Canto, Mexico | 1:20:49 |
| 1987 | Maurizio Damilano, Italy | 1:20:45 |
| 1991 | Maurizio Damilano, Italy | 1:19:37 |
| 1993 | Valentin Massana, Spain | 1:22:31 |
| 1995 | Michele Didoni, Italy | 1:19:59 |
| 1997 | Daniel Garcia, Mexico | 1:21:43 |
| 1999 | Ilya Markov, Russia | 1:23:34 |
| 2001 | Roman Rasskazov, Russia | 1:20:31 |

### 50-KILOMETER WALK

| | | |
|---|---|---|
| 1983 | Ronald Weigel, E Germany | 3:43:08 |
| 1987 | Hartwig Gauder, E Germany | 3:40:53 |
| 1991 | Aleksandr Potashov, USSR | 3:53:09 |
| 1993 | Jesus Angel Garcia, Spain | 3:41:41 |
| 1995 | Valentin Kononen, Finland | 3:43:42 |
| 1997 | Robert Korzeniowski, Poland | 3:44:46 |
| 1999 | German Skurygin, Russia | 3:44:23 |
| 2001 | Robert Korzeniowski, Poland | 3:42:08 |

### 4 X 100-METER RELAY

| | | |
|---|---|---|
| 1983 | United States (Emmit King, Willie Gault, Calvin Smith, Carl Lewis) | 37.86 |
| 1987 | United States (Lee McRae, Lee McNeil, Harvey Glance, Carl Lewis) | 37.90 |
| 1991 | United States (Andre Cason, Leroy Burrell, Dennis Mitchell, Carl Lewis) | 37.50 WR |
| 1993 | United States (Jon Drummond, | 37.48 |

WR=World record.  *Ben Johnson, Canada, disqualified.

## Men *(Cont.)*

### 4 X 100-METER RELAY *(CONT.)*

|  | Andre Cason, Dennis Mitchell, Leroy Burrell) |  |
|---|---|---|
| 1995 | Canada (Robert Esmie, Glenroy Gilbert, Bruny Surin, Donovan Bailey) | 38.31 |
| 1997 | Canada (Robert Esmie, Glenroy Gilbert, Bruny Surin, Donovan Bailey) | 37.86 |
| 1999 | United States (Jon Drummond, Tim Montgomery, Brian Lewis, Maurice Greene) | 37.59 |
| 2001 | United States (Mickey Grimes, Bernard Williams, Dennis Mitchell, Tim Montgomery) | 37.96 |

### 4 X 400-METER RELAY

| 1983 | USSR (Sergei Lovachev, Alecksandr Troschilo, Nikolay Chernyetski, Viktor Markin) | 3:00.79 |
|---|---|---|
| 1987 | United States (Danny Everett, Rod Haley, Antonio McKay, Butch Reynolds) | 2:57.29 |
| 1991 | Great Britain (Roger Black, Derek Redmond, John Regis, Kriss Akabusi) | 2:57.53 |
| 1993 | United States (Andrew Valmon, Quincy Watts, Butch Reynolds, Michael Johnson) | 2:54.29 WR |
| 1995 | United States (Marlon Ramsey, Derek Mills, Butch Reynolds, Michael Johnson) | 2:57.32 |
| 1997 | United States (Jerome Young, Antonio Pettigrew, Chris Jones, Tyree Washington) | 2:56.47 |
| 1999 | United States (Jerome Davis, Antonio Pettigrew, Angelo Taylor, Michael Johnson) | 2:56.45 |
| 2001 | United States (Leonard Byrd, Antonio Pettigrew, Derrick Brew, Angelo Taylor) | 2:57.54 |

### HIGH JUMP

| 1983 | Gennadi Avdeyenko, USSR | 7 ft 7¼ in |
|---|---|---|
| 1987 | Patrik Sjoberg, Sweden | 7 ft 9¾ in |
| 1991 | Charles Austin, United States | 7 ft 9¾ in |
| 1993 | Javier Sotomayor, Cuba | 7 ft 10½ in |
| 1995 | Troy Kemp, Bahamas | 7 ft 9¼ in |
| 1997 | Javier Sotomayor, Cuba | 7 ft 9¼ in |
| 1999 | Vyacheslav Voronin, Russia | 7 ft 9¼ in |
| 2001 | Martin Buss, Germany | 7 ft 8¾ in |

### POLE VAULT

| 1983 | Sergei Bubka, USSR | 18 ft 8¼ in |
|---|---|---|
| 1987 | Sergei Bubka, USSR | 19 ft 2¼ in |
| 1991 | Sergei Bubka, USSR | 19 ft 6¼ in |
| 1993 | Sergei Bubka, Ukraine | 19 ft 8¼ in |
| 1995 | Sergei Bubka, Ukraine | 19 ft 5 in |
| 1997 | Sergei Bubka, Ukraine | 19 ft 8½ in |
| 1999 | Maksim Tarasov, Russia | 19 ft 9 in |
| 2001 | Dmitri Markov, Australia | 19 ft 10¼ in |

### LONG JUMP

| 1983 | Carl Lewis, United States | 28 ft ¾ in |
|---|---|---|
| 1987 | Carl Lewis, United States | 28 ft 5¼ in |
| 1991 | Mike Powell, U.S. | 29 ft 4½ in WR |
| 1993 | Mike Powell, United States | 28 ft 2¼ in |
| 1995 | Ivan Pedroso, Cuba | 28 ft 6½ in |
| 1997 | Ivan Pedroso, Cuba | 27 ft 7½ in |
| 1999 | Ivan Pedroso, Cuba | 28 ft 1 in |
| 2001 | Iván Pedroso, Cuba | 27 ft 6¾ in |

### TRIPLE JUMP

| 1983 | Zdzislaw Hoffmann, Poland | 57 ft 2 in |
|---|---|---|
| 1987 | Khristo Markov, Bulgaria | 58 ft 9½ in |
| 1991 | Kenny Harrison, United States | 58 ft 4 in |
| 1993 | Mike Conley, United States | 58 ft 7¼ in |
| 1995 | Jonathan Edwards, G.B. | 60 ft ¼ in WR |
| 1997 | Yoelvis Quesada, Cuba | 58 ft 6¾ in |
| 1999 | Charle Michael Friedek, Ger. | 57 ft 8½ in |
| 2001 | Jonathan Edwards, G. Britain | 58 ft 9½ in |

### SHOT PUT

| 1983 | Edward Sarul, Poland | 70 ft 2¼ in |
|---|---|---|
| 1987 | Werner Günthör, Switz. | 72 ft 11¼ in |
| 1991 | Werner Günthör, Switz. | 71 ft 1¼ in |
| 1993 | Werner Günthör, Switz. | 72 ft 1 in |
| 1995 | John Godina, United States | 70 ft 5¼ in |
| 1997 | John Godina, United States | 70 ft 4¼ in |
| 1999 | C.J. Hunter, United States | 71 ft 6 in |
| 2001 | John Godina, United States | 71 ft 9 in |

### DISCUS THROW

| 1983 | Imrich Bugar, Czechoslovakia | 222 ft 2 in |
|---|---|---|
| 1987 | Juergen Schult, E Germany | 225 ft 6 in |
| 1991 | Lars Riedel, Germany | 217 ft 2 in |
| 1993 | Lars Riedel, Germany | 222 ft 2 in |
| 1995 | Lars Riedel, Germany | 225 ft 7 in |
| 1997 | Lars Riedel, Germany | 224 ft 10 in |
| 1999 | Anthony Washington, U.S. | 226 ft 8 in |
| 2001 | Lars Riedel, Germany | 228 ft 9 in |

### HAMMER THROW

| 1983 | Sergei Litvinov, USSR | 271 ft 3 in |
|---|---|---|
| 1987 | Sergei Litvinov, USSR | 272 ft 6 in |
| 1991 | Yuriy Sedykh, USSR | 268 ft |
| 1993 | Andrey Abduvaliyev, Tajikistan | 267 ft 10 in |
| 1995 | Andrey Abduvaliyev, Tajikistan | 267 ft 7 in |
| 1997 | Heinz Weis, Germany | 268 ft 4 in |
| 1999 | Karsten Kobs, Germany | 263 ft 3 in |
| 2001 | Szymon Kiólkowski, Poland | 273 ft 7 in |

### JAVELIN

| 1983 | Detlef Michel, E Germany | 293 ft 7 in |
|---|---|---|
| 1987 | Seppo Räty, Finland | 274 ft 1 in |
| 1991 | Kimmo Kinnunen, Finland | 297 ft 11 in |
| 1993 | Jan Zelezny, Czech Republic | 282 ft 1 in |
| 1995 | Jan Zelezny, Czech Republic | 293 ft 11 in |
| 1997 | Marius Corbett, S Africa | 290 ft 0 in |
| 1999 | Aki Parviainen, Finland | 293 ft 8 in |
| 2001 | Jan Zelezny, Czech Republic | 304 ft 5 in |

### DECATHLON

| 1983 | Daley Thompson, G. Britain | 8666 pts |
|---|---|---|
| 1987 | Torsten Voss, E Germany | 8680 pts |
| 1991 | Dan O'Brien, United States | 8812 pts |
| 1993 | Dan O'Brien, United States | 8817 pts |
| 1995 | Dan O'Brien, United States | 8695 pts |
| 1997 | Tomás Dvorák, Czech Rep. | 8837 pts |
| 1999 | Tomás Dvorák, Czech Rep. | 8744 pts |
| 2001 | Tomás Dvorák, Czech Rep. | 8902 pts |

WR=World record.

## Women

### 100 METERS

| | | |
|---|---|---|
| 1983 | Marlies Gohr, E Germany | 10.97 |
| 1987 | Silke Gladisch, E Germany | 10.90 |
| 1991 | Katrin Krabbe, Germany | 10.99 |
| 1993 | Gail Devers, United States | 10.82 |
| 1995 | Gwen Torrence, United States | 10.85 |
| 1997 | Marion Jones, United States | 10.83 |
| 1999 | Marion Jones, United States | 10.70 |
| 2001 | Zhanna Pintusevich-Block, Ukraine | 10.82 |

### 200 METERS

| | | |
|---|---|---|
| 1983 | Marita Koch, E Germany | 22.13 |
| 1987 | Silke Gladisch, E Germany | 21.74 |
| 1991 | Katrin Krabbe, Germany | 22.09 |
| 1993 | Merlene Ottey, Jamaica | 21.98 |
| 1995 | Merlene Ottey, Jamaica | 22.12 |
| 1997 | Zhanna Pintusevich, Ukraine | 22.32 |
| 1999 | Inger Miller, United States | 21.77 |
| 2001 | Marion Jones, United States | 22.39 |

### 400 METERS

| | | |
|---|---|---|
| 1983 | Jarmila Kratochvilova, Czech. | 47.99 |
| 1987 | Olga Bryzgina, USSR | 49.38 |
| 1991 | Marie-José Pérec, France | 49.13 |
| 1993 | Jearl Miles, United States | 49.82 |
| 1995 | Marie-José Pérec, France | 49.28 |
| 1997 | Cathy Freeman, Australia | 49.77 |
| 1999 | Cathy Freeman, Australia | 49.67 |
| 2001 | Amy Mbacke Thiam, Senegal | 49.86 |

### 800 METERS

| | | |
|---|---|---|
| 1983 | Jarmila Kratochvilova, Czech. | 1:54.68 |
| 1987 | Sigrun Wodars, E Germany | 1:55.26 |
| 1991 | Lilia Nurutdinova, USSR | 1:57.50 |
| 1993 | Maria Mutola, Mozambique | 1:55.43 |
| 1995 | Ana Quirot, Cuba | 1:56.11 |
| 1997 | Ana Quirot, Cuba | 1:57.14 |
| 1999 | Ludmila Formanová, Czech Rep. | 1:56.68 |
| 2001 | Maria Mutola, Mozambique | 1:57.17 |

### 1,500 METERS

| | | |
|---|---|---|
| 1983 | Mary Slaney, United States | 4:00.90 |
| 1987 | Tatyana Samolenko, USSR | 3:58.56 |
| 1991 | Hassiba Boulmerka, Algeria | 4:02.21 |
| 1993 | Dong Liu, China | 4:00.50 |
| 1995 | Hassiba Boulmerka, Algeria | 4:02.42 |
| 1997 | Carla Sacramento, Portugal | 4:04.24 |
| 1999 | Svetlana Masterkova, Russia | 3:59.53 |
| 2001 | Gabriela Szabo, Romania | 4:00.57 |

### 3,000 METERS

| | | |
|---|---|---|
| 1983 | Mary Slaney, United States | 8:34.62 |
| 1987 | Tatyana Samolenko, USSR | 8:38.73 |
| 1991 | Tatyana Dorovskikh, USSR | 8:35.82 |
| 1993 | Qu Yunxia, China | 8:28.71 |

### 5,000 METERS

| | | |
|---|---|---|
| 1995 | Sonia O'Sullivan, Ireland | 14:46.47 |
| 1997 | Gabriela Szabo, Romania | 14:57.68 |
| 1999 | Gabriela Szabo, Romania | 14:41.82 |
| 2001 | Olga Yegorova, Russia | 15:03.39 |

### 10,000 METERS

| | | |
|---|---|---|
| 1987 | Ingrid Kristiansen, Norway | 31:05.85 |
| 1991 | Liz McColgan, Great Britain | 31:14.31 |
| 1993 | Wang Junxia, China | 30:49.30 |
| 1995 | Fernanda Ribeiro, Portugal | 31:04.99 |
| 1997 | Sally Barsosio, Kenya | 31:32.92 |
| 1999 | Gete Wami, Ethiopia | 30:24.56 |
| 2001 | Derartu Tulu, Ethiopia | 31:48.81 |

*400 meters short.

### MARATHON

| | | |
|---|---|---|
| 1983 | Grete Waitz, Norway | 2:28:09 |
| 1987 | Rosa Mota, Portugal | 2:25:17 |
| 1991 | Wanda Panfil, Poland | 2:29:53 |
| 1993 | Junko Asari, Japan | 2:30:03 |
| 1995 | Manuela Machado, Portugal | 2:25:39* |
| 1997 | Hiromi Suzuki, Japan | 2:29.48 |
| 1999 | Jong Song-Ok, N Korea | 2:26:59 |
| 2001 | Lidia Simon, Romania | 2:26.01 |

### 100-METER HURDLES

| | | |
|---|---|---|
| 1983 | Bettine Jahn, E Germany | 12.35 |
| 1987 | Ginka Zagorcheva, Bulgaria | 12.34 |
| 1991 | Lyudmila Narozhilenko, USSR | 12.59 |
| 1993 | Gail Devers, United States | 12.46 |
| 1995 | Gail Devers, United States | 12.68 |
| 1997 | Ludmila Engquist, Sweden | 12.50 |
| 1999 | Gail Devers, United States | 12.37 |
| 2001 | Anjanette Kirkland, United States | 12.42 |

### 400-METER HURDLES

| | | |
|---|---|---|
| 1983 | Yekaterina Fesenko, USSR | 54.14 |
| 1987 | Sabine Busch, E Germany | 53.62 |
| 1991 | Tatyana Ledovskaya, USSR | 53.11 |
| 1993 | Sally Gunnell, Great Britain | 52.74 WR |
| 1995 | Kim Batten, United States | 52.61 |
| 1997 | Nezha Bidouane, Morocco | 52.97 |
| 1999 | Daimi Pernia, Cuba | 52.89 |
| 2001 | Nezha Bidouane, Morocco | 53.34 |

### 10-KILOMETER WALK

| | | |
|---|---|---|
| 1987 | Irina Strakhova, USSR | 44:12 |
| 1991 | Alina Ivanova, USSR | 42:57 |
| 1993 | Sari Essayah, Finland | 42:59 |
| 1995 | Irina Stankina, Russia | 42:13 |
| 1997 | Annarita Sidoti, Italy | 42:56 |

### 20-KILOMETER WALK

| | | |
|---|---|---|
| 1999 | Hongyu Liu, China | 1:30:50 |
| 2001 | Olimpiada Ivanova, Russia | 1:27.48 |

### 4 X 100-METER RELAY

| | | |
|---|---|---|
| 1983 | E Germany (Silke Gladisch, Marita Koch, Ingrid Auerswald, Marlies Gohr) | 41.76 |
| 1987 | United States (Alice Brown, Diane Williams, Florence Griffith, Pam Marshall) | 41.58 |
| 1991 | Jamaica (Dalia Duhaney, Juliet Cuthbert, Beverley McDonald, Merlene Ottey) | 41.94 |
| 1993 | Russia (Olga Bogoslovskaya, Galina Malchugina, Natalya Voronova, Irina Privalova) | 41.49 |
| 1995 | United States (Celena Mondie-Milner, Carlette Guidry, Chryste Gaines, Gwen Torrence) | 42.12 |
| 1997 | United States (Chryste Gaines, Marion Jones, Inger Miller, Gail Devers) | 41.47 |
| 1999 | Bahamas (Sevatheda Fynes, Chandra Sturrup, Pauline Davis-Thompson, Debbie Ferguson) | 41.92 |
| 2001 | United States (Kelli White, Chryste Gaines, Inger Miller, Marion Jones) | 41.71 |

### 4 X 400-METER RELAY

| | | |
|---|---|---|
| 1983 | E Germany (Kerstin Walther, Sabine Busch, Marita | 3:19.73 |

## Women *(Cont.)*

### 4 X 400-METER RELAY *(CONT.)*

| | | |
|---|---|---|
| | Koch, Dagmar Rubsam) | |
| 1987 | E Germany (Dagmar | 3:18.63 |
| | Neubauer, Kirsten Emmelmann, | |
| | Petra Müller, Sabine Busch) | |
| 1991 | USSR (Tatyana Ledovskaya, | 3:18.43 |
| | Lyudmila Dzhigalova, Olga | |
| | Nazarova, Olga Bryzgina) | |
| 1993 | United States (Gwen Torrence, | 3:16.71 |
| | Maicel Malone, Natasha | |
| | Kaiser-Brown, Jearl Miles) | |
| 1995 | United States (Kim Graham, | 3:22.39 |
| | Rochelle Stevens, Camara | |
| | Jones, Jearl Miles) | |
| 1997 | Germany (Anke Feller, Uta | 3:20.92 |
| | Rohlander, Anja Rucker, Grit | |
| | Breuer) | |
| 1999 | Russia (Tatyana Chebykina, | 3:21.98 |
| | Svetlana Goncharenko, Olga | |
| | Kotylarova, Natalya Nazarova) | |
| 2001 | Jamaica (Sandie Richards, | 3:20.65 |
| | Catherine Scott, Debbie Ann | |
| | Parris, Lorraine Fenton) | |

### HIGH JUMP

| | | |
|---|---|---|
| 1983 | Tamara Bykova, USSR | 6 ft 7 in |
| 1987 | Stefka Kostadinova, Bulgaria | 6 ft 10¼ in |
| 1991 | Heike Henkel, Germany | 6 ft 8¾ in |
| 1993 | Ioamnet Quintero, Cuba | 6 ft 6¼ in |
| 1995 | Stefka Kostadinova, Bulgaria | 6 ft 7 in |
| 1997 | Hanne Haugland, Norway | 6 ft 6¼ in |
| 1999 | Inga Babakova, Ukraine | 6 ft 6¼ in |
| 2001 | Hestrie Cloete, S Africa | 6 ft 6¾ in |

### POLE VAULT

| | | |
|---|---|---|
| 1999 | Stacy Dragila, U.S. | 15 ft 1 in EWR |
| 2001 | Stacy Dragila, United States | 15 ft 7 in |

### LONG JUMP

| | | |
|---|---|---|
| 1983 | Heike Daute, E Germany | 23 ft 10¼ in |
| 1987 | Jackie Joyner-Kersee, U.S. | 24 ft 1¾ in |
| 1991 | Jackie Joyner-Kersee, U.S. | 24 ft ¼ in |
| 1993 | Heike Drechsler, Germany | 23 ft 4 in |
| 1995 | Fiona May, Italy | 22 ft 10¾ in |
| 1997 | Lyudmila Galkina, Russia | 23 ft 1¾ in |
| 1999 | Niurka Montalvo, Spain | 23 ft 2 in |
| 2001 | Fiona May, Italy | 23 ft ½ in |

WR=World record. EWR=equals world record.

### TRIPLE JUMP

| | | |
|---|---|---|
| 1993 | Ana Biryukova, Russia | 49 ft 6 ¼ in WR |
| 1995 | Inessa Kravets, Ukraine | 50 ft 10¼ in WR |
| 1997 | S. Kasparkova, Czech Rep. | 49 ft 10½ in |
| 1999 | Paraskevi Tsiamíta, Greece | 48 ft 10 in |
| 2001 | Tatyana Lebedeva, Russia | 50 ft ½ in |

### SHOT PUT

| | | |
|---|---|---|
| 1983 | Helena Fibingerova, Czech. | 69 ft ¾ in |
| 1987 | Natalya Lisovskaya, USSR | 69 ft 8¼ in |
| 1991 | Zhihong Huang, China | 68 ft 4¼ in |
| 1993 | Zhihong Huang, China | 67 ft 6 in |
| 1995 | Astrid Kumbernuss, Germany | 69 ft 7½ in |
| 1997 | Astrid Kumbernuss, Germany | 67 ft 11½ in |
| 1999 | Astrid Kumbernuss, Germany | 65 ft 1½ in |
| 2001 | Yanina Korolchik, Belarus | 67 ft 7½ in |

### HAMMER THROW

| | | |
|---|---|---|
| 1999 | Mihaela Melinte, Romania | 246 ft 9 in |
| 2001 | Yipsi Moreno, Cuba | 231 ft 9 in |

### DISCUS THROW

| | | |
|---|---|---|
| 1983 | Martina Opitz, E Germany | 226 ft 2 in |
| 1987 | Martina Hellmann, E Germany | 235 ft |
| 1991 | Tsvetanka Khristova, Bulgaria | 233 ft |
| 1993 | Olga Burova, Russia | 221 ft 1 in |
| 1995 | Ellina Zvereva, Belarus | 225 ft 2 in |
| 1997 | Beatrice Faumuina, New Zeal. | 219 ft 3 in |
| 1999 | Franka Dietzsch, Germany | 223 ft 7 in |
| 2001 | Natalya Sadova, Russia | 224 ft 11 in |

### JAVELIN

| | | |
|---|---|---|
| 1983 | Tiina Lillak, Finland | 232 ft 4 in |
| 1987 | Fatima Whitbread, G.B. | 251 ft 5 in |
| 1991 | Demei Xu, China | 225 ft 8 in |
| 1993 | Trine Hattestad, Finland | 227 ft |
| 1995 | Natalya Shikolenko, Belarus | 221 ft 8 in |
| 1997 | Trine Hattestad, Norway | 225 ft 8 in |
| 1999 | Mirela Manjani-Tzelili, Greece | 220 ft 1 in |
| 2001 | Osleidys Menéndez, Cuba | 228 ft 1 in |

### HEPTATHLON

| | | |
|---|---|---|
| 1983 | Ramona Neubert, E Germany | 6714 pts |
| 1987 | Jackie Joyner-Kersee, U.S. | 7128 pts |
| 1991 | Sabine Braun, Germany | 6672 pts |
| 1993 | Jackie Joyner-Kersee, U.S. | 6837 pts |
| 1995 | Ghada Shouaa, Syria | 6651 pts |
| 1997 | Sabine Braun, Germany | 6739 pts |
| 1999 | Eunice Barber, France | 6861 pts |
| 2001 | Yelena Prokhorova, Russia | 6694 pts |

## *Track and Field News* Athlete of the Year

Each year (since 1959 for men and since 1974 for women) *Track and Field News* has chosen the outstanding athlete in the sport.

### MEN

| Year | Athlete | Event |
|---|---|---|
| 1959 | Martin Lauer, W Germany | 110H/Decath |
| 1960 | Rafer Johnson, United States | Decathlon |
| 1961 | Ralph Boston, United States | Long jump |
| 1962 | Peter Snell, New Zealand | 800/1,500 |
| 1963 | C. K. Yang, Taiwan | Decath/PV |
| 1964 | Peter Snell, New Zealand | 800/1,500 |
| 1965 | Ron Clarke, Australia | 5K/10K |
| 1966 | Jim Ryun, United States | 800/1,500 |
| 1967 | Jim Ryun, United States | 1,500 |
| 1968 | Bob Beamon, United States | Long jump |
| 1969 | Bill Toomey, United States | Decathlon |
| 1970 | Randy Matson, United States | Shot put |

| Year | Athlete | Event |
|---|---|---|
| 1971 | Rod Milburn, United States | 110H |
| 1972 | Lasse Viren, Finland | 5K/10K |
| 1973 | Ben Jipcho, Kenya | 1,500/5K/ST |
| 1974 | Rick Wohlhuter, United States | 800/1,500 |
| 1975 | John Walker, New Zealand | 800/1,500 |
| 1976 | Alberto Juantorena, Cuba | 400/800 |
| 1977 | Alberto Juantorena, Cuba | 400/800 |
| 1978 | Henry Rono, Kenya | 5K/10K/ST |
| 1979 | Sebastian Coe, Great Britain | 800/1,500 |
| 1980 | Edwin Moses, United States | 400H |
| 1981 | Sebastian Coe, Great Britain | 800/1,500 |
| 1982 | Carl Lewis, United States | 100/200/LJ |
| 1983 | Carl Lewis, United States | 100/200/LJ |
| 1984 | Carl Lewis, United States | 100/200/LJ |

**MEN (CONT.)**

| Year | Athlete | Event |
|---|---|---|
| 1985 | Said Aouita, Morocco | 1,500/5000 |
| 1986 | Yuri Syedikh, USSR | Hammer |
| 1987 | Ben Johnson, Canada | 100 |
| 1988 | Sergei Bubka, USSR | Pole vault |
| 1989 | Roger Kingdom, United States | 110H |
| 1990 | Michael Johnson, United States | 200/400 |
| 1991 | Sergei Bubka, CIS | Pole vault |
| 1992 | Kevin Young, United States | 400H |
| 1993 | Noureddine Morceli, Algeria | 1,500/mile/3K |
| 1994 | Noureddine Morceli, Algeria | 1,500/mile/3K |
| 1995 | Haile Gebrselassie, Ethiopia | 5K/10K |
| 1996 | Michael Johnson, United States | 200/400 |
| 1997 | Wilson Kipketer, Denmark | 800 |
| 1998 | Haile Gebrselassie, Ethiopia | 5K/10K |
| 1999 | Hicham El Guerrouj, Morocco | 1,500/Mile |
| 2000 | Virgilijus Alekna, Lithuania | Discus |

**WOMEN**

| Year | Athlete | Event |
|---|---|---|
| 1974 | Irena Szewinska, Poland | 100/200/400 |
| 1975 | Faina Melnik, USSR | Shot/Discus |
| 1976 | Tatyana Kazankina, USSR | 800/1,500 |
| 1977 | R. Ackermann, E Germany | High jump |
| 1978 | Marita Koch, E Germany | 100/200/400 |

**WOMEN (CONT.)**

| Year | Athlete | Event |
|---|---|---|
| 1979 | Marita Koch, E Germany | 100/200/400 |
| 1980 | Ilona Briesenick, E Germany | Shot put |
| 1981 | Evelyn Ashford, United States | 100/200 |
| 1982 | Marita Koch, E Germany | 100/200/400 |
| 1983 | J. Kratochvilova, Czechoslovakia | 200/400/800 |
| 1984 | Evelyn Ashford, United States | 100 |
| 1985 | Marita Koch, E Germany | 100/200/400 |
| 1986 | Jackie Joyner-Kersee, U.S. | LJ/Hept |
| 1987 | Jackie Joyner-Kersee, U.S | 100H/LJ/Hept |
| 1988 | Florence Griffith Joyner, U.S. | 100/200 |
| 1989 | Ana Quirot, Cuba | 400/800 |
| 1990 | Merlene Ottey, Jamaica | 100/200 |
| 1991 | Heike Henkel, Germany | High jump |
| 1992 | Heike Drechsler, Germany | Long Jump |
| 1993 | Wang Junxia, China | 1.5K/3K/10K |
| 1994 | Jackie Joyner-Kersee, U.S. | 100H/LJ/Hept |
| 1995 | Sonia O'Sullivan, Ireland | 1,500/3K/5K |
| 1996 | Svetlana Masterkova, Russia | 800/1,500 |
| 1997 | Marion Jones, United States | 100/200/LJ |
| 1998 | Marion Jones, United States | 100/200/LJ |
| 1999 | Gabriela Szabo, Romania | 1,500/5,000 |
| 2000 | Marion Jones, United States | 100/200/LJ |

## Marathon World Record Progression

### Men

| Record Holder | Time | Date | Site |
|---|---|---|---|
| John Hayes, United States | 2:55:18.4 | 7-24-08 | Shepherd's Bush, London |
| Robert Fowler, United States | 2:52:45.4 | 1-1-09 | Yonkers, NY |
| James Clark, United States | 2:46:52.6 | 2-12-09 | New York City |
| Albert Raines, United States | 2:46:04.6 | 5-8-09 | New York City |
| Frederick Barrett, Great Britain | 2:42:31 | 5-26-09 | Shepherd's Bush, London |
| Harry Green, Great Britain | 2:38:16.2 | 5-12-13 | Shepherd's Bush, London |
| Alexis Ahlgren, Sweden | 2:36:06.6 | 5-31-13 | Shepherd's Bush, London |
| Johannes Kolehmainen, Finland | 2:32:35.8 | 8-22-20 | Antwerp, Belgium |
| Albert Michelsen, United States | 2:29:01.8 | 10-12-25 | Port Chester, NY |
| Fusashige Suzuki, Japan | 2:27:49 | 3-31-35 | Tokyo |
| Yasuo Ikenaka, Japan | 2:26:44 | 4-3-35 | Tokyo |
| Kitei Son, Japan | 2:26:42 | 11-3-35 | Tokyo |
| Yun Bok Suh, Korea | 2:25:39 | 4-19-47 | Boston |
| James Peters, Great Britain | 2:20:42.2 | 6-14-52 | Chiswick, England |
| James Peters, Great Britain | 2:18:40.2 | 6-13-53 | Chiswick, England |
| James Peters, Great Britain | 2:18:34.8 | 10-4-53 | Turku, Finland |
| James Peters, Great Britain | 2:17:39.4 | 6-26-54 | Chiswick, England |
| Sergei Popov, USSR | 2:15:17 | 8-24-58 | Stockholm |
| Abebe Bikila, Ethiopia | 2:15:16.2 | 9-10-60 | Rome |
| Toru Terasawa, Japan | 2:15:15.8 | 2-17-63 | Beppu, Japan |
| Leonard Edelen, United States | 2:14:28 | 6-15-63 | Chiswick, England |
| Basil Heatley, Great Britain | 2:13:55 | 6-13-64 | Chiswick, England |
| Abebe Bikila, Ethiopia | 2:12:11.2 | 6-21-64 | Tokyo |
| Morio Shigematsu, Japan | 2:12:00 | 6-12-65 | Chiswick, England |
| Derek Clayton, Australia | 2:09:36.4 | 12-3-67 | Fukuoka, Japan |
| Derek Clayton, Australia | 2:08:33.6 | 5-30-69 | Antwerp, Belgium |
| Rob de Castella, Australia | 2:08:18 | 12-6-81 | Fukuoka, Japan |
| Steve Jones, Great Britain | 2:08:05 | 10-21-84 | Chicago |
| Carlos Lopes, Portugal | 2:07:12 | 4-20-85 | Rotterdam, Netherlands |
| Belayneh Dinsamo, Ethiopia | 2:06:50 | 4-17-88 | Rotterdam, Netherlands |
| Ronaldo Da Costa, Brazil | 2:06:05 | 9-20-98 | Berlin, Germany |
| Khalid Khannouchi, Morocco | 2:05:42 | 10-24-99 | Chicago |

### Women

| Record Holder | Time | Date | Site |
|---|---|---|---|
| Dale Greig, Great Britain | 3:27:45 | 5-23-64 | Ryde, England |
| Mildred Simpson, New Zealand | 3:19:33 | 7-21-64 | Auckland, New Zealand |
| Maureen Wilton, Canada | 3:15:22 | 5-6-67 | Toronto |
| Anni Pede-Erdkamp, W Germany | 3:07:26 | 9-16-67 | Waldniel, W Germany |

## Marathon World Record Progression (Cont.)

### Women (Cont.)

| Record Holder | Time | Date | Site |
|---|---|---|---|
| Caroline Walker, United States | 3:02:53 | 2-28-70 | Seaside, OR |
| Elizabeth Bonner, United States | 3:01:42 | 5-9-71 | Philadelphia |
| Adrienne Beames, Australia | 2:46:30 | 8-31-71 | Werribee, Australia |
| Chantal Langlace, France | 2:46:24 | 10-27-74 | Neuf Brisach, France |
| Jacqueline Hansen, United States | 2:43:54.5 | 12-1-74 | Culver City, CA |
| Liane Winter, W Germany | 2:42:24 | 4-21-75 | Boston |
| Christa Vahlensieck, W Germany | 2:40:15.8 | 5-3-75 | Dülmen, W Germany |
| Jacqueline Hansen, United States | 2:38:19 | 10-12-75 | Eugene, OR |
| Chantal Langlace, France | 2:35:15.4 | 5-1-77 | Oyarzun, France |
| Christa Vahlensieck, W Germany | 2:34:47.5 | 9-10-77 | Berlin, W Germany |
| Grete Waitz, Norway | 2:32:29.9 | 10-22-78 | New York City |
| Grete Waitz, Norway | 2:27:32.6 | 10-21-79 | New York City |
| Grete Waitz, Norway | 2:25:41.3 | 10-26-80 | New York City |
| Grete Waitz, Norway | 2:25:29 | 4-17-83 | London |
| Joan Benoit Samuelson, United States | 2:22:43 | 4-18-83 | Boston |
| Ingrid Kristiansen, Norway | 2:21:06 | 4-21-85 | London |
| Tegla Loroupe, Kenya | 2:20:47 | 4-19-98 | Rotterdam, Netherlands |
| Tegla Loroupe, Kenya | 2:20:43 | 9-26-99 | Berlin |
| Naoko Takahashi, Japan | 2:19:46 | 9-30-01 | Berlin |

## Boston Marathon

The Boston Marathon began in 1897 as a local Patriot's Day event. Run every year but 1918 since then, it has grown into one of the world's premier marathons.

### Men

| Year | Winner | Time | Year | Winner | Time |
|---|---|---|---|---|---|
| 1897 | John J. McDermott, United States | 2:55:10 | 1939 | Ellison M. (Tarzan) Brown, United States | 2:28:51 |
| 1898 | Ronald J. McDonald, United States | 2:42:00 | 1940 | Gerard Cote, Canada | 2:28:28 |
| 1899 | Lawrence J. Brignolia, United States | 2:54:38 | 1941 | Leslie Pawson, United States | 2:30:38 |
| 1900 | James J. Caffrey, Canada | 2:39:44 | 1942 | Bernard Joseph Smith, United States | 2:26:51 |
| 1901 | James J. Caffrey, Canada | 2:29:23 | 1943 | Gerard Cote, Canada | 2:28:25 |
| 1902 | Sammy Mellor, United States | 2:43:12 | 1944 | Gerard Cote, Canada | 2:31:50 |
| 1903 | John C. Lorden, United States | 2:41:29 | 1945 | John A. Kelley, United States | 2:30:40 |
| 1904 | Michael Spring, United States | 2:38:04 | 1946 | Stylianos Kyriakides, Greece | 2:29:27 |
| 1905 | Fred Lorz, United States | 2:38:25 | 1947 | Yun Bok Suh, Korea | 2:25:39 |
| 1906 | Timothy Ford, United States | 2:45:45 | 1948 | Gerard Cote, Canada | 2:31:02 |
| 1907 | Tom Longboat, Canada | 2:24:24 | 1949 | Karl Gosta Leandersson, Sweden | 2:31:50 |
| 1908 | Thomas Morrissey, United States | 2:25:43 | 1950 | Kee Yong Ham, Korea | 2:32:39 |
| 1909 | Henri Renaud, United States | 2:53:36 | 1951 | Shigeki Tanaka, Japan | 2:27:45 |
| 1910 | Fred Cameron, Canada | 2:28:52 | 1952 | Doroteo Flores, Guatemala | 2:31:53 |
| 1911 | Clarence H. DeMar, United States | 2:21:39 | 1953 | Keizo Yamada, Japan | 2:18:51 |
| 1912 | Mike Ryan, United States | 2:21:18 | 1954 | Veikko Karvonen, Finland | 2:20:39 |
| 1913 | Fritz Carlson, United States | 2:25:14 | 1955 | Hideo Hamamura, Japan | 2:18:22 |
| 1914 | James Duffy, Canada | 2:25:01 | 1956 | Antti Viskari, Finland | 2:14:14 |
| 1915 | Edouard Fabre, Canada | 2:31:41 | 1957 | John J. Kelley, United States | 2:20:05 |
| 1916 | Arthur Roth, United States | 2:27:16 | 1958 | Franjo Mihalic, Yugoslavia | 2:25:54 |
| 1917 | Bill Kennedy, United States | 2:28:37 | 1959 | Eino Oksanen, Finland | 2:22:42 |
| 1918 | No race | | 1960 | Paavo Kotila, Finland | 2:20:54 |
| 1919 | Carl Linder, United States | 2:29:13 | 1961 | Eino Oksanen, Finland | 2:23:39 |
| 1920 | Peter Trivoulidas, Greece | 2:29:31 | 1962 | Eino Oksanen, Finland | 2:23:48 |
| 1921 | Frank Zuna, United States | 2:18:57 | 1963 | Aurele Vandendriessche, Belgium | 2:18:58 |
| 1922 | Clarence H. DeMar, United States | 2:18:10 | 1964 | Aurele Vandendriessche, Belgium | 2:19:59 |
| 1923 | Clarence H. DeMar, United States | 2:23:37 | 1965 | Morio Shigematsu, Japan | 2:16:33 |
| 1924 | Clarence H. DeMar, United States | 2:29:40 | 1966 | Kenji Kimihara, Japan | 2:17:11 |
| 1925 | Chuck Mellor, United States | 2:33:00 | 1967 | David McKenzie, New Zealand | 2:15:45 |
| 1926 | John C. Miles, Canada | 2:25:40 | 1968 | Amby Burfoot, United States | 2:22:17 |
| 1927 | Clarence H. DeMar, United States | 2:40:22 | 1969 | Yoshiaki Unetani, Japan | 2:13:49 |
| 1928 | Clarence H. DeMar, United States | 2:37:07 | 1970 | Ron Hill, England | 2:10:30 |
| 1929 | John C. Miles, Canada | 2:33:08 | 1971 | Alvaro Mejia, Colombia | 2:18:45 |
| 1930 | Clarence H. DeMar, United States | 2:34:48 | 1972 | Olavi Suomalainen, Finland | 2:15:39 |
| 1931 | James (Hinky) Henigan, United States | 2:46:45 | 1973 | Jon Anderson, United States | 2:16:03 |
| 1932 | Paul de Bruyn, Germany | 2:33:36 | 1974 | Neil Cusack, Ireland | 2:13:39 |
| 1933 | Leslie Pawson, United States | 2:31:01 | 1975 | Bill Rodgers, United States | 2:09:55 |
| 1934 | Dave Komonen, Canada | 2:32:53 | 1976 | Jack Fultz, United States | 2:20:19 |
| 1935 | John A. Kelley, United States | 2:32:07 | 1977 | Jerome Drayton, Canada | 2:14:46 |
| 1936 | Ellison M. (Tarzan) Brown, United States | 2:33:40 | 1978 | Bill Rodgers, United States | 2:10:13 |
| 1937 | Walter Young, Canada | 2:33:20 | 1979 | Bill Rodgers, United States | 2:09:27 |
| 1938 | Leslie Pawson, United States | 2:35:34 | 1980 | Bill Rodgers, United States | 2:12:11 |

# Boston Marathon *(Cont.)*

| Year | Winner | Time | Year | Winner | Time |
|------|--------|------|------|--------|------|
| 1981...Toshihiko Seko, Japan | | 2:09:26 | 1972...Nina Kuscsik, United States | | 3:10:36 |
| 1982...Alberto Salazar, United States | | 2:08:52 | 1973...Jacqueline A. Hansen, United States | | 3:05:59 |
| 1983...Gregory A. Meyer, United States | | 2:09:00 | 1974...Miki Gorman, United States | | 2:47:11 |
| 1984...Geoff Smith, England | | 2:10:34 | 1975...Liane Winter, W Germany | | 2:42:24 |
| 1985...Geoff Smith, England | | 2:14:05 | 1976...Kim Merritt, United States | | 2:47:10 |
| 1986...Rob de Castella, Australia | | 2:07:51 | 1977...Miki Gorman, United States | | 2:48:33 |
| 1987...Toshihiko Seko, Japan | | 2:11:50 | 1978...Gayle Barron, United States | | 2:44:52 |
| 1988...Ibrahim Hussein, Kenya | | 2:08:43 | 1979...Joan Benoit, United States | | 2:35:15 |
| 1989...Abebe Mekonnen, Ethiopia | | 2:09:06 | 1980...Jacqueline Gareau, Canada | | 2:34:28 |
| 1990...Gelindo Bordin, Italy | | 2:08:19 | 1981...Allison Roe, New Zealand | | 2:26:46 |
| 1991...Ibrahim Hussein, Kenya | | 2:11:06 | 1982...Charlotte Teske, W Germany | | 2:29:33 |
| 1992...Ibrahim Hussein, Kenya | | 2:08:14 | 1983...Joan Benoit, United States | | 2:22:43 |
| 1993...Cosmas N'Deti, Kenya | | 2:09:33 | 1984...Lorraine Moller, New Zealand | | 2:29:28 |
| 1994...Cosmas N'Deti, Kenya | | 2:07:15 | 1985...Lisa Larsen Weidenbach, United States | | 2:34:06 |
| 1995...Cosmas N'Deti, Kenya | | 2:09:22 | 1986...Ingrid Kristiansen, Norway | | 2:24:55 |
| 1996...Moses Tanui, Kenya | | 2:09:16 | 1987...Rosa Mota, Portugal | | 2:25:21 |
| 1997...Lameck Aguta, Kenya | | 2:10:34 | 1988...Rosa Mota, Portugal | | 2:24:30 |
| 1998...Moses Tanui, Kenya | | 2:07:34 | 1989...Ingrid Kristiansen, Norway | | 2:24:33 |
| 1999...Joseph Chebet, Kenya | | 2:09:52 | 1990...Rosa Mota, Portugal | | 2:25:24 |
| 2000...Elijah Lagat, Kenya | | 2:09:47 | 1991...Wanda Panfil, Poland | | 2:24:18 |
| 2001...Lee Bong-Ju, Korea | | 2:09:43 | 1992...Olga Markova, Russia | | 2:23:43 |
| | | | 1993...Olga Markova, Russia | | 2:25:27 |

## Women

| Year | Winner | Time |
|------|--------|------|
| 1966...Roberta Gibb, United States | | 3:21:40* |
| 1967...Roberta Gibb, United States | | 3:27:17* |
| 1968...Roberta Gibb, United States | | 3:30:00* |
| 1969...Sara Mae Berman, United States | | 3:22:46* |
| 1970...Sara Mae Berman, United States | | 3:05:07* |
| 1971...Sara Mae Berman, United States | | 3:08:30* |

| Year | Winner | Time |
|------|--------|------|
| 1994...Uta Pippig, Germany | | 2:21:45 |
| 1995...Uta Pippig, Germany | | 2:25:11 |
| 1996...Uta Pippig, Germany | | 2:27:12 |
| 1997...Fatuma Roba, Ethiopia | | 2:26:23 |
| 1998...Fatuma Roba, Ethiopia | | 2:23:21 |
| 1999...Fatuma Roba, Ethiopia | | 2:23:25 |
| 2000...Catherine Ndereba, Kenya | | 2:26:11 |
| 2001...Catherine Ndereba, Kenya | | 2:23:53 |

Note: Over the years the Boston course has varied in length. The distances have been 24 miles, 1,232 yards (1897–1923); 26 miles, 209 yards (1924–1926); 26 miles, 385 yards (1927–1952); and 25 miles, 958 yards (1953–1956). Since 1957, the course has been certified to be the standard marathon distance of 26 miles, 385 yards. (*Unofficial.)

# New York City Marathon

## MEN

| Year | Winner | Time |
|------|--------|------|
| 1970...Gary Muhrcke, United States | | 2:31:38 |
| 1971...Norman Higgins, United States | | 2:22:54 |
| 1972...Sheldon Karlin, United States | | 2:27:52 |
| 1973...Tom Fleming, United States | | 2:21:54 |
| 1974...Norbert Sander, United States | | 2:26:30 |
| 1975...Tom Fleming, United States | | 2:19:27 |
| 1976...Bill Rodgers, United States | | 2:10:10 |
| 1977...Bill Rodgers, United States | | 2:11:28 |
| 1978...Bill Rodgers, United States | | 2:12:12 |
| 1979...Bill Rodgers, United States | | 2:11:42 |
| 1980...Alberto Salazar, United States | | 2:09:41 |
| 1981...Alberto Salazar, United States | | 2:08:13 |
| 1982...Alberto Salazar, United States | | 2:09:29 |
| 1983...Rod Dixon, New Zealand | | 2:08:59 |
| 1984...Orlando Pizzolato, Italy | | 2:14:53 |
| 1985...Orlando Pizzolato, Italy | | 2:11:34 |
| 1986...Gianni Poli, Italy | | 2:11:06 |
| 1987...Ibrahim Hussein, Kenya | | 2:11:01 |
| 1988...Steve Jones, Great Britain | | 2:08:20 |
| 1989...Juma Ikangaa, Tanzania | | 2:08:01 |
| 1990...Douglas Wakiihuri, Kenya | | 2:12:39 |
| 1991...Salvador Garcia, Mexico | | 2:09:28 |
| 1992...Willie Mtolo, S Africa | | 2:09:29 |
| 1993...Andres Espinosa, Mexico | | 2:10:04 |
| 1994...German Silva, Mexico | | 2:11:21 |
| 1995...German Silva, Mexico | | 2:11:00 |
| 1996...Giacomo Leone, Italy | | 2:09:54 |
| 1997...John Kagwe, Kenya | | 2:08:12 |
| 1998...John Kagwe, Kenya | | 2:08:45 |
| 1999...Joseph Chebet, Kenya | | 2:09:14 |
| 2000...Abdelkhader El Mouaziz, Morocco | | 2:10:09 |

## WOMEN

| Year | Winner | Time |
|------|--------|------|
| 1970...No finisher | | |
| 1971...Beth Bonner, United States | | 2:55:22 |
| 1972...Nina Kuscsik, United States | | 3:08:41 |
| 1973...Nina Kuscsik, United States | | 2:57:07 |
| 1974...Katherine Switzer, United States | | 3:07:29 |
| 1975...Kim Merritt, United States | | 2:46:14 |
| 1976...Miki Gorman, United States | | 2:39:11 |
| 1977...Miki Gorman, United States | | 2:43:10 |
| 1978...Grete Waitz, Norway | | 2:32:30 |
| 1979...Grete Waitz, Norway | | 2:27:33 |
| 1980...Grete Waitz, Norway | | 2:25:41 |
| 1981...Allison Roe, New Zealand | | 2:25:29 |
| 1982...Grete Waitz, Norway | | 2:27:14 |
| 1983...Grete Waitz, Norway | | 2:27:00 |
| 1984...Grete Waitz, Norway | | 2:29:30 |
| 1985...Grete Waitz, Norway | | 2:28:34 |
| 1986...Grete Waitz, Norway | | 2:28:06 |
| 1987...Priscilla Welch, Great Britain | | 2:30:17 |
| 1988...Grete Waitz, Norway | | 2:28:07 |
| 1989...Ingrid Kristiansen, Norway | | 2:25:30 |
| 1990...Wanda Panfiil, Poland | | 2:30:45 |
| 1991...Liz McColgan, Scotland | | 2:27:23 |
| 1992...Lisa Ondieki, Australia | | 2:24:40 |
| 1993...Uta Pippig, Germany | | 2:26:24 |
| 1994...Tegla Loroupe, Kenya | | 2:27:37 |
| 1995...Tegla Loroupe, Kenya | | 2:28:06 |
| 1996...Anuta Catuna, Romania | | 2:28:18 |
| 1997...Franziska Rochat-Moser, Switzerland | | 2:28:43 |
| 1998...Franca Fiacconi, Italy | | 2:25:17 |
| 1999...Adriana Fernandez, Mexico | | 2:25:06 |
| 2000...Ludmila Petrova, Russia | | 2:25:45 |

# World Cross-Country Championships

Conducted by the International Amateur Athletic Federation (IAAF), this meet annually brings together the best runners in the world at every distance from the mile to the marathon to compete in the same cross-country race.

## Men

| Year | Winner | Winning Team | Year | Winner | Winning Team |
|------|--------|--------------|------|--------|--------------|
| 1973 | Pekka Paivarinta, Finland | Belgium | 1988 | John Ngugi, Kenya | Kenya |
| 1974 | Eric DeBeck, Belgium | Belgium | 1989 | John Ngugi, Kenya | Kenya |
| 1975 | Ian Stewart, Scotland | New Zealand | 1990 | Khalid Skah, Morocco | Kenya |
| 1976 | Carlos Lopes, Portugal | England | 1991 | Khalid Skah, Morocco | Kenya |
| 1977 | Leon Schots, Belgium | Belgium | 1992 | John Ngugi, Kenya | Kenya |
| 1978 | John Treacy, Ireland | France | 1993 | William Sigei, Kenya | Kenya |
| 1979 | John Treacy, Ireland | England | 1994 | William Sigei, Kenya | Kenya |
| 1980 | Craig Virgin, United States | England | 1995 | Paul Tergat, Kenya | Kenya |
| 1981 | Craig Virgin, United States | Ethiopia | 1996 | Paul Tergat, Kenya | Kenya |
| 1982 | Mohammed Kedir, Ethiopia | Ethiopia | 1997 | Paul Tergat, Kenya | Kenya |
| 1983 | Bekele Debele, Ethiopia | Ethiopia | 1998 | Paul Tergat, Kenya | Kenya |
| 1984 | Carlos Lopes, Portugal | Ethiopia | 1999 | Paul Tergat, Kenya | Kenya |
| 1985 | Carlos Lopes, Portugal | Ethiopia | 2000 | Mohammed Mourhit, Belgium | Kenya |
| 1987 | John Ngugi, Kenya | Kenya | 2001 | Mohammed Mourhit, Belgium | Kenya |

## Women

| Year | Winner | Winning Team | Year | Winner | Winning Team |
|------|--------|--------------|------|--------|--------------|
| 1973 | Paola Cacchi, Italy | England | 1988 | Ingrid Kristiansen, Norway | USSR |
| 1974 | Paola Cacchi, Italy | England | 1989 | Annette Sergent, France | USSR |
| 1975 | Julie Brown, United States | United States | 1990 | Lynn Jennings, United States | USSR |
| 1976 | Carmen Valero, Spain | USSR | 1991 | Lynn Jennings, United States | Kenya |
| 1977 | Carmen Valero, Spain | USSR | 1992 | Lynn Jennings, United States | Kenya |
| 1978 | Grete Waitz, Norway | Romania | 1993 | Albertina Dias, Portugal | Kenya |
| 1979 | Grete Waitz, Norway | United States | 1994 | Helen Chepngeno, Kenya | Portugal |
| 1980 | Grete Waitz, Norway | USSR | 1995 | Derartu Tulu, Ethiopia | Kenya |
| 1981 | Grete Waitz, Norway | USSR | 1996 | Gete Wami, Ethiopia | Kenya |
| 1982 | Maricica Puica, Romania | USSR | 1997 | Derartu Tulu, Ethiopia | Ethiopia |
| 1983 | Grete Waitz, Norway | United States | 1998 | Sonia O'Sullivan, Ireland | Kenya |
| 1984 | Maricica Puica, Romania | United States | 1999 | Gete Wami, Ethiopia | Ethiopia |
| 1985 | Zola Budd, England | United States | 2000 | Derartu Tulu, Ethiopia | Ethiopia |
| 1986 | Zola Budd, England | England | 2001 | Paula Radcliffe, Great Britain | Kenya |
| 1987 | Annette Sergent, France | United States | | | |

# Notable Achievements

## Longest Winning Streaks

### MEN

| Event | Name and Nationality | Streak | Years |
|-------|---------------------|--------|-------|
| 100 meters | Bob Hayes, United States | 49 | 1962–64 |
| 200 meters | Manfred Gemar, Germany | 41 | 1956–60 |
| 400 meters | Michael Johnson, United States | 58 | 1989–97 |
| 800 meters | Mal Whitfield, United States | 40 | 1951–54 |
| 1,500 meters | Hicham El Guerrouj, Morocco | 23 | 1996–00 |
| 1,500 meters/mile | Steve Ovett, Great Britain | 45 | 1977–80 |
| Mile | Herb Elliott, Australia | 35 | 1957–60 |
| Steeplechase | Gaston Roelants, Belgium | 45 | 1961–66 |
| 5,000 meters | Emil Zátopek, Czechoslovakia | 48 | 1949–52 |
| 10,000 meters | Emil Zátopek, Czechoslovakia | 38 | 1948–54 |
| Marathon | Frank Shorter, United States | 6 | 1971–73 |
| 110-meter hurdles | Jack Davis, United States | 44 | 1952–55 |
| 400-meter hurdles | Edwin Moses, United States | 107 | 1977–87 |
| High jump | Ernie Shelton, United States | 46 | 1953–55 |
| Pole vault | Bob Richards, United States | 50 | 1950–52 |
| Long jump | Carl Lewis, United States | 65 | 1981–91 |
| Triple jump | Adhemar da Silva, Brazil | 60 | 1950–56 |
| Shot put | Parry O'Brien, United States | 116 | 1952–56 |
| Discus throw | Ricky Bruch, Sweden | 54 | 1972–73 |
| Hammer throw | Imre Nemeth, Hungary | 73 | 1946–50 |
| Javelin throw | Janis Lusis, USSR | 41 | 1967–70 |
| Decathlon | Bob Mathias, United States | 11 | 1948–56 |

## Longest Winning Streaks *(Cont.)*

### WOMEN

| Event | Name and Nationality | Streak | Years |
|---|---|---|---|
| 100 meters | Merlene Ottey, Jamaica | 56 | 1987–91 |
| 200 meters | Irena Szewinska, Poland | 38 | 1973–75 |
| 400 meters | Irena Szewinska, Poland | 36 | 1973–78 |
| 800 meters | Ana Fidelia Quirot, Cuba | 36 | 1987–90 |
| 1,500 meters | Paula Ivan, Romania | 15 | 1988–91 |
| 1,500 meters/mile | Paula Ivan, Romania | 19 | 1988–90 |
| 3,000 meters | Mary Slaney, United States | 10 | 1982–84 |
| 10,000 meters | Ingrid Kristiansen, Norway | 5 | 1985–87 |
| Marathon | Katrin Dörre, E Germany | 10 | 1982–86 |
| 100-meter hurdles | Annelie Ernhardt, E Germany | 44 | 1972–75 |
| 400-meter hurdles | Ann-Louise Skoglund, Sweden | 18 | 1981–83 |
| High jump | Iolanda Balas, Romania | 140 | 1956–67 |
| Long jump | Tatyana Shchelkanova, USSR | 19 | 1964–66 |
| Shot put | Nadezhda Chizhova, USSR | 57 | 1969–73 |
| Discus throw | Gisela Mauermeyer, Germany | 65 | 1935–42 |
| Javelin throw | Ruth Fuchs, E Germany | 30 | 1972–73 |
| Multi | Heide Rosendahl, W Germany | 15 | 1969–72 |

## Most Consecutive Years Ranked No. 1 in the World

### MEN

| No. | Name and Nationality | Event | Years |
|---|---|---|---|
| 11 | Sergei Bubka, Ukraine | Pole vault | 1984–94 |
| 9 | Viktor Saneyev, USSR | Triple jump | 1968–76 |
| 8 | Bob Richards, United States | Pole vault | 1949–56 |
| 8 | Ralph Boston, United States | Long jump | 1960–67 |

### WOMEN

| No. | Name and Nationality | Event | Years |
|---|---|---|---|
| 9 | Iolanda Balas, Romania | High jump | 1958–66 |
| 8 | Ruth Fuchs, E Germany | Javelin | 1972–79 |
| 7 | Faina Melnick, USSR | Discus throw | 1971–77 |

## Major Barrier Breakers

### MEN

| Event | Mark | Name and Nationality | Date | Site |
|---|---|---|---|---|
| sub 10-second 100 meters | 9.95 | Jim Hines, United States | Oct. 14, 1968 | Mexico City |
| sub 20-second 200 meters | 19.83 | Tommie Smith, United States | Oct. 16, 1968 | Mexico City |
| sub 45-second 400 meters | 44.9 | Otis Davis, United States | Sept. 6, 1960 | Rome |
| sub 1:45 800 meters | 1:44.3 | Peter Snell, New Zealand | Feb. 3, 1962 | Christchurch, New Zealand |
| sub four minute mile | 3:59.4 | Roger Bannister, Great Britain | May 6, 1954 | Oxford |
| sub 3:50 mile | 3:49.4 | John Walker, New Zealand | Aug. 12, 1975 | Göteborg, Sweden |
| sub 13-minute 5,000 meters | 12:58.39 | Said Aouita, Morocco | July 22, 1986 | Rome |
| sub 27:00 10,000 meters | 26:58.38 | Yobes Ondieki, Kenya | July 10, 1993 | Oslo |
| sub 13-second 110-meter hurdles | 12.93 | Renaldo Nehemiah, United States | Aug. 19, 1981 | Zurich |
| sub 50-second 400-meter hurdles | 49.5 | Glenn Davis, United States | June 29, 1956 | Los Angeles |
| 7' high jump | 7' ⅝" | Charles Dumas, United States | June 29, 1956 | Los Angeles |
| 8' high jump | 8' | Javier Sotomayor, Cuba | July 29, 1989 | San Juan |
| 60' triple jump | 60' ¼" | Jonathan Edwards, Great Britain | Aug. 7, 1995 | Göteborg, Sweden |
| 20' pole vault | 20' | Sergei Bubka, USSR | March 15, 1991 | San Sebastian, Spain |
| 70' shot put | 70' 7¼" | Randy Matson, United States | May 5, 1965 | College Station, Texas |
| 200' discus throw | 200' 5" | Al Oerter, United States | May 18, 1962 | Los Angeles |
| 300' (new) javelin | 300' 1" | Steve Backley, Great Britain | Jan. 25, 1992 | Auckland, New Zealand |
| 9,000-pt decathlon | 9026 | Roman Sebrle, Czech Republic | May 27, 2001 | Gotzis, Austria |

## Major Barrier Breakers *(Cont.)*
### WOMEN

| Event | Mark | Name and Nationality | Date | Site |
|---|---|---|---|---|
| sub 11-second 100 meters | 10.88 | Marlies Oelsner, E Germany | July 1, 1977 | Dresden |
| sub 22-second 200 meters | 21.71 | Marita Koch, E Germany | June 10, 1979 | Karl Marxstadt, E Germany |
| sub 50-second 400 meters | 49.9 | Irena Szewinska, Poland | June 22, 1974 | Warsaw |
| sub 2:00 800 meters | 1:59.1 | Shin Geum Dan, N Korea | Nov. 12, 1963 | Djakarta |
| sub 4:00 1,500 meters | 3:56.0 | Tatyana Kazankina, USSR | June 28, 1976 | Podolsk, USSR |
| sub 4:20 mile | 4:17.55 | Mary Decker, United States | Feb. 16, 1980 | Houston |
| sub 15:00 5,000 meters | 14:58.89 | Ingrid Kristiansen, Norway | June 28, 1984 | Oslo |
| sub 30:00 10,000 meters | 29:31.78 | Wang Junxia, China | Sept. 8, 1993 | Beijing |
| sub 2:30 marathon | 2:27:33 | Grete Waitz, Norway | Oct. 21, 1979 | New York City |
| sub 2:20 marathon | 2:19:46 | Naoko Takahashi, Japan | Sept. 30, 2001 | Berlin |
| sub 13-second 100-meter hurdles | 12.9 | Karin Balzer, E Germany | Sept. 5, 1969 | Berlin |
| 6' high jump | 6' | Iolanda Balas, Romania | Oct. 18, 1958 | Budapest |
| 15' pole vault | 15 ½" | Emma George, Australia | March 14, 1998 | Melbourne |
| 70' shot put | 70' 4½" | Nadyezhda Chizhova, USSR | Sept. 29, 1973 | Varna, Bulgaria |
| 200' discus throw | 201' | Liesel Westermann, W Germany | Nov. 5, 1967 | Sao Paulo |
| 200' javelin throw | 201' 4" | Elvira Ozolina, USSR | Aug. 27, 1964 | Kiev |
| first 7,000-point heptathlon | 7,148 | Jackie Joyner-Kersee, U.S. | July 6–7, 1986 | Moscow |

## Olympic Accomplishments

**Oldest Olympic gold medalist**—Patrick (Babe) McDonald, United States, 42 years, 26 days, 56-pound weight throw, 1920.
**Oldest Olympic medalist**—Tebbs Lloyd Johnson, Great Britain, 48 years, 115 days, 1948 (bronze), 50K walk.
**Youngest Olympic gold medalist**—Barbara Jones, United States, 15 years 123 days, 1952, 4 x 100 relay.
**Youngest gold medalist in individual event**—Ulrike Meyfarth, W Germany, 16 years, 123 days, 1972, high jump.

## World Record Accomplishments*

**Most world records equaled or set in a day**—6, Jesse Owens, United States, 5-25-35, (9.4 100 yards; 26' 8¼" long jump; 20.3 200 meters and 220 yards; and 22.6 220-yard hurdles and 200-meter hurdles.
**Most records in a year**—10, Gunder Hägg, Sweden, 1941–42, 1,500 to 5,000 meters.
**Most records in a career**—35, Sergei Bubka, 1983–94, pole vault indoors and out.
**Longest span of record setting**—11 years, 20 days, Irena Szewinska, Poland, 1965–76, 200 meters.
**Youngest person to set a set world record**—Carolina Gisolf, Holland, 15 years, 5 days, 1928, high jump, 5' 3⅜".
**Youngest man to set a world record**—John Thomas, United States, 17 years, 355 days, 1959, high jump, 7' 1¼".
**Oldest person to set world record**—Carlos Lopes, Portugal, 38 years, 59 days, marathon, 2:07:12.
**Greatest percentage improvement**—6.59, Bob Beamon, United States, 1968, long jump.
**Longest lasting record**—long jump, 26' 8¼", Jesse Owens, United States, 25 years, 79 days (1935–60).
**Highest clearance over head, men**—23¼", Franklin Jacobs, United States (5' 8"), 1978.
**Highest clearance over head, woman**—12¾", Yolanda Henry, United States (5' 6"), 1990.

*Marks sanctioned by the IAAF.

# Swimming

Telstra
Dolphins

**Australia's Ian Thorpe**

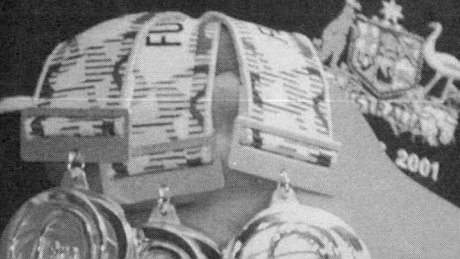

2001

# Aussies Rule

## Australia bested depleted U.S. teams at both the controversy-filled worlds and the discombobulated Goodwill Games

### BY MARK BECHTEL

O N THE WHOLE, the setting for the first world championships of the new millennium did little to remind those on hand that the 21st century had arrived. Competitors swam in three temporary plastic pools in Fukuoka, Japan—one in a convention center, one in a parking lot and one on a tennis court. And while the main pool drew raves from the competitors, the electronic timing devices failed repeatedly. In fact, the timing system's glitches nearly overshadowed the growing rivalry between the Americans, who won the most medals at the 2000 Olympics, and the Australians, who talked much smack after handing the Yanks their first loss in the 400-meter freestyle relay in Sydney.

The tension peaked in the women's 800-meter freestyle relay, when the Australian team touched the wall first but were subsequently disqualified when it was determined that a team member had jumped into the pool in celebration before the last-placed team had finished the race. The Americans, who finished second,

were also disqualified, for an illegal change. But they seemed to make a compelling case that the touchpad had malfunctioned. A poolside video review led to the U.S. being unofficially reinstated, but when the third-place British team protested, a FINA appeals committee upheld both disqualifications and awarded the gold to the Brits— some 15 hours after the conclusion of the race. It was one of three relays in which a U.S. team was disqualified. (Australian coach Don Talbot described FINA's handling of the decision, appropriately enough, as a "kangaroo court.")

While the women's relay was being sorted out, Australian Ian Thorpe was setting his third world record of the meet, in the 200-meter freestyle. In Sydney, Thorpe narrowly lost the 200 free to Pieter van den Hoogenband of the Netherlands, and the two were again neck-and-neck after the first 100 meters. Over the last length of the temporary pool, though, Thorpe kicked on his afterburners and pulled away to win by six feet. "It came down to conditioning," said van den Hoogenband. "Thorpe was in such

**At the worlds, Ervin (right) set a new American record while winning the 100 free.**

good shape tonight." The 18-year-old set a personal best in every race he swam—the 100-, 200-, 400- and 800-meter freestyles and three relays. Thorpe had a hand in six of the Aussies' 13 gold medals, which was four more than the Americans won.

"The Americans have been Number 1 for a long time, and I'll make no bones about it, we want to beat them, and we did just that," said Talbot. "It's fabulous, and it makes me feel great." But on its official Web site, USA Swimming claimed victory, pointing out that the Yanks won the overall medal count and the team points race. "I'm a purist," countered Talbot. "I operate on the gold standard. I'll take golds any day."

There was no such debate at the Goodwill Games in Brisbane, which used a dual-meet, round-robin format that, while it left little room for argument about results, did leave a lot to be desired. The United States, Australia, a European all-star team and a World all-star team comprised a competition that was roundly described as boring, even farcical—Thorpe swam backstroke on the medley relay.

Petria Thomas, the Australian who ignited controversy in Fukuoka by jumping into the pool before the completion of the 800-meter relay, was the top scorer in three events. Talbot, who left his post after the Goodwill Games, was tossed, fully clothed, into the pool after the meet. Before he had a chance to dry himself, he was singing his team's praises. "We were Number 1 at the world

championships— regardless of what the Americans say," he said. "And we're Number 1 again here too."

The U.S. women won silver, and the men won bronze, but they did have a reasonable excuse for their failure to win gold. The teams they fielded at both the Goodwill Games and in Japan were missing several big names. The worlds were held 10 months after the Olympics, and with several top names opting to sit out, many titles went undefended. The list of American no-shows in Fukuoka included Lenny Krayzelburg, Gary Hall Jr., Tom Dolan, Jenny Thompson and Dara Torres. "It's been kind of a roller coaster week, both in respect to our performances and the distractions related to the timing system," said U.S. coach Dennis Pursley at the worlds. "We're pleased that although a lot of things did not go our way, the team maintained their enthusiasm. We had more upset winners on this team than any I can remember."

The brightest American stars in Japan were Anthony Ervin of Phoenix, who secured his place as the sport's top sprinter when he won both the 50- and 100-meter freestyle, and Michael Phelps, a 16-year-old sensation from Baltimore, who shattered the world record in the 200 fly, going 1:54.58. A glitchy touchpad delayed Ervin's victory a few moments, but when his official time (48.33) went up on the board, it edged van den Hoogenband's, as well as the 13-year-old U.S. record. While Ervin's time might in turn be bested someday, the mark is certain to stand as a pool record forever, since the pool it was set in was dismantled after the meet.

As workers carted off the pieces of the deck—and the electronic touchpads that caused so many problems—no one seemed disappointed to see them go, and no one asked for a souvenir.

## 2000–2001 Major Competitions

### Men

#### U.S. OPEN
##### Auburn, AL, November 20–Dec.2 2000

| | | |
|---|---|---|
| 50 free | Michael Picotta, N Coast | 22.36 |
| 100 free | Michael Picotta, N Coast | 48.51 |
| 200 free | Michael Kiedel, Unat. | 1:48.18 |
| 400 free | Richardo Monaserio, Florida | 3:48.92 |
| 1,500 free | Robert Margalis, St. Petersburg | 15:03.04 |
| 100 back | Andrew Davidson, Excel | 54.43 |
| 200 back | Romain Barnier, Unat. | 1:58.99 |
| 100 breast | Ed Moses, Curl-Burke | 59.70 |
| 200 breast | Ed Moses, Curl-Burke | 2:11.22 |
| 100 fly | Zsolt Gaspar, S Carolina | 54.10 |
| 200 fly | Greg Reeves, Florida | 1:58.01 |
| 200 IM | Honza Vitazka, Unat. | 1:58.35 |
| 400 IM | Robert Margalis, St. Petersburg | 4:15.70 |
| 400 m relay | Auburn A | 3:42.97 |
| 400 f relay | University of Alabama | 3:22.79 |
| 800 f relay | Auburn A | 7:27.08 |

#### FINA DIVING WORLD CUP
##### Fukuoka, Japan, July 22–28, 2001

| | | |
|---|---|---|
| 1-m spgbd | Wang Feng, China | 444.03 |
| 3-m spgbd | Dmitry Sautin, Russia | 725.82 |
| Platform | Tian Lang, China | 688.77 |
| 3-m sync | Peng/Wang, China | 342.63 |
| 10-m sync | Tian/Hu, China | 361.41 |

#### FINA WORLD CHAMPIONSHIPS
##### Fukuoka, Japan, July 22–28, 2001

| | | |
|---|---|---|
| 50 free | Anthony Ervin, United States | 22.09 |
| 100 free | Anthony Ervin, United States | 48.33† |
| 200 free | Ian Thorpe, Australia | 1:44.06 WR |
| 400 free | Ian Thorpe, Australia | 3:40.17 WR |
| 1,500 free | Grant Hackett, Australia | 14:34.56 WR |
| 50 back | Randall Bal, United States | 25.34 |
| 100 back | Matt Welsh, Australia | 54.31† |
| 200 back | Aaron Peirsol, United States | 1:57.13† |
| 50 breast | Oleg Lisogor, Ukraine | 27.52 |
| 100 breast | Roman Sloudnov, Russia | 1:00.16 |
| 200 breast | Brendan Hansen, U.S. | 2:10.69† |
| 100 fly | Lars Frolander, Sweden | 52.10† |
| 200 fly | Michael Phelps, U.S. | 1:54.58 WR |
| 200 IM | Massimiliano Rosolino, Italy | 1:59.71 |
| 400 IM | Alessio Boggiatto, Italy | 4:13.15 |
| 400 m relay | Australia | 3:35.35 |
| 400 f relay | Australia | 3:14.10† |
| 800 f relay | Australia | 7:04.66 WR |

#### U.S. NATIONAL CHAMPIONSHIPS
##### Austin, TX, March 27–April 1, 2001

| | | |
|---|---|---|
| 50 free | Anthony Ervin, Phoenix Swim Club | 22.18 |
| 100 free | Anthony Ervin, Phoenix Swim Club | 48.99 |
| 200 free | Klete Keller, Southern Cal | 1:48.89 |
| 400 free | Robert Margalis, Mission Viejo | 3:48.72 |
| 800 free | Chad Carvin, Mission Viejo | 7:56.39 |
| 1,500 free | Erik Vendt, Southern Cal | 15:13.00 |
| 100 back | Aaron Peirsol, Irvine Novas | 54.80 |
| 200 back | Aaron Peirsol, Irvine Novas | 1:56.56 |
| 100 breast | Glenn Moses, Curl-Burke | 1:00.29* |
| 200 breast | Glenn Moses, Curl-Burke | 2:10.40 |
| 100 fly | Ian Crocker, Texas | 52.46 |
| 200 fly | Michael Phelps, N Baltimore | 1:54.92 |
| 200 IM | Tom Wilkens, Santa Clara | 2:01.58 |
| 400 IM | Erik Vendt, Southern Cal | 4:14.19 |
| 400 m relay | Irvine Novas | 3:46.79 |
| 400 f relay | Irvine Novas | 3:23.80 |
| 800 f relay | Southern Cal | 7:28.47 |

#### GOODWILL GAMES
##### Brisbane, Australia, August 29–Sept. 9 2001

| | | |
|---|---|---|
| 50 free | Bartosz Kizierowski, Poland | 22.36 |
| 100 free | Michael Klim, Australia | 48.81 |
| 200 free | Grant Hackett, Australia | 1:47.95 |
| 400 free | Ian Thorpe, Australia | 3:45.40 |
| 1500 free | Grant Hackett, Australia | 15:01.25† |
| 50 back | Bartosz Kizierowski, Poland | 25.63 |
| 100 back | Matthew Welsh, Australia | 54.81 |
| 200 back | Ray Hass, Australia | 1:59.95 |
| 50 breast | Jarrod Marrs, United States | 28.50 |
| 100 breast | Kosuke Kitajima, Japan | 1:01.76 |
| 200 breast | Terence Parkin, S Africa | 2:13.21 |
| 50 fly | Geoff Huegill, Australia | 23.63† |
| 100 fly | Michael Klim, Australia | 52.51† |
| 200 fly | Tom Malchow, United States | 1:55.27† |
| 200 IM | Thomas Wilkens, United States | 2:02.05 |
| 400 IM | Thomas Wilkens, United States | 4:17.93 |
| 400 m relay | Australia | 3:16.32 |
| 400 f relay | Australia | 3:38.26† |

*American record. †Meet record. WR World record.

## Women

### U.S. OPEN
#### Auburn, AL November 20–Dec.2 2000

| | | |
|---|---|---|
| 50 free | Christina Swindle, Miami | 25.17 |
| 100 free | Christina Swindle, Miami | 54.89 |
| 200 free | Rachel Komisarz, Unat. | 1:59.75 |
| 400 free | Janelle Atkinson, Florida | 4:07.43 |
| 800 free | Janelle Atkinson, Florida | 8:29.13 |
| 100 back | Nicole Mackey, Aquazot | 1:00.51 |
| 200 back | Jamie Reid, Puyallup Aquatic | 2:09.47 |
| 100 breast | Megan Quann, Puyallup Aquatic | 1:07.25† |
| 200 breast | Megan Quann, Puyallup Aquatic | 2:26.16 |
| 100 fly | Rachel Komisarz, Unat. | 59.34 |
| 200 fly | Jamie Reid, Puyallup Aquatic | 2:10.21 |
| 200 IM | Maggie Bowen, Auburn | 2:11.30 |
| 400 IM | Maggie Bowen, Auburn | 4:38.82 |
| 400 m relay | Auburn A | 4:09.42 |
| 400 f relay | Auburn A | 3:45.85 |
| 800 f relay | Florida A | 8:11.46 |

### FINA DIVING WORLD CUP
#### Fukuoka, Japan July 22–28, 2001

| | | |
|---|---|---|
| 1-m spgbd | Blythe Hartley, Canada | 300.81 |
| 3-m spgbd | Jingling Guo, China | 596.67 |
| Platform | Mian Xu, China | 532.65 |
| 3-m sync | Wu/Guo, China | 347.31 |
| 10-m sync | Duan/Sang, China | 329.94 |

### FINA WORLD CHAMPIONSHIPS
#### Fukuoka, Japan July 22–28, 2001

| | | |
|---|---|---|
| 50 free | Inge DeBruijn, Netherlands | 24.47 |
| 100 free | Inge DeBruijn, Netherlands | 54.18 |
| 200 free | Giaan Rooney, Australia | 1:58.57 |
| 400 free | Yana Klochkova, Ukraine | 4:07.30 |
| 800 free | Hannah Stockbauer, Germany | 8:24.66 |
| 50 back | Haley Cope, United States | 28.51 |
| 100 back | Natalie Coughlin, United States | 1:00.37 |
| 200 back | Diana Mocanu, Romania | 2.09.94 |
| 50 breast | Xuejuan Luo, China | 30.84 |
| 100 breast | Xuejuan Luo, China | 1:07.18† |
| 200 breast | Agnes Kovacs, Hungary | 2:24.90 |
| 50 fly | Inge DeBruijn, Netherlands | 25.90 |
| 100 fly | Petria Thomas, Australia | 58:27 |
| 200 fly | Petria Thomas, Australia | 2:06.73† |
| 200 IM | Martha Bowen, United States | 2:11.93 |
| 400 IM | Yana Klochkova, Ukraine | 4:36.98 |
| 400 m relay | Australia | 4:07.30 |
| 400 f relay | Germany | 3:39.80 |
| 800 f relay | Great Britain | 7:58.69 |

### U.S. NATIONAL CHAMPIONSHIPS
#### Austin, TX March 27–April 2, 2001

| | | |
|---|---|---|
| 50 free | Tammie Stone, Texas Aquatics | 25.11 |
| 100 free | Colleen Lanne, Texas | 55.20 |
| 200 free | Lindsay Benko, Trojan SC | 1:59.81 |
| 400 free | Ashley Chandler, Sun Devils | 4:12.06 |
| 800 free | Diana Munz, Lake Erie Silver | 8:32.20 |
| 1,500 free | Diana Munz, Lake Erie Silver | 16:27.74 |
| 100 back | Natalie Coughlin, Terrapins | 1:01.32 |
| 200 back | Jamie Reid, Puyallup Aquatic | 2:13.34 |
| 100 breast | Kristy Kowal, Georgia | 1:08.25 |
| 200 breast | Kristy Kowal, United States | 2:26.57 |
| 100 fly | Natalie Coughlin, Terrapins | 59.40 |
| 200 fly | Kaitin Sandeno, NGSU Gators | 2:10.95 |
| 200 IM | Maggie Bowen, Auburn | 2:16.41 |
| 400 IM | Kaitlin Sandeno, United States | 4:42.98 |
| 400 m relay | Southern Cal A | 4:14.35 |
| 400 f relay | Texas A | 3:45.44 |
| 800 f relay | Southern Cal A | 8:14.90 |

### GOODWILL GAMES
#### Brisbane, Australia August 29–Sept. 9 2001

| | | |
|---|---|---|
| 50 free | Inge de Bruijn, Netherlands | 25.00† |
| 100 free | Sarah Ryan, Australia | 55.13† |
| 200 free | Lindsay Benko, United States | 1:59.71 |
| 400 free | Jingweng Tang, China | 4:11.40 |
| 800 free | Yana Klochkova, Ukraine | 8:38.51 |
| 50 back | Haley Cope, United States | 28.89† |
| 100 back | Mai Nakamura, Japan | 1:01.46 |
| 200 back | Clementine Stoney, Australia | 2:13.54 |
| 50 breast | Brooke Hanson, Australia | 31.91† |
| 100 breast | Brooke Hanson, Australia | 1:09.25 |
| 200 breast | Beatrice Caslaru, Romania | 2:28.61 |
| 50 fly | Inge de Bruijn, Netherlands | 26.48† |
| 100 fly | Martina Moravcova, Slovakia | 58.28 |
| 200 fly | Maki Mita, Japan | 2:09.15 |
| 200 IM | Beatrice Caslaru, Romania | 2:14.91 |
| 400 IM | Yana Klochkova, Ukraine | 4:41.12 |
| 400 m relay | Australia | 4:03.96 |
| 400 f relay | Europe | 3:42.40 |

*American record. †Meet record. WR World record.

# World and American Records Set in 2001

## Men

| Event | Mark | Record Holder | Date | Site |
|-------|------|---------------|------|------|
| 50 free | 21.64 | Alexander Popov, Russia (W) | 6-16-00 | Moscow |
| 100 free | 47.84 | Pieter van den Hoogenband, Netherlands (W) | 9-19-00 | Sydney |
| | | Anthony Ervin (A) | 7-27-01 | Fukuoka |
| 200 free | 1:44.06 | Ian Thorpe, Australia (W) | 7-25-01 | Fukuoka |
| 400 free | 3:40.17 | Ian Thorpe, Australia (W) | 7-22-01 | Fukuoka |
| 400 free | 7:39.16 | Ian Thorpe, Australia (W) | 7-24-01 | Fukuoka |
| 1500 free | 14:34.56 | Grant Hackett, Australia (W) | 7-29-01 | Fukuoja |
| 100 breast | 59.94 | Roman Sloudnov, Russia (W) | 7-23-01 | Fukuoka |
| | 1:00.29 | Ed Moses, United States (A) | 3-28-01 | Austin |
| 100 fly | 52.25 | Ian Crocker, United States (A) | 7-26-01 | Fukuoka |
| 200 fly | 1:54.58 | Michael Phelps (W, A) | 7-24-01 | Fukuoka |
| 4 x 200 freestyle relay | 7:04.66 | Australia (W): (Ian Thorpe, Michael Klim, Bill Kirby,Todd Pearson) | 7-29-01 | Fukuoka |

## Women

| Event | Mark | Record Holder | Date | Site |
|-------|------|---------------|------|------|
| 200 breast | 2:22.99 | Hui Qi, China (W) | 4-13-01 | Hangzhou, China |

W= world record. A= American record.

## A FINA Mess

Thanks to a faulty timing system and blundering FINA officials, the women's 4 x 200-meter relay at the world championships produced three winners and wasn't resolved for 15 hours. On the evening of July 25, 2001, the Australians touched the wall first, followed by the U.S. and Great Britain. FINA officials immediately disqualified the Aussies for jumping into the pool to celebrate before last-place Italy had finished. Then they DQ'd the U.S. team when the automatic timing system indicated that the second American swimmer, Cristina Teuscher, had left the blocks .06 of a second before her teammate Natalie Coughlin had touched the wall. (Rules permit a difference of up to .03 of a second.) That timing system, however, had been malfunctioning all evening—FINA had adjusted 10 finish times up to that point in the competition based on video evidence from a backup system.

Later that night, poolside referee Andriy Vlaskov of the Ukraine consulted the video, found Teuscher had left the blocks only .01 before Coughlin touched and reinstated the U.S. team, giving the Americans the gold. The next morning a FINA appeals jury refused to view the video, overturned Vlaskov's decision and gave the gold to Great Britain. "We've gone from third to second to first to second to first," said British swimmer Karen Legg, "so I'm a bit knackered."

FINA spokesman Sam Ramsamy, an IOC member from South Africa, clumsily defended FINA's actions at a press conference the following night, and Australian coach Don Talbot called the decision makers a "kangaroo court." USA Swimming president Dale Neuberger said his federation would appeal the case to the Court of Arbitration for Sport in Lausanne.

# FOR THE RECORD·Year by Year

## MEN

### Freestyle

| Event | Time | Record Holder | Date | Site |
|---|---|---|---|---|
| 50 meters | 21.64 | Alexander Popov, Russia (W) | 6-16-00 | Moscow |
| | 21.76 | Gary Hall Jr. (A) | 8-15-00 | Indianapolis |
| 100 meters | 47.84 | Pieter van den Hoogenband (W) Netherlands | 9-19-00 | Sydney |
| | 48.33 | Anthony Ervin (A) | 7-27-01 | Fukuoka, Japan |
| 200 meters | 1:44.06 | Ian Thorpe, Australia (W) | 7-25-01 | Fukuoka, Japan |
| | 1:46.73 | Josh Davis (A) | 9-18-00 | Sydney |
| 400 meters | 3:40.17 | Ian Thorpe, Australia (W) | 7-22-01 | Fukuoka, Japan |
| | 3:47.00 | Klete Keller (A) | 9-16-00 | Sydney |
| 800 meters | 7:39.16 | Ian Thorpe, Australia (W) | 7-24-01 | Fukuoka, Japan |
| | 7:52.45 | Sean Killion (A) | 7-27-87 | Clovis, CA |
| 1,500 meters | 14:34.56 | Grant Hackett, Australia (W) | 7-29-01 | Fukuoka, Japan |
| | 14.56.81 | Chris Thompson (A) | 9-23-00 | Sydney |

### Backstroke

| Event | Time | Record Holder | Date | Site |
|---|---|---|---|---|
| 50 meters | 24.99 | Lenny Krayzelburg (W, A) | 8-28-99 | Sydney |
| 100 meters | 53.60 | Lenny Krayzelburg (W, A) | 8-24-99 | Sydney |
| 200 meters | 1:55.87 | Lenny Krayzelburg (W, A) | 8-27-99 | Sydney |

### Breaststroke

| Event | Time | Record Holder | Date | Site |
|---|---|---|---|---|
| 100 meters | 59.94 | Roman Sloudnov, Russia (W) | 7-23-01 | Fukuoka, Japan |
| | 1:00.29 | Ed Moses (A) | 3-28-01 | Austin |
| 200 meters | 2:10.16 | Mike Barrowman (W, A) | 7-29-92 | Barcelona |

### Butterfly

| Event | Time | Record Holder | Date | Site |
|---|---|---|---|---|
| 100 meters | 51.81 | Michael Klim, Australia (W) | 12-12-99 | Canberra, Australia |
| | 52.25 | Ian Crocker(A) | 7-26-01 | Fukuoka, Japan |
| 200 meters | 1:54.58 | Michael Phelps (W, A) | 7-24-01 | Fukuoka, Japan |

### Individual Medley

| Event | Time | Record Holder | Date | Site |
|---|---|---|---|---|
| 200 meters | 1:59.36 | Jani Sievinen, Finland (W) | 9-11-94 | Rome |
| | 1:59.77 | Tom Dolan (A) | 9-21-00 | Sydney |
| 400 meters | 4:11.76 | Tom Dolan (W, A) | 9-17-00 | Sydney |

### Relays

| Event | Time | Record Holder | Date | Site |
|---|---|---|---|---|
| 400-meter medley | 3:33.73 | United States (W,A) (Lenny Krayzelburg, Ed Moses, Ian Crocker, Gary Hall Jr) | 9-23-00 | Sydney |
| 400-meter freestyle | 3:13.67 | Australia (W) (Ian Thorpe, Michael Klim, Ashley Callus, Chris Fydler) | 9-16-00 | Sydney |
| | 3:13.86 | United States (A) (Anthony Ervin, Neil Walker, Jason Lezak, Gary Hall Jr | 9-16-95 | Sydney |
| 800-meter freestyle | 7:04.66 | Australia (W) (Ian Thorpe, Michael Klim, Bill Kirby, Grant Hackett) | 7-27-01 | Fukuoka, Japan |
| | 7:12.51 | United States (A) (Troy Dalbey, Matt Cetlinski, Doug Gjertsen, Matt Biondi) | 9-21-88 | Seoul |

Note: Records through Sept. 23, 2000.

## WOMEN

### Freestyle

| Event | Time | Record Holder | Date | Site |
|---|---|---|---|---|
| 50 meters | 24.13 | Inge de Bruijn, Netherlands (W) | 9-22-00 | Sydney |
| | 24.63 | Dana Torres (A) | 9-23-00 | Sydney |
| 100 meters | 53.77 | Inge de Bruijn, Netherlands (W) | 9-20-00 | Sydney |
| | 54.07 | Jenny Thompson (A) | 8-14-00 | Indianapolis |
| 200 meters | 1:56.78 | Franziska van Almsick, Germany (W) | 9-5-94 | Rome |
| | 1:57.90 | Nicole Haislett (A) | 7-27-90 | Barcelona |
| 400 meters | 4:03.85 | Janet Evans (W, A) | 9-22-88 | Seoul |
| 800 meters | 8:16.22 | Janet Evans (W, A) | 8-20-89 | Tokyo |
| 1,500 meters | 15:52.10 | Janet Evans (W, A) | 3-26-88 | Orlando, FL |

### Backstroke

| Event | Time | Record Holder | Date | Site |
|---|---|---|---|---|
| 50 meters | 28.78 | Sandra Volker, Germany (W) | 6-12-99 | Monte Carlo |
| | 28.49 | Natalie Coughlin (A) | 7-23-01 | Fukuoka, Japan |
| 100 meters | 1:00.16 | Cihong He, China (W) | 9-10-94 | Rome |
| | 1:00.18 | Natalie Coughlin (A) | 7-28-01 | Fukuoka, Japan |
| 200 meters | 2:06.62 | Krisztina Egerszegi, Hungary (W) | 8-26-91 | Athens, Greece |
| | 2:08.60 | Betsy Mitchell (A) | 6-27-86 | Orlando, FL |

### Breaststroke

| Event | Time | Record Holder | Date | Site |
|---|---|---|---|---|
| 50 meters | 30.83 | Penelope Heyns, S Africa (W) | 8-28-99 | Sydney |
| | 31.34 | Megan Quann (A) | 8-11-00 | Indianapolis |
| 100 meters | 1:06.52 | Penelope Heyns, S Africa (W) | 8-23-99 | Sydney |
| | 1:07.05 | Megan Quann (A) | 9-18-00 | Sydney |
| 200 meters | 2:22.99 | Hui Qi (W) | 4-13-01 | Hangzhou, China |
| | 2:24.56 | Kristy Kowal (A) | 9-21-00 | Sydney |

### Butterfly

| Event | Time | Record Holder | Date | Site |
|---|---|---|---|---|
| 50 meters | 25.64 | Inge de Bruijn, Netherlands (W) | 5-27-00 | Sheffield, England |
| | 26.50 | Dana Torres (A) | 8-9-00 | Indianapolis |
| 100 meters | 56.61 | Inge de Bruijn, Netherlands (W) | 9-17-00 | Sydney |
| | 57.58 | Dara Torres (A) | 8-9-00 | Indianapolis |
| 200 meters | 2:05.81 | Susan O'Neill (W) | 5-17-00 | Sydney |
| | 2:05.88 | Misty Hyman (A) | 9-20-00 | Sydney |

### Individual Medley

| Event | Time | Record Holder | Date | Site |
|---|---|---|---|---|
| 200 meters | 2:09.72 | Yanyan Wu, China (W) | 10-17-97 | Shanghai |
| | 2:11.91 | Summer Sanders (A) | 7-30-92 | Barcelona |
| 400 meters | 4:33.59 | Yana Klochkova, Ukraine (W) | 9-16-00 | Sydney |
| | 4:37.58 | Summer Sanders (A) | 7-26-92 | Barcelona |

### Relays

| Event | Time | Record Holder | Date | Site |
|---|---|---|---|---|
| 400-meter medley | 3:58.30 | United States (W, A) (BJ Bedford, Megan Quann, Jenny Thompson Dana Torres) | 9-23-00 | Sydney |
| 400-meter freestyle | 3:36.61 | United States (W, A) (Jenny Thompson, Courtney Shealy, Dara Torres, Amy Van Dyken) | 9-16-00 | Sydney |
| 800-meter freestyle | 7:55.47 | E Germany (W) (Manuela Stellmach, Astrid Strauss, Anke Mohring, Heike Friedrich) | 8-18-87 | Strasbourg, France |
| | 7:57.61 | United States (A) (Christina. Teuscher, Ellen Stonebraker, Lindsay Benko, Jenny Thompson) | 8-26-99 | Sydney |

Venues: Belgrade, 1973; Cali, Colombia, 1975; W Berlin, 1978; Guayaquil, Equador, 1982; Madrid, 1986; Perth, Australia, 1991; Rome, 1994; Perth, Australia, 1998.Fukuoka, Japan, 2001

## MEN

### 50-meter Freestyle

| 1986 | Tom Jager, United States | 22.49‡ |
|---|---|---|
| 1991 | Tom Jager, United States | 22.16‡ |
| 1994 | Aleksandr Popov, Russia | 22.17 |
| 1998 | Bill Pilczuk, United States | 22.29 |
| 2001 | Anthony Ervin, USA | 22.09 |

### 100-meter Freestyle

| 1973 | Jim Montgomery, United States | 51.70 |
|---|---|---|
| 1975 | Andy Coan, United States | 51.25 |
| 1978 | David McCagg, United States | 50.24 |
| 1982 | Jorg Woithe, E Germany | 50.18 |
| 1986 | Matt Biondi, United States | 48.94 |
| 1991 | Matt Biondi, United States | 49.18 |
| 1994 | Aleksandr Popov, Russia | 49.12 |
| 1998 | Aleksandr Popov, Russia | 48.93‡ |
| 2001 | Anthony Ervin, USA | 48.33‡ |

### 200-meter Freestyle

| 1973 | Jim Montgomery, United States | 1:53.02 |
|---|---|---|
| 1975 | Tim Shaw, United States | 1:52.04‡ |
| 1978 | Billy Forrester, United States | 1:51.02‡ |
| 1982 | Michael Gross, W Germany | 1:49.84 |
| 1986 | Michael Gross, W Germany | 1:47.92 |
| 1991 | Giorgio Lamberti, Italy | 1:47.27‡ |
| 1994 | Antti Kasvio, Finland | 1:47.32 |
| 1998 | Michael Klim, Australia | 1:47.41 |
| 2001 | Ian Thorpe, Australia | 1:44.06* |

### 400-meter Freestyle

| 1973 | Rick DeMont, United States | 3:58.18‡ |
|---|---|---|
| 1975 | Tim Shaw, United States | 3:54.88‡ |
| 1978 | Vladimir Salnikov, USSR | 3:51.94‡ |
| 1982 | Vladimir Salnikov, USSR | 3:51.30‡ |
| 1986 | Rainer Henkel, W Germany | 3:50.05 |
| 1991 | Joerg Hoffman, Germany | 3:48.04‡ |
| 1994 | Kieran Perkins, Australia | 3:43.80* |
| 1998 | Ian Thorpe, Australia | 3:46.29 |
| 2001 | Ian Thorpe, Australia | 3:40.17* |

### 1,500-meter Freestyle

| 1973 | Stephen Holland, Australia | 15:31.85 |
|---|---|---|
| 1975 | Tim Shaw, United States | 15:28.92‡ |
| 1978 | Vladimir Salnikov, USSR | 15:03.99‡ |
| 1982 | Vladimir Salnikov, USSR | 15:01.7/‡ |
| 1986 | Rainer Henkel, W Germany | 15:05.31 |
| 1991 | Joerg Hoffman, Germany | 14:50.36* |
| 1994 | Kieran Perkins, Australia | 14:50.52 |
| 1998 | Grant Hackett, Australia | 14:51.70 |
| 2001 | Grant Hackett, Australia | 14:34.56* |

### 100-meter Backstroke

| 1973 | Roland Matthes, E Germany | 57.47 |
|---|---|---|
| 1975 | Roland Matthes, E Germany | 58.15 |
| 1978 | Bob Jackson, United States | 56.36‡ |
| 1982 | Dirk Richter, E Germany | 55.95 |
| 1986 | Igor Polianski, USSR | 55.58‡ |
| 1991 | Jeff Rouse, United States | 55.23‡ |
| 1994 | Martin Lopez Zubero, Spain | 55.17‡ |
| 1998 | Lenny Krayzelburg, United States | 55.00‡ |
| 2001 | Matt Welsh, Australia | 54.31‡ |

### 200-meter Backstroke

| 1973 | Roland Matthes, E Germany | 2:01.87‡ |
|---|---|---|
| 1975 | Zoltan Varraszto, Hungary | 2:05.05 |
| 1978 | Jesse Vassallo, United States | 2:02.16 |
| 1982 | Rick Carey, United States | 2:00.82‡ |
| 1986 | Igor Polianski, USSR | 1:58.78‡ |
| 1991 | Martin Zubero, Spain | 1:59.52 |
| 1994 | Vladimir Selkov, Russia | 1:57.42‡ |

### 200-meter Backstroke (Cont.)

| 1998 | Lenny Krayzelburg, United States | 1:58.84 |
|---|---|---|
| 2001 | Aaron Peirsol, USA | 1:57.13‡ |

### 100-meter Breaststroke

| 1973 | John Hencken, United States | 1:04.02‡ |
|---|---|---|
| 1975 | David Wilkie, Great Britain | 1:04.26‡ |
| 1978 | Walter Kusch, W Germany | 1:03.56‡ |
| 1982 | Steve Lundquist, United States | 1:02.75‡ |
| 1986 | Victor Davis, Canada | 1:02.71 |
| 1991 | Norbert Rozsa, Hungary | 1:01.45* |
| 1994 | Norbert Rozsa, Hungary | 1:01.24‡ |
| 1998 | Frederik Deburghgraeve, Belgium | 1:01.34 |
| 2001 | Roman Sloudnov, Russia | 1:00.16 |

### 200-meter Breaststroke

| 1973 | David Wilkie, Great Britain | 2:19.28‡ |
|---|---|---|
| 1975 | David Wilkie, Great Britain | 2:18.23‡ |
| 1978 | Nick Nevid, United States | 2:18.37 |
| 1982 | Victor Davis, Canada | 2:14.77* |
| 1986 | Jozsef Szabo, Hungary | 2:14.27‡ |
| 1991 | Mike Barrowman, United States | 2:11.23* |
| 1994 | Norbert Rozsa, Hungary | 2:12.81 |
| 1998 | Kurt Grote, United States | 2:13.40 |
| 2001 | Brendan Hansen, United States | 2:10.69‡ |

### 100-meter Butterfly

| 1973 | Bruce Robertson, Canada | 55.69 |
|---|---|---|
| 1975 | Greg Jagenburg, United States | 55.63 |
| 1978 | Joe Bottom, United States | 54.30 |
| 1982 | Matt Gribble, United States | 53.88‡ |
| 1986 | Pablo Morales, United States | 53.54‡ |
| 1991 | Anthony Nesty, Suriname | 53.29‡ |
| 1994 | Rafal Szukala, Poland | 53.51 |
| 1998 | Michael Klim, Australia | 52.25‡ |
| 2001 | Lars Frolander, Sweden | 52.10‡ |

### 200-meter Butterfly

| 1973 | Robin Backhaus, United States | 2:03.32 |
|---|---|---|
| 1975 | Bill Forrester, United States | 2:01.95‡ |
| 1978 | Mike Bruner, United States | 1:59.38‡ |
| 1982 | Michael Gross, E Germany | 1:58.85‡ |
| 1986 | Michael Gross, E Germany | 1:56.53‡ |
| 1991 | Melvin Stewart, United States | 1:55.69* |
| 1994 | Denis Pankratov, Russia | 1:56.54 |
| 1998 | Denys Sylantyev, Ukraine | 1:56.61 |
| 2001 | Michael Phelps, United States | 1:54.58* |

### 200-meter Individual Medley

| 1973 | Gunnar Larsson, Sweden | 2:08.36 |
|---|---|---|
| 1975 | Andras Hargitay, Hungary | 2:07.72 |
| 1978 | Graham Smith, Canada | 2:03.65* |
| 1982 | Aleksandr Sidorenko, USSR | 2:03.30‡ |
| 1986 | Tamás Darnyi, Hungary | 2:01.57‡ |
| 1991 | Tamás Darnyi, Hungary | 1:59.36* |
| 1994 | Jani Sievin, Finland | 1:58.16* |
| 1998 | Marcel Wouda, Netherlands | 2:01.18 |
| 2001 | Massimiliano Rosolino, Italy | 1:59.71 |

### 400-meter Individual Medley

| 1975 | Andras Hargitay, Hungary | 4:32.57 |
|---|---|---|
| 1978 | Jesse Vassallo, United States | 4:20.05* |
| 1982 | Ricardo Prado, Brazil | 4:19.78* |
| 1986 | Tamás Darnyi, Hungary | 4:18.98‡ |
| 1991 | Tamás Darnyi, Hungary | 4:12.36* |
| 1994 | Tom Dolan, United States | 4:12.30* |
| 1998 | Tom Dolan, United States | 4:14.95 |
| 2001 | Alessio Boggiatto, Italy | 4:13.15 |

* World record. ‡Meet record.

### 400-meter Medley Relay

| | | |
|---|---|---|
| 1973 | United States (Mike Stamm, John Hencken, Joe Bottom, Jim Montgomery) | 3:49.49 |
| 1975 | United States (John Murphy, Rick Colella, Greg Jagenburg, Andy Coan) | 3:49.00 |
| 1978 | United States (Robert Jackson, Nick Nevid, Joe Bottom, David McCagg) | 3:44.63 |
| 1982 | United States (Rick Carey, Steve Lundquist, Matt Gribble, Rowdy Gaines) | 3:40.84* |
| 1986 | United States (Dan Veatch, David Lundberg, Pablo Morales, Matt Biondi) | 3:41.25 |
| 1991 | United States (Jeff Rouse, Eric Wunderlich, Mark Henderson Matt Biondi) | 3:39.66‡ |
| 1994 | United States (Jeff Rouse, Eric Wunderlich, Mark Henderson, Gary Hall) | 3:37.74‡ |
| 1998 | Australia (Matt Welsh, Phil Rogers, Robin Backhaus, Rick Klatt, Jim Montgomery) | 3:37.98 |
| 2001 | Australia(Matt Welsh, Ian Thorpe, Geoff Huegill, Regan Harrison) | 3:35.35 |

### 400-meter Freestyle Relay

| | | |
|---|---|---|
| 1973 | United States (Mel Nash, Joe Bottom, Jim Montgomery, John Murphy) | 3:27.18 |
| 1975 | United States (Bruce Furniss, Jim Montgomery, Andy Coan, John Murphy) | 3:24.85 |
| 1978 | United States (Jack Babashoff, Rowdy Gaines, Jim Montgomery, David McCagg) | 3:19.74 |
| 1982 | United States (Chris Cavanaugh, Robin Leamy, David McCagg, Rowdy Gaines) | 3:19.26* |
| 1986 | United States (Tom Jager, Mike Heath, Paul Wallace, Matt Biondi) | 3:19.89 |
| 1991 | United States (Tom Jager, Brent Lang, Doug Gjertsen, Matt Biondi) | 3:17.15‡ |
| 1994 | United States (Jon Olsen, Josh Davis, Ugur Taner, Gary Hall Jr.) | 3:16.90‡ |
| 1998 | United States (Bryan Jones, Jon Olsen, Bradley Schumacher, Gary Hall Jr.) | 3:16.69† |
| 2001 | Australia(Michael Klim, Ian Thorpe, Todd Pearson, Ashley Callus) | 3:14.10† |

### 800-meter Freestyle Relay

| | | |
|---|---|---|
| 1973 | United States (Kurt Krumpholz, Robin Backhaus, Rick Klatt, Jim Montgomery) | 7:33.22* |
| 1975 | W Germany (Klaus Steinbach, Werner Lampe, Hans Joachim Geisler, Peter Nocke) | 7:39.44 |
| 1978 | United States (Bruce Furniss, Billy Forrester, Bobby Hackett, Rowdy Gaines) | 7:20.82 |
| 1982 | United States (Rich Saeger, Jeff Float, Kyle Miller, Rowdy Gaines) | 7:21.09 |
| 1986 | E Germany (Lars Hinneburg, Thomas Flemming, Dirk Richter, Sven Lodziewski) | 7:15.91‡ |

| | | |
|---|---|---|
| 1991 | Germany (Peter Sitt, Steffan Zesner, Stefan Pfeiffer, Michael Gross) | 7:13.50‡ |
| 1994 | Sweden (Christer Waller, Tommy Werner, Lars Frolander, Anders Holmertz) | 7:17.34 |
| 1998 | Australia (Daniel Kowalski, Grant Hackett, Ian Thorpe, Anthony Rogis) | 7:12.48† |
| 1998 | Australia (Daniel Kowalski, Grant Hackett, Ian Thorpe, Anthony Rogis) | 7:12.48† |
| 2001 | Australia (Michael Klim, Ian Thorpe, William Kirby, Grant Hackett) | 7:04.66* |

## WOMEN

### 50-meter Freestyle

| | | |
|---|---|---|
| 1986 | Tamara Costache, Romania | 25.28* |
| 1991 | Zhuang Yong, China | 25.47 |
| 1994 | Le Jingyi, China | 24.51* |
| 1998 | Amy Van Dyken, United States | 25.15 |
| 2001 | Inge DeBruijn, Netherlands | 24.47 |

### 100-meter Freestyle

| | | |
|---|---|---|
| 1973 | Kornelia Ender, E Germany | 57.54 |
| 1975 | Kornelia Ender, E Germany | 56.50 |
| 1978 | Barbara Krause, E Germany | 55.68‡ |
| 1982 | Birgit Meineke, E Germany | 55.79 |
| 1986 | Kristin Otto, E Germany | 55.05‡ |
| 1991 | Nicole Haislett, United States | 55.17 |
| 1994 | Le Jingyi, China | 54.01* |
| 1998 | Jenny Thompson, United States | 54.95 |
| 2001 | Inge DeBruijn, Netherlands | 54.18 |

### 200-meter Freestyle

| | | |
|---|---|---|
| 1973 | Keena Rothhammer, United States | 2:04.99 |
| 1975 | Shirley Babashoff, United States | 2:02.50 |
| 1978 | Cynthia Woodhead, United States | 1:58.53* |
| 1982 | Annemarie Verstappen, Netherlands | 1:59.53‡ |
| 1986 | Heike Friedrich, E Germany | 1:58.26‡ |
| 1991 | Hayley Lewis, Australia | 2:00.48 |
| 1994 | Franziska Van Almsick, Germany | 1:56.78* |
| 1998 | Claudia Poll, Costa Rica | 1:58.90 |
| 2001 | Giaan Rooney, Australia | 1:58.57 |

### 400-meter Freestyle

| | | |
|---|---|---|
| 1973 | Heather Greenwood, United States | 4:20.28 |
| 1975 | Shirley Babashoff, United States | 4:22.70 |
| 1978 | Tracey Wickham, Australia | 4:06.28* |
| 1982 | Carmela Schmidt, E Germany | 4:08.98 |
| 1986 | Heike Friedrich, E Germany | 4:07.45 |
| 1991 | Janet Evans, United States | 4:08.63 |
| 1994 | Yang Aihua, China | 4:09.64 |
| 1998 | Chen Yan, China | 4:06.72 |
| 2001 | Yana Klochkova, Ukraine | 4:07.30 |

* World record; ‡Meet record.

## WOMEN *(Cont.)*

### 800-meter Freestyle

1973....Novella Calligaris, Italy — 8:52.97
1975....Jenny Turrall, Australia — 8:44.75‡
1978....Tracey Wickham, Australia — 8:24.94‡
1982....Kim Linehan, United States — 8:27.48
1986....Astrid Strauss, E Germany — 8:28.24
1991....Janet Evans, United States — 8:24.05‡
1994....Janet Evans, United States — 8:29.85
1998....Brooke Bennett, United States — 8.28.71
2001....Hannah Stockbauer, Germany — 8:24.66

### 100-meter Backstroke

1973....Ulrike Richter, E Germany — 1:05.42
1975....Ulrike Richter, E Germany — 1:03.30‡
1978....Linda Jezek, United States — 1:02.55‡
1982....Kristin Otto, E Germany — 1:01.30‡
1986....Betsy Mitchell, United States — 1:01.74
1991....Krisztina Egerszegi, Hungary — 1:01.78
1994....He Cihong, China — 1:00.57
1998....Lea Maurer, United States — 1:01.16
2001....Natalie Coughlin, United States — 1:00.37

### 200-meter Backstroke

1973....Melissa Belote, United States — 2:20.52
1975....Birgit Treiber, E Germany — 2:15.46*
1978....Linda Jezek, United States — 2:11.93*
1982....Cornelia Sirch, E Germany — 2:09.91*
1986....Cornelia Sirch, E Germany — 2:11.37
1991....Krisztina Egerszegi, Hungary — 2:09.15‡
1994....He Cihong, China — 2:07.40
1998....Roxanna Maracineanu, France — 2:11.26
2001.... Diana Mocanu, Romania — 2.09.94

### 100-meter Breaststroke

1973....Renate Vogel, E Germany — 1:13.74
1975....Hannalore Anke, E Germany — 1:12.72
1978....Julia Bogdanova, USSR — 1:10.31*
1982....Ute Geweniger, E Germany — 1:09.14‡
1986....Sylvia Gerasch, E Germany — 1:08.11*
1991....Linley Frame, Australia — 1:08.81
1994....Samantha Riley, Australia — 1:07.96*
1998....Kristy Kowal, United States — 1:08.42
2001....Xuejuan Luo, China — 1:07.18‡

### 200-meter Breaststroke

1973....Renate Vogel, E Germany — 2:40.01
1975....Hannalore Anke, E Germany — 2:37.25‡
1978.... Lina Kachushite, USSR — 2:31.42*
1982....Svetlana Varganova, USSR — 2:28.82†
1986....Silke Hoerner, E Germany — 2:27.40*
1991....Elena Volkova, USSR — 2:29.53
1994....Samantha Riley, Australia — 2:26.87‡
1998....Agnes Kovacs, Hungary — 2:25.45†
2001....Agnes Kovacs, Hungary — 2:24.90

### 100-meter Butterfly

1973....Kornelia Ender, E Germany — 1:02.53
1975....Kornelia Ender, E Germany — 1:01.24*
1978....Joan Pennington, United States — 1:00.20‡
1982....Mary T. Meagher, United States — 59.41‡
1986....Kornelia Gressler, E Germany — 59.51
1991....Qian Hong, China — 59.68
1994....Liu Limin, China — 58.98‡
1998....Jenny Thompson, United States — 58.46†
2001....Petria Thomas, Australia — 58:27

### 200-meter Butterfly

1973....Rosemarie Kother, E Germany — 2:13.76‡
1975....Rosemarie Kother, E Germany — 2:15.92
1978....Tracy Caulkins, United States — 2:09.87*
1982....Ines Geissler, E Germany — 2:08.66‡
1986....Mary T. Meagher, United States — 2:08.41‡
1991....Summer Sanders, United States — 2:09.24
1994....Liu Limin, China — 2:07.25‡
1998....Susie O'Neill, Australia — 2:07.93‡
2001....Petria Thomas, Australia — 2:06.73‡

### 200-meter Individual Medley

1973....Andrea Huebner, E Germany — 2:20.51
1975....Kathy Heddy, United States — 2:19.80
1978....Tracy Caulkins, United States — 2:14.07*
1982....Petra Schneider, E Germany — 2:11.79
1986....Kristin Otto, E Germany — 2:15.56
1991....Li Lin, China — 2:13.40
1994....Lu Bin, China — 2:12.34‡
1998....Wu Yanyan, China — 2:10.88
2001....Martha Bowen, United States — 2:11.93

### 400-meter Individual Medley

1973....Gudrun Wegner, E Germany — 4:57.71
1975....Ulrike Tauber, E Germany — 4:52.76‡
1978....Tracy Caulkins, United States — 4:40.83*
1982....Petra Schneider, E Germany — 4:36.10*
1986....Kathleen Nord, E Germany — 4:43.75
1991....Lin Li, China — 4:41.45
1994....Dai Guohong, China — 4:39.14
1998....Chen Yan, China — 4:36.66
2001....Yana Klochkova, Ukraine — 4:36.98

### 400-meter Medley Relay

1973....E Germany (Ulrike Richter, Renate Vogel, Rosemarie Kother, Kornelia Ender) — 4:16.84
1975....E Germany (Ulrike Richter, Hannelore Anke, Rosemarie Kother, Kornelia Ender) — 4:14.74
1978....United States (Linda Jezek, Tracy Caulkins, Joan Pennington, Cynthia Woodhead) — 4:08.21‡
1982....E Germany (Kristin Otto, Ute Gewinger, Ines Geissler, Birgit Meineke) — 4:05.8*
1986....E Germany (Kathrin Zimmermann, Sylvia Gerasch, Kornelia Gressler, Kristin Otto) — 4:04.82
1991....United States (Janie Wagstaff, Tracey McFarlane, Crissy Ahmann-Leighton, Nicole Haislett) — 4:06.51
1994....China (He Cihong, Dai Guohong, Liu Limin, Lu Bin) — 4:01.67*
1998....United States (Kristy Kowal, Lea Maurer, Jenny Thompson, Amy Van Dyken) — 4:01.93
2001....Australia (Dyana Calub, Sarah Ryan, Petria Thomas, Leisel Jones) — 4:07.30

### 400-meter Freestyle Relay

1973....E Germany (Kornelia Ender, Andrea Eife, Andrea Huebner, Sylvia Eichner) — 3:52.45
1975....E Germany (Kornelia Ender, Barbara Krause, Claudia Hempel, Ute Bruckner) — 3:49.37

## WOMEN (Cont.)

### 400-meter Freestyle Relay (Cont.)

1978....United States (Tracy Caulkins,   3:43.43*
Stephanie Elkins, Joan Pennington,
Cynthia Woodhead)

1982....E Germany (Birgit Meineke,   3:43.97
Susanne Link, Kristin Otto,
Caren Metschuk)

1986....E Germany (Kristin Otto,   3:40.57*
Manuela Stellmach, Sabine
Schulze, Heike Friedrich)

1991....United States (Nicole Haislett,   3:43.26
Julie Cooper, Whitney Hedgepeth,
Jenny Thompson)

1994....China (Le Jingyi, Ying Shan,   3:37.91*
Le Ying, Lu Bin)

1998....United States (Catherine Fox, Lindsey   3:42.11
Farella, Melanie Valerio, B.J. Bedford)

2001....Germany (Petra Dallman,   3:39.58
Antje Buschschulter, Katrin Meissner,
Sandra Volkner)

\* World record; ‡Meet record.

### 800-meter Freestyle Relay

1986....E Germany (Manuela   7:59.33*
Stellmach, Astrid Strauss,
Nadja Bergknecht, Heike Friedrich)

1991....Germany (Kerstin Kielgass,   8:02.56
Manuela Stellmach, Dagmar Hase,
Stephanie Ortwig)

1994....China (Le Ying, Yang Alhua,   7:57.96
Zhou Guabin, Lu Bin)

1998....Germany (Silvia Szalai, Antje   8:02.56
Buschschulte, Janina Goetz,
Franziska Van Almsick)

2001....Great Britain (Nicola Jackson,   7:58.69
Janine Belton, Karen Legg,
Karen Pickering)

# World Diving Championships

## MEN

### 1-meter Springboard

| | Pts |
|---|---|
| 1991........Edwin Jongejans, Netherlands | 588.51 |
| 1994........Evan Stewart, Zimbabwe | 382.14 |
| 1998........Yu Zhuocheng, China | 417.54 |
| 2001........Wang Feng, China | 444.03 |

### 3-meter Springboard

| | Pts |
|---|---|
| 1973........Phil Boggs, United States | 618.57 |
| 1975........Phil Boggs, United States | 597.12 |
| 1978........Phil Boggs, United States | 913.95 |
| 1982........Greg Louganis, United States | 752.67 |
| 1986........Greg Louganis, United States | 750.06 |
| 1991........Kent Ferguson, United States | 650.25 |
| 1994........Wu Zhuocheng, China | 655.44 |
| 1998........Dmitry Sautin, Russia | 746.79 |
| 2001........Dmitry Sautin, Russia | 725.82 |

### Platform

| | Pts |
|---|---|
| 1973........Klaus Dibiasi, Italy | 559.53 |
| 1975........Klaus Dibiasi, Italy | 547.98 |
| 1978........Greg Louganis, United States | 844.11 |
| 1982........Greg Louganis, United States | 634.26 |
| 1986........Greg Louganis, United States | 668.58 |
| 1991........Sun Shuwei, China | 626.79 |
| 1994........Dmitry Sautin, Russia | 634.71 |
| 1998........Dmitry Sautin, Russia | 750.90 |
| 2001........Tian Lang, China | 688.77 |

### 3-meter Synchronized

| | Pts |
|---|---|
| 1998........China (Sun Shuwei, Tian Liang) | 313.50 |
| 2001........China (Bo Peng, Kenan Wang) | 342.63 |

### 10-meter Synchronized

| | |
|---|---|
| 1998........China (Xu Hao, Yu Zhuocheng) | 326.34 |
| 2001........China (Jian Tian, Jia Bu) | 361.41 |

## WOMEN

### 1-meter Springboard

| | Pts |
|---|---|
| 1991........Gao Min, China | 478.26 |
| 1994........Chen Lixia, China | 279.30 |
| 1998........Irina Lashko, Russia | 296.07 |
| 2001........Blythe Hartley, Canada | 300.81 |

### 3-meter Springboard

| | Pts |
|---|---|
| 1973........Christa Koehler, E Germany | 442.17 |
| 1975........Irina Kalinina, USSR | 489.81 |
| 1978........Irina Kalinina, USSR | 691.43 |
| 1982........Megan Neyer, United States | 501.03 |
| 1986........Gao Min, China | 582.90 |
| 1991........Gao Min, China | 539.01 |
| 1994........Tan Shuping, China | 548.49 |
| 1998........Yulia Pakhalina, Russia | 544.62 |
| 2001........Jingling Guo, China | 596.67 |

### Platform

| | Pts |
|---|---|
| 1973........Ulrike Knape, Sweden | 406.77 |
| 1975........Janet Ely, United States | 403.89 |
| 1978........Irina Kalinina, USSR | 412.71 |
| 1982........Wendy Wyland, United States | 438.79 |
| 1986........Chen Lin, China | 449.67 |
| 1991........Fu Mingxia, China | 426.51 |
| 1994........Fu Mingxia, China | 434.04 |
| 1998........Olena Zhupyna, Ukraine | 550.41 |
| 2001........Mian XU, China | 532.65 |

### 3-meter Synchronized

| | Pts |
|---|---|
| 1998..........Russia (Irina Lashko, Yulia Pakhalina) | 282.30 |
| 2001........China (Minxia Wu, Jingjing Guo) | 347.31 |

### 10-meter Synchronized

| | Pts |
|---|---|
| 1998..........Ukraine (O. Zhupyna, S. Serbina) | 278.28 |
| 2001........China (Qing Duan, Xue Sang) | 329.94 |

# U.S. Olympic Champions

## Men

### 50-METER FREESTYLE

| | | |
|---|---|---|
| 1988 | Matt Biondi | 22.14* |
| 2000 | Gary Hall Jr. and Anthony Ervin | 21.98 |

### 100-METER FREESTLYE

| | | |
|---|---|---|
| 1906 | Charles Daniels | 1:13.4 |
| 1908 | Charles Daniels | 1:05.6* |
| 1912 | Duke Kahanamoku | 1:03.4 |
| 1920 | Duke Kahanamoku | 1:00.4 |
| 1924 | John Weissmuller | 59.0‡ |
| 1928 | John Weissmuller | 58.6‡ |
| 1948 | Wally Ris | 57.3‡ |
| 1952 | Clarke Scholes | 57.4 |
| 1964 | Don Schollander | 53.4‡ |
| 1972 | Mark Spitz | 51.22* |
| 1976 | Jim Montgomery | 49.99* |
| 1984 | Rowdy Gaines | 49.80‡ |
| 1988 | Matt Biondi | 48.63‡ |

### 200-METER FREESTYLE

| | | |
|---|---|---|
| 1904 | Charles Daniels | 2:44.2 |
| 1906–1964 | Not held | |
| 1972 | Mark Spitz | 1:52.78* |
| 1976 | Bruce Furniss | 1:50.29* |

### 400-METER FREESTYLE

| | | |
|---|---|---|
| 1904 | Charles Daniels (440 yds) | 6:16.2 |
| 1920 | Norman Ross | 5:26.8 |
| 1924 | John Weissmuller | 5:04.2‡ |
| 1932 | Buster Crabbe | 4:48.4‡ |
| 1936 | Jack Medica | 4:44.5‡ |
| 1948 | William Smith | 4:41.0‡ |
| 1964 | Don Schollander | 4:12.2* |
| 1968 | Mike Burton | 4:09.0‡ |
| 1976 | Brian Goodell | 3:51.93* |
| 1984 | George DiCarlo | 3:51.23‡ |

### 1,500-METER FREESTYLE

| | | |
|---|---|---|
| 1920 | Norman Ross | 22:23.2 |
| 1948 | James McLane | 19:18.5 |
| 1952 | Ford Konno | 18:30.3‡ |
| 1968 | Mike Burton | 16:38.9‡ |
| 1972 | Mike Burton | 15:52.58‡ |
| 1976 | Brian Goodell | 15:02.40* |
| 1984 | Michael O'Brien | 15:05.20 |

### 100-METER BACKSTROKE

| | | |
|---|---|---|
| 1912 | Harry Hebner | 1:21.2 |
| 1920 | Warren Kealoha | 1:15.2 |
| 1924 | Warren Kealoha | 1:13.2‡ |
| 1928 | George Kojac | 1:08.2* |
| 1936 | Adolph Kiefer | 1:05.9‡ |
| 1948 | Allen Stack | 1:06.4 |
| 1952 | Yoshi Oyakawa | 1:05.4‡ |
| 1976 | John Naber | 55.49* |
| 1984 | Rick Carey | 55.79 |
| 1996 | Jeff Rouse | 54.10 |
| 2000 | Lenny Krayzelburg | 53.60‡ |

### 200-METER BACKSTROKE

| | | |
|---|---|---|
| 1964 | Jed Graef | 2:10.3* |
| 1976 | John Naber | 1:59.19* |
| 1984 | Rick Carey | 2:00.23 |
| 1996 | Brad Bridgewater | 1:58.54 |
| 2000 | Lenny Krayzelburg | 1:56.76‡ |

### 100-METER BREASTSTROKE

| | | |
|---|---|---|
| 1968 | Donald McKenzie | 1:07.7‡ |
| 1976 | John Hencken | 1:03.11* |
| 1984 | Steve Lundquist | 1:01.65 * |
| 1992 | Nelson Diebel | 1:01.50‡ |

### 200-METER BREASTSTROKE

| | | |
|---|---|---|
| 1924 | Robert Skelton | 2:56.6 |
| 1948 | Joseph Verdeur | 2:39.3‡ |
| 1960 | William Mulliken | 2:37.4 |
| 1972 | John Hencken | 2:21.55 |
| 1992 | Mike Barrowman | 2:10.16* |

### 100-METER BUTTERFLY

| | | |
|---|---|---|
| 1968 | Douglas Russell | 55.9‡ |
| 1972 | Mark Spitz | 54.27* |
| 1976 | Matt Vogel | 54.35 |
| 1992 | Pablo Morales | 53.32 |

### 200-METER BUTTERFLY

| | | |
|---|---|---|
| 1956 | William Yorzyk | 2:19.3‡ |
| 1960 | Michael Troy | 2:12.8* |
| 1968 | Carl Robie | 2:08.7 |
| 1972 | Mark Spitz | 2:00.70* |
| 1976 | Mike Bruner | 1:59.23* |
| 1992 | Melvin Stewart | 1:56.26 |
| 2000 | Tom Malchow | 1:55.35‡ |

### 200-METER INDIVIDUAL MEDLEY

| | | |
|---|---|---|
| 1968 | Charles Hickcox | 2:12.0‡ |

### 400-METER INDIVIDUAL MEDLEY

| | | |
|---|---|---|
| 1964 | Richard Roth | 4:45.4* |
| 1968 | Charles Hickcox | 4:48.4 |
| 1976 | Rod Strachan | 4:23.68* |
| 1996 | Tom Dolan | 4.:14.90 |
| 2000 | Tom Dolan | 4:11.76‡ |

### 3-METER SPRINGBOARD DIVING

| | | |
|---|---|---|
| 1920 | Louis Kuehn | 675.4 points |
| 1924 | Albert White | 696.4 |
| 1928 | Pete Desjardins | 185.04 |
| 1932 | Michael Galitzen | 161.38 |
| 1936 | Richard Degener | 163.57 |
| 1948 | Bruce Harlan | 163.64 |
| 1952 | David Browning | 205.29 |
| 1956 | Robert Clotworthy | 159.56 |
| 1960 | Gary Tobian | 170.00 |
| 1964 | Kenneth Sitzberger | 159.90 |
| 1968 | Bernard Wrightson | 170.15 |
| 1976 | Philip Doggs | 619.05 |
| 1984 | Greg Louganis | 754.41 |
| 1988 | Greg Louganis | 730.80 |

### PLATFORM DIVING

| | | |
|---|---|---|
| 1904 | George Sheldon | 12.66 points |
| 1920 | Clarence Pinkston | 100.67 |
| 1924 | Albert White | 97.46 |
| 1928 | Pete Desjardins | 98.74 |
| 1932 | Harold Smith | 124.80 |
| 1936 | Marshall Wayne | 113.58 |
| 1948 | Sammy Lee | 130.05 |
| 1952 | Sammy Lee | 156.28 |
| 1960 | Robert Webster | 165.56 |
| 1964 | Robert Webster | 148.58 |
| 1984 | Greg Louganis | 576.99 |
| 1988 | Greg Louganis | 638.61 |

* World record. ‡ Meet (Olympic) record.

## Women

### 50-METER FREESTYLE

| | | |
|---|---|---|
| 1996 | Amy Van Dyken | 24.87 |

### 100-METER FREESTLYE

| | | |
|---|---|---|
| 1920 | Ethelda Bleibtrey | 1:13.6* |
| 1924 | Ethel Lackie | 1:12.4 |
| 1928 | Albina Osipowich | 1:11.0‡ |
| 1932 | Helene Madison | 1:06.8‡ |
| 1968 | Jan Henne | 1:00.0 |
| 1972 | Sandra Neilson | 58.59‡ |
| 1984 | Carrie Steinseifer | 55.92 |
| | Nancy Hogshead | 55.92 |

### 200-METER FREESTYLE

| | | |
|---|---|---|
| 1968 | Debbie Meyer | 2:10.5‡ |
| 1984 | Mary Wayte | 1:59.23 |
| 1992 | Nicole Haislett | 1:57.90 |

### 400-METER FREESTYLE

| | | |
|---|---|---|
| 1924 | Martha Norelius | 6:02.2‡ |
| 1928 | Martha Norelius | 5:42.8* |
| 1932 | Helene Madison | 5:28.5* |
| 1948 | Ann Curtis | 5:17.8‡ |
| 1960 | Chris von Saltza | 4:50.6 |
| 1964 | Virginia Duenkel | 4:43.3‡ |
| 1968 | Debbie Meyer | 4:31.8‡ |
| 1984 | Tiffany Cohen | 4:07.10‡ |
| 1988 | Janet Evans | 4:03.85* |

### 800-METER FREESTYLE

| | | |
|---|---|---|
| 1968 | Debbie Meyer | 9:24.0‡ |
| 1972 | Keena Rothhammer | 8:53.86* |
| 1984 | Tiffany Cohen | 8:24.95‡ |
| 1988 | Janet Evans | 8:20.20‡ |
| 1992 | Janet Evans | 8:25.52 |
| 1996 | Brooke Bennett | 8:27.89 |
| 2000 | Brooke Bennett | 8:19.67 |

### 100-METER BACKSTROKE

| | | |
|---|---|---|
| 1924 | Sybil Bauer | 1:23.2‡ |
| 1932 | Eleanor Holm | 1:19.4 |
| 1960 | Lynn Burke | 1:09.3‡ |
| 1964 | Cathy Ferguson | 1:07.7* |
| 1968 | Kaye Hall | 1:06.2* |
| 1972 | Melissa Belote | 1:05.78‡ |
| 1984 | Theresa Andrews | 1:02.55 |
| 1996 | Beth Botsford | 1:01.19 |

### 200-METER BACKSTROKE

| | | |
|---|---|---|
| 1968 | Pokey Watson | 2:24.8‡ |
| 1972 | Melissa Belote | 2:19.19* |

### 100-METER BREASTSTROKE

| | | |
|---|---|---|
| 1972 | Catherine Carr | 1:13.58* |
| 2000 | Megan Quann | 1:07.05 |

### 200-METER BREASTSTROKE

| | | |
|---|---|---|
| 1968 | Sharon Wichman | 2:44.4‡ |

### 100-METER BUTTERFLY

| | | |
|---|---|---|
| 1956 | Shelley Mann | 1:11.0‡ |
| 1960 | Carolyn Schuler | 1:09.5‡ |
| 1964 | Sharon Stouder | 1:04.7* |
| 1984 | Mary T. Meagher | 59.26 |
| 1996 | Amy Van Dyken | 59.13 |

### 200-METER BUTTERFLY

| | | |
|---|---|---|
| 1972 | Karen Moe | 2:15.57* |
| 1984 | Mary T. Meagher | 2:06.90‡ |
| 1992 | Summer Sanders | 2:08.67 |
| 2000 | Misty Hyman | 2:05.88‡ |

### 200-METER INDIVIDUAL MEDLEY

| | | |
|---|---|---|
| 1968 | Sharon Wichman | 2:44.4‡ |
| 1984 | Tracy Caulkins | 2:12.64‡ |

### 400-METER INDIVIDUAL MEDLEY

| | | |
|---|---|---|
| 1964 | Donna De Varona | 5:18.7‡ |
| 1968 | Claudia Kolb | 5:08.5‡ |
| 1984 | Tracy Caulkins | 4:39.24 |
| 1988 | Janet Evans | 4:37.76 |

### 3-METER SPRINGBOARD DIVING

| | | |
|---|---|---|
| 1920 | Aileen Riggin | 539.9 points |
| 1924 | Elizabeth Becker | 474.5 |
| 1928 | Helen Meany | 78.62 |
| 1932 | Georgia Coleman | 87.52 |
| 1936 | Marjorie Gestring | 89.27 |
| 1948 | Victoria Draves | 108.74 |
| 1952 | Patricia McCormick | 147.30 |
| 1956 | Patricia McCormick | 142.36 |
| 1968 | Sue Gossick | 150.77 |
| 1972 | Micki King | 450.03 |
| 1976 | Jennifer Chandler | 506.19 |

### PLATFORM DIVING

| | | |
|---|---|---|
| 1924 | Caroline Smith | 33.2 points |
| 1928 | Elizabeth Becker Pinkston | 31.6 |
| 1932 | Dorothy Poynton | 40.26 |
| 1936 | Dorothy Poynton Hill | 33.93 |
| 1948 | Victoria Draves | 68.87 |
| 1952 | Patricia McCormick | 79.37 |
| 1956 | Patricia McCormick | 84.85 |
| 1964 | Lesley Bush | 99.80 |
| 2000 | Laura Wilkinson | 543.75 |

* World record; ‡ Meet (Olympic) record.

# Notable Achievements

## Barrier Breakers

### MEN

| Event | Barrier | Athlete and Nation | Time | Date |
|---|---|---|---|---|
| 100 Freestyle | 1:00 | Johnny Weissmuller, United States | 58.6 | 7-9-22 |
| 100 Freestyle | :50 | James Montgomery, United States | 49.99 | 7-25-76 |
| 200 Freestyle | 2:00 | Don Schollander, United States | 1:58.8 | 7-27-63 |
| 200 Freestyle | 1:50 | Sergei Kopliakov, USSR | 1:49.83 | 4-7-79 |
| 400 Freestyle | 4:00 | Rick DeMont, United States | 3:58.18 | 9-6-73 |
| 400 Freestyle | 3:50 | Vladimir Salnikov, USSR | 3:49.57 | 3-12-82 |
| 800 Freestyle | 8:00 | Vladimir Salnikov, USSR | 7:56.49 | 3-23-79 |
| 1500 Freestyle | 15:00 | Vladimir Salnikov, USSR | 14:58.27 | 7-22-80 |
| 100 Backstroke | 1:00 | Thompson Mann, United States | 59.6 | 10-16-64 |
| 200 Backstroke | 2:00 | John Naber, United States | 1:59.19 | 7-24-76 |
| 200 Breaststroke | 2:30 | Chester Jastremski, United States | 2:29.6 | 8-19-61 |
| 100 Butterfly | 1:00 | Lance Larson, United States | 59.0 | 6-29-60 |
| 200 Butterfly | 2:00 | Roger Pyttel, E Germany | 1:59.63 | 6-3-76 |

### WOMEN

| Event | Barrier | Athlete and Nation | Time | Date |
|---|---|---|---|---|
| 100 Freestyle | 1:00 | Dawn Fraser, Australia | 59.9 | 10-27-62 |
| 200 Freestyle | 2:00 | Kornelia Ender, E Germany | 1:59.78 | 6-2-76 |
| 400 Freestyle | 4:30 | Debbie Meyer, United States | 4:29.0 | 8-18-67 |
| 800 Freestyle | 10:00 | Jane Cederqvist, Sweden | 9:55.6 | 8-17-60 |
| 800 Freestyle | 9:00 | Ann Simmons, United States | 8:59.4 | 9-10-71 |
| 1500 Freestyle | 20:00 | Ilsa Konrads, Australia | 19:25.7 | 1-14-60 |
| | 16:00 | Janet Evans, United States | 15:52.10 | 3-26-88 |
| 200 Backstroke | 2:30 | Satoko Tanaka, Japan | 2:29.6 | 2-10-63 |
| 100 Butterfly | 1:00 | Christiane Knacke, E Germany | 59.78 | 8-28-77 |
| 400 Individual Medley | 5:00 | Gudrun Wegner, E Germany | 4:57.51 | 9-6-73 |

## Olympic Achievements

### MOST INDIVIDUAL GOLDS IN SINGLE OLYMPICS

#### MEN

| No. | Athlete and Nation | Olympic Year | Events |
|---|---|---|---|
| 4 | Mark Spitz, United States | 1972 | 100, 200 Free; 100, 200 Fly |

#### WOMEN

| No. | Athlete and Nation | Olympic Year | Events |
|---|---|---|---|
| 4 | Kristin Otto, E Germany | 1988 | 50, 100 Free; 100 Back; 100 Fly |
| 3 | Debbie Meyer, United States | 1968 | 200, 400, 800 Free |
| 3 | Shane Gould, Australia | 1972 | 200, 400 Free; 200 IM |
| 3 | Kornelia Ender, E Germany | 1976 | 100, 200 Free; 100 Fly |
| 3 | Janet Evans, United States | 1988 | 400, 800 Free; 400 IM |
| 3 | Krisztina Egerszegi, Hungary | 1992 | 100, 200 Back; 400 IM |
| 3 | Michelle Smith, Ireland | 1996 | 400 Free; 200, 400 IM |
| 3 | Inge de Bruijn, Netherlands | 2000 | 50, 100 Free; 100 Fly |

## Olympic Achievements *(Cont.)*

### MOST INDIVIDUAL OLYMPIC GOLD MEDALS, CAREER

#### MEN

| No. | Athlete and Nation | Olympic Years and Events |
|---|---|---|
| 4 | Charles Meldrum Daniels, United States | 1904 (220, 440 Free); 1906 (100 Free) 1908 (100 Free) |
| 4 | Roland Matthes, E Germany | 1968 (100, 200 Back); 1972 (100, 200 Back) |
| 4 | Mark Spitz, United States | 1972 (100, 200 Free; 100, 200 Fly) |

#### WOMEN

| No. | Athlete and Nation | Olympic Years and Events |
|---|---|---|
| 4 | Kristin Otto, E Germany | 1988 (50 Free; 100 Free, Back and Fly) |
| 4 | Janet Evans, United States | 1988 (400, 800 Free; 400 IM); 1992 (800 Free) |
| 4 | Krisztina Egerszegi, Hungary | 1992 (100, 200 Back; 400 IM); 1996 (200 Back) |

**Most Olympic Gold Medals in a Single Olympics, Men—**7, Mark Spitz, United States, 1972: 100, 200 Free; 100, 200 Fly; 4 x 100, 4 x 200 Free Relays; 4 x 100 Medley Relay.
**Most Olympic Gold Medals in a Single Olympics, Women—**6, Kristin Otto, E Germany, 1988: 50, 100 Free; 100 Back; 100 Fly; 4 x 100 Free Relay; 4 x 100 Medley Relay.
**Most Olympic Medals in a Career, Men—**11, Matt Biondi, United States: 1984 (one gold), '88 (five gold, one silver, one bronze), '92 (two gold, one silver); 11, Mark Spitz, United States: 1968 (two gold, one silver, one bronze), '72 (seven gold).
**Most Olympic Medals in a Career, Women—**10, Jenny Thompson, United States: 1992 (two gold, one silver), 1996 (three gold), 2000 (three gold, one bronze); 8, Dawn Fraser, Australia: 1956 (two gold, one silver), '60 (one gold, two silver), '64 (one gold, one silver); 8, Kornelia Ender, E Germany: 1972 (three silver), '76 (four gold, one silver); 8, Shirley Babashoff, United States: 1972 (one gold, two silver); '76 (one gold, four silver).
**Winner, Same Event, Three Consecutive Olympics—**Dawn Fraser, Australia, 100 Freestyle, 1956, '60, '64; Krisztina Egerszegi, Hungary, 200 Back, 1988, '92, '96.
**Youngest Person to Win an Olympic Diving Gold—**Marjorie Gestring, United States, 1936, 13 years, 9 months, springboard diving.
**Youngest Person to Win an Olympic Swimming Gold—**Krisztina Egerszegi, Hungary, 1988, 14 years, one month, 200 backstroke.

## World Record Achievements

**Most World Records, Career, Women—**42, Ragnhild Hveger, Denmark, 1936–42.
**Most World Records, Career, Men—**32, Arne Borg, Sweden, 1921–29.
**Most Freestyle Records Held Concurrently—**5, Helene Madison, United States, 1931–33; 5, Shane Gould, Australia, 1972.
**Most Consecutive Lowerings of a Record—**10, Kornelia Ender, E Germany, 100 Freestyle, 7-13-73 to 7-19-76.
**Longest Duration of World Record—**19 years, 359 days, 1:04.6 in 100 Free, Willy den Ouden, Netherlands.

World slalom and
overall champ Janica
Kostelic of Croatia

# Skiing

# Peaks and Valleys

## The unflappable Janica Kostelic has known them both in her short, eventful career

### BY MARK BECHTEL

JANICA KOSTELIC began the 2000–01 skiing season without much ambition. "I didn't have any goals," the Croat teenager said. Her modesty was understandable. In December 1999, she crashed while training for a downhill event in St. Moritz, and after a six-hour operation on her right knee, her doctor told her father, Ante, that she would never ski competitively again.

It had been a devastating blow for the entire Kostelic family. Ante spent much of the mid-1990s in a van with Janica and her older brother, Ivica, driving from slope to slope as the two kids trained for what they hoped would be stellar skiing careers. The Croatian Ski Federation offered little fiscal help, so Ante scrambled to make money any way he could, including by gambling in casinos. On many nights Janica slept in the van while the men slept on glaciers under the stars. Ivica's career has been marred by a pair of bad crashes, lending a sick sense of déjà vu to Janica's misfortune.

Her 1999 season had gotten off to a fantastic start. She had regained 33 pounds during the summer—after nearly withering away in '98 because of her distaste for most of the food she encountered on tour. "My mother is a very good cook," she said. Well nourished, she won the first two slalom races of '99—including one by 1.78 seconds, the largest margin of victory in 31 years—before the debacle at St. Moritz. She resumed training in May 2000 but had another operation in June, which meant she didn't take a full-speed run until the season-opening giant slalom in Sölden, Austria. Her knee hurt constantly, but Janica decided that sitting out another year wasn't an option. "If I had missed a whole year, I would never have made it back to the top," she said. "I have to race with a lot of pain in my knee, but that's the only way I can do it."

A slalom specialist, she finished 12th in the GS in Sölden, prompting Ante to tell her, "This year you're going to win the World Cup." Sure enough, Janica was unbeatable in the slalom and good enough in the other disciplines to forge a run at the overall title. But her season was not without its difficulties. After winning the first seven slalom races of the season—and extending her winning streak in the event to nine—she had a disastrous world championship. She fell in the slalom portion of the combined event and finished fifth in the regular slalom. The criticism she received was so harsh that Ante told a newspaper that his daughter was quitting at the end of the season to study physical education in college and "have friends that she never had the chance to meet due to her ski career."

But Janica bounced back the next weekend, winning a record 10th-straight World Cup slalom race. The streak evoked a typically understated reaction from the winner: "It's nothing special, but now everybody will remember my name." Three weeks later, in Are, Sweden, at the final World Cup event of the season, Janica became the fourth teenager to win the overall title. Renate Goetschl of Austria fell in both the first run of the giant slalom and during her best event, the downhill, giving the title to Kostelic. "I don't like to let my feelings out," Janica said. "I'm happy, but today is today, and life will be going up and down. Sometimes you're happy, sometimes you're unhappy. I was happy, but also sorry for Renate, because I know how she feels."

Kostelic's reserved celebration stood in marked contrast to the men's overall champion, Hermann Maier, who celebrated ecstatically when he clinched the title. In addition to the overall crown and the giant slalom, the Austrian eked out titles in the downhill and the Super G at Are. Maier won the same four championships in 1999–2000, but his 2000–01 season was more impressive. The Hermannator equaled Sweden's Ingemar Stenmark's 22-year-old record of 13 wins in a season—and probably would have broken it had bad weather not forced the cancellation of six races.

While Kostelic scraped out her title by dominating the slalom, Maier coasted to his championship by excelling in every discipline. That fact wasn't lost on the 19-year-old, whose vow not to rest on her laurels has to have her competitors worried. "My father was the best coach in the world before, and he is now," she said. "I want points in all four disciplines."

## A Legend's Ill-fated Return

Seventeen years after winning an Olympic gold medal and 12 years after retiring, 41-year-old U.S. skiing legend Bill Johnson decided to make a run at the 2002 U.S. Olympic team. On March 22 the comeback came to a gruesome end when he crashed face-first during a downhill race in Montana. He underwent four hours of surgery to relieve pressure on his brain and to repair his tongue, which was nearly severed in the accident. In May 2001, during a press conference at a hospital in Oregon, Johnson said that he planned to ski

**Johnson soared to gold in Sarajevo, but no longer remembers it.**

again, but it looks unlikely. Saddest of all, as a result of his quest to regain the happiest time of his life, Johnson can no longer remember striking gold in Sarajevo.

# FOR THE RECORD · 2000-2001

## World Cup Alpine Racing Season Results

### Men

| Date | Event | Site | Winner |
|------|-------|------|--------|
| 10-29-00 | Giant Slalom | Sölden, Austria | Hermann Maier, Austria |
| 11-17-00 | Giant Slalom | Park City, Utah | Michael von Grünigen, Switz |
| 11-19-00 | Slalom | Park City, Utah | Heinz Schilchegger, Austria |
| 11-25-00 | Downhill | Lake Louise, Alberta | Stephan Eberharter, Austria |
| 11-26-00 | Super G | Lake Louise, Alberta | Hermann Maier, Austria |
| 12-2-00 | Downhill | Vail/Beaver Creek, Colorado | Hermann Maier, Austria |
| 12-3-00 | Super G | Vail/Beaver Creek, Colorado | Frederik Nyberg, Sweden |
| 12-9-00 | Downhill | Val D'Isere, France | Hermann Maier, Austria |
| 12-10-00 | Giant Slalom | Val D'Isere, France | Hermann Maier, Austria |
| 12-11-00 | Slalom | Sestriere, Italy | Hans-Petter Buraas, Norway |
| 12-16-00 | Downhill | Val D'Isere, France | Alessandro Fattori, Italy |
| 12-17-00 | Giant Slalom | Val D'Isere, France | Michael von Grünigen, Switz |
| 12-19-00 | Slalom | Madonna di Campiglio, Italy | Matt Mario, Austria |
| 12-21-00 | Giant Slalom | Bormio, Italy | Christoph Gruber, Austria |
| 1-6-01 | Giant Slalom | Les Arcs, France | Michael von Grünigen, Switz |
| 1-9-01 | Giant Slalom | Adelboden, Switzerland | Hermann Maier, Austria |
| 1-14-01 | Slalom | Wengen, Switzerland | Benjamin Raich, Austria |
| 1-19-01 | Super G | Kitzbühel, Austria | Hermann Maier, Austria |
| 1-20-01 | Downhill | Kitzbühel, Austria | Hermann Maier, Austria |
| 1-21-01 | Slalom | Kitzbühel, Austria | Benjamin Raich, Austria |
| 1-23-01 | Slalom | Schladming, Austria | Benjamin Raich, Austria |
| 1-27-01 | Downhill | Garmisch-Partenkirchen, Germany | Fritz Strobl, Austria |
| 1-28-01 | Super G | Garmisch-Partenkirchen, Germany | Christoph Gruber, Austria |
| 2-15-01 | Giant Slalom | Shigakogen, Japan | Hermann Maier, Austria |
| 2-17-01 | Slalom | Shigakogen, Japan | Pierrick Bourgeat, France |
| 2-18-01 | Slalom | Shigakogen, Japan | Pierrick Bourgeat, France |
| 3-2-01 | Downhill | Kvitfjell, Norway | Hermann Maier, Austria |
| 3-3-01 | Downhill | Kvitfjell, Norway | Stephan Eberharter, Austria |
| 3-4-01 | Super G | Kvitfjell, Norway | Hermann Maier, Austria |
| 3-8-01 | Downhill | Are, Sweden | Hermann Maier, Austria |

### Women

| Date | Event | Site | Winner |
|------|-------|------|--------|
| 10-28-00 | Giant Slalom | Sölden, Austria | Martina Ertl, Germany |
| 11-16-00 | Giant Slalom | Park City, Utah | Sonja Nef, Switzerland |
| 11-18-00 | Slalom | Park City, Utah | Janica Kostelic, Croatia |
| 11-24-00 | Super G | Aspen, Colorado | Michaela Dorfmeister, Austria |
| 11-25-00 | Slalom | Aspen, Colorado | Janica Kostelic, Croatia |
| 11-30-00 | Downhill | Lake Louise, Alberta | Petra Haltmeyer, Germany |
| 12-1-00 | Downhill | Lake Louise, Alberta | Isolde Kostner, Italy |
| 12-2-00 | Super G | Lake Louise, Alberta | Renate Götschl, Austria |
| 12-6-00 | Super G | Val D'Isere, France | Regine Cavagnoud, France |
| 12-9-00 | Giant Slalom | Sestriere, Italy | Michaela Dorfmeister, Austria |
| 12-10-00 | Slalom | Sestriere, Italy | Janica Kostelic, Croatia |
| 12-16-00 | Downhill | St. Moritz, Switzerland | Brigitte Obermoser, Austria |
| 12-17-00 | Downhill | St. Moritz, Switzerland | Renate Götschl, Austria |
| 12-19-00 | Giant Slalom | Sestriere, Italy | Sonja Nef, Switzerland |
| 12-20-00 | Slalom | Sestriere, Italy | Janica Kostelic, Croatia |
| 12-28-00 | Slalom | Semmering, Austria | Janica Kostelic, Croatia |
| 12-30-00 | Giant Slalom | Semmering, Austria | Sonja Nef, Switzerland |
| 1-6-01 | Giant Slalom | Maribor, Slovenia | Sonja Nef, Switzerland |
| 1-13-01 | Downhill | Haus in Ennstal, Austria | Renate Götschl, Austria |
| 1-13-01 | Super G | Haus in Ennstal, Austria | Regine Cavagnoud, France |
| 1-14-01 | Slalom | Flachau, Austria | Janica Kostelic, Croatia |
| 1-19-01 | Downhill | Cortina, Italy | Isolde Kostner, Italy |
| 1-20-01 | Super G | Cortina, Italy | Regine Cavagnoud, France |
| 1-21-01 | Giant Slalom | Cortina, Italy | Sonja Nef, Switzerland |
| 1-26-01 | Slalom | Ofterschwang, Germany | Janica Kostelic, Croatia |
| 2-18-01 | Slalom | Garmisch-Partenkirchen, Germany | Janica Kostelic, Croatia |
| 2-24-01 | Downhill | Lenzerheide, Switzerland | Kirsten Clark, United States |
| 2-25-00 | Super G | Lenzerheide, Switzerland | Isolde Kostner, Italy |
| 3-9-00 | Super G | Are, Sweden | Corinne Rey-Bellet, Switzerland |

# World Cup Alpine Racing Final Standings

## Men

### OVERALL

| | Pts |
|---|---|
| Hermann Maier, Austria | 1,618 |
| Stephan Eberharter, Austria | 875 |
| Lasse Kjus, Norway | 866 |
| Benjamin Raich, Austria | 865 |
| Michael von Gruenigen, Switz | 743 |
| Heinz Schilchegger, Austria | 730 |
| Kjetil André Aamodt, Norway | 668 |
| Josef Strobl, Austria | 527 |
| Frederik Nyberg, Sweden | 475 |
| Didier Cuche, Switzerland | 473 |

### DOWNHILL

| | Pts |
|---|---|
| Hermann Maier, Austria | 576 |
| Stephan Eberharter, Austria | 562 |
| Fritz Strobl, Austria | 402 |
| Hannes Trinkl, Austria | 313 |
| Lasse Kjus, Norway | 301 |
| Franco Cavegn, Switzerland | 290 |
| Silvano Beltrametti, Switz. | 266 |
| Werner Franz, Austria | 236 |
| Peter Rzehak, Austria | 213 |
| Josef Strobl, Austria | 196 |

### SLALOM

| | Pts |
|---|---|
| Benjamin Raich, Austria | 545 |
| Heinz Schilchegger, Austria | 414 |
| Mario Matt, Austria | 406 |
| Pierrick Bourgeat, France | 368 |
| Hans-Petter Buraas, Norway | 340 |
| Jure Kosir, Slovenia | 300 |
| Kjetil André Aamodt, Norway | 291 |
| Kilian Albrecht, Austria | 247 |
| Rainer Schoenfelder, Austria | 226 |
| Mitja Kunc, Slovenia | 226 |

### GIANT SLALOM

| | Pts |
|---|---|
| Hermann Maier, Austria | 622 |
| Michael von Greunigen, Switz. | 612 |
| Erik Schlopy, United States | 350 |
| Benjamin Raich, Austria | 320 |
| Heinz Shilchegger, Austria | 316 |
| Marco Büchel, Liechtenstein | 305 |
| Frederik Nyberg, Sweden | 300 |
| Lasse Kjus, Norway | 241 |
| Andreas Schifferer, Austria | 185 |
| M. Blardone, Italy | 185 |

### SUPER G

| | Pts |
|---|---|
| Hermann Maier, Austria | 420 |
| Christoph Gruber, Austria | 246 |
| Josef Strobl, Austria | 228 |
| Stephan Eberharter, Austria | 208 |
| Werner Franz, Austria | 182 |
| Didier Cuche, Switzerland | 177 |
| Hannes Trinkl, Austria | 148 |
| Lasse Kjus, Norway | 143 |
| Frederik Nyberg, Sweden | 129 |
| Kjetil André Aamodt, Norway | 124 |

## Women

### OVERALL

| | Pts |
|---|---|
| Janica Kostelic, Croatia | 1,256 |
| Renate Götschl, Austria | 1,189 |
| Regine Cavagnoud, France | 1,105 |
| Sonja Nef, Switzerland | 1,060 |
| Michaela Dorfmeister, Austria | 923 |
| Isolde Kostner, Italy | 895 |
| Martina Ertl, Germany | 776 |
| Corinne Rey-Bellet, Switzerland | 744 |
| Carole Montillet, France | 702 |
| Brigitte Obermoser, Austria | 669 |

### DOWNHILL

| | Pts |
|---|---|
| Isolde Kostner, Italy | 596 |
| Renate Götschl, Austria | 455 |
| Regine Cavagnoud, France | 360 |
| Carole Montillet, France | 297 |
| Brigitte Obermoser, Austria | 295 |
| Melanie Turgeon, Canada | 275 |
| Petra Haltmayer, Germany | 215 |
| Corinne Rey-Bellet, Switzerland | 212 |
| Michaela Dorfmeister, Austria | 210 |
| Megan Gerety, United States | 204 |

### SLALOM

| | Pts |
|---|---|
| Janica Kostelic, Croatia | 824 |
| Sonja Nef, Switzerland | 384 |
| Martina Ertl, Germany | 346 |
| Karin Koellerer, Austria | 340 |
| Laure Pequegnot, France | 317 |
| Christel Saioni, France | 311 |
| Kristina Koznick, United States | 300 |
| Hedda Berntsen, Norway | 293 |
| Trine Bakke, Norway | 245 |
| Anja Paerson, Sweden | 235 |

### GIANT SLALOM

| | Pts |
|---|---|
| Sonja Nef, Switzerland | 676 |
| Anja Paerson, Sweden | 408 |
| Michaela Dorfmeister, Austria | 341 |
| Karen Putzer, Italy | 297 |
| Corinne Rey-Bellet, Switzerland | 265 |
| Martina Ertl, Germany | 260 |
| Brigitte Obermoser, Austria | 238 |
| Allison Forsyth, Canada | 226 |
| Janica Kostelic, Croatia | 204 |
| Ylva Nowen, Sweden | 162 |

### SUPER G

| | Pts |
|---|---|
| Regine Cavagnoud, France | 577 |
| Renate Götschl, Austria | 466 |
| Carole Montillet, France | 405 |
| Melanie Turgeon, Canada | 364 |
| Michaela Dorfmeister, Austria | 332 |
| Isolde Kostner, Italy | 281 |
| Corrine Ray-Bellet, Switzerland | 267 |
| Mojca Suhadolc, Slovenia | 162 |
| Martina Ertl, Germany | 156 |
| Petra Haltmayer, Germany | 153 |

## Event Descriptions

**Downhill:** A speed event entailing a single run on a course with a minimum vertical drop of 500 meters (800 for men's World Cup) and very few control gates.
**Slalom:** A technical event in which times for runs on two courses are totaled to determine the winner. Skiers must make many quick, short turns through a combination of gates (55–75 gates for men, 40–60 for women) over a short course (140–220-meter vertical drop for men, 120–180 for women).
**Combined:** An event in which scores from designated slalom and downhill races are combined to determine finish order.

**Giant Slalom:** A faster technical event with fewer, more broadly spaced gates than in the slalom. Times for runs on two courses with vertical drops of 250–400 meters for men and 250–300 meters for women are combined to determine the winner.
**Super Giant Slalom:** A speed event that is a cross between the downhill and the giant slalom.
**Parallel Slalom:** A technical event that combines slalom and giant slalom turns.

## FIS World Championships

### Sites

| | |
|---|---|
| 1931 .........................Mürren, Switzerland | 1936 .........................Innsbruck, Austria |
| 1932 .........................Cortina d'Ampezzo, Italy | 1937 .........................Chamonix, France |
| 1933 .........................Innsbruck, Austria | 1938 .........................Engelberg, Switzerland |
| 1934 .........................St. Moritz, Switzerland | 1939 .........................Zakopane, Poland |
| 1935 .........................Mürren, Switzerland | |

### Men

#### DOWNHILL

| | |
|---|---|
| 1931 | Walter Prager, Switzerland |
| 1932 | Gustav Lantschner, Austria |
| 1933 | Walter Prager, Switzerland |
| 1934 | David Zogg, Switzerland |
| 1935 | Franz Zingerle, Austria |
| 1936 | Rudolf Rominger, Switzerland |
| 1937 | Émile Allais, France |
| 1938 | James Couttet, France |
| 1939 | Hans Lantschner, Germany |

#### SLALOM

| | |
|---|---|
| 1931 | David Zogg, Switzerland |
| 1932 | Friedrich Dauber, Germany |
| 1933 | Anton Seelos, Austria |
| 1934 | Franz Pfnür, Germany |
| 1935 | Anton Seelos, Austria |
| 1936 | Rudi Matt, Austria |
| 1937 | Émile Allais, France |
| 1938 | Rudolf Rominger, Switzerland |
| 1939 | Rudolf Rominger, Switzerland |

### Women

#### DOWNHILL

| | |
|---|---|
| 1931 | Esme Mackinnon, Great Britain |
| 1932 | Paola Wiesinger, Italy |
| 1933 | Inge Wersin-Lantschner, Austria |
| 1934 | Anni Rüegg, Switzerland |
| 1935 | Christel Cranz, Germany |
| 1936 | Evie Pinching, Great Britain |
| 1937 | Christel Cranz, Germany |
| 1938 | Lisa Resch, Germany |
| 1939 | Christel Cranz, Germany |

#### SLALOM

| | |
|---|---|
| 1931 | Esme Mackinnon, Great Britain |
| 1932 | Rösli Streiff, Switzerland |
| 1933 | Inge Wersin-Lantschner, Austria |
| 1934 | Christel Cranz, Germany |
| 1935 | Anni Rüegg, Switzerland |
| 1936 | Gerda Paumgarten, Austria |
| 1937 | Christel Cranz, Germany |
| 1938 | Christel Cranz, Germany |
| 1939 | Christel Cranz, Germany |

## FIS World Alpine Ski Championships

### Sites

| | |
|---|---|
| 1950 .........................Aspen, Colorado | 1985 .........................Bormio, Italy |
| 1954 .........................Are, Sweden | 1987 .........................Crans-Montana, Switzerland |
| 1958 .........................Badgastein, Austria | 1989 .........................Vail, Colorado |
| 1962 .........................Chamonix, France | 1991 .........................Saalbach-Hinterglemm, Austria |
| 1966 .........................Portillo, Chile | 1993 .........................Morioka-Shizukuishi, Japan |
| 1970 .........................Val Gardena, Italy | 1996 .........................Sierra Nevada, Spain |
| 1974 .........................St. Moritz, Switzerland | 1997 .........................Sestriere, Italy |
| 1978 .........................Garmisch-Partenkirchen, W Germany | 1999 .........................Vail, Colorado |
| 1982 .........................Schladming, Austria | 2001 .........................St. Anton, Switzerland |

# FIS World Alpine Ski Championships *(Cont.)*

## Men

### DOWNHILL

| | |
|---|---|
| 1950.............Zeno Colo, Italy | 1985.............Pirmin Zurbriggen, Switzerland |
| 1954.............Christian Pravda, Austria | 1987.............Peter Müller, Switzerland |
| 1958.............Toni Sailer, Austria | 1989.............Hansjörg Tauscher, W Germany |
| 1962.............Karl Schranz, Austria | 1991.............Franz Heinzer, Switzerland |
| 1966.............Jean-Claude Killy, France | 1993.............Urs Lehmann, Switzerland |
| 1970.............Bernard Russi, Switzerland | 1996.............Patrick Ortlieb, Austria |
| 1974.............David Zwilling, Austria | 1997.............Bruno Kernen, Switzerland |
| 1978.............Josef Walcher, Austria | 1999.............Hermann Maier, Austria |
| 1982.............Harti Weirather, Austria | 2001.............Hannes Trinkl, Austria |

### SLALOM

| | |
|---|---|
| 1950.............Georges Schneider, Switzerland | 1985.............Jonas Nilsson, Sweden |
| 1954.............Stein Eriksen, Norway | 1987.............Frank Wörndl, W Germany |
| 1958.............Josl Rieder, Austria | 1989.............Rudolf Nierlich, Austria |
| 1962.............Charles Bozon, France | 1991.............Marc Girardelli, Luxembourg |
| 1966.............Carlo Senoner, Italy | 1993.............Kjetil André Aamodt, Norway |
| 1970.............Jean-Noël Augert, France | 1996.............Alberto Tomba, Italy |
| 1974.............Gustavo Thoeni, Italy | 1997.............Tom Stiansen, Norway |
| 1978.............Ingemar Stenmark, Sweden | 1999.............Lasse Kjus, Norway |
| 1982.............Ingemar Stenmark, Sweden | 2001.............Mario Matt, Austria |

### GIANT SLALOM

| | |
|---|---|
| 1950.............Zeno Colo, Italy | 1987.............Pirmin Zurbriggen, Switzerland |
| 1954.............Stein Eriksen, Norway | 1989.............Rudolf Nierlich, Austria |
| 1958.............Toni Sailer, Austria | 1991.............Rudolf Nierlich, Austria |
| 1962.............Egon Zimmermann, Austria | 1993.............Kjetil André Aamodt, Norway |
| 1966.............Guy Périllat, France | 1996.............Alberto Tomba, Italy |
| 1970.............Karl Schranz, Austria | 1997.............Michael von Grünigen, Switzerland |
| 1974.............Gustavo Thoeni, Italy | 1999.............Marco Büchel, Liechtenstein |
| 1978.............Ingemar Stenmark, Sweden | 2001.............Michael von Grünigen, Switzerland |
| 1982.............Steve Mahre, United States | |
| 1985.............Markus Wasmaier, W Germany | |

### COMBINED

| | |
|---|---|
| 1982.............Michel Vion, France | 1993.............Lasse Kjus, Norway |
| 1985.............Pirmin Zurbriggen, Switzerland | 1996.............Marc Girardelli, Luxembourg |
| 1987.............Marc Girardelli, Luxembourg | 1997.............Kjetil André Aamodt, Norway |
| 1989.............Marc Girardelli, Luxembourg | 1999.............Kjetil André Aamodt, Norway |
| 1991.............Stefan Eberharter, Austria | 2001.............Kjetil André Aamodt, Norway |

### SUPER G

| | |
|---|---|
| 1987.............Pirmin Zurbriggen, Switzerland | 1997.............Atle Skaardal, Norway |
| 1989.............Martin Hangl, Switzerland | 1999.............Hermann Maier, Austria |
| 1991.............Stefan Eberharter, Austria | .............Lasse Kjus, Norway |
| 1993.............Cancelled due to weather | 2001.............Daron Rahlves, United States |
| 1996.............Atle Skaardal, Norway | |

## Women

### DOWNHILL

| | |
|---|---|
| 1950.............Trude Beiser-Jochum, Austria | 1985.............Michela Figini, Switzerland |
| 1954.............Ida Schopfer, Switzerland | 1987.............Maria Walliser, Switzerland |
| 1958.............Lucile Wheeler, Canada | 1989.............Maria Walliser, Switzerland |
| 1962.............Christl Haas, Austria | 1991.............Petra Kronberger, Austria |
| 1966.............Erika Schinegger, Austria | 1993.............Kate Pace, Canada |
| 1970.............Annerösli Zryd, Switzerland | 1996.............Picabo Street, United States |
| 1974.............Annemarie Moser-Pröll, Austria | 1997.............Hilary Lindh, United States |
| 1978.............Annemarie Moser-Pröll, Austria | 1999.............Renate Götschl, Austria |
| 1982.............Gerry Sorensen, Canada | 2001.............Michaela Dorfmeister, Austria |

## Women *(Cont.)*

### SLALOM

| | | | | |
|---|---|---|---|---|
| 1950............Dagmar Rom, Austria | 1985............Perrine Pelen, France |
| 1954............Trude Klecker, Austria | 1987............Erika Hess, Switzerland |
| 1958............Inger Bjornbakken, Norway | 1989............Mateja Svet, Yugoslavia |
| 1962............Marianne Jahn, Austria | 1991............Vreni Schneider, Switzerland |
| 1966............Annie Famose, France | 1993............Karin Buder, Austria |
| 1970............Ingrid Lafforgue, France | 1996............Pernilla Wiberg, Sweden |
| 1974............Hanni Wenzel, Liechtenstein | 1997............Deborah Compagnoni, Italy |
| 1978............Lea Sölkner, Austria | 1999............Trine Bakke, Norway |
| 1982............Erika Hess, Switzerland | 2001............Anja Paerson, Sweden |

### GIANT SLALOM

| | |
|---|---|
| 1950............Dagmar Rom, Austria | 1985 ....................Diann Roffe, United States |
| 1954............Lucienne Schmith-Couttet, France | 1987 ....................Vreni Schneider, Switzerland |
| 1958............Lucile Wheeler, Canada | 1989 ....................Vreni Schneider, Switzerland |
| 1962............Marianne Jahn, Austria | 1991 ....................Pernilla Wiberg, Sweden |
| 1966............Marielle Goitschel, France | 1993 ....................Carole Merle, France |
| 1970............Betsy Clifford, Canada | 1996 ....................Deborah Compagnoni, Italy |
| 1974............Fabienne Serrat, France | 1997 ....................Deborah Compagnoni, Italy |
| 1978............Maria Epple, W Germany | 1999 ....................Anita Wachter, Austria |
| 1982............Erika Hess, Switzerland | 2001 ....................Sonja Nef, Switzerland |

### COMBINED

| | |
|---|---|
| 1982 ....................Erika Hess, Switzerland | 1993 ....................Miriam Vogt, Germany |
| 1985 ....................Erika Hess, Switzerland | 1996 ....................Pernilla Wiberg, Sweden |
| 1987 ....................Erika Hess, Switzerland | 1997 ....................Renate Götschl, Austria |
| 1989 ....................Tamara McKinney, United States | 1999 ....................Pernilla Wiberg, Sweden |
| 1991 ....................Chantal Bournissen, Switzerland | 2001 ....................Martina Ertl, Germany |

### SUPER G

| | |
|---|---|
| 1987 ....................Maria Walliser, Switzerland | 1996 ....................Isolde Kostner, Italy |
| 1989 ....................Ulrike Maier, Austria | 1997 ....................Isolde Kostner, Italy |
| 1991 ....................Ulrike Maier, Austria | 1999 ....................Alexandra Meissnitzer, Austria |
| 1993 ....................Katja Seizinger, Germany | 2001 ....................Regine Cavagnoud, France |

Note: The 1995 FIS World Alpine Ski Championships were postponed to 1996 due to lack of snow.

## Not So Sweet Victory

For the past decade Norway's Kari Traa was the finest freestyle skier never to win a world or Olympic title. Traa was a respected technician who seemed primed to rule the moguls event if she could muster more speed over the bumps and better extension on her jumps. In January 2001 in Whistler, B.C., after winning her first moguls world championship, Traa, 27, admitted that she had known the problem all along but couldn't stomach the remedy. It is, after all, devilishly hard to fight off a chocolate craving. "I lost some chocolate and lost some pounds," said Traa, who began cutting back in 1999 and, that winter, after dropping 20 pounds from her 5'6", 170-pound frame, won her second World Cup season title in dual moguls. "Now I'm moving not so much fat."

This was no bite-sized habit. There was hot chocolate, baked chocolate, dark chocolate, white chocolate, cookies, cakes, brownies. "Look, some people like whiskey," said Traa, a bronze medalist at the 1998 Nagano Games. "I like chocolate. I still eat it, but as a reward."

The restraint has helped propel Traa to the top of the World Cup standings. Asked which form of her favorite confection she would use to celebrate her triumph, Traa would not bite. "I can't tell you," she said. "I must guess myself."

—Brian Cazeneuve

# World Cup Season Title Holders

## Men

### OVERALL

| | |
|---|---|
| 1967 .....................Jean-Claude Killy, France | 1985 .....................Marc Girardelli, Luxembourg |
| 1968 .....................Jean-Claude Killy, France | 1986 .....................Marc Girardelli, Luxembourg |
| 1969 .....................Karl Schranz, Austria | 1987 .....................Pirmin Zurbriggen, Switzerland |
| 1970 .....................Karl Schranz, Austria | 1988 .....................Pirmin Zurbriggen, Switzerland |
| 1971 .....................Gustavo Thoeni, Italy | 1989 .....................Marc Girardelli, Luxembourg |
| 1972 .....................Gustavo Thoeni, Italy | 1990 .....................Pirmin Zurbriggen, Switzerland |
| 1973 .....................Gustavo Thoeni, Italy | 1991 .....................Marc Girardelli, Luxembourg |
| 1974 .....................Piero Gros, Italy | 1992 .....................Paul Accola, Switzerland |
| 1975 .....................Gustavo Thoeni, Italy | 1993 .....................Marc Girardelli, Luxembourg |
| 1976 .....................Ingemar Stenmark, Sweden | 1994 .....................Kjetil André Aamodt, Norway |
| 1977 .....................Ingemar Stenmark, Sweden | 1995 .....................Alberto Tomba, Italy |
| 1978 .....................Ingemar Stenmark, Sweden | 1996 .....................Lasse Kjus, Norway |
| 1979 .....................Peter Lüscher, Switzerland | 1997 .....................Luc Alphand, France |
| 1980 .....................Andreas Wenzel, Liechtenstein | 1998 .....................Hermann Maier, Austria |
| 1981 .....................Phil Mahre, United States | 1999 .....................Lasse Kjus, Norway |
| 1982 .....................Phil Mahre, United States | 2000 .....................Hermann Maier, Austria |
| 1983 .....................Phil Mahre, United States | 2001 .....................Hermann Maier, Austria |
| 1984 .....................Pirmin Zurbriggen, Switzerland | |

### DOWNHILL

| | |
|---|---|
| 1967 .....................Jean-Claude Killy, France | 1984 .....................Urs Raber, Switzerland |
| 1968 .....................Gerhard Nenning, Austria | 1985 .....................Helmut Höflehner, Austria |
| 1969 .....................Karl Schranz, Austria | 1986 .....................Peter Wirnsberger, Austria |
| 1970 .....................Karl Schranz, Austria | 1987 .....................Pirmin Zurbriggen, Switzerland |
| Karl Cordin, Austria | 1988 .....................Pirmin Zurbriggen, Switzerland |
| 1971 .....................Bernhard Russi, Switzerland | 1989 .....................Marc Girardelli, Luxembourg |
| 1972 .....................Bernhard Russi, Switzerland | 1990 .....................Helmut Höflehner, Austria |
| 1973 .....................Roland Collumbin, Switzerland | 1991 .....................Franz Heinzer, Switzerland |
| 1974 .....................Roland Collumbin, Switzerland | 1992 .....................Franz Heinzer, Switzerland |
| 1975 .....................Franz Klammer, Austria | 1993 .....................Franz Heinzer, Switzerland |
| 1976 .....................Franz Klammer, Austria | 1994 .....................Marc Girardelli, Luxembourg |
| 1977 .....................Franz Klammer, Austria | 1995 .....................Luc Alphand, France |
| 1978 .....................Franz Klammer, Austria | 1996 .....................Luc Alphand, France |
| 1979 .....................Peter Müller, Switzerland | 1997 .....................Luc Alphand, France |
| 1980 .....................Peter Müller, Switzerland | 1998 .....................Andreas Schifferer, Austria |
| 1981 .....................Harti Weirather, Austria | 1999 .....................Lasse Kjus, Norway |
| 1982 .....................Steve Podborski, Canada | 2000 .....................Hermann Maier, Austria |
| Peter Müller, Switzerland | 2001 .....................Hermann Maier, Austria |
| 1983 .....................Franz Klammer, Austria | |

### SLALOM

| | |
|---|---|
| 1967 ...............Jean-Claude Killy, France | 1984 ...............Marc Girardelli, Luxembourg |
| 1968 ...............Domeng Giovanoli, Switzerland | 1985 ...............Marc Girardelli, Luxembourg |
| 1969 ...............Jean-Noël Augert, France | 1986 ...............Rok Petrovic, Yugoslavia |
| 1970 ...............Patrick Russel, France | 1987 ...............Bojan Krizaj, Yugoslavia |
| Alain Penz, France | 1988 ...............Alberto Tomba, Italy |
| 1971 ...............Jean-Noël Augert, France | 1989 ...............Armin Bittner, W Germany |
| 1972 ...............Jean-Noël Augert, France | 1990 ...............Armin Bittner, W Germany |
| 1973 ...............Gustavo Thoeni, Italy | 1991 ...............Marc Girardelli, Luxembourg |
| 1974 ...............Gustavo Thoeni, Italy | 1992 ...............Alberto Tomba, Italy |
| 1975 ...............Ingemar Stenmark, Sweden | 1993 ...............Tomas Fogdof, Sweden |
| 1976 ...............Ingemar Stenmark, Sweden | 1994 ...............Alberto Tomba, Italy |
| 1977 ...............Ingemar Stenmark, Sweden | 1995 ...............Alberto Tomba, Italy |
| 1978 ...............Ingemar Stenmark, Sweden | 1996 ...............Sebastien Amiez, France |
| 1979 ...............Ingemar Stenmark, Sweden | 1997 ...............Thomas Sykora, Austria |
| 1980 ...............Ingemar Stenmark, Sweden | 1998 ...............Thomas Sykora, Austria |
| 1981 ...............Ingemar Stenmark, Sweden | 1999 ...............Thomas Stangassinger, Austria |
| 1982 ...............Phil Mahre, United States | 2000 ...............Kjetil André Aamodt, Norway |
| 1983 ...............Ingemar Stenmark, Sweden | 2001 ...............Benjamin Raich, Austria |

## Men *(Cont.)*

### GIANT SLALOM

| | |
|---|---|
| 1967 ..............Jean-Claude Killy, France | 1985 ..............Marc Girardelli, Luxembourg |
| 1968 ..............Jean-Claude Killy, France | 1986 ..............Joël Gaspoz, Switzerland |
| 1969 ..............Karl Schranz, Austria | 1987 ..............Joël Gaspoz, Switzerland |
| 1970 ..............Gustavo Thoeni, Italy | Pirmin Zurbriggen, Switzerland |
| 1971 ..............Patrick Russel, France | 1988 ..............Alberto Tomba, Italy |
| 1972 ..............Gustavo Thoeni, Italy | 1989 ..............Pirmin Zurbriggen, Switzerland |
| 1973 ..............Hans Hinterseer, Austria | 1990 ..............Ole-Cristian Furuseth, Norway |
| 1974 ..............Piero Gros, Italy | Günther Mader, Austria |
| 1975 ..............Ingemar Stenmark, Sweden | 1991 ..............Alberto Tomba, Italy |
| 1976 ..............Ingemar Stenmark, Sweden | 1992 ..............Alberto Tomba, Italy |
| 1977 ..............Heini Hemmi, Switzerland | 1993 ..............Kjetil André Aamodt, Norway |
| Ingemar Stenmark, Sweden | 1994 ..............Christian Mayer, Austria |
| 1978 ..............Ingemar Stenmark, Sweden | 1995 ..............Alberto Tomba, Italy |
| 1979 ..............Ingemar Stenmark, Sweden | 1996 ..............Michael von Grünigen, Switzerland |
| 1980 ..............Ingemar Stenmark, Sweden | 1997 ..............Michael von Grünigen, Switzerland |
| 1981 ..............Ingemar Stenmark, Sweden | 1998 ..............Hermann Maier, Austria |
| 1982 ..............Phil Mahre, United States | 1999 ..............Michael von Grünigen, Switzerland |
| 1983 ..............Phil Mahre, United States | 2000 ..............Hermann Maier, Austria |
| 1984 ..............Ingemar Stenmark, Sweden | 2001 ..............Hermann Maier, Austria |
| Pirmin Zurbriggen, Switzerland | |

### SUPER G

| | |
|---|---|
| 1986 ..............Markus Wasmeier, W Germany | 1994 ..............Jan Einar Thorsen, Norway |
| 1987 ..............Pirmin Zurbriggen, Switzerland | 1995 ..............Peter Runggaldier, Italy |
| 1988 ..............Pirmin Zurbriggen, Switzerland | 1996 ..............Atle Skaardal, Norway |
| 1989 ..............Pirmin Zurbriggen, Switzerland | 1997 ..............Luc Alphand, France |
| 1990 ..............Pirmin Zurbriggen, Switzerland | 1998 ..............Hermann Maier, Austria |
| 1991 ..............Franz Heinzer, Switzerland | 1999 ..............Hermann Maier, Austria |
| 1992 ..............Paul Accola, Switzerland | 2000 ..............Hermann Maier, Austria |
| 1993 ..............Kjetil André Aamodt, Norway | 2001 ..............Hermann Maier, Austria |

### COMBINED

| | |
|---|---|
| 1979 ..............Andreas Wenzel, Liechtenstein | 1991 ..............Marc Girardelli, Luxembourg |
| 1980 ..............Andreas Wenzel, Liechtenstein | 1992 ..............Paul Accola, Switzerland |
| 1981 ..............Phil Mahre, United States | 1993 ..............Marc Girardelli, Luxembourg |
| 1982 ..............Phil Mahre, United States | 1994 ..............Kjetil André Aamodt, Norway |
| 1983 ..............Phil Mahre, United States | 1995 ..............Marc Girardelli, Luxembourg |
| 1984 ..............Andreas Wenzel, Liechtenstein | 1996 ..............Günther Mader, Austria |
| 1985 ..............Andreas Wenzel, Liechtenstein | 1997 ..............Kjetil André Aamodt, Norway |
| 1986 ..............Markus Wasmeier, W Germany | 1998 ..............Werner Franz, Austria |
| 1987 ..............Pirmin Zurbriggen, Switzerland | 1999 ..............Kjetil André Aamodt, Norway |
| 1988 ..............Hubert Strolz, Austria | 2000 ..............Kjetil André Aamodt, Norway |
| 1989 ..............Marc Girardelli, Luxembourg | Lasse Kjus, Norway |
| 1990 ..............Pirmin Zurbriggen, Switzerland | 2001 ..............Lasse Kjus, Norway |

## Women

### OVERALL

| | |
|---|---|
| 1967 ..............Nancy Greene, Canada | 1985 ..............Michela Figini, Switzerland |
| 1968 ..............Nancy Greene, Canada | 1986 ..............Maria Walliser, Switzerland |
| 1969 ..............Gertrud Gabl, Austria | 1987 ..............Maria Walliser, Switzerland |
| 1970 ..............Michèle Jacot, France | 1988 ..............Michela Figini, Switzerland |
| 1971 ..............Annemarie Pröll, Austria | 1989 ..............Vreni Schneider, Switzerland |
| 1972 ..............Annemarie Pröll, Austria | 1990 ..............Petra Kronberger, Austria |
| 1973 ..............Annemarie Pröll, Austria | 1991 ..............Petra Kronberger, Austria |
| 1974 ..............Annemarie Moser-Pröll, Austria | 1992 ..............Petra Kronberger, Austria |
| 1975 ..............Annemarie Moser-Pröll, Austria | 1993 ..............Anita Wachter, Austria |
| 1976 ..............Rosi Mitermaier, W Germany | 1994 ..............Vreni Schneider, Switzerland |
| 1977 ..............Lise-Marie Morerod, Switzerland | 1995 ..............Vreni Schneider, Switzerland |
| 1978 ..............Hanni Wenzel, Liechtenstein | 1996 ..............Katja Seizinger, Germany |
| 1979 ..............Annemarie Moser-Pröll, Austria | 1997 ..............Pernilla Wiberg, Sweden |
| 1980 ..............Hanni Wenzel, Liechtenstein | 1998 ..............Katja Seizinger, Germany |
| 1981 ..............Marie-Thérèse Nadig, Switzerland | 1999 ..............Alexandra Meissnitzer, Austria |
| 1982 ..............Erika Hess, Switzerland | 2000 ..............Renate Götschl, Austria |
| 1983 ..............Tamara McKinney, United States | 2001 ..............Janica Kostelic, Croatia |
| 1984 ..............Erika Hess, Switzerland | |

## Women *(Cont.)*

### DOWNHILL

| | |
|---|---|
| 1967 ...............Marielle Goitschel, France | 1985 ...............Michela Figini, Switzerland |
| 1968 ...............Isabelle Mir, France & Olga Pall, Austria | 1986 ...............Maria Walliser, Switzerland |
| 1969 ...............Wiltrud Drexel, Austria | 1987 ...............Michela Figini, Switzerland |
| 1970 ...............Isabelle Mir, France | 1988 ...............Michela Figini, Switzerland |
| 1971 ...............Annemarie Pröll, Austria | 1989 ...............Michela Figini, Switzerland |
| 1972 ...............Annemarie Pröll, Austria | 1990 ...............Katrin Gutensohn-Knopf, Germany |
| 1973 ...............Annemarie Pröll, Austria | 1991 ...............Chantal Bournissen, Switzerland |
| 1974 ...............Annemarie Moser-Pröll, Austria | 1992 ...............Katja Seizinger, Germany |
| 1975 ...............Annemarie Moser-Pröll, Austria | 1993 ...............Katja Seizinger, Germany |
| 1976 ...............Brigitte Totschnig, Austria | 1994 ...............Katja Seizinger, Germany |
| 1977 ...............Brigitte Totschnig-Habersatter, Austria | 1995 ...............Picabo Street, United States |
| 1978 ...............Annemarie Moser-Pröll, Austria | 1996 ...............Picabo Street, United States |
| 1979 ...............Annemarie Moser-Pröll, Austria | 1997 ...............Renate Götschl, Austria |
| 1980 ...............Marie-Thérèse Nadig, Switzerland | 1998 ...............Katja Seizinger, Germany |
| 1981 ...............Marie-Thérèse Nadig, Switzerland | 1999 ...............Renate Götschl, Austria |
| 1982 ...............Marie-Cecile Gros-Gaudenier, France | 2000 ...............Regina Haeusl, Germany |
| 1983 ...............Doris De Agostini, Switzerland | 2001 ...............Isolde Kostner, Italy |
| 1984 ...............Maria Walliser, Switzerland | |

### SLALOM

| | |
|---|---|
| 1967 ...............Marielle Goitschel, France | 1985 ...............Erika Hess, Switzerland |
| 1968 ...............Marielle Goitschel, France | 1986 ...............Roswitha Steiner, Austria |
| 1969 ...............Gertrud Gabl, Austria | Erika Hess, Switzerland |
| 1970 ...............Ingrid Lafforgue, France | 1987 ...............Corrine Schmidhauser, Switzerland |
| 1971 ...............Britt Lafforgue, France | 1988 ...............Roswitha Steiner, Austria |
| 1972 ...............Britt Lafforgue, France | 1989 ...............Vreni Schneider, Switzerland |
| 1973 ...............Patricia Emonet, France | 1990 ...............Vreni Schneider, Switzerland |
| 1974 ...............Christa Zechmeister, W Germany | 1991 ...............Petra Kronberger, Austria |
| 1975 ...............Lise-Marie Morerod, Switzerland | 1992 ...............Vreni Schneider, Switzerland |
| 1976 ...............Rosi Mittermaier, W Germany | 1993 ...............Vreni Schneider, Switzerland |
| 1977 ...............Lise-Marie Morerod, Switzerland | 1994 ...............Vreni Schneider, Switzerland |
| 1978 ...............Hanni Wenzel, Liechtenstein | 1995 ...............Vreni Schneider, Switzerland |
| 1979 ...............Regina Sackl, Austria | 1996 ...............Elfi Eder, Austria |
| 1980 ...............Perrine Pelen, France | 1997 ...............Pernilla Wiberg, Sweden |
| 1981 ...............Erika Hess, Switzerland | 1998 ...............Ylva Nowen, Sweden |
| 1982 ...............Erika Hess, Switzerland | 1999 ...............Sabine Egger, Austria |
| 1983 ...............Erika Hess, Switzerland | 2000 ...............Spela Pretnar, Slovenia |
| 1984 ...............Tamara McKinney, United States | 2001 ...............Janica Kostelic, Croatia |

### GIANT SLALOM

| | |
|---|---|
| 1967 ...............Nancy Greene, Canada | 1985 ...............Maria Keihl, W Germany |
| 1968 ...............Nancy Greene, Canada | Michela Figini, Switzerland |
| 1969 ...............Marilyn Cochran, United States | 1986 ...............Vreni Schneider, Switzerland |
| 1970 ...............Michèle Jacot, France | 1987 ...............Vreni Schneider, Switzerland |
| Françoise Macchi, France | Maria Walliser, Switzerland |
| 1971 ...............Annemarie Pröll, Austria | 1988 ...............Mateja Svet, Yugoslavia |
| 1972 ...............Annemarie Pröll, Austria | 1989 ...............Vreni Schneider, Switzerland |
| 1973 ...............Monika Kaserer, Austria | 1990 ...............Anita Wachter, Austria |
| 1974 ...............Hanni Wenzel, Liechtenstein | 1991 ...............Vreni Schneider, Switzerland |
| 1975 ...............Annemarie Moser-Pröll, Austria | 1992 ...............Carole Merle, France |
| 1976 ...............Lise-Marie Morerod, Switzerland | 1993 ...............Carole Merle, France |
| 1977 ...............Lise-Marie Morerod, Switzerland | 1994 ...............Anita Wachter, Austria |
| 1978 ...............Lise-Marie Morerod, Switzerland | 1995 ...............Vreni Schneider, Switzerland |
| 1979 ...............Christa Kinshofer, W Germany | 1996 ...............Martina Ertl, Germany |
| 1980 ...............Hanni Wenzel, Liechtenstein | 1997 ...............Deborah Compagnoni, Italy |
| 1981 ...............Marie-Thérèse Nadig, Switzerland | 1998 ...............Martina Ertl, Germany |
| 1982 ...............Irene Epple, W Germany | 1999 ...............Alexandra Meissnitzer, Austria |
| 1983 ...............Tamara McKinney, United States | 2000 ...............Michaela Dorfmeister, Austria |
| 1984 ...............Erika Hess, Switzerland | 2001 ...............Sonja Nef, Switzerland |

### SUPER G

| | |
|---|---|
| 1986 ...............Maria Kiehl, W Germany | 1991 ...............Carole Merle, France |
| 1987 ...............Maria Walliser, Switzerland | 1992 ...............Carole Merle, France |
| 1988 ...............Michela Figini, Switzerland | 1993 ...............Katja Seizinger, Germany |
| 1989 ...............Carole Merle, France | 1994 ...............Katja Seizinger, Germany |
| 1990 ...............Carole Merle, France | 1995 ...............Katja Seizinger, Germany |

## Women *(Cont.)*

### SUPER G *(CONT.)*

| | |
|---|---|
| 1996 ...............Katja Seizinger, Germany | 1999 ...............Alexandra Meissnitzer, Austria |
| 1997 ...............Hilde Gerg, Germany | 2000 ...............Renate Götschl, Austria |
| 1998 ...............Katja Seizinger, Germany | 2001 ...............Regine Cavagnoud, France |

### COMBINED

| | |
|---|---|
| 1979 ...............Annemarie Moser-Pröll, Austria | 1990 ...............Anita Wachter, Austria |
| Hanni Wenzel, Liechtenstein | 1991 ...............Sabine Ginther, Austria |
| 1980 ...............Hanni Wenzel, Liechtenstein | 1992 ...............Sabine Ginther, Austria |
| 1981 ...............Marie-Thérèse Nadig, Switzerland | 1993 ...............Anita Wachter, Austria |
| 1982 ...............Irene Epple, W Germany | 1994 ...............Pernilla Wiberg, Sweden |
| 1983 ...............Hanni Wenzel, Liechtenstein | 1995 ...............Pernilla Wiberg, Sweden |
| 1984 ...............Erika Hess, Switzerland | 1996 ...............Anita Wachter, Austria |
| 1985 ...............Brigitte Oertli, Switzerland | 1997 ...............Pernilla Wiberg, Sweden |
| 1986 ...............Maria Walliser, Switzerland | 1998 ...............Hilde Gerg, Germany |
| 1987 ...............Brigitte Oertli, Switzerland | 1999 ...............Hilde Gerg, Germany |
| 1988 ...............Brigitte Oertli, Switzerland | 2000 ...............Renate Götschl, Austria |
| 1989 ...............Brigitte Oertli, Switzerland | 2001 ...............Janica Kostelic, Croatia |

# World Cup Career Victories

## Men

### DOWNHILL

| | |
|---|---|
| 25 | Franz Klammer, Austria |
| 19 | Peter Müller, Switzerland |
| 15 | Franz Heinzer, Switzerland |

### SLALOM

| | |
|---|---|
| 40 | Ingemar Stenmark, Sweden |
| 35 | Alberto Tomba, Italy |
| 16 | Marc Girardelli, Luxembourg |

### GIANT SLALOM

| | |
|---|---|
| 46 | Ingemar Stenmark, Sweden |
| 19 | *Michael von Grünigen, Switz |
| 15 | Alberto Tomba, Italy |

### SUPER G

| | |
|---|---|
| 16 | *Hermann Maier, Austria |
| 10 | Pirmin Zurbriggen, Switzerland |
| 7 | Marc Girardelli, Luxembourg |

### COMBINED

| | |
|---|---|
| 11 | Phil Mahre, United States |
| | Pirmin Zurbriggen, Switzerland |
| | Marc Girardelli, Luxembourg |

*Active in 2001.

## Women

### DOWNHILL

| | |
|---|---|
| 36 | Annemarie Moser-Pröll, Austria |
| 17 | Michela Figini, Switzerland |
| 16 | Katja Seizinger, Germany |

### SLALOM

| | |
|---|---|
| 33 | Vreni Schneider, Switzerland |
| 21 | Erika Hess, Switzerland |
| 15 | Perrine Pelen, France |

### GIANT SLALOM

| | |
|---|---|
| 21 | Vreni Schneider, Switzerland |
| 16 | Annemarie Moser-Pröll, Austria |
| 14 | Anita Wachter, Austria |
| | Lise-Marie Morerod, Switzerland |

### SUPER G

| | |
|---|---|
| 16 | Katja Seizinger, Germany |
| 12 | Carole Merle, France |
| 4 | Alexandra Meissnitzer, Austria |
| | Regine Cavagnoud, France |

### COMBINED

| | |
|---|---|
| 8 | Hanni Wenzel, Lichtenstein |
| 7 | Annemarie Moser-Pröll, Austria |
| | Brigitte Oertli, Switzerland |

# U.S. Olympic Gold Medalists

## Men

| Year | Winner | Event |
|---|---|---|
| 1980 ...............Phil Mahre | | Combined |
| 1984 ...............Bill Johnson | | Downhill |
| 1984 ...............Phil Mahre | | Slalom |
| 1994 ...............Tommy Moe | | Downhill |

## Women

| Year | Winner | Event |
|---|---|---|
| 1948 ...............Gretchen Fraser | | Slalom |
| 1952 ...............Andrea Mead Lawrence | | Slalom |
| 1952 ...............Andrea Mead Lawrence | | Giant Slalom |
| 1972 ...............Barbara Ann Cochran | | Slalom |
| 1984 ...............Debbie Armstrong | | Giant Slalom |
| 1994 ...............Diann Roffe-Steinrotter | | Super G |
| 1998 ...............Picabo Street | | Super G |

# Figure Skating

**World champion
Evgeny Plushenko
of Russia**

# Double Double

## For the second year in a row, Michelle Kwan swept the U.S. and world titles

### BY MERRELL NODEN

**N**O NEED to check your calendar: It only *seems* as if Michelle Kwan has been around for decades. In a sport of ephemeral hummingbirds who delight us with dramatic flitting flights of fancy across the ice before they burn out with injuries or stress, she is a rarity, demonstrating not only the surpassing grace we've come to expect from her, but uncommon staying power too.

Since winning her first national title in 1996, at age 15, Kwan has racked up four more U.S. championships and four world titles. Though she will probably go to the Salt Lake City Winter Olympics as the favorite to win the gold medal that eluded her in Nagano, Kwan is as far from a lock as a front-runner can be. She would inspire more confidence if she were not still skating astride the sport's oldest fault line, the divide between artistry and athleticism. Her skating is universally praised for its elegance and expressiveness, but it will take more than those qualities to beat her chief rival, Irina Slutskaya of Russia, who regularly lands far more difficult jumps than Kwan even attempts.

In January 2001, at the U.S. Nationals in Boston's FleetCenter, Kwan beat a women's field that was remarkably strong despite the absence of up-and-comers like Naomi Nari Nam, Deanna Stellato and Sasha Cohen, all of whom were injured. After skating a nearly perfect short program, Kwan showed why her fans watch her with their fingers crossed. In the freestyle she downsized a planned triple toe–triple toe combination to a double-double, the sort of compromise that won't cost her with American judges but almost certainly will with international ones, who want to see greater athleticism—and get it from skaters like Slutskaya.

The qualms about the difficulty of her program notwithstanding, Kwan is far ahead of her male teammates. It was a lousy year for the American men. The FleetCenter ice somehow seemed more slippery than usual. SPORTS ILLUSTRATED'S E.M. Swift dubbed the men's competition a "Boston Ass-over-Teakettle Party," while *Boston Globe* writer John Powers compared the inept proceedings to "a drunken all-skate on the Frog Pond."

Two-time defending champion Michael

**Despite her four world titles, Kwan will be only a slight favorite at the 2002 Olympics.**

HEINZ KLUETMEIER

Weiss performed as if the spirits of Moe, Larry and Curly were wrestling in his limbs. After placing first in the short program, Weiss fell twice during the freestyle, stepped out of his jumps twice and failed to land even one combination. Tim Goebel, whose 11th-place finish at the worlds last year meant that the U.S. could not take the full complement of three skaters to the worlds this year, landed just one of the three combination jumps he'd planned. So woeful was the field that Goebel made the U.S. team, along with veteran Todd Eldredge, returning to competition after two years of touring.

While the American men stumbled, the Russians raised the stakes. At the world championships in March in Vancouver, there was no doubt as to who was the most electrifying skater. It wasn't three-time defending champion Alexei Yagudin, who turned his ankle while jogging and then turned in his worst performance in years, failing on jump after jump. No, the star was Yagudin's former training partner, Evgeny Plushenko. After finishing a disappointing fourth at the worlds in 2000, Plushenko arrived in Vancouver unbeaten in 2001. With his spidery arms and long blond hair flying out behind him, Plushenko so entranced the crowd that it booed when no judge awarded him a 6.0. Flexible enough to perform a Biellmann spin (in which the skater reaches back and holds his skate blade), the 18-year-old Russian landed his trademark quadruple toe loop, triple toe loop, double loop combination early and then fed off the crowd's excitement. Yagudin was lucky to finish second, and Eldredge was delighted to finish third, at 29 the oldest man in 70 years to medal at the worlds. Goebel's fourth-place finish guaranteed the U.S. another skater in Salt Lake City.

The U.S. resumed its run of disappointing performances in both pairs and dance, where the teams of Kyoka Ina and John Zimmerman and Naomi Lang and Peter Tchernyshev finished seventh and ninth, respectively. The Italian team of Barbara Fusar-Poli and Maurizio Margaglio won Italy's first gold at the worlds, in dance, and the Canadian duo of Jamie Salé and David Pelletier, who won the pairs competition, gave the Vancouver crowd an excuse to go nuts.

Kwan was also impressive, producing the kind of gritty performance that proved she isn't all pretty icing. Trailing Slutskaya after the short program, Kwan nailed seven triples and a triple-triple combination when she needed it. She finished by shouting, "Yes!" and pumping her fists. "I was gutsy," she said later. "I just let myself go."

Slutskaya, skating next, tried valiantly to catch her and might have but for botching a second three-jump combination. Still, Slutskaya became the first woman to land a triple Salchow, triple loop, double toe loop combination in competition, eliciting a collective gasp from the crowd. Behind Kwan and Slutskaya came Sarah Hughes, an uncommonly poised 15-year-old from Great Neck, N.Y., who has now improved from seventh to fifth to third in her three worlds.

So Kwan will arrive in Utah as the favorite over Slutskaya, with the knowledge that the last four Olympic titlists were reigning world champions. But to finally grab Olympic gold, Kwan will have to let herself go again.

# FOR THE RECORD 2001

Vancouver, March 19–25

### Women

1........Michelle Kwan, United States
2........Irina Slutskaya, Russia
3........Sarah Hughes, United States

### Men

1.........Evgeny Plushenko, Russia
2.........Alexei Yagudin, Russia
3.........Todd Eldredge, United States

### Pairs

1........Jamie Salé and David Pelletier, Canada
2........Elena Berezhnaya and Anton Sikharulidze, Russia
3........Xue Shen and Hongo Zhao, China

### Dance

1.........Barbara Fusar-Poli and Maurizio Margaglio, Italy
2.........Marina Anissina and Gwendal Peizerat, France
3.........Irina Lobacheva and Ilia Averbukh, Russia

## World Figure Skating Championships Medal Table

| Country | Gold | Silver | Bronze | Total |
|---|---|---|---|---|
| Russia | 3 | 4 | 1 | 8 |
| United States | 1 | 0 | 2 | 3 |
| France | 1 | 1 | 1 | 3 |
| China | 0 | 1 | 1 | 2 |
| Canada | 1 | 1 | 0 | 2 |
| Italy | 1 | 1 | 0 | 2 |
| Lithuania | 0 | 0 | 1 | 1 |

## Champions of the United States

Boston, January 14–21

### Women

1......................Michelle Kwan, Los Angeles FSC
2......................Sarah Hughes, SC of New York
3......................Angela Nikodinov, All year FSC

### Men

1......................Timothy Goebel, Winterhurst FSC
2......................Todd Eldredge, Detroit SC
3......................Matthew Savoie, Illinois Valley FSC

### Pairs

1. ......................Kyoko Ina and John Zimmerman, SC of New York/Birmingham FSC
2......................Tiffany Scott and Philip Dulebohn, Colonial FSC and Univeristy of Del FSC
3......................Danielle Hartsell and Steve Hartsell, Detroit SC

### Dance

1. ......................Naomi Lang and Peter Tchernyshev, Detroit SC
2......................Tanith Belbin and Benjamin Agosto, Detroit SC
3......................Jessica Joseph and Brandon Forsyth, Detroit SC and The SC of Boston

**Guts and Glory**

While winning the U.S. nationals in Boston, Michelle Kwan was, well, utterly Kwanlike—elegant, confident, smooth—but it was her flawless triple toe, triple toe combination that allowed her to edge her nemesis, Russia's Irina Slutskaya, who'd beaten Kwan three times in the previous 13 months. In winning her fourth world title in six years, Kwan earned a psychologically important victory, since the last four ladies' Olympic gold medalists have gone into the Games as the reigning world champion. "I was gutsy," Kwan said. "I did everything I planned."

## Skating Terminology*

### Basic Skating Terms

**Edges:** The two sides of the skating blade, on either side of the grooved center. There is an inside edge, on the inner side of the leg; and an outside edge, on the outer side of the leg.

**Free Foot, Hip, Knee, Side, etc.:** The foot a skater is not skating on at any one time is the free foot; everything on that side of the body is then called "free." (See also "skating foot.")

**Free Skating (Freestyle):** A 4- or 5-minute competition program of free-skating components, choreographed to music, with no set elements. Skating moves include jumps, spins, steps and other linking movements.

**Skating Foot, Hip, Knee, Side, etc.:** Opposite of the free foot, hip, knee, side, etc. The foot a skater is skating on at any one time is the skating foot; everything on that side of the body is then called "skating."

**Toe Picks (Toe Rakes):** The teeth at the front of the skate blade, used primarily for certain jumps and spins.

**Trace, Tracing:** The line left on the ice by the skater's blade.

### Jumps

**Waltz:** A beginner's jump, involving half a revolution in the air, taken from a forward outside edge and landed on the back outside edge of the other foot.

**Toe Loop:** A one-revolution jump taken off from and landed on the same back outside edge. This jump is similar to the loop jump except that the skater kicks the toe pick of the free leg into the ice upon takeoff, providing added power.

**Toe Walley:** A jump similar to the toe loop, except that the takeoff is from the inside edge.

**Flip:** A jump taken off with the toe pick of the free leg from a back inside edge and landed on a back outside edge, with one in-air revolution.

**Lutz:** A toe jump similar to the flip, taken off with the toe pick of the free leg from a backward outside edge. The skater enters the jump skating in one direction, and concludes the jump skating in the opposite direction. Usually performed in the corners of the rink. Named after inventor Alois Lutz, who first landed the jump in Vienna, 1918.

**Salchow:** A one-, two- or three-revolution jump. The skater takes off from the back inside edge of one foot and lands backwards on the outside edge of the right foot, the opposite foot from which the skater took off. Named for its originator and first Olympic champion (1908), Sweden's Ulrich Salchow.

**Axel:** A combination of the waltz and loop jumps, including one-and-a-half revolutions. The only jump begun from a forward outside edge, the Axel is landed on the back outside edge of the opposite foot. Named for its inventor, Norway's Axel Paulsen.

### Spins

**Spin:** The rotation of the body in one place on the ice. Various spins are the back, fast or scratch, sit, camel, butterfly and layback.

**Camel Spin:** A spin with the skater in an arabesque position (free leg at right angles to the leg on the ice).

**Flying Camel Spin:** A jump spin ending in the camel-spin position.

**Flying Sit Spin:** A jump spin in which the skater leaps off the ice, assumes a sitting position at the peak of the jump, lands and spins in a similar sitting position.

### Pair Movements/Techniques

**Death Spiral:** One of the most dramatic moves in figure skating. The man, acting as the center of a circle, holds tightly to the hand of his partner and pulls her around him. The woman, gliding on one foot, achieves a position almost horizontal to the ice.

**Lifts:** The most spectacular moves in pairs skating. They involve any maneuver in which the man lifts the woman off the ice. The man often holds his partner above his head with one hand.

**Throws:** The man lifts the woman into the air and throws her away from him. She spins in the air and lands on one foot.

**Twist:** The man throws the woman into the air. She spins in the air (either a double- or triple-twist), and he catches her at the landing.

*Compiled by the United States Figure Skating Association.

## World Champions

### Women

| | |
|---|---|
| 1906 | Madge Sayers-Cave, Great Britain |
| 1907 | Madge Sayers-Cave, Great Britain |
| 1908 | Lily Kronberger, Hungary |
| 1909 | Lily Kronberger, Hungary |
| 1910 | Lily Kronberger, Hungary |
| 1911 | Lily Kronberger, Hungary |
| 1912 | Opika von Meray Horvath, Hungary |
| 1913 | Opika von Meray Horvath, Hungary |
| 1914 | Opika von Meray Horvath, Hungary |
| 1915–21 | No competition |
| 1922 | Herma Plank-Szabo, Austria |
| 1923 | Herma Plank-Szabo, Austria |
| 1924 | Herma Plank-Szabo, Austria |
| 1925 | Herma Jaross-Szabo, Austria |
| 1926 | Herma Jaross-Szabo, Austria |
| 1927 | Sonja Henie, Norway |
| 1928 | Sonja Henie, Norway |
| 1929 | Sonja Henie, Norway |
| 1930 | Sonja Henie, Norway |
| 1931 | Sonja Henie, Norway |
| 1932 | Sonja Henie, Norway |
| 1933 | Sonja Henie, Norway |
| 1934 | Sonja Henie, Norway |
| 1935 | Sonja Henie, Norway |
| 1936 | Sonja Henie, Norway |
| 1937 | Cecilia Colledge, Great Britain |
| 1938 | Megan Taylor, Great Britain |
| 1939 | Megan Taylor, Great Britain |
| 1940–46 | No competition |
| 1947 | Barbara Ann Scott, Canada |
| 1948 | Barbara Ann Scott, Canada |
| 1949 | Alena Vrzanova, Czechoslovakia |
| 1950 | Alena Vrzanova, Czechoslovakia |
| 1951 | Jeannette Altwegg, Great Britain |
| 1952 | Jacqueline duBief, France |
| 1953 | Tenley Albright, United States |
| 1954 | Gundi Busch, W Germany |
| 1955 | Tenley Albright, United States |
| 1956 | Carol Heiss, United States |
| 1957 | Carol Heiss, United States |

## Women *(Cont.)*

| | |
|---|---|
| 1958 | Carol Heiss, United States |
| 1959 | Carol Heiss, United States |
| 1960 | Carol Heiss, United States |
| 1961 | No competition |
| 1962 | Sjoukje Dijkstra, Netherlands |
| 1963 | Sjoukje Dijkstra, Netherlands |
| 1964 | Sjoukje Dijkstra, Netherlands |
| 1965 | Petra Burka, Canada |
| 1966 | Peggy Fleming, United States |
| 1967 | Peggy Fleming, United States |
| 1968 | Peggy Fleming, United States |
| 1969 | Gabriele Seyfert, E Germany |
| 1970 | Gabriele Seyfert, E Germany |
| 1971 | Beatrix Schuba, Austria |
| 1972 | Beatrix Schuba, Austria |
| 1973 | Karen Magnussen, Canada |
| 1974 | Christine Errath, E Germany |
| 1975 | Dianne DeLeeuw, Netherlands |
| 1976 | Dorothy Hamill, United States |
| 1977 | Linda Fratianne, United States |
| 1978 | Annett Poetzsch, E Germany |
| 1979 | Linda Fratianne, United States |
| 1980 | Annett Poetzsch, E Germany |
| 1981 | Denise Biellmann, Switzerland |
| 1982 | Elaine Zayak, United States |
| 1983 | Rosalynn Sumners, United States |
| 1984 | Katarina Witt, E Germany |
| 1985 | Katarina Witt, E Germany |
| 1986 | Debi Thomas, United States |
| 1987 | Katarina Witt, E Germany |
| 1988 | Katarina Witt, E Germany |
| 1989 | Midori Ito, Japan |
| 1990 | Jill Trenary, United States |
| 1991 | Kristi Yamaguchi, United States |
| 1992 | Kristi Yamaguchi, United States |
| 1993 | Oksana Baiul, Ukraine |
| 1994 | Yuka Sato, Japan |
| 1995 | Chen Lu, China |
| 1996 | Michelle Kwan, United States |
| 1997 | Tara Lipinski, United States |
| 1998 | Michelle Kwan, United States |
| 1999 | Maria Butyrskaya, Russia |
| 2000 | Michelle Kwan, United States |
| 2001 | Michelle Kwan, United States |

## Men

| | |
|---|---|
| 1896 | Gilbert Fuchs, Germany |
| 1897 | Gustav Hugel, Austria |
| 1898 | Henning Grenander, Sweden |
| 1899 | Gustav Hugel, Austria |
| 1900 | Gustav Hugel, Austria |
| 1901 | Ulrich Salchow, Sweden |
| 1902 | Ulrich Salchow, Sweden |
| 1903 | Ulrich Salchow, Sweden |
| 1904 | Ulrich Salchow, Sweden |
| 1905 | Ulrich Salchow, Sweden |
| 1906 | Gilbert Fuchs, Germany |
| 1907 | Ulrich Salchow, Sweden |
| 1908 | Ulrich Salchow, Sweden |
| 1909 | Ulrich Salchow, Sweden |
| 1910 | Ulrich Salchow, Sweden |
| 1911 | Ulrich Salchow, Sweden |
| 1912 | Fritz Kachler, Austria |
| 1913 | Fritz Kachler, Austria |
| 1914 | Gosta Sandhal, Sweden |
| 1915–21 | No competition |
| 1922 | Gillis Grafstrom, Sweden |
| 1923 | Fritz Kachler, Austria |
| 1924 | Gillis Grafstrom, Sweden |
| 1925 | Willy Bockl, Austria |
| 1926 | Willy Bockl, Austria |
| 1927 | Willy Bockl, Austria |
| 1928 | Willy Bockl, Austria |
| 1929 | Gillis Grafstrom, Sweden |
| 1930 | Karl Schafer, Austria |
| 1931 | Karl Schafer, Austria |
| 1932 | Karl Schafer, Austria |
| 1933 | Karl Schafer, Austria |
| 1934 | Karl Schafer, Austria |
| 1935 | Karl Schafer, Austria |
| 1936 | Karl Schafer, Austria |
| 1937 | Felix Kaspar, Austria |
| 1938 | Felix Kaspar, Austria |
| 1939 | Graham Sharp, Great Britain |
| 1940–46 | No competition |
| 1947 | Hans Gerschwiler, Switzerland |
| 1948 | Dick Button, United States |
| 1949 | Dick Button, United States |
| 1950 | Dick Button, United States |
| 1951 | Dick Button, United States |
| 1952 | Dick Button, United States |
| 1953 | Hayes Alan Jenkins, United States |
| 1954 | Hayes Alan Jenkins, United States |
| 1955 | Hayes Alan Jenkins, United States |
| 1956 | Hayes Alan Jenkins, United States |
| 1957 | David W. Jenkins, United States |
| 1958 | David W. Jenkins, United States |
| 1959 | David W. Jenkins, United States |
| 1960 | Alan Giletti, France |
| 1961 | No competition |
| 1962 | Donald Jackson, Canada |
| 1963 | Donald McPherson, Canada |
| 1964 | Manfred Schneldorfer, W Germany |
| 1965 | Alain Calmat, France |
| 1966 | Emmerich Danzer, Austria |
| 1967 | Emmerich Danzer, Austria |
| 1968 | Emmerich Danzer, Austria |
| 1969 | Tim Wood, United States |
| 1970 | Tim Wood, United States |
| 1971 | Andrej Nepela, Czechoslovakia |
| 1972 | Andrej Nepela, Czechoslovakia |
| 1973 | Andrej Nepela, Czechoslovakia |
| 1974 | Jan Hoffmann, E Germany |
| 1975 | Sergei Volkov, USSR |
| 1976 | John Curry, Great Britain |
| 1977 | Vladimir Kovalev, USSR |
| 1978 | Charles Tickner, United States |
| 1979 | Vladimir Kovalev, USSR |
| 1980 | Jan Hoffmann, E Germany |
| 1981 | Scott Hamilton, United States |
| 1982 | Scott Hamilton, United States |
| 1983 | Scott Hamilton, United States |
| 1984 | Scott Hamilton, United States |
| 1985 | Aleksandr Fadeev, USSR |
| 1986 | Brian Boitano, United States |
| 1987 | Brian Orser, Canada |
| 1988 | Brian Boitano, United States |
| 1989 | Kurt Browning, Canada |
| 1990 | Kurt Browning, Canada |
| 1991 | Kurt Browning, Canada |
| 1992 | Viktor Petrenko, CIS |
| 1993 | Kurt Browning, Canada |

## Men *(Cont.)*

| | |
|---|---|
| 1994..................Elvis Stojko, Canada | 1998..................Aleksei Yagudin, Russia |
| 1995..................Elvis Stojko, Canada | 1999..................Aleksei Yagudin, Russia |
| 1996..................Todd Eldredge, United States | 2000..................Aleksei Yagudin, Russia |
| 1997..................Elvis Stojko, Canada | 2001..................Evgeny Plushenko, Russia |

## Pairs

| | |
|---|---|
| 1908...........Anna Hubler, Heinrich Burger, Germany | 1963...........Marika Kilius, Hans-Jurgen Baumler, W Germany |
| 1909...........Phyllis Johnson, James H. Johnson, Great Britain | 1964...........Marika Kilius, Hans-Jurgen Baumler, W Germany |
| 1910...........Anna Hubler, Heinrich Burger, Germany | 1965...........Ljudmila Protopopov, Oleg Protopopov, USSR |
| 1911...........Ludowika Eilers, Walter Jakobsson, Germany/Finland | 1966...........Ljudmila Protopopov, Oleg Protopopov, USSR |
| 1912...........Phyllis Johnson, James H. Johnson, Great Britain | 1967...........Ljudmila Protopopov, Oleg Protopopov, USSR |
| 1913...........Helene Engelmann, Karl Majstrik, Germany | 1968...........Ljudmila Protopopov, Oleg Protopopov, USSR |
| 1914...........Ludowika Jakobsson-Eilers, Walter Jakobsson-Eilers, Finland | 1969...........Irina Rodnina, Alexsei Ulanov, USSR |
| 1915–21 .....No competition | 1970............Irina Rodnina, Alexsei Ulanov, USSR |
| 1922...........Helene Engelmann, Alfred Berger, Germany | 1971...........Irina Rodnina, Sergei Ulanov, USSR |
| 1923...........Ludowika Jakobsson Eilers, Walter Jakobsson-Eilers, Finland | 1972...........Irina Rodnina, Sergei Ulanov, USSR |
| 1924...........Helene Engelmann, Alfred Berger, Germany | 1973...........Irina Rodnina, Aleksandr Zaitsev, USSR |
| 1925...........Herma Jaross-Szabo, Ludwig Wrede, Austria | 1974...........Irina Rodnina, Aleksandr Zaitsev, USSR |
| 1926...........Andree Joly, Pierre Brunet, France | 1975...........Irina Rodnina, Aleksandr Zaitsev, USSR |
| 1927...........Herma Jaross-Szabo, Ludwig Wrede, Austria | 1976...........Irina Rodnina, Aleksandr Zaitsev, USSR |
| 1928...........Andree Joly, Pierre Brunet, France | 1977...........Irina Rodnina, Aleksandr Zaitsev, USSR |
| 1929...........Lilly Scholz, Otto Kaiser, Austria | 1978...........Irina Rodnina, Aleksandr Zaitsev, USSR |
| 1930...........Andree Brunet-Joly, Pierre Brunet-Joly, France | 1979...........Tai Babilonia, Randy Gardner, United States |
| 1931...........Emilie Rotter, Laszlo Szollas, Hungary | 1980...........Maria Cherkasova, Sergei Shakhrai, USSR |
| 1932...........Andree Brunet-Joly, Pierre Brunet-Joly, France | 1981...........Irina Vorobieva, Igor Lisovsky, USSR |
| 1933...........Emilie Rotter, Laszlo Szollas, Hungary | 1982...........Sabine Baess, Tassilio Thierbach, E Germany |
| 1934...........Emilie Rotter, Laszlo Szollas, Hungary | 1983...........Elena Valova, Oleg Vasiliev, USSR |
| 1935...........Emilie Rotter, Laszlo Szollas, Hungary | 1984...........Barbara Underhill, Paul Martini, Canada |
| 1936...........Maxi Herber, Ernst Bajer, Germany | 1985...........Elena Valova, Oleg Vasiliev, USSR |
| 1937...........Maxi Herber, Ernst Bajer, Germany | 1986...........Ekaterina Gordeeva, Sergei Grinkov, USSR |
| 1938...........Maxi Herber, Ernst Bajer, Germany | 1987...........Ekaterina Gordeeva, Sergei Grinkov, USSR |
| 1939...........Maxi Herber, Ernst Bajer, Germany | 1988...........Elena Valova, Oleg Vasiliev, USSR |
| 1940–46 .....No competition | 1989...........Ekaterina Gordeeva, Sergei Grinkov, USSR |
| 1947...........Micheline Lannoy, Pierre Baugniet, Belgium | 1990...........Ekaterina Gordeeva, Sergei Grinkov, USSR |
| 1948...........Micheline Lannoy, Pierre Baugniet, Belgium | 1991...........Natalia Mishkutienok, Artur Dmitriev, USSR |
| 1949...........Andrea Kekessy, Ede Kiraly, Hungary | 1992...........Natalia Mishkutienok, Artur Dmitriev, CIS |
| 1950...........Karol Kennedy, Peter Kennedy, United States | 1993...........Isabelle Brasseur, Lloyd Eisler, Canada |
| 1951...........Ria Baran, Paul Falk, W Germany | 1994...........Evgenia Shishkova, Vadim Naumov, Russia |
| 1952...........Ria Baran Falk, Paul Falk, W Germany | 1995...........Radka Kovarikova, Rene Novotny, Czech Republic |
| 1953...........Jennifer Nicks, John Nicks, Great Britain | 1996...........Marina Eltsova, Andrey Buskhov, Russia |
| 1954...........Frances Dafoe, Norris Bowden, Canada | 1997...........Mandy Wötzel, Ingo Steuer, Germany |
| 1955...........Frances Dafoe, Norris Bowden, Canada | 1998...........Jenni Meno, Todd Sand, United States |
| 1956...........Sissy Schwarz, Kurt Oppelt, Austria | 1999...........Elena Berezhnaya, Anton Sikharulidze, Russia |
| 1957...........Barbara Wagner, Robert Paul, Canada | 2000...........Maria Petrova and Aleksei Tikhonov, Russia |
| 1958...........Barbara Wagner, Robert Paul, Canada | 2001      Jamie Salé and David Pelletier, Canada |
| 1959...........Barbara Wagner, Robert Paul, Canada | |
| 1960...........Barbara Wagner, Robert Paul, Canada | |
| 1961...........No competition | |
| 1962...........Maria Jelinek, Otto Jelinek, Canada | |

### Dance

| | |
|---|---|
| 1950 ...........Lois Waring, Michael McGean, United States | 1973 ...........Ljudmila Pakhomova, Aleksandr Gorshkov, USSR |
| 1951 ...........Jean Westwood, Lawrence Demmy, Great Britain | 1974 ...........Ljudmila Pakhomova, Aleksandr Gorshkov, USSR |
| 1952 ...........Jean Westwood, Lawrence Demmy, Great Britain | 1975 ...........Irina Moiseeva, Andreij Minenkov, USSR |
| 1953 ...........Jean Westwood, Lawrence Demmy, Great Britain | 1976 ...........Ljudmila Pakhomova, Aleksandr Gorshkov, USSR |
| 1954 ...........Jean Westwood, Lawrence Demmy, Great Britain | 1977 ...........Irina Moiseeva, Andreij Minenkov, USSR |
| 1955 ...........Jean Westwood, Lawrence Demmy, Great Britain | 1978 ...........Natalia Linichuk, Gennadi Karponosov, USSR |
| 1956 ...........Pamela Wieght, Paul Thomas, Great Britain | 1979 ...........Natalia Linichuk, Gennadi Karponosov,USSR |
| 1957 ...........June Markham, Courtney Jones, Great Britain | 1980 ...........Krisztina Regoeczy, Andras Sallai, Hungary |
| 1958 ...........June Markham, Courtney Jones, Great Britain | 1981 ...........Jayne Torvill, Christopher Dean, Great Britain |
| 1959 ...........Doreen D. Denny, Courtney Jones, Great Britain | 1982 ...........Jayne Torvill, Christopher Dean, Great Britain |
| 1960 ...........Doreen D. Denny, Courtney Jones, Great Britain | 1983 ...........Jayne Torvill, Christopher Dean, Great Britain |
| 1961 ...........No competition | 1984 ...........Jayne Torvill, Christopher Dean, Great Britain |
| 1962 ...........Eva Romanova, Pavel Roman, Czechoslovakia | 1985.............Natalia Bestemianova, Andrei Bukin, USSR |
| 1963 ...........Eva Romanova, Pavel Roman, Czechoslovakia | 1986.............Natalia Bestemianova, Andrei Bukin, USSR |
| 1964 ...........Eva Romanova, Pavel Roman, Czechoslovakia | 1987.............Natalia Bestemianova, Andrei Bukin, USSR |
| 1965 ...........Eva Romanova, Pavel Roman, Czechoslovakia | 1988.............Natalia Bestemianova, Andrei Bukin, USSR |
| 1966 ...........Diane Towler, Bernard Ford, Great Britain | 1989.............Marina Klimova, Sergei Ponomarenko, USSR |
| 1967 ...........Diane Towler, Bernard Ford, Great Britain | 1990.............Marina Klimova, Sergei Ponomarenko, USSR |
| 1968 ...........Diane Towler, Bernard Ford, Great Britain | 1991...............Isabelle Duchesnay, Paul Duchesnay, France |
| 1969 ...........Diane Towler, Bernard Ford, Great Britain | 1992.............Marina Klimova, Sergei Ponomarenko, CIS |
| 1970 ...........Ljudmila Pakhomova, Aleksandr Gorshkov, USSR | 1993.............Renee Roca, Gorsha Sur, United States |
| 1971 ...........Ljudmila Pakhomova, Aleksandr Gorshkov, USSR | 1994 ...........Oksana Grishuk, Evgeny Platov, Russia |
| 1972 ...........Ljudmila Pakhomova, Aleksandr Gorshkov, USSR | 1995 ...........Oksana Grishuk, Evgeny Platov, Russia |
| | 1996 ...........Oksana Grishuk, Evgeny Platov, Russia |
| | 1997 ...........Oksana Grishuk, Evgeny Platov, Russia |
| | 1998 ...........Anjelika Krylova and Oleg Ovsyannikov, Russia |
| | 1999 ...........Anjelika Krylova and Oleg Ovsyannikov, Russia |
| | 2000 ...........Marina Anissina and Gwendal Peizerat, France |
| | 2001      Barbara Fusar-Poli and Maurizio Margaglio, Italy |

## Champions of the United States

The championships held in 1914, 1918, 1920 and 1921 under the auspices of the International Skating Union of America were open to Canadians, although the competitions were considered to be United States championships. Beginning in 1922, the championships have been held under the auspices of the United States Figure Skating Association.

### Women

| | |
|---|---|
| 1914 ...........Theresa Weld, SC of Boston | 1931 ...........Maribel Y. Vinson, SC of Boston |
| 1915–17 .....No competition | 1932 ...........Maribel Y. Vinson, SC of Boston |
| 1918............Rosemary S. Beresford, New York SC | 1933 ...........Maribel Y. Vinson, SC of Boston |
| 1919 ...........No competition | 1934 ...........Suzanne Davis, SC of Boston |
| 1920 ...........Theresa Weld, SC of Boston | 1935 ...........Maribel Y. Vinson, SC of Boston |
| 1921 ...........Theresa Weld Blanchard, SC of Boston | 1936 ...........Maribel Y. Vinson, SC of Boston |
| 1922 ...........Theresa Weld Blanchard, SC of Boston | 1937 ...........Maribel Y. Vinson, SC of Boston |
| 1923 ...........Theresa Weld Blanchard, SC of Boston | 1938 ...........Joan Tozzer, SC of Boston |
| 1924 ...........Theresa Weld Blanchard, SC of Boston | 1939 ...........Joan Tozzer, SC of Boston |
| 1925 ...........Beatrix Loughran, New York SC | 1940 ...........Joan Tozzer, SC of Boston |
| 1926 ...........Beatrix Loughran, New York SC | 1941 ...........Jane Vaughn, Philadelphia SC & HS |
| 1927 ...........Beatrix Loughran, New York SC | 1942 ...........Jane Vaughn Sullivan, Philadelphia SC & HS |
| 1928 ...........Maribel Y. Vinson, SC of Boston | 1943............Gretchen Van Zandt Merrill, SC of Boston |
| 1929 ...........Maribel Y. Vinson, SC of Boston | 1944............Gretchen Van Zandt Merrill, SC of Boston |
| 1930 ...........Maribel Y. Vinson, SC of Boston | |

### Women *(Cont.)*

| | |
|---|---|
| 1945...........Gretchen Van Zandt Merrill, SC of Boston | 1974 ...........Dorothy Hamill, SC of New York |
| 1946...........Gretchen Van Zandt Merrill, SC of Boston | 1975 ...........Dorothy Hamill, SC of New York |
| 1947...........Gretchen Van Zandt Merrill, SC of Boston | 1976 ...........Dorothy Hamill, SC of New York |
| 1948...........Gretchen Van Zandt Merrill, SC of Boston | 1977 ...........Linda Fratianne, Los Angeles FSC |
| 1949 ...........Yvonne Claire Sherman, SC of New York | 1978 ...........Linda Fratianne, Los Angeles FSC |
| 1950 ...........Yvonne Claire Sherman, SC of New York | 1979 ...........Linda Fratianne, Los Angeles FSC |
| 1951 ...........Sonya Klopfer, Junior SC of New York | 1980 ...........Linda Fratianne, Los Angeles FSC |
| 1952...........Tenley E. Albright, SC of Boston | 1981 ...........Elaine Zayak, SC of New York |
| 1953...........Tenley E. Albright, SC of Boston | 1982 ...........Rosalynn Sumners, Seattle SC |
| 1954...........Tenley E. Albright, SC of Boston | 1983 ...........Rosalynn Sumners, Seattle SC |
| 1955...........Tenley E. Albright, SC of Boston | 1984 ...........Rosalynn Sumners, Seattle SC |
| 1956...........Tenley E. Albright, SC of Boston | 1985 ...........Tiffany Chin, San Diego FSC |
| 1957...........Carol E. Heiss, SC of New York | 1986 ...........Debi Thomas, Los Angeles FSC |
| 1958...........Carol E. Heiss, SC of New York | 1987 ...........Jill Trenary, Broadmoor SC |
| 1959...........Carol E. Heiss, SC of New York | 1988 ...........Debi Thomas, Los Angeles FSC |
| 1960...........Carol E. Heiss, SC of New York | 1989 ...........Jill Trenary, Broadmoor SC |
| 1961 ...........Laurence R. Owen, SC of Boston | 1990 ...........Jill Trenary, Broadmoor SC |
| 1962...........Barbara Roles Pursley, Arctic Blades FSC | 1991 ...........Tonya Harding, Carousel FSC |
| 1963...........Lorraine G. Hanlon, SC of Boston | 1992 ...........Kristi Yamaguchi, St Moritz ISC |
| 1964...........Peggy Fleming, Arctic Blades FSC | 1993 ...........Nancy Kerrigan, Colonial FSC |
| 1965...........Peggy Fleming, Arctic Blades FSC | 1994 ...........Tonya Harding, Portland FSC |
| 1966...........Peggy Fleming, City of Colorado Springs | 1995 ...........Nicole Bobek, Los Angeles FSC |
| 1967 ...........Peggy Fleming, Broadmoor SC | 1996 ...........Michelle Kwan, Los Angeles FSC |
| 1968...........Peggy Fleming, Broadmoor SC | 1997 ...........Tara Lipinski, Detroit SC |
| 1969 ...........Janet Lynn, Wagon Wheel FSC | 1998 ...........Michelle Kwan, Los Angeles FSC |
| 1970...........Janet Lynn, Wagon Wheel FSC | 1999 ...........Michelle Kwan, Los Angeles FSC |
| 1971 ...........Janet Lynn, Wagon Wheel FSC | 2000 ...........Michelle Kwan, Los Angeles FSC |
| 1972...........Janet Lynn, Wagon Wheel FSC | 2001 ...........Michelle Kwan, Los Angeles FSC |
| 1973...........Janet Lynn, Wagon Wheel FSC | |

### Men

| | |
|---|---|
| 1914 ...........Norman M. Scott, WC of Montreal | 1952 ...........Dick Button, SC of Boston |
| 1915–17 .....No competition | 1953 ...........Hayes Alan Jenkins, Cleveland SC |
| 1918 ...........Nathaniel W. Niles, SC of Boston | 1954 ...........Hayes Alan Jenkins, Broadmoor SC |
| 1919 ...........No competition | 1955 ...........Hayes Alan Jenkins, Broadmoor SC |
| 1920 ...........Sherwin C. Badger, SC of Boston | 1956 ...........Hayes Alan Jenkins, Broadmoor SC |
| 1921 ...........Sherwin C. Badger, SC of Boston | 1957 ...........David Jenkins, Broadmoor SC |
| 1922 ...........Sherwin C. Badger, SC of Boston | 1958 ...........David Jenkins, Broadmoor SC |
| 1923 ...........Sherwin C. Badger, SC of Boston | 1959 ...........David Jenkins, Broadmoor SC |
| 1924 ...........Sherwin C. Badger, SC of Boston | 1960 ...........David Jenkins, Broadmoor SC |
| 1925 ...........Nathaniel W. Niles, SC of Boston | 1961 ...........Bradley R. Lord, SC of Boston |
| 1926 ...........Chris I. Christenson, Twin City FSC | 1962 ...........Monty Hoyt, Broadmoor SC |
| 1927 ...........Nathaniel W. Niles, SC of Boston | 1963 ...........Thomas Litz, Hershey FSC |
| 1928 ...........Roger F. Turner, SC of Boston | 1964 ...........Scott Ethan Allen, SC of New York |
| 1929 ...........Roger F. Turner, SC of Boston | 1965 ...........Gary C. Visconti, Detroit SC |
| 1930 ...........Roger F. Turner, SC of Boston | 1966 ...........Scott Ethan Allen, SC of New York |
| 1931 ...........Roger F. Turner, SC of Boston | 1967 ...........Gary C. Visconti, Detroit SC |
| 1932 ...........Roger F. Turner, SC of Boston | 1968 ...........Tim Wood, Detroit SC |
| 1933 ...........Roger F. Turner, SC of Boston | 1969 ...........Tim Wood, Detroit SC |
| 1934 ...........Roger F. Turner, SC of Boston | 1970 ...........Tim Wood, City of Colorado Springs |
| 1935 ...........Robin H. Lee, SC of New York | 1971 ...........John Misha Petkevich, Great Falls FSC |
| 1936 ...........Robin H. Lee, SC of New York | 1972 ...........Kenneth Shelley, Arctic Blades FSC |
| 1937 ...........Robin H. Lee, SC of New York | 1973 ...........Gordon McKellen Jr., SC of Lake Placid |
| 1938 ...........Robin H. Lee, Chicago FSC | 1974 ...........Gordon McKellen Jr., SC of Lake Placid |
| 1939 ...........Robin H. Lee, St Paul FSC | 1975 ...........Gordon McKellen Jr., SC of Lake Placid |
| 1940 ...........Eugene Turner, Los Angeles FSC | 1976 ...........Terry Kubicka, Arctic Blades FSC |
| 1941 ...........Eugene Turner, Los Angeles FSC | 1977 ...........Charles Tickner, Denver FSC |
| 1942 ...........Robert Specht, Chicago FSC | 1978 ...........Charles Tickner, Denver FSC |
| 1943 ...........Arthur R. Vaughn Jr., Philadelphia SC & HS | 1979 ...........Charles Tickner, Denver FSC |
| 1944–45 .....No competition | 1980 ...........Charles Tickner, Denver FSC |
| 1946 ...........Dick Button, Philadelphia SC & HS | 1981 ...........Scott Hamilton, Philadelphia SC & HS |
| 1947 ...........Dick Button, Philadelphia SC & HS | 1982 ...........Scott Hamilton, Philadelphia SC & HS |
| 1948 ...........Dick Button, Philadelphia SC & HS | 1983 ...........Scott Hamilton, Philadelphia SC & HS |
| 1949 ...........Dick Button, Philadelphia SC & HS | 1984 ...........Scott Hamilton, Philadelphia SC & HS |
| 1950 ...........Dick Button, SC of Boston | 1985 ...........Brian Boitano, Peninsula FSC |
| 1951 ...........Dick Button, SC of Boston | 1986 ...........Brian Boitano, Peninsula FSC |
| | 1987 ...........Brian Boitano, Peninsula FSC |

## Men *(Cont.)*

| | |
|---|---|
| 1988 ...........Brian Boitano, Peninsula FSC | 1995 ...........Todd Eldredge, Detroit SC |
| 1989 ...........Christopher Bowman, Los Angeles FSC | 1996 ...........Rudy Galindo, St Moritz ISC |
| 1990 ...........Todd Eldredge, Los Angeles FSC | 1997 ...........Todd Eldredge, Detroit SC |
| 1991 ...........Todd Eldredge, Los Angeles FSC | 1998 ...........Todd Eldredge, Detroit SC |
| 1992 ...........Christopher Bowman, Los Angeles FSC | 1999 ...........Michael Weiss, Washington FSC |
| 1993 ...........Scott Davis, Broadmoor SC | 2000 ...........Michael Weiss, Washington FSC |
| 1994 ...........Scott Davis, Broadmoor SC | 2001 ...........Timothy Goebel, Winterhurst FSC |

## Pairs

1914 ......Jeanne Chevalier, Norman M. Scott, WC of Montreal
1915–17.No competition
1918 ......Theresa Weld, Nathaniel W. Niles, SC of Boston
1919 ......No competition
1920 ......Theresa Weld, Nathaniel W. Niles, SC of Boston
1921 ......Theresa Weld Blanchard, Nathaniel W. Niles, SC of Boston
1922 ......Theresa Weld Blanchard, Nathaniel W. Niles, SC of Boston
1923 ......Theresa Weld Blanchard, Nathaniel W. Niles, SC of Boston
1924 ......Theresa Weld Blanchard, Nathaniel W. Niles, SC of Boston
1925 ......Theresa Weld Blanchard, Nathaniel W. Niles, SC of Boston
1926 ......Theresa Weld Blanchard, Nathaniel W. Niles, SC of Boston
1927 ......Theresa Weld Blanchard, Nathaniel W. Niles, SC of Boston
1928 ......Maribel Y. Vinson, Thornton L. Coolidge, SC of Boston
1929 ......Maribel Y. Vinson, Thornton L. Coolidge, SC of Boston
1930 ......Beatrix Loughran, Sherwin C. Badger, SC of New York
1931 ......Beatrix Loughran, Sherwin C. Badger, SC of New York
1932 ......Beatrix Loughran, Sherwin C. Badger, SC of New York
1933 ......Maribel Y. Vinson, George E. B. Hill, SC of Boston
1934 ......Grace E. Madden, James L. Madden, SC of Boston
1935 ......Maribel Y. Vinson, George E. B. Hill, SC of Boston
1936 ......Maribel Y. Vinson, George E. B. Hill, SC of Boston
1937 ......Maribel Y. Vinson, George E. B. Hill, SC of Boston
1938 ......Joan Tozzer, M. Bernard Fox, SC of Boston
1939 ......Joan Tozzer, M. Bernard Fox, SC of Boston
1940 ......Joan Tozzer, M. Bernard Fox, SC of Boston
1941 ......Donna Atwood, Eugene Turner, Mercury FSC/Los Angeles FSC
1942 ......Doris Schubach, Walter Noffke, Springfield Ice Birds
1943 ......Doris Schubach, Walter Noffke, Springfield Ice Birds
1944 ......Doris Schubach, Walter Noffke, Springfield Ice Birds
1945 ......Donna Jeanne Pospisil, Jean-Pierre Brunet, SC of New York
1946 ......Donna Jeanne Pospisil, Jean-Pierre Brunet, SC of New York

1947 ......Yvonne Claire Sherman, Robert J. Swenning, SC of New York
1948 ......Karol Kennedy, Peter Kennedy, Seattle SC
1949 ......Karol Kennedy, Peter Kennedy, Seattle SC
1950 ......Karol Kennedy, Peter Kennedy, Broadmoor SC
1951 ......Karol Kennedy, Peter Kennedy, Broadmoor SC
1952 ......Karol Kennedy, Peter Kennedy, Broadmoor SC
1953 ......Carole Ann Ormaca, Robin Greiner, SC of Fresno
1954 ......Carole Ann Ormaca, Robin Greiner, SC of Fresno
1955 ......Carole Ann Ormaca, Robin Greiner, St Moritz ISC
1956 ......Carole Ann Ormaca, Robin Greiner, St Moritz ISC
1957 ......Nancy Rouillard Ludington, Ronald Ludington, Commonwealth FSC/ SC of Boston
1958 ......Nancy Rouillard Ludington, Ronald Ludington, Commonwealth FSC/ SC of Boston
1959 ......Nancy Rouillard Ludington, Ronald Ludington, Commonwealth FSC
1960 ......Nancy Rouillard Ludington, Ronald Ludington, Commonwealth FSC
1961 ......Maribel Y. Owen, Dudley S. Richards, SC of Boston
1962 ......Dorothyann Nelson, Pieter Kollen, Village of Lake Placid
1963 ......Judianne Fotheringill, Jerry J. Fotheringill, Broadmoor SC
1964 ......Judianne Fotheringill, Jerry J. Fotheringill, Broadmoor SC
1965 ......Vivian Joseph, Ronald Joseph, Chicago FSC
1966 ......Cynthia Kauffman, Ronald Kauffman, Seattle SC
1967 ......Cynthia Kauffman, Ronald Kauffman, Seattle SC
1968 ......Cynthia Kauffman, Ronald Kauffman, Seattle SC
1969 ......Cynthia Kauffman, Ronald Kauffman, Seattle SC
1970 ......Jo Jo Starbuck, Kenneth Shelley, Arctic Blades FSC
1971 ......Jo Jo Starbuck, Kenneth Shelley, Arctic Blades FSC
1972 ......Jo Jo Starbuck, Kenneth Shelley, Arctic Blades FSC
1973 ......Melissa Militano, Mark Militano, SC of New York
1974 ......Melissa Militano, Johnny Johns, SC of New York/Detroit SC
1975 ......Melissa Militano, Johnny Johns, SC of NY/ Detroit SC

## Pairs *(Cont.)*

| | |
|---|---|
| 1976 | Tai Babilonia, Randy Gardner, Los Angeles FSC |
| 1977 | Tai Babilonia, Randy Gardner, LA FSC |
| 1978 | Tai Babilonia, Randy Gardner, Los Angeles FSC/Santa Monica FSC |
| 1979 | Tai Babilonia, Randy Gardner, Los Angeles FSC/Santa Monica FSC |
| 1980 | Tai Babilonia, Randy Gardner, Los Angeles FSC/Santa Monica FSC |
| 1981 | Caitlin Carruthers, Peter Carruthers, SC of Wilmington |
| 1982 | Caitlin Carruthers, Peter Carruthers, SC of Wilmington |
| 1983 | Caitlin Carruthers, Peter Carruthers, SC of Wilmington |
| 1984 | Caitlin Carruthers, Peter Carruthers, SC of Wilmington |
| 1985 | Jill Watson, Peter Oppegard, LA FSC |
| 1986 | Gillian Wachsman, Todd Waggoner, SC of Wilmington |
| 1987 | Jill Watson, Peter Oppegard, Los Angeles FSC |
| 1988 | Jill Watson, Peter Oppegard, Los Angeles FSC |
| 1989 | Kristi Yamaguchi, Rudy Galindo, St Mortiz ISC |
| 1990 | Kristi Yamaguchi, Rudy Galindo, St Mortiz ISC |
| 1991 | Natasha Kuchiki, Todd Sand, Los Angeles FSC |
| 1992 | Calla Urbanski, Rocky Marval, U of Delaware FSC/SC of New York |
| 1993 | Calla Urbanski, Rocky Marval, U of Delaware FSC/SC of New York |
| 1994 | Jenni Meno, Todd Sand, Winterhurst FSC/Los Angeles FSC |
| 1995 | Jenni Meno, Todd Sand, Winterhurst FSC/Los Angeles FSC |
| 1996 | Jenni Meno, Todd Sand, Winterhurst FSC/Los Angeles FSC |
| 1997 | Kyoko Ina, Jason Dungjen, SC of New York |
| 1998 | Kyoko Ina, Jason Dungjen, SC of New York |
| 1999 | Danielle Hartsell, Steve Hartsell, Detroit SC |
| 2000 | Kyoko Ina and John Zimmerman, SC of New York/Birmingham FSC |
| 2001 | Kyoko Ina and John Zimmerman, SC of New York/Birmingham FSC |

## Dance

| | |
|---|---|
| 1914 | Waltz: Theresa Weld, Nathaniel W. Niles, SC of Boston |
| 1915–19 | No competition |
| 1920 | Waltz: Theresa Weld, Nathaniel W. Niles, SC of Boston; Fourteenstep: Gertrude Cheever Porter, Irving Brokaw, New York SC |
| 1921 | Waltz and Fourteenstep: Theresa Weld Blanchard, Nathaniel W. Niles, SC of Boston |
| 1922 | Waltz: Beatrix Loughran, Edward M. Howland, New York SC/SC of Boston; Fourteenstep: Theresa Weld Blanchard, Nathaniel W. Niles, SC of Boston |
| 1923 | Waltz: Mr. & Mrs. Henry W. Howe, New York SC; Fourteenstep: Sydney Goode, James B. Greene, New York SC |
| 1924 | Waltz: Rosaline Dunn, Frederick Gabel, New York SC; Fourteenstep: Sydney Goode, James B. Greene, New York SC |
| 1925 | Waltz and Fourteenstep: Virginia Slattery, Ferrier T. Martin, New York SC |
| 1926 | Waltz: Rosaline Dunn, Joseph K. Savage, New York SC; Fourteenstep: Sydney Goode, James B. Greene, New York SC |
| 1927 | Waltz and Fourteenstep: Rosaline Dunn, Joseph K. Savage, New York SC |
| 1928 | Waltz: Rosaline Dunn, Joseph K. Savage, New York SC; Fourteenstep: Ada Bauman Kelly, George T. Braakman, New York SC |
| 1929 | Waltz and Original Dance combined: Edith C. Secord, Joseph K. Savage, SC of New York |
| 1930 | Waltz: Edith C. Secord, Joseph K. Savage, SC of New York; Original: Clara Rotch Frothingham, George E. B. Hill, SC of Boston |
| 1931 | Waltz: Edith C. Secord, Ferrier T. Martin, SC of New York |
| 1931 *(Cont.)* | Original: Theresa Weld Blanchard, Nathaniel W. Niles, SC of Boston |
| 1932 | Waltz: Edith C. Secord, Joseph K. Savage, SC of New York; Original: Clara Rotch Frothingham, George E. B. Hill, SC of Boston |
| 1933 | Waltz: Ilse Twaroschk, Frederick F. Fleishmann, Brooklyn FSC; Original: Suzanne Davis, Frederick Goodridge, SC of Boston |
| 1934 | Waltz: Nettie C. Prantel, Roy Hunt, SC of New York; Original: Suzanne Davis, Frederick Goodridge, SC of Boston |
| 1935 | Waltz: Nettie C. Prantel, Roy Hunt, SC of New York |
| 1936 | Marjorie Parker, Joseph K. Savage, SC of New York |
| 1937 | Nettie C. Prantel, Harold Hartshorne, SC of New York |
| 1938 | Nettie C. Prantel, Harold Hartshorne, SC of New York |
| 1939 | Sandy Macdonald, Harold Hartshorne, SC of New York |
| 1940 | Sandy Macdonald, Harold Hartshorne, SC of New York |
| 1941 | Sandy Macdonald, Harold Hartshorne, SCNY |
| 1942 | Edith B. Whetstone, Alfred N. Richards, Jr, Philadelphia SC & HS |
| 1943 | Marcella May, James Lochead Jr., Skate & Ski Club |
| 1944 | Marcella May, James Lochead Jr., Skate & Ski Club |
| 1945 | Kathe Mehl Williams, Robert J. Swenning, SC of New York |
| 1946 | Anne Davies, Carleton C. Hoffner Jr., Washington FSC |
| 1947 | Lois Waring, Walter H. Bainbridge Jr., Baltimore FSC/Washigton FSC |
| 1948 | Lois Waring, Walter H. Bainbridge Jr., Baltimore FSC/Washington FSC |
| 1949 | Lois Waring, Walter H. Bainbridge Jr., Baltimore FSC/Washington FSC |
| 1950 | Lois Waring, Michael McGean, Baltimore FSC |

## Dance *(Cont.)*

1951 ......Carmel Bodel, Edward L. Bodel,
St Moritz ISC
1952 ......Lois Waring, Michael McGean,
Baltimore FSC
1953 ......Carol Ann Peters, Daniel C. Ryan,
Washington FSC
1954 ......Carmel Bodel, Edward L. Bodel, St Moritz ISC
1955 ......Carmel Bodel, Edward L. Bodel,
St Moritz ISC
1956 ......Joan Zamboni, Roland Junso,
Arctic Blades FSC
1957 ......Sharon McKenzie, Bert Wright,
Los Angeles FSC
1958 ......Andree Anderson, Donald Jacoby, Buffalo SC
1959 ......Andree Anderson Jacoby, Donald Jacoby,
Buffalo SC
1960 ......Margie Ackles, Charles W. Phillips Jr.,
Los Angeles FSC/Arctic Blades FSC
1961 ......Diane C. Sherbloom, Larry Pierce,
Los Angeles FSC/WC of Indianapolis
1962 ......Yvonne N. Littlefield, Peter F. Betts,
Arctic Blades FSC/ Paramount, CA
1963 ......Sally Schantz, Stanley Urban,
SC of Boston/Buffalo SC
1964 ......Darlene Streich, Charles D. Fetter Jr.,
WC of Indianapolis
1965 ......Kristin Fortune, Dennis Sveum,
Los Angeles FSC
1966 ......Kristin Fortune, Dennis Sveum, Los Angeles FSC
1967 ......Lorna Dyer, John Carrell, Broadmoor SC
1968 ......Judy Schwomeyer, James Sladky,
WC of Indianapolis/Genesee FSC
1969 ......Judy Schwomeyer, James Sladky,
WC of Indianapolis/Genesee FSC
1970 ......Judy Schwomeyer, James Sladky,
WC of Indianapolis/Genesee FSC
1971 ......Judy Schwomeyer, James Sladky,
WC of Indianapolis/Genesee FSC
1972 ......Judy Schwomeyer, James Sladky,
WC of Indianapolis/Genesee FSC
1973 ......Mary Karen Campbell, Johnny Johns,
Lansing SC/Detroit SC
1974 ......Colleen O'Connor, Jim Millns, Broadmoor
SC/ City of Colorado Springs
1975 ......Colleen O'Connor, Jim Millns, Broadmoor SC

1976 ......Colleen O'Connor, Jim Millns,
Broadmoor SC
1977 ......Judy Genovesi, Kent Weigle,
SC of Hartford/Charter Oak FSC
1978 ......Stacey Smith, John Summers,
SC of Wilmington
1979 ......Stacey Smith, John Summers,
SC of Wilmington
1980 ......Stacey Smith, John Summers,
SC of Wilmington
1981 ......Judy Blumberg, Michael Seibert,
Broadmoor SC/ISC of Indianapolis
1982 ......Judy Blumberg, Michael Seibert,
Broadmoor SC/ISC of Indianapolis
1983 ......Judy Blumberg, Michael Seibert,
Pittsburgh FSC
1984 ......Judy Blumberg, Michael Seibert,
Pittsburgh FSC
1985 ......Judy Blumberg, Michael Seibert,
Pittsburgh FSC
1986 ......Renee Roca, Donald Adair,
Genesee FSC/Academy FSC
1987 ......Suzanne Semanick, Scott Gregory,
U of Delaware SC
1988 ......Suzanne Semanick, Scott Gregory,
U of Delaware SC
1989 ......Susan Wynne, Joseph Druar,
Broadmoor SC/Seattle SC
1990 ......Susan Wynne, Joseph Druar,
Broadmoor SC/Seattle SC
1991 ......Elizabeth Punsalan, Jerod Swallow,
Broadmoor SC
1992 ......April Sargent, Russ Witherby,
Ogdensburg FSC/U of Delaware FSC
1993 ......Renee Roca, Gorsha Sur, Broadmoor SC
1994 ......Elizabeth Punsalan, Jerod Swallow,
Broadmoor SC/Detroit SC
1995 ......Renee Roca, Gorsha Sur, Broadmoor SC
1996 ......Elizabeth Punsalan, Jerod Swallow, Detroit SC
1997 ......Elizabeth Punsalan, Jerod Swallow, Detroit SC
1998 ......Elizabeth Punsalan, Jerod Swallow, Detroit SC
1999 ......Naomi Lang, Peter Tchernyshev, Detroit SC
2000.......Naomi Lang, Peter Tchernyshev, Detroit SC
2001.......Naomi Lang, Peter Tchernyshev, Detroit SC

# U.S. Olympic Gold Medalists

## Women

1956 ...........................................Tenley Albright
1960 ...............................................Carol Heiss
1968 ..........................................Peggy Fleming

1976 ........................................Dorothy Hamill
1992 .......................................Kristi Yamaguchi
1998 ...........................................Tara Lipinski

## Men

1948 ..........................................Richard Button
1952 ..........................................Richard Button
1956 ....................................Hayes Alan Jenkins

1960 .......................................David W. Jenkins
1984 ..........................................Scott Hamilton
1988 ..............................................Brian Boitano

# Special Achievements

Women successfully landing a triple Axel in competition:
  Midori Ito, Japan, 1988 free-skating competition at Aichi, Japan.
  Tonya Harding, United States, 1991 U.S. Figure Skating Championship.
Men successfully landing three quadruple jumps in competition:
  Timothy Goebel, United States, 1999 Skate America, Colorado Springs (two Salchows and one toe loop).

# Miscellaneous Sports

**Overage Little Leaguer Danny Almonte**

# Exposed

## One pitcher dominated the Little League World Series so thoroughly, he seemed too good to be true—and he was

### BY MERRELL NODEN

YOGI BERRA sure got this one wrong: Long after Nobuhisa Baba singled to left in the bottom of the sixth to give the Kitasuna league of Tokyo a dramatic 2–1 win over a team from Apopka, Fla., the 2001 Little League World Series was not yet over. Far from it. The interesting stuff was only just beginning. And with each ensuing day, long after Baba and his teammates had flown home to Japan, suspicions about the age of Danny Almonte, a fireball pitcher ostensibly from the Bronx, multiplied and soured. The story reminded us once more of the ugly need to win that corrupts what was once, presumably, a game played for fun by children, not manipulated for glory by grasping adults.

Little League Baseball has faced this sort of bad news before, most notably in 1992, when a team from the Philippines was found to have recruited players from outside local league boundaries. But this latest incident felt more tawdry—and avoidable—since it turned out that the Rolando Paulino league, for whose All-Star team Almonte pitched, had been caught breaking the rules twice in the past three years and that its founder and namesake had been banned from Little League

ball in Latin America for using six overage players in a 1988 Caribbean tournament. Indeed, suspicions were so strong that earlier this year a group from Staten Island paid a private investigator $10,000 to find evidence of the league's cheating, though none was found.

Of course, the whole episode would have been far more embarrassing had the New Yorkers won the whole thing: But no one could get around the rules mandating rest for young arms, and with Almonte neutralized at centerfield, the Apopka team got its revenge, beating the Rolando Paulino team 8–2 in the U.S. championship. Six days later, prompted by a SPORTS ILLUSTRATED investigation that turned up multiple birth records, officials in the Dominican Republic ruled that Almonte was not 12 but 14, and hence ineligible.

"Clearly, adults have used Danny Almonte and his teammates in a most contemptible and despicable way," said Little League CEO Stephen Keener, announcing that his organization was banning both Paulino and Felipe Almonte, Danny's father, from any further involvement in Little League.

The scandal drowned out news of some

AP PHOTO/ROBERT SPENCER

imaginative changes at the world series. After 52 years in which the number of teams had held steady at eight, the size of the field doubled this year, to 16. It included a delightful team from Moscow, thrilled to be included even though they lost their three games by a cumulative score of 12–1. Another change was the opening of a second stadium, Little League Volunteers Stadium, which seats 5,000. The title game, on Aug. 26, was the first to be televised in prime time, starting at 6:30 p.m. And for the first time, a woman, Flora Stansbury of Seneca, Mo., umped behind home plate during the championship game.

From the start, though, it was the team from New York City that generated the most excitement in Williamsport. Certainly they were sentimental favorites. Made up of boys whose families relocated to the Bronx and northern Manhattan from the baseball-rich islands of Puerto Rico and the Dominican Republic, the Rolando Paulino All-Stars did not even have their own field until earlier this year, when Merrill Lynch and a nonprofit group called Take the Field built one for them at South Bronx High School.

But in the lanky Almonte, the Bronx Baby Bombers, as they came to be known, had a fearsome weapon. His fastball was clocked at over 70 miles per hour, which, given the 46-foot distance from home plate to the pitcher's rubber in Little League, looks like a 92-plus mph pitch would to a major league batter standing more than 60 feet away. Offsetting his heater with a sharp

curve and a changeup, Almonte was almost unhittable. In his team's round-robin opener, against Apopka, he pitched the first perfect game in world series play since 1957, striking out the first 15 batters he faced as his team beat Apopka 5–0. The only balls hit fair by Apopka were two sixth-inning bunts.

But the Apopka kids were resilient, regrouping to sweep the rest of their round-robin games and win a shot at revenge against the Bronx team. While Apopka was routing Rolando Paulino in the U.S. championship game, Kitasuna edged a team from Curaçao, Netherlands Antilles, 2–1 on Atsushi Mochizuki's two-run, walk-off homer in the bottom of the sixth.

A crowd of 44,800 that included George W. Bush, the first U.S. president to have played Little League ball, was treated to a superb championship game. Apopka scored first, when Andrew Cobb scored from second on Jeff Lovejoy's bloop single to left. The Florida team wouldn't score again, due largely to the glovework of Kitasuna shortstop Takaaki Ohno, who twice stopped bullets and had the presence of mind to cut down the lead runner at home. Kitasuna rallied in the bottom of the sixth, and after Yuusuke Nomura crossed home with the winning run, the entire team sprinted out to centerfield, where they threw themselves to the ground and bowed before the bust of Howard J. Lamade, who donated the land for the stadium.

The next morning, the media focus quickly shifted full force to Almonte. Among the more stunning revelations was the fact that Danny had not attended school since arriving in the U.S. in June 2000. What had this 14-year-old boy been doing while his peers were in school? "Eating and playing ball," said his father. Surely, everyone seemed to agree, that isn't enough to sustain a boy, whether he's 12 or 14. But will anyone remember that lesson next time?

## Archery

### National Men's Champions

| | | | |
|---|---|---|---|
| 1879...Will H. Thompson | 1910...Henry Richardson | 1947...Jack Wilson | 1978...Darrell Pace |
| 1880...L.L. Pedinghaus | 1911...Dr. Robert Elmer | 1948...Larry Hughes | 1979...Rick McKinney |
| 1881...F.H. Walworth | 1912...George Bryant | 1949...Russ Reynolds | 1980...Rick McKinney |
| 1882...D.H. Nash | 1913...George Bryant | 1950...Stan Overby | 1981...Rick McKinney |
| 1883...Col. Robert Williams | 1914...Dr. Robert Elmer | 1951...Russ Reynolds | 1982...Rick McKinney |
| 1884...Col. Robert Williams | 1915...Dr. Robert Elmer | 1952...Robert Larson | 1983...Rick McKinney |
| 1885...Col. Robert Williams | 1916...Dr. Robert Elmer | 1953...Bill Glackin | 1984...Darrell Pace |
| 1886...W.A. Clark | 1919...Dr. Robert Elmer | 1954...Robert Rhode | 1985...Rick McKinney |
| 1887...W.A. Clark | 1920...Dr. Robert Elmer | 1955...Joe Fries | 1986...Rick McKinney |
| 1888...Lewis Maxson | 1921...James Jiles | 1956...Joe Fries | 1987...Rick McKinney |
| 1889...Lewis Maxson | 1922...Dr. Robert Elmer | 1957...Joe Fries | 1988...Jay Barrs |
| 1890...Lewis Maxson | 1923...Bill Palmer | 1958...Robert Bitner | 1989...Ed Eliason |
| 1891...Lewis Maxson | 1924...James Jiles | 1959...Wilbert Vetrovsky | 1990...Ed Eliason |
| 1892...Lewis Maxson | 1925...Dr. Paul Crouch | 1960...Robert Kadlec | 1991...Ed Eliason |
| 1893...Lewis Maxson | 1926...Stanley Spencer | 1961...Clayton Sherman | 1992...Alan Rasor |
| 1894...Lewis Maxson | 1927...Dr. Paul Crouch | 1962...Charles Sandlin | 1993...Jay Barrs |
| 1895...W.B. Robinson | 1928...Bill Palmer | 1963...Dave Keaggy Jr. | 1994...Jay Barrs |
| 1896...Lewis Maxson | 1929...Dr. E.K. Roberts | 1964...Dave Keaggy Jr. | 1995...Justin Huish |
| 1897...W.A. Clark | 1930...Russ Hoogerhyde | 1965...George Slinzer | 1996...Richard (Butch) |
| 1898...Lewis Maxson | 1931...Russ Hoogerhyde | 1966...Hardy Ward |     Johnson |
| 1899...M.C. Howell | 1932...Russ Hoogerhyde | 1967...Ray Rogers | 1997...Richard (Butch) |
| 1900...A.R. Clark | 1933...Ralph Miller | 1968...Hardy Ward |     Johnson |
| 1901...Will H. Thompson | 1934...Russ Hoogerhyde | 1969...Ray Rogers | 1998...Victor Wunderle |
| 1902...Will H. Thompson | 1935...Gilman Keasey | 1970...Joe Thornton | 1999...Victor Wunderle |
| 1903...Will H. Thompson | 1936...Gilman Keasey | 1971...John Williams | 2000...Richard (Butch) |
| 1904...George Bryant | 1937...Russ Hoogerhyde | 1972...Kevin Erlandson |     Johnson |
| 1905...George Bryant | 1938...Pat Chambers | 1973...Darrell Pace | 2001...Richard (Butch) |
| 1906...Henry Richardson | 1939...Pat Chambers | 1974...Darrell Pace |     Johnson |
| 1907...Henry Richardson | 1940...Russ Hoogerhyde | 1975...Darrell Pace | |
| 1908...Will H. Thompson | 1941...Larry Hughes | 1976...Darrell Pace | |
| 1909...George Bryant | 1946...Wayne Thompson | 1977...Rick McKinney | |

### National Women's Champions

| | | | |
|---|---|---|---|
| 1879...Mrs. S. Brown | 1909...Harriet Case | 1939...Belvia Carter | 1972...Ruth Rowe |
| 1880...Mrs. T. Davies | 1910...J.V. Sullivan | 1940...Ann Weber | 1973...Doreen Wilber |
| 1881...Mrs. A.H. Gibbes | 1911...Mrs. J.S. Taylor | 1941...Ree Dillinger | 1974...Doreen Wilber |
| 1882...Mrs. A.H. Gibbes | 1912...Mrs. Witwer | 1946...Ann Weber | 1975...Irene Lorensen |
| 1883...Mrs. M.C. Howell |     Tayler | 1947...Ann Weber | 1976...Luann Ryon |
| 1884...Mrs. H. Hall | 1913...Mrs. P. Fletcher | 1948...Jean Lee | 1977...Luann Ryon |
| 1885...Mrs. M.C. Howell | 1914...Mrs. B.P. Gray | 1949...Jean Lee | 1978...Luann Ryon |
| 1886...Mrs. M.C. Howell | 1915...Cynthia Wesson | 1950...Jean Lee | 1979...Lynette Johnson |
| 1887...Mrs. A.M. Phillips | 1916...Cynthia Wesson | 1951...Jean Lee | 1980...Judi Adams |
| 1888...Mrs. A.M. Phillips | 1919...Dorothy Smith | 1952...Ann Weber | 1981...Debra Metzger |
| 1889...Mrs. A.M. Phillips | 1920...Cynthia Wesson | 1953...Ann Weber | 1982...Luann Ryon |
| 1890...Mrs. M.C. Howell | 1921...Mrs. L.C. Smith | 1954...Laurette Young | 1983...Nancy Myrick |
| 1891...Mrs. M.C. Howell | 1922...Dorothy Smith | 1955...Ann Clark | 1984...Ruth Rowe |
| 1892...Mrs. M.C. Howell | 1923...Norma Pierce | 1956...Carole Meinhart | 1985...Terri Pesho |
| 1893...Mrs. M.C. Howell | 1924...Dorothy Smith | 1957...Carole Meinhart | 1986...Debra Ochs |
| 1894...Mrs. Albert Kern | 1925...Dorothy Smith | 1958...Carole Meinhart | 1987...Terry Quinn |
| 1895...Mrs. M.C. Howell | 1926...Dorothy Smith | 1959...Carole Meinhart | 1988...Debra Ochs |
| 1896...Mrs. M.C. Howell | 1927...Mrs. R. Johnson | 1960...Ann Clark | 1989...Debra Ochs |
| 1897...Mrs. J.S. Baker | 1928...Beatrice | 1961...Victoria Cook | 1990...Denise Parker |
| 1898...Mrs. M.C. Howell |     Hodgson | 1962...Nancy | 1991...Denise Parker |
| 1899...Mrs. M.C. Howell | 1929...Audrey Grubbs |     Vonderheide | 1992...Sherry Block |
| 1900...Mrs. M.C. Howell | 1930...Audrey Grubbs | 1963...Nancy | 1993...Denise Parker |
| 1901...Mrs. C.E. | 1931...Dorothy |     Vonderheide | 1994...Judy Adams |
|     Woodruff |     Cummings | 1964...Victoria Cook | 1995...Jessica Carlson |
| 1902...Mrs. M.C. Howell | 1932...Ilda Hanchette | 1965...Nancy Pfeiffer | 1996...Janet Dykman |
| 1903...Mrs. M.C. Howell | 1933...Madelaine Taylor | 1966...Helen Thornton | 1997...Janet Dykman |
| 1904...Mrs. M.C. Howell | 1934...Desales Mudd | 1967...Ardelle Mills | 1998...Janet Dykman |
| 1905...Mrs. M.C. Howell | 1935...Ruth Hodgert | 1968...Victoria Cook | 1999...Denise Parker |
| 1906...Mrs. E.C. Cook | 1936...Gladys Hammer | 1969...Doreen Wilber | 2000...Karen Scavatto |
| 1907...Mrs. M.C. Howell | 1937...Gladys Hammer | 1970...Nancy Myrick | 2001...Kathie Loesch |
| 1908...Harriet Case | 1938...Jean Tenney | 1971...Doreen Wilber | |

# Chess

## World Champions

### FIDE

| | |
|---|---|
| 1866–94 | Wilhelm Steinitz, Austria |
| 1894–1921 | Emanuel Lasker, Germany |
| 1921–27 | Jose Capablanca, Cuba |
| 1927–35 | Alexander Alekhine, France |
| 1935–37 | Max Euwe, Holland |
| 1937–47 | Alexander Alekhine, France |
| 1948–57 | Mikhail Botvinnik, USSR |
| 1957–58 | Vassily Smyslov, USSR |
| 1958–59 | Mikhail Botvinnik, USSR |
| 1960–61 | Mikhail Tal, USSR |
| 1961–63 | Mikhail Botvinnik, USSR |

### FIDE

| | |
|---|---|
| 1963–69 | Tigran Petrosian, USSR |
| 1969–72 | Boris Spassky, USSR |
| 1972–75 | Bobby Fischer, United States |
| 1975–85 | Anatoly Karpov, USSR |
| 1985–93 | *Garry Kasparov, USSR |
| 1994–98 | Anatoly Karpov, Russia |
| 1999– | Alexander Khalifman, Russia |

*Kasparov stripped of title by FIDE in 1993; title vacant until '94.

### Professional Chess Association

| | |
|---|---|
| 1993– | Garry Kasparov |

## United States Champions

| | | | | | |
|---|---|---|---|---|---|
| 1857–71 | Paul Morphy | 1961–62 | Larry Evans | 1988 | Michael Wilder |
| 1871–76 | George Mackenzie | 1962–68 | Bobby Fischer | 1989 | Roman |
| 1876–80 | James Mason | 1968–69 | Larry Evans | | Dzindzichashvili |
| 1880–89 | George Mackenzie | 1969–72 | Samuel Reshevsky | | Stuart Rachels |
| 1889–90 | Samuel Lipschutz | 1972–73 | Robert Byrne | | Yasser Seirawan |
| 1890 | Jackson Showalter | 1973–74 | Lubomir Kavale | 1990 | Lev Alburt |
| 1890–91 | Max Judd | | John Grefe | 1991 | Gata Kamski |
| 1891–92 | Jackson Showalter | 1974–77 | Walter Browne | 1992 | Patrick Wolff |
| 1892–94 | Samuel Lipschutz | 1978–80 | Lubomir Kavalek | 1993 | Alex Yermolinsky |
| 1894 | Jackson Showalter | 1980–81 | Larry Evans | | A. Shabalov |
| 1894–95 | Albert Hodges | | Larry Christiansen | 1994 | Boris Gulko |
| 1895–97 | Jackson Showalter | | Walter Browne | 1995 | Patrick Wolff |
| 1897–1906 | Harry Pillsbury | 1981–83 | Walter Browne | | Nick DeFirmian |
| 1906–09 | Vacant | | Yasser Seirawan | | Alexander Ivanov |
| 1909–36 | Frank Marshall | 1983 | Roman | 1996 | Alex Yermolinsky |
| 1936–44 | Samuel Reshevsky | | Dzindzichashvili | 1997 | Alex Yermolinsky |
| 1944–46 | Arnold Denker | 1983 | Larry Christiansen | 1998 | Alex Yermolinsky |
| 1946–48 | Samuel Reshevsky | | Walter Browne | 1999 | Boris Gulko |
| 1948–51 | Herman Steiner | 1984–85 | Lev Alburt | 2000 | Joel Benjamin |
| 1951–54 | Larry Evans | 1986 | Yasser Seirawan | 2001 | Joel Benjamin |
| 1954–57 | Arthur Bisguier | 1987 | Joel Benjamin | | |
| 1957–61 | Bobby Fischer | | Nick DeFirmian | | |

# Curling

## World Men's Champions

| Year | Country, Skip | Year | Country, Skip | Year | Country, Skip |
|---|---|---|---|---|---|
| 1972 | Canada, Crest Melesnuk | 1982 | Canada, Al Hackner | 1992 | Switzerland, Markus Eggler |
| 1973 | Sweden, Kjell Oscarius | 1983 | Canada, Ed Werenich | 1993 | Canada, Russ Howard |
| 1974 | U.S., Bud Somerville | 1984 | Norway, Eigil Ramsfjell | 1994 | Canada, Rick Folk |
| 1975 | Switzerland, Otto Danieli | 1985 | Canada, Al Hackner | 1995 | Canada, Kerry Burtnyk |
| 1976 | U.S., Bruce Roberts | 1986 | Canada, Ed Luckowich | 1996 | Canada, Jeff Stoughton |
| 1977 | Sweden, Ragnar Kamp | 1987 | Canada, Russ Howard | 1997 | Sweden, Peter Lindholm |
| 1978 | U.S., Bob Nichols | 1988 | Norway, Eigil Ramsfjell | 1998 | Canada, Wayne Middaugh |
| 1979 | Norway, Kristian Soerum | 1989 | Canada, Pat Ryan | 1999 | Scotland, Hammy McMillan |
| 1980 | Canada, Rich Folk | 1990 | Canada, Ed Werenich | 2000 | Canada, Greg McAulay |
| 1981 | Switzerland, Jurg Tanner | 1991 | Scotland, David Smith | 2001 | Sweden, Peter Lindholm |

## World Women's Champions

| Year | Country, Skip | Year | Country, Skip | Year | Country, Skip |
|---|---|---|---|---|---|
| 1979 | Switzerland, Gaby Casanova | 1985 | Canada, Linda Moore | 1993 | Canada, Sandra Peterson |
| 1980 | Canada, Marj Mitchell | 1986 | Canada, Marilyn Darte | 1994 | Canada, Sandra Peterson |
| 1981 | Sweden, Elisabeth Hogstrom | 1987 | Canada, Pat Sanders | 1995 | Sweden, Elisabet Gustafson |
| 1982 | Denmark, Marianne Jorgenson | 1988 | Germany, Andrea Schopp | 1996 | Canada, Marilyn Bodogh |
| 1983 | Switzerland, Erika Mueller | 1989 | Canada, Heather Houston | 1997 | Canada, Sandra Schmirler |
| 1984 | Canada, Connie Lallberte | 1990 | Norway, Dordi Nordby | 1998 | Sweden, Elisabet Gustafson |
| | | 1991 | Norway, Dordi Nordby | 1999 | Sweden, Elisabet Gustafson |
| | | 1992 | Sweden, Elisabet Johanssen | 2000 | Canada, Kelley Law |
| | | | | 2001 | Canada, Colleen Jones |

# Curling (Cont.)

## U.S. Men's Champions

| Year | Site | Winning Club | Skip |
|---|---|---|---|
| 1957 | Chicago, IL | Hibbing, MN | Harold Lauber |
| 1958 | Milwaukee, WI | Detroit, MI | Douglas Fisk |
| 1959 | Green Bay, WI | Hibbing, MN | Fran Kleffman |
| 1960 | Chicago, IL | Grafton, ND | Orvil Gilleshammer |
| 1961 | Grand Forks, ND | Seattle, WA | Frank Crealock |
| 1962 | Detroit, MI | Hibbing, MN | Fran Kleffman |
| 1963 | Duluth, MN | Detroit, MI | Mike Slyziuk |
| 1964 | Utica, NY | Duluth, MN | Robert Magle Jr. |
| 1965 | Seattle, WA | Superior, WI | Bud Somerville |
| 1966 | Hibbing, MN | Fargo, ND | Joe Zbacnik |
| 1967 | Winchester, MA | Seattle, WA | Bruce Roberts |
| 1968 | Madison, WI | Superior, WI | Bud Somerville |
| 1969 | Grand Forks, ND | Superior, WI | Bud Somerville |
| 1970 | Ardsley, NY | Grafton, ND | Art Tallackson |
| 1971 | Duluth, MN | Edmore, ND | Dale Dalziel |
| 1972 | Wilmette, IL | Grafton, ND | Robert Labonte |
| 1973 | Colorado Springs, CO | Winchester, MA | Charles Reeves |
| 1974 | Schenectady, NY | Superior, WI | Bud Somerville |
| 1975 | Detroit, MI | Seattle, WA | Ed Risling |
| 1976 | Wausau, WI | Hibbing, MN | Bruce Roberts |
| 1977 | Northbrook, IL | Hibbing, MN | Bruce Roberts |
| 1978 | Utica, NY | Superior, WI | Bob Nichols |
| 1979 | Superior, WI | Bemidji, MN | Scott Baird |
| 1980 | Bemidji, MN | Hibbing, MN | Paul Pustovar |
| 1981 | Fairbanks, AK | Superior, WI | Bob Nichols |
| 1982 | Brookline, MA | Madison, WI | Steve Brown |
| 1983 | Colorado Springs, CO | Colorado Springs, CO | Don Cooper |
| 1984 | Hibbing, MN | Hibbing, MN | Bruce Roberts |
| 1985 | Mequon, WI | Wilmette, IL | Tim Wright |
| 1986 | Seattle, WA | Madison, WI | Steve Brown |
| 1987 | Lake Placid, NY | Seattle, WA | Jim Vukich |
| 1988 | St. Paul, MN | Seattle, WA | Doug Jones |
| 1989 | Detroit, MI | Seattle, WA | Jim Vukich |
| 1990 | Superior, WI | Seattle, WA | Doug Jones |
| 1991 | Utica, NY | Madison, WI | Steve Brown |
| 1992 | Grafton, ND | Seattle, WA | Doug Jones |
| 1993 | St. Paul, MN | Bemidji, MN | Scott Baird |
| 1994 | Duluth, MN | Bemidji, MN | Scott Baird |
| 1995 | Appleton, WI | Superior, WI | Tim Somerville |
| 1996 | Bemidji, MN | Superior, WI | Tim Somerville |
| 1997 | Seattle,WA | Langdon, ND | Craig Disher |
| 1998 | Bismarck, SD | Stevens Pt., WI | Paul Pustovar |
| 1999 | Duluth, MN | Superior, WI | Tim Somerville |
| 2000 | Ogden, UT | Wisconsin3 | Craig Brown |
| 2001 | Madison, WI | Washington | Jason Larway |

## U.S. Women's Champions

| Year | Site | Winning Club | Skip |
|---|---|---|---|
| 1977 | Wilmette, IL | Hastings, NY | Margaret Smith |
| 1978 | Duluth, MN | Wausau, WI | Sandy Robarge |
| 1979 | Winchester, MA | Seattle, WA | Nancy Langley |
| 1980 | Seattle, WA | Seattle, WA | Sharon Kozal |
| 1981 | Kettle Moraine, WI | Seattle, WA | Nancy Langley |
| 1982 | Bowling Green, OH | Oak Park, IL | Ruth Schwenker |
| 1983 | Grafton, ND | Seattle, WA | Nancy Langley |
| 1984 | Wauwatosa, WI | Duluth, MN | Amy Hatten |
| 1985 | Hershey, PA | Fairbanks, AK | Bev Birklid |
| 1986 | Chicago, IL | St Paul, MN | Gerri Tilden |
| 1987 | St Paul, MN | Seattle, WA | Sharon Good |
| 1988 | Darien, CT | Seattle, WA | Nancy Langley |
| 1989 | Detroit, MI | Rolla, ND | Jan Lagasse |
| 1990 | Superior, WI | Denver, CO | Bev Behnke |
| 1991 | Utica, NY | Houston, TX | Maymar Gemmell |
| 1992 | Grafton, ND | Madison, WI | Lisa Schoeneberg |
| 1993 | St Paul, MN | Denver, CO | Bev Behnke |
| 1994 | Duluth, MN | Denver, CO | Bev Behnke |
| 1995 | Appleton, WI | Madison, WI | Lisa Schoeneberg |
| 1996 | Bemidji, MN | Madison, WI | Lisa Schoeneberg |

# Curling *(Cont.)*

## U.S. Women's Champions *(Cont.)*

| Year | Site | Winning Club | Skip |
|------|------|------|------|
| 1997 | Seattle, WA | Arlington, WI | Patti Lank |
| 1998 | Bismarck, SD | Wilmette, IL | Kari Erickson |
| 1999 | Duluth, MN | Madison, WI | Patti Lank |
| 2000 | Ogden, UT | Nebraska | Amy Wright |
| 2001 | Madison, WI | Illinois | Kari Erickson |

# Cycling

## Professional Road Race World Champions

| | |
|---|---|
| 1927 ....Alfred Binda, Italy | 1956 ....Rik Van Steenbergen, Belg. |
| 1928 ....George Ronsse, Belgium | 1957 ....Rik Van Steenbergen, |
| 1929 ....George Ronsse, Belgium |      Belgium |
| 1930 ....Alfred Binda, Italy | 1958 ....Ercole Baldini, Italy |
| 1931 ....Learco Guerra, Italy | 1959 ....Andre Darrigade, France |
| 1932 ....Alfred Binda, Italy | 1960 ....Rik van Looy, Belgium |
| 1933 ....George Speicher, France | 1961 ....Rik van Looy, Belgium |
| 1934 ....Karel Kaers, Belgium | 1962 ....Jean Stablenski, France |
| 1935 ....Jean Aerts, Belgium | 1963 ....Bennoni Beheyt, Belgium |
| 1936 ....Antonio Magne, France | 1964 ....Jan Janssen, Holland |
| 1937 ....Elio Meulenberg, Belgium | 1965 ....Tommy Simpson, England |
| 1938 ....Marcel Kint, Belgium | 1966 ....Rudi Altig, West Germany |
| No competition 1939–45 | 1967 ....Eddy Merckx, Belgium |
| 1946 ....Hans Knecht, Switzerland | 1968 ....Vittorio Adorni, Italy |
| 1947 ....Theo. Middelkamp, Holland | 1969 ....Harm Ottenbros, |
| 1948 ....Alberic Schotte, Belgium |      Netherlands |
| 1949 ....Henri Van Steenbergen, | 1970 ....J.P. Monseré, Belgium |
|      Belgium | 1971 ....Eddy Merckx, Belgium |
| 1950 ....Alberic Schotte, Belgium | 1972 ....Marino Basso, Italy |
| 1951 ....Ferdinand Kubler, | 1973 ....Felice Gimondi, Italy |
|      Switzerland | 1974 ....Eddy Merckx, Belgium |
| 1952 ....Heinz Mueller, Germany | 1975 ....Hennie Kuiper, Holland |
| 1953 ....Fausto Coppi, Italy | 1976 ....Freddy Maertens, Belgium |
| 1954 ....Louison Bobet, France | 1977 ....Francesco Moser, Italy |
| 1955 ....Stan Ockers, Belgium | 1978 ....Gerri Knetemann, Holland |

| |
|---|
| 1979 ....Jan Raas, Holland |
| 1980 ....Bernard Hinault, France |
| 1981 ....Freddy Maertens, Belgium |
| 1982 ....Giuseppe Saronni, Italy |
| 1983 ....Greg LeMond, |
|      United States |
| 1984 ....Claude Criquielion, Belgium |
| 1985 ....Joop Zoetemelk, Holland |
| 1986 ....Moreno Argentin, Italy |
| 1987 ....Stephen Roche, Ireland |
| 1988 ....Maurizio Fondriest, Italy |
| 1989 ....Greg LeMond, |
|      United States |
| 1990 ....Rudy Dhaenene, Belgium |
| 1991 ....Gianni Bugno, Italy |
| 1992 ....Gianni Bugno, Italy |
| 1993 ....Lance Armstrong, |
|      United States |
| 1994 ....Luc LeBlanc, France |
| 1995 ....Abraham Olano, Spain |
| 1996 ....Johan Museeuw, Belgium |
| 1997 ....Laurent Brochard, France |
| 1998 ....Oskar Camenzind, Switz |
| 1999 ....Oscar Gomez Freire, Spain |
| 2000 .....Romans Vainsteins, Latvia |

## Tour DuPont Winners

| Year | Winner | Time |
|------|--------|------|
| 1989 | Dag Otto Lauritzen, Norway | 33 hrs, 28 min, 48 sec |
| 1990 | Raul Alcala, Mexico | 45 hrs, 20 min, 9 sec |
| 1991 | Erik Breukink, Holland | 48 hrs, 56 min, 53 sec |
| 1992 | Greg LeMond, United States | 44 hrs, 27 min, 43 sec |
| 1993 | Raul Alcala, Mexico | 46 hrs, 42 min, 52 sec |
| 1994 | Viatcheslav Ekimov, Russia | 47 hrs, 14 min, 29 sec |
| 1995 | Lance Armstrong, United States | 46 hrs, 31 min, 16 sec |
| 1996 | Lance Armstrong, United States | 48 hrs, 20 min, 5 sec |

Note: Race not held since 1996.

## Tour de France Winners

| Year | Winner | Time |
|------|--------|------|
| 1903 | Maurice Garin, France | 94 hrs, 33 min |
| 1904 | Henry Cornet, France | 96 hrs, 5 min, 56 sec |
| 1905 | Louis Trousselier, France | 110 hrs, 26 min, 58 sec |
| 1906 | Rene Pottier, France | Not available |
| 1907 | Lucien Petit-Breton, France | 158 hrs, 54 min, 5 sec |
| 1908 | Lucien Petit-Breton, France | Not available |
| 1909 | Francois Faber, Luxembourg | 157 hrs, 1 min, 22 sec |
| 1910 | Octave Lapize, France | 162 hrs, 41 min, 30 sec |
| 1911 | Gustave Garrigou, France | 195 hrs, 37 min |
| 1912 | Odile Defraye, Belgium | 190 hrs, 30 min, 28 sec |
| 1913 | Philippe Thys, Belgium | 197 hrs, 54 min |
| 1914 | Philippe Thys, Belgium | 200 hrs, 28 min, 48 sec |
| 1915–18 | No race | |
| 1919 | Firmin Lambot, Belgium | 231 hrs, 7 min, 15 sec |
| 1920 | Philippe Thys, Belgium | 228 hrs, 36 min, 13 sec |
| 1921 | Leon Scieur, Belgium | 221 hrs, 50 min, 26 sec |

## Tour de France Winners *(Cont.)*

| Year | Winner | Time |
|------|--------|------|
| 1922 | Firmin Lambot, Belgium | 222 hrs, 8 min, 6 sec |
| 1923 | Henri Pelissier, France | 222 hrs, 15 min, 30 sec |
| 1924 | Ottavio Bottechia, Italy | 226 hrs, 18 min, 21 sec |
| 1925 | Ottavio Bottechia, Italy | 219 hrs, 10 min, 18 sec |
| 1926 | Lucien Buysse, Belgium | 238 hrs, 44 min, 25 sec |
| 1927 | Nicolas Frantz, Luxembourg | 198 hrs, 16 min, 42 sec |
| 1928 | Nicolas Frantz, Luxembourg | 192 hrs, 48 min, 58 sec |
| 1929 | Maurice Dewaele, Belgium | 186 hrs, 39 min, 16 sec |
| 1930 | Andre Leducq, France | 172 hrs, 12 min, 16 sec |
| 1931 | Antonin Magne, France | 177 hrs, 10 min, 3 sec |
| 1932 | Andre Leducq, France | 154 hrs, 12 min, 49 sec |
| 1933 | Georges Speicher, France | 147 hrs, 51 min, 37 sec |
| 1934 | Antonin Magne, France | 147 hrs, 13 min, 58 sec |
| 1935 | Romain Maes, Belgium | 141 hrs, 32 min |
| 1936 | Sylvere Maes, Belgium | 142 hrs, 47 min, 32 sec |
| 1937 | Roger Lapebie, France | 138 hrs, 58 min, 31 sec |
| 1938 | Gino Bartali, Italy | 148 hrs, 29 min, 12 sec |
| 1939 | Sylvere Maes, Belgium | 132 hrs, 3 min, 17 sec |
| 1940–46 | No race | |
| 1947 | Jean Robic, France | 148 hrs, 11 min, 25 sec |
| 1948 | Gino Bartali, Italy | 147 hrs, 10 min, 36 sec |
| 1949 | Fausto Coppi, Italy | 149 hrs, 40 min, 49 sec |
| 1950 | Ferdi Kubler, Switzerland | 145 hrs, 36 min, 56 sec |
| 1951 | Hugo Koblet, Switzerland | 142 hrs, 20 min, 14 sec |
| 1952 | Fausto Coppi, Italy | 151 hrs, 57 min, 20 sec |
| 1953 | Louison Bobet, France | 129 hrs, 23 min, 25 sec |
| 1954 | Louison Bobet, France | 140 hrs, 6 min, 5 sec |
| 1955 | Louison Bobet, France | 130 hrs, 29 min, 26 sec |
| 1956 | Roger Walkowiak, France | 124 hrs, 1 min, 16 sec |
| 1957 | Jacques Anquetil, France | 129 hrs, 46 min, 11 sec |
| 1958 | Charly Gaul, Luxembourg | 116 hrs, 59 min, 5 sec |
| 1959 | Federico Bahamontes, Spain | 123 hrs, 46 min, 45 sec |
| 1960 | Gastone Nencini, Italy | 112 hrs, 8 min, 42 sec |
| 1961 | Jacques Anquetil, France | 122 hrs, 1 min, 33 sec |
| 1962 | Jacques Anquetil, France | 114 hrs, 31 min, 54 sec |
| 1963 | Jacques Anquetil, France | 113 hrs, 30 min, 5 sec |
| 1964 | Jacques Anquetil, France | 127 hrs, 9 min, 44 sec |
| 1965 | Felice Gimondi, Italy | 116 hrs, 42 min, 6 sec |
| 1966 | Lucien Aimar, France | 117 hrs, 34 min, 21 sec |
| 1967 | Roger Pingeon, France | 136 hrs, 53 min, 50 sec |
| 1968 | Jan Janssen, Netherlands | 133 hrs, 49 min, 32 sec |
| 1969 | Eddy Merckx, Belgium | 116 hrs, 16 min, 2 sec |
| 1970 | Eddy Merckx, Belgium | 119 hrs, 31 min, 49 sec |
| 1971 | Eddy Merckx, Belgium | 96 hrs, 45 min, 14 sec |
| 1972 | Eddy Merckx, Belgium | 108 hrs, 17 min, 18 sec |
| 1973 | Luis Ocana, Spain | 122 hrs, 25 min, 34 sec |
| 1974 | Eddy Merckx, Belgium | 116 hrs, 16 min, 58 sec |
| 1975 | Bernard Thevenet, France | 114 hrs, 35 min, 31 sec |
| 1976 | Lucien Van Impe, Belgium | 116 hrs, 22 min, 23 sec |
| 1977 | Bernard Thevenet, France | 115 hrs, 38 min, 30 sec |
| 1978 | Bernard Hinault, France | 108 hrs, 18 min |
| 1979 | Bernard Hinault, France | 103 hrs, 6 min, 50 sec |
| 1980 | Joop Zoetemelk, Netherlands | 109 hrs, 19 min, 14 sec |
| 1981 | Bernard Hinault, France | 96 hrs, 19 min, 38 sec |
| 1982 | Bernard Hinault, France | 92 hrs, 8 min, 46 sec |
| 1983 | Laurent Fignon, France | 105 hrs, 7 min, 52 sec |
| 1984 | Laurent Fignon, France | 112 hrs, 3 min, 40 sec |
| 1985 | Bernard Hinault, France | 113 hrs, 24 min, 23 sec |
| 1986 | Greg LeMond, United States | 110 hrs, 35 min, 19 sec |
| 1987 | Stephen Roche, Ireland | 115 hrs, 27 min, 42 sec |
| 1988 | Pedro Delgado, Spain | 84 hrs, 27 min, 53 sec |
| 1989 | Greg LeMond, United States | 87 hrs, 38 min, 35 sec |
| 1990 | Greg LeMond, United States | 90 hrs, 43 min, 20 sec |
| 1991 | Miguel Induráin, Spain | 101 hrs, 1 min, 20 sec |
| 1992 | Miguel Induráin, Spain | 100 hrs, 49 min, 30 sec |
| 1993 | Miguel Induráin, Spain | 95 hrs, 57 min, 9 sec |
| 1994 | Miguel Induráin, Spain | 103 hrs, 38 min, 38 sec |
| 1995 | Miguel Induráin, Spain | 92 hrs, 44 min, 59 sec |

# Cycling (Cont.)

## Tour de France Winners (Cont.)

| Year | Winner | Time |
|------|--------|------|
| 1996 | Bjarne Riis, Denmark | 95 hrs, 57 min, 16 sec |
| 1997 | Jan Ullrich, Germany | 100 hrs, 30 min, 35 sec |
| 1998 | Marco Pantani, Italy | 92 hrs, 49 min, 46 sec |
| 1999 | Lance Armstrong, United States | 91 hrs, 32 min, 16 sec |
| 2000 | Lance Armstrong, United States | 92 hrs, 33 min, 8 sec |
| 2001 | Lance Armstrong, United States | 86 hrs, 17 min, 28 sec |

# Sled Dog Racing

## Iditarod

| Year | Winner | Time | Year | Winner | Time |
|------|--------|------|------|--------|------|
| 1973 | Dick Wilmarth | 20 days, 00:49:41 | 1988 | Susan Butcher | 11 days, 11:41:40 |
| 1974 | Carl Huntington | 20 days, 15:02:07 | 1989 | Joe Runyan | 11 days, 05:24:34 |
| 1975 | Emmitt Peters | 14 days, 14:43:45 | 1990 | Susan Butcher | 11 days, 01:53:23 |
| 1976 | Gerald Riley | 18 days, 22:58:17 | 1991 | Rick Swenson | 12 days, 16:34:39 |
| 1977 | Rick Swenson | 16 days, 16:27:13 | 1992 | Martin Buser | 10 days, 19:17:15 |
| 1978 | Dick Mackey | 14 days, 18:52:24 | 1993 | Jeff King | 10 days, 15:38:15 |
| 1979 | Rick Swenson | 15 days, 10:37:47 | 1994 | Martin Buser | 10 days, 13:02:39 |
| 1980 | Joe May | 14 days, 07:11:51 | 1995 | Doug Swingley | 9 days, 02:42:19 |
| 1981 | Rick Swenson | 12 days, 08:45:02 | 1996 | Jeff King | 9 days, 05:43:13 |
| 1982 | Rick Swenson | 16 days, 04:40:10 | 1997 | Martin Buser | 9 days, 08:30:45 |
| 1983 | Dick Mackey | 12 days, 14:10:44 | 1998 | Jeff King | 9 days, 05:52:26 |
| 1984 | Dean Osmar | 12 days, 15:07:33 | 1999 | Doug Swingley | 9 days, 14:31:19 |
| 1985 | Libby Riddles | 18 days, 00:20:17 | 2000 | Doug Swingley | 9 days, 00:58:06 |
| 1986 | Susan Butcher | 11 days, 15:06:00 | 2001 | Doug Swingley | 9 days, 19:55:50 |
| 1987 | Susan Butcher | 11 days, 02:05:13 | | | |

# Fishing

## Saltwater Fishing Records

| Species | Weight | Where Caught | Date | Angler |
|---------|--------|--------------|------|--------|
| Albacore | 88 lb 2 oz | Gran Canaria, Canary Islands | Nov 19, 1977 | Siegfried Dickemann |
| Amberjack, greater | 155 lb 12 oz | Bermuda | Aug 16, 1992 | Larry Trott |
| Amberjack, Pacific | 104 lb | Baja California, Mexico | July 4, 1984 | Richard Cresswell |
| Angler | 126 lb 12 oz | Sognefjorden Hoyanger, Norway | July 4, 1996 | Gunnar Thorsteinsen |
| Barracuda, great | 85 lb | Christmas Island, Kiribati | April 11, 1992 | John W. Helfrich |
| Barracuda, Mexican | 21 lb | Phantom Isle, Costa Rica | Mar 27, 1987 | E. Greg Kent |
| Barracuda, pickhandle | 25 lb 5 oz | Scottburgh, Natal, South Africa | July 3, 1996 | Demetrios Stamatis |
| Bass, barred sand | 13 lb 3 oz | Huntington Beach, California | Aug 29, 1988 | Robert Halal |
| Bass, black sea | 10 lb 4 oz | Virginia Beach, Virginia | Jan 1, 2000 | Allan P. Paschall |
| Bass, European | 20 lb 14 oz | Cap d'Agde, France | Sept. 8, 1999 | Robert Mari |
| Bass, giant sea | 563 lb 8 oz | Anacapa Island, California | Aug 20, 1968 | James D. McAdam Jr. |
| Bass, striped | 78 lb 8 oz | Atlantic City, New Jersey | Sep 21, 1982 | Albert R. McReynolds |
| Bluefish | 31 lb 12 oz | Hatteras Inlet, North Carolina | Jan 30, 1972 | James M. Hussey |
| Bonefish | 19 lb | Zululand, South Africa | May 26, 1962 | Brian W. Batchelor |
| Bonito, Atlantic | 18 lb 4 oz | Faial Island, Azores | July 8, 1953 | D.G. Higgs |
| Bonito, Pacific | 21 lb 3 oz | Malibu, California | July 30, 1978 | Gino M. Picciolo |
| Cabezon | 23 lb | Juan De Fuca Strait, Washington | Aug 4, 1990 | Wesley Hunter |
| Cobia | 135 lb 9 oz | Shark Bay, Australia | July 9, 1985 | Peter W. Goulding |
| Cod, Atlantic | 98 lb 12 oz | Isle of Shoals, New Hampshire | June 8, 1969 | Alphonse Bielevich |
| Cod, Pacific | 35 lb | Unalaska Bay, Alaska | June 16, 1999 | Jim Johnson |
| Conger | 133 lb 4 oz | South Devon, England | June 5, 1995 | Vic Evans |
| Dolphinfish | 88 lb | Highbourne Cay, Bahamas | May 5, 1998 | Richard D. Evans |
| Drum, black | 113 lb 1 oz | Lewes, Delaware | Sep 15, 1975 | Gerald M. Townsend |
| Drum, red | 94 lb 2 oz | Avon, North Carolina | Nov 7, 1984 | David Deuel |
| Eel, American | 9 lb 4 oz | Cape May, New Jersey | Nov 9, 1995 | Jeff Pennick |
| Eel, marbled | 36 lb 1 oz | Durban, South Africa | June 10, 1984 | Ferdie van Nooten |
| Flounder, southern | 20 lb 9 oz | Nassau Sound, Florida | Dec 23, 1983 | Larenza W. Mungin |
| Flounder, summer | 22 lb 7 oz | Montauk, New York | Sep 15, 1975 | Charles Nappi |
| Grouper, Warsaw | 436 lb 12 oz | Destin, Florida | Dec 22, 1985 | Steve Haeusler |
| Halibut, Atlantic | 355 lb 6 oz | Valevag, Norway | Oct 20, 1997 | Odd Arve Gunderstad |

## Saltwater Fishing Records *(Cont.)*

| Species | Weight | Where Caught | Date | Angler |
|---|---|---|---|---|
| Halibut, California | 58 lb 9 oz | Santa Rosa Island, California | June 26, 1999 | Roger W. Borrell |
| Halibut, Pacific | 459 lb | Dutch Harbor, Alaska | June 11, 1996 | Jack Tragis |
| Jack, crevalle | 58 lb 6 oz | Barro do Kwanza, Angola | Dec 10, 2000 | Nuno Abohbot p.da Silva |
| Jack, horse-eye | 29 lb 8 oz | Ascencion Island, S Atlantic Ocean | May 28, 1993 | Mike Hanson |
| Jack, Pacific crevalle | 39 lb | Playa Zancudo, Costa Rica | Mar 3, 1997 | Ingrid Callaghan |
| Jewfish | 680 lb | Fernandina Beach, Florida | May 20, 1961 | Lynn Joyner |
| Kawakawa | 29 lb | Isla Clarion, Mexico | Dec 17, 1986 | Ronald Nakamura |
| Lingcod | 69 lb 3 oz | Waterfall Resort, Alaska | Aug 18, 1999 | Rizwan Sheikh |
| Mackerel, cero | 17 lb 2 oz | Islamorada, Florida | Apr 5, 1986 | G. Michael Mills |
| Mackerel, king | 93 lb | San Juan, Puerto Rico | Apr 18, 1999 | Steve Perez Graulau |
| Mackerel, narrowbarred | 99 lb | Natal, South Africa | Mar 14, 1982 | Michael J. Wilkinson |
| Mackerel, Spanish | 13 lb | Ocracoke Inlet, North Carolina | Nov 4, 1987 | Robert Cranton |
| Marlin, Atlantic blue | 1,402 lb 2 oz | Vitoria, Brazil | Feb 29, 1992 | Paulo R.A. Amorim |
| Marlin, black | 1,560 lb | Cabo Blanco, Peru | Aug 4, 1953 | A.C. Glassell Jr. |
| Marlin, Pacific blue | 1,376 lb | Kaaiwi Point, Hawaii | May 31, 1982 | J.W. de Beaubien |
| Marlin, striped | 494 lb | Tutukaka, New Zealand | Jan 16, 1986 | Bill Boniface |
| Marlin, white | 181 lb 14 oz | Vitoria, Brazil | Dec 8, 1979 | Evandro Luiz Caser |
| Permit | 56 lb 2 oz | Fort Lauderdale, Florida | June 30, 1997 | Thomas Sebestyen |
| Pollock | 50 lb | Salstraumen, Norway | Nov 30, 1995 | Thor Magnus-Lekang |
| Pompano, African | 50 lb 8 oz | Daytona Beach, Florida | Apr 21, 1990 | Tom Sargent |
| Roosterfish | 114 lb | La Paz, Mexico | June 1, 1960 | Abe Sackheim |
| Runner, blue | 11 lb 2 oz | Dauphin Island, Alaska | June 28, 1997 | Stacey M. Moiren |
| Runner, rainbow | 37 lb 9 oz | Isla Clarion, Mexico | Nov 21, 1991 | Tom Pfleger |
| Sailfish, Atlantic | 141 lb 1 oz | Luanda, Angola | Feb 19, 1994 | Alfredo de Sousa Neves |
| Sailfish, Pacific | 221 lb | Santa Cruz Island, Ecuador | Feb 12, 1947 | C.W. Stewart |
| Seabass, white | 83 lb 12 oz | San Felipe, Mexico | Mar 31, 1953 | L.C. Baumgardner |
| Seatrout, spotted | 17 lb 7 oz | Ft. Pierce, Florida | May 11, 1995 | Craig F. Carson |
| Shark, bigeye thresher | 802 lb | Tutukaka, New Zealand | Feb 8, 1981 | Dianne North |
| Shark, blue | 454 lb | Martha's Vineyard, Massachusetts | July 19, 1996 | Pete Bergin |
| Shark, grter hammrhd | 991 lb | Sarasota, Florida | May 30, 1982 | Allen Ogle |
| Shark, Greenland | 1,708 lb 9 oz | Trondheimsfjord, Norway | Oct 18, 1987 | Terje Nordtvedt |
| Shark, porbeagle | 507 lb | Caithness, Scotland | Mar 9, 1993 | Christopher Bennet |
| Shark, shortfin mako | 1,115 lb | Black River, Mauritius | Nov 16, 1988 | Patrick Guillanton |
| Shark, tiger | 1,780 lb | Cherry Grove, South Carolina | June 14, 1964 | Walter Maxwell |
| Shark, tope | 72 lb 12 oz | Parengarenga Harbor, N.Z. | Dec 19, 1986 | Melanie B. Feldman |
| Shark, white | 2,664 lb | Ceduna, Australia | Apr 21, 1959 | Alfred Dean |
| Skipjack, black | 26 lb | Baja California, Mexico | Oct 23, 1991 | Clifford K. Hamaishi |
| Snapper, cubera | 121 lb 8 oz | Cameron, Louisiana | July 5, 1982 | Mike Hebert |
| Snook, common | 53 lb 10 oz | Parismina Ranch, Costa Rica | Oct 18, 1978 | Gilbert Ponzi |
| Spearfish, Mediterr. | 90 lb 13 oz | Madeira Island, Portugal | June 2, 1980 | Joseph Larkin |
| Spearfish, Atlantic | 127 lb 13 oz | Puerto Rico, Gran Canaria, Spain | May 20, 1999 | Paul Cashmore |
| Spearfish, shortbill | 74 lb 8 oz | Bay of Islands, New Zealand | Mar 16, 1999 | Leonie Kai Patterson |
| Swordfish | 1,182 lb | Iquique, Chile | May 7, 1953 | L. Marron |
| Tarpon | 283 lb 4 oz | Sherbro Island, Sierra Leone | Apr 16, 1991 | Yvon Victor Sebag |
| Tautog | 25 lb | Ocean City, New Jersey | Jan 20, 1998 | Anthony Monica |
| Tilapia, Mozambique | 2 lb 8 oz | Delray Beach, Florida | Nov 10, 1997 | Nick Cardella |
| Trevally, bigeye | 31 lb 8 oz | Poivre Island, Seychelles | Apr 23, 1997 | Les Sampson |
| Trevally, giant | 145 lb 8 oz | Maui, Hawaii | Mar 28, 1991 | Russell Mori |
| Tuna, Atlantic bigeye | 392 lb 6 oz | Puerto Rico, Gran Caneria, Spain | July 25, 1996 | Dieter Vogel |
| Tuna, blackfin | 45 lb 8 oz | Key West, Florida | May 4, 1996 | Sam J. Burnett |
| Tuna, bluefin | 1,496 lb | Aulds Cove, Nova Scotia | Oct 26, 1979 | Ken Fraser |
| Tuna, longtail | 79 lb 2 oz | Montague Island, New South Wales, Australia | Apr 12, 1982 | Tim Simpson |
| Tuna, Pacific bigeye | 435 lb | Cabo Blanco, Peru | Apr 17, 1957 | Russel Lee |
| Tuna, skipjack | 45 lb 4 oz | Baja California, Mexico | Nov 16, 1996 | Brian Evans |
| Tuna, southern bluefin | 348 lb 5 oz | Whakatane, New Zealand | Jan 16, 1981 | Rex Wood |
| Tuna, yellowfin | 388 lb 12 oz | San Benedicto Is, Mexico | Apr 1, 1977 | Curt Wiesenhutter |
| Tunny, little | 35 lb 2 oz | Cape de Garde, Algeria | Dec 14, 1988 | Jean Yves Chatard |
| Wahoo | 158 lb 8 oz | Loreto, Baja California, Mexico | June 10, 1996 | Keith Winter |
| Weakfish | 19 lb 2 oz | Jones Beach Inlet, New York | Oct 11, 1984 | Dennis Rooney |
|  |  | Delaware Bay, Delaware | May 20, 1989 | William E. Thomas |
| Yellowtail, California | 80 lb 11 oz | Alijos Rocks, Baja Calif., Mexico | Nov 12, 1998 | Brian Buddell |
| Yellowtail, southern | 114 lb 10 oz | Tauranga, New Zealand | Feb 5, 1984 | Mike Godfrey |

## Freshwater Fishing Records

| Species | Weight | Where Caught | Date | Angler |
|---|---|---|---|---|
| Barramundi | 83 lb 7 oz | Lake Tinaroo, N Queensl'd, Aus. | Sept 23, 1999 | David Powell |
| Bass, largemouth | 22 lb 4 oz | Montgomery Lake, Georgia | June 2, 1932 | George W. Perry |
| Bass, rock | 3 lb | York River, Ontario | Aug 1, 1974 | Peter Gulgin |
| Bass, shoal | 8 lb 12 oz | Apalatchicola River, Florida | Jan 28, 1995 | Carl W. Davis |
| Bass, smallmouth | 10 lb 14 oz | Dale Hollow, Tennessee | April 24, 1969 | John T. Gorman |
| Bass, Suwannee | 3 lb 14 oz | Suwannee River, Florida | Mar 2, 1985 | Ronnie Everett |
| Bass, white | 6 lb 13 oz | Orange, Virginia | July 31, 1989 | Ronald Sprouse |
| Bass, whiterock | 27 lb 5 oz | Greers Ferry Lake, Arkansas | Apr 24, 1997 | Jerald Shaum |
| Bass, yellow | 2 lb 9 oz | Waverly, Tennessee | Feb 27, 1998 | John Chappell |
| Bluegill | 4 lb 12 oz | Ketona Lake, Alabama | Apr 9, 1950 | T.S. Hudson |
| Bowfin | 21 lb 8 oz | Florence, South Carolina | Jan 29, 1980 | Robert Harmon |
| Buffalo, bigmouth | 70 lb 5 oz | Bastrop, Louisiana | Apr 21, 1980 | Delbert Sisk |
| Buffalo, black | 63 lb 6 oz | Mississippi River, Iowa | Aug 14, 1999 | Jim Winter |
| Buffalo, smallmouth | 82 lb 3 oz | Athens Lake, Georgia | June 6, 1993 | Randy Collins |
| Bullhead, brown | 6 lb 1 oz | Waterford, New York | Apr 26, 1998 | Bobby Triplett |
| Bullhead, yellow | 4 lb 4 oz | Mormon Lake, Arizona | May 11, 1984 | Emily Williams |
| Burbot | 18 lb 11 oz | Angenmanalren, Sweden | Oct 22, 1996 | Margit Agren |
| Carp | 75 lb 11 oz | Lac de St. Cassien, France | May 21, 1987 | Leo van der Gugten |
| Catfish, blue | 111 lb | Tennesee River, Alabama | July 5, 1996 | William P. McKinley |
| Catfish, channel | 58 lb | Santee-Cooper Reservoir, SC | July 7, 1964 | W.B. Whaley |
| Catfish, flathead | 123 lb 9 oz | Elk City Reservoir, Indep., KS | May 14, 1998 | Ken Paulie |
| Catfish, white | 18 lb 14 oz | Inverness, Florida | Sep 21, 1991 | Jim Miller |
| Char, Arctic | 32 lb 9 oz | Tree River, Canada | July 30, 1981 | Jeffrey Ward |
| Crappie, white | 5 lb 3 oz | Enid Dam, Mississippi | July 31, 1957 | Fred L. Bright |
| Dolly Varden | 19 lb 4 oz | Unnamed River, Alaska | Sept 4, 1998 | Gary D. Ordway |
| Dorado | 51 lb 5 oz | Corrientes, Argentina | Sep 27, 1984 | Armando Giudice |
| Drum, freshwater | 54 lb 8 oz | Nickajack Lake, Tennessee | Apr 20, 1972 | Benny E. Hull |
| Gar, alligator | 279 lb | Rio Grande River, Texas | Dec 2, 1951 | Bill Valverde |
| Gar, Florida | 9 lb 7 oz | Lake Lawne, Orlando, Florida | Mar 25, 2001 | Patrick A. McDaniel |
| Gar, longnose | 50 lb 5 oz | Trinity River, Texas | July 30, 1954 | Townsend Miller |
| Gar, shortnose | 5 lb 12 oz | Rend Lake, Illinois | July 16, 1995 | Donna K. Willmert |
| Gar, spotted | 9 lb 12 oz | Lake Mexia, Texas | Apr 7, 1994 | Rick Rivard |
| Grayling, Arctic | 5 lb 15 oz | Katseyedie River, Northwest Territories | Aug 16, 1967 | Jeanne P. Branson |
| Inconnu | 53 lb | Pah River, Alaska | Aug 20, 1986 | Lawrence Hudnall |
| Kokanee | 9 lb 6 oz | Okanagan Lake, Vernon, BC | June 18, 1988 | Norm Kuhn |
| Muskellunge | 67 lb 8 oz | Hayward, Wisconsin | July 24, 1949 | Cal Johnson |
| Muskellunge, tiger | 51 lb 3 oz | Lac Vieux-Desert, WI, MI | July 16, 1919 | John Knobla |
| Peacock, speckled | 27 lb | Rio Negro, Brazil | Dec 4, 1994 | Gerald (Doc) Lawson |
| Perch, Nile | 230 lb | Lake Nasser, Egypt | Dec 20, 2000 | William Toth |
| Perch, white | 4 lb 12 oz | Messalonskee Lake, Maine | June 4, 1949 | Mrs. Earl Small |
| Perch, yellow | 4 lb 3 oz | Bordentown, New Jersey | May 1865 | C.C. Abbot |
| Pickerel, chain | 9 lb 6 oz | Homerville, Georgia | Feb 17, 1961 | Baxley McQuaig Jr. |
| Pike, northern | 55 lb 1 oz | Lake of Grefeern, W Germany | Oct 16, 1986 | Lothar Louis |
| Redhorse, greater | 9 lb 3 oz | Salmon River, Pulaski, New York | May 11, 1985 | Jason Wilson |
| Redhorse, silver | 11 lb 7 oz | Plum Creek, Wisconsin | May 29, 1985 | Neal Long |
| Salmon, Atlantic | 79 lb 2 oz | Tana River, Norway | 1928 | Henrik Henriksen |
| Salmon, Chinook | 97 lb 4 oz | Kenai River, Alaska | May 17, 1985 | Les Anderson |
| Salmon, chum | 35 lb | Edye Pass, Canada | July 11, 1995 | Todd A. Johansson |
| Salmon, coho | 33 lb 4 oz | Pulaski, New York | Sep 27, 1989 | Jerry Lifton |
| Salmon, pink | 13 lb 1 oz | Ontario, Canada | Sep 23, 1992 | Ray Higaki |
| Salmon, sockeye | 15 lb 3 oz | Kenai River, Alaska | Aug 9, 1987 | Stan Roach |
| Sauger | 8 lb 12 oz | Lake Sakakawea, North Dakota | Oct 6, 1971 | Mike Fischer |
| Shad, American | 11 lb 4 oz | Connecticut River, Massachusetts | May 19, 1986 | Bob Thibodo |
| Sturgeon, white | 468 lb | Benicia, California | July 9, 1983 | Joey Pallotta III |
| Sunfish, green | 2 lb 2 oz | Stockton Lake, Missouri | June 18, 1971 | Paul M. Dilley |
| Sunfish, redbreast | 1 lb 12 oz | Suwannee River, Florida | May 29, 1984 | Alvin Buchanan |
| Sunfish, redear | 5 lb 7 oz | Diverson Canal, Georgia | Nov 6, 1998 | Amos M. Gay |
| Tigerfish, giant | 97 lb | Zaire River, Kinshasa, Zaire | July 9, 1988 | Raymond Houtmans |
| Trout, Apache | 5 lb 3 oz | Apache Reservation, Arizona | May 29, 1991 | John Baldwin |
| Trout, brook | 14 lb 8 oz | Nipigon River, Ontario | July 1916 | W.J. Cook |
| Trout, brown | 40 lb 4 oz | Heber Springs, Arkansas | May 9, 1992 | Howard L. Collins |
| Trout, bull | 32 lb | Lake Pond Oreille, Idaho | Oct 27, 1949 | N.L. Higgins |
| Trout, cutthroat | 41 lb | Pyramid Lake, Nevada | Dec 1925 | John Skimmerhorn |
| Trout, golden | 11 lb | Cook's Lake, Wyoming | Aug 5, 1948 | Charles S. Reed |

## Freshwater Fishing Records (Cont.)

| Species | Weight | Where Caught | Date | Angler |
|---|---|---|---|---|
| Trout, lake | 72 lb | Great Bear Lake, Northwest Territories | Aug 19, 1995 | Lloyd Bull |
| Trout, rainbow | 42 lb 2 oz | Bell Island, Alaska | June 22, 1970 | David Robert White |
| Trout, tiger | 20 lb 13 oz | Lake Michigan, Wisconsin | Aug 12, 1978 | Pete M. Friedland |
| Walleye | 25 lb | Old Hickory Lake, Tennessee | Aug 2, 1960 | Mabry Harper |
| Warmouth | 2 lb 7 oz | Yellow River, Holt, Florida | Oct 19, 1985 | Tony D. Dempsey |
| Whitefish, lake | 14 lb 6 oz | Meaford, Ontario | May 21, 1984 | Dennis Laycock |
| Whitefish, mountain | 6 lb 7 oz | Shasta Lake, California | June 13, 2001 | James W. Schmidt |
| Whitefish, broad | 9 lb | Tozitna River, Alaska | July 17, 1989 | Al Mathews |
| Whitefish, round | 6 lb | Putahow River, Manitoba | June 14, 1984 | Allan J. Ristori |
| Zander | 25 lb 2 oz | Trosa, Sweden | June 12, 1986 | Harry Lee Tennison |

# Greyhound Racing

## Annual Greyhound Race of Champions Winners*

| Year | Winner (Sex) | Affiliation/Owner | Year | Winner (Sex) | Affiliation/Owner |
|---|---|---|---|---|---|
| 1982 | DD's Jackie (F) | Wonderland Park/ R.H. Walters Jr. | 1988 | BB's Old Yellow (M) | Supplemental (Southland)/ Margie Bonita Hyers |
| 1983 | Comin' Attraction (F) | Rocky Mt. Greyhound Park/ Bob Riggin | 1989 | Osh Kosh Juliet (F) | Tampa Greyhound Track/ William F. Pollard |
| 1984 | Fallon (F) | Tampa Greyhound Track/ E.J. Alderson | 1990 | Daring Don (M) | Interstate Kennel Club/ Perry Padrta |
| 1985 | Lady Delight (F) | Lincoln Greyhound Park/ Julian A. Gay | 1991 | Mo Kick (M) | Flagler Greyhound Track/ Eric M. Kennon |
| 1986 | Ben G Speedboat (M) | Multnomah Kennel Club/ Louis Bennett | 1992 | Dicky Vallie (M) | Dairyland Greyhound Track/ George Benjamin |
| 1987 | ET's Pesky (F) | Supplemental (Flagler)/ Emil Tanis | 1993 | Mega Morris (M) | Jacksonville Kennel Club/ Ferrell's Kennel |

* The Greyhound Race of Champions has not been held since 1993.

# Gymnastics

## World Champions
### MEN
### All-Around

| Year | Champion, Nation | Year | Champion, Nation | Year | Champion, Nation |
|---|---|---|---|---|---|
| 1903 | Joseph Martinez, France | 1938 | Jan Gajdos, Czechoslovakia | 1983 | Dimitri Bilozertchev, USSR |
| 1905 | Marcel Lalue, France | 1950 | Walter Lehmann, Switzerland | 1985 | Yuri Korolev, USSR |
| 1907 | Joseph Czada, Czechoslovakia | 1954 | Valentin Mouratov, USSR Victor Chukarin, USSR | 1987 | Dimitri Bilozertchev, USSR |
| 1909 | Marcos Torres, France | 1958 | Boris Shaklin, USSR | 1989 | Igor Korobchinsky, USSR |
| 1911 | Ferdinand Steiner, Czechoslovakia | 1962 | Yuri Titov, USSR | 1991 | Grigori Misutin, CIS |
| 1913 | Marcos Torres, France | 1966 | Mikhail Voronin, USSR | 1993 | Vitaly Scherbo, Belarus |
| 1922 | Peter Sumi, Yugoslavia F. Pechacek, Czechoslovakia | 1970 | Eizo Kenmotsu, Japan | 1994 | Ivan Ivankov, Belarus |
| 1926 | Peter Sumi, Yugoslavia | 1974 | Shigeru Kasamatsu, Japan | 1995 | Li Xiaoshuang, China |
| 1930 | Josip Primozic, Yugoslavia | 1978 | Nikolai Andrianov, USSR | 1997 | Ivan Ivankov, Belarus |
| 1934 | Eugene Mack, Switzerland | 1979 | Alexander Ditiatin, USSR | 1999 | Nicolae Krukov, Russia |
|  |  | 1981 | Yuri Korolev, USSR |  |  |

### Pommel Horse

| Year | Champion, Nation | Year | Champion, Nation | Year | Champion, Nation |
|---|---|---|---|---|---|
| 1930 | Josip Primozic, Yugoslavia | 1958 | Boris Shaklin, USSR | 1978 | Zoltan Magyar, Hungary |
| 1934 | Eugene Mack, Switzerland | 1962 | Miroslav Cerar, Yugoslavia | 1979 | Zoltan Magyar, Hungary |
| 1938 | Michael Reusch, Switzerland | 1966 | Miroslav Cerar, Yugoslavia | 1981 | Michael Mikolai, East Germany Li Xiaoping, China |
| 1950 | Josef Stalder, Switzerland | 1970 | Miroslav Cerar, Yugoslavia |  |  |
| 1954 | Grant Chaguinjan, USSR | 1974 | Zoltan Magyar, Hungary |  |  |

## World Champions (Cont.)
### MEN (Cont.)
### Pommel Horse (Cont.)

| Year | Champion, Nation | Year | Champion, Nation | Year | Champion, Nation |
|---|---|---|---|---|---|
| 1983 | Dmitri Bilozertchev, USSR | 1991 | Valeri Belenki, USSR | 1994 | Marius Urzica, Romania |
| 1985 | Valentin Moguilny, USSR | 1992 | Pae Gil Su, North Korea | 1995 | Li Donghua, Switzerland |
| 1987 | Zsolt Borkai, Hungary | | Vitaly Scherbo, CIS | 1996 | Pae Gil Su, North Korea |
| | Dmitri Bilozertchev, USSR | | Li Jing, China | 1997 | Valeri Belenki, Germany |
| 1989 | Valentin Moguilny, USSR | 1993 | Pae Gil Su, North Korea | 1999 | Alexei Nemov, Russia |

### Floor Exercise

| Year | Champion, Nation | Year | Champion, Nation | Year | Champion, Nation |
|---|---|---|---|---|---|
| 1930 | Josip Primozic, Yugoslavia | 1970 | Akinori Nakayama, Japan | 1989 | Igor Korobchinsky, USSR |
| 1934 | Georges Miesz, Switzerland | 1974 | Shigeru Kasamatsu, Japan | 1991 | Igor Korobchinsky, USSR |
| 1938 | Jan Gajdos, Czechoslovakia | 1978 | Kurt Thomas, United States | 1993 | Grigori Misutin, Ukraine |
| 1950 | Josef Stalder, Switzerland | 1979 | Kurt Thomas, United States | 1994 | Vitaly Scherbo, Belarus |
| 1954 | Valentin Mouratov, USSR | | Roland Brucker, GDR | 1995 | Vitaly Scherbo, Belarus |
| | Masao Takemoto, Japan | 1981 | Yuri Korolev, USSR | 1996 | Vitaly Scherbo, Belarus |
| 1958 | Masao Takemoto, Japan | | Li Yuejui, Chi | 1997 | Alexei Nemov, Russia |
| 1962 | Nobuyuki Aihara, Japan | 1983 | Tong Fei, China | 1999 | Alexei Nemov, Russia |
| | Yukio Endo, Japan | 1985 | Tong Fei, China | | |
| 1966 | Akinori Nakayama, Japan | 1987 | Lou Yun, China | | |

### Rings

| Year | Champion, Nation | Year | Champion, Nation | Year | Champion, Nation |
|---|---|---|---|---|---|
| 1930 | Emanuel Loffler, Czechoslovakia | 1970 | Akinori Nakayama, Japan | 1989 | Andreas Aguilar, West Germany |
| 1934 | Alois Hudec, Czechoslovakia | 1974 | N. Andrianov, USSR | 1991 | Grigory Misutin, USSR |
| 1938 | Alois Hudec, Czechoslovakia | | D. Grecu, Rom. | 1992 | Vitaly Scherbo, CIS |
| 1950 | Walter Lehmann, Switzerland | 1978 | Nikolai Andrianov, USSR | 1993 | Yuri Chechi, Italy |
| 1954 | Albert Azarian, USSR | 1979 | Alexander Ditiatin, USSR | 1994 | Yuri Chechi, Italy |
| 1958 | Albert Azarian, USSR | 1981 | Alexander Ditiatin, USSR | 1995 | Yuri Chechi, Italy |
| 1962 | Yuri Titov, USSR | 1983 | Dimitri Bilozertchev, USSR | 1996 | Yuri Chechi, Italy |
| 1966 | Mikhail Voronin, USSR | 1985 | Li Ning, China | 1997 | Yuri Chechi, Italy |
| | | | Yuri Korolev, USSR | 1999 | Zhen Dong, China |
| | | 1987 | Yuri Korolev, USSR | | |

### Parallel Bars

| Year | Champion, Nation | Year | Champion, Nation | Year | Champion, Nation |
|---|---|---|---|---|---|
| 1930 | Josip Primozic, Yugoslavia | 1979 | Bart Conner, United States | 1992 | Li Jin, China |
| 1934 | Eugene Mack, Switzerland | 1981 | Koji Gushiken, Japan | | Alexei Voropaev, CIS |
| 1938 | Michael Reusch, Switzerland | | Alexandr Ditiatin, USSR | 1993 | Vitaly Scherbo, Belarus |
| 1950 | Hans Eugster, Switzerland | 1983 | Vladimir Artemov, USSR | 1994 | Huang Liping, China |
| 1954 | Victor Chukarin, USSR | | Lou Yun, China | 1995 | Vitaly Scherbo, Belarus |
| 1958 | Boris Shaklin, USSR | 1985 | Sylvio Kroll, East Germany | 1996 | Rustam Sharipov, Ukraine |
| 1962 | Miroslav Cerar, Yugoslavia | | Valentin Moguilny, USSR | 1997 | Zhang Jinjing, China |
| 1966 | Sergei Diamidov, USSR | 1987 | Vladimir Artemov, USSR | 1999 | Joo-Hyung Lee, S Korea |
| 1970 | Akinori Nakayama, Japan | 1989 | Li Jing, China | | |
| 1974 | Eizo Kenmotsu, Japan | | Vladimir Artemov, USSR | | |
| 1978 | Eizo Kenmotsu, Japan | 1991 | Li Jing, China | | |

### High Bar

| Year | Champion, Nation | Year | Champion, Nation | Year | Champion, Nation |
|---|---|---|---|---|---|
| 1930 | Istvan Pelle, Hungary | 1978 | Shigeru Kasamatsu, Japan | 1994 | Vitaly Scherbo, Belarus |
| 1934 | Ernst Winter, Germany | 1979 | Kurt Thomas, United States | 1995 | Andreas Wecker, Germany |
| 1938 | Michael Reusch, Switzerland | 1981 | Alexander Takchev, USSR | 1996 | Jesús Carballo, Spain |
| 1950 | Paavo Aaltonen, Finland | 1983 | Dimitri Bilozertchev, USSR | 1997 | Jani Tanskanen, Finland |
| 1954 | Valentin Mouratov, USSR | 1985 | Tong Fei, China | 1999 | Jesus Carballo, Spain |
| 1958 | Boris Shaklin, USSR | 1987 | Dimitri Bilozertchev, USSR | | |
| 1962 | Takashi Ono, Japan | 1989 | Li Chunyang, China | | |
| 1966 | Akinori Nakayama, Japan | 1991 | Li Chunyang, China | | |
| 1970 | Eizo Kenmotsu, Japan | | R. Buechner, Germ | | |
| 1974 | Eberhard Gienger, West Germany | 1992 | Grigori Misutin, CIS | | |
| | | 1993 | Sergei Kharkov, Russia | | |

## World Champions *(Cont.)*

### MEN *(Cont.)*

## Vault

| Year | Champion, Nation | Year | Champion, Nation | Year | Champion, Nation |
|------|------------------|------|------------------|------|------------------|
| 1934 | Eugene Mack, Switzerland | 1978 | Junichi Shimizu, Japan | 1992 | Yoo Ok Youl, South Korea |
| 1938 | Eugene Mack, Switzerland | 1979 | Alexander Ditiatin, USSR | 1993 | Vitaly Scherbo, Belarus |
| 1950 | Ernst Gebendinger, Switzerland | 1981 | Ralf-Peter Hemmann, East Germany | 1994 | Vitaly Scherbo, Belarus |
| 1954 | Leo Sotornik, Czechoslovakia | 1983 | Arthur Akopian, USSR | 1995 | G. Misutin, Ukraine |
| 1958 | Yuri Titov, USSR | 1985 | Yuri Korolev, USSR | | A. Nemov, Russia |
| 1962 | Premysel Krbec, Czechoslovakia | 1987 | Lou Yun, China Sylvio Kroll, East Germany | 1996 | Alexei Nemov, Russia |
| 1966 | Haruhiro Yamashita, Japan | 1989 | Joreg Behrend, East Germany | 1997 | Sergei Fedorchenko, Kazakhstan |
| 1970 | Mitsuo Tsukahara, Japan | 1991 | Yoo Ok Youl, South Korea | 1999 | Xiaopeng Li, China |
| 1974 | Shigeru Kasamatsu, Japan | | | | |

### WOMEN

## All-Around

| Year | Champion, Nation | Year | Champion, Nation | Year | Champion, Nation |
|------|------------------|------|------------------|------|------------------|
| 1934 | Vlasta Dekanova, Czechoslovakia | 1970 | Ludmilla Tourischeva, USSR | 1991 | Kim Zmeskal, United States |
| 1938 | Vlasta Dekanova, Czechoslovakia | 1974 | Ludmilla Tourischeva, USSR | 1993 | Shannon Miller, United States |
| | | 1978 | Elena Mukhina, USSR | 1994 | Shannon Miller, United States |
| 1950 | Helena Rakoczy, Poland | 1979 | Nelli Kim, USSR | 1995 | Lilia Podkopayeva, Ukraine |
| 1954 | Galina Roudiko, USSR | 1981 | Olga Bicherova, USSR | 1997 | Svetlana Khorkina, Russia |
| 1958 | Larissa Latynina, USSR | 1983 | Natalia Yurchenko, USSR | 1999 | Maria Olaru, Romania |
| 1962 | Larissa Latynina, USSR | 1985 | Elena Shoushounova, USSR Oksana Omeliantchik, USSR | | |
| 1966 | Vera Caslavska, Czechoslovakia | 1987 | Aurelia Dobre, Romania | | |
| | | 1989 | Svetlana Bouguinskaia, USSR | | |

## Floor Exercise

| Year | Champion, Nation | Year | Champion, Nation | Year | Champion, Nation |
|------|------------------|------|------------------|------|------------------|
| 1950 | Helena Rakoczy, Poland | 1979 | Emilia Eberle, Romania | 1992 | Kim Zmeskal, United States |
| 1954 | Tamara Manina, USSR | 1981 | Natalia Ilenko, USSR | 1993 | Shannon Miller, United States |
| 1958 | Eva Bosakava, Czechoslovakia | 1983 | Ecaterina Szabo, Romania | 1994 | Dina Kochetkova, Russia |
| 1962 | Larissa Latynina, USSR | 1985 | Oksana Omeliantchik, USSR | 1995 | Gina Gogean, Romania |
| 1966 | Natalia Kuchinskaya, USSR | 1987 | Elena Shoushounova, USSR Daniela Silivas, Romania | 1996 | Gina Gogean, Romania |
| 1970 | Ludmilla Tourischeva, USSR | 1989 | Svetlana Bouguinskaia, USSR Daniela Silivas, Romania | 1997 | Gina Gogean, Romania |
| 1974 | Ludmilla Tourischeva, USSR | 1991 | Cristina Bontas, Romania Oksana Tchusovitina, USSR | 1999 | Andreea Raducan, Romania |
| 1978 | Nelli Kim, USSR Elena Mukhina, USSR | | | | |

## Uneven Bars

| Year | Champion, Nation | Year | Champion, Nation | Year | Champion, Nation |
|------|------------------|------|------------------|------|------------------|
| 1950 | Gertchen Kolar, Austria Anna Pettersson, Sweden | 1979 | Ma Yanhong, China Maxi Gnauck, East Germany | 1991 | Gwang Suk Kim, North Korea |
| 1954 | Agnes Keleti, Hungary | 1981 | Maxi Gnauck, East Germany | 1992 | Lavinia Milosivici, Romania |
| 1958 | Larissa Latynina, USSR | 1983 | Maxi Gnauck, East Germany | 1993 | Shannon Miller, United States |
| 1962 | Irina Pervuschina, USSR | 1985 | Gabriele Fahnrich, East Germany | 1994 | Luo Li, China |
| 1966 | Natalia Kuchinskaya, USSR | 1987 | Daniela Silivas, Romania Doerte Thuemmler, East Germany | 1995 | Svetlana Khorkina, Russia |
| 1970 | Karin Janz, East Germany | 1989 | Fan Di, China Daniela Silivas, Romania | 1996 | Svetlana Khorkina, Russia |
| 1974 | Annelore Zinke, East Germany | | | 1997 | Svetlana Khorkina, Russia |
| 1978 | Marcia Frederick, United States | | | 1999 | Svetlana Khorkina, Russia |

## World Champions *(Cont.)*
### WOMEN *(Cont.)*
### Balance Beam

| Year | Champion, Nation |
|------|------------------|
| 1950 | Helena Rakoczy, Poland |
| 1954 | Keiko Tanaka, Japan |
| 1958 | Larissa Latynina, USSR |
| 1962 | Eva Bosakova, Czechoslovakia |
| 1966 | Natalia Kuchinskaya, USSR |
| 1970 | Erika Zuchold, East Germany |
| 1974 | Ludmilla Tourischeva, USSR |

| Year | Champion, Nation |
|------|------------------|
| 1978 | Nadia Comaneci, Romania |
| 1979 | Vera Cerna, Czechoslovakia |
| 1981 | Maxi Gnauck, East Germany |
| 1983 | Olga Mostepanova, USSR |
| 1985 | Daniela Silivas, Romania |
| 1987 | Aurelia Dobre, Romania |
| 1989 | Daniela Silivas, Romania |
| 1991 | Svetlana Boguinskaia, USSR |

| Year | Champion, Nation |
|------|------------------|
| 1992 | Kim Zmeskal, United States |
| 1993 | Lavinia Milosovici, Romania |
| 1994 | Shannon Miller, United States |
| 1995 | Mo Huilan, China |
| 1996 | Dina Kochetkova, Russia |
| 1997 | Gina Gogean, Romania |
| 1999 | Elena Zamolodchikova, Russia |

### Vault

| Year | Champion, Nation |
|------|------------------|
| 1950 | Helena Rakoczy, Poland |
| 1954 | T. Manina, USSR |
| | Anna Pettersson, Sweden |
| 1958 | Larissa Latynina, USSR |
| 1962 | Vera Caslavska, Czechoslovakia |
| 1966 | Vera Caslavska, Czechoslovakia |
| 1970 | Erika Zuchold, East Germany |

| Year | Champion, Nation |
|------|------------------|
| 1974 | Olga Korbut, USSR |
| 1978 | Nelli Kim, USSR |
| 1979 | Dumitrita Turner, Romania |
| 1981 | Maxi Gnauck, East Germany |
| 1983 | Boriana Stoyanova, Bulgaria |
| 1985 | Elena Shoushounova, USSR |
| 1987 | Elena Shoushounova, USSR |
| 1989 | Olesia Durnik, USSR |
| 1991 | Lavinia Milosovici, Romania |

| Year | Champion, Nation |
|------|------------------|
| 1992 | Henrietta Onodi, Hungary |
| 1993 | Elena Piskun, Belarus |
| 1994 | Gina Gogean, Romania |
| 1995 | L. Podkopayeva, Ukraine |
| | Simona Amanar, Rom. |
| 1996 | Gina Gogean, Romania |
| 1997 | Simona Amanar, Romania |
| 1999 | Jie Ling, China |

## National Champions
### MEN
### All-Around

| Year | Champion |
|------|----------|
| 1963 | Art Shurlock |
| 1964 | Rusty Mitchell |
| 1965 | Rusty Mitchell |
| 1966 | Rusty Mitchell |
| 1967 | Katsuzoki Kanzaki |
| 1968 | Yoshi Hayasaki |
| 1969 | Steve Hug |
| 1970 | Makoto Sakamoto |
| | Mas Watanabe |
| 1971 | Yoshi Takei |
| 1972 | Yoshi Takei |
| 1973 | Marshall Avener |
| 1974 | John Crosby |
| 1975 | Tom Beach |
| | Bart Conner |

| Year | Champion |
|------|----------|
| 1976 | Kurt Thomas |
| 1977 | Kurt Thomas |
| 1978 | Kurt Thomas |
| 1979 | Bart Conner |
| 1980 | Peter Vidmar |
| 1981 | Jim Hartung |
| 1982 | Peter Vidmar |
| 1983 | Mitch Gaylord |
| 1984 | Mitch Gaylord |
| 1985 | Brian Babcock |
| 1986 | Tim Daggett |
| 1987 | Scott Johnson |
| 1988 | Dan Hayden |
| 1989 | Tim Ryan |
| 1990 | John Roethlisberger |

| Year | Champion |
|------|----------|
| 1991 | Chris Waller |
| 1992 | John Roethlisberger |
| 1993 | John Roethlisberger |
| 1994 | Scott Keswick |
| 1995 | John Roethlisberger |
| 1996 | Blaine Wilson |
| 1997 | Blaine Wilson |
| 1998 | Blaine Wilson |
| 1999 | Blaine Wilson |
| 2000 | Blaine Wilson |
| 2001 | Sean Townsend |

### Floor Exercise

| Year | Champion |
|------|----------|
| 1963 | Tom Seward |
| 1964 | Rusty Mitchell |
| 1965 | Rusty Mitchell |
| 1966 | Dan Millman |
| 1967 | Katsuzoki Kanzaki |
| | Ron Aure |
| 1968 | Katsuzoki Kanzaki |
| 1969 | Steve Hug |
| | Dave Thor |
| 1970 | Makoto Sakamoto |
| 1971 | John Crosby |
| 1972 | Yoshi Takei |
| 1973 | John Crosby |
| 1974 | John Crosby |

| Year | Champion |
|------|----------|
| 1975 | Peter Korman |
| 1977 | Ron Galimore |
| 1978 | Kurt Thomas |
| 1979 | Ron Galimore |
| 1980 | Ron Galimore |
| 1981 | Jim Hartung |
| 1982 | Jim Hartung |
| 1983 | Mitch Gaylord |
| 1984 | Peter Vidmar |
| 1985 | Mark Oates |
| 1986 | Robert Sundstrom |
| 1987 | John Sweeney |
| 1988 | Mark Oates |
| | Charles Lakes |

| Year | Champion |
|------|----------|
| 1989 | Mike Racanelli |
| 1990 | Bob Stelter |
| 1991 | Mike Racanelli |
| 1992 | Gregg Curtis |
| 1993 | Kerry Huston |
| 1994 | Jeremy Killen |
| 1995 | Daniel Stover |
| 1996 | Jay Thornton |
| 1997 | Jason Gatson |
| 1998 | Jason Gatson |
| 1999 | Jason Gatson |
| 2000 | Blaine Wilson |
| 2001 | Sean Townsend |

# Gymnastics *(Cont.)*

## National Champions *(Cont.)*

### MEN *(Cont.)*

### Pommel Horse

| Year | Champion | Year | Champion | Year | Champion |
|------|----------|------|----------|------|----------|
| 1963 | Larry Spiegel | 1977 | Gene Whelan | 1990 | Patrick Kirksey |
| 1964 | Sam Bailie | 1978 | Jim Hartung | 1991 | Chris Waller |
| 1965 | Jack Ryan | 1979 | Bart Conner | 1992 | Chris Waller |
| 1966 | Jack Ryan | 1980 | Jim Hartung | 1993 | Chris Waller |
| 1967 | Paul Mayer/Dave Doty | 1981 | Jim Hartung | 1994 | Mihai Begiu |
| 1968 | Katsuoki Kanzaki | 1982 | Jim Hartung | 1995 | Mark Sohn |
| 1969 | Dave Thor | 1983 | Bart Conner | 1996 | Josh Stein |
| 1970 | Mas Watanabe | 1984 | Tim Daggett | 1997 | John Roethlisberger |
| 1971 | Leonard Caling | 1985 | Phil Cahoy | 1998 | John Roethlisberger |
| 1972 | Sadao Hamada | 1986 | Phil Cahoy | 1999 | John Roethlisberger |
| 1973 | Marshall Avener | 1987 | Tim Daggett | 2000 | John Roethlisberger |
| 1974 | Marshall Avener | 1988 | Kevin Davis | 2001 | Brett McClure |
| 1975 | Bart Conner | 1989 | Kevin Davis | | |

### Rings

| Year | Champion | Year | Champion | Year | Champion |
|------|----------|------|----------|------|----------|
| 1963 | Art Shurlock | 1975 | Tom Beach | 1989 | Scott Keswick |
| 1964 | Glen Gailis | 1977 | Kurt Thomas | 1990 | Scott Keswick |
| 1965 | Glen Gailis | 1978 | Mike Silverstein | 1991 | Scott Keswick |
| 1966 | Glen Gailis | 1979 | Bart Conner | 1992 | Tim Ryan |
| 1967 | Fred Dennis | 1980 | Jim Hartung | 1993 | John Roethlisberger |
| | Don Hatch | 1981 | Jim Hartung | 1994 | Scott Keswick |
| 1968 | Yoshi Hayasaki | 1982 | Jim Hartung | 1995 | Paul O'Neill |
| 1969 | Fred Dennis | | Peter Vidmar | 1996 | Kip Simons |
| | Bob Emery | 1983 | Mitch Gaylord | 1997 | Blaine Wilson |
| 1970 | Makoto Sakamoto | 1984 | Jim Hartung | 1998 | Jeff Johnson |
| 1971 | Yoshi Takei | 1985 | Dan Hayden | 1999 | Blaine Wilson |
| 1972 | Yoshi Takei | 1986 | Dan Hayden | 2000 | Blaine Wilson |
| 1973 | Jim Ivicek | 1987 | Scott Johnson | 2001 | Sean Townsend |
| 1974 | Tom Weeder | 1988 | Dan Hayden | | |

### Vault

| Year | Champion | Year | Champion | Year | Champion |
|------|----------|------|----------|------|----------|
| 1963 | Art Shurlock | 1977 | Ron Galimore | 1990 | Lance Ringnald |
| 1964 | Gary Hery | 1978 | Jim Hartung | 1991 | Scott Keswick |
| 1965 | Brent Williams | 1979 | Ron Galimore | 1992 | Trent Dimas |
| 1966 | Dan Millman | 1980 | Ron Galimore | 1993 | Bill Roth |
| 1967 | Jack Kenan | 1981 | Ron Galimore | 1994 | Keith Wiley |
| | Sid Jensen | 1982 | Jim Hartung/Jim Mikus | 1995 | David St. Pierre |
| 1968 | Rich Scorza | 1983 | Chris Reigel | 1996 | Blaine Wilson |
| 1969 | Dave Butzman | 1984 | Chris Reigel | 1997 | Blaine Wilson |
| 1970 | Makoto Sakamoto | 1985 | Scott Johnson | 1998 | Brent Klaus |
| 1971 | Gary Morava | | Mark Oates | 1999 | Guard Young |
| 1972 | Mike Kelley | 1986 | Scott Wilbanks | 2000 | Blaine Wilson |
| 1973 | Gary Morava | 1987 | John Sweeney | 2001 | Jason Furr |
| 1974 | John Crosby | 1988 | John Sweeney/Bill Paul | | |
| 1975 | Tom Beach | 1989 | Bill Roth | | |

### Parallel Bars

| Year | Champion | Year | Champion | Year | Champion |
|------|----------|------|----------|------|----------|
| 1963 | Tom Seward | 1970 | Makoto Sakamoto | 1979 | Bart Conner |
| 1964 | Rusty Mitchell | 1971 | Brent Simmons | 1980 | Phil Cahoy/Larry Gerard |
| 1965 | Glen Gailis | 1972 | Yoshi Takei | 1981 | Bart Conner |
| 1966 | Ray Hadley | 1973 | Marshall Avener | 1982 | Peter Vidmar |
| 1967 | Katsuoki Kanzaki | 1974 | Jim Ivicek | 1983 | Mitch Gaylord |
| | Tom Goldsborough | 1975 | Bart Conner | 1984 | Peter Vidmar |
| 1968 | Yoshi Hayasaki | 1977 | Kurt Thomas | | Mitch Gaylord |
| 1969 | Steve Hug | 1978 | Bart Conner | | Tim Daggett |

## National Champions *(Cont.)*

### MEN *(Cont.)*

### Parallel Bars *(Cont.)*

| Year | Champion | Year | Champion |
|------|----------|------|----------|
| 1985 | Tim Daggett | 1990 | Trent Dimas |
| 1986 | Tim Daggett | 1991 | Scott Keswick |
| 1987 | Scott Johnson | 1992 | Jair Lynch |
| 1988 | D. Hayden/K. Davis | 1993 | Chainey Umphrey |
| 1989 | Conrad Voorsanger | 1994 | Steve McCain |

| Year | Champion |
|------|----------|
| 1995 | John Roethlisberger |
| 1996 | Jair Lynch |
| 1997 | Blaine Wilson |
| 1998 | Blaine Wilson |
| 1999 | Jason Gatson |
| 2000 | Trent Wells |
| 2001 | Sean Townsend |

### High Bars

| Year | Champion |
|------|----------|
| 1963 | Art Shurlock |
| 1964 | Glen Gailis |
| 1965 | Rusty Mitchell |
| 1966 | Katsuzoki Kanzaki |
| 1967 | Katsuzoki Kanzaki |
|  | Jerry Fontana |
| 1968 | Yoshi Hayasaki |
| 1969 | Rich Grisby |
| 1970 | Makoto Sakamoto |
| 1971 | Yoshi Takei |
| 1972 | Tom Lindner |
| 1973 | John Crosby |
| 1974 | Brent Simmons |
| 1975 | Tom Beach |

| Year | Champion |
|------|----------|
| 1977 | Kurt Thomas |
| 1978 | Kurt Thomas |
| 1979 | Yoichi Tomita |
| 1980 | Jim Hartung |
| 1981 | Bart Conner |
| 1982 | Mitch Gaylord |
| 1983 | Mario McCutcheon |
| 1984 | Peter Vidmar |
|  | Tim Daggett |
|  | Mitch Gaylord |
| 1985 | Dan Hayden |
| 1986 | D. Hayden/D. Moriel |
| 1987 | David Moriel |
| 1988 | Dan Hayden |
| 1989 | Tim Ryan |

| Year | Champion |
|------|----------|
| 1990 | Trent Dimas |
|  | Lance Ringnald |
| 1991 | Lance Ringnald |
| 1992 | Jair Lynch |
| 1993 | Steve McCain |
| 1994 | Scott Keswick |
| 1995 | John Roethlisberger |
| 1996 | Bill Roth |
| 1997 | Douglas Stibel |
| 1998 | Jason Gatson |
| 1999 | Jamie Natalie |
| 2000 | Trent Wells |
|  | Jamie Natalie |
| 2001 | Daniel Diaz-Luong |

### WOMEN

### All-Around

| Year | Champion |
|------|----------|
| 1963 | Donna Schanezer |
| 1965 | Gail Daley |
| 1966 | Donna Schanezer |
| 1968 | Linda Scott |
| 1969 | Joyce Tanac |
|  | Schroeder |
| 1970 | Cathy Rigby McCoy |
| 1971 | Joan Moore Gnat |
|  | Linda Metheny |
|  | Mulvihill |
| 1972 | Joan Moore Gnat |
|  | Cathy Rigby McCoy |
| 1973 | Joan Moore Gnat |
| 1974 | Joan Moore Gnat |
| 1975 | Tammy Manville |

| Year | Champion |
|------|----------|
| 1976 | Denise Cheshire |
| 1977 | Donna Turnbow |
| 1978 | Kathy Johnson |
| 1979 | Leslie Pyfer |
| 1980 | Julianne McNamara |
| 1981 | Tracee Talavera |
| 1982 | Tracee Talavera |
| 1983 | Dianne Durham |
| 1984 | Mary Lou Retton |
| 1985 | Sabrina Mar |
| 1986 | Jennifer Sey |
| 1987 | Kristie Phillips |
| 1988 | Phoebe Mills |
| 1989 | Brandy Johnson |
| 1990 | Kim Zmeskal |

| Year | Champion |
|------|----------|
| 1991 | Kim Zmeskal |
| 1992 | Kim Zmeskal |
| 1993 | Shannon Miller |
| 1994 | Dominique Dawes |
| 1995 | Dominique Moceanu |
| 1996 | Shannon Miller |
| 1997 | Vanessa Adler |
|  | Kristy Powell |
| 1998 | Kristen Maloney |
| 1999 | Kristen Maloney |
| 2000 | Elise Ray |
| 2001 | Tasha Schwikert |

### Vault

| Year | Champion |
|------|----------|
| 1963 | Donna Schanezer |
| 1965 | Gail Daley |
| 1966 | Donna Schanezer |
| 1968 | Terry Spencer |
| 1969 | Joyce Tanac |
|  | Schroeder |
|  | Cleo Carver |
| 1970 | Cathy Rigby McCoy |
| 1971 | Joan Moore Gnat |
|  | Adele Gleaves |
| 1972 | Cindy Eastwood |
| 1973 | Roxanne Pierce |
|  | Mancha |
| 1974 | Dianne Dunbar |
| 1975 | Kolleen Casey |

| Year | Champion |
|------|----------|
| 1976 | Debbie Wilcox |
| 1977 | Lisa Cawthron |
| 1978 | Rhonda Schwandt |
|  | Sharon Shapiro |
| 1979 | Christa Canary |
| 1980 | J. McNamara/B. Kline |
| 1981 | Kim Neal |
| 1982 | Yumi Mordre |
| 1983 | Dianne Durham |
| 1984 | Mary Lou Retton |
| 1985 | Yolanda Mavity |
| 1986 | Joyce Wilborn |
| 1987 | Rhonda Faehn |
| 1988 | Rhonda Faehn |
| 1989 | Brandy Johnson |

| Year | Champion |
|------|----------|
| 1990 | Brandy Johnson |
| 1991 | Kerri Strug |
| 1992 | Kerri Strug |
| 1993 | Dominique Dawes |
| 1994 | Dominique Dawes |
| 1995 | Shannon Miller |
| 1996 | Dominique Dawes |
| 1997 | Vanessa Atler |
| 1998 | Dominique Moceanu |
| 1999 | Vanessa Atler |
| 2000 | Kristen Maloney |
| 2001 | Mohini Bhardwaj |

# Gymnastics *(Cont.)*

## National Champions *(Cont.)*
### WOMEN *(Cont.)*

## Uneven Bars

| Year | Champion |
|---|---|
| 1963 | Donna Schanezer |
| 1965 | Irene Haworth |
| 1966 | Donna Schanezer |
| 1968 | Linda Scott |
| 1969 | Joyce Tanac Schroeder Lisa Nelson |
| 1970 | Roxanne Pierce Mancha |
| 1971 | Joan Moore Gnat |
| 1972 | Cathy Rigby McCoy |
| 1973 | Roxanne Pierce Mancha |
| 1974 | Diane Dunbar |
| 1975 | Leslie Wolfsberger |

| Year | Champion |
|---|---|
| 1976 | Leslie Wolfsberger |
| 1977 | Donna Turnbow |
| 1978 | Marcia Frederick |
| 1979 | Marcia Frederick |
| 1980 | Marcia Frederick |
| 1981 | Julianne McNamara |
| 1982 | Marie Roethlisberger |
| 1983 | Julianne McNamara |
| 1984 | Julianne McNamara |
| 1985 | Sabrina Mar |
| 1986 | Marie Roethlisberger |
| 1987 | Melissa Marlowe |
| 1988 | Chelle Stack |
| 1989 | Chelle Stack |
| 1990 | Sandy Woolsey |

| Year | Champion |
|---|---|
| 1991 | Elisabeth Crandall |
| 1992 | Dominique Dawes |
| 1993 | Shannon Miller |
| 1994 | Dominique Dawes |
| 1995 | Dominique Dawes |
| 1996 | Dominique Dawes |
| 1997 | Kristy Powell |
| 1998 | Elise Ray |
| 1999 | Jamie Dantzscher Jennie Thompson |
| 2000 | Elise Ray |
| 2001 | Katie Heenan |

## Balance Beam

| Year | Champion |
|---|---|
| 1963 | Leissa Krol |
| 1965 | Gail Daley |
| 1966 | Irene Haworth Linda Scott |
| 1968 | Linda Scott |
| 1969 | Lonna Woodward |
| 1970 | Joyce Tanac Schroeder |
| 1971 | Linda Metheny Mulvihill |
| 1972 | Kim Chace |
| 1973 | Nancy Thies Marshall |
| 1974 | Joan Moore Gnat |
| 1975 | Kyle Gayner |
| 1976 | Carrie Englert |

| Year | Champion |
|---|---|
| 1977 | Donna Turnbow |
| 1978 | Christa Canary |
| 1979 | Heidi Anderson |
| 1980 | Kelly Garrison-Steves |
| 1981 | Tracee Talavera |
| 1982 | Julianne McNamara |
| 1983 | Dianne Durham |
| 1984 | Pam Bileck Tracee Talavera |
| 1986 | Angie Denkins |
| 1987 | Kristie Phillips |
| 1985 | Kelly Garrison-Steves |
| 1988 | Kelly Garrison-Steves |
| 1989 | Brandy Johnson |
| 1990 | Betty Okino |

| Year | Champion |
|---|---|
| 1991 | Shannon Miller |
| 1992 | Kerri Strug Kim Zmeskal |
| 1993 | Dominique Dawes |
| 1994 | Dominique Dawes |
| 1995 | Doni Thompson Monica Flammer |
| 1996 | Dominique Dawes |
| 1997 | Kendall Beck |
| 1998 | Dominique Moceanu |
| 1999 | Vanessa Atler |
| 2000 | Alyssa Beckerman Amy Chow |
| 2001 | Tasha Schwikert |

## Floor Exercise

| Year | Champion |
|---|---|
| 1963 | Donna Schanezer |
| 1965 | Gail Daley |
| 1966 | Donna Schanezer |
| 1968 | Linda Scott |
| 1970 | Cathy Rigby McCoy |
| 1971 | Linda Metheny Mulvihill |
| 1972 | Joan Moore Gnat |
| 1973 | Joan Moore Gnat |
| 1974 | Joan Moore Gnat |
| 1975 | Kathy Howard |
| 1976 | Carrie Englert |
| 1977 | Kathy Johnson |
| 1978 | Kathy Johnson |

| Year | Champion |
|---|---|
| 1979 | Heidi Anderson |
| 1980 | Beth Kline |
| 1981 | Michelle Goodwin |
| 1982 | Amy Koopman |
| 1983 | Dianne Durham |
| 1984 | Mary Lou Retton |
| 1985 | Sabrina Mar |
| 1986 | Yolanda Mavity |
| 1987 | Kristie Phillips |
| 1988 | Phoebe Mills |
| 1989 | Brandy Johnson |
| 1990 | Brandy Johnson |
| 1991 | Kim Zmeskal Dominique Dawes |
| 1992 | Kim Zmeskal |

| Year | Champion |
|---|---|
| 1993 | Shannon Miller |
| 1994 | Dominique Dawes |
| 1995 | Dominique Dawes |
| 1996 | Dominique Dawes |
| 1997 | Lindsay Wing |
| 1998 | Vanessa Atler |
| 1999 | Elise Ray |
| 2000 | Kristen Maloney |
| 2001 | Tabitha Yim |

# Handball

## National Four-Wall Champions

### MEN

| | | | |
|---|---|---|---|
| 1919 .....Bill Ranft | 1940 .....Joe Platak | 1961 .....John Sloan | 1982 .....Naty Alvarado |
| 1920 .....Max Gold | 1941 .....Joe Platak | 1962 .....Oscar Obert | 1983 .....Naty Alvarado |
| 1921 .....Carl Haedge | 1942 .....Jack Clemente | 1963 .....Oscar Obert | 1984 .....Naty Alvarado |
| 1922 .....Art Shinners | 1943 .....Joe Platak | 1964 .....Jimmy Jacobs | 1985 .....Naty Alvarado |
| 1923 .....Joe Murray | 1944 .....Frank Coyle | 1965 .....Jimmy Jacobs | 1986 .....Naty Alvarado |
| 1924 .....Maynard Laswe | 1945 .....Joe Platak | 1966 .....Paul Haber | 1987 .....Naty Alvarado |
| 1925 .....Maynard Laswe | 1946 .....Angelo Trutio | 1967 .....Paul Haber | 1988 .....Naty Alvarado |
| 1926 .....Maynard Laswe | 1947 .....Gus Lewis | 1968 .....Stuffy Singer | 1989 .....Poncho Monreal |
| 1927 .....George Nelson | 1948 .....Gus Lewis | 1969 .....Paul Haber | 1990 .....Naty Alvarado |
| 1928 .....Joe Griffin | 1949 .....Vic Hershkowitz | 1970 .....Paul Haber | 1991 .....John Bike |
| 1929 .....Al Banuet | 1950 .....Ken Schneider | 1971 .....Paul Haber | 1992 .....Octavio Silveyra |
| 1930 .....Al Banuet | 1951 .....Walter Plakan | 1972 .....Fred Lewis | 1993 .....David Chapman |
| 1931 .....Al Banuet | 1952 .....Vic Hershkowitz | 1973 .....Terry Muck | 1994 .....Octavio Silveyra |
| 1932 .....Angelo Trutio | 1953 .....Bob Brady | 1974 .....Fred Lewis | 1995 .....David Chapman |
| 1933 .....Sam Atcheson | 1954 .....Vic Hershkowitz | 1975 .....Fred Lewis | 1996 .....David Chapman |
| 1934 .....Sam Atcheson | 1955 .....Jimmy Jacobs | 1976 .....Fred Lewis | 1997 .....Octavio Silveyra |
| 1935 .....Joe Platak | 1956 .....Jimmy Jacobs | 1977 .....Naty Alvarado | 1998 .....David Chapman |
| 1936 .....Joe Platak | 1957 .....Jimmy Jacobs | 1978 .....Fred Lewis | 1999 .....David Chapman |
| 1937 .....Joe Platak | 1958 .....John Sloan | 1979 .....Naty Alvarado | 2000 .....David Chapman |
| 1938 .....Joe Platak | 1959 .....John Sloan | 1980 .....Naty Alvarado | 2001 .....Vince Munoz |
| 1939 .....Joe Platak | 1960 .....Jimmy Jacobs | 1981 .....Fred Lewis | |

### WOMEN

| | | | |
|---|---|---|---|
| 1980 .....Rosemary Bellini | 1986 .....Peanut Motal | 1992 .....Lisa Fraser | 1998 .....Lisa Fraser |
| 1981 .....Rosemary Bellini | 1987 .....Rosemary Bellini | 1993 .....Anna Engele | 1999 .....Anna Christoff |
| 1982 .....Rosemary Bellini | 1988 .....Rosemary Bellini | 1994 .....Anna Engele | 2000 .....Priscilla |
| 1983 .....Diane Harmon | 1989 .....Anna Engele | 1995 .....Anna Engele | Shumate |
| 1984 .....Rosemary Bellini | 1990 .....Anna Engele | 1996 .....Anna Engele | 2001 .....Anna Christoff |
| 1985 .....Peanut Motal | 1991 .....Anna Engele | 1997 .....Lisa Fraser | |

## National Three-Wall Champions

### MEN

| | | | |
|---|---|---|---|
| 1950 .....Vic Hershkowitz | 1964 .....Marty Decatur | 1978 .....Fred Lewis | 1992 .....John Bike |
| 1951 .....Vic Hershkowitz | 1965 .....Carl Obert | 1979 .....Naty Alvarado | 1993 .....Eric Klarman |
| 1952 .....Vic Hershkowitz | 1966 .....Marty Decatur | 1980 .....Lou Russo | 1994 .....David Chapman |
| 1953 .....Vic Hershkowitz | 1967 .....Carl Obert | 1981 .....Naty Alvarado | 1995 .....David Chapman |
| 1954 .....Vic Hershkowitz | 1968 .....Marty Decatur | 1982 .....Naty Alvarado | 1996 .....Vince Munoz |
| 1955 .....Vic Hershkowitz | 1969 .....Marty Decatur | 1983 .....Naty Alvarado | 1997 .....Vince Munoz |
| 1956 .....Vic Hershkowitz | 1970 .....Steve August | 1984 .....Naty Alvarado | 1998 .....Vince Munoz |
| 1957 .....Vic Hershkowitz | 1971 .....Lou Russo | 1985 .....Vern Roberts | 1999 .....Vince Munoz |
| 1958 .....Vic Hershkowitz | 1972 .....Lou Russo | 1986 .....Vern Roberts | 2000 .....Vince Munoz |
| 1959 .....Jimmy Jacobs | 1973 .....Paul Haber | 1987 .....Vern Roberts | 2001 .....Vince Munoz |
| 1960 .....Jimmy Jacobs | 1974 .....Fred Lewis | 1988 .....Jon Kendler | |
| 1961 .....Jimmy Jacobs | 1975 .....Lou Russo | 1989 .....John Bike | |
| 1962 .....Oscar Obert | 1976 .....Lou Russo | 1990 .....Vince Munoz | |
| 1963 .....Marty Decatur | 1977 .....Fred Lewis | 1991 .....John Bike | |

### WOMEN

| | | | |
|---|---|---|---|
| 1981 .....Allison Roberts | 1987 .....Rosemary Bellini | 1993 .....Anna Engele | 1999 .....Allison Roberts |
| 1982 .....Allison Roberts | 1988 .....Rosemary Bellini | 1994 .....Anna Engele | 2000 .....Priscilla Shumate |
| 1983 .....Allison Roberts | 1989 .....Rosemary Bellini | 1995 .....Allison Roberts | 2001 .....Anna Christoff |
| 1984 .....Rosemary Bellini | 1990 .....Rosemary Bellini | 1996 .....Anna Engele | |
| 1985 .....Rosemary Bellini | 1991 .....Rosemary Bellini | 1997 .....Allison Roberts | |
| 1986 .....Rosemary Bellini | 1992 .....Anna Engele | 1998 .....Anna Christoff | |

## World Four-Wall Champions

| | |
|---|---|
| 1984 ..................Merv Deckert, Canada | 1994 ..................David Chapman, United States |
| 1986 ..................Vern Roberts, United States | 1997 ..................John Bike Jr., United States |
| 1988 ..................Naty Alvarado, United States | 2000 ..................David Chapman, United States |
| 1991 ..................Pancho Monreal, United States | |

# Lacrosse

## United States Club Lacrosse Association Champions

| | | |
|---|---|---|
| 1960 ......Mt. Washington Club | 1974 ......Long Island Athletic Club | 1988 ......Maryland Lacrosse Club |
| 1961 ......Baltimore Lacrosse Club | 1975 ......Mt. Washington Club | 1989 ......LI-Hofstra Lacrosse Club |
| 1962 ......Mt. Washington Club | 1976 ......Mt. Washington Club | 1990 ......Mt. Washington Club |
| 1963 ......University Club | 1977 ......Mt. Washington Club | 1991 ......Mt. Washington Club |
| 1964 ......Mt. Washington Club | 1978 ......Long Island Athletic Club | 1992 ......Maryland Lacrosse Club |
| 1965 ......Mt. Washington Club | 1979 ......Maryland Lacrosse Club | 1993 ......Mt. Washington Club |
| 1966 ......Mt. Washington Club | 1980 ......Long Island Athletic Club | 1994 ......LI-Hofstra Lacrosse Club |
| 1967 ......Mt. Washington Club | 1981 ......Long Island Athletic Club | 1995 ......Mt. Washington Club |
| 1968 ......Long Island Athletic Club | 1982 ......Maryland Lacrosse Club | 1996 ......LI-Hofstra Lacrosse Club |
| 1969 ......Long Island Athletic Club | 1983 ......Maryland Lacrosse Club | 1997 ......LI-Hofstra Lacrosse Club |
| 1970 ......Long Island Athletic Club | 1984 ......Maryland Lacrosse Club | 1998 ......LI-Hofstra Lacrosse Club |
| 1971 ......Long Island Athletic Club | 1985 ......LI-Hofstra Lacrosse Club | 1999 ......New York Athletic Club |
| 1972 ......Carling | 1986 ......LI-Hofstra Lacrosse Club | 2000 ......Team Toyota (Baltimore) |
| 1973 ......Long Island Athletic Club | 1987 ......LI-Hofstra Lacrosse Club | 2001 ......LI Lacrosse Club |

## National Lacrosse League Champions*

| | | |
|---|---|---|
| 1987 ......Baltimore Thunder | 1992 ......Buffalo Bandits | 1997 ......Rochester Knighthawks |
| 1988 ......New Jersey Saints | 1993 ......Buffalo Bandits | 1998 ......Philadelphia Wings |
| 1989 ......Philadelphia Wings | 1994 ......Philadelphia Wings | 1999 ......Toronto Rock |
| 1990 ......Philadelphia Wings | 1995 ......Philadelphia Wings | 2000 ......Toronto Rock |
| 1991 ......Detroit Turbos | 1996 ......Buffalo Bandits | 2001 ......Philadelphia Wings |

*Indoor league formerly known as the Eagle Pro Box Lacrosse League, and the Major Indoor Lacrosse League.

## Major League Lacrosse*

2001 .....Long Island Lizards

*Outdoor league.

# Little League Baseball

## Little League World Series Champions

| Year | Champion | Runner-Up | Score | Year | Champion | Runner-Up | Score |
|---|---|---|---|---|---|---|---|
| 1947 | Williamsport, PA | Lock Haven, PA | 16–7 | 1975 | Lakewood, NJ | Tampa, FL | 4–3 |
| 1948 | Lock Haven, PA | St. Petersburg, FL | 6–5 | 1976 | Tokyo, Japan | Campbell, CA | 10–3 |
| 1949 | Hammonton, NJ | Pensacola, FL | 5–0 | 1977 | Kao-Hsuing, Taiwan | El Cajun, CA | 7–2 |
| 1950 | Houston, TX | Bridgeport, CT | 2–1 | 1978 | Pin-Tung, Taiwan | Danville, CA | 11–1 |
| 1951 | Stamford, CT | Austin, TX | 3–0 | 1979 | Hsien, Taiwan | Campbell, CA | 2–1 |
| 1952 | Norwalk, CT | Monongahela, PA | 4–3 | 1980 | Hua Lian, Taiwan | Tampa, FL | 4–3 |
| 1953 | Birmingham, AL | Schenectady, NY | 1–0 | 1981 | Tai-Chung, Taiwan | Tampa, FL | 4–2 |
| 1954 | Schenectady, NY | Colton, CA | 7–5 | 1982 | Kirkland, WA | Hsien, Taiwan | 6–0 |
| 1955 | Morrisville, PA | Merchantville, NJ | 4–3 | 1983 | Marietta, GA | Barahona, D.Rep. | 3–1 |
| 1956 | Roswell, NM | Merchantville, NJ | 3–1 | 1984 | Seoul, S. Korea | Altamonte Sgs, FL | 6–2 |
| 1957 | Monterrey, Mex. | LaMesa, CA | 4–0 | 1985 | Seoul, S. Korea | Mexicali, Mex. | 7–1 |
| 1958 | Monterrey, Mex. | Kankakee, IL | 10–1 | 1986 | Tainan Park, Taiwan | Tucson, AZ | 12–0 |
| 1959 | Hamtramck, MI | Auburn, CA | 12–0 | 1987 | Hua Lian, Taiwan | Irvine, CA | 21–1 |
| 1960 | Levittown, PA | Ft. Worth, TX | 5–0 | 1988 | Tai-Chung, Taiwan | Pearl City, HI | 10–0 |
| 1961 | El Cajon, CA | El Campo, TX | 4–2 | 1989 | Trumbull, CT | Kaohsiung, Taiwan | 5–2 |
| 1962 | San Jose, CA | Kankakee, IL | 3–0 | 1990 | Taipei, Taiwan | Shippensburg, PA | 9–0 |
| 1963 | Granada Hills, CA | Stratford, CT | 2–1 | 1991 | Tai-Chung, Taiwan | San Ramon Vly, CA | 11–0 |
| 1964 | Staten Island, NY | Monterrey, Mex. | 4–0 | 1992* | Long Beach, CA | Zamboanga, Phil. | 6–0 |
| 1965 | Windsor Locks, CT | Stoney Creek, Can. | 3–1 | 1993 | Long Beach, CA | David Chiriqui, Pan. | 3–2 |
| 1966 | Houston, TX | W. New York, NJ | 8–2 | 1994 | Maracaibo, Venez. | Northridge, CA | 4–3 |
| 1967 | West Tokyo, Japan | Chicago, IL | 4–1 | 1995 | Tainan, Taiwan | Sprint, TX | 17–3 |
| 1968 | Osaka, Japan | Richmond, VA | 1–0 | 1996 | Kao-Hsuing, Taiwan | Cranston, RI | 13–3 |
| 1969 | Taipei, Taiwan | Santa Clara, CA | 5–0 | 1997 | Guadalupe, Mex. | Mission Viejo, CA | 5–4 |
| 1970 | Wayne, NJ | Campbell, CA | 2–0 | 1998 | Toms River, NJ | Kashima, Japan | 12–9 |
| 1971 | Tainan, Taiwan | Gary, IN | 12–3 | 1999 | Osaka, Japan | Phenix City, AL | 5–0 |
| 1972 | Taipei, Taiwan | Hammond, IN | 6–0 | 2000 | Maracaibo, Venez. | Bellaire, TX | 3–2 |
| 1973 | Tainan City, Taiwan | Tucson, AZ | 12–0 | 2001 | Tokyo, Japan | Apopka, FL | 2–1 |
| 1974 | Kao-Hsuing, Taiwan | El Cajun, CA | 7–2 | | | | |

*Long Beach declared a 6–0 winner after the international tournament committee determined that Zamboanga City had used players that were not within its city limits.

# Motor Boat Racing

## American Power Boat Association Gold Cup Champions

| Year | Boat | Driver | Avg MPH | Year | Boat | Driver | Avg MPH |
|------|------|--------|---------|------|------|--------|---------|
| 1904 | Standard (June) | Carl Riotte | 23.160 | 1955 | Gale V | Lee Schoenith | 99.552 |
| 1904 | Vingt-et-Un II (Sep) | W. Sharpe Kilmer | 24.900 | 1956 | Miss Thriftaway | Bill Muncey | 96.552 |
| 1905 | Chip I | J. Wainwright | 15.000 | 1957 | Miss Thriftaway | Bill Muncey | 101.787 |
| 1906 | Chip II | J. Wainwright | 25.000 | 1958 | Hawaii Kai III | Jack Regas | 103.000 |
| 1907 | Chip II | J. Wainwright | 23.903 | 1959 | Maverick | Bill Stead | 104.481 |
| 1908 | Dixie II | E.J. Schroeder | 29.938 | 1960 | No race | — | — |
| 1909 | Dixie II | E.J. Schroeder | 29.590 | 1961 | Miss Century 21 | Bill Muncey | 99.678 |
| 1910 | Dixie III | F.K. Burnham | 32.473 | 1962 | Miss Century 21 | Bill Muncey | 100.710 |
| 1911 | MIT II | J.H. Hayden | 37.000 | 1963 | Miss Bardahl | Ron Musson | 105.124 |
| 1912 | P.D.Q. II | A.G. Miles | 39.462 | 1964 | Miss Bardahl | Ron Musson | 103.433 |
| 1913 | Ankle Deep | Cas Mankowski | 42.779 | 1965 | Miss Bardahl | Ron Musson | 103.132 |
| 1914 | Baby Speed Demon II | Jim Blackton & Bob Edgren | 48.458 | 1966 | Tahoe Miss | Mira Slovak | 93.019 |
| 1915 | Miss Detroit | Johnny Milot & Jack Beebe | 37.656 | 1967 | Miss Bardahl | Bill Shumacher | 101.484 |
| | | | | 1968 | Miss Bardahl | Bill Shumacher | 108.173 |
| 1916 | Miss Minneapolis | Bernard Smith | 48.860 | 1969 | Miss Budweiser | Bill Sterett | 98.504 |
| 1917 | Miss Detroit II | Gar Wood | 54.410 | 1970 | Miss Budweiser | Dean Chenoweth | 99.562 |
| 1918 | Miss Detroit II | Gar Wood | 51.619 | | | | |
| 1919 | Miss Detroit III | Gar Wood | 42.748 | 1971 | Miss Madison | Jim McCormick | 98.043 |
| 1920 | Miss America I | Gar Wood | 62.022 | 1972 | Atlas Van Lines | Bill Muncey | 104.277 |
| 1921 | Miss America I | Gar Wood | 52.825 | 1973 | Miss Budweiser | Dean Chenoweth | 99.043 |
| 1922 | Packard Chriscraft | J.G. Vincent | 40.253 | | | | |
| 1923 | Packard Chriscraft | Caleb Bragg | 43.867 | 1974 | Pay 'n Pak | George Henley | 104.428 |
| 1924 | Baby Bootlegger | Caleb Bragg | 45.302 | 1975 | Pay 'n Pak | George Henley | 108.921 |
| 1925 | Baby Bootlegger | Caleb Bragg | 47.240 | 1976 | Miss U.S. | Tom D'Eath | 100.412 |
| 1926 | Greenwich Folly | George Townsend | 47.984 | 1977 | Atlas Van Lines | Bill Muncey | 111.822 |
| | | | | 1978 | Atlas Van Lines | Bill Muncey | 111.412 |
| 1927 | Greenwich Folly | George Townsend | 47.662 | 1979 | Atlas Van Lines | Bill Muncey | 100.765 |
| | | | | 1980 | Miss Budweiser | Dean Chenoweth | 106.932 |
| 1928 | No race | | | | | | |
| 1929 | Imp | Richard Hoyt | 48.662 | 1981 | Miss Budweiser | Dean Chenoweth | 116.932 |
| 1930 | Hotsy Totsy | Vic Kliesrath | 52.673 | | | | |
| 1931 | Hotsy Totsy | Vic Kliesrath | 53.602 | 1982 | Atlas Van Lines | Chip Hanauer | 120.050 |
| 1932 | Delphine IV | Bill Horn | 57.775 | 1983 | Atlas Van Lines | Chip Hanauer | 118.507 |
| 1933 | El Lagarto | George Reis | 56.260 | 1984 | Atlas Van Lines | Chip Hanauer | 130.175 |
| 1934 | El Lagarto | George Reis | 55.000 | 1985 | Miller American | Chip Hanauer | 120.643 |
| 1935 | El Lagarto | George Reis | 55.056 | 1986 | Miller American | Chip Hanauer | 116.523 |
| 1936 | Impshi | Kaye Don | 45.735 | 1987 | Miller American | Chip Hanauer | 127.620 |
| 1937 | Notre Dame | Clell Perry | 63.675 | 1988 | Miss Circus Circus | Chip Hanauer & Jim Prevost | 123.756 |
| 1938 | Alagi | Theo Rossi | 64.340 | | | | |
| 1939 | My Sin | Z.G. Simmons Jr. | 66.133 | 1989 | Miss Budweiser | Tom D'Eath | 131.209 |
| 1940 | Hotsy Totsy III | Sidney Allen | 48.295 | 1990 | Miss Budweiser | Tom D'Eath | 143.176 |
| 1941 | My Sin | Z.G. Simmons Jr. | 52.509 | 1991 | Winston Eagle | Mark Tate | 137.771 |
| 1942–45 | | No race | — | 1992 | Miss Budweiser | Chip Hanauer | 136.282 |
| 1946 | Tempo VI | Guy Lombardo | 68.132 | 1993 | Miss Budweiser | Chip Hanauer | 141.195 |
| 1947 | Miss Peps V | Danny Foster | 57.000 | 1994 | Smokin' Joe Camel | Mark Tate | 145.260 |
| 1948 | Miss Great Lakes | Danny Foster | 46.845 | 1995 | Miss Budweiser | Chip Hanauer | 149.160 |
| 1949 | My Sweetie | Bill Cantrell | 73.612 | 1996 | PICO American Dream | Dave Villwock | 149.328 |
| 1950 | Slo-Mo-Shun IV | Ted Jones | 78.216 | 1997 | Miss Budweiser | Dave Villwock | 129.366 |
| 1951 | Slo-Mo-Shun V | Lou Fageol | 90.871 | 1998 | Miss Budweiser | Dave Villwock | 140.309 |
| 1952 | Slo-Mo-Shun IV | Stan Dollar | 79.923 | 1999 | Miss PICO | Chip Hanauer | 152.591 |
| 1953 | Slo-Mo-Shun IV | Joe Taggart & Lou Fageol | 99.108 | 2000 | Miss Budweiser | Dave Villwock | 162.850 |
| 1954 | Slo-Mo-Shun IV | Joe Taggart & Lou Fageol | 92.613 | 2001 | Miss Tubby's Subs | Michael Hanson | 140.519 |

## Unlimited Hydroplane Racing Association Annual Champion Drivers

| Year | Driver | Boat | Wins | Year | Driver | Boat | Wins |
|------|--------|------|------|------|--------|------|------|
| 1947 | Danny Foster | Miss Peps V | 6 | 1976 | Bill Muncey | Atlas Van Lines | 5 |
| 1948 | Dan Arena | Such Crust | 2 | 1977 | Mickey Remund | Miss Budweiser | 3 |
| 1949 | Bill Cantrell | My Sweetie | 7 | 1978 | Bill Muncey | Atlas Van Lines | 6 |
| 1950 | Dan Foster | Such Crust/DaphneX | 2 | 1979 | Bill Muncey | Atlas Van Lines | 7 |
| 1951 | Chuck Thompson | Miss Pepsi | 5 | 1980 | Dean Chenoweth | Miss Budweiser | 5 |
| 1952 | Chuck Thompson | Miss Pepsi | 3 | 1981 | Dean Chenoweth | Miss Budweiser | 6 |
| 1953 | Lee Schoenith | Gale II | 1 | 1982 | Chip Hanauer | Atlas Van Lines | 5 |
| 1954 | Lee Schoenith | Gale V | 4 | 1983 | Chip Hanauer | Atlas Van Lines | 3 |
| 1955 | Lee Schoenith | Gale V/Wha Hoppen | 1 | 1984 | Jim Kropfeld | Miss Budweiser | 6 |
| 1956 | Russ Schleeh | Shanty I | 3 | 1985 | Chip Hanauer | Miller American | 5 |
| 1957 | Jack Regas | Hawaii Kai III | 5 | 1986 | Jim Kropfeld | Miss Budweiser | 3 |
| 1958 | Mira Slovak | Bardah/Miss Buren | 3 | 1987 | Jim Kropfeld | Miss Budweiser | 5 |
| 1959 | Bill Stead | Maverick | 5 | 1988 | Tom D'Eath | Miss Budweiser | 4 |
| 1960 | Bill Muncey | Miss Thriftway | 4 | 1989 | Chip Hanauer | Miss Circus Circus | 3 |
| 1961 | Bill Muncey | Miss Century 21 | 4 | 1990 | Chip Hanauer | Miss Circus Circus | 6 |
| 1962 | Bill Muncey | Miss Century 21 | 5 | 1991 | Mark Tate | Winston/Oberto | 3 |
| 1963 | Bill Cantrell | Gale V | 0 | 1992 | Chip Hanauer | Miss Budweiser | 7 |
| 1964 | Ron Musson | Miss Bardahl | 4 | 1993 | Chip Hanauer | Miss Budweiser | 7 |
| 1965 | Ron Musson | Miss Bardahl | 4 | 1994 | Mark Tate | Smokin' Joe Camel | 2 |
| 1966 | Mira Slovak | Tahoe Miss | 4 | 1995 | Mark Tate | Smokin' Joe Camel | 4 |
| 1967 | Bill Schumacher | Miss Bardahl | 6 | 1996 | Dave Villwock | PICO American Dream | 6 |
| 1968 | Bill Schumacher | Miss Bardahl | 4 | 1997 | Mark Tate | Close Call | 1 |
| 1969 | Bill Sterett Sr. | Miss Budweiser | 4 | 1998 | Dave Villwock | Miss Budweiser | 8 |
| 1970 | Dean Chenoweth | Miss Budweiser | 4 | 1999 | Dave Villwock | Miss Budweiser | 8 |
| 1971 | Dean Chenoweth | Miss Budweiser | 2 | 2000 | Dave Villwock | Miss Budweiser | 6 |
| 1972 | Bill Muncey | Atlas Van Lines | 6 | 2001 | Dave Villwock | Miss Budweiser | 1 |
| 1973 | Mickey Remund | Pay 'n Pak | 4 | | | | |
| 1974 | George Henley | Pay 'n Pak | 7 | | | | |
| 1975 | Billy Schumacher | Weisfield's | 2 | | | | |

## Unlimited Hydroplane Racing Association Annual Champion Boats

| Year | Boat | Owner | Wins | Year | Boat | Owner | Wins |
|------|------|-------|------|------|------|-------|------|
| 1970 | Miss Budweiser | Little-Friedkin | 4 | 1987 | Miss Budweiser | Bernie Little | 5 |
| 1971 | Miss Budweiser | Little-Friedkin | 2 | 1988 | Miss Budweiser | Bernie Little | 4 |
| 1972 | Atlas Van Lines | Joe Schoenith | 6 | 1989 | Miss Budweiser | Bernie Little | 4 |
| 1973 | Pay 'n Pak | Dave Heerensperger | 4 | 1990 | Miss Circus Circus | Bill Bennett | 6 |
| 1974 | Pay 'n Pak | Dave Heerensperger | 7 | 1991 | Miss Budweiser | Bernie Little | 4 |
| 1975 | Pay 'n Pak | Dave Heerensperger | 5 | 1992 | Miss Budweiser | Bernie Little | 7 |
| 1976 | Atlas Van Lines | Bill Muncey | 5 | 1993 | Miss Budweiser | Bernie Little | 7 |
| 1977 | Miss Budweiser | Bernie Little | 3 | 1994 | Miss Budweiser | Bernie Little | 4 |
| 1978 | Atlas Van Lines | Bill Muncey | 6 | 1995 | Miss Budweiser | Bernie Little | 5 |
| 1979 | Atlas Van Lines | Bill Muncey | 7 | 1996 | PICO Amer. Dream | Fred Leland | 6 |
| 1980 | Miss Budweiser | Bernie Little | 5 | 1997 | Miss Budweiser | Bernie Little | 5 |
| 1981 | Miss Budweiser | Bernie Little | 6 | 1998 | Miss Budweiser | Bernie Little | 8 |
| 1982 | Atlas Van Lines | Fran Muncey | 5 | 1999 | Miss Budweiser | Bernie Little | 8 |
| 1983 | Atlas Van Lines | Muncey-Lucero | 3 | 2000 | Miss Budweiser | Bernie Little | 6 |
| 1984 | Miss Budweiser | Bernie Little | 6 | 2001 | Miss Budweiser | Bernie Little | 1 |
| 1985 | Miller American | Muncey-Lucero | 5 | | | | |
| 1986 | Miss Budweiser | Bernie Little | 3 | | | | |

# Polo

## United States Open Polo Champions

| | | | |
|---|---|---|---|
| 1904 ......Wanderers | 1934 ......Templeton | 1961 ......Milwaukee | 1983 ......Ft. Lauderdale |
| 1905–09..Not contested | 1935 ......Greentree | 1962 ......Santa Barbara | 1984 ......Retama |
| 1910 ......Ranelagh | 1936 ......Greentree | 1963 ......Tulsa | 1985 ......Carter Ranch |
| 1911 ......Not contested | 1937 ......Old Westbury | 1964 ......Concar Oak | 1986 ......Retama II |
| 1912 ......Cooperstown | 1938 ......Old Westbury | Brook | 1987 ......Aloha |
| 1913 ......Cooperstown | 1939 ......Bostwick Field | 1965 ......Oak Brook– | 1988 ......Les Diables |
| 1914 ......Meadow Brook | 1940 ......Aknusti | Santa Barbara | Bleus |
| Magpies | 1941 ......Gulf Stream | 1966 ......Tulsa | 1989 ......Les Diables |
| 1915 ......Not contested | 1942–45...Not contested | 1967 ......Bunntyco– | Bleus |
| 1916 ......Meadow Brook | 1946 ......Mexico | Oak Brook | 1990 ......Les Diables |
| 1917–18..Not contested | 1947 ......Old Westbury | 1968 ......Midland | Bleus |
| 1919 ......Meadow Brook | 1948 ......Hurricanes | 1969 ......Tulsa Greenhill | 1991 ......Grant's Farm |
| 1920 ......Meadow Brook | 1949 ......Hurricanes | 1970 ......Tulsa Greenhill | Manor |
| 1921 ......Great Neck | 1950 ......Bostwick | 1971 ......Oak Brook | 1992 ......Hanalei Bay |
| 1922 ......Argentine | 1951 ......Milwaukee | 1972 ......Milwaukee | 1993 ......Gehache |
| 1923 ......Meadow Brook | 1952 ......Beverly Hills | 1973 ......Oak Brook | 1994 ......Aspen |
| 1924 ......Midwick | 1953 ......Meadow Brook | 1974 ......Milwaukee | 1995 ......Outback |
| 1925 ......Orange County | 1954 ......C.C.C.– | 1975 ......Milwaukee | 1996 ......Outback |
| 1926 ......Hurricanes | Meadow Brook | 1976 ......Willow Bend | 1997 ......Isla Carroll |
| 1927 ......Sands Point | 1955 ......C.C.C. | 1977 ......Retama | 1998 ......Esque |
| 1928 ......Meadow Brook | 1956 ......Brandywine | 1978 ......Abercrombie & | 1999 ......Outback |
| 1929 ......Hurricanes | 1957 ......Detroit | Kent | 2000 ......Outback |
| 1930 ......Hurricanes | 1958 ......Dallas | 1979 ......Retama | 2001 ......Outback |
| 1931 ......Santa Paula | 1959 ......Circle F | 1980 ......Southern Hills | |
| 1932 ......Templeton | 1960 ......Oak Brook– | 1981 ......Rolex A & K | |
| 1933 ......Aurora | C.C.C. | 1982 ......Retama | |

## Top-Ranked Players

The United States Polo Association ranks its registered players from minus 2 to plus 10 goals, with 10-Goal players being the game's best. At present, the USPA recognizes ten 10-Goal and seven 9-Goal players:

### 10-GOAL

Mariano Aguerre (Greenwich)
Michael Azzaro (San Antonio)
Adolfo Cambiaso (Palm Beach)
Guillermo Gracida Jr. (Palm Beach)
Bautista Heguy (Palm Beach)
Ignacio Heguy (Palm Beach)
Eduardo Heguy (Palm Beach)
Marcos Heguy (Palm Beach)
Sebastian Merlos (Aiken)
Juan Ignacio Merlos (Aiken)

### 9-GOAL

Javier Novillo Astrada (Palm Beach)
Miguel Novillo Astrada (Palm Beach)
Lucas Criado (Palm Beach)
Hector Galindo (Palm Beach)
Carlos Gracida (Palm Beach)
Alberto Heguy (Palm Beach)
Adam Snow (Langdon Road)

## Rodeo Days

Every December the Old West mixes it up with the gold-chain gang, and the result is pure Americana, a blend of patriotic fervor, nostalgia, prayer, danger, entertainment, big money and sports. The National Finals Rodeo in Las Vegas is 10 nights of the top cowboys on the best livestock competing for the biggest purses. The bucking events (bareback, saddle bronc and bull) become battles of attrition, as the cowboys' bodies begin to break down from the beating the animals dole out. By the last few performances, competitors with broken bones, separated shoulders and wired jaws are literally strapping themselves on. The bulls don't care how tired and sore the riders are, how near Christmas it is—they only want to buck them off. Then they want to kill them. The clowns try to prevent that. Bodies get thrown pretty high in the confusion. If all goes exactly right, the cowboy gets a paycheck at the end of the day. Usually he just gets applause. No contracts. No guarantees. No excuses.

—E.M. Swift

## Professional Rodeo Cowboys Association World Champions

### All-Around

| | | | |
|---|---|---|---|
| 1929....Earl Thode | 1949....Jim Shoulders | 1967....Larry Mahan | 1985....Lewis Feild |
| 1930....Clay Carr | 1950....Bill Linderman | 1968....Larry Mahan | 1986....Lewis Feild |
| 1931....John Schneider | 1951....Casey Tibbs | 1969....Larry Mahan | 1987....Lewis Feild |
| 1932....Donald Nesbit | 1952....Harry Tompkins | 1970....Larry Mahan | 1988....Dave Appleton |
| 1933....Clay Carr | 1953....Bill Linderman | 1971....Phil Lyne | 1989....Ty Murray |
| 1934....Leonard Ward | 1954....Buck Rutherford | 1972....Phil Lyne | 1990....Ty Murray |
| 1935....Everett Bowman | 1955....Casey Tibbs | 1973....Larry Mahan | 1991....Ty Murray |
| 1936....John Bowman | 1956....Jim Shoulders | 1974....Tom Ferguson | 1992....Ty Murray |
| 1937....Everett Bowman | 1957....Jim Shoulders | 1975....Tom Ferguson | 1993....Ty Murray |
| 1938....Burel Mulkey | 1958....Jim Shoulders | 1976....Tom Ferguson | 1994....Ty Murray |
| 1939....Paul Carney | 1959....Jim Shoulders | 1977....Tom Ferguson | 1995....Joe Beaver |
| 1940....Fritz Truan | 1960....Harry Tompkins | 1978....Tom Ferguson | 1996....Joe Beaver |
| 1941....Homer Pettigrew | 1961....Benny Reynolds | 1979....Tom Ferguson | 1997....Dan Mortensen |
| 1942....Gerald Roberts | 1962....Tom Nesmith | 1980....Paul Tierney | 1998....Ty Murray |
| 1943....Louis Brooks | 1963....Dean Oliver | 1981....Jimmie Cooper | 1999....Fred Whitfield |
| 1944....Louis Brooks | 1964....Dean Oliver | 1982....Chris Lybbert | 2000....Joe Beaver |
| 1947....Todd Whatley | 1965....Dean Oliver | 1983....Roy Cooper | |
| 1948....Gerald Roberts | 1966....Larry Mahan | 1984....Dee Picket | |

### Saddle Bronc Riding

| | | | |
|---|---|---|---|
| 1929....Earl Thode | 1949....Casey Tibbs | 1967....Shawn Davis | 1985....B. Gjermundson |
| 1930....Clay Carr | 1950....Bill Linderman | 1968....Shawn Davis | 1986....Bud Munroe |
| 1931....Earl Thode | 1951....Casey Tibbs | 1969....Bill Smith | 1987....Clint Johnson |
| 1932....Peter Knight | 1952....Casey Tibbs | 1970....Dennis Reiners | 1988....Clint Johnson |
| 1933....Peter Knight | 1953....Casey Tibbs | 1971....Bill Smith | 1989....Clint Johnson |
| 1934....Leonard Ward | 1954....Casey Tibbs | 1972....Mel Hyland | 1990....Robert Etbauer |
| 1935....Peter Knight | 1955....Deb Copenhaver | 1973....Bill Smith | 1991....Robert Etbauer |
| 1936....Peter Knight | 1956....Deb Copenhaver | 1974....John McBeth | 1992....Billy Etbauer |
| 1937....Burel Mulkey | 1957....Alvin Nelson | 1975....Monty Henson | 1993....Dan Mortensen |
| 1938....Burel Mulkey | 1958....Marty Wood | 1976....Monty Henson | 1994....Dan Mortensen |
| 1939....Fritz Truan | 1959....Casey Tibbs | 1977....Bobby Berger | 1995....Dan Mortensen |
| 1940....Fritz Truan | 1960....Enoch Walker | 1978....Joe Marvel | 1996....Billy Etbauer |
| 1941....Doff Aber | 1961....Winston Bruce | 1979....Bobby Berger | 1997....Dan Mortensen |
| 1942....Doff Aber | 1962....Kenny McLean | 1980....Clint Johnson | 1998....Dan Mortensen |
| 1943....Louis Brooks | 1963....Guy Weeks | 1981....B. Gjermundson | 1999....Billy Etbauer |
| 1944....Louis Brooks | 1964....Marty Wood | 1982....Monty Henson | 2000....Billy Etbauer |
| 1947....Carl Olson | 1965....Shawn Davis | 1983....B. Gjermundson | |
| 1948....Gene Pruett | 1966....Marty Wood | 1984....B. Gjermundson | |

### Bareback Riding

| | | | |
|---|---|---|---|
| 1932....Smoky Snyder | 1951....Casey Tibbs | 1968....Clyde Vamvoras | 1985....Lewis Feild |
| 1933....Nate Waldrum | 1952....Harry Tompkins | 1969....Gary Tucker | 1986....Lewis Feild |
| 1934....Leonard Ward | 1953....Eddy Akridge | 1970....Paul Mayo | 1987....Bruce Ford |
| 1935....Frank Schneider | 1954....Eddy Akridge | 1971....Joe Alexander | 1988....Marvin Garrett |
| 1936....Smoky Snyder | 1955....Eddy Akridge | 1972....Joe Alexander | 1989....Marvin Garrett |
| 1937....Paul Carney | 1956....Jim Shoulders | 1973....Joe Alexander | 1990....Chuck Logue |
| 1938....Pete Grubb | 1957....Jim Shoulders | 1974....Joe Alexander | 1991....Clint Corey |
| 1939....Paul Carney | 1958....Jim Shoulders | 1975....Joe Alexander | 1992....Wayne Herman |
| 1940....Carl Dossey | 1959....Jack Buschbom | 1976....Joe Alexander | 1993....Deb Greenough |
| 1941....George Mills | 1960....Jack Buschbom | 1977....Joe Alexander | 1994....Marvin Garrett |
| 1942....Louis Brooks | 1961....Eddy Akridge | 1978....Bruce Ford | 1995....Marvin Garrett |
| 1943....Bill Linderman | 1962....Ralph Buell | 1979....Bruce Ford | 1996....Mark Garrett |
| 1944....Louis Brooks | 1963....John Hawkins | 1980....Bruce Ford | 1997....Eric Mouton |
| 1947....Larry Finley | 1964....Jim Houston | 1981....J.C. Trujillo | 1998....Mark Gomes |
| 1948....Sonny Tureman | 1965....Jim Houston | 1982....Bruce Ford | 1999....Lan LaJeunesse |
| 1949....Jack Buschbom | 1966....Paul Mayo | 1983....Bruce Ford | 2000....Jeffrey Collins |
| 1950....Jim Shoulders | 1967....Clyde Vamvoras | 1984....Larry Peabody | |

### Professional Rodeo Cowboys Association World Champions *(Cont.)*

#### Bull Riding

| | | | |
|---|---|---|---|
| 1929....John Schneider | 1948....Harry Tompkins | 1967....Larry Mahan | 1986....Tuff Hedeman |
| 1930....John Schneider | 1949....Harry Tompkins | 1968....George Paul | 1987....Lane Frost |
| 1931....Smokey Snyder | 1950....Harry Tompkins | 1969....Doug Brown | 1988....Jim Sharp |
| 1932....John Schneider | 1951....Jim Shoulders | 1970....Gary Leffew | 1989....Tuff Hedeman |
| 1932....Smokey Snyder | 1952....Harry Tompkins | 1971....Bill Nelson | 1990....Jim Sharp |
|      John Schneider | 1953....Todd Whatley | 1972....John Quintana | 1991....Tuff Hedeman |
| 1933....Frank Schneider | 1954....Jim Shoulders | 1973....Bobby Steiner | 1992....Cody Custer |
| 1934....Frank Schneider | 1955....Jim Shoulders | 1974....Don Gay | 1993....Ty Murray |
| 1935....Smokey Snyder | 1956....Jim Shoulders | 1975....Don Gay | 1994....Daryl Mills |
| 1936....Smokey Snyder | 1957....Jim Shoulders | 1976....Don Gay | 1995....Jerome Davis |
| 1937....Smokey Snyder | 1958....Jim Shoulders | 1977....Don Gay | 1996....Terry West |
| 1938....Kid Fletcher | 1959....Jim Shoulders | 1978....Don Gay | 1997....Scott Mendes |
| 1939....Dick Griffith | 1960....Harry Tompkins | 1979....Don Gay | 1998....Ty Murray |
| 1940....Dick Griffith | 1961....Ronnie Rossen | 1980....Don Gay | 1999....Mike White |
| 1941....Dick Griffith | 1962....Freckles Brown | 1981....Don Gay | 2000....Cody Hancock |
| 1942....Dick Griffith | 1963....Bill Kornell | 1982....Charles Sampson | |
| 1943....Ken Roberts | 1964....Bob Wegner | 1983....Cody Snyder | |
| 1944....Ken Roberts | 1965....Larry Mahan | 1984....Don Gay | |
| 1947....Wag Blessing | 1966....Ronnie Rossen | 1985....Ted Nuce | |

#### Calf Roping

| | | | |
|---|---|---|---|
| 1929....Everett Bowman | 1949....Troy Fort | 1967....Glen Franklin | 1985....Joe Beaver |
| 1930....Jake McClure | 1950....Toots Mansfield | 1968....Glen Franklin | 1986....Chris Lybbert |
| 1931....Herb Meyers | 1951....Don McLaughlin | 1969....Dean Oliver | 1987....Joe Beaver |
| 1932....Richard Merchant | 1952....Don McLaughlin | 1970....Junior Garrison | 1988....Joe Beaver |
| 1933....Bill McFarlane | 1953....Don McLaughlin | 1971....Phil Lyne | 1989....Rabe Rabon |
| 1934....Irby Mundy | 1954....Don McLaughlin | 1972....Phil Lyne | 1990....Troy Pruitt |
| 1935....Everett Bowman | 1955....Dean Oliver | 1973....Ernie Taylor | 1991....Fred Whitfield |
| 1936....Clyde Burk | 1956....Ray Wharton | 1974....Tom Ferguson | 1992....Joe Beaver |
| 1937....Everett Bowman | 1957....Don McLaughlin | 1975....Jeff Copenhaver | 1993....Joe Beaver |
| 1938....Burel Mulkey | 1958....Dean Oliver | 1976....Roy Cooper | 1994....Herbert Theriot |
| 1939....Toots Mansfield | 1959....Jim Bob Altizer | 1977....Roy Cooper | 1995....Fred Whitfield |
| 1940....Toots Mansfield | 1960....Dean Oliver | 1978....Roy Cooper | 1996....Fred Whitfield |
| 1941....Toots Mansfield | 1961....Dean Oliver | 1979....Paul Tierney | 1997....Cody Ohl |
| 1942....Clyde Burk | 1962....Dean Oliver | 1980....Roy Cooper | 1998....Cody Ohl |
| 1943....Toots Mansfield | 1963....Dean Oliver | 1981....Roy Cooper | 1999....Fred Whitfield |
| 1944....Clyde Burk | 1964....Dean Oliver | 1982....Roy Cooper | 2000....Fred Whitfield |
| 1947....Troy Fort | 1965....Glen Franklin | 1983....Roy Cooper | |
| 1948....Toots Mansfield | 1966....Junior Garrison | 1984....Roy Cooper | |

#### Steer Wrestling

| | | | |
|---|---|---|---|
| 1929....Gene Ross | 1949....Bill McGuire | 1967....Roy Duvall | 1985....Ote Berry |
| 1930....Everett Bowman | 1950....Bill Linderman | 1968....Jack Roddy | 1986....Steve Duhon |
| 1931....Gene Ross | 1951....Dub Phillips | 1969....Roy Duvall | 1987....Steve Duhon |
| 1932....Hugh Bennett | 1952....Harley May | 1970....John W. Jones | 1988....John W. Jones |
| 1933....Everett Bowman | 1953....Ross Dollarhide | 1971....Billy Hale | 1989....John W. Jones |
| 1934....Shorty Ricker | 1954....James Bynum | 1972....Roy Duvall | 1990....Ote Berry |
| 1935....Everett Bowman | 1955....Benny Combs | 1973....Bob Marshall | 1991....Ote Berry |
| 1936....Jack Kerschner | 1956....Harley May | 1974....Tommy Puryear | 1992....Mark Roy |
| 1937....Gene Ross | 1957....Clark McEntire | 1975....F. Shepperson | 1993....Steve Duhon |
| 1938....Everett Bowman | 1958....James Bynum | 1976....Tom Ferguson | 1994....Blaine Pederson |
| 1939....Harry Hart | 1959....Harry Charters | 1977....Larry Ferguson | 1995....Ote Berry |
| 1940....Homer Pettigrew | 1960....Bob A. Robinson | 1978....Byron Walker | 1996....Chad Bedell |
| 1941....Hub Whiteman | 1961....Jim Bynum | 1979....Stan Williamson | 1997....Brad Gleason |
| 1942....Homer Pettigrew | 1962....Tom Nesmith | 1980....Butch Myers | 1998....Mike Smith |
| 1943....Homer Pettigrew | 1963....Jim Bynum | 1981....Byron Walker | 1999....Mickey Gee |
| 1944....Homer Pettigrew | 1964....C.R. Boucher | 1982....Stan Williamson | 2000....Frank Thompson |
| 1947....Todd Whatley | 1965....Harley May | 1983....Joel Edmondson | |
| 1948....Homer Pettigrew | 1966....Jack Roddy | 1984....John W. Jones | |

## Professional Rodeo Cowboys Association World Champions *(Cont.)*

### Team Roping

| | | |
|---|---|---|
| 1929....Charles Maggini | 1949....Ed Yanez | 1969....Jerold Camarillo | 1989....Jake Barnes |
| 1930....Norman Cowan | 1950....Buck Sorrels | 1970....John Miller | 1990....Allen Bach |
| 1931....Arthur Beloat | 1951....Olan Sims | 1971....John Miller | 1991....Bob Harris |
| 1932....Ace Gardner | 1952....Asbury Schell | 1972....Leo Camarillo | 1992....Clay O. Cooper |
| 1933....Roy Adams | 1953....Ben Johnson | 1973....Leo Camarillo | 1993....Bobby Hurley |
| 1934....Andy Jauregui | 1954....Eddie Schell | 1974....H.P. Evetts | 1994....Jake Barnes |
| 1935....Lawrence Conltk | 1955....Vern Castro | 1975....Leo Camarillo |  Clay O. Cooper |
| 1936....John Rhodes | 1956....Dale Smith | 1976....Leo Camarillo | 1995....Bobby Hurley |
| 1937....Asbury Schell | 1957....Dale Smith | 1977....Jerold Camarillo |  Allen Bach |
| 1938....John Rhodes | 1958....Ted Ashworth | 1978....Doyle Gellerman | 1996....Steve Purcella |
| 1939....Asbury Schell | 1959....Jim Rodriguez Jr. | 1979....Allen Bach |  Steve Northcott |
| 1940....Pete Grubb | 1960....Jim Rodriguez Jr. | 1980....Tee Woolman | 1997....Speed Williams |
| 1941....Jim Hudson | 1961....Al Hooper | 1981....Walt Woodard |  Rich Skelton |
| 1942....Verne Castro | 1962....Jim Rodriguez Jr. | 1982....Tee Woolman | 1998....Speed Williams |
|  Vic Castro | 1963....Les Hirdes | 1983....Leo Camarillo |  Rich Skelton |
| 1943....Mark Hull | 1964....Bill Hamilton | 1984....Dee Pickett | 1999....Speed Williams |
|  Leonard Block | 1965....Jim Rodriguez Jr. | 1985....Jake Barnes |  Rich Skelton |
| 1944....Murphy Chaney | 1966....Ken Luman | 1986....Clay O. Cooper | 2000....Speed Williams |
| 1947....Jim Brister | 1967....Joe Glenn | 1987....Clay O. Cooper |  Rich Skelton |
| 1948....Joe Glenn | 1968....Art Arnold | 1988....Jake Barnes | |

### Steer Roping

| | | |
|---|---|---|
| 1929....Charles Maggini | 1948....Everett Shaw | 1967....Jim Bob Altizer | 1986....Jim Davis |
| 1930....Clay Carr | 1949....Shoat Webster | 1968....Sonny Davis | 1987....Shaun Burchett |
| 1931....Andy Jauregui | 1950....Shoat Webster | 1969....Walter Arnold | 1988....Shaun Burchett |
| 1932....George Weir | 1951....Everett Shaw | 1970....Don McLaughlin | 1989....Guy Allen |
| 1933....John Bowman | 1952....Buddy Neal | 1971....Olin Young | 1990....Phil Lyne |
| 1934....John McEntire | 1953....Ike Rude | 1972....Allen Keller | 1991....Guy Allen |
| 1935....Richard Merchant | 1954....Shoat Webster | 1973....Roy Thompson | 1992....Guy Allen |
| 1936....John Bowman | 1955....Shoat Webster | 1974....Olin Young | 1993....Guy Allen |
| 1937....Everett Bowman | 1956....Jim Snively | 1975....Roy Thompson | 1994....Guy Allen |
| 1938....Hugh Bennett | 1957....Clark McEntire | 1976....Marvin Cantrell | 1995....Guy Allen |
| 1939....Dick Truitt | 1958....Clark McEntire | 1977....Buddy Cockrell | 1996....Guy Allen |
| 1940....Clay Carr | 1959....Everett Shaw | 1978....Sonny Worrell | 1997....Guy Allen |
| 1941....Ike Rude | 1960....Don McLaughlin | 1979....Gary Good | 1998....Guy Allen |
| 1942....King Merrit | 1961....Clark McEntire | 1980....Guy Allen | 1999....Guy Allen |
| 1943....Tom Rhodes | 1962....Everett Shaw | 1981....Arnold Felts | 2000....Guy Allen |
| 1944....Tom Rhodes | 1963....Don McLaughlin | 1982....Guy Allen | |
| 1945....Everett Shaw | 1964....Sonny Davis | 1983....Roy Cooper | |
| 1946....Everett Shaw | 1965....Sonney Wright | 1984....Guy Allen | |
| 1947....Ike Rude | 1966....Sonny Davis | 1985....Jim Davis | |

Note: In 1945–46 champions were crowned only in Steer Roping.

# Rowing

## National Collegiate Rowing Champions

### MEN'S EIGHT

| | | |
|---|---|---|
| 1985 ...............Harvard | 1991 ...............Pennsylvania | 1997 ...............Washington |
| 1986 ...............Wisconsin | 1992 ...............Harvard | 1998 ...............Princeton |
| 1987 ...............Harvard | 1993 ...............Brown | 1999 ...............California |
| 1988 ...............Harvard | 1994 ...............Brown | 2000 ...............California |
| 1989 ...............Harvard | 1995 ...............Brown | 2001 ...............California |
| 1990 ...............Wisconsin | 1996 ...............Princeton | |

### WOMEN'S EIGHT

| | | |
|---|---|---|
| 1979 ...............Yale | 1987 ...............Washington | 1995 ...............Princeton |
| 1980 ...............California | 1988 ...............Washington | 1996 ...............Brown |
| 1981 ...............Washington | 1989 ...............Cornell | 1997 ...............Washington |
| 1982 ...............Washington | 1990 ...............Princeton | 1998 ...............Washington |
| 1983 ...............Washington | 1991 ...............Boston University | 1999 ...............Brown |
| 1984 ...............Washington | 1992 ...............Boston University | 2000 ...............Brown |
| 1985 ...............Washington | 1993 ...............Princeton | 2001 ...............Washington |
| 1986 ...............Wisconsin | 1994 ...............Princeton | |

# Rugby Union

## National Men's Club Championship

| Year | Winner | Runner-Up | Year | Winner | Runner-Up |
|------|--------|-----------|------|--------|-----------|
| 1979 | Old Blues (CA) | St. Louis Falcons | 1991 | Old Mission Beach AC | Washington |
| 1980 | Old Blues (CA) | St. Louis Falcons | 1992 | Old Blues (CA) | Mystic River (MA) |
| 1981 | Old Blues (CA) | Old Blue (NY) | 1993 | Old Mission Beach AC | Milwaukee |
| 1982 | Old Blues (CA) | Denver Barbos | 1994 | Old Mission Beach AC | Life College (GA) |
| 1983 | Old Blues (CA) | Dallas Harlequins | 1995 | Potomac Athletic Club | Old Mission Beach |
| 1984 | Dallas Harlequins | Los Angeles | 1996 | Old Mission Beach AC | Old Blues (CA) |
| 1985 | Milwaukee | Denver Barbos | 1997 | Gentlemen of Aspen | Old Blue (NY) |
| 1986 | Old Blues (CA) | Old Blue (NY) | 1998 | Gentlemen of Aspen | Old Blue (NY) |
| 1987 | Old Blues (CA) | Pittsburgh | 1999 | Gentlemen of Aspen | Golden Gate (CA) |
| 1988 | Old Mission Beach AC | Milwaukee | 2000 | Gentlemen of Aspen | Hayward Griffins |
| 1989 | Old Mission Beach AC | Philly/Whitemarsh | 2001 | San Mateo | New York AC |
| 1990 | Denver Barbos | Old Blues (CA) | | | |

## National Men's Collegiate Championship

| Year | Winner | Runner-Up | Year | Winner | Runner-Up |
|------|--------|-----------|------|--------|-----------|
| 1980 | California | Air Force | 1992 | California | Army |
| 1981 | California | Harvard | 1993 | California | Air Force |
| 1982 | California | Life College | 1994 | California | Navy |
| 1983 | California | Air Force | 1995 | California | Air Force |
| 1984 | Harvard | Colorado | 1996 | California | Penn St |
| 1985 | California | Maryland | 1997 | California | Penn St |
| 1986 | California | Dartmouth | 1998 | California | Stanford |
| 1987 | San Diego State | Air Force | 1999 | California | Penn St |
| 1988 | California | Dartmouth | 2000 | California | Wyoming |
| 1989 | Air Force | Long Beach | 2001 | California | Penn St |
| 1990 | Air Force | Army | | | |
| 1991 | California | Army | | | |

## World Cup Championship

| Year | Winner | Runner-Up | Year | Winner | Runner-Up |
|------|--------|-----------|------|--------|-----------|
| 1987 | New Zealand | France | 1995 | South Africa | New Zealand |
| 1991 | Australia | England | 1999 | Australia | France |

# Rugby League

## American National Rugby League Champions

| Year | Winner | Runner-Up |
|------|--------|-----------|
| 1998 | Glen Mills Bulls | Philadelphia Bulldogs |
| 1999 | Glen Mills Bulls | New Jersey Sharks |
| 2000 | Glen Mills Bulls | Philadelphia Fight |
| 2001 | Glen Mills Bulls | Media Mantarays |

## World Cup Championship

| Year | Winner | Runner-Up | Host |
|------|--------|-----------|------|
| 1954 | Great Britain | France | France |
| 1957 | Australia | International Team | Australia |
| 1960 | Great Britain | International Team | England |
| 1968 | Australia | France | Australia–New Zealand |
| 1970 | Great Britain | Australia | England |
| 1972 | Australia | Great Britain | France |
| 1975 | Australia | England | Worldwide |
| 1977 | Australia | Great Britain | Australia–New Zealand |
| 1985–88 | Australia | New Zealand | Worldwide |
| 1989–92 | Australia | Great Britain | Worldwide |
| 1995 | Australia | England | Great Britain |
| 2000 | Australia | New Zealand | G Britain-Ireland-France |

# Sailing

## America's Cup Champions

### SCHOONERS AND J-CLASS BOATS

| Year | Winner | Skipper | Series | Loser | Skipper |
|------|--------|---------|--------|-------|---------|
| 1851 | America | Richard Brown | | | |
| 1870 | Magic | Andrew Comstock | 1–0 | Cambria, Great Britain | J. Tannock |
| 1871 | Columbia (2–1) | Nelson Comstock | 4–1 | Livonia, Great Britain | J.H. Woods |
| | Sappho (2–0) | Sam Greenwood | | | |
| 1876 | Madeleine | Josephus Williams | 2–0 | Countess of Dufferin, Canada | J.E. Ellsworth |
| 1881 | Mischief | Nathanael Clock | 2–0 | Atalanta, Canada | Alexander Cuthbert |
| 1885 | Puritan | Aubrey Crocker | 2–0 | Genesta, Great Britain | John Carter |
| 1886 | Mayflower | Martin Stone | 2–0 | Galatea, Great Britain | Dan Bradford |
| 1887 | Volunteer | Henry Haff | 2–0 | Thistle, Great Britain | John Barr |
| 1893 | Vigilant | William Hansen | 3–0 | Valkyrie II, Great Britain | William Granfield |
| 1895 | Defender | Henry Haff | 3–0 | Valkyrie III, Great Britain | William Granfield |
| 1899 | Columbia | Charles Barr | 3–0 | Shamrock I, Great Britain | Archie Hogarth |
| 1901 | Columbia | Charles Barr | 3–0 | Shamrock II, Great Britain | E.A. Sycamore |
| 1903 | Reliance | Charles Barr | 3–0 | Shamrock III, Great Britain | Bob Wringe |
| 1920 | Resolute | Charles F. Adams | 3–2 | Shamrock IV, Great Britain | William Burton |
| 1930 | Enterprise | Harold Vanderbilt | 4–0 | Shamrock V, Great Britain | Ned Heard |
| 1934 | Rainbow | Harold Vanderbilt | 4–2 | Endeavour, Great Britain | T.O.M. Sopwith |
| 1937 | Ranger | Harold Vanderbilt | 4–0 | Endeavour II, Great Britain | T.O.M. Sopwith |

### 12-METER BOATS

| Year | Winner | Skipper | Series | Loser | Skipper |
|------|--------|---------|--------|-------|---------|
| 1958 | Columbia | Briggs Cunningham | 4–0 | Sceptre, Great Britain | Graham Mann |
| 1962 | Weatherly | Bus Mosbacher | 4–1 | Gretel, Australia | Jock Sturrock |
| 1964 | Constellation | Bob Bavier & Eric Ridder | 4–0 | Sovereign, Australia | Peter Scott |
| 1967 | Intrepid | Bus Mosbacher | 4–0 | Dame Pattie, Australia | Jock Sturrock |
| 1970 | Intrepid | Bill Ficker | 4–1 | Gretel II, Australia | Jim Hardy |
| 1974 | Courageous | Ted Hood | 4–0 | Southern Cross, Australia | John Cuneo |
| 1977 | Courageous | Ted Turner | 4–0 | Australia | Noel Robins |
| 1980 | Freedom | Dennis Conner | 4–1 | Australia | Jim Hardy |
| 1983 | Australia II | John Bertrand | 4–3 | Liberty, United States | Dennis Conner |
| 1987 | Stars & Stripes | Dennis Conner | 4–0 | Kookaburra III, Australia | Iain Murray |

### 60-FOOT CATAMARAN vs 133-FOOT MONOHULL

| Year | Winner | Skipper | Series | Loser | Skipper |
|------|--------|---------|--------|-------|---------|
| 1988 | Stars & Stripes | Dennis Conner | 2–0 | New Zealand | David Barnes |

### 75-FOOT MONOHULL (IACC)

| Year | Winner | Skipper | Series | Loser | Skipper |
|------|--------|---------|--------|-------|---------|
| 1992 | America[3] | Bill Koch | 4–1 | Il Moro di Venezia, Italy | Paul Cayard |
| 1995 | Black Magic I | Russell Coutts | 5–0 | Young America, United States | Dennis Conner |
| 2000 | New Zealand | Russell Coutts | 5–0 | Luna Rossa, Italy | Francesco de Angelis |

Note: Winning entries have been from the United States every year but three: In 1983 an Australian vessel won, and in 1995 and 2000 a vessel from New Zealand won.

# Shooting World Champions

## Men

### 50M FREE RIFLE PRONE
1947 .....O. Sannes, Norway
1949 .....A.C. Jackson, U.S.
1952 .....A.C. Jackson, U.S.
1954 .....G. Boa, Canada
1958 .....M. Nordquist
1962 .....K. Wenk, W Germany
1966 .....D. Boyd, U.S.
1970 .....M. Fiess, S. Africa
1974 .....K. Bulan, Czechoslovakia
1978 .....A. Allan, Great Britain
1982 .....V. Danilschenko, USSR
1986 .....S. Bereczky, Hungary
1990 .....V. Bochkarev, USSR
1994 .....Venjie Li, China
1998 .....Thomas Tamas, U.S.
1999 .....Thomas Tamas, U.S.
2000 .....Siarhei Martynau, Belarus

### AIR RIFLE
1966 .....G. Kümmet, W Germany
1970 .....G. Kusterman, W Germ.
1974 .....E. Pedzisz, Poland
1978 .....O. Schlipf, W. Germany
1979 .....K. Hillenbrand
1981 .....F. Bessy, France
1982 .....F. Rettkowski, E Germ.
1983 .....P. Heberle, France
1985 .....P. Heberle, France
1986 .....H. Riederer, W Germany
1987 .....K. Ivanov, USSR
1989 .....J. P. Amet, France
1990 .....H. Riederer, W Germany
1994 .....Boris Polak, Israel
1998 .....Artem Khadjibekov, Russia
1999 .....Jozef Gonci, Slovakia
2000 .....Artem Khadjibekov, Russia

### THREE POSITION RIFLE
1966 .....M. Thompson, U.S.
1970 .....M. Thompson Murdock, U.S.
1974 .....A. Pelova, Bulgaria
1978 .....W. Oliver, U.S.
1982 .....M. Helbig, E Germany
1986 .....V. Letcheva, Bulgaria
1990 .....V. Letcheva, Bulgaria
1994 .....A. Maloukhina, Russia
1998 .....Sonja Pfeilschifter, Germany
1999 .....Sonja Pfeilschifter, Germany
2000 .....Hong Shan, China

### AIR RIFLE
1970 .....V. Cherkasque, USSR
1974 .....T. Ratkinova, USSR
1978 .....W. Oliver, U.S.
1979 .....K. Monez, U.S.
1981 .....S. Romaristova, USSR
1982 .....S. Lang, W Germany
1983 .....M. Helbig, E Germany
1985 .....E. Forian, Hungary
1986 .....V. Letcheva, Bulgaria
1987 .....V. Letcheva, Bulgaria
1989 .....V. Letcheva, Bulgaria

### AIR RIFLE (Cont.)

### MEN'S TRAP
1929 .....De Lumniczer, Hungary
1930 .....M. Arie, U.S.
1931 .....Kiszkurno, Poland
1933 .....De Lumniczer, Hungary
1934 .....A. Montagh, Hungary
1935 .....R. Sack, W Germany
1936 .....Kiszkurno, Poland
1937 .....K. Huber, Finland
1938 .....I. Strassburger, Hungary
1939 .....De Lumniczer, Hungary
1947 .....H. Liljedahl, Sweden
1949 .....F. Rocchi, Argentina
1950 .....C. Sala, Italy
1952 .....P.J. Grossi, Argentina
1954 .....C. Merlo, Italy
1958 .....F. Eisenlauer, U.S.
1959 .....H. Badravi, Egypt
1961 .....E. Mattarelli, Italy
1962 .....W. Zimenko, USSR
1965 .....J.E. Lire, Chile
1966 .....K. Jones, U.S.
1967 .....G. Rennard, Belgium
1969 .....E. Mattarelli, Italy
1970 .....M. Carrega, France
1971 .....M. Carrega, France
1973 .....A. Andrushkin, USSR
1974 .....M. Carrega, France
1975 .....J. Primrose, Canada
1977 .....E. Azkue, Spain
1978 .....E. Vallduvi, Spain
1979 .....M. Carrega, France
1981 .....A. Asanov, USSR
1982 .....L. Giovonnetti, Italy
1983 .....J. Primrose, Canada
1985 .....M. Bednarik, Czechoslovakia

## Women
1990 .....E. Joc, Hungary
1994 .....Sonja Pfeilschifter, Germany
1998 .....Sonja Pfeilschifter, Germany
1999 .....Sonja Pfeilschifter, Germany
2000 .....Sonja Pfeilschifter, Germany

### SPORT PISTOL
1966 .....N. Rasskazova, USSR
1970 .....N. Stoljarova, USSR
1974 .....N. Stoljarova, USSR
1978 .....K. Dyer, U.S.
1982 .....P. Balogh, Hungary
1986 .....M. Dobrantcheva, USSR
1990 .....M. Logvinenko, USSR
1994 .....Soon Hee Boo, S Korea
1998 .....Yieqing Cai, China
1999 .....Soon Hee Boo, S Korea
2000 .....Lalita Vauhleuskaya, Belarus

### AIR PISTOL
1970 .....S. Carroll, U.S.
1974 .....Z. Simonian, USSR
1978 .....K. Hansson, Sweden
1979 .....R. Fox, U.S.
1981 .....N. Kalinina, USSR

### AIR PISTOL (Cont.)

### MEN'S TRAP (Cont.)
1986 .......M. Bednarik, Czechoslovakia
1987 .....D. Monakov, USSR
1989 .....M. Venturini, Italy
1990 .....J. Damne, E Germany
1994 .....Dmitriy Monakov, Ukraine
1995 .....Giovanni Pellielo, Italy
1998 .....Giovanni Pellielo, Italy
1999 .....Joao Rebelo, Portugal
2000 .....Michael Diamond, Australia

### THREE POSITION RIFLE
1929 .....O. Ericsson, Sweden
1930 .....Petersen, Denmark
1931 .....Amundson, Norway
1933 .....De Lisle, France
1935 .....Leskinnen, Finland
1937 .....Mazoyer, France
1939 .....Steigelmann, Germany
1947 .....I.H. Erben, Sweden
1949 .....P. Janhonen, Finland
1952 .....Kongshaug, Norway
1954 .....A. Bugdanov, USSR
1958 .....Itkis, USSR
1962 .....G. Anderson, U.S.
1966 .....G. Anderson, U.S.
1970 .....Parkhimovitch, USSR
1974 .....L. Wigger, U.S.
1978 .....E. Svensson, Sweden
1982 .....K. Ivanov, USSR
1986 .....P. Heinz, W Germany
1990 .....E. C. Lee, S Korea
1994 .....P. Kurka, Czech Republic
1998 .....Jozef Gonci, Slovakia
1999 .....Jozef Gonci, Slovakia
2000 .....Jozef Gonci, Slovakia

1982 .....M. Dobrantcheva, USSR
1983 .....K. Bodin, Sweden
1985 .....M. Dobrantcheva, USSR
1986 .....A. Völker, E Germany
1987 .....J. Brajkovic, Yugoslavia
1989 .....N. Salukvadse, USSR
1990 .....Jasna Sekaric, Yugoslavia
1994 .....Jasna Sekaric, IOP
1998 .....Dorisuren Munkhbayar, Mongolia
1999 .....Nino Salukvadze, Georgia
2000 .....Luna Tao, China

# Softball

## U.S. Champions—Men
### MAJOR FAST PITCH

| | |
|---|---|
| 1933.........J.L. Gill Boosters, Chicago | 1968.........Clearwater (FL) Bombers |
| 1934.........Ke-Nash-A, Kenosha, WI | 1969.........Raybestos Cardinals, Stratford, CT |
| 1935.........Crimson Coaches, Toledo, OH | 1970.........Raybestos Cardinals, Stratford, CT |
| 1936.........Kodak Park, Rochester, NY | 1971.........Welty Way, Cedar Rapids, IA |
| 1937.........Briggs Body Team, Detroit | 1972.........Raybestos Cardinals, Stratford, CT |
| 1938.........The Pohlers, Cincinnati | 1973.........Clearwater (FL) Bombers |
| 1939.........Carr's Boosters, Covington, KY | 1974.........Gianella Bros, Santa Rosa, CA |
| 1940.........Kodak Park, Rochester, NY | 1975.........Rising Sun Hotel, Reading, PA |
| 1941.........Bendix Brakes, South Bend, IN | 1976.........Raybestos Cardinals, Stratford, CT |
| 1942.........Deep Rock Oilers, Tulsa | 1977.........Billard Barbell, Reading, PA |
| 1943.........Hammer Air Field, Fresno | 1978.........Billard Barbell, Reading, PA |
| 1944.........Hammer Air Field, Fresno | 1979.........McArdle Pontiac/Cadillac, Midland, MI |
| 1945.........Zollner Pistons, Fort Wayne, IN | 1980.........Peterbilt Western, Seattle |
| 1946.........Zollner Pistons, Fort Wayne, IN | 1981.........Archer Daniels Midland, Decatur, IL |
| 1947.........Zollner Pistons, Fort Wayne, IN | 1982.........Peterbilt Western, Seattle |
| 1948.........Briggs Beautyware, Detroit | 1983.........Franklin Cardinals, Stratford, CT |
| 1949.........Tip Top Tailors, Toronto | 1984.........California Kings, Merced, CA |
| 1950.........Clearwater (FL) Bombers | 1985.........Pay'n Pak, Seattle |
| 1951.........Dow Chemical, Midland, MI | 1986.........Pay'n Pak, Seattle |
| 1952.........Briggs Beautyware, Detroit | 1987.........Pay'n Pak, Seattle |
| 1953.........Briggs Beautyware, Detroit | 1988.........TransAire, Elkhart, IN |
| 1954.........Clearwater (FL) Bombers | 1989.........Penn Corp, Sioux City, IA |
| 1955.........Raybestos Cardinals, Stratford, CT | 1990.........Penn Corp, Sioux City, IA |
| 1956.........Clearwater (FL) Bombers | 1991.........Guanella Brothers, Rohnert Park, CA |
| 1957.........Clearwater (FL) Bombers | 1992.........Natl Health Care Disc, Sioux City, IA |
| 1958.........Raybestos Cardinals, Stratford, CT | 1993.........Natl Health Care Disc, Sioux City, IA |
| 1959.........Sealmasters, Aurora, IL | 1994.........Decatur Pride, Decatur, IL |
| 1960.........Clearwater (FL) Bombers | 1995.........Decatur Pride, Decatur, IL |
| 1961.........Sealmasters, Aurora, IL | 1996.........Green Bay All-Car, Green Bay, WI |
| 1962.........Clearwater (FL) Bombers | 1997.........Green Bay All-Car, Green Bay, WI |
| 1963.........Clearwater (FL) Bombers | 1998.........Meierhoffer-Fleeman, St. Joseph, MO |
| 1964.........Burch Tool, Detroit | 1999.........Decatur Pride, Decatur, IL |
| 1965.........Sealmasters, Aurora, IL | 2000.........Meierhoffer, St. Joseph, MO |
| 1966.........Clearwater (FL) Bombers | 2001.........Frontier Players Casino, St. Joseph, MO |
| 1967.........Sealmasters, Aurora, IL | |

### SUPER SLOW PITCH

| | |
|---|---|
| 1981.........Howard's/Western Steer, Denver, NC | 1992.........Ritch's Superior, Windsor Locks, CT |
| 1982.........Jerry's Catering, Miami, FL | 1993.........Ritch's Superior, Windsor Locks, CT |
| 1983.........Howard's/Western Steer, Denver, NC | 1994.........Bell Corp, Tampa, FL |
| 1984.........Howard's/Western Steer, Denver, NC | 1995.........Lighthouse/Worth, Stone Mt., GA |
| 1985.........Steele's Sports, Grafton, OH | 1996.........Ritch's Superior, Windsor Locks, CT |
| 1986.........Steele's Sports, Grafton, OH | 1997.........Ritch's Superior, Windsor Locks, CT |
| 1987.........Steele's Sports, Grafton, OH | 1998.........Lighthouse/Worth, Stone Mt., GA |
| 1988.........Starpath, Monticello, KY | 1999.........Team Easton, Wilmington, NC |
| 1989.........Ritch's Salvage, Harrisburg, NC | 2000.........Team TPS, Louisville, KY |
| 1990.........Steele's Silver Bullets, Grafton, OH | |
| 1991.........Sunbelt/Worth, Centerville, GA | |

## ONE MORE SIGN OF THE APOCALYPSE

*Cheryl Reeves, 19, of Levittown, Pa., is suing her former softball pitching coach for more than $100,000, claiming, among other things, that she suffered anguish and the loss of earning capacity because he taught her an illegal pitch.*

## U.S.Champions—Men *(Cont.)*

### MAJOR SLOW PITCH

| | |
|---|---|
| 1953..........Shields Construction, Newport, KY | 1978..........Campbell Carpets, Concord, CA |
| 1954..........Waldneck's Tavern, Cincinnati | 1979..........Nelco Mfg Co., Oklahoma City |
| 1955..........Lang Pet Shop, Covington, KY | 1980..........Campbell Carpets, Concord, CA |
| 1956..........Gatliff Auto Sales, Newport, KY | 1981..........Elite Coating, Gordon, CA |
| 1957..........Gatliff Auto Sales, Newport, KY | 1982..........Triangle Sports, Minneapolis |
| 1958..........East Side Sports, Detroit | 1983..........No. 1 Electric & Heating, Gastonia, NC |
| 1959..........Yorkshire Restaurant, Newport, KY | 1984..........Lilly Air Systems, Chicago |
| 1960..........Hamilton Tailoring, Cincinnati | 1985..........Blanton's, Fayetteville, NC |
| 1961..........Hamilton Tailoring, Cincinnati | 1986..........Non-Ferrous Metals, Cleveland |
| 1962..........Skip Hogan A.C., Pittsburgh | 1987..........Starpath, Monticello, KY |
| 1963..........Gatliff Auto Sales, Newport, KY | 1988..........Bell Corp/FAF, Tampa, FL |
| 1964..........Skip Hogan A.C., Pittsburgh | 1989..........Ritch's Salvage, Harrisburg, NC |
| 1965..........Skip Hogan A.C., Pittsburgh | 1990..........New Construction, Shelbyville, IN |
| 1966..........Michael's Lounge, Detroit | 1991..........Riverside Paving, Louisville, KY |
| 1967..........Jim's Sport Shop, Pittsburgh | 1992..........Vernon's, Jacksonville, FL |
| 1968..........County Sports, Levittown, NY | 1993..........Back Porch/Destin Roofing, Destin, FL |
| 1969..........Copper Hearth, Milwaukee | 1994..........Riverside RAM/Taylor Bros., Louisville, KY |
| 1970..........Little Caesar's, Southgate, MI | 1995..........Riverside/RAM/Taylor/TPS, Louisville, KY |
| 1971..........Pile Drivers, Virginia Beach, VA | 1996..........Bell 2/Robert's/Easton, Orlando, FL |
| 1972..........Jiffy Club, Louisville, KY | 1997..........Long Haul/TPS, Albertville, MN |
| 1973..........Howard's Furniture, Denver, NC | 1998..........Chase Mortgage/Easton, Wilmington, NC |
| 1974..........Howard's Furniture, Denver, NC | 1999..........Gasoline Heaven/Worth, Commack, NY |
| 1975..........Pyramid Cafe, Lakewood, OH | 2000..........Long Haul/TPS, Albertville, MN |
| 1976..........Warren Motors, Jacksonville, FL | 2001..........New Construction, Shelbyville, IN |
| 1977..........Nelson Painting, Oklahoma City | |

## Shadow of Doubt

Lance Armstrong shouldn't hold his breath waiting for a congratulatory phone call from Greg LeMond, the only other American to have won the Tour de France. "To be honest, I haven't watched any of the Tour this year," LeMond said in late July 2001 from his home in suburban Minneapolis. "I've been fishing for the last three weeks in Montana, so I don't know very much about what's going on."

But as LeMond spoke, it became clear that he believes he knows more than a little about what's going on. "I was deeply saddened," he said, "to hear about Lance's relationship with Dr. Michele Ferrari," who is awaiting trial in Italy on charges of providing riders with erythropoietin (EPO), a banned substance that increases red blood cell count. On the eve of the Tour, *The Sunday Times* of London reported that Armstrong had visited Ferrari five times since March 1999. "Have I been tested by him, gone there and consulted on certain things?" Armstrong told the paper. "Perhaps."

Visits prove nothing, of course. Armstrong has been among the most frequently drug-tested riders over the last three years and has never failed a test. He describes Ferrari as a friend he came to know in the "small community" of cycling, and at a press conference on July 23 he called him "a fair man and an innocent man.... Let there be a trial."

There will be a trial. Among the names likely to arise is that of Kevin Livingston, Armstrong's former *domestique* and friend, whose name appears in confiscated files of the good doctor, according to *The Sunday Times*. "I wish with all my heart that the story is the way he [Armstrong] tells it," said LeMond. "Ferrari is a cancer in sports, and it's sad that Lance has had a five-year relationship with him. I would have all the praise in the world for Lance if I thought he was clean, but until Dr. Ferrari's trial, we can't know for sure. It sounds like I'm bitter or jealous about Lance Armstrong, but I'm not."

—Austin Murphy

# Softball *(Cont.)*

## U.S. Champions—Women

### MAJOR FAST PITCH

| | |
|---|---|
| 1933..........Great Northerns, Chicago | 1968..........Raybestos Brakettes, Stratford, CT |
| 1934..........Hart Motors, Chicago | 1969..........Orange (CA) Lionettes |
| 1935..........Bloomer Girls, Cleveland | 1970..........Orange (CA) Lionettes |
| 1936..........Nat'l Screw & Mfg., Cleveland | 1971..........Raybestos Brakettes, Stratford, CT |
| 1937..........Nat'l Screw & Mfg., Cleveland | 1972..........Raybestos Brakettes, Stratford, CT |
| 1938..........J.J. Krieg's, Alameda, CA | 1973..........Raybestos Brakettes, Stratford, CT |
| 1939..........J.J. Krieg's, Alameda, CA | 1974..........Raybestos Brakettes, Stratford, CT |
| 1940..........Arizona Ramblers, Phoenix | 1975..........Raybestos Brakettes, Stratford, CT |
| 1941..........Higgins Midgets, Tulsa | 1976..........Raybestos Brakettes, Stratford, CT |
| 1942..........Jax Maids, New Orleans | 1977..........Raybestos Brakettes, Stratford, CT |
| 1943..........Jax Maids, New Orleans | 1978..........Raybestos Brakettes, Stratford, CT |
| 1944..........Lind & Pomeroy, Portland, OR | 1979..........Sun City (AZ) Saints |
| 1945..........Jax Maids, New Orleans | 1980..........Raybestos Brakettes, Stratford, CT |
| 1946..........Jax Maids, New Orleans | 1981..........Orlando (FL) Rebels |
| 1947..........Jax Maids, New Orleans | 1982..........Raybestos Brakettes, Stratford, CT |
| 1948..........Arizona Ramblers, Phoenix | 1983..........Raybestos Brakettes, Stratford, CT |
| 1949..........Arizona Ramblers, Phoenix | 1984..........Los Angeles Diamonds |
| 1950..........Orange (CA) Lionettes | 1985..........Hi-Ho Brakettes, Stratford, CT |
| 1951..........Orange (CA) Lionettes | 1986..........Southern California Invasion, Los Angeles |
| 1952..........Orange (CA) Lionettes | 1987..........Orange County Majestics, Anaheim, CA |
| 1953..........Betsy Ross Rockets, Fresno | 1988..........Hi-Ho Brakettes, Stratford, CT |
| 1954..........Leach Motor Rockets, Fresno | 1989..........Whittier (CA) Raiders |
| 1955..........Orange (CA) Lionettes | 1990..........Raybestos Brakettes, Stratford, CT |
| 1956..........Orange (CA) Lionettes | 1991..........Raybestos Brakettes, Stratford, CT |
| 1957..........Hacienda Rockets, Fresno | 1992..........Raybestos Brakettes, Stratford, CT |
| 1958..........Raybestos Brakettes, Stratford, CT | 1993..........Redding Rebels, Redding, CA |
| 1959..........Raybestos Brakettes, Stratford, CT | 1994..........Redding Rebels, Redding, CA |
| 1960..........Raybestos Brakettes, Stratford, CT | 1995..........Redding Rebels, Redding, CA |
| 1961..........Gold Sox, Whittier, CA | 1996..........California Commotion, Woodland Hills, CA |
| 1962..........Orange (CA) Lionettes | 1997..........California Commotion, Woodland Hills, CA |
| 1963..........Raybestos Brakettes, Stratford, CT | 1998..........California Commotion, Woodland Hills, CA |
| 1964..........Erv Lind Florists, Portland, OR | 1999..........California Commotion, Woodland Hills, CA |
| 1965..........Orange (CA) Lionettes | 2000..........Phoenix Storm, Phoenix |
| 1966..........Raybestos Brakettes, Stratford, CT | 2001..........Phoenix Storm, Phoenix |
| 1967..........Raybestos Brakettes, Stratford, CT | |

### MAJOR SLOW PITCH

| | |
|---|---|
| 1959..........Pearl Laundry, Richmond, VA | 1981..........Tifton (GA) Tomboys |
| 1960..........Carolina Rockets, High Pt, NC | 1982..........Richmond (VA) Stompers |
| 1961..........Dairy Cottage, Covington, KY | 1983..........Spooks, Anoka, MN |
| 1962..........Dana Gardens, Cincinnati | 1984..........Spooks, Anoka, MN |
| 1963..........Dana Gardens, Cincinnati | 1985..........Key Ford Mustangs, Pensacola, FL |
| 1964..........Dana Gardens, Cincinnati | 1986..........Sur-Way Tomboys, Tifton, GA |
| 1965..........Art's Acres, Omaha | 1987..........Key Ford Mustangs, Pensacola, FL |
| 1966..........Dana Gardens, Cincinnati | 1988..........Spooks, Anoka, MN |
| 1967..........Ridge Maintenance, Cleveland | 1989..........Canaan's Illusions, Houston |
| 1968..........Escue Pontiac, Cincinnati | 1990..........Spooks, Anoka, MN |
| 1969..........Converse Dots, Hialeah, FL | 1991..........Kannan's Illusions, San Antonio, TX |
| 1970..........Rutenschruder Floral, Cincinnati | 1992..........Universal Plastics, Cookeville, TN |
| 1971..........Gators, Ft. Lauderdale, FL | 1993..........Universal Plastics, Cookeville, TN |
| 1972..........Riverside Ford, Cincinnati | 1994..........Universal Plastics, Cookeville, TN |
| 1973..........Sweeney Chevrolet, Cincinnati | 1995..........Armed Forces, Sacramento, CA |
| 1974..........Marks Brothers Dots, Miami | 1996..........Spooks, Anoka, MN |
| 1975..........Marks Brothers Dots, Miami | 1997..........Taylor's Major Slow Pitch, Glendale, MD |
| 1976..........Sorrento's Pizza, Cincinnati | 1998..........Lakerettes, Conneaut Lake, PA |
| 1977..........Fox Valley Lassies, St. Charles, IL | 1999..........Lakerettes, Conneaut Lake, PA |
| 1978..........Bob Hoffman's Dots, Miami | 2000..........Premier Motor Sports, Pittsboro, NC |
| 1979..........Bob Hoffman's Dots, Miami | 2001..........Shooters/Nike, Orlando, FL |
| 1980..........Howard's Rubi-Otts, Graham, NC | |

## All-Around World Champions
### MEN

| | | |
|---|---|---|
| 1891 .....Joseph F. Donoghue, U.S. | 1935 .....Michael Staksrud, Nor. | 1973 .....Göran Claeson, Sweden |
| 1893 .....Jaap Eden, Netherlands | 1936 .....Ivar Ballangrud, Norway | 1974 .....Sten Stensen, Norway |
| 1895 .....Jaap Eden, Netherlands | 1937 .....Michael Staksrud, Nor. | 1975 .....Harm Kuipers, Netherlands |
| 1896 .....Jaap Eden, Netherlands | 1938 .....Ivar Ballangrud, Norway | 1976 .....Piet Kleine, Netherlands |
| 1897 .....Jack K. McCulloch, Can. | 1939 .....Birger Wasenius, Finland | 1977 .....Eric Heiden, U.S. |
| 1898 .....Peder Ostlund, Norway | 1947 .....Lassi Parkkinen, Finland | 1978 .....Eric Heiden, U.S. |
| 1899 .....Peder Ostlund, Norway | 1948 .....Odd Lundberg, Norway | 1979 .....Eric Heiden, U.S. |
| 1900 .....Edvard Engelsaas, Nor. | 1949 .....Kornel Pajor, Hungary | 1980 .....Hilbert van der Duin, Neth. |
| 1901 .....Franz F. Wathan, Finland | 1950 .....Hjalmar Andersen, Nor. | 1981 .....Amund Sjobrand, Norway |
| 1904 .....Sigurd Mathisen, Norway | 1951 .....Hjalmar Andersen, Nor. | 1982 .....Hilbert van der Duin, Neth. |
| 1905 .....C. Coen de Koning, Neth. | 1952 .....Hjalmar Andersen, Nor. | 1983 .....Rolf Falk-Larssen, Nor. |
| 1908 .....Oscar Mathisen, Norway | 1953 .....Oleg Goncharenko, USSR | 1984 .....Oleg Bozhev, USSR |
| 1909 .....Oscar Mathisen, Norway | 1954 .....Boris Shilkov, USSR | 1985 ......Hein Vergeer, Netherlands |
| 1910 .....Nikolai Strunnikov, Russia | 1955 .....Sigvard Ericsson, Swe. | 1986 .....Hein Vergeer, Netherlands |
| 1911 .....Nikolai Strunnikov, Russia | 1956 .....Oleg Goncharenko, USSR | 1987 .....Nikolai Guliaev, USSR |
| 1912 .....Oscar Mathisen, Norway | 1957 .....Knut Johannesen, Nor. | 1988 .....Eric Flaim, U.S. |
| 1913 .....Oscar Mathisen, Norway | 1958 .....Oleg Goncharenko, USSR | 1989 .....Leo Visser, Netherlands |
| 1914 .....Oscar Mathisen, Norway | 1959 .....Juhani Järvinen, Finland | 1990 .....Johann Olav Koss, Nor. |
| 1922 .....Harald Strom, Norway | 1960 .....Boris Stenin, USSR | 1991 .....Johann Olav Koss, Nor. |
| 1923 .....Klas Thunberg, Finland | 1961 .....Henk van der Grift, Neth. | 1992 .....Roberto Sighel, Italy |
| 1924 .....Roald Larsen, Norway | 1962 .....Viktor Kosichkin, USSR | 1993 .....Falko Zandstra, Neth. |
| 1925 .....Klas Thunberg, Finland | 1963 .....Jonny Nilsson, Sweden | 1994 .....Johann Olav Koss, Nor. |
| 1926 .....Ivar Ballangrud, Norway | 1964 .....Knut Johannesen, Nor. | 1995 .....Rintje Ritsma, Netherlands |
| 1927 .....Bernt Evensen, Norway | 1965 .....Per Ivar Moe, Norway | 1996 .....Rintje Ritsma, Netherlands |
| 1928 .....Klas Thunberg, Finland | 1966 .....Kees Verkerk, Neth. | 1997 .....Ids Postma, Netherlands |
| 1929 .....Klas Thunberg, Finland | 1967 .....Kees Verkerk, Neth. | 1998 .....Ids Postma, Netherlands |
| 1930 .....Michael Staksrud, Nor. | 1968 .....Fred Anton Maier, Nor. | 1999 .....Rintje Ritsma, Netherlands |
| 1931 .....Klas Thunberg, Finland | 1969 .....Dag Fornaes, Norway | 2000.......Gianni Romme, Netherlands |
| 1932 .....Ivar Ballangrud, Norway | 1970 ....Ard Schenk, Netherlands | 2001......Rintje Ritsma, Netherlands |
| 1933 .....Hans Engnestangen, Nor. | 1971 .....Ard Schenk, Netherlands | |
| 1934 .....Bernt Evensen, Norway | 1972 .....Ard Schenk, Netherlands | |

### WOMEN

| | | |
|---|---|---|
| 1936 .....Kit Klein, U.S. | 1964 .....Lidia Skoblikova, USSR | 1985 .....Andrea Schöne, GDR |
| 1937 .....Laila Schou Nilsen, Nor. | 1965 .....Inga Artamonova, USSR | 1986 .....Karin Kania-Enke, GDR |
| 1938 .....Laila Schou Nilsen, Nor. | 1966 .....Valentina Stenina, USSR | 1987 .....Karin Kania, GDR |
| 1939 ....Verné Lesche, Finland | 1967 .....Stien Kaiser, Netherlands | 1988 .....Karin Kania, GDR |
| 1947 .....Verné Lesche, Finland | 1968 .....Stien Kaiser, Netherlands | 1989 ....Constanze Moser, GDR |
| 1948 .....Maria Isakova, USSR | 1969 .....Lasma Kauniste, USSR | 1990 .....Jacqueline Börner, GDR |
| 1949 .....Maria Isakova, USSR | 1970 .....Atje Keulen-Deelstra, Neth. | 1991 .....Gunda Kleemann, Ger. |
| 1950 .....Maria Isakova, USSR | 1971 .....Nina Statkevich, USSR | 1992 .....Gunda Niemann-Kleemann, Germany |
| 1951 .....Eevi Huttunen, Finland | 1972 .....Atje Keulen-Deelstra, Neth. | |
| 1952 .....Lidia Selikhova, USSR | 1973 .....Atje Keulen-Deelstra, Neth. | 1993 .....Gunda Niemann, Germany |
| 1953 .......Khalida Shchegoleeva, USSR | 1974 .....Atje Keulen-Deelstra, Neth. | 1994 .....Emese Hunyady, Austria |
| 1954 .....Lidia Selikhova, USSR | 1975 .....Karin Kessow, GDR | 1995 .....Gunda Niemann, Germany |
| 1955 .....Rimma Zhukova, USSR | 1976 .....Sylvia Burka, Canada | 1996 ......Gunda Niemann, Germany |
| 1956 .....Sofia Kondakova, USSR | 1977 .....Vera Bryndzej, USSR | 1997 ......Gunda Niemann, Germany |
| 1957 .....Inga Artamonova, USSR | 1978 .....Tatiana Averina, USSR | 1997 ......Gunda Niemann, Germany |
| 1958 .....Inga Artamonova, USSR | 1979 .....Beth Heiden, U.S. | 1998 ......Gunda Niemann, Germany |
| 1959 .....Tamara Rylova, USSR | 1980 .....Natalia Petruseva, USSR | 1999 ......Gunda Niemann, Germany |
| 1960 .....Valentina Stenina, USSR | 1981 .....Natalia Petruseva, USSR | 2000 .....Claudia Pechstein, Ger. |
| 1961 .....Valentina Stenina, USSR | 1982 .....Karin Busch, GDR | 2001 .....Anni Friesinger, Germany |
| 1962 .....Inga Artamonova, USSR | 1983 .....Andrea Schöne, GDR | |
| 1963 .....Lidia Skoblikova, USSR | 1984 .....Karin Enke-Busch, GDR | |

# Squash

## National Men's Champions

| HARD BALL | | HARD BALL *(Cont.)* | | SOFT BALL | |
|---|---|---|---|---|---|
| Year | Champion | Year | Champion | Year | Champion |
| 1907 | John A. Miskey | 1957 | Henri R. Salaun | 1983 | Kenton Jernigan |
| 1908 | John A. Miskey | 1958 | Henri R. Salaun | 1984 | Kenton Jernigan |
| 1909 | William L. Freeland | 1959 | Benjamin H. Heckscher | 1985 | Kenton Jernigan |
| 1910 | John A. Miskey | 1960 | G. Diehl Mateer Jr. | 1986 | Darius Pandole |
| 1911 | Francis S. White | 1961 | Henri R. Salaun | 1987 | Richard Hashim |
| 1912 | Constantine Hutchins | 1962 | Samuel P. Howe III | 1988 | John Phelan |
| 1913 | Morton L. Newhall | 1963 | Benjamin H. Heckscher | 1989 | Will Carlin |
| 1914 | Constantine Hutchins | | | 1990 | Syed Jafry |
| 1915 | Stanley W. Pearson | 1964 | Ralph E. Howe | 1991 | Hector Barragan |
| 1916 | Stanley W. Pearson | 1965 | Stephen T. Vehslage | 1992 | Phil Yarrow |
| 1917 | Stanley W. Pearson | 1966 | Victor Niederhoffer | 1993 | Phil Yarrow |
| 1918–19 | No tournament | 1967 | Samuel P. Howe III | 1994 | Roberto Rosales |
| 1920 | Charles C. Peabody | 1968 | Colin Adair | 1995 | A. Martin Clark |
| 1921 | Stanley W. Pearson | 1969 | Anil Nayar | 1996 | Mohsen Mir |
| 1922 | Stanley W. Pearson | 1970 | Anil Nayar | 1997 | A. Martin Clark |
| 1923 | Stanley W. Pearson | 1971 | Colin Adair | 1998 | A. Martin Clark |
| 1924 | Gerald Roberts | 1972 | Victor Niederhoffer | 1999 | David McNeely |
| 1925 | W. Palmer Dixon | 1973 | Victor Niederhoffer | 2000 | A. Martin Clark |
| 1926 | W. Palmer Dixon | 1974 | Victor Niederhoffer | 2001 | Damian Walker |
| 1927 | Myles Baker | 1975 | Victor Niederhoffer | | |
| 1928 | Herbert N. Rawlins Jr. | 1976 | Peter Briggs | | |
| 1929 | J. Lawrence Pool | 1977 | Thomas E. Page | | |
| 1930 | Herbert N. Rawlins Jr. | 1978 | Michael Desaulniers | | |
| 1931 | J. Lawrence Pool | 1979 | Mario Sanchez | | |
| 1932 | Beckman H. Pool | 1980 | Michael Desaulniers | | |
| 1933 | Beckman H. Pool | 1981 | Mark Alger | | |
| 1934 | Neil J. Sullivan II | 1982 | John Nimick | | |
| 1935 | Donald Strachan | 1983 | Kenton Jernigan | | |
| 1936 | Germain G. Glidden | 1984 | Kenton Jernigan | | |
| 1937 | Germain G. Glidden | 1987 | Frank J. Stanley IV | | |
| 1938 | Germain G. Glidden | 1988 | Scott Dulmage | | |
| 1939 | Donald Strachan | 1989 | Rodolfo Rodriquez | | |
| 1940 | A. Willing Patterson | 1990 | Hector Barragan | | |
| 1941 | Charles M.P. Britton | 1991 | Hector Barragan | | |
| 1942 | Charles M.P. Britton | 1992 | Hector Barragan | | |
| 1943–45 | No tournament | 1985 | Kenton Jernigan | | |
| 1946 | Charles M.P. Britton | 1986 | Hugh LaBossier | | |
| 1947 | Charles M.P. Britton | 1993 | Hector Barragan | | |
| 1948 | Stanley W. Pearson Jr. | 1994 | Hector Barragan | | |
| 1949 | H. Hunter Lott Jr. | 1995 | W. Keen Butcher | | |
| 1950 | Edward J. Hahn | 1996 | W. Keen Butcher | | |
| 1951 | Edward J. Hahn | 1997 | Rob Hill | | |
| 1952 | Harry B. Conlon | 1998 | Rob Hill | | |
| 1953 | Ernest Howard | 1999 | Rob Hill | | |
| 1954 | G. Diehl Mateer Jr. | 2000 | Thomas Harrity | | |
| 1955 | Henri R. Salaun | 2001 | Rob Hill | | |
| 1956 | G. Diehl Mateer Jr. | | | | |

# Squash (Cont.)

## National Women's Champions

| HARD BALL | | HARD BALL *(Cont.)* | | SOFT BALL | |
|---|---|---|---|---|---|
| Year | Champion | Year | Champion | Year | Champion |
| 1928 | Eleanora Sears | 1965 | Joyce Davenport | 1983 | Alicia McConnell |
| 1929 | Margaret Howe | 1966 | Betty Meade | 1984 | Julie Harris |
| 1930 | Hazel Wightman | 1967 | Betty Meade | 1985 | Sue Clinch |
| 1931 | Ruth Banks | 1968 | Betty Meade | 1986 | Julie Harris |
| 1932 | Margaret Howe | 1969 | Joyce Davenport | 1987 | Diana Staley |
| 1933 | Susan Noel | 1970 | Nina Moyer | 1988 | Sara Luther |
| 1934 | Margaret Howe | 1971 | Carol Thesieres | 1989 | Nancy Gengler |
| 1935 | Margot Lumb | 1972 | Nina Moyer | 1990 | Joyce Maycock |
| 1936 | Anne Page | 1973 | Gretchen Spruance | 1991 | Ellie Pierce |
| 1937 | Anne Page | 1974 | Gretchen Spruance | 1992 | Demer Holleran |
| 1938 | Cecile Bowes | 1975 | Ginny Akabane | 1993 | Demer Holleran |
| 1939 | Anne Page | 1976 | Gretchen Spruance | 1994 | Demer Holleran |
| 1940 | Cecile Bowes | 1977 | Gretchen Spruance | 1995 | Ellie Pierce |
| 1941 | Cecile Bowes | 1978 | Gretchen Spruance | 1996 | Demer Holleran |
| 1942–46 | No tournament | 1979 | Heather McKay | 1997 | Demer Holleran |
| 1947 | Anne Page Homer | 1980 | Barbara Maltby | 1998 | Latasha Khan |
| 1948 | Cecile Bowes | 1981 | Barbara Maltby | 1999 | Demer Holleran |
| 1949 | Janet Morgan | 1982 | Alicia McConnell | 2000 | Latasha Khan |
| 1950 | Betty Howe | 1983 | Alicia McConnell | 2001 | Shabana Khan |
| 1951 | Jane Austin | 1984 | Alicia McConnell | | |
| 1952 | Margaret Howe | 1985 | Alicia McConnell | | |
| 1953 | Margaret Howe | 1986 | Alicia McConnell | | |
| 1954 | Lois Dilks | 1987 | Alicia McConnell | | |
| 1955 | Janet Morgan | 1988 | Alicia McConnell | | |
| 1956 | Betty Howe Constable | 1986 | Alicia McConnell | | |
| 1957 | Betty Howe Constable | 1987 | Alicia McConnell | | |
| 1958 | Betty Howe Constable | 1988 | Alicia McConnell | | |
| 1959 | Betty Howe Constable | 1989 | Demer Holleran | | |
| 1960 | Margaret Varner | 1990 | Demer Holleran | | |
| 1961 | Margaret Varner | 1991 | Demer Holleran | | |
| 1962 | Margaret Varner | 1992 | Demer Holleran | | |
| 1963 | Margaret Varner | 1993 | Demer Holleran | | |
| 1964 | Ann Wetzel | 1994 | Demer Holleran | | |

Note: Tournament not held since 1994.

**Squashed**

In the summer of 2001, the Women's International Squash Players Association formally banned its members from wearing thong bikinis during play. Britain's Vicky Botwright, the world's 19th-ranked player, had been pressing to wear a sports bra and thong during competition. "We are a minority sport," said Botwright. "Any interest is good interest."

# Triathlon

## Ironman Championship

| Year | MEN Winner | Time | Year | WOMEN Winner | Time |
|------|------------|------|------|--------------|------|
| 1978 | Gordon Haller | 11:46 | 1978 | No finishers | |
| 1979 | Tom Warren | 11:15:56 | 1979 | Lyn Lemaire | 12:55 |
| 1980 | Dave Scott | 9:24:33 | 1980 | Robin Beck | 11:21:24 |
| 1981 | John Howard | 9:38:29 | 1981 | Linda Sweeney | 12:00:32 |
| 1982 | Scott Tinley | 9:19:41 | 1982 | Kathleen McCartney | 11:09:40 |
| 1982 | Dave Scott | 9:08:23 | 1982 | Julie Leach | 10:54:08 |
| 1983 | Dave Scott | 9:05:57 | 1983 | Sylviane Puntous | 10:43:36 |
| 1984 | Dave Scott | 8:54:20 | 1984 | Sylviane Puntous | 10:25:13 |
| 1985 | Scott Tinley | 8:50:54 | 1985 | Joanne Ernst | 10:25:22 |
| 1986 | Dave Scott | 8:28:37 | 1986 | Paula Newby-Fraser | 9:49:14 |
| 1987 | Dave Scott | 8:34:13 | 1987 | Erin Baker | 9:35:25 |
| 1988 | Scott Molina | 8:31:00 | 1988 | Paula Newby-Fraser | 9:01:01 |
| 1989 | Mark Allen | 8:09:15 | 1989 | Paula Newby-Fraser | 9:00:56 |
| 1990 | Mark Allen | 8:28:17 | 1990 | Erin Baker | 9:13:42 |
| 1991 | Mark Allen | 8:18:32 | 1991 | Paula Newby-Fraser | 9:07:52 |
| 1992 | Mark Allen | 8:09:09 | 1992 | Paula Newby-Fraser | 8:55:29 |
| 1993 | Mark Allen | 8:07:46 | 1993 | Paula Newby-Fraser | 8:58:23 |
| 1994 | Greg Welch | 8:20:27 | 1994 | Paula Newby-Fraser | 9:20:14 |
| 1995 | Mark Allen | 8:20:34 | 1995 | Karen Smyers | 9:16:46 |
| 1996 | Luc Van Lierde | 8:04:08 | 1996 | Paula Newby-Fraser | 9:06:49 |
| 1997 | Thomas Hellriegel | 8:33:01 | 1997 | Heather Fuhr | 9:31:43 |
| 1998 | Peter Reid | 8:24:20 | 1998 | Natascha Badmann | 9:24:16 |
| 1999 | Luc Van Lierde | 8:17:17 | 1999 | Lori Bowden | 9:13:02 |
| 2000 | Peter Reid | 8:21:01 | 2000 | Natascha Badmann | 9:26:17 |

Note: The Ironman Championship was contested twice in 1982.
Sites: Waikiki Beach (1978–79); Ala Moana Park (1980); Kailua-Kona (since 1981).

## U.S. Triathlon National Champions*

| Year | MEN Winner | Year | MEN (CONT.) Winner | Year | WOMEN Winner | Year | WOMEN (CONT.) Winner |
|------|------------|------|---------------------|------|--------------|------|----------------------|
| 1984 | Scott Molina | 1995 | Jeff Devlin | 1984 | Beth Mitchell | 1991 | Karen Smyers |
| 1985 | Scott Molina | 1996 | Jeff Devlin | 1985 | Linda Buchanan | 1992 | Karen Smyers |
| 1986 | Scott Molina | 1997 | Cameron Wydoff | 1986 | Kirsten Hanssen | 1993 | Karen Smyers |
| 1987 | Mike Pigg | 1998 | Hunter Kemper | 1987 | Kirsten Hanssen | 1994 | Karen Smyers |
| 1988 | Mike Pigg | 1999 | Hunter Kemper | 1988 | Colleen Cannon Kaushansky | 1995 | Karen Smyers |
| 1989 | Ken Glah | 2000 | Marcel Viffian | 1989 | Jan Ripple | 1996 | Susan Latshaw |
| 1990 | Scott Molina | 2001 | Hunter Kemper | 1990 | Karen Smyers | 1997 | Sian Welch |
| 1991 | Mike Pigg | | | | | 1998 | Siri Lindley |
| 1992 | Mike Pigg | | | | | 1999 | Barb Lindquist |
| 1993 | Bill Braun | | | | | 2000 | Joanna Zeiger |
| 1994 | Scott Molina | | | | | 2001 | Karen Smyers |

*Olympic distances: 1.5 km swim, 40km bike, 10km run.

# Volleyball

## World Champions
### MEN

| Year | Winner | Runner-up | Site |
|------|--------|-----------|------|
| 1949 | Soviet Union | Czechoslovakia | Prague |
| 1952 | Soviet Union | Czechoslovakia | Moscow |
| 1956 | Czechoslovakia | Soviet Union | Paris |
| 1960 | Soviet Union | Czechoslovakia | Rio de Janeiro |
| 1962 | Soviet Union | Czechoslovakia | Moscow |
| 1966 | Czechoslovakia | Romania | Prague |
| 1970 | East Germany | Bulgaria | Sofia, Bulgaria |
| 1974 | Poland | Soviet Union | Mexico City |
| 1978 | Soviet Union | Italy | Rome |
| 1982 | Soviet Union | Brazil | Buenos Aires |
| 1986 | United States | Soviet Union | Paris |
| 1990 | Italy | Cuba | Rio de Janeiro |
| 1994 | Italy | Netherlands | Athens |
| 1998 | Italy | Yugoslavia | Tokyo |

# Volleyball (Cont.)

## World Champions (Cont.)
### WOMEN

| Year | Winner | Runner-up | Site |
|------|--------|-----------|------|
| 1952 | Soviet Union | Poland | Moscow |
| 1956 | Soviet Union | Romania | Paris |
| 1960 | Soviet Union | Japan | Rio de Janeiro |
| 1962 | Japan | Soviet Union | Moscow |
| 1966 | Japan | United States | Prague |
| 1970 | Soviet Union | Japan | Sofia, Bulgaria |
| 1974 | Japan | Soviet Union | Mexico City |
| 1978 | Cuba | Japan | Rome |
| 1982 | China | Peru | Lima, Peru |
| 1986 | China | Cuba | Prague |
| 1990 | Soviet Union | China | Beijing |
| 1994 | Cuba | Brazil | Sao Paulo, Brazil |
| 1998 | Cuba | China | Osaka, Japan |

## U.S. Men's Open Champions—Gold Division

| Year | Champion |
|------|----------|
| 1928 | Germantown, PA YMCA |
| 1929 | Hyde Park YMCA, IL |
| 1930 | Hyde Park YMCA, IL |
| 1931 | San Antonio, TX YMCA |
| 1932 | San Antonio, TX YMCA |
| 1933 | Houston, TX YMCA |
| 1934 | Houston, TX YMCA |
| 1935 | Houston, TX YMCA |
| 1936 | Houston, TX YMCA |
| 1937 | Duncan YMCA, IL |
| 1938 | Houston, TX YMCA |
| 1939 | Houston, TX YMCA |
| 1940 | Los Angeles AC, CA |
| 1941 | North Ave. YMCA, IL |
| 1942 | North Ave. YMCA, IL |
| 1943–44 | No championships |
| 1945 | North Ave. YMCA, IL |
| 1946 | Pasadena, CA YMCA |
| 1947 | North Ave. YMCA, IL |
| 1948 | Hollywood, CA YMCA |
| 1949 | Downtown YMCA, CA |
| 1950 | Long Beach, CA YMCA |
| 1951 | Hollywood, CA YMCA |
| 1952 | Hollywood, CA YMCA |
| 1953 | Hollywood, CA YMCA |
| 1954 | Stockton, CA YMCA |
| 1955 | Stockton, CA YMCA |
| 1956 | Hollywood, CA YMCA Stars |
| 1957 | Hollywood, CA YMCA Stars |
| 1958 | Hollywood, CA YMCA Stars |
| 1959 | Hollywood, CA YMCA Stars |
| 1960 | Westside JCC, CA |
| 1961 | Hollywood, CA YMCA |
| 1962 | Hollywood, CA YMCA |
| 1963 | Hollywood, CA YMCA |
| 1964 | Hollywood, CA YMCA Stars |
| 1965 | Westside JCC, CA |
| 1966 | Sand & Sea Club, CA |
| 1967 | Fresno, CA VBC |
| 1968 | Westside JCC, Los Angeles, CA |
| 1969 | Los Angeles, CA YMCA |
| 1970 | Chart House, San Diego |
| 1971 | Santa Monica, CA YMCA |
| 1972 | Chart House, San Diego |
| 1973 | Chuck's Steak, Los Angeles |
| 1974 | UC Santa Barbara, CA |
| 1975 | Chart House, San Diego |
| 1976 | Malibu, Los Angeles |
| 1977 | Chuck's, Santa Barbara |
| 1978 | Chuck's, Los Angeles |
| 1979 | Nautilus, Long Beach CA |
| 1980 | Olympic Club, San Francisco |
| 1981 | Nautilus, Long Beach CA |
| 1982 | Chuck's, Los Angeles |
| 1983 | Nautilus Pacifica, CA |
| 1984 | Nautilus Pacifica, CA |
| 1985 | Molten/SSI Torrance, CA |
| 1986 | Molten, Torrance, CA |
| 1987 | Molten, Torrance, CA |
| 1988 | Molten, Torrance, CA |
| 1989 | Not held |
| 1990 | Nike, Carson, CA |
| 1991 | Offshore, Woodland Hills, CA |
| 1992 | Creole Six Pack, Elmhurst, NY |
| 1993 | Asics, Huntington Beach, CA |
| 1994 | Asics/Paul Mitchell, Hunt. Beach, CA |
| 1995 | Shakter, Belagarad, Ukraine |
| 1996 | POL-AM-VBC, Brooklyn, NY |
| 1997 | Canuck Stuff VBC, Calgary |
| 1998 | T-Town, Tulsa, OK |
| 1999 | Los Angeles Athletic Club, Los Angeles |
| 2000 | Paul Mitchell, Huntington Beach, CA |
| 2001 | Los Angeles Athletic Club, Los Angeles |

## U.S. Women's Open Champions—Gold Division

| | |
|---|---|
| 1949 | Eagles, Houston |
| 1950 | Voit #1, Santa Monica, CA |
| 1951 | Eagles, Houston |
| 1952 | Voit #1, Santa Monica, CA |
| 1953 | Voit #1, Los Angeles |
| 1954 | Houstonettes, Houston, TX |
| 1955 | Mariners, Santa Monica, CA |
| 1956 | Mariners, Santa Monica, CA |
| 1957 | Mariners, Santa Monica, CA |
| 1958 | Mariners, Santa Monica, CA |
| 1959 | Mariners, Santa Monica, CA |
| 1960 | Mariners, Santa Monica, CA |
| 1961 | Breakers, Long Beach, CA |
| 1962 | Shamrocks, Long Beach, CA |
| 1963 | Shamrocks, Long Beach, CA |
| 1964 | Shamrocks, Long Beach, CA |
| 1965 | Shamrocks, Long Beach, CA |
| 1966 | Renegades, Los Angeles |
| 1967 | Shamrocks, Long Beach, CA |
| 1968 | Shamrocks, Long Beach, CA |
| 1969 | Shamrocks, Long Beach, CA |
| 1970 | Shamrocks, Long Beach, CA |
| 1971 | Renegades, Los Angeles |
| 1972 | E Pluribus Unum, Houston |
| 1973 | E Pluribus Unum, Houston |
| 1974 | Renegades, Los Angeles |
| 1975 | Adidas, Norwalk, CA |
| 1976 | Pasadena, TX |
| 1977 | Spoilers, Hermosa, CA |
| 1978 | Nick's, Los Angeles |
| 1979 | Mavericks, Los Angeles |
| 1980 | NAVA, Fountain Valley, CA |
| 1981 | Utah State, Logan, UT |
| 1982 | Monarchs, Hilo, HI |
| 1983 | Syntex, Stockton, CA |
| 1984 | Chrysler, Palo Alto, CA |
| 1985 | Merrill Lynch, AZ |
| 1986 | Merrill Lynch, AZ |
| 1987 | Chrysler, Pleasanton, CA |
| 1988 | Chrysler, Hayward, CA |
| 1989 | Plymouth, Hayward, CA |
| 1990 | Plymouth, Hayward, CA |
| 1991 | Fitness, Champaign, IL |
| 1992 | Nick's Kronies, Chicago |
| 1993 | Nick's Fishmarket, Chicago |
| 1994 | Nick's Fishmarket, Chicago |
| 1995 | Kittleman/Branfield's/Nick's, Chi. |
| 1996 | Pure Texas Nuts, Austin, TX |
| 1997 | Kittleman/Branfield's/Nick's, Chi. |
| 1998 | The Exterminators, Barrington, IL |
| 1999 | Dominican Dream Team, Santo Domingo, D.R. |
| 2000 | Dominican Dream Team II, Santo Domingo, D.R. |
| 2001 | Dominican Dream Team III, Santo Domingo, D.R. |

# Wrestling

## United States National Champions

### 1983

**FREESTYLE**

| | |
|---|---|
| 105.5 | Rich Salamone |
| 114.5 | Joe Gonzales |
| 125.5 | Joe Corso |
| 136.5 | Rich Dellagatta* |
| 149.5 | Bill Hugent |
| 163 | Lee Kemp |
| 180.5 | Chris Campbell |
| 198 | Pete Bush |

**FREESTYLE (Cont.)**

| | |
|---|---|
| 220 | Greg Gibson |
| Hvy | Bruce Baumgartner |
| Team | Sunkist Kids |

**GRECO-ROMAN**

| | |
|---|---|
| 105.5 | T.J. Jones |
| 114.5 | Mark Fuller |
| 125.5 | Rob Hermann |

**GRECO-ROMAN (Cont.)**

| | |
|---|---|
| 136.5 | Dan Mello |
| 149.5 | Jim Martinez |
| 163 | James Andre |
| 180.5 | Steve Goss |
| 198 | Steve Fraser* |
| 220 | Dennis Koslowski |
| Hvy | No champion |
| Team | Minn. Wrestling Club |

### 1984

**FREESTYLE**

| | |
|---|---|
| 105.5 | Rich Salamone |
| 114.5 | Charlie Heard |
| 125.5 | Joe Corso |
| 136.5 | Rich Dellagatta* |
| 149.5 | Andre Metzger |
| 163 | Dave Schultz* |
| 180.5 | Mark Schultz |
| 198 | Steve Fraser |

**FREESTYLE (Cont.)**

| | |
|---|---|
| 220 | Harold Smith |
| Hvy | Bruce Baumgartner |
| Team | Sunkist Kids |

**GRECO-ROMAN**

| | |
|---|---|
| 105.5 | T.J. Jones |
| 114.5 | Mark Fuller |
| 136.5 | Dan Mello |

**GRECO-ROMAN (Cont.)**

| | |
|---|---|
| 149.5 | Jim Martinez* |
| 163 | John Matthews |
| 180.5 | Tom Press |
| 198 | Mike Houck |
| 220 | No champion |
| Hvy | No champion |
| Team | Adirondack 3-Style, WA |

### 1985

**FREESTYLE**

| | |
|---|---|
| 105.5 | Tim Vanni |
| 114.5 | Jim Martin |
| 125.5 | Charlie Heard |
| 136.5 | Darryl Burley |
| 149.5 | Bill Nugent* |
| 163 | Kenny Monday |
| 180.5 | Mike Sheets |
| 198 | Mark Schultz |

**FREESTYLE (Cont.)**

| | |
|---|---|
| 220 | Greg Gibson |
| 286 | Bruce Baumgartner |
| Team | Sunkist Kids |

**GRECO-ROMAN**

| | |
|---|---|
| 105.5 | T.J. Jones |
| 114.5 | Mark Fuller |
| 125.5 | Eric Seward* |

**GRECO-ROMAN (Cont.)**

| | |
|---|---|
| 136.5 | Buddy Lee |
| 149.5 | Jim Martinez |
| 163 | David Butler |
| 180.5 | Chris Catallo |
| 198 | Mike Houck |
| 220 | Greg Gibson |
| 286 | Dennis Koslowski |
| Team | U.S. Marine Corps |

## United States National Champions *(Cont.)*

### 1986

**FREESTYLE**
105.5 .......Rich Salamone
114.5 .......Joe Gonzales
125.5 .......Kevin Darkus
136.5 .......John Smith
149.5 .......Andre Metzger*
163 .........Dave Schultz
180.5 .......Mark Schultz
198 .........Jim Scherr
220 .........Dan Severn

**FREESTYLE** *(Cont.)*
286 .........Bruce Baumgartner
Team .......Sunkist Kids (Div. I)
           Hawkeye Wrestling
           Club (Div. II)

**GRECO-ROMAN**
105.5 .......Eric Wetzel
114.5 .......Shawn Sheldon
125.5 .......Anthony Amado

**GRECO-ROMAN** *(Cont.)*
136.5 .......Frank Famiano
149.5 .......Jim Martinez
163 .........David Butler*
180.5 .......Darryl Gholar
198 .........Derrick Waldroup
220 .........Dennis Koslowski
286 .........Duane Koslowski
Team .......U.S. Marine Corps (Div. I)
           U.S. Navy (Div. II)

### 1987

**FREESTYLE**
105.5 .......Takashi Irie
114.5 .......Mitsuru Sato
125.5 .......Barry Davis
136.5 .......Takumi Adachi
149.5 .......Andre Metzger
163 .........Dave Schultz*
180.5 .......Mark Schultz
198 .........Jim Scherr
220 .........Bill Scherr

**FREESTYLE** *(Cont.)*
286 .........Bruce Baumgartner
Team .......Sunkist Kids (Div. I)
           Team Foxcatcher (Div. II)

**GRECO-ROMAN**
105.5 .......Eric Wetzel
114.5 .......Shawn Sheldon
125.5 .......Eric Seward
136.5 .......Frank Famiano

**GRECO-ROMAN** *(Cont.)*
149.5 .......Jim Martinez
163 .........David Butler
180.5 .......Chris Catallo
198 .........Derrick Waldroup*
220 .........Dennis Koslowski
286 .........Duane Koslowski
Team .........U.S. Marine Corp (Div. I)
           U.S. Army (Div. II)

### 1988

**FREESTYLE**
105.5 .......Tim Vanni
114.5 .......Joe Gonzales
125.5 .......Kevin Darkus
136.5 .......John Smith*
149.5 .......Nate Carr
163 .........Kenny Monday
180.5 .......Dave Schultz
198 .........Melvin Douglas III
220 .........Bill Scherr

**FREESTYLE** *(Cont.)*
286 .........Bruce Baumgartner
Team .......Sunkist Kids (Div. I)
           Team Foxcatcher (Div. II)

**GRECO-ROMAN**
105.5 .......T.J. Jones
114.5 .......Shawn Sheldon
125.5 .......Gogi Parseghian*
136.5 .......Dalen Wasmund

**GRECO-ROMAN** *(Cont.)*
149.5 .......Craig Pollard
163 .........Tony Thomas
180.5 .......Darryl Gholar
198 .........Mike Carolan
220 .........Dennis Koslowski
286 .........Duane Koslowski
Team .......U.S. Marine Corps (Div. I)
           Sunkist Kids (Div. II)

### 1989

**FREESTYLE**
105.5 .......Tim Vanni
114.5 .......Zeke Jones
125.5 .......Brad Penrith
136.5 .......John Smith
149.5 .......Nate Carr
163 .........Rob Koll
180.5 .......Rico Chiapparelli
198 .........Jim Scherr*
220 .........Bill Scherr

**FREESTYLE** *(Cont.)*
286 .........Bruce Baumgartner
Team .......Sunkist Kids (Div. I)
           Team Foxcatcher (Div. II)

**GRECO-ROMAN**
105.5 .......Lew Dorrance
114.5 .......Mark Fuller
125.5 .......Gogi Parseghian
136.5 .......Isaac Anderson

**GRECO-ROMAN** *(Cont.)*
149.5 .......Andy Seras*
163 .........David Butler
180.5 .......John Morgan
198 .........Michial Foy
220 .........Steve Lawson
286 .........Craig Pittman
Team .......U.S. Marine Corps (Div. I)
           Jets USA (Div. II)

### 1990

**FREESTYLE**
105.5 .......Rob Eiter
114.5 .......Zeke Jones
125.5 .......Joe Melchiore
136.5 .......John Smith
149.5 .......Nate Carr
163 .........Rob Koll
180.5 .......Royce Alger
198 .........Chris Campbell*
220 .........Bill Scherr

**FREESTYLE** *(Cont.)*
286 .........Bruce Baumgartner
Team .......Sunkist Kids (Div. I)
           Team Foxcatcher (Div. II)

**GRECO-ROMAN**
105.5 .......Lew Dorrance
114.5 .......Sam Henson
125.5 .......Mark Pustelnik
136.5 .......Isaac Anderson

**GRECO-ROMAN** *(Cont.)*
149.5 .......Andy Seras
163 .........David Butler
180.5 .......Derrick Waldroup
198 .........Randy Couture*
220 .........Chris Tironi
286 .........Matt Ghaffari
Team .......Jets USA (Div. I)
           California Jets (Div. II)

*Outstanding wrestler.

## United States National Champions (Cont.)

### 1991

**FREESTYLE**
105.5 ......Tim Vanni
114.5 ......Zeke Jones
125.5 ......Brad Penrith
136.5 ......John Smith*
149.5 ......Townsend Saunders
163 ..........Kenny Monday
180.5 ......Kevin Jackson
198 ..........Chris Campbell
220 ..........Mark Coleman

**FREESTYLE (Cont.)**
286 ..........Bruce Baumgartner
Team .......Sunkist Kids (Div. I)
    Jets USA (Div. II)

**GRECO-ROMAN**
105.5 ......Eric Wetzel
114.5 ......Shawn Sheldon
125.5 ......Frank Famiano
136.5 ......Buddy Lee

**GRECO-ROMAN (Cont.)**
149.5 ......Andy Seras
163 ..........Gordy Morgan
180.5 ......John Morgan*
198 ..........Michial Foy
220 ..........Dennis Koslowski
286 ..........Craig Pittman
Team .......Jets USA (Div. I)
    Sunkist Kids (Div. II)

### 1992

**FREESTYLE**
105.5 ......Rob Eiter
114.5 ......Jack Griffin
125.5 ......Kendall Cross*
136.5 ......John Fisher
149.5 ......Matt Demaray
163 ..........Greg Elinsky
180.5 ......Royce Alger
198 ..........Dan Chaid
220 ..........Bill Scherr

**FREESTYLE (Cont.)**
286 ..........Bruce Baumgartner
Team .......Sunkist Kids (Div. I)
    Team Foxcatcher (Div. II)

**GRECO-ROMAN**
105.5 ......Eric Wetzel
114.5 ......Mark Fuller
125.5 ......Dennis Hall
136.5 ......Buddy Lee*

**GRECO-ROMAN (Cont.)**
149.5 ......Rodney Smith
163 ..........Travis West
180.5 ......John Morgan
198 ..........Michial Foy
220 ..........Dennis Koslowski
286 ..........Matt Ghaffari
Team .......NY Athletic Club (Div. I)
    Sunkist Kids (Div. II)

### 1993

**FREESTYLE**
105.5 ......Rob Eiter
114.5 ......Zeke Jones
125.5 ......Brad Penrith
136.5 ......Tom Brands
149.5 ......Matt Demaray
163 ..........Dave Schultz*
180.5 ......Kevin Jackson
198 ..........Melvin Douglas
220 ..........Kirk Trost

**FREESTYLE (Cont.)**
286 ..........Bruce Baumgartner
Team .......Sunkist Kids (Div. I)
    Team Foxcatcher (Div. II)

**GRECO-ROMAN**
105.5 ......Eric Wetzel
114.5 ......Shawn Sheldon
125.5 ......Dennis Hall*
136.5 ......Shon Lewis

**GRECO-ROMAN (Cont.)**
149.5 ......Andy Seras
163 ..........Gordy Morgan
180.5 ......Dan Henderson
198 ..........Randy Couture
220 ..........James Johnson
286 ..........Matt Ghaffari
Team .......NY Athletic Club (Div. I)
    Sunkist Kids (Div. II)

### 1994

**FREESTYLE**
105.5 ......Tim Vanni
114.5 ......Zeke Jones
125.5 ......Terry Brands
136.5 ......Tom Brands
149.5 ......Matt Demaray
163 ..........Dave Schultz
180.5 ......Royce Alger
198 ..........Melvin Douglas
220 ..........Mark Kerr

**FREESTYLE (Cont.)**
286 ..........Bruce Baumgartner*
Team .......Sunkist Kids (Div. I)
    Team Foxcatcher (Div. II)

**GRECO-ROMAN**
105.5 ......Isaac Ramaswamy
114.5 ......Shawn Sheldon
125.5 ......Dennis Hall
136.5 ......Shon Lewis

**GRECO-ROMAN (Cont.)**
149.5 ......Andy Seras*
163 ..........Gordy Morgan
180.5 ......Dan Henderson
198 ..........Derrick Waldroup

**GRECO-ROMAN (Cont.)**
220 ..........James Johnson
286 ..........Matt Ghaffari
Team .......Armed Forces (Div. I)
    NY Athletic Club (Div. II)

### 1995

**FREESTYLE**
105.5 ......Rob Eiter
114.5 ......Lou Rosselli
125.5 ......Kendall Cross*
136.5 ......Tom Brands
149.5 ......Matt Demaray
163 ..........Dave Schultz
180.5 ......Kevin Jackson
198 ..........Melvin Douglas
220 ..........Kurt Angle

**FREESTYLE (Cont.)**
286 ..........Bruce Baumgartner
Team .......Sunkist Kids (Div. I)
    Team Foxcatcher (Div. II)

**GRECO-ROMAN**
105.5 ......Isaac Ramaswamy
114.5 ......Shawn Sheldon
125.5 ......Dennis Hall*
136.5 ......Van Fronhofer

**GRECO-ROMAN (Cont.)**
149.5 ......Heath Sims
163 ..........Matt Lindland
180.5 ......Marty Morgan
198 ..........Michial Foy
220 ..........James Johnson
286 ..........Rulon Gardner
Team .......Armed Forces (Div. I)
    Sunkist Kids (Div. II)

*Outstanding wrestler.

## United States National Champions (Cont.)

### 1996

**FREESTYLE**
105.5 ......Rob Eiter
114.5 ......Lou Rosselli
125.5 ......Kendall Cross
136.5 ......Tom Brands
149.5 ......Townsend Saunders
163 ..........Kenny Monday
180.5 ......Les Gutches*
198 ..........Melvin Douglas
220 ..........Kurt Angle

**FREESTYLE (Cont.)**
286 ..........Bruce Baumgartner
Team .......Sunkist Kids (Div. I)
                  NY Athletic Club (Div. II)

**GRECO-ROMAN**
105.5 ......Mujaahid Maynard
114.5 ......Shawn Sheldon
125.5 ......Dennis Hall*
136.5 ......Shon Lewis

**GRECO-ROMAN (Cont.)**
149.5 ......Rodney Smith
163 ..........Keith Sieracki
180.5 ......Marty Morgan
198 ..........Michial Foy
220 ..........John Oostendrop
286 ..........Matt Ghaffari
Team .......Armed Forces (Div. I)
                  Sunkist Kids (Div. II)

### 1997

**FREESTYLE**
110 ..........Kanamti Soloman
119 ..........Zeke Jones
127.75 .....Terry Brands
138.75 .....Carl Kolat
152 ..........Lincoln McIlravy*
167.5 ......Dan St. John
187.25 .....Les Gutches
213.75 .....Melvin Douglas

**FREESTYLE (Cont.)**
275.5 ......Tom Erikson
Team .......Sunkist Kids (Div. I)
                  NY Athletic Club (Div. II)

**GRECO-ROMAN**
110 ..........Mark Yanagihara
119 ..........Broderick Lee
127.75 .....Dennis Hall

**GRECO-ROMAN (Cont.)**
138.75 .....Kevin Bracken
152 ..........Chris Saba
167.5 ......Miguel Spencer
187.25 .....Dan Henderson
213.75 .....Randy Couture*
275.5 ......Rulon Gardner
Team .......Armed Forces (Div. I)
                  NY Athletic Club (Div. II)

### 1998

**FREESTYLE**
119 ..........Sam Henson
127.75 .....Tony Purler
138.75 .....Shawn Charles
152 ..........Lincoln McIlravy
167.5 ......Steve Marianetti
187.25 .....Les Gutches*
213.75 .....Melvin Douglas

**FREESTYLE (Cont.)**
286 ..........Tolly Thompson
Team .......Sunkist Kids (Div. I)
                  NY Athletic Club (Div. II)

**GRECO-ROMAN**
119 ..........Shawn Sheldon
127.75 .....Dennis Hall
138.75 .....Shon Lewis

**GRECO-ROMAN (Cont.)**
152 ..........Chris Saba
167.5 ......Matt Lindland
187.25 .....Dan Niebuhr*
213.75 .....Jason Klohs
286 ..........Matt Ghaffari
Team .......Armed Forces (Div. I)
                  Sunkist Kids (Div. II)

### 1999

**FREESTYLE**
119 ..........Lou Rosselli
127.75 .....Terry Brands
138.75 .....Cary Kolat
152 ..........Lincoln McIlravy
167.5 ......Joe Williams
187.25 .....Les Gutches
213.75 .....Dominic Black

**FREESTYLE (Cont.)**
286 ..........Stephen Neal*
Team .......Sunkist Kids (Div. I)
                  NY Athletic Club (Div. II)

**GRECO-ROMAN**
119 ..........Steven Mays
127.75 .....Dennis Hall
138.75 .....Glen Nieradka

**GRECO-ROMAN (Cont.)**
152 ..........David Zuniga
167.5 ......Matt Lindland
187.25 .....Quincey Clark
213.75 .....Randy Couture
286 ..........Dremiel Byers*
Team .......Minnesota Storm (Div. I)
                  Sunkist Kids (Div. II)

### 2000

**FREESTYLE**
119 ..........Sammie Henson
127.75 .....Keyy Boumans
138.75 .....Cary Kolat
152 ..........Lincoln McIlravy
167.5 ......Brandon Slay*
187.25 .....Les Gutches
213.75 .....Melvin Douglas

**FREESTYLE (Cont.)**
286 ...... Kerry McCoy
Team .......Sunkist Kids (Div. I)
                  NY Athletic Club (Div. II)

**GRECO-ROMAN**
119 ..........Brandon Paulson
127.75 .....Dennis Hall
138.75 .....Kevin Bracken

**GRECO-ROMAN (Cont.)**
152 ..........Heath Sims
167.5 ......Matt Lindland
187.25 .....Quincey Clark*
213.75 .....Jason Gleasman
286 ..........Rulon Gardner
Team .......Armed Forces (Div. I)
                  Sunkist Kids (Div. II)

*Outstanding wrestler.

## United States National Champions *(Cont.)*
### 2001

**FREESTYLE**

119 .........Eric Akin
127.75 .....Eric Guerrero
138.75 .....Bill Zadick
152 .........Ramico Blackmon
167.5 .......Joe Williams
187.25 .....Cael Sanderson*
213.75 .....Dominic Black

**FREESTYLE *(Cont.)***

286 .........Kerry McCoy
Team .......Sunkist Kids (Div. I)
New York AC (Div. II)

**GRECO-ROMAN**

119 .........Jeff Cervone
127.75 .....Dennis Hall
138.75 .....Kevin Bracken

**GRECO-ROMAN *(Cont.)***

152 .........Marcel Cooper
167.5 .......Keith Sieracki
187.25 .....Matt Lindland*
213.75 .....Garrett Lowney
286 .........Rulon Gardner
Team .......Army (Div. I)
Sunkist Kids (Div. II)

*Outstanding wrestler.

## Knight Life

PlayStation is passé. Dominoes are dead. Card games are so five minutes ago. The latest locker room activity for jocks with downtime: chess. Among the pros who've been known to sacrifice a pawn or two are NBA players Steve Smith, Erick Strickland and Chris Webber, North Carolina basketball guard Joe Forte, big league pitchers Rick Reed and Pete Harnisch, and nearly the entire roster of the Knicks. (Larry Johnson is considered the most avid player on the team, Latrell Sprewell the best.)

Why are athletes suddenly seeing the world in black and white? "There are parallels between chess and sports strategy," says Forte. "Different pieces have different strengths. Outthinking your opponent applies in both areas." For Johson the game's appeal is simpler: "I picked it up for relaxation. I can sit down, get into the game and escape."

Of course, pro athletes haven't necessarily adopted all the formal playing customs usually associated with the rarefied game. Knicks forward Kurt Thomas is an unabashed trash talker when he pulls up to a board, and Harnisch doesn't exactly respect his opponent's fallen men. "When he captures your pieces," says Joe Ausanio, a former major league reliever who's now a member of the United States Chess Federation, "he puts them in his nose."

Alex Rodriguez of the
Texas Rangers

# The Sports Market

# Star System

## Increasingly, the powers that be in sports business are staking their financial futures on individual, bankable stars

### BY HANK HERSCH

**K**EYNOTE ADDRESS:
2001 Convention of Sports Executives
Rancho Mirage, Calif.
SPEAKER:
Herb Goldengoos, Chairman,
ProfliGate Pictures

"Ladies and gentlemen, I am delighted to be here today—in fact, I would be delighted to be *anywhere* today after the news I received mere moments ago: ProfliGate's new picture, *One Million Years B.C. II*, starring Britney Spears, has set a record for opening-week grosses in Japan. Thank you very much, thank you. I'm sure you all know how that sort of financial windfall feels—except maybe you folks at the WNBA and MLS tables. Don't look grim. Hey, profitability doesn't happen overnight—or even after five years, in some cases. (Our accountants know some wonderful write-off opportunities for you guys. We'll talk later.)

"Your flattering decision to invite me to speak only underscores what has become increasingly obvious to us in the motion picture industry: that more and more the sports world is, as it were, stealing pages from our playbook. Both of us have limited resources; you have budgets and salary caps, we have a fiduciary responsibility to our shareholders. The question we both face is, What are we going to spend our money on? Now more than ever it seems, we have arrived at the same answer.

"Say a producer wants me to green-light a nine-figure picture. The first thing I want to know is, Who's going to play the lead? I don't care if the screenplay's by Woody and Spike and Shakespeare, if I can't bill Julia or Brad or Harrison—or even Britney—it's going to be awfully hard to say yes. It may cost me 20 percent of my budget to sign a marquee name, but having one guarantees me a strong opening week and a good chance of at least breaking even. The same principle applies for

JOHN BIEVER

*betting* on Tiger, because when he isn't on the leader board people are far less likely to tune in. Last year TV audiences dropped precipitously for those Tour events he didn't enter. Remember when Tiger was asked if he deserved a percentage of the new television contract? 'In a perfect world I would,' he said. If he worked in Hollywood, he would, too.

"So would Michael Jordan. Just think about it: The return of a bald 38-year-old means NBC and TNT will agree to pony up significantly bigger bucks for the TV rights than they would have without His Airness in the league. The NBA has the best labor deal in sports, and kids all over the world are firing up three-pointers, but the league's value swings radically on the whim of one guy—one superstar.

"Remember when Jordan was looking into buying the Hornets in 1999?

you. After all, sports is entertainment, right? And the biggest stars provide the most entertainment.

"The TV pooh-bahs certainly get it, don't you? When six of you from different networks shelled out $850 million in July for the rights to the PGA Tour from 2003 to '06—a 45 percent increase over the current $575 million deal—you weren't buying tight shots of curling 30-foot putts and slacks that look like test patterns. You were paying for the greatest draw in sports, Tiger Woods. Actually, you were

Do you think the referendum to build a new arena in Charlotte would have failed if he had owned the team? If there had been even a remote chance he might suit up in that god-awful teal and play for Charlotte? Would the Grizzlies have moved from Vancouver to Memphis if they had a player as charismatic as Vince Carter, who re-signed in the off-season to stay with the league's lone remaining Canadian franchise, the Toronto Raptors?

"I know what some of you are thinking—especially you, Donald Sterling, with

**Incomplete: LA quarterback Tommy Maddox and the XFL failed to connect with fans.**

BRAD MANGIN

your revolving door of Clippers over in Los Angeles: You don't need stars to make money if you keep your overhead low. After all, Reebok has whittled its list of upper-echelon hoops pitchmen to one—Allen Iverson—dumping such stars as Shaquille O'Neal along the way. (Of course, one of those celebs, Shawn Kemp, got canned in 2000 after he called his

Reeboks the "worst" shoes of his 11-year career. The company was paying him $11.2 million at the time.) As Reebok CEO Paul Fireman put it, 'It takes heavy spending and marketing to bring a celebrity to light.'

"Then in August, Reebok poured an estimated $175 million into a 10-year deal to become the exclusive supplier and marketer of warmup gear and game uniforms for the NBA, the WNBA and the NBA's new developmental league, the NBDL.

Reebok needed this deal to stay on equal footing—so to speak—with Nike, which has nearly 70 percent of the NBA players wearing its shoes, and the fact that Reebok held tight to Iverson indicates that it hasn't given up on the idea of star power. How else do you explain the company's signing Wimbledon and U.S. Open champ Venus Williams to a five-year, $40 million endorsement package, the largest ever for a female athlete? "We want to show her as a lifestyle icon," said the company's chief marketing officer, Angel Martinez.

"Stars provide instant credibility. Our good friend Vince McMahon, the WWF impresario, found that out the hard way. He's bright, he's bold, and in a matter of months he dropped a $35 million bundle on his brainchild, the XFL. Few sports leagues in history got as much attention before a game had been played as the XFL did—thanks largely to Vince's ability to titillate the media. He promoted less rigid rules and more scantily clad cheerleaders than the NFL; he put Minnesota governor Jesse Ventura—who also happens to be a former WWF wrestler—in the broadcast booth; he secured a prime-time slot on NBC and deployed more cameras at XFL games than Spielberg used to re-create D Day. 'We're going to show you the snot coming out of a lineman's nose,' he promised.

"An astounding 10 percent of the nation's homes tuned in to the XFL opener. By the second week viewership fell by half; the third week, by another 25 percent. The problem wasn't the cheerleaders' outfits or the linemen's effluvia—it was the atrocious caliber of play. The only guy to make a name for himself literally made a name for himself: Rod Smart, a Las Vegas Outlaws running back, who chose to put HE HATE ME on the back of his jersey—for reasons truly clear only to him. After 12 weeks and oceans of red ink, McMahon and his TV partners pulled the plug.

"Vince would have been wise to funnel some of the dough he put into production values into players' salaries. The same can hardly be said, however, of the man I per-

sonally consider the sports executive of the year in 2001: Texas Rangers owner Tom Hicks. Take a bow, Tom. Hey, you guys at the Minnesota Twins table, there's no call for that scoffing; commissioner Bud Selig, you can stop sarcastically waving your white handkerchief. There will always be those who don't like trendsetters, Tom, and what you did on Dec. 11, 2000, will have huge implications for the game you love.

"For on that date you signed free-agent Alex Rodriguez to a 10-year, $252 million contract—the most lucrative deal in sports history and more than twice as much money as any baseball team had ever guaranteed a player. And what did you get for that staggering sum? You got a bilingual 25-year-old with boyish good looks who delivers slugging numbers unheard of for a shortstop—Can you tell I have A-Rod on my Rotisserie team?—and you also got a fixture in the middle of the diamond around which to market and build. The contract was way more than any other team offered Rodriguez, but you could afford it because of your 15-year, $550 million TV deal with Fox Sports to televise the Rangers and your hockey team, the Dallas Stars. In fact, because of those rights fees and the increased ticket sales, you believe the Rangers will be turning a profit next season.

"More amazing, you sold Rodriguez on playing in Arlington despite an inept pitching staff and an aging lineup, both of which dragged your club to the bottom of the standings despite A-Rod's stellar season. And you persuaded him to forego out clauses after three years and six years, saying, 'If I'm going to sign this player, I want to do it for a long time.' Maybe this deal will force revenue sharing among the 30 teams; maybe no one will want to sit next to you at the owners' meetings. Whatever happens, you're a shrewd operator in my book.

"And by the way, Tom, do you have a number for Rodriguez's agent? I've got a project—it's sort of *Scarface* meets *American Pie*—that I think would be perfect for Alex."

## Major League Baseball
Address:    245 Park Avenue
    New York, NY 10167
Telephone: (212) 931-7800
Commissioner: Bud Selig
Chief Operating Officer: Paul Beeston
Senior VP, Public Relations: Richard Levin
www.majorleague baseball.com

## Major League Baseball Players Association
Address:    12 East 49th Street, 24th Floor
    New York, NY 10017
Telephone: (212) 826-0808
Executive Director: Donald Fehr
Director of Communications: Greg Bouris
Director of Licensing: Judy Heeter
www.bigleaguers.com

## Anaheim Angels
Address:    P.O. Box 2000
    Anaheim, CA 92803
Telephone: (714) 940-2000
Stadium (Capacity): Edison International Field of
Anaheim (45,050)
Owner: Walt Disney Company
General Manager: Bill Stoneman
Manager: Mike Scioscia
Vice President of Communications: Tim Mead
www.angelsbaseball.com

## Arizona Diamondbacks
Address:    401 East Jefferson Street
    Phoenix, AZ 85001
Telephone: (602) 462-6500
Stadium (Capacity): Bank One Ballpark (49,033)
Managing General Partner: Jerry Colangelo
General Manager: Joe Garagiola Jr.
Manager: Bob Brenly
Director of Public Relations: Mike Swanson
www.azdiamondbacks.com

## Atlanta Braves
Address:    P.O. Box 4064
    Atlanta, GA 30302
Telephone: (404) 522-7630
Stadium (Capacity): Turner Field (50,091)
Vice Chrmn./Sr. Advisor of Time Warner/AOL: Ted Turner
Executive VP & General Manager: John Schuerholz
Manager: Bobby Cox
Director of Public Relations: Jim Schultz
www.atlantabraves.com

## Baltimore Orioles
Address:    Oriole Park at Camden Yards
    333 W Camden Street
    Baltimore, MD 21201
Telephone: (410) 685-9800
Stadium (Capacity): Oriole Park at Camden Yards
(48,876)
Chairman of the Board/CEO: Peter G. Angelos
Vice Chairman/COO: Joseph E. Foss
Manager: Mike Hargrove
Director of Public Relations: Bill Stetka
www.theorioles.com

## Boston Red Sox
Address:    4 Yawkey Way
    Fenway Park
    Boston, MA 02215
Telephone: (617) 267-9440
Stadium (Capacity): Fenway Park (33,993)
CEO: John Harrington
Executive VP and GM: Daniel F. Duquette
Manager: Joe Kerrigan
Vice President, Public Affairs: Dick Bresciani
www.theredsox.com

## Chicago Cubs
Address:    Wrigley Field
    1060 West Addison
    Chicago, IL 60613
Telephone: (773) 404-2827
Stadium (Capacity): Wrigley Field (39,056)
President and CEO: Andrew B. MacPhail
Executive VP of Business Operations: Mark McGuire
Manager: Don Baylor
Director of Media Relations: Sharon Panozzo
www.cubs.com

## Chicago White Sox
Address:    Comiskey Park
    333 West 35th Street
    Chicago, IL 60616
Telephone: (312) 674-1000
Stadium (Capacity): Comiskey Park (46,943)
Chairman: Jerry Reinsdorf
General Manager: Kenny Williams
Manager: Jerry Manuel
Director of Publc Relations: Scott Reifert
www.whitesox.com

## Cincinnati Reds
Address:    100 Cinergy Field
    Cincinnati, OH 45202
Telephone: (513) 421-4510
Stadium (Capacity): Cinergy Field (40,007)
CEO/General Partner: Carl Lindner
COO: John L. Allen
General Manager: James G. Bowden
Managing Executive: John L. Allen
Manager: Bob Boone
Director of Media Relations: Rob Butcher
www.cincinnatireds.com

## Cleveland Indians
Address:    Jacobs Field
    2401 Ontario Street
    Cleveland, OH 44115-4003
Telephone: (216) 420-4200
Stadium (Capacity): Jacobs Field (43,368)
President and CEO: Lawrence J. Dolan
Executive VP and General Manager: Mark Shapiro
Manager: Charlie Manuel
Vice President, Public Relations: Bob DiBiasio
www.indians.com

## Colorado Rockies
Address:    2001 Blake Street
    Denver, CO 80205
Telephone: (303) 292-0200
Stadium (Capacity): Coors Field (50,449)
Chairman, President and CEO: Jerry D. McMorris
Executive VP of Business Operations: Keli McGregor
General Manager and Executive VP: Dan O'Dowd
Manager: Buddy Bell
Senior Director of Public Relations: Jay Alves
www.coloradorockies.com

## Detroit Tigers
Address:    Comerica Park
    2100 Woodward Avenue
    Detroit, MI 48201
Telephone: (313) 962-4000
Stadium (Capacity): Comerica Park (40,120)
Owner and President: Mike Ilitch
Manager: Phil Garner
Director of Communications: John Hahn
www.detroittigers.com

### Florida Marlins
Address:      2267 Dan Marino Boulevard
              Miami, FL 33056
Telephone: (305) 626-7400
Stadium (Capacity): Pro Player Stadium (36,331)
Chairman: John W. Henry
President and General Manager: Dave Dombrowski
Manager: Tony Perez
VP of Communications/Broadcasting: Ron Colangelo
www.floridamarlins.com

### Houston Astros
Address:      P.O. Box 288
              Houston, TX 77001
Telephone: (713) 259-8000
Stadium (Capacity): Enron Field (40,950)
Chairman: Drayton McLane
General Manager: Gerry Hunsicker
Manager: Larry Dierker
Director of Media Relations: Warren Miller
www.astros.com

### Kansas City Royals
Address:      P.O. Box 419969
              Kansas City, MO 64141
Telephone: (816) 921-8000
Stadium (Capacity): Kauffman Stadium (40,793)
Owner and Chairman of the Board: David D. Glass
General Manager: Allard Baird
Manager: Tony Muser
Vice President, Communications: Charlie Seraphin
www.kcroyals.com

### Los Angeles Dodgers
Address:      1000 Elysian Park Avenue
              Los Angeles, CA 90012-1199
Telephone: (323) 224-1500
Stadium (Capacity): Dodger Stadium (56,000)
Managing Partner, Chairman and CEO: Robert Daly
President and COO: Bob Graziano
General Manager: Dave Wallace
Manager: Jim Tracy
Director Media Relations/Publicity: John Olguin
www.dodgers.com

### Milwaukee Brewers
Address:      1 Brewers Way
              Milwaukee, WI 53214
Telephone: (414) 902-4400
Stadium (Capacity): Miller Park (41,900)
President and CEO: Wendy Selig-Prieb
Senior VP and GM: Dean Taylor
Manager: Davey Lopes
Director of Media Relations: Jon Greenberg
www.milwaukeebrewers.com

### Minnesota Twins
Address:      34 Kirby Puckett Place
              Minneapolis, MN 55415
Telephone: (612) 375-1366
Stadium (Capacity): Hubert H. Humphrey
  Metrodome (48,678)
Owner: Carl Pohlad
General Manager: Terry Ryan
Manager: Tom Kelly
Manager of Media Relations: Sean Harlin
www.twinsbaseball.com

### Montreal Expos
Address:      P.O. Box 500 Station M
              Montreal, Quebec H1V 3P2 Canada
Telephone: (514) 253-3434
Stadium (Capacity): Olympic Stadium (46,500)
Chairman and CEO: Jeffrey H. Loria
Vice President and General Manager: Jim Beattie

### Montreal Expos *(Cont.)*
Manager: Jeff Torborg
Director, Media Relations: Peter Loyello
www.montrealexpos.com

### New York Mets
Address:      Shea Stadium
              123-01 Roosevelt Ave.
              Flushing, NY 11368
Telephone: (718) 507-6387
Stadium (Capacity): Shea Stadium (56,521)
Chairman: Nelson Doubleday
President and Chief Executive Officer: Fred Wilpon
Senior VP and General Manager: Steve Phillips
Manager: Bobby Valentine
Director of Media Relations: Jay Horwitz
www.mets.com

### New York Yankees
Address:      Yankee Stadium
              Bronx, NY 10451
Telephone: (718) 293-4300
Stadium (Capacity): Yankee Stadium (57,746)
Principal Owner: George Steinbrenner
Chief Operating Officer: Lonn Trost
VP/General Manager: Brian Cashman
Manager: Joe Torre
Director of Media Relations: Rick Cerone
www.yankees.com

### Oakland Athletics
Address:      7000 Coliseum Way
              Oakland, CA 94621
Telephone: (510) 638-4900
Stadium (Capacity): Network Associates Coliseum
(43,662)
Owners: Steve Schott and Ken Hofmann
President: Michael Crowley
General Manager: Billy Beane
Manager: Art Howe
Baseball Information Manager: Mike Selleck
www.oaklandathletics.com

### Philadelphia Phillies
Address:      P.O. Box 7575
              Philadelphia, PA 19101-7575
Telephone: (215) 463-6000
Stadium (Capacity): Veterans Stadium (62,418)
Chairman: Bill Giles
President: David P. Montgomery
Vice President and General Manager: Ed Wade
Manager: Larry Bowa
Vice President, Public Relations: Larry Shenk
www.phillies.com

### Pittsburgh Pirates
Address:      P.O. Box 7000
              Pittsburgh, PA 15212
Telephone: (412) 323-5000
Stadium (Capacity): PNC Park (37,898)
CEO and Managing General Partner: Kevin McClatchy
General Manager: Dave Littlefield
Manager: Lloyd McClendon
Director of Media Relations: Jim Trdinich
www.pirateball.com

### St. Louis Cardinals
Address:      Busch Stadium/ 250 Stadium Plaza
              St. Louis, MO 63102
Telephone: (314) 421-3060
Stadium (Capacity): Busch Stadium (49,814)
President: Mark Lamping
Senior Vice President and GM: Walt Jocketty
Manager: Tony LaRussa
Director of Media Relations: Brian Bartow
www.stlcardinals.com

## San Diego Padres
Address:     P.O. Box 122000
                San Diego, CA 92112
Telephone: (619) 283-4494
Stadium (Capacity): Qualcomm Stadium (66,307)
Chairman: John Moores
General Manager: Kevin Towers
Manager: Bruce Bochy
Director of Media Relations: Glenn Geffner
www.padres.com

## San Francisco Giants
Address:     24 Willie Mays Plaza
                San Francisco, CA 94107
Telephone: (415) 972-2000
Stadium (Capacity): Pacific Bell Park (41,341)
President/Managing General Partner: Peter Magowan
General Manager: Brian Sabean
Manager: Dusty Baker
Vice President, Communications: Bob Rose
www.sfgiants.com

## Seattle Mariners
Address:     P.O. Box 4100
                Seattle, WA 98104
Telephone: (206) 346-4000
Stadium (Capacity): SAFECO Field (47,116)
Chairman and CEO: Howard Lincoln
General Manager: Pat Gillick
Manager: Lou Piniella
Director of Baseball Information: Tim Hevly
www.seattlemariners.com

## Tampa Bay Devil Rays
Address:     One Tropicana Drive
                St. Petersburg, FL 33705
Telephone: (727) 825-3137
Stadium (Capacity): Tropicana Field (44,397)
Managing General Partner/CEO: Vincent J. Naimoli
Senior VP and General Manager: Chuck Lamar
Manager: Hal McRae
Vice President, Public Relations: Rick Vaughn
www.devilray.com

## Texas Rangers
Address:     P.O. Box 90111
                Arlington, TX 76004
Telephone: (817) 273-5222
Stadium (Capacity): The Ballpark in Arlington (49,115)
Owner: Thomas O. Hicks
General Manager: Doug Melvin
Manager: Jerry Narron
Senior VP, Communications: John Blake
www.texasrangers.com

## Toronto Blue Jays
Address:     SkyDome
                1 Blue Jays Way, Suite 3200
                Toronto, Ontario M5V 1J1 Canada
Telephone: (416) 341-1000
Stadium (Capacity): SkyDome (45,100)
Presiden/CEO: Paul Godfrey
Senior Vice President/GM: Gord Ash
Manager: Buck Martinez
Vice President, Media Relations: Howard Starkman
www.bluejays.com

# Pro Football Directory

## National Football League
Address:     280 Park Avenue
                New York, NY 10017
Telephone: (212) 450-2000
Commissioner: Paul Tagliabue
www.nfl.com

## NFL Players Association
Address:     2021 L Street, N.W.
                Washington, D.C. 20036
Telephone: (202) 463-2200
Executive Director: Gene Upshaw
Director of Communications: Carl Francis
www.nflpa.org

## Arizona Cardinals
Address:     P.O. Box 888
                Phoenix, AZ 85001
Telephone: (602) 379-0101
Stadium (Capacity): Sun Devil Stadium (73,377)
President and Owner: Bill Bidwill
General Manager: Bob Ferguson
Head Coach: Dave McGinnis
Director of Public Relations: Paul Jensen
www.azcardinals.com

## Atlanta Falcons
Address:     4400 Falcon Park Way
                Flowery Branch, GA 30542
Telephone: (770) 965-3115
Stadium (Capacity): Georgia Dome (71,228)
President: Taylor W. Smith
VP of Football Operations: Ron Hill
Coach: Dan Reeves
Director of Communications: Aaron Salkin
www.atlantafalcons.com

## Baltimore Ravens
Address:     11001 Owings Mills Blvd.
                Owings Mills, MD 21117
Telephone: (410) 654-6200
Stadium (Capacity): PSINet Stadium (69,084)
Owner/CEO: Art Modell
President/COO: David Modell
Coach: Brian Billick
VP of Public Relations: Kevin Byrne
www.ravenszone.net

## Buffalo Bills
Address:     One Bills Drive
                Orchard Park, NY 14127
Telephone: (716) 648-1800
Stadium (Capacity): Ralph Wilson Stadium (73,967)
Chairman: Ralph C. Wilson Jr.
General Manager: Tom Donohoe
Coach: Gregg Williams
Vice President of Communications: Scott Berchtold
www.buffalobills.com

## Carolina Panthers
Address:     Ericsson Stadium
                800 South Mint St.
                Charlotte, NC 28202
Telephone: (704) 358-7000
Stadium (Capacity): Ericsson Stadium (73,250)
Founder and Owner: Jerry Richardson
President: Mark Richardson
Coach: George Seifert
Director of Communications: Charlie Dayton
www.panthers.com

## Chicago Bears
Address:     1000 Football Drive
             Lake Forest, IL 60045
Telephone: (847) 295-6600
Stadium (Capacity): Soldier Field (66,944)
Chairman: Michael McCaskey
President/CEO: Ted Phillips
Coach: Dick Jauron
Director of Public Relations: Scott Hagel
www.chicagobears.com

## Cincinnati Bengals
Address:     One Paul Brown Stadium
             Cincinnati, OH 45202
Telephone: (513) 621-3550
Stadium (Capacity): Paul Brown Stadium (65,393)
President: Mike Brown
Executive Vice President: Katherine Blackburn
Coach: Dick LeBeau
Director of Public Relations: Jack Brennan
www.bengals.com

## Cleveland Browns
Address:     76 Lou Groza Boulevard
             Berea, OH 44017
Telephone: (440) 891-5000
Stadium (Capacity): Cleveland Browns Stadium
(73,200)
Owner: Alfred Lerner
Exec. VP/Dir. of Football Operations: Dwight Clark
Coach: Butch Davis
Exec. Director of Publicity/Media Rel.: Todd Stewart
www.clevelandbrowns.com

## Dallas Cowboys
Address:     One Cowboys Parkway
             Irving, TX 75063
Telephone: (972) 556-9900
Stadium (Capacity): Texas Stadium (65,639)
Owner, President and General Manager: Jerry Jones
Coach: Dave Campo
Public Relations Director: Rich Dalrymple
www.dallascowboys.com

## Denver Broncos
Address:     13655 Broncos Parkway
             Englewood, CO 80112
Telephone: (303) 649-9000
Stadium (Capacity): INVESCO Field at Mile High
(76,125)
President and Chief Executive Officer: Pat Bowlen
General Manager: Neal Dahlen
Coach: Mike Shanahan
Director of Media Relations: Jim Saccomano
www.denverbroncos.com

## Detroit Lions
Address:     1200 Featherstone Road
             Pontiac, MI 48342
Telephone: (248) 335-4131
Stadium (Capacity): Pontiac Silverdome (80,311)
Owner/Chairman: William Clay Ford
President/CEO: Matt Millen
Coach: Marty Mornhinweg
Director of Media Relations: Matt Barnhart
www.detroitlions.com

## Green Bay Packers
Address:     1265 Lombardi Avenue
             Green Bay, WI 54304
Telephone: (920) 496-5700
Stadium (Capacity): Lambeau Field (60,890)
President: Bob Harlan
Executive VP/GM/Coach: Mike Sherman
Executive Director of Public Relations: Lee Remmel
www.packers.com

## Indianapolis Colts
Address:     P.O. Box 535000
             Indianapolis, IN 46253
Telephone: (317) 297-2658
Stadium (Capacity): RCA Dome (56,127)
Owner and Chief Executive Officer: Jim Irsay
President: Bill Polian
Senior Executive Vice President: Pete Ward
Coach: Jim Mora
Vice President of Public Relations: Craig Kelley
www.colts.com

## Jacksonville Jaguars
Address:     One Alltel Stadium Place
             Jacksonville, FL 32202
Telephone: (904) 633-6000
Stadium (Capacity): Alltel Stadium (73,000)
Owner: J. Wayne Weaver
Vice President and CFO: Bill Prescott
Senior VP of Football Operations: Michael Huyghue
Coach: Tom Coughlin
Executive Director of Communications: Dan Edwards
www.jaguars.com

## Kansas City Chiefs
Address:     One Arrowhead Drive
             Kansas City, MO 64129
Telephone: (816) 920-9300
Stadium (Capacity): Arrowhead Stadium (79,451)
Founder: Lamar Hunt
CEO, President and General Manager: Carl Peterson
Coach: Dick Vermeil
Public Relations Director: Bob Moore
www.kcchiefs.com

## Miami Dolphins
Address:     7500 S.W. 30th Street
             Davie, FL 33314
Telephone: (954) 452-7000
Stadium (Capacity): Pro Player Stadium (75,540)
Chairman of the Board/Owner: H. Wayne Huizenga
President and COO: Eddie J. Jones
VP of Player Personnel: Rick Spielman
Head Coach: Dave Wannstedt
VP Media Relations: Harvey Greene
www.miamidolphins.com

## Minnesota Vikings
Address:     9520 Viking Drive
             Eden Prairie, MN 55344
Telephone: (952) 828-6500
Stadium (Capacity): HHH Metrodome (64,121)
Owner: Red McCombs
President: Gary Woods
Coach: Dennis Green
Public Relations Director: Bob Hagan
www.vikings.com

## New England Patriots
Address:     Foxboro Stadium
             60 Washington St.
             Foxboro, MA 02035
Telephone: (508) 543-8200
Stadium (Capacity): Foxboro Stadium (60,292)
Owner and Chairman: Robert K. Kraft
Vice Chairman: Jonathan Kraft
Senior VP and COO: Andy Wasynczuk
Coach: Bill Belichick
VP of Player Development/
Community Relations: Donald Lowery
www.patriots.com

## New Orleans Saints
Address:     5800 Airline Highway
             Metairie, LA 70003
Telephone: (504) 733-0255
Stadium (Capacity): Louisiana Superdome (70,054)
Owner: Tom Benson
GM of Football Operations: Randy Mueller
Head Coach: Jim Haslett
Director of Media Relations: Greg Bensel
www.neworleanssaints.com

## New York Giants
Address:     Giants Stadium
             East Rutherford, NJ 07073
Telephone: (201) 935-8111
Stadium (Capacity): Giants Stadium (79,469)
President and co-CEO: Wellington T. Mara
Chairman and co-CEO: Preston Robert Tisch
Senior VP and General Manager: Ernie Accorsi
Coach: Jim Fassel
Vice President of Communications: Pat Hanlon
www.giants.com

## New York Jets
Address:     1000 Fulton Avenue
             Hempstead, NY 11550
Telephone: (516) 560-8100
Stadium (Capacity): Giants Stadium (80,062)
Owner: Robert Wood Johnson IV
Director of Player Personnel: Dick Haley
Coach: Herman Edwards
VP of Public Relations: Frank Ramos
www.newyorkjets.com

## Oakland Raiders
Address:     1220 Harbor Bay Parkway
             Alameda, CA 94502
Telephone: (510) 864-5000
Stadium (Capacity): Oakland-Alameda County
  Coliseum (62,500)
President of the General Partner: Al Davis
Coach: Jon Gruden
Executive Assistant: Al LoCasale
Director of Public Relations: Mike Taylor
www.raiders.com

## Philadelphia Eagles
Address:     NovaCare Complex
             1 NovaCare Way
             Philadelphia, PA 19145
Telephone: (215) 463-2500
Stadium (Capacity): Veterans Stadium (65,352)
Chairman: Jeffrey Lurie
President: Joe Banner
Exec. VP of Football Operations/Coach: Andy Reid
Football Media Services Coordinator: Derek Boyko
www.philadelphiaeagles.com

## Pittsburgh Steelers
Address:     3400 South Water Street
             Pittsburgh, PA 15203
Telephone: (412) 432-7800
Stadium (Capacity): Heinz Field (64,450)
President: Dan Rooney
Director of Football Operations: Kevin Colbert
Coach: Bill Cowher
Director of Communications: Ron Wahl
www.steelers.com

## St. Louis Rams
Address:     One Rams Way
             St. Louis, MO 63045
Telephone: (314) 982-7267
Stadium (Capacity): Trans World Dome (66,000)
Owner and Chairman: Georgia Frontiere
Vice Chairman and Owner: Stan Kroenke

## St. Louis Rams *(Cont.)*
President: John Shaw
Coach: Mike Martz
Director of Public Relations: Rick Smith
www.stlouisrams.com

## San Francisco 49ers
Address:     4949 Centennial Boulevard
             Santa Clara, CA 95054
Telephone: (408) 562-4949
Stadium (Capacity): 3Com Park (69,734)
Owner: Denise DeBartolo-York
President: Peter Harris
Director/Owner's Rep.: John York
General Manager: Terry Donahue
Coach: Steve Mariucci
Public Relations Director: Kirk Reynolds
www.49ers.com

## Tampa Bay Buccaneers
Address:     One Buccaneer Place
             Tampa, FL 33607
Telephone: (813) 870-2700
Stadium (Capacity): Raymond James Stadium (66,321)
Owner: Malcolm Glazer
General Manager: Rich McKay
Coach: Tony Dungy
Director of Communications: Reggie Roberts
www.buccaneers.com

## Washington Redskins
Address:     21300 Redskins Park Drive
             Ashburn, VA 20147
Telephone: (703) 478-8900
Stadium (Capacity): Fedex Field (86,484)
Owner: Daniel M. Snyder
VP of Player Personnel: John Schneider
Coach/Dir. of Football Operations: Marty
Schottenheimer
Director of Public Relations: Michelle Tessier
www.redskins.com

## San Diego Chargers
Address:     Qualcomm Stadium
             4020 Murphy Canyon Road
             San Diego, CA 92123
Telephone: (858) 874-4500
Stadium (Capacity): Qualcomm Stadium (70,000)
Chairman: Alex G. Spanos
President/Vice Chairman: Dean A. Spanos
General Manager: John Butler
Coach: Mike Riley
Director of Public Relations: Bill Johnston
www.chargers.com

## Seattle Seahawks
Address:     11220 N.E. 53rd Street
             Kirkland, WA 98033
Telephone: (425) 827-9777
Stadium (Capacity): Husky Stadium (68,589)
Owner: Paul Allen
President: Bob Whitsitt
Coach/GM: Mike Holmgren
VP of Administration and Communications: Gary Wright
Director of Public Relations: Dave Pearson
www.seahawks.com

## Tennessee Titans
Address:     460 Great Circle Road
             Nashville, TN 37228
Telephone: 615-565-4000
Stadium (Capacity): Adelphia Coliseum (68,498)
President: Jeff Diamond
General Manager: Floyd Reese
Coach: Jeff Fisher
Director of Media Relations: Robbie Bohren
www.titansonline.com

## Other Leagues

### Canadian Football League
Address:  110 Eglinton Avenue West, 5th floor
Toronto, Ontario M4R1A3 Canada
Telephone: (416) 322-9650
Commissioner: Michael R. Lysko
Senior VP, Business Operations/Treasurer: James E. Grundy
VP of Communications: Shawn Lackie
www.cfl.ca

### NFL EUROPE
Address:  280 Park Avenue
New York, NY 10017
Telephone: (212) 450-2000
President: Bill Peterson (London)
Chief Operating Officer: Dan Margoshes (London)
Director of Communications: David Tossel
www.nfleurope.com

# Pro Basketball Directory

## National Basketball Association

### National Basketball Association
Address:  645 Fifth Avenue
New York, NY 10022
Telephone: (212) 826-7000
Commissioner: David Stern
Deputy Commissioner: Russell Granik
Sr. VP of Communications: Brian McIntyre
www.nba.com

### National Basketball Association Players Association
Address:  1700 Broadway
Suite 1400
New York, NY 10019
Telephone: (212) 655-0880
Executive Director: William Hunter
www.nbapa.com

### Atlanta Hawks
Address:  One CNN Center, South Tower
Atlanta, GA 30303
Telephone: (404) 827-3800
Arena (Capacity): Philips Arena (19,445)
Owner: Ted Turner
President: Stan Kasten
VP and General Manager: Pete Babcock
Coach: Lon Kruger
VP of Communications: Arthur Triche
www.hawks.com

### Boston Celtics
Address:  151 Merrimac Street
Boston, MA 02114
Telephone: (617) 523-6050
Arena (Capacity): FleetCenter (18,624)
Owner and Chairman of the Board: Paul Gaston
General Manager: Chris Wallace
Coach: Jim O'Brien
Director of Media Relations: Bill Bonsiewicz
www.celtics.com

### Charlotte Hornets
Address:  100 Hive Drive
Charlotte, NC 28217
Telephone: (704) 357-0252
Arena (Capacity): Charlotte Coliseum (19,925)
Owners: George Shinn and Ray Wooldridge
Coach: Paul Silas
VP of Public Relations: Harold Kaufman
www.hornets.com

### Chicago Bulls
Address:  1901 W. Madison Street
Chicago, IL 60612
Telephone: (312) 455-4000
Arena (Capacity): United Center (21,711)

### Chicago Bulls *(Cont.)*
Chairman: Jerry Reinsdorf
Executive VP of Basketball Operations: Jerry Krause
Coach: Tim Floyd
Senior Director of Media Services: Tim Hallam
www.bulls.com

### Cleveland Cavaliers
Address:  One Center Court
Cleveland, OH 44115
Telephone: (216) 420-2000
Arena (Capacity): Gund Arena (20,562)
Chairman: Gordon Gund
Senior VP and GM: Jim Paxson
Coach: John Lucas
Sr. Director of Communications/PR: Bob Price
www.cavs.com

### Dallas Mavericks
Address:  2500 Victory Avenue
Dallas, TX 75201
Telephone: (214) 665-4660
Arena (Capacity): American Airlines Center (19,200)
Owner: Mark Cuban
General Manager and Head Coach: Don Nelson
Director of Player Personnel: Donn Nelson
Sr. VP of Marketing/Communications: Matt Fitzgerald
www.dallasmavericks.com

### Denver Nuggets
Address:  Pepsi Center
1000 Chopper Circle
Denver, CO 80204
Telephone: (303) 405-1100
Arena (Capacity): Pepsi Center (19,099)
Owner: E. Stanley Kroenke
President/Coach: Dan Issel
Media Relations Director: Tommy Sheppard
www.nuggets.com

### Detroit Pistons
Address:  The Palace of Auburn Hills
Two Championship Drive
Auburn Hills, MI 48326
Telephone: (248) 377-0100
Arena (Capacity): The Palace of Auburn Hills (22,076)
Owner: William M. Davidson
President of Basketball Operations: Joe Dumars
Coach: Rick Carlisle
VP of Public Relations: Matt Dobek
www.palacenet.com

## National Basketball Association *(Cont.)*

### Golden State Warriors
Address:    1011 Broadway
            Oakland, CA  94607-4019
Telephone: (510) 986-2200
Arena (Capacity): The Arena in Oakland
  (19,596)
Owner and CEO: Christopher Cohan
General Manager: Garry St. Jean
Coach: Dave Cowens
Director of Public Relations: Raymond Ridder
www.gs-warriors.com

### Houston Rockets
Address:    Two Greenway Plaza, Suite 400
            Houston, TX  77046
Telephone: (713) 627-3865
Arena (Capacity): Compaq Center (16,285)
Owner: Leslie Alexander
Chief Operating Officer: George Postolos
General Manager: Carroll Dawson
Coach: Rudy Tomjanovich
Director of Team Communications: Nelson Luis
www.rockets.com

### Indiana Pacers
Address:    125 S. Pennsylvania Street
            Indianapolis, IN  46204
Telephone: (317) 917-2500
Arena (Capacity): Conseco Fieldhouse (18,345)
Owners: Melvin Simon and Herbert Simon
President: Donnie Walsh
General Manager: David Kahn
Head Coach: Isiah Thomas
Media Relations Director: David Benner
www.pacers.com

### Los Angeles Clippers
Address:    The Staples Center
            1111 S. Figueroa Street - St. 1100
            Los Angeles, CA  90015
Telephone: (213) 742-7500
Arena (Capacity): The Staples Center (18,964)
Owner: Donald T. Sterling
Vice President of Basketball Operations: Elgin Baylor
Coach: Alvin Gentry
Vice President of Communications: Joe Safety
www.clippers.com

### Los Angeles Lakers
Address:    555 North Nash Street
            El Segundo, CA  90245
Telephone: (310) 426-6000
Arena (Capacity): The Staples Center (18,997)
Owner: Dr. Jerry Buss
General Manager: Mitch Kupchak
Coach: Phil Jackson
Director of Public Relations: John Black
www.lakers.com

### Memphis Grizzlies
Address:    60 Madison Street
            10th Floor
            Memphis  TN 38103
Telephone: (901) 205-1234
Arena (Capacity): The Pyramid (19,423)
Owner: Michael E. Heisley
President of Basketball Operations: Dick Versace
General Manager: Billy Knight
Coach: Sidney Lowe
Director of Media Relations: Kirk Clayborn
www.grizzlies.com

### Miami Heat
Address:    American Airlines Arena
            601 Biscayne Boulevard
            Miami, FL  33132
Telephone: (786) 777-4328
Arena (Capacity): American Airlines Arena (16,500)
Managing General Partner: Micky Arison
Executive Emeritus: Pauline Winick
President and Coach: Pat Riley
President/GM of Basketball Operations: Randy Pfund
VP of Sports Media Relations: Tim Donovan
www.heat.com

### Milwaukee Bucks
Address:    The Bradley Center
            1001 N. Fourth Street
            Milwaukee, WI  53203
Telephone: (414) 227-0500
Arena (Capacity): The Bradley Center (18,717)
Owner: Herb Kohl
General Manager: Ernie Grunfeld
Coach: George Karl
Public Relations Director: Cheri Hanson
www.bucks.com

### Minnesota Timberwolves
Address:    600 First Avenue North
            Minneapolis, MN  55403
Telephone: (612) 673-1600
Arena (Capacity): Target Center (19,006)
Owner: Glen Taylor
VP of Basketball Operations: Kevin McHale
Coach: Phil (Flip) Saunders
Director of Communications: Kent Wipf
www.timberwolves.com

### New Jersey Nets
Address:    Nets Champion Center
            390 Murray Hill Parkway
            East Rutherford, NJ  07073
Telephone: (201) 935-8888
Arena (Capacity): Continental Airlines Arena (20,049)
Principal Owner: Lewis Katz
President/General Manager: Rod Thorn
Coach: Byron Scott
Director of Public Relations: Gary Sussman
www.njnets.com

### New York Knickerbockers
Address:    Madison Square Garden
            Two Pennsylvania Plaza
            New York, NY  10121
Telephone: (212) 465-5867
Arena (Capacity): Madison Square Garden (19,763)
Owner: ITT/Sheraton and Cablevision
Chairman of MSG/President and CEO of Cablevision:
James Dolan
Team President/General Manager: Scott Layden
Coach: Jeff Van Gundy
Vice President of Public Relations: TBA
www.nyknicks.com

## National Basketball Association *(Cont.)*

### Orlando Magic
Address:    Two Magic Place
8701 Maitland Summit Blvd.
Orlando, FL 32810
Telephone: (407) 916-2400
Arena (Capacity): TD Waterhouse Centre (17,248)
Owner: Rich DeVos
Senior Executive Vice President: Pat Williams
General Manager: John Gabriel
Coach: Glenn "Doc" Rivers
Director of Communications: Joel Glass
www.orlandomagic.com

### Philadelphia 76ers
Address:    First Union Center
3601 South Broad Street
Philadelphia, PA 19148
Telephone: (215) 339-7600
Arena (Capacity): First Union Center (20,444)
Head Coach and Vice President of Basketball
  Operations: Larry Brown
General Manager: Billy King
Executive Vice President: Dave Coskey
Senior Director of Communications: Karen Frascona
www.sixers.com

### Phoenix Suns
Address:    P.O. Box 1369
Phoenix, AZ 85001
Telephone: (602) 379-7900
Arena (Capacity): America West Arena (19,023)
Chairman/CEO and Managing General Partner: Jerry Colangelo
President: Bryan Colangelo
Coach: Scott Skiles
VP of Basketball Communications: Julie Fie
www.suns.com

### Portland Trail Blazers
Address:    One Center Court
Suite 200
Portland, OR 97227
Telephone: (503) 234-9291
Arena (Capacity): Rose Garden Arena (19,980)
Chairman of the Board: Paul Allen
President and General Manager: Bob Whitsitt
Coach: Maurice Cheeks
Director of Sports Communications: Sue Carpenter
www.blazers.com

### Sacramento Kings
Address:    One Sports Parkway
Sacramento, CA 95834
Telephone: (916) 928-0000
Arena (Capacity): ARCO Arena (17,317)
Owners: Joe and Gavin Maloof
President of Basketball Operations: Geoff Petrie
Coach: Rick Adelman
Director of Media Relations: Troy Hanson
www.kings.com

### San Antonio Spurs
Address:    Alamodome
100 Montana
San Antonio, TX 78203
Telephone: (210) 554-7787
Arena (Capacity): Alamodome (34,215)
Chairman: Peter Holt
Head Coach and General Manager: Gregg Popovich
Director of Media Services: Tom James
www.spurs.com

### Seattle SuperSonics
Address:    351 Elliott Avenue West
Suite 500
Seattle, WA 98119
Telephone: (206) 281-5847
Arena (Capacity): KeyArena (17,072)
Owner: The Basketball Club of Seattle, LLC
Chairman: Howard Schultz
President/CEO: Wally Walker
General Manager: Rick Sund
Coach: Nate McMillan
Director of Public Relations: Marc Moquin
www.supersonics.com

### Toronto Raptors
Address:    40 Bay Street, Suite 400
Toronto, Ontario M5J 2X2 Canada
Telephone: (416) 815-5600
Arena (Capacity): Air Canada Centre (19,800)
Owner: Maple Leaf Sports and Entertainment, Ltd.
Senior VP and General Manager: Glen Grunwald
Coach: Lenny Wilkens
Manager of Media Relations: Jim Labumbard
www.raptors.com

### Utah Jazz
Address:    301 West So. Temple
Salt Lake City, UT 84101
Telephone: (801) 575-7800
Arena (Capacity): Delta Center (19,911)
Owner: Larry H. Miller
President: Dennis Haslam
VP of Basketball Operations: Kevin O'Connor
Coach: Jerry Sloan
Director of Media Relations: Kim Turner
www.utahjazz.com

### Washington Wizards
Address:    601 F Street NW
Washington D.C. 20004
Telephone: (202) 661-5000
Arena (Capacity): MCI Center (20,674)
Owner: Abe Pollin
General Manager and Vice President: Wes Unseld
President of Basketball Operations: Michael Jordan
Coach: Doug Collins
Director of Public Relations: Maureen Nasser
www.nba.com/wizards

## Women's National Basketball Association

### Women's National Basketball Association
Address: 645 Fifth Avenue
New York, NY 10022
Telephone: (212) 688-9622
President: Valerie B. Ackerman
Director of Sports Communications: Maureen Coyle
www.wnba.com

### Charlotte Sting
Address: 3308 Oak Lake Boulevard
Suite B
Charlotte, NC 28208
Telephone: (704) 357-0252
Arena (Capacity): Charlotte Coliseum (12,843)
Executive Vice President: Sam Russo
Coach: Anne Donovan
Vice President of Public Relations: Harold Kaufman
www.charlottesting.com

### Cleveland Rockers
Address: Gund Arena
One Center Court
Cleveland, OH 44115
Telephone: (216) 420-2000
Arena (Capacity): Gund Arena (20,500)
Chairman: Gordon Gund
President, Business Division: James C. Boland
Coach: Dan Hughes
Director of Media Relations: Ed Markey
www.clevelandrockers.com

### Detroit Shock
Address: 2 Championship Drive
Auburn Hills, MI 48326
Telephone: (248) 377-0100
Arena (Capacity): The Palace of Auburn Hills (19,000)
Managing Partner: William Davidson
President: Tom Wilson
Head Coach: Greg Williams
Director of Media Relations: Dennis Sampier
www.detroitshock.com

### Houston Comets
Address: Two Greenway Plaza, Suite 400
Houston, TX 77046-3865
Telephone: (713) 627-9622
Arena (Capacity): The Compaq Center (16,285)
President: Leslie L. Alexander
Coach and General Manager: Van Chancellor
Director of Team Communications: Tim Frank
www.houstoncomets.com

### Indiana Fever
Address: 125 S. Pennsylvania Street
Indianapolis, IN 46204
Telephone: (317) 917-2500
Arena (Capacity): Conseco Field House (18,345)
President: Donnie Walsh
Chief Operating Officer: Kelly Kraus Koupf
Coach: Nell Fortner
Director of Media Relations: Tom Savage
www.wnba.com/fever

### Los Angeles Sparks
Address: 555 Nash Street
El Segundo, CA 90tktk
Telephone: (310) 330-2434
Arena (Capacity): Staples Center (18,997)
Chairman: Dr. Jerry Buss
General Manager: Virginia (Penny) Toller

### Los Angeles Sparks *(Cont.)*
Coach: Michael Cooper
Media Relations Director: Krystal Shipp
www.lasparks.com

### Minnesota Lynx
Address: Target Center
600 First Avenue North
Minneapolis, MN 55403
Telephone: (612) 673-8400
Arena (Capacity): Target Center (19,006)
Chief Operating Officer: Roger Griffith
General Manager/Coach: Brian Agler
Public Relations Manager: Mike Cristaldi
www.wnba.com/lynx

### New York Liberty
Address: Two Penn Plaza
New York, NY 10121
Telephone: (212) 465-5867
Arena (Capacity): Madison Square Garden (19,763)
GM and Vice President: Carol Blazejowski
Coach: Richie Adubato
VP of Marketing and Communications: Amy Scheer
www.nyliberty.com

### Orlando Miracle
Address: Two Magic Place
8701 Maitland Summit Boulevard
Orlando, FL 32810
Telephone: (407) 916-2400
Arena (Capacity): TD Waterhouse Centre (17,306)
Chairman: Rich DeVos
President: Bob Van der Weide
General Manager/ Coach: Carolyn Peck
Director of Media Relations: Katherine Wu
www.orlandomiracle.com

### Miami Sol
Address: American Airlines Arena
601 Biscayne Blvd.
Miami, FL 33132
Telephone: (786) 577-4328
Arena (Capacity): American Airlines Arena (10,412)
Senior Director of Operations: Kim Stone
General Manager/ Coach: Ron Rothstein
Media Relations Manager: Alan Hancock
www.miami-sol.com

### Phoenix Mercury
Address: 201 East Jefferson Street
Phoenix, AZ 85004
Telephone: (602) 514-8333
Arena (Capacity): America West Arena (17,623)
Chairman and CEO: Jerry Colangelo
President: Bryan Colangelo
Coach: Cynthia Cooper
Media Relations Director: Tami Scott
www.phoenixmercury.com

### Portland Fire
Address: One Center Court
Suite 150
Portland, OR 97227
Telephone: (503) 235-9291
Arena (Capacity): The Rose Garden (19,980)
Chairman: Paul Allen
Vice President of Business Operations: Sandi Bittler
General Manager/ Coach: Linda Hargrove
Director of Communications: Jill Wiggins
www.firebasketball.com

## Women's National Basketball Association *(Cont.)*

### Sacramento Monarchs

Address:     One Sports Parkway
             Sacramento, CA  95834
Telephone: (916) 455-4647
Arena (Capacity): ARCO Arena (17,317)
Managing General Partner: Jim Thomas
President: John Thomas
General Manager: Jerry Reynolds
Coach: Maura McHugh
Manager of Media Relations: Jennifer Norris
www.sacramentomonarchs.com

### Seattle Storm

Address:     351 Elliott Avenue West
             Suite 500
             Seattle, WA 98119
Telephone: (206) 281-5800
Arena (Capacity): Key Arena (12,000)
Owners: The Basketball Club of Seattle LLC
President and CEO: Wally Walker
General Manager/ Coach: Lin Dunn
Director, Media Relations: Valerie O'Neil
www.wnba.com/storm

### Utah Starzz

Address:     301 W. South Temple
             Salt Lake City, UT 84101
Telephone: (801) 325-7827
Arena (Capacity): Delta Center (8,916)
Owner: Larry H. Miller
President: Dennis Haslam
Coach: Candi Harvey
Media Relations Manager: Erin Bodily
www.utahstarzz.com

### Washington Mystics

Address:     MCI Center
             601 F Street, NW
             Washington, DC 20004
Telephone: (202) 661-5000
Arena (Capacity): MCI Center (19,093)
Chairman: Abe Pollin
President: Susan O'Malley
Coach: Tom Maher
Director, Public Relations: Sashia Jones
www.washingtonmystics.com

# Hockey Directory

### National Hockey League

Address:     1251 Avenue of the Americas
             47th floor
             New York, NY  10020-1198
Telephone: (212) 789-2000
Commissioner: Gary Bettman
President of NHL Enterprises: Ed Horne
Executive VP and Dir. of Hockey Operations: Colin Campbell
VP of Media Relations: Frank Brown
www.nhl.com

### National Hockey League Players Association

Address:     777 Bay Street, Suite 2400
             Toronto, Ontario M5G 2C8 Canada
Telephone: (416) 313-2300
Executive Director: Bob Goodenow
www.nhlpa.com

### Mighty Ducks of Anaheim

Address:     Arrowhead Pond of Anaheim
             2695 Katella Avenue
             Anaheim, CA  92806
Telephone: (714) 940-2900
Arena (Capacity): Arrowhead Pond of Anaheim (17,174)
Chairman and Governor: Tony Tavares
President and General Manager: Pierre Gauthier
Coach: Bryan Murray
Manager of Communications: Alex Gilchrist
www.mightyducks.com

### Atlanta Thrashers

Address:     1 CNN Center
             P.O. Box 15538
             Atlanta, GA 30348
Telephone: (404) 827-5300
Arena (Capacity): Philips Arena (18,545)
Owner: AOL/Time Warner

### Atlanta Thrashers *(Cont.)*

President and Governor: Stan Kasten
VP and General Manager: Don Waddell
Coach: Curt Fraser
Director of Public Relations: Tom Hughes
www.atlantathrashers.com

### Boston Bruins

Address:     One FleetCenter, Suite 250
             Boston, MA  02114-1303
Telephone: (617) 624-1900
Arena (Capacity): FleetCenter (17,565)
Owner and Governor: Jeremy M. Jacobs
Alternative Governor and President: Harry Sinden
VP/General Manager and Alt. Governor: Mike O'Connell
Coach: Robbie Ftorek
Director of Media Relations: Heidi Holland
www.bostonbruins.com

### Buffalo Sabres

Address:     HSBC Arena
             One Seymour H. Knox III Plaza
             Buffalo, NY  14203
Telephone: (716) 855-4100
Arena (Capacity): HSBC Arena (18,690)
Chairman of the Board: John J. Rigas
CEO: Tim J. Rigas
General Manager: Darcy Regier
Coach: Lindy Ruff
VP of Communications: Michael Gilbert
www.sabres.com

## Calgary Flames

Address:     Pengrowth Saddledome
             555 Saddledome Rise, SE
             Calgary, Alberta T2G 2W1
Telephone: (403) 777-2177
Arena (Capacity): Pengrowth Saddledome (17,158)
Owners: Harley N. Hotchkiss, N. Murray Edwards, Alvin G. Libin, Allan P. Markin, J.R. "Bud" McCaig, Byron J.Seaman, Daryl K. Seaman
President and CEO: Ken King
VP/General Manager: Craig Button
Coach: Greg Gilbert
Director of Communications: Peter Hanlon
www.calgaryflames.com

## Carolina Hurricanes

Address:     1400 Edwards Mill Road
             Raleigh, NC 27607
Telephone: (919) 467-7825
Arena (Capacity): Entertainment and Sports Arena (18,730)
Owner: Peter Karmanos
CEO and General Manager: Jim Rutherford
VP/Assistant General Manager: Jason Karmanos
Coach: Paul Maurice
Director of Public Relations: Jerry Higgins
www.carolinahurricanes.com

## Chicago Blackhawks

Address:     United Center
             1901 W. Madison Street
             Chicago, IL 60612
Telephone: (312) 455-7000
Arena (Capacity): United Center (20,500)
President: William W. Wirtz
Senior Vice President: Robert Pulford
General Manager: Mike Smith
Coach: Brian Sutter
Public Relations Director: Jim DeMaria
www.chicagoblackhawks.com

## Colorado Avalanche

Address:     Pepsi Center
             1000 Chopper Circle
             Denver, CO 80204
Telephone: (303) 405-1100
Arena (Capacity): Pepsi Center (18,007)
Owner and Governor: E. Stanley Kroenke
Alt. Governor, President and General Manager: Pierre Lacroix
Coach: Bob Hartley
VP of Communications and Team Services: Jean Martineau
www.coloradoavalanche.com

## Columbus Blue Jackets

Address:     200 West Nationwide Boulevard
             Columbus, OH 43215
Telephone: (614) 246-4625
Arena (Capacity): Nationwide Arena (18,136)
Owner: John H. McConnell
President and General Manager: Doug MacLean
Coach: Dave King
Director of Communications: Todd Sharrock
www.bluejackets.com

## Dallas Stars

Address:     211 Cowboys Parkway
             Irving, TX 75063
Telephone: (972) 831-2401
Arena (Capacity): American Airlines Center (18,532)

## Dallas Stars *(Cont.)*

Owner: Thomas O. Hicks
General Manager: Bob Gainey
Coach: Ken Hitchcock
Director of Media Relations: Larry Kelly
www.dallasstars.com

## Detroit Red Wings

Address:     Joe Louis Arena
             600 Civic Center Drive
             Detroit, MI 48226
Telephone: (313) 396-7544
Arena (Capacity): Joe Louis Arena (19,983)
Owner and Governor: Mike Ilitch
Senior Vice President/Alt. Governor: Jim Devellano
General Manager: Ken Holland
Head Coach: Scott Bowman
Director of Public Relations: John Hahn
www.detroitredwings.com

## Edmonton Oilers

Address:     11230 110th Street
             Edmonton, Alberta T5G 3H7
Telephone: (780) 414-4000
Arena (Capacity): Skyreach Centre (16,839)
Owner: Edmonton Investors Group
Governor: Cal Nichols
President and Alt. Governor: Patrick LaForge
General Manager: Kevin Lowe
Coach: Craig MacTavish
VP of Public Relations, Hockey: Bill Tuele
www.edmontonoilers.com

## Florida Panthers

Address:     1 Panther Parkway
             Sunrise, FL 33323
Telephone: (954) 835-7000
Arena (Capacity): National Car Rental Center (19,250)
Chairman of the Board/CEO: Alan Cohen
President, General Manager, and Governor: William A. Torrey
Coach: Duane Sutter
Director of Broadcasting and Communications: Mike Hanson
www.floridapanthers.com

## Los Angeles Kings

Address:     The Staples Center
             1111 South Figueroa Street
             Los Angeles, CA 90037
Telephone: (213) 742-7100
Arena (Capacity): The Staples Center (18,118)
Owners: Philip Anschutz and Edward P. Roske Jr.
President and Governor: Tim Leiweke
Vice President and GM: Dave Taylor
Coach: Andy Murray
Director of Media Relations: Mike Altieri
www.lakings.com

## Minnesota Wild

Address:     317 Washington Street
             St. Paul, MN, 55102
Telephone: (651) 602-6000
Arena (Capacity): Excel Energy Center (18,064)
Chairman: Bob Naegele Jr.
General Manager: Doug Risebrough
Coach: Jacques Lemaire
VP of Communications/Broadcasting: Bill Robertson
www.wild.com

## Montreal Canadiens

Address:    Molson Centre
            1260 de la Gauchetiere West
            Montreal, Quebec H3B 5E8 Canada
Telephone: (514) 932-2582
Arena (Capacity): Molson Centre (21,273)
Owner: George N. Gillett Jr.
President and Governor: Pierre Boivin
General Manager: Andre Savard
Coach: Michel Therrien
Director of Communications: Donald Beauchamp
www.canadiens.com

## Nashville Predators

Address:    Gaylord Entertainment Center
            501 Broadway
            Nashville, TN 37203
Telephone: (615) 770-2300
Arena (Capacity): Gaylord Entertainment Center
(17,113)
Owner, Chairman and Governor: Craig Leipold
President, COO: Jack Diller
Executive VP of Hockey Operations/GM: David Poile
Coach: Barry Trotz
VP of Communications/Development: Gerry Helper
www.nashvillepredators.com

## New Jersey Devils

Address:    Continental Airlines Arena, PO Box 504
            East Rutherford, NJ 07073
Telephone: (201) 935-6050
Arena (Capacity): Continental Airlines Arena (19,040)
Owner: Puck Holdings
CEO, President and GM: Lou Lamoriello
Coach: Larry Robinson
Director of Public Relations: Jeff Altstadter
www.newjerseydevils.com

## New York Islanders

Address:    1535 Old Country Road
            Plainview, NY 11803
Telephone: (516) 501-6700
Arena (Capacity): Nassau Coliseum (16,297)
Owners: Charles Wong and Sanjay Kumar
Co-Chairman and Alt. Governor: Edward Milstein
Senior VP of Operations and Alt. Governor: Michael J.
Picker
General Manager: Mike Milbury
Coach: Peter Laviolette
VP of Communications: Chris Botta
www.newyorkislanders.com

## New York Rangers

Address:    Madison Square Garden
            2 Pennsylvania Plaza
            New York, NY 10121
Telephone: (212) 465-6000
Arena (Capacity): Madison Square Garden (18,200)
Owner: Cablevision
President and General Manager: Glen Sather
Coach: Ron Low
VP of Public Relations: John Rosasco
www.newyorkrangers.com

## Ottawa Senators

Address:    The Corel Centre
            1000 Palladium Drive
            Ottawa, Ontario K2V 1A5 Canada
Telephone: (613) 599-0250
Arena (Capacity): The Corel Centre (18,500)
Founder: Bruce M. Firestone
Chairman and Governor: Rod Bryden

## Ottawa Senators *(Cont.)*

President and Chief Executive Officer: Roy Mlakar
General Manager: Marshall Johnston
Coach: Jacques Martin
VP of Communications: Phil Legault
www.ottawasenators.com

## Philadelphia Flyers

Address:    First Union Center
            3601 South Broad Street
            Philadelphia, PA 19148
Telephone: (215) 465-4500
Arena (Capacity): First Union Center (19,541)
Majority Owner: Comcast Spectacor
Chairman: Ed Snider
President and General Manager: Bob Clarke
Coach: Bill Barber
Director of Public Relations: Zack Hill
www.philadelphiaflyers.com

## Phoenix Coyotes

Address:    ALLTEL Ice Den
            9375 East Belle Road
            Scottsdale, AZ 85260
Telephone: (480) 473-5600
Arena (Capacity): America West Arena (16,210)
Chairman and CEO: Steve Ellman
Managing Partner: Wayne Gretzky
General Manager: Michael Barnette
Coach: Bob Francis
VP of Media and Player Relations: Richard Nairn
www.phoenixcoyotes.com

## Pittsburgh Penguins

Address:    Mellon Arena
            66 Mario Lemieux Place
            Pittsburgh, PA 15219
Telephone: (412) 642-1300
Arena (Capacity): Mellon Arena (16,958)
Owner: Mario Lemieux (Lemieux Ownership Group)
General Manager: Craig Patrick
Coach: Ivan Hlinka
Director of Media Relations: Steve Bovino
www.pittsburghpenguins.com

## St. Louis Blues

Address:    Savvis Center
            1401 Clark Avenue
            St. Louis, MO 63103
Telephone: (314) 622-2500
Arena (Capacity): Savvis Center (19,022)
President and Chief Executive Officer: Mark Sauer
Senior VP and General Manager: Larry Pleau
Coach: Joel Quenneville
Director of Media Relations: Frank Buomono
www.stlouisblues.com

## San Jose Sharks

Address:    Compaq Center at San Jose
            525 West Santa Clara Street
            San Jose, CA 95113
Telephone: (408) 287-7070
Arena (Capacity): Compaq Center at San Jose
(17,496)
Owners: George and Gordon Gund
Executive VP and General Manager: Dean Lombardi
Coach: Darryl Sutter
Director of Media Relations: Ken Arnold
www.sjsharks.com

## Tampa Bay Lightning
Address: 401 Channelside Drive
Tampa, FL 33602
Telephone: (813) 229-2658
Arena (Capacity): Ice Palace (19,758)
Owner: Palace Sports & Entertainment/Bill Davidson and David Hermelin
CEO and Governor: Tom Wilson
President and Alt. Governor: Ron Campbell
Senior VP & General Manager: Rick Dudley
Coach: John Tortorella
VP of Public Relations: Bill Wickett
www.tampabaylightning.com

## Toronto Maple Leafs
Address: Air Canada Centre
40 Bay Street - St. 400
Toronto, Ontario M5J 2X2 Canada
Telephone: (416) 815-5500
Arena (Capacity): Air Canada Centre (18,819)
Chairman of the Board: Steve A. Stavro
President: Ken Dryden
Coach/GM: Pat Quinn
Director of Media Relations: Pat Park
www.mapleleafs.com

## Vancouver Canucks
Address: General Motors Place/800 Griffiths Way
Vancouver, B.C. V6B 6G1
Telephone: (604) 899-4600
Arena (Capacity): General Motors Place (18,422)
Chairman and Governor: John E. McCaw Jr.
President and CEO: Stanley McCammon
Chief Operating Officer: David Cobb
President and GM: Brian Burke
Coach: Marc Crawford
Manager of Media Relations: Chris Brumwell
www.canucks.com

## Washington Capitals
Address: 401 Ninth Street, NW
Suite 750
Washington, DC 20004
Telephone: (202) 266-2200
Arena (Capacity): MCI Center (18,672)
Owners: Ted Leonsis, Raul Fernandez and Michael Jordan
Owner and President: Richard M. Patrick
VP and General Manager: George McPhee
Coach: Ron Wilson
Senior VP of Business Operations: Declan J. Bolger
www.washingtoncaps.com

# College Sports Directory

## NATIONAL COLLEGIATE ATHLETIC ASSOCIATION (NCAA)
Address: 700 W. Washington Street
P.O. Box 6222
Indianapolis, IN 46206-6222
Telephone: (317) 917-6222
President: Cedric Dempsey
Director of Public Relations: Wallace I. Renfro
www.ncaa.org

## ATLANTIC COAST CONFERENCE
Address: P.O. Drawer ACC
Greensboro, NC 27417-6724
Telephone: (336) 854-8787
Commissioner: John Swofford
Asst. Com. of Media Relations: Brian Morrison
www.theacc.com

## Clemson University
Address: P.O. Box 31
Clemson, SC 29633
Nickname: Tigers
Telephone: (864) 656-2114
Football Stadium (Capacity): Clemson Memorial Stadium (81,474)
Basketball Arena (Capacity): Littlejohn Coliseum (11,020)
President: James F. Barker
Athletic Director: Bobby Robinson
Football Coach: Tommy Bowden
Basketball Coach: Larry Shyatt
Sports Information Director: Tim Bourret
www.clemsontigers.com

## Duke University
Address: P.O. Box 90557
Durham, NC 27708
Nickname: Blue Devils
Telephone: (919) 684-2633
Football Stadium (Capacity): Wallace Wade Stadium (33,941)
Basketball Arena (Capacity): Cameron Indoor Stadium (9,314)

## Duke University (Cont.)
President: Nan Keohane
Athletic Director: Joe Alleva
Football Coach: Carl Franks
Men's Basketball Coach: Mike Krzyzewski
Women's Basketball Coach: Gail Goestenkors
Sports Information Director: Jon Jackson
www.goduke.com

## Florida State University
Address: P.O. Box 2195
Tallahassee, FL 32316
Nickname: Seminoles
Telephone: (850) 644-1403
Football Stadium (Capacity): Doak S. Campbell Stadium (80,000)
Basketball Arena (Capacity): Leon County Civic Center (12,200)
President: Sandy D'Alemberte
Athletic Director: Dave Hart
Football Coach: Bobby Bowden
Basketball Coach: Steve Robinson
Sports Information Director: Rob Wilson
www.seminoles.com

## Georgia Tech
Address: 150 Bobby Dodd Way
Atlanta, GA 30332
Nickname: Yellow Jackets
Telephone: (404) 894-5445
Football Stadium (Capacity): Bobby Dodd Stadium at Grant Field (46,000)
Basketball Arena (Capacity): Alexander Memorial Coliseum at McDonald's Center (10,000)
President: G. Wayne Clough
Athletic Director: David Braine
Football Coach: George O'Leary
Basketball Coach: Paul Hewitt
Director of Communications: Mike Stamus
www.ramblinwreck.com

## University of Maryland

Address: P.O. Box 295
College Park, MD 20741-0295
Nickname: Terrapins
Telephone: (301) 314-7064
Football Stadium (Capacity): Byrd Stadium (48,055)
Basketball Arena (Capacity): Cole Fieldhouse
(14,500)
President: Dr. C.D. Mote, Jr.
Athletic Director: Deborah A. Yow
Football Coach: Ralph Friedgen
Basketball Coach: Gary Williams
Sports Information Director: David Haglund
www.umterps.com

## University of North Carolina

Address: P.O. Box 2126
Chapel Hill, NC 27515
Nickname: Tar Heels
Telephone: (919) 962-2123
Football Stadium (Capacity): Kenan Memorial
Stadium (60,000)
Basketball Arena (Capacity): Dean E. Smith Center
(21,572)
Chancellor: Dr. James Moeser
Athletic Director: Dick Baddour
Football Coach: John Bunting
Men's Basketball Coach: Matt Doherty
Women's Basketball Coach: Sylvia Hatchell
Sports Information Director: Steve Kirschner
www.tarheelblue.com

## North Carolina State University

Address: Box 8501
Raleigh, NC 27695
Nickname: Wolfpack
Telephone: (919) 515-2102
Football Stadium (Capacity): Carter-Finley Stadium
(51,500)
Basketball Arena (Capacity): Entertainment and
Sports Arena (19,722)
Chancellor: Dr. Marye Anne Fox
Athletic Director: TBA
Football Coach: Chuck Amato
Basketball Coach: Herb Sendek
Asst. Media Relations Director: Bruce Winkworth
www.gopack.com

## University of Virginia

Address: P.O. Box 3785
Charlottesville, VA 22903
Nickname: Cavaliers
Telephone: (804) 982-5500
Football Stadium (Capacity): Carl Smith Center,
Home of David A. Harrison III Field at Scott Stadium
(61,500)
Basketball Arena (Capacity): University Hall (8,457)
President: John Casteen III
Athletic Director: Craig Littlepage
Football Coach: Al Groh
Men's Basketball Coach: Pete Gillen
Women's Basketball Coach: Debbie Ryan
Sports Information Director: Rich Murray
www.virginiasports.com

## Wake Forest University

Address: P.O. Box 7426
Winston-Salem, NC 27109
Nickname: Demon Deacons
Telephone: (336) 758-5640
Football Stadium (Capacity): Groves Stadium (31,500)
Basketball Arena (Capacity): Lawrence Joel Veterans
Memorial Coliseum (14,407)
President: Dr. Thomas K. Hearn Jr.
Athletic Director: Ron Wellman
Football Coach: Jim Grobe
Basketball Coach: Skip Prosaer
Media Relations Director: Dean Buchan
www.wakeforestsports.com

## BIG EAST CONFERENCE

Address: 222 Richmond St, Suite 110
Providence, RI 02903
Telephone: (401) 272-9108
Commissioner: Michael A. Tranghese
Associate Commissioner for PR: John Paquette
www.bigeast.com

## Boston College

Address: Conte Forum 321
Chestnut Hill, MA 02467
Nickname: Eagles
Telephone: (617) 552-3004
Football Stadium (Capacity): Alumni Stadium (44,500)
Basketball Arena (Capacity): Silvio O. Conte Forum (8,606)
President: Rev. William P. Leahy, S.J.
Athletic Director: Gene DeFilippo
Football Coach: Tom O'Brien
Basketball Coach: Al Skinner
Sports Information Director: Michael Enright
www.bceagles.com

## University of Connecticut

Address: 2095 Hillside Road
Storrs, CT 06269-3078
Nickname: Huskies
Telephone: (860) 486-3531
Football Stadium (Capacity): Memorial Stadium (16,200)
Basketball Arena (Capacity): Harry A. Gampel
Pavilion (10,027)
President: Philip E. Austin
Athletic Director: Lew Perkins
Football Coach: Randy Edsall
Men's Basketball Coach: Jim Calhoun
Women's Basketball Coach: Geno Auriemma
Sports Information Director: Tim Tolokan
www.uconnhuskies.com
Note: Division I-A football.

## Georgetown University

Address: McDonough Arena
Box 571124
Washington, DC 20057-1124
Nickname: Hoyas
Telephone: (202) 687-2492
Football Stadium (Capacity): Kehoe Field (2,400)
Basketball Arena (Capacity): MCI Center (26,000)
President: Rev. John J. De Gidia
Athletic Director: Joseph Lang
Football Coach: Robert Benson
Basketball Coach: Craig Esherick
Sports Information Director: Mike Tuberosa, (Men's
basketball) Bill Shapland
www.guhoyas.com
Note: Division I-AA football.

## University of Miami

Address: 5821 San Amaro Drive
Coral Gables, FL 33146
Nickname: Hurricanes
Telephone: (305) 284-3244
Football Stadium (Capacity): Orange Bowl (72,319)
Basketball Arena (Capacity): Miami Arena (15,388)
President: Donna E. Shalala
Athletic Director: Paul Dee
Football Coach: Larry Coker
Basketball Coach: Perry Clark
Sports Information Director: Bob Burda
www.hurricanesports.com

## University of Pittsburgh

Address: Dept. of Athletics; P.O. Box 7436
Pittsburgh, PA 15213-0436
Nickname: Panthers
Telephone: (412) 648-8240
Football Stadium (Capacity): Heinz Field (65,000)
Basketball Arena (Capacity): Fitzgerald Field House
(6,798), Pittsburgh Civic Arena (17,159)
Chancellor: Mark A. Nordenberg
Athletic Director: Steven Pederson
Football Coach: Walt Harris
Basketball Coach: Ben Howland
Sports Information Director: E.J. Borghetti
www.pittsburghpanthers.com

## Providence College

Address: 549 River Avenue
Providence, RI 02918
Nickname: Friars
Telephone: (401) 865-2272
Basketball Arena (Capacity): Providence Civic
Center (12,993)
President: Rev. Philip A. Smith, O.P.
Athletic Director: John Marinatto
Basketball Coach: Tim Welsh
Sports Information Director: Arthur Parks
www.friars.com
Note: No football program.

## Rutgers University

Address: 83 Rockefeller Road
Piscataway, NJ 08854-7005
Nickname: Scarlet Knights
Telephone: (732) 445-8053
Football Stadium (Capacity): Rutgers Stadium (42,000)
Basketball Arena (Capacity): Louis Brown Ctr (8,500)
President: Dr. Francis L. Lawrence
Athletic Director: Bob Mulcahy III
Football Coach: Greg Schiano
Men's Basketball Coach: Gary Waters
Women's Basketball Coach: C. Vivian Stringer
Sports Information Director: John Wooding
scarletknights.com [no www.]

## St. John's University

Address: 8000 Utopia Parkway; Jamaica, NY 11439
Nickname: Red Storm
Telephone: (718) 990-6367
Football Stadium (Capacity): DaSilva Mem. Field (3,000)
Basketball Arena (Capacity): Alumni Hall (6,008),
Madison Square Garden (19,876)
President: Rev. Donald J. Harrington, C.M.
Athletic Director: Edward J. Manetta Jr.
Football Coach: Bob Ricca
Basketball Coach: Mike Jarvis
Sports Information Director: Dominic Scianna
www.redstormsports.com
Note: Division I-AA football.

## Seton Hall University

Address: 400 South Orange Avenue
South Orange, NJ 07079
Nickname: Pirates
Telephone: (973) 761-9493
Basketball Arena (Capacity): Walsh Gymnasium
(2,600), Continental Airlines Arena (20,029)
President: Monsignor Robert T. Sheeran
Athletic Director: Jeff Fogelson
Basketball Coach: Louis Orr
Sports Information Director: Marie Wozniak
www.shupirates.com
Note: No football program.

## Syracuse University

Address: Manley Field House
Syracuse, NY 13244-5020
Nickname: Orangemen
Telephone: (315) 443-2608
Football Stadium (Capacity): Carrier Dome (52,000)
Basketball Arena (Capacity): Carrier Dome (32,000)
Chancellor: Dr. Kenneth Shaw
Athletic Director: Jake Crouthamel
Football Coach: Paul Pasqualoni
Basketball Coach: Jim Boeheim
Sports Information Director: Sue Cornelius Edson
www.suathletics.com

## Temple University

Address: Vivacqua Hall, 4th Floor
1700 North Broad Street
Philadelphia, PA 19122-0842
Nickname: Owls
Telephone: (215) 204-7445
Football Stadium (Capacity): Veterans Stadium (66,592)
Basketball Arena (Capacity): Apollo of Temple (10,224)
President: Dr. David Adamany
Athletic Director: Dave O'Brien
Football Coach: Bobby Wallace
Basketball Coach: John Chaney
Sports Information Director: Brian Kirschner
www.owlsports.com
Note: Plays football in Big East, basketball in Atlantic 10
Conference.

## Villanova University

Address: 800 Lancaster Avenue
Villanova, PA 19085
Nickname: Wildcats
Telephone: (610) 519-4110
Football Stadium (Capacity): Villanova Stadium (12,000)
Basketball Arena (Capacity): The Pavilion (6,500),
First Union Spectrum (18,060), First Union Center
(22,000)
President: Rev. Edmund Dobbin, O.S.A.
Athletic Director: Vince Nicastro
Football Coach: Andy Talley
Basketball Coach: Steve Lappas
Sports Information Director: Dean Kenefick
www.villanova.com
Note: Division I-AA football.

## Virginia Tech
Address:     Jamerson Athletic Center
             Blacksburg, VA 24061
Nickname: Hokies
Telephone: (540) 231-6726
Football Stadium (Capacity): Lane Stadium/Worsham
  Field (51,907)
Basketball Arena (Capacity): Cassell Coliseum
  (10,052)
President: Charles Steger
Athletic Director: Jim Weaver
Football Coach: Frank Beamer
Basketball Coach: Ricky Stokes
Sports Information Director: Dave Smith
www.hokiesportsinfo.com

## West Virginia University
Address:     P.O. Box 0877
             Morgantown, WV 26507-0877
Nickname: Mountaineers
Telephone: (304) 293-2821
Football Stadium (Capacity): Mountaineer Field (63,500)
Basketball Arena (Capacity): WVU Coliseum (14,000)
President: David Hardesty
Athletic Director: Ed Pastilong
Football Coach: Rich Rodriguez
Basketball Coach: Gale Catlett
Sports Information Director: Shelley Poe
www.wvu.edu/~sports

## BIG TEN CONFERENCE
Address:     1500 West Higgins Road
             Park Ridge, IL 60068
Telephone: (847) 696-1010
Commissioner: James E. Delany
Associate Commissioner: Mark Rudner
www.bigten.org

## University of Illinois
Address:     1700 S 4th Street
             Champaign, IL 61820
Nickname: Fighting Illini
Telephone: (217) 333-1391
Football Stadium (Capacity): Memorial Stadium (70,904)
Basketball Arena (Capacity): Assembly Hall (16,450)
President: James Stukel
Athletic Director: Ronald Guenther
Football Coach: Ron Turner
Men's Basketball Coach: Bill Self
Sports Information Director: Kent Brown
www.fightingillini.com

## Indiana University
Address:     Assembly Hall
             1001 E. 17th Street
             Bloomington, IN 47408-1590
Nickname: Hoosiers
Telephone: (812) 855-2421
Football Stadium (Capacity): Memorial Stadium (52,354)
Basketball Arena (Capacity): Assembly Hall (17,357)
President: Myles Brand
Athletic Director: Michael S. McNeely
Football Coach: Cam Cameron
Basketball Coach: Mike Davis
Sports Information Director: Jeff Fanter
www.athletics.indiana.edu

## University of Iowa
Address:     157 Carver-Hawkeye Arena
             Iowa City, IA 52242
Nickname: Hawkeyes
Telephone: (319) 335-9411
Football Stadium (Capacity): Kinnick Stadium (70,397)
Basketball Arena (Capacity): Carver-Hawkeye (15,500)
President: Mary Sue Coleman
Athletic Director: Robert Bowlsby
Football Coach: Kirk Ferentz
Men's Basketball Coach: Steve Alford
Women's Basketball Coach: Lisa Bluder
Sports Information Director: Phil Haddy (Men's),
  Matt Weitzel, Tony Wirt (Women's Asst. Directors)
www.hawkeyesports.com

## University of Michigan
Address:     1000 S. State Street
             Ann Arbor, MI 48109
Nickname: Wolverines
Telephone: (734) 763-4423
Football Stadium (Capacity): Michigan
  Stadium (107,501)
Basketball Arena (Capacity): Crisler Arena (13,562)
President: Lee Bollinger
Athletic Director: William C. Martin
Football Coach: Lloyd Carr
Basketball Coach: Tommy Amaker
Sports Information Director: Bruce Madej
www.mgoblue.com

## Michigan State University
Address:     401 Olds Hall
             East Lansing, MI 48824
Nickname: Spartans
Telephone: (517) 355-2271
Football Stadium (Capacity): Spartan Stadium (72,027)
Basketball Arena (Capacity): Jack Breslin Student
  Events Center (15,085)
President: M. Peter McPherson
Athletic Director: Clarence Underwood
Football Coach: Bobby Williams
Basketball Coach: Tom Izzo
Sports Information Director: John Lewandowski
www.msuspartans.com

## University of Minnesota
Address:     208 Bierman Athletic Building
             516 15th Ave SE
             Minneapolis, MN 55455
Nickname: Golden Gophers
Telephone: (612) 625 4090
Football Stadium (Capacity): Hubert H. Humphrey
  Metrodome (64,172)
Basketball Arena (Capacity): Williams Arena (14,625)
President: Mark Yudof
Athletic Director: Tom Moe
Football Coach: Glen Mason
Basketball Coach: Dan Monson
Sports Information Director: Bill Crumley
www.gophersports.com

## Northwestern University

Address:     1501 Central Street
             Evanston, IL 60208
Nickname: Wildcats
Telephone: (847) 491-7503
Football Stadium (Capacity): Ryan Field (47,130)
Basketball Arena (Capacity): Welsh-Ryan Arena (8,117)
President: Henry S. Bienen
Athletic Director: Rick Taylor
Football Coach: Randy Walker
Basketball Coach: Bill Carmody
Sports Information Director: Mike Wolf
www.nusports.com

## Ohio State University

Address:     410 Woody Hayes Drive
             St. John Arena, Room 124
             Columbus, OH 43210
Nickname: Buckeyes
Telephone: (614) 292-6861
Football Stadium (Capacity): Ohio Stadium (102,075)
Basketball Arena (Capacity): Jerome Schottenstein
  Center (19,500)
President: William Kirwin
Athletic Director: Andy Geiger
Football Coach: Jim Tressel
Basketball Coach: Jim O'Brien
Sports Information Director: Steve Snapp
www.ohiostatebuckeyes.com

## Penn State University

Address:     101D Bryce Jordan Center
             University Park, PA 16802
Nickname: Nittany Lions
Telephone: (814) 865-1757
Football Stadium (Capacity): Beaver Stadium (106,537)
Basketball Arena (Capacity): Bryce Jordan Center
  (15,261)
President: Dr. Graham Spanier
Athletic Director: Tim Curley
Football Coach: Joe Paterno
Men's Basketball Coach: Jerry Dunn
Women's Basketball Coach: Rene Portland
Sports Information Director: Jeff Nelson
www.gopsusports.com

## Purdue University

Address:     Mackey Arena, Room 15
             West Lafayette, IN 47907
Nickname: Boilermakers
Telephone: (765) 494-3200
Football Stadium (Capacity): Ross-Ade Stadium
  (67,331)
Basketball Arena (Capacity): Mackey Arena (14,123)
President: Martin C. Jishke
Athletic Director: Morgan Burke
Football Coach: Joe Tiller
Basketball Coach: Gene Keady
Sports Information Director: Tom Schott
www.purdue.edu/sports

## University of Wisconsin

Address:     1440 Monroe Street
             Madison, WI 53711
Nickname: Badgers
Telephone: (608) 262-1811
Football Stadium (Capacity): Camp Randall
  Stadium (76,129)
Basketball Arena (Capacity): Kohl Center (17,142)
Chancellor: John Wiley
Athletic Director: Pat Richter
Football Coach: Barry Alvarez
Basketball Coach: Bo Ryan
Sports Information Director: Justin Doherty
www.uwbadgers.com

## BIG 12 CONFERENCE

Address:     2201 Stemmons Freeway, 28th floor
             Dallas, TX 75207
Telephone: (214) 742-1212
Commissioner: Kevin Weiberg
Director of Media Relations: Bo Carter
www.big12sports.com

## Baylor University

Address:     150 Bear Run
             Waco, TX 76711
Nickname: Bears
Telephone: (254) 710-1234
Football Stadium (Capacity): Floyd Casey
  Stadium (50,000)
Basketball Arena (Capacity): Ferrell Center (10,284)
President: Robert Sloan
Athletic Director: Tom Stanton
Football Coach: Kevin Steele
Basketball Coach: Dave Bliss
Sports Information Director: Scott Stricklin
www.gobaylorbears.com

## University of Colorado

Address:     Campus Box 357
             Boulder, CO 80309
Nickname: Buffaloes
Telephone: (303) 492-5626
Football Stadium (Capacity): Folsom Field (51,808)
Basketball Arena (Capacity): Coors Event
  Center (11,198)
President: Elizabeth Hoffman
Athletic Director: Dick Tharpe
Football Coach: Gary Barnett
Men's Basketball Coach: Ricardo Patton
Women's Basketball Coach: Ceal Barry
Sports Information Director: David Plati
www.cubuffs.com

## Iowa State University

Address:    1800 S. Fourth Street
    Jacobson Building
    Ames, IA 50011
Nickname: Cyclones
Telephone: (515) 294-3372
Football Stadium (Capacity): Jack Trice Stadium
(43,000)
Basketball Arena (Capacity): James H. Hilton
Coliseum (14,092)
President: Dr. Gregory L. Geoffroy
Athletic Director: Bruce Van De Velde
Football Coach: Dan McCarney
Men's Basketball Coach: Larry Eustachy
Women's Basketball Coach: Bill Fennelly
www.cyclones.com

## University of Kansas

Address:    Allen Field House, Room 104
    Lawrence, KS 66045
Nickname: Jayhawks
Telephone: (785) 864-3417
Football Stadium (Capacity): Memorial
Stadium (50,250)
Basketball Arena (Capacity): Allen Field
House (16,300)
Chancellor: Robert Hemenway
Athletic Director: Dr. Allen Bohl
Football Coach: Terry Allen
Men's Basketball Coach: Roy Williams
Women's Basketball Coach: Marian Washington
Sports Information Director: Doug Vance
www.kuathletics.com

## Kansas State University

Address:    1800 College Ave., Suite 144
    Manhattan, KS 66502
Nickname: Wildcats
Telephone: (785) 532-6735
Football Stadium (Capacity): KSU Stadium-Wagner
Field (50,000)
Basketball Arena (Capacity): Bramlage Coliseum
(13,500)
President: Dr. Jon Wefald
Athletic Director: Tim Weiser
Football Coach: Bill Snyder
Basketball Coach: Jim Wooldridge
Sports Information Director: Doug Dull
www.kstatesports.com

## University of Missouri

Address:    P.O. Box 677
    Columbia, MO 65205
Nickname: Tigers
Telephone: (573) 882-3241
Football Stadium (Capacity): Faurot Field/Memorial
Stadium (62,000)
Basketball Arena (Capacity): Hearnes Center (13,300)
Chancellor: Dr. Richard Wallace
Athletic Director: Michael F. Alden
Football Coach: Gary Pinkel
Basketball Coach: Quin Snyder
Sports Information Director: Chad Moller
www.mutigers.com

## University of Nebraska

Address:    116 South Stadium
    Lincoln, NE 68588
Nickname: Cornhuskers
Telephone: (402) 472-2263
Football Stadium (Capacity): Memorial
Stadium (72,918)
Basketball Arena (Capacity): Bob Devaney Sports
Center (13,500)
President: L. Dennis Smith
Athletic Director: Bill Byrne
Football Coach: Frank Solich
Basketball Coach: Barry Collier
Sports Information Director: Chris Anderson
www.huskers.com

## University of Oklahoma

Address:    180 W. Brooks, Room 235
    Norman, OK 73019
Nickname: Sooners
Telephone: (405) 325-8231
Football Stadium (Capacity): Memorial Stadium/Owen
Field (75,004)
Basketball Arena (Capacity): Lloyd Noble
Center (11,100)
President: David Boren
Athletic Director: Joe Castiglione
Football Coach: Bob Stoops
Men's Basketball Coach: Kelvin Sampson
Women's Basketball Coach: Sherri Coale
Sports Media Relations Director: Mike Prusinski
www.soonersports.com

## Oklahoma State University

Address:    424 Squires Street
    Stillwater, OK 74078
Nickname: Cowboys
Telephone: (405) 707-7830
Football Stadium (Capacity): Lewis Field (50,614)
Basketball Arena (Capacity): Gallagher-Iba
Arena (6,381)
President: Dr. James Halligan
Athletic Director: Terry Don Phillips
Football Coach: Bob Simmons
Basketball Coach: Eddie Sutton
Sports Information Director: Steve Buzzard
www.okstate.edu

## University of Texas

Address:    P.O. Box 7399; Austin, TX 78713
Nickname: Longhorns
Telephone: (512) 471-7437
Football Stadium (Capacity): Darrell K. Royal/Texas
Memorial Stadium (80,216)
Basketball Arena (Capacity): Erwin Special Events
Center (16,231)
Chancellor: Larry Faulkner
Athletic Director (M): DeLoss Dodds
Athletic Director (W): Jody Conradt
Football Coach: Mack Brown
Basketball Coach: Rick Barnes
Sports Information Directors: (M) John Bianco, (W)
Jody Conradt
www.texassports.com

## Texas A&M University

Address: John Koldus Building, Room 222
College Station, TX 77843-1228
Nickname: Aggies
Telephone: (979) 845-5725
Football Stadium (Capacity): Kyle Field (80,600)
Basketball Arena (Capacity): Reed Arena (12,500)
President: Dr. Ray Bowen
Athletic Director: Wally Groff
Football Coach: R.C. Slocum
Basketball Coach: Melvin Watkins
Sports Information Director: Alan Cannon
www.aggieathletics.com

## Texas Tech University

Address: Box 43021
Lubbock, TX 79409
Nickname: Red Raiders
Telephone: (806) 742-2770
Football Stadium (Capacity): Jones SBC Stadium
(50,500)
Basketball Arena (Capacity): United Spirit Arena (15,000)
President: Dr. David Schmidly
Athletic Director: Gerald Myers
Football Coach: Mike Leach
Men's Basketball Coach: Bob Knight
Women's Basketball Coach: Marsha Sharp
Sports Information Director: Kent Partridge
www.texastech.com

## BIG WEST CONFERENCE

Address: 2 Corporate Park, Suite 206
Irvine, CA 92606
Telephone: (949) 261-2525
Commissioner: Dennis Farrell
Publicity Director: Mike Daniels
www.bigwest.org

## Boise State University

Address: 1910 University Drive
Boise, ID 83725
Nickname: Broncos
Telephone: (208) 426-1288
Football Stadium (Capacity) Lyle Smith Field (30,000)
Basketball Arena (Capacity): BSU Pavilion (13,000)
President: Dr. Charles Ruch
Athletic Director: Gene Bleymaier
Football Coach: Dirk Koetter
Basketball Coach: Rod Jensen
Sports Information Director: Max Corbet
www.broncosports.com

## Cal Poly

Address: One Grand Avenue
San Luis Obispo, CA 93407
Nickname: Mustangs
Telephone: (805) 756-6531
Football Stadium (Capacity): Mustang Stadium (8,500)
Basketball Arena (Capacity): Mott Gym (3,200)
President: Dr. Warren J. Baker
Athletic Director: John McCutcheon
Football Coach: Larry Welsh
Basketball Coach: Jeff Schneider
Sports Information Director: Jason Sullivan
www.gopoly.com

## University of California–Irvine

Address: Intercollegiate Athletics, Crawford Hall
903 West Peltason
Irvine, CA 92697
Nickname: Anteaters
Telephone: (949) 824-6931
Basketball Arena (Capacity): Bren Event Center (5,000)
Chancellor: Ralph Cicerone
Athletic Director: Dan Guerrero
Basketball Coach: Pat Douglass
Sports Information Director: Bob Olson
www.athletics.uci.edu
Note: No football program.

## University of California–Santa Barbara

Address: Department of Athletics
1000 Robertson Gymnasium
Santa Barbara, CA 93106-7211
Nickname: Gauchos
Telephone: (805) 893-3428
Basketball Arena (Capacity): Thunderdome (6,000)
Chancellor: Henry Yang
Athletic Director: Gary Cunningham
Basketball Coach: Bob Williams
Sports Information Director: Bill Mahoney
www.ucsbgauchos.com
Note: No football program.

## California State University–Fullerton

Address: 800 North State College Boulevard
P.O. Box 6810
Fullerton, CA 92834-6810
Nickname: Titans
Telephone: (714) 278-3970
Basketball Arena (Capacity): Titan Gym (3,500)
President: Dr. Milton A. Gordon
Athletic Director: TBA
Basketball Coach: Donny Daniels
Sports Information Director: Mel Franks
sports.fullerton.edu [no www in this URL]
Note: No football program.

## University of Idaho

Address: Kibbie Activities Center
P.O. Box 442302
Moscow, ID 83844-2302
Nickname: Vandals
Telephone: (208) 885-0211
Football Stadium (Capacity): Martin Stadium (37,600);
Kibbie Dome (16,000)
Basketball Arena (Capacity): Cowan Spectrum (7,000)
President: Dr. Bob Hoover
Athletic Director: Mike Bohn
Football Coach: Tom Cable
Basketball Coach: Leonard Perry
Sports Information Director: Becky Paull
www.uiathletics.com

## Long Beach State University

Address: 1250 Bellflower Boulevard
Long Beach, CA 90840-7701
Nicknames: 49ers, The Beach
Telephone: (562) 985-7565
Basketball Arena (Capacity): The Pyramid (5,000)
President: Dr. Robert C. Maxson
Athletic Director: Bill Shumard
Basketball Coach: Wayne Morgan
Sports Information Director: Steve Janisch
www.longbeachstate.com
Note: No football program.

## University of Nevada–Reno

Address: Legacy Hall
Athletic Department MS: 232
Reno, NV 89557-0110
Nickname: Wolf Pack
Telephone: (775) 784-6900 x263
Football Stadium (Capacity): Mackay Stadium
(31,545)
Basketball Arena (Capacity): Lawlor Event Center
(11,200)
President: Dr. John Lilley
Athletic Director: Chris Ault
Football Coach: Chris Tormey
Basketball Coach: Trent Johnson
Director of Media Services: Jamie Klund
www.nevadawolfpack.com

## New Mexico State University

Address: Department of Athletics, MSC 3145
P.O. Box 30001
Las Cruces, NM 88003
Nickname: Aggies
Telephone: (505) 646-4126
Football Stadium (Capacity): Aggie Memorial
Stadium (30,343)
Basketball Arena (Capacity): Pan American
Center (13,071)
President: Dr. Jay Gogue
Athletic Director: Brian Faison
Football Coach: Tony Samuel
Basketball Coach: Lou Henson
Sports Information Director: Sean Johnson
www.nmstatesports.com

## University of North Texas

Address: P.O. Box 311397
Denton, TX 76203-1397
Nickname: Eagles, Mean Green
Telephone: (940) 565-2662
Football Stadium (Capacity): Fouts Field (30,500)
Basketball Arena (Capacity): Super Pit (10,032)
President: Dr. Norval Pohl
Athletic Director: Rick Villarreal
Football Coach: Darrell Dickey
Basketball Coach: Johnny Jones
Sports Information Director: Eric Capper
www.unt.edu/meangreen

## University of the Pacific

Address: 3601 Pacific Avenue
Stockton, CA 95211
Nickname: Tigers
Telephone: (209) 946-2472
Basketball Arena (Capacity): Alex G. Spanos
Center (6,150)
President: Dr. Donald DeRosa
Athletic Director: Lynn King
Basketball Coach: Bob Thomason
Director, Athletic Media Relations: Mike Millerick
www.pacifictigers.com
Note: No football program.

## Utah State University

Address: 7400 Old Main Hill
Logan, UT 84322-7400
Nickname: Aggies
Telephone: (435) 797-1850
Football Stadium (Capacity): Romney Stadium (30,257)
Basketball Arena (Capacity): The Dee Glen Smith
Spectrum (11,000)
President: Dr. Kermit L. Hall

## Utah State University *(Cont.)*

Athletic Director: Rance Pugmire
Football Coach: Mick Dennehy
Basketball Coach: Stew Morrill
Sports Information Director: Mike Strauss
www.utahstateaggies.com

## CONFERENCE USA

Address: 35 East Wacker Drive, Suite 650
Chicago, IL 60601
Telephone: (312) 553-0483
Comissioner: Michael Slive
Media Relations Director: Brian Teter
www.c-usasports.org

## University of Alabama–Birmingham

Address: Bartow Arena
617 13th Street South
Birmingham, AL 35294
Nickname: Blazers
Telephone: (205) 934-7252
Football Stadium (Capacity): Legion Field (83,091)
Basketball Arena (Capacity): Bartow Arena (8,500)
President: Dr. Ann Reynolds
Athletic Director: Herman Frazier
Football Coach: Watson Brown
Men's Basketball Coach: Murry Bartow
Women's Basketball Coach: Jeannie Milling
Sports Information Director: Grant Shingleton
www.uabsports.com

## University of Cincinnati

Address: 309 Lawrence Hall
Cincinnati, OH 45221-0021
Nickname: Bearcats
Telephone: (513) 556-5191
Football Stadium (Capacity): Nippert Stadium (35,000)
Basketball Arena (Capacity): Myrl Shoemaker
Center (13,176)
President: Dr. Joseph A. Steger
Athletic Director: Bob Goin
Football Coach: Rick Minter
Basketball Coach: Bob Huggins
Assistant A. D. /Media Relations: Tom Hathaway
www.ucbearcats.com

## DePaul University

Address: 2323 North Sheffield Avenue
Chicago, IL 60614
Nickname: Blue Demons
Telephone: (773) 325-7525
Basketball Arena (Capacity): Allstate Arena (18,000)
President: Rev. John P. Minogue, C.M.
Athletic Director: Bill Bradshaw
Basketball Coach: Pat Kennedy
Sports Information Director: Scott Reed
www.depaulbluedemons.com
Note: No football program.

## University of Houston

Address: 3100 Cullen Boulevard
Houston, TX 77204
Nickname: Cougars
Telephone: (713) 743-9370
Football Stadium (Capacity): Robertson Stadium (33,000)
Basketball Arena (Capacity): Hofheinz Pavilion (8,479)
Chancellor and President: Dr. Arthur Smith
Athletic Director: TBA
Football Coach: Dana Dimel
Basketball Coach: Ray McCallum
Sports Information Director: Chris Burkhalter
www.uhcougars.com

## University of Louisville

Address:      Athletic Department,
              Student Activities Center
              Louisville, KY 40292
Nickname: Cardinals
Telephone: (502) 852-6581
Football Stadium (Capacity): Papa John's Cardinal
  Stadium (42,000)
Basketball Arena (Capacity): Freedom Hall (18,865)
President: Dr. John Shumaker
Athletic Director: Tom Jurich
Football Coach: John L. Smith
Basketball Coach: Rick Pitino
Sports Information Director: Kenny Klein
www.uoflsports.com

## Marquette University

Address:      P.O. Box 1881
              Milwaukee, WI 53201-1881
Nickname: Golden Eagles
Telephone: (414) 288-7447
Basketball Arena (Capacity): Bradley Center (19,150)
President: Rev. Robert A. Wild, S.J.
Athletic Director: Bill Cords
Basketball Coach: Tom Crean
Sports Information Director: John Farina
www.gomarquette.com
Note: No football program.

## University of Memphis

Address:      570 Normal Street, Room 203
              Memphis, TN 38152-3730
Nickname: Tigers
Telephone: (901) 678-2337
Football Stadium (Capacity): Liberty Bowl Memorial
  Stadium/Rex Dockery Field (62,380)
Basketball Arena (Capacity): The Pyramid (20,142)
President: Dr. Shirley Raines
Athletic Director: R.C. Johnson
Football Coach: Tommy West
Basketball Coach: John Calipari
Director of Athletic Media Relations: Bob Winn
www.gotigersgo.com

## University of North Carolina–Charlotte

Address:      9201 University City Boulevard
              UNC–Charlotte
              Student Activity Center
              Charlotte, NC 28223-0001
Nickname: 49ers
Telephone: (704) 687-4937
Basketball Arena (Capacity): Dale F. Halton Arena (9,000)
Chancellor: James H. Woodward
Athletic Director: Judy W. Rose
Basketball Coach: Bobby Lutz
Sports Information Director: Tom Whitestone
www.charlotte49ers.com
Note: No football program.

## Saint Louis University

Address:      3672 West Pine Mall Road
              St. Louis, MO 63108
Nickname: Billikens
Telephone: (314) 977-2524
Basketball Arena (Capacity): Savvis Center (20,000)
President: Rev. Lawrence Biondi, S.J.
Athletic Director: Doug Woolard
Basketball Coach: Lorenzo Romar
Sports Information Director: Doug McIlhagga
www.slubillikens.com
Note: No football program.

## University of South Florida

Address:      4202 East Fowler Ave., PED 214
              Tampa, FL 33620
Nickname: Bulls
Telephone: (813) 974-2125
Football Stadium (Capacity): Raymond James
  Stadium (41,400)
Basketball Arena (Capacity): Sun Dome (10,411)
President: Judy Genshaft
Athletic Director: Lee Roy Selmon
Football Coach: Jim Leavitt
Basketball Coach: Seth Greenberg
Sports Information Director: John Gerdes
www.gousfbulls.com

## University of Southern Mississippi

Address:      P.O. Box 5161
              Hattiesburg, MS 39406
Nickname: Golden Eagles
Telephone: (601) 266-4503
Football Stadium (Capacity): M.M. Roberts
  Stadium (33,000)
Basketball Arena (Capacity): Reed Green
  Coliseum (8,095)
President: Aubrey Lucas
Athletic Director: Richard Giannini
Football Coach: Jeff Bower
Basketball Coach: James Green
Sports Information Director: Mike Montoro
www.southernmiss.com

## Tulane University

Address:      James Wilson Jr. Center for
              Intercollegiate Athletics
              New Orleans, LA 70118
Nickname: Green Wave
Telephone: (504) 865-5501
Football Stadium (Capacity): Louisiana Superdome
  (72,675)
Basketball Arena (Capacity): Fogelman Arena (3,600)
President: Scott Cowen
Athletic Director: Rick Dickson
Football Coach: Chris Scelfo
Basketball Coach: Shawn Finney
Sports Information Director: Donna Turner
www.tulanegreenwave.com

## IVY LEAGUE

Address:      330 Alexander Street
              Princeton, NJ 08544
Telephone: (609) 258-6426
Executive Director: Jeff Orleans
Publicity Director: Brett Hoover
www.ivyleaguesports.com

## Brown University

Address:      235 Hope Street
              Providence, RI 02912
Nickname: Bears
Telephone: (401) 863-2219
Football Stadium (Capacity): Brown Stadium (20,000)
Basketball Arena (Capacity): Paul Bailey Pizzitola
  Memorial Sports Center (3,100)
President: Ruth Simmons
Athletic Director: David Roach
Football Coach: Phil Estes
Basketball Coach: Glen Miller
Sports Information Director: Christopher Humm
www.brownbears.com

## Columbia University
Address:     Dodge Physical Fitness Center
              3030 Broadway
              New York, NY 10027
Nickname: Lions
Telephone: (212) 854-2534
Football Stadium (Capacity): Lawrence A. Wien
  Stadium at Baker Field (17,000)
Basketball Arena (Capacity): Levien Gymnasium (3,400)
President: Dr. George Rupp
Athletic Director: Dr. John Reeves
Football Coach: Ray Tellier
Basketball Coach: Armond Hill
Director of Athletic Communications: Al Langer
www.gocolumbialions.com

## Cornell University
Address:     Teagle Hall, Campus Road
              Ithaca, NY 14853-6501
Nickname: Big Red
Telephone: (607) 255-3752
Football Stadium (Capacity): Schoellkopf Field (25,597)
Basketball Arena (Capacity): Newman Arena (4,473)
President: Hunter R. Rawlings III
Athletic Director: J. Andrew Noel Jr.
Football Coach: Tim Pendergast
Basketball Coach: Steve Donahue
Sports Information Director: Laura Stange
www.cornellbigred.com

## Dartmouth College
Address:     6083 Alumni Gym
              Hanover, NH 03755-3512
Nickname: Big Green
Telephone: (603) 646-2465
Football Stadium (Capacity): Memorial Field (20,416)
Basketball Arena (Capacity): Leede Arena (2,100)
President: James Wright
Athletic Director: Richard G. Jaeger
Football Coach: John Lyons
Basketball Coach: Dave Faucher
Sports Information Director: Kathy Slattery
www.dartmouth.edu/athletics

## Harvard University
Address:     65 North Harvard St.; Murr Center
              Boston, MA 02163
Nickname: Crimson
Telephone: (617) 495-2206
Football Stadium (Capacity): Harvard Stadium (30,898)
Basketball Arena (Capacity): Lavietes Pavilion (2,198)
President: Lawrence H. Summers
Athletic Director: Robert L. Scalise
Football Coach: Tim Murphy
Basketball Coach: Frank Sullivan
Sports Information Director: John Veneziano
http://www.athletics.harvard.edu

## University of Pennsylvania
Address:     Weightman Hall South
              235 South 33rd Street
              Philadelphia, PA 19104-6322
Nickname: Quakers
Telephone: (215) 898-6128
Football Stadium (Capacity): Franklin Field (52,958)
Basketball Arena (Capacity): The Palestra (8,700)
President: Dr. Judith Rodin
Athletic Director: Steven Bilsky
Football Coach: Al Bagnoli
Basketball Coach: Fran Dunphy
Director, Athletic Communications: Carla Shulzberg
www.pennathletics.com

## Princeton University
Address:     P.O. Box 71
              Jadwin Gym
              Princeton, NJ 08544
Nickname: Tigers
Telephone: (609) 258-3568
Football Stadium (Capacity): Princeton Stadium
  (30,000),
Basketball Arena (Capacity): Jadwin Gym (7,230)
President: Shirley Tilghman
Athletic Director: Gary D. Walters
Football Coach: Roger Hughes
Basketball Coach: John Thompson III
Sports Information Director: Jerry Price
www.goprincetontigers.com

## Yale University
Address:     Box 208216
              New Haven, CT 06520
Nickname: Bulldogs, Elis
Telephone: (203) 432-1456
Football Stadium (Capacity): Yale Bowl (64,269)
Basketball Arena (Capacity): John J. Lee
  Amphitheater (3,100)
President: Richard C. Levin
Athletic Director: Tom Beckett
Football Coach: Jack Siedlecki
Basketball Coach: James Jones
Sports Information Director: Steve Conn
www.yale.edu/athletics

## MID-AMERICAN CONFERENCE
Address:     24 Public Square 15th floor
              Cleveland, OH 44113
Telephone: (216) 566-4622
Commissioner: Rick Chryst
Director of Communications: Gary Richter
www.mac-sports.com

## Ball State University
Address:     2000 University Avenue
              Muncie, IN 47306
Nickname: Cardinals
Telephone: (765) 285-8242
Football Stadium (Capacity): Ball State University
  Stadium (21,581)
Basketball Arena (Capacity): John Worthen Arena
  (11,500)
President: Dr. Blaine Brownell
Athletic Director: Andrea Seger
Football Coach: Bill Lynch
Basketball Coach: Tim Buckley
Assistant Athletic Director: Joe Hernandez
www.bsu.edu/sports

## Bowling Green University
Address:     Perry Stadium East
              Bowling Green, OH 43403
Nickname: Falcons
Telephone: (419) 372-7075
Football Stadium (Capacity): Doyt L. Perry Stadium
  (30,599)
Basketball Arena (Capacity): Anderson Arena (5,000)
President: Dr. Sidney A. Ribeau
Athletic Director: Paul Krebs
Football Coach: Gary Blackney
Basketball Coach: Dan Dakich
Sports Information Director: J.D. Campbell
www.bgsufalcons.com

## Central Michigan University
Address:     Rose Center
             Mount Pleasant, MI 48859
Nickname: Chippewas
Telephone: (517) 774-3277
Football Stadium (Capacity): Kelly/Shorts
  Stadium (30,199)
Basketball Arena (Capacity): Rose Arena (5,200)
President: Michael Rao
Athletic Director: Herb Deromedi
Football Coach: Mike DeBord
Basketball Coach: Jay Smith
Sports Information Director: Fred Stabley Jr.
www.cmuchippewas.com

## Eastern Michigan University
Address:     371 Convocation Center
             Ypsilanti, MI 48197
Nickname: Eagles
Telephone: (734) 487-1050
Football Stadium (Capacity): Rynearson
  Stadium (30,200)
Basketball Arena (Capacity): Convocation Center
  (8,857)
President: Sam Kirpatrick
Athletic Director: Dr. David L. Diles
Football Coach: Jeff Woodruff
Basketball Coach: Jim Boone
Sports Information Director: Jim Streeter
www.emich.edu/goeagles

## Kent State University
Address:     P.O. Box 5190
             Kent, OH 44242
Nickname: Golden Flashes
Telephone: (330) 672-2110
Football Stadium (Capacity): Dix Stadium (30,520)
Basketball Arena (Capacity): Memorial Athletic and
  Convocation Center (6,327)
President: Dr. Carol A. Cartwright
Athletic Director: Laing Kennedy
Football Coach: Dean Pees
Basketball Coach: Stan Heath
Sports Information Director: Will Roleson
www.kent.edu/athletics

## Miami University
Address:     230 Millett Hall
             Oxford, OH 45056
Nickname: Red Hawks
Telephone: (513) 529-3113
Football Stadium (Capacity): Yager Stadium (30,012)
Basketball Arena (Capacity): Millett Hall (9,200)
President: Dr. James Garland
Athletic Director: Joel Maturi
Football Coach: Terry Hoeppner
Basketball Coach: Charlie Coles
Sports Information Director: Mike Harris
www.redhawks.com

## Ohio University
Address:     P.O. Box 689; Convocation Center
             Athens, OH 45701-2979
Nickname: Bobcats
Telephone: (740) 593-1174
Football Stadium (Capacity): Don Peden
  Stadium (40,000)
Basketball Arena (Capacity): Convocation
  Center (13,000)
President: Dr. Robert Glidden
Athletic Director: Thomas Boeh

## Ohio University *(Cont.)*
Football Coach: Brian Knorr
Basketball Coach: Tim O'Shea
Director of Sports Information: Jim Stephan
www.ohiobobcats.com

## University of Toledo
Address:     2801 W. Bancroft St.
             Toledo, OH 43606
Nickname: Rockets
Telephone: (419) 530-4920
Football Stadium (Capacity): Glass Bowl (26,248)
Basketball Arena (Capacity): Savage Hall (9,000)
President: Dr. Daniel Johnson
Interim Athletic Director: Mike Karabin
Football Coach: Tom Amstutz
Basketball Coach: Stan Joplin
Sports Information Director: Paul Helgren
www.utrockets.com

## Western Michigan University
Address:     Read Field House
             Kalamazoo, MI 49008
Nickname: Broncos
Telephone: (616) 387-4138
Football Stadium (Capacity): Waldo Stadium (30,200)
Basketball Arena (Capacity): University Arena (5,800)
President: Dr. Elson Floyd
Athletic Director: Kathy Beauregard
Football Coach: Gary Darnell
Basketball Coach: Robert McCullum
Sports Information Director: Daniel Jankowski
www.wmubroncos.com

## PACIFIC-10 CONFERENCE
Address:     800 S. Broadway, Suite 400
             Walnut Creek, CA 94596
Telephone: (925) 932-4411
Commissioner: Thomas C. Hansen
Publicity Director: Jim Muldoon
www.pac-10.com

## University of Arizona
Address:     106 McHale Center
             Tuscon, AZ 85721
Nickname: Wildcats
Telephone: (520) 621-4163
Football Stadium (Capacity): Arizona Stadium (57,803)
Basketball Arena (Capacity): Lute & Bobbi Olson
Court at McHale Center (14,454)
President: Dr. Peter Likins
Athletic Director: Jim Livengood
Football Coach: John Mackovic
Basketball Coach: Lute Olson
Sports Information Director: Tom Duddleston Jr.
www.arizcats.com

## Arizona State University
Address:     ICA Building, Room 105
             Tempe, AZ 85287-2505
Nickname: Sun Devils
Telephone: (602) 965-6592
Football Stadium (Capacity): Sun Devil Stadium (74,186)
Basketball Arena (Capacity): Wells Fargo Arena
  (14,198)
President: Lattie F. Coor
Athletic Director: Gene Smith
Football Coach: Dirk Koetter
Basketball Coach: Rob Evans
Director, Sports Media Relations: Mark Brand
www.thesundevils.com

## University of California at Berkeley
Address:  210 Memorial Stadium
Berkeley, CA 94720
Nickname: Golden Bears
Telephone: (510) 642-5363
Football Stadium (Capacity): Memorial Stadium (75,028)
Basketball Arena (Capacity): Haas Pavilion (12,172)
Chancellor: Robert Berdahl
Athletic Director: Stephen Gladstone
Football Coach: Tom Holmoe
Basketball Coach: Ben Braun
Sports Information Director: Herb Benenson
www.calbears.com

## University of California at Los Angeles
Address:  P.O. Box 24044
Los Angeles, CA 90024-0044
Nickname: Bruins
Telephone: (310) 206-7870
Football Stadium (Capacity): Rose Bowl (91,136)
Basketball Arena (Capacity): Pauley Pavilion (12,819)
Chancellor: Albert Carnesale
Athletic Director: Peter T. Dalis
Football Coach: Bob Toledo
Basketball Coach: Steve Lavin
Sports Information Director: Marc Dellins
www.uclabruins.com

## University of Oregon
Address:  Len Casanova Athletic Center
2727 Leo Harris Parkway
Eugene, OR 97401
Nickname: Ducks
Telephone: (541) 346-4481
Football Stadium (Capacity): Autzen Stadium (41,698)
Basketball Arena (Capacity): McArthur Court (9,078)
President: David Frohnmayer
Athletic Director: Bill Moos
Football Coach: Mike Bellotti
Basketball Coach: Ernie Kent
Director of Media Services: David Williford
www.goducks.com

## Oregon State University
Address:  Gill Coliseum
Corvallis, OR 97331
Nickname: Beavers
Telephone: (541) 737-3720
Football Stadium (Capacity): Reser Stadium (35,362)
Basketball Arena (Capacity): Gill Coliseum (10,400)
President: Dr. Paul Risser
Athletic Director: Mitch Barnhart
Football Coach: Dennis Erickson
Basketball Coach: Ritchie McKay
Sports Information Director: Hal Cowan
www.osubeavers.com

## University of Southern California
Address:  HER-203A
3501 Watt Way
Los Angeles, CA 90089-0602
Nickname: Trojans
Telephone: (213) 740-8480
Football Stadium (Capacity): Los Angeles Memorial
Coliseum (92,000)
Basketball Arena (Capacity): Los Angeles Sports
Arena (16,161)
President: Dr. Steven Sample
Athletic Director: Mike Garrett
Football Coach: Pete Carroll
Basketball Coach: Henry Bibby
Sports Information Director: Tim Tessalone
www.usctrojans.com

## Stanford University
Address:  Arrillaga Family Sports Center
Stanford, CA 94305
Nickname: Cardinal
Telephone: (650) 723-4418
Football Stadium (Capacity): Stanford Stadium (85,500)
Basketball Arena (Capacity): Maples Pavilion (7,391)
President: Dr. John Hennessy
Athletic Director: Dr. Ted Leland
Football Coach: Tyrone Willingham
Men's Basketball Coach: Mike Montgomery
Women's Basketball Coach: Tara Van Derveer
Director, Sports Media Relations: Gary Migdol
www.gostanford.com

## University of Washington
Address:  UW Media Relations
Graves Building, Box 354070
Seattle, WA 98195-4070
Nickname: Huskies
Telephone: (206) 543-2230
Football Stadium (Capacity): Husky Stadium (72,500)
Basketball Arena (Capacity): Bank of America Arena
at Heck Edmonson Pavilion (10,000)
President: Richard L. McCormick
Athletic Director: Barbara Hedges
Football Coach: Rick Neuheisel
Basketball Coach: Bob Bender
Sports Information Director: Jim Daves
www.gohuskies.com

## Washington State University
Address:  P.O. Box 641602
Pullman, WA 99164-1602
Nickname: Cougars
Telephone: (509) 335-2684
Football Stadium (Capacity): Martin Stadium (37,600)
Basketball Arena (Capacity): Friel Court (12,058)
President: V. Lane Rawlins
Athletic Director: Jim Sterk
Football Coach: Mike Price
Basketball Coach: Paul Graham
Sports Information Director: Rod Commons
www.wsucougars.com

## SOUTHEASTERN CONFERENCE
Address:  2201 Richard Arrington Boulevard North
Birmingham, AL 35203
Telephone: (205) 458-3000
Commissioner: Roy Kramer
Publicity Director: Charles Bloom
www.secsports.org

## University of Alabama
Address:  P.O. Box 870391
323 Paul Bryant Drive
Tuscaloosa, AL 35487
Nickname: Crimson Tide
Telephone: (205) 348-6084
Football Stadium (Capacity): Bryant-Denny Stadium
(83,818)
Basketball Arena (Capacity): Coleman
Coliseum (15,043)
President: Dr. Andrew Sorensen
Athletic Director: Mal Moore
Football Coach: Dennis Franchione
Men's Basketball Coach: Mark Gottfried
Women's Basketball Coach: Rick Moody
Sports Information Director: Larry White
www.rolltide.com

## University of Arkansas
Address: Broyles Athletic Center
Fayetteville, AR 72701
Nickname: Razorbacks
Telephone: (501) 575-2751
Football Stadium (Capacity): Donald W. Reynolds
Razorback Stadium (72,000); War Memorial Stadium
(53,727)
Basketball Arena (Capacity): Bud Walton Arena (19,200)
Chancellor: Dr. John White
Athletic Director: Frank Broyles
Football Coach: Houston Nutt
Basketball Coach: Nolan Richardson
Sports Information Director: Kevin Trainor
www.hogwired.com

## Auburn University
Address: P.O. Box 351
Auburn, AL 36831-0351
Nickname: Tigers
Telephone: (334) 844-9800
Football Stadium (Capacity): Jordan Hare Stadium (86,063)
Basketball Arena (Capacity): Beard-Eaves Memorial
Coliseum (13,500)
Interim President: William Walker
Athletic Director: David Housel
Football Coach: Tommy Tuberville
Men's Basketball Coach: Cliff Ellis
Women's Basketball Coach: Joe Ciampi
Sports Information Director: Meredith Jenkins
www.auburn.edu/athletics

## University of Florida
Address: P.O. Box 14485
Gainesville, FL 32604
Nickname: Gators
Telephone: (352) 375-4683
Football Stadium (Capacity): Ben Hill Griffin Stadium
at Florida Field (84,000)
Basketball Arena (Capacity): Stephen C. O'Connell
Center (12,000)
Interim President: Dr. Charles Young
Athletic Director: Jeremy Foley
Football Coach: Steve Spurrier
Men's Basketball Coach: Billy Donovan
Women's Basketball Coach: Carol Ross
Sports Information Director: John Humenik
www.gatorzone.com

## University of Georgia
Address: P.O. Box 1472
Athens, GA 30603-1472
Nickname: Bulldogs
Telephone: (706) 542-1621
Football Stadium (Capacity): Sanford Stadium (86,520)
Basketball Arena (Capacity): Stegman Coliseum
(10,523)
President: Dr. Michael F. Adams
Athletic Director: Vince Dooley
Football Coach: Mark Richt
Men's Basketball Coach: Jim Harrick
Women's Basketball Coach: Andy Landers
Sports Information Director: Claude Felton
www.georgiadogs.com

## University of Kentucky
Address: 23 Memorial Coliseum
Lexington, KY 40506-0019
Nickname: Wildcats
Telephone: (859) 257-3838
Football Stadium (Capacity): Commonwealth
Stadium (67,530)
Basketball Arena (Capacity): Rupp Arena (23,000)
President: Dr. Lee Todd
Athletic Director: Larry Ivy
Football Coach: Guy Morriss
Basketball Coach: Orlando (Tubby) Smith
Sports Information Director: Brooks Downing
www.ukathletics.com

## Louisiana State University
Address: P.O. Box 25095
Baton Rouge, LA 70894
Nickname: Fighting Tigers
Telephone: (225) 388-8226
Football Stadium (Capacity): Tiger Stadium (91,600)
Basketball Arena (Capacity): Pete Maravich
Assembly Center (14,164)
Chancellor: Dr. Mark Emmert
Athletic Director: Skip Bertman
Football Coach: Nick Saban
Men's Basketball Coach: John Brady
Women's Basketball Coach: Sue Gunter
Sports Information Director: Michael Bonnette
www.lsusports.net

## University of Mississippi
Address: P.O. Box 217
University, MS 38677
Nickname: Rebels
Telephone: (662) 915-7522
Football Stadium (Capacity): Vaught-Hemingway
Stadium/Hollingsworth Field (45,577)
Basketball Arena (Capacity): C.M. "Tad" Smith
Coliseum (8,700)
Chancellor: Dr. Robert C. Khayat
Athletic Director: John Schafer
Football Coach: David Cutcliffe
Basketball Coach: Rod Barnes
Sports Information Director: Langston Rogers
www.olemisssports.com

## Mississippi State University
Address: P.O. Box 5308
Starkville, MS 39762
Nickname: Bulldogs
Telephone: (662) 325-2703
Football Stadium (Capacity): Scott Field (40,656)
Basketball Arena (Capacity): Humphrey Coliseum (10,500)
President: Malcolm Portera
Athletic Director: Larry Templeton
Football Coach: Jackie Sherrill
Basketball Coach: Rick Stansbury
Sports Information Director: Mike Nemeth
www.mstateathletics.com

## University of South Carolina
Address:    Rex Enright Athletic Center
            1300 Rosewood Drive
            Columbia, SC 29208
Nickname: Gamecocks
Telephone: (803) 777-5204
Football Stadium (Capacity): Williams-Brice
  Stadium  (80,250)
Basketball Arena (Capacity): Frank McGuire
  Arena (12,401)
President: Dr. John Palms
Athletic Director: Dr. Mike McGee
Football Coach: Lou Holtz
Basketball Coach: Dave Odom
Sports Information Director: Kerry Tharp
www.uscsports.com

## University of Tennessee
Address:    P.O. Box 15016
            Knoxville, TN 37901
Nickname: Volunteers
Telephone: (865) 974-1212
Football Stadium (Capacity): Neyland Stadium (104,079)
Basketball Arena (Capacity): Thompson-Boling Arena
  and Assembly Center (24,535)
President: Eli Fly
Athletic Director: Doug Dickey
Football Coach: Phillip Fulmer
Men's Basketball Coach: Buzz Peterson
Women's Basketball Coach: Pat Summitt
Sports Information Directors: (M) Bud Ford,
  (W) Debby Jennings
www.utsports.com

## Vanderbilt University
Address:    P.O. Box 120158
            Nashville, TN 37212
Nickname: Commodores
Telephone: (615) 322-4121
Football Stadium (Capacity): Vanderbilt Stadium
  (42,000)
Basketball Arena (Capacity): Memorial Gym (15,311)
Chancellor: E. Gordon Gee
Athletic Director: Todd Turner
Football Coach: Woody Widenhofer
Men's Basketball Coach: Kevin Stallings
Sports Information Director: Rod Williamson
www.vucommodores.com

## WESTERN ATHLETIC CONFERENCE
Address:    9250 East Costilla Avenue, Suite 300
            Englewood, CO 80112
Telephone: (303) 799-9221
Commissioner: Karl Benson
Publicity Director: Jeff Hurd
www.wacsports.com

## Air Force
Address:    2169 Field House Drive
            USAF Academy, CO 80840-9500
Nickname: Falcons
Telephone: (719) 333-2313
Football Stadium (Capacity): Falcon Stadium (52,480)
Basketball Arena (Capacity): Clune Arena (6,002)
Superintendent: Lt. Gen. John R. Dallager
Athletic Director: Col. Randall W. Spetman
Football Coach: Fisher DeBerry
Basketball Coach: Joe Scott
Sports Information Director: Troy Garnhart
www.airforcesports.com

## Brigham Young University
Address:    30 Smith Field House
            Provo, UT 84602
Nickname: Cougars
Telephone: (801) 378-4911
Football Stadium (Capacity): Cougar Stadium (65,000)
Basketball Arena (Capacity): Marriott Center (23,000)
President: Merrill J. Bateman
Athletic Director: Val Hale
Football Coach: Gary Crowton
Basketball Coach: Steve Cleveland
Sports Information Directors: Brett Pyne/Jeff Reynolds
www.byucougars.edu

## Colorado State University
Address:    McGraw Athletic Center
            Moby Arena
            Fort Collins, CO 80523
Nickname: Rams
Telephone: (970) 491-5300
Football Stadium (Capacity): Hughes Stadium (30,000)
Basketball Arena (Capacity): Moby Arena (8,745)
President: Dr. Albert C. Yates
Athletic Director: Jeffrey Hathaway
Football Coach: Sonny Lubick
Basketball Coach: Dale Layer
Sports Information Director: Gary Ozello
www.csurams.com

## Fresno State University
Address:    5305 N. Campus Drive, Room 153
            Fresno, CA 93740-8020
Nickname: Bulldogs
Telephone: (559) 278-2509
Football Stadium (Capacity): Bulldog
  Stadium (41,031)
Basketball Arena (Capacity): Selland Arena (10,182)
President: Dr. John Welty
Interim Athletic Director: Scott Johnson
Football Coach: Pat Hill
Basketball Coach: Jerry Tarkanian
Sports Information Director: Steve Weakland
www.gobulldogs.com

## University of Hawaii
Address:    1337 Lower Campus Road
            Honolulu, HI 96822-2370
Nickname: Warriors
Telephone: (808) 956-7523
Football Stadium (Capacity): Aloha Stadium (50,000)
Basketball Arena (Capacity): Stan Sheriff Center (10,225)
President: Dr. Kenneth Mortimer
Athletic Director: Hugh Yoshida
Football Coach: June Jones
Basketball Coach: Riley Wallace
Sports Information Director: Lois Manin
www.uhathletics.hawaii.edu

## University of Nevada at Las Vegas
Address:    4505 Maryland Parkway
            Las Vegas, NV 89154-0004
Nickname: Rebels
Telephone: (702) 895-3207
Football Stadium (Capacity): Sam Boyd Stadium (36,800)
Basketball Arena (Capacity): Thomas & Mack Center (18,500)
President: Dr. Carol C. Harter
Athletic Director: Charles Cavagnaro
Football Coach: John Robinson
Basketball Coach: Charlie Spoonhour
Sports Information Director: Andy Grossman
www.unlvrebels.com

## University of New Mexico
Address:     UNM South Complex
             Albuquerque, NM  87131-0041
Nickname: Lobos
Telephone: (505) 925-5500
Football Stadium (Capacity): University Stadium (37,000)
Basketball Arena (Capacity): University Arena (18,018)
President: Dr. William Gordon
Athletic Director: Rudy Davalos
Football Coach: Rocky Long
Basketball Coach: Fran Fraschilla
Sports Information Director: Greg Remington
www.golobos.com

## Rice University
Address:     P.O. Box 1892 MS548
             Houston, TX 77251-1892
Nickname: Owls
Telephone: (713) 348-4034
Football Stadium (Capacity): Rice Stadium (70,000)
Basketball Arena (Capacity): Autry Court (5,000)
President: Malcolm Gillis
Athletic Director: Bobby May
Football Coach: Ken Hatfield
Basketball Coach: Willis Wilson
Sports Information Director: Bill Cousins
www.riceowls.com

## San Diego State University
Address:     5500 Campanile Drive
             San Diego, CA 92182-4313
Nickname: Aztecs
Telephone: (619) 594-5547
Football Stadium (Capacity): Qualcomm
  Stadium (71,400)
Basketball Arena (Capacity): Cox Arena (12,414)
President: Dr. Stephen Weber
Athletic Director: Rick Bay
Football Coach: Ted Tollner
Basketball Coach: Steve Fisher
Sports Information Director: Kevin Klintworth
www.goaztecs.com

## San Jose State University
Address:     One Washington Square
             San Jose, CA 95192-0062
Nickname: Spartans
Telephone: (408) 924-1217
Football Stadium (Capacity): Spartan Stadium (30,578)
Basketball Arena (Capacity): Event Center (5,000)
President: Dr. Robert L. Caret
Athletic Director: Chuck Bell
Football Coach: Fitz Hill
Basketball Coach: Steve Barnes
Sports Information Director: Lawrence Fan
www.sjsuspartans.com

## Southern Methodist University
Address:     SMU Box 750216
             Dallas, TX 75275-0216
Nickname: Mustangs
Telephone: (214) 768-2883
Football Stadium (Capacity): Gerald J. Ford Stadium
  (32,000)
Basketball Arena (Capacity): Moody Coliseum (8,998)
President: R. Gerald Turner
Athletic Director: Jim Copeland
Football Coach: Mike Cavan
Basketball Coach: Mike Dement
Sports Information Director: Chris Walker
www.smumustangs.com

## University of Texas at El Paso
Address:     201 Baltimore
             El Paso, TX 79902
Nickname: Miners
Telephone: (915) 747-5347
Football Stadium (Capacity): Sun Bowl (52,000)
Basketball Arena (Capacity): Don Haskins Center (11,500)
President: Dr. Diana Natalicio
Athletic Director: Bob Stull
Football Coach: Gary Nord
Basketball Coach: Jason Rabedeaux
Sports Information Director: Jeff Darby
http://athletics.utep.edu (no www)

## Texas Christian University
Address:     Box 297600
             Fort Worth, TX 76129
Nickname: Horned Frogs
Telephone: (817) 257-7969
Football Stadium (Capacity): Amon G. Carter
  Stadium (46,000)
Basketball Arena (Capacity): Daniel-Meyer Coliseum (7,200)
Chancellor: Dr. Michael R. Ferrari
Athletic Director: Eric Hyman
Football Coach: Gary Patterson
Basketball Coach: Billy Tubbs
Sports Information Director: Steve Fink
www.gofrogs.com

## University of Tulsa
Address:     600 S. College
             Tulsa, OK  74104-3189
Nickname: Golden Hurricane
Telephone: (918) 631-2395
Football Stadium (Capacity): Skelly Stadium (40,385)
Basketball Arena (Capacity): Donald W. Reynolds
  Center (8,300)
President: Dr. Robert Lawless
Athletic Director: Judy MacLeod
Football Coach: Keith Burns
Basketball Coach: John Philips
Sports Information Director: Don Tomkalski
www.tulsahurricane.com

## University of Utah
Address:     1825 E. South Campus Drive, Front
             Salt Lake City, UT 84112-0900
Nickname: Utes
Telephone: (801) 581-8171
Football Stadium (Capacity): Rice-Eccles Stadium (45,634)
Basketball Arena (Capacity): Jon M. Huntsman
  Center (15,000)
President: Dr. Bernie Machen
Athletic Director: Dr. Chris Hill
Football Coach: Ron McBride
Basketball Coach: Rick Majerus
Sports Information Director: Liz Abel
www.utahutes.com

## University of Wyoming

Address:     P.O. Box 3414
                Laramie, WY 82071-3414
Nickname: Cowboys
Telephone: (307) 766-2256
Football Stadium (Capacity): War Memorial Stadium
  (33,500)
Basketball Arena (Capacity): Arena-Auditorium (15,028)
President: Dr. Philip Dubois
Athletic Director: Lee Moon
Football Coach: Vic Koenning
Basketball Coach: Steve McClain
Sports Information Director: Kevin McKinney
http://www.wyomingathletics.com

## INDEPENDENTS

### Army

Address:     639 Howard Road
                West Point, NY 10996
Nickname: Black Knights
Telephone: (914) 938-3303
Football Stadium (Capacity): Michie Stadium (39,929)
Basketball Arena (Capacity): Christl Arena (5,043)
Superintendent: Lt. Gen. William J. Lennox Jr.
Athletic Director: Rick Greenspan
Football Coach: Todd Berry
Basketball Coach: Pat Harris
Asst. Athletic Dir. for Media Relations: Bob Baretta
www.goARMYsports.com
Note: Plays football in Conference USA, basketball in
Patriot League.

### East Carolina University

Address:    Ward Sports Medicine Building
             Greenville, NC 27858-4353
Nickname: Pirates
Telephone: (252) 328-4600
Football Stadium (Capacity): Dowdy-Ficklen (43,000)
Basketball Arena (Capacity): Williams Arena (7,500)
Chancellor: William V. Muse
Athletic Director: Michael A. Hamrick
Football Coach: Steve Logan
Basketball Coach: Bill Herrion
Asst. Athletic Dir. for Media Relations: Norm Reilly
www.ecupirates.com

## Navy

Address:     566 Brownson Road, Ricketts Hall
                Annapolis, MD 21402
Nickname: Midshipmen
Telephone: (410) 293-2340
Football Stadium (Capacity): Navy-Marine Corps
  Memorial Stadium (30,000)
Basketball Arena (Capacity): Alumni Hall (5,700)
Superintendent: John Ryan, USN
Athletic Director: Jack Lengyel
Football Coach: Charlie Weatherbie
Basketball Coach: Don DeVoe
Sports Information Director: Scott Strasemeier
www.navy sports.com
Note: Plays football as independent, basketball in Patriot League.

### University of Notre Dame

Address:     112 Joyce Center
                Notre Dame, IN 46556
Nickname: Fighting Irish
Telephone: (219) 631-7516
Football Stadium (Capacity): Notre Dame Stadium (80,232)
Basketball Arena (Capacity): Joyce Athletic and
  Convocation Center (11,418)
President: Rev. Edward A. Malloy, CSC
Athletic Director: Dr. Kevin White
Football Coach: Bob Davie
Men's Basketball Coach: Michael Brey
Women's Basketball Coach: Muffet McGraw
Sports Information Director: John Heisler
www.und.com

## Tiger, Tiger Burning Bright

After Clemson sophomore defensive lineman Nick Eason tied for the team lead in sacks during the 2000–01 season, with seven, he tore his right Achilles tendon in December during a practice for the Gator Bowl. He pursued his rehab so aggressively that he started and made four tackles in the 2001–02 season opener against Central Florida, albeit at a new position—tackle instead of end. But it's off the field where Eason really shines. He is the first Clemson athlete in any sport to receive the ACC Top Six Award for community service three years in a row, in recognition of his talks and reading sessions with grammar school children. Moreover, he graduated on Aug. 11, 2001, needing only three years to do so, another first for a Clemson football player. "He is what a college player is supposed to be," says Tigers defensive coordinator Reggie Herring.

# Olympic Sports Directory

## United States Olympic Committee
Address:    Olympic House
            1 Olympic Plaza
            Colorado Springs, CO  80909
Telephone: (719) 632-5551
Acting CEO: Scott Blackmun
Managing Director for Media Relations and
  Programs: Mike Moran
www.usolympicteam.com

## U.S. Olympic Training Centers
Address:    1 Olympic Plaza
            Colorado Springs, CO  80909
Telephone: (719) 632-5551
Director: John Smith
Address:    421 Old Military Road
            Lake Placid, NY 12946
Telephone: (518) 523-2600
Director: Jack Favro
Address:    2800 Olympic Parkway
            Chula Vista, CA 91915
Telephone: (619) 656-1500
Director: Patrice Milkovich
www.olympic.org

## International Olympic Committee
Address:    Chateau de Vidy
            Case Postale 356
            CH-1007 Lausanne, Switzerland
Telephone: 41-21-621-6111
President: Jacques Rogge
Director General: Francois Carrard
www.olympic.org

## Salt Lake Organizing Committee for the Olympic Winter Games
Address:    299 South Main Street, Suite 1300
            Salt Lake City, UT  84111
Telephone: (801) 212-2002
President/CEO: Mitt Romney
Director of Media Relations: Caroline Shaw
(XIX Winter Games; Feb 8–24, 2002)
www.saltlake2002.com

## Athens Olympic Organizing Committee for the 2004 Summer Games
Address:    7 Kifissias Avenue
            115 23 Athens, Greece
Telephone: 30 1 2004 000
President: Gianna Angelopoulos-Daskalaki
Head of Communications and Media: Serafim Kotrotsos
(XXVII Summer Games; Aug 11–29, 2004)
www.athens.olympic.org

## U.S. Olympic Organizations

### National Archery Association (NAA)
Address:    1 Olympic Plaza
            Colorado Springs, CO  80909
Telephone: (719) 578-4576
President: Mark Miller
Executive Director: Rick Mack
Media Relations: Desiree Freiherr
www.usarchery.org

### USA Badminton (USAB)
Address:    1 Olympic Plaza
            Colorado Springs, CO 80909
Telephone: (719) 578-4808
President: Don Chew
Executive Director: Dan Cloppas
Media Contact: Barb Kissick
www.usabadminton.org

### USA Baseball
Address:    Hi Corbett Field
            3400 East Camino Campestre
            Tucson, AZ  85716
Telephone: (520) 327-9700
President: Lindsay Burbage
Executive Director/CEO: Paul V. Seiler
Director of Media Relations: David Fanucchi
www.usabaseball.com

### USA Basketball
Address:    5465 Mark Dabling Blvd.
            Colorado Springs, CO 80918
Telephone: (719) 590-4800
President: Tom Jannstedt
Executive Director: Jim Tolley
Assistant Executive Director for Public Relations:
  Craig Miller
www.usabasketball.com

### U.S. Biathlon Association (USBA)
Address:    29 Ethan Allen Avenue
            Colchester, VT 05446
Telephone: (802) 654-7833
President: Lyle Nelson
Executive Director: Stephen R. Sands
Media Contact: Anita Hall
www.usbiathlon.com

### U.S. Bobsled and Skeleton Federation
Address:    P.O. Box 828
            Lake Placid, NY 12946
Telephone: (518) 523-1842
President: Jim Morris
Executive Director: Matt Roy
Media and PR Director Director: Julie Urbansky
www.usabobsledandskeleton.org

### USA Bowling
Address:    5301 South 76th Street
            Greendale, WI 53129
Telephone: (414) 421-9008
President: Elaine Hagin
Executive Director: Gerald Koenig
Communications Director: Sarah Krainert
www.bowl.com

### USA Boxing, Inc.
Address:    1 Olympic Plaza
            Colorado Springs, CO 80909
Telephone: (719) 578-4506
President: Dr. Robert Voy
Executive Director: Mike Stone
Director of PR and Media: Bill Kellick
www.usaboxing.org

## U.S. Olympic Organizations *(Cont.)*

### U.S. Canoe and Kayak Team
Address:  P.O. Box 789
Lake Placid, NY 12946
Telephone: (518) 523-1855
Interim President: Anne Blanchard
Executive Director: Lisa Fish
Public Relations Director: Doug Haney
www.usacanoekayak.org

### USA Cycling
Address:  1 Olympic Plaza
Colorado Springs, CO 80909
Telephone: (719) 578-4581
President: Mike Plant
Executive Director and Chief Executive Officer:
Lisa Voight
Director of Communications: Patrice Quintero
www.usacycling.org

### United States Diving, Inc. (USD)
Address:  Pan American Plaza, Suite 430
201 South Capitol Avenue
Indianapolis, IN 46225
Telephone: (317) 237-5252
President: William Walker
Executive Director: Todd Smith
Director of Communications: Kelly Servizzi
www.usdiving.org

### U.S. Equestrian Team (USET)
Address:  Pottersville Rd.
Gladstone, NJ 07934
Telephone: (908) 234-1251
Executive Director: Robert C. Standish
Director of Communications: Joanna Smith
www.uset.org

### U.S. Fencing Association (USFA)
Address:  1 Olympic Plaza
Colorado Springs, CO 80909
Telephone: (719) 578-4511
President: Don Alperstein
Executive Director: Michael Massik
Media Relations Director: Cynthia Bent
www.usafencing.org

### U.S. Field Hockey Association (USFHA)
Address:  1 Olympic Plaza
Colorado Springs, CO 80909-5773
Telephone: (719) 578-4567
President: Sharon Taylor
Executive Director: Jane Betts
Sport and Public Information Director:
Howard Thomas
www.usfieldhockey.com

### U.S. Figure Skating Association
Address:  20 First Street
Colorado Springs, CO 80906
Telephone: (719) 635-5200
President: Phyllis Howard
Executive Director: John LeFevre
Communications Coordinator: Bob Dunlop
www.usfsa.org

### USA Gymnastics
Address:  Pan American Plaza, Suite 300
201 South Capitol Avenue
Indianapolis, IN 46225
Telephone: (317) 237-5050
Chairman of the Board: Ron Froehlich
President: Robert Colarossi
Director of Public Relations: Steve Penny
www.usa-gymnastics.org

### USA Hockey
Address:  1775 Bob Johnson Drive
Colorado Springs, CO 80906
Telephone: (719) 576-8724
President: Walter L. Bush, Jr.
Executive Director: Doug Palazzari
Coordinator, Media Relations: Chuck Menke
www.usahockey.com

### United States Judo, Inc. (USJ)
Address:  1 Olympic Plaza Suite 202
Colorado Springs, CO 80909
Telephone: (719) 578-4730
President: Dr. Ronald Tripp
Executive Director: William Rosenberg

### U.S. Luge Association (USLA)
Address:  35 Church Street
Lake Placid, NY 12946
Telephone: (518) 523-2071
President: Doug Bateman
Executive Director: Ron Rossi
Public Relations Manager: Jon Lundin
www.usaluge.org

### U.S. Modern Pentathlon Association
Address:  8610 Broadway, Suite 260
San Antonio, TX 78217
Telephone: (210) 822-1206
President: Ralph Bender
Executive Director: Robert Marbut Jr.
www.usmpa.home.texas.net

### U.S. Racquetball Association
Address:  1685 West Uintah
Colorado Springs, CO 80904
Telephone: (719) 635-5396
President: Otto Dietrich
Executive Director: Luke St. Onge
Public Relations Coordinator: Ryan John
www.usra.org

### USA Roller Sports
Address:  4730 South Street
P.O. Box 6579
Lincoln, NE 68506
Telephone: (402) 483-7551
President: George Kolibaba
Executive Director: Louis Marciani
Communications Director: Bill Wolf
www.usacrs.com

## U.S. Olympic Organizations (Cont.)

### U.S. Rowing
Address:     Pan American Plaza, Suite 400
             201 South Capitol Avenue
             Indianapolis, IN 46225
Telephone: (317) 237-5656/ 1 (800) 314-4769
President: Lawrence Terry
Executive Director: John Dane
Press Contact: Brett Johnson
www.usrowing.org

### U.S. Sailing Association
Address:     P.O. Box 1260
             Portsmouth, RI 02871
Telephone: (401) 683-0800
President: Dave Rosekrans
Interim Executive Director: William Placke
Communications Director: Penny Piva Rego
Olympic Yachting Director: Jonathan R. Harley
www.ussailing.org

### USA Shooting
Address:     1 Olympic Plaza
             Colorado Springs, CO  80909
Telephone: (719) 578-4670
President of the Board: Stevan B. Richards
Executive Director: Robert K. Mitchell
Director of Marketing: Bob Groate
www.usashooting.com

### U.S. Ski and Snowboard Association
Address:     P.O. Box 100
             Park City, UT  84060
Telephone: (435) 649-9090
Chairman: Jim McCarthy
President and CEO: Bill Marolt
V.P. of Communications and Media: Tom Kelly
Media Services Coordinator: Scott Flanders
www.usskiteam.com

### U.S. Soccer Federation (USSF)
Address:     1801-1811 South Prairie Avenue
             Chicago, IL 60616
Telephone: (312) 808-1300
President: Robert Contiguglia
Secretary General: Dan Flynn
Director of Communications: Jim Moorhouse
www.us-soccer.com

### Amateur Softball Association (ASA)
Address:     2801 N.E. 50th Street
             Oklahoma City, OK 73111
Telephone: (405) 424-5266
President: TBA
Executive Director: Ron Radigonda
Director of Communications: Brian McCall
www.softball.org

### U.S. Speed Skating
Address:     P.O. Box 450639
             Westlake OH 44145
Telephone: (440) 899-0128
President: Fred Benjamin
Executive Director: Katie Marquard
Public Relations Director: Nick Paulenich
Publicity telephone: (810) 212-2350
www.usspeedskating.org

### U.S. Swimming, Inc. (USS)
Address:     1 Olympic Plaza
             Colorado Springs, CO  80909
Telephone: (719) 578-4578
President: Dale Neuburger
Executive Director: Chuck Wielgus
Public Relations Director: Mary Wagner
www.usa-swimming.org

### U.S. Synchronized Swimming, Inc. (USSS)
Address:     Pan American Plaza, Suite 901
             201 South Capitol Avenue
             Indianapolis, IN 46225
Telephone: (317) 237-5700
President: Betty Hazle
Executive Director: Debbie Hesse
Media Relations: Brian Eaton
www.usasynchro.org

### U.S. Table Tennis Association (USTTA)
Address:     1 Olympic Plaza
             Colorado Springs, CO 80909
Telephone: (719) 578-4583
Executive Director: Dwight Johnson
President: Sheri Pittman
Director of Media and PR: Debbie Doney
www.usatt.org

### U.S. Taekwondo Union (USTU)
Address:     1 Olympic Plaza, Suite 405
             Colorado Springs, CO  80909
Telephone: (719) 578-4632
President: Sang Lee
Executive Director: R. Jay Warwick
Media and Communications Director: Chris Condron
www.ustu.org

### USA Team Handball
Address:     1 Olympic Plaza
             Colrado Springs, CO 80909
Telephone: (719) 575-4036
President: Bob Djokovich
Executive Director: Mike Cavanaugh
www.usateamhandball.org

### U.S. Tennis Association
Address:     70 West Red Oak Lane
             White Plains, NY 10604
Telephone: (914) 696-7000
President: Marvin Heller
Executive Director: Richard D. Ferman
Director of Communications: Andrea Jayson
www.usta.com

### USA Track & Field (formerly TAC)
Address:     1 RCA Dome, Suite 140
             Indianapolis, IN 46225
Telephone: (317) 261-0500
President: Bill Roe
Chief Executive Officer: Craig A. Masback
Communications Coordinator: Melissa Beasley
www.usatf.org

# Olympic Sports Directory (Cont.)

## U.S. Olympic Organizations (Cont.)

**USA Volleyball**
Address:     715 South Circle Drive
              Colorado Springs, CO 80910
Telephone: (719) 228-6800
President: Albert M. Monaco Jr.
Executive Director: Kerry Klostermann
Coordinator of Marketing and Comm.:Cecil Bleiker
www.usavolleyball.org

**United States Water Polo (USWP)**
Address:     1685 West Uintah
              Colorado Springs, CO 80904
Telephone: (719) 634-0699
President: Rich Foster
Executive Director: Bruce J. Wigo
Director of Media and Marketing: Eric Tittmeyer
www.usawaterpolo.com

**USA Weightlifting**
Address:     1 Olympic Plaza
              Colorado Springs, CO  80909
Telephone: (719) 578-4508
President: Dennis Snethen
Executive Director and Media Contact: Jim Fox
www.usaweightlifting.org

**USA Wrestling**
Address:     6155 Lehman Drive
              Colorado Springs, CO 80918
Telephone: (719) 598-8181
President: Bruce Baumgartner
Executive Director: Rich Bender
Director of Communications: Gary Abbott
www.usawrestling.org

## Affiliated Sports Organizations

**Amateur Athletic Union (AAU)**
Address:     Walt Disney World Resort; P.O. Box 10000
              Lake Buena Vista, FL 32830-1000
Telephone: (407) 934-7200
President: Bobby Dodd
Media Contact: Melissa Wilson
www.aausports.org

**U.S. Curling Association (USCA)**
Address:     1100 Center Point Drive
              P.O. Box 866
              Stevens Point, WI 54481
Telephone: (715) 344-1199
President: Peggy Hatch
Executive Director: David Garber
Communications Director: Rick Patzke
www.usacurl.org

**USA Karate Federation**
Address:     1300 Kenmore Boulevard
              Akron, OH 44314
Telephone: (330) 753-3114
President: George Anderson
www.usakarate.org

**U.S. Orienteering Federation**
Address:     P.O. Box 1444
              Forest Park, GA 30298
Telephone: (404) 363-2110
President: Chuck Ferguson
Executive Director: Robin Shannonhouse
Marketing and Public Relations VP: Sherry Litasi
Publicity telephone: (303) 694-4914
www.us.orienteering.org

**U.S. Squash Racquets Association**
Address:     23 Cynwyd Road
              P.O. Box 1216
              Bala Cynwyd, PA 19004
Telephone: (610) 667-4006
President: Eben Hardie III
Vice President: Kevin Jernigan
www.uss-squash.org

**USA Trampoline and Tumbling**
Address:     1309 Tahoka Road
              Brownfield, TX 79316
Telephone: (806) 637-8670
President: Paul Parilla
Executive Director: Ann Sims
www.usa-gymnastics.org

**USA Triathlon**
Address:     3595 East Fountain Boulevard, Suite F-1
              Colorado Springs, CO 80910
Telephone: (719) 597-9090
President: Mike Highfield
Executive Director: Steve Locke
Communications Director: B. J. Hoeptner
www.usatriathlon.org

**USA Waterski**
Address:     1251 Holy Cow Road
              Polk City, FL 33868
Telephone: (863) 324-4341
President: Andrea Plough
Executive Director: Steve McDermeit
Public Relations Manager: Scott Atkinson
www.usawaterski.org

# Miscellaneous Sports Directory

**Championship Auto Racing Teams (CART)**
Address:     755 West Big Beaver Road, Suite 800
              Troy, MI 48084
Telephone: (248) 362-8800
President and CEO: Joseph F. Heitzler
VP of Corporate Communications: Ron Richards
www.cart.com

**Indy Racing League**
Address:     4565 West 16th Street
              Indianapolis, IN  46222
Telephone: (317) 484-6526
President and Founder: Tony George
Manager of Media Relations: Ron Green
www.indyracing.com

# Miscellaneous Sports Directory

## Professional Sports Car Racing, Inc.
Address:     14175 Icot Blvd., Suite 300
             Clearwater, FL 33760
Telephone: (727) 533-0503
Managing Director: H. Doug Robinson
www.professionalsportscar.com

## National Association for Stock Car Auto Racing (NASCAR)
Address:     1801 W International Speedway Blvd.
             Daytona Beach, FL 32114-1243
Telephone: (904) 253-0611
President: Mike Helton
Director of Communications Worldwide: John Griffin
www.nascar.com

## National Hot Rod Association
Address:     2035 East Financial Way
             Glendora, CA 91741
Telephone: (626) 914-4761
President: Tom Compton
Director of Communications: Denny Darnell
www.nhra.com

## Professional Women's Bowling Association
Address:     7171 Cherryvale Boulevard
             Rockford, IL 61112
Telephone: (815) 332-5756
Tournament Director: Wyatt Slaughter
Media Director: Darlene Priscilla
www.pwba.com

## Professional Bowlers Association LLC
Address:     999 Third Avenue, Suite 8210
             Seattle, WA 98104
Telephone: (206) 332-9688
Commissioner: Anne Hamilton
Public Relations Director: Dan McConnell
www.pba.com

## U.S. Chess Federation
Address:     3054 Route 9 W
             New Windsor, NY  12553
Telephone: (845) 562-8350
Executive Director: George De Feis
Media Relations: Joan DuBois
www.uschess.org

## International Game Fish Association
Address:     300 Gulf Stream Way
             Dania Beach, FL 33004
Telephone: (954) 927-2628
President: Mike Leech
www.igfa.org

## Ladies Professional Golf Association
Address:     100 International Golf Drive
             Daytona Beach, FL 32124
Telephone: (386) 274-6200
Commissioner: Ty Votaw
Director of Communications: Leslie King
www.lpga.com

## PGA Tour
Address:     112 PGA Tour Boulevard
             Ponte Vedra Beach, FL 32082
Telephone: (904) 285-3700
Commissioner: Timothy W. Finchem
Senior VP of Communications: Bob Combs
www.pgatour.com

## Professional Golfers' Association of America
Address:     100 Avenue of the Champions
             Box 109601
             Palm Beach Gardens, FL 33410-9601
Telephone: (561) 624-8400
President: Jack Connelly
Director of Public Relations: Julius Mason
www.pgaonline.com

## United States Golf Association
Address:     P.O. Box 708, Golf House
             Liberty Corner Road
             Far Hills, NJ 07931-0708
Telephone: (908) 234-2300
President: Dr. Trey Holland
Director of Communications: Craig Smith
www.usga.org

## U.S. Handball Association
Address:     2333 North Tucson Boulevard
             Tucson, AZ  85716
Telephone: (520) 795-0434
Executive Director: Vern Roberts
Director of Public Relations: Mark Carpenter
www.ushandball.org

## Breeders' Cup Limited
Address:     2525 Harrodsburg Road
             PO Box 4230
             Lexington, KY 40504
Telephone: (859) 223-5444
President: D. G. Van Clief Jr.
Media Relations Director: James Gluckson
Director of Marketing: Damon Thayer
www.breederscup.com

## The Jockeys' Guild, Inc.
Address:     P.O. Box 250
             Lexington, KY 40588-0250
Telephone: (859) 259-3211
Chairman of the Board: Tomey Swan
Public Relations: TBA
www.jockeysguild.com

## Thoroughbred Racing Associations of America
Address:     420 Fair Hill Drive, Suite 1
             Elkton, MD 21921
Telephone: (410) 392-9200
President: Chris Scherf
www.tra-online.com

## National Thoroughbred Racing Association
Address:     444 Madison Avenue, Suite 503
             New York, NY 10022
Telephone: (212) 907-9280
VP of NTRA Communications: Chip Tuttle
www.ntra.com

## United States Trotting Association
Address:     750 Michigan Avenue
             Columbus, OH 43215
Telephone: (614) 224-2291
Executive Vice President: Fred J. Noe
Director of Publicity: John Pawlak
www.ustrotting.com

## Iditarod Trail Committee
Address:     P.O. Box 870800; Wasilla, AK  99687
Telephone: (907) 376-5155
Executive Director: Stan Hooley
Race Director: Joanne Potts
www.iditarod.com

## U.S. Lacrosse
Address:  113 W University Parkway
          Baltimore, MD 21210
Telephone: (410) 235-6882
Executive Director: Steven B. Stenersen
www.lacrosse.org

## Little League Baseball, Inc.
Address:  P.O. Box 3485
          Williamsport, PA 17701
Telephone: (570) 326-1921
President & CEO: Stephen D. Keener
Communications & Marketing Director: Jud Rogers
www.littleleague.org

## U.S. Polo Association
Address:  771 Corporate Drive, Suite 505
          Lexington, KY 40503
Telephone: (859) 219-1000
Executive Director: David Cummings
Media Contact: Merle Jenkins
www.uspolo.org

## American Powerboating Association
Address:  P.O. Box 377
          Eastpointe, MI 48021
Telephone: (810) 773-9700
Executive Administrator: Gloria Urbin
www.APBA.org

## Professional Rodeo Cowboys Association
Address:  101 Pro Rodeo Drive
          Colorado Springs, CO 80919
Telephone: (719) 593-8840
Commissioner: Steven J. Hatchell
Director of Communications: Steve Fleming
www.prorodeo.com

## USA Rugby Football Union
Address:  3595 East Fountain Boulevard
          Colorado Springs, CO 80910
Telephone: (719) 637-1022
President: Anne Barry
Chair, Communications Committee: Patrick J. O'Connor
Chair, Collegiate & Membership Committee: Bill Sexton
www.usarugby.org

## The United Soccer Leagues
Address:  14497 North Dale Mabry Highway, Ste 201
          Tampa, FL 33618
Telephone: (813) 963-3909
President and A-League Commissioner: Francisco Marcos
Director of Public Relations:Gerald Barnhart
www.unitedsoccerleagues.com

## Major League Soccer
Address:  110 East 42nd Street, Suite 1000
          New York, NY 10017
Telephone: (212) 687-1400
Commissioner: Don Garber
Director of Communications: Dan Courtemanche
www.mlsnet.com

## Major Indoor Soccer League
Address:  1175 Post Road East
          Westport, CT 06880
Telephone: (330) 455-4625
Commissioner: Steve Ryan
Director of Media Relations: Greg Bibb
www.misl.net

## Women's United Soccer Association
Address:  1120 Avenue of the Americas/ 6th Floor
          New York, NY 10036
Telephone: (212) 869-8558
Commissioner: Tony DiCicco
Director of Public Relations: Shaun May
www.wusa.com

## Association of Tennis Professionals Tour
Address:  201 ATP Tour Boulevard
          Ponte Vedra Beach, FL 32082
Telephone: (904) 285-8000
Chief Executive Officer: Mark Miles
VP of Comm. and Media Relations: Greg Sharko
www.atptour.org

## COREL WTA Tour (Women's Tennis)
Address:  1266 East Main Street, 4th floor
          Stamford, CT 06902-3546
Telephone: (203) 978-1740; (727) 895-5000
Chief Executive Officer: Bart McGuire
Director of Communications: Christopher DeMaria
www.sanexwta.com

## Association of Volleyball Professionals
Address:  1600 Rosecrans Avenue
          Suite 330, Building 7
          Manhattan Beach, CA 90266
Telephone: (310) 426-8000
Public Relations: Debbie Rubio, The Robbins Group
  (818) 776-1244
www.avptour.com

# MINOR LEAGUES

## Baseball (AAA)

## National Association of Professional Baseball Leagues
Address:  201 Bayshore Drive S.E.
          St. Petersburg, FL 33731
Telephone: (727) 822-6937
President: Mike Moore
Director of Media Relations: Jim Ferguson
www.minorleaguebaseball.com

## International League
Address:  55 South High Street, Suite 202
          Dublin, OH 43017
Telephone: (614) 791-9300
President: Randy Mobley
www.ilbaseball.com

## Pacific Coast League
Address:  1631 Mesa Avenue
          Colorado Springs, CO 80906
Telephone: (719) 636-3399
President: Branch Rickey
www.pclbaseball.com

## Mexican League
Address:  Angela Pola #16
          Col. Periodista, C.P. 11220
          Mexico D.F.
Telephone: 011-525-557-10-07
Manager of Operations: Nestor Alva Brito
President: Jose Orozco Topete
www.imb.com.mx

### MINOR LEAGUES *(Cont.)*
### Hockey

#### American Hockey League
Address:     1 Monarch Place Suite 2400
             Springfield, MA 01144
Telephone: (413) 781-2030
President, CEO & Treasurer: David A. Andrews
Director of Hockey Operations: Jim Mill
Director of Comm. & Media Relations: Bret Stothart
www.theahl.com

## Halls of Fame Directory

### National Baseball Hall of Fame and Museum
Address:     P.O. Box 590/25 Main Street
             Cooperstown, NY 13326
Telephone: (607) 547-7200
President: Dale Petroskey
Senior Vice President: Bill Haase
V.P. of Communications and Education: Jeff Idelson
www.baseballhalloffame.org

### Naismith Memorial Basketball Hall of Fame
Address:     1150 West Columbus Avenue
             Springfield, MA 01105
Telephone: (413) 781-6500
COO: John L. Doleva
Senior Director of Marketing Communications: Kim Lee
www.hoophall.com

### International Bowling Museum and Hall of Fame
Address:     111 Stadium Plaza
             St. Louis, MO 63102
Telephone: (314) 231-6340
Executive Director: Gerald Baltz
Communications Director: Jim Baer
www.bowlingmuseum.com

### National Boxing Hall of Fame
Address:     1 Hall of Fame Drive
             Canastota, NY 13032
Telephone: (315) 697-7095
President: Donald Ackerman
Executive Director: Edward Brophy
www.ibohf.com

### Professional Football Hall of Fame
Address:     2121 George Halas Drive NW
             Canton, OH 44708
Telephone: (330) 456-8207
Executive Director: John Bankert
Vice President of Public Relations: Joe Horrigan
www.profootballhof.com

### LPGA Hall of Fame
Address:     100 International Golf Drive
             Daytona Beach, FL 32124
Telephone: (904) 274-6200
Commissioner: Ty Votaw
Communications Director: Leslie King
www.lpga.com

### Hockey Hall of Fame
Address:     30 Yonge Street BCE Place
             Toronto, Ontario  Canada M5E 1X8
Telephone: (416) 360-7735
Chairman: William Hay
President & COO: Jeff Denomme
VP of Marketing and Communications: Craig Baines
www.hhof.com

### National Museum of Racing and Hall of Fame
Address:     191 Union Avenue
             Saratoga Springs, NY 12866
Telephone: (518) 584-0400
Executive Director: Peter Hammell
Assistant Director: Catherine Maguire
Communications Officer: Richard Hamilton
www.racingmuseum.org

### National Soccer Hall of Fame
Address:     Wright Soccer Campus
             18 Stadium Circle
             Oneonta, NY 13820
Telephone: (607) 432-3351
President: Will Lunn
www.soccerhall.org

### International Swimming Hall of Fame
Address:     1 Hall of Fame Drive
             Fort Lauderdale, FL 33316
Telephone: (954) 462-6536
President: Dr. Samuel J. Freas
Media Contact: Preston Levi
www.ishof.org

### International Tennis Hall of Fame
Address:     194 Bellevue Avenue
             Newport, RI 02840
Telephone: (401) 849-3990
Executive Vice President and COO: Mark Stenning
Marketing Manager: Kat Anderson
www.tennisfame.com

### National Track & Field Hall of Fame
Address:     216 Ft. Washington Avenue
             The Armory Foundation
             New York, NY 10032
Telephone: (317) 261-0500
Chief Executive Officer: Craig Masback
Director of Communications: Jill Geer
www.usatf.org
Note: Expected opening in New York, Nov 2002.

# Awards

GERARD RANCINAN

## Athlete Awards

### Sports Illustrated Sportsman of the Year

| | | | |
|---|---|---|---|
| 1954 | Roger Bannister, Track and Field | 1982 | Wayne Gretzky, Hockey |
| 1955 | Johnny Podres, Baseball | 1983 | Mary Decker, Track and Field |
| 1956 | Bobby Morrow, Track and Field | 1984 | Mary Lou Retton, Gymnastics |
| 1957 | Stan Musial, Baseball | | Edwin Moses, Track and Field |
| 1958 | Rafer Johnson, Track and Field | 1985 | Kareem Abdul-Jabbar, Pro Basketball |
| 1959 | Ingemar Johansson, Boxing | 1986 | Joe Paterno, Football |
| 1960 | Arnold Palmer, Golf | 1987 | Athletes Who Care: |
| 1961 | Jerry Lucas, Basketball | | Bob Bourne, Hockey |
| 1962 | Terry Baker, Football | | Kip Keino, Track and Field |
| 1963 | Pete Rozelle, Pro Football | | Judi Brown King, Track and Field |
| 1964 | Ken Venturi, Golf | | Dale Murphy, Baseball |
| 1965 | Sandy Koufax, Baseball | | Chip Rives, Football |
| 1966 | Jim Ryun, Track and Field | | Patty Sheehan, Golf |
| 1967 | Carl Yastrzemski, Baseball | | Rory Sparrow, Pro Basketball |
| 1968 | Bill Russell, Pro Basketball | | Reggie Williams, Pro Football |
| 1969 | Tom Seaver, Baseball | 1988 | Orel Hershiser, Baseball |
| 1970 | Bobby Orr, Hockey | 1989 | Greg LeMond, Cycling |
| 1971 | Lee Trevino, Golf | 1990 | Joe Montana, Pro Football |
| 1972 | Billie Jean King, Tennis | 1991 | Michael Jordan, Pro Basketball |
| | John Wooden, Basketball | 1992 | Arthur Ashe, Tennis |
| 1973 | Jackie Stewart, Auto Racing | 1993 | Don Shula, Pro Football |
| 1974 | Muhammad Ali, Boxing | 1994 | Bonnie Blair, Speed Skating |
| 1975 | Pete Rose, Baseball | | Johann Olav Koss, Speed Skating |
| 1976 | Chris Evert, Tennis | 1995 | Cal Ripken Jr, Baseball |
| 1977 | Steve Cauthen, Horse Racing | 1996 | Tiger Woods, Golf |
| 1978 | Jack Nicklaus, Golf | 1997 | Dean Smith, College Basketball |
| 1979 | Terry Bradshaw, Pro Football | 1998 | Mark McGwire, Sammy Sosa, Baseball |
| | Willie Stargell, Baseball | 1999 | U.S. Women's Soccer Team |
| 1980 | U.S. Olympic Hockey Team | 2000 | Tiger Woods, Golf |
| 1981 | Sugar Ray Leonard, Boxing | | |

### Associated Press Athletes of the Year

| | MEN | WOMEN |
|---|---|---|
| 1931 | Pepper Martin, Baseball | Helene Madison, Swimming |
| 1932 | Gene Sarazen, Golf | Babe Didrikson, Track and Field |
| 1933 | Carl Hubbell, Baseball | Helen Jacobs, Tennis |
| 1934 | Dizzy Dean, Baseball | Virginia Van Wie, Golf |
| 1935 | Joe Louis, Boxing | Helen Wills Moody, Tennis |
| 1936 | Jesse Owens, Track and Field | Helen Stephens, Track and Field |
| 1937 | Don Budge, Tennis | Katherine Rawls, Swimming |
| 1938 | Don Budge, Tennis | Patty Berg, Golf |
| 1939 | Nile Kinnick, Football | Alice Marble, Tennis |
| 1940 | Tom Harmon, Football | Alice Marble, Tennis |
| 1941 | Joe DiMaggio, Baseball | Betty Hicks Newell, Golf |
| 1942 | Frank Sinkwich, Football | Gloria Callen, Swimming |
| 1943 | Gunder Haegg, Track and Field | Patty Berg, Golf |
| 1944 | Byron Nelson, Golf | Ann Curtis, Swimming |
| 1945 | Bryon Nelson, Golf | Babe Didrikson Zaharias, Golf |
| 1946 | Glenn Davis, Football | Babe Didrikson Zaharias, Golf |
| 1947 | Johnny Lujack, Football | Babe Didrikson Zaharias, Golf |
| 1948 | Lou Boudreau, Baseball | Fanny Blankers-Koen, Track and Field |
| 1949 | Leon Hart, Football | Marlene Bauer, Golf |
| 1950 | Jim Konstanty, Baseball | Babe Didrikson Zaharias, Golf |
| 1951 | Dick Kazmaier, Football | Maureen Connolly, Tennis |
| 1952 | Bob Mathias, Track and Field | Maureen Connolly, Tennis |
| 1953 | Ben Hogan, Golf | Maureen Connolly, Tennis |
| 1954 | Willie Mays, Baseball | Babe Didrikson Zaharias, Golf |
| 1955 | Hopalong Cassidy, Football | Patty Berg, Golf |
| 1956 | Mickey Mantle, Baseball | Pat McCormick, Diving |
| 1957 | Ted Williams, Baseball | Althea Gibson, Tennis |
| 1958 | Herb Elliott, Track and Field | Althea Gibson, Tennis |
| 1959 | Ingemar Johansson, Boxing | Maria Bueno, Tennis |
| 1960 | Rafer Johnson, Track and Field | Wilma Rudolph, Track and Field |
| 1961 | Roger Maris, Baseball | Wilma Rudolph, Track and Field |
| 1962 | Maury Wills, Baseball | Dawn Fraser, Swimming |
| 1963 | Sandy Koufax, Baseball | Mickey Wright, Golf |
| 1964 | Don Schollander, Swimming | Mickey Wright, Golf |
| 1965 | Sandy Koufax, Baseball | Kathy Whitworth, Golf |
| 1966 | Frank Robinson, Baseball | Kathy Whitworth, Golf |

## Associated Press Athletes of the Year (Cont.)

| | MEN | WOMEN |
|---|---|---|
| 1967 | Carl Yastrzemski, Baseball | Billie Jean King, Tennis |
| 1968 | Denny McLain, Baseball | Peggy Fleming, Skating |
| 1969 | Tom Seaver, Baseball | Debbie Meyer, Swimming |
| 1970 | George Blanda, Pro Football | Chi Cheng, Track and Field |
| 1971 | Lee Trevino, Golf | Evonne Goolagong, Tennis |
| 1972 | Mark Spitz, Swimming | Olga Korbut, Gymnastics |
| 1973 | O.J. Simpson, Pro Football | Billie Jean King, Tennis |
| 1974 | Muhammad Ali, Boxing | Chris Evert, Tennis |
| 1975 | Fred Lynn, Baseball | Chris Evert, Tennis |
| 1976 | Bruce Jenner, Track and Field | Nadia Comaneci, Gymnastics |
| 1977 | Steve Cauthen, Horse Racing | Chris Evert, Tennis |
| 1978 | Ron Guidry, Baseball | Nancy Lopez, Golf |
| 1979 | Willie Stargell, Baseball | Tracy Austin, Tennis |
| 1980 | U.S. Olympic Hockey Team | Chris Evert Lloyd, Tennis |
| 1981 | John McEnroe, Tennis | Tracy Austin, Tennis |
| 1982 | Wayne Gretzky, Hockey | Mary Decker, Track and Field |
| 1983 | Carl Lewis, Track and Field | Martina Navratilova, Tennis |
| 1984 | Carl Lewis, Track and Field | Mary Lou Retton, Gymnastics |
| 1985 | Dwight Gooden, Baseball | Nancy Lopez, Golf |
| 1986 | Larry Bird, Pro Basketball | Martina Navratilova, Tennis |
| 1987 | Ben Johnson, Track and Field | Jackie Joyner-Kersee, Track and Field |
| 1988 | Orel Hershiser, Baseball | Florence Griffith Joyner, Track and Field |
| 1989 | Joe Montana, Pro Football | Steffi Graf, Tennis |
| 1990 | Joe Montana, Pro Football | Beth Daniel, Golf |
| 1991 | Michael Jordan, Pro Basketball | Monica Seles, Tennis |
| 1992 | Michael Jordan, Pro Basketball | Monica Seles, Tennis |
| 1993 | Michael Jordan, Pro Basketball | Sheryl Swoopes, Basketball |
| 1994 | George Foreman, Boxing | Bonnie Blair, Speed Skating |
| 1995 | Cal Ripken Jr, Baseball | Rebecca Lobo, Basketball |
| 1996 | Michael Johnson, Track and Field | Amy Van Dyken, Swimming |
| 1997 | Tiger Woods, Golf | Martina Hingis, Tennis |
| 1998 | Mark McGwire, Baseball | Se Ri Pak, Golf |
| 1999 | Tiger Woods, Golf | U.S. Women's Soccer Team |
| 2000 | Tiger Woods, Golf | Marion Jones, Track and Field |

## James E. Sullivan Award

Presented annually by the AAU to the athlete who "by his or her performance, example and influence as an amateur, has done the most during the year to advance the cause of sportsmanship."

| 1930 | Bobby Jones, Golf | 1963 | John Pennel, Track and Field |
|---|---|---|---|
| 1931 | Barney Berlinger, Track and Field | 1964 | Don Schollander, Swimming |
| 1932 | Jim Bausch, Track and Field | 1965 | Bill Bradley, Basketball |
| 1933 | Glenn Cunningham, Track and Field | 1966 | Jim Ryun, Track and Field |
| 1934 | Bill Bonthron, Track and Field | 1967 | Randy Matson, Track and Field |
| 1935 | Lawson Little, Golf | 1968 | Debbie Meyer, Swimming |
| 1936 | Glenn Morris, Track and Field | 1969 | Bill Toomey, Track and Field |
| 1937 | Don Budge, Tennis | 1970 | John Kinsella, Swimming |
| 1938 | Don Lash, Track and Field | 1971 | Mark Spitz, Swimming |
| 1939 | Joe Burk, Rowing | 1972 | Frank Shorter, Track and Field |
| 1940 | Greg Rice, Track and Field | 1973 | Bill Walton, Basketball |
| 1941 | Leslie MacMitchell, Track and Field | 1974 | Rich Wohlhuter, Track and Field |
| 1942 | Cornelius Warmerdam, Track | 1975 | Tim Shaw, Swimming |
| 1943 | Gilbert Dodds, Track and Field | 1976 | Bruce Jenner, Track and Field |
| 1944 | Ann Curtis, Swimming | 1977 | John Naber, Swimming |
| 1945 | Doc Blanchard, Football | 1978 | Tracy Caulkins, Swimming |
| 1946 | Arnold Tucker, Football | 1979 | Kurt Thomas, Gymnastics |
| 1947 | John B. Kelly Jr, Rowing | 1980 | Eric Heiden, Speed Skating |
| 1948 | Bob Mathias, Track and Field | 1981 | Carl Lewis, Track and Field |
| 1949 | Dick Button, Skating | 1982 | Mary Decker, Track and Field |
| 1950 | Fred Wilt, Track and Field | 1983 | Edwin Moses, Track and Field |
| 1951 | Bob Richards, Track and Field | 1984 | Greg Louganis, Diving |
| 1952 | Horace Ashenfelter, Track and Field | 1985 | Joan B. Samuelson, Track and Field |
| 1953 | Sammy Lee, Diving | 1986 | Jackie Joyner-Kersee, Track and Field |
| 1954 | Mal Whitfield, Track and Field | 1987 | Jim Abbott, Baseball |
| 1955 | Harrison Dillard, Track and Field | 1988 | Florence Griffith Joyner, Track |
| 1956 | Pat McCormick, Diving | 1989 | Janet Evans, Swimming |
| 1957 | Bobby Morrow, Track and Field | 1990 | John Smith, Wrestling |
| 1958 | Glenn Davis, Track and Field | 1991 | Mike Powell, Track and Field |
| 1959 | Parry O'Brien, Track and Field | 1992 | Bonnie Blair, Speed Skating |
| 1960 | Rafer Johnson, Track and Field | 1993 | Charlie Ward, Football, Basketball |
| 1961 | Wilma Rudolph, Track and Field | 1994 | Dan Jansen, Speed Skating |
| 1962 | Jim Beatty, Track and Field | 1995 | Bruce Baumgartner, Wrestling |

## James E. Sullivan Award *(Cont.)*

| | |
|---|---|
| 1996 .............................Michael Johnson, Track and Field | 1999 ..............................Kelly and Coco Miller, Basketball |
| 1997 .............................Peyton Manning, Football | 2000 ..............................Rulon Gardner, Wrestling |
| 1998 ..............................Chamique Holdsclaw, Basketball | |

## *The Sporting News* Sportsman of the Year

| | |
|---|---|
| 1968 ...........................Denny McLain, Baseball | 1985 ...........................Pete Rose, Baseball |
| 1969 ...........................Tom Seaver, Baseball | 1986 ...........................Larry Bird, Pro Basketball |
| 1970 ...........................John Wooden, Basketball | 1987 ...........................No award |
| 1971 ...........................Lee Trevino, Golf | 1988 ...........................Jackie Joyner-Kersee, Track and Field |
| 1972 ...........................Charles O. Finley, Baseball | 1989 ...........................Joe Montana, Pro Football |
| 1973 ...........................O.J. Simpson, Pro Football | 1990 ...........................Nolan Ryan, Baseball |
| 1974 ...........................Lou Brock, Baseball | 1991 ...........................Michael Jordan, Pro Basketball |
| 1975 ...........................Archie Griffin, Football | 1992 ...........................Mike Krzyzewski, Basketball |
| 1976 ...........................Larry O'Brien, Pro Basketball | 1993 ...........................Pat Gillick/Cito Gaston, Baseball |
| 1977 ...........................Steve Cauthen, Horse Racing | 1994 ...........................Emmitt Smith, Pro Football |
| 1978 ...........................Ron Guidry, Baseball | 1995 ...........................Cal Ripken Jr, Baseball |
| 1979 ...........................Willie Stargell, Baseball | 1996 ...........................Joe Torre, Baseball |
| 1980 ...........................George Brett, Baseball | 1997 ...........................Michael Jordan, Basketball |
| 1981 ...........................Wayne Gretzky, Hockey | 1998 ...........................Mark McGwire, Baseball |
| 1982 ...........................Whitey Herzog, Baseball | 1999 ...........................New York Yankees, Baseball |
| 1983 ...........................Bowie Kuhn, Baseball | 2000 ...........................Kurt Warner/ |
| 1984 ...........................Peter Ueberroth, LA Olympics | Marshall Faulk, Football |

## United Press International Male and Female Athlete of the Year

| MEN | WOMEN |
|---|---|
| 1974...............................Muhammad Ali, Boxing | Irena Szewinska, Track and Field |
| 1975...............................Joao Oliveira, Track and Field | Nadia Comaneci, Gymnastics |
| 1976...............................Alberto Juantorena, Track and Field | Nadia Comaneci, Gymnastics |
| 1977...............................Alberto Juantorena, Track and Field | Rosie Ackermann, Track and Field |
| 1978...............................Henry Rono, Track and Field | Tracy Caulkins, Swimming |
| 1979...............................Sebastian Coe, Track and Field | Marita Koch, Track and Field |
| 1980...............................Eric Heiden, Speed Skating | Hanni Wenzel, Alpine Skiing |
| 1981...............................Sebastian Coe, Track and Field | Chris Evert Lloyd, Tennis |
| 1982...............................Daley Thompson, Track and Field | Marita Koch, Track and Field |
| 1983...............................Carl Lewis, Track and Field | Jarmila Kratochvilova, Track and Field |
| 1984...............................Carl Lewis, Track and Field | Martina Navratilova, Tennis |
| 1985...............................Steve Cram, Track and Field | Mary Decker Slaney, Track and Field |
| 1986...............................Diego Maradona, Soccer | Heike Drechsler, Track and Field |
| 1987...............................Ben Johnson, Track and Field | Steffi Graf, Tennis |
| 1988...............................Matt Biondi, Swimming | Florence Griffith Joyner, Track and Field |
| 1989...............................Boris Becker, Tennis | Steffi Graf, Tennis |
| 1990...............................Stefan Edberg, Tennis | Merlene Ottey, Track and Field |
| 1991...............................Michael Jordan, Pro Basketball | Monica Seles, Tennis |
| 1992...............................Mario Lemieux, Hockey | Monica Seles, Tennis |
| 1993...............................Michael Jordan, Pro Basketball | Steffi Graf, Tennis |
| 1994...............................Nick Price, Golf | Bonnie Blair, Speed Skating |
| 1995...............................Cal Ripken Jr, Baseball | Steffi Graf, Tennis |

Note: Award not given since 1995.

## Dial Award

Presented by the Dial Corporation to the male and female national high school athlete/scholar of the year.

| BOYS | GIRLS |
|---|---|
| 1979...............................Herschel Walker, Football | No award |
| 1980...............................Bill Fralic, Football | Carol Lewis, Track and Field |
| 1981...............................Kevin Willhite, Football | Cheryl Miller, Basketball |
| 1982...............................Mike Smith, Basketball | Elaine Zayak, Skating |
| 1983...............................Chris Spielman, Football | Melanie Buddemeyer, Swimming |
| 1984...............................Hart Lee Dykes, Football | Nora Lewis, Basketball |
| 1985...............................Jeff George, Football | Gea Johnson, Track and Field |
| 1986...............................Scott Schaffner, Football | Mya Johnson, Track and Field |
| 1987...............................Todd Marinovich, Football | Kristi Overton, Water Skiing |
| 1988...............................Carlton Gray, Football | Courtney Cox, Basketball |
| 1989...............................Robert Smith, Football | Lisa Leslie, Basketball |
| 1990...............................Derrick Brooks, Football | Vicki Goetze, Golf |
| 1991...............................Jeff Buckey, Football, Track and Field | Katie Smith, Basketball, Volleyball, Track |
| 1992...............................Jacque Vaughn, Basketball | Amanda White, Track and Field, Swimming |
| 1993...............................Tiger Woods, Golf | Kristin Folkl, Basketball |
| 1994...............................Taymon Domzalski, Basketball | Shannon Miller, Gymnastics |
| 1995...............................Brent Abernathy, Baseball | Shea Ralph, Basketball |
| 1996...............................Grant Irons, Football | Grace Park, Golf |
| 1997...............................Ronald Curry, Football | Michelle Kwan, Figure Skating |

Note: Award not given since 1997.

# Profiles

WALTER IOOSS JR.

**Hall of Fame quarterback John Unitas**

# Profiles

**Henry Aaron** (b. 2-5-34): Baseball OF. "Hammerin' Hank." Alltime leader in HR (755) and RBI (2,297); third in hits (3,771). 1957 MVP. Led league in HR and RBI four times each, runs scored three times, hits and batting average twice. No. 44, he had 44 homers four times. Had 40+ HR eight times; 100+ RBI 11 times; .300+ average 14 times. All-Star 24 times . Career span 1954–76; jersey number retired by Atlanta and Milwaukee.

**Kareem Abdul-Jabbar** (b. 4-16-47): Born Lew Alcindor. Basketball C. Alltime leader points scored (38,387), field goals attempted (28,307), field goals made (15,837); second alltime blocked shots (3,189); third alltime rebounds (17,440). Won six MVP awards (1971–72, 1974, 1976–77, 1980). Career scoring average was 24.6, rebounding average 11.2. Ten-time All-Star, All-Defensive team five times. 1970 Rookie of the Year. Played on six championship teams; was playoff MVP in 1971, 1985. Career span 1969–88 with Milwaukee, Los Angeles. Also played on three NCAA championship teams with UCLA; tournament MVP 1967–69; Player of the Year two times.

**Affirmed** (b. 2-21-75, d. 1-12-01): Thoroughbred race horse. Triple Crown winner in 1978 with jockey Steve Cauthen aboard. Trained by Laz Barrera.

**Andre Agassi** (b. 4-29-70): Tennis player. Won 1999 French Open to become one of five players in history who have won all four Grand Slams. Won '92 Wimbledon, '94 and '99 U.S. Opens and '95, '00 and '01 Australian Opens. Ranked No. 1 in 1995 and again in '99.

**Troy Aikman** (b. 11-21-66): Football QB. MVP of Super Bowl XXVII, in which he completed 22 of 30 passes for 273 yards and four TDs with no interceptions. Led Cowboys to victory in Super Bowls XXVIII and XXX. Retired after 2000 season as a result of a series of concussions. Spent entire career (1989–2000) with Dallas Cowboys.

**Michelle Akers** (b. 2-1-66): Soccer player. Charter member of U.S. women's national team. Scored first goal ever for U.S. women's team on 8-21-85 against Denmark. Second alltime leading scorer in U.S. women's national team history. Member of Women's World Cup champion team in 1991, '99, and third-place team in '95. Member of Olympic champion team in 1996. Battled chronic fatigue syndrome.

**Tenley Albright** (b. 7-18-35): Figure skater. Gold medalist at 1956 Olympics, silver medalist at 1952 Olympics. World champion two times (1953, 1955) and U.S. champion five consecutive years (1952–56).

**Grover Cleveland Alexander** (b. 2-26-1887, d. 11-4-50): Baseball RHP. Tied for third alltime in career wins (373), second in shutouts (90). Won 30+ games three times, 20+ games six other times. Set rookie record with 28 wins in 1911. Career span 1911–30 with Philadelphia (NL), Chicago (NL), St. Louis (NL).

**Vasili Alexeyev** (b. 1942): Soviet weightlifter. Gold medalist at two consecutive Olympics in 1972, 1976. World champion eight times.

**Muhammad Ali** (b. 1-17-42): Born Cassius Clay. Boxer. Heavyweight champion three times (1964–67, 1974–78, 1978–79). Stripped of title in 1967 because he refused to serve in the Vietnam War. Career record 56–5 with 37 KOs. Defended title 19 times. Also light heavyweight gold medalist at 1960 Olympics.

**Phog Allen** (b. 11-18-1885, d. 9-16-74): College basketball coach. Ninth alltime in coaching wins (746); .739 career winning percentage. Won 1952 NCAA championship. Spent most of his career from 1920 to '56 with Kansas.

**Bobby Allison** (b. 12-3-37): Auto racer. Third alltime in NASCAR victories (84) at the time of his retirement. Won Daytona 500 three times (1978, 1982, 1988). NASCAR champion in 1983.

**Naty Alvarado** (b. 7-25-55): Mexican-born handball player. "El Gato (The Cat)." Won a record 11 U.S. pro four-wall handball titles, starting in 1977.

**Lance Alworth** (b. 8-3-40): Football WR. "Bambi" led AFL in receiving in 1966, '68 and '69. 200+ yards in a game five times in career, a record. Gained 100+ yards in a game 41 times. In 1965 gained 1,602 yards receiving. Career span 1962–70 with San Diego and 1971–72 with Dallas. Elected to Pro Football Hall of Fame 1978.

**Gary Anderson** (b. 7-16-59): Football K. Four-time Pro Bowl kicker (1983, '85, '93, '98). NFL's alltime leading scorer (2,060 pts). Made league record 40 consecutive FGs in 1997–98 season. Made every field goal and extra point attempt during the 1998–99 season.

**Sparky Anderson** (b. 2-22-34): Baseball manager. Only manager to win World Series in both leagues (Cincinnati, 1975–76, Detroit, 1984); only manager to win 100 games in both leagues. Elected to Hall of Fame in 2000.

**Willie Anderson** (b. 1880, d. 1910): Scottish golfer. Won U.S. Open four times (1901 and an unmatched three straight, 1903–05). Also won four Western Opens between 1902 and 1909.

**Mario Andretti** (b. 2-28-40): Auto racer. The only driver in history to win the Daytona 500 (1967), the Indy 500 (1969) and a Formula One world championship (1978). Second alltime in CART victories (52). Twelve career Formula One victories. USAC/CART champion four times (consecutively 1965–66, 1969, 1984).

**Earl Anthony** (b. 4-27-38, d. 8-14-01): Bowler. Won PBA National Championship six times, more than any other bowler (consecutively 1973–75, 1981–83) and Tournament of Champions two times (1974, 1978). First bowler to top $1 million in career earnings. Bowler of the Year six times (consecutively 1974–76, 1981–83). Won 41 career PBA titles.

**Said Aouita** (b. 11-2-60): Track and field. Moroccan set world records in 2,000 meters (4:50.81 in 1987), and 5,000 meters (12:58.39 in 1987). 1984 Olympic champion in 5,000; 1988 Olympic third place in 800.

**Al Arbour** (b. 11-1-32): Hockey D-coach. Led NY Islanders to four consecutive Stanley Cup championships (1980–83). Also played on three Stanley Cup champions: Detroit, Chicago and Toronto, from 1953 to 1971.

**Eddie Arcaro** (b. 2-19-16, d. 11-14-97): Horse racing jockey. The only jockey to win the Triple Crown two times (aboard Whirlaway in 1941, Citation in 1948). Rode Preakness Stakes winner (1941, 1948, consecutively 1950–51, 1955, 1957) and Belmont Stakes winner (consecutively 1941–42, 1945, 1948, 1952, 1955) six times each and Kentucky Derby winner five times (1938, 1941, 1945, 1948, 1952). 4,779 career wins.

**Nate Archibald** (b. 9-2-48): Basketball player. "Tiny" only by NBA standards at 6' 1", 160 pounds. Drafted by Cincinnati in 1970. Led NBA in scoring (34.0) and assists (11.4) in 1972–73. First team, all-NBA in 1973, '75 and '76. MVP of NBA All-Star Game in 1981. Retired in 1984.

**Alexis Arguello** (b. 4-19-52): Nicaraguan boxer. Won world titles in three weight classes: featherweight, super featherweight and lightweight. Won first title, WBA featherweight, on 11-23-74 when he KO'd Ruben Olivares in 13. Career record: 88–8, 64 KO.

**Henry Armstrong** (b. 12-12-12, d. 10-24-88): Boxer. Champion in three different weight classes: featherweight, welterweight, and lightweight. Career record 145-20-9 with 98 KOs (27 consecutively, 1937–38) from 1931 to 1945.

**Lance Armstrong** (b. 9-18-71): Cyclist. Three-time Tour de France winner (1999, '00, '01). Two-time winner of Tour DuPont (1995, '96). Won 1993 world championships. Recovered from testicular cancer to win 1999 Tour de France title.

**Arthur Ashe** (b. 7-10-43, d. 2-6-93): Tennis player. First black man to win U.S. Open (1968, as an amateur), Australian Open (1970) and Wimbledon singles titles (1975). 33 career tournament victories. Member of Davis Cup team 1963–78; captain 1980–85.Stadium at the United States Tennis Center, home of the U.S. Open, named in his honor.

**Assault** (b. 1943, d. 1971): Thoroughbred race horse. Horse of the Year for 1946 when he won the Triple Crown. Won Kentucky Derby by eight lengths; Preakness by a neck over Lord Boswell; and the Belmont by three lengths from Natchez. Trained by Max Hirsch.

**Red Auerbach** (b. 9-20-17): Basketball coach-executive. 938 career wins. Coached Boston from 1946 to 1965, winning nine championships, eight consecutively. Had .662 career winning percentage, with 50+ wins eight consecutive seasons. Also won seven championships as general manager.

**Hobey Baker** (b. 1-15-1892, d. 12-21-18): Sportsman. Member of both college football and hockey Halls of Fame. College hockey and football star at Princeton, 1911–14. Fighter pilot in World War I, died in plane crash. College hockey Player of the Year award named in his honor.

**Seve Ballesteros** (b. 4-9-57): Spanish golfer. Notorious scrambler. Won British Opens in 1979, '84 and '88. Won Masters in 1980 and '83.

**Ernie Banks** (b. 1-31-31): Baseball SS-1B. "Mr. Cub." Won two consecutive MVP awards, in 1958–59. 512 career HR. League leader in HR, RBI two times each; career batting average of .274; 40+ HR five times; 100+ RBI eight times. Second-most HR by a shortstop with 47 in 1958. Career span 1953–71 with Chicago.

**Roger Bannister** (b. 3-23-29): Track and field. British runner broke the four-minute mile barrier, running 3:59.4 on 5-6-54.

**Red Barber** (b. 2-17-08, d. 10-22-92): Sportscaster. TV-radio baseball announcer was the voice of Cincinnati, Brooklyn and NY Yankees. His expressions, such as "sitting in the catbird seat," "pea patch" and "rhubarb," captivated audiences from 1934 to 1966.

**Charles Barkley** (b. 2-20-63): Basketball F. "The Round Mound of Rebound." Eleven-time All-Star. One of only four NBA players to amass 20,000 points, 10,000 rebounds, and 4,000 assists. Named one of

NBA's greatest 50 players. Leading scorer on the 1992 Olympic team. League MVP for 1992–93 season. Played for Philadelphia, Phoenix, Houston. Career averages: 22.2 ppg, 11.7 rpg.

**Rick Barry** (b. 3-28-44): Basketball F. Only player in history to win scoring titles in NBA (San Francisco, 1967) and ABA (Oakland, 1969). Second alltime highest free throw percentage (.900). Led league in free throw percentage six times, steals and scoring one time each. Career scoring average 23.2. Five-time All-Star. 1975 playoff MVP with Golden State. 1966 Rookie of the Year. Career span 1967–79.

**Carmen Basilio** (b. 4-2-27): Boxer. Won titles in two classes, welterweight and middleweight. Won welterweight title by TKO of Tony DeMarco in 12 rounds on 6-10-55. Won and then lost middleweight title in two 15-round fights with Ray Robinson. Made three unsuccessful bids to regain middle title. *The Ring* Fighter of the Year for 1957. Career record: 55–16–7, 26 KOs.

**Sammy Baugh** (b. 3-17-14): Football QB-P. Led league in passing six times and punting four times, a record. Also holds record for highest career punting average (45.1) and highest season average (51.0 in 1940). Career span 1937–52 with Washington. Three-time All-America with Texas Christian.

**Elgin Baylor** (b. 9-16-34): Basketball F. Fourth alltime highest scoring average (27.4), scored 23,149 points. Averaged 30+ points three consecutive seasons (1960-63). Ten-time All-Star. 1959 Rookie of the Year. Played in eight Finals without winning championship. Career span 1958–71 with Los Angeles. MVP of 1958 NCAA tournament with Seattle.

**Bob Beamon** (b. 8-29-46): Track and field. Gold medalist in long jump at 1968 Olympics with world record jump of 29' 2½" that stood until 1991.

**Franz Beckenbauer** (b. 9-11-45): West German soccer player. Captain of 1974 World Cup champions and coach of 1990 champions. Also played for NY Cosmos from 1977 to 1980.

**Boris Becker** (b. 11-22-67): German tennis player. The youngest male player to win a Wimbledon singles title, at age 17 in 1985. Won three Wimbledon titles (consecutively 1985–86, 1989), one U.S. Open (1989) and one Australian Open title (1991). Led West Germany to two consecutive Davis Cup victories (1988–89).

**Chuck Bednarik** (b. 5-1-25): Football C-LB. Last of the great two-way players, was named All-Pro at both center and linebacker. Missed only three games in 14 seasons with Philadelphia from 1949-62. Two-time All-America at Pennsylvania.

**Clair Bee** (b. 3-2-1896, d. 5-20-83): Basketball coach. Originated 1-3-1 defense, helped develop three-second rule, 24-second clock. Won 82.7 percent of games as coach for Rider College and Long Island University. Coach, Baltimore Bullets, 1952–54. Author, 23-volume Chip Hilton series for children, 21 nonfiction sports books.

**Jean Beliveau** (b. 8-31-31): Hockey C. Won MVP award twice (1956, 1964), playoff MVP in 1965. Led league in assists three times, goals two times and points once. 507 career goals, 712 assists. All-Star six times. Played on 10 Stanley Cup champions with Montreal from 1950 to 1971.

**Bert Bell** (b. 2-25-1895, d. 10-11-59): Football executive. Second NFL commissioner (1946–59). Also owner of Philadelphia (1933–40) and Pittsburgh (1941–46). Proposed the first college draft in 1936.

**James (Cool Papa) Bell** (b. 5-17-03, d. 3-7-91): Baseball OF. Legendary foot speed—according to Satchel Paige could flip light switch and be in bed before room was dark. Hit .392 in games against white major leaguers. Career span 1922–46 with many teams of the Negro Leagues, including the Pittsburgh Crawfords and the Homestead Grays. Inducted in the Hall of Fame in 1974.

**Lyudmila Belousova/Oleg Protopov** (no dates of birth available): Soviet figure skaters. Won Olympic gold medal in pairs competition in 1964 and 1968. Won four consecutive World and European championships (1965–68) and eight consecutive Soviet titles (1961–68).

**Deane Beman** (b. 4-22-38): Commissioner of the PGA Tour 1974–94. Won British Amateur title in 1959 and U.S. Amateur titles in 1960 and 1963.

**Johnny Bench** (b. 12-7-47): Baseball C. MVP in 1970, 1972; World Series MVP in 1976; Rookie of the Year in 1968. 389 career HR. League leader in HR two times, RBI three times. Career span 1967–83 with Cincinnati. Elected to Hall of Fame in 1989.

**Patty Berg** (b. 2-13-18): Golfer. Alltime women's leader in major championships (16), third alltime in career wins (57). Won Titleholders Championship and Western Open seven times each, the most of any golfer. Also won U.S. Women's Amateur (1938) and U.S. Women's Open (1946).

**Yogi Berra** (b. 5-12-25): Baseball C. Played on 10 World Series winners. Alltime Series leader in games, at-bats, hits and doubles. MVP in 1951 and consecutively 1954–55. 358 career HR. Career span 1946–63, '65. Managed pennant-winning Yankees (1964) and Mets (1973).

**Jay Berwanger** (b. 3-19-14): College football RB. Won the first Heisman Trophy and named All-America with Chicago in 1935.

**Raymond Berry** (b. 2-27-33): Football E. Led NFL in receiving 1958–60. In 13-season career, caught 631 passes, 68 for TDs. Career span 1955–67, all with Baltimore Colts. Coached New England Patriots from 1984–89 with 51–41 record.

**George Best** (b. 5-22-46): Northern Ireland soccer player. Led Manchester United to European Cup title in 1968. Named England's and Europe's Player of the Year in 1968. Played in North American Soccer League for Los Angeles (1976–78), Fort Lauderdale (1978–79) and San Jose (1980–81). Frequent troubles with alcohol and gambling shadowed career.

**Abebe Bikila** (b. 8-7-32, d. 10-25-73): Track and field. Ethiopian barefoot runner won consecutive gold medals in the marathon at Olympics, in 1960 and 1964.

**Fred Biletnikoff** (b. 2-23-43): Football WR. In 14 pro seasons caught 589 passes for 8,974 yards and 76 TDs. In 1971 led NFL receivers with 61 catches; in '72 led AFC with 58. Career span 1965–78, all with Raiders. Elected to Pro Football Hall of Fame in 1988.

**Dmitri Bilozerchev** (b. 12-22-66): Soviet gymnast. Won three gold medals at 1988 Olympics. Made comeback after shattering his left leg into 44 pieces in 1985. Two-time world champion (1983, '87). At 16, became youngest to win all-around world championship title in 1983.

**Dave Bing** (b. 11-24-43): Basketball G. NBA Rookie of Year in 1967. Led NBA in scoring (27.1) in 1968.

MVP NBA All-Star game in 1976. In 12-year career from 1967–78, most of it with Detroit Pistons, averaged 20.3 points. Averaged 24.8 points a game in four years at Syracuse.

**Matt Biondi** (b. 10-8-65): Swimmer. Winner of five gold medals, one silver medal and one bronze medal at 1988 Olympics. Won one gold and one silver at 1992 Olympics.

**Larry Bird** (b. 12-7-56): Basketball F. Won three consecutive MVP awards (1984–86) and two playoff MVP awards (1984, 1986). Rookie of the Year (1980) and All-Star nine consecutive seasons. Led league in free throw percentage four times. Averaged 20+ points 10 times. Career span 1979–92 with Boston. Named College Player of the Year in 1979 with Indiana State. 1997–98 NBA Coach of the Year in first year as coach of Indiana Pacers.

**Bonnie Blair** (b. 3-18-64): Speed skater. Won gold medal in 500 meters and bronze medal in 1,000 meters at 1988 Olympics and gold medals in both events in 1992 and '94. 1989 World Sprint champion. Winner of 1992 Sullivan Award. *Sports Illustrated* Sportswoman of the Year, 1994.

**Toe Blake** (b. 8-21-12, d. 5-17-95): Hockey LW and coach. Second alltime highest winning percentage (.634) and sixth in wins (500). Led Montreal to eight Stanley Cup championships from 1955 to 1968 (consecutively 1956–60, 1965–66, '68). Also MVP and scoring leader in 1939. Played on two Stanley Cup champions with Montreal from 1932 to 1948.

**Doc Blanchard** (b. 12-11-24): College football FB. "Mr. Inside." Teamed with Glenn Davis to lead Army to three consecutive undefeated seasons (1944–46) and two consecutive national championships (1944–45). Won Heisman Trophy and Sullivan Award in 1945. All-America three times.

**George Blanda** (b. 9-17-27): Football QB-K. Alltime leader in seasons played (26), games played (340), and PAT's (943); second in points scored (2,002); kicked 335 field goals. Passed for 26,920 career yards and 236 touchdowns. Tied record with seven touchdown passes on Nov. 19, 1961. Player of the Year two times (1961, 1970). Retired at age 48, the oldest to ever play. Career span 1949–75 with Chicago, Houston, Oakland.

**Fanny Blankers-Koen** (b. 4-26-18): Track and field. Dutch athlete won four gold medals at 1948 Olympics, in 100 meters; 200 meters; 80-meter hurdles; and 400-meter relay. She also set world records in high jump (5' 7¼" in 1943), long jump (20' 6" in 1943) and pentathlon (4,692 points in 1951).

**Wade Boggs** (b. 6-15-58): Baseball 3B. Won five batting titles (1983, consecutively 1985–88); had .350+ average five times, 200+ hits seven times. Won World Series with 1996 Yankees. Career span 1982–99 with Boston, New York Yankees, Tampa Bay; .328 career average, 3,010 hits.

**Nick Bolletieri** (b. 7-31-31): Tennis coach. Since 1976, has run Nick Bolletieri Tennis Academy in Bradenton, Fla. Former residents of the academy include Andre Agassi, Monica Seles and Jim Courier.

**Barry Bonds** (b. 7-24-64): Baseball OF. Broke single-season home run record on Oct 5, 2001, belting his 71st of the year. Finished with 73. Also produced .863 slugging percentage that season, and 177 walks, breaking two of Babe Ruth's records, the first of which had stood since 1920. One of three players to top 40 homers (42) and 40 steals (40) in same season (1996).

Three-time National League MVP (1990, '92, '93); Career span 1986–92 with Pirates; 1993– with Giants. Father Bobby had solid 14-year MLB career, mostly with Giants.

**Bjorn Borg** (b. 6-6-56): Swedish tennis player. Third alltime in Grand Slam singles titles (11—tied with Rod Laver). Set modern record by winning five consecutive Wimbledon titles (1976–80). Won six French Open titles (consecutively 1974–75, 1978–81). Reached U.S. Open final four times, but title eluded him. 65 career tournament victories. Led Sweden to Davis Cup win in 1975.

**Julius Boros** (b. 3-3-20, d. 5-28-94): Golfer. Won U.S. Opens in 1952 at Northwood CC in Dallas and in 1963 at The Country Club in Brookline, Mass. Won 1968 PGA Championship at Pecan Valley CC, San Antonio, when 48 years old, making him oldest winner of a major ever. Led PGA money list in 1952 and '55.

**Mike Bossy** (b. 1-22-57): Hockey RW. In 1978 set NHL rookie scoring record of 54 goals. Scored 50 or more each of first nine seasons, totaling 573 goals and 1,126 points in 10 seasons (1977–78 through 1986–87) with New York Islanders. Elected to Hall of Fame in 1991.

**Ralph Boston** (b. 5-9-39): Track and field. Long jumper won medals at three consecutive Olympics: gold in 1960, silver in '64, bronze in '68.

**Ray Bourque** (b. 12-28-60): Hockey D. Highest scoring defenseman in NHL history (1,579 pts). Won Norris Trophy as NHL's top defenseman five times. Played in 19 consecutive All-Star games. No. 77. Career span 1979–00 with Boston Bruins; 2000–01 with Colorado Avalanche. Won first and only Stanley Cup in 2001.

**Scotty Bowman** (b. 9-18-33): Alltime leader in regular-season wins (1,193) and playoff wins (207). Has won eight Stanley Cups; coached Montreal, St. Louis, Buffalo, and Detroit. Won Jack Adams Award, Coach of the Year, 1976–77.

**Bill Bradley** (b. 7-28-43): Basketball F. Played on two NBA championship teams with New York from 1967 to '77. Player of the Year and NCAA tournament MVP in 1965 with Princeton; All-America three times; Sullivan Award winner in 1965. Rhodes scholar. U.S. Senator (D-NJ) 1979–96.

**Terry Bradshaw** (b. 9-2-48): Football QB. Played on four Super Bowl champions (consecutively 1974–75, 1978–79); named Super Bowl MVP two consecutive seasons (1978–79). 212 career touchdown passes; 27,989 yards passing. Player of the Year in 1978. Career span 1970–83 with Pittsburgh.

**George Brett** (b. 5-15-53): Baseball 3B-1B. MVP in 1980 with .390 batting average; three batting titles, in 1976, '80, '90; and .300+ average 11 times. Led league in hits and triples three times. Reached 3,000-hit mark in 1992. Career span 1973–93, with Kansas City. Career totals: 3,153 hits; 317 HR; 1,595 RBI; batting average .305. Elected to Hall of Fame in 1999.

**Bret Hanover** (b. 1962, d. 1993): Horse. Son of Adios. Won 62 of 68 harness races and earned $922,616. Undefeated as two-year-old. From total of 1,694 foals, he sired winners of $61 million and 511 horses that have recorded sub-2:00 performances.

**Lou Brock** (b. 6-18-39): Baseball OF. Second alltime in career stolen bases (938); second highest single-season steals total (118) of modern era. Led league in steals eight times, with 50+ steals 12 consecutive seasons. Alltime World Series leader in steals (14—tied with Eddie Collins); hit .391 in World Series play. 3,023

career hits. Career span 1961–64 Chicago (NL), 1964–79 St. Louis.

**Jim Brown** (b. 2-17-36): Football FB. 126 career touchdowns; 12,312 career rushing yards. Led league in rushing a record eight times. His 5.2 yards per carry average is the best ever. Player of the Year four times (consecutively 1957–58, '63, '65) and Rookie of the Year in 1957. Rushed for 1,000+ yards in seven seasons, 200+ yards in four games, 100+ yards in 54 other games. Career span 1957–65 with Cleveland; never missed a game. All-America in both football and lacrosse at Syracuse.

**Paul Brown** (b. 9-7-08, d. 8-5-91): Football coach. Led Cleveland to 10 consecutive championship games. Won four consecutive AAFC titles (1946–49) and three NFL titles (1950, consecutively 1954–55). Coached Cleveland from 1946 to 1962; became first coach of Cincinnati, 1968–75, and then general manager. Career coaching record 222-113-9. Also won national championship with Ohio State in 1942.

**Avery Brundage** (b. 9-28-1887, d. 5-5-75): Amateur sports executive. President of International Olympic Committee 1952–72. Served as president of U.S. Olympic Committee 1929–53. Also president of Amateur Athletic Union 1928–35. Member of 1912 U.S. Olympic track and field team.

**Paul (Bear) Bryant** (b. 9-11-13, d. 1-26-83): College football coach. Alltime Division I-A leader in wins (323). Won six national championships (1961, consecutively 1964–65, 1973, consecutively 1978–79) with Alabama. Career record 323–85–17, including four undefeated seasons. Won 15 bowl games. Career span 1945–82 with Maryland, Kentucky, Texas A&M, Alabama.

**Sergei Bubka** (b. 12-4-63): Track and field. Ukrainian pole vaulter was gold medalist at 1988 Olympics. Only five-time world outdoor champion in any event (1983, '87, '91, '93, '95). First man to vault 20 feet, set world indoor record of 20' 2" on 2-21-93 and world outdoor record of 20' 1½", set on 9-20-92.

**Buck Buchanan** (b. 9-10-40): Football DT. Career span 1963–75 with Kansas City Chiefs. Elected to Pro Football Hall of Fame 1990.

**Don Budge** (b. 6-13-15, d. 1-26-00): Tennis player. First player to achieve the Grand Slam, in 1938. Won two consecutive Wimbledon and U.S. singles titles (1937–38), one French and one Australian title (1938).

**Dick Butkus** (b. 12-9-42): Football LB. Recovered 25 opponents' fumbles, third most in history. Selected for Pro Bowl eight times. Career span 1965–73 with Chicago. All-America two times with Illinois. Award recognizing the outstanding college linebacker named in his honor.

**Dick Button** (b. 7-18-29): Figure skater. Gold medalist at two consecutive Olympics in 1948, 1952. World champion five consecutive years (1948–52) and U.S. champion seven consecutive years (1946–52). Sullivan Award winner in 1949.

**Walter Byers** (b. 3-13-22): Amateur sports executive. First director of NCAA, served from 1952 to 1987.

**Frank Calder** (b. 11-17-1877, d. 2-4-43): Hockey executive. First commissioner of NHL, served from 1917 to 1943. Rookie of the Year award named in his honor.

**Walter Camp** (b. 4-7-1859, d. 3-14-25): Football pioneer. Played for Yale in its first football game vs. Harvard on Nov. 17, 1876. Proposed rules such as 11 men per side, scrimmage line, center snap, yards and downs. Founded the All-America selections in 1889.

**Roy Campanella** (b. 11-19-21; d. 6-26-93): Baseball C. Career span 1948–57, ended when paralyzed in car crash. MVP in 1951, 1953, 1955. Played on five pennant winners; 1955 World Series winner with Brooklyn Dodgers.

**Earl Campbell** (b. 3-29-55): Football RB. 9,407 career rushing yards; gained 1,934 yards rushing in 1980; 19 TDs rushing in 1979. Led league in rushing three consecutive seasons. Player of the Year two consecutive seasons (1978–79). Rookie of the Year in 1978. Career span 1978–85 with Houston, New Orleans. Won Heisman Trophy with Texas in 1977.

**John Campbell** (b. 4-8-55): Canadian harness racing driver. Alltime leading money winner with over $100 million in earnings. Leading money winner each year 1986–90.

**Billy Cannon** (b. 2-8-37): Football RB. Led Louisiana State to national championship in 1958 and won Heisman Trophy in 1959. Signed contract in both NFL (Los Angeles) and AFL (Houston). Houston won lawsuit for his services. Played in six AFL championship games with Houston, Oakland, Kansas City. Career span 1960–70. Served three-year jail term for 1983 conviction on counterfeiting charges.

**Jose Canseco** (b. 7-2-64): Baseball OF. One of three players to top 40 homers (42) and 40 steals (40) in same season (1988). AL MVP in 1988, when he also batted .307 with 124 RBI. AL Rookie of the Year in 1986, hitting 33 home runs and driving in 117 runs.

**Harry Caray** (b. 3-1-17, d. 2-18-98): Sportscaster. TV-radio baseball announcer 1945–97 with St. Louis (NL), Oakland, Chicago (AL) and Chicago (NL). Achieved celebrity status on Cubs' superstation WGN by singing "Take Me Out to the Ball Game" with Wrigley Field fans.

**Rod Carew** (b. 10-1-45): Baseball 2B-1B. Won seven batting titles (1969, consecutively 1972–75, 1977–78). Had .328 career average, 3,053 career hits, and .300+ average 15 times. 1977 MVP; 1967 Rookie of the Year. Career span 1967–85; jersey number (29) retired by Minnesota and Anaheim.

**Steve Carlton** (b. 12-22-44): Baseball LHP. Second in career strikeouts (4,136). Four Cy Young awards (1972, '77, '80, '82). 329 career wins; won 20+ games six times. League leader in wins four times, innings pitched and strikeouts five times each. Struck out 19 batters in one game in 1969. Career span 1965–88 with St. Louis, Philadelphia and four other teams in last two years.

**JoAnne Carner** (b. 4-21-39): Golfer. Won 42 titles, including U.S. Women's Opens in 1971 and '76 and du Maurier Classic in 1975 and '78. LPGA top earner in 1974 and 1982–83. LPGA Player of the Year in 1974 and 1981–82. Won five Vare Trophies (1974–75 and 1981–83).

**Joe Carr** (b. 10-22-1880; d. 5-20-39): Football administrator. Instrumental in forming American Professional Football Association in 1920. President of AAFA from 1922 to '39.

**Don Carter** (b. 7-29-26): Bowler. Won All-Star Tournament four times (1952, 1954, 1956, 1958) and PBA National Championship in 1960. Voted Bowler of the Year six times (consecutively 1953–54, 1957–58, 1960, 1962).

**Alexander Cartwright** (b. 4-17-1820, d. 7-12-1892): Baseball pioneer. Credited with setting the basic rules of baseball: bases 90 feet apart, nine men per side,

three strikes per out and three outs per inning. On June 19, 1846, in what is often cited as the first baseball game, his New York Knickerbockers lost to the New York Nine 23–1 at Elysian Fields in Hoboken, NJ.

**Billy Casper** (b. 6-24-31): Golfer. Famed putter. Won 51 PGA tournaments. PGA Player of Year in both 1966 and '70. Won Vardon Trophy in 1960, '63, '64, '65 and '68. Won the U.S. Open twice, in 1959 at Winged Foot in Mamaroneck, New York, and in 1966 in 18-hole playoff over Arnold Palmer at Olympic Club, San Francisco. Beat Gene Littler in 18-hole playoff to win 1970 Masters.

**Tracy Caulkins** (b. 1-11-63): Swimmer. Won three gold medals at 1984 Olympics. Won 48 U.S. national titles, more than any other swimmer, from 1978 to 1984. Also won Sullivan Award in 1978.

**Steve Cauthen** (b. 5-1-60): Jockey. In 1978 became youngest jockey to win Triple Crown, aboard Affirmed. First jockey to top $6 million in season earnings (1977). *Sports Illustrated* Sportsman of Year for 1977. Moved to England in 1979; rode Epsom Derby winners Slip Anchor (1985) and Reference Point (1987).

**Evonne Goolagong Cawley** (b. 7-31-51): Tennis player. Won four Australian Open titles from 1974 through '77; won '71 French Open; won Wimbledon in 1971 and '80. Runner-up four straight years at U.S. Open (1973–76), which she never won.

**Bill Chadwick** (b. 10-10-15): Hockey referee. Spent 16 years as a referee despite vision in only one eye. Developed hand signals to signify penalties. Also former television announcer for the New York Rangers.

**Wilt Chamberlain** (b. 8-21-36, d. 10-12-99): "The Big Dipper." "The Stilt." Basketball C. Alltime leader in rebounds (23,924) and rebounding average (22.9). Alltime season leader in points scored (4,029 in 1962), scoring average (50.4 in 1962), rebounding average (27.2 in 1961) and field goal percentage (.727 in 1973). Set records for most points (100 in 1962) and rebounds (55 in 1960) in a game. Third in career points (31,419); second most field goals made (12,681). Four MVP awards (1960, consecutively 1966–68); playoff MVP in 1972 and 1960 Rookie of the Year. Seven-time All-Star. 30.1 career scoring average. Career span 1959–72 with Philadelphia, Los Angeles. College Player of the Year in 1957 at Kansas.

**Colin Chapman** (b. 1928, d. 12-16-83): Auto racing engineer. Founded Lotus race and street cars, designing the first Lotus racer in 1948. Introduced the monocoque design for Formula One cars in 1962 and ground effects in 1978.

**Julio Cesar Chavez** (b. 7-12-62): Boxer. Career record: 103-5-2. Held titles as junior welterweight, lightweight and super featherweight.

**Gerry Cheevers** (b. 12-7-40): Hockey goalie. Goaltender for Stanley Cup-winning Boston Bruins teams of 1970 and '72. In 12 seasons with Boston had 230-94-74 record with a goals against average of 2.89. Also coached Bruins from 1980–84, with 204-126-46 record. Elected to Hall of Fame 1985.

**Cigar** (b. 1990): Thoroughbred race horse. Tied Citation's American-record 16-race win-streak with a win on 7-13-96. Won $4 million Dubai World Cup on 3-27-96.

**Citation** (b. 4-11-45, d. 8-8-70): Thoroughbred race horse. Triple Crown winner in 1948 with jockey Eddie Arcaro aboard. Trained by Ben A. Jones.

**King Clancy** (b. 2-25-03, d. 11-6-86): Hockey D. Four-time All-Star. Coach, Montreal Maroons, Toronto.

Also referee. Trophy named in his honor, recognizing leadership qualities and contribution to community.

**Jim Clark** (b. 3-4-36, d. 4-7-68): Scottish auto racer. Twenty-five career Formula 1 victories. Formula 1 champion two times (1963, 1965). Won Indy 500 in 1965. Named Indy 500 Rookie of the Year in 1963. Killed during competition in 1968 at age 32.

**Bobby Clarke** (b. 8-13-49): Hockey C. Won MVP award three times (1973, consecutively 1975–76). 358 career goals, 852 assists. Scored 100+ points three times. Played on two consecutive Stanley Cup champions (1974–75) with Philadelphia. Career span 1969 to 1984. Also general manager with Philadelphia 1984–90, Minnesota 1991–92, Florida 1993–94, and Philadelphia since 1994.

**Roger Clemens** (b. 8-4-62): Baseball RHP. Has struck out a record 20 batters in one game on two occasions. Won five Cy Young awards (1986, '87, '91, '97, '98), most by any pitcher. Also 1986 MVP. League leader in ERA six times, wins and strikeouts four times each. Won Triple Crown of pitching in 1997 and '98. Career span 1984–96 with Boston, 1997–98 with Toronto; 1999– with Yankees.

**Roberto Clemente** (b. 8-18-34, d. 12-31-72): Baseball OF. Killed in plane crash while still an active player. Had 3,000 career hits and .317 career average. Won four batting titles; .300+ average 13 times. 1966 MVP; 1971 World Series MVP. Twelve consecutive Gold Gloves; led league in assists five times. Career span 1955–72 with Pittsburgh.

**Ty Cobb** (b. 12-18-1886, d. 7-17-61): Baseball OF. Alltime leader in batting average (.366), second in runs scored (2,245) and hits (4,189); fourth most stolen bases (892). 1911 MVP and 1909 Triple Crown winner. Twelve batting titles. Had .400+ average three times, .350+ average 13 other times; 200+ hits nine times. Led league in hits seven times, steals six times and runs scored five times. Career span 1905–28 with Detroit and Philadelphia.

**Mickey Cochrane** (b. 4-6-03, d. 6-28-62): Baseball C. Second highest career batting average among catchers (.320). MVP in 1928, 1934. Had .300+ average eight times. Career span 1925–37 with Philadelphia and Detroit.

**Sebastian Coe** (b. 9-29-56): Track and field. British runner was gold medalist in 1,500 meters and silver medalist in 800 meters at two consecutive Olympics in 1980, 1984. Set world record in 800 meters (1:41.73 in 1981) and 1,000 meters (2:12.18 in 1981). Served in Parliament after his running career.

**Eddie Collins** (b. 5-2-1887, d. 3-25-51): Baseball 2B. Alltime leader among second basemen in games, chances and assists; led league in fielding nine times. 3,311 career hits; .333 career average; .330+ average 12 times. 743 career stolen bases; alltime co-leader in World Series steals (14—tied with Lou Brock); alltime leader in single-game steals (six, twice). 1914 MVP. Career span 1906–30 with Philadelphia, Chicago.

**Nadia Comaneci** (b. 11-12-61): Romanian gymnast. First ever to score a perfect 10 at Olympics (on uneven parallel bars in 1976). Won three gold, two silver and one bronze medal at 1976 Olympics. Also won two gold and two silver medals at 1980 Olympics.

**David Cone** (b. 1-2-63): Baseball P. Won 20 games in 1988 and again in '98 to set ML record for longest stretch between 20-win seasons. Pitched in four World Series for Toronto and New York. Tossed baseball's 14th perfect game on Yogi Berra Day at Yankee Stadium, 7-18-99, with Berra and Don Larsen in attendance. Won 1994 AL Cy Young award. Career span since 1986 with Kansas City, NY Mets, Toronto, NY Yankees, Boston.

**Dennis Conner** (b. 9-16-42): Sailing. Captain of three America's Cup winners (1980, '87,'88).

**Maureen Connolly** (b. 9-17-34, d. 6-21-69): Tennis player. "Little Mo." First woman to achieve the Grand Slam, in 1953. Won the U.S. singles title in 1951 at age 16. Thereafter lost only four matches before retiring in 1954 because of a broken leg caused by a riding accident. Was never beaten in singles at Wimbledon, winning three consecutive titles (1952–54). Won three consecutive U.S. singles titles (1951–53) and two consecutive French titles (1953–54). Also won Australian title (1953).

**Jimmy Connors** (b. 9-2-52): Tennis player. Alltime men's leader in tournament victories (109). Held men's No. 1 ranking a record 160 consecutive weeks (7-29-74 through 8-16-77). Won five U.S. Open singles titles on three different surfaces (grass 1974, clay 1976, hard 1978, consecutively 1982–83). Won two Wimbledon singles titles (1974, '82) further apart than anyone since Bill Tilden. Also won 1974 Australian Open title. Reached Grand Slam final seven other times.

**Jim Corbett** (b. 9-1-1866; d. 2-18-33): Boxer. "Gentleman Jim." Invented jab. Fight with Australian Peter Jackson on 5-21-1891 ruled no contest when neither could continue into 62nd round. Won heavyweight title on 9-7-1892 with a KO of John Sullivan in 21 rounds; it was first heavyweight title fight using gloves. Lost title when KO'd by Bob Fitzsimmons in 14 on 3-17-1897, then lost two bids to regain it against Jim Jeffries. Career record: 11-4-2, 7 KOs, 2 ND.

**Angel Cordero** (b. 11-8-42): Jockey. Sixth alltime in wins (7,057) and seventh in earnings ($164,561,227). Led yearly earnings three times, in 1976 and 1982–83, winning Eclipse Awards in the last two years.

**Howard Cosell** (b. 3-25-18, d. 4-23-95): Sportscaster. Lawyer–turned–TV-radio sports commentator in 1953. Best known for his work on "Monday Night Football." His nasal voice and "tell it like it is" approach made him a controversial figure.

**James (Doc) Counsilman** (b. 12-28-20): Swimming coach. Coached Indiana from 1957 to 1990. Won six consecutive NCAA championships (1968–73). Career record 287-36-1. Coached U.S. men's team at Olympics in 1964, '76. Swam English Channel in 1979 at age 58.

**Count Fleet** (b. 3-24-40, d. 12-3-73): Thoroughbred race horse. Triple Crown winner in 1943 with jockey Johnny Longden aboard. Trained by Don Cameron.

**Yvan Cournoyer** (b. 11-22-43): Hockey RW. "The Roadrunner" had 428 goals and 435 assists during his 15-season career with the Montreal Canadiens. Had 25 or more goals in 12 straight seasons. Played on 10 Stanley Cup championship teams. Elected to Hall of Fame in 1982.

**Margaret Smith Court** (b. 7-16-42): Australian tennis player. Alltime leader in Grand Slam singles titles (24) and total Grand Slam titles (62). Achieved Grand Slam in 1970 and mixed doubles Grand Slam in 1963 with Ken Fletcher. Won 11 Australian singles titles (consecutively 1960–66, 1969–71, '73), five French titles (1962, '64, consecutively 1969–70, '73), 5 U.S. titles (1962, '65, consecutively 1969–70, '73) and three Wimbledon titles ('63, '65, '70). Also won 19 Grand Slam doubles titles and 19 mixed doubles titles.

**Bob Cousy** (b. 8-9-28): Basketball G. League leader in assists eight consecutive seasons. Averaged 18+ points and named to All-Star team 10 consecutive seasons. 1957 MVP. Played on six championship teams with Boston from 1950 to 1969. Finished career with 6,955 assists; in 1958 had 28 assists in a single game. Also played on 1947 NCAA championship team with Holy Cross.

**Dave Cowens** (b. 10-25-48): Basketball C. NBA co-Rookie of Year in 1971. NBA MVP for 1973. All-Star game MVP in 1973. Career span 1970–71 through 1982–83, all but the last year with the Boston Celtics. Coached Charlotte Hornets 1996–99. Named head coach of Golden State in 2000. Elected to Hall of Fame in 1991.

**Ben Crenshaw** (b. 1-11-52): Golfer. Legendary putter. Won Masters in 1984 and '95. Captain of 1999 U.S. Ryder Cup team.

**Johan Cruyff** (b. 4-25-47): Dutch soccer player. Led Ajax Amsterdam to three European Cup titles, and guided the Netherlands to the 1974 World Cup final, a 2–1 loss to Germany.

**Larry Csonka** (b. 12-25-46): Football RB. In 11 seasons rushed 1,891 times for 8,081 yards (4.3 per carry) and 64 TDs. MVP of Super Bowl VIII, when he rushed 33 times for a then Super Bowl–record 145 yards in Miami's 24–7 defeat of Minnesota. Career span 1968–74, '79 with Miami Dolphins; 1976–78 with New York Giants. Elected to Hall of Fame in 1987.

**Billy Cunningham** (b. 6-3-43): Basketball player and coach. Averaged 24.8 points a game at North Carolina. In nine seasons (1965–66 through 1975–76) with Philadelphia 76ers, averaged 20.8 points per game. All-NBA first team 1969, '70 and '71. In eight seasons as Sixers coach went 454–196 in regular season, 66–39 in playoffs and won NBA title in 1983. Elected to Hall of Fame in 1985.

**Bjørn Dæhlie** (b.6-19-67): Norwegian skier. Legendary cross-country skier won a Winter Olympics–record eight gold medals over three Games from 1992 to '98. Won a total of 12 Olympic medals and more than 40 World Cup races.

**Chuck Daly** (b. 7-20-30): Basketball coach. Won two consecutive championships with Detroit (1989–90). Won 50+ games four consecutive seasons. Coach of 1992 Olympic team. Career span as pro coach 1983–92 with Pistons; 1992–94 with New Jersey; 1997–99 with Orlando.

**Damascus** (b. 1964, d. 1995): Thoroughbred race horse. After finishing third in 1967 Kentucky Derby, won the Preakness, the Belmont, the Dwyer, the American Derby, the Travers, the Woodward and others—12 of 16 starts. Unanimous Horse of the Year in 1967.

**Stanley Dancer** (b. 7-25-27): Harness racing driver. Only driver to win the Trotting Triple Crown two times (Nevele Pride in 1968, Super Bowl in 1972). Also won Pacing Triple Crown driving Most Happy Fella in 1970. Won The Hambletonian four times (1968, '72, '75, '83). Driver of the Year in 1968.

**Tamas Darnyi** (b. 6-3-67): Hungarian swimmer. Gold medalist in 200-meter and 400-meter individual medleys at 1988 and '92 Olympics. Won both events at World Championships in 1986 and '91. Set world records in these events at 1991 Championships (1:59.36 and 4:12.36).

**Al Davis** (b. 7-4-29): Football executive. Owner and general manager of Raiders since 1963. Team has won three Super Bowl championships (1976, '80, '83).

Served as AFL commissioner in 1966; helped negotiate AFL–NFL merger.

**Ernie Davis** (b. 12-14-39, d. 5-18-63): Football RB. Won Heisman Trophy in 1961, the first black man to win the award. All-America three times at Syracuse. First selection in 1962 NFL draft, but became fatally ill with leukemia and never played professionally.

**Glenn Davis** (b. 12-26-24): College football HB. "Mr. Outside." Teamed with Doc Blanchard to lead Army to three consecutive undefeated seasons (1944–46) and two consecutive national championships (1944–45). Won Heisman Trophy in 1946. Named All-America three times.

**John Davis** (b. 1-12-21, d. 7-13-84): Weightlifter. Gold medalist at two consecutive Olympics, 1948, '52. World champion six times.

**Terrell Davis** (b. 10-28-72): Football RB. Became the fourth player to run for more than 2,000 yards in a season when he gained 2,008 yards for the Denver Broncos in 1998. Led Denver to back-to-back Super Bowl wins (1998–99) and won Super Bowl MVP award in '98. Rushed for over 1,000 yards in each of his first four seasons, but suffered career-threatening knee injuries in 1999, '00, and '01.

**Pete Dawkins** (b. 3-8-38): Football RB. Starred at Army 1956–58. Won Heisman Trophy 1958. Was first captain of cadets, class president, top five percent of class academically and football team captain; first man to do all four at West Point. Did not play pro football. Attended Oxford on Rhodes scholarship, won two Bronze Stars in Vietnam, rose to brigadier general before leaving Army to become investment banker. Made unsuccessful run for Senate from New Jersey in 1988.

**Len Dawson** (b. 6-20-35): Football QB. MVP of Super Bowl IV, a 23–7 victory against Minnesota. Threw 239 TDs in his career. Career span 1957–75, the last 13 seasons with Kansas City Chiefs. Elected to Hall of Fame in 1987.

**Dizzy Dean** (b. 1-16-11, d. 7-17-74): Baseball RHP. 1934 MVP with 30 wins. League leader in strikeouts, complete games four times each. 150 career wins. Arm trouble shortened career after 134 wins by age 26. Career span 1930–41 and 1947 with St. Louis and Chicago Cubs.

**Dave DeBusschere** (b. 10-16-40): Basketball F. NBA First Team Defense six straight seasons, 1969–74. Member of NBA champion New York Knicks in 1970 and '73. Career span 1962–63 through middle of 1968–69 season with Detroit Pistons; through 1973–74 with Knicks. Youngest coach (24) in NBA history. Elected to NBA Hall of Fame in 1982.

**Pierre de Coubertin** (b. 1-1-1863, d. 9-2-37): Frenchman called the father of the Modern Olympics. President of International Olympic Committee from 1896 to 1925.

**Oscar De La Hoya** (b. 2-4-73): Boxer. Won lightweight, super lightweight and welterweight titles. 34–2 with 27 KOs. Won lightweight gold medal at 1992 Olympics in Barcelona.

**Jack Dempsey** (b. 6-24-1895, d. 5-31-83): Boxer. Heavyweight champ (1919–26), lost title to Gene Tunney and rematch in the famed "long count" bout in 1927. Career record 62-6-10 with 49 KOs from 1914 to '28.

**Gail Devers** (b. 11-19-66): Track and field sprinter-hurdler. Won 100 at 1992 and '96 Olympics. Successfully completed 100m/100h double at 1993 World Championships, winning 100 in 10.82 and 100 hurdles in American record 12.46. Also won '93 world indoor title in 60 (6.95). Battled Graves disease.

**Klaus Dibiasi** (b. 10-6-47): Italian diver. Gold medalist in platform at three consecutive Olympics (1968, '72, '76) and silver medalist at 1964 Olympics.

**Eric Dickerson** (b. 9-2-60): Football RB. Alltime season leader in yards rushing (2,105 in 1984), fourth in career yards rushing (13,259). Rushed for 1,000+ yards in seven consecutive seasons; 100+ yards in 61 games, including 12 times in 1984. Led league in rushing four times. Rookie of the Year in 1983. Career span with the Los Angeles Rams, Indianapolis, L.A. Raiders and Atlanta Falcons.

**Bill Dickey** (b. 6-6-07 d. 11-12-93): Baseball C. Lifetime average .313. Hit 202 career home runs. Played on 11 AL All-Star teams. In eight World Series, hit five homers and 24 RBI. Career span 1928–43 and 1946, all with the New York Yankees. Inducted to Hall of Fame 1954.

**Harrison Dillard** (b. 7-8-23): Track and field. Only man to win Olympic gold medal in sprint (100 meters in 1948) and hurdles (110 meters in 1952). Sullivan Award winner in 1955.

**Joe DiMaggio** (b. 11-25-14 d. 3-8-99): Baseball OF. "The Yankee Clipper." Tremendous all-around talent. Record 56-game hitting streak in 1941. MVP in 1939, 1941, 1947. Had .325 career batting average; .300+ average 11 times; 100+ RBI nine times. League leader in batting average, HR, and RBI two times each. Played on 10 World Series winners with NY Yankees. Career span 1936–51.

**Mike Ditka** (b. 10-18-39): Football TE–Coach. NFL Rookie of the Year in 1961. Named to five Pro Bowls. Made 427 catches for 5,812 yards and 43 TDs. Career span 1961 to '72 with Bears, Eagles and Cowboys. Recorded 127–101 record as head coach of the Bears and Saints. Coach of Bears team that won Super Bowl XX, 46–10 over New England. Elected to Hall of Fame 1988.

**Tony Dorsett** (b. 4-7-54): Football RB. Rushed for 12,739 yards on 2,936 career attempts. Rushed for 1,000+ yards in eight seasons. Set record for longest run from scrimmage with 99-yard touchdown run on 1-3-83. Scored 91 career touchdowns. Named Rookie of the Year in 1977. Career span 1977–88 with Dallas, Denver. Also won Heisman Trophy in 1976, leading Pittsburgh to national championship. Graduated as alltime NCAA leader in yards rushing and was first man to break 6,000-yard barrier (6,082).

**Abner Doubleday** (b. 6-26-1819, d. 1-26-1893): Civil War hero incorrectly credited as the inventor of baseball in Cooperstown, NY, in 1839.

**Clyde Drexler** (b. 6-22-62): Basketball G. Nicknamed "The Glide" for his smooth play. Member of U.S. "Dream Team" that won 1992 Olympic gold medal. Career span 1984–1994 with Portland Trail Blazers and 1995–98 with Houston Rockets, with whom he won his first NBA title in 1995. Head coach at University of Houston from 1998–00.

**Ken Dryden** (b. 8-8-47): Hockey G. Goaltender of the Year five times (1973, consecutively 1976–79). Playoff MVP as a rookie in 1971, maintained rookie status and named Rookie of the Year in 1972. Led league in goals against average five times. Career record 258-57-74, including 46 shutouts. Career 2.24 goals against average is the modern record. Four playoff shutouts in 1977. Played on six Stanley Cup champions with Montreal from 1970 to 1979.

**Don Drysdale** (b. 7-23-36, d. 7-3-93): Baseball RHP. Led NL three times in strikeouts (1959, '60, '62) and once in wins (1962). Won 1962 Cy Young Award with 25–9 mark. In 1968 pitched six straight shutouts en route to major league record—broken in 1988 by Orel Hershiser—of 58 consecutive scoreless innings. Career record of 209–166, with 2,484 K's and ERA of 2.95. Career span 1956–69, all with Dodgers. Inducted into Hall of Fame 1984.

**Tim Duncan** (b. 4-25-76): Basketball C. Won 1998 rookie of the year award and named first-team All-NBA, only ninth rookie in league history to be so honored. First-team All-NBA and first-team All-Defensive NBA in '99, when he also won Spurs to NBA title and was named Finals MVP. Career span since 1997 with San Antonio.

**Roberto Duran** (b. 6-16-51): Panamanian boxer. Champion in three different weight classes: lightweight (1972–79), welterweight (1980, lost rematch to Sugar Ray Leonard in famous "no más" bout) and junior middleweight (1983–84).

**Leo Durocher** (b. 7-27-05, d. 10-7-91): Baseball manager. "Leo the Lip." Said "Nice guys finish last." Managed three pennant winners and 1954 World Series winner. Won 2,008 games in 24 years. Led Brooklyn 1939–46; New York 1948–55; Chicago 1966–72; and Houston 1972–73.

**David Duval** (b. 11-9-71): Golfer. Won 2001 British Open. Set record for tour earnings in a single season with $2.6 million in 1998, when he also won Vardon Trophy for lowest scoring average (69.13). Won 1997 Tour Championship, four tournaments in 1998. Four-time all-America at Georgia Tech.

**Tomás Dvorák** (b. 5-11-72): Czech decathlete. Broke Dan O'Brien's seven-year-old decathlon world record by 103 points on 7-4-99 in Prague, amassing 8,994 points. Won decathlon bronze medal at Atlanta in '96.

**Eddie Eagan** (b. 4-26-1898, d. 6-14-67): Only American athlete to win gold medal at Summer and Winter Olympic Games (boxing 1920, bobsled '32).

**Alan Eagleson** (b. 4-24-33): Hockey labor leader. Founder of NHL Players' Association and its executive director from 1967–92. Pleaded guilty on 1-6-98 to three counts of fraud and theft involving players' insurance premiums; served six months of an 18-month jail sentence. Resigned from Hall of Fame 3-25-98.

**Dale Earnhardt** (b. 4-29-52, d. 2-18-01): Auto racer. "The Intimidator." NASCAR champion seven times (1980, 1986–87, 1990–91, 1993–94). Won 1998 Daytona 500. Died in crash on the final lap of the 2001 Daytona 500.

**Stefan Edberg** (b. 1-19-66): Swedish tennis player. Won two Wimbledon singles titles (1988, '90), two Australian Open titles (1985, '87) and two U.S. Open titles (1991, '92). Led Sweden to three Davis Cup victories (consecutively 1984–85, '87).

**Gertrude Ederle** (b. 10-23-06): Swimmer. First woman to swim the English Channel, in 1926. Swam 21 miles from France to England in 14:39. Also won three medals at the 1924 Olympics.

**Jason Elam** (b. 3-8-70): Football K. Tied Tom Dempsey's 28-year-old NFL record for the longest field goal with a 63-yard boot on 10-25-98 against Jacksonville.

**Hicham El Gerrouj** (b. 9-14-74): Track and field. Morrocan runner broke world record in mile on 7-7-99, clocking 3:43.13 to trim 1.26 seconds from six-year-old previous record. Performance was his fourth world records, in addition to indoor mile, indoor 1,500 and outdoor 1,500.

**Herb Elliott** (b. 2-25-38): Track and field. Australian runner was gold medalist in 1960 Olympic 1,500 meters in world record 3:35.6. Also set world mile record of 3:54.5 in 1958. Undefeated at 1,500 meters/mile in international competition. Retired at 22.

**Ernie Els** (b.10-17-69): South African golfer. Two-time U.S. Open winner (1994, '97); first foreign-born player to win the event twice since Alex Smith in 1910.

**John Elway** (b. 6-28-60): Football QB. First player taken in 1983 NFL draft. Topped 3,000 yards passing every season from 1985–91. One of two NFL QBs with more than 50,000 passing yards (51,475); 300 career TD passes. Famous for last-minute drives. Won back-to-back Super Bowls (XXXII and XXXII) after three previous Super Bowl losses. Career span 1983–99 with Denver Broncos.

**Roy Emerson** (b. 11-3-36): Australian tennis player. Second alltime in Grand Slam singles titles (12). Won six Australian titles, five consecutively (1961, 1963–67), two consecutive Wimbledon titles (1964–65), two U.S. titles (1961, '64) and two French titles (1963, '67). Also won 13 Grand Slam doubles titles.

**Kornelia Ender** (b. 10-25-58): East German swimmer. Won four gold medals at 1976 Olympics and three silver medals at 1972 Olympics.

**Julius Erving** (b. 2-22-50): Basketball F. "Dr. J." His combined ABA and NBA career points (30,026) rank fourth alltime. Career scoring average of 24.2. Averaged 20+ points 14 consecutive seasons. Won four MVP awards, consecutively 1974–76, '81; playoff MVP 1974, '76. All-Star nine times. Led league in scoring three times. Played on three championship teams, with New York (ABA) and Philadelphia (NBA). Career span 1971 to 1986. Elected to Hall of Fame in 1993.

**Phil Esposito** (b. 2-20-42): Hockey C. "Espo." First to break the 100-point barrier (126 in 1969). 1,590 career points, 717 goals, and 873 assists. Led league in goals six consecutive seasons, points five times and assists three times. Won MVP award two times (1969, 1974). Scored 30+ goals 13 consecutive seasons and 100+ points six times. All-Star six times. Career span 1963–81 with Chicago, Boston, NY Rangers.

**Tony Esposito** (b. 4-23-43): Hockey goalie. Brother of Phil. A five-time All-Star during 16-season NHL career, almost all of it with the Chicago Blackhawks. Career GAA of 2.92. Won or shared Vezina Trophy three times. Elected to Hall of Fame in 1988.

**Janet Evans** (b. 8-28-71): Swimmer. Competed in 1988, '92 and '96 Olympics, winning three gold medals in '88 and one in '92. Set world record in 400-meter freestyle (4:03.85 in 1988), 800-meter freestyle (8:16.22 in 1989) and 1,500-meter freestyle (15:52.10 in 1988). Sullivan Award winner in 1989.

**Lee Evans** (b. 2-25-47): Track and field. Gold medalist in 400 meters at 1968 Olympics with world record time of 43.86, which stood until 1988.

**Chris Evert** (b. 12-21-54): Also Chris Evert Lloyd. Tennis player. Second alltime in tournament victories (157). Tied for fourth alltime in women's Grand Slam singles titles (18). Won at least one Grand Slam singles title every year from 1974 to '86. Won seven French Open titles (1974–75, 1979–80, '83, 1985–86), six U.S. Open titles (1975–77, 1978, 1980, 1982), three Wimbledon titles

(1974, 1976, 1981) and two Australian Open titles (1982, 1984). Reached Grand Slam finals 16 other times. Reached semifinals at 52 of her last 56 Grand Slams.

**Weeb Ewbank** (b. 5-6-07, d. 11-17-98): Football coach. Only coach to win titles in both the NFL and AFL. Coached Baltimore Colts to classic overtime defeat of New York Giants in 1958 and New York Jets to their stunning 16–7 win over Baltimore in Super Bowl III. Career record of 134-130-7. Career span 1954–62 with Colts and 1963–73 with Jets. Elected to Hall of Fame in 1978.

**Patrick Ewing** (b. 8-5-62): Basketball C. 1986 Rookie of the Year with New York. 20+ points per game average in 13 of 15 seasons with Knicks. Played on three NCAA final teams with Georgetown (1982, 1984–85); tournament MVP in 1984. All-America three times.

**Nick Faldo** (b. 7-18-57): British golfer. Three-time winner of Masters (1989–90, consecutively, 1996) and British Open (1987, 1990, 1992).

**Juan Manuel Fangio** (b. 6-24-11, d. 7-17-95): Argentine auto racer. 24 Formula 1 victories in just 51 starts. Formula 1 champion five times, the most of any driver (1951, consecutively 1954–57). Retired in 1958.

**Brett Favre** (b.10-10-69): Football QB. Sixth quarterback in NFL history to throw for more than 3,000 yards in five consecutive seasons. Won NFL MVP award three years in a row (1995–97). Led Packers to victory in Super Bowl XXXI. Career span 1991 with Atlanta, since '92 with Green Bay.

**Bob Feller** (b. 11-3-18): Baseball RHP. League leader in wins six times, strikeouts seven times, innings pitched five times. Pitched three no-hitters and 12 one-hitters. 266 career wins; 2,581 career strikeouts. Won 20+ games six times. Served four years in military during career. Career span 1936–41, 1945–56 with Cleveland.

**Tom Ferguson** (b. 12-20-50): Rodeo. First to top $1 million in career earnings. All-Around champion six consecutive years (1974–79).

**Enzo Ferrari** (b. 2-8-1898, d. 8-14-88): Auto racing engineer. Team owner since 1929, he built first Ferrari race car in Italy in 1947 and continued to preside over Ferrari race and street cars until his death. In 68 years of competition, Ferrari's cars have won over 5,000 races.

**Herve Filion** (b. 2-1-40): Harness racing driver. Alltime leader in career wins (more than 14,000). Driver of the Year 10 times, more than any other driver (consecutively 1969–74, 1978, 1981, 1989).

**Rollie Fingers** (b. 8-25-46): Baseball RHP. Won 107 games in relief in his career; 341 career saves. 1981 Cy Young and MVP winner; 1974 World Series MVP. Saved six World Series games in his career. Career span 1968–85 with Oakland, San Diego, Milwaukee.

**Bobby Fischer** (b. 3-9-43): Chess. World champion from 1972 to 1975, the only American to hold title. Never played competitive chess during his reign. Forfeited title to Anatoly Karpov by refusing to play him.

**Carlton Fisk** (b. 12-26-47): Baseball C. Alltime HR leader among catchers (352) and second in games caught (2,226). 376 career HR, including a record 75 after age 40. Rookie of the Year in 1972 and All-Star 11 times. Hit dramatic 12th-inning HR to win Game 6 of 1975 World Series. Career span 1969–93 with Boston, Chicago (AL). Elected to Hall of Fame in 2000.

**Emerson Fittipaldi** (b. 12-12-46): Brazilian auto racer. Won Indy 500 in 1989 and '93. Won CART championship in 1989. Formula 1 champion two times (1972, 1974).

**James Fitzsimmons** (b. 7-23-1874, d. 3-11-66): Horse racing trainer. "Sunny Jim." Trained two Triple Crown winners (Gallant Fox in 1930, Omaha in 1935). Trained six Belmont Stakes winners (1930, 1932, consecutively 1935–36, 1939, 1955), four Preakness Stakes winners (1930, 1935, 1955, 1957) and three Kentucky Derby winners (1930, 1935, 1939).

**Peggy Fleming** (b. 7-27-48): Figure skater. Olympic champion 1968. World champion (1966–68) and U.S. champion (1964–68).

**Curt Flood** (b. 1-18-38, d. 1-20-97): Baseball OF. Refused to be traded after 1969 season, challenging baseball's reserve clause. Supreme Court rejected his plea, but baseball was eventually forced to adopt free agency system. Won seven consecutive Gold Gloves from 1963 to 1969. Career batting average of .293. Career span 1956–69 with St. Louis.

**Whitey Ford** (b. 10-21-26): Baseball LHP. Alltime World Series leader in wins, losses, games started, innings pitched, hits allowed, walks and strikeouts. 236 career wins, 2.75 ERA. Alltime leader career winning percentage (.690—tied with Dave Foutz). Led league in wins and winning percentage three times each; ERA, shutouts, innings pitched two times each. 1961 Cy Young winner and World Series MVP. Career span 1950, 1953–67 with New York Yankees.

**Forego** (b. 1970, d. 8-27-97): Thoroughbred race horse. Horse of the Year in 1974 (won 8 of 13 starts); '75 (won 6 of 9); and '76 (won 6 of 8). Finished fourth in 1973 Kentucky Derby. Over six years won 34 of 57 starts and $1,938,957.

**George Foreman** (b. 1-22-48): Boxer. Heavyweight champion (1973–74). Retired in 1977, but returned to the ring in 1987. At age 45, KO'd Michael Moorer to regain heavyweight title. Also heavyweight gold medalist at 1968 Olympics.

**Dick Fosbury** (b. 3-6-47): Track and field. Gold medalist in high jump at 1968 Olympics. Introduced back-to-the-bar style of high jumping, called the "Fosbury Flop."

**Jimmie Foxx** (b. 10-22-07, d. 7-21-67): Baseball 1B. Won three MVP awards, consecutively 1932–33, 1938. Fourth alltime highest slugging average (.609), with 534 career HR; hit 30+ HR 12 consecutive seasons, 100+ RBI 13 consecutive seasons. Won Triple Crown in 1933. Led league in HR four times, batting average two times. Career span 1925–45 with Philadelphia, Boston.

**A.J. Foyt** (b. 1-16-35): Auto racer. Alltime leader in Indy Car victories (67). Won Indy 500 four times (1961, 1964, 1967, 1977), Daytona 500 one time (1972), 24 Hours of Daytona two times (1983, 1985) and 24 Hours of LeMans one time (1967). USAC champion seven times, more than any other driver (consecutively 1960–61, 1963–64, 1967, 1975, 1979).

**William H.G. France** (b. 9-26-09, d. 6-7-92): Auto racing executive. Founder of NASCAR and president from 1948 to 1972, succeeded by his son Bill Jr. Builder of Daytona and Talladega speedways.

**Dawn Fraser** (b. 9-4-37): Australian swimmer. First swimmer to win gold medal in same event at three consecutive Olympics (100-meter freestyle in 1956, 1960, 1964). First woman to break the one-minute barrier at 100 meters (59.9 in 1962).

**Joe Frazier** (b. 1-12-44): Boxer. "Smokin' Joe." Heavyweight champion (1970–73). Best known for his three epic bouts with Muhammad Ali. Career record 32-4-1 with 27 KOs from 1965 to 1976. Also heavyweight gold medalist at 1964 Olympics.

**Walt Frazier** (b. 3-29-45): Basketball G. "Clyde." Point guard on championship Knick teams of 1970 and '73. First team All-Star in 1970, '72, '74 and '75. First team All Defense every year from 1969–1975. Averaged 18.9 points per game in 13-season NBA career. Elected to Hall of Fame in 1986.

**Frankie Frisch** (b. 9-9-1898, d. 3-12-73): Baseball IF. "The Fordham Flash." Led NL in hits in 1923 (223). Hit over .300 13 seasons. Scored 100+ runs seven times. Drove in 100+ runs three times. Career .316 batting average. Career span 1919–26 with New York Giants and 1927–37 with St. Louis Cardinals' "Gashouse Gang." NL MVP in 1931. Elected to Hall of Fame in 1947.

**Dan Gable** (b. 10-25-48): Wrestler. Gold medalist in 149–pound division at 1972 Olympics. Also NCAA champion two times (in 1968 at 130 pounds, in 1969 at 137 pounds). Coached Iowa to NCAA championship 15 times (consecutively 1978–86, 1991–93 and 1995–97).

**Clarence Gaines** (b. 5-21-23): College basketball coach. "Bighouse." Retired after 1992–93 season with 828 career wins in 46 seasons at Division II Winston-Salem State since 1947.

**John Galbreath** (b. 8-10-1897, d. 7-20-88): Horse racing owner. Owner of Darby Dan Farms from 1935 until his death and of baseball's Pittsburgh Pirates from 1946 to 1985. Only man to breed and own winners of both the Kentucky Derby (Chateaugay in 1963 and Proud Clarion in 1967) and the Epsom Derby (Roberto in 1972).

**Gallant Fox** (b. 3-23-27, d. 11-13-54): Thoroughbred race horse. Triple Crown winner in 1930 with jockey Earle Sande aboard. Trained by James Fitzsimmons. The only Triple Crown winner to sire another Triple Crown winner (Omaha in 1935).

**Don Garlits** (b. 1-14-32): Auto racer. "Big Daddy." Has won 35 National Hot Rod Association Top Fuel events. Won three NHRA Top Fuel points titles (1975, 1985–86). First Top Fuel driver to surpass 190 mph (1963), 200 mph (1964), 240 mph (1973), 250 mph (1975) and 270 mph (1986). Credited with developing rear-engine dragster.

**Haile Gebrselassie** (b. 4-18-73): Track and field. Ethiopian distance runner reclaimed the world record in the 10,000 meters on 6-1-98 in Hengelo, Neth., clocking 26:22.75, and in the 5,000, running 12:39.36 in Helsinki on 6-13-98. Won gold medal in 10,000 meters in 1996 Games at Atlanta.

**Lou Gehrig** (b. 6-19-03, d. 6-2-41): Baseball 1B. "The Iron Horse." Second alltime in consecutive games played (2,130), leader in grand slam HR (23), third in RBI (1,995) and slugging average (.632). MVP in 1927, 1936; won Triple Crown in 1934. .340 career average; 493 career HR. 100+ RBI 13 consecutive seasons. Led league in RBI five times and HR three times. Played on seven World Series winners with New York Yankees. Died of disease since named for him. Career span 1923–39.

**Bernie Geoffrion** (b. 2-16-31): Hockey RW. "Boom Boom" for his powerful slapshot. Won Hart Memorial Trophy for 1960–61. Scored 393 goals and 429 assists in 16 seasons (1950–51 through 1967–68), the first 14 with the Montreal Canadiens, the final two with the New York Rangers. Elected to Hall of Fame 1972.

**Eddie Giacomin** (b. 6-6-39): Hockey goalie. "Fast Eddie" led NHL goalies in games won for three straight seasons. Shared Vezina Trophy for 1970–71. Career GAA of 2.82. Career span 1965–75 with the New York Rangers and 1975–78 with Detroit Red Wings.

**Althea Gibson** (b. 8-25-27): Tennis player. Won two consecutive Wimbledon and U.S. singles titles (1957–58), the first black player to win these tournaments. Also won one French Open singles title (1956).

**Bob Gibson** (b. 11-9-35): Baseball RHP. 1968 Cy Young and MVP award winner with modern National League–best ERA (1.12) and second in shutouts (13). Also 1970 Cy Young award winner. Record holder for most strikeouts in a World Series game (17); Series MVP in 1964, 1967. Won 20+ games five times. 251 career wins; 3,117 strikeouts. Pitched no-hitter in 1971. Career span 1959–75 with St. Louis.

**Josh Gibson** (b. 12-21-11, d. 1-20-47): Baseball C. "The Black Babe Ruth." Couldn't play in major leagues because of racial barrier. Credited with 950 HR (75 in 1931, 69 in 1934) and .350 batting average. Had .400+ average two times. Career span 1930–46 with Homestead Grays, Pittsburgh Crawfords.

**Kirk Gibson** (b. 5-28-57): Baseball OF. Played on two World Series champions (Detroit in 1984 and Los Angeles in 1988). Hit dramatic pinch-hit HR in ninth inning to win Game 1 of 1988 series. MVP in 1988. Career span 1979–94 with Detroit, LA, KC, Pitt. Also starred in baseball and football at Michigan State.

**Frank Gifford** (b. 8-16-30): Football RB. NFL Player of Year in 1956 when he rushed for 819 yards and caught 51 passes. Played in seven Pro Bowls. Retired for one season after ferocious hit by Chuck Bednarik. Career span 1952–60 and 1962–64, all with New York Giants. Elected to Hall of Fame in 1977.

**Rod Gilbert** (b. 7-1-41): Hockey RW. Played 16 seasons, all with the New York Rangers (1960–61 through 1977–78), and had 406 goals and 615 assists. Elected to Hall of Fame 1982.

**Sid Gillman** (b. 10-26-11): Football coach. Developed wide-open, pass-oriented style of offense, introduced techniques for situational player substitutions and the study of game films. Won AFL championship (1963) with Los Angeles/San Diego Chargers. Career span 1955–59 Los Angeles Rams; 1960 Los Angeles Chargers; 1961–69 San Diego; 1973–74 Houston. Lifetime record 124-101-7.

**Pancho Gonzales** (b. 5-9-28, d. 7-3-95): Tennis player. Won two consecutive U.S. singles titles (1948–49). In 1969, at age 41, beat Charlie Pasarell 22–24, 1–6, 16–14, 6–3, 11–9 in longest Wimbledon match ever (5:12).

**Jeff Gordon** (b. 8-4-71): Auto racer. Three-time NASCAR Winston Cup champion (1995, '97, '98). Youngest Winston Cup Series champion in the modern era, having won his first title at age 24. Won at least 10 times in three straight seasons (1996–98), and won 13 times in 1998, both modern records.

**Shane Gould** (b. 11-23-56): Australian swimmer. Won three gold medals, one silver and one bronze at 1972 Olympics. Set 11 world records over 23-month period beginning in 1971. Held world record in five freestyle distances ranging from 100 meters to 1,500 meters in late 1971 and 1972. Retired at age 16.

**Steffi Graf** (b. 6-14-69): German tennis player. Achieved the Grand Slam in 1988. Won four Australian Open singles titles (1988–90, '94), seven Wimbledon

titles (1988–89, 1991–93, '95–96), six French Open titles (1987, '88, '93, '95, '96 and '99) and five U.S. Open titles (1988–89, '93 and '95–96). Held the No. 1 ranking a record 186 weeks; Aug. 17, 1987 through March 10, 1991. Gold medalist at 1988 Olympics. Second in alltime Grand Slam singles titles (22).

**Otto Graham** (b. 12-6-21): Football QB. Led Cleveland to 10 championship games in his 10-year career. Played on four consecutive AAFC champions (1946–49) and three NFL champions (1950, consecutively 1954–55). Combined league totals: 23,584 yards passing, 174 touchdown passes. Player of the Year two times (1953, 1955). Led league in passing six times. Career span 1946–55.

**Red Grange** (b. 6-13-03, d. 1-28-91): Football HB. "The Galloping Ghost." All-America three consecutive seasons with Illinois (1923–25), scoring 31 touchdowns in 20-game collegiate career. Signed by George Halas of Chicago in 1925, attracted sellout crowds across the country. Established the first AFL with manager C.C. Pyle in 1926, but league folded after one year. Career span 1925–34 with Chicago, New York.

**Rocky Graziano** (b. 6-7-22, d. 5-22-90): Boxer. Middleweight champion from 1947 to 1948. Career record 67–13. Endured three brutal title fights against Tony Zale, with Zale winning by KO in 1946 and 1948, and Graziano winning by KO in 1947.

**Hank Greenberg** (b. 1-1-11, d. 9-4-86): Baseball 1B. 331 career HR (58 in 1938). MVP in 1935, 1940. League leader in HR and RBI four times each. Fifth alltime highest slugging average (.605). 100+ RBI seven times. Career span 1933-41, 1945-47 with Detroit, Pittsburgh.

**Joe Greene** (b. 9-24-46): Football DT. "Mean Joe." Anchored Pittsburgh's famed "Steel Curtain" defense. Selected for Pro Bowl 10 times. Played on four Super Bowl champions (consecutively 1974–75, 1978–79). Career span 1969 to 1981.

**Maurice Greene** (b. 7-23-74): Track and field. Set world record for 100 meters (9.79) on 6-16-99 in Athens. Won Olympic gold medals in Sydney in the 100 meters and the 4x100 relay.

**Forrest Gregg** (b. 10-18-33): Football OT/G. Played in then-record 188 straight games from 1956 through 1971. Named all-NFL eight straight years starting in 1960. Career span 1956–71, most of it with Green Bay Packers. Played on winning Packer team in first two Super Bowls. Inducted into Hall of Fame in 1977.

**Wayne Gretzky** (b. 1-26-61): Hockey C. "The Great One." Most dominant player in history. Alltime scoring leader in points (2,795), assists (1,910), and goals (885). Alltime single-season scoring leader in points (215 in 1986), goals (92 in 1982) and assists (163 in 1986). Has won MVP award nine times, more than any other player (consecutively 1980-87, 1989). Led league in assists 16 times, scoring 11 times, goals five times. Scored 200+ points four times, 100+ points 10 other times; 70+ goals four consecutive seasons, 50+ goals five other times; 100+ assists 11 consecutive seasons. Playoff MVP two times (1985, 1988). Played on four Stanley Cup champions with Edmonton from 1978 to 1988. Traded to Los Angeles on Aug. 9, 1988, then to St. Louis Feb. 1996. Moved as a free agent to NY Rangers before 1996–97 season. Wore uniform No. 99, which entire NHL retired when Gretzky ended career after '99 season.

**Bob Griese** (b. 2-3-45): Football QB. Career span 1967–80 with Miami Dolphins. Played in three straight

Super Bowls, 1971–73. Quarterback of 1972 Dolphin team that went 17–0. Won Super Bowl VII and VIII. In 14 seasons completed 1,926 passes for 25,092 yards and 192 TDs. Elected to Hall of Fame in 1990.

**Florence Griffith Joyner** (b. 12-21-59, d. 9-21-98): Track and field. Won three gold medals (100 meters, 200 meters, 4x100-meter relay) at 1988 Olympics; Set world record in 100 (10.49) in 1988 and in 200 (21.34) at the 1988 Olympics. Sullivan Award winner in 1988.

**Ken Griffey Jr.** (b. 11-21-69): Baseball OF. Hit 56 home runs in back-to-back seasons (1997–98). Hit career home run No. 450 on 8-9-01 to become, at 31 years 261 days, the youngest to reach the milestone. Won AL MVP award in 1997, when he hit .304 with 56 HRs and 147 RBI. Father Ken Sr. starred with Cincinnati Reds in 1970s.

**Archie Griffin** (b. 8-21-54): College football RB. Only player to win the Heisman Trophy two times (consecutively 1974-75), with Ohio State. Eighth alltime NCAA career yards rushing (5,177). Professional career span 1976-83 with Cincinnati; totaled 2,808 yards rushing and 192 receptions.

**Lefty Grove** (b. 3-6-00, d. 5-22-75): Baseball LHP. 300 career wins and fourth alltime highest winning percentage (.680). League leader in ERA nine times, strikeouts seven consecutive seasons. Won 20+ games eight times. 1931 MVP. Career span 1925-41 with Philadelphia, Boston.

**Tony Gwynn** (b. 5-9-60): Baseball OF. Won eight batting titles (1984, consecutively 1987–89, 1994–97). League leader in hits six times, with .300+ average 16 times, 200+ hits five times. Career span since 1982 with San Diego. Reached 3,000 career hits in 1999.

**Walter Hagen** (b. 12-21-1892, d. 10-5-69): Golfer. Third alltime leader in major championships (11). Won PGA Championship five times (1921, consecutively 1924–27), British Open four times (1922, 1924, consecutively 1928–29) and U.S. Open two times (1914, 1919). Won 40 career tournaments.

**Marvin Hagler** (b. 5-23-54): Boxer. "Marvelous." Middleweight champion (1980–87). Career record 62-3-2 with 52 KOs from 1973 to 1987. Defended title 13 times.

**George Halas** (b. 2-2-1895, d. 10-31-83): Football owner and coach. "Papa Bear." Alltime leader in seasons coaching (40) and second in wins (324). Career record 324-151-31 intermittently from 1920 to 1967. Remained as owner until his death. Chicago won a record seven NFL championships during his tenure.

**Glenn Hall** (b. 10-3-31): Hockey goalie. "Mr. Goalie" was an All-Star goalie in 11 of his 18 seasons. Set record for consecutive games by a goaltender, with 502, and ended career with goals against average of 2.51. Won or shared Vezina Trophy three times. Career span 1952–53 through 1970–71.

**Charles Haley** (b. 1-6-64): Football DE. Only player in NFL history to be a member of five Super Bowl champions, two with San Francisco (1989, '90) and three with Dallas (1993, '94 and '96). Career span 1986–99. Recorded 100.5 career sacks.

**Mia Hamm** (b. 3-17-72): Soccer player. Alltime leading scorer in U.S. women's national team history. Member of Women's World Cup champion team in 1991, '99, and third-place team in '95. Member of Olympic champion team in 1996. Debuted with national team against China on 8-3-87 as its youngest player ever, at age 15.

**Arthur B. (Bull) Hancock** (b. 1-24-10, d. 9-14-72): Horse racing owner. Owner of Claiborne Farm and arguably the greatest breeder in history. For 15 straight years, from 1955 to 1969, a Claiborne stallion led the sire list. Foaled at Claiborne Farm were four Horses of the Year (Kelso, Round Table, Bold Ruler and Nashua).

**Tom Harmon** (b. 9-28-19, d. 3-17-90): Football RB. Won Heisman Trophy in 1940 with Michigan. Triple-threat back led nation in scoring and named All-America two consecutive seasons. Awarded Silver Star and Purple Heart in World War II. Played in NFL with Los Angeles (1946–47).

**Franco Harris** (b. 3-7-50): Football RB. Rushed for 12,120 yards and 91 touchdowns. Gained 1,000+ yards in eight seasons, 100+ yards in 47 games. Scored 100 career touchdowns. Selected for Pro Bowl nine times. Rookie of the Year in 1972. Played on four Super Bowl champions (consecutively 1974–75, 1978–79) with Pittsburgh. Super Bowl MVP in 1974. Holds Super Bowl record for career rushing yards (354). Made the "Immaculate Reception" to win 1972 playoff game against Oakland. Career span 1972–83 with Pittsburgh. Elected to the Hall of Fame in 1990.

**Leon Hart** (b. 11-2-28): Football DE. Won Heisman Trophy in 1949, the last lineman to win the award. Played on three national champions with Notre Dame (consecutively 1946–47, 1949) and the Irish went undefeated during his four years (36-0-2). Also played on three NFL champions with Detroit. Career span 1950-57.

**Bill Hartack** (b. 12-9-32): Horse racing jockey. Rode five Kentucky Derby winners (1957, 1960, 1962, 1964, 1969), three Preakness Stakes winners (1956, 1964, 1969) and one Belmont Stakes winner (1960).

**Doug Harvey** (b. 12-19-24, d. 12-26-90): Hockey D. Defensive Player of the Year seven times (consecutively 1954–57, 1959–61). Led league in assists in 1954. All-Star 10 times. Played on six Stanley Cup champions with Montreal from 1947 to 1968.

**Dominik Hasek** (b. 1-29-65): Czech hockey G. Two-time NHL MVP (1997, 98) with Buffalo; six-time Vezina Trophy winner (1994–95, 1997–99, '01) as top goalie in league. Led NHL with a 1.95 goals-against average in 1993–94, the first sub-2.00 GAA since Bernie Parent in 1974. Topped that with 1.87 GAA in 1998–99. Guided Czech Republic to Olympic gold medal in 1998 at Nagano. Career span 1990–92 with Chicago, 1992–01 with Buffalo. Traded to Detroit in July 2001.

**Billy Haughton** (b. 11-2-23, d. 7-15-86): Harness racing driver. Won the Pacing Triple Crown driving Rum Customer in 1968. Won The Hambletonian four times (1974, consecutively 1976-77, 1980).

**John Havlicek** (b. 4-8-40): Basketball F/G. Member of Ohio State team that won 1960 NCAA title. "Hondo" averaged 20.8 points per game over 16-season NBA career, all with Boston. First team NBA All-Star in 1971, '72, '73 and '74. Member of eight Celtic teams that won NBA title. Playoff MVP 1974. Elected to Hall of Fame in 1983.

**Elvin Hayes** (b. 11-17-45): Basketball C. 1968 *Sporting News* College Player of Year as Houston senior. Averaged 21.0 points per game over 16-season NBA career. Led NBA in scoring (28.4) in 1969 and in rebounding in 1970 (16.9 per game) and '74 (18.1). First team All-NBA in 1975, '77 and '79. Elected to Hall of Fame in 1989.

**Woody Hayes** (b. 2-14-13, d. 3-12-87): College football coach. Won national championship three times

(1954, 1957, 1968) and Rose Bowl four times. Career record 238-72-10, including four undefeated seasons, with Ohio State from 1951 to 1978. Forced to resign after striking an opposing player during 1978 Gator Bowl.

**Marques Haynes** (b. 10-3-26): Basketball G. Known as "The World's Greatest Dribbler." Beginning in 1946 barnstormed more than four million miles throughout 97 countries for the Harlem Globetrotters, Harlem Magicians, Meadowlark Lemon's Bucketeers, Harlem Wizards.

**Thomas Hearns** (b. 10-18-58): Boxer. "Hit Man." Champion in four weight classes: welterweight, super welterweight, middleweight and light heavyweight. Career record: 57–4–1 with 45 KOs.

**Eric Heiden** (b. 6-14-58): Speed skater. Won five gold medals at 1980 Olympics. World champion three consecutive years (1977–79). Won Sullivan Award in 1980.

**Carol Heiss** (b. 1-20-40): Figure skater. Gold medalist at 1960 Olympics, silver medalist at 1956 Olympics. World champion five consecutive years (1956–60) and U.S. champion four consecutive years (1957–60). Married 1956 gold medalist Hayes Jenkins.

**Rickey Henderson** (b. 12-25-57): Baseball OF. Career leader in stolen bases, walks and runs; modern single-season stolen base record holder (130 in 1982). Led league in steals 11 times. 1990 MVP. Alltime leader in lead-off HRs. Became 25th member of 3,000-hit club on Oct. 7, 2001. Career span since 1979 with Oakland, NY Yankees, Toronto, Anaheim, San Diego, NY Mets, and Seattle.

**Sonja Henie** (b. 4-8-12, d. 10-12-69): Norwegian figure skater. Gold medalist at three consecutive Olympics (1928, 1932, 1936). World champion 10 consecutive years (1927–36).

**Orel Hershiser** (b. 9-16-58): Baseball RHP. Alltime leader most consecutive scoreless innings pitched (59 in 1988). Cy Young Award winner in 1988 and World Series MVP. Career span 1983–94, Los Angeles; 1995–97, Cleveland; 1998, San Francisco; 1999, NY Mets.

**Foster Hewitt** (b. 11-21-02, d. 4-22-85): Hockey sportscaster. In 1923, aired one of hockey's first radio broadcasts. Became the voice of hockey in Canada on radio and later television. Famous for the phrase, "He shoots ... he scores!"

**Tommy Hitchcock** (b. 2-11-00, d. 4-19-44): Polo. 10-goal rating 18 times in his 19-year career from 1922 to 1940. Killed in plane crash in World War II.

**Lew Hoad** (b. 11-23-34): Australian tennis player. Won two consecutive Wimbledon singles titles (1956–57). Also won French title and Australian title in 1956, but failed to achieve the Grand Slam when defeated at Forest Hills by countryman Ken Rosewall.

**Ben Hogan** (b. 8-13-12, d. 7-25-97): Golfer. Third alltime in career wins (63). Won U.S. Open four times (1948, consecutively 1950–51, 1953), the Masters (1951, 1953) and PGA Championship (1946, 1948) two times each and British Open once (1953). PGA Player of the Year four times (1948, consecutively 1950-51, 1953).

**Marshall Holman** (b. 9-29-54): Bowler. Won 21 PBA titles between 1975 and 1988. Had leading average in 1987 (213.54) and was named PBA Bowler of the Year.

**Nat Holman** (b. 10-18-1896, d. 2-12-95): College basketball coach. Only coach in history to win NCAA and NIT championships in same season, in 1950 with CCNY; 423 career wins, a .689 winning percentage.

**Larry Holmes** (b. 11-3-49): Boxer. Heavyweight champion (1978–85). Career record 67–6 with 43 KOs from 1973 to 1999. Defended title 21 times.

**Lou Holtz** (b. 1-6-37): Football coach. Coached Notre Dame to national championship in 1988 with 12–0 record and a 34–21 win over West Virginia in Fiesta Bowl. 11-8-2 career record in bowl games. Career span 1969–71 at William & Mary (13–20); 1972–75 at N.C. State (33-12-3); 1977–83 at Arkansas (60-21-2); 1984–85 at Minnesota (10–12); 1986–96 at Notre Dame (100-30-2); and 1999– South Carolina (8–15).

**Evander Holyfield** (b. 10-19-62): Boxer. Only man to win the heavyweight title four times. Won heavyweight crown Oct. 25, 1990 when he beat James (Buster) Douglas in Las Vegas. Fought three epic bouts with Riddick Bowe and two memorable fights with Mike Tyson (Tyson was disqualified in the rematch for biting Holyfield's ears.) Career record: 37–4–1, 25 KOs.

**Red Holzman** (b. 8-10-20; d. 11-13-98): Basketball coach. Led New York Knicks to NBA title in 1970 and '73. NBA Coach of the Year in 1970. Member of Rochester team that won NBA title in both 1946 (in NBL) and '51. After two-year coaching stints in Milwaukee and St. Louis, coached New York Knicks from 1968–82. Elected to Hall of Fame in 1985.

**Harry Hopman** (b. 8-12-06, d. 12-27-85): Australian tennis coach. As nonplaying captain, led Australia to 15 Davis Cup titles between 1950 and 1969. Mentor to Lew Hoad, Ken Rosewall, Rod Laver and John Newcombe.

**Willie Hoppe** (b. 10-11-1887, d. 2-1-59): Billiards. Won 51 world championship matches from 1904 to 1952.

**Rogers Hornsby** (b. 4-27-1896, d. 1-5-63): Baseball 2B. Second alltime in career batting average (.358), won seven batting titles, including with .424 average in 1924. 200+ hits seven times; .400+ average three times and .300+ average 12 other times. Led league in slugging average nine times. Triple Crown winner in 1922, 1925; MVP award winner in 1925, 1929. Career span 1915–37 with St. Louis (NL), New York (NL), Boston, Chicago (NL).

**Paul Hornung** (b. 12-23-35): Football RB–K. Led league in scoring three consecutive seasons, including a record 176 points in 1960 (15 touchdowns, 15 field goals, 41 extra points). Player of the Year in 1961. Career span 1957–66 with Green Bay. Suspended for 1963 season by Pete Rozelle for gambling. Also won Heisman Trophy in 1956 with Notre Dame.

**Gordie Howe** (b. 3-31-28): Hockey RW. Second alltime in goals (801), first in years played (26) and games (1,767). Finished career with 1,850 points and 1,049 assists. Won MVP award six times (consecutively 1952–53, 1957–58, 1960, 1963). Led league in scoring six times, goals five times and assists three times. Scored 40+ goals five times, 30+ goals 13 other times, 100+ points three times. All-Star 12 times. Played on four Stanley Cup champions with Detroit from 1946 to 1971. Teamed with sons Mark and Marty in the WHA with Houston and New England from 1973 to 1979, in NHL with Hartford in 1980.

**Carl Hubbell** (b. 6-22-03, d. 11-21-88): Baseball LHP. 253 career wins. MVP in 1933, 1936. League leader in wins and ERA three times each. Won 24 consecutive games from 1936 to 1937. Struck out Ruth, Gehrig, Foxx, Simmons and Cronin consecutively in

1934 All-Star game. Pitched no-hitter in 1929. Career span 1928–43 with New York Giants.

**Sam Huff** (b. 10-4-34): Football LB. Made 30 interceptions. Career span 1956–69 with New York Giants and Washington Redskins. Elected to Hall of Fame in 1982.

**Bobby Hull** (b. 1-3-39): Hockey LW. "The Golden Jet." Led league in goals seven times and points three times. 610 career goals. Scored five times, 30+ goals eight other times. Won MVP award two consecutive seasons (1965–66). Son Brett won MVP award in 1991, the only father and son to be so honored. All-Star 10 times. Career span 1957–72 with Chicago, 1973–80 with Winnipeg of WHA.

**Brett Hull** (b. 8-9-64): Hockey RW. Son of Bobby Hull. Won Hart Memorial Trophy for 1990–91 season. Scored Stanley Cup–winning goal for Dallas in third overtime of Game 6 against Buffalo in 1999. Career span 1986–87 with Calgary Flames; 1987–98 with St. Louis Blues; 1998–01 with Dallas Stars.

**Jim (Catfish) Hunter** (b. 4-8-46, d. 9-9-99): Baseball RHP. 1974 Cy Young award winner. Won 20+ games five consecutive seasons. Led league in wins and winning percentage two times each, ERA one time. 250+ innings pitched eight times. Pitched perfect game in 1968. Member of five World Series champions for Oakland and New York Yankees. Career span 1965–79.

**Don Hutson** (b. 1-31-13, d. 6-26-97): Football WR. Fourth alltime in touchdown receptions (99). Led league in pass receptions eight times, receiving yards seven times and scoring five consecutive seasons. Caught at least one pass in 95 consecutive games. Player of the Year two consecutive seasons (1941–42). Career span 1935–45 with Green Bay.

**Hank Iba** (b. 8-6-04; d. 1-15-93): College basketball coach. Coached Oklahoma A&M (which became Oklahoma State) from 1934 to 1970. Team won NCAA titles in 1945 and '46. 767 career wins is fourth alltime behind Dean Smith, Adolph Rupp and Jim Phelan.

**Jackie Ickx** (b. 1-1-45): Belgian auto racer. Won the 24 Hours of LeMans a record six times (1969, consecutively 1975–77, 1981–82) before retiring in 1985.

**Punch Imlach** (b. 3-15-18, d. 12-1-87): Hockey coach. 467 wins. With Toronto from 1958 to 1969. Won four Stanley Cup championships (consecutively 1962–64, 1967).

**Miguel Induráin** (b. 7-16-64): Cyclist. Won an unprecedented five consecutive Tours de France (1991–95).

**Juli Inkster** (b.6-24-60): Golfer. Became only the second woman ever to win all four of the LPGA's modern majors when she won the LPGA Championship on 6-27-99; finished eagle-birdie-birdie for a 6-under 65 and a four-stroke victory. Inducted to LPGA Hall of Fame in 1999.

**Bo Jackson** (b. 11-30-62): Baseball OF and Football RB. Only person in history to be named to baseball All-Star game and football Pro Bowl game. 1985 Heisman Trophy winner at Auburn. First pick in 1986 NFL draft by Tampa Bay, but opted to play baseball at Kansas City. 1989 All-Star game MVP. Signed with football's LA Raiders in 1988. Retired 1994 following hip replacement surgery.

**Joe Jackson** (b. 7-16-1889, d. 12-5-51): Baseball OF. "Shoeless Joe." Third alltime highest career batting average (.356), with .300+ average 11 times. One of

the "Eight Men Out" banned from baseball for throwing 1919 World Series. Career span 1908–20 with Cleveland, Chicago.

**Phil Jackson** (b. 9-17-45): Basketball F-Coach. Coached the Lakers to their second straight NBA Championship in 2001, his eighth as a coach. Won six titles as coach of the Chicago Bulls ('91, '92, '93, '96, '97, '98). Best winning percentage in NBA history (668–234, .741). Spent 13 years as a scrappy forward in the NBA, winning an NBA title with the Knicks in 1973.

**Reggie Jackson** (b. 5-18-46): Baseball OF. "Mr. October." Alltime leader in World Series slugging percentage (.755). 1977 Series MVP, hit three HR in final game on three consecutive pitches. 563 career HR total is eighth alltime. Led league in HR four times. 1973 MVP. Alltime strikeout leader (2,597). In a 12-year period played on 10 first-place teams, five World Series winners. Career span 1967–87 with Oakland, Baltimore, New York and California. Inducted to baseball Hall of Fame in 1993.

**Bruce Jenner** (b. 10-28-49): Track and Field. Set then-world decathlon record (8,634) in winning gold medal at 1976 Olympics. Sullivan Award winner in 1976.

**John Henry** (b. 1975): Thoroughbred race horse. Sold as yearling for $1,100, the gelding was Horse of the Year in 1981 and in 1984 and retired with then-record $6,597,947 in winnings.

**Ben Johnson** (b. 12-30-61): Track and field. Canadian sprinter set world record in 100 meters (9.83 in 1987). Won event at 1988 Olympics in 9.79, but gold medal revoked for failing drug test. Both world records revoked for steroid usage. Suspended for life after testing positive for elevated testosterone level at an indoor meet in Montreal on 1-17-93.

**Earvin (Magic) Johnson** (b. 8-14-59): Basketball G. Retired Nov. 7, 1991 after being diagnosed with HIV, the virus that causes AIDS. Returned to Lakers Feb '96 at age 36. Finished career second alltime in assists (10,141); alltime playoff leader in assists (2,346) and steals (358). MVP award three times (1987, consecutively 1989–90) and playoff MVP in 1980, '82 and '87. Played on five championship teams with Los Angeles since 1979. All-Star eight consecutive seasons. League leader in assists four times, steals two times, free throw percentage once. Also won NCAA championship and named tournament MVP in 1979 with Michigan State.

**Jack Johnson** (b. 3-31-1878, d. 6-10-46): Boxer. First black heavyweight champion (1908-15). Career record 78-8-12 with 45 KOs from 1897 to 1928.

**Jimmy Johnson** (b. 7-16-43): Football coach. Led the Cowboys from 1–15 in 1989, his first season in Dallas, to a 52–17 win over the Buffalo Bills in the Super Bowl XXVII just four seasons later. Also coached Super Bowl XXVIII champion Cowboys. Head coach at Oklahoma State from 1979–83 and Univ. of Miami 1984–88. Johnson's Hurricanes won national championship in 1987. Succeeded Don Shula as Miami Dolphins coach, Jan. '96.

**Michael Johnson** (b. 9-13-67): Track and field. First man to win gold medals in both the 200 and 400 at the Olympics (1996). Broke 17-year-old 200-meter world record (from 19.72 to 19.66) in '96 U.S. Olympic trials, then further lowered mark to 19.32 at Atlanta. Repeated in the 400 meters at the 2000 Sydney Games. Anchored U.S. 4x400 team at 1993 World Championship to world record of 2:54.29 with fastest ever relay carry of 42.97.

**Walter Johnson** (b. 11-6-1887, d. 12-10-46): Baseball RHP. "Big Train." Alltime leader in shutouts (110), second in wins (416), fourth in losses (279) and third in innings pitched (5,914). His 2.17 career ERA and 3,509 career strikeouts are eighth best alltime.. MVP in 1913, 1924. Won 20+ games 12 times. League leader in strikeouts 12 times, ERA five times, wins six times. Pitched no-hitter in 1920. Career span 1907–27 with Washington.

**Ben A. Jones** (b. 12-31-1882, d. 6-13-61): Horse racing trainer. Trained Triple Crown winner (Whirlaway in 1941). Trained six Kentucky Derby winners, more than any other trainer (1938, 1941, 1944, consecutively 1948–49, 1952), two Preakness Stakes winners (1941, 1944) and one Belmont Stakes winner (1941).

**Bobby Jones** (b. 3-17-02, d. 12-18-71): Golfer. Achieved golf's only recognized Grand Slam in 1930. Second alltime in major championships (13). Won U.S. Amateur five times, more than any golfer (consecutively 1924–25, 1927–28, 1930), U.S. Open four times (1923, 1926, consecutively 1929–30), British Open three times (consecutively 1926–27, 1930) and British Amateur (1930). Also designed Augusta National course, site of the Masters, and founded the tournament. Winner of Sullivan Award in 1930.

**K.C. Jones** (b. 5-25-32): Basketball G-coach. Member of eight straight NBA-championship Boston Celtic teams in his nine season career from 1958–59 through 1966–67. Averaged 7.4 points and 4.3 assists per game. Coached Celtics from 1983–84 through 1987–88, with 308–102 regular season record and 65–37 playoff record with NBA titles in 1984 and '86.

**Robert Trent Jones** (b. 6-20-06, d. 6-14-00): English-born golf course architect designed or remodeled over 500 courses, including Baltusrol, Hazeltine, Oak Hill and Winged Foot. In the mid-60s five straight U.S. Opens were played on courses designed or remodeled by Jones.

**Roy Jones Jr.** (b.1-16-69): Boxer. Won silver medal at the 1988 Olympics in Seoul despite dominating his South Korean opponent in the final. Decision commonly called worst in Olympic boxing history. Awarded Val Barker Trophy as outstanding boxer of '88 Games. Won titles at middleweight, super middleweight and light heavyweight as a professional. Career record: 45–1, 36 KOs.

**Sam Jones** (b. 6-24-33): Basketball G. Played 12 seasons with Boston Celtics (1958–69), who won NBA title every year from 1959–66, plus 1968 and '69. Averaged 17.7 points per game. Elected to Hall of Fame in 1983.

**Michael Jordan** (b. 2-17-63): Basketball G. "Air." Arguably greatest player of all time. Led Bulls to six NBA titles (consecutively, 1991–93; 1996–98). Retired after 1997–98 season with alltime highest regular season scoring average (31.5) and most points scored in a playoff game (63 in 1986). Guided Bulls to an NBA-record 72 wins in 1995–96. Led league in scoring a record 10 seasons; led in steals three times. League MVP in 1988, 1991–92, '96 and '98; Finals MVP in 1991–93 and 1996–98; Rookie of the Year in 1985. All-Star team six consecutive seasons, All-Defensive team five consecutive seasons. Career span 1984–93, 1995–98 and 1996–98; with Chicago. Announced retirement on 10-6-93; returned in March 1995. College Player of the Year in 1984. Played on NCAA title team with North Carolina in 1982. Member of gold medal-winning 1984 and '92 Olympic teams. Ended his second retirement on

9-25-01, when, at age 38, he rejoined the NBA to play for the Washington Wizards.

**Jackie Joyner-Kersee** (b. 3-3-62): Track and field. Gold medalist in heptathlon and long jump at 1988 Olympics and in the former at the 1992 Olympics. Set heptathlon world record (7,291 points) at 1988 Olympics. Also won silver medal in heptathlon at 1984 Games and bronze in long jump at 1992 and '96 Olympics. Sullivan Award winner in 1986.

**Alberto Juantorena** (b. 3-12-51): Track and field. Cuban was gold medalist in 400 meters and 800 meters at 1976 Olympics.

**Wang Junxia** (b. 1963): Chinese distance runner. Broke four existing world records over six days in Sept. 1993. Broke 10,000 (29:31.78) on Sept 8; ran 1,500 in 3:51.92 in finishing second to countrywoman Qu Yunxia's world record of 3:50.46 on Sept 11; ran 3,000 record of 8:12.19 in heats on Sept 12 and lowered it to 8:06.11 on Sept 13. Won gold in 5,000 and silver in 10,000 at 1996 Olympics.

**Sonny Jurgensen** (b. 8-23-34): Football QB. In 18 seasons completed 2,433 of 4,262 pass attempts for 32,224 yards and 255 TDs. Led NFL in passing both 1967 and '69. Career span 1957–1974 with Philadelphia Eagles and Washington Redskins. Elected to Hall of Fame in 1983.

**Duke Kahanamoku** (b. 8-24-1890, d. 1-22-68): Swimmer. Won a total of five medals (3 gold and two silver) at three Olympics in 1912, 1920, 1924. Introduced the crawl stroke to America. Surfing pioneer and water polo player. Later sheriff of Honolulu.

**Al Kaline** (b. 12-19-34): Baseball OF. 3,007 career hits and 399 career HR. As a 20-year-old in 1955, became youngest player to win batting title, with .340 average. Had .300+ average nine times. Played in 18 All-Star games. Career span 1953–74 with Detroit.

**Anatoly Karpov** (b. 5-23-61): Soviet chess player. First world champion to receive title by default, in 1975, when Bobby Fischer chose not to defend his crown. Champion until 1985 when beaten by Garry Kasparov. Recognized by FIDE as champion in 1994.

**Garry Kasparov** (b. 4-13-63): Born Garik Weinstein. Chess player. World champion from 1985 to 1993 when stripped of title by FIDE. Won six-game series against IBM computer, Deep Blue, in 1996. Lost to improved version of Deep Blue in 1997.

**Kip Keino** (b. 1-17-40): Track and field. Kenyan was gold medalist in 1,500 meters at 1968 Olympics and in steeplechase at 1972 Olympics.

**Jim Kelly** (b. 2-14-60): Football QB. Led NFL in passing in 1990 (219 of 346 for 2,829 yards and 24 TDs). In 11 seasons completed 2,874 of 4,779 attempts for 35,467 yards and 237 TDs. Career span 1983–85 with Houston Gamblers (USFL), 1986–96 with Buffalo Bills. Led Bills to four straight Super Bowls, all losses.

**Kelso** (b. 1957, d. 1983): Thoroughbred race horse. Gelding was Horse of the Year five straight years (1960–64). Finished in the money in 53 of 63 races. Career earnings $1,977,896.

**Harmon Killebrew** (b. 6-29-36): Baseball 3B-1B. 573 career HR total is sixth most alltime. 100+ RBI nine times, 40+ HR eight times. League leader in HR six times and RBI four times. 1969 MVP. 100+ walks and strikeouts seven times each. Career span 1954-75 with Washington, Minnesota.

**Jean Claude Killy** (b. 8-30-43): French skier. Won three gold medals at 1968 Olympics. World Cup overall champion two consecutive years (1967-68).

**Ralph Kiner** (b. 10-27-22): Baseball OF. Third to Babe Ruth in alltime HR frequency (7.1 HR every 100 at bats). 369 career HR. Led league in HR seven consecutive seasons, with 50+ HR two times; 100+ RBI and runs scored in same season six times; 100+ walks six times. Career span 1946–55 with Pittsburgh, Chicago (NL), and Cleveland.

**Billie Jean King** (b. 11-22-43): Tennis player. Won a record 20 Wimbledon titles, including six singles titles (consecutively 1966–68, 1972–73, 1975). Won four U.S. singles titles (1967, consecutively 1971–72, 1974), and singles titles at Australian Open (1968) and French Open (1972). Won 27 Grand Slam doubles titles—total of 39 Grand Slam titles is third alltime. Helped found the women's pro tour in 1970, serving as president of the Women's Tennis Association two times. Helped form Team Tennis.

**Nile Kinnick** (b. 7-9-18, d. 6-2-43): College football RB. Won the Heisman Trophy in 1939 with Iowa. Premier runner, passer and punter was killed in plane crash during routine Navy training flight. Stadium in Iowa City named in his honor.

**Tom Kite** (b. 12-9-49): Golfer. Led PGA in scoring average in 1981 (69.80) and '82 (70.21). PGA Player of Year in 1989, when he won a then-record $1,395,278. Shook reputation for failing to win the big ones by winning 1992 U.S. Open at windy Pebble Beach.

**Franz Klammer** (b. 12-3-54): Austrian alpine skier. Greatest downhiller ever. Gold medalist in downhill at 1976 Olympics. Also won four World Cup downhill titles (1975–78).

**Bob Knight** (b. 10-25-40): College basketball coach. Longtime Indiana coach who was fired in 2000 after a series of controversial disputes with the media, ex-players, students, and the university. Hired to lead Texas Tech in 2001. Won three NCAA championships with Indiana in 1976, 1981, 1987. Coached U.S. Olympic team to gold medal in 1984. 763 career wins and .725 career winning percentage. Career span since 1966 with Army, Indiana and Texas Tech.

**Olga Korbut** (b. 5-16-55): Soviet gymnast. First ever to complete backward somersault on balance beam. Won three gold medals at 1972 Olympics.

**Johann Olav Koss** (b.10-29-68): Speed Skater. Norwegian won three gold medals at 1994 Olympics in Lillehammer, with world records in the 1,500, 5,000 and 10,000 meters. Won 1,500 meter gold medal and 10,000 meter silver medal in 1992 Games at Albertville.

**Sandy Koufax** (b. 12-30-35): Baseball LHP. Cy Young Award winner three times (1963, consecutively 1965-66); and MVP in 1963; World Series MVP in 1963, 1965. Pitched one perfect game, four no-hitters. League leader in ERA five consecutive seasons, strikeouts four times. Won 25+ games three times. Career record 165–87, with 2.76 ERA. Career span 1955–66 with Brooklyn/Los Angeles.

**Jack Kramer** (b. 8-1-21): Tennis player. Won two consecutive U.S. singles titles (1946–47) and one Wimbledon title (1947). Also won six Grand Slam doubles titles. Served as executive director of Association of Tennis Professionals from 1972 to 1975.

**Ingrid Kristiansen** (b. 3-21-56): Track and field. Norwegian runner is only person—male or female—to hold world records in 5,000 meters (14:37.33 set in

1986), 10,000 meters (30:13.74 set in 1986) and marathon (2:21:06 set in 1985, a record that still stands). Also won Boston Marathon two times (1986, 1989) and New York City Marathon once (1989).

**Bob Kurland** (b. 12-23-24): College basketball player. 6' 10¼" center on Oklahoma A&M teams that won NCAA titles in 1945 and '46. Consensus All-America and NCAA tournament MVP in both 1945 and '46. Led nation in scoring in '46. His habit of swatting shots off rim led to creation of goaltending rule in 1945. Won gold medals in both 1948 and '52 Olympics. Turned down lucrative pro offers, playing instead for Phillips 66 Oilers AAU team.

**Michelle Kwan** (b. 7-7-80): Figure skater. Three-time U.S. champion (1996, '98, '99), two-time world champion (1996, '98); silver medalist in 1998 Olympics at Nagano.

**Rene Lacoste** (b. 7-2-05, d. 10-12-96): French tennis player. "The Crocodile." One of France's "Four Musketeers" of the 1920s. Won three French singles titles (1925, 1927, 1929), two consecutive U.S. titles (1926–27) and two Wimbledon titles (1925, 1928). Also designed casual shirt with embroidered crocodile that bears his name.

**Marion Ladewig** (b. 10-30-14): Bowler. Won All-Star Tournament eight times (consecutively 1949–52, 1954, 1956, 1959, 1963) and WPBA National Championship once (1960). Also voted Bowler of the Year nine times (consecutively 1950–54, 1957–59, 1963).

**Guy Lafleur** (b. 9-20-51): Hockey RW. Won MVP award two consecutive seasons (1977–78), playoff MVP in 1977. Scored 50+ goals and 100+ points six consecutive seasons. Led league in points scored three consecutive seasons, goals and assists one time each. 560 career goals, 793 assists. Played on five Stanley Cup champions with Montreal from 1971 to 1985.

**Curly Lambeau** (b. 4-9-1898; d. 6-1-65): Football QB and coach. Quarterback for Packers team in early 1920s. Record of 212-106-21 in his 29 seasons (1921–49) as Packer coach, winning three NFL titles in 1929–31.

**Jack Lambert** (b. 7-8-52): Football LB. Anchored Pittsburgh's famed "Steel Curtain" defense. Selected for Pro Bowl nine times. Played on four Super Bowl champions (consecutively 1974–75, 1978–79) with Pittsburgh from 1974 to 1984. Elected to Hall of Fame 1990.

**Jake LaMotta** (b. 7-10-21): Boxer. "The Bronx Bull." Subject of *Raging Bull*, a film by Martin Scorsese, starring Robert DeNiro. Won middleweight title by knocking out Marcel Cerdan in 10 on 6-16-49. Lost title to Ray Robinson, who KO'd him in 13 on 2-13-51. Career record: 83–19–4, 30 KOs.

**Kenesaw Mountain Landis** (b. 11-20-1866, d. 11-25-44): Baseball's first and most powerful commissioner from 1920 to 1944. By banning the eight "Black Sox" involved in the fixing of the 1919 World Series, he restored public confidence in the integrity of baseball.

**Tom Landry** (b. 9-11-24, d. 2-12-00): Football coach. Third alltime in wins (270). The first coach in Dallas history, from 1960 to 1988. Led team to 13 division titles, seven championship games and five Super Bowls. Won two Super Bowl championships (1971, 1977). Career record 270-178-6.

**Dick (Night Train) Lane** (b. 4-16-28): Football DB. Third alltime in interceptions (68) and second in interception yardage (1,207). Set record with 14

interceptions as a rookie in 1952. Career span 1952–65 with Los Angeles, Chicago Cardinals, Detroit.

**Joe Lapchick** (b. 4-12-00, d. 8-10-70): Basketball C–coach. One of the first big men in basketball, member of New York's Original Celtics. Coached St. John's (1936–47, 1956–65) winning four NIT Tournaments. Coached New York Knicks, 1947–56.

**Steve Largent** (b. 9-28-54): Football WR. Retired as alltime leader in pass receptions (819), and TD receptions (100). 177 consecutive games with reception, 10 seasons with 50+ receptions and eight seasons with 1,000+ yards receiving. Career span 1976–89 with Seattle. Oklahoma congressman since 1994.

**Don Larsen** (b. 8-7-29): Baseball RHP. Pitched only perfect game in World Series history, for the NY Yankees on Oct. 8, 1956, beating the Dodgers 2–0; named World Series MVP. Career span 1953–67 for many teams.

**Tommy Lasorda** (b. 9-22-27): Baseball manager. Spent nearly his entire minor and major league career in Dodgers organization as a pitcher, coach and manager. Managed Dodgers 1977–96, winning four pennants and two World Series (1981, 1988). Only three men managed one baseball team longer. Coached U.S. Olympic baseball team to the gold medal at the 2000 Sydney Games.

**Rod Laver** (b. 8-9-38): Australian tennis player. "Rocket." Only player to achieve the Grand Slam twice (as an amateur in 1962 and as a pro in 1969). Third alltime in men's Grand Slam singles titles (11—tied with Bjorn Borg). Won four Wimbledon titles (consecutively 1961–62, 1968–69), three Australian titles (1960, '62, '69), two U.S. titles (1962, '69) and two French titles (1962, '69). Also won eight Grand Slam doubles titles. First player to earn $1 million in prize money. 47 career tournament victories. Member of undefeated Australian Davis Cup team from 1959 to '62.

**Andrea Mead Lawrence** (b. 4-19-32): Skier. Gold medalist in slalom and giant slalom at 1952 Olympics.

**Bobby Layne** (b. 12-19-26; d. 12-1-86): Football QB. Led Detroit Lions to NFL championships in both 1952 and '53. In 1952 led NFL in every passing category. Career span 1948–62, most with the Detroit Lions. Elected to Hall of Fame in 1967.

**Sammy Lee** (b. 8-1-20): Diver. Gold medalist at two consecutive Olympics (highboard in 1948, 1952); bronze medalist in springboard at 1948 Olympics. Won the 1953 Sullivan Award. Also 1960 U.S. Olympic diving coach.

**Jacques Lemaire** (b. 9-7-45): Hockey C–Coach. As center for Montreal Canadiens from 1967–68 through 1978–79 was part of eight Stanley Cup winning teams. Over 12 seasons, all with Montreal, scored 366 goals and had 469 assists. Elected to Hall of Fame in 1984. Coached Canadiens 1983–85 and N.J. Devils 1993–98. Named first coach of expansion Minnesota Wild in 2000.

**Mario Lemieux** (b. 10-5-65): Hockey C. Won MVP award in 1988, '93, '96. Playoff MVP in 1991. Led league in points five seasons and goals scored three seasons, assists one season. Scored 40+ goals and 100+ points six consecutive seasons, including 85 goals and 199 points in 1989. Rookie of the Year in 1985. Won 1992–93 scoring title despite sitting out six weeks to receive treatment for Hodgkin's disease, a form of cancer. Sat out 1994–95 season, returned in '95–96 to lead league in scoring and become second fastest player to score 500 career goals. Awarded

ownership of Penguins in a settlement in 1999, and returned to the ice in 2001, when he scored 35 goals in 43 games. Career span 1984–94, 1995–97, 2001 with Pittsburgh.

**Greg LeMond** (b. 6-26-61): Cyclist. First American to win Tour de France; won event three times (1986, consecutively 1989–90). Recovered from hunting accident to win in 1989.

**Ivan Lendl** (b. 3-7-60): Tennis player. Second alltime men's most career tournament victories (94). Won three consecutive U.S. Open singles titles (1985–87) and three French Open titles (1984, consecutively 1986–87). Also won two consecutive Australian Open titles (1989–90). Reached Grand Slam final nine other times.

**Suzanne Lenglen** (b. 5-24-1899, d. 7-4-38): French tennis player. Lost only one match from 1919 to her retirement in 1926. Won six Wimbledon singles and doubles titles (consecutively 1919–23, 1925). Won six French singles and doubles titles (consecutively 1920–23, 1925–26).

**Sugar Ray Leonard** (b. 5-17-56): Boxer. Champion in five weight classes: welterweight, junior middle-weight, middleweight, super middleweight and light heavyweight. Career record 36-3-1 with 25 KOs from 1977 to 1997, including comeback loss to Hector Camacho at the age of 41. Also light welterweight gold medalist at 1976 Olympics.

**Carl Lewis** (b. 7-1-61): Track and field. Held world record for 100 meters (9.86), set on 8-25-91 at World Championships in Tokyo. Duplicated Jesse Owens's feat by winning four gold medals at 1984 Olympics (100 and 200 meters, 4x100-meter relay and long jump). Also won two gold medals (100 meters, long jump) and one silver (200 meters) at 1988 Olympics and two gold medals (long jump, 4x100 relay) at 1992 Olympics. Sullivan Award winner in 1981. Won 1996 Olympic long jump gold at age 35, giving him nine career gold medals and making him just the second track and field athlete (along with Al Oerter) to win four golds in a single event.

**Nancy Lieberman-Cline** (b. 7-1-58): Basketball G. Three-time All-America at Old Dominion. Player of the Year (1979, 1980). Olympian, 1976, and selected for 1980 team, but quit because of Moscow boycott. Promoter of women's basketball, played in WPBL, WABA. First woman to play basketball in a men's professional league (USBL), in 1986. Joined WNBA in 1997, retired in '98 to become GM/coach of the Detroit Shock.

**Bob Lilly** (b. 7-26-39): Football DT. Dallas Cowboys' first ever draft pick, first Pro Bowl player and first all-NFL choice. Made all-NFL eight times. Career span 1961–74, all with Cowboys. Elected to Hall of Fame in 1980.

**Tara Lipinski** (b. 6-10-82): Figure skater. In 1998 at Nagano eclipsed Sonja Henie as the youngest individual Winter Olympic champion in history when, at 15, she won the women's figure skating gold medal. Also won U.S. and world championships in 1997.

**Sonny Liston** (b. 5-8-32, d. 12-30-70): Boxer. Heavyweight champion from 1962 to 1964. Won title by KO of Floyd Patterson on 9-25-62. Lost title when TKO'd by Cassius Clay (Muhammad Ali) on 2-25-64 and then lost rematch on 5-25-65 when KO'd in first round. Career record: 50–4, 39 KOs.

**Vince Lombardi** (b. 6-11-13, d. 9-3-70): Football coach. Highest alltime winning percentage (.740). Career record 105-35-6. Won five NFL championships and two consecutive Super Bowl titles with Green Bay from 1959 to 1967. Coached Washington in 1969. Super Bowl trophy named in his honor.

**Johnny Longden** (b. 2-14-07): Horse racing jockey. Rode Triple Crown winner Count Fleet in 1943. 6,032 wins.

**Nancy Lopez** (b. 1-6-57): Golfer. LPGA Player of the Year four times (consecutively 1978–79, 1985, 1988). Winner of LPGA Championship three times (1978, 1985, 1989). Member of the LPGA Hall of Fame.

**Greg Louganis** (b. 1-29-60): Diver. Gold medalist in platform and springboard at two consecutive Olympics in 1984, 1988. World champion five times (platform in 1978, 1982, 1986; springboard in 1982, 1986). Also Sullivan Award winner in 1984.

**Joe Louis** (b. 5-13-14, d. 4-12-81): Boxer. "The Brown Bomber." Longest title reign of any heavyweight champion (11 years, nine months) from June 1937 through March 1949. Career record 63–3 with 49 KOs from 1934 to 1951. Defended title 25 times.

**Jerry Lucas** (b. 3-30-40): Basketball F. Star at Ohio State. *Sporting News* College Player of Year in both 1961 and '62. In 1960 member of both NCAA championship team and gold-medal winning U.S. Olympic team. Averaged over 20 points and 20 rebounds a game for college career. NBA Rookie of Year in 1964. In 11 NBA seasons averaged 17 points a game. Elected to Hall of Fame in 1979.

**Sid Luckman** (b. 11-21-16, d. 7-5-98): Football QB. Played on four NFL champions (consecutively 1940–41, 1943, 1946) with Chicago. Player of the Year in 1943. Tied record with seven touchdown passes on 11-14-43. All-Pro six times. 137 career touchdown passes. Career span 1939–50. Also All-America with Columbia.

**Jon Lugbill** (b. 5-27-61): Whitewater canoe racer. Won five world singles titles from 1979 to 1989.

**Hank Luisetti** (b. 6-16-16): Basketball F. The first player to use the one-handed shot. All-America at Stanford three consecutive years from 1936–38.

**D. Wayne Lukas** (b. 9-2-35): Horse racing trainer. Former college basketball coach and quarter horse trainer. Trained three Horses of the Year, Lady's Secret in 1986, Criminal Type in 1990, and Charismatic in 1999. Won 1988 Kentucky Derby with a filly, Winning Colors. Won 1994 Preakness and Belmont with Tabasco Cat. Won all three Triple Crown races in 1995, with Thunder Gulch (Kentucky Derby and Belmont) and Timbor County (Preakness). Won 1999 Derby and Preakness with Charismatic.

**Connie Mack** (b. 2-22-1862, d. 2-8-56): Born Cornelius McGillicuddy. Baseball manager. Managed Philadelphia for 50 years (1901–50) until age 87. All-time leader in games (7,755), wins (3,731) and losses (3,948). Won nine pennants and five World Series (1910–11, 1913, 1929–30).

**Greg Maddux** (b. 4-14-66): Baseball P. Won unprecedented fourth consecutive Cy Young Award in 1995, when he was 19–2 with a 1.63 ERA and led the Atlanta Braves to their first World Series title. Career span 1986–92 Chicago (NL), 1993– Atlanta.

**Larry Mahan** (b. 11-21-43): Rodeo. All-around champion six times (consecutively 1966–70, 1973).

**Frank Mahovlich** (b. 1-10-38): Hockey LW. Winner of Calder Trophy for top rookie for 1957–58 season. In 18 NHL seasons with Toronto Maple Leafs, Detroit Red

Wings and Montreal Canadiens, had 533 goals and 570 assists. Played for six Stanley Cup winners. Elected to Hall of Fame 1981.

**Phil Mahre** (b. 5-10-57): Skier. Gold medalist in slalom at 1984 Olympics (twin brother Steve won silver medal). World Cup champion three consecutive years (1981–83).

**Joe Malone** (b. 2-28-1890, d. 5-15-69): Hockey F. "Phantom Joe." Led the NHL in its first season, 1917–18, with 44 goals in 20 games with Montreal. Led league in scoring two times (1918, 1920). Holds NHL record with most goals scored, single game (7) in 1920.

**Karl Malone** (b. 7-24-63): Basketball F. "The Mailman." Second in NBA history in points scored (32,919). Eleven-time first-team All-Star. All-Star MVP, 1989, 1993 (shared with John Stockton). All-Rookie team, 1986. League MVP in 1997 when he led Jazz to NBA Finals and in 1999 when he averaged 23.8 PPG. Member of 1992 and '96 Olympic teams. Career span since 1985 with Utah.

**Moses Malone** (b. 3-23-55): Basketball C. Second alltime in free throws made (8,531), fifth in rebounds (16,212) and fifth in points scored (27,409). three MVP awards in 1979, consecutively 1982–83; playoff MVP in 1983. 4-time All-Star. Led league in rebounding six times, five consecutively. Career span 1976–95 with Houston, Philadelphia, Washington, Atlanta, Milwaukee, San Antonio.

**Hermann Maier** (b.12-7-72): Austrian skier. Recovered from spectacular crash in the downhill to win two gold medals at 1998 Olympics in Nagano. Won 1998 Super G, Giant Slalom and overall World Cup season titles.

**Man o' War** (b. 1917, d. 1947): Thoroughbred race horse. Won 20 of 21 races 1919–20. Only loss was in 1919 in Sanford Stakes to Upset. Passed up Derby but won both Preakness and Belmont. Winner of $249,465. Sire of War Admiral, 1937 Triple Crown winner.

**Mickey Mantle** (b. 10-20-31, d. 8-13-95): Baseball OF. Won three MVP awards, consecutively 1956–57 and 1962; won Triple Crown in 1956. 536 career HR. Greatest switch hitter in history. Played in 20 All-Star games. Alltime World Series leader in HR (18), RBI (40) and runs scored (42). No. 7 was a member of seven World Series winners with NY Yankees. Career span 1951–68.

**Diego Maradona** (b. 10-30-60): Argentine soccer player. Led Argentina to 1986 World Cup victory and to 1990 World Cup finals. Led Naples to Italian League titles (1987, 1990), Italian Cup (1987) and to UEFA Cup title (1989). Throughout 1980s often acknowledged as best player in the world. Tested positive for cocaine and suspended by FIFA and Italian Soccer Federation for 15 months in March 1991. Failed drug test in 1994 World Cup and suspended before second round.

**Pete Maravich** (b. 6-22-47, d. 1-5-88): Basketball G. "Pistol Pete." Alltime NCAA leader in points scored (3,667), scoring average (44.2) and games scoring 50+ points (28, including two Division I record 69 points in 1970). Alltime season leader in points scored (1,381) and scoring average (44.5) in 1970. College Player of the Year in 1970. NCAA scoring leader and All-America three consecutive seasons from 1968 to 1970 with Louisiana State. Also led NBA in scoring in 1977. Averaged 20+ points eight times. All-Star two times. Career span 1970–79 with Atlanta, New Orleans/Utah, Boston.

**Gino Marchetti** (b. 1-2-27): Football DE. Played in Pro Bowl every year from 1955 to '65, except 1958 when he broke right ankle tackling Frank Gifford in Colts' 23–17 win over the Giants. Career span 1952–66, almost all with Baltimore Colts. Inducted into Hall of Fame in 1972.

**Rocky Marciano** (b. 9-1-23, d. 8-31-69): Boxer. Heavyweight champion (1952–56). Career record 49–0 with 43 KOs from 1947 to 1956. Only heavyweight to retire as undefeated champion.

**Juan Marichal** (b. 10-24-37): Baseball RHP. 243 career wins, 2.89 career ERA. Won 20+ games six times; 250+ innings pitched eight times; 200+ strikeouts six times. Pitched no-hitter in 1963. Career span 1960–75, mostly with San Francisco. Elected to Hall of Fame in 1983.

**Dan Marino** (b. 9-15-61): Football QB. Set alltime season record for yards passing (5,084) and touchdown passes (48) in 1984. Passed for 4,000+ yards five other seasons. Player of the Year in 1984. Career totals: 61,361 yards passing, 420 touchdown passes, first alltime in both categories. Career span 1983–00 with Miami.

**Roger Maris** (b. 9-10-34, d. 12-14-85): Baseball OF. Broke Babe Ruth's alltime season HR record with 61 in 1961. Won consecutive MVP awards and led league in RBI 1960–61. Career span 1957–68 with Kansas City, New York (AL), St. Louis.

**Billy Martin** (b. 5-16-28, d. 12-25-89): Baseball 2B–manager. Volatile manager was hired and fired by Minnesota, Detroit, Texas, New York Yankees (five times!) and Oakland from 1969 to 1988. Won World Series with Yankees as manager in 1977 and as player four times.

**Pedro Martinez** (b. 10-25-71): Baseball P. Won his third Cy Young award in 2000: 18–6, 1.74 ERA, 284 K's. Became second pitcher to win Cy Young Awards in both leagues when he went 23–4 with 2.07 ERA for Boston in '99. Dominican righthander went 17–8 with a 1.90 ERA and 305 strikeouts for Montreal in 1997 to win first Cy Young. First pitcher in 25 years to have more than 300 Ks and ERA below 2.00. Started '99 All-Star Game and was named MVP after striking out first four batters.

**Eddie Mathews** (b. 10-13-31, d. 2-18-01): Baseball 3B. 512 career HR and 30+ HR nine consecutive seasons. League leader in HR two times, walks four times. Career span 1952–68 with Milwaukee.

**Christy Mathewson** (b. 8-12-1880, d. 10-7-25): Baseball RHP. Third alltime most wins (373, tied with Grover Alexander) and shutouts (79); career ERA 2.13. Led league in wins five times; won 30+ games four times and 20+ games nine other times. Led league in ERA and strikeouts five times each. Pitched two no-hitters. Pitched three shutouts in 1905 World Series. Career span 1900–16 with New York. Played one game for Reds in 1916.

**Bob Mathias** (b. 11-17-30): Track and field. At age 17, youngest to win gold medal in decathlon at 1948 Olympics. First decathlete to win gold medal at consecutive Olympics (1948, 1952). Also won Sullivan Award in 1948.

**Ollie Matson** (b. 5-1-30): Football RB. Versatile runner totalled 12,884 combined yards rushing, receiving and kick returning. Scored 73 career touchdowns, including a 105-yard kickoff return on Oct. 14, 1956, the second longest ever. Career span 1952–66 with Chicago Cardinals, Los Angeles, Detroit, Philadelphia. Also won bronze medal in 400 meters at 1952 Olympics. Elected to Hall of Fame in 1972.

**Roland Matthes** (b. 11-17-50): German swimmer. Gold medalist in 100-meter and 200-meter backstroke at two consecutive Olympics (1968, 1972). Set 16 world records from 1967 to 1973.

**Don Maynard** (b. 1-25-37): Football WR. Retired in 1973 as the NFL's alltime leading receiver. In 15 seasons, 10 with the New York Jets, caught 633 passes for 11,834 yards and 88 TDs. Averaged 18.7 yards per catch for career. In 1967 and '68 led AFL with average of 20.2 and 22.8 yards per catch. Elected to Hall of Fame in 1987.

**Willie Mays** (b. 5-6-31): Baseball OF. "Say Hey Kid." MVP in 1954, 1965; Rookie of the Year in 1951. Third alltime most HR (660), with 50+ HR two times, 30+ HR nine other times. 100+ RBI 10 times; 100+ runs scored 12 consecutive seasons. 3,283 career hits. Led league in stolen bases four consecutive seasons. 30 HR and 30 steals in same season two times and first man in history to hit 300+ HR and steal 300+ bases. Won 11 consecutive Gold Gloves; set record for career putouts by an outfielder and league record for total chances. His catch in the 1954 World Series off the bat of Vic Wertz called the greatest ever. Career span 1951–73 with New York and San Francisco Giants, New York Mets.

**Bill Mazeroski** (b. 9-5-36): Baseball 2B. Hit dramatic ninth-inning home run in Game 7 to win 1960 World Series, first of only two Series' to end on a home run. Also a great fielder, won Gold Glove eight times. Led league in assists nine times, double plays eight times and putouts five times. Inducted to Hall of Fame in 2001.

**Joe McCarthy** (b. 4-21-1887, d. 1-3-78): Baseball manager. Alltime highest winning percentage among managers for regular season (.615). First manager to win pennants in both leagues (Chicago (NL), 1929, New York (AL), 1932). From 1926 to 1950 his teams won seven World Series and nine pennants.

**Mark McCormack** (b. 11-6-30): Sports marketing agent. Founded International Management Group in 1962. Also author of best-selling business advice books.

**Pat McCormick** (b. 5-12-30): Diver. Gold medalist in platform and springboard at two consecutive Olympics (1952, 1956). Also won Sullivan Award in 1956.

**Willie McCovey** (b. 1-10-38): Baseball 1B. Led NL in HRs three times (1963, '68, '69) and in RBI twice (1968–69). 521 career homers. .270 career average. Hit 18 grand slams. Rookie of Year 1959. NL MVP in 1969. Career span 1959–73 and 1977–80 with San Francisco Giants, 1974–76 with San Diego Padres and 1976 with Oakland A's. Elected to Hall of Fame in 1986.

**John McEnroe** (b. 2-26-59): Tennis player. Won four U.S. Open singles titles (consecutively 1979–81, 1984) and three Wimbledon titles (1981, consecutively 1983–84). Also won eight Grand Slam doubles titles. Third alltime men's most career tournament victories (77). Led U.S. to five Davis Cup victories (1978–79, 1981–82, 1992).

**John McGraw** (b. 4-7-1873, d. 2-25-34): Baseball manager. Second alltime in games (4,801) and wins (2,784). Guided New York Giants to three World Series titles and 10 pennants from 1902 to 1932.

**Mark McGwire** (b. 10-1-63): Baseball 1B. Broke Roger Maris's 37-year-old single-season HR record with 70 in 155 games in 1998; record broken by Barry Bonds in 2001. Rookie of the Year in 1987, when he hit rookie record 49 home runs. Hit 30+ HR 12 times, 40+ HR six times, 50+ HR four straight years (1996–99). Member of 1984 U.S. Olympic baseball team. Career span 1986–97 Oakland; since 1997 with St. Louis.

**Denny McLain** (b. 3-29-44): Baseball RHP. Last pitcher to win 30+ games in a season (Detroit, 1968); won 20+ games two other times. Won two consecutive Cy Young Awards (1968–69). Led league in innings pitched two times. Served 2½-year jail term for 1985 conviction of extortion, racketeering and drug possession. Re-entered prison in 1997 on fraud conviction. Career span 1963–72.

**Mary T. Meagher** (b. 10-27-64): Swimmer. "Madame Butterfly." Won three gold medals at 1984 Olympics (100-meter butterfly, 200-meter butterfly and 400-medley relay). In 1981 set world records in 100-meter butterfly (57.93) and 200-meter butterfly (2:05.96).

**Rick Mears** (b. 12-3-51): Auto racer. Has won Indy 500 four times (1979, '84, '88, '91) and been CART champion three times (1979, consecutively 1981–82). Named Indy 500 Rookie of the Year in 1978.

**Eddy Merckx** (b. 1945): Belgian cyclist. Won five Tours de France, including four in a row (1969–72).

**Mark Messier** (b. 1-18-61): Hockey C. Two-time Hart Trophy (MVP) winnner; won Stanley Cups with Edmonton (1984, '85, '87, '88 and '90) and NY Rangers (1994). Among top five alltime in points, top 10 in goals, assists. Career span 1979–91 Edmonton, 1991–96 NY Rangers, 1997–00 Vancouver, 2000–01 Rangers.

**Cary Middlecoff** (b. 1-6-21, d. 9-1-98): Golfer. Also a dentist. Won 40 PGA tournaments, including 1955 Masters and U.S. Opens in 1949 and '56. Won 1956 Vardon Trophy.

**George Mikan** (b. 6-18-24): Basketball C. Averaged 20+ points per game and made All-Star team six consecutive seasons. Led league in scoring three times, rebounding once. Played on five championship teams in six years (1949–54) with Minneapolis. Also played on 1945 NIT championship team with DePaul. All-America three times. Served as ABA Commissioner from 1968 to 1969.

**Stan Mikita** (b. 5-20-40): Hockey C. Won MVP award two consecutive seasons (1967–68). 926 career assists, 1,467 career points. Led league in assists four straight seasons and scoring four times. 541 career goals. All-Star six times. Career span 1958–80 with Chicago.

**Del Miller** (b. 7-5-13; d. 8-19-96): Harness racing driver. Raced in eight decades, beginning in 1929, the longest career of any athlete. Won The Hambletonian in 1950.

**Marvin Miller** (b. 4-14 17): Labor negotiator. Union chief of MLB Players Association from 1966 to 1984. Led strikes in 1972 and '81. Negotiated five labor contracts that increased minimum salary and pension fund, allowed for agents and arbitration, and brought about the end of the reserve clause and the start of free agency.

**Art Monk** (b. 12-5-57): Football WR. Fourth alltime in pass receptions (940 for 12,721 and 68 TDs). 106 catches in 1984 was then NFL single season record. Career span 1980–93 with Redskins, 1993–95 with New York Jets, 1995 with Eagles.

**Earl Monroe** (b. 11-21-44): Basketball G. "The Pearl" played 13 seasons (1968–80) with the Baltimore Bullets and New York Knicks. NBA Rookie of Year in 1968. Member of 1973 NBA championship Knicks team. Averaged 18.8 points a game. Elected to Hall of Fame 1989.

**Joe Montana** (b. 6-11-56): Football QB. Second alltime highest-rated passer (92.3); fifth in completions (3,409); retired with 40,551 passing yards and 273 touchdown passes. Won four Super Bowl championships (1981, 1984, consecutively 1988–89) with San Francisco. Named Super Bowl MVP three times (1981, 1984, 1989). Player of the Year in 1989. Also led Notre Dame to national championship in 1977. Career span 1979–92 with San Francisco, 1993–94 Kansas City. Elected to Hall of Fame in 2000.

**Carlos Monzon** (b. 8-7-42, d. 1-8-95): Argentine boxer. Longest title reign of any middleweight champion (6 years, nine months) from Nov. 1970 through Aug. 1977. Career record 89-3-9 with 61 KOs from 1963 to 1977. Won 82 consecutive bouts from 1964 to 1977. Defended title 14 times. Retired as champion.

**Helen Wills Moody** (b. 10-6-05, d. 1-1-98): Tennis player. Third alltime in women's Grand Slam singles titles (19). Her eight Wimbledon titles are second most alltime (consecutively 1927–30, 1932–33, 1935, 1938). Won seven U.S. titles (consecutively 1923–25, 1927–29, 1931) and four French titles (consecutively 1928–30, 1932). Also won 12 Grand Slam doubles titles.

**Archie Moore** (b. 12-13-16 d. 12-9-98): Boxer. Longest title reign of any light heavyweight champion (9 years, one month) from Dec. 1952 through Feb. 1962. Career record 199-26-8 with an alltime record 145 KOs from 1935 to 1965. Retired at age 52.

**Davey Moore** (b. 11-1-33; d. 3-23-63): Boxer. Won featherweight title by KO of Kid Bassey in 13 on 3-18-59. Five successful defenses of title, before losing it on 3-21-63 to Sugar Ramos who KO'd him in 10. Died two days after fight of brain damage suffered during fight. Career record: 58–7–1, 30 KOs.

**Noureddine Morceli** (b. 2-20-70). Algerian track and field middle distance runner. Set world record for mile (3:44.39) in Rieti, Italy, on 9-5-93. Set world record for 1,500 (3:28.86) on 9-5-92. World champion at 1,500 in both 1991 and '93. Finished a shocking seventh at 1992 Olympics, but won gold medal in '96 at Atlanta. Only man ever to rank first in the world at 1,500/mile four straight years (1990–93).

**Joe Morgan** (b. 9-19-43): Baseball 2B. Won two consecutive MVP awards in 1975–76. Fourth alltime in career walks (1,865). 689 stolen bases. Led league in walks four times. 100+ walks and runs scored eight times each; 40+ stolen bases nine times. Won five Gold Gloves. Second alltime in games played by 2nd baseman (2,527). Career span 1963–84 with Houston, Cincinnati, San Francisco, Philadelphia and Oakland.

**Willie Mosconi** (b. 6-27-13; d. 9-16-93): Pocket billiards player. Won world title a record 15 straight times between 1941 and 1957. Once pocketed 526 balls without a miss.

**Edwin Moses** (b. 8-31-55): Track and field. Gold medalist in 400-meter hurdles at two Olympics, in 1976, '84 (U.S. boycotted '80 Games); bronze medalist at '88 Olympics. Set four world records in 400-meter hurdles (best of 47.02 set on 8-31-83). Won 122 consecutive races from 1977 to 1987. Won Sullivan Award in 1983.

**Marion Motley** (b. 6-5-20 d. 6-27-99): Football FB. All-time AAFC leader in yards rushing (3,024). Led NFL in rushing once. Combined league totals: 4,712 yards rushing, 39 touchdowns. Played for four consecutive

AAFC champions (1946–49) and one NFL champion (1950). Career span with Cleveland 1946–1953.

**Shirley Muldowney** (b. 6-19-40): Drag racer. First woman to win the Top Fuel championship, which she won three times (1977, 1980, 1982).

**Anthony Munoz** (b. 8-19-58): Football OT. Probably the greatest tackle ever. Made Pro Bowl a record-tying 11 times. Career span 1980–92 with the Cincinnati Bengals. Elected to Hall of Fame 1998.

**Isaac Murphy** (b. 4-16-1861, d. 2-12-1896): Horse racing jockey. Top jockey of his era, Murphy, who was black, won three Kentucky Derbys (aboard Buchanan in 1884, Riley in 1890 and Kingman in 1891).

**Eddie Murray** (b. 2-24-56): Baseball 1B. 100+ RBI six seasons and 30+ HRs five seasons. Retired with 3,255 hits, 504 HRs and 1,917 RBI. Alltime leader in RBI by switch hitter. Career span 1977–88, '96 with Baltimore Orioles; 1989–91, '97 with Los Angeles; 1992–93 with New York Mets; 1994–96 with Cleveland; 1997 with Anaheim.

**Jim Murray** (b. 12-29-19; d. 8-16-98): Sportswriter. Won Pulitzer Prize in 1990. Named Sportswriter of the Year 14 times. Columnist for *Los Angeles Times* 1961–98.

**Ty Murray** (b. 10-11-69): Rodeo cowboy. All-around world champion, 1989–94. Set single-season earnings record, 1990 ($213,771). Rookie of the Year, 1988. At 20 in 1989, became youngest man ever to win national all-around title.

**Stan Musial** (b. 11-21-20): Baseball OF–1B. "Stan the Man." Had .331 career batting average and 475 career HR. MVP award winner 1943, 1946, 1948. Fourth alltime in hits (3,630) and third in doubles (725). Won seven batting titles. Led league in hits six times, slugging average five times, doubles eight times. Had .300+ batting average 17 times, 200+ hits six times, 100+ RBI 10 times, and 100+ runs scored 11 times. 24-time All-Star. Career span 1941–63 with St. Louis.

**John Naber** (b. 1-20-56): Swimmer. Won four gold medals and one silver medal at 1976 Olympics. Sullivan Award winner in 1977.

**Bronko Nagurski** (b. 11-3-08, d. 1-7-90): Football FB. Punishing runner played on three NFL champions (1932, '33, '43) with Bears. 2,778 career yards, 1930–37 and 1943 with Chicago.

**James Naismith** (b. 11-6-1861, d. 11-28-39): Invented basketball in 1891 while an instructor at YMCA Training School in Springfield, Mass. Refined the game while a professor at Kansas from 1898 to 1937. Hall of Fame is named in his honor.

**Joe Namath** (b. 5-31-43): Football QB. "Broadway Joe." Super Bowl MVP in 1968 after he guaranteed victory for AFL. 173 career touchdown passes. Led league in yards passing three times, including 4,007 yards in 1967. Player of the Year,1968; Rookie of the Year, 1965. Career span 1965–77 with NY Jets, LA Rams.

**Ilie Nastase** (b. 7-19-46): Romanian tennis player. "Nasty" for his unruly deportment on court. Beat Arthur Ashe to win 1972 U.S. Open title. Won 1973 French Open. Twice Wimbledon runner-up (to Stan Smith in 1972 and Bjorn Borg in '76).

**Martina Navratilova** (b. 10-18-56): Tennis player. Fourth in women's Grand Slam singles titles (18—tied with Chris Evert). Won a record nine Wimbledon titles, including six consecutively (1978–79, 1982–87, '90). Won four U.S. Open titles (consecutively 1983–84,

1986–87), three Australian Open titles (1981, '83, '85) and two French Open titles (1982, '84). Reached Grand Slam final 13 other times. Also won 38 Grand Slam doubles titles. Her total of 56 Grand Slam titles is second alltime to Margaret Court's. Set mark for longest winning streak with 74 matches in 1984. Also won the doubles Grand Slam in 1984 with Pam Shriver. Won 109 consecutive doubles matches with Shriver from 1983–85.

**Byron Nelson** (b. 2-14-12): Golfer. Won the Masters (1937, 1942) and PGA Championship (1940, 1945) two times each and U.S. Open once (1939). Won 52 career tournaments, including 11 consecutively in 1945.

**Ernie Nevers** (b. 6-11-03, d. 5-3-76): Football FB. Set alltime pro single game record for points scored (40) and touchdowns (six) on 11-28-29. Career span 1926–31 with Duluth, Chicago. Also a pitcher with St. Louis, surrendered two of Babe Ruth's 60 home runs in 1927. All-America at Stanford, earned 11 letters in four sports.

**John Newcombe** (b. 5-23-44): Australian tennis player. Won three Wimbledon singles titles (1967, consecutively 1970–71), two U.S. titles (1967, 1973) and two Australian Open titles (1973, 1975). Also won 17 Grand Slam doubles titles.

**Pete Newell** (b. 8-31-15): College basketball coach. Despite coaching only 13 seasons, 1947 through 1960, was first coach to win NIT, NCAA and Olympic crowns. Led Univ. of San Francisco to 1949 NIT title, Cal to 1959 NCAA title, and the 1960 U.S. Olympic basketball team that included Jerry Lucas, Oscar Robertson and Jerry West to gold medal. Overall collegiate coaching record of 234–123.

**Jack Nicklaus** (b. 1-21-40): Golfer. "The Golden Bear." Alltime leader in major championships (20). Second alltime in career wins (70). Won Masters six times, more than any player (1963, consecutively 1965–66, '72, '75, '86—at age 46, the oldest player to win event), PGA Championship five times (1963, '71, '73, '75, '80), U.S. Open four times (1962, '67, '72, '80), British Open three times (1966, '70, '78) and U.S. Amateur twice (1959, '61). PGA Player of the Year five times (1967, consecutively 1972–73, 1975–76). Also NCAA champion with Ohio State in 1961.

**Ray Nitschke** (b. 12-29-36 d. 3-8-98): Football LB. Defensive signal-caller for the great Packer teams of the '60s. Voted Packer MVP by teammates after 1967 season. MVP of the 1962 NFL title game. Career span 1958–72 with Green Bay Packers.

**Chuck Noll** (b. 1-5-32): Football coach. Led Pittsburgh to four Super Bowl victories in six years (1975, '76, '79, '80). Retired in 1991 after 23 years and 209 wins.

**Greg Norman** (b. 2-10-55): Golfer. "The Shark" led PGA in winnings in 1986, '90, 1995–96. Won Vardon Trophy twice, 1989–90. Won two British Opens (1986, '93) but is almost as famous for his heartbreaking misses. Beaten at the 1986 PGA when Bob Tway holed out a sand shot at '87 Masters when Larry Mize chipped in from a downhill lie. Blew a six-stroke, third-round lead to lose to Nick Faldo by five shots at 1996 Masters. PGA Player of the Year 1996.

**James D. Norris** (b. 11-6-06, d. 2-25-66): Hockey executive. Owner of Detroit from 1933 to 1943 and Chicago from 1946 to 1966. Teams won four Stanley Cup championships (consecutively 1936–37, '43, '61). Defensive Player of the Year award named in his honor. Also a boxing promoter, operated International Boxing Club from 1949 to 1958.

**Paavo Nurmi** (b. 6-13-1897, d. 10-2-73): Track and field. Finnish middle- and long-distance runner won a total of nine gold medals at three Olympics in 1920, '24, '28.

**Matti Nykänen** (b. 7-17-63): Finnish ski jumper. Three-time Olympic gold medalist. Won 90-meter jump (1984, '88) and 70-meter jump (1988). World champion on 90-meter jump in 1982. Won four World Cups (1983, '85, '86, '88).

**Dan O'Brien** (b. 7-18-66): Track and field decathlete. Won world decathlon title in 1991, '93 and '95. Set world decathlon record of 8,891 in Talence, France, on 9-4/5-92, that stood for seven years. Heavily favored to win 1992 Olympic decathlon but missed making U.S. team when he no-heighted in pole vault at U.S. Olympic Trials. Won gold medal at 1996 Olympics in Atlanta.

**Parry O'Brien** (b. 1-28-32): Track and field. Shot-putter who revolutionized the event with his "glide" technique and won Olympic gold medals in 1952 and '56, silver in '60. Set 10 world records from 1953 to 1959, topped by a put of 63' 4" in '59. Sullivan Award winner in 1959.

**Al Oerter** (b. 8-19-36): Track and field. Gold medalist in discus at four consecutive Olympics (1956, '60, '64, '68), setting Olympic record each time. First to break the 200-foot barrier, throwing 200' 5" in 1962.

**Sadaharu Oh** (b. 5-20-40): Baseball 1B in Japanese league. 868 career HR in 22 seasons for the Tokyo Giants. Led league in HR 15 times, RBI 13 times, batting five times and runs 13 consecutive seasons. Awarded MVP nine times; won two consecutive Triple Crowns and nine Gold Gloves.

**Hakeem Olajuwon** (b. 1-21-63): Basketball C. From Nigeria. Alltime NBA career leader in blocked shots (3,740). All-NBA First Team 1987–89, '93–94. League MVP in 1994 as he led Houston to NBA title (repeated in '95). Led NCAA in field goal percentage, rebounding and blocked shots in 1984 at Houston. Career span since 1985 with the Rockets. Member of 1996 U.S. Olympic team.

**Merlin Olsen** (b. 9-15-40): Fooball DT. Part of LA Rams "Fearsome Foursome" defensive line. Named to Pro Bowl 14 straight times. Career span 1962–76, all with LA Rams. Elected to Hall of Fame 1982.

**Omaha** (b. 1932, d. 1959): Thoroughbred race horse. Won Triple Crown in 1935. Trained by Sunny Jim Fitzsimmons.

**Mark O'Meara** (b. 1-13-57): Golfer. Won Masters and British Open in 1998. Tour rookie of the year in 1981; won 1979 U.S. Amateur.

**Shaquille O'Neal** (b. 3-6-72): Basketball C. "Shaq." Top pick of Orlando Magic in 1992 NBA draft. NBA Rookie of the Year 1993. Led league in scoring in '95 and 2000, and in field goal percentage '98, '99, '00 and '01. Member of 1996 U.S. Olympic team. Was named MVP of the regular season, All-Star game, and playoffs in 1999–2000. Led NCAA in blocked shots in 1992, with 5.23 a game; averaged 4.58 over his 90-game, three-year career. Career with Orlando Magic 1992–96, Los Angeles lakers 1996–present. Won NBA titles with Lakers in 2000 and 2001.

**Bobby Orr** (b. 3-20-48): Hockey D. Defensive Player of the Year more than any other player, eight consecutive seasons (1968-75). Won MVP award three consecutive seasons (1970-72), playoff MVP two times (1970, '72). Also Rookie of the Year in 1967. Led

league in assists five times and scoring two times. Career span 1966–77 with Boston.

**Mel Ott** (b. 3-2-09, d. 11-21-58): Baseball OF. 511 career HR, 1,861 RBI, .304 batting average. League leader in HR and walks six times each. 100+ RBI nine times and 100+ walks ten times. Career span 1926–47 with New York Giants.

**Jim Otto** (b. 1-5-38): Football C. Number 00 started every game (210) in his 15-year career (1960–74) with the Oakland Raiders. Inducted to Hall of Fame in 1980.

**Kristin Otto** (b. 1966): German swimmer. Won six gold medals for East Germany at 1988 Olympics.

**Jesse Owens** (b. 9-12-13, d. 3-31-80): Track and field. Gold medalist in four events (100 meters and 200 meters; 4x100-meter relay and long jump) at 1936 Olympics. At the 1935 Big 10 championship set or equaled four world record in 70 minutes, including 100 yards, long jump, 220-yard low hurdles and 220 dash.

**Alan Page** (b. 8-7-45): Football DT. First defensive player to be named NFL Player of the Year, in 1972. Career span 1967–78 with Minnesota Vikings and 1978–81 with Chicago Bears. Now sits on Minnesota Supreme Court.

**Satchel Paige** (b. 7-7-06, d. 6-8-82): Baseball RHP. Alltime greatest black pitcher, didn't pitch in major leagues until 1948 at age 42 with Cleveland. Oldest pitcher in major league history at age 59 with Kansas City in 1965. Pitched in the Negro leagues from 1926 to 1950 with Birmingham Black Barons, Pittsburgh Crawfords and Kansas City Monarchs. Estimated career record is 2,000 wins, 250 shutouts, 30,000 strikeouts, 45 no-hitters. Said "Don't look back. Something may be gaining on you."

**Se Ri Pak** (b. 9-28-77): South Korean golfer. Named 1998 LPGA Rookie of the Year for a season in which she won both the first major she entered, the LPGA Championships, and the U.S. Open.

**Arnold Palmer** (b. 9-10-29): Golfer. Fourth alltime in career wins (60). Won the Masters four times (1958, 1960, 1962, 1964), British Open two consecutive years (1961–62) and U.S. Open (1960) and U.S. Amateur (1954) once each. PGA Player of the Year two times (1960, 1962). The first golfer to surpass $1 million in career earnings. Also won Seniors Championship two times (1980, 1984) and U.S. Senior Open once (1981).

**Jim Palmer** (b. 10-15-45): Baseball RHP. 268 career wins, 2.86 ERA. Won three Cy Young Awards (1973, consecutively 1975–76). Won 20+ games eight times. Led league in wins three times, innings pitched four times, ERA two times. Never allowed a grand slam HR. Pitched on six World Series teams with Baltimore, including shutout at age 20. Pitched no-hitter in 1969. Career span 1965–84.

**Bernie Parent** (b. 4-3-45): Hockey G. Alltime leader for wins in a season (47 in 1974). Goaltender of the Year, playoff MVP, league leader in wins, goals against average and shutouts two consecutive seasons (1974–75). Career record 270-197-121, including 55 shutouts. Career 2.55 goals against average. Tied record of four playoff shutouts in 1975. Played on two consecutive Stanley Cup champions (1974–75). Career span 1965–79 with Philadelphia.

**Brad Park** (b. 7-6-48): Hockey D. Seven-time All-Star. In 17 seasons with the New York Rangers, Boston Bruins and Detroit Red Wings (1968–69 through 1984–85) scored 213 goals and had 683 assists. Elected to Hall of Fame 1988.

**Jim Parker** (b. 4-3-34): Football T/G. Winner of 1956 Outland Trophy as Ohio State senior. Blocked for Johnny Unitas. All-NFL four times at guard, four times at tackle. Career span 1957–67, all with Baltimore Colts. Inducted to Hall of Fame in 1973.

**Joe Paterno** (b. 12-21-26): College football coach. Second alltime in wins in Division I-A (322). Has won two national championships (1982, 1986) with Penn State since 1966. Career record 322-90-3, including five undefeated seasons. Has also won 20 bowl games.

**Lester Patrick** (b. 12-30-1883, d. 6-1-60): Hockey coach. Led NY Rangers to three Stanley Cup championships (1928, '33, '40). Originated the NHL's farm system and developed playoff format.

**Floyd Patterson** (b. 1-4-35): Boxer. Heavyweight champion two times (1956-59, 1960-62). First heavyweight to regain title, in rematch with Ingemar Johansson. Career record 55-8-1 with 40 KOs from 1952 to 1972. Also middleweight gold medalist at 1952 Olympics.

**Walter Payton** (b. 7-25-54, d. 11-1-99): Football RB. "Sweetness." Alltime leader in yards rushing (16,726). Gained 1,000+ yards rushing in 10 seasons. Third alltime in rushing touchdowns (110). 125 career touchdowns. Gained a record 275 yards on 11-20-77, against Minnesota. Selected for Pro Bowl nine times. Player of the Year two times (1977, 1985). Led league in rushing five consecutive seasons. Career span 1975–87 with Chicago.

**Pelé** (b. 10-23-40): Born Edson Arantes do Nascimento. Brazilian soccer player. Soccer's great ambassador. Played on three World Cup winners with Brazil (1958, 1962, 1970). Helped promote soccer in U.S. by playing with NY Cosmos from 1975 to 1977. Scored 1,281 goals in 22 years.

**Willie Pep** (b. 9-19-22): Boxer. Featherweight champion two times (1942-48, 1949-50). Lost title to Sandy Saddler, won it back in rematch, then lost it to Saddler again. Career record 230-11-1 with 65 KOs from 1940 to 1966. Won 73 consecutive bouts from 1940 to 1943. Defended title nine times.

**Gil Perreault** (b. 11-13-50): Hockey C. NHL Rookie of the Year in 1970–71. Played 17 seasons, all with Buffalo Sabres. Scored 512 goals and had 814 assists in career. Elected to Hall of Fame in 1990.

**Fred Perry** (b. 5-18-09, d. 2-2-95): British tennis player. Won three consecutive Wimbledon singles titles (1934–36), the last British man to win the tournament. Also won three U.S. titles (consecutively 1933–34, '36), one French title (1935) and one Australian title (1934).

**Gaylord Perry** (b. 9-15-38): Baseball RHP. First pitcher to win Cy Young Award in both leagues (Cleveland 1972, San Diego 1978). 314 career wins, 3,534 strikeouts. 20+ wins five times; 200+ strikeouts eight times; 250+ innings pitched 12 times. Pitched no-hitter in 1968. Admitted to throwing a spitter. Career span 1962–83 with eight teams.

**Bob Pettit** (b. 12-12-32): Basketball F. First player in history to break 20,000-point barrier (20,880 career points scored). 26.4 career scoring average; 16.2 rebound avg. MVP in 1956, 1959; Rookie of the Year in 1955. All-Star 10 consecutive seasons. Led league in scoring two times, rebounding once. Career span 1954–64 with St. Louis.

**Richard Petty** (b. 7-2-37): Auto racer. Alltime leader in NASCAR victories (200). Daytona 500 winner (1964, '66,

'71, consecutively 1973–74, '79, '81) and NASCAR champion (1964, 1967, consecutively 1971–72, 1974–75, '79) seven times each, the most of any driver. First stock car racer to reach $1 million in earnings. Son of Lee Petty, three-time NASCAR champion (1954, consecutively 1958–59). Retired after 1992 season.

**Laffit Pincay Jr.** (b. 12-29-46): Jockey. Only jockey with more than 9,000 career victories. Among the top money-winners of all time, with more than $215,000,000 in career earnings. Won five Eclipse Awards as outstanding jockey. Rode one Kentucky Derby winner (Swale), and three Belmont winners (Conquistador Cielo, Cavaet, Swale).

**Scottie Pippen** (b. 9-25-65): Basketball F. Won six NBA titles with Chicago Bulls (consecutively 1991–1993, and 1996–1998). Tied NBA record with seven three-pointers against Utah in Game 3 of '97 Finals. Member of 1992 and '96 gold medal-winning U.S. Olympic basketball teams. Career span 1987–99 with Chicago, 1999 Houston, since 1999 with Portland.

**Jacques Plante** (b. 1-17-29, d. 2-27-86): Hockey G. First goalie to wear a mask. Third alltime in wins (435) and second lowest modern goals against average (2.38). Goaltender of the Year seven times, more than any other goalie (consecutively 1955–59, 1961, 1968). Won MVP award in 1961. Led league in goals against average eight times, wins six times and shutouts four times. Was on six Stanley Cup champions with Montreal from 1952 to 1962 and played for four other teams until retirement in 1972.

**Gary Player** (b. 11-1-35): South African golfer. Won the Masters (1961, '74, '78) and British Open (1959, '68, '74) three times each, PGA Championship two times (1962, '72) and U.S. Open (1965). Also won Seniors Championship three times (1986, '88, '90) and U.S. Senior Open two consecutive years (1987–88).

**Sam Pollock** (b. 12-15-25): Hockey executive. As general manager of Montreal from 1964 to 1978 won nine Stanley Cup championships (1965–66, 1968–69, '71, '73, 1976–78).

**Denis Potvin** (b. 10-29-53): Hockey D. Seven-time All-Star during 15-season career (1973–74 through 1987–88), all with New York Islanders. Won Calder Trophy for 1973–74 season. Won Norris Trophy three times. Captained Islanders to four Stanley Cup championships. Elected to Hall of Fame in 1991.

**Mike Powell** (b. 11-10-63): Track and field. Long jumper broke Bob Beamon's 23-year-old world record at 1991 World Championships in Tokyo with a jump of 29' 4½". Won silver in 1992 Olympics.

**Steve Prefontaine** (b. 1-25-51, d. 5-30-75): Track and field. Distance runner killed in car accident at age 24. Held every American record from 2,000 meters to 10,000 meters at the time of his death. At age 21, finished fourth in the 5,000 at the 1972 Olympics in Munich after holding lead with less than 600 meters to go.

**Annemarie Moser-Pröll** (b. 3-27-53): Austrian skier. Gold medalist in downhill at 1980 Olympics. World Cup overall champion six times, more than any other skier (consecutively 1971–75, '79).

**Alain Prost** (b. 2-24-55): French auto racer. Alltime leader in Formula 1 victories (51). Formula 1 champion four times (consecutively 1985–86, '89, '93).

**Jack Ramsay** (b. 2-21-25): Basketball coach. Coached 11 seasons at St. Joseph's University, with 234–72 record. Overall record of 864–783 as NBA coach. Coach of NBA champion 1977 Portland Trail Blazers. Elected to Hall of Fame 1992.

**Jean Ratelle** (b. 10-3-40): Hockey C. In 21-season career (1960–61 through 1980–81) with the New York Rangers and Boston Bruins, scored 491 goals and had 776 assists. Twice won Lady Byng Trophy. Elected to Hall of Fame in 1985.

**Willis Reed** (b. 6-25-42): Basketball C. Played 10 seasons (1965–74), all with the New York Knicks. Career average of 18.7 points a game. NBA Rookie of Year in 1965. Playoff MVP of both Knick championship teams, in 1970 and '73. NBA MVP in 1970. Elected to Hall of Fame in 1981.

**Harold Henry (Pee Wee) Reese** (b. 7-23-18 d. 8-14-99): Baseball SS. Played for six pennant-winning Dodger teams. Led NL in runs scored in 1949, with 132. Elected to Hall of Fame in 1984.

**Mary Lou Retton** (b. 1-24-68): Gymnast. Won one gold, one silver and two bronze medals at 1984 Olympics.

**Grantland Rice** (b. 11-1-1880, d. 7-13-54): Sportswriter. Legendary figure during sport's Golden Age of the 1920s. Wrote "For when the one great Scorer comes/ To write against your name/ He writes not that you won or lost/ But how you played the game." Also named the 1924–25 Notre Dame backfield the "Four Horsemen."

**Jerry Rice** (b. 10-13-62): Football WR. Alltime leader in touchdowns (186), touchdown receptions (176), receptions (1,290), receiving yards (19,1341) and in consecutive games with a TD reception (13 in 1988). Player of the Year in 1987 and led league in scoring (138 points on 23 touchdowns). Super Bowl MVP in 1989 with record 215 receiving yards on 11 catches. Also set Super Bowl record with three touchdown receptions in 1990 and in 1995. Career span 1985–01 with San Francisco 49ers, 2001–present with Oakland Raiders.

**Henri Richard** (b. 2-29-36): Hockey C. "The Pocket Rocket." Won 11 Stanley Cup championships with Montreal. Four-time All-Star. Career span 1955–75.

**Maurice Richard** (b. 8-4-21, d. 5-27-00): Hockey RW. "The Rocket." First player ever to score 50 goals in a season, in 1945. Led league in goals five times. 544 career goals. MVP in 1947. All-Star eight times. Tied playoff game record for most goals (five on March 23, 1944). Won eight Stanley Cups with Montreal 1942–59.

**Bob Richards** (b. 2-2-26): Track and field. The only pole vaulter to win gold medal at two consecutive Olympics (1952, 1956). Also won Sullivan Award in 1951.

**Branch Rickey** (b. 12-20-1881, d. 12-9-65): Baseball executive. Integrated major league baseball in 1947 by signing Jackie Robinson to contract with Brooklyn Dodgers. Conceived minor league farm system in 1919 at St. Louis; instituted batting cage and sliding pit.

**Pat Riley** (b. 3-20-45): Basketball coach. Most career playoff wins (155). Coached Los Angeles to four championships, two consecutively, from 1981 to 1989. 60+ wins seven times (four times consecutively), 50+ wins five other times. Coach of the Year in 1990, '93 and '97. Led New York Knicks to NBA Finals in 1994, then left three weeks later to become coach and part owner of Miami Heat.

**Cal Ripken Jr.** (b. 8-24-60): Baseball SS–3B. Broke Lou Gehrig's record for most consecutive games played (2,131) on Sept. 5, 1995; streak ended at 2,632 games on Sept. 20, 1998. Set record for consecutive

errorless games by a shortstop (95 in 1990). MVP in 1983 and '91. Rookie of the Year in 1982. Hit 20+ HRs in 10 consecutive seasons; elected to 19th All-Star game in 2001.

**Glenn (Fireball) Roberts** (b. 1-20-31, d. 7-2-64): Auto racer. Won 34 NASCAR races. Died as a result of fiery accident in World 600 at Charlotte Motor Speedway in May 1964. At time of his death had won more major races than any other driver in NASCAR history.

**Oscar Robertson** (b. 11-24-38): Basketball G. "The Big O." 9,887 career assists; 26,710 points, 25.7 ppg. MVP in 1964, All-Star nine consecutive seasons and 1961 Rookie of the Year. Led league in assists six times, free throw percentage two times. Averaged 30+ points six times in seven seasons, 20+ points four other times. Only player in history to average a season triple-double (1961). Career span 1960–72 with Cincinnati, Milwaukee. Also College Player of the Year, All-America and NCAA scoring leader three consecutive seasons from 1958 to 1960 with Cincinnati. Third all-time NCAA highest scoring average (33.8); seventh most points scored (2,973).

**Brooks Robinson** (b. 5-18-37): Baseball 3B. Alltime leader in assists, putouts, double plays and fielding average among 3rd basemen. Won 16 consecutive Gold Gloves. Led league in fielding average a record 11 times. MVP in 1964—led league in RBI—and MVP in 1970 World Series. Career span 1955–77 with Baltimore.

**David Robinson** (b. 8-6-65): Basketball C. *Sporting News* Player of the Year in 1987. Led college players in 1986 in both rebounding (13.0) and blocked shots (5.91). 1990 NBA Rookie of the Year. Led NBA in rebounding 1991 (13.0), in scoring in '94 (29.8) and in blocked shots in '92, when he was named Defensive Player of the Year. Named NBA MVP in 1995. Member of 1988, '92 and '96 Olympic teams. Career span since 1989 with San Antonio. Won NBA title with Spurs in '99.

**Eddie Robinson** (b. 2-13-19): College football coach. Retired with alltime college record 408 career wins through 1941–97 at Division I-AA Grambling State.

**Frank Robinson** (b. 8-31-35): Baseball OF–manager. Only player to win MVP awards in both leagues (Cincinnati, 1961, Baltimore, 1966). Won Triple Crown and World Series MVP in 1966. Rookie of the Year in 1956. Fourth in career HR (586). 30+ HR 11 times; 100+ RBI six times; 100+ runs scored eight times (led league three times). Had .300+ batting average nine times. Became first black manager in major leagues, with Cleveland in 1975. Career span as player 1956–76. Career span as manager 1975–77 with Cleveland; 1981–84 with San Francisco; 1988–91 with Baltimore.

**Jackie Robinson** (b. 1-13-19, d. 10-24-72): Baseball 2B. Broke the color barrier as first black player in major leagues in 1947 with Brooklyn Dodgers. 1947 Rookie of the Year; 1949 MVP with .342 batting average to lead league. Had .311 career batting average. Led league in stolen bases two times; stole home 19 times. Played on six pennant winners in 10 years with Brooklyn. Elected to Hall of Fame in 1962. No. 42 retired by every team in the major leagues.

**Larry Robinson** (b. 6-2-51): Hockey D. Twice won Norris Trophy as NHL's top defenseman. Career span 1972–73 through 1991–92, all but the last three with the Montreal Canadiens. Member of six Montreal teams that won Stanley Cup. Awarded Conn Smythe Trophy as MVP of 1978 Stanley Cup. Coached New Jersey to Stanley Cup in 2000.

**Sugar Ray Robinson** (b. 5-3-21, d. 4-12-89): Born Walker Smith Jr. Boxer. Called best pound-for-pound boxer ever. Welterweight champ (1946–51) and middleweight champ five times. Career record: 174-19-6 with 109 KOs from 1940–65. Won 91 consecutive bouts from 1943–51. Fifteen losses came after age 35.

**Knute Rockne** (b. 3-4-1888, d. 3-31-31): College football coach. Won national championship three times (1924, consecutively 1929–30). Alltime highest winning percentage (.881). Career record 105-12-5, including five undefeated seasons, with Notre Dame from 1918 to 1930.

**Bill Rodgers** (b. 12-23-47): Track and field. Won the Boston and New York City marathons four times each between 1975 and 1980.

**Dennis Rodman** (b. 5-13-61): Basketball F. NBA Defensive Player of the Year 1990, '91. First player to win seven consecutive rebounding titles; won NBA titles with Detroit 1989 and '90 and Chicago 1996–98. Career span 1986–93 with Detroit, '93–95 with San Antonio, '95–98 with Chicago, '99 with LA, and '00 with Dallas.

**Chi Chi Rodriguez** (b. 10-23-35): Golfer. Led senior money list for 1987 ($509,145). Won eight events during PGA career that began in 1960.

**Art Rooney** (b. 1-27-01; d. 8-25-88): Owner of Pittsburgh Steelers. Bought team in 1933 and ran it until his death in 1988. Elected to Hall of Fame in 1964.

**Murray Rose** (b. 1-6-39) Australian swimmer. Won three gold medals (including 400- and 1,500-meter freestyle) at 1956 Olympics. Also won one gold, one silver and one bronze medal at 1960 Olympics.

**Pete Rose** (b. 4-14-41): Baseball OF-IF. "Charlie Hustle." Alltime leader in hits (4,256), games played (3,562) and at bats (14,053); second in doubles (746); fourth in runs scored (2,165). Had .303 career average and won three batting titles. Averaged .300+ 15 times, 200+ hits and 100+ runs scored each 10 times. Led league in hits seven times, runs scored four times, doubles five times. 1963 Rookie of the Year; 1973 MVP; 1975 World Series MVP. Had 44-game hitting streak in 1978. Played in 17 All-Star games, starting at five different positions. Career span 1963–86 with Cincinnati, Philadelphia and Montreal. Manager of Cincinnati from 1984 to 1989. Banned from baseball for life by Commissioner Bart Giamatti in 1989 for betting activities. Served five-month jail term for tax evasion in 1990. Ineligible for Baseball Hall of Fame.

**Ken Rosewall** (b. 11-2-34): Australian tennis player. Won Grand Slam singles titles at ages 18 and 35. Won four Australian titles (1953, '55, consecutively 1971–72), two French titles (1953, '68) and two U.S. titles (1956, '70). Reached four Wimbledon finals, but title eluded him.

**Art Ross** (b. 1-13-1886, d. 8-5-64): Hockey D–coach. Improved design of puck and goal net. Manager-coach of Boston, 1924–45, won Stanley Cup, 1938–39. The Art Ross Trophy is awarded to the NHL scoring champion.

**Donald Ross** (b. 1873, d. 4-26-48): Scottish-born golf course architect. Trained at St. Andrews under Old Tom Morris. Designed over 500 courses, including Pinehurst No. 2 course and Oakland Hills.

**Patrick Roy** (b. 10-5-65): Hockey G. Alltime leader in career wins for a goalie (484). Won Vezina Trophy three times. Won Conn Smythe Trophy three times (1986, '93, '01). Career span 1984–95 Montreal, '95– Colorado.

**Pete Rozelle** (b. 3-1-26, d. 12-6-96): Football executive. Fourth NFL commissioner, served from 1960 to 1989. During his term, league expanded from 12 to 28 teams. Created Super Bowl in 1966 and negotiated merger with AFL. Devised plan for revenue sharing of lucrative TV monies among owners. Presided during players' strikes of 1982, '87.

**Wilma Rudolph** (b. 6-23-40, d. 11-12-94): Track and field. Gold medalist in three events (100 , 200 and 4 x 100-meter relay) at 1960 Olympics. Also won Sullivan Award in 1961.

**Adolph Rupp** (b. 9-2-01, d. 12-10-77): College basketball coach. Second alltime in NCAA wins (876) and third highest winning percentage (.822). Won four NCAA championships: consecutively 1948–49, '51, '58. Career span 1930–72 with Kentucky.

**Amos Rusie** (b. 5-3-1871, d. 12-6-42): Baseball RHP. Fastball was so intimidating that in 1893 the pitching mound was moved back 5' 6" to its present distance of 60' 6". Led league in strikeouts and walks five times each. Career record 246–174, 3.07 ERA with New York (NL) from 1889–1901.

**Bill Russell** (b. 2-12-34): Basketball C. Won MVP award five times (1958, consecutively 1961–63, '65). Played on 11 championship teams, eight consecutively, with Boston (1957, 1959–66, 1968–69). Player-coach 1968–69 (league's first black coach). Second alltime in career rebounds (21,620) and second highest rebounding average (22.5); second-highest single-game rebounding total (51 in 1960). Led league in rebounding four times. Also played on two consecutive NCAA championship teams with San Francisco in 1955–56; tournament MVP in 1955. Member of gold medal-winning 1956 Olympic team.

**Babe Ruth** (b. 2-6-1895, d. 8-16-48): Born George Herman Ruth. Baseball P–OF. Most dominant player in history. Alltime leader in slugging average (.690), HR frequency (8.5 HR every 100 at bats); second in career HR (714), RBI (2,211), and walks (2,056). Second-highest single-season slugging average (.847 in 1920). 1923 high .342 career batting average and 2,873 hits. 60 HR in 1927, 50+ HR three other times and 40+ HR seven other times; 100+ RBI and 100+ walks 13 times each; 100+ runs scored 12 times. Second alltime in World Series HR (15), including his "called shot" off Charlie Root in 1932. Began career as a pitcher for Boston Red Sox: 94 career wins and 2.28 ERA. Won 20+ games two times; ERA leader in 1916. Played on 10 pennant winners, seven World Series winners (three with Boston, four with New York). Sold to Yankees in 1920 (Boston hasn't won World Series since). Career span 1914–35.

**Nolan Ryan** (b. 1-31-47): Baseball RHP. Alltime leader in strikeouts (5,714), walks (2,795). Pitched seven no-hitters. League leader in strikeouts 11 times, walks eight times, shutouts three times, ERA two times. 300+ strikeouts six times, including season record of 383 in 1973. 324 career wins. Career span 1966–93 with New York (NL), California, Houston, Texas. Elected to Hall of Fame 1999.

**Jim Ryun** (b. 4-29-47): Track and field. Youngest ever to run under four minutes for the mile (3:59.0 at 17 years, 37 days). Set two world records in mile (3:51.3 in 1966 and 3:51.1 in 1967) and one in 1,500 (3:33.1 in 1967). Plagued by bad luck at Olympics; won silver medal in 1968 1,500 meters despite mononucleosis; was bumped and fell in 1972. Won Sullivan Award in 1967.

**Toni Sailer** (b. 11-17-35): Austrian skier. Won gold medals in 1956 Olympics in slalom, giant slalom and downhill, the first skier to accomplish the feat.

**Juan Antonio Samaranch** (b. 7-17-20): Amateur sports executive. From 1980 to 2001, Spaniard served as president of International Olympic Committee.

**Pete Sampras** (b. 8-12-71): Tennis player. First player in ATP rankings history to hold No. 1 ranking for six consecutive years. Won seventh Wimbledon title in 2000 to surpass Roy Emerson's record of 12 Grand Slam singles titles.

**Joan Benoit Samuelson** (b. 5-16-57): Track and field. Gold medalist in first ever women's Olympic marathon (1984). Won Boston Marathon two times (1979, 1983). Sullivan Award winner in 1985.

**Barry Sanders** (b. 7-16-68): Football RB. Alltime NCAA season leader in yards rushing (2,628 in 1988). Won Heisman Trophy in 1988 at Oklahoma State. Entered NFL in 1989 with Detroit and named Rookie of the Year. Gained 1,000+ yards rushing in each of his 10 seasons. Retired abruptly in 1999, ranked second alltime in career rushing yards (15,269). Third player to rush for over 2,000 yards (2,053 in 1997). Led league in rushing in 1990, '94 and 1996–97.

**Gene Sarazen** (b. 2-27-02 d. 5-13-99): Golfer. Won PGA Championship three times (consecutively 1922-23, 1933), U.S. Open two times (1922, 1932), British Open once (1932) and the Masters once (1935). His win at the Masters included golf's most famous shot, a double eagle on the 15th hole of the final round to tie Craig Wood (Sarazen then won the playoff). Won 38 career tournaments. Also won Seniors Championship two times (1954, 1958). Pioneered the sand wedge in 1930.

**Glen Sather** (b. 9-2-43): Hockey coach and general manager. As coach, third alltime in career winning percentage (.616). 464 regular season wins. Led Edmonton to four Stanley Cup championships (consecutively 1984–85, 1987–88) from 1979 to 1989 and 1993–94. Also played for six teams from 1966 to 1976.

**Terry Sawchuk** (b. 12-28-29): Hockey G. Alltime leader in shutouts (103); second in wins (447). Career 2.52 goals against average. Goaltender of the Year four times (consecutively 1951–52, 1954, 1964). Led league in wins and shutouts three times and goals against average two times. Rookie of the Year in 1950. Tied record of four playoff shutouts in 1952. Played on four Stanley Cup champions with Detroit and Toronto from 1949 to 1969.

**Gale Sayers** (b. 5-30-43): Football RB. Alltime leader in kickoff return average (30.6). Scored 56 career touchdowns, including a rookie record 22 in 1965. Led league in rushing and gained 1,000+ yards rushing two times. Averaged five yards per carry. Rookie of the Year in 1965. Tied record with six rushing touchdowns on Dec. 12, 1965. Career span 1965–71 with Chicago cut short due to knee injury. Also All-America two times with Kansas.

**Dolph Schayes** (b. 5-19-28): Basketball player. College star at NYU. In 1960 became first NBA player to reach 15,000 career points. Also first NBA player to play in 1,000 games. Led NBA in free throw percentage three times, and shot .843 for his career. Over stretch of 10 years played in 706 consecutive games. Elected to Hall of Fame 1972.

**Bo Schembechler** (b. 4-1-29): Football coach. In 21 seasons at Michigan from 1969–89, had a 194-48-5 record. Overall college coaching went 234-65-8.

**Mike Schmidt** (b. 9-27-49): Baseball 3B. Won three MVP awards (1980, '81, '86). 548 career HR, ninth alltime. Led league in HR eight times, slugging average five times and RBI, walks and strikeouts four times

each. 40+ HR three times, 30+ HR 10 other times; 100+ RBI nine times, 100+ runs scored seven times, 100+ strikeouts 12 times and third in career strikeouts (1,883). 100+ walks seven times. Won 10 Gold Gloves. Career span 1972–89 with Philadelphia. Elected to the Hall of Fame in 1995.

**Don Schollander** (b. 4-30-46): Swimmer. Won four gold medals (including 100- and 400-meter freestyle) at 1964 Olympics; won one gold and one silver medal at 1968 Olympics. Also won Sullivan Award in 1964.

**Dick Schultz** (b. 9-5-29): Amateur sports executive. Second executive director of the NCAA, served from 1987 to '93. Also served as athletic director at Cornell (1976–81) and Virginia (1981–87).

**Seattle Slew** (b. 1974): Thoroughbred race horse. Horse of the Year for 1977, when he won the Triple Crown, winning the Kentucky Derby by 1¾ lengths; the Preakness by 1½; and the Belmont by 4. In three-year career from 1976–78, won 14 of 17 starts.

**Tom Seaver** (b. 11-17-44): Baseball RHP. "Tom Terrific." 311 career wins. 2.86 ERA. Cy Young Award winner three times (1969, 1973, 1975) and Rookie of the Year 1967. Fifth alltime in career strikeouts (3,640). Led league in strikeouts five times, winning percentage four times and wins and ERA three times each. Won 20+ games five times; 200+ strikeouts 10 times. Struck out 19 batters in one game in 1970, including the final 10 in succession. Pitched no-hitter in 1978. Career span 1967–86 with New York Mets, Cincinnati, Chicago White Sox, Boston.

**Secretariat** (b. 3-30-70, d. 10-4-89): Thoroughbred race horse. Triple Crown winner in 1973 with jockey Ron Turcotte aboard. Trained by Lucien Laurin.

**Katja Seizinger** (b. 5-10-72): German skier. Won downhill gold medals in 1994 at Lillehammer and '98 at Nagano. Won Giant Slalom bronze medal at Nagano. 1998 World Cup champion in downhill, Super G and overall. 32 World Cup victories in downhill and Super G.

**Monica Seles** (b. 12-2-73): Tennis player. Won three consecutive French Open singles titles (1990-92), four Australian Open titles (1991–93, '96) and two U.S. Open titles (1991–92). Seles's 1993 season ended on April 30 when she was stabbed in the back by Gunther Parche while seated during a changeover in a tournament in Hamburg, Germany; also missed 1994 season. Returned to tennis in 1995, reached U.S. Open final.

**Bill Sharman** (b. 5-25-26): Basketball G. First team All-Star four straight years 1956–59. Led NBA in free throw percentage every year from 1953–57, and in 1959 and '61. All-Star Game MVP in 1955. NBA Coach of the Year in 1972, when his Lakers won NBA title. Elected to Hall of Fame in 1974.

**Wilbur Shaw** (b. 10-31-02, d. 10-30-54): Auto racer. Won Indy 500 three times in four years (1937, consecutively 1939-40). AAA champion two times (1937, 1939). Also pioneered the use of the crash helmet after suffering skull fracture in 1923 crash.

**Patty Sheehan** (b. 10-27-56): Golfer. Won back-to-back LPGA championships, 1983–84. Won 1992 and '94 U.S. Women's Opens, '93 LPGA title, '96 Nabisco. 1983 LPGA Player of Year. Vare Trophy winner in 1984. Qualified for Hall of Fame in 1993.

**Fred Shero** (b. 10-23-25, d. 11-24-90): Hockey coach. Fourth alltime highest winning percentage (.612, regular season). Led Philadelphia to two Stanley Cup championships (1974-75). Also coached NY Rangers. Played defense for NY Rangers, 1947–50.

**Bill Shoemaker** (b. 8-19-31): Horse racing jockey. Second alltime in wins (8,833). Rode Belmont Stakes winner five times (1957, 1959, 1962, 1967, 1975), Kentucky Derby winner four times (1955, 1959, 1965, 1986—at age 54, the oldest jockey to win Derby) and Preakness Stakes winner two times (1963, 1967). Also won Eclipse Award in 1981.

**Eddie Shore** (b. 11-25-02, d. 3-16-85): Hockey D. Won MVP award four times (1933, consecutively 1935–36, 1938). All-Star seven times. Played on two Stanley Cup champions with Boston from 1926 to 1940.

**Frank Shorter** (b. 10-31-47): Track and field. Gold medalist in marathon at 1972 Olympics, the first American to win the event since 1908. Olympic silver medalist in 1976 marathon. Sullivan Award winner in 1972.

**Jim Shoulders** (b. 5-13-28): Rodeo. Sixteen career titles. All-Around champion five times (1949, consecutively 1956–59).

**Don Shula** (b. 1-4-30): Football coach. Alltime leader in wins (347). Won two consecutive Super Bowl championships (1972–73) with Miami, including NFL's only undefeated season in 1972. Also reached Super Bowl four other times. Career span 1963–70 with Baltimore, 1970–95 Miami.

**Al Simmons** (b. 5-22-02; d. 5-26-56): Baseball OF. "Bucketfoot Al" for hitting stance. Named AL MVP for 1929, when he led league with 157 RBI. Led league in batting average in 1930 (.381) and '31 (.390). Lifetime average of .334 with 307 homers. Career span 1924–44 with a variety of teams, but mostly Philadelphia A's. Elected to Hall of Fame in 1953.

**O.J. Simpson** (b. 7-9-47): Given name Orenthal James. "Juice" Football RB. 11,236 career yards rushing. Gained 1,000+ yards rushing five consecutive seasons, including then-record 2,003 yards in 1973. Player of the Year three times (consecutively 1972–73, 1975). Led league in rushing four times. Gained 200+ yards rushing in a game a record six times, including 273 rush on Nov. 25, 1976. Scored 61 career touchdowns, including 23 in 1975. Also won Heisman Trophy with USC in 1968.

**Sir Barton** (b. 1916, d. 1937): Thoroughbred. In 1919, before they were linked as the Triple Crown, became first horse to win the Kentucky Derby, the Preakness and the Belmont. Won eight of 13 starts as 3-year-old.

**George Sisler** (b. 3-24-1893, d. 3-26-73): Baseball 1B. His 257 hit total in 1920 season is alltime major league record. League leader in hits two times, banged out 200+ hits six times. Won two batting titles, including with .420 average in 1922; averaged .400+ two times and .300+ 11 other times. Had 2,812 career hits and a .340 lifetime batting average. Career span 1915–30 with St. Louis.

**Mary Decker Slaney** (b. 8-4-58): Track and field. American record holder in five events ranging from 800 to 3,000 meters. Won 1,500 and 3,000 meters at World Championships in 1983. Lost chance for medal at 1984 Olympics when she tripped and fell after contact with Zola Budd. Won Sullivan Award in 1982. Competed in 1996 Olympics at age 37.

**Bruce Smith** (b. 6-18-63): Football DE. Second alltime in NFL sacks. Played in four consecutive Super Bowls with the Bills (1991–94), all losses. Career span 1985–00 with Buffalo, 2000–01 with Washington.

**Dean Smith** (b. 2-28-31): College basketball coach. Alltime leader in wins (879); sixth alltime highest winning percentage (.776). Alltime most NCAA

tournament appearances (27), reached Final Four 11 times. Won NCAA championship in 1982 and '93. Coached 1976 Olympic team to gold medal. Career span 1962–97 with North Carolina. 1997 *Sports Illustrated* Sportsman of the Year.

**Emmitt Smith** (b. 5-15-69): Football RB. Led NFL in rushing in 1991, '92 , '93 and '95. Then-record 25 TDs in 1995. Rushed for 108 yards in 52–17 Cowboys win over Bills in Super Bowl XXVII. Rushed for 132 yards and named MVP of Super Bowl XXVIII, a 30–13 Dallas victory over Buffalo. Career span since 1990 with Cowboys.

**Ozzie Smith** (b. 12-26-54): Baseball SS. "The Wizard of Oz." May be the best defensive shortstop in history. Holds alltime record for most assists in a season among shortstops (621 in 1980). Career double-play and assist leader among shortstops. 14-time All-Star. Won 13 consecutive Gold Gloves. Career span 1978–96 with San Diego, St. Louis.

**Red Smith** (b. 9-25-05, d. 1-15-82): Sportswriter. Won Pulitzer Prize in 1976. After Grantland Rice, the most widely syndicated sports columnist. His literary essays appeared in the *NY Herald Tribune* from 1945 to 1971 and the *NY Times* from 1971 to 1982.

**Stan Smith** (b. 12-14-46): Tennis. Won 39 tournaments in career, including 1972 Wimbledon in five sets over Ilie Nastase. Won 1971 U.S. Open over Jan Kodes and amateur version of U.S. Open in 1969. 1970 won inaugural Grand Prix Masters. Inducted to Tennis Hall of Fame in 1987.

**Tommie Smith** (b. 6-5-44): Track and field. Sprinter won 1968 Olympic 200 meters in world record of 19.83, then was expelled from Olympic Village, along with bronze medalist John Carlos, for raising black-gloved fist and bowing head during playing of national anthem to protest racism in U.S.

**Conn Smythe** (b. 2-1-1895, d. 11-18-80): Hockey executive. As general manager with Toronto from 1929 to 1961 won seven Stanley Cup championships (1932, '42, '45, consecutively 1947–49, '51). Award for playoff MVP named in his honor.

**Sam Snead** (b. 5-27-12): Golfer. Alltime leader in career wins (81). Won the Masters (1949, '52, '54) and PGA Championship (1942, '49, '51) three times each and British Open (1946). Runner-up at U.S. Open four times, but title eluded him. PGA Player of the Year in 1949. Won Seniors Championship six times, more than any golfer (1964–65, '67, '70, 1972–73).

**Peter Snell** (b. 12-17-38): Track and field. New Zealand runner was gold medalist in 800 meters at two consecutive Olympics in 1960, '64. Also gold medalist in 1,500 meters at 1964 Olympics. Twice broke world mile record; broke world 800 record once.

**Duke Snider** (b. 9-19-26): Baseball OF. Career .295 average, 407 HR and 1,333 RBI. Hit 40+ HR five consecutive seasons and 100+ RBI six times. Also led league in runs scored three consecutive seasons. Played on six pennant winners with the Brooklyn Dodgers. World Series total of 11 HR and 26 RBI are NL best. Career span 1947–64.

**Sammy Sosa** (b. 11-12-68): Baseball RF. Followed Mark McGwire in eclipsing Roger Maris's single-season HR mark in 1998. Lost HR race to McGwire that season but won MVP with .308 average, 66 HR, 134 runs, 158 RBI. In 2001, became first man to hit 60+ home runs in three seasons. Career span 1989 with Texas; 1989–91 with Chicago White Sox; 1992– with Chicago Cubs.

**Javier Sotomayor** (b. 10-13-67): Track and field. Cuban high jumper broke the 8-foot barrier with world record jump of 8' 0" in 1989. Set record of 8' ½" in 7-27-93 in Salamanca, Spain.

**Warren Spahn** (b. 4-23-21): Baseball LHP. Alltime leader in games won for a lefthander (363): 20+ wins 13 times. League leader in wins eight times (five seasons consecutively), complete games nine times (seven seasons consecutively), strikeouts four consecutive seasons, innings pitched four times and ERA three times. 1957 Cy Young award. 63 career shutouts. Pitched two no-hitters after age 39. Career span 1942–65, all but last year with Boston Braves, Milwaukee.

**Tris Speaker** (b. 4-4-1888, d. 12-8-58): Baseball OF. Alltime leader in doubles (792), fifth in hits (3,514) and fifth in batting average (.345). One batting title (.386 in 1916), but .375+ average six times and .300+ average 12 other times. League leader in doubles eight times, hits two times and HR and RBI one time each. 200+ hits four times, 40+ doubles 10 times and 100+ runs scored seven times. MVP in 1912. Career span 1907–28 with Boston, Cleveland.

**Michael Spinks** (b. 7-13-56): Boxer. 1976 Olympic middleweight champion. Won world light heavyweight title on 7-18-81. Defended it five times and consolidated light heavy titles with decision over Dwight Braxton on 3-18-83. Defended four more times. Won heavyweight title on 9-22-85 in decision over Larry Holmes. Lost title to Mike Tyson in 91 seconds on 6-27-88.

**Mark Spitz** (b. 2-10-50): Swimmer. Won a record seven gold medals (two in freestyle, two in butterfly, three in relays) at 1972 Olympics, setting world record in each event. Also won two gold medals and one silver and one bronze medal at 1968 Olympics. Sullivan Award winner in 1971.

**Amos Alonzo Stagg** (b. 8-16-1862, d. 3-17-65): College football coach. 314 career wins. Won national title with Chicago in 1905. Coach of the Year with Pacific in 1943 at age 81. Five undefeated seasons. Career span 1892 to 1946. Only person elected to both college football and basketball Halls of Fame. Played in the first basketball game in 1891.

**Willie Stargell** (b. 3-6-40, d. 4-9-01): Baseball OF–1B. "Pops" achieved a 1979 MVP triple crown, winning NL regular season, playoff and World Series MVP awards. Led NL in homers in 1971 and '73. Hit 475 career homers. Drove in 1,540 runs. Had .282 career batting average. Played all 21 seasons with the Pirates. Elected to Hall of Fame in 1988.

**Bart Starr** (b. 1-9-34): Football QB. Played on three NFL champions (consecutively 1961–62, '65) and first two Super Bowl champions (1966–67) with Green Bay. Also named MVP of first two Super Bowls. Player of the Year in 1966. Led league in passing three times. Also coached Green Bay to 53-77-3 record from 1975 to 1983.

**Roger Staubach** (b. 2-5-42): Football QB. Won Heisman Trophy with Navy as a junior in 1963. Served four-year military obligation before turning pro. Led Dallas to six NFC Championships, four Super Bowls and two Super Bowl titles (1971, '77). Player of the Year and Super Bowl MVP in 1971. Also led league in passing four times. Career span 1969–79.

**Jan Stenerud** (b. 11-26-42): Football K. Scored 1,699 career NFL points. Converted 373 field goals in 558 attempts. Career span 1967–79 with Kansas City Chiefs, 1980–83 with Green Bay Packers and 1984–85 with Minnesota Vikings. First pure kicker inducted to Hall of Fame, 1991.

**Casey Stengel** (b. 7-30-1890, d. 9-29-75): Baseball manager. "The Ol' Perfesser." Managed New York Yankees to 10 pennants and seven World Series titles (five consecutively) in 12 years from 1949 to 1960. Alltime leader in World Series games (63), wins (37) and losses (26). Platoon system was his trademark strategy, Stengelese his trademark language ("You could look it up."). Managed New York Mets from 1962 to 1965. Jersey number (37) retired by Yankees and Mets.

**Ingemar Stenmark** (b. 3-18-56): Swedish skier. Gold medalist in slalom and giant slalom at 1980 Olympics. World Cup overall champion three consecutive years (1976–78).

**Woody Stephens** (b. 9-1-13 d. 8-22-98): Horse racing trainer. Trained two Kentucky Derby winners (Cannonade, who won the 100th Derby in 1974 and Swale in 1984) and five straight Belmont winners from 1982–86, starting with 1982 Horse of the Year Conquistador Cielo.

**David Stern** (b. 9-22-42): Fourth NBA commissioner. Has served since 1984. Oversaw unprecedented growth of league. Owners rewarded him with five-year, $40-million contract extension in 1996.

**Jackie Stewart** (b. 6-11-39): Scottish auto racer. Fifth alltime in Formula 1 victories (27); Formula 1 champion three times (1969, '71, '73). Also Indy 500 Rookie of the Year in 1966. Retired in 1973.

**Payne Stewart** (b. 1-3-57, d. 10-25-99): Golfer. Two-time U.S. Open champion (1991, '99), also won 1989 PGA Championship. Killed in plane crash.

**John Stockton** (b. 3-26-62): Basketball G. Alltime leader in assists (14,503) and steals (2,976). Set single-season assist record of 1,164 in 1990–91. Led NBA in assists a record nine consecutive times, 1988–96. Ten-time All-Star, consecutively 1989–97, 2000. Co-MVP (with Karl Malone) of 1993 All-Star Game. Member of 1992 and '96 Olympic teams. Career span since 1984 with Utah.

**Picabo Street** (b. 4-3-71): Skier. Won silver medal in downhill at 1994 Olympics in Lillehammer and gold in Super G at '98 Games in Nagano. World Cup downhill champion in 1995 and '96. Nine career World Cup victories.

**John L. Sullivan** (b. 10-15-1858, d. 2-2-18): Boxer. Last bareknuckle champion. Heavyweight title holder (1882–92), lost to Jim Corbett. Career record 38-1-3 with 33 KOs from 1878 to 1892.

**Paul Tagliabue** (b. 11-24-40): Football executive. Fifth NFL commissioner, has served since 1989.

**Anatoli Tarasov** (b. 1918, d. 6-23-95): Hockey coach. Orchestrated Soviet Union's emergence as a hockey power. Won nine consecutive world amateur championships (1963–71) and three Olympic gold medals in 1964, '68, '72.

**Fran Tarkenton** (b. 2-3-40): Football QB. Hall of Famer retired with 342 touchdown passes, 47,003 yards passing, 6,467 pass attempts and 3,686 pass completions. Player of the Year in 1975. Career span 1961–78 with Minnesota, NY Giants.

**Lawrence Taylor** (b. 2-4-59): Football LB. Revolutionized the linebacker position. Ended 1993 season as the alltime leader in sacks. Also named to Pro Bowl a record 10 consecutive seasons. Player of the Year in 1986. Played on two Super Bowl champions with New York Giants (1986, '90). Career span 1981–93 with Giants. Elected to Hall of Fame 1999.

**Isiah Thomas** (b. 4-30-61): Basketball G. Member of Indiana University team that won 1981 NCAA title. Point guard for Detroit Pistons 1982–94. All-NBA First Team 1984, '85 and '86. NBA All-Star Game MVP both 1984 and '86. Led NBA in assists (13.9) in 1984–85. Fifth alltime in assists (9,061). Member of Pistons team that won NBA title in both 1989 and '90. GM of Toronto Raptors 1995–97. Named head coach of Indiana Pacers in 2000.

**Thurman Thomas** (b. 5-15-66): Football RB. Led AFC in rushing both 1990 (1,297 yards) and '91 (1,407). Career span 1988–00 with Buffalo Bills., 2000–01 with Miami Dolphins.

**Daley Thompson** (b. 7-30-58): Track and field. British decathlete was gold medalist at two consecutive Olympics in 1980, '84. At 1984 Olympics set world record (8,847 points) that lasted eight years.

**John Thompson** (b. 9-2-41): College basketball coach. Coached at Georgetown (1973–99), where he mentored Patrick Ewing, Alonzo Mourning and Dikembe Mutombo. Won NCAA title in 1984, runner-up in '82 and '85.

**Bobby Thomson** (b. 10-25-23): Baseball OF. Hit dramatic ninth-inning playoff home run to win NL pennant for New York Giants on Oct. 3, 1951. The Giants came from 13½ games behind the Brooklyn Dodgers on Aug. 11 to win the pennant on Thomson's three-run homer off Ralph Branca in the final game of the three-game playoff.

**Jim Thorpe** (b. 5-28-1888, d. 3-28-53): Sportsman. Gold medalist in decathlon and pentathlon at 1912 Olympics. Played pro baseball with New York (NL) and Cincinnati 1913–19, and pro football with several teams 1919–26. Also All-America two times with Carlisle.

**Dick Tiger** (b. 8-14-29; d. 12-14-71): Nigerian boxer. Born Richard Ihetu. Two-time middleweight champ, also won light heavyweight title Fighter of the Year for 1962 and '65. Elected to Boxing Hall of Fame 1974.

**Bill Tilden** (b. 2-10-1893, d. 6-5-53): Tennis player. "Big Bill." Won seven U.S. singles titles, six consecutively (1920–25, '29) and three Wimbledon titles (consecutively 1920–21, '30). Also won six Grand Slam doubles titles. Led U.S. to seven consecutive Davis Cup victories (1920–26).

**Ted Tinling** (b. 6-23-10, d. 5-23-90): British tennis couturier. The premier source of women's tennis fashion, from Suzanne Lenglen to Steffi Graf—most notable creation: the frilled lace panties worn by Gorgeous Gussy Moran at Wimbledon in 1949.

**Y.A. Tittle** (b. 10-24-26): Football QB. Threw 33 TD passes in 1962 and in '63 led league in passing, completing 221 of 367 attempts for 3,145 yards and 36 TDs. Career span 1948–64, mostly with San Francisco 49ers and New York Giants. Inducted into Hall of Fame 1971.

**Jayne Torvill/Christopher Dean** (b. 10-7-57/ b. 7-27-58): British figure skaters. Won four consecutive ice dancing world championships (1981–84) and Olympic ice dancing gold medal (1984). Won world professional championships in 1985. Won Olympic ice dancing bronze in 1994.

**Vladislav Tretiak** (b. 4-25-52): Hockey G. Led USSR to gold medals at Olympics in 1972, '76, '84. Played on 13 world amateur champions from 1970 to 1984.

**Lee Trevino** (b. 12-1-39): Golfer. Won U.S. Open (1968, '71), British Open (consecutively 1971–72) and PGA Championship (1974, '84) two times each. PGA

Player of the Year in 1971. Also won U.S. Senior Open in 1990. First Senior $1 million season.

**Emlen Tunnell** (b. 3-29-25, d. 7-23-75): Football S. Alltime leader in interception return yardage with 1,282 and second in interceptions (79). All-Pro nine times. Career span 1948–61 with New York Giants and Green Bay.

**Gene Tunney** (b. 5-25-1897, d. 11-7-78): Boxer. Heavyweight champion (1926–28). Defeated Jack Dempsey two times, including famous "long count" bout. Career record 65-2-1 with 43 KOs from 1915 to 1928. Retired as champion.

**Ted Turner** (b. 11-19-38): Sportsman. Skipper who successfully defended the America's Cup in 1977. Also owner of the Atlanta Braves since 1976 and Hawks since '77. Founded the Goodwill Games in 1986.

**Mike Tyson** (b. 6-30-66): Boxer. Youngest heavyweight champion at 20 years old in 1986. Held title until knocked out by James (Buster) Douglas on 2-10-90. Convicted of rape in 1992, released from prison in 1995. Lost WBA title to Evander Holyfield on 11-9-96. In one of boxing's more bizarre episodes, disqualified from rematch on 6-28-97 for biting Holyfield's ears. Career record: 48–3, 41 KOs.

**Johnny Unitas** (b. 5-7-33): Football QB. 47 consecutive games throwing touchdown pass (1956–60); 290 career touchdown passes; 40,239 career passing yards. Led league in touchdown passes four consecutive seasons. Player of the Year three times (1959, '64, '67). Career span 1956–72 with Baltimore, San Diego.

**Al Unser Sr.** (b. 5-29-39): Auto racer. Won Indy 500 four times (1970, '71, '78, '87). Retired with 39 career CART victories. USAC/CART champion three times (1970, '83, '85). Brother of Bobby.

**Bobby Unser** (b. 2-20-34): Auto racer. Won Indy 500 three times (1968, '75, '81). Retired with 35 career victories. USAC champion twice (1968, '74). Brother of Al Sr.

**Harold S. Vanderbilt** (b. 7-6-1884, d. 7-4-70): Sailor. Owner and skipper who successfully defended the America's Cup three consecutive times, in 1930, '34 and '37.

**Glenna Collett Vare** (b. 6-20-03, d. 2-2-89): Golfer. Won U.S. Women's Amateur six times, more than any golfer (1922, '25, consecutively 1928–30, '35).

**Bill Veeck** (b. 2-9-14, d. 1-2-86): Baseball owner. From 1946 to 1980, owned ballclubs in Cleveland, St. Louis (AL), Chicago (AL). In 1948, Cleveland became baseball's first team to draw two million in attendance. That year Veeck integrated AL by signing Larry Doby and then Satchel Paige. A brilliant promoter, Veeck sent midget Eddie Gaedel up to bat for St. Louis in 1951.

**Guillermo Vilas** (b. 8-17-52): Tennis. Argentine won 50 straight matches in 1977. In '77 won French Open, where he beat Brian Gottfried, and the U.S. Open, where he beat Jimmy Connors. Also won Australian Open twice, 1978–79.

**Lasse Viren** (b. 7-22-49): Track and field. Finnish runner was gold medalist in 5,000 and 10,000 meters at two consecutive Olympics (1972, '76).

**Virginia Wade** (b. 7-10-45): Tennis. Beloved in Britain, Wade won three major titles, most notably Wimbledon in 1977, its centenary year, where she triumphed over Betty Stove. Also won 1968 U.S. Open, '72 Australian Open, and doubles titles in '73 at the Australian, French and U.S. Opens, all with Margaret Smith Court.

**Honus Wagner** (b. 2-24-1874, d. 12-6-55): Baseball SS. Had .327 career batting average, 3,415 hits and eight batting titles. Averaged .300+ 15 consecutive seasons. Led league in RBI four times, with 100+ RBI nine times. Third alltime in triples (252) and league leader in doubles eight times. 703 career stolen bases, league leader in steals five times. Career span 1897–1917 with Pittsburgh.

**Grete Waitz** (b. 10-1-53): Track and field. Norwegian runner won New York City Marathon a record nine times (consecutively 1978–80, 1982–86, '88). Won the women's marathon at the 1983 World Championship.

**Jersey Joe Walcott** (b. 10-31-14, d. 2-25-94): Boxer. Heavyweight champion from 1951 to 1952. Won title at age 37 on fifth attempt before surrendering it to Rocky Marciano. Later became sheriff of Camden, NJ.

**Doak Walker** (b. 1-1-27, d. 9-27-98): Football HB. Led league in scoring two times, his first and final seasons. All-Pro five times. Played on two consecutive NFL champions (1952–53) with Detroit. Career span 1950 to 1955. Also won Heisman Trophy as a junior in 1948. All-America three consecutive seasons with SMU.

**Herschel Walker** (b. 3-3-62): Football RB. Won Heisman Trophy in 1982 with Georgia. Turned pro by entering USFL with New Jersey. Gained 7,000+ rushing yards and scored 61 touchdowns in three seasons before league folded. Entered NFL in 1986 with Dallas and led league in rushing yards in 1988 (1,514).

**Bill Walsh** (b. 11-30-31): Football coach. "The Genius." Led San Francisco to three Super Bowl wins, after the 1981, '84, '88 seasons. Career record with 49ers 102-63-1. Developed short-passing game.

**Bill Walton** (b. 11-5-52): Basketball C. College Player of the Year three consecutive seasons (1972–74). Played on two NCAA championship teams (1972–73) with UCLA; tournament MVP twice (1972–73). Sullivan Award winner in 1973. NBA MVP in 1978, playoff MVP in '77. Led league in rebounding and blocks in 1977. Career span 1974–86 with Portland, San Diego, Boston.

**War Admiral** (b. 1934, d. 1959): Thoroughbred race horse. A son of Man o' War, won Triple Crown and Horse of the Year honors in 1937.

**Paul Warfield** (b. 11-28-42): Football WR. Caught 427 passes for 8,565 yards and 85 TDs. Played on two Super Bowl–winning Miami Dolphins teams. Career span 1964–77, all with Cleveland Browns except for 1970–74 with Miami Dolphins. Inducted into Hall of Fame 1983.

**Glenn (Pop) Warner** (b. 4-5-1871, d. 9-7-54): College football coach. Third alltime in wins (319). Won three national championships with Pittsburgh (1916, '18) and Stanford (1926). Career record 319-106-32 with six teams from 1896 to 1938.

**Tom Watson** (b. 9-4-49): Golfer. Winner of British Open five times (1975, '77, '80, consecutively 1982–83), the Masters two times (1977, '81) and U.S. Open once (1982). PGA Player of the Year six times, more than any golfer (consecutively 1977–80, '82, '84).

**Dick Weber** (b. 12-23-29): Bowler. Won All-Star Tournament four times (consecutively 1962–63, 1965–66). Voted Bowler of the Year three times (1961, '63, '65). Won 31 career PBA titles.

**Johnny Weismuller** (b. 6-2-04, d. 1-21-84): Swimmer. Won three gold medals (including 100- and 400-meter freestyle) at 1924 Olympics and two gold medals at '28 Olympics. Also played Tarzan in the movies.

**Jerry West** (b. 5-28-38): Basketball G. 10 time All-Star; All-Defensive Team four times; 1969 playoff MVP. Led league in assists and scoring one time each. Career span 1960–72 with Los Angeles. Currently executive vice president of Lakers. Also NCAA tournament MVP in 1959. All-America two times with West Virginia. Played on 1960 gold medal-winning Olympic team.

**Whirlaway** (b. 4-2-38, d. 4-6-53): Thoroughbred race horse. Triple Crown winner in 1941 with jockey Eddie Arcaro aboard. Trained by Ben A. Jones.

**Byron (Whizzer) White** (b. 6-8-17): Football RB. Led NFL in rushing two times (Pittsburgh in 1938, Detroit in '40). Led NCAA in scoring and rushing with Colorado in 1937; named All-America. United States Supreme Court justice 1962–93.

**Reggie White** (b. 12-19-62): Football DE. Alltime leader in sacks. Signed with Green Bay in 1993 for $17 million over four years. Member of Green Bay's 1997 Super Bowl championship team. Career span: 1984 with Memphis Showboats (USFL), 1985–92 with Philadelphia, 1993–99 with Packers, 2000– 01 with Carolina.

**Charles Whittingham** (b. 4-13-13 d. 4-20-99): Thoroughbred race horse trainer. "Bald Eagle" after losing hair to tropical disease in World War II. Led yearly earnings list for trainers from 1970–73 consecutively; in 1975; and in 1981–82 consecutively. Won three Eclipse Awards and trained two Horses of the Year (Ack Ack in 1971 and Ferdinand in '87).

**Kathy Whitworth** (b. 9-27-39): Golfer. Alltime LPGA leader with 88 tour victories, including six majors. Won LPGA Championship in 1967, '71 and '75. Won Titleholders Championship (extinct major) in 1965 and '66. Won Western Open (extinct major) in 1967. Won Vare Trophy every year from 1965–72, except '68. LPGA Player of Year from 1966–69 and 1971–73.

**Hoyt Wilhelm** (b. 7-26-23): Baseball RHP. Hall of Famer. Threw knuckleball until age 48. Career 2.52 ERA, 227 saves. Hit home run in his first at bat (never hit another) and pitched no-hitter in 1958. Career span 1952–72 with nine teams.

**Bud Wilkinson** (b. 4-23-15 d. 2-9-94): Football coach. Alltime NCAA leader in consecutive wins (47, 1953–57). Won three national championships (1950, consecutively 1955–56) with Oklahoma, where he coached from 1947 to 1963. Won Orange Bowl four times and Sugar Bowl two times. Career record 145-29-4, including four undefeated seasons. Also coached with St. Louis of NFL in 1978–79.

**Billy Williams** (b. 6-15-38): Baseball OF. "Sweet Swinging." NL Rookie of the Year for 1961. Hit 426 career home runs. Drove in 1,475 runs. Lifetime average of .290. Named to six NL All-Star teams. Career span 1959–74 with Chicago Cubs, 1975–76 with Oakland A's. Elected to Hall of Fame in 1987.

**Ted Williams** (b. 8-30-18): Baseball OF. "The Splendid Splinter." Last player to hit .400 (.406 in 1941). MVP in 1946, '49 and Triple Crown winner in 1942, '47. Sixth in career batting average (.344), third in walks (2,019) and second in slugging average (.634). 521 career HR. League leader in batting average and runs scored six times each, RBI and HR four times each. Had .300+ average 15 consecutive seasons; 100+ RBI and runs scored nine times each; 30+ HR eight times; and 100+ walks 11 times. Lost nearly five seasons to military service. Career span 1939–42 and 1946–60 with Boston.

**Hack Wilson** (b. 4-26-1900; d. 11-23-48): Baseball OF. Stood 5' 6" but weighed 210. Had five astounding seasons 1926–30. Best was 1930 when he hit .356, scored 146 runs, hit a NL record 56 homers and drove in 190, which is still the major league record. Career span 1923–34 with several teams. Elected to Hall of Fame in 1979.

**Dave Winfield** (b. 10-3-51): Baseball OF. Drafted out of Univ. of Minnesota for both pro basketball and football. Led NL in RBI in 1979 (118). In 1992, first 40-year-old to get 100+ RBI, with 108. Hit clutch double to win 1992 World Series. Got 3,000th hit, off Dennis Eckersley, on 9-16-93. Career span 1973–80 with San Diego; 1981–90 with Yankees; 1990–91 with California; 1992 with Toronto; 1993–94 with Minnesota; and 1995 with Cleveland. Inducted into hall of Fame in 2001.

**Major W.C. Wingfield** (b. 10-16-1833, d. 4-18-12): British tennis pioneer. Credited with inventing the game of tennis, which he called "Sphairistike" or "sticky" and patented in February 1874.

**Colonel Matt Winn** (b. 6-30-1861, d. 10-6-49): General manager of Churchill Downs from 1904 until his death; made Kentucky Derby premier U.S. race.

**Katarina Witt** (b. 12-3-65): East German figure skater. Gold medalist at 1984 and '88 Olympics. Also world champion four times (consecutively 1984–85, 1987–88).

**John Wooden** (b. 10-14-10): College basketball coach. First member of basketball Hall of Fame as coach and player. Coached UCLA to 10 NCAA championships in 12 years (consecutively 1964–65, 1967–73, 1975). Record winning streak of 88 games (1971–74). 664 career wins and third highest career winning percentage (.804). Career span 1949–75 with UCLA.1932 College Player of the Year at Purdue.

**Tiger Woods** (b. 12-30-75): Golfer. Won three straight U.S. Junior Amateur titles (1991–93), three straight U.S. Amateur titles (1994–96), then took the PGA tour by storm, winning six of his first 21 tournaments, including the 1997 Masters. There, he was the youngest winner ever, scoring a record-low 270, and winning by the widest margin in tournament history, 12 strokes. 1996 *Sports Illustrated* Sportsman of the Year. Became the youngest player to win all four major tournaments ('99 PGA, '00 U.S. Open, '00 British Open). Holds tournament record for best scores at Masters, U.S. Open, and British Open. Won the '01 Masters, completing an unofficial Grand Slam by winning four consecutive Grand Slam tournaments.

**Mickey Wright** (b. 2-14-35): Golfer. Second alltime in career wins (82) and major championships (13; tied with Louise Suggs). Won U.S. Open four times (consecutively 1958-59, 1961, 1964), LPGA Championship four times (1958, consecutively 1960–61, '63), Western Open three times (consecutively 1962–63, '66).

**Kristi Yamaguchi** (b.7-12-71): Figure skater. Olympic champion in 1992. Back-to-back world champion (1991–92).

**Cale Yarborough** (b. 3-27-40): Auto racer. Won Daytona 500 four times (1968, '77, consecutively 1983–84). 83 career victories. Also NASCAR champion three consecutive years (1976–78).

**Carl Yastrzemski** (b. 8-22-39): Baseball OF. "Yaz." 3,419 career hits, 452 HR. 1967 MVP and Triple Crown winner. Three batting titles, including .301 in 1968, lowest ever to win. Second alltime in games played (3,308) and fifth in walks (1,845). Career span 1961–83 with Boston.

**Cy Young** (b. 3-29-1867, d. 11-4-55): Baseball RHP. Alltime leader in wins (511), losses (315), innings pitched (7,354⅔) and complete games (749); fourth in shutouts (76). Had 2.63 career ERA. Pitched three no-hitters, including a perfect game in 1904. Career span 1890–1911 with Cleveland, Boston.

**Steve Young** (b. 10-11-61): Football QB. Highest rated passer in NFL history, with 96.8 rating. Led 49ers to victory in Super Bowl XXIX of which he was MVP. Two-time NFL MVP (1992 and '94). Career span 1984 with LA Express of the USFL, 1985–86 with Tampa Bay, and 1987–00 with San Francisco.

**Robin Yount** (b. 9-16-55): Baseball OF–SS. Became Brewers shortstop at 18. Won 1982 AL MVP when he hit .331 with 29 homers. 3,142 career hits. Shoulder injury caused move to outfield in 1984. Career span 1974–93, all with the Brewers. Elected to Hall of Fame 1999.

**Steve Yzerman** (b. 5-9-65): Hockey C. Won back-to-back Stanley Cups with Red Wings (1997, '98). Won Conn Smythe trophy in 1998. Scored 100+ points six consecutive seasons (1987–88 through 1992–93). Career span since 1983 with Detroit.

**Babe Didrikson Zaharias** (b. 6-26-14, d. 9-27-56): Sportswoman. Gold medalist in 80-meter hurdles and javelin throw at 1932 Olympics; also won silver medal in high jump (her gold medal jump was disallowed for using the then-illegal western roll). Became a golfer in 1935 and won 12 major titles, including U.S. Open three times (1948, 1950, 1954—a year after cancer surgery). Also helped found the LPGA in 1949.

**Tony Zale** (b. 5-29-13, d. 3-20-97): Boxer. Born Anthony Zaleski. "The Man of Steel." Two-time middleweight champ. Fought Rocky Graziano for title three times in 21 months, winning twice. 67-18-2 with 44 KOs. Elected to Boxing Hall of Fame 1958.

**Emil Zatopek** (b. 9-19-22): Track and field. Czech runner became only athlete to win gold medal in 5,000 and 10,000 meters and marathon, at 1952 Olympics. Also gold medalist in 10,000 meters at '48 Olympics.

**Zinedine Zidane** (b. 6-23-72): French soccer player. "Zizou." Led France to 1998 World Cup title; scored two goals in 3–0 win over Brazil in the final. Led Juventus to 1998 Italian League title and to '98 European Cup final. 1998 FIFA World Player of the Year. Led France to 2000 European Championship.

GEORGE TIEDEMANN

# Obituaries

**Tommie Agee, 58, baseball player.** Centerfielder for the 1969 "Miracle Mets," Agee is famous for his Game 3 heroics during the '69 World Series: two scintillating catches—commonly ranked among the best in World Series history—and a leadoff homer against the favored Baltimore Orioles. His 12-year career included seasons with Cleveland, the White Sox, the Mets, Houston and St. Louis. He retired with 130 home runs, 433 RBI and a lifetime average of .255. Agee threw out a ceremonial pitch at Shea before Game 4 of the 2000 Subway Series.

In New York, of a heart attack, Jan. 21, 2001.

**Earl Anthony, 63, bowler.** With a delivery so reliable he was nicknamed "the machine," Hall of Famer Anthony became the sport's first million-dollar man. He was named Bowler of the Year consecutively from 1974 to '76 and from 1981 to '83. His record of 41 career wins still stands.

*SI*'s Alexander Wolff writes:

"Earl Anthony made pocket money as a kid by setting up pins in a bowling alley. His knack for knocking them down as an adult made him the first bowler to earn $1 million during his career.... [He] dominated bowling when bowling dominated Saturday-afternoon television. He won 10 titles in the majors. 'Earl made our broadcasts,' former ABC host Chris Schenkel said, recalling the 36-year stretch that made the Professional Bowlers Tour one of the longest-running and highest-rated sports series in television history.

"That appeal might seem hard to fathom today. With his nerdy hair and Poindexter glasses, Anthony would go over only in a hip-to-be-square sense. Nonetheless, even as bowling has all but disappeared from the airwaves, it has come back in vogue in other ways of late, and a trio of Microsoft millionaires recently bought the PBA tour. They're doing their best to make the sport cool again. They have paid down the tour's debt, raised its purses, granted stock options to the bowlers and raided Nike for marketing executives who are trying to reinvent pro bowling.

"It's hard to imagine Anthony on this newfangled PBA tour. Square Earl liked to say, 'You can't ever be too slow to the line.' Taciturn, indistractibly focused, a junkballer who was always recalibrating speed and spin, he'd be the analog oddball at Digital City Lanes. The poky style that made Anthony an immortal only underscores how bowling's golden age belonged to another era entirely—and how daunting a task the PBA tour's new proprietors face."

In New Berlin, Wis., of injuries sustained from falling down a flight of stairs, Aug. 14, 2001.

**Chris Antley, 34, jockey.** Antley, who stood 5'3" in his riding gear, became the first jockey to win nine races in one day, on Oct. 31, 1987. In a 16-year career, he won 3,480 races, and his mounts amassed more than $92 million. Although his death was initially suspected as a homicide, a final autopsy report concluded that foul play was not involved.

*SI*'s Mark Beech writes:

"Chris Antley was one of the most enigmatic figures in horse racing. Undeniably brilliant and engaging at the track, he was maddeningly erratic and withdrawn away from it, often disappearing for long stretches to wage battles with depression, weight gain and cocaine abuse. 'He had Howard Hughes qualities,' says Drew Mollica, Antley's agent in the late 1980s. 'Professionally

he was an angel, but he could disappear and go stealth very quickly.' When Antley piloted Charismatic to the brink of the Triple Crown in 1999, he seemed to have put his troubles behind him, but that wasn't the case. He missed four months of 1999 with a knee injury, and when he returned to racing in February 2000, he struggled with his diet. In March he split with his agent of four years, Ron Anderson, and soon thereafter, claiming he was 10 pounds over his racing weight of 117, he walked away from the track.

"In April, Antley married Natalie Jowett, an ABC Sports producer he had met during his pursuit of the '99 Triple Crown. Sources close to Antley say the marriage left him wondering if there might be more to life than riding horses. On the backstretch, however, there were rumors that Antley had again succumbed to drugs. In 1998 he had pleaded guilty to a charge of being under the influence of a controlled substance, and in July 2000 he was found guilty on a drunk-driving charge. Pasadena police said that twice this fall they made contact with him, in September regarding a possible narcotics violation and in October for unspecified reasons.

"With two Kentucky Derby victories and more than 3,000 winners, Antley's place in racing history is secure. Sadly, he won't be around to attend to the most important of his legacies. Natalie Antley was scheduled to deliver their child, a baby girl, in late December. 'He was a perfect rider,' says Mollica. 'This is a tragic end to a very tortured and tormented life.'"

In Pasadena, Calif., of multiple drug intoxication, Dec. 2, 2000.

**Eraste Autin, 18, college football player.** An incoming freshman at Florida, Autin collapsed after a voluntary preseason workout, slipped into a coma and died a week later. The 6'2", 250-pound fullback rushed for 700 yards and scored 12 touchdowns in his senior year at St. Thomas More High in Lafayette, La.

In Gainesville, Fla., from complications related to heatstroke, July 25, 2001.

**Lou Boudreau, 84, baseball player–manager.** Cleveland legend Boudreau had his best season as a player in 1948, when he hit .355, swatted 18 home runs and drove in 106 runs for the Indians—the Associated Press named him Male Athlete of the Year. He was inducted into the Hall of Fame in 1970 and was also a radio commentator for the Cubs for nearly 30 years.

*SI*'s Mark Bechtel writes:

"The idea seems preposterous now—a 24-year-old shortstop sweet-talking an owner into handing him the manager's job—but it wasn't always so. In November 1941, before the biggest concern of a player with 2½ years of major league experience was whether he was eligible for arbitration as a 'super two,' Lou Boudreau convinced Cleveland owner Alva Bradley that he was ready to become the youngest manager in baseball history. No mere stopgap, Boudreau ... managed and played short for the Indians for nine more years and, in 1948, led them to the World Series title, their last to date.

"'Everything about the game then was more conducive to player-managers,' says Mariners skipper Lou Piniella. 'There were no pregame meetings with trainers and doctors. There wasn't as much travel. There was little media attention. And these days no one needs the supplemental money to get by.' (In 1942 Boudreau got $5,000 for playing and $20,000 for managing.)

"Playing while managing had other advantages. When Boudreau the manager made a call, he knew he had Boudreau the player to cover his back. After the Indians finished the 1948 regular season tied with the Red Sox, Boudreau chose rookie Gene Bearden over Bob Feller and Bob Lemon to start the one-game playoff at Fenway. Bearden beat Boston 8–3; it helped that Boudreau went 4 for 4 with two homers.

"Cleveland went on to defeat the Braves in six games, making Boudreau the only man to manage a World Series winner in the same year he was named MVP. Safe to say, that's a feat that won't be repeated anytime soon."

In Olympia Fields, Ill., of cardiac arrest, Aug. 10, 2001.

**Sir Donald Bradman, 92, cricketer.** With an astonishing scoring average of 99.94 during 52 international test matches—more than 50 percent higher than his nearest rival—Bradman, an Australian, was widely hailed as the greatest batsman of all time. His utter dominance in the 1930s and '40s—when he scored nearly 7,000 runs for his national team—is recognized as one of the sport's unparalleled accomplishments.

In Adelaide, Australia, from complications due to pneumonia, Feb. 25, 2001.

**John Cooper, 77, race car designer.** Cooper, who founded the Cooper Car Co. in 1946 with his father, was responsible for the rear-engine configuration that revolutionized Formula One racing in the 1950s. The pair's cars won the F/1 constructors' title in 1959 and '61. While rear-mounted engines became the standard for the industry, the Coopers' racing version of the classic Mini achieved pop cult status—celebrity owners included Paul McCartney, John Lennon and Peter Sellers. In 2000, Cooper was awarded a CBE, or Commanders of the Order of the British Empire, for his services to the motor industry.

In Worthing, England, of cancer, Dec. 24, 2000.

**Devaughn Darling, 18, college football player.** Complaining of chest pains, Darling collapsed and died shortly after an early-morning offseason training session with Florida State. Both he and his twin brother had been diagnosed with a sickle-cell blood condition, but no definitive cause of death was named in the linebacker's autopsy report. The Florida State team physician theorized that "cardiac arrhythmia" might have been the cause. The native of Sugar Land, Texas, was credited with 11 tackles in seven games as a member of special teams in 2000.

In Tallahassee, Fla., of unknown causes, Feb. 26, 2001.

**Didi, 71, soccer player.** A Brazilian soccer legend who valued artful passing, ball control and skill over brute force and endless running, Didi—born Valdir Pereira—led his country to World Cup titles in 1958 and 1962. He began his career in 1943 with Rio de Janiero's Sao Cristovao club. In 1950, he was the first player to score at the massive Maracana, a stadium built for the 1950 World Cup. In 1958 the midfielder was named the World Cup's Most Valuable Player as he guided a 17-year-old prodigy named Pelé through his national-team debut. Didi (pronounced GEE-gee), who scored 21 goals in 74 international games, summed up his philosophy by saying, "It's the ball that needs to run, not the player." After becoming a coach in 1966, Didi led teams in Argentina, Peru, Turkey, Saudi Arabia and his native Brazil. His crowning moment as a coach came when he led Peru to the 1970 World Cup quarterfinals, where they lost 4–2 to eventual champion Brazil. "He was eulogized by Pelé, who said simply, "For him, playing football was as easy as peeling an orange."

In Rio de Janiero, of liver failure, May 12, 2001.

**Dale Earnhardt, 49, stock car driver.** One of the most daring race car drivers in NASCAR history, seven-time Winston Cup champion Dale Earnhardt was ultimately claimed by the sport he helped define when he lost control of his Chevrolet Monte Carlo in Turn 4 of the final lap of the Daytona 500 and slammed into a wall at more than 170 mph. Arguably the most popular star in stock car racing, Earnhardt racked up 76 victories in 676 Winston Cup races. He had a record 20 Top 10 finishes in Winston Cup season points races. Earnhardt's career prize-money total of $41,639,662 is the most of any NASCAR driver.

*SI*'s Mark Bechtel writes:

"In losing Earnhardt, NASCAR didn't just lose the best driver stock car racing had seen. It also lost its heart and soul, the one thing it had that no other sport could claim: a superstar the average blue-jean-wearing fan could identify with. 'Dale was the Michael Jordan of our sport,' said H.A. (Humpy) Wheeler, president of Lowe's Motor Speedway near Charlotte. Earnhardt's appeal was so broad because nearly everyone could find something to like about him. Front-runners cheered him on as he won seven Winston Cup championships, equaling the record set by Richard Petty. Underdogs appreciated how he had worked his way up from humble beginnings, tinkering with cars in a makeshift garage that his dad, Ralph, a short-track whiz, built in the barn behind the family's house on Sedan Avenue in Kannapolis, N.C. Sentimental types loved watching him goof around with his namesake, 26-year-old NASCAR driver Dale Jr. Then there were the tough guys, the ones who couldn't get enough of the way he refused to let anyone slow him down on the way to his destination. 'I think everybody in the country is angry about having to drive in urban areas,' said Wheeler in 1995. 'They hate the traffic with a passion. Earnhardt drives through traffic too. And he won't put up with anything. He's going to get through. That's what they want to do—but they can't. So Earnhardt is playing out their fantasies.'

"As a teen, Earnhardt picked up the nickname Ironhead, a play on his father's nickname, Ironheart. A high school dropout, Dale was married at 17 and began racing for grocery money. He described himself as 'wild and crazy, young and dumb,' but he was forced to get his act together when Ralph died of a heart attack while working on a carburetor in his garage in 1973. Dale, then 22, essentially took over his dad's car and made enough of a name for himself on the short tracks of North Carolina that he earned a NASCAR ride and in 1979 was the Winston Cup Rookie of the Year.

"As the years passed, Earnhardt matured, but that's not to say he mellowed on the track. In 1987 he won 11 races—three after bumping the leader out of the way. Sometime around 1989 he swapped the moniker Ironhead for the Intimidator, and he did his best to live up to the name.

"When athletes—especially ones in their mid-40s—start to decline, they aren't supposed to bounce back. But after finishing eighth in the Winston Cup standings in '98 and seventh in '99, Earnhardt made a serious run in 2000 at his eighth championship, finishing second, 265 points behind champion Bobby Labonte. Two factors contributed heavily to his resurgence. He had back surgery in December '99 to correct the lingering effects of a nasty crash at Atlanta Motor Speedway earlier that year, and Dale Jr. spent the season driving a Winston Cup car owned by his old man.

"For much of Earnhardt's career, the 2½-mile Daytona tri-oval defined him. He won 34 races at the track, but until '98 he had never won the big one. He had come close, losing on the last lap three times between 1993 and '96. However, until he won in '98—and produced a stuffed gibbon in Victory Lane, declaring, 'I'm here, and I've got that goddam monkey off my back!'—he was known for two things: being the best superspeedway racer of all time and being unable to win the biggest superspeedway race.

"Though he excelled at restrictor-plate racing, he loathed both the device mandated by NASCAR to reduce speeds on some of its tracks and the type of racing it produced. He offered this bit of advice last summer to drivers who complained that they were going too fast: 'If you're not a race driver, stay the hell home. Don't come here and grumble about going too fast. Get the hell out of the race car if you've got feathers on your legs or butt. Put a kerosene rag around your ankles so the ants won't climb up there and eat that candy ass.'

"The 76th and final win of Earnhardt's career came in a restrictor-plate race in October, the Winston 500 in Talladega, Ala.

"'It's hard to say how long you should drive,' Earnhardt said last summer. 'Some people hang on too long just trying to get one last victory. For me, racing is in my blood. It's who I am. Right now I think I can win championships and go after it as hard as I ever have. It will be tough getting out of the car for the last time, but I'll know when to do it.'"

In Daytona Beach, Fla., of severe neck and skull injuries sustained in a crash during the Daytona 500, Feb. 18, 2001.

**Stan Fox, 48, race car driver.** Fox was perhaps best known for his miraculous recovery from a catastrophic, career-ending six-car wreck on the first lap of the 1995 Indianapolis 500, in which his car was nearly sheared in half and he was thrown legs-first into the wall. He regained consciousness five days later and left the hospital a month after that. Fox's career had begun in 1972 and he made eight starts at the Indy 500, with a career-best finish of seventh, as a rookie in 1987. His midget-car career was more successful, with 19 wins in 184 starts and Copper World Midget division titles in 1980, '90 and '93. He was killed in a head-on crash on a desolate stretch of road 200 miles south of Auckland, New Zealand, where he was—ironically—working on head-injury support units.

In New Zealand, of injuries sustained in an automobile accident, Dec. 18, 2000.

**Werner Fricker, 65, U.S. soccer executive.** A prominent figure in the revitalization of American soccer, Fricker was president of the U.S. Soccer Federation from 1984 to 1990. Born in the former Yugoslavia and of German and Hungarian descent, Fricker sought to unite a disorganized U.S. soccer tradition. He emigrated to Pennsylvania, played on the U.S. Olympic team in 1964 and led his local team to victory in the National Amateur Cup the following year. In 1992 he was elected to the National Soccer Hall of Fame. The current USSF leadership has said that without Fricker's efforts, the U.S. would not have hosted the World Cup in 1994. Two years later, Major League Soccer kicked off its inaugural season, and in 1999 the U.S. hosted the Women's World Cup. The Women's United Soccer Association

launched in 2001. Fricker, whose real-estate development company thrived in suburban Pennsylvania, reportedly never accepted a salary for his work with USSF.

In Horsham, Pa., of cancer, May 30, 2001.

**Eddie Futch, 90, boxing trainer.** Futch, a Golden Gloves lightweight champ who once sparred with Joe Louis as an amateur, trained 20 world champions in his seven-decade, Hall of Fame career. He was a legendary cornerman, with his first champion in 1959 (welterweight Don Jordan) and his last in 1997 (light heavyweight Montell Griffin). Futch trained five heavyweight champions: Joe Frazier, Larry Holmes, Michael Spinks, Trevor Berbick and Riddick Bowe.

"There was nothing bad about Eddie Futch," said promoter Lou DiBella. "He cared about the kids. He cared about the sport. He was the best of the best."

In Las Vegas, Nev., of natural causes, Oct. 10, 2001.

**Joe Gilliam Jr., 49, football player.** One of the first black quarterbacks to start in the NFL, Gilliam played for the Pittsburgh Steelers from 1972, when he joined the club as an 11th-round draft pick from Tennessee State, to 1975, when he was cut, probably due to substance abuse. He won a starting position in 1974, and threw for 1,274 yards and four touchdowns before being replaced by Terry Bradshaw. After his slide into drug addiction, Gilliam became homeless and said he lived under a bridge in a cardboard box for two years. He played in the USFL in the 1980s. He appeared to have gotten his life back on track in the late '90s, claiming he'd been drug free for three years. In 2000 he established a football camp for boys and girls at his alma mater and became an advocate for drug and alcohol abstinence.

In Nashville, of an apparent heart attack, Dec. 25, 2000.

**Marty Glickman, 83, broadcaster.** A football and track star at Syracuse, Glickman was a victim of anti-Semitism during the 1936 Olympics in Berlin, where he was yanked from the 400-meter relay team for fear that a Jew on a winning relay team would embarrass the Nazis. He went on to a pioneering, distinguished career in sports broadcasting for several networks. The onetime voice of New York's Giants, Jets and Knicks, Glickman influenced generations of broadcasters with his work behind the mike and as a consultant for NBC, HBO, MSG Network and SportsChannel.

SI asked colleagues and protégés of Glickman's to describe what they learned from him.

Marv Albert: "There should be a course taught in journalism schools entitled Marty Glickman, the way you might study Fellini in film school. He set the terminology for basketball play-by-play. On radio it was very precise. Right side of the lane. Left side, top of the key. Right baseline. He would always drum into me, 'What kind of shot is it? Is it a running one-hander? Is it a jumper from 15 along the baseline? Does he drive, stop, jump, shoot? Be precise because you're providing the eyes for the listener.'"

Bob Costas: "When I started in the early 1980s, I said to him, 'I look so much younger than I am,' which was a standing joke around NBC. 'What can I do to counteract that?' He said, 'Have you ever heard an older person who talks really fast? Hardly ever. Try to slow down and have a more measured pace.' That was good advice. It gave me a little more authority."

Gayle Sierens (first female NFL announcer): "He was a great believer in less is more. He thought that one of the great mistakes announcers make is talking too much. He always said, 'It's not about you.' He also stressed giving down and distance and time remaining. Every time they moved the chains he wanted me talking about down and distance."

Bill Walton: "I was cursed with severe stuttering until I was 28 years old. Marty Glickman taught me how to speak. The tips he gave me almost 20 years ago I still apply every day: Slow down your thoughts; think about what you are saying now, not three or four sentences ahead. Chew sugarless gum to strengthen the muscles in your jaw and to get your mouth moving. Read out loud; it doesn't matter what the subject is, just do it a lot. When you are comfortable doing that, move in front of the mirror and watch yourself as others will see you speaking. Become a teacher—to anyone, anywhere, on any subject you know."

In New York, of complications from heart bypass surgery, Dec. 14, 2000.

**Lou Groza, 76, football player.** The NFL Player of the Year in 1954, Groza, a kicker and a lineman, remains the Cleveland Browns leading scorer, with 1,349 points—including one touchdown in 1951. He played 21 seasons for the Browns (1946 to '67), signing 21 one-year contracts. He was selected for the Pro Bowl nine times and played in nine NFL championship games, four of which he and his Browns won. He led the NFL in field goals in five seasons, a record that still stands. College football's annual top kicker is presented with the Lou Groza Award.

*SI*'s Paul Zimmerman writes:

"Paul Brown called him 'my Louie.' He was 'one of Dad's favorites,' says Bengals president Mike Brown, son of Paul, the legendary Browns coach. 'Louie's word was solid. You could count on him.' Groza had been one of Brown's prize recruits at Ohio State, a big guy for that era (6'3", 240 pounds) with remarkable agility. He played tackle on the freshman team in 1941, before World War II ended his college career. In '45 Groza was serving in a medical unit on Okinawa when he received a couple of footballs from Brown along with a reminder to 'work on your kicking.' After the war, Brown invited Groza to join his franchise in the nascent All-America Football Conference. That's how Groza, who still had three years of college eligibility left, became a Cleveland Brown. The team won the league championship in each of the AAFC's four years of existence, and four NFL titles from 1950 to Groza's retirement in '67.

"Groza's kicking earned him his nickname, the Toe, and got him into the Hall of Fame. But he was also a six-time All-Pro tackle who was perfect for Brown's revolutionary pass-protection scheme called cup blocking, in which the linemen picked up the men to their outside, forming a protective cup for quarterback Otto Graham. 'Fast on his feet, able to glide and shuffle, just what scouts look for in a pass-blocking tackle nowadays,' says Mike Brown. 'Plus Louie could run.' Especially downfield: On his kickoffs he was often the first man in for the tackle.

"It's a picture that smacks of antiquity: the kicker who doubled as a lineman, and a fine one at that. 'It's more efficient now,' says Brown, 'but maybe the game lost something when it went to the pure kickers.' With Groza's death it lost a whole lot more."

In Middleburg Heights, Ohio, of a heart attack, Nov. 29, 2000.

**Victor Kiam, 74, football owner.** Kiam gained notice as the star of commercials for his Remington Products Company, genially promising viewers that the company's shaver "shaves as close as a blade, or your money back!" He was also the majority owner of the New England Patriots from 1988 to '92, a period that saw three coaches, a dismal record of 21–43 and no playoff appearances. His family retains a majority stake in Remington.

In Stamford, Conn., from a heart condition, May 27, 2001.

**Stephen Malcolm, 30, soccer player.** A defender with the Jamaican national team, Stephen (Shorty) Malcolm played in 91 international matches. He was a member of the Reggae Boyz 1998 World Cup team, and started against Argentina and Japan in France that year. He was traveling home from an exhibition match against Bulgaria when the vehicle in which he was riding, driven by teammate Theodore Whitmore, flipped after hitting an embankment.

In Trelawny, Jamaica, of injuries sustained in a car accident, Jan. 28, 2001.

**Eddie Mathews, 69, baseball player.** Considered the game's best third baseman in the 1950s and early '60s, Mathews was, in Ty Cobb's estimation, one of only three or four players blessed with a "perfect swing." In his 17-year career, he won the NL home run title twice (1953 and '59), was a nine-time All-Star and was the only man to have played for the Braves in Boston, Milwaukee and Atlanta. He also played for the Astros and the Tigers, winning the World Series with Detroit in his final season. Mathews served a brief stint as manager of the Braves and held several positions with the Milwaukee Brewers and the Oakland A's.

*SI*'s Walter Bingham writes:

"As a Hall of Famer and one of only 16 players to hit 500 home runs, Eddie Mathews has a secure place in baseball history. But Mathews, also holds a special place in *SI*'s history—as the athlete featured on the cover of our first issue, dated Aug. 16, 1954.

"At the time Mathews was one of baseball's most promising young sluggers, but his prowess was incidental to his being on the cover. Sid James, *SI*'s first managing editor, wanted to run a red-blooded sports photograph on that first issue, in contrast to some of the effete cover subjects—like dogs and sailboats—that were to follow. No story in that first issue accompanied the cover shot, only a short box on the contents page that identified Mathews and declared the scene 'baseball's classic home plate tableau.'

"The selection of Mathews for our inaugural cover was, in retrospect, fortuitous, for he embodied many traits we would come to celebrate: poise, teamwork, durability, all-around excellence. Mathews went on to hit 40 home runs in 1954, and together with his more celebrated teammate, Hank Aaron, formed the one-two punch that led the Braves to a World Series title in '57 and a National League pennant in '58. Mathews ended his career with 512 homers and was elected to the Hall of Fame in '78. 'It's funny,' he told *SI* in 1999. 'When that picture was taken, I didn't think of it—or myself—as anything special. SPORTS ILLUSTRATED and me, we were nuthins.' "

In San Diego, of complications from pneumonia, Aug. 18, 2001.

**Tyrone McGriff, 41, football player.** McGriff was a three-time Division I-AA All-America with Florida A&M and a member of its national championship teams in 1977 and '78. He made the NFL All-Rookie team in 1980 with the Steelers, playing three seasons in the NFL and, later, three seasons in the USFL.

In Melbourne, Fla., from complications after a heart attack, Dec. 9, 2000.

**Al McGuire, 72, basketball player, coach and broadcaster.** The multitalented McGuire played for the New York Knicks (1951–54) and the Baltimore Bullets (1954–55) and coached three college teams, most notably Marquette, which he led to the NCAA championship in 1977, his last game. He then became a television analyst until 2000. He was named Coach of the Year by four major sportswriting organizations in 1971 and was inducted into the Basketball Hall of Fame in 1992.

*SI* 's Alexander Wolff writes:

"We could recite the details of the life of Al McGuire, but he wouldn't want us to. McGuire didn't believe in details. He blithely forgot names, of players in games he telecast and of those on his own team. Jerome Whitehead, a star of McGuire's 1977 NCAA champion Marquette team, was forever Whitehorse. So was Whitehead's father, a minister who must have frowned upon realizing that White Horse is a brand of Scotch. But both Whiteheads surely knew the futility of correcting the man whose rules for life and basketball had been formed in the taverns and playgrounds of Rockaway Beach, N.Y. Forever fuzzy on the particulars, McGuire never erred in the broad strokes. When he said, 'Just show me the numbers,' he didn't mean that literally, only that what interested him was the metaphorical bottom line.

" 'He had a gift for seeing the wonder and the goodness of God's creation, sometimes in the most unlikely places, and for sharing his delight in that discovery with those around him,' Robert Wild, the Jesuit priest who is Marquette's president, said after McGuire's death. Wild was no doubt referring to the coach's habit of telling lunch companions, 'If the waitress has dirty ankles, the chili's terrific.'

"McGuire quit right after he and Whitehorse won that NCAA title 24 years ago, so his basketball legacy requires some brushing up on. He'll be remembered for his sensibility, including that picturesque urban argot of which Dick Vitale's is wincingly derivative. He was without peer as a game coach. 'I don't know basketball,' he said. 'I feel basketball. Drop me in the middle of a game, and I could manage it by the ebb and flow.'

"He won his title because the button-down guy on the other bench, North Carolina's Dean Smith—who lost a lead after ordering his Tar Heels into a four-corners delay—didn't understand what McGuire did: that basketball resists excessive organization. He had the cojones and self-possession to walk away from the summit of the clipboard racket in midlife.

"McGuire didn't let details encumber him. He didn't let basketball do so, either."

In Milwaukee, of a blood disorder, Jan. 26, 2001.

**John McKay, 77, football coach.** The irascible leader of the Southern Cal football program for 15 years, McKay also coached the NFL's Tampa Bay Buccaneers for nine seasons. In 1984, he moved to the Bucs front office, becoming president of the franchise. Also popular on the speaking circuit, he made 286 appearances one year. McKay was twice voted college coach of the year.

*SI* 's Ivan Maisel writes:

"John McKay's appointment as USC football coach in 1960 helped usher in the golden age of Southern California sports. Like Walter O'Malley, who had brought his Dodgers to Los Angeles two years earlier, McKay realized the significance of the country's westward migration in the postwar years. Seeing a burgeoning talent pool, McKay recruited almost exclusively in his backyard. On his 1967 national championship team, 69 of 78 players came from the L.A. area.

"McKay won three other national titles with the Trojans, in 1962, '72 and '74. The USC job was his first as head coach, and he proved to be a natural in the spotlight. His quick wit and cool demeanor made him a star in a town full of stars. (Johnny Carson and Frank Sinatra were among his buddies.) To get his players loose before a big game, McKay once told them, 'We ought to keep in mind that there are over 600 million Chinese who don't care whether we win or lose.' Another time, he jogged onto the field before a game in South Bend singing the Notre Dame fight song.

"At heart, however, McKay was a fierce competitor. After the Irish routed his Trojans 51–0 in 1966, he vowed he would never again lose to Notre Dame. He nearly pulled it off, going 6-1-2 in his final nine games against the Irish. McKay was also a tactical innovator: With his modified I formation, in which the tailback started seven yards behind the line and agile linemen pulled out in front of him to block, he created one of the college game's most powerful running attacks. It's no coincidence that Mike Garrett (1965) and O.J. Simpson (1968) won Heismans playing tailback for McKay.

"McKay left USC in 1975 to become the first coach of the Tampa Bay Buccaneers. Though it took him nearly two seasons to win a game, he had the Bucs playing for the NFC title in his fourth year, a feat he took in stride. 'A genius in the National Football League,' McKay said with typical deflection, 'is a guy who won last week.' "

In Tampa, Fla., from kidney failure due to complications from diabetes, June 10, 2001.

**Murray Murdoch, 96, hockey player.** The oldest living Stanley Cup champion (1926), Murdoch had 84 goals and 192 points in 508 games from 1926 to '37 for the New York Rangers. He became a coach after his NHL career and led Yale to 278 victories as coach from 1938 to '65, setting a school record that was broken by Tim Taylor in 2000. Murdoch won the Lester Patrick Trophy in 1974 for contributions to American hockey.

In Pawley's Island, S.C., from unknown causes, May 17, 2001.

**Bobbi Olson, 65, college basketball administrator.** Olson, beloved by players and fans alike as a pillar of the Arizona basketball program, was the wife of head coach Lute Olson for 47 years. They met at Augsburg College in Minneapolis and were married on Nov. 27, 1953. Olson, born Roberta Rae Russell, was an integral part of the Arizona program, often attending recruiting trips with her husband, making pancakes for recruits when they visited the Arizona campus and traveling with the team. She was a mother of five and a grandmother of 13.

In Tucson, from complications related to ovarian cancer, Jan. 1, 2001.

**Charley Pell, 60, college football coach.** As a player, Pell was a two-way lineman on Bear Bryant's first national title team at Alabama (1961). As coach at Clemson from 1977 to '78, he was 18-4-1, and at Florida from 1979 to '84, he was 33-26-3. He resigned after the third game of the 1984 season, when the NCAA hit the Florida program with nearly 60 sanctions for rules violations. Pell accepted responsibility for the infractions.

In Gadsden, Ala., from cancer, May 29, 2001.

**Lowell Perry, 66, football pioneer and public figure.** The NFL's first black coach of the modern era, Perry was a star player at Michigan in the 1950s. He joined the Pittsburgh Steelers in 1956 as a player and was moved to the receivers coaching staff the following year. According to the NFL, Perry became the first black football commentator when CBS hired him in 1966. In 1973, he was named manager of a Chrysler plant in Michigan, becoming one of the first blacks to head a major auto facility. President Ford tapped Perry to run the Equal Employment Opportunity Commission two years later. And in 1991, Michigan Gov. John Engler appointed Perry head of the state labor department.

In Southfield, Mich., from complications related to cancer, Jan. 7, 2001.

**Bill Rigney, 83, baseball player, coach and executive.** A consummate baseball professional for 60 years, Rigney worked in the national pastime as a player, manager, coach, scout, broadcaster and executive. He started his career in the Pacific Coast League, playing for the Oakland Oaks from 1938 until he entered the Navy in 1943. After the war, he joined the New York Giants as an infielder and utility player. He played for New York for 10 years, making the NL All-Star team in 1948 and playing on the "Miracle of Coogan's Bluff" pennant-winning team of 1951. Nicknamed "the Cricket," Rigney was immortalized more for his relentless bench-chatter than for his stats. His 18-year coaching career included two stints with the Giants—he was the last manager at the Polo Grounds and the first in San Francisco—as well as the Los Angeles and California Angels and the Minnesota Twins. He led the Angels to 70 victories in their first season, 1961, and was named American League Manager of the Year the following year. He was a special assistant and commentator for the Oakland A's when he died.

In Walnut Creek, Calif., from heart disease and pneumonia, Feb. 20, 2001.

**Bekzat Sattarkhanov, 20, Olympic boxer.** Sattarkhanov, of Kazakhstan, won the featherweight gold medal at the 2000 Sydney Games by defeating Ricardo (Rocky) Juarez of the U.S.

In the Shumkent region of Kazakstan, from injuries sustained in an automobile accident, Dec. 31, 2000.

**Willie Stargell, 61, baseball player.** The heart and soul of "The Family"—the 1979 World Series champion Pirates—Stargell played for 21 seasons in Pittsburgh, amassing 474 homers, 2,232 hits, 1,540 RBIs and a career average of .282. He was credited with uniting black and white players in the Pirates organization with his inspiring leadership and affable demeanor. As captain, he awarded cloth gold stars to his teammates—who stitched them onto their caps—for individual accomplishments. Renowned for his power-hitting, Stargell was the first batter to hit a ball out of Dodger Stadium in L.A. Of the 18 home runs in 45 years clubbed over the roof of Pittsburgh's Forbes Field, seven came off Stargell's bat.

*SI* asked members of the formidable Pirates teams from the 1970s about their memories of the Hall of Fame slugger:

Phil Garner, second baseman: "He had an unbelievable fire to play, but his emotions never got out of control. One time we were in St. Louis, and Darold Knowles came into a tie game and struck Willie out on a changeup. Willie came back to the dugout and said, 'I'll hit that changeup later.' Sure enough, in the

ninth inning, Knowles throws him a change, and Willie hits it into the upper tier. And he comes back to the dugout very calmly and puts his helmet and bat away and takes a seat."

Richie Hebner, third baseman: "He was always a teacher. For the past couple of years, during spring training, Willie gave a speech to all the Pirates' minor league kids. It was impressive. He said, 'Don't think you're here as a number or just another player. Everyone's goal should be to wear a Pittsburgh Pirates uniform.' You could hear a pin drop."

Dave Parker, rightfielder: "He was my baseball father. That's why I called him Pops. In '78 I told the Pirates that the only way I would re-sign was if they brought Pops back too."

"Bill Robinson, leftfielder: "Willie wasn't one to brag, but every time we'd go to Philadelphia, he'd point to a seat way, way, way up in the rightfield stands and say, 'I hit Jim Bunning up there.' He was always pulling for you. Other guys would ask him, 'Should I take a pitch?' and Willie would say, 'Hit like you live—hard.'"

In Wilmington, N.C., from a stroke, April 9, 2001.

**John Steadman, 73, sportswriter.** With a career that spanned 50 years for such publications as Baltimore's *News-Post, News-American, The Evening Sun* and *The Sun*—as well as a three-year stint in the mid-1950s in the Baltimore Colts' front office—Steadman attended every NFL game played by a Baltimore team from 1950 to December 2000: 719 straight. He was also one of a small number of sportswriters to have covered every Super Bowl prior to the 2001 game. He was posthumously given the 2001 Red Smith Award for major contributions to sports journalism, in June 2001.

In Baltimore, from complications related to cancer, Jan. 1, 2001.

**Korey Stringer, 27, football player.** After complaining of heat exhaustion the previous day, Stringer collapsed on the second afternoon of the Minnesota Vikings' training camp. He had just completed a 2½-hour workout in temperatures that reached a heat index of 110°. The 6'4", 335 pound All-Pro offensive tackle died early the next morning, prompting an inquest by league officials into training procedures. Stringer was entering his seventh pro season.

*SI*'s Steve Rushin writes:

"I always liked Korey Stringer, but only for his hair, which exploded from his head in minidreadlocks, like novelty spring snakes from an opened can, and for the way—in his purple Vikings uniform top—he put me in mind of a hip-hop Barney the Dinosaur. Beyond that, I knew almost nothing about the Minnesota offensive tackle until he died, and I learned that he had lived year-round in Bloomington. That's my hometown, and the place where all my friends and I had become, like it or not, permanently em-Purpled. The Vikings of today, while I rooted for them, were not real. They were cartoons, almost literally so in the case of Stringer, with the Barney build and Sideshow Bob hair. I admired the preposterous talent of wide receiver Randy Moss, but was put off by his arrogance, which appeared to be equally outsized.

"Those shallow assumptions changed when Stringer, in essence, worked himself to death in practice and, hours later, Moss stepped to a microphone to remember his friend. He got only as far as this halting reminiscence: 'After the games I'd see his wife and son in the lounge … ' Then grief bent him double like a jackknife, and Moss was led away from the podium, sobbing. In that instant, two comic-book figures stepped off the page and became—for the first time in my eyes—fully human.

"In the days following his death, news reports revealed Stringer to be the best-liked player in the Vikings' locker room. The compliments were not the customary kindnesses that eulogists grant to anyone who hasn't been convicted of crimes against humanity. A caller to a Twin Cities radio station told of Stringer's stopping, after a Vikings game, to help the fan change a tire. While visiting a youth football program in his hometown of Warren, Ohio, Stringer retrieved from his truck his $15,000 Pro Bowl check and—on an impulse—endorsed it over to the organization. He was father to three-year-old Kodie, so the 335-pound Stringer sat on his Bloomington porch on Halloween and insisted that timid children take more candy from the bowl: Take a 'Korey handful,' he told trick-or-treaters.

"He was, in other words, exceedingly difficult to dislike. Tom Powers of the *Saint Paul Pioneer Press* recalled a tense postgame locker room in which Moss lashed out at reporters who were waiting at his locker after a shower. 'Why don't you go over there and watch Big K get dressed?' Moss told the throng. To which Big K replied, 'Have to put a dollar in the G-string if you want to watch. I'm not going to perform for free.' Everyone—reporters and Moss alike—roared.

" 'The hardest thing I had to do was ask him to be a tough guy,' Vikings offensive line coach Mike Tice said of Stringer at Friday's memorial. 'He was a sweetheart. He was a teddy bear. He was a little kid.'

"Evidently Stringer tried at one time to be more menacing, getting a tattoo that read FTW (F--- the World). But he didn't have it in him, and Stringer began to tell people that the tat really stood for Find the Way. He seems to have done so before saying goodbye. Or not goodbye, really, for Stringer never said that. In parting, he always said, 'Peace.' "

In Mankato, Minn., of heatstroke sustained during a training session, Aug. 1, 2001.

**Mickey Trotman, 26, soccer player.** Trotman, a native of Trinidad & Tobago who attended the Univeristy of Mobile on a scholarship, played for the Dallas Burn and the Miami Fusion of MLS, as well as the A-League's Lehigh Valley, Riverboat Gamblers and Rochester clubs. He scored the goal that gave Trinidad and Tobago a 2–1 win over Costa Rica in overtime in the quarterfinals of the 2000 CONCACAF Gold Cup. Trotman scored nine goals in 24 appearances for T&T.

Near Arima, Trinadad, from injuries sustained in an automobile accident, Oct. 10, 2001.

**Dan Turk, 38, football player.** During a 15-year NFL career, Turk, a center, played for Pittsburgh, Tampa Bay, the Raiders and Washington. With Washington from 1997 to '99, he, along with his brother Matt, made the first brother-to-brother, long-snapper-to-punter combo in NFL history.

In Ashburn, Va., from complications related to cancer, Dec. 23, 2000.

**Rashidi Wheeler, 22, college football player.** Wheeler, a Northwestern safety, collapsed during preseason conditioning drills and died an hour later. Although diagnosed as a chronic asthmatic, the senior had played with the condition since high school and had passed a physical the previous month.

In Evanston, Ill., from bronchial asthma , Aug. 3, 2001.

**Emil Zatopek, 78, Olympic runner.** Zatopek, of Czechoslovakia, was arguably the greatest distance runner of all time. He won the 5,000 meters, the 10,000 meters and the marathon at the 1952 Olympics in Helsinki, a feat that remains unmatched. In 1975 he was awarded the U.N.'s Pierre de Coubertin Prize for promoting Fair Play. The International Amateur Athletic Federation honored him posthumously with the Golden Honor of Merit, usually given to heads of state, in recognition of his achievements. Zatopek was given a State funeral by the Czech Republic.

*SI*'s Leigh Montville writes:

"There was nothing else to do, so he ran. The Nazis had taken control of his country in 1939, tanks in the streets, jackboots marching in the dead of night.

" 'There were no dances,' he explained on a February day in 1990 in his pleasant little house on a hill on the outskirts of Prague. 'Social gatherings were not allowed. Every night there was a curfew at sunset.'

"He had found his sport late, at almost 19, when the director of the shoe factory where he worked forced him to run a Sunday-afternoon race. Finishing second in the first race of his life, he wondered how good he could become. The Nazis unknowingly gave him perfect conditions. 'If there is luxury, there is the danger of degeneration,' Zatopek said. 'Sit behind the wheel of a car, and a man gains time but loses condition. There was no car. I ran instead. Look at the distance champions today. They are mostly Africans. Runners from underdeveloped countries. They are not softened by luxury.'

"He ran to work. He ran home. He ran everywhere … he ran in place, miles and miles in one spot. He ran in combat boots because he thought that would make him feel faster on a race day, with the boots removed. He ran wearing a gas mask to see if it helped control his breathing. He ran more mileage than anyone else was running. He ran through all of World War II.

"At the 1948 Olympics in London, peace restored, Zatopek, now a member of the new Czechoslovakian army, came away with a gold medal and a wife. The medal was for the 10,000 meters, the first gold ever won by a Czechoslovakian runner; the wife was Dana Ingrova, who had finished seventh in the javelin, also for Czechoslovakia. [He won silver in the 5,000 meters also.]

"In 1952 at Helsinki they became one of the great athletic couples of all time. In the midst of Emil's three gold medals in eight days—the press calling him the Human Locomotive—Dana won a gold in the javelin. Three gold medals for one man! Another for his wife! All this was unprecedented.

"Zatopek retired after the 1956 Olympics in Melbourne, where he was sixth in the marathon. In 1968, Zatopek and his wife were at the front of the [reform] movement. They addressed crowds in Wenceslas Square. They signed The Manifesto of 2000 Words against the Soviet Union. When the Soviet troops and tanks arrived, the signers of the manifesto were punished.

"Zatopek was forced out of the army, expelled from the Communist Party. The only job he could find for a time was with a surveying team, living in a trailer, digging ditches and carrying large bags of cement. For most of the next 22 years, until the second Czechoslovakian revolution, the world was told that the country's most famous athlete was 'not available.'

" 'I think sometimes about our lives, Emil's and mine,' Dana said, three months into the second revolution. 'They have been like this….'

"She ran her hand through the air, up and down, up and down, describing a roller coaster. At the finish, her husband next to her on the couch, available again, her hand was held high."

In Prague, after a stroke, Nov. 21 2000.

# 2002 Major Events

## JANUARY

| | |
|---|---|
| Major College Bowl Games | Jan 1 & 2 |
| Rose Bowl/National Championship | Jan 3 |
| U.S. Figure Skating Championships | Jan 6–13 |
| NFL Wild-Card Playoffs | Jan 12 & 13 |
| NFL Divisional Championships | Jan 19 & 20 |
| Australian Open Tennis | Jan 14–27 |
| NFL Conference Championships | Jan 27 |

## FEBRUARY

| | |
|---|---|
| Millrose Games | Feb 1 |
| NHL All-Star Game | Feb 2 |
| Super Bowl XXXVI | Feb 3 |
| AFC-NFC Pro Bowl | Feb 9 |
| 2002 Olympic Winter Games | Feb 9–22 |
| NBA All-Star Game | Feb 10 |
| Daytona 500 | Feb 17 |

## MARCH

| | |
|---|---|
| PBA World Championship | Feb 26–Mar 3 |
| U.S. Indoor Track and Field Championships | March 1–2 |
| The Players Championship | March 20–24 |
| NCAA Women's Basketball Final Four | March 29–31 |
| Major League Soccer Season Begins | March 30* |
| NCAA Men's Basketball Final Four | March 30–April 1 |

## APRIL

| | |
|---|---|
| Baseball Opening Day | April 2 |
| Masters Tournament | April 11–14 |
| Boston Marathon | April 15 |
| Stanley Cup Playoffs Begin | April 17 |
| NBA Playoffs Begin | April 20 |

## MAY

| | |
|---|---|
| Kentucky Derby | May 4 |
| Preakness | May 18 |
| Indianapolis 500 | May 26 |

## JUNE

| | |
|---|---|
| World Cup | May 31–June 30 |
| French Open Tennis | May 27–June 9 |
| NBA Finals Begin | June 2 |
| Stanley Cup Finals Begin | June 4 |
| Belmont Stakes | June 8 |
| U.S. Open Golf | June 13–16 |
| NBA Draft | June 26 |

## JULY

| | |
|---|---|
| Wimbledon Tennis | June 24–July 7 |
| Baseball All-Star Game | July 9 |
| British Open Golf | July 18–21 |
| Tour de France | July 6–28 |

## AUGUST

| | |
|---|---|
| Brickyard 400 | Aug 4 |
| PGA Championship | Aug 15–18 |
| College Football Season Begins | Aug 24 |

## SEPTEMBER

| | |
|---|---|
| U.S. Open Tennis | Aug 26–Sept 8 |
| NFL Season Begins | Sept 8 |
| Ryder Cup | Sept 27–29 |

## OCTOBER

| | |
|---|---|
| NHL Season Begins | Oct 2* |
| World Series Begins | Oct 19* |
| Breeders' Cup | Oct 26* |
| MLS Cup 2002 | Oct 27* |
| NBA Regular Season Begins | Oct 29* |

## NOVEMBER

| | |
|---|---|
| Women's Tennis Tour Championships | Oct 28–Nov 3* |
| New York Marathon | Nov 3 |
| The President's Cup | Nov 7–10 |
| Tennis Masters Cup | Nov 11–17 |

## DECEMBER

| | |
|---|---|
| Heisman Trophy Presentation | Dec 14 |
| Major College Bowl Games Begin | Dec 19 |

* Approximate date.